BAKER ENCYCLOPEDIA *of* PSYCHOLOGY &COUNSELING

SECOND EDITION

Edited by
DAVID G. BENNER
&PETER C. HILL

Baker Books
A Division of Baker Book House Co
Grand Rapids, Michigan 49516

Published by Baker Books
a division of Baker Book House Company
P.O. Box 6287, Grand Rapids, MI 49516-6287

Printed in the United States of America

Library of Congress Cataloging-in-Publication Data
is on file at the Library of Congress, Washington, D.C.

ISBN: 0-8010-2100-6

For information about academic books, resources for Christian leaders, and all new releases available from Baker Book House, visit our web site:
http://www.bakerbooks.com

Preface to Second Edition

Serious work on the relationship of psychology to Christian theology and faith has gained a great deal of momentum in the past 25 years. During that time, both the *Journal of Psychology and Christianity* and the *Journal of Psychology and Theology* had their beginnings and have grown into important publication outlets for work on this interface. Over the same years we have witnessed the development of the Christian Association for Psychological Studies into a vital international association of Christian mental health professionals and have also seen the birth of a new organization, the American Association of Christian Counselors. Pastoral care and counseling has also grown in sophistication and rigor, with an increasing number of publications and conferences dedicated to applications of psychological theory and practice to pastoral settings. Christian counseling has also experienced an enormous development, both in number of practitioners as well as in the vision that directs such work.

All of this has meant that *Baker Encyclopedia of Psychology,* published in 1985 and rapidly embraced as the first comprehensive treatment of psychology from a Christian point of view, has been for several years much in need of revision. Developments within the field of psychology over the last decade have also, of course, demanded such a revision. Treatment approaches have been tested in the fire of research evaluation and some have been found wanting. Consequently, these approaches have not been included in this revised edition. Changes in the classification and understanding of the major psychological disorders, especially in the light of the 1994 publication of the fourth edition of the *Diagnostic and Statistical Manual of Mental Disorders* (*DSM-IV*), have also required extensive changes to these articles. The same is true of articles on psychological development, social behavior, and personality.

Another major difference between the present edition and the previous one is the much more extensive attention given in the present edition to pastoral care and counseling. Implications for pastoral care are noted in many articles, and a large number of new articles exploring issues of particular interest to clergy are contained in this edition. These articles should also be of interest to Christian counselors and mental health practitioners as well as students preparing for work in any of these fields.

The present edition also contains a much more elaborate network of links between articles. This includes a substantially increased number of cross references (entries that lead to other articles) as well as listings of related articles to be found at the conclusion of the article. References and suggested additional readings have also been revised and extended. It is our hope that these changes will build on the strengths of the first edition while making this revision of even more use to an even larger number of people.

Once again, we wish to acknowledge and thank the authors who have worked with us in preparing this revision, with a special sense of gratitude to those who took on special writing assignments near the end of the project. All have performed admirably in helping to produce this updated volume. We have been extremely fortunate to reinvolve most of the authors from the first edition and are delighted to welcome a number of new ones. Drawn from the ranks of both academicians and practitioners, the authors are mostly psychologists but also include a number of pastors, psychiatrists, social workers, and Christian counselors. Together, they include most of the major contributors to the current dialogue regarding the relationship of psychology and Christianity. They are identified at the end of each article, the only exception being short definitional articles which are the work of the editors. Authors are also listed on pages 9–13 with brief biographical data.

This work would not have been possible without the support of a great number of people. Principal among them we would like to acknowledge Jim Weaver, the Editorial Director for Academic and Reference Books at Baker Book House. We wish to recognize the support provided by our institutions, Redeemer College and Grove City College. We also wish to thank our wives, Juliet Benner and Carol Hill, for their superb patience and understanding during what has been a long and arduous, but also meaningful and fulfilling process. Our hope and prayer is that the reader will greatly benefit from this second edition.

Preface to First Edition

This book was born out of an awareness of the need for a comprehensive treatment of psychology from a Christian point of view. The rapidly expanding body of knowledge in psychology has led to the publication of a number of encyclopedias in recent years, each written from one viewpoint or more usually from several. None of these, however, has been written from a Christian perspective, identifying the issues and applications of particular importance from that perspective and suggesting ways of evaluating the concepts, theories, and research findings in light of biblical teachings. This volume fills that void.

First and foremost this is an encyclopedia, factually presenting the major current findings and theories in the field. Thus it presents psychology in its own terms. Second, many articles also contain an explicit biblical or theological perspective. This is broadly evangelical, though it is much less monolithic and narrowly defined than it would be if all articles had been written by one author. I made no effort to force my viewpoint on the articles, preferring instead to allow contributors the liberty to speak for themselves. This work derives its strength from numerous authors writing on their areas of expertise and from their individual Christian perspectives.

Although providing representative coverage of important aspects of the entire field, this volume focuses on the areas of personality, psychopathology (psychological problems), psychotherapy and other treatment approaches, major systems and theories of psychology, and the psychology of religion. These areas interest Christians the most and are often crucial in efforts to relate psychology and Christianity. Approximately 80 percent of the 1,050 articles in this volume fall in these areas, the remaining ones being divided among social psychology, developmental psychology, and general experimental psychology. The goal for all articles has been to be both readily understandable to nonpsychologists and useful to psychologists and other mental health professionals.

The encyclopedia was designed around the topics identified in the category index. For example, articles in the category "Psychopathology" include 184 disorders found in the third edition of the *Diagnostic and Statistical Manual of Mental Disorders*, 99 symptoms and reactions, and 25 general topics. The category "Treatment Approaches and Issues" contains 149 articles on different approaches, and 34 on general issues involved in treating psychological problems.

Although planned topically, articles appear in alphabetical order. The topical index, which includes all articles, helps the reader find articles of interest. Cross references within and at the end of articles also lead the reader to related articles. These references are identified by capital letters. Bibliographies identify books and articles for further reading. These may include References (sources cited in the article) and Additional Readings (sources not cited but recommended).

An encyclopedia is only as good as its contributors. I have been extremely fortunate to enlist most of the major scholars involved in current discussions of the relationship between psychology and Christianity. Drawn from the ranks of both academicians and practitioners, they are mostly psychologists. Some, however, specialize in psychiatry, social work, and pastoral care. Authors are identified at the end of each article. Short definitional articles lacking an author's name are mine.

Considerable help in preparing this volume has come from a wide circle of friends and colleagues. I wish to acknowledge the invaluable help of my secretary and editorial assistant, Marcy Bump, who worked with me from the earliest stages to the book's completion. Thanks go to my graduate assistants, Toby Drew, Tom Gill, David Dunkerton, John Robertson, and Melody Patterson, for technical and research support. Special thanks also go to Walter Elwell, who provided the initial idea for the project; Allan Fisher, the Baker Book House editor whose experience with similar projects enabled him to provide much guidance and assistance; and Jean Hager of the Word Works, who provided invaluable help as the copyeditor. Finally, I most appreciate the love and support of Juliet and Sean, who shared a husband and father with this project.

Contributor List

Naji Abi-Hashem. Ph.D., Licensed Clinical Psychologist, Minirth–Meier New Life Clinics.

LeRoy Aden. Ph.D., Professor Emeritus of Pastoral Care, Lutheran Theological Seminary.

Ihsan Al-Issa. Ph.D., Professor of Psychology, University of Calgary.

Elizabeth M. Altmaier. Ph.D., Associate Professor, Division of Counselor Education, University of Iowa.

David E. Anderson. Ph.D., Associate Professor of Psychology, Bethel College, St. Paul, Minnesota.

Susan L. Aoki. M.A., Children's Minister, Pasadena Covenant Church, Pasadena, California.

Wayne T. Aoki. Ph.D., Assistant Professor of Psychology, Fuller Theological Seminary.

Donald S. Aultman. Ed.D., Vice Chancellor, Church of God, School of Ministry.

William W. Austin. Psy.D., Private Practice, Chicago, Illinois.

Timothy J. Aycock. Ph.D., Licensed Psychologist, A New Start Counseling Center.

Aloysius Balawyder. Ph.D., Retired Professor of History, St. Francis Xavier University.

Stanley N. Ballard. Ph.D., Professor and Chairman, Department of Psychology, Cedarville College.

Clark E. Barshinger. Ph.D., Director and Owner, Cherry Hill Center for Counseling and Psychotherapy.

Toby E. Basalla. B.A., Computer Consultant, Pittsburgh, Pennsylvania.

Rodney L. Bassett. Ph.D., Professor of Psychology, Roberts Wesleyan College.

James R. Beck. Ph.D., Professor of Counseling, Denver Seminary.

David G. Benner. Ph.D., Professor of Psychology, Redeemer College.

C. Markham Berry. M.D., Retired Psychiatrist and Writer.

William G. Bixler. Ph.D., Clinical Psychologist, Private Practice.

Jeffrey P. Bjorck. Ph.D., Associate Professor of Psychology, Fuller Theological Seminary.

Tannis J. Blair. M.A., Research Assistant, Casey Family Services.

Martin Bolt. Ph.D., Professor of Psychology, Calvin College.

Alexander H. Bolyanatz. Ph.D., Assistant Professor of Anthropology, Wheaton College.

Bruce E. Bonecutter. Ph.D., Clinical Director, Genesis Therapy Center and Alternative Behavior Treatment Center.

Timothy A. Boyd. Psy.D., Associate Professor of Social Work and Psychology, Roberts Wesleyan College.

Jay L. Brand. Ph.D., Research Psychologist, Ideation Haworth, Inc., Holland, Michigan.

Jeffrey M. Brandsma. Ph.D., Professor, Psychology Section Chief, and Director of Clinical Psychology Training, Medical College of Georgia.

Helen Bray-Garretson. Ph.D., Clinical Psychologist, Housatonic Center for Mental Health.

T. L. Brink. Ph.D., Coordinator, Psychology Program, Crafton Hills College.

David W. Brokaw. Ph.D., Assistant Professor of Psychology, Azusa Pacific University.

Christine J. Bruun. Ph.D., Chair, Department of Psychology, Rockford College.

Rodger K. Bufford. Ph.D., Professor and Director of Research and Integration, George Fox University.

Richard E. Butman. Ph.D., Professor of Psychology, Wheaton College.

Eric M. Butter. M.A., Doctoral Candidate, Bowling Green State University.

Contributor List

Alphonese F. X. Calabrese. Ph.D., Executive Director, Christian Institute for Psychotherapeutic Studies, Hicksville, New York.

Paul Cameron. Ph.D., Chairperson, Institute for the Scientific Investigation of Sexuality, Lincoln, Nebraska.

Clark D. Campbell. Ph.D., Associate Professor and Chair, Psychology Department, George Fox University.

Michael A. Campion. Ph.D., Senior Therapist, Campion, Barrow & Associates Clinical Assistant Professor of Psychology Internal Medicine, University of Illinois.

Sally Schwer Canning. Ph.D., Assistant Professor of Psychology, Wheaton College.

Steven A. Cappa. Psy.D., Assistant Professor of Counseling, Denver Seminary.

John D. Carter. Ph.D., Dean of Doctoral Studies, Trinity College of Graduate Studies/Private Practice.

James F. Cassens. Ph.D., Cassens and Associates, P.C., Park Ridge, Illinois.

John R. Cheydleur. Ph.D., Program Development Officer, Adult Rehabilitation Centers Command, The Salvation Army.

Mary Franzen Clark. Ed.D., Associate Director, Alpha Psychological Services, Livonia, Michigan.

Paul W. Clement. Ph.D., Clinical Psychologist, Psychology Resource Consultants.

Bonnidell Clouse. Ph.D., Professor of Educational and School Psychology, Indiana State University.

John Henry Coe. Ph.D., Associate Professor of Psychology, Biola University.

Gary R. Collins. Ph.D., President, American Association of Christian Counselors.

Arlo D. Compaan. Ph.D., Co-director and Clinical Psychologist, Tolentine Personal Resource Center.

David M. Cook. Ph.D., Clinical Psychologist, Private Practice.

Kaye V. Cook. Ph.D., Professor of Psychology, Gordon College.

Mark Coppenger. Ph.D., Associate Professor of Philosophy, Wheaton College.

Mark P. Cosgrove. Ph.D., Professor of Psychology, Taylor University.

John H. Court. Ph.D., Director of Counseling, Tabor College.

Michael D. Cozzens. Ph.D., Associate Professor and Director of Academic Affairs, International School of Theology.

Frederic C. Craigie, Jr. Ph.D., Clinical Psychologist and Behavioral Sciences Coordinator, Maine-Dartmouth Family Practice Residency.

James R. David. Ph.D., Adjunct Associate Professor, National Catholic School of Social Service, Catholic University of America.

Creath Davis. M.Div., Executive Director, Christian Concern Foundation, Dallas, Texas.

Jerry E. Davis. Ph.D., Associate Professor of Psychology and Director, Graduate Counseling Program, Indiana Wesleyan University.

Matthew J. Davis. B.S., Research Assistant, Brigham Young University.

Daniel H. Decker. M.A., Licensed Professional Counselor, Private Practice.

Edward E. Decker, Jr. Ph.D., Professor and Director of Graduate Programs, Oral Roberts University.

A. Robert Denton. Ph.D., Director, Victim Assistance Program, Furnace Street Mission, Akron, Ohio.

Helen M. DeVries. Ph.D., Associate Professor of Psychology, Wheaton College.

Quentin R. DeYoung. Ph.D., Emeritus Professor of Psychology, Chapman College.

Frederick A. DiBlasio. Ph.D., Professor, University of Maryland at Baltimore.

John B. Dilley. Ed.D., Private Practice, West Des Moines, Iowa.

Charles D. Dolph. Ph.D., Professor of Psychology, Cedarville College.

Warren C. Drew. Psy.D., USAF Medical Center, Wright-Patterson Air Force Base.

Michelle L. Dykstra. Ph.D., Assistant Professor of Psychology, George Fox University.

Brian E. Eck. Ph.D., Department Chair and Director of Clinical Programs, Azusa Pacific University.

William L. Edkins. Psy.D., Clinical Psychologist, Private Practice.

Dan Egli. Ph.D., Licensed Clinical Psychologist, Private Practice.

J. Harold Ellens. Ph.D., Professor Emeritus, Christian Association for Psychological Studies, International.

Craig W. Ellison. Ph.D., Professor of Counseling and Urban Ministries of Alliance Theological Seminary/Executive Director, Agape Counseling and Training Services.

Ronald Enroth. Ph.D., Professor of Sociology, Westmont College.

Truman G. Esau. M.D., Medical Director, Old Orchard Hospital, Chicago, Illinois.

C. Stephen Evans. Ph.D., Professor of Philosophy, Calvin College.

Kirk E. Farnsworth. Ph.D., Vice President and Executive Director, CRISTA Counseling Service.

Larry N. Ferguson. Ph.D., Psychologist, Link Care Center.

John G. Finch. Ph.D., Consulting Psychologist, Gig Harbor, Washington.

Geraldine E. Forsberg. Ph.D., Assistant Professor of Communication, Trinity Western University.

James D. Foster. Ph.D., Professor of Psychology and Dean of the School of Natural and Behavioral Sciences, George Fox University.

Michelle L. Freeman. B.A., Student, Grove City College.

David J. Frenchak. D.Min., Center for Life Skills, Chicago.

Elizabeth A. Gassin. Ph.D., Assistant Professor of Psychology, Olivet Nazarene University.

Kathleen A. Gathercoal. Ph.D., Associate Professor of Psychology, George Fox University.

Eugene S. Gibbs. Ed.D., Associate Professor of Christian Education and Director of Doctoral Studies, Ashland Theological Seminary.

Dennis L. Gibson. Ph.D., Wheaton Counseling Associates, Wheaton, Illinois.

Norman Giesbrecht. Ph.D., Research Consultant, Insight Research and Consulting, Calgary, Alberta, Canada.

Joan B. Goldsmith. B.A., Certified Public Accountant.

W. Mack Goldsmith. Ph.D., Professor of Psychology, Emeritus, California State University, Stanislaus.

Julia Pecnik Grimm. Ph.D., Assistant Professor, State University of New York College at Fredonia.

James D. Guy, Jr. Ph.D., Professor and Dean, School of Psychology, Fuller Theological Seminary.

Todd W. Hall. Ph.D., Assistant Professor of Psychology, Biola University.

John A. Hammes. Ph.D., Professor of Psychology, University of Georgia.

Brent A. Hanson. M.S., Associate Psychotherapist and Director of Dissociative Disorder Treatment, and Licensed Clinical Professional Counselor, Campion, Barrow & Associates.

Linda B. Hardy. D.O., Assistant Professor of Psychiatry and Director of Medical Student Education, Department of Psychiatry, Medical College of Georgia.

Kelly R. Harkcom. B.A., Psychology Paraprofessional, Jeffrey L. Lenshower (private practice).

Charles E. Henry. Ph.D., Vice President, VMS Realty, Chicago, Illinois.

Kelly J. Hetrick. M.A., Student, Westminster Theological Seminary.

Terry L. Hight. M.A., Student, Virginia Commonwealth University.

Peter C. Hill. Ph.D., Professor of Psychology, Grove City College.

William Colyn Hill. Ph.D., Northwestern University.

Elizabeth L. Hillstrom. Ph.D., Associate Professor of Psychology, Wheaton College.

Kenneth A. Holstein. Ph.D., Bell Labs, Lisle, Illinois.

Ralph W. Hood, Jr. Ph.D., Professor, University of Tennessee at Chattanooga.

Keith A. Houde. Ph.D., Togus VA Hospital/Private Practice.

Gary S. Hurd. Ph.D., Assistant Professor of Psychiatry, Medical College of Georgia.

John A. Ingram. Ph.D., Associate Professor of Psychology, Biola University.

Cedric B. Johnson. Ph.D., Psychologist, Fred Gross Christian Therapy Program and Cedric Johnson Seminars.

Eric L. Johnson. Ph.D., Associate Professor, Northwestern College.

Lucie R. Johnson. Ph.D., Professor of Psychology, Bethel College, St. Paul, Minnesota.

Ronald B. Johnson. Ph.D., Midlands Psychological Association, Lodi, Wisconsin.

Theodore M. Johnson. Ph.D., Philhaven Hospital, Lebanon, Pennsylvania.

G. Archie Johnston. Ed.D., Ph.D., Executive Director, California Behavioral Science Institute, San Francisco.

Dawn R. Jones. B.S., Student, Virginia Commonwealth University.

Stanton L. Jones. Ph.D., Provost, Wheaton College.

Brenda Joscelyne. M.A., Student, University of South Africa.

Allan M. Josephson. M.D., Chief of Child, Adolescent and Family Psychiatry and Professor of Psychiatry, Medical College of Georgia.

Robert H. Joss. Ph.D., Professor of Forensic Psychology, Gordon College/Forensic Psychologist, Psychological Consulting Services.

Donald M. Joy. Ph.D., Professor of Human Development and Family Studies, Asbury Theological Seminary.

Richard D. Kahoe. Ph.D., Christian Haven Homes, Wheatfield, Illinois.

Duane Kauffmann. Ph.D., Professor of Psychology, Goshen College.

Cherie L. Kelly. M.A., Student, Frostbury State University.

Tracy Kempton. Ph.D., Assistant Professor and Associate Director, Child Inpatient Unit, Medical College of Ohio.

Amy E. King. M.A., Student, University of Texas–Pan American.

William T. Kirwan. D.Min., Ph.D., Psychiatric Associates, St. Louis, Missouri.

Wendy Kliewer. Ph.D., Assistant Professor of Psychology, Virginia Commonwealth University.

Haddon Klingberg, Jr. Ph.D., President, Klingberg Family Centers, New Britain, Connecticut.

Chris Koch. Ph.D., Assistant Professor of Psychology, George Fox University.

Jane Kopas. Ph.D., Associate Professor of Theology, University of Scranton.

Roksana Korchynsky. M.A., Student, Bowling Green State University.

Russell D. Kosits. M.A., Milieu Therapist, Western Psychiatric Institute and Clinic, Pittsburgh, Pennsylvania.

Ronald L. Koteskey. Ph.D., Professor of Psychology, Asbury College.

Kevin R. Kracke. Ph.D., Director of Children and Adolescent Services, Central Kansas Mental Health Center/Associate Professor of Psychology, Marymount College of Kansas.

Michael J. Lambert. Ph.D., Professor of Psychology, Brigham Young University.

Reginald Larkin. Ph.D., University of Texas at Austin.

Lojan E. LaRowe. Ph.D., Co-owner, Cherry Hill Center for Counseling & Psychotherapy.

John A. Larsen. Ph.D., Director of Consultation and Education, Midwest Christian Counseling Center, Kansas City, Missouri.

Michael D. Lastoria. Ed.D., Director of Counseling Services, Houghton College.

Kathleen M. Lattea. M.A., Psychotherapist, Westview Psychological Services.

Katherine Rankin Leung. B.A., Student, Fuller Theological Seminary.

Philip C. Lewis. M.D., Chairman, Department of Psychiatry, Tripler Army Medical Center.

Earl A. Loomis, Jr. M.D., Professor of Child and Adolescent Psychiatry, Medical College of Georgia.

Heather Looy. Ph.D., Assistant Professor of Psychology, The King's University College.

Joe W. Lund. Ph.D., Professor of Psychology, Taylor University.

H. Newton Malony. Ph.D., Senior Professor of Psychology, Fuller Theological Seminary.

Michael W. Mangis. Ph.D., Associate Professor and Master's Program Coordinator, Wheaton College.

Leonardo M. Marmol. Ph.D., Professor of Psychology, George Fox University.

Grant L. Martin. Ph.D., Psychologist, Private Practice, Seattle, Washington.

Rod A. Martin. Ph.D., Professor of Psychology, University of Western Ontario.

Michael L. Marvin. Ph.D., Clinical Psychologist, Federal Prison System, Lompoc, California.

George Matheson. Ph.D., Chief of Psychology, Etobicoke General Hospital, Rexdale, Ontario, Canada.

Jacqueline E. M. McCreary. M.A., Training Coordinator, Senior, Virginia Commonwealth University.

Micah L. McCreary. Ph.D., Assistant Professor of Psychology, Virginia Commonwealth University.

Donald S. McCulloch. Ph.D., Nova University.

M. E. McCurdy.

John M. McDonagh. Ph.D., Psychologist, Private Practice, Cold Spring Harbor, New York.

Marvin J. McDonald. Ph.D., Associate Professor of Psychology, Augustana University College.

Jocelyn Shealy McGee. M.S.G., Administrative Coordinator for the Center for Aging Resources, Fuller Theological Seminary.

Rodney B. McKean. Ph.D., First Alliance Church, Tucson, Arizona.

D. Douglas McKenna. Ph.D., Research Psychologist, Personnel Decisions Institute, Minneapolis, Minnesota.

Clinton W. McLemore. Ph.D., President, Relational Dynamics Institute, Inc., Sierra Madre, California.

Mark R. McMinn. Ph.D., Dr. Arthur P. Rech and Mrs. Jean May Rech Professor of Psychology and Director of the Doctoral Progam in Clinical Psychology, Wheaton College.

Mary Jo Meadow. Ph.D., Professor of Psychology and Religious Studies, Mankato State University/Resources for Ecumenical Spirituality.

Katheryn Rhoads Meek. Psy.D. Candidate, Wheaton College.

J. Trevor Milliron. Ph.D. Candidate, Fuller Theological Seminary.

Brenda Nowlin Mitchell. M.A., M.Div., Chaplain, Holy Cross Medical Center and UCLA Medical Center.

Frank J. Moncher. Ph.D., Professor of Psychiatry and Health Behavior, Medical College of Georgia.

Gary W. Moon. Ph.D., President, Psychological Studies Institute.

Ronald W. Moslener. D.Min., Assistant Professor of Psychology, Geneva College.

Dan Motet. Ph.D., Private Practice, Honolulu, Hawaii.

Gail P. Nagel. B.S., Student, Fuller Theological Seminary.

S. Bruce Narramore. Ph.D., Distinguished Professor of Psychology, Biola University.

Cynthia Jones Neal. Ph.D., Associate Professor and Chair, Psychology Department, Wheaton College.

Douglas Needham. Ph.D., Assistant Professor of Psychology, Redeemer College.

Melvin R. Nelson. Ph.D., Private Practice, Wauwatosa, Wisconsin.

Joseph K. Neumann. Ph.D., Clinical Psychologist, Medical Center, Mountain Home, Tennessee.

Mary Ann Norfleet. Ph.D., Clinical Professor of Psychiatry and Behavioral Sciences, Stanford University.

Wayne D. Norman. Ph.D., Professor of Psychology, Redeemer College.

Gary J. Oliver. Ph.D., Clinical Director, Southwest Counseling Associates.

Steve R. Osborne. Ph.D., Senior Research Scientist, Allen Corporation of America, Dallas, Texas.

Les Parrott, III. Ph.D., Associate Professor of Psychology and Director, Center for Relationship Development, Seattle Pacific University.

Leslie Parrott. Ed.D., Co-director, Center for Relationship Development, Seattle Pacific University.

E. Mansell Pattison. M.D., Professor and Chairman, Department of Psychiatry and Health Behavior, Medical College of Georgia.

P. Pecheur.

Kristin M. Perrone-Shea. M.S., Doctoral Candidate, Virginia Commonwealth University.

Peggy Perry. M.S.W., Department of Psychiatry, University of Kentucky.

Donn W. Peters. Psy.D., Presbyterian Counseling Center, Salt Lake City, Utah.

Contributor List

Ronald Philipchalk. Ph.D., Professor and Chair, Department of Pschology, Trinity Western University.

Harry L. Piersma. Ph.D., Director of Counseling Services, Michigan State University.

Eric P. Pitts. B.A., Student, Slippery Rock University.

James E. Plueddemann. Ph.D., Chairman and Associate Professor of Educational Ministries, Wheaton College.

David Powlison. Ph.D., Editor, *Journal of Biblical Counseling.*

Avie J. Rainwater, III. Ph.D., Director of Behavioral Medicine and Associate Professor of Family Medicine and Psychiatry (MUSC), McLeod Family Medicine Residency Program.

Katherine Pollock Rankin. Ph.D. Candidate, Fuller Theological Seminary.

Carole A. Rayburn. Ph.D., Clinical, Consulting, and Research Psychologist, Private Practice.

Teri K. Reisser. M.S., MFCC Intern, Thousand Oaks Counseling Group, Thousand Oaks, California.

J. Roberto Reyes. Ph.D., Assistant Professor of Family Studies and Director of the Latino Partnership Program, Messiah College.

Dennis R. Ridley. Ph.D., Research Associate, Department of Human Service Studies, Cornell University.

Jennifer S. Ripley. B.A., Student, Virginia Commonwealth University.

Robert C. Roberts. Ph.D., Professor of Philosophy and Psychological Studies, Wheaton College.

J. H. Robertson.

Mícheál D. Roe. Ph.D., Professor and Chair, Department of Psychology, Seattle Pacific University.

Gale H. Roid. Ph.D., Associate Professor of Psychology, George Fox University.

Charlotte Rosenak. Ph.D., Psychologist, Christian Psychological Services.

Christopher H. Rosik. Ph.D., Psychologist and Assistant Clinical Director, Link Care Center.

Ronald H. Rottschafer. Ph.D., Clinical Psychologist, Private Practice.

Timothy J. Runkel. Ph.D., Consulting Psychologist, Zion, Illinois.

Steven J. Sandage. Ph.D., Assistant Professor of Psychology, Bethel Seminary.

Randolph K. Sanders. Ph.D., Clinical Psychologist/Executive Director, Christian Association for Psychological Studies.

John A. Sanford. .M.Div., Certified Jungian Analyst, Private Practice, San Diego, California.

Onas C. Scandrette. Ed.D., Emeritus Professor of Psychology, Wheaton College.

John D. Scanish. Psy.D., New Life Counseling Center, Louisville, Kentucky.

David C. Schutz. M.D., Assistant Clinical Professor of Psychiatry, Loyola University Medical School.

Donna Lynne Schuurman. Ed.D., Northern Illinois University.

Winston Seegobin. Ph.D., Assistant Professor of Psychology, Messiah College.

Kevin S. Seybold. Ph.D., Professor of Psychology, Grove City College.

Virginia K. Seybold. RNC, BSN, Butler Memorial Hospital, Butler, Pennsylvania.

Leigh S. Shaffer. Ph.D., Professor of Sociology and Interim Coordinator of Institutional Research, West Chester University.

Rebecca A. Sheaffer. B.S., Student, Indiana Wesleyan University.

Bethyl J. Shepperson. Psy.D., Claremont Psychological Services.

Vance L. Shepperson. Ph.D., Associate Adjunct Professor, California Graduate Institute, California State University at Los Angeles.

Paul N. Shultz. M.A., Student, University of North Carolina.

Dale Simpson. Ph.D., Clinical Director, Family Life Counseling Services, Bryan, Texas.

Stan Skarsten. D.S.W., Stan Skarsten Counseling, Toronto, Ontario, Canada.

Darrell Smith. Ph.D., Director, Dogwood Hill Counseling Center.

Gary Scott Smith. Ph.D., Professor of Sociology, Grove City College.

John M. Smith, IV. B.A., Financial Advisor, American Express, Inc.

Mark Stanton. Ph.D., Associate Professor of Psychology, Azusa Pacific University.

Daryl H. Stevenson. Ph.D., Professor of Psychology, Houghton College.

Carey R. Stites. B.A., Training and Support Specialist, Sughrue, Mion, Zinn, Macpeak, and Seas, PLLC, Washington, DC.

Howard Stone. Ph.D., Professor of Pastoral Theology and Pastoral Counseling, Texas Christian University.

Eric K. Sweitzer. Ph.D., Director, Charis Counseling Center.

Joseph Eugene Talley. Ph.D., ABPP, Assistant Clinical Professor, Duke University.

Siang-Yang Tan. Ph.D., Professor of Psychology, Fuller Theological Seminary.

Glenn C. Taylor. M.Th., M.Ed., General Director, Younge Street Mission, Adjunct Faculty, Ontario Theological Seminary.

E. Warren Throckmorton. Ph.D., Director of College Counseling and Associate Professor of Psychology, Grove City College.

Nancy Stiehler Thurston. Psy.D., Assistant Professor of Psychology, Fuller Theological Seminary.

Randie L. Timpe. Ph.D., Professor of Psychology and Associate Dean of Instruction, Mount Vernon Nazarene College.

Jay M. Uomoto. Ph.D., Clinical Director and Neuropsychologist, The Shepherd Center.

H. A. Van Belle. Ph.D., Associate Professor of Psychology, The King's University College.

Hendrika Vande Kemp. Ph.D., Professor of Psychology, Fuller Theological Seminary.

James H. Vander May. M.A., F.T.E.P., Chairperson, Activity Therapy Department, Pine Rest Christian Hospital, Grand Rapids, Michigan.

Bryan Van Dragt. Ph.D., Private Practice, Gig Harbor, Washington.

Henry A. Virkler. Ph.D., Professor of Psychology, Palm Beach Atlantic College.

Paul C. Vitz. Ph.D., Professor of Psychology, New York University.

Harold Wahking. D.Min., Retired, St. Petersburg, Florida.

Edwin R. Wallace, IV. M.D., Research Professor of Bioethics, University of South Carolina.

Andrew J. Weaver. Ph.D., Clinical Psychologist, Hawaii State Hospital.

Richard Welsh. M.S.W., Professor of Clinical Social Work in Psychiatry, University of Kentucky Medical Center.

Gary L. Welton. Ph.D., Associate Professor of Psychology, Grove City College.

Floyd Westendorp. M.D., Professor of Psychiatry, Michigan State University.

William T. Weyerhaeuser. Ph.D., Private Practice, Gig Harbor, Washington.

Frances J. White. Ph.D., Professor of Psychology Emerita, Wheaton College.

Katherine Hsu Wibberly. Ph.D., MH/MR Prevention Specialist, District 19 Community Services Board.

Frank B. Wichern, Sr. Ph.D., Clinical Psychologist/ Associate Professor, Amber University.

Rod Wilson. Ph.D., Counseling Staff, Missionary Health Institute, Teaching Elder, Forest Brook Bible Chapel.

William P. Wilson. M.D., Director, Institute of Christian Growth.

Everett L. Worthington, Jr. Ph.D., Professor of Psychology, Virginia Commonwealth University.

Mark A. Yarhouse. Psy.D., Assistant Professor of Psychology, Regent University.

Paul D. Young. Ph.D., Professor and Chair, Psychology Department, Houghton College.

Category Index

Fields of Specialization and Professional Organizations

Eminent Contributors

Category Index

Learning, Cognition, and Intelligence

Sexuality, Marriage, and Family

Category Index

Psychopathology

General

Category Index

Obesity
Pica
Sleep Disorders
Somnambulism

Symptoms

Acalculia
Aggression
Agitation
Agnosia
Agraphia
Alexia
Amok
Amusia
Anhedonia
Anniversary Depression
Anosognosia
Anxiety
Aphasia
Apraxia
Automaticity
Belle Indifference
Blocking
Catalepsy
Cataplexy
Circumstantiality
Clang Association
Compulsion
Confabulation
Cotard's Syndrome
Crying
Decompensation
Delirium Tremens
Delusion
Dereistic Thinking
Disorientation
Displacement
Dissociation
Doubt
Envy
Erotomania
Excuse Making
False Memory Syndrome
Fear
Flight into Health
Flight of Ideas
Folie a Deaux
Grief
Guilt
Hallucination
Hopelessness
Hypertension
Hypoactivity
Idea of Reference
Juvenile Delinquency
Learned Helplessness
Lie Detection
Logorrhea
Loneliness
Loosening of Associations
Loss and Separation
Lying
Magical Thinking
Malingering
Mania
Masturbation
Megalomania

Menopause
Midlife Crisis
Monoideism
Nail Biting
Narcissism
Neologism
Nervous Breakdown
Neurosis, Experimental
Nightmare
Obesity
Obsession
Oligophrenia
Omnipotence, Feelings of
Pain
Panic Attack
Paranoia
Perseveration
Pica
Poverty of Speech
Pressure of Speech
Pseudocyesis
Pyromania
Rebellion, Adolescent
Rehearsal, Obsessional
Scapegoating
Self-Destructive Behavior
Shame
Shyness
Somnambulism
Splitting
Stress
Stupor
Suffering
Suicide
Syncope
Temper Tantrum
Tension
Trauma
Ulcers
Verbigeration
Vertigo
Visions and Voices
Word Salad
Workaholism

Treatment

Individual Therapies

Actualizing Therapy
Adlerian Psychotherapy
Adolescent Therapy
Antabuse Therapy
Applied Behavioral Analysis
Assertiveness Training
Autogenic Therapy
Aversion Therapy
Behavior Modification
Behavior Therapy
Biblical Counseling
Biocentric Therapy
Bioenergetic Analysis
Biofeedback Training
Biopsychosocial Therapy
Cancer Counseling
Child Therapy
Christian Counseling and
    Psychotherapy

Cognitive-Behavior Therapy
Conditioning, Operant
Confrontation in Therapy
Coping Skills Therapies
Daseinsanalysis
Direct Psychoanalysis
Ego-State Therapy
Electroconvulsive Therapy
Existential Psychology and
    Psychotherapy
Feminist Psychotherapy
Financial Counseling
Flooding
Genetic Counseling
Geriatric Psychotherapy
Gestalt Therapy
Grief Therapy
Growth Counseling
Guidance
Holistic Health and Therapy
Hypnosis
Hypnotherapy
Infertility Counseling
Integrity Therapy
Interpersonal Diagnosis
Jungian Analysis
Life Skills Counseling
Logotherapy
Multimodal Therapy
Narcotherapy
Neurolinguistic Programming
Nouthetic Counseling
Object Relations Theory
Object Relations Therapy
Pastoral Care and Counseling, Role
    Conflicts in
Pastoral Counseling
Person-Centered Therapy
Phenomenological Therapy
Post-Abortion Counseling
Primal Therapy
Problem-Solving Therapy
Provocative Therapy
Psychedelic Therapy
Psychoanalysis: Technique
Psychoanalytic Psychotherapy
Psychodrama
Psychopharmacology
Psychosynthesis
Rational-Emotive Therapy
Reality Therapy
Reconstructive Psychotherapy
Reeducative Psychotherapy
Regressive Therapy
Short-Term Anxiety-Provoking
    Therapy
Short-Term Dynamic Psychotherapy
Short-Term Therapies
Solution-Focused Therapy
Spirituotherapy
Structural Integration
Supportive Psychotherapy
Systematic Desensitization
Tranquilizer
Transactional Analysis
Vocational Counseling
Will Therapy

Category Index

Group Therapies

Alcoholics Anonymous
Assertiveness Training
Gestalt therapy
Group Psychotherapy
Psychoanalytic Group Therapy
Psychodrama
Theme-Centered Interactional
    Groups

Couple, Family, and System Therapies

Behavioral Family Therapy
Behavioral Marital Therapy
Conjoint Family Therapy
Contextual Family Therapy
Creative Aggression Therapy
Cybernetic Theory
Family Group Therapy
Family Systems Therapy
Family Therapy: Overview
Financial Counseling
Functional Family Therapy
Infertility Counseling
Interfaith Marriage Counseling
Interracial Marriage Counseling
Marital Contract Therapy
Marriage Counseling
Marriage Enrichment
Mediation/Conciliation
Multiple Family Therapy
Multiple Impact Therapy
Premarital Counseling
Problem-Centered Family Systems
Psychoanalytic Family Therapy
Sex Therapy
Social Network Intervention
Strategic Therapy
Structural Family Therapy
Symbolic-Experiential Family
    Therapy
Therapeutic Community
Triadic-Based Family Therapy

Techniques

Abreaction
Abstinence, Therapeutic Rule of
Advice Giving
Alexander Technique
Automatic Writing
Auxiliary Chair Technique
Bibliotherapy
Catharsis
Cognitive Restructuring
Communication Skills Training
Concretizing Technique
Congruence
Contingency Contracting
Contracts, Therapeutic Use of
Cotherapy
Counterconditioning
Covert Modeling
Covert Sensitization
Detriangulation
Double Bind
Double Technique

Dreams, Therapeutic Use of
Electroencephalography
Empathy
Experiential Focusing
Family Choreography
Family Sculpture Technique
Free Association
Game Analysis
Gestalt Techniques
Homework in Psychotherapy
Humor
Imagery, Therapeutic Use of
Immediacy
Interpretation
Life Script
Lithium Therapy
Lobotomy
Mediation/Conciliation
Milieu Therapy
Mutual Storytelling Technique
Narcotherapy
Overcorrection
Paradoxical Intervention
Psychoanalysis: Technique
Psychosurgery
Quid pro Quo
Rational Disputation
Reframing Technique
Rehabilitation
Reinforcement, Self
Relaxation Training
Response Cost Contingency
Role Playing
Script Analysis
Self-Disclosure, Therapist
Self-Instruction
Self-Monitoring
Social Influence Therapy
Structural Analysis
Techniques of Christian
    Counseling
Telephone Therapy
Therapeutic Double Bind
Therapeutic Recreation
Thought Stopping
Time-out
Token Economy
Unconditional Positive Regard
Video Feedback in Therapy

Other

Alcoholics Anonymous
Communication Skills Training
Computer Applications in Mental
    Health
Conflict Management
Crisis Intervention
Exorcism
Faith Healing
Feminist Psychotherapy
Group Homes
Holistic Health and Therapy
Human Relations Training
Human Resource Training and
    Development
Inner Healing
Interview

Managed Care
Meditation
Moral Therapy
Mutual Help Groups
Paraprofessional Therapy
Prayer, Use of in Counseling
Scream Therapy

General Issues

Acting Out
Advice Giving
Biopsychosocial Rehabilitation
Burnout
Career Development and Guidance
Catharsis
Computer Applications in Mental
    Health
Confession
Confidentiality
Consultation and Referral
Counseling and Psychotherapy:
    Biblical Themes
Counseling and Psychotherapy:
    Overview
Counseling and Psychotherapy:
    Theological Themes
Countertransference
Cross-Cultural Therapy
Culture and Psychotherapy
Differential Diagnosis
Dix, Dorothea Lynde
Eclecticism in Psychotherapy
Fees for Psychotherapy
Flight into Health
Forgiveness
Holy Spirit, Role in Counseling
Insight in Psychotherapy
Insurance: Health and Mental
    Health
Law and Psychological Practice
Lay Counseling
Limit Setting in Psychotherapy
Malpractice
Managed Care
Moral and Ethical Issues in
    Treatment
Normalization in Human Services
Paraprofessional Therapy
Physical Contact in Therapy
Placebo Effects in Therapy
Prognosis
Psychic Healing
Psychosomatic Factors in Health
    and Illness
Psychosurgery
Psychotherapy, Effectiveness of
Record Keeping
Resistance in Psychotherapy
Screen Memory
Spiritual and Religious Issues in
    Therapy
Supervision in Psychotherapy
Training in Counseling and
    Psychotherapy
Transference
Unconditional Positive Regard
Values and Psychotherapy

Category Index

Abnormal Psychology. A branch of psychology that deals with mental illness, its classification, the theories to explain it, and the methods used for treating it. Abnormal psychology attempts to answer what abnormality means, how we know that someone is abnormal, how he or she became abnormal, and how we can change abnormal behavior. Undergraduate courses in abnormal psychology, given in most universities and colleges, are particularly useful for students who aim at pursuing careers as clinical psychologists, psychiatrists, psychiatric social workers, psychiatric nurses, and medical sociologists and anthropologists.

The Definition of Abnormality. Many definitions have been suggested for abnormality. The statistical definition considers behavior abnormal if it is infrequent or uncommon in the general population. Statistically abnormality is a deviation from the average. However, not all deviations from the average are regarded as abnormal (e.g., geniuses deviate from average intelligence); only deviations in an undesirable direction are abnormal, and social judgment is needed to determine the desirability of behavior. Abnormality may be defined as a violation of social norms, which are the standards and rules of behavior in society. Another definition considers behavior abnormal if it causes personal distress. Personal suffering and discomfort may be caused by depression and anxiety and therefore are regarded as abnormal. Abnormality is also defined in terms of disability and dysfunction when the individual is unable to achieve his or her goals and when there is occupational, social, and family maladjustment (e.g., phobias or alcoholism). One definition of abnormality that applies to severe pathology is lack of contact with reality: the person misperceives the environment (hearing voices) or misinterprets the social environment (thinking he or she is Jesus Christ or that the CIA is planning to kill him or her). In this case the person is considered psychotic or schizophrenic. Psychotic behavior is incomprehensive and irrational.

It appears that no single definition of abnormality applies to all types of mental illness because no general characteristic is shared by all abnormal behavior; believing that one is Jesus Christ, having social anxiety during social interactions, and having intrusive obsessive thoughts have nothing in common.

Theories of Abnormality. Historical Explanations. The ancients sometimes attributed mental illness to physical causes. For example, Egyptian and Greek physicians reported that hysteria which was characterized by physical symptoms (epileptic-like fits, pains, headaches, dizziness, paralysis, blindness) was caused by the movement of the uterus to other parts of the body.

Archaeologists have found skulls with characteristic holes, called trephines, that seem to have been chipped off by stone instruments. Trephining might have been performed to provide exit for the demons or evil spirits. To treat hysteria the priest or shaman might use aromatic substances to entice the wandering uterus to its proper place or drive it away from other parts of the body by unpleasant fumigations.

Another common explanation of madness was that evil spirits had possessed individuals and controlled their behavior. Some persons with religious or magical powers were believed to be able to free the individual from these spirits. The treatment of demonic possession used exorcism, a ritual by which the demons were expelled from the body. A priest or a shaman tried to communicate with the spirit, make it identify itself, and persuade it to leave its victim.

During the medieval era in Western Europe, epidemics of madness, such as dancing manias, involved hundreds of people who danced continuously until they were exhausted. Animal possession—for example, lycanthropy, in which a group of people believed that they were wolves—was also widespread.

In the history of humanity hospitals have been a relatively recent invention. Among the ancients the care of the mentally ill was left to the family, and violent patients were restrained.

During the Middle Ages, hospitals were started as religious institutions. One example is the Priory of St. Mary of Bethlehem, founded in London in 1243; it later became the notorious Bethlehem Hospital

(Bedlam), where patients were chained to the walls or kept on long leashes.

The fifteenth and sixteenth centuries saw the conversion of the leprosariums in Europe into mental institutions. From the sixteenth century mental hospitals changed from religious to social institutions to protect society and keep social order. The government rather than the church became responsible for the administration of mental institutions.

In the seventeenth and eighteenth centuries mental illness was conceived as the loss of reason, in contrast to the religious view of considering it as the loss of one's soul to the devil. This is the period when the inhumane treatment of the mentally ill and animalism became dominant. Animalism, the belief in a similarity between animals and mad people, led to the perception of the mentally ill as violent and dangerous, thus justifying the restraint and harsh treatment of patients. This Age of Reason may be contrasted with the era during which Christian brotherly love of the weak and poor contributed positively to the care of the mentally ill in monasteries.

In the second half of the eighteenth century Philippe Pinel reacted against cruelty to patients at La Bicêtre hospital in Paris and started humane treatment by unshackling patients. About the same period, what is now known as moral treatment had started on a religious basis in England. In 1796 William Tuke, a Quaker, established the York Retreat (the word *retreat* was used to avoid the stigma of labels such as *madhouse* or *insane asylum*), where kindness to patients and the value of work were emphasized. Modeled on the British experience, the Friends Asylum at Frankford, Pennsylvania, was established in 1817.

In the middle of the eighteenth century Franz Anton Mesmer suggested that diseases such as epilepsy and hysteria are caused by an imbalance of a magnetic fluid in the body. Illness, he believed, could be cured by restoring the balance of this fluid. Mesmerism continued to be practiced in Europe and the United States but later came to be known as hypnotism (*see* Hypnosis). Jean-Martin Charcot, a French neurologist during the nineteenth century, was a major figure in the study of hypnosis. While at La Salpetrière in Paris, he tried to distinguish hysteria from other neurological disorders by using hypnosis. If, for example, patients could move their paralyzed arm under hypnosis, they were diagnosed as having hysteria rather than a neurological disorder.

Biomedical Theory. Normality is considered to be health and abnormality, sickness. This perspective explains abnormality as a physical malfunction such as a chemical or an anatomical defect. It also uses medical terminology such as syndrome (symptoms occurring together), etiology (cause), and treatment.

The application of physical etiologies to abnormal behavior had been encouraged by both historical and contemporary events and discoveries. A large number of patients in mental institutions in the early 1900s had general paresis, which is charac-terized by grandiose ideas, loss of memory, and paralysis. In 1897 Krafft-Ebing found a link between syphilis and general paresis. This discovery supported the view that mental illness is caused by physical factors.

Genetic research also provided evidence that mental illness, not unlike physical illness, could be inherited. For example, many studies of twins from Europe, Japan, and the United States demonstrated that identical twins have a concordance (i.e., both are schizophrenic) rate of about 50%, while fraternal twins have a concordance of 10%. Since identical twins share the same genes, genetic factors seem to contribute to the development of and vulnerability to schizophrenia.

Research in the biochemistry of mental illness has also supported the biomedical theory. For example, evidence shows an excess of dopamine in the brain of some schizophrenic patients. Dopamine is a neurotransmitter, a chemical that transmits nerve impulses from one nerve cell to the next, and drugs that reduce the symptoms of schizophrenia also lower the amount of dopamine in the brain.

The biomedical perspective also considers neuroanatomical disorders of the brain in the etiology of mental illness. For example, evidence shows that abnormalities in the frontal lobes and brain ventricles as well as neuronal degeneration, particularly in the cortex, are detectable in some schizophrenic patients. Thus the evidence that mental illness is similar to physical illness comes from four sources: germs, genes, biochemical deficiency, and anatomical cerebral abnormalities.

Biomedical treatment consists of the use of antipsychotics, antidepressants, lithium, and antianxiety drugs. Many physical treatments such as electroconvulsive therapy, brain surgery, insulin shock, and cocktails of drugs were tried in treating schizophrenia. In the 1950s, however, Delay and Denker used a new antihistamine, chlorpromazine, that had been synthesized for hay fever. Patients who were given this drug became calm and lost their delusions. This initiative had started a revolution in psychiatry and the development of drugs called neuroleptics or psychotropics in the treatment of schizophrenia. However, these antipsychotic drugs produced side effects such as irregular heartbeat, low blood pressure, uncontrolled fidgeting, and rigidity of facial muscles. The worst side effect, tardive dyskinesia, such as involuntary sucking and smacking the lips, is caused by the effect of the drug on the brain's control of movement.

Antidepressant drug treatment was discovered by chance. A new drug, iproniazid—a monoamine oxidase inhibitor (MAO)—was tried on tubercular patients and was found to bring euphoria and to elevate patients' moods, relieving their depression. When iproniazid was to be found toxic and even lethal, it was replaced by milder antidepressants called tricyclics. The newest antidepressant, Prozac (fluoxetine), has similar effects but produces fewer side effects. The tricyclics, like the MAO inhibitors, can be lethal; some of their side effects are cardiac problems, mania, confusion, memory loss, and fatigue. Although Prozac produces less drowsiness, dry mouth, or sweating, it tends to cause more nausea, nervousness, and insomnia.

Lithium is used in the treatment of bipolar disorder. In 1947 Cade found that the urine of his manic patients made guinea pigs twitch, shiver violently, and die. But when the guinea pigs were injected with lithium, they became calm and survived. Cade then found that lithium is effective in treating manic patients. Lithium has a marked effect on the manic episodes of the majority of patients. However, its use has to be monitored, since it is potentially toxic and can be lethal.

An antianxiety drug, Miltown (meprobamate), had been used in the mid-1950s to treat anxiety. Librium (chlordiazepoxide) replaced Miltown and became the most frequently used drug until it was replaced by Valium (diazepam). These drugs do not have as strong side effects as antipsychotics or antidepressants. However, unlike the other drugs, antianxiety drugs may be addictive, and their potency tends to decrease the longer they are used. In all psychiatric drug treatments, symptoms return when patients stop taking medication.

Psychoanalytical Theory. The father of psychoanalytical theory is Sigmund Freud, whose theory of abnormality is concerned with conscious or unconscious psychological forces that affect the mind. These forces are often in conflict with each other, and unless the conflicts are resolved they will result in abnormal behavior. Three topics, the development of personality, the structure of personality, and psychoanalysis, are important components of psychoanalytical theory.

In the development of personality people pass through five psychosexual stages from birth to maturity. Freudians use the term *sexuality* to describe not only adult sexual character but also a sexual energy that exists at birth (*libido*, the Latin word for desire or lust) and is associated with many pleasurable activities, including feeding in infancy. At the oral stage (to age 2) the mouth and feeding are the source of satisfaction. At the anal stage (ages 2–4) the anal region and toilet training become the focus of attention. At the phallic stage (ages 3–6) stimulation of the genitals is the source of pleasure. This stage is associated with intense sexual rivalry with the parent of the same sex for the love of the parent of the opposite sex. This conflict is called the oedipus complex (from the Greek tragedy of Oedipus, who unknowingly killed his father and married his mother). Children normally resolve this conflict by identifying with the same-sex parent and obtain sexual satisfaction through marriage. Children become asexual (i.e., not interested in sex) during the latency stage (ages 6–12), which leads to the genital stage and adult heterosexual maturity.

According to Freud, personality has three components: the id, which is controlled by the pleasure principle and aims to achieve immediate biological needs; the ego, which is guided by the reality principle that enables the individual to achieve acceptable goals; and the superego, which represents the ideals of society and directs behavior toward morality and religion. Both the id and the superego put continuous pressure on the ego to achieve their goals. The ego has to protect itself by using defense mechanisms: Repression is used by the ego to push impulses (sexual, aggressive) into the unconscious, so that the person becomes unaware of them; projection attributes one's own impulses or desires to others because they are not acceptable to the superego (I hate you is changed into you hate me); reaction formation converts one's impulses into their opposite (I hate you is changed into I love you); regression is to return to behavior of an earlier age (temper tantrums); rationalization is inventing reasons for behavior and ignoring the real ones; displacement is transferring unacceptable emotions from one target to another (father beats son, son beats the cat); identification is to incorporate the characteristics and behavior of others (a child walks, talks, and thinks like his father).

As a method of treatment psychoanalysis aims at reducing repression, making the patient conscious of early childhood experience. In order to lift repression, analysts use free association, dream analysis, and analysis of defenses. In free association patients lie comfortably on a couch and are asked to say whatever comes to mind. In dream analysis it is assumed that sleep weakens ego defenses that repress threatening and unacceptable material. During dreaming, such material becomes distorted and appears in a symbolic form; for example, a woman concerned with sexual advances may dream of being attacked by savages with spears (spears are a phallic symbol). The analyst interprets the behavior and verbalization of the patient, so that a woman's concern with the appearance of her nose may be interpreted as a manifestation of penis envy. It is hoped that during analysis the patient reaches a stage of transference in which attitudes and emotions toward significant others (parent or spouse) are directed toward the analysis. This process will end with catharsis (reliving previously experienced emotions) and the disappearance of symptoms.

Behavioral and Cognitive Theories. The behavioral or learning perspective is based on experimental laboratory studies and measurement. Its emphasis is on behavior and environmental influences. Three approaches to learning have become popular during the second half of the twentieth century: classical conditioning, which is identified with Ivan Pavlov (*see* Conditioning, Classical); operant conditioning, with B. F. Skinner (*see* Conditioning, Operant); and Modeling or observational learning, with Albert Bandura.

Pavlov was a physiologist interested in the process of digestion and in the study of salivation. He had serendipitously found that dogs not only salivated when food was put in their mouths but also responded to its sight and smell and the footsteps of the attendant who brought the food to them. He started a laboratory experiment in which the sound of a bell, which does not initially elicit salivation, was associated with meat powder he put in the mouths of the dogs. He called the meat powder the conditioned stimulus and the salivation the unconditioned response. When he later sounded the bell alone (conditioned stimulus, or CS), it elicited salivation (conditioned response, or CR). This procedure became known as classical conditioning.

In 1920 Watson and Rayner applied classical conditioning by developing rat phobia in an 11-month-old boy. Initially the boy was fond of the rat and played with it. In the study Watson and Rayner banged an iron bar with a hammer whenever the boy reached for the rat. The association of banging (unconditioned stimulus, or UCS) of the iron bar with the rat (CS) resulted in fear (CR) of the rat. This experiment became the basis of explaining the development of phobias and other abnormal responses in terms of classical conditioning.

Operant conditioning deals with motor and verbal responses. The basic principle of operant conditioning is that the frequency of these responses increases when they are followed by reinforcement and decreases (is extinguished) when reinforcement is withdrawn. Operant conditioning has been often used in the behavior modification of children and the rehabilitation of chronic schizophrenics.

Learning can be achieved by observing others (modeling). We learn to avoid dangerous animals by observing them harming others. We also can learn vicariously (indirectly) by verbal instructions (written or spoken); for example, many children's fears are learned this way (fear of darkness, animals, and strangers).

Behavior therapy relies on several methods. In counterconditioning fears can be eliminated by associating the feared stimulus with another one that is pleasant. For example, a boy's fear of rabbits was eliminated by associating the rabbit with food.

Systematic desensitization is another technique based on the principle of reciprocal inhibition, which states that when there are two incompatible responses, the stronger one inhibits the weaker one. Relaxation is incompatible with anxiety, for one cannot be relaxed and anxious at the same time. Therefore, those who have fears and anxieties are first trained to relax. With the help of the therapist, patients are asked to compile a list of fearful objects and situations, including the object of their phobia, and then to arrange the contents of this list from those least anxiety-arousing to those most anxiety-arousing. In order to desensitize the patients, they are asked to relax and then imagine these situations, starting with the least anxiety-arousing stimuli.

In modeling the patient is asked to observe a fearless model. For example, in the case of snake phobia, the model handles snakes without showing fear or anxiety. In extinction the treatment consists of with-drawing reinforcement from unwanted behavior; for example, withdrawing attention from a baby during a tantrum.

Another method used to activate schizophrenic patients in hospital wards is called token economy. Patients are given a specified number of tokens when they carry out certain behaviors in the hospital ward (make their beds, clean their rooms). These tokens can later be exchanged with a variety of reinforcement. In contrast, aversive conditioning is used to eliminate abnormal behavior. An attractive stimulus or behavior is paired with an unpleasant stimulus. Drinking, for example, is associated with an electric shock.

Cognition refers to mental functions involved in processing information in the environment such as perception, recognition, conceiving, judging, and reasoning. Cognitive psychologists emphasize thoughts, beliefs, expectations, and memories that mediate behavior. They consider irrational beliefs to be the cause of abnormal behavior. Beck suggested logical errors that are related to abnormalities: arbitrary inference, when a conclusion is reached contrary to evidence or with no evidence at all (a frown on the face of a stranger may lead to the conclusion that the stranger is disgusted with the patient and therefore she becomes depressed); overgeneralization, when the patients make unjustified generalizations based on a single incident (after one failure patients may believe that they will never succeed again, or after a single dog attack patients may believe that all dogs are dangerous); magnification, when the meaning and significance of an event is exaggerated (an unpleasant body sensation is considered a sign of fatal disease).

Cognitive therapy emphasizes how patients perceive, label, and view their problem and the meaning they assign to it. The patients' feelings and emotions are considered to be the result of these cognitive processes. Both Beck and Albert Ellis, who pioneered cognitive therapy, suggested that patients' problems are the result of irrational views of reality and that patients should be helped to see the illogical way in which they distort reality. Therapy should result in replacing rational with irrational beliefs. For example, a woman who believes that she should be loved by everybody is frustrated by her failure to please everybody and consequently becomes depressed. In therapy such a belief is substituted with the belief that many people love the patient and that she cannot please everybody. Cognitive therapy is particularly useful in the treatment of depression.

Psychological Assessment. Psychologists use different procedures to understand people and diagnose their abnormal behavior. The procedures used have to be reliable; they must be stable and give the same results on repeated use. They must also be valid; that is, they should be useful for the purpose for which they were intended (in this case, to help solve the patient's problems or treat the illness). Psychological assessment may take the form of clinical interview, in which the clinician meets and talks with the patient. In an unstructured interview both the psychologist or the psychiatrist and the clients are free to raise any topic they like. In a structured interview the interviewer has prepared a specific interview schedule.

A second method of assessment is by psychological testing. Some tests, such as the draw-a-person test or the Rorschach test, are unstructured or projective. Others take the form of structured psychological inventories: the Minnesota Multiphasic Personality Inventory, or MMPI, whose 550 items assess a wide range of normal or abnormal characteristics, and various intelligence tests. A third method of assessment is through behavioral observation.

In behavioral assessment therapists may keep records of the behavior to be modified. The clients may also record their own behavior and report it to the therapist. In psychophysiological measurements psychophysiologists assess physiological reactions such as heart rate, muscle tension, blood flow in various parts of the body, and brain waves while subjects are experiencing certain emotions (depression, fear) or are carrying out certain activities. In neurological measurements the neuropsychologist assesses how certain brain dysfunctions affect thought, emotion, and behavior. One well-known group of neurological tests is the Halstead-Reiten Test Battery, which is used to diagnose brain damage and locate the area that has been affected.

Additional Readings

American Psychiatric Association. (1994). *Diagnostic and statistical manual of mental disorders* (4th ed.). Washington, DC: Author.

Barlow, D. H., & Durand, V. M. (1995). *Abnormal psychology: An integrative approach*. Pacific Grove, CA: Brooks/Cole.

Davison, G. C., & Neale, J. M. (1996). *Abnormal psychology* (Rev. 6th ed.). New York: Wiley.

Rosenhan, D. L., & Seligman, M. E. P. (1995). *Abnormal psychology* (3rd ed.). New York: Norton.

Sue, D., Sue, D., & Sue, A. (1994). *Understanding abnormal behavior* (4th ed.). Boston: Houghton Mifflin.

I. AL-ISSA

See MENTAL ILLNESS, MODELS OF; PSYCHOPATHOLOGY IN PRIMITIVE CULTURES; PSYCHOLOGY, HISTORY OF; CLASSIFICATION OF MENTAL DISORDERS.

Abortion. *See* POSTABORTION COUNSELING.

Abortion Counseling. *See* POSTABORTION COUNSELING.

Abraham, Karl (1877–1925). Pioneer German psychoanalyst and founder of the Berlin Society of Psychoanalysis (1908). Abraham was born in Bremen into a well-established and highly cultured Jewish family. His father gave up being a teacher of Hebrew religion for economic reasons, and Karl early abandoned the Jewish faith. His writings reflect no interest in religion, this being in marked contrast to his friend and mentor, Sigmund Freud.

Following the standard German preparatory education Abraham received his medical degree from the University of Freiburg in 1901. Thereafter he became deeply interested in philology and linguistics, and he learned to speak five languages, read several others, and even analyzed some patients in English.

Abraham's first position was at Burgholzi Mental Hospital in Zurich. He became assistant to Eugen Bleuler and studied with Carl Gustav Jung, who in 1907 introduced him to Freud. In that same year Abraham published his first paper, which began with the phrase "according to Freud." It was a prophetic beginning. Abraham, among all Freud's disciples, never deviated either from personal loyalty to Freud or from the classical principles of psychoanalysis. However, he was soon alienated by Jung's personality and by what he saw as Jung's threats to the scientific status of psychoanalysis. Despite Freud's pleadings the two men were never reconciled, and Abraham soon left Zurich to establish a practice in Berlin. This practice flourished, and among his analysands were several who became respected analysts, including Karen Horney, Sandor Rado, Helene Deutsch, Melanie Klein, and two American physicians, James Glover and Edward Glover. Thus Abraham brought to the fledgling psychoanalytic movement considerable prestige, and his contributions have lasted far beyond his own brief lifetime.

Abraham's total literary output was fewer than 700 pages, consisting of 4 short books and 49 papers, all but 8 of which dealt with the theory and practice of psychoanalysis. Nevertheless, he made important contributions to the psychology of sexuality, character development, myths, dreams, symbolism, and folk psychology. His most important theoretical contribution was his delineation of the etiology and dynamics of bipolar disorder.

Q. R. DE YOUNG

Abreaction. A psychotherapeutic process wherein previously repressed feelings are brought to conscious awareness and given expression. These feelings are usually associated with past traumatic experiences. Their expression, therefore, is usually accompanied by considerable emotional discharge. Getting rid of these pent-up emotions may provide the patient with insight into the causes of unrealistic or immature behavior and allow these behaviors to be modified or eliminated.

Reliving the repressed experiences is sometimes aided by hypnosis or by drugs such as sodium amytal (*see* Narcotherapy). Specialized techniques in Gestalt therapy, primal therapy, and psychodrama are also often useful in achieving abreaction.

The method used to bring about abreaction is called catharsis. Abreaction refers to the end result. Abreaction and catharsis are, however, often used synonymously.

G. A. JOHNSTON

See CATHARSIS; EMOTION.

Abstinence, Sexual. Contrary to popular opinion, refraining from sexual activity is not psychologically harmful. Sexual energy can be strong, but its expression is not essential for maintaining physical or emotional health.

Sexual abstinence is the only foolproof way to avoid both unwanted pregnancies and sexually transmitted diseases (STDs). However, trying to force abstinence on sexually active persons for these reasons will almost certainly fail.

Sexual abstinence is not normative for human beings. For most people sexual partnership and family life are the best choices. Although sexual abstinence can be a healthy way of life for spiritual reasons, some motives for it are faulty.

Various fears of or repugnance for sexuality lead to abstinence in some people. Such sexual abstinence is usually not psychologically healthy. All who practice abstinence out of such motives are best served by counseling that will relieve their misperceptions or troubled emotions.

Some people refrain from sex out of fear of the opposite sex. Some have been abused as children and shun sexuality because it brings up painful emotions that have not been adequately processed. Others refrain because of fear of disease or pregnancy. People with excessively puritanical upbringing may equate sexuality with evil or dirtiness. Their disinclination to sexual activity is also not healthy.

Some people choose sexual abstinence for moral reasons. Those who consider all sexual activity outside of marriage sinful usually try to practice abstinence. Most often this is temporary until they marry. Those who remain unmarried but consider abstinence the moral choice may have periods of great conflict over their desires.

Moral demands sometimes make sexual expression within marriage problematic. Sometimes sexual activity during pregnancy is contraindicated. For health reasons women ought to refrain from sexual activity for some weeks after giving birth. Those who consider contraception immoral must practice periodic abstinence to avoid inopportune pregnancies. Known carriers of sexually transmitted diseases may need to be abstinent out of consideration for a disease-free spouse.

Choosing sexual abstinence as a lifelong option for spiritual reasons holds a venerable place in many world religions. When the motive is to have more time either for spiritual practice or to serve other people, it can be a positive and life-fulfilling choice.

Monasteries and convents have long existed for those who retire from worldly activity to live lives of prayer. Some develop deep concern for and sensitivity to the suffering in the world and live truly self-sacrificial lives in prayer for others. Some sisterhoods and brotherhoods that practice sexual abstinence are devoted to missions of special service to others, such as teaching or nursing. Freedom from family responsibilities makes one's entire life available for a chosen service.

While failing to relieve sexual tension is not harmful, dishonesty with oneself about sexual feelings and urges can be. People unable to recognize their sexual urges may be pushed to act upon them without realizing what is moving them until they pass the point of stopping. Some who try to stay sexually abstinent by distorting awareness of their urges fail; they may resort to abusive or hidden ways of relieving sexual tensions.

Abstinence is easiest when motives for it are appropriate and one is in touch with what one is feeling. Those practicing either permanent or temporary abstinence for wholesome motives must be honest with themselves about sexual feelings and attractions if they are to be healthily abstinent.

M. J. MEADOW

See SEXUALITY; CELIBACY; POSTABORTION COUNSELING; PREMARITAL COUNSELING.

Abstinence, Therapeutic Rule of. Therapeutic abstinence is activity of the therapist's carefully refraining from meeting the unconscious infantile emotional demands of patients, thus allowing patients to project their own feelings upon the therapist. Abstinence is central to the process of psychoanalytic technique, but it is used in some form in all systems of therapy.

When people submit themselves to the care of a psychotherapist, they come to the therapeutic setting with mixed feelings. Patients seemingly come to therapy seeking to be cured or improved, but generally they are full of shame, desperately afraid of being discovered, and afraid of change. Therapy patients both want to change and want not to change. Patients consciously will ask for advice and seek to change, but unconsciously they wish to avoid personal change and wish for the world to change to accommodate their unrealistic expectations and fantasies. Unconsciously or consciously patients will seek to have the therapist meet these unrealistic desires and thus protect these desires from the onslaught of reality. The psychoanalytic approach proposes that the therapist refrain from meeting these emotional demands but help patients to understand them and have an unencumbered opportunity to see the unrealistic nature of these desires.

The strictest application of the rule of abstinence results in the analyst not responding to (gratifying) any of the patient's attempts to relate socially. Thus Brenner (1976) advises against shaking hands or engaging in social conversation or other social amenities within therapy. Colby (1951) moderates this absolute rule by saying that the therapist is a person as well as a therapist and that rigid attempts to avoid social and practical interaction with the patient artificially induce feelings of rejection rather than bring them to the surface. Colby agrees, however, that there is a temptation for the therapist to be seduced by patient's personal interest in them. While the patient's seducing includes sexuality, it is not exclusively sexual. More often patients want the therapist to agree with them and seek this agreement by covert seduction and overt asking for approval. Experts disagree as to how to deal with patients' questions; some (e.g., Greenson, 1967) believe that all questions are rhetorical and hence seductive, while others (e.g., Glickauf-Hughes & Chance, 1995) suggest that the therapist carefully differentiate among patients' questions, answering those that are practical in nature. The therapist's own narcissistic needs, including the need to be seen as kind, reasonable, and beneficent, often make it difficult to resist such attempts to enter into a neurotic alliance rather than a therapeutic alliance with patients.

References

Brenner, C. (1976). *Psychoanalytic technique and psychic conflict.* New York: International Universities Press.

Colby, K. M. (1951). *A primer for psychotherapists.* New York: Ronald.

Glickauf-Hughes, C., & Chance, S. (1995). Answering clients' questions. *Psychotherapy, 32* (3), 375–380.

Greenson, R. (1967). *The technique and practice of psychoanalysis* (Vol. 1). Madison, CT: International Universities Press.

R. B. JOHNSON

See PSYCHOANALYSIS: TECHNIQUE; PSYCHOANALYSIS: THEORY; PSYCHOANALYTIC PSYCHOTHERAPY.

Abuse and Neglect. Child maltreatment is any interaction or lack of interaction between a child and a caregiver that results in nonaccidental harm to the child's physical and developmental state. Maltreatment can be divided further into physical and sexual abuse, physical neglect, and emotional maltreatment.

Physical abuse is characterized by use of force or aggression in discrete episodes, often accompanied by parental anger.

Physical neglect is the lack of adequate nurturing experiences, as evidenced by inadequate hygiene, nutrition, educational opportunities, medical care, or supervision. The definition of neglect is subjective in that it involves varying community standards regarding what is essential for a child's well-being and future development.

Sexual abuse includes interactions with an adult in which the child is being used for the sexual stimulation of an adult (the focus here will be upon nonfamilial sexual abuse; incest is described in a separate entry).

Emotional maltreatment covers verbal or nonverbal interactions (e.g., rejection) that negatively impact a child's developmental needs and frequently occurs coincident with other forms of maltreatment.

In addition to clinical definitions, legal statutes are important. All 50 United States have three sets of laws regarding maltreatment: reporting laws specifying who and what must be reported; civil codes regarding placement decisions; and criminal codes defining criminal maltreatment.

Professionals are mandated to report suspected maltreatment. Reporting laws focus on the observable consequences of maltreatment as opposed to making judgments regarding parental intent. However, because great variability exists in the phrasing of these laws, one should consult local statutes for precise definitions and provisions regarding the need to report maltreatment.

In addition clinicians should acquire skills to recognize signs of child abuse, discuss ambiguous cases with colleagues, and establish relationships with local child protective service agencies.

When one is required to report abuse, it is important to maintain the therapeutic relationship with the family by continuing to engage them in treatment and by assisting them through the investigations. While legal statutes define discrete categories based upon the nature of the act and observable consequences, it may be most useful for the clinician to view maltreatment on a continuum of caretaking practices ranging from competent and loving care to abuse.

Scope of the Problem. Although the actual incidence and prevalence of maltreatment are difficult to state definitively, abuse is clearly a critical social problem. Reports of suspected abuse and neglect have been increasing yearly, and abuse-related deaths are now a leading cause of child mortality. Data from reported cases indicate that 1% to 5% of children in the United States have been maltreated, indicating that well over one million children are maltreated each year (Cicchetti & Carlson, 1989). The vast majority of incidents (up to 90%) occur in the child's home. Since these figures represent only reported cases, the actual incidence is likely higher.

Historical Perspective. Although recent evidence indicates that child maltreatment is increasing, from a broader historical perspective there has been marked improvement in the treatment of children. The Bible alludes to infanticide (e.g., Matt. 2:16) and the ritual sacrifice of children (Josh. 6:26; 1 Kings 16:34; 2 Chron. 28:3), which continued in practice into the Middle Ages. Sexual exploitation of children was a part of ancient religious ceremonies and initiation rights.

However, child advocacy has a long history as well. Jewish, Christian, and Muslim doctrines command against infanticide. Beginning in the early centuries a.d., government (e.g., Empress Faustina) and church (e.g., Council of Nicea) established orphanages and asylums for children who were abandoned.

In modern times the first recorded case of prosecution of child abuse led to the Protective Services Act and the Cruelty to Children Act in New York State and the founding of the Society for the Prevention of Cruelty to Children in the 1870s.

However, substantial further advances did not occur until the middle of the twentieth century, when medical doctors began suspecting intentional maltreatment of children. The professional literature expanded when Kempe and his colleagues (Kempe, Silverman, Steele, Droegemueller, & Silver, 1962) first described the battered child syndrome. In 1974 the federal government enacted the Child Abuse Prevention and Treatment Act, which served as a catalyst to expand research and intervention efforts.

Correlates of Maltreatment. Three specific categories of characteristics have been related to the occurrence of maltreatment: caretaker variables, child variables, and sociocultural variables. Each of these influences the occurrence of maltreatment as background contributors to pervasive maltreatment as well as contributes to discrete incidents of maltreatment. Furthermore, these factors interact with each other to result in an episode of maltreatment.

Physical Abuse. In abusive families the primary contributors to maltreatment appear to be parental characteristics and adverse social circumstances, with child characteristics playing a secondary role. The immediate caregiver factors related to abuse include the need for control and ineffective discipline. The background factors that are related to the occurrence of abuse include personality or emotional problems (e.g., low tolerance for frustration, impulsiveness, rigidity, depression, compulsiveness), knowledge deficits (e.g., inappropriate strategies of discipline, poor coping skills, and unrealistic expectations of the child), errors in perception (e.g., misattributions about the child's behavior), and other personal problems (e.g., substance abuse, poor health). A caregiver's own developmental history (e.g., having experienced abuse) is a potential antecedent to aberrant child-rearing practices, though many individuals who were maltreated as children parent competently. Parents who are young and single are at increased risk for abusing due to social isolation, economic deprivation, and stress secondary to rearing children without consistent help.

Three types of children are at increased risk for abuse: those with physical or psychological disorders (e.g., congenital anomalies, mental retardation); those with difficult temperaments (e.g., irritable, impulsive, hyperactive); and those who are identified with a hated person or situation (e.g., ex-spouse, unwanted pregnancy, stepchild). The child's immediate contribution to an abuse episode is commonly noncompliance or impulsive behavior. Demographic data suggest that children under the age of four and in large families are at increased risk for abuse.

Socioeconomic status (SES) is the primary sociocultural variable related to abuse. Stress factors related to SES, such as poverty, crowding, frequent moves, unemployment, and unavailability of day care, contribute to caretakers being less patient, sensitive, and resourceful in responding to their children. While lower SES increases the risk of abuse, abuse occurs in all strata of society. The immediate social factor that precipitates a discrete incident of abuse is often a stressful event, which, in the context of a difficult child and few parental coping resources, results in a violent response. A culture that tolerates increasing levels of violence (e.g., corporal punishment in schools, violence in the media) is likely to have a permissive effect on child-abuse occurrences.

Physical Neglect. Physical neglect has less direct impact on a child and is more difficult to detect than physical abuse is, but its effects are significant and can be lethal because of its pervasive, enduring nature. Neglect typically involves a poor, socially isolated, and chaotic family in which the immediate needs for survival preoccupy the family to an extent that the child's basic care—food, clothes, shelter, and medical care—is not provided.

Caregiver characteristics implicated in neglect include personality disorders, inadequate knowledge of development, chronic patterns of social isolation, and deviant subcultural identification. Sociocultural characteristics include poverty, larger multiproblem families, poor housing and living conditions, and low education and employment levels. While middle- and upper-class families may maltreat in other ways, they tend to have enough resources to prevent the neglect that occurs primarily in lower-income families.

Sexual Abuse. Finkelhor (1984) has summarized conditions that predispose toward molestation perpetrated by a nonfamily member. First, there must be the motivation to abuse. This can arise from a perpetrator's arrested emotional development, need to control others, unconscious reenactment of childhood trauma, or misattention to arousal cues, and social factors such as masculine requirements to be dominant or to sexualize emotional needs. Second, one must overcome internal inhibitions. This can follow from a perpetrator's problems with controlling impulses, senility, or psychosis, and social factors such as child pornography, weak criminal sanctions, or tolerance of deviance while intoxicated. Third, external inhibitors must be overcome. This can occur through lack of supervision of children or poor social support. Finally, the child's resistance must be overcome. This can occur with children who are emotionally insecure or deprived or who are not taught about sexual abuse.

Sequelae to Maltreatment. Maltreated children are at greater risk of developing emotional and behavioral problems because their social, emotional, and cognitive development is interrupted or inadequately facilitated. The impact of maltreatment is influenced by its duration, frequency, and severity, age of onset and termination, the perpetrator's gender and relationship to the child, and the presence of multiple forms of maltreatment.

Physically abused children have lower academic achievement and show the immediate consequences of physical injury, aggressiveness, and psychological problems such as hopelessness, depression, and low self-worth. As adolescents and adults these children show increased levels of violence that threaten any possibility of forming healthy relationships. Substance abuse, self-injurious or suicidal behavior, and depression are also common sequelae, while cognitive ability, the absence of brain trauma, and family strengths moderate the long-term impact of abuse.

Physically neglected children have shown immediate consequences of withdrawal, depression, lower intellectual functioning, and behavior problems. Long-term consequences include difficulties with attachment and developing relationships, as well as mastery of other developmental tasks. These children grow up socially isolated, stressed, and at risk for seeking out deviant peer groups.

Sexually abused children have shown immediate consequences of passivity and compliance, anger and aggression, mistrust, and hypersexualized behavior. Consequences can be greatly impacted by the reaction of parents and legal proceedings upon disclosure of the abuse. Long-term consequences include problems in three major areas: emotional reactions and self-perceptions (e.g., depression, self-injury, anxiety, low self-esteem); interpersonal relating and sexuality (e.g., social isolation, difficulty with trusting others, indiscriminate attachments); and social functioning (e.g., substance abuse, prostitution).

Intervention. The first intervention in child maltreatment is generally a report to the child protective services system. Many of the factors that predispose individuals to parenting problems are increased as a result of being identified as having maltreated a child (e.g., self-esteem is lowered, isolation is increased), a fact that makes remediation even more difficult. It is critical that the services to support children and families be commensurate with the stress that charges, inquiries, and labeling will inevitably bring. The present system, however, is designed primarily for protection rather than assistance.

Primary prevention efforts to decrease the risk of maltreatment would be most effective if begun prenatally. The provision of adequate health care, parenting information, community resources, and assistance in developing healthy social support would decrease risk of maltreatment. Services must be presented in a manner that is culturally sensitive, nonthreatening, and consistent with the stated needs of these families. Social support provides feedback to parents about their parenting, clarifies expectations about children, and helps with concrete tasks (e.g., outside contacts provide respite from continual interaction that may fuel impulsive, abusive behavior). Support also enables parents to control impulses through meeting their emotional needs and thus allowing appropriate attention to their children.

Intervention following the identification of maltreatment usually means removal of the child from the parents and placement in a children's home or foster care. Children tend to improve emotionally and behaviorally, but the solution is temporary and costly. When to return the children is a vexing problem. Recent efforts have focused on maintaining the child in the home. First, economic assistance and linkages to social services are necessary to help the family utilize other treatments most effectively. Next, intensive therapeutic and support services utilize an intensive, case-manager approach that allows access to many sources of economic and educational support, with the continued option of out-of-home placement for limited progress. Components of these approaches include group therapy and support groups (e.g., Parents Anonymous), home visitation, and parent education. Home visits provide parental support and instruction in child management and stimulation, leading to improved child-rearing skills and adjustment in parents when the intervention is sufficiently prolonged (one to three years) and a sound therapeutic alliance is formed with the parent. Group education impacts parental knowledge and attitudes, especially when a broad scope of material (e.g., child development, anger management), which includes information specific to the stress in parents' lives, is presented.

With some environmental stabilization, traditional psychotherapies can have an effect. There are inherent difficulties in initiating therapy with families who have maltreated their children. However, efforts should be made to address individual caregiver problems and family system problems. Individual therapy should address general emotional disturbance and specific issues of caregivers who were abused as children. Referrals for treatment of substance abuse may be indicated. Family therapy is an important intervention not only for improving parent-child relationships but also for addressing problems of marital discord or spousal abuse. Assisting parents in relating to their children in appropriately nurturing ways can decrease children's opposition, which is often fueled by their non-nurturant experiences with parents. Finally, teaching the child to adhere to rules and develop self-control would decrease the risk of abuse.

Therapists who consider the Christian viewpoint must be clear about their role: to protect the child, to preserve the family, and to promote the healthy growth of each of the individuals within the family. When working with Christian families whose primary discipline is to not spare the rod (Prov. 13:24), encouraging a broader understanding of the biblical teaching on child guidance and nurturing (Prov. 19:18, 22:6, 29:17; Eph. 6:4) as well as explaining the benefits of nurturing relationships for each family member's growth may be useful.

References

Cicchetti, D., & Carlson, V. (1989). *Child maltreatment: Theory and research on the causes and consequences of child abuse and neglect.* New York: Cambridge.

Finkelhor, D. (1984). *Child sexual abuse: New theories and research.* New York: Free Press.

Kempe, H. C., Silverman, F. N., Steele, B. F., Droegemueller, W., & Silver, H. K. (1962). The battered child syndrome. *Journal of the American Medical Association, 181,* 4–11.

Additional Reading

Walker, C. E., Bonner, B. L., & Kaufman, K. L. (1988). *The physically and sexually abused child: Evaluation and treatment.* New York: Pergamon.

F. J. MONCHER AND A. JOSEPHSON

See INCEST; TRAUMA; DOMESTIC VIOLENCE; CHILD ABUSE.

Abuse, Child. *See* ABUSE AND NEGLECT.

Abuse, Spouse. *See* ABUSE AND NEGLECT.

Academy of Religion and Mental Health (ARMH). The National Academy of Religion and Mental Health was chartered in Pennsylvania on 14 July 1954. In 1957 the designation *National* was dropped. George Christian Anderson, an Episcopal clergyman, founded ARMH to provide educational opportunities to clergy of all faiths on the relationship between medicine and religion and to educate physicians, social scientists, and psychiatrists on the dynamics of religion. A second purpose was to establish ecumenical programs on religion and mental health in cooperation with medical and social scientists. Student fellowships were also offered. ARMH emphasized local chapter meetings and published a monthly *Academy Reporter* (after 1972, the *Institutes Reporter*). By 1967 members totaled 3,200 and represented 35 countries.

An early grant from the National Institute of Mental Health (NIMH) funded a five-year ARMH project on clergy education at three universities: Loyola/Chicago (Roman Catholic), Harvard (Protestant), and Yeshiva (Jewish). Funded by the Josiah Macy, Jr., Foundation, ARMH sponsored a symposium series on philosophical issues related to religion and health. Proceedings of these symposia were published by ARMH, Fordham University, and New York University. These volumes include *Religion, Science, and Mental Health* (1959), *Religion in the Developing Personality* (1960), *Religion, Culture and Mental Health* (1961), *The Place of Value Systems in Medical Education* (1961), *Research in Religion and Health: Selected Projects and Methods* (1963), *Moral Values in Psychoanalysis* (1963), *Today's Youth and Moral Values* (1969), Meissner's *Annotated Bibliography in Religion and Psychology* (1961), and Bier's *Psychological Testing for Ministerial Selection* (1970).

In the 1960s ARMH became increasingly professional in both organization and activities. It sponsored "Conversations in Medical Ethics" for Philadelphia's 2,500 medical students, helped set up a number of Community Mental Health centers, consulted with the World Council of Churches in planning its 1964 Geneva meeting of psychiatrists and clergy, helped plan the Institute of Religion and Medicine in London, and conducted workshops for United States army chaplains at 25 posts. Charles E. Bergman, executive secretary, presided over the 1972 merger of ARMH with the American Foundation of Religion and Psychiatry and its Blanton-Peale Graduate Institute. The *Journal of Religion and Health (JRH)* was launched in 1961, and through 1993 it was edited by Harry C. Meserve. *JRH* is now published by Human Sciences Press, with Ann Belford Ulanov and Barry Ulanov assuming the editorial role in 1994.

Additional Readings

Anderson, G. C. (1967). The Academy's development program. *Journal of Religion and Health, 6,* 259–268.
Appel, K. E. (1965). Academy of Religion and Mental Health: Past and future. *Journal of Religion and Health, 4,* 207–216.
Tompkins, H. J. (1961). Present and future. *Journal of Religion and Health, 1,* 68–77.

H. VANDE KEMP

Acalculia. A learning or language disturbance in which the person cannot perform arithmetic operations. This inability to calculate mathematically is the result of a loss of capacity for numerical ideation, often associated with brain injury or disease. Of three types of acalculia, two are associated with speech and verbalization disturbances. One type involves the loss of previous ability to grasp the meaning of symbols or to write numbers and figures. A second type is anarithmia, a disturbance in the actual performance of arithmetic operations. A third type involves the inability to spatially organize numbers, so that the person cannot read or understand what is read. Acalculia is found in persons with brain lesions. It is also associated with spatial dyslexia, spatial agnosia, sensorikinetic apraxia, somatospatial apractognosia, and some oculomotor disorders.

D. L. SCHUURMAN

See LEARNING DISABILITY.

Acculturation. *Theoretical Roots.* In the mid-1930s, the Social Science Research Council appointed a subcommittee on acculturation composed primarily of scholars in the field of anthropology. These scholars were charged with the task of defining and examining the dimensions of this concept (Olmedo, 1979). The subcommittee, composed of Redfield, Linton, and Herskovitz (1936), came to define acculturation as "a phenomenon which result when groups of individuals having different cultures come into continuous first hand contact with subsequent changes in the original pattern of either or both groups" (cited in Olmedo, 1979).

Since then, most research on acculturation has been done from an anthropological perspective. The primary focus was on the study of acculturation of Third-World countries to industrialized Western societies. In the United States, most of the early research emphasized the process of acculturation of

Native Americans to European culture. Acculturation research with other ethnic groups was done by sociologists who were primarily interested in examining issues of minority or race relations (Olmedo, 1979).

In the mid-1960s and early 1970s, psychologists began to study the concept of acculturation in their search for better methods of equipping clinicians for the task of cross-cultural psychotherapy. Acculturation within this framework was defined as a series of changes of intrapsychic mechanisms such as changes in perceptions, attitudes, and cognitive processes of the individual (cited in Olmedo, 1979). This perspective has yielded the current emphasis on the area of "ethnic identity development."

Marin (1992, 236), for instance, defines acculturation as "a process of attitudinal and behavioral changes undergone by individuals who reside in multi-cultural societies." In this definition Marin emphasizes a multilevel approach that stresses primarily the examination of outward behaviors. The first level, the superficial level, is one in which "the learning and forgetting of facts that are parts of the individual's cultural history or tradition takes place" (Marin, 1992, 237). At this level the person starts changing eating habits, consuming less ethnic foods, and observing fewer special holidays from his or her country of origin. The second level is the intermediate level. Here, behaviors that seem to be at the core of a person's social life start to change. The most significant of them is the change in language preference. We also find other predictors, such as names given to children, preference for English-speaking radio and television programs rather than programs in their native language, and the ethnicity of their spouse and friends. Finally, at the third level, the significant level, changes take place in terms of the person's values and norms. The constructs that help the individual define his or her worldview begin to change. Marin provides an example in discussing the difference between the regard of individualism versus collectivism. "Latino cultural values, for instance, encourage positive interpersonal relationships and discourages competitive and assertive interaction, also known as 'simpatia.' As the person experiences acculturation, that value might become less central to the individual" (Marin, 1992, 238–239).

Evaluation. Researchers have argued that changes at the third level may be difficult to measure. An individual could hold to a combination of values that may include those values from the host country and those of his or her country of origin. As a result, researchers have seen the need to evaluate the methodology involved in measuring acculturation and advocate for the use of multidimensional measures (e.g., Mendoza, 1989; Rogler, Cortes, & Malgady, 1991; Feliz-Ortiz, Newcomb, & Myers, 1994). These researchers would argue that the process of acculturation is more than assimilating into the dominant culture. Instead, it is a process by which individuals

retain, at varying levels, both their ethnic identity and that of the host culture.

For practitioners, however, the use of levels in conceptualizing acculturation can be helpful in bridging the gap between the social and psychological elements present in the concept. In developing programs, it provides an initial assessment of the needs of subgroups among larger minority groups. It also provides a larger context in understanding individual differences within familial patterns of interaction. For instance, knowing the level to which immigrant parents have acculturated may help counselors better understand the parents' expectations in their relationships to their children.

References

Feliz-Ortiz, M., Newcomb, M. D., & Myers, H. (1994). A multidimensional measure of cultural identity for Latino and Latina adolescents. *Hispanic Journal of Behavioral Sciences, 16,* 99–115.

Marin, G. (1992). Issues in the measurement of acculturation among Hispanics. In K. F. Geisinger (Ed.), *Psychological testing of Hispanics.* Washington, DC: American Psychological Association.

Mendoza, R. H. (1989). An empirical scale to measure type and degree of acculturation in Mexican adolescents and adults. *Journal of Cross-Cultural Psychology, 20,* 372–385.

Olmedo, E. L. (1979). Acculturation: A psychometric perspective. *American Psychologist, 34,* 1061–1070.

Redfield, R., Linton, R., & Herskovits, M. T. (1936). Memorandum for the study of acculturation. *American Anthropologist, 38,* 149–152.

Rogler, L. H., Cortes, D. E., & Malgady, R. C. (1991). Acculturation and mental health status among Hispanics: Convergence and new directions for research. *American Psychologist, 46,* 585–597.

J. R. REYES

See CROSS-CULTURAL PSYCHOLOGY; ETHNIC IDENTITY DEVELOPMENT.

Achievement, Need for. Murray's (1938) taxonomy of human motivation included the need for achievement, conceived as a desire for significant accomplishment, for mastering skills or ideas, and for attaining a high standard. To assess an individual's motivational concerns Murray designed the Thematic Apperception Test (TAT), in which the respondent is presented with ambiguous pictures and is asked to write a brief story about each. Presumably these invented stories reflect the respondent's own needs. Although the TAT has shortcomings, it continues to be the instrument often used to assess the achievement motive.

Studies indicate that people with high achievement motivation achieve more than others do. They are more successful in school, particularly in courses that are perceived as relevant to their future career, and are more persistent in completing college degrees, holding their jobs, and maintaining their marriages (McCall, 1994). They are better able to delay gratification and are more likely to persist on a difficult task. Research on outstanding athletes, scholars, and artists indicates that success is more a matter of high motivation, self-discipline, and commitment than a matter of natural talent.

People who vary in achievement motivation also differ in the explanations they give for their own successes or failures. Individuals high in achievement need take personal responsibility for success and perceive themselves as high in ability. They may attribute failures to insufficient effort. In contrast, people with a low need for achievement have a tendency to attribute their success to external factors such as ease of the task or good luck. They may attribute failure to a personal lack of ability.

Atkinson (1964) proposed one of the most influential theories of achievement motivation. He suggested that in every achievement-related situation both the need to achieve success and the need to avoid failure are aroused. A person's behavior is determined not only by the relative strength of these motives but also by the expectancy and the incentive value of success and failure.

One of the predictions derived from Atkinson's theory is that people high in achievement motivation will prefer tasks of intermediate difficulty rather than those that are very easy or difficult. Research has confirmed this prediction. In one study investigators measured how far subjects chose to stand from the target when playing a ring-toss game. Those high in achievement motivation stood at an intermediate distance at which the game was challenging but not impossible. Other studies have also indicated that people with high need for achievement may set challenging but realistic goals. Some have argued that tasks of intermediate ability provide the performer with the most information about his or her competence.

McClelland (1961) has attempted to explain the economic development of societies in terms of achievement motivation. He reasoned that the link Ernst Weber saw between the Protestant Reformation and the growth of capitalism was mediated by a changed pattern of child-rearing practices that encouraged independence and the need for achievement. In an important study McClelland determined the achievement scores of different societies through an analysis of their written material, particularly of children's readers, and related these scores to the societies' economic growth as assessed through such indices as electric power consumption. Results indicated that an increase in the achievement need of a society preceded economic development, while decreases in achievement motivation were followed by subsequent economic decline. Other studies suggest there may be negative consequences when a society emphasizes achievement. For example, achievement scores also correlate with psychophysiological disorders.

Early research found that achievement motivation did not predict the behavior of females as well as that of males. Although different explanations have been offered for this finding, the most intriguing has been that women may be motivated to avoid success. Presumably they have learned from childhood that achievement is unfeminine and thus leads to social rejection. While initial research seemed to indicate that the motive to avoid success was greater in women than in men, more recent studies have failed to replicate this finding. Some psychologists have suggested that women are not necessarily motivated by a fear of success itself but that both males and females may have a set of expectations regarding the negative consequences that may occur if they deviate from accepted sex-role norms.

Psychologists have generally viewed the need for achievement as a learned motive, with parents playing a major role in shaping their children's later strivings. Parents may foster achievement motivation through independence training by setting high but realistic standards for their children and by being appreciative of their children's successes. As a result of such training, children are likely to associate achievement with positive emotions, to attribute their accomplishments to their own competence, and to develop higher expectations for themselves. Possible differences in childrearing may help explain why firstborn children tend to be high achievers, while later-borns tend to have greater social skills and to be more accepting of new ideas. Achievement motivation has been raised in adults through special training in the creation of success fantasies and through role-playing exercises.

References

Atkinson, J. W. (1964). *An introduction to motivation.* Princeton, NJ: Van Nostrand.

McCall, R. B. (1994). Academic underachievers. *Current Directions in Psychological Science, 3,* 15–19.

McClelland, D. (1961). *The achieving society.* Princeton, NJ: Van Nostrand.

Murray, H. A. (1938). *Exploration in personality.* New York: Oxford University Press.

M. BOLT

See MOTIVATION; PERSONALITY; COOPERATION AND COMPETITION.

Achievement Age. The relationship between age of achievement, as established by standard achievement tests, and chronological age. Achievement tests are distinguished from intelligence tests in that they measure the amount of information or skill an individual has acquired from past learning rather than the general capacity to learn and behave adaptively.

Achievement Tests. A measure of proficiency in a specific area obtained by testing performance or knowledge in that area. Many writers have attempted to distinguish among ability, achievement, and aptitude tests. Most agree that in the main the achievement test measures past learning, the ability test measures an individual's present status, and the aptitude test estimates future performance. While such distinctions among the three types of tests are useful, there remains a considerable amount of overlap (Anastasi, 1988).

Achievement tests measure the effect of some kind of training, narrow or broad. For example, an instructor may conduct a two-day instructional unit on the Battle of Vicksburg and then give a test that measures what students learned about the battle. Many achievement tests, however, measure a much broader area, such as high school mathematics or college German. Those tests that measure school performance or vocational training are the most popular.

Achievement tests are used for many vocational and educational purposes. Governmental agencies and industry utilize achievement tests to evaluate job applicants. Students in educational settings can receive helpful feedback on their educational progress from the results of achievement tests, even though critics assert that discouraging results can have a detrimental effect on future achievement.

Achievement tests of the survey type will give the student a single score; a diagnostic achievement test will yield several scores, helping the pupil identify various discrete strengths and weaknesses; and a readiness achievement test will tell the pupil if he or she is prepared to enter the next level of training in that field (Reynolds & Kamphaus, 1990). Teachers and instructors can often obtain valuable information regarding the effectiveness of their teaching. A final educational use of achievement tests involves administrative evaluations. School officials can gauge the effectiveness of various curricula, the value of supplemental programs, or the benefit of allocating funds by the achievement scores of pupils.

A vast array of standardized achievement tests is available. The *Mental Measurements Yearbook* is the best source for information on each test's reliability and validity, age range, topics covered, scoring procedures, and cost (Kramer & Conoley, 1992). This volume also includes major reviews by test construction experts as well as bibliographic citations of research regarding the tests. Many publishers offer an age-graded series of achievement batteries that can be used by a school district over a span of years on the same group of pupils.

During the 1970s a major movement by advocates of minority and disadvantaged children began to question the validity of testing, including achievement tests. Because the results of achievement tests are often used as a criterion for further education, children who have suffered from educational deficits tend to suffer discrimination. Some have advocated the use of criterion-referenced achievement tests rather than norm-referenced tests as a way of minimizing the discriminating aspects of achievement tests (Reynolds & Kamphaus, 1990). Other researchers are exploring cultural-specific achievement tests.

References

Anastasi, A. (1988). *Psychological testing* (6th ed.). New York: Macmillan.

Kramer, J. J., & Conoley, J. C. (Eds.). (1992). *The eleventh mental measurements yearbook*. Lincoln: University of Nebraska Press.

Reynolds, C. R., & Kamphaus, R. W. (Eds.). (1990). *Handbook of psychological and educational assessment of children: Intelligence and achievement*. New York: Guilford.

Additional Readings

Herrnstein, R. J., & Murray, C. A. (1994). *The bell curve: Intelligence and class structure in American life*. New York: Free Press.

Jacoby, R., & Glauberman, N. (Eds.). (1995). *The bell curve debate*. New York: Times Books.

J. R. BECK

See PSYCHOLOGICAL MEASUREMENT.

Acrocephaly. A birth disorder characterized by severe mental retardation and an exceptionally high skull. It is believed to be caused by a dominant gene.

See MENTAL RETARDATION.

Act Psychology. Two competitive schools dominated nineteenth-century German psychology. Act psychology, the less rigorous approach, was advocated by Franz Brentano (1838–1917) at Vienna and by Carl Stumpf (1848–1936), his student, at Berlin. The rival school, structuralism, was centered in the work of Wilhelm Wundt at Leipzig. While Brentano and Wundt agreed on making psychology a science, they defined the subject matter and its method differently. Wundt conceived of psychology as the experimental study of the contents (structure) of consciousness, while Brentano stressed it as an empirical study of the act of experiencing.

For Brentano act psychology is the view that every mental event referred to an event other than itself. This process of referring defined the subject matter of psychology and took the act-forms of ideating, judging, and feeling. Attention was directed toward understanding the nature and process of referring. This stood in opposition to Wundt's assertion that psychology is directed toward the elements of the object that was experienced.

Brentano suggested the act of perceiving color is mental, while color itself is a physical quality. The act of perceiving cannot occur without the object, but the act is more than a simple reflection of the physical properties of the object. The sensory content of a color is different from the act of sensing color. The act of sensing is meaningless without something being sensed, yet the act is more than the objective qualities. The subjective act is dependent on the experiencer, not solely on the experience.

Wundtian introspection was a highly structured, disciplined experimental technique. Orthodox introspection was a trained method in which the reporter was instructed to guard against committing the cardinal sin of stimulus error. Rather than reporting the experience of an apple as an apple, one was to report its objective, contentual properties of intensity, protensity, and extensity. But to the act psychologists this trained approach destroyed the act. Stumpf favored using native or naïve introspection, introspection as it occurred in common folk.

Due to Wundt's prodigious publication rate, structuralism won out as the leading German psychology in the latter decades of the nineteenth century. However, the influence of act psychology did not die out. Brentano's doctrine made a positive impact on his students, who included Stumpf, Christian von Ehrenfels, and Sigmund Freud. Edmund Husserl, one of Stumpf's students, founded the philosophy of phenomenology. Other of Stumpf's students, Max Wertheimer, Kurt Koffka, and Wolfgang Köhler, were instrumental in founding Gestalt Psychology. The tenets of act psychology are found in the works of Fritz Heider, Kurt Lewin, and Carl Rogers. Act psychology was antecedent to Gestalt, psychoanalytic, and phenomenological psychologies.

R. L. TIMPE

See PSYCHOLOGY, HISTORY OF.

Acting Out. The concept of acting out was first developed by Sigmund Freud to describe the tendency of patients in psychoanalysis to respond to unconscious conflicts by action. Instead of remembering and understanding, the individual circumvents insight by reliving the repressed emotional experiences through direct discharge of tension. Acting out is therefore a defense against the unconscious conflict. It also frequently serves as resistance against the therapeutic process.

An example of acting out would be the man who reacts to his unconscious hostility to his father with aggression toward his boss. This behavior begins or intensifies when therapy starts to focus on the unconscious conflict. When these feelings are acted out upon the person of the therapist, it is called transference. Acting out that occurs within the therapy situation is referred to as acting in. Although it is still a defense against remembering and verbalizing, it is generally seen as closer to symbolization or verbal expression and is therefore easier to work with. It is also less disruptive to therapy because it can be observed by the therapist and analyzed.

Acting out does not occur only in psychoanalysis. However, many therapies fail to deal with its defensive functions, and some may even encourage it. The term *acting out* is often applied indiscriminately to all aggressive or antisocial behavior. Such usage has led to a confused understanding of the concept.

D. G. BENNER

See RESISTANCE IN PSYCHOTHERAPY.

Active Imagination Technique. *See* IMAGERY, THERAPEUTIC USE OF.

Activity Therapy. *See* EXPRESSIVE THERAPY.

Actualization. *See* SELF-ACTUALIZATION.

Actualizing Therapy. Socrates claimed that the destiny of humans is the "perfection of the soul." By that he meant that humans are invested by their Creator with a magnificent and nearly infinite set of creative potentials for growth in body, mind, and spirit. The reason for the life of every person, he thought, is the grateful and thoughtful actualization of all those productive possibilities for humanness. Believing human personality to be essentially rational in nature, he concluded that the way to self-actualization is through thoughtful and rational living.

In modern psychology the challenge of self-actualization has not been championed so much by the rationalists as by those who have assumed that human personality is essentially emotional and dynamic in nature. Abraham Maslow brought the notion of self-actualization back into focus with his work on the hierarchy of human needs and his study of self-actualized individuals (1954). It was left for Shostrom to translate these ideas into a system of therapy, which he has done in *Man the Manipulator* (1967). His more recent work, *Actualizing Therapy* (1976), contains the most systematic presentation of the theory and practice of this approach.

Shostrom views actualizing therapy as a creative synthesis of many schools of theory and practice in psychotherapy (Shostrom & Montgomery, 1981). From conjoint family therapy he took the emphasis on the feeling polarities of anger-love and strength-weakness. From client-centered or person-centered therapy comes the focus on feelings and the importance of the therapist's nonjudgmental respect for the client. From Gestalt therapy Shostrom took the focus on the client's awareness in the here and now, and from bioenergetic analysis he took the focus on the client's body as a primary diagnostic and therapeutic tool. This sort of borrowing from other traditions was facilitated by Shostrom's close personal relationship with the founders of these approaches as well as with Maslow, Rollo May, Victor Frankl, and Albert Ellis. These relationships, as well as Shostrom's personal synthetic style, account for the broad and integrative quality of his approach.

Actualizing therapy deals systematically with the problem of helping people become more actualizing. It may be conducted within individual or group therapy. It can also function within the framework of any school of therapeutic preference. When it is offered within a group format, the emphasis is on the perception and expression of inner feelings, thoughts, needs, strengths, and weaknesses that function in the self and others. The intent is to achieve honesty and growth-inducing coping responses to one's inner world and outer world. Individual therapy endeavors to achieve the same process with a therapist.

The actualizing therapy model sees the client moving through eight stages from manipulator to self-actualizer and instigator of self-actualization in others. Persons may enter therapy at any stage of their own self-actualization. They should then experience some growth in self-actualization, and they may leave therapy at any one of the stages at which they are functioning.

The actualizing process consists, according to Shostrom, of "aiding the person to become aware of core pain, to express feelings that have been rigidly held back, to experiment with actualizing behaviors, body awareness and feeling expression, . . . [and] to develop a sense of core trust in being oneself" (Shostrom & Montgomery, 1981, p. 7). This process is facilitated by twelve basic therapeutic strategies. Caring as unconditional positive regard or as care-filled confrontation addresses active and passive manipulators respectively. Ego strengthening develops the thinking, feeling, and perceptive ability of the client in positive directions, enhancing the belief that he or she is capable of coping. Behavior modification is usefully employed in this regard. Reflection of feeling involves the reexpression, in fresh words, of the essential attitudes expressed by the client. Reflection of experience involves observing the client's nonverbal behavior and feeding back certain information in order to expand the client's self-awareness. This technique is most effective for focusing on contradictions between verbal and nonverbal behavior.

Interpersonal analysis clarifies for the client how he or she misperceives and manipulates the therapist and others. The client is also confronted with the relationship-defeating games he or she plays. Pattern analysis, a corollary to interpersonal analysis, examines the client's self-defeating coping techniques. Therapy identifies alternative constructive patterns that may be chosen. Reinforcement is a process of therapeutic rewards for socially adaptive, self-actualizing behavior. Healthy responses replace bad psychological habits and bring rewarding gains. Self-disclosure is the process in which the therapist as wounded healer acknowledges his or her own defenses and pathologies and incarnates the evidence that life can be lived wholesomely despite these. Value reorienting helps the patient to choose more functionally operational values, and reexperiencing is the process of reviewing past perceptions and their pathological consequences, so that their impact on the present may be acknowledged and they can be changed. Body-awareness techniques assist the client in learning to attend to the messages from the body, and interpretation is the therapist's way of presenting hypotheses about relationships that should serve to bring a new perspective on familiar behavior.

Actualizing therapy contrasts with the medical model of psychotherapy, which moves a patient from illness to normalcy, in that it expresses the expectation of moving the person beyond mere elimination of symptoms to growth. Shostrom developed the Personal Orientation Inventory (Shostrom, 1963) to measure growth in self-actualization. This instrument has proven useful in providing an objective measure of the client's level of actualization as well as positive guidelines for growth during therapy. It has also been useful in researching the effectiveness of actualizing therapy. In one study Shostrom and Knapp (1966) showed actualizing therapy to be effective in helping clients become more emotionally spontaneous and expressive, less interpersonally withdrawn, more competent in effective time use, more present oriented, more inner directed, and less socially constrained. Compared to other therapeutic processes the patient's achievement was more that of growth than mere cure of symptoms. Shostrom's judgment is that actualizing therapy is most effective with normal or mildly disturbed individuals. It has not been used extensively with severely neurotic or psychotic persons.

The perspective of actualizing therapy expresses well the essential elements of Judeo-Christian anthropology. As imagers of God we are described in the Bible as endowed with majestic and immense potential for growth, creativity, productivity, and communion. Humans are a little lower than heavenly beings, according to Psalm 8. Humans, then, are destined to magnificent growth in the actualization of their full range of possibilities as divine imagers. Illness is anything that obstructs or curtails that growth. To be in a state of such curtailment is to be sick. Health is the state of being self-actualized or of being at a place on the continuum of self-actualization appropriate to one's stage in life. Healing is any process that removes the curtailment of growth. Therapy is any formal strategy for the production or enhancement of the healing process. Therefore, Paul can say with confidence that the whole creation is standing on tiptoe, waiting for the children of God to come into their own.

References

Maslow, A. H. (1954). *Motivation and personality.* New York: Harper & Row.

Shostrom, E. L. (1963). *Personal orientation inventory.* San Diego: EdITS.

Shostrom, E. L. (1967). *Man the manipulator.* Nashville: Abingdon.

Shostrom, E. L. (1976). *Actualizing therapy.* San Diego: EdITS.

Shostrom, E. L., & Knapp, R. R. (1966). The relationship of a measure of self-actualization (POI) to a measure of pathology (MMPI) and to therapeutic growth. *American Journal of Psychotherapy, 20,* 193–202.

Shostrom, E. L., & Montgomery, D. (1981). Actualizing therapy. In R. Corsini (Ed.), *Handbook of innovative psychotherapies.* New York: Wiley.

J. H. ELLENS

See Counseling and Psychotherapy: Overview; Humanistic Psychology; Self-Actualization.

Acute Stress Disorder. Almost all people experience some psychological symptoms and disruption following exposure to extreme traumatic events. Natural or manmade disasters, severe motor vehicle accidents, violent personal assaults, and a variety of other profoundly threatening events almost universally result in some degree of psychological numbing and temporary disorganization. When the magnitude of psychological disruption in the wake of acute trauma leads to significant impairment in functioning, however, a diagnosis of acute stress disorder may be made. A new diagnostic category in the fourth edition of the American Psychiatric Association *Diagnostic and Statistical Manual of Mental Disorders (DSM-IV)*, acute stress disorder refers to symptoms and reactions to trauma that are clinically significant and pathological but do not meet the criteria for the diagnosis of the more chronic Posttraumatic Stress Disorder (PTSD).

Acute stress disorder follows exposure to events involving actual or threatened death, serious injury, or significant psychological peril. Symptomatic reactions, according to *DSM-IV*, include numbing, detachment, or other expressions of decreased responsiveness to surroundings; reexperience of the traumatic event through images, thoughts, dreams, or flashbacks; avoidance of people, places, activities, or other stimuli that trigger recollections of the trauma; significant anxiety or increased arousal; and clinically significant disruption of important areas of functioning or the pursuit of tasks (such as seeking help or support) necessary to restore such functioning. These reactions must occur within four weeks of the trauma and last for a maximum of four weeks. Following this period, continuing symptoms suggest a diagnosis of posttraumatic stress disorder.

There are considerable variations among people in terms of developing acute stress disorder in reaction to trauma and in terms of eventually developing PTSD. Greater intensity and duration of trauma exposures are fairly consistently associated with a greater likelihood of developing stress disorders. Individual characteristics such as childhood history, economic status, previous pathology and concurrent psychiatric problems, intellectual and educational attainment, coping skills, availability of social support, and personality patterns have been suggested to influence the development of stress disorders. People whose vocations bring them into frequent contact with traumatic situations, such as police, firefighters, emergency medical services workers, and military personnel, are also considered to be at higher risk.

Perhaps the most comprehensive theoretical model of acute stress disorder is provided by Rahe (1993). He proposes a six-step process in which perceptions of life events, psychological defense mechanisms, psychophysiological responses, coping approaches, and beliefs about illness and health care together determine the likelihood of illness in reaction to significant acute stress.

There have been efforts to prevent the development of stress disorders through education about trauma and team development among groups of people with likely exposure to trauma. Once traumatic events have taken place, treatment strategies concentrate on mobilizing psychological support, problem-focused crisis intervention, culturally endorsed rituals, and "emotional first aid" (Lundin, 1994). Perhaps the core of treatment for significant acute stress has been trauma debriefing (Mitchell & Everly, 1993), which encourages trauma victims or caregivers to talk about their experiences in supportive group settings.

Religious commitment and practices can offer trauma victims a framework for finding meaning in struggles and a sense of comfort and assurance in the face of uncontrollable events. For many people of faith, healing takes place best amid the fellowship and support of fellow believers. Writing in the Christian recovery tradition, Brende (1991) proposes that spiritual healing (restoring contact with God, healing shame and self-doubt, healing lost innocence and idealism, learning to forgive, and practicing regular prayer or meditation) complements physical, emotional, and family healing approaches for survivors of acute traumatic episodes.

References

American Psychiatric Association. (1994). *Diagnostic and statistical manual of mental disorders* (4th ed.). Washington, DC: Author.

Brende, J. O. (1991). *Trauma recovery for victims and survivors.* Columbus, GA: Trauma Recovery Publications.

Lundin, T. (1994). The treatment of acute trauma: Posttraumatic stress disorder prevention. *Psychiatric Clinics of North America, 17,* 385–391.

Mitchell, J. T.; & Everly, G. S., Jr. (1993). *Critical incident stress debriefing.* Ellicott City, MD: Chevron.

Rahe, R. H. (1993). Acute versus chronic post-traumatic stress disorder. *Integrative Physiological and Behavioral Science, 28* (1), 46–56.

F. C. Craigie, Jr.

See Anxiety Disorders.

Adjustment Disorders. A diagnostic category included in the *Diagnostic and Statistical Manual of Mental Disorders* (*DSM-IV*; American Psychiatric Association, 1994). The diagnosis is given to individuals who have a significant amount of difficulty dealing with stressful life events. People who qualify for this diagnosis find themselves significantly impaired in their social, occupational, or academic lives or react in a way that is considered excessive by an objective observer.

A stressful life event can be defined as any situation that places a significant demand on an individual's coping resources. This definition is broad enough to cover both negative and positive events. An experience of abuse, a divorce, or the loss of a job could qualify as a stressful event, but so could getting married, going to college, or a promotion.

Adjustment disorders are considered to be among the least severe of all psychiatric diagnoses. If an individual meets the criteria for a more severe diagnosis, such as an anxiety disorder or a mood disorder, the diagnosis of adjustment disorder is inappropriate. Consider, for example, an individual whose reaction to divorce includes low mood, poor concentration, poor appetite, lack of enjoyment in previously enjoyed activities, lack of energy, and thoughts of death. Although there is a clear reaction to a stressful life event, the symptoms are severe enough to warrant the more serious diagnosis of major depressive episode. Therefore it is likely that the diagnosis of adjustment disorder would not be given.

There is a degree of subjectivity involved in the diagnosis of adjustment disorder. The reaction to the stressor must be significant, but one person's assessment of significance is bound to differ from that of another. An analysis of the person's social, occupational, or academic life is therefore utilized to decrease this subjectivity. Sudden manifestations of abusive behavior, extreme isolation, or neglect of parental duties might be examples of impaired social functioning. Missing deadlines or developing patterns of tardiness on the job may indicate impairment of occupational functioning. Sudden declines in school performance or increased conflict with teachers may be evidences of impaired academic functioning.

If the person's social, occupational, and academic functioning is not impaired, the diagnosis of adjustment disorder may still be given if the reaction to the life event is considered excessive. For example, an individual experiencing chronic sleeplessness after being promoted may receive this diagnosis, even though his or her work performance does not suffer.

Approaches to the treatment of this disorder are nearly as widely varied as the types of stressful life events that can cause an adjustment disorder. Generally speaking, however, support and direction are given so that clients can solve the problems on their own. Treatment may not be necessary due to the fact that these disorders tend to improve spontaneously without intervention. Medication is rarely needed (Sperry & Carlson, 1996).

Those of the Christian faith seem to be uniquely equipped to handle an adjustment disorder. Rather than seeing the stressful life event as an haphazardly occurring incident, the Christian believes that God is working out "everything in conformity with the purpose of his will" (Eph. 1:11b, NIV). Realizing that it is God's purpose for his children to share in his holiness (Heb. 12:10), the Christian joyfully endures the hardship as discipline (Heb. 12:7). Brought to an end of his or her own sufficiency, God's child is enabled to look up, taste of God's sufficiency, and

proclaim, "The LORD is my light and my salvation—whom shall I fear?" (Ps. 27:1, NIV).

References

American Psychiatric Association. (1994). *Diagnostic and statistical manual of mental disorders* (4th ed.). Washington, DC: Author.

Sperry, L., & Carlson, J. (Eds.). (1996). *Psychopathology and psychotherapy: From DSM-IV diagnosis to treatment* (2nd ed.). Washington, DC: Accelerated Development.

R. D. KOSITS

Adler, Alfred (1870–1937). The major developer of the concepts of inferiority feeling, social interest, lifestyle, and fictional goals, Adler was also the founder of the theory of personality known as individual psychology. His life, especially his early childhood, portrays many of the concepts he later developed.

Adler was the second child in a large Jewish family. His mother appears to have embodied what her son later referred to as the martyr complex: gloomy and self-sacrificing. His father was cheerful and self-confident, and Alfred strongly identified with him. The senior Adler believed in avoiding both punishment and overt physical affection with his children, but he believed in giving them encouragement. As a prosperous grain merchant he could afford to provide his family with a suburban rather than a ghetto residence. The children grew up influenced more by Viennese than by Jewish culture.

Adler's childhood was marred by several close encounters with death and disease. When he was three, a younger brother died in the next bed. When he was five, he contracted pneumonia and barely survived. Twice he was in street accidents. One of his earliest childhood memories was of sitting on a bench, incapacitated by rickets, while an athletic older brother played. In school he tasted defeat several times. He could not draw well and had to repeat an arithmetic class. One counselor told his father that the boy should be apprenticed to a shoemaker. One day Alfred figured out an arithmetic problem that could not be solved by anyone. He told the teacher, felt proud, and from then on did well in math. His later school years were remarkable for the number of friends that he made.

At a political rally Adler met Raissa Epstein, the daughter of Russian intelligentsia, who had come to Vienna to complete her education. When she returned home, Adler scraped together enough money to visit her in Russia. He married her in 1897. A strong-willed woman with a social background different from Adler's, Raissa influenced her husband's positive views on the equality of women. Although the marriage had a few conflicts, it served as the basis for Adler's positive view of monogamous matrimony. Two of their four children became psychiatrists.

Adler received his medical degree in 1895. He first specialized in ophthalmology but broadened his practice to general medicine. His interest in psychiatry grew around the turn of the century, but he maintained his general practice until after the First World War. From his clinic in a lower-middle-class neighborhood he worked with a broad range of patients and diseases. This experience convinced him that the organic and psychological dimensions of disease are not separate and that many individuals' special mental or physical abilities arise as overcompensations for childhood inferiorities.

After the war he was given the special task of establishing a system of guidance clinics for youth. Every child from 6 to 14 was screened, and those with learning disabilities, emotional disturbances, or behavioral problems received counseling. This project reduced the level of delinquency and served to convince Adler of the importance of child-rearing practices.

Adler never considered himself a pupil or a disciple of Sigmund Freud. He first heard Freud lecture in 1899 and was invited to join the latter's discussion group in 1902. Adler was never psychoanalyzed, as were the other members of the inner circle. Nevertheless, the general practitioner won the respect of the early psychoanalysts and was selected as the editor of their journal and elected president of the Vienna Psychoanalytic Society. Adler's intellectual independence led to a widening rift with Freud. Early in 1911 Adler delivered three lectures to the Vienna society. He clearly enumerated the differences that set him apart from Freud. The subsequent discussion factionalized the group into a Freudian majority and an Adlerian minority. The former group declared that Adler's views were not psychoanalytic and the latter group withdrew, forming the Society for Free Psychoanalysis, which later became known as the Society for Individual Psychology. Freud and Adler remained on poor terms from then on.

Although individual psychology has religious implications, little is known about Adler's personal views on religion. He has been accused of being a radical atheist, but he had himself baptized a Protestant at age 34. This could have been due to a conversion experience, but more likely it was an attempt to escape the vestiges of Judaism, which he consistently criticized. Adler was socialist and attended rallies and discussion groups in his student days. His first publication, *A Health Book for the Tailor Trade*, in 1898, proposed sweeping social reforms to improve workers' environments at home and work.

Adler was a lively public speaker who richly sprinkled his lectures with clinical anecdotes. However, his writings suffered because he never mastered the rules of formal scholarship. There were insufficient allusions to knowledge in other disciplines. For this reason, of all the early psychological theorists Freud remained the most remembered and Adler has been the most rediscovered. Since Adler wrote many books, articles, and pamphlets, the repetition of content is enormous. Two posthumously compiled anthologies (Adler, 1956, 1964) give a sufficient introduction to his writings.

References

Adler, A. (1956). *The individual psychology of Alfred Adler*. New York: Basic.
Adler, A. (1964). *Superiority and social interest*. Evanston, IL: Northwestern University Press.

Additional Reading

Sperber, M. (1974). *Masks of loneliness: Alfred Adler in perspective*. New York: Macmillan.

T. L. BRINK

See INDIVIDUAL PSYCHOLOGY; ADLERIAN PSYCHOTHERAPY.

Adlerian Psychology. See EGO PSYCHOLOGY; INDIVIDUAL PSYCHOLOGY.

Adlerian Psychotherapy. "It would not be easy to find another author from which so much has been borrowed from all sides without acknowledgment than Adler" (Ellenberger, 1970, p. 645). Decades after Alfred Adler's death, thinkers are positing ideas similar to Adler's without apparent awareness of his work. cognitive-behavior therapy and rational-emotive therapy view personality and approach psychotherapy much as did Adler yet have not derived their theories from his body of work. Adlerians regard this as proof that Adler drew his concepts from a well of truth self-evident to any alert student who takes an uncomplicated, common-sense approach to understanding human nature.

Psychology textbooks routinely list Adler as a dissident disciple of Sigmund Freud. Adler's disciples view his years with Freud (ca. 1902–1911) as a collegial relationship of two genius physicians in search of psychological truth. They attribute the subsequent dominance of Freud's ideas to his more voluminous writing, his greater elegance of expression, and his choice to orient to the intelligentsia of the medical profession. Adler opted instead to popularize his views. He wrote rather loosely organized materials for the lay public and eschewed jargon in favor of common-sense terms.

Theoretical Roots. The primary precursor who shaped Adler's views was the philosopher Vaihinger (1924). Vaihinger taught that none of us can know truth exactly; we all formulate our own approximations of reality and then live by these fictions as if they represent the truth. Adler expanded this basic idea into his concept of lifestyle, by which he meant the particular arrangement of convictions each person establishes early in life concerning self, others, and reality (*see* Style of Life). Adler emphasized lifestyle as something a person uses rather than something the person possesses. He called it the person's unique law of movement. His view of the uniqueness and holistic cohesiveness of each individual's personality resulted in the name individual psychology for his school of thought.

Theory of Psychotherapy. To the Adlerian therapist the primary problem with any person seeking therapy is low social interest. The neurotic preoccupied with striving for glory thus evades the normal tasks of life: love and sexual adjustment, work, and friendship. The primary goal of therapy is to arouse the patient's social interest or sense of commonality with all fellow humans, who by the nature of human limitations need each other's cooperation in order to live.

Adlerian therapists function as educators. In supportive therapy they identify and build on strengths the client already shows. They encourage the person to use those talents for the benefit of other persons. In more intensive therapy they seek to identify and revise crippling perceptions of self, others, and the world in the client's lifestyle. Since there is no perfect cognitive map for people to follow, the goal of lifestyle revision is to replace big mistakes with smaller ones.

Process of Psychotherapy. From the first contact Adlerians work to establish a friendly relationship with their clients. They make themselves models to follow in being humorous rather than anxious, unimpressed by their own mistakes rather than perfectionistic, and curious rather than defensive about flaws in thinking or acting. They realize as educators that much of what clients take away with them will be caught rather than taught. Adlerian therapists are seldom sphinxlike and passive; they are usually active and talkative.

Many Adlerians do a formal lifestyle assessment early in therapy. Part of this assessment focuses on the family constellation in which the person grew up. Adlerians ask more about birth order and sibling relationships than do therapists of most other persuasions, who tend to emphasize parental influences in the person's childhood.

A second aspect of lifestyle assessment is early recollections, which Adlerians use as a projective technique. Analyzing these much as they do dreams, therapists distill themes that indicate what directions of movement a client considers important vis-à-vis the tasks of life.

Therapists make this assessment an actively therapeutic process. They involve clients thoroughly in refining the final, written lifestyle formulation. They offer an interpretation and ask, "Does that seem to fit you?" Clients who say, "Yes, that's me," take responsibility for the guidelines they follow in living. In reviewing the lifestyle assessment findings over the course of one- to three-hour-long therapy sessions, therapists teach that people form their fundamental beliefs about life, themselves, and other persons early in life as they strive to find a place of significance in their families of origin. Thereby therapists set the stage for future repeated references to cognitions and the purpose they serve for the client's felt sense of security and significance.

Adlerian therapists rely largely on interpretations to promote insight. Insight implies that a person grasps some bit of self-knowledge with the zest of an "aha" experience. This energizes behavioral change in the direction of social interest. An interpretation of a thought or an action ideally should illuminate its purpose and dynamic effects as well as the use the client makes of it. Purpose, movement, and use, three central Adlerian constructs, are thus the three criteria for a good interpretation. For example, an interpretation may sound something like this: "You use your tears as water power to arouse sympathy in others, to get them to excuse you from tasks you agreed to take on but at which you don't want to look inadequate. A skill you began using with your mother long ago you still use today even with your own grown children."

The Adlerian typically embeds such an interpretation in good-natured humor and in back-and-forth talk with the client. An interpretation like the preceding example might arise in a group setting in which the therapist comments on a client's here-and-now behavior. One such group setting that Adlerians like involves multiple therapists with one client.

Long before the cognitive-behavior therapies flourished in the late 1970s, Adlerians directed their clients to do tasks outside of therapy that would change their beliefs, feelings, and habits. They often assigned roles for clients to play: as if they were successful, as if they were beautiful, or courageous, or happy, or whatever clients said they lacked.

Adler loved paradoxical tactics. He often prescribed that clients do more of some resistant action they were already doing, so that they could continue resisting him only by doing less of the prescribed action. For example, a depressed client who was hardly doing anything more than getting out of bed each day might ask desperately at the end of the first interview, "Doctor, what can I do until next time?" Adler characteristically might answer, "Don't do anything you don't want to do."

Adler is reported to have said that neurosis is, in a word, vanity. Both he and Karen Horney repeatedly cited the godlike strivings behind the neurotic's vain search for glory. In this they echo biblical views of pride as the central human sin (Gen. 3:5; Isa. 14:14).

Adler saw no basic clash between his views and those of Christian theology. He wrote that individual psychology and religion have things in common, often in thinking, in feeling, in willing, but always with regard to the perfection of humankind (Adler, 1979, p. 281). This comment comes out of 37 pages of exchange between Adler and a Lutheran clergyman, Ernst Jahn. Adler agreed heartily with Christian teachings that we must love our neighbors as ourselves. His concept of social interest was the bedrock of his own humanistic rather than theistic faith.

References

Adler, A. (1979). *Superiority and social interest: A collection of later writings* (3rd ed.) (H. L. Ansbacher & R. W. Ansbacher, Eds.). New York: Norton.

Ellenberger, H. F. (1970). *The discovery of the unconscious.* New York: Basic.

Vaihinger, H. (1924). *The philosophy of "as if."* New York: Harcourt, Brace.

Additional Readings

Adler, A. (1924). *The practice and theory of individual psychology.* New York: Harcourt, Brace.

Mosak, H. H. (1979). Adlerian psychotherapy. In R. J. Corsini (Ed.), *Current psychotherapies* (2nd ed.). Itasca, IL: Peacock.

D. L. GIBSON

See COUNSELING AND PSYCHOTHERAPY: OVERVIEW.

Adolescence. There is no universally accepted definition of adolescence. The particular definitions, however, generally agree that adolescence begins with puberty and ends with the assumption of certain adult roles, including some degree of financial independence. This definition implies that adolescence was absent until the turn of the century, because all children who were capable of accepting some responsibility for the family were expected to do so. The definition also implies that adolescence is becoming longer as more teens and young adults rely on parents for significant economic support in terms of housing or educational expenses. In practice teens consider adolescence to end at 18, whereas parents still have some doubts when their progeny reach the age of 21.

Troubled Years or Troubled People? Many parents dread the onset of the teen years. Will their beloved, compliant children suddenly turn into rebellious youth?

Storm and Stress. Adolescence traditionally has been described as a time of storm and stress, a period of upheaval, passion, and rebellion against authority (Adams, Gullotta, & Markstrom-Adams, 1994). Certainly some teens do have difficulty during these years. Estimates are that between 10% and 20% of teens experience this storm and stress (Powers, Hauser, & Kilner, 1989). However, estimates indicate that about the same percentage of children and adults suffer such difficulties. Hence the evidence does not suggest that adolescence is a time of particular hardship. Nevertheless, 10–20% is a significant number of individuals. Why do these individuals experience the trauma of adolescence?

Continuity. As a general rule difficulties do not suddenly arise in adolescence. Those adolescents who struggle with peer pressure, sexuality, or drug use tend to be the same individuals who were troubled and experienced difficulty in childhood. Concerning peer pressure, Elkind (1994) says that peer groups are not inherently problematic. Rather, certain teens turn to troubled peers because of a lack of healthy parental relationships. Concerning drug use, Shedler and Block (1990) conclude, on the basis of studying their sample from age 4 to age 18, that drug abuse is the natural next step for troubled children rather than the result of peer pressure.

Most scholars consider adolescence to be a time of continuity. Troubled children act out their difficulties, whereas healthy children use the opportunities for growth and positive development. There are no guarantees as to how a child will turn out, but the rule is that one can predict adolescent behavior on the basis of childhood behavior.

Current Trends. After years of struggle psychologists seem to have concluded that adolescence is not a time of particular difficulty. This conclusion, however, has come at a time in which trends look rather pessimistic. Since the mid-1970s the overall health and well-being of adolescents have declined. There have been increases in adolescent morbidity, suicide, depression, crime, unplanned pregnancy, substance abuse, sexually transmitted diseases, and behavioral and emotional problems (Compas, Hinden, & Gerhardt, 1995). Elkind (1988) suggests that these numbers are due not to problems of adolescence per se but to inadequate parenting. These numbers have also increased for children, and the increases are of great concern but do not contradict the previous point. When adolescents experience trauma, it is usually a continuation of problems from childhood years, some of which may be due to poor parenting practices in society.

Puberty and Sexuality. The secular trend that has occurred over the last century has resulted in children's entering puberty at earlier ages. The average age has decreased by about three years during this century. Of course, some individuals develop somewhat before the average age, and others are behind. What is the effect of early versus late maturation?

Early versus Late Maturation. For males early maturation seems to be advantageous. Because our society places great value on athletic pursuits and because males who experience puberty sooner develop bulk and height at a younger age, males who mature early tend to become popular leaders among their peers.

For females early maturation seems to be less advantageous. These girls look like young women, even though they are still girls. They are faced with sexual innuendoes and pressures sooner than their peers, before they are ready to cope. As a result these females are more likely to become sexually active and pregnant than their peers. There is some debate over whether average or late development is the most beneficial for females.

Sexual Behavior. At the same time the age of puberty is decreasing and the age at marriage is increasing, resulting in a longer gap between sexual maturity and relationship commitment. This has resulted in increases of adolescent sexual behavior and teenage pregnancy.

Little research has been conducted on questions about the meaning and experience of sexuality during adolescence. It is hypothesized that adolescent sexuality is more self-focused than adult sexuality. According to Erikson's (1968) stages of psychosocial development, adolescents are at the identity stage, during which they have to answer the question, Who am I as an individual, apart from my family and other groups to which I belong? The self-centered nature of this question implies that relationships, including sexual ones, are primarily for the benefit of the self. Sexual experiences may address the question of what it means to be male or female, for example.

Others have noted that what adolescents ultimately seek is to establish meaningful relationships (Elkind, 1988). If they have weak role models from their parents, they tend to assume that one can quickly create these relationships through shared sexual experiences rather than understanding that there is no shortcut to good relationships.

Most of the research (Brooks-Gunn & Furstenberg, 1989) has focused on two questions: what predicts the age at which individuals become sexually active, and what predicts inconsistent use of birth control? The authors list about a dozen correlates to answer each question.

Of note are the findings concerning the role of religious belief. Research has shown that the highest level of premarital intercourse occurs among teens with no religious affiliation. Research also shows that one correlate of the irregular use of contraceptives is a fundamentalist Protestant affiliation. The first finding indicates that religious training does somewhat reduce adolescent sexual behavior. However, when adolescent sexual behavior does occur for those with a fundamentalist Protestant affiliation, they are more likely to get pregnant.

Cognitive Development. According to Jean Piaget's theory of cognitive development, the adolescent has moved through the preliminary stages (sensorimotor, preoperational, and concrete operational) and has reached the final stage of formal operational thought. The adolescent can think hypothetically, abstractly, and scientifically. This does not, however, imply that the adolescent is yet as rational as the adult.

The adolescent now has the ability to consider the perspectives of others, having grown beyond the egocentrism of the preoperational stage. Yet it seems as if the adolescent returns to egocentrism in practice. Adolescents fall prey to the imaginary audience. They tend to assume that other people are thinking about the same things they are, and what they are usually thinking about is self. If I am preoccupied in thinking about myself and I assume that you are thinking about the same thing I am, then you must also be thinking about me. Hence I assume that everyone else is just as interested in me as I am, creating the imaginary audience.

The result of the imaginary audience is the personal fable. If everyone is concerned about me and constantly thinking about me, then I must be uniquely special. These two concepts, the imaginary audience and the personal fable, create the problem of the illusion of invulnerability. Because I am uniquely special on this earth, I do not need to worry about bad things happening to me. Other people get killed in accidents because of alcohol or get infected with sexually transmitted diseases, but that will not happen to me. This adolescent risk taking produces a high fatality rate from accidents, the leading cause of death during this age, especially for males.

Religious and political beliefs tend to be rather immature during the adolescent years. Teens may be committed to a religious party or a particular belief system, but this commitment is usually because they have accepted or rebelled against what they have been told by parents or peers. It is typically in the young adult years that these beliefs are internalized.

The Identity Crisis. According to Erikson (1968), adolescents face the crisis of identity versus role confusion. By crisis he does not imply storm and stress. He uses the term *crisis* for every age group, when a critical point is reached. The task during the teen years is to establish a personal identity that is separate from parents and peers. This is a Western concept. Eastern cultures do not consider this a logical goal, as one's identity is a part of the significant groups to which one belongs.

Crisis and Commitment. According to Marcia (1966), achieving one's identity requires two steps. First, one must go through the crisis, which is a period of questioning what one has been told by parents and peers. This questioning is at a hypothetical level: What if my parents were wrong about . . . or What if society were wrong about norms against . . . These hypothetical questions require formal operational thinking. Hence one must be a formal operational thinker before experiencing the identity crisis (Erikson, 1968).

After experiencing the crisis, in time one begins to establish a system of beliefs and choices. One becomes committed to a particular career choice and to certain religious and political beliefs. These commitments tend to look similar to the parents' commitments, although there will be some differences due to cultural influences. Those who have undergone the crisis and made resultant commitments will have achieved an identity.

According to this theory, the questioning time is a necessary one. One cannot make internalized commitments without considering alternatives. This process is a part of the Amish culture, for example, in which they give their teens a time to experience "English" life before making a choice to remain with or leave the church. To the extent that this model is correct, churches need to avoid giving adolescents the message that it is wrong to ask questions. If our teens get the message that they are weak when they question our belief system, we will create rebellion rather than assist our teens.

In addition to the identity achieved status, Marcia (1966) defined three other identity states. The individual who has neither experienced a crisis nor made a commitment is in a state of identity diffusion. This is where all teens begin their process. Most teens have moved beyond this level before completing high school. Another identity state is termed moratorium. This describes those individuals who are currently in the state of crisis but who have not yet made commitments. The other state is termed identity foreclosure. These individuals have formed commitments without having experienced a crisis. They have accepted values and choices of other people, usually parents or peers. This can be a dead end for some. For others it will eventually give way to a state of moratorium, leading to identity achievement.

Negative Identity and Delinquency. It is possible to go through a crisis and form commitments that are inconsistent with the values of society. One might achieve an identity of a criminal, for example. Delinquency, in fact, is an excellent example. Will a juvenile delinquent establish the negative identity of a criminal? Or is the juvenile simply questioning the standards of society as a part of a healthy crisis? Compas, Hinden, and Gerhardt (1995) suggest that the former involves a trajectory of chronic poor adjustment, the result of childhood problems. The latter, however, occurs when a healthy adolescent experiments with new roles before returning to a positive identity. Hence we return to the original observation that serious adolescent problems tend to follow from serious childhood problems. Nevertheless there are many exceptions, so that we cannot assume a positive or negative outcome when working with adolescents.

References

Adams, G. R., Gullotta, T. P., & Markstrom-Adams, C. (1994). *Adolescent life experiences* (3rd ed.). Pacific Grove, CA: Brooks/Cole.

Brooks-Gunn, J., & Furstenberg, Jr., F. F. (1989). Adolescent sexual behavior. *American Psychologist, 44,* 249–257.

Compas, B. E., Hinden, B. R., & Gerhardt, C. A. (1995). Adolescent development: Pathways and processes of risk and resilience. *Annual Review of Psychology, 46,* 265–293.

Elkind, D. (1988). *The hurried child: Growing up too fast too soon* (Rev. ed.). Reading, MA: Addison-Wesley.

Elkind, D. (1994). *A sympathetic understanding of the child: Birth to sixteen* (3rd ed.). Boston: Allyn & Bacon.

Erikson, E. H. (1968). *Identity: Youth and crisis.* New York: Norton.

Marcia, J. E. (1966). Development and validation of ego-identity status. *Journal of Personality and Social Psychology, 3,* 551–558.

Powers, S. I., Hauser, S. T., & Kilner, L. A. (1989). Adolescent mental health. *American Psychologist, 44,* 200–208.

Shedler, J., & Block, J. (1990). Adolescent drug use and psychological health: A longitudinal inquiry. *American Psychologist, 45,* 612–630.

G. L. WELTON

See LIFE SPAN DEVELOPMENT; PSYCHOSEXUAL DEVELOPMENT; PSYCHOSOCIAL DEVELOPMENT; COGNITIVE DEVELOPMENT; MORAL DEVELOPMENT.

Adolescent Therapy. With the recent advances in biological psychiatry many exciting changes are occurring in the treatment of adolescent patients. Some of these findings challenge long-standing theoretical concepts of certain aspects of psychopathology and consequently the treatment of adolescents with these clinical pictures.

One of these advances is the development of the Dexamethasone Suppression Test (DST), which is proving to be of great benefit in identifying depression in children and adolescents (Poznanski, Carroll, Banegas, Cook, & Grossman, 1982). It is difficult to diagnose depression in adolescents on a clinical basis, since the behavior that they utilize to cope with their depression often masks the depression itself. These patients traditionally have been treated with psychotherapy and/or behavioral therapy. Current data derived from use of the DST suggest that these patients should be treated with antidepressants concomitantly with psychological therapies.

Another biological advance is a clearer delineation of panic disorders (Sheehan, 1982). The new findings indicate that panic disorders may manifest first by a clinical picture previously called separation anxiety or school phobia. These clinical syndromes were perceived as purely psychological phenomena and classified as neurosis. The new data suggest that this may be a distinct biological syndrome with phobias as a byproduct. The studies also suggest that the best treatment is specific antidepressant medications rather than psychotherapy, which has been utilized in the past with minimal benefits.

These illustrations support the need for a comprehensive evaluation prior to beginning any treatment. The essential components of this evaluation include a developmental and family history as well as a history of the present problem. A second component includes a physical examination, a mental status examination, and biological tests such as the DST and other endocrine tests. The third component of the evaluation is psychological testing. Which tests are to be utilized depends on the nature of the problem.

Treatment of adolescents should be carried out by a team that has representatives from the medical, social, and psychological disciplines. If all components are not addressed, the results will be inadequate. If each component is addressed in isolation, one representative may work against another or the adolescent can manipulate one representative against another. All members of the treatment team must collaborate, with one member serving as the primary therapist whose responsibility is to orchestrate the therapeutic input of the team members. The team members need not all be from the same agency. For example, the biological input may be from the adolescent's family physician, while much of the social input, as well as psychological evaluations, can come from teachers, a school social worker, and a school psychologist. If an adolescent comes for therapy, another member of the family often has been or is being seen by another social agency. It is important to have a collaborative relationship with this agency.

A variety of treatment modalities are available in the treatment of adolescents. No one of these needs to be used in isolation, nor is one invariably the preferred treatment. Rather, the multidisciplinary team generally utilizes a combination of treatment modalities under close coordination of the primary therapist. The most common treatment modalities are behavioral, biological, social, and psychotherapy. This article will focus on psychotherapy with adolescents.

Therapist Qualifications. Work with adolescents requires somewhat different qualifications from those required for work with adults, since most adolescents do not come to therapy of their own accord. Rather, they are coerced by the family, the schools, or the court. A second reason for this difference lies in the dynamics of adolescents. Adolescents generally are in a state of strong ambivalence between dependence and independence, and this conflict is closely linked with their self-esteem. This often makes the therapeutic relationship difficult to establish and accounts for the powerful transference and countertransference features encountered in treatment.

The therapist must be able to develop a warm, friendly relationship in which rapport is established as soon as possible. The therapist must also be able to accept the adolescent as he or she is. It is also important that the therapist be able to establish a feeling of permissiveness in the relationship so the adolescent feels free to express his or her feelings. The therapist must be alert to feelings and be able to reflect them in such a manner that insight is gained. The therapist must also maintain respect for the ability the adolescent has for solving his or her own problems if given the opportunity. Consequently adolescents must be helped to realize that it is their responsibility to institute changes. Finally, the therapist must be able to assist adolescents in setting limits, in order to anchor the therapy to the world of reality and to make adolescents aware of their responsibility in the relationship as well as responsibility for all their behavior.

Short-Term Therapy. Most psychotherapy with adolescents is relatively brief, either by design or because of premature termination. However, brief therapy is often both successful and the treatment of choice due to the nature of adolescence and the types of problems that lead adolescents to seek help. Adolescence is a time of rapid growth and maturation; consequently much of the behavior patterns of this period is not a fixed part of their personality. This makes adolescent problems adaptable to change, often rather rapid change.

One form of brief psychotherapy frequently utilized is advice and provision of an organizational framework. This consists of assessing the problem and providing concrete advice, especially to the family. The approach enables the patient and family to place an ill-defined vagueness about what is wrong into a well-formulated problem with structure, a framework that enables them to find their own solution to the problem. It not only assists the family in coping with the present problem and making appropriate resolutions but also helps mobilize them to cope with subsequent problems in an adapted fashion that leads to positive resolution. The approach is most effective when it enables the family's current anxieties and preoccupations to be placed in a relevant conceptual framework in which they are able to see their own positive qualities that will assist them in successfully coping with the stress. This approach is most successful when dealing with an adolescent showing a healthy response to a self-limiting problem but where, due to misjudgment on the part of the family, a self-perpetuating state of anxiety appears to be established with the prospect of a prolonged disturbance from which the family cannot extricate themselves.

This approach accomplishes two therapeutic tasks. First, through the family assessment process the family members are able to hear each other out and ventilate their feelings, consequently altering their communication network. Second, it assures the family that the behavior of the adolescent is a variation of normality and can be self-limiting, provided that the family's anxieties do not perpetuate it.

The second brief psychotherapeutic approach is crisis intervention, an intermediate approach between advice and the provision of structure and insight-oriented psychotherapy. Crises usually arise when persons are confronted by important life problems from which they cannot escape and that they cannot solve in their usual coping manner. The cause of the crisis can be internal (i.e., physiological or psychological) or environmental. Adolescents' crises generally are not as dramatic as those of adults; therefore agencies tend not to be as responsive. During crisis adolescents tend to reach out more readily and are much more easily influenced; consequently it is a good time to make a significant impact. The timing is important. It is during the second phase of a crisis—during the time of increasing tension and disorganization—that an individual is most susceptible to seeking help and making changes.

Crisis intervention is reality-based and focuses on the present, utilizing new problem-solving techniques to bring about resolution. In crisis intervention one does not seek insights into the how or why of the problem but rather focuses on mechanisms for surmounting the difficulties. It is important to provide a supportive environment that aids in problem resolution or a structure that allows decisions to be made.

Medication and hospitalization should never be utilized as solutions to a problem but rather as means to assist in mobilizing inner resources. These treatments may postpone problem solving or lead to premature closure. However, either one must be used in order to protect the individual, the family, the social agency, or the therapist or when it provides the necessary means to mobilize inner resources.

Long-Term Therapy. Long-term insight-oriented psychotherapy should be utilized only by experienced therapists who have a comprehensive knowledge of both psychodynamics and normal growth and development. It is utilized with adolescents who have experienced long-term problems. It must be understood that the insight produced through this approach is not necessarily curative. However, it does frequently alleviate stress and misery and often serves to establish continuity and a sense of order in the individual's life. The insight gained from such an experience ideally will also bring mastery of the problems the adolescent is experiencing. Some of the common goals in long-term psychotherapy include achievement of age-appropriate maturation, improved object relationships, improved capacity to tolerate frustration, improvement of reality testing, a modification of defenses and reduction of anxiety, removal of fixations, and the recovery of repressed memories.

Certain components of long-term psychotherapy are common to all such therapies regardless of theoretical orientation. These include concern, the provision of a stress-surmounting structure, the provision of a corrective emotional experience, interpretation, and limit setting.

Concern enables the therapist to maintain an interest in the adolescent until the adolescent acquires insight that allows therapeutic intervention. It permits intimacy without being intrusive. It permits the therapist to be accepting and respectful of the adolescent yet free to state his or her own views.

Provision of a stress-surmounting structure involves establishing an environment that is safe for both the therapist and the adolescent. The therapist is responsible for providing the language and concepts for the adolescent to use, as well as the interpretation, confrontations, and necessary controls. Much of the adolescent's anxiety regarding psychotherapy can be relieved by having a comprehensive understanding of the rules of the game.

Provision of a corrective emotional experience can best be accomplished by assisting the adolescent in disentangling his or her feelings and helping him or her to understand them. This is especially true with respect to ambivalence toward significant adults in his or her life. Often the best timing for addressing these issues is when the therapist experiences similar reactions of the adolescent toward the therapist.

The goal of interpretation is insight and learning new, more adaptive ways of coping with anxiety and conflicts. The therapist must be aware of the patient's anxiety and of his or her general coping mechanisms, as well as the quality of his or her object relations. The communication of the interpretations must be in language that is meaningful to the adolescent; it must be given in an acceptable dose so that it does not precipitate more anxiety than is necessary to facilitate in developing the patient's own solution. Interpretations of transference should be made very cautiously with adolescents.

It is of utmost importance for the therapist working with adolescents to set limits through controls and confrontations. Many inexperienced therapists want someone else to set the controls and let them do the therapy, since they want to maintain emotional rapport with the patient. However, this is always counterproductive. Setting limits assists in ego development by inhibiting direct primitive expression of aggression. Also, if limits are not set during the session, the therapist may be preoccupied with self-defense rather than with conducting therapy. A passive, nondirective approach by the therapist leads to treatment failure. Limit setting does not imply rejection of the adolescent but rather rejection of the deed along with expectations of the adolescent.

All long-term therapy is a learning experience. This is facilitated by three factors. First, learning through conditioning takes place by means of the repetitive working through of material. Second, the patient develops an awareness of the connection between motivation and behavior, diminishing the gap that exists between one's emotional and intellectual life. Third and most important is that learning occurs by the adolescent identifying with the psychotherapist.

References

Poznanski, E. O., Carroll, B. J., Banegas, M. C., Cook, S. C., & Grossman, J. A. (1982). The dexamethasone suppression test in prepubertal depressed children. *American Journal of Psychiatry, 139,* 321–324.

Sheehan, D. V. (1982). Panic attacks and phobias. *The New England Journal of Medicine, 307,* 156–158.

Additional Readings

Evans, J. (1982). *Adolescent and pre-adolescent psychiatry.* New York: Grune & Stratton.

Holmes, D. J. (1964). *The adolescent in psychotherapy.* Boston: Little, Brown.

Malmquist, C. P. (1978). *Handbook of adolescence.* New York: Aronson.

Meeks, J. E. (1980). *The fragile alliance: An orientation to the outpatient psychotherapy of the adolescent* (2nd ed.). Huntington, NY: Krieger.

F. WESTENDORP

See COUNSELING AND PSYCHOTHERAPY: OVERVIEW.

Adoption. In 1992 approximately 127,000 children were adopted in the United States (Flango & Flango, 1995). The demand for infant adoptions has increased especially among older, two-career couples who have delayed starting a family. While good statistics are scarce, the National Committee for Adoption estimates that approximately 40,000 healthy, newborn infants are available for adoption per year (Gilman, 1987). This is well below the number of couples on waiting lists across the country. About 5% of unwed pregnant teenagers consider adoption, with the majority choosing to keep their babies due to the acceptance of single parenting. Based on data from 26 states, 42% of all adoptions are by stepparents, frequently of older children (Flango & Flango, 1995).

Adoption has also received increased attention because many states are turning to adoption as a means of decreasing the burden upon the social services system of caring for abused and neglected children (*see* Abuse and Neglect). There also has been increasing publicity regarding the plight of children in war-torn countries, leading many Americans to pursue international adoptions, which, according to the U.S. Immigration and Naturalization Service, have doubled between 1981 and 1987 to almost 10,000 adoptions.

Pastors are encountering an increasing need to counsel both the challenge of unplanned or unwanted pregnancies and the grief of infertility (*see* Infertility Counseling). This has placed many pastors and churches in the middle of the adoption process. Furthermore, the family focus of many churches provides a convenient and fruitful network for making adoptive connections.

Type of Adoption. When a couple decides they are interested in adoption, the first decision they must make is whether to utilize the services of an agency, either public or private, or pursue an independent adoption. This decision is significant, as the type of children available, the criteria of desirable parents, the costs, and the risks vary with each method. As most agencies do not permit couples to be involved with more than one agency at a time, couples need to do considerable research before they begin their adoption applications.

Approximately 15% of adoptions are managed through public adoption agencies (Flango & Flango, 1995). This percentage is low due primarily to the small numbers of infants, especially Caucasian infants, who come through these agencies. Children are typically older, ages three and up, boys, and minorities, predominantly African-American. Furthermore, they are often classified as special needs children due to emotional problems or physical or mental disabilities or because they are part of a sibling group and must be adopted together.

Public agencies have criteria for describing desirable adoptive parents. Some of these include marriage of at least two years' duration; documented infertility; one stay-at-home parent; minimum levels of income; racial and/or religious match with the adoptive child; the mother or both parents under the age of 40; a maximum number of siblings; and no children in the home younger than the adoptee. These formal and informal guidelines used by social workers have been criticized and have undergone review and revision in many states.

The definition of the ideal family has changed with changing values in our society. Furthermore, the large numbers of older children awaiting homes have necessitated an expansion of the pool of "desirable" adoptive parents. Many states now allow for single-parent adoptions, including single men, and the upper age limit is being raised. Federal legislation now mandates agencies to permit cross-racial adoption if the biological parents approve. Through the 1980 Adoption Assistance and Child Welfare Act, funds are available to assist families adopting special needs children.

Adoptions through public agencies are considered low risk in that most children have been fully relinquished by their biological parents before the child is placed in the adoptive home. Because social workers have been involved with the biological parents, there is less recourse for the biological parents to change their minds and seek a reversal of the relinquishment. The legal system usually allows three to six months during which the biological parents may appeal to get their child back. After one year most adoptions are legally finalized, leaving little recourse for biological parents to reverse the court's decision. At this point the best interests of the child will outweigh the parental rights of the biological parents.

Adoptions are also handled through private, nonprofit agencies. Many private agencies have an established network of referrals from lawyers, physicians, and churches to match prospective parents and children. Unlike public agencies, these agencies frequently involve the biological parents in selecting potential adoptive parents for their infant. Furthermore, they frequently specialize in infant adoptions, with the majority of clients being Caucasian. Agencies such as Bethany Christian Services in Grand Rapids, Michigan, seek out Christian families and are often referred biological mothers who desire a Christian home for their infants. Costs through a private agency typically run between $5,000 and $10,000. International agency adoptions frequently cost more.

Private agencies also have criteria for evaluating prospective adoptive parents. In Christian agencies a pastoral letter of support is needed. Many private agencies have specialized their networks of referrals for specific groups of children. For example, Holt International (headquartered in Eugene, Oregon, and with branches in other states) specializes in overseas children, Homes for Black Families in Detroit focuses on African-American children and families, and Downey Side in Massachusetts and New York specializes in adolescent adoptions.

A third process for adoptions is through a private attorney acting as an intermediary and facilitating the legal paperwork. Prospective parents initiate this process by either contacting an attorney who specializes in adoptions or finding their own match by announcing publicly to friends, physicians, and relatives their interest in adopting an infant. Many will also place ads in the local newspaper. Adoptive matches occur through this informal network. Fees to lawyers and accommodation expenses for the biological mother typically cost $10,000 or more.

Independent adoptions often entail more risk in that the biological mother may not have received any counseling or social-work intervention prior to releasing her child. Consequently her decision to relinquish her infant may lack careful consideration and certainty. Although they are uncommon, adoption scams have taken advantage of desperate couples. Legal counsel is often needed to clarify the legal parameters of any financial arrangements.

The Adoption Process. After a significant amount of paperwork, a home study is conducted. The home study is usually performed by a social worker who verifies the suitability of the home environment in meeting basic safety codes as well as assesses the psychological stability of the parents. The home study is ordered by the court upon receiving a petition for adoption.

During the 1960s questions were raised regarding the legitimacy of a policy of secrecy regarding adoption and withholding information about the circumstances of a child's birth. Open adoptions entail the involvement of both biological and adoptive parents in the upbringing of the child. The biological parents' involvement may be only an interview with the parents, or they may send Christmas and birthday greetings or receive regular updates on the child's development. Contemporary social work theory suggests that an open and nonsecretive approach to adoption decreases any negative stigma, satisfies the natural curiosity and right of a child to know his or her history, and allows for a healthier integration of all of their past in identity development (Gross, 1993).

Common Issues for Adopted Families. When does one tell a child that he or she is adopted? Parents are encouraged to speak of adoption as soon as their child becomes verbal and openly discuss it with friends and relatives before that time. Many parents will frame adoption as "you're special because we chose you." Furthermore, deliberate use of the concept of adoption in a variety of settings will enhance an easy comfort with the word. Adopting pets, adoption of close friends into the family, and God's adoption of all people as his children are examples.

How does one handle a child's desire to meet the biological parents? Many adopted children, especially adolescents, will want to know what their biological parents are like and if there is a physical resemblance. State laws vary regarding the age at which an adoptee may have access to adoption records, though this is typically set at the age of majority. Care must be taken in respecting the privacy of biological parents. An intermediary, such as the original adoption agency, may be helpful in both searching for biological parents and laying the groundwork for a meeting. The psychological impact upon the adoptee will depend upon the quality of relationships within the adoptive family and the maturity of the child. Children usually know that their parents are the ones who nurtured and cared for them.

How does one explain why the biological parents placed the child for adoption? Many parents do not know the answer to this question. One explanation is that the biological mother had many problems and could not adequately care for the infant. Therefore, out of love for the child, she made the difficult choice of giving that child to someone who could care for him or her.

Adoption of children is a growing phenomenon of contemporary family life. This is a response to problems of infertility as well as a deliberate humanitarian response to the plight of many orphaned children both in this country and abroad. This resonates with much in Christian thought regarding God's adoption of us as children and heirs, as well as the mysterious mixture of the sacrificial suffering by one party leading to the joy of life experienced by another.

References

Flango, V. E., & Flango, C. R. (1995). How many children were adopted in 1992? *Child Welfare, 74*, 1018–1031.

Gilman, L. (1987). *The adoption resource book*. New York: Harper & Row.

Gross, H. (1993). Open adoption: A research-based literature review and new data. *Child Welfare, 72*, 269–284.

Additional Readings

Bartholet, E. (1993). *Family bonds: Adoption and the politics of parenting*. Boston: Houghton Mifflin.

McKelvey, C. A., & Stevens, J. (1994). *Adoption crisis: The truth behind adoption and foster care*. Golden, CO: Fulcrum.

W. T. AOKI AND S. L. AOKI

See PARENTING.

Advice Giving. Mental health professionals have always been ambivalent about the role of advice in counseling, particularly of advice directed toward the client's personal life. Counseling models that pursue long-term personality change have generally eschewed advice giving, while theories seeking short-term or immediate change value it. With the trend toward short-term treatment, the role of more active and change-oriented techniques such as advice giving will probably increase. It remains important, therefore, for all in the helping professions to consider the advantages and disadvantages of personal advice giving in counseling.

Among the advantages of advice to counselees is the fact that they often desire and even expect to be advised by a counselor. Counselors who give advice may seem more caring and invested in the counselee, while resistance to giving advice can make the counselor appear detached and aloof. For certain populations, cultures, or age groups advice giving may be necessary to develop a sense of respect and trust. Though the myth of the objective, value-free counselor has been abandoned, the truth remains that the professional, as an outside observer, sometimes has a broader perspective on the individual's situation. The professional has advanced training and the experience of helping people in similar situations. The counselee may have every right to expect the therapist to offer the wisdom and insight gained from that experience.

Many people seeking counsel from a professional are facing crises or decisions when they are least prepared. Though the counselor's goal may be to help them think through ramifications of a decision, clients may remain severely limited in their insight or decision-making ability. Some people have grown so accustomed to being helpless in such situations that they are unable to see any options. This may especially be true when counselees are in danger from others in their lives. Others in the counselee's life may also be dramatically affected by that person's choices and behavior. When children or others may be harmed by the counselee's choices, the counselor may have a responsibility to give advice.

There is clearly a place for advice in some counseling situations. The long-standing resistance to advice giving in the helping professions, however, has grown out of the many possible risks of advising counselees. First and most obvious, advice can foster dependency. Autonomy is often overrated, but for those who need to develop greater independence, advice will usually be countertherapeutic. Advice often flows from the desire of both the counselor and the counselee to alleviate pain or to relieve the tension of taking responsibility for oneself. Pain has its constructive purposes, and advice may directly subvert them. It may provide short-term relief but do nothing toward the permanent growth that the individual seeks. Advice therefore may best be restricted to situations in which short-term relief is a more appropriate goal than long-term change.

Advice can be dangerous because of the temptations it presents to the counselor. Every person in the role of a helper has felt the temptation to quickly fix a situation. When we succumb to impatience we cheat the other of the chance to be listened to and to come to and own his or her own decision. It is too easy to give advice out of a desire to appear clever and wise. Such strokes to our own egos are addictive enough that we might find more opportunities to give advice than are necessary. Even if the advice was given to help persons through a time of crisis, after the crisis passes they may feel they were not given the opportunity to find and rely on their own reserves of strength.

Advice from the counselor often gives the illusion of objectivity when the counselor may have the least objective view of anyone. The counselor may not have all the facts. If we have heard only or primarily one side of a dispute, for example, we will certainly have a biased view of the situation. More often than we would like to admit, however, the counselor has personal motives and agendas. None of us is immune to the urge to impose our own view onto others, especially when their situations, decisions, or issues are similar to our own. Even if counselees have the best intentions they cannot help but give a one-sided perspective—their own. It is too easy to be trapped into giving the advice that individuals want and will then use to club someone else, with the added clout that a professional agrees with their perspective.

In many cases advice will feel disrespectful to counselees, even though they may ask for it. Those who want to develop confidence in making decisions or facing painful situations often want only to be heard and helped in thinking through their options. Advice may only confirm their suspicion that their perspective will not be heard and that another perspective will be imposed on them. When the counselor is unfamiliar with the other's situation advice can appear especially insensitive. This begs the question of whether we are ever adequately familiar with another's situation. Perhaps, as scriptural wisdom would suggest, we should pause before giving advice.

M. W. Mangis

See Counseling and Psychotherapy: Overview.

Affairs. In an affair a married person begins to allow someone other than his or her spouse to meet emotional and eventually sexual needs that should be met only by one's spouse. An affair is not synonymous with adultery (i.e., a sexual relationship with someone other than one's spouse), for people can commit adultery without developing an emotional relationship (e.g., a sexual encounter with a prostitute), and the early stages of many affairs do not include adultery.

There are a number of ways of understanding the reasons people become involved in affairs (Virkler, 1992). First, some people develop unhealthy personality styles (personality disorders) that make them vulnerable to affairs. Among these personality styles that often predispose a person to unfaithfulness are the narcissistic, histrionic, borderline, and antisocial personality disorders.

Second, sexual addictions often lead to infidelity. In a sexual addiction a person begins to use sexual encounters as a person with a developing alcohol addiction uses alcohol, that is, to deal with more and more of the stresses of everyday life (Carnes, 1983, 1989). Thus the person with a sexual addiction begins to search for a sexual experience when bored, lonely, anxious, frustrated, or depressed. It might be more accurate to say that those with sexual addictions are likely to have series of adulterous encounters rather than affairs, since they generally have many partners rather than develop an emotional and sexual relationship with one individual.

Third, as people go through life they face a number of developmental situations. When they do not resolve these successfully, the lack of resolution may lead to an emotional state (anxiety, anger, dissatisfaction, loneliness) that makes them vulnerable to the temptation of an affair. Examples of such developmental situations include making the transition from romantic love to commitment love during the early months of marriage; learning to negotiate differences in ways that result in both marital partners feeling counted; pregnancy, birth of the first child, and mothering; extraordinary stress at work for either partner; being away from home too much; rejection or failure; success; and midlife crises.

Fourth, people also become involved in affairs because they are exposed to temptation-filled situations for which they are inadequately prepared or in which they do not set wise boundaries. Affairs that fall into this category have been given names such as the friendship affair, the office affair, and the people-helper affair. The majority of affairs start as friendships, often well-meaning and innocent friendships, and move toward an emotional and sexual attachment so gradually and sometimes so unconsciously that the persons involved may not be aware that the relationship is changing until significant transformation has occurred.

Fifth, some people become involved in affairs because of unconscious, unrealistic, or uncommunicated expectations they hold. Everyone enters marriage with many expectations, some verbalized, others unverbalized, and some of which they may not be consciously aware. When people have unconscious or unverbalized expectations, their partners sometimes may not meet them, and they become dissatisfied with the marriage. At other times people enter marriage with unrealistic expectations (e.g., that honeymoon fever will last forever, or that if my partner really loves me, he or she will know what I want without my having to ask). When those expectations are not met, a person may feel dissatisfied with the marriage, believing that something fundamental is missing from the relationship, and be tempted to start looking elsewhere. When someone has an affair, it does not always indicate a defect in the faithful partner or in the marriage.

Sixth, there are a number of situations in which the faithful partner can produce a situation that makes the person who eventually becomes unfaithful more vulnerable. One of these is when the faithful partner fails to meet realistic, communicated requests of the spouse. Scripture clearly teaches that we are to be loving and gentle with each other and that marital partners should meet each other's companionship and sexual needs. While failure to do so does not justify adultery, it does increase a partner's vulnerability when someone else shows the warmth, respect, or compassion that had been requested from the spouse.

Seventh, each person has ego needs. Harley's research (1986) suggests that the top five ego needs of men and women are usually different. Women's top five needs, according to Harley, are for affection, conversation, honesty and openness, financial support, and commitment to family. Men's top five needs are sexual fulfillment, recreational companionship, an attractive spouse, domestic support (managing the home well), and admiration. Men and women generally try to show love to their spouse in the way they want to be loved, without realizing their spouse has different priorities of ego needs. As a result men and women sometimes do not meet their spouse's ego needs well, causing an emotional void that leaves the spouse more vulnerable to temptation.

Eighth, almost any psychopathology in the faithful partner, if it is extreme enough, can frustrate that person's partner and make him or her vulnerable to having an affair. Examples include paranoid personality disorder, obsessive-compulsive personality disorder (extreme perfectionism that keeps normal human needs from being met), substance abuse, physical or emotional abuse, or chronic passive-aggressiveness. For reasons that are not totally clear, codependency also seems to encourage infidelity in the partner but probably for different reasons than the above.

We know from Scripture that a person can be "a man after God's own heart" and still fall into adultery. It is wise to remember Ellen Williams's words (cited in Peterson, 1983, p. 79): "If you are thinking to yourself, 'An affair could never happen to me,' you are in trouble. To believe we are immune leaves us wide open and unprotected."

References

Carnes, P. (1983). *Out of the shadows: Understanding sexual addiction.* Minneapolis: Compcare.

Carnes, P. (1989). *Contrary to love: Helping the sexual addict.* Minneapolis: Compcare.

Harley, W. (1986). *His needs, her needs: Building an affair-proof marriage.* Old Tappan, NJ: Revell.

Peterson, J. (1983). *The myth of the greener grass.* Wheaton, IL: Tyndale House.

Virkler, H. A. (1992). *Broken promises: Understanding, healing and preventing affairs in Christian marriages.* Dallas: Word.

H. A. VIRKLER

See COUNSELING AND PSYCHOTHERAPY: OVERVIEW.

Affect. A term often used loosely as a synonym for feeling, emotion, or mood. A more precise definition places affect closest to feeling, additionally requiring, however, that the feeling state be observable. It should be distinguished from mood, which is a more pervasive and often longer-lasting state. Common examples of affect are anger, sadness, and joy.

In describing an individual's affective functioning, clinicians frequently employ the dimensions of range, stability, and appropriateness. The range of affects experienced may be either broad or constricted. Although there is considerable variability between people, normal affective functioning usually involves the expression of a range of affects with variability in facial expression, voice quality, and body movements. Restrictions of this may show in terms of either a limited range of affects experienced or a reduction in the intensity of their expression. The stability of an individual's affects describes the persistence of affective states. Affect is labile when it is characterized by rapid and abrupt changes. The appropriateness of affect describes the concordance between the individual's speech or thoughts and the affect.

D. G. BENNER

See EMOTION.

Affective Disorders. *See* MOOD DISORDERS.

Affiliation, Need for. Research clearly indicates that human beings have a pervasive tendency to seek out the company of others. People in every society form groups. In an extensive review of the literature, Baumeister and Leary (1995) conclude that "human beings are fundamentally and pervasively motivated by a need to belong, that is, by a strong desire to form and maintain enduring interpersonal relationships." Clearly they form social relationships in the absence of any special set of eliciting circumstances or ulterior motives and will invest considerable time and effort in fostering those relationships.

The need to associate and interact with other people is perhaps most evident in reactions to isolation. After reviewing the anecdotal accounts of those alone at sea or locked in solitary confinement, Schachter (1959) concluded that "one of the consequences of isolation appears to be a psychological state which in its extreme form resembles a full-blown anxiety attack" (p. 12). Children raised in institutions with minimal social contact or locked away at home become withdrawn, frightened, and speechless. Adults who are ostracized may become depressed.

Berscheid (1985) reported that when people were asked, What is necessary for your happiness? or What makes your life meaningful? most people first mention satisfying close relationships with family, friends, or romantic partners. One 16-nation survey found that separated and divorced people were half as likely as married people to declare themselves very happy. Those who lack strong social bonds experience higher rates of both mental and physical illness. In the United States, mortality rates for all causes of death are consistently higher for divorced, single, and widowed individuals. Although there are many possible explanations for this relationship other than affiliation, efforts to control for other variables have found a persistent, independent, and robust effect of social relations.

Clearly God created us interdependent, not self-sufficient; social, not isolated: "It is not good for the man to be alone" (Gen. 2:18, NIV). Many psychologists have argued that we are innately social creatures. Those working from an evolutionary perspective have argued that social bonding increased our ancestors' survival rate. It kept children close to their caregivers, and those adults who formed groups gained protection from predators and enemies. If those who affiliated survived and reproduced most successfully, their genes would in time predominate. Some psychologists, however, have regarded the motive to affiliate to be a learned need. According to this view, infants may come to associate other persons, particularly their parents, with the satisfaction of basic needs for food, warmth, and security. As a result of these repeated pairings most children

learn to seek out the company of others. Presumably when others have not been a source of pleasure in early life, the child may develop as a loner who prefers to engage in relatively solitary activity.

Several attempts have been made to measure individual differences in the need to affiliate. The concept was included in Murray's (1938) list of motives and, like the need for achievement, has been measured with the Thematic Apperception Test (TAT). More recently Mehrabian (1970) designed a scale consisting of 31 statements to assess the need for affiliation. Research on individual differences in affiliation need has indicated that interpersonal behavior may vary as a function of the strength of the motive. Not only are those high in this need more likely to initiate conversation and to attempt to establish friendship, but also they seem to have a greater desire to be accepted and liked by others.

External threat seems to influence the desire to affiliate. In a series of classic experiments Schachter (1959) tested the hypothesis that fear may be an important determinant of affiliation. Female subjects were led to believe that after a ten-minute delay, in which the necessary equipment would be set up, they would receive either painful electric shocks or mild, virtually painless stimulation. Each subject was then allowed to choose whether she wanted to wait alone or with some of the other subjects. In the low-fear condition only one-third of the women desired to wait with others, while in the high-fear condition two-thirds of the women preferred to wait with others. Other research has confirmed that fear increases the desire to affiliate.

References

Baumeister, R. F., & Leary, M. R. (1995). The need to belong: Desire for interpersonal attachments as a fundamental human motivation. *Psychological Bulletin, 117,* 497–529.

Berscheid, E. (1985). Interpersonal attraction. In G. Lindzey & E. Aronson (Eds.), *The handbook of social psychology.* New York: Random House.

Mehrabian, A. (1970). The development and validation of measures of affiliative tendency and sensitivity to rejection. *Educational and Psychological Measurement, 30,* 417–428.

Murray, H. A. (1938). *Explorations in personality.* New York: Oxford University Press.

Schachter, S. (1959). *The psychology of affiliation.* Stanford, CA: Stanford University Press.

M. BOLT

See NEEDS; SOCIAL PSYCHOLOGY; PERSONALITY; COOPERATION AND COMPETITION.

Aggression. Cain's murder of his brother Abel is the Bible's first recorded incidence of aggression (Gen. 4). Since then aggression, hostility, and violence typify significant social problems. Understanding aggression's nature is made problematic because of a heterogeneous multiplicity of causes existing at intrapersonal, interpersonal, cultural, and neurobiological levels. Aggression takes multiple forms. In instrumental aggression, aggression functions as a means to achieve an end. In hostile aggression, aggression reciprocates other aggression. In games of aggression, instigation escalates until there is injury. Defensive aggression promotes protective action when one is confronted with a threat.

The core definition of aggression is the intention to inflict physical harm on another person. Surrounding the core are related abuses: inflicting psychological harm, fantasies that envision inflicting pain, and a disregard of consequences from individual actions that harm the larger group. Considering the origins and consequences of aggression is essential to solving the social problems of violence (e.g., assault, homicide, rape), racial hostilities, family discord, and war.

Three threads run through the definition as intent to inflict injury. First, the intention may originate from emotional arousal, particularly negative responses like anger and frustration. Second, the person's intention to harm provides motivational energy. Accidental harming of another, although unfortunate, is not considered aggression. Third, if the instigation is sufficiently intense and if the situation permits, the motivational element is enacted in behavior that harms the other individual. The primary target is the person who originally induced the negative emotion, or a displaced target may provide a safer object. The injury may be physical (e.g., a slap) or psychological (e.g., sarcasm or innuendo). Aggression may be motivated by self-protection or as a response to threat. Aggression involves motivational complexity.

Intrapersonal Origins. The origin of some aggression lies in innate personality factors. In the 1920s Sigmund Freud sought to understand World War I atrocities. He concluded that humans are driven by two instincts: eros (the drive to life) and thanatos (the drive toward death). Aggression is a displaced or turned-around death wish. Much socialization seeks to displace or sublimate the death wish and aggression.

A second internal approach that considers aggression as instinctual is the ethnological theory of Lorenz (1966). Intraspecies aggression and fighting serve to distribute the species over a greater territory. Greater territory provides more resources with which to ensure the survival of the species, as only the strongest mate. Interspecies aggression is merely predation or defense. Morris (1967) popularized and applied this approach to humans. However, Montagu (1976) critiqued the scientific data and concluded that there is little evidence for aggression being an instinct in humans, a view most behavioral scientists share.

A third intrapersonal theory is hedonistic. Dollard, Miller, Doog, Mowrer, and Sears (1939) proposed the frustration-aggression hypothesis in which frustration always led to aggression; aggression always resulted from frustration. The relationship between the two is linear. Frustration is defined as a blocked goal response and aggression as intended harm. This restrictive view was later modified to suggest that frustrations lead to the instigation of aggression rather than overt acts. The effects of frustration are strongest when the individual is attacked rather than the goal blocked, when the frustration is unexpected and arbitrary, when aggressive stimuli are present, or when aggression might be rewarded.

The catharsis hypothesis derived from the frustration-aggression concept. Acting on one's aggression cleansed one of accumulated aggressive instigation. Vicariously participating in aggression (e.g., watching aggression on television) diminished subsequent aggression. Experimental evidence has been mixed and inconsistent (Middlebrook, 1980).

Interpersonal Origins. Certain environmental cues trigger aggression. Berkowitz (1962) theorized that individuals are conditioned to act aggressively when certain cues are present. Classical conditioning was believed to be responsible for teaching aggressive responses (*see* Conditioning, Classical). Conditioning occurs in social contexts as symbols for aggression are communicated from individual to individual. In Berkowitz's view certain symbols (e.g., weapons) trigger aggression. In a classic study Berkowitz and LePage (1967) demonstrated that the presence of a gun increased the level of aggression.

Bandura (1973) developed an alternate view. According to social learning theory, two separate aspects of learning affect the production of aggression (*see* Learning, Social). Aggression, like most complex behaviors, is first learned by imitation. Whether this learning leads to aggressive action depends upon the anticipated consequences. Vicarious reinforcement of aggression leads to aggression in the imitators; vicarious punishment for aggression suppresses aggression in imitators.

The perspectives of Berkowitz and Bandura noted that aggression has not only interpersonal and social consequences (i.e., injury to another human) but interpersonal and social origins as well. Aggression is communicated and taught in socialization, especially when prevailing sex roles equate maleness and aggressiveness.

Other observations strengthen this view. Aggression and violence operate as subcultural norms (e.g., in military units, professional contact sports, juvenile gangs). Aggressive norms manifest themselves under intense economic competition for limited resources. The economic competition hypothesis predicts aggression is probable to the extent that the rival group is seen as hostile and dissimilar and to the extent that resources are limited and unjustly distributed (e.g., strikes, wars). This aggression is strengthened if the restraining forces against aggression are reduced (e.g., anonymity as a factor in looting or shared guilt in gang violence). Deindividuation and depersonalization of other groups' members serve to justify aggression. Frustration and emotional arousal also operate as personal instigating forces in these group interactions.

These approaches do not provide an altogether adequate explanation for violence as a transaction (e.g., domestic violence, personal abuse, or war). Toch (1969) explained that aggression is a predictable sequence: one member of a dyad is provoked and confronts the other. The other reacts defensively and counterattacks. The argument escalates to other issues. If the confrontation-escalation sequence is not halted, the verbal dispute results in physical attack. The provocation-confrontation-escalation stages explain domestic disputes and international incidents.

Social and Clinical Syndromes. Western cultures socialize males to be aggressive through sex-typing mechanisms of imitation, identification, and reinforcement (Maccoby & Jacklin, 1974). Recent studies link genetic and hormonal factors in males to aggression. Testosterone functions not only as a hormone of sexual pursuit but also as the hormone for aggression in males (Carlson, 1994). A close derivative of the androgen has a similar effect in females.

Others have hypothesized that aggression may be linked to abnormalities of the Y chromosome. A chromosomal aberration found in some males is the existence of an additional Y chromosome, making the genotype XYY. Several studies have found that the incidence of XYY males is greater in prison populations than in the population at large. The XYY inmates are more likely to be charged with violent crimes against persons than with property crimes like burglary and forgery.

Disturbances involving aggression characterize both the personality that is undercontrolled and the one that is overcontrolled. In the undercontrolled personality inhibitions against aggression are weak, so that the individual reacts impulsively when provoked. Aggression in the undercontrolled is no surprise. But when the silent, introverted individual erupts in a violent display of anger, everyone is horrified and questions how it happened. Megargee (1966) suggested that the expression of emotion is normally inhibited in this overcontrolled individual. The person stores up aggression over a long time. At some point the inhibitory brake fails and the individual explodes in a violent outburst. The outburst is often disproportional to the triggering event. Both personalities have not learned the ability to handle aggression-arousing emotions in socially acceptable ways.

Horney (1937) advanced another clinical hypothesis linking personality to hostility and anxiety. Hostility stems from a sense of injustice and unfairness in life. The connection between hostility and injustice seems particularly acute in males and is exacerbated if in the male's socialization there is no differentiation between various negative emotions: frustration, fear, anger, or anxiety. Anger and hostility become the undifferentiated response to any situation that arouses an unpleasant or negative emotion in cultures and family units that expect males not to cry and rely on punitive and authoritarian discipline styles.

Aggression is a perverse and pervasive phenomenon covering a wide gamut, from indirect expression in racial jokes and gossip to direct expression in crimes of passion and international warfare. Accounts of its origins range from instinctual and genetic predispositions to cultural conditioning; personality dynamics play a prominent role.

References

Bandura, A. (1973). *Aggression: A social learning analysis.* Englewood Cliffs, NJ: Prentice-Hall.

Berkowitz, L. (1962). *Aggression.* New York: McGraw-Hill.

Berkowitz, L., & LePage, A. (1967). Weapons as aggression-eliciting stimuli. *Journal of Personality and Social Psychology, 7,* 202–207.

Carlson, N. R. (1994). *Physiology of behavior* (5th ed.). Boston: Allyn & Bacon.

Dollard, J., Miller, N. E., Doog, L. W., Mowrer, O. H., & Sears, R. R. (1939). *Frustration and aggression.* New Haven, CT: Yale University Press.

Horney, K. (1937). *The neurotic personality of our time.* New York: Norton.

Lorenz, K. (1966). *On aggression.* New York: Harcourt, Brace, & World.

Maccoby, E., & Jacklin, C. (1974). *The psychology of sex differences.* Stanford, CA: Stanford University Press.

Megargee, E. (1966). Undercontrolled and overcontrolled personality types in extreme antisocial aggression. *Psychological Monographs, 80* (3), whole no. 611.

Middlebrook, P. (1980). *Social psychology and modern life* (2nd ed.). New York: Knopf.

Montagu, A. (1976). *The nature of human aggression.* New York: Oxford University Press.

Morris, D. (1967). *The naked ape.* New York: McGraw-Hill.

Toch, H. (1969). *Violent men: An inquiry into the psychology of violence.* Chicago: Aldine.

R. L. Timpe

See Anger; Social Psychology; Personality.

Aging. *See* Geriatric Psychotherapy; Gerontology; Life Span Development.

Agitation. A state of anxiety and marked restlessness manifested by psychomotor activities such as pacing, insomnia, handwringing, continuous talking, and constant movement. Feelings of worthlessness and hopelessness are often present, and in severe cases of agitated depression, talk of death or suicide is observed frequently.

Agnosia. The loss of ability to recognize a symbol despite intact functioning of the sense organs. Nonrecognition of linguistic symbols, auditory or visual, is classified as aphasia. The term *agnosia* therefore is reserved for nonlinguistic symbols. The most common agnosias are astereognosis or tactile agnosia (the inability to identify familiar objects by touch), visual agnosia (the inability to recognize familiar visual symbols), and auditory agnosia (the inability to recognize familiar noises or melodies).

Agnosia is usually the result of neurological damage or disease.

See DEMENTIA.

Agoraphobia. An abnormal or exaggerated dread of being in open spaces. The person suffering from agoraphobia is panic-stricken even at the thought of going outdoors and usually remains at home.

See PHOBIC DISORDERS.

Agraphia. A subdivision of aphasia, agraphia is the state of being unable to communicate one's thoughts or ideas in writing. The inability may involve individual letters or entire words and phrases. While it is commonly attributed to cerebral disorders, agraphia may also be psychically or emotionally induced as a result of melancholic inhibition.

AIDS. Acquired Immunodeficiency Syndrome (AIDS) is a fatal medical condition in which a person's immune system is suppressed, leaving him or her vulnerable to a variety of infections that people with healthy immune systems will usually be able to fight. AIDS is characterized by extreme weight loss, cognitive and motor dysfunction, various viral, fungal, and bacterial infections, and a number of cancers and pneumonia. It is believed that any one or a combination of these illnesses will result in death.

Most research suggests that AIDS is the direct result of being infected with the Human Immunodeficiency Virus (HIV). HIV is a retrovirus that primarily infects the T-helper cells of the immune system. The loss of T-cells will eventually manifest in the immune suppression associated with AIDS. The virus is thought to have a variable incubation period such that when they contract HIV, most people are not symptomatic or complain of flulike symptoms that disappear quickly. People infected with HIV can be asymptomatic for five to ten years. Eventually the immune system of HIV-infected individuals will become suppressed by the virus and they will start demonstrating symptoms of AIDS, such as viral infections, rare forms of cancer, or pneumonia. People infected with HIV die because their suppressed immune system cannot protect them from these illnesses.

HIV is transmitted by blood, semen, vaginal fluid, and (rarely) breast milk. HIV is not transmitted by water, air, saliva, or casual contact. Transmission of HIV may occur by any activity in which blood, semen, or vaginal fluid is exchanged between a person who is HIV-infected and someone who is not. This includes injecting drugs using shared needles with someone who is infected or having oral, vaginal, or anal sex with someone who is infected. A baby who is exposed to the blood of an HIV-infected mother during pregnancy or delivery or who has been exposed to infected breast milk is at risk. Anyone receiving blood products, such as in a transfusion, is also at risk. However, routine testing of the blood supply in the United States since 1985 has greatly limited the risk of transmission via blood transfusions.

The most common way that HIV is transmitted is through sexual contact. Any sexual behavior that involves the exchange of semen, vaginal fluids, and/or blood may result in transmitting HIV from an infected person to a previously uninfected person. The risk of transmission can be greatly reduced if latex condoms are used during sexual activities. The only way to surely protect against HIV infection is to refrain from having sexual contact with anyone whose HIV status is unknown. Since 1988 massive AIDS education programs have been undertaken to promote safe sex and abstinence as well as to educate the public about HIV and AIDS. AIDS awareness programs are targeting adolescents and youth in an effort to curb the dramatic increases of infection in teenagers and young adults.

Researchers have developed tests that can accurately diagnose someone who has been infected with HIV. The most commonly used and accurate test for HIV is a test for antibodies that the body mobilizes to fight the virus. These antibodies develop 6 to 12 weeks after a person has contracted the virus; thus this test may not identify a person who has been infected within the 3 months prior to testing. It is recommended that people who believe they may have come in contact with the blood, semen, or vaginal fluids of someone who is known to be infected with HIV, or whose HIV status is unknown, should be tested after the incubation period has passed.

AIDS is a pandemic that crosses all geographic boundaries and affects every segment of the population. Worldwide 4.5 million cases of AIDS have been diagnosed, with close to another 20 million people being infected with HIV. AIDS first appeared in the United States in the early 1980s and had reached pandemic proportions by 1985. Initially it was thought that the virus infected only high-risk groups such as homosexual and bisexual men, intravenous drug users, and recipients of blood transfusions, because it was in these groups that high rates of HIV infection occurred. However, AIDS is now the primary cause of death among all persons between 25 and 44. HIV infection rates are disproportionately higher among African-Americans and Hispanics when compared to infection rates among whites.

People who are infected with HIV are living longer than at any other time during the epidemic. Increasing biomedical research is focusing on developing pharmacological treatments that directly attack HIV to inhibit its proliferation and its destruction of the immune system. One of the most common drugs used is zidovudine (AZT), which works by inhibiting an enzyme necessary for HIV replication. Zidovudine works in slowing HIV growth but may have a number of side effects, including bone marrow suppression. Other medical interventions focus on preventing or treating the various diseases that are usually protected against by a healthy immune response. Prophylactic treatments for such common illnesses associated with AIDS as *Pneumocystis carinii* pneumonia are started early in the course of HIV infection to assist an already deteriorating immune system. The most promising treatment for prolonging the lives of HIV-infected people is the combination of zidovudine with other drugs that assist in destroying HIV's replicating enzymes and drugs that help to prevent opportunistic bacterial or viral infections and cancers. Much has been learned about HIV and AIDS in the first 15 years of the epidemic, and advances in treatment continue to emerge.

The experience of psychological distress over the course of HIV infection differs markedly among people. Responses to HIV infection range from extreme anxiety to an immobilizing melancholy. Psychological distress usually subsides after notification of infection, being followed by an adjustment phase that is punctuated by various events over the course of infection. Such milestones include seeking treatment for immunosuppression, seeking treatment for opportunistic infections, and various end-of-life activities such as drafting a will. Some individuals react with anger, despair, guilt, or confusion at any of these milestones. Suicidal ideation and attempts are reported to be higher among individuals infected with HIV when compared to the general population, with greatest risk for suicide occurring during the early stages of infection. As a person learns of his or her immune system failing, becomes diagnosed with an opportunistic illness, or experiences the death from AIDS of someone close, he or she will likely experience marked distress and suicidal ideation. The psychological adjustment of a person infected with HIV can be expected to change unpredictably with each significant life episode related to the illness.

HIV or AIDS also has a significant emotional impact on loved ones. Not only attempting to negotiate the grief associated with the dying of a family member, spouse, or friend, loved ones often also take on a physically and emotionally taxing role as primary caregiver for an individual dying of AIDS. Spouses or other people close to a person in the late stages of AIDS may be handling the difficult notion that they too are infected with HIV. In the death of their loved one, they see their own end.

The Christian community has responded variably to the AIDS crisis. Initially AIDS carried a stigma associated with homosexuality. Some church leaders considered AIDS to be God's punishment on homosexuals for their sins of sexual deviance and referenced the plague of the end days (Rev. 6:8). However, such radically misguided theological perspectives as this are not representative of how the church has reacted to the AIDS crisis. In a growing number of cases the church has reacted with the same gentleness and charity Christ bestowed on the lepers of his time (Cambridge, 1993).

Following the diagnosis of HIV infection or AIDS, people have been shown to have dramatic psychological reactions and shifts in meaning, purpose, and values (Schaefer & Coleman, 1992). The church is in a position to offer spiritual direction and support to both the individual who has been infected and his or her caregiver; it is a calling of the church to assist in any way it can in the course of this human tragedy. The church can offer comfort and assist in facing the fear of death (Heb. 2:14–15).

References

Cambridge, B. S. (1993). Women and HIV disease. In T. Eidson (Ed.), *The AIDS caregiver's handbook*. New York: St. Martin's.

Schaefer, S., & Coleman, E. (1992). Shifts in meaning, purpose, and values following a diagnosis of human immunodeficiency virus (HIV) infection among gay men. *Journal of Psychology and Human Sexuality, 51,* 13–29.

Additional Reading

Kalichman, S. C. (1995). *Understanding AIDS: A guide for mental health professionals*. Washington, DC: American Psychological Association.

E. M. BUTTER

See SEXUALLY TRANSMITTED DISEASES.

Alcohol Abuse and Dependence. Humans have used, abused, and become dependent upon alcohol from the time of earliest recorded history. Until about five hundred years ago alcoholic beverages were made by fermenting organic juices, with a natural maximum alcohol content of 14%. Then Europeans developed distilled spirits, with an alcohol content of up to 99%.

Noah is shown to have become drunk (Gen. 9), and various ancient cultures record both the use and abuse of alcohol. The Book of Proverbs admonishes the reader not to abuse alcohol (Prov. 23:29–35).

The Roman philosopher Seneca was aware of the difference between alcohol abuse and alcohol dependence. He "distinguished sharply between 'a man who is drunk' and one 'who has no control over himself . . . who is accustomed to get drunk, and is a slave to the habit'" (Keller, 1976, p. 1698).

According to the Alcohol, Drug Abuse and Mental Health Administration, more than 7 million Americans are estimated to be alcohol abusers, and 10.5 million people are affected by alcoholism. Alcohol is a factor in 50% of all traffic fatalities. Hospital emergency room studies implicate alcohol in 22% of home injuries, 16% of on-the-job injuries, and 56% of fights leading to hospital treatment (Alcohol, Drug Abuse and Mental Health Administration, 1989, p. 2).

Definition and Diagnostic Criteria. The World Health Organization (1977) defined alcohol dependence syndrome as "a state, psychic and usually also physical, resulting from taking alcohol, characterized by behavioral and other responses that always include a compulsion to take alcohol on a continuous or periodic basis in order to experience its psychic effects, and sometimes to avoid the discomfort of its absence; tolerance may or may not be present."

In 1994 the American Psychiatric Association (APA) updated its diagnostic criteria for alcohol-related problems in a way that clearly differentiates among alcohol intoxication, abuse, and dependency. This is particularly helpful for pastors and other Christian workers who seek to understand how the sin of drunkenness and the disease of alcoholism relate to each other (American Psychiatric Association, 1994, pp. 181–197).

Alcohol Intoxication. The APA (1994) does not define a single use of alcohol leading to intoxication as alcohol abuse. However, while not labeling intoxication as sin, the APA describes the effects of intoxication as "clinically significant maladaptive behavioral changes," such as "inappropriate sexual or aggressive behavior, mood changes, impaired judgment, impaired social or occupational functioning [accompanied by] slurred speech, incoordination, unsteady gait [up to and including] coma" (p. 197).

Life Patterns Related to Alcohol Abuse. As seen by the APA (1994), "the identifying characteristic of alcohol *abuse* is a maladaptive *pattern* . . . manifested by recurrent and significant adverse consequences" (p. 182). Alcohol abusers may have poor school and job performance, neglect their children or homes, operate vehicles while drunk, or initiate family violence yet not show the three key signs of alcohol dependence. While such persons have a chronic sinful life pattern, they may not have the disease of alcoholism.

Diagnosis of Alcohol Dependence. There are seven professional diagnostic criteria for all types of substance dependence, including alcohol dependence (American Psychiatric Association, 1994). The three leading indicators for a diagnosis of alcohol dependence are evidence of tolerance, symptoms of withdrawal, and a pattern of compulsive use. Physical tolerance as related to alcohol means the need or ability to drink increasing amounts of liquor to get the same effect. It can also mean that individuals no longer get obviously drunk with the same amount of alcohol that used to make them intoxicated. Many maintenance alcoholics have high tolerance levels yet do not appear to be drunk.

Physical withdrawal from alcohol is defined as including at least two of the following: "sweating or pulse rate greater than 100, increased hand tremor, insomnia, nausea or vomiting, transient . . . hallucinations, psychomotor agitation, anxiety, and/or grand mal seizures" (American Psychiatric Association, 1994, p. 198).

Compulsive use of alcohol means that alcohol is often taken in larger amounts over a longer period of time than planned. The alcohol-dependent person does not have the ability to be a moderate drinker, although this individual does have the ability to be abstinent, with the help of Jesus Christ, a supportive church family, and a recovery fellowship such as Alcoholics Anonymous or Overcomers Outreach.

The APA (1994) sets forth four additional criteria for substance dependence, including alcohol dependence: "unsuccessful efforts to cut down or control substance use, a great deal of time spent in activities to obtain, use, or recover from the effects of the substance, important social, occupational or recreational activities are given up or reduced . . . and . . . continued [use] despite recurrent physiological or psychological problems [caused by it]."

Presumed Causes. There are agreed-upon professional standards for defining the differences among alcohol use, intoxication, abuse, and dependence. However, in spite of significant research in this field, major differences of opinion remain regarding the presumed causes of alcoholism. The field has not become substantially more unified than it was in 1959, when Mann, a leader in alcohol research and treatment, wrote, "Almost everyone who has given it any thought at all, has had an opinion on the cause of alcoholism. These opinions, however, have differed widely. The temperance groups held that alcohol was the cause, and the only cause. The wet groups, not only the dispensers of liquor, but drinkers as well, have held that the cause lay in the individual drinker's own deliberate abuse of the privilege of drinking. A third major opinion held that alcoholism was caused entirely by the drinker's lack of will power or character" (Mann, 1959, p. 11).

How one understands the cause(s) of alcoholism will greatly influence the preferred approach to treatment. Differing approaches to understanding the etiology of alcoholism may be loosely grouped into three categories: physical models, moral models, and pain-based models.

Physical Models. Alcoholics Anonymous (1989), the largest and most successful self-help program for alcoholics, understands alcoholism to be physically based and defines it as "an illness, a progressive illness, which can never be cured, but which, like some other illnesses, can be arrested. Going one step further, many AA's feel that the illness represents the combination of a physical sensitivity to alcohol, plus a mental obsession with drinking which, regardless of consequences, cannot be broken by will power alone" (p. 4). This approach, pioneered by Jellinek (Jellinek & Haggard, 1942, pp. 4–5), is called the disease model of alcoholism.

Some genetic studies, most notably that regarding the dopamine D2 postsynaptic receptor gene published in the *Journal of the American Medical Association* (Blum et al., 1990), have suggested specific genetic causes for up to 69% of alcoholics. Other biochemical researchers have noted various brain differences between alcoholics and nonalcoholics but attributed these to a progressive degeneration of brain function due to prolonged alcohol abuse. Adoption studies, which isolate physical inheritance from sociological factors, have shown alcoholism rates up to three times as high in adopted-away sons of alcoholic parents as compared with adopted-away sons of nonalcoholic parents. Studies of the inherited transmission of alcoholism in women have been less conclusive (Svikis, Velez, & Pickens, 1994, p. 195).

Moral Models. The effective contribution of faith-based ministries to the reclamation of alcoholics and other addicts, such as the services provided by the members of the International Union of Gospel Missions, the Salvation Army's 119 Adult Rehabilitation Centers, and the extensive network of Teen Challenge residential programs, is often overlooked by non-Christian professionals. The religious understanding of the cause(s) and treatment of addictions, including alcoholism, is often labeled moral or, more negatively, moralistic.

However, there are two significantly different types of moral models regarding the use of alcohol and other addictive substances. One model is a conservative, abstinence-based model that is usually but not always religious in nature, the dry moral model. This model suggests that no one should use these substances, even if they are fortunate enough not to become addicted. Some evangelical versions of this model define all use of beverage alcohol as sin even for nonaddicted individuals, sometimes adding that as Christians we accept social responsibility for the failures of others due to our example (1 Cor. 8:6–13).

In contrast to the dry moral model, the wet moral model of alcoholism is a moderation-based rather than abstinence-based approach. This model asserts that the nonabusive use of beverage alcohol and other intoxicating substances (such as marijuana, if it were legal) is legitimate and even beneficial. Primary support for this model comes from the alcoholic beverage industry, some religiously liberal groups, and most moderate nonaddicted drinkers. Scientific rationale for this model is presented by some behavioral psychological theorists who postulate that immoderate drinking is due to problems in intrinsic or extrinsic reinforcement and/or the failure to learn appropriate coping responses to limit alcohol intake.

The moralism of the dry moral model lies in its assumption that those who cannot or will not drink moderately are demonstrating a basic failure to exercise will power and personal responsibility. In this model the goodness or badness of the use of various mood-altering substances is determined solely by the responsibility that the user takes for moderate use under appropriate circumstances. Therefore, those persons who are able to control their use are seen as responsible (good) persons. Those persons who are unable to control their use are seen as irresponsible (bad) persons. No social responsibility is accepted by the moderate users for the anguish and torment that accrues to the immoderate users.

Pain-Based Models. The dominant secular psychological approach to the causes of alcoholism is the medical model used in both inpatient and outpatient therapy. The medical model is actually a psychological rather than a biochemical model. The primary premise of this model is that beverage alcohol is being misused in an attempt to self-medicate in order to cover up underlying psychological stress, which may stem from childhood development problems, sexual abuse, adult experiences of failure, or other unresolved emotional experiences or unconscious needs.

A study by the Research Institute on Addictions in Buffalo, New York, showed that 42% of adult alcoholism patients had experienced either sexual abuse or severe physical violence as children. Physical abuse was reported by 33% of the women and 29% of the men, while sexual abuse was reported by 49% of the women and 11% of the men (Windle, 1996, p. 9). Addiction psychologists Hemfelt and Fowler (1990, pp. 18–19) suggest that the first two steps of the addictions cycle are "(1) pain, and (2) reaching out to an addictive agent, such as work, food, sex, alcohol, or dependent relationships to salve our pain."

A more holistic, pain-based healing model is being explored by some Christian psychologists and pastors who work regularly with alcoholics. This model combines psychodynamic insights with biblical understandings of spiritual woundedness and sin into a Christian conceptual framework for understanding alcoholism and recovery (Arterburn & Stoop, 1992).

Treatment Approaches. During the last 30 years a somewhat standard process for middle-class alcoholism treatment has developed: intervention—group persuasion by family members, employer, or clergy to enter treatment; detoxification—3 to 5 days of medical or social treatment eliminating alcohol and/or other drugs from the body, followed by treatment—21 to 28 days of hospitalization, including individual and group therapy and introduction to Alcoholics Anonymous; and followup—1 to 2 years of outpatient counseling, along with regular participation in a self-help group for recovering alcoholics.

However, because there is such a difference in understanding of the cause(s) of alcoholism, there is also substantial variation in what approach is used during the process of alcoholism treatment. The Joint Commission on Accreditation of Hospitals (JCAH), after investigating the most effective treatments for alcoholism, stated, "[The hospital alcoholism treatment] staff need not be committed to any particular thought or philosophy" (Joint Commission on Accreditation of Hospitals, 1974, p. 4).

In a separate review the New York State Division of Alcoholism (1975, p. 24) defined alcoholism as "a complex illness whose etiology is currently not understood." While recommending eight categories of service (such as 24-hour emergency services or outpatient clinics), this task force was unable to define any favored treatment modality, stating, "while alcoholic persons share a common illness, their needs and responses to care often differ."

These differences among alcoholics and the documented differences in response to varied treatment approaches mean that treatment strategies are often selected by treatment providers on the basis of individual beliefs about the causes of alcoholism and the hope for reversal or remission of its effects.

Two different Alcoholics Anonymous approaches, a new physically based treatment, the conversionist dry and behaviorist wet moral models, and two psychodynamic medical and healing models are reviewed below.

Two Different Alcoholics Anonymous (AA) Approaches. All members of AA attend regular meetings to learn "a simple program that has proved effective for thousands of other men and women" (Alcoholics Anonymous, 1989, p. 4). Although AA believes alcoholism to have a physical origin, neither of these approaches is biophysical, since AA understands that an alcoholic will always be physiologically addicted, even when in recovery and not using alcohol for many years. Interviews with hundreds of AA attenders show that they do not all interpret the "simple program" the same way, and they can be roughly classified into two groups regarding their understanding of the effective sobriety-producing agent present in Alcoholics Anonymous.

While AA literature promotes a 12-step program of recovery, many persons who have attended AA seem to have comprehended only a fellowship model. "Alcoholics Anonymous, the most successful organization involved in the treatment of the alcoholic, has made fellowship a cornerstone in their efforts to help the individual. We must do the same, no matter how difficult, if we are going to help our alcoholic" (Dunn, 1986, p. 83). A familiar AA slogan is "people, places and things." The idea of this slogan is that a person stays sober by spending his time in AA and with sober AA people instead of at the bar. Although this is a somewhat fragile prescription, many people have begun their sobriety in just this way. However, this is not the complete 12-step model of the AA literature. Still, many people believe they are working the AA program when they are working this fellowship model rather than a 12-step model. In a sense these people are following psychological behavior theory. They have not changed their intrinsic motivators, but they have changed their extrinsic behavioral reinforcers.

The complete AA 12-step model is much more complex than that of mere fellowship with sober companions. The 12 steps may be loosely listed as admission of powerlessness over alcohol and openness to spiritual factors (steps 1–3); internalization of moral factors in self-control (steps 4–6), repentance toward God and rediscovery of personal responsibility (steps 7–9), and the spiritual maintenance steps (steps 10–12) (Hemfelt & Fowler, 1990, pp. 18–19).

Therefore, when Alcoholics Anonymous or other 12-step-based organizations begin to work with a person, they are offering neither medical treatment nor fellowship and support. They are offering a new, spiritually based way of life. Although the AA program is not specifically Christian or even religious,

it can lead to a strong, vibrant Christian life when appropriate pastoral support and biblically integrated recovery materials (Arterburn & Stoop, 1992; Hemfelt & Fowler, 1990) are provided to the recovering person.

Physically Based Treatment Approaches. Although many researchers, including the National Institute on Alcohol Abuse and researcher Theodore Reich, a psychiatric geneticist at Washington University, are "convinced that there is a pharmacogenetics of alcoholism" (Holden, 1991, p. 163), there has been no vaccine or any other medical cure. However, in 1995 the Food and Drug Administration (FDA) approved the use of the drug Naltrexone as the "first pharmacologic agent for alcoholism in 47 years" (Enos, 1995, p. 2). Preliminary research shows that Naltrexone reduces the pleasurable effect of alcohol and may reduce alcohol consumption. Caution in the prescription of Naltrexone is still indicated, since the drug is approved for use only in conjunction with an alcoholism treatment program and not in the absence of other psychological, social, or spiritual interventions.

Two Different Moral Treatment Approaches. As described by its proponents, the dry moral model treatment approach has less to do with morality and legalism than with the power of religious conversion to Jesus Christ. This conversionist (and sometimes, deliverance) approach emphasizes the power of God to release one from the sinful bondage to alcohol, the redemption of the cross, the fellowship with God's people on earth, and the reward of heaven as powerful stimulants to sobriety. This approach has been highly effective in promoting an initial release from alcohol use and abuse, and the conversionist dry moral model's emphasis upon lifelong abstinence is seen as protecting the physiologically addicted person from relapse and backsliding. However, the most effective faith-based alcoholism programs also have residential components with behavioral limits, linkages with strong, caring church fellowships, psychological support where appropriate, and educational and vocational opportunities for those who need them.

The wet moral model, by comparison, places a strong emphasis on the positive value of moderate drinking, with the following therapeutic implication: "a person is not cured of the liquor habit until he can take a drink without going into an alcoholic binge" (Richardson & Woolfolk, 1954, p. 109). This absolutist condemnation of both those who are alcohol dependent and those who are alcohol abstinent has been maintained by some apparently responsible theorists, although the most highly publicized research project for creating moderate drinkers from those previously addicted ended in complete failure: "In the 1970's, two American psychologists, Mark and Linda Sobel, claimed to be able to teach hospitalized alcoholics how to control their drinking. A subsequent independent followup of these supposedly happy controlled drinkers showed just the opposite. The vast majority were rehospitalized for alcoholism, arrested for alcohol related crimes, divorced, seriously ill from alcohol induced diseases or dead" (Kirk, 1995, p. 5).

Although there are some anecdotal accounts of individual alcohol abusers who have apparently become moderate drinkers, the limited studies of moderation programs have usually been conducted by those attempting to operate and promote those programs rather than by independent researchers. One example is a RAND Corporation study that "claimed to find that a quarter of its sample of alcoholics was capable of normal drinking. But the further work showed that only a tiny fraction of the sample could sustain patterns of lower consumption over longer periods. Most subjects, if they did not try to remain completely sober, were drinking dangerously and destructively" (Kirk, 1995, p. 5).

In spite of recurrent theoretical proposals and uncritical media publicity for experimental moderation programs, no substantial body of research evidence supports the idea that alcohol-dependent drinkers can be trained to increase their will power and refusal skills ("know when to say when") to reduce their drinking patterns to moderate levels on a lifetime basis. What appears to be good advice for the moderate drinker has not been proven helpful for the addicted alcoholic. It remains possible, however, that a small minority of alcohol abusers may be able to alter their drinking patterns to moderate use without becoming abstinent.

Pain-Based Treatment Approaches. Two different pain-based models share the common psychodynamic assumption that addiction to alcohol is primarily a symptom of underlying pain. The pain-based medical model is not the same as the disease model, since its causal assumptions are psychological rather than biological in nature.

The medical model, which is rooted in humanistic psychology, assumes that people are born good and would, in a perfect world, grow up with healthy egos and would not become addicted. However, psychological pain, in the form of emotional or physical childhood neglect, sexual abuse, or other psychosocial stressors, has become internalized and unresolved and results in the symptom of alcoholism and/or other addictions. Individual insight therapy and psychodynamic group therapy are recommended to bring the damaged emotions and unresolved conflicts to the surface. This awareness will, it is proposed, result in the addiction becoming no longer necessary. This model does not take a specific position on the value of abstinence versus moderation, although individual therapists may emphasize one or the other.

The healing model is also a pain-based model. The understanding of the etiology of addiction is similar to or even identical to that of the medical model, except that this model acknowledges the universality of original sin rather than assumes the inherent goodness of the human race. A major difference between the two models is in the arena of treatment. Psychodynamic insight is valued in both models, but the healing model attempts to heal the emotional woundedness that insight reveals, through prayer therapy (in this model's more intellectual form) or by using specific words or symbolic acts of spiritual deliverance (in this model's more concrete and active form). The healing model shares some language forms and theological presuppositions with the dry moral conversionist model, but its treatment approaches are more graduated and share similarities with the medical model. A strong emphasis on the relational value of acceptance into the church as a loving family of God is also a characteristic of this approach. The healing model usually promotes abstinence from alcohol rather than moderation.

Pastoral Prevention and Intervention. While the family is undoubtedly the most effective force in a child's life for prevention of alcohol abuse and dependence, school- and church-based alcohol prevention educational programs may augment positive family influence. The largest national program in public schools is Drug Abuse Resistance Education (D.A.R.E.), which presents information about addictive substances and exposes manipulative advertising in an effort to counterbalance the pressures placed on children to drink and use drugs. An effective Christian group program for grade-school children, used by an increasing number of churches, is the "Confident Kids" program developed by the National Association for Christian Recovery (NACR) in Yorba Linda, California (Kondracki, 1995, pp. 20–21).

Pastors and other Christian workers seeking to determine whether an adult who drinks is alcohol-dependent may find it helpful to use the CAGE questionnaire developed by the Center for Alcohol Studies at the University of North Carolina. There are four basic questions: Ever feel the need to *C*ut down on drinking? Ever feel *A*nnoyed by critics of drinking? Ever been *G*uilty about drinking? Ever take an *E*ye-opener drink in the morning? Positive answers to one or more of these questions have been shown to have an 86% correlation with more extensive diagnostic criteria for alcohol dependence (Liskow et al., 1995, pp. 277–281).

Pastors may be tempted to refer a person experiencing alcohol problems to a family doctor; however, a 1982 poll taken by the American Medical Association shows that 71% of physicians feel either incompetent or ambivalent about treating alcoholism (Lewis, 1989, p. 8). Therefore, it is recommended that pastors identify a residential or outpatient resource in the community that is staffed by persons who have specific experience in working with alcoholism.

For those churches wishing to form a Christian 12-step recovery group for believers, similar to AA but church-based and focused specifically on Jesus Christ, information is available from Overcomers Outreach in La Habra, California. This organization has a network of more than 1,800 church-sponsored groups in the United States (Bartosch, 1993, pp. 2–7).

References

Alcohol, Drug Abuse and Mental Health Administration. (1989, March/April). Alcoholism. *ADAMHA News*, 2–4.

Alcoholics Anonymous. (1989). *44 Questions*. New York: AA General Service Conference.

American Psychiatric Association. (1994). *Diagnostic and statistical manual of mental disorders* (4th ed.). Washington, DC: Author.

Arterburn, S., & Stoop, D. (1992). *The life recovery Bible*. Wheaton, IL: Tyndale House.

Bartosch, B. (1993). *Chemical dependency, compulsive behaviors and codependency within the church*. La Habra, CA: Overcomers Outreach.

Blum, K., Noble, E. P., Sheridan, P. J., Montgomery, A., Ritchie, T., Jagadeeswaren, P., Nogami, H., Briggs, A. H., & Cohen, J. B. (1990). Allelic association of human dopamine D2 receptor gene in alcoholism. *Journal of the American Medical Association*, 263 (15), 2055–2060.

Dunn, J. G. (1986). *God is for the alcoholic*. Chicago: Moody.

Enos, G. A. (1995, April 24). Researchers: Naltrexone use requires knowing possible pitfalls. *Alcoholism and Drug Abuse Weekly*, 7 (17), 2.

Hemfelt, R., & Fowler, R. (1990). *Serenity: A companion for 12-step recovery*. Nashville: Nelson.

Holden, C. (1991). Probing the complex genetics of alcoholism. *Science*, *251*, 163–164.

Jellinek, E. M., & Haggard, H. W. (1942). *Alcohol explored*. Garden City, NY: Doubleday.

Joint Commission on Accreditation of Hospitals. (1974). *Accreditation manual for alcoholism programs*. Chicago: Author.

Keller, M. (1976). The disease concept of alcoholism revisited. *Journal of Studies on Alcohol*, *37*, 1694, 1698, 1717.

Kirk, C. H. (1995). The fallacy of the moderate-drinking argument. *Alcoholism and Drug Abuse Weekly*, 7 (48), 5.

Kondracki, L. (1995). Recovery for kids. *Steps*, *6* (3), 20–21.

Lewis, D. C. (1989). Putting training about alcohol and other drugs into the mainstream. *Alcohol Health and Research World*, *13* (1), 8.

Liskow, B., et al. (1995). Validity of the CAGE questionnaire in screening for alcohol dependence in a walk-in (triage) clinic. *Journal of Studies on Alcohol*, *56* (3), 277–281.

Mann, M. (1959). *New primer on alcoholism*. New York: Rinehart & Co.

New York State Division of Alcoholism. (1975). *Report of the state wide planning effort of alcohol problems*. Albany: Author.

Richardson, E. R., & Woolfolk, J. T. (1954). *Drink and stay sober*. New York: Bridgehead.

Svikis, D. S., Velez, M. L., & Pickens, R. N. (1994, fall). Genetic aspects of alcohol use and alcoholism in women. *Alcohol Health and Research World*, 192–196.

Windle, M. (1966, January 11). Many alcoholics abused as children. *Substance Abuse Funding News*, 9.

World Health Organization. (1977). *International classification of diseases*. Ann Arbor, MI: Author.

J. R. CHEYDLEUR

See CULTURE AND ALCOHOL.

Alcohol-Induced Disorders. According to the American Psychiatric Association (APA), many

American men (60%) and women (30%) have had "one or more alcohol-related adverse life events" such as drunk driving or missing school or work due to a hangover. In addition many adults have been alcohol-dependent (8%) or alcohol abusers (5%) during their lives (American Psychiatric Association, 1994, pp. 194, 202). The negative effects of alcohol use include social problems, medical disorders, alcohol abuse and dependence, and neurological or psychological disorders.

Alcohol-Related Social Problems. A recent study of American college students showed that "more than a quarter of the nation's students are chronic abusers of alcohol," and another study found that "25% of all college dropouts are connected to alcohol problems" (Beneson, 1990, p. 10). From 20% to 36% of suicide victims are alcohol abusers, and the use of guns in connection with suicide also correlates with increased alcohol use (Roizen, 1982, pp. 179–219). Alcohol is a factor in 80% of domestic disputes (*see* Domestic Violence). Alcohol-dependent men are three times as likely to physically abuse their wives as those who are not alcohol-dependent (Jenish, 1993, p. 37).

Crime is often alcohol-related, with 40% of state prison inmates under the influence of alcohol when they committed their crimes. Also, 68% of manslaughter convictions and 62% of assault convictions are alcohol-related (Landers, 1990). Research by the United States Department of Health and Human Services shows that alcohol is "implicated in the four leading causes of accidental death in the United States: motor vehicle crashes, falls, drownings, and fires and burns." Alcohol is involved in 50% of deaths due to traffic crashes, 24% of deaths due to falls, 38% of deaths by drowning, and 64% of deaths due to fires and burns (U.S. Department of Health and Human Services, 1990, pp. 163–167).

Alcohol-Related Medical Disorders. Alcohol is related in one-fourth of medical problems leading to hospitalization (Landers, 1990). Alcohol abuse increases the risk of seizure up to 20 times and is the leading cause of liver disease. Also, 46% of cirrhosis deaths in men and 15% in women are caused by heavy drinking. Various infectious illnesses as well as certain cancers are more common in alcohol-dependent individuals due to alcohol's effect on the immune system. These include pneumonia, tuberculosis, diarrhea, skin and soft tissue infections, urinary tract infections, and sexually transmitted diseases (Christner, 1993, pp. 19–24, 25).

Another problem associated with alcohol is fetal alcohol syndrome (FAS). More than one thousand infants are born mentally retarded each year due to FAS, which decreases Intelligence Quotient from an average of 90–109 (normal) to an average of 68. FAS is due to the use of alcohol by pregnant women (Anstett, 1991).

Other conditions "frequently associated with an alcohol related diagnosis" are "thiamin deficiency, varicose veins, spinocerebellar disease, hypothermia, diseases of the pancreas, coagulation defects, deficiency of B complex components, and gastrointestinal hemorrhage" (U.S. Department of Health and Human Services, 1990, p. 21).

Alcohol Abuse and Dependence. The American Psychiatric Association identifies the two primary alcohol use disorders as alcohol abuse and alcohol dependence. Two related alcohol-induced disorders are alcohol intoxication and alcohol withdrawal (American Psychiatric Association, 1994, p. 195). These four primary classes of alcohol problems are described in Alcohol Abuse and Dependence.

Alcohol-Induced Neurological and Psychological Disorders. In its *Diagnostic and Statistical Manual* (1994) the American Psychiatric Association describes ten alcohol-induced mental disorders.

Alcohol Intoxication Delirium. In delirium there is a reduced awareness of the environment and reduced ability to focus attention. Features may include inability to retrieve recent memories, language problems, problems with writing, and time and place disorientation. Delirium usually develops rapidly when it is related to alcohol intoxication (pp. 130–131).

Alcohol Withdrawal Delirium. Symptoms of delirium due to withdrawal from chronic alcohol abuse may include visual, tactile, or auditory hallucinations. Symptoms usually begin about 4 to 12 hours after alcohol use has been stopped and usually peak on the second day but improve substantially by the fifth day. This condition is often called delirium tremens or DTs (pp. 131–132, 198).

Alcohol-Induced Persisting Dementia. Dementia includes memory impairment and multiple cognitive defects. Four common symptoms are Aphasia (a deterioration of language function), Apraxia (the impaired mental ability to execute motor activities), Agnosia (an inability to identify objects), and executive function disturbance (a group of problems in planning, sequencing, or stopping complex behaviors). Possible nonalcohol causes of dementia include Parkinson's Disease and Alzheimer's Disease (pp. 133–138).

Alcohol-Induced Persisting Amnestic Disorder. Amnestic disorder is a memory disturbance usually characterized by the inability to learn and recall new information. Nonalcohol physical causes include trauma to the head or stroke. Psychiatric causes include dementia and delirium (pp. 161–162).

Alcohol-Induced Psychotic Disorder with Delusions or Hallucinations. Psychotic disorder may occur during alcohol intoxication or withdrawal when there are prominent hallucinations or delusions that are perceived as real by the subject and that are not caused by any other underlying psychotic disorder. If a person has hallucinations or delusions but knows that they are not real, if the symptoms occur only in a delirium, or if the symptoms are not greater than those normally experienced during alcohol intoxication or withdrawal, this diagnosis is inappropriate (pp. 310–315).

Alcohol-Induced Mood Disorder. A mood disorder may be depressed, with diminished interest and/or pleasure, manic (elevated and expansive), or mixed (irritable and changing back and forth). This diagnosis is made when a person is currently experiencing either alcohol intoxication or alcohol withdrawal and the mood disturbances are not better accounted for by some other form of mood disorder (pp. 370–375).

Alcohol-Induced Anxiety Disorder. Alcohol-induced anxiety disorder is characterized by excessive worry but does not always have a single diagnostic focus such as panic, social phobia, physical problems, or separation anxiety. Symptoms are directly related to alcohol intoxication or withdrawal and are not better accounted for by another condition (pp. 439–444).

Alcohol-Induced Sexual Dysfunction. Alcohol intoxication may cause decreased sexual interest and problems with sexual arousal. A diagnosis of alcohol-induced sexual dysfunction is made when there is marked personal distress due to sexual difficulty related specifically to alcohol intoxifcation (pp. 516–522).

Alcohol-Induced Sleep Disorder. Insomnia is the most common form of this disorder. During alcohol intoxication, a sedative effect is produced for about three to four hours, but later the alcohol increases restless sleep, wakefulness, and anxiety-laden dreams. Sleep is also grossly disturbed during alcohol withdrawal. Symptoms may persist up to a month (pp. 602–607).

Summary. A number of medical, social, and mental problems are caused by or made more severe by heavy alcohol use. The addictive effects of alcohol are well documented, as are the neurological and psychological effects of a number of alcohol-related disorders.

References

American Psychiatric Association. (1994). *Diagnostic and statistical manual of mental disorders* (4th ed.). Washington, DC: Author.

Anstett, P. (1991, April 17). Fetal alcohol syndrome brings problems for life. *Detroit Free Press,* pp. 1A+.

Beneson, L. (1990, March 25). Alcoholism and crime. *Newsday,* pp. 10+.

Christner, A. M. (1993). Heavy drinking still major cause of liver disease. *Reference guide to addiction counseling* (2nd ed.). Providence, RI: Manisses Publications.

Jenish, D. (1993, July 19). The battlefield of addiction. *Maclean's,* pp. 36–39.

Landers, R. K. (1990, September 7). Dealing with the dangers of alcohol. *Editorial Research Reports,* 510–522.

Roizen, J. (1982). Estimating alcohol involvement in serious events. *Alcohol Consumption and Related Problems.* Washington, DC: National Institute on Alcohol Abuse and Alcoholism.

U.S. Department of Health and Human Services. (1990). *Seventh special report to the U.S. Congress on alcohol and health.* Washington, DC: Author.

J. R. CHEYDLEUR

See ALCOHOL ABUSE AND DEPENDENCE.

Alcoholics Anonymous (AA). A nonprofit voluntary self-help organization of current and former alcoholics whose aim is to help themselves and others overcome their problem of alcoholism. The first AA group was founded in Akron, Ohio, by a stockbroker and a physician in 1935. The broker, known to AA as Bill W., traced his sobriety to being confronted by a friend who had achieved sobriety by "getting religion." Bill W. could not accept the idea of God, though he could accept a "Universal Mind or Spirit of Nature," so his friend challenged him to "choose your own conception of God" (Alcoholics Anonymous, 1939, p. 22). Thus Bill W. came to see that "it was only a matter of being willing to believe in a power greater than myself. Nothing more was required of me to make my beginning" (p. 22).

The concept of loss of control over alcohol and that of the efficacious belief in a Higher Power of the person's choosing form the foundation of AA's 12 steps to recovery. Alcoholics begin these steps by admitting their loss of control over alcohol and their lives and by believing that a Higher Power can restore them to sanity. Persons are encouraged to make a "decision to turn [their] will and [their] lives over to God" *as they understand him* (p. 71); to make a moral inventory of themselves; to admit to God, self, and others those defects found; to be ready for God to remove those defects; and to ask him to do so. They are to list all persons they have harmed, be willing to make restitution to all, and to proceed to make restitution where appropriate. Finally, the recovering alcoholics are to improve their conscious contact with their Higher Power through prayer and meditation. This spiritual awakening is to result in reaching out to help other struggling alcoholics.

The only requirement for involvement in AA is a desire to stop drinking. Typical problem drinkers might attend their first AA meeting during a period of discouragement or defeat. AA meetings are usually structured to include recovering alcoholics, who identify themselves by only their first names. Several members will then give a testimonial of their struggle with alcoholism and their pilgrimage in the AA program. The troubled drinker can ask for more assistance after the meeting. If he or she is serious about stopping drinking, a recovering alcoholic will volunteer to be the person's sponsor, someone who can be called on for advice and guidance and, of particular importance, who can guide the person through AA's 12 steps. An integral part of the person's recovery program is continued attendance at AA meetings.

Members of AA strictly adhere to a disease conceptualization of alcohol abuse, defining themselves as alcoholics who have the disease alcoholism. Alcoholics are seen as being different from normal individuals. While the alcoholic might have been able to control his or her drinking earlier in life, that person at some point comes to lose control over alcohol consumption, thus becoming an alcoholic. This loss of control is most cogently summarized in the frequently heard AA adage, "one drink, one drunk." The disease is viewed as permanent and as progressive and irreversible. It may be halted in its course by abstinence, but upon any alcohol consumption the alcoholic will reinitiate the chain of abusive drinking at the same level at which he or she became abstinent unless the 12 steps are started over again. Alcoholics who are sober are termed "recovering alcoholics" rather than "recovered alcoholics," since the former implies that the disease has been arrested in its progress rather than cured or reversed.

AA grew enormously in its popularity in the first few decades following its founding, and its members have exerted tremendous effects upon the views of American society regarding the problem of alcoholism. Today there are said to be about 40,000 chapters throughout the world, with membership estimated at one million men and women.

The effectiveness of AA is difficult to gauge. Recovery rates of up to 90% have been claimed. Several factors make the estimation of effectiveness problematic. First, recovery rates differ with differing definitions of success, and no consensus has been achieved on a single definition. Second, success rates are drastically influenced by the parameters set for the population to be studied. Does one include only those who commit themselves to the AA program (a select group), or should all drinkers who have ever attended an AA meeting constitute the sample? Finally, AA meetings and philosophies have been absorbed as supports for many alcoholism treatment programs that also include other treatment methods. How are alcoholics going through these programs to be considered when studying the effectiveness of AA?

Elements of AA philosophy and practice are compelling parallels to Christian faith and practice: submission to God, confession of and restitution for wrongdoing, reliance upon God for the shaping of Personality and behavior, and diligent prayer and meditation to facilitate personal contact with God. These parallels have led many orthodox believers to unequivocally endorse AA.

There are, however, fundamental problems in drawing too close parallels between AA and the evangelical Christian faith. AA was established and its basic philosophies set under the influence of modernist theological thought (Kurtz, 1979), and this influence is strongly reflected in its prescribed belief system. AA adherents are encouraged to believe in a transcendent entity of their own choice. This flexibility in choice of a faith object suggests a basic confidence in faith as faith rather than confidence in faith based on a reliable and benevolent transcendent Being. Also consistent with classical liberal thought is the assumption that the Higher Power is known only through its felt impact and not through external referents such as inspired Scriptures. A third major problem concerns the concept of powerlessness over alcohol. While Scripture addresses the influence of environmental events upon persons (e.g., the exhortations to avoid contact with immorality), we are not pronounced powerless over these influences. In Scripture the description of drunkenness as a moral problem implies responsibility for refraining from alcohol abuse. It appears that AA would state that a recovering alcoholic is responsible for refraining from taking the first drink but cannot be held responsible for subsequent drinking over which he or she has no control. This philosophy is responsible in part for the prevalent conceptualization of alcoholism as a disease rather than a moral or a legal problem. Finally, AA appears to be a religious way of life, including a conversion (Kurtz, 1979, p. 184). The question is whether such a system should be regarded as a secularized religion not incompatible with orthodox faith or as a potentially dangerous mix of near-truth and untruth.

References

Alcoholics Anonymous. (1939). *Alcoholics Anonymous.* New York: Works Publishing Co.
Kurtz, E. (1979). *Not God: A history of Alcoholics Anonymous.* Center City, MN: Hazelden Educational Services.

S. L. JONES

See MUTUAL HELP GROUPS.

Alcoholism. *See* ALCOHOL ABUSE AND DEPENDENCE; CULTURE AND ALCOHOL.

Alexander Technique. A method of improving the use of the body by modifying what Reich has called the muscular armor. The technique was developed by Frederick Alexander, an Australian actor, who discovered that his periodic voice loss while performing was caused by tension in his neck and rib cage. His self-treatment consisted in changing his muscular-skeletal habits through careful awareness of faulty existing patterns and the practice of new ones. This was the birth of the Alexander technique.

The technique is quite simple. The patient gives commands to his own body (e.g., "Let the neck muscles loosen and lengthen") while the therapist uses his hands to assist the body in complying with the command. Neck and head muscles receive the first attention, as Alexander felt that if an individual's head is balanced properly on the spine, the rest of the muscular-skeletal system can then be balanced more easily.

Fritz Perls was greatly influenced by Alexander in his development of Gestalt Therapy. Bioenergetic analysis and other body therapies are the most common psychotherapy systems utilizing the Alexander technique. It is also often used in the training of actors, and general medicine has shown some interest in the technique for the treatment of stress disorders.

Additional Reading

Barlow, W. (1973). *The Alexander technique.* New York: Knopf.

D. G. BENNER

See BIOENERGETIC ANALYSIS.

Alexia. The loss of ability to read, thought to be caused by a cortical lesion.

See READING DISABILITIES.

Alliance for the Mentally Ill (AMI). A group of national, state, and local organizations dedicated to providing support and education to families of the mentally ill while advocating for improvement in the treatment and quality of life for persons with a chronic mental illness. AMI began in 1979 as a grassroots self-help movement by families who had severely mentally ill relatives, and it currently welcomes relatives of the mentally ill, persons with a mental illness, and mental health professionals.

Local and state chapters are affiliated through the National Alliance for the Mentally Ill (NAMI), which provides coordination for referrals, publications, advocacy efforts, and conferences. Weekly or monthly chapter meetings offer educational programs and the opportunity for personal sharing typical of most self-help groups. Telephone support is offered between meetings.

Meetings provide opportunities to express feelings of anxiety, frustration, guilt, and isolation in caring for a mentally ill relative. They also develop a sense of community and a network of social relationships, and they facilitate learning from others coping with similar concerns. Psychoeducational presentations by health care professionals and pamphlets, books, and videotapes help inform members on the latest medications and treatments, working with the legal system, responding to crises, and accessing social services. These efforts seek to reduce stigma, improve family functioning, and increase the awareness of mental health professionals to the needs of AMI families.

AMI groups have developed a powerful legislative advocacy and are the largest lobbying group at the state and national levels for supportive legislation and increased funding of mental health research and services.

Through the *Religious Outreach Network*, which provides literature and speakers for use in churches, AMI seeks to help congregations understand and support the mentally ill and their families.

B. E. ECK

Alloplasty. An adaptation to a stressful situation by altering or manipulating one's external environment. It is contrasted to autoplasty, which is adaptation through changing oneself. The most common forms of alloplasty are flight and defensive behaviors.

Allport, Gordon Willard (1897–1967). American psychologist who established personality as a legitimate psychological study and resurrected the American psychology of religion.

Born in Montezuma, Indiana, Allport was the last of four sons of physician John Edwards Allport, who soon moved his practice to Ohio. Gordon's maternal grandmother was a founder of Free Methodism; his mother, Nellie Wise Allport, strongly influenced his quest for ultimate religious answers. Gordon finished Cleveland public schools in 1915.

Floyd Allport, later an eminent social psychologist, suggested that his brother follow him to Harvard University. Gordon did and stayed there the rest of his life, save seven years. He earned his A.B. in economics and philosophy in 1919. Gordon was inclined toward social service but took an opportunity to teach one year at Robert College in Constantinople (now Istanbul). Unexpectedly comfortable with teaching, he accepted a fellowship to return to Harvard. His doctoral thesis (1922) was titled "An Experimental Study of the Traits of Personality: With Special Reference to the Problem of Social Diagnosis." His first article, also on personality traits, was coauthored with Floyd in 1921. After graduating, Allport studied for two years in Germany and England. The German experience enabled him to interpret German psychology to America and to assist in the immigration of many academic refugees from Nazism.

At Harvard (1924–1926) Allport taught the first recorded personality course offered in America. He delivered his first professional paper, "What Is a Trait of Personality?" while at Dartmouth College, where he taught for the next four years. He returned to Harvard in 1930.

Allport is best known as a personality theorist. As indicated by his thesis and initial papers, he held a trait view of personality, but, emphasizing the uniqueness of individuals, he stressed personal dispositions over common traits. Nonetheless he collaborated on two popular tests of common traits: the A-S Reaction Study (his second and final publication with Floyd) and A Study of Values. Allport used the term *proprium* for his central concept of Self. He believed that an individual's conscious thinking and present life are more important for personality and behavior than the unconscious and childhood or other historical events. He posited his principle of functional autonomy of motives in *Personality: A Psychological Interpretation* (1937). The concept holds that adult motives may develop from basic drives of infancy and childhood, but they become self-sustaining and no longer depend on the baser motives. *Personality* was one of two 1937 books that stimulated teaching about personality in psychology curricula. It was standard reading in personality until Allport's 1961 revision, *Pattern and Growth in Personality.*

Although personality theory was Allport's primary intellectual love, half of his work was in social psychology. Research in mass communication led to work on rumors and morale during World War II, including a daily newspaper feature countering harmful war rumors. Attitudes in general and prejudice in particular were prolonged concerns, with *The Nature of Prejudice* (1954) the germinal work in the field.

As an undergraduate Allport had tried to replace childhood dogmas with a humanistic religion. Soon that position appeared to "exalt one's own intellect and affirm only a precarious man-made set of values. . . . Humility and some mysticism, I felt, were indispensable for me" (1968, p. 382). He became an Episcopalian, active in Boston's Church of the Advent.

Allport wrote little on psychology of religion before the 1940s, when seven articles (10% of his publications for the decade) had religious implications. That rate increased to 22% in the 1960s. *The Individual and His Religion* (1950), more than any other work, reopened American psychology to a serious study of religion.

Allport wrote, "A narrowly conceived science can never do business with a narrowly conceived religion" (1950, p. x). He brought to religious studies the openness he demanded for personality theory, never forsaking the quest for ultimate meanings his mother set him on. In a mature religion, he said, a belief is heuristic—"held tentatively until it can be confirmed or until it helps us discover a more valid belief" (1950, p. 81).

Mature faith also has a "derivative yet dynamic nature" (1950, p. 71). Its motivations are separate from the organic cravings that underlie the religious life; "a mature religious sentiment supplies its own driving power, and becomes dynamic in its own right" (1950, pp. 71–72). This statement simply applies functional autonomy to religion. As early as 1946, Allport's studies of prejudice found churchgoers to be more prejudiced than the nonreligious. This apparent violation of the Christian principle of brotherhood received further attention in *The Nature of Prejudice.* Allport gradually transformed his distinction between immature and mature religion into concepts of extrinsic and intrinsic religion, which became the most influential constructs in the new American psychology of religion. His last research paper (1968, pp. 237–268) presented these widely used measures. The larger number of extrinsic, immature, self-serving churchgoers tended to be prejudiced; the intrinsic minority were relatively free from prejudice.

Allport served as president of the American Psychological Association (1939), the Eastern Psychological Association (1943), and the Society for the Psychological Study of Social Issues (1944); he received the American Psychological Foundation gold medal and the American Psychological Association distinguished scientific contribution award. He edited the *Journal of Personality and Social Psychology* (1938–1949), helped found the interdisciplinary Department of Social Relations at Harvard (1946), and in 1966 was appointed the first Richard Cabot Professor of Social Ethics at the university. The bibliography in *The Person in Psychology* cites almost 250 publications.

References

Allport, G. W. (1937). *Personality: A psychological interpretation.* New York: Holt.

Allport, G. W. (1950). *The individual and his religion.* New York: Macmillan.

Allport, G. W. (1954). *The nature of prejudice.* Reading, MA: Addison-Wesley.

Allport, G. W. (1961). *Pattern and growth in personality.* New York: Holt, Rinehart & Winston.

Allport, G. W. (1968). *The person in psychology.* Boston: Beacon.

R. D. KAHOE

See PSYCHOLOGY OF RELIGION; RELIGIOUS ORIENTATION; PREJUDICE; PERSONALITY.

Altered States of Consciousness. *See* CONSCIOUSNESS.

Altruism. *See* HELPING BEHAVIOR.

Alzheimer's Disease. A common form of dementia that affects approximately 20 million people worldwide (between 2% and 4% of the population over age 65). Typically striking a person in the seventh or eighth decade, Alzheimer's disease (AD) appears first as memory impairment and then slowly, over seven or more years, progresses to affect multiple cognitive abilities (e.g., agnosia, disturbance in planning, organizing, sequencing), personality, language (e.g., aphasia), social/occupational functioning, and motor skills (e.g., apraxia), eventually leading to death. In latter stages individuals might experience a complete loss of ability to function and become bedridden and mute. The annual cost of AD is thought to be over $60,000,000,000 dollars in the United States alone. While a diagnosis of AD can be made only when other possible causes of dementia (e.g., cardiovascular, metabolic, and infectious disorders) have been ruled out, current criteria for diagnosis correctly identify the disease in more than 85% of patients (Friedland, 1993).

Neuropathological correlates present in this neurodegenerative disorder include neurofibrillary tangles (neuron cell bodies filled with paired helical filaments) and senile plaques (degenerating brain tissue surrounding a core of beta-amyloid). The brain areas involved include the hippocampus, neocortical association areas, basal nucleus, and gray matter in other cerebral areas. In addition to these morphological changes, deficiencies in the neurotransmitters acetylcholine and serotonin have been noted.

A number of causes of AD have been advanced. At various times aluminum, poor circulation, deficient immune reactions, and viruses have been proposed as etiological factors in AD; however, current research is concentrating on the genetic contribution to the disease. Putative risk factors for AD include a family history of dementia, Parkinson's disease, or Down's syndrome, which suggests that a genetic factor is implicated. Molecular genetic studies have identified a number of chromosomes that seem to be involved in the development of AD (St. George-Hyslop, 1993). The possibility that chromosome 21 carries genes for AD pathology is suggested by the clinical and pathological evidence of AD in individuals with Down's syndrome (Trisomy 21). Also, the amyloid precursor protein (APP) gene is located on chromosome 21, and when this protein is improperly metabolized in the brain, beta-amyloid builds up and leads to the amyloid core of senile plaques. It appears then that mutations of the APP gene on chromosome 21 are a contributing factor to AD.

Another chromosome apparently involved in AD is chromosome 19. The protein Apolipoprotein E (ApoE) is involved in the transport of cholesterol, and the gene for this protein is encoded on chromosome 19. A version of this gene (ApoE-4) is a suspect in the development of AD pathology. Recently scientists have also identified genes on chromosomes 14 and 1 that are linked to AD etiology. These studies make it clear that there is a genetic contribution to AD and suggest that environmental agents, such as toxic metals and infections, play a relatively minor role in the development of AD.

The finding that various genes are implicated in AD has led to the development of physiological diagnostic tests that look for these genes. One such test indicates whether an individual has the ApoE-4 version of the apolipoprotein gene or some other form. While the test cannot currently predict whether a person who is symptom-free will eventually develop Alzheimer's, it can help a clinician distinguish among possible diseases and diagnose AD in a person who is already suffering from dementia. Other recently developed tests have been praised for their simplicity and usefulness. The eyedrop test, administered during the early stages of cognitive impairment, reveals a loss of the neurotransmitter acetylcholine; positron emission tomography (PET) scanning can expose subtle neuropathological changes well in advance of symptoms. An additional test measures beta-amyloid levels in cerebrospinal fluid.

Many of the treatments for AD center around restoring neurotransmitter (e.g., acetylcholine) function by increasing the synthesis and release of the transmitter, by protecting the transmitter from breakdown, or by acting at the transmitter receptor site (Allen & Burns, 1995). The first drug used in the treatment of AD was Cognex (tacrine), which improves cognition in some patients but has side effects that limit its usefulness. Other drugs with similar modes of action are being tested clinically. Treatments to prevent the development of neurofibrillary tangles or senile plaques are also under development.

References

Allen, N. H. P., & Burns, A. (1995). The treatment of Alzheimer's disease. *Journal of Psychopharmacology, 9,* 43–56.

Friedland, R. P. (1993). Alzheimer's disease: Clinical features and differential diagnosis. *Neurology, 43,* S45–S51.

St. George-Hyslop, P. H. (1993). Recent advances in the molecular genetics of Alzheimer's disease. *Clinical Neuroscience, 1,* 171–175.

Additional Reading

Kolb, B., & Whishaw, I. Q. (1990). *Fundamentals of human neuropsychology* (3rd ed.). New York: Freeman.

K. S. Seybold

See Genetic and Biochemical Factors in Psychopathology.

Ambiguity, Intolerance of. Daily living presents countless issues and situations that are difficult to understand and in which appropriate courses of action are unclear. We are all called upon to respond to complicated interpersonal relationships, new technology, unforeseen turns of events, controversial political questions, and a host of other challenges that require adjustment and creativity in the face of uncertainty.

Tolerance of ambiguity is a personality variable that refers to people's level of comfort and response style in dealing with unclear situations. In a seminal article for research in this area, Budner (1962) defines intolerance of ambiguity as "the tendency to perceive (i.e., interpret) ambiguous situations as sources of threat." Tolerance of ambiguity is defined as "the tendency to perceive ambiguous situations as desirable."

Ambiguous situations, according to Budner, may be characterized by three features. Situations may be ambiguous because they are novel, presenting new or unfamiliar cues. Situations may be ambiguous because they are complex, requiring comprehension of a large amount of information. Situations may also be ambiguous because they are contradictory or insoluble, having elements that do not fit together in clearly organized or logical ways.

Budner developed an intolerance of ambiguity rating scale that has been the methodological cornerstone of research in this area. His scale solicits ratings of subjects' experience of discomfort or threat in the face of ambiguity in terms of both perceptions and feelings (e.g., "Often the most interesting and stimulating people are those who don't mind being different and original") and in terms that point more directly to behavior (e.g., "A good job is one where what is to be done and how it is to be done are always clear").

Budner's subsequent research, as well as that by his successors, reveals some patterns of association of intolerance of ambiguity with other personality variables. Intolerance of ambiguity, for instance, has been both theoretically and empirically associated with measures of conventionality and authoritarianism. It has also been associated with other personality variables, among them cautiousness, dogmatism, and mental rigidity. Tolerance of ambiguity has been associated with unconventionality, daring, individualism, mental flexibility, openness to new ideas, and originality. Intolerance of ambiguity may also be related to career choice, with some data suggesting that students in the arts are more tolerant of ambiguity than students in business and that physicians in primary care specialties such as family medicine are more tolerant of ambiguity than physicians in surgery, radiology, and anesthesiology.

It is not clear whether intolerance of ambiguity changes during the course of life. Some research that examines intolerance of ambiguity in people of different ages reports a fair amount of stability over time. At least one longitudinal study (Helson & Wink, 1992), however, describes increases in tolerance of ambiguity among middle-aged women over a period of ten years. Beginning in their early forties, women displayed these changes together with decreases in dependence and self-criticism and increases in confidence and decisiveness.

There has been lively conceptual and research interest in the relationship of tolerance of ambiguity with religious commitment and practice. In this setting the discussion has focused on the role of religion in reducing uncertainty about the meaning of challenging life struggles and events. Religious commitment, it is argued, provides explanations that help people interpret and make sense of suffering, death, injustice, and other such existential puzzles. A number of authors have suggested, therefore, that the extent of people's religious commitment and activity should be associated with their need to reduce ambiguity and create certainty in dealing with life events.

There is modest support for this proposition. In his original research Budner (1962) reported some association of intolerance of ambiguity with belief in a divine power and with attendance at religious services. He also reported association of tolerance of ambiguity with self-questioning of religious beliefs. Subsequent research has suggested that religious converts and members of religious cults may be more intolerant of ambiguity than are other religious and nonreligious people. Data from converts and cult members are explained in terms of their having more urgent needs than other people for nonambiguous ways of interpreting the complexities of life.

In a landmark study of value priorities and religiosity in four Western religions, Schwartz and Huismans (1995) found support for a number of hypotheses about uncertainty and religious experience. Studying Israeli Jews, Dutch Protestants, Spanish Catholics, and Greek Orthodox, they reported correlations of religious commitment with a number of values (such as security, tradition, and conformity) that were considered to preserve social order and protect individuals against uncertainty. They found negative correlations of religious commitment with a number of values (such as stimulation and self-direction) that were considered to threaten social order and increase individual uncertainty.

Such analyses, however, capture something less than a full picture of the variety of religious experience. Some groups, reflected in the Western religious tradition by such denominations as Unitarian/Universalists and the Society of Friends, give clear priority to openness and dialogue about alternative ideas and to the social gospel of political and economic change. It might be expected that individuals with greater tolerance of ambiguity would be drawn to such denominations. Pargament, Johnson, Echemendia, and Silverman (1985) found that American church members with greater tolerance of ambiguity were more satisfied and involved with churches judged to be more open to different points of view and change; members who were less tolerant of ambiguity were more satisfied and involved with churches judged to be less open to different points of view and change.

Observations such as these raise an important conceptual issue. Much of the research assumes that intolerance and tolerance of ambiguity fall on a continuum, with intolerance being bad and movement toward tolerance being good. However, as we accept involvement with churches with "less openness to different points of view and change" as a legitimate expression of religious faith (as one might also accept surgery as a legitimate choice of medical specialty), we move more toward a conceptual model that views intolerance and tolerance of ambiguity as different but legitimate styles or preferences in approaching the world. Some people accordingly might show more comfort and success in relating to a narrower field of possibilities, with other people showing more comfort and success relating to larger fields of possibility. The challenge for future research that follows from this model is to find neutral, nonpejorative language with which to describe the "narrower field" style. Gerrity, DeVellis, and Earp (1990) take a step in this direction by reframing the concept as "affective reaction to uncertainty."

For the individual Christian, life holds no shortage of ambiguity and uncertainty. Health status, family relationships, job and financial matters, social and political choices, and church involvement all require adjustment to situations that defy complete understanding and control. Christians might consider several guidelines in facing uncertainty. First, they should choose activities that match their comfort with ambiguity. A Christian who prefers the "narrower field" style, for instance, would probably function better as an accountant than as a labor negotiator. Second, they should cultivate skills for making responsible and effective choices in ambiguous situations. Even in the absence of clear-cut choices, some approaches are better than others. Christians must develop skills to make the best financial, social, and other decisions as possible in view of their value systems. Third, Christians should take care to define success less in terms of particular outcomes than in terms of faithfulness. Expressing words of reconciliation and forgiveness cannot guarantee that a severed relationship can be restored, but it can result in a sense of integrity and peace. Finally, Christians can abide in the assurances of such scriptural sources as Matthew 6, Romans 8, and Philippians 4 that the Lord is always and inalterably present to believers during the uncertainties of life.

References

Budner, S. (1962). Intolerance of ambiguity as a personality variable. *Journal of Personality, 30,* 29–50.

Gerrity, M. S., DeVellis, R. F., & Earp, J. A. (1990). Physicians' reactions to uncertainty in patient care. *Medical Care, 28* (8), 724–736.

Helson, R., & Wink, P. (1992). Personality change in women from the early 40's to the early 50's. *Psychology and Aging, 7* (1), 46–55.

Pargament, K. I., Johnson, S. M., Echemendia, R. J., & Silverman, W. H. (1985). The limits of fit: Examining the implications of person-environment congruence within different religious settings. *Journal of Community Psychology, 13,* 20–30.

Schwartz, S. H., & Huismans, S. (1995). Value priorities and religiosity in four Western religions. *Social Psychology Quarterly, 58* (2), 88–107.

F. C. Craigie, Jr.

See Religion and Personality; Authoritarian Personality; Personality.

Ambition. The strong desire for achievement or success, ambition is viewed psychodynamically as a defense against shame. Success proves that there is no need for shame. Apart from these psychoanalytic speculations there has been little systematic study of ambition. The closely related concept of need for achievement has, however, been extensively studied.

See Achievement, Need for.

Ambivalence. The psychic activity whereby a person has two apparently opposite, contradictory, or paradoxical feelings. The experience of ambivalence can be normal and rewarding or pathological and damaging, depending on the depth to which one integrates infantile demands and resolves childhood conflicts. It is important for a maturing person to accept that everything in life has two sides, and the more important matters in life, like loving and the incarnation, are highly paradoxical.

Traditional psychoanalytic understanding (Fenichel, 1945) proposes that the origin of ambivalence is in infancy; the infant develops or has by nature ambivalent feelings because its primary function is eating. Eating is viewed as ambivalent in that it is both aggressive (biting, sucking) and receptive (swallowing). Fenichel and others (Klein, 1975) suggest that this aggressiveness while eating is the seed of the adult experience of hate and aggression and this receiving (swallowing, digesting) is the origin of adult love and tenderness. As the individual moves from infancy to late childhood, those early ambivalent feelings can develop into active loving and giving on the one hand or aggression or protection on the other.

Psychoanalysts further suggest that the manner in which the infant relates to its environment, most importantly the mother, predicts relationships in adult life. The infant's primary object in early life is the food it ingests, milk, and this primary object is represented by the mother's breast or breast substitute. As the infant develops in relating to this primary breast object, so will it relate as an adult. Some persons remain fixated at the so-called anal-retentive stage of infancy in their personal psychology and become greedy and passive in adult life. Such neurotic persons tend to cling to others as their primary means of loving and do not progress to a more fully developed capacity to love by giving and receiving. Jealousy can originate in this early retentive stage due to ambivalent, loving and hating, feelings. Such concepts as the oedipus complex and penis envy proposed by Sigmund Freud and developed by his followers are classic examples of ambivalence in early childhood. In the oedipus complex the child loves the opposite-sex parent and hates or envies the same-sex parent. Fenichel believes that envy is more prominent in women than in men because it originates in penis envy and the sense of being "incomplete, and hence feeling ambivalent about being female."

Psychoanalysts also believe that most adult sexual disorders result from unresolved childhood ambivalent feelings. Thus homosexuality, as viewed by classical dynamicists, is related to the anal eroticism characteristic of the second year of life, as the rectum ambivalently is used both to retain and to reject feces. In infancy feces become ambivalently loved objects, first retained, then expelled, and adult homosexuality similarly shows desires for reception and expulsion. Other evidence of ambivalence predominating in homosexuality is seen in the love and hatred of men in adult life, a result, it is suggested, of desire for intimacy with an unavailable father and a resulting hatred of the father. The passive submission to another male is an unconscious desire to rob him of his masculinity and is a displacement of the homosexual's ambivalent feelings.

Compulsive neurosis is seen by analysts as failure to mature beyond an infantile perfectionism in which ambivalent feelings are neurotically resolved by making the world perfect instead of accepting the inevitability of mistakes, misunderstandings, and errors. Excessive altruism is similarly seen as a denial of one's natural anger and defense as well as evidence of poor integration of love and aggression. Excessive inhibitions are allegedly evidences that early conflicts (e.g., sexual fantasies) have been denied or repressed. Phobias represent a lack of acceptance of one's normal fears and compensating aggressive/angry tendencies.

Jacobsen (1971) suggests that depression, schizophrenia, and psychopathy originate in ambivalence because in all of these disturbances the person is first ambivalent toward other people and then toward oneself, leaving the person unable to love well or hate well. The subtle arrogance of depression is that "someone should take care of me because I deserve it," but the depressive appears humiliated by having not learned to love a person without devouring the person. The depressive's inability to devour his or her love object is depressing. Paranoid persons, accurately perceiving the unconscious desires of others, fail to see their own aggressive tendencies.

The most devastating element of unresolved infantile ambivalence for adequate adult functioning is the retention of separate hate and love. Persons who fail to understand the basic nature of ambivalence in adult life continue to believe that there are good people and bad people, and this goodness or badness is largely defined according to the pleasure they induce. Neurotic people have not synthesized their own love and aggressiveness enough to see both good and bad in everyone.

Ambivalence, adequately developed and accepted, can be the hallmark of the mature person. The acceptance of one's sinful nature as well as one's capacity to love is the basic ingredient of adult humility and happiness. Paul certainly understood his own ambivalence in calling himself the "chief of sinners" as well as a righteous person, and Jesus' asking us to "hate . . . mother and father" (Luke 14:26) in order to follow him calls for mature Christian ambivalence.

References

Fenichel, O. (1945). *The psychoanalytic theory of neuroses.* New York: Norton.

Jacobsen, E. (1971). *Depression.* New York: International Universities Press.

Klein, M. (1975). *Love, guilt, and separation and other works, 1921–1945.* New York: Delacorte.

R. B. JOHNSON

See PSYCHOSEXUAL DEVELOPMENT; PSYCHOANALYTIC PSYCHOLOGY.

American Association of Christian Counselors (AACC). An organization of professional, pastoral, and lay counselors who are committed to strengthening the church internationally by building excellence and unity in Christian counseling.

The organization was founded in 1985 and grew to seven hundred members before it was transferred to new leadership in 1991. A new board of advisors was formed, including prominent leaders in Christian counseling; the quarterly cassette tapes (known as *Counseltapes*) were improved in quality; and the official AACC publication was redesigned, upgraded, and produced as a new magazine, *Christian Counseling Today.* Soon this was joined by a newsletter *(Christian Counseling Connection),* a quarterly publication that reviews recent counseling books *(Christian Counseling Resource Review),* and a professional marriage and family journal. In addition the *Journal of Psychology and Theology (JPT)* has become an official AACC publication.

As membership has grown to more than 17,000, so have the services to members. A Law and Ethics Commission was established and a new code of ethics developed. A program for liability insurance was made available to members in 1993. A book service has been established to enable members to purchase counseling books at discounted prices. Regional conferences were begun in the spring of 1994 with steadily increasing attendance, a Congress on the Family was held in 1995 (in partnership with Focus on the Family), and a partnership has been established with Tyndale House Publishers to produce a series of AACC-Tyndale books. A computerized and Christian version of the fully standardized adjective check list (ACL) is available for members for use as a test in their counseling work, and AACC has produced both a series of videos and several software packages for use by Christian counselors. As interest has grown internationally, AACC has given birth to an International Association of Christian Counselors and a not-for-profit AACC Foundation, established to raise funds to provide for the production of resources and training for counselors internationally.

AACC seeks to be a service organization, guided by the Holy Spirit in bringing together Christian counselors who are committed to their churches and dedicated to becoming more effective, Christ-honoring, biblically sensitive people helpers. The AACC statement of purpose is a concise summary of its reason for existence: "The AACC exists to encourage and promote excellence in counseling worldwide; disseminate information, educational resources, and counseling aids; stimulate interaction and mutual encouragement between counselors; encourage the integration of counseling principles with biblical theology; inspire the highest levels of counselor training; contribute to the strengthening of families; and bring honor to Jesus Christ."

G. R. COLLINS

See ASSOCIATION FOR CLINICAL PASTORAL EDUCATION; PASTORAL COUNSELING; CHRISTIAN PSYCHOLOGY; CHRISTIAN ASSOCIATION OF PSYCHOLOGICAL STUDIES.

American Association of Pastoral Counselors (AAPC). This association was formally organized in 1964 in response to the need for standards for involvement of religious organizations in mental health care. Since that time the association has provided leadership in pastoral counseling practice and training, criteria for religious institutions in pastoral counseling ministry, and coordination with other mental health professionals.

AAPC establishes standards for training and supervision in pastoral counseling. Fulfillment of these standards leads to certification of individuals for practice as pastoral counselors and accreditation of institutions that provide counseling service and education. The association also provides opportunities for continuing education, professional dialogue, and ongoing consultation.

AAPC defines a pastoral counselor as a minister who practices counseling at an advanced level, integrating religious resources with insights from the behavioral sciences. Three basic kinds of individual membership are available: certified, affiliate, and training. Certified membership requires B.A. and M.Div. degrees, good standing in a recognized denomination or faith group, one unit of Clinical Pastoral Education in an accredited center, three years as a minister, and 375 hours of pastoral counseling together with 125 hours of supervision of that counseling. Affiliate and training membership standards are less stringent.

C. DAVIS

See ASSOCIATION FOR CLINICAL PASTORAL EDUCATION; PASTORAL COUNSELING; PASTORAL CARE.

American Board of Professional Psychology (ABPP). The American Board of Professional Psychology, Inc., was originally incorporated as the American Board of Examiners in Professional Psychology in 1947. The board was established in cooperation with the American Psychological Association, and a motivating factor in its initiation was psychology's increasing participation in professional and clinical practice. According to the current bylaws, the purposes of the board are to conduct examinations for those applying for a diploma, to award diplomas and maintain a registry of diplomates, to serve the public welfare by providing lists of certified specialists to appropriate individuals and agencies, and to serve the public welfare by sponsoring programs to enhance quality specialty services.

Since the 1980s the number of specialty areas under the board's umbrella has more than doubled. For many years the ABPP diploma was awarded in the areas of clinical, counseling, school, and industrial/organizational psychology. Currently diplomas are awarded in the additional specialties of behavioral psychology, clinical neuropsychology, family psychology, forensic psychology, and health psychology. The ABPP Board of Directors oversees general standards of quality for all specialties, but the credentialing process is primarily defined and administered by specialty boards.

Any psychologist must meet basic requirements to be eligible for the ABPP boards. These include a doctoral degree from a recognized program in psychology, completion of two to three years of postdoctoral experience, and licensure appropriate to the state in which the psychologist practices. All diplomate candidates additionally undergo a rigorous examination process that includes submission of work samples for review by appropriate specialists, as well as an oral examination.

American Board of Professional Psychology (ABPP)

The credentialing process for the ABPP diploma is voluntary. Whereas licensure laws are created within states to assure that individual psychologists have the basic knowledge and skills to serve the public, ABPP diploma credentialing has been developed to certify individual psychologists as specialists who have demonstrated advanced competence.

H. L. PIERSMA

See AMERICAN PSYCHOLOGICAL ASSOCIATION; PSYCHOLOGIST.

American Psychiatric Association. A rising tide of humanism at the end of the eighteenth century gave rise to the moral treatment of the insane. An outgrowth of this movement was the establishment of mental hospitals, usually founded and financed by the state. When enough of these hospitals had been established in the United States, the superintendents of these institutions found it desirable to assemble to discuss their mutual problems and to share their discoveries. The prime movers of the first meeting were Samuel B. Woodward of Massachusetts and Francis T. Stribling of Virginia. The first meeting was held in Philadelphia on 16 October 1844. This group became known as the Association of Medical Superintendents of American Institutions for the Insane, later renamed the American Medico-Psychological Association and finally the American Psychiatric Association.

Since its inception the association has worked to improve hospital design and construction, the training of physicians and mental health professionals, medical jurisprudence, and the understanding of the causes, prevention, and treatment of mental disease. As was the case in the rest of medicine, little real progress was made until the turn of the twentieth century.

The American Psychiatric Association has instigated and promoted community psychiatry, leading to the current emphasis on community care. It has encouraged better understanding of mentally ill prisoners, leading to increased utilization of psychiatrists in prisons. It has insisted on better management of delinquent children, leading to the development of the specialty of child psychiatry. It has encouraged the treatment of psychologically disturbed soldiers, leading to the Veterans Administration assuming responsibility for their care.

The American Psychiatric Association has also encouraged research. Its annual meetings and journal *(American Journal of Psychiatry)* have provided a forum in which research findings are disseminated to the profession. It has also been a leader in the education of physicians, nurses, psychologists, and social workers. It has encouraged the development of competence in psychiatry by participating in the approval of training programs and the establishment of the American Board of Psychiatry and Neurology, a certifying agency, and by requiring continuing education for all its members. Undergraduate medical education has not been neglected, for the association has insisted on the inclusion of adequate psychiatric education for all physicians.

W. P. WILSON

See PSYCHIATRIST.

American Psychological Association (APA). The world's largest association of psychologists, the American Psychological Association was founded in 1892 at Clark University in Worcester, Massachusetts, under the leadership of G. Stanley Hall. There were 31 charter members from whom Hall was elected president, and 7 members were elected to a council. By World War I the membership numbers had grown to about 400, and by World War II there were more than 3,000 members. The Public Affairs Office indicates that APA membership now includes more than 142,000 researchers, educators, clinicians, consultants, and students (although the 1996 membership directory lists approximately 126,000 individuals). The phenomenal membership increase reflects the growth of psychology as an academic and applied discipline.

As stated in the first article of the organization's bylaws, the purpose of the APA is "to advance psychology as a science, as a profession, and as a means of promoting human welfare." APA has created the Science Directorate as a way of enhancing psychology as a science. The Science Directorate develops programs and publications to encourage the exchange of ideas and research findings and to provide psychologists an edge in securing financial resources for research. APA also sponsors a science advocacy program administered by its Public Policy Office that not only advocates federal support for psychological research but also informs policymakers about issues related to scientific psychology.

APA has also created the Practice Directorate to promote psychology as a professional practice. The Practice Directorate works with members of the United States Congress on federal legislative initiatives and regulations regarding the availability of psychological care, provides information to help the field develop an efficient health care delivery system, represents psychologists in various settings such as the public health sector, and helps the public by establishing programs for special at-risk populations and by educating consumers on important mental health issues.

The Public Interest Directorate promotes the application of psychology as a science and profession to the advancement of human welfare by providing expertise on social issues (e.g., the establishment of a Commission on Violence and Youth and the sponsorship of a 1994 conference on women's health) and by educating the public on various mental and physical health-related issues (e.g., educational workshops employing a model curricula by the HIV Office for Psychology Education). Directorate activities include research, training, and advocacy through program and policy development, especially on social issues that may put people in disadvantaged positions (such as equal opportunities for those with physical disabilities); homelessness; gay and lesbian issues; violence; women's issues; ethnic minority concerns; AIDS; issues facing children, youth, and families; and workplace issues. As a result the Public Interest Directorate often develops controversial policy that many members of APA may not agree with.

The APA currently has 49 divisions, each with a focus on some combination of research, public interest, or professional aspect of psychology. Each division develops its own bylaws and governance structure and operates somewhat independently from the governing body of the APA, the Council of Representatives. Each division is assigned a number (currently ranging from numbers 1 to 51; there are no divisions 4 and 11), determined chronologically by when the division was approved by the APA, with division members responsible for providing a name. Many of the lower-numbered divisions (i.e., those established relatively early) have rather general names (e.g., Division 1—General Psychology; Division 3—Experimental Psychology; Division 7—Developmental Psychology), while the more recently established higher-numbered divisions have names with a more specific focus reflecting contemporary issues (e.g., Division 44—Society for the Psychological Study of Lesbian and Gay Issues; Division 47—Exercise and Sport Psychology; Division 51—The Society for the Psychological Study of Men and Masculinity). Division 36 is the Psychology of Religion division (*see* Psychologists of Religion). A complete listing of all divisions may be obtained from the APA Public Affairs Office. Individuals may choose to be a member of as many divisions as they like. Division membership is not necessary for APA membership; APA membership is not necessary for division membership but is necessary to hold a division office.

APA is the world's largest association publisher in psychology. The association publishes 27 peer-reviewed journals, including the *American Psychologist*, the official journal of the APA. APA also publishes 10 abstract periodicals, including *Psychological Abstracts* and *Psychoanalytic Abstracts*, with the other abstracts designated by the prefix *PsycSCAN* (e.g., *PsycSCAN: Clinical Psychology*). Membership dues provide subscriptions to the *American Psychologist* and the association's newsletter, the *APA Monitor*.

Membership status generally requires a doctoral degree, though a master's degree with one year of professional experience qualifies an individual to be an associate member. Members who present evidence of outstanding contribution or performance in the field of psychology may be nominated by an APA division and elected by the APA Council of Representatives to become Fellows of APA. Affiliate membership status is granted to nationals in other countries, high school teachers, and undergraduate or graduate students.

P. C. HILL

See AMERICAN PSYCHOLOGICAL SOCIETY.

American Psychological Society (APS). As a result of continuing tensions between academic psychologists and practitioners within the American Psychological Association (APA), a new organization of psychologists was formed in 1988. Named the American Psychological Society, the group's purpose is to advance a scientifically oriented psychology in both research and application. Beginning with a membership of approximately five hundred and providing an alternative for research psychologists who believe that the APA is too oriented toward the concerns of psychological practitioners, the society grew to more than fifteen thousand members as of 1995. As part of its commitment to advancing a psychology that is scientifically oriented, APS publishes two journals, *Psychological Science* and *Current Directions in Psychological Science*, meant to bring to both psychologists and nonpsychologists a sample of the broad range of scholarly research that is conducted in contemporary psychology. APS also plays a leading role in educating the United States Congress on the importance of scientific psychology and in lobbying for funds directed specifically toward basic behavioral research.

K. S. SEYBOLD

See PSYCHOLOGIST; AMERICAN PSYCHOLOGICAL ASSOCIATION.

Ames, Edward Scribner (1870–1958). Professor, pastor, author, and psychologist of religion, Ames was born in Eau Claire, Wisconsin. His father, Lucius Ames, frequently moved the family to pastor churches of the growing Disciples of Christ. A practical, common-sense, nontheological faith pervaded the home.

Ames received his A.B. (1889) and A.M. (1891) from Drake University, his B.D. from Yale Divinity School (1892), and his Ph.D. in philosophy from the University of Chicago (1895). He then taught at Chicago's Disciples Divinity House (1895–1897) and at Butler University in Indianapolis (1897–1900).

From 1900 to 1940 Ames ministered to the Hyde Park Church of Christ (later renamed University Church of Disciples of Christ). He had been a charter member of the six-year-old church, still under one hundred members, when he accepted the challenge of a liberal, university community congregation. It grew fivefold and erected a new sanctuary under his leadership. During the same period Ames was associated with the University of Chicago until his retirement in 1935 and with Disciples Divinity House (1927–1945).

With no thought of university service when he came to the Hyde Park church, Ames almost immediately began teaching at the University of Chicago's philosophy department, which included psychology and education. His appointment expanded to two-thirds time. The works of William James and anthropologists' writings on religion led Ames to introduce probably the first psychology of religion course in 1905. Teaching, reading, and forging ideas in the practicum of the pastorate produced the widely regarded *Psychology of Religious Experience* (1910). Ames wrote six more books and contributed to at least four others.

Ames emphasized the roles of symbol and ceremony and the centrality of mystical experience in religion. He was convinced that scientific and psychological analyses enriched faith: "Reflection helps religious practice to be sane and precious, showing its true function and importance. . . . Psychology and philosophy of religion renew religion. A religion without their benefit will not satisfy a modern critical mind" (Ames, 1959, p. 96).

References

Ames, E. S. (1910). *The psychology of religious experience.* New York: Houghton-Mifflin.

Ames, V. M. (Ed.). (1959). *Beyond theology: The autobiography of Edward Scribner Ames.* Chicago: University of Chicago Press.

R. D. KAHOE

See PSYCHOLOGY OF RELIGION.

Amnestic Disorders. According to the *DSM-IV,* amnestic disorders are characterized by memory impairment due to the physiological effects of a medical condition or the lasting effects of medications, abused drugs, or toxins. To be diagnosed with an "amnestic disorder due to a general medical condition," individuals must manifest difficulty in learning new information or recalling what was previously learned (anterograde and retrograde amnesia respectively). These persons must also show impairment in and a deterioration from a previous level of social and/or occupational functioning. Diagnosis requires that delirium and dementia be ruled out and that a direct link be established between the medical condition and the memory disturbance. Amnestic disorders of this nature that last for one month or less are further classified as transient, while disorders characterized by memory impairment lasting more than one month are labeled chronic.

Medical conditions often linked to amnestic disorders include head trauma, tumors, oxygen deprivation, strokes, herpes encephalitis, severe hypoglycemia, and surgical procedures. Epileptic convulsions and restricted blood flow to the brain are most often responsible for transient amnestic disorders.

The *DSM-IV* diagnostic criteria for a "substance-induced persisting amnestic disorder" include impairment in memory and a deterioration in functioning similar to that noted in amnestic disorders due to general medical conditions, as well as the exclusion of delirium and dementia as diagnoses. This diagnosis further requires that symptoms last longer than the substance intoxication or withdrawal. A direct connection must also be established between the substance in question and the memory impairment.

One of the most common substance-induced disorders is alcohol persisting amnestic disorder, also known as Korsakoff's syndrome. This disorder is caused by a thiamine deficiency resulting from long-term heavy alcohol consumption (Wise & Gray, 1994). Individuals with Korsakoff's syndrome demonstrate complete anterograde amnesia, while some remote memories persist. Early in the course of this syndrome, confabulation is common, as well as variable losses of insight and initiative (Wise & Gray, 1994).

Benzodiazepine persisting amnestic disorder is another common substance-induced amnestic disorder caused by the popular antianxiety agent, benzodiazepine (Wise & Gray, 1994). This amnestic disorder results in anterograde amnesia following administration of the medication and subsequent impairment in memory consolidation and retrieval. Intravenous administration (e.g., presurgical) and high dosages are associated with the greatest degree of memory impairment (Wise & Gray, 1994). However, lower doses of benzodiazepines, administered long term, can cause gradual memory impairment, especially in elderly populations.

Benson and McDaniel (1991) note that the treatment for amnestic disorders is generally focused on their apparent cause. However, there is no effective treatment for many of the causes. Treatment is usually aimed at reducing further memory loss. Occasionally treatment leads to improvement.

The treatment for amnestic disorders due to medical conditions focuses on treating the underlying medical condition (Benson & McDaniel, 1991). Medical interventions to manage brain tumors may temporarily lead to improvement in memory. The regulation of blood sugar levels may enhance memory function in individuals with hypoglycemia. When memory impairment is attributed to strokes, treatment of cardiovascular disease and preventative measures to decrease the risk of atherosclerosis (hardening of the arteries) may be helpful in reducing further memory loss and may lead to a reduction in memory impairment. In some instances (e.g., head trauma, seizure disorders) the greatest memory impairment will be noted at the time of the brain insult, with the possibility of some gradual improvement over time.

In individuals with substance-induced amnestic disorders, removal of the offending substance may lead to some memory improvement (Benson & McDaniel, 1991). For example, it has been recommended that all alcohol-dependent individuals be routinely treated with thiamine nutritional supplements (e.g., B-complex vitamins) and abstinence from alcohol. While some individuals with Korsakoff's syndrome demonstrate considerable improvement over time, there is rarely a dramatic reversal of their memory impairment.

Benson and McDaniel (1991) note that clear prescriptions for treatment are not available due to our limited understanding of specific amnestic disorders. Behavioral treatments are often indicated in helping individuals compensate for their memory losses. Relaxation training and stress management can be used to sharpen attention and focus on information to be learned. Memory prostheses (e.g., checklists, prompters) may also be helpful. The efficacy of internal memory aids (e.g., imagery, mnemonics) has not been conclusively demonstrated. Pharmacological interventions have produced only marginal results, although researchers remain hopeful (Benson & McDaniel, 1991).

References

Benson, D. F., & McDaniel, K. D. (1991). Memory disorders. In W. D. Bradley, R. B. Daroff, G. M. Fenichel, & C. D. Marsden (Eds.), *Neurology in clinical practice* (Vol. 2). Boston: Butterworth-Heinemann.
Wise, M. G., & Gray, K. F. (1994). Delirium, dementia, and amnestic disorders. In R. E. Hales, S. C. Yudofsky, & J. A. Talbott (Eds.), *The American Psychiatric Press textbook of psychiatry* (2nd ed.). Washington, DC: American Psychiatric Press.

J. P. GRIMM

See DISSOCIATIVE AMNESIA.

Amok. A culture-specific syndrome of Malay in which an individual attacks murderously anyone he encounters. This state of frenzy continues until the individual collapses. Running amok has frequently been thought to be a manifestation of psychomotor epilepsy. Others have viewed it as hysterical behavior.

See PSYCHOPATHOLOGY IN PRIMITIVE CULTURES; DISSOCIATIVE TRANCE DISORDER.

Amusia. The loss of ability for either perception or reproduction of vocal or musical sounds. Motor amusia involves the memory and interpretation of melodies, so that a person loses the ability to play an instrument or reproduce tunes. Sensory amusia is characterized by an inability to recognize tunes. The person may be able to reproduce notes but cannot understand what he or she is singing or playing. Amusia may be a result of a tumor, blood clot, or lesion in the temporal lobe of the brain.

Amytal Interview. *See* NARCOTHERAPY.

Anaclitic Depression. First described by Spitz, anaclitic depression refers to the syndrome observed in infants separated from their mothers for long periods of time. The infant initially gives indications of distress. However, after approximately three months of separation the infant begins to withdraw,

and psychological contact after this point is progressively more and more difficult.

See MATERNAL DEPRIVATION; REACTIVE ATTACHMENT DISORDER OF INFANCY.

Anal Stage. According to Sigmund Freud, the anal stage is the second stage of a child's psychological development, consisting of approximately the period between 18 and 30 months.

See PSYCHOSEXUAL DEVELOPMENT.

Analytical Psychology. A school of psychology founded in 1913 by Carl Gustav Jung following the break of his close association with Sigmund Freud. Jung named his approach analytical psychology to distinguish it from Freud's psychoanalysis. Analytical psychology has had a significant impact in the areas of personality theory, psychology of religion, and psychotherapy.

Theoretical Roots. Trained as a psychiatrist, Jung sought knowledge in sources beyond empirical science, including art, religion, anthropology, and mythology. In fact Jung's interest in the religious dimension of the psyche contributed to his break with Freud. Jung believed psychology should be the study of the soul, and analytical psychology embraces the existential themes of meaning and purpose.

Jung stands in the humanistic tradition by viewing the soul as having an inherent drive toward wholeness and self-realization. Analytical psychology emphasizes personal experience, and Jung studied his own dreams and visions. Jung was a student of comparative religions and was especially intrigued by the union of opposites in Eastern religions. Jung's interest in the synthesis of opposites was also influenced by Hegel's process philosophy. His central concept of individuation, or the process of becoming a self, involved the union of opposites in the psyche.

Jung found a parallel for his ideas about the process of individuation in alchemy, the medieval precursor to modern chemistry. Alchemy involved the transformation of base metals into precious ones, and Jung viewed this as symbolic of the transformation of the psyche.

The ancient Hellenistic gnostics were another important source of inspiration for Jung. Gnosticism derives its name from *gnosis,* or mystical knowledge. The gnostic emphasis on dualistic opposites provided Jung with further symbolic representation of the development of the psyche through individuation. Jung also studied and wrote about paranormal experiences and the occult (Jung, 1961).

Personality. Jung described the psyche as the total personality. The psyche has both a conscious and an unconscious dimension. The ego is the center of consciousness and the unifying force of the psyche.

Jung identified four main functions of consciousness: the thinking function, concerned with objectivity and rationality; the feeling function, sensitive to subjective values; the sensing function, attentive to the way things feel, sound, smell, and appear; and the intuitive function, perceiving deeper meaning at an unconscious level. The ego tends to embrace one of these modes as the superior function during the first half of development.

The basic personality dimensions in Jung's system are extraversion and introversion and describe contrasting directions of a person's psychic energy (*see* Introversion-Extraversion). The extraverted person is externally oriented toward the social world, whereas the introverted person turns inward. An individual's psychological type is based on the superior function combined with either the extraverted or introverted attitude. The less developed functions of the psyche exert influence on the unconscious and may begin to emerge in a compensatory manner during the second half of development.

The more significant dimension of the psyche in analytical psychology is the unconscious, which is divided into two parts: the personal unconscious and the collective unconscious. The personal unconscious corresponds to Freud's notion of the unconscious and consists of all the material from one's lifetime, including objectionable memories that have been repressed and indifferent memories or impressions outside conscious awareness. Complexes are emotional ideas that lie within the personal unconscious and are split off from consciousness through traumatic influences. A complex can assume an independent and fragmentary personality, which can exert a positive or a negative influence on the psyche.

The concept of the collective unconscious is one of the most unique contributions of analytic psychology. The collective unconscious makes up the bulk of the psychic iceberg and is the primary source of creativity and wisdom. The collective unconscious reflects not personal experiences but is the repository of the latent memories and accumulated experiences of the human species. Jung arrived at the concept of the collective unconscious through struggling with the premodern belief in spiritual forces, such as gods and devils, which he observed across many cultures (Maddi, 1980). Jung chose the collective unconscious as a way of locating such beliefs in the symbolic expressions of the psyche rather than in an external supernatural order.

Archetypes. Within the collective unconscious are archetypes, which are universal mental structures or "forms without content." Jung developed the idea of archetypes from observing recurring symbols in dreams, religions, and myths that have appeared in various cultures throughout the centuries. The dreams and fantasies of Jung's patients convinced him of the reality of symbolic images that could not be traced to personal experiences.

The principal archetypes that reflect human experience include the persona, the shadow, the anima or the animus, the mother, the child, the wise old man, and the self. The persona is the mask people wear to manage social impressions. Jung suggested that the process of self-realization entails distinguishing between one's public persona and one's real self.

The shadow is the negative or dark side of our personality that usually remains hidden and undeveloped. The first step of individuation involves recognizing and integrating one's shadow in order to release the need to project the shadow upon others.

The anima is the unconsciously feminine side of a male, which is yielding, nurturing, and intuitive. The animus is the unconscious masculine side of a female, which is driving, aggressive, and disciplined. Jung believed wholeness is promoted through accepting both dimensions of one's personality.

The mother archetype represents all that is benign and helpful as well as secret and seductive. The wise old man is the archetype of meaning, wisdom, and cleverness. The child archetype signifies the potential of future development of the personality.

The self is the most important archetype and is the center of personality between the conscious and unconscious dimensions of the psyche. Jung thought mandalas, which are elaborate circular designs, best symbolize the self. The transcendent function of the psyche serves to unify the opposing trends within the personality and facilitate the transition to a higher attitude.

Archetypes manifest themselves in various ways but particularly through dreams. Dreams serve the compensatory function of allowing the unconscious to influence the conscious mind. For example, through dreams a female can understand and incorporate into consciousness the archetype of animus, which may have formerly controlled her if left outside consciousness. Dreams serve to provide the conscious ego with additional information and can alter the structure of the ego. One purpose of dream analysis in analytical psychology is to understand what functions a dream or a dream series has and to incorporate that into the conscious ego (*see* Dreams, Therapeutic Use of).

Personal Adjustment. Jung viewed personality development as a process across the life span. Self-realization and wholeness are ideals that move the psyche toward individuation rather than goals that are normally achieved in one's lifetime. According to Jung, personal adjustment is facilitated by trusting the unconscious and bringing the archetypes into proper balance. Problems of personal adjustment result from attempts by the psyche to compensate for a one-sided view of life. Jung believed that psychological symptoms could be understood as the unconscious trying to correct the imbalance caused by a repressed dimension of the personality.

Individuation stresses the Jungian value on growing in self-knowledge. Precisely when individuation takes place continues to be a matter of discussion in analytical psychology. Initially Jung postulated that it occurred only in the latter half of life. Most analytical psychologists now understand that individuation processes are evident in early childhood and that these processes are blocked by pathological influences. If these processes are not blocked, individuating experiences may occur early in life. If, however, psychic energy is used to reinforce the ego rather than to identify and develop the self, these experiences are not reinforced or integrated, contributing to a more dramatic experience of individuation in the latter half of life.

Jung viewed adulthood as the time when developmental concerns shift from the material to the spiritual. Late in his career Jung proposed the principle of synchronicity to refer to simultaneous events or coincidences that are not causally related, such as thinking of an old friend and having that person arrive unexpectedly. The principle of synchronicity suggests that the collective unconscious expresses archetypes in multiple simultaneous events that are beyond scientific explanation. Jung was willing to embrace a sense of mystery absent from most schools of psychology and was particularly interested in phenomena such as telepathy, clairvoyance, and the paranormal.

Analytical psychology views myth as an important element of human development. Individual consciousness is only a manifestation of a larger whole. Myth, defined as that which has always been believed everywhere by everyone, provides a link to the symbols of the collective unconscious.

Analytic Therapy. The primary therapeutic goal of analytical psychology is for the client to become aware of the unconscious so he or she may gain insight into the specific structures and dynamics that emerge out of the unconscious, especially through the self archetype. The creativity of the unconscious is released through symbols. The individual's identity shifts from ego to self as unconscious structures are integrated into consciousness. Jung did not specify a particular treatment methodology.

Evaluation. Jung noted that both analysis and pastoral care are concerned with the cure of souls. Analytical psychology offers a more positive appraisal of the psychological value of religion, spirituality, and mysticism than do most of the traditional schools of psychology. For Jung religion and spirituality are instinctual aspects of human nature. Episcopalians Kelsey (1968) and Sanford (1987) have integrated analytical psychology and Christianity.

Jung can be commended for seeking to recover an appreciation for the symbolic and the experiential dynamics of religion. Analytical psychology as a system of psychology is among the most comprehensive, as Jung displayed a vast knowledge of disciplines in the sciences and humanities.

Jung's embrace of religion has also been questioned. Jung tends to reduce spiritual realities to the psychological by suggesting that notions about God and other spiritual matters are archetypal projections of the collective unconscious. While Jung claimed that the theological truth of metaphysical realities was outside his realm as a psychologist, his worldview

has been described as resting upon the pantheism of Eastern religions. Jung comes close to proposing a rival religion to Christianity, evidenced by the inspiration he drew from gnosticism, which has traditionally been a challenge to Christianity.

Jung's preference for subjective experience suggests little appreciation for the historical traditions of religion. Christian theology places more importance on the content and rational dimension of belief than does analytical psychology.

Analytical psychology emphasizes the individual growing in self-knowledge. In this sense Jung has been criticized for being too individualistic (Jones & Butman, 1991) and for failing to value relationships and community. A Christian understanding of human nature seems to require a stronger appreciation for relationships with God and others than an exclusive focus on the introspective path of individuation.

Jung's ambiguous view of evil has also been debated by Christians (Griffin, 1986; Sanford, 1988). Jung speaks of evil as part of the shadow archetype that needs to be integrated into the self. Jung also articulated a gnostic view of God as both good and evil and suggested making the Trinity into a quaternity to include Satan in the Godhead. The Christian faith states that in God there is no darkness (1 John 1:5). The path to wholeness and to holiness is through God's forgiveness in Christ. The cross and resurrection of Christ represent the victory of good over evil, not the ultimate union of good and evil.

References

Griffin, E. (1986). Analytical psychology and the dynamics of human evil: A problematic case in the integration of psychology and theology. *Journal of Psychology and Theology, 14,* 269–277.

Jones, S. L., & Butman, R. E. (1991). *Modern psychotherapies: A comprehensive Christian appraisal.* Downers Grove, IL: InterVarsity Press.

Jung, C. G. (1961). *Memories, dreams, and reflections.* New York: Random House.

Kelsey, M. (1968). *Christo-psychology.* New York: Crossroad.

Maddi, S. (1980). *Personality theories: A comparative analysis* (4th ed.). Homewood, IL: Dorsey.

Sanford, J. A. (1987). *The kingdom within: The inner meaning of Jesus' sayings.* New York: Harper & Row.

Sanford, J. A. (1988). The problem of evil in Christianity and analytical psychology. In R. L. Moore (Ed.), *Carl Jung and Christian spirituality.* New York: Paulist.

Additional Readings

Jung, C. G. (1953–1979). *The collected works of C. G. Jung* (20 vols.). (H. Read, M. Fordham, & G. Adler, Eds.). (R. F. C. Hull, Trans.). Princeton, NJ: Princeton University Press.

Jung, C. G. (1964). *Man and his symbols.* New York: Dell.

Noll, R. (1994). *The Jung cult: Origins of a charismatic movement.* Princeton, NJ: Princeton University Press.

S. J. SANDAGE

See JUNG, CARL GUSTAV; JUNGIAN ANALYSIS.

Androgyny. The English term *androgyny* is derived from the combination of two Greek words, *andros* (man) and *gyne* (woman), and traditional use refers to individuals who possess simultaneously a high degree of stereotypically masculine and feminine behavioral characteristics. Androgyny is a recurrent theme in literature and religion over the centuries (Kaplan & Sedney, 1980). Carl Gustav Jung was one of the first psychotherapists to recognize both masculine and feminine qualities in the same person. He identified the feminine part of a man as anima and the masculine in a woman as animus and emphasized the integration of these inherent cross-gender characteristics in order to achieve personal wholeness or individuation.

A segment of current understanding of androgyny does not require that an androgynous person be one who possesses both masculine and feminine behavioral characteristics but rather is an individual who does not rely on gender as a cognitive organizing principle (Bem, 1984). A broader definition is offered by Cook (1985), who views the term denoting a "body of psychological theory . . . that recognizes masculinity and femininity as independent psychological domains desirable for both sexes" (p. 20). She adds that androgyny should not be equated with either sexual emancipation, absence of sex-role identification, or physical hermaphroditism or bisexuality.

A review of the literature suggests numerous benefits for individuals who are identified as androgynous persons. They possess greater levels of independence, affection, assertiveness, and understanding (Bem, 1974); higher self-esteem (Spence, Helmreich, & Stapp, 1975); more mature self-descriptions (Block, 1973); and more adaptive and flexible behavior skills (Bem, 1974). Androgyny is considered a highly desirable state of being, and "perhaps the androgynous person will come to define a more human standard of psychological health" (Bem, 1974, p. 162).

Psychological androgyny has its critics. Some argue that masculinity rather than androgyny promotes healthy psychological functioning, at least in the United States' culture (e.g., Taylor & Hall, 1982). These authors maintain that it is a misconception that an androgynous person is healthiest; this misconception leads to a false assumption that problems with current sex-role definitions are rooted within the psyche instead of societal structures. Sampson (1977) considers androgyny to be too individualistically oriented and proposes that the androgynous person is part of a larger system and is one whose individual synthesis is shaped by the collective social structure. Murphy (1994), who views androgyny in light of Alfred Adler's concept of social interest, has reached a similar conclusion. The feminist attitude, as reflected definitively by Lott (1981), asserts that labeling behaviors of androgynous persons in terms of masculine and feminine reinforces the association between gender and behavior, an association that would best be eliminated.

According to the Genesis story, androgyny is implied to exist in God, and this androgynous quality was an intrinsic part of the original human being (Gen. 1:26–27; 2:21–23). Viewed from a more traditional perspective, biblical assertions suggest that God is an androgynous person. For example, the maternal concern of God for people shows in "the LORD . . . my God . . . will cover [me] with his feathers, and under his wings [I] will find refuge" (Ps. 91:1–4, NIV). The same maternal theme is observed in Jesus' declaration: "O Jerusalem, Jerusalem . . . how often I have longed to gather your children together as a hen gathers her chicks under her wings" (Matt. 23:37, NIV). Too, certain biblical personalities could be identified as androgynous. Two examples are Deborah, who was the leader of Israel during a difficult and male-dominated period (Judg. 4–5), and the apostle Paul, self-described as "gentle . . . like a mother caring for her little children" (1 Thess. 2:7, NIV). Furthermore, the equality or oneness of persons without gender-based identity is implied to be the ideal state in the family of God (e.g., Gal. 3:28).

References

Bem, S. L. (1974). The measurement of psychological androgyny. *Journal of Consulting and Clinical Psychology, 42,* 155–162.

Bem, S. L. (1984). Androgyny and gender schema theory: A conceptual and empirical integration. *Nebraska Symposium on Motivation, 32,* 179–226.

Block, J. H. (1973). Conceptions of sex role: Some cross-cultural and longitudinal perspectives. *American Psychologist, 28,* 512–526.

Cook, E. P. (1985). *Psychological androgyny.* New York: Pergamon.

Kaplan, A. G., & Sedney, M. A. (1980). *Psychology and sex roles: An androgynous perspective.* Boston: Little, Brown.

Lott, B. (1981). A feminist critique of androgyny: Toward the elimination of gender attributions for learned behavior. In C. Mayo & N. M. Henly (Eds.), *Gender and nonverbal behavior.* New York: Springer-Verlag.

Murphy, P. J. (1994). Social interest and psychological androgyny: Conceptualized and tested. *Individual Psychology, 50,* 18–30.

Sampson, E. (1977). Psychology and the American ideal. *Journal of Personality and Social Psychology, 35,* 767–782.

Spence, J. T., Helmreich, R. L., & Stapp, J. (1975). Ratings of self and peers on sex role attributes and their relation to self-esteem and conceptions of masculinity and femininity. *Journal of Personality and Social Psychology, 32,* 29–39.

Taylor, M. C., & Hall, J. A. (1982). Psychological androgyny: Theories, methods, and conclusions. *Psychological Bulletin, 92,* 347–366.

D. SMITH

See GENDER IDENTITY; SEXUALITY.

Anger. An intense emotional reaction, sometimes directly expressed in overt behavior and sometimes remaining a largely unexpressed feeling. Anger is not a disease but rather a social event that has meaning in terms of the implicit social contract between persons. There is little debate about whether anger has the potential to be harmful to oneself. Far greater concern, however, is expressed about aggression, the destructive behavior that is one kind of response to angry feelings. Finding effective ways to help others deal with anger requires careful diagnostic considerations and knowledge of a wide variety of alternative coping strategies (see Miller & Jackson, 1995).

There is a large body of lay and professional literature related to anger and anger management. This literature clearly reflects our society's ambivalence and confusion about angry feelings. Growing awareness of the problems of physical, sexual, and verbal abuse has contributed to heightened sensitivity and an improved knowledge base about this often misunderstood emotion (see Lerner, 1985; Cosgrove, 1988). This article will present three major theories about anger and will discuss appropriate ways to effectively deal with angry feelings.

Especially prominent in the popular literature is the assumption that anger can best be understood using a hydraulic model (Lorenz, 1966). Lorenz suggests that anger is instinctual. If it is not discharged it will accumulate from within like water behind a dam. In other words, anger must be viewed internally rather than examined contextually. Although there is evidence to suggest that aggression may be influenced by heredity, chemical imbalances, and brain diseases (see Myers, 1983), this position probably represents a distortion of the relationship between repressed anger and certain psychophysiological disorders (see Meyer & Deitsch, 1996). Careful work by Tavris (1982), a social psychologist, has seriously challenged the assumptions related to the hydraulic model. Warren (1983) is not as quick to dismiss such thinking, nor are other Christian authors like Cerling (1974) or Pederson (1974). Perhaps this reflects their convictions that there is an appropriate place for the healthy expression of anger, an ethical question that is especially important in conservative Christian circles, where it is often taught that anger is a sin and that its direct expression should be avoided at all costs. The far more common assumption is that expressing one's anger is an inherent right (i.e., it is usually related to a strong sense of entitlement and possessive power).

A second broad theory about anger contends that frustration creates anger (see Berkowitz, 1978). This theory holds that when appropriate aggressive cues are present, anger may be released as aggression (verbal or physical) or turned inward against oneself. Frustration is inevitable in the human experience, and the greater the gap between one's expectations and one's achievements, the more likely one is to become angry. Especially vulnerable to such frustrations are those persons who drive themselves hard and set increasingly high expectations for themselves and others and who by nature are intensely competitive. Since the 1980s this theory has been more directly applied to larger groups of in-

dividuals who feel invisible, ignored, or marginalized in an affluent and materialistic society (see Kotlowitz, 1991). Much of the research on cognitive strategies in psychotherapy (see Ellis & Harper, 1975) tends to support this theory. Hart (1979) presents a popular Christian version of this position.

A final major view contends that anger is a socially learned behavior (Bandura, 1979). Like other emotions, anger occurs according to lawful principles. This position is well documented in the research literature (see Miller & Jackson, 1995). Albert Bandura, for example, has observed that socialization of angry feelings is affected by experience and by observing others' success with aggressive behavior. Anger is understood as a state of arousal that can be experienced differently depending on how the model's success is perceived.

In contrast to the instinctual theorizing of the hydraulic model, the social learning model asserts that we internalize behaviors that we have seen effectively utilized in the external environment (see Learning, Social). Such theorizing is certainly not incompatible with contemporary psychodynamic formulations of anger (see Lerner, 1985) that focus on the social-relational milieu rather than reinforcing contingencies of the environment. If anger is a particular response to arousal, one can learn to redirect it into affection, Humor, or compassion. Humans have the capacity to rechannel unacceptable impulses (e.g., the desire to aggress) into acceptable, even creative actions (see Jones & Butman, 1991). Gandhi and Martin Luther King, Jr., are two frequently cited examples of individuals who put anger to such socially constructive uses.

Implicit in the professional literature on anger is the assumption that a frequent source of anger is the sense of demand or obligation. Some persons feel unloved, unworthy, and often angry, and their unrealistic expectations for self and others contribute to diminished self-esteem and frustration (see Ellison, 1983). Fearful and anxious, such individuals are more likely to lash out at those who do not give them what they feel is rightly owed. Self-protective strategies develop lest others discover their anger and punish them or reject them. In this dance, anger may be disowned but indirectly expressed in cynicism, sarcasm, projection, or more directly in explosive episodes. Destructive repressive mechanisms develop and become firmly entrenched, keeping these individuals from experiencing and owning their anger and denying them the opportunity to explore it, seek to understand it, confess it when necessary, experience healing, and seek reconciliation whenever possible. Lerner's (1985) discussion of these dynamics is especially insightful and helpful.

There are many possible sources of anger and aggression. The skilled and sensitive agent of change would be wise to look closely at possible situational variables (e.g., obstacles to goal attainment), thought patterns (e.g., a tendency to misinterpret life events), organic variables (e.g., alcohol or substance abuse), responses to anger (e.g., a pattern of responding when overaroused), and consequences of anger-related behavior (e.g., what needs or wants are met in responding this way). Miller and Jackson (1995) offer many practical suggestions for sharpening one's diagnostic skills in this area.

Anger is a complex emotional reaction, and clinicians must be cautioned against implementing techniques that fail to reflect an appreciation for the many factors that can cause or maintain it. Explosive outbursts may have an initial calming effect on the individual, but in the long run they tend to reduce inhibition and may even facilitate the expression of aggressive behaviors (see Intermittent Explosive Disorder). Such outbursts are often imitated by others if the results obtained by such behaviors are deemed successful. In contrast, there is a need in all societies to acknowledge and affirm role models who exhibit nonaggressive ways of expressing their feelings. The tremendous emphasis being placed on assertiveness training seems directly related to the need to teach and reinforce incompatible and competing behaviors (see Augsburger, 1973). Learning to recognize one's own feelings and those of others can be helpful, but knowing how best to respond to anger and aggression requires a good repertoire of communication and conflict-management skills (see Cosgrove, 1988). Minimizing aversive stimulation, rewarding nonaggressive behavior, and eliciting reactions that are incompatible with anger are the major strategies that have been suggested in the literature for several decades (see Myers, 1983). Learning to constructively deal with anger is a peacemaking process that can require great patience, reflective listening, and knowledge of the major alternative strategies.

For the Christian self-control is an important fruit of the Spirit. Perhaps anger can best be understood as a sign or symbol that something has gone awry internally and/or interpersonally. Honest Christianity calls us to reckon with truth about ourselves and each other and with God (McLemore, 1984). When we learn to deal effectively with our own anger or assist others in finding healthy ways to express their own ambivalent and confusing feelings, perhaps we are helping each other to develop a growing capacity to accept God's love for us and to experience that love in ways that will allow us to more truthfully respond to each other with greater compassion and sensitivity.

References

Augsburger, D. (1973). *Caring enough to confront*. Scottdale, PA: Herald.

Bandura, A. (1979). The social learning perspective: Mechanisms of aggression. In H. Toch (Ed.), *Psychology of crime and criminal justice*. New York: Holt, Rinehart, & Winston.

Berkowitz, L. (1978). Whatever happened to the frustration-aggression hypothesis? *American Behavioral Scientist, 21*, 691–708.

Cerling, C. E. (1974). Anger: Musing of a theologian/psychologist. *Journal of Psychology and Theology, 2* (1), 12–17.

Cosgrove, M. (1988). *Counseling for anger*. Dallas: Word.

Ellis, A., & Harper, H. (1975). *A new guide to rational living* (Rev. ed.). Englewood Cliffs, NJ: Prentice-Hall.

Ellison, C. W. (1983). *Your better self*. San Francisco: Harper & Row.

Hart, A. (1979). *Feeling free*. Old Tappan, NJ: Revell.

Jones, S., & Butman, R. (1991). *Modern psychotherapies*. Downers Grove, IL: InterVarsity Press.

Kotlowitz, A. (1991). *There are no children here*. Garden City, NY: Anchor Books.

Lerner, H. G. (1985). *The dance of anger*. New York: Harper & Row.

Lorenz, K. (1966). *On aggression*. New York: Harcourt, Brace, & World.

McLemore, C. (1984). *Honest Christianity*. Philadelphia: Westminster.

Miller, W., & Jackson, K. (1995). *Practical psychology for pastors* (2nd ed.). Englewood Cliffs, NJ: Prentice-Hall.

Meyer, R., & Deitsch, S. (1996). *The clinician's handbook* (4th ed.). Boston: Allyn & Bacon.

Myers, D. (1983). *Social psychology*. New York: McGraw-Hill.

Pederson, J. E. (1974). Some thoughts on the biblical view of anger. *Journal of Psychology and Theology, 2* (3), 210–215.

Tavris, C. (1982). *Anger: The misunderstood emotion*. New York: Simon & Schuster.

Warren, N. C. (1983). *Make anger be your ally*. Garden City, NY: Doubleday.

R. E. BUTMAN

See AGGRESSION; EMOTION; PERSONALITY.

Angyal, Andras (1902–1960). One of the major proponents of the holistic point of view in psychology. As a European Angyal shared in the phenomenological tradition of his time, and his thinking concerning human nature, health and illness, and death resembles that of contemporary existential writers.

Born in Hungary, Angyal spent his youth in rural Transylvania. He received his Ph.D. in psychology from the University of Vienna in 1927 and an M.D. from the University of Turin in 1932. After coming to the United States in 1932, he focused his early research on the physiological and psychological aspects of schizophrenia. Angyal's first book, *Foundations for a Science of Personality* (1941), developed a detailed conceptual framework for approaching each personality problem from a consistently organismic, holistic standpoint. A major shift in emphasis occurred in 1945, when he focused his efforts entirely on his private practice in Boston. Although he continued to write and lecture, his primary interest remained his therapeutic work with neurotics. His final and perhaps most important work was *Neurosis and Treatment: A Holistic Theory* (1965), published posthumously. This summarized his conceptualizations based on his many years in clinical practice.

Angyal developed an intricate theory of personality and neurosis that avoids a mind-body, subject-object dichotomy. Instead life is viewed as a continuous interplay of organismic and environmental influences. Two observable forces, autonomy and homonomy, constantly interact to direct a person's behavior. Autonomy refers to the striving for control over one's environment. Homonomy refers to the striving to be a part of something larger than self. Neurosis is a way of life resulting from a self-protective isolation that has grown out of an individual's anxiety and diffidence caused by early traumatic experiences during the individuation process.

Angyal advocated a therapeutic stance that seeks to make holistic interpretations that uncover the patient's patterns of isolation, conflict, and anxiety. More than leading one to insight, such interpretations attempt to return the patient to a healthy real self by carefully unearthing and fostering the repressed healthy pattern that existed prior to the development of the neurosis.

Angyal considered religion to be an important aspect of the human experience. He was particularly interested in the aspects of human existence expressed by the wide variety of religious philosophies and worldviews present in numerous cultures, and through these he countered attempts to dispel the importance of religious beliefs and experience that characterized much of the scientific writing of his time.

References

Angyal, A. (1941). *Foundations for a science of personality.* New York: The Commonwealth Fund.
Angyal, A. (1965). *Neurosis and treatment: A holistic theory* (E. Hanfmann & R. M. Jones, Eds.). New York: Wiley.

J. D. GUY, JR.

See ORGANISMIC THEORY.

Anhedonia. The absence of pleasure in acts that are normally found pleasurable, such as sexual activity, intellectual stimulation, and athletic involvement. In general a person loses enjoyment for previously pleasurable activities and appears apathetic, emotionally flat, and indifferent. Anhedonia can be a symptom of depression and is frequently observed in schizophrenia.

See EMOTION; DEPRESSION; SCHIZOPHRENIA.

Animal Experimentation. The use of animals in research has a distinguished history marked by progress toward a better understanding of disease and development of vaccines and medications. Without the use of animal subjects, this progress would not have been possible. Even though humans are used as subjects more often than animals, there are several advantages in using animal subjects. First, manipulations that are unethical for humans can be performed on animals; second, an animal's life span is typically much shorter, allowing for longitudinal studies; third, greater genetic and environmental control can be exercised over animals, thus improving the internal validity of the research; and finally, animals are readily available and most are bred specifically for research purposes.

Progress has been made since the 1970s by scientists, including psychologists, in understanding AIDS, anxiety disorders, Alzheimer's disease, Parkinson's disease, schizophrenia, depressive disorders, learning and memory, and recovery from spinal cord trauma, to mention just a few of the areas in which animal experimentation has played a major role. In spite of these advances, some people question the morality of using animals for research purposes. The objections often center around the number of animals used in research, the treatment of the animals in laboratories, and the rights of animals to be free from human exploitation.

Of the many ways animals are used by humans, less than 0.5% are used for research; of these, approximately 90% are rodents. The animals used are protected by laws as well as by guidelines established by federal agencies such as the National Institutes of Health (NIH). In addition scientists are careful to protect their animal subjects because valid data are obtained only when subjects are properly handled and cared for during the experiment. The opponents of animal use often refer to the rights of the animal. This emphasis on animal rights distorts the traditional Judeo-Christian view of humanity's sovereignty over nature (including animals), an ethic that has led to a robust animal welfare movement in the United States.

Animal experimentation is necessary to gain knowledge of medical diseases as well as human psychological function. The extent to which results from animal studies can be generalized to humans must be considered; however, without the use of animals as subjects, little advancement would be seen in understanding human behavior or the physical and mental disorders that impair so many people.

K. S. SEYBOLD

See COMPARATIVE PSYCHOLOGY; PSYCHOLOGY, METHODS OF.

Animal Psychology. *See* COMPARATIVE PSYCHOLOGY.

Anniversary Depression. "Anniversary depression" is a descriptive phrase for emotions people experience periodically for years after a painful loss. They begin to dread the approach of the date and may become increasingly depressed. They may mentally and emotionally relive the event to a degree that parallels posttraumatic stress disorder (PTSD).

The most common trauma-forming roots of anniversary depression include a child's death, suicide, divorce, death in a tragic accident, betrayal by a spouse, and loss of one's job. Every survivor of such a loss does not develop anniversary depression, but those who do usually have deep emotional and spiritual issues to resolve.

The death of a young child almost always stirs parents and relatives to form grief patterns that recur at each anniversary. The family grieves over what would have been happening had the child lived: "This year our child would be starting first grade" or "This year our teenager would be graduating from high school." Another root of grief is unresolved guilt. A family member may believe that if more had been done, the person would not have committed suicide. Another person may have unreleased rage at the person whose death still feels like a betrayal of the survivor.

Sometimes survivors cling to depression as an unconscious way of avoiding another issue in their lives. A parent might talk openly about a deceased child and be defensive if asked about his or her neglect of surviving children and spouse. The person may be intensely angry at God for letting the tragedy happen and yet be afraid to confess that anger for fear that God will punish someone who feels that way. If the depression is severe there may have been a history of depression before the trauma, and the loss therefore exacerbates the depression more than causes it.

There are many Christian teachings for people suffering from anniversary depression. The basic need is a heartfelt experience of God's grace (Eph. 2:5), freely given, overflowing, more than we can hold, a gift of love (Luke 6:38). This means that God loves us in spite of our sinfulness (Rom. 5:6–8). The more aware we are that everyone sins (Rom. 3:23) and that we are not unusual in our shortcomings, the more grace we can experience. The experience of God's grace gives us hope. Christian hope is rooted in the character of God; hope is a trust that God loves us, forgives us, calls us to service, and has given us the gift of eternal life. The more we trust in the character of God, the more empowered we are to bring to God our sadness, rage, guilt, and fear about a tragic loss. Through confession (1 John 1:8–9) to God of what we truly feel, we move toward reconciliation with God and any others who have wronged us. This spiritual discipline is the primary path to the healing of anniversary depression.

Most major losses trigger grief during the first year afterward such as on a first birthday, first Christmas, first wedding anniversary, and first anniversary of the loss. Many churches once posted the names of deceased members and then removed those names at the end of the year to suggest that the grief be largely put aside. This was a clear encouragement to people to grieve yet not as those who have no hope (1 Thess. 4:13). A sign of healing and new hope is when the recall of the loss becomes mild and more sentimental than depressive.

H. Wahking

See Depression.

Anointing. The ceremonial act of anointing in the Old Testament was used to set apart or to consecrate someone or something. In the preparation for worship, the priest and his garments were anointed with a specific sacred oil (e.g., Exod. 29:21). Rubbing or pouring of oil on the head was used to install kings into their positions as God's chosen rulers, also known as the anointed of God. Jesus Christ was referred to as the Anointed One.

Anointing with oil is also used for spiritual healing of the sick. This is not a medical treatment but a ceremonial consecration of the sick person and prayer by the elders for healing (James 5:14). The mental health professional is wise to recommend that clients seek out the elders of their church to receive this blessing. Sometimes clients present obvious physical problems and at other times have a physical sickness that promotes mental health disturbances (e.g., depression resulting from thyroid disease). Some therapists and clients believe that mental health disorders are illnesses that qualify for the anointing of oil and prayer by the elders, whether or not physical etiology or symptoms are present.

Another use of the term *anointing* is when God bestows the power of the Holy Spirit on an individual for a specific purpose. The anointing is a consecration of the individual by God for a temporary service or permanent ministry (Isa. 61:1; Zech. 4:14). God anointed Jesus with the Holy Spirit and with power for the purposes of healing and casting out demons (Acts 10:38). Similarly God anoints certain Christians with special power from the Holy Spirit for the gift of healing (1 Cor. 12:9, 28). Therapists may receive spontaneous anointings from God through the Holy Spirit that enable them to address or bring healing to specific client problems. In addition a therapist may be anointed in a more permanent fashion, as would be the case for the therapist anointed to bring healing in cases of sexual abuse.

F. A. DiBlasio

See Pastoral Counseling; Religious Resources in Psychotherapy.

Anorexia Nervosa. Although this disorder was first noted in the literature by Richard Morton in 1689, W. W. Gull in England (1873) provided the name and established the major diagnostic criteria still in use. Unlike its name implies, this is not a disorder of appetite. Rather, it is the fear of gaining weight, with the accompanying misperception that one is grotesquely fat. This perception persists even in the presence of indisputable evidence to the contrary. Anorexics most commonly seem to be more concerned about gaining weight than losing weight. Many anorexics report normal sensations of hunger and are frequently preoccupied with food, so much so that they do a great deal of cooking, baking, or gathering of cookbooks. The loss of appetite does not occur until late in the starvation process.

In addition to the fear of gaining weight, individuals with anorexia may exercise excessively in order to burn calories, eat inordinately small portions of food, take an extremely long time to eat, avoid public scrutiny by eating in private, be prone to wearing loose-fitting clothes, have a tendency toward being perfectionistic, have difficulty accepting their own faults and failures, and be preoccupied with social opinion. Thus the disorder is much more than an eating disorder, since it influences the individual's life in myriad ways.

The onset of anorexia nervosa seems to be multifactoral. The predisposing factors or precipitating influences may be related to individual genetics and characteristics, family patterns of functioning, and social/cultural influences. It has been reported that approximately 80% of all adolescent girls have been on a diet by the time they have reached age 18. In light of the fact that 90% of the sufferers of anorexia nervosa are females, this suggests that social and cultural elements are highly influential when predisposing one to weight loss. Certain family characteristics also appear to be consistent with the onset of anorexia nervosa. They are enmeshment with family members, overprotection, rigidity of family rules, and a lack of conflict resolution. Some researchers contend that family characteristics are not so much precipitants of the anorexia as characteristics that may result in having a seriously ill child. In either case these issues may need to be addressed during the therapeutic intervention with the anorexic.

Other experts believe that since the onset of anorexia nervosa is typically during the adolescent years, the initiating factors are crisis-related. Accompanying the weight loss is the postponement of menses and possibly hypothalamic dysfunction. Medical complications may arise from laxative abuse and self-induced vomiting. For those individuals in the later stages of the starvation process who frequently use vomiting or laxatives to rid themselves of unwanted calories, the following must be monitored: hematologic indices; electrolytes; and hepatic, cardiac, and renal functioning.

The younger the age of onset and treatment, the better the prognosis. Individuals who also suffer from bulimia usually have a much poorer prognosis than those who do not. Individuals who have both anorexia nervosa and bulimia have frequently been associated with borderline character structures. Some researchers have found a high incidence of sexual abuse in those individuals who later develop anorexia nervosa. Though the disorder is relatively rare in males, it is likely to be an indication of severe psychopathology.

Along with the medical complications, psychosocial complications also arise. Anorexics frequently become social isolates, which only confirms their deep sense of self-loathing and unacceptability. Many become meticulous and perfectionistic as a means of reclaiming some self-worth or as an attempt to establish some artificial boundaries within the family. One 16-year-old anorexic kept her bedroom meticulously clean and was an excellent student. She did not easily achieve good grades, so she spent a great deal of time studying; this was a way to obtain excellent marks as well as establish her autonomy within the family.

Many anorexics also display compulsive patterns of exercise and an obsession with the topic. Some report a sense of power, mastery, and control that becomes equated with losing weight. For them this sense of mastery is a pocket of control that establishes them as important, providing some sense of autonomy and self-esteem.

Bruch (1973) in her classic work relates anorexia nervosa to severe ego deficits, which she called perceptual and conceptual disturbances. They are distortion of body image; distortion of internal states and sensations (such as hunger, satiety, and emotion); and the pervasive sense of personal ineffectiveness. Bruch notes that anorexics truly believe they are overweight even though they are visibly emaciated. She maintains that realistic body image is a precondition for recovery of anorexia. Bruch further contends that anorexics have difficulty correctly identifying and labeling different physical cues (i.e., hunger) and emotional states (sadness). Many will report feeling full after a few bites of food or even report satiation by watching others eat. In addition she maintains that for the most part they feel interpersonally inept. Quite often anorexics maintain robotlike obedience and rigid conformity to parental standards and have limited ability to assert themselves interpersonally. According to Bruch, these deficits are a result of dysfunctional interactional patterns that arose between a parent and an infant.

Others, such as Garfinkel and Garner (1982), see anorexia nervosa as a multidimensional disorder, viewing it as a heterogeneous disorder with a multidetermined nature. It is a consequence and interaction of those factors (individual, familial, and cultural) that predispose one to the disorder; a precipitating event that brings about the onset of the disorder; and factors within either the individual and/or family that maintain or sustain the disorder.

According to Garfinkel and Garner (1982), each of the three clusters needs to be addressed in the course of treatment. Thus therapy may include medical maintenance, nutritional counseling, individual therapy, family therapy, behavior therapy, rational-emotive therapy, or group therapy in order to address those factors that predisposed, precipitated, or are functioning to sustain the disorder. This may best proceed from a multidisciplinary perspective, which should include a physician, nutritionist, psychiatric social worker, psychiatric nurse, dietitian, and clinical psychologist. Their cooperative effort is most significant for cases on the inpatient ward. Some research has indicated that antidepressant medication may be helpful in managing what may be an underlying affective disorder with the anorexia nervosa.

References

Bruch, H. (1973). *Eating disorders.* New York: Basic.

Garfinkel, P. E., & Garner, D. M. (1982). *Anorexia nervosa: A multidimensional perspective.* New York: Brunner/Mazel.

K. R. KRACKE

See BULIMIA NERVOSA; EATING DISORDERS.

Anosognosia. A denial or nonrecognition of physical illness in one's own body. Its most common manifestations are cases of blindness or deafness. Phantom limb (*see* Phantom Response) has been described as a transitory form of anosognosia. This unawareness of sickness or disease may be a method of adaptation to stress that enables a person to cope by denying the illness. It is also interpreted as a defense mechanism that serves to make the victim of an illness feel better about himself. In some cases the denial is based on a view of sickness as failure or weakness.

D. L. SCHUURMAN

See DENIAL; CONVERSION DISORDER; SOMATIZATION DISORDER.

Antabuse Therapy. Antabuse is one trade name for the generic compound disulfiram. It was first used in the treatment of alcohol abuse in the late 1940s after it was noted that patients taking the drug exhibited an extremely unpleasant physical reaction following ingestion of any product containing alcohol.

The symptoms of a typical disulfiram-alcohol reaction for a person on a daily regimen of the drug begin within 15 minutes after alcohol ingestion. The symptoms typically appear in the following order: flushing, sweating, heart palpitation, hyperventilation, decreased blood pressure, nausea, vomiting, and drowsiness. The intensity and duration of symptoms depend on the daily dosage of disulfiram ingested, the amount of alcohol consumed, and individual physiological variables.

When disulfiram was first introduced, physicians administered much larger doses than is common today, and manifestations of the dangerous side effects were much more common. These side effects, which can occur even at lower doses, include psychosis and degeneration of peripheral neural fibers. Extreme reactions, caused by individual hypersensitivity or by larger doses of disulfiram or alcohol, can result in psychosis, shock, or cardiac arrest. Most authorities feel, however, that when properly administered, disulfiram is a relatively safe drug to use as an adjunct to the treatment of alcohol abuse.

There is still some question as to the mode of effect of disulfiram. It is well established that disulfiram blocks the metabolism of alcohol in the liver at a point when a major alcohol byproduct is a toxin. The buildup of this toxin may directly cause the symptoms of the reaction. It is also possible that when it is combined with alcohol, the drug has other effects involving the central nervous system. Evidences for these secondary modes of action are just beginning to accumulate.

When it was introduced, disulfiram was viewed by many as a cure for alcoholism. It then became popular to use it as the primary ingredient in a fear-conditioning treatment of alcohol abuse. Following this model, abusive drinkers were put on large doses of disulfiram and then made to repeatedly drink alcohol to induce multiple reactions. Repeated experiences of reaction were viewed as necessary to condition a fear of drinking. This view of the utility of disulfiram is now in disfavor, with most professionals considering disulfiram a helpful component of a comprehensive, psychologically based treatment program. Taking disulfiram is viewed as a form of self-control whereby patients are able to decide once daily whether to drink during the next 24 hours, rather than having to make constant decisions on a moment-by-moment basis. It is seen as an excellent temporary way to limit impulsive drinking, thus giving other aspects of the treatment program the opportunity to be effective. The goal is the eventual termination of the use of disulfiram. Some empirical evidence suggests that use of disulfiram does increase the effectiveness of psychological treatment of alcohol abuse (Kwentus & Major, 1979). It should be noted that antabuse therapy is opposed by most members of Alcoholics Anonymous, as it is seen as a continuance of the pattern of reliance upon chemical substances by the recovering alcoholic.

Reference

Kwentus, J., & Major, L. (1979). Disulfiram in the treatment of alcoholism. *Journal of Studies in Alcohol, 40,* 428–446.

S. L. JONES

See ALCOHOL ABUSE AND DEPENDENCE.

Anthropology, Psychological. Anthropology is the scientific study of humanity. It is one of the most comprehensive academic disciplines. Like psychology, it has developed a broad spectrum of interests not sharply distinguishable from other fields already engaged in the study of humans. Anthropology overlaps with and draws from other sister disciplines including archaeology, sociology, religion, psychology, and cultural studies.

Anthropology as a separate field gradually emerged during the nineteenth century. It mainly focuses on the comparison of societies with each other, especially the more traditional and preliterate ones. It specializes in the observation, study, and analysis of peoples' customs, activities, traditions, languages, spirituality, norms, behaviors, belief systems, physical conditions, family structure, social bonding, and worldviews. The subdisciplines of anthropology are naturally consistent with and scholarly relevant to many fields of psychology, like sociocultural anthropology, physical anthropology, and psychological anthropology.

The history of cultures is what most anthropological theories seek to explain. The method commonly used for investigation and research is fieldwork. The anthropologist lives within the target community passively observing or, when appropriate, actively participating, possibly without disturbing the cultural dynamics of people's lives he or she is trying to study. Fieldwork procedures and methodologies greatly vary, depending on the anthropologist's theory and past experience, the nature and location of the community, the prior knowledge about the particular people group, and the intent of the research project.

Many anthropological findings and insights are very useful to the Christian professional who is engaged in cross-cultural psychology, counseling, or missions. They can help us avoid mistakes done in the past and virtually provide us with better understanding and reliable tools to carry on our Christian services in more sensitive and effective ways.

N. ABI-HASHEM

See CROSS-CULTURAL PSYCHOLOGY.

Antisocial Personality Disorder. The disordered personality who is also a criminal, commonly called a psychopath or sociopath, has always been a profound challenge both to therapists and to the judiciary. The empathic responsibility to identify with the patient often stands in direct opposition to the obligation to support the moral integrity of the community. The entire community is ambivalent about whether this much abused yet very defensive population should be treated or punished. Both judges and therapists are instructed to control the offender, yet both are repeatedly told treatment is futile and recidivism is inevitable. Of all the personality disorders this one, defined by hostility to civility itself, pleads with us most poignantly to understand and manage.

History. Whiteley (1975) gives an excellent review of the long history of the antisocial personality disorder, showing how existing social attitudes and general ideas of what makes people behave the way they do influence the labels and conceptual models over time. How do we explain this person who cuts such a devastating swath, wounding so many who try to respond lovingly to profound loneliness, yet a person who apparently feels no sorrow, no guilt, and no personal anxiety and even fails to learn from punishment?

Much of the literature focuses on moral depravity, seeking defects and their causes in failed social learning (*see* Learning, Social). But Link, Scherer, and Byrne (1977) have demonstrated that the sociopath is probably more aware of moral imperatives than are other borderlines.

Lack of anxiety also seemed an explanation until Vaillant (1984) described a unique and severe anxiety that surfaced when these patients were incarcerated "and could not run away." Under such constraint, he saw no distinction between the sociopath and any other low-functioning borderline personality, beyond their law breaking. If one can get to know the sociopath well enough, the structural deficits and defenses appear identical to those of the borderline. Seeing them this way lifts some of the mystery and hopelessness surrounding sociopaths.

Diagnosis. Considering criminal behavior alone as a diagnostic criterion has pitfalls. The most important of these pitfalls is that other psychopathology can present as law breaking as well. Many schizophrenics, some manic-depressives, and hysterics are brought to therapists by the police. None of these need the added stigma of psychopathy. Ruling out psychosis (which may be treatable) and finding the fundamental borderline structural pathology are critical for accurate diagnosis.

Distinctive features have been identified in the families of sociopaths, especially in fathers who have a higher incidence of criminality, alcoholism, and violence. Vaillant also noted that many mothers were terrified by the anxiety of their presociopathic children and taught them to avoid or deny their anxiety at any cost. But other narcissists and borderlines have fathers who are alcoholic and violent and have mothers who spoil this child because she fears anxiety.

Seeking a biological, genetic loading in sociopathy has come in and out of fashion as social scientists become less or more interested in such causes. Genetic research is strongly suggestive but far from conclusive. More recently biological markers, especially in brain neurotransmitters, have been investigated intensely, perhaps because sociopathy and substance abuse often occur together. The serotonin system seems distinctly implicated at least in the impulsiveness of borderlines and in the explosiveness of the sociopath (Siever & Trestman, 1993).

Management. Before deciding on how to manage these difficult patients, a distinction must be made between the criminal psychopath and the con man. Cleckley's (1941) influential study considered the two interchangeable, and in practice many criminals have the extraordinary gifts of the con. But seeing the usual con man who rarely is incarcerated as a male histrionic personality disorder or as one who organizes reality by a gamelike drama and becomes anxious when the action stops makes him more understandable and treatable than the sociopath.

Management almost inevitably means working in or with the justice system. Prisons and parole systems are usually not helpful. But should the prison systems use fewer and clearer rules, rewards, and discipline more rigidly and consistently, recidivism would improve. Incarceration itself, ordinarily considered a block to effective psychotherapy, can become a graphic model of the reality these patients must learn to face and handle. For difficult offenders especially, a rigid, disciplined environment is more helpful than one more permissive.

Many other sociopaths are committed to treatment as a condition of parole. The threat of reimprisonment in the hands of the therapist makes countertransference more difficult. But as a reality that must be adjusted to, it can become a practical issue of therapy.

Treatment. Treatment should follow that recommended for the borderline. Groups are considerably more effective than individual therapy. To be most effective, therapy should focus sharply on behavioral control of anxiety arousal as well as the addictive nature of their offending and on confronting the cognitions characteristically underlying the defenses of this group. A modified Alcoholics Anonymous group with a 12-step program can also provide a direct, group-supported method of monitoring and teaching healthy living principles.

If individual therapy is available to support the group, it should focus on the difficulties that step by step led to offending. Each of these can then, with the oversight of the group, be written into a clear, comprehensive relapse prevention plan. The plan can then be the focus of any therapy or follow-up groups in prison and on parole. The temptation of many therapists is to drift into insight-oriented techniques, but these, however skillfully done, are counterproductive with sociopaths except as insight is used to inform a cognitive-behavioral base.

Outcome. In the classic, *Deviant Children Grow Up,* Robins (1966) presents a detailed, long-term follow-up of delinquent children. Multiple or severe offenses committed in childhood, plus neurological signs such as hyperactivity, are indicators of poor outcome. An excellent review (Whiteley, 1975) of outcome of treatment in many circumstances and methods describes a disorder that tends over time to become less intense, at least less subject to criminal actions. Some 40% of all sociopaths, dropping to under 20% of those with more severe pathology, get better over time. These figures come from public records and do not indicate whether the bruising of families and friends improves. Prognosis is discouraging. However, cognitive-behavioral regimens have not been tried either extensively or long enough to fairly evaluate. Initially this approach seems promising, at least in a subgroup of sex offenders.

References

Cleckley, H. M. (1941). *The mask of sanity.* St. Louis: Mosby.

Link, N. F., Scherer, S. E., & Byrne, P. N. (1977). Moral judgment and moral conduct in the psychopath. *Canadian Psychiatric Association Journal, 22,* 341–346.

Robins, L. N. (1966). *Deviant children grow up: A sociological and psychiatric study of sociopathic personality.* Baltimore: Williams & Wilkins.

Siever, L., & Trestman, R. L. (1993). The serotonin system and aggressive personality disorder. *International Clinical Psychopharmacology, 8 Supplement 2,* 33–39.

Vaillant, G. E. (1984). Sociopathy as a human process. *Archives of General Psychiatry, 32,* 178–183.

Whiteley, J. S. (1975). The psychopath and his treatment. *British Journal of Psychiatry, 9,* 159–169.

C. M. BERRY

See PERSONALITY DISORDERS.

Anxiety. Feelings of anxiety are among the most common emotions experienced by humans. One can easily postulate that both Adam and Eve experienced anxiety when they became aware of their nakedness and hid themselves from God (Gen. 3:7–8). They had a vague sense that something was wrong. While they did not yet know this change of circumstance was due to sin, they did know it was not pleasing to God and naively attempted to hide. One can imagine they experienced nervous energy as they sewed fig leaves into clothing for themselves. It is easy to imagine they had ruminative thoughts about what was happening and what would occur when they came face to face with God. For the first time in the history of humanity there was a sense of vulnerability and an apprehension that something bad was about to occur; these emotions characterize the phenomenon of anxiety. It is important to remember that this is a state of emotional experience that is contrary to what God wanted for people (Isa. 48:18).

Anxiety is psychologically experienced as a combination of looming dread or impending danger and a vague uneasiness. There are also associated symptoms of mild agitation, racing thoughts, impaired sleep, and difficulty in calming oneself. There are parallel physiological experiences of sustained muscle tension and/or trembling, increased heart rate, and disturbed breathing—either as hyperventilation (i.e., breathing too fast) or as a tendency to hold one's breath. These characteristics produce a sense of heightened awareness or alertness that frequently disturbs concentration, memory, and a person's ability to feel emotionally comfortable. These psychological and physiological responses combine to make anxiety a psychophysiological disturbance.

The first encounter with this experience is termed separation anxiety, which is developmentally normal around six to nine months of age and is characterized by a fear of strangers or of separating from one's home or the persons to whom the child is attached. This may reoccur at any time during childhood or adolescence, but it is commonly associated with significant milestones, such as starting elementary or junior high school.

Anxiety can be relatively brief and situational, termed an adjustment disorder in the *DSM-IV* (American Psychiatric Association, 1994), or more prolonged and diffuse, as in the case of generalized anxiety disorder. The physiological symptoms of heightened arousal associated with anxiety can prompt a panic attack that may or may not be associated with agoraphobia. As a unique entity, agoraphobia is a feeling of powerlessness and a fear that one might lose control if he or she ventures from a

safe environment. This is different from social phobia, which is a fear of having to engage in social interactions. Through conditioning a person can become fearful of almost anything and experience
anxiety when confronted with that particular thing
or situation; this is called a specific phobia.

Freud's (1936) work crystallized the concept of
anxiety as a psychological entity. He postulated that
anxiety is either objective (e.g., reality-based) or neurotic in origin (Freud, 1933). The latter category is
exemplified by various expressions of general, free-
floating dread or apprehension that typifies what
Freud called the "neurotic lifestyle." Ever the prag-
matist, Freud saw reality-based anxiety as a feeling
born from those experiences that we have learned
are best to avoid. A chronic low self-esteem that
makes me too nervous to effectively drive my car for
fear that I might cause a crash would be a superego-
based anxiety. A nervousness that is based upon how
others might perceive and judge my driving would
be a neurotic anxiety that might make my driving
an automobile ineffective. Being hesitant to drive because I was in a car crash two weeks ago might, however, be an example of reality-based anxiety.

Existential theorists, however, differ with Freud
and do not see anxiety as an intrapsychic struggle.
Rather, they look at this phenomena as being a result
of humanity's struggle for meaning and being. From
a Christian perspective this creates problems, since
the existentialists see humanity as its own metric.
Without a solid, shared foundation of meaning (e.g.,
the Scriptures), humans, in this view, are doomed
to struggle with the questions of how a life can be
lived responsibly and authentically.

Anxiety states are related to physical changes
within the individual. This includes both parasympathetic and sympathetic activities of the autonomic
nervous system. These changes are related to the
flight-or-fight reaction, seen in such processes as rapid
heart rate, increased perspiration, increased blood
pressure, and coolness in the bodily extremities. Other
evidences include increased muscle tension as the person consciously or unconsciously prepares to meet
the threat from the environment. Epinephrine and
norepinephrine are secreted by the pituitary-adreno-
cortical system, and evidence shows that anxious individuals maintain increased levels of these metabolic
changes for longer periods of time (Martin, 1971). The
role of nature versus nurture comes strongly into play
regarding the psychophysiological aspects of anxiety.
The data are clear that anxious individuals tend to
have children who are more anxious. However, the
degree of relative contribution of heredity versus
learning is not clear. Even twin studies bring inconclusive results (Klein & Rabkin, 1981).

There is considerable overlap between anxiety and
many other psychological problems. However, anxiety must be clearly differentiated from fear, which
is an anxiety about a specific thing and is contrasted
with general anxiety, which is a pervasive and diffuse
sense of being worried.

A second area of overlap is with depression.
Clancy, Knoyes, Honeak, and Slymen (1979) found
approximately five years between the onset of anxiety and the development of depression. This led
Lesse (1982) to develop a position that anxiety is
the primary response to stress and leads to a continuum development of depression. This was postulated as a stress-anxiety-depression axis. Many researchers, however, have postulated that anxiety and
depression are separate entities (Roth, Gruney, &
Garside, 1972), and others see anxiety and depression as co-existent factors (Van Valkenburg, Akiskal,
Puzantian, & Rosenthal, 1984). Considerable other
work has been done to tie anxiety to a biological perspective, drawing upon anxiety as the prototypical
reaction to stress (Friedman, Clark, & Gershon,
1992). This work is built upon the stress-diataesis
model. In this conceptualization stress (with anxiety
being the most common manifestation) precipitates
a disorder to which an individual is predisposed (see
Marlow, 1988, for a review).

The overlap between anxiety disorders and personality disorders is a broad area of study that has,
as is typical with more broad-based mental health
symptoms, a variety of clarifying and then contradicting findings. The major area of difficulty is that
in the presence of an Axis I disorder, assessment of
Axis II pathology is likely to be distorted. Roth,
Gruney, and Garside (1972) found anxious patients
had a higher incidence of maladaptive personality
traits than do depressed patients. Utilizing a self-
psychology conceptualization of borderline disruption, Conte, Plutchik, and Karasu (1980) found borderline disordered patients to have higher levels of
anxiety than do normals. However, Synder and Pitts
(1988) found borderline and dysthymic patients
tended to not differ on certain measures of anxiety.
It has been suggested and empirically supported
that antisocial personality disorder patients have
lower levels of anxiety and are less responsive to
stress than normals (Speilberger, Kling, & O'Hagan,
1978). Only 24% of antisocial disorder patients were
found to have anxious symptoms (Weiss et al., 1983)
as compared to other personality disorders, which
have been found to have an incidence as high as 58%
positive for anxiety (Friedman, Shear, & Frances,
1987). What does seem to be a fairly consistent finding, however, is that the co-existence of anxiety and
personality disorders is suggestive of a negative
prognosis (Stein, Hollander, & Skodol, 1993).

The cognitive-behavioral perspective, the favored
school of thought among newly trained psychologists, considers anxiety to be the process of either
behavioral conditioning, internal appraisals of situations, or some combination of both.

Paul and Berstein (1973) have hypothesized two
distinctive types of anxiety. The first is conditioned
anxiety, which is a product of learning theory and
classical conditioning (*see* Conditioning, Classical).
A particular event or object becomes anxiety-
provoking because it has been paired with unpleas-

ant circumstances and gains the ability to provoke the anxiety independent of the circumstance. Such anxieties are not easily distinguished because individuals attempt to avoid or escape these anxiety-producing situations or stimulants. Thus there is little natural opportunity for the anxiety-producing power of the situation or item to have its provocative impetus eroded.

The second type of anxiety is termed by Lazarus and Launier (1978) as a reactive anxiety and is typified by the person's appraisal of his or her circumstance. How a person judges a threat and the capacity to cope or avoid the threat creates the extent of the anxiety. There is much pragmatic value in this view, since this theory well incorporates environmental/external threats to safety (i.e., the sight of flames and the smell of smoke in a restaurant) by misappraisals of demands on the person (e.g., "I must do perfectly on the exam or my life is over"), by real or perceived skill deficits (e.g., "I'm so shy, I'll probably make a fool of myself on this day"), or by any process whereby the perceived demands on the person taxes or exceeds the person's perceived capacity to cope.

This explanation of anxiety, however, is not well equipped to deal with what might be termed normal or purposeful anxieties. For example, as a person struggles with alienation from God, he or she may appropriately feel anxious. Yet this can be termed, in a cognitive-behavioral perspective, as an irrational belief. Irrational beliefs are too frequently defined merely in terms of their failure to enhance survival or pleasure rather than their compatibility to transcendent and eternal truth.

Among Christians there is a wide range of views about anxiety. At one end of the continuum, some Christian writers are almost indistinguishable from existentialists via their emphasis on humanity's search for identity, self, meaning, and the search to reduce existential angst. These writers seem to de-emphasize both Scripture and the idea of a personal God who holds answers for the human condition. On the other end of the spectrum are the writers who focus upon the sense of fear and doubt of God's provision, calling people to repentance, deliverance, and an end to anxiety through prayer and meditation. In that humans were created perfect, we can trace all problems to the fall from grace as a result of sin. However, it may be simplistic to say that, since this is the case, one should simply call the troubled person to a changed life. This approach tends to favor the concept of repentance, which is a discrete event or decision, and ignores the ongoing process of sanctification whereby a person learns, on a daily if not hourly basis, how to be in fellowship with a loving God and to live accordingly. There are writers in the middle of this continuum who accept a Christian ideal of life as free from worry as well as the fact of fallenness in ourselves and creation. For these individuals neurotic anxiety may be viewed as ultimately the result of sin, but whose sin and

how the sin should be dealt with are often unclear. These writers argue that even though anxiety may not be desirable, the way to eliminate it is not repression and denial but rather acceptance of our anxious feelings as real and, ultimately, looking to the Scripture and Jehovah Rapha as a healing God.

Although the Bible is silent about unconscious mechanisms of anxiety, fewer things are clearer in Scripture than Jesus' views regarding worry and earthly care. In Matthew 6:25–32 Jesus announces that because of God's love and omnipotence, worry is a needless waste of energy. The implication is that only God can run the world, so worrying about things not under our control is senseless. Jesus also contrasted two categories of experiences we can focus upon: the material and the spiritual. Both masters cannot be served simultaneously. One focus leads to worry and care, the other to peace. The emotional consequences of the two choices are predictable.

Paul was an intense man who at times experienced fear and trembling (1 Cor. 2:3). Yet he echoes Jesus' position regarding uselessness of worry. In Philippians 4:6 he urges readers to "be anxious for nothing" (NASB) and entreats us instead to prayer with thanksgiving. Peter joins Paul's call, exhorting us to humble ourselves before a mighty God, "casting all your anxiety upon Him, because He cares for you" (1 Peter 5:7, NASB). As it was with the Israelites (e.g., 1 Sam. 17:47), our "battles are the LORD'S." If God is for us, why should we fear (Rom. 8:31)? Yet knowing this intellectually is only the first step. Following insight, the Holy Spirit must work within believers to produce God's peace, which is a result of the relationship with God and not of positive thinking or some other cognitive technique.

According to the Scriptures, our attention should be fixed upon the ultimate spiritual realities. More than three hundred biblical passages tell us not to fear. Narcissistic self-preoccupation, besides being unnecessary and unrealistic, is a form of self-reliance, and self-reliance is, according to Scripture, sin. The consequences of seeking God's kingdom and righteousness first is that our needs are guaranteed to be met (Matt. 6:33). When we seek anything other than God as first priority in our lives, the meeting of our needs is not assured. Seeking Jehovah God first, however, produces the realities of the kingdom of God.

References

American Psychiatric Press. (1994). *Diagnostic and statistical manual of mental disorders* (4th ed.). Washington, DC: Author.

Clancy, J., Knoyes, R., Honeak, P. R., & Slymen, D. J. (1979). Secondary depression in anxiety neurosis. *Journal of Nervous and Mental Diseases, 166*, 846–850.

Conte, H. R., Plutchik, R., & Karasu, T. (1980). A self-report borderline scale: Discriminative validity and preliminary norms. *Journal of Nervous and Mental Diseases, 168*, 428–435.

Freud, S. (1933). *New introductory lectures on psycho-analysis*. New York: Norton.

Freud, S. (1936). *The problem of anxiety*. New York: Norton.

Friedman, C., Shear, M. K., & Frances, A. (1987). *DSM-III* personality disorders in panic patients. *Journal of Personality Disorders, 1*, 132–135.

Friedman, E. S., Clark, D. B., & Gershon, S. (1992). Stress, anxiety and depression: Review of biologic, diagnostic, and nosologic issues. *Journal of Anxiety Disorders, 6*, 337–363.

Klein, D. F., & Rabkin, J. G. (Eds.). (1981). *Anxiety: New research and changing concepts*. New York: Raven.

Lazarus, R. S., & Launier, R. (1978). Stress-related transactions between person and environment. In L. A. Previn & M. Lewis (Eds.), *Perspectives in interactional psychology*. New York: Plenum.

Lesse, S. (1982). The relationship of anxiety to depression. *American Journal of Psychotherapy, 36*, 332–348.

Marlow, D. H. (1988). Current models of panic disorder and a view from emotion theory. In A. J. Frances and R. E. Hales (Eds.), *Review of psychiatry*. Washington, DC: American Psychiatric Press.

Martin, B. (1971). *Anxiety and neurotic disorders*. New York: Wiley.

Paul, G. L., & Bernstein, D. A. (1973). *Anxiety and clinical problems*. Morristown, NJ: General Learning Press.

Roth, M., Gruney, C., & Garside, R. F. (1972). Studies in the classification of affective disorders: The relationship between anxiety states and expressive illness—I. *British Journal of Psychiatry, 121*, 147–161.

Speilberger, C. D., Kling, J. K., & O'Hagan, E. S. J. (1978). Dimensions of psychopathic personality: Antisocial behavior and anxiety. In R. D. Hair and D. Shalling (Eds.), *Psychopathic behavior: Approaches to research*. Chichester, NY: Wylie and Sons.

Stein, D. J., Hollander, E., & Skodol, A. E. (1993). Anxiety disorder and personality disorders: A review. *Journal of Personality Disorders, 7*, 87–104.

Synder, S., & Pitts, W. M. (1988). Characterizing anxiety in the *DSM-III* borderline personality disorder. *Journal of Personality Disorders, 2*, 93–101.

Van Valkenburg, C., Akiskal, H. S., Puzantian, V., & Rosenthal, T. (1984). Anxious depressions: Clinical, family history, and naturalistic outcome—comparisons with panic and major depressive disorders. *Journal of Affective Disorders, 6*, 67–82.

Weiss, J. M., Davis, D., Hedlund, J. L., et al. (1983). The dysphoric psychopath: A comparison of 524 cases of antisocial personality disorder with matched controls. *Comprehensive Psychiatry, 24*, 355–369.

A. J. Rainwater III

See Fear; Emotion; Phobic Disorders.

Anxiety Disorders. Although all anxiety disorders share common features, they can be divided by four defining characteristics. Regardless of the intensity of symptoms, separation anxiety, adjustment disorder with anxious mood, substance-induced anxiety, and anxiety associated with a general medical condition are all situation- or event-specific and typically are relatively brief in duration.

Disorders that are highly defined by a component of fear include specific phobia, social phobia, panic attacks, and agoraphobia. In each of these the person experiences anxiety in response to fear of a unique thing or a particularly undesired outcome.

Ruminative and perseverative thoughts or actions that focus on unique events, specific emotional responses, diffuse physiological sensations, and/or negative consequences typify obsessive-compulsive disorder, posttraumatic stress disorder (or its precursor, acute stress disorder). The persistent and circular nature of these thoughts, sensations, or behaviors can have a broad impact on a person's life.

Generalized anxiety disorder is the remaining diagnosis that accounts for diffusely defined and more broadly experienced anxiety occurrences. The believer has a distinct advantage in overcoming anxiety through victory in Christ (1 John 5:4–5), who teaches us to be anxious for nothing (Phil. 4:6–7) and to dwell in his peace (John 14:27).

A. J. Rainwater III

Aphasia. A general term for language disturbance, both in expression and interpretation, due to brain lesions. Types of aphasia include amnestic aphasia (difficulty in finding the correct name for an object), auditory aphasia (word deafness), central aphasia (semantic disintegration—sometimes called jargon aphasia), global aphasia (total aphasia due to major destruction of the left hemisphere's frontaltemporal region), motor aphasia (difficulty in speech expression), semantic aphasia (inability to grasp meaning of words), sensory aphasia (difficulty in using the senses to perceive speech), and visual aphasia (the inability to recognize words).

P. C. Hill

See Communication Disorders.

Apostasy. In the Christian tradition apostasy refers to the process of turning away from Christianity and from one's relationship with God. It is considered an egregious sin (2 Peter 2:20–21), synonymous with falling away from the faith and rebellion. The term *apostasy* is rarely used in the Bible (e.g., in the NASB only Jer. 2:19; 5:6; 2 Thess. 2:3); however, the concept can be found throughout Scripture.

The first apostasy occurred in heaven (Jude 6), but Adam and Eve's primal sin became the first human apostasy. From the wanderings of the exodus to the fall of the monarchies of Judah and Israel, apostasy among the Old Testament people of God was a continual problem. Christ taught that some would receive God's word gladly at first, only to fall away later in response to temptation or affliction (Matt. 13:21). The early church witnessed the falling away of some disciples (John 6:66; 1 John 2:19), including Judas, Hymenaeus and Alexander (1 Tim. 1:19–20), and Demas (2 Tim. 4:10). Apostasy has been a tragic reality in the history of God's people. With regard to the future, both Christ and the apostles warned that a great apostasy is coming which will precede the day of the Lord (Matt. 24:9–12; 2 Thess. 2:2–3; 1 Tim. 4:1–3; 2 Tim. 4:4).

The danger of apostasy comprises a main theme of the Book of Hebrews (Hughes, 1977). The author admonishes the readers to beware lest they possess evil, unbelieving hearts that lead them away from God (Heb. 3:12). He argues for the possibility that one can fall away even after one has been enlightened, tasted of the powers of the age to come, been made a partaker of the Holy Spirit (Heb. 6:4–5), and sanctified (Heb. 10:29). The author urgently warns against apostasy because once persons have fallen away "it is impossible to renew them again to repentance" (Heb. 6:6, nasb), since they recrucify Christ and dishonor his sacrificial death (Heb. 6:6; 10:29). The state of those who turn away from God's salvation is worse than if they had never known it (2 Peter 2:20–21).

Such teaching has been the source of much theological and pastoral controversy over the centuries. The possibility of apostasy has been thought to undermine or contradict God's sovereign grace in salvation. As a result some have argued that true Christians can lose their salvation, whereas others have argued that the passages about apostasy have relevance only to false Christians. Berkouwer (1958) believed that the Scriptures teach neither extreme. Many Scriptures make clear that God will lead his believing people to glory (Pss. 23:6; 55:22; John 10:27–28; Phil. 1:6). Faith and God's sovereign grace are not mutually exclusive but correlative. The admonitions to persevere and to avoid shipwreck are necessary and applicable to believers because it is only through perseverance in faith and obedience that they will arrive in glory (Matt. 24:13; Rom. 2:7; cf. the "if" passages: John 15:6–7; 1 Cor. 15:2; Col. 1:23), a glory to which they have been ordained (Rom. 8:29–30). As Berkouwer stated: "Anyone who takes away any of this tension, this completely earnest admonition, this many-sided warning, from the doctrine of the perseverance of the saints would do the Scriptures a great injury, and would cast the Church into the error of carelessness and sloth" (p. 110). God sovereignly preserves true believers through faith; therefore the warnings of apostasy must be taken seriously.

The issue of apostasy is a living one for pastors and Christian counselors. Depressed believers sometimes feel that they have committed the unpardonable sin or have become apostate. They may benefit from a careful consideration of the (imperfect) evidence that they are believers: for example, they are concerned about God; apostates are not. They may also need to be encouraged to continue to trust in God's forgiving grace. Their sins and need for forgiveness should be taken seriously, but they will need corrective biblical teaching if their consciences are overly burdened or scrupulous. Christians who are living in evident sin (e.g., idolatry, adultery, homosexuality; 1 Cor. 6:9–10) and are unrepentant need to be warned that they are placing their souls in jeopardy and are in danger of being cut off (2 Tim.

2:12). "It is a terrifying thing to fall into the hands of the living God" (Heb. 10:31, nasb).

Richard Baxter (1673/1990), one of the great Puritan pastors, discussed some signs of growing apostasy: when sin's delights are continually greater than the pleasures of holiness; when repentance is put off; when legitimate admonitions of others are resisted; when sin becomes easy and conscience offers no argument; and when sin is mentally and verbally defended. Baxter then offers some topics for meditation to help call the person back: consider that such a course brings hell into the present; recall the misery and folly of the non-Christian life; the guilt of the apostate is greater than any; God continues to demonstrate his love with his daily mercies; and one should not forsake the best friend one has ever had. Though God knows who is beyond repentance, humans never do, so the counselor's response should always be to encourage faith in the God of all grace.

References

Baxter, R. (1990). *The practical works of Richard Baxter: Vol. 1. A Christian directory.* Ligonier, PA: Soli Deo Gloria. (Original work published 1673)

Berkouwer, G. C. (1958). *Faith and perseverance.* Grand Rapids, MI: Eerdmans.

Hughes, P. E. (1977). *A commentary on the epistle to the Hebrews.* Grand Rapids, MI: Eerdmans.

Additional Reading

Grudem, W. (1994). *Systematic theology: An introduction to biblical doctrine.* Grand Rapids, MI: Zondervan.

E. L. JOHNSON

See DOUBT; RELIGIOUS DEVELOPMENT; RELIGIOUS EXPERIENCE; FAITH; CHRISTIAN GROWTH.

Applied Behavioral Analysis. Applied behavioral analysis has its historical origins in operant conditioning and the experimental analysis of behavior. B. F. Skinner introduced the basic concepts of operant conditioning (*see* Conditioning, Operant) in *The Behavior of Organisms* (1938). He insisted that observable behavior is the proper concern of psychology and that individual variability in behavior can be accounted for in terms of environmental variables without making reference to unobservables such as thoughts or feelings. He did not deny the presence of covert processes; he denied that they are necessary in giving an account of what controls behavior.

Although Skinner was an experimental psychologist who investigated the behavior of rats and pigeons within the laboratory, he also had serious interest in the application of his methods and conceptual models to humans. Ten years after he published his first book, he wrote *Walden Two*. This novel described a psychological utopia set in the contemporary United States. The story provocatively illustrated an experimental community in which human problems were solved by a scientific technology of behavior. This book inflamed the imaginations of many readers, some of whom established experimental communities based on Skinnerian principles.

Fifteen years after publishing his first book on operant conditioning Skinner wrote *Science and Human Behavior*. In this work he tried to illustrate how to account for complex human processes in terms of environmental factors. Among the topics covered were self-control, thinking, the self, social behavior, government, religion, psychotherapy, education, and cultures. The book was a catalyst for many investigators and theorists. Skinner's approach to psychology was distinctive in at least two ways. First, he insisted on the possibility and importance of analyzing even the most complex behaviors in terms of their publicly observable controlling variables. Second, he insisted on studying individuals rather than data averaged across groups of subjects. This focus on the individual led to research designs and methodologies not used by most other psychological investigators.

At least partially because the Skinnerian approach to research was different from that used by most other psychologists, journal editors were often not receptive to publishing articles by operant investigators. In 1957 this publishing problem was alleviated by the introduction of the *Journal of the Experimental Analysis of Behavior*. The title of this new journal communicated the essence of operant conditioning. Skinner's followers were committed to analyzing behaviors of individual animals or persons by systematically manipulating those variables that may have a controlling influence. Rather than first developing a comprehensive theory and then experimentally testing the validity of the theory, the operant investigators were committed to gather experimental data, determine trends in those data, and repeatedly replicate those trends before articulating laws or principles.

Another landmark in the development of the experimental analysis of behavior was the publication of Sidman's *Tactics of Scientific Research* in 1960. Prior to this there had been no comprehensive text explaining how to conduct intensive experimental studies on individual subjects. Sidman's book made the concepts and procedures of the experimental analysis of behavior available to a broader audience.

At the same time these methodological advances were occurring, other researchers were beginning to explore means of applying the procedures that had been developed with rats and pigeons to people and their problems in living. These early explorations were part of the beginning of a major movement within education, medicine, and psychology.

Behavior Modification and Behavior Therapy. Beginning in the 1950s an increasing number of researchers became interested in applying the experimental analysis of behavior to real problems. For example, Bijou and Baer of the University of Washington analyzed the behavior of developmentally disabled persons as well as that of normal children. In the process of experimentally analyzing what variables controlled the individual's behavior, they discovered ways of helping the person behave more effectively or appropriately. Persons responsible for the care of individuals with problems did not want simply to know what environmental variables control what behaviors. They wanted a psychological technology that could be used to strengthen appropriate behaviors and to weaken inappropriate behaviors. They wanted methods for changing behavior in the natural environment rather than in the laboratory. They were interested in behavior modification.

In the 1950s other investigators began to explore how to apply findings and procedures discovered in learning laboratories to alleviate the kinds of problems faced by clinical psychologists and psychiatrists. Lazarus and Wolpe were two such persons. They began their clinical research in South Africa, and both eventually came to the United States, where they continued their work. They too were interested in focusing on observable behavior. Since they were psychotherapists, they were responsible for treating their patients. As clinicians they had a natural interest in therapy. A combination of these two concepts produced behavior therapy.

Although early behavior therapists such as Lazarus and Wolpe seemed to emphasize the concepts of theorists such as Clark Leonard Hull and Ivan Pavlov more than those of Skinner, there was no fundamental incompatibility in the approaches of the behavior modifiers and the behavior therapists. Behavior modifiers tended to be persons who had come out of operant conditioning laboratories. Behavior therapists tended to be persons who had trained and worked in mental health settings and then turned to findings from laboratory research for help in treating their patients more effectively.

Most contemporary behaviorally oriented psychological practitioners treat behavior modification and behavior therapy as synonyms. Whether they are talking about modification or therapy, the emphasis is placed on interventions and their outcome. In contrast, applied behavioral analysis places the emphasis on analyzing what environmental variables control a given behavior rather than focusing primarily on outcome.

Strategies for Analyzing Behavior Change. Behavioral analysts have developed a large number of strategies for evaluating the effects of environmental variables on individual subjects. The strategies are usually referred to as single-subject, N = 1, or intensive experimental designs. The best known single-subject strategy is the ABAB design. Each letter represents a treatment phase, with A usually indicating baseline or nontreatment conditions and B indicating treatment conditions. Each phase lasts a number of days, weeks, or sometimes months. The investigator records the subject's behavior throughout each phase. At least five to ten observations are normally made within each phase. Following the initial baseline phase the investigator introduces a treatment for a period of time equal to that of the first baseline period. Assuming the treated behavior changes during intervention, the next step is to restore the original baseline conditions. The target behavior typically worsens during this third phase. The final phase is a return to intervention. If the applied researcher can systematically increase and then decrease the target behavior as the conditions are changed from phase to phase, experimental control is demonstrated and a controlling variable is identified.

Another widely used single-subject design is the multiple baseline strategy. For example, a behavior analyst may begin by observing three behaviors (such as on task, raising hand before speaking, and disruptiveness) in the same subject without applying any treatment. Then the investigator may apply an intervention to on task while keeping the other two behaviors on baseline conditions. If only one task improves and the other two behaviors stay the same, there is evidence that the treatment controlled the behavior. Next the analyst can apply the treatment to both on task and raising hand but not to disruptiveness. If raising hand then improves but disruptiveness does not, additional evidence accrues regarding the impact of the treatment. Finally, the investigator can apply the intervention to disruptiveness. If disruptiveness then improves, still more evidence is obtained about the power of the intervention.

A basic concept underlying the preceding designs is replication. Treatment effects are replicated within a single subject. Then those effects are replicated across many subjects taken one at a time. When the same effects can be repeatedly demonstrated within and across individuals, experimental control is demonstrated.

Applications. Interest in adapting the concepts and procedures of the experimental analysis of behavior to practical problems grew rapidly during the 1960s. This interest led to a new journal in 1968, *The Journal of Applied Behavior Analysis.* Its purpose as stated in the initial issue was "primarily for the original publication of reports of experimental research involving applications of the analysis of behavior to problems of social importance."

Applied behavioral analysts have spent much time determining what factors enhance or hinder academic performance. They have investigated variables that control classroom behavior—sustained attention, disruptiveness, handwriting, hyperactivity, learning disabilities, doing homework, tardiness, truancy, and underachieving.

Another focus has been health-related behaviors, including drug addictions, alcoholism, asthma, headaches, smoking, auto accidents, high blood pressure, pain, cerebral palsy, adjusting to deafness, diabetes, exercise, nutrition, obesity, rumination in infants, self-injurious behavior, recovery from head injuries, and chronic vomiting.

A third area of exploration has been social and relational skills, including altruism, assertiveness, isolate behavior, marriage, parenting, oppositional children, cooperative play, sexual behavior, sexual deviations, and sharing.

Behavioral analysts have identified ways to affect a wide range of personal problems, including aggression, anxiety, articulation disorders, autistic behavior, snoring, child molesting, excessive crying, delusions, enuresis, encopresis, echolalia, gambling, gender identity problems, head banging, homosexuality, incontinence, insomnia, phobias, stuttering, stealing, throwing tantrums, thumb sucking, tics, and difficulties in toilet training.

Applied behavioral analysis has also been used to identify ways of promoting athletic performance, energy conservation, Creativity, driver safety, personal goal setting, happiness, job interviewing skills, prayer, room-cleaning behavior, self-care, swimming, time management, and work output.

Effectiveness. Applied behavioral analysis is not a set of treatment techniques. It is an approach to analyzing the impact of any environmental variable that might influence behavior. Psychological treatments constitute one broad category of environmental variables. Applied behavioral analysis has been useful in evaluating the effects of a wide range of treatments. Behavioral analysts have clearly demonstrated the possibility and value of experimentally analyzing which interventions are most effective for a particular type of psychological problem.

Applied behavioral analysis bridges the gap between traditional laboratory research and clinical practice by merging experimental research with practical problem solving. The development of single-subject experimental designs has made it possible to do controlled research with individual subjects in their own homes, schools, playgrounds, offices, athletic fields, or hospital rooms. This particular approach seems to have some effect on most problem areas to which applied psychologists have paid attention.

P. W. CLEMENT

See BEHAVIORAL PSYCHOLOGY; BEHAVIOR THERAPY.

Applied Psychology. The human mind seems to have a need to organize and name the parts of its world. For example, we name ourselves, our pets, and our occupations. One way to name psychologists is to use the distinction between applied and basic psychology. Applied psychologists typically are interested in helping people, while basic psychologists are interested in understanding people.

The problem with the distinction is that it represents a dimension rather than two discrete categories. Almost all psychologists reflect a blend of applied and basic orientations. In addition today's esoteric laboratory finding may become tomorrow's solution to an important human problem. Therefore, although naming psychologists as basic or applied may satisfy a human need, it can distort our understanding of psychologists and what they do.

With these qualifications in mind, this article will discuss two current areas of psychological study that are bearing significant applied fruit but have basic roots: the psychology of the courtroom and behavioral medicine. Both areas are new and rapidly growing and both hold the potential for producing wide-ranging changes in people's lives.

Forensic Psychology. As psychologists have entered the courtroom they have focused on at least three issues: eyewitness testimony, "irrelevant" attributes of the defendant affecting judgments of guilt or innocence, and the dynamics of jury deliberation.

The major contribution of psychologists regarding eyewitness testimony probably has been to disabuse us of the notion that people are walking videotape machines. A basic Gestalt principle is that when faced with an event, such as a crime, people interpret, organize, and transform what they experience. Among other things this means that we tend to see what we expect to see, perhaps going beyond the facts to produce a more understandable and organized picture of what happened. Researchers have even found that how we recall an event may alter our memories (Loftus, 1979). Thus, biased questioning of a witness may distort a witness's memory or testimony (e.g., "Wasn't it true that the defendant spoke to the victim in an angry tone of voice?"). One of the more curious findings in this literature is that eyewitness confidence is more related to the personality of the eyewitness than the accuracy of the testimony.

Research into the impact of defendant attributes suggests that jurors are affected by more than the facts of a case. For example, pretty defendants are less likely to be judged guilty than ugly ones (Cash, 1981). Presumably jurors and people in general attribute fairly positive characteristics to beautiful people. However, there is a limit to the benefits of beauty. If a defendant uses his or her good looks in the commission of a crime (e.g., swindling a lonely person), then jurors seem to be less understanding (Sigall & Ostrove, 1975).

The study of jury deliberations is a natural extension of the research in group dynamics. For example, the group polarization effect is the tendency of group members to become more extreme in their position following group discussion. This suggests that a jury that might have been willing to convict on a lesser charge before deliberation may be more willing to convict on a more severe charge following deliberation.

Behavioral Medicine. A second major application of psychology is behavioral medicine. It has been argued (Miller, 1983) that before the introduction of antibiotics, medicine had no inherently therapeutic methods or substances. In other words, people were healed through medical interventions because they believed in medicine (placebo effects). This suggests that the human mind has tremendous power to heal or to damage the human body. If this is so, then there is room for the application of psychology in the world of medicine.

One possible application is in the area of patient compliance with a doctor's requests. Oftentimes a patient is asked to take medicine or participate in a therapeutic process that will have long-term benefits and short-term costs. The classic example is the use of medication to reduce high blood pressure. In the long run the patient may be protected from a heart attack or stroke, but the immediate consequences of the medication include tiredness and other side effects. Under these conditions patients often do not follow doctors' orders. Psychology could be helpful in making doctors more persuasive.

A second area of application concerns the relationship between personality and health. For example, researchers have found that anger-prone individuals who are time-pressured and task-oriented (the Type A personality) are more likely to secrete hormones that contribute to the narrowing of blood vessels than are their more relaxed counterparts. Another complication for stressed individuals is the growing literature suggesting that stress can lead to suppression of the immune system of the body.

Finally, psychology has provided specific technologies for medicine. For example, biofeedback allows patients to consciously control "involuntary" processes. Blood flow to the hands can be increased to avoid migraine headaches. Heart irregularities can be reduced. Brain activity can be controlled to promote relaxation.

Psychology has much to say about important areas of our lives. These contributions and insights often begin as part of basic psychology and evolve into significant tools for applied psychology. An interesting question for Christians is the extent to which techniques derived within one philosophical framework can be used by people who reject that framework. For example, many behavior modification techniques were developed by researchers committed to a deterministic worldview. Can these techniques be used, apart from their philosophical roots, by Christians who embrace a free will perspective?

References

Cash, T. F. (1981). Physical attractiveness. An annotated bibliography of theory and research in the behavior sciences (Ms. 2370). *Catalog of Selected Documents in Psychology, 11,* 83.

Loftus, E. F. (1979). *Eyewitness testimony.* Cambridge, MA: Harvard University Press.

Miller, N. E. (1983). Behavioral medicine. Symbiosis between laboratory and clinic. In M. R. Rosenzweig & L. W. Porter (Eds.), *Annual Review of Psychology* (Vol. 34). Palo Alto, CA: Annual Review.

Sigall, H., & Ostrove, N. (1975). Beautiful but dangerous. Effects of offender attractiveness and nature of the crime on juridic judgment. *Journal of Personality and Social Psychology, 31,* 410–414.

R. L. BASSETT

See FORENSIC PSYCHOLOGY; HEALTH PSYCHOLOGY; INDUSTRIAL/ORGANIZATIONAL PSYCHOLOGY; CLINICAL PSYCHOLOGY; POPULAR PSYCHOLOGY.

Apraxia. The impairment of learned purposeful movement that is not attributable to paralysis or other motor or sensory disorder. In apraxia of gait, for example, the individual has difficulty in coordinating limb movements necessary for walking. There is currently no comprehensive understanding of the causes of apraxia. It is undoubtedly related to neurological lesions. However, the specific areas of the brain involved remain unclear.

See SOMATIZATION DISORDER.

Aptitude Tests. An aptitude test is a standardized battery designed to produce a score predictive of future performance in a given area. An aptitude is generally defined as a capacity to acquire proficiency in a specific or general area after training. For example, a person's potential to become an automobile mechanic could be measured by a mechanical aptitude test. Or a high school senior's potential to do well in college could be measured by a scholastic aptitude battery. The former is a type of specific aptitude testing, the latter a general aptitude test.

Aptitudes are one kind of ability. An ability is a present, actual capacity to perform a certain task. One's current ability to perform certain manual dexterity tasks with speed and precision might also be an aptitude for future high performance in mechanics once training is obtained. A test of manual dexterity would be called an ability test if the aim were to measure current functioning, an aptitude test if the intent were to predict future performance in mechanics, or an achievement test if the intent were to measure the adequacy of past learning or training (Friedenberg, 1995).

The development of aptitude testing was one of the early achievements of psychology as a discipline. The initial impetus came during World War I, when it became necessary to identify men with the potential to become pilots. The success of the Otis-based Army Alpha tests of aptitude in directions, arithmetic, practical judgment, synonyms, disarranged sentences, number series, analogies, and general information launched a new field of aptitude testing. The development of correlation coefficients gave this infant science a much stronger means of identifying how closely two sets of numbers are related to one another than had previously been possible. Thus research could proceed to identify correlations between various tasks needed in the performance of certain jobs and simple tests that might be good predictors of such performance.

The theory behind aptitude testing assumes that all individuals differ. The differences may be congenital, acquired, physical, or mental. The theory is supported by the fact that training often highlights the natural differences among people to perform certain tasks and that some people do not seem to achieve well in certain tasks no matter how well they have been trained.

Aptitude tests are frequently used in schools (Gellman, 1995). Another major use of aptitude testing is in industry, where present or future employees are tested for potential achievement in various skills. The General Aptitude Test Battery is a widely used battery of tests emphasizing the measurement of motor skills needed in various nonprofessional occupations.

The major criticisms of aptitude tests revolve around their questionable predictive value for long-term performance and problems in test construction. Critics claim that most aptitude testing should be abandoned due to these and other problems (Kline, 1993).

References

Gellman, E. S. (1995). *School testing: What parents and educators need to know.* Westport, CT: Praeger.

Friedenberg, L. (1995). *Psychological testing: Design, analysis, and use.* Boston: Allyn & Bacon.

Kline, P. (1993). *The handbook of psychological testing.* London: Routledge.

J. R. BECK

See PSYCHOLOGICAL MEASUREMENT.

Archetypes. As described by Jung, archetypes are inborn images or encapsuled symbols that suggest the most fundamental motifs and themes of human existence. The same archetypes exist in people of all times and from all places. Thus the archetypes form what Jung called the collective unconscious, the deepest, most primitive stratum of the human mind, and as such it is hidden from us. Therefore pure pictures of archetypes remain masked from full awareness.

However, representations of archetypes are available through symbols and metaphors, particularly as revealed in fairy tales, legends, myths, and folklore. These representations are distorted by both the culture and the personal histories of authors or storytellers. Culture and personal history serve as filters through which the image of an archetype must pass. Therefore archetypes are best glimpsed through symbols that distill the commonalties of similar legendary figures across different cultures. The wise old man, the trickster, the great earth mother, and the hero are examples of such distillations.

Jung found these characters in every culture. The stories of King Arthur, Columbus, Odysseus, George Washington, and Rama (the hero warrior of Hindu scriptures) are all variations on the theme of the hero. In the Bible David fits this role well.

Jung observed archetypes to be active forces in the lives of his patients and in his own life. In a sense the archetypes represent the many potential aspects of the self or the numerous subpersonalities common to every personality. Thus a part of each of us wishes to see the self as questing heroically, and therefore we can identify with stories of those who act this role to the utmost. A person who cannot identify at all with a particular archetype may have alienated that part of the self. This prevents harmonious functioning of the various components of the personality and may cause psychological problems.

The concept of an archetype was not new with Jung. He viewed St. Augustine's *ideaes principales* as the equivalent. Plato's forms, described as existing before, above, and apart from all actual things, are similar to archetypes. Most familiar in the Christian tradition is the *imago Dei,* or image of God, which is imprinted in every person. This is the God archetype. We also have many other images imprinted in our minds. The Christian task in this framework is to make the God image dominant in the personality and to weave together archetypes representing all other parts of the self, including the less palatable aspects, under the image of God within us.

J. E. TALLEY

See ANALYTICAL PSYCHOLOGY; JUNG, CARL GUSTAV.

Aristotle (384–322 B.C.). A student of Plato who eventually broke with his master on a number of key issues. Specifically Aristotle contended that the forms that Plato had accepted existed not separately from the physical world but only as the essential structures of that world. Aristotle's philosophy dominated the late medieval period, and many of his ideas and insights continue to be lively centers of controversy. Among his many achievements Aristotle virtually invented formal logic.

The general tendency of Aristotle's psychology is away from Plato's dualistic separation of soul and body toward a more unified view of the "soul as the form of the body," the two together forming one substance. Aristotle viewed the main functions of the soul as the nutritive, the perceptive, the power to initiate movement, and the power to reason. These he arranged in a hierarchy, with lower forms of life sharing the lower functions but only humans fully possessing the power to reason. This laid the basis for his famous definition of man as a rational animal.

In an obscure passage in *On the Soul* Aristotle distinguished between an active and a passive intellect or reason and stated that the active intellect is in some sense separable and, when separated, is eternal. This passage enabled Christian Aristotelians like Thomas Aquinas to interpret Aristotle as allowing for personal immortality. Other commentators, such as Averroes, interpreted the active intellect as identical with a universal or divine reason, a view that does not allow for personal immortality.

Aristotle taught that all human beings aim at happiness, which is therefore the supreme good, but he denied that happiness could be equated with pleasure in a hedonistic fashion. For Aristotle the good for anything involves the fulfillment of its nature or actuality; hence happiness for humans is found in actualizing the characteristic functions of the soul. Since a person's most distinctive characteristic is seen as reason, the happy life is a rational one. Practically this requires moral virtue, which consists in developing habits of choosing the mean course between extremes. The highest form of happiness, for Aristotle, was the life of theoretical reason, the disinterested contemplation of truth, a life that is lived most perfectly by God.

C. S. EVANS

See PSYCHOLOGY, HISTORY OF.

Art Therapy. See EXPRESSIVE THERAPY.

Artificial Insemination. A technique whereby sperm, obtained by masturbation, is placed by a syringe into the vagina. The first recorded artificial insemination was performed at Jefferson Medical College in Philadelphia in 1884.

Artificial insemination can occur by one of three variations of a process. Artificial insemination donor (AID) refers to mechanically introducing sperm into a woman from a man other than her husband. Artificial insemination homologous (AIH) refers to a similar process using the husband's sperm. A third form of artificial insemination involves mixing the husband's sperm with a donor's and is referred to as biseminal artificial insemination (BAI). Artificial insemination of a donor's sperm is the most common procedure and it has become a $160,000,000 industry.

Artificial insemination is employed when a couple desires a child and the husband is infertile or when the husband is a carrier of a serious hereditary disease such as Huntington's chorea or Hoffman's atrophy. The process is effective about 60% of the time. This compares to 75% of couples who conceive after six months of unprotected intercourse. Usually one or two inseminations are performed per cycle in the fertilization effort.

Currently between 60,000 and 80,000 women are artificially inseminated in Canada and the United States.

There are several concerns involving artificial insemination. The most obvious possible complication is infection caused by contaminated sperm or venereal infection, including viruses, parasites, bacteria, gonorrhea, and human immune deficiency virus (HIV). The chance of disease is lessened when the donors are carefully screened.

Psychological complications following artificial insemination may include a husband subconsciously feeling threatened, inferior, or jealous of the unknown donor. Couples may also experience a loss of libido. Such complications can be lessened by careful screening by the physician and psychologist. The psychologist assists in analyzing the dynamics of the couple's relationship and helps them carefully explore the reasons they want a child. The psychologist can also help them consider why they wish to choose artificial insemination over adoption as a means of obtaining a child.

Ethical issues also must be considered. Should lesbians and single mothers be artificially inseminated? At least three thousand fatherless babies are born each year, contributing to the number of broken families and negating legitimate male responsibility. The possibility of genetic selection or manipulation can occur as a result of artificial insemination if the procedure is used on a large scale.

Currently there is a lack of adequate legislation to cover artificial insemination. This means that the area is open to litigation that may occur from complications such as chromosomal abnormalities, infection, and congenital disease. There may also be grounds for complaint if the couple believes the child's appearance is too different from that of the father or if there has been a break in confidentiality.

Artificial insemination is not an issue dealt with directly in the Bible. Physical adultery is not involved in the procedure; therefore, it is a question of one's motivation rather than the physical act. A couple should be in total agreement regarding the decision and should be clear as to the reasons for their choice of artificial insemination over adoption or continuing without children.

Additional Readings

Looking for a donor to call Dad. (1995, June 18). *The New York Times Magazine*, 28–35.

Waltzer, H. (1982). Psychological and legal aspects of artificial insemination (A.I.D.): An overview. *American Journal of Psychotherapy, 76*, 91–102.

Zoldbrod, A. (1988). The emotional distress of the artificial insemination patient. *Medical Psychotherapy: An International Journal, 1*, 161–172.

M. A. CAMPION

See INFERTILITY COUNSELING.

Artificial Intelligence. *See* INTELLIGENCE, ARTIFICIAL.

Assertiveness Training. Assertiveness training was most popular in the 1960s and 1970s. While it is less popular as a specific approach to personal growth now, many of the ideas developed then continue to be repeated in books on communication, conflict resolution, and leadership training. Assertive discipline is also widely taught to teachers in primary and secondary schools. Assertiveness, properly understood, is compatible with the biblical concept of speaking the truth in love and so continues to be relevant for Christians. Three groups who can particularly benefit from assertiveness training are those who are shy, codependent, or have difficulty managing anger.

Assertiveness can be divided into two broad sets of skills: relationship-enhancement skills (sometimes called positive assertion) and self-protective skills. Relationship-enhancement skills include the ability to give encouragement; receive compliments; initiate, maintain, and end conversations comfortably; express love and affection appropriately; and deepen friendships.

Assertive self-protective skills include the ability to state one's feelings, beliefs, wishes, attitudes, or rights; disagree with someone else's point of view comfortably; refuse requests or demands that conflict with one's priorities; defend oneself against unfair or inaccurate accusations; express anger or annoyance assertively; deal with someone else's anger and annoyance comfortably and nondefensively; and make reasonable requests of others.

Assertiveness training does not have one uniform format. Some steps often included in the training process include the following.

(1) Helping counselees learn to identify the possible response styles that are available. Response styles include passivity, aggressiveness, passive-aggressiveness, manipulation, and assertion.

(2) Helping counselees identify which of those styles they use. It is common for people to vary their style in different contexts. For example, some people are assertive when dealing with their children but become passive (nonassertive) when dealing with adult peers or authority figures.

(3) Having counselees examine how they developed the particular response styles they use. Often the recognition that they learned to use a specific style (usually from a parent) frees them to realize that they can learn a different style.

(4) Helping counselees become convinced that an assertive response style is healthier than being passive, aggressive, passive-aggressive, or manipulative. Research has shown that some people will become more assertive by being taught assertive skills. However, counselees are more likely to become assertive if they are first convinced that assertiveness is an effective way to relate and then are taught assertive skills. For most Christians this cognitive reframing process needs to include the fact that assertiveness is not only healthy but also biblically permissible and preferable to other response styles.

(5) Helping counselees identify specific contexts and ways they wish to change their response style.

(6) Teaching counselees a variety of assertive techniques, since various situations call for different approaches. Techniques that can be taught include those needed to make an initial assertive request, broken record, sorting issues, disagreeing, emphasizing thoughts or feelings, redefining, negative inquiry, negative assertion, and repeating the action line.

(7) When counselees initially become assertive, others will sometimes show respect and make requested changes. However, a few people will try to detour the newly assertive person back to one's former nonassertive role. Thus it is important to prepare counselees for these detouring attempts and to give them methods to resist being manipulated or intimidated.

(8) Assertive people can harm relationships unless they also are taught the importance of, and skills

associated with, negotiation. Negotiation (developing workable compromises) can include finding a mutually satisfying alternative, developing a quid pro quo contract, taking turns, temporarily separating, allowing an involved third party to decide, and positive yielding.

(9) Teaching nonverbal assertive behavior that reinforces the verbal message. Since an estimated 80% of the impact of a message depends on one's nonverbal behavior, it is important to teach the counselee assertive nonverbal behavior that parallels the verbal message he or she is sending. Nonverbal behavior includes eye contact, voice volume and tone, gestures, distance, clothing and grooming, facial expressions, and timing and pacing.

Unless one has only small attitudinal or behavioral adjustments to make, making major changes in one's level of assertiveness by reading a book only is difficult. Significant changes in attitudes and skills can be learned most effectively in either one-to-one role plays with a counselor or in a group setting. These changes will probably occur more frequently if people have a safe environment (such as an assertiveness training group) in which they can experiment with new response styles and receive feedback and affirmation regarding the changes they are making.

Assertiveness training can probably benefit Christians in several ways as long as one does not adopt every aspect of the assertiveness movement without reflection. For example, Matthew 18:15–17 recommends assertively attempting to restore broken relationships rather than allowing frustration to cause resentment and emotional distance (the context both before and after these passages is speaking about restoration of relationships, suggesting that verses 15–17 be interpreted with this in mind).

The phrase "speaking the truth in love" (Eph. 4:15) suggests a balance that is neither passive nor aggressive. Perhaps the strongest biblical passage endorsing assertiveness is Ephesians 4:26–32 (NIV), which says, "In your anger do not sin [do not be aggressive]. Do not let the sun go down while you are still angry [do not be passive]." Verses 31–32 then go on to list the range of passive-aggressive emotions that can result when people fail to deal with their anger constructively and says that Christians are to put away all of these feelings.

Proverbs contains several prohibitions against angry (aggressive) behavior, and the New Testament clearly says that resentment and unforgiveness, the hallmark of the passive-aggressive person, are not to be part of the believer's life (Matt. 6:12–15; Mark 11:25; Eph. 4:32). By learning to deal with interpersonal difficulties assertively rather than aggressively or passive-aggressively, Christians can learn to avoid these kinds of behavior that are prohibited in Scripture.

Some Christians reject assertiveness because they equate a passive response style with the humility and giving up of personal rights that seem to be encouraged in Scripture. Several arguments can be made against this type of thinking. First, it is impossible to be the leaders God calls parents to be unless we are assertive. David and Eli are powerful biblical examples of what can happen when adults are passive (i.e., permissive) parents. Second, the person who tries to be passive (long-suffering) in the face of continued abuse often becomes passive-aggressive as the abuse and consequent hurt continue over months or years. Third, codependency can be found in both men and women, but it is more commonly found in women. While most Christian women who are codependent are so because they believe this is a biblical response, their behavior may have unbiblical consequences that they do not anticipate. For example, a codependent woman often encourages her husband to become increasingly insensitive to her needs and increasingly abusive. She models for her sons that it is acceptable for men to treat their wives this way. She models for her daughters that this is normal, expected behavior between husbands and wives. Recognition of these facts may help passive Christians see that honest, caring assertiveness leads to healthier, more Christlike families than does passivity.

However, Christians will probably not want to adopt all that is in the assertiveness literature. A primary goal for the non-Christian is self-actualization; in contrast, the Christian's primary goal is building God's kingdom in the hearts of people. Therefore Christians are sometimes called to suspend expression of their own needs or desires in order to be a testimony to the nonbelievers (Matt. 5:38–48) or to build up fellow believers (Rom. 14:1–21). Second, assertiveness may only help a person become a more polite narcissist. The biblical message is that Christian living is much more than polite narcissism. We are to strive to become as concerned about the needs of others as we are about ourselves (Phil. 2:3–8). Third, assertiveness rarely encourages people to examine their motives for being assertive. James 3:13–4:4 reminds us that often our frustrations arise because we have selfish, overly self-centered motives. In these cases the biblical answer is not assertiveness but examination and modification of our motives.

H. A. VIRKLER

See BEHAVIOR THERAPY; BEHAVIORAL PSYCHOLOGY; AGGRESSION.

Association of Christian Therapists (ACT). The Association of Christian Therapists, an international Roman Catholic organization, open to all Christian denominations, was founded in 1975 at Mount Augustine, Florida. In 1996 it had a membership of about 1,200, of which 25% are non-Roman Catholic. It is an association of health care professionals, particularly physicians, nurses, psychiatrists, psychologists, social workers, administrators, clergy, counselors, and pastoral ministers, who believe and promote the healing love of Jesus Christ in their professional work. The mission of ACT is to empower those in the healing professions in the spirit and truth of Jesus Christ through prayer, through support of one another, and in the sharing of gifts.

The five founders of ACT were Francis MacNutt, Ph.D.; Barbara Schlieman, R.N.; Father Paul Schaff; Jean Hill, M.A.; and Father Alfred Fredette, Ph.D. Fredette, with the assistance of Grey nuns at St. Vincent Medical Centre, Toledo, Ohio, was instrumental in drawing up the constitution, suggesting a name for the organization, accepting the caduceus (a medical symbol representing physical and psychological healing) as the logo of the association, and having the state of Ohio recognize ACT as a charitable organization.

Conferences provide the members with opportunities to learn more about Christian healing as it is applicable to health care professions. At the same time these conferences give members an opportunity to become more whole as they grow in holiness and become freer instruments of God's healing power. Members are frequently reminded that they are wounded healers who cannot do much unless they take on the characteristics of compassion and love of the divine heart of Jesus.

The first ACT conference was held at Tampa, Florida, in March 1976. Cardinal Leon Joseph Suenens, the unofficial protector of the Catholic charismatic renewal, was present along with 56 others. Suenens encouraged the newly founded organization and cautioned its members against extremism and pseudomiracles.

ACT is divided into regions; 75% are in the United States and the remainder in 18 other countries. Three of the 48 regions have conferences of their own. From 1976 to 1996 there were 26 international conferences. For five years (1977–1982) two international conferences were held, one in the eastern part of the United States and one in the western part. On each day of a conference, Roman Catholic mass is celebrated. Each conference has several guest speakers who focus on a given theme. During the conferences such gifts of the Holy Spirit as tongues, prophecy, and healing are exercised. Prayer teams and the sacrament of reconciliation are available. Generally there is also a healing service at each conference.

The members of the association are called to be visible signs of God's desire to heal and restore his people. They serve the whole body of Christ by sharing gifts and by being open to the giftedness of others. They are encouraged to evangelize by healing, thus bringing people into the saving knowledge of the healing Jesus. Their ministry is based on the foundation of the Word of God. At all times the members are asked to be models in their personal and professional lives by actively cooperating with God's healing plan.

From the head office one can obtain the *History of ACT, The Journal of Christian Healing*, and the newsletter *InterACT*.

A. BALAWYDER

For Further Information

Association of Christian Therapists. 329 Prince George Street, Laurel, MD 20707.

See CHRISTIAN COUNSELING AND PSYCHOTHERAPY; CHRISTIAN ASSOCIATION OF PSYCHOLOGICAL STUDIES; AMERICAN ASSOCIATION OF CHRISTIAN COUNSELORS.

Association for Clinical Pastoral Education. An ecumenical, interfaith association composed of clinical pastoral educators, theological school representatives, representatives of church agencies, health and welfare institutions, and interested individuals. The purposes of the association are to define standards for clinical pastoral education; accredit clinical pastoral education centers; certify supervisors; promote clinical pastoral education as a part of theological education and as continuing education for ministry; and provide conferences, publications, and research opportunities for its members.

Clinical pastoral education can be described best as professional education for ministry. It brings theological students and ministers into supervised encounter with persons in crisis. Out of an intense involvement with persons in need and the feedback from peers and teachers, students develop new awareness of themselves as persons and of the needs of those to whom they minister. From theological reflection on specific human experiences they gain new understanding of the human situation. Within the interdisciplinary team process of helping persons they develop skills in interpersonal and interprofessional relationships. There are more than 350 clinical pastoral education centers throughout the United States.

C. DAVIS

See AMERICAN ASSOCIATION OF CHRISTIAN COUNSELORS; PASTORAL COUNSELING; AMERICAN ASSOCIATION OF PASTORAL COUNSELORS.

Associationism. While historians of psychology seldom ascribe to associationism the status of a school, its adherents worked from a common point of view and saw the major problems of psychology in the same way (Heidbreder, 1933). The classical principles of association were postulated by Aristotle in partial response to two related paradoxes articulated in Plato's *Meno:* "We cannot learn anything *new* unless we already know it (by some other means), and we cannot know *anything* unless we have already learned (come to know) it" (Weimer, 1973, p. 16). Aristotle felt that memory processes are explainable through processes of association. These follow the laws of similarity, contrast, and contiguity. When one thing is recalled, the recall is usually followed by the recall of another thing that is like it, different from it, or accompanied by it in the original experience. From the differences between Plato and Aristotle emerged two lines of explanation in philosophy and psychology: explanations based on mental faculties (*see* Faculty Psychology) and explanations based on processes of association.

Associationism had its roots in British empiricism. Thomas Hobbes distinguished between regulated, orderly "trains of thought" and those that were unguided and without design. John Locke coined the phrase "association of ideas," viewing ideas as either simple or complex and arising in either sensation or reflection. The compounding of complex out of simple ideas is one of the operations of the mind, and errors of understanding result from wrong connections. George Berkeley, the Anglican Bishop of Cloyne, was more explicit in his assertion that "ideas are associated when they are connected in experience" (Watson, 1968, p. 194). Berkeley described simultaneous and successive association and distinguished among association by similarity, causality, and co-existence. Abstract ideas result from particular ideas becoming associated with one general idea. David Hume marked the culmination of this phase when he argued that causality is a special case of resemblance (similarity) and spatial and temporal contiguity.

Associationism as a school was founded by David Hartley, who published its systematic principles in the first part of his *Observations on Man* in 1749. Hartley emphasized the principle of contiguity as an explanation for the passage from sensation to idea and from one idea to another. He formulated parallel laws for mental and bodily associations and posited a controversial physiological psychology based on Newton's theory of vibrations to account for the neurophysiology of sensation, motion, and ideation.

The Scottish psychologists tended to oppose both the extreme empiricism and associationism of the British. The work of James Mill epitomized the notion of association as an essentially additive principle. He asserted that all complex associations can be analyzed into multiple elementary associations and that the notion of their compounding is an absurdity. He also specified conditions of association and criteria for specifying associative strength. In his assertion that words accrue their meaning by association, he articulated an associative theory of meaning later much elaborated in Edward Titchener's context theory. John Stuart Mill rejected the atomistic, additive associationism of his father and stressed the mind's activity. He also asserted that the combination of mental elements gives rise to quality not present in the originals, thus articulating what Wilhelm Wundt later termed "creative synthesis." Bain systematized the classical associationist position at its apex, added his own ideas on creativity and repetition, and made associationism the basis for the newly emerging physiological psychology. Spencer added an evolutionary touch by claiming that complex traits in the human race evolved in the same way that the complex ideas evolved from simple ones in individuals.

While Aristotle's associationism involved a clear rejection of the soul and the transcendent, this antitheological bias did not extend to all these psychologists. Hartley was "a zealous champion of scriptural authority and seriously concerned with theological teachings" (Klein, 1970, p. 616). Associationism also had a strong influence on nineteenth-century theological education. Psychology was at that time included in the college curriculum as mental philosophy, a course generally taught by the college president, who was usually trained for the Christian ministry.

References

Heidbreder, E. (1933). *Seven psychologies.* New York: Appleton-Century-Crofts.
Klein, D. B. (1970). *A history of scientific psychology.* New York: Basic.
Watson, R. I. (1968). *The great psychologists: From Aristotle to Freud* (2nd ed.). Philadelphia: Lippincott.
Weimer, W. B. (1973). Psycholinguistics and Plato's paradoxes of the *Meno. American Psychologist, 28* (1), 15–33.

H. VANDE KEMP

See PSYCHOLOGY, HISTORY OF.

Asthma. A disorder characterized by recurrent periods of breathlessness, wheezing, and coughing. The experience of being unable to breathe results from a narrowing of the large and/or small airways in the lungs that can be caused by muscle spasms, mucus secretion, mucus plugs, or a swelling of lung tissue. These may be triggered by a multitude of factors, including allergens, seasonal changes, exercise, dust, pollen, and animal dander. Some authorities view emotional perturbation as another trigger.

The presence of psychosomatic factors in asthma has been the subject of much controversy. According to Ferguson and Taylor (1981), there is no clear and convincing evidence that a direct correlation exists between asthma and psychosocial influences. However, others (Knapp, Mathe, & Vachon, 1976) have found research that has linked psychological factors such as stress, environmental changes, and learned responses to quantifiable pulmonary changes. Opponents of the psychosomatic theory question if small but statistically significant changes in pulmonary action due to psychosocial factors are massive enough to produce or exacerbate the clinical symptoms of asthma. In light of the equivocal evidence to date, it may be best to view asthma as a disorder with multiple interactional factors, psychological influences possibly being one of these.

Medical treatment generally consists of the use of oral bronchodilators, inhaled bronchodilators, and corticosteroids, the latter being used only when necessary because of their numerous and adverse side effects. When the asthma is not controlled by an adequate medical regimen, emotional factors are frequently involved in the exacerbation of the symptoms. For example, Liebman, Minuchin, and Baker (1974) contend that poorly controlled asthma in children is perpetuated but not necessarily caused by chronic, unresolved conflicts in the family.

Relaxation, airways, biofeedback, and systematic desensitization have shown positive results in decreasing breathlessness. Even more conclusively these approaches have been found to decrease the anxiety associated with the panic of an asthma attack. Behavior modification, group therapy, individually oriented psychoanalytic psychotherapy, and family therapy are all being used with favorable results. Because these therapies are reporting some positive outcomes, their use could be a valuable adjunctive therapy in the medical management of this debilitating disorder.

References

Ferguson, J., & Taylor, C. (1981). *The comprehensive handbook of behavioral medicine* (Vol. 2). New York: SP Medical and Scientific Books.

Knapp, P., Mathe, A., & Vachon, L. (1976). Psychosomatic aspects of bronchial asthma. In E. Weiss & M. Segal (Eds.), *Bronchial asthma: Mechanisms and therapeutics.* Boston: Little, Brown.

Liebman, R., Minuchin, S., & Baker, L. (1974). The use of structural family therapy in the treatment of intractable asthma. *American Journal of Psychiatry, 131,* 535–540.

K. R. KRACKE

See HEALTH PSYCHOLOGY.

Attachment Theory and Disorders. Attachment theory draws on the works of Bowlby (1969, 1973, 1980) as the primary theorist and Ainsworth (1969, 1985; Ainsworth, Bleher, Walters, & Wall, 1978) as the principal researcher, as well as a host of other researchers seeking to further refine and validate the concepts. Bowlby received psychoanalytic training in London in the 1930s. He was trained with the Kleinians, and this experience influenced him greatly. In Melanie Klein's version of psychoanalysis primary importance is placed upon the child's inner life; real experiences are given an inferior place in the psychological economy of the child. This emphasis greatly disturbed Bowlby and many others, most notably Donald Woods Winnicott. Discussions were vociferous and often acrimonious. As a result the London institute was severed into three camps, and Bowlby left looking for more compassionate theoretical ground.

Bowlby's theory posits that the kind and quality of early infant attachments are of fundamental importance for development. Human infants, according to Bowlby, depend upon human adult caregivers in order to develop into mature adults. Infants, he says, are equipped with attachment-seeking behaviors that are designed to engage the adult caregiver. Smiling, cooing, and crying are among those behaviors. The attachment system, made up of adult caregiver, child, and the relationship between them, is a homeostatic system analogous to other homeostatic systems in the body (*see* Homeostasis). The infant experiences a need signaled by anxiety, cries, and is responded to by the caregiver. The infant experiences a concomitant decrease in anxiety (i.e., is soothed). Bowlby believed, contra Sigmund Freud and Klein, that this need the infant experiences does not primarily serve the purpose of drive reduction (i.e., hunger or pain) but is designed to engage the caregiver in a nurturing relationship. Bowlby's theory strongly implies human relationship is the primary need. The basic need has three aspects: proximity maintenance, seeking a safe haven, and seeking a secure base.

The process of attachment takes an average of two to three years and results in a goal-corrected partnership in which the child develops an "internal working model" of the relationship between himself or herself and the caregiver. Developmentally the infant moves from a complete dependence on the physical presence of the caregiver, through various phases of independence, to an interdependent relationship that is characterized by, among other things, the ability to tolerate physical absence (delay gratification) by calling upon the internal working model for soothing. This internal working model has striking similarity to Jean Piaget's concept of schema (Piaget, 1955) and the object relations concept of an internalized object relation (Mitchell, 1988). Disruptions in attachment formation are met with protest, which involves crying, active searching for the caregiver, and resistance to others' soothing efforts. Protest is followed by despair, which is characterized by passivity, sadness, and sometimes depression. Emotional detachment, which is characterized by aloofness, is the final response. Each of these responses and the whole sequence are seen as adaptive. The crying and searching of protest are meant to reestablish proximity. Because continued demonstrations of protest will attract negative attention and will likely exhaust the infant, a period of inactivity allows for rest and recuperation. Detachment makes possible the resumption of daily tasks. Bowlby observed that even short-lived separations have long-lasting effects on the child. Subsequent research has also observed that while the infant may have opportunity for many attachments, he or she generally forms selective attachments, choosing one or at most a few selected people for close attachments (Shaffer & Emerson, 1964).

Research on Bowlby's theory by Ainsworth (Ainsworth, et al., 1978) described three attachment styles. These attachment styles are described upon the basis of how the children coped with the initial anxiety of making attachment and then dealt with the later anxiety of separation as well as with reunification. Securely attached children cried when their mothers left, were easily comforted when they returned, and engaged in active exploration of the day-care room while they were present, using their mothers as secure bases. These mothers were seen as responsive, and a reciprocal cueing relationship had been developed.

Anxious/ambivalently attached children were clingy and afraid to explore the room from the beginning. They cried profusely upon separation and were difficult to console. When their mothers returned they sought them out but were often observed to arch themselves away from the mothers when being held. Mothers of these children were seen as inconsistent caregivers but tended to give mixed signals, behaviorally and emotionally, rewarding dependence while verbally punishing it.

Anxious/avoidantly attached children gave the impression of independence, explored the room without using their mothers as bases, seemed not to be affected by their leaving, and snubbed their mothers upon their return. These children were pseudomature. Mothers of these children were judged to be inconsistent in caregiving but tended to reward independence. About 60% of the American children fell into secure categories, 15% fell into ambivalent, and 25% fell into the avoidant category. Subsequent research (Main & Solomon, 1990) has defined a fourth style, that of disorganized/disoriented. In these children there is an absence of a coherent strategy for making attachments and managing the anxiety of separation. It has also been suggested that attachment in this style is of good quality but has been disrupted and present sporadically, making it difficult for the child to develop a consistent internal working model.

Attachment researchers have long known that attachment styles are relatively stable over the lifetime, but they have puzzled as to exactly what insecurely attached children look like as adults. Main, a student of Ainsworth, asked adults what they remembered about their childhood experiences. She found these remembrances to be a powerful predictor of adult attachment styles (Main, Kaplan, & Cassidy, 1985). Four adult attachment styles were defined. Adults who were seen to be autonomously attached easily remembered experiences with their parents. They seemed self-reliant, objective, and able to incorporate painful memories within their balanced remembrances. Adults who seemed indifferent to their early attachments remembered little of their childhood but would recall contradictory memories when the researcher probed, held idealized views of their parents, were often detached as adults, and presented themselves as strong and capable. Main et al. labeled these as dismissive of early attachments and surmised that they were from anxious/avoidant attachments histories. Some adults seemed to be preoccupied with early attachments. Their memories were confused and incoherent. They were flooded with negative memories. They were subject to anger, depression, despair, feelings of worthlessness, and dependency. These children were viewed to be from anxious/ambivalent attachments. The disorganized attachment style as an adult was typically found in children who were victims of abuse or who lost parents early and subsequently had a parade of caregivers.

Kirkpatrick (1992) has suggested that much of the research in Psychology of Religion could be interpreted in attachment terms. He observes "that the availability and responsiveness of an attachment figure, who serves alternatively as a haven and a secure base, separation from whom would cause considerable distress, is a fundamental dynamic underlying Christianity and many other theistic religions" (p. 6). In terms of attachment theory humanity is already separated from God, experiencing despair and emotional detachment of various degrees. Attachment theory then would describe the various manifestations of separation behavior as recapitulations of former attachment styles. If we are securely attached, we welcome God back into our lives. If we are insecurely attached, we engage in avoidant or ambivalent behaviors. Others have yet to develop, due to previous trauma, a consistent working attachment model and remain in the throes of disorganization and disorientation. Reed (1978) noted that "every form of attachment behavior, and of the behavior of the attachment figure, identified by Bowlby, has its close counterpart in the images of the relationship between Israel (or the worshipper) and God which we find in for example the Psalms" (p. 32). An older study of Protestant hymns by Young (1926) found a theme in one-third of the hymns to be the powerful and loving protector who shields humanity from all harm. It would be an interesting study to see if Protestant Christian hymnody has maintained this focus, developed into a more adult version, or regressed.

Kirkpatrick (1992, 1994) analyzes two hypotheses regarding child and adult attachments. The compensation hypothesis says that humans compensate for attachment deficits in later life. Therefore where one child had emotionally absent parents she or he may develop relationships with more responsive parental figures in adult life. This suggests that God could be related to as a compensatory attachment figure. Most likely this would show up in choice of marriage partners, where insecurely attached people would seek securely attached partners. It is obvious that insecurely attached persons would seek relationships with securely attached ones, but would securely attached persons seek relationships with insecurely attached persons? This arrangement might give the securely attached person a sense of power and importance, allowing him or her to identify with God and act as God would in saving the unfortunate one.

The correspondence hypothesis suggests that adult attachments correspond in kind and quality to the attachment of childhood. This means that the adult relationship with God would bear a striking resemblance to the child's relationship with his or her parents. Securely attached children should display securely attached patterns with other adults and God. Avoidantly attached persons should tend toward atheism or agnosticism or to hold an intellectual belief in God as available and responsive but have contradictory experiences. The management of this dissonance would be the psychological task of life for this person. Ambivalently attached persons might be found to have a clingy, dependent relationship with God, holding on to God with all means possible while wanting to punish God for being absent.

With regard to empirical support for these two hypotheses Kirkpatrick (1994) reports, "All of the data supporting the correspondence hypothesis are cross-sectional, and suggest that at a given time, people tend to hold essentially parallel models with respect to human and divine relationships. The data supporting the compensation hypothesis are either longitudinal or approximations of longitudinal data (based on retrospective reports), and show that insecure attachment predict religious conversion (and related variables) at a later point in time. There is nothing necessarily paradoxical about these pattern of findings" (p. 254).

References

Ainsworth, M. D. S. (1969). Object relations, dependency and attachment: A theoretical review of the infant-mother relationship. *Child Development, 40,* 969–1025.

Ainsworth, M. D. S. (1985). Attachments across the life-span. *Bulletin of the New York Academy of Medicine, 61,* 792–812.

Ainsworth, M. D. S., Bleher, M. C., Walters, E., & Wall, S. (1978). *Patterns of attachment: A psychological study of the strange situation.* Hillsdale, NJ: Erlbaum.

Bowlby, J. (1969). *Attachment and loss: Vol. 1. Attachment.* New York: Basic.

Bowlby, J. (1973). *Attachment and loss: Vol. 2. Separation: Anxiety and anger.* New York: Basic.

Bowlby, J. (1980). *Attachment and loss: Vol. 3. Loss.* New York: Basic.

Kirkpatrick, L. A. (1992). An attachment-theory approach to the psychology of religion. *The International Journal for the Psychology of Religion, 2* (1), 3–28.

Kirkpatrick, L. A. (1994). The role of attachment in religious belief and behavior. *Personal Relationships, 5,* 239–265.

Main, M., Kaplan, N., & Cassidy, J. (1985). Security in infancy, childhood and adulthood: A move to the level of representation. *Monographs for the Society of Research in Child Development, 50* (1–2, Serial no. 209), 66–104.

Main, M., & Solomon, J. (1990). Procedures for identifying infants as disorganized/disoriented during the Ainsworth Strange Situation. In M. T. Greenberg, D. Cicchetti, & E. M. Cummings (Eds.), *Attachment in the preschool years.* Chicago: University of Chicago Press.

Mitchell, S. (1988). *Relational concepts in psychoanalysis.* Cambridge, MA: Harvard University Press.

Piaget, J. (1955). *The child's construction of reality.* London: Routledge & Kegan Paul.

Reed, B. (1978). *The dynamics of religion: Process and movement in Christian churches.* London: Darton, Longman & Todd.

Shaffer, H. R., & Emerson, P. E. (1964). The development of social attachments in infancy. *Monographs of the society for research on child development, 29* (3 Serial 94).

Young, K. (1926). The psychology of hymns. *The Journal of Abnormal and Social Psychology, 20,* 391–406.

D. W. Peters

See Loss and Separation.

Attention. A mental process of focusing on a specific portion of the total stimulation impinging on a person. Attention allows people to actively detect and experience what is important in the myriad of stimuli. The process of attention may be unconscious or conscious, such as when one scans memory for a familiar person's name.

The internal determinants of a person's attention include experience, ongoing behavior, and physiological condition. External determinants of attention include the repetition, size, movement, intensity, novelty, contrast, and complexity of stimuli. In all these factors affecting attention the reticular activating system, a network of cells extending from the upper part of the spinal cord to the brain stem, plays an important role in alerting the brain to process sensory information. Recent positron emission tomography (PET) scan studies of human attention show different cortical brain areas of increased activity depending on where and to what attention has been directed (Corbetta, Meizin, Shulman, & Petersen, 1993).

Selective attention has been explained in terms of a hypothetical filter located in the brain. The filter is presumably interposed between the initial sensory registration and later stages of perceptual analysis. If information is of some value to the person, it is allowed through the attention filter, where it can then be further analyzed and stored in memory. Related to the filter theory of attention is the deviant filter theory. This theory holds that schizophrenics are the victims of a malfunctioning filter system that floods the brain with more signals than it can handle, thus producing the delusions that characterize schizophrenic behavior.

It is obvious that people experience or attend to only a small fraction of the total neural activity in the brain at any moment. This shows that conscious awareness is only a small part but a very important part of total brain activity. Much of the information processing in the human mind is apparently subconscious. This does not detract from the conscious self but frees up the conscious self to function more efficiently. In their shifting of attention people are apparently able to separate some aspects of their consciousness from their total brain activity. This fact does not necessarily imply a dualistic view of the person, but it does limit the usefulness of reductionistic, materialistic views that equate personality with neural activity.

Reference

Corbetta, M., Meizin, F., Shulman, G., & Petersen, S. (1993). A PET study of visuospatial attention. *Journal of Neuroscience, 13,* 1202–1226.

M. P. Cosgrove

See Cognitive Psychology; Mind-Brain Relationship; Physiological Psychology.

Attention Deficit/Hyperactivity Disorder. This disorder (ADHD) has had many alternative labels, including attention deficit disorder (ADD), minimal brain dysfunction, hyperkinetic syndrome, and developmental hyperactivity. This syndrome appears in early childhood and may have a lifelong course. Research findings show a primary deficit in the ability to inhibit responding, to delay responding, or to tolerate externally imposed delays in behavior once a task is begun.

Students with ADHD do not see the value in working hard at school, and academic achievement is often below the student's measured Intelligence. Sustained mental effort tends to be inherently punishing. Conflict with parents and teachers is common. Compared to most individuals of the same age there is more variability in the ADHD person's behavior across situations and time. Classrooms and other group settings requiring sustained attention to task produce much more symptomatic behavior than one-to-one situations, novel settings, or situations in which the person receives frequent feedback or reinforcement.

As of 1994 the American Psychiatric Association recognized three types of ADHD: combined type, predominantly inattentive type, and predominantly hyperactive-impulsive type.

There are nine criteria for diagnosing the inattentive type. Six or more of these must have been often or very often true for at least six months in order to make a diagnosis of ADHD. These criteria are that the person fails to give close attention to details or makes careless mistakes in schoolwork, work, or other activities; has difficulty sustaining attention in tasks or play activities; does not seem to listen when spoken to directly; does not follow through on instructions and fails to finish schoolwork, chores, or duties in the workplace; often has difficulty organizing tasks and activities; avoids, dislikes, or is reluctant to engage in tasks that require sustained mental effort; loses things necessary for tasks or activities, such as school assignments, pencils, books, or tools; is easily distracted by extraneous stimuli; and is forgetful in daily activities.

There are also nine criteria for the hyperactive-impulsive type. As with inattention, six or more of these must have been true often or very often for at least six months in order to make a diagnosis of ADHD. Six of these relate to hyperactivity: the person fidgets with hands or feet or squirms in seat; leaves seat in classroom or in other situations in which remaining seated is expected; runs about or climbs excessively in situations in which it is inappropriate or has subjective feelings of restlessness; has difficulty playing or engaging in leisure activities quietly; is on the go or acts as if driven by a motor; and talks excessively. The final three criteria in this set cover impulsivity: the person blurts out answers before questions have been completed, has difficulty waiting for his or her turn, and interrupts or intrudes on others.

The diagnosis of ADHD also requires that some of the symptoms appeared before age seven, that the symptoms impair functioning in at least two settings (e.g., school and home), that there must be impairment in social, academic, or occupational functioning that is clinically significant, and that the symptoms are not caused by another mental or physical disorder.

For children and adolescents at least six criteria within both sets of nine must be met to make the diagnosis of ADHD, combined. Experts on ADHD have not reached consensus on making the diagnosis in adults; however, evidence exists that suggests when an adult meets at least four of the criteria in a given set, making the ADHD diagnosis is appropriate. Gathering retrospective data on the adult's behavior in childhood can be helpful in clarifying whether the diagnosis is appropriate.

Regardless of the age of the patient, personal history and current symptoms form the basis for making the diagnosis. Particularly for children and adolescents many questionnaires are available to help in determining whether ADHD is present. Common clinical practice calls for using multiple informants to fill out a variety of such measures. No medical laboratory tests are useful in diagnosing ADHD. Psychological tests are also of little value in making the diagnosis. Many computerized tests for measuring sustained attention to task are available, but most of these do not appear to be helpful in discriminating ADHD from other disorders.

Inattention, fidgeting, overactivity, and impulsivity are common in young children. They are also often present in children with lower intelligence who are placed in academic settings that do not match their ability or in intellectually gifted children who are understimulated. In addition the symptoms of inattention, hyperactivity, and impulsivity can appear in a number of other disorders. Although there is some overlap in some of the symptoms that define ADHD and these other disorders, the diagnostic criteria in use as of the mid-1990s are sufficiently clear to discriminate among these disorders.

Comorbidity refers to the phenomenon in which persons with one disorder have a greater-than-chance probability of having one or more other disorders. ADHD has a number of comorbidities. Up to 85% of ADHD children have at least one other diagnosable behavioral, emotional, or learning disability. They also have more minor physical anomalies, wet the bed more frequently, have more physical accidents, manifest greater sleep problems, and have more aches and pains than other children. They are most at risk for oppositional, defiant, and antisocial behavior problems. ADHD appears to raise the risk of substance abuse, job failure, marital discord, and divorce, but longitudinal studies suggest that it is comorbid oppositional, defiant, and aggressive behavior that places the child at high risk for serious problems in later life rather than the ADHD symptoms themselves.

ADHD is the most frequent referral problem to clinics and professionals that serve children and adolescents with behavioral or psychological problems in the United States. It occurs across cultures and socioeconomic levels. This disorder is diagnosed substantially more often in boys than in girls. There appears to be a significant hereditary contribution to the appearance of the disorder. If a child's parent had ADHD, the child has more than a 50% chance of having the disorder. The basic problem does not seem to be a problem in attention; rather, it is an impairment in cortical regulation of response inhibition and impulse control.

The effective treatment of ADHD children is multifaceted. Drugs are typically one part of the treatment regimen. From 70% to 90% of ADHD children benefit from one of the psychostimulants: methylphenidate, amphetamine, and pemoline. Available evidence indicates that adolescents and adults also benefit from stimulant medication.

Although individual play therapy or psychotherapy has no demonstrated helpfulness in treating ADHD, other psychological interventions are recommended. Parent training is standard practice (*see* Parent Training Programs). This training covers many points. The child's difficulties are not a result of faulty parenting. The symptoms will make parenting difficult, demanding, and complex. Parenting that includes writing and managing parent-child contingency contracts will be helpful. These contracts identify what the parents want the child to do and not to do as well as the specific consequences the child will receive for the desired behaviors. Catching the child being good, delivering rewards immediately and frequently after good behavior, and using mild punishments such as time out and response cost are some of the keys to success.

Psychological consultation with the child's teacher is also important. The purpose of this consultation is to identify what educational services will benefit the student and to establish a contingency management program at school similar to the one used by the parents at home. The home and school programs are often linked by the teacher's sending home a daily report on the child's behavior and academic performance. This report allows the parents to reinforce good behavior that occurs at school. Academic tutoring by adults or peers is often helpful.

Direct therapeutic work by mental health professionals includes social skills training; coaching in goal setting, in self-monitoring of progress toward goals, in making plans to reach one's goals, and in using timers, checklists, organizers, and other tools for self-management; and family therapy.

In dealing with ADHD in adolescents, all of the procedures outlined may be used, but there is value in emphasizing the self-control strategies, including cognitive-behavior therapy. When the patient is an adult, self-regulation approaches also are relevant. Marital therapy by a professional experienced in treating ADHD may be helpful.

Various experts have proposed the value of a number of other treatments without providing adequate scientific evidence of their effectiveness. Among these treatments that do not have empirical validity are eliminating food additives or sugar from the diet, the use of megavitamins and mineral supplements, taking anti-motion sickness medication, antifungal medication combined with a low-sugar diet, biofeedback targeting brain waves, sensory integration training, the chiropractic neural organization technique (applied kinesiology), and optometric training.

Additional Readings

Barkley, R. A. (1990). *Attention-deficit hyperactivity disorder: A handbook for diagnosis and treatment*. New York: Guilford.

Weiss, G., & Hechtman, L. T. (1993). *Hyperactive children grown up: ADHD in children, adolescents, and adults* (2nd ed.). New York: Guilford.

For Further Information

ADHD Report. The Guilford Press, 72 Spring Street, New York, NY 10012.

Attention! The Magazine of Children and Adults with Attention Deficit Disorders. CH.A.D.D., 499 NW 70th Avenue, Suite 109, Plantation, FL 33317. (305) 587-3700.

Brakes: The Interactive Newsletter for Kids with ADHD. Brunner/Mazel, 19 Union Square West, New York, NY 10003.

P. W. Clement

See Learning Disability.

Attitude. Identified by the preeminent social psychologist Gordon Allport (1935) as "the most distinctive and indispensable concept in contemporary American social psychology" (p. 198), the concept of attitude continues to be a major focus of theoretical development. Such developments have also allowed researchers to apply the attitude concept to a number of domains of interest, particularly in the field of social psychology (e.g., prejudice, conformity, attitudes toward social issues).

Attitude may be defined as "a psychological tendency that is expressed by evaluating a particular entity with some degree of favor or disfavor" (Eagly & Chaiken, 1993, p. 1). This definition suggests that attitudes involve some sort of internal state that lasts for at least a brief period of time (a psychological tendency), that this internal state employs some standard of goodness and badness (an evaluation), and that something is the object of the evaluation (an entity). People may thus hold attitudes toward any discriminable event in their environment, including themselves.

Researchers consider attitudes to be unobservable; we may observe the results and possibly the causes of attitudes, but we cannot observe attitudes directly. For example, we may observe that someone subscribes to a politically conservative publication and votes for a conservative candidate. In such a case the attitudinal object may be political conservatism, and we may infer that this individual has a favorable attitude toward such conservatism. Even though we may label this person a conservative, we cannot say that we have observed his or her attitude. This distinction is important in that inferences are subject to greater error than direct observations.

Major Theoretical Conceptions. *Cognitive Approach.* According to this view, beliefs are the primary components of attitudes. An individual may hold any number of beliefs toward an entity that links that entity with either a positive or a negative attribute. If the cluster of beliefs tends to involve more positive than negative attributes, then the resulting attitude may be reasonably favorable. However, the overall attitude toward the object will also be influenced by the value of the attribute as well as the subjective probability (the degree to which the person believes in the link between the object and the attribute) of the belief. Thus the single belief that smoking (an entity) causes lung cancer (an attribute) may be enough to counter a large number of positive beliefs related to smoking (e.g., smoking makes people popular, makes people look older, calms nerves) but only if the attribute is highly valued and if the subjective probability is high. When attitudes involve the self, particularly as a predictor of behavior (such as the decision to smoke cigarettes), attitude determination may also be influenced by the degree to which the subjective probability is personalized (i.e., the degree to which I believe that my cigarette smoking could give me lung cancer).

Functional Approach. This perspective, once the dominant view of attitudes, has fallen into disfavor largely because it is of limited value in understanding the underlying processes of attitudes. Yet this approach provides the opportunity to apply the attitudinal concept to a variety of experiential domains in that a given attitude may have affective functions (e.g., protection of self-esteem), cognitive functions (e.g., categorization of experiences into that which is good and bad), and expressive functions (e.g., determining appropriate means of communication). For example, a prejudicial attitude toward another group may function in a way to make one feel superior (affect), to simplify experiences into the "good us" and "bad them" categories (cognition), and to justify the use of racial epithets (expression).

Behavioral Approach. This approach, sometimes referred to as an undifferentiated view, defines attitude as nothing but an evaluative position, and the origin of an attitude as the accretion of experience. Principles of classical and operant conditioning are at work to influence the attitude. For example, if an object (cigarette smoking) is repeatedly associated with a negative attribute (lung cancer), then the association is assumed to produce a negative attitude toward the object. While this approach may be of benefit in treating a behavior that is closely related to the attitude, such as that done through behavior modification techniques, many researchers believe that awareness of the association is often necessary; therefore, the cognitive approach is more useful in understanding underlying processes of attitudes.

Religious Experience as Attitudes. Attitudes are central to religious experience. Hill and Bassett (1992) suggest that the spiritual and mental aspects of humanity, often expressed through the term *heart*, involve the attitude concept. Hill (1994) has introduced what he calls an "attitude process model" whereby religious experiences are differentiated between religious attitudes that occur spontaneously, are inescapable, and lack reflection, and religious attitudes that require attention and are reflective in nature. The premise of this research is that the study of attitudes and attitude change has much to offer in understanding religious experience, even as it has much to offer the entire discipline of psychology.

References

Allport, G. W. (1935). Attitudes. In C. Murchison (Ed.), *Handbook of social psychology.* Worcester, MA: Clark University Press.

Eagly, A. H., & Chaiken, S. (1993). *The psychology of attitudes.* Ft. Worth, TX: Harcourt Brace Jovanovich.

Hill, P. C. (1994). Toward an attitude process model of religious experience. *Journal for the Scientific Study of Religion, 33* (4), 303–314.

Hill, P. C., & Bassett, R. L. (1992). Getting to the heart of the matter: What the social-psychological study of attitudes has to offer the psychology of religion. In M. L. Lynn & D. O. Moberg (Eds.), *Research in the social scientific study of religion* (Vol. 4). Greenwich, CT: JAI Press.

P. C. HILL

See PREJUDICE; SOCIAL INTEREST; ATTITUDE-BEHAVIOR RELATIONSHIPS.

Attitude Assessment. Research on attitudes has recently enjoyed renewed attention. Research testing new theories of attitude has tended to utilize indirect measures of attitude, inferring attitudinal properties from such measures as the response times to answer questions in interviews or the ability to recall attitude-related information from memory. But direct empirical assessments of particular attitudes continue to emphasize the use of paper-and-pencil instruments such as indexes and scales. Most experts advocate the use of carefully constructed and validated composite measures (Babbie, 1995). Among the wide variety of available techniques for attitude assessment, three have received widespread acceptance: Thurstone scales, Guttman scales, and Likert scales.

Thurstone scaling consists of a number of statements expressing sentiments across the range of possible attitudes toward an issue. These statements are carefully chosen in pretesting to represent equal-appearing intervals between attitude positions, making each statement analogous to a unit mark on a yardstick. Respondents indicate their attitudes by choosing the one statement that best describes their feelings about the attitude object.

Guttman scaling takes advantage of the fact that attitudes expressed in concrete situations often show cumulative patterns. For example, a person's attitude toward abortion could be determined by asking respondents to indicate whether they would agree to a woman's right to an abortion if the woman were unmarried, if she were pregnant as a result of rape, or if her health were seriously endangered. Since it is likely that a respondent who would approve of abortion for unmarried women would also approve of abortions under more extenuating circumstances, a score indicating the most extenuating circumstance in which abortion could be approved would allow all of the person's other opinions to be reconstructed as well.

Likert scaling is perhaps the most familiar. It consists of a set of statements of belief accompanied by a Likert response format—strongly agree, agree, no opinion, disagree, strongly disagree. Each Likert response is given an integer value called a rating (e.g., strongly agree equals five points, agree equals four points, etc.), and a respondent's scale score is determined by summing the ratings for each statement.

Descriptions of these and other techniques are available in Babbie (1995); detailed instructions for developing and validating each type of scale is found in Fishbein (1967).

References

Babbie, E. (1995). *The practice of social research* (7th ed.). Belmont, CA: Wadsworth.
Fishbein, M. (Ed.). (1967). *Readings in attitude theory and measurement*. New York: Wiley.

L. S. SHAFFER

See PSYCHOLOGICAL MEASUREMENT; PERSONALITY ASSESSMENT.

Attitude-Behavior Relationships. Research on attitudes, which lost momentum during the period of social psychology's crisis of confidence, has recently enjoyed renewed attention (Eagly, 1992; Olson & Zanna, 1993). Attitude had been historically the most important explanatory concept in social psychology because researchers focused on social learning as the primary source of social behavior, and attitude was the most conspicuous product of social learning (*see* Learning, Social). From the time that attitudes were first measured by Louis Leon Thurstone until the 1960s, the research paradigm for social psychologists consisted of developing reliable and valid measures of general attitudes such as prejudice and using those scales to predict specific behaviors. However, critical reviews of these studies, such as Wicker (1969), concluded that attitudes are relatively weak predictors of overt behavior with reported correlations between measures of attitude and behavior rarely exceeding 0.3. As a result social psychologists began to speak of an attitude-behavior problem, and the perceived failure of attitude theory was one of the strongest reasons for the crisis of confidence.

While there is still no consensus concerning a conceptual definition of the concept of attitude (Olson & Zanna, 1993), most definitions include the following elements. Foremost, attitudes are evaluative feelings individuals have formed about social objects, and attitude measurement techniques generally include the dimension of evaluation in some way. Also, the attitudes studied by social psychologists have typically been social attitudes (attitudes held by many people or groups) rather than idiosyncratic, personal attitudes. Attitudes are always directed toward something (a group, an individual, a place, or a practice), which is called the attitude object. Finally, most social psychologists describe attitudes as having three components: a cognitive component (beliefs or ideas), the evaluative component (feelings of being favorable or unfavorable toward the attitude object), and a behavioral component (tendencies of approach or avoidance of contact with the attitude object).

The presumed correlation between evaluative feelings and social motivation is at the heart of historical theory of attitude-behavior relationships. The classical view of attitudes can be described as follows. Attitudes are formed in the context of daily social interaction in a variety of ways, including direct experience with the attitude object and verbal transmission of beliefs and evaluations of the attitude object. Attitudes, once formed, were presumed to be a relatively enduring predisposition to respond to a general class of attitude objects. The explanatory power of attitudes was presumed to be broad because of the generalized motives they created; knowing individuals' attitudes would make it possible to predict their overt social behavior in a variety of situations.

However, researchers identified two problems with the original research paradigm that led to immediate improvements in understanding the effect of attitudes on behavior. The first was the realization that general attitudes are more likely to predict aggregations of acts relevant to the attitude rather than any particular single act. For example, a measure of religiosity may correlate poorly with a variable such as church attendance but may correlate highly with a multiple-act index including attendance with other variables such as financial contributions and levels of church activity. The second was that attitudes are only one factor among many that can influence particular social behaviors and that it was necessary to construct more complex models to predict single acts. One valuable contribution was the theory of reasoned action (Fishbein & Ajzen, 1975) in which attitudes directly affect individuals' intentions to perform a particular act.

Several studies have shown a strong link between predictions from behavioral intentions to specific acts, derived in part from the individual's attitudes. Other factors have been shown to increase the predictive validity of attitudes. One useful factor is the actor's attitude toward performing the behavior itself, as opposed to the actor's attitude toward the attitude object. For example, an actor may demonstrate a prejudiced attitude toward members of an outgroup but not express that attitude with rude behavior against a member of that group if the actor abhors rudeness. Another factor, called a subjective norm, refers to actors' perception of what is expected of them in a situation by significant others such as a friend or a spouse. A third factor is actors' evaluations of the consequences of performing a particular action. More recently researchers have begun to examine the role of the actors' perceptions of their own ability to control their behavior in a given situation. Predictions made from these expanded models are usually much better than predictions made from measures of attitude alone.

References

Eagly, A. H. (1992). Uneven progress: Social psychology and the study of attitudes. *Journal of Personality and Social Psychology, 63* (5), 693–710.

Fishbein, M., & Ajzen, I. (1975). *Belief, attitude, intention and behavior: An introduction to theory and research.* Reading, MA: Addison-Wesley.

Olson, J. M., & Zanna, M. P. (1993). Attitudes and attitude change. *Annual Review of Psychology, 44,* 117–154.

Wicker, A. W. (1969). Attitude versus actions: The relationship of verbal and overt behavioral responses to attitude objects. *Journal of Social Issues, 25* (4), 41–78.

L. S. SHAFFER

See PERSONALITY; ATTITUDE; COGNITIVE DISSONANCE.

Attraction. *See* INTERPERSONAL ATTRACTION; AFFILIATION, NEED FOR; LOVE.

Attribution Theory. To understand and interpret the behavior of people is a goal not only for psychologists; each person attempts to make sense of the world and this involves gaining knowledge of both one's self and others. People often question their own true motives behind certain behaviors or ask why another person acts the way he or she does. Psychologists have thus involved themselves in the study of causality, not in a purely logical sense as philosophers have done, but rather in terms of how and why ordinary people make the causal inferences they do. Such inferences have been studied within the framework of what has been called attribution theory.

The observation of behavior must necessarily be the first step in the attribution process. Such an observation can be of one's self (i.e., one can both be an actor and an observer of his or her own behavior) or of others. Not all behavior, at least in theory, is meaningful for an attributional inference because not all behavior is judged to be the product of an intention. Routine or involuntary actions are not as meaningful to the observer since attributions of intention for such actions are ambiguous. Research suggests, however, that "meaningless" behavior, such as routinized or involuntary actions, still may be attributed as meaningful by observers. For example, Jones and Harris (1967) discovered that participants in their experiment believed a speaker privately held the position publicly advocated (in this case, defending Fidel Castro), even when they were informed that the speaker was assigned the position.

Attribution theory is not a monolithic theory but rather is a group of somewhat loosely structured theoretical models, or at least propositions, that constitute a conceptual framework. These models, presented systematically in the form of research hypotheses that have proved remarkably fruitful for social psychological investigation, focus on common questions people ask when observing behavior.

Theoretical Models. Heider's Naive Psychology. Attribution theory evolved in the 1960s as a product of the theoretical writings of Heider (1958), who analyzed the "commonsense psychology" by which people explain everyday social events. However, because not everyone has access to the principles of scientific psychology to explain behavior, the average person is what Heider called a naive psychologist. In their naive analyses of behavior, people employ two general attributional categories: internal causes (i.e., personal dispositions) and external causes (i.e., situational factors). In reality this either-or nature of ascribing causality is not quite so black-and-white. Many behaviors are caused by a combination of dispositional and situational factors, and therefore causal inferences may be in error. Attribution theorists are particularly interested in how both dispositional and situational factors are used in making causal judgments.

Causal Attribution. Kelley (1973) suggests that the attributor makes inferences in response to the covariation between some observed behavior (an observed effect) and three possible causes of the effect: persons (either self or others), entities (objects present in relation to the behavior), and the context (specific situations). By covariation, Kelley means that we note some relationship or association between the observed behavior and some set of conditions involving these three possible causes. If, for example, we observe over time at the local comedy club that individual X (a person) consistently laughs only at comedian Y (an entity) and no other comedian, then we may determine that comedian Y causes the observed effect (laughing). This is an entity attribution in that the laughter was distinctive to and consistent with this particular comedian. We will be even more confident in attributing laughter to the comedian if others also laugh at comedian Y (i.e., high consensus).

If, however, we observe that individual X laughs (high consistency) at virtually any comedian (low distinctiveness), we may conclude that the observed effect is due to X's jovial nature (especially if others think the comedians are not very humorous—low consensus). This is a person attribution. But if we notice that X's laughing behavior is unique that particular evening in that normally X does not laugh at any comedian (low consistency), we may think that X is in an unusually good mood or has had too much to drink. This is a context attribution. So the degree to which we see another's behavior reflecting an internal disposition (a person attribution) or an external situation (either an entity or a context attribution) depends on the unique configuration of distinctiveness, consistency, and consensus information.

Dispositional Factors. Sometimes we are confident in inferring other people's intentions and dispositions because these characteristics correspond closely to their actions. Jones and Davis's (1965) theory of correspondent inferences suggests that high correspondence more likely occurs when the person is engaged in unusual behavior given the circumstances of the situation. For example, we may see the frequent smile of the athlete in the midst of intense competition as a reflection of a truly pleasant disposition. In contrast, when we are approached by a smiling car salesperson, we may attribute the smile only to his or her desire to sell a car.

High correspondence between the behavior and underlying personal characteristics is also more likely when the observed behavior produces noncommon consequences (i.e., consequences different from which alternative actions would produce). For instance, we may infer that the student athlete who chooses college A, known for both its athletic and academic program, over college B, known only for its athletic program, places importance on academics, since that is the noncommon effect. The common effect, a good athletic program, does not tell us much about what is important to this student athlete unless, of course, it too is a noncommon effect between selecting college A over college C.

Jones and Davis (1965) maintain that we see situational factors merely as prescriptions for behavior and only as behavior deviates from these constraints ("out of role" behavior) does a person's behavior tell us much about underlying personality characteristics. They suggest that if a plausible cause, whether situational or dispositional, for a given behavior is already known, people often discount or ignore other contributing causes. So, if a teacher knows that a particular student went to a party the night before the exam, the student's poor exam performance may be seen only as a function of party-going. Several researchers, however, have found evidence of insufficient discounting: observers have been found to attribute an individual's behavior to dispositional factors, even when the situational demands provide a sufficient explanation for the behavior.

Attributional Bias. People frequently make the reasonable attributions predicted by the theoretical models. But what is equally important and often more intriguing are the attributional errors we make. One such error, the insufficient discounting of dispositional factors in light of situational demands, has already been highlighted. This particular bias has become known as the fundamental attribution error, named so in part because it is so pervasive

and irresistible and in part because it colors our explanations of the world in such basic, yet important, ways.

Why do we tend to underestimate situational determinants of behavior? First, it should be pointed out that this tendency is not equally likely in all cultures, and even as part of highly individualistic western cultures (where it is more frequently found), we are far less likely to make the fundamental attribution error if we are explaining our own behavior rather than someone else's. That is, we are less prone to see ourselves as clumsy and to blame the uneven sidewalk or tree root when tripping than when we observe the same behavior in someone else. Such a tendency may reflect at times a "defensive attribution" (Bradley, 1978), whereby one is less likely to blame the self, in contrast to blaming others for the same negative behavior. Bradley suggests that such self-protective attributions (including the reversed tendency of generously crediting the self for positive behaviors) are most likely to occur when behavior is public and produces high ego involvement. At other times, however, the fundamental attribution error may result from different perspectives and levels of situational awareness. Research (Carver & Scheier, 1978) shows that we tend to overestimate the effects of whatever it is upon which we are focused. As observers of others, our primary focus is on them as individuals, and we may not be finely attuned to situational forces; as observers of ourselves as actors, our focus is elsewhere and we may be more aware of situational factors at work.

Another common attributional bias is what psychologists refer to as false consensus. Researchers have documented the considerable tendency to view one's own behavioral choices and judgments as overly common and appropriate to existing circumstances. Such distortions exist in part because people selectively expose themselves to the influence of others by associating primarily with those who share similar values, interests, and perspectives. Therefore, it is not unusual that both sides of a social issue think that their position is majority-held.

Religious Attributions. Spilka and McIntosh (1995) see attributional processes at the heart of religious experience by suggesting that "religious experience refers to a cognitive-emotional state in which the experiencer's understandings involve attributions or references to religious figures, roles, or powers" (p. 422), thus supporting Proudfoot and Shaver's (1975) claim that "attribution theory is attractive to the student of religion because . . . it deals directly with a person's interpretation of his own experience" (p. 322). Spilka, Shaver, and Kirkpatrick (1985) maintain that three basic needs or desires of people—a sense of meaning, a sense of control over outcomes, and a need for self-esteem—not only are evident throughout the attribution process but are often met through a religious meaning-belief system. Suggesting that "causal explanation is a hallmark of religion" (p. 1), these authors contend that an attributional theoretical framework provides a useful approach to the study of religious explanation.

References

Bradley, G. W. (1978). Self-serving biases in the attribution process: A reexamination of the fact or fiction question. *Journal of Personality and Social Psychology, 36* (1), 56–71.

Carver, C. S., & Scheier, M. F. (1978). Self-focusing effects of dispositional self-consciousness, mirror presence, and audience presence. *Journal of Personality and Social Psychology, 36,* 324–332.

Heider, F. (1958). *The psychology of interpersonal relations.* New York: Wiley.

Jones, E. E., & David, K. E. (1965). From acts to dispositions: The attributional process in person perception. In L. Berkowitz (Ed.), *Advances in experimental social psychology* (Vol. 2). New York: Academic Press.

Jones, E. E., & Harris, V. A. (1967). The attribution of attitudes. *Journal of Experimental Social Psychology, 3,* 1–24.

Kelley, H. H. (1973). The process of causal attribution. *American Psychologist, 28,* 107–128.

Proudfoot, W., & Shaver, P. (1975). Attribution theory and the psychology of religion. *Journal for the Scientific Study of Religion, 14,* 317–330.

Spilka, B., & McIntosh, D. N. (1995). Attribution theory and religious experience. In R. W. Hood, Jr. (Ed.), *Handbook of religious experience.* Birmingham, AL: Religious Education Press.

Spilka, B., Shaver, P., & Kirkpatrick, L. A. (1985). A general attribution theory for the psychology of religion. *Journal for the Scientific Study of Religion, 24* (1), 1–20.

P. C. Hill

See Person Perception; Self-Perception Theory; Social Psychology.

Authoritarian Personality. In the aftermath of World War II many social scientists attempted to explain how individuals or whole societies could resort to such intense prejudicial and aggressive attitudes as were demonstrated by the fascist forces of Europe. Though many theories and lines of research have been developed, few have received as much attention as the theory of the authoritarian personality. In *The Authoritarian Personality* the authors proposed the notion that a certain personality type is especially prone to develop and display prejudicial and/or aggressive attitudes and behaviors (Adorno, Frenkel-Brunswik, Levinson, & Sanford, 1950). Such individuals seem particularly predisposed to engage in scapegoating, or blaming their personal or societal difficulties on a certain class of people or an ethnic or religious minority.

For Adorno and his colleagues there are four major characteristics that, taken together, help define the authoritarian personality. The first is that of fascism. They define fascism as a trait in which a person focuses upon the importance of demonstrating respect for and showing obedience to established authority persons and structures. The leader or master is all-important, all-powerful, and all-good and should be accorded due honor and respect.

A person with fascist tendencies is likely to show blind and unquestioning devotion and loyalty to his or her leader (whether it be a führer, president, premier, king, commanding officer, or an older sibling) and to be outraged at hearing criticism of this leader. The fascist person is overly influenced by the position of authority itself. No honor can be greater than to have served the authority well and to have been faithful to the end to all of the leader's commands and wishes; the virtue comes in having served authority for authority's sake.

Another tendency of fascist individuals is to divide the world's people into two rather simplistic groups. The "good" group serves authority well and is physically, spiritually, and morally strong. The "bad" group consists of immoral, crooked, and feeble-minded people who can never be trusted, who never learned respect and reverence for tradition, and who are responsible for most of the world's problems.

Finally, there is a tendency in fascism to enjoy and respect symbols of power, authority, and mass conformity—guns, swords, flags, insignias, uniforms.

The second major characteristic of the authoritarian personality is the tendency toward ethnocentrism. An ethnocentric attitude holds that one group or culture or nation is best, and all others are inferior. Political pluralism and ethnic or religious diversity are not societal qualities to be admired or desired.

Third, the authoritarian personality tends to be quite anti-Semitic. Such an individual is likely to possess many stereotypes of Jews (e.g., "Jewish power and control in money matters is far out of proportion to the number of Jews in the total population") and is likely to blame "the Jewish element" for a myriad of social and economic problems.

Fourth, the person with an authoritarian personality is seen by Adorno as being politically and economically conservative. This person will believe in the notion that determination and hard work are the only requirements for success in life (ignoring racial or gender barriers), that "children should be taught the value of money," and that tradition is usually superior to innovation in both the political and economic arenas.

Adorno and his associates established a paper-and-pencil inventory of authoritarianism and used the tool to isolate authoritarian individuals for research and study. One important finding is that subjects with authoritarian personalities tend to have grown up in homes characterized by strict and punitive child-rearing practices; the subjects often report that their fathers in particular demanded obedience and unquestioning loyalty.

Lest Americans think that authoritarianism was to be found only in Hitler's Germany, many theorists have pointed to the United States' own brand of authoritarianism. For example, it has been suggested that the Ku Klux Klan, many individuals in the nation's intelligence and/or military agencies, and many Americans in general seem to demonstrate several traits of the authoritarian personality (the trait of anti-Semitism may be broadened to include scapegoating of any cultural, religious, ethnic, or gender group, be they Catholics, blacks, illegal aliens, gays, feminists). Individuals who possess such a personality constellation have even been portrayed as major characters on popular television programs, such as Archie Bunker in *All in the Family* or Major Frank Burns in *M*A*S*H**.

The popularity of many of the religious cults in America has been explained in part by the ability of charismatic and power-oriented leaders to capture the hearts and minds of potential followers who have an authoritarian bent. Of even greater concern to many Christians is the opinion expressed in some quarters that elements of the new right in American politics and religion represent a special kind of Christian authoritarianism in which blind devotion and loyalty are accorded to fast-speaking preachers as much as, if not more than, to Christ himself.

The concept of and the research on the authoritarian personality is not without its critics. One concern, for example, is that the existing research presupposes only a right-wing authoritarian personality. Could there not also be a political and religious left-wing counterpart personality type? Finally, social scientists who study so-called authoritarian personality individuals might be somewhat prejudiced themselves in the way they describe the personality traits of their subjects; the authoritarian person is often described as being "intolerant of ambiguity" and "rigid." Perhaps others might see such a person as being "decisive" and "stable."

Reference

Adorno, T. W., Frenkel-Brunswik, E., Levinson, D., & Sanford, R. N. (1950). *The authoritarian personality*. New York: Harper & Row.

D. E. ANDERSON

See PREJUDICE; AMBIGUITY, INTOLERANCE OF; DOGMATISM; PERSONALITY; POWER.

Autistic Disorder. Autistic disorder is characterized by devastating impairments in a young child's communication and language skills, disinterest in social interaction, and preference for repetitive, stereotyped behaviors. Although it is usually present in infancy, no physical indicators or hard neurological signs facilitate an accurate neurological diagnosis before the age of three. Early signs of autism include lack of eye contact, failure to cuddle with affection, and nonreciprocal smiling patterns. Children may not speak or may be unable to carry on a meaningful conversation, other than making requests to get their own needs fulfilled. Autistic children may engage in idiosyncratic verbalizations, especially echolalia or the repeating of recently heard or preferred idiosyncratic phrases without prosody or communicative intent. When left to themselves, autistic children frequently become absorbed into stereotyped actions, especially spinning objects, body rocking, and flapping their hands. They are repetitive specialists and can sustain attention on their preferred activities for hours but will actively resist changes in their routines or rituals.

Autistic disorder occurs at a rate of 2 to 5 cases per 10,000 individuals and is more likely to be present in males than in females at a ratio of 4 to 1. At this time there is no definitive test for autism. Amniocentesis has not yet identified any chromosomal or chemical predictor of autism. Diagnosis occurs on the basis of symptom profiles and elimination of competing diagnoses such as deafness or expressive language disorders. Neither is there full consensus in research and theory about the causes of autistic disorder.

Early infantile autism was first labeled by Kanner in 1943 from his clinical work with a sample of 11 children. The term *autism* had first been used by Eugen Bleuler in 1919 to describe the withdrawal from the outside world seen in adult schizophrenics. Early theory focused on whether autism should be viewed as a childhood version of schizophrenia. However, autism seems to follow a more uniform course than the pattern of remission and relapse in schizophrenia and is essentially marked by the absence of fantasy, play, and hallucinations, while schizophrenics complain of excessive and confusing internal images. In the psychoanalytic thought of Bettelheim, the disorder is caused by attachment trauma in infancy, the so-called refrigerator parents who cannot respond nurturantly to their children. However, research suggests that parents of autistic children are not significantly different from parents of any severely chronically ill child.

Although the causal mechanisms have not been isolated, it is believed that the disorder originates early in neonatal brain development. The developing brain sustains some damage, perhaps mediated by maternal illness, chemical toxins, viral agents, environmental pollutants, or genetic susceptibility that affects its continued growth. As a consequence the central nervous system substrata necessary for processing complex perceptual information, especially information critical for establishing social reciprocity, does not mature through infancy. Self-stimulation through kinesthetic actions seems to help the children regulate their arousal and soothe their perceptual processing disturbance so that they can feel calm.

Children do not outgrow autism or the concomitant mental retardation. Better prognosis is marked by the presence of language before the age of five, ability to benefit from observational learning (imitation), absence of severe symptoms such as self-injury and aggression, and ability to demonstrate intelligence with an intelligence quotient above 50. Most autistic persons are unable to manage rudimentary skills of daily living and require substantial supervision and care through their adult years.

Treatment is more effective if it occurs as early as possible with a focus on language, functional communication, and motivational assessment. Medication may be useful for management of behavioral outbursts and mood disturbances but does not resolve the core symptoms of autistic disorder. The innovative technique of facilitated communication teaches autistic persons to use keyboards as language tools and has been useful for some autistic people. Intervention typically consists of efforts to teach adaptive skills, manage disruptive behavior, and communicate for self-advocacy purposes so that persons with autistic disorder can care for themselves in as independent a way as possible.

H. BRAY-GARRETSON

See REACTIVE ATTACHMENT DISORDER OF INFANCY.

Autoeroticism. Usually defined as self-stimulation of any kind short of orgasm. Some have differentiated this from masturbation, which has historically been defined as self-stimulation to the point of orgasm. In contemporary discussion, however, these words are often used interchangeably, along with others like self-exploration, self-pleasuring, and self-arousal. The distinction between any of these terms no longer seems helpful either clinically or theoretically.

R. E. BUTMAN

See SEXUALITY.

Autogenic Therapy. Prominent approach among the therapies oriented toward the treatment of both psychological and physical aspects of the person. Autogenic therapy is much more popular in Europe and Japan than in the United States, and many of the empirical studies of its effectiveness have been published in non-English professional journals. Autogenic therapy bears many similarities to relaxation training, hypnotherapy, biofeedback, and meditation techniques.

Autogenic therapy (or training) has its roots in studies of hypnotic suggestion and autohypnosis in Germany at the turn of the century. Schultz and Luthe (1969), the major proponents of autogenic training, attempted to remove what were seen as the negative aspects of hypnotherapy (i.e., the passivity and dependence of the patient on the therapist) from the suggestion process by developing standardized procedures for self-suggestion. Their final result was a series of six standardized self-suggestion exercises that combine suggestion of the experience of calmness or peace with suggestion of particular physical experience related to absence of anxiety. Examples of such suggestions are heaviness and warmth in the extremities, regulation of cardiac activity and respiration, abdominal warmth, and cooling of the forehead (Ramsay, Wittkower, & Warnes, 1976). A typical single script might have patients suggesting to themselves three times, "My right arm is very heavy," followed by the suggestion, "I am completely calm." This whole sequence may then be repeated a number of times. The exercises are to be practiced regularly by the patient and integrated into the person's normal daily routine.

Autogenic therapy is most frequently applied to anxiety-based psychosomatic disorders such as peptic ulcers, ulcerative colitis, a number of psychologically based cardiovascular disorders (including angina pectoris, paroxysmal tachycardia, and essential hypertension), migraine and tension headaches, and asthma. The clinical efficacy of autogenic therapy is difficult to judge. When compared to other variants of relaxation training, autogenic training seems to be as effective as other methods. Autogenic therapy is probably a useful adjunct to the psychotherapeutic treatment of anxiety-based disorders, though it is unquestionably not as efficacious as other methods when used as the sole treatment modality. Some form of relaxation training can provide substantial benefit in the treatment of psychosomatic disorders and is likely to be of use as an adjunct in the treatment of other anxiety disorders.

References

Ramsay, R. A., Wittkower, E. D., & Warnes, H. (1976). Treatment of psychosomatic disorders. In B. B. Wolman (Ed.), *The therapist's handbook.* New York: Van Nostrand.
Schultz, J. H., & Luthe, W. (1969). *Autogenic therapy.* New York: Grune & Stratton.

S. L. JONES

See RELAXATION TRAINING.

Automatic Writing. Writing that is carried out without conscious control or with attention concentrated on content rather than on the act of writing itself. Automatic writing is one of the more frequently used ideomotor signaling systems in hypnosis, whereby the hypnotized individual is able to provide feedback about internal events, thus allowing the hypnotist to tailor future suggestions. Following trance induction, which includes the elements of a relaxed body, greater susceptibility to suggestion, and a focused concentration, the hypnotic subject is directed to an acute awareness of sensations in the limbs, particularly the writing hand. With paper and pen in hand, the individual is encouraged to begin writing, or even doodling or scribbling, with a focus not on the process of writing but rather on the content of what is being written.

Sometimes the term has been used as a related phenomenon to parapsychology. Here it is believed that the mind of one person may communicate through mechanical writing across place or time to another individual or group.

P. C. HILL

See HYPNOSIS; HYPNOTHERAPY.

Automaticity. A term used to describe cognitive processes that require neither attention nor effort and therefore do not consume cognitive capacity, which is believed to be limited. The concept is useful in understanding two basic types of phenomenon (Isen & Diamond, 1989): when we do something without awareness or effort, such as driving the usual route to work where little or no attention is given to signs or making turns, and when our attention is irresistibly captured, even when doing something else, such as when we hear someone mention our name in a crowded room despite our engagement in a separate conversation.

In contrast, the term *controlled processing* is often used to describe that which requires attention, such as learning new material, and decreases the cognitive capacity for other processing. Shiffrin and Dumais (1981) identify 13 distinguishing characteristics between automatic and controlled cognitive processing. In contrast to controlled processes, automatic processes do not use general cognitive processing resources; cannot be ignored; tend to run to completion; tend to occur in units with fixed beginning and ending points; show greater improvement with practice; are relatively difficult to modify; can operate parallel to other thoughts; are less likely to require long-term memory storage; can increase performance level on complex tasks; generally occur in response to situations that are unambiguous; may operate with less awareness; allow attention to be less focused and therefore can be divided among many inputs; and are no less simple than controlled processes (this criterion is listed because other researchers have suggested that simplicity is a defining characteristic of automaticity, but Shiffrin and Dumais suggest otherwise).

Many skills that at some point require a great deal of effort may become automated (Bloom, 1986). For example, learning to drive a car, especially one with a standard transmission, requires a great deal of effort, yet most experienced drivers are not even aware of utilizing their many necessary skills. Other examples of automaticity include reading, where the experienced reader, unlike the individual learning to read, can ignore individual letters and read words by sight. Reading eventually becomes so automated for most individuals that even sight words are processed automatically; in turn this frees the individual to read for meaning and to employ critical thinking. Other common examples of automaticity include riding a bicycle, touch typing, playing musical instruments, and the various skills used in sports activities.

Developing automaticity is often necessary to reach top-level performance in a field that requires specific talents. Bloom (1986) studied outstanding achievers under the age of 35 in six fields: concert piano, sculpture, professional tennis, Olympic swimming, research mathematics, and research neurology. On average these individuals were spending 25 hours a week learning and practicing their skill for 16 years (and none less than 12 years). Even after

becoming outstanding performers, many reported the need to overlearn particular aspects of their skill repertoire, practicing as much as 50 hours per week. Most performers, especially in music and sports, began at an early age. But even those in cognitive fields and sculpture began early to learn content and skills that were relevant to their chosen field.

Researchers have begun to apply the concept of automaticity to attitudes, suggesting that attitudes toward some objects may become so ingrained that the attitude may be present and may even be expressed with little or no conscious awareness. Promising research on the automatic activation of attitudes has led Hill (1994) to suggest that attitude automaticity may be an underlying process involved in religious experience and may be a useful way of conceptualizing and measuring religious commitment.

References

Bloom, B. S. (1986). Automaticity: The hands and feet of genius. *Educational Leadership, 43,* 5–11.

Hill, P. C. (1994). Toward an attitude process model of religious experience. *Journal for the Scientific Study of Religion, 33* (4), 303–314.

Isen, A. M., & Diamond, G. A. (1989). Affect and automaticity. In J. S. Uleman & J. A Bargh (Eds.), *Unintended thought.* New York: Guilford.

Shiffrin, R. M., & Dumais, S. T. (1981). The development of automatism. In J. R. Anderson (Ed.), *Cognitive skills and their acquisition.* Hillsdale, NJ: Erlbaum.

P. C. Hill

Autonomy, Functional. According to Gordon Allport's principle of functional autonomy, motives or behaviors can become independent of their origins. Persons who learned frugality during their childhood years of economic depression and who continue its practice in spite of present prosperity illustrate this principle.

Autoplasty. The process of adapting to stress by changing oneself intrapsychically. It is contrasted to alloplasty, which involves adaptation through the manipulation of external factors in the environment. In some cases autoplasty is a normal and healthy process, as in psychoanalytic treatment or other methods of internal change. Autoplasty can also be a neurotic adjustment to stress, as evidenced in symptom formation or psychosomatic disorders.

Auxiliary Chair Technique. The auxiliary chair, or empty chair, is used in Psychodrama to represent a person or thing significant to the protagonist. The protagonist vividly fantasizes the image in the chair and encounters it. Unspoken thoughts and feelings are vented, yielding a cathartic release (*see* Catharsis). This technique is particularly useful if the protagonist chooses not to use auxiliary egos to play the role of the person or thing.

The auxiliary chair technique is similar to the empty chair used in Gestalt therapy, where it is referred to as the "hot seat." The basic difference is in application. Psychodramatists encourage the protagonist to confront persons, things, and self. The Gestalt therapist uses the hot seat to help the client encounter parts and dimensions of the self.

J. H. VANDER MAY

See GESTALT TECHNIQUES; GESTALT THERAPY.

Aversion Therapy. Aversion therapy uses a number of techniques and stimuli to weaken or eliminate undesirable responses such as deviant sexual behavior and substance abuse. In theory punishment is used to directly reduce the frequency of undesired behaviors through contingent presentation or removal of a stimulus, while aversion, or aversive counter-conditioning, seeks to change the undesirable response indirectly by altering the functions of the discriminative and reinforcing stimuli. In practice this distinction is somewhat blurred, since many aversion procedures have both punishing and stimulus-altering effects.

In some forms of aversion, no behavior need occur. Rather, the discriminative and reinforcing stimuli that maintain the problem behavior (e.g., sight or smell of alcohol, deviant sexual stimuli) are presented to the person, and an unpleasant stimulus (e.g., electric shock) is presented simultaneously. The discriminative and reinforcing stimuli acquire the properties of the aversive stimulus through association. The goal is to weaken the link between the controlling conditioned stimulus (e.g., children) and undesired response (e.g., sexual arousal). Wolpe's theory of reciprocal inhibition provides one explanation for this process. Wolpe theorizes that arousing a strong competing response such as nausea or fear inhibits the undesired response.

Aversion uses electrical shock; chemical and olfactory stimuli such as emetine hydrochloride (which causes nausea and vomiting); valeric acid (which smells like rotten eggs) and ammonia; covert sensitization by aversive imagery; and shame induction (McAnulty & Adams, 1992). The ideal stimulus is one that permits rapid onset, prompt termination, controlled intensity, and quick recovery so that repeated trials may be administered in a brief time. Electric shock and noxious smells are readily controlled in these ways, but drugs are not. Drug administration also requires medical personnel and sometimes hospitalization, is medically contraindicated for many individuals, and may have side effects that impair conditioning. Shock is widely applicable except for persons with heart conditions. For all these reasons shock replaced drugs as the principal aversion technique in the 1970s. More recently covert sensitization has become preferred.

Aversion takes three basic forms: escape training, avoidance training, and presenting the unpleasant stimulus without permitting either escape or avoid-

ance. Often escape training is used initially, then modified into avoidance training.

In escape training the target stimulus is presented; then an unpleasant stimulus such as electric shock occurs. After brief exposure to the two stimuli, the individual escapes from the stimuli by making a specified response. For example, a transvestite is given an article of women's clothing to put on and then administered electric shock. Once the clothing is removed, shock is terminated.

In avoidance training the individual is presented with the stimulus that elicits the problem behavior. If an avoidance response is made quickly enough, the aversion stimulus is avoided. The avoidance response typically removes the stimulus for the undesired response. For example, turning off pictures of women's clothing quickly enough may avoid shock for a fetishist. An advantage of the avoidance procedure is that the client learns to be anxious in the presence of the target stimulus and is positively reinforced for actively avoiding it.

Covert sensitization is a form of aversive counterconditioning in which the client imagines an unpleasant event following the undesired stimulus response complex rather than experiencing overt aversive stimulation. For example, persons may imagine taking a large bite of hot fudge sundae topped with whipped cream and nuts and then imagine becoming grossly fat, unable to fit into their clothes, and socially ostracized. In the avoidance phase they imagine becoming increasingly anxious as they approach the ice cream shop. They then imagine turning away and experiencing immediate relief.

Effectiveness of Aversion. Research on the outcomes of aversion treatments has produced mixed results. Aversion is quite effective with transvestism and fetishism. Aversion techniques are the most common approach to treatment of pedophilia. Aversion with sexual reconditioning has shown favorable short-term effects with pedophiliacs, but reductions of long-term recidivism have not been demonstrated. Results with homosexuality are modest; they are better for homosexuals voluntarily seeking treatment and for those with prior heterosexual experience. Aversion has been found effective with transvestites and fetishists with prior heterosexual experience; and a few gender identity problems also show favorable outcomes (McAnulty & Adams, 1992).

The effectiveness of aversion with sexual deviations is influenced by a number of factors. Most studies have used electrical aversion; smell aversion shows promise and has been widely adopted but needs further study. Although drug aversion studies have sometimes yielded promising results, shock and unpleasant smells are more commonly used with sexual behaviors. A major concern with sexual disorders is the need to assess sexual arousal to appropriate heterosexual stimuli. When appropriate sexual arousal patterns are absent or weak, developing or strengthening them is essential to lasting effects of aversion.

Electrical aversion does not appear effective for alcohol abuse. Nausea aversion is generally effective for several months, but as time passes an increasing percentage of clients resume drinking. Compliance may be as low as 20% when voluntary; thus administration in a supervised setting is important. Additional treatment of psychosocial problems is widely recommended and may help to maintain gains. In a recent review Emmelkamp concludes "aversive therapy, if applied at all, should be part of a more comprehensive cognitive-behavioral program" (Emmelkamp, 1994, p. 400).

Covert sensitization is appealing for both theoretical and practical reasons. Covert sensitization appears promising for those who can visualize well and are well motivated. However, there remains a lack of clear empirical evidence of treatment effectiveness for covert sensitization when it is used alone. Thus it should be used as part of a more comprehensive approach that also addresses the psychosocial aspects of the problem behavior. Adams notes that a number of biblical teachings are consistent with the idea of replacing responses rather than simply eliminating them (Adams, 1973).

Ethical Issues. Aversion therapy has often been opposed on ethical and moral grounds. However, aversive consequences are a natural feature of the social and physical world. Behaviors treated by aversion usually produce immediate rewards followed by delayed pain. For example, the sexual gratifications of paraphilias are immediate, but the costs of broken relationships and sexually transmitted diseases are delayed. Aversion therapy helps persons forego immediate rewards so they can avoid these delayed aversive events.

Guidelines for aversion emphasize informed consent and minimal exposure to painful stimuli. Persons voluntarily seeking treatment respond better than those sent by the courts or family members. For both these reasons, use of aversion on reluctant patients is questionable. The individual will avoid treatment if the experience is sufficiently unpleasant. Aversion to the target stimulus or elimination of the problem behavior must thus be accomplished without causing aversion to treatment.

Research evidence indicates that problem behaviors are most effectively eliminated when constructive alternatives are developed simultaneously. This raises two concerns. First, many (especially laypersons) use aversion techniques without establishing suitable alternatives; developing these is essential. Second, problems arise in selecting alternatives, especially for sexual behaviors like homosexuality, voyeurism, and transvestism. From a Christian perspective most sexual activity outside of marriage is unacceptable, and alternative goals have not been clearly articulated. For many sexual contact appears to have become a sole form of intimacy. Erotic intimacy substitutes for familial, fraternal, and spiritual closeness. The biblical concept of love suggests a direction for consideration. Learning to experience and express love, especially God's love, may be the key.

Reorientation treatment of homosexual behavior is highly controversial and is not widely practiced. Since 1973 homosexuality has not been considered a mental disorder by the American Psychiatric Association. Some contend that any sexual reorientation treatment is abusive, a result of homophobia—fear of and hostility toward homosexuality. Others, such as Nicolosi (1991), contend that reorientation treatment can be ethically conducted within the guidelines of informed consent when it is consistent with the values and goals of the individual seeking treatment.

Summary. Aversion therapy uses aversive counterconditioning and covert sensitization to eliminate undesired behaviors. Research indicates that aversion is effective for some problems and under some conditions. Because of legal, ethical, and practical concerns, covert sensitization has gradually become the preferred approach, at least for outpatient psychotherapy. Empirical support is limited for covert sensitization alone but indicates that more comprehensive treatment packages that include covert sensitization along with strengthening of desired alternative responses are quite effective. The precise contribution of covert sensitization in these treatment approaches is not known. Finally, as applied to sexual behavior, aversion therapy poses a number of unique problems from a Christian perspective.

References

Adams, J. E. (1973). *The Christian counselor's manual.* Grand Rapids, MI: Baker.

Emmelkamp, P. M. G. (1994). Behavior therapy with adults. In A. E. Bergin & S. L. Garfield (Eds.), *Handbook of psychotherapy and behavior change* (4th ed.). New York: Wiley.

McAnulty, R. D., & Adams, H. E. (1992). Behavior therapy with paraphilic disorders. In S. M. Turner, K. M. Calhoun, & H. E. Adams (Eds.), *Handbook of clinical behavior therapy.* New York: Wiley.

Nicolosi, J. (1991). *Reparative therapy of male homosexuality: A new clinical approach.* Northvale, NJ: Aronson.

R. K. BUFFORD

See PUNISHMENT; COGNITIVE-BEHAVIOR THERAPY; BEHAVIOR THERAPY.

Avoidant Personality Disorder. The person diagnosed as having this disorder displays, as the name suggests, an avoidance of interpersonal relationships. The diagnostic features include low self-esteem, social withdrawal, restraint within intimate relationships, hypersensitivity to rejection, and an unwillingness to enter relationships unless guaranteed open acceptance. Such persons devalue their achievements and become overly concerned with their personal shortcomings. They withdraw from social opportunity because of marked fear of being rejected, belittled, shamed, or humiliated. The slightest disapproval from someone devastates them and may cause self-anger for failing to relate effectively.

Avoidant personality disorder results in depression, anxiety, and self-anger. Impairment in social relationships may preclude marriage or meaningful relationships. Occupational goals may not be met if job interaction requires interpersonal involvement. At best job performance will be impaired due to social withdrawal.

Differential Diagnosis. A key difference between avoidant personality disorder and schizoid personality disorder is that while the latter involves social isolation, it is without a desire for social interaction. The individual with an avoidant personality disorder strongly desires acceptance and affection from others and is very sensitive to criticism.

Avoidance disorders should also be considered as a differential diagnosis with regard to social phobia. A person diagnosed as avoidant personality disorder is anxious in all social situations, and the anxiety is more intense with greater impairment. There is also more commonality with other psychopathology when compared to social phobias.

Avoidance disorder of childhood or adolescence, 18 years and under, has similar features to the adult version. It may develop as early as 2 ½ years of age and may become chronic and continue into adulthood. Children with this disorder are inhibited in normal psychosexual activity, are unassertive, experience severe interference with social functioning with peers, and lack self-confidence. They desire affection and acceptance but are preoccupied with rejection or criticism. They have more satisfying relationships with family members and others with whom they are very familiar. The problem is noticed when it comes to relationships outside the family or outside close, familiar friendships.

Separation anxiety in children differs from avoidant personality disorder in that the former is due to separation from home or a special person rather than fear of contact with strangers. Schizoid disorder of childhood or adolescence differs in that there is little or no desire for social interaction. In the case of overanxious disorder, the anxiety is not limited to social contact with strangers and therefore is not focused on a specific situation or object.

Treatment. Treatment is difficult because it requires individuals with avoidant personality disorder to meet a stranger for therapy. When they do come for treatment, it is usually at the encouragement of a family member. The treatment of choice often is family therapy. Whether or not the person has left home, family therapy helps the avoidant person to understand his or her response pattern and move toward increased healthy social contacts.

Individual therapy is often an important part of the total treatment process. A major goal of individual therapy is to build a therapeutic relationship in order to gain insight into the dynamics of the problem. Group therapy is also helpful in that it provides social interaction with strangers in a protected environment. It thus serves as a testing ground for new behavior under the protection of the group leader.

Chemotherapy may be appropriate in some cases if the depression and anxiety are severely impairing the therapy process. Drug therapy must be approached with caution because it can easily be used as a means of further avoiding relationships by retreating into dependency on medication.

Additional Reading

Millon, T. (1991). Avoidant personality disorder: A brief review of issues and data. *Journal of Personality Disorders, 5,* 353–362.

M. A. CAMPION

See PERSONALITY DISORDERS.

Bb

Bandura, Albert (1925–). Known for his development of a social learning theory of personality and abnormal behavior. Bandura grew up in the hamlet of Mundare in northern Alberta. His undergraduate study was done at the University of British Columbia, and at his graduation in 1949 he received the Bolocan Award in psychology.

Influenced by the presence of Kenneth Spence at the University of Iowa, Bandura chose that institution for graduate study. The Iowa program emphasized theories of learning and rigorous experimentation. Following completion (1952) of his Ph.D. in clinical psychology under the direction of Arthur Benton, Bandura took a postdoctoral internship at the Wichita Guidance Center. He joined the Stanford University faculty in 1954 and has remained there since, except for one year at the Center for Advanced Studies in Behavioral Science.

When Bandura went to Stanford, he brought with him interest in learning and in abnormal behavior. Under the influence of Robert Sears he began investigation of social learning and aggression with his first doctoral student, Richard Walters, culminating in their books on aggression and personality. Further studies of observational learning and symbolic modeling led to several more books. More recent work involves self-regulatory mechanisms and self-precepts of efficacy. He is currently involved in study of the mechanisms by which self-referent thought mediates action and affective arousal.

Bandura's professional activities and awards have been numerous. Among the more prominent ones are serving on the editorial boards of about 20 journals, editing the Social Learning Theory series for Prentice-Hall, receiving a Guggenheim Fellowship and a Distinguished Scientist Award from the American Psychological Association's Division 12 in 1972, being elected president of the association in 1974, receiving the J. McKeen Cattell award in 1977, and being elected president of the Western Psychological Association in 1981.

R. K. BUFFORD

See SOCIAL LEARNING THEORY; MODELING; SELF-EFFICACY.

Bedwetting. *See* ENURESIS.

Beers, Clifford Whittingham (1876–1943). Founder of the mental hygiene movement. After his graduation from Yale University in 1900 Beers suffered a "mental breakdown" at the age of 24. He attempted suicide by jumping from a fourth-floor window. After a year of depression he was committed to the Hartford Retreat. In 1902 he experienced feelings of exaltation and decided to describe these feelings, writing at a rate of 12 feet of manila wrapping paper an hour. An assistant physician confiscated the manuscript, and Beers spent 21 nights in a straitjacket in a padded cell. Later he was transferred to the Connecticut State Hospital at Middletown and was released in September 1903.

Beers resolved to write about his experiences and to organize a movement to help the mentally ill. He knew that he had to prove his sanity, so he married and took a position in business. His autobiography, *A Mind That Found Itself,* describes his experiences. William James read the manuscript in 1906 and wrote a letter of approval that became part of the introduction when the book was published in 1908. Beers also enlisted the aid of Adolf Meyer, a leading psychiatrist. Meyer suggested that the movement be called mental hygiene. In May 1908 Beers founded the Connecticut Society for Mental Hygiene, the first such organization in the United States. In 1909 he founded the National Commission for Mental Hygiene and became its secretary. In 1928 he organized the American Foundation for Mental Hygiene and was its secretary until his death.

Beers also helped Clarence Hincks found the Canadian National Committee for Mental Hygiene in 1918 and the International Committee for Mental Hygiene in 1920. He organized the first International Congress on Mental Hygiene in 1930. His work to help the mentally ill and to prevent mental illness had a worldwide impact.

R. L. KOTESKEY

See PSYCHOLOGY, HISTORY OF.

Behavior Disorders. *See* Disruptive Behavior Disorders.

Behavior Modification. Behavior modification is "learning with a particular intent, namely clinical treatment and change" (Ullmann & Krasner, 1965, p. 1). Initially behavior modification referred largely to operant techniques and behavior therapy to respondent techniques. As early as 1965 the terms *behavior modification* and *behavior therapy* were used interchangeably (O'Donohue & Krasner, 1995). With publication of the journal *Behavior Research and Therapy* in 1963 and the founding of the Association for the Advancement of Behavior Therapy, behavior therapy became a general term for all of these techniques. Thus *behavior therapy* will be used in this discussion.

Behavior therapy is "the most influential therapy of the second half of the twentieth century" (O'Donohue & Krasner, 1995, p. xii). According to Krasner, 15 streams of research and theory contributed to its development. Among them were Wolpe's theory of reciprocal inhibition and B. F. Skinner's theory of positive reinforcement. Behavior therapy is often considered a simple-minded approach; behavior therapists are chided for thinking they can change the world with a supply of M&Ms. However, behavior theory is complex. It draws on many streams of theory and research and is applied to widely varied human problems.

Based on classical or respondent conditioning, behavior therapy emphasizes changing troublesome behavior directly rather than altering hypothesized internal processes (*see* Conditioning, Classical). Three basic principles are that learning theory provides the foundation; environmental events or stimuli control the problem behavior; changing events in the environment will change the problem behavior.

Behavior therapy uses a variety of techniques to weaken or extinguish undesired responses, develop or strengthen desired responses, bring responses under stimulus control so that they occur only as desired, and weaken or extinguish conditioned eliciting stimuli that produce troublesome emotional responses. Interventions include shaping and strengthening assertive responses; extinction and use of aversive techniques or punishment to weaken troublesome behaviors such as tantrums, aggression, and substance abuse; shaping desired responses such as attending school, performing assignments, giving correct responses, and the like; self-management (by rewarding desired responses; for example, taking a break after a difficult task or keeping a record of exercise and reporting it to a friend); and desensitization, implosion, and flooding to eliminate learned fear responses.

Recent Trends. Recent developments in behavioral approaches include the emergence in the 1970s of the social learning principles of imitation, modeling, and vicarious processes. Cognitive-behavioral models became common in the 1980s. O'Donohue

and Krasner (1995), however, consider the term *cognitive-behavioral* an oxymoron because it seeks to bring together emphases on internal processes (cognitions) and external behavior, approaches they view as antithetical. Further, they note that "behavior therapy in its original paradigm included variables that are now labeled as 'cognitive' such as feelings, thoughts, and so on; hence to add this new adjective is redundant, misleading, and unnecessary" (p. 20).

Perhaps the most significant development, however, has been the gradual emergence of integrative models combining elements of psychodynamic, behavioral, cognitive, and experiential approaches. Controversy will continue, although the integrative trend likely foreshadows emergence of a new paradigm.

Outcome Research. Outcome research provides support for the effectiveness of exposure desensitization for phobias and obsessive-compulsive disorders; behavioral and cognitive-behavioral interventions have been effective for depression, panic attacks and agoraphobia, social phobia, tension headaches, chronic pain, and bulimia. Behavioral approaches to marital therapy have been effective but seem to work best when combined with elements from other approaches. Finally, behavioral family interventions, along with maintenance on neuroleptics, have been shown to reduce relapse rates in schizophrenics (Emmelkamp, 1994). Outcome research on behavior therapy has generally been supportive but has strengthened the move toward integrative models.

Christian Perspectives. Behavior modification has had mixed reception in the Christian community. The chief concerns arise from behaviorism, the philosophical position of Skinner and many of his colleagues. Behaviorism is a philosophy or worldview that assumes materialism, reductionism, determinism, scientism, naturalism, evolution, and uniformity (see Collins, 1977). It often accompanies behavioral theory. Determinism is of particular concern to Christians. Christian theology holds that humans have some degree of personal choice along with accountability. Bufford (1981) argues that causality and choice form a paradox: both causality and choice are affirmed by Christian theology. Thus neither complete freedom nor determinism fits with most Christian perspectives (*see* Determinism and Free Will).

Another concern is that some behaviorists, notably Skinner, adamantly oppose punishment. Skinner holds that punishment is temporary and produces harmful emotional side effects. Bufford (1981) affirms this but points out that Skinner's view is inconsistent with the behavioral data. The data suggest punishment is effective and has both beneficial and undesirable side effects. Further, punishment parallels reinforcement, which also has temporary effects and emotional consequences. A Christian worldview is compatible in most respects with behavior therapy; many parallels exist with biblical teachings. For example, God uses reward (Heb.

11:6) and punishment (Heb. 12:6) and encourages us to be careful about social influence processes (Prov. 22:24).

References

Bufford, R. K. (1981). *The human reflex: Behavioral psychology in biblical perspective.* San Francisco: Harper & Row.

Collins, G. R. (1977). *The rebuilding of psychology.* Wheaton, IL: Tyndale House.

O'Donohue, W., & Krasner, L. (1995). *Theories of behavior therapy: Exploring behavior change.* Washington, DC: American Psychological Association.

Emmelkamp, P. M. G. (1994). Behavior therapy with adults. In A. E. Bergin & S. L. Garfield (Eds.), *Handbook of psychotherapy and behavior change* (4th ed.). New York: Wiley.

Ullmann, L. P., & Krasner, L. (Eds.). (1965). *Case studies in behavior modification.* New York: Holt, Rinehart, & Winston.

R. K. Bufford

See Applied Behavioral Analysis; Learning; Behavioral Psychology.

Behavior Therapy. A term applied to an exceptionally broad group of approaches to enhancing human welfare. The terms *behavior therapy* and *behavior modification* are increasingly regarded as synonymous. For simplicity only the former term will be used here.

History. The rise of behaviorism in the first half of the twentieth century set a stage for an application of this perspective to the clinical practice of psychology and psychiatry. The philosophy of behaviorism provided a view of persons as exclusively physical beings who necessarily act in accordance with universal behavioral laws and a view of science that eschewed all knowledge not empirically verifiable. Applications of operationistic, quantitative, experimental scientific methods in psychology produced what were seen as remarkable advances in scientific knowledge about animal and human behavior.

The typical practices of clinical psychology and psychiatry at this time were also influential in the rise of behavior therapy because of their disparity with academic psychology. Kazdin (1982) called the predominant model of this time the "intrapsychic disease" approach. This approach tends to look for psychological disease processes underlying behavioral symptoms. Further, this view encourages the search for symptom syndromes (or clusters), implying a common underlying cause for each syndrome. Treatment approaches based on these conceptions (e.g., psychoanalysis) were preeminent during this period.

Kazdin (1982) has documented that many treatment methods essentially behavioral in practice had been used before 1900. For example, Lancaster in the early 1800s developed and used what was essentially a token economy system for the classroom, and Brissaud developed a precursor to systematic desensitization in the 1890s. Use of expressly behavioral methods of treatment began to increase steadily in the first half of the 1900s. Watson, Jones, and others worked at conditioning and deconditioning fear. The Russian psychologist Kantorovich and Americans Voegtlin and Lemere used aversive shock conditioning to treat alcoholics. In his *Conditioned Reflex Therapy* (1949) Salter proposed conceptualizations of and treatment methods for abnormal behavior that were based primarily on Pavlovian conditioning models of habit.

In 1952 Hans Eysenck published his famous article in which he argued that there was no convincing evidence that psychotherapy as commonly practiced produced any benefits for clients above that which would normally accrue to them without formal treatment. This article scandalized the professional community and became a rallying point for the search for more effective (behavioral) methods for treating maladjustment.

Major developments began to emerge on three continents in the 1950s. In South Africa, Wolpe began to report his pioneering development of systematic desensitization for the treatment of anxiety-based disorders. In Britain, Eysenck, Rachman, and others at Maudsley Hospital in London were vigorous proponents of behavioral treatment methods similar to Wolpe's. In the United States an increasing number of applications of operant methods were reported. Ayllon, Lindsley, and B. F. Skinner worked with the psychotic inpatients, and Bijou, Staats, and Ferster did pioneering work with disturbed children.

The behavior therapy movement grew rapidly in the 1960s and 1970s. The character of the movement evolved remarkably with its growth. The publication of Albert Bandura's influential *Principles of Behavior Modification* (1969) marked an increased openness to the consideration of mediational variables and highlighted the diversity of views that might be called behavioral. Lindsley and Skinner in the United States and Lazarus in South Africa were the first to use the term *behavior therapy* in the 1950s. The first behavior therapy journal began publication in 1963; now more than 15 journals are devoted to that one topic, and many others publish a substantial number of behavioral articles. A large number of books on the approach have been published. Most graduate schools of psychology teach specialized courses in the practice of behavior therapy, and several major national and international associations exist for the promotion of behavior therapy, the largest of which is the Association for the Advancement of Behavior Therapy. Given their relatively recent development, it is remarkable that Smith (1982) showed that behavioral and cognitive-behavioral orientations are together the most frequent orientation of practicing psychologists who identify themselves as adhering to a specific approach.

The influence of behavior therapy has been on a plateau of sorts. The approach continues to show impressive outcome results with many discrete forms of psychopathology, such that recent compendiums of the most thoroughly empirically validated treatment techniques in applied psychology tend to be dominated by behavior therapy and cognitive therapy methods. Nevertheless, there have been few major breakthroughs in treatment methods in the last 15 years (see Bellack, Hersen, & Kazdin, 1990). There is less confidence today among behavior therapists that this paradigm will produce the grand unifying theory of human personality than there was in the approach's infancy.

Distinctives. Erwin (1978) struggled to define behavior therapy and came to the surprising but compelling conclusion that "no such definition is possible because behavior therapies do not share a set of illuminating defining properties" (p. 38). He proposed rather that a group of characteristics tends to be associated with what we call behavior therapy approaches. The more of these characteristics an approach exhibits, the more likely the approach is to be considered behavioral. The following list of characteristics is derived from Erwin (1978) and O'Leary and Wilson (1987).

First, behavior therapy is fundamentally oriented toward the alleviation of human suffering and the promotion of human growth. Second, it is a psychological rather than a biological form of intervention. Third, it is usually used to modify problem behaviors directly rather than to modify hypothesized psychological disorders. For example, the behavior therapist will attempt to modify a person's unassertive behavior directly rather than by exploring a hypothesized inferiority complex. Fourth, behavior therapy emphasizes current determinants of behavior rather than historical antecedents. If a problem is shown to be clearly related to a series of childhood events, the behavior therapist will focus on how these events are active in the person's life rather than concentrate on retrospection. Fifth, behavior therapy can be used sequentially (i.e., different problems in the same person tend to be viewed as independent, thus allowing for different methods to be brought sequentially to bear on each problem). Sixth, assessment, problem conceptualization, and treatment are individualized. In behavior therapy diagnostic groupings are used at most for economy of communication; the behavior therapist tends to doubt that such categorizations are the best way to group disorders, questioning whether they represent real species. Seventh, the therapist's role in relation to the client is that of behavior change consultant. Eighth, many behavior therapy techniques are closely related at least on a metaphorical level to classic learning theory research. Finally, behavior therapists are typically committed to an applied experimental science approach to clinical practice. Empirical confirmation of treatment effectiveness is emphasized and is the major criterion for judging the value of a technique.

Agras et al. (1979), noting that modern behavior therapy cannot be considered monolithic, differentiated four major perspectives on behavior therapy. The first they termed applied behavioral analysis. This approach is most heavily influenced by Skinner's operant psychology. Its practitioners emphasize the alteration of the functional relationships between overt behaviors and their antecedents and consequences. Intensive analysis of individual cases is the major form of empirical investigation utilized.

The second school was labeled the neobehavioristic mediational S-R model. Typified by Eysenck, Wolpe, and Rachman, this perspective tends to emphasize classical conditioning processes (to which S-R refers) while also using operant methods. Neobehavioristic mediational refers to the willingness of its adherents (unlike Skinnerians) to use hypothesized intervening psychological states in their conceptualizations (e.g., fear, anxiety). Their treatment techniques frequently assume the reality of mental events (e.g., systematic desensitization assumes that the person can really imagine a feared scene). These mental events are, however, viewed as being another type of causally determined behavior that operates according to the same laws of conditioning as all other forms of behavior.

The final two groups are dominant in contemporary behavior therapy. The third major group is the social learning or social cognitive group. Exemplified by Bandura and Mischel, this approach suggests that operant and classical conditioning processes occur primarily via cognitive mediation. Beliefs, thoughts, perceptions, and other cognitive processes are viewed as major determinants of behavior. Modeling and other forms of vicarious learning (learning by indirect rather than direct experience) are emphasized. Humans are assumed to be capable of limited self-direction, in that people can exert some control over the environmental and cognitive determinants of behavior (*see* Social Learning Theory).

The fourth major perspective is cognitive-behavior therapy. This perspective was inspired by Albert Ellis's rational-emotive therapy. Mahoney, Meichenbaum, Beck, and others drew from Ellis the emphasis on cognition as a major influence upon behavior but attempted to develop more broadly applicable and less philosophically loaded methods for changing human cognition. The differences between these last two perspectives is primarily one of emphasis on thoughts and behavior, with this last group almost exclusively emphasizing the mediating cognitive variables that are frequently described as an internal dialogue. There are numerous close connections between this last group and the burgeoning cognitive therapy movement.

Practice of Behavior Therapy. In her or his relationship with the client the behavior therapist is primarily a consultant in behavior change who serves as a supporter and motivator in the process of change, as a resource on clarifying the problem and designing change strategies, and as a model of more functional behavior. Therapy usually begins with behavioral assessment, in which the attempt is made to understand clients' unique problems in light of their current psychological and environmental determinants (see Behavioral Assessment). Treatment is carefully tailored to the results of the assessment process. Since client problems are frequently complex, treatment tends to be multifaceted.

The process of treatment varies with the specific orientation of the behavior therapist and the problems of the client. Applied behavior analysts are likely to use such techniques as material or social reinforcement, punishment, shaping, time out, token economies, prompting, and contingency contracting. Applied behavior analysis seems to be most widely used with mentally retarded persons, children, and institutionalized populations. Neobehavioristic mediational S-R therapists utilize conditioning techniques such as systematic desensitization, flooding, covert sensitization, and aversive conditioning. The first two techniques are widely used with anxiety-based disorders (phobias, obsessive-compulsive disorders, impotence) whenever a stimulus for the anxiety can be identified. The latter two are used to create aversions to stimuli in order to decrease the occurrence of such problem behaviors as sexual deviations and drug or alcohol abuse.

Social learning therapists emphasize methods that utilize modeling and competency building—such as training in coping skills, social skills, assertiveness, and communication skills—to deal with social interaction difficulties, anxiety-based disorders, and depression. Self-control is also a focus in this model; it can be taught by teaching the skills of self-monitoring, self-evaluating, and self-consequencing behavior. Cognitive-behavior therapists frequently use such exclusively cognitive methods as cognitive restructuring, problem solving, thought stopping, or covert sensitization. These cognitive-behavioral methods are used particularly in treating affective disorders (anxiety, depression, and anger), stress disorders, and pain; in children they are used to decrease impulsivity and increase academic skills.

There are few purists in any of these schools, and almost all the techniques listed for one group are used by practitioners in the other groups. The overall effectiveness of behavior therapy is difficult to judge. Some suggest that it is no better than other approaches. Reports suggest that it is extremely valuable in the treatment of specific anxiety disorders, behavior and cognitive disorders of childhood, interpersonal skill deficits, unipolar depression, sexual dysfunction, stress reactions, and schizophrenia (in tandem with pharmacotherapy).

Views of Human Nature. A major distinctive of the behavioral view of human nature is its emphasis on universal processes of human change, in contrast to other schools' emphasis on universal psychological structures, stages of development, or motivations. Because the laws of learning are emphasized,

there is greater readiness to appreciate the idiosyncratic nature of human life. Behavior therapists are less likely to emphasize commonalities of experience (e.g., Carl Rogers's proposed tendency toward self-actualization) but rather to focus on the way in which learning can lead to the development of practically any pattern of human behavior imaginable, depending upon the person's learning history and biological potential.

Second, the behavioral view of humankind (except perhaps for the applied behavior analysis group) is interactional in nature; that is, it gives serious consideration to both personal and environmental (physical and social) determinants of human behavior. To the behavior therapist dynamic views of personality underemphasize the pervasive effect that external events have upon persons. They believe instead that behavior originates primarily from intrapsychic causes.

In the most general terms the behavior therapist views people in terms of their "person variables" (Mischel, 1973), their biological heritage, and their environment. Person variables (also termed organismic variables or learning history) include the person's acquired response capacities, expectancies, and the myriad of other cognitive variables. Biological variables include physical assets and deficits, physiologically based emotional responsiveness, and conditionability. Social and physical environmental variables must be considered at all levels, from the most immediate and specific (the parent reinforcing the noncompliant child's misbehavior with attention) to the most broad and indirect (e.g., culture and language). If the pressure cooker is a metaphor for understanding human behavior from a psychoanalytic perspective, then we might say that behavior therapists would use the computer as a metaphor for understanding the human person. Input (environmental variables) is processed through the software (person variables), which is built upon the existing hardware (biological variables) to produce the behavioral output.

Most behavior therapists would argue that humans are hedonistic in nature. Behavior therapy therefore is maximally responsive to requests to end or decrease suffering and to promote growth toward greater pleasure and enjoyment of life. Behavior therapists have no a priori model of optimal human functioning toward which clients are led. On one hand this allows them greater flexibility in attending to client complaints, since they have no prior commitments to a concrete definition of normality. On the other hand this inevitably leads behavior therapy to be pathology-oriented, especially in its research literature, because people typically come for treatment wanting relief from a specific problem or problem complex.

Conclusion. Erwin (1978) has suggested that behavior therapy neither needs nor is consistent with philosophical behaviorism, which was part of its ancestry. Many Christians reject behavior therapy on the basis of its presumed close association with philosophical behaviorism (with its unacceptable commitments to materialism, determinism, and ethical relativism), though such a connection is debatable and has little to do with the practice and effectiveness of the approach. The behavioral emphasis on the potential for beneficial change of one's thoughts and actions is consistent with a scriptural emphasis on similar changes as critical to sanctification (Rom. 12:1–2; Eph. 4:20–32). Biblical injunctions to avoid bad company (1 Cor. 15:33) and to build the community of believers (1 Thess. 5:11–22) show an environmental as well as intrapersonal focus of Christian faith. In the Scriptures habit is a theme of human life (Heb. 5:13–14). The ever-present reductionism of behavioral analysis, however, can undermine our understanding of such critical human capacities as love and will, as when the former is described in terms of reinforcement history and the latter as the possession of self-management skills. More fundamentally the Scriptures suggest that both behavior and thoughts issue out of the heart, which is that central part of human life allied to or in rebellion against the Lord God. For the behavior therapist thoughts and actions are purely functional; there is no human capacity akin to the biblical doctrine of the heart. Overall the behavior therapies warrant serious study by the Christian counselor (for a more detailed evaluation, see Jones & Butman, 1991).

References

Bellack, A. S., Hersen, M., & Kazdin, A. E. (Eds.). (1990). *International handbook of behavior modification and therapy* (2nd ed.). New York: Plenum.

Erwin, E. (1978). *Behavior therapy: Scientific, philosophical, and moral foundations.* New York: Cambridge University Press.

Eysenck, H. J. (1952). The effects of psychotherapy: An evaluation. *Journal of Consulting and Clinical Psychology, 16,* 319–324.

Jones, S. L., & Butman, R. E. (1991). *Modern psychotherapies: A comprehensive Christian appraisal.* Downers Grove, IL: InterVarsity Press.

Kazdin, A. E. (1982). History of behavior modification. In A. S. Bellack, M. Hersen, & A. E. Kazdin (Eds.), *International handbook of behavior modification.* New York: Plenum.

Mischel, W. (1973). Toward a cognitive social learning reconceptualization of human personality. *Psychological Review, 80,* 252–283.

O'Leary, K. D., & Wilson, G. T. (1987). *Behavior therapy: Application and outcome.* Englewood Cliffs, NJ: Prentice-Hall.

Salter (1949). *Conditioned reflex therapy: The direct approach to the reconstruction of personality.* New York: Creative Age Press.

Smith, D. (1982). Trends in counseling and psychotherapy. *American Psychologist, 37,* 802–809.

S. L. JONES

See BEHAVIORAL PSYCHOLOGY; APPLIED BEHAVIORAL ANALYSIS.

Behavioral Assessment. Advocates of behavior modification and behavior therapy in the 1960s and earlier had departed widely from the mainstream of clinical and counseling psychology. They attacked not only the dominant conceptions of human personality and treatment but also the predominant modes of psychological assessment, claiming that unreliable and frequently invalid methods of assessment and diagnosis were used. They also claimed that assessment was intrapsychically oriented and thus tended to ignore important environmental causes of behavior, and that traditional assessment looked for symptoms of underlying disturbance rather than dealing with the person's behavior as behavior. The result of this was diagnostic judgment that had little to do with shaping subsequent treatment.

Behavioral assessment was proposed as an alternative system to more traditional techniques. Its major distinctives are associated with a greater concern for an individualized formulation of the problems and assets of the client as opposed to a description of the client in terms of broad diagnostic categories. More balanced attention is given to environmental determinants of the problems, focusing on what is causing and maintaining the behavior. This also involves a primary focus on the present rather than the past. Finally, an attempt is made in behavioral assessment to define the problem of the client in concrete, observable terms. Given these distinctives, it was hoped that behavioral assessment would be more directly relevant to the development of a comprehensive treatment plan to alleviate the focal distress of the client.

The process of behavioral assessment can be understood best by distinguishing between the information that the assessment is designed to generate and the methods used to gather information. Regarding the former, Goldfried and Davidson (1994) distinguished four major classes or variables that must be carefully assessed. The first is the maladaptive behavior itself. What characteristics or qualities of the behavior lead to it being labeled a problem? How can the problem be concretely defined so that it can be monitored throughout treatment? Second, the antecedent environmental stimuli related to the problem must be assessed. Under what environmental conditions does the problem occur and not occur? Third, the behavior analyst looks at the organismic variables. What personality variables are related to the occurrence of the problem behavior? The behavior therapist looks especially at the distinctive ways in which the client is interpreting his or her world that might be related to the occurrence of the problem. Finally, the behavior therapist looks at consequence variables—the results of the client's problem and nonproblem behaviors. Generally the ways in which the client's maladaptive behavior is reinforced by events in his or her life and the way in which more adaptive behavior is not reinforced or perhaps even punished are closely examined.

Many methods of gathering these data have been used. The most widely used technique is the clinical interview. The client is asked to be specific about the nature of the problem behavior and the factors relating to or causing it. Clients also might be observed directly to uncover relevant information. This observation might take place in natural settings (e.g., observing a troubled couple in their home or an emotionally disturbed child in the classroom) or in contrived settings (e.g., when the client is asked to role play a situation in which the problem would occur or an attempt is made to observe the maladaptive behavior in the therapist's office). Psychophysiological recordings might be taken to provide additional information about the physiological dimension of the client's responses. The therapist might instruct the client in the nature of the relevant information that would be beneficial to planning treatment and then help the client keep careful self-monitoring records to yield usable data. Finally, self-report methods might be used, with these techniques ranging from specially constructed behavioral inventories that ask about the occurrence of specific behaviors (e.g., feared stimulus inventories, assertive behavior inventories, marital behavior inventories) to use of the more empirically validated psychological tests.

The overall goal of behavioral assessment is to gather specific, concrete information that will be maximally relevant to planning treatment. Behavioral assessment is no longer as distinct from other broadly accepted assessment approaches. With the increased societal emphasis on professional accountability, most assessment approaches are becoming more problem-oriented and require higher levels of empirical validity for specific assessment methods. The most important criticism of behavioral assessment is that with all of the emphasis on empirical validation of technique, the behavior therapist still uses largely unvalidated assessment methods. The primary diagnostic tool of the behavior therapist is the old standby of mental health practice, the clinical interview. Many of the existing self-report instruments are psychometrically crude, with little attention paid until recently to assuring that they measure what they purport to measure. Behavior therapists have also developed complex systems for rating behavior but again have only recently begun to examine the validity of these systems. The field of behavioral assessment provides an alternative to many forms of traditional assessment; its distinctiveness, however, flows more from its theoretical base than from any firm empirical demonstrations of its superiority (Mash & Hunsley, 1990).

References

Goldfried, M. R., & Davidson, G. C. (1994). *Clinical behavior therapy*. New York: Wiley Interscience.

Mash, E. J., & Hunsley, J. (1990). Behavioral assessment: A contemporary approach. In A. S. Bellack, M. Hersen, & A. E. Kazdin (Eds.), *International handbook of behavior modification and therapy* (2nd ed.). New York: Plenum.

S. L. JONES

See APPLIED BEHAVIORAL ANALYSIS; BEHAVIOR THERAPY; PSYCHIATRIC ASSESSMENT; PSYCHOLOGICAL MEASUREMENT.

Behavioral Family Therapy. As with all forms of family therapy, the major purpose of behaviorally oriented family therapy is to help the family become a better-functioning interdependent group. Ideally this should result in improved communication, autonomy, and individuation, greater empathy, more flexible and effective parental leadership, reduced conflict, increased individual symptom improvement, and greater individual task improvement. The key differences in the varied approaches to family therapy are in how theorists and therapists conceptualize the interactional variables and suggest that specific interventions can best bring about desirable changes (see Goldenberg & Goldenberg, 1991).

Since the 1980s this particular tradition of clinical problem identification and problem solving has combined behavioral, cognitive-behavioral, and social learning modalities (see Jones & Butman, 1991). Great emphases are placed on establishing concrete and observable goals, the realignment of the contingencies of social reinforcement in the family system, the modeling and shaping of healthy prosocial interactional patterns, and the maintenance of a sharp focus on an explicit contract between the therapist and family members. As might be expected within this tradition, the therapist is viewed as a coach, facilitator, teacher, or trainer. It is assumed that by restructuring their interpersonal environments, family members will learn how to act more effectively with each other (Lieberman, 1970).

Diagnosis follows logically from contemporary cognitive-behavioral theory. Therapists carefully study patterns of reinforcement, extinction, or punishment in family systems. They attempt to make implicit goals collaborative and explicit. Their clinical interactions tend to focus on reinforcing desirable behaviors rather than negative, attention-getting behaviors. Modeling and shaping healthy communication and conflict-management skills are deemed especially important. More recently the literature has focused on the need to strengthen the repertoire of coping skills for family members as they face together the challenges of everyday living. Historically this approach tended to focus on treatment of the noncompliant behaviors of strong-willed children and adolescents, often at the risk of neglecting important structural and systemic variables that might be contributing to dysfunctional family processes (see Corey, 1996).

Behavioral family therapy has become especially influential because theorists and therapists alike have taken the need for outcome-based research seriously. In most other traditions of family therapy the link between theory and technique has been weak, making it difficult to develop a clear, rational basis for choosing one intervention over and against others. Whether the focus is on parent training, working with juvenile delinquents, improving marital or family communication patterns, or treating psychosexual dysfunctions, different expressions of behavioral family therapy share a strong conviction that learning principles can be directly applied to the clinical context.

Deceptively simple upon initial examination, behavioral family therapy has matured into a highly sophisticated collection of strategies and interventions that aspire to nothing less than restructuring the interpersonal environments of families. It can be a refreshing contrast to some of the excesses of individualistic approaches to people helping (see Jones & Butman, 1991). Behavioral family therapy takes seriously the need for firm parental coalitions and appropriate generational boundaries. When this approach can move families in directions increasingly characterized by grace, empowerment, and a mature covenant, families can become oases of encouragement and support in a world characterized by far too much cynicism and negativity (see Balswick & Balswick, 1987). When applied in a mechanical and reductionist fashion, behavioral family therapy runs the risk of becoming a victim of its own success. This once minority position has done a remarkable job of integrating behavioral and cognitive perspectives into a wide variety of important applications. It will become even more influential in this era of managed care (see Meyer & Deistch, 1996).

References

Balswick, J., & Balswick, J. (1987). A theological basis for family relationships. *Journal of Psychology and Christianity*, 6 (3), 37–49.

Corey, G. (1996). *Theory and practice of counseling and psychotherapy* (5th ed.). Pacific Grove, CA: Brooks/Cole.

Goldenberg, I., & Goldenberg, H. (1991). *Family therapy: An overview* (3rd ed.). Pacific Grove, CA: Brooks/Cole.

Jones, S., & Butman, R. (1991). *Modern psychotherapies*. Downers Grove, IL: InterVarsity Press.

Lieberman, R. P. (1970). Behavioral approaches to family therapy. *American Journal of Orthopsychiatry*, 40, 106–118.

Meyer, R., & Deitsch, S. (1996). *The clinician's handbook*. Boston: Allyn & Bacon.

R. E. Butman

See Family Therapy: Overview; Behavior Therapy.

Behavioral Marital Therapy. Behavioral marital therapy (BMT) approaches the treatment of distressed couples using the principles of both behavioral and social learning theory to understand problems and bring about change. Behavioral theory assumes that environmental reinforcers (contingencies of reinforcement) shape and maintain behaviors. Problem behaviors can be changed if the contingencies of reinforcement that maintain those behaviors are removed and more preferred behaviors are given increased levels of reinforcement.

BMT contends that the behavior of both partners in a marital relationship will be strengthened, weakened, or modified by current environmental contingencies, especially those involving the other spouse. Past learning history cannot be changed. Rather, the emphasis in BMT is to change the contingencies in the current environment that maintain or support negative behaviors. The couple is the unit of assessment and treatment, since individual behaviors are interactive and highly contingent on the response of the spouse. BMT attempts to use the reinforcement value of spouses for each other to effect changes in behavior.

Social learning theory maintains that all behaviors are learned through multiple interactions with the social environment. Over time both rewarding and punishing interactions will occur. If the rate of exchange is positive (i.e., higher levels of rewarding than punishing responses), then the relationship will be viewed positively. If the rate of exchange is negative (i.e., higher levels of punishing responses), then the relationship will be viewed negatively. Several studies exploring behavior exchanges between distressed and nondistressed couples support these assumptions by finding that distressed couples engage in fewer reinforcing and more punishing behaviors; are particularly reactive to negative behaviors; and rely on negative and aversive control tactics.

Perceptions of a relationship can be made more positive if the ratio of positive to negative interactions is increased or at least made more balanced (reciprocal). This principle of reciprocity suggests that individuals enter and stay in intimate relationships for as long as that relationship is adequately satisfying in its rate of rewards and costs. Marital satisfaction is conceptualized as a function of a cost/benefit ratio with spouses tending to exchange positive and negative behaviors at about the same rate. BMT attempts to maximize satisfaction and minimize dissatisfaction in a couple's interactions by increasing the benefits (rate of rewards) and decreasing the costs (rate of punishment).

The bank account model of marital exchange suggests that couples build up deposits of positive or negative interactions over time that determine their perspective on the relationship. The more "money" in the account, the longer the couple can go before having to balance the account. Thus couples with a long history of negative interactions may experience more difficulty overcoming the significant deficit in rewarding interactions that have built up over the years than couples with more recent onset of marital dissatisfaction.

The goal of BMT is to isolate the problem behaviors and then create a means for changing them. Therapy is perceived as a collaborative process in which couple and therapist work together to achieve commonly agreed upon goals. Treatment is usually brief and maintains a focus on current behaviors rather than past history. Assessment is an important component of treatment both initially and throughout the course of treatment. Behavioral assessment emphasizes direct behavioral observation, functional analysis, and the systematic monitoring of new skills and behaviors. Contracts are an essential component in BMT and are used to target therapeutic goals and to facilitate behavioral change.

The process of therapy generally follows a sequential pattern. The initial phase consists of assessment of the problem, identification of specific behaviors for change, and development of a therapy contract outlining the course and goals of treatment to which both couple and therapist agree. Treatment does not begin until both spouses agree to the terms of the therapy contract. Once this has been accomplished, the therapist moves to the intervention phase of treatment.

The treatment phase consists of several types of interventions. The first type of intervention focuses on structuring and increasing the number of positive behavior exchanges between the couple. This intervention is usually attempted early in treatment to create a positive environment for change. A typical example of this type of intervention would be caring days in which couples are taught to act as if they care for each other on designated days by carrying out small, specific, positive behaviors. The assumption is that changes in behavior open the way to changes in feelings. Another example would be an assignment to "catch your spouse doing something nice," which helps shift focus to positive rather than negative behaviors. The effect of these interventions tends to be immediate but short-term.

The second type of intervention focuses on systematic skill acquisition. Through structured exercises couples are taught to increase their skills in communication and problem solving. For example, in communication skills training couples are taught how to express emotions appropriately and how to listen actively to their partners. The goal is to reduce and clarify misunderstandings that arise in interactions and to increase appropriate expression of feeling. The skill-building process progresses through several steps, including instruction about the skill, behavioral rehearsal of the skill, feedback about the performance of the skill, and homework to practice the skill.

The third type of intervention seeks changes in behavior through the use of marital contracting. Contracts seek to make explicit the expectations and consequences of specific behaviors in the marital relationship. In drawing up a contract a couple specifies the behaviors each desires the other to perform more frequently and the rewards that the recipient is willing to provide for the performance of those specific behaviors. Thus each spouse agrees both to give and to receive pleasing behaviors. Contracts need to be agreed upon by both partners to be effective in inducing behavioral change.

More recently BMT has included a final phase of treatment focusing on generalization and maintenance of skills. Initially the therapist is active and directive in teaching and reinforcing the learning of new skills. Eventually, however, couples must be able to function without the reinforcement of the therapist. The therapist's influence must gradually fade so that couples can maintain the changes without needing the therapist's support. Several approaches to enhancing generalization of gains have been suggested, including gradual spacing of sessions and use of booster sessions at regularly scheduled intervals.

BMT is one of the most thoroughly researched approaches to marital therapy. Results indicate that the most durable effects are most likely to occur if communication and problem-solving skills are added to simple behavior exchange interventions. Studies of BMT outcome report that at the end of treatment about two-thirds of couples improve substantially, while about half improve to the "happily married" range on measures of marital satisfaction. Six-month and one-year follow-ups continue to show high rates of positive effects of treatment.

However, data indicate that by a two-year follow-up, about 30% of couples who responded positively to treatment will have suffered a recurrence of marital problems. These findings emphasize the need for BMT to develop better interventions for maintaining gains and preventing recurrence. Several studies have found that the best prognosis for positive outcome is associated with couples who are actively engaged during the session, have the ability to form a collaborative working relationship with the therapist and each other, and comply with homework.

The major weakness of BMT stems from an absence of a model of healthy marital functioning and the potential for a mechanistic, deterministic approach to therapy that fails to individualize treatment. The major strength lies in its documented effectiveness in teaching new skills and its ability to effect significant behavioral changes in couples' patterns of interaction.

Additional Readings

Goldstein, A., Krasner, L., & Garfield, S. (1993). *Marital therapy: A behavioral-communications approach*. Boston: Allyn & Bacon.

Holtzworth-Munroe, A., & Jacobson, N. (1991). Behavioral marital therapy. In A. Gurman & D. Kniskern (Eds.), *Handbook of family therapy* (Vol. 2). New York: Brunner/Mazel.

H. M. DeVries

See Marriage Counseling; Behavior Therapy.

Behavioral Medicine. *See* HEALTH PSYCHOLOGY.

Behavioral Psychology. Behavioral psychology is concerned with the conditions involved in development, maintenance, and control of the behavior of individuals and other organisms. Behavioral approaches have been developed in many areas of applied psychology. These raise a number of issues important from a Christian perspective.

History. Behavioral psychology grew out of laboratory studies of learning that began in the late nineteenth century. Applications of behavioral psychology to human problems are more recent, beginning around 1950 under the influence of B. F. Skinner and his colleagues. Most theories of personality, psychopathology, and psychotherapy can be divided into three to five broad schools. Lyddon (1995) proposes four models, based on Pepper's root metaphor or world hypothesis (ontology, or nature of reality) theory: formism, mechanism, contextualism, and organicism (pp. 71–72). Behavioral psychology is based on the mechanistic metaphor. Of contemporary theories, behavioral psychology is most clearly rooted in empirical research.

Ivan Pavlov, the Russian physiologist, was one of the earliest contributors to modern behavior theory. Pavlov's original work involved the study of the digestive system in dogs. He noticed that the dogs secreted saliva upon the sight of food as well as when food was placed in their mouths. Pavlov soon found that the presence of the lab attendant produced salivation and that ringing a bell or sounding a tone also quickly came to produce salivation if these events immediately preceded giving food. Pavlov's discovery came to be known as classical, respondent, or Pavlovian conditioning (*see* Conditioning, Classical).

John B. Watson, an American psychologist and an avowed materialist, soon learned of Pavlov's work. Watson vigorously objected to such concepts as mind, consciousness, volition, and emotion. He believed that psychology should be the science of directly observable behavior. Watson adopted the conditioned reflex method of Pavlov and played a major role in further development of behavioral psychology. Watson emphasized comparative psychology; he was firmly convinced that principles of animal behavior could be extended to higher-order animals and to humans.

A contemporary of Watson, Edward Lee Thorndike shared Watson's naturalistic and mechanistic approach to comparative psychology. Thorndike also believed psychology should be a science of observable behavior, developed through rigorous experimentation. From his studies of cats in puzzle boxes, Thorndike concluded learning takes place by trial and error. He developed the law of effect, which states that responses followed by reinforcement will be repeated while responses followed by nonreinforcement or by punishment will not recur. Guthrie, Clark Leonard Hull, Edward Chace Tolman, and others made significant contributions to the psychology of learning. Skinner is widely known for his work on reinforcement, which extended Thorndike's law of effect.

Skinner, an intrepid individualist, went his own way even though it was inconsistent with that of prominent theorists of his time. Skinner coined the term *operant.* He studied operant behavior through ingenious laboratory techniques that he developed. Skinner and his students contributed prolifically to the growing knowledge of operant behavior. Watson had conceived respondent behavior as the sole form of learned response. Under Skinner's influence respondent behavior came to be seen as a minor form of behavior, with most behavior considered operant.

Modern Behavior Theory. Behavior theory divides behavior into two classes, respondents and operants. Respondents are behaviors elicited or controlled primarily by preceding events. They are involuntary, involving the autonomic nervous system and the smooth muscles and glands. Respondents occur automatically following their eliciting stimulus unless the organism is exhausted or incapacitated; thus respondents are sometimes referred to as reflexive. Initially respondents are under control of a limited range of stimulus events determined by biological and genetic factors. Through presenting a new stimulus followed by the eliciting stimulus, new eliciting stimuli can be developed. This process is known as respondent or Pavlovian conditioning. Conditioned respondents can be eliminated by presenting the conditioned stimulus in the absence of the natural eliciting stimulus until the organism ceases to respond; this process is called respondent extinction.

The range of respondent behavior is limited. First, respondents are determined by biological factors; the responses are given with the biological characteristics of the organism. Second, learning brings the existing respondents under control of the new stimulus; no new responses are developed. Third, conditioned stimuli lose their eliciting capability very quickly. Fourth, most behavior is not respondent.

Operant behavior involves the organism acting on the environment to produce an effect. Operants are controlled primarily by events that follow them, called consequences. However, once the response-consequence relationship has been established, the response can then be brought under control of preceding events, called discriminative stimuli. The process is called stimulus control. Since much of human behavior is operant, the principles of operant behavior are extremely important in understanding human behavior.

Respondent behavior is measured primarily in terms of the latency or delay between presentation of stimulus and occurrence of the response and the intensity or magnitude of the response. Operant behavior, because of its greater complexity, is measured in several ways: rate or frequency, latency, duration, and intensity or amplitude. Rate or frequency is by far the most common measure, but the preferred measure of an operant depends substantially on the aspect of behavior that is of concern. Tantrums, for example, are often measured in terms of duration and intensity as well as frequency.

Operant behaviors are also determined by the biological characteristics of the organism: for example, pigs do not fly. However, operant behavior is vastly more variable than respondent behavior, and the initial number of operants is much larger as well. Operant behaviors include such behaviors as walking, throwing, grasping, chewing, swallowing, talking, and thinking. Virtually all behavior involving the skeletal muscles is operant.

Operant learning involves a variety of processes. Complex operant performances involve integrated sets of basic response units under precise stimulus control. Playing the piano involves common finger, hand, and arm movements. But the intricate control over the precise location, intensity, and timing of the movements requires extensive training. Complex operants are formed from basic operants by the processes of operant learning, which include strengthening and weakening of responses by altering their consequences, shaping, establishing stimulus control, and chaining.

The most basic operant processes are those that increase or decrease the frequency of a response: reinforcement, extinction, and punishment. Presenting a stimulus following a response with the result that the response increases in strength (rate or frequency increases, latency decreases) is termed positive reinforcement. Removing a stimulus following a response with the result that the response increases in strength is termed negative reinforcement. Presenting a stimulus following a response with the result that the response decreases in strength is termed punishment. The process of weakening a response through removing a stimulus that follows it is sometimes termed response cost. Extinction weakens an operant by eliminating the reinforcement that previously maintained the response.

In shaping, the form or topography of a response is progressively altered from an existing form to a desired form. This is accomplished through systematically reinforcing successively closer approximations to the desired performance. For example, in teaching a child to say "daddy" one might begin by reinforcing the vocalization *da-da-da* and then gradually shift to reinforcing only two-syllable vocalizations: "da-da." Gradually reinforcement would be provided only when the "da-dee" sequence occurred. Similar processes are involved in developing driving skills and in athletic or dance performance.

Operant stimulus control is developed by presenting a stimulus before a response. When the stimulus reliably predicts that a particular consequence will follow the response, the response gradually comes under control of the stimulus. Bringing the vocalization *daddy* under stimulus control, for example, involves reinforcing the vocalization *daddy* only when Daddy is present or when objects or events related to Daddy occur. For a young child, if the word *hot* reliably predicts pain when an object is touched, the child soon learns to avoid touching objects when Mom or Dad says "hot."

Discrete response elements are linked into integrated sequences by chaining. Through this process longer and more complex sequences of behavior may be developed. The example of saying "da-dee" is an example of an elementary chain composed of two response elements. Reciting the Pledge of Allegiance is a more complex example of an operant chain in which the entire pledge eventually becomes linked into a complex performance.

Since the 1970s it has become clear that operant and respondent processes continuously interact in an intricate fashion. Traditional distinctions between operant and respondent behavior also have become blurred. Operant-respondent interactions can be seen in at least four ways. First, the consequences following operant responses—reinforcement, punishment, and extinction—both affect the frequency of the preceding operant and simultaneously elicit various respondent behaviors. When Johnny runs an errand, Mother's comment "Thank you, Johnny, that's a good boy" not only strengthens Johnny's errand running but also produces pleasant emotional respondents.

Operants and respondents also interact through setting conditions, stimulus-response interactions that, simply because they have occurred, affect a wide range of subsequent stimulus-response interactions. There are many kinds of setting conditions: being ill, having eaten a good meal, smashing one's thumb with a hammer, and so on. When Johnny's mother compliments him for errand running, the resulting emotional responses will affect his response to other people and events for a time. Imagine what might have occurred if Mother had instead shouted, "Johnny, you dummy, you never get things right." The emotional effects thus elicited are an integral part of each operant-consequence interaction. Depending on which of these interactions has just occurred, Johnny's response to a wide range of events can be dramatically altered.

A third area of interaction involves operant conditioning of respondents. Miller and his colleagues demonstrated that autonomic nervous system functions such as peripheral vascular dilation, heart rate, blood pressure, and kidney output can be influenced by operant conditioning. While the precise mechanisms involved are a subject of controversy, these findings blur the distinction that has traditionally been held between operants and respondents (see Turner, Calhoun, & Adams, 1992).

A fourth area of overlap is species-specific behavior. Species-specific behaviors include such phenomena as imprinting in young ducklings. Species-specific behaviors involve a relatively permanent or lasting effect from a single learning experience during a critical time period in the development of the organism. Because they are so unusual, some theorists consider them a third type of learning.

Finally, emotions are thought of as respondent by many behavioral psychologists. Thus they are presumed to be automatically elicited by stimulus events that precede them. However, much of what we normally consider emotion is actually operant. Hitting, kicking, throwing objects, and so on are operants. Tantrums and emotional outbursts illustrate the complex intertwining of operant and respondent processes. Interventions must take such complexities into account.

Applications. Early application studies were isolated and had little impact. In the 1920s Watson and Rayner studied conditioning of fear responses, and Jones studied the elimination of conditioned fear. Other early work included the development of the negative practice technique by Dunlap and the principles of reconditioning developed by Guthrie and supported by the research of Jersild and Holmes conducted in 1935. Around 1950, Dollard, Miller, and Mowrer contributed to relating psychoanalytic concepts to learning theory. Skinner's *Science and Human Behavior* (1953), although largely theoretical, clearly advocated application of behavior theory to practical human concerns. In the 1950s two additional books were published, and journal articles applying behavioral principles to human problems began to appear more regularly. At the same time a number of psychologists whose primary identification was as researchers began shifting their research from basic to more applied concerns.

By 1968 the interest in behavior modification and behavior therapy had become sufficiently widespread that the first journal devoted exclusively to this subject, the *Journal of Applied Behavior Analysis*, was started. In the ensuing years research in applied behavior theory grew phenomenally. By 1980 several journals had appeared that addressed a broad range of applied behavioral research. Behavior theory has been applied to institutionalized retarded and psychotic persons, children in public schools, outpatient psychotherapy with adults and children, prisons, business and industry, and other settings. The scope of behaviors addressed is equally broad, including elimination of problem behaviors like tantrums, establishment of basic social skills such as toileting and education, and social concerns such as conservation of resources and litter reduction. Behavior principles have even been applied in Christian education and pastoral ministries (Bufford, 1981).

Many applications of behavioral techniques have been developed, including assertiveness training; social skills training; aversion therapy for alcohol and drug abuse and for sexual offenders; token economies for use with children, institutionalized psychotics, and retarded persons; systematic desensitization, flooding, and relaxation training for elimination of anxiety and phobias; and biofeedback for control of such bodily processes as temperature, blood pressure, and heart rate (Craighead, Craighead, Kazdin, & Mahoney, 1994; Emmelkamp, 1994; Kazdin, 1994; Turner, Calhoun, & Adams, 1992).

Issues from a Christian Perspective. Numerous parallels can be found between biblical teachings and behavior principles (Bufford, 1981). The reinforcement principle is consistent with the biblical teaching that one must work to eat and that the laborer is worthy of his hire. Biblical teachings about social influence indicate that association with wise persons or with foolish or angry persons results in learning their ways; these are paralleled by Bandura's (1986) concepts of modeling and vicarious learning. Biblical teachings that self-control is desirable and manifests the working of the Holy Spirit are at least partially comparable to the behavioral emphasis on self-control.

But while many parallels exist, behavioral psychology is highly controversial for Christians. Most of the controversy surrounds the philosophy or worldview (religion) of behaviorists rather than the science or application of behavioral psychology. Worldview issues include the assumptions of materialistic reductionism, scientism, naturalism, determinism, and evolution by many behaviorists. Christians also object to common behavioral views of the nature of humanity and to the focus in early behavioral work on overt motor behavior to the exclusion of mental, emotional, and relational aspects of behavior (Cosgrove, 1982). Some Christians also object to the behavioral emphasis on reinforcement or reward. Finally, at times empirical findings have been reported that seem contrary to biblical teachings, such as the findings that led Skinner and others to conclude that punishment is both ineffective and undesirable (Bufford, 1982).

Many behavioral psychologists are materialistic reductionists who view persons as nothing but complex animals. Christians object because they believe persons are created in the image of God, although humans clearly share with other animals the characteristics of eating, sleeping, begetting after our own kind, and dying. However, one can study the behavior of persons as material beings in relationship to their environment without assuming material existence is the entire story (e.g., see Koteskey, 1991). Thus reductionism is not intrinsic to behavioral psychology.

Another criticism of behavioral psychology is its implicit scientism. Scientism is the view that science is the only legitimate way of knowing. It discounts intuition and experience and explicitly rejects biblical revelation. However, it is possible to view science as a legitimate approach without making it the sole means of knowledge.

Naturalism limits reality to the natural order. Implicit in reductionism and scientism, naturalism is a common assumption among those who do not believe in a creator God. While rejecting naturalism, Christians affirm the existence of physical creation, which God pronounced as "good."

For many Christians the common behavioral assumption of determinism is the most objectionable. Christians affirm free will or choice. In its strongest form, free will is postulated as an uncaused cause of human behavior. Free will is problematic for science since it implies that human behavior is not predictable. Determinism suggests that responsible choice is an illusion and that all behavior is solely the result of material causes. Both free will and determinism are inconsistent with biblical teaching (*see* Determinism and Free Will).

The New Testament uses freedom in terms of one's relationship to God in Christ: "The New Testament idea of freedom is thus linked to the Old Testament idea, which sees freedom as connected to God as giver; this freedom is a freedom from the bondage of sin and its inescapable compulsion. 'Liberation from the compulsion to sin . . . opens up the hitherto impossible possibility of serving God'" (Bufford, 1981, p. 49). God foreknows and foreordains all things; thus from God's perspective they are completely predictable. God alone is free from external causes. Christian freedom involves not so much physical freedom from events and consequences as spiritual freedom from the penalty, power, and (ultimately) presence of sin. Slavery to sin and its consequences is contrasted with freedom to serve God and receive his blessings.

Another common behavioral assumption is evolution. Evolution is generally seen as antithetic to creation, although some Christians postulate theistic evolution. It is possible to view humans as both unique and similar to animals without assuming evolution. If persons and other animals are made by a common creator to share a common environment, we can expect similarities in structure, function, and behavior.

In many ways materialistic reductionism, naturalism, and, to a large degree, scientism and determinism are intricately interrelated. Once one is committed to a naturalistic worldview that rejects the notion of a creator God, these assumptions are easily adopted, especially for persons involved in academic communities where they are widespread and rarely discussed or subjected to critical examination and where such examination may be quickly labeled "unscientific" (cf. VanLeeuwen, 1982). Along with behaviorists, psychologists who adhere to the other major theoretical systems also typically make these assumptions. However, it is possible to adopt behavioral theory and methods while holding a Christian worldview. Conversely, it is possible to hold un-Christian worldviews whether or not one advocates behavioral theory.

Objections have also been raised regarding the behavioral emphasis on reward; some have equated reward with bribery. However, reward is a common theme in Scripture. We are told that God rewards those who diligently seek him and that on his return his reward will be with him. Similarly, the elder who serves well is worthy of a double reward. Scripture teaches that one must work in order to eat and that laziness leads to want.

Behavioral psychology is also faulted for neglecting the central essence of humanity. The Bible is clear in its teaching that persons function as unified wholes. Biopsychosocial and spiritual wholism is consistent with a behavioral perspective that emphasizes the role of what one does but strikes a balance and thus takes exception with early forms of behavior theory that tend to deemphasize the role of thinking, feeling, and relating. Recent developments extend behavior theory to include these aspects.

A final consideration is the effectiveness and desirability of punishment. Skinner and many behaviorists contend that punishment is ineffective and that it has a number of harmful side effects. Bufford (1982) shows that while Skinner's conclusions were plausible in the 1940s, subsequent data clearly indicate that punishment works. Though the direction of effects is opposite, reinforcement and punishment are otherwise similar: both alter the frequency of behavior; in both cases the effects are normally reversible but under extreme conditions may be permanent; both affect emotional behavior; generalization occurs with both; problems may arise from attempts to circumvent the contingent relationship between behavior and consequences for both reinforcement (theft) and punishment (unauthorized escape and counteraggression). To be consistent one must conclude either that both work or that neither is effective.

Christians believe that God created and continuously sustains the universe and that God's normal method of working in the world is through the world processes that he created and sustains. The naturalistic viewpoint of many behavioral psychologists holds that events may be explained completely in terms of natural causes. Christians believe that most events in the created order can be explained at two levels: first in terms of natural (or creational) cause and then in terms of divine activity. Miracles are a special class of events, at least some of which may be explainable only in terms of divine activity (e.g., creation ex nihilo); by their very definition they do not follow world principles and thus cannot be the subject of or ruled out by science. Thus science, the study of the created order, is one method of knowing and understanding the way in which God normally works. As such, science in general and behavioral psychology in particular pose no insurmountable problem for a Christian worldview.

Summary and Conclusions. Behavioral psychology has long raised concerns for Christians. However, most of the objections raised to behavioral psychology have focused on the worldview of many behavioral psychologists rather than on behavioral psychology as a science or on behavioral applications. Modern science emerged in the context of a Christian worldview that acknowledged God as creator and God's mandate to persons to exercise stewardship over the earth (Hooykaas, 1972). Stewardship requires us to understand the functioning of the world and implies that it is orderly. Behavioral psychology as a method for understanding human and animal functioning is largely consistent with a Christian worldview.

Early behavioral psychology ignored thinking, feeling, and relating. Recently behavioral psychology has begun to address these aspects of behavior as well as motor activities.

As an underlying premise, the notion that God is the source of all truth suggests that there is in principle consistency between good science and good biblical interpretation. While the worldview of many behavioral psychologists is incompatible with a biblical worldview, behavioral psychology per se is fundamentally consistent with Christian beliefs.

References

Bandura, A. (1986). *Social foundations of thought and action*. Englewood Cliffs, NJ: Prentice-Hall.

Bufford, R. K. (1981). *The human reflex: Behavioral psychology in biblical perspective*. San Francisco: Harper & Row.

Bufford, R. K. (1982). Behavioral views of punishment: A critique. *Journal of the American Scientific Affiliation, 34*, 135–144.

Cosgrove, M. P. (1982). *B. F. Skinner's behaviorism: An analysis*. Grand Rapids, MI: Zondervan.

Craighead, L. W., Craighead, W. E., Kazdin, A. E., & Mahoney, M. J. (1994). *Cognitive and behavioral interventions: An empirical approach to mental health problems*. Boston: Allyn & Bacon.

Emmelkamp, P. M. G. (1994). Behavior therapy with adults. In A. E. Bergin and S. L. Garfield (Eds.), *Handbook of psychotherapy and behavior change*. New York: Wiley.

Hooykaas, R. (1972). *Religion and the rise of modern science*. Grand Rapids, MI: Eerdmans.

Kazdin, A. E. (1994). Psychotherapy for children and adolescents. In A. E. Bergin and S. L. Garfield (Eds.), *Handbook of psychotherapy and behavior change*. New York: Wiley.

Kotesky, R. L. (1991). *Psychology from a Christian perspective* (2nd ed.). Washington, DC: University Press of America.

Lyddon, W. J. (1995). Forms and facets of constructivist psychology. In R. A. Neimeyer & M. J. Mahoney (Eds.), *Constructivism in psychotherapy*. Washington, DC: American Psychological Association.

Skinner, B. F. (1953). *Science and human behavior*. New York: Free Press.

Turner, S. M., Calhoun, K. S., & Adams, H. E. (1992). *Handbook of clinical behavior therapy*. New York: Wiley.

VanLeeuwen, M. S. (1982). *The sorcerer's apprentice: A Christian looks at the changing face of psychology*. Downers Grove, IL: InterVarsity Press.

R. K. BUFFORD

Behavioral Science. Behavioral science encompasses a number of disciplines that seek to describe, understand, and beneficially influence human experience. It has its origins in the rise of the behavioral movement in the early twentieth century.

John B. Watson, an early behavioral psychologist, rejected previous approaches to human understanding because he considered them to be too subjective and qualitative. Rather, he argued, the study of human experience should focus on overt, measurable behavior and should utilize the methods of natural science. Watson, along with a great many methodological heirs, sought to use controlled scientific investigations to isolate factors, chiefly environmental influences, that might teach or condition people to behave as they do.

Behavioral science has broadened considerably since Watson's time, addressing cognitive, emotional, and even faith factors, in addition to overt behavior. It still holds the central assumption, however, that empirical research is the basis of both theory development and practical applications. Behavioral scientists today may be found conducting basic science research on biological influences on behavior, doing descriptive or experimental human research with individuals or groups, or engaging in a variety of research-based applications in clinical, community, educational, industrial, forensic, and pastoral settings.

F. C. CRAIGIE, JR.

Behaviorism. *See* BEHAVIORAL PSYCHOLOGY.

Being/Becoming Relationship. An important intellectual tension throughout the history of Western thought is between philosophies of being and of becoming. Leahey (1992) traces the roots of this conflict to the pre-Socratic period and Parmenides of Elea (fl. 475 B.C.) and Heraclitus of Ephesus (fl. 500 B.C.). Parmenides articulated the philosophy of being and argued that eternal truths exist in the realm of pure being, apart from the changing nature of the physical world. Heraclitus proposed the philosophy of becoming and viewed reality as continually changing. He became famous for saying that a person never steps into the same river twice.

Western thought came to be dominated by the philosophy of being through the influence of Plato and Aristotle (Worthington, 1984). Plato suggested that eternal forms exist and are unchanging. Aristotle believed universals exist and can be discovered. The philosophy of being posited stability at the core of reality, which fit with the emergence of the Judeo-Christian worldview.

The philosophy of being was undermined in the eighteenth century through the influence of Hegel. Hegel denied that absolute truth exists and instead proposed the concept of the dialectic. The process of discovering truth, said Hegel, is one of becoming. In the nineteenth century, Marx applied Hegel's dialectic to political philosophy, and Darwin popularized the evolutionary paradigm in biology. In the twentieth century Einstein's theory of relativity further advanced the philosophy of becoming in science.

American psychology has increasingly adopted the philosophy of becoming. William James advocated studying the processes of adaptation rather than the content of consciousness. In the 1950s Carl Rogers integrated the philosophy of becoming into his theory of counseling, which emphasizes the process of self-actualization. Developmental psychology adopted the evolutionary paradigm to study the processes of change across the life span. In the psychology of religion Batson and Ventis (1982) were influenced by the process philosophy of becoming in formulating their open-ended religious orientation called "quest." The field of family therapy is also largely process-oriented.

Classic Christian theology stresses the unchangeable attributes of God. The Scriptures portray God as the absolute Being whose promises and commandments are not subject to change. Jesus is also unchanging (Heb. 13:8). "Being" is an important theme for a Christian worldview, yet becoming is also a theme in Scripture. Sanctification is a process of becoming more like Christ. By following Christ, the eternal Word, one becomes more fully human.

References

Batson, C. D., & Ventis, W. L. (1982). *The religious experience: A social-psychological perspective*. New York: Oxford University Press.

Leahey, T. H. (1992). *A history of psychology: Main currents in psychological thought* (3rd ed.). Englewood Cliffs, NJ: Prentice-Hall.

Worthington, E. L., Jr. (1984). The impact of psychology's philosophy of continual change on evangelical Christianity. *Journal of the American Scientific Affiliation*, 36, 3–8.

S. J. SANDAGE

See EXISTENTIAL PSYCHOLOGY AND PSYCHOTHERAPY.

Belle Indifference. A term originally used by Pierre Janet to characterize the appearance of unconcern manifested by hysterical patients toward their physical symptoms. Instead of anxiety there is an air of calm indifference. This may be a coping mechanism in that it can bring secondary gains of attention and sympathy that may help the individual cope with the conflict.

See CONVERSION DISORDER.

Bender-Gestalt Test. The Bender Visual Motor Gestalt Test, commonly known as the Bender-Gestalt test, is widely used by clinicians as a screening device for the assessment of brain damage. It is often included in a standard psychological test battery along with a measure of general Intelligence (e.g., the Wechsler Adult Intelligence Scale), one or more projective tests (e.g., the Thematic Apperception Test or the Rorschach), and an objective test of personality (e.g., the Minnesota Multiphasic Personality Inventory).

The study of the behavioral effects of brain damage deeply interests clinicians for several reasons.

First, they want to describe more precisely the cognitive or perceptual loss that often accompanies organic impairment. Second, they administer tests of perceptual-motor integration or spatial visualization like the Bender-Gestalt to determine whether or not brain damage (also called organicity) exists. Third, clinicians need to assess the possibility that cerebral dysfunction might be a contributing factor in the client's clinical symptoms.

The test itself was first introduced in 1938 by Bender and reflected psychology's concern at that time with Gestalt perceptual theory. The test consists of nine simple geometric designs that are shown to the subject one at a time and are removed after the subject has reproduced them. A number of objective scoring systems have been developed for both children and adults (Marley, 1982). Some clinicians, however, prefer to score the results intuitively, both as a measure of brain damage and as a type of projective device. In the latter, the individual's approach to the task is hypothesized to reflect a certain cognitive and perceptual style.

To successfully complete the task the subject must evidence visual acuity and adequate motor control. If these can be assumed, errors in reproduction would be attributed to cerebral impairment. An exception would have to be made, however, for an individual who reproduces the figures in an impulsive and haphazard manner. This is highly relevant information, but it more often reflects the person's style of approach to the task at hand. With young children immaturity can be a significant factor as well. The sensitive and intuitive clinician is often able to discern the relevance of these factors for differential diagnosis.

Classic errors on the test include rotation of the geometric designs, partial reproduction, and perseveration (the individual draws more than is in the stimulus design). The frequency of these errors is thought to be a rough measure of the type and degree of cerebral dysfunction.

There is an impressive body of research on the Bender-Gestalt test. It is a moderately reliable and valid screening device for the assessment of cerebral dysfunction. Recently there have been attempts to increase its validity by using a background interference procedure whereby the subject is asked to reproduce the designs on paper that already has randomly drawn curved black lines (Maloney & Ward, 1976).

If, after using this test in conjunction with additional tests and observational data, the clinician suspects the possibility of brain damage, he or she should consider referral to a neuropsychologist who is familiar with the Halstead-Reitan Test Battery, a promising approach to assessing the complex effects of damage to the brain. This should help refine or rule out the diagnosis. A referral to a neurologist should also be considered. Careful assessment is prerequisite for most effective psychotherapeutic interventions.

References

Maloney, M. P., & Ward, M. P. (1976). *Psychological assessment*. New York: Oxford University Press.

Marley, M. L. (1982). *Organic brain pathology and the Bender-Gestalt test*. New York: Grune & Stratton.

R. E. BUTMAN

See NEUROPSYCHOLOGICAL ASSESSMENT; PSYCHOLOGICAL MEASUREMENT; PERSONALITY ASSESSMENT.

Bereavement. *See* GRIEF; LOSS AND SEPARATION.

Biblical Anthropology. The study of the biblical view of humanity has been somewhat confusing, since a multitude of terms is used to refer to humanity. *Soul, spirit, body, heart,* and *mind* are a few of the key words that refer to people in their psychospiritual functioning. In the past much debate has centered on the so-called dichotomistic versus the trichotomistic models of humans. However, more recent biblical scholarship suggests that any time the Bible speaks of an aspect of humanity (soul, spirit, or mind) it is always talking about the whole person (Berkouwer, 1962). People are never fragmented or divided into parts; they are always viewed as a totality. This distinctive separates biblical thought from Greek thought, in which knowledge was seen as cognitive; to the Greeks, the accumulation of facts was something that could be abstractly discussed apart from the knower or the context of a personal commitment to that knowledge by the knower. Biblical thought knows nothing of such an idea but sees knowledge as something to be acted upon and demanding commitment by the person. Thus in the Bible *mind* and its ability to know refers to a response that involves the whole person.

It seems clear that the key biblical term for the psychospiritual nature of persons is *heart*. More than any other biblical term *heart* refers to the absolute inner center of humans. All the other biblical terms may often be used interchangeably with heart. They may give a different light on people in totality, but they do not indicate a part of them that is separate from or not included in their hearts. A brief examination of a few of these other terms will help interpret the biblical concept of heart.

Soul, Spirit, and Mind. The words *soul* (*nephesh; psuche*) and *spirit* (*ruah; pneuma*) are often used as parallel expressions and probably should be viewed as synonymous. Matthew 27:50 (NIV) reads, "And when Jesus had cried out again in a loud voice, he gave up his spirit [*pneuma*]." However, in John 10:17 Jesus says, "The reason my Father loves me is that I lay down my life [*psuche*]—only to take it up again" (NIV). Here both *soul* and *spirit* refer to the laying down and giving up of Christ's life and seem to be used interchangeably.

It should be noted that the highest experiences of life can be ascribed to either the soul or the spirit. In John 12:27 (NIV) Jesus said, "Now my heart [*psuche*]

is troubled, and what shall I say? 'Father, save me from this hour'?" In contrast, John 13:21 (NIV) says, "After he had said this, Jesus was troubled in spirit [*pneuma*], and testified, 'I tell you the truth, one of you is going to betray me.'" To attempt to differentiate soul and spirit based on these examples would be extremely difficult. Those who make a distinction suggest that *soul* refers to the individual's personal life, while *spirit* refers to the principle of life—the sense of a person being a spiritual being.

With the term *mind (nous; dianoia)* we find the same emphasis. The total person is always in view. In Deuteronomy 6:5 (NIV) God says, "Love the LORD your God with all your heart and with all your soul and with all your strength." There was no technical word in Hebrew for the mind, so we have the word *strength*. In repeating this commandment Jesus says in Matthew 22:37 (NIV), "Love the Lord your God with all your heart and with all your soul and with all your mind [*dianoia*]." Clearly his reference to loving God with the mind implies the whole personality is to be committed to an intimate and personal relationship with God.

Heart. Heart is emphasized as the center, the core of psychospiritual life. "Above all else, guard your heart, for it is the wellspring of life" (Prov. 4:23, NIV). In some of his harshest teachings Jesus rebuked the Pharisees, and in doing so he picks up the theme of the heart as central to human personality: "But the things that come out of the mouth come from the heart, and these make a man 'unclean.' For out of the heart come evil thoughts, murder, adultery, sexual immorality, theft, false testimony, slander" (Matt. 15:18–19, NIV). The heart represents the ego or the person. "Thus the heart is supremely the one center in man to which God turns, in which the religious life is rooted, which determines moral conduct" (Kittel, 1976, p. 608). Brandon notes that the heart is the source of motives, the seat of passions, the center of the thought processes, and the spring of conscience. He further notes that this incorporates what is now meant by the cognitive, affective, and volitional elements of personality (Brandon, 1967).

It is interesting to note that the uses of *heart* that refer to thinking, feeling, and acting are balanced enough to represent nearly equal emphases. The heart can then be said to contain cognition, affect, and volition. Delitzsch (1867/1977) states that the heart is the center of the pneumatico-psychical life, the life of thought and perceptions, the life of will and desire, and the life of feelings and affections. According to Scripture, the heart is the seat not only of emotion but also of the will and thought; all three spiritual activities converge in the heart (Delitzsch, 1867/1977, p. 307).

This biblical perspective underlines the importance of the heart and its key role in Christian life and thought. It is upon the heart that God looks (1 Sam. 16:7), with the heart that we believe unto salvation (Rom. 10:10), and from the heart that obedience springs (Rom. 6:17). The heart is wicked and evil (Jer. 17:9), and the heart is the internal source for all that is external in us (Luke 6:45). As the center of the person, the internal source of one's life, it is the core and seat of emotions, the center of emotional reaction, feeling, and sensitivity. The full spectrum of emotions, from joy to depression and from love to hatred, are ascribed to the heart. Says Delitzsch, "The heart is the laboratory and place of issue of all that is good and evil in thoughts, words and deeds" (1867/1977, p. 148).

If God views the heart as the central influence in the Christian life, then how is the heart transformed from being "deceitful above all things" to "white as snow"? Perhaps no more important question can be asked in philosophy as well as in psychology. The biblical answer is clear. The heart is changed only through relationship with Jesus Christ. All theology that deals with a person's change, salvation, sanctification, and glorification ultimately focuses upon the simple relationship that an individual can have with Christ. Neither the heart nor the person is ever changed in any other way. Evidence for this cardinal truth can be seen throughout Scripture. In the Old Testament only a personal relationship with Jehovah, the covenant God, changed a person. David says, "Create in me a pure heart, O God, and renew a steadfast spirit within me" (Ps. 51:10, NIV), and again, "Search me, O God, and know my heart; test me and know my anxious thoughts" (Ps. 139:23, NIV). The primacy of the heart is also set forth in Ezekiel. God says, "I will give them an undivided heart and put a new spirit in them; I will remove from them their heart of stone and give them a heart of flesh" (Ezek. 11:19, NIV). Paul repeats the same thinking in the New Testament (Eph. 4:16–19).

Implications for Psychology. This meaning of the biblical use of *heart* has several implications for the study of psychology. First is the emphasis on the hiddenness of the heart. It is presented as that which lies at the root of thinking, feeling, and acting, the core of people's psychic processes. Its depth and unknowability strongly hint at the modern concept of the unconscious. This is substantiated by David's prayer, "Search me, O God, and know my heart; . . . and see if there is any offensive way in me" (Ps. 139:23–24, NIV). Again, "The heart is deceitful above all things and beyond cure. Who can understand it?" (Jer. 17:9, NIV). The primacy of the intellect versus the primacy of the inner person or one's heart needs to inform the direction of Christian thought in psychology.

Second, the heart shows the importance of affect or feeling. The power of feelings is easily observable clinically, but to have the Bible point to emotions and feelings as an important part of people is significant. Since Christians have often tended to downplay emotions or make them subordinate to other functions, biblical teaching about the heart stands as a corrective against such views.

Third, the importance of relationships can be seen by the fact that the heart is changed only by relationship with Christ. This emphasis is found throughout the Bible, and it too has tended to be overlooked in Christian thought. The heart calls relationships to the fore in any discussion of Christian theology or psychology.

Fourth, the heart serves to inform us about the use of psychological thought. If a person's chief areas of functioning are knowing, being, and doing, it can be seen that cognition, feeling, and behavior correspond closely to these. Therapy should therefore involve all three if it is to be biblical.

Last, the heart must be the core that corresponds to the modern concept of identity. Cognition would emphasize self-image or one's rational view of himself. Affect would emphasize self-esteem or one's feeling about worth, value, or image. Volition would emphasize self-control or one's ability to control impulses and feelings. The biblical emphasis on heart suggests that all three components would apply to persons as observers of themselves. Thus a comprehensive psychology of identity must include self-image, self-esteem, and self-control mechanisms and structures.

References

Berkouwer, G. C. (1962). *Man: The image of God.* Grand Rapids, MI: Eerdmans.

Brandon, S. G. F. (1967). *Jesus and the zealots.* New York: Scribner's.

Delitzsch, F. J. (1977). *A system of biblical psychology* (2nd ed.). Grand Rapids, MI: Baker. (Original work published 1867)

Kittel, G. Kardia. (1976). In G. Kittel (Ed.), *Theological dictionary of the New Testament* (Vol. 3). Grand Rapids, MI: Eerdmans.

W. T. KIRWAN

See PERSONALITY; RELIGION AND PERSONALITY.

Biblical Counseling. The current biblical counseling (BC) movement began with the publication of Adams's (1970) *Competent to Counsel* (though its theological roots can be traced throughout church history as one of the historical responses to the integration of faith and learning, cf. Niebuhr, 1951). Adams sought to call and equip conservative Protestant pastors to counsel with demonstrable competency from the standpoint of the distinctive knowledge system of Reformed orthodoxy. This professional and intellectual agenda, catalyzed in part by critics of psychiatry such as Thomas Szasz and Orval Hobart Mowrer, flew in the face of the modern psychotherapeutic professions. Throughout the 1970s a vigorous turf war ensued between Adams and the evangelical psychotherapy community. By the 1980s the BC movement was largely isolated from the discussions of counseling in the evangelical mainstream.

The BC message and practicality provoked strong reaction, winning many pastors and alienating others. It promised that by doing better what pastors did best—expositing and applying the Bible—they might prove competent to counsel. As in any movement, fault lines, or differences in emphasis, appeared among allies. In the 1980s three main strands emerged within the BC movement, though people in each group continued to work cooperatively.

First, Adams's original emphases were carried forward by the National Association of Nouthetic Counseling (NANC), which emphasized the counseling activities of local church pastors. NANC tended toward a brisk, didactic, confrontational style, largely focusing on concrete behavioral change (this included authors such as John MacArthur and Wayne Mack). Second, John Broger's Biblical Counseling Foundation (BCF) emphasized laypersons and discipleship. BCF did not offer formal counseling but an extended, structured Bible study aiming at personal growth. Third, John Bettler's Christian Counseling and Educational Foundation (CCEF), along with Westminster Theological Seminary, emphasized training counseling specialists, both pastors and laypersons. CCEF's counseling tended to explore motives and belief systems and placed greater emphasis on the counselor's relationship to the counselee. Other authors include Ed Welch, David Powlison, and Paul Tripp and various contributors to the *Journal of Biblical Counseling.* Each strand differed in its attitude toward the environing evangelical psychotherapy community. NANC was overtly polemical and dismissive toward integrationists; BCF disagreed with integrationists but ignored them; CCEF interacted with integrationists and even reworked its model in the light of criticisms.

Three well-known psychologists—Larry Crabb, Martin Bobgan, and Henry Brandt—stand outside the BC movement but are often perceived as being part of it. In general they agree with the BC position that the Scriptures are the source of a comprehensive counseling model and that all nonorganic problems in living are moral-spiritual. But Crabb's view of the underlying dynamics of human nature (psychological needs for significance and security) put him at odds with biblical counselors, who perceive his work as a synthesis of humanistic psychology and Scripture. Crabb viewed the BC position's emphases on behavior change and confrontation as legalistic. (*see* Legalism). Bobgan's failures of intellectual integrity and civility discredited him among biblical counselors; from Bobgan's perspective, the BC movement was a dangerous "psychoheresy" because it imported psychological ideas and practices under the guise of biblical Christianity. Brandt participated with Adams in the late 1960s and 1970s but distanced himself on account of the polemicism.

Major Themes. Six organizing ideas unify the BC movement. First, it asserts that the Bible supplies all the formative ingredients for a comprehensive counseling model (the theoretical view of the human dilemma and its resolution in Christ, a wise and flexible counseling methodology, the institu-

tional locus for counseling practice, and the intellectual tools both to critique and profit from secular research and theory). Though most counselors in the BC movement accept common grace and the contributions of the biological and social sciences (e.g., experimental psychology, neuropsychology) insofar as they are descriptive, they tend to reject psychology in its therapeutic form and prescriptive role, particularly to the degree that standards of psychological health and dysfunction are defined from studies of human nature that explicitly avoid issues of sin and redemption in Christ.

Second, the BC movement insists that sin in all its dimensions and consequences is the primary and specific factor in the etiology of those personal and interpersonal problems that necessitate counseling. Though there may be some disagreement on specifics, biblical counseling at its best views sin as both external (words, deeds, strategies) and internal (motives, beliefs, attitudes, distortions of conscience and identity). It considers numerous situational factors as partly responsible for temptation and suffering, though within a context of God's sovereignty (including general life hardships, physiological factors, shaping influences from the sociocultural milieu, being sinned against, the devil).

Third, the BC position insists that Jesus Christ's multifaceted gospel brings the truth and power of God's redemptive love to resolve both sin and suffering. The goal of counseling is to help remake people in the image of Jesus, to sanctify sinners, and to sustain sufferers. Biblical counseling closely analyzes how sin and misery define the problem because it seeks to bring Christ to counselees in word, deed, and example. Biblical counseling is evangelistic with non-Christians, because when problems are understood in their depth and concreteness, Christ alone is the solution.

Fourth, the BC position believes that the biblical authors both teach and model methods of ministry adaptable to the varying needs of humankind. That methodology includes many things: the personal qualities of the counselor, demonstrable love for those counseled, probing exploration of the experience and responses of strugglers, and various forms of constructive and grace giving speech, and helping counselees identify and move toward specific change in belief and action that will address and redress their problems.

Fifth, according to the BC movement, counseling is preeminently the ministry of the church. Though the church often fails—pastors can be incompetent and their education inadequate, communities can be cold or censorious—yet Scripture indicates that the church is where counseling will come into its own. The church alone can offer the blend of both pastoral authority and every-member mutuality, the dynamics of both individual and corporate growth, the possibility of both remedial and proactive counseling.

Sixth, the BC position affirms that counseling should reflect the work of God who searches all hearts. The biblical counselor is to expose the plausible facades of secular models and discern the outworking of idolatry and falsehood at work in the church and counselee.

Major Concerns. The BC movement positions itself against three major social and intellectual movements: first, the twentieth-century secular psychologies that sought to systematically destroy the biblical understanding that human life and its problems exist *coram Deo* (before God); second, the mainline pastoral counseling movement (beginning in the 1920s and coming to full flower around 1950 with Seward Hiltner and others) which was thought to have harmfully inculcated the churches with the secular psychologies of Carl Rogers and others; and third, the evangelical psychotherapy movement (begun in the 1950s, consolidated institutionally in the 1970s, and became a major power in the church in the 1980s), which attempted to integrate the modern psychologies into conservative Protestantism. In the words of the BC position, these integrationists have mediated to the church an ethos of psychotherapeutic professionalism and many short-lived and unsound syntheses of Scripture and psychology. The BC position adds a fourth problem that it believes stands in the background of these three: the dearth of counseling skills and wisdom among both pastorate and laity, and the failure of the Christian mind to think carefully and theologically about the problems in living and the tasks of counseling.

Evaluation of the BC Position. The BC position aroused a strong response among evangelical psychotherapists. It struck a nerve by challenging secularity and calling the integrationist community to biblical fidelity. It might well be credited with influencing the community in a more conservative direction theologically.

However, a number of nuanced disagreements emerged between many integrationists and various proponents of the BC position. As is true of most ideological stances or positions, including the integrationists' view, there is no one BC position as to all the details and nuances. The preceding account has tried to get at the heart of the view, but, as with most traditions, the proponents fall along a continuum with respect to the many of the more subtle and even less subtle dimensions of the view. One must keep this in mind when examining the various critiques by the integrationists, for they may apply to one BC adherent and not another. Many critiques back and forth are mere caricatures of the positions and do little justice to particular viewpoints. As one distinguished BC proponent expressed it, often more heat than light is generated by these critiques.

Since we do not have space to do justice in a critique of the various BC proponents, it might be helpful to merely set forth how the debate in fact has been framed by the integrationists and BC proponents. The issues most central to the debate tend to focus around concerns of common grace, the impact of the fall, and the nature of science and professional issues related to counseling. Perhaps these controversies can be framed within the following interrelated discussions: whether science or clinical psychology can provide prescriptive insights for living (wisdom) by means of observing nature, particularly human nature; the extent to which the unregenerate can understand and profit from these insights; the parameters, role, and nature of therapy for the unbeliever in light of his or her ability or inability to benefit from God's wisdom in the Scriptures or science; the nature of counseling with respect to an individual's past, being sinned against, personal responsibility, the time element involved in therapy and the degree to which counseling is directive, confrontive, nondirective, and client-oriented; and the proper emphasis and reliance upon agents of change in counseling such as the Scriptures, the prayer, wisdom gained from nature, the Holy Spirit, the therapeutic relationship, human choice, and the underlying dynamics of the heart. In some cases, differences may be more about professional issues of skill and emphasis than about absolute differences over theory. In other cases, there may be some real conflicts over the truth of fundamental theoretical issues. In both cases, the disagreements are much more nuanced and subtle than is often admitted or understood by either side. The integrationist and BC adherent who together penned these words can attest to the truth of this oversight.

Additional Readings

Adams, J. (1970). *Competent to counsel.* Grand Rapids, MI: Zondervan.

Adams, J. (1979). *Theology of Christian counseling.* Grand Rapids, MI: Zondervan.

Bobgan, M. (1994). *Against biblical counseling—for the Bible.* Santa Barbara, CA: EastGate.

Broger, J. (1994). *Self-confrontation.* Nashville: Nelson.

The Journal of Biblical Counseling. Glenside, PA: Christian Counseling & Educational Foundation.

MacArthur, J., & Mack, W., eds. (1994). *Introduction to biblical counseling.* Dallas: Word.

Powlison, D. (1988). Crucial issues in contemporary biblical counseling. *Journal of Pastoral Practice, 9* (3), 53–78.

D. POWLISON AND J. H. COE

See CHRISTIAN COUNSELING AND PSYCHOTHERAPY; PASTORAL COUNSELING; PASTORAL CARE; RELIGIOUS RESOURCES IN PSYCHOTHERAPY; NOUTHETIC COUNSELING.

Biblical Psychology. *See* CHRISTIAN PSYCHOLOGY.

Biblical View of Persons. *See* BIBLICAL ANTHROPOLOGY.

Bibliotherapy. The term, from the transliteration of the two Greek words *biblion* (book) and *therapeuo* (healing or therapy), means literally "book therapy" (Smith, 1990, p. 146). The term refers generically to use of literary materials as a treatment technique aimed at repairing psychological disorder or inducing change toward growth.

Discussions and research in this area focus most often on printed material (books, biography, stories), but diversification of media makes a discussion of books alone too limited; mediatherapy might be a more appropriate and relevant term (Smith, 1990). Innovative programs involving theater, movies, television, and other single or combined media presentations are used as adjuncts to or substitutes for therapy. However, these applications have not been explored thoroughly in the literature. Thus bibliotherapy as the use of printed matter will be the focus here, but this discussion should hold for other forms of media as well.

Bibliotherapy has long historical roots. Sclabassi (1980) notes that the concept of growth through reading is an ancient one. Shiryon (1977) has observed that "literatherapy" has its roots in the Old Testament. The concept of bibliotherapy as understood today dates back to the emergence of the mental health professions. Benjamin Rush in the early 1800s and Alfred Adler in the early 1900s were pioneers in the use of bibliotherapeutic methods. Steinmetz's (1930) reported case studies of bibliotherapy with delinquent boys in the first quarter of this century represents one of the first formal accounts. Throughout the 1930s and 1940s articles such as Steinmetz's, although not experimental, established a foundation for bibliotherapy. More recently the cause of bibliotherapy has been given added impetus through groups such as the Association of Mental Health Librarians and the Bibliotherapy Roundtable (Smith & Burkhalter, 1987).

There are two major approaches to bibliotherapy: the didactic and the catalytic. These can be identified respectively with cognitive-behavioral approaches to therapy versus psychodynamic approaches. The didactic approach attempts to facilitate change by providing information helpful in analyzing problems, formulating new approaches to problem resolution, and motivating the reader to implement and evaluate change procedures. Glasgow and Rosen (1979) have reviewed self-help behavior therapy manuals that are but one subgroup of literature in this area. These works are generally intended to be used by the reader without professional help, but many behavior therapists use them on an adjunct basis during the process of behavior therapy. A survey of the self-help section of any bookstore reveals an array of such materials. Didactic books have been developed in areas such as fear reduction, weight reduction, smoking cessation, enhancement of assertive responding and social skill, parenting and child management, physical fitness, sexual dysfunction, marital enrichment, depression, and problem drinking (Smith & Burkhalter, 1987; Jamison & Scogin, 1995).

Catalytic bibliotherapy is substantially different, involving the use primarily of imaginative literature for the purpose of facilitating identification, cathar-sis, and insight on the part of the client (Pardeck, 1994; Sclabassi, 1980; Schrank & Engels, 1981). Identification with book or story characters can reduce the client's sense of isolation from others due to perceived uniqueness of his or her problems and can pave the way for catharsis. Catharsis, or therapeutic release of affect, can occur as the reader vicariously shares the powerful experiences of the literary characters. Finally, insight occurs as parallels between the reader and story characters are explored. Catalytic bibliotherapy has been used with children and adults, individually or in groups, as an elective adjunct to therapy and as a mainstay of the therapeutic content. Schrank and Engels (1981) reviewed the research in this area and concluded that positive recommendations for bibliotherapy far exceed conclusive demonstrations of its merit but judge that "catalytic bibliotherapy can be effective for developing assertiveness, attitude change, helper effectiveness, self-development, and therapeutic gains" (p. 145).

Although adequate guidelines for selecting, using, and evaluating bibliotherapy are lacking, some attempts have been made (Brammer & Shostrom, 1982; Gladding & Gladding, 1991; Gould, Clum, & Shapiro, 1993; Jamison & Scogin, 1995; Smith, 1990).

The effectiveness of bibliotherapy remains a speculative issue. Surveys of different groups of therapists (Atwater & Smith, 1982; Smith & Burkhalter, 1987) have shown that bibliotherapy is a potentially useful but underdeveloped approach to enhancing human growth. Riordan and Wilson (1989) reviewed research literature on bibliotherapy, found conflicting results, and concluded that bibliotherapy appears to be a popular research tool while remaining less convincing as a treatment modality, with the weight of research evidence confirming its value as an adjunct to counseling and psychotherapy.

References

Atwater, J. M., & Smith, D. (1982). Christian therapists' utilization of bibliotherapeutic resources. *Journal of Psychology and Theology, 10*, 230–235.

Brammer, L. M., & Shostrom, E. L. (1982). *Therapeutic psychology* (4th ed.). Englewood Cliffs, NJ: Prentice-Hall.

Gladding, S. T., & Gladding, C. (1991). The ABCs of bibliotherapy for school counselors. *The School Counselor, 39*, 7–13.

Glasgow, R. E., & Rosen, G. M. (1979). Self-help behavior therapy manuals: Recent developments and clinical usage. *Clinical Behavior Therapy Review, 1* (1), 1–20.

Gould, R. A., Clum, G. A., & Shapiro, D. (1993). The use of bibliotherapy in treatment of panic: A preliminary investigation. *Behavior Therapy, 24*, 241–252.

Jamison, C., & Scogin, F. (1995). The outcome of cognitive bibliotherapy with depressed adults. *Journal of Consulting and Clinical Psychology, 63*, 644–650.

Pardeck, J. T. (1994). Bibliotherapy: An innovative approach for helping children. *Contemporary Education, 65*, 191–193.

Riordan, R. J., & Wilson, L. S. (1989). Bibliotherapy: Does it work? *Journal of Counseling and Development, 67,* 506–508.

Schrank, F. A., & Engels, D. W. (1981). Bibliotherapy as a counseling adjunct: Research findings. *Personnel and Guidance Journal, 60* (3), 143–147.

Sclabassi, S. H. (1980). Bibliotherapy. In R. Herink (Ed.), *The psychotherapy handbook.* New York: New American Library.

Shiryon, M. (1977). Biblical roots of literatherapy. *Journal of Psychology and Judaism, 2,* 3–11.

Smith, D., & Burkhalter, J. K. (1987). The use of bibliotherapy in clinical practice. *Journal of Mental Health Counseling, 9,* 184–190.

Smith, D. (1990). *Integrative therapy.* Grand Rapids, MI: Baker.

Steinmetz, N. (1930). Books and the discipline problem boy. *Library Journal, 55,* 814–815.

D. SMITH AND S. L. JONES

See BEHAVIOR THERAPY.

Binet, Alfred (1857–1911). Pioneer in the development of intelligence tests. Born in Nice, France, Binet obtained a law degree from the Lycée Saint-Louis in 1878, but his real interest was in the biological sciences. Even while studying law he was attracted to the Salpétrière Hospital, where he was influenced by Jean-Martin Charcot. He studied medicine and began a career in medical research. In 1890 he obtained a degree in the natural sciences, and in 1894 he earned his doctorate in science with a thesis on the insect nervous system.

In 1889 Binet and Henri Beaunis founded the first experimental psychology laboratory in France. When Beaunis retired in 1895, Binet became director of the laboratory. That same year the two men founded the first French psychology journal, *Psychological Year,* with Beaunis as editor. This became the major vehicle for publication of Binet's research on intelligence. Binet himself became editor in 1897 and continued his research on intelligence until his death.

Binet conducted research in several areas, but he is most widely known for his development of intelligence tests. In the late 1880s and early 1890s he used tests measuring sensory and motor capacities but soon realized that these did not measure intellect. He then began to use tasks to measure attention, comprehension, memory, judgment, and other capacities. In 1903 he published his most important work, *The Experimental Study of Intelligence.*

In 1904 the Minister of Public Instruction in Paris appointed a commission to recommend procedures by which mentally retarded children could benefit from their education. Binet and Théodore Simon (a psychiatrist) were commissioned to develop a test that would pick out children who would not profit from the regular classroom. Such children could then be put in special classes. The first measuring scale of intelligence (1905) had 30 items arranged in order of increasing difficulty. The second one (1908) had 59 tasks grouped at age levels from 3 to 13 years. This test has been revised several times, standardized in different countries, and is still widely used today.

In addition to his work in intelligence Binet published such important works as *The Psychology of Reasoning* (1886), *Changes in Personality* (1892), *Intellectual Weariness* (1898), and *Suggestibility* (1900). Although he was productive in many areas, the concept of mental age was his most lasting contribution. That concept was later used by others to determine an intelligence quotient, the IQ. IQ tests became very popular during the first half of the twentieth century.

R. L. KOTESKEY

See STANFORD-BINET INTELLIGENCE SCALE; INTELLECTUAL ASSESSMENT.

Binswanger, Ludwig (1881–1966). Ludwig Binswanger was born in Kreuzlingen, Switzerland, into a family distinguished for generations for famous physicians and psychiatrists. He followed the career path of other members of his family, including both his grandfather and father, and earned his medical degree at the University of Zurich in 1907 (May, Angel, & Ellenberger, 1958). Binswanger interned in Zurich under the tutelage of Eugen Bleuler and was a resident at the Psychiatric Clinic for Nervous Diseases of Jena University, where his uncle, Otto Binswanger, served as mentor. He then joined his father, Robert, at the Sanatorium Bellevue in Kruzlingen in 1908 and subsequently succeeded his grandfather and father respectively as Chief Medical Director of the sanatorium. He resigned the role of Chief Medical Director in 1956 but remained active there for the remainder of his career.

Binswanger was one of the major pioneers and proponents of existential psychology. He wrote extensively on this topic but is known best in the United States for *Sigmund Freud: Reminiscences of a Friendship* (1958), *The Existential Analysis School of Thought* (1958), *The Case of Ellen West: An Anthropological-Clinical Study* (1958), and *Being-in-the-World* (1963).

Binswanger applied themes of existential philosophy, especially the thoughts of Martin Heidegger (e.g., *Analysis of Being* or *Daseins Analytics*), to psychology and psychiatry. The approach was called existential analysis and represented study of the essential meaning and characteristics of being human. Central to this orientation to psychotherapy is the concept of being-in-the-world, which seeks to describe the whole of a person's existence. Each person develops his or her own world design or mode of being-in-the-world. Being-in-the-world consists of three simultaneous aspects of reality: The *Umwelt* (world around) represents biological or physical reality that surrounds the individual; the *Mitwelt* (with-world) refers to the social or human environment; and the *Eigenwelt* (own-world) depicts the person's relationship to self.

Binswanger, as is typical of existential exponents, rejected positivism, rigid determinism, and materialism. He viewed human beings as free and completely responsible for their own choices and way of being-in-the-world. Becoming is important to human development; the person is ever free to become more than one is in the moment and to transcend opposing forces and realize full possibilities of being. The person who refuses to become remains static. Neurotic and psychotic symptoms develop, which indicate a refusal to grow or become. The goal in life is authentic existence; therefore, allowing dominance by others or yielding to environmental forces leads to lack of freedom and inauthentic existence.

The therapy process in existential analysis seeks to help individuals with disordered modes of being to reconstruct the inner world of existence so they can affirm personal freedom, assume responsibility for making new decisions, and design an authentic way of being-in-the-world.

References

Binswanger, L. (1958). *Sigmund Freud: Reminiscences of a friendship*. New York: Grune & Stratton.

Binswanger, L. (1958). The existential analysis school of thought. In R. May, E. Angel, & H. F. Ellenberger (Eds.), *Existence: A new dimension in psychiatry and psychology*. New York: Basic.

Binswanger, L. (1958). The case of Ellen West: An anthropological-clinical study. In R. May, E. Angel, & H. F. Ellenberger (Eds.), *Existence: A new dimension in psychiatry and psychology*. New York: Basic.

Binswanger, L. (1963). *Being-in-the-world*. New York: Basic.

May, R., Angel, E., & Ellenberger, H. F. (Eds.). (1958). *Existence: A new dimension in psychiatry and psychology*. New York: Basic.

D. SMITH

See EXISTENTIAL PSYCHOLOGY AND PSYCHOTHERAPY.

Biocentric Therapy. In the 1960s Nathaniel Branden developed a system of psychology and therapy in response to the limitations of the deterministic view evident in both psychoanalysis and behaviorism. Called biocentric therapy (biologically oriented and life-centered), this cognitive and experiential approach has its roots in the philosophies of Aristotle and Rand (1964) and stresses the importance of fully actualizing all of humans' capacities to achieve maturity and maintain mental health.

Basic to Branden's thinking is the belief that the individual plays a vital and active role in his or her personal psychological development and achievement of self-esteem. The essential elements in this self-creative process are the ability to reason, the decision either to use that faculty or to suppress it, and the conscious and subconscious value judgments that influence one's emotions and behavior. Anything that blocks or distorts one's reason, volition, values, and emotions results in maladaptive behavior and decreased self-esteem. In biocentric therapy the failure to achieve a healthy sense of self-esteem is the basis for all neurotic disorders, and symptoms are viewed as undesirable solutions to real problems.

The goal of therapy (Branden, 1969, 1971) is to improve the thinking process and to eliminate the blocks to awareness so that new alternatives become available. Biocentric therapy makes use of a wide variety of techniques such as psychodrama, hypnosis, homework assignments, and breathing exercises that are meant to incorporate the best aspects of both cognitive and emotive therapies in dealing with the whole person. Unique to biocentric therapy is the use of sentence completion tasks, which serve as a powerful tool in eliciting a client's repressed feelings and images and which bring about a reintegration of cognitive and affective experience.

According to Branden, the more one is aware of all aspects of oneself and the world outside, the better one can responsibly function to meet unique needs and enhance well-being. Throughout his works he stresses the survival value of the virtues of rationality, independence, honesty, integrity, justice, productiveness, and pride. However, he defines all of these in terms of the objectivist's ethics of rational self-interest, which hold that every person is an end in himself or herself and that attaining one's own happiness is one's highest moral purpose. There is no room in this philosophy for self-sacrifice or for the dynamics of faith, as reason in the pursuit of self-interest is the only reality.

References

Branden, N. (1969). *The psychology of self-esteem*. Los Angeles: Nash.

Branden, N. (1971). *The disowned self*. Los Angeles: Nash.

Rand, A. (1964). *The virtue of selfishness*. New York: New American Library.

W. C. DREW

See SELF-ACTUALIZATION.

Bioenergetic Analysis. A form of psychotherapy founded by Alexander Lowen. Lowen was a student of Reich, who was a contemporary of Sigmund Freud and the originator of body psychotherapy. Lowen continued the work of Reich in the analysis of bodily-muscular expressions of mental illness and in the development of techniques for releasing those tensions.

Bioenergetic Theory. In the theory of body psychotherapy it is believed that the person experiences the reality of the world primarily through the body (Lowen, 1975). The sense of individual identity stems from a feeling of contact with the body. Without openness to bodily feeling and attitudes, a person becomes split into a disembodied spirit or mind and an increasingly inflexible, deadened body (Lowen, 1967).

The problem in mental illness, according to body psychotherapy, is the tendency to repress or implode (i.e., to hold within and refuse to express) viscerally experienced feeling. The source of this repression is the growing child's desire to avoid the loss of love by conforming to what the child perceives to be the expectations of others. The child relies upon his or her mind to figure out what is expected and then attempts to perform those behaviors that will ensure love. A result of this process is that the cerebral cortex struggles to gain control over the naturally experienced body emotion. The intelligence of the individual is funneled into ego, and the ego is increasingly split off from the needs and experiences of the body. This split is viewed as neurotic, since mind (the cognitive functions) and body (the visceral feelings and responses) are one unitary process.

The result of long-term repression of bodily experience in favor of adaptation to the demands of society can be rigidification of the body. This is referred to as increasing muscular armor. Muscular armoring is accompanied by physical tension and the experience of deadness and isolation. Increasingly the cerebral cortex censors and controls as much of the experience of life as possible. Knowledge becomes increasingly intellectual, cut off from the inner depths of the person.

Control becomes key in the life of such individuals. They are turned inward. Thoughts and fantasies replace feeling and action. Exaggerated mental activity substitutes for contact with the real world, and belief systems replace aliveness. Faith, hope, and love are increasingly superstitious, pietistic, legalistic, and/or authoritarian. Belief becomes objectified rather than experienced from within. Interpersonal relationships also suffer as other people become objects to be navigated around in life rather than persons to be intimately engaged. The rich inner life of emotions is squeezed to a trickle except for moments of sentimentally or vicariously experienced strong emotion, such as through films, sports, and mass behavior.

Bioenergetic analysis attempts to alleviate this alienation between ego and body and thereby assist clients in their pursuit of faith and happiness. According to Lowen, faith comes from the heart, which is literally surrounded by flexible and nonrigid muscles. Thus the pursuit of faith and happiness entails releasing tension throughout the body.

Bioenergetic analysis also theorizes that different childhood developmental experiences result in different types of muscular armoring and thereby different personality or character types. Lowen devoted much attention to the analysis of and the therapeutic intervention with the different character types (Lowen, 1958). For example, masochism is characterized by intense muscular tension, often resulting in muscle spasms and pain. Other character types include the hysterical, the schizoid, the "rigid character structures," and the oral. In each of these different character types childhood developmental issues differ, and the resulting muscular armoring, in both its intensity and location in the body, also differs. The different character types are treated therapeutically in different ways.

Bioenergetic Therapy. Therapy in bioenergetic analysis centers on increasing the internal unity of body and psyche. Body psychotherapy is a combination of physical exercises, catalytic therapist touch, and traditional verbal interactions. The physical exercises are aimed at stretching, relaxing, and opening the tensions in the body so that the deeper emotions and repressed memories of the individual can be reintegrated.

At times the therapist will encourage the patient to express some emotion strongly. This might take the form of pounding on a pillow with a tennis racket to release anger long denied expression. The expression of feeling in a physical way begins the reintegrative process of allowing the ego and the body to once again communicate freely. To Lowen this is the beginning of faith and the emergence of true self. Feelings may emerge that at first seem to be unjustified or irrational but which, upon closer examination, become understandable and logical.

Evaluation. One of the major strengths of bioenergetic analysis is its attempt to avoid sterile and passive verbal reflections that can characterize traditional psychotherapy and to utilize the dramatic power of integrating body experience in therapy. One of the major criticisms of body psychotherapies is the tendency among some practitioners to be antiintellectual. The client can be encouraged into emotional experiences and bodily movement without much sense of their purpose or meaning. The release of emotion in the therapy process can be seen as an end in itself rather than a purposeful step in the unification of mind and body. This can lead to valuing the expression of feelings regardless of the social context or interpersonal impact. Another criticism of body psychotherapy is that it can create an unnecessary amount of confusion and disorientation. During the de-armoring process it is important that sufficient direction, nurturance, and support be given. During this stage patients are vulnerable to confusing or even harmful impulses and inputs in their lives.

Bioenergetic analysis and other body psychotherapies have relevant concepts for Christian culture. Throughout the history of Christianity there has been a tendency to disconnect the Christian faith from the body and to reduce the Christian message to abstract theology. A theology that flows only from a detached intellect is more likely to be a statement of the status quo than a compassionate, courageous spirituality. The Pharisees, for example, were condemned not for carnal sins but for an egoistic perversion of the truth in which the letter rather than the heart of the law was worshiped.

Knowledge, Lowen argues, is a surface phenomenon and belongs to the ego, while truth flows through the whole being. We are advised in Ephesians 5 to know the love of God though it is beyond knowledge. Lowen postulates that knowledge becomes understanding when it is coupled with feeling. The Scriptures argue that the devil knows the truth and yet does not embrace it. Sin and faith are holistic realities, not just physical and mental realities. Faith and life become integrated because the person is integrated, body and soul.

References

Lowen, A. (1958). *Physical dynamics of character structure.* New York: Grune & Stratton.

Lowen, A. (1967). *The betrayal of the body.* New York: Macmillan.

Lowen, A. (1970). *Pleasure.* New York: Coward-McCann.

Lowen, A. (1975). *Bioenergetics and the language of the body.* New York: Coward, McCann & Geoghegan.

C. E. BARSHINGER AND L. E. LaROWE

See PHYSICAL CONTACT IN THERAPY; PRIMAL THERAPY.

Biofeedback Training. Biofeedback training consists of reporting back to individuals, through instrumentation, information about their physiological functions in order to help them modify or regulate their biological responses. The goals are twofold: to develop increased physiological self-awareness in order to control specific internal functions and to transfer that control from therapy to other areas of one's life.

Self-regulation through such techniques as progressive relaxation and autogenic training was developed 50 years before clinical biofeedback training, but the clinical results were not well substantiated until instrumentation was developed to record the data. This prevented biofeedback training from making an impact on psychology and medicine until the l960s. Since then biofeedback training has emerged as a new frontier in the treatment of stress diseases but only continued up to the late 1980s, when the popularity of the use of various instruments to measure physiological responses diminished.

Most modern medical textbooks attribute between 50% and 80% of all diseases to psychosomatic or stress-related origins. Stress causes inappropriate heightening of arousal that includes increased heart rate, muscle tension, blood pressure, palm sweating, and peripheral vascular constriction. In many cases there is also rapid respiration. This stress reaction is theorized as a contributing factor to many serious diseases.

The underlying principle behind biofeedback is that stress and nonstress states cannot exist in the human organism at the same moment. Biofeedback training uses such instruments as the electromyograph, skin surface thermometer, and electrodermalgraph (or galvanic skin response) to help train individuals to monitor and reduce their stress levels.

The immediate feedback, either by a tone or a light or by observing a needle on a panel, allows patients to immediately know if they are relaxing or becoming more tense.

The electromyograph measures the electronic activity of muscles. Electrodes are attached to various parts of the body (e.g., to the forehead and/or back of the neck in the treatment of tension headaches). The instrument has been shown to be quite successful in the treatment of tension headaches and has shown some promise in the treatment of generalized tension (Katkin & Goldband, 1980). The thermal unit measures skin (peripheral) temperature. The sensors are usually attached to the fingertips. As the smooth muscles around peripheral blood vessels dilate during relaxation, the skin temperature rises. The thermal unit is frequently used in the treatment of migraine headaches, Raynaud's disease, and hypertension (Fuller, 1977). The electrodermalgraph measures the level of skin conductance. It is used to show the client areas of stress that need to be dealt with, such as fear, anger, or anxiety. It also can be used to aid the therapist in creating a hierarchy for systematic desensitization and guided imagery.

The stress management program asks individuals to initiate physiological change through focusing their attention on their biological functioning. Many times this is accomplished through relaxation exercises that focus on relaxing various parts or the whole body. The instrumentation gives feedback as to the effectiveness of the relaxation effort.

Not all patients respond to biofeedback training, nor should all individuals be considered for such treatment. The training aspects of treatment can be discouraging, especially to individuals who expect a quick cure. Persons suffering from myocardial infarction or diabetes should not be considered for biofeedback training on an outpatient basis. Psychological conditions in the psychotic range, especially paranoia, are also inappropriate for biofeedback training.

Although the most frequent applications of biofeedback training have been to stress-related disorders, other applications have emerged. Biofeedback has become a central focus of behavioral medicine (*see* Health Psychology) and has shown much promise in such areas as muscular rehabilitation, epilepsy control, panic attack, phobias, sleep disorders, peptic ulcers, Tourette's disorder, and the treatment of cardiac dysfunction (Miller-Laurence, 1989). Some research seems to suggest that biofeedback training may be even more successful in these areas than in the more traditional psychological areas such as anxiety reduction (Katkin & Goldband, 1980).

With this trend, quality control in training and practice becomes an increasing problem. The Biofeedback Society of America began in 1981 to administer a certification test to biofeedback personnel. Although this is a step in the right direction, therapists continue to adopt biofeedback procedures with minimal training and no certification.

References

Fuller, G. D. (1977). *Biofeedback*. San Francisco: Biofeedback Press.

Katkin, E. S., & Goldband, S. (1980). Biofeedback. In F. Kanfer & A. Goldstein (Eds.), *Helping people change* (2nd ed.). New York: Pergamon.

Miller-Laurence, M. (1989, November). What biofeedback does (and doesn't) do. *Psychology Today, 23,* 22–24.

M. A. CAMPION

See STRESS; TENSION; BEHAVIOR THERAPY.

Biopsychosocial Rehabilitation. A multimodel, multidisciplinary, and integrated approach first defined by Engel (1980) and expanded by Liberman (1988) and others for the treatment of biologically based psychological disorders.

Coordinating the efforts of psychiatrists, psychologists, and social workers, this interdisciplinary approach seeks the rehabilitation of the whole person by targeting all areas impacted by a mental illness. Therapeutically this approach addresses the biological through appropriate use of medications; the psychological through behavioral self-management, problem solving, and skill development; and the social through development of social and vocational skills with community involvement. Providing support, education, encouragement, and in vivo practice of learned skills, interventions have as a goal that each person achieves his or her highest possible level of autonomous living, work, and socialization in the community. Although this approach has been used to successfully treat phobias, panic disorders, obsessive-compulsive disorders, and eating disorders, its primary use has been in the treatment of psychotic disorders, including schizophrenia, schizoaffective, bipolar, and major depression with psychotic features.

Common core concepts and values of biopsychosocial rehabilitation are consistent with a biblical understanding of persons: their need for relatedness and their role in the world. Concepts and values related to personhood include a central commitment to developing each individual's capabilities to the fullest extent, facilitating one's adaptation to environmental realities or adapting social and physical environments to the person's capabilities, building upon a person's strengths while improving competencies, and increasing self-esteem while restoring hope.

Concepts and values associated with our need for relatedness involve the development of one's social and recreational life by training in social skills, resocialization programs, and sponsoring social clubs. Finally, concepts and values related to the person's place in the world include a commitment to each person's vocational potential. Work is viewed as providing the income to permit autonomy, structuring of time and space, broadening of social contacts, provision of a recognizable societal role, and facilitating activity and involvement.

The integrity and value of each person are supported through the belief that the person's own values, experiences, feelings, ideas, and goals shape the direction of treatment and that each person should be actively involved in his or her own care.

References

Engel, G. L. (1980). The clinical application of the biopsychosocial model. *American Journal of Psychiatry, 137,* 535–544.

Liberman, R. P. (1988). Psychiatric rehabilitation of chronic mental patients. Washington, DC: American Psychiatric Press.

B. E. ECK

See REHABILITATION.

Biopsychosocial Therapy. The term *biopsychosocial* was made prominent by Engel (1977, 1978, 1980), a long-time professor of psychiatry and medicine at the University of Rochester School of Medicine. In Engel's use of the term and that of most subsequent commentators, "biopsychosocial" refers more to a model of understanding people rather than to a specific approach to therapy.

Engel points out that health care has been dominated for generations by a biomedical model of people and of disease. The biomedical model, he argues, is dualistic (separating mind from body and psychological from somatic) and reductionistic (assuming that all the complexities of human experience are ultimately understandable in terms of their smallest component parts and processes) and leads caregivers to be preoccupied with the body in a way that neglects the human experiences of patients as people. A heart attack, according to this model, would be understood primarily in terms of events at the levels of cells, tissues, and organ systems.

As an alternative, Engel proposes a systems-based model that incorporates biological and psychosocial variables. The biopsychosocial model holds that it is necessary to consider a hierarchy of mutually-influential systems from cells and tissues, to the nervous system, to the experience and behavior of persons, and to interpersonal, family, and community events in order to understand people adequately. Conceptualizing and addressing a heart attack, from a biopsychosocial perspective, involves biomedical events as well as health beliefs and health-related behaviors of the patient, interactions of the patient with other people in family, social, and professional roles, and resources and values of the health care system and the larger community.

The thinking that drives the biopsychosocial model has a number of implications for mental health and pastoral care. First, the biological arena remains an important part of the whole system and should not be overlooked. Biological effects on psychological status may take a number of forms, including

- genetic influences and biological predispositions. Research with large populations of people, for instance, reveals that close biological relatives of people with a variety of psychological disorders (such as schizophrenia, depression, and alcohol abuse [*see* Alcohol Abuse and Dependence]) are more likely to develop these disorders themselves than would otherwise be expected. While people cannot change their inherited biology, they may be encouraged to make lifestyle choices (e.g., in patterns of alcohol use) that take their inherited biology into account.

- mental health effects of medical illness. A number of medical conditions (progressive neurological disorders, cerebrovascular disease, certain vitamin deficiencies, endocrine conditions, viral infections, and some cancers, among others) can have direct physiological effects on mental health status.

- toxic and chemical effects. Exposure to a variety of environmental toxins, such as lead and mercury, and chemicals, such as alcohol and other drugs of abuse, produces psychological effects.

- psychological effects of health behaviors. A number of health behaviors (such as aerobic exercise, appropriate nutrition, prayer or meditation, and adequate sleep) that affect the biology of people have psychological effects and benefits.

- benefits of medical treatment of psychological disorders. There are good data on the beneficial effects of drug treatment of a number of psychological disorders, such as schizophrenia, bipolar disorders, and depression.

Second, a large number of psychological and social variables may be considered as part of the process of understanding people and helping them to move toward health. Examples of such variables include

- personal qualities and psychological characteristics. temperament, self-esteem, and self-efficacy, patterns of beliefs and styles of thinking . . . and almost countless other psychological patterns and constructs . . . help to provide some explanatory framework about how people make choices and live their lives.

- stress and coping. The presence of environmental challenges and the styles and resources with which people seek to adapt to these challenges.

- health beliefs. The assumptions of people about what constitutes illness and health and what is helpful and necessary in moving between the two.

- culture. The beliefs and practices that arise from cultural traditions, that further serve to define appropriate behavior and sometimes to prescribe healing approaches.

- social and family support. Substantial psychological literature demonstrates that the presence of social and community support and positive family relationships can exert a protective and healing effect on health and mental health status.

Third, the biopsychosocial model may be understood to include spiritual and religious variables. Although relatively little writing about the biopsychosocial model has made this connection, there is a great deal of information in psychological and medical literature (e.g., Gartner, Larson, & Allen, 1991; Hill & Butter, 1995) about the health and mental health benefits of spiritual and religious beliefs and practices. This literature suggests that a number of dimensions of spirituality, including ceremonies, sacraments, and rituals; prayer and devotional practices; community; understanding and pursuit of meaning and purpose; and relationships with God offer contributions toward the health and wellness of people.

Therapy that derives from the biopsychosocial model takes all of these variables into account. The therapist carefully considers, with the client, the roles that biological, psychosocial, and spiritual variables may play in the development of distress and in opportunities for healing. For the person of faith this comprehensive approach should feel familiar and comfortable insofar as it reflects and supports the journey toward wholeness and *shalom*.

References

Engel, G. L. (1977). The need for a new medical model: A challenge for biomedicine. *Science, 196*, 129–136.

Engel, G. L. (1978). The biopsychosocial model and the education of health professionals. *Annals New York Academy of Sciences, 310*, 169–181.

Engel, G. L. (1980). The clinical application of the biopsychosocial model. *American Journal of Psychiatry, 137* (5), 535–544.

Gartner, J., Larson, D. B., and Allen, G. D. (1991). Religious commitment and mental health: A review of the empirical literature. *Journal of Psychology and Theology, 19* (1), 6–25.

Hill, P. C., and Butter, E. M. (1995). The role of religion in promoting physical health. *Journal of Psychology and Christianity, 14* (2), 141–155.

F. C. CRAIGIE, JR.

See FAMILY THERAPY: OVERVIEW.

Biosocial Theory. The comprehensive, integrated formulation of human behavior developed by Gardner Murphy. It is comprehensive in its reliance on diverse data bases, including clinical experience, physiological and animal experimentation, and social science research. Murphy strove to use all reliable empirical data. It is integrated to the extent that Murphy attempted to specify the interrelations and interdependencies of the biological and social substrata of behavior.

By biosocial Murphy meant "what is biological is at the same time social" (Murphy, 1947, p. 138). Biological processes have antecedent and consequent social impact. "The only thing that can be socialized is a biological process, and in man most biological processes are to some degree socialized" (Murphy, 1947, p. 139). Most biological events can be visibly altered by social control.

Personality denotes affective and volitional qualities that distinguish persons from one another and general characteristics that distinguish persons from nonpersons. The latter is the focus of Murphy's major theoretical interest, though he did not deny individual differences. To Murphy personality can be studied at three levels of complexity: personality as distinct individuals, personality as structured whole with defined parts, and personality as structured organism-environment field in which the components of each interact. Biosocial theory considers personality at the highest level of complexity. Murphy developed his propositions logically, methodically, and meticulously. As a consequence he has been called a "theorist's theoretician."

Murphy conceived of personality as having its prime mover in a biological field. The organic systems of the body are tension or energy systems with complex interactions designed to achieve homeostasis. Energy moves from an area of excess to one of deficit in response to changing needs and environments. A hierarchy of interdependent organs exists to ensure survival. Each organic system (e.g., sympathetic nervous system) is responsive to endogenous needs, needs of other systems, and exogenous stimulation. Organic needs involve the visceral needs for food, water, or air, activity needs of exploration and preservation, and needs to avoid pain, death, and threats. Needs operate to motivate behavior and are produced from the interplay of inner and outer pressures. Murphy's theory of personality is essentially a motivational one (cf. Abraham Maslow's hierarchy of needs).

Biosocial theory can be considered in light of five major postulates: field theory wherein the person is an organism in a time and space energy system; evolutionary development following the homogeneous to heterogeneous to structured organization sequence; canalization as the process by which needs become more specific when satisfied in a specific manner; autism, by which cognitive processes work in concert with need satisfaction; and feedback, which provides a basis for testing reality and avoiding self-deception.

Following the Gestalt heritage of Kurt Lewin, Murphy believed the person to be a nodal point in an energy field. This field theory is a "psychological approach which regards the barrier between individual and environment as indefinite and unstable, and requires the consideration of an organism-environment field whose properties are studied as field properties" (Murphy, 1947, p. 986). The perceptual redefinition of organism and environment results from the exchange of materials through the skin and other membranes. The same relation holds between the person and the social environment, in which social forces become internalized and the person alters the environment.

Human development follows the three-stage evolutionary theory advocated by Herbert Spencer. In this view the organism begins as a homogeneous, undifferentiated unit, but specialized structures form to accomplish specialized functions. The second stage is one in which the organism is composed of heterogeneous units with unique roles. The third stage is marked by further specialization in structure-function relations, with special structures performing the function of integrating the others (central nervous system and self). This integrating mechanism maintains the structural unity of the whole. This conception of development is applied to biological development from ovum through senescence. It is also descriptive of cognitive development as theorized by Jean Piaget and of socialization of individuals into substructures of society.

Social differentiation is accomplished largely through conditioning and canalization. C. S. Sherrington (1857–1952) had asserted that responses are of two major types, preparatory or consummatory, each modifiable through specific forms of learning. Murphy held that conditioning applied only to preparatory responses (e.g., Pavlov's dog, which salivated in anticipation of meat powder) and that conditioning is reversible, subject to extinction. However, consummatory responses (e.g., eating, drinking, sexual behavior) are canalized. Once canalized stimuli are associated with the consummatory response, they cannot be modified or extinguished (cf. Gordon Allport's functional autonomy). Murphy borrowed Pierre Janet's term *canalization* to describe the "process by which general motives . . . tend, upon repeated experience, to become more easily satisfied through the action of the specific satisfier than of others of the same general class" (Murphy, 1949, p. 162). Canalization forms the basis of acquired tastes. The choice of satisfier goes to the familiar one, so that a progressive shift is made in preference to specific means of satisfaction. Murphy asserted that those preferences do not change much once they are formed.

The life of the organism is geared toward need satisfaction. Canalization makes certain satisfiers more emotionally appealing or desirable than others. To maintain internal integrity cognitive processes are altered to conform to emotional predispositions regarding satisfiers. Murphy termed this tendency *autism* and defined it as "the movement of cognitive processes in the direction of need satisfaction" (1949, p. 980). Feelings are justified in thinking, in that "the best is the norm" (1949, p. 377) and "needs keep ahead of percepts" (1949, p. 378). This autistic-type thinking is evidenced in rigid and defensive reactions (cf. Freudian rationalization). To prevent autistic self-deception from destroying it, the organism tests its percepts against reality.

In summary, Murphy's concept of personality is that it is a point in a biological and social field. It draws and returns energy to that field, being interdependent with the field. Personality development is a process of progressive differentiation. The future of human personality is positive, provided conflicts are resolved (Murphy, 1953).

References

Murphy, G. (1947). *Personality: A biosocial approach to origins and structures.* New York: Harper & Brothers.

Murphy, G. (1949). *Historical introduction to modern psychology* (Rev. ed.). New York: Harcourt, Brace.

Murphy, G. (1953). *Human potentialities.* New York: Association Press.

R. L. TIMPE

See MURPHY, GARDNER.

Bipolar Disorder. Bipolar disorder, formerly called manic–depressive illness, is one of several disorders known as mood disorders. Mania and depression alone or in combination are the hallmarks of the mood disorders. Mania is characterized by a feeling of euphoria in which the individual has grandiose ideas, exhibits boundless energy, needs little sleep, and exhibits great self-assurance. While in a manic state people's thoughts race, they speak too fast, and they demonstrate poor judgment. Manics may impulsively spend too much money, commit sexual indiscretions, and alienate people with their irritability and impatience. Hypomania refers to a milder form of mania that is an excessive amount of elation but does not significantly impair the individual's life.

Depression can be characterized by many symptoms, including feelings of worthlessness, guilt, and sadness. When one is depressed, life seems empty and overwhelming. The depressed individual has difficulty concentrating, cannot make decisions, lacks confidence, and cannot enjoy activities that previously were pleasurable. Physical symptoms may include gaining or losing weight, sleeping too much or too little, agitation, or lethargy. Depressed individuals may be preoccupied with death or suicide. They may believe that they have committed the unpardonable sin and that loved ones would be better off without them.

Bipolar disorder is so named because those afflicted with it experience both mania and depression, in contrast to those with unipolar disorders, who experience only one extreme, usually depression. Bipolar disorders are categorized into two types, Bipolar I and Bipolar II. In Bipolar I the individual experiences both mania and depression; in Bipolar II the individual experiences hypomania and depression. Mania or hypomania is the key to diagnosing bipolar disorder. A person who experiences a manic state even once is presumed to have bipolar disorder. Manic and depressive states may immediately precede or follow one another or may be separated by long time intervals, and the individual may have more episodes of one pole than the other. Some individuals, known as rapid cyclers, will experience four or more episodes per year.

The age of onset for bipolar disorder is younger than for unipolar depression and usually begins in the late teens or twenties but seldom begins after age 40. In some cases it is preceded by a disorder named cyclothymia, which is a milder form of mood disorder, characterized by marked moodiness and mood swings for at least two years. Bipolar disorder is a chronic disorder and even with treatment less than half of the individuals who experience it go five years without a manic or a depressive episode. People with bipolar are at risk for suicide in the depressive phase and are more prone to accidental death in the manic phase due to impulsiveness and poor judgment.

The causes of bipolar disorder are unclear, but it is probably determined by multiple factors. Family and adoption studies have consistently indicated a genetic predisposition toward mood disorders. First-degree relatives of persons with bipolar disorder are much more likely than the general population to experience bipolar depression, unipolar depression, and anxiety. At this point, however, there is no clear evidence that a particular gene is linked to the transmission of bipolar disorder; instead it seems that a family history increases vulnerability to several disorders.

Neurotransmitters in the brain have been widely investigated and are very likely involved in bipolar disorder but in complex and interactional ways not yet understood. The relationship between neurotransmitters and the hormones secreted by the hypothalamus, pituitary, and adrenal glands seems to be significant. There is also speculation that bipolar disorder may be related to circadian rhythms because some people with bipolar disorder are especially light-sensitive and show abnormalities in sleep patterns such as entering REM sleep too quickly, dreaming intensely, and missing the deeper stages of sleep.

Stressful life events may precipitate episodes of mania or depression but do not seem to be the primary cause of bipolar disorder. Psychosocial factors such as attributional style, learned helplessness, attitudes, and interpersonal relationships all seem to be correlated with bipolar disorder but have not been identified as causes; they are often the result of having such a disorder. It seems that a genetic vulnerability coupled with stressful psychological and sociocultural events may result in bipolar disorder.

Three primary treatment modalities are most frequently used for bipolar disorder. Medication is commonly used, especially lithium. For reasons not yet fully understood, lithium reduces the frequency of episodes, and many persons with bipolar disorder are maintained on lithium for long periods. Lithium levels must be carefully monitored through blood tests, and there may be side effects such as weight gain, lethargy, and kidney malfunction. Because of the side effects of medication and because they miss the energy of hypomania and manic states, people with bipolar disorder may discontinue their medications. The newer antidepressants that affect serotonin levels are often used, but there is some suspicion that they may contribute to more rapid cycling. Antiseizure medication, such as carbamazepine, is also being used.

A second treatment approach that is sometimes used is electroconvulsive therapy (ECT). This approach is used only in severe cases in which uncontrollable behavior or the threat of suicide makes it impossible to wait the two to three weeks for medication to take effect. ECT, used to treat people who have not responded to other forms of treatment, is often effective but is subject to side effects: temporary short-term memory loss and confusion immediately after treatment.

Psychotherapy is the third treatment approach. While many psychotherapeutic approaches have been tried, cognitive therapy and interpersonal therapy are currently the most popular. Cognitive therapy focuses on identifying and correcting faulty thinking and attributional styles, so that the client can gain cognitive control of emotions. Interpersonal therapy focuses on developing the skills to identify and resolve interpersonal conflicts, which frequently accompany bipolar disorder. Both of these psychotherapies are highly structured and short-term. Many people receive a combination of both medication and psychotherapy to stabilize them and prevent relapse.

In addition to addressing the potential causes of bipolar disorder, psychotherapists help people cope with a number of problems that arise in living with the disorder. One is the difficulty of living with interruptions to one's life that manic and depressive states bring. People may be too ill to work or parent and may even be hospitalized. Another problem is undoing or coping with inappropriate behavior that was performed during a manic state, when the individual may have recklessly spent money, made grandiose promises, or said inappropriate things. A third common problem is dealing with negative reactions and the distrust of family, friends, and coworkers who have been affected by the individual's extreme mood swings. Taking medication regularly is a struggle for some people, a struggle that is compounded by the tendency for people in a manic or hypomanic state to feel that they do not need medication. People with bipolar disorder deal with the constant anxiety that their feelings may spin out of control. They often feel powerless and as though their illness is in control and may take over any time. There is also the question of why God allows people to go through such struggles. People with bipolar disorder need therapists who help them exercise cognitive control over their emotions, recognize when they are getting too high or too low, manage interpersonal relationships, cope with life stresses, and understand how to accept and live successfully with bipolar disorder.

C. D. DOLPH

See MOOD DISORDERS.

Birth Order. The ordinal position of the child within the family has been studied extensively, and researchers conclude that a number of personality characteristics can be linked to order of birth. Being the oldest child or the youngest child or a child in between affects the psychological relationship the child has with parents and siblings. As each child comes into the family, he or she is given a special place in the family constellation and is treated accordingly. The characteristics attributed to children in each of the three positions—oldest, middle, youngest—will not apply to every child, but they will hold true generally for the population.

Galton (1869) was among the first to record that men of genius are more apt to be firstborns, a conclusion supported by studies since that time, including Terman's (1925) well-known observation of almost 1,500 very bright children. The firstborn has an edge in experience and competence (Toman, 1993), is more apt to be listed in *Who's Who*, and is more likely to become a doctor, a lawyer, or an astronaut and to show leadership ability. Other characteristics include superior language ability, higher achievement motivation, a greater sense of responsibility, and a sensitivity to social expectations. On the negative side firstborns are less warm and more anxious than their siblings, are more apt to be brought to the attention of mental health professionals (Abram & Coie, 1981), are sometimes bossy, and tend to feel superior to other people.

These characteristics, both positive and negative, are attributed to the fact that parental concern and attention are greater for the first child than for later-born children. More pressure is put on the oldest child to achieve and to act responsibly. Parents are excited when the first child arrives, but they also are tense and feel personally responsible for the kind of adult the child will become. More directives are given to this child to ensure successful development, giving him or her the incentive to do well but also creating anxiety when things go badly. The superior language skill exhibited by firstborns is directly related to the fact that the first child has adults as models of speech whereas later-born children imitate siblings as well as parents.

The middle child is any child between the first and the last, and although less research has been done on the middle child than on either the oldest or the youngest, it is generally agreed that the middle child is sociable, well-liked, adapts to new situations easily, and is seldom spoiled. Middle children also make better marriage partners. However, their easygoing manner and diplomatic ways are in contrast to their general lack of self-esteem. These are the "sandwich kids" who are bossed by an older brother or sister and have to vie for the attention given to the baby. Often they are lost in the shuffle, and their self-concept suffers accordingly. This is more apt to occur if the middle child is a second female (Jacobs & Moss, 1976). The more relaxed attitude of the parents to the second child contributes to the child's gregarious nature yet takes its toll in fewer accomplishments and lower self-esteem. It would seem that parents should spend more time with the middle child, showing affection and finding ways to appreciate the child's unique abilities.

The youngest child is usually more dependent, less mature, and less oriented to parental and peer approval than are older brothers and sisters. Being the youngest means no one will ever take his or her place, and the child can continue to enjoy the attention reserved for the last one in the family. Parents tend to be less exacting, less punitive, and less demanding with the youngest, and sometimes parents are too weary to work with this child as they did with the others, giving the child the reputation of being spoiled. This greater permissiveness on the part of parents makes the child more difficult to live with and is a source of irritation to siblings, who feel discriminated against when rules do not apply to all alike. Yet because of the increased freedom, the youngest may become the inventive one in the family, going in a direction quite different from the others.

Part of the confusion in studies on birth order comes because other variables affect the outcome. The sex of the child, the spacing between children, the education of the parents, the socioeconomic status of the family, and the family size are all relevant and must be taken into account. However, controlling for these factors is difficult, especially when the very nature of the topic mandates that the research method be observational rather than experimental. As one might expect, the only girl in a family of boys and the only boy in a family of girls will be given a special place regardless of ordinal position.

The spacing between children also has an effect on the child. There is more sibling rivalry and a greater bid for parental attention if children are close to one another in age, whereas a space of six or seven years may mean that a later-born child is raised in much the same way as the oldest child and so will take on the same characteristics as the oldest child. The education of the parents and the socioeconomic status of the family also affect child-rearing procedures. If the family income changes appreciably between the first child and the last, this may make a difference. Overall family size also has repercussions, larger families being more strict and expecting children to take more responsibility than do smaller families.

Although research on birth order is relatively recent, an understanding of personality characteristics as related to ordinal position has been known for centuries. In the parable Jesus told of the prodigal son (Luke 15:11–32), the behavior and attitude of the older brother were typically those one would expect from the oldest child, whereas the actions of the younger brother were not surprising in the light of the fact that he was the younger one. Mosaic law gave the firstborn male a status not shared by any other child, and because he was "the firstborn of your

sons" he was to be given to the Lord (Exod. 22:29) and blessed with a double portion of the inheritance. What Jesus was saying in the parable of the prodigal son is that every child has worth, even the youngest who may take a wrong turn. Every child is a part of the family of God and will be welcomed into that family by the Father.

References

Abram, R. S., & Coie, J. D. (1981). Maternal reactions to problem behaviors and ordinal position of child. *Journal of Personality, 49,* 450–467.

Galton, F. (1869). *Hereditary genius: An inquiry into its laws and consequences.* London: Macmillan.

Jacobs, B. S., & Moss, H. A. (1976). Birth order and sex of sibling as determinants of mother-infant interaction. *Child Development, 47,* 315–322.

Terman, L. M. (1925). *Genetic studies of genius.* Stanford, CA: Stanford University Press.

Toman, W. (1993). *Family constellation: Its effect on personality and social behavior.* New York: Springer.

B. Clouse

See Personality; Life Span Development; Individual Psychology.

Birth Trauma. The experience of being born is a unique experience in the life of a human being. Psychoanalytic theories suggest that all anxiety and pleasure may originate in this experience called birth trauma.

While the fetus is in the safety, warmth, and care of the uterus, the experience is presumably pleasant or at least peaceful. All bodily functions are cared for to such an extent that it does not even have to breathe for itself. There is little or no variation in temperature, and the fetus has hardly any need for activity requiring energy. Conjecture is that there is either no thinking and feeling or that these functions are so primitive as to be nonexistent.

During the birth process the fetus experiences more change in a matter of the relatively few hours of labor than it has experienced during the nine months of incubation. The new elements of light, sound, cold, and absence of contact might bring fear to the newborn. Gone forever are the constant contact of the mother's uterus, 98° warmth, and near-perfect protection and provision.

Freud (1936) believed that all anxiety of adult life is due to this flooding with stimulation in the absence of adequate defense apparatus. Thus Freud viewed all attempts to reduce anxiety as symbolic of returning to the warmth and safety of the womb. Anxiety, which is a symptom of displeasure, is evidence of the adult feeling separate from the mother.

Pleasure is felt whenever there is a creation of a womblike experience or a reminder of the safety of the womb. Thus, according to Rank (1929), the mourning for a lost loved one represents the desire to join the dead person, as death, like the womb, is safe. Likewise, the playing of hide-and-seek by children is symbolic of the womb in that when hiding, one is alone, crouched as if in a fetal position, and covered.

Thumb sucking, rocking, wetting, soiling, and clinging may all be symbolic of the care of the womb. When symptoms impair daily functioning, anxiety is indicated, which in turn points to the trauma of birth.

The concept of birth trauma has been most closely associated with the writings of Rank. Most psychoanalytic theorists agree with Rank that birth is probably the most important psychological event in life. His assumption that all anxiety and pleasure are related to the birth experience has, however, not been so widely accepted.

References

Freud, S. (1936). *The problem of anxiety.* New York: Norton.
Rank, O. (1929). *The trauma of birth.* New York: Harcourt, Brace.

R. B. Johnson

See Primal Therapy.

Bisexuality. The sexual orientation of individuals who are sexually attracted and/or sexually involved with both women and men. Those individuals who label themselves bisexual are considered to be part of a group of sexual minorities that also includes gays, lesbians, and transgendered people. It is important to note that individuals may or may not label themselves bisexual in a way that is congruent with their sexual behavior. People may engage in bisexual behavior while not conceiving of themselves as having a bisexual identity (i.e., a person may have sex with both men and women but does not call himself or herself bisexual). People who report having had sexual experiences with both men and women are not rare, being more common than those who define themselves as a sexual minority. It is estimated that about 25% of males have participated in bisexual behavior, while only 2% of males are thought to be exclusively homosexual and even fewer are thought to ascribe to the label of bisexual (Weinberg, Williams, & Pryor, 1994).

Of those sexual minorities identifying themselves as having a bisexual orientation, some may maintain sexual relationships with both women and men simultaneously, or they may be involved exclusively with one gender or the other at any given time. Bisexuals may marry someone of the opposite gender or may have long-term, committed, monogamous relationships with someone of the same gender.

Speculations about the causes of bisexuality, though not as prolific, are as varied as the speculations about the causes of homosexuality. It is now generally accepted that sexual orientation is not a personal choice but instead is determined by a variety of biological and/or environmental factors. Genetic and neurobiological evidence suggesting that sexual orientation is at least in part biologically determined is increasing as more sophisticated and technologically advanced research designs are used. Many theorists adopt a learning model and suggest that early childhood experiences and/or a person's initial sexual experiences greatly impact sexual preference. Though the determinants of sexuality continue to evade researchers, sexual orientation is a complicated human trait that seems to involve both learned and biological components.

Weinberg, Williams, and Pryor (1994) present a model of bisexual identity formation and emphasize that bisexuality is a potential sexual orientation for everyone, as Sigmund Freud and Alfred Kinsey posited earlier in this century. According to their model, sexuality is determined by interactions of sexual behavior, social factors, and historical factors such as AIDS or the gay rights movement. These authors suggest that bisexuals are initially confused by their sexual attraction to and involvement with both men and women. This period of confusion may span years and will culminate when individuals find the label *bisexual* and are comfortably able to apply it to themselves. As people become more self-accepting, they will settle into the identity of being a bisexual. Bisexuals who have successfully settled on their identity may have an exclusive heterosexual or homosexual relationship but still refer to themselves as bisexual. Weinberg, Williams, and Pryor (1994) suggest that bisexuals nonetheless will continue to experience doubts and uncertainty about their sexual identity primarily resulting from a lack of social validation.

This continued state of confusion is just one of the psychological costs of the bisexual experience. In addition sexual minorities must endure various social and psychological strains. Having been rejected by the heterosexual and homosexual communities, friends, and family, bisexuals may lack social support. Being members of a somewhat ostracized and stigmatized minority, bisexuals may be at greater risk for experiencing psychological distress such as depression. Depending upon their sexual behavior, bisexuals may be at great risk for contracting AIDS. The focus of therapeutic interventions with sexual minority clients is generally to build social support and personal acceptance and to begin the task of admitting their sexual orientation to friends and family (Paul, 1996).

Despite these factors, Weinberg, Williams, and Pryor (1994) found that 80% of bisexuals do not regret living their lives with a bisexual orientation. This satisfaction with their orientation may in part be influenced by a shift toward monogamy among bisexuals. Monogamous relationships (as opposed to open relationships, in which bisexual individuals may have both a male and a female partner) tend to be less complicated, more stable, and more supportive (Paul, 1996).

Traditional Christian thought views bisexual behavior as deviant practice that should not be acted out. This thought rests on the biblical notion that sexual behavior outside of the marital union between a man and a woman is sin (Lev. 18:22; 20:13). Some Christian therapists who are operating under this traditional assumption purport to cure sexual minorities (Pattison & Pattison, 1980). However, Haldeman (1991) points out that the "cure" obtained by these therapeutic interventions involves teaching sexual minorities to resist acting on same-sex attractions but does not eliminate sexual attraction to members of the same sex.

As sexual mores and values are changing, so are biblical interpretations and church doctrines regarding sexuality. The view that the only appropriate sexual behavior is between a married man and woman has been challenged recently in a number of mainstream churches in the United States, including Lutheran, Episcopal, and Presbyterian denominations. This matter will continue to face the church in years to come (Spong, 1988).

References

Haldeman, D. C. (1991). Sexual orientation conversion therapy for gay men and lesbians: A scientific examination. In J. C. Gonsiorek & J. D. Weinrich (Eds.), *Homosexuality: Research implications for public policy*. Newbury Park, CA: Sage.

Pattison, E., & Pattison, M. (1980). Ex-gays: Religiously-mediated change in homosexuals. *American Journal of Psychiatry, 137*, 1553–1562.

Paul, J. P. (1996). Bisexuality: Exploring/exploding the boundaries. In R. C. Savin-Williams & K. M. Cohen (Eds.), *The lives of lesbians, gays, and bisexuals*. New York: Harcourt Brace.

Spong, J. S. (1988). *Living in sin: A bishop rethinks human sexuality*. New York: HarperCollins.

Weinberg, M. S., Williams, C. J., & Pryor, D. W. (1994). *Dual attraction: Understanding bisexuality*. New York: Oxford University Press.

E. M. BUTTER

See GENDER IDENTITY; SEXUALITY.

Black Issues in Psychology and Pastoral Care. This article will first focus on key definitions and concepts. Second, issues of class and history will be summarized. Third, issues of power in the black community will be discussed. Fourth, gender issues and sex-role stereotypes will be presented. Fifth, issues to be considered when ministering to African-American Christians will be presented.

Definitions of Key Concepts. Christian ministry with black Americans can be greatly enhanced by clarifying several important concepts. Three key concepts that affect ministry with African-Americans are race, culture, and ethnicity. Race refers to groupings based on physical characteristics and genetic origins; thus race can have different cultures and ethnic groups within it. Culture can be conceptualized as the thoughts, beliefs, practices, and behaviors of a people in the areas of history, religion, organization (social, economic, or political), and collective production. Culture is passed on to group members from one generation to the next. Ethnicity often refers to a group's social and cultural heritage.

The term *visible minority group* is also important when ministering to African-Americans. It is used to draw a distinction between groups whose minority status is clearly visible at all times, such as African-Americans, and those whose minority status is more easily hidden or overlooked, such as Jews.

Issues of Class and History. Socioeconomic status is another variable that deserves careful consideration. Individuals adopt different values and views of the world depending on their economic resources, type of employment, future aspirations, and educational level. Minority group members are more likely to live in poverty and are less likely to be included in the middle class. Observations about minority cultures in the United States that relate to social class and economic factors are thus often confused with elements that relate to ethnicity. This problem has been especially relevant when ministering to African-Americans.

The issue of acculturation is also relevant to ministry with black Americans. Black families might be considered to be bicultural. That is, black Americans are generally socialized into both the standard culture in the United States and the cultural patterns of West Africa. The black family's history of oppression is also an important background factor. Black Americans' oppression can be categorized into four historical periods: preslavery, slavery, postslavery, and post-1940s. These categories provide a context for discussing the influences of the larger social context on African-Americans. During these four periods, African-Americans lost their kinship system and were subjected to political, economic, judicial, and social dependency. They were and still are frequently stigmatized and portrayed and treated as less than human. As a result black Americans are very sensitive and attuned to issues of oppression and discrimination as they occur in interpersonal and employment situations, as well as to potential discrimination in courts of law, by the police, and by other public servants. Black Americans are also sensitive to discrimination in securing land, credit, jobs, public relief, and social welfare. The experience of racism means that this sensitivity to oppression and discrimination has been labeled as healthy cultural distrust (Thomas & Sillen, 1993). Thus it may be important to assess the level of the oppression the individual or family is experiencing.

Power and the Black Community. Power and power differentials inside and outside of the home are other issues that affect black families. It is important to recognize the power held by the person(s) one is ministering to. The issue of power influences vulnerability, role responsibility, and burnout among black family members. The issue of power is particularly important to discuss when conducting pre-marriage, marriage, or couple- or other gender-based counseling. Some black gender role issues originated with slavery and continue to affect gender relations. For example, under the American system of slavery, male slaves were not allowed to function as providers or women as nurturers in their own families. Rather, they were forced to work for slave owners and to nurture the children of their masters. Furthermore, privileges and rights of African slaves were regulated and controlled by others when they were allowed to marry. Consequently, as with all Americans, power issues in marital relationships are important matters to be addressed with African-American families. Women's issues and men's issues continue to be important matters among African-Americans.

Gender Issues and Sex-Role Stereotypes. Women in the African-American community are subjected to similar prejudice and discrimination encountered by white females in the United States. In this respect understanding the social context of sex stereotyping when working with African-American females is vital. However, it is also important to note that African-American females have the added load of contending with racial issues as a result of their visible minority status. A critical racial issue is the issue of image and beauty. The standard of beauty in America is straight hair, light skin, thin build, and fine facial features. African-American women are often the antithesis to this standard.

African-American males deal with unique issues. Men throughout the history of American society have been assigned the responsibility of taking care of their families, especially economically. African-American men, however, have been relegated to low-paying work and often have been unable to financially provide for their families. The economic disenfranchisement of African-American males has negatively affected the black man's individual and group esteem. It has also affected the way black men are viewed by the black family and by society at large. It has perpetuated a victim system wherein racial discrimination prevents black men from finding employment, unemployment and underemployment lead to poverty and stress, family poverty and stress cause individual problems, black individuals cannot give to their communities, and black communities are unable to give to, provide for, and protect their citizens (Pinderhughes, 1982).

Sex-role stereotypes exist within the African-American community; however, they have not traditionally been made public. African-American men and women tend to work on an egalitarian level. This equal status between the sexes is often illustrated in their marriages as well. Understanding the basic egalitarian attitude of most African-American men and women is useful when dealing with marital problems.

Gender issues and sex-role stereotypes can also be observed in African-American child-rearing practices. Most child rearing among African-Americans is characterized by a strict, no-nonsense parenting style. Traditionally African-American boys are socialized to be confrontive, because of the cultural belief that they need to be selectively assertive and acquiescent. African-American girls are more likely to be socialized toward domestication. It is generally believed that African-American families of lower economic resources are much harsher disciplinarians than are middle-class families.

Ministry with Black Americans. Ministry with African-Americans can be a rewarding endeavor when the minister or counselor is aware of issues such as class, power, ethnicity, gender, and child-rearing practices. Four specific issues are to be addressed when ministering with African-Americans. Help African-Americans to connect their strong Christian beliefs with the black church tradition of social change and social justice. Black Christians can be liberated by assuming the position that God is concerned with their liberation, poverty, and justice. Help black Americans realize and understand how oppression is operating in their lives. Is the oppression they are experiencing primary or secondary? At the primary level the oppressor is physically present, there is a power differential, and there is a differential access to resources. At the secondary level the oppressor is not present, the oppressed take on the characteristics of the oppressor, and oppression is internalized. Help black families identify and operationalize their unique strengths: their strong kinship bonds, strong work orientation, flexibility of family roles, strong achievement orientation, and strong religious values. Help black families recognize that their gender-role challenges can typically be addressed by distinguishing between women's issues and gender issues, by examining the issue of black male oppression and black female oppression, by understanding how power is misused and abused in the home, by understanding that black men have as much at stake in resolving black gender issues as black women, and by understanding how marital and gender issues effect child-rearing practices.

Ministry with black families can facilitate individual, family, and community growth. Ministers and counselors who are knowledgable, sensitive, and aware of these issues will be better equipped to help black Americans obtain health and combat social ills.

References

Pinderhughes, E. (1982). Afro-American families and the victim system. In M. McGoldrick, J. K. Pearce, & J. Giordano (Eds.), *Ethnicity and family therapy*. New York: Guilford.

Thomas, A., & Sillen, S. (1993). *Racism and psychiatry.* Secaucus, NJ.

Additional Readings

Akbar, N. (1984). *The chains and images of psychological slavery*. Jersey City, NJ: New Mind Productions.

Boyd-Franklin, N. (1989). *Black families in therapy: A multisystems approach*. New York: Guilford.

Johnson, S. D., Jr. (1990). Toward clarifying culture, race, and ethnicity in the context of multicultural counseling. *Journal of Multicultural Counseling and Development*, *18*, 41–50.

Lincoln, C. E., & Mamiya, L. H. (1990). *The black church and the African-American experience*. Durham, NC: Duke University Press.

Peters, M. F., & Massey, G. (1983). Mundane extreme environmental stress in family stress theories: The case of black families in white America. *Marriage and Family Review*, *6*, 193–218.

M. L. McCreary and D. R. Jones

See Psychology, History of; Pastoral Care; Pastoral Counseling; Culture and Psychotherapy; Cross-Cultural Therapy; Ethnic Identity.

Blended Family. A blended family is formed by the merging through official or common-law marriage of two or more family remnants of previous marriages or family constellations. At least one of the spouses has been in a parental role in a previous family system and brings to the blended family a child or children from that union. Blended families vary considerably in composition. The children may belong to the wife or husband by a previous family union or may be theirs by the present arrangement. Inasmuch as custody is ordinarily awarded to the mother, the typical blended unit consists of a wife, her children, and the husband, whose children, if he has any, reside with their mother (*see* Child Custody).

With the growing popularity of joint custody and the rising number of serial family relationships, blended family configurations are becoming increasingly varied and complex. Many children now belong to two households, dividing their time equally between both. In some families children from two or more previous marriages retain their paternal surnames. Hence, numerous last names may be used within the same family, affecting the bonding and identity formation process significantly.

Blended families may be extended families with exponentially complicated structures, though the term is normally used mainly to refer to newly formed nuclear families that are made up of integrated subsystems from previous family units. The principal challenge of the blended family is to develop into a cohesive unit. Yet it must be defined by boundaries that allow appropriate contact with what frequently is a large, disjointed network of relatives in the new extended family. These families must negotiate several critical developmental tasks in order to coalesce.

One task faced by all the members is the mourning of the lost families they represent. Family failures and breakup are severe emotional trauma, and this loss requires substantial grieving if one is to be prepared for investment in new relationships. Blended families frequently arise from relationships motivated by the rebound from former relationships in an effort to escape the pain of the loss, loneliness, and shame about failure. Though one may have accepted cognitively the termination of a previous family union by death or divorce, the new relationship symbolizes the old loss and failure. Out of loyalty to the new relationship one may repress that grief/loss but that merely constipates and subverts the residual grief. It will surface in some destructive way at a later point.

This grief experience may be particularly true for children, who often grieve long after the family breakup. This is seen in the persistent longing to be reunited with the absent parent and in the enduring fantasy that the child's mother and father will eventually remarry. It is also manifested in the refusal of some children to form a relationship in the new family constellation or with the stepparent. Unfinished grief tends to skew the child's loyalty toward the natural parent exclusively. This usually produces destructive counterforces in the entire family constellation. Unresolved grief is poison to the blended family. It produces intrafamilial tension and siphons off emotional energy that could otherwise be channeled into strengthening family relationships. Professional help is frequently needed to resolve this type of mourning because of its insidious character.

A critical developmental task for spouses is to form a strong marital bond. Continued contact with the ex-spouse and former in-laws, for example, in the course of normal child visitation, can be disruptive to developing the new spousal relationship. Issues of jealousy, trust, and loyalty are easily activated by these continuing contacts. Yet the cornerstone of the blended family is the quality of the new spousal union. Moreover, one dimension of this spousal union is the development of a co-parent partnership of care for each other's children that is strong enough to withstand repeated counterforce dynamics injected by the children, who are likely still to have their own unresolved and pathological agenda to act out or resolve. Children accept the stepparent more readily if their natural parent demonstrates unwavering commitment to the spousal relationship and its long-term viability. Children often create conflict between the parent and stepparent, maneuvering for the natural parent's support. Feelings of loyalty and guilt on the part of the parent, particularly regarding having failed the child by failing in the earlier relationship, tempt the parent to side with the child against the new spouse. This kind of triangulation is always destructive.

Maintaining a "mine/yours" view of the children undermines the stepparent–stepchild relationship. It places the stepparent in the untenable position of having to borrow authority from the natural parent when dealing with stepchildren. This obstructs the process of true blending between the new spouses as well as between all the members of the new family constellation. Triangulation produces divisiveness.

Moreover, building functional stepsibling relationships is complicated by the fact that the ordinal position among siblings and the entire structure of the genogram for the new family will change extensively with the merging of the family remnants into the blended family. Rivalry with siblings may decrease as that family remnant closes ranks for this new experience, but stepsibling rivalry often increases, painfully changing the roles, identities, and self-perceptions of all the children (*see* Sibling Rivalry). A related issue for blended families with adolescent or young adult progeny living in the home as part of the family constellation is the fact that children who could be dating are living together as siblings. Sexual boundaries are usually weak, as blended families may not have well-established inherent incest taboos. Conflict and rivalry are ways in which teenage stepsiblings define boundaries to protect themselves from the anxiety and threat of excessive intimacy. Many blended families achieve well-adjusted and harmonious relationships, though the usual critical adjustment time frame is two to four years.

Additional Reading

Frydenger, T., & Frydenger, A. (1984). *The blended family*. Grand Rapids, MI: Zondervan.

J. H. ELLENS AND J. A. LARSEN

See DIVORCE; CHILD CUSTODY; FAMILY SYSTEMS THEORY; FAMILY COMMUNICATIONS THEORY.

Bleuler, Eugen (1857–1939). Swiss psychiatrist who has had a profound influence on the development of the dynamic view of psychopathology. Born in Zollikon, Bleuler served as the director of the Burgholzli Hospital in Zurich from 1889 until 1927, succeeding August Forel. Burgholzli was the first mental hospital to accept psychoanalysis as a means of treatment, due in large part to the work of Bleuler, along with Carl Gustav Jung and Ludwig Binswanger.

Like most of his contemporaries, Bleuler considered mental illness to be primarily an organic process. However, unlike others of his day, he did not endeavor to explain the neuropathology of mental illness itself but rather the meaning of the symptoms as the result of psychological events. Bleuler combined Emil Kraepelin's systematic classification of mental illness with Sigmund Freud's dynamic approach to the unconscious to redefine psychosis, aligning himself with neither a purely organic nor a psychoanalytic model.

In 1911 Bleuler coined the term *schizophrenia* to replace Kraepelin's *dementia praecox*, disagreeing with Kraepelin's belief that premature dementia is the ultimate outcome and viewing schizophrenia as a group of treatable psychotic reactions rather than one distinct and incurable disease. He used the term *schizophrenia* (from Greek words meaning split mind) to describe the dissociation of thoughts and affects that he observed in these patients.

Bleuler considered the primary symptoms of schizophrenia to be disturbances of affect, volition, and associations, viewing the symptoms described by Kraepelin (hallucinations, delusions, negativism, and stupor) as secondary. He observed the inappropriate expression of affect and the circumstantial and tangential verbal associations of these patients and noted that certain psychotics seemed to experience the simultaneous presence of two opposing tendencies (i.e., love and hate) more intensely than did normals or neurotic patients, a condition that he termed ambivalence. He also coined the term *autistic thinking* to describe the schizophrenic patient's primitive cognitive processes, which are characterized by wishful symbolic thinking rather than conformity to logic or reality. Thus Bleuler's system of schizophrenia is often referred to as the four As: disturbances in affect and associations, autism, and ambivalence. Bleuler divided schizophrenia into four basic subtypes—catatonic, hebephrenic, and paranoia (described by Kraepelin), and schizophrenia simplex.

Although Bleuler's 1911 monograph *Dementia Praecox or the Group of Schizophrenias* was not translated into English until 1950, his *Textbook of Psychiatry,* published in 1923, became well known and helped to disseminate his ideas. Bleuler is best remembered for his contributions in the field of schizophrenia, and many of his theories and observations remain clinically relevant in the dynamic understanding of this mental disorder.

L. B. HARDY

Blocking. A sudden obstruction of speech in the middle of a thought or sentence, to which no specific external influence can be ascribed. Following the interrupted action the person may indicate inability to find words to express himself or herself, is unable to explain why, and cannot remember what he or she has been saying prior to the obstruction. The inhibited train of thought may be a reaction to the emergence of unconscious material of a threatening nature. A temporary form may occur in healthy individuals who are suddenly overcome by powerful feelings. Blocking is also referred to as thought obstruction or thought deprivation.

D. L. SCHUURMAN

See MEMORY; AMNESTIC DISORDERS.

Body Dysmorphic Disorder. People who are repulsed by certain aspects of their own physical appearance suffer from body dysmorphic disorder. Their preoccupation with minor or imagined flaws becomes so consuming that they are unable to respond to daily social and occupational responsibilities. Although any body part can be the focus of concern, women are most likely to complain about thighs, abdomen, breast size, buttocks, skin, hips, and facial features while men are most likely to complain about scars, abdomen, physical injuries, head hair, height, upper body size, hands, and facial features. Most individuals with significant body image disturbance engage in repetitive and ritualistic behaviors such as checking themselves in mirrors, excessive grooming, skin picking, hiding the imagined defect, and seeking nearly continuous reassurance from others. Individuals with body dysmorphic disorder may avoid social interactions of all types for fear of feeling shamed by their perceived disfigurement, which they believe is obvious to anyone who glances their way.

Body dysmorphic disorder, also known as dysmorphophobia, dermatological hypochondriasis, and body image disorder, seems to be as common in men as in women and is likely underdiagnosed and undertreated in both. Body dysmorphic disorder is not diagnosed when body hatred is limited to excessive fear of fatness and distortions of body size estimations as evident in anorexia or bulimia nervosa or when related to the body discomfort experienced in gender identity disorder. Body image disturbances of varying severities often occur among patients with atypical major depression, obsessive-compulsive disorder, social phobia, delusional disorder with somatic focus, and among patients seeking cosmetic surgery or dermatological treatments.

Because body dysmorphic disorder as a diagnosis is still in the process of refinement as a distinct diagnostic entity, research has been limited to clinical case reports and small sample studies. Available information suggests, however, that body dysmorphic disorder begins in adolescence when social and cultural pressures for physical beauty and body attractiveness are felt most keenly and when body changes themselves are dramatic and prominent. Patients often identify critical incidents of being teased, criticized, or humiliated by family members, teachers, peers, or passersby as key in the onset of the disorder. Without effective intervention, compulsive symptoms increase in intensity over the course of years, and social fears may render the individual unable to enter even minimally interactive public situations, not to mention relationships of a more intimate nature.

Body image therapy includes desensitization procedures to decrease anxiety focused on the flaw, cognitive-behavior therapy strategies for coping with intrusive or irrational thoughts of body dissatisfaction, and behavioral plans for changing social avoidance patterns. Case study reports suggest that serotonin reuptake inhibitors may be effective in treatment of body dysmorphic disorder. From a broader perspective of prevention, it is important that the values of society, especially those promoted by the fashion and media industries, be confronted whenever possible as contributing to the current epidemic of body image disturbances. For young people the need to be attractive, as defined by society's rigid definition of beauty, far too often overpowers the positive self-regard rooted in the development of good judgment and values, competency at school or work, compassion for others, and the growth of moral character and spiritual gifts.

H. BRAY-GARRETSON

Body Image. Body image is the mental representation of one's physical body. This mental representation includes perceptions individuals have of their physical characteristics as well as their attitudes regarding their bodies. Behavioral patterns are also related to body image in that perceptions and attitudes will influence behavior. For example, an individual with a negative body image may perceive his or her body in a distorted way, may feel dissatisfied with its appearance, and may engage in behavior that minimizes its perceived negative qualities.

An understanding of body image disturbance is necessary in order to diagnose many clinical disorders. It is common, however, for some body image disturbance to exist among normal, nonclinical populations. Women in particular show a high degree of dissatisfaction with their body size and shape. This dissatisfaction is possibly related to the association of thinness with beauty, wealth, and happiness. Due to the prevalence of such a value system in Western society, women who do not achieve the ideal thinness often feel unattractive and inadequate.

The *Diagnostic and Statistical Manual of Mental Disorders* (*DSM-IV;* American Psychiatric Association, 1994), identifies a number of disorders that involve distorted perceptions of the physical body. Body dismorphic disorder is characterized by a persistent preoccupation with an imagined defect in appearance or by exaggerated concern about a slight defect. These concerns cause significant distress in important areas of daily functioning. Individuals may socially withdraw from situations in which their imagined defect would be noticed by others. Correcting the perceived abnormality by plastic surgery may even be considered.

According to the *DSM-IV,* the eating disorders anorexia nervosa and bulimia nervosa involve a disturbance in the experience of one's body or an excessive concern about one's body shape or size. Individuals with these disorders seem to associate self-worth with thinness and may resort to such extreme measures as excessive exercise, purging, or starvation in an attempt to achieve the ideal physique. Despite their sometimes severely emaciated state, sufferers of anorexia nervosa often perceive themselves as much larger than their ideal. Similarly, sufferers of bulimia nervosa may perceive themselves as being obese even when they are of normal weight.

Truly obese individuals who have a realistic perception of their physical appearance may demonstrate social withdrawal due to dissatisfaction with their bodies.

Some other disorders that are not as commonly thought of in connection with body image disturbance are in fact significantly related to it. Gender identity disorder is characterized by discomfort with one's gender and physical sexual characteristics. Due to this dissatisfaction individuals may attempt to alter their physical characteristics in order to resemble those of the opposite sex.

Numerous pathologies exist that are not necessarily characterized by body image disturbance but may be associated with it. Depression and low self-esteem often exist in conjunction with disorders such as anorexia nervosa, more obviously related to distorted body image. Delusional disorder of the somatic subtype involves the delusion that one has some physical defect or illness. Schizophrenics may report a variety of psychotic bodily perceptions such as the feeling that body parts have changed shape or disappeared or that they have exchanged bodies with other individuals. Persons with neurological abnormalities, especially stroke victims, may demonstrate neglect of certain body areas or confusion surrounding the use, shape, or size of particular body parts. Individuals with amputated limbs often report the phantom limb phenomenon (*see* Phantom Response), sensing pain in the amputated limb as if it were still attached to the body.

Various strategies have been developed to assess body image. Self-report questionnaires ask respondents to reveal the extent to which they agree with such statements as "I am satisfied with the shape of my body." One particular questionnaire, the body cathexis scale, requires respondents to indicate ways in which they would like to change various areas of their body. In other cases projective techniques attempt to access body attitudes that are not as readily available to the conscious mind. For example, a respondent's sketch of a human figure may be interpreted as reflecting the attitude toward his or her own body. Similarly, responses to the Rorschach inkblots may be analyzed for references to underlying body image attitudes. The perceptions that individuals have of their actual physical appearance can be measured by showing them a variety of body silhouettes and having them identify which they feel they resemble most. Although such measurement techniques are useful in identifying body image distortions in the general population, clinical populations require a more sensitive and comprehensive approach. Structured interviews are highly effective in diagnosing disorders related to body image disturbance.

Reference

American Psychiatric Association. (1994). *Diagnostic and statistical manual of mental disorders* (4th ed.). Washington, DC: Author.

T. J. BLAIR

See SELF-PERCEPTION THEORY; SELF-ESTEEM.

Body Language. Body language is symbolic nonverbal behavior by one organism that is designed to convey meaning to another organism. It includes physical movements, postures, gestures, and facial expressions that communicate feelings, attitudes, judgments, intentions, or relationship states. The human face particularly and the entire body in general are remarkably capable of an immense range and type of expressions and communications. Comparably, the entire human body participates in the communicative process through the various forms of body language that range from obvious, stereotyped patterns to subtle expressions of thought and feeling.

Body language is the primary form of nonverbal communication and, with varying levels of conscious awareness, human beings use it virtually continuously. However, since most body language is unconsciously generated, it is often regarded to significantly if unintentionally reveal the real feelings and intentions of the inner person of the communicator, even when that perception contradicts or stands in tension with what the sender (*see* Communication) is expressing verbally. Indeed, it is commonly regarded as a direct communication of the unconscious mind and thus a more candid form of communication than verbal language, which is generally calculated to express what we believe our hearers want or ought to hear (*see* Communication, Nonverbal).

Body language tends to be culture–specific in most of its semiotic values. Every therapist has witnessed the patient who expresses with vigor all the words that would convey evidence of love and care to the spouse while sitting in the clinical chair in a posture that expresses articulately through body language the defensiveness, rage, and distancing he or she really feels. The body language is more persuasive in such a situation than the words. Instances like that are obvious indications of the power of body language but both more subtle and even more precise vocabularies of body language also surface in human function, as recent research in the body language science of kinesics has shown (Lowen, 1972, 1973).

Therapists must learn to read body language well, but it is also a great aid to all human relationships for everyone to learn well and read sensitively the meaning of this symbolic behavior. To do so broadens and deepens communication, opens more significant forms of relationship, and enhances the certainty and security with which we can build bonding and communion with each other. Body language vocabularies vary by culture and subculture and to some extent from person to person. They always involve a relatively high degree of subjective interpretation. Thus it is dangerous to draw simplistic or stereotyped conclusions from body language alone, apart from a sensitive reading of the entire picture of verbal and nonverbal expression, including any patterns of nonverbal behavior other than body language. All this must be carefully interpreted in its cultural context. Therapists generally consider the significance of their own body language, since it is the case that though patients may not be focused upon that, subliminally some awareness of it will inevitably and significantly enter into and thus influence the therapeutic experience.

References

Lowen, A. (1972). *The betrayal of the body*. New York: Macmillan, Collier Books.
Lowen, A. (1973). *The language of the body*. New York: Macmillan, Collier Books.

J. H. ELLENS

See COMMUNICATION, NONVERBAL.

Body Therapies. *See* BIOENERGETIC ANALYSIS; PRIMAL THERAPY.

Boisen, Anton Theophilus (1876–1965). Founder of the clinical pastoral education movement. Born in Bloomington, Indiana, where his father was a professor of modern languages at Indiana University, Boisen graduated from Indiana University in 1897 but could not find a teaching position. The next 24 years of his life were ones of struggle and frustration. He entered graduate school in 1897 but suffered a severe anxiety attack on Easter morning of 1898. He was a part-time teacher of German and French, attended the Yale School of Forestry, and entered the Forestry Service in 1905. He attended Union Theological Seminary from 1908 to 1911, served churches in Kansas and Maine, did surveys for the church, spent time in Europe with the United States army, and was unable to find a pastorate when he returned to the United States in 1919.

In October 1920 Boisen suffered a psychotic episode and spent 15 months in mental hospitals. After he recovered, he began an experiment in religious ministry to the mentally ill. In July 1924 he began as chaplain at Worcester State Hospital in Massachusetts. He also wanted to train seminary students in such work, and in 1925 he had his first four students, the beginning of the clinical training movement. He became chaplain at Elgin State Hospital in Illinois in 1931 and lived there the rest of his life. He retired officially from Elgin in 1938 and taught for three years but returned to Elgin for research and writing.

Boisen's major books are *Exploration of the Inner World* (1936), *Religion in Crisis and Custom* (1945), and his autobiography, *Out of the Depths* (1960), which details five psychotic episodes occurring between 1908 and 1935. He describes these as problem-solving experiences, leaving him not worse but better. Much of his original thinking came from his efforts to test the insights formed during these periods of acute conflict. Out of these experiences has come the clinical pastoral education movement (*see* Association for Clinical Pastoral Education). In 1930 the Council for the Clinical Training of Theological Students was incorporated.

Boisen used clinical case studies, sociological surveys, and his own experiences as a participant observer keeping company with the patients and staff of the old custodial mental hospital. He made contributions to psychology, religion, and the psychology of religion. He is more often remembered for his idiosyncrasies and schizoid personality than for his contributions—contributions made both because of and in spite of his personal experience of mental illness.

R. L. KOTESKEY

See CLINICAL PASTORAL EDUCATION; PASTORAL CARE; PASTORAL COUNSELING.

Borderline Personality Disorder. A complex of emotional storms, erratic behavior, and marked disturbances in relationships based on gross distortions of images of self and intimate others. This disorder became recognized with its inclusion in *DSM-III*. Planners considered calling it the unstable personality disorder, a name closer to its clinical presentation than considering it on a border between psychosis and neurosis.

Symptoms cluster first around affective swings similar to but more severe than those of the narcissist, from abject terror or panic to blinding rage; second, around interpersonal relationships that radically oscillate between clinging dependency and abusiveness; and third, around distorted cognitions that tend briefly to become psychotic in circumstances of injury or rage, while still maintaining a certain amount of reality testing between the storms. These characteristics, to one degree or another, are noted in all other personality disorders when they are severe enough. Unique to the borderline is a peculiar inner emptiness, a rapidly escalating tension, an impulsivity, and self-mutilating actions such as wrist slashing.

Although the diagnosis has been used only recently by anyone other than psychoanalysts, the patients have been around a long time. These individuals cut a wide swath of misery in society, leave a series of shattered innocent lives scattered in their wakes, and devastate those who have the misfortune to fall in love with them or be related to them. Psychologists began to identify a group of clients with striking overelaborated affect and psychoticlike responses on the Rorschach. Psychoanalysts noted severe, psychoticlike regressions in free association in some patients with totally unpredictable responses to interpretations. Criminologists found them fairly normal people who occasionally commit heinous crimes but who are not typical sociopaths. Hospital staffs noted outbursts with trivial provocation, deceptive manipulation, and a failure to establish an effective therapeutic relationship. Psychotherapists noticed this as well, finding themselves dealing with a series of outlandish crises, fights, self-inflicted wounds, and unrelenting trouble.

Lumping these people together as borderlines created what seemed a wastebasket term for troublesome patients. The category soon accrued hostility also, since the borderline inevitably induces feelings of helplessness and retaliatory rage in caretakers who respond to their overwhelming need and then find themselves under attack when help is proffered.

Still, in a few years the borderline diagnosis became widely recognized; a need to understand and help these people and those who are injured by them soon followed. Now it has elicited more attention in the literature, better descriptions, and more understanding than any other personality disorder.

Diagnosis. Although the borders of the borderline remain a little hazy, instruments like Gunderson's Diagnostic Interview for Borderlines provide some help (Gunderson & Singer, 1975). The Borderline Personality Disorder Scale of Perry and Vaillant (1989) and Kernberg's (1975) structural interview for borderline personality organization have discriminated the borderline from other affective and personality disorders sufficiently well to help with research. Now the etiology, psychopathology, and more recently biology and genetics of the disorder are better understood.

Yet the symptoms that best discriminate the borderline are also the most puzzling. To treat such symptoms, the features one needs most to understand include explosive affect, interpersonal conflict, and fragmented identity. These all occur also in the narcissistic personality disorder, but in the borderline these distortions are much more severe and create more chaos than the milder pathology at the narcissistic level.

If one listens attentively to the patient's description of an explosive response to some injury or threat, the curve of arousal ascends quickly beyond the limits of normal upset and their internal mental images, or objects of self and significant others, change radically. The caring helper or lover becomes the vicious abuser, the self-image of a grandiose lord of all or the favored child becomes a worthless castoff, a helpless victim. The rage from such thoughts pours oil on the fires of the arousal, and an apparently unprovoked explosion results. When the arousal is at its peak the borderline's cognitions become psychotic, displaying a flow of primary process thinking. Kernberg (1975) considers this unveiling under stress of a primitive substrate as "still the most important single structural indicator of borderline personality organization." This abrupt switch from "good self"-"good other" to "bad self"-"bad other," or splitting, can be observed directly. Much the same thing happens in all personality disorders, but when they are less severe, the cognitions are less primitive and the results less destructive. As splitting becomes more widespread, normal controls on behavior weaken and are overcome, and the verbal violence of the narcissist becomes the physical abuse often seen in the borderline.

These explosive feeling states result from threatened separations from caregivers of any kind. What feels to the borderline like abject abandonment produces heart-rending appeals for closeness. Closeness then arouses the terrors of engulfment, vulnerability, and loss of control. Such explosions and long, empty loneliness between them destroys empathy, and borderlines lose hope of ever knowing self or anyone else. They often remember their past as constant depression, relieved only by activities carefully chosen to excite or soothe without threatening injury.

Etiology. From the start theorists have considered that some constitutional flaw might explain the excessive arousal of the borderline to perceived injuries, especially those of early life. More recently this research has studied anxiety regulation itself. Family studies, genetic research, and neurochemical studies begin to suggest that borderlines constitutionally experience psychic injury more explosively and more intensely, with less regulatory control on their arousal mechanism than normal people. Should one or both parents have a similar disorder, as is often the case, the growing child not only sustains more injuries but also gets no instruction or modeling in how one handles explosive feelings. With the support and discipline of good parenting, many narcissistic or even borderline children have less pathology and are more responsive to therapy in adulthood.

Description. The clinical picture of borderline structural pathology is colored by the personality type. The "bad hysteric," the psychopath, and the more pathological paranoid personalities present differently but are borderline in their psychic structure. The personality type also gives us hints as to the kinds of injuries that are most damaging. Temperamental differences, for instance in aggressiveness, also color the particular defenses chosen. Nevertheless, the explosive affect and distinctive structural defects are common to all, and these must be understood and addressed at either the narcissistic or borderline level if the patient is to be helped.

Treatment. A number of modalities have been proposed to treat the borderline. All have been reported to be helpful, but none has gained a consensus. Borderlines respond to firm, clear discipline, provided the consequences of disobedience are painful, immediate, and certain. With individual therapy to help them process and learn from punishment it becomes even more helpful. The most rational approach to the structural pathology begins with a discussion of the arousal process itself. Most borderlines are aware of the terrible storms of depressing anxiety that darken their lives but are unaware that their arousals far exceed those of normal people. To understand this and to learn that their problems come from their own responses and thinking rather than from others can helpfully adjust their perspective. With their cooperation, a behavioral program like that used in anger management can begin. Along with these approaches, cognitive techniques can address their wildly distorted, split thinking. Something like a 12-step program can begin to teach them to live more normally and responsively.

For this kind of work groups are by far the most effective instrument for borderlines. Often a certain amount of individual therapy is necessary to get them in the group and keep them there. Anyone, however experienced, who undertakes individual psychotherapy should be alert to the dangerous countertransferences of borderline treatment. To protect the therapist, it is wise to seek supervision should treatment go on for long.

Medication. Medications have not been predictably helpful to the borderline condition as a whole but can modify individual symptoms. Should impulsiveness be a problem, a major tranquilizer or anticonvulsant can be helpful. To regulate affect, tranquilizers have long been shown to be helpful for some, and the newer antidepressants show promise. However, any of these can produce a paradoxical response, in which case stimulants are occasionally helpful. Regulating medication in the borderline requires not only great skill but also a level of cooperation in the patient that is not always available.

Prognosis. Over the years, the core structural difficulties of the borderline change little without treatment. The explosive bursts tend to ameliorate with time and experience, even to the point where these people might become less of a "problem." However, borderlines rarely if ever become happy people.

References

Gunderson, J. G., & Singer, M. T. (1975). Defining borderline patients: An overview. *The American Journal of Psychiatry, 132,* 1–10.

Kernberg, O. (1975). *Borderline conditions and pathological narcissism.* New York: Aronson.

Perry, J. C., & Vaillant, G. S. (1989). Personality disorders. In H. J. Kaplan & B. J. Sadock (Eds.), *Comprehensive textbook of psychiatry.* Baltimore: Williams & Wilkins.

Additional Reading

Kohut, H. (1977). *The restoration of the self.* New York: International Universities Press.

C. M. BERRY

See PERSONALITY DISORDERS.

Boredom. The feeling of unpleasantness and restlessness experienced by an individual who desires to do something but does not know what. In mild forms boredom results from prolonged exposure to an unchanging environment (such as repetitive, monotonous tasks) or from an absence of external stimulation. More pathological forms exist in the presence of external stimulation and are experienced as the inability to become stimulated.

The psychodynamic understanding of boredom assumes that it represents a defense against some unacceptable drive. Fenichel (1953) suggests that it is a state of excitement in which the aim is repressed. Accordingly, bored persons are looking for distraction from their disruptive and unacceptable unconscious urges.

Reference

Fenichel, O. (1953). On the psychology of boredom. In H. Fenichel & D. Rappaport (Eds.), *The collected papers of Otto Fenichel.* New York: D. Lewis.

D. G. BENNER

Boring, Edwin Garrigues (1886–1968). Experimental psychologist and historian of psychology. Born in Philadelphia, Boring received a degree in engineering from Cornell University in 1908. He returned to Cornell for an M.A. degree in psychology in 1912 and a Ph.D. in 1914. He taught at Cornell from 1911 to 1918 and at Clark University from 1919 to 1922; then he began his long career at Harvard. He taught at Harvard from 1922 until his retirement in 1957 and was director of the psychological laboratory there from 1924 to 1949. Under his direction the departments of psychology and philosophy were separated in 1934, and in 1945 the divisions of experimental and physiological psychology were separated from those of social and clinical psychology.

Boring was an experimental psychologist in the broadest sense of the term. Between 1912 and 1929 he published research on audition, animal behavior, dementia praecox, educational psychology, organ and alimentary sensations, thermal sensitivity, the psychology of testimony, cutaneous sensations, psychophysics, vision, sleep, psychometrics, statistics, psychological examining, intelligence, facial expression, psychic research, the psychology of science, olfaction, and memory.

This wide background prepared Boring to write *A History of Experimental Psychology* in 1929, which became the definitive work on the history of psychology. Revised in 1950, it continued to be a leading textbook in the history of psychology in U.S. colleges and universities. He became the leading historian of psychology, also publishing *Sensation and Perception in the History of Experimental Psychology* (1942). He emphasized an intertwined *Zeitgeist* and Great Man theory of history.

In addition to the history of psychology, Boring wrote much on epistemology. Two of his students selected his most important papers and classified them into five categories: history; the psychology of science, the problem of how the beliefs and motivations of the scientist help or hinder scientific progress; the scientific method, especially operationism; the mind-body problem; and the communication of science, the psychological and strategic problems of criticism.

Boring served as co-editor of the *American Journal of Psychology.* He was one of the founders of *Contemporary Psychology: A Journal of Reviews,* and was its editor for the first six years. In his regular monthly feature, "CP Speaks," he called attention to a variety of current issues, many of them the problems of the psychology of communicating science.

R. L. KOTESKEY

See PSYCHOLOGY, HISTORY OF.

Boundary Issues in Pastoral Care. Clergy have many roles in ministry that require intentional boundary or limit setting. It is important that pastors be clear about their strengths and limitations in all aspects of ministry, but especially pastoral care. Surveyed pastors indicate that they feel counseling is the third most important role in ministry, followed by preaching and teaching, and that their ministry involves heavy demands for mental health services. Members of the local church have high expectations of pastors as counselors. When 758 members of the United Methodist Church were asked to name the essential skills for effective ministry, pastoral care also ranked third, this time identified only after preaching and administration. This article discusses some of the structures that pastors need to put in place to effectively set boundaries and develop a responsible pastoral care ministry.

It is important to define and understand the pastoral care role as that of a supportive counselor who will help a person or a family attempt to solve problems for a limited time (two to five sessions). Pastors should avoid doing long-term psychotherapy unless they have the clinical training and the community of faith has affirmed that specialized ministry. Long-term treatment requires extensive education and clinical supervision; most problematic, pastors have a dual relationship as leader or surrogate parental figure within the extended family of a religious community. In all mental health professions, treating a friend or family member is explicitly unethical. The role of the parish-based clergy needs to be defined as skilled facilitator in the mental health network, not as treating psychotherapist. Most pastors say they do not attempt long-term counseling with parishioners and limit their help to a few sessions of problem solving.

If a member of the clergy is going to offer adequate pastoral care with a brief counseling approach as well as guide those who need extended counseling to appropriate help, the pastor needs to know how to do two things well: how to accurately identify the presenting problems and how to access available community resources.

First, it is critical that clergy recognize mental health problems, particularly mental health emergencies such as suicide and major depression, substance abuse, psychosis, domestic violence, child and elder abuse, and psychological trauma. Even though many pastors recognize their need for more effective counseling skills, many report they are unlikely to seek additional training in counseling. The church needs to begin to more effectively train pastors to be able to recognize mental health problems, especially emergencies, and to mandate these screening skills as a part of training for ministry. On a hopeful note, pastors who feel greater competence as counselors are more willing to seek outside assistance for their personal and family problems and are much less prone to alienation and burnout. Apparently those who trust in their ability to help others are more likely to seek help for themselves as well as enjoy a greater satisfaction in ministry.

Second, responsible pastoral care requires clergy to learn to work with mental health specialists. Pastors should develop a working relationship with at least one, preferably several, mental health professionals who have a comprehensive knowledge of the mental health services in the community and are willing to work as a colleague. Pastors should seek out mental health specialists who are open to people of faith and have some appreciation of the scientific fact that religious commitment can be a positive coping resource. Members of the clergy should not be timid. They should interview the mental health specialist on the telephone before referring a person in need. They should ask the specialists direct questions to assess skill level, expertise, and fee schedule. Pastors should ask detailed questions about experience, training, and education. What sorts of cases have they worked with in the past? What specialties do they have? How do they develop a treatment plan for various situations? How easily can they be located in a crisis? Are they willing to do some low-fee work? Clergy should keep a record of available providers to refer to in an emergency.

Finally, sexual issues are an important area in which clergy need to set very clear boundaries. Sexual behavior with someone a pastor serves in pastoral ministry is unethical and immoral as well as spiritually and psychologically damaging to the individual. Although we do not have clear studies telling us the rate of sexual misconduct among clergy, we do know that about 1 in 20 male psychotherapists has been found to act in a sexual way toward his female clients. These counselors were most likely to act sexually toward clients when they were in dysfunctional marriages, recently separated or divorced, and in highly stressful situations. Pastors who are emotionally vulnerable need to pay extra attention to sexual issues in their ministry. Pastors who are sexually attracted to someone they are counseling will need to seek consultation from a wise colleague in ministry or a mental health specialist. They will need to develop a plan of self-examination and good self-care practices that can reduce stress. Working with people in emotional distress but in isolation, without good self-care practices and a good support system, will place pastors at higher risk of sexual misconduct.

Additional Readings

Benner, D. G. (1992). *Strategic pastoral counseling.* Grand Rapids, MI: Baker.

Childs B. H. (1990). *Short-term pastoral counseling.* Nashville: Abingdon.

Fortune, M. (1989). *Is nothing sacred? When sex invades the pastoral relationship.* New York: Harper.

Miller, R. W., & Jackson, K. A. (1995). *Practical psychology for pastors.* Englewood Cliffs, NJ: Prentice-Hall.

Orthner, D. K. (1986). *Pastoral counseling: Caring and caregivers in the United Methodist Church.* Nashville: The

General Board of Higher Education and Ministry of The United Methodist Church.

Switzer, D. (1986). *The minister as the crisis counselor.* Nashville: Abingdon.

Weaver, A. J. (1995). Has there been a failure to prepare and support parish-based clergy in their role as front-line community mental health workers? A review. *The Journal of Pastoral Care, 49* (2),129–149.

A. J. WEAVER

See PASTORAL CARE; PASTORAL COUNSELING.

Brain and Human Behavior. The idea that the brain is uniquely involved in behavior is taken for granted today. What behavior can be performed without a functioning brain? However, the position that the brain is implicated in behavior defined in the broadest possible sense (i.e., overt motor behavior, thoughts, feelings, perceptions, awareness, desires) is also true, if not as widely accepted. No human thought, emotion, wish, or motor action is conceivable without brain activity.

Early Greek philosophers disagreed as to whether the brain or the heart is the location of behavior. The hypothesis that the brain controls behavior prevailed eventually, in part because of empirical observations showing that nerves travel from the sense organs to the brain, not the heart. The acceptance of this hypothesis led to an attempt to localize various functions in specific brain areas.

The exact number of nerve cells, called neurons, in the human nervous system is unknown, but estimates range between 100 and 1,000 billion. The postulate that individual neurons are the primary signaling elements in the nervous system was developed by the Spanish histologist Santiago Ramón y Cajal and is known as the neuron doctrine. These neurons are arranged into functioning groups and are interconnected, forming a vast net through which they communicate with each other and the rest of the body (Kandel, Schwartz, & Jessell, 1995, pp. 6–8).

The brain, along with the spinal cord, composes what is called the central nervous system (CNS). Any cell, neural or nonneural, in the brain or spinal cord is part of the CNS. Together with the peripheral nervous system (PNS), which consists of cranial nerves (those nerves that leave the brain) and spinal nerves (those nerves that leave the spinal cord), the CNS exercises control over even the most complex human behavior.

Regions of the Central Nervous System. The adult human CNS is typically organized into four main divisions: the spinal cord, the hindbrain, the midbrain, and the forebrain.

The Spinal Cord. The spinal cord extends from the base of the skull and is protected by the vertebral column. Approximately the diameter of a little finger and 42–45 cm long, the spinal cord sends out motor neurons for both voluntary and involuntary movements and collects sensory information from the

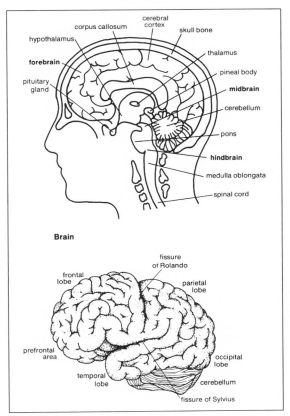

figure 1 Brain

trunk and limbs of the body. The spinal cord is also the site for certain stereotyped motor reflexes such as the knee-jerk reflex. Thus the spinal cord acts as a pathway to and from the brain, a road over which much but not all of the brain's control over behavior is accomplished.

The spinal cord is segmented, and from these segments come 31 pairs of spinal nerves that exit the cord and travel to various parts of the body. These nerves are mixed (i.e., they carry both sensory and motor messages), but the information is divided into sensory and motor components at the spinal cord itself. Sensory information enters the cord along the dorsal (top or back) surface while motor information leaves the cord along the ventral (front) surface. A further division within the spinal cord is seen in the manner in which information to or from the brain is carried along clearly defined ascending (sensory) and descending (motor) paths.

The Hindbrain. The hindbrain is composed of three main structures: the medulla oblongata, the pons, and the cerebellum. The medulla oblongata, or medulla, is the extension of the spinal cord into the brain itself and is organized in a manner similar to the spinal cord. Centers for cardiovascular regulation and respiration are located in the medulla.

Moving in an anterior (toward the head) direction, the next principal structure is the pons, which protrudes from the ventral surface of the brainstem. The pons (Latin for bridge) contains relay areas connecting the cerebral hemispheres to the cerebellum. The pons also contains neurons involved in sleep and arousal.

Lying on top of the brainstem dorsal to the pons and medulla, the cerebellum (little brain) is involved in equilibrium, postural control, and coordinated movement (e.g., standing, walking, playing the cello). The cerebellum receives input from sensory systems and integrates this information with data regarding muscle movements directed by the brain. Recent evidence also indicates that the cerebellum is involved in some forms of learning and cognition. Specific cells located in the cerebellum are necessary for classical conditioning to occur, and neuroimaging studies indicate that the cerebellum is also involved in cognitive functions such as attention shifting, mental fluency, and timing. The cerebellum has also recently been implicated in disorders such as dyslexia and autism.

The Midbrain. Anterior to the pons lies the midbrain, which consists of several regions involved in eye movements, sleep and arousal, attention, motor behavior, and various vital reflexes.

The Forebrain. The forebrain is composed of several structures, most of which are bilateral structures (i.e., they are located in both sides or hemispheres of the brain). The first of these structures is the thalamus. Almost all sensory and motor information going to the cerebral cortex passes through and is processed by the thalamus, which is located roughly in the center of the brain and thus makes a good reference point. Damage to the thalamus, which typically occurs due to vascular accidents, can result in loss of somatic sensation in the contralateral (opposite side) body and head.

Just below the thalamus is the hypothalamus, which is involved in emotional and somatic functions and controls the behaviors necessary for survival (e.g., feeding and drinking). Its connections with other brain areas are intricate and widespread but can be organized into three major categories: interconnections with motor and sensory areas in the brainstem and spinal cord, outputs to the pituitary gland, and interconnections with the limbic system. One area of the hypothalamus, the suprachiasmatic nucleus (SCN), is believed to operate as a biological clock in humans, helping to regulate the normal cyclical pattern of much of our behavior. Sleeping, arousal, and temperature regulation are just a few of the behaviors that follow a daily, rhythmical pattern.

Another area in the hypothalamus is the medial forebrain bundle (MFB), the so-called reward center. Electrical stimulation of these cells is considered reinforcing or rewarding in both animals and humans. Other hypothalamic areas include nuclei (groups of cells) involved in feeding and satiety. The exact influence these nuclei have over eating is not simple, but they clearly exert some control over these necessary behaviors.

The hypothalamus is also involved in sexual behavior, and evidence has linked some cells in the hypothalamus to sexual orientation (LeVay, 1991). While this evidence is controversial (Byne & Parsons, 1993), it does represent a developing area of research in brain-behavior relationships.

Behavior is influenced by hormones, and hormone release is ultimately controlled by the hypothalamus via its connections to the pituitary gland, the master gland of the body, which lies just below the hypothalamus. The hypothalamus communicates with the pituitary both chemically and neurally to influence the ultimate release of specific hormones.

The pineal body, which sits just posterior (toward the tail) to the thalamus and is not bilaterally represented, controls seasonal rhythms by secreting a chemical called melatonin. Melatonin has received attention as a substance used to help induce sleep. While the exact mechanism of action is unknown, the pineal does seem to exercise some control over the biological clock(s) of the body.

The cerebral hemispheres are the largest region of the brain and consist of several structures, including the limbic system and the basal ganglia. The basal ganglia are a group of cells buried within the hemispheres that are involved in the control of movement. Specific structures composing the basal ganglia are the caudate nucleus, the globus pallidus, and the putamen. Damage to the basal ganglia results in unintentional movements and disturbances of muscle tone. Parkinson's disease results from the death of cells within the midbrain that send messages to the basal ganglia (*see* Parkinson's Disease). Another disease resulting from degeneration of the basal ganglia, particularly in the caudate nucleus, is Huntington's disease, a hereditary disorder that affects movement and cognition and is ultimately fatal.

The limbic system consists of several structures and is responsible for motivation, emotion, and learning and memory. It has widespread connections with both cortical areas and with the hypothalamus. There is no universal agreement on which brain structures compose the limbic system; however, there is agreement that two principal structures of the limbic system are the amygdala and the hippocampus. The amygdala is important in emotional behavior. Tumors of the amygdala or surrounding tissue can produce aggressive, violent behavior. The hippocampus is involved primarily in learning and memory. Damage to the hippocampus produces amnesia (*see* Amnestic Disorders), in particular a type of amnesia in which declarative memory is lost. Declarative memory, or knowledge, is memory for facts and data that are directly accessible to conscious recollection; it is often contrasted with procedural memory, which is knowledge of how to do certain skills, knowledge that is typically spared in amnesia.

The cerebral hemispheres are covered by a convoluted surface called the cerebral cortex. The convolutions consist of sulci (small grooves), fissures (large grooves), and gyri (bulges between sulci), and result in nearly two-thirds of the surface area of the cortex (a total of 2.5 square feet in humans) being hidden in the grooves.

The surface of the cerebral cortex is divided into four lobes, each lobe containing areas specialized for a particular function. The frontal lobe extends from the frontal pole to the central sulcus (or fissure of Rolando) and laterally to the lateral sulcus (or fissure of Sylvius), and it contains the primary motor area. A map, or homunculus (Latin for little person), of the entire body is laid out onto this cortical area. A neural impulse originating in particular cells of this motor area will produce muscular movement in the corresponding portion of the body. Also in the frontal lobe is an area of cortex specialized for language, Broca's area. This speech center, used in speech production, is located only in one hemisphere, the left hemisphere in most people. A third area found in the frontal lobe is the prefrontal area, which is concerned with what is generally described as personality.

Posterior to the fissure of Rolando is the parietal lobe, which contains the primary somatosensory cortex. Again, the entire body is laid out onto this cortex, and somatosensory stimulation originating in a particular body area will ultimately terminate in the corresponding cells of the somatosensory cortex. In addition parts of the parietal lobe are involved in language comprehension (again, usually the left parietal lobe), spatial orientation, and perception.

Lying on the back surface of the cerebral cortex is the occipital lobe, the location for the primary visual cortex and higher-order visual processing areas. The final lobe, the temporal lobe, is found on the side of the cerebral cortex and contains the primary auditory cortex and parts of the limbic system.

The two cerebral hemispheres do not function independently; they are connected via several structures called commissures, the largest of which is the corpus callosum. The corpus callosum connects corresponding anatomical sites in the two hemispheres. Cutting the corpus callosum yields the so-called split-brain preparation in which the two hemispheres do not share information and thus appear to act independently. This procedure is sometimes performed to treat intractable epilepsy (*see* Epilepsy).

The Peripheral Nervous System. The CNS communicates with the rest of the body via cranial and spinal nerves that make up the peripheral nervous system. The PNS is composed of two general systems, the somatic nervous system, which receives information from the sensory organs and controls movement of the skeletal or voluntary muscles, and the autonomic nervous system, which regulates smooth (or involuntary) muscles, cardiac muscle, and the glands of the body. Smooth muscles are found in blood vessels to control constriction, in the

eyes to control pupil dilation and lens accommodation, and around various organs of the body such as the bladder.

The autonomic nervous system is in turn divided into two roughly complementary branches: the sympathetic and parasympathetic divisions. The sympathetic division is involved in the expenditure of energy, for example, the changes in the body necessary for fight or flight. These changes include an increase in blood pressure and heart rate, a rise in blood sugar, and increased blood flow to the muscles (Carlson, 1994, p. 102). The parasympathetic division is involved in activities that increase the storage of energy in the body (rest and digest), for example, gastrointestinal motility and salivation. The sympathetic and parasympathetic systems generally have opposite effects on the organs they serve. The sympathetic system increases heart rate while the parasympathetic system decreases heart rate; pupils dilate due to sympathetic activity and constrict as a result of parasympathetic action.

The brain also controls behavior through its effects on the endocrine glands. The endocrine glands, such as the gonads, thyroid gland, and adrenal glands, release chemical messengers called hormones into the general circulation of the body. The secretion of these hormones from the endocrine glands is controlled by the pituitary gland located at the base of the hypothalamus. The hypothalamus communicates with the pituitary both directly, through neurons that originate in the hypothalamus and terminate in the pituitary, and indirectly via chemicals that travel from the hypothalamus to the pituitary through a special circulatory system linking the two structures.

When either neural or chemical signals reach the pituitary, it in turn releases a particular chemical that enters the bloodstream and eventually reaches the appropriate endocrine gland, or target. The gland will then secrete its hormone into the general circulation. For example, under stressful conditions the hypothalamus releases a chemical called corticotropin releasing factor (CRF), which travels to the pituitary causing it to secrete the adrenocorticotropic hormone (ACTH). ACTH travels via the general circulation to the adrenal gland where, in response to ACTH, another hormone, cortisol, is secreted. Cortisol helps prepare the body to fight stress by, for example, increasing blood flow and stimulating the breakdown of protein into glucose for energy.

Current Research Areas in Brain-Behavior Relationships. An important area of investigation in neuroscience is the manner in which the brain influences health. If the brain controls all behavior, how can the brain influence behavior that promotes either health or illness? One of the leading causes of death in the United States is cardiovascular disease (e.g., heart attacks and strokes). Risk factors for cardiovascular disease include high blood pressure and high cholesterol in the blood. Another risk factor seems to be the manner in which a person responds to a potential stressor (Carlson, 1994, p. 363). Both animal and human studies show that those subjects who demonstrate the strongest negative reaction to a potential stressor have the highest risk of cardiovascular disease. Evidence suggests that some of this negative reaction might be due to a hyperreactive hypothalamus. Such an abnormality could affect health via the type of mechanism whereby ACTH and cortisol are released in larger than normal amounts in all types of situations.

An additional potential risk factor for cardiovascular disease is personality. Some evidence has suggested that Type A personality (competitive, impatient, hostile) is correlated with several other risk factors. For example, the Type A pattern is more likely to be found among smokers, those who have high blood pressure, and those with high blood cholesterol levels (Carlson, 1994, p. 364).

Another way the brain can influence behavior and health is through its effect on the immune system. The immune system's function is to protect us from infection, and the immune reactions of the body involve various cell types that communicate with each other (Carlson, 1994, pp. 365–366). While the immune system normally protects the body, it can cause harm. The reactions produced by the system can attack healthy cells, leading to autoimmune diseases such as rheumatoid arthritis, multiple sclerosis, and diabetes mellitus. In addition stress directly suppresses the immune system by way of the secretion of cortisol from the adrenal gland, which is controlled by the brain (through CRF).

A second major area of research in brain-behavior relationships is the study of how abnormal behaviors, such as the hallucinations and delusions found in schizophrenia, are produced by the brain. Many disorders that have traditionally been classified as psychological (e.g., depression, schizophrenia, and anxiety) have biological bases. Neuroscientists and physiological psychologists are trying to elucidate how the brain generates these behaviors and what that generation can tell us about normal brain activity and normal brain-behavior relationships.

The brain is involved in all human behavior. Whether the behavior is abnormal (e.g., hallucination) or normal (e.g., the perception of actual auditory stimuli), it could not occur without a functioning brain. In addition our ability to love, get angry, dream, worship, learn, move, have self-awareness, remember what happened yesterday or 25 years ago, or plan what we will do tomorrow is impossible without our brain. Much of what we are as humans results from brain activity, and it is because of the brain's importance that the 1990s has been designated by the United States Congress as The Decade of the Brain.

References

Byne, W., & Parsons, B. (1993). Human sexual orientation: The biologic theories reappraised. *Archives of General Psychiatry, 50,* 228–239.

Carlson, N. R. (1994). *Physiology of behavior* (5th ed.). Boston: Allyn & Bacon.

Kandel, E. R., Schwartz, J. H., & Jessell, T. M. (1995). *Essentials of neural science and behavior.* Norwalk, CT: Appleton & Lange.

LeVay, S. (1991). A difference in hypothalamic structure between heterosexual and homosexual men. *Science, 253,* 1034–1037.

Additional Readings

Bear, M. F., Connors, B. W., & Paradiso, M. A. (1996). *Neuroscience: Exploring the brain.* Baltimore: Williams & Wilkins.

Finger, S. (1994). *Origins of neuroscience: A history of explorations into brain function.* New York: Oxford University Press.

Nolte, J. (1993). *The human brain: An introduction to its functional anatomy* (3rd ed.). St. Louis: Mosby Year Book.

K. S. Seybold

See Neuropsychology.

Brain Injuries. A brain injury, more commonly referred to as traumatic brain injury (TBI), is an acquired condition in which damage to brain tissue occurs due to mechanical forces being applied to the head. In acceleration injuries, a moving object strikes a stationary head, resulting in brain tissue damage. In a deceleration injury, a head that is in motion is stopped by a stationary object. Brain injuries are considered open when an object penetrates the skull (e.g., a bullet wound to the head or an object striking the skull, depressing the skull material into the brain cortex itself). A closed TBI occurs when significant motion of the head results in brain damage or when the head is struck without any penetration into the cortex.

Brain tissue damage can be due to diffuse axonal injury, which occurs when acceleration or deceleration forces create movements of the brain within the skull, resulting in shearing of the neuronal axons across the cerebral cortex. Diffuse axonal injury renders the person unconscious. Focal contusions occur after TBI and are bruises in the brain tissue in which increased blood and fluid collect, similar to what is normally seen in bruises of the hand or arm. In mildest form contusions are limited to increased fluid or edema in the area of damage. In more severe contusions there is more pure blood in the damaged area, and this is known as a hemorrhage or hematoma.

The most common areas of brain tissue damage are the frontal lobe regions of both the right and left cerebral hemispheres and the forward portions of the right and left temporal lobes. This situation arises due to the location of the frontal and temporal lobes, which ride on regions of the skull that have bony ridges. With acceleration or deceleration forces being applied to the head, the brain will move across these bony ridges in the frontal and temporal regions, resulting in a greater frequency of axonal damage and contusions in these areas.

Traumatic brain injuries are graded in levels of severity most commonly by the Glasgow Coma Scale (Teasdale & Jennett, 1974). This scale is administered by medical personnel such as emergency medical technicians or paramedics at the scene of an accident and by medical staff during a patient's early emergency trauma treatment. The scale measures the patient's best verbal response, eye response, and motor movement. The scale runs from a low of 3 to a high of 15. Patients with scores between 13 and 15 are graded as a mild TBI. Those with scores between 9 and 12 are considered moderate, and from 3 to 8 as severe.

Large epidemiological studies (Kalsbeek, McLauren, Harris, & Miller, 1981; Kraus, 1978) have found that the incidence of TBI is 200 per 100,000 in the population. This totals approximately 500,000 new traumatic brain injuries per year, of whom 20% die. Another 10% to 20% survive with severe impairments that prevent independent living, and up to another 20% have deficits that permanently interfere with daily living skills. About two-thirds of all TBIs are mild. Motor vehicle accidents account for approximately 50% of all traumatic brain injuries in the United States, followed by falls of various types. More than twice as many males than females sustain such injuries, with the greatest number occurring in the 15-to-24 age range.

Common physical consequences of TBI include changes in vision, smell, taste, and hearing. Motor problems such as paralysis, numbing, and sensation changes can occur, as can changes in balance and gait. Seizure disorders are an increased risk after TBI. Cardinal cognitive problems include language disturbances, short-term memory disorders, problems with visual and spatial analytic ability, impaired alertness, difficulties with sustained auditory and visual attention, and changes in abstract reasoning. Deficits in self-awareness and self-monitoring are common. Difficulties with impulse control, temper outbursts, and initiating new activities are problematic. Major depressive disorder occurs in about one-third of patients with TBI within the first year postinjury.

Systems of care are available for individuals with TBI. These range from rehabilitation medicine services within large medical centers to free-standing specialty rehabilitation hospitals and programs in the community (Uomoto & McLean, 1989).

References

Kalsbeek, W., McLauren, R., Harris, B., & Miller, J. (1981). The national head and spinal cord injury survey: Major findings. *Journal of Neurosurgery, 53*, 19–31.

Kraus, J. (1978). Epidemiologic features of head and spinal cord injury. *Advances in Neurology, 19*, 261–279.

Teasdale, G., & Jennett, B. (1974). Assessment of coma and impaired consciousness. A practical scale. *Lancet, 2*, 81–84.

Uomoto, J. M., & McLean, A. (1989). The care continuum in traumatic brain injury rehabilitation. *Rehabilitation Psychology, 34*, 71–79.

J. M. UOMOTO

Brainwashing. The emergence and increased visibility of New Age Cults and other religious movements since the late 1960s have engendered considerable discussion and debate regarding allegations of brainwashing and mind control on the part of these new cultic groups. The controversy, at both professional and popular levels, centers on whether certain techniques are employed consciously or unconsciously by cults and self-improvement groups, with detrimental outcomes.

The term *brainwashing* is a useful though scientifically imprecise concept that refers to the systematic manipulation of social and psychological influences, in a particular environment, to achieve attitudinal and behavioral change. Such synonymous terms as thought reform, coercive persuasion, resocialization, and mind control are frequently used in the literature.

According to the research findings of sociologists, psychologists, and other mental health professionals, authoritarian groups employ recruitment and indoctrination procedures that effectively induce behavioral and cognitive changes in new recruits. Such changes involve a gradual process of breaking down and transformation resulting in diminished personal autonomy, increased dependency, and the assumption of a new identity and worldview. Psychospiritual conditioning mechanisms used by cults destabilize an individual's sense of self and affect members' ability to fully exercise independent judgment. Members are subjected to intense indoctrination pressures, which include the manipulation of commitment mechanisms so that new converts assume a posture of unswerving loyalty to the organization and unquestioning obedience to the leadership.

It should be noted that not all groups that use some form of mind control implement their manipulative techniques in the same way or to the same extent. There is considerable variation within individual cults and across groups.

The brainwashing view of cult recruitment posits that new adherents are isolated from the outside world in order to minimize contacts with persons holding conflicting views as well as to reinforce commitment to the group and its particular worldview. External ties with all familiar social support systems, including family, friends, and former church connections, are usually severed. Especially evident is the disruption of normal family bonds and the redefinition of past frames of reference. The cult becomes the convert's new spiritual family.

Members are placed into a socially and psychologically dependent state in which decision making is minimal. Leaders maintain a taut organizational structure by suppressing dissent and managing group loyalty. The convert is able to function relatively independently and securely within the cult's social and ideological structure but is often dysfunctional outside the totalistic milieu.

In addition to residential isolation and the suppression of alternative views, control-oriented cults are also characterized by a vigorous regime of work, fund-raising, recruitment, and participation in various sorts of ritual. When this intense level of activity and the resulting sensory deprivation (particularly sleep) is combined with a low-protein diet, limited self-reflection, reduced privacy, and a highly idealistic orientation, the thought reform potential of any given group becomes increasingly plausible. This is especially true when strong affective ties are encouraged toward a living person who is the charismatic leader/inspirator of the group.

Many of the newer cultic movements, especially the Eastern mystical groups, stress the use of various forms of psychospiritual technology in order to achieve desired altered states of consciousness. These conditioning mechanisms include meditation, repetitive chanting, and various forms of yoga. They are employed to eliminate all consciously directed thought and to heighten awareness levels. From the Christian perspective such spiritual technologies also open the individual to the possibility of demonic involvement.

Brainwashing cults, by using techniques of environmental and interpersonal manipulation, are able to foster an unquestioning devotion to the cause. Themes of sacrifice and renunciation are common. True believers must be willing to sacrifice a college education, a career, or even a potential mate for the good of the group. An austere living arrangement and disengagement from the outside world may be called for. In some groups new names and a new manner of dress are cultural insignia that identify a newly found lifestyle.

Thought reform is reinforced by the threat of sanctions should one ever consider leaving the group. Fear, guilt, and various forms of psychospiritual intimidation are effective means of ensuring conformity and limiting defections. Physical punishment is rare but not unknown. Dissenters are viewed as rebellious detractors from the cause and are encouraged to submit their individual wills to group goals.

Critics of the brainwashing argument maintain that it is a simplistic concept with little scientific evidence to support its claims. Such critics point to the absence of physical coercion in virtually all the major religious cults and to the fact that voluntary exit from these groups is not uncommon. They argue that the manipulation that undoubtedly occurs in cults has been exaggerated and is nothing more than extensions of basic principles of group dynamics and psychological conditioning that are routinely applied in less emotionally charged situations. The accusation of brainwashing, it is claimed, is applied to unfamiliar new religions by those who disapprove of such groups and fear them or by those seeking a scapegoat, including parents who are no longer able to exert influence over their offspring.

It is difficult for the Christian observer to remain neutral and value-free in the face of accumulating evidence of the destructiveness of cults on human lives. Certainly the Scriptures make frequent reference to spiritual brainwashing as a device commonly employed by God's adversary, Satan. It should not be surprising, then, that false teachers and self-appointed spiritual masters have achieved considerable success in undermining and subverting the autonomy of many people who have joined cults.

Additional Readings

Lifton, R. J. (1989). *Thought reform and the psychology of totalism*. Chapel Hill: University of North Carolina Press.

Singer, M. (1995). *Cults in our midst*. San Francisco: Jossey-Bass.

Tobias, M. L., & Lalich, J. (1994). *Captive hearts, captive minds*. Alameda, CA: Hunter House.

R. ENROTH

See ATTITUDE-BEHAVIOR RELATIONSHIPS; COMPLIANCE.

Breuer, Josef (1842–1925). A highly respected and successful Viennese neurologist-scientist whose considerable contributions tend to be veiled in the shadow of Sigmund Freud. Freud himself credited Breuer with the creation of psychoanalysis. However, even before their collaboration Breuer had made fundamental and far-reaching discoveries in mammalian physiology.

Breuer was influenced by the *Zeitgeist* of the physicalistic science then dominating the medical faculty of the University of Vienna. A skeptic, Breuer described himself as one who had religious needs but found himself utterly unable to satisfy them within the faith of popular religion. Although his writings reveal little interest in religion, he was neither irreligious nor antireligious.

Breuer early manifested a talent for experimental science. With Ewald Hering, he identified the mechanism regulating respiration. A second major contribution was his elucidation of the differing functions of the labyrinth. Over a 40-year period he published some 20 purely physiological articles. But his primary loyalty was to his large and lucrative practice, serving the illustrious and the indigent alike.

Freud's acquaintance with Breuer, an older and highly respected physician in Vienna, came as a result of his fascination with Breuer's reported treatment of a hysterical young woman named Anna O. To Breuer's great surprise he found that, after the patient reported the details of the onset of her hysterical symptoms (paralysis as well as sight and speech disturbances), these symptoms disappeared. His treatment evolved from this discovery and placed a major emphasis on catharsis and hypnosis, techniques of much interest to Freud at this early point in the development of psychoanalysis.

In the course of his work Breuer arrived at two important principles that were to become the cornerstone of psychoanalysis. First, neurotic symptoms arise from unconscious processes. Second, these symptoms disappear when their causes are made conscious through verbalization. Freud and Breuer published their observations in "Psychic Mechanisms in Hysteria" (1893) and their practical and theoretical conclusions in *Studies on Hysteria* (1895). Psychoanalysis and a new era of psychotherapy were born.

In his obituary of Breuer, Freud expressed regret that Breuer's brilliance had been directed toward psychopathology for only a brief time. All the eulogies published after Breuer's death emphasize that the range and depth of his cultural interests were as unusual and important as his medical and scientific accomplishments.

Q. R. DeYoung

See Psychoanalytic Psychology.

Brief Psychotic Disorder. In *DSM-IV* (American Psychiatric Association, 1994) brief psychotic disorder replaces and expands on the former brief reactive psychosis to include all transitory psychotic episodes that last at least one day but less than one month and from which there is a complete return to previous levels of functioning.

The disorder is characterized by a sudden onset of at least one of the following psychotic symptoms: delusions, hallucinations, disorganized or incoherent speech, or grossly disorganized or catatonic behavior. To clarify the context in which these symptoms occur the diagnosis is amended by one of the following specifiers: with marked stressor(s), symptoms develop shortly after and apparently in response to one or more events that would be markedly stressful to almost anyone; without marked stressor(s), symptoms do not appear to be temporally related to a stressor; and with postpartum onset, symptoms occur within four weeks after childbirth.

Brief psychotic disorder appears most frequently when persons are in their late twenties or their thirties. People typically experience emotional turmoil or overwhelming confusion in response to the psychotic symptoms. They may need protection from the consequences of poor judgment, misunderstanding what is real, or acting on their delusions. There is an increased risk of life-threatening behaviors and a high potential for suicide.

Brief psychotic disorder must be distinguished from culturally sanctioned patterns of behavior. For instance, hearing voices or seeing visions during religious ceremonies or practices, where these are a part of the person's religious tradition, would not be considered abnormal. Brief psychotic disorder is also distinguished from other psychotic disorders on the basis of time and context. If symptoms last for less than one day or more than one month, if they occur in the context of a medical condition, substance use, or a mood disorder, or if they are intentionally produced, this diagnosis is not made.

Initial treatment seeks to protect persons from self-harm through suicidal gestures or dangerous risk-taking behaviors. A period of brief hospitalization may be required to help them stabilize, reduce confusion, and initiate a short-term course of antipsychotic medications. Follow-up psychotherapy (individual, family, and/or marital as indicated) is essential to facilitate understanding of the experience, repair interpersonal relationships, and evaluate what stressors or conditions were involved. A full return to previous levels of activity is indicated, and with the support of professionals and family members this episode can be placed in its rightful context.

Reference

American Psychiatric Association. (1994). *Diagnosis and statistical manual of mental disorders* (4th ed.). Washington, DC: Author.

B. E. Eck

See Psychotic Disorders.

Brief Therapy. *See* Short-Term Therapies.

Briquet's Syndrome. *See* Somatization Disorder.

Broadspectrum Psychotherapy. An expression that denotes an openmindedness regarding the practice of psychotherapy. It has more to do with attitude than with preference for any particular theoretical orientation. Some psychotherapists are likely to consider the term synonymous with eclecticism. Although the same basic frame of reference characterizes both eclecticism and broadspectrum therapy, the latter tends to be more precise in conceptualization, to be treated more systematically, and to possess greater breadth and comprehensiveness.

Multidimensionality in problem analysis or diagnosis and treatment modalities is the central theme of broadspectrum therapy. A stronger emphasis is usually placed on the applied and practical aspects than on the philosophical and theoretical issues. A major assumption is that the best clinical treatment is provided when the presenting problem is defined from the widest possible perspective and interventions are made by carefully selecting appropriate methods and strategies from a storehouse of well-refined techniques. The methodological options are dictated by an accurate diagnosis, an integration of the various components of the problem situation, and a compatibility of the techniques with the personality of both the therapist and the client.

Broadspectrum therapy has been articulated most clearly by Lazarus (1971, 1976) under the term *multimodal therapy*. Other advocates of the broadspectrum approach, though they might not use the specific term to describe their position, include Ivey (Ivey & Simek-Downing, 1980) and Goldfried (1982).

References

Goldfried, M. R. (1982). *Converging themes in psychotherapy.* New York: Springer.

Ivey, A. E., & Simek-Downing, L. (1980). *Counseling and psychotherapy.* Englewood Cliffs, NJ: Prentice-Hall.

Lazarus, A. A. (1971). *Behavior therapy and beyond.* New York: McGraw-Hill.

Lazarus, A. A. (1976). *Multimodal behavior therapy.* New York: Springer.

D. SMITH

Bruner, Jerome Seymour (1915–). Best known as a child psychologist who has had significant impact on the field of education. Born in New York, Bruner completed the Ph.D. degree in psychology at Harvard in 1941 after completing a bachelor's degree at Duke in 1937.

Bruner's first interests in psychology were animal perception and learning. These interests shifted to human psychology with the outbreak of World War II. During the war Bruner studied human perceptions and propaganda, and he wrote his doctoral thesis on Nazi propaganda techniques. He served with General Eisenhower's headquarters, working on psychological warfare.

After the war Bruner returned to Harvard, where he began his work on children's perceptions. His studies indicated that needs and values strongly influence human perceptions. Bruner soon became a main force in cognitive psychology, and by 1960 he had helped establish the Center for Cognitive Studies at Harvard.

After Russia launched *Sputnik* in 1957, America placed new emphasis on education. Various types of experts were consulted, and Bruner became involved in educational psychology. In 1960 he wrote *The Process of Education,* in which he makes his famous statement, "Any subject can be taught effectively in some intellectually honest way to any person at any stage of development." He was quickly misquoted and criticized as saying that anything could be taught to anybody regardless of the person's age.

Bruner's hypothesis was based upon the concept of structure. He maintained that any subject matter or field of knowledge has an inherent structure and that normally a person learns the structure of a subject before learning all the propositional details of the subject. His ideas can be illustrated by how a person learns the rules of grammar. Most four-year-olds can select the proper case for a pronoun, depending on whether it is the subject or the object of the sentence. There are dozens of other rules of grammar that four-year-olds can use appropriately in speech, and thus they could be said to know those rules of grammar. However, few if any know the rules as stated propositionally. Bruner calls the first

level of knowledge "intuitive knowledge" of the subject matter, in this case of grammar. He suggests that we should learn how children intuitively learn the structure of various subjects before they learn those subjects verbally, and then we should design curriculum and instruction in order to coordinate with this natural way of learning.

Bruner also came to be known for his emphasis on inquiry, problem solving, and discovery as modes of school learning. This emphasis led him to develop an elementary school curriculum called "Man: A Course of Study," in which the entire curriculum is based around answering the question, What is human about humans?

In 1963 Bruner received the Distinguished Scientific Award by the American Psychological Association, and in 1965 he was elected president of the association. In 1972 he left Harvard and took up a new post at Oxford University in England.

R. B. MCKEAN

Bulimia. *See* BULIMIA NERVOSA; EATING DISORDERS.

Bulimia Nervosa. An eating disorder characterized by recurrent episodes of binge eating followed by behaviors to prevent weight gain and to find relief from the binge behavior. A person with bulimia nervosa exhibits a preoccupation with food and often binges in secret. A binge is an amount of food that is definitely larger than most people would eat during a similar period of time and under similar circumstances (e.g., most people will overeat on holidays). Bingers also exhibit a lack of control over eating during the episode, calorie intake varying from 3,000 to 40,000 per episode. To qualify diagnostically under *DSM-IV,* binges occur at least twice a week for three months, but they can occur as often as ten times per day. Incidence of this disorder is unknown, since it is secretive and is kept hidden due to fear or shame. Bulimia nervosa often begins in teenage years, but recorded incidences range from ages 5 to 70.

Binge episodes are followed by several forms of purging. Vomiting can be induced by inserting a finger or other object down the throat. After some time vomiting may no longer need to be induced. The person will check that all the intake has been vomited before purging is completed. Feelings immediately afterward are relief, power, of being able to overeat but avoid the consequences, of "winning," and of fooling everyone. One young woman reported, "It's the only thing my father can't control." These feelings are positively reinforcing and help to explain why the disorder continues. However, negative feelings such as self-depreciation, self-hatred, fear of discovery, Guilt, and being out of control, follow the positive ones. Bulimics often promise never to do this again.

Other forms of purging include laxatives (typically 2 to 30 laxatives per use), diuretics, diet pills, or enemas. These methods do not achieve weight loss, but still the sense of getting rid of the intake is satisfying and reinforcing. Nonpurging methods include excessive exercise (up to five hours per day), which can be rationalized as fitness. Fasting, an attempt to make up for the excessive intake, is self-defeating in that it triggers binge eating again when the person feels starved.

Physical ramifications of binging followed by purging can include swollen salivary glands, broken blood vessels in the eyes, ruptured stomach, esophageal tears, dehydration, electrolyte imbalance (which jeopardizes heart function), and malnutrition. Because vomit erodes the enamel on the inside of the teeth, one eight-year bulimic reports dental repairs costing $10,000.

Bulimia nervosa has several causative factors. One biological factor points to serotonin in the brain and its regulation of satiety and food preferences as well as in regulation of impulses. Approximately 85% of bulimic patients suffer from hypoglycemia (low blood sugar), which may contribute to the urge to binge; over time the behavior develops addictive qualities. A multilevel model for the etiology of bulimia nervosa includes social, cultural, family, and personal factors: society overvalues thinness, and obesity is highly stigmatized; bulimic families express greater anger, aggression, and conflict (without conflict resolution skills), indirect communication, lack of support, and lack of economy; overattention to food and weight in the family (degree of symptoms is associated with occurrence among mothers and sisters); overconcern with pleasing others; strong peer group influences to be attractive (thin), to gain approval of other females, and to attract boyfriends; sense of ineffectiveness and low interoceptive awareness, generating high anxiety; a disconnection from unpleasant feelings by diverting attention to food (Pike, 1995). Bulimics may display other impulsive behaviors such as drinking, sexual promiscuity, kleptomania, spending sprees, and drug use.

Treatment involves a multifocused approach. The therapist needs to braid the addiction component, the personality disorder if present, women's issues (such as sexist attitudes and behavior), health problems, family of origin issues, and how they all relate to the bulimia. The psychotherapist (a specialist with minimally 30 hours of training in eating disorders) is the base of the team. Bulimics will treat therapists the same way they treat food—a love/hate relationship. Because of the need to please, it may seem rapport is well established, but this must never be taken for granted. If there is an Axis II of borderline personality, even more caution must be given to rapport. The therapist takes a detailed report of a binge/purge episode so he or she can accurately and nonjudgmentally view the experience from the patient's perspective and determine the feelings associated with the episode and the problems it solves. At the same time the therapist must respect the adjustive value to bulimics, realizing they have not been able to meet their needs in other ways.

When rapport is established, referral is made to the medical team for necessary tests. If depression or sleep disorder coexists, the physician can recommend medications. If tests reveal physical problems (such as hypoglycemia), the dietitian is introduced to design a personalized food program. Bulimics will not fully comply at first, but any compliance will help stabilize them to some degree, and the therapist can distinguish organic from psychological symptoms. The therapist can highlight the bulimic's increased feelings of control and stability produced from the food program (for example, a lower food "drive"), so it can become self-reinforcing.

Treatment, averaging two years, will focus on reaching patients' goals for control over their own lives, safe relationships, and incorporating affect in more effective ways so that the bulimia will not be needed. They will eventually learn that what comes out of their mouths can produce more security than the binging/purging. Family of origin issues will be addressed (higher-than-average reports of physical, emotional, and/or sexual abuse, among other issues) to see how bulimia has been used to deal with such issues. Food and feelings will be separated enough so feelings can be incorporated into their choice-making behavior until food is depowered and can be used normally, and the drive to eat for emotional purposes is abated.

Reference

Pike, K. M. (1995). Bulimic symptomatology in high school girls. *Psychology of Women Quarterly, 19,* 373–396.

For Further Information

ANAD. National Association of Anorexia Nervosa and Associated Disorders, P.O. Box 7, Highland Park, IL 60035. (708) 831-3438.
NEDO. National Eating Disorders Organization, 6655 South Yale Ave., Tulsa, OK 74136. (918) 481-4044.
Eating Disorders Review (bimonthly newsletter). Gurze Books, P.O. Box 2238, Carlsbad, CA 92018.

M. F. CLARK

See ANOREXIA NERVOSA; EATING DISORDERS.

Burnout. A state of fatigue or frustration resulting from devotion to a way of life or a relationship that has failed to produce the expected reward (Freudenberger & Richelson, 1980). Freudenberger, a New York psychologist, was the first to use the 1960s drug-culture term *burned out* to describe the process of physical and emotional depletion resulting from various harmful work-related conditions experienced by the professional staff of health care agencies (Guy, 1984). This concept was then applied to a wide variety of individuals in the helping professions (Farber, 1983).

Burnout is considered to be a process rather than a state or a condition. Popular use of the term has equated or confused it with the experience of generalized stress or anxiety. In actuality the experience of burnout is a much more serious, chronic, and debilitating condition. It is typically a gradual decline in job performance and a noticeable decrease in pleasure derived from interpersonal relationships. The symptoms can include cognitive, affective, behavioral, physical, and relational changes in functioning (Guy, 1984). There may be an increase in rigid, intolerant, and pessimistic thinking. Some people report the onset of depression, fearfulness, irritability, self-doubt, and withdrawal. This is often followed by a decrease in productivity and an increase in aggressive, reckless behavior. Other people experience chronic fatigue, exhaustion, and increased illness, with a heightened susceptibility to muscular pain and gastrointestinal illnesses. There is typically a pattern of increased withdrawal, isolation, paranoia, and relationship difficulties. This wide array of symptoms hinders accurate identification of this syndrome, particularly since it appears to affect each individual in a uniquely different way.

Since burnout is more of a process than a specific state of mind, it is difficult to assess its incidence. However, it is thought to be more prevalent among those in the helping professions. For example, studies of counselors and psychotherapists estimate that as many as 15% to 20% suffer from moderate to high levels of burnout. More conservative estimates place the incidence at around 6% among mental health professionals (Farber, 1985). Its prevalence among the general population has yet to be determined.

In understanding the process that leads to the onset of burnout, it is helpful to remember that it is a gradually increasing condition that results from unmediated, unrelenting stress and dissatisfaction wherein an individual's personal resources are chronically overwhelmed by the demands of the environment within which she or he functions (Guy, 1984). The cumulative impact of a variety of stressors leads to a feeling of despair and exhaustion. This understanding of the phenomenon of burnout distinguishes it from moments of frustration, distress, or disappointment and also differentiates it from career dissatisfaction.

A number of factors contribute to the onset of burnout. Personality characteristics may predispose individuals to this malady. For example, those who tend to be overly idealistic, dedicated, and people-oriented often have unrealistically high expectations that lead to disillusionment. People who tend to be controlling, authoritarian, and withdrawn may be more vulnerable to burnout. Those with high affiliation needs and a particularly strong longing for intimacy and closeness may experience repeated disappointment and eventual burnout. It is also possible that significant life events and unexpected changes can contribute to a growing sense of failure or discouragement that spins into something more chronic and serious. Farber (1983) identifies four major work-related factors that contribute to burnout: role ambiguity, role conflict, role overload, and inconsequentiality. A lack of clarity about a worker's status and goals, the experience of inconsistent and inappropriate demands, an overwhelming increase in the amount of responsibility assigned to the individual, and a growing sense of being unimportant or impotent can lead to an experience of burnout.

A number of steps can be taken to reduce the tendency toward burnout. The first step is to become educated about the etiology and progression of this syndrome. This permits prevention and early identification of the problem. Personal psychotherapy can assist with understanding and managing the personality characteristics that increase the predisposition to burnout. Pursuing nurturing, honest relationships with significant others outside of work allows for honest feedback and assessment of personal functioning as well as replenishment of emotional resources. The importance of adequate social support networks cannot be overestimated. Proper attention to physical health and exercise are also important factors for mitigating against this syndrome. The pursuit of hobbies, avocational interests, and community involvements can bring balance and vitality to life. Finally, and perhaps most importantly, an open, honest assessment of spiritual well-being and Christian commitment enables one to invite God to explore motives, expose sin, and empower the Christian to fulfill his or her mission. By reaffirming dependence on God and obedience to God's calling, the believer is able to release to the workings of providence the ultimate responsibility for the challenges that lie ahead.

References

Farber, B. A. (1983). *Stress and burnout in the human services professions.* New York: Pergamon.

Farber, B. A. (1985). The genesis, development, and implications of psychological-mindedness in psychotherapists. *Psychotherapy, 22,* 170–177.

Freudenberger, H. J., & Richelson, G. (1980). *Burnout: The high cost of high achievement.* Garden City, NY: Anchor Books.

Guy, J. D. (1984). *The personal life of the psychotherapist.* New York: Wiley.

J. D. GUY, JR.

See STRESS.

Bystander Intervention. *See* HELPING BEHAVIOR.

California Psychological Inventory. Harrison Gough developed the California Psychological Inventory (CPI) for the purpose of measuring folk concepts of personality—traits that are so much a part of our personal and social experience that they are symbolized in the natural language of virtually all cultures and societies. The CPI focuses on the positive or normal aspects of personality rather than the negative or pathological. Although popularity is not an indicator of a test's scientific merit, the 1,362 CPI references in Buros's *Mental Measurement Yearbook* (eds. 5–8) attest to its practical utility in a wide variety of research and applied settings.

The CPI is composed of 480 true-false items that are scored as 18 separate scales. Items ask the respondent to report typical feelings, behaviors, opinions, and attitudes toward moral, ethical, and family concerns. To facilitate the interpretation of the scales, Gough clusters them into four classes. Class I includes the dominance, capacity for status, sociability, social presence, self-acceptance, and sense of well-being scales. Responsibility, socialization, self-control, tolerance, good impression, and communality are the scales in Class II. Class III measures are achievement via conformance, achievement via independence, and intellectual efficiency. Class IV scales include psychological-mindedness, flexibility, and femininity.

The CPI can be administered individually or in groups and takes about one hour for most people to complete. Although the test has been used with individuals ranging in age from 12 to 70, its content is most appropriate for high-school students through young adults. Scoring is done either by hand with templates or by using several available computer scoring services. Standardized scores based on normative samples of more than six thousand men and seven thousand women are reported in profile form. The CPI manual (Gough, 1975) and the handbook (Megargee, 1972) provide detailed instructions for the interpretation of each scale and the overall profile.

Evidence for the psychometric quality of the CPI scales ranges from very strong to nonexistent, depending upon the scale in question. Test-retest reliabilities with intervals up to one year range from .38 (communality) to .87 (tolerance). The CPI handbook gives a review of validity studies. While several of the scales need research attention, it should be noted that the socialization, dominance, sociability, and achievement via conformance scales are among the most well-validated measures in the personality test literature.

The CPI's uniqueness as a general personality test lies in its method of construction. As in the Minnesota Multiphasic Personality Inventory and the Strong-Campbell Interest Inventory, CPI items were selected according to their correlation with an external criterion. For example, items that differentiate high versus low socioeconomic status respondents were selected for the capacity for status scale. Scales that will predict real-life behaviors are the goal of this procedure. In settings where prediction of such behaviors from common personality traits is desired, the CPI merits serious consideration.

References

Buros, O. K. (Ed.). (1938–1978). *Mental measurements yearbook* (Eds. 5–8). Highland Park, NJ: Gryphon.

Gough, H. G. (1975). *Manual for the California psychological inventory*. Palo Alto, CA: Consulting Psychologists Press.

Megargee, E. I. (1972). *The California psychological inventory handbook*. San Francisco: Jossey-Bass.

D. D. MCKENNA

See PERSONALITY ASSESSMENT; PSYCHOLOGICAL MEASUREMENT.

Campbell, Joseph. Joseph Campbell (1904–1987) was to mythology what Sigmund Freud was to psychology. At thirty, he went to Woodstock and spent the next four years reading the classics. In 1934 he accepted a teaching position at Sarah Lawrence College, where he stayed until he retired in 1972. He edited numerous works on mythology from many different sources and wrote such well-known books as *The Hero with a Thousand Faces* (1947), *The Masks* *of God* (1959), *The Mystic Image* (1975), *The Way of the Animal Powers* (1983), and *The Inner Reaches of Outer Space* (1985). After his death, PBS broadcast Stuart Brown's *The Hero's Journey: The World of Joseph Campbell* and Bill Moyers's *Joseph Campbell and the Power of Myth*. These programs won Campbell a large posthumous following.

For Campbell mythology was a study of the depths, both the inner depths of human beings and the outer depths of the world, indeed of the cosmos. Campbell, with Carl Jung, saw in archetypal images (*see* Archetypes) universal themes that illumine both personal and multicultural existence. His favorite image was that of the hero, but he also found in fire and water, birth and death, darkness and light, father and mother timeless images that reveal the wonders of existence to the sensitive soul.

Campbell was suspicious of both conceptual thought and institutional systems. He believed that concepts bog down in ideology and that institutions tend to protect the status quo. Myths penetrate below both to deal with the experiential, the affective, the symbolic; in short, matters of the heart that have to do with the "ground from which all human life springs" (Cousineau, 1990).

Campbell posited a close relation between myths and dreams. He thought that both are revelatory of the self and beyond that are revelatory of our culture and the world. But Campbell also distinguished between them: dream is fashioned by the particular concerns of the dreamer while a myth gives expression to the concerns of humanity. Campbell is more descriptive: A dream is a "personalized myth," while a myth is a "depersonalized dream."

The image of the hero was of special interest to Campbell because he saw in the image the challenge of life to leave the old and to embrace the new, that is, to die and to be reborn. Typically the hero goes through three stages: the call to adventure, the initiation into a new state, and a return to reconstruct some part of the old order. Campbell himself went through this process many times, because he always remained open to new thoughts and experiences. He lived the life of a hero but was humble enough to eschew the title.

Campbell has expanded our knowledge of the nature and function of myth. Even more important, he has validated the language of myth in an age that puts a premium on mathematical or scientific discourse.

Reference

Cousineau, P. (Ed.). 1990. *The hero's journey: The world of Joseph Campbell.* New York: Harper.

Additional Reading

Maher, J. M., & Briggs, D. (Eds.). (1988). *An open life: Joseph Campbell in conversation with Michael Toms.* Burdett, NY: Larson Publications.

L. ADEN

Canadian Association for Pastoral Education. Copublisher of *The Journal of Pastoral Care*, this is the only organization in Canada that is responsible for training, certifying, and accrediting supervised pastoral education.

See CLINICAL PASTORAL EDUCATION; PASTORAL COUNSELING; PASTORAL CARE.

Cancer Counseling. Recent medical advances have improved the treatment of cancer so significantly that many patients who have been diagnosed with cancer will survive their treatment and go on to experience a return to health. These improvements in cancer treatment have paralleled an increased expectation on the part of the American public that cancer can be treated and, in many cases, cured. Unfortunately, the best outcomes for cancer treatment are with early diagnosis; public health workers know that many people delay seeking treatment once they recognize an early warning sign of cancer (i.e., a lump in a woman's breast, a hacking cough, bloody stools). However, the most likely scenario in counseling patients with cancer is that their disease is treatable. Thus, patients face two tasks in adapting to cancer: coping with the stresses involved in their treatment, and coping with life after treatment as it is changed by their illness.

During treatment, patients will experience a range of painful procedures and distressing treatment-related side effects. There will be procedures for diagnosis, such as bone marrow aspirations, and for treatment, such as chemotherapy and radiation therapy. Typical side effects are loss of appetite, nausea and vomiting, skin changes, hair loss, extreme fatigue, and depression. Patients also face a range of psychological issues, including confronting the possibility of dying, handling the costs of treatment, informing family and friends, and assisting children in understanding and accepting the parent's illness and treatment. It is not surprising that cancer and its treatment is a highly stressful series of events. Indeed, Weisman and Worden (1976–1977) considered the first 100 days following diagnosis to be an "existential crisis."

When counseling cancer patients, it is important to keep in mind that levels of distress are initially quite high, then taper to lower levels of distress over time. Thus, initial counseling tasks are for the counselor to work with the client to mobilize resources to reduce the initial distress and increase the likelihood of successful coping. These coping resources may be tangible in nature, such as providing assistance in clarifying insurance coverage for treatments or arranging altered work schedules with an employer, or planning for a congregation or friends to bring meals into the home. These coping resources may also be emotional, such as providing support for the family and sending cards and letters to the patient in the hospital. They may also be spiritual in nature, such as having the congregation pray for the patient and family, providing targeted Bible study material for the family, and visiting the patient in the hospital. During this initial time, it is important to keep the patient's and family's confidence level high and to concentrate on tangible outcomes.

Over time, the stress of cancer and its treatment may result in poorer adjustment by the patient than desired. Senescu (1963) offered the following conditions as indicative of potential poor adjustment: 1) when the patient's emotional reactions interfere with treatment by preventing the patient from seeking treatment or complying with treatment, 2) when the patient's emotional response causes more pain and distress than the disease itself, 3) when the patient's emotional response interferes with accomplishing daily tasks, and 4) when the patient's emotional reactions are manifested as psychiatric symptoms (e.g., distortion of reality, hallucinations). In these cases, referral for evaluation for more intense professional treatment seems warranted.

More likely, cancer patients will complete their treatments and return home to face an additional series of stressors. At this time, counseling can be considered task-oriented or process-oriented. Within a task facilitation approach, the counselor should focus on specific tasks that need attention. For example, families can learn to change dressings, assist the patient in physical therapy exercises, or monitor food and liquid intake. It is important that both the patient and the family have accurate information on the patient's condition. A lack of information can cause patients needless grief if relatives and family avoid the patient for fear of "catching" cancer. A critical task is to provide a network of social support for the patient, particularly in the family but also in the patient's wider social circles. At this point in time, many patients report that friends avoid contact with them because they "don't know what to say." Increasing the likelihood of social contacts is very important, and the pastor himself or herself should be a frequent visitor to the home.

Counseling which focuses on process may deal with several types of issues. First is the need for patients to be able to "tell their stories," to relate at some length the facts of the treatment and their current lives and their responses. There are self-esteem needs as well, particularly if the patient is cut off from normal sources of self-esteem such as work, parenting, and leisure activities. Finally, there are process issues having to do with fear of dying and the management of that fear. Keeping hope alive among patients appears to be a crucial aspect of psychosocial care (Cassileth, 1979).

Social support has been cited as a critical concern. Recent research on social support and its role in helping people cope with a variety of stressors (Cutrona, 1990) has revealed that "matching" types of social support to the stressor results in the best outcomes. A counselor should therefore consider the type of stress when facilitating the best type of support. As an example, chemotherapy is an uncontrollable stressor; therefore, the best type of support is instrumental (such as providing information) and esteem support (reassurance of competence and ability).

In summary, while issues of death and dying may be relevant for cancer patients, issues of growth and adjustment are also important to consider. Within these issues are tasks that can be facilitated by the counselor among the patient and his or her family and psychological adjustment processes that can be initiated for the patient by the counselor.

References

Cassileth, B. R. (Ed.) (1979). *The cancer patient.* Philadelphia: Lea & Febiger.
Cutrona, C. (1990). Stress and social support—in search of optimal matching. *Journal of Social and Clinical Psychology, 9,* 3–14.
Senescu, R. A. (1963). The development of emotional complications in the patient with cancer. *Journal of Chronic Diseases, 16,* 813–832.
Weisman, A. D., & Worden, J. W. (1976–77). The existential plight in cancer: Significance of the first 100 days. *Psychiatry in Medicine, 7,* 1–15.

E. M. ALTMAIER

See HEALTH PSYCHOLOGY.

Cannon, Walter Bradford (1871–1945). Physiologist whose research on physiological factors in motivation and emotion is important for psychology. Born in Prairie du Chien, Wisconsin, Cannon's early education was in the public schools of Milwaukee and St. Paul, but his father took him out of school because he was not applying himself. After two years of work in a railroad office, Cannon returned to school with a new appreciation for it and completed high school in three years. He won a Harvard scholarship and graduated *summa cum laude* in 1896. He received his M.D. from Harvard in 1900 and taught there from 1899 to 1942.

Cannon introduced the concept of homeostasis and believed that organisms are motivated to maintain themselves at an optimal level of functioning. In his peripheral (or local) theory of motivation, stimuli such as stomach contractions or dryness of the mouth prompt searching for food and water. When homeostasis is restored, messages from the periphery stop, and the organism is no longer motivated. His most important book on this is *The Wisdom of the Body* (1932). Although such local factors cannot account for all motivation, they have some effect.

In *Bodily Changes in Pain, Hunger, Fear, and Rage* (1915) Cannon reported his work on the emergency functions of the sympathetic nervous system. Critical of the James-Lange theory of emotion, he and Bard proposed an alternative theory of emotion in an attempt to explain the behavior of brain-damaged cats. Cannon and Bard suggested that the thalamus or hypothalamus contains centers for the emotions; these are responsible for organizing both the autonomic responses and the overt behavior patterns in rage. These centers also stimulate the cerebral cortex to give rise to the conscious experience of emotion.

R. L. KOTESKEY

See EMOTION; MOTIVATION.

Capgras Syndrome. First described in 1923 by the French psychiatrist Capgras, this syndrome is the delusional belief that other individuals are not themselves but imposters or doubles. French psychiatrists consider the syndrome a disorder in itself. In the United States it has generally been viewed as a part of the paranoid schizophrenic disorder. It has also been reported in organic disorders and affective psychotic disorders.

See SCHIZOPRHENIA.

Career Development and Guidance. A behavioral science and profession dedicated to vocational selection and career adjustment. Career development and guidance was born early in the twentieth century. With the Industrial Revolution sweeping changes came to the world of work. Large factories replaced homes and small workshops as manufacturing centers. Educational and political privileges, which had once belonged largely to the upper class, spread to the growing middle class. Machines displaced some jobs, but other workers found new job opportunities with machinery. Both workers and employers had to adjust to a new, cold, and impersonal relationship. In addition many people lived and worked under harsh conditions in the expanding industrial cities.

But the rise of industrialization in the late 1800s also sparked a spirit of reform to compensate for the new impersonal systems of urban life. In this spirit Parsons, a young American engineer deeply committed to social change, introduced the world to the field of vocational guidance in 1908. Parsons's book, *Choosing a Vocation*, published in 1909, was followed by the First National Conference on Vocational Guidance in 1910. Several speakers, including the president of Harvard University, called on science to take this new field seriously. It did. The incorporation of the National Vocational Guidance Association (NVGA) came in 1913. By 1921 the NVGA had defined vocational guidance as "the process of assisting the individual to choose an occupation, prepare for it, enter upon, and progress in it. [Vocational counseling] is concerned primarily with helping individuals make decisions and choices involved in planning a future and building a career—decisions and choices necessary in effecting satisfactory vocational adjustment" (Myers, 1941, p. 3). Since that time the work of career development

theorists has concentrated on the theoretical development of occupational choice.

Theories of occupational choice place an emphasis on assessing the interests and abilities of the worker. Parsons's original work blossomed into a theory of occupational choice known as the trait and factor theory. This theory incorporates the three facets of "personal analysis, job analysis, and matching through scientific advising for occupational choice making" (Brown, et al., 1984, p. 8). Vocational psychologists associated with the University of Minnesota furthered this model and propelled it into the mainstream through the development of aptitude tests and personality inventories. Trait and factor theory is the foundational model of career development work in a majority of college and university career centers as well as in larger, more established programs such as the Veterans Administration (VA), the YMCA, and the Jewish Vocational Services.

Career psychologist Holland's theory of occupational choice emerged in the 1950s and is still used extensively in contemporary vocational counseling. Holland's (1985) theory of occupational choice is based on personality as expressed through interests and career fit. At the heart of his theory are the following assumptions: most people can be categorized as one of six personality types; there are six kinds of work environments; people search for environments that will allow them to express their skills, abilities, and values; our behavior is determined by an interaction between our personality and the character of our work environment (Holland, 1985).

The six basic personality types that Holland used to categorize people and environments are realistic, involving physical activity that requires strength, skill, and coordination (i.e., farming, surveying, mechanical tasks, forestry); investigative, involving critical thinking, creative observation, investigation and organization of physical, biological, and cultural phenomena rather than socially oriented activities (i.e., mathematics, chemistry, and physics); artistic, involving creative self-expression and unsystematic, unordered, emotional interaction with physical, verbal, or human materials to produce art forms or products (i.e., writing, acting, music, art); social, involving interpersonal activities focused on curing, enlightening, training, and developing people (i.e., social work, vocational counseling, teaching); enterprising, involving persuasive and influential verbal activities focused on obtaining power and status (i.e., sales, politics, entrepreneurship); and conventional, involving ordered and systematic activities to obtain organizational goals (i.e., accounting, clerical work).

Holland's approach enables individuals to make occupational choices that result in congruence between their personality and their working environment. Holland postulates that increased levels of congruence lead to increased levels of stability, achievement, and fulfillment in vocational life. To that end Holland has developed the *Self-Directed Search* and the companion resource *The Occupations Finder*, which matches the personality codes with 456 occupations classified by the same three type codes. His theory of career personality has also been incorporated into a widely used career assessment tool, the Strong Interest Inventory.

Unlike the theory of occupational choice, which points to an already established personality, career development theories emphasize the process of personal and personality development as the determining factor in vocational choice. It was also in the 1950s that interest in occupational choice from a developmental perspective emerged. Super is perhaps the preeminent figure in developmental career theory in the 1990s, and he promotes a "loosely unified set of theories dealing with specific aspects of career development, taken from developmental, differential, social, personality, and phenomenological psychology and held together by self-concept and learning theory" (Super, 1990, p. 199). Super's theory, rather than being limited only to occupation, encompasses six major life roles: homemaker, worker, citizen, leisurite, student, and child. Each of these roles plays a part of varying importance over the developmental life span of an individual and is a significant factor in the development of career maturity. Super's construct of career maturity involves a constellation of physical, psychological, and social characteristics. Career maturity incorporates the elements of planning, exploration, information, decision making, and reality orientation as an individual moves through the passages of childhood, adolescence, and adulthood.

References

Brown, D., Brooks, L., Roe, A., Lunneborg, P., Weinrach, S., Bordin, E., Hotchkiss, H., Ginzberg, E., Super, D., Mitchell, L., Krumboltz, J., Tiedeman, D., & Miller-Tiedeman, A. (1984). *Career choice and development*. San Francisco: Jossey-Bass.

Holland, J. L. (1985). *Making vocational choices: A theory of personalities and work environments* (2nd ed.). Englewood Cliffs, NJ: Prentice-Hall.

Myers, G. E. (1941). *Principles and techniques of vocational guidance*. New York: McGraw-Hill.

Parsons, F. (1909). *Choosing a vocation*. Boston: Houghton Mifflin.

Super, D. E. (1990). A life-span, life-space approach to career development. In D. Brown and L. Brooks, *Career choice and development: Applying contemporary theories to practice* (2nd ed.). San Francisco: Jossey-Bass.

L. PARROTT

See VOCATIONAL COUNSELING.

Case Study Method. Next to introspection, the oldest research technique in psychology. In sociology, anthropology, political science, and history, case studies can be done on organizations, movements, and events. In psychology, however, case studies are done on individual people. The most common form of the case study in psychology is the clinical report. The data come from the clinician's direct contact with the patient: interviews, testing (laboratory, paper and pencil, oral, and projective), the course of treatment (e.g., medication, behavioral, psychotherapy), and the patient's improvement (i.e., immediate and follow-up).

Another form of case study is the biography, which relies primarily upon sources that are documents or testimony given by third parties. Erik Erikson's studies of Luther and Gandhi and Sigmund Freud's studies of Leonardo and Schreber are of this biographical format, since these historical figures were not patients of the psychoanalysts.

A case study remains qualitative (i.e., using narrative format), even though it may include some quantified data. Like all qualitative research, case studies are best for illustrating a point (e.g., how to diagnose or treat a patient) or for exploring possible explanations rather than for confirming a hypothesis about the cause of a disorder or the effectiveness of a treatment. A good case study is objective, comprehensive, and unbiased. Many case studies are written in a way so as to justify the actions of the writer: The patient got better, therefore proving that my diagnosis and treatment plans were correct. When large numbers of subjects are available and variables can be identified and quantified, the survey is a more appropriate research technique. When an independent variable can be manipulated, the experiment is a more appropriate research technique. Many behaviorists have demonstrated that even when limited to one human subject, experimental manipulations can take place over time in pretest/posttest designs.

Further Readings

Kratochwill, T. R. (1992). Single case study research design and analysis: An overview. In T. R. Kratochwill & J. R. Levin (Eds.), *Single case research design and analysis*. Hillsdale, NJ: Erlbaum.

Yin, R. (1994). *Case study research: Methods and design*. Newbury Park, CA: Sage.

T. L. BRINK

See PSYCHOLOGY, METHODS OF.

Castration Complex. In psychoanalytic theory the castration complex is a normal part of the process of psychosexual development for both males and females. It is hypothesized to be most prominent during the oedipal crisis, which occurs in late infancy, beginning at approximately age three and usually lasting until age six or seven. It is assumed that the manner in which the castration complex is handled determines in large part the adequacy of the resolution of the oedipus complex; failure to resolve this latter complex is hypothesized to lie at the root of adult neurotic disorders.

Sigmund Freud assumed that children of both sexes believe that everyone is born with a penis. When the female child discovers that she does not have one and that boys do, she responds with what he called penis envy and blames her mother for her deprivation. This is felt to lead to the onset of the oedipal crisis as she then moves her primary attachment from her mother to her father. For the male child the discovery that some people (girls) do not have a penis is assumed to confirm his own fear that he might lose his, just as in the past he lost other valued possessions. In particular he fears that his father might inflict this on him as punishment for his secret incestuous longings for his mother (the oedipus complex). Thus in the male the castration complex is assumed to lead to the resolution of the oedipus complex in that the male represses his oedipal longings and moves to a primary attachment to and identification with his father.

D. G. BENNER

See PSYCHOSEXUAL DEVELOPMENT; OEDIPUS COMPLEX.

Catalepsy. A spontaneous or hypnotically induced trancelike state in which an individual maintains a semirigid or rigid physical posture. It is a disorder of the muscular system. The two types of catalepsy are waxy (or flexible, sometimes called *flexibitas cerea*) and rigid. In waxy catalepsy a person assumes postures that someone else places him or her in. Limbs can be positioned and the individual will maintain the position until he or she is moved by another. In rigid catalepsy the person assumes self-selected postures and is resistant to changing them. Catalepsy is most common in catatonic schizophrenia, epilepsy, and hysteria, and it may also occur as a result of organic brain damage. It is often associated with amphetamine toxicity.

D. L. SCHUURMAN

Cataplexy. A temporary attack of paralysis or powerlessness provoked by an emotional experience or intense excitement. The physical loss of muscle tone results in a collapse of the body, most commonly triggered by laughter but also by anger or anxiety. Cataplexy is associated with narcoleptic attacks.

Catharsis. The word, which comes from the Greek, means purification. Aristotle used it to refer to the emotional purgation that spectators experience while viewing a tragic play. Many of the healing rituals of primitive peoples (e.g., demonic exorcism) involve an emotional intensity that seems to be followed by a sense of release and restoration to normal functioning. The same tendencies could be found in Franz Anton Mesmer's "animal magnetism" cures. For almost two hundred years religious conversion in some Protestant groups has been accompanied by a great emotional outpouring and sometimes followed by dramatic behavioral changes (*see* Ecstatic Religious Experiences).

In the nineteenth century Allen treated agitated patients at his asylum by allowing them to ramble (accompanied by an attendant) and to scream in the forest the whole day. The greatest advance in the application of catharsis to the treatment of mental disorder occurred at the close of the nineteenth century, when Sigmund Freud and Josef Breuer used hypnosis to remove hysterical symptoms. Although French alienists had used these techniques for more than a decade, Freud must be credited with developing the theoretical framework for understanding the therapeutic value of abreaction. The early psychoanalytic model was homeostatic and hydraulic (*see* Homeostasis). The mind was viewed as a steam kettle or water balloon. If too much emotional pressure builds up, the vessel may become stretched out of shape, spring a leak, or rupture. The abreaction obtained during therapy serves to discharge excessive tension and return emotional pressure to tolerable levels.

Although the homeostatic, hydraulic understanding of catharsis has persisted, the nature of the abreacted emotions and degree of reliance on catharsis have varied widely in psychotherapy. Freud, who understood catharsis as a discharge of painful memories from early childhood, abandoned the technique of hypnosis for free association and began to understand cure in terms of insight and ego strengthening. Otto Rank and Janov (*see* Primal Therapy) developed their forms of psychotherapy by emphasizing the need to have a catharsis of painful early memories. Rank later moved away from this when he replaced his emphasis on the birth trauma with that of the need to strengthen the will. Reich conceived of catharsis as sexual orgasm and emphasized physiological factors, especially muscular rigidities. Bioenergetic analysis continues this emphasis. Since the 1940s catharsis has been an essential feature of several popular therapies, including Gestalt therapy, psychodrama, and encounter groups. While these approaches include catharsis of feelings in general, including those resulting from sexual experiences and painful memories, the focus is frequently on ventilating anger.

There are several problems with the reliance on catharsis in psychotherapy. One is that the proof of its efficacy is founded more on metaphor, analogy, introspection, and anecdotal case studies than on carefully designed experiments. A difficulty is that the therapists who are quite skilled in cathartic therapy are usually not precise designers of quantitative research. Indeed, the operational definitions of catharsis have been imprecise and varied. One researcher may use galvanic skin response (GSR) measurements while another employs raters who evaluate the patient's degree of emotional intensity in a taped therapy session. The measurements of the criteria for treatment success have likewise varied between physiological measures (e.g., blood pressure) and subjective reports made by patients or therapists. The area of catharsis research in which there have been several well-designed studies has been that of anger and aggression (verbal or physical catharsis). The weight of the evidence is that catharsis, in whatever form, does not reduce the likelihood of future anger and aggression. The notion that adolescents participating in vigorous contact sports (e.g., football) reduce or rechannel their aggression has been largely refuted.

In general neither catharsis nor its hydraulic way of understanding human mental processes has been popular with cognitive or behavioral psychologists. The former reject the concept of emotion as something that can be stored in favor of seeing emotion as a by-product of cognitive structures. Many cognitive therapists would agree that the controlled expression of hostility may be therapeutic, but because it only enhances the perception of control and power, not because of emotional discharge per se. The behaviorists also reject the model's emphasis on unobservable, internal processes. Many behaviorists echo William James's concern that emotional discharge may become habit forming rather than purgative. Although one form of behavioral modification, flooding, involves great emotional intensity, the behaviorists describe its efficacy in terms of classical extinction.

Debriefing Vietnam veterans with posttraumatic stress disorder (PTSD) can yield painful reminiscences, but is this an essential part of the process of treatment? Perhaps the best example of long-buried repressed traumatic memories can be found in the aging survivors of the Nazi Holocaust. Neither catharsis nor recovery of repressed memories seems to be required for all patients to go on and live healthy and productive lives. Recently developed techniques, such as eye movement desensitization and reprocessing (EMDR) show that emotionally traumatic events can be dealt with from a behavioral perspective.

Until there is improvement in both the quantity and quality of research on the use of catharsis in psychotherapy, therapists must proceed with caution. Catharsis may be useful, though it is only rarely essential, and it is certainly not a self-sufficient treatment. Catharsis may be most appropriate in the kinds of patients that Freud and Breuer saw: somatoform and dissociative disorders. Many therapists have found that bereaved patients seem to benefit from abreaction. It is usually best that the therapist permit the patient to engage in intense emotional expression rather than compel it or contend that it is a requirement for cure. Catharsis seems to work best when the patient believes in its therapeutic value and has great faith in the therapist. One danger of catharsis is that the therapist and/or patient may come to see it as the purpose of therapy rather than an adjunct. Another danger of catharsis is that it leaves patients in a highly vulnerable state. In order to protect them against the possibilities of becoming psychiatric casualties, it is important to provide them with a supportive therapist or group.

Additional Readings

Brink, T. L. (Ed.). (1994). *Holocaust survivors' mental health*. New York: Haworth.

Jackson, S. W. (1994). Catharsis and abreaction in the history of psychological healing. *Psychiatric Clinics of North America, 17*, 471–491.

Nichols, M. P., & Zax, M. (1977). *Catharsis in psychotherapy*. New York: Gardner.

Shapiro, F. (1995). *Eye movement desensitization and reprocessing*. New York: Guilford.

Tavris, C. (1982). *Anger: The misunderstood emotion*. New York: Simon & Schuster.

T. L. BRINK

See EMOTION.

Cathexis. In psychoanalytic terminology cathexis signifies a concentration of psychic energy upon some person or object. This concept plays a central role in the process of psychosexual development where psychological maturation is traced in terms of shifting patterns of cathexes.

Cattell, James McKeen (1860–1944). Pioneer in testing and practical application of psychology. Born in Easton, Pennsylvania, where his father was professor of classics at Lafayette College, Cattell received his bachelor's degree from Lafayette in 1880. After graduate study at Göttingen, Leipzig, and Johns Hopkins, he returned to Leipzig to receive his doctorate in 1886.

Cattell was lecturer at the University of Pennsylvania, Bryn Mawr College, and Cambridge University. He received the first professorship of psychology in the world at the University of Pennsylvania in 1888. In 1891 he became professor and head of the department at Columbia University. After longtime difficulties with the administration, Cattell was dismissed from Columbia in 1917 because of his pacifist activities. He never took another academic appointment but devoted himself to the public promotion of psychology and the other sciences.

Although he did studies on reaction time, Cattell's major early interest was in individual differences. He developed a rank order method of evaluating persons, was the first psychologist to teach statistics in his course, and coined the term *mental tests* in 1890. He also conducted research in association, perception, reading, and psychophysics.

Although his bibliography includes 167 items, Cattell is most widely remembered as an editor, creating channels to disseminate psychological information. He was cofounder of the *Psychological Review*, *Psychological Monographs*, and *Psychological Index*. He bought *Science* in 1894, and five years later it became the official journal of the American Association for the Advancement of Science. He published *Popular Science Monthly*, which became

Scientific Monthly, and was editor of *School and Society* and the *American Naturalist*. Between 1906 and 1938 he edited six editions of *American Men of Science*. He also founded *Leaders of Education* and the *Directory of American Scholars*. In 1921 he organized the Psychological Corporation to promote the application of psychology to industry and make it available to the public through psychologists.

R. L. KOTESKEY

Cattell, Raymond Bernard (1905–1998). Developer of the trait approach to personality. Cattell was born in Staffordshire, England, and received his B.S. degree in chemistry and physics from the University of London in 1924. He changed to psychology because of his concern for social ills, and in 1929 he received his Ph.D. from the University of London, where he studied under Charles Spearman.

From 1928 to 1937 Cattell held a variety of jobs in psychology because there were few full-time jobs for psychologists in England. He lectured at Exeter University and set up a psychological service and clinic in Leicester while he continued to conduct research and write. Finally, in 1937, he was offered a full-time position in the United States. He went to Columbia University in 1937, Clark University in 1938, Harvard University in 1941, and became research professor at the University of Illinois in 1945. He retired in 1973 and is currently visiting professor at the University of Hawaii.

Cattell sees personality as a structure of traits that can be identified by using the method of factor analysis on data gathered from masses of human subjects. He distinguishes between surface and source traits, environmental-mold and constitutional traits, ability and temperament traits, and dynamic traits in individuals. He also proposes a concept, syntality, that refers to traits characteristic of a group of people.

Cattell's writings include 30 books and 350 journal articles, making him one of the most prolific of personality theorists. His major works include *Personality and Motivation Structure and Measurement* (1957) and *The Scientific Analysis of Personality* (1965) as well as two handbooks he edited, *Handbook of Multivariate Experimental Psychology* (1966) and *Handbook of Modern Personality Theory* (1977). In 1973 he established the nonprofit Institute for Research on Morality and Self-Realization, through which he hopes to integrate his interest in science with social and religious concerns.

R. L. KOTESKEY

See FACTOR THEORIES OF PERSONALITY; PERSONALITY; PERSONALITY ASSESSMENT; SIXTEEN PERSONALITY FACTOR QUESTIONNAIRE.

Celibacy. The deliberate abstinence from marital or sexual intimacy.

Old Testament and Judaism on Celibacy. Celibacy has a long history in Christianity, but virtually no precedent in Judaism. Rather, marriage and child-bearing are high-priority religious values in the Jewish community. The Hebrew understanding based upon Genesis 2:24 implied that the norm for man and woman was marital unity in a one-flesh relationship in which the creation mandate of subduing creation and populating the earth would be realized. Various Christian theologians, commenting on this, go so far as to relate the image of God to this male-female dynamic (cf. Barth,1958; Jewett, 1975). The Genesis account clearly indicates that the first man was in a relationally needy state in the original creation despite the fact of harmony between him and God ("It is not good that the man is alone," Gen. 2:18ff.). From the Old Testament's perspective, the original creation state of man required a human companion to help stay potential loneliness.

Furthermore, even though the sacred duties of priests (Lev. 21:1–15) and the rigorous ascetic requirements placed on Nazirites (Num. 6:1–21) detailed many abstinences, there is no hint of celibacy. Proverbs, in fact, discusses much of its wisdom within a familial matrix of parents, spouses, and children, and is aware of the dysfunction and suffering in a problematic marriage as well as in the case of the "unloved woman" (Prov. 30:23).

Later, rabbinical law required priests and religious leaders to be married. Josephus reports that celibacy was practiced among the Essene groups, yet rabbinic law prevented the unmarried from holding public office. Celibacy was evidently tolerated among the Jews on rare occasions. In the Talmud Ben Azzai wrote: "My soul is fond of the Law; the world will be perpetuated by others" (Yev. 63b). Even here celibacy is tolerated only because the scholar is so fully absorbed in his sacred world and is not experiencing sexual temptation. Apparently, in the Jewish understanding religious maturity and perfection was thought to be reached primarily in the married state. Other conditions were less than optimal insofar as the human required a human companion to avoid loneliness.

New Testament Teaching on Celibacy. The teaching and the practice of Jesus provide the basis on which the early church gives a new focus and emphasis upon celibacy. On the one hand, the teachings of Jesus consistently echo the "one flesh" quality of marriage (Matt. 19:4–6), and he was fond of the metaphor of weddings, in obvious reference to his activity and mission (Matt. 9:15). Beyond these metaphoric images, but consistent with them, is the vision of the eschaton as culminating in a marriage banquet, a spotless bride dressed up for her husband (Rev. 19:7–9; 21:2; 22:1–7). Thus, in Jesus there are combined the princely groom and the pure and spotless bride, the church. They are temporarily separated (since the Ascension) but will be reunited in eternity. All of this suggests the image of "one flesh" as an important metaphor and experience from Eden to the eternal kingdom.

On the other hand, Jesus Christ lived and died single, thus seeming to validate celibacy by his personal practice. And his teachings contain terse sayings which seem to put family and marital obligations in perspective as second to the Kingdom of God, though often contenders for ultimate loyalty. The excuse of having married a wife is not sufficient to draw back from following him (Luke 14:20). "Leaving all" to follow Jesus suggests that the single life style is, however, perhaps more adapted to being a disciple. One must not even hold back to care for the burial of members of the family (Matt. 8:21; Luke 9:59). Yet some of the apostles, perhaps all, were married (Matt. 8:14; 1 Cor. 9:5). Given the Hebrew context, his reply to the Sadducees that there was to be no marriage or giving in marriage in the Kingdom of Heaven must have come as a surprise and hinted at the fact that human companionship was only an analogy or a "type" of the relationship between the people of God and God that is to come with the end of ages.

Only once does Jesus address the issue of celibacy directly. In Matthew 19, in the content of responding to the question about divorce, Jesus expounded on the miracle of the sexual bond which, he said, should be protected at all costs ("Therefore what God has joined together, let man not separate," Matt. 19:6). This new insight, that marriage is absolutely permanent, led the disciples to exclaim, "If this is the situation between a husband and wife, it is better not to marry" (19:10). This exchange sets the stage for Jesus to speak of celibacy. First he stated that "not everyone can accept this teaching." What is unclear is whether he is referring to his own words about the permanence of marriage or to his disciples' expression of their fear of being permanently married and their statement that it is better not to marry. Either way, he then cites three kinds of "eunuchs": 1) those who were born sexually dysfunctional, hence eunuchs without capability of reproduction; 2) those who were made eunuchs by the surgeon's knife, sexually altered usually for the purpose of being house-hold domestic servants; and 3) those who "have made themselves eunuchs" for the sake of the kingdom of heaven. Then he ends with, "Not everyone can receive this teaching, only the one to whom it has been given" (19:11). This seems to indicate a new possibility for Kingdom living unknown to the Jews whereby the human need for fulfillment and companionship could be fulfilled apart from spousal intimacy.

Paul, who could not have been a member of the Sanhedrin without being married, condoned marriage for church leaders (1 Tim. 3:2), but held up his present unmarried state as the better way of consecrating oneself to the work of God (1 Cor. 7:26–35). Paul's bottom line for justifying marriage has a different emphasis than the elegance of the creation account: "But if they cannot control themselves, they should marry, for it is better to marry than to burn with passion" (1 Cor. 7:9ff.). Even in his discussion in Ephesians 5 of the role of marriage and the spiritual parallels between the woman's and man's role and the relationship between Christ and the church, he indicates that the whole point of the marital one-flesh relationship was primarily that of being a finite "type" of the relationship between the believer and God. Pentecost inaugurates the church into the new eschaton whereby the kingdom of God comes, not in its fullness, but into the hearts of God's people whereby the indwelling Spirit brings union with Christ and his body. Here is the beginning of the culmination of history in which human loneliness and need for a companion comes to its climax: the very sharing of one's psychological states with a loving God in perfect harmony. It turns out that nothing short of union with God can meet the deep and continual need of love that we all have has since the creation of Adam. Thus, Pentecost presents the church with new horizons of possibilities for relationships, anticipating the fullness of the Kingdom of God when "God may be all in all" (1 Cor. 15:28). This is the final end or telos of all persons. Although it is still legitimate in this age to participate in the old order of marriage and there is no merit to celibacy in itself, nevertheless, the New Testament envisions celibacy as an opportunity to model human teleology and destiny in union with the Spirit.

Church History. Based on the teaching of Jesus and Paul, parts of the early and later Roman Catholic Church formulated the requirement of celibacy for clergy in the church. By the fourth century most of the bishops from Greece, Egypt, and Europe either had remained unmarried or had placed their wives in monasteries upon being consecrated bishop. During the first three hundred years, however, deacons and priests married.

Canon 33 of the Council of Elvira (ca. 305) reads: "We decree that all bishops, priests, and deacons, and all clerics engaged in the ministry are forbidden entirely to live with their wives and to beget children: whoever shall do so shall be deposed from the clerical dignity." Hosius of Cordova brought celibacy to the Council of Nicaea hoping to make it the law of the clergy in general. When the council refused to enact such a law, the popes decreed it: Damascus I, Siricius, Innocent I, and Leo I required celibacy and dissolution of marriages of all clergy. Gregory VII, pope at the zenith of the Hildebrandine reform, made every effort to establish celibacy for all clergy. But actual adherence to sexual and marital abstinence was still far from universal. It was the Council of Trent (1545–1563) which clarified that celibacy is the law of the church and not the law of God. Today, the Roman Catholic case for celibacy is based on the desire to devote oneself to the service of God. Celibacy also serves to protect against the potential conflict of priority between family and ministry.

Early Protestantism in many ways returned to the Jewish pattern of a married priesthood, and it was common for the Reformers, most of whom were trained as Roman priests, to marry soon after separating themselves from the Roman church. Zwingli, Luther, Cranmer, and Calvin each married. The Lutheran, Anglican, and Calvinist focus has consistently been on the quality and structure of family life. Each parsonage or rectory has felt a clear obligation to display a model of the Christian marriage, family, and home.

Even so, in the late twentieth century there is renewed interest in celibacy for the sake of the kingdom of God. Perhaps it has developed due to unusually high-risk vocations, ethical considerations regarding population control, and general fear of marital commitment in light of skyrocketing divorce rates. Thus, it is important to distinguish between celibacy for Jesus' sake and mere singleness experienced by choice or by failure to find a relationship that leads to marriage. Singleness, a rising phenomenon among young adults in North America, tends to be characterized by sexual promiscuity. This modern tendency should serve as a reminder of Jesus' caution that only those who are able should attempt to take the lonely road, and of Paul's concern that those with high sexual appetite should marry rather than burn. The rising number of singles and previously married adults may signify for us the trend toward privatism, toward isolation, and thus away from fulfillment through responsible relationships. Jesus accepts the continuance of the Creation Mandate and its high view of the "one flesh" spousal relationship. Nevertheless, that same Jesus, author of the Great Commission and initiator of Pentecost, opened new horizons of ministry for those choosing to live as celibates in union with God the Spirit—a foretaste for all of the world to come.

Additional Readings

Barth, K. (1958). *Kirchliche dogmatik*, Vol. III. Trans. J. W. Edwards, O. Bussey and H. Knight. Edinburgh: T. & T. Clark.

Blenkinsopp, J. (1968). *Celibacy, ministry, church.* New York: Herder & Herder.

Frein, G. H. (Ed.). (1968). *Celibacy: The necessary option.* New York: Herder & Herder.

Hermand, P. (1965). *The priest: Celibate or married.* New York: Libra.

Jewett, P. (1975). *Man as male and female: A study in sexual relationships from a theological point of view.* Grand Rapids, MI: Eerdmans.

Lea, H. C. (1957). *The history of sacerdotal celibacy in the Christian church.* New York: Russell & Russell.

Thurian, M. (1959). *Marriage and celibacy.* London: SCM Press.

J. H. Coe and D. M. Joy

See Sexuality.

Central Nervous System. *See* Brain and Human Behavior.

Cerebral Hemispheric Specialization. *See* Brain and Human Behavior.

Certification. *See* Counseling and Psychotherapy: Overview; Licensure.

Character Disorder. *See* Personality Disorders.

Charcot, Jean-Martin (1825–1893). The leading French neurologist and psychiatrist of his time. Becoming a professor of pathological anatomy in 1878 and later director, Charcot made the Salpétrière Hospital in Paris the first postgraduate institute for psychiatric education.

Charcot was widely acclaimed for his research in localization of function in cerebral disease and hysteria. By means of his experiments in hypnosis, he distinguished hysterical phenomena from organic neurological disorders. Although he believed, as did most of his contemporaries, that hysteria has a neurological basis and is due to degenerative changes of the brain, he also believed that the symptoms manifested in hysteria are also psychogenic in origin and are produced by a specific set of ideas held by the patient. By the same token he reasoned that hysterical symptoms could be cured by ideas. The basic theory of disassociation originated with Charcot's teachings that the stream of consciousness breaks up into diverse elements in cases of hysteria.

In 1885 Sigmund Freud went to Paris to study with Charcot. He was most impressed by Charcot's innovative approach to hysteria through the use of hypnosis. As a result of Charcot's influence, Freud became deeply interested in the problem of hysteria and came to believe that the phenomenon is genuine. Charcot was able to precipitate hysterical paralysis, seizures, and other symptoms through hypnotic suggestion. Freud returned to Vienna in 1886 with the intention of giving up his laboratory studies so that he might devote all of his time to the clinical practice of neurology.

Because of Charcot's prestige at the Salpétrière, hypnosis soon acquired wide popularity, together with an equal amount of opposition from the medical profession. Charcot was the first modern physician to make a serious attempt to treat emotional disorders on an individual psychotherapeutic basis.

G. A. Johnston

See Hypnosis.

Charismatic Experience. *See* Dissociative Trance Disorder; Ecstatic Religious Experience; Religious Experience.

Child Abuse. All too often the cries of children take on a sinister significance. The muffled screams of terror can be the result of deliberately broken bones or burns from a cup of scalding coffee or a lighted cigarette. The silent tears may flow from spleens ruptured by repeated blows or skin welted and bruised by whippings. Children also cry from the pain of inflamed sexual organs or a neglected body starved to sickness. Emotional scars such as the inability to trust is an additional indicator of pain in victimized children.

Millions of children are abused or neglected each year. Estimates of physical abuse range from more than 300,00 to almost 1,500,000. As many as 400,000 children are sexually abused. A range of 700,000 to 1,200,000 million children are physically or educationally neglected. Homicide is one of the five leading causes of child mortality in the United States. In addition to the more than 2,000 homicide deaths reported by the Federal Bureau of Investigation (FBI) each year, there are perhaps 1,200 child abuse and neglect fatalities not included in the FBI total.

Abused children are found at all socioeconomic levels. The overall incidence rates are similar for city, suburban, and rural communities.

Since time immemorial children have been treated with incredible cruelty. Children were tortured, burned, terrorized, and flogged in the name of discipline. Infants were dipped in ice water and rolled in snow in order to harden them, as well as buried alive with their dead parents.

Parents have been "beating the devil" out of their children since colonial times. Parents have exposed children to weather or starved or abandoned them in order to avoid the burden of rearing them or having to divide property among too many heirs.

In both the Old and New Testaments we read about the abuse of children. Pharaoh advised the Hebrew midwives to kill every Hebrew boy (Exod. 1:16), and when that scheme did not work, he demanded all boys be thrown into the river (Exod. 1:22). In the New Testament accounts King Herod, hoping to eliminate the Messiah, ordered all boys in and around Bethlehem under the age of two to be killed (Matt. 2:16).

The first obvious consequence of child abuse is the physical damage ranging from cuts and bruises to broken bones and internal injuries to death. Estimates are that almost 318,000 children suffer serious or moderate physical injuries in one year as a result of physical abuse, neglect, or sexual abuse.

A child's physical and intellectual development is influenced by the type and severity of injuries and trauma stemming from victimization. Examples are a greater vulnerability to illness and further injury coming from prior abuse. Susceptibility to sexually transmitted diseases is a growing concern for victims of sexual abuse. Anemia and its related aspects of apathy, poor learning ability, listlessness, and exhaustion are common in abused children. It is also possible that lower intelligence quotients, poorer language skills, and reduced achievement levels can result from chronic abuse.

There is strong evidence that victimization has significant repercussions on children's mental health. For example, sexually abused children have a nearly fourfold lifetime risk for psychiatric disorders and a threefold risk for substance abuse.

Abuse is a profoundly disruptive, disorienting, and destructive experience for children. The progression of self-mastery, developmental stages, and relationship with others is altered and disrupted by the abusive experiences. Symptoms such as irritability, school truancy, behavior problems, poor classroom performances, health complaints, sexual promiscuity, running away from home, and lying are common in victimized children. Depression, panic disorders, dissociative disorders, and suicide attempts can also result from chronic abuse.

Two additional consequences are very important. A history of victimization increases the likelihood that someone will become a perpetrator of crime, violence, or abuse. For example, an extremely high percentage of convicted child abusers were themselves abused as children. An important qualification is that victims are not necessarily prone to repeat their own form of victimization. However, there is ample evidence that a victim of childhood abuse is more likely to grow up and victimize others.

In the case of childhood sexual abuse, there is some evidence that women who were abused tend to select mates who are likely to abuse them and sexually exploit their children. While these mothers may not abuse their children, they are more likely to marry men who will.

Another form of abuse arises when children live in homes where domestic violence prevails. The child may not be a direct victim of beating but sees the mother suffer at the hands of her husband or partner. There will still be negative effects on the child. Pain will continue to be a constant companion. Ten to 30% of children live in violent homes. These children suffer the same consequences as do other victims.

Treatment is crucial for abused children. The majority will need some type of medical and/or psychological help. One in three children who come from homes where domestic violence is present will need treatment.

The first order of business in treatment is to stop the violence. This may involve legal procedures to remove the perpetrator, followed by social, economic, and emotional actions. Counselors need to support the family through the crisis, locate financial and medical support, assist in job training for the displaced parent, and teach coping skills.

Therapy and education are needed for the victim and the family. Issues of self-blame, trust, identity, and empowerment often are crucial. Victims often need help in learning how to interact socially, to express their feelings in interpersonal situations, and to be more empathic. Many of these children have negative thought patterns, accompanied by depression and feelings of helplessness. They need new positive and healthy ways to think.

The second focus of treatment is to break the cycle of violence. We need to find ways to become a less violent society, although this is not a simple task. Limiting violent television and encouraging parents to avoid violent toys and games is a start. Most importantly, parents need to model and teach children nonviolent ways to deal with anger. Issues relating to spouse abuse and its effects on children need attention. Abused children need parents to learn how to discipline in effective but nonviolent ways (*see* Child Discipline).

Preventing abuse is also a priority. History tells us this is a major endeavor. We need more research on prevention. We must develop new methods for teaching conflict resolution and find ways for everyone to have some sense of empowerment, productivity, and need fulfillment. Above all we must speak to the vacuum that exists in all persons. Until people bring God and the person of Jesus Christ into their lives, nothing will change.

Additional Readings

Finkelhor, D., & Dziuba-Leatherman, J. (1994). Victimization of children. *American Psychologist, 49* (3), 173–183.

MacFarlane, K., & Waterman, J. (1986). *Sexual abuse of young children.* New York: Guilford.

Martin, G. L. (1987). *Counseling for family violence and abuse.* Dallas: Word.

Adler, T. (1991, December). Abuse within families emerging from closet. *APA Monitor,* 16.

G. L. Martin

See Abuse and Neglect.

Child Custody. Almost half of all marriages now end in divorce. The most frequent and major issues in these dissolutions are property rights and child custody. Disputes concerning the custody of children are among the most difficult and troubling decisions to adjudicate. Often the court is asked to choose between custody alternatives that are either equally good or equally not in the best interests of the child. Such is the case if two parents who claim to love their children appear to be equally flawed and equally capable.

Judges in custody disputes are faced with the task of making decisions that will determine the future of innocent children. To help with the process the courts will often ask the assistance of expert witnesses. It is into these highly charged emotional settings that the mental health professional contributes an opinion. The goal is to do a comprehensive job of evaluation and reporting so as to serve the needs of the children who are already experiencing high levels of stress (Schutz, Dixon, Lindenberger, & Ruther, 1989).

Background. Prior to the eighteenth century, the social role definitions of parental responsibilities gave fathers complete legal control over their families. Children were considered the father's property.

In 1817 the English parliament established a change in the social status of children by instituting the doctrine of *parens patriae.* This doctrine held that the Crown should defend the rights of those who had no other protection. Although it did not happen often, for the first time in history the father's rights over his children could be superseded.

The presumption that fathers had priority over mothers, unless the father could be shown to be unfit, continued until the early 1900s. By the 1920s the courts had shifted to favor maternal custody based on the "tender years" doctrine. The mother's care was seen as necessary and more important than paternal care for the development of children through the early years of life. The courts reflected this rise in social status of mothers, so that by the mid-1900s about 90% of the cases were settled in favor of women. This altered the burden of proof so that the father had to prove the mother to be unfit in order to gain custody (Derdeyn, 1976; Sorensen & Goldman, 1990).

In the 1970s the pendulum became more centered as the courts began to recognize the standard of the "best interest of the child." This presumption suggests a more sex-neutral stance. This idea was codified in the Uniform Marriage and Divorce Act of 1970 and has since been adopted by all states in the U.S. The act states that "the court shall determine custody in accordance with the best interest of the child." All relevant factors are to be considered, including the wishes of the child's parent(s), as well as the child; the child's interaction and interrelationships with other family members; the child's adjustment to school, home, and community; the mental and physical health of all persons involved; and the presence of potential violence or abuse. The court is not to consider any conduct of the present or proposed custodian that does not affect the relationship to the child.

The 1980s marked a growing trend to recognize and encourage joint custody. It is permitted in every state, and the majority of states have statutes that specifically recognize it. The premise for joint custody is to keep both parents actively involved in the life of the child. While it appears to be a sensible idea, the conflicts that bring a couple to divorce also make it difficult for most divorcing parents to cooperate and communicate about the logistics of joint custody. Research has not supported the assumption that joint custody will promote cooperation between previously conflicted parents (Simmons & Meyer, 1986).

The legal community is still looking for a child custody process that is just, fair, and equitable and that minimizes the emotional trauma of the participants. The United States court system is based on the adversarial form of presenting a case in both criminal and civil action, and some scholars argue that the adversary system is the worst conceivable method for resolving child-custody disputes (Gardner, 1989). Mediation has been proposed as an alternative to the adversarial approach. While mediation takes time and skill, it can be cost-effective and less traumatic than a court battle.

The Value of Expert Opinion. The mental health professional can be an asset to the court. Four categories of assistance seem to be relevant: discovering, articulating, highlighting, and analyzing (Litwack, Gerber, & Fenster, 1980).

Through interviews and testing the counselor can identify and then bring to the attention of the court the feelings, attitudes, and personality traits of the children in the custody dispute. Patterns of interaction among all family members that are not otherwise evident to the court can be discovered. Requests for custody can stem from anger, manipulation, power, control, or bargaining issues. The evaluation can help bring these dynamics to light.

Another function of the mental health professional can be to articulate to the court emotions and beliefs the family members may find difficult to express. Most children have trouble expressing their true feelings and experiences. After interviewing the child a trained professional may be able to articulate more precisely those thoughts and feelings for the court.

The witness can serve the function of bringing to the court's attention factors and observations that are relevant but otherwise might have been neglected and given too little weight. A psychological witness can also apply psychological logic to aspects of the evidence before the court to help it discern the implications of that evidence. The witness can articulate the reasons the various custody alternatives are likely to affect the specific circumstances of the case. The expert will enable the court to better weigh all the factors that are relevant to the court's ultimate decision.

For many reasons the court-appointed role of impartial examiner is far superior to that of an advocate. There are many guidelines for responding to requests from a parent for declarations when serving as a therapist for the child. It is important to maintain the distinction that the evaluator provides information for the court to make the final decision. The ultimate decisions regarding custody issues are not made by the evaluator. Further, this state of affairs is reached only because the parents have been unable to decide responsibility for their child's future.

Evaluation Process. Conducting a custody evaluation includes an initial meeting to establish the evaluator's neutrality and role as advocate for the child. The first phase of the custody evaluation is this initial meeting with parents and their legal representatives in which structure, focus, and agreement between parties are established. The evaluator's role as an advocate for the child should be highlighted. The focus of the evaluation is upon identifying the needs of the child and how best to match the strengths of each parent to meet those needs. A provisions document, which clearly states the terms, conditions, and agreements for the custody evaluation, is necessary. This is given to the parties at the initial inquiry to explain the evaluation process.

The second phase is data gathering. Clinical interviews, testing, observations, and corroborative contacts are used to acquire the necessary information about the needs of the child and the various characteristics of the parents.

The third phase is the preparation of the conclusions and recommendations. The prime purpose of the evaluation is to recommend a custody plan in which there is the best possible match between the respective parent's strengths and the child's needs. This goodness of fit exists when the demands and expectations of the parents are compatible with the child's personality, abilities, and needs. When there is such a good fit, healthy development can be assumed (Martin, 1992).

References

Derdeyn, A. (1976). Child custody contests in historical perspective. *The American Journal of Psychiatry, 133,* 1369–1376.

Gardner, R. A. (1989). *Family evaluation in child custody mediation, arbitration, and litigation.* Cresskil, NJ: Creative Therapeutics.

Litwack, T. R., Gerber, G. L., & Fenster, C. A. (1980). The proper role of psychology in child custody disputes. *Journal of Family Law, 18* (2), 269–300.

Martin, G. L. (1992). *Critical problems in children and youth.* Dallas: Word.

Schutz, B. M., Dixon, E. B., Lindenberger, J. C., & Ruther, N. J. (1989). *Solomon's sword: A practical guide to conducting child custody evaluations.* San Francisco: Jossey-Bass.

Simmons, V., & Meyer, K. G. (1986). The child custody evaluation: Issues and trends. *Behavioral Sciences & the Law, 4* (2), 37–156.

Sorensen, E. D., & Goldman, J. (1990). Custody determinations and child development. *Journal of Divorce, 13* (4), 53–67.

G. L. MARTIN

See DIVORCE; BLENDED FAMILY; FORENSIC PSYCHIATRY; FORENSIC PSYCHOLOGY.

Child Custody Evaluations. When a marriage fails and the parents are unwilling to agree regarding the custody of their children, the court will intervene by ordering an evaluation of the parents and the children. The purpose of a child-custody evaluation is to determine what is in the best interests of the children, not the parents. The goal of such an evaluation is to assist the parents in forming agreements and to provide a written report to the attorneys representing the parents and to the judge who ordered the evaluation. This report will summarize levels of parental agreement and the evaluator's recommendations for residential placement, sole versus joint custodial arrangements, and the specifics of a visitation schedule for weekends, overnights, holidays, birthdays, and summer vacations.

At times a parent will hire his or her own evaluation so that the evaluator can be available both to present a report or as an advocate in a court hearing or a trial. Usually one parent will, out of anger, refuse to honor the other parent's request for an independent assessment, so child-custody evaluations typically follow a direct order of the court.

In an evaluation the parents are interviewed alone and together for several sessions. The parents are asked to describe their history of interaction with each other and the children and the beliefs they hold about love, discipline, and patterns of child care. Each parent will maximize his or her own skills and denigrate those of the other parent. Strong, deliberate structuring and intervention by the evaluator are needed to prevent endless bickering and exaggerated claims.

It is useful to administer to the parents a questionnaire such as the Adult-Adolescent Parenting Inventory. This instrument provides information in four areas: knowledge of how children develop; the ability to empathize with the needs and feelings of children; the ability to find alternatives to corporal punishment; and skill at avoiding use of the children to satisfy one's personal needs for care.

If the parents demonstrate personality problems that may impair their ability as parents, the evaluator may administer a personality test such as the Millon Clinical Multiaxial Inventory II or the Minnesota Multiphasic Personality Inventory II. Since these tests are typically scored by computer the results are objective and avoid arguments in court.

Each child should be interviewed alone and with each parent. The child is asked about his or her perceptions of family life; how love is shown; who disciplines and how; the kind of things done together, including play, talk, fun, and homework; and the kind of fears and worries each child has. Children generally are willing to talk candidly, despite possible coaching by one or both parents. Direct quotes are extremely valuable in formulating recommendations in the report as to the wisdom of either parent as primary custodial caregiver. Depending on age, each child should be asked what thoughts he or she has had about living with either parent.

Psychological tests are extremely useful to check on parental claims, child exaggerations, or observer bias. The Bricklin Perceptual Scales measure a child's perception of each parent in areas of parental competence, parental support, follow-up consistency, and admirable character traits. Judges are very interested in these objective test scores. Personality tests such as the Children's Apperception Test and the Kinetic Family Drawing Test are also useful in demonstrating each child's needs, desires, level of maturity, degree of emotional pain, and depth of bonding with each parent. The final report should include all of these data.

R. H. ROTTSCHAFER

See PARENTING.

Child Discipline. Discipline is "teaching children character, self-control, and moral behavior." Discipline is perhaps the greatest child-rearing challenge for parents because parents have a heavy investment in its outcome. They may not desire the same effects as other parents (e.g., one couple might desire obedient children whereas another couple might desire children committed to social action), but discipline is practiced for the results it produces, and it is often hard to know what qualities of discipline bring about the desired effects.

Discipline is not the same thing as punishment. Behavioral psychologists define punishment as inflicting pain or other negative effects for the sake of reducing a particular behavior, whereas discipline reorients behavior in more positive directions. Behaviorists have documented that punishment tends to be less effective than discipline, because punishment tends to make an organism anxious and reduces its ability to learn from a particular event.

Contemporary parents, particularly Christians, wonder whether spanking is effective discipline. Many modern psychological experts are against spanking, and yet Christian parents would like to have children who love and serve God, who exercise restraint in their own behavior, and who are loving and generous, and many believe that spanking is an important tool in this training. Advocates of spanking argue that Scripture recommends spanking (see, e.g., Prov. 13:24; 22:15), whereas critics believe that the "rod" in these verses refers to discipline in general, not spanking specifically. Further, many opponents of spanking believe that spanking models aggression and teaches children that hitting is acceptable if one is bigger (see, e.g., Larzelere, 1993). They may also believe that spanking used indiscriminately is child abuse and potentially has the same negative effects (Heggen, 1993): feelings of self-blame and powerlessness, inappropriate mechanisms of self-protectiveness, and an inability to trust others and God. Spanking used wrongly can have these effects and, if parents choose to spank, they should follow certain guidelines.

Spank sparingly. Spanking is a strong reaction to behavior and should be used only when absolutely necessary.

Spank for carefully selected behavior. Husbands and wives together develop a "spanking contract" that describes which behaviors elicit spanking and why. Typically parents choose to spank when children place themselves in physical danger or when a child is clearly, willfully, and defiantly disobedient. Parents should use mild instances of limit testing to develop negotiation skills. For example, when a child asks for more cookies by saying "two" when Dad says "one," Dad may say, "You can have two cookies but not until after dinner," thus modeling for the child a strategy to resolve conflicts positively. This spanking contract should also summarize the goals of spanking. Spanking and discipline in general should not be to break a child's spirit but to channel his or her God-given abilities for responsibility and service.

Never spank in anger. Spanking is a potentially abusive act and should be used only when one is able to think rationally and act wisely. By waiting, the parent can discipline the child thoughtfully and model self-control, one lesson the parent wants the child to learn.

Spank less often as children age. Most developmental psychologists recommend spanking, if used at all, be discontinued by five to six years of age, because it contributes to strong feelings of shame and powerlessness. Teenagers should never be spanked because their developing sense of sexuality can be significantly compromised by spankings.

Disciplinary techniques in addition to spanking include distraction, particularly for young or impulsive children; time out (i.e., removing a child from the scene of conflict); offering choices (for preschool children, no more than two); logical consequences, when discipline matches the misbehavior in nature and intensity; and rewards for prosocial behaviors. The specific discipline used is less important than the ongoing relationship between parent and child.

Effective discipline follows certain guidelines.

Discipline warmly, consistently, as soon as possible, and in proportion to the misbehavior. Delayed discipline is less effective in changing behavior, and discipline that is too severe triggers anger and resentment and encourages parents not to enforce the discipline.

Use inductive reasoning. Explanations help the child understand why certain behaviors are wrong and that wrong behavior brings consequences to the one who misbehaves and to the victim.

Expect restitution. Correcting damage helps children pay attention to the consequences and recognize cause-and-effect relationships.

Adapt discipline to the age of the child. Parents should exercise the most control in the preschool years; the school-age years should be a time of "coregulation" (Maccoby, 1984) when parents exercise general supervision and children take increasing control of their moment-to-moment self-regulation; during the adolescent years, parents should delegate more responsibilities for self-management to their teenagers and spend less time in teaching them how to act (Balswick & Balswick, 1989).

Disciplinary style is one aspect of a dynamic, contextual relationship between parent and child(ren) (Lee, 1991). One classic study (Baumrind, 1977) describes the characteristics of children whose parents practice one of three parenting styles. Authoritarian parents try to control their children's behavior and attitudes and make them conform to a set and usually absolute standard of conduct. They demand respect, often by indiscriminate, excessive punishment. In comparison to peers parented by other styles, their children tend to be more moody, more anxious, and more vulnerable to stress.

Permissive parents, in contrast, are warm and loving but do not set clear limits for their children. They make few demands on their children, allowing them to regulate their own activities as much as possible. Their children tend to experience low self-esteem, to have limited abilities for self-control and self-monitoring, and to be less happy and well adapted in adulthood than the children of authoritative parents.

Authoritative parents are warm and consistent, providing clear guidelines for positive behavior. They discipline by focusing on the issues rather than by instilling fear of punishment or by threatening withdrawal of love. They use inductive reasoning (Mussen & Eisenbergberg, 1977), in which they explain why the child's behavior is inappropriate and expect their children to make restitution for any harm they have caused (even if only by saying "sorry"). Their children are more obedient because these parents inspire respect and attachment and their children tend to internalize disciplinary standards. Even as early as the preschool years, the children of authoritative parents tend to be the most self-reliant, self-controlled, self-assertive, exploratory, and content of all children; in school, these children are the high achievers.

No parent is totally consistent or functions at the highest level all the time. Yet parents tend to be relatively consistent in their warmth, their investment in caregiving, and their degree of control as their children mature. Further, authoritative styles may be more conducive to raising thoughtful, responsible children but, in communities in which children are at high physical risk, authoritarian styles may better protect children from the dangers of the streets, particularly when they are young. Finally, parents may not discipline each of their children in the same way. Miedzian (1991) documents that parents discipline boys less carefully than girls, and, when this is true, the behavior of boys is less moral as a result.

These and other studies indicate that warm, consistent caregiving, with clear rules, inductive reasoning, and restitution for wrongdoing are most effective in stimulating children to become mature moral agents (*see* Moral Development). For Christians much of the content of inductive reasoning is biblically based. A Christian might say, for example, that we do not hurt other people because we would not want to be hurt ourselves; instead we are to love and respect one another (Matt. 7:12).

Discipline may be the most demanding task of parenthood, but parenting is discipleship and good parenting makes a difference in children's sense of self, in their mastery of their world, and in their moral and faith development. The results are worth the effort.

References

Balswick, J. O., & Balswick, J. K. (1989). *The family: A Christian perspective on the contemporary home*. Grand Rapids, MI: Baker.

Baumrind, D. (1977). Some thoughts about childrearing. In S. Cohen & T. Comiskey (Eds.), *Child development: Contemporary perspectives*. Itasca, IL: Peacock.

Heggen, C. H. (1993). *Sexual abuse in Christian homes and churches*. Scottdale, PA: Herald.

Larzelere, R. E. (1993). Response to Oosterhuis: Empirically justified uses of spanking: Toward a discriminating view of corporal punishment. *Journal of Psychology and Theology, 21* (2), 142–147.

Lee, C. (1991). Parenting as discipleship: A contextual motif for Christian parent education. *Journal of Psychology and Theology, 19* (3), 268–277.

Maccoby, E. E. (1984). Middle childhood in the context of the family. In W. A. Collins (Ed.), *Development during middle childhood*. Washington, DC: National Academy.

Miedzian, M. (1991). *Boys will be boys: Breaking the link between masculinity and violence*. New York: Doubleday.

Mussen, P., & Eisenbergberg, N. (1977). *Roots of caring, sharing, and helping: The development of prosocial behavior in children*. San Francisco: Freeman.

K. V. COOK

See PARENTING; DISRUPTIVE BEHAVIOR DISORDERS.

Child Management. *See* COGNITIVE DEVELOPMENT; DISRUPTIVE BEHAVIOR DISORDERS; MORAL DEVELOPMENT; PARENT TRAINING PROGRAMS.

Child Therapy. Estimates of the numbers of children needing mental health services in the United States range from 8% to 22%, with conservative estimates around 12%. Despite these numbers and the long-term impact of early life problems, only one-third of these children receive the services they need (Weisz & Weiss, 1993).

For those who do, treatment takes place in a variety of inpatient, outpatient, and school settings and addresses a wide array of problems. The broad categories of internalizing versus externalizing encompass most problems referred for treatment. Internalizing problems (e.g., worries and sadness) are characterized by an inward focus and excessive inhibition. Externalizing problems (e.g., lying and tantrums) share an external focus and involve insufficient restraint. The greatest proportion of children referred to clinics present with externalizing problems.

Although more than two hundred specific therapies for children have been identified (Kazdin, 1988), most therapists employ strategies consistent with one or more of the psychodynamic, behavioral, or cognitive approaches. The diverse group of therapies categorized as psychodynamic share the assumption that early childhood conflicts involving significant others are at the heart of psychological problems. Traditional psychoanalytic techniques were first adapted for children by Anna Freud and Melanie Klein. Their early means of interpreting play themes replaced the adult techniques of free association and dream analysis (*see* Dreams, Therapeutic Use of).

The psychodynamic school now incorporates a number of variations on early psychoanalytic themes.

Some important elements of psychodynamic therapies include a focus on insight, emotional working through of conflicts, and labeling and release of emotions. Many practitioners place a high value on the therapeutic relationship's potential to provide the child with a corrective emotional experience. Self psychologists like Kohut focus on empathic understanding of the child's emotions and seek to create an emotional holding environment in which the child can attach and appropriately separate from a significant object. These relationship experiences are thought to foster the previously impeded development of the child's ability to differentiate reality from fantasy and self from other and to participate in successful relationships.

In contrast to this approach, behavioral and cognitive therapies attend more to current behaviors and thought processes than early experience and insight into unconscious conflicts. Behavioral therapies are based on the shared belief that both adaptive and maladaptive behaviors are acquired or changed through lawful learning processes that occur as the child interacts with the environment. The orientation is a multifaceted one encompassing operant conditioning, classical conditioning, cognitive-behavioral principles, and social learning theory. Most contemporary child therapists identifying with this orientation incorporate contributions from all four of these paradigms.

The therapists' focus is on the function of beliefs and behaviors in the child's environment. The function of a behavior (e.g., crying before school) is identified by examining the antecedent and consequent setting events (antecedent: parent preoccupied and rushing to get ready for the day; consequent: parent verbally reassures and hugs child). Once a thorough understanding of controlling stimuli is achieved, a hypothesis is generated (i.e., crying elicits positive attention from the parent). The therapist can then design environmental modifications that would increase, decrease, eliminate, redirect, or originate more desirable beliefs and behaviors (parent will preemptively provide verbal and physical attention in the morning routine).

Evidence for the general effectiveness of child therapies has been mounting. Strong support exists for the efficacy of child-focused interventions for a variety of problems. Researchers have turned their attentions to the relative effectiveness of various forms of child therapy and the effect of therapist and client characteristics on the success of treatment. Research in these areas is difficult to summarize briefly and is generally inconclusive. Some tentative conclusions include the possible superiority of behavioral therapies over other modalities; female adolescents may benefit more from therapy than do male adolescents; and paraprofessional therapists may be more effective than students and professionals except in treating internalizing problems. Finally, the idea that child culture effects the therapy process is well accepted by practitioners and researchers. A cultural compatibility hypothesis has been formulated that links success in therapy to a match between intervention characteristics and client cultural characteristics (Tharp, 1991). Further investigation is needed in all these areas related to the effectiveness of child therapy.

Regardless of specific therapy characteristics, all child-focused treatments must accommodate the developmental abilities and limitations of their clients. Children are qualitatively different from adults in the ways they perceive, express their understanding, and interact with the world around them. Their stage of development in thinking, language, and social relationships will strongly influence how children experience the activities involved in therapy.

Exhaustive coverage of relevant child development information is not possible here. Those involved in helping relationships with children should become educated in areas related to children's reliance on context, perceptions of others, memory, symbolic thought, and the differentiation of appearance and reality. A firm understanding of changes that occur in these domains from preschool through adolescence will assist child interventionists in molding their behavior to maximize treatment effectiveness.

Hugh and Baker (1990) describe some of the elements of developmentally sensitive interactions with children. Some of their guidelines for therapists are summarized:

1. Combine open-ended questions with non-leading specific questions and extenders like "mmm" and "oh."
2. Avoid asking questions the child knows you know the answers to—children tend not to answer these with any depth.
3. Reduce the complexity of questions by simplifying language, shortening question length, providing response options, or using concrete referents like pictures or toys.
4. Reduce the complexity of the response required by using concrete referents the child may point to or props to enact their answers.
5. Avoid questions requiring thinking about thinking (e.g., "do you understand?") with young children. Ask them to explain what has been said or create a task to test comprehension.
6. Many children would be uncomfortable with the amount of eye contact expected in adult-focused therapy. Reduce such expectations by interacting obliquely via writing, drawing, or the use of objects like clay or dolls.
7. Capitalize on play as the young child's natural mode of expression by providing realistic props for dramatic play.
8. Children's perceptions of self and others are globalized and polarized. They are likely to equate bad feelings or behavior with bad people

and be threatened by direct questions in these areas. Try suggesting that many children feel that way, asking about what another child might feel, or framing questions that assume "bad" behavior (e.g., "What do the kids in your house fight about?").

9. Children's memory abilities leave them open to suggestibility. When it is important to reduce the likelihood of suggestion, open-ended questions and reconstructive strategies such as the use of props to enact situations are most appropriate.
10. Asking a child specific, evaluative questions about relationships is often unproductive. A description of familiar routines (e.g., dinner time) can provide the context to elicit important information about other people in the child's life.

References

Hugh, J. N., & Baker, D. B. (1990). *The clinical child interview*. New York: Guilford.

Kazdin, A. E. (1988). *Child psychotherapy: Developing and identifying effective treatments.* Elmsford, NY: Pergamon.

Tharp, R. G. (1991). Cultural diversity and treatment of children. *Journal of Consulting and Clinical Psychology, 59* (6), 799–812.

Weisz, J. R., & Weiss, B. (1993). *Effects of psychotherapy with children and adolescents.* In A. E. Kazdin (Series Ed.), *Developmental clinical psychology and psychiatry* (Vol. 27). Newbury Park, CA: Sage.

S. S. CANNING

See ADOLESCENT THERAPY.

Childhood Memories. *See* FALSE MEMORY SYNDROME.

Children and War. *See* WAR, PSYCHOLOGICAL EFFECTS OF.

Christian Association for Psychological Studies (CAPS). An international society of Christians in the psychological and helping professions. CAPS is concerned with the interface between Christianity and the behavioral sciences at both theoretical and applied levels, educational and research opportunities that advance the mental health disciplines as avenues of ministry in and to the world, fellowship among Christians in psychological and related disciplines, and the spiritual, emotional, and professional well-being of members. The association is committed to exploring the relationship between Christian faith and responsible professional life and work, between theology and psychology, between the church and the scientific and academic institutions, and between wholesome spirituality and psychological health.

CAPS had its roots in a conference on Christianity, psychology, and psychiatry held in 1954 at Calvin College in Grand Rapids, Michigan. The small group of Christian psychologists, psychiatrists, pastoral counselors, and educators who organized and conducted the conference decided to make it an annual event, a practice that has continued. In addition the group decided to form an association, and in 1956 the conference committee approved a proposed constitution for the Christian Association for Psychological Studies. The constitution was formally adopted the next year.

In the early years CAPS published the proceedings of its annual conventions. From 1974 to 1981 it replaced these proceedings with a quarterly professional journal, *The Bulletin of CAPS*, which in turn was replaced in 1982 by the *Journal of Psychology and Christianity*. The journal publishes articles on clinical, research, and theoretical topics and is overseen by a board of editors. The journal also includes reviews of important books in the field. Several hundred college and university libraries worldwide subscribe to the journal.

From its beginnings CAPS has grown to become a respected international organization with more than two thousand members scattered throughout the United States, Canada, and 25 other countries. The United States and Canadian membership is divided into six different geographic regions. Each of the six regions conducts its own conferences and activities and has its own regional director.

CAPS members represent a variety of disciplines. Regular members hold graduate degrees and/or professional certification and include psychologists, marriage and family therapists, professional counselors, pastoral counselors, psychiatrists, professors and researchers, social workers, psychiatric nurses, and others. Associate membership is open to students and lay counselors.

Members of CAPS adhere to a statement of faith that, as presented in the organization's bylaws, requires "belief in God, the Father, who creates and sustains us; Jesus Christ, the Son, who redeems and rules us; the Holy Spirit, who guides us personally and professionally, through God's inspired Word, the Bible, our infallible guide of faith and conduct, and through the communion of Christians." In addition members agree to the CAPS *Statement of Ethical Guidelines*. This statement, adopted in 1992, sets forth a set of ethical ideals for the conduct of members. The guidelines are aimed at helping members in conducting their professional or pastoral services. They are also meant as an encouragement to CAPS members reaching out to other members in distress.

Over the years CAPS has developed a number of materials that benefit members and the profession. In addition to the journal, the organization also publishes an *International Directory* that provides a listing of and pertinent information about each CAPS member. CAPS also prints a regular newsletter that contains news and interviews. The organization continues to hold national, regional, and local conferences to provide opportunities for continuing education and dissemination of new ideas.

National and regional conventions typically feature nationally recognized experts in the field, clinical teaching workshops, theoretical and research papers, and discussion forums and seminars on pertinent topics. An award program for student papers and other research is a frequent feature of conventions. From time to time the organization has also been involved in book and video publishing. For example, a CAPS video series features noted Christian therapists demonstrating their work.

CAPS is a nonprofit, member-supported association. It is governed by a fully functioning board of directors who represent the regions of CAPS and the professional entities within CAPS. An executive director directs the day-to-day activities of the organization at the discretion of the board. The board holds regular business meetings, and elections and referendums are regularly placed before the membership.

R. K. SANDERS AND J. H. ELLENS

See CHRISTIAN PSYCHOLOGY; PASTORAL COUNSELING; AMERICAN ASSOCIATION OF CHRISTIAN COUNSELORS.

Christian Counseling and Psychotherapy. People cannot agree on the definition of Christian counseling, but they know when they experience it. Theologians and psychotherapists likewise cannot define Christian counseling to everyone's satisfaction. On one hand controversy rages about whether Christian counseling is Christian (Adams, 1970; Bobgan & Bobgan, 1985). On the other hand, critics think that some of what passes for Christian counseling—prayer with clients, Scripture reading and interpretation, and direct advice about what to do—is Christian, but they question whether it is counseling.

Critics on both sides correct excesses by some Christian counselors. As a Christian counselor, I have seen examples of those excesses, and I believe we need to be called into conformity with Scripture by the critics. Despite the excesses, the criticisms do not invalidate the enterprise of a legitimate, God-centered, Scripture-consistent Christian counseling. There are answers to the criticisms, though this forum is not the place to discuss them at length. (For some answers see the integration literature: Bouma-Prediger, 1990; Carter & Narramore, 1979; Farnsworth, 1982; Foster & Bolsinger, 1990; Foster, Horn, & Watson, 1988; Jones & Butman, 1991.) Criticisms of Christian counseling have proliferated in recent years, and the field is in need of a current apologetic that meets the criticisms.

Beliefs and Values of the Therapist. *Personal Devotion to Jesus Christ.* A Christian counselor should be expected to be Christian—that is, the therapist should have a vibrant personal relationship with God through Jesus Christ and the work of the Holy Spirit. A Christian counselor should seek to further that relationship through Bible reading and study, prayer, spiritual disciplines, and seeking to discern the will of God.

Can either a non-Christian or a person who gives intellectual assent to Christianity without embracing a personal faith do Christian counseling? Yes. The client can benefit because of the work of the Holy Spirit apart from the counselor or even in spite of the counselor, in the same way that a nonbelieving or nonfaith-filled pastor might be the conduit of genuine faith passing from God to a parishioner. However, the chances of Christian counseling occurring are increased to the extent that the counselor has a vibrant personal faith.

Personal Adherence to Biblical Beliefs and Values. It is assumed that the Bible is the true written Word of God and is Christians' final rule for faith and practice. To the extent that the counselor attempts to conform his or her personal beliefs and values to the Bible, the counselor affects the client and does more Christian counseling than were the counselor not to attempt to conform to the Bible. It is assumed that the character of a Christian therapist can be healing (apart from any counseling techniques) if the Christian counselor forms a personal, trusting relationship with the client.

Subjection to the Lordship of Christ. Subjecting the theory of therapy to the lordship of Christ involves examining each of the following to make sure that one's position is consistent with Scripture.

1. View of the person. The person can be viewed as a psychospiritual unity of body and soul (or body, soul, and spirit, depending on one's theology), created in the image of God (as a relational, rational, creative, loving being designed to be eternally in relationship with the triune God), and sinful by human nature in thought, word, and deed and thus in need of redemption (Benner, 1985). Benner discusses the adequacy of then-current Christian approaches to counseling in terms of a biblical anthropology and identifies four approaches to the roles and tasks of the counselor: reductionists, dualists, alternativists, and specialists (see Benner, 1985, for this discussion).

2. Conceptualizations about the cause of problems. Causes of problems exist on many levels from distal (i.e., the ultimate distal cause of all problems being the fall of humans) to intermediate (personality traits or behavioral repertoires) to proximal (external events, cognition, unconscious impulses and conflicts, the prompting of the Holy Spirit, and the like). Because behavior is multiply determined, counselors cannot identify all relevant causes for problematic behavior. They must choose which causes to focus on. This choice places a special call on the counselor to examine his or her theoretical system to insure that the conceptualization is subjected to the lordship of Christ.

3. Assumptions about how the counselor can stimulate change.

4. Goals of therapy. Goals should include both psychological and spiritual goals, though in different proportions depending on the setting, theory of the therapist, expectations and preferences of the client, and restrictions of the setting. For example, in the pastoral setting the client approaches the pastor for counseling because the pastor is Christian or at least with the clear knowledge that the pastor is a representative of the church. That pastor will violate the expected contract between client and counselor to the extent that the pastor ignores spiritual growth and focuses solely on psychological problem solving or growth. In the same way a client who attends secular professional counseling usually does not expect to receive Christian counseling and will likely feel a violation of trust if the counselor overtly promotes spiritual growth. When a client attends professional counseling with an explicitly Christian psychotherapist, the therapist should attend to psychological growth, spiritual growth, and problem solving.

5. Techniques of change.

Beliefs and Values of the Client. *Beliefs.* Christians necessarily believe some things about religion. Those beliefs are codified as doctrines in the church, and clients can check the orthodoxy of their beliefs against church doctrines. Not every client will be doctrinally correct. We will probably find, when we see God face to face, that no set of church doctrines is completely correct either, so we, as fellow sojourners with clients, should maintain an attitude of humility about the doctrinal correctness of our clients' beliefs. That is not to say that we should not (perhaps) intervene when a client's beliefs are causing harm, but our calling as a counselor is not to make sure that the client's theology is completely in harmony with our own.

Beliefs and Values Differ. Values are beliefs to which we assign importance. A person may believe in God but not value that belief. What beliefs people value seems to make a bigger impact on their behavior than what they believe. Knowing a person believes in Christ as his or her personal Savior may not predict much of the person's behavior if the person does not value that belief more than he or she values other, competing beliefs. Thus a key concept in what makes up Christian counseling is the Christian commitment (value) of the client.

Clients Who Are Not Christians. Can a therapist do Christian counseling with a client who is not a Christian? Effective counseling—the elimination or amelioration of the presenting problem or personality change that permits the client to experience less distress from problems—*can* be done in such cases. It is unlikely that Christian counseling will often occur in such an instance because the client will not be viewing counseling from a Christian worldview and may resent any expression of the therapist's Christian beliefs and values during counseling.

The Christian counselor's ability to expose his or her Christian values, without seeming to impose those values on the client, will be crucial to the therapeutic relationship. Ethical considerations are unclear. Most Christians would not object to a therapist sensitively sharing his or her Christian values with a non-Christian client. However, suppose that your child went to a school counselor who is a New Age enthusiast. Would you appreciate the New Age counselor sharing his or her values with your vulnerable child? Although I trust my children's Christian foundation, I would not appreciate the counselor sharing New Age spirituality with my child. I would prefer to have the counselor refer my child to a Christian. If I am consistent, how can I share my Christian beliefs with non-Christian clients unless circumstances are extremely unusual or they ask me directly? Unusual situations do occur. The work of the Holy Spirit is powerful if counselors are prayerfully involved with their clients' lives. The Holy Spirit might make a way to open doors to Christian counseling even with a nonbeliever.

The Setting. The counseling setting shapes clients' expectations of counseling. That setting figures into the implicit or explicit contract between the client and counselor about what will happen in counseling. Setting consists of the following considerations:

1. Type of agency.
2. Office decor. Plaques, certificates of membership, diplomas from Christian universities or graduate programs, licenses, and other physical objects might inform the client about the counselor and shape expectations.
3. The interpersonal setting; that is, expectations that occur because of a referral. What a referral source says about the counselor can shape expectations, sometimes inaccurately, because a former client might have different needs than the new client and thus might have been exposed to more or less explicit Christianity from the counselor than will the new client.
4. What is explicitly said in counseling. In-session and pretherapy information can focus expectations on Christian or non-Christian processes.
5. The counselor's reputation in the community. A counselor who has a fine reputation as a Christian speaker might be expected to be overt with his or her Christianity during counseling, and the client might be disappointed if the counselor did not address topics with an explicit Christian focus.

A Difficult Question. Suppose a counselor is personally devoted to a saving relationship with Jesus, devoutly holds Christian beliefs and values, and adheres to counseling theory that has scrupulously filtered out assumptions, propositions, and techniques of change that do not adhere to biblical principles. Further, suppose the counselor counsels a devoted Christian client. Afterward, the client cannot discern the therapist's beliefs or values and, if asked, would not say that Christian counseling occurred. Did the therapist do Christian counseling? The therapist might say yes, citing his or her Christian beliefs and values and the consistency of his or her approach with Scripture. But the client might say no because no one mentioned any Christian belief, practice, or goal.

Some Definitions of Christian Counseling. Collins (1988, 1993) defines Christian counseling: "Attempts to define or describe Christian counseling tend to emphasize the *person* who does the helping, the *techniques* or skills that are used, and the *goals* that counseling seeks to reach. From this perspective the Christian counselor is

- a deeply committed, Spirit guided (and Spirit filled) servant of Jesus Christ
- who applies his or her God-given abilities, skills, training, knowledge, and insights
- to the task of helping others move to personal wholeness, interpersonal competence, mental stability, and spiritual maturity.

Christian counselors are committed believers, doing their best to help others, with the help of God. Such a definition includes believers who come from different theological perspectives, use different approaches to counseling, and have different levels of training and experience" (Collins, 1993, p. 21).

Jones and Butman (1991) likewise define Christian counseling in terms of the person, techniques, and goals of counseling. They begin by considering what Christ's call on any vocation is. They conclude that the claims of the gospel express themselves in the areas of character and concern of the person and structure and content of the work. In Christian farming, they argue, the gospel speaks strongly to the character and concern of the Christian farmer but is almost silent about the structure and content of the work. In Christian ministry, however, the gospel speaks strongly about both the character and concern of the Christian and about the structure and content of the work. Jones and Butman characterize counseling as closer to ministry than to farming; thus the structure and content of counseling must be closely modeled after Christian ministry.

Jones and Butman (1991) describe the character of a Christian who is a Christian counselor. They suggest that he or she be an exemplar of various offices of God—paraclete (a helper who comes alongside the counselee), reconciler, healer, source of wisdom. Further, the Christian counselor should exhibit certain character traits: compassion, servanthood, community, accountability, transparency, love, stewardship, holiness, wisdom, integrity, and depth of spirituality.

Throughout their book Jones and Butman attempt to exhibit how one might judge and adapt secular theories of counseling according to a standard that makes them consistent with the Bible. In doing so they analyze theories according to philosophical assumptions, models of personality, models of abnormality, models of health, models of psychotherapy, and demonstrated effectiveness. For Jones and Butman (1991) Christian psychotherapy is counseling done by a Christian using a theory that has been subjected to rigorous theological scrutiny and modified to be consistent with Christian principles as understood within the theologically conservative Protestant Christian tradition.

Considering Collins (1993) and Jones and Butman (1991), we might define Christian counseling using a wide net (as did Collins) or a narrow net (as did Jones and Butman). Collins's definition is lacking in that it deals only with the counselor's perspective. In Collins's definition Christian counseling is counseling done by a Christian who uses unspecified abilities to bring about the therapist's good intentions. Jones and Butman agree that Christian counseling must be done by a Christian (they describe wonderfully what that means), and they prescribe rigid content analysis to determine whether the intentions of the therapist are indeed good. As a theologically conservative Protestant Christian, I agree with their analysis of appropriate standards by which I judge my theory of therapy, but I am concerned about the inclusiveness of their definition of Christian counseling. More accurately they describe theologically conservative Protestant Christian counseling.

Yet Another Imperfect Definition of Christian Counseling. To remedy the deficiency in both Collins's and Jones and Butman's definitions (i.e., that only the character, skills, theory, and techniques of the counselor were considered), I offer yet another imperfect definition of Christian counseling: Christian counseling is an explicit or implicit agreement between a counselor who is a Christian and a client for the provision of help for a client, in which the counselor not only has at heart the client's psychological welfare but also the client's Christian spiritual welfare and tries to promote those goals through counseling methods, and the client can trust the counselor not to harm and to try to help the client psychologically or spiritually.

There are several implications of this definition. First, once the agreement is accepted, explicit mention of Christian concepts, principles, beliefs, and values may take place on a continuum from not at all to continual. The extent of explicit mention of Christian concepts, principles, beliefs, and values will be determined in large part by the psychological and theological theory of the counselor, the ex-

pectations and language system of the client, and the constraints and freedoms of the setting.

Second, the Christian therapist's examination of his or her theory in light of biblical principles and the attempt to adjust the theory to not be inconsistent with biblical principles is a necessary result of the commitment to protect the Christian welfare of the client. Correct theology is necessary, but correct theology is not the defining characteristic of Christian therapy. As Christians, we want to be theologically correct. Yet, as fallible humans, we need the humility to know that we will never be perfectly correct in our theology. Christian counseling may have some error, just as the Reformed, Baptist, or Wesleyan traditions may have some error and yet still be Christian and useful at promoting Christian spiritual growth. An explicit theory of Christian therapy is important because it makes doing Christian therapy easier, especially if the theory is complete and specifies how to arrive at an explicitly Christian therapy contract with the client.

Third, whether Christian counseling is being done cannot be discerned by examining counseling outcomes. Psychodynamic therapy is psychodynamic therapy even if a client does not change according to psychodynamic theory. The same is true of any theory of counseling; it is never judged as being doctrinally correct according to its success. Nor is evangelism judged as doctrinally correct based on whether every person is converted. If a person witnesses in faith to a nonbeliever or a pastor preaches and a nonbeliever hears, and if the nonbeliever rebels and opposes Christianity more than was true prior to the witness or preaching, the Christianity of the witness or preacher is not condemned. Christian counseling cannot be condemned if its clients do not become more spiritually mature, as long as some of them become more spiritually mature.

Brief Evaluation of Some Christian Theories. *How Christian Counselors Classify Themselves.* Jones, Watson, and Wolfram (1992) surveyed alumni of programs participating in the Rech conference (*N* = 640). Participants chose what they considered to be their primary theoretical orientation, and they could identify any number of secondary orientations. Based on primary orientations (secondary orientations also reported within parentheses), most identified eclectic (28%, 26%), psychodynamic or psychoanalytic (21%, 39%), cognitive-behavioral or cognitive (17%, 69%), and family systems or family strategic (9%, 61%) as the orientation they identified with. Participants in this study were not representative of all Christian counselors, and Jones, Watson, and Wolfram did not include Christian professionals from programs that were not explicitly Christian, pastors, pastoral counselors, or lay counselors—all of whom might be Christian counselors.

Psychodynamic Theories. Many Christian counselors embrace the psychoanalytically informed theoretical tradition, in which most counselors advocate minimal value intrusion in therapy. The therapist should strive to be a blank screen so that client projection is uncontaminated. If a therapist suggests that he or she is a Christian (and thus makes a tacit or an explicit agreement to Christian counseling with a client), psychoanalytically informed counselors might suspect that therapy might be negatively affected. Some continuum of counselor value exposure exists—from none permissible to use of a vague label as "Christian." Research evidence for effectiveness of Christian psychodynamic therapy has not been systematically presented.

Cognitive Theories. Two versions of Christian cognitive therapy have been tested. One version (Propst, 1980, 1988; Propst, Ostrom, Watkins, Dean, & Mashburn, 1992) resembles that of Beck, and the other (Johnson, 1993; Johnson & Ridley, 1992; Johnson et al., 1994; Pecheur & Edwards, 1984) is more like that of Albert Ellis. Both have been found to be modestly effective, primarily with moderately depressed people.

Integrative, Transtheoretical, or Eclectic Theories. Integrative or eclectic therapies are generally hard to test because different counselors use different rules for integration and thus end with different systems of therapy. Theorists must articulate the theories carefully (i.e., Smith, 1990) before they test. No experimental evidence of the effectiveness of integrative or eclectic Christian therapies exists.

Pastoral Counseling Theories. Benner (1992) suggested a model for brief, strategic, time-limited, spiritually focused pastoral counseling. For pastors, pastoral counseling is embedded in the larger context of pastoral care, which in turn is part of the larger pastoral ministry, including preaching and administering. Pastoral counseling generally is brief and uses more ecclesiastically based techniques (e.g., prayer, Scripture references, explicit evangelism, and the like) than does professional counseling. Such counseling has been found to be effective (see one control group in Propst et al., 1992).

Narrative Approaches. In recent years narrative approaches to therapy have become more numerous within psychology (McAdams, 1988; O'Hanlon, 1994; Vitz, 1992a, 1992b). Narrative approaches understand humans as creating stories or narratives that give events connectedness and meaning. When people have problems, narrative therapists seek to help them construct new narratives that help them deal more effectively with their lives and experience less distress. Vitz (1992a, 1992b) argues that narrative approaches are congruent with Christian worldviews and thus merit development.

Lay Counseling Theories. Tan (1985, 1991) surveyed the status of lay counseling within the church and compiled numerous resources to fuel the lay counseling movement. Since the mid-1980s the lay counseling movement has expanded dramatically. One reason has been the growth of the megachurch, in which it is impossible for pastors to meet all the psychological needs of parishioners through individual counseling. To help troubled parishioners, megachurches have often appointed a minister to coordinate a lay counseling program that provides training in counseling to parishioners. This equips the saints to meet needs of others within the church. Lay counseling has generally been found to be effective relative to professional counseling (see Christensen & Jacobson, 1994, for a review; see Boan & Owens, 1985; Harris, 1985; Walters, 1987, for investigations of Christian programs).

Marital Therapy and Family Counseling. The most frequent problem seen by religious counselors is marital distress (Benner, 1992). Numerous theoretical expositions of Christian marital therapies have been proposed (see Worthington, 1994, for nine summaries). In light of the prevalence of the problem and the surfeit of supposed solutions, one might think that empirical research on the efficacy of religious marital counseling would be a garden of delight. Instead it is a wasteland (Worthington, Shortz, & McCullough, 1993). Family problems are almost as frequently presented to religious counselors as are marital problems, and the empirical research on family problems and family therapy with religious people is likewise sparse. There has not even been an investigation of the extent of family counseling with religious clients.

Brief Solution-Focused Therapies. Solution-focused therapies, arising from family therapy, have become popular in the mid-1990s with the increasing importance of managed mental health care and its emphasis on brief treatment. As of 1995 the Christian community has only one book-length description of solution-focused therapies (Dillon, 1992), and it provides only brief summaries of secular approaches.

Adequacy of the Theories as Theories. Most approaches to counseling, especially within the Christian literature, are models, not theories. A theory is an explanatory system that ties together data and conceptual frameworks within a unified scheme. It is a set of propositions that describe the connections among constructs in the theory and that connect constructs with supportive data.

Approaches to Christian counseling are models that outline an approach to counseling. The only theoretical approach that could be considered a Christian theory is Christian cognitive therapy, which is the only approach on which anything resembling research has been done. Lay counseling paradoxically may have more research than any approach besides Christian cognitive therapy. Christian psychodynamic approaches have a large amount of unsystematic empirical evidence but have not been systematically tested for efficacy. If any theory is to adduce evidence of its adequacy as a theory, it must import evidence from secular theory and research.

Christian counseling stands in the gap between the secular and Christian world. Christian counseling is not adequate as a secular approach to counseling because it has rarely been subjected to empirical scrutiny and the constructs do not meet rigorous criteria to qualify as a theory. Christian counseling does not please everyone in the Christian community precisely because it smacks too much of the secular society, and critics of Christian counseling seem worried that too much of the world is imported into the lives of vulnerable Christians. Despite being in the breach, Christian counseling continues to be widely practiced.

References

Adams, J. E. (1970). *Competent to counsel*. Nutley, NJ: Presbyterian & Reformed.

Benner, D. G. (1985). Christian counseling. In D. G. Benner (Ed.), *Baker encyclopedia of Christian psychology*. Grand Rapids, MI: Baker.

Benner, D. G. (1992). *Strategic pastoral counseling: A short-term structured model*. Grand Rapids, MI: Baker.

Boan, D. M., & Owens, T. (1985). Peer ratings of lay counselor skill as related to client satisfaction. *Journal of Psychology and Christianity, 4* (1), 79–81.

Bobgan, M., & Bobgan, D. (1985). *How to counsel from Scripture*. Chicago: Moody.

Bouma-Prediger, S. (1990). The task of integration: A modest proposal. *Journal of Psychology and Theology, 18*, 21–31.

Carter, J. D., & Narramore, B. (1979). *The integration of psychology and theology: An introduction*. Grand Rapids, MI: Zondervan.

Christensen, A., & Jacobson, N. S. (1994). Who (or what) can do psychotherapy: The status and challenge of nonprofessional therapies. *Psychological Science, 5*, 8–14.

Collins, G. R. (1988). *Christian counseling: A comprehensive guide*. Dallas: Word.

Collins, G. R. (1993). *The biblical basis of Christian counseling for people helpers: Relating the basic teachings of Scripture to people's problems*. Colorado Springs, CO: NavPress.

Dillon, D. (1992). *Short-term counseling*. Dallas: Word.

Farnsworth, K. E. (1982). The conduct of integration. *Journal of Psychology and Theology, 10*, 308–319.

Foster, J. D., & Bolsinger, S. A. (1990). Prominent themes in evangelical integration literature. *Journal of Psychology and Theology, 18*, 3–12.

Foster, J. D., Horn, D. A., & Watson, S. (1988). The popularity of integration models, 1980–1985. *Journal of Psychology and Theology, 16*, 3–14.

Harris, J. (1985). Non-professionals as effective helpers for pastoral counselors. *Journal of Pastoral Care, 39*, 165–172.

Johnson, W. B. (1993). Christian rational-emotive therapy: A treatment protocol. *Journal of Psychology and Christianity, 12* (3), 254–261.

Johnson, W. B., Devries, R., Ridley, C. R., Pettorini, D., & Peterson, D. R. (1994). The comparative efficacy of Christian and secular rational-emotive therapy with Christian clients. *Journal of Psychology and Theology, 22*, 130–140.

Johnson, W. B., & Ridley, C. R. (1992). Brief Christian and non-Christian rational emotive therapy with depressed Christian clients: An exploratory study. *Counseling and Values, 36*, 220–228.

Jones, S. L., & Butman, R. (1991). *Modern psychotherapies: A comprehensive Christian appraisal*. Downers Grove, IL: InterVarsity Press.

Jones, S. L., Watson, E. J., & Wolfram, T. J. (1992). Results of the Rech Conference survey on religious faith and professional psychology. *Journal of Psychology and Theology, 20*, 147–158.

McAdams, D. P. (1988). *Power, intimacy and the life story*. New York: Guilford.

O'Hanlon, B. (1994). The third wave: The promise of narrative. *Family Therapy Networker, 18* (6), 18–29.

Pecheur, D. R., & Edwards, K. J. (1984). A comparison of secular and religious versions of cognitive therapy with depressed Christian college students. *Journal of Psychology and Theology, 12*, 45–54.

Propst, L. R. (1980). The comparative efficacy of religious and nonreligious imagery for the treatment of mild depression in religious individuals. *Cognitive Therapy and Research, 4*, 167–178.

Propst, L. R. (1988). *Psychotherapy within a religious framework: Spirituality in the emotional healing process*. New York: Human Sciences.

Propst, L. R., Ostrom, R., Watkins, P., Dean, T., & Mashburn, D. (1992). Comparative efficacy of religious and nonreligious cognitive-behavioral therapy for the treatment of clinical depression in religious individuals. *Journal of Consulting and Clinical Psychology, 60*, 94–103.

Smith, D. (1990). *Integrative therapy: A comprehensive approach to methods and principles of counseling and psychotherapy*. Grand Rapids, MI: Baker.

Tan, S.-Y. (Ed.). (1985). Lay Christian counseling [Special issue]. *Journal of Psychology and Christianity, 6* (2).

Tan, S.-Y. (1991). *Lay counseling: Equipping Christians for a helping ministry*. Grand Rapids, MI: Zondervan.

Vitz, P. C. (1992a). Narratives and counseling: I. From analysis of the past to stories about it. *Journal of Psychology and Theology, 20*, 11–19.

Vitz, P. C. (1992b). Narratives and counseling: II. From stories of the past to stories of the future. *Journal of Psychology and Theology, 20*, 20–27.

Walters, R. P. (1987). A survey of client satisfaction in a lay counseling program. *Journal of Psychology and Christianity, 6* (2), 62–69.

Worthington, E. L., Jr. (Ed.). (1994). Christian marriage counseling [Special issue]. *Journal of Psychology and Christianity, 13* (2).

Worthington, E. L., Jr., Shortz, J. L., & McCullough, M. E. (1993). A call for emphasis on scholarship on Christian marriage and marriage counseling. *Journal of Psychology and Christianity, 12* (1), 13–23.

E. L. WORTHINGTON, JR.

See SPIRITUAL AND RELIGIOUS ISSUES IN THERAPY; CHRISTIAN PSYCHOLOGY.

Christian Education. *See* RELIGIOUS DEVELOPMENT.

Christian Growth. Of keen interest to a growing number of psychologists has been the issue of adult growth and maturation. One has only to examine recent editions of any standard text in developmental psychology to see the striking increase in the number of pages devoted to study of such an intrinsically interesting and relevant topic (*see* Life Span Development). Recent texts in the psychology of religion (see Paloutzian, 1996; Wulff, 1991) likewise reflect this emphasis, especially as it relates to an understanding of faith development, mature religion, or psychospiritual well-being. Perhaps this is a good time for careful reflection on the relationship between spiritual and psychological maturity and the processes of growth in each. Efforts by Malony (1978, 1983), Carter (1974a, 1974b), Oakland (1974), and Nouwen (1972) did much to facilitate this integrative dialogue.

Mature Religion. A major work by Strunk (1965) has attempted to define mature religion, a task that is needed in order to give a sense of perspective to the maturation of faith and reason. He sees religion as a dynamic organization of cognitive-affective-conative factors, thereby suggesting that the characteristics of mature religion could be analyzed in terms of beliefs, feelings, and actions. Mature religious beliefs are characterized by lack of contamination by childish wishes; deep involvement in the world in terms of one's attitudes; a high awareness of one's convictions; the belief in the existence of a being greater than oneself; and comprehensiveness and articulation of those beliefs in a manner that serves well in the search for meaning. Religious feelings that are mature, according to Strunk, are characterized by profound experiences of mystical oneness resulting in feelings of wonder and awe, elation and freedom. Mature religious actions are characterized by good integration with the religious factors of the psyche; the presence of love as a comprehensive action with productiveness, humility, and responsibility as natural signs of this love; and a dynamic balance between commitment and tentativeness. Strunk believes that in the analysis of mature religion one will find these factors dynamically organized both horizontally and in depth, yielding a religious motive of master proportion. He argues that individuals will not be mature or immature but will fall on a continuum between the two.

According to Strunk (1965), the questions the Christian helper should be asking are, What am I doing to foster my own religious growth and development? What am I doing to foster that maturation process in the persons with whom I work? How are the religious organizations and systems of which I am a part facilitating necessary development at the local and communal levels?

Strunk's theory focuses more on process than content variables, perhaps underestimating the relevance of certain essential beliefs and convictions in the integrative quest, a serious concern that has been raised in the literature (see Jones & Butman, 1991). The work of Malony and his colleagues at Fuller Theological Seminary has provided a major alternative to Strunk's typology of mature religion, resulting in sophisticated psychometric instruments (both interview and self-report formats) that do an especially good job of balancing both the content and application of beliefs (see Malony, 1995). They certainly have the potential for clinical application in working with persons of faith pending further refinement of the existing measures (called the Religious Status Interview and Religious Status Inventory).

Faith Development. Fowler (1981) has written the seminal work on the stages of faith development through which the faith aspect of a human life may pass. Nearly every article or book written on faith development since his initial book is a modification or revision of his model (see Parks, 1986). Fowler sees moral and faith development as progressing through invariant and sequential transitions. He is careful not to confuse faith with a creedal statement but rather sees faith as answering a basic question, On what do you set your heart? He sees faith as an active mode of being and committing, with a strong social-relational component. Specific content is far less important to Fowler than the manner in which an individual makes sense of ultimate meanings in life. Ideally, then, our faith should be dynamic, evolving, and interactional, not static and primarily cognitive. It is not surprising that his approach is often characterized as stressing civility rather than conviction, and thereby eroding confidence in our collective ability to achieve consensus on essential beliefs (see Coles, 1990).

Building on a theoretical foundation of Erik Erikson, Jean Piaget, and Lawrence Kohlberg, Fowler (1981) presents a six-stage model of faith development that clearly reflects these significant psychosocial, cognitive, and moral theorists. Stage 1, intuitive-projective, is the fantasy-filled, imitative phase in which the child can be powerfully and permanently influenced by other models and their visible faith. Stage 2, mythic-literal, is the stage in which individuals begin to make personal the beliefs, observances, and stories that symbolize their belonging to their community support systems. This is followed by Stage 3, synthetic-conventional, which provides a coherent orientation in the midst of a more complex and diverse range of involvements. It synthesizes values and information; it provides a basis for identity and outlook. It is a conformist stage in that it is acutely tuned to the expectations and judgments of others and does not yet have enough independence to construct and maintain an autonomous perspective.

Stage 4, individualistic-reflective, is marked by a double development. The self, previously sustained in its identity and faith by a network of significant others, now claims an identity no longer built by the composite of one's roles or the internalized meanings of others. Fowler suggests that "self (identity) and outlook (world view) are differentiated from those of others and become acknowledged factors in the reactions, interpretations and judgments one makes of self and others" (p. 182). Stage 5, conjunctive, involves the integration of much that was suppressed or unrecognized in the interest of Stage 4's self-certainty. Faith in this stage reunites symbolic power with conceptual meaning. Stage 6, universalizing, is a disciplined making real and tangible the "imperatives of absolute love and justice of which Stage 5 has partial apprehensions. The self at Stage 6 engages in spending and being spent for the transformation of presenting reality in the direction of transcendent actuality" (p. 200). Implicit in Fowler's work is the assumption that the quality of one's faith community can facilitate or retard this process throughout the life span. Faith development cannot occur in isolation.

Fowler has a high view of persons, one that places the quest for meaning at the core of human existence. He also makes a valuable contribution to the discussion of faith development by offering an important perspective on the critical distinction between faith and creed. Much of the research by conservative Christians has been crippled by a rather predictable tendency to equate the two. Although we must be careful not to see all of faith development in terms of invariant sequential stages or to use a stage model to categorize persons in a legalistic and reductionistic manner, the idea of somewhat universal development milestones has enormous intrinsic appeal. A more recent and perhaps integrative formulation (see Groeschel, 1992) recognizes the inherent and somewhat limiting tendencies of stage models. Still, the stage models force us to reflect on how we can help others go deeper, a theme that can be found throughout the explosion of literature on spiritual formation (see Gangel & Wilhoit, 1994).

Psychospiritual Wholeness. The existing literature on spiritual and psychological health suggests that the following qualities seem to characterize the psychospiritually whole person: a strong religious faith commitment expressed both individually and corporately; the ability to resist silencing or pressures to conform; a small circle of intimate friends; a deep appreciation of God's handiwork; the ability to generate novel solutions to problems (i.e., creativity); self-acceptance and openness to others; the desire and the ability to confront others openly, directly, and honestly; a good balance between the rational and the emotional; involvement in helping those less fortunate than oneself; interdependence; good decision-making ability; a tolerance for ambiguity in life; a high level of moral development; and a belief that one's actions make a difference and that one is not the victim of forces beyond one's control. These criteria should be undergirded by a clearly articulated and well-formulated Christian worldview.

Probably no one meets these criteria all the time. We are limited by our own finiteness, fallenness, and humanness. Spiritual maturity, not unlike psychological normality, is perhaps best viewed as a batting average (i.e., nobody can bat a 1.000 for an entire season). While we can reasonably expect that a deeply internalized faith commitment will enhance a person's well-being, we cannot expect Christians to become fully self-actualized or sanctified (McLemore, 1982). The doctrine of sin implies the impossibility of such perfection. That alone should make us cautious in making strong judgments about the character of others. Rather, our energies should

be geared toward creating opportunities and settings in which spiritual growth and development can be maximized and regression or stagnation can be minimized (see Ortberg, 1995). The skillful administration of grace and truth by discerning and nurturing Christian communities and their individual representatives have an important part in the process of growing more fully developed Christians (see Gangel & Wilhoit, 1993).

References

Carter, J. D. (1974a). Maturity: Psychological and biblical. *Journal of Psychology and Theology, 2,* 89–96.
Carter, J. D. (1974b). Personality and Christian maturity: A process congruity model. *Journal of Psychology and Theology, 2,* 190–201.
Coles, R. (1990). *Harvard diary.* New York: Crossroad.
Fowler, J. (1981). *Stages of faith.* San Francisco: Harper & Row.
Gangel, K., & Wilhoit, J. (Eds.). (1993). *The Christian educator's handbook of adult education.* Wheaton, IL: Victor.
Gangel, K., & Wilhoit, J. (Eds.). (1994). *The Christian educator's handbook on spiritual formation.* Wheaton, IL: Victor.
Groeschel, B. (1992). *Spiritual passages.* New York: Crossroad.
Jones, S., & Butman, R. (1991). *Modern psychotherapies.* Downers Grove, IL: InterVarsity Press.
Malony, H. N. (1978). *Understanding your faith.* Nashville: Abingdon.
Malony, H. N. (Ed.). (1983). *Wholeness and holiness.* Grand Rapids, MI: Baker.
Malony, H. N. (1995). *The psychology of religion for ministry.* New York: Paulist.
McLemore, C. W. (1982). *The scandal of psychotherapy.* Wheaton, IL: Tyndale House.
Nouwen, H. J. (1972). *The wounded healer.* Garden City, NY: Doubleday.
Oakland, J. (1974). Self-actualization and sanctification. *Journal of Psychology and Theology, 2,* 202–209.
Ortberg, J. (1995). Rethinking the kingdom of God: The work of Dallas Willard and some applications to psychotherapeutic practice. *Journal of Psychology and Christianity, 4,* 306–317.
Parks, S. (1986). *The critical years.* San Francisco: Harper & Row.
Paloutzian, R. (1996). *Invitation to the psychology of religion* (2nd ed.). Boston: Allyn & Bacon.
Strunk, O. (1965). *Mature religion.* New York: Abingdon.
Wulff, D. M. (1991). *Psychology of religion.* New York: Wiley.

R. E. BUTMAN

See FAITH; RELIGIOUS HEALTH AND PATHOLOGY; RELIGIOUS DEVELOPMENT.

Christian Psychology. Although the term is not widely used (Myers and Jeeves, 1987, and Philipchalk, 1988 are exceptions), "Christian psychology" refers to a movement within psychology that seeks to integrate biblical doctrines with scientific and applied aspects of psychology. The movement's critical focus is to reconceptualize psychology in such a way as to be consistent with the tenets of an orthodox, Protestant worldview. However, the general purpose is broader than purely cognitive reconceptualization; theological and psychological insights are applied to bolster one's personal faith and deeds (Farnsworth, 1985b).

Secularized Psychology. The late nineteenth and early twentieth centuries witnessed the gradual but complete secularization of concepts about personality that had theological origins (Roback, 1952). During the first half of the twentieth century psychologists were more disposed to discuss sexual matters than religion (except for William James and Gordon Allport). In spite of recent antipathy between psychologists and theologians, there is a close historical link between them. The Latin term *persona*, from which the English term *personality* developed, denoted both the mask used to indicate a particular theatrical role and the real self or actor. *Persona* suggested that the inner nature may be split from outward action. But the Latin word *religio* meant a binding or fastening, especially in the form of reverence or fear of a more powerful being. Thus the person had internal integrity because of the religious nature of personality (Oates, 1973).

The ancient Greeks used two words to portray human nature. *Psyche* originally denoted the breath or spirit that distinguished the animate from the inanimate. Later it developed connotations of soul and mind, and the study of psychology ensued. *Pneuma* was a close parallel to psyche; *pneuma* referred to life but in its relationship to the eternal. From the study of *pneuma* came theology; religion was a human expression of *pneuma*. The secularization of *psyche* inevitably led to the development of psychology as a discipline distinct from philosophy and theology.

The language of psychology was also desacralized at other points. The Hebrews used the word *nepesh* to describe the whole person, a union of inner and outer aspects. In the Old Testament *nepesh* is commonly translated *soul*. However, when *soul* gradually developed connotations of transcendency and eternity, psychologists adopted the term *self* to refer to human wholeness. Self to the holistic psychologists is essentially the rebirth in a desacralized form of the Hebraic concept of soul, and the will became secularized (Kantor, 1963; Roback, 1952).

Integration of Psychology and Christianity. Christian psychology originates from a drive to construct a more adequate psychology by reconnecting the severed relationships with theology; the drive embodies a desire to adopt the best of science and faith. The goal is to integrate faith and reason by linking theology and science. The reassertion of biblical orthodoxy as the basis of one's science is a reaction to modern psychology's endorsement of the religion of secular humanism (Collins, 1977; Vitz, 1977). Although the relationship between theology and psychology has been strained and is one of mutual suspicion and denigration, this need not be the case (Ellison, 1972). Thus the task in integration is "to learn to think Christianly about psychology" (Farnsworth, 1985a, p. 82).

The attempt to integrate psychology and theology springs from a belief in "the unity of truth" (Holmes, 1985). The task of integration involves explicitly relating truth discovered through general or natural revelation to that disclosed in special or biblical revelation, of interrelating knowledge gained from the world and knowledge gained from the Word. Critical are the issues regarding the nature of reality and the nature of knowledge. The conflict between science and theology at this point stems from variations in original assumptions. The naturalistic, objective, and inductive biases of scientists are juxtaposed to the supernaturalistic, subjective, and deductive premises of the theologian. The integration movement begins with fundamental assumptions concerning the locus and methodology of truth: God is the source of all truth, no matter where it is found (Holmes, 1987); God is the source of all truth no matter how it is found (Timpe, 1980; Farnsworth, 1985b).

To the integrationist, natural revelation supports special revelation. That is, if God is consistent, as the Scriptures suggest (e.g., Mal. 3:6), then knowledge based in revelation, replication, reason, and intuition should be complementary. Underlying this approach is a faith statement common to scientist and theologian alike: the laws that govern the operation of the world are discoverable.

Models of Integration. Carter and Narramore (1979) were among the first to describe integration strategies. They suggested four basic strategies with sacred and secular versions. Perhaps the oldest and most familiar description is the against model, in which psychology and theology are portrayed as mortal enemies. Each defines one exclusive approach to truth (empiricism versus revelation), one cause for human discomfort and misfortune (environmental conditioning versus sin), and one solution to problems (psychotherapy versus salvation).

The of model holds that humans are moral-spiritual creatures not reducible to a collection of naturalistic forces. Humans are fundamentally good, and whatever pain is experienced is attributed to environmental or psychological factors rather than sin. Psychological insights aid persons in spiritual development. In the secular version human personality tends to be deified (the religion of psychology), while in the sacred version (the psychology of religion) the divine is desupernaturalized.

In the parallels model psychology and theology are distinct disciplines with separate goals, contents, and methods of inquiry to describe different dimensions of human nature. Spiritual dimensions constitute the province of theology, while physical and social dimensions concern psychology. Psychological insights parallel those of theology, but neither discipline purports to offer a comprehensive description of human totality. In one respect psychology and theology have chosen to limit the focus of their study; both attempt to conceptualize the given aspects of human nature (Jeeves, 1976).

Psychology originates etymologically from two Greek words, *psyche* and *logos,* so that literally psychology is human words about life and personality. The term *theology* comes from the Greek *theos* and *logos.* Theology is human words about God. Individuals who favor the parallels model suggest that psychology and theology are theory and conceptualization, regardless of the source of evidence. Psychology and theology are free to change when new facts are discovered or when old facts are reinterpreted. Humans are not obliged to act as psychologists have constructed them, nor is God obligated to correspond to theological ideas.

Moreover, the parallelists have defined different goals. Psychology is often described as the science that seeks to understand, predict, and control behavior. Following the scientific model has had the effect of limiting study to regular, lawful, and aggregate events. Aided regularly by divine revelation via the Scriptures, theology has sought to reason and deduce the nature of God and his laws. The focus in theology is often on unique, one-time events (e.g., incarnation, miracles). Psychology may be described as a science that tells the how of personal motivation and social relationships, whereas theology explains the why of creation and redemption (Jeeves, 1976; Timpe, 1980). Psychology is horizontal; theology is vertical in perspective. Each discipline couches its insights in separate linguistic conventions. Furthermore, the parallel model holds that the Bible was inspired to be not a science book but rather history (i.e., the story about God's redemptive efforts to save his people). As history it contains all truth necessary for an individual's salvation.

According to Carter and Narramore (1979), the integrates model is to be preferred, since it is the most comprehensive. Psychology is not treated as a system of thought about human nature but rather about the actuality of created humanness. In like fashion theology is more than a body of thought about God; it takes on the character (or caricature) of cosmology. Knowledge is not pigeonholed into discipline-defined units, but all sources of knowledge are interrelated into one body of truth. Of necessity the integrationist must be competently knowledgeable in both fields and then be able to transcend the traditional limits of each. These latter two groups have been described by Evans (1982) as the limiters and the Christianizers respectively.

The work of Farnsworth has provided fresh and additional perspectives to the integration task. Farnsworth (1981) described two possible arenas for integration. Critical integration is a cognitive reassessment of psychological assumptions and propositions from the foundations of a Christian worldview (i.e., a thinking integration of psychology and theology), while embodied integration applies biblical and psychological insights to Christian living and deeds (i.e., a heartfelt integration of psychology and Christian faith). He also described five methodologies for integration: credibility, convertibility, conformability, compatibility, and complementarity (Farnsworth, 1982, 1985b). According to the credibility model, psychological insights are given significance only when they are screened through the sieve of theology and specific biblical texts. The convertibility model takes theological insights and converts them into psychological terminology. In the conformability model, the assumptive bases upon which a psychology is to be built must conform to a Christian worldview (the review of critical integration). The compatibility model notes the common parallels and correlations between psychological and theological findings. The complementarity model notes the differences and relates them in an organized manner. But for Farnsworth the integration must eventually evidence itself in life applications.

Levels of Integration. Integration may occur at several levels (Larzalere, 1980). The broadest level of analysis is worldview. These foundational assumptions are faith statements, since neither psychology nor theology can prove the correctness of its assertions about reality's nature. Embedded within the worldview is the second level of special assumptions pertaining to content and methodologies. Most tension between psychology and theology occurs at these two levels.

Foundational presuppositions in large measure determine the shape of the superstructure (i.e., theory). The central and nonnegotiable assumption for the Christian psychologist is that God exists and is Creator-source of all truth and power. Furthermore, God has chosen to reveal to humans individually and collectively some of his nature through the created world, through inspired Scripture, and through Jesus Christ as the agent of creation and redemption. Positions on peripheral assumptions may vary. The central assumption deals with the Christian in Christian psychology while the peripheral assumptions may reflect Christian psychologies. Peripheral assumptions address issues like the mind-brain relation, the nature-nurture controversy, the pervasiveness of sin, and determinism and free will. Integrationists take a position on each, however implicit or explicit, but peripheral assumptions remain secondary and subservient to the central supernatural one.

The third level of analysis is that of theoretical proposition and hypothesis. The fourth and final level constitutes data. While conflict between psychology and theology may exist at these levels, it is not as pronounced as at the first two levels.

The late 1970s and early 1980s saw a flurry of activity focused on macrointegration. In macrointegration theorists sought to integrate psychology and theology by specifically addressing the assumptive foundations of varying worldviews held by the psychology and theology under review. Since these broad-brush efforts, integration adherents have engaged in microintegration, in which the integration efforts focus on forming, researching, and revising specific hypotheses. This process parallels a similar development of personality theory in which early notable theorists developed broad theories (from about 1890 to 1960). Since then personality research efforts have been more directed to specific hypotheses; theories take on less grand design but are more focused.

Examples of Macrointegration. Conflict between psychology and theology is most prominent at the worldview and special assumptions levels. The credo of the secular psychologist is "I believe in the efficacy of empiricism, the divinity of determinism, the reality of relativism, the revelation of reductionism, and the necessity of naturalism" (adapted from Collins, 1977). Collins (1977) spent considerable time and effort addressing the issues of worldview and special assumptions. He found the traditional behavioral assumptions of empiricism, determinism, relativism, reductionism, and naturalism problematic in an integration of psychology and theology (*see* Psychology, Presuppositions of). Since these do not correspond well with traditional theological tenets, he suggested the faulty assumptive foundations be rebuilt. He proposed specific revisions to each of these problematic assumptions that were truer to theological insights while they built on science's strength.

While the work of Collins was at the worldview level, Koteskey (1983, 1991) addressed the general theoretical level. The integrative mechanism he employed is a variant of Schaeffer's (1968) view that God is personal and infinite. Humans are like God in having personality (soul, spirit), but a chasm exists between God the Creator and created humankind relative to infiniteness. Thus the personal dimension emphasizes the ways that humans mirror God's image and differ from animals, while the infinite aspects point to human-divine differences and a commonality with animals. In this way perspectives and ideas from structuralism, Gestalt psychology, and humanistic psychology illustrate likenesses between the divine and human. Behaviorism and functionalism point to the similarities of humans and animals, while psychoanalysis marks how unlike God humans are.

Koteskey's (1983) position is not that psychology and theology need to be integrated, but that theology (i.e., Schaeffer's discussion of the personal and infinite dimensions) should serve to integrate a fragmented secular psychology. The content areas in psychology are ordered into this pattern. For example, physiological studies in structure, motivation, emotion, sensation, and conditioning describe similarities between humans and animals. Godlikeness is seen in the areas of perception, cognition, and cognitive aspects of motivation, emotion, and social relationships. Psychiatric disorders can be ordered similarly. Organic mental disorders, disorders appearing in childhood or adolescence, somatoform disorders, phobic disorders, psychosexual disorders, and anxiety disorders are at the animal end of the continuum. Personality disorders, paranoid disorders, schizophrenic disorders, narcissism, and affective disorders are failures to achieve human potential at the Godlike end of the continuum.

At the general theoretical level Bufford (1981) examined behavioral psychology and its relation to Scripture. His basic position is that there is little in behavioral psychology and its practice (i.e., methodological behaviorism as a way of knowing and changing) to contradict biblical understanding. However, when behavioral psychology takes a more radical view (i.e., radical or metaphysical behaviorism), the naturalistic and reductionistic premises pose problems at the philosophic level for a classical theologian. This tension is due in large measure to Platonic dualism, with an exaggeration of supernaturalism by theologians of the Middle Ages and a corresponding exaggeration of naturalism by Enlightenment scientists. Neither exaggeration is consistent with the biblical record.

Bufford conceptualized causation of events in an intriguing way. The two causes, divine and natural, could be either present or absent. When these are combined into a 2 x 2 matrix, 4 possible types of causation emerge. When both divine and natural causes are absent, there is chaos. When divine cause is absent but natural cause is present, a naturalistic explanation is given. If a supernatural cause is present and a natural cause is absent, there is said to exist a supernatural explanation or miracle (e.g., creation ex nihilo). Providential explanation is the divine employing natural mechanisms as sources of causality. The Christian scientist or psychologist must endorse the providential explanation, since chaos and miracles are not predictable, nor are they recurring events. Natural explanations must also be ruled out on the basis of the assumption of divine causation. Bufford contended that this behavioral view is consistent with the Westminster Confession of Faith.

Examples of Microintegration. Several writers have attempted to present Christian perspectives on specific hypotheses. Both Custance (1980) and Jones (1981) argued that there is biblical and scientific support for a dualistic solution to the mind-brain problem. Their hypothesis is a modernization of Cartesian interactionism. Citing the works of Penfield, Eccles, Sperry, and Popper, they asserted that consciousness cannot be equated with brain state and that full humanness in the biblical perspective is described only when physical and mental dimensions of the person are recognized. Furthermore, human dignity has its fullest meaning when the physical and spiritual (i.e., mental) dimensions are viewed as God's creation. However,

Myers (1978) reviewed the same literature and holds a monistic (i.e., holistic) view of human nature in which mental conditions (e.g., thoughts, feelings, and beliefs) are identical to brain states.

At the data level Myers (1978, 1980) reported a remarkable parallel between experimental studies in social psychology and biblical concepts. It seems that pride (i.e., undue concern for self) is manifested in a number of self-serving biases. From a theological point of view pride distorts the way the individual responds to experience in the world. Similar processes are reported in laboratory experiments. Persons attribute positive consequences to their own good action but blame environmental forces for bad outcomes. The individual claims freedom and responsibility when the outcomes are good but avoids personal freedom and responsibility when outcomes are bad. Self-serving biases induce individuals to change attitudes and values to be consistent with behavior, because attitudes are derived from behavior.

Other work on microintegration has focused on applied topics as diverse as self-esteem, child rearing, discipline, mental health, human sexuality, and stress management.

Christian psychology meets all the criteria to be considered a school or a system. Its general perspective and theoretical assumptions have been articulated. It is an explicit institutional goal in graduate psychology programs, including those at Fuller Theological Seminary, Rosemead School of Professional Psychology at Biola University, Wheaton College, and George Fox College. Integration is a significant undergraduate activity in colleges affiliated with the Coalition of Christian Colleges and Universities. The importance of the undergraduate aspect was highlighted by devoting a special issue of the *Journal of Psychology and Theology* to undergraduate education (winter 1995). In the undergraduate curriculum integration takes place by using the combined strategies of modeling one's personal faith, discussing Christian topics, and assigning readings concerning Christian topics, as well as in fully integrated courses (Dykstra, Foster, Kleiner, & Koch, 1995).

Professional organizations also emphasize the integration of psychology and religion: the Christian Association for Psychological Studies, American Scientific Affiliation, and Psychologists Interested in Religious Issues (Division 36 of the American Psychological Association). Several professional journals publish integration works (e.g., *Journal of Psychology and Theology, Journal of Psychology and Christianity, Journal of the American Scientific Affiliation*).

The concern for a Christian psychology is active and broad-based. Myers (1995, p. 247) summarized cogently the significant dimensions of the integration: "Faith motivates science. . . . Faith mandates skeptical scrutiny. . . . [In addition it means] being true to one's deepest convictions and values, . . . giving psychology to the church, . . . relating psychological and religious descriptions of human nature, . . . studying determinants of religious experience, . . . [and] studying religion's effect."

References

Bufford, R. K. (1981). *The human reflex: Behavioral psychology in biblical perspective.* San Francisco: Harper & Row.

Carter, J. D., & Narramore, B. (1979). *The integration of psychology and theology.* Grand Rapids, MI: Zondervan.

Collins, G. R. (1977). *The rebuilding of psychology.* Wheaton, IL: Tyndale House.

Custance, A. C. (1980). *The mysterious matter of mind.* Grand Rapids, MI: Zondervan.

Dykstra, M. L., Foster, J. D., Kleiner, K. A., & Koch, C. J. (1995). Integrating across the psychology curriculum: A content review approach. *Journal of Psychology and Theology, 23,* 277–288.

Ellison, C. W. (1972). Christianity and psychology: Contradictory or complementary? *Journal of the American Scientific Affiliation, 24,* 131–134.

Evans, C. S. (1982). *Preserving the person.* Grand Rapids, MI: Zondervan.

Farnsworth, K. E. (1981). *Integrating psychology and theology: Elbows together but hearts apart.* Washington, DC: University Press of America.

Farnsworth, K. E. (1982). The conduct of integration. *Journal of Psychology and Theology, 10,* 308–319.

Farnsworth, K. E. (1985a). Furthering the kingdom in psychology. In A. F. Holmes (Ed.), *The making of a Christian mind: A Christian world view and the academic enterprise.* Downers Grove, IL: InterVarsity Press.

Farnsworth, K. E. (1985b). *Wholehearted integration: Harmonizing psychology and Christianity through word and deed.* Grand Rapids, MI: Baker.

Holmes, A. F. (1985). Toward a Christian view of things. In A. F. Holmes (Ed.), *The making of a Christian mind: A Christian world view and the academic enterprise.* Downers Grove, IL: InterVarsity Press.

Holmes, A. F. (1987). *The idea of a Christian college* (Rev. ed.). Grand Rapids, MI: Eerdmans.

Jeeves, M. A. (1976). *Psychology and Christianity.* Downers Grove, IL: InterVarsity Press.

Jones, D. G. (1981). *Our fragile brains.* Downers Grove, IL: InterVarsity Press.

Kantor, J. R. (1963). *The scientific evolution of psychology* (Vol. 2). Chicago: Principia.

Koteskey, R. L. (1983). *General psychology for Christian counselors.* Nashville: Abingdon.

Koteskey, R. L. (1991). *Psychology from a Christian perspective* (2nd ed.). Washington, DC: University Press of America.

Larzalere, R. E. (1980). The task ahead: Six levels of integration of Christianity and psychology. *Journal of Psychology and Theology, 8,* 3–11.

Myers, D. G. (1978). *The human puzzle.* San Francisco: Harper & Row.

Myers, D. G. (1980). *The inflated self.* New York: Seabury.

Myers, D. G. (1995). Teaching, texts, and values. *Journal of Psychology and Theology, 23,* 244–247.

Myers, D. G., & Jeeves, M. A. (1987). *Psychology through the eyes of faith.* San Francisco: Harper & Row.

Oates, W. E. (1973). *The psychology of religion.* Waco, TX: Word.

Philipchalk, R. P. (1988). *Psychology and Christianity* (Rev. ed.). Lanham, MD: University Press of America.

Roback, A. A. (1952). *History of psychology and psychiatry.* New York: Philosophical Library.

Schaeffer, F. A. (1968). *The God who is there.* Downers Grove, IL: InterVarsity Press.

Timpe, R. L. (1980). Assumptions and parameters for developing Christian psychological systems. *Journal of Psychology and Theology, 8,* 230–239.

Vitz, P. C. (1977). *Psychology as religion.* Grand Rapids, MI: Eerdmans.

R. L. TIMPE

See CHRISTIAN COUNSELING AND PSYCHOTHERAPY.

Christian Psychology, Graduate Programs. One of the byproducts of efforts to integrate psychology with the Christian faith has been the establishment and growth of a number of psychology graduate programs with a Christian emphasis. This discussion will focus on those programs offered through departments or schools of psychology and will not include pastoral counseling or pastoral psychology programs found in many seminaries. For individuals entering the pastorate, such seminary programs may be the most useful.

For people desiring graduate study in either a Christian or a secular program, it is important to choose the degree that represents the credentials needed for employment. Though doctoral degrees have traditionally provided more flexibility in the marketplace, it is unclear what effects managed health care will have on the market for individuals with either doctoral or master's training.

Doctoral Programs. The doctoral degree has been traditionally recognized as the basic credential for entering the field of psychology. There are three doctoral degree options to consider. The doctor of philosophy (Ph.D.) degree is offered by most university-based psychology departments that train in the scientist-practitioner model. People who want to hold academic positions as teachers and researchers should obtain the Ph.D. Some clinical practitioner employers will also show a preference for the Ph.D. The doctor of psychology (Psy.D.) is the degree offered by some university-based psychology departments or independent schools of professional psychology (such as the California School of Professional Psychology) that train with a professional model. All things being equal, this degree program will provide more clinical skill training but less research training than the Ph.D. The doctor of education (Ed.D.) is the degree granted by a university-based education department, usually with a research emphasis. Among Christian graduate programs only the Ph.D. and the Psy.D. options are available. The following list of programs is representative of available programs and is not exhaustive.

- Fuller Theological Seminary (Pasadena, CA). Ph.D. and Psy.D. in clinical psychology; Ph.D. in marriage and family therapy; Ph.D. in marriage and family studies; and doctor of marriage and family therapy (DMFT). Fuller also offers a master's degree in marriage and family therapy.
- George Fox College (Newberg, OR). Psy.D. in clinical psychology.
- Rosemead School of Psychology (part of Biola University, La Mirada, CA). Ph.D. and Psy.D. in clinical psychology.
- Wheaton College (Wheaton, IL). Psy.D. in clinical psychology. Wheaton also offers a master's degree in clinical psychology.

Master's Programs. The major distinction in master's-level training is whether the program offers a terminal master's degree, which is designed to prepare the student for a specific occupation that requires only a master's degree for entry-level employment, or a nonterminal master's degree, which is designed to allow the student to transfer credits into a doctoral program in the same department or institution. However, the word *nonterminal* sometimes is used to describe programs that offer only the master's degree but are designed to provide training that will allow the student to transfer to a doctoral program at another institution. The master of arts (M.A.) versus master of science (M.S.) distinction does not appear to be important. Many programs, including Christian programs, may emphasize the terminal or nonterminal degree but will allow the student to customize his or her program according to interests and future plans. In addition to Fuller and Wheaton, a representative but not exhaustive list of Christian programs at the master's level includes:

- Geneva College (Beaver Falls, PA). M.A. in professional psychology (may be designed as either a terminal or nonterminal degree).
- Psychological Studies Institute (Atlanta, GA). M.A. in clinical psychology. Through a cooperative arrangement with the Georgia School of Professional Psychology, the M.A. degree is from the GSPP with a diploma in Christian counseling from the Institute. Students are then eligible to be considered for the Psy.D. program at GSPP.

P. C. HILL

See CHRISTIAN PSYCHOLOGY.

Christian Psychology, Key Figures. Any brief compilation of key figures does a disservice to the hundreds of dedicated Christian psychologists working in university, clinical, and pastoral settings. This article selectively identifies and categorizes some psychologists who have represented the field to the general population.

Historical Figures. Jay Adams, Ph.D. in speech (University of Missouri) and a postdoctoral fellow in psychology (University of Illinois), is the director of advanced studies and practical theology at Westminster Theological Seminary in Escondido, California. He has taught at Westminster Seminary in Philadelphia and developed nouthetic counseling, an approach that confronts the client with Scripture to produce behavioral change. His books include *Competent to Counsel* and *The Christian Counselor's Manual*.

Clyde Narramore, Ed.D. (Columbia University), was the founding president of the Rosemead School of Psychology and is currently founder, director, and president of the Narramore Christian Foundation in Rosemead, California. Using an insight-oriented approach to clients, he has written a number of books, including *The Encyclopedia of Psychological Problems* and *The Psychology of Counseling*.

Wayne E. Oates, Th.D. (Southern Baptist Theological Seminary), is professor of psychiatry and behavioral science at the University of Louisville School of Medicine. He has taught at Southern Baptist Theological Seminary and received the Distinguished Service Award of the American Association of Pastoral Counselors. He takes a phenomenological and developmental approach to his clients and has written more than 20 books, including *The Psychology of Religion, When Religion Gets Sick*, and *New Dimensions in Pastoral Care*.

Paul Tournier, a Swiss physician, psychotherapist, and lay theologian, was involved in international meetings on the Christian faith and medical practice at the Ecumenical Institute in Switzerland. He took an interpersonal approach to his clients and has authored more than 30 articles and books, among them *The Strong and the Weak, The Healing of Persons*, and *The Meaning of Persons*.

Howard Clinebell, Ph.D. in psychology of religion (Union Theological Seminary), was professor of pastoral counseling at the School of Theology, Claremont, California. He takes a human growth and potential orientation to his clients. His publications include *Basic Types of Pastoral Counseling, Growth Counseling: New Tools for Clergy and Laity*, and *Growth Groups*.

Contemporary Clinical. Gary Collins, Ph.D. in clinical psychology (Purdue University), was professor of psychology and chairman of the Division of Pastoral Counseling and Psychology at Trinity Evangelical Divinity School and is currently associated with Liberty University. His educative approach makes clients into disciples. Among his articles and books are *The Rebuilding of Psychology* and *Overcoming Anxiety*.

Lawrence J. Crabb, Ph.D. in clinical psychology (University of Illinois), is the founder and director of the Institute of Biblical Counseling in Morrison, Colorado. He has served as professor at Colorado Christian University and chair of the department of counseling, Grace Theological Seminary. He developed biblical counseling, which changes client's thinking to a biblically based belief system and way of life. He has authored many books, including *Inside Out* and *Effective Biblical Counseling*.

Frank B. Minirth, M.D. (University of Arkansas), is assistant professor of pastoral ministries at Dallas Theological Seminary and is president of Minirth-Meier Clinics. He has authored many books, including *Happiness Is a Choice* and *You Can Measure Your Health*.

Paul D. Meier, M.D. (University of Arkansas), is assistant professor of pastoral ministries at Dallas Theological Seminary and is vice president of Minirth-Meier Clinics. His books include *Christian Child Rearing and Personality Development, Happiness Is a Choice*, and *You Can Avoid Divorce*.

S. Bruce Narramore, Ph.D. in clinical psychology (University of Kentucky), is professor of psychology, Rosemead School of Psychology/Biola University. He has authored *Help! I'm a Parent: A Guide to Child Rearing, You're Someone Special, No Condemnation*, and other books.

Contemporary Academics. David G. Benner, Ph.D. in clinical psychology (York University), is professor of psychology at Redeemer College. He has written extensively on the relationship of Christian faith and psychotherapy (*Psychotherapy in Christian Perspective* and *Care of Souls)*, and is editor of the *Baker Encyclopedia of Psychology and Counseling*.

Craig W. Ellison, Ph.D. (Wayne State University), is professor of psychology and urban studies, Alliance Theological Seminary and Nyack College, New Jersey. He has extensively researched the influence of religious factors on mental health and written a number of books and articles, including *Your Better Self, Self-Esteem*, and *Modifying Man: Implications and Ethics*.

C. Steven Evans, Ph.D. (Yale University), is professor of philosophy at Calvin College. A Kierkegaard scholar, he has argued for the role of the self and human personhood in the science of psychology in a wide range of books and articles, including *Preserving the Person*.

Stanton L. Jones, Ph.D. (Arizona State University), is provost at Wheaton College and Wheaton Graduate School. He has researched and written on the integration of therapy models with a Christian worldview and edited *Psychology and the Christian Faith: An Introductory Reader*.

Donald M. McKay, Ph.D. (University of London) in physics, was professor of communications at Keele University in England. He specialized in brain physiology and information theory and applies this to the integration of science and the Christian faith in numerous articles and books, including *The Clockwork Image* and *Room for Freedom and Action in a Mechanistic Universe*.

David G. Myers, Ph.D. (University of Iowa), is professor of psychology at Hope College in Holland, Michigan. He has researched and written extensively on the relationship of social psychology to the Christian faith. His books include *Social Psy-*

chology, Psychology, the Human Puzzle, and *The Human Connection*.

Contemporary Pastoral. David Augsburger, Ph.D. in pastoral psychotherapy and family therapy (School of Theology at Claremont), is professor of pastoral care at the Associated Mennonite Biblical Seminaries. He has written extensively on interpersonal relationships. The *Caring Enough to Confront* series is part of his published work.

David A. Seamands, M.Div. (Drew Theological Seminary) and M.A. (Hartford Seminary Foundation), is pastor emeritus of pastoral ministries and counselor in residence at Asbury Theological Seminary in Wilmore, Kentucky. He has written extensively on the role of God's grace and healing in helping Christians overcome psychological problems; his books include *Healing of Memories*, *Healing for Damaged Emotions*, and *Healing Grace*.

H. Norman Wright, M.R.E. (Fuller Theological Seminary) and M.A. in clinical psychology (Pepperdine University), has served as the director of the graduate department of marriage and family therapy at Talbot School of Theology/Biola University. He has written extensively on marriage and family relationships. Among his many books are *Communication: Key to Your Marriage* and *Seasons of a Marriage*.

B. E. ECK

See CHRISTIAN PSYCHOLOGY.

Christian Psychology, Professional Journals. The dialogue between psychology and Christian faith has a long history. Since the early 1970s, however, the effort to explore the interface between psychology and the Christian faith has greatly intensified. "Integration" has been the dominant term to describe the efforts in exploring this relationship. It is in this context that organizations like the Christian Association for Psychological Studies (CAPS) experienced phenomenal growth, Christian graduate programs in psychology were established, and professional journals with a Christian emphasis were born. Of several professional journals (i.e., journals that are written by professionals to professionals, usually by author submission that is then subject to peer review) that report studies in some way involving religious experience, two are most explicit in identifying themselves as journals that explore the relationship between psychology and Christianity: the *Journal of Psychology and Christianity* and the *Journal of Psychology and Theology*. Though clearly there are similarities between the two journals, each has its own set of distinctive characteristics. A third journal, *Marriage and Family: A Christian Journal*, focuses on marriage and family issues and interventions. With all three journals, articles are submitted to a peer review process. In addition to publishing articles, all three journals have book review sections.

The *Journal of Psychology and Christianity (JPC)* is a quarterly publication of the Christian Association for Psychological Studies with all members of CAPS receiving the journal as a benefit of membership, though individuals and libraries may subscribe to the journal. The contents page of each issue states that the *JPC* is "designed to provide scholarly interchange among Christian professionals in the psychological and pastoral professions." The *JPC* has a clear clinical orientation, given that CAPS consists primarily of clinicians, though submissions on nonclinical topics are welcome and are frequently published. Theoretical, research, and applied articles are all considered for publication. Authors need not be a member of CAPS to have their articles published. Every other *JPC* issue (each summer and winter issue) is devoted to a special topic and is guest edited by an expert on the topic. The *JPC* is indexed or abstracted in a number of databases (including Psych-INFO) listed on the contents page.

The *Journal of Psychology and Theology (JPT)*, subtitled "An Evangelical Forum for the Integration of Psychology and Theology," says on its inside cover that its purpose is "to communicate recent scholarly thinking on the interrelationships of psychological and theological concepts and to consider the application of these concepts to a variety of professional settings. The major intent of the editors is to place before the evangelical community articles that have bearing on the nature of humankind from a biblical perspective." The journal is published quarterly through the Rosemead School of Psychology at Biola University in La Mirada, California, and is also sponsored by the American Association of Christian Counselors (AACC). The *JPT* is indexed or abstracted in a large number of databases listed on the inside of the front cover.

Marriage and Family: A Christian Journal is also sponsored by the AACC. Related professional publications include journals in the area of pastoral counseling (e.g., *Journal of Pastoral Counseling*, *Journal of Pastoral Practice*, *Pastoral Care*, and *Pastoral Psychology*), journals that integrate psychology and religion in general (e.g., *Counseling and Values*, *Journal of Religion and Health*), and journals that investigate religion from a social scientific perspective (e.g., *Journal for the Scientific Study of Religion*, *Review of Religious Research*).

P. C. HILL

See CHRISTIAN PSYCHOLOGY.

Chronic Illness. An illness becomes chronic when it persists past six months in duration. There are strong similarities in how individuals respond to prolonged suffering, regardless of whether the condition is medical or psychological. The primary effect of the process of being ill is a negative shift in the person's self-concept. Any robustness the person felt prior to becoming ill can be replaced with a sense of fragility, vulnerability, and fear. While every person reacts differently, the typical psychological response to continued illness includes depression, anxiety, disturbed sleep, decreased mental stamina, decreased appetite, decreased libido, worry, powerlessness, fear, defeatism, and hopelessness.

Slow, steady progress is often not appreciated by the patient who has become accustomed to feeling bad and is overwhelmed by the constant nature of the illness. In a nonpsychotic fashion individuals can misinterpret daily experiences when their perception is so influenced by discomfort and reduced functioning. Minor changes can be seen as major setbacks, or significant problems can be minimized through denial. Such diminution of emotional functioning can negatively impact how well the patient cooperates with those who are trying to bring healing. Noncompliance with treatments robs patients of opportunities to become well. As they continue to feel reduced in body and/or mind, and, quite often, spirit, it can become difficult for patients to exert the necessary psychological and physiological energy to engage in health-promoting behaviors. Patients may not avail themselves of prescribed therapies or get adequate strength-building, motion-increasing exercise. They may not get adequate nutrition. The dangerous consequence of not having the psychological presence to engage in healing behavior or activity is the negative impact it has on the chronic condition one is trying to overcome. This can become a self-perpetuating negative cycle in which disordered psychological functioning leads to prolonged chronicity, which leads to further decrements in psychological status.

Not only the patient is affected by a chronic illness, however. There is consequence for the entire family. The family system can be dramatically disrupted. All members of the family go through shock, disbelief, and feelings of helplessness as they see their loved one struggle. This causes them to interact and react differently with the ill family member, a change that can further disturb the psychological equilibrium of the patient. The patient may feel abandoned, smothered, or controlled by family members. Work and sleep schedules of family members are often disrupted as they are called upon to provide needed assistance; this can create negative emotions within these support persons. The illness of a child has different dynamics from that of an adult.

Not only the patient but the entire family must also struggle with related spiritual issues. Believers who struggle to get by each day find it either difficult or impossible to attend church functions. They are at great risk of becoming unchurched (Heb. 10:25) and not being spiritually fed (1 Thess. 5:11). It is the rare church that can or will sustain support and create impromptu fellowship in a lengthy illness. It is hard to find meaning in trials (Ps. 25:17) such as a continued illness. It is frustrating to seek healing that sometimes comes slowly regardless of the best intentions of the health care providers and the earnest-

ness of the prayers offered by family and church (James 5:14). If one can be sustained (Ps. 41:3), however, the Scriptures tell us the Lord is faithful to heal (James 5:15).

Recovery from a prolonged illness is quite different from recovery from a minor illness. There may be financial disability, reintegration to work or school, and a need for previously ill persons to reclaim their wellness. Sick role behaviors may be slow to fall away.

If the illness has ended in death the survivors will have the added stress of grief to work through, life insurance policies to execute, remaining health care bills to satisfy, and lives to redefine without the loved one. For the Christian who has died, there is eternal health and joy in the presence of the Lord. For the family there are pieces of shattered, neglected lives to piece back together. The family of a believer can take comfort in knowing their loved one is released, but this does not mean those who remain will immediately return to normal. All surviving members must afford time to allow each other to heal and regain strength as they support one another (Phil. 2:4).

A. J. Rainwater III

See Health Psychology.

Chronic Illness, Pastoral Care of. By age 65 nearly 80% of the population in the United States has at least one chronic illness. Most of the deaths in the United States are attributable to chronic illness. Acute infectious diseases that used to kill many people at an early age have for the most part been conquered. The diseases that are more likely to strike in middle and advanced age, such as heart disease, cancer, and stroke, are now much more treatable. People who experience these diseases are, with good medical care, likely to live for years after the onset of the disease. As people live longer they tend to collect chronic illnesses that may limit them but do not prove quickly fatal.

With the aging of the baby boom generation, pastors should be prepared for the surge in demand for pastoral care of the chronically ill. Pastors should understand the nature of the illness, the patient's initial response, and the needs of the patient over the years of living with chronic illness. Pastors must realize that ministering to the chronically ill requires a flexible, enduring approach.

When a chronic illness first strikes, people are usually stunned. Then they go through a period of instability and disorganization that may include denial and avoidance, alternating with panic and despair. During the early stages they need emotional support, hope, and information to quell their racing thoughts and fears. It is important for pastors to gain a basic understanding of the illness so that they can properly anticipate and evaluate their parishioner's behavior and needs. Heart attacks and heart surgery are often followed by depression. Advanced Parkinson's disease is sometimes accompanied by paranoid ideas and hallucinations. Pastors who know some of the symptoms of these diseases are better prepared to minister and less confused and intimidated by their parishioner's emotions and behaviors. They are less likely to mistake symptoms of illness for spiritual problems.

Pastors should approach parishioners suffering from chronic illnesses with a long-term plan, because the adjustments to chronic illness are made over a long span of time. After the initial crisis and diagnosis patients must adjust to their illness. The most notable and difficult change is living with new limits. Some of the limits that may result from chronic illness include dependence on medication or medical treatments, embarrassing personal hygiene problems such as incontinence or catheters, restricted mobility, and institutionalization. People need help and encouragement over months and sometimes years to make those difficult adjustments and to learn to live graciously with their illness-imposed limits.

During this time of adjustment to chronic illness, people need to regain a sense of control. They have lost their health and have been subjected to medical treatments and lifestyle changes that they did not want or anticipate. They usually feel out of control and sometimes hopeless. Pastors can help them get back into control by reviewing their value and purpose in life. People often go through a period in which they do not want to live "like this" (with the illness and its limits). They need to be reminded that God has a plan and purpose for them. The pastor can help them to focus on what they can do rather than on what they cannot do. This is a good time for pastors to emphasize the value of the spiritual disciplines such as prayer and meditation as active ministries in which the chronically ill may participate and be effective.

Pastors are also vital in establishing and maintaining social networks for parishioners with chronic illness. In the initial crisis phase of an illness people may get visits from pastors, friends, and church members; once the crisis passes the social support usually diminishes quickly. The elderly, people who are homebound and unable to attend church, and the institutionalized are the most likely to be lonely and socially neglected. Pastors should remind their congregations to provide ongoing support for their ill members and to organize regular visitation teams, and they themselves should continue to visit and minister.

Pastors must realize that psychological and spiritual development is a lifelong process; it does not cease at adolescence or in early adulthood. Even elderly persons with chronic illnesses face many important developmental tasks. Some of the important developmental tasks that the chronically ill face include making sense of their lives, talking about their losses, learning to live with limits, learning to be graciously dependent, reviewing their lives, completing unfinished business, getting right with others (which may include confessing or forgiving), and preparing to die. Pastors who are sensitive to the psychological and spiritual needs can have a rich ministry in helping the chronically ill to mature through their illness. Pastoral visits of this nature over the course of months and years often yield relationships that are very spiritual and meaningful for both parties.

C. D. DOLPH

See PAIN.

Circadian Rhythms. Daily rhythms in basic physiological processes and behavior. These regular variations, evident across the plant and animal kingdoms, are called circadian rhythms (Latin *circa*, about, and *dies*, day) because of their approximate 24-hour cyclical nature. Examples of such diurnal changes include variations in cell division, liver and kidney functions, pressure and composition of the blood, body temperature, rate of drug uptake, hormone production, sensory acuity, reaction time, learning, efficiency, drive intensity, and response to noxious stimuli.

Although it was once thought that daily rhythms are the direct result of environmental events, such as day and night, current understanding is that such events act as time cues (German *Zeitgeber*, time-giver) that may regulate or even reset an ongoing rhythm. Day and night and temperature changes are two such important cues. In the absence of these, as when an organism is exposed to constant low levels of light, the cycles continue in a free-running state with a fixed period. Humans, for example, develop a sleeping/waking cycle of about 25 hours.

It has been argued that if environmental events act only as time cues, then organisms may possess internal clocks as regulators for cyclical behavior. The suprachiasmatic nucleus (SCN) of the hypothalamus is postulated as one primary biological clock. Fibers from the retina of the eye project to the SCN providing light/dark information. It is not clear, however, what mechanism within the SCN provides the time base. Results of animal and plant research suggest a genetic component to the pattern of circadian rhythms. Organisms raised from eggs under constant light and temperature conditions will still spontaneously display circadian rhythms.

The existence of circadian rhythms is important in human behavior. The natural day/night cycle acts as a *Zeitgeber* for waking and sleeping, with most people being active for about 16 hours and inactive for 8 hours. Digestion, hormone secretion, body temperature, and metabolic rates vary regularly within this pattern. However, if the pattern is disrupted by moving rapidly across a number of time zones, missing sleep over an extended period of time, or constantly changing shiftwork conditions, then problems may arise. Individuals often report problems in terms of feelings of lassitude and lowered arousal. Depressive symptoms may occur with extended disruption. It has been speculated that the normal cycling of a number of biological patterns becomes desynchronized. As a result hormonal, metabolic, and activity patterns are disrupted.

Some investigators have proposed that affective disorders may result from a disturbance in circadian rhythms, specifically a phase advance of the mechanisms controlling REM sleep. REM sleep deprivation is employed as a temporary adjustment to reset the system and to alleviate the depressive symptoms. It has also been reported that the effectiveness of a number of medications varies with time of day.

W. D. NORMAN

See SLEEP AND DREAMING.

Circumstantiality. Speech that is indirect and encumbered with unnecessary details and parenthetical remarks. Unlike loosening of associations, an absence of a meaningful connection between the various parts of the sentence, circumstantial speech is organized and the speaker never loses sight of the original focus of the conversation. The problem is that the speaker fails to suppress extraneous thoughts and the essential message gets lost. Circumstantiality is frequently seen in schizophrenia and compulsive personality disorder. It also sometimes occurs in epileptic dementia.

Civil Commitment. *See* FORENSIC PSYCHIATRY.

Clang Association. Nonsensical talk on the basis of an association of words or ideas by superficial sound similarity. In manic states (*see* Mania) and schizophrenia the rapid speech is considered part of a thought disturbance (*see* Flight of Ideas). Without any apparent meaning the individual carries on a one-way conversation; for example, he may say, "We went to the land . . . there was a band . . . bang, bang . . . dam broke . . . we caught kites."

Clark, Walter Houston (1902–1994). Known for his contributions to the advancement of the scientific study of religion and more specifically for his work in the psychology of religion.

Clark took his Ph.D. degree at Harvard University in 1944, studying under Gordon Allport. His doctoral dissertation was a study of the moral rearmament doctrine of the Oxford Group, a social movement of interest both to social psychology and to religious studies. Using a case study approach, Clark studied the manner in which the movement contributed to the personal religiosity of its members. He served as professor of psychology and dean of the Hartford School of Religious Education at the Hartford Seminary Foundation and later as profes-

sor of the psychology of religion at Andover Newton Theological Seminary, from which he retired in 1969.

Clark was one of the founders of the Society for the Scientific Study of Religion, serving as a member of the editorial board of the *Journal for the Scientific Study of Religion* and serving the society in various capacities, including its presidency in 1964. He also chaired the committee on research of the Religious Education Association, which convened a commission in 1961 to provide methodological guidelines for researchers of religious phenomena. The publication resulting from the work of this commission has been widely influential in guiding empirical research since the 1970s.

Clark has produced many articles and book reviews in the area of psychology of religion, but he is best remembered for three books. The first, *The Oxford Group, Its History and Significance* (1951), was an elaboration of his doctoral dissertation. *The Psychology of Religion* (1958) was a textbook updating and reconceptualizing the whole field. This book also presented a concerted plea for greater methodological rigor in psychology of religion research. His best-known book, *Chemical Ecstasy: Psychedelic Drugs and Religion* (1969), was also his most controversial. In this book he explored the relationship between religious and drug-induced experience. Clark's arguments in support of the value of mystical experience, including drug-induced mystical states, were provocative and led to accusations that the book was merely a defense of Timothy Leary and illicit drugs.

L. S. SHAFFER

See PSYCHOLOGISTS OF RELIGION.

Classification of Mental Disorders. For the religious-ethical person, the concept of mental disorder is closely associated with the disorder introduced into the whole of nature as a result of the fall or an imbalance in a harmonious system. As Berkouwer (1962) has observed, the fall left each human being living in an imperfect body (nature) within an imperfect environment (nurture). Other consequences include disrupted relationships with God, other humans, and even with oneself. The apostle Paul classifies some of the resulting disorders in 1 Corinthians 6 and Galatians 5. Paul's list includes adultery, idolatry, hatred, envy, murder, and drunkenness.

Christians acknowledge this personal and universal state of disorder. Everyone is disordered to some degree. The understanding of interactions among biological, psychological, social, spiritual/moral factors that create various types and degrees of disorder in cognitive, emotional, and interpersonal domains is the purpose of classifying mental disorders. Both science and Scripture see "mental" as a systemic set of interactions among mind, body, society, and soul. The use of the term *mental disorder* is an anachronistic term from Cartesian mind/body dualism. We now use interactive factor models of mental styles, including normal and abnormal. At some point along a continuum from normal and healthy to highly disordered, we define a point of mental disorder. The psychiatric community defines mental disorder in the *Diagnostic and Statistical Manual of Mental Disorders-IV* (*DSM-IV;* American Psychiatric Association, 1994) as "a clinically significant behavioral or psychological syndrome or pattern that occurs in an individual and that is associated with present distress (e.g., a painful symptom or disability, i.e., impairment in one or more important areas of functioning) or with a significantly increased risk of suffering death, pain, disability, or an important loss of freedom. In addition, this syndrome or pattern must not be merely an expectable and culturally sanctioned response to a particular event, for example, the death of a loved one. Whatever the original cause, it must currently be considered a manifestation of a behavioral, psychological, or biological dysfunction in the individual. Neither deviant behavior (e.g., political, religious, or sexual) nor conflicts that are primarily between the individual and society are mental disorders unless the deviance or conflict is a symptom of a dysfunction in the individual as described above" (pp. xxvi, xxvii).

Ethical and Scientific Accountability. A good system for the classification of mental disorders reliably and accurately describes, organizes, and codes all known mental disorders. It ranks the relative degree to which a patient suffers from the disorder. Classification of mental disorders is not intended to label people (i.e., "a borderline" or "an alcoholic"). In classifying mental disorders, we should be precise from the highest standards of science and ethics (see American Psychological Association, 1992, especially Ethical Standard 2, "Evaluation, Assessment, or Intervention" and Ethical Standard 7, "Forensic Activities"). One ethical and scientific practice is to assume psychological normality until one is able to justify a diagnosis of mental disorder. Assume the person is normal, and then prove this assumption wrong. Some "normal" character styles put a person easily out of order with themselves, with other people, and with God. The usual meaning of "mental disorder" is at an extreme of mental, behavioral, or social style. Labeling such extremes requires scientific specificity and ethical caution when that labeling is applied to persons.

The purpose of classifying disorders is to construct treatment interventions that are appropriate and effective for that particular disorder. It is tempting to see the diagnosis as an end (e.g., the best diagnostic label) rather than as a means to an end (e.g., empowering the patient). If a diagnosis is not made, treatment proceeds aimlessly and the patient is harmed. If an accurate diagnosis is made but does not lead to delivering the best available treatment for that disorder, the patient's problems are labeled, and the patient is harmed by neglect.

Adequate data collection is essential for making responsible diagnostic judgments. Psychodiagnostic systems differ on the data from which diagnosis is drawn or on how to weight different aspects of this data. Most systems, however, gather data in three multidimensional systems: Cross-time monitors the patient or gets a history from the patient and the patient's support system (family, clergy, community professionals); Multimodal considers biological, psychological, social, and spiritual aspects; Multimeasure uses structured or standardized interviews, observations, and formal tests.

Clinicians need to have a solid knowledge base of these multidimensional systems even while specializing in treatments focused on one dimension. Lack of understanding leads to missed diagnoses and treatment that damages the patient.

History and Development of Classification Systems. Classification of mental disorders date as far back as 2600 B.C., when clinical descriptions of histrionic and melancholic behavior appear in Egyptian literature. However, the scientific understanding of psychopathology developed very little over the next four thousand years (*see* Abnormal Psychology). The first official system developed in the United States was prepared for the census in 1840. It contained only one category for "mental disorder" with subcategories of "insane" (psychotic) and "idiot" (retarded). Many old concepts about classifying mental disorder are still evidenced in current cultural and subcultural settings. These old classification ideas can have damaging consequences for the patient and the professional working within the patient's culture.

The first major effort at classification of mental disorders was that of the German psychiatrist Kraepelin, *Textbook of Psychiatry* (1883). Kraepelin identified two major disorders: Dementia praecox (schizophrenia) and manic-depressive psychosis (*see* Bipolar Disorder). His textbook underwent eight revisions over the next 40 years and is the foundational work for modern classification.

Two world wars brought a need for more precision in diagnosis, for screening recruits, draftees, and factory workers, and for developing syndrome-specific treatments for soldiers suffering from mental disorders. For example, in World War I the treatments for "shell shock" were likely to be different if soldiers came from a healthy mental state to their experience of the horrors of trench war than if they were known to be previously psychoneurotic. In mental health treatment, the practice of adjusting the treatment of situationally induced mental disorders (states) to the longer-term style (traits) is an old, respected one.

From 1940 to 1951 the *Standard Nomenclature of Diseases of the Psychobiological Unit* of the U.S. military was the major system in use. It had three major sections: Mental Deficiencies; Mental Disorders, including psychosis, psychoneurosis, and primary behavior disorder; and Organic Diseases Affecting Mental Functioning.

The first *Diagnostic and Statistical Manual of Mental Disorders (DSM)*, the *DSM-I* of the American Psychiatric Association was published only recently in the history of science, in 1952. It was the standard until 1968. *DSM-I* was researched and codified by only one psychiatrist. Its revision, the *DSM-II* (1968), was the work of a committee of respected psychiatrists. Both *DSM-I* and *DSM-II* were researched and developed by only one profession, psychiatry, and assumed a disease model. Both are qualitative and subjective rather than quantitative and objective in description of mental disorders.

The *DSM-III* (1980), *DSM-III-Revised* (1987), and the *DSM-IV* (1994) were rigorously researched and are more objective in criteria than were previous large-scale mental health classification systems. *DSM-III* and *DSM-IV* used multidisciplinary research and clinical input along with extensive ongoing field trials in the development and refinement of diagnostic classifications. They attempt to link the largely North American-based system with the mental health classification system used in the *International Classification of Diseases*, in both its ninth and upcoming tenth revisions *(ICD-9, ICD-10)*. More international research is needed to increase professional communication and increase knowledge of the effects of such phenomena as culture and genetic inheritance on mental health. The training section of the *DSM-IV* is useful for all students and professionals. The American Psychiatric Association offers other training and clinical tools, such as a computer software program called Electronic *DSM-IV*™, which works the clinician through the rigorous diagnostic Decision Trees for Differential Diagnosis listed in Appendix A of the *DSM-IV*.

After the development of the *DSM-III*, good clinical scientist/practitioner standards required that the patient be evaluated and diagnosed on several salient dimensions. These dimensions are called axes. Each of these axes represents a different domain of information. The *DSM-IV* has five axes; the first three focus on problems of the individual, and the last two focus on problems of the individual's interaction with the world. Axis I contains most of the major mental disorders that are the focus of treatment during an episode of care, such as the depressions, the anxiety disorders, and the psychoses. Axis II contains mental disorders that are of long-standing duration, specifically personality disorders and mental retardation. Axis III contains information about general medical conditions, especially factors that interact with the mental disorders on Axes I and II. (My practice is to quote the patient's physician on Axis III, since I did not make the medical diagnosis.) Axis IV describes the psychosocial contextual problems in which the patient's problems have developed. The diagnostician should be aware that these contextual problems are understood to be external to the patient rather than being caused by the patient's psychopathology. These context variables would be used in ruling out the diagnosis of normal personality under extraordinary pressure(s) or in understanding why a mental disorder may be exacerbated by situational stress. Axis V is a global assessment of the patient's ability to function in the world. There are separate criteria for adult functioning and child/adolescent functioning on Axis V. Axis V is global and is only a rough measure of function. Multiple diagnosis may be appropriate on Axes I through IV, and explanatory comments may be appropriate on any of the axes. It is useful to note which diagnosis is primary (the reason that the patient is seeking treatment at this time) and which is secondary to this episode of treatment (background information, i.e., a patient suffering from borderline personality disorder [secondary] who seeks training in affect management and communication for depression [primary]).

Throughout the *DSM-IV,* specific criteria are outlined that may rule in or rule out a diagnosis. The criteria are scientifically specific and follow a clear decision tree with an "if this, then consider that; if not, then consider this other . . ." format. Mastery of the diagnostic criteria and the decision trees in Appendix A of the *DSM-IV* are essential skills in using the *DSM-IV.* A diagnosis for an adult patient in a day hospitalization program might be

- Axis I: Mood Disorder: Bipolar II Disorder (recurrent major depressive episodes with hypomanic episodes), minimally responsive to mood stabilizing medication—Primary.
- Axis II: Paranoid Personality Disorder: increasing fears, some plausible, some more delusional, focused on a former (ten years ago) boss and the patient's corporate conspiracy beliefs.
- Axis III: Recent Physical "Age Appropriate X All Systems"/M. A. Jones, M.D. at the University Outpatient Clinic. Patient smokes 20 filtered cigarettes a day; both patient and spouse report alcohol abstinence and patient attending Alcoholics Anonymous (AA) meetings twice a week.
- Axis IV: Economic Problems: Patient's current company has restructured and the patient's job remains, but at fewer hours per week.
- Axis V: GAF = 35 for the past two months, following the announcement of the restructuring.

The *DSM-IV* diagnostic system offers a succinct overview of the patient within the biological, psychological, and social complexity of the human condition. It is a secular system; no attempt is made to determine the patient's moral or spiritual functioning. The religious psychologist might add scales such as VI—Morals/Values and VII—Current Personal Spiritual Beliefs and Style.

Alternate Approaches. From the introduction of *DSM-I* to the present, the *DSM* system has been the dominant mental disorder classification system in North America and has influenced international classification systems. The *DSM* system is not the only system. Alternative systems grew out of different assumptions and emphases in biopsychosocial interactions. Responsible clinical practice works to integrate the *DSM-IV* with these alternate approaches. Widely respected clinical handbooks (e.g., Barlow, 1985, 1988; Bellack & Hersen, 1990) provide chapter subsections written by experts that use alternative diagnostic system emphasis such as "Psychodynamic Perspective"; "Cognitive Behavioral Perspective"; "Interpersonal Perspective"; and "Psychopharmacological Perspective." Each of these focused perspectives summarizes a particular subset of the clinical diagnostic research literature. The main alternate classification systems include the following.

Biological Systems. The basic notion in these diagnostic systems is that mental disorders have such strong genetic codes and/or biophysiological components that they should be considered primarily brain disorders. Theorists in this tradition usually do not claim that biological explanations will account for all mental disorders but often do suggest that far more is determined by biophysiology than our current science can identify. Great strides have been made by university and pharmaceutical company researchers in identifying which neurotransmitters play the major roles in specific clusters of diagnosis (e.g., the selective serotonergic reuptake inhibitors [SSRI] in treating many depressive or anxiety-based disorders).

Theorists in this tradition use the *DSM-IV*, family history, and structured interviewing regarding the patient's experience and functioning to classify and prescribe the most helpful psychotropic medications currently available. The vast majority of biological specialists work as a team or refer to specialists in psychological and social treatments. The notion is that once the biological basis of behavior is set to its best balance, all the learned dysfunctional cognitions, emotions, and interpersonal manipulations of the patient can receive treatment.

Specific sequencing for the timing of biological-psychological and social interventions are of considerable research interest.

Phenomenological and Humanistic Systems. This collection of approaches to diagnosis includes phenomenological, existential, humanist, and narrative traditions within psychology. A basic tenet of these systems is that each individual is unique and that attempts to know (diagnose) the individual must not rob the individual of uniqueness. Grouped classification systems are eschewed or are used only as sources for descriptive language in understanding the individual's experience within his or her life domain. Persons are to be treated as persons, not as categories, classifications, or diseases. To the humanist, it is more important to know what kind of a person has the symptom than to know the symptom's detailed classification. The task for the diagnostician in these systems is to experience the world as closely as possible to the way(s) the patient (called the client) experiences it. This tradition has important influence in ethical and religious views of diagnosis.

Cognitive Systems. The essence of this system's classification of mental disorders is that learned or habitual thinking errors result in disturbances in problem solving and emotional experience for the patient. The greater in quality and quantity the cognitive error(s), the greater the disordered psychological and social life of the patient. These cognitive approaches have become clinically useful and are widely taught. They are preferred by most managers of health insurance plans.

Cognitive therapists focus heavily on errors in thinking. Both the content of thought and the logic used in organizing that thought can be sources of errors. These therapists use concepts from linguistics, logic, and hermeneutics in diagnosis and treatment. Diagnosis leads directly into correcting the patient through "rethinking" or therapy homework designed to help the patient experience the benefit of changing beliefs. This form of therapy, along with behavioral forms of therapy, is often called directive psychotherapy as opposed to nondirective, in which the patient, not the therapist, sets the pace of their discovery and change.

Behavioral Systems. Behavioral assessment and applied behavioral analysis have been important alternative diagnostic systems. Applying classical and operant conditioning analysis to diagnosis and treatment has benefited the profession. Behavioral analysis systems, such as those developed by Kanfer and Schefft (1988), have proven beneficial in understanding and treating a wide range of psychopathology. Behavior is often not as controlled by purposeful thought as we humans would like to believe. We are quite conditioned by life history and environmental reinforcers in ways only rationalized, minimized, and confused by cognitive process (thinking errors). A careful behavioral assessment followed by assigned behavioral regimen is efficacious for persons suffering from such diverse symptoms as the flashbacks of posttraumatic stress disorder (PSTD) or management of distracting schizophrenic hallucinations.

Behavioral systems are most frequently combined with cognitive systems and are referred to as cognitive-behavioral psychotherapy. In fact the terms are now most often used in conjunction. However, they have different diagnostic and clinical assumptions. Some clinicians are understandably concerned that the pressure to quickly and economically manage persons with mental disorders will push these cognitive-behavioral or directive approaches toward a doctrinaire, dogmatic scientology. That is, patients will be told to correct their thinking errors (told what and how to believe). Combine this with the rapid effects of psychopharmacological medication, and worries of an Orwellian *1984* managed society emerge. These are powerful diagnostic and clinical tools and like any tool can be used to an extreme.

Multidimensional Systems. Leary is often praised for constructing a valid, useful multidimensional diagnostic model for defining and measuring the continuum between normal and abnormal personality. Leary's (1957) system posited two intersecting axes: Love—Hate and Dominance—Submission. A patient's more enduring personality style can be plotted on the quadrants of this two-by-two system. Indeed, the robust and clinically useful multidimensional diagnostic systems of Millon (Millon, 1969; Millon & Davis, 1995) and McLemore and Benjamin (1979) stem from Leary's theoretical and empirical work on interpersonal diagnosis. Much of family systems theory and much of the empirically robust five-factor model of personality emerge from the multidimensional systems approach to understanding both normal and abnormal personality.

Millon's system is the best known multidimensional diagnostic system and has been widely supported both clinically and empirically. His basic framework has three intersecting dimensions: *Severity of Disturbance*: mild-moderate-severe X *Interpersonal Goals in Gaining Reward or Avoiding Punishment:* independent, dependent, ambivalent, and detached X *Style of Pursuing Interpersonal Goals:* active, passive, or alternating.

The accumulated body of empirical research literature on personality structure or personality traits consistently defines five factors with related subfactors contributing to these main five factors. The five-factor theory of personality structure is empirically supported and describes normal as well as disordered personality styles. It has gained wide acceptance as a diagnostic tool for both normal and abnormal personality assessment. Costa and Widiger's (1994) book does a good job of informing the reader of general and specific applications of this empirically based theory. The basic factors and subfactors are *Neuroticism:* anxiety, angry hostility, depression, self-consciousness, impulsivity, vulnerability; *Extroversion:* warmth, gregariousness, assertiveness, activity, excitement seeking, positive emotions; *Openness:* fantasy, aesthetics, feelings, actions, ideas, values; *Agreeableness:* trust, straightforwardness, altruism, competence, modesty, tendermindedness; *Conscientiousness:* competence, order, dutifulness, achievement striving, self-discipline, deliberation.

The multidimensional systems hold much promise as tools for reliably and accurately diagnosing mental and interpersonal disorders. They lead more directly to informing the patient of specific skills needed to be learned in order to have a more functional and balanced life.

The *DSM-IV* has combined some of each of these alternative systems of diagnosis into its five axes.

It remains a disease-model classification system, which does not offer many principles for integrating the biopsychosocial and spiritual aspects of human existence. It attempts to be as strictly descriptive and as nontheoretical as possible.

A great deal has been gained in the refinements of the *DSM* systems. The alternative systems continue to offer fertile research and clinical assistance to the modern diagnostician.

References

American Psychiatric Association. (1994). *Diagnostic and statistical manual of mental disorders* (4th ed.). Washington, DC: Author.

American Psychological Association. (1992). Ethical principles of psychologists and code of conduct. *American Psychologist, 47,* 1597–1611.

Barlow, D. H. (1988). *Anxiety and its disorders: The nature and treatment of anxiety and panic.* New York: Guilford.

Barlow, D. H. (Ed.). (1985). *Clinical handbook of psychological disorders.* New York: Guilford.

Bellack, A. S., & Hersen, M. (Eds.). (1990). *Handbook of comparative treatments for adult disorders.* New York: Wiley.

Berkouwer, G. C. (1962). *Man: The image of God.* Grand Rapids, MI: Eerdmans.

Costa, T., & Widiger, T. A. (Eds.). (1994). *Personality disorders and the five-factor model of personality.* Washington, DC: American Psychological Association Press.

Kanfer, F., & Schefft, B. K. (1988). *Guiding the process of therapeutic change.* Champaign, IL: Research Press.

Leary, T. (1957). *Interpersonal diagnosis of personality.* New York: Ronald Press.

McLemore, C., & Benjamin, L. (1979). Whatever happened to interpersonal diagnosis? A psychosocial alternative to *DSM-III. American Psychologist, 34,* 17–34.

Millon, T. (1969). *Modern psychopathology.* Philadelphia: Saunders.

Millon, T., & Davis, R. D. (1995). *Disorders of personality: DSM-IV and beyond* (2nd ed.). New York: Wiley.

B. E. BONECUTTER

See ABNORMAL PSYCHOLOGY; MENTAL ILLNESS, MODELS OF.

Claustrophobia. The fear of confinement, of being locked or trapped in enclosed places such as elevators, classrooms, boats, planes, or narrow streets. This phobia may represent fear of yielding to a desired temptation, or it may serve as a type of self-inflicted punishment for giving in to an ego dystonic temptation. Most commonly it is a reaction based on a combination of both fear and punishment.

See PHOBIC DISORDERS.

Clergy, Personal and Family Issues. There is a growing body of study on the personal and family issues related to being in the ministry, much of it identifying the unique stressors and demands that are inherent in the pastoral role. Although there are numerous rewards and satisfactions in pastoring, much attention has been directed to the personal hazards of the profession and to the concomitant fallout for the families of clergy. In recent years pastors have been under a high degree of scrutiny, which has often been accompanied by a climate of intolerance. Increased public awareness of clergy misconduct and jaundiced media portrayals of clergy have resulted in a growing cynicism toward the profession. Despite these obstacles, many persons pursue their call to serve.

A number of stress factors are inherent in the professional ministry, although these stressors affect each person differently. Eight stress factors are summarized in the following discussion.

Life in the Fishbowl. Because the work of clergy is often highly visible and the clergyperson is expected to be a model of exemplary behavior, pastors often feel as if their lives are under constant scrutiny. They experience a loss of their privacy. A common pastoral complaint relates to having parishioners intrude into their private lives, often with a sense of entitlement to the pastor's time. The ability to set boundaries is a necessary but neglected skill for many pastors. Limiting one's availability can conflict with a pastor's desire to be readily accessible for the needs of parishioners, generate guilt feelings, and meet with criticism from those who expect that a pastor should be on call 24 hours a day.

Role Ambiguity and Role Strain. Most pastors perform multiple roles covering three main functions: teaching, administrating, and counseling. Aspects of this work may include public speaking, managing volunteers, leading groups, overseeing music or Christian education programs, managing finances, counseling individuals, couples, and families, and supervising staff operations. A pastor may be expected to be competent in each role, an expectation that can generate high levels of role strain. Seminary training equips pastors for some of the aspects of their work more than others; a pastor may need additional training or experience to achieve competency in other role functions. In addition pastors often experience a sense of ambiguity about their role performance due to a lack of clear job descriptions and reasonable job parameters. If the clergy position is poorly defined it is tempting to try to fill vacuums in leadership or service by self-effort rather than by delegating responsibility or setting limits.

Expectations. Clergy are subject to high performance and character expectations both from themselves (internal) and from others (external). They are vulnerable to centering their self-worth in their pastoral image with the generated result of performance anxiety. A combination of internal and external expectations can drive clergy to overload and overfunction (trying to do too much for too many). Neglecting personal and family needs, with a reluctance to take personal days and vacations, can result.

It is difficult for clergy to be authentic about their personal struggles when they are being ide-alized and fear falling off the pedestal. Because congregations are involved in many hiring and firing decisions, pastors often live with the threat of forced termination. The expectations of congregational members can reflect their own family backgrounds, with the result that pastors are often subject to projections of unresolved needs and conflicts.

Isolation and Loneliness. Pastors often describe a sense of isolation, experiencing a limitation in the availability of people with whom they can discuss the complexities and frustrations of their job. It can be difficult to be transparent and to develop relational closeness with members of the congregation due to fears of exposure or the appearance of favoritism. It may also be difficult to be open with other pastors when there is a sense of inadequacy or negative comparison. Denominational structures provide varying degrees of support systems, but they are often limited. It is easy to adopt the Lone Ranger mentality and to avoid relational accountability. Support systems for pastors have been limited, but a growing number of organizations have begun to address the question, Who pastors the pastor? *Leadership* magazine has published an annual list of organizations that provide a range of support services for clergy and their families. There has also been a yearly conference for those involved in such ministries, Caregiver's Forum. Other groups and denominations also have developed resources for pastors and their families.

Congregational Dynamics. Congregations are made up of people with diverse backgrounds, a range of personal strengths and weaknesses, and different personality dynamics. Each congregation has its own history, with part of that history being congregational relations to pastors and their families. In addition to an understanding of individual and family emotional functioning, a pastor needs to have an awareness of system dynamics in order to enlist congregational cooperation. Lack of functional congregational relationships has been a major cause for pastoral attrition.

Finances. The salary structure for pastors usually is not commensurate with other professions of similar education and training. A significant number of pastors struggle to support themselves on their salary, and a number take a second job to supplement their income. Being dependent on decisions regarding salary and benefits from church leaders, who may be under the overall authority of the pastor, presents a conundrum for many pastors. In a significant number of cases clergy find that they have insufficient resources when they retire. Lack of funding for continuing education can inhibit professional growth.

Sexuality. Situations of pastoral sexual misconduct have received much attention from the media. Pastors are subject to similar vulnerabilities as others in the helping professions. Isolated counseling sessions, pastoral marriages that have suffered from negative effects of pastoral life, and a sense of entitlement fueled by hours of meeting others' needs at the cost of personal emotional exhaustion are a few of the factors that may be catalytic for sexual misconduct.

Effects on Family. Clergy families deal with the same issues as other families, but they have a unique set of factors that impinge upon them. Blackmon (1990) has noted that clergy have an intense emotional interlock between work and home, which is perhaps more intense for them than for any other profession, and encourages clergy families to find a balance between their connectedness to their congregations and their separateness from them.

One of the most common frustrations of clergy spouses relates to the pattern of frequent relocations, with many feeling as if the frequency of uprootings interferes with their ability to develop long-term emotional closeness. It is a common experience to have people in the congregation maintain an emotional distance, viewing the pastoral family as temporary. Lack of privacy, feeling inhibited to express individuality, feeling as if it is necessary to please everyone, feeling as if they are treated differently, and feeling a pressure to be a model can negatively affect clergy spouses. They suffer when their spouse comes under criticism but often feel as if they need to keep their responses internal. Another common pressure is the congregational expectation that the clergy spouse is unpaid staff and should perform certain tasks in the church. An effect of congregational expectations on clergy spouses is a tendency to feel as if they are defined by their husband's or wife's profession.

When pastors are overworking, their spouses may feel as if they are competing with the church for time and attention. If this is framed as an interference with "the Lord's work," there is usually a high degree of guilt for the spouse. A tension usually exists if a pastor seeks to pastor his or her own family, as this typically presents an enmeshment of roles. Finding a stable and trustworthy extrafamilial support system to depend upon can be a difficult task for the spouse.

There are similar dynamics at play for clergy children. The scrutiny they frequently experience can engender a feeling of living in the glass house, and clergy children are often measured against a different standard, which can generate an exaggerated self-consciousness (Lee, 1990). Developing a defense of overcompliance or the opposite, rebelliousness, are too frequent means of coping with the pressures to conform.

Conclusion. Being in the ministry is one of the most challenging professions in our society. It requires relating to a group of people on a human level, while at the same time trying to maintain an intimate relationship with God that would enable one to speak for God. It involves addressing the complex needs of people whose lives reflect the social dysfunctions of our time. It also necessitates developing wisdom to navigate through the numerous stress factors discussed. It is a calling that requires an empowerment from above.

References

Blackmon, R. (1990, December). Family concerns for the minister. *Theology News and Notes Fuller Theological Seminary,* 4.

Lee, C. (1990, December). Growing up in a glass house. *Theology News and Notes Fuller Theological Seminary,* 17.

T. A. BOYD

See SPIRITUAL AND RELIGIOUS ISSUES IN THERAPY; MARITAL HEALTH AND PATHOLOGY; FAMILY PSYCHOLOGY.

Client-Centered Therapy. *See* PERSON-CENTERED THERAPY.

Clinical Pastoral Education. Clinical pastoral education (CPE) is a method of education and training for clergy that utilizes three specific educational approaches. These are the development of pastoral skills, the ability to reflect theologically on specific human situations, and clinical supervision.

Taking place primarily within what is known as a small process group, a group in which there is an open agenda to discuss the experience of each person in his or her ministry situation, each CPE participant develops a learning contract. This contract includes a commitment for four hundred hours of training (one unit) within a variety of settings. Traditionally, however, CPE training occurs within a hospital setting and emphasizes an interfaith dialogue.

The development of this approach to clergy education is an outgrowth of the historic traditions of pastoral care: sustaining, guiding, reconciling, and healing. As more became known about persons through what were at the turn of the twentieth century the new fields of psychology and psychiatry, physicians, clergy, and seminary professors joined together to learn from each other about ministering to the whole person and to teach others what they had learned. It was their contention that medicine, science, and theology are concerned about the same thing, the human soul, although from different perspectives.

Central to these efforts, which were initially centered in New England, were physicians such as William Keller and Richard Cabot. Clergy included Anton Boisen, who suffered periodic bouts of mental illness and learned firsthand the lack of adequate or knowledgeable ministry in the hospital setting, and Russell L. Dicks. Seminary administrators and professors included A. B. Mercer, Joseph Fletcher, George Albert Coe, and Carroll Wise.

Three theological themes emerged from this dialogue and persist today: the living human document; the incarnational presence; the patient as teacher. Persons who complete CPE training are committed to being present when other persons are in crucial human need. They emphasize face-to-face encounters that result in what are known as open interviews. This approach to interpersonal interaction focuses on what is occurring between two people in their encounter in the present. Further, persons who have been a part of CPE training are committed to continuous supervision and to faithful teamwork.

Since 1967, when accurate statistics began to be recorded, it is estimated that 75,000 persons have taken at least one unit of CPE. Of these, approximately 20,000 have pursued some form of specialized ministry such as the chaplaincy or pastoral counseling, 50,000 are in parish ministry or seminary teaching, and 5,000 have gone another direction.

E. E. DECKER, JR.

For Further Information

Association for Clinical Pastoral Education, Inc.
Decatur, Georgia
www.acpe-edu.org.

See PASTORAL CARE; PASTORAL COUNSELING.

Clinical Psychology. During and immediately after World War II a critical shortage of psychiatrists brought more and more psychologists into the arena of applied mental health services. Psychologists had already developed a reputation as testing specialists in the decades preceding the Second World War, but it was only in the aftermath of this war that they were accorded anything like true parity with psychiatrists in the practice of psychotherapy and established themselves as fully autonomous mental health practitioners.

The identity struggles of clinical psychologists have had both positive and negative consequences. On the negative side, some psychologists show what seems to be a cavalier disregard for the medical expertise of psychiatrists, who are without question the mental health professionals best equipped to handle psychiatric hospitalizations, psychotropic medications, and physical evaluations. On the positive side, as a direct result of clinical psychology's successful battle for professional independence, the general public has access to professionals who are equipped to render high-quality helping services grounded in behavioral science.

While the psychiatrist is unquestionably master of the physical domain and is often the expert best suited to manage psychiatric emergencies, clinical psychologists also have unique qualifications. For one thing, whereas psychiatrists ordinarily are not trained in the logic and methods of psychological science, all psychologists from reputable training programs have had extensive training in psychological research. Specific areas in which this empirical orientation affects their work include the construction and validation of assessment methods such as psychological tests, the study of treatment regimens such as hospital programs, and the analysis of organizational structures. This training also equips and encourages them to evaluate rigorously the effectiveness of all psychological treatments. Psychologists, therefore, are typically less reliant on intuition and more likely to be tough-minded about what they do.

Another unique qualification possessed by the clinical psychologists relates to the extensive background in psychology gained through four years of undergraduate and four to six years of graduate study. The study and practice of medicine ordinarily has little if anything to do with the ability of one human being to help another through psychological means. Freud himself believed that, because of the differences in thought forms between psychological and physiological disciplines, medical training was a obstacle that had to be overcome in order to provide good psychological treatment.

Clinical psychologists are engaged in a wide variety of activities, ranging from management consulting to working in pain clinics. However, the principal activities of clinical psychologists usually concern the diagnosis and treatment of mental disorders. While many psychologists take exception to terms such as "diagnosis" and "treatment," viewing them as archaic metaphors from psychiatry's medical heritage, it cannot be doubted that clinical psychology is focally concerned with understanding and alleviating human psychological misery.

Although a number of persons with master's degrees are regarded by their respective states as clinical psychologists, most members of the American Psychological Association (APA) regard the possession of an earned doctorate in psychology from an accredited institution as a critical criterion. Furthermore, this doctorate will ideally have been earned in an APA-approved clinical training program. Such programs demand at least one year of internship work beyond preinternship level "clerkships," and most states require an additional year of clinical experience beyond the doctorate for licensure.

It should be noted that the American Psychological Association has expressly disapproved of persons with doctorates in nonclinical areas simply doing an internship and then representing themselves as clinical psychologists. The import of this disapproval is to highlight the special educational requirements for clinical specialization.

The major journals of interest to clinical psychologists, and those in which they tend most often to publish, are *Journal of Abnormal Psychology, Journal of Consulting and Clinical Psychology, Professional Psychology Psychotherapy: Theory, Research and Practice*, and a number of behavioral psychology journals, most notably *Behavior Research & Therapy*.

Regarding the relationship of clinical psychology to Christianity, it must first be said that the doing of good in any form is, at very least, a vehicle for the expression of common grace. Clinical psychologists minister to human hurts, miseries, and tragedies. It must also be said, in the interest of candor, that while clinical psychology is grounded in and informed by behavioral science, psychotherapy is heavily saturated with applied philosophy. Stated differently, the conduct of verbal psychotherapy is an art form that relies on science, philosophy, and at least an unspoken theology.

The belief systems and values held by therapists are bound to influence clients (*see* Values and Psychotherapy). The idea of an ethically neutral psychotherapy is quite simply naive (London, 1964). At the same time, the psychological results produced even by atheistic therapists must not be disparaged. Indeed, it may sometimes be difficult to decide whether to have a loved one treated by a professionally incompetent believer or a competent unbeliever. While this issue is unlikely to confront those who live in urban areas, it does arise for persons who live in rural areas. The power of persuasion that psychotherapists sometimes seem to hold over clients must be considered in this decision.

It is vitally necessary, at this juncture, for Christians to embrace what is good within clinical psychology and to use it in every way they can to augment the well-being of persons. At the same time, the danger of psychology becoming a new religion for many people, as it seems to have done for some (Vitz, 1977), is a danger that should not be ignored.

References

London, P. (1964). *The modes and morals of psychotherapy.* New York: Holt, Rinehart & Winston.
Vitz, P. (1977). *Psychology as religion.* Grand Rapids: Eerdmans.

Additional Readings

Garfield, S. L. (1974). *Clinical psychology: The study of personality and behavior.* Chicago: Aldine.
Goldenberg, H. (1977). *Contemporary clinical psychology.* Monterey, Calif.: Brooks/Cole.
Korchin, S. J. (1976). *Modern clinical psychology.* New York: Basic Books.
Weiner, I. B. (Ed.). (1976). *Clinical methods in psychology.* New York: Wiley-Interscience.

C. W. McLemore

See Psychologist; Psychology, History of; Psychology as Religion.

Clinical Social Work. The field of social work has undergone a transformation since the 1970s. Earlier in its evolution social work was defined by three different methods: social casework, social group work, and community organization, with each seen as having distinct goals and activities. The practice of clinical social work was generally equated with the methods of social casework, and the two terms were used interchangeably. Since the 1970s, however, the theory base of social work has adopted a generalist model. Modern generalist social work training, as prescribed by the Council of Social Work Education (CSWE), prepares practitioners to make interventions at three levels: the micro level (with individual and families), the mezzo or midlevel (with organizations and formal groups), and the macro level (with the community and society). In the generalist model the clinician role is only one of a number of roles a social worker may take in addition to being a broker, an advocate, a social reformer, an educator, and a mediator. The generalist social worker is expected to maintain a dual focus, helping specific clients and their systems to change as well as addressing the larger social issues that impact those clients.

Some persons in the field have been critical of clinical social work practitioners, feeling that clinicians tend to take an overly individualized approach and that social work's heritage of fighting poverty and discrimination is being compromised or abandoned. Another aspect of the tension in the field relates to the issue of agency-based versus private practice, with some feeling that the agency is the only appropriate practice venue for social workers.

Although there are a number of competing theories of social work practice, the ecological systems perspective has gained wide support. The ecological perspective is essentially a social systems model that emphasizes the hallmark of social work identity, the person in environment. The ecological perspective has an underlying philosophical view that human beings are adaptive and in continuous transaction with their environments. By understanding the context of clients' behavior, one can understand how they have created their own particular "ecological fit" (Germain, 1991). The social workers' interventions are based, therefore, upon the clients' strengths, helping them to achieve mastery over their environment. Social workers are to empower their clients, both individually and collectively, by helping them to use their own problem-solving capacities.

Clinical social work, also called direct practice, has as its general focus the personal (intrapsychic) and social (interpersonal) adjustment of individuals and families. One of the key functions of the clinician is to thoroughly assess the cognitive, affective, and behavioral problems of clients, with emphasis on the larger social context of the clients' difficulties, as well as clients' strengths and resources. Some of the standard assessment tools used by the social worker are ecomaps, genograms, extended social histories, and P-I-E (Person-In-Environment) charts. Clinical social workers draw from a wide variety of practice theories and intervention techniques and practice in a range of settings, including schools, businesses or corporations, clinics, hospitals, correctional facilities, rehabilitation centers, social agencies, residential homes and institutions, and private practices.

The largest professional organization is the National Association of Social Workers (NASW), which was founded in 1955. The NASW, in addition to maintaining standards and ethical guidelines, also provides some regulation to clinical social workers through a clinical registry, by sponsoring conferences and by supporting regulations concerning licensing and third-party payments to social workers. States vary in their regulation of social work practice, with most having some form of registration or licensure. A parallel organization, committed to promoting a Christian worldview in social work, is the North American Association of Christians in Social Work (NACSW). Formed in 1955, NACSW publishes a journal, sponsors workshops and conferences, and provides an opportunity for fellowship.

Reference

Germain, C. B. (1991) *Human behavior in the social environment: An ecological view.* New York: Columbia University Press.

For Further Information

North American Association of Christians in Social Work, Box 7090, St. Davids, PA 19087-5777.

T. A. BOYD

See SOCIAL WORK.

Codependency. A relational style characterized by unhealthy bonding, repression, compulsions, poor social image, and a sense of duty and obligation. Codependency (CDPC) is an irrational involvement with another party where denial, imbalance, disruptive behaviors, and low self-esteem shape the relationship. The codependent person is usually driven by a intense need to connect with and a deep desire to belong to a significant other (person, object, system, or entity), yet at the same time is compelled by an unconscious motive to control the outcomes of that relationship.

CDPC is a behavioral pattern, personality trait, and psychosocial feature that reflects major needs, undefined boundaries, self-doubts, confusion of roles, and massive clinging. It typically displays fluctuation of mood, polarization of attitudes, vacillation between extremes, and, at times, constant change of positions. The person usually has a strong need to smooth conflicts and tensions, rescue those in trouble, avoid embarrassment and shame, readily fix problematic situations, control outside events, take full responsibility for people's actions and behaviors, and constantly try to keep the peace or harmony at any price.

CDPC is also characterized by a compulsive tendency to make difficult relationships work. That is usually done by dismissing serious character flaws and covering up destructive patterns of behavior and, thus, contributing indirectly to the addiction, acting out, or psychopathology. The codependent person is totally absorbed in and completely obsessed with the other(s). He or she has a strong wish to make life better and others feel good all the time. CDPC is best described as an addiction to relationships. Its object could be people, substances, situations, events, ideas, or set of ideals. It is simply a partnership in dependency.

Similar to chemically dependent personality, codependents are indirect, reactive, complaining, difficult to reason with, pleasing, and demanding at once. They are disagreeable, guilt producing, caretakers, easily crushed, overprotective, vulnerable, yet set in their own ways. They virtually help create CDPC around them in people with whom they closely interact. Codependents can be reactionaries. They overreact or underreact but seldom rationally act.

CDPC is a habitual system of thinking, feeling, and behaving. It is when a person develops a close and dependent relationship with someone else who has an addiction. Addiction could be understood as losing control over a certain activity, behavior, habit, or the use of a substance. In fact, some of the mental, emotional, and spiritual symptoms present in an addict and a substance abuser seem to appear in the non-alcoholic or non-chemically dependent individual. Terms like co-addict, para-alcoholic, or non-abuser were used before the emergence of the term *codependent*.

Originally, CDPC referred to persons whose lives were affected by someone who was an addict (like a family member). However, it could also apply to those who are professionally involved with and trying to help the addict, like healthcare providers, teachers, co-workers, clergy, social workers, and psychotherapists (Fausel, 1988; Williams, Bissell, & Sullivan, 1991). CDPC could be direct or indirect, active or passive. It could be limited to one particular relationship at a given time, or be chronic and progressive with age, contaminating more relationships and affecting a larger group of people.

So much has been written on CDPC, mostly from a popular perspective and to lay audiences. It has a broad meaning or connotation and certainly is still lacking an accurate and comprehensive definition. CDPC is mostly self- or peer-diagnosed. The person is usually guided by a myth or an illusion that by entering into an enmeshed and closely monitored relationship and by becoming a vital part of another person's life or family unit, together they can meet all of their emotional needs, make all of their difficult decisions, find the appropriate solutions, and maintain a smooth and predictable life. To accomplish these goals, they usually try to manipulate the dynamics of the relationship, control the surrounding events, and disregard major faults, multiple red flags, and many alarming signals.

When a relationship is solely exclusive and is relied upon as the main source of personal identity, safety, contentment, and stability, then this relationship can be classified as CDPC. Although, there may be some elements of genuine care, support, concern, and affection in codependent relationships, most of them involve serious exploitation. It is not uncommon to find symbiotic partnerships in which two or more people use each other in an unhealthy way to sustain their functioning and, by doing so, they ultimately feed into each other's deficiencies and pathology.

CDPC is motivated by a wishful thinking like "if I work hard enough to connect and merge with my significant other, then my life will be safe, secure, meaningful, and happy." Furthermore, "if I control all important details and predict all significant outcomes, then nothing bad will happen." By entertaining such omnipotent wishes, the codependents are in fact trying to play "god" and often their concept of and relationship with the real God is distorted.

Codependents' unhealthy attachment and symbiotic relationship normally stem from their irrational expectations, childish desires, and, at times, infantile wishes that all their internal and emotional needs for safety, comfort, and happiness can be nicely met and all unpleasant, painful, and conflictual situations of life can be totally avoided. Their perception of interpersonal realities tends to be considerably distorted and assessment of their own personal abilities tends to be significantly skewed.

The codependent has many blind spots, many of which are crippling to self and others: the constant enabling behavior, desiring to fix everybody else's problems, making excuses for other people's mistakes, and struggling with high anxiety, indecisiveness, and poor self-concept. Only healthy exposures and sound therapy could uncover these spots and begin to heal, repair, and recover the person's mind and soul. Existentially speaking, such individuals seem to carry a heavy load of perceived worries, feel substantial emptiness, suffer from major uncertainties, lack a clear sense of self, and struggle with a strong feeling of meaninglessness (as one client declared, "I seem to be walking around with a big hole in my stomach"). Codependents subject themselves to someone else's opinion, mood, perception, needs, and approval. They easily become tormented by other people's reactions. They seem to be constantly searching for the missing pieces and essential ingredients in life.

Codependents have mixed the concepts of dependence and independence and have certainly confused interdependence with enmeshment and fusion. While a purely dependent personality lives a life which is mostly determined or conditioned by others, codependent people seem to equally depend on and mutually condition each other. An extreme example of being codependent is when the person tries to become responsible for not only other people's emotional needs, comfort, and welfare, but also for their irresponsible behaviors—in other words, becoming responsible for other people's irresponsibilities.

Another feature of codependents is that they initially draw some pleasure or satisfaction from enabling each other. With time, however, this activity stops being rewarding and codependents start to feel depleted, exhausted, and increasingly empty. This adds to their frustration and disappointment and eventually drives them to either intensify their desperate efforts to further engage the significant other or to completely rebel, abandon, and run away from that relationship.

Similar to other popular, vague, or overly used terminology (like being dysfunctional, borderline, depressed, or lacking boundaries), CDPC has somewhat become another psychological basket case category or common label which is easily being assigned to people who experience common troubles with interpersonal relationships. Some theorists and specialized therapists have recently tried to establish CDPC as a separate diagnosis. They claim that CDPC can have its own criteria and cluster of symptoms (Cermak, 1986; O'Brien & Gaborit, 1992). However, CDPC is still best recognized as a semi-professional term, more popular than scientific, describing certain relational patterns, personality style, and a broad interpersonal phenomenon. CDPC is not yet an established disorder by itself like other diagnostic criteria which are based on empirical research or extensive clinical observations.

Martin and Piazza (1995), for example, conducted a research study on 207 women from six mental health facilities, all of whom were officially labeled as "codependent." The authors concluded that CDPC was not a separate disorder but was indicative of women presenting with combined personality disorders or showing situational adaptive mechanisms. Essentially, the concept of CDPC has gained a lot attention and publicity in self-help circles but not in health sciences (Bell, 1995). There have been some questions about the validity of its hypothesized syndrome and criticism of CDPC as a disease model. Although there is basic agreement on its general characteristics, solid theoretical foundations, specific behavioral criteria, and physical symptomatology are, however, still lacking. In addition, empirical research is needed to examine its underlying assumptions and to formulate a clear operational definition.

The concept of CDPC has become inflated, resulting in a language used to describe all sorts of psychosocial problems. This may have negative implications for counseling. Therapists should verify, challenge, and soften the term with self-diagnosed clients. Furthermore, this may have serious implications for cross-cultural encounters. What is considered dysfunctional or abnormal in one culture may be totally acceptable and normal in another. So, when dealing with different subcultures, minorities, or ethnic groups, its essential to carefully listen and learn and consciously avoid quick interpretations, conclusions, or diagnoses. Some therapeutic suggestions or interventions that are effective within the Anglo-American society may be in conflict with other cultural backgrounds that value closer communities and familism (cf. Inclan & Hernandez, 1992). Anderson (1994) argued that the individual identity tends to be lost in the label and the CDPC model encourages alienation from rather than connection with the family of origin.

Generally, what is known about codependent people is that they become highly invested in and focused upon the significant other(s). They neglect the unfolding of their own unique lives and direct themselves toward their significant other. According to Shockley (1994), in order to overcome the obstacles of CDPC one must engage in interdisciplinary tasks. The most effective treatment rests in a global approach of indepth counseling, support groups, and spiritual guidance.

Currently, there are numerous support groups, books, tapes, literature, and twelve-step recovery programs, ranging from highly professional to self-help approaches, that are sponsored by many Christian organizations, churches, and agencies. These resources and services are available to those people who are struggling with similar conditions and seem unable to break the CDPC cycle alone.

The Bible repeatedly calls us to be anchored, solid, and balanced people. The Scriptures encourage us to cultivate maturity, both on the individual and interpersonal levels, and to develop a strong sense of personhood in Christ. The following are foundational marks of a healthy self:

- Having the capacity to be alone and be content.
- Establishing a good balance between independence and dependence (a functional interdependence).
- Possessing a well-defined personal boundary and a clear sense of self.
- Stopping the habit of peace-keeping (accommodating, pleasing, avoiding) and learning the virtue of peace-making (addressing, facing, challenging) (cf. Matt. 5:9).
- Maintaining a healthy balance between giving and receiving, caring and letting go.
- Ability to mean what one says and to say what one means. Christ's teaching clearly conveyed that principle, "Let your yes be yes and your no be no" (Matt. 5: 37).
- Developing a constructive style for conflict resolution and stress management.
- Becoming aware of self and others. Being in touch with deep emotional needs and being observant of personal patterns and surrounding cues.
- Embracing one's full humanity including the shadow, potential for failure, and set of weaknesses and vulnerabilities. Seeking close relationships with other healthy, positive, and mature people.

- Realistically evaluating personal qualities. Avoiding the common tendency of underestimating or overestimating oneself.
- Learning to be proactive instead of being passive, responsive, or merely reactive. Taking initiation, setting goals, pursuing interests, fulfilling potentials, and positively acting upon life.

References

Anderson, S. C. (1994). A critical analysis of the concept of codependency. *Social Work, 39,* 677–685.

Bell, J. (1995). "Co-dependency: A critical review": Comment. *Drug and Alcohol Review, 14,* 240–241.

Cermak, T. L. (1986). Diagnostic criteria for codependency. *Journal of Psychoactive Drugs, 18,* 15–20.

Fausel, D. F. (1988). Helping the helper heal: Co-dependency in helping professionals. *Journal of Independent Social Work, 3,* 35–45.

Inclan, J., & Hernandez, M. (1992). Cross-cultural perspectives and codependence: The case of poor Hispanics. *American Journal of Orthopsychiatry, 62,* 245–255.

Martin, A. L., & Piazza, N. J. (1995). Codependency in women: Personality disorder or popular descriptive term? *Journal of Mental Health Counseling, 17,* 428–440.

O'Brien, P. E., & Gaborit, M. (1992). Codependency: A disorder separate from chemical dependency. *Journal of Clinical Psychology, 48,* 129–136.

Shockley, G. A., (1994). Overcoming the obstacles of co-dependency: An interdisciplinary task. *Journal of Spiritual Formation, 15,* 103–108.

Williams, E., Bissell, L., & Sullivan, E. (1991). The effects of co-dependence on physicians and nurses. *British Journal of Addiction, 86,* 37–42.

Suggested Reading

Beattie, M. (1987). *Codependent no more: How to stop controlling others and start caring for yourself.* Center City, MN: Hazelden.

Cloud, H. (1992). *Changes that heal: How to understand your past to ensure a healthier future.* Grand Rapids, MI: Zondervan.

Cowan, G., Bommersbach, M., & Curtis, S. R. (1995). Codependency, loss of self, and power. *Psychology of Women Quarterly, 19,* 221–236.

Hemfelt, R., Minirth, F., & Meier, P. (1989). *Love is a choice: Recovery for codependent relationships.* Nashville, TN: Thomas Nelson.

Riordan, R. J., & Simone, D. (1993). Codependent Christians: Some issues for church-based recovery groups. *Journal of Psychology and Theology, 21,* 158–164.

NAJI ABI-HASHEM

See AFFILIATION, NEED FOR; COMPLIANCE; CONFORMITY; CROSS-CULTURAL PSYCHOLOGY; DOMINANCE; LEARNED HELPLESSNESS; MATURITY; PEACE, INNER; SELF-CONCEPT; SELF-DISCLOSURE; SELF-ESTEEM; DEPENDENCY.

Coe, George Albert (1862–1951). One of the most important contributors to religious education in the United States. Coe was born in Mendon, New York, and was educated at the University of Rochester,

Boston University School of Theology, and the University of Berlin. His academic career spanned five decades and included faculty appointments at the University of Southern California, Northwestern University, Union Theological Seminary, and finally at Teachers College of Columbia University, from which he retired in 1927. His retirement was honored by a special edition of *Religious Education*, but retirement did not terminate his productivity. Two of his most notable books, *What Is Christian Education* (1929) and *What Is Religion Doing to Our Consciences*, were published after his retirement. In all Coe published 11 books, nearly 60 book reviews, and more than 250 articles.

Coe was one of the founders of the Religious Education Association in 1903 and was generally recognized as the leader of that movement. His view of Christian education was quite broad; he argued that it is a process of systematic, critical study of interpersonal relationships guided by two theological assumptions: the existence of God (conceived as the "Great Valuer of persons") and the infinite value of the individual (which Coe specifically identified as the teaching of Christ). Yet Coe avoided being dogmatic in his views and encouraged constructive debate among various theological views. He remained active in the Religious Education Association throughout his life and was honorary president of that body at the time of his death.

Coe is perhaps best known for his pioneering study of the psychology of religion. *The Psychology of Religion* dealt with issues in the methodology of the fields. His best-known work, *The Spiritual Life: Studies in the Science of Religion* (1900), is often mentioned along with the contemporary work of William James and James Leuba as one of the seminal books in that field. In this work Coe analyzed the cases of 27 converts and tried to explain the character of their conversion experiences with the psychological theories of the day. On the basis of his cases Coe related sudden, striking conversions to an active "subliminal self" and suggested that such conversions usually occur in people who are emotionally suggestible, passive, and show a tendency toward automisms. Coe's work in the psychology of religion remains influential to this day.

L. S. SHAFFER

See PSYCHOLOGY OF RELIGION.

Cognitive-Behavior Therapy. Cognitive-behavior therapy has continued to grow in prominence as a school of psychotherapy or counseling both among secular (e.g., Dobson and Craig, 1996; Persons, 1989) as well as Christian therapists (Tan, 1987; also see Craigie & Tan, 1989; McMinn, 1991; Propst, 1988; Tan & Ortberg, 1995; Wright, 1986).

Cognitive-behavior therapy was defined by Kendall and Hollon (1979) as "a purposeful attempt to preserve the demonstrated efficiencies of behavior modification within a less doctrinaire context, and to incorporate the cognitive activities of the client in the efforts to produce therapeutic change" (p. 1). It is more correct to use the term *cognitive-behavioral therapies*, since there are about a dozen major approaches to cognitive-behavior therapy (see Dobson & Block, 1988). They include rational-emotive therapy (Ellis), cognitive therapy (Beck), self-instructional training (Meichenbaum), anxiety management training, problem-solving therapy, stress inoculation training (Meichenbaum), systematic rational restructuring, personal science (Mahoney), rational behavior therapy, self-control therapy, and structural psychotherapy (Guidano & Liotti).

However, there are still at least six basic tenets foundational to any cognitive-behavioral therapy. Kendall and Bemis (1983) listed them: "(1) the human organism responds primarily to cognitive representations of their environments . . . ; (2) most human learning is cognitively mediated; (3) thoughts, feelings, and behaviors are causally interrelated; (4) attitude, expectancies, attributions, and other cognitive activities are central to producing, predicting, and understanding psychopathological behavior and the effects of therapeutic interventions; (5) cognitive processes can be cast into testable formulations that are easily integrated with behavioral paradigms, and it is possible and desirable to combine cognitive treatment strategies with enactive techniques and behavioral contingency management; and (6) the task of the cognitive-behavioral therapist is to act as diagnostician, educator, and technical consultant who assesses maladaptive cognitive processes and works with the client to design learning experiences that may remediate these dysfunctional cognitions and the behavioral and affective patterns with which they correlate" (pp. 565–566).

Cognitive-behavior therapy therefore focuses on how problem thinking and problem behavior affect problem feelings like depression, anxiety, and anger. It attempts to change such problem feelings by modifying problem thinking and behavior. Cognitive techniques include cognitive restructuring of negative, irrational, extreme, maladaptive thinking, imagery strategies, and coping self-talk. Behavioral techniques include relaxation training, desensitization, flooding, assertiveness or social skills training, external contingency management, and modeling.

The different approaches to cognitive-behavior therapy can be generally classified into three major categories (Mahoney & Arnkoff, 1978): cognitive restructuring (e.g., rational-emotive therapy, cognitive therapy, and self-instructional training); coping skills therapy (e.g., anxiety management training and stress-inoculation training); and problem-solving therapies (e.g., problem-solving therapy and personal science).

Recent Developments and Contemporary Issues. A number of recent developments and contemporary issues in cognitive-behavior therapy have been reviewed by Tan (1987) and will be briefly summarized and updated here. First, self-efficacy theory, originally developed by Bandura (1977, 1986), has continued to play a central role in explaining the effects of different cognitive-behavioral interventions, despite theoretical and methodological criticisms. Self-efficacy refers to the conviction that one can successfully execute the behavior required to produce a certain outcome. Self-efficacy expectations will therefore determine one's persistence and ultimate success in coping with threats. Bandura's self-efficacy theory asserts that psychological interventions of whatever type are effective because they serve as a means of creating and strengthening such expectations of self-efficacy or personal mastery in specific situations.

Second, the literature on dealing with client resistance, facilitating treatment adherence, and relapse prevention has grown, reflecting the development of cognitive-behavioral strategies for effective handling of such crucial therapeutic issues (e.g., Marlatt & Gordon, 1985; Meichenbaum & Turk, 1987).

Third, cognitive-behavior therapy has been used with a greater variety of clinical populations other than adults, such as children, adolescents, and the elderly (e.g., a book on cognitive-behavioral play therapy, Knell, 1993). Cognitive-behavior therapy has also been applied to borderline personality disorder (Linehan, 1993) as well as other personality disorders (Beck et al., 1990), substance abuse (Beck, Wright, Newman, & Liese, 1993), marital problems (Epstein & Baucom, 1988), family of origin problems (Bedrosian & Bozicas, 1994), schizophrenic disorders (Perris, 1989), and severely disturbed inpatients (Wright, Thase, Beck, & Ludgate, 1993).

Fourth, in a related cognitive-behavior therapy has achieved a prominent place in behavioral medicine, or more specifically clinical health psychology, as an effective intervention for a number of physical or medical conditions, including chronic pain (Keefe, Dunsmore, & Burnett, 1992; Tan & Leucht, 1997).

Fifth, strategies and measures for cognitive-behavioral assessment have become more sophisticated and comprehensive (Segal & Shaw, 1988), including the need to pay more attention to motivational and interpersonal contexts such as the cognitive-interpersonal cycle (Safran & Segal, 1990).

Sixth, there has been more caution in clinical decision making as well as client and therapist judgments, due to a greater awareness of the biases and shortcomings inherent in human information processing. Suggestions have also been offered for reducing such biases (Turk & Salovey, 1988).

Seventh, cognitive-behavior therapists have dealt more openly with treatment failures and negative outcome in therapy, reflecting to an extent the maturing of this particular approach to therapy.

Finally, the importance of integrating affect and cognition, or feelings and thoughts, has been emphasized. In particular cognitive-behavior therapists have recently paid more attention to the need for eliciting hot cognitions or affect-laden thoughts rather than cold or rational, affect-free cognitions (see Greenberg & Safran, 1987). A closely related development has been a greater recognition of the need to explore past events and understand the developmental or structural context of maladaptive, dysfunctional cognitive schemas or ways of thinking that often have their roots in early childhood experiences (e.g., see Guidano & Liotti, 1983). Such experiences may give rise to "early maladaptive schemas" (Young, 1990) that may play a crucial role in the development of personality disorders.

A Biblical Approach to Cognitive-Behavior Therapy. After pointing out several limitations and criticisms of secular cognitive-behavior therapy, Tan (1987) provided the following guidelines for conducting a Christian, biblical approach to cognitive-behavior therapy that is more broad-based. One guideline is to emphasize the primacy of agape love and the need to develop a warm, genuine, and empathic relationship with the client that is collaborative. Therapists must deal more adequately with the past, especially unresolved developmental issues or childhood experiences, with the judicious use of inner healing prayer or healing of memories where appropriate (see Tan & Ortberg, 1995). They must also pay special attention to the meaning of spiritual, experiential, and mystical aspects of faith and life and not overemphasize the rationalistic dimension. The possibility of demonic involvement in some cases should also be seriously considered. Therapists can use biblical truth and not relativistic, empirically oriented values in conducting cognitive restructuring and behavioral change interventions to modify problem thinking and behaviors. They can also emphasize the Holy Spirit's ministry in producing inner healing and cognitive, behavioral, and emotional change. Prayer and the Scriptures as God's Word will be crucial in this process.

It is useful to pay more attention to larger contextual factors such as familial, societal, religious, and cultural influences and use community and church resources more. Therapists may use only those techniques that are consistent with biblical truth, morality, and ethics and not simplistically use whatever techniques work. They can reaffirm biblical perspectives on suffering, including the possibility of the "blessings of mental anguish" or the "dark night of the soul," with the ultimate goal of therapy being holiness or Christlikeness (Rom. 8:29) and not necessarily temporal happiness. They can utilize rigorous outcome research methodology before making definitive conclusions about the superiority (not just the general effectiveness) of cognitive-behavior therapy, whether Christian or secular.

Cognitive therapy has not been found to be superior to interpersonal therapy for depression. However, the empirical support is solid for the overall effectiveness of cognitive-behavioral treatments for depression, chronic pain, panic disorder with and without agoraphobia, generalized anxiety disorder, and social phobia (American Psychological Association Division of Clinical Psychology, 1995; also see Robins & Hayes, 1993). While research support for the greater efficacy of religious or Christian cognitive-behavior therapy with Christian clients is growing (e.g., Propst, Ostrom, Watkins, Dean, & Mashburn, 1992), it is not always consistent (e.g., Johnson, DeVries, Ridley, Pettorini, & Peterson, 1994; Pecheur & Edwards, 1984). Further research is needed.

Conclusion. Cognitive-behavior therapy is now an established school of psychotherapy with much empirical support for its efficacy with a number of psychological disorders such as depression, anxiety, and chronic pain. A more broad-based, biblical approach to cognitive-behavior therapy has been developed by various Christian therapists, and it appears to be particularly helpful with Christian clients.

References

American Psychological Association, Division of Clinical Psychology, Task Force on Promotion and Dissemination of Psychological Procedures. (1995). Training in and dissemination of empirically-validated psychological treatments: Report and recommendations. *The Clinical Psychologist, 48*, 3–23.

Bandura, A. (1977). Self-efficacy: Toward a unifying theory of behavioral change. *Psychological Review, 84*, 191–215.

Bandura, A. (1986). *Social foundations of thought and action: A social cognitive theory.* Englewood Cliffs, NJ: Prentice-Hall.

Beck, A. T., Freeman, A., et al. (1990). *Cognitive therapy of personality disorders.* New York: Guilford.

Beck, A. T., Wright, F. D., Newman, C. F., & Liese, B. S. (1993). *Cognitive therapy of substance abuse.* New York: Guilford.

Bedrosian, R. C., & Bozicas, G. D. (1994). *Treating family of origin problems: A cognitive approach.* New York: Guilford.

Craigie, F. C., Jr., & Tan, S.-Y. (1989). Changing resistant assumptions in Christian cognitive-behavioral therapy. *Journal of Psychology and Theology, 17*, 93–100.

Dobson, K. S., & Block, L. (1988). Historical and philosophical bases of the cognitive-behavioral therapies. In K. S. Dobson (Ed.), *Handbook of cognitive-behavioral therapies.* New York: Guilford.

Dobson, K. S., & Craig, K. D. (Eds.). (1996). *Advances in cognitive-behavioral therapy.* Thousand Oaks, CA: Sage.

Epstein, N., & Baucom, D. (1988). *Cognitive-behavioral marital therapy.* New York: Brunner/Mazel.

Greenberg, L. S., & Safran, J. D. (1987). *Emotion in psychotherapy.* New York: Guilford.

Guidano, V. F., & Liotti, G. (1983). *Cognitive processes and emotional disorders.* New York: Guilford.

Johnson, W. B., DeVries, R., Ridley, C. R., Pettorini, D., & Peterson, D. R. (1994). The comparative efficacy of Christian and secular rational-emotive therapy with Christian clients. *Journal of Psychology and Theology, 22*, 130–140.

Keefe, F. J., Dunsmore, J., & Burnett, R. (1992). Behavioral and cognitive-behavioral approaches to chronic pain: Recent advances and future directions. *Journal of Consulting and Clinical Psychology, 60*, 528–536.

Kendall, P. C., & Bemis, K. M. (1983). Thought and action in psychotherapy: The cognitive-behavioral approaches. In M. Hersen, A. E. Kazdin, & A. S. Bellack (Eds.), *The clinical psychology handbook.* New York: Pergamon.

Kendall, P. C., & Hollon, S. D. (Eds.). (1979). *Cognitive-behavioral interventions: Theory, research, and procedures.* New York: Academic.

Knell, S. M. (1993). *Cognitive-behavioral play therapy.* Northvale, NJ: Aronson.

Linehan, M. M. (1993). *Cognitive-behavioral treatment of borderline personality disorder.* New York: Guilford.

Mahoney, M. J., & Arnkoff, D. B. (1978). Cognitive and self-control therapies. In S. L. Garfield & A. E. Bergin (Eds.), *Handbook of psychotherapy and behavior change* (2nd ed.). New York: Wiley.

Marlatt, G. A., & Gordon, J. R. (Eds.). (1985). *Relapse prevention: Maintenance strategies in the treatment of the addictive behaviors.* New York: Guilford.

McMinn, M. R. (1991). *Cognitive therapy techniques in Christian counseling.* Dallas: Word.

Meichenbaum, D., & Turk, D. C. (1987). *Facilitating treatment adherence: A practitioner's guidebook.* New York: Plenum.

Pecheur, D., & Edwards, K. J. (1984). A comparison of secular and religious versions of cognitive therapy with depressed Christian college students. *Journal of Psychology and Theology, 12*, 45–54.

Perris, C. (1989). *Cognitive therapy and the schizophrenic disorders.* New York: Guilford.

Persons, J. B. (1989). *Cognitive therapy in practice: A case formulation approach.* New York: Norton.

Propst, L. R. (1988). *Psychotherapy in a religious framework: Spirituality in the emotional healing process.* New York: Human Sciences.

Propst, L. R., Ostrom, R., Watkins, P., Dean, T., & Mashburn, D. (1992). Comparative efficacy of religious and nonreligious cognitive-behavioral therapy for the treatment of clinical depression in religious individuals. *Journal of Consulting and Clinical Psychology, 60*, 94–103.

Robins, C. J., & Hayes, A. M. (1993). An appraisal of cognitive therapy. *Journal of Consulting and Clinical Psychology, 61*, 205–214.

Safran, J. D., & Segal, Z. V. (1990). *Interpersonal process in cognitive therapy.* New York: Basic.

Segal, Z. V., & Shaw, B. F. (1988). Cognitive assessment: Issues and methods. In K. S. Dobson (Ed.), *Handbook of cognitive-behavioral therapies.* New York: Guilford.

Tan, S.-Y. (1987). Cognitive-behavior therapy: A biblical approach and critique. *Journal of Psychology and Theology, 15*, 103–112.

Tan, S. Y., & Leucht, C. A. (1997). Cognitive-behavioral therapy for clinical pain control: A 15-year update and its relationship to hypnosis. *International Journal of Clinical and Experimental Hypnosis, 45*, 396–416.

Tan, S.-Y., & Ortberg, J., Jr. (1995). *Understanding depression.* Grand Rapids, MI: Baker.

Turk, D., & Salovey, P. (Eds.). (1988). *Reasoning, inference, and judgment in clinical psychology.* New York: Free Press.

Wright, H. N. (1986). *Self-talk, imagery and prayer in counseling.* Waco, TX: Word.

Wright, J. H., Thase, M. E., Beck, A. T., & Ludgate, J. W. (Eds.). (1993). *Cognitive therapy with inpatients.* New York: Guilford.

Cognitive-Behavior Therapy

Young, J. E. (1990). *Cognitive therapy for personality disorders: A schema-focused approach*. Sarasota, FL: Professional Resource Exchange.

S.-Y. TAN

See BEHAVIOR THERAPY.

Cognitive Development. Between the 1950s and the 1970s psychology experienced a dramatic transformation from a field of study focused on the mechanistic theory of behaviorism, with its emphasis on rewards and punishments provided by the external environment, to focus on the meaningfulness of human action and the more constructivist theories of cognition. In his classic text of cognitive psychology Neisser (1967) defined cognition as "the processes by which the sensory input is transformed, reduced, elaborated, stored, recovered, and used" (p. 4). The development of cognition then refers to changes in our abilities to acquire or process information.

The field of cognitive psychology is currently dominated by two approaches: information processing approaches and Piagetian theories. Information processing approaches to cognition use the computer as a model for how people handle information. From this analogy cognitive development can be seen as reflecting changes in the hardware (e.g., the capacity of memory systems and the speed of processing) or software (e.g., children's ability to use strategies or other learning devices). These models use multistore models of memory (the model of Atkinson and Shiffrin, 1968). Each stage except long-term memory has limited capacity. As children develop their capacity and speed of processing increases. Strategies (the software) are the goal-directed operations used to aid task performance. They include rehearsal, categorization to enhance recall, comparison to sharpen differences, and imagery to aid memory. Most children with age become increasingly adept and flexible with strategy use. A few children are production-deficient. These children do not produce as many strategies spontaneously, use strategies as appropriately, or use multiple strategies as adeptly as do other children their age. Production-deficient children may sometimes be taught to employ strategies more efficiently.

A new information processing model for cognitive development has recently been proposed by Brainerd and Reyna (1993). Believing that people prefer to think, reason, and remember by processing inexact, fuzzy memory representations rather than working on exact representations, Brainerd and Reyna (1993) propose that memory is based on "fuzzy representations (senses, patterns, gists) in combination with construction rules that operate on those representations" (p. 50). Fuzzy-trace theory explains why eyewitness testimony is notoriously inexact and suggestible (see, e.g., Ceci & Bruck, 1993).

Sternberg (1985) has proposed a radically different information processing model of development, componential theory. In his model he defines three components (or processes that act on internal representations of objects or symbols): metacomponents, which monitor task performance; performance components, which encode and manage stimulus information; and knowledge-acquisition components, which are involved in acquiring new knowledge.

The second common approach to cognitive development, Piagetian theory, is complex and difficult to summarize (for a highly readable review, see Flavell, 1963). Jean Piaget considered human development as biological. Thus cognitive development follows the same process of epigenesis, of biological unfolding with maturity, as other abilities in humans and animals. The cognitive system is, however, strikingly active, selecting and processing environmental information, constructing knowledge rather than passively receiving knowledge in its senses.

The smallest units of organized information are schemas, internal representations of external reality. These schemas match reality more or less well and are continuously in the process of being adapted to better match the external world. This adaptation process involves assimilation, or interpreting new objects or events in terms of earlier schema, and accommodation, or modifying older schema or building new schema to reflect new events or objects. Piaget believed that play is virtually pure assimilation and that imitation is primarily accommodation. Although they are defined distinctively, Piaget considered every behavior to consist of the dynamic interrelationship between these two processes.

Piaget described cognitive development using four stages. Often called cognitive-developmental theory, his model has been used to describe development in a range of behaviors (see, e.g., Kohlberg's [1964] theory of moral development and Fowler's [1981] theory of faith development). Cognitive-developmental theorists argue that changes in cognition modify other behaviors such as morality, that development is best described by characterizing the structure of cognition, and that cognition and its correlated behaviors develop in stages. Further, these stages are hierarchical (i.e., stage 2 is more complex and biologically more mature than stage 1), universal (i.e., everyone goes through the same stages), and invariant (i.e., the stages must occur in order).

The first stage of development according to Piaget is the sensorimotor stage, the period from birth to 2 years of age, when intelligence evolves from infants' actions on their environment. Object permanence (i.e., recognizing that an object that is out of sight nevertheless continues to exist), imitation (i.e., being able to reproduce observed actions), and symbolic abilities (language and play) develop in the sensorimotor stage. Piaget divides this stage into six substages, during which the child becomes increasingly able, for example, to imitate actions (i.e., first repeating behaviors it has just produced, then repeating behaviors of which it is capable, then copying new behaviors, then copying behaviors at a later time or in a different place). During the second stage, the preoperational stage (ages 2 to 7 years), intelligence is symbolic, expressed via language and play, permitting children to compare events or objects, even when the referents are out of sight. Thought is intuitive rather than logical and egocentric rather than flexible (i.e., it reflects the child's own perspective rather than another's). The third stage, the concrete operational stage (ages 7 to 11 years), is marked by concrete reasoning and symbolic logical reasoning abilities. During the formal operational stage (ages 11 to 16 years) children are able to make and test hypotheses. They are capable of metacognition (i.e., to think about thinking) and abstract thinking.

It is difficult to overemphasize the importance of Piaget's theory of cognitive development, as most cognitive theorists begin with it. Because of him, we see children not as "ill-formed adults on the edges of society" but as having distinctive characteristics in their own right and being active in their own development.

Critics of Piaget's theory have challenged his theory on several grounds. Some have argued that he underestimated children's abilities. For example, Piaget suggested that children develop the ability to imitate toward the end of the sensorimotor period, whereas others have documented imitative abilities in newborn children (see Meltzoff & Moore, 1977). Also, Piaget suggested that children are egocentric until the concrete operational stage (ages 7–11), whereas Flavell (1988) and others have documented earlier emerging perspective-taking abilities. These abilities form the basis for theory of mind, observable in children by four to five years of age. (Theory of mind refers to children's ability to understand that the perceptions, knowledge, and thoughts of others are different from their own.)

Other critics have argued for the existence of a later stage in cognitive development beginning about age 20 to 25, the emergence of mature reflective judgment, or reasoning about the basis for knowledge when solving ill-structured problems (Kitchener, Lynch, Fischer, & Wood, 1993).

Yet other critics have argued that Piaget described development as domain-general (i.e., all cognitive abilities reorganize at once) when a more domain-specific model is more accurate. Thus, Fischer (1980) has blended Piagetian theory and Skinnerian behaviorism by arguing that skills develop as the result of interaction between the child and the environment (a Piagetian assumption) and that the environment determines which skills (or sets of actions, both physical and mental) will be developed (a behavioral assumption). Although Fischer agrees with Piaget that skills emerge in an in-

variant developmental progression, he argues that only optimal environments produce optimal performance. Further, Fischer has summarized Piaget's six substages of the sensorimotor period into four, which have been found to match biological changes in the neuronal organization of infants. Case (1978) has similarly merged Piagetian and information processing theory by arguing that children become increasingly efficient at processing information and suggesting that development consists of stages. Nevertheless he believes that development is more heterogeneous than Piaget argued, with important differences between and within individuals in how cognitive structures are formed.

Finally, a large group of theorists, including many information processing theorists, have challenged Piaget's assumption that development is primarily discontinuous or stagelike. When one watches one child, development appears continuous. That is, this child's cognitive abilities seem to mature progressively with age. When one compares many children, however, the parallels in their abilities at the same age are often striking, supporting a discontinuous model. In fact development is probably both continuous and discontinuous, and Piagetian and information processing theories are not necessarily mutually exclusive.

Both Piagetian and information processing theories make assumptions about human behavior that Christians need to evaluate. Information processing theories reinforce observations that children do indeed grow and mature and that there is a great deal of similarity between our abilities and interests as children and as adults (continuity). At the same time, although this theory has contributed immensely to our knowledge, information processing theorists view humans as passive recipients of information. This more mechanistic view of humans does not do justice to our Godlikeness, in which we exercise rational abilities and act on our environment in accordance with our perception of God's will.

Piagetian theory emphasizes our active, constructive nature, thereby emphasizing our Godlikeness. Thus we are called to believe for ourselves, not to be passive recipients of the beliefs of other people. Further, contrary to many people's assumptions, the belief that humans construct their view of reality is not necessarily unbiblical. As Christians, we agree that belief requires a personal encounter with knowledge (i.e., a personal relationship with Jesus Christ), active questioning, and a conversion that has rational as well as emotional components. Although this perspective argues that people construct their own understanding of reality, it does not necessarily imply that absolute truth does not exist. Rather, as Christians we believe that "all truth is God's truth" and is observable by Christians and non-Christians alike. As we study the world, our search for subjective knowledge leads us to construct schemas that approximate objective, ontological truth. In biblical terms, we are called to understand God better and to "grow" as Jesus did (Luke 2:52) with the promise that we will one day see God face to face.

References

Atkinson, R. C., & Shiffrin, R. M. (1968). Human memory: A proposed system and its control processes. In K. W. Spence & J. T. Spence (Eds.), *The psychology of learning and motivation: Advances in research and theory* (Vol. 2). New York: Academic.

Brainerd, C. J., & Reyna, V. F. (1993). Domains of fuzzy trace theory. In M. L. Howe & R. Pasnak (Eds.), *Emerging themes in cognitive development: Foundations* (Vol. 1). New York: Springer-Verlag.

Case, R. (1978). Intellectual development from birth to adulthood: A Neo-Piagetian investigation. In R. S. Siegler (Ed.), *Children's thinking: What develops?* Hillsdale, NJ: Erlbaum.

Ceci, S. J., & Bruck, M. (1993). Suggestibility of the child witness: A historical review and synthesis. *Psychological Bulletin, 113,* 403–439.

Fischer, K. W. (1980). A theory of cognitive development: The control and construction of hierarchies of skills. *Psychological Review, 87,* 477–531.

Flavell, J. H. (1988). The development of children's knowledge about mind: From cognitive connections to mental representations. In J. W. Astington, P. L. Harris, & D. R. Olson (Eds.), *Developing theories of mind.* Cambridge: Cambridge University Press.

Flavell, J. H. (1963). *The developmental psychology of Jean Piaget.* Princeton, NJ: Van Nostrand.

Fowler, J. W. (1981). *Stages of faith: The psychology of human development and the quest for meaning.* San Francisco: Harper & Row.

Kitchener, K. S., Lynch, C. L., Fischer, K. W., & Wood, P. K. (1993). Developmental range of reflective judgment: The effect of contextual support and practice on developmental stage. *Developmental Psychology, 29,* 893–906.

Kohlberg, L. (1964). Development of moral character and moral ideology. In M. L. Hoffman & L. W. Hoffman (Eds.), *Review of child development research* (Vol. 1). New York: Russell Sage Foundation.

Meltzoff, A. N., & Moore, M. K. (1977). Imitation of facial and manual gestures by human neonates. *Science, 198,* 75–78.

Neisser, U. (1967). *Cognitive psychology.* New York: Meredith.

Sternberg, R. J. (1985). *Beyond IQ: A triarchic theory of human intelligence.* Cambridge: Cambridge University Press.

K. V. Cook

See Thinking; Intelligence; Culture and Cognition; Cognitive Psychology; Moral Development.

Cognitive Dissonance. In the 1950s Leon Festinger proposed the theory of cognitive dissonance, which had a greater impact on social psychology than any theory except attribution theory. Festinger observed that when an individual held a cognition (e.g., belief or expectation) that was later disconfirmed, the individual held the cognition more strongly afterward. Festinger studied a religious group that predicted the world's end on a particular day. Anticipating the end, which included a daring rescue from outer space, they sold all possessions and waited on a mountaintop. When the predicted end and rescue failed, they held their beliefs more strongly. These findings stimulated Festinger (1957, 1964) to examine the cognitive and social factors in belief and behavior change.

As the prototype of cognitive consistency theories, cognitive dissonance theory is simple. Its implications are provocative and widespread. An individual holds beliefs or cognitions that do not fit with each other (e.g., I believe the world will end, and the world did not end as predicted). Nonfitting beliefs give rise to dissonance, a hypothetical aversive state the individual is motivated to reduce or at least not increase. The aversive stimulation initiates changes in the individual's behavior (e.g., undoing) or beliefs (e.g., the world was saved because of our fervent prayer) or limits exposure to discrepant information.

Cognitions relate to other cognitions in three ways: they may be irrelevant, dissonant, or consonant. Dissonance exists between two beliefs when one is the opposite of the other, yet both are held simultaneously; consonant relations exist when one belief follows from the other. Dissonance may arise from logically inconsistent beliefs, when beliefs are against the prevailing cultural mores, or when beliefs are inconsistent with past experience.

The amount of dissonance indicates the importance of the beliefs to the person. Beliefs that are held strongly are capable of arousing more dissonance than are less important beliefs. When the dissonance level rises to equal the resistance of the least resistant element, that element will change and the dissonance will be reduced.

Dissonance may be reduced by changing behavior, altering a belief, or adding a new one. When the person makes a decision where the alternate choices each have positive and negative aspects, dissonance may result from the decision. Dissonance will be greater when the decision is important and when the unchosen alternative is attractive. This may lead to revoking the decision, denigrating the unchosen one, and postdecision justification.

The theory has generated much research by advocates and opposition. Research has addressed the role of volition and commitment, the ability to tolerate dissonance, and the limits under which the theory works best. It has been applied to self-persuasion, forced compliance, exposure to information, and social support. It has been used in cognitive psychotherapies to initiate personal change. Its attraction seems to lie in counterintuitive predictions.

References

Festinger, L. (1957). *A theory of cognitive dissonance.* Stanford, CA: Stanford University Press.

Festinger, L. (1964). *Conflict, decision and dissonance.* Stanford, CA: Stanford University Press.

R. L. TIMPE

See ATTITUDE; ATTITUDE-BEHAVIOR RELATIONSHIPS.

Cognitive Psychology. "Cognitive psychology attempts to understand the basic mechanisms governing human thought, and these mechanisms are important in understanding the types of behavior studied by other social science fields. . . . Cognitive psychology studies the foundation on which all other social sciences stand" (Anderson, 1985, p. 4).

Cognitive psychology is concerned with the nature of human intelligence and how people think (Anderson, 1985). Thus cognitive psychologists have been interested in how people acquire, store, and use knowledge. In the process of acquiring knowledge, people must examine information within the environment, selecting important information while discarding that which is unimportant. Thus perception and attention are significant areas of investigation in cognitive psychology. People must also be able to express their knowledge. Therefore, language, reading, and writing have become important areas of research within cognitive psychology.

Brief Historical Review. From Plato's and Aristotle's thoughts on reasoning to Alfred Binet's work on intelligence and Hermann Ebbinghaus's work on memory, much of psychology in its earliest stages was concerned with cognition, as was much of the early experimental research in psychology. Hermann Helmholtz conducted research on nerve conduction, sensation, and perception, including color vision and audition. Ernst Weber demonstrated systematic relationships between stimulation and sensation using the idea of a just noticeable difference. Gustav Fechner extended Weber's work to show that arithmetic variations in just noticeable differences are due to geometric variations of stimulus intensity. Penfield electrically stimulated the cortex of human subjects to confirm that different areas of the brain exist for processing motor, sensory, visual, and auditory information. The first psychology lab was established by Wilhelm Wundt in 1879 in order to discover the basic elements of thought and to determine laws governing the combination of basic elements into complex mental processes and experiences.

The dominance of behaviorism during the early 1900s caused cognition to be a neglected area of study. However, the advent of the computer in the 1950s and 1960s provided a new metaphor for explaining human cognitive processing. Cognitive processes were now discussed in terms of information processing (Norman, 1976) and the brain was compared to a computer. Miller's (1956) paper discussed the limitations of short-term processing, which allowed researchers such as Atkinson and Shiffrin (1971) to develop a two-store model of memory. In addition Sperling's (1960) research using brief presentations indicated that a sensory store exists and holds a relatively large amount of sensory information for an extremely brief period of time. Information not moved from the sensory store to short-term memory is lost. Thus the current cognitive description of memory was formed: information is transferred from the sensory store to working memory, where it is processed and either stored or discarded.

Although some writers refer to the current period as the cognitive revolution (e.g., Ashcraft, 1989), others claim that a revolution did not take place. They suggest instead that cognitive psychology reemerged (e.g., Hintzman, 1993). Friman, Allen, Kerwin, and Larzelere (1993) searched citations from leading journals between 1979 and 1988 and found that while cognitive psychology has become more popular, no paradigm shift (Kuhn, 1970) has displaced behaviorism. It may be most accurate to view the current popularity of cognitive psychology as a reemergence of cognitive psychology instead of a revolution.

A key to the reemergence of cognitive psychology was the first cognitive psychology text (Neisser, 1967), in which the author devoted 6 chapters to attention and perception and only 4 to memory, thinking, and language. The emphasis on attention and perception is not surprising, given the perceptual roots of much of the early experimental research in psychology. However, a review of recent texts in cognitive psychology shows a different emphasis. In general only 1 or 2 chapters are devoted to attention and perception, while 9 to 11 chapters are devoted to memory, thinking, and language. How knowledge is represented in memory is of growing concern, especially since the development of neural network modeling (e.g., Haberlandt, 1994; Kellog, 1995). The findings within cognitive psychology are also being applied to other areas of psychology (e.g., Ellis & Hunt, 1993). For example, cognitive processing in social contexts (i.e., social cognition) is becoming an increasingly popular area of research (Smith, 1994). Further, practical applications highlighted in texts show among other things how cognitive psychology impacts the courtroom with research on eyewitness testimony (e.g., Loftus, 1986) or how it can be used to enhance learning among those with learning deficits (e.g., Merzenich, et al., 1996).

Cognitive psychologists use a variety of tasks to assess cognitive processing and ability. Recall tasks require that a subject reproduce information previously learned. In recognition tasks subjects must discriminate between the target (information presented previously) and distractors (new information). Judgment tasks are often used to determine the structure of knowledge. Judgment tasks ask "which occurred more recently" or "which is a more representative member of this category." How prior or subsequent learning impacts current learning and what information is retained over time are studied with transfer tasks. Concept-learning tasks require that subjects generalize learned concepts to new stimuli. This type of task is useful for determining how people learn and apply concepts in a laboratory setting. Knowledge-based learning tasks, however, parallel concept-learning tasks but are used for examining the structure of real-world knowledge about objects, events, and groups (Bower & Clapper, 1991). Response time and the number of items correctly identified are common measures in cognitive research.

Language is typically studied using three different types of tasks. First, judgment tasks require subjects to make judgments about word strings according to a criterion specified by the experimenter. Production tasks use utterances of a subject to examine pronunciation, intonation, and pauses in order to study the processes related to the production of speech. Third, reception tasks ask subjects to respond to speech or text in order to examine their understanding of the message.

Finally, there is a differentiation between cognitive psychology and cognitive science. Cognitive psychology incorporates contributions from a variety of subdisciplines within psychology (e.g., attention, perception, memory, thinking, language). Cognitive science integrates cognitive psychology with other disciplines (e.g., philosophy, linguistics, artificial intelligence, neuroscience, and to a lesser degree anthropology, social psychology, economics, and statistical decision making).

References

Anderson, J. R. (1985). *Cognitive psychology* (2nd ed.). New York: Freeman.

Ashcraft, M. H. (1989). *Human memory and cognition*. New York: HarperCollins.

Atkinson, R. C., & Shiffrin, R. M. (1971). The control of short-term memory. *Scientific American, 224,* 82–90.

Bower, G. H., & Clapper, J. P. (1991). Experimental methods in cognitive science. In M. I. Posner (Ed.), *Foundations of cognitive science*. Cambridge, MA: MIT Press.

Ellis, H. C., & Hunt, R. R. (1993). *Fundamentals of cognitive psychology*. Madison, WI: Brown & Benchmark.

Friman, P. C., Allen, K. D., Kerwin, M. L. E., & Larzelere, R. (1993). Changes in modern psychology: A citation analysis of the Kuhnian displacement theory. *American Psychologist, 48,* 658–664.

Haberlandt, K. (1994). *Cognitive psychology*. Boston: Allyn & Bacon.

Hintzman, D. L. (1993). Twenty-five years of learning and memory: Was the cognitive revolution a mistake? In D. E. Meyer & S. Kornblum (Eds.), *Attention and Performance 14*. Cambridge, MA: MIT Press.

Kellog, R. T. (1995). *Cognitive psychology*. Thousand Oaks, CA: Sage.

Kuhn, T. S. (1970). *The structure of scientific revolutions* (2nd ed.). Chicago: University of Chicago Press.

Loftus, E. F. (1986). Ten years in the life of an expert witness. *Law and Human Behavior, 10,* 241–263.

Merzenich, M. M., Jenkins, W. M., Johnston, P., Schreiner, C., Miller, S. L., & Tallal, P. (1996). Temporal processing deficits of language-learning impaired children ameliorated by training. *Science, 271,* 77–81.

Miller, G. A. (1956). The magical number seven, plus or minus two: Some limits on our capacity for processing information. *Psychological Review, 63,* 81–97.

Neisser, U. (1967). *Cognitive psychology*. New York: Appleton-Century-Crofts.

Norman, D. A. (1976). *Memory and attention: An introduction to human information processing* (2nd ed.). New York: Wiley.

Smith, E. R. (1994). Social cognition contributions to attribution theory and research. In P. G. Devine, D. L. Hamilton, & T. M. Ostrom (Eds.), *Social cognition: Impact on social psychology*. San Diego, CA: Academic.

Sperling, G. A. (1960). The information available in brief visual presentation. *Psychological Monographs, 74* (Whole No. 498).

C. KOCH

See ATTENTION; SENSATION AND PERCEPTION; INTELLIGENCE; PROBLEM SOLVING; LANGUAGE DEVELOPMENT; MEMORY.

Cognitive Restructuring. This technique, refined primarily by Goldfried (Goldfried & Goldfried, 1980), translates Albert Ellis's rational-emotive therapy into a social learning framework. Many behavior therapists have seen the utility of Ellis's conceptualization of psychopathology and psychotherapy, especially with anxiety disorders, but have been wary of the system because of its heavy philosophical trappings and because of Ellis's advocacy of a rather combative model of therapist influence. At the theoretical level Goldfried grounded the concept of irrational ideation in the broader experimental literature dealing with cognitive mediation of stress reactions and the social learning concept of expectancy.

Goldfried conceptualized the process of cognitive restructuring as involving four steps. First, the therapist helps the client recognize how unrealistic thoughts can be when one is emotionally upset. The therapist also discusses with the client how such beliefs can become so habitual that the client is no longer aware of these automatic thoughts. Second, the therapist helps the client recognize the obvious irrationality of some exaggerated unrealistic beliefs that the therapist supposes might be relevant to the client's distress. The client is frequently asked to role-play being a therapist who is persuading a client of the irrationality of the exaggerated unrealistic beliefs. The third step is to help the client see the unrealistic thoughts that cause his or her own distress. At this stage Socratic questioning, requests for evidence in support of specific beliefs, and examination of the long-term implications of the client's way of thinking may be used to help the client see the relationship between his or her thoughts and distress. The final stage of the process is to help the client think more realistically when confronted with problem situations. Role-playing practice is the primary mode of change.

The importance of cognitive restructuring as a distinct approach or technique has steadily diminished in light of major advances and changes in cognitive therapy.

Reference

Goldfried, M. R., & Goldfried, A. P. (1980). Cognitive change methods. In F. H. Kanfer & A. P. Goldstein (Eds.), *Helping people change* (2nd ed.). New York: Pergamon.

S. L. JONES

See COGNITIVE-BEHAVIOR THERAPY.

Cognitive Science. *See* INTELLIGENCE, ARTIFICIAL.

Cognitive Style. *See* CULTURE AND COGNITION.

Cognitive Therapy. *See* COGNITIVE-BEHAVIOR THERAPY.

Cohabitation. Christian counselors are accustomed to seeing a couple's cohabitation, living together though unmarried, as a moral issue. It is important for the professional to know, however, that it is a significant psychological issue as well. Since the mid-1980s a spate of research has appeared, and few areas of psychological research show such robust findings. Couples who cohabit before marriage are consistently found to have a significantly higher incidence of divorce than those who do not. This relationship has been demonstrated repeatedly despite the fact that early research in this area was usually predicated on the hypothesis that cohabitation would prove to be a helpful precursor to marriage. There is now little question in the literature that cohabitation is a good predictor of divorce, regardless of whether individuals marry the person they lived with. Nevertheless, census data show cohabitation to continue to increase as a precursor to and an alternative to marriage.

The most consistent explanations for the correlation of cohabitation with divorce center around the type of people who choose to cohabit and the effects of cohabitation itself. Those who choose to cohabit differ from those who marry without living together. Since cohabitation is a lifestyle that deviates from traditional societal and religious mores, those who flout those standards are less likely to feel bound by similar standards against divorce. Cohabitation also gives a false sense of security to the couple that they have already experienced what marriage will be like, leaving them shocked and disappointed. Cohabitors are found to exhibit less commitment to relationships, less happiness in their relationships, and poorer relationships with their parents (Nock, 1995).

Men and women differ in their reasons for cohabiting. Men tend to view cohabitation as convenient, particularly in the availability of sex. Men who cohabit are also less religious and have more accepting attitudes toward rape than those who do not (Huffman, Chang, Rausch, & Schaffer, 1994). Women who cohabit are more traditional in their attitudes toward relationships, regarding cohabitation as a step toward marriage. This difference in attitudes creates a power imbalance and may leave cohabiting women at greater risk of physical violence (Huffman, et al., 1994).

In addition to exhibiting a different set of values and dynamics prior to cohabiting, couples who live together show effects from cohabitation itself. Of particular note to Christian counselors is the effect on religious participation. In one longitudinal study religious beliefs and cohabitation demonstrated a reciprocal effect (Thornton, Axinn, & Hill, 1992). Lower levels of religiosity in mothers and children correlated with higher rates of cohabitation, as expected. However, after the effects of prior differences were controlled for, cohabitation also showed an effect on religious affiliation. Cohabiting decreased religious attendance from precohabiting levels while entering marriage without living together increased religious attendance.

References

Huffman, T., Chang, K., Rausch, P., & Schaffer, N. (1994). Gender differences and factors related to the disposition toward cohabitation. *Family Therapy, 21* (3), 171–184.
Nock, S. L. (1995). A comparison of marriages and cohabiting relationships. *Journal of Family Issues, 16* (1), 53–76.
Thornton, A., Axinn, W. G., & Hill, D. H. (1992). Reciprocal effects of religiosity, cohabitation, and marriage. *American Journal of Sociology, 98* (3), 628–651.

M. W. MANGIS

See MARITAL COMPATIBILITY.

Colitis. An inflammation of the lining of the large intestine. This condition is a form of chronic inflammatory disorder of the colon referred to as chronic nonspecific ulcerative colitis. Another, less common type of inflammatory bowel condition is called Crohn's disease of the colon. In both, small ulcers form throughout the lining of the colon, but they tend to be deeper in Crohn's disease. The incidence of ulcerative colitis is not high; about 250,000 Americans suffer from it. Colitis occurs across all ages from children to older adults but is most common in people aged 15 to 40.

The major symptom of colitis is frequent bloody diarrhea, which may be accompanied by stomach pain or cramps, fever, fatigue, and loss of weight. Complications may be local, such as perforation of the wall of the colon, or systemic, such as anemia, vitamin deficiencies, arthritis, or skin lesions.

The causes of colitis are unknown. Possibilities are genetic, bacterial, or viral, allergic reactions, immune mechanisms, or most likely, some combination of these factors. Many people with colitis are depressed and have feelings of hopelessness and despair. They may exhibit underlying hostility with unexpressed chronic resentment. It is not clear whether these emotions contribute to the development of colitis or whether they may be a response to being ill.

Mild attacks of colitis can be treated on an outpatient basis; acute attacks are usually treated in the hospital, where the inflammation can be controlled and nutritional losses can be replaced. In addition to bed rest, treatment often includes only clear liquids for food and intravenous feedings to replace lost fluids. This also allows the bowel to rest. In order to correct anemia, blood transfusions are required for those who have extensive bleeding. Corticosteroids are sometimes administered to reduce inflammation, pain, and fever. Steroid medication is gradually reduced over a two- to six-month period, although some people need to take it indefinitely. Sulfasalazine is given concurrently with the steroid medication. Surgery is required for perforation, severe bleeding, or failure to improve after two to three weeks of intensive medical treatment. Psychotherapy is sometimes prescribed to provide emotional support and to treat depression if it is present.

Colitis is a highly variable condition. About three-fourths of the people who develop colitis have recurrences, with 10 to 15 years elapsing before the next attack. Others have chronic and unremitting symptoms over long periods of time. Most have periods of good health interspersed with intermittent symptoms. If the condition is properly treated, the prognosis is favorable.

M. A. NORFLEET

Collective Unconscious. In Jungian or analytical psychology the unconscious division of the psyche consists of two distinct domains or levels. One level is composed of a more or less superficial layer of repressed and/or forgotten contents that have been derived from personal experience. This part of the personality is referred to as the personal unconscious. The other domain of the unconscious is a much deeper layer that does not derive from personal experience and is not a personal acquisition but is inborn or inherited. This domain of the psyche is known as the collective unconscious and owes its existence totally and exclusively to heredity.

The term *collective* expresses Jung's belief that, in contrast to the personal psyche that is individually acquired or developed, part of the unconscious has contents and modes of behavior that are nearly the same everywhere in all individuals. The collective unconscious can be viewed as being impersonal, supraindividual, and objective due to its belonging to all members of the human species.

While the personal unconscious is made up of complexes or feeling-toned trains of thought, the collective unconscious consists of archetypes. Archetypes are preexistent, inherited dispositions to apperceive typical or nearly universal situations and figures.

They are not inherited ideas but a priori possibilities phylogenetically transmitted from one generation to the next. Archetypes are not determined innately in terms of specific contents but only in regard to their form. The archetype itself is empty and purely formal, only a possibility of representation in consciousness. These preexistent forms lie deeply in the unconscious and require cultural influence to activate and symbolically structure or clothe them in order to attain conscious reality. There are as many archetypes as there are typical situations in life, and when a situation occurs that corresponds to a given archetype, that archetype becomes activated and takes color from the individual consciousness in which it appears. Thus the contents of an archetype develop from being filled out with the material of conscious experiences.

Archetypes can be seen from two points of view. On the one hand they are predispositions to have certain experiences. This suggests the notion of potential without any concrete or measurable existence. On the other hand archetypes may be considered as idea-forms that can become a part of actual experience. These two perspectives complement each other, since an individual cannot have experience without the preexisting potential for such. For example, the mother archetype requires an experience of a mother in order to take definite shape; but at the same time there must be the innate potential to have this experience.

The collective unconscious, with its storehouse of archetypes, contains the building forms and blueprint for the entire personality and the whole of life. As the archetypes for the ego—persona, shadow, anima/animus, self—become activated, symbolized, and actualized, the person matures and moves toward the individuated state.

The philosophical roots of archetypes can be detected in such sources as Plato's conception of the universal Idea as supraordinate and preexistent to all phenomena and Immanuel Kant's categories of meaning. From a theological perspective Irenaeus, a leader in the early years of Christianity, alluded to archetypes in his belief that the Creator of the world fashioned things according to preexisting patterns or archetypes. This theme is seen in God's giving instructions to Moses concerning the construction of the tabernacle according to an already existing pattern (Exod. 25; Heb. 8:1–5).

Additional Readings

Jung, C. G. (1954–1991). *The collected works of C. G. Jung.* (22 vols.). Princeton, NJ: Princeton University Press.

Jung, C. G. (1959). *The archetypes and the collective unconscious.* New York: Pantheon.

Jung, C. G. (1964). *Man and his symbols.* Garden City, NY: Doubleday.

D. SMITH

See ANALYTICAL PSYCHOLOGY; JUNG, CARL GUSTAV.

Colorblindness. Colorblindness, or color deficiency, refers to any condition in which a person has difficulty distinguishing colors. Most forms of color deficiency are hereditary and involve the cones in the retina of the eye. Cones are receptors that transduce light energy into neural activity, thus preserving information about wavelength, which is necessary for color perception. Three categories of cones register different wavelength ranges: long (perceived as red), medium (green), and short (blue). Combinations of activity across the three cone types permit the perception of the whole spectrum of colors.

Monochromatism is a rare condition in which there are no functioning cones. Monochromats can perceive only shades of gray and thus are truly colorblind. They also have poor visual acuity and are sensitive to strong light.

Dichromats have only two functioning categories of cones instead of three. Dichromatism is a recessive trait inherited through a gene on the X chromosome. Therefore it is more common in males, who have only one X chromosome, than in females, who have two. There are three forms of dichromatism, each corresponding to loss of one type of cone. Protanopia involves insensitivity to long wavelengths of light, causing inability to distinguish reds. Protanopes see only blues and yellows. Deuteranopes are insensitive to medium wavelengths of light, causing inability to perceive greens. Like protanopes, they perceive only blues and yellows. Both protanopia and deuteranopia occur in about 1% of males and 0.01 to 0.02% of females. Tritanopia involves the loss of the short-wavelength cones and is very rare. Tritanopes perceive the world in bluish-greens and reds.

Other forms of color deficiency are more subtle and complex, such as anomalous trichromatism. Another example is achromatopsia, which involves the inability to perceive color due to malfunctions in the brain. Achromatopsia can be inherited or acquired through injury, inflammation, or disease. The existence of achromatopsia reveals that color is processed in the brain, not the eyes, and that color perception occurs through mechanisms separate from those that produce the perception of shade, contour, and movement.

While color deficiencies are not considered debilitating, there are many situations in which color distinctions are important. Tasks such as choosing clothing, identifying traffic signals, or reading colored text often require normal color vision. Psychologists are just beginning to explore the cognitive and social-emotional implications of color deficiencies.

H. LOOY

See SENSATION AND PERCEPTION.

Commitment. The avowed or inferred binding dedication to a relationship based on a willful promise. Commitment is maintained by a moral obligation to loyally persist in spite of obstacles, costs, or alternative possibilities. Whether in love, friendship, marriage, work, career, moral life, or religion, commitment is a profoundly important human activity. While it is certainly related to love, it is not the same as love.

Commitment may stem from internal factors, such as feelings of respect, affection, and liking. It may stem from shared interests, mutual obligations and responsibilities or religious convictions. Or it may stem from such external factors as family expectations, pressure from friends, social considerations, or business or financial interests and concerns. From a religious point of view commitment is viewed as the most important aspect of a marriage. Christian orthodoxy, for example, finds that duty or obligation must be regarded as more important than emotional ties (Bellah, Madsen, Sullivan, Swindler, & Tipton, 1985).

Commitment, regardless of its motivational source, serves as a stabilizing influence in a relationship, and its quality is measured in terms of three basic standards. Duration refers to how long a person is willing to give unreserved love and support to another. Time span, however, has little to do with the quality of a relationship, which is also important to commitment. This is measured in the second stabilizing influence, intensity. This refers to the strength of feeling and depth of concern for the partner. Just as enduring relationships may be shallow, brief encounters may be intense, so this quality too is not enough. Priority must also be a part of commitment. This is the extent to which the relationship takes precedence over other matters. In essence commitment is measured by the value placed on the relationship and the willingness to take the responsibility for maintaining it.

Like braids of a rope, duration, intensity, and priority combine to hold a relationship together. In a two-month longitudinal study of dating couples, the commitment they expressed at the beginning of the study was the best single predictor of whether they were together at the end of the study (Hendrick, Hendrick, & Adler, 1988). Commitment was a better predictor of endurance of the relationship than either investments made in the relationship or satisfaction with the relationship. However, for those couples who increase their commitment to their spouse, there is generally a greater number of expressions of love and fewer marital problems.

Research has revealed that persons frequently maintain their commitment to a marriage by devaluing potential alternative partners. It has been shown, for example, that compared to individuals who left a marriage, persons who stayed in a relationship evaluated alternative partners more negatively, were less attracted to alternatives than less committed persons, and did not base their commitment solely on satisfaction with the current relationship. The absence of perceived alternatives strengthens commitment.

Closely linked with commitment is the concept of investment, derived from exchange notions. Investments can be emotional or material or may involve the sheer quantity of time put into a relationship. Investments are important to commitment because a greater investment size increases the likely success of a commitment. Both the absence of perceived alternatives and a relatively consistent increase in investments strengthen individual commitment. However, even a strong individual commitment is not enough to guarantee the longevity of a relationship. For commitment to last, it must be mutual.

Partners in a relationship often are not equally committed to building the relationship. Waller (1951) refers to this as "the principle of least interest," pointing out that the person with the least interest in the relationship is more likely to exploit the other. The person with the least commitment may dictate and manipulate the development of the relationship because he or she will not be so badly hurt if the relationship ends. This unequal commitment poses a trap for the unwary who venture into intimate relationships. But having just roughly equal degrees of commitment is not enough. Relationships require a high degree of commitment from each partner; otherwise neither person is likely to devote the time and effort needed to sustain the relationship.

References

Bellah, R., Madsen, R., Sullivan, W. M., Swindler, A., & Tipton, S. M. (1985). *Habits of the heart: Individualism and commitment in American life.* Berkeley: University of California Press.

Hendrick, S. S., Hendrick, C., & Adler, N. L. (1988). Romantic relationships: Love, satisfaction, and staying together. *Journal of Personality and Social Psychology, 54,* 980–988.

Waller, W. (1951). *The family: A dynamic interpretation.* New York: Dryden.

L. Parrott III

See Cognitive Dissonance; Dogmatism.

Communication. Communication is behavior designed to exchange meaning between organisms. Language is likely the loveliest dimension of human nature, indeed, of all communicating organisms, but it is also complicated. Through language humans can hurt but also heal, manipulate but share the meaning of life, express sickness and sin but also praise God and share the consolation of the gospel. A person's ability to share with another person genuine sensations and insights regarding the meaning of things surely is the epitome of God's image reflected in our humanness. Language is the channel of communication and may take the form of verbal or nonverbal expression (*see* Communication, Nonverbal). Verbal language has two forms: oral-aural (speech) symbols and pictographic (written) symbols. Both allow communication because they have culturally agreed-upon meaning. The science that studies the process by which meaning is turned into symbols or symbolic behavior for communicating that meaning to another is called semiotics.

Language is useful because it allows us to communicate a broad range of experience and ideas that may be profound and complex. Through language the communicator is able to create in the receiver a cognitive and emotive experience like that which the communicator experiences (Hayakawa, 1949). The communicator or sender of the message experiences a subconscious affective sensation that he or she wishes to incite in the receiver. There is considerable question whether the communicator transfers to the receiver a "package of meaning" through the channel of language or whether, as Kant thought, the meaning percept is already latently present in the receiver and is stimulated into experience by the impact of the language upon the receiver (Keltner, 1969).

The communication process is structured in terms of the dynamics of who says what to whom, in what channel, and with what effect. In that process numerous elements function in an interactive manner (Ellens, 1979, 1987, 1990; see also Ross, 1974). Within the sender the emotive need is sensed. The psyche progressively raises that sensation as a notion or a budding thought to the conscious level and shifts it into the cognitive arena. The cognitive function of the person evaluates the need sensation and the idea it generates, beginning the process of conceptualizing a formal concept. The concept is then shaped into a thought construct that in the mind may be either pictorially or linguistically conceptualized, depending in part upon whether the person is right- or left-hemisphere dominant. In its verbal expression as well, the message may be formulated in either pictorial or oral-aural (visual or vocal) form. The concept is loaded onto a sentence as freight is loaded onto a sequence of train cars. That sentence may be formulated and expressed in either written (visual, pictorial) or spoken (vocal, oral-aural) form. That sentence must carry to the receiver the meaning freight of the sender's affective sensation and cognitive message. The formal thought is encoded in language and ready for expression. The encoded percept is broadcast in the language channel to the receiver. That person's receptor grasps the signal, decodes the symbology of the language, interprets the cognitive material, and registers it in the psyche.

In this total process a number of subprocesses are functioning. As the sender is sensing, encoding, and broadcasting the message, he or she is also experiencing an intrinsic feedback loop by which each stage of the sender's experience is being internally evaluated. This evaluation is influenced by previously stored memory, rational reflection, learned defenses, and the monitoring that the superego and frontal lobes bring to bear upon the matter. Moreover, as the broadcasting of the message is in process, an extrinsic feedback loop is also functioning by which the sender is evaluating the setting and responses of the receiver and the communications environment and is modifying the message accordingly. The same may be said conversely about the receiver.

The communication process is never free from distraction. This is referred to as static. Static may be generated by incongruence between the sender's verbal and nonverbal language (see Communication, Nonverbal), offensive elements in the language, noise or uncongenial activities in the environment, or negative behavior on the part of the receiver. Static is usually an activity or a condition that emotionally overloads some aspect of the communication process. This aspect then attracts all the attention and takes energy away from the main message. If a preacher used scatological language in a sermon, the congregation would remember the scatology rather than the sermon. This is because the scatology would incite emotions of great intensity that would absorb all the energy and attention that should be concentrated on the sermon. Thus the scatology is static in the communication system and obstructs communication.

It is evident therefore that at numerous junctures in any communication process, breakdown can occur. It may occur in the sender or the receiver at each of the points of perception transition: the sender may not be able to raise the unconscious sensation to the conscious level, or translate the conscious percept into a formal concept or the concept into a thought and the thought into a sentence to be broadcast to the receiver; the sender and receiver may speak different languages and thus communicate in incompatible channels; or the receiver may experience dysfunction at each of those same junctures in the decoding and digesting process. Our cultures are filled with jargon and are vocationally and therefore linguistically tribalized. Few of us "speak the same language" as those around us. In such a situation sender and receiver have different, tribalized, communication channels and cannot therefore communicate as easily as we pretend or assume.

Finally, it is clear from this understanding of communication theory and operations, for example, why the first chapter of the epistle to the Hebrews emphasizes the importance of God's shift in history from speaking to humanity in the sermons of the prophets to God's incarnate visit in the person of Jesus of Nazareth. Dialogic communication is more effective than monologic. Therefore, a visit is better than a lecture (Wheelwright, 1954; see also Berry, 1985; Buber, 1955, 1958). Also, a combined and coherent verbal and nonverbal communication is more efficient than an exclusively verbal one. This is evident in Jesus' teaching being combined with ministries of healing. Thirdly, the communication mission of the believing community is to incarnate the gospel in word and deed, since that heals humans most effectively and enlightens them best (Ellens, 1970a, 1970b, 1973, 1974a, 1974b; see also Wheelwright, 1962).

References

Berry, D. L. (1985). *Mutuality, the vision of Martin Buber*. Albany: State University of New York.

Buber, M. (1955). *Between man and man*. Boston: Beacon.

Buber, M. (1958). *I and thou*. New York: Scribners.

Ellens, J. H. (1970a). Communication as healing. *The Reformed Journal, 20* (7), 9ff.

Ellens, J. H. (1970b). Creative worship. *Proceedings of the Seventeenth Annual Convention, Christian Association for Psychological Studies*, 37–44.

Ellens, J. H. (1973). Psychological dynamics of worship. *Journal of Psychology and Theology, 1* (4), 10–19.

Ellens, J. H. (1974a). A theology of communication: Putting the question. *Journal of Psychology and Theology, 2* (2), 132–139.

Ellens, J. H. (1974b). Preaching and worship. *Federation Messenger, 45* (1), 5ff.

Ellens, J. H. (1979). The psychodynamics of mass communication. *Journal of Psychology and Theology, 7* (3), 192–201.

Ellens, J. H. (1987). *Psychotheology: Key issues*. Pretoria: UNISA.

Ellens, J. H. (1990). Communication. In R. Hunter (Ed.), *Dictionary of pastoral care and counseling*. Nashville, TN: Abingdon.

Hayakawa, S. I. (1949). *Language in thought and action*. New York: Harcourt, Brace.

Keltner, J. W. (1969). *Interpersonal speech communication*. Belmont, CA: Wadsworth.

Ross, R. S. (1974). *Persuasion*. Englewood Cliffs, NJ: Prentice-Hall.

Wheelwright, P. E. (1954). *The burning fountain*. Bloomington: Indiana University Press.

Wheelwright, P. E. (1962). *Metaphor and reality*. Bloomington: Indiana University Press.

J. H. ELLENS

See FAMILY COMMUNICATIONS THEORY.

Communication, Nonverbal. Nonverbal communication is symbolic nonverbal behavior designed to exchange meaning between organisms. Much of what is said of verbal communication (see Communication), both regarding theory and operations, applies as well to nonverbal communication. Nonverbal language involves symbolic expressions that may or may not be accompanied by verbal language. Nonverbal language, frequently referred to as body language (see Body Language), includes posture, facial expression, limb movements, dress, proximity to others, orientation toward another person, nonverbal sounds, and other symbolic behaviors (Ellens, 1990; see also Lowen, 1972, 1973). Nonverbal language can express meaning, attitude, feeling, and intent. Usually our nonverbal language reinforces what we are communicating verbally; however, our physical expressions may contrast with what we are saying and belie a deeper truth about our true feelings or thoughts that is being edited out of our verbal language because we wish to give our hearer a different impression than our real perceptions or because we do not wish to convey our real feelings, attitude, or judgment.

Nonverbal language elements, such as gestures, posture, and dress, work as tools for the exchange of meaning just as words do in spoken or written verbal language. Some of these symbolic elements seem to be inherently human and thus cross-cultural and universal. These include symbolic behavior such as crying when expressing grief or smiling when expressing joy. Other nonverbal language elements seem to be learned, and these function for us because a given culture has achieved a general agreement about what their meanings are. The meaning of shaking hands, kissing upon greeting one another, rubbing noses, or shaking one's head is culture-specific, a learned language, and not universal or inherently human. But much of our nonverbal human language we have in common with a number of the other higher mammals.

In every verbal communication process nonverbal communication is also at work, if only in the tone of one's voice, the volume and pitch of one's expression, or the style of one's handwriting. The most obvious way in which nonverbal communication is taking place in such a setting is in the activation of the internal and external feedback loops that help us modulate our communication. The internal feedback loop takes place within our minds and psyches as we process our feelings and ideas, namely, our potential message, through our memory bank, our evaluation system, and our moral reasoning and reflection (see Communication). The external feedback loop projects from our minds to take in our exterior environment and evaluates the conditions out there for the expression and reception of our message. There is general agreement among communication scientists and psychologists that nonverbal communication is a more direct expression of the feeling world of the sender than is his or her verbal communication.

There are good reasons for this. In the employment of verbal communication an unconscious sensation in the affective field is raised to the conscious level, turned into a cognitive construct, and translated into verbal language. During this process both the internal and external feedback loops are activated. This causes us to adapt our verbal message, as it finally gets expressed, so that it fits the perceived situation in the external environment, such as the attitude of those to whom we are going to communicate. Similarly, we adapt our verbal expression to the perceived situation evidenced by the internal feedback loop as it reflects our memory and judgment regarding previous similar communication needs and situations. In our expressions of nonverbal communication there is far less of this pre-editing, self-reflective, and analytic process going on. Our body language usually reflects our affective states, feelings, and at-

titudes directly from our unconscious world without adaptation by our conscious reflection. Thus in nonverbal communication, we do not so extensively edit our feeling needs, states, and expressions in terms of rational evaluation of the data produced by our internal and external feedback loops as we do in the highly reflective process of verbal communication. So nonverbal language seems to be a more direct expression of the needs and notions of the unconscious mind than is verbal language, forging a more direct link between psyche, symbolic encoding, and expression. However, since some nonverbal language is culturally conditioned and therefore learned, there must also be a cognitive element in the process linking sensation to some symbolic encoding and its nonverbal expression.

This characteristic of nonverbal communication, as direct and relatively unedited spontaneous expression of the unconscious, subconscious, and conscious affective world reinforces the idea that communication is less the conveyance of a package of information from the sender to the receiver and more a symbolic behavior that incites or awakens in the receiver information already latent in him or her, requiring only the stimulation of the sender's symbol, nonverbal or verbal, to bring it to life.

Because nonverbal communication is less consciously edited and hence less contrived and because its semiotic value depends upon symbolic behavior rather than rational, verbal explanation, it almost inevitably lacks some of the cognitive level precision of expression that humans are able to achieve in verbal communication. Conversely, the psychological impact of nonverbal behavior is frequently significantly more powerful than that of verbal communication because, whether it is precisely understood or not, it incites in the receiver an immediate and direct affective level response that is usually commensurate in size and force with the expression of the sender (DeVito, 1970). There is a danger at the heart of this fact. Nonverbal communication is usually psychologically forceful, even when it is subtly expressed. Thus when it communicates imprecisely it may convey to the receiver quite a different message than that intended, even unconsciously, by the sender. At the same time, as it incites a response of equivalent force from the receiver, the impact of the misunderstanding expands exponentially, rather than merely arithmetically, in action and reaction. More family distress, marital crises, and international wars result from this phenomenon than from any other matter in human affairs.

References

DeVito, J. A. (1970). *The psychology of speech and language: An introduction to psycholinguistics.* New York: Random House.

Ellens, J. H. (1990). Communication. In R. Hunter (Ed.), *Dictionary of pastoral care and counseling.* Nashville, TN: Abingdon.

Lowen, A. (1972). *The betrayal of the body*. New York: Macmillan, Collier Books.

Lowen, A. (1973). *The language of the body*. New York: Macmillan, Collier Books.

J. H. ELLENS

See FAMILY COMMUNICATIONS THEORY.

Communication Disorders. Communication disorders include problems with expressive language (conveying meaning through speaking or sign language), receptive language (understanding words or sentences), phonology (producing appropriate speech sounds), and fluency (stuttering). *DSM-IV* (American Psychiatric Association, 1994) classifies disorders of reading and writing as learning disorders.

In communication disorders the problems are more severe than can be explained by mental retardation, sensory deficit (e.g., hearing difficulty), disorder of the muscles of speech, or environmental deprivation (e.g., extreme poverty or being shut away from interaction with other people). Clinicians should also diagnose cautiously if children are from bilingual homes, as the necessity of searching through two sets of vocabulary may produce their apparent slowness. Following *DSM-IV*, communication disorders are diagnosed when the problems interfere with social communication or achievement in job or school.

Most communication disorders are developmental, appearing during early childhood or adolescence. Some are acquired following a period of normal development, due to damage to the brain. Acquired communication disorders may occur at any age. Although *DSM-IV* focuses on children's communication disorders, researchers often use the term to describe communication problems acquired in adulthood.

People with expressive language disorder score more poorly on standardized tests of ability to express themselves in a language than they do on nonverbal intelligence tests or tests of understanding language. They show symptoms in three additional areas: poverty of speech, such as limited vocabulary, difficulty learning or finding words, and use of short, simple sentences; grammatical anomalies, such as deleting small words or parts of sentences and odd sequencing of words; and slow language development. Children with expressive language disorder seem willing, even eager, to use language effectively, but their efforts are frustrated. Even when they learn new words, they then forget words they previously knew.

Some children with expressive language disorder demonstrate cluttering. They speak extremely rapidly but neither fluently nor accurately, and it is difficult to impossible to understand what they are saying.

The developmental form of expressive language disorder affects between 3% and 5% of children. Boys are more likely to have the disorder than girls.

Children who have family members with any of the communication or learning disorders have a higher risk of developing expressive language problems. About half of children with this disorder completely recover by late adolescence, and most of the rest improve to the point that they can function normally.

Children with expressive language disorder do not appear to have problems understanding what others say to them. Children who do have difficulty understanding will also have difficulty expressing themselves and may be diagnosed with mixed receptive-expressive language disorder. They have difficulties understanding sentences, words, or specific types of words. This receptive problem may appear only in careful testing, or it may show up as confusion, lack of attention, failing to follow directions, not taking turns in conversation, or difficulty staying on a topic.

Mixed receptive-expressive language disorder is less common than the expressive type, and it is more common in boys and in relatives of people with the disorder. Many children will recover by late adolescence, but a significant proportion experience lifelong difficulties.

Children with either of these language disorders will have difficulty in school, and they may be diagnosed with a learning disorder.

The causes of developmental language disorders are not known. Since many people with developmental language disorders also have EEG abnormalities or anomalies of brain structure (found in CAT scans or postmortem examinations) and since the disorders tend to occur in families, the problem may arise from biological differences in the brain. Brain damage is clearly the cause of most forms of acquired language disorders.

Children with a pervasive developmental disorder, such as autistic disorder, may have the symptoms of a language disorder. Because they have additional symptoms, however, they should be diagnosed only with the pervasive developmental disorder.

The usual treatment provides specialized education to address the language difficulties. Since some children with language problems are socially isolated, supportive counseling may be necessary to strengthen their self-esteem and teach ways to connect with peers.

Phonological disorder, formerly known as developmental articulation disorder, is characterized by problems in making and discriminating speech sounds. Sounds may be made incorrectly, left out entirely, or used in the wrong place. The difficulty may interfere with the child's ability to understand differences between words.

Some children with this disorder speak reasonably clearly, while others cannot be understood. The most common symptom is lisping, followed by difficulty pronouncing the sounds *l, r, s, z, th*, and *ch*. People with the disorder may use correct sounds but in the wrong order. Incorrect order of sounds may change the word to a different word or may produce humorous or incomprehensible nonwords.

Specific causes, such as hearing impairment, cleft palate, or cerebral palsy explain only a minority of cases of phonological disorder. Between 2% and 3% of children may have phonological difficulties. It is more common in boys and in some forms follows a family pattern. Clinicians should not diagnose phonological disorder, however, when dialect produces unusual speech sounds.

Children with mild forms of phonological disorder may recover, without treatment, by age eight. Speech therapy is completely effective in almost all cases.

Stuttering is a disturbance of fluency and timing of speech. People with this disorder may repeat or prolong speech sounds, pause either within a word or while trying to say a word, or insert unrelated words into a sentence. They are keenly aware of their difficulty and may use circumlocutions (substituting phrases for difficult words). They may coach themselves aloud, commenting on the difficulty they are having and suggesting coping tactics.

Since stuttering is more severe in stressful situations, people with this disorder may avoid public speaking, job interviews, or telephones. Many people who stutter, however, have no difficulty when singing, reading aloud, or talking to pets.

Nearly all people who stutter begin symptoms before age 10. The symptoms develop gradually, in episodes, and vary in degree. As children become aware that they have a problem, anxiety may make the symptoms worse. However, most will develop tactics to deal with the symptoms, and up to 60% recover without treatment. An additional 20% will recover with treatment, typically by age 16. Stuttering is usually chronic for those who do not recover before adulthood.

Fewer than 1% of children and adolescents stutter, but 75% of them are boys. The gender ratio and the fact that stuttering is more common in relatives of people with a language disorder suggest a genetic cause. Some researchers have proposed that a delay in auditory information processing contributes to stuttering by disrupting the synchronization between what the person says and hears. Hearing one's words slightly after they are spoken, instead of at the same time, may cause just enough confusion to produce stuttering.

Communication disorders acquired in adulthood are usually due to brain damage from strokes, injury, or poisoning. Many of them, such as Broca's aphasia and global aphasia, fit well into *DSM-IV* as expressive language disorders. Others, such as Wernicke's aphasia and pure word deafness, show comprehension difficulties (receptive problems) but fluent speech. *DSM-IV* does not have a category for language disorders that affect comprehension but not expression.

Researchers include another set of acquired problems under the heading of communication disorders: emotional communication disorders. Communication of emotion involves both understanding and expression. It is done not with words but with facial expression, tone of voice, posture, and gesture.

Disruption of emotional expression by damage to the right hemisphere of the brain may produce indifferent or euphoric emotional expressions. Patients with damage to the left hemisphere, however, may convey appropriate sadness and despair about their problem. Damage to the right hemisphere impairs comprehension of emotion conveyed in tone of voice or facial expression. However, some patients are able to express emotion but not comprehend emotional cues, while others can comprehend cues but not express emotion.

Reference

American Psychiatric Association. (1994). *Diagnostic and statistical manual of mental disorders* (4th ed.). Washington, DC: Author.

P. D. YOUNG

Communication Skills Training. Programs that teach people skills for communicating with each other have become a conspicuous part of popular applied psychology. These programs usually are directed toward married or engaged couples, parents, teachers, employers, managers, or lay and professional counselors. Two conspicuous training programs with widely publicized textbooks typify the field. One is Parent Effectiveness Training (Gordon, 1970), with its offshoots for teachers and for leaders in business and government. The other is the Couples Communication Program (Miller, Nunnally, & Wackman, 1979).

Parent Effectiveness Training rests on the cornerstone of emphatic listening skills Gordon learned from his mentor, Carl Rogers. The Rogerian imprint shows throughout the communication training literature, including that for counselors (Carkhuff, 1969) and for encounter group participants (Egan, 1973).

The format for a Parent Effectiveness Training course includes ten weekly sessions two or three hours long for up to a dozen persons. The instructor follows a course outline replete with exercises for the class members to use in role playing problem situations. The pinnacle skill is active listening. That means I as receiver say back to you, the sender, in my own words what I sense you have just communicated to me in your words and nonverbal feeling tone. When your behavior bothers me, I use the second skill: confrontation. This involves what are called "I-messages," so named because they start with the nonjudgmental self-disclosure of "I," rather than the critic's rapier "you."

Parent Effectiveness Training emphasizes hearing the messages of a partner or child who is not necessarily committed to the communication process. By contrast, the Couples Communication Program stresses telling one's messages to a cooperating partner (e.g., spouse) so as to help that partner understand one. The approach places heavy emphasis on self-disclosure and on the distinction between content and process (i.e., what we say and how we say it). Instructors typically lead groups of about four couples in four weekly three-hour sessions. The couples practice skills in front of the group, using actual issues between them. The leader keeps the emphasis on learning the skill rather than on solving particular problems.

Marriage enrichment programs of many kinds also emphasize communication skills. Like the other training programs, they do not rehabilitate the sick but aim to make good relationships better. The prototype is Marriage Encounter, which is conducted in an intense weekend experience using written dialogues between spouses. This technique controls the flow of words, so that eye contact and voice tones do not intimidate shy partners or inflame conflictual ones.

Although research on the effectiveness of these programs is minimal, typically participants look back on the training sessions as rich experiences. But they quickly apologize for not having followed through as diligently as they intended. They generally seem to approach everyday situations with the confidence of knowing they can draw on the skills they have filed away if problems arise. Trained couples committed to not separating or divorcing return to carefully using the structures they learned as a kind of portable referee when things get sticky between them The key ingredient in the effectiveness of these programs is not the skill but the will to use the skill.

References

Carkhuff, R. R. (1969). *Helping and human relations* (Vols. 1 & 2). New York: Holt, Rinehart.

Egan, G. *Face to face.* (1973). Monterey, CA: Brooks/Cole.

Gordon, T. (1970). *Parent effectiveness training.* New York: Wyden.

Miller, S., Nunnally, E. W., & Wackman, D. B. (1975). Minneapolis: Interpersonal Communication Programs.

D. L. Gibson

See Marriage Enrichment; Parent Training Programs.

Community Mental Health. A public service delivery system providing a variety of services to persons with diagnosable mental illnesses or at risk for the development of psychological problems. About 20% of mental health services in the United States have been estimated to be provided by this system (Freedman, 1990). Emerging in the 1960s, community mental health represented an innovation in mental health services. The unique character of community mental health as it was originally conceived is best understood in the context of the evolving conceptualization and treatment of the mentally ill in the United States.

Community mental health and community psychology were nearly synonymous in their early histories. This has become less the case as community mental health took shape as a service delivery system struggling with stringent political and fiscal realities and community psychology developed as an important academic and applied discipline.

Historical Origins of Community Mental Health. During the colonial period mental illness was understood as possession by the devil or the result of excessive bile in the system. Prayers, threats, and punishment or blood-letting, purging, and blistering constituted most of the available treatment. Persons displaying unusual behaviors were kept locked at home, jailed, or put in almshouses.

By the eighteenth and nineteenth centuries conceptualizations of illness were changing, and the hospital emerged as the primary psychiatric service available for the mentally ill. These asylums were viewed by many with zealous optimism for their potential to cure psychopathology. The Quakers were influential developers of treatment during this period, founding one of the earliest institutions exclusively for the mentally ill. Services were based on the principles of moral treatment articulated by William Tuke in England.

Although some mentally ill persons still languished in jails or other nontreatment institutions during this time, growth in the number of asylum residents increased steadily. Eventually the intractability of illnesses plaguing many of these residents became more apparent and previous hopes for wholesale cures withered. Overcrowding, limitations in treatment, and abuse of patients led to advocacy efforts and subsequent reforms in policies and practices. Some new service delivery models emerged, such as the first outpatient hospital.

A large variety of societal influences converged in the twentieth century to enable the emergence of the community mental health system. The mental hygiene movement of the late nineteenth and early twentieth centuries reflected a growing belief in the role of environment and early childhood experience on the development and treatment of mental illness. The advent of new medical technologies such as electroconvulsive shock therapy and psychotropic medications like Elavil and Thorazine increased psychiatrists' effectiveness in treating chronic mental illnesses. Public concern over the scope of mental health problems in the United States shot up as higher than expected numbers of mental disorders were identified during screening for military service in World War II and as psychological casualties returned from that war. The ideals embodied by humanism, the emerging philosophy of the midcentury, set an atmosphere of optimism and an increasing priority on respect for personal rights and human dignity, especially for groups thought to be particularly vulnerable.

Community Mental Health's Beginnings. By the mid-1950s Congress had established a Joint

Commission on Mental Illness and Health. The commission studied a wide variety of issues such as the scope of mental illnesses, availability of treatment, public attitudes, and future direction for services. In 1963 President John F. Kennedy revealed a new agenda for the nation's mental health care system. The Community Mental Health Centers Construction Act passed later that year.

This act outlined a plan for communities to be divided into catchment areas for the purpose of delivering comprehensive, federally funded mental health services. More than two thousand of these centers were originally envisioned. Each catchment area would devise its own plan for services based on an individualized assessment of needs within the communities. Contrary to the state hospital approach, centers were to coordinate services from a variety of agencies to offer inpatient, outpatient, and partial hospitalization services, 24-hour emergency services, and community education.

In contrast to the traditional psychiatric model, services were to reflect an underlying philosophy of comprehensiveness, coordination, and continuity of care. Accessibility of services was to be paramount in order that persons with mental illness could be cared for within their own communities. Center governance was designed to include community members on the boards, reflecting the desire to empower neighborhood citizens by encouraging community responsibility and authority. Finally, the centers were charged to help prevent the incidence and severity of mental health problems in the community. Toward this end the community education was meant to extend services to less severely affected clients and those who might not otherwise seek treatment through one of the centers.

By 1980 only about seven hundred community mental health centers were in existence. Not only had the number of catchment centers fallen short of the original goal, but also certain groups such as rural dwellers, minorities, migrant workers, and the elderly were not being adequately served under existing federal funding levels. Despite these realities government funding declined and more cuts loomed. The Reagan administration drastically reduced federal funds for mental health services and transferred allocations to states via block grants. Pressure in the states to reduce tax expenditures and support other demanded services contributed to the failure of many communities to provide full mental health services to their citizenry.

Shore (1992) argues that the failure of the community mental health movement to produce a comprehensive service delivery system with well-established treatment effectiveness is due more to the lack of commitment to funding than a lack of commitment within the field or limitations in the model itself. Declines in funding and public support and drastic changes in the health care system have exerted considerable pressure on community mental health centers to increase caseloads and

shift their focus and strategies of service delivery to those who can pay.

Recent Developments. In spite of these trends a number of developments in the delivery of community mental health services are worth noting. Models of psychosocial rehabilitation such as assertive community treatment are expanding drop-in center and traditional casework approaches to include practical living skills training that occurs in the client's natural environment. Vocational rehabilitation efforts, which were successful in placing mentally ill individuals in jobs, have evolved to include on-site job training designed to promote long-term job retention. Creative relationships between hospitals and community-based programs have been identified in which some hospitals have adopted community mental health methods to reach out to the neighborhoods around them with new programs (Stein, 1992).

At the level of clinical services, increasing appreciation for the importance of culture has built. This trend has contributed to some extent to an examination of the overdiagnosis of psychopathology in minority groups, the effect of like- versus unlike-race practitioners on clients, and problems in the goodness of fit of assessment and treatment methods for culturally unique populations. One resulting innovation has been the incorporation into treatment of culturally indigenous modes of healing such as storytelling and the use of traditional rituals and folk healers.

Outside the more traditional community mental health delivery system, the National Institute of Mental Health (NIMH) has sponsored a number of initiatives designed to strengthen public, community-based mental health services. Projects such as the Community Support Program and the Human Resource Development Program have been devoted to improving opportunities and services for clients, training professionals, and seeking to team the resources of academic institutions with community agencies (Wohlford, Myers, & Callan, 1993).

Money for prevention has not always been available through community mental health channels. However, significant advances in prevention have been made by community psychologists and researchers and practitioners in other fields. Promising programs that target a wide variety of problems such as delinquency or risk factors like poverty and divorce have been developed and evaluated.

One last development to be noted is the rise in influence of consumer movements concerned with mental health issues. One of these, the National Alliance for the Mentally Ill (NAMI), deserves special mention. NAMI is made up of family members of the mentally ill and persons with mental illness. They are joined by friends and professionals with the goals of providing support, education, and advocacy for this community. NAMI's influence has been felt on the national level, where it has helped to increase funding for research on mental illnesses and to influence how professionals are trained to work with these populations.

References

Freedman, A. M. (1990). Mental health programs in the United States: Idiosyncratic roots. *International Journal of Mental Health, 18* (3), 81–98.

Shore, M. F. (1992). Community mental health: Corpse or phoenix? Personal reflections on an era. *Professional Psychology: Research and Practice, 23* (4), 257–262.

Stein, L. I. (1992). *Innovative community mental health programs.* In H. R. Lamb (Series Ed.), *New Directions for Mental Health Services: No. 56.* San Francisco: Jossey-Bass.

Wohlford, P., Myers, H. F. & Callan, J. E. (1993). *Serving the seriously mentally ill: Public-academic linkages in services, research, and training.* Washington, DC: American Psychological Association.

Additional Reading

Dana, R. H. (1981). *Human services for cultural minorities.* Baltimore: University Park Press.

S. S. CANNING

Community Psychology. Community psychology grew in part out of the social reform movement of the 1960s and has emerged as an important voice in psychology. Many professionals are drawn to community psychology because it represents an alternative to traditional clinical psychology. The work of the community psychologist "is focused on improving community life for all citizens, in preventing disorder, and in promoting psychological well-being in the population" (Heller, Price, Reinharz, Riger, & Wandersman, 1984, p. 5). Toward this end community psychologists develop education and prevention programs, organize community members to effectively accomplish their goals, and attempt to conduct and disseminate research in a way that is relevant to all members of a community.

Historical Context and Philosophical Assumptions. Although the Swampscott Conference in May 1965 has been described as marking the beginning of community psychology, it will be helpful to look at a number of factors that facilitated its growth. According to Heller et al. (1984), the emergence of the community psychology perspective can be thought of in terms of dramatic changes in three domains: values, professional conceptualization, and research/practice.

First, the community psychology perspective emerged as part of the social reform movement of the 1960s. This movement promoted awareness of a number of social problems, including gender and racial discrimination and the state of the poor and homeless. As a result of this effort to highlight social concerns, a growing number of psychologists recognized that their work involves value choices. These choices often include whether or not psychologists advocate for change at the local and/or national level. In addition many psychologists began to question which problems a limited number of mental health professionals should focus upon, as well as which specific interventions should be employed to promote change.

A second way of thinking about the emergence of community psychology is to think of how it was "part of the conceptual reorientation occurring within clinical psychology" (Heller et al., 1984, p. 14). A number of factors led to this conceptual reorientation, including challenges to the psychoanalytic perspective (which emphasized intrapsychic psychopathology), challenges to the medical model of psychopathology (that emotional disturbances result from a disease, which must be treated by trained professionals), and increased use and demonstrated efficacy of psychotropic medications for the treatment of severe mental illnesses. In addition President John F. Kennedy helped to pass the Community Mental Health Centers Construction Act in 1963, which provided financial support to community centers developed to provide education and outpatient care to the mentally ill (*see* Community Mental Health). Although intended as alternatives to institutionalization, these centers would later be criticized by community psychologists for not being sufficiently different from treatment facilities operating from a clinical psychology perspective, as many services took the form of remedial care of the individual. The Swampscott Conference marked the beginning of many meetings of psychologists interested in promoting change within the field of psychology (in addition to social and political change), and in 1967 the American Psychological Association officially recognized Division 27 (Community Psychology). Interest in community psychology led to a conceptual shift away from treatment to prevention and away from a focus upon the individual to an ecological perspective related to how environment influences behavior.

A third facet is to see community psychology leading to new areas for research and practice. Heller et al. (1984) discuss this in the context of social policy decisions that can be affected by research. Community psychologists not only are challenged to become increasingly aware of social policy issues but also work to develop interventions that provide a strong scientific basis for change. This involvement in social policy and politics also requires community psychologists to be familiar with the reality of multiple political pressures that have an impact on community decision making. Community psychologists also are concerned about the relationship between research and action, so that interventions are based on informative evaluations based on the expressed needs of a community. Assessments from a community psychology perspective include variables such as personal and community resources, strengths and proficiencies, identification of the needs of a community, and alternative taxonomies to the *Diagnostic and Statistical Manual* (American Psychiatric Association, 1994).

Conceptual Distinctives. As has been suggested, a number of conceptual emphases distinguish community psychology from traditional clinical psychology. These include an emphasis on prevention, an ecological perspective, mechanisms for alternative service delivery, wellness, and collaborative partnerships.

Prevention. Community psychologists are concerned that remedial interventions are offered too late. In contrast to treating disorders, community psychologists argue for preventing individuals or communities from developing a problem. Community psychologists distinguish among primary, secondary, and tertiary prevention. Primary prevention is designed to prevent a disorder from occurring, and those who implement such a program usually target all members of a community. One benefit of primary prevention is that all members of a group receive the intervention, which reduces the stigma often associated with mental health interventions. However, the drawback to this approach is that large-scale programs spend money on individuals in the community who do not need the intervention. Secondary prevention targets at-risk individuals. The benefit to secondary prevention is that it can be more cost-effective than primary prevention, as only those believed to be at risk will receive the intervention. Community psychologists are concerned, however, with the impact of labeling someone as at risk, as the social stigma can be great. Tertiary prevention is concerned to mitigate the impact of an existing disorder.

There are additional typologies of prevention. For example, some community psychologists refer to systems-centered, person-centered, and situation-centered prevention programs. Systems-centered prevention is designed to produce change at the systems level (e.g., school or neighborhood). Person-centered prevention targets key individuals who have an impact on others, such as parents or teachers. Situation-centered prevention is similar conceptually to secondary prevention because the psychologist identifies a situation that places people at risk and intervenes to change characteristics of the situation itself (e.g., addressing the stress associated with providing care to a family member with Alzheimer's disease).

Ecological Perspective. Community psychologists are concerned to take an ecological perspective, which involves assessing ways the environment influences the individual. Vincent and Trickett (1983) identify four basic ecological principles: interdependence, cycling of resources, succession, and adaptation. The concept of interdependence suggests that the social environment is a dynamic system, so that change in one part of the system will lead to change among the other parts of the system. Cycling of resources refers to ways in which a community defines, develops, utilizes, and distributes its resources. Community psychologists are concerned to identify the positive, potential use of resources already available in a community. Succession refers to predictable changes in the environment that are brought about by the community to establish stability. Succession also refers to important historical events that played a role in the development of the environment, as well as the various mechanisms that facilitate future change and development. The concept of adaptation means that any system seeks equilibrium. Broadly understood, adaptation includes not only how individuals adapt to their environment but also the characteristics of the environment that promote or constrain certain behaviors.

Alternative Service Delivery. Community psychologists have criticized ways in which psychologists have traditionally provided services. For example, Reissman (1990) argues against the clinical model, which he sees as individual psychotherapy emphasizing training, knowledge, specialization, and underlying "scientific" analysis. Reissman argues for a "prosumer" model characterized by self-help and peer counseling, a model that destigmatizes help receiving, empowers the help-receiver, and expands resources in a cost-effective manner. He argues that help is best received when all members of a group receive help (thereby reducing the stigma); those who receive help have control over the intervention; the help-receiver is a member of a self-help group; help is provided while training someone to become a helper; those who receive and provide help are similar (e.g., peer helping or group therapy); the situation is temporary; and providing and receiving help is a part of the overall spirit or philosophy of the system in which the help is provided.

Wellness. Wellness is a broad concept, and, according to Cohen (1991), it involves "having a sense of control over one's fate, a feeling of purpose and belongingness, and a basic satisfaction with oneself and one's existence" (p. 404). Cohen argues that professionals can promote wellness by addressing four different but related concepts: competence, resilience, social system modification, and empowerment. Competence "means doing well the things that a person's givens and life role suggest that she or he *should* be doing" (p. 406). Competency includes the strengths and skills necessary to respond to a given demand responsibly and effectively. Community psychologists argue that as psychologists identify existing competencies and promote their use, community members will be less vulnerable to problems later in life.

Resiliency refers to how some individuals under profound stress manage to adapt and succeed in life. Community psychologists are cautious not to equate adaptive behavior with emotional health, as many in a community may be able to function under stress but still experience depression or anxiety, for example. At the same time, because some people are apparently resilient to significant levels of stress, community psychologists are concerned to understand resiliency so they can promote it in others and so they can consider ways to utilize resilient individuals as treatment agents themselves.

In addition to identifying and shoring up qualities in individuals, the community psychologist is concerned with social systems modification, which refers to promoting change in social systems, especially those "in which people have significant interactions over long time periods" (Cohen, 1991, p. 407). Community psychologists are concerned to identify social systems that influence people and to initiate changes that allow for social settings to accomplish their goals while promoting wellness among community members.

Empowerment refers to finding ways to help people "to gain control over their lives, on the assumption that doing so will reduce problems in living and enhance wellness" (Cohen, 1991, p. 407). Broadly understood, empowerment involves efforts to increase others' choices and options, sense of control over their life, access to resources, self-efficacy, experiences of active participation, and ability to critique the status quo and express the critique constructively. Community psychologists also recognize that empowerment occurs within domains; one can feel empowered in certain domains and not others (e.g., at work but not at home, or as a parent but not as a spouse).

Collaborative Partnerships. Collaborative partnerships refer to citizen participation and collaborative relationships between people who bring different strengths and weaknesses to research and practice. On the one hand are community researchers who have the training to facilitate research, develop a needs assessment, carry out an intervention, and so on. On the other hand are those who bring resources such as community membership or gatekeeper status and who can identify needs, clarify goals, and facilitate change. From a community psychology perspective these individuals work together in a collaborative partnership to identify the needs in a community and to promote change at a level that is deemed satisfactory to all.

In addition to all of its conceptual distinctives, community psychology is also known for its respect for diversity, collaborative relationships with other disciplines (e.g., sociology, political science), and efforts to promote a sense of belonging in the community.

Critique. Those who take a community psychology perspective offer strong arguments for their position, including the gap between the availability of professional care and the demand for services. At the same time some professionals have raised concerns as to the accuracy of the claims of some community psychologists and have called for greater clarity concerning what professionals know and do not know about the efficacy and scope of primary prevention programs. In addition it may be argued that community psychology remains a loose collection of concepts and not a clearly defined theoretical approach.

However, community psychology has had an impact on emerging trends in psychology, including family systems models and other models that emphasize person-environment influences, the importance of removing constraints, and relational aspects of disorders. A community psychology perspective also cautions clinicians about the stigma attached to diagnoses. Furthermore, this perspective has probably had an impact on the science and practice of psychology to the extent that the profession has taken seriously the social and political realities within which people live.

Perhaps one of the greatest strengths of community psychology is its emphasis on the interdependence of persons in community and the related concern for responsibility to others. Such a perspective is consistent with a biblical view of community, responsibility, and justice. For example, the biblical vision of *shalom* refers to one's enjoyment of a right relationship to God, the world, others, and ourselves. As Wolterstorff (1983) reminds us, justice is an integral part of shalom because shalom is concerned to achieve an ethical community: "If individuals are not granted what is due them, if their claim on others is not acknowledged by those others, if others do not carry out their obligations to them, then shalom is wounded. . . . Shalom cannot be secured in an unjust situation by managing to get all concerned to feel content with their lot in life" (p. 71). A community psychology perspective reminds us of possible and actual injustices within systems, and the church may benefit from creative ways of incorporating a perspective that attempts to enhance well-being through its emphasis on strengthening competencies, promoting justice, and fostering a shared sense of community.

References

American Psychiatric Association. (1994). *Diagnostic and statistical manual of mental disorders* (4th ed.). Washington, DC: Author.

Cohen, E. (1991). In pursuit of wellness. *American Psychologist, 46* (4), 404–408.

Heller, K., Price, R., Reinharz, S., Riger, S., & Wandersman, A. (1984). *Psychology and community change: Challenges of the future* (2nd ed.). Pacific Grove, CA: Brooks/Cole.

Reissman, F. (1990). Restructuring help: A human services paradigm for the 1990s. *American Journal of Community Psychology, 18* (2), 221–230.

Vincent, T., & Trickett, E. (1983). Preventive interventions and the human context: Ecological approaches to environmental assessment and change. In R. Felner, L. Jason, J. Moritsugu, & S. Farber (Eds.), *Preventive psychology: Theory, research and practice.* New York: Pergamon.

Wolterstorff, N. (1983). *Until justice and peace embrace.* Grand Rapids, MI: Eerdmans.

M. A. YARHOUSE

See PREVENTION OF PSYCHOLOGICAL DISORDERS.

Comparative Psychology. In the nineteenth century two theories of evolution made important contributions to the development of comparative psychology. The first was the theory of Jean Baptiste de Lamark (1744–1829), a French naturalist who believed in the inheritance of acquired characteristics made during the lifetime of an animal. The second and more influential theory was that of Charles Darwin (1809–1882), the English naturalist who proposed natural selection as the mechanism whereby species differentiate. One result of Darwin's theory was that man was placed on a continuum of lower to higher organisms: a physiological, behavioral, and mental continuum.

Simple comparisons between human and animal capabilities go back to Aristotle, and an interest in animal mind was demonstrated by physiologists before evolutionary theory. Evolutionary theory, however, changed the type of questions that were asked by physiologists. Animal thinking per se was still a concern, but animals were also studied to identify relationships between various species as well as to reveal insights into human behavior and thinking. Consequently a genuine comparative psychology developed.

Using primarily an anecdotal method, Darwin's friend George Romanes (1848–1894) applied evolutionary theory to the study of behavior and mental capabilities. In *Animal Intelligence* (1883) Romanes studied the abilities of a number of species in an attempt to trace the evolution of the mind. C. Lloyd Morgan (1852–1936) objected to Romanes's projecting mental traits onto animals. In his *Introduction to Comparative Psychology* (1894), from which the field derived its name, Morgan formulated what has since been known as Morgan's canon, that is, inferences of animal thinking should be no more than is required to explain an animal's behavior.

In addition to the study of animal consciousness or mind, early comparative psychologists were also interested in animal learning. Not all psychologists who used animals as subjects were comparative psychologists, however. Many times animals were used for convenience, not to make truly comparative analyses among a variety of species thought to be related phylogenetically. As a result true comparisons were often neglected. Only a few species (e.g., rats and pigeons) were extensively studied by these animal psychologists and then in artificial laboratory settings. Also, the emphasis on learned behaviors meant that the study of instinctive behaviors was largely ignored. Thus the field of comparative psychology suffered as behavioral psychology, represented by Clark Leonard Hull, B. F. Skinner, and others prospered. In the mid-twentieth century, however, the work of ethologists such as Konrad Lorenz (1903–1989) and Niko Tinbergen (1907–1988) brought greater attention to the study of behavior in a naturalistic setting and increased interest in some of these previously neglected topics.

Comparative psychology today is closely tied to biology, especially the areas of behavioral genetics and ethology. Other areas of biology that influence comparative psychology are behavioral endocrinology, embryology, and sociobiology, the study of how social behaviors are controlled by genes.

Additional Reading

Hilgard, E. R. (1987). *Psychology in America: A historical survey.* New York: Harcourt Brace Jovanovich.

K. S. SEYBOLD

Competition. *See* ACHIEVEMENT, NEED FOR; COOPERATION AND COMPETITION.

Complex. A group of ideas or memories that are repressed but have a strong emotional charge. This term was first used extensively by Carl Gustav Jung, who called his approach "a psychology of complexes." In psychoanalytic thought the complex is always partially unconscious even though the content of the complex may be partially conscious. Nonpsychoanalytic writers sometimes use the term to refer to overemphasized ideas, without any implication of unconscious source.

Compliance. The art of getting someone to do a favor. Sometimes this process involves only a straightforward request. However, psychologists have become particularly interested in this process of making a request more powerful by adding subtle social pressures. Of these more manipulative techniques the majority fall into one of two categories: methods that rely on making multiple requests and methods that take advantage of our notions of fairness.

Of the multiple-request techniques the most common is probably the foot in the door. With this technique the request of real interest is preceded by a smaller and less costly request. For example, successful panhandlers often lead into a request for money by first asking for directions or the time of day. Having complied with the first request, the target is then more vulnerable to the second and more important request. In Christian circles evangelists may conclude a service by first asking people to raise their hands if they have "experienced God working in their lives." This initial request to raise hands may then be followed by a request to come forward for prayer and counseling. Such an approach to encouraging people to come forward may be effective at least in part because it represents a foot-in-the-door compliance technique.

Another multiple-request technique is the door in the face. Someone using this technique begins with an outrageously large request. When the target refuses (as expected), the person counters with a more modest request (the request of real interest). Because the solicitor appears to compromise, the target feels pressure to reciprocate by agreeing with the smaller request. Suppose a Christian wants to invite a non-Christian friend to a special program at church but anticipates that the non-Christian might be resistant. The Christian could begin by inviting the non-Christian to a week-long retreat. When the non-Christian refuses, the Christian could then follow up the first request with an invitation to attend the special program. The Christian has just used the door in the face.

The second category of compliance techniques takes advantage of our notions of fairness. It has long been acknowledged that favors beget favors. When someone does us a favor, our notion of fairness typically obligates us to reciprocate. We are more vulnerable to a request from the person who has done us a favor. It is not uncommon for Christian organizations to offer gifts to those who contact the organization. If the gift is accompanied with a request for funds, then the organization is using a compliance technique.

Another example of a technique that takes advantage of our notions of fairness is guilt induction. If we feel we have harmed someone, we become more vulnerable to a request from that person. By saying yes to that request we may be attempting to restore equity, make ourselves feel better, or make ourselves look better. I still remember a summer day when I was fantasizing about playing in the World Series and hitting a home run. On my backswing I connected with my playmate Billy's mouth, knocking out his two front teeth. At that moment I felt terrible and I would have done anything for Billy (I think I offered him my two front teeth). Charitable organizations often accompany requests for donations with graphic depictions of human hurt and suffering. To the extent that we feel part of this world and thus at least indirectly a part of the problem, we may be induced through guilt to donate.

A thought-provoking issue for Christians is the extent to which compliance techniques, particularly the more manipulative ones, should be used in evangelism and fund raising. An easy answer is to assume that those who use manipulative techniques are interested in selfish gain. However, a more serious look at the issue forces one to acknowledge that there are good-hearted Christians who use manipulative techniques to advance the kingdom of God. Certainly Christians are not called to be incompetent for Christ. Christians should use effective methods and techniques for advancing the kingdom. Yet, how far is too far when it comes to using compliance techniques? Basinger and Bassett (1982) suggest that such techniques go too far when they violate people's capacities as image bearers. Being created in the image of God means, among other things, that we have the capacity for responsible choice. When manipulation leads people into something they do not understand or they regret, then that capacity for responsible choice has been compromised and manipulation has gone too far.

Reference

Basinger, D., & Bassett, R. L. (1982). Ye shall be manipulators of men. *Eternity, 33* (7–8), 20–23.

R. L. BASSETT

See OBEDIENCE.

Compulsion. An urge to perform an act or ritualized series of acts that, if it is not completed, leads to intolerable anxiety. Hence the urge feels irresistible. The anxiety, according to psychoanalytic theorists, is the result of ideas or desires that are unacceptable to the person but are nevertheless surfacing into conscious awareness. The compulsion serves to defend against the anxiety by displacing attention from the unacceptable ideas or desires onto the irrational but acceptable compulsion. Allaying anxiety serves to reinforce the performance of the act, thus making its repetition even more likely. An example of compulsion is individuals who feel forced to wash their hands every time they touch anything. Compulsions are characteristic of obsessive-compulsive disorder and may also be seen in schizophrenia.

J. E. TALLEY

See OBSESSIVE-COMPULSIVE DISORDER; OBSESSION.

Compulsive Personality Disorder. *See* OBSESSION; OBSESSIVE-COMPULSIVE DISORDER.

Computer Applications in Mental Health. The use of computers as a tool in mental health settings has gained attention since the early 1970s. Most of the early work with computers featured computer-assisted instruction, computerized adaptive testing, or computer software for statistical analysis. Punch cards and cumbersome programs soon gave way to more user-friendly and inexpensive opportunities for mental health professionals with the development and widespread use of personal computers. Current developments include computerized networking, therapeutic uses of the Internet, and virtual reality technology.

Computer-Assisted Instruction and Research. Computer use became widespread in universities in the 1980s. Previously the expense of using computers in instruction outweighed the benefits. As the price of computers and software has continued to decline, their use has become more standard in university and research settings. The most frequent use of computers in these settings is statistical packages to analyze data. Most colleges and universities now incorporate some computer orientation in their statistics and experimental methods courses. Research on mental health treatments has become reliant on computers for analysis of results as well as for data collection in some settings. Software has been written for research projects or college course instruction and is available from many publishing companies as well as software companies.

Computerized Testing. Computerized testing began in the assessment of intelligence (e.g., Wechsler Adult Intelligence Scale), psychological functioning (e.g., Minnesota Multiphasic Personality Inventory), and achievement (e.g., Scholastic Aptitude Test), but more recent developments have used attitudinal measures and affective measures (Koch, Dodd, & Fitzpatrick, 1990). Primary advantages to computerized testing have been the ease of analysis of results and software's ability to adapt in testing based on the respondent's previous answers to questions. Scores can be computed and stored by the computer, helping to easily establish the reliability and validity of the instrument. Assessment reports can be printed and tailored to individuals.

Computers in Psychotherapy. The use of computers in therapeutic settings is being discussed. Some practitioners have found computer applications that are effective and impressive. Many centers with multiple mental health workers use computers for networking among therapists and for file maintenance. Clarke and Schoech (1994) found a computer-assisted therapeutic game useful with adolescents with impulse control difficulties. They found that use of the program transferred impulse control beyond computer games and that clients were cooperative with the computer game format. Other practitioners have used computers for measuring outcomes of therapy. The CASPER system is used with clients at a university-based counseling center (McCullough, Farrell, & Longabaugh, 1986). In a typical use of CASPER, a measure is taken at intake, midway through treatment, and at termination. This system's data can then be used to plan for the future of the center based on clientele, tailor the training of practicum students, assist with diagnosis, and analyze the effectiveness of treatments.

Critics wonder if computer applications in psychotherapy may be limited by the functioning of the client, wherein clients who are severely depressed or delusional would have difficulty concentrating on computer programs. In addition the observations of the counselor cannot currently be replaced by computers.

New and Upcoming Directions for Computers in Mental Health. The future of computers in mental health is a frontier full of possibilities and discoveries. Innovations are being developed in many areas of computer applications. Virtual reality technology may be one of the next applications of computers in mental health. Applications for virtual reality in education and rehabilitation are particularly being investigated. New developments suggest that individuals with physical disabilities will be able to use virtual reality to increase their functioning. Research is underway to make this idea a reality (Baker-Van Den Goorbergh, 1994; Bailey, 1994). Virtual reality treatment for individuals with phobias (Rothbaum, Hodges, Kooper, & Opdyke, 1995)

or in need of interpersonal skill training (Muscott & Gifford, 1994) is also underway as some of the first investigations in virtual reality psychotherapy.

The use of the Internet in psychotherapy is already underway. A scan of the major Internet sites reveals therapists around the country setting up websites for therapeutic services. Group therapy could take on a whole new meaning with online chat rooms. Quality therapy could become available for individuals living in remote areas around the world. Online supervision could be made available to mental health professionals. In addition psychoeducational materials could be accessed through interactive Internet sites to help in prevention and coping with mental health difficulties.

Difficulties with these new technologies still exist. Some critics argue that encouraging hallucinations through virtual reality as a form of treatment may be harmful for some clients and encourage them to seek escape as an option for coping. As the world becomes increasingly computer-oriented, person-to-person interaction may become less frequent. It remains to be seen whether computer-oriented interaction will be preferred, or if society will prioritize person-to-person contact in mental health. It also remains to be seen if mental health practitioners will adapt to computer applications in their therapeutic practices.

Conclusion. The ethics of the uses of computers in mental health settings is a subject that has yet to be developed in the literature. Ethical guidelines, particularly for some of the newest applications such as Internet sites, are not formalized (Meier & Geiger, 1986). Analysis of the effectiveness and the ethical obligations of mental health workers using computers should be formalized. How mental health professionals will utilize future applications of computers as tools for mental health remains to be seen.

References

Baker-Van Den Goorbergh, L. (1994). Language impaired children. *Computers and Language Analysis: Theory and Practice, 10*, 329–348.

Bailey, D. M. (1994). Technology for adults with multiple impairments: A trilogy of case reports. *American Journal of Occupational Therapy, 48*, 341–345.

Clarke, B., & Schoech, D. (1994). A computer assisted therapeutic game for adolescents: Initial development and comments. *Computers in Human Services, 11*, 121–140.

Koch, W. R., Dodd, B. G., & Fitzpatrick, S. J. (1990). Computerized adaptive measurements of attitudes. Special issue: Computerized testing. *Measurement & Evaluation in Counseling & Development, 23*, 20–30.

McCullough, L., Farrell, A. D., & Longabaugh, R. (1986). The development of a microcomputer-based mental health information system. *American Psychologist, 41*, 207–214.

Meier, S. T., & Geiger, S. M. (1986). Implications of computer-assisted testing and assessment for professional practice and training. Special issue: Computer applications in testing and assessment. *Measurement & Evaluation in Counseling & Development, 19*, 29–34.

Muscott, H. S., & Gifford, T. (1994). Virtual reality and social skill training for students with behavior disorders: Application challenges and promising practices. *Education and Treatment of Children, 17,* 417–434.

Rothbaum, B. O., Hodges, L. F., Kooper, R., & Opdyke, D. (1995). Effectiveness of computer generated graded exposure in the treatment of acrophobia. *American Journal of Psychiatry, 152,* 626–628.

J. S. RIPLEY

Concept Formation. *See* COGNITIVE PSYCHOLOGY.

Conciliation. *See* CHILD CUSTODY EVALUATIONS; MEDIATION/CONCILIATION.

Concretizing Technique. Concretization, a technique of psychodrama, involves the use of sculpting (*see* Family Choreography; Family Sculpture Technique) to describe the dynamics involved in interaction. Much of the content for concretizations comes from symbolic language used by the person to describe his or her plight. The spatial dimension is seen in the nearness of the person to significant others. High and low often represent power and weakness. The others in the scene are sculpted according to their relationship with the person.

An example of the concretizing technique is a scene in which a person feels alienated and powerless in the presence of a parent. The individual might assume a 20-foot distance and be on his or her knees. The parent (played by another member of the psychodrama group) might stand on a chair and point derisively.

In a more general way the concretizing technique is also used within other therapeutic traditions when the therapist asks for concrete details to move a highly abstract and generalized discussion toward specifics. Therapists must also model this dimension through their own use of concrete and specific terminology. When they avoid vagueness and ambiguity, clients tend to do the same.

J. H. VANDER MAY

Condensation. In psychoanalysis condensation refers to the process whereby a single idea in consciousness contains all the emotion associated with a number of unconscious ideas. The single idea, word, or phrase is described as overcathected in that it has attached to it the psychic energy of all the fused ideas. This process is best seen in dreams, in which details in the dream are each condensations of a number of unconscious elements. The dream itself, therefore, is a condensation of a vast complex of unconscious ideas.

See DEFENSE MECHANISMS.

Conditioning, Avoidance. In avoidance conditioning the occurrence of an aversive event is postponed or prevented by performing the appropriate response prior to its onset. Most laboratory studies of avoidance conditioning have used the following procedure. A stimulus, such as a light, is presented some time (e.g., 30 seconds) before the presentation of the aversive event (e.g., painful electric shock). If the appropriate avoidance response is performed during the light and prior to the aversive event, shock does not occur, the light is terminated, and there is a pause of specified length before the light is presented again. If the avoidance response is not performed, shock is presented.

A critical factor in the acquisition of an avoidance response is the nature of the response itself. For example, rats readily learn to press a lever for food pellets, but a lever-press avoidance response is acquired very slowly and sometimes incompletely. Alternatively, rats rapidly acquire a running response to avoid shock. Aversive stimuli often elicit innate defensive behavior. If the required avoidance response is compatible with the general form of the defensive behavior, then it normally will be learned easily. Otherwise learning may occur slowly or not at all.

Variables that affect avoidance conditioning, other than the nature of the response, include the interval between the onset of the conditioned stimulus and the presentation of the aversive event, the interval between successive conditioning trials, intensity of the aversive event, the nature of the conditioning stimulus, the type of organism (e.g., rat, pigeon), whether or not the aversive event can be escaped, and, if so, the nature of the escape response.

Apart from laboratory investigations of avoidance conditioning the learned ability to avoid potentially harmful situations is clearly adaptive; for many animal species such learning is critical to their survival. For humans the effects of avoidance learning go well beyond mere survival. Most people learn to avoid unpleasant social situations and to adapt their behavior to avoid the potentially aversive consequences of unlawful, immoral, or unacceptable social behavior.

The outcome of avoidance learning, however, is not always adaptive. Phobias—extreme, irrational fears—often result in maladaptive or debilitating avoidance behavior. For example, a person with a chronic fear of hospitals may avoid seeking needed medical help. Avoidance responses also may generalize beyond the original situation. For example, a child who has experienced aversive (emotional) consequences because of failing a particular academic subject may try to avoid school altogether. Finally, avoidance learning may limit future behavioral flexibility. That is, avoidance learning may have originally taken place under a set of circumstances that no longer exists. However, inappropriate avoidance behavior may be maintained because the avoidance response itself prevents the person from coming into contact with new contingencies.

Fortunately, maladaptive avoidance behavior often is corrected naturally by the behavioral consequences that exist in our everyday lives. In more extreme cases (e.g., phobias) some form of behavioral therapy may be required.

S. R. OSBORNE

See LEARNING.

Conditioning, Classical. Classical, or respondent, conditioning represents a simple form of learning that results from the pairing of stimuli. In a well-known experiment Ivan Pavlov, who was studying the digestion of dogs, noticed an unusual phenomenon. A metronome that was associated with the placement of food in the dogs' mouths caused the dogs to salivate in much the same manner as did the food itself. This simple observation became the basis for the theory of classical conditioning.

Some stimuli have an innate ability to elicit a response; that is, they automatically produce a response without any special training or previous experience. Such a stimulus is termed an unconditioned stimulus and the response it elicits is termed an unconditioned response. Eye blinks to a puff of air, knee jerks to taps below the kneecap, perspiration to warm temperatures, and salivation to food are all examples of unconditioned responses and stimuli.

If a stimulus that normally has no effect on behavior is repeatedly paired with an unconditioned stimulus, it will come to elicit the same response as the unconditioned stimulus, even if presented in its absence. The previously neutral stimulus is then called a conditioned stimulus, the response a conditioned response, and the process itself classical conditioning. For example, if a tone (neutral stimulus) is repeatedly paired with a puff of air (unconditioned stimulus) to the eye, the tone will become a conditioned stimulus and elicit the eye-blink reflex even if the air puff is not presented. Similarly a neutral stimulus, after sufficient pairing with a painful electric shock, can come to elicit an emotional fear response similar to that elicited by the shock.

Conditioned responses can be classified according to the type of unconditioned stimulus used and the nature of the response that is conditioned. An unconditioned stimulus is appetitive if it is generally attractive to the organism (e.g., food) and aversive if it is generally unpleasant (e.g., a loud noise). Responses are classified as skeletal if they involve the musculature of the body, organic if they involve internal organs, and glandular if they involve the glands. All these types of conditioning have been demonstrated in the laboratory. A conditioned response also can be developed if the unconditioned stimulus is presented at regular and predictable time intervals (temporal conditioning). In this case the time interval separating successive presentations of the unconditioned stimulus comes to serve as the conditioned stimulus.

Classical conditioning has many properties that are important in determining how it affects behavior. First, conditioned responses tend to be anticipatory. When a conditioned response is fully conditioned it typically precedes the occurrence of the unconditioned stimulus or occurs before the unconditioned stimulus would have been presented. Therefore, the conditioned response is not simply a substitute for the unconditioned response but a particular learned reaction in its own right. Second, conditioned responses generalize from one stimulus to another. Stimuli that are similar to the conditioned stimulus will elicit the conditioned response; the greater the similarity, the greater the likelihood that generalization will occur. For example, in an early experiment a young infant was conditioned by repeatedly pairing a white rat with a sudden loud noise. Eventually the white rat came to elicit a fear response similar to that produced by the noise. However, fear responses also were elicited by other white, furry objects (e.g., a white rabbit) even though these objects had never been paired with the loud noise.

A third property of classical conditioning is that discriminations between stimuli can be developed. Discriminations are the behavioral opposites of generalizations; they enable an organism to narrow the range of generalization. The process can be demonstrated by the following example: If the conditioned stimulus (white rat) is presented with the unconditioned stimulus (loud noise) and a similar stimulus (white rabbit) is presented without the unconditioned stimulus, the conditioned response (fear reaction) that initially occurred to both stimuli will soon become more frequent to the conditioned stimulus that is paired with the unconditioned stimulus and the fear response to the other stimulus will eventually cease.

Finally, conditioned responses are not necessarily permanent. If the conditioned stimulus is repeatedly presented without the unconditioned stimulus, it will eventually lose its power to elicit the conditioned response. The number of unpaired presentations required for this extinction process to occur depends upon, among other things, the strength of the original conditioning.

The implications of classical conditioning extend far beyond the laboratory curiosity of learning psychologists. The conditioned reflex is regarded by many as the basic building block of behavior. Moreover, the critical conditions necessary for conditioning to occur are present in the normal environment of every person.

The role of classical conditioning in our lives is not trivial. Simple conditioned responses make a significant contribution to our behavior. For example, people close their eyes when something is about to hit them in the face, and they flinch when threatened by a blow. Many internal body reactions also are partially controlled by a wide variety of conditioned stimuli. These stimuli have functional significance in preparing us for events to come. The heart rate and blood pressure change and increased adrenaline flow that characterize fear are often elicited by stimuli that are not inherently threatening. Such stimuli acquire their power through conditioning.

Classical conditioning procedures also form the basis of some psychotherapies. Systematic desensitization is one method psychologists have developed for overcoming such undesirable, long-lasting emotional responses as phobias. The objective of desensitization is to condition the patient to relax in the presence of anxiety-arousing stimuli. Because relaxation and anxiety are incompatible, as the patient learns to relax he or she simultaneously learns not to be anxious. Although the success rate of desensitization depends on the specific anxiety, systematic desensitization has been shown to be an effective treatment and is a standard approach of most behavioral clinicians.

S. R. Osborne

See Learning; Behavioral Psychology.

Conditioning, Higher-Order. Within classical conditioning there are many ways in which a neutral stimulus can acquire conditioning properties. One method, known as higher-order conditioning, involves pairing two or more stimuli in a situation in which an unconditioned stimulus is not directly involved.

The standard conditions under which classical conditioning normally occurs consist of the repeated pairing of a neutral stimulus (e.g., a tone) with an unconditioned stimulus (e.g., food) so that the previously neutral stimulus comes to elicit a response similar to the one elicited by the unconditioned stimulus.

In higher-order conditioning a second neutral stimulus is repeatedly paired with an established conditioned stimulus. After a number of pairings the neutral stimulus will elicit the same response as the conditioned stimulus, even though the new stimulus has never been paired with the unconditioned stimulus. For example, the tick of a metronome when paired with the presentation of food will eventually elicit a salivation response similar to that elicited by the sight of food itself. If the sound of the metronome is then preceded by a second stimulus (e.g., a light) this stimulus initially will have no effect on the salivation response. However, after repeated pairings of the light and the sound of the metronome without any presentation of food, the light alone will come to elicit the salivation response. This process of higher-order conditioning has been demonstrated with as many as three conditioned stimuli, counting backward from the unconditioned stimulus.

The importance of higher-order conditioning is that it shows that conditioning can take place in situations in which an unconditioned stimulus is not directly involved. It also highlights the complex relationships that can be developed between stimuli through the conditioning process.

S. R. Osborne

See Learning.

Conditioning, Operant. Learning based on the relationship among a discriminative stimulus, a response, and a reinforcer, plus those variables that affect the power of a reinforcer. A discriminative stimulus is a cue that signals what reinforcer is likely to be delivered when a particular response occurs. The response in operant conditioning consists of emitted behaviors. Emitted behaviors are actions that technically are known as operants. Reinforcers are stimuli that are produced by an operant and that change the rate of that operant (*see* Reinforcement).

An example of operant conditioning would be the employee who works with extra diligence and enthusiasm when the boss is in the office. The presence of the boss is the discriminative stimulus and the extra productivity in work is the operant, or response. The reinforcer in this example would be the boss's approval (perhaps expressed in a smile or a greeting) or at least the absence of the boss's disapproval, which could be expressed in dismissal or reprimand.

Skinner introduced the basic concepts of operant conditioning to the psychological world in *The Behavior of Organisms* (1938). His system and the type of behavior that he studied may be contrasted with that of Ivan Pavlov. Pavlov focused on reflexive responses, which are elicited by stimuli that immediately precede them (*see* Conditioning, Classical). Skinner labeled such reflexive responses respondent behaviors.

Operant conditioning involves a process analogous to Darwinian natural selection. In operant conditioning behaviors that are reinforced by the environment survive; behaviors that are not reinforced by the environment do not survive. Since operant conditioning focuses on actions and since actions constitute that category of behavior of most importance to human behavior, the way the environment "selects" behaviors has great significance.

In order to study behavior an investigator must choose a particular measure. Early in his career Skinner chose rate as his primary response measure. Much of his work has used simple responses such as pecks by a pigeon or lever presses by a rat. To study such behaviors in laboratory animals Skinner developed what he called the operant chamber; most of the rest of the psychological world has referred to the operant chamber as the Skinner box.

Researchers have used the Skinner box to explore the effects of reinforcers on operants. There are two basic types of reinforcers: positive and negative. Positive reinforcers are stimuli that will strengthen a response if the response produces the reinforcer. Examples are food, water, or sexual stimulation. Negative reinforcers are stimuli that will strengthen a response if the response removes the reinforcer. Examples are a loud noise, extremes of temperature, or an electric shock. These are examples of primary reinforcers; these reinforcers are relatively universal in their effects and they do not acquire their power through prior learning.

Secondary reinforcers, in contrast, are conditioned or learned reinforcing stimuli. Words of praise are commonly used secondary reinforcers. Behaviors either producing or removing positive or negative reinforcers involve four basic reinforcement contingencies: positive reinforcement, negative reinforcement, punishment type I, and punishment type II. Positive reinforcement is the name of the contingency when an action produces a positive reinforcer. For example, when the rat presses the lever, the dispenser drops a pellet of food in the animal's food dish. Actions that produce positive reinforcers are strengthened. Negative reinforcement occurs when an action removes a negative reinforcer. For example, a cat escapes an electric shock by jumping from the shocked side to the safe side of a shuttle box. Actions that remove negative reinforcers are strengthened.

Punishment type I is the contingency in which an action produces a negative reinforcer. For example, when a toddler runs into the street, the parent spanks the child. The effects of punishment type I are not the opposite of those for reinforcement. Punishment type I may temporarily suppress an operant, but the organism is not likely to stop responding permanently. Punishment type II is the contingency in which an action removes a positive reinforcer. Examples of this contingency are when an operant produces a fine or time out from positive reinforcers. Actions that produce a response cost or time out tend to be weakened (see Punishment).

In addition to these four contingencies, a fifth possibility exists: the organism acts, but the actions do not produce or remove any effective reinforcers. Such a situation is labeled extinction. Actions that have been effectively reinforced but are then switched to extinction conditions tend to decrease in rate. Actions that have been effectively punished but are then switched to extinction conditions tend to increase in rate.

The power of a reinforcer is affected by operations such as depriving the organism of the reinforcer, satiating the organism on the reinforcer, administering certain drugs, applying physical restraints, noncontingently administering positive or negative reinforcers, and providing or removing choices.

Previous reinforcement, punishment, and extinction contingencies are not the only events that can alter response rates. The motivational operations mentioned above as well as age, emotional arousal, illness, and rest may alter response rates.

Investigators of operant conditioning have spent much time determining the effects of different schedules of reinforcement (see Reinforcement, Schedule of). The most common have involved continuous reinforcement schedules, fixed-interval schedules, variable-interval schedules, fixed-ratio schedules, and variable-ratio schedules. Each schedule of reinforcement produces a distinctive pattern of responding. Variable-ratio schedules tend to produce the highest rates of responding. In addition to these commonly used schedules of reinforcement there are a number of more complex schedules.

Research on operant conditioning has covered a wide range of problems. Among the generic issues explored have been discrimination, differentiation, and generalization. Discrimination research focuses on the role of cues (discriminative stimuli) in operant conditioning. Discriminative stimuli signal whether a particular response will produce a particular reinforcer. Differentiation of a response refers to the shaping of a response pattern by making reinforcement contingent on gradual changes in one dimension of responding. Generalization refers to one of many processes: stimulus generalization, response generalization, temporal generalization, subject generalization, or combinations of two or more of these processes.

Operant conditioning developed concurrently with a particular approach to psychological research is known as the experimental analysis of behavior. This approach emphasizes the intensive study of single subjects rather than comparing groups of subjects. Operant conditioning and the experimental analysis of behavior have had a profound impact on applied psychology. The earliest attempts to apply operant conditioning to problems in the real world occurred in the 1950s. By the 1960s applied behavior analysis was being practiced in a wide range of human service settings, including mental hospitals, schools, institutions for developmentally disabled persons, correctional facilities, rehabilitation medicine, and special education. Programmed instruction, teaching machines, and behavior modification are direct outgrowths of operant conditioning.

Reference

Skinner, B. F. (1938). *The behavior of organisms.* New York: Appleton-Century.

P. W. Clement

See Applied Behavior Analysis; Learning; Skinner, Burrhus Frederic; Behavioral Psychology.

Conditions of Worth. *See* Person-Centered Therapy; Rogers, Carl Ransom; Self-Congruence; Self-Defeating Behavior; Unconditional Positive Regard.

Conduct Disorders. *See* Disruptive Behavior Disorders.

Confabulation. The unconscious act of replacing memory gaps by fantasizing experiences with no basis in fact. The gaps are replaced by confabulations, which are narrated in elaborate detail with specific events and real people. Confabulations differ from delusions in that the props of the stories are real, but the experiences themselves never took place. The individual believes his or her stories are factual and will stick emphatically to them. Unconscious motives are evident in that the individual seems to hide embarrassment over a memory loss by inventing fabrications. Confabulation is found in organic brain diseases and principally in Korsakoff's syndrome.

D. L. Schuurman

See False Memory Syndrome; Memory.

Confession. The professionals most often sought for assistance in easing the pain of human anguish and guilt are psychotherapists and the clergy (Frank, 1973). As their roles in the healing process are examined, one may ask how certain tasks of the psychotherapist differ from those of a priest hearing a confession and granting absolution (Jung, 1938). Such reflections raise at least three basic questions: What are confession and psychotherapy? How is confession comparable to psychotherapy? Can these two be brought together into a single, more efficient method? (Worthen, 1983).

One of the great mysteries of faith is the process of redemption and reconciliation. At the heart of God is the desire to forgive, making confession and forgiveness spiritual exercises that can transform lives (see Foster, 1988; Willard, 1988). The Scriptures clearly call us to practice confession on a regular basis, both as a private matter between the individual and God and as a corporate discipline between believers (Stott, 1965).

Yet practicing confession is often a difficult discipline to implement in our lives, partly because, as Bonhoeffer (1954) has noted, we often have fellowship with one another as believers and as devout people, but rarely do we have fellowship with each other when we despair and lapse into sinful patterns. Consequently we are prone to "spiritual impression management" (Smedes, 1982)—that is, we attempt to conceal our sinfulness from each other, pretending not to be subject to the same deeply engrained deceitful habits (see Shuster, 1987). In our desire to maintain fellowship we fail to recognize that we are living in lies and hypocrisy. The obvious alternative is to recognize that we are a fellowship of sinners needing to hear the unconditional call of God's love and needing to confess our neediness and sins before God as well as our brothers and sisters in Christ.

Confession has been understood differently throughout the course of church history. Within the Catholic or Anglo-Catholic traditions it is usually perceived as a sacrament that should be experienced rather often. This ministry of reconciliation, it is argued, is "exercised through the care each Christian has for others, through the common prayer of Christians assembled for public worship, and through the priesthood of the Church and its ministers declaring absolution" (*Book of Common Prayer*, 1979, p. 446). The content of a confession is usually deemed a sacred trust and must under no circumstances be broken. Outside these liturgical traditions it would be difficult to describe the many different ways in which confession is publicly and/or privately practiced. As Worthen (1983) describes it, it involves first that the sinner acknowledge that a serious sin has been committed and has become troubling to the conscience. Genuine contrition is expressed (i.e., the sinner expresses a strong resolve not to repeat the sin). Second, the confession is heard by a deacon, an elder, or a priest, depending on the context and tradition. Third, there is the willing performance of some task (penance) imposed as compensation—or more accurately, as a token of good faith to accept the consequences of sin.

In the orthodox Jewish tradition a special day was set aside for confession in which amends were to be made to the person against whom sin had been committed and from whom the offender desired and needed to receive forgiveness (see Smedes, 1984).

In the Reformed tradition the authority of all believers to receive the confession of sin and forgive it in the name of Jesus Christ (John 20:23) was stressed, thereby lessening the emphasis placed on the more formal institution of priest-mediated confession.

Foster (1988) calls this authority a great gift for the people of God and a tremendous opportunity to manifest God's grace that we dare not withhold from others. Confession is seen as an essential responsibility of all believers who desire to restore right relationships between individuals and their Maker. And as Bonhoeffer (1954) has noted, hearing such confession is the greatest service of listening that God has committed to us, a sacred trust that is built on a solid foundation of truly listening to one another on lesser and often mundane subjects.

Psychotherapy is usually viewed as a process in which a trained clinician helps clients resolve emotional difficulties, develop more constructive attitudes, and alter their behaviors in the direction of becoming more independent, self-fulfilled, growth-directed individuals (Goldenberg, 1973). Both confession and individually oriented therapy, then, are potentially intimate, one-to-one interpersonal relationships with the aim of reducing subjective distress and the potential of restoring emotional and/or spiritual health. Confession, however, tends to stress conscious motivation and recall, whereas both classical and contemporary psychoanalytic formulations aim at finding whether unconscious dynamics might be influencing current functioning (see Jones & Butman, 1991). Perhaps the goals might be the same, but the processes whereby the goals are attained can differ significantly. As Menninger (1973) has noted, psychotherapists tend to be profoundly ambivalent about words like "confession," "repentance," or "sin," more often than not avoiding them entirely (*see* Sin, Psychological Consequences of). Whereas persons of faith usually understand sin as turning from God, breaking a code of morality, or failing to live up to God's standards as stated in Scripture, clinicians are more prone to think in terms of constructs like "narcissism," "self-absorption," or a "Swiss cheese conscience" (i.e., no lasting concerns about the legitimate needs/wants of others). guilt or shame may be viewed differently (see Narramore, 1974).

Humanistic theorists and therapists tend to be especially bothered by serious discussion of sin and its consequences, perhaps because they so often deal with the developmental affects of rigid and authoritarian family systems and are thereby inclined to be more permissive in their clinical interactions (see Jones & Butman, 1991).

How one conceptualizes the problems of human anguish and guilt has profound implications for diagnosis (e.g., Is it sin or an addiction?), treatment (e.g., locus of control, responsibility for the cure, type of treatment to be recommended), and prevention (e.g., What is a meaningful and truly satisfying philosophy of life?).

In comparing the literature on confession and psychotherapy, Worthen (1983) suggests several conclusions. First, there seems to be more of an emphasis on restoration to the community with confession than in traditional psychotherapy. Second, penance, especially in the Roman Catholic or Anglo-Catholic tradition, is based on an almost universally accepted set of procedures. Psychotherapy can make no such claims about alleviating human anguish and guilt. Third, the priest-confessor generally views the individual and corporate consequences of sin as a root cause of much human unhappiness. The psychotherapist sees the etiology and maintenance of psychopathology as complex phenomena requiring careful and ongoing assessment throughout treatment. Perhaps confession more often deals with the evil of human freedom, whereas psychotherapy tends to deal with the results of human compulsions and the vicious cycles of repetition and conditioning.

Another key difference might be that confession is most often seen as necessary for dealing with willful misdeeds, whereas psychotherapy more often deals with the consequences of less conscious motivations. Compared to the priest-confessor, the psychotherapist is less likely to be concerned with meeting the immediate needs of penitents for reconciliation and restoration to fellowship but far more likely to be concerned about looking for root causes of the problems, a process that can be long and agonizingly difficult for the client. Psychotherapists tend to be neutral about making judg-

ments about problems in living, whereas the priest-confessor is expected to take a firm stance about moral rightness or wrongness.

Few would view psychotherapy as an ordained context in which to fully experience forgiveness of sin and the ministry of reconciliation. It can, however, do much to free individuals from certain compulsions that make it difficult to abstain from and to repent of sin. Whereas confession tends to see intention as the core and basic cause of sin, psychotherapy is more likely to view the motivation of the external act as the individual's inability to cope with inherited or acquired vulnerabilities, unusually high levels of stresses, or both. Suffice it to say that there is a considerable amount of discussion about which techniques in either pastoral care or professional psychotherapy are most appropriate in alleviating anguish and guilt or whether religious beliefs should be addressed (see Oden, 1984).

A potential resolution to this perceived conflict is possible. With mutual respect for both confession and psychotherapy, a new direction may be found. It is not enough, for example, to quote Scripture to a brother or sister in Christ after one hears a confession. The listener must encounter and speak to each individual in such a way that the message of God's grace and forgiveness for sins is clearly stated and is made relevant for that individual's needs. Confession of sin, followed by constructive change and repentance, can certainly contribute toward the wholeness of the person. Psychotherapy can assist the person in developing the psychological freedom to respond to the environment in more intentional and responsible ways. Confession has the potential to assist the person in developing greater spiritual freedom to respond to others and to God. Together these separate but potentially complementary functions can assist the Christian in the process of becoming oneself in truth before God and others.

Many who have written on confession have pointed to the important role of personal preparation in being able properly to hear the confession of another. By coming to grips with the sin that nailed Jesus to the cross, we will realize that nothing anyone could say or do should disturb us to the point we could never even conceive of hearing that person's honest confession. Bonhoeffer (1954) calls this learning to live under the cross. Such a commitment will truly convey to others that it is safe to come to us and that we can receive anything they could reveal. We thereby demonstrate by our listening and response that we understand and that we do not need to tell others such privileged information. In other words, we must prepare for this sacred ministry by earning the right to be trusted by those who come to us in godly sorrow. By living under the cross, we approach the other person as an equal, resisting the temptation to control or "straighten out" that individual. What is needed is acceptance and understanding. Toward that end we should pray for a deeper spiritual commitment in ourselves, so that when we are with the other we will radiate Christ's life and light (i.e., we will act in such a way that our presence demonstrates the love and forgiving grace of God). As both Foster (1988) and Willard (1988) warn, we must discipline ourselves to be quiet and pray for the other, both during the confession and afterward.

Confession brings an end to pretense; we are all equals under the cross. By more openly confessing our sin, we allow ourselves to more fully know the forgiving and empowering grace of Christ. True confession requires real commitment and honesty. True confession leads to potential changes in thought, affect, and behavior. Surely confession is a grace that needs to be practiced more often in the church (see Gangel & Wilhoit, 1994).

References

Book of common prayer. (1979). New York: The Church Hymnal Corporation.

Bonhoeffer, D. (1954). Life together. New York: Harper & Row.

Foster, R. (1988). Celebration of discipline (Rev. ed.). San Francisco: Harper San Francisco.

Frank, J. (1973). Persuasion and healing (Rev. ed.). Baltimore: Johns Hopkins University Press.

Gangel, K., & Wilhoit, J. (Eds.). (1994). The Christian educator's handbook on spiritual formation. Wheaton, IL: Victor.

Goldenberg, H. (1973). Contemporary clinical psychology. Monterey, CA: Brooks/Cole.

Jones, S., & Butman, R. (1991). Modern psychotherapies. Downers Grove, IL: InterVarsity Press.

Jung, C. G. (1938). Psychology and religion. New Haven, CT: Yale University Press.

Menninger, K. A. (1973). What ever happened to sin? New York: Hawthorn.

Narramore, S. B. (1974). Guilt: Where theology and psychology meet. Journal of Psychology and Theology, 1, 18–25.

Oden, T. (1984). Care of souls in the classic tradition. Philadelphia: Fortress.

Shuster, M. (1987). Power, pathology, paradox: The dynamics of evil and good. Grand Rapids, MI: Zondervan.

Smedes, L. B. (1982). How can it be all right when everything is all wrong? San Francisco: Harper & Row.

Smedes, L. B. (1984). Forgive and forget. San Francisco: Harper & Row.

Stott, J. (1965). Confess your sins. Waco, TX: Word.

Willard, D. (1988). The spirit of the disciples. New York: Harper & Row.

Worthen, V. (1983). Psychotherapy and Catholic confession. In H. N. Malony (Ed.), Wholeness and holiness. Grand Rapids, MI: Baker.

R. E. BUTMAN

See SPIRITUAL AND RELIGIOUS ISSUES IN THERAPY; RELIGIOUS RESOURCES IN PSYCHOTHERAPY.

Confidentiality. Confidentiality is broadly defined as the ethical responsibility of mental health professionals to hold in confidence information shared by clients in the course of psychotherapy or other professional work. This article will examine confidentiality primarily with reference to guidelines developed by the American Psychological Association (1992). However, other mental health professions have also developed standards regarding confidentiality.

To better understand confidentiality, it is helpful to distinguish it from other frequently encountered related concepts: privacy, privileged communication, and informed consent. Ethical principles concerning confidentiality are based on privacy, which means that individuals have a right to privacy regarding to what degree information about themselves should be available to others, such as employers and governmental agencies. In the therapeutic relationship individuals voluntarily provide personal and private information to the therapist. However, clients' rights to the privacy of this information are protected by ethical guidelines regarding confidentiality.

Privileged communication is a legal term, referring to the fact that clients hold the right to have information shared in professional relationships withheld from legal proceedings. Thus a therapist could not ordinarily be compelled to provide information gained in the course of psychotherapy. However, clients may waive this privilege if they believe the release of such information may serve their best interests. For example, clients undergoing a divorce may release their rights to privileged communication and ask that information shared in therapy be released in custody proceedings. In some states judges are allowed to override privileged communication between therapist and client if there are compelling legal factors. In such instances psychologists may face a dilemma in that ethical standards regarding confidentiality may conflict with legal rulings that involuntarily waive clients' rights to privileged communication.

A third concept, informed consent, is a broad ethical principle that encourages psychologists to discuss as early as possible with clients all relevant information about treatment and/or assessment procedures. As part of informed consent psychologists are bound by their guidelines (American Psychological Association, 1992) to discuss the limits of confidentiality, particularly under which circumstances confidentiality may be breached.

There is much controversy within the profession of psychology regarding circumstances under which it is appropriate to breach confidentiality. Some psychologists hold to a standard of absolute confidentiality. That is, under no circumstances would they concur that they should be compelled to provide information gained in the therapeutic relationship to outside parties—whether the outside parties be legal officials, employers, or third-party payers. However, the majority of psychologists and current APA ethical standards (1992) recognize that in some instances certain considerations may override customary confidentiality standards. One prominent example is the Tarasoff ruling (Stone, 1976). In this case it was ruled that therapists have a duty to warn third parties when a client has revealed information in therapy that would lead the therapist to conclude that a third party is in imminent danger. In the Tarasoff ruling a psychologist was held legally liable for not informing a third party of the murderous threats made by the therapist's client. The third party was subsequently killed by the client.

In other instances psychologists' commitment to absolute confidentiality is tempered by either ethical guidelines or legal standards. APA guidelines (1992) state that psychologists may disclose confidential information when mandated or permitted by law. Most states have explicit statutes that require psychologists to inform appropriate authorities should they have reason to suspect child abuse. APA guidelines also suggest that psychologists may break confidentiality when clients are in imminent danger of harm to themselves or others. If a client were actively suicidal, the psychologist would be ethically obligated to pursue reasonable means of protecting the client from self-harm.

This article has focused on confidentiality as related primarily to the client-therapist relationship in individual therapy. Ethical and legal considerations are even more complex regarding confidentiality in group, marital, and family therapy (Margolin, 1982). With the coming of the electronic/computer age, confidentiality issues with regard to client records have also become more problematic. Finally, managed care has had a major impact on the nature of confidentiality between client and therapist. Corcoran and Winslade (1994) provide an excellent commentary on how managed care has affected the confidentiality of the psychotherapeutic relationship.

References

American Psychological Association. (1992, December). Ethical principles of psychologists and code of conduct. *American Psychologist.*

Corcoran, K., & Winslade, W. J. (1994). Eavesdropping on the 50-minute hour: Managed mental health care and confidentiality. *Behavioral Sciences and the Law, 12,* 351–365.

Margolin, G. (1982). Ethical and legal considerations in marital and family therapy. *American Psychologist, 37,* 788–801.

Stone, A. A. (1976). The Tarasoff decisions: Suing therapists to safeguard society. *Harvard Law Review, 90,* 358–378.

H. L. Piersma

See Counseling and Psychotherapy: Overview; Moral and Ethical Issues in Treatment.

Conflict. A prominent construct in clinical, motivational, and social psychology, conflict is usually defined as the simultaneous existence of mutually exclusive or opposite desires or response tendencies. It may be intrapsychic, interpersonal, or mental.

In clinical psychology conflict concepts are present in the theories of Sigmund Freud and Karen Horney. Several types of conflict were considered by Freud. One of the biological impulses, eros (e.g., sexual motivation) or thanatos (e.g., aggression), may confront the prevailing social reality. Libidinal impulses (i.e., id) demand a type of gratification deemed inappropriate by society. Furthermore, libidinal impulses may bid for expression only to be thwarted by the moral censoring of the superego. Ego defense mechanisms are strategies to resolve intrapsychic conflict. They permit the expression of libidinal energy in forms tolerable to one's moral training or social convention.

In Horney's view basic conflict is intrapsychic tension due to competing neurotic trends (e.g., the need for autonomy and independence versus the need for a partner to take over one's life). Basic conflict may stem from incompatible images of self, particularly the idealized self versus the despised real self. Central conflict is an intrapsychic conflict between the healthy, constructive forces of the real self and the neurotic obsessions of the idealized self. In either case conflict is an underlying force in the etiology of neuroses.

Much of the motivational analysis of conflict originated in Lewin's (1938) field theory. The direction and strength of forces comprise a vector. When two vectors are balanced (e.g., same strength) but are directed in opposite directions, a state of conflict is said to exist. Lewin posited three types of conflict. In the approach-approach conflict an individual experiences two attractive but mutually exclusive goals. Equilibrium is, however, unstable. Movement toward one resolves the conflict, because the equilibrium is upset.

The avoidance-avoidance conflict is more serious. The person experiences two goals, both of which are aversive, but one must be chosen. The equilibrium is stabilized at the point between the goals at which the avoidant forces are equal. At this point there is little movement; the conflict remains unresolved.

In the approach-avoidance conflict one goal object has both positive and negative aspects. The person is both drawn to and repulsed by the goal object. The approach-avoidance conflict has a stable equilibrium point where the positive and negative forces balance. However, the goal object is never experienced.

Building on the work of Lewin, Miller (1959) gathered extensive experimental evidence regarding the nature of conflict. He found that the closer the organism is to the goal, the stronger the motivation; he termed this a gradient. The avoidance gradient was found to be steeper than the approach gradient. In approach-avoidance conflicts, when the organism is far from the goal, the approach tendency is stronger and the organism approaches the goal. However, as the organism approaches the goal, the avoidance tendency becomes stronger. The approach stops when the avoidance gradient overtakes the approach gradient. At that point equilibrium is achieved.

A more complicated form of approach-avoidance conflict is typical of most conflict situations. The double approach-avoidance conflict involves two goal objects, both of which have positive and negative aspects. For example, one might be shopping for a new home. One house is spacious, prestigious, and expensive; the other less spacious and less prestigious but more affordable.

Miller further demonstrated that when two incompatible responses are in conflict (e.g., approach or avoidance), the stronger motivation occurs. In the case of approach drives, deprivation of the goal object served to strengthen the drive.

The only serious challenge to Miller's theory is that of Maher (1966). Maher questioned the concept of intersecting approach and avoidance gradients, presuming instead that approach and avoidance gradients are parallel. Conflict exists when the relative strengths of these gradients are indistinguishable. Maher also suggested that feedback cues, rather than distance per se, produced the avoidance and approach gradients. However, to date Miller's analysis appears to have more support than Maher's.

Conflict can be interpersonal as well as intrapersonal. Social psychologists consider conflict to exist when persons in dyads or groups have variant aims. Satisfactory functioning of the group is contingent on resolving conflict through the process of negotiation. Mixed motives exist when one person in the dyad desires to cooperate while the other one views the situation as competitive. A conflict spiral emerges as one person uses a threat to induce conformity and the other responds with a counterthreat.

In summary, conflict is the existence of divergent aims or goals within the person or group. It is normally expected that conflict be resolved or reduced, especially for healthy functioning. The nature of the conflict is determined by the positive and/or negative aspects of the goal object.

References

Lewin, K. (1938). *The conceptual representation and measurement of psychological forces.* Durham, NC: Duke University Press.

Maher, B. A. (1966). *Principles of psychopathology.* New York: McGraw-Hill.

Miller, N. E. (1959). Liberalization of basic S-R concepts. In S. Koch (Ed.), *Psychology* (Vol. 2). New York: McGraw-Hill.

R. L. Timpe

See Cooperation and Competition.

Conflict Management. Conflict can be either intrapersonal or interpersonal. Intrapersonal conflict occurs when an individual experiences real or imag-

ined incompatibility among needs, goals, or roles. Interpersonal conflict, which will be emphasized here, has been defined as a perceived divergence of interest among individuals, groups, or organizations (Pruitt & Rubin, 1986; Worchel & Lundgren, 1991).

Conflict can have both positive and negative consequences. Conflict between Jewish and Christian leaders in the New Testament resulted in the apostles' imprisonment and martyrdom. It also, however, resulted in the spreading of Christianity beyond Jerusalem (Acts 8). Conflict between Paul and Barnabas over the role of John Mark produced interpersonal strife but resulted in two missionary teams rather than one (Acts 15). Conflict is often the impetus for change.

The recognition that conflict has both positive and negative consequences and the recognition that sometimes conflict may not be solvable imply that the goal should be conflict management rather than conflict resolution. Although both terms are often used, an emphasis on managing conflict may be more productive (Worchel & Lundgren, 1991).

There are five general procedures for managing conflict (see Carnevale & Pruitt, 1992). The most common, perhaps, is avoidance. This method may be functional as a short-term means of allowing emotions to cool but is often used as an inadequate long-term solution because the parties have a fear of the negative consequences of conflict. As a result they are not able to benefit from more adaptive conflict management.

The second procedure is the use of struggle, which can have many obvious negative consequences. Struggle includes any use of physical force to exert one's will on others.

A third procedure is arbitration. This involves asking a third party to make a binding decision, such as in our judicial system. The two young mothers sought arbitration when they brought their babies, one alive and one dead, to King Solomon, asking him to arbitrate the conflict (1 Kings 3). The apostle Paul instructed Christians to seek out arbitrators from within the church rather than from the state (1 Cor. 6; see Thomas, 1994, for additional biblical examples).

A fourth procedure is negotiation, in which the two parties discuss their interests and goals as they try to reach a mutually beneficial solution. If they bring in a third party with the limited role of facilitating discussion, then it would be an example of the fifth procedure, mediation (*see* Mediation/Conciliation).

The consequences of conflict are most beneficial when the parties seek a win-win solution. Although it is not always attainable, this ideal goal is one in which the parties are able to maximize their mutual benefit. By emphasizing underlying interests, concentrating on long-term consequences, and employing cooperative strategies, the parties may be able to achieve mutual benefit.

More frequently, however, parties in conflict think in win-lose terms. Your gain is at my expense; your loss is my gain. Although this type of structure often occurs, it is also frequently only a perception and an assumption. It may be possible to trade off on low-priority issues or to generate new proposals that maximize joint benefit.

The most negative consequences result from a lose-lose approach to conflict. People following this contentious approach say, "We don't care what it costs us; we are going to make you suffer." Both parties lose from such an approach.

Conflict theory and research have been more successful in describing conflict escalation than in prescribing methods of conflict management and de-escalation. Nevertheless, there have been several noteworthy approaches.

Classic research by Sherif and Sherif (1953) demonstrated the effectiveness of a superordinate goal. When conflicting parties are forced to work interdependently in order to accomplish a goal and achieve success in reaching that goal, preexisting differences become less problematic.

The graduated and reciprocated initiatives in tension reduction model (GRIT; see Lindskold, 1978) provides another approach. One side makes an initial series of minor cooperative gestures. As soon as the other side reciprocates, the first side follows with a corresponding move, creating a de-escalation spiral that mistrust and suspicion would otherwise have made impossible.

References

Carnevale, P. J., & Pruitt, D. G. (1992). Negotiation and mediation. *Annual Review of Psychology, 43,* 531–582.

Lindskold, S. (1978). Trust development, the GRIT proposal, and the effects of conciliatory acts on conflict and cooperation. *Psychological Bulletin, 85,* 772–793.

Pruitt, D. G., & Rubin, J. Z. (1986). *Social conflict: Escalation, stalemate, and settlement.* New York: Random House.

Sherif, M., & Sherif, C. W. (1953). *Groups in harmony and tension.* New York: Harper & Row.

Thomas, M. E. (1994). *Resolving disputes in Christian groups.* Winnipeg, MAN: Windflower.

Worchel, S., & Lundgren, S. (1991). The nature of conflict and conflict resolution. In K. G. Duffy, J. W. Grosch, & P. V. Olczak (Eds.), *Community mediation: A handbook for practitioners and researchers.* New York: Guilford.

G. L. WELTON

See COOPERATION AND COMPETITION.

Conformity. The change in an individual's beliefs or behavior as a result of group pressure. This failure to remain independent of social influence may have negative consequences—for example, when it leads people to violate their own moral principles—but it also is an important force for social stability. Social chaos would occur without some agreement on what is appropriate behavior. Psychologists have studied the extent to which people conform, their reasons for doing so, and the factors that influence their responses.

Sherif (1935) reported experiments that dramatically demonstrate how a person's judgments may be influenced by others. His studies utilized an optical illusion known as the autokinetic effect, in which a pinpoint of light shown in a darkened room appears to move. Sherif placed solitary individuals in the room and asked them to estimate the movement of the light. In this highly ambiguous situation individual judgments varied greatly. When Sherif brought the subjects together in small groups to repeat the task, they soon developed a common norm regarding the light's movement. Subjects who were again asked to make their judgments alone continued to adhere to the group norm.

Asch (1956) asked groups of subjects to perform a simple visual discrimination task in which they indicated which of three vertical lines drawn on a card was closest in length to a comparison line. In each group all but one of the subjects were confederates who had been instructed by the experimenter to make incorrect judgments on certain trials. The real subject responded to the examiner's questions after most of the confederates had made their judgments. Asch reported that when the confederates unanimously agreed on an obviously incorrect judgment, the subjects conformed in approximately 37% of their choices. Only 25% of the subjects remained independent and never conformed to the majority.

Research has revealed two reasons why people conform. A person may be influenced by others because their statements and actions provide guides to understanding reality. When others are used as a source of information, their influence will be pervasive and is likely to change both a person's beliefs and behavior. A second reason why a person may conform is the desire to avoid rejection or to gain approval. Groups often reject those who consistently deviate. When a person conforms to avoid rejection, the influence of others may be less pervasive and produce temporary changes in behavior but no change in belief.

Many studies have sought to identify factors that influence the extent to which people conform. For example, when the group is unanimous, as was true in Asch's initial study, people find resisting group pressure is particularly difficult. If just one ally is present, they are significantly less likely to conform. Viewing another's dissent, even when it is wrong, can increase the observer's independence. As the number of group members exerting pressure rises to approximately five persons, conformity also increases. Beyond this level increasing size produces little effect. The more cohesive a group, the greater its influence over its members. People are more likely to conform to those perceived as attractive, expert, or of high status. They are more likely to conform when they must respond publicly than privately, and having made a public commitment, they hesitate to change it.

While early studies indicated that females may conform more than males, subsequent research has not found strong differences in conformity between the sexes. However, cultural values do influence conformity. Compared to people in individualistic societies, those in collectivist countries are more responsive to social influence. Such variations suggest that people can be socialized to be more or less conforming. Specific personality characteristics are only moderately related to conformity. For example, higher self-esteem has been associated with less conformity, but the relationship is not as strong as might be expected.

While the degree to which people conform is often surprising, research also indicates that a person may resist being influenced. People are not puppets, and when social pressure becomes blatant, they may act to restore their freedom. This may be expressed in an increased liking for the choice the group seeks to prohibit. Resistance is particularly strong when the issue is important and when people believe they have a right to choose for themselves. Studies also suggest that while people do not want to appear too different from others, they do not want to appear too similar either. They may resist influence in an attempt to maintain their distinctiveness and sense of individuality.

References

Asch, S. E. (1956). Studies of independence and conformity. *Psychological Monographs, 7* (9, Whole No. 416).

Sherif, M. (1935). A study of some social factors in perception. *Archives of Psychology, 187,* 60.

Additional Reading

Ross, L., & Nisbett, R. E. (1991). *The person and the situation.* New York: McGraw-Hill.

M. BOLT

See OBEDIENCE; COMPLIANCE.

Confrontation in Therapy. An active intervention tool by which the therapist brings a client into contact with an issue. Like questions, probes, and directives, confrontation is noninterpretive. Confrontation is different from less active interventions such as interpretations, reflections, and restatements. When a confrontation is made, the therapist offers a one-sided observation. An interpretation, by way of contrast, is a shared discovery between the therapist and client.

The use of confrontation in therapy is analogous to its use in other interpersonal relationships. Confrontation is most effective when it is conducted in an atmosphere of mutual trust and openness. The timing of confrontation is critical. Its overuse may lead to client passivity, as might be the case if confrontation were overused in a friendship.

Jesus frequently used confrontation in his relationships and was also confrontive when dealing with people in need. His use of confrontation serves as a good model for the counselor.

The more directive and active therapies advocate a greater use of confrontation. All advocates of confrontation emphasize the need to be accurate and discerning in its use. One danger in the therapeutic use of confrontation is that the therapist may assume an authoritarian role or a condemnatory stance toward the client. A major benefit of confrontation is its facility in helping the severely disturbed or the decompensating client.

Garner (1970) proposed a model called confrontation problem-solving therapy. The therapist confronts the client with some aspect of the client's behavior. This is followed by a question to determine the client's understanding of the reaction to the confrontation. The goal is to foster good reality testing.

Confrontation is also essential to the theory of Adams (1970). Adams builds his view of counseling around the Greek word *nouthesis,* defined as a caring confrontation. The aim of nouthetic confrontation is to effect change in the counselee by encouraging greater conformity to the principles of Scripture (*see* Nouthetic Counseling).

In the analytic therapies confrontation is an auxiliary intervention used mainly when interpretation is unfeasible or insufficient. For example, analysts use confrontation in the face of acting out, in emergencies, or when a client is decompensating. Analysts feel that confrontation has limitations because it deals with surface resistance and defenses and it interrupts the flow of a session.

Confrontation is also central to many group therapies that advocate helping clients encounter previously unknown personality facets. In this sense confrontation is more than an intellectual interaction; it is a substantive emotional interaction.

References

Adams, J. E. (1970). *Competent to counsel.* Grand Rapids, MI: Baker.

Garner, H. H. (1970). *Psychotherapy: Confrontation problem-solving technique.* St. Louis: Green.

Additional Reading

Hoffman, J. C. (1979). *Ethical confrontation in counseling.* Chicago: University of Chicago Press.

J. R. BECK

See COUNSELING AND PSYCHOTHERAPY: OVERVIEW.

Congregational Dynamics. The church is charged with achieving heavenly goals through human vessels. The Bible gives specific directives as to how Christians are to relate to each other in the church precisely because human nature, especially human behavior in groups, can so easily disrupt smooth group functioning toward the goals of worship, edification, evangelism, and mission. An examination of congregational dynamics must address theology of the church, social psychology, typical church group dynamics, and pastoral management of flock potential and problems.

Church Theology. Commissioned to glorify God by advancing the gospel on earth, early church leaders had authority to protect the truth and lead members into greater conformity with it. Using biblical teachings on godly behavior as the rule, norms about church relations are developed and taught by pastors and elders with authority to enforce discipline on individuals threatening their own personal well-being as well as group mission by their unscriptural attitudes and actions (De Koster, 1984). Generally agreed-upon norms include active agape love and service toward one another, respect for church leaders' authority, telling the truth in love, avoiding gossip, pursuing peace, and mutual accountability.

Social Psychology. Findings from the field of social psychology contribute to an understanding of how people in groups (such as church leaders and congregants) experience forces that work both for and against adherence to these norms. Being in the presence of a group can increase task performance, increase dominant (trained) responses, and increase compliance with norms. Group therapy literature (see Yalom, 1975) shows the positive effects of a cohesive group: hope for desired change, modeling healthy behavior, sharing successful problem-solving skills, and a sense of belonging and affirmation leading to improved self-esteem.

Organizational studies (see Covey, 1990) show how team building can create synergy—a process whereby the group accomplishes greater and more creative results than an individual through the combination of talents.

However, group influence can also cause effects contrary to church goals: decreased individual accountability (anonymity breeds release from responsibility); increased psychological reactivity (a state of arousal related to concerns about group approval); group think (concurrence becomes more important than consideration of alternative views); and cult indoctrination (an authoritarian leader uses group pressure to force compliance with selfish aims; see Myers, 1993).

Congregational Dynamics—The Healing Community. When church leadership and norms are biblical, group dynamics operate in the way intended by the Creator God who knows we are made of dust and understands the way humans operate in groups. The power of group influence is channeled for the advance of Christ's kingdom. The church body becomes a healing community. Pastors cast a godly vision for the church that members own and pursue without reactive rebellion. Pastors work in concert with elders for the good of the body, eschewing power plays. Leaders provide a living lesson of progressive sanctification. Members evidence grace in cooperation and in conflict: esteeming others over themselves and showing mercy to the weaker members, yet confronting face to face in love. In this environment believers are able to confess failures and receive discipling help, then treat others with the grace they have experienced, and finally move boldly into leadership with group support. There is an ever-widening circle of influence as nonbelievers are reached and see the power of love lived out in a biblical community.

Congregational Dynamics—Conflict. Conflict is normal and healthy in any group striving for close fellowship as well as high goals. Positively managed along biblical rules of engagement, conflict can increase communication, prevent wrong turns, and foster creativity of programs. Common areas of church conflict include theology, leadership, tradition, direction, handling of people issues, and personalities. However, when a conflict spills well beyond reasonable limits, becomes rancorous, or gets stuck in long-term bitterness, it is likely that personal issues of individuals are at issue.

Every experienced church leader knows the too-familiar pattern of church conflict due to individuals' past baggage. Members who have not dealt with family wounds see intent to hurt in leaders' actions and react with displaced anger. Pastors and elders who have not learned their own trigger points can cause or exacerbate turmoil. Abetted by the devil, the disgruntled individual takes the easy path: make the "enemy" all bad and yourself all good; gather other malcontents (often with similar past issues) to buttress your case; gossip, slander, and tear down; berate, accuse, and demand; sulk and play the aggrieved victim. A small issue becomes a large one as the original group gathers other members who assume where there is smoke there is fire. Bible passages are hurled, with both sides unable to remove the log in their own eye.

Pastoral Management. Pastors must realize that management is a crucial component of their job, and facing important issues head on and early reduces the risk of several negative results (Buzzard, 1983). Pastors want to avoid church splits, compromising the gospel truth, getting co-opted, and damaging members of the flock. They also want to avoid or ignore conflict, most of them having a nurturing versus a fighting bent. Sometimes a resistant individual or family must be confronted and possibly leave the church in order to preserve the ongoing mission of the larger group. When pastors realize that addressing conflict biblically protects the flock they are called to shepherd, they are motivated to learn how to resolve conflict.

Pastors who are skilled in conflict resolution use standard tools of listening with neutrality, negotiating for a win-win resolution, compromising on nonessentials, and unifying around shared vision. Calling in a reconciliation team is especially helpful when rifts are long-standing, broad, or resistant to in-house efforts. When appropriate, a simple acknowledgment of hurt and honest request for forgiveness can heal small disputes (Shelley, 1993).

With recalcitrant conflicts pastors have many management options. First, congregants must be taught three basic rules of disagreement: contribute your opinion at meetings in an appropriate manner—disagree without being disagreeable; discuss your concerns about the vote or decision of the body directly with the people involved without spreading the dispute; if you cannot stay on the team, go to another body where you can support the vision.

Though attacks on a pastor's motives and ministry are extremely painful, following six Cs of conflict can decrease the total anguish. First, clarify: Ask, Are you saying you can't support this decision? Many fights are avoided by clearing up misunderstandings at the start. Second, pour cold water on small issues. Troubled parishioners too often are allowed to become bigger than life when everyone jumps to their cry of Fire! Third, cast light all over a legitimate concern. Never take anonymous complaints and never allow fear of discomfort to preclude discussion. Fourth, confront complaining congregants early and with witnesses. This step is counterintuitive to many young pastors but prevents debilitating turmoil for the body and pastor. Fifth, call for a healthy choice on the part of the grumblers: "John, I hope we can resolve this and work effectively together again, but if you can't I release you to find another body you can support in which to serve our Lord." Finally, carry on with the ministry Christ has given, shaking the dust, remembering the flock who are still following, and working through the wounds with God's help.

References

Buzzard, L. (1983). War and peace in the local church. *Leadership, 4*, 20–30.

Covey, S. R. (1990). *Principle-centered leadership.* New York: Summit.

De Koster, L. (1984). In W. A. Elwell (Ed.), *Evangelical dictionary of theology.* Grand Rapids, MI: Baker.

Myers, D. G. (1993). *Social psychology* (4th ed.). New York: McGraw-Hill.

Shelley, M. (Ed.). (1993). Conflict. *Leadership, 14* (1).

Yalom, I. D. (1975). *The theory and practice of group psychotherapy* (2nd ed.). New York: Basic.

K. M. Lattea

See Group Dynamics.

Congruence. As developed by Rogers (1957) congruence refers to an accurate matching of experience, awareness, and communication. It can be illustrated by a hungry infant who is crying. The baby experiences hunger at the visceral level, is fully aware of being hungry, and communicates the discomfort of hunger.

Incongruence can be illustrated by a man engaged in an argument whose face is flushed, whose voice is raised, and who shakes his finger at his opponent but denies being angry. It seems clear that at the physiological level the man is experiencing anger. His denial of anger may be due to lack of awareness of his experience or unwillingness to communicate his experience. In either case there is not an accurate matching of experience, awareness, and communication.

The concept of incongruence can also be used to describe a discrepancy between the perceived self (self-concept) and the experiencing self. For example, a woman may cherish the concept of being a good tennis player but may experience frequent defeats by mediocre players. Logically this should cause the woman to revise her self-concept downward with respect to her tennis-playing ability. However, if skill at tennis is an important part of her self-concept, the woman may cling to this belief in spite of her experience. A number of stratagems may be used to maintain this faulty self-concept. She may quit playing tennis, thus becoming the "retiring champ," or she may play only weak opponents, thus continuing to win.

Congruence on the part of the therapist has been found to be one of the three important therapist interpersonal factors in the success of psychotherapy, the other two being empathy and nonpossessive warmth. These three factors are often referred to as the therapeutic triad. Congruence in the context of psychotherapy means that the therapist is fully aware of the feelings he or she experiences and is able to communicate them to the client if appropriate. According to Rogers (1961), if the therapist is experiencing persistent negative feelings toward the client, it may be necessary to communicate these feelings to the client. For example, to maintain congruence among experience, awareness, and communication the therapist may have to say, "I may be wrong, but I have the feeling that you are not being honest with me." In a summary of eight studies related to the therapeutic effectiveness of congruence, Truax and Mitchell (1971) found that in seven of the studies overall combined outcome measures favored the hypothesis, while none of the overall combined measures were against the hypothesis.

Rogers (1961) believes that congruence is as important in other interpersonal relationships as it is in psychotherapy. He has suggested as a general law of interpersonal relationships: the greater the congruence of experience, awareness, and communication on the part of one individual, the more the ensuing relationship will involve "a tendency toward reciprocal communication with a quality of increasing congruence; a tendency toward more mutually accurate understanding of the communications; improved psychological adjustment and functioning in both parties; and mutual satisfaction in the relationship" (p. 344).

References

Rogers, C. R. (1957). The necessary and sufficient conditions of therapeutic personality change. *Journal of Consulting Psychology, 21,* 95–103.

Rogers, C. R. (1961). *On becoming a person*. Boston: Houghton Mifflin.

Truax, C. B., & Mitchell, K. M. (1971). Research on certain therapist skills in relation to process and outcome. In A. E. Bergin & S. L. Garfield (Eds.), *Handbook of psychotherapy and behavior change*. New York: Wiley.

O. Scandrette

See Rogers, Carl Ransom; Person-Centered Therapy.

Conjoint Family Therapy. A model of therapy in which a therapist sees family members together when one of them, usually a troublesome child, is identified as the one needing help. The term is most strongly identified with Satir (1967).

Satir took her training in social work, which has a larger-than-the-individual emphasis. In 1959 she brought that perspective to the Mental Research Institute in Palo Alto, California, where she collaborated with Jackson, Bateson, Watzlawick, and others associated with the communications theory of psychopathology and family systems functioning. Harry Stack Sullivan's earlier work on interpersonal theories of personality significantly influenced this group's leading force, Jackson.

Satir identified with the optimistic, experiential humanism referred to as the "third force" in mid-twentieth-century American psychology. She was one of three remarkable therapists (with Fritz Perls and Milton Erickson) studied by the founders of neurolinguistic programming, Bandler and Grinder. These two astute observers reduced Satir's effective actions to descriptive terms. *Changing with families* (Bandler, Grinder, & Satir, 1976) semantically analyzed key verbal sequences that Satir used to clarify communications between members of a dysfunctional family system.

In her view of human nature Satir emphasizes that all behavior, no matter how distorted, aims at preserving and enhancing self-esteem. Virtually synonymous with self-esteem is a person's sense of being esteemed, validated, welcomed, and responded to congruently by others. Therefore, behavior that society regards as "sick, crazy, stupid, or bad" is really a message signaling distress and requesting help. Everyone can learn to communicate feelings more effectively and thus escape his or her psychic prisons.

Satir calls her model of therapy a growth model, in contrast to the medical model and the sin model. She caricatures the latter as a critical, moralistic model; it lacks the element of good news that the Bible announces for persons whose values, beliefs, and attitudes make them incongruent with the blueprint by which a loving God created them.

Satir is evidently antichurch, since she sees Christianity causing more guilt than is good for people. She regards pathology as dysfunctional communication by individuals within families and cultures. In this she comes close to the profound insight expressed by an Old Testament prophet: "I am a man of unclean lips and live among a people of unclean lips" (Isa. 6:5).

Illness in a person derives from inadequate methods of communicating in that person's intimate relationships. It follows that the goal of therapy is to improve those methods. That means putting into clear, direct words messages that have been delivered in the past by unclear and indirect nonverbal gestures and nuances. Most of these transactions have been outside the awareness of the participants, so they could never talk about them. Therapists make the covert overt.

One of the primary topics that people can learn to talk about is differentness. Therapists work to immunize family members against the jarring effects of discovering that loved ones think, feel, perceive, and desire in ways different from themselves. A therapist "raises their capacity to give and minimizes their sensitivities to painful subjects, thereby decreasing the necessity for defenses" (Satir, 1967, p. 165).

The conjoint therapist concentrates especially on reducing the threat of blame, so as to build "a safe, understanding framework within which child and mates will be able to comment on what they see and hear" (Satir, 1967, p. 132). Achieving this safety is a primary step toward uncovering the root of all family problems—discord in the husband-wife relationship.

In her role as therapist Satir actively manages the sessions. She structures the first two to four sessions by taking a family chronology. She questions relentlessly and specifically, often repeating her questions as if a little slow to catch on. This repetition simplifies and clarifies what had previously been to the family confusing, overwhelming aspects of their lives.

Absolutely opposed to any hint of faultfinding, Satir speaks of the identified patient's "pain" and says that the whole family hurts. She thus shifts the investigative aspect of therapy from that of a policeman seeking to arrest a villain to that of a curious child seeking to solve a puzzle. She spreads ownership of the problem to the family. She further fosters a "we" orientation in positive ways by citing the strengths of the family, especially the storms they have already weathered in their history. She highlights the relationship-seeking intention behind even the most hurtful actions. At the end of the first interview she assigns each family member to make it known when pleased by what another member does.

Conjoint family therapy is primarily a means for fostering more enjoyable and productive relationships among persons living or working together in systems. Management relations, marriage enrichment, and premarital counseling increasingly use concepts that Satir and her colleagues advocate.

References

Bandler, R., Grinder, J., & Satir, V. (1976). *Changing with families*. Palo Alto, CA: Science and Behavior Books.

Satir, V. *Conjoint family therapy* (Rev. ed.). (1967). Palo Alto, CA.: Science and Behavior Books.

D. L. GIBSON

See FAMILY THERAPY: OVERVIEW; FAMILY COMMUNICATIONS THEORY.

Conscience. The set of personality processes involved in evaluating oneself by one's accepted ideals or standards. Beyond this broad definition, however, there is little agreement on the precise meaning and nature of conscience. Psychological theorists shape their understanding and definition of conscience to fit their theoretical framework. Fromm (1947), for example, spoke of an infantile, fear-based, authoritarian conscience and a more mature, rational, and sensitive humanistic conscience. Allport (1955) wrote of the generic conscience that enhances one's life, and Freud (1923/1927) drew a general parallel between his concept of the superego and conscience.

Theologians also differ in their understanding of conscience. Pierce (1955, p. 111), for example, sees conscience as God-given and the punitive functions of conscience as "the internal counterpart and complement of the wrath" of God. In contrast, Bavinck (1898) and Bonhoeffer (1959) view conscience as a result of the fall and as carrying out fallen humanity's attempt to know good and evil apart from God and to solve its moral dilemma on its own. Aquinas views conscience as a dimension of self-knowledge, of one's human potential to be fully human and failings thereof.

Conscience in the Bible. The Old Testament has no word fully equivalent to conscience. The Hebrew *leb* (generally translated heart), however, is sometimes used to refer to the functions the New Testament calls conscience. Conscience *(syneideesis)* is used 31 times in the New Testament, but nowhere is it clearly defined. Its functions include bearing witness to or evaluating oneself in relation to a standard (Rom. 1:32); assuring one of consistent, integrative living (2 Tim. 1:3); motivating constructively (Rom. 13:5; Acts 2:16); inhibiting unnecessarily (1 Cor. 8:4–8); and producing feelings of guilt and self-condemnation (1 John 3:19–20).

The first three functions of conscience are God-given. As moral beings we are created with the capacity to observe ourselves and to live consistently and responsibly out of a motivation of love. At times, however, the conscience can also needlessly inhibit and become the source of self-punitive, destructive emotions of guilt. Although some assume these functions are also the work of God, Scripture indicates they are not, at least in the life of the believer. Paul speaks of those with a weak conscience that is overly restrictive (1 Cor. 8:7). And John indicates that condemnation is not God-given (1 John 3:20). The biblical doctrines of the atonement and justification make it clear that the believer's sins

have already been paid for and that the Christian is no longer under condemnation (Rom. 8:1). These emotions of guilt are reserved for the unrepentant, and then only as a destructive result of an impaired relationship with God and not as a motivation to repent. Only the possibility of knowing God's love and forgiveness motivates an individual toward repentance or godly sorrow. Seen in this light, the condemnation of a guilty conscience actually involves a denial of the efficacy of the atonement. It constitutes an additional, self-inflicted penalty or payment for one's sins.

Biblically, conscience functions a great deal like the law. Prior to salvation it serves the useful purposes of showing us a standard to reach for, acting as a schoolmaster (Gal. 3:24), giving moral structure to society (Exod. 21:1–31:18), showing us our failures within an awareness of God's wrath evident to human consciousness in natural revelation with corresponding feelings of anxiety (Rom. 1:18–20, 32), and driving us to despair and consequently to God's grace (Rom. 5:20–21). After salvation, however, the Christian must learn to relate to conscience in an entirely different manner, just as she or he does to the law. The attempt to merit acceptance or avoid punishment by living up to the demands of conscience can be as much a legalistic process as the attempt to merit God's approval by living up to the law (*see* Legalism). This effort to merit approval and avoid the condemnation of conscience must be replaced by the following: a wise transformation of an misinformed conscience, a humble openness to the dictates of a well-formed conscience, resulting in inner congruity or incongruity, the latter requiring repentance; and a profound awareness in the Spirit—motivated by love, modeled by the church—that Christ has taken our condemnation and that we are now acceptable through him.

The Development of Conscience. The processes we know as conscience develop out of the complex interaction between one's God-given moral potential, which is rooted in the image of God and progressively unfolds with the development of one's cognitive capacities; one's own desires and attempts to merit self-acceptance and avoid punishment; and the impact of socializing agents, particularly parents. Although the Bible does not elaborate extensively on humanity's moral nature but more on the result as good character, it does describe us as moral beings, created in the image of God with some sense of the potentials of moral development and attending awareness of psychological congruity or incongruity depending upon our development. This fundamental moral nature provides the ability for the individual to profit from the socializing process and to develop a set of moral values.

Beyond humanity's innate moral propensity, the unique shape of one's conscience is highly influenced by one's interaction with significant socialization agents. This takes place through the process of internalization. From early childhood children take in, or internalize, the ideals and expectations of parents and significant others because they fear parental punishment, rejection, or shame if they fall short and because they love and admire these significant adults. In the first five years of life parents are the main source of these expectations. As children grow older, they increasingly look to other authorities and to peers and broader social standards for the ideals they adopt.

As these ideals and expectations are internalized and merged with one's innate moral awareness and individual desires, they come together to form what is generally called the ideal self or the ego ideal. This set of ideals becomes the standard by which one judges himself or herself. These deep beliefs may or may not be congruent with the truth about human moral potential. In the case of inappropriate models and internalization, the dictates of conscience form a dilemma for the person. To act against conscience is to violate one's own psychological functioning which is designed to lead the individual into the good and to avoid evil. Yet, to follow the dictates of an ill-informed conscience may lead to a life of unnecessary suffering and moral ruin. In such cases, a slow and wise process of transformation in the context of truth and a relationship with a loving community and the Holy Spirit are required.

Thus it appears that the biblical model of conscience maintains that there is a natural, built-in capacity for discerning right and wrong, good and bad, that can be well-informed (when it is in accordance with human nature or the intended way we were created) or ill-informed (when it is contrary to human nature), depending upon a person's environment and development. While children are taking in their parents' values and standards they also internalize the corrective attitudes of significant others. When parents rely on angry, punitive corrections, children tend to take in these corrective attitudes as their own. As these punitive attitudes merge with the child's inherent sense of moral justice, they form the essential ingredients of punitive emotions of guilt generally called neurotic or false guilt. In this case, the person's development and environment have hindered the growth of a healthy or natural conscience as intended by God. Rather, it is misinformed and thus does not serve the child well. By contrast, when children take in predominantly loving disciplinary attitudes, those attitudes merge with the child's inherent moral sense and love to form a set of love-based corrective attitudes. These comprise natural feelings and awareness which are sometimes referred to as true guilt and are developmentally analogous to godly sorrow, a work of the Spirit in the heart of the believer. In this case, conscience has formed in accord with human nature and God's intention for fallen humanity.

With the completion of this process the development of the broad outlines of conscience is largely finished. Individuals have a set of standards, the perceptual ability to evaluate themselves (to bear witness), and two sets of corrective attitudes they can use to motivate themselves.

Pathologies of Conscience. Problems of conscience grow naturally out of disturbances in the function of conscience described above. Some people have problems with the functioning of conscience because they develop inadequate standards. They may have failed to internalize acceptable standards, or they may have repressed their inherent moral nature and developed antisocial or sociopathic personality styles because they have inappropriate values or a fundamental difficulty relating to others in an empathic manner. Or they may have internalized rigid, unnatural and narrow standards that inhibit unnecessarily, cause neurotic problems, and do not allow a creative and assertive style of life.

Others develop problems because of inappropriate corrective attitudes and emotions. Internalization of punitive corrective attitudes can result in the severe guilt emotions found in depressive and obsessive-compulsive personalities, the two guilt neuroses. The failure to internalize loving corrective attitudes which are at the root of an inability to love and experience empathy can lead to a lack of concern for others and consequently antisocial behavior.

Psychotherapy of Problems of Conscience. An understanding of the processes involved in the development of conscience also provides direction for resolving problems of conscience. Effective therapy needs to give attention to the development and adequacy of both one's standards and one's corrective attitudes. People who have developed rigid, unnatural neurotic standards need to rework these. Those who have repressed or failed to internalize biblically and socially appropriate values need to develop these. And people who have developed self-punitive guilt feelings need to internalize the truth that they are forgiven and accepted by God and can give up their own self-punishment. In each case this is most effectively carried out within the context of a meaningful personal relationship with the Holy Spirit and a modeling, loving community such as the church who communicate the love and forgiveness of God to the heart and conscience of the believer. These relationships based upon forgiveness provide an emotional bond to help effect deep changes in one's personal values rather than merely an intellectual change of standards.

References

Allport, G. (1955). *Becoming: Basic considerations for a psychology of personality*. New Haven, CT: Yale University Press.

Bavinck, H. (1898). *Gereformerde Dogmatiek* (Vol. 3). Kampen: Bos.

Bonhoeffer, D. (1959). *Creation and fall*. New York: Macmillan.

Freud, S. (1927). *The ego and the id*. London: Hogarth. (Original work published 1923)

Fromm, E. (1947). *Man for himself*. New York: Rinehart.

Pierce, C. A. (1955). *Conscience in the New Testament.* London: SCM.

Additional Reading

Narramore, B. (1984). *No condemnation: Rethinking guilt and motivation.* Grand Rapids, MI: Zondervan.

S. B. NARRAMORE AND J. H. COE

See GUILT; SUPEREGO; SHAME; PSYCHOANALYTIC PSYCHOLOGY.

Consciousness. Consciousness is a fundamental aspect of every human's experience, yet it is also exceptionally difficult to describe adequately. It encompasses not only our ability to be aware of many things (objects or events in our environment, bodily sensations, thoughts, images, memories, feelings, and emotions) but also our ability to think about the things we are aware of, making judgments about them, determining their meaning and importance. At a higher level it also includes our ability to reflect upon the fact that we have such abilities (to know that we know) and to question how or why we should have them. Human consciousness also includes self-awareness and a sense of agency, the perception that we are independent, conscious beings, with a past, present, and future, who can make plans, exercise judgment, solve problems, create new things, live mostly the way we choose, and control the contents of our own conscious awareness.

Since consciousness is such a defining feature of human life, one might expect the study of conscious awareness to lie at the heart of psychology. However, this is not the case. The topic was a prominent issue for the first psychologists, but it did not retain its prominence for long because it is difficult to study and is difficult to reconcile with materialistic views of human nature. Materialists deny the existence of a spiritual realm or human spirits, assert that all life came into being by chance through evolution, depict humans as highly evolved animals, and believe that all human capacities arise solely from the physical operations of the brain. Attributes like self-awareness, human choice, and conscious agency are difficult to explain with a reductionistic model of this type. For these reasons the study of consciousness was largely neglected until the late 1960s.

William James (1890/1983) provided some foundations for a psychology based on the study of conscious experience in *Principles of Psychology*. His insights were astute. His list of higher attributes of consciousness included subjectivity (every thought belongs to a personal self and is expressed in terms of "I feel," "I believe"), change (the contents of consciousness change constantly in a deliberate rather than a passive way), and continuity (awareness flows smoothly from one thought, event, or feeling to the next without interruption or noticeable breaks, even closing the gap between waking and sleeping). Consciousness is selective (we attend to only a small portion of the events or thoughts that are potentially available) and intentional (we think objectively, separating what we are thinking about from ourselves). James acquired these insights by a process of introspection, examining his own conscious experiences and comparing them to experiences reported by others. His work was well received but failed to generate a following, primarily because introspection seemed to many to be a weak and limiting technique.

Investigators also veered away from James's introspective approach because they were persuaded that the only way to progress in psychology was to adopt the methods that were rapidly advancing knowledge in chemistry and physics. However, this approach also created tensions because there are fundamental differences between physical and psychological variables that limit the usefulness of physical techniques.

Physical variables produce observable physical effects that are unambiguously measurable. They also affect one another in predictable, lawful ways. (A chemist can repeatedly combine measured quantities of A and B and always obtain a predictable amount of C.) By contrast, psychological (conscious) experiences are private and directly observable only by the person who has them. Thus conscious experiences can be studied only indirectly through verbal reports. In addition interesting psychological variables (e.g., perceptions, memories, moods, aggression, love) are attributes of complex, living, conscious agents, not of simple, inanimate, physical objects. As such they are likely to be strongly influenced by the agent's attitudes and conscious choices as well as an experimenter's manipulations. Such factors can seriously compromise the use of physical science methods in psychology.

Some of the early researchers recognized these constraints and restricted their study to conscious processes that seemed closely tied to physical events in the brain. For instance, Ernst Weber and Gustav Fechner used scientific methods to study sensation and successfully discovered lawful relationships between various physical stimuli and the sensations these produced (*see* Psychophysics). Others, like Edward Titchener, who did not heed the constraints, did not fare so well.

Titchener proposed that conscious experience is constructed from a limited number of "elements" (simple sensory experiences and feelings) that combine in lawful ways to produce more complex precepts and ideas, much as atoms combine into molecules. He also believed that the elements of experience can be discovered through the process of introspection (carefully recording one's elemental sensations and feelings) and that it is possible to deduce the laws of combination once the elements of experience are identified. Titchener's approach (known as structuralism) proved unproductive and embarrassing and was soon abandoned. Its failure underscored the difficulty of applying the methods of physical science to the study of conscious experience, cast doubt on the efficacy of introspection, and helped set the stage for radical behaviorism.

In 1913 John B. Watson argued forcibly for behaviorism, an approach that would establish psychology as an empirical science by limiting study to variables that are physical and measurable (e.g., environmental events and behaviors). To justify their elimination of conscious experience from psychology, radical behaviorists embraced a view of mind and brain called epiphenomenalism. This position acknowledges the existence of conscious experience but also asserts that conscious experiences are produced entirely by the brain and play no role in controlling the actions of the body. According to this position, our sense of conscious agency is an illusion and all of our conscious experiences are merely byproducts of brain activity. By taking this position behaviorists tried to get rid of the problem of human agency by denying that it exists.

Psychologists of the time wanted psychology to be a strong (physical) science and endorsed the prevailing materialistic/evolutionary views of human nature, so Watson's arguments prevailed and behaviorism rapidly became the dominant paradigm in American psychology. It remained dominant through the 1960s but gradually lost power as cognitive psychology and humanism gained in prominence. During the reign of behaviorism, "mentalist" subjects like consciousness, introspection, attention, mental imagery, dreaming, and hypnosis were rarely mentioned in textbooks or in the psychological literature. Now, however, after a long period of banishment they are back and are once more considered respectable topics.

Two groups of psychologists currently are interested in conscious experience. Cognitive psychologists, who are materialists and still rely heavily on physical data wherever possible, are particularly interested in decision making, problem solving, mental imagery, perception, and memory, and a few have ventured into studies of hypnosis (Hillstrom, 1988) or altered states of consciousness (Farthing, 1992). Psychologists in the second group are interested in conscious awareness itself and in mind-brain relationships. They also study altered states of consciousness, near-death and out-of-body experiences, paranormal events, and other topics that suggest that humans may be more than just physical beings. Many in this group are sympathetic with Eastern or New Age beliefs, which posit that humans and everything else are essentially spiritual in nature. Psychologists in this latter group have adopted the word *consciousness* to describe their field of interests (Ornstein, 1977; Pelletier, 1978; Tart, 1969). So far there is no obvious representation of the Christian perspective in this area of study.

Human consciousness is a complex and provocative subject that addresses some fundamental questions about human nature. It currently encompasses three main areas of study: mind/brain relationships, altered states of consciousness, and conscious versus subconscious mental operations. Since these are all lengthy topics, only a few of the noteworthy developments in these areas will be summarized here.

Mind/Brain Relationships. Humans have been curious about the origins of mindedness (conscious awareness, sense of self, agency, language, cognitive, and creative capabilities) for a very long time. Explanations for these phenomena fall into three major categories: materialistic monism or materialism, spiritual monism (also known as idealism), and dualism. Materialists believe that humans are only physical and that our qualities of mindedness are ultimately produced by the brain. Spiritual monists maintain that humans and everything else are composed of a universal spiritual substance (part of "God"). In this view conscious qualities are a property of the spiritual substance from which we are formed. (Many idealists also believe that the physical appearance of humans and objects is an illusion.) Dualists believe that humans are composed of both body and spirit and that unique qualities of human mindedness are probably imparted by the spirit or perhaps by the human brain and spirit working as a unit.

Two developments in this area are worthy of mention. One is an increasing interest in idealism or spiritual monism. As noted, this view is appealing to psychologists who are sympathetic with Eastern or New Age views of human nature. The second development is the continuing evolution in materialistic thinking. In the 1920s most behaviorists endorsed epiphenomenalism. Many materialists later shifted to a more defensible position known as identity theory. This theory postulates that mind and brain are one and the same and that qualities of mindedness are what humans experience while their brains are at work at various tasks. On the surface this view appears to allow materialists to have their cake and eat it too. If self and brain are one and the same, then it is permissible to speak of a self/brain that can make choices and control actions. This position also implies that in principle one should be able to understand consciousness by studying physical events in the brain.

However, identity theory also has its problems. Events in the brain (impulses, transmitter release, electrical excitation) are different in kind from events of the mind (thoughts, feelings, sensations), and it is impossible to show that there is a one-to-one correspondence between them.

There is also evidence that suggests thoughts can produce measurable changes in brain activity, which implies that thoughts (activities of the mind) and the brain are two different things. In light of such difficulties many materialists have shifted their position again. In the newer perspective mind and brain are different things; however the mind "arises" from the brain. This position is not far from inter-active dualism (which also posits a separate "mind" and brain), and it also raises some difficult questions. How could the brain give rise to a separate entity, mind, which then somehow acquires the power to influence the brain, even using it for its own ends?

Altered States of Consciousness. Altered states can be produced by a variety of agents, including sleep, drugs, sensory deprivation, hypnosis, Eastern meditative techniques, psychosis, and others. It is worth noting that even though these various states differ in many respects, they also have important commonalities. They all impair critical thinking, memory, and the ability to distinguish between what is real and unreal, while making people hypersuggestible and opening the door for all sorts of imaginary or visionary experiences. They can also impart a profound sense of realism, truthfulness, and spiritual significance to the events that unfold, whether the experiences have any basis in reality (e.g., sensing holiness and spiritual light emanating from a peach and falling to one's knees to worship the peach when a person is under the influence of LSD). "Spiritual" experiences that occur in altered states of consciousness can be deceptive (Hillstrom, 1995; *see* Ecstatic Religious Experiences).

Conscious versus Nonconscious Mental Operations. This is currently an active area of research in cognitive psychology. Some of the topics of interest include selective attention (the process by which our minds or brains select portions of incoming sensory information to attend to while ignoring the rest), episodic memory (memory for personal episodes in one's life) and how this can be disrupted by some types of brain injury, and impression formation (the nonconscious manner in which we process cues from body language or facial expressions to obtain impressions about another person's friendliness, motives, or competence). Cognitive psychologists are also researching the many automatic cognitive and sensory-motor programs that enable us to carry out skilled activities such as driving, typing, knitting, walking, or automatically decoding the meaning of spoken or written words with little conscious effort.

References

Farthing, G. W. (1992). *The psychology of consciousness.* Englewood Cliffs, NJ: Prentice-Hall.

Hillstrom, E. L. (1995). *Testing the spirits.* Downers Grove, IL: InterVarsity Press.

James, W. (1983). *The principles of psychology.* Cambridge: Harvard University Press. (Original work published 1890)

Ornstein, R. E. (1977). *The psychology of consciousness* (2nd ed.). New York: Harcourt Brace Jovanovich.

Pelletier, K. R. (1978). *Toward a science of consciousness.* New York: Dell.

Tart, C. T. (1969). *Altered states of consciousness.* New York: Wiley.

E. L. HILLSTROM

See MIND-BRAIN RELATIONSHIP; SELF; PERSONHOOD; TRANSPERSONAL PSYCHOLOGY.

Constitutional Personality Theory. Primarily attributed to the work of William Herbert Sheldon, this theory is part of the general study of constitutional psychology, or the relationship between one's physiological and psychological composition. The term "constitution" in the medical literature, though imprecise, refers to the general biological makeup of the organism that at least partially determines the individual's reaction, successful or unsuccessful, to environmental demands. From Hippocrates to the present, numerous attempts have been made to link constitution with behavior.

Investigations during the 1920s by the German psychiatrist Ernst Kretschmer on the relationship between body build and mental disorder provided the basis for Sheldon's (1944; Sheldon & Stevens, 1942) work. The value of Kretschmer's work was limited by the restricted nature of his sample (i.e., only people with mental disorders). Sheldon's typology not only included a broader sample but also involved a more sophisticated measurement system than that used by Kretschmer and other predecessors. Sheldon and his associates searched for regularities in the physiques of thousands of nude male college students (from photographs) and in personality trait dimensions. They (Sheldon, Hartl, & McDermott, 1949) concluded that three general body types express predictable personality patterns: endomorphs, with a relative predominance of fatty tissue, are more sociable, complacent, and expressive of feelings; mesomorphs, with a relative predominance of muscle, bone, and connective tissue, are more adventurousness, competitive, energetic, and favor activities that require boldness or courage; and ectomorphs, with a predominately slender and fragile build, are more inhibited and sensitive.

Much of Sheldon's research has been criticized on methodological grounds. For example, Sheldon himself, along with his research colleagues, made the physical and psychological ratings rather than relying on independent raters. Other more methodologically sound studies (Cortes & Gatti, 1965; Yates & Taylor, 1978), by either utilizing independent raters or by having investigators rate the somatotypes and then asking the subjects to independently assess their own personality characteristics, have produced evidence partially supporting Sheldon's theory.

The corroborative evidence is, however, primarily correlational in nature, and there is little direct confirmation of Sheldon's biological position. As an alternative to Sheldon's genetic hypothesis, social learning theory proposes that the relation between physiological and psychological characteristics is the result of learning. That is, people learn and maintain through the media and through social contacts certain stereotypes about the kinds of personality traits associated with specific body builds.

These stereotypes are often transmitted to children, who learn to incorporate, based on their own body concepts, the expected personality characteristics into their own self-concept.

The primary shortcomings of Sheldon's theory are therefore twofold. First, though his measurement system was an improvement over an earlier work, his technique was still too imprecise and subjective to assess personality characteristics in a scientific manner. Second, research supporting the theory is limited and only correlational in nature, thereby not conclusively confirming or even testing Sheldon's biological position. Yet Sheldon's theory is valuable to the extent that the fundamental ideas underlying modern typologies in psychological trait theories, such as those proposed by Raymond Bernard Cattell and Hans Jurgen Eysenck, can be found in his work.

References

Cortes, J. B., & Gatti, F. M. (1965). Physique and self-descriptions of temperament. *Journal of Consulting Psychology, 29,* 432–439.

Sheldon, W. H. (1944). Constitutional factors in personality. In J. M. Hunt (Ed.), *Personality and the behavior disorders.* New York: Ronald.

Sheldon, W. H., & Stevens, S. S. (1942). *The varieties of temperament.* New York: Harper & Row.

Sheldon, W. H., Hartl, E. M., & McDermott, E. (1949). *Varieties of delinquent youth: An introduction to constitutional psychiatry.* New York: Harper & Row.

Yates, J., & Taylor, J. (1978). Stereotypes for somatotypes: Shared beliefs about Sheldon's physiques. *Psychological Reports, 43,* 777–778.

P. C. HILL

See PERSONALITY.

Consultation and Referral. The concepts of consultation and referral refer to the processes through which professional assistance is obtained. The two terms are often used interchangeably in lay and professional circles. They share the following basic steps that any caregiver, professional or lay person, should take in helping people to obtain appropriate professional care: recognize that there is a need, determine the general nature of the need, determine what resources and/or interventions may be required to meet the need, assess whether one possesses the necessary competencies or qualifications to properly meet the need, seek professional assistance when the need exceeds one's ability to appropriately meet the need, and collaborate as needed and requested with the referral resource or consultant in addressing the need.

There are some generally held distinctions between the consultation and referral processes. Referral typically refers to a lay caregiver (e.g., pastor, teacher, family member, or friend) recommending that someone in need should pursue professional evaluation and intervention from a trained mental health care provider (e.g., psychologist, psychiatrist, or one of various types of trained counselors).

Consultation typically refers to the act of one professional consulting with another professional when additional or different expertise is required. A consultant is typically involved in two situations: when there is a need for a second professional opinion on diagnosis or treatment strategy or when there is a need to obtain specialized evaluation (e.g., psychoeducational testing by a psychologist to evaluate for a possible learning problem underlying a teenager's failure in school, as part of a community-based or church-based counseling program for substance abuse and behavioral problems) or when there is a need to implement some adjunctive intervention (e.g., a family physician or a psychiatrist prescribing medication for a depressed husband adjunct to ongoing psychotherapy with a psychologist for a complicated bereavement after the traumatic death of his wife).

In professional-to-professional consultation the professional requesting consultative assistance from another professional will often stay involved as a primary care provider for the person in need during and after whatever more specialized or adjunctive care is being provided by the consultant. For example, a marriage and family counselor might suspect that the lack of progress in counseling with a particular family is the result of a possible personality disorder in one of the parents. In such a case the counselor may seek out consultation from a clinical psychologist who evaluates the parent, diagnoses the suspected disorder, and initiates adjunctive psychotherapy with the parent while the family counselor continues to conduct the family counseling, coordinating care as needed with the psychologist.

Professional consultation is often requested if an organization or agency is the client. A psychologist, for example, may be called on to consult with a church's ministerial staff and lay leaders in handling suspected child abuse involving one of the leaders in the youth program and in developing policy to more effectively deal with similar situations in the future. The client in need would be the church and its leaders. If mental health services for individuals involved in the crisis are needed and/or if the church needs to have the employee evaluated for risk management purposes, the consulting psychologist would assist the church to refer these needs to other properly qualified professionals.

Lay caregivers should establish and maintain an ongoing relationship with a properly trained, well-credentialed, trustworthy, and respected mental health professional in their area who can serve reliably as their referral and consultation resource person. This professional should be licensed for the independent practice of one of the mental health disciplines, should be readily accessible, and should have good connections with the professional community. This professional should be a highly trained generalist rather than a specialist in one narrow area of practice. The lay caregiver should be sufficiently informed about and supportive of this professional's personal beliefs and values and professional practices so as to assist referred people to be properly informed consumers. Lay caregivers should compassionately but assertively assist people they are trying to refer to creatively work through the real and imagined barriers to obtaining professional assistance, such as barriers related to cost, geographic and time convenience, stereotypes about mental health professionals or their methods, and people who pursue psychological services.

As in all types of health care, the interests of people needing psychological or psychiatric services are best served if they can be initially evaluated and triaged by the most highly trained and experienced professional to which they have access. A mental health provider trained and licensed at the doctoral level (i.e., Ph.D. or Psy.D. psychologist or psychiatrist) is the best person to assess and treat mental health needs. They should readily refer to other less highly trained and less costly professionals as needed, such as a well-qualified master's-degree-level mental health counselor, clinical social worker, or marriage and family therapist.

A plethora of kinds of counselors has sprung up in recent years in the United States, especially within the Christian community. Many are well trained and properly credentialed. Others are not. To avoid inadvertently referring someone to inadequate or unqualified care, always verify qualifications by looking up the professional's name in one of several respected national registries of mental health care providers at a local university library, or ask a professional resource person for assistance. Although it is not a guarantor of competence, the most highly respected resource for finding well-qualified psychologists in the United States, and the listing most insurance companies use to determine adequacy of training and experience for psychological providers, is the National Register for Health Care Providers in Psychology.

The economics of modern health insurance make it increasingly difficult for people in need to obtain access to or adequate reimbursement for quality mental health services in general and especially those within a Christian worldview. The referring caregiver, therefore, is in a unique position to assist those they refer to properly value and prioritize their needs, evaluate available options and alternatives, and assist them to make the necessary personal sacrifices of time, emotional energy, and money to make possible appropriate professional mental health care.

D. M. COOK

Consulting Psychology. In the past this term has referred more to one of several functions of psychology rather than to a type of psychologist. More recently, however, it has been used by some professionals to depict their total identity. Caplan (1970) has described consultation as the service given to a person who seeks help on a given problem by a specialist who has expert knowledge in the area of concern but who is not directly involved in the situation.

Two trends have contributed to the emergence of consulting psychology as a professional specialty subfield. The first is the growing awareness that the need for treatment is far greater than can ever be met by mental health professionals. Thus even in the 1960s consultation became one of the essential services that community mental health centers were required to provide. The second is the new awareness among many varied organizations that their effectiveness can be improved by consultation. It is now the rule rather than the exception for governmental, private, business, and service groups to routinely employ consultants in their work.

The role of the mental health consultant should be differentiated from that of friend or therapist. Consultants are experts with specific knowledge rather than friends with general interests. Furthermore, the consultant is not and does not become the primary therapist. It is the consultant's intent to enlighten the situation from a specialized viewpoint in order that the person or group may become better informed, function more effectively, and acquire skills for use in the future.

Caplan (1970) has identified four types of mental health consultation: client-centered case consultation, in which the focus of the interaction is the individual who is being treated for a problem; consultee-centered case consultation, in which the focus of the interaction is the therapist providing the treatment; program-centered administrative consultation, in which the focus of the interaction is the organization providing the service; and consultee-centered administrative consultation, in which the focus of the interaction is the individual administrator of the service program.

Organizational consultation is much broader than mental health consultation in that the psychologist is perceived as an expert in human behavior in general, not just in human psychopathology and its treatment. Organizations are understood to be the primary social units in which individuals achieve status and identity. Consultant psychologists see their work as efforts to enhance change in these social systems in order that they may accomplish their goals more successfully while fulfilling their members' lives more completely. Thus they perceive themselves as organizational development specialists and advise groups on a wide range of problems relating both to the processes through which they function and the practical methods they use to achieve their goals. They engage in problem analysis, training, conflict management, personnel selection, and program planning, to name only a few of their roles.

Reference

Caplan, G. (1970). *The theory and practice of mental health consultation*. New York: Basic.

Additional Readings

Blake, R. R., & Mouton, J. S. (1976). *Consultation*. Reading, MA: Addison-Wesley.

Lippitt, G., & Lippitt, R. (1978). *The consulting process in action*. La Jolla, CA: University Associates.

Schein, E. H. (1969). *Process consultation*. Reading, MA: Addison-Wesley.

H. N. MALONY

See APPLIED PSYCHOLOGY; INDUSTRIAL/ORGANIZATIONAL PSYCHOLOGY.

Consumer Psychology. An applied field of psychology rooted in the concerns of those who attempt to market products and services. The relevant topics and issues include advertising, sales, customer satisfaction, brand loyalty, decision making, and product development. Although the academic study of consumer behavior is usually housed at the department of marketing in a school of business, it frequently incorporates knowledge and research techniques from economics, sociology, and anthropology, as well as psychology. Social psychology may contribute the most to this field, but the study of sensation and perception, conditioning (classical and operant), modeling, memory, motivation, and personality is also relevant.

The main message that scholars in this field have for sales and advertising professionals is, Never assume that you know the customer: do research! The potential consumer is the subject of this research. Independent variables include the six Ps of marketing: product, packaging, promotional campaigns, places of distribution, price, and purchasing options. The dependent variable is how the potential customers respond: how much of the product is purchased?

There are three main research techniques in consumer behavior. Focus groups are qualitative: potential consumers are interviewed in order to understand what their concerns might be, what they are looking for in a product, what kinds of promotions they would find appealing or offensive, and most importantly, how they go about making the purchase decision. Surveys can be conducted using quantifiable questionnaires or information taken from archives such as credit histories or purchase records. These let marketers know how the purchase of one product might be associated with the purchase of other products or background variables (e.g., zip code of residence, television programs regularly viewed, whether the customer is more likely to be on the Internet). Experiments can be conducted either in laboratory conditions or in the field (e.g., running one advertising campaign in Cincinnati and comparing its results with that of another campaign run in St. Louis). New technology allows researchers to measure whether a television is on, who is watching, or (in the laboratory) how well an advertisement captures the attention as measured by a tracking of eye movements or brain metabolism.

The marketplace is not monolithic but highly segmented. The success of a product or promotion depends upon its ability to find a niche and succeed there. Demographic segmentation is based upon measurable socioeconomic background factors (e.g., age, gender, residence, education, income). Psychographic segmentation was developed principally by the followers of Abraham Maslow and attempts to divide the marketplace along the lines of personality types. Benefit segmentation focuses on developing a product and promotional campaign geared to the potential customers' understanding of what they need. When all of these segmentations are put together, the marketer knows that the segment of the market interested in new luxury cars is not the same segment as those who are looking for parts to fix up old cars, and there must be an emphasis on different advertisements in different media: *match the product with the customer in medium and message.*

Marketing and consumer psychology is also relevant to nonprofit organizations, for their success is also linked with serving an identified constituency (i.e., market segment). Building a successful practice as a clinical psychologist, building a congregation of a church, or running an effective political campaign for the local school board all depend on these marketing techniques.

Additional Readings

Assael, H. (1995). *Consumer behavior and marketing action* (6th ed.). Belmont, CA: Wadsworth.

Bearden, W. O. (1993). *Handbook of marketing scales*. Thousand Oaks, CA: Sage.

Kassarjian, H. H., & Robertson, T. S. (1991). *Handbook of consumer behavior*. Englewood Cliffs, NJ: Prentice-Hall.

O'Shaugnhessy, J. (1992). *Explaining buyer behavior: Central concepts and philosophy of science issues*. New York: Oxford University Press.

Wilkie, W. L. (1993). *Consumer behavior* (3rd ed.). New York: Wiley.

T. L. BRINK

Consumerism. A primary characteristic of postmodern society in which individuals excessively attend to acquiring, assimilating, using, experiencing, and creating various objects or simulations of objects. Research in regard to consumerism is extensive and includes analyses of the cultural, economic, psychological, sociological, and ethical aspects of consumption.

Consumerism has developed simultaneously with other economic, political, and social changes. In North America a revolutionary social transformation has taken place during the twentieth century. This transformation has included a shift away from an industrial society to a consumer society, a shift from production to consumption, and a shift from a literacy-based society to an image-based society. Understanding changes in culture is essential to understanding consumerism (Firat & Venkatish, 1995).

A significant factor related to postmodern cultural dynamics is the advent of image-centered media. Visual media such as photography, film, television, video, and computers have radically transformed all aspects of human life. These media have altered production by replacing the production of real objects with simulations and have also altered consumption. Instead of purchasing real objects, people can purchase simulated objects. Instead of consuming real experiences, people often consume simulations of experiences (Rifkin, 1970).

Visual media not only have altered consumption but also have changed the nature of the consumer. To a large extent visual media have influenced and shaped the consumer mentality. This mentality is characterized by the desire to get rather than give, to spend rather than save, and to have all perceived needs met instantly. Structures are created to meet these desires. Automatic teller machines deliver instant cash, drive-through restaurants provide fast food, and beepers, cell phones, and e-mail enable instant communication. In this present-focused culture consumers have a hard time setting long-term goals, planning for the future, or learning from the past.

Along with changes in mentality fostered by visual media, there have also been changes in intellectual processes, some of which Ellul (1985) has described. People are moving away from rational, logical, reflective ways of thinking to emotional, intuitive, reactive ways of thinking. Visual images are needed in order to set thought in motion, and concrete thinking is favored over abstract analytical thought. These changes in intellectual processes cannot help but affect the nature of consumerism.

Research directed at understanding consumerism is important to psychologists for theoretical insight and important to businesses and corporations for pragmatic reasons. Three significant aspects of consumer research relate to the values and lifestyles of consumers, motivations for consumption, and decision-making processes involved in consumption.

The values and lifestyles of consumers have been analyzed by developmental psychologists. Through research called values and lifestyles (VALS), researchers have divided the population into nine distinct categories based on their psychographics. The nine categories include "survivors and sustainers," who because of poverty are not upwardly mobile. Belongers are fairly conservative in their spending. Achievers and emulators are outer-directed and success-oriented people. I-am-me, experiential, and societally conscious individuals are inner-directed and oriented to personal growth. There are inte-grated individuals who are ready for leadership positions. This research is used by advertisers and marketers so that they can better understand their target audiences (Vivian, 1991).

Other research has focused on motivations for purchasing products. There are numerous reasons why people believe possessions are of value. Possessions have utilitarian value or enjoyment value, represent interpersonal ties, are connected to individual identity, have financial value, and contribute to a person's status or appearance (Richins, 1994). This research helps us to understand the psychological complexity of consumer behavior.

Tybout and Artz (1994) have reviewed literature on how consumers process information and how such processing affects judgments and decision making. Among the factors influencing a consumer's decision to buy are the person's gender and age, prior knowledge about the product, the context in which an advertisement appears, and the mood associated with an advertisement.

Businesses and corporations also monitor individual spending patterns. Detailed records are kept of where people spend, when they buy, and what they purchase. Centralized computer databases, bank records, credit cards, Social Security numbers, and numerous other technologies assist in consumer surveillance. Invasion of privacy and the reinforcement of social divisions are only two of the potential dangers (Lyon, 1994).

Other dangers associated with consumerism include compulsive consumption and addictions (Hirschman, 1992), self-conceptions based on cultural standards (Thompson & Hirschman, 1995), indebtedness, and living in a fantasy world.

It is important for Christians to learn how to respond to consumerism. In order to do this biblically, we need to understand the nature, problems, and dynamics of consumerism. We need to examine our priorities and values to see if they are in alignment with biblical priorities and values. We also need to develop biblical ethics in order to understand right from wrong. Christians need to learn how to think critically, biblically, and with discernment in an age of consumerism.

References

Ellul, J. (1985). *The humiliation of the word*. Grand Rapids, MI: Eerdmans.

Firat, A. F., & Venkatish, A. (1995). Liberatory postmodernism and the reenchantment of consumption. *Journal of Consumer Research, 22,* 239–267.

Hirschman, E. (1992). The consciousness of addiction: Toward a general theory of compulsive consumption. *Journal of Consumer Research, 19,* 155–179.

Lyon, D. (1994). *The electronic eye: The rise of surveillance society*. Minneapolis: University of Minnesota Press.

Richins, M. L. (1994). Valuing things: The public and private meanings of possessions. *Journal of Consumer Research, 21,* 504–521.

Rifkin, J. (1970). *Time wars: The primary conflict in human history*. New York: Harper & Row.

Thompson, C., & Hirschman, E. C. (1995). Understanding the socialized body: A poststructuralist analysis of consumers' self-conceptions, body images, and self-care practices. *Journal of Consumer Research, 22,* 139–153.

Tybout, A. M., & Artz, N. (1994). Consumer psychology. *Annual Review of Psychology, 45,* 131–169.

Vivian, J. (1991). *The media of mass communication.* Needham Heights, MA: Allyn & Bacon.

G. E. FORSBERG

Contextual Family Therapy. This approach understands human existence as primarily relational, emphasizing the ties that bind all ontic (as opposed to functional) relationships. It is rooted in the Judeo-Christian tradition, and its proponents have sought to integrate family theory and the biblical theologies of both Old and New Testaments. Other roots lie in object relations theory.

Boszormenyi-Nagy and Spark (1973), the first major expositors of this position, stressed the invisible fibers of loyalty commitments that sustain family networks. All family members keep track of their perceptions of the balances of give and take in past, present, and future. A trustworthy early environment inevitably engenders indebtedness. If the child cannot repay benefits received from parents, an emotional debt accumulates. When indebtedness is heavy, the adult child is unable to transfer loyalty from the parents and the family of origin to a new relationship, and marital commitment suffers. In the future the marital commitment will be in conflict with loyalty to the offspring as the parents seek ethical balance in the new generation. Vertical and horizontal loyalty commitments often conflict, so that the loyalty owed to previous or subsequent generations (parents, grandparents, and children) competes with loyalty owed to husband or wife, brothers and sisters, friends and peers.

The contextual family therapist assesses family dynamics on four dimensions: facts, those aspects provided by destiny, such as ethnic identity, adoption, survivorship, illness, sex, and religious identity; psychology, the individual dimension, which takes into account the psychodynamic factors of drives, psychic development, object relations, and inner experience; transactions or power alignments, those aspects emphasized by the structural and systems family theorists; and relational ethics, concerned with the "balance of equitable fairness between people, . . . the long-term preservation of an oscillating balance among family members, whereby the basic interests of each are taken into account by the others" (Boszormenyi-Nagy & Ulrich, 1981, p. 160). The emphasis on relational ethics is unique to the contextual approach. Entitlement and indebtedness are among the existential givens of life, and relationships are trustworthy only to the extent that they allow the facing of these ethical concerns.

The most basic of the existential givens is the fact of one's birth. We do not ask to be born, yet we are born into a family that inherits the invisible loyalties of countless preceding generations. Another given is the wish of every family member to establish trustworthy relationships. The assumption by therapists of adversary relationships within families violates the basic urge toward relational justice. The family is strengthened by moves toward trustworthiness and weakened by moves away from it. Thus high levels of individual merit, accumulated by supporting the interests of others, contribute to the health of the whole family.

The concept of legacy relates to the family's bookkeeping system, which tracks the debts and entitlements contributed by legacy, to which the child must adapt. One's actual entitlement is composed both of one's natural due as parent and child and of what one has come to merit. It is also existentially given that the legacies ascribed to different children in one family may be unequal. Legacy expectations are perceived by family members as ethical imperatives much more powerful than mere wishes or needs. The currency in which relational debts are paid is also dictated by the family: options available to a member of one family may not be available to a member of another family or to another member of the same family. Enlarging the range of options is one of the tasks of the contextual family therapist.

Contextual family therapists are gravely concerned about loyalty splits that allow a child to offer loyalty to one parent only at the expense of the other. It is imperative that in a situation of divorce and remarriage children not be asked to renounce loyalty to the noncustodial parent. Children are also damaged by parents who are unwilling to accept payments on the child's debt. When no repayment is acceptable, the child enters into new relationships with no emotional energy to contribute: that which is given to the mate or friend will be regarded as stolen from the parents. The tragic component of legacy is that "patterns shall be repeated, against unavailing struggle, from one generation to the next" in a revolving slate (Boszormenyi-Nagy & Ulrich, 1981, p. 166). Accounts must be settled where they were engendered, and it is critical that one's unfinished business with parents, brothers, and sisters be resolved before one enters into marriage, where legacies are compounded.

Family pathology results from relational exploitation. Examples include secret marriage contracts in which partners act out each other's negative aspects; the scapegoating of a child to bear the family's pain; the parentification of a child to provide its parents with the nurturance they never received from their parents; and relational corruption, in which persons believe that they are entitled to be unfair to all others, because they were never on the receiving end of a truly nurturing relationship.

In contextual family therapy the goal is always to move the marital partners and family members in the direction of ethical relationships. By involving members of the extended family the chains of invisible loyalty and legacy can be loosened, allowing individuals to give up symptoms and creating new options. The therapist takes a stance of multidirected partiality, taking into account the concerns of all family members, since "no family member can alone judge whether the ledger is in balance" (Boszormenyi-Nagy & Ulrich, 1981, p. 164). Where there has been pain and destruction, the goal is exoneration, "lifting the load of culpability" from the guilty person (Boszormenyi-Nagy & Krasner, 1986, p. 416). Contextual therapists avoid the loyalty conflicts inherent in traditional individual psychotherapy, in which the therapist often challenges the client's loyalty to the parents.

Krasner and her co-workers (Krasner & Joyce, 1992; Krasner & Shapiro, 1979) have integrated contextual therapy in rabbinic and Christian settings. Contextual family therapy is based on an "enlightenment ethic" (Dueck, 1992, p. 197) that can be integrated with Christian theology to develop an approach that stresses "fidelity, community, commitment, upward striving, and a reliance on a higher power that in turn fuels the process of responsible relatedness and interdependence" (Vande Kemp, 1987, p. 293). Contextual family therapy affirms the Christian values of trust, mutuality, and justice (Roberts, 1991).

References

Boszormenyi-Nagy, I., & Krasner, B. (1986). *Between give and take: A clinical guide to contextual therapy.* New York: Brunner/Mazel.

Boszormenyi-Nagy, I., & Spark, G. M. (1973). *Invisible loyalties.* New York: Harper & Row.

Boszormenyi-Nagy, I., & Ulrich, D. N. (1981). Contextual family therapy. In A. S. Gurman & D. P. Kniskern (Eds.), *Handbook of family therapy.* New York: Brunner/Mazel.

Dueck, A. C. (1992). Metaphors, models, paradigms, and stories in family therapy. In H. Vande Kemp (Ed.), *Family therapy: Christian perspectives.* Grand Rapids, MI: Baker.

Krasner, B., & Joyce, A. (1992). Between truth and trust: Elements of direct address. In H. Vande Kemp (Ed.), *Family therapy: Christian perspectives.* Grand Rapids, MI: Baker.

Krasner, B. R., & Shapiro, A. (1979). Trustbuilding initiatives in the rabbinic community. *Conservative Judaism, 33,* 3–21.

Roberts, R. C. (1991). Mental health and the virtues of community: Christian reflections on contextual therapy. *Journal of Psychology and Theology, 19,* 319–333.

Vande Kemp, H. (1987). Relational ethics in the novels of Charles Williams. *Family Process, 26,* 283-294.

H. VANDE KEMP

See FAMILY THERAPY: OVERVIEW.

Contingency Contracting. A technique used primarily in behavior therapy, by which an agreement is made between two or more parties and then formalized into a contract (written or verbal but always explicit). This contract specifies the behaviors required of the parties to the contract and spells out the consequences that are to follow those behaviors.

Behaviorists believe that behavior is in large part a function of environmental consequences of the behavior. Contracts are thus a means of clarifying and ordering in a systematic way the consequences of the client's actions. Contracts may focus on the interactions between therapist and client (e.g., specifying consequences for succeeding at agreed-upon changes in the client's behavior), interactions between spouses (e.g., specifying mutual responsibilities in the marriage and the consequences for reneging on those responsibilities), and between parent and child (e.g., defining responsibilities and privileges of the child, including loss of privileges following failure to meet responsibilities). These examples are the most common areas of use for contingency contracts. The use of a contract presupposes, first, the capacity of all parties involved to understand the details of the contract and, second, that the behaviors in question can be adequately defined and the appropriate consequences provided.

S. L. JONES

See BEHAVIOR THERAPY; APPLIED BEHAVIORAL ANALYSIS.

Contracts, Therapeutic Use of. Believing that no productive outcomes arise from therapy that does not work toward specific goals, therapists of several different theoretical orientations employ treatment goals as a contract for therapy. Such contracts sometimes also specify the role or responsibilities of both therapist and client, although a statement of mutually acceptable goals is the most common ingredient. Gestalt, transactional, and behavioral therapists most commonly employ such treatment contracts, but their use is not limited to these modalities of therapy. Their use in these approaches is consistent with the generally active role of the therapist. Contracts are thus often employed by therapists who might also utilize homework or other structured assignments.

See HOMEWORK IN PSYCHOTHERAPY.

Control Group. Those subjects in an experiment who do not receive the experimental treatment but who are otherwise as similar to subjects in the experimental group as possible. The experimental group are those subjects who receive the experimental treatment. The results are then interpreted by comparing the degree and direction of the effect on the experimental subjects to that of the control subjects.

See PSYCHOLOGY, METHODS OF; EXPERIMENTAL GROUP.

Conversion. Webster's dictionary suggests that conversion means to "turn around, transform, or change the characteristics of something." The word is sometimes used to refer to general personality or behavioral changes, such as those that result from education or psychotherapy. However, conversion refers most often to religious experiences in which attitudes or actions are dramatically altered, as when Paul was converted on the Damascus road or more recently when Malcolm Muggeridge converted to Roman Catholicism.

These illustrations refer to the distinction between inner and outer conversion as suggested by some theorists. Often the joining of a given church or religious group (termed outer conversion) is mistaken for a radical change of perception and outlook (termed inner conversion). Although both may occur simultaneously, they are not necessarily synonymous. Gordon (1967) noted this fact in studying converts by marriage to the Jewish faith. Often these are cultural conversions rather than genuine transformations of outlook. Many persons attest that they participated in outer conversion when they joined the church in early adolescence and that inner conversion followed later.

Whereas outer conversion refers to a formal action of identifying with a given faith, inner conversion refers to a newly acquired sense of inner security, unity, peace, and meaning such as is exemplified by Paul. James (1902) gave the classic definition of this experience: "To be converted, to be regenerate, to receive grace, to experience religion, to gain an assurance, are so many phrases which denote the process, gradual or sudden, by which a self hitherto divided, and consciously wrong, inferior and unhappy, becomes unified and consciously right, superior and happy, in consequence of its firmer hold upon religious realities" (p. 157). James's definition has provided many of the themes that have been investigated by psychologists since the beginning of this century. These themes have included whether conversion is a process or an event; the preconversion mental state; and the nature of the inner change that occurs in conversion.

Conversion as Process or Event? James considered conversion to be "a process, gradual or sudden," whereas many religionists have thought of it as a specific event occurring at a given time. In fact many have used the word to apply only to those who can point to a time and place at which they were born again in a manner similar to that recommended to Nicodemus by Jesus (John 3:3) and exemplified by Paul (Acts 9). However, James contended that these events were part of a process and used the term *conversion* to apply to both those who could and those who could not point to a specific moment of decision.

Healthy and Sick Converts. James contended that the self-awareness of both sudden and gradual converts was preceded by a period of preparation,

whether the individuals were conscious of it or not. He paired up sudden conversions with sick persons and gradual conversions with healthy personalities. There was no bias toward the healthy-minded in James's theory. He perceived them as weaker than their sick-minded counterparts because they were unable to bear prolonged suffering in their minds and consequently had a tendency to deny conflict and to see things optimistically. They engaged in what the psychoanalysts call repression in an effort to avoid inner turmoil. This led the healthy-minded to affirm a given type of religion, the idealistic, positive kind, and to be unaware of the time when they adopted such an outlook. James described these persons as gradual converts or as once-born persons.

Sick-minded individuals had a stronger congenital temperament. These persons were more realistic about themselves and about the world. They were able to perceive enigmas, injustices, hypocrisies, and evils. They agonized over problems in themselves in the fashion of which Paul spoke: "For what I do is not the good I want to do; no, the evil I do not want to do—this I keep on doing. . . . What a wretched man I am! Who will rescue me from this body of death?" (Rom. 7:19, 24, NIV). From a psychoanalytic point of view they had enough ego strength to keep opposing impulses in consciousness. They were not neurotic in the sense that they remained aware of the conflict. The resolution of their dilemmas typically came suddenly, and the immediate release that occurred prompted James to term these twice-born persons.

James did not make the distinctions among levels of consciousness that were later clarified by analytic theorists. However, he did suggest that sick-minded converts were more aware of their unconscious minds than were healthy-minded persons. Nevertheless, there was a sense in which he considered the sick-minded persons predisposed toward morbidity and an inability to trust either themselves or the universe. Whereas they were able to tolerate conflict better than healthy-minded persons, they also tended to remain weak and fearful after the experience and to rely too intensely on divine power. This tendency toward self-depreciation and immature dependence was characteristic of much religious experience that Sigmund Freud was later to criticize and denigrate.

Process of Conversion. A model that encompasses both gradual and sudden conversions has been proposed by Tippett (1977). It includes both periods of time and points in time in alternating sequence. Initially there is a period of growing awareness, in which the individual becomes conscious of the possibilities of a given faith answer to problems of life but sees them as peripheral to his or her own concerns. This is tantamount to saying that the answers of faith that are later affirmed by the convert must first become a part of the mind at a subliminal level. This is usually the result of cultural contact with one or more religions.

This period of growing awareness is succeeded by a point of realization, at which time the potential convert becomes aware that the faith to which she or he will later accede is not merely an idea but a possibility. Tippett contends that there is such a moment even though persons may not be able to pinpoint it. This is tantamount to saying that the cultural context that had been a backdrop for the thinking of the convert becomes somewhat more focal and results in fleeting ideas that the faith could have some personal meaning in the future.

This point of realization is succeeded by a period of consideration during which individuals wrestle with the dilemmas they face and also interact with others who have found an answer to these same problems. Persons become active seekers during this period and place themselves in settings where the faith that will later be affirmed is talked about and acted upon. As Tippett notes, the change that will later be made is never a change from no faith to a faith but a change from this faith to that faith. The ideas of faith come to the foreground in the mental life of the individual during this time. They compete with other options on an equal basis even though they do not dominate as they will in the future.

This period of consideration ends with a point of encounter for the gradual as well as the sudden convert, according to Tippett. Again, although the sudden convert may have a public event to which he or she can point, there is a day on which the gradual convert also felt sure of the faith that he or she espouses. However it comes about, at this point most persons would say a conversion has occurred. Often this experience is accompanied by a sense that a problem has been solved and that peace and security have come. The supposed psychological processes that occur at this point will be discussed later in this article. Suffice it to say that a point at which the faith takes over and the individual decisively changes his or her outlook on life does happen and that many persons can indicate the time and place at which this occurs. This means that faith is no longer one among several options cognitively, but it takes over and dominates the other possibilities that the individual was considering as answers to dilemmas.

Although both Tippett and James consider conversion to be a process, Tippett proposes a sequence of events that occur after the point of encounter as well as before it. James also writes about these but calls them "saintliness" rather than conversion. This is an important distinction because Tippett is more aware of the absolute meaning of conversion as complete change of life. He is aware that this by no means occurs because a person has made a decision to accept a given faith, which is only the beginning of a change that will itself take time. The point of encounter may signify a turning around or a stopping of going in one direction, but it does not signify that a person has reversed the past to the point where new life is a reality.

These considerations led Tippett to propose another period in the conversion process after the point of encounter. There is a period of incorporation during which the new convert is socialized into the new faith. For example, the public confession of faith, typical for the sudden convert, is often followed by a period of training and consultation during which the individual both reconsiders the meaning of the decision and learns more about the religion to which he or she desires to belong. This is followed by a rite of passage such as baptism and joining the church, which signifies that the person is now a part of the faith in both its public and private dimensions. Furthermore, after a person has become a new member of the faith group, obligations and opportunities are provided as means whereby the individual can grow in faith. This maturation process is sometimes ritualized into pressure to reach a new point of development and receive a second blessing, which may express itself in such ways as speaking in tongues and healing powers. Tippett considers this process of growth in faith and practice to be an integral part of conversion. The new faith takes over the mental and physical life of the individual and becomes the dominant life force by which the person exists. Only when this is so can conversion be thought to have fully occurred.

Two contemporary communication theorists (Lofland & Stark, 1965) have translated Tippett's model into terms of traditional Christian categories, which include God's action, the role of the Christian evangelist, and the response of the convert. They begin with God's general revelation whereby persons are aware of a supreme Being but have no effective knowledge of the gospel. This leads to the proclamation of Jesus as Savior, which is God's special revelation and which leads to an initial awareness of the Christian faith. As the proclaimer begins to influence and persuade the soon-to-be-convert, a grasp of the fundamentals and implications of the gospel begins to grow. Soon the individual begins to have a positive attitude toward the gospel and toward the evangelist. This results in a decision to act, after which the convert repents and places his or her faith in Christ. God's role then becomes that of regeneration, and the convert both becomes and begins to become the new creature in Christ.

After this God's role becomes one of sanctification and the role of the evangelist one of support and cultivation. During this time and throughout the rest of life the convert evaluates his or her decision, is incorporated into the church, grows in Christian knowledge and behavior, begins to daily commune with God, identifies personal gifts of ministry, and begins to witness to others and to engage in social action. This total process is conversion in the same sense that it is for Tippett. It retains an acknowledgment that there is both a point in time at which a person changes direction and a period of time both preceding and succeeding this event wherein a person grows toward the full meaning of conversion.

The Preconversion Mental State. Several psychologists other than James have studied this phenomenon. At the turn of the twentieth century much attention was given to the experience of adolescence, which was thought to be accompanied by much stress and strain. Hall (1905) postulated in his theory of recapitulation that each individual goes through the experience of the race and that adolescence is parallel to primitive society. Because conversion often occurs during this period, it was natural that it was conceived to be a distinctively adolescent phenomenon. Erik Erikson later proposed adolescence to be a unique period of identity formation during which persons are especially open to a reconsideration of the meaning and purpose of life. Thus it would seem natural that many conversions would occur in this period during which persons are struggling for independence and are looking for new authority in their lives.

Hall, one of the early pioneers in both developmental psychology and the psychology of religion, offered an apology for the Christian faith based on his understanding of the crucial nature of the adolescent experience (Hall, 1905). Along with many other theorists he suggested that humans were created innocent and altruistic but became self-centered in the experience of growing up. During adolescence persons began to see both the limits and the possibilities of living selfishly and became torn but attracted by their egotistic tendencies. Their greed turns them against the altruism with which life began. No amount of reason or appeal to conscience changes persons from this greedy track, according to Hall. Only the Christian gospel with its story of a God who loved persons enough to die for them can break through this barrier and open persons up to the possibilities of loving again. Hall considered the gospel the most powerful psychological force in converting persons from a life of selfishness to the life of love for which they were created. He offered a psychodynamic explanation wherein the persuasive force of the gospel is powerful enough to interrupt all other mental forces in the conversion process during adolescence.

Whereas Hall conceived the process of Christian conversion as healthy and normal, Freud (1928) suggested that religious conversion is a sign of psychopathology. For Freud, affirming religious faith is a sign that one has resolved psychosexual conflicts inappropriately. Although religion as a mass neurosis is better than individual neuroses, it is still abnormal and immature. Persons should face evil in themselves and in the world in a rational manner. They should solve problems with scientific pragmatism rather than dependent faith.

Salzman (1966), while agreeing with Freud in his basic model, suggested that there can be progressive as well as regressive conversions. Progressive conversions would result in courage and faithful action, while regressive conversions would result in self-doubt and dependency. Progressive conversions would seem to be what Hall had in mind in his contention that the Christian faith makes persons more loving.

In an alternate understanding of the place of psychopathology in conversion, Boisen (1936) contended that there is an affinity between mental illness and religious experience. He suggested that both the mentally ill and the sincerely religious are likely to be deeper thinkers than the average person. They experience the crisis of life at its most intense and deepest level. He compared the fantasies of psychosis with the supernatural stories of faith and concluded that they are similar. He concluded that some persons come through these experiences with religious conversions while others go the way of mental illness. Unlike Freud, he did not consider the experience itself as abnormal. Quite the contrary, it was a sign of greater depth of personality.

Changes Occurring Through Conversion. James felt that the event of conversion resulted in a shift of mental energy so that it was concentrated in one area of the mind and withdrawn from another. He felt this accounted for the intensity of the feelings and thoughts that accompanied the experience. He contended that there is no such thing as a unique religious emotion and that the feelings differ from normal experience in degree rather than in kind.

An alternative explanation for these phenomena was proposed by Sargant (1957), who compared conversion to brainwashing. Using the Pavlovian model of conditioning-crisis-breakdown-reorientation, he suggested that the individual is worked into a hyperemotional state he termed "transmarginal inhibition," during which the nerve endings become so exhausted that the individual borders on hysteria and becomes hypersuggestible. At this point the individual becomes more susceptible to ideas that he or she would resist in a normal mental state. This is coupled with a suppression of previously held beliefs. The new faith is acted upon in a dramatic manner and becomes the new conditioned stimulus for behavior.

Sargant's theory equates the influence process that leads persons to conversion with brainwashing. He is thus negative in his evaluation and suggests that such influence processes have negative value for society in that they induce pathology and dependence. Although many would agree with his evaluation as it applies to some mass meetings, it should be noted that he makes no distinction between the process and the positive results that often occur in people's lives from such experiences.

From a more positive perspective Oden (1966) has equated healing in psychotherapy with the process of conversion. Oden contends that God's grace is always available to humans in that he unconditionally accepts them and has infinite positive regard toward them. Wherever persons experience this, either from a therapist or an evangelist, the result is the same. Persons cease being self-centered, self-protective, defensive, and easily led into wrongdoing. They begin to appreciate anew the purpose for which they were uniquely created and that they have been denying. They discover again the power that is given them to love and to live without pretense. They gain courage to risk and to be loving. They have been converted.

On the question of the life changes resulting from conversion, once again James offered a model for evaluating as well as explaining these phenomena. He concluded that conversion integrates the personality around a dominant motive. He believed that conversion is the process whereby a divided self becomes unified. His dictum that religion should be judged by its fruits rather than its roots was a way of saying that if conversion results in a less conflicted, less indecisive, less troubled person, then it is valuable regardless of whether it occurs in a sick or a healthy mind. His *Varieties of Religious Experience* is replete with accounts of lives in which this unification resulted from religious conversion. James was describing in behavioral terms the phenomenon referred to in Scripture as the "new creation" (2 Cor. 5:17). The gospel accounts of Zacchaeus, Nicodemus, and the woman at the well are prime biblical examples of James's description. Charles Colson is representative of many modern examples of lives that have been radically changed by conversion in the manner James depicted.

Ideally the person should feel inwardly less anxious, less confused, more in control, and more energized. The purpose and meaning of life should be clearer. Outwardly the person should become more unselfish, more loving, more just, and more merciful. However, research suggests that typically these life changes are far less radical than might be anticipated. If James was correct in suggesting that conversion should be evaluated in terms of the degree to which these changes occur, then far too many conversions fall short of the ideal. However, if Paul is correct (Rom. 7), these changes are less important than James might have presumed, at least from God's point of view. The juxtaposition of sin and grace in the Pauline model implies that salvation is less an achievement and more a gift and that righteousness, the biblical term for James's changes, is ascribed to the believer rather than characteristic of her or him. Furthermore, from a psychological point of view the dilemma of achieving one's life goals of love and justice remains a problem even after conversion. These goals are better conceived as possible when they are understood as the gifts of grace rather than the expectations by which our salvation is proven.

More empirically, Gorsuch, a social psychologist, has concluded that we cannot expect change of mind, the typical kind of change that occurs in conversion, to generalize fully to other types of behavior such as overt actions of love and mercy (Gorsuch & Malony, 1976). Behavioral change will most likely generalize to other similar types of behavior and will less likely generalize to dissimilar kinds of acts. Thus attitudes and thoughts and feelings will predictably change more than interpersonal behaviors. But, apart from whether change should or should not occur, from a strictly psychological point of view it would not be expected as much for some behaviors as for others.

One of the most recent reconceptualizations of the conversion experience has been that of Richardson (1979), who has proposed that we think less of conversion from a "preordained" than an "interactive" point of view. Taking the conversion of Paul as a focus, he suggested that the preordained model sees the event as planned by God in such a manner that it is predispositional from a psychological and presituational from a sociological perspective.

A corrective to these points of view might be to conceive of Paul's experience on the Damascus road less as beginning there and more as continuing for a prolonged period of seclusion in which he probably conversed with Jesus again and again. Paul's experience was no surprise to him but instead came as the result of long years of searching for the meaning of life. He knew the language of faith long before he met the Messiah on the road to Damascus. Paul's dramatic experience with Jesus was but the first of many times that Paul renewed his faith and grew in his understanding of the Good News that changed his life. Finally, in regard to behavioral changes that resulted from the experience, Paul reported "I die every day" (1 Cor. 15:31, NIV), as if to say his struggle with sin in his life was an ongoing struggle. He grew in grace throughout his life and in many new circumstances.

This interactive view of the changes that occur puts the experience of conversion in a sound sociopsychological as well as theological perspective. It preserves the power of God as well as the activity of persons in the conversion process. It allows for conceiving the behavior change in conversion more as a change of direction than a total change of life.

References

Boisen, A. (1936). *The exploration of the inner world*. Chicago: Willett, Clark.

Freud, S. (1928). *The future of an illusion*. New York: Liveright.

Gordon, A. (1967). *The nature of conversion*. Boston: Beacon.

Gorsuch, R. L., & Malony, H. N. (1976). *The nature of man*. Springfield, IL: Thomas.

Hall, G. (1905). *Adolescence*. New York: Appleton.

James, W. (1902). *The varieties of religious experience*. New York: Doubleday.

Lofland, J., & Stark, R. (1965). Becoming a world saver: A theory of conversion to a deviant perspective. *American Sociological Review*, 30, 862–875.

Oden, T. C. (1966). *Kerygma and counseling*. Philadelphia: Westminster.

Richardson, J. T. (1979, May). *A new paradigm for conversion research*. Paper presented at the International Society for Political Psychology, Washington, DC.

Salzman, L. (1966, September). Types of religious conversion. *Pastoral Psychology*, 8–20.

Sargant, W. (1957). *Battle for the mind*. Garden City, NY: Doubleday.

Tippett, A. (1977). Conversion as a dynamic process in Christian mission. *Missiology, 5* (2), 203–221.

Additional Reading

Johnson, C., & Malony, H. N. (1982). *Christian conversion: Biblical and psychological perspectives*. Grand Rapids, MI: Zondervan.

H. N. Malony

See Psychology of Religion; Christian Growth; Religious Development.

Conversion Disorder. The primary feature of conversion disorder is the presence of symptoms or deficits affecting voluntary motor or sensory function that appear to have a neurological or other medical origin and are not intentionally produced (American Psychiatric Association, 1994). Symptoms of pain and sexual dysfunction are specifically excluded. The symptoms also cause considerable distress in important areas of the individual's life and are frequently associated with extreme psychological distress (e.g., military combat, severe child abuse). Typical conversion symptoms include blindness, paralysis, aphonia (loss of voice), uncontrolled vomiting, tics, and seizures.

Conversion disorder occurs from childhood to old age. The disorder is more common in rural areas, among the less educated and lower socioeconomic groups. The disorder is diagnosed two to five times more frequently among women. Military personnel who have combat exposure have a higher risk of the disorder than does the general public. Unresolved grief is common in persons who have conversion reactions. About one in three individuals with this disorder have a current or previous neurological or general medical condition. Preexisting mental health problems can predispose an individual to this disorder. The most common are histrionic, antisocial, and dependent personality disorder, major depression, anxiety disorders, schizophrenia, and somatization disorder. About one in three patients with conversion reactions also have somatization disorder.

Several hypotheses have been suggested to explain the etiology of conversion reaction. According to the psychodynamic theory, conversion reaction is a result of anxiety caused by unconscious psychological conflict. Other theories have suggested that a conversion reaction is a nonverbal communication that is used when direct verbal communications are not acceptable. Some experts point out that some of the symptoms may have a symbolic or functional aspect; for example, the mother who goes "blind" after viewing her murdered child because she cannot bear to see more. Secondary gains are common in conversion disorder. Secondary gains are extraneous benefits such as increased attention from others as a result of being hospitalized.

From 1% to 3% of patients served by an outpatient mental health facility have conversion disorder as the focus of treatment. For psychiatric hospital patients with conversion disorder without a coexisting neurological or other medical problem, nine out of ten recovered with specialized treatment and 75% remained well a year later. A good prognosis is associated with acute onset, presence of a clearly defined identified stressor, a short period of time from onset, early treatment, and no coexisting medical condition. A favorable outcome appears to depend most on the person's psychological strengths and personality type. Individuals with conversion reaction may show la belle indifference (i.e., a lack of anxiety or other emotional response to the symptom; *see* Belle Indifference) or may react in a dramatic manner.

One theoretical example of conversion disorder is seen in a 25-year-old committed Christian and member of a police bomb squad who becomes paralyzed in his legs after surviving a terrorist bombing in which he had only minor physical injuries. Three of his colleagues were killed in the explosion. He felt deep survivor's guilt, believing that he was somehow responsible for the death of his friends, as their bodies had protected him from much of the force of the explosion. He felt trapped by guilt, shame, fear, and a plaguing sense of failure that he should have done more to save his friends. He felt he deserved a greater personal injury since his friends died. In this theoretical case the young policeman's conversion reaction is an involuntary attempt to resolve his severe psychological conflicts.

It will be important when treating this patient to provide a safe, caring environment to facilitate the gradual decrease of symptoms. Relaxing and reassuring the patient are crucial. Treatment would involve a nonconfrontational, noninterpretative, supportive psychotherapy that would allow the policeman to ventilate his painful feelings. Since he is a committed person of faith, Christian practices such as prayer and confession should be encouraged to facilitate the grief process and explore his self-punishing reaction (*see* Prayer, Therapeutic Use of). A knowledgeable clergy person could be of great help in this case working collaboratively with the mental health professionals. Physical therapy that prevented disuse and atrophy needs to be used. Working at resolving the policeman's overall problems as well as eliminating the conversion reaction is the best approach.

Reference

American Psychiatric Association. (1994). *Diagnostic and statistical manual of mental disorders* (4th ed.). Washington, DC: Author.

Additional Readings

Benner, D. G. (1992). *Strategic pastoral counseling: A short-term structured model.* Grand Rapids, MI: Baker.

Dale, N., & Witztum, E. (1991). Short-term strategic treatment in traumatic conversion reaction. *American Journal of Psychotherapy, 45* (3), 335–347.

Ford, C. V., & Folks D. G. (1985). Conversion disorder: An overview. *Psychosomatics, 26,* 371–383.

Guggenheim, G. F., & Smith, G. R. (1995). Somatoform disorders. In H. I. Kaplan and B. J. Sadock (Eds.), *Comprehensive textbook of psychiatry* (Vol. 1, 6th ed.). Baltimore: Williams & Wilkins.

Viederman, M. (1991). Somatoform and factitious disorders. In R. Michels, A. M. Copper, & S. B. Guze et al., (Eds.), *Psychiatry,* (2nd ed.). Philadelphia: Lippincott.

A. J. WEAVER

See SOMATOFORM DISORDERS.

Cooperation and Competition. Few persons would disagree that in the West we live in a society that encourages a spirit of competition. From basking in the glory of being number one to driving out competitors in the name of economic survival, competition appears to be a way of life. To what extent is this sense of competition healthy and necessary, and to what extent does it undermine social well-being? Classical economic thought has maintained that the interests of society are not only harmonious with but even rely upon the competitive interests of the individual. Yet much contemporary social science suggests that the individual's best interest, which may require a competitive spirit, often conflicts with the interests of society and that it may be wise to transform such situations into an atmosphere calling for a spirit of cooperation.

Kauffmann (1991) reminds us that competitive imagery of running and fighting was frequently used in the Pauline epistles. For instance, Paul speaks of all the runners running a race but only one getting the prize (1 Cor. 9:24), and therefore we should run in such a way as to get the prize (v. 25). Kauffmann correctly points out, however, that Paul's analogy is somewhat misleading in that it may foster an image of what social psychologists refer to as a zero-sum competitive situation; that is, the thrill of victory is experienced at the expense of someone else's agonizing defeat. For one to gain the prize (or the promotion, election, team victory) means that somebody else must lose.

The real competition that Paul is speaking of is not interpersonal but intrapersonal in nature. One's attainment of God's favor is not at somebody else's expense but involves an internal struggle and eventually a claim that can be made by all.

The frequent interpersonal experiences of competition and cooperation will be discussed primarily within the context of a group setting. Since a group, however, can be as few as two people exerting influence on each other, the discussion of both cooperation and competition can be understood as dynamics involving not only formally established groups such as appointed or elected committees, teammates of an organized sport, boards of directors, and faculty members but also entailing informal groups such as friends, spouses, business partners, classmates, and co-workers. Cooperation and competition influence the quality of interpersonal relationships within a group and such relationships in turn play an important role in group cohesiveness and productivity.

The Tragedy of the Commons. Social-psychological researchers have long been interested in studying interpersonal behavior where long-term interests are served by cooperation but short-term gains are best achieved through the competitive spirit of self-interest. Such dilemmas in real-life situations frequently center around issues threatening social well-being such as waste recycling, pollution control, and depletion of natural resources. The question left to answer is how to reconcile self-interest (for example, using chemical fertilizers to enhance the appearance of one's lawn and increase the value of one's property) with societal need (the necessity of reducing pollutants).

Perhaps this social dilemma is best illustrated by social ecologist Garrett Hardin's notion of the "tragedy of the commons." The commons are public pasturelands and the tragedy is that each individual shepherd is motivated to add as many sheep as possible to the herd, even if it means that if other shepherds do the same, the result will be serious overgrazing and all the shepherds will be hurt. Of course, the message here is that abuse of the resources available to all will occur when people are concerned only about their own self-interest and do not accept personal responsibility for what is commonly shared.

The Prisoner's Dilemma. Psychologists have used laboratory games to study such social dilemmas. Perhaps the most frequently used game for research purposes is some variant of what has been called the prisoner's dilemma. Imagine how you would respond to the following dilemma. You are one of two suspects working in tandem who are being questioned separately by a district attorney (DA) about a crime that has been committed. You are both guilty, but the DA has only enough evidence to convict both of you of a lesser crime. So the DA, hoping to achieve a conviction for the more serious offense, offers an incentive for each of you to privately confess. If you confess, there are two possibilities: your cohort does not confess, you are granted immunity, and the DA now has enough evidence to convict your partner of the more serious offense (the best possible scenario for you but the worst for your partner); or your cohort also confesses and each receives a moderate sentence for the lesser offense (a good scenario for neither you nor your partner). If you do not confess, there are also two possibilities: your cohort confesses, is granted immunity, and the DA now has enough evidence to convict you of the more serious offense (the worst scenario for you but the best for your partner); or your cohort does not confess and each receives a light sentence for the lesser offense (the second best scenario for you and the best scenario for the partnership).

What would you do? If you are like most people, you will confess. In this situation, not confessing is the more cooperative approach with your partner while confessing is placing self-interest first, even at the expense of your partner. Typical reasoning goes something like this: If I confess, the worst possible case is receiving a moderate sentence (if my partner confesses) and I may go free (if my partner does not confess), plus I avoid the most severe sentence (by not confessing when my partner confesses). But here is the catch. Both prisoners will think the same way and hence both will receive a moderate sentence. If both had cooperated with each other and *not* confessed, both would receive a light sentence. By protecting self-interest, both partners lose.

Variations of this dilemma have been developed around more common issues, such as negotiating for bonus points in a college course. Each variant of the game is structured such that each party is potentially better off on an individual basis by not cooperating. The results of this research are consistent: by mutually not cooperating, both parties suffer more than if they had cooperated.

Is Competition Ever Healthy? Competitive interactions need not lead inevitably to social conflict. Many competitive interactions are begun with agreed-upon and socially acceptable purposes such as organized sporting events, board games, and friendly contests used to motivate high levels of individual or group performance. However, both research and personal experience show that even such friendly uses of competition can set the stage for social conflict. It is easy for invidious comparison to occur in competitive situations. Such comparisons may lead people to attribute negative intentions or motives to their opponent in casual interactions, spousal relationships, athletic events, or international negotiations.

In spite of the negative consequences often associated with competition, it is used widely as a motivator in schools, churches, and other organizations, particularly in Western society. This use seems based on the assumption that competitive rewards are more effective in stimulating learning and group performance. Much research shows that cooperative situations generally motivate individual learning and group performance as well as competitive or individualistic situations and often do so with more positive effects on personal feelings and relationships.

Why Do People Compete? If competition often undermines social well-being and is ultimately less productive than cooperation, at least in some circumstances, why is it that people have such a strong

tendency to compete? Other than the answer provided by social dilemma research, that competition appears to best serve our own interests, a number of theoretical frameworks may help explain the proclivity to compete.

First, competition provides the motivation that some people find necessary to optimally complete a task. The elementary school teacher may find that some students are more motivated to complete an assignment if it involves some sort of competition. Generally competition increases motivation, but more so for people who have a strong need to achieve. Atkinson's (1977) model of achievement motivation categorizes people according to the strength of their need to achieve as well as their fear of failure and predicts that people with a high need for achievement will be most likely to compete with people they perceive to be similar in ability. Research on social facilitation (Zajonc, 1965) suggests that a person with a strong need for achievement who may already be highly competitive will become more so in the presence of spectators, whereas someone who shies away from competition will become even less competitive in front of an audience.

Whether we compete or cooperate may also be examined in light of social exchange theory (Chadwick-Jones, 1976). The idea here is that we unconsciously structure our social relationships in such a way that we try to maximize our social benefits while minimizing social costs. At times we may recognize that it is to our benefit to cooperate rather than compete. If we are confident that our partner in the prisoner's dilemma will cooperate (i.e., not confess), then we too may choose not to confess.

The tendency to compete may also be understood in terms of social comparison processes. Social comparison theory (Festinger, 1954) suggests that competition with similar others serves the function of self-evaluation and that we can arrive at a more precise assessment of our abilities through competing with others.

Encouraging Cooperation. Competitive interactions can be transformed to have fewer negative social consequences. Given the general superiority of cooperative interactions, a key method involves constructing cooperative situations to replace competitive ones. For example, teachers can make grades dependent on the performance of cooperative work groups in which individuals must work together to reach their common goals.

Especially for non-zero-sum situations (i.e., where for each winner there does not have to be a loser), psychologists have discovered the value of open and honest communication between competing and often conflicting parties. The focus on honesty and openness is important, since communication can also be used for deceptive purposes. Hence, modes of unilateral influence, such as threats, persuasion, and sometimes even promises, are generally less effective than two-way communication. Communication that enhances awareness of the nature of the interdependency and that clarifies perceptions, goals, and values is more likely to yield cooperative solutions.

References

Atkinson, J. W. (1977). Motivation for achievement. In T. Blass (Ed.), *Personality variables in social behavior.* Hillsdale, NJ: Erlbaum.

Chadwick-Jones, J. K. (1976). *Social exchange theory: Its structure and influence in social psychology.* New York: Academic Press.

Festinger, L. (1954). A theory of social comparison processes. *Human Relations, 7,* 117–140.

Kauffmann, D. (1991). *My faith's OK, your faith's NOT: Reflections on psychology and religion.* (Available from Duane Kauffmann, Dept. of Psychology, Goshen College, Goshen, IN 46526)

Zajonc, R. B. (1965). Social facilitation. *Science, 149,* 269–274.

P. C. HILL

See CONFLICT; CONFLICT MANAGEMENT; ACHIEVEMENT, NEED FOR; AFFILIATION, NEED FOR.

Coping. Coping has received increasing attention in the past several decades. Although there is not complete agreement about what coping means, a widely accepted definition was developed by Lazarus and his colleagues. In their view coping involves "constantly changing cognitive and behavioral efforts to manage specific external and/or internal demands that are appraised as taxing or exceeding the resources of the person" (Lazarus & Folkman, 1984, p. 141). This view of coping emanates from a view of stress as a transactional concept. That is, stress is not seen as something external to individuals (such as death or divorce), nor is it seen as the responses our bodies have to external or internal demands (such as rapid heart rate, sweaty palms, or ulcers). Stress is a person's perception that his or her resources are not adequate to deal with circumstances. Coping, then, refers to what people do to deal with this condition of stress and does not include all responses an individual makes to his or her environment.

Lazarus and Folkman (1984) also note that coping is a process—a conscious process—rather than a one-time action. Individuals will typically engage in a variety of behaviors over the course of a stressful circumstance to manage their responses to the situation. Further, their responses will probably affect their circumstances, leading to further action by the individual. Thus the individual and the environment affect one another. Lazarus recognized that our values, commitments, and personal resources will affect how we handle stressful situations and that stressful situations also come with their own unique constraints. Another distinguishing point about this definition is that coping is not equated with mastery. That is, coping involves

efforts to manage stress. Attempts to manage stress will involve a wide variety of cognitive and behavioral strategies, which can be categorized broadly as problem-focused (attempts to fix the source of the problem) and emotion-focused (attempts to deal with the emotional responses to the situation). Sometimes these efforts are successful; sometimes they are not.

Since the early 1980s a number of instruments have been developed to assess coping efforts. Currently the most accepted measure for use with adults is the 60-item COPE (Carver, Scheier, & Weintraub, 1989). This instrument improves on prior measures of coping because it is theoretically driven and captures a wide array of coping activity. Additionally the COPE moves beyond the simplistic distinctions between problem- and emotion-focused coping efforts. The 15 coping scales included in the COPE are active coping, planning, suppression of competing activities, restraint coping, seeking social support for instrumental reasons (help with solving a problem), seeking emotional support, focusing on and venting emotions, use of humor, behavioral disengagement, mental disengagement, denial, acceptance, positive reinterpretation and growth, use of drugs or alcohol to disengage, and turning to religion. The inclusion of turning to religion as a coping scale is interesting because this facet of individuals' lives has been ignored by many academic psychologists.

In part to address the lack of information on religious coping in the scientific literature, Pargament and his colleagues (1988) developed a measure to assess three distinct problem-solving styles, each involving a different relationship between the individual and God. These styles vary on two key dimensions underlying the individual's relationship with God: the locus of responsibility for the problem-solving process and the level of activity in the problem-solving process. Individuals with a self-directing style believe it is their responsibility, not God's, to solve problems and therefore take an active problem-solving stance. This style is not anti-religious but rather views God as giving people the freedom and resources to direct their own lives. In contrast, individuals with a deferring style believe it is God's responsibility to solve problems; therefore they are passive in their problem-solving efforts. Individuals who believe that they and God share responsibility for problem solving and therefore are both active in seeking solutions have a collaborative style.

Perhaps the main reason to pay attention to coping research is that not all coping responses are equally beneficial. Dozens of studies involving adults and children dealing with a wide range of stressful circumstances have found that active coping (trying to change the source of the problem, considering alternatives, thinking about the situation in a positive light) is related to better mental and physical well-being, while passive coping (avoiding thinking about or taking action regarding the problem) is associated with less adaptive outcomes. In more detailed analyses Mattlin, Wethington, and Kessler (1990) attempted to determine the benefit of different coping strategies for stressful life events of different types (e.g., illness, death of a loved one, practical problems, interpersonal relationship difficulties). They found that avoidance coping was associated with higher rates of anxiety and depression in nearly every circumstance. Reappraisal (thinking about the situation differently) led to higher anxiety when dealing with practical problems but led to lower depression when coping with the death of a loved one. Religious coping was most beneficial for persons coping with the deaths of loved ones.

Hathaway and Pargament (1990) demonstrated that the type of religious coping used makes a difference. Intrinsically religious persons may use either collaborative or deferring religious coping styles. However, a collaborative style is associated with higher competence (having higher self-esteem, trusting others more), while a deferring style is associated with lower competence. This suggests that it is important to assess religious coping carefully rather than assuming all religious persons cope the same way.

In other work Pargament et al. (1990) examined the types of religious coping efforts and resources that are helpful, harmful, or irrelevant to church members dealing with significant negative events. They found that those who involved religion in dealing with their most serious negative event, believing that God is just and benevolent, experiencing God as a supportive partner in coping, participating in religious rituals such as church attendance and prayer, and seeking spiritual and personal support through religion, were associated with better mental health and favorable outcomes of the event.

Current research on coping is focused in several directions. First, there is a continuing interest in describing when some coping strategies are beneficial and when they are not. Second, scientists are trying to understand the factors that influence choice of coping strategies, particularly among children and adolescents. For example, the role that parents play in this process is being investigated. Third, the role of appraisals (evaluations of how threatening a situation is to one's well-being) in the coping process is gaining increasing attention.

References

Carver, C. S., Scheier, M. F., & Weintraub, J. K. (1989). Assessing coping strategies: A theoretically based approach. *Journal of Personality and Social Psychology, 56*, 267–283.

Hathaway, W. L., & Pargament, K. I. (1990). Intrinsic religiousness, religious coping, and psychosocial competence: A covariance structure analysis. *Journal for the Scientific Study of Religion, 29*, 423–441.

Lazarus, R. S., & Folkman, S. (1984). *Stress, appraisal, and coping.* New York: Springer.

Mattlin, J. A., Wethington, E., & Kessler, R. C. (1990). Situational determinants of coping and coping effectiveness. *The Journal of Health and Social Behavior, 31*, 103–122.

Pargament, K. I., Ensing, D., Falgout, K., Olsen, H., Reilly, B., Van Haitsma, K., & Warren, R. (1990). God help me: (I): Religious coping efforts as predictors of the outcomes to significant negative life events. *American Journal of Community Psychology, 18*, 793–824.

Pargament, K. I., Kennell, J., Hathaway, W., Grevengoed, N., Newman, J., & Jones, W. (1988). Religion and the problem-solving process: Three styles of coping. *Journal for the Scientific Study of Religion, 27*, 90–104.

W. KLIEWER

Coping Skills Therapies. Coping skills treatments have their conceptual grounding in behavior therapy. However, they developed during a shift in emphasis in behavioral treatments away from environmental controls toward self-control (Bandura, 1969). Coping skills therapies are oriented toward two goals. The first is for the client to adopt a conceptual model of his or her problem that emphasizes the possibility of successful coping. The second is for the client to learn an array of techniques to use in the problem situation. Thus the role of the counselor is that of a coach-facilitator: teaching coping techniques, assigning homework (*see* Homework in Psychotherapy), and analyzing both successful and unsuccessful applications of the techniques so as to foster increasingly independent use of them by the client.

Coping skills treatments are based on a model of dysfunction that has three assumptions. First, it is assumed that people develop both adaptive and maladaptive feelings and responses through their cognitive processes. In stressful situations, what people believe about the situations can have as much influence on their responses as the situations themselves. According to Lazarus and Folkman (1984), if we appraise a potentially stressful situation as one that exceeds our coping resources, we will feel threatened and respond accordingly. In contrast, if we believe we have the means to cope with the situation, it may still be stressful, but we will feel challenged and cope more successfully. These two types of appraisals—threat versus challenge—will result in dramatically different approaches to the stressful situation.

The second assumption behind coping skills treatments is that these cognitive processes (thoughts, feelings, beliefs) are learned according to the same rules that govern the acquisition of behavior and can therefore be unlearned. This assumption is the link between coping skills treatments and their behavior therapy antecedents.

The third assumption is that the task of the therapist is to determine, in a collegial manner with the client, the nature of the stressful situations, the nature of the cognitive processes that are affecting the client's responses, and the best manner to assist the client in acquiring new cognitive processes and behavioral outcomes. Thus the therapist is an educator, a coach, and a facilitator.

Several different treatment approaches all fit under the label of coping skills treatments. These treatments share the goal of providing training to clients in a repertoire of skills that will facilitate adjustment to stressful situations. The four approaches most commonly considered are covert modeling, coping skills training, anxiety management training, and stress inoculation training.

The distinguishing feature of covert modeling is that a client mentally rehearses the desired behavior (e.g., making an assertive request) prior to the situation in which the behavior will be used. This procedure is common among athletes, who use mental preparation and visualization to enhance performance. It has been demonstrated to be successful in overcoming specific fears, such as social anxiety and interpersonal anxiety. This covert, or imaginal, rehearsal is also a feature of coping skills training, a variant of systematic desensitization where clients do not stop visualizing a scene when anxious but rather begin visualizing themselves coping in the situation or relaxing away the anxiety. Thus clients practice relaxation responses while imagining aspects of the stressful situation. Anxiety management training also uses visualization by the clients. However, this treatment approach has the client visualize different scenes, some unrelated to the actual fear, to develop a generalized coping response. This coping response is then linked to the stressful situation through practice.

The most articulated coping skill treatment, one with considerable research support, is stress inoculation training (Meichenbaum, 1974, 1985). Stress inoculation has three distinct phases of treatment. During the first phase, the counselor and client collaborate in developing a model of the client's presenting problem that defines the problem in cognitive (thoughts), affective (feelings), and behavioral terms. Thus a client with chronic pain will come to see the pain as more than just painful stimuli. Rather the client will understand pain as encompassing the client's thoughts about the pain ("I can't stop this pain, I am helpless"), feelings (depression), and behaviors (muscular tension, avoidance, sick role behaviors). In this first phase, clients are also taught to see the problem in stages: an anticipation stage, a stage in which the stressor is confronted and handled, a stage oin which the stressor becomes overwhelming; and a stage in which the event is reviewed and analyzed. Each stage will have its own matching skills.

The second phase involves the client learning an array of coping skills, depending on the nature of the presenting problem. Chronic pain patients, for example, might be taught relaxation approaches, attention-diversion techniques, and appraisal processes. For all of the skills, there is an underlying emphasis on preparation, planning, and coping applications.

Each of these techniques is presented, rehearsed in the session, and assigned for homework (the third phase). In the last phase, the client's use of the skills is monitored. Changes are made as necessary in which skills are used in which stage. The client is also given opportunities to apply the new skills in different settings to increase the generalizability of coping.

Research on coping skills treatments has been rapidly increasing in the contemporary emphasis on effective treatment outcomes. The most recent listing of empirically validated treatments (Chambless et al., 1996) contains several entries that are oriented toward coping skills and also identifies stress inoculation training as a treatment that has received empirical validation. The nature of coping skills treatment suggests its use for clients with focused problems, in a short-term context, who have a minimal degree of pathology, and who are motivated to change.

An emphasis on cognitive processes as mediating the effects of the environment on behavior does not conflict with a biblical view of humans as rational persons capable of volitional acts. Additionally, the emphasis on responsibility for coping corresponds to a Christian emphasis on self-responsibility. In spite of many Christians' concern over behavior modification (e.g., Kauffman, 1977), there seems to be an increasing acceptance of therapies that are cognitive-behavioral in nature. Given the promise of these treatments, such acceptance appears warranted.

References

Bandura, A. (1969). *Principles of behavior modification.* New York: Holt, Rinehart, & Winston.

Chambless, D. L., Sanderson, W. C., Shoham, V., Johnson, S. B., Pope, K. S., Crits-Christoph, P., Baker, M., Johnson, B., Woody, S. R., Sue, S., Beutler, L., Williams, D. A., & McCurry, S. (1996). An update on empirically validated therapies. *The Clinical Psychologists 49* (2), 5–18.

Kauffman, D. (1977). Behaviorism, psychology, and Christian education. *The Bulletin of CAPS, 3,* 17–21.

Lazarus, R. S., & Folkman, S. (1984). *Stress, appraisal, and coping.* New York: Springer.

Meichenbaum, D. (1974). *Cognitive behavior modification.* Morristown, NJ: General Learning Press.

Meichenbaum, D. (1985). *Stress inoculation training.* Elmsford, NY: Pergamon.

E. M. Altmaier

See Cognitive-Behavior Therapy; Life Skills Counseling.

Coprophilia. A condition in which erotic arousal or orgasm is dependent on the smell, taste, or sight of feces. Generally found among men, the incidence is low, with few reported cases. When coprophilia is noted it is often associated with prostitution or homosexual acts.

In some cases smearing or eating feces is part of the act. An individual derives sexual arousal when another person defecates on the body or is watched while defecating. Often the fantasy life is involved: an individual imagines feces during the sexual act. This is said to enhance the sexual involvement.

No clear factors are associated with the development of coprophilia. Various case histories have indicated that small children saw the mother or father defecate and drew some pleasure from it. Some theorists suggest that the origins of coprophilia may be in mammalian hygiene whereby infants are licked clean. Why this would continue into adulthood and fixate on feces is unclear.

Psychoanalysts view coprophilia as a carryover from the anal stage when retention or expulsion of fecal material is hypothesized to produce intense sexual stimulation. Sometimes the interest in the product is transferred to other objects where no conscious connection is seen. In coprophilia, however, the feces themselves continue to provide erotic fantasies or arousal.

Treatment will include group therapy where persons are able to learn from each other how to control or regulate the behavior. A cure is difficult because the behavior often goes undetected and is easily hidden.

L. N. Ferguson

Coronary Heart Disease. The terms *cardiovascular disease* (CD) and *coronary heart disease* (CHD) are often used interchangeably. The major cause of CD is atherosclerosis, which is commonly known as hardening of the arteries. This occurs with age, to some extent. It is caused by deposits of cholesterol, fats, calcium, and other products in the blood; these deposits (plaque) build up inside the arteries and block blood flow. Plaque buildup can cause bleeding (hemorrhage) or blood clots (thrombi), resulting in heart attack or stroke.

CHD is the primary cause of death for both men and women in the United States. It is the most common form of heart disease. Seven million Americans have CHD, and a half million die from heart attacks caused by CHD every year. CHD is caused by a narrowing and/or clogging of the coronary arteries supplying the heart. Prevention is important, since many of the risk factors (including high blood pressure, smoking, overweight, high cholesterol, and lack of physical activity) can be controlled by a healthy lifestyle.

When coronary arteries are narrow or clogged, they cannot provide enough blood and oxygen to the heart. This causes pain called angina or a heart attack if the blood is totally cut off. High levels of cholesterol can build up on arterial walls and cause clogging; this decreases or blocks blood flow to the heart. This can begin as early as childhood and increases with age. Hereditary factors influence this process, along with high blood pressure, high cholesterol levels, and smoking. Being overweight increases a person's likelihood of having high blood pressure and increased cholesterol. Therefore it is important to get regular exercise and to eat a well-balanced, low-fat diet with high proportions of fruits, vegetables, and whole grains. It is also important not to smoke. Practicing this type of healthy lifestyle is a significant means of decreasing the risk for developing CHD.

Chest pain or shortness of breath are the most common signs of CHD, although some people have no symptoms. Physicians have a variety of tests for determining if a person has CHD. Treatment may consist of changes in lifestyle and medications. Surgery or other procedures such as angioplasty may be required for some cases. Surgery does not cure. It relieves symptoms. Lifelong treatment and management of lifestyle are necessary for the person who has CHD.

Personality factors related to heart disease have been studied for more than twenty years. People who are more prone to heart disease are often overly competitive and work under a sense of time urgency in an attempt to meet deadlines, and they may be impatient and quick to anger. Everyday expressions and folk sayings recognize the close link between the heart and psychological states. The disappointed are referred to as downhearted or brokenhearted; when happy, one's heart leaps for joy; when frightened, one's heart stands still; it goes out to those for whom one has compassion; and the heart is given in love. Proverbs notes, "A merry heart maketh a cheerful countenance," and "He that is of a merry heart hath a continual feast" (Prov. 15:13, 15, KJV).

People with CHD are often unaware of their feelings, but they tend to show chronic anxiety and hostility. Both of these emotions activate the sympathetic nervous system, which in turn increases the body's output of adrenalin. These physiological changes prepare a person to run from danger or fight an attacker, and they were protective in ancient times when a person might be attacked by a wild animal or a warring tribe. We do not usually run or fight, but the body prepares for this when we feel threatened, and it stays in a continual state of arousal when these feelings are present. An increase in fear, anxiety, anger, or other activating emotions causes the heart to work harder. For example, persons who do not like their job or their employer may stay in a frustrating situation for years because they are afraid of losing their job if they speak out and because they fear they will not secure as good a job if they quit. The chronic stress of fear and frustration can contribute to high blood pressure, heart pains, or other cardiovascular problems.

In addition to the lifestyle changes mentioned previously, people with heart disease are often taught to relax and to become more patient and less competitive. This seems to help lower the incidence of heart attacks. In contrast to telling people to slow down, treatment programs teach people active ways of coping with stress. They learn to feel in control rather than feeling helpless, as they might if they just "take it easy." In addition to relaxation skills, people learn more constructive means of communicating so they can express feelings, wants, and needs directly rather than indirectly or competitively.

As scientists learn more about changing the behaviors related to cardiac disease, people will be able to focus more accurately on what they must do to prevent heart disease. In the meantime, people can positively influence their own cardiovascular health by learning to cope more effectively with stress and by adopting a healthy way of living with attention to diet and exercise.

M. A. NORFLEET

See HEALTH PSYCHOLOGY

Correlation. A statistical expression of the degree of relationship between two or more variables. Correlation coefficients vary between +1.00 and -1.00, 0.00 indicating the absence of any correlation and +1.00 and -1.00 indicating a perfect positive or negative relationship. Perfect correlations are seldom found in experiments. Positive correlations are found when an increase in one variable leads to an increase in the other. If an increase in one variable leads to a decrease in the other, the correlation is negative.

See PSYCHOLOGY, METHODS OF.

Cotard's Syndrome. A rare delusional state identified by the French neurologist Jules Cotard (1840–1887). In this psychotic state, characterized by anxiety, depression, and suicidal tendencies, the patient believes reality has ceased to exist and that he or she no longer has a body.

Cotherapy. Over the course of many years there have been varying levels of interest in involving two professionals in a particular therapeutic setting. This has been called cotherapy, multiple therapy, cooperative psychotherapy, and three-cornered therapy. The most common form of cotherapy involves two therapists engaged simultaneously in a given therapeutic context, such as individual, marital, family, or group psychotherapy. As early as 1930 Adler reported success in using cotherapy to treat dysfunctional families (Adler, 1930). This technique was later used by others for marital, group, and individual psychotherapy, with almost universal claims of success but little empirical data to substantiate such reports (Holt & Greiner, 1976).

Cotherapy has been used for a wide variety of reasons. Sometimes it is used with the intent of simplifying the therapeutic task. For example, cotherapy is often utilized in the treatment of severely dysfunctional families, marital couples, and psychotic patients because it is believed or hoped that this will reduce the difficulty of the therapeutic task.

Although this position lacks strong empirical support, several reasons for the belief exist. Psychodynamically oriented therapists believe that the use of cotherapists reduces the intensity of the transference (distorted perceptions) by dispersing it among the two clinicians, thereby facilitating the treatment of severely disturbed patients. Others feel that the added strength and support of a second therapist help to balance the power of control, preventing more regressive forms of acting out within the session. Finally, some believe that in cotherapy one therapist is always available to be objective and thereby more helpful while the other is involved in a moment of confrontation or heightened emotion.

Cotherapy is often used by a wide variety of therapists who believe that the use of two therapists, particularly when they are of the opposite sex, facilitates communication and thereby encourages exploration of family issues and early conflicts. Cotherapy is also used for training, supervision, and consultation. It is viewed as a particularly valuable way to provide carefully monitored on-the-job training. Since psychotherapists in training learn through a mentoring process, cotherapy is an important tool in helping them develop good technique.

The use of cotherapy can be successful for all concerned when the therapists are of equal status, competence, and sensitivity. Cotherapists who are comfortable and open with each other, respectful and courteous, and mutually concerned with the needs of the patient can have a profoundly valuable therapeutic impact.

References

Adler, A. (1930). *The education of children.* New York: Greenberg.
Holt, M., & Greiner, D. (1976). Co-therapy in the treatment of families. In P. J. Guerin (Ed.), *Family therapy.* New York: Gardner.

J. D. GUY, JR.

See COUNSELING AND PSYCHOTHERAPY: OVERVIEW.

Counseling and Psychotherapy: Biblical Themes. Counseling and psychotherapy as currently practiced generally involve prescheduled, time-limited encounters between a counselor/therapist and a client in order to provide help for the latter. Scripture offers no evidence of such a systematic approach to this activity. However, the Bible does speak of counsel and counselors and offers abundant evidence of encounters within the community of God's people designed to provide instruction, admonition, correction, encouragement, and comfort. The principles guiding such encounters continue to be valid for contemporary counselors and therapists. Salient biblical themes as set forth in the Old Testament, in the ministry of our Lord, and in the New Testament epistles are briefly surveyed.

Old Testament. A key word is the verb *ya'ats* (to advise, counsel, purpose, devise), its participle, *yo'ets* (counselor), and its cognate nouns, *'etsah* (counsel, purpose) and *mo'etsah* (counsel, plan). These words often describe the activity of political or military counselors such as Ahithophel (2 Sam. 16:15–17:14). One text states that "any advice Ahithophel gave . . . was accepted as though it were the very word of God" (2 Sam. 16:23, TEV). Non-Israelite kings such as Pharaoh (Isa. 19:11) and Artaxerxes also had counselors.

As Jeremiah 18:18 suggests, the counselor's task was not that of the priest or Levite who taught the law, nor was it the prophetic task of serving as God's mouthpiece. Rather, in situations where there were no explicit divine directives the wise counselor assessed the situation, considered the options, and helped the counselee select the best of these. Several passages illustrate the nature of these counseling activities. Jethro offered advice to his son-in-law, Moses, regarding the best way to handle the administrative aspects of leading Israel (Exod. 18:13–26). The prophet Nathan offered Bathsheba advice on what steps to take to save her life and Solomon's at the time of Adonijah's coup (1 Kings 1:12). Among the Levitical gatekeepers, Zechariah ben-Shelemiah is described as a wise counselor (1 Chron. 26:14). Several passages in Proverbs highlight the wisdom of seeking advice from a group of counselors (i.e., a council) when conducting affairs of state (Prov. 11:14; 15:22; 24:6).

As mentioned, counselors must assess situations and determine the best course of action. But what norms should guide such decisions? The Bible explicitly claims to provide guidelines that will lead to wise thinking and successful living (e.g., Deut. 4:5–6; 6:1–3; Prov. 1:1–7). But Scripture itself also implies that human beings have been tasked with further studying God's creation in order to better understand it. Israel's sages observed and pondered human behavior and discovered valid principles for successful living (e.g., Prov. 23:29–35; 24:30–34). Conclusions that are based on accurate human observation will not contradict God's Word but may well illuminate and illustrate basic scriptural principles of broad application. A good counselor will seek to understand principles revealed in Scripture and gained through the study of human behavior and will utilize them in setting goals and strategies for counseling.

The story of Job's counselors contains a salutary warning against attempts to rigidly apply sound theology to a specific situation when not all the facts are known. Although a man reaps what he sows (Gal. 6:7), Job's calamities were not the consequence of wrongdoing on his part. His friends, of course, thought otherwise. God indicated his anger at the misrepresentation he suffered at the hands of Job's counselors: "You have not spoken of me what is right" (Job 42:8). In light of this, humility needs to be exercised in counseling/psychotherapy, because counselors' knowledge is always limited. Thus it is important for counselors/therapists to rely on the Holy Spirit, in conjunction with their knowledge, for direction and guidance.

Jesus' Ministry. One of the prophetic titles given to our Lord is that of Wonderful Counselor (Isa. 9:6). No merely human counselor can hope to equal his insight into the human psyche (John 2:24–25) or his divine authority. Yet many principles of counseling are illustrated by his encounters. A word that is used frequently to describe his encounters with others is the word *splachnizomai* (to have pity, show mercy, feel sympathy). The *splachna* are the entrails, the inner organs, and the verb describes a profound emotional response to another's need. Jesus experienced compassion for a leper (Mark 1:41), for the crowds that attended his itinerant ministry (Matt. 9:36), for two blind men (Matt. 20:34), for a hungry multitude that had not eaten for three days (Matt. 15:34; Mark 8:2), and for the widow at Nain mourning the death of her only son (Luke 7:13). Although Jesus' compassion was often in response to a concrete and readily visible need, it was also elicited by the "harassed and helpless" multitudes whom Jesus saw "as sheep without a shepherd" (Matt. 9:36; cf. Mark 6:34). He perceived their emotional and spiritual bankruptcy and responded to it. It is noteworthy that Jesus' compassion for those in need habitually moved him to act on their behalf.

Compassion is a critical element in the contemporary counseling process. It parallels in some senses the current psychotherapeutic concept of empathy, which has been demonstrated to be one of the key factors of successful therapeutic outcome. Just as Jesus' compassion for people moved him to help them in some way, compassion for clients helps counselors to maintain a positive therapeutic alliance and to act in a therapeutic manner. Empathy is one of the most important elements in communicating acceptance to clients and thus a necessary foundation for counseling or psychotherapy.

In the parable of the good Samaritan (Luke 10:30–37) *splanchnizomai* expresses the desire to use all of one's resources to help another at the crucial moment. In the parable of the prodigal son (Luke 15:11–32) *splanchnizomai* expresses the strongest type of merciful or loving reaction (Esser, 1975). Counseling and psychotherapy are likewise characterized by the counselor using all of his or her available resources within the psychotherapy context to help a client.

The meaning of *splanchnizomai* in the parable of the prodigal son is particularly instructive for counseling. Therapists' reactions to their clients often have a powerful impact on them, particularly when clients' sin and psychopathology have personally impinged on the therapist. In such situations therapists need to demonstrate, as much as is humanly possible, the type of reaction described by *splanchnizomai*. In other words, they need to accept clients in light of their sin and psychopathology rather than retaliating in some manner. Just as the father's merciful reaction represents God's grace in the story of the prodigal son, a therapist's merciful reaction to a client can be a powerful, concrete manifestation of God's grace.

Other counseling techniques and principles are illustrated in the Gospel accounts. These include the use of probing questions (e.g., "Why do you call me good?" [Mark 10:18]), gentle confrontation of wrongdoing (John 4:16–18; 8:10–11), seeking agreement on the purpose or goals of the encounter ("What do you want me to do for you?" [Mark 10:51]; "do you want to get well?" [John 5:6]), and answering questions with questions as means of clarifying the intent of the questioner (Mark 10:27–33; Luke 10:25–37).

New Testament Epistles. Several terms in the New Testament that occur most frequently in the Pauline epistles capture important aspects of the counselor's task. *Parakaleo* (to summon, invite, exhort, encourage, implore, ask) is a common verb in the New Testament. The associated noun, *paraklesis* (encouragement, exhortation, appeal, comfort, consolation), is found 29 times. The root idea of these words is to be called *(kaleo)* in or alongside *(para)* another in order to provide help. The required help may take several forms ranging from comfort or consolation to encouragement or exhortation. The picture of being called alongside captures the idea of the therapeutic alliance necessary for a successful outcome in counseling. The sense of "comfort" is found especially in 2 Corinthians 1:3–7, where Paul describes the process of comforting others with the comfort received from God.

Paramytheomai (to encourage, cheer up, console) and its cognate nouns *paramythia* and *paramythion* (encouragement, comfort, consolation) reinforce the idea of helping those experiencing sorrow. In 1 Thessalonians 2:12 Paul reminds his readers that when he visited Thessalonica he comforted them. In 1 Thessalonians 5:14 Paul urges the whole church to encourage the timid. Then as now, sorrow is an integral part of human existence; giving comfort was a crucial part of Paul's missionary activity and of the life of the young church.

Providing comfort, encouragement, and exhortation are also key components of the contemporary counseling process. Clients seek counseling because they are hurting and need the comfort and encouragement of another human being. A principle that can be drawn from 2 Corinthians 1:3–7 is that counselors need to be strengthened themselves in order to have the needed emotional resources to comfort their clients. As clients receive comfort from counseling, their emotional resources are replenished; this increases their ability to tolerate frustration and pain and to deal with problems in life. Comforting in the sense of addressing cheering words to a client may or may not be helpful in psychotherapy; sometimes comforting involves communicating an understanding of a client's suffering rather than speaking positive words. Giving comfort and encouragement to clients is a key therapeutic component and one function of the body of Christ.

Noutheteo is derived from *nous* (mind) and *tithemi* (put) and describes the exertion of influence on the mind, implying that there is some resistance (Selter, 1975). In contrast to *didasko* (to teach or instruct), which refers to guidance of the intellect, *noutheteo* is concerned with the will and feelings of a person. Although *noutheteo* may carry a secondary sense of to chastise, Selter (1975) points out that this meaning does not occur in the New Testament. In the Septuagint it is used in the active sense of to instruct (Job 4:3). In the New Testament the verb is found only in Paul's letters and Acts 20:31, where Luke is reporting one of Paul's speeches. Paul reminds the Ephesian elders that he never stopped warning each of them night and day with tears (Acts 20:31). Likewise, he warns the Corinthian church, addressing them as his "dear children" (1 Cor. 4:14). Even though he needed to correct them, he did so out of love and for their own good. In Colossians 1:28 and 3:16 *noutheteo* is paired with *didasko* in connection with the proclamation of Christ. The goal of admonishing and teaching is maturity in Christ (Col. 1:28).

Noutheteo captures much of the counseling process. Counseling always involves dealing with resistance to change. Moreover, counselors largely address their clients' will and feelings. Like Paul, therapists seek to influence their clients toward growth and maturity. Sometimes this involves admonishing and instructing to provide a corrective (1 Thess. 5:14; 2 Thess. 3:15). Paul's motivation for admonishing his people is clear—it is not to shame them (1 Cor. 4:14) but rather to bring them to maturity in Christ (Col. 1:28). Exerting influence, admonishing, and instructing are part of the counseling/psychotherapy process but should always be done out of concern for the client's welfare with the ultimate goal of promoting maturity.

References

Esser, H. H. (1975). s.v. Mercy. In C. Brown (Ed.), *New international dictionary of New Testament theology.* Grand Rapids, MI: Zondervan.

Selter, F. (1975). s.v. Exhort, Warn, Console, Rebuke. In C. Brown (Ed.), *New international dictionary of New Testament theology.* Grand Rapids, MI: Zondervan.

T. W. HALL AND P. C. LEWIS

See CHRISTIAN COUNSELING AND PSYCHOTHERAPY; COUNSELING AND PSYCHOTHERAPY: THEOLOGICAL THEMES.

Counseling and Psychotherapy: Overview. Responsible Christian professionals acknowledge a necessary relationship between the art of Christian living and that of psychotherapy and counseling. They recognize that behind those applied arts is an essential interaction between the science of theology and the science of psychology, each science forming and informing the other.

There are five levels at which the two sciences interact: theory formulation, research methodology, data base, clinical application, and internal personal perception. At each level the two sciences interact specifically within the anthropology that is functioning in each science. More specifically, it is the personality theory in that anthropology which is the focus of the interaction of the two sciences.

Since Christians acknowledge that all truth is God's truth, no matter who finds it or where it is found, the information derived from both psychology and theology is taken with equal seriousness. God's self-revelation in the data of Scripture and spiritual experience, as well as in the data of the material universe are both sought diligently to ensure the maximum constructive interaction between theology and psychology. The concern in this is not to integrate the two sciences but to acknowledge that each, as science, has its own domain, universe of discourse, and data base and must be carried out in the light of or from the perspective of the other.

In this perspectival model (Ellens, 1982) which acknowledges that the science of biblical theology examines the special revelation in Scripture and the science of psychology examines the general revelation in creation, the development of sound personality theory and psychotherapy models requires careful attention to the cardinal themes of both psychology and theology. In the art of counseling and psychotherapy those theological themes have clear-cut and palpable import.

Principles and Themes. The first theological principle for counseling and psychotherapy is that godliness or Christian authenticity requires thorough responsibility. To be a Christian counselor or therapist means first to be the best therapist it is possible to be. The second principle is that Christian and professional authenticity requires incarnation in the person of the therapist of that grace-shaped redemptive quality which reflects how God is disposed toward humans and how God designs humans to be disposed toward each other. To be a Christian counselor or therapist means to be God's incarnation for the patient or client, as Jesus Christ is for all of us in everything necessary to our redemption.

Eight theological themes crucially shape a Christian personality theory and counseling or psychotherapy. The first is grace: radical, unconditional, and universal. In the creation story humans are never referred to as children or servants of God but are depicted as compatriots, collaborators, and coequals of God in the kingdom enterprise. That royal status is not abrogated by the fall. The *proto-evangelium* (Gen. 3:15) affirms that, whereas God recognized that the human predicament had changed and therefore that the divine redemptive strategy had to change, the objective remained the same. Humans exist to grow into the divinely ordered destiny of full-orbed personhood, in the image of God. To ensure that, God's disposition is not one of judgment but of unconditional acceptance of humans as we are, for the sake of what we can become. It is a disposition of grace, freedom, and affirmation. That covenant is "for the healing of the nations." It

renders irrelevant all strategies of religious legalism, psychological defensiveness, and self-justification. Grace is God's ambition for all humanity; it cuts through to the center of our alienation and disorder, and outflanks all our techniques for creating a conditional relationship with God and each other.

The second theme is alienation. The fallenness of humanity is obvious. Its psychological consequences are evident everywhere. Humans are as children thrust out of the maternal womb and unable to catch hold of our father's hand. The biblical story of the fall depicts the spiritual and psychological disorders caused by this experience. The confusion of identity, role, focus, and relationship pervades life like that confusion attendant upon all birth trauma and adolescent disengagement. That is undoubtedly why the biblical account of the fall spontaneously seems so authentic. In the face of generic human fallenness and alienation life becomes an endeavor at anxiety reduction. Most human strategies for that, and for increasing control and security, are pathogenic compensatory strategies. All religion is such an anxiety reduction strategy. Apart from the Judeo-Christian type of grace theology, other religious strategies and practices merely increase the human sense of alienation and disorder because they provide only strategies for self justification. Unconditional grace cuts through that pathogenesis and affirms humans as God compatriots, in spite of ourselves. Even in Judeo-Christian history there have been frequent reversions to pagan conditionalism, but the essence of grace theology transcends that.

The third theme is therefore the biblical theology of personhood. From the biblical tradition of the Yahwist, through the theology of the prophets, to the gospel incarnated in Jesus' way of handling people, it is clear that humans are unconditionally cherished by God. Human personhood is rooted in the fact that we are created as imagers of God and arbitrarily assigned the status of coequals with God in keeping the garden kingdom. So human persons have only two potential conditions: to be in a posture which rings true to that God-given status and, therefore, to self; or to be inauthentic, alienated from God and our own true destiny, and suffering and dissonance and disease inherent to our inauthenticity. In all that, since God is God and grace is grace, God remains preoccupied with human need, not naughtiness; with human failure of destiny more than of duty; and with our redeemed potential, not our wretched past. Health then means not merely absence of disease but freedom and affirmation for growth to our destiny. We are free in spite of ourselves, to be what we are for the sake of what we can become before the face of God.

The fourth theme is sin, the failure to achieve authenticity to self and full-orbed personhood as God's person. Sin is a distortion and distraction to lesser achievements. Nothing can compensate for it. One can only be converted from it. Repentance is the only solution: turning from our pathogenic compensatory behavior to acceptance of God's unconditional acceptance of us. God's law, then, is not a threat but a constitution for the life of the kingdom, wholeness in the whole person. Having freed us by his grace, God simply waits for us to achieve the self-actualization which expresses the regal status of God compatriot. Sin is "falling short of his glory," his glorious destiny for us true selfhood as imagers and compatriots of God.

The fifth theme is discipline and discipleship. It is the endeavor of beginning down the way of grace: forgiveness and acceptance of self and others and unconditional caring for self and others. It is not structuring life in a controlled legalism of personal purity and piety designed to gain credit with God. Discipleship is a troth with self and God to incarnate that divine grace dynamic that infuses the universe. It is a troth to forsake all other *foci* and keep only to the kingdom destiny of God imager, compatriot, and incarnator of grace.

The sixth theme is that of the suffering servant and wounded healer. Nouwen (1972) suggests that there are five doors through which God and the Christian can touch humans: the woundedness of Jesus of Nazareth, of the world, of a given generation, of the individual patient, and of the healer. Grace, growth, and healing are communicated, through the brokenness of the healer, to the person to be healed. The humanness and brokenness of both must be affirmed. The healer's role is not to remove the pain of life but to interpret it. The evidence in the healer of woundedness and pain and of the constructive uses and endurance of it helps to heal the patient. The wounded healer can become the model and the sign of hope, of the risk taking inherent in growth and healing.

The seventh theme is celebration. People who can be grateful can be healthy. People who cannot be grateful cannot be healthy in body, mind, psyche, or spirit. They do not have access to the psychological and spiritual machinery of health. The Christian life is the celebration that springs spontaneously from gratitude. The Bible makes it clear that Christianity is not a command to be obeyed, a burden to be labored under, nor an obligation to be met. It is an opportunity to be seized, a relief to be celebrated, and a salvation to be savored. The celebration of gratitude may take the form of the childlike posture of prayer or the exhilarated reflective enjoyment of God's providence.

The eighth theme is mortality. The Bible gives little impetus to the perfectionist notions that building the kingdom will eliminate mortality. It affirms the world's brokenness and pathology and that we are dying persons in a world of malignancy as well as of magnificence. It is acceptable to age, wrinkle, weaken, become more dependent, and even die. Maturation, not youthfulness, is the focus of meaning. People needing healing need to feel in their counselors the Christian realization that it is a supportable and perhaps even a celebratable condition to be a human mortal before the face of God.

Implications for Therapy. The consequences of these themes for counseling and psychotherapy are direct and practical. First, they imply that the patient possesses a pre-established identity, arbitrarily imputed by God in grace. The patient is, in spite of himself or herself, an image bearer of God. That identity needs to be recovered. Therapy is the process of recovering it and propelling the patient into the certified and secure destiny of purposeful self-realization as imager and compatriot of God. That may not be overtly explained in therapy but will be implicit in the perspective, goals, expectations, and values inherent in the therapist's incarnational role.

Second, the themes of grace-shaped identity, growth, healing, and destiny introduce into the therapeutic milieu dynamics which can erode neurotic guilt, remorse, grief, hopelessness, self-pity, compulsivity, and rigidity of personality. The Christian perspective potentially decreases the need for the self-defeating processes of denial and self-justification as well as the various compensatory reactions so often produced by them. The biblical perspective frees the patient and the therapist for self-acceptance and a life style of dignity. It is a perspective shaped by God's unconditional positive regard for humans.

Third, the Christian perspective removes the anxiety of the therapy responsibility for the therapist and thus decreases the degree of iatrogenic psychopathology (i.e., therapist induced psychopathology). It also affords a base for wholesome transference and countertransference and frees the therapist to be human and healthily humorful.

Fourth, the Christian perspective can reduce the anxiety and distraction of the patient. This may come by means of the sense of relief and affirmed self-esteem implied in the fact that his or her worthiness is imputed and inherent rather than a worthiness earned and dependent upon his or her health, behavior, or effectiveness in therapy.

Fifth, this Christian perspective of freedom and affirmation expands the potential for risk taking toward growth by its constructive anxiety reduction value. It affords relief from constraints that distract the patient from Christian self-actualization. It releases persons to accept humanness and mortality, and thereby it mollifies that ultimate threat which stands behind all pathology: the fear of death, meaninglessness, and annihilation.

Theology and faith are cognitive emotive processes. Their function for good or ill is relevant to all cognitive and emotive disorders, even those of an organic or body chemistry source. Therefore, concerns about theological perspective, faith commitment, religious experience, and spiritual maturity are vital therapeutic issues. The concern to be a *Christian* professional is a crucial one.

J. H. Ellens

References

Ellens, J. H. (1982). *God's grace and human health*. Nashville: Abingdon.

Nouwen, H. J. (1972). *The wounded healer*. Garden City, New York: Doubleday.

See MORAL AND ETHICAL ISSUES IN TREATMENT; PSYCHOLOGY AS RELIGION; VALUES AND PSYCHOLOGY; PHILOSOPHICAL PSYCHOLOGY.

Counseling and Psychotherapy: Theological Themes.

Responsible Christian professionals acknowledge a necessary relationship between the art of Christian living and that of psychotherapy and counseling. They recognize that behind those applied arts is an essential interaction between the science of theology and the science of psychology, each science forming and informing the other.

The two sciences interact at five levels: theory formulation, research methodology, database, clinical application, and internal personal perception. At each level the two sciences interact specifically within the anthropology that is functioning in each science. More specifically the personality theory in that anthropology is the locus of the interaction of the two sciences.

Since Christians acknowledge that all truth is God's truth, no matter who finds it or where it is found, the information derived from both psychology and theology is taken with equal seriousness. God's self-revelation in the data of Scripture and spiritual experience as well as in the data of the material universe are both sought diligently to ensure the maximum constructive interaction between theology and psychology. The concern is not to integrate the two sciences but to acknowledge that each, as science, has its own domain and universe of discourse and database and must be carried out in the light of or from the perspective of the other.

In this perspectival model (Ellens, 1982), which acknowledges that the science of biblical theology examines the special revelation in Scripture and the science of psychology examines the general revelation in creation, the development of sound personality theory and psychotherapy models requires careful attention to the cardinal themes of both psychology and theology. In the art of counseling and psychotherapy those theological themes have clear-cut and palpable import.

Principles and Themes. The first theological principle for counseling and psychotherapy is that godliness or Christian authenticity requires thorough responsibility. To be a Christian counselor or therapist means first to be the best therapist it is possible to be. The second principle is that Christian and professional authenticity requires incarnation in the person of the therapist of that grace-shaped redemptive quality that reflects how God is disposed toward humans and how God designs humans to be disposed toward each other. To be a Christian counselor or therapist means to be God's incarnation for the patient or client, as Jesus Christ is for all of us in everything necessary to our redemption.

Eight theological themes crucially shape a Christian personality theory and counseling or psychotherapy. The first is grace: radical, unconditional, and universal. In the creation story humans are never referred to as children or servants of God but are depicted as compatriots, colaborers, and coequals of God in the kingdom enterprise. That royal status is not abrogated by the fall. The protoevangelium (Gen. 3:15) affirms that, whereas God recognized that the human predicament had changed and therefore that the divine redemptive strategy had to change, the objective remained the same. Humans exist to grow into the divinely ordered destiny of full-orbed personhood, in the image of God. To ensure that, God's disposition is one not of judgment but of unconditional acceptance of humans as we are, for the sake of what we can become. It is a disposition of grace, freedom, and affirmation. That covenant is for the healing of the nations. It renders irrelevant all strategies of religious legalism, psychological defensiveness, and self-justification. Grace is God's ambition for all humanity; it cuts through to the center of our alienation and disorder and outflanks all our techniques for creating a conditional relationship with God and each other.

The second theme is alienation. The fallenness of humanity is obvious. Its psychological consequences are evident everywhere. Humans are as children thrust out of the maternal womb and unable to catch hold of our father's hand. The biblical story of the fall depicts the spiritual and psychological disorders caused by this experience. The confusion of identity, role, focus, and relationship pervades life like that confusion attendant upon all birth trauma and adolescent disengagement (*see* Adolescence). That is undoubtedly why the biblical account of the fall seems so authentic. In the face of generic human fallenness and alienation life becomes an endeavor at anxiety reduction. Most human strategies for that and for increasing control and security are pathogenic compensatory strategies. All religion is such an anxiety-reduction strategy. Apart from the Judeo-Christian grace theology, all other religions increase the human sense of alienation and disorder because they provide only strategies for self-justification. Unconditional grace cuts through that pathogenesis and affirms humans as God-compatriots, in spite of ourselves. Even in Judeo-Christian history there have been frequent reversions to pagan conditionalism, but the essence of grace theology transcends that.

The third theme is therefore the biblical theology of personhood. From the biblical tradition of the Yahwist, through the theology of the prophets, to the gospel incarnated in Jesus' way of handling people, it is clear that humans are unconditionally cherished by God. Personhood is rooted in the fact that we are created as imagers of God and arbitrarily assigned the status of coequal with God in keeping the garden kingdom. So persons have only two potential conditions: to be in a posture that rings true to that God-given status and therefore to self; or to be inauthentic, alienated from God and our own true destiny and suffering the dissonance and disease inherent to our inauthenticity. In all that, since God is God and grace is grace, God remains preoccupied with human need, not naughtiness; human failure of destiny more than duty; and with our redeemed potential, not our wretched past. Health then means not merely absence of disease but freedom and affirmation for growth to our destiny. We are free in spite of ourselves, to be what we are, for the sake of what we can become before the face of God.

The fourth theme is sin, the failure to achieve authenticity to self and the full-orbed personhood in Christ. Sin is a distortion and distraction to lesser achievements. Nothing can compensate for it. One can only be converted from it. Repentance is the only solution: turning from our pathogenic compensatory behavior to acceptance of God's unconditional acceptance of us. God's law, then, is not a threat but a constitution for the life of the kingdom, wholeness in the whole person. Having freed us by his grace, God waits for us to achieve the self-actualization that expresses the regal status of God-compatriot. Sin is "falling short of his glory," his glorious destiny for us—true selfhood as imagers and compatriots of God.

The fifth theme is discipline and discipleship. It is the endeavor of beginning down the way of grace: forgiveness and acceptance of self and others and unconditional caring for self and others. It is not structuring life in a controlled legalism of personal purity and piety designed to gain credit with God. Discipleship is a troth with self and God to incarnate that divine grace dynamic that infuses the universe. It is a troth to forsake all other foci and keep only to the kingdom destiny of God imager, compatriot, and incarnator of grace.

The sixth theme is that of the suffering servant or wounded healer. Nouwen (1972) suggests that there are four doors through which God and the Christian can touch humans: the woundedness of the world, of a given generation, of the individual, and of the healer. Grace, growth, and healing are communicated through the brokenness of the healer to the person to be healed. The humanness and brokenness of both must be affirmed. The healer's role is not to remove the pain of life but to interpret it. The evidence in the healer of woundedness and pain and of the constructive uses and endurance of it helps to heal the patient. The wounded healer can become the model and the sign of hope, of the risk taking inherent in growth and healing.

The seventh theme is celebration. People who can be grateful can be healthy. People who cannot be grateful cannot be healthy. They do not have access to the psychological and spiritual machinery of health. The Christian life is celebration. The Bible makes it clear that Christianity is not a command to be obeyed, a burden to be labored under, or an obligation to be met. It is an opportunity to be seized, a relief to be celebrated, and a salvation to be savored. The celebration of gratitude may take the form of the childlike posture of prayer or the exhilarated, reflective enjoyment of God's providence.

The eighth theme is mortality. The Bible gives little impetus to the perfectionist notions that building the kingdom will eliminate mortality. It affirms the world's brokenness and pathology and that we are dying persons in a world of malignancy as well as of magnificence. It is acceptable to age, wrinkle, weaken, become more dependent, and die. Maturation, not youthfulness, is the focus of meaning. People needing healing need to feel in their counselors the Christian realization that it is a supportable and perhaps even a celebratable condition to be a human mortal before the face of God.

Implications for Therapy. The consequences of these themes for counseling and psychotherapy are direct and practical. First, they imply that the patient possesses a preestablished identity, arbitrarily imputed by God in his grace. The patient is, in spite of himself or herself, an image bearer of God. That identity needs to be recovered. Therapy is the process of recovering it and propelling the patient into the certified and secure destiny of purposeful self-realization as imager and compatriot of God. That may not be overtly explained in therapy but will be implicit in the perspective, goals, expectations, and values inherent in the therapist's incarnational role.

Second, the themes of grace-shaped identity, growth, healing, and destiny introduce into the therapeutic milieu dynamics that can erode neurotic guilt, remorse, grief, hopelessness, self-pity, compulsivity, and rigidity of personality. The Christian perspective potentially decreases the need for the self-defeating processes of denial and self-justification as well as the various compensatory reactions so often produced by them. The biblical perspective frees the patient and the therapist for self-acceptance and a lifestyle of dignity. It is a perspective shaped by God's unconditional positive regard for humans.

Third, the Christian perspective removes the anxiety of the therapy responsibility for the therapist and so decreases the degree of iatrogenic psychopathology (i.e., therapist-induced psychopathology). It also affords a base for wholesome transference and countertransference and frees the therapist to be human and healthily humorful (*see* Humor).

Fourth, the Christian perspective can reduce the anxiety and distraction of the patient. This may come by means of the sense of relief and affirmed self-esteem implied in the fact that his or her worthiness is imputed and inherent rather than earned and dependent upon his or her health or behavior.

Fifth, this Christian perspective of freedom and affirmation expands the potential for risk taking toward growth by its constructive anxiety-reduction value. It affords relief from constraints that distract the patient from Christian self-actualization. It releases persons to accept humanness and mortality, and thereby it mollifies that ultimate threat that stands behind all pathology: the fear of death, meaninglessness, and annihilation.

Theology and faith are cognitive-emotive processes. Their functions for good or ill are relevant to all cognitive and emotive disorders, even those of an organic or body chemistry source. Therefore, concerns about theological perspective, faith commitment, religious experience, and spiritual maturity are vital therapeutic issues. The concern to be a Christian professional is a crucial one.

References

Ellens, J. H. (1982). *God's grace and human health.* Nashville: Abingdon.

Nouwen, H. J. (1972). *The wounded healer.* Garden City, NY: Doubleday.

J. H. ELLENS

See CHRISTIAN COUNSELING AND PSYCHOTHERAPY; COUNSELING AND PSYCHOTHERAPY: BIBLICAL THEMES.

Counseling Psychology. Counseling psychology is one of the four traditional specialty areas of professional psychology, the other three being clinical psychology, school psychology, and industrial-self-organizational psychology. The American Psychological Association recognizes these distinct specialties by accrediting their graduate training programs. Additionally, the American Board of Professional Psychology awards diplomate status to outstanding practitioners in each specialty area. Counseling psychology overlaps with each of the three traditional areas to some extent. There are also new specialty areas, such as health psychology and neuropsychology, that are seeking recognition by the American Psychological Association, having already been recognized as an area of practice by the American Board of Professional Psychology. Counseling psychologists have been active in these new specialty areas as well, and have engaged in research and practice that have applied counseling psychology to areas new for counseling psychologists.

However, as noted by Gelso and Fretz (1992), counseling psychology is distinguished from other areas of practice by its emphasis on five unifying themes. First is an emphasis on individuals who possess relatively adequate functioning as opposed to an emphasis on individuals who are seriously disturbed. Second is attention to areas of assets and strengths compared to attention to areas of deficit. Third is an emphasis on interventions that are relatively brief and educational in nature, including prevention, rather than an emphasis on long-term relationship-oriented psychotherapy. Fourth is a blended focus on understanding the person in his or her environment rather than considering only the person or only the environment. Fifth is an emphasis on problems faced by virtually everyone across the life span: problems of development (*see* Life Span Development), decision making, adjustment, and transition.

The distinction between clinical psychology and counseling psychology is often a puzzling one. Indeed, as will be discussed later, there has been a blending of areas of practice between these two specialties over time. However, as defined by the *Specialty Guidelines for the Delivery of Services by Clinical Psychologists*, the goals of clinical psychology services are to "understand, predict, and alleviate intellectual, emotional, psychological, and behavioral disability and discomfort" (American Psychological Association, 1981, p. 642). Thus clinical psychology, in contrast to counseling psychology, focuses on individual pathology or disturbance and uses remedial techniques to remove or alleviate dysfunction.

History. This distinction between clinical psychology and counseling psychology is easily understood in light of the histories of the specialties. When clinical psychology developed in medical settings, the primary task of the specialty was to do assessment and provide diagnoses for patients who would then receive therapy from psychiatrists. However, after World War II, with the development of various types of psychotherapy, clinical psychologists began to be trained in the delivery of therapeutic services as well as in conducting assessment. Their services were still delivered in medical or inpatient psychiatric settings (although some clinical psychologists were independent practitioners), and their patients were still primarily persons with severe psychological disturbances.

Clinical psychology and counseling psychology came into being officially in 1946 as charter divisions (Divisions 12 and 17 respectively) of the newly merged American Psychological Association and the American Association for Applied Psychology. Counseling psychology's division was then entitled Counseling and Guidance. This name reflected the common interests among early counseling psychologists who were primarily employed as faculty in colleges and universities and who were active in developing models of vocational decision making. The primary focus of counseling psychology was vocational guidance and counseling (*see* Vocational Counseling), and many counseling psychologists who were charter members of Division 17 were also active in the American College Personnel Association, whose members were involved in student personnel work in colleges and universities, and in the National Vocational Guidance Association, whose members were involved in providing vocational guidance in secondary schools.

During the 1950s, the division changed its name to the Division of Counseling Psychology, and its members became known as counseling psychologists. Funding for doctoral training programs became available through the Veterans Administration, and these programs were developed with the goal of the doctoral degree as the minimal level of training. A later invitational conference at Greyston Center further contributed to the development of the specialty by providing a common definition and by separating counseling psychology from the related but separate practice of counseling, which was also developing during this time (Thompson & Super, 1964).

Counseling psychology as a specialty rapidly expanded through the 1960s and 1970s. Many graduates took positions in newly developing graduate training programs and in counseling centers and the Veterans Administration system. The increased availability of positions led to a dramatic increase in the number of training programs. During this same time, there was a rapid proliferation of research on the process of counseling, on supervision and training, on issues of testing and measurement, and on vocational psychology and career counseling. This research was published in journals such as the *Journal of Counseling Psychology,* the *Journal of Vocational Behavior,* and *The Counseling Psychologist.*

Current Status. In the late 1970s through the 1980s, changing population trends and altered marketplace finances led to a period of rapid change in the specialty. For the first time, counseling psychologists began to seek positions in community mental health centers and in individual and group practice settings where they directly competed with clinical psychologists for jobs for which counseling psychologists believed they had comparable training. Further, the practice of counseling and clinical psychology came to blend, and several prominent counseling psychologists questioned the ongoing viability of counseling psychology as a distinct specialty (Fitzgerald & Osipow, 1986).

This state of affairs came about for several reasons. First, the accreditation criteria of the American Psychological Association contained basic educational requirements that served to make training in clinical psychology and counseling psychology more comparable than had originally been the case. Second, clinical psychology had begun to respond to criticisms of its own focus and redefined its role to include clients whose concerns were less pathological and more developmental and treatments that were short-term and educational in nature. The growth of behavioral therapies at this time was a great influence on this redefinition. Counseling psychology, in a parallel fashion, had expanded its treatments beyond vocational decision making to include psychotherapy, behavior therapy, marriage and family counseling, and other more clinical procedures as a means of reaching the goal of facilitating normal growth and development. Third,

counseling psychologists were beginning to be more active in the consideration of private practice issues of credentials, licensing, and third party payment (insurance reimbursement for health care services such as diagnosis and therapy).

As these pressures, generated by changes in the specialty, intensified, there has been a corresponding growth of conflict within counseling psychology about its rightful role in psychology (e.g., Fretz & Mills, 1980). During the 1980s, there was increased attention to defining areas of unity among counseling psychologists. Two sets of white papers were published, one defining the role of counseling psychology in the 1980s (Whiteley, Ragan, Harmon, Fretz, and Taney, 1984) and the other defining what counseling psychology should encompass in the year 2000 (Whiteley, & Fretz, 1980). A third national conference on counseling psychology, the Georgia Conference, was held in 1987. Over 180 counseling psychologists formed five task groups to prepare recommendations for the specialty in areas such as education and training, research, and professional practice (Rudd, Weisberg, & Gazda, 1988).

In all of these activities, counseling psychology unified around several themes: maintaining a scientific basis for practice (including emphasizing the scientist-practitioner model in graduate training), continuing an emphasis on positive mental health, promoting mental health at the level of groups as well as individuals, and considering development across the life span. These common themes were continued into the 1990s, and were expanded to include an emphasis on providing services to clients in a multicultural and multiracial society. Part of this latter emphasis means increasing competence on the part of counselors in providing treatment for clients of varying races, socioeconomic backgrounds, religions, and other conditions of individual differences.

Future Trends. For any specialty to continue its viability, certain criteria need to be met. A specialty area of practice indicates that the knowledge base has increased to the point where specification of training and state-of-the-art practices can be articulated. Counseling psychology has faced a series of difficult questions in this regard. Should counseling psychology continue to affirm its roots in vocational guidance? Should counseling psychology broaden its usual practices to include treating seriously pathological clients with intensive psychotherapy? Or is there a middle ground of practice that reaffirms counseling psychology's traditional emphasis of building on a client's strengths but expands service delivery to a variety of different settings, such as medical settings? Many counseling psychologists believe the latter is the best choice.

The Division of Counseling Psychology has responded to these pressures in establishing formal sections, groups of counseling psychologists who share interests in applications and/or research. The first two sections to be approved were those focusing on Women and Health Psychology. Other sections are Independent Practice, Vocational Psychology, Ethnic and Racial Diversity, and Lesbian, Gay, and Bisexual Awareness. Thus the interest in diversity among clients is clearly evident in the developing sections.

Many practitioners see counseling psychology as growing in its involvement with other areas as well. Some of these are the psychological, social, and vocational rehabilitation of the chronically and severely disabled; the development and delivery of mental health services for underserved populations (e.g., rural, elderly, minority); outreach activities such as consultation and prevention; and research relating to these new directions. However, in all of the new applications, counseling psychology has maintained a clear focus on several core values articulated by Hurst (1989). First, within the specialty is a deep sense of respect for persons. Second, scientists and practitioners have a healthy interdependence. Third, there is a respect for conditions of diversity. And fourth, there is a common cause of facilitating growth processes in persons and environments.

References

American Psychological Association. (1981). Specialty guidelines for the delivery of services by clinical psychologists. *American Psychologist 36,* 640–651.

Fitzgerald, L. F., & Osipow, S. H. (1986). An occupational analysis of counseling psychology: How special is the specialty? *American Psychologist, 41,* 535–544.

Fretz, B. R., & Mills, D. H. (1980). Professional certification in counseling psychology. *The Counseling Psychologist, 9,* 2–17.

Gelso, C. J., & Fretz, B. R. (1992). *Counseling psychology.* New York: Holt, Rinehart, & Winston.

Hurst, J. C. (1989). Counseling psychology—A source of strength and pride in the ties that bind. *The Counseling Psychologist, 17,* 147–160.

Rudd, S. S., Weisberg, N., & Gazda, G. M. (1988). Looking to the future: Themes from the third national conference for counseling psychology. *The Counseling Psychologist, 16,* 423–430.

Thompson, A. S., & Super, D. E. (Eds.). (1964). *The professional preparation of counseling psychologists: Report of the 1964 Greyston Conference.* New York: Teachers College, Columbia University, Bureau of Publications.

Whiteley, J. N., & Fretz, B. R. (Eds.). (1980). *The present and future of counseling psychology.* Monterey, CA: Brooks/Cole.

Whiteley, J. N., Kagan, N., Harmon, L. W., Fretz, B. R., & Tanney, F. (Eds.). (1984). *The coming decade in counseling psychology.* Alexandria, VA: American Association for Counseling and Development.

E. M. ALTMAIER

See CLINICAL PSYCHOLOGY; COMMUNITY PSYCHOLOGY; APPLIED PSYCHOLOGY.

Counselor Training. *See* TRAINING IN COUNSELING AND PSYCHOTHERAPY.

Counterconditioning. In counterconditioning a maladaptive response is eliminated by establishing a new response in the presence of the stimulus that initially controlled occurrence of the maladaptive response. In a classical study crying in the presence of a rabbit was eliminated by feeding the fearful child and gradually bringing the rabbit into the child's proximity while he ate.

The critical components in counterconditioning are the maladaptive stimulus-response pattern and a new stimulus-response interaction. This new pattern is usually developed through replacing the maladaptive response with a more acceptable response—in other words, response substitution. By contrast, punishment and extinction weaken present responses without developing alternative responses to the controlling stimulus.

Although it is rarely discussed in recent behavioral literature, counterconditioning is a basic process underlying many behavior therapy techniques, including such procedures as covert sensitization, differential reinforcement of alternative behavior, aversion therapy, systematic and in vivo desensitization, assertiveness training, and sex therapy.

Despite neglect of the concept, there is general agreement that the research evidence indicates that replacing problem behaviors with adaptive behaviors is an effective treatment approach. An interesting parallel noted by Adams is that a number of biblical teachings suggest the value of replacing sinful practices with godly behavior (Adams, 1973, pp. 176–216).

Reference

Adams, J. E. (1973). *The Christian counselor's manual.* Grand Rapids, MI: Baker.

R. K. BUFFORD

See BEHAVIOR THERAPY.

Countertransference. The subjective experience of the therapist during the course of a therapeutic relationship with a patient. This clinical concept has been discussed primarily in psychoanalytic literature, but it occurs in the course of any relationship. The term was first used by Sigmund Freud (1910/ 1946; 1910/1946) to describe the unconscious conflicts and feelings of the psychoanalyst that are evoked by the patient. Largely through his own self-analysis, Freud identified the key role of the unconscious in human personality. He observed how conflicted and traumatic aspects of relationships from one's past are disavowed and repressed into the unconscious psyche. In the course of psychoanalyzing patients' neurotic symptoms, he found that these repressed relationships from the past, with accompanying fantasies and impulses, were at the base of the symptoms and would surface in the relationship with the analyst. He called this reaction to the analyst transference. Countertransference involves the analyst's unconscious, repressed, and conflicted infantile relationships that surface in reaction to the patient in general or in reaction to the patient's transference.

The significance of the countertransference is that the analyst needs to become aware of these reactions in order to deal with them, thereby avoiding acting them out toward the patient in a potentially destructive interaction. The implication of this early understanding of countertransference is that it is dangerous and aberrant, a sign of something unanalyzed in the analyst that should not be there. The analyst's own primitive reactions belong more in their own training analysis or self-analysis than in the consulting room.

There are many serious problems with this view of countertransference. It poses an unrealistic standard for analysts and contradicts analytic theory by implying that anyone, including an analyst, can be free of reactions that carry a myriad of unconscious infantile and conflicted impulses and internal relationships. Racker (1972) notes that it is a myth to think of analysis as an interaction between a sick person and a healthy one. As a result of this myth there developed an ideal of the detached analyst whose only appropriate feeling is to have a distant concern for the patient; anything else is to be overcome (Heimann, 1949/1981).

A problem related to this mythical view of countertransference is that therapists might experience anxiety or guilt regarding countertransference feelings to the extent that they would avoid the full awareness of the countertransference experience. This would only assure that the anxiety or guilt-laden experience of the analyst would go underground and become inaccessible for self-analysis. This could result in acting out these feelings toward the patient. Thus the moralistic view of countertransference as something wrong and dangerous can foster the perils against which it warns.

In the late 1940s a more realistic view of the analyst and the therapeutic relationship started to appear in the literature. There was an acknowledgment that the analyst responds to the patient on all levels of personality at the same time, from id, ego, and superego, including infantile self and disturbed internal parental objects (Racker, 1972). Little (1951) suggests countertransference cannot be avoided but only observed and analyzed.

In 1949 Heimann introduced a radical but remarkably useful idea: that countertransference be utilized by the therapist to understand the patient's experience. She called it an instrument of research into the patient's unconscious that emanates from the analyst's unconscious understanding of the patient.

Racker's work (1972) on the subject explains the mechanisms involved in how the countertransference reflects the analyst's unconscious understanding of the patient. It starts with the analyst's openness to truly empathizing and identifying with the patient's internal experience, including even symbiotic identification. For example, a moment of strong anxiety or anger the analyst experienced in a session might reflect something the patient is feeling but cannot yet express in words. He calls this concordant identification in that the analyst is unconsciously aligning each level of his or her personality, ego, id, and superego, with the corresponding level in the patient. In order to help the analyst truly understand, the patient might unconsciously treat the analyst as someone from the patient's past. In turn the analyst would feel treated as such and might start feeling toward the patient just like the patient's object from the past. For instance, the analyst might feel critical of the patient's steps toward autonomy as the patient had experienced a parent's reacting to him or her. This would be the therapist's complementary identification felt in the countertransference.

These recent developments in comprehending countertransference have great clinical usefulness. Regardless of one's therapeutic approach, transference and countertransference occur. Psychoanalytical literature suggests that countertransference be valued as the instrument par excellence for understanding and even resolving psychic pain. The patient's ability to communicate his or her most painful, disturbing affects and relationships, unconsciously and largely without words, to the therapist, and the therapist's capacity to deeply and unconsciously experience these as his or her own, are profound and might be described as one of the most truly intimate and spiritual aspects of the therapeutic relationship. To the extent that the patient's pain and needs are traumatic, he or she has not been able to psychically digest or mentalize them so that they cannot be communicated in words. Thus the patient must rely on presenting the analyst with some disturbing emotional experience in order to be understood. This requires the therapist to be aware of the trauma in the countertransference and at times to stand it and digest it for the patient instead of reacting like the original parent or engaging with the patient in a nonproductive, maladaptive response to it.

The countertransference can even be a kind of neurosis suffered by the therapist for the patient (Tower, 1956). This might involve the therapist digesting something that has been indigestible for the patient or detoxifying something that has been too toxic for the patient to allow himself or herself to experience, much less resolve. In this way the therapist, with all of his or her own past and present conflicts and inner world, can join the patient's inner reality and create a unique emotional experience (Kernberg, 1965) that can lead to insight and transformation in the patient and often in the therapist (Searles, 1986).

References

Freud, S. (1946). The future prospects of psychoanalytic therapy. *Collected papers*. London: Hogarth. (Original work published 1910)

Freud, S. (1946). The dynamics of the transference. *Collected papers*. London: Hogarth. (Original work published 1910)

Heimann, P. (1981). On countertransference. In R. Langs (Ed.), *Classics in psychoanalytic technique*. Northvale, NJ: Aronson. (Original work published 1949)

Kernberg, O. F. (1965). Countertransference. *Journal of the American Psychoanalytic Association, 13*, 38–56.

Little, M. (1951). Countertransference and the patient's response to it. *International Journal of Psychoanalysis, 32*, 32–40.

Racker, H. (1972). The meaning and uses of countertransference. *Journal of the American Psychoanalytic Association, 4*, 224–255.

Searles, H. F. (1986). *My work with borderline patients*. Northvale, NJ: Aronson.

Tower, L. E. (1956). Countertransference. In R. Langs (Ed.), *Classics in psychoanalytic technique*. Northvale, NJ: Aronson.

W. L. EDKINS

See TRANSFERENCE.

Courage. Courage appears in Isaiah in the list of the gifts of the Holy Spirit that rest upon the Messiah. Traditional Christian spirituality recognizes it as a cardinal or key virtue. Some forms of courage are among the attitudes that Galatians says are a sign of being in the Spirit. Other spiritual traditions also recognize the importance of this quality.

The Holy Spirit's gift of courage, called strength or fortitude, is the ability to do what must be done. Misunderstood, it can lead to arguments about grace and works. However, without effective choices, without maintaining good effort, moral rectitude and spiritual growth will not happen. Tanquerey said that courage gives energy to the will so it can do great things with joy and fearlessness in spite of any obstacles.

Religious responsibilities call for various degrees of courage. It takes courage to avoid the easy but immoral choice. It takes courage to speak for what one ought speak. It takes courage to discipline and govern oneself. Some life tasks may require heroic courage.

Effective courage is less an attitude of forced heroism than a use of psychologically skillful means to orient oneself toward doing what must be done. This article discusses psychologically sound methods that will develop courage. These means produce behavioral dispositions that make courageous behavior flow easily when required.

Work on disordered personal attitudes and conduct is needed for courage. One can expel negative attitudes such as resentment and self-pity by cultivating their opposites. Practicing gratitude or surrender can end feelings of deprivation or resentment. Incompatible opposing actions help eliminate wrong behavior (e.g., combating stinginess with generosity). Envy can be overcome by celebrating others' good fortune and speaking of their good qualities. This method is much more effective than forcing courageous rejection of attitudes to be eliminated.

Inner revulsion toward unwanted behavior helps stop it. Moral sensitivity helps one recognize and want to shrink away from unworthy conduct. Moral conscientiousness makes one dread doing anything that will cause harm or suffering. However, one must be careful to develop revulsion toward the conduct and not oneself.

Another method is deliberately diverting attention from negativity. The diversion must be carefully chosen so one does not find oneself in an even worse situation. Sometimes watching disordered attitudes and behavior move through oneself, not analyzing them, is helpful. States like anger, sadness, or jealousy frequently lose their strength if they are carefully observed rather than fed with thought.

These methods require overcoming the notion that one must openly express emotional states. Impulsively acting may feel courageous, but the opposite is true. Patience builds courage. Being reactive encourages aroused states to stay. One must recognize them, not denying feelings, but need not act on them. Often saying no to oneself is the better choice. When some action is necessary, waiting until feelings are under control is effective.

Appealing objects easily draw out desire or greed—the point of advertising—and unappealing objects some form of aversion: anger, fear, or sadness. Sense restraint is thus a major help in preventing disordered states. Uncontrolled senses take in many experiences that can trigger latent negative tendencies and draw out unhelpful behavior. Sense restraint does not require retiring from life; however, wisely choosing sensory input protects one's vulnerability. Carelessness is easy, but the courage to refuse minor unwholesome experiences prepares one for harder refusals.

Psychologists have shown that attitudes follow behavior. People tend to bring attitudes into line with behavior, whether the behavior is chosen or imposed. This understanding supported forced racial integration; living and working with others changes attitudes toward them. One can thus prompt good action by doing things that reflect and support it. One can also deliberately cultivate attitudes of reverence for what deserves respect and caring about others' problems. The courage to act in difficult situations involving these attitudes will be available.

One can also choose experiences that draw out wholesome attitudes. Seeing good in others helps one feel kindly toward them. Whether one focuses on what is wrong or right about others is largely habit, and habits can be changed. Being willing to see suffering draws out compassion. One need not feel heroic; one becomes turned toward compassion. To cultivate generosity, one can vow to act on every serious thought of giving. Being aware of and encouraging wholesome states becomes heroic cooperation with grace.

Forcing or chiding oneself or feeling brave are not especially helpful in developing courage. Needed courage comes from regularly training oneself to make correct behavior habitual, regardless of the situations in which one finds oneself.

M. J. MEADOW

Covert Modeling. A cognitive process in which individuals change response patterns through imagining themselves engaging in the desired responses rather than by observing another person model the responses. Since these new responses are weak, even at the imaginal level, it is essential that they be reinforced in order to strengthen and maintain them. This reinforcement normally is self-administered. Covert modeling thus involves a combination of modeling and self-control procedures, all conducted internally in the form of thought and fantasy.

Although covert modeling is a fairly new concept, it has been used in assertiveness training, development of athletic skills, and enhancement of reading comprehension. Research on its effectiveness has been encouraging, although the number of well-controlled studies is quite small.

A basic limitation with covert modeling is that it requires prior exposure to the desired behaviors in some manner, such as by instructions or by observing a live model. Thus covert modeling is effective in releasing responses already available to the individual, such as assertive responses that are inhibited by unrealistic expectations of social responses to them, but it is not effective for teaching new responses. A second limitation is that the performance must ultimately come under reinforcement control of events mediated by the environment, much as with other self-control procedures. Finally, it seems a bit strained to term this process modeling, since it does not involve observing another's behavior.

R. K. BUFFORD

See MODELING; SELF-CONTROL; COGNITIVE-BEHAVIOR THERAPY.

Covert Sensitization. A form of aversion therapy in which a covert response such as a thought or an image is followed by an imagined aversive event. An individual may imagine himself relaxing in front of the television and eating a large bowl of hot buttered popcorn, enjoying the smell and taste; he then imagines the rolls of fat accumulating around his waist, having to buy new clothes, and being rejected by his girlfriend because of his weight. In covert sensitization the cognitive elements of the stimulus-response sequence rather than overt responses and external stimuli are dealt with. The goal is to block the thoughts and fantasies that precede undesired overt behaviors and increase their probability.

Although it is possible for an individual to self-administer covert sensitization, it is more common for covert sensitization to be conducted in a structured therapy interaction. Relaxation procedures often are used to heighten the relief following termination of the imagined aversive stimulus.

Covert sensitization has been employed with homosexuality, pedophilia, obesity, and smoking. Initial studies of its effectiveness have been encouraging.

Covert sensitization offers some advantages over aversion therapy. Since the events are imagined, pictures, slides, projectors, shock apparatus, and other equipment are not required.

However, covert sensitization has two disadvantages. First, because the scenes, behavior, and aversive stimulation are imagined, they are not amenable to precise control. Second, there is the problem of finding a suitable aversive stimulus that the individual is able to imagine. Since most behaviors that are candidates for this approach are highly motivated, intrinsically reinforcing, and under strong stimulus control, it is essential to locate a powerful aversive stimulus.

Finally, covert sensitization shares a limitation common to all the aversive procedures: the failure to establish alternative and more desirable forms of behavior. For this reason some theorists object categorically to all forms of aversive procedures. The majority of professionals, however, agree that the preferred intervention strategy is to use aversion procedures in conjunction with procedures designed to establish positive alternative behaviors. In many applications of covert sensitization the individual terminates the aversive scene and then imagines initiating an alternative, more desirable response.

R. K. BUFFORD

See AVERSION THERAPY; BEHAVIOR THERAPY.

Creative Aggression Therapy. A skill-building, educative type of short-term endeavor originated by Bach (Bach & Goldberg, 1974). The approach tends to be highly structured and requires the therapist to be active and flexible, shifting from role to role as teacher, cajoler, coach, referee, and antagonist. It is built on the assumptions that nice people get themselves into emotional trouble by blocking the expression of negative emotions such as anger and rage; people change by doing something different rather than by gaining insight into something different; the verbal and physical expression of negative affect acts as a curative change agent within the client.

According to Bach, current Western culture emphasizes the prohibition of anger. As a result of not being allowed to directly vent their aggression many individuals pay a heavy price: depression (or anger indirectly expressed at one's psyche), psychosomatization (anger indirectly expressed at one's own body), passive-aggressive lifestyles (anger indirectly expressed toward others), impulsive lifestyles (anger indirectly breaking out through action rather than through talking), and psychotic behavior (anger vented toward others that is simultaneously disqualified through "crazy talk," so that one cannot be held responsible for the anger). This premise is extended further to a political level on which the escalating level of violence within cities and between nations is viewed as a partial product of our cultural proscription of clean, direct expression of anger between individuals.

Much of creative aggression therapy is based on an avoidance learning paradigm. It is hypothesized that many individuals are afraid of the disastrous consequences that will certainly follow the direct expression of anger. One learns as a small child that it is not smart to be directly angry at one's parents; they are far more powerful and wield a vast array of positive and negative reinforcers not available to the child. As an adult, this avoidance of the expression of anger becomes an anachronistic albatross around one's neck. However, as long as one avoids aggression, one will never learn that the contingencies have changed and that it is now more safe to vent anger.

From this perspective it does little good to inform an individual that he or she is angry. It is assumed that at some level the client already knows about this anger. The knowledge of that internal state of being without appropriate doing produces an iatrogenic effect: the individual becomes more and more furious without finding any way of releasing that aggressive feeling directly. Insight does not prove to be curative from this point of view. Instead the client needs to be taught how to directly vent aggressive feelings in an appropriate fashion.

The creative aggression therapist will typically operate in the following fashion. First, one teaches clients (individuals, couples, or families) something of the theoretical perspective; second, one instructs these clients regarding the mechanics of how to appropriately discharge aggression using a ritualistic type of procedure, assertiveness skills, and/or a fair fight format; third, one sends the clients home to practice the new skill; and fourth, one follows up on the new learning by rewarding progress verbally or with other prearranged reinforcers in future sessions.

As an example of aggressive ritual, a couple might be encouraged to stand nose to nose and scream vindictives simultaneously. In this fashion neither can hear the other and both can experience a catharsis. In a similar way an individual might be encouraged to vent anger by pounding on a pillow with fists or a bataca bat. While physically pounding, the client might also be encouraged to scream out his or her anger toward an imagined significant other in that person's current or past experience.

Creative aggression therapy is best known by many for its fair fight ritual. A fair fight is useful both for families who are sufficiently inhibited so that they never risk a cross word and for families whose constantly destructive uproar pattern needs to be contained by appropriate structuring. When using the fair fight the therapist determines who is the heavyweight and who is the lightweight in the relationship (i.e., who is most and least powerful). The lightweight is given the job of setting a time and place for the fight when the couple is least stressed and most relaxed. Once the appointment is made, the couple is instructed to initially keep within a 15- to 20-minute limit. Each individual defines for the therapist and partner what are sensitive areas, or zaps, not to be mentioned (e.g., "You act just like your mother when you say that!"). A zap tolerance for each person is established beyond which the fight is terminated even if the time limit is not completed. Once the fight has finished, the couple is given fight style score sheets to rate each other. These score sheets assign values to each of 10 different dimensions thought to be critical in fighting.

This type of therapy has distinct potential applicability within that Christian sector where aggressive displays of behavior are thought to be unspiritual. The Christian therapist is faced with the task of teaching clients to "be angry and sin not" (Eph. 4:26). The danger in this therapy lies in encouraging undisciplined, inappropriate lashing out toward others in a destructive manner; the benefit lies in more open, honest communication between intimates. Thus, as in most therapy, discernment and good judgment on the part of the therapist are essential.

Reference

Bach, G., & Goldberg, H. (1974). *Creative aggression*. Garden City, NY: Doubleday.

V. L. Shepperson

See Aggression; Anger; Assertiveness Training.

Creativity. Creativity in human endeavors is our counterpart to God's marvelous creative activity in fashioning the material and spiritual universes, sustaining them by his providence, and directing them to their appointed ends. To define creativity is exceedingly difficult. It is easier to formulate the question than to discern how to craft a meaningful answer (Sebba & Boers, 1987). To speak of creativity means to suggest a process of human cogitation and craft that goes beyond the usual means for dealing with our internal and external environment. Creativity enlarges human experience in surprising ways, thus liberating us from the constraints of conditioned responses and usual choices. It fulfills the human longing or search for a new object, state of experience, or state of existence. This process seems to be more than mere uniqueness, originality, or surprise in problem solving. Creativity must be distinguished from these in that, though they may be prerequisites for creativity, they do not constitute its essence (Arieti, 1976).

Creativity has been variously described as the product of genius or of mere randomness and generalization from an accumulation of data. The concept of genius accounts for the achievements of creativity as coming from superior intelligence that perceives generalizations others do not see or from divine inspiration, the muses, or an unexplainable capacity to see significance in the apparently irrelevant. The notion of randomness and generalization as its source tends to explain creativity in behaviorist terms. In fact, creativity seems to be less mysterious than the genius view suggests and less trivial than the behaviorists would have us believe (Weisberg, 1986).

Gardner developed a model of creativity that assumes that humans possess seven types of intelligence ranging from musical to self-perceptive intelligence. These operate within domains of individual expertise and fields of communal expectation or possibility. Within these fields the current state of the art in any domain and the community expectation and support are crucial to the enhancement of the creative breakthrough (Gardner, 1993). Increasingly the research on creativity is moving from early psychoanalytic preoccupation with issues of consciousness and the unconscious to wholistic models combining the dynamics of cognitive and affective function in creativity (Damasio, 1994).

Thus creativity has been defined in many ways, depending upon the theoretical and operational perspective of the researcher. Stein (1975) cryptically distilled the discussion by defining creativity as a process that results in a novel product or an idea that is accepted as useful by some significant group of people. A key point in this definition is that a creative product or an idea must be more than merely novel or original. Creativity occurs within real-world settings and is thus subject to various constraints. For example, creative scientific acts must either contribute to new theories or advance established theories in such a way that fellow scientists who are qualified to judge will acknowledge that the contribution is functional but remarkably innovative. These decisions depend on more or less established criteria, explicitly or tacitly applied. Controversy and change in these standards can occur, occasionally resulting in belated assessments that creativity has occurred. However, solitary appraisals are of little note unless they are validated by a significant group of people. Creativity does not occur in a social vacuum.

This definition also suggests complexity. Creativity involves both the private perception and thinking of individuals during its genesis (i.e., intrapersonal dynamics) and the broader social setting in which products and ideas are introduced and tested (i.e., interpersonal dynamics). Many discussions of creativity focus on only one of these aspects. It is necessary to use the broad framework implied by this definition to evaluate creativity.

Not surprisingly, theories of creativity have been likened to the fabled blind men who described the same elephant in radically different ways (Yamamoto, 1965). The differences stem in large measure from theorists' identification with one of the major systems of psychology. As the following survey reveals, each makes provocative and valid contributions to our understanding of the matter.

Associationist Approach. This approach arose from the theory that dominated psychology until the early 1970s, namely, associationism, which explains the acquiring of behavior in terms of associations or bonds between stimuli and responses. In this view the problem of creativity is to explain how responses that are only weakly associated with a given situation (e.g., creative solutions to a newly encountered problem) are evoked. This approach is somewhat related to behaviorist and conditioned response theory. A well-known example is Maier's problem in which two strings are suspended from above, more than an arm's length apart. Subjects are required to tie them together using no more than a few simple available implements. The solution is to create a pendulum and so to swing one string nearer the other. Exposure to instruments to be used in atypical ways enhances the likelihood of solution.

The associationist approach makes detailed analyses of experimental situations and practical suggestions for facilitating solutions in such situations. An outgrowth of the approach is an idea also associated with the group technique known as brainstorming. This technique encourages the rapid production of a large number of proposed solutions to a problem with a minimum of criticism. An associative explanation is that when a larger number of responses to the same stimulus are made in rapid succession, stereotyped, uncreative, conditioned responses are used up first, allowing weaker, remote associations to appear. These enhance the likelihood of creative solutions.

This perspective has lost influence despite its usefulness in some experimental situations. Perhaps the greatest difficulty is the need to make enormous leaps from the experimental setting to creativity in art, science, engineering, and so forth. Additionally, the assumption that the basic elements of creative acts consist of associations to environmental stimuli appears overly restrictive in the light of other perspectives.

Psychometric Approach. The psychometric approach of Guilford and others has stimulated much research, particularly the measurement of creative performance and the identification of intellectual abilities that influence it (Guilford, 1950, 1959). Psychometric refers to the research tool employed. Paper-and-pencil tests are devised to measure separate facets of creative performance (e.g., subjects are asked to name unusual uses for a brick and other common objects). Scores on these tests (e.g., the number of nonstandard uses for a brick) are correlated to discover to what degree the tests measure the same or different things. A statistical technique known as factor analysis reveals underlying patterns in the ways various tests are correlated, and these suggest the intellectual abilities or other traits that best explain individual differences on test scores.

Probably the most significant avenue of research stemming from this approach relates to the distinction between creativity and intelligence. Guilford proposed that creativity, like intelligence, is not simple but is rather a domain consisting of a host of divergent thinking abilities. However, the issue of whether creative abilities are distinct from intelligence as traditionally measured became doubtful when tests designed to measure these abilities were found to be at least as highly related to intelligence scores as they are to each other. This contrasts to the subtests of an intelligence test battery, which tend to be highly correlated. But other investigators found that when the context of evaluation normally associated with test taking is relaxed and time restrictions removed, performance becomes more consistent across divergent thinking tests. To recall the argument of associative theorists, removal of these artificial restrictions allows more creative responses to appear after the stereotyped ones are used up.

Findings such as these supported the argument that there is a creativity domain, measured by divergent thinking tests, that is distinct from intelligence. Indeed, good divergent thinkers proved different in many ways from those high in intelligence quotient (IQ) alone (e.g., in social adjustment and occupational preference). But are these performances associated with complex, long-term, or outstanding examples of creativity? While controversy on this issue continues, it is clear that other personality variables comparatively ignored in this approach are also relevant.

Psychoanalytic Approaches. Psychoanalysts beginning with Sigmund Freud have preoccupied themselves with the internal dynamics of creative persons and frequently tried to relate creativity and abnormal behavior. For Freud (1916) creative works, like cultural achievements in general, are suspect. They arise from the artist's attempt to derive gratification in fantasy, like a child in play. Unlike his followers, Freud presumed only to illumine motives behind the creative work, not the shape taken by the work itself.

Psychoanalysts since Freud generally have taken a less cynical view of creativity. Kris (1952) theorized that creative works evidence not neurotic trends within the creator but rather a mature form of adaptation that he called "regression in the service of the ego." This is an ability or a tendency to relax the boundaries of the ego, or conscious self, to permit material not accessible to conscious recall to influence the creative work. Similarly, Schachtel (1959) proposed that creative work demands a mature form of perception characterized by radical openness to experience. The value of these capacities for creativity stems from the greater availability of material

often barred from conscious awareness. These ideas call attention to interference with the creative process due to a certain inflexibility, an overinsistence on keeping a conscious grip on oneself. They also suggest that creative artists succeed in part through eliciting uncharacteristic modes of awareness in their audiences.

Cognitive-Development Approach. Other psychologists place creativity in the perspective of cognitive development. Werner (1957) described an invariant sequence in development. Infants can make little differentiation between themselves and the external world; their various psychological processes, sensory, affective, motoric, and the like, lack organization or differentiation from one another. For example, objects are first perceived as inseparable from the feelings they evoke in infants. By adulthood the individual clearly separates between the technical properties of objects and internal psychological processes. A great deal of empirical work supports the notion that creativity is marked by flexible functioning or integration of the developmentally mature and developmentally primitive modes of perception. The similarity between this idea and the psychoanalytic concept of regression in the service of the ego is obvious. However, here the emphasis is on a developmentally ordered sequence of stages rather than on unconscious sources of creative ideas. The cognitive-developmental approach may be faulted, however, for not having enough to say about other types of development such as social, affective, and personality development.

An Integrative Model. This overview reveals much theoretical ferment and pluralism. An integrative theory or model may therefore be premature. However, some broad dimensions that any comprehensive theory must account for can be sketched. There is some consensus regarding a number of these dimensions, and without keeping them in view, theorizing is likely to flounder over merely semantic difficulties.

First, creativity can be studied in relation to at least four components: process, product, person, and situation. As the survey revealed, specific theories are involved with some components more than others. For example, the associative approach is more concerned with situational analysis than are the other approaches. Gardner is concerned with individual function, intelligence, domains, fields, and support communities. When attention is focused on only one area, there is greater consensus at least in regard to description. For example, the creative process is described in much the same terms regardless of the approach. Wallas (1926) describes four stages of the creative process: prior preparation, incubation or relaxing of conscious effort, illumination or discovery, and verification or testing of the result. While slight variations have been proposed, these stages are still frequently cited. There is also consensus regarding what creative persons are like. Their attributes include flexibility and productivity of ideas; uniqueness and originality of ideas and perceptions; intuitiveness, empathy, and perceptual openness; preference for complexity; independence of judgment; and aesthetic sensitivity.

A second dimension is the field of endeavor. Although there is surprising consistency in the description of both creative processes and persons regardless of field, it appears likely that different fields place different demands on creative work (Gardner, 1993). Roe (1952) has elucidated such differences among the branches of science while Gardner addresses the entire spectrum of the sciences and the arts or humanities.

Third, the level of creativity is crucial. Many key studies used subjects selected for their high level of creativity. Still unclear is the relationship that exists between creativity on this level and that on lower or even higher levels. One suggestion is that while creativity and intelligence may be meaningfully separated at lower levels, eminent accomplishment depends on a happy coincidence of both.

Finally, the relationship between divine and human creativity should be considered. The biblical narrative indicates that we are made in God's image: movers, shakers, deciders, creators. That characteristic common to God and humans, the divine or image-bearing quality indicated in Genesis, is the ability and desire to create. The parallels between human and divine creativity are striking. Godly persons create with a humble eye of gratitude to God's infinite potential for aesthetic, gracious, and providential creativity (Ellens, 1982).

References

Arieti, S. (1976). *Creativity: The magic synthesis.* New York: Basic Books.

Damasio, A. R. (1994). *Descartes' error, emotion, reason, and the human brain.* New York: Putnam.

Ellens, J. H. (1982). *God's grace and human health.* Nashville, TN: Abingdon.

Freud, S. (1916).

Gardner, H. (1993). *Creating minds, an anatomy of creativity.* New York: HarperCollins, Basic Books.

Guilford, J. P. (1950). Creativity. *American Psychologist, 5,* 444–454.

Guilford, J. P. (1959). Traits of creativity. In H. H. Anderson (Ed.), *Creativity and its cultivation.* New York: Harper.

Kris, E. (1952). *Psychoanalytic explorations in art.* New York: International Universities Press.

Roe, A. (1952). *The making of a scientist.* New York: Dodd, Mead.

Schachtel, E. G. (1959). *Metamorphosis.* New York: Basic Books.

Sebba, H., & Boers, H. (1987). *Creativity, lectures of Gregor Sebba.* Atlanta: Scholars Press.

Stein, M. I. (1975). *Stimulating creativity.* New York: Academic Press.

Wallas, G. (1926). *The art of thought.* New York: Harcourt, Brace.

Weisberg, R. W. (1986). *Creativity, genius and other myths.* New York: Freeman.

Werner, H. (1957). *Comparative psychology of mental development.* New York: International Universities Press.

Yamamoto, K. (1965). Research Frontier: "Creativity"—A blind man's report on the elephant. *Journal of Counseling Psychology, 12,* 428–434.

J. H. ELLENS AND D. R. RIDLEY

See INTELLIGENCE; THINKING.

Creativity Tests. Creativity is a theoretical concept in psychology that is defined in a variety of ways and thus is measured with a variety of methods. Since these methods are often fraught with problems of reliability and validity, tests of creativity need to be applied and interpreted with much caution.

Traditional measurement approaches to creativity have included achievement performed, ratings of specific productions, prediction of future creative behavior from biographical information, and tests of divergent thinking. An even wider variety of tests is being developed or adapted to creativity research to correspond with the lessened emphasis on logical, rational thinking and the greater interest in insight and intuitive processes. For example, the focus of current research includes such topics as transcendental meditation, image making, and incubation. Even so, divergent thinking tests continue to be the most widely applied and researched.

Many divergent thinking measures originate in Guilford's model, in which divergent production is performed on a variety of contents with a variety of outcomes (Guilford & Merrifield, 1960). Divergent thinking does not lead to a single correct answer but goes off in a multitude of directions, leading to numerous solutions. For example, tests such as Guilford's Creativity Tests for Children and Torrance's Tests of Creative Thinking include items requiring the examinee to provide as many meanings as possible for ambiguous words (e.g., hand), to propose possible outcomes for novel situations (e.g., if people flew rather than walked), and to produce pictures combining geometric figures (e.g., a boat, using squares and triangles only). Responses are evaluated according to fluency, flexibility, originality, and elaboration.

Although they are used extensively, measures of divergent thinking have been criticized for their questionable predictive validity, their reliance on time, and their failure to acknowledge the importance of convergence in creative productions. That is, to be recognized as creative, processes and/or products must conform to some social expectations.

Reference

Guilford, J. P., & Merrifield, P. R. (1960). *Structure of the intellect model.* Los Angeles: University of Southern California.

M. D. ROE

See CREATIVITY; THINKING; PSYCHOLOGICAL MEASUREMENT; PERSONALITY ASSESSMENT.

Cretinism. A congenital condition associated with complete absence or defective functioning of secretion in the thyroid gland. Mental and physical development is retarded, and the disease becomes evident in approximately the sixth month of life. A disturbance in the central nervous system, skeleton, and skin leads to general underdevelopment, distorted posture and gait, and a bloated appearance. Other symptoms include lethargy, defective speech and hearing, apathy, protrusion of the tongue, and thickening of the features. The cause of cretinism is unknown, but it is thought to be related to birth injuries, an iodine deficiency, or infectious diseases in childhood. The use of iodized salt in the first six months of life has reduced the incidence and severity of the disease.

D. L. SCHUURMAN

See MENTAL RETARDATION.

Crime and Mental Disorder. Through the Middle Ages criminal behavior was variously considered as either a serious character flaw or moral departure from standard societal or religious norms, a sin, or the result of demonic possession of the person. Exorcisms through torture and witch-hunts were common. With the advent of the Enlightenment scientists turned their attention to explaining human behaviors in other terms. An Italian physician by the name of Cesare Lombroso (1891) proposed a theory of criminality based on the physical characteristics of persons. Performing autopsies on men who were executed for heinous crimes, Lombroso found certain abnormalities of physiognomy that he thought were causative of the behavior of the men he examined. Such things as asymmetry of the ears, pointed heads, retreating foreheads, bushy eyebrows that met over the bridge of the nose were traits that he considered as "ape like," indicating that these men were somehow "subhuman" and therefore physically preconditioned to behave violently.

Lombroso's early theories have been discredited, but the search for the etiology of criminality in genetics has not abated to this day. Several years ago the search for the connection between violence and the presence of an extra Y chromosome in the DNA of men incarcerated for violent crimes was popular. That too has been discredited (Denno, 1996), but the search continues. In February of 1995, the Ciba Foundation held in London a "Symposium on Genetics of criminal and antisocial behavior," attended by geneticists from all over the world. The proceedings were published by John Wiley & Sons in 1996 under the title of *Genetics of Criminal and Antisocial Behaviour.*

The study of criminality as the result of mental illness arises with the M'Naghten case. On January 20, 1843, Daniel M'Naghten shot the secretary of the Prime Minister of England. His testimony was that he was acting under "orders from God." The plea made on his behalf was of "not guilty by reason of insanity" (for a transcript of the case see Blau, 1984, pp. 372ff.). The NGRI plea, as it has become known in forensics, has been codified in all states and continues to be used in courts. The assumption in both English common law and U.S. case law is that when a person is mentally ill, he or she is not responsible before the law for actions that do not conform to the mandates of law. Such persons are distinguished from criminals otherwise motivated. Such persons are not condemned to prisons for punishment, but committed to psychiatric facilities for treatment.

The concept that the connection between criminal behavior and mental illness is a legitimate point of argument in courts is exemplified by the publication by the American Bar Association of a 532-page manual entitled *ABA Criminal Justice Mental Health Standards.* This document, approved by the ABA House of Delegates, published in 1986 and revised in 1989, lays out definitions, procedures and principles for bringing up defenses related to mental illness in all the courts of the land.

Different schools and theories of psychology offer different explanations for antisocial behaviors, some based on intellectual deficiency and others on developmental lags and neuropsychologists speak of injuries or failure of maturation of the prefrontal cortex of the brain of these individuals.

The interaction of genetic inheritance and environmental factors often become the subject of adjudication in criminal trials. Many studies have been published on how criminal behaviors run in families (Bohman, 1996; Cairns, 1996). A case in point was the trial of Stephen Mobley in Hall County, Georgia. On February 17, 1991, Mobley shot the manager of a Domino's Pizza parlor in the process of robbing it. At his trial defense attorneys attempted to present the family tree of the defendant showing a history of violence, aggression, and behavioral disorders in Mobley's family. They also claimed the defendant suffered a deficiency of enzymic activity of monoamine oxidase A. The court refused to admit the evidence on the basis that the genetic or familial connection with criminality had not achieved the level of scientific acceptance to make it admissible. Mobley was convicted and sentenced to death (Denno, 1996).

Courts are willing to admit evidence of serious mental illness for defenses in felony cases, but tend to resist admitting defenses based on other conditions clinicians associate with mental illness such as alcoholism, drug addiction and post-traumatic stress disorders. The popular press often carries stories of outrageous defenses proposed to excuse criminal behavior, ranging from the effects of sugar products to allegations of prior abuse perpetrated on the criminals as reasons why persons behave violently. Harvard Law professor Alan M. Dershowitz has recently published *The abuse excuse and other cop-outs, sob stories, and evasions of responsibility* (1994) which catalogs multiple attempts to exculpate criminal behavior by allegations that ultimately relate to conditions that clinicians often treat under the heading of mental disorders. While there is research to show a connection between crime and mental disorders, the excessive use of the presence of psychological dysfunction in persons accused of criminal behavior as a defense from responsibility points to a generalized deterioration in society of the value of personal responsibility.

References

Author. (1989) *ABA Criminal justice mental health standards.* Washington, DC: American Bar Association.

Author. (1996). *Genetics of criminal and antisocial behaviour.* Ciba Foundation Symposium 194. Chichester, England: John Wiley & Sons.

Blau, T. (1984). *The psychologist as expert witness.* New York: John Wiley & Sons.

Bohman, M. (1996). Predisposition to criminality: Swedish adoption studies in retrospect. In *Genetics of criminal and antisocial behaviour.* Chichester, England: John Wiley & Sons.

Cairns, R. B. (1996). Aggression from a developmental perspective: Genes, environments and interactions. In *Genetics of criminal and antisocial behaviour.* Chichester, England: John Wiley & Sons.

Denno, D. W. (1996). Legal implications of genetics and crime research. In *Genetics of criminal and antisocial behaviour.* Chichester, England: John Wiley & Sons.

Dershowitz, A. M. (1994). *The abuse excuse and other copouts, sob stories, and evasions of responsibility.* Boston, MA: Little, Brown & Co.

Lombroso, C. (1891). *Men of genius.* New York: Walter Scott.

L. M. MARMOL

See FORENSIC PSYCHIATRY; FORENSIC PSYCHOLOGY.

Criminal Insanity. *See* FORENSIC PSYCHIATRY.

Criminal Responsibility. *See* FORENSIC PSYCHIATRY.

Crisis Family Therapy. *See* ABUSE AND NEGLECT.

Crisis Hotline. *See* TELEPHONE THERAPY.

Crisis Intervention. A short-term therapeutic approach to the common human experience of emotional crisis, crisis intervention has become increasingly popular among mental health professionals. It has its roots in the work of Lindemann (1944), who developed a program to aid in the healthy resolution of the grief of the survivors and relatives of those who perished in the Coconut Grove nightclub fire in 1943. During the 1940s and 1950s, when little professional attention was given to crisis intervention, Caplan (1964) and his colleagues followed up Lindemann's work, advancing the understanding of crisis and its healthy resolution. Since the middle 1960s—spurred by the community mental health movement, increased consumer demand, and limited professional resources—the helping professions have turned more and more to crisis intervention as an effective mode of providing care for those in emotional crisis.

In theory and practice crisis intervention is still developing. It is strongly eclectic, corralling insights and techniques from a variety of mental health disciplines. At the heart of its current theory and application is Caplan's (1964) concept of homeostasis. Borrowed from physiology, the term, as understood in crisis theory, refers to the healthy balance between the emotional and cognitive experience and functioning of individuals, allowing them to relate effectively to their environment.

Each person has a homeostatic stability that is normal. However, a person constantly faces situations that disrupt that homeostasis. These "emotionally hazardous situations" (Caplan, 1964)—changes in environment, interpersonal relationships, or oneself that entail loss and are perceived as negative—give rise to painful emotions, sometimes accompanied by decreased cognitive ability. In the face of this stress the person calls forth habitual coping mechanisms, both conscious and unconscious, and problem-solving activities in an effort to restore homeostasis. If a person fails to restore homeostasis, an emotional crisis may ensue.

Because individuals cannot tolerate stress indefinitely, emotional crises have a limited life span, usually resolving themselves within four to six weeks (Caplan, 1964). If the person receives help and learns new, effective coping skills, the crisis will resolve healthily, strengthening him or her for future events. In the absence of help or of acquiring effective coping skills, the crisis resolution will be maladaptive, leaving the individual more vulnerable to similar crises in the future.

Crises are a normal part of life and are not in themselves an indication of psychopathology. Everyone, even the well-adjusted, experiences emotional crises in stressful situations for which coping behaviors are weak or absent. Crises may be triggered by relatively predictable developmental events—life transitions such as birth, adolescence, and old age—and by more unpredictable situational upsets such as illness, unemployment, divorce, or moving to a new home. Crises always involve either actual or symbolic conflicts with a significant other person. Developmental and situational changes lead to crisis when they reawaken unresolved conflicts and traumas from the past.

Because of the limited duration of crises, crisis intervention, to be effective, must take place as soon as possible after the precipitating event. The goal of crisis intervention is to restore the person as quickly as possible to at least a pre-crisis level of functioning, whether or not that level was ideal. Solving all the client's problems, restructuring personality, bringing about major changes, and resolving deep-seated, long-standing conflicts—goals common to long-term therapy—are outside the scope of crisis intervention. Any gains in those areas are considered a therapeutic bonus, not a goal to be pursued.

In crisis a person is more open than usual to receiving help and support from others and learning new ways of functioning. The therapist's role is to guide the client, over the four- to six-week duration of the crisis, toward an adaptive resolution. Unlike long-term, insight-oriented therapy, in which the therapist may be passive and maintain a professional distance, crisis intervention calls for an active, personal encounter. The therapist must be direct and flexible enough to use a variety of techniques.

The therapist provides hope and support to the client, presenting himself or herself as interested, caring, and willing to understand and help. Through empathy the therapist both communicates support and helps the client to ventilate and understand those negative emotions that prevent him or her from coping with the situation, thereby restoring some cognitive mastery.

Since the goal of therapy is to restore the client's own functioning, the therapist, while supportive, does not foster dependency but seeks to mobilize the client's internal strengths and external resources (e.g., family or friends) in defining the problem, identifying the event that precipitated the crisis, addressing and at least partially resolving the underlying conflict that has made the client vulnerable to that event, and planning ways of dealing with the situation. In the process the therapist seeks to help the client avoid learning or using maladaptive coping responses; learn new, adaptive coping skills; reconcile himself or herself both emotionally and intellectually to the changes brought about by the crisis; and anticipate and plan for future similar situations.

The focus of therapy is the present situation, not the historical origin of the client's conflicts. Attention is given to past events only as they relate to the current crisis, helping the client to understand and act in the present situation. In the course of therapy the therapist gradually shifts responsibility for dealing with the problem to the client, building his or her hope, independence, and self-esteem. When crisis intervention is successful, the client's anxiety is replaced with genuine hope for the future as supportive interpersonal relationships are strengthened and he or she gradually regains the capacity for independently planning ways to meet needs.

Crisis intervention offers one way of answering Scripture's call to help those in need. Its balance between supportive help and encouragement of the client's independent functioning is reminiscent of Paul's teaching that we are to bear one another's burdens, yet each is responsible to carry his or her own load when he or she is able (Gal. 6:2, 4–5). Its emphasis on hope is also consistent with Scripture's teaching on coping with difficulty (Rom. 5:3–5; James 1:2).

References

Caplan, G. (1964). *Principles of preventive psychiatry.* New York: Basic.

Lindemann, E. (1944). Symptomatology and management of acute grief. *American Journal of Psychiatry, 101,* 141–148.

Additional Readings

Aguilera, D., & Messick, J. (1982). *Crisis intervention, theory and methodology* (4th ed.). St. Louis: Mosby.

Baldwin, B. A. (1979). Crisis intervention: An overview of theory and practice. *The Counseling Psychologist, 8* (2), 43–52.

Ewing, C. P. (1978). *Crisis intervention as psychotherapy.* New York: Oxford University Press.

F. J. WHITE

Cross Dressing. *See* TRANSVESTIC FETISHISM.

Critical Period. *See* SENSITIVE PERIOD.

Cross-Cultural Psychology. A combined field of knowledge (psychosociocultural) that incorporates the study, observation, and analysis of human behaviors, community dynamics, and relational phenomena across cultures. This field of interest takes into consideration cultural mediators and compares personal conditions, communal structures, and sets of ideals among different cultures that guide human behavior.

The emphasis on cross-cultural psychology has emerged during the second half of the twentieth century. It resulted from the activities of many thinkers and clinicians in culturally diverse communities and several developing countries. It integrates a variety of areas from different spheres and applied disciplines and promotes the investigation and comparison of several cultures and subcultures. Anthropology has traditionally played that role by focusing mainly on the study of more isolated and remote cultures. However, the emphasis has shifted lately to pluralistic societies and modern communities, and especially mixed environments and complex living.

During the last decade, this new emerging trend, both in academia and the work place, has been trying to emphasize the cultural reality of contemporary society. Businesses, human resources, medical sciences, public schools, social services, and other helping agencies are heightening the awareness of their staff and employees to the cultural aspects of their communities. The interest in global and international affairs is remarkably increasing. The mass media and many popular periodicals are addressing the importance of the new cultural reality. This reflects the shape and nature of several populations and subcultures, those currently evolving or already established. Many graduate schools have introduced at least one course or seminar on cross-cultural issues in their curriculum designed especially for their field of study. Many academic textbooks in psychology now include a chapter on cross-cultural aspects. Graduate programs in clinical and counseling psychology have already begun to require cross-cultural exposure and training. In fact, few programs have recently created a subspecialty, an emphasis, or a proficiency in ethnic and minority studies.

Cross-cultural adaptation takes place when a person or a family moves to a new environment or unfamiliar setting. It is the process of mental adjustment and internal modification that enables the person or family unit to become better equipped for living and functioning in that new milieu or under different cultural circumstances. In the helping professions, caregivers are normally more comfortable and least anxious when dealing with people or groups from the same backgrounds and with whom they share similar values and world views. Cross-cultural psychotherapy, therefore, could be defined as a counseling relationship where two or more involved individuals differ from each other with respect to race, gender, faith, experience, symbols, practices, or lifestyle. Existentially speaking, every encounter is a cross-cultural encounter. It usually has a profound impact on all the parties involved, so that people leave the encounter, not exactly the same as before, but somewhat transformed in the process.

In regard to empirical research, cross-cultural psychology is concerned with topics like the relationship between language and cognition, perception, mental health and illness, personality types, development, communication, testing and measurement, and organization. Although there is a pressing need to accurately observe, analyze, and research the differences among cultures or subcultures, at many times these activities are affected by the common tendency to overestimate and overhighlight or underestimate and totally ignore these differences. Along this line, Triandis (1993) emphasized that the contrasts provided among mainstream psychology, cross-cultural psychology, and pluralistic human sciences are greatly exaggerated and, in some instances, inaccurate. Therefore, in order to avoid further polarization, generalization, or fragmentation, the psychological culture, or more precisely, *the culture of psychology* itself must be frequently examined, evaluated, and reviewed in order to remain realistic, adequate, healthy, and relevant.

When observing, comparing, or studying certain phenomena across cultures, or even across families from different backgrounds, it is essential not to rate the cultures on a hierarchical scale (e.g., advanced vs. primitive, superior vs. inferior, civilized vs. backward, high vs. low, rich vs. poor). Such ratings reflect value judgments and ignore each culture's traditional style, linguistic expressions, set of values, unique customs, and normative qualities. Furthermore, each culture has its stored wisdom and inherent richness as well as its social problems and pathologies.

It is possible, however, to compare certain attributes among different cultures and societies without collectively labeling, categorizing, or diagnosing them. Some examples would be aspects related to physical health, density of population, concepts of self and family, environmental resources, political systems, level of communication, social stability, work ethics, spiritual commitment, and degree of connectivity and brotherhood versus privacy and individualism (Levinson, 1994).

The questions that need to be addressed are not only limited to how cultural factors can be detected and their impact on people and institutions measured, but also how cross-cultural adjustments are made and cross-cultural communications facilitated. How can psychology effectively cross the culture? How can its theoretical concepts, practical tools, and common expertise be appropriate, operational, and contributory in a different setting? In other words, how can psychology cross the boundaries of countries, minorities, diverse populations, ethnic groups, and various communities and remain helpful, reasonable, and meaningful? What really happens when psychology as a discipline and a helping profession (both as an art and science, theory and practice) crosses cultural lines?

The challenge that is facing psychology as a field of knowledge and human service is that it must grow broader, more flexible, adaptable, and global in its nature, scope, and function. That is, psychology has to become less Western and more international in order to be relevant and survive well into the 21st century (cf. Abi-Hashem, 1997; Kitayama & Markus, 1995; Landrine, 1992).

Because most of the modern psychological studies, publications, observation, and research have been done in the West, there is a need to conduct similar investigations and collect insights about the human nature and sociocultural condition from around the world. Obviously, many theories, approaches, ideas, methods, and therapeutic modalities need to be modified, adjusted, or even changed before they are applied to the new setting. Otherwise, old and past mistakes will be repeated by transporting concepts, tools, and methodologies from one place to another and imposing them on the new hosting culture, people group, or minority (Abi-Hashem, 1991; Augsburger, 1986). Unfortunately, this happened far too often, not only in the fields of psychology and counseling (for example, introducing purely Western theories, techniques, and interventions into a non-Western society), but also in fields of business (marketing goods and products for the mere sake of financial benefits), education (transporting curriculum and training programs without consultation with local leaders or any material modification) (cf. Goldstein, 1993), and missions (spreading Western Christianity, worship styles, and church functions as if they are the biblical model) (cf. Lawton, 1997). Those practices can be dangerous, lead to colonization and modernization by the dominant culture (at times, "Westoxification"), and cause considerable damage to the local psychosocial and spiritual identity (Huntington, 1996). Consequently, what is acceptable and relevant in one culture may be totally unacceptable and irrelevant in another culture.

Although Western psychology has contributed a great deal to the body of knowledge, its applicability is limited in the developing countries because of its individualistic orientation, lack of conceptual totals, and inappropriate emphasis on narrow aspects of human living (Sinha, 1990). Most certainly, multicultural perspectives give psychology the potency to reassess itself (cf. Matsumoto, 1996). It helps reveal how the psychology's tendency toward monocultural universalism has undermined its aims and functions as a science of human behavior and promoter of human welfare (Fowers & Richardson, 1996).

What exactly is a *culture?* How are cultures best defined? Is there any accurate and comprehensive definition of culture? Although, there have been many great attempts to define its concept, there is still no single precise, articulate, or complete definition of culture. Cultures are hard to define. Invariably, they are fascinating phenomena. They are better felt than defined and better experienced than explained.

Culture is a design of life. It can be understood as a way of feeling, acting, and believing. It is the knowledge of the community or the people group stored for future use (Hesselgrave , 1984). Culture shapes the life of the community and in return is shaped by the community itself. It is, at the same time, the cause and the outcome, the source and the product. Cultures have an abstract and a concrete element to them. They are, at once, tangible and symbolic, moral and temporal. They represent connectivity with the past and continuity into the future.

Culture is both a content and a process. It consists of tradition and change. The heart of a culture involves language, religion, values, traditions, and customs (Huntington, 1996). Whatever profoundly affects the mental and emotional status of people, directly or indirectly, be it literature, customs, industry, government, means of communication, transportation, social system, level of comfort, environmental stress, and spirituality are all elements of culture. In that context, the definition of psychology is not only limited to "the scientific study of human behavior and mental processes" (Hilgard et al., 1971), but also includes the study and mediation of communal life, cultural heritage, and spiritual phenomena (as relating to God and the supernatural). Paul Tillich (1959) saw culture as the form of religion and religion as the substance of culture. He disconfirmed the dualism of culture and spiritual life. Tillich wrote, "Every religious act, not only in organized religion, but in the most intimate movement of the soul, is culturally formed" (p. 42).

Is there a Christian view of culture? What is considered to be a sound theological perspective of culture? There is certainly a need to develop a balanced biblical approach to culture and an adequate theological understanding of human nature, communal life, and social interactions. Furthermore, there is a need to reconcile the more traditional views with the modern and technological views of culture.

From a psychological and spiritual perspective, culture is a way of operating in life. It is a design of life under God. It is a way of developing intellectual, communal, and aesthetic values and finding ways of meaningfully and experientially expressing them. So in practice, the Christian ministry is an attempt to help people move deeper in the love of God and further toward the kingdom of God. Although the helpers themselves are agents of reconciliation and healing (cf. Lingenfelter, 1996), they still are under the rule of God. That remarkable fact and outstanding reality shapes the *culture* of all Christian-helping professions and provides an immeasurable source of divine presence, wisdom, comfort, and grace.

New terminology has been emerging to describe these cross-cultural phenomena, like multiculturalism, ethnicity, cultural adaptation, intercultural studies, multinationalism, internationalization, acculturation, deculturation, hosting culture, majority versus minority culture, racial harmony, sociocultural aspects, culture shock, people groups, ethnic minority, subcultures, cultural awareness, cultural diversity, and cultural relativism. In addition, new terms are replacing old stereotypes, like *internationals* instead of *foreigners,* and *developing* countries instead of *third world* countries.

The recent past years and decades have witnessed the birth of several international associations and culturally oriented periodicals, like the *Journal of Cross-Cultural Psychology*, *International Journal of Psychology*, and *Cross-Cultural Studies*. Agencies, Councils, and societies like the International Association for Cross-Cultural Psychology, World Federation for Mental Health, and International Council of Psychologists, hold an annual congress or symposium in a different part of the world.

Therapists, pastors, missionaries, educators, physicians, and members of the helping professions cannot avoid crossing cultural lines. In fact, they are called to be students of culture. In that context they deeply learn about human nature, history, and authentic condition. Coote and Stott (1980) emphasized that God is the supreme communicator and the ultimate cross-cultural expert and we should take other people's cultures seriously as God has taken our culture seriously. The incarnational ministry of Christ is our model and guide in this endeavor. We need to discover how Christ crossed the culture(s), what strategies Christ used, and how can we apply these profound insights and approaches to our counseling service and soul care ministry.

The following are suggestions and guidelines designed to help the professional cross the culture and effectively deal with people from different backgrounds:

- Be open to learn about the norms, values, faith, and traditions of the other person or group of people.
- Acknowledge the obvious differences between you and them. Gently ask if they have any concerns about relating to or working with you.

- If people belong to an ethnic or racial minority, acknowledge the reality of hardship, stereotype, and even discrimination they may face.

- Make an effort to be culturally sensitive in your comments and in your interpretations of behavior.

- Do not be afraid of silence. Be careful not to interpret politeness, slow disclosure, repetition, indirectiveness, low expressiveness, and not enough eye contact as defensiveness, high resistance, or emotional disturbances.

- Do not be offended by their lack of modern refinement or non-Western mannerism.

- Avoid generalization. Do not label, e.g., "You Black . . . Arab . . . Latino . . . people." Watch the non-verbal dimensions. Listen to their signals, cues, and style of communication. Do not impose on them your ideas, solutions, values, or cultural preferences.

- Inquire gently. Allow enough time. And be patient. Do not demand information or put pressure on them to quickly and completely describe their heritage, struggles, habits, or needs.

- Be faithful to what you learn from them. They internally expect you to remember and honor that information.

- Try to find out the individual's degree of acculturation. Detect any existing tension between the individual and the family, the community, or the hosting culture. Discover any confusion of roles, conflict of norms, and division of loyalties (splitting) between home culture and larger society. Help them navigate well within their cultural setting.

- Realize that people from certain minorities and subcultures (non-Westerners in general) have substantial tolerance for pain and suffering. They do not expect you to fix their problems or provide a quick relief and immediate resolution to their struggles.

- Develop the skills and sensitivity to discern what is culturally normal and what is psychologically abnormal, in other words, detect the difference between what is cultural and what is pathological.

- Build a desire to discover God's image in the person you are dealing with and to value that inherent potential and profound quality.

- Allow yourself to learn, grow, and be changed as a result of such encounters. Enjoy the depth and richness of these experiences.

- Rely on God's wisdom and presence with you as you endeavor to serve across the cultures and effectively minister to a great variety and quality of people.

References

Abi-Hashem, N. (1991). Cross-cultural counseling: An aspect of missions. *Search, 20,* 36–45.

Abi-Hashem, N. (1997). Reflections on international perspectives in psychology. *American Psychologist, 52,* 569–570.

Augsburger, D. W. (1986). *Pastoral counseling across cultures.* Philadelphia, PA: Westminster.

Coote, R. T., & Stott, J. R. W. (Eds.). (1980). *Down to earth: Studies in Christianity and culture.* Grand Rapids, MI: Eerdmans.

Fowers, B. J., & Richardson, F. C. (1996). Why is multiculturalism good? *American Psychologist, 51,* 609–621.

Goldstein, S. B. (1993). Cross-cultural psychology as a curriculum transformation resource. *Teaching of Psychology, 22,* 228–232.

Hesselgrave, D. J. (1984). *Counseling cross-culturally: An introduction to theory and practice for Christians.* Grand Rapids, MI: Baker.

Hilgard, E. R., Atkinson, R. C., & Atkinson, R. L. (1971). *Introduction to psychology* (5th ed.). New York: Hartcourt Brace Jovanovich.

Huntington, S. P. (1996). The West: Unique, not universal. *Foreign Affairs, 75,* 29–46.

Kitayama, S., & Markus, H. R. (1995). Culture and self: Implications for internationalizing psychology. In N. R. Goldberger & J. B. Veroff (Eds.), *The culture and psychology reader.* New York: New York University.

Landrine, H. (1992). Clinical implications of cultural differences. *Clinical Psychology Review, 12,* 401–415.

Lawton, K. A. (1997, May). Faith without borders: How the developing world is changing the face of Christianity. *Christianity Today, 41,* 39–49.

Levinson, D. (1994). *Ethnic relations: A cross-cultural study.* Santa Barbara, CA: ABC Clio.

Lingenfelter, S. G. (1996). *Agents of transformation: A guide for effective cross-cultural ministry.* Grand Rapids, MI: Baker.

Matsumoto, D. R. (1996). *Culture and psychology.* Pacific Grove, CA: Brooks/Cole.

Sinha, D. (1990). Applied cross-cultural psychology and the developing world. *International Journal of Psychology, 25,* 381–386.

Tillich, P. (1959). *Theology of culture.* New York: Oxford University.

Triandis, H. C. (1993). On the place of culture in psychological science. *International Journal of Psychology, 28,* 249–250.

Suggested Reading

Atkinson, D. R., Morten, G., & Sue, D. W. (1993). *Counseling American minorities: A cross-cultural perspective* (4th ed.). Madison, WI: W.C. Brown.

Berry, J. W., Poortinga, Y. H., & Pandy, J. (Eds.). (1997). *Handbook of cross-cultural psychology* (2nd ed.). Boston, MA: Allyn & Bacon.

Bouvy, A. M., Van de Vijver, F. J. R., Boski, P., & Schmitz, P. G. (Eds.). (1994). *Journeys into cross-cultural psychology.* Amsterdam, Netherlands: Swets & Zeitlinger.

Brown, D. E. (1991). *Human universals.* Philadelphia, PA: Temple University.

Hesselgrave, D. J. (1991). *Communicating Christ cross-culturally* (2nd ed.). Grand Rapids, MI: Zondervan.

Iwawaki, S., Kashima, Y., & Leung, K. (Eds.). (1992). *Innovations in cross-cultural psychology.* Amsterdam, Netherlands: Swets & Zeitlinger.

Kagitcibasi, C., & Berry, J. W. (1989). *Cross-cultural psychology: Current research and trends.* Istanbul, Turkey: Bogazici University.

Kraft, C. H. (1979). *Christianity in culture.* Maryknoll, NY: Orbis.

La Belle, T. J., & Ward, C. R. (1996). *Ethnic studies and multiculturalism.* New York: State University of New York.

Leong, F. T. L. (1996). Toward an integrative model for cross-cultural counseling and psychotherapy. *Applied and Preventive Psychology, 5,* 189–209.

Myers, M. K. (1987). *Christianity confronts culture: A strategy for crosscultural evangelism.* Grand Rapids, MI: Academie/Zondervan.

Pedersen, P. (1987). *Handbook of cross-cultural counseling and therapy.* Westport, CT: Greenwood.

Pedersen, P. B., Draguns, J. G., Lonner, W. J., & Trimble, J. E. (Eds.). (1989). *Counseling across cultures* (3rd ed.). Honolulu, HI: University of Hawaii.

Stott, J. R. W. (1978). *Christian counter-culture.* Downer's Grove, IL: Inter Varsity.

N. Abi-Hashem

See Acculturation; Affiliation, Need for; Anthropology, Psychological; Cross-Cultural Therapy; Culture and Cognition; Culture and Psychopathology; Culture and Psychotherapy; Self-Esteem; Social Psychology; Stereotype.

Cross-Cultural Therapy. There is a sense in which all psychotherapy is a cross-cultural experience, since there are likely to be many differences between therapist and client, many of which can be thought of as cultural. Triandis (1995) has defined culture as the entire humanmade parts of the environment. Culture is to humans what a program is to a computer, to society what memory is to individuals. However, in psychological literature the term "cross-cultural therapy" has become a term of art to indicate situations in which the differences between therapist and client are defined in terms of race, ethnicity, gender, language, or lifestyles. It is in that sense that this article approaches the subject.

The psychological theories, assessment instruments, and therapeutic techniques taught in U.S. universities, seminaries, and professional schools of psychology come from a European/Caucasian cultural context. The U.S. is more and more becoming a pluralistic society in which co-exist a variety of cultures and languages. It behooves the therapist or pastoral counselor to be sensitive to these cultural differences lest he or she run the risk of misdiagnosing as pathology what may be due to different cultural norms.

The seminal work of Kluckhohn and Strodtbeck (1961), which delineated a framework for contrasting cultural values, is as relevant today as when it was first published. It continues to be cited in recent books on cross-cultural psychology. Kluckhohn and Strodtbeck proposed a five question paradigm for ranking cultures: What is the nature of humans? What is the relation of persons to nature? What is the preferred time orientation? What is the mode of orientation or activity valued? What are the relational structures? There is not sufficient space in this article to explore these questions in depth, but it takes only a cursory look to see that Americans value the subjugation of nature while other cultures attempt to achieve harmony and subjugation to nature. American culture as a whole values the present and future over the past, doing over being, and collateral relations over hierarchical ones.

Triandis (1995) divides cultures along the lines of individualism versus collectivism. The former he calls idiocentrism, the latter allocentrism. Contrasting values of each line up as follows: competitive versus cooperative; independent self versus interdependent self; emphasis on self-reliance versus emphasis on security; non-conformity versus conformity and self-sacrifice; emphasis on own needs versus needs of the community; emphasis on attitudes versus emphasis on norms. It is not hard to see that U.S. "standard" culture, which is to say white, middle-class, Protestant, is an idiocentric culture. This would not be an issue in psychotherapy except that at least 20% of the population come from allocentric cultures.

Of course these are generalities, and there are multiple individual variations, but as Sue and Sue (1990) have pointed out, "generalizations are necessary for us to use; without them, we would become inefficient creatures" (p. 47). The point is not to allow the generalities to become stereotypes. The authors define stereotypes as "rigid preconceptions we hold about all people who are members of a particular group, whether it be defined along racial, religious, sexual, or other lines. The belief in a perceived characteristic of the group is applied to all members without regard for individual variations. The danger of stereotypes is that they are impervious to logic or experience" (pp. 47–48).

For the clinician, the concern is to be open to allow clients define the parameters of their own value systems, which are culturally determined and may be different from those of the therapist. The therapist needs to be accepting of different value and cultural systems without prejudging the acceptability of such. The therapeutic interventions should be applied taking these different contexts into account. For example, the analytical and psychodynamic approach of nondirectiveness may frustrate persons of Asian or Hispanic cultures, who expect the doctor to make prescriptions for behavior and offer specific advice to solve their problems. The other side of that coin would be when the therapist assumes the ethnic person is still living by the old cultural values when he or she may be significantly acculturated to U.S. life and would be offended by being treated as someone "from the old country."

Howard (1991) wrote that "life is the stories we live by, psychopathology is stories gone mad, psychotherapy is an exercise in story repair." This dictum is most valuable when it is applied in the context of cross-cultural therapy. We need to let the client tell us his or her story and how he or she sees life. This story comes from their cultural context and is the result of the synthesis the person has made of ancestral upbringing, educational experience, and their interpretation of the dominant culture and how it has impinged on his or her life, bringing that person to the problems of the present for which he or she consults the therapist.

The culturally sensitive therapist needs to be aware of his or her own values, attitudes, biases, and feelings about minority persons. Therapists must be comfortable in the presence of persons different from themselves and be willing to let the client educate them about the client's cultural background. They need to understand that assumptions of major theories need to be translated into the context of different cultures and that there are culture-specific definitions of illness. Above all, the culturally sensitive therapist must be aware of the role of oppression and poverty in the etiology of mental illness. Often the therapist must engage in institutional interventions on behalf of their ethnic clients, sometimes out of the office.

There was a time when pastoral counselors and Christian therapists assumed that if the ethnic person is a Christian, there were no cultural differences because of a common faith. This assumption needs to be revised. Third-World Christian theologians are educating us about the different ways in which the Bible can be contextualized into other cultures. Thus we need to be sensitive to cultural differences that exist even among those within the faith.

References

Howard, G. S. (1991). A narrative approach to thinking, cross-cultural psychology, and psychotherapy. *American Psychologist, 46,* 187–197.

Kluckhohn, F. R., & Strodtbeck, F. L. (1961). *Variations in value orientation.* Evanston, IL: Row, Peterson.

Sue, D. W., & Sue, D. (1990). *Counseling the culturally different: Theory and practice* (2nd ed.). New York: Wiley.

Triandis, H. C. (1995). *Individualism and collectivism.* Boulder CO.: Westview.

L. M. MARMOL

See CROSS-CULTURAL PSYCHOLOGY; BLACK ISSUES IN PSYCHOLOGY AND PASTORAL CARE.

Crowd Behavior. A crowd can be described as a great number of persons gathered in one geographical area with at least one characteristic in common. It is a large assembly of people closely congregated or pressed together in a compact place without any specific order. In this massive concentration of persons, which is temporarily assembled with one or more commonalities, the individuality of the participants is unrecognized and rather submerged within the larger group.

In any given crowd, the collection of people normally influence and interact with each other and moreover begin to act together. A crowd may gather to form opinions, to protest, to assign leaders, to entertain itself, or to create a new movement. However, there are other types of crowd which are well organized, having clear purpose, planned schedule, and set of activities. These may result in a meaningful experience for the participants (e.g., gatherings in lecture halls, church buildings, sports stadiums, etc . . .). These regular social behaviors are not the main focus of this discussion, though this article will occasionally compare and contrast them with unconventional crowd behaviors.

The theory of crowd psychology was refined in Europe, especially in France, at the beginning of this century. Gustave Le Bon was a pioneer in articulating the dynamics of a crowd phenomenon as an essential element in social behavior. In his famous *The crowd*, published in 1895 (original French edition *Psychologie des foules*), he emphasized that the world was entering an "era of crowds." He observed a radical difference between the individual's psyche, which is reasonable, peaceful, and conscious and that of the crowd, which is spontaneous, irrational, and subconscious. Gustave Le Bon affirmed that the heat generated by a crowd fuses individuals with each other into a common sentiment, blurs their personality differences, and propels them to an enthusiastic behavior that is sometimes constructive and heroic and sometimes destructive and violent. Le Bon described a phase where the crowd would enter into a state of trance or hypnotism due to the fixation of attention, strong suggestion, undifferentiated mental condition, and intense propagation of emotional flow among the participants.

Gabriel Tarde, another French theorist, built upon Le Bon's discovery of "the natural crowd" and amplified his notions considerably. Tarde became interested in the study of *masses* and *mass culture*. He talked about artificial versus organized crowds. Tarde drew an important distinction between the physically proximate crowd, which is characterized by intimate connections, and the dispersed public characterized by a pure ideological cohesion. Masses, which are institutionalized crowds, must be capable of creativity, he affirmed. This is possible when there is an accomplished leader who becomes the driving engine behind the system. Suggestibility, imitation, affective and cognitive uniformity, and submission to the leader(s) are forces which shape the crowd's mind and behavior.

Many social theorists perceive the crowd behavior as characterized by several phenomena. They occur when the *coactors* begin to experience a decreased sense of self-awareness, an increased sense of collective interaction, and a higher sensitivity to surrounding cues. The first phenomenon is a heightened level of physiological arousal. The social facilitation effect has been used to explain the energizing influence a crowd normally has on the individual. The second is diffusion of personal responsibility. And the third characteristic is deindividuation, where a person experiences a greater sense of personal anonymity.

To understand the forms of collective behavior we need to consider and examine three essential questions: How does crowd behavior differ from everyday social behavior? Under what conditions does collective behavior emerge? What accounts for the coordination of collective behavior?

Although it is difficult to always make a clear distinction, there are basic differences between normal everyday institutionalized behavior and collective behavior of compact crowd. The first is well established and based on enduring relationships, norms, and predictability. It usually reflects routine and stability. The second is neither temporally nor spatially routinized. It is characterized by emergent norms, obsessive preoccupations, and unpredicted behaviors. It is most likely unscheduled, unstructured, and unconventional in nature.

For a collective behavior to emerge, at least three conditions must exist: (a) conduciveness, (b) situational strains, and (c) mobilization. In terms of coordination of collective behavior, it has been hypothesized that some crowds form patterns of behavior quicker than others. This could be due to a faster identification process, stronger suggestibility, or greater homogeneity among participants.

Christ was not mislead, intimidated, or overly enthused by the crowd. He did not allow the multitude to change His mind or attitude, to alter His teachings or convictions, nor to influence His purposes or mission. At the same time, however, Christ related well to the masses and knew precisely and intimately the crowds' mind. He was sensitive to their needs and was aware of their dynamics, underlying causes, and group formations. He was able to see beyond their overt crowd behaviors to the inner core of the assembled people.

The Scriptures reveal Christ responding to the crowd in a variety of ways. His reactions were consistently based upon His own timing, internal feelings, sense of priorities, perceptions of events, and connection with God the Father. He taught the crowd (Matt. 5:1–2; Luke 5:3), was followed and surrounded by great multitude (Luke 8:4; 23:27), was deeply moved with compassion when he saw the multitude distressed like sheep without a shepherd (Matt. 9:36), completely avoided the crowds (Mark 1:35–37; Luke 4:42; John 6:15), received and talked to the crowd (Luke 9: 10–12), was pressed by compact crowds (Luke 5:1; 8:42b), challenged the angry and violent crowd and walked out of their midst (John 7:43–44; 8:59), fed the multitude (Matt. 14:15–20), confronted the crowd who came to arrest Him at night (Mark 14:43, 48), and amazed the crowds and filled them with great and marvelous surprises (Matt. 9:33).

N. Abi-Hashem

See Group Dynamics; Crowding, Effects of.

Crowding, Effects of. Crowding refers to the sensation of being pressed into a small space insufficient for one's activities and threatening to one's own comfort. Crowding can have either positive or negative effects on people. Some crowded situations may enhance an experience while other crowded conditions make the experience unpleasant.

The study of crowding examines the relationship between high-density environments and stress reactions exhibited by people. One aspect that can cause a feeling of discomfort is the invasion of personal space. The term *social density* represents the number of other people with whom a person may share a certain space or a closed area. It could be inside density, i.e., the number of individuals per room, house, or dwelling place, and outside density, that is, the number of individuals per acre, land, or territory.

Crowding, then, is an experiential state based upon the effect of density. It is a psychological variable reflecting the way people believe or expect density will affect them. One factor that amplifies the negative effect of crowding is the individual's increased need for personal space and privacy. North Americans generally require more personal space than many other nationalities, including several European populations.

The negative consequences of crowding are more obvious on vulnerable individuals and those who struggle with severe anxiety, poor self-image, and high level of insecurities. Greater personal space is also required by authoritarian, aggressive, or violent people. In terms of general performances, it has been observed that crowding has little or no effect on simple and minor tasks. However, it may considerably affect performance on major and complex tasks. In most situations, men need more personal space than women. Normally, males tend to be more sensitive, more stressed, and even react more aggressively in high social density than females. Men often tend to keep a larger and protective space between themselves while women often tend toward closeness, touching, and minimum space.

People may typically experience less stress and therefore reduce the negative impact of crowding if (1) they are forewarned ahead of time about the crowded situation they are about to enter, (2) they are able to change their perception of the environment and believe they have more control over the situation, and (3) they are distracted by another event or environmental factor within the setting.

Social psychologists and ecologists try to study not only the effect of crowding and personal space on people but also the effect of noise and architectural features. For example, loud, intermittent, and uncontrollable noises will eventually have adverse effects. With regards to the architectural design, it has been reported that crowded living spaces, poor living conditions, and some high-rise buildings have been associated with certain psychological problems.

Many non-Western cultures and less industrialized societies still tolerate high-density living and close spatial proximity. What is crowded and stressful in one culture may totally be expected and normal in another. As the sense of community and close family ties are declining in Western society, the need for personal space and privacy is dramatically increasing. On the other hand, a strong emphasis on personal space and privacy usually leads to isolation, loneliness, lack of involvement, and a lessened sense of belonging.

N. Abi-Hashem

See Crowd Behavior; Group Dynamics.

Crying. Crying is probably the most demonstrative means of expressing one's feelings, particularly the feelings of sadness and joy. Both sadness and joy generate from love.

The Bible has no fewer than 510 references to crying and uses at least 11 words in New Testament Greek to describe crying. In the Bible God says that the blood of Abel cried out from the ground after Cain murdered Abel (Gen. 4:10), and it is noteworthy that the Scriptures end with the apostle John's assurance that God "will wipe every tear from [our] eyes. . . ; there will be no more . . . mourning or crying or pain" (Rev. 21:4, NIV).

The Old Testament story replete with references to crying is that of Joseph's reconnecting with his estranged family. When he first recognized his long-lost brothers, Joseph is said to have "wept so loudly that the Egyptians heard him, and Pharaoh's household heard about it" (Gen. 45:2, NIV). As the story unfolds, however, this crying out of joy extends to his brothers, his father, Israel, and the household, and leads to Joseph's weeping at his father's funeral. While there is ample scriptural evidence of crying out of the experience of sorrow, it is important to note that the Bible sees crying as a broadly based human experience, including Delilah's manipulative crying (Judg. 14:16–17), and among other human experiences there is a "time to weep" (Eccl. 3:4). Jesus experienced this time to weep at the loss of his friend, when he was "deeply moved in spirit and troubled" and wept (John 11:33, 35, NIV).

Psychologists (Lowen, 1972) regard genuine crying to be a natural reflection of love in the form of joy when one has something or someone loved or sorrow when one experiences the loss of that person or thing. A recent phenomenon in the literature has been the idea that not only is it important to cry but also it is particularly important for men to learn to do so. Christian authors (Dalbey, 1988) and secular authors (Moore & Gillette, 1990) have suggested that men learn the value of crying, and none other than General Norman Schwarzkopf not only cried publicly but also said that it is acceptable for men to cry. One Christian author has suggested that because crying is more socially acceptable for women than for men, women tend to cry when they are sad, hurt, afraid, or angry, thus making it difficult for a man to understand a woman's tears, whereas men are inclined to express these feelings with anger, making it equally difficult for a woman to understand a man's anger.

Biological research (Tornick, 1986) has shown that tears of emotion are chemically different from tears caused by intrusions into the eyes (e.g., onion fumes). The fact that crying can display such a wide array of feelings makes its centrality in the human experience undebatable, adding to the zoological observation that no animals are known to cry (with the exception of crocodiles, who "cry" when they eat their prey).

Psychological researchers and theorists have set out a variety of proposals for the reasons humans cry and otherwise display sorrow and grief. Bowlby (1980), in a seminal work regarding attachment, separation, and loss, tries to explain the seemingly protracted amount of crying and sadness sometimes expressed by adults as a remnant of a childhood filled with the repeated experience of crying at some kind of loss with the hope and sometimes the experience of retrieving what was lost (see Separation and Loss). In other words, crying and grief may be an unconscious attempt to get back what has been lost. While crying may not retrieve the lost item, person, or idea, it sometimes engenders sympathy and replacement for what has been lost. This idea that crying generates out of a childhood experience suggests that crying may be either a natural experience to cope with loss or a vain attempt to manipulate the world into returning to the person whatever has been lost. It is known that even in children there is a great difference in people's inclination to cry: some young children seem temperamentally inclined to more crying while others seem to cope with loss without many tears.

There is general agreement that parental constraints on their children's tendency to cry is deleterious. While much has been made of helping men to learn to cry, there are many childhoods filled with futile and abusive statements such as, "Don't cry or I'll give you something to cry about." Children should be encouraged to express the breadth of their feelings, regardless of the feeling or its expression, but this encouragement need not be accompanied by indulgence. Of the many unknown factors related to crying is the apparent phenomenon that adults but not children are inclined to cry tears of joy, possibly suggesting that adults suppressed too many tears as children, thus allowing for especially emotional times to surface old feelings mixed with new ones.

References

Bowlby, J. (1980). *Loss: Sadness and depression.* New York: Basic.

Dalbey, G. (1988). *Healing the masculine soul.* Dallas: Word.

Lowen, A. (1972). *Depression and the body.* New York: Penguin.

Moore, R. T., & Gillette, D. (1990). *King, warrior, magician, lover.* San Francisco: Harper & Row.

Tornick. E. (1986). Infant communicative intent: The infant's reference to serial interaction. In R. E. Stark (Ed.), *Language behavior in infancy and early childhood*. New York: Elsevier.

R. B. JOHNSON

See DEPRESSION; EMOTION.

Cults. Religious cults are not a new phenomenon on the human scene. Since the late 1960s, however, there seems to have been an upsurge in the growth of new religious movements, aberrational Christian groups, and self-improvement cults. Although most of these cultic movements have emerged in the West, many of them have been heavily influenced by an Eastern or a mystical worldview. This is true not only of the specifically religious movements but also of those groups that claim to be nonreligious in nature and whose stated objective is personal transformation or the realization of human potential.

The definition of the term *cult* depends largely on the frame of reference of the definer. Most definitions stress the unconventional and nonnormative dimensions of the word. There is usually negative connotation and stigma associated with its usage. Most cults are groups that are outside the mainstream of the prevailing, established religious tradition of any given society. Cult members view themselves as a minority group who share a common vision and who are dedicated to a person, an ideology, or a cause.

A psychological approach to cults includes a consideration of group dynamics (especially leader-follower roles), recruitment and indoctrination practices, the assumption by a member of a new identity and its management by the group, and the various methods of thought control that characterize the more extreme cultic groups.

A theological approach to the identification of a cult focuses on the group's belief system and its relation to a standard of Christian orthodoxy. From this perspective a cult is a religious movement that has doctrines and/or practices that conflict with the teachings of biblical Christianity. Primary focus is on issues of truth and error as theologically defined.

Cult Membership: Predisposing Factors. Any serious consideration of cult dynamics must include an examination of the reasons people are attracted to cults and the factors that make some people more vulnerable to cultic involvement than others. While there is always a danger in generalizing, the existing literature suggests that certain patterns characterize the recruitment/joining process.

The target population for most recruitment efforts by cults is young adults. Persons in this age group are frequently experiencing changes in their lives and are in various stages of transition. Cult converts are usually ordinary people who are experiencing specific and transitory difficulties in life.

They may be disenchanted with a sociopolitical cause, suffering from academic frustration, or encountering career uncertainty or job dissatisfaction. There may be a recent history of disruption in relationships, such as a breakup with a boyfriend or girlfriend or spouse. Typically they tend to come from middle- and upper-middle-class surroundings.

Prospective cult members are also individuals who can be characterized as seekers—people who are searching for religious experiences and for truth. The person who joins a cult often has a nominal religious background or no religious background. Those individuals who are attracted to aberrational Christian groups frequently are young Christians lacking in discernment skills or members of evangelical churches who become dissatisfied or disillusioned with their traditional church life.

Emotional and interpersonal factors predispose some people to cult membership. Among the converts to cults are those individuals who show some evidence of developmental and emotional problems over time. This type of recruit also has frequently experienced some kind of disjuncture in family relations, such as conflict with parents.

Cults appeal to persons who are experiencing a sense of personal inadequacy, loneliness, or disappointment with life. There are also those individuals who exhibit strong dependency needs and who are attracted to the totalistic and communal groups in which decision making is minimal and life's basic necessities are provided. Contact with the larger society is regulated and the demands of conventional existence can be by-passed or at least deferred.

Cults also appeal to people who have a strongly idealistic orientation. Such people sincerely desire to be a part of a group or organization that is focused on change—personal transformation or societal change. To join such a group is to affiliate with a cause, to become linked with a network of true believers who are determined to achieve their objectives.

Commitment Mechanisms. Among the most significant psychological dynamics at work in the cultic milieu are the various commitment mechanisms that help bind members to the group and that militate against easy departure.

Most cultic organizations exercise control over members by requiring total loyalty to the group, its particular ideology, and its leaders. Often legitimate and acceptable biblical concepts such as loyalty and commitment are completely redefined and distorted to suit the needs of the leaders.

Another effective commitment mechanism involves the suspension of supportive ties with the member's precult life, a severing of ties with families, friends, and all other familiar social support networks. There is a dying to the past, a conscious distancing of oneself from the outside world and its attendant evils.

Themes of sacrifice and investment pervade the cultic lifestyle. There is frequently a willingness to forsake family, education, or career in order to advance the objectives of the group. Whether the decision to invest all of one's energy and material resources in the group is a decision freely entered into is a matter of controversy. Critics contend that informed consent is not always fully operative in totalistic cults and that considerable psychological and spiritual pressure is exerted on members to be committed to the group to a point beyond what is normative for conventional religious organizations.

Fervent commitment to the group is also enhanced by a deliberate devaluing of the individual in favor of the group. Drastic personality shifts are often observed in individuals who become involved with cults. The person tends to be more rigid and less autonomous. The individual personality is submerged in the group and a collective orientation predominates. A new spiritual family often replaces the natural family.

Along with the adoption of a new lifestyle and the acquisition of a new identity is the assumption of a radically new worldview. Ideological conversion, however, usually is secondary to the gratification of basic human needs represented by the act of joining. Most individuals are attracted to cultic groups because of the need for acceptance, community, fellowship, a sense of belonging, and a need for purpose and direction rather than by the particular ideological propaganda of the group. Cults are successful because they meet human needs.

The nature and scope of the indoctrination process vary from group to group. Some cults have rather elaborate theological systems; others are unsophisticated in this area. Indoctrination is almost always wedded to elitist thinking: we alone possess the truth.

There is considerable debate among scholars and other observers as to whether the subjugation of the individual member's will to the requisites of the cult involves the loss or diminishment of personal autonomy. Cult critics maintain that, especially in the more totalistic groups, members' ability to think for themselves and to make independent decisions is impaired.

Cult defenders claim that allegations of brainwashing and thought control leveled at new religious movements are questionable and unfounded. Scholars are divided as to whether such charges are substantiated. Concepts of brainwashing and mind control are said to be vague and elusive. Some observers maintain that whatever manipulative techniques may be present in the controversial groups are extensions of basic principles of psychological conditioning and group dynamics.

Leadership Dynamics. Many feel that the most crucial factor in any approach to the psychology of cults is the role played by leaders. In the newer cultic movements as well as in the cults of the past there is always a single, living person who is the founder/leader of the group and who occupies a position of respect and prominence within the organization. Almost without exception, cult leaders are highly authoritarian and extract from their followers a loyalty and devotion that are probably due to a combination of awe, charisma, and psychospiritual intimidation.

Some evidence indicates that charismatic cult leaders are insecure individuals who need to exercise power over people and who find it easier to do so within a tightly structured environment. There is some debate as to whether their motives include any or all of the following: exploiting members for financial gain; political ambition; ego need for recognition and acceptance; genuine religious conviction that their own role is central to truth and the unfolding of history; the building of self-serving religious empires.

There are those who argue that cult leaders exhibit varying degrees of psychopathology, particularly paranoia. The latter trait is linked with the frequent assertion by leaders that they and their movements are targets of attack and persecution by the media, parents, governmental agencies, and anticult activists.

In some cultic organizations the leader is granted special sexual access to the membership. Besides the sexual and material benefits that accrue to the role of leader, ego needs are satisfied by virtue of the special status accorded leaders, not the least of which is the realization that one is recognized as a spiritual master, a religious pioneer, even a messianic figure.

Postcult Adjustment. Most cults employ highly sophisticated techniques for inducing behavioral change and conversion to their ideological systems. The life situation of most cult members is all-encompassing and highly intense. It therefore follows that the period following separation from the cult is often traumatic and unsettling. Sensitivity to the special problems of former members is especially needed by helping professionals who might be called on for counseling.

The early transition period following the cult experience is frequently characterized by episodes of depression and feelings of confusion. There is often uncertainty and indecisiveness regarding the future and feelings of anger and embarrassment about the past. Former members need to understand their particular vulnerabilities and that they were not abnormal or strange because of their entry into an unconventional religious group.

The reconstruction activity following the cult experience is incomplete if it fails to deal with the spiritual vacuum resulting from the exit from the group. The Christian counselor should be especially sensitive to the possibility of spiritual burnout that frequently characterizes the ex-member. A relationship of trust must be established in view of the likelihood of extreme distrust of religious authority of any kind. The individual therapist, like the Christian church at large, must be an agent of healing, restoration, and reconciliation.

Additional Readings

Enroth, R. (Ed.). (1983). *A guide to cults & new religions.* Downers Grove, IL: InterVarsity Press.

Langone, M. D. (Ed.). (1993). *Recovery from cults.* New York: Norton.

Singer, M. (1995). *Cults in our midst.* San Francisco: Jossey-Bass.

R. Enroth

See Brainwashing.

Culture and Alcohol. Alcoholic beverages may serve a wide range of functions across cultures—social organization, recreation, religious and symbolic functions—but its excessive use results in devastating social and physical effects. A major cross-cultural finding is that addiction to alcohol and problem drinking seems to be rare outside certain societies of Western civilization (Mandelbaum, 1965; Barry, 1982; Heath, 1986). In many societies where drinking is customary and drunkenness is common, people do not develop withdrawal symptoms or compulsive drinking. The adverse outcomes of the use of alcohol seem to be mediated by sociocultural factors. The occurrence of pathology in a substantial proportion of the people of a society may be related to the presence of each of three conditions: motivation to drink, which causes people to crave severe intoxication; cultural permissiveness and encouragement of alcohol intoxication; and the availability of sufficient alcohol.

The agricultural economic base in Western nations can produce as much alcohol as the population is physiologically capable of consuming. Accordingly the differences in the drinking customs among these nations seem to be influenced more by variations in social control than by availability of alcohol, thus requiring the study of attitudes, values, and behavior associated with drinking.

The importance of sociocultural factors in relation to drinking may be illustrated by the contrast between Jews and Irish-Americans. Bales (1946) emphasized Orthodox Jewish intrafamilial introduction of children to wine in a sacred ritual context, in contrast with the Irish pattern in which children are not supposed to drink but in adolescence have to prove their manhood in the secular context of the pub.

Since the 1970s, however, a decrease in religious orthodoxy, which had weakened the ritual significance of drinking and loosened family ties, thus undermining parental norms for moderation, had changed the stereotype of Jewish drinking (Blume & Dropkin, 1980; Blume, Dropkin, & Sokolow, 1980). Earlier Snyder (1958) reported that drinking problems are rare among Orthodox Jews and progressively more frequent among Conservative, Reform, and secular Jews. In Israel it was long reported that problem drinking was rare except among Yemenites (Hes, 1970). Could understanding the Jewish attitude toward drinking and teaching it to the public lead to moderation and prevent problem drinking in Western nations? Muslim countries, where the religion dictates a complete abstinence, are known for low rates of alcoholism. However, problems related to drinking are increasing in Muslim countries such as Kuwait, where strict prohibition is practiced (Bilal & El-Islam, 1985; Bilal & Angelo-Khattar, 1989).

Ethnic sensitivity to the short-term physiological effects of alcohol may demonstrate the interaction between biological and cultural factors. Response to alcohol, which is indicated by intense facial flushing, increased heart rate, and activation of the sympathetic nervous system, is found more among Mongoloids than Caucasoids. Intense response to alcohol is found among Japanese, Taiwanese, Koreans, the Eastern Cree tribe of North American Indians, and Chinese, but this effect is not a universal characteristic of this large racial category. Sensitivity to alcohol may have contributed to the absence of alcohol consumption aboriginally among most North American Indian tribes and rarity of heavy drinking among the Chinese. However, heavy drinking has characterized many Mongoloid nations (Japanese, Koreans, American Indians) since the introduction of distilled spirits by Europeans (Yamamoto, Eng-Kung, Chung-Kyoon, & Keh-Ming, 1988).

Differences in drinking patterns among nations may result in different alcohol-related pathology, as indicated by the rates of liver cirrhosis. Murphy (1982) ranked countries in terms of cirrhosis of the liver related to alcohol consumption. He found that nearly all high-ranking countries are wine drinking (Chile, Mexico, France), while the low-ranking ones are not (Iceland, Ireland, England, and Wales). The main difference between wine-drinking and other alcohol-consuming societies is that the former regard wine as part of their daily nourishment, to be taken mainly at meals, while the latter tend to regard alcohol as an aid to recreation, mostly consumed outside mealtimes. One result is the quantity consumed per capita tends to be considerably higher in wine-drinking nations than in those that depend on beer and spirits, and mortality rates from cirrhosis and from other aspects of alcoholism are a simple function of the amount of alcohol consumed (a correlation of 0.85 between mortality from cirrhosis and per capita consumption of alcohol among 17 countries). However, there are some exceptions. Noble found that Austria, which is compared with Italy, has 38% less alcohol consumption but 14% more mortality from cirrhosis. Regional variations (16 regions) in France indicate an inverse relationship between absolute alcohol consumed and death rates from alcoholism and cirrhosis of the liver ($r = -0.69$). Two areas in the north (Normandy plus Brittany and Alsace) had the highest death rates and the lowest consumption. Four areas in the south had the lowest death rates but an above-average consumption. Southern France is more similar to Italy in its drinking pattern than the northern part of France.

References

Bales, R. F. (1946). Cultural differences in rates of alcoholism. *Quarterly Journal of Studies on Alcohol, 6*, 480–499.

Barry, H., III (1982). Cultural variations in alcohol abuse. In I. Al-Issa (Ed.), *Culture and psychopathology*. Baltimore: University Park Press.

Bilal, A. M., & Angelo-Khattar, M. (1989). Correlates of alcohol-related casualties in Kuwait. *Acta Psychiatrica Scandinavica, 71*, 1–4.

Bilal, A. M., & El-Islam, M. F. (1985). Some clinical and behavioural aspects of patients with alcohol dependence problems in Kuwait psychiatric hospital. *Alcohol & Alcoholism, 20*, 57–62.

Blume, S. B., & Dropkin, D. (1980). The Jewish alcoholic: An unrecognized minority? *Journal of Psychiatric Treatment Evaluation, 2*, 1–4.

Blume, S. B., Dropkin, D., & Sokolow, L. (1980). The Jewish alcoholic: A descriptive study. *Alcohol, Health & Research World, 4*, 21–26.

Heath, D. B. (1986). Drinking and drunkenness in transcultural perspective. Part I. *Transcultural Psychiatric Research Review, 23*, 7–42.

Hes, J. P. (1970). Drinking in a Yemenite rural settlement in Israel. *British Journal of Addiction, 65*, 293–296.

Mandelbaum, D. B. (1965). Alcohol and culture. *Current Anthropology, 6*, 281–293.

Murphy, H. B. M. (1982). *Comparative psychiatry: The international and intercultural distribution of mental illness*. Berlin: Springer.

Snyder, C. R. (1958). *Alcohol and Jews*. Glencoe, IL: Free Press.

Yamamoto, J., Eng-Kung, Y., Chung-Kyoon, L., & Keh-Ming, L. (1988). Alcohol abuse among Koreans and Taiwanese. In L. H. Towle & T. C. Harford (Eds.), *Cultural influences and drinking patterns: A focus on Hispanic and Japanese populations*. Washington, DC: National Institute of Alcohol Abuse & Alcoholism.

I. Al-Issa

See Alcohol Abuse and Dependence.

Culture and Cognition. Straddling the nexus of anthropology and psychology, the set of interests labeled culture and cognition generally consists of attempts to answer three related questions: Is there a relationship between cultural variability and cognitive differences? If there is a relationship between culture and cognition, can either one be seen as more of an independent variable? What are the panhuman characteristics of culture and cognition that serve as substrata for cultural variability and cognitive differences?

Cognition can be thought of as the processes by which humans acquire, store, transform, and use information about the world (cf. Cole & Scribner, 1974, p. 2). Culture is the set of shared understandings, beliefs, and values that reside in people's minds. At one level the culture and cognition rubric is overly discriminatory: culture is a cognitive phenomenon, and cognition describes culture as a guide for human behavior. But the reality is that the two-part label represents the dual—that is, anthropological and psychological—nature of the genealogy of the endeavor to answer the three questions above. Anthropologists interested in these questions are known as cognitive anthropologists; psychologists with overlapping interests are cross-cultural psychologists. Recently, however, the divergence has changed trajectory so that a new discipline, cognitive science, makes use of the advantages of both disciplinary traditions, as well as linguistics.

Historical Roots. In 1858 William Gladstone noted the paucity of color terms in Homeric Greek and concluded that the ancient Greeks were incapable of seeing the world in the panorama of color that English speakers did. Similar results and conclusions were generated by members of the Cambridge expedition to the Torres Straits (between Australia and New Guinea) in 1899 (Rivers, 1901). The assumption was that language reflected cognitive structures: people cannot say what they cannot think, nor can they think what they cannot say.

Anthropology before the turn of the twentieth century was struggling to explain cultural variation. Evolutionary models seemed to be the best available explanations: differences exist because at any time societies reside on different levels as they move toward greater complexity. By the early years of the twentieth century, evolutionary explanations were rejected and particularistic explanations, championed by Franz Boas, became more fashionable. These particularistic explanations were functional and ahistorical in nature: a particular society was seen to have the cultural understandings and degree of social complexity that it did not because it was inexorably on its way to being something bigger and better but because for those people, living in that place, at that time, the culture and social structure in place were the most useful. Thus anthropology began to view its raison d'être as demonstrating that cultural variation was adaptive. Many of the data used within this paradigm were linguistic; the index of cultural variation was linguistic variation. *Pace* Sigmund Freud, language was and still is seen by anthropologists as the royal road to cognition.

Psychology for its part was rent by the dichotomy between the burgeoning intrapsychic determinism of Freud and the extrapsychic determinism of the stimulus-response school. Cognition, as the mental handling of information, was irrelevant for psychodynamic psychology and a mere byproduct for the behaviorists. Jean Piaget began developing his universal stages of cognitive development in the 1920s. Standing above the psychoanalytic-behaviorist split, Piaget held that the cultural milieu of a child affected her or his cognitive development, such as acquiring the principle of conservation. In a vivid demonstration Price-Williams, Gordon, and Ramirez (1969) showed that some Mexican children, when shown two balls of clay, asserted that the amount of clay changes when one of the balls is rolled into a sausage shape in front of them. Children who live in pottery-making families, however, recognized that the amount of clay does not change just because the shape changes.

Soviet psychologist Vygotsky also attempted to overcome the split in the 1920s and 1930s by focusing on childhood socialization (and so was consistent with the psychoanalytic approach) and experience (thus satisfying the behavioral mavens). Vygotsky, who has recently been rediscovered by American psychological anthropologists (see, for example, Miller & Hoogstra, 1992), argued that certain types of thought—that is, cognition—can be transmitted to children only via language (1934 [1987], 1978).

Since Vygotsky's era, doctrinaire Freudianism has fallen into disrepute and behaviorism has been done in by the computer. (Since computers could be programmed to be more than stimulus-response machines, how much more so the minds that program them?) Language, however, still takes center stage as the manifestation par excellence of cognition. The three questions of culture and cognition began for research purposes to take this shape: Is there a relationship between cultural variability and linguistic differences? If there is a relationship between culture and language, can either one be seen as more of an independent variable? and What are the panhuman characteristics of culture and language that serve as substrata for cultural variability and linguistic differences?

Cultural Variability and Linguistic Differences.
The collaborative work of Sapir and Whorf is the fundamental concept. The Sapir-Whorf hypothesis (called an axiom by Hill and Mannheim [1992]) is a statement of linguistic determinism: linguistic categories affect the way in which people see the world; differences in language are commensurate with differences in perception and cognition. For example, in Sursurunga, a language spoken in New Ireland in the South Pacific, nouns are classed as either alienable or inalienable. The word for same-sex sibling, *tuang*, is part of the inalienable noun class, while the words for spouse (*wák* and *pup* for wife and husband respectively) are alienable. Sursurunga speakers view this as a reasonable distinction, since one's siblings are inherently kin but spouses are acquired later in life and furthermore can be replaced.

A corollary of the Sapir-Whorf hypothesis would be that these linguistic/cognitive differences result in differences in perception and behavior. Kay and Kempton (1984) conducted an experiment to find out how much difference in perception and behavior results from linguistic/cognitive difference. Their conclusion is that the differences are present but not significant.

The Relationship between Culture and Language.
At present the question, Which comes first, the word or the idea? is undergoing scrutiny. Lucy's recent work (1993a, 1993b) is an attempt to reformulate or modernize the Sapir-Whorf hypothesis. He starts by unhitching cognition and language, stating that "the mere presence or absence of a specific grammatical category alone is not a sufficient basis for inferring a possible influence on thought" (1993b, p. 103). For Lucy linguistic classification and cognitive classification cannot be assumed to be the same thing, and he suggests that the intervening variable is habitual behavior. Linguistic categories are assumed to parallel cognitive categories only if the linguistic categories are salient in everyday living. In the Sursurunga example, Lucy would argue that since the linguistic categories are used on a daily basis, they can be expected to be indexical of cognitive/conceptual distinctions: "[D]ifferences in morphosyntactic structure have detectable effects on thought about reality" (1993b, p. 266). Sursurunga terminology for body parts would not be expected, according to Lucy, to represent salient conceptual differences. The Sursurunga term for neck or throat (*pongon*) is alienable, while the word for head (*lulun*) is inalienable. Since this linguistic distinction is almost never relevant to everyday life, it does not represent a cognitive difference.

The Panhuman Characteristics of Culture and Language.
Earlier treatments of cultural, linguistic, and cognitive differences toyed with the idea that some languages and conceptual systems were unable to use (Lévy-Bruhl, 1923, 1926) or saw no utility in (Sahlins, 1995) Western logic and reasoning.

Three strands of argumentation for the existence of significant panhuman cognitive similarities neutralize this sort of thinking. The first is the research on color terminology, exemplified by Berlin and Kay's *Basic Color Terms* (1969). Berlin and Kay showed that while the number of color terms varied across languages, the systematicity of the terminologies were universal: in languages with only three color terms, the colors that the terms represented were (in English) black, white, and red. Languages with four terms use these three plus either green or yellow. Languages with five terms use green and yellow. There are, then, universal and probably biological antecedents of the cognition of color.

A second strand is the work of Hutchins, an anthropologist, who worked on the Trobriand Islands in the South Pacific. He showed that the dialogue of disputes, usually over land, used the same types of reasoning found elsewhere, including modus ponens and modus tollens forms of inference (1980). More recently Hutchins (1994) has shown how Micronesian mariners, by using a navigational concept that assumes that the canoe stands still while islands move past it, generate extremely accurate conceptual maps of the islands and atolls in the region. In the face of Trobriand litigation and Micronesian navigation, claims that there are qualitative differences between Western and non-Western thought are ill-conceived.

The third strand returns us to languages. Bickerton, building on Chomsky's ideas about a universal grammar, has suggested that the basic human syntactic template is subject-verb-object (SVO). Bickerton (1990) argues on the basis of Creoles and Pidgins that SVO is the default option, although other patterns can be learned relatively easily. Consider, for example, English-speaking children, who quickly learn to handle SVO statements such as "I want a cookie" but encounter trouble when English requires VSO for questions: children are inclined to say, "What the cookie taste like?" rather than "What does the cookie taste like?" The auxiliary verb *does* prior to the subject *cookie* is counterintuitive to the child because, according to Bickerton, it is not consistent with the SVO pattern. If there is a universal default syntax, as Bickerton's data suggest, then the source is likely to be neurological, and neuroscience, along with psychology and anthropology, are important components of the contemporary discipline of cognitive science and the study of culture and cognition.

Evaluation. Contemporary studies of culture and cognition rely heavily on a model of the human mind as a machine—or, more to the point, a very sophisticated computer. While cognition is seen to have emergent qualities (e.g., even a computer recognizes that sometimes a whole is more than the sum of its parts), the mind is less often viewed in this way. Perhaps the fundamental question for Christians is, Where in this extremely complex machine is the conscience? the soul?

The limitations of linguistic determinism and linguistic relativity, coupled with the ongoing research into the universals of human cognition, are consistent with the biblical implications for a fundamental human nature. Furthermore, the integrity of linguistic and cultural systems as discrete *ethnoi* can be found to be consistent with biblical counsel. The implications of the field of culture and cognition are importantly but not exclusively missiological. The transmission of the gospel cannot be undertaken simplemindedly; linguistic and conceptual variation can shroud the message, but the universals of cognition suggest that no cultural system is incommensurate with the gospel. Translators and exegetes ought to consider the cognitive/conceptual milieu in which the Scriptures originated. Did, following Lucy, for example, the aorist tense in Greek qualify as a linguistic category that has behavioral and therefore conceptual relevance? How much does the male pronoun for God affect English speakers' perceptions of God? Are the hearts in "heartburn," "heartache," "heartfelt," "heartily," "heartless," and "inviting Jesus into my heart" all related at some conceptual level to English speakers?

There is much research to be done on culture and cognition, whether it is done under the auspices of the nascent cognitive science or within the conventional parameters of anthropology and psychology. The search for human universals, eschewed for much of the twentieth century, is likely to occupy us as we enter the next one.

References

Berlin, B., & Kay, P. (1969). *Basic color terms.* Berkeley: University of California Press.

Bickerton, D. (1990). *Language and species.* Chicago: University of Chicago Press.

Cole, M., & Scribner, S. (1974). *Culture and thought.* New York: Wiley.

Hill, J. & Mannheim, B. (1992). Language and world view. *Annual Review of Anthropology, 21,* 381–406.

Hutchins, E. (1980). *Culture and inference.* Cambridge, MA: Harvard University Press.

Hutchins, E. (1994). *Cognition in the wild.* Cambridge, MA: MIT Press.

Kay, P., & Kempton, W. (1984). What is the Sapir-Whorf Hypothesis? *American Anthropologist, 86,* 64–79.

Lévy-Bruhl, L. (1923). *Primitive mentality.* New York: Macmillan.

Lévy-Bruhl, L. (1926). *How natives think.* London: Allen & Unwin.

Lucy, J. A. (1993a). *Grammatical categories and cognition.* Cambridge: Cambridge University Press.

Lucy, J. A. (1993b). *Language diversity and thought.* Cambridge: Cambridge University Press.

Miller, P. J., & Hoogstra, L. (1992). Language as tool in the socialization and apprehension of cultural meanings. In T. Schwartz, G. M. White, & C. A. Lutz (Eds.), *New directions in psychological anthropology.* Cambridge: Cambridge University Press.

Price-Williams, D. R., Gordon, W., & Ramirez, M. (1969). Skill and conservation. *Developmental Psychology, 1,* 769–783.

Rivers, W. H. R. (1901). Introduction and vision. In A. C. Haddon (Ed.), *Report of the Cambridge anthropological expedition to the Torres Straits* (Vol. 2). Cambridge: Cambridge University Press.

Sahlins, M. (1995). *How "natives" think.* Chicago: University of Chicago Press.

Vygotsky, L. (1978). *Mind in society.* Cambridge, MA: Harvard University Press.

Vygotsky, L. (1987). *Thinking and speech.* N. Minick (Trans.). New York: Plenum. (Original work published 1934)

Additional Reading

Dunlop, C. E. M., & Fetzer, J. H. (1993). *Glossary of cognitive science.* New York: Paragon House.

A. H. BOLYNATZ

See COGNITIVE DEVELOPMENT.

Culture and Psychopathology. Culture refers to the humanmade part of the environment, consisting of its physical aspects such as roads and buildings as well as its symbolic aspects such as beliefs, norms, values, and myths. Five basic questions have formed the theoretical and research foundation of the area of culture and psychopathology (Marsella, 1993): How do sociocultural factors affect the etiology of mental illness and interact with biological, psychological, and environmental factors in influencing psychopathology? How do sociocultural factors influence the definition of normality and abnormality? What are the sociocultural variations in the classification and diagnosis of psychopathology? What are the sociocultural variations in the rates of psychopathology? And what are the sociocultural variations in the experience, manifestation, course, and outcome of psychopathology?

The medical view suggests that, similar to physical illness, psychopathology is universal and the rates of mental illness are the same regardless of the sociocultural background. Early in this century Emil Kraepelin, the father of modern psychiatry, traveled to Southeast Asia and other parts of the world and observed that mental illness as known in the West, such as dementia praecox (his term for schizophrenia) and bipolar disorder, exists in non-Western countries. Kraepelin had a biological orientation, which led to the conclusion that Western disease entities are universal.

The medical perspective is concisely expressed by Berne (1959), who found that patients were similar in the type of diagnosis they received but varied in their symptoms in mental hospitals he visited in several tropical African countries, the United States, and Australia. He concluded that "clinically, differences can be treated as mere dialects or accents of a common language; the Italian schizophrenic speaks schizophrenic with an Italian accent; the Siamese manic speaks manic with a Siamese accent" (Berne, 1959, p. 108). In 1976 Jane M. Murphy reported in *Science* results of community studies of the rates of mental illness among Canadian villagers (18%), the Eskimos (19%), and members of the Yoruba tribe in Nigeria (15%) in order to demonstrate similarity in the rates of psychopathology despite wide differences between these cultures.

In contrast to the medical perspective, the proponents of the sociocultural approach accept the concept of cultural relativity as a guide for research. Cultural relativity implies that each culture has its own mental disorders, and normality and abnormality are defined within a specific social and cultural context. The classical version of this approach was expressed in the 1930s by anthropologist Ruth Benedict, who suggested that what is regarded as abnormal in one culture may be considered normal or may constitute highly desired behavior in another culture. Whereas psychiatrists believe that the diagnostic system of mental disorders can be universally applied regardless of culture, the cultural relativists, who are mainly anthropologists, emphasize that diagnosis should not be divorced from understanding the habits and beliefs of the group and that psychopathology should be viewed within a social system.

One notion that became popular among proponents of the cultural approach is that complex Euro-American cultures cause serious mental illness; simple preliterate cultures are free of neuroses or psychoses. It is implied that advances in civiliza-

tion increase tension as well as the rates of mental illness. This notion has its origin in the nature cult of the eighteenth century, which attributed the increase of insanity in Europe to a degeneration from a golden age of natural virtue and idealized the noble savage who had been in previous generations free of greed, egotism, envy, and the like.

The concept of the noble savage in the study of culture and psychopathology is consistent with anthropological reports in the 1920s and 1930s; for example, the well-adjusted Trobriand Islanders described by Malinowski and the contrast between the carefree Samoan adolescents and the storm and stress of European and American youth made by Mead. In *Civilization and Its Discontents* (1930), Sigmund Freud conceptualized neurosis as the result of a conflict between instincts and the repressive processes of civilization; individuals are better off in a simpler culture with fewer restrictions on their instincts. A survey of cross-cultural research by Benedict and Jack in 1954 does not support the hypothesis that a non-Western lifestyle provides an immunity against mental illness; the major psychoses occur in all human societies.

An intermediate position between the medical and the cultural approaches suggests that psychopathology is comparable across cultures but variable in its incidence and expression. Both common cross-cultural patterns and local cultural differences in psychiatric syndromes coexist. The extreme views of the medical or cultural relativity perspective are rarely accepted by contemporary researchers.

During the last four decades the study of culture and psychopathology passed from a previous era of speculation on and description of the exotic behavior of non-Western people to the objective collection of data and the use of sophisticated methodology. Research and general information on the relationship between culture and mental illness have now been published from almost every corner of the globe, representing researchers from both Western and non-Western nations (Al-Issa, 1995). The following sections discuss the relationship between culture and some major subtypes of pathology, namely, schizophrenia and depression.

Schizophrenia. Early studies by anthropologists suggest that chronic psychosis and schizophrenia are rare among some tribes, but these reports were based on small populations. More recent studies of large samples of communities report that schizophrenia is everywhere, but sociocultural factors may reduce or increase the risk for the illness. Among contemporary low-risk groups studied are the Hutterites, the South Pacific Tongans, and the Taiwan aboriginal tribes. These three groups are from contrasting cultural backgrounds with no common genetic or cultural heritage except that they share a communal style of living. In contrast, high-risk groups studied are the Irish and the Istrians (in Croatia). These two groups also have no common genetic or cultural background. However, both had experienced centuries of resented domination by a neighboring power and extensive overseas emigrations. These massive emigrations may raise the question of whether the high rates of schizophrenia in the Republic of Ireland or Croatia are due to selection: the schizophrenics remain in the home country while the more healthy grasp opportunities abroad.

Cultural effects on the content of symptoms of schizophrenia tend to be superficial and may reflect only secondary features of the disease. For example, some familiarity with European history or Christianity is necessary for arriving at the delusion that one is Napoleon or Christ. A common delusion among Western patients is that of being controlled by rays or electricity, but this is found only among Westernized Africans. South American Indians who move to the cities develop delusions of radio waves and secret police instead of the more traditional delusions about saints, witchcraft, and jungle spirits. Hospitalized schizophrenic patients are less violent and aggressive in India, Africa, and Japan than are those in the West. Catatonic rigidity, negativism, and stereotyped behavior are more often reported in India than in other countries. Differences in the contents of symptoms are found among schizophrenics in Western nations as well; for example, Irish patients show preoccupation with sin and guilt related to sex, but this is not true of Italian patients, who are more emotionally expressive (elation, overtalkativeness, grinning, laughing, assaultiveness).

A diagnostic label like schizophrenia carries a different meaning even to psychiatrists trained in quite similar cultures such as Britain and the United States. Cooper et al. (1972) found that identical patients were five times more likely to be diagnosed as schizophrenic by American than by British psychiatrists. American psychiatrists tend to have a broader concept of schizophrenia and see more severe pathology in their patients.

The International Pilot Study of Schizophrenia (World Health Organization, 1979) found that schizophrenia has better outcome among Nigerian and Indian patients than among British, Czechoslovakian, Danish, and American samples. It is still not known why non-Western patients who receive less medication than their Western counterparts recover faster from schizophrenia, but support from social networks such as the extended family and the tolerance of deviance in the culture may facilitate the social recovery of patients.

Depression. The term *depression* may be used to describe a normal reaction to loss, a symptom of a disorder, or the disorder itself. Thus cross-cultural studies of depression raise the question whether one is dealing with normal depressive mood or mental illness; and variations in the rates of depressive disorder in Western and non-Western cultures may reflect confusion in the meaning of this term.

Early studies suggest that true depression is rare or even nonexistent in some parts of Africa and Asia; if the disorder occurs, it tends to be relatively mild with a short duration and with no guilt feelings or suicide. Recent studies, however, suggest that true depression in non-Western patients may appear in some other form; for example, patients may emphasize the physical aspects of their trouble to such an extent that they would not see a psychiatrist, or if they are seen by a psychiatrist, their condition may be considered a physical rather than a depressive illness. Later studies reported high rates of depression among non-Western patients. Depression is found to be the most common mental illness among women who seek help in shrines in rural Ghana. Leighton et al. (1963) compared the results of two field surveys of depression using the same procedure in Nigeria and Canada; depressive symptoms were about four times more common among the Nigerian sample than among the Canadian sample.

An opinion survey of psychiatrists in 30 countries reveals that depression is present in widely different cultures. The survey indicates that the most common form of depressive illness includes the following symptoms: a mood of depression or dejection, diurnal mood change (e.g., more depressed in the morning than in the evening), insomnia with early morning waking, diminution of interest in the social environment, and fatigue. Other symptoms seem to be reported as less than frequent in some cultures: weight loss (Scandinavia), despondency and hopelessness (West Africa), and loss of sexual interest (Japan). Self-depreciation and guilt feelings were reported as the most frequent among devout Roman Catholic communities and rare among Muslims and Hindus. However, it is unclear from the data whether the association is truly with Christian belief or with modern European civilization, which had influenced Roman Catholic communities.

Other attempts to find links between religion and depression were inconclusive. For example, a higher prevalence of depression in Jews than in Christians was found in hospital admissions in New York, but studies in Israel did not reveal such a trend. Eaton and Weil (1955) found higher rates of depressive illness with guilt feelings among the Hutterites, but patriarchal family structure and community pressure on the individual rather than religious beliefs are felt to be contributory factors to the development of both depression and guilt feelings. However, religious beliefs may influence both the conception and treatment of depression among the Hutterites. Symptoms of depression are not considered as an illness but as a socially patterned expression called *anfechtung*, meaning temptation by the devil; it is believed that the victims are suffering because they have sinned and questioned basic religious beliefs. Confession is expected to restore the patient to God's favor. The Hutterite way of life seems to provide an atmosphere within which emotionally disturbed members are encouraged to function within the limits of their handicaps and thus avoid the negative effects of institutionalization such as extreme social withdrawal and mental deterioration.

Low rates of suicide are consistently reported among Asian and African patients (Al-Issa, 1995). One explanation of these low rates is the low feeling of guilt and self-depreciation of depressive patients. Another explanation of low rates in some countries such as the Irish Republic and Muslim countries concerns the condemnation of suicide by Roman Catholicism and Islam respectively. However, when suicide is considered as a sin in a culture, this may result in its underreporting. One may also wonder about other Christian countries in which suicide is considered a sin but the rates of suicide tend to be high.

The validity of the concept of depression has been questioned by many researchers (Kleinman & Good, 1985). It has been suggested that Western psychiatry attempts to medicalize human suffering by considering depression as an illness. It has been pointed out that depressive mood is considered as a normal religious sentiment among Iranians (Good, Good, & Moradi, 1985), and the symptoms of depression such as hopelessness and loss of a sense of pleasure are not considered abnormal by a Buddhist (Obeyesekere, 1985).

References

Al-Issa. I. (1995). *Handbook of culture and mental illness: An international perspective*. Madison, WI: International Universities Press.

Berne, E. (1959). Difficulties of comparative psychiatry. *American Journal of Psychiatry, 116*, 104–109.

Cooper, S., Kendell, R., Gurland, B., Sharpe, L., Copeland, J., & Simon, R. (1972). *Psychiatric diagnosis in New York and London: A comparative study of mental hospital admission*. London: Oxford University Press.

Eaton, J., & Weil, R. (1955). *Culture and mental disorders*. New York: Free Press.

Good, J. B., Good, M. D., & Moradi, R. (1985). The interpretation of Iranian depressive illness and dysphoric affect. In A. Kleinman & B. Good (Eds.), *Culture and depression*. Los Angeles: University of California Press.

Kleinman, A., & Good, B. (1985). *Culture and depression*. Los Angeles: University of California Press.

Leighton, D. C., Harding, J. C., Macklin, D. B., Macmillan, A. M., & Leighton, A. H. (1963). *The character of danger: Psychiatric symptoms in selected communities*. New York: Basic.

Marsella, A. J. (1993). Sociocultural foundations of psychopathology: An historical overview of concepts, events and pioneers prior to 1970. *Transcultural Psychiatric Research Review, 30*, 97–142.

Obeyesekere, G. (1985). Depression, Buddhism and the work of culture in Sri Lanka. In A. Kleinman & B. Good (Eds.), *Culture and depression*. Los Angeles: University of California Press.

World Health Organization. (1979). *Schizophrenia: An international follow-up study*. New York: Wiley.

I. Al-Issa

See Psychopathology in Primitive Cultures.

Culture and Psychotherapy. There are universal elements in all kinds of healing practices: faith in the therapist, active participation of the clients and their families, the authority figure and warm personality of the therapist, and the facilitation of emotional arousal as a prerequisite of changes in attitudes and behavior during therapy (Wittkower & Warnes, 1974). However, in culturally diverse North American and European societies, Western systems of psychotherapy are culturally biased against people whose values differ from those of the dominant group. There are many ways in which the processes and goals of Western psychotherapy could become biased against those who are culturally different (Sue & Sue, 1990).

First, Western psychotherapy is individual-centered, in a one-to-one relationship encouraging the clients to take responsibility for their own affairs. In many societies the basic psychosocial unit is not the individual but the family, the group, and the community; the identity of individuals is defined within the context of the family and the group. Many important personal decisions are carried out by the family and the group. Thus clients from these communalistic societies may give the impression that they are dependent and irresponsible. The goal of therapy in these situations is to encourage interdependence rather than independence of clients (Chaleby, 1992). Such different orientations may influence the affective response of the client. In traditional societies that emphasize group orientation, the most dominant affective response to wrongdoing is shame rather than guilt, which is usually shown by persons in an individualistic society.

Second, psychotherapy works best with individuals who are verbal and able to express their thoughts and feelings clearly. The word *alexithymia* (Greek: *a*, lack; *lexis*, word; *thymos*, emotion) is used to describe a disturbance characterized by inability of psychotherapy clients to verbalize their emotions or to elaborate on their fantasies. Such clients are usually rejected as unsuitable candidates for psychotherapy. Many cultural minorities tend not to value verbalization, which they consider a manifestation of assertiveness. In many cultures (e.g., Japanese) children are taught not to speak unless they are spoken to. Verbal communication usually flows from those of higher prestige and status to those of lower prestige and status. While the expression of emotions is encouraged in Western psychotherapy, restraint of feelings may be highly valued in other cultures. Control of emotions and feelings may be considered a sign of maturity rather than inhibition or lack of spontaneity (e.g., among Hispanics and Asian cultures).

Third, insight or understanding the causes of one's abnormal behavior may not be highly valued by many culturally different groups. When persons in China become depressed or anxious, they are advised to avoid the thoughts that cause their distress. People from lower socioeconomic classes may be more concerned with family and occupational problems (feeding the family, finding a job) rather than with understanding them.

Finally, self-disclosure, as characterized by openness and intimacy and the revelation of personal or social problems, may not be acceptable for culturally different people, since such problems reflect not only on the individual but also on the family. In communal societies (Asian-Americans, American Indians, and Hispanics) the individual is trained not to reveal personal matters to strangers. African-Americans are particularly distrustful of the white therapist and are reluctant to disclose themselves because of the discrimination they have experienced through racism. The white therapist is not conceived of as a person of good will but rather as an agent of society who may use the information against them.

In considering cultural differences in the psychotherapy situation, it is important that white middle-class psychotherapists become aware of their own values as well as those of their culturally different clients, modifying their procedures to accommodate these clients. For example, Chaleby (1992) reported that in an authoritarian Muslim society the psychotherapist has to take a directive approach in dealing with patients' practical problems, giving more attention to teaching problem-solving techniques within the community context. The patient is encouraged to conform and be socially responsible rather than be independent from the norms of the community or have insights into his or her problems. The therapist also uses religious beliefs for cognitive restructuring: clients' thoughts are changed within the framework of Muslim religious beliefs, and Muslim rules of complete abstinence are utilized in the therapeutic situation when one deals with alcoholism or drug addiction. Although new culturally specific techniques may be needed with minorities (Ramirez, 1991), this should not rule out the use of traditional psychotherapy (Wohl, 1995).

In contrast to Western psychotherapy, altered states of consciousness involving dreams, mystical experience, shamanistic ecstasy, and dissociation states are frequently used for therapy in non-Western cultures (Prince, 1980). Dreams are used in diagnosis in Western Africa, where disturbed women dream of killing their children; they are then diagnosed as witches who must confess their evil witchcraft in order to be healed of their symptoms. A sick person among the Australian aborigines, for example, may dream of a supernatural visitation and be cured. Almost all major world religions prescribe exercises of meditation techniques aimed at achieving mystical experiences. Since the 1970s transcendental meditation, a method in the practice of yoga, has been used by Western therapists as a means to improve physical and mental health and to reduce stress (Benson, 1991; Nystul, 1987). Shamanic ecstasy is a visionary state in which the healer's "soul" journeys out of the body to the upper world of spirits or to the underworld of demons to obtain information about the illness of the patient or to search for the patient's lost soul. Singing, drumming, and smoking culminate in the shaman's falling into an unconscious state. After a few minutes to an hour, the shaman regains consciousness and reports on the journey. The shamans' contact with the realm of spirits enhances their suggestive power and endows them with enormous prestige.

Finally, dissociation states are often utilized in non-Western therapeutic systems. Dissociation states are achieved through dancing and music or may follow a period of starvation and/or over-breathing that culminates in convulsive jerks and unconsciousness. Both healer and patient may experience dissociation during the therapeutic sessions. The spirit speaks through the healer (the medium), whereas the dissociated patient experiences catharsis—that is, acting out forbidden emotions and behavior (aggressive, sadistic, or cross-gender behavior). Cult ceremonies, such as in the Zar cult in Ethiopia or Pentecostal services in Africa and Caribbean countries, seem to be widely used for therapeutic purposes in non-Western cultures.

Many elements are involved in the therapeutic effects of these non-Western healing procedures (Wittkower & Warnes, 1974): fears of an unknown origin are rationalized (e.g., "Sponos, the smallpox god, has inflicted this on you"); suggestion by a prestigious traditional healer results in the repression of stressful conflicts; projection of personal wickedness onto malicious deities; displacement of sin or sickness on a scapegoat or a sacrificial animal; displacement of aggression by killing an animal rather than a person; and penance by sacrifice.

References

Benson, H. (1991). Mind/body interactions including Tibetan studies. In the Dalai Lama, H. Benson, R. A. F. Thurman, H. E. Gardner, and D. Goleman (Eds.), *Mindscience: An East-West dialogue.* Boston: Wisdom.

Chaleby, K. (1992). Psychotherapy with Arab patients, toward a culturally oriented technique. *The Arab Journal of Psychiatry, 3,* 16–27.

Nystul, M. S. (1987). Transcendental meditation. In R. J. Corsini (Ed.), *Concise encyclopedia of psychology.* New York: Wiley.

Prince, R. (1980). Variations in psychotherapeutic procedures. In H. C. Triandis & J. G. Draguns (Eds.), *Handbook of cross-cultural psychology* (Vol. 6). Boston: Allyn & Bacon.

Ramirez, M. (1991). *Psychotherapy and counseling with minorities.* New York: Pergamon.

Sue, D. W., & Sue, D. (1990). *Counseling the culturally different* (2nd ed.). New York: Wiley.

Wittkower, E. D., & Warnes, H. (1974). Cultural aspects of psychotherapy. *Psychotherapy and Psychosomatics, 24,* 303–310.

Wohl, J. (1995). Traditional individual psychotherapy and ethnic minorities. In J. F. Aponte, R. Y. Rivers, & J. Wohl (Eds.), *Psychological interventions and cultural diversity.* Boston: Allyn & Bacon.

I. Al-Issa

See Cross-Cultural Psychology; Cross-Cultural Therapy; Black Issues in Psychology and Pastoral Care.

Cybernetic Theory. In 1946 mathematician Norbert Wiener coined the term *cybernetics* to describe the study of control and communication in animal, human, machine, and organizational systems. The term, from the Greek *kybernetes*, meaning steersman, captures a key concept in cybernetic theory—feedback. Control and communication in many systems are possible because some aspect of the system's output feeds back and regulates the process. Positive feedback reinforces the process while negative feedback opposes it. Negative feedback makes possible another process, homeostasis, the maintenance of equilibrium or preset levels of some condition. The same principles that describe how a thermostat works with the heating and cooling systems in a home to maintain a constant temperature have been used to describe hormonal and population control. Along with physiologist Arturo Rosenblueth, Wiener developed a cybernetic model of the human nervous system.

Cybernetic theory involves a nontraditional concept of causality. The linear view in which event A causes event B is replaced with one in which A causes B, which may cause a change in A, and so on. Self-maintenance, self-autonomy, and self-reference play a key role in cybernetic theory.

In clinical psychology cybernetic theory was first adopted by family therapists as a way to describe control and communication problems in the family. It was used by biological psychologists and neuropsychologists as an explanatory model for physiological and neural processes. Cybernetic theory no longer stands as a separate discipline; its concepts have been absorbed into areas such as systems and general systems theory, information theory, automata theory, and systems engineering.

W. D. Norman

See Intelligence, Artificial; Family Systems Theory.

Cyclothymic Disorder. According to the *DSM-IV* (American Psychiatric Association, 1994), this is a chronic, fluctuating mood disturbance involving numerous periods of both hypomanic and depressive symptoms. These prominent alterations of mood and activity are not of sufficient severity and duration to meet the criteria for a major depressive episode, manic episode, or mixed episode. The pattern of chronicity must last for at least two years with adults (one year with children or adolescents), during which the individual cannot be without symptoms for more than two months at a time. Differential diagnosis must rule out schizoaffective, schizophrenic, schizophreniform, or delusional disorders. The symptoms must cause clinically significant distress or impairment in social, occupational, or other important areas of functioning. The diagnostician must also decide that the symptoms cannot be better explained by the direct physiological effects of a drug or medication or a general medical condition (e.g., hyperthyroidism).

Clinicians traditionally assumed that this disorder was rare, but recent evidence (Meyer & Deitsch, 1996) suggests that it is at least moderately common—0.4% to 1% in the general population, with a 15% to 50% risk of such persons later developing some form of bipolar disturbance. The usual age for onset is adolescence or early adulthood. Many factors can contribute to the development and maintenance of this disorder, including situational factors (e.g., stress and trauma), thought patterns (e.g., rigid and irrational beliefs), organic variables (e.g., chemical imbalances or substance abuse), behavioral factors (e.g., limited social skills or pattern of withdrawal), and consequential factors (e.g., reinforcement of depression or ignoring more adaptive behavior) (see Miller & Jackson, 1995).

It is generally assumed that an individual has at least one acquired or inherited vulnerability (diathesis) that interacts with specific stressors to cause the disorder. Theoreticians and therapists usually agree that no single model best explains the etiology and maintenance of this particular expression of mood disturbance (see Comer, 1995). Few would doubt, however, the need to carefully consider the potential contribution of biochemical and genetic factors in addition to the usual personal, interactional, and situational variables.

Treatment for cyclothymic disorder tends to follow strategies designed for the major affective disorders (see Meyer & Deitsch, 1996). The hypomanic phase of cyclothymia usually is not severe enough to warrant significant intervention. It tends to be viewed as the relief stage from the more prominent depressive periods. The latter is treated with a wide variety of cognitive-behavioral and interpersonal techniques, including stress reduction, cognitive restructuring, self-monitoring, contingency management, and lifestyle modification (see Miller & Jackson, 1995). Chemotherapy may be indicated for more serious depressive and hypomanic periods, but it is not used as often as it is with the major affective disorders. Because of the risk of the cyclothymic disorder developing into a more serious bipolar disturbance, the clinician should carefully monitor the symptoms throughout treatment and consider lithium therapy when indicated. When the hypomanic symptoms become troublesome, it may be necessary to teach the client and extended family ways to modify negative behavioral habits. As Goodwin and Jamison (1990) suggest, this may include helping hypomanic clients to focus their plans and activities, reinforce them for staying on task, and encouraging them to honor their interpersonal commitments.

With reference to matters of faith, standard psychotherapeutic and integrative approaches may be used in the treatment of the milder forms of cyclothymic disorder (see Jones & Butman, 1991). It is imperative to note, however, that a person's mood and behavior are strongly influenced by the reactions of others. Strategies that acknowledge and reinforce more adaptive interactional patterns in cyclothymic clients are critical for successful treatment and eventual recovery. Depressed clients need support and encouragement when they take risks and are growing as well as when they are discouraged and demoralized. Otherwise the clinician can get caught in a vicious cycle of depression and rescue, thereby inadvertently reinforcing depressed behavior.

References

American Psychiatric Association. (1994). *Diagnostic and statistical manual of mental disorders* (4th ed.). Washington, DC: Author.

Comer, R. (1995). *Abnormal psychology* (2nd ed.). New York: Freeman.

Goodwin, F., & Jamison, D. (1990). *Manic-depressive illness.* New York: Oxford University Press.

Jones, S., & Butman, R. (1991). *Modern psychotherapies.* Downers Grove, IL: InterVarsity Press.

Meyer, R., & Deitsch, S. (1996). *The clinician's handbook* (4th ed.). Boston: Allyn & Bacon.

Miller, W., & Jackson, K. (1995). *Practical psychology for pastors* (2nd ed.). Englewood Cliffs, NJ: Prentice-Hall.

R. E. BUTMAN

See DEPRESSION; MOOD DISORDERS.

Dd

Dance Therapy. *See* EXPRESSIVE THERAPY.

Dangerousness, Assessment of. *See* FORENSIC PSY-CHIATRY.

Daseinsanalysis. A method of existential psychotherapy developed by the Swiss psychiatrist Medard Boss. Analyzed by Sigmund Freud, Boss then studied under such eminent psychoanalysts as Reich, Jones, and Karen Horney before beginning private practice as a psychoanalyst at the age of 32. As a result of a personal friendship with existential philosopher Martin Heidegger, he gradually moved from classical Freudian thought toward an existential psychology. His method of therapy focused on the individual's existence or his specific way of being-in-the-world *(dasein)*.

> *See* EXISTENTIAL PSYCHOLOGY AND PSYCHO-THERAPY.

Daydreaming. A form of mental activity that, although it is nearly universal in human experience, has eluded systematic investigation until fairly recently. One reason for this is that daydreams are so personal, private, and often fleeting that they are difficult to study with objective methods. Nevertheless, considerable progress has been made through the convergence of data from different methods, yielding clues to the functions of daydreaming, how it changes over development, what conditions favor its expression, individual differences, and its relation to mental health.

Daydreaming is characterized by a shift of attention away from ongoing activity in the immediate environment toward one's internal thoughts and images. These may include more or less imaginary persons and sequences of events. Accompanying these experiences, commonly called fantasies or reveries, is usually some affect, often pleasure or excitement. Daydreaming tends to be thought of as a form of irresponsibility or even mental instability showing an inability to cope with life's circumstances. However, this stereotype must be questioned in light of current research.

Sigmund Freud contributed substantially to this common view of daydreaming as irresponsibility or even a sign of mental disorder. Although he acknowledged that daydreams can represent preparation for action, he felt that in most cases they represent a neurotic avoidance of action. In essence psychoanalytic theory states that all thought and imagination grow out of instinctive desires. These are in conflict with reality constraints and must therefore be suppressed. However, if a person lacks an acceptable outlet for these desires, he or she may find a substitute fulfillment in fantasy. The daydreamer derives pleasure vicariously through the exploits of fantasy characters.

The cognitive-affective view of Singer (1975) emphasizes a much more positive, adaptive interpretation of daydreaming. It is also derived from a much broader research base than was Freud's view. Singer views daydreaming as essentially a trial action. It is a process whereby individuals anticipate and plan for a range of possible future actions without committing themselves in action.

Despite the unrealistic quality of many daydreams, the content is practical. Surveys reveal that daydreaming is reported by virtually every category of persons, regardless of age, status, or sociocultural background. Most daydreams are future-oriented (although elderly persons often report reminiscent daydreams as well), and they deal with possible actions bearing some relation to the daydreamer's circumstances. Frequently there is a definite correlation between the content of early daydreams and actual accomplishments, suggesting that they helped the individual prepare and plan for future roles.

The cognitive-affective interpretation of daydreaming rests on Tomkins's (1962) theory of emotions, in which the individual is viewed according to the analogy of information processing. People are oriented toward understanding the environment and thus tend to assimilate new information into categories that have worked for them in the past. However, information that is very novel can evoke fear. The positive character of daydreams or fantasies lies in their permitting one to anticipate and deal with possible future situations and thus conquer debilitating fears at the same time.

Relaxed states of awareness, such as just before falling asleep, are often times of increased daydreaming. However, a surprising amount of daydreaming occurs during periods of mental productivity through a kind of time-sharing, or rapid shifting of attention and mood. Experiments have also shown that eye shifting occurs frequently when questions are posed that demand reflection. Apparently in some mental activity attention must be diverted away from the task in order to attend to one's private store of associations. As in daydreaming, the process is adaptive to the situation.

Singer's research has provided a good deal of support for a positive interpretation of daydreaming. He has shown that daydreaming is frequently adaptive. His research also suggests that daydreaming can under some circumstances even be associated with decreased reliance on drugs and less resort to aggression (1975).

The psychoanalytic interpretation is not well supported. Daydreams do not appear to automatically reduce the level of a need such as aggression through substitute fulfillment. According to the psychoanalytic view, one might expect television portrayals of violence to reduce tendencies toward aggression. On the contrary, people tend to respond more aggressively under certain conditions following the televised portrayals. This and other evidence suggests that daydreaming is not well explained as discharge of pent-up emotion. Therefore, whatever positive benefits might accrue from the activity are probably better explained as a consequence of shifting one's mood and attention toward future possibilities.

Christians can be challenged to take a broad view of daydreaming as one capacity that God has given us for our good. The lack of an obvious, immediate return on the investment should not necessarily cause one to scorn the activity as unprofitable. In this regard one recalls the scorn of Joseph's brothers ("Behold, this dreamer cometh," Gen. 37:19, KJV) in contrast with God's favor upon Joseph.

References

Singer, J. L. (1975). *The inner world of daydreaming.* New York: Harper & Row.
Tomkins, S. S. (1962). *Affect, imagery, consciousness* (2 vols.). New York: Springer.

D. R. RIDLEY

See IMAGERY, THERAPEUTIC USE OF; COGNITIVE PSYCHOLOGY.

Death and Dying. Life is animate being, and once it begins it inexorably leads to death. Death is a cessation of life, an irreversible state that is characterized by the cessation of all those processes that sustain life.

Life begins with conception, an event that is the starting point of its trajectory. At conception an organism possesses all the potential that it will ever have, although growth is necessary for the realiza-

tion of the potential. The process of growth continues to a point called maturity. At maturity the organism can maintain its integrity of replacing cells that are injured and die. This capacity to replace cells is, however, finite, and in time the process of repair cannot continue. At this point the organism reaches the senium. As growth decelerates, decay accelerates. The accelerating decay in time comprises the function of the cardiovascular and nervous system. As adequate functioning of these two systems is essential for life; the failure of either results in death.

Many things can interrupt the trajectory of life. Spontaneous or induced abortion, trauma, infection, cancer, or other diseases can occur during the period of growth and end life prematurely. These interruptions to a great extent determine life expectancy. In prehistory life was short. Disease or trauma ended life at an average age of 18 years. Even in ancient Greece and Rome one could not expect to live beyond 20 to 22 years. At the time of the colonization of America life expectancy had not increased beyond 35 years. The major prolongation has occurred in the twentieth century, rising from 47 years at the turn of the century to 71 years in 1971. This has since increased to just less than 80 years. This dramatic change has occurred because of the control of infectious disease through a variety of public health and treatment interventions.

Medical Death. Throughout the centuries the determination of death was simple. If a person fell unconscious someone would feel for the pulse, determine whether there was breathing, and look at the pupils. If there was no pulse or breath and the pupils were fixed, death was considered to have occurred. These criteria were called the heart-lung criteria. Over time physicians have been given the primary responsibility for determining death.

In recent years medicine has developed techniques to resuscitate and sustain life after a person has appeared clinically dead. These techniques have sustained the function of vital organs so that persons may appear dead even though their hearts continue to beat and their vital organs continue to function well enough to keep the largest part of the cells of the body alive. Although there is the appearance of life these persons are insensate and do not carry on the intellectual functions that characterize life. It has therefore been necessary to establish new criteria for a kind of death that is called brain death.

Brain death has been the subject of much discussion, a discussion that is the outgrowth of the need to determine the point at which life support systems can be discontinued with the certainty that there is no hope for life. With the advent of transplant surgery, first with kidney and later with heart and liver transplants, the need for definite criteria to determine brain death increased if transplantation was to be successful. As a result a study was conducted at the Harvard Medical School to establish criteria for brain death. A subsequent cooperative study conducted in several institutions further refined the criteria. They are unreceptivity and unresponsivity, no spontaneous or stimulated movements or breathing, no reflexes, and a flat electroencephalogram in the absence of drug intoxication and hypothermia. (The flat electroencephalogram indicates the absence of brain metabolic activity.)

When a patient meets these criteria for 24 hours or when there is obviously no hope, such as in traumatic lesions of the brain that are irremediable, brain death has occurred. When it is determined that brain death has occurred according to these criteria, it is permissible to discontinue life support systems and to harvest organs for transplant. Most countries in the Western world have enacted legislation to legally define brain death. The medical profession and the law have become increasingly comfortable with the concept of brain death.

Some Non-Christian Views of Death. The secular world and medicine have viewed death as an enemy, something to be avoided at all costs but that is nevertheless accepted as inevitable. Most persons have conflicts about dying. Some are afraid of "not being," being a coward, being punished, or being in pain. Others dislike the interruptions of their goals or are concerned about the impact of their death on their survivors. Scientific humanism, a philosophy to which most physicians subscribe, sees death as dissolution and destruction.

Since physicians see death as an enemy, their entire training and clinical efforts are directed toward the preservation of life. As a result physicians and other medical personnel are forced to maintain a detached concern for the dying and a matter-of-fact attitude about death.

Ancient Greeks, following Plato's teaching, believed in immortality of the soul. In their view the preexistent soul resumed its incorporeal existence after separation from the body and ascended toward truth through the process of education. Hindus and Buddhists teach that humans are caught on the wheel of circumstance and are born, suffer, and die only to start the cycle again in reincarnation. The only way to escape is to merge into the ultimate, an act accomplished through meditation, good works, or both. These latter religions deny death.

Muslims believe in an afterlife. They believe that there are rewards and punishments in the afterlife and that good works and obedience to the Quran result in rewards.

Judeo-Christian Views of Death. In Judaism and Christianity death is an enemy and is related to sin. It is the outgrowth of human rebellion. Because of Adam's and Eve's rejection of God's command, people have been appointed to die. Early Old Testament writings indicate that the body decayed and the soul ceased to be (Pss. 6:5; 88:10–12). Later, in the writings of the prophets, there was hope of resurrection (Isa. 26:19; Dan. 12:12). In the New Testament resurrection is not just a hope; it is a reality attested by the reality of Jesus' resurrection (John 5:28–29; 1 Cor. 15:1–32).

In the New Testament death is contrasted to life so that time and eternity have different dimensions. In life there is conflict; in eternity there is harmony. In life there is strife; in eternity there is peace. In life and eternity there are other contrasting qualities such as work versus rest, search versus discovery, suffering versus wholeness, faith versus doubt, yearning versus fulfillment, and imperfection and brokenness versus wholeness. In eternity there is no separation, and knowledge is complete.

These qualities are to be attained at the resurrection, which is to occur at the establishment of the new order. Souls are to sleep until it occurs. The Scriptures are, however, not clear as to when this new order is to be established. Jesus' promise to the thief ("today you will be with me in paradise") suggests an immediate transition. Paul seems to have held a similar view, although in his description of the return of Christ he notes that the dead will be raised to life at the sound of the last trumpet. Paul believed that the return of Christ was imminent. In the teaching of both Jesus and Paul there is a retention of the unity of the body, soul, and spirit, although the resurrection body has different dimensions from the one occupied in time.

The early church fathers held to the resurrection view of death, although Origen accepted the Platonic view. Tertullian was the first to propose a purgatory, in which prejudgment was to occur before the doomsday judgment. Augustine supported this view, which in time became the doctrine of the church. Interestingly enough, the doctrine is in accord with the Greek Platonic view instead of the apocalyptic view of Jesus and Paul. It was made the official doctrine of the Roman Catholic Church by the Council of Trent.

The Protestant view as set forth by Luther and Calvin denied the existence of purgatory and affirmed the reality of the resurrection. Protestant doctrinal positions are either vague or do not speak to the whereabouts of the soul from death until the resurrection, at which time the destiny of every soul to life or death will be decreed.

Dying. Every person comes to the knowledge that death is final and inevitable. When this realization occurs, whether in the process of meditating on one's life, when faced with imminent death, or when a loved one dies, there is the development of what is known as death anxiety. Death anxiety is separate and distinct from general anxiety. It occurs when it is impossible to discern the meaning of death.

There is extensive literature on this subject. The data are at times confusing because studies relating religiosity to death anxiety report conflicting results. Most of the reports do show a correlation between Christian faith and a reduction of death anxiety. The primary instruments used to determine the role of religion in reducing or increasing death anxiety are religiosity scales; that is, the stronger the faith of the person, the less the anxiety. Christians who are very religious, as evidenced by frequent church attendance and being born again, have less death anxiety. A critical study, however, reveals that spirituality, not religiosity, is a primary factor in reducing death anxiety. The terminally ill, mentally ill, and aged do not have more death anxiety than those who are not ill or aged, although one author reported less anxiety in highly religious, terminally ill persons. Those who are likely to have high levels are uninvolved with life with no well-defined purpose in life and those who are highly motivated to achievement (*see* Achievement, Need for).

Muslims and Jews tend to have less death anxiety if they have a strong faith and practice it.

Death anxiety can progress to a despair of death, one of the existential predicaments that human beings must face. Despair of death occurs if a person cannot discern meaning when he or she examines his or her life and then contemplates his or her certain death. Such despair can be a moment or a way of life.

When death is imminent, persons have needs that, if they are not met, can result in despair. These needs are to control pain, to retain dignity and self-worth as they participate in decisions that determine outcomes, and to receive love and affection from others in the environment. The despair that occurs is characterized by depression and feelings of hopelessness, helplessness, and withdrawal. The emotional trajectory of death has been described by Kübler-Ross (1969). Her five stages of dying are denial, anger, bargaining, depression, and acceptance. Other investigators have not confirmed her findings. In contrast, they find that initially there are two general responses to imminent death—despair and withdrawal.

The response to death by those who survive the loss of a loved one is grief. Grief is resolved by the decathexis of the lost love object. This process is accomplished by mourning. Facilitation of mourning is accomplished by talking about the death of the loved one to sympathetic listeners, and if the mourner is a Christian, by committing the eternal destiny of the dead person to God and surrendering one's love for the person to him. The empty spot in life can be filled with God's love.

Reference

Kübler-Ross, E. (1969). *On death and dying.* New York: Macmillan.

Additional Readings

Brooks, D. (1974). *Dealing with death.* Nashville: Broadman.

Gatch, M. M. (1969). *Death.* New York: Seabury.

Pressman, P., Lyons, J. S., Larson, D. B., & Gartner, J. (1992). Religion anxiety and fear of death. In J. F. Schumacher (Ed.), *Religion and mental health.* New York: Oxford University Press.

Schulz, R. (1978). *The psychology of death, dying and bereavement.* Reading, MA: Addison-Wesley.

W. P. Wilson

See Loss and Separation; Grief; Anxiety.

Decision Making. Cognitive psychologists and clinical psychologists have contributed to our understanding of decision making. Cognitive psychologists have investigated normative models and optimal decision strategies based on statistical concepts, and clinical psychologists have examined models and techniques applicable to their clients' needs.

Making a decision is often difficult because each alternative usually has many attributes, some attractive and some unattractive, and the optimal alternative rarely excels over the others. If a certain attribute is unattractive, the decision maker must either exclude the alternative or continue to consider it because its other attributes are attractive and compensate for the unattractive attribute. For example, a person may buy an expensive house because of its proximity to his or her workplace.

Compensatory models of decision making allow for a positive attribute to compensate for a negative attribute; an example is an additive model. An additive model considers attractive and unattractive attributes and calculates a score for each alternative. When confronted with a decision, people should list the advantages and disadvantages of each alternative. Each advantage is valued as +1 and each disadvantage as –1. If any attribute is particularly important, it is valued proportionately more heavily (e.g., a +3 or –3). Then the values for each alternative are summed; the highest positive value belongs to the best alternative.

Psychologists also study noncompensatory models, in which unattractive attributes exclude the alternative altogether. The advantage of these models is that they require no calculations. Tversky's 1972 model, called elimination by aspects, suggests that we no longer consider an alternative if an attribute of that alternative fails to meet some criterion. For example, if a couple is planning a vacation and can spend only one thousand dollars, they will first exclude those vacations that cost more than one thousand dollars. By selecting attributes and rejecting those not satisfying a certain criterion, they will gradually exclude alternatives until there remains a single alternative that meets all criteria. The decision depends on the order in which the attributes are considered. The likelihood of evaluating a particular attribute depends on its importance. An attribute judged to be important is likely to be selected for evaluation early in the process. This order of evaluation is critical; for example, if price is one of the last attributes considered, our travelers might have excluded all vacations costing under one thousand dollars early in the process.

Another noncompensatory model is the conjunctive model, which requires that every attribute of an alternative meet some criteria before the alternative is selected. It differs from elimination by aspects because people finish considering one alternative before they consider another. We will select the first alternative that satisfies all criteria. The conjunctive model involves a satisfying search.

Simon (1976) claimed that because of fatigue and time and knowledge limitations, we are frequently unable to consider several alternatives; consequently we often do not select the best alternative but instead settle for a good one—one that satisfies all minimum criteria.

From a statistical perspective the best decision is one that maximizes gain and minimizes loss. One technique that achieves this is the maximum expected value model (Coombs, Dawes, & Tversky, 1970). This model assumes that in every decision there are two or more alternatives and that each alternative has one or more consequences. Each consequence has a probability of occurrence and an overall value that can be positive (a gain) or negative (a loss). The expected value (EV) for each alternative is calculated by multiplying the probability of each of its consequences by its corresponding value and adding these products. The alternative with the more positive EV will be the best (and selected) alternative. However, because people do not always know the actual values and probabilities of certain events, the model does not always correctly predict behavior. For example, gamblers play games that have negative EVs; people buy insurance in spite of its negative EV.

With the subjective expected utility model, Payne (1973) modified the concept of expected value to make it more descriptive of actual behavior. Payne changed the value of a consequence to its utility. Utility is the subjective value of a consequence, or what the outcome is actually worth to the person. If someone enjoys gambling, gambling has utility apart from any money won or lost. People buy insurance because they appreciate the peace of mind that its purchase brings. Payne also replaced probabilities with subjective probabilities, or what people believe the probability of an outcome is. Subjective expected utility is calculated the same way as expected value, replacing probabilities with subjective probabilities and values with utilities. Because Payne's model is based on subjective information, it is more predictive of people's behavior than is the expected value model.

Sometimes important decisions are based on a single criterion. For example, people in difficulty may consult a doctor or lawyer recommended by a trusted friend and follow whatever course of action is suggested. Sometimes people use a single moral precept as their only rule when deciding to help someone in trouble (Schwartz, 1970). If they realize that someone needs help, they give it without any deliberation. They may think it immoral to consider anything else.

Some problems treated by counselors either originated with or are increased by poor decisions or a reluctance to make decisions. Janis and Mann (1977) demonstrated the benefits of teaching clients better decision-making skills. Clients can benefit by being taught to recognize the potential consequences of events, to consider more alternatives and their consequences (to prevent making a decision without sufficient deliberation), to develop skill and

confidence in their ability to make decisions, and to learn to accept and live with potential negative consequences of decisions. Some successful intervention techniques include decision counseling, the use of systematic balance sheets, outcome psychodrama, and emotional inoculation against postdecisional regret (see Janis & Mann, 1977, for further clinical applications).

References

Coombs, C. H., Dawes, R. M., & Tversky, A. (1970). *Mathematical psychology: An elementary introduction.* Englewood Cliffs, NJ: Prentice-Hall.

Janis, I. L., & Mann, L. (1977). *Decision making.* New York: Free Press.

Payne, J. W. (1973). Alternative approaches to decision making under risk. *Psychological Bulletin, 80,* 439–453.

Schwartz, S. (1970). Moral decision making and behavior. In J. Macaulay & L. Berkowitz (Eds.), *Altruism and helping behavior.* New York: Academic.

Simon, H. A. (1976). *Administrative behavior: A study of decision-making processes in administrative organization* (3rd ed.). New York: Free Press.

Tversky, A. (1972). Elimination by aspects: A theory of choice. *Psychological Review, 79,* 281–299.

D. Needham

See Thinking; Cognitive Psychology.

Decision Making, Group. The effects of interpersonal interaction on the processes and outcomes arrived at by persons defined as a group. Since definitions of the term *group* include the provision that the persons forming the assemblage have influence on one another, the task of those studying group decision making is to understand how personal and interpersonal factors affect group functioning. Group decision making has stimulated considerable research interest by social scientists, especially by the branch of psychology known as social psychology.

For group members the presence of others may stimulate and energize (a phenomenon called social facilitation), or inhibit and suppress (phenomena called social loafing and self-censorship). On the one hand the arousal associated with social facilitation contributes to the critical mass of ideas required to elevate the quality of group discourse to an optimum level. The stimulation and energy provided by a supportive group may lead to novel and creative ideas (a process termed brainstorming) whose synthesis may lead to a group decision of superior quality. Ironically on the other hand group decisions make it difficult to identify the contributions of any single group member, a situation that may tempt group members to social loafing (which means they work less hard than they would if working alone). Only when members feel they have a unique contribution to make or find the task challenging and involving will they put forth an optimum effort.

Research has shown that communication within a group may be inhibited if group members focus immediate attention on the shortcomings of ideas suggested by group members. The inhibition that results from critical comments from group members means that some points that would lead to a more satisfactory decision are suppressed (referred to as self-censorship). Self-censorship may also lead to a group decision that contains weakness or error, since those who might expose that weakness are afraid to share their concerns.

When the inhibition of group communication is accompanied by strong pressure toward conformity, avoidance of opposing points of view, and certainty that the group is invulnerable to aversive consequences, the group members have fallen victim to the phenomenon labeled groupthink (Janis, 1983). Groupthink leads to faulty group decisions because the focus is on group unity and uniformity and not on reaching the best decision.

Research has also shown that group decisions may be polarized; that is, the group decision may be more extreme than the individual positions held by group members. If group members are leaning toward a more liberal or risky position, the group outcome is polarized in that direction, a phenomenon termed the risky shift. A conservative shift may occur if the original tendencies of the group are in that direction; however, the group decision is likely to be more conservative than the position of any individual.

Group process strategies affect efficiency and satisfaction with decisions. The decision strategy labeled consensus requires time and member patience and can be made difficult or impossible by the presence of a single obstinate group member. True consensus, however, generates satisfaction and support for decisions by group members. Many groups use voting to reach decisions; however, group members on the losing side of the vote may be dissatisfied and fail to support the group decision.

Leaders can increase commitment to group process and decision by assuring that all group members are involved; involvement leads to greater satisfaction with the group and its decisions. Leaders may be counterproductive if they err on the side of either domination or laxity. Excessive control results in groups whose members are reluctant to share their views and who are afraid to decide against the wishes of the leader. Too little direction can produce group meetings that deteriorate into aimless and nonproductive chatter that produces weak decisions.

Reference

Janis, I. (1983). *Groupthink* (2nd ed. rev.). Boston: Houghton Mifflin.

Additional Reading

Myers, D. (1993). *Social psychology* (4th ed.). New York: McGraw-Hill.

D. KAUFFMANN

See THINKING; COGNITIVE PSYCHOLOGY.

Decompensation. A breakdown in the operation of defense systems that previously maintained the person's optimal psychic functioning. An example of such a breakdown of the defense system is a relapse in the schizophrenic patient.

See DEFENSE MECHANISMS.

Defense Mechanisms. However negative Sigmund Freud may have been toward religion, no honest and competent scholar can deny the monumental contributions he made to psychological thought. Among his greatest achievements was the careful way in which he documented the complexity of the human heart. Freud, the founder of psychoanalysis and consequently of all psychodynamic approaches to psychotherapy, systematically studied the incredibly subtle ways in which people try to fool themselves and others. Psychological defense mechanisms can be viewed as forms of dishonesty.

Freud ignored the moral implications of his insights by claiming that defense mechanisms are by definition unconscious. The person defending is neither aware of the defensive process nor purposely invoking it. According to the orthodox Freudian view, if the person is aware of what he or she is doing, one cannot correctly speak of the operation of a defense. Thus, while repression is one of the cardinal Freudian defenses, suppression—consciously putting material out of one's mind—is not.

From the vantage point of contemporary behavioral science, defense mechanisms are a subset of a broader class of phenomena: coping strategies. They are those coping strategies we engage in without awareness, in order to keep ourselves from experiencing anxiety. Anxiety is prompted by unwanted thoughts, feelings, and impulses. To prevent or bind our anxieties, we try to keep these thoughts from entering consciousness.

There has been much debate among psychodynamically oriented theorists over which of the defense mechanisms is primary, the progenitor of all the others. While some have contended that the prototypical defense is projection and others have suggested that it is denial, the traditional psychoanalytic view has stressed repression. Accordingly, repression is said to be the most primitive of all the defenses. It is the simple exclusion from awareness of troubling psychic contents.

A psychological disorder in which repression can be seen pivotally to operate is a panic attack. People with this diagnosis have acute attacks of anxiety, often quite severe, which seem not to be triggered by any specific event. They sweat, shake, have rapid heartbeats, and so on. Typically and significantly, such persons have little understanding of what underlies their anxiety. Psychotherapy usually reveals that the person is troubled by certain ideas, sentiments, or inclinations that he or she does not want to face. The anxiety attacks occur when repression fails to keep these unwanted contents completely out of consciousness.

Closely related to repression is denial. While many clinicians use the two terms interchangeably, there is a technical difference between them. Repression is keeping from awareness that which is inside one's own psyche. Denial is refusing to admit into awareness that which comes from one's environment—what others say or do. Some people, for instance, will not acknowledge even to themselves that someone else is behaving in an unfriendly manner. They are said, unkindly, to be too stupid to be insulted. In reality their failure to comprehend hostility has nothing to do with their intellectual endowment or the lack of it. Another example would be the husband or wife who does not see what all the neighbors can—that his or her spouse is involved with someone else.

Projection is refusing to come to terms with our own attributes (e.g., anger or lust) by seeing them in others but not in ourselves. On days when one feels irritable, for example, others may seem excessively irritable. Sometimes disturbed persons will claim that others are trying to seduce them when such persons are merely projecting their own libidinal inclinations. Although we usually project unfavorable characteristics onto others, it is also possible to see in them our own favorable qualities, such as trustworthiness and valor.

Rationalization is the process of trumping up justifications for what we do, think, and feel. Rationalizations are excuses, offered sometimes to others but perhaps more often to ourselves. The businessperson who, sensing potential advantage, unethically dissolves a partnership may view himself or herself as taking this action for a good reason, perhaps the incompetence of the disenfranchised partner. A more primitive example of rationalization is the delinquent who maintains that he stole the car because its owner left the keys in the ignition.

Intellectualization is closely related to rationalization and involves the substitution of safe intellectual concerns for dangerous ideas and impulses. Acting almost as verbal magic, intellectualization is an attempt to control the world and to cope with inner conflicts through thinking. Intellectualization prevents us from turning our attention toward unpleasant mental material (e.g., feelings of injury, grief, or anger). People who intellectualize often seem to others to have no feelings. In actuality such feelings they do have are defensively blocked out by excessive cogitation.

While intellectualization involves an exaggerated reliance on words—thinking is carried along on a train of words—isolation is the defense of compartmentalizing troublesome aspects of our mental life without doing a lot of thinking. Upsetting mental conflicts can be stripped of their emotional power by separating them from their natural affective significance. These conflicts become detached from the rest of the personality.

Dissociation is a related defense that involves splitting off some aspect of ourselves. Sleepwalking is a well-known form of dissociation. A less well-known form is fugue, in which a person may suddenly travel to another city, amnesic with respect to his or her ongoing life, and begin another existence. One patient, for example, would blank out and find herself in a phone booth, many miles from home, telephoning the police.

Undoing is the attempt to nullify or cancel out the significance of an earlier action. Everyday apologies often serve an undoing function. We say "I'm sorry" to make it almost as if we had not done whatever it is for which we claim to be repentant. One advantage of such apologies is that they make us less likely to pay for the social consequences of our actions. A more pathological form of undoing can be seen in Lady Macbeth's washing the imaginary blood from her hands. Undoing can take a compulsive form. Pathological repentances are also extreme versions of undoing.

Reaction formation is the substitution in consciousness of what is unconsciously true. Schoolchildren provide us with a particularly charming example of reaction formation when, embarrassed by their budding romantic sentiments, they suddenly "hate" members of the opposite sex. Adamant social reformers are also sometimes defending against their own deeper wishes and impulses. Note, however, that one should not assume that a defense is necessarily operating in all social reform. Not all persons who crusade against pornography can be said to be enacting psychological defenses against their own lust. Reaction formation is also used to defend against anger. Sometimes, for example, we witness people whom we know to be quite angry acting inordinately nice.

Ambivalence is regarded as a defensive maneuver by certain theorists. Preventing ourselves from making psychic or behavioral commitments by endlessly posing reasons "why not" is a common strategy for guarding against the anxiety that often attends commitment. As soon as one thinks of doing such and such, reasons for doing the opposite may come to mind. Dialectic thinking is characteristic of intelligent human beings, but it can become a way of life—a way to avoid making a mistake.

Displacement is attaching to a neutral object mental contents that were originally attached to someone or something else. The person who kicks the dog on the way into the house is probably angry at a boss or co-worker. Parents often take out on children what they feel toward each other. The payoff in displacement is obvious. Telling off one's boss can be hazardous. Fighting openly with one's spouse can also lead to more retaliation than children are immediately able to mete out.

Identification can operate as a defense against one's own powerlessness or lack of perceived virtue. An especially tragic example of identification is when prisoners of war internalize the antisocial values of their captors. Beyond such tangible payoffs as avoiding torture or acquiring more rations, identification with the aggressor serves to diffuse the awfulness of the experience as well as to bind one's own dangerous counteraggressive impulses. Most identifications are far less dramatic. Children growing up normally identify with their parents, one result of which is internalization of the parents' values.

Identification is sometimes closely tied up with another defense, compensation. Our culture is replete with stories of skinny or afflicted youths turning themselves, through herculean efforts, into wonders of athletic prowess. Teddy Roosevelt is one example. Compensation is ordinarily used as a defense against felt inadequacy.

Although most treatises on defense mechanisms do not discuss mania, frenetic activity is probably used by many people to ward off a lurking depression. One theory of psychotically manic individuals is that they too are using activity as a defense against depression. Activity may serve to distract one from inner misery.

Freud maintained that there is at least one defense mechanism that is usually constructive: sublimation. This is the changing of baser desires into socially acceptable ones. An example would be the artist who takes out his aggression by constructing highly creative and aesthetic paintings. A more neurotic form of sublimation is the individual who makes up for lack of marital intimacy by working 16 hours a day instead of having an affair.

Depending on the literature one reads, lists of defense mechanisms vary from just a few to more than 20. This article discusses those that are common to most lists. Theorists making finer discriminations among the defenses also write about other mechanisms, such as insulation, substitution, projective identification, introjection, and incorporation.

It is important to keep in mind that defense mechanisms are metaphors. Mental health professionals often forget this and regard the classical defenses almost as physical realities. In fact defenses are models, approximate representations of how human beings deal with anxiety-provoking material.

Additional Readings

Fenichel, O. (1945). *The psychoanalytic theory of neurosis*. New York: Norton.
Freud, A. (1937). *The ego and the mechanisms of defense*. London: Hogarth.
Laughlin, H. P. (1979). *The ego and its defenses* (2nd ed.). New York: Aronson.

C. W. McLemore

See Coping Skills Therapies; Anxiety; Psychoanalytic Psychology; Psychoanalytic Psychotherapy.

Deindividuation. A condition in which one's identifiability is decreased and internal constraints against certain actions are more likely to be abandoned, resulting in behavior that a person might otherwise not engage in. Examples of deindividuated behavior can be found in both common and uncommon experiences such as doing more tricking than treating on Halloween or ridiculing a referee at a basketball game to encouraging an individual to jump from a high-rise building (as did a group of ordinary citizens in New York City in 1984) or engaging in a public lynching. The experience of deindividuation is most likely to occur in group situations that foster anonymity and in which the individual loses a sense of self-awareness and evaluation apprehension (Myers, 1990).

The key factor underlying the deindividuated state is the person's sense of physical anonymity. In a study conducted on Halloween (Diener, Fraser, Beaman, & Kelem, 1976), anonymous children were more likely to take extra candy than what was allowed by a homeowner who left the room than were children who were asked to identify themselves by name and address. Other experiments (see Myers, 1990) suggest that even wearing uniforms under some conditions may foster deindividuated behavior. This may help explain what is often described as the brutal behavior engaged in by law enforcement officials. But this does not mean that deindividuation always displays the seamy side of human nature. The uniform that represents prosocial behavior, such as a nurse's uniform, may produce a deindividuated state that encourages even more humane behavior.

The nature and function of the group are also important factors. If groups have clearly identifiable normative behavior that is antisocial in nature and the group's structure protects the person from individual accountability, then it may be easy for the individual to engage in a behavior that would otherwise be unthinkable. If the person's individual identity is heightened, there is a greater sense of evaluation apprehension (i.e., the sense that I am being evaluated by others) that is sometimes lost in the context of group behavior. The behavior itself now belongs to the group. Perhaps the most poignant example of the group's power to weaken individual identity is that which is found in street gangs, though the group need not require formal membership (witness the deindividuating influence often experienced by rabid fans at a sports arena).

References

Diener, E., Fraser, S. C., Beaman, A. L., & Kelem, R. T. (1976). Effects of deindividuation variables on stealing among Halloween trick-or-treaters. *Journal of Personality and Social Psychology, 33,* 178–183.
Myers, D. G. (1990). *Social psychology* (3rd ed.). New York: McGraw-Hill.

P. C. Hill

See Individuation; Life Span Development.

Déjà Vu. The illusion of familiarity. The individual experiencing this encounters some new situation with the distinct feeling of having had the same experience previously. It is an illusion not of the senses but of memory. It occurs in healthy, normal individuals, particularly in a state of exhaustion, but more frequently in neurotics and psychotics. Sigmund Freud suggested that the déjà vu feelings correspond to the memory of an unconscious fantasy. Others have viewed it as an example of generalization from past experience. Plato took it as evidence of a previous existence.

D. G. BENNER

Delinquency. *See* JUVENILE DELINQUENCY.

Delirium. A psychiatric syndrome of transient disorganization of cognitive and perceptual functions due to metabolic disturbance of the central nervous system. Delirious patients are confused because something is wrong with the brain's functioning. Some terms that are used almost synonymously with delirium are acute brain syndrome, acute confusional state, and toxic psychosis.

The patient may initially complain of several of the following symptoms: irritability, restlessness, fatigue, hypersensitivity to light and noise, disturbing dreams, or brief hallucinations. Examination of the patient may discover a cognitive impairment that can range from mild disorientation to a complete insensibility. Consciousness is disturbed in terms of reduced clarity of awareness of the environment and reduced ability to focus, sustain, or shift attention. Memory is faulty, especially for the recall of recent events. If given instructions for a specific task, the patient will have difficulty in maintaining attention and directing thought in a purposive manner.

The cause of delirium is always organic: the disturbances of central nervous system metabolism brought on by general medical conditions, poisons, or drug side effects or withdrawal. Surgery, burns, head trauma, seizure, AIDS, cerebral vascular accident, and malnutrition can make a patient delirious. The range of poisons that can induce delirium is wide: plants, mushrooms, venom from reptile bites or insect stings, industrial chemicals (e.g., bromides, solvents, glue, exhaust fumes). Medications for arthritis and hypertension are frequent offenders. Central anticholinergic syndrome is a rare complication of heterocyclic antidepressants. Drugs that can induce delirium include alcohol, LSD, and PCP. Persons addicted to alcohol, sedatives, and tranquilizers (e.g., diazepam) may experience delirium during withdrawal.

About a fifth of all general hospital patients become delirious, and this proportion rises to half of the aged patients. This is due to the combination of the reduced ability of the aging body to tolerate medications and the fact that the average nursing home patient ingests more than four prescription medications daily. Infections leading to a high fever are common in many medical inpatients. Dehydration brought on by vomiting and diarrhea is frequently found in medical patients. The failure of organs, such as the liver, kidneys, pancreas, thyroid, or parathyroids can also induce delirium. Any tissue abnormality around the brain (e.g., tumor, abscess, cyst) can exert a pressure, making the patient delirious. Environmental causes (e.g., temperature extremes, toxins) are also possible causal agents. Nutritional disturbances can bring on delirium. Deficiencies in B vitamins or an overabundance of A or D can occur. Potassium metabolism, which may be upset by medication for controlling hypertension, is another culprit.

The diagnosis of delirium is twofold. The first step is to verify that the patient is merely delirious rather than suffering from some other psychiatric disorder. Schizophrenia, anxiety, and mania share one or more symptoms with delirium, but the overlap is not as great as the key differences. Delirium has a more severe overall cognitive impairment. Delirium has a greater symptom overlap with dementia; *DSM-IV* criteria suggest that the diagnosis of delirium is made only when symptoms could not be better accounted for by a preexisting or evolving dementia. What distinguishes between these organic brain syndromes is that delirium has a more rapid onset, hallucinations, disturbed sleep cycle, and fluctuating course. These disorders are not mutually exclusive and can co-exist simultaneously. Perhaps a third of demented aged admitted to psychiatric hospitals have delirium superimposed on a preexisting dementia.

The second diagnostic step involves confirmation of an organic etiology. Medical records indicating known diseases, prescriptions, and allergies are most helpful. So are reports about the onset and course. When external data are not sufficient, laboratory investigations can usually find the cause.

The prognosis for delirium is usually favorable. Most patients recover from the organic cause and regain normal brain functioning. If recovery does not take place, the most likely course is a progression to stupor, coma, and death. If there is neither recovery nor death, then it is likely that the diagnosis of delirium was in error.

Management of delirium is usually best accomplished in a medical environment, with the most important factor being the elimination of the underlying organic cause. If the body's own recuperative powers are not sufficient, medication or surgery might be required. Needs for sleep, nutrition, comfort, and fluid must be met. The optimal environment for recovery is a quiet, well-lighted room and the provision of orienting and reassuring information. Any attempt at psychotherapy should be within this context and be supportive and directive.

Additional Reading

Lipowski, Z. J. (1990). *Delirium: Acute confusional states.* New York: Oxford University Press.

T. L. BRINK

See DEMENTIA.

Delirium Tremens. An acute brain syndrome characterized by terrifying hallucinatory delirium and tremors of the hands, tongue, and lips. Caused by alcohol or drug intoxication, delirium tremens rarely occurs before the age of 30 and follows at least a three- to four-year history of alcoholism or drug addiction. It was first named and described by Thomas Sutton in 1813. Delirium tremens may occur any time in chronic alcoholism but usually follows a prolonged drinking spree or infection.

The initial signs of delirium tremens include rapid pulse, confusion, headache, fever, loss of appetite, nausea, perspiration, and dehydration. The delirium that follows may last from three to six days and frequently involves visual hallucinations, particularly of animals like snakes or rats. Auditory hallucinations are generally of a derogatory nature, with references to persecution or castration. The resulting memory impairment and disorientation may lead to suicide or homicide. The alcoholic's emotional state may waver from panic, anxiety, and terror to complete indifference. Often the delirium is followed by a deep sleep and amnesia, and the person returns to the same cycle of alcohol or drug abuse. Repeated alcohol intoxication leads to nuclear destruction of nerve cells and death. If the condition is untreated, mortality rate may be as high as 15%, although this is now rare. However, death can occur suddenly as a result of hypothermia or vascular collapse.

D. L. SCHUURMAN

See ALCOHOL-INDUCED DISORDERS.

Delusion. A false belief based on incorrect inference about reality that is firmly sustained despite what almost everyone else believes and incontrovertible evidence to the contrary (*DSM-IV*; American Psychiatric Association, 1994). Delusions are usually a sign of psychosis, since people hold them tenaciously regardless of reality and how these beliefs affect themselves or others.

Delusions are usually classified as bizarre (fragmented, poorly formed ideas) or systematized (fixed, elaborate ideas related to a few false beliefs). Bizarre delusions, such as "someone removed my heart and replaced it with an alien's heart," are usually associated with schizophrenia. Systematized delusions, such as "the FBI is monitoring me," are usually associated with delusional disorder or paranoid personality disorder. Bizarre delusions generally respond better to treatment (medication and a structured, therapeutic environment), while systematized delusions are often refractory to treatment.

There are several types of delusions: persecutory (I am being cheated or harassed), jealous (my spouse is being unfaithful), reference (events, objects, or persons have special relevance to me), grandiose (I have unusual importance or power), erotomanic (although she won't admit it, she is deeply in love with me), and somatic (something is wrong with my throat). Delusions of persecution and jealousy are the most common.

Several causes of delusions have been proposed, but no one cause has been found to trigger all or most delusions. Projection and reaction formation are the central defense mechanisms characteristic of delusional patients. It is believed that these patients reduce their anxiety by projecting their own impulses and fears onto others. The result is that they have to control others or distance themselves to maintain decreased anxiety. Many experts believe that delusions are developed as a way to explain strange or anomalous experiences. One school of thought suggests that delusional patients have normal reasoning processes, based on a false premise about an anomalous experience. The other school maintains that these patients utilize flawed reasoning processes.

Reference

American Psychiatric Association. (1994). *Diagnostic and statistical manual of mental disorders* (4th ed.). Washington, DC: Author.

C. D. CAMPBELL

See DELUSIONAL DISORDER.

Delusional Disorder. Delusional disorder is one among several types of psychotic disorders, all of which involve grossly impaired reality testing. The core feature of delusional disorder is one or more nonbizarre delusions that last for at least one month. These delusions involve situations that could plausibly happen in life. Apart from the direct impact of the delusion, persons with this disorder appear normal to others and are able to function adequately in everyday life. If the person has a mood episode (such as depression) while having delusions, it must be relatively brief in order to warrant the delusional disorder diagnosis. The delusions must not be directly caused by substance use or a general medical condition in order to fit the criteria for this diagnosis.

There are seven types of delusional disorders. In the erotomanic type, the person erroneously believes that someone is in love with her or him. The love object often is someone famous and/or of higher status than the individual. Celebrities are plagued by letters, phone calls, and even stalking by people with erotic delusions.

People with grandiose delusions believe that they possess special talents, powers, or identities (such as having found a cure for cancer or that they are Albert Einstein). Grandiose delusions sometimes have religious content such as a conviction that one is Jesus Christ or a special messenger from God.

Jealous delusions involve unfounded suspicions that a spouse or lover is unfaithful. So-called evidence of infidelity is construed through grossly faulty logic. A person with this type of disorder may go so far as to hire a private detective to spy on one's spouse.

The persecutory type is the most prevalent kind of delusional disorder. In this type the person is convinced that others are plotting against him or her to cheat, poison, malign, or otherwise harm that person. In retaliation for these fantasized attacks or insults, such persons often get litigious and repeatedly file lawsuits against imagined offenders.

A somatic type of delusion involves a person's distortion of bodily functions or sensations. Such a person may be convinced that she has contracted AIDS in a swimming pool, despite negative medical test results and the extreme implausibility of her belief.

When more than one type of delusion is present, a mixed type of delusional disorder is diagnosed. An unspecified type of this disorder is diagnosed when the nature of the delusional belief cannot be determined.

In considering a diagnosis of delusional disorder, it is important to take into account the person's religious and cultural background. Some religions and cultures have beliefs that are sanctioned throughout the community but that would be considered delusional outside of it. An example of this would be the virgin birth of Jesus and his bodily resurrection after he died. These are core beliefs for many within the Christian faith. However, these beliefs might appear delusional to someone who had no knowledge of Christian doctrines.

The cause of this disorder is unknown, and its treatment is notoriously difficult due to the deeply ingrained nature of the delusions. A treatment plan must first and foremost involve gaining the person's trust and establishing a therapeutic alliance. The therapist must respond empathically to the person without buying into the delusion. This is best done by reflecting concern over feelings of frustration, Fear, inadequacy, or loneliness that the person suffers as a byproduct of the delusion.

Concern for the safety of the patient and others must be considered early in treatment, as a number of the types of delusional disorder involve a propensity for Violence. In the erotomania and jealous subtypes, there is a danger that the patient might murder the love object in extreme circumstances. The persecutory type also involves the potential use of violence in retaliation for fantasized mistreatment by others. It may be necessary for a victim of such a person to obtain a restraining order for protection. Psychiatric hospitalization might also be necessary if the person is in clear danger of harming someone.

It is useful to refer the person for a medication evaluation as soon as possible in treatment, while being careful not to shatter the fragile bond of trust between patient and clinician. Antipsychotic and antianxiety medications have a good track record of relieving symptoms of this disorder.

Supportive therapy for delusional disorder aims toward a goal of helping patients adjust better to their environment rather than trying to cure the disorder itself. Social isolation is often a result of people finding the patient's delusions disconcerting. Therefore, in supportive therapy the patient is encouraged to refrain from discussing the delusional beliefs with others. Coping mechanisms such as humor, relaxation training, and assertiveness training are other useful techniques to work on in supportive therapy.

N. S. THURSTON

See PSYCHOTIC DISORDERS.

Dementia. A deterioration of mental condition. Dementia usually occurs in later life, though rarer cases of presenile dementia are diagnosed. Terms that are used synonymously with dementia are chronic brain syndrome, organic mental syndrome, and senile confusional state.

The incidence of dementia is less than 10% of persons over age 65 but perhaps a quarter of those over age 80 and half of all nursing home patients. Dementia is not the most common mental disorder in later life (that is depression), nor should it be considered an inevitable concomitant of aging. Many individuals are able to preserve cognitive functioning into their ninth decade.

The onset of most cases of dementia tends to be gradual. The first mental changes may be heightened rigidity, suspiciousness, crankiness, or depression. As the disorder progresses, deficits in short-term memory become pronounced. Patients may be able to recall in great detail what happened years ago but be unable to remember the answers to a question given five minutes ago. One woman in a nursing home could remember how to play a song she had learned in a Prohibition-era honky tonk, but when the other residents applauded and asked for another song, she played it again. The ability to follow instructions also decreases, leading to the consternation of the patient's caregivers. Disorientation in time develops: the patient does not know which day of the week it is. Then comes disorientation in place: the patient may get lost, even in familiar territory. The patient may develop aphasias, apraxias, perseveration, and/or social withdrawal. In later stages the recognition of significant others may be lost, along with bowel and bladder functions. Death usually occurs when the patient loses the ability to swallow.

Dementia is different in kind rather than degree from the forgetfulness of which most elders complain. Benign senescent forgetfulness is an age-associated memory impairment that does not have a serious prognostic implication. Neither is dementia analogous to a second childhood. Childish playfulness stems from a lack of knowledge about proper adult roles, whereas demented elders may manifest such behavior because of impaired memory, confusion, or sensory/motor limitations. Some nursing home patients may act more like children if the staff rewards such behavior with attention, especially affection.

More than 50 different diseases can bring about dementia. Huntington's chorea is due entirely to the presence of a single dominant gene. Creutzfeld-Jakob disease is caused by viral infection, perhaps due to the consumption of insufficiently cooked bovine brain. Kuru, a viral infection in Melanesia, may be spread by ritual cannibalism. Hydrocephalus is excessive pressure of cerebrospinal fluid in the ventricles, impairing the functioning of the cortex. Chronic alcohol abuse, tertiary syphilis (general paresis), AIDS, encephalitis, subdural hemotoma, Parkinson's Disease, intracranial neoplasm, head trauma, and meningitis are other possible causes.

The majority of the demented geriatric patients suffer from Alzheimer's Disease (also known as senile dementia of the Alzheimer type), which results in specific degenerative diseases in the brain's tissues. A similar though rarer disorder is Pick's disease, which usually affects people in their fifties and is located primarily in the frontal and temporal lobes. These changes can be observed postmortem or via computerized tomography.

Before 1980 it was assumed that the principal cause of dementia is cerebral arteriosclerosis, a hardening of the brain's arteries that results in less oxygen being supplied to the brain's tissues. The current consensus is that diminished blood flow is a significant causal factor in only a minority of dementia cases of later life. Reduced oxygen may be more a symptom of reduced cortical functioning rather than its cause. A greater cause of dementia posed by the vascular system may be multi-infarct dementia—many tiny strokes that have the combined impact of diminishing cognitive ability without bringing on the paralysis characteristic of the larger strokes.

The diagnosis of dementia cannot be based solely upon the patient's complaints of a failing memory. There is no correlation between the self-reported memory capacity and memory capacity as indicated by objective tests. Many of the elders who complain the most about diminishing memory are well within the normal range but suffer from depression. Some thoroughly demented patients perceive no difficulty with their memories.

The first step should be brief psychological screening tests. Use of the Bender-Gestalt, Intelligence Quotient test scales, or other tests devised for other purposes or other age groups should be avoided. Questions that test the capacity for orientation in space and time are useful. The ability to draw a clock face with its hands and dial is useful. Focusing the examination on short-term memory tends to neutralize some of the confounding variables and give a truer indication of dementia. Many of these tests (e.g., the Mental Status Questionnaire or the Folstein Mini Mental Status Exam) have a greater sensitivity than specificity: it is more likely that some normal elders will be misdiagnosed as having dementia than that seniles will score in the normal range.

Whenever these screening tests suggest the presence of dementia, a comprehensive neurological examination is appropriate.

One diagnostic difficulty is to distinguish organically based dementia from a pseudodementia due to depression. Dementia is usually characterized by a gradual onset, while depression may have a rapid progression of symptoms in the wake of environmental stress or loss. Depressed patients are more likely to complain of memory loss and give "don't know" answers. Purely demented patients are more likely to attempt to conceal cognitive deficits or to give ludicrous answers rather than admit that they do not know the answer. One complication for the differential diagnosis of depression is that self-rating scales (e.g., the Geriatric Depression Scale) may lose their validity as senile confusion increases: the patient may be unable to understand the questions. Another problem with differential diagnosis is that the two disorders are not mutually exclusive. Awareness of cognitive decline can produce a depressive reaction, and a sizable minority of early-stage dementia patients develop a clinically significant depression.

Another possibility is that the cognitive impairments are the result of a delirium or an amnestic disorder rather than dementia. This may be the case with many confused elders admitted to general hospitals. What is needed is a knowledge of the details about the onset, course, and laboratory testing. The complicating factors are that delirious patients cannot take memory tests and these disorders are not mutually exclusive.

Even with computerized tomography and spinal taps, the diagnosis of dementia is far from exact. Some patients are falsely labeled as demented, while other cases might go unnoticed until autopsy.

Treatment for dementia can be both medical and psychosocial. About a fifth of dementia patients have a treatable organic cause (e.g., hydrocephalus, which is treatable by surgery). The use of medications has been much debated. While some patients report some benefit from tacrine or Hydergine, some report side effects from the former and most report little benefit from the latter. Another controversial issue is the use of psychiatric medications (e.g., antidepressants, antipsychotics) with dementia patients. In many nursing homes the antidepressants are probably underutilized while the antipsychotics are often given to diminish behaviors that the staff may find objectionable or inconvenient.

Psychotherapy, especially in groups, can be a help in reducing depression and in getting patients to make maximum utilization of remaining memory potential. Therapeutic milieus that seek to motivate, stimulate, and orient the patient can be highly successful. Another perspective on comprehensive treatment is to focus on the needs of caregivers in the family: they need support and consolation for the stress and sacrifices they undergo. Families that opt for institutionalization may need help in resolving guilt feelings.

Additional Readings

Albert, M. L., & Knoefel, J. E. (1994). *Clinical neurology of aging* (2nd ed.). New York: Oxford University Press.

Emery, V. O. B., & Oxman, T. E. (Eds.). (1994). *Dementia: Presentations, differential diagnosis and nosology.* Baltimore: Johns Hopkins University Press.

Fitten, L. J. (Ed.). (1994). *Dementia and cognitive impairments.* New York: Springer.

Terry, R., Katzman, R., & Bick, K. L. (Eds.). (1993). *Alzheimer disease.* New York: Raven.

T. L. Brink

See Delirium; Gerontology.

Dementia Praecox. The term, coined in 1857, originated from a term signifying a psychosis with a poor prognosis, often ending in complete deterioration and incurability. Dementia refers to a mental disorder, and praecox refers to the origin of the disorder in early life, frequently adolescence. Included under this term are the symptom complexes of catatonia, hebephrenia, and paranoia. Although some European psychiatrists continue to use dementia praecox to describe an incurable type of schizophrenia, the term is largely obsolete following Eugen Bleuler's introduction of the term *schizophrenia* in 1911.

D. L. Schuurman

See Schizophrenia.

Demonic Influence, Sin, and Psychopathology. *Cosmology.* Wagner (1988, pp. 30–35) describes some concepts first brought to public attention by Paul G. Hiebert, a missiologist at Trinity Evangelical Divinity School. Hiebert compares the cosmology of most Westerners with that of much of the rest of the world. Secular Westerners usually believe in a single-tiered (naturalistic) universe only. Christian Westerners typically believe in a two-tiered universe, with God and other supernatural forces inhabiting the upper story and human beings occupying the lower story. In contrast, most other cultures believe in a three-tiered universe; the middle story represents the sphere in which the interaction between humans and supernatural beings occurs. This is not primarily an external combat between supernatural and natural beings but an interaction that occurs intrapsychically. Much of what happens in human life is believed to occur in this middle story.

Hiebert makes the point that this three-tiered cosmology is truer to biblical reality than is the two-tiered one. Christian growth, according to Scripture, occurs as a result of the influence of the Holy Spirit living within us. Likewise, Christians struggle "not against flesh and blood, but against the rulers, against the authorities, against the powers of this dark world and against the spiritual forces of evil in the heavenly realms" (Eph. 6:12, NIV). The spiritual weapons and armor described in Ephesians 6:13–18 refer to cognitive truths that Christians can use to refute the theological mistruths that Satan and his forces attempt to insert into our minds. Thus, according to God's Word, much of our Christian experience and non-Christians' experiences as well occur in the middle story.

Diagnostic Implications. The *Diagnostic and Statistical Manual of Mental Disorders* (*DSM-IV*; American Psychiatric Association, 1994) contains the most comprehensive description of mental illness available. Psychopathology (mental illness) is conceptualized in the *DSM-IV* in a one-tiered universe. Christian counselors usually believe in a two-tiered universe, but because most are trained from a secular perspective their diagnoses often remain functionally one-tiered. Yet, if the three-tiered cosmology is correct, this has significant implications for our conceptualization of psychopathology. Such a model would suggest that much of what we call abnormal behavior is not simply a result of developmental events occurring within the natural universe. Instead, abnormality may be a result of the interaction between developmental events occurring at the natural level and Satan (using a combination of our sin natures, the attraction of the world's system of thinking, and demonic agents) trying to draw people away from God. Thus a biblical model of illness, both physical and psychological/spiritual illness, suggests that it can come from disease occurring in the natural realm, sin (the combined effects of our sin nature and the influence of the world's value system), and demonic forces (often interacting with one or both of these sources).

The Reality and Activity of Demons. In recent years some Christian theologians have attempted to demythologize the Bible's teaching on demons and demonic involvement in human life or have otherwise characterized it as prescientific, superstitious thinking. However, the New Testament includes more than one hundred references to the existence of demons; it is clear that Jesus taught that demons are real and that they cause a variety of physical and mental disorders.

Some Christians believe that Satan and Satan's demons were bound at the time of Christ's death and resurrection. Nevertheless, many New Testament passages teach that Satan and demons continue to be active; they deceive human beings (1 Tim. 4:1; 1 John 4:1–3), seek to blind humans to God's truth (2 Cor. 4:3–4), and promote both legalism (Gal. 3:1–3; 1 Tim. 4:1–8) and immoral living (1 John 3:8; Jude 4). Thus while some demons may be confined (Jude 6; 2 Peter 2:4), others appear to have access to earth's inhabitants (Eph. 3:10; 6:12) and will continue their activities until Christ casts them into the abyss at the end of the age (Rev. 20:1–3).

Levels of Demonic Influence. Scripture suggests four levels of demonic involvement in human temptation. These levels represent a continuum ranging from no demonic involvement to significant involvement.

No Involvement. Scripture makes it clear that temptations may come from our sinful nature without demonic intervention (Jer. 17:9; Mark 7:21–23; James 1:14–15). In such cases our sin nature takes a natural desire, one that is often good when it occurs in moderation and within God's defined limits, and turns it into something evil. In addition to our sin natures, the persuasion of the world's system of thinking can lead us into sin without direct demonic involvement.

Demonic Temptation. Scripture speaks of a second category of temptation that is demonic in its origin. Christ was tempted directly by Satan (Matt. 4:1–11). Likewise, Satan apparently tempted Ananias to lie (Acts 5:3). He incited David to take a census in Israel in a way that displeased God (1 Chron. 21:1). Paul reminds believers that they battle against evil supernatural forces (Eph. 6:10–18), and thus must be fully equipped with appropriate spiritual weapons.

It seems likely that sometimes yielding to one's sinful human impulses (the first category) provides an opening for demonic temptation (this category). For example, David's pride in the growing strength of Israel probably made him more easily vulnerable to Satan's temptation to take a census for the wrong reasons. Judas's love of money made him susceptible to Satan's temptation to betray Jesus. Scripture repeatedly affirms that the practice of yielding to sin makes one less able to resist its temptations (e.g., John 8:34). Yielding to sinful temptations arising from one's own nature may make one increasingly susceptible to demonic temptation as well.

Demonic Oppression. A more intense level of demonic involvement in human life is called by various authors demonic influence, demonic oppression, demonic subjection, or demonic obsession. Demons are believed to exert considerable influence over a person's life short of actual possession (Unger, 1971, p. 113). Oppression may be a mild form of subjection that goes unnoticed for years until a particular event uncovers it. It may also refer to a state in which the person is continually surrounded and harassed by the powers of darkness (Koch, 1971, p. 32).

Unger (1971, p. 114) summarizes the biblical data regarding manifestations of demonic oppression as blindness and hardness of heart toward the gospel (2 Cor. 4:4), apostasy and doctrinal corruption (1 Tim. 4:1), and indulging in sinful, defiling behavior (2 Peter 2:1–12). Scripture also mentions that demonic oppression can result in physical illness (e.g., Luke 13:10–16).

It could be argued that for the most part symptoms that result from demonic temptation or demonic oppression are not qualitatively different from symptoms that result from our sin natures and the temptation of the world system. It appears that the role of demons in these situations is to intensify the temptations or symptoms coming from those sources rather than to produce unique symptoms. It is primarily in the case of demon possession that some unique symptoms are produced.

White (1990, p. 150) suggests four means by which he believes people become demonically oppressed. These are habitual moral compromise, such as involvement in the occult, nurturing bitterness or hatred, persistent sexual sin, or fleshly indulgence; family involvement in the occult; victimization by others (incest, rape, violence, exposure to satanic rituals); or ministry activity that draws attention away from Satan.

Demon Possession. In several instances where demon possession is described in Scripture, no specific symptoms are mentioned. When specific symptoms are mentioned they include possessed individuals manifesting supernormal strength; going about naked; being unable to speak, hear, or see; experiencing self-destructive convulsions with symptoms such as rigidity, foaming at the mouth, and teeth grinding; and making statements that suggest that one has supernatural knowledge. Sometimes the symptoms caused by the demon are continuously present. In other instances the manifestation of the demon's presence is episodic.

While some persons have questioned whether demon possession continues, many missionaries who work in countries where demonic (idol) worship is prevalent testify that demon possession continues to exist there with symptoms quite similar to the biblical descriptions (e.g., Nevius, 1968; Peters, 1976; Tippett, 1976). Possession appears to occur as a result of idol worship, occult involvement, spells cast by another person, or receiving healing through sorcery (Koch, 1971). Possession is sometimes by a single demon and sometimes by multiple demons.

Christians debate whether believers can be possessed. A growing number of conservative writers believe that the biblical data do not clearly answer this issue and that therefore we should look to human experience to help us decide it. Many accounts from experienced missionaries around the world and from ministers in the United States who specialize in spiritual warfare ministries assert that possession can occur in believers. In 1952 Unger wrote in *Biblical Demonology* that he believes Christians cannot be demon possessed. However, he later reported that he received so many letters from missionaries all over the world documenting this kind of occurrence that he came to believe that it does happen (1971, p. 117). Other writers who agree with this conclusion include C. Fred Dickason (chair of the theology department at Moody Bible Institute and author of *Demon Possession and the Christian* [1987]), Neil T. Anderson (former chair of the practical theology department at Talbot School of Theology and author of *The Bondage Breaker* [1993]), Mark Bubeck (author of *The Adversary* [1975] and *Overcoming the Adversary* [1984]), and Thomas White (director of Frontline Ministries and author of *The Believer's Guide to Spiritual Warfare* [1990]). The common means by which this seems to happen is through believers arrogantly attacking demons (cf. Jude 9) or through habitual sin.

Some Christian writers have objected to translating *daimonizomai* as demon possessed, preferring instead to use the word *demonized* to refer to those whose symptoms fit into this category. *Daimonizomai* means to have a demon, to be possessed by a demon, or to be exercised by or under the control of a demon. Therefore the translators of both the New American Standard Bible and the New International Version have generally translated the word as demon possessed.

Three objections have been raised to the use of this phrase. First, it connotes to some people the idea of ownership, and Christians, even when they are being demonically harassed, belong to Christ, not to Satan. Second, there is an important difference in the Holy Spirit's residence within a believer and demonic residence. The Holy Spirit always comes as an invited guest, while Satan and his demons often come uninvited to try to harass or control a person. Third, since the Holy Spirit lives within the believer, it seems conceptually impossible to believe that a demon or demons could live there also.

The first two arguments make valid points. With regard to the third, when Scripture talks about the Holy Spirit or a demonic spirit within a person this is probably a metaphor suggesting influence or control over that person, since human spatial considerations apply to neither God nor demons. Thus there is not an inherent contradiction in recognizing that Satan and his demons may at times try to replace the loving influence the Holy Spirit has on a believer's personality with their own control or that there may be a struggle between the Holy Spirit and a demon.

Since some people have these concerns about the use of the term *demon possessed*, there may be value in using the words *demonized* or *demonic control* rather than *demon possessed* when talking with them. Most biblical writers still use the term *demon possession*, since it does seem to have a clearer meaning to the general public than does the term *demonized*. For example, even though Dickason strongly argues for the use of "demonization" rather than "demon possession," his book title remains *Demon Possession and the Christian* (1987).

An Amplified Model of Mental Illness.
What would a model of mental illness that included the possibility of demonization look like? The following schema proposes eight tentative categories. These eight categories are not assumed to be a full statement of all causes, and they are not assumed to operate independently of each other. Abnormal behavior can be caused by psychopathology from two or more of these categories acting synergistically.

First, some mental illnesses such as schizophrenia, bipolar disorder, obsessive-compulsive disorder, and attention deficit/hyperactivity disorder appear to have a significant genetic component that predisposes people to have one or more episodes or chronic occurrence of these particular illnesses.

Second, people sometimes develop mistaken beliefs as a result of their human finiteness. Human beings may come to mistaken interpretations or mistaken conclusions because they do not see all the data or because they do not correctly analyze it. Or they may misinterpret data because the only human examples they had available to them did not model a correct way of understanding or responding to that part of their experience.

Third, psychopathology may also be a result of lack of knowledge about how to deal with situations—social situations, academic situations, work situations, marital situations. Sometimes people lack the skills that they need to respond effectively to life. Lack of skills or knowledge may also keep a person from moving to a new developmental stage, even though this would be chronologically appropriate.

Fourth, psychopathology may also be the result of lack of awareness of one's thoughts, feelings, or goals. In this situation, rather than thinking the situation through so that conscious decisions about one's behavior can be made, internal processes, feelings, or goals may be acted out. Examples might include all of the impulse control disorders and histrionic personality disorder. A related situation can occur if persons have conflicting, mutually exclusive goals of which they are not fully aware or that they do not know how to resolve, so their behavior expresses that ambivalence.

A fifth factor that can produce unhealthy or undesirable behavior is our sin nature; that is, our self-centeredness, our desire to be god of our own lives. Our sin nature causes us to take healthy needs or drives (normal physical needs for food, shelter, and enjoyment) and distort them through overemphasis or misdirection. For example, the lust of the flesh is an improper satisfaction of a natural desire. The lust of the eyes refers to a desire to obtain possessions that has grown to a willingness to exploit or steal from others to obtain those possessions. The pride of life represents the legitimate desire to achieve taken to a point where one has a consuming desire to achieve, even at the expense of others (1 John 2:16).

Sixth, the traumas that some people experience—emotional abuse, physical abuse, sexual abuse, or some other assault or crisis—can cause psychopathology. Besides the naturally occurring results of these traumas, those who have had many years experience in spiritual warfare consistently say that these kinds of developmental situations regularly become a means of entry for demonic temptation or oppression. The exact mechanism of how this occurs has not been clearly defined, and it may vary from individual to individual. For some the trauma may become the means by which Satan tempts people to become bitter. For others it may have damaged their ability to believe they can meet their emotional needs in healthy ways. As a result they have become overly dependent, seductive, aggressive, or passive-aggressive in a mistaken attempt to meet their needs for security and significance. Others may have experienced the trauma as both anxiety-producing and stimulating, and they develop a habit of seeking out that kind of experience whenever they become lonely, depressed, or anxious.

Seventh, Satan is the author of the world's system of thinking and encourages people to develop mistaken beliefs about what goals they need to reach to achieve happiness (e.g., possessions, fame, power, or pleasure). Satan also encourages people to develop mistaken beliefs about how best to reach those goals (e.g., through lying, deception, stealing, or infidelity). We as individuals can incorporate those mistaken beliefs either because we see them modeled in the world system or through mistaken interpretations we make as we grow up in our families. Satan and Satan's demons work in two ways to accomplish this: indirectly by influencing the world system and directly by suggesting thoughts to us (e.g., 1 Chron. 21:1; Acts 5:3). Satan may also in some way blind us to the error of the mistaken beliefs he has persuaded us to accept (2 Cor. 4:4; James 3:15). These would be the categories labeled as examples of demonic temptation and oppression.

Eighth, in some situations abnormal behavior may be the result of demon possession. Possession may be less frequent in the United States than in other countries that have many pagan religions. It is not implausible to believe that Satan and demons adapt their strategies to the prevailing culture. In a culture where the majority of people no longer believe in the reality of demons, outright demon possession may be counterproductive to Satan's strategy. It seems probable that in the United States more abnormal behavior may be the result of nonsupernaturally caused psychopathology, sin, demonic temptation, and oppression than is due to demon possession.

Some abnormal behavior may be the result of the synergistic effect of two or more of these factors. For example, Satan or demons may attack the Christian suffering from major depression and may use the vulnerability caused by the major depression to convince the believer that salvation has been lost or the unpardonable sin committed or that salvation was never really obtained. Treatment with antidepressants alone may be sufficient to remove the vulnerability that enabled Satan to successfully attack, but treatment with antidepressants followed by biblical cognitive therapy to reaffirm the believer's position in Christ may be an even more thorough treatment for such a person.

Differential Diagnosis. If the single-story model of the universe is correct, then all abnormal behavior can be understood fully by examining the natural factors surrounding it. If the two-story model of the universe is correct, then the diagnostic question becomes one of asking whether the abnormal behavior is due to natural or supernatural forces and treating it accordingly. If the three-story model described by Hiebert is correct and a significant amount of human behavior is a result of the interaction between humans in the natural realm interacting with good and evil supernatural beings, then the diagnostic questions become considerably more complex. They could include the following: Is this abnormal behavior primarily a result of nonmoral natural processes? Is this abnormal behavior primarily a result of one's personal sin nature, as influenced by the world's system of values? Alternatively, is Satan using either our sin nature or the world's system to tempt us? Is this abnormal behavior primarily a result of demonic oppression or possession? Is this abnormal behavior the result of an interaction between natural psychological processes, both nonmoral and sin-based, and the impact of supernatural beings interacting with those processes? (Since *DSM-IV* assumes that all psychopathology occurs in the first category, it is of limited help in answering these questions.)

How do we decide whether the psychopathology we are dealing with best fits into the third and fourth categories versus the first and second categories? The technical process we are considering is called differential diagnosis; that is, trying to decide whether the psychopathology we are examining best fits into one category or another. One possible answer in trying to differentiate supernatural versus natural causation would be to suggest that we act similarly although not identically to the way we would when trying to make other medical or psychological diagnoses that are confined to the natural realm. This would include taking a history, analyzing the constellation of presenting symptoms, observing epiphenomena or related activity within the person's social system, and evaluating the person's response to treatment.

History taking would focus on the person's spiritual history and involvement with the occult and on immediate precursors of the present situation. Many who write in this area emphasize that even casual interactions with occult practices may result in long-standing effects. It is also important to investigate family involvement in the occult as far back as three or four generations. Evidence of occult involvement in the past does not prove that the present problem has demonic components but increases the probability that it may be so. An analysis of the immediate precursors to the present situation may be helpful in differentiating role-enactment behaviors from genuine possession.

Role enactment refers to the possibility that, if persons are experiencing unusual physical or psychological symptoms and are told that these symptoms indicate that they are demonically oppressed or possessed, they may believe this and may enact the role of a demonized person as they understand it. This may make the process of differential diagnosis more complicated.

Some writers have concluded that diagnosis of demon possession based on symptom analysis is indeterminate, since each individual symptom found in demon possession is also found in some kind of mental illness. Such a conclusion seems unnecessarily pessimistic. In most diseases the combination of symptoms rather than any single symptom is the basis of a diagnostic decision. Thus while various mental illnesses share one or two symptoms in common with demon possession, none shares the entire symptom complex.

The symptom complex may be described in terms of physical symptoms, psychological symptoms, and spiritual symptoms. Few people will manifest all the symptoms, but available evidence suggests that most will exhibit several from each category (as in most diagnoses in *DSM-IV*). Physical symptoms often include preternatural (more than natural) strength; change in facial demeanor, usually to one of intense hatred and evil; change in voice tone and pitch (usually the voice deepens and becomes harsher or takes on a mocking tone); epileptic-like convulsions with attendant symptoms; and anesthesia to pain.

Psychological symptoms may include clairvoyance (seeing things that could not be seen through normal means); telepathy (communication from one mind to another by other than normal means); the ability to predict the future; the ability to speak in languages not known by the possessed person; clouding of consciousness while in the trance state; and amnesia for things that happened while in the trance state.

An extremely important diagnostic question is, "Is there present an identifiable, alien force of evil separate from personality that responds negatively to the authority of Christ and the presence of his Spirit?" (White, 1990, p. 151). This "alien force of evil" is not the result of a single human personality splitting (as in dissociative identity disorder [formerly multiple personality disorder]), nor is it a result of a delusional process (as in schizophrenia or bipolar disorder).

Spiritual changes may include a significant change in moral character; becoming verbally or physically aggressive; falling into a trance if someone prays; and an inability to say Jesus' name reverently or to affirm that he is God's Son in the flesh (1 John 4:1–2).

An important epiphenomenon of diagnostic significance in demon possession is that possession is often accompanied by poltergeist (noisy ghosts) phenomena. These may include such things as unexplainable noises, furniture or household goods inexplicably overturned, pungent odors, and showers of damp earth.

If the preceding criteria do not yield a diagnosis, the person's response to treatment may also be used diagnostically. If standard psychotherapy or medication does not produce expected results and there is reason to expect demonic involvement (op-pression or possession), a deliverance session might be considered if the client gives permission.

Levels of Treatment. If the four categories of causes of psychopathology (see the section on differential diagnosis) are valid, then treatment should be related to what is causing that person's psychopathology. These four categories are used for initial conceptualization only, with the recognition that in life multiple causes often interact.

Category One. If the abnormal behavior is primarily a result of nonmoral natural processes, then standard secular biological and psychological therapies may be the treatments of choice.

Category Two. Sometimes the abnormal behavior may be primarily a result of one's sin nature as influenced by the world's value system. When this is the case, some secular therapy techniques may be helpful (empathy skills, insight-oriented techniques) to help persons recognize the mistaken beliefs or mistaken goals they have adopted. Sometimes these beliefs can be replaced using cognitive-behavioral methods, complemented by confession, repentance, and forgiveness as appropriate. Thus many irrational thoughts or dysfunctional thoughts that rational-emotive and cognitive-behavioral therapists attempt to help their clients dispute and replace may have their origin in the work of Satan, either directly or indirectly. While secular cognitive therapy may correctly identify some of the beliefs that cause psychopathology, often Scripture will give different content to dispute with those dysfunctional beliefs than that found in secular psychology. For example, people develop psychopathology when they base their self-acceptance on the opinions of others or by trying to attain perfect performance. Secular psychotherapy can point out the unhealthiness of this kind of thinking and can suggest healthier thought processes. But the Christian therapist can point to the healthiest basis for self-acceptance; namely, that God has completely forgiven us, the price for all our inadequacies and sins has been fully paid, and God has totally accepted us and adopted us into God's family. Because God accepts us, even with our imperfections, we can accept ourselves.

When a person is being tempted by a demonic spirit, often the temptation will be to sins originating within our sin nature. The intensity of the temptation may be increased by the involvement of a demonic spirit. The recommended scriptural response is to "resist the devil and he will flee from you." This can be done by confronting Satan with scriptural truths as Christ did when he was tempted by Satan in the desert (Matt. 4:1–11). This is an example of cognitive self-talk (disputing), but the content of the disputing self-talk has decidedly biblical content. If we have already succumbed to temptation, then to our resistance we should add the steps of recognition, confession, repentance, and replacement (James 4:7–10).

Category Three. Psychopathology from this source refers to both demonic oppression and possession. The biblical response to demonic oppression appears to be binding demons (i.e., in the authority of Jesus commanding the evil spirits to no longer harass, oppress, or blind a person to spiritual realities). When people are demon possessed, exorcism or casting out of demons *(ekballo)* seems to be the recommended biblical response.

Category Four. When psychopathology is due to a combination of nonmoral biological or psychological processes, sin, or some elements of demonic temptation, oppression, or possession, then it seems reasonable that the use of a combination of the preceding methods would be appropriate.

If psychopathology does occur in what Hiebert calls the middle tier, this may explain why changing one's thinking patterns via Christian therapy versus exposure to deliverance ministry plus discipleship training may at times produce similar results but by different pathways. For example, Christian therapy that helps a client change one's thinking may make that person a less attractive target for demonic temptation or oppression, even though no specific deliverance methods were used. Conversely, deliverance plus discipleship training may result in expulsion of demons and preventing relapses into the thinking and behavioral patterns that made demonic temptation or oppression possible. This may explain why some ministers report success treating a wide variety of what appear to be *DSM-IV* disorders with deliverance followed by discipleship training (e.g., Dickason, 1987, pp. 279–291; Anderson, 1993, pp. 57, 75, 154, 192, 203–205), whereas Christian therapists experience success in treating people with those same kinds of disorders using approaches that have a much stronger Christian psychological emphasis and that do not include specific deliverance methods.

This might also suggest that therapy combining a recognition that we are working in the middle tier, where both psychopathology due to natural processes and demonic temptation, oppression, or possession reside, might be a helpful paradigm. For example, the Christian who was reared in an environment where he or she received little validation may grow up to have low self-esteem. Satan or demons may use that naturally produced psychopathology to keep the Christian in bondage to low self-esteem and prevent the individual from experiencing the abundant life that Christ wishes for him or her. Those false beliefs can be attacked using secular cognitive methods alone. A more effective attack may use cognitive methods that have their basis in scriptural truth. The oppression that Satan may be causing could be attacked by using deliverance methods alone (binding Satan's ability to blind the Christian from the realities that are true of Satan) but probably could be more effectively dealt with by rebuking Satan, learning the method of cognitive disputing using biblical truth, and experiencing God's acceptance as mediated through the acceptance of a Christian therapist.

Spiritual Warfare Methods. *Jesus' Method.* Jesus' exorcism method was powerful, direct, and brief.

Jesus frequently cast demons out of persons with a single word: Go. At other times he used a longer command: Come out of him. Jesus' longest recorded exorcism was "You deaf and mute spirit, I command you, come out of him and never enter him again" (Mark 9:25, NIV). Jesus commanded his followers to continue the ministry of exorcism and empowered them to do so. Their instructions were to cast out demons in his name.

There is no instruction given that Christian exorcists must force the demon to name itself so that they can exorcise it by name, although this is a common practice among those who carry on deliverance ministries. On at least one occasion the biblical record indicates that exorcism was done without the presence or cooperation of the person possessed (Mark 7:25–30). The Bible does admonish those involved in a deliverance ministry to have a firm faith in Jesus' power to exorcise the demon and to prepare for exorcism by prayer (Mark 9:17–29). Scripture also warns that attempting to exorcise demons in Jesus' name is dangerous for unbelievers (Acts 19:13–16).

Contemporary Deliverance Methods. Following is a list of suggestions commonly made by Christians actively involved in deliverance ministries in the twentieth century.

1. Remember that the power to exorcise demons lies in Jesus' name, not in a prescribed procedure or ritual.
2. Faith in Jesus' ability to exorcise demons and prayer beforehand are important preparations.
3. Self-examination and godly living are essential. More than one would-be exorcist has been embarrassed by a demon publicly revealing his or her private sins.
4. Exorcism should be done by a group of believers whenever possible.
5. When the possessed person tells the demon that he or she wants the demon to leave it hastens the deliverance process.
6. The possessed person should make a full confession of sins, pray a prayer of renunciation, and make a clean break with sin by burning occult books and breaking mediumistic contacts or friendships.
7. More than one demon may possess a person simultaneously. It is important that all demons be cast out before the exorcism process is stopped.
8. Sometimes deliverance prayers must continue over a period of time (e.g., a few weeks) before the process is complete.
9. Relapses can occur after exorcism. There are reports of demons reentering a believer because of lapses into pre-Christian ways of living. Therefore exorcised persons should fill their lives with Bible reading and the Holy Spirit.
10. A follow-up support group of two or more people who can meet regularly for prayer and fellowship is recommended.

Anderson's Model. Anderson (1993, pp. 215–235) has some thoughtful comments on the practice of deliverance. He recommends that deliverance should be based more on the teachings of the epistles than the Gospels. Most people involved in deliverance ministry command the demon to name itself and then command it to leave. What follows is sometimes a dramatic power struggle, with the demon resisting and the exorcist commanding. The person inhabited may sometimes lapse into unconsciousness during the struggle, and Anderson states that he has seen people be physically injured during such struggles (p. 216).

Anderson recommends instead that the counselor prepare the person by having an intake interview, similar to that done by professional counselors, in which they together explore the problems the person is experiencing. If the problem appears to be related to demonic oppression or possession, he recommends that the counselor correct any distorted views the person may have about God or what he or she is experiencing. He then recommends that the counselor bind the demon by the authority of Christ, commanding the demon not to speak to or inflict any harm on the counselee and to release the counselee from any bondage under which it has put that person. Anderson then leads the counselee through a series of prayers in which the counselee rejects any sins that may have allowed him or her to become possessed. Ultimately the counselee rather than the counselor commands the spirit to leave and never return.

Professional Licensure Considerations. Despite the writings of Peck (1985, 1992), a psychiatrist who believes in the legitimacy of both demons and exorcism, state licensure boards tend to take a dim view of deliverance done by licensed mental health practitioners (*see* Licensure). As a result some Christian practitioners who believe that demonic oppression or possession may sometimes be part of their clients' psychopathology refer persons whom they believe need deliverance to a trusted nonlicensed person or couple who has deliverance ministry gifts. Care should be taken in selecting such a person, since the mental health professional could still be considered liable for making the referral if difficulties were to develop during the deliverance process. It may be worthwhile finding a person or couple who are open to using the approach described by Anderson (1993), since the counselee takes greater personal responsibility for the timing and intensity of the process itself. Thus this approach may reduce the chances of physical or psychological trauma occurring during the deliverance sessions.

References

American Psychiatric Association. (1994). *Diagnostic and statistical manual of mental disorders* (4th ed.). Washington, DC: Author.

Anderson, N. T. (1993). *The bondage breaker: Overcoming negative thoughts, irrational feelings, habitual sins.* Eugene, OR: Harvest House.

Bubeck, M. (1975). *The adversary.* Chicago: Moody.

Bubeck, M. (1984). *Overcoming the adversary.* Chicago: Moody.

Dickason, C. F. (1987). *Demon possession and the Christian: A new perspective.* Wheaton, IL: Crossway.

Koch, K. (Ed.). (1971). *Occult bondage and deliverance.* Grand Rapids, MI: Kregel.

Nevius, J. L. (1968). *Demon possession* (8th ed.). Grand Rapids, MI: Kregel.

Peck, M. S. (1985). *People of the lie: The hope for healing human evil.* New York: Touchstone.

Peck, M. S. (1992). *Further along the road less travelled.* New York: Peregrine.

Peters, G. W. (1976). Demonism on the mission field. In J. W. Montgomery (Ed.), *Demon possession.* Minneapolis: Bethany Fellowship.

Tippett, A. R. (1976). Spirit possession as it relates to culture and religion. In J. W. Montgomery (Ed.), *Demon possession.* Minneapolis: Bethany Fellowship.

Unger, M. F. (1971). *Demons in the world today.* Wheaton, IL: Tyndale House.

Wagner, C. P. (1988). *The third wave of the Holy Spirit.* Ann Arbor, MI: Vine.

White, T. B. (1990). *The believer's guide to spiritual warfare.* Ann Arbor, MI: Vine.

H. A. VIRKLER

See PASTORAL CARE; PASTORAL COUNSELING; SPIRITUAL AND RELIGIOUS ISSUES IN THERAPY; RELIGION AND PERSONALITY; HOLY SPIRIT, ROLE IN COUNSELING.

Denial. An unconscious mental mechanism in which refusal to perceive or admit the existence of something serves as an ego defense against some unpleasant, unacceptable aspect of reality. Thus when some internal or external perception is judged by the unconscious ego as potentially threatening, the perception or memory of that reality is filtered out of conscious awareness. This process generally operates within a weak ego, functioning most successfully in the denial of painful or threatening internal realities. Denial, also known as negation in the psychological literature, is seen in the example of a woman faced with the news of her impending death from cancer, who believes that there must be some mistake, that such an event could not be happening to her.

R. LARKIN

See DEFENSE MECHANISMS.

Dependency. There is nothing inherently wrong with being dependent on others. Healthy interdependent relationships, however, differ dramatically from enmeshed or symbiotic relationships. When one's psychological need for security in adulthood rests almost exclusively on the approval of others, it may best be viewed as pathological dependency. Environments that do not encourage appropriate self-expression or that demand total compliance with the whims and wishes of authoritarian leaders (*see* Authoritarian Personality) can thwart the development of any strong sense of self in the context of important social support systems.

Healthy cooperation and reciprocal relationships are the foundation of human social life; the Christian community ought to be characterized by the many ways in which we love the brothers and sisters. Yet truly dependent people in the pejorative sense are characterized by a willingness to allow others to assume major responsibility for their lives. In a diagnostic sense, this may develop into what the *DSM-IV* (American Psychiatric Association, 1994) calls a dependent personality disorder, characterized by a pervasive need to cling to stronger personalities who are all too willing to make most important decisions for them (see Meyer & Deitsch, 1996). Such individuals tend to be characterized in the literature as naive and unassertive, seldom willing to take any initiative in social situations. Although they may appear to be content in their one-sided relationships, it is often at the cost of any consistent expression of their own personality. Widiger and Costa (1994) maintain that such dependency may represent an extreme exaggeration of the traditional feminine role. Not being in such a dependent relationship may lead to symptoms of anxiety and depression, perhaps not unrelated to fears of abandonment. As Willis (1982) understands it, pathological dependency may reflect an almost infantile refusal to accept responsibility for managing one's life, making decisions, and acting on them.

Dependency begins developmentally in the familial context and is eventually shaped by the larger social network. A measure of dependency is normal and natural throughout childhood, but as the person grows and develops, it can be distorted in an effort to mold oneself to gain the approval of others at great cost to one's personhood. Persons remain dependent because they crave security or prefer to engage in self-protective and anxiety-reducing strategies to allow themselves to remain childlike. Pathological dependency is the failure to grow up psychosocially, cognitively, and interpersonally.

All persons who desire to promote growth and wholeness in others must come to grips with the subtle and overt ways people hang on to outside sources of affirmation, identity, and security. Certain parental, leadership, interactional, and teaching styles are potentially antidevelopmental in that they fail to foster any degree of healthy autonomy and interdependence (see Gangel & Wilhoit, 1993). As the clinician knows, deeply ingrained habits develop, and abandoning these can be an intensely painful and anxiety-producing experience. Since helping clients develop a strong sense of self is an implicit goal in most models of people helping (see Jones & Butman, 1991), clinicians must sensitize their clients to the freedom and responsibility that is theirs and cultivate within them a sincere desire to develop more of their own inner resources for problem solving. Their choices must become their own choices within the context of the communities of which they are a part. With-

out coercion or manipulation they must be helped to develop a more adequate philosophy of life, so that authentic living can increasingly replace their fearful self-protectiveness (McLemore, 1984).

Few would doubt that assertiveness training is indicated in the treatment of pathological dependency. In a clinical or helping relationship, however, there are dangers that must be faced. It can be tempting for clinicians to use the therapeutic relationship to serve their own dependency needs and thereby to retard the development of their clients. Freeing clients to choose and to take full responsibility for decisions can certainly be anxiety-producing for therapists (see Fromm-Reichman, 1950). While therapists maintain a nurturing and nonjudgmental stance, clear limits must be set so that new forms of pathological dependency do not develop in the clinical context. Integrated persons live by their own internalized standards that reflect the virtues that their communities cherish. What clients take from their therapists must be incorporated within the fabric of their own unique personalities rather than becoming yet another expression of internalized dominance. More specifically for the Christian, holy values need to be fully assimilated so that they become part and parcel of one's being rather than yet another expression of concern about surface behavior (see Roberts, 1993). We as Christians are called first and foremost to follow Christ, not those who would seek to control, dominate, or exploit basic trust and respect for one's own personhood.

References

American Psychiatric Association. (1994). *Diagnostic and statistical manual of mental disorders* (4th ed.). Washington, DC: Author.

Fromm-Reichman, F. (1950). *Principles of intensive psychotherapy*. Chicago: University of Chicago Press.

Gangel, K., & Wilhoit, J. (1993). *The Christian educator's handbook on adult education*. Wheaton, IL: Victor.

Jones, S., & Butman, R. (1991). *Modern psychotherapies*. Downers Grove, IL: InterVarsity Press.

McLemore, C. (1984). *Honest Christianity*. Philadelphia: Westminster.

Meyer, R., & Deitsch, S. (1996). *The clinician's handbook* (4th ed.). Boston: Allyn & Bacon.

Roberts, R. (1993). *Taking the word to heart*. Grand Rapids, MI: Eerdmans.

Widiger, T., & Costa, P. (1994). Personality and personality disorders. *Journal of Abnormal Psychology, 103,* 78–91.

Willis, E. (1982). The politics of dependency. *Ms., 7,* 181–214.

R. E. Butman

See CODEPENDENCY.

Dependent Personality Disorder. The diagnostic criteria for dependent personality disorder include lack of self-confidence, allowing others to assume responsibility for one's life, difficulty expressing disagreement, exaggerated fear of being unable to care for oneself, volunteering to do things that are unpleasant to obtain nurturance and support, seeking an excessive amount of advice to make everyday decisions, and the inability to function independently. Such individuals feel inadequate and helpless and put their own needs second so as to avoid offending the person on whom they are dependent. They believe that if they offend that person they will be rejected, leaving them to rely on themselves. Thus they will even suffer humiliation and physical abuse from a mate or a parent in order not to lose the relationship. They are preoccupied with the thought of being abandoned. They urgently seek another relationship if their current support system ends. If they are married, their spouses will assume all responsibility regarding where they live, who they should be friends with, and what job they should take.

Physical illness in childhood may contribute to the development of this disorder. Such children allow their parents to decide who they should play with, how to spend their free time, and what they should wear. Dependent personality is diagnosed more frequently in women, but the prevalence rates may be similar among males and females.

Persons with a dependent personality disorder are impaired in social relationships. Their contacts become limited to only the person on whom they are dependent and the individuals who are acquaintances of that person. There are also vocational limitations. Dependent persons have difficulty making decisions and asserting themselves, and the autonomous functioning required by some jobs poses impossible demands.

Persons with this disorder will often benefit from insight therapy. The goal is to help them gain an understanding of how the disorder developed and learn to utilize assertive skills (see Assertiveness Training). The person on whom the client is dependent, such as a parent or a mate, should also participate in the therapeutic process. Such persons need to understand how they can encourage the client to gain self-confidence and independence. These persons may also need the dependent relationship in order to meet their own needs, and this need must be addressed in therapy.

Freedom in Jesus Christ is a key concept to be developed in persons suffering from dependent personality disorder. Trusting Christ for care and provision helps them develop healthy relationships with others. If anxiety and depression interfere with therapy, medication may also be a helpful component of a total treatment approach.

M. A. CAMPION

See PERSONALITY DISORDERS.

Dependent Variable. The predicted variable in an experiment, usually representing an abstract concept or hypothetical construct, that is some well-defined and measurable belief, sentiment, intention, or behavior. The value assumed by the dependent variable is hypothesized to be dependent upon the value of the independent variable (the predictor variable). Thus a change in the independent variable is expected to produce a resulting change in the dependent variable. The dependent variable may be influenced by extraneous variables, and therefore control procedures should be implemented.

P. C. HILL

See PSYCHOLOGY, METHODS OF.

Depersonalization Disorder. Depersonalization disorder is one of the dissociative disorders. The dissociative disorders are characterized by alterations, usually a separation or splitting, in consciousness, memory, or identity. Depersonalization involves an alteration in one's conscious experience of one's self and environment. Depersonalization symptoms, which are common, must be distinguished from depersonalization disorder, which is rare.

Symptoms of Depersonalization. Depersonalization is characterized by a sense of alienation and estrangement from one's self. Self and the environment may appear dreamlike and unreal. Persons who have experienced depersonalization may report feelings of being outside one's body and observing it from a distance. These people may also report feeling detached, numb, mechanical, disjointed, or dead inside. Some feel as though they are floating. While these feelings are unpleasant, depersonalization is usually accompanied by diminished rather than heightened emotion.

Depersonalization is marked by a qualitative change in experiencing. It is as though consciousness dissociates from the body and the person steps outside the physical boundaries of the body. The person's ability to perceive self and the environment is not grossly impaired, but the perceptions do not feel right. The external world may seem strange or unreal. Although the person may have a difficult time communicating what was experienced during the episode of depersonalization, the report may be distinguished from the hallucination of a psychotic because the content is organized, accurate as to the physical details of the setting, and free from delusional content. The person with depersonalization disorder does not demonstrate the extreme anxiety and disorganization of the psychotic or schizophrenic person. Mild to moderate anxiety or depression sometimes accompanies depersonalization.

Symptoms of depersonalization but not depersonalization disorder may be secondary to many other medical or psychological disturbances. Symptoms of depersonalization are frequently reported in anxiety disorders, schizophrenia, drug and alcohol intoxication and withdrawal, and epilepsy. In each of the preceding cases depersonalization is incidental to other significant disorders and depersonalization disorder would not be diagnosed.

Depersonalization Disorder. Depersonalization disorder is diagnosed only when the person's symptoms are unaccompanied by any evidence of another significant psychological or medical problem. While depersonalization disorder may be accompanied by some anxiety or depression, the anxiety and depression are alone insufficient to warrant a diagnosis other than depersonalization disorder. Persons with depersonalization disorder are not psychotic. They do not lose touch with reality, although their experience of reality may be episodically altered. In addition, the diagnosis of depersonalization disorder is not made unless the symptoms are severe enough to impair social relationships or occupational competence.

Depersonalization disorder occurs most frequently among adolescents and young adults. It tends to run an intermittent but chronic course. Episodes of depersonalization tend to be elicited by stress. Depersonalization disorder does not appear to result in marked personality deterioration, and persons may function adequately between episodes. Symptomatology probably diminishes with age and adjustment. Sex differences in the incidence of depersonalization disorder have not been reliably established.

Normal persons may infrequently experience some symptoms of depersonalization. It has been speculated that many adolescents and young adults experience mild and temporary depersonalization when under stress. A study of persons in life-threatening situations revealed that many experienced some temporary symptoms of depersonalization. The life-after-death experiences that are being reported and are beginning to receive research scrutiny seem to be a type of depersonalization experience.

As ubiquitous as symptoms of depersonalization are, depersonalization disorder is a seldom diagnosed and little understood problem. The cause is unknown. Most theories have suggested that depersonalization reflects difficulties during development, either in infants' failure to develop a unified sense of self and world or adolescents' inability to forge a coherent identity and assume healthful roles in family and society, possibly due to trauma.

Treatment of depersonalization disorder has also varied widely and depends largely on the theoretical orientation of the clinician. Many medications have been tried, although there is still considerable interest in the use of antidepressants. Supportive psychotherapy has been frequently used, with mixed results. Behavioral approaches have included recording symptoms, stress management, relaxation, and assertiveness training. Milieu therapy has been recommended for adolescents in an attempt to help them develop a sense of identity. In spite of these recommendations there has been little research on the treatment of depersonalization disorder, and a clearly superior method of treatment has yet to be determined.

C. D. DOLPH

See DISSOCIATIVE DISORDERS.

Depression. Depression has been called the common cold of mental illnesses. Current estimates from the National Institutes of Mental Health (NIMH) suggest that each year more than 11,000,000 people in the United States suffer from this illness. A national study (Kessler, 1994) of more than 8,000 people aged 15 to 54 found a lifetime rate of 17% for major depression (21% among women and 13% among men) and a rate of 5% when people were asked whether they had been depressed in the previous month. If these statistics remain accurate, one of every five women and one of every eight men will suffer from major depression during their lifetime. In addition, a recent cross-national comparison (Cross National Collaborative Group, 1992) compiling the data of 12 studies from nine countries, and involving interviews with 43,000 people, indicated that the major rate of depression has risen steadily in much of the world during the twentieth century. In response to the increasing prevalence of depression in the United States and elsewhere, research efforts have been focusing more attention than ever before on the causes and treatment for depression.

However, the term *depression* needs more explanation. The current psychiatric glossary of mental illnesses, the *Diagnostic and Statistical Manual of Mental Disorders,* published by the American Psychiatric Association (1994) and commonly referred to as *DSM-IV,* lists major depression as only one of a larger related cluster of mood disorders. Suffice it to say depression differs greatly among people in its symptomatology, severity, and duration. Major depression and the associated mood disorders are further defined in the following section.

Depression also should be distinguished from what many of us experience as a bad mood, or from the normal grief reaction to the loss of a loved one or loved object. Bad moods, which often diminish during the course of a day or two, and normal grief, which may last beyond a period of a year, usually do not consistently interfere with work, friendships, family life, and physical health. More serious depression, however, sometimes referred to as clinical depression, interferes with and disrupts a person's job and relational life. The usual amounts of cheering up, exercise, prayer, vitamins, or vacation leave have little or no impact on this form of depression. People with clinical depression need to get proper treatment, which usually includes medication, psychotherapy, or a combination of both.

Depression and the Mood Disorders. The *DSM-IV* lists major depression, bipolar disorder, dysthymic disorder, and cyclothymic disorder as the primary disorders of mood. Major depression, also called unipolar depression, is identified by sad, empty, or hopeless feelings; slowed physical and cognitive behavior, including cognitive disorientation; changes in weight, appetite, and sleeping patterns; diminished interest or pleasure in activities and time spent with friends; and occasional to frequent thoughts of death and suicide. The presence of several of these symptoms for a period exceeding two weeks and a marked change from previous functioning are sufficient criteria for a diagnosis of a major depressive episode. Psychotic symptoms (delusions or hallucinations) are not common but do occur in about 15% of patients with major depression. According to one recent study (Update, 1994) the average major depression lasts four months. More than half of the people with one depressive episode will have a second, and 80% of people with two episodes will have a third.

Bipolar disorder, popularly called manic depression, is identified by alternating cycles of depression and manic elation. The length of cycle, the degree to which either depression or mania is present during a cycle, and the frequency of shifting between moods vary considerably in a bipolar disorder. The manic phase, when it is extreme, often resembles some forms of schizophrenia. As a result it can be very difficult to accurately diagnose a bipolar disorder at the onset. Manic phase symptoms include increased energy, inappropriate excitement or irritability, increased talking or moving, promiscuous sexual behavior, racing thoughts, impulsive behavior, and poor judgment, such as spending sprees or unrealistic plans or goals. These symptoms are often accompanied by grandiose thoughts and an inflated self-esteem.

Dysthymia and cyclothymia are related to major depression and bipolar disorder respectively in that each resembles a less severe but more chronic form of the latter. These disorders may be likened to a low-grade infection. For example, individuals diagnosed with a dysthymic disorder may never feel really good; they may go through the motions of daily life for years with little pleasure or enthusiasm. A cyclothymic disorder, by contrast, involves numerous periods of manic symptoms coupled with numerous periods of depressive symptoms. These symptoms are present for at least two years, but they are not as intense, nor do they meet all of the criteria for a classic bipolar illness.

Seasonal affect disorder, popularly known as SAD, is another closely related condition. SAD is a major depressive or bipolar disorder that recurs with a distinct seasonal pattern, excluding the obvious effect of seasonal related psychosocial stressors. This form of depression has been related to the brightness and duration of daylight, and in some cases has been successfully treated with artificial light therapy combined with medication.

The *DSM-IV* outlines each of these disorders in the section entitled mood disorders and supplies the more detailed criteria required for accurate diagnosis and treatment. A complete diagnosis involves careful attention to the onset, duration, and frequency of symptoms as well as accompanying features. When these factors are taken into account, there exist twelve distinct different forms of mood disorders. A copy of the *DSM-IV* should be available at a local library or Community Mental Health agency.

In addition to the *DSM-IV*, several well-known pencil-and-paper inventories can assist in the diagnosis of depression. Beck's Inventory for Measuring Depression (Beck, 1967), Zung's Self-Rating Depression Scale (Zung, 1973), and the Hamilton Rating Scale for Depression (Hamilton, 1960) are among the most common. The first two are self reporting, while the latter uses the scoring of two independent raters. In general these instruments are best used as screening tools or in conjunction with a clinical examination. They are not intended as a primary means of diagnosing major depressive illness.

Theories of Depression. Many general theories have been developed to explain how early family life, learning and cognition, social circumstances, and biology might produce a clinical depression. The best known are psychodynamic, behavioral, cognitive, systemic (family), and biological theories.

Psychodynamic Theories. These theories stress the resultant anger present when early dependency needs are frustrated (see Fenichel, 1945). Dependency needs can be unmet or frustrated in several ways. A child may experience actual or perceived parental rejection through autocratic and rigid parenting, experience the loss of a parent (especially mother) at an early age through death or divorce, or experience abusive or neglectful parenting (*see* Abuse and Neglect). Whatever the cause, intense feelings of loss and anger can result. At early ages children are not consciously aware of anger. If partial awareness is experienced, there still remains the problem of directing anger in a nondestructive manner. The frustration over unmet needs cannot be directed at the object of the anger but rather is directed to the inward or introjected image of that person. This is because the lost love object is either no longer available or is too threatening a figure. This introjected image is a part of the self in analytical terms, but it has yet to be adequately assimilated into the life of the individual. Consequently a loss or stressful experience in later life may reactivate the anger and cause a kind of delayed grief. The accompanying self-criticism and guilt (i.e., "anger is bad") are often expressed through symptoms of depression.

Fenichel (1945) also noted that dependency plays a major role in a psychodynamic understanding of depression. Depressive individuals are very dependent, showing a desire to passively meet needs and to react violently when such needs are frustrated. Depressive individuals interact with others in clinging or helpless ways that induce others to take care of them. This childlike dependency or helpless and hopeless pattern that follows the loss of a loved one or object is a postulate in most psychological theories of depression. Consequently psychodynamic treatment for depression will include an exploration of past events to discover unresolved painful experiences and the resultant anger that appears to be related to depressive symptoms.

Behavioral Theories. The nature of response patterns in an individual's behavioral repertoire is emphasized in this theory. Depression is described as a lowered frequency of adjustive responses to daily life. Compared to the normal person's responses to life, the depressed person's responses are fewer and slower. The depressed person may sit silently for long periods or perhaps stay in bed all day. The time taken to reply to a question may be longer than usual, and speaking, walking, or carrying out routine tasks will also occur at a slower pace. By its very nature such behavior will lead to a reduction in gratification. The depressed person's repertoire is also a passive one. It is marked by the effort to escape or avoid any uncomfortable or aversive social consequences.

Ferster (1973) suggests that a depressive response pattern can be elicited by a number of events: a high level of exposure to aversive events and the need to avoid aversive situations (e.g., consider the situation of the biblical character Job or Jonah); a low level of positive reinforcement (i.e., "no news is not always good news"); a sudden decrease in reinforcement from a significant source that has controlled a large amount of behavior (e.g., retirement or the death of a loved one); repeated exposure to a situation that requires much effort to gain even a little reinforcement (e.g., living under unrealistically high standards of performance); and the expression of anger that annoys other people and consequently denies the individual positive reinforcement. Since all of us experience some of these situations from time to time, the frequency and duration of these aversive experiences will distinguish people who are vulnerable to depression.

Furthermore, it is important to note that not everyone who is vulnerable to depression will become depressed. Behavioral theorists describe a cycle of depressive behaviors that tends to perpetuate itself. The low availability of reinforcement leads to depressive symptoms, which in turn lead to social avoidance, which ultimately perpetuates even lower levels of reinforcement. Consequently successful treatment for depression will break into this process at some point and reverse its downward spiral. The primary goal of behavior therapy for depression is to help the depressed person increase the frequency of positive adjustive behavior and ultimately restore much needed reinforcement.

Cognitive Theories. Depression is best described in these theories as a disorder of thinking. The philosopher Epictetus wrote that "men are not moved by things, but the view which they take of them." Ellis (1962) believes that most emotional disturbances arise from faulty thought processes. The depressed person has distorted beliefs about life that are sustained by automatic thoughts submerged in partial awareness. These thoughts are brief and may be only a word or two, yet they appear with regularity and create a form of negative self-talk that gives a running commentary on one's immediate experiences. This negative talk has its roots in what Beck (1976, p. 84) described as a cognitive triad of depression consisting of a negative view of the world, a negative concept of the self, and a negative appraisal of the future. The triad represents the essence of a depressed person's faulty thinking. All of us have some characteristic distortions in our thinking, but depressed persons consistently see the world, themselves, and the future through dark-colored glasses.

One common cognitive distortion is polarized thinking, or the all or nothing approach to life. A student may believe that a grade of A is the only acceptable grade. Consequently a grade of B or C is grouped with grades of D and lower. Grades then come in only two forms: acceptable (A) or unacceptable (B and lower). Other common cognitive distortions are usually identified through the therapy process. The treatment of depression with cognitive therapy will include the discovery and challenge of faulty thinking or distortions anywhere they are found.

A second major cognitive theory of depression is learned helplessness. Seligman (1975) formulated the concept based on a discovery involving animal research. Animals underwent a series of painful experiences (shocks) from which they could not escape. After repeated exposure to the experiments, the animals gave up even trying to escape and reduced their behavior to passive whimpering. When they were placed in trial runs where escape was a possibility, the animals believed they could not influence their environment (escape) and accepted the shocks. Applied to human behavior, learned helplessness is that state in which the individual comes to believe that nothing can be done about a present painful experience. For example, if a teacher were to pull grades out of a hat and assign them to students at random, the students would soon learn that nothing they did by way of work or study would influence their grade. It is easy to see how a person faced with this scenario might develop depressive symptoms. Perhaps readers can think of a few situations where people may feel they have little or no control. Successful therapy, directed toward reducing learned helplessness, must assist people in discriminating between controllable situations from those which are beyond one's control.

Systemic Theories. These theories interpret individual behavior, including depression, to be a function of one's interaction within the larger system (family). Applied mostly to the field of family therapy, depressive symptoms in a family member would be considered a sign that the entire family has an ailment. Consequently a member of a family who is experiencing depression is acting as a spokesperson for the family. A child's depression may be linked to a stressful marital relationship; a mother's depression may be linked to the children's leaving home and the father's preoccupation with work; a father's depression may be related to the unresolved grief accumulated over several past generations within his own family of origin.

An important distinction of systemic theories when compared to individual theories is the emphasis upon circular causality (see Watzlawick, Beavin, & Jackson, 1967, p. 46). In other words, individual behavior is more often a product of the interactions of an individual with other members of a shared system that comprise a series of never-ending feedback loops (i.e., member A influences member B, who influences A, who in turn influences B). For example, a young adult's efforts to leave home may make one parent anxious. The parent responds by attempting to move closer emotionally to the child. The child, who at this developmental stage of life needs greater independence, reacts by pushing further away from the parent. The parent becomes more anxious and increases efforts at moving closer to the child. If the anxious parent's efforts are successful in thwarting the child's natural move toward independence, depression may arise as a symptom in the child. Add family members C, D, and E to the equation, and the possibilities become myriad. This circular model is in contrast to the linear approaches of causation used in most individually oriented theories (e.g., A causes B causes C). Therefore, depression in a family member is seen as the entire family's response to the peculiar stressors of that family. Systems therapy will consider the symptom of depression within the context of the family and be directed at changing the interactions between family members that will eliminate the need for one of its members to be symptomatic. This type of reasoning can be applied to other individual symptoms, so that systemic thinking can be a way of interpreting other mental disorders.

Biological Theories. The role of genetic factors and brain chemistry is normally considered in these theories. Evidence for a genetic basis of mood disorders is largely supplied through comparison studies of monozygotic (identical) and dizygotic (fraternal) twins. Identical twins show a high rate of concordance with bipolar illness but a lower rate with unipolar depression when compared to fraternal twins. For example, Price (1968) found that in 66 of 97 pairs of identical twins, when one twin was diagnosed with a bipolar illness, so was the other. However, fraternal twins showed identical diagnosis in only 27 of 119 pairs. Moreover, the concordance levels for unipolar depression are even less for both identical and fraternal twins. The implication is that genetic factors play a stronger role in the causation of bipolar depression.

While it is generally agreed that genetic factors are linked to depressive illness, the mechanism responsible for the link is less clear. It is currently believed that genes exert their influence primarily by altering or modifying biochemical activity in the brain. The most prominent biochemical theory is the catecholamine hypothesis (see Adams, 1982, p. 418). According to this theory, depressive illness is associated with the amount of neurotransmitters (chemical substances) available at the synapse (a gap between neurons) site. The essence of brain activity is the firing of electrochemical impulses across neurons (nerve cells). Neurotransmitters facilitate this activity in the brain. Between 35 to 40 neurotransmitters have been identified in neuron activity. The availability of three of these appears to be closely related to depression. An insufficient amount of the catecholamines norepinephrine and dopamine or the idolamine serotonin at the synapse site has been strongly linked to depression. Conversely, an excessive amount of these may help explain the manic features in a bipolar disorder. The current antidepressant medications have the effect of increasing the availability of one or more of these neurotransmitters at the synapse.

Other Related Causes. Brandt (1988, p. 189) states that certain dysfunctions of the endocrine system can be chief sources of depression. Specific failures of the thyroid gland (hypothyroidism), the adrenal glands (affecting sodium and electrolyte balance), and pancreas (hypoglycemia) have all been related to the onset of depression. A thorough medical examination is usually recommended before diagnosing major depression and undertaking lengthy psychotherapy or treatment with antidepressants.

Lack of nutrition also can be an overlooked cause of depressive symptoms, and laboratory tests can identify specific vitamin deficiencies. Multiple vitamin and mineral (usually in megadoses) and amino acid supplements can be useful in such cases. The picture is complicated by the fact that depression can also contribute to nutritional deficiency. Emotional distress interferes with the proper absorption of vitamins, minerals, and amino acids, which in turn alter the availability of neurotransmitters. The question of which comes first is not an easy one to address and goes beyond the nutritional deficiency debate. Even when biochemical abnormalities are found to be causal agents in a person's depression, it is difficult to determine if depressed thinking has caused the biochemical changes or whether the chemical imbalances cause the depressed thinking.

Reviewing the numerous theories and related causes of depression might lead the reader to wonder which, if any, are the correct ones. Each theory explains depressive illness from a particular vantage point, and each related cause has supportive evidence. Furthermore, treatments based upon each have had some success in treating those suffering from depression. Each theory also has its limitations; none satisfactorily accounts for all manifestations of the mood disorders. As a result most experts believe in a biopsychosocial causation of depression. This means that the symptoms of depression are most likely caused by a combination of biological, psychological, and social factors, each of which contributes to a final common pathway to depression.

Treatment for Depression. The standard treatments for mood disorders are psychotherapy, medication (antidepressants), and electroconvulsive therapy (ECT, sometimes called shock therapy). It is difficult to specify psychotherapy techniques that are consistently superior in the treatment of depression. Perhaps this is because psychotherapy cannot be reduced to mere techniques but is best described as part science and part art. The chemistry between a client and therapist may have as much to do with successful treatment as the particular techniques employed by the therapist. The NIMH recently undertook what may have been the most careful comparative study (Update, 1995) of psychotherapy in history. Patients with major depression were assigned to one of four treatments: an antidepressant, a placebo, interpersonal therapy, and cognitive therapy. Interpersonal therapists emphasize the immediate social context of depression and the depressed person's relationships with other people. Cognitive therapists, as mentioned earlier, focus on correcting faulty thinking. Patients in all four groups improved; however, there was some indication that the combination of medication and some form of therapy was more effective than medication alone. Most experts believe that medication combined with a course of counseling offers the best possibility for successful treatment. It should be remembered that most research of this sort is conducted only on major depressive illness. Further research is needed to study the effectiveness of treatments for the other mood disorders (e.g., bipolar disorder or dysthymia).

Three main classes of medications are currently used for the treatment of depression: the tricyclics (TCAs), which increase the availability of norepinephrine and serotonin at the neuron synapse; monoamine oxidase inhibitors (MAOIs), which increase transmitter norepinephrine and dopamine; and the most recent addition, the selective serotonin reuptake inhibitors (SSRIs), which increase the availability of serotonin at nerve endings. Each has been shown to be generally effective in the treatment of depression. The differences between these medications arise mostly in experienced side effects. It is important to remember that each of these medications acts idiosyncratically with the users. For example, individuals taking the same tricyclic antidepressant (there are several available) may experience different side effects. Also, MAOIs, while effective, can produce a dangerous rise in blood pressure when taken at the same time as tyramine, a substance found in cheese, red wine, and other foods. All TCAs, if taken in an overdose of ten times the daily prescription, can be lethal. These drawbacks have led to the popularity of the newly released SSRIs, currently available under the popular names Prozac, Zoloft, and Paxil. These are not lethal if taken in over-

dose, and the noted side effects are fewer and less severe for the SSRIs. Contrary to popular opinion, none of the antidepressants is habit forming. They do not cause euphoria, and they will do little more than offer a few temporary side effects if taken by a person who is not depressed.

Physicians and psychiatrists normally prescribe antidepressants for a period of four to six months to a year. If one medication proves ineffective or its side effects are unacceptable, the doctor will likely prescribe another antidepressant. There is some trial and error involved in finding the most effective antidepressant, since at this time it is not known whether one is experiencing a depression related to a deficiency of serotonin, norepinephrine, or dopamine.

There are several other means of increasing the availability of neurotransmitters associated with depression. They are often overlooked because they are common and practical: proper exercise and nutrition. Proper exercise decreases vulnerability to the effects of stress (which deplete neurotransmitters), and proper nutrition provides the natural manufacturing of essential neurotransmitters. Brandt (1988, pp. 247–266) offers a guide to vitamin and food supplements that may assist one in overcoming depression. These obvious means of maintaining our physical and mental health need to be taken seriously when normal functioning has been disrupted.

Electroconvulsive Therapy. ECT is accomplished by passing an electric current through the brain to create an artificial epileptic seizure (the rapid firing of neurons throughout the brain). The procedure was introduced in 1938 and admittedly has not received a great deal of public support. In novels and films (e.g., *One Flew Over the Cuckoo's Nest*) it has been associated with attempts to subdue subversives. Discomfort with the convulsions occurred during the seizures, the severity of which would sometimes cause sprains and bone fractures. Drugs are now administered to make the patient comfortable and to relax the muscles. The procedure is painless and relatively safe. ECT is most often used for severely depressed patients who do not respond to other forms of treatment. Its effectiveness has also been shown on a limited basis for mania and schizophrenia. ECT may be the choice of treatment for some patients who cannot take medications for health reasons.

Pastoral Counseling and Spiritual Help. Medieval counselors saw depression as a sin to be fled. Current popular opinion among Christian counselors varies from treating depression as primarily a spiritual problem (Adams, 1970; LaHaye, 1974; Lloyd-Jones, 1965; Solomon, 1971) to considering it more an affliction of the body-mind that eventually oppresses the spirit of its victim (Minirth & Meier, 1978; White, 1982). The matter is further complicated by widely differing opinions on the nature of the spiritual life. Those who believe that the primary stumbling blocks to a healthy spiritual life are manifested in the subtle lies of this world will be careful to search the Scriptures and life for signs of the pure, holy, and true. Those who conceptualize spiritual health in terms of overcoming spiritual oppression may consider depression as an attack from the evil one.

White (1982, chap. 10), a Christian psychiatrist, believes that it is difficult to know if and when a person's depression is mainly a spiritual matter. He cites the case of a man who was relieved of depression through an understanding of the grace of God. Yet he added that "among the thousands of patients I have treated . . . he is the only seriously depressed person whose psychological needs were met by a spiritual understanding. More frequently I see spiritual understanding restored by psychiatric treatment" (p. 201). White acknowledges the importance of humans as spiritual beings created in the image of God and considers clinical depression a malady that often distorts one's spiritual understanding. It may also be impractical if not impossible to distinguish a spiritual depression from one caused by stress, disrupted affectional bonds, genetic vulnerability, or physiological imbalances. Efforts at separating the body and soul have led to much confusion throughout history, and the same is true when attempting to explain depression as an either/or phenomenon.

However, Brandt (1988) suggests three spiritual sources of depression: God-Void or the loss of an illusion, God-Neglect or the loss of fellowship, and God-Confusion or the loss of peace. Although these are problems of spiritual content, Brandt considers them ultimately the result of wrong thinking (p. 94). This may explain the popularity among many Christian counselors of the cognitive approach to depression. A number of Christian authors (e.g., Crabb, 1977; Backus & Chapian, 1980) have published popular helps for depression using a cognitive approach that allows for the use of Scripture as a guide to remedy the spiritual sources of depression.

White (1982) further reminds pastoral counselors of their important role in counseling a depressed person. It is the role of a patient encourager. The pastor is in a unique position to assist depressed persons in the congregation in fighting off the debilitating guilt that often accompanies depression. Moreover, this guilt is intensified by the idea that spiritual people do not become depressed. The pastor can help explain the numerous causes of depression and its ability to hold people almost helplessly within its grasp. Referrals for professional help can also be an important part of the pastor's role as caregiver. If depression has its roots in helplessness and hopelessness, the pastor can surely be a messenger of hope.

References

Adams, H. E. (1982). *Abnormal psychology.* Dubuque, IA: Brown.

Adams, J. (1970). *Competent to counsel.* Grand Rapids, MI: Baker.

American Psychiatric Association. (1994). *Diagnostic and statistical manual of mental disorders* (4th ed.). Washington, DC: Author.

Backus, W., & Chapian, M. (1980). *Telling yourself the truth.* Minneapolis: Bethany Fellowship.

Beck, A. T. (1967). *Depression: Causes and treatment.* Philadelphia: University of Pennsylvania Press.

Beck, A. T. (1976). *Cognitive therapy and the emotional disorders.* New York: International Universities Press.

Brandt, F. M. J. (1988). *Victory over depression.* Grand Rapids, MI: Baker.

Crabb, L. (1977). *Effective biblical counseling.* Grand Rapids, MI: Zondervan.

Cross National Collaborative Group. (1992). The changing rate of major depression: Cross National Comparisons. *Journal of the American Medical Association, 268,* 3098–3105.

Ellis, A. (1962). *Reason and emotion in psychotherapy.* New York: Lyle Stuart.

Fenichel, O. (1945). *The psychoanalytic theory of neurosis.* New York: Norton.

Ferster, C. B. (1973). A functional analysis of depression. *American Psychologist, 28,* 857–870.

Hamilton, M. (1960). A rating scale for depression. *Journal of Neurology and Psychiatry, 23,* 56–62.

Kessler, R. C. (1994). The national comorbidity survey of the United States. *International Review of Psychiatry, 6,* 365–376.

LaHaye, T. (1974). *How to win over depression.* Grand Rapids, MI: Zondervan.

Lloyd-Jones, D. M. (1965). *Spiritual depression: Its causes and cures.* Grand Rapids, MI: Eerdmans.

Minirth, F. B., & Meier, P. (1978). *Happiness is a choice.* Grand Rapids, MI: Baker.

Price, J. S. (1968). The genetics of depressive disorder. In A. Copper & A. Walk (Eds.), Recent developments in affective disorders. *British Journal of Psychiatry, Special Publication 2.*

Seligman, M. (1975). *Helplessness: On depression, development, and death.* San Francisco: Freeman.

Solomon, C. R. (1971). *Handbook to happiness: A guide to victorious living and effective counseling.* Wheaton, IL: Tyndale House.

Update on Mood Disorders: Part I. (1994, December). *The Harvard Mental Health Letter, 11* (6), 1–4.

Update on Mood Disorders: Part II. (1995, January). *The Harvard Mental Health Letter, 11* (7), 1–4.

Watzlawick, P. A., Beavin, J. H., & Jackson, D. D. (1967). *Pragmatics of human communication.* New York: Norton.

White, J. (1982). *The masks of melancholy.* Downers Grove, IL: InterVarsity Press.

Zung, W. K. (1973). From art to science: The diagnosis and treatment of depression. *Archives, 29,* 328–337.

For Further Information

The National Public Education Campaign on Clinical Depression. The nation's five leading mental health advocacy organizations have joined forces to raise awareness about clinical depression as a mental illness. Provides free brochures from the National Mental Health Association. (1-800-228-1114)

Depression/Awareness, Recognition, and Treatment Program (DART), National Institute of Mental Health. The federal government's public education campaign to raise awareness about depression and encourage depressed people to seek help. Provides free brochures in English and Spanish. (1-800-421-4211)

National Depressive and Manic-Depressive Association (NDMDA). A national membership organization representing and coordinated by people with depressive and bipolar illness. Offers patient support groups, advocacy, and educational brochures. (1-800-82-ND-MDA)

M. D. LASTORIA

See PESSIMISM; SUICIDE.

Depressogenic Attribution Style. A cognitive personality characteristic of how one habitually explains the causes of bad events involving the self. Of particular interest to psychologists is the depressogenic explanatory (or attributional) style. Also known as a helpless or pessimistic explanatory style, many researchers are convinced that the depressogenic explanatory style is a key in understanding disruptions in motivation, cognition, and emotion, especially following an experience with some uncontrollable event (*see* Learned Helplessness).

When people experience negative events, they are likely to ask why the events occurred as they did. Their answer to this "why me?" question, their explanatory style, will influence not only how they react to the event, but also their expectations for future behavior in relation to the event.

Explanatory style involving the self appears to be a function of three important dimensions. The first issue is the stability factor. To what extent is the causal explanation reflecting a long-lasting or stable self-characteristic and to what extent is the characteristic unstable, suggesting a transient cause? The second important dimension in the "why me?" search for causality is the global factor. A causal explanation can be global in that it can influence many outcomes or it can be specific by influencing only the outcome currently under focus. The third consideration is the locus factor, ranging from an internal to eternal focus. The causal explanation may involve something about the individual (the internal explanation) or about something external to the individual.

The person burdened with a depressogenic explanatory style is the person who scores high on stability, globality, and internality in reaction to a negative event. Research suggests that people who demonstrate a depressogenic style in reaction to negative events unfortunately do not employ the same style when good things happen to them. So, in relation only to negative (especially uncontrollable) events, the person who thinks "it's me, it happens every time, it appears in everything I get involved in" is the pessimist who may demonstrate learned helplessness.

The Attributional Style Questionnaire (see Peterson, 1991; Peterson, Maier, & Seligman, 1993) is the primary instrument developed to measure explanatory style. It consists of twelve scenarios, six positive and six negative, to which respondents are asked to rate the events described in each scenario along the stable, global, and locus dimensions.

References

Peterson, C. (1991). The meaning and measurement of explanatory style. *Psychological Inquiry, 2,* 1–10.

Peterson, C., Maier, S. F., & Seligman, M. E. P. (1993). *Learned helplessness: A theory for the age of personal control.* New York: Oxford.

P. C. HILL

See ATTRIBUTION THEORY.

Deprogramming. *See* CULTS.

Depth Perception. Depth perception is the ability to see objects as three-dimensional. The perception of depth by a two-dimensional detector, the retina, is the result of the synthesis of binocular and monocular cues. Binocular cues result from differences in the images received by our eyes, which are about 2 ½ inches apart. The brain uses this retinal disparity to make depth judgments. A second binocular cue is convergence, which refers to cues received from the muscles that control the eyes. As objects approach the face the eyes turn toward each other and the angle of convergence provides information used in perceiving depth.

While binocular cues are important when objects are close, information from binocular cues diminishes with distance as retinal disparity becomes insignificant and there is little or no convergence of the eyes. For more distant perceptions we rely on monocular cues, which do not depend on retinal disparity or convergence. Monocular cues include linear perspective, the appearance that parallel lines converge with distance; overlap, which occurs when nearer objects partially cover more distant objects; and relative height, the fact that objects higher in the visual field are perceived as more distant.

Additional Reading

Gibson, E. J., & Walk, R. D. (1960, April). The "visual cliff." *Scientific American,* pp. 64–71.

J. D. FOSTER

Depth Psychology. Systems of psychology that address the realm of the unconscious rather than just the conscious aspect of mental life. The term is used much more frequently in Europe, less frequently in England and the United States. Some authors equate it with psychoanalysis. More broadly understood, it also includes the systems of individual psychology, analytical psychology, and much of European existential psychology.

See SENSATION AND PERCEPTION.

Dereistic Thinking. A thought process that deviates from the normal laws of logic, reality, and experience. An example is the person who believes he is Jesus Christ. Such mental activity, characteristic of autistic and schizophrenic thinking, is called dereistic in that it is out of harmony with the facts.

See INDIVIDUAL PSYCHOLOGY; ANALYTICAL PSYCHOLOGY; EXISTENTIAL PSYCHOLOGY AND PSYCHOTHERAPY.

Descartes, René (1596–1650). French philosopher and mathematician who is justly renowned as the father of modern philosophy. Descartes's importance for psychology lies in his promulgation of a dualistic view of the person, in which the true self is viewed as an immaterial soul that is distinct from the body. Though his position is widely rejected in the twentieth century, Descartes's formulation of the mind/body problem continues to be a starting place for contemporary discussions of the issue.

Descartes lived in a period of scientific upheaval and social change. He attempted to overcome the resulting threat of skepticism by a method of doubting all beliefs that were not truly certain. The one thing that he felt could withstand such a doubt was his own consciousness of himself as a conscious being. Hence he laid down *Cogito, ergo sum* (I think, therefore I am) as the ultimate foundation for knowledge. Descartes reasoned that even if all his perceptual experience was illusory, even if he had no body, at least he must exist as the subject of the illusory perceptions.

From this basis Descartes argued that he, as "thinking thing" or soul, must be an immaterial substance, distinct from any body. His argument is as follows: Whatever can be clearly and distinctly conceived as separate could exist separately (at least by God's omnipotence). Descartes can clearly and distinctly conceive himself as a conscious being (soul) existing separately from a body (e.g., existing even if his body is a perceptual illusion). Therefore, soul and body could exist separately. Since whatever can exist separately is distinct, therefore soul and body are distinct.

This argument, even if it is sound, proves only that soul and body are separable, not that they are separate, a position we might call minimal dualism. Minimal dualism is a position many Christians have accepted for theological reasons, and it continues to be a defensible philosophical position. However, Descartes went on to assume that soul and body are separate and to postulate that soul or mind interacts causally with the body. The difficulty in understanding and explaining such interaction has led many people to accept parallelism, which denies any interaction, or to reject dualism altogether.

Descartes's conception of thinking was a very broad one, encompassing such diverse forms of mental activity as doubting, perceiving, willing, imagining, and feeling. Although the soul was thought of as a free spiritual entity, the body was conceived by

Descartes as "extended stuff" that operates in a machinelike manner. At some places Descartes suggested that animals are purely physical machines that lack consciousness. Contrary to his intentions, this suggestion that apparently conscious behavior in animals could be explained in mechanistic terms eventually led to the suggestion that consciousness in humans could be explained along the same lines. This discussion of animals highlights the poor fit of Cartesianism, which draws such a sharp line between the human and the subhuman, with evolutionary theory. Contemporary dualists have usually been emergentists, who attempt to work out a view of consciousness that allows more continuity with the higher animals.

C. S. EVANS

See MIND-BRAIN RELATIONSHIP.

Descriptive Psychology/Psychiatry. The descriptive approach to psychology or psychiatry is based on the study and classification of behavior without attempts to explain why the behavior occurs. It contrasts with the dynamic approach (*see* Dynamic Psychology), which focuses on the underlying causes of behavior.

In psychology the descriptive approach had its beginnings in Germany with the work of Franz Brentano (1838–1917). Brentano opposed structuralism as an approach to psychology and became the founder of its major contemporary rival, act psychology.

In psychiatry the descriptive approach is most commonly associated with the work of Emil Kraepelin. Kraepelin was also a German, and in spite of the overlap of their lives, there is no clear indication that he and Brentano had any awareness of each other or the similarities of their approaches. Kraepelin's classification of psychopathologies was in essence a descriptive approach. His assumption was that groups of symptoms that occur regularly together should be regarded as a specific psychopathology. This approach remains in current classifications of mental disorders, *DSM-IV*.

D. G. BENNER

Desensitization. *See* CLASSIFICATION OF MENTAL DISORDERS; DYNAMIC PSYCHOLOGY; SYSTEMATIC DESENSITIZATION.

Determinism and Free Will. The question of whether or not a person's choice of behavior is free, and to what extent, has plagued thinkers for centuries. Each answer has its defenders and critics. The position supporting free will or free-choice behavior has been called libertarianism (D'Angelo, 1968) or voluntarism (Hammes, 1971). Freedom here refers to the absence of intrinsic necessity in the performance of an act. That is, given alternatives among which to choose, one can select freely, without coercion. Freedom in behavior does not mean absence of causality. The libertarian does not contend that human behavior is uncaused but rather that there is a cause (the self) that can operate in a free manner to produce effects (choices).

Freedom is not the same as variance, as some would contend (Boring, 1957). The statistical variability of accumulative behavioral responses, referred to as the standard deviation of a distribution, does not constitute human freedom. Animals lower than humans, even the earthworm, possess behavioral variability. However, the voluntarist does not attribute freedom to such behavior. Human freedom can induce variability, but the presence of variability does not necessarily infer freedom.

Certain prerequisite conditions must be met before a free choice is possible. The first is awareness, or a normal state of attention. A second condition is deliberation. The person must have opportunity to consider choices of action prior to decision. When awareness and deliberation are lacking, either in degree or in entirety, there is corresponding attenuation of freedom and responsibility—for example, in actions of a retarded person or a psychotic, and in spontaneous emotional impulses (Hammes, 1971).

Evidence for Free Will. Various kinds of evidence have been adduced to support freedom in human choices. First, there is the capacity for voluntary attention, the act of directing the focal point of awareness to some object (Bittle, 1945). At this moment the reader's attention is on this page. Since the present behavior is deliberate, the state of attention is called voluntary. If, however, a sudden noise were to draw this attention aside, the interruption would illustrate involuntary attention. The fundamental awareness that attention is at times under personal control and in other instances is not demonstrates human freedom and is the basis for differentiating the two states of attention. The experience of intentionality itself is evidence for freedom and is a basic theme of humanistic-existential authors.

Libertarians also point to the experience of moral consciousness and conscience to support their belief in freedom (Bittle, 1945). The experience of guilt is indicative of the fundamental awareness that in the area of moral behavior one can be responsible for evil acts that need not have been done or that could have been freely avoided. The experience of guilt is so universal that persons lacking such feelings are diagnosed as psychopathic. Libertarians also cite the experience of moral effort in support of the conviction of human freedom (Dworkin, 1970), as well as personal achievement and the pride of accomplishment (Hammes, 1971).

Another argument in defense of free will is the conviction "I could have done otherwise" (D'Angelo, 1968). For the libertarian this statement means, "If I had so freely chosen, I would have done otherwise." It would seem the original statement could be compatible with determinism, if interpreted to mean, "If the determining conditions were different, I could have chosen otherwise" (Lamont, 1967). However, the belief in free will is based on the grounds of practical experience, whereas the determinist's objections are primarily theoretical and therefore not as weighty (Dworkin, 1970).

Another defense of freedom of choice is based on the observation of indeterminacy at the subatomic level. As expressed in the Heisenberg principle, which points out that it is impossible to make a simultaneous determination of the position and momentum of atomic particles, this indeterminacy is understood to be in the very fabric of nature rather than mere uncertainty or limitation in knowledge (Bube, 1971). However, libertarians vary on this interpretation of Heisenberg.

Determinist Objections to Free Will. Determinism has been classified by some observers into hard determinism and soft determinism. Hard determinists assert that freedom is illusory, that every event has a cause and is predictable, and that all human acts occur necessarily as effects of causes. Soft determinists attempt to introduce some element of freedom while still recognizing determinism. Humanistic-existential writers such as Rollo May and Carl Rogers are sometimes placed in the category of soft determinism. Others disagree with this division within determinism. They consider soft determinism an evasion of the issue and logically reducible to either libertarianism or hard determinism. Hard determinism has been presented in a number of different ways. Each will be examined here, followed by the libertarian's response.

A primary objection to freedom is that of skeptic determinism. The common basis for testimony of freedom is awareness, or the consciousness of this capability. Skeptic determinism strikes at the root of this conviction by asserting consciousness to be an invalid informational source. For example, an amputee may attribute sensation to a foot no longer present; a straight stick placed partly in water appears bent, although it is not. In both instances the skeptic contends that consciousness has lied.

However, the converse is true. Past learning accounts for the discrepancy between fact and judgment in the first example, and in the second example advantage has been taken of the structure of the human eye, which does not naturally correct for refraction of light in two media. The skeptic therefore attempts to use abnormal settings to discredit the testimony of consciousness in normal circumstances. A similar argument would be that if a blind person cannot see, no one can.

A more critical reply to skeptics, however, concerns the validity of their own positiveness. Can they doubt the trustworthiness of consciousness while using that consciousness as a basis for their doubt? Obviously not. Skeptics, in removing the basis for the validity of any doubt, consequently discredit their own. They can only hold to a doubt that is in itself doubtful.

A second form of determinism, cause-effect determinism, is based on law and predictability. It is contended that freedom is a conclusion based on ignorance of the causes actually present but unknown. These causes act necessarily to produce behavior as an effect. In response voluntarists concede that all behavior is caused but disagree that all causes act necessarily to produce effects. In the instance of free choice they contend that the person, as cause, freely initiates effects (behavior). Furthermore, the principle of causality states that effects are necessarily brought about by causes but does not demand that all causes necessarily act to produce effects. Neither is predictability a problem for libertarians, for a person may and usually does choose to act consistently, since by nature we are ordered human beings. A person freely choosing to lead a good moral life, for example, can be predicted to act in ways consistent with this resolve. Predictability, being compatible with both freedom and determinism, cannot be used as an argument against freedom.

A third expression of determinism is mechanistic determinism. This grows out of the monistic view that humans are merely complex machines whose mental processes are neurological only, reducible to physiochemical forces subject to the determining laws of matter. However, the evidence that mind and brain are distinct within humans, and that the mind cannot be reduced to matter, makes possible the exercise of freedom in human behavior (*see* Mind-Brain Relationship).

Fourth is biogenetic determinism. Heredity, temperament, glands, and emotions are supposedly the architects of human personality and the dictators of action. Sociobiology is a contemporary example of the emphasis on genetic structure as a determinant of character traits and presumably choice behavior as well. Libertarians respond that these factors are not self-evidently deterministic and can be considered influences rather than determinants.

A fifth variety of determinism is based on learning theory and could be termed stimulus-response determinism. This is illustrated by Ivan Pavlov and other classical conditioning learning theorists (*see* Conditioning, Classical). Conditioned behavior is sometimes used to arrive at the sweeping generalization that all human behavior is conditioned and that consequently freedom is precluded. However, some learning patterns require concentrated effort (e.g., learning to play golf or mastering algebra). The attempt to reduce all human learning to simple conditioning is, in the opinion of libertarians, arbitrary and unwarranted.

A closely related but broader theory is that of reinforcement determinism. This is illustrated by B. F. Skinner and other operant conditioning learning theorists. Whatever reinforces behavior determines its repetition. However, the fact that reinforced behavior is repeated does not necessarily infer a determined relationship. It is only logical for one to choose pleasurable experiences over unpleasant ones. Knowledge of the action taken sheds no light on whether or not the choice was free or determined.

Wider still is the theory of sociocultural determinism, the view that behavior is shaped by forces such as home, school, church, and community. These environmental variables purportedly indoctrinate individuals and structure their choice behavior. For example, slums are said to breed criminals. Clarence Darrow believed prisoners could not help being criminals, just as those outside of jail could not help but be there (Dworkin, 1970). Skinner contends human behavior can be engineered and controlled through cultural design. Libertarians would respond that social forces should be considered as influences rather than determinants of behavior. Criminals come from high as well as from low socioeconomic levels, and good citizens as well as delinquents emerge from slum conditions. Although socioeconomic factors most certainly limit the kind and number of available opportunities, the choice among these alternatives can nonetheless be free (Hammes, 1978).

An eighth objection to free will is motivational determinism. This is expressed by the statement The stronger motive prevails. Neo-Gestalt field theorists illustrate this position (Lewin, 1935). The fault in motivational determinism is that the prevailing motive is not labeled until after the decision is made. Thus no matter what alternative is selected, determinists would designate it as the stronger one. To do so proves nothing. The knowledge that a decision has been made gives no information on whether there was freedom or lack of freedom existing prior to the decision.

Another example offered by motivational determinists is that of reactive inhibition. After a person has pressed a red-light button for a hundred trials and has then been given the opportunity to push a light button other than red, it can be predicted that the individual will invariably select the alternative, which was thereby necessitated, according to determinists. (The reader may have recognized reactive inhibition as a term equivalent to monotony.) A repetitive behavior pattern will usually induce the impulse or tendency to alternate activity, a response natural to life forms, one which has survival value and which in humans may even be consciously experienced. Even in such circumstances, however, voluntarists would consider these behavioral tendencies to be influences rather than compulsive determinants.

Unconscious motivation is used as the basis for a ninth objection to freedom, termed unconscious determinism. This is illustrated by Sigmund Freud. Some psychoanalysts, on the evidence of unconscious defense mechanisms, deny freedom of choice. Even though on the conscious level humans are convinced of freedom, it is contended that there are unconscious forces unknowingly manipulating the decision-making process.

The defect in this line of reasoning is that the unconscious, being unconscious, is unknowable. Voluntarists could argue that the unconscious force of the rejected alternative was actually the stronger, and the chooser exerted great self-effort in the decision to overcome that option. Since the role of motivation below the level of awareness is an unknowable variable, it is arbitrary to assign various strengths of influence to one alternative over another. Unconscious motivation, therefore, cannot be used to prove or disprove freedom of choice.

A tenth theory of determinism involves the relationship between God and humans and can be called theological determinism. Three variants of this perspective are creationistic determinism, omniscient determinism, and predestination, based respectively on God's creative power, his knowledge, and his will.

Creationistic determinism is based on the law of causality, which states that effects are utterly dependent on their causes. If so, it follows that a person (as an effect) created by God (the cause) would be completely dependent upon the Creator in all human activity, including decision behavior. According to this idea a person is a divinely manipulated puppet.

Defenders of human freedom consider this view to be an unnecessary application of a law in the physical world to the world of the spiritual. In the material cosmos it is true that effects are completely dependent upon and determined by their causes. But is it not possible that different cause-effect relations exist on the nonmaterial, or spiritual, level? God could, if he so desired, create in his image a being with free will, utterly dependent upon him for existence but nonetheless possessing the capacity for freedom of choice. In no way would this concept do violence to the laws governing the material universe. Freedom exists as an immaterial, or spiritual, behavior pattern, since such activity is a function of the mind, itself immaterial. It could thus be argued that God created humans not just to be but rather to be free.

A second expression of theological determinism is omniscient determinism. Since God is all-knowing, he knows every human choice before it is made. Consequently it is contended that his knowledge determines that choice. The problem here lies in a person's inability to experience outside of time, since the human creature is time-bound and can experience events only as they occur. God, being independent of time, is not so bound. However, we can understand by analogy how his knowledge need not be causative. A person, having seen a football game and then reviewing it on film, could predict during the film exactly what the players would do next. If one were not bound by time, he or she could also have predicted the play at the time of watching the actual game. In neither instance would such knowledge be the cause of the players' reactions.

Therefore, it should be apparent that knowledge of behavior, even divine knowledge, is not necessarily the cause of that behavior. God could, if he so desired, control human activities completely. The question is not whether God possesses this power; it is rather whether his knowledge alone predetermines human choice.

A final variant of theological determinism is predestination, the position that God chooses those to be saved. Although both Luther and Calvin, representative of this view, believed in free will in everyday choice activity, they did not extend this ability to the matter of cooperating in personal salvation. Moreover, Luther believed in single predestination, the saving of the just, whereas Calvin held to double predestination, which included the eternal perdition of the reprobate. Predestination, however, is compatible with human freedom if it is interpreted to mean the promise of salvation to those who freely respond to God's redemptive grace. Since we are dealing with matters of Christian faith, determinists and voluntarists will be divided in accordance with their understanding of divine redemption.

Alternative Approaches. In addition to libertarianism and determinism, there are two other options in the argument over free will. There are those who believe the controversy to be an unresolvable paradox with which one must learn to live, and there are others who consider the controversy a pseudoproblem, reducible to semantic confusion. Some have applied Bohr's principle of complementarity, borrowed from physics, to the freedom-determinism controversy. According to this view both perspectives, being complementary, are true. Such attempts have been described as reconciliationism (Berofsky, 1966). However, voluntarists perceive the problem as involving contradictions, not mere complementarities, and resolvable only in terms of one side or the other.

The linguistic analyst sees the solution in terms of describing behavior in diverse languages, descriptions that present different aspects unrelated to each other (Barbour, 1966). Thus humans can supposedly be both determined and free in the same behavioral act, dependent on whether they are being described in terms of spectator language (determinism) or actor language (voluntarism). However, this approach would appear to evade the issue. For example, the preference of a scientist for spectator language or of an existentialist for actor language is irrelevant to the objective, ontological nature of the act, which in itself is independent of any descriptive language.

Resembling linguistic analysis is the multilevel systems approach (Bube, 1971), which contends that description on one level may be deterministic and yet on another level be indeterministic. All such approaches deny the determinism-free will problems. However, for reasons already considered in this article, many observers conclude that a real controversy exists, one that cannot be dismissed easily and one that requires resolution.

References

Barbour, I. G. (1966). *Issues in science and religion.* Englewood Cliffs, NJ: Prentice-Hall.

Berofsky, B. (Ed.). (1966). *Free will and determinism*. New York: Harper & Row.

Bittle, C. (1945). *The whole man: Psychology*. Milwaukee: Bruce.

Boring, E. G. (1957). When is behavior pre-determined? *Scientific Monthly, 84*, 189–196.

Bube, R. H. (1971). *The human quest*. Waco, TX: Word.

D'Angelo, E. (1968). *The problem of freedom and determinism*. Columbia: University of Missouri Press.

Dworkin, G. (1970). *Determinism, free will, and moral responsibility*. Englewood Cliffs, NJ: Prentice-Hall.

Hammes, J. A. (1971). *Humanistic psychology*. New York: Grune & Stratton.

Hammes, J. A. (1978). *Human destiny: Exploring today's value systems*. Huntington, IN: Our Sunday Visitor.

Lamont, C. (1967). *Freedom of choice affirmed*. New York: Horizon.

Lewin, K. (1935). *A dynamic theory of personality*. New York: McGraw-Hill.

J. A. HAMMES

See PHILOSOPHICAL PSYCHOLOGY.

Detriangulation. The process of family therapy by which a triangle (three people stuck in repetitious maladaptive patterns of interaction) is broken up. This can occur by the removal of one member of the triangle, as in the case of an adolescent who leaves home for college. Where removal of an individual is not feasible, detriangulation can be brought about by realigning relationships among the three. This process involves moving from enmeshment to interdependence. Because behavior patterns within triangles are frequently rigid and because the emotional forces among the three are so powerful, psychotherapy may be needed to effect a complete detriangulation.

J. A. LARSEN

See TRIANGLE; FAMILY SYSTEMS THEORY; FAMILY SYSTEMS THERAPY.

Developmental Coordination Disorder. The *DSM-IV* (American Psychiatric Association, 1994) recognizes four diagnostic criteria for developmental coordination disorder. The essential feature is a marked impairment in the development of motor coordination. Performance in daily activities that require this coordination is substantially below what is expected in accordance with the person's measured intelligence and chronological age. This may be displayed by marked delays in achieving usual childhood milestones (e.g., sitting, walking, crawling, clapping hands, tying shoelaces, buttoning shirts, zipping pants), dropping things, "clumsiness," poor performance in sports activities, or poor handwriting.

The diagnosis is made only if the disturbance in the first criteria significantly interferes with academic achievement or activities of daily living. The coordination difficulties can be diagnosed only if they are not due to a general medical condition (e.g., cerebral palsy, hemiplegia, or muscular dystrophy) and do not meet criteria for a pervasive developmental disorder. If mental retardation is present, the motor difficulties are beyond those usually associated with it.

The indications of the disorder vary depending upon age and development. Young children, for example, may demonstrate clumsiness and delays in accomplishing developmental motor milestones, as stated earlier. Older children may demonstrate difficulties with the motor aspects of assembling puzzles, playing catch, building models, and printing or handwriting.

Delays in other nonmotor milestones are problems that are commonly associated with developmental coordination disorder. Associated disorders may include phonological disorder, expressive language disorder, and mixed receptive-expressive language disorder.

Developmental coordination disorder must be distinguished from other motor impairments that are due instead to a general medical condition. Problems in coordination may be associated with specific neurological disorders such as cerebral palsy and progressive lesions of the cerebellum. In these cases, though, there is definite neural damage and abnormal findings on neurological examination.

A diagnosis of developmental coordination disorder is not given if the criteria are met for a pervasive development disorder. Individuals with attention-deficit/hyperactivity disorder (ADHD) may fall, bump into things, or knock things over, but this is usually due to distractibility and impulsiveness rather than to a motor impairment. If criteria for both disorders are met, both diagnoses can be given.

The prevalence of developmental coordination disorder has been estimated to be as high as 6% in the age range of 5 to 11 years. The diagnosis of the disorder usually occurs when the child first attempts certain tasks such as running, holding a spoon and knife, buttoning clothing, or playing ball games. Its course is variable. In some cases, the difficulties in coordination continue throughout adolescence and into adulthood.

Reference

American Psychiatric Association. (1994). *Diagnostic and statistical manual of mental disorders* (4th ed.). Washington, DC: Author.

K. R. HARKCOM

Developmental Psychology. This branch of psychology is concerned with the aspects of animal and human behavior that change from conception to death and with the processes that account for these changes. The length of time required for mature development is in relation to the position of the species on the phylogenetic scale, higher forms of life taking longer to reach reproductive capacity than lower forms.

The processes that account for behavioral change include growth, maturation, and learning. Growth is primarily quantitative and is seen in an increase in size. As children grow older, they also get bigger. Maturation is a more nebulous term but generally is used in connection with the unfolding of genetic potential. Programmed within every organism is a sequence and direction of behavior needed to adapt to the environment. What sets humankind apart from all other forms of life is a biological given that provides for intellectual, emotional, social, moral, and spiritual attainments not seen in any other species. The worth of the human infant is based not on competencies present at birth but on possibilities that will be realized as the child matures.

Learning connotes relatively permanent changes in behavior as the result of experience. All beings are influenced by the environment and learn as they are rewarded and punished. People learn not only by the consequences of their actions but also by imitating others and by responding to verbal instruction. Concept formation, problem solving, and language acquisition allow for complex understandings that enrich life and render the human experience unique. All three processes of development may combine to produce a given behavior. Playing basketball, for example, is possible only after the body has increased in size, muscles have matured, and the proper way to handle the ball has been learned. Psychologists who hold a behaviorist position tend to emphasize the role of learning in development, whereas psychologists who take a humanistic view are more apt to stress the potential within each person.

Development proceeds in a series of stages that correspond with chronological age. Infancy, early childhood, middle childhood, adolescence, early adulthood, middle age, and old age make up the major groupings. The research focus traditionally has been on the child rather than on the adult. Changes occur more quickly in the young and are easier to observe and record. Furthermore, the earlier stages are critical in that they take place during the formative years and affect successive stages. However, the more recent interest in the life span has produced considerable information on developmental processes during middle age and old age (Friedan, 1993). Each period is unique, representing the optimal age for the development of specific skills, cognitions, and personality characteristics (*see* Life Span Development).

All development is an interaction of heredity and environment (*see* Heredity and Environment in Human Development). The fetus is affected not only by genes inherited from the parents but also by an intrauterine environment that is sensitive to whether the expectant mother smokes, consumes alcohol, is malnourished, or contracts particular diseases such as rubella (German measles). The extent and nature of the insult to the developing organism depend on the characteristic that is changing most rapidly at the time. For example, European babies born with deformed limbs in the 1950s were so afflicted because their mothers took Thalidomide during the early weeks of pregnancy when limb buds were forming.

The emphasis of American psychology has been on the environment rather than on heredity, especially after the child is born. It is attractive to the Western mind to believe that with proper care and education every child can become a happy and useful adult. Attention given to individual differences present at birth that restrict the limits of development in such areas as intelligence (Herrnstein & Murray, 1994) and temperament (Thomas & Chess, 1977) has met considerable resistance.

The Scriptures present a number of comparisons between the development of the child and development in the Christian life. Salvation is described as a new birth (John 3:1–8) and spiritual growth as a consequence of feeding on "the pure spiritual milk [of the Word]" (1 Peter 2:2, NIV). Parents are enjoined to diligently teach their children the commandments of God (Deut. 6:6–7), since the early formative years affect the direction and pattern of behavior as children grow older (Prov. 22:6). Growing up in Christ brings new understanding and communications (Eph. 4:18, 29), development that for the Christian will someday be complete when "we shall be like him" (1 John 3:2, NIV).

References

Friedan, B. (1993). *The fountain of age.* New York: Simon & Schuster.
Herrnstein, R. J., & Murray, C. A. (1994). *The bell curve: Intelligence and class structure in American life.* New York: Free Press.
Thomas, A., & Chess, S. (1977). *Temperament and development.* New York: Brunner/Mazel.

B. Clouse

Deviant Behavior. See Life Span Development.

Dewey, John (1859–1952). The life of John Dewey is an example of his theory. He was influenced by the rural democratic Vermont environment, and he in turn did much to modify the environment of education in the United States.

Dewey was born in Burlington, Vermont, the son of a grocery store owner. His deeply pious mother required that he attend Sunday school and church services and properly observe the sabbath. Dewey reacted against this training and rejected the supernaturalism of his mother. He felt the idea of God hindered creative intelligence. After attending the University of Vermont, he taught high school for three years, then began doctoral studies at Johns Hopkins in 1882. He studied under Gordon S. Hall, became interested in the writings of Hegel, and wrote his dissertation on Immanuel Kant.

In 1884 Dewey became an instructor of psychology and philosophy at the University of Michigan. Ten years later he took over the chair of philosophy, psychology, and pedagogy at the University of Chicago, where he began a philosophical shift from Hegel's idealism to a pragmatic instrumentalism. He saw ideas as instruments for solving problems encountered in the environment. Nature, he believed, is ultimate reality, and people find meaning in the present.

Dewey's educational psychology was tested and developed in the laboratory school he and his wife began in Chicago. This was a functional psychology that focused on all aspects of the student as the student worked to adjust to the environment. Schools must begin with the interest of the child and provide opportunity for the child to interact between doing and thinking. While Dewey reacted against the content transmission of traditional schools, he also reacted against the kind of progressive education that failed to teach the disciplined use of intelligence.

In 1904 Dewey moved to Columbia University, where he was associated for the next 47 years. He attracted thousands of students and published enough books and articles to fill 125 pages of bibliography.

Dewey believed that maturing people are constantly faced with challenges from the environment, challenges that stimulate the use of intelligent action by the individual, which in turn promotes more maturity. Problems in experience are the stimuli that generate interest in growing.

While Dewey wrote little about therapy techniques, it would not be unreasonable to assume that he would advocate the exploration of problems through intelligent action. He had faith in the self-correcting process of creative intelligence. The counselor probably would help the individual articulate and analyze a problem situation, help the individual to project possible courses of action, and allow the individual to act, then help the person to scrutinize the consequence of the action. Since Dewey believed that people grow and mature when they interact with a community of inquiries, he most likely would facilitate problem solving in groups.

Dewey is often rejected by evangelical Christians because of his antipathy toward supernaturalism and special revelation. He rejected institutional religious dogma of any kind. Yet several aspects of his psychology seem consistent with Scripture and may be helpful to Christians. First, as the Christian struggles to find a view of the person that takes into account both the image of God and fallen human nature, Dewey can give valuable insight. His psychology would not accept a mechanistic view of the person, nor would he accept a romantic view that overlooks the selfishness of the child.

Second, to better understand the process of maturity we can learn from Dewey's psychological understanding of growth. Scripture illustrates God's use of the problem-posing experiences to stimulate maturity. Often God's chosen people were given difficulties that encouraged them to learn by reflecting on the consequences of their actions.

Some of Dewey's views of human nature and his views on the process of growth can be helpful to the Christian psychologist. While Christians need to beware of his antisupernaturalism, we can learn from Dewey as we seek to promote Christian growth.

J. E. PLUEDDEMANN

See ABNORMAL PSYCHOLOGY.

Dextrality-Sinistrality. See HANDEDNESS.

Dicks, Russell L. (1906–1965). Russell Dicks was born in Stillwater, Oklahoma, orphaned at the age of 15, and worked his way through high school, the University of Oklahoma, and Union Theological Seminary (B.D.). Hospitalization for tuberculosis in an injured elbow inspired his lifelong interest in pastoral care. Ordained a Methodist minister in 1933, Dicks served chaplaincies at Massachusetts General Hospital in Boston (1933–1938), Presbyterian Hospital in Chicago (1938–1941), and Wesley Memorial Hospital in Chicago (1944–1948). He also served as associate professor of pastoral care at Duke University (1948–1958) and as director of the Central Florida Counseling Center in Orlando (1958–1965).

After completing Clinical Pastoral Education (CPE) through the Council for Clinical Training in Boston, Dicks was an early chaplain supervisor for CPE. He routinely recorded his prayers and made word-for-word transcriptions of his pastoral calls, teaching students to prepare such verbatims in clinical training and using verbatims as illustrations in textbooks on pastoral care and counseling. Dicks's emphasis on the direct encounter challenged Anton Boisen's approach that utilized detailed case histories of the patient's physical and emotional development. Dicks pioneered in the preparation of devotional material for those in distress based on an empathic understanding of their special needs: selected prayers and reports are included in *Comfort Ye My People* (1947) and *My Faith Looks Up* (1949). With Richard C. Cabot, Dicks wrote the first book on pastoral care in illness, *The Art of Ministering to the Sick* (1936).

Dicks was a founder of the Institute of Pastoral Care in Boston in 1944; one of the first CPE trainers to analyze pastoral case material in a magazine for pastors; and the first to edit a magazine for laypersons on religion in relation to health and healing. Some of his books, including *When You Call on the Sick* (1938) and *Who is My Patient?* (1941), were written specifically for the laity. Dicks founded and edited *Religion and Health*, a short-lived periodical (1952–1956) distributed to churches, hospitals, and clergy; served on the editorial board of *Pastoral Psychology*; and was general editor of the Pastoral Aid Series for Westminster Press. In *Toward Health and Wholeness* (1960), Dicks discusses eight pairs of destructive and healing emotions: anxiety/faith, hostility/joy, guilt/self-awareness, despair/hope, loneliness/love, pain/courage, boredom/creative work, and rejection/acceptance. In 1963 he published *Premarital Guidance* and *Principles and Practices of Pastoral Care.*

Additional Reading

The man of the month: Russell L. Dicks. (1952, November). *Pastoral Psychology, 3* (28), 6, 66.

H. VANDE KEMP

Differential Diagnosis. The process of determining which of a number of similar-appearing disorders a patient has, while ruling out those which do not apply (Gallatin, 1982). In reality this is an extremely difficult task, particularly when the disorder is emotional rather than physical. In order to better understand the complexity of this task, it is necessary first to briefly review the purpose and technique of diagnostic formulation.

When a therapist is confronted with an individual seeking psychotherapy in order to find solutions to problems, relief from distressing symptoms, or guidance in formulating meaningful short- and long-range goals, a diagnostic formulation is sometimes helpful in assessing current functioning as well as in treatment planning. Rather than providing a snapshot of the present emotional state, a thorough diagnostic formulation serves as a roadmap that outlines the entire journey, past and present, as well as provides information on the likely directions of future functioning. This formulation takes into account constitutional factors that may have predisposed an individual toward certain forms of psychopathology, past significant traumatic experiences, and particular factors of interest in the early family environment. This information leads to what is called a genetic diagnosis, a summary of early, possibly predisposing, factors and forces that have formed the background for the present problems. A thorough diagnostic formulation may also include a dynamic diagnosis, which is typically a summary of the mechanisms and techniques unconsciously employed to manage anxiety and enhance self-esteem (Kolb & Brodie, 1982). The dynamic formulation focuses on the pattern of human transactions, resultant intrapsychic structures, and possible unresolved conflicts that have led to rigid, ineffective, self-defeating patterns of thought and behavior. Finally, a thorough diagnostic formulation includes a clinical diagnosis, a recognized system of classification that provides general information regarding associated symptoms, probable course, prognosis, and useful methods of treatment. *DSM–IV* is the nationally recognized classification system in the United States. It is when trying to determine the appropriate clinical diagnosis that the issue of differential diagnosis becomes paramount.

DSM-IV contains 20 major classifications and more than 200 specific disorders. Due to the similarity of symptoms and their sometimes vague and confusing presentation, determining the appropriate diagnosis can be a difficult task. (For example, it may be difficult to differentially diagnose a conversion versus organic or psychophysiological disorder, dissociative versus malingering or organic-mental disorder, dissociative identity disorder versus schizophrenia, affective versus organic-mental disorder, or affective disorder versus schizophrenia. It may also be difficult to determine whether the underlying personality structure is that of a borderline, narcissistic, or histrionic personality.) Differential diagnoses are sometimes made on the basis of symptoms described, history of previous functioning, response to treatment, psychological test data, neurological exam data, physical exam data, presence or absence of current stressors, family history, and current level of functioning.

Studies of the accuracy of differential diagnosis have demonstrated such decisions to be often inaccurate and unreliable. For example, in one study there was less than 40% agreement concerning the diagnoses in a group of psychiatric inpatients (Beck, Ward, Mendelsohn, Mock, & Rebaugh, 1962). While attempts to differentiate among major diagnoses (such as psychosis versus nonpsychosis) ranged as high as 70% to 85% in agreement (Gallatin, 1982), more narrow differential diagnoses, such as the specific form of schizophrenia or affective disorder, resulted in embarrassingly little agreement beyond that expected by pure chance. Even more interesting, although 80% agreement could be obtained when clinicians indicated that they were certain of the diagnosis, the infrequency of such moments of certainty and the low level of agreement at other times seriously undermine confidence in either the reliability or validity of present diagnostic systems for accurate differential diagnosis.

Why is differential diagnosis so difficult? Several reasons are typically given. Some attribute it to failure to apply uniform methods for collecting data in the interview process, as well as a lack of quantification of principal symptoms and signs recorded by different interviewers (Kolb & Brodie, 1982). Others attribute it to the complexity, ambiguity, and uncertainty inherent in the available diagnostic classification systems such as the *DSM–IV* (Gallatin, 1982). Still others point out the inherent complexity of sorting through confusing, vaguely presented symptoms reported by the patient (Woodruff, Goodwin, & Guze, 1974).

It is encouraging to note reports of improving reliability in differential diagnosis with the adoption of *DSM–IV.* However, regardless of how precise classifications become, the ambiguity of emotional problems and symptoms, as well as variance in the styles and experience of clinicians, will continue to make differential diagnosis a difficult task fraught with errors.

References

American Psychiatric Association. (1994). *Diagnostic and statistical manual of mental disorders* (4th ed.). Washington, DC: Author.

Beck, A. T., Ward, C. H., Mendelsohn, M., Mock, J. E., & Rebaugh, J. K. (1962). Reliability of psychiatric diagnosis. *American Journal of Psychiatry, 119*, 351.

Gallatin, J. E. (1982). *Abnormal psychology.* New York: Macmillan.

Kolb, L. C., & Brodie, H. K. (1982). *Modern clinical psychiatry* (10th ed.). Philadelphia: Saunders.

Woodruff, R. A., Goodwin, D. W., & Guze, S. B. (1974). *Psychiatric diagnosis.* New York: Oxford University Press.

J. D. GUY, JR.

See CLASSIFICATION OF MENTAL DISORDERS.

Differential Psychology. Differential psychology is "the objective and quantitative investigation of individual differences in behavior" (Anastasi, 1958, p. 1). As a branch of psychology it examines the types, amounts, antecedents, and consequences of differences, whether between individuals or groups (e.g., races, species, or sexes). Measurement of differences is a key concern, as are the related issues of reliability and validity. As a consequence differential psychologists rely on statistical theory, particularly correlational and normative statistics. For this reason differential psychology has sometimes been called quantitative psychology.

Differential psychology is best contrasted with general psychology (Cronbach, 1957). General psychology (e.g., experimental) studies individuals for the purpose of formulating general laws describing how individuals are alike. Differential psychology (e.g., ethnic, psychometric, genetic, comparative, or individual) asks how individuals differ. These branches employ different research strategies. The controlled experiment in which the psychologist manipulates one variable (independent variable) to determine its effect on another variable (dependent variable) while all other influences are constant is the method adopted by the general psychologist. But differential psychologists conduct multiple measurements on variables under nature's control to determine their interrelations.

The forte of general psychology is the discovery of general laws of behavior through the methods of isolation and control. Differential psychology searches out reliable relationships between variables through correlational methods such as factor analysis. In general psychology individual differences are considered to be noise and become a significant component in the composition of experimental error. General psychologists attempt to minimize individual differences through controlling experiential histories and using powerful treatments. Differential psychologists seek to maximize individual differences, an approach that increases the reliability of their measurements. Maximizing variance and using large samples become important in using the normal distribution.

Differential psychology may have originated in Adolph Quetelet's (1796–1874) application of the normal curve to biological and social data. Previously it had been applied only in the physical sciences. Quetelet coined the phrase *l'homme moyen* (the average person) to indicate that when measurements are taken from a large, randomly selected sample, they approach the normal distribution with a concentration of scores near the mean and only a few extreme cases.

Francis Galton applied the normal curve to hereditary genius and other individual differences such as reaction time and sensory thresholds; he conducted his research in his famous Anthropometric Laboratory. He developed the concepts of correlation and regression toward the mediocre (i.e., mean). The symbol r, signifying correlation, came from regression. Karl Pearson (1857–1936) developed the present statistical formula, product-moment correlation, to measure Galton's concept.

Further developments came from James McKeen Cattell, who coined the phrase *mental test*. Cattell investigated reaction time as a significant part of mental abilities. The study of reaction time stemmed from an incident at Greenwich Observatory. The royal astronomer Maskelyne dismissed Kinnebrook for observing stellar movements a consistent one-half second later than himself. Other contributions to differential psychology include Alfred Binet's and Simon's work on intelligence testing, Charles Edward Spearman's two-factor theory of intelligence, Louis Leon Thurstone's theory of primary mental abilities, and Raymond B. Cattell's factor analytic work on personality and mental abilities.

In recent years differential psychologists have concentrated on personality and intellectual differences. However, a number of other domains have been examined in the past. These include a study of the nature-nurture controversy, psychological differences between the sexes, and age and class differences.

References

Anastasi, A. (1958). *Differential psychology* (3rd ed.). New York: Macmillan.

Cronbach, L. J. (1957). The two disciples of scientific psychology. *American Psychologist, 12*, 671–684.

R. L. TIMPE

See PERSONALITY ASSESSMENT; PSYCHOLOGICAL MEASUREMENT.

Direct Decision Therapy. A loosely formed approach to counseling and psychotherapy founded by Greenwald (1967, 1973). It has its roots in psychoanalytic theory, in which Greenwald was originally trained, but it tends to be open-minded and eclectic in nature. The approach has not achieved the status of a major system of psychotherapy. It appears to be little known and remains primarily the interest of its founder.

Greenwald defines direct decision therapy as a brief therapy that is in essence a philosophy of living. The main objective is to help individuals make decisions to change their lives. "Direct" has reference to the fact that clients are made aware that they indeed are making decisions in therapy as well as in everyday living. "Decision" depicts the choices that can be made regarding alternative behaviors, ways of organizing information, or modes of perceiving the world.

Direct decision therapy is built on some basic assumptions about human beings and their behavior. People are free to decide and change. Yet there exists the tendency to remain and act like infants in the desire to be taken care of. But with professional guidance individuals have the ability to deal with their problems, make constructive choices, and take charge of their lives.

An individual lifestyle is shaped by the decisions one makes. Basic decisions include deciding to be perfect, to be different, to suffer, to please, to live or die, to be indecisive, to be nonexpressive of feelings, to be "crazy" or "normal," and so forth. It follows that problems in living—psychoses, depression, homosexuality, anger, loneliness—are the consequences of an individual's decisions. Environmental influences do serve to condition certain problems, but decision making accounts for most of the causation. Organic conditions such as congenital defects and mental retardation impede adaptive decisions.

Direct decision therapy places a strong emphasis on the relationship between the therapist and the client. The therapeutic encounter is marked by the therapist's authenticity, honesty, and nonjudgmental attitude. The therapist also seeks to have an empathic understanding of the client and his or her problem, to respect the individual as a person, to provide an accepting atmosphere for therapy, and to demonstrate consistently the firm belief in the client's ability to decide and change for the better.

A set of essential guidelines is followed to give structure to the procedures in the therapy process. The client first is asked to state the problem clearly. Next the client is guided in examining past decisions that have helped to create and maintain the problem. Third, the payoffs for each of the decisions are identified. Fourth, a profile is sketched of the context in which the original decision was made. Then the client identifies and explores alternatives to the past decisions. After identifying alternative options, the client is asked to choose one of the alternatives and to decide to put it into practice. The therapist's encouragement and support are used to reinforce the client's carrying out of the decision.

A wide variety of therapeutic methods and strategies are used to supplement the decision-making model. Examples of the eclectic blend are psychoanalytic free association, Gestalt, behavior modification, paradoxical intervention, humor, and hypnosis.

Direct decision therapy is offered by the founder as a therapy that is applicable to the gamut of problems in living. However, Greenwald himself seems to have a penchant for cases of sexual deviancy. Perhaps this stems from his original research with female prostitutes. While the decision-making paradigm appears to be down-to-earth and useful, the approach lacks depth and comprehensiveness. Also, the Christian counselor or therapist is likely to look askance at Greenwald's free-spirited and sometimes risqué style of doing therapy. The appealing qualities of direct decision therapy are its simplicity, practicality, and stress on the therapist as a genuine, self-disclosing person.

References

Greenwald, H. (1967). *Active psychotherapy*. New York: Atherton.

Greenwald, H. (1973). *Decision therapy*. New York: Wyden.

D. SMITH

See SHORT-TERM THERAPIES.

Direct Psychoanalysis. Therapeutic approach developed by Rosen in his attempt to understand and communicate directly with the unconscious of psychotic patients. It utilizes in modified form many of the psychoanalytic insights and techniques in an effort to make them most useful for work with psychotics.

Rosen's approach is based on the assumption that the behavior of the psychotic patient, no matter how bizarre it may appear, is an attempt to communicate. The challenge for the therapist is to understand the logic of the unconscious in an attempt to decode the psychotic communication. In essence the treatment consists of having the patient relive early traumatic experiences with the mother. In this process the therapist attacks the patient's delusions. Thus, for example, if a patient claims he is God, Rosen might say "Prove it." Or he might squeeze the hand of a mute patient until she screams and then use this to prove to her that she can communicate vocally.

Rosen adopted the term *direct psychoanalysis* to contrast his approach to that of Sigmund Freud, whose classical method he saw as too indirect for work with psychotics. He reports his procedures to be quite successful, but the majority of psychoanalysts remain skeptical about his methods and their effectiveness.

D. G. BENNER

See PSYCHOANALYSIS: TECHNIQUE.

Disability. It is estimated that 36,000,000, or 14.5% of the 246,000,000 people living in the United States, have some form of disability (Adams & Benson, 1991). Disability may broadly be defined as "limitation(s) in human actions or activities due to physical or mental impairment(s)" (LaPlante, 1992, p. 1).

Types of physical disability include mobility impairment, sensory loss, disfigurement, chronic pain, and long-term illness. Mental disabilities include mental retardation, learning disability, and chronic mental illness (Creamer, 1995). Hidden disabilities include but are not limited to learning disability, brain injury, chronic fatigue, diabetes, chemical sensitivities, allergies, and epilepsy.

The experiences of disability are varied. Disabilities may be temporary or permanent. They may affect all aspects of a person's life or may cause only minor inconveniences. A disability can be relatively stable or can become worse over time. Some disabilities improve with time, in conjunction with appropriate treatment. Disabilities may be caused by accident, illness, or genetics. Some individuals acquire disabilities at birth, while others develop a disability during the course of life (Creamer, 1995).

Appropriate terminology is essential to an accurate understanding and positive attitude regarding disability. "Disability" is a general term used for a functional limitation that interferes with abilities such as walking, hearing, seeing, or learning. It may refer to a physical, sensory, or mental condition. "Handicap" describes a condition or barrier imposed by society, the environment, or oneself. "Handicap" may be used for citing laws and situations, but is it not an appropriate term to describe a disability or a person with a disability. It is essential to emphasize personhood and ability over disability and limitation and to avoid equating the person with his or her disability. Thus it is more appropriate to say "people who are blind" or "a woman with arthritis" than to say "the blind," or "she is an arthritic" (Research & Training Center on Independent Living, 1990).

The Americans with Disabilities Act of 1990 (ADA) is the world's first comprehensive civil rights act for people with disabilities. It is a federal antidiscrimination law that ensures that people with disabilities have equal opportunity and access. It is comprised of four Titles: Title I—equal employment opportunity; Title II—nondiscrimination in state and local government services; Title III—public accommodations and commercial facilities; and Title IV—telecommunications. Religious organizations are legally exempt from the accessibility requirements of the ADA (Section 307).

Section 504 of the Rehabilitation Act of 1973 prohibits discrimination in any programs or activities that receive federal financial assistance. Title II of the ADA extends the nondiscriminatory requirements of Section 504 to include programs and activities of all state and local governments, whether or not they receive federal financial assistance.

A psychology of disability must include an understanding of the psychological and social impact of disability on the person with the disability, the family, and others in relationship with the person with a disability. An understanding of the psychological mindset, understanding, and attitudes of individuals and society toward disability is also needed.

Accurate empathy is essential to the understanding, support, and treatment of persons with a disability. Empathic understanding implies that the therapist is able to sense the client's feelings as if they were his or her own, without becoming lost and overwhelmed in those feelings. Empathy is not objective knowledge about the client; it "is a deep and subjective understanding of the client with the client" (Corey, 1986, p. 109). Two essential aspects of empathy are intellectual identification of oneself with another through knowledge and understanding and emotional identification of oneself with another, through the ability to feel with another.

Rehabilitation is a multidisciplinary endeavor, aimed at integrating and meeting the holistic needs of a person with physical, sensory, or mental disability. Clinical and behavioral psychology by itself is not adequate to address the life picture of a person with a disability. Perspectives from economics, sociology, history, anthropology, and politics are needed as a backdrop for the accurate understanding of psychological issues such as grief, loss, trauma, sexuality, and life adjustment (Stubbins, 1991). A rehabilitation team may include general and specialist physicians, physical, occupational, and recreation therapists, social workers, psychologists, caregivers, family members, nursing personnel, vocational rehabilitation counselors, health care equipment providers, nutritionists, and other resources as needed.

Coping with disability often raises the theological issues of suffering, healing, and faith, the problems of pain and evil, and the perceived absence of God. The counselor, whatever her or his individual beliefs, should approach these issues with profound sensitivity so as to impart grace and comfort rather than guilt and shame.

References

Adams, P. F., & Benson, V. (1991). Current statistics from the National Health Interview Survey, 1990. *Vital Health Statistics, 10* (181), 1–112.

Corey, G. (1986). *Theory and practice of counseling and psychotherapy* (3rd ed.). Monterey, CA: Brooks/Cole.

Creamer, D. (1995). Finding God in our bodies: Theology from the perspective of people with disabilities, Part I. *Journal of Religion in Disability & Rehabilitation, 2* (1), 27–42.

LaPlante, M. P. (December, 1992). How many Americans have a disability? *Disability Statistics Abstract, 5,* 1–4.

The Research & Training Center on Independent Living. (1990). *Guidelines for reporting and writing about people with disabilities* (3rd ed.). Lawrence: University of Kansas Press.

Stubbins, J. (1991). The interdisciplinary status of rehabilitation psychology. In R. P. Marinelli & A. E. Dell Orto (Eds.), *The psychological and social impact of disability.* New York: Springer.

Additional Readings

Journal of Religion in Disability & Rehabilitation (spring 1994 to present, quarterly). W. A. Blair & D. D. Blair (Eds.). Binghamton, NY: Haworth Pastoral Press.

Marinelli, R. P., & A. E. Dell Orto (Eds.). (1991). *The psychological and social impact of disability*. New York: Springer.

Rolland, J. S. (1994). *Families, illness, & disability: An integrative treatment model*. New York: Basic.

G. P. NAGEL

See NORMALIZATION IN HUMAN SERVICES; COMMUNITY PSYCHOLOGY.

Disagreement, Handling of. *See* CONFLICT MANAGEMENT.

Discernment, Spiritual. In 1 Corinthians 12:10 it is written that the Holy Spirit gives to some individuals the discerning of spirits: the wisdom in making keen judgments, the ability to discriminate and perceive with insight, and to recognize or identify good and evil in a separate and distinct way. Spiritual discernment is a subjective and experiential ability to understand and interpret a religious experience and spiritual condition. The seeker of God, in humility and love, desires to be led by the Spirit in all ways (Gal. 5:18; Rom. 8:14). This religious experience strengthens the awareness of believers as "the children of God" (Rom. 8:14–17), forming a dependency and interactive communication with God through prayer and action.

Closely connected to spiritual discernment, especially when the community and its life are involved, is the spirit of prophecy. The Christian community is warned in 1 Thessalonians 5:19–22 to take care not to quench the Spirit or despise prophesyings. In all matters, refraining from all evil and testing or proving of everything to ensure that it is good (i.e., of God) is essential. When individuals depend on their own fallible knowledge and abilities, failing to recognize that all power comes from God, they are led into falsehood, temptation, false pride, and a breach in communication with God and divine will. Only constant reliance upon God can make possible the understanding of good and evil, should God choose to imbue an individual with such a gift or experience. Slipping on the rocks of pride and independence from God, even momentarily, caused one as devout as Moses to lose his spiritual balance and to forfeit entering the promised land with his people. Peter, momentarily taking his eyes off of Jesus and focusing instead on the boisterous wind and his fear of slipping, lost his footing in the water and began to sink. Only when he once again looked to Jesus was he connected to the divine and able to discern the good (strong faith in God) and evil (doubting God's salvific grace; Matt. 14:27–31).

Although the Old Testament does not speak of spiritual discernment in that terminology, it describes the intervention of prophetic interpretation and the presence of God in directing the Jewish community and its daily life. Guidelines were set by which people might judge the validity of what prophets spoke (Deut. 18:21–23).

Discriminating between the Spirit of God and a counterfeit, evil spirit involves a judgment by discerners of their fruits or what their actions bring about. Where the true Spirit is present, the spiritual discerner has taken much care, through the help of God, to be pure, moral, a devout believer, trustworthy, loving of others, generous, loyal, temperate, and peace-loving. For the Christian, acknowledging Jesus Christ as Lord and Savior comes from the teaching and guidance of the Spirit (1 Cor. 3:3). Then, choosing to live in the Spirit and to follow the leading of the Spirit, certain individuals are able to discern the direction in which the Spirit guides. Paul, speaking of the transforming power of the Spirit to renew the mind so that the person might discern the will of God, what is good, pleasing, and perfect (Rom. 12:2), describes the development of a Christian into a spiritual person who is then able to judge all things. In this way people who are given the gift or awareness by the Spirit are allowed to share in God's wisdom on some matters. Extreme humility is required, since in no way is the created ever to equate ability to discern with being equal to the Creator. This was the grievous sin of Lucifer.

Discernment of evil could come about through sincere prayer, a dedicated spiritual life, and a strong desire to stay close to God and under divine protection from evil. Focusing so much on the good and thus on God allows the individual to see the contrast of good and evil. However, where there is sin and self-seeking, there will be distortion of purpose and thinking. Satan will be able to deceive, making the ungodly appear acceptable and attractive to the superficially righteous.

A possible serious error that some religious leaders may make concerns not only correctly discerning spiritual gifts of other believers, including spiritual discernment, but also encouraging such gifts and their sharing and not envying those with keen insight in detecting good from evil. Scripture tells us that in the last days women and children will prophesy and that, if God's people do not bear witness for Christ as Savior, the very rocks would speak out for him. Such prophesying and witnessing require spiritual discernment of good and evil and of the sacred and the secular. The survival of the community of believers depends on at least some of its members remaining in close relationship with God to discern and instruct others in the divine life and holy goals.

C. A. RAYBURN

See SPIRITUAL AND RELIGIOUS ISSUES IN PSYCHOTHERAPY.

Disorientation. A breakdown in the awareness and understanding of time, people, and places. Temporal effects include an impairment in individuals' understanding of where they are in time and space. They also lose perception of who they are and of their body image. Disorientation occurs in psychosis, organic conditions, mental disorders such as hallucinations and delusions, and neurotic disorders such as hysterical fugue.

Displacement. The unconscious transference of emotional charge or symbolic significance from one object or set of ideas to another. This ego defense process serves to protect against the threat or pain of associating the feelings or meanings with their original ideas. This may be seen in the case of a schizophrenic patient who has displaced all the anxiety and emotion originally associated with his conflicted relationship to his mother onto a word, phrase, or mental image apparently unrelated to his mother, reacting to that idea as he otherwise would react to mother. Displacement may also operate toward the self, as when anger at another is turned inward. This results in irrational self-denigration, depression, guilt, and perhaps suicidal impulses.

Displacement may also refer to the redirection of id impulses. This would be seen when sexual impulses, denied direct genital satisfaction, find expression through talking about intimate sexual matters. This form of displacement, called Sublimation, is viewed by psychoanalysts as a healthy and often socially constructive activity.

R. LARKIN

See DEFENSE MECHANISMS.

Disruptive Behavior Disorders. The disruptive behavior disorders are a category of psychological disorders specific to childhood and include attention deficit/hyperactivity disorder (ADHD), oppositional defiant disorder (ODD), and conduct disorders (CD). The latter two have much in common and will be discussed here. The predominant thinking is that CD is the result of untreated or uninterrupted ODD.

The primary symptoms of both ODD and CD include a disruption in socially appropriate behaviors, which causes distress to others. ODD, according to *DSM-IV* (American Psychiatric Association, 1994), includes "a pattern of negativistic, hostile, and defiant behavior" and must be represented by at least four of these symptoms occurring often: loses temper, argues with adults, actively defies or refuses to comply with adults' requests or rules, deliberately annoys people, blames others for his or her mistakes or misbehavior, is touchy or easily annoyed by others, is angry and resentful, is spiteful or vindictive.

Children and adolescents with CD, according to *DSM-IV,* perform "a repetitive and persistent pattern of behavior in which the basic rights of others or major age-appropriate societal norms or rules are violated." Such demonstrations fall into four categories: aggression to people and animals (including bullying, threatening, or intimidating others, initiating physical fights, use of a weapon, physical cruelty to people or animals, stealing with confrontation of victim, or forced sexual activity), destruction of property (including fire setting with intent of damage, other deliberate destruction of others' property), deceitfulness or theft (breaking into house, car, or building, conning others, stealing without confrontation such as shoplifting), and serious violations of rules (such as staying out at night without parental permission, running away from home overnight, truancy from school).

These disorders have been a focus of much research. There is no debate over the evidence that both ODD and CD seem to run in families; rather the debate centers on the mode of transmission across generations. Compared to other families, parents of children who have ODD and CD have been shown to be more likely to use discipline less consistently, to be poorer at supervision of their children, to use harsh and abusive methods of discipline, to be more rejecting of their children, and at times to reinforce antisocial behavior by their children. This familial link, however, seems to extend beyond the parenting skills of the parents. Research has strongly supported the relationship between childhood behavior problems and one or more parents having antisocial personality disorder, the adult equivalent and/or perhaps result of ODD and CD. The question then becomes whether the child learned or inherited this maladaptive behavioral pattern. Plenty of evidence exists for the learning paradigm, but some also exists for the genetic transmission. For instance, some studies have shown a relationship between children adopted at birth who have ODD and CD and their biological parents (and not their adoptive parents) having antisocial personality disorder. Studies that have examined identical twins who were reared apart have also supported a genetic link to these disorders. Finally, other factors that have been shown to be related to ODD and CD include early trauma such as abuse, neglect, and separation from parents (*see* Abuse and Neglect). Family conflict and divorce are also potentially important contributors, although again, one has to consider whether a third factor led to both the conflict/divorce and the behavior problems.

Children with ODD or CD who are not treated are at considerable risk of graduating to criminal and/or antisocial behavior as adults. In general the younger the age of onset and greater the number of symptoms, the worse the prognosis for the child. Other risk factors include lower intellectual abilities and achievement, peer rejection, less parental supervision, and coexisting diagnosis of ADHD. Children who develop behavioral symptoms in conjunction with depression have a better prognosis of recovering if the depression is treated.

In cases of ODD and CD, treatment must focus on others in the child's environment, especially parents, who must think in terms of long-term management. Children with ODD and CD typically have personality styles that steer them toward limit testing, risk, and being in control. In order to successfully treat, parents must learn how to manage the difficulties that their child presents day in and day out, possibly for as long as they have guardianship over them. Parents who hope that their child's problems can be "cured" with a bout of therapy are in danger of being badly disappointed. However, the prognosis is promising for children whose parents can master the necessary skills.

Reference

American Psychiatric Association. (1994). *Diagnostic and statistical manual of mental disorders* (4th ed.). Washington, DC: Author.

T. KEMPTON

See CHILD DISCIPLINE.

Dissociation. Dissociation occurs when there is a disruption in the normal integrative functions of consciousness, which may include behavior, affect, sensation, and knowledge. Dissociation is generally considered to exist on a continuum (Putnam, 1989). Normal dissociative experiences of everyday life include being absorbed in a movie or daydreaming. Certain religious practices, such as glossolalia, may also represent a normal variant of dissociative experience within certain faith communities. The most extreme pathological form of dissociation occurs in dissociative identity disorder.

In pathological dissociation psychic material is pushed out of the ego's awareness to the side or back of the mind. The material is not, however, unconscious. It is merely dissociated ego, which may be rational, organized, and coherent in its own right. This phenomenon has been described as a vertical split (Hilgard, 1977), in contrast to a horizontal split, in which aspects of the psyche are considered to be repressed and submerged in the unconscious. Pathological forms of dissociation are widely considered to be traumatically induced. Studies of combat veterans and child abuse survivors renewed modern interest in dissociation (Herman, 1992). These groups reported high levels of posttraumatic stress disorder (PTSD), a condition that researchers now know to include dissociative symptomology.

References

Herman, J. L. (1992). *Trauma and recovery.* New York: Basic.
Hilgard, E. R. (1977). *Divided consciousness: Multiple controls in human thought and action.* New York: Wiley.
Putnam, F. W. (1989). *Diagnosis and treatment of multiple personality disorder.* New York: Guilford.

C. H. ROSIK

See DEFENSE MECHANISMS.

Dissociative Amnesia. The essential feature of dissociative amnesia is a sudden inability to recall important personal information, usually of a traumatic or stressful nature, that is too extensive to be explained by ordinary forgetfulness and is not associated with a general medical condition. Most commonly the missing personal information concerns the individual's identity and can include name, age, marital status, occupational information, and personal life history. The person's fund of general knowledge typically is intact. This helps to differentiate the disorder from medical conditions, in which general information is usually the first to be lost and personal information is preserved until the end. Individuals with dissociative amnesia are normally aware of the fact that they are unable to recall important personal information.

Several types of dissociative amnesia have been described in the literature according to the nature of the disturbance in recall. Localized amnesia involves a failure to recall all events occurring during a circumscribed period of time. This is considered to be the most common form of dissociative amnesia. Selective amnesia is a failure to recall some but not all of the events during a circumscribed period of time. Generalized amnesia involves a failure of recall for important personal information that encompasses the person's life. This form most commonly presents to the police or in hospital emergency rooms. In continuous amnesia recall for events subsequent to a specific time up to and including the present is impaired. Finally, systematized amnesia is a loss of memory for specific categories of information, such as all memory relating to one's family or a particular person.

Dissociative amnesia can be found in any age group, from young children to adults. The onset of the disorder is usually sudden and often occurs following a traumatic experience. Only a single episode of amnesia may be reported, although two or more episodes are not uncommon. Unusual somatic sensations, dizziness, headaches, or feelings of depersonalization may be reported. The reported duration of the events that cannot be recalled may be minutes to years but usually does not last more than several days. Recovery is frequently spontaneous. Dissociative amnesia needs to be distinguished from dissociative fugue, which involves a sudden, unexpected travel away from one's home or customary place of work, accompanied by an inability to recall the past and confusion about personal identity or adoption of a new identity.

C. H. ROSIK

See DISSOCIATIVE DISORDERS.

Dissociative Disorders. Dissociation is defined by *DSM-IV* as "a disruption in the normally integrative functions of consciousness, memory, identity, or perception of the environment" (American Psychiatric Association, 1994, p. 766). Although mild dissociative features are common in childhood and adolescence, severe dissociative symptoms are recognized to be consequences of trauma. Understood in this way, dissociation can be seen to be a defense against trauma and as such is used by survivors of abuse and other psychologically traumatic events as a means of coping with overwhelming anxiety and pain. Recent work by Steinberg (1985) has identified a cluster of five core dissociative symptoms—amnesia, depersonalization, derealization, identity confusion, and identity alteration.

Amnesia is either the inability to recall important personal information or the total lack of awareness of what has transpired in a significant block of recent time. People with amnesia report gaps in their memory. Sometimes described as lost time, these gaps can range from a few seconds to years.

Depersonalization is an alteration in a person's perception or experience of self; for example, feeling detached from the self as if one were an outside observer of one's self. It may also manifest itself in terms of a feeling that the self is strange or unreal, feeling like one is in a dream, or feeling like a robot. Depersonalization is difficult to describe, and persons experiencing this dissociative symptom often describe their experience in "as if" terms (i.e., "I feel as if I am a robot").

Derealization involves an alteration in the perception or experience of the external world that is reported as feeling strange or unreal. Often this takes the form of sensing a loss of familiarity with one's physical or interpersonal environment. Friends and relatives may be experienced as strange or unfamiliar, as may be one's home or place of work.

Identity confusion describes a state of uncertainty, puzzlement, or conflict regarding personal identity. Persons with dissociative disorders often report confusion about who they really are or may have difficulty maintaining a feeling of inner cohesion or continuity.

Identity alteration refers to the assumption of different identities. Examples of this include the use of different names, the experience of self as a plurality, and rapid and often dramatic changes in behavior that are often accompanied by amnesia for events experienced under alternate personality states.

Cultural sensitivity is important in evaluating dissociative disorders because dissociative states are a common and accepted expression of cultural activities or religious experiences in many societies. *DSM–IV* notes that dissociative symptoms should be judged as pathological only when they lead to significant distress, impairment, or help-seeking behavior. Dissociative trance disorder is not currently included among the official diagnoses of *DSM–IV* but is under study for inclusion in subsequent revisions of the classification system. As currently understood it involves an involuntary trance state that is not accepted by the person's culture as a normal part of cultural or religious practice and that causes significant distress or functional impairment. It is often experienced and described as a possession state.

DSM–IV includes four major dissociative disorders: dissociative amnesia, dissociative fugue, dissociative identity disorder, and depersonalization disorder. A fifth disorder, dissociative disorder not otherwise specified, refers to disorders in which dissociative symptoms are present and predominant but that do not meet the criteria for any of the other four specific dissociative disorders.

References

American Psychiatric Association. (1994). *Diagnostic and statistical manual of mental disorders* (4th ed.). Washington, DC: Author.

Steinberg, M. (1985). *Structured clinical interview for DSM–III–R dissociative disorders (SCID–D)*. Washington, DC: American Psychiatric Association.

D. G. BENNER

See DEPERSONALIZATION DISORDER; FUGUE; DISSOCIATIVE FUGUE; DISSOCIATIVE AMNESIA; DISSOCIATIVE IDENTITY DISORDER; DISSOCIATIVE TRANCE DISORDER.

Dissociative Fugue. The unexpected travel of a person who cannot later recall the trip. Dissociative fugue is classified among the dissociative disorders in the *DSM-IV.* In a dissociative state the affected person temporarily is unable to integrate all the elements of personality into a unified whole; the result is fragmentation, dissociation, or splitting. Other dissociative disorders are dissociative amnesia, dissociative identity disorder, and depersonalization disorder (Cohen, Berzoff, & Elin, 1995).

A fugue is a flight: in music, of notes and melody; in psychopathology, of persons and personalities. The sufferer may assume a new identity while on his or her trip and be genuinely unable to recall the former, true identity. An elaborate or full-blown example of psychogenic fugue would include the person assuming a bolder, more outgoing personality during the fugue state than would normally be characteristic of that person. More often, however, the fugue state is relatively short. Dissociative fugue "usually consists of a single, nonrecurrent episode" (Steinberg, 1995, p. 275).

A famous historical example of fugue is the story of Ansel Bourne as reported by William James (1890). Bourne was a lay minister in Rhode Island who traveled in 1887 to Norristown, Pennsylvania. There he lived for six weeks as the owner of a variety store under the name of Mr. Brown. James's description of this historical case illustrates many of the same features currently used by the *DSM-IV* to diagnose dissociative fugue.

The fugue condition is quite rare, although it tends to be seen more frequently during war or after a natural disaster. Often a severe stressor or trauma such as a serious level of marital discord or a profound personal rejection is connected with onset. Technically a fugue state can be differentiated from other similar pathologies by careful observation. For example, persons in fugue states are unaware that they have forgotten anything, whereas psychogenic amnesiacs are well aware that true identity is beyond recall. Also, the casual observer of a newcomer to town who may actually be in a fugue state will not necessarily suspect that something is drastically wrong. People who observe sleepwalkers, in contrast, can usually detect something amiss in their behavior. If the travel is nonpurposeful, unsophisticated, and appears to be aimless wandering, an organic mental disorder is the more likely diagnosis. Dissociative fugue can be feigned so that the distinction between a genuine fugue state and malingering is difficult to make.

Current standards require four criteria, all of which must be present in order to make a diagnosis of dissociative fugue: sudden unexpected travel with retrograde amnesia; confusion surrounding one's identity and/or assumption of a new identity while in the fugue; not a part of the dissociative identity disorder, some form of substance abuse, or a medical condition; and symptoms causing significant distress or impairment.

Individuals with recurrent fugue states should be considered for the dissociative identity disorder diagnosis. Benign forms of fugue (that are thus not diagnosable) include the familiar experience reported by many people of not being able to reconstruct the exact details of how one arrived at a freeway exit or a destination.

Treatment cannot commence until the true identity of the fugue victim is established. Gradual reexposure to the normal environment plus careful therapy to help the victim learn more constructive pressure-coping strategies will enhance recovery. Recurrences are rare.

References

Cohen, L. M., Berzoff, J. M., & Elin, M. R. (Eds.). (1995). *Dissociative identity disorder: Theoretical and treatment controversies*. Northvale, NJ: Aronson.

James, W. (1890). *Principles of psychology*. New York: Dover.

Steinberg, M. (1995). *Handbook for the assessment of dissociation*. Washington, DC: American Psychiatric Press.

J. R. Beck

See Dissociative Disorders.

Dissociative Identity Disorder. Dissociative identity disorder (DID), formerly known as multiple personality disorder (MPD), is one of five dissociative disorders identified in the fourth edition of the *Diagnostic and Statistical Manual of Mental Disorders (DSM-IV)* published by the American Psychiatric Association (1994). Common to all dissociative disorders is capacity to segregate and isolate chunks of experience to protect oneself from painful memories or events. Minor forms of dissociation such as daydreaming are considered normal and common, but more severe forms such as DID are considered to be psychiatric disorders. Those with DID compartmentalize their experiences and coping responses into separate personality states, referred to as alter personalities. Although DID can cause social and occupational deficits, it is also important to recognize the dissociative defenses of DID as adaptive (Ludwig, 1983). Dissociation is often the psychological tool used to survive traumatic and horrifying childhood events.

Although the phenomenon of dissociation can be traced back as far as 400 B.C., contemporary discussions of dissociation and multiple personalities originated with Pierre Janet, Morton Prince, and William James in the late 1800s and early 1900s. The splitting of self into alter personalities was studied in the laboratory, although without adequate experimental conditions and controls, and was commonly discussed among those interested in mental health until the 1930s. As behaviorism and psychoanalysis gained momentum, and as the diagnosis of schizophrenia increased, discussions of dissociation and reported cases of multiple personality disorder almost disappeared from the scientific literature. In recent years, as cognitive explanations for psychopathology have again become more prevalent, interest in dissociative phenomena has been renewed. Multiple personality disorder was renamed dissociative identity disorder with the publication of the *DSM-IV.*

Clinical Presentation. In the context of a relatively safe adult environment, memories that have previously been sealed off and personified in an alter personality sometimes escape their normal boundaries and invade other aspects of consciousness. Troubling dreams, black-out periods, and vague feelings of depression or anxiety often bring people with DID to treatment. In some cases those with DID have been diagnosed and treated for other psychological disorders such as major depression or schizophrenia before being correctly diagnosed. Many times the primary personality is unaware of the alter personalities until after the diagnosis is made.

The *DSM-IV* includes four diagnostic criteria for DID. First, the individual must experience two or more distinct personality states, each with a stable pattern of perceiving and relating to self and others. For example, a woman known as Terri to most of her friends and co-workers may also have an alter personality named Ellen. Whereas Terri is docile and dependent, Ellen may be audacious and offensive. Terri and Ellen share the same body, although they write, speak, and behave differently. Although this example suggests only two personalities, many people with DID have many more than two alter personalities. Second, at least two of the personality states have repeatedly taken control of the client's behavior. Terri may have black-out periods during which Ellen goes to parties, gets drunk, and acts impulsively. Ellen, in contrast, may always be aware of Terri's behavior but have little power to take control until Terri is feeling overwhelmed with the social demands of a novel situation. Third, there must be significant memory gaps that cannot be explained by normal forgetfulness. Terri may see many people around town who seem to know her well, yet she cannot recall ever meeting them. Ellen may have no recollections prior to the age of ten years. Fourth, DID is not diagnosed if the condition can be attributed to substance abuse or a medical condition.

Etiology. Although various causes for DID have been considered and explored, the most consistent finding is severe, repetitive childhood trauma. More than 80% of DID clients report being sexually abused as children, most commonly in the form of incest (Putnam, Guroff, Silberman, Barban, & Post, 1986). The abuse usually comes from a parent or primary caregiver. The majority of DID clients also report being physically abused and experiencing extreme neglect (*see* Abuse and Neglect). A relatively high proportion (about 40%) report being witness to a violent death; 20% report being raised in extreme poverty. Although the idea is controversial, many believe that cultic or ritual abuse is a frequent cause of DID.

Most children have a rich capacity to imagine, and when this imaginary capacity is coupled with severe trauma it can lead to a dissociative defense system to protect the child from pain. Extreme trauma keeps children from developing a consistent sense of self that transcends a variety of situations and contexts.

Assessment and Treatment. Assessing DID can be quite difficult for at least three reasons. First, the one with DID often does not know about the alter personalities and might be quite surprised to hear the diagnosis of DID. Second, a safe therapeutic relationship is usually required before alter personalities make themselves known to the counselor. Such a relationship often requires many weeks or months of treatment, thus deferring an accurate diagnosis until relatively late in the treatment relationship. Some short-term therapies may start and finish without the alter personalities revealing themselves. Third, some people have been improperly diagnosed with DID by therapists who are overly zealous to diagnose dissociative disorders or cultic ritual abuse, resulting in widespread concern about misdiagnosis and false memories. It is essential that counselors and psychotherapists avoid suggesting DID, even when some initial symptoms suggest dissociative phenomena are occurring. The most reliable way to diagnose DID is to have a conversation with an alter personality at the client's initiative without prior suggestion or discussion of DID.

As with most psychological disorders, a variety of treatments have been proposed for DID. The common themes of various treatment approaches include a safe and trusting therapeutic relationship, understanding the struggle for control that occurs among various alters, the importance of uncovering secrets from the past, and properly handling transference and countertransference. Many people with DID have an alter personality with the capacity to look objectively at the various alters and thereby help their therapists understand the personality system. This type of alter is referred to as the internal self-helper. Many forms of therapy for DID call upon the counselor to identify and collaborate with the internal self-helper as early as possible in the treatment relationship. The ultimate goal of treatment is to integrate the various aspects of personality that have been compartmentalized by dissociative defenses.

Those with DID often experience spatial metaphors to understand their various personalities. For example, in the middle of treatment the client may perceive each alter to live in a separate room inside his or her body. Ideally the metaphor will shift throughout the treatment process so that ultimately the various alter personalities are in a common room making decisions together and cooperatively.

Considerations for Christians. Whereas most therapists perceive all alter personalities to play a vital role in adaptive functioning and thus work to integrate all personalities in the process of treatment, a number of Christian authors and therapists have suggested that some alters may be demonic in nature and should be expelled from the personality. Although DID is not specifically described in Scripture, there is ample evidence that Jesus believed in demonic possession and often cast demons out of troubled people (see, e.g., Matt. 8:32; Mark 1:34; Luke 11:14).

If demons are sometimes part of the personality system in DID clients, then it is untenable from a Christian perspective to work toward integrating all the alter personality states into the final integrated self. This creates the difficult task of determining which if any of the alter personalities are demonic in nature or influenced by demonic activity. It also challenges Christian counselors to develop a theological position on the possibility of demon possession and/or demon oppression with Christian clients. Friesen (1992) suggests that supernatural influences should at least be considered when the alter personality feels like an external intruder to the client and schizophrenia has been ruled out. He further suggests that supernatural influences are likely if the alter is repulsed by Christian symbols or the name of Jesus, the client shows indication of supernatural abilities such as telepathy, or an evil presence is sensed by people other than the client.

Another issue of particular interest to pastors and Christian counselors is the relationship between cultic ritual abuse and DID. In the absence of firm evidence from law enforcement agencies, there is increasing skepticism about the prevalence of cult-related ritual abuse. Nonetheless, some compelling clinical evidence suggests that ritual abuse does occur and is related to DID (Young, Sachs, Braun, & Watkins, 1991). The prevalence of ritual abuse remains unknown. Because many with dissociative disorders are quite suggestible and because of the high risks associated with false memories of abuse, counselors must be cautious not to plant ideas of cultic or ritual abuse by asking leading questions or making direct suggestions. McMinn and Wade (1995) found that Christian counselors were no more likely than nonreligious psychologists to diagnose DID, and they were only slightly more likely to attribute their clients' symptoms to cultic ritual abuse.

References

American Psychiatric Association. (1994). *Diagnostic and statistical manual of mental disorders* (4th ed.). Washington, DC: Author.

Friesen, J. G., Jr. (1992). Ego-dystonic or ego-alien: Alternate personality or evil spirit? *Journal of Psychology and Theology, 20,* 197–200.

Ludwig, A. M. (1983). The psychobiological functions of dissociation. *American Journal of Clinical Hypnosis, 26,* 93–99.

McMinn, M. R., & Wade, N. G. (1995). Beliefs about the prevalence of Dissociative Identity Disorder, sexual abuse, and ritual abuse among religious and nonreligious therapists. *Professional Psychology: Research and Practice, 26,* 257–261.

Putnam, F. W., Guroff, J. J., Silberman, E. K., Barban, L., & Post, R. M. (1986). The clinical phenomenology of multiple personality disorder: A review of 100 recent cases. *Journal of Clinical Psychiatry, 47,* 285–293.

Young, W. C., Sachs, R. G., Braun, B. G., & Watkins, R. T. (1991). Patients reporting ritual abuse in childhood: A clinical syndrome. Report of 37 cases. *Child Abuse and Neglect, 15,* 181–189.

Additional Readings

Bloch, J. P. (1991). *Assessment and treatment of multiple personality and dissociative disorders.* Sarasota, FL: Professional Resource.

Putnam, F. W. (1989). *Diagnosis and treatment of multiple personality disorder.* New York: Guilford.

Rogers, M. L. (Ed.). (1992). Satanic ritual abuse: The current state of knowledge. *Journal of Psychology and Theology, 20,* 175–305. [Special issue]

Ross, C. A. (1989). *Multiple personality disorder: Diagnosis, clinical features, and treatment.* New York: Wiley.

Yapko, M. D. (1994). *Suggestions of abuse.* New York: Simon & Schuster.

M. R. McMinn

See DISSOCIATIVE DISORDERS.

Dissociative Trance Disorder. The main characteristic of this disorder is an involuntary state of trance that is not accepted by the person's culture as a normal part of a collective cultural or religious practice and that causes clinically significant distress or functional impairment. At present dissociative trance disorder is not an official diagnostic category of the *DSM-IV,* but it is proposed as a new category in order to stimulate more research that will further refine the criteria. This disorder was developed in part so as not to pathologize the vast number of dissociative experiences that occur cross-culturally as part of common religious and cultural practices. However, there are instances in which individuals involved in culturally normative trance or possession trance states develop symptoms that cause distress and impairment and that would fall under the domain of dissociative trance disorder.

This proposed new diagnosis has two subtypes: trance and possession trance. The term *trance* generally connotes a mental state in which the individual is not reflectively conscious of mental contents and/or of salient features of the environment for a prolonged period of time. Trance states are differentiated from possession trance states, with the former involving an alteration but not replacement of embodied identity, whereas the latter signifies a partial or full replacement of embodied identity and amnesia. There was much professional discussion as to whether possession trance is a cultural expression of dissociative identity disorder (DID). However, this reductionistic assumption was questioned on several grounds (Begelman, 1993; Cardena, 1992; Coons, 1993). Possession trance, in contrast to DID, typically involves displays of special knowledge, physical contortions, and blasphemy; appears unrelated to early physical and/or sexual abuse; usually has an acute or subacute course of occurrence; involves few alternate identities experienced as external to the individual; and shows important commonalities cross-culturally, such as flailing of limbs and unusual vocalizations.

References

Begelman, D. A. (1993). Possession: Interdisciplinary roots. *Dissociation, 6,* 201–212.

Cardena, E. (1992). Trance and possession as dissociative disorders. *Transcultural Psychiatric Research Review, 29,* 287–300.

Coons, P. M. (1993). The differential diagnosis of possession states. *Dissociation, 6,* 213–221.

C. H. Rosik

See DISSOCIATIVE DISORDERS.

Divine Guidance. *See* GUIDANCE, DIVINE.

Divorce. The legal ending of a marriage. The United States exhibits the highest rate of divorce in the civilized world. It is estimated that between 40% and 50% of current first marriages will end in divorce. Although the divorce rate has been steadily on the rise for the last one hundred years, it now appears that the divorce rate has leveled off beginning in the 1980s and continuing to the present. Divorce statistics are not uniform across all demographic categories. For instance, divorces are more common in black than in white families. Age at marriage is inversely related to divorce rate; thus the younger the age at marriage, the more likely the couple is to divorce. Educational attainment is also related to divorce rate, although in a nonlinear way: lower divorce rates occur for people who have finished either high school or college, while noncompletion of either high school or college is associated with higher divorce rates. Income is also inversely related to divorce rate. That is, the higher one's income, the less likely is divorce to occur.

It does not appear that Americans are disillusioned about marriage in general; statistics show that five out of six divorced men remarry while three out of four divorced women remarry. The likelihood that children will be involved in the divorce seems to be rising as well. It appears that parents are less likely to stay together for the sake of the children than had been the case in previous years. Children do at times, however, serve as a deterrent: rates of divorce for families with a preschool child are about half those of families with no children. This disparity disappears when school-aged children are considered. Children in some cases are even associated with an increased divorce rate. This occurs for families in which the child was born prior to the marriage and in stepfamilies that include stepchildren. Each year in the United States, more than one million children experience parental divorce. About half of those children will go through this experience a second time. Thus divorce marks only one of possibly many significant family transitions that millions of children endure. Ramifications occur with these transitions, for both children and adults, and perspectives sometimes differ among Christians, the general public, and scholarly research.

As noted earlier, the divorce rate has shown a steady increase in this century. Before the Reformation in the sixteenth century, divorce in Europe was controlled by religious governance and could be granted only on grounds of adultery, cruelty, or heresy. During this time divorce was rarely granted. Gradually thereafter, control was shifted from religious to civil. In the early days of America, both marriage and divorce were controlled by the Puritan government. Divorce was extremely difficult to obtain when the church controlled this decision.

However, divorce continued to be very rare even after government began to take over. Divorce was governed by strict laws that required that the requesting party present evidence to the court demonstrating the fault of the partner. This was common practice into the twentieth century; however, around this time the courts had to respond to the increasing numbers of divorce petitions being filed, which they did by becoming less restrictive in their interpretation of and holding to the law. Despite the relaxing of legal standards, no significant change in divorce law occurred until 1970, at which time California's no-fault divorce law was enacted. Similar laws now exist in all fifty states. The more dramatic rise in divorce rates in the most recent two to three decades is often attributed to these legislative enactments and other frequently cited culprits such as the events of the 1960s and the self-centeredness of the population. In the broader picture, however, the trend has been for the divorce rate to rise steadily over the last one hundred years.

The more dramatic recent increase in the number of divorces has coincided with a radical change in attitudes toward divorce. It is impossible to tell whether the change in public acceptance of divorce preceded or followed the increase in frequency of divorce. One study conducted between 1962 and 1980 documented the shift in attitudes toward approval by respondents irrespective of age, religion, religiosity, education, income, work history, and family size. However, the impact of one's religious affiliation is interesting; Roman Catholics initially were more disapproving of divorce, but this was not the case in the later years of the study. Thus Catholicism did not seem to be related to continuing to hold more negative views on divorce. Fundamentalists, however, seemed to change their attitudes toward divorce less than did the other categories of respondents. Also associated with less attitude change was frequency of church attendance. One can assume from these findings that among the most conservative Christian groups and among those who attend services most regularly, divorce continues to meet with disapproval, with attitudes not changing in line with those of the general public (Thornton, 1985).

The reasons behind this unchanging view may be found in the Bible. It is clear from Scripture that God created and honors marriage, intending it to be a lifelong state. References from both the Old and New Testaments uphold this view of marriage. Genesis 2:24 (NIV) states, "For this reason a man will leave his father and mother and be united to his wife, and they will become one flesh." Paul states in at least two places (Rom. 7:2; 1 Cor. 7:39) that husband and wife are bound to each other as long as they both live.

Divorce appears to be a clear departure from God's intention for human marriage. However, allowances for particular situations are discussed in Scripture. In the Old Testament, provisions for divorce were described as accommodations to the "hardness" of people's hearts rather than a permissible option (Matt. 19:8). In fact, the word *hate* is used in Malachi: "'I hate divorce,' says the LORD God of Israel" (Mal. 2:16, NIV). Jesus' teaching makes it clear that divorce is not to be considered the solution to marital problems. In Matthew 19:6 and Mark 10:6–9, Jesus commands that man is not to take apart a union that has been covenanted before God. An exception to God's forbiddance of divorce is cited in Matthew 5:32 and 19:9, in which Jesus says that a man is not to divorce his wife unless the wife is guilty of fornication. The Greek word used for this sexual sin refers not to a single instance of extramarital intercourse but rather means habitual sexual immorality. Thus it appears that Jesus was not saying that an extramarital adulterous encounter should provide an excuse for one to get rid of one's partner; rather, ongoing and unrepentant adulterous behavior is the only basis upon which a Christian is permitted to seek a divorce.

In another scriptural passage, believers are taught that they may allow an unbelieving partner to leave (1 Cor. 7:15). However, in no place in Scripture is the partner permitted to put out or request that the unbelieving spouse leave. Thus the moral question about the permissibility of divorce can be addressed by serious study of such passages.

The emotional issue of divorce, however, is a different dilemma. Within the American population, most adults are familiar with one or more divorce situations that have been traumatic for those involved. The popular opinion leans toward dwelling on its negative impact. Aside from common opinion, however, it is an area that has been quite thoroughly researched. As such, it is important to examine these findings in order to make more helpful predictions and suggestions.

Divorce is a different experience for families. Sometimes it involves a move; at other times it does not. Sometimes it results in less time spent with one parent, while other divorces mean the absence of one parent. Divorce sometimes results in a reduction of interparental conflict, but other times it does not. Financial changes after divorce vary widely. Stepparents may become involved, siblings may be separated, parental lifestyles may change. Suddenly there may be two sets of rules in two households rather than one. Thus the effect of divorce on children is not one that can be uniformly described. Multiple factors are influential, including family financial status, level of interparental conflict, relationship of the child to each parent, as well as the personality of the child. When the effects of divorce on children are studied, children from divorced homes are typically shown to have more problems in such areas as acting out behavior, oppositionality, school grades, and truancy, as well as more difficulties with anxiety and depression. Furthermore, research generally has supported the notion that children who experience divorce become adults who are less well adjusted than are their peers from intact families. While research generally finds that children who have experienced divorce do worse in many areas than children from intact families, the relationship between the two is tempered by multiple other factors. Perhaps most important among these factors is the level of interparental conflict.

Children from high-conflict intact homes have been repeatedly shown to have more problems in multiple areas than do children from low-conflict divorced homes, leading some researchers to conclude that the conflict between parents rather than the divorce leads to children's difficulties. Several studies have demonstrated a relationship between conflict in intact marriages and the severity or frequency of behavior problems in children. This means that the greater the level of marital turmoil, the more severe and/or frequent are the behavior problems of the children of the marriage. Furthermore, this relationship appears when considering intact marriages, predivorce conflict, and postdivorce conflict. The strongest associations between marital (both pre- and postdivorce) fighting and child problems occurs for child externalizing problems. Examples of such problems include aggression, noncompliance, and delinquency. Some association has also been found, however, for marital conflict and child symptoms of anxiety and depression. Researchers also frequently cite the negative changes in children's academic performance relative to marital conflict.

Numerous other factors have been considered in the question of how a child is likely to adjust following a divorce. Among these are the child's adjustment prior to the divorce, changes in financial status following the divorce, social supports available to the child, adjustment of the parents, and relationship of the child to each parent. Negative status of these variables generally leads to more difficulties following divorce. Positive status of these variables may provide protection to the child who is experiencing the breakup of the parental marriage. Parents, then, can actively contribute to the lessening of impact on their children. For example, parents can try to concentrate on building and maintaining good relationships with their children, and this may help to cushion the blow of the divorce. Consequently many children are able to navigate safely through a divorce and experience relatively little emotional impact. Research also tends to conclude that the initial negative impact of divorce on children is not nearly as obvious two or more years after the event. Although again some children seem to be scarred by their experience, most seem to adapt to the changes in a reasonable period of time. The influence of parents in their relationship to the child as well as their own ability to continue uninterrupted and effective parenting throughout this time is perhaps the most important factor in the ability of the child to adequately adjust.

This chore of concentrating on the child, however, is often difficult for the adults to accomplish, as they are often too involved in their own anger, grief, and other emotional experiences to devote the additional energy to perceive and meet the needs of their children. Numerous theories have been advanced in an attempt to explain the process of adjustment that is experienced by adults who divorce. At this time there is no overwhelming support for any one of these theories. Most involve approximately five stages, beginning with the period before separation and including denial or disillusionment and emotional divorce. Many theories describe anger as being the next stage, also usually occurring before separation. At the decision and physical movement to separation, various possible stages and their emotional sequelae are posited; among the most common are bargaining, depression, guilt, and regret. From separation to the legal divorce, adults may go through a period of mourning, focus on oneself and a restructuring of one's lifestyle and identity. The final stage occurs after the finalization of the divorce and is described in terms of adjustment, acceptance, and autonomy. Every divorce is different and could vary both in the order of accomplishing each adjustment stage as well as the degree to which each is accomplished. Many divorced adults, especially those for whom divorce was not the preference, may have difficulty getting beyond the stage of anger and regret. In such cases retaliation can become a way of coping with one's feelings, and this then promotes negative relationships among all family members, with children being the worst victims of the fallout.

In such cases the assistance of a therapist could be beneficial. Counseling for adults as well as children who are experiencing the turmoils of family disruption can help the members learn to communicate more effectively and in less blaming ways, enable children as well as adults to express their feelings about what is happening, help family members cope with the changes, and perhaps most importantly, ensure that children are not victimized in the process.

Divorce is a negative phenomenon of society. It is impossible to escape emotional wounds for the adults who are divorcing, their family members, and their children. The conclusion of the vast amounts of research that have been conducted on this subject, however, is that even though there is a negative effect when divorce occurs, both for the divorcing adults and for the children involved, this effect, considering all divorce participants and not only those who have sought clinical help, is weak and tempered by many changeable factors. This stands in contrast to much of what is heard from a Christian perspective, which tends to dwell on the damage that occurs as a result of divorce. While we should not minimize or justify divorce based on research evidence, we should correspondingly not use emotional arguments to decry divorce. Rather, our consideration of whether divorce is morally permissible in any particular situation should be based on the biblical guidelines we have been given. We also need to remember the Christian character attributes of love, forgiveness, and empathy when dealing with those who are going through marital transitions. The biblical appropriateness of the divorce is an extremely important factor; but in addition we should make use of the research that is readily available to assist families in the most helpful ways possible.

Reference

Thornton, A. (1985). Changing attitudes toward separation and divorce: Causes and consequences. *American Journal of Sociology, 90* (4), 856–872.

T. KEMPTON

See BLENDED FAMILY; LOSS AND SEPARATION.

Dix, Dorothea Lynde (1802–1887). A major force in mental health reform, Dorothea Dix has a secure place in the history of psychology. She was born in Hampden, Maine. Her parents treated her so harshly that she left them to live with her grandparents in Boston. At the age of 14 she began teaching school in Worcester, and by the age of 20 she was running a school that catered to the daughters of prominent Bostonians.

Soon Dix was the victim of recurring attacks of tuberculosis. During this time, from 1824 to 1840, she wrote stories and books for children. She became financially independent when she received her inheritance from her grandmother. In 1841 she began teaching a Sunday school class for women prisoners in Boston. She was horrified at the neglect and brutality and the mixing of the mentally ill and the retarded with criminals.

Between 1841 and 1881 Dix aroused the public and the state legislatures to an awareness of the inhuman treatment of the mentally ill. New Jersey was first to respond by building a hospital for the mentally ill in 1848. More than 20 states built or enlarged more than 30 state mental hospitals. Dix directed the opening of 2 institutions in Canada, reformed the asylum system in Scotland, and brought about reform in 14 other countries.

During the Civil War Dix organized the nursing forces of the Northern armies. Later she heard of the dangerous shores of Sable Island, Newfoundland, visited the region, and persuaded officials to provide life-saving boats. A resolution presented by Congress in 1901 described her as "among the noblest examples of humanity in all history."

R. L. KOTESKEY

See ABNORMAL PSYCHOLOGY.

Dogmatism. Rokeach, in *The Open and Closed Mind* (1960), promoted the concept of dogmatism in psychology. His Dogmatism Scale popularized research on the subject, with hundreds of published studies relating dogmatic tendencies to attitude, personality, and behavior variables, including religion.

Political extremes associated with World War II inspired the concept of the authoritarian personality, with an emphasis on conservative, fascistic authoritarianisms. Rokeach observed that liberalisms can also take authoritarian or dogmatic forms.

Rokeach based the Dogmatism Scale on theories of belief systems and communication. Any message includes both relevant and irrelevant information. Relevant facts concern the immediate issue. Irrelevant facts include the source of the message, authority figures, rewards and punishments for alternative actions, and relationships of these to current belief systems, defenses, and motivations. Rokeach said open-minded people discriminate and respond primarily to relevant information. Dogmatic (closed-minded) persons tend to respond instead to irrelevant factors, such as the authority and personal needs. Dogmatics see the world as relatively threatening and hold narrow, future-oriented (rather than broad) time perspectives. They are prone to hold beliefs in isolation, without logical integration; they tend strongly to reject and be ill-informed about alternative belief systems.

Rokeach's theory and research related individual closed-mindedness to difficulties in expressing ambivalent feelings about one's parents and (by a defensive constriction) a dearth of influence by adults outside the family. Other research relates origins of open-mindedness to higher social class, larger family size, and later birth order.

Rokeach (1960) related situational threat to dogmatism in a study of 12 Roman Catholic ecumenical councils (A.D. 325–1563). The degree of threat or heresy prompting each council was strongly related to dogmatism of the resulting canons. Sales (1972) studied economic threat in relation to religious conversion in two studies (nationwide, 1920–1939; Seattle, WA, 1961–1970). Times of economic prosperity were associated with more conversions to nonauthoritarian denominations and economic depression with conversions to dogmatic faiths.

Subsequent research supports dogmatism as generalized authoritarianism—left and right, political and religious. Churchgoers tend to be more dogmatic than the nonreligious, but radical atheists are also dogmatic. Dogmatism is associated with racial prejudice, sex-role stereotypes, and rejection of unconventional music. More dogmatic personalities tend to reflect low self-esteem, anxiety, needs to receive support from others, defensiveness, impatience, timidity, conformity, and general maladjustment and instability (Vacchiano, Strauss, & Schiffman, 1968). Research on individual dogmatism continues at a reduced pace; in the decade 1985–1994 *Psychological Abstract* periodical citations decreased from ten annually in the first part of the decade to four in the last half.

In a different, less studied sense dogmatism can be seen as a stage of religious development. Dogmatism tends to accompany an extrinsic, self-serving religion but is unrelated to degree of intrinsic or committed religious orientation. Insofar as mature faith develops out of a self-serving religion, dogmatism may be a typical phase of faith development. Theories of Lawrence Kohlberg, Fowler, and Loevinger (development of moral judgment, faith, and ego, respectively) all include rigidly held beliefs and reliance on authority at early developmental stages. In the growth of a personal religious faith, openness to relevant new information tends to replace defensive reliance on authority as the faith becomes more committed, mature, and secure.

References

Rokeach, M. (1960). *The open and closed mind*. New York: Basic.

Sales, S. M. (1972). Economic threat as a determinant of conversion rates in authoritarian and nonauthoritarian churches. *Journal of Personality and Social Psychology, 23*, 420–428.

Vacchiano, R. B., Strauss, P. S., & Schiffman, D. C. (1968). Personality correlates of dogmatism. *Journal of Consulting and Clinical Psychology, 32*, 83–85.

R. D. Kahoe

See Authoritarian Personality; Ambiguity, Intolerance of; Religion and Personality; Religious Orientation; Commitment.

Domestic Violence. Acts within a family unit that have threatening or violent aspects; that result in injury, whether physical or emotional; that have a lack of consent on the part of the victim; and that are excessive or inappropriate to the situation. At one time domestic violence referred primarily to physical abuse toward children or the wife. The current definition of domestic violence includes the emotional components and has been extended to any situation in which a family member is harmed. The most common types are violence by parents to children, violence by a husband to a wife, and violence by adult children to elderly parents. Current legal standards require mental health professionals to report any incidence of abuse or violence to the appropriate authorities if it involves children or the elderly. Counselors should consult local and state codes for exact provisions.

Many definitions of domestic violence abound and focus on everything from the nature of the act itself to the physical and psychological impact and to the community standards regarding appropriate conduct. In communities with large immigrant and refugee populations, what is considered abuse in the dominant society is seen as normal in the cultural group. This presents many problems for definition, legal action, intervention, and treatment. Awareness of cross-cultural issues, if one is working with families from such groups, is critical. For example, the police were called to a scene where a teenager was "tied" to a tree and "beaten" with a rod. The belief was that the child was possessed by spirits that needed persuasion to leave. This was considered the appropriate way to deal with this problem within this ethnic group. This causes a cultural clash and must be dealt with sensitively.

The person who is the target of the violence is referred to as the victim. The person who acts is the abuser or the perpetrator. The acts themselves are referred to as abuse. These terms help depersonalize the situation and make it easier to identify abuse but also may make intervention cold and impersonal. A counselor must balance the person and the act to avoid becoming too emotional or too unemotional when working with any part of the system.

Four types of abuse may be clustered under domestic violence. Each has its own dynamic. All four, however, affect a victim, resulting in fear, threat, and violence. The first type is neglect: the basic necessities of life, such as food, shelter, or medical attention, are withheld from the victim. Whether a child or an elderly adult, these victims are usually unable to cope for themselves and rely on the family to provide the basics. The second type is physical abuse. The perpetrator hits, pushes, whips, bites, punches, slaps, or burns the victim, resulting in injuries that are left on the body. Some are visible wounds, such as bruises; others are internal, such as broken bones or hemorrhaging. Children and wives are the most common victims. The third type is sexual abuse. Whenever a person is tricked, trapped, forced, or bribed into a sexual act, this is considered abuse. This is called incest in the family. It may occur toward a spouse or even toward an elderly parent. The fourth type is emotional abuse. It occurs when parents take no interest in their child. Parents are emotionally unavailable to the child or may belittle and yell at the child. This could occur toward the elderly as well.

The Christian response to domestic violence arises from the concern for human beings who have experienced sin and need to know the comfort and love of God. For victims, trust has been violated, dignity stepped on, and lives twisted because someone did something that should not have been done. They will carry scars and wounds throughout their life that could affect others with whom they interact. These are people who desire to be whole and healthy but may not be able to do so. Deception, hypocrisy, anger, and exploitation have developed and impact everyone. Healthy families work together to face life's challenges. Abusive families are unable to do so. The abuser or perpetrator often has been a victim and is now passing on this abuse. Instead of love there is lust or hate. Instead of caring there is exploitation. This person is a prisoner of sin and often denies or minimizes the offense. To address all these concerns we need to understand the causes and effects of domestic violence and then look at interventions.

Domestic Violence toward Children. Child sexual abuse is the most frequent form of violence on children, followed by physical abuse. Some forms of sexual abuse and emotional abuse are more insidious and seldom are expressed until the child is an adult. Both boys and girls are victims, with girls predominating. As many as one out of three girls may be sexually abused, while one out of eight males may be abused. Stepfathers are five times more likely to abuse than are natural fathers. There is no clear evidence of the prevalence of each type of violence. The most noted in news would be physical violence or sexual abuse; sometimes neglect or deprivation reaches the news.

Families differ in their composition, history, and stability. Thus many factors might be involved in the causes or background of domestic violence. Family size, class, economic status, education, spiritual background and beliefs, and personal background are influences. Situational stress may increase the likelihood of violence, but a problem of inadequacy seems to underlie most violence. Limited child-rearing knowledge, lower tolerance, and misattributions about a child's motivation for behaving are three areas in which inadequacy arises.

The effects of violence toward children are both short-term and long-term. Short-term effects are seen in lower school grades, rebellious behavior, passivity, or any other acting out or withdrawing pattern. Family tension increases. This becomes a problem at home and for the community that now must respond to the problems. Broken homes, gangs, and juvenile delinquency are all a part of this problem. Long-term effects are seen when these children grow up and become parents themselves. The same patterns are played out in their relationships and marriages. It is known that abused children are more likely to become abusers. They learned to deal with anger, conflict, power, and hurts in unhealthy ways and usually pass this on through their relationships.

Interventions at this level include therapy, legal involvement, and protection of the victims. Depending on the nature of the abuse, the family may work together to heal or may be required to function in foster settings to aim at personal healing.

Domestic Violence toward a Spouse. Wife battering and to a lesser degree husband battering occurs when one spouse uses physical force on the other. The most frequent abuser is the angry male who cannot control his intense emotion and beats, hits, slaps, or kicks his wife. Often these abusive relationships replay childhood experiences. The male may have grown up with an angry father and codependent mother. In some cases the male had a domineering mother and weak father. In either case the husband has not learned how to express his fear, inadequacy, or anger in healthy ways. Feeling threatened and overwhelmed, he strikes out to control the situation. His emotions get out of control. After this explosion he becomes remorseful, guilty, and ashamed. Promises are made, and tears are shed. A period of pleasantness follows, until some minor upset occurs to start the pattern again.

Many wives report emotional and verbal abuse, but these are less visible than physical violence. Wives learn to either tolerate the abuse or leave the marriage. When physical abuse occurs, the women are in a bind. To report the incident and press charges could mean incarceration for the husband and loss of income or family support for the woman. These fears sometimes lead to the wife taking the blame and hoping all will work out.

Interventions are usually remedial, meaning shelter and assistance are given wives and families after an abusive situation in which injury or threats have occurred. Counseling, anger management, and family intervention are necessary. It is not clear to what extent sexual addictions play in violence, but the nature of the addictive cycle is similar to alcohol and may lead to the same type of anger and resentments.

Domestic Violence toward the Elderly. As the population of elderly increases and people live longer, it has been noted that many older adults are being cared for by their adult children. In cases where another caretaker has been assigned, such as a relative or a rest home, that becomes the family setting. Neglect is the major type of abuse. Confined to a home and surrendering income to the caretaker, the elderly individual literally becomes a prisoner. Little research reports on incidence, but enough is known to warrant legal requirements that mental health workers report any such abuse.

Unresolved issues between parents and child may be the main reason for this abuse. As the elderly parent becomes more needy of care, the stress of care can become overwhelming. Roles are reversed. If cognitive and physical deterioration occur, such as with Alzheimer's disease, constant attention to the needs can be tiring and demanding. A lack of skill in relating to an elderly person can be guilt-producing to the child, especially if the parent is demanding or critical.

Home health care, support groups, adequate physical examination, and outside placements can help to reduce senior abuse. This can be an extremely difficult issue to deal with because of the bind that we are in when we want to show respect to our parents but also must be firm and understanding of their loss of cognitive abilities.

Intervention. There are three levels of intervention for domestic violence. First is alleviation. When any form of violence is observed or identified, it must be reported and dealt with. In brutal forms of violence, incarceration results. At other times counseling, anger management, education, and training may be employed. Shelters for battered women, foster homes for children, and special homes for seniors are available to remove the victim from the problem. Second is prevention. Within the community and church, educational efforts to increase awareness or skills are employed. Healthy family living is fostered. Third is growth. This refers to those who have been victims or who have come from abusive families to deal with and process their pain and hurts. Numerous books on inner healing have helped many people identify and grow through dysfunctional pasts.

Dealing with the deeper issues of guilt and shame are necessary for both victim and perpetrator. It is often believed that victims are able to heal, but that the abuser may be stuck for life. Denial and avoidance are so common that it is difficult to see long-term growth.

As counselors or therapists, our attitudes and experiences with domestic violence will certainly color our effectiveness as interveners. Applying scriptural and psychological knowledge can allow us to be better counselors to those who seek our help.

L. N. FERGUSON

See VICTIMS OF VIOLENT CRIMES.

Dominance. The concept of dominance implies the notions of authority, control, and power. The dynamic which is involved in any state of dominance is manifested when one function or figure determines the terms and conditions under which all other functions or figures must operate. To be dominant means to be in a position of superior influence or mastery, commanding and prevailing over many structures, entities, or people.

In order to adequately understand the concept of dominance, one ought to consider other similar yet not merely identical concepts like authority, power, and aggression. Forceful and arrogant authority is typically viewed as intimidating and destructive while acceptable and legitimate authority is viewed as rightful and productive. When individuals possess formal authority and are assigned power justly, they are able to rationally demonstrate the appropriateness of their actions, opinions, or decisions and meet the demands of the situation. Therefore, they can fulfill the moral and ethical standards required and reflect the transparent truths involved.

Legitimate power is based on competence, respect, and wisdom while illegitimate power is based on coercion, irrationality, and manipulation. According to the frustration-aggression hypothesis, when people are frustrated by inner tensions and conflicts or are deprived of essential needs they tend to act aggressively and display hostile behavior. In the world of animals, fighting and competing for food, mates, and territory is a clear attempt to achieve security and dominance.

Domination can be achieved by force (subduing people), money (purchasing followers), or mental persuasion (changing people's convictions). Sometimes, dominant leaders are treated like gods and in some cases are officially elevated and worshiped (e.g., Roman emperors; also cf. Daniel 3). Ultimately, the freedom to participate or choose is better understood and practiced in the context of power, control, and authority.

From a Darwinian evolutionistic view, the dominant species or function, outside or inside the organism, regulates the conditions essential for its survival and therefore competes for the resources and controls of that given environment. From a sociological perspective, the concept of dominance refers to the exercise of power by certain member(s) of society or the local community through performing key functions and controlling the lifeline of that community. In addition, political dominance is the influence practiced by a central government usually located in a particular town or city, extending its rule and supervision over large geographic areas both near and far, although it usually diminishes with long and extended distances. Likewise, dominance is the rule or reign of a strong and powerful nation over a small and less autonomous nation.

In the world of business and economics, dominance is manifested by the managerial hierarchy, division of labor, distribution of responsibilities, and executive decisions which impact the employees and consumers alike. Dominance is found within families and interpersonal relationships, as well, and is manifested in the powerful dynamic of superordination versus subordination (e.g., child-parent and male-female relations).

The right to lead or practice authoritative dominance and the freedom to follow or show devotion must be based on a voluntary response to the natural gift of leadership, called charisma. Historically, those figures who abused power had significant internal insecurities, stored aggressions, and hidden deprivations. The crippling fear of abandonment, severe anxieties, history of past abuses, and lack of personal value are some deeply rooted psychological reasons why individuals reach high positions, exercise control over others, and abuse the power entrusted to them.

An effective leader, master, or executive is someone who is people oriented, rational, egalitarian, visionary, sensitive, and fulfills the group needs. Christ's view of greatness and power is in sharp contrast with the materialistic models (Mark 10:42–44; Luke 22:25–26). Christians are mainly called to acknowledge the positive rule of God. Both the general and special revelations marvelously point to God's remarkable dominion over creation and all existence (e.g., 1 Chron. 29:11; Pss. 19:1; 103:19–22; 108:1–5; 136:1–9; 145; Jude 24–25). The true believers who have a living and dynamic faith are disciples of the kingdom of God. They are responsible and accountable to God, yet they surely enjoy God's provision, protection, and personal presence.

N. ABI-HASHEM

See NEEDS; PERSONALITY.

Double Bind. The double bind hypothesis was first formulated to describe a communication phenomenon observed in schizophrenic families (Bateson, Jackson, Haley, & Weakland, 1956). The elements of the double bind include two or more people having repeated experiences in an important relationship, at least one of whom is sending messages with a primary injunction coupled with a secondary injunction that conflicts at a different level. There is additionally a perceived inability to escape from the relationship or comment on the incongruity. Reactions to this pattern of communication include anxiety, ambivalence, defensiveness, withdrawal, paranoia, shifts between concrete and abstract thinking, and disqualification of the other, the message, or the self. The double bind proposes to explain and underlie several of the symptoms of schizophrenia, and it was thought to have a progressive and cumulative effect on psychic functioning.

As an example, a mother has a fear of intimacy and dislikes children but, through the defense mechanism of reaction formation, shows loving behavior toward her child. The child is in a double bind;

if he discriminates accurately, he will realize that his primary love object and best hope for survival does not love him or does so ambivalently at best. If he does not discriminate accurately, he will approach her and be rebuffed by more or less conscious hostility. If he then withdraws, she will punish him verbally because the withdrawal indicates that she is not a loving mother. In this situation the child cannot win. The only escape from this situation is to talk with the mother about the bind, but the child is unable to do so because of a lack of language skills or a history of punishment. Thus over time this child fails to learn to talk about these binds. He too begins to give distorted messages, feels ambivalent, does not do well outside his family, and eventually becomes symptomatic.

The best theoretical formulation of this hypothesis has been in terms of a conflict of logical types, a paradox involving the inappropriate use of concepts drawn from two different conceptual levels or categories but sent in the same message (Gootnick, 1973). This understanding has often proved to be too abstract; that is, it is too easily extended to areas where in fact it has no logical explanatory power, even though it seems applicable. Thus it has been difficult conceptually and empirically to specify accurately what is indeed a double bind and to predict whether the effects will be negative or positive. However, the hypothesis remains useful with regard to generating research and sensitizing clinicians to communicational subtleties in family interaction patterns. Thus it has directly contributed to the popularity of family therapy, particularly in the area of distorted communication, but no longer is it seen to have an explanatory or therapeutic utility with schizophrenics per se. It has also come to play an important conceptual role in some forms of hypnotherapy, especially those associated with the work of Milton Erickson. Likewise, building on the previous work of Victor Frankl, Weeks and L'Abate (1982) have developed an approach called paradoxical psychotherapy in which the double bind plays a prominent role.

References

Bateson, F., Jackson, D. D., Haley, J., & Weakland, H. H. (1956). Toward a theory of schizophrenia. *Behavioral Science, I,* 251–264.

Gootnick, A. T. (1973). The double-bind hypothesis: A conceptual and empirical review. *Journal Supplement Abstract Service,* 3.

Weeks, G. R., & L'Abate, L. (1982). *Paradoxical psychotherapy.* New York: Brunner/Mazel.

J. M. BRANDSMA

See PARADOXICAL INTERVENTION.

Double Technique. The double technique, used in psychodrama, involves a person (the double) whose purpose it is to mirror the protagonist (the one being helped) and facilitate the expression of unsaid feelings and thoughts. The double begins by mirroring the body of the protagonist and then seeks information about who the protagonist is and what he or she is feeling. This information assists the double in enlarging on the role and speaking what is not being spoken. Often during the psychodrama the double is directed to become a specific part of the protagonist—for example, self-condemning, confused, nurturing. Although it is most commonly employed in group settings, this technique is also useful for individual therapy. Doubling does require some training and experience in psychodramatic methods.

J. H. VANDER MAY

See PSYCHODRAMA.

Doubt. A state of mind characterized by an absence of either assent or dissent to a certain proposition. It is a suspension of commitment to belief or disbelief, either because the evidence pro and con is evenly balanced (positive doubt) or because evidence is lacking for either side (negative doubt, exemplified by the apostle Thomas). Doubt is thus an integral part of each person's belief system, since it is impossible for anyone to believe or disbelieve with complete certainty all propositions of which he or she is aware. Yet in spite of the natural occurrence of doubt in human cognition, many people view doubt as a negative mindset to be avoided if at all possible.

Doubt is a topic of interest to scholars from three academic disciplines. Philosophers study doubt because of its epistemological implications in relation to knowledge, truth, and awareness of existence. Theologians are concerned with doubt because it often occurs as a prelude to belief or as a precursor of disbelief. Psychologists investigate doubt because of the emotions that often accompany it (anxiety, depression, or fear) and because in certain pathologies doubt can become obsessional and debilitating.

Doubt, Unbelief, and Ambivalence. One can differentiate between doubt and unbelief. Unbelief is a positive conviction of falsity regarding an issue and hence is a form of belief. Doubt does not imply a belief in a contrary position; it is simply being unconvinced. If, however, doubt becomes pervasive and dominates the thinking of a person regarding all issues, it is more appropriately called skepticism or definitive doubt. The skeptic despairs of ever knowing truth with certainty.

One can also distinguish doubt from ambivalence. Ambivalence is a state of mind characterized by the concurrent presence of two or more differing feelings toward the same object. Indecisiveness and vacillation, although related to doubt, refer more to a lack of commitment to a proposition or to a frequent change of opinion. Ambivalence in massive quantities is classically seen as a primary indicator of schizophrenia, whereas massive doubt is more often a part of obsessional disorders.

One can differentiate between normal doubt and abnormal doubt chiefly by the degree to which the doubt impairs daily living. Doubt is normal when it does not dominate a person's thinking, when it is overshadowed by stable beliefs, and when the goal of the doubt is resolution into belief or disbelief. Doubt is also normal when employed, as René Descartes advocated, for the purpose of seeking truth. Normal doubt is a type of mental clarification and can help a person better organize his or her beliefs. Developmental theorists have noted several phases of life when doubts are characteristically found: in adolescence, when the teenager moves from childhood credulity toward a personalized belief system, and in the middle years, when issues of competence and direction predominate (Grant, 1974). Abnormal doubt, unlike normal doubt, focuses on issues having little consequence or issues without grave implications of error.

Religious Doubt. Religious doubt has been a concern of believers from biblical days to the present. In the garden of Eden the serpent used doubt as a tool to move Eve from a position of belief to one of disobedience. Abraham, Job, and David all had times of doubt that were painful yet growth-producing. The best-known example of doubt in the Bible is Thomas, who was absent when Jesus made a postresurrection appearance to the ten apostles. Jesus showed the ten his hands and his side (John 20), evidence that dispelled their doubt as to his identity. When told of Jesus' appearance, Thomas replied that he would not believe until he too had seen the evidence. Eight days later Jesus reappeared, showed Thomas his wounds, and made a gracious plea for faith.

By way of contrast, Jesus consistently condemned unbelief wherever he found it. Jesus presumably tolerated doubt because it was a transitory, nonpermanent state of mind, whereas he condemned unbelief because it was a fixed decision often accompanied by hardness of heart. Guinness (1976) cautions, however, that Scripture sometimes uses the word *unbelief* to refer to doubt (Mark 9:24). Hence exegetical care is needed when interpreting the Bible's teachings regarding doubt.

Doubt is a problem in theological systems committed to inscripturated truth. For example, evangelical Christians are generally not tolerant of doubt if it is prolonged, unyielding, and centered on cardinal truths. Doubt is not so much a problem in liberal theologies since truth in those systems is more relative and less certain. Thus the conservative Christian community sees doubt as risky and dangerous, whereas the liberal Christian community sees doubt as a sign of healthy intellectual inquiry. Some psychologists of religion even see doubt, particularly as envisioned within a questing religious orientation (see Batson, Schoenrade, & Ventis, 1993), as an indication of religious maturity.

Normal doubt tends to appear when a person's belief system "does not protect the individual in his life experiences and from its more painful states" (Halfaer, 1972, p. 216). Doubt is resolved into belief or disbelief in any of four ways: through conversion, through liberalization, through renewal, or through emotional growth. Individuals can construct rigid defenses designed to ensure belief and prevent doubt at all costs such as sometimes occurs in cults that discourage any reexamination of beliefs.

Doubt and Psychopathology. In psychopathology doubt often occurs as a prominent symptom in the obsessive-compulsive disorders. Earlier in the twentieth century a special diagnostic category was created called *folie du doute,* or doubting mania. The disorder was described as an extreme self-consciousness and a preoccupation with hesitation and doubt. The condition was frequently considered progressive and incurable. Eventually the disorder was seen as but one variety of an obsessive-compulsive disorder, since the doubting mania was accompanied by overconscientiousness, fears of contamination, and other obsessive-compulsive characteristics.

The obsessive doubter is one whose symptoms have taken a cognitive rather than a predominantly behavioral form. In other words, the doubter is usually more obsessive than compulsive, although the dynamics behind either form is similar. The obsessive doubter usually centers his or her thinking on some imponderable issue that is just beyond the pale of provability. For example, the doubter may fret over issues of existence (Do I really exist?) or over issues of reality (Did I actually put a stamp on the letter I just mailed?). As a doubter becomes more and more proficient in his or her ruminations, an elaborate network of essentially futile mental operations develops.

If the obsessive doubter is religious, the doubts will likely involve issues of God's existence, God's involvement in human affairs, salvation, security, and one's eternal state. Doubters who are serious students of Scripture will find an ample supply of issues that qualify for obsessive doubting, issues essentially unanswerable or imponderable. For example, the obsessive doubter who reads Jesus' statement, "If anyone is ashamed of me and my words, the Son of Man will be ashamed of him" (Luke 9:26, NIV), may worry about a specific time of embarrassment or shame in the past. Soon all confidence and security disappear, and the doubter fears eternal damnation.

There are several characteristics of the teachings of Jesus that seem to aggravate the obsessive doubter (Beck, 1981). Jesus frequently used themes of exclusivity (Matt. 10:33), absoluteness (Luke 18:22), abstractness (Mark 9:43, 45), impossibility (Mark 10:25), and prohibition (Luke 13:28). Any of these themes can aggravate the obsessive's tendency to be overconscientious, rigid, and concrete, resulting in doubts.

Professional help is indicated in cases of obsessive doubting (Salzman, 1980). If treatment commences soon enough in the process, the prognosis is generally favorable. Therapy can help the sufferer to learn new channels for coping with anxiety and new patterns of effective decision making.

Doubt can be a valuable part of one's life if its goal is resolution and if it results in deeper commitment to existing beliefs and less commitment to extraneous or harmful presuppositions (Pruyser, 1974). All belief has about it a feeling of resolved doubt. Hence as the doubter moves toward belief, his or her life is enriched by the resulting relief and satisfaction.

References

Batson, C. D., Schoenrade, P., & Ventis, W. L. (1993). *Religion and the individual: A social-psychological perspective.* New York: Oxford University Press.

Beck, J. R. (1981). Treatment of spiritual doubt among obsessing evangelicals. *Journal of Psychology and Theology, 9,* 224–231.

Grant, V. W. (1974). *The roots of religious doubt and the search for security.* New York: Seabury.

Guinness, O. (1976). *In two minds: The dilemma of doubt and how to resolve it.* Downers Grove, IL: InterVarsity Press.

Halfaer, P. M. (1972). *The psychology of religious doubt.* Boston: Beacon.

Pruyser, P. W. (1974). *Between belief and unbelief.* New York: Harper & Row.

Salzman, L. (1980). *Treatment of the obsessive personality.* New York: Aronson.

J. R. Beck

See Faith; Religious Development; Christian Growth.

Down's Syndrome. A type of mental retardation caused by an extra chromosome, resulting in a moderate to severe level of general retardation. Measurable intelligence quotients could range from 20 to 55.

First described by J. Langdon-Down in 1866, this syndrome was initially called mongolism due to the resemblance in facial appearance to members of the Mongolian race. Later it was discovered that the syndrome is caused by an extra chromosome (no. 21) which triples instead of pairing. Known as trisomy 21, or Down's syndrome after the discoverer, this leaves 47 chromosomes instead of the normal 46. While we know that this extra chromosome is responsible for Down's syndrome, we do not yet know how it has its effect.

This widely known, common form of retardation is the result of cell division and is not inherited. Either parent may contribute the chromosome. It is known that the occurrence of this syndrome increases from about 1 in every 1,000 births to mothers age 20 years, to 25 per 1,000 births for women age 35, to about 88 per 1,000 births to mothers age 49.

It is not clear why the mother's age is associated with the syndrome. It is possible that the mother's eggs, which are all present at her birth, have been exposed to more environmental agents or stresses. Perhaps hormonal changes in midlife influence the process.

There is little evidence to show that the father's age is involved. If so, it is not significant until the father is in the mid-fifties.

Down's syndrome is characterized by almond-shaped eyes that slant upward, a small nose with a low bridge, and a furrowed tongue that protrudes because the mouth is small and has a low roof. The head may be flattened in the back. The ears are small and sometimes the tops are folded a little. The nose is also flattened and wide. The child is often short. These children are often born with heart problems, a susceptibility to colds and pneumonia, and more susceptibility to Alzheimer's disease as they age. Less than 60% of Down's syndrome children live more than 5 years after birth. The approximate life span of the remainder is 35 to 40 years.

Down's syndrome children are usually good-natured, happy, affectionate, socially well adjusted, and playful. They can usually do most things that any young child can do, such as walking, talking, dressing themselves, and being toilet trained. However, they do these things a little later than other children. Considerable care is necessary for many of these individuals. While some are capable of learning normal skills to contribute in various jobs and some marry, most are too retarded to live alone responsibly.

L. N. FERGUSON

See MENTAL RETARDATION.

Dreams. *See* SLEEP AND DREAMING.

Dreams, Therapeutic Use of. Since Sigmund Freud (1900/1913) published *The Interpretation of Dreams,* depth psychologists and dynamic psychotherapists have regarded dreams as meaningful. In contemporary clinical practice theories and techniques of dream interpretation are included in a broad spectrum of therapies and comprise an extensive literature.

Freud. Freud distinguished between manifest dream (the story) and latent dream (the hidden meaning). Latent dream is transformed into manifest dream through four essential mechanisms Freud labeled dreamwork. In condensation dream elements are overdetermined, with each element in the manifest dream representing several elements of latent content, and vice versa. In displacement the psychic intensity or emotional content of dream thoughts is focused on nonessential aspects of the dream, with the most important content of the latent dream masked in the manifest dream. In dramatization psychic regression occurs in dreams, which are primarily visual and auditory experiences, and logical relationships between ideas must be expressed through spatial or temporal proximity or through fusing several features. Similarity may be represented through identification and causal relationships by making one group of elements follow another, one dream scene fading into another. Opposition and contradiction are depicted through inverting two corresponding elements or scenes. In secondary revision or elaboration dream processes are altered as they are perceived by consciousness; dream fragments are transformed into a whole by inserting connecting words or scenes during recollection or retelling of the dream. The process of free association, designed to unveil underlying conflicts, constitutes a reversal of this process.

Symbolization is the most popularized aspect of Freud's dream theory, with much emphasis on fixed sexual symbols. When the association between symbol and idea symbolized appear widely discrepant, Freud attributes this to the work of the censor, an ego function designed to protect the dreamer's sleep. The censor distorts the dream's meaning so much that it is seldom discernible merely through intuition. For Freud the ultimate meaning of the dream lay in the fulfillment of a wish, a notion E. Jones (1931) extended to nightmares. Dream interpretation, because it unearthed secret, disguised wishes, was regarded as the royal highway to the unconscious.

Adler and Jung. Major shifts in the depth psychology of dreaming came with the work of Freud's early disciples. Adler (1925) emphasized the unity of personality, with dreams revealing the person's lifestyle (*see* Adler, Alfred). Dream symbols are protective devices defending the dreamer from life's threatening problems, and the dream is a forward-looking rehearsal for life, a compensation for inferiority feelings. Dreams produce emotions that carry over into waking life, bringing adaptation.

Carl Gustav Jung, relying on the rich traditions of mythology, mandala symbolism, and alchemy, shifted the focus to the transpersonal level, with dreams providing clues to the nature of the collective unconscious. Dreams often have a dramatic structure that includes exposition, development, culmination, and resolution. Manifest contents must be taken seriously, as they give an accurate picture of the dreamer's psychological state. The dream serves much like a building facade that carefully observes the architect's plan and provides major clues to the interior arrangement: the manifest dream *is* the dream, containing the whole meaning. For Freud's analytical method of free association, Jung substituted a synthetic-hermeneutic method in which the therapist gradually leads the client through the realm of the unconscious, where one encounters the various archetypes of the ego (persona and shadow), the soul (anima and animus), the spirit (old wise man and magna mater), and the self (mandala, quaternity, and other symbols of individuation). Jung approaches the dream as an anthropologist or a linguist approaches a text in an unknown language, not by trying to get behind it to its real meaning but by learning to read it.

The function of the dream is compensation, "balancing and comparing different data or points of view so as to produce an adjustment or a rectification" (Jung, 1974, pp. 73–74). When we begin to interpret a dream, we should consider what conscious attitude it might compensate. In discussing how compensation takes place in dreams, Jung considers three possibilities. If the conscious attitude toward a life situation is primarily one-sided, the dream will take the opposite side. If the conscious position is more mediate, the dream will present mild variations. If the conscious attitude is adequate, the dream will reinforce this tendency, identifying with it and emphasizing it.

Using the patient's dreams as a guide, the therapist seeks for a balancing of conscious and unconscious factors in the patient's life, thus leading to mental health. Daniel (Dan. 4:10–16) offers a compensatory view in the interpretation of the dream of Nebuchadnezzar. The dream tree is personified as the dreaming king himself. The dream points to the king's megalomania, which actually developed into psychosis, a result that reflects a lack of harmony between the conscious and the unconscious.

Other Major Theorists of the Early and Middle Twentieth Century. Therapists developed alternative methods to Freud's free association very early in the history of psychotherapy. Prince (1910) utilized free association as well as dissociation of the dreamer into various states of consciousness through hypnosis to retrieve various layers of the dream's meaning. Erikson (1954) accepted Jung's emphasis on manifest content and took an epigenetic view of dreams, insisting that dreams are normal processes, often analyzing dream series as a means for resolving developmental conflicts and encouraging dreamers to work out their conflicts in real-world relationships. Stekel (1943) also focused on the dream's ability to reveal life conflicts. Silberer (1955) analyzed both latent and manifest content, using both free association and direct interpretation. He felt the dream is a clue to emotionally valenced material: material and functional dream symbols reveal what and how a person is thinking, somatic symbols disclose bodily states.

Lowy (1942) connected dreams with psychoaffective homeostasis: dream interpretation uses intuition and induction to focus on the entire dream picture, and the symbols must be interpreted on their own terms. Hall and Van de Castle (1966) collected data on the contents of thousands of dreams, to which they applied a psychoanalytically based interpretation that often focused on entire dream series. C. S. Hall regards dreams as wish fulfillments, but the symbols are regarded as expressive rather than distorting. French and Fromm (1964) assumed that dreaming serves the purpose of seeking solutions to interpersonal problems: past and present experiences converge on the focal conflict presented in the dream. Their functional analysis relies on direct symbol translation, literal symbol interpretation, and the therapist's intuitive imagination.

Ullman (1961) integrates sleep research into his dream theory, noting that the dream helps maintain an optimal level of vigilance. Like Jung, he focuses on the capacity for revelation and the autobiographical truth that is possible because sleeping consciousness is far less defensive than waking consciousness. Boss (1958), taking an existential, phenomenological stance, insists on experiencing dreams rather than studying or interpreting them. A similar stance is taken by Caligor and May (1968) and Erich Fromm (1951). R. M. Jones (1970), who systematically integrates dream physiology with dream psychology, applies the preceding theories to the analysis of one dream, providing a comparative set of interpretations. Bonime (1962) provides a social and interpersonal theory of dream symbolism and interpretation that incorporates much of the dream literature and integrates it with unique contributions to the general theory of psychotherapy.

Specialized Literature. Fosshage and Loew (1987) summarize the object-relational, Gestalt (see Downing, 1973), and phenomenological approaches to dream interpretation. Other specialized perspectives include the intersubjective (Atwood & Stolorow, 1984), the culturalist (Bonime, 1962), and family dream analysis (Bynum, 1993).

Dream interpretation is also applied to a variety of special clinical situations. Natterson (1980) includes chapters on the dream in schizophrenia, manic-depressive psychosis, and depressive personality; in obsessive, dissociative, regressed, psychosomatic, and traumatic states; in perversion and acting out disturbances; and in suicidal clients. The investigation and treatment of posttraumatic dreams began with Rivers (1923), whose creative therapy with World War I veterans challenged Freud's wish-fulfillment theory. Recent work on nightmares is summarized in Lansky (1992), and specific research on post-traumatic nightmares is found in Lansky (1995). Special attention has been given to children's dreams by Foulkes (1982) and Catalano (1990).

Dreams and Spirituality. Contemporary dream theorists, especially the Jungians, acknowledge the spiritual potential of dreams. Meseguér (1960) incorporates dreams into every phase of spiritual direction. The classics by Kelsey (1968) and Sanford (1968) both focus on the numinous quality of dreams and their ability to reveal the state of one's relationship to God. Boss (1958) states that dreams offer the possibility of "living in relation to a Being whom we call God or gods" (p. 141) and notes that the more the religious relationship is destroyed in waking life, the more significant a role it plays in dreams. He regards these dream experiences as "numinous," providing "direct appearances of the Divine revealed in the light of the dreamer's existence" (p. 149). J. A. Hall (1993) classifies the variety of forms dream images of God may take. Daim (1954/1963) focuses on the dream's potential to reveal objects of fixation and "dislocation" of the heart;

their resurrection symbolism reveals the goal of salvation. Frankl (1975) regards the dream as a revelation of the dreamer's struggle to be reconnected with God and fellow humans. A broad range of approaches to spirituality and dreams is integrated in Savary, Berne, and Williams (1984), and a cross-cultural perspective is provided by Bulkeley (1994).

References

Adler, A. (1925). *The practice and theory of individual psychology*. London: Routledge & Kegan Paul.

Atwood, G. E., & Stolorow, R. (1984). *Structures of subjectivity*. Hillsdale, NJ: Analytic.

Bonime, W. (1962). *The clinical use of dreams*. New York: Basic.

Boss, M. (1958). *The analysis of dreams* (A. J. Pomerans, Trans.). New York: Philosophical Library.

Bulkeley, K. (1994). *The wilderness of dreams. Exploring the religious meaning of dreams in modern western culture*. Albany: State University of New York.

Bynum, E. B. (1993). *Families and the interpretation of dreams*. New York: Harrington Park/Haworth.

Caligor, L., & May, R. (1968). *Dreams and symbols: Man's unconscious language*. New York: Basic.

Catalano, S. (1990). *Children's dreams in clinical practice*. New York: Plenum.

Daim, W. (1963). *Depth psychology and salvation* (K. F. Reinhardt, Trans.). New York: Ungar. (Original work published 1954)

Downing, J. J. (1973). *Dreams and nightmares: A book of Gestalt therapy sessions*. New York: Harper & Row.

Erikson, E. H. (1954). The dream specimen of psychoanalysis. In R. Knight & C. Friedman (Eds.), *Psychoanalytic psychiatry and psychology*. New York: International Universities Press.

Fosshage, J. L., & Loew, C. (1987). *Dream interpretation: A comparative study* (Rev. ed.). New York: PMA.

Foulkes, D. (1982). *Children's dreams: Longitudinal studies*. New York: Wiley.

Frankl, V. (1975). *The unconscious god: Psychotherapy and theology*. New York: Simon & Schuster.

French, T. M., & Fromm, E. (1964). *Dream interpretation: A new approach*. New York: Basic.

Freud, S. (1913). *The interpretation of dreams* (A. A. Brill, Trans.). New York: Macmillan. (Original work published 1900)

Fromm, E. (1951). *The forgotten language: An introduction to the understanding of dreams, fairy tales, and myths*. New York: Grove.

Hall, C. S., & Van de Castle, R. L. (1966). *The content analysis of dreams*. New York: Appleton-Century-Crofts.

Hall, J. A. (1993). *Unconscious Christian: Images of God in dreams* (D. J. Meckel, Ed.). New York: Paulist.

Jones, E. (1931). *On the nightmare*. London: Hogarth.

Jones, R. M. (1970). *The new psychology of dreaming*. New York: Grune & Stratton.

Jung, C. G. (1974). *Dreams*. Princeton, NJ: Princeton University Press.

Kelsey, M. T. (1968). *Dreams, the dark speech of the spirit: A Christian interpretation*. Garden City, NY: Doubleday.

Lansky, M. R. (Ed.). (1992). *Essential papers on dreams*. New York: New York University.

Lansky, M. R. (1995). *Posttraumatic nightmares: Psychodynamic explorations*. Hillsdale, NJ: Analytic.

Lowy, S. (1942). *Foundations of dream interpretation*. London: Kegan Paul.

Meseguér, P. (1960). *The secret of dreams*. London: Burns and Oates.

Prince, M. (1910). The mechanism and interpretation of dreams. *Journal of Abnormal Psychology, 5*, 139–195.

Natterson, J. (Ed.). (1980). *The dream in clinical practice*. New York: Aronson.

Rivers, W. H. R. (1923). *Conflict and dream*. London: Kegan Paul, Trench, Trubner.

Sanford, J. A. (1968). *Dreams: God's forgotten language*. Philadelphia: Lippincott.

Savary, L. M., Berne, P. H., & Williams, S. K. (1984). *Dreams and spiritual growth: A Christian approach to dreamwork*. New York: Paulist.

Silberer, H. (1955). The dream. *Psychoanalytic Review, 42*, 361–387.

Stekel, W. (1943). *The interpretations of dreams* (2 vols.). (E. & C. Paul, Trans.). New York: Liveright.

Ullman, M. (1961). Dreaming, altered states of consciousness, and the problem of vigilance. *Journal of Nervous and Mental Disease, 133*, 519–535.

H. VANDE KEMP

See SLEEP AND DREAMING; PSYCHOANALYSIS: TECHNIQUE.

Drive. An aroused state resulting from a biological need. The concept of drive is a major one in the field of motivation. When an animal or a person is deprived of essentials, such as food, water, or air, it is said to be in a state of physiological need. This need state leads to the state of arousal known as the drive state. The energized drive state then pushes the organism to do something to reduce the need. After the need is satisfied, the drive subsides.

Although Sigmund Freud used the German word *Trieb* similarly in 1915, Woodworth first used the word *drive* to describe this hypothetical force or energy in 1918. Within a few years nearly all psychologists believed in some form of the drive concept. The logic of drive theory was advanced by Walter Bradford Cannon's concept of homeostasis introduced in 1932. According to Cannon, whenever the internal physiological conditions deviate from their normal state, a state of disequilibrium is set up and the body attempts to return to an equilibrium.

Drive theory reached its fullest development in Clark Leonard Hull's learning theory in 1943. Hull said there were many sources of drive, but they all contributed to the total pool of arousal. The resulting drive energized behavior but did not direct it. Instead the direction came from the habits operating in the given situation. The drive simply multiplied the habits present at the time. When the drive was reduced following response to a stimulus, the connection between that stimulus and response was strengthened.

In 1948 Miller showed that fear could become a learned drive. Rats learned to press a lever or turn a wheel when the only drive present was the fear of the box in which the rats had been shocked. Escaping from the box led to learning to make the pressing or turning response. Psychologists then began proposing all kinds of learned secondary drives, such as a drive for money and a drive for achievement. The concept of homeostasis was essentially broadened to include psychological as well as physiological imbalances.

During the 1950s psychologists began to question the drive theory as a means of explaining all kinds of behavior. They realized that organisms are not pushed into activity just by internal drives. External stimuli, called incentives, also play an important part in determining behavior. People may not even be hungry until they smell the food cooking. They may eat more dessert if it tastes good, even though they are full from dinner. People and animals are not only pushed (drives) but pulled (incentives) as well.

The mechanistic philosophy underlying the original drive concept is outmoded. Most psychologists do not hold the idea that people or even animals are inert and have to be driven into activity. They see movement as intrinsic to life. However, the word *drive* continues to be used. Drive theory does help explain some behavior, but it is not adequate as a complete theory of motivation as many psychologists tried to make it in the 1940s.

R. L. KOTESKEY

See MOTIVATION.

Drug Addiction. *See* SUBSTANCE-USE DISORDERS.

Drugs, Therapeutic Use of. *See* PSYCHOPHARMACOLOGY.

DSM-IV. The standard abbreviation for the *Diagnostic and Statistical Manual of Mental Disorders*, fourth edition (1994). Prepared and published by the American Psychiatric Association, *DSM-IV* is the standard classification system for mental disorders used in North America.

See CLASSIFICATION OF MENTAL DISORDERS.

Dual-Career Marriage. Rapaport and Rapaport (1969) coined the term *dual-career family* to describe families headed by a heterosexual married couple in which each spouse has a career requiring a high degree of commitment or training. Dual-career marriage has become increasingly common since the 1970s (Apostal & Helland, 1993). Most married women with children are employed (67%), and growing numbers of women consider their careers to be central to their identity (Gilbert, 1994).

Types of Dual-Career Marriages. Gilbert (1994) identified three marital patterns for dual-career couples: conventional, modern, and role sharing. In the conventional dual-career marriage pattern the wife retains full responsibility for household work and parenting. In the modern pattern both spouses share parenting responsibility, but the wife

takes more responsibility for household work than does the husband. In the role-sharing pattern partners share parenting and household work equally. Gilbert (1994) proposes a number of personal (e.g., attitudes, values), relationship (e.g., power, partner support), and environmental (e.g., work situation) factors that influence the way the partners combine career and family roles. Scanzoni (1975) theorized that dual-career marriages, in which husband and wife share equally in the rights and duties of marriage, are closer and more satisfying than are less egalitarian marriages.

Research on Dual-Career Marriage. Much research on dual-career couples has focused on specific outcome variables such as work-family conflict, marital adjustment, or division of household responsibility (Swanson, 1992). Duxbury and Higgins (1991) examined gender differences in work-family conflict and found that the marriage relationship was more likely to be affected by conflict at the husband's workplace than by conflict at the wife's workplace. Spillover theory is often used to explain how work influences family life, with positive spillover (e.g., satisfaction and stimulation at work) promoting high satisfaction at home and negative spillover (e.g., conflict at work) decreasing satisfaction at home.

Hardesty and Betz (1980) examined the relationships of career salience, attitudes toward women, and demographic and family characteristics to marital adjustment in dual-career couples. In all couples both husband and wife reported high levels of marital adjustment, modern attitudes toward women, and moderate levels of career salience, with family interests ranked more important than career interests. High educational level of the wife and greater combined income were related to higher levels of marital adjustment.

Apostal and Helland (1993) examined commitment and role changes for dual-career couples. All of the couples studied had a strong ideological commitment to the dual-career lifestyle. Role changes for domestic tasks were low (with wives taking primary responsibility). Role changes for nondomestic activities were higher. For example, wives reported role changes in personal identity and community participation.

Swanson (1992) briefly reviewed literature on multiple roles and issues for dual-career couples. Much of the research on multiple roles has focused on women and has examined mental health effects. Studies of both members of dual-career couples generally indicate positive effects of wives' career participation on men's career and marital and family satisfaction and indicate that similar issues exist for both African-American and Caucasian dual-career couples. Swanson also found that women's career involvement is related to more equality. Variables such as number of hours spent at work, number of children, and type of career also influenced the distribution of power and responsibility in marriages.

Clinical Issues for Dual-Career Couples. Jordan, Cobb, and McCully (1989) identified areas for special focus when working with dual-career couples: working styles, stressors of the work environment, household and child-care tasks, and personal issues. Jordan and colleagues recommended interventions for clinicians working with dual-career couples. Interventions such as goals and values clarification, communication training, negotiation and contracting skills training, and time-management and stress-management techniques are recommended.

References

Apostal, R. A., & Helland, C. (1993). Commitment to and role changes in dual career families. *Journal of Career Development, 20,* 121–129.

Duxbury, L. E., & Higgins, C. A. (1991). Gender differences in work-family conflict. *Journal of Applied Psychology, 76,* 60–74.

Gilbert, L. A. (1994). Current perspectives on dual-career families. *Current Directions in Psychological Science, 3,* 101–105.

Hardesty, S. A., & Betz, N. E. (1980). The relationships of career salience, attitudes toward women, and demographic and family characteristics to marital adjustment in dual-career couples. *Journal of Vocational Behavior, 17,* 242–250.

Jordan, C., Cobb, N., & McCully, R. (1989). Clinical issues of the dual-career couple. *Social Work, 32,* 29–32.

Rapaport, R., & Rapaport, R. N. (1969). The dual-career family: A variant pattern of social change. *Human Relations, 22,* 3–30.

Scanzoni, J. (1975). Sex roles, economic factors and marital solidarity in black and white marriages. *Journal of Marriage and the Family, 37,* 130–145.

Swanson, J. L. (1992). Vocational behavior 1989–1991: Lifespan career development and reciprocal interaction of work and nonwork. *Journal of Vocational Behavior, 41,* 101–161.

K. M. Perrone

See Marital Health and Pathology; Marital Types.

Dunbar, Helen Flanders (1902–1959). Flanders Dunbar, "the mother of holistic medicine" (Stevens & Gardner, 1982, p. 93) and matriarch of clinical pastoral education (CPE), was born 14 May 1902 in Chicago. Dunbar earned her B.A. at Bryn Mawr (1923), where she studied psychology of religion with James Leuba. She earned advanced degrees in theology (B.D., Union Theological Seminary, 1927), medicine (M.D., Yale, 1930), and philosophy (M.A. & Ph.D., Columbia, 1924 & 1929). Her dissertation applied biblical exegesis to the interpretation of Dante's *Divine Comedy* and demonstrated that "religion and science are not antagonistic but complementary through symbolism" (Powell, 1974, p. 91). An Ely-Eby Landon fellowship for advanced theological studies took her to the University of Vienna for the 1929–1930 year, during which she completed a medical subinternship and studied at Zurich's Burghölzli Clinic.

In 1925 Dunbar was one of the four students in the summer class that launched Anton Boisen's CPE training program at Worcester State Hospital. In 1930 Dunbar became medical director of the Council for the Clinical Training of Theological Students, working with executive secretary Seward Hiltner to establish CPE in theological seminaries and serving through the turbulent debates between the Boston and New York factions in the 1930s (see Holifield, 1983). Her departure from the council was due in part to her Freudian and Reichian ideas: her husband, Theodore Wolfe, both translated and advocated Reich's work. Dunbar also directed the Joint Committee on Religion and Medicine of the New York Academy of Medicine (1931–1936).

In the early 1930s Dunbar completed her residency and served as an instructor at Columbia Medical College. As director of the psychosomatic research program (1932–1949), she conducted holistic evaluations of more than 1,600 patients at the Columbia-Presbyterian Hospital that established the relationship between "personality constellation" and psychosomatic disorder. This work led Dunbar to publish several classics in the field: *Emotions and Bodily Changes* (1935), *Psychosomatic Diagnosis* (1943), *Mind and Body: Psychosomatic Medicine* (1947), *Psychiatry and the Medical Specialties* (1959). Dunbar founded the American Society for Research in Psychosomatic Problems (American Psychosomatic Society) and its journal, *Psychosomatic Medicine,* which she also edited (1939–1947). Dunbar was also an instructor at the New York Psychoanalytic Institute (1941–1949). Twice married, Dunbar died by drowning 21 August 1959.

References

Holifield, E. B. (1983). *A history of pastoral care in America.* New York: Abingdon.

Powell, R. C. (1974). *Healing and wholeness: Helen Flanders Dunbar (1902–1959) and an extra-medical origin of the American psychosomatic movement, 1906–1936.* Ann Arbor, MI: Xerox University Microfilms, 75–2415.

Stevens, G., & Gardner, S. (1982). *The women of psychology.* Vol. II. Cambridge, MA: Schenckman.

H. Vande Kemp

Dying. *See* Death and Dying.

Dying, Pastoral Care of. A specialized type of ministry to dying individuals and their families, relatives, and friends. The caring pastor is a symbol of religious faith and an active spiritual life. Around the death experience, his or her presence and tangible ministry are much appreciated and welcomed by all communities and cultures. The pastor represents assurance, comfort, and hope in a time of great uncertainty, transition, and need.

Death and dying have been a major focus in religious education, human services, spiritual ministry, and helping professions for decades. Both the physical death (cessation of bodily functions) and the theological death (separation from God) have been the center of much thought and attention in biblical literature.

Dying is a process. It is similar, in some ways, to other major processes of life. Care for the dying is in the heart of pastoral ministry. People need pastoral contact. It is a central part of the Christian call and an essential way of showing incarnational love. The dying process affects the psychosocial roles and attitudes of the people involved. An understanding of thanatology is essential for the helping professional who comes in frequent contact with the dying persons.

The dying person looks to the pastor for assurance of faith, company in the midst of fears and loneliness, help in communicating with his or her family, perhaps for the last time, guidance in reflecting on the quality of life, and, finally, comfort in a major transition as the self prepares to leave the body and the familiar physical world. Also, survivors look to their pastor for help with family arrangements, funeral and burial planning, as well as personal decisions and social demands. The minister needs to be prepared to serve as a major support system for a long while after the death, especially when the survivor is an older widow(er).

For some individuals, death is the worst aspect of life. They try to avoid any reminder of it at any cost. In certain families, death is never discussed. Some children grow up naive in this area, having to create their own unrealistic concepts of separation, loss, and mortality. They become protected from the real experiences of life and, too often, are left alone to develop their own distorted views of death.

People's view of death is shaped by their cultural background, religious beliefs, community heritage, social norms, personal philosophy, and individual worldview. Some view death as a real stranger, an ugly disturber, or an aggressive intruder into normal living. They perceive it as the ultimate problem and serious enemy of life. Others view death, including pain and suffering, as integral parts of life. They possess a natural ability to integrate its reality with the broader reality of existence, and, therefore, reconcile the concept of dying with the idea of living. To them, death virtually gives meaning to life.

Western societies tend to perceive death as an enemy which must be conquered or as an obstacle which must be overcome. Modern medical sciences, especially, try to go to a great extent in order to stop, reverse, or control the dying process. Perhaps health care providers tend to view death as a failure or a defeat. They indirectly, or unconsciously, engage in a war against it, employing sophisticated technologies and powerful medications possibly more than the average dying patient can bear.

In the mind of the dying person and his or her family members or loved ones, the pastor is an agent of genuine comfort, spiritual guidance, and existential stability as they, together, go through significant mental and emotional adjustments. In their mind, the pastor represents both a spiritual connection with the after-life and a supportive social agency. As the condition of the dying progresses further and death becomes inevitable, family and friends normally begin to feel closer to each other and to their minister. Therefore, they start to look forward to his or her presence, receive his or her guidance, increasingly rely on his or her judgment, and depend on his or her nurture and soul care.

The pastor is usually called upon to help in making crucial decisions involving moral, medical, ethical, and familial issues. The situation can be highly charged and complex. For example, they need to decide whether to continue treatment in the case of a terminal illness, to remove life-support machines from an unconscious family member (young or old), or to bring the dying person home from the hospital for his or her last days. Reasonable suggestions, sound interventions, adequate care, and appropriate resolutions may be, at times, difficult to formulate and achieve especially when there is tension in the family, opposing views among the professionals, and conflictual feelings toward the dying person.

The clergy, like any other helping professional, may find himself or herself in the midst of an intense situation, a major accident, a sudden loss, or a social crisis. Besides being knowledgeable and ready to help spiritually and existentially (with meaningful Scripture readings and compassionate prayers), ministers should acquaint themselves with the issues related to grief, loss, bereavement, terminal illnesses, biomedical ethics, family dynamics, crisis intervention, stress management, and conflict resolution. It is essential to realize that the pastor is not dealing only with one dying individual but with a circle of family members, relatives, and close friends (and at times, even adversaries) in whom the anticipated death has stirred a host of issues, emotions, behaviors, and attitudes.

So, caring for the dying person means also caring for those who are around him or her who perhaps are equally affected by the process of death. The pastor may succeed, at times, in helping facilitate the intense emotions, express the deep thoughts, and disclose the unresolved matters and, by doing so, helping family members reach some resolution and closure. The pastor may witness healing of past wounds, relief from current tensions, and emergence of fresh communication, transparency, and mutual forgiveness. He or she may be instrumental in causing substantial emotional cleanliness, spiritual renewal, or a marvelous sense of bonding, closeness, and affection. All this usually leads to a smooth ending, significant relief, and a peaceful death.

However, this is not the case all the time. In many instances, the death occurs without any possibility for peace, closure, or resolution. Instead, people become highly resistant, more divided, and deeply resentful as they drift further apart, perhaps not to see each other again. Therefore, the minister must not place high expectations on himself or herself or on the situation but rather he or she should realistically deal with such unfortunate losses, major disappointments, and missed opportunities.

Finally, the caring pastor ought to face his or her own mortality and become at ease with his or her own dying process. Being able to accept one's progressive or final death and prepare oneself, ahead of time, to grieve, let go, and say good-bye, is a virtue and a sign of emotional maturity. This helps make the pastor a more refined person, a more seasoned professional, and a more effective people helper as he or she cares for both the living and the dying. In addition, the pastor's role is to heighten other people's awareness of death and to teach them about healthy grieving so they can better face their future separations and losses.

Additional Readings

Aiken, L. R. (1991). *Dying, death, and bereavement* (2nd ed.). Boston, MA: Allyn & Bacon.
Cox, G. R., & Fundis, R. J. (Eds.). (1992). *Spiritual, ethical and pastoral aspects of death and bereavement* [Death, value, and meaning series]. Amityville, NY: Baywood.
Mauritzen, J. (1988). Pastoral care for the dying and bereaved. *Death Studies, 12*, 111–122.
Parry, J. K. (Ed.). (1990). *Social work practice with the terminally ill: A transcultural perspective.* Springfield, IL: Charles C. Thomas.

N. Abi-Hashem

See Death And Dying.

Dynamic Psychology. This branch of psychology encompasses the various psychologies of motivation as they emphasize the role of the will, affects, and the unconscious rather than the psychophysiological components. Dynamic psychology emerged independently in several different countries, at different periods, and includes such schools as psychoanalysis and purposive psychology as well as the dynamic psychologies proper. Its principal source lies in the work of Sigmund Freud as well as that of Anton Mesmer, Jean-Martin Charcot, Bernheim, and Pierre Janet. Another source lies in the act psychologies of Leibnitz, Herbart, Brentano, and others, with the notion of active ideas or motives being basic to the conflict and psychological mechanisms of motivation. A third source lies in the motivational doctrine of hedonism, which can be traced from Hobbes through John Locke and Hartley to Bentham and the Mills (*see* John Stuart Mill), culminating in Edward Lee Thorndike's law of effect and Freud's pleasure principle.

Four elements are basic to all dynamic psychologies (Roback, 1952, p. 248): the analysis of motives rather than causes, thus shifting the emphasis from how to why; a shift of interest from cognition to affect; an interest in drives, instincts, and complexes; a rejection of the introspective method in favor of clinical material as a base for inference. Most dynamic psychologists also share the assumption that one drive can be changed into another without the conscious effort of the individual, as epitomized in Freud's mechanisms of sublimation and conversion. Freud adopted the concept of the unconscious and constructed a personality theory based on unconscious psychic tensions that were often sexual in nature. The unconscious was conceived as active, striving, and powerful, and repression was viewed as evidence of the deep-seated conflict between the ego and unconscious desires. While Freud was primarily an affectional dynamist, Prince was an ideational dynamist, retaining the role of cognition in the psyche. Giving a dynamic turn to abnormal psychology, Prince illuminated the process of dissociation and the phenomenon of multiple personality, studied hallucinations and visions, and elaborated a doctrine of purpose and meaning. A motivational emphasis was retained in the neo-Freudian psychologies.

While Freud was probably the greatest dynamist, McDougall rates a close second. As early as 1923 he pleaded for a purposive behaviorism, of which his hormic psychology was a prime example. McDougall asserted that there was "an end or purpose which goads us on to action without any real knowledge of its nature, although a dim or vague foresight or prescience may be there" (Roback, 1952, p. 259). He called his dynamisms instincts, urges, and finally propensities. Instincts, being goal directed, consisted of the liberation of energy guiding the organism toward a goal. Adopting McDougall's concept of purposive behaviorism, Edward Chace Tolman's learning theory included many purposive terms (demands, goal objects, and means-end readiness) and assumed that purpose could be observed. Holt's cognitive psychology was also purposive. Holt termed the dynamic principle a wish and spoke of both negative and positive purposes, though these were conceived in causal rather than teleological terms.

The dynamic psychologies proper include those of Woodworth, Kurt Lewin, and Henry Alexander Murray. Woodworth began using the phrase *dynamic psychology* around 1910 and probably coined the term. His dynamism consisted in his belief that the organism is an important intervening variable between the stimulus and response and that the organism's activity might be seen in its conscious processes as well as in its behavior. Lewin regarded the person as a locomotor organism whose desires could be represented as valences and vectors that push the person toward or away from objects. He used the concept of tension to describe motivations and needs. Murray articulated his dynamic theory in terms of needs, presses, themas, and regnancies, and formulated a list of needs very similar to McDougall's list of instincts.

Also in the dynamic camp is Gordon Allport, who defined personality as the dynamic organization within the individual of those psychophysical systems that determine his or her unique adjustments to the environment.

Of special interest to the Christian psychologist is the dynamic psychology of Moore (1948), the Benedictine monk who became a leader in the psychology department at the Catholic University in Washington, D.C. Moore blended dynamic psychology, functional psychology, the techniques of factor analysis, and the traditional Thomistic psychology. Dynamic psychology also inspired the integrationist efforts of Seward Hiltner (1972), who states that "theological doctrines themselves always exist in a dynamic relationship, containing tensions and equilibriums and the temptation to distortion" (p. 201). Dynamic psychology stands in contrast to descriptive psychology and psychiatry, which focuses on a classification of behaviors without regard for motives or other underlying dynamics.

References

Hiltner, S. (1972). *Theological dynamics*. Nashville: Abingdon.

Moore, T. V. (1948). *The driving forces of human nature and their adjustment*. New York: Grune & Stratton.

Roback, A. A. (1952). *History of American psychology*. New York: Library Publishers.

H. VANDE KEMP

See DESCRIPTIVE PSYCHOLOGY/PSYCHIATRY.

Dyslexia. A disorder manifested by difficulty in learning to read despite conventional instruction, adequate intelligence, and sociocultural opportunity. It is frequently constitutional in origin being more prevalent among "first-degree biological relatives of individuals with Learning Disorders" (American Psychiatric Association, 1994, p. 49).

The term *dyslexia* generally is not used unless reading performance is two grade levels below that of age mates or the child performs at two standard deviations below the reading achievement expected for his or her performance on an IQ test. In some educational circles there is opposition to using the term for fear a child will be labeled. However, if the problem is not recognized, the child may be unfairly criticized for not trying hard enough.

Dyslexia affects millions, and 5% to 10% of all children have severe difficulties. Males are four times as vulnerable as females, and there is a higher proportion among left-handed and mixed-dominance individuals than among right-dominance persons (*see* Handedness). Because students with dyslexia cannot store word images in the brain, writing and spelling are also adversely affected, interfering with academic achievement. In time all areas of study may show a decline. Other activities of daily living that require reading skills, such as grocery shopping or understanding road signs, may also prove difficult.

Additional problems sometimes accompany dyslexia. High activity level, impaired coordination, lack of impulse control, inattentiveness, resistance to social demands, poor memory, and emotional difficulties are more prevalent in those with the disorder than in those not having the disorder. Delinquency is also more apt to occur.

A number of famous men such as Leonardo da Vinci, Albert Einstein, Thomas Edison, Woodrow Wilson, Nelson Rockefeller, and General George S. Patton have been diagnosed as having had dyslexia. Thousands of lesser-known men and women have also led full and productive lives. With proper understanding and special educational techniques the diagnosis of dyslexia need not be frightening.

Brain scans of extremely dyslexic children using magnetic resonance imaging (MRI) have shown that the area involved in "phonological coding, language comprehension, and auditory perception" is smaller than in normal children (Adler, 1989, p. 7). Several scientists are narrowing their search for a dyslexia gene to either chromosome 6 or chromosome 15.

References

Adler, T. (1989, November). Brain's language area is abnormal in disabled. *Science Monitor*, p. 7.

American Psychiatric Association. (1994). *Diagnostic and statistical manual of mental disorders* (4th ed.). Washington, DC: Author.

B. CLOUSE

See LEARNING DISABILITY.

Dyspareunia. A medical term for painful sexual intercourse. It is usually used in reference to women (as it is here) rather than men.

The pain experienced during penile-vaginal intercourse may have physical or emotional bases. If the dyspareunia is physically based, it is often brought about by a semiperforated hymen, ulceration of the fourchette, urethritis, vaginitis, and other inflammatory conditions in the pelvis (Taber, 1940).

If, after physical examination by a physician, no organic basis for the presence of dyspareunia is found, the condition is generally assumed to be emotionally based. It is frequently referred to as functional dyspareunia, referring to disorders that are without known organic basis.

Pain at the beginning of intercourse generally indicates an absence of vaginal lubrication. Lubrication and swelling of the vaginal canal normally begin less than one minute after the beginning of sexual stimulation. The lack of lubrication is generally due to a lack of sexual desire on the part of the wife, fear of becoming pregnant even though sexual desire is present, or other emotionally based resistances to experiencing sexual excitement (Hinsie & Campbell, 1970).

Functional dyspareunia may be symptomatically overcome by using various lubrication jellies. Establishing the capacity for natural vaginal lubrication and swelling, which will eliminate painful intercourse, is very difficult, since the requisite vasocongestion is governed by the parasympathetic portion of the autonomic nervous system, which is beyond conscious, decisional control (*see* Inhibited Sexual Arousal).

As with other aspects of human sexual response, the presence of painful intercourse may vary in frequency, duration, and degree. There is generally no overt marital discord to account for the lack of vaginal lubrication. The absence of vaginal lubrication and swelling associated with functional dyspareunia is sometimes labeled general sexual dysfunction.

No definitive figures are available for the incidence rate of dyspareunia. Some approximation is contained in a study by Biggerstaff, David, and Lloyd (1982). Upon taking a sexual history of one hundred consecutive women presenting themselves for routine gynecologic examination, they found that 17% had no organic basis for their reported dyspareunia while 7% had gynecologic pathology upon examination.

Overcoming functional dyspareunia may be accomplished by spending more time in sexual play prior to insertion of the penis. Coaching the couple would involve advice to enjoy present feelings rather than focusing on intercourse itself. Penetration should not be attempted until it is ascertained that adequate lubrication is present. No direct conscious effort by the wife should be made to lubricate; allowing sexual excitement to occur will spontaneously bring about the desired lubrication.

It is suggested that wives experiencing difficulty with lubrication and accompanying painful intercourse use the female superior position and insert the husband's penis into the vagina only when she is sufficiently aroused and adequately lubricated. Using the weight of her body to slowly introduce the penis into her vagina gives the wife greater control and reduces fear of pain or discomfort (Hartman & Fithian, 1974).

Wives should be counseled to not accept dyspareunia as an untreatable condition. Whether organically or emotionally based, it is subject to resolution. As in the treatment of most sexual dysfunctions, the crucial process involves relaxed touching without pressure or demand for sexual performance or intercourse. It is a paradoxical situation—like the Christian sayings, "It is in giving that we receive" and "It is in dying that we are born to eternal life." We will become sexually aroused if we do not consciously strive for it to happen.

References

Biggerstaff, E. D., David, J. R., & Lloyd, A. J. (1982). Female sexual dysfunction incidence rate in a military medical center. *Medical Bulletin, 39* (6), 17–21.

Hartman, W. E., & Fithian, M. A. (1974). *Treatment of sexual dysfunction.* New York: Aronson.

Hinsie, L. E., & Campbell, R. J. (1970). *Psychiatric dictionary* (4th ed.). New York: Oxford University Press.

Taber, C. W. (1940). *Taber's cyclopedic medical dictionary.* Philadelphia: Davis.

J. R. DAVID

See SEXUAL PAIN DISORDERS.

Dysthymic Disorder. The essential feature of this disorder is a chronic disturbance of mood involving depression and loss of interest and pleasure. Under older terminology the disorder was called neurasthenia or depressive neurosis. It is differentiated from the more serious depressive disorder, major depressive episode, on the basis of severity and duration of symptoms.

See DEPRESSION.

Ee

Eating Disorders. Eating disorders manifest a wide range of weight and food issues experienced by both men and women. They symbolize serious emotional and physical problems that can have life-threatening consequences. The most effective treatment is psychotherapy with an eating disorder specialist, combined with medical, dietary, and in the case of bulimia, dental services. Length of treatment will vary depending on the severity, chronicity, ego and coping skills, absence or presence of personality disorders, and availability of support systems. If hospitalization is necessary, a specialized eating disorder unit is best (such as Remuda Ranch, a Christian-based residential treatment center in Arizona).

There are three diagnostic groups. They are not exclusive of each other in that patients may move from one type of eating disorder to another.

Anorexia nervosa is evidenced primarily by self-starvation and severe body image distortion. Rituals involving food are compulsive, and the person fears losing control if rituals are broken.

Bulimia nervosa is characterized by usually secretive cycles of binging (two binges per week to up to ten per day), consisting of 2,000 to 40,000 calories per binge, followed by purging by vomiting, use of laxatives, diet pills, diuretics, excessive exercise, or fasting.

Compulsive eating consists of recurrent episodes of binge eating, a loss of control over food, and using food to numb affect.

Understanding eating disorders requires a multilevel model combining psychological, interpersonal, social, and physiological factors. Feelings of inadequacy, depression, anxiety, loneliness, troubled family backgrounds, lack of identity, and split affect can contribute. Eating disorders help some people cope with painful emotions, to feel as if they are in control when they have no other method to do so.

Christian counselors need to pay particular attention to the fact that the person with the eating disorder not only will treat people like they treat food (for example, anorexics resist letting people in in much the same way they disallow food—for fear of becoming out of control or fat) but also will respond to God similarly (for example, anorexics may be fearful of "letting the Holy Spirit in" to lead their lives when the only one they trust to lead their lives is themselves). Thus any incorporation of spiritual issues needs to correlate to the metaphor of the eating disorder—with anorexics, stress the choices they have, that God is empathetic, and that God is not capricious; with bulimics, stress God's consistency, unconditional acceptance, and security; with compulsive overeaters, stress God's balance, control, love, and relational boundaries.

For Further Information

ANAD. National Association of Anorexia Nervosa and Associated Disorders, P.O. Box 7, Highland Park, IL 60035. (708) 831-3438.

NEDO. National Eating Disorders Organization, 6655 South Yale Ave., Tulsa, OK 74136. (918) 481-4044.

Eating Disorders Review (bimonthly newsletter). Gurze Books, P.O. Box 2238, Carlsbad, CA 92018.

M. F. CLARK

See ANOREXIA NERVOSA; BULIMIA NERVOSA.

Ebbinghaus, Hermann (1850–1909). Pioneer in the study of memory. Born in Barmen, Germany, Ebbinghaus studied history and philosophy at Bonn, Berlin, and Halle between 1867 and 1870. He received his doctorate in philosophy in 1873 from Bonn after serving in the army during the Franco-Prussian War. For the next seven years he lived as a private scholar, visiting England and France, where he became acquainted with Gustav Fechner's work.

In 1880 Ebbinghaus began teaching at the University of Berlin. He became professor in 1886 and remained at Berlin until 1894, when he accepted the chair of philosophy at Breslau. In 1905 he went to Halle, where he remained until his death. He founded or expanded laboratories at all three universities.

The best known of Ebbinghaus's accomplishments is his experimentation on memory. He invented the nonsense syllable in an attempt to get verbal material without previous associations. With the combinations of three letters (consonant, vowel, consonant) he developed 2,300 meaningless syllables that he could use in memory studies. He served as his own subject in his experiments and memorized hundreds of lists. His results have been verified by other research and are still cited in general psychology texts.

Although Wilhelm Wundt had stated that it was not possible to experiment on the higher mental processes, Ebbinghaus opened up this new field. He applied Fechner's methods of psychophysics to memory rather than just to sensation. He also devised a sentence completion test as a method of mental measurement.

Ebbinghaus was a careful researcher, but his desire to check, recheck, and revise his work resulted in fewer publications and fewer promotions for him than for many of his colleagues. His classic book *On Memory* (1885) is still frequently cited more than a century after its publication. He also published a successful general textbook, *The Principles of Psychology* (1902), and a more popular text, *A Summary of Psychology* (1908). In 1890 he was cofounder of the *Journal of Psychology and Physiology of the Sense Organs*, a journal publishing experiment different from those done by the structuralists at Leipzig.

Ebbinghaus made no theoretical contributions, did not create a formal system, had no important disciples, and did not found a school, but his research findings have stood the test of time. He brought objectivity, quantification, and experimentation to the study of learning and memory. The nonsense syllable has been widely used in the study of memory; however, psychologists have found that such materials do have associations, so they are used less today.

R. L. KOTESKEY

See MEMORY.

Echolalia. A pathological reaction characterized by the mechanical imitation of the speech of another. The repetitive echoing of words or phrases tends to be persistent, and the tone is mumbling, mocking, or stilted. In some cases there is guarded hostility, perhaps as a regressive childhood behavior. Echolalia is not to be confused with habitual repetition of questions. In echolalia a person may reply to the statement, "It's a rainy day outside," with the words, "Rainy day outside, rainy day outside." The reaction is noted in organic mental disorders, catatonic schizophrenia, Pick's disease, Alzheimer's Disease, and some pervasive mental disorders.

Echopraxia. A pathological reaction and a common symptom in catatonic schizophrenia in which a person acts as a mirror image of another by imitating movements. The term is reserved for those with brain disease or functional psychosis. The imitation of actions of another is known as echokinesis, and the imitation of the gestures of another is echomimia.

Eclecticism in Psychotherapy. Psychotherapy as a formal and systematic practice has its roots in the late 1800s and early 1900s. The work of Sigmund Freud (1856–1939) is often cited as the beginning of contemporary psychotherapy, but it would be erroneous to give him sole credit for founding the profession. Ellenberger (1970) affirms that Pierre Janet (1859–1947) founded the first system of dynamic psychiatry. Janet in turn had been trained by the most renowned neurologist at the time, Jean-Martin Charcot (1825–1893). Freud himself studied with Charcot. Josef Breuer (1842–1925), in the opinion of Arlow (1995), originated psychoanalysis proper through his sharing with Freud the hypnotic procedure he used in the treatment of a female hysteric. Still, Freud had both a major role in the development of psychoanalytic psychotherapy and influence on the works of others (e.g., Alfred Adler, Carl Gustav Jung, Otto Rank, and Wilhelm Reich) who proceeded to launch their own schools of psychotherapy.

Since the founding of Freudian psychoanalysis and the various neo-Freudian spin-offs, there has been a proliferation of theoretical approaches to psychotherapy. Each new system of therapy has faulted to some degree all of its predecessors and claimed a status superior to them on one ground or another. Although adherence to a particular school of psychotherapy formerly appeared to be more prestigious, an increasing number of psychotherapists have shown a disenchantment with exclusive systems of psychotherapy and a preference for an eclectic orientation that combines the essential principles and methods of various theories about human behavior to develop a more comprehensive approach to therapy.

The word *eclectic* has its origin in the Greek verbal root *eklego*, a composite of *ek* (from or out of) and *lego* (to pick, choose, or select). "Eclectic" literally means to pick out or to select from. It is hard to improve on the basic definition of eclecticism offered by English and English: "The selection and orderly combination of compatible features from diverse sources, sometimes from otherwise incompatible theories and systems; the effort to find valid elements in all . . . theories and to combine them into a harmonious whole. The resulting system is open to constant revision even in its major outings" (1958, p. 168). Although the term *integration* appears to be more descriptive of the current trend away from exclusive systems of psychotherapy, the focus here is on eclecticism in the traditional perspective.

Brief History. Theoretical eclecticism is not a new phenomenon in either psychology or the practice of psychotherapy. James (1907/1975) sought to bring together the thoughts of tender-minded rationalists and tough-minded empiricists via the pragmatic method. He considered pragmatism as being a mediator and reconciler that eschewed fixed principles, rigid dogma, pretense of finality in truth, and closed systems. He viewed it as marked by openness and a flexible empiricist attitude that invites the application of any and all principles, concepts, and methods that can be assimilated, validated, corroborated, and verified in reality.

Woodworth (1931) referred to himself as a middle-of-the-roader who maintained that each school or system makes its special contribution to the whole of psychology and believed that none of them is ideal. For a half-century Woodworth encouraged rapprochement of overtly competitive factions.

Allport (1964, 1968) was a self-described polemic-eclectic who was theoretically open yet prepared to challenge any psychological idol. His concept of a theoretical system was "one that allows for truth wherever found, one that encompasses the totality of human experience and does full justice to the nature of man" (1968, p. 406).

Numerous eclectic approaches to psychotherapy have been developed since the 1940s. The psychobiology of Meyer (1948) is generally accepted as the first serious attempt at an eclectic psychotherapy. Meyer wanted an integration of the psychological, sociological, and biological dimensions of human behavior. He insisted on a comprehensiveness that included the life history of the individual, a thorough diagnosis of the clinical situation, and the application of a variety of techniques that fitted the person and the problem presented.

Dollard and Miller (1950) endeavored to integrate the psychoanalytic concepts of Freud, learning theory, and cultural influences. Their aim was "to combine the vitality of psychoanalysis, the vigor of the natural science laboratory, and the facts of culture" (p. 3).

Wolberg (1954) made an initial effort to extract methods from the field of psychoanalysis, psychobiology, psychiatric interviewing, casework, and therapeutic counseling and to blend these into an eclectic system of methodology. He has broadened the scope of the inclusions in subsequent editions of *The Technique of Psychotherapy*.

For more than 30 years the late Fredrick Thorne was the prince of the eclectics. He wrote prolifically on eclecticism, and each of his several major works is encyclopedic in content. A quote from his *Psychological Case Handling* well illustrates his position: "to collect and integrate all known methods of personality counseling and psychotherapy into an eclectic system which might form the basis of standardized practice; . . . to be rigidly scientific . . . [with] no priority given to any theoretical viewpoint or school . . . [but] to analyze the contributions of all existing schools and fit them together into an integrated system . . . [that] combines the best features of all methods" (Thorne, 1968, vol. 1, p. vi).

The *Therapeutic Psychology* of Brammer and Shostrom, published first in 1960 and now available in the fourth edition (1982), is a landmark in the evolution of eclectic psychotherapy. They use the term *emerging eclecticism* to define their efforts to develop a comprehensive and dynamic perspective on personality structure and change as a basis for clinical practice. They assimilate extractions from psychoanalytic, humanistic, existential-phenomenological, and behavioral approaches to form a multidimensional system of therapy.

Another substantial work on eclectic theory, *Beyond Counseling and Psychotherapy* by Carkhuff and Berenson, appeared in 1967. These authors sought to build around a central core of facilitative conditions an armamentarium of clinical methods judged to be compatible with the facilitative core. The methods were derived from client-centered, existential, behavioral, trait-factor, and psychoanalytic orientations.

The work of Lazarus (1967, 1976, 1989) represents a more recent and substantial effort to craft an eclectic psychotherapy that he has labeled "multimodal therapy" that espouses a technical rather than a theoretical emphasis. While it is atheoretical, his technically eclectic therapy is firmly rooted in behavioral principles, social learning theory, and cognitive theory. Lazarus draws less extensively from general systems theory and communications theory.

Several other psychotherapists have presented excellent eclectic themes, though these have been less substantial in nature than those already cited. A sample of these titles includes *Psychological Counseling* (Bordin, 1968), *Psychobehavioral Counseling and Therapy* (Woody, 1971), *A Primer of Eclectic Psychotherapy* (Palmer, 1980), *Psychotherapy: An Eclectic Approach* (Garfield, 1980), *Eclectic Psychotherapy: A Systematic Approach* (Beutler, 1983), and *Modern Eclectic Therapy: A Functional Orientation to Counseling and Psychotherapy* (Hart, 1983).

Criticism. A mixed audience exists regarding eclecticism in counseling and psychotherapy. On the one hand there are those who hold that eclecticism is essential for a psychotherapy approach that is open, comprehensive, flexible, and truly adaptable to the unique needs of clients and their diversity of presenting problems (e.g., Allport, 1964; Carkhuff & Berenson, 1967; Beutler, 1983; Lazarus, 1989). On the other hand some therapists, including those who endorse eclecticism, believe that this is often the therapeutic preference of lazy, unscientific, and irresponsible individuals who opt for an undisciplined and poorly crafted collection of concepts, principles, and methods (Hart, 1983; Ivey & Simek-Downing, 1980; Lazarus & Beutler, 1993; Patterson, 1986).

Current Status. Survey research findings indicate that a growing number of psychotherapists identify with an eclectic orientation (Garfield & Kurtz, 1976; Jensen, Bergin, & Greaves, 1990; Smith, 1982). At the same time, a stronger preference appears to be shown for integration than for eclecticism per se (Jensen, Bergin, & Greaves, 1990). Three current trends can be detected in continued movement away from exclusive schools and systems of psychotherapy. One is in the direction of theory-oriented integration in which labels such as "dynamic eclectics," "systems eclectics," "cognitive eclectics," and "technical eclectics" are descriptive (Jensen, Bergin, & Greaves, 1990). A second trend is toward an atheoretical approach that is systematic, prescriptive, and technical (Lazarus & Beutler, 1993). The third trend could be described as Christian psychotheology that represents a rapidly expanding movement to integrate traditional Christian values, biblical truths, and psychological principles and methods. Two notable indices of the increased status of eclecticism and integration are the formation of the Society for the Exploration of Psychotherapy and founding of the *Journal of Integrative and Eclectic Psychotherapy*.

References

Allport, G. W. (1964). The fruits of eclecticism: Bitter or sweet? *Acta Psychologica, 23*, 27–44.

Allport, G. W. (1968). *The person in psychology*. Boston: Beacon.

Arlow, J. A. (1995). Psychoanalysis. In R. J. Corsini & D. Wedding (Eds.), *Current psychotherapies* (5th ed.). Itasca, IL: Peacock.

Beutler, L. E. (1983). *Eclectic psychotherapy: A systematic approach*. New York: Pergamon.

Bordin, E. S. (1968). *Psychological counseling* (2nd ed.). New York: Appleton-Century-Crofts.

Brammer, L. M., & Shostrom, E. L. (1982). *Therapeutic psychology* (4th ed.). Englewood Cliffs, NJ: Prentice-Hall.

Carkhuff, R. R., & Berenson, B. G. (1967). *Beyond counseling and psychotherapy*. New York: Holt, Rinehart, & Winston.

Dollard, J., & Miller, N. E. (1950). *Personality and psychotherapy*. New York: McGraw-Hill.

Ellenberger, H. F. (1970). *The discovery of the unconscious*. New York: Basic.

English, H. B., & English, A. C. (1958). *A comprehensive dictionary of psychological and psychoanalytic terms*. New York: Longmans, Green.

Garfield, S. L. (1980). *Psychotherapy: An eclectic approach*. New York: Wiley.

Garfield, S. L., & Kurtz, R. (1976). Clinical psychologists in the 1970s. *American Psychologist, 31*, 1–9.

Hart, J. T. (1983). *Modern eclectic therapy: A functional orientation to counseling and psychotherapy*. New York: Pergamon.

Ivey, A. E., & Simek-Downing, L. (1980). *Counseling and psychotherapy*. Englewood Cliffs, NJ: Prentice-Hall.

James, W. (1975). *Pragmatism*. Cambridge, MA: Harvard University Press. (Original work published 1907)

Jensen, J. P., Bergin, A. E., & Greaves, D. W. (1990). The meaning of eclecticism: New survey and analysis of components. *Professional Psychology: Research and Practice, 21*, 124–130.

Lazarus, A. A. (1967). In support of technical eclecticism. *Psychological Reports, 21*, 415–416.

Lazarus, A. A. (1976). *Multimodal behavior therapy*. New York: Springer.

Lazarus, A. A. (1989). *The practice of multimodal therapy* (Updated ed.). Baltimore: Johns Hopkins University Press.

Lazarus, A. A., & Beutler, L. E. (1993). On technical eclecticism. *Journal of Counseling and Development, 71*, 381–385.

Meyer, A. (1948). *The common sense psychiatry of Dr. Adolf Meyer*. New York: McGraw-Hill, 1948.

Palmer, J. O. (1980). *A primer of eclectic psychotherapy*. Monterey, CA: Brooks/Cole.

Patterson, C. H. (1986). *Theories of counseling and psychotherapy* (4th ed.). New York: Harper & Row.

Smith, D. (1982). Trends in counseling and psychotherapy. *American Psychologist, 37*, 802–809.

Thorne, F. (1968). *Psychological case handling* (2 vols.). Brandon, VT: Clinical Psychology Publishing.

Wolberg, L. R. (1954). *The technique of psychotherapy*. New York: Grune & Stratton.

Woodworth, R. S. (1931). *Contemporary schools of psychology*. New York: Ronald.

Woody, R. H. (1971). *Psychobehavioral counseling and therapy*. New York: Appleton-Century-Crofts.

Additional Readings

Lazarus, A. A., Beutler, L. E., & Norcross, J. C. (1992). The future of technical eclecticism. *Psychotherapy, 29*, 11–20.

Shostrom, E. L. (1976). *Actualizing therapy*. San Diego, CA: EDits.

Smith, D. (1975). *Integrative counseling and psychotherapy*. Boston: Houghton Mifflin.

D. Smith

See Counseling and Psychotherapy: Overview.

Ecstatic Religious Experiences. Ecstatic experiences play important roles in many Christian and non-Christian traditions. Other committed believers and religious subcultures find no need for such expressions.

Scope. Religious ecstasies (notably speaking in tongues or glossolalia) are recorded in the New Testament, and some are reported throughout church history. The most consistent expressions, however, have been within the Pentecostal movement, beginning in the first decade of the twentieth century, with influences from southern black Christian traditions. Starting about 1960 ecstatic experiences, especially glossolalia, have found expression in Roman Catholic and mainstream Protestant churches.

Perhaps the prototype of ecstatic religion is the possession Trance in African animism, Haitian vodou (voodoo), and numerous other folk religions. Possession trance refers to an alternation of personality, consciousness, or will that is attributed to possession by an alien spirit, which might be the spirit of an animal or another person. In some primitive cultures possession trance is cultivated as an important part of the religious expression. Sometimes possession is seen as an experience to be avoided or terminated, as in Roman Catholic exorcism rites. In some Pentecostal, charismatic, and black churches glossolalia, shouting, dancing, and fainting are interpreted as manifestations of possession by the Holy Spirit—that is, as possession trance. Others consider them gifts of the Spirit or blessings. Almost invariably, though, such experiences are perceived as supernatural or beyond mere human will—in psychological terms, a trance or an altered or alternative state of consciousness.

Automatic writing, as claimed by some prophets and religious founders, has trancelike if not overtly ecstatic features. Much snake handling, fire handling, and fire walking are similarly trancelike and/or ecstatic. Some faith healing rituals and mystical experiences involve ecstasy and, especially in mysticism, altered states of consciousness, but they have significantly different religious functions and psychological causes or dynamics.

Functions. Considerable speculation and some firm evidence indicate that ecstatic religion functions in part as a compensation or outlet for frustrated or conflicting needs. Possession trance is more likely to occur in societies that have rigid, fixed status distinctions, including slavery. Trance behavior represents a safety valve for stresses caused by such social rigidities (Bourguignon, 1976). Pentecostalism has made its greatest inroads in American lower classes and in African countries that have anxiety-producing status differences and class conflicts. Glossolalia is often associated with anxiety states and a need to discharge built-up tension, and it is related to personality measures that give credence to this function (Smith, 1976).

A related function, beyond mere compensation, is personality integration. Do ecstatic experiences prove therapeutic to their anxious and frustrated subjects? Ritualized possession trance does not solve any of the social differences that spawn it, but it can give new structure and meaning to individual lives (Bourguignon, 1976). It is hard to separate the ecstatic expressions themselves from the belief and social support system of which they are a part. Most studies of glossolalia suggest that the total religious context, not just the ecstatic experience, is redemptive. Nonetheless, the emotional release and personal interpretations of ecstasies are part of the religious system that provides hope and meaning to many desperate lives.

Probably the most fundamental function of ecstatic religious experiences was suggested by James: "Beliefs are strengthened whenever automatisms corroborate them. Incursions from beyond the transmarginal have a peculiar power to increase conviction" (1902, p. 372). Speaking in tongues or other public display of so-called irrational behavior irrevocably sets people apart from secular society, affirming their religious identities and belief systems. In the 1960s the disruption of traditional Roman Catholic practices by Vatican Council II changes and the secular drift of liberal Protestant denominations set the stage for the need to reaffirm spiritual identity and dependency. Visions, automatic writing, and other charismatic gifts have lent credence and impetus to the revelations of major religious leaders for centuries. Sometimes ecstasy functions as testimony to unbelievers of God's power. Appalachian Holiness fire handlers avow that their purpose is to convince sinners of God's power and produce repentance. Miracles in both Testaments frequently served these belief functions.

Dynamics of Ecstasy. To the uninitiated, religious ecstasies often look like psychiatric disorder—hysteria, Schizophrenia, or even perhaps epilepsy. Consequently most serious psychological studies of the ecstasies have used personality measures like the Minnesota Multiphasic Personality Inventory (MMPI). The results have been minimal and sometimes inconsistent. Glossolalists, the most widely studied group, and snake handlers have usually shown fewer signs of pathology than do nonecstatic religious groups. In general they show somewhat different personality patterns but no greater indication of personality disorder per se. Ecstasy practitioners tend to be less socially conforming and more pleasure-oriented—that is, less inhibited and more expressive. They usually show signs of lower autonomy and more dependence on other individuals, especially trusted religious leaders. They are more trusting in general. Hysteria—the MMPI scale indicating tendency to express inner conflicts through physical means—consistently has not been related to ecstatic behaviors. As a group glossolalists are apparently less intelligent and lower in educational levels than are comparable nonglossolalists (Smith, 1976).

Glossolalists frequently have experienced some personal stress or crisis (financial reversal, family or personal illness, marital discord) not long before they first spoke in tongues (Kildahl, 1972; Smith, 1976). A few studies have failed to find this effect. Perhaps it may be that in groups who use glossolalia in a more playful manner, the gift is less likely to be related to stress, anxiety, or other psychiatric factors.

To a substantial extent religious ecstasy is more a matter of learning than of psychiatry. People who grow up in a culture or church where such experiences are routine are imprinted to accept and enact such behaviors at an appropriate age and circumstance. Social learning has been explicitly observed for possession trance in Haitian vodou. Children who hear adults talk about the clan's favorite possessing spirits accept the spirits as virtually part of the extended family. Discussion and observation of the rites leading up to trance teach the children how to induce the trances and how to respond when in them (Bourguignon, 1976). Similar observations could surely be made in Pentecostal churches.

More individualized learning is sometimes observed. While glossolalia is not learned in the way one learns a foreign language, coaching has been noted at charismatic meetings—for example, "Come on now. Speak out. You're still begging. There you are. Keep talking. Come on. Hallelujah. He's praying a new language" (Samarin, 1969). Once an individual has experienced glossolalia, possession trance, or Pentecostal ecstatic expressions, these can be repeated with relative ease in the appropriately sanctioned religious setting.

Glossolalic utterances have frequently been claimed as real foreign tongues that the speaker has not learned. Scientifically verifiable, firsthand reports of such events have not been produced. Nor do glossolalic utterances show linguistic characteristics common to human languages.

Expression of trancelike religious ecstasies resembles hypnosis. Induction has been related to loud, rhythmic, repetitious, and/or stupefying music and other environmental and physical factors—a hot, stuffy room high in carbon dioxide, social isolation, and fasting (Aylland, 1962).

Other unconscious factors undoubtedly play roles in glossolalia. Christian tongues speaking sometimes occurs spontaneously, without explicit social modeling or learning but probably never without knowledge of such events in the New Testament record. Occurrence of glossolalia also in non-Christian religions and in psychosis suggests that the structure of the central nervous system enables nonrational use of language. The brain appears to have neurological structures that promote development of a natural language, given normal linguistic experience in a family or human community. Similarly various neural inhibitions, disinhibitions, and "switches" controlling them are consistent with current knowledge of the central nervous system. These brain mechanisms are probably involved in the practice of speaking in tongues.

Psychologists increasingly recognize various altered states of consciousness, and they frequently consider trancelike religious ecstasies from this perspective. Fire walking and handling fire in many religious traditions can involve a trance state or altered state of consciousness. Southern Appalachian Holiness fire handlers report an anointing that enables them to expose bodily parts to intense flames and heat for up to 15 seconds without pain or burning. The anointing is variously described by practitioners: "Just don't feel much at all. I get numb. Feels like my skin crawls." "A shield comes down over me. I know when it's around me. It's cold inside. My hands get numb and cold" (Kane, 1974, p. 119).

Hypnotic experiments spanning more than half a century demonstrate psychological control of heat pain. With few exceptions, hypnotic suggestion eliminates or minimizes the effects of heat stimuli applied to a limb. Similarly, given the suggestion that the experimenter's finger is a red-hot iron, the finger can produce pain and blisters like those normally produced by heat. When subjects are hypnotized to be insensitive to heat pain, their blood vessels constrict in the affected body parts, and they report numbness and coldness strikingly similar to reports by anointed Holiness fire handlers. Given either hypnosis or spiritual motivation, the central nervous system can control the effects of intense heat for as long as 15 seconds.

Every religious experience occurs in the context of an individual who is at once a physical, psychological, and social as well as spiritual being. Ecstatic religious experiences in particular serve a variety of functions, some primarily religious, some more psy-chological. Each such occurrence is grounded in a human personality with distinctive individual and cultural experiences, with neurological capabilities that are not fully understood. No single dynamic, cause, or factor explains any form of ecstatic religious experience. Even taken together they do not fully account for any individual's ecstatic behavior or feelings. Psychologists slowly and imperfectly seek better to understand and explain these factors and their interacting effects on human behavior. However, no psychological explanation, however complete, can explain away or determine the spiritual value of any religious experience.

References

Aylland, A., Jr. (1962). "Possession" in a revivalistic Negro church. *Journal for the Scientific Study of Religion, 1,* 204–213.

Bourguignon, E. (1976). *Possession*. San Francisco: Chandler & Sharp.

James, W. (1978). *The varieties of religious experience*. Garden City, NY: Image Books. (Original work published 1902)

Kane, S. M. (1974). Holiness fire handling in Southern Appalachia. In J. D. Photiadis (Ed.), *Religion in Appalachia*. Morgantown: West Virginia University.

Kildahl, J. P. (1972). *The psychology of speaking in tongues*. New York: Harper & Row.

Samarin, W. J. (1969). Glossolalia as learned behavior. *Canadian Journal of Theology, 15,* 60–64.

Smith, D. S. (1976). Glossolalia: The personality correlates of conventional and unconventional subgroups. Doctoral dissertation, Rosemead Graduate School of Psychology. (University Microfilms No. 77–21,537)

R. D. KAHOE

See RELIGIOUS HEALTH AND PATHOLOGY; RELIGIOUS EXPERIENCE; DISSOCIATIVE TRANCE DISORDER.

ECT. *See* ELECTROCONVULSIVE THERAPY.

Ectomorph. In Sheldon's system of constitutional types the ectomorph is a person with a thin, frail, and angular body. This body type, comparable to Kretschmer's asthenic type, is contrasted to the endomorph and mesomorph types. Sheldon's research suggested that ectomorphs tend to be restrained, inhibited, and self-conscious.

See CONSTITUTIONAL PERSONALITY THEORY.

Educational Psychology. Educational psychology deals with learning and cognition and the conditions that influence them, particularly within educational settings; the psychological development, social relationships, and adjustment found within educational settings. The attention of educational psychology has broadened to encompass nontraditional subjects and contexts—that is, those lying outside the institution and age boundaries most frequently associated with education of the young. Interests in lifelong learning and on learning in work and other nonstandard educational settings are but two examples of these expanding boundaries. The study of cognitive outcomes associated with school curricula is now only one concern, albeit the major one, among others. Attitudes, career awareness, and creativity are also prized outcomes. While continuing to focus primarily on school learning and instruction, educational psychology includes many other considerations relevant to teaching and learning.

Considering its full scope, disparities among characterizations of the field do not seem surprising. For some it is a branch of applied psychology, the goal of which is to identify the educationally relevant concepts and findings of psychology and demonstrate their applications, much as engineering uses basic principles of physics to solve practical problems. Others place more emphasis on educational psychology as a discipline in its own right.

The roots of this ambiguity go back to the establishment of educational psychology as a scientifically respectable discipline by Edward Lee Thorndike around 1900 to 1910. This beginning was actually a manifesto promising that laws of learning would be identified and education would be founded at last upon a secure scientific foundation. Thorndike's positive contributions were his insistence on objective, empirical methods and his stress on the role of environmental influences. These set the field forever apart from armchair philosophizing about learning. However, in retrospect the price of this rigor was methodological narrowness and an impoverished view of the learner and the learning process. This view, which saw learning in terms of forming bonds between stimuli and responses, was enormously significant in stimulating the behaviorist school of psychology. Although many practical applications eventually resulted from this movement—techniques of behavior modification and programmed instruction, to name only two—the major consequence was failure to fulfill the original promise of a science of education. It also led to a widening gap between theory and experimentation on the one hand and educational practice on the other. Educational psychologists were placed in the position of trying to bridge this gap; hence the confusion as to what their role should be.

Another significant activity of many educational psychologists is the testing of individual differences, particularly intelligence and special abilities, and identifying their components. The testing movement does not fit the preceding characterization, since tests have gained their prominence primarily as a response to urgent practical needs—for example, selection and placement in education, industry, and the military. The thriving test industry demonstrates the popularity of tests for many practical purposes. Nonetheless, testing has not in general been undergirded with a psychological theory of learning and performance, and thus the gap between theory and practice in educational psychology has not been significantly closed by this movement.

The dominant theoretical force in educational psychology is cognitive psychology. This approach is concerned with the neglected hyphen in the stimulus-response formulation—the active, internal mental processes of thinking, remembering, or problem solving that underlie instruction and learning. Modern computers have provided powerful tools for simulating many complex mental operations and testing the model's correspondence to human subjects' performance. The view of the learner as an active information processor has also spurred a great deal of experimental research resulting in an enriched understanding of reading, mathematical comprehension, the acquisition of subject matter competence, and more.

A closely related phenomenon has been the ascendancy of cognitive developmental psychology under the influence of Jean Piaget, Bruner, and others. The interaction between cognitive developmental stages and instruction has been of paramount interest.

Finally, the field of testing and individual differences is undergoing a great deal of ferment through the impact of these developments. Several trends now challenge the static view of individual differences as permanent fixtures to which instruction must accommodate. First, intellectual abilities are being closely analyzed to reveal the actual mental operations that contribute to test performance. Second, achievement tests are being designed as adjuncts to instruction, to facilitate learning rather than merely report the results of previous learning. Mastery learning, as this approach is called, suggests that many individual differences, regarded as fixed when tests are used to classify students, diminish sharply when tests are used as learning devices. A third trend is the analysis of ways in which learners' attributes do appear to make a difference in the type of instruction that is optimal. The focus here is on students' typical cognitive processes and how they interact with instruction (i.e., a conceptual grasp of what is happening rather than formula prescriptions for different types of students).

Educational psychology can now be identified, with more justification than heretofore, as a distinctive field of inquiry with many potential implications for practice. However, the field still has not developed into the kind of prescriptive science Thorndike envisioned, and few can say confidently that it will do so in the foreseeable future.

Although the Bible does not explicitly set forth principles of educational psychology, when one reads it with educational psychology in mind, numerous points of contact emerge. For instance, Jesus as the teacher par excellence demonstrated in his manner of teaching several important principles. One is that of engaging the active curiosity of listeners by asking probing questions ("Who do you say that I am?" or "To what shall I liken the kingdom of God?"). Jesus' model would seem to support the current cognitive emphasis more than a strictly behavioral emphasis. Another principle is illustrated by his patient nurturance of learning, extending over his three-year ministry and coordinated with the readiness of his disciples to receive his teaching. Finally, Jesus dealt with the whole person, not with cognitive understanding alone. In this respect a strictly cognitive approach may eventually turn out to look as impoverished as the stimulus-response approach now looks from the perspective of cognitive instructional psychology.

D. R. RIDLEY

See SCHOOL PSYCHOLOGY; COGNITIVE PSYCHOLOGY.

Edwards, Jonathan (1703–1758). Because of the tremendous influence of his theological system, his development of a comprehensive understanding of human nature, and his analysis of the nature of conversion and religious experience, the views of Jonathan Edwards had a significant impact on the origins of psychology in America. Influenced by the work of the Cambridge platonists, John Newton, Hume, and especially John Locke, Edwards published treatises, essays, and sermons to defend the First Great Awakening of the 1730s and 1740s against its many critics and to defend the Calvinist tenets of the sovereignty of God and the total depravity and helplessness of human beings.

Edwards, who sought to unite Lockean empiricism with the theology of Augustine and Calvin, conceived of people as a unity composed of a closely interdependent body and soul. He argued that the mind contains two principal components: understanding (which included the functions of sensation, imagination, memory, and judgment) and will. The will, according to Edwards, is the faculty by which the mind chose. The mind chooses in accordance with its inclinations, and inclinations are based on two primary affections: liking, which gives rise to desire, hope, joy, and gratitude, and disliking, which produces fear, anger, grief, and hatred. Edwards's rejection of the separate and independent operation of the faculties of the mind and his argument that human acts involve the total personality have been appealing to many modern psychologists.

Edwards's main contribution to psychology is through his detailed analysis of religious conversion and spiritual experience. He sought to show that all human perception, including Christian faith, involves both rational and emotional components. Unlike his Puritan predecessors, he insisted that both reason and volition are crucial to salvation. In *A Faithful Narrative of the Surprising Work of God* (1737) he carefully described various types and stages of the conversion experience. His examination of religious phenomenology in *A Treatise Concerning the Religious Affections* (1746) is equaled only by James's *The Varieties of Religious Experience* (1901). In this treatise Edwards devised criteria for distinguishing genuine piety from delusionary and

deceptive feelings and behavior and argued that holy affections, especially a thirst for God that produces works in accord with God's law, are a vital part of the true Christian life. Edwards argued persuasively that an intimate relationship with God constitutes the greatest possible fulfillment of human personality. Convinced that an empirical examination of human nature could be very fruitful, he carefully scrutinized and delineated the basis of religious knowledge and the Christian spiritual life. These contributions have led one investigator to argue that Edwards is the "most profound and influential expositor" of an indigenous American psychology before William James (Blight, 1984, p. 98).

Reference

Blight, J. G. (1984). Jonathan Edwards' theory of the mind. In J. Brozek (Ed.), *Explorations in the history of psychology in the United States*. London: Associated University Presses.

G. S. SMITH

EEG. See ELECTROENCEPHALOGRAPHY.

Ego. The technical usage of the term (Latin, I) has been around for quite some time in psychology. As early as 1867 William Griesinger, who published a text in psychiatry, and a French contemporary, Durand, used the term to describe the conscious areas of personality that have to do with self-control and self-observation. They viewed pathology as occurring when a vast discrepancy exists between what a person is in his or her unconscious and in his or her conscious ego. About the same time Meynert, a German psychiatrist, also developed a theory of personality based on the psychology of the ego.

One of Meynert's students, Sigmund Freud, went on to revolutionize psychiatry with his psychoanalytic theory of the ego. Freud avoided using the Latin *ego* in his theory but accepted the term used by his mentors, the German *Das Ich* (the I). This is remarkable because it demonstrates his intent to use the term in a way that was consistent with the technical, psychiatric definition of ego at that time, namely, the self-conscious, controlling aspect of personality. As Freud worked with his patients he expanded this concept of the ego and saw it as part of a topographical model of the mind. In this model he viewed the conscious ego as a repressor that overlays unconscious forbidden memories and impulses that might seek to surface into consciousness.

However, by the time Freud wrote his monumental work on the structure of the psyche, *The Ego and the Id*, in 1923, he significantly expanded the role of the ego in mental functioning. Instead of using ego to refer loosely to consciousness, he more clearly defined it as a mental structure comprising those aspects of the psyche that function to regulate the interaction between the demands of external reality and the demands of internal instinctual drives. The ego arises out of the raw instinctual mass of the id. Through the impact of the external world the child learns the prominence of the reality principle: that instinctual gratification and pleasure must at times be postponed or relinquished and that the realities of consequences must be taken into account. Thus the ego is made up of the aspects of mental life that have become tamed, in that it seeks to achieve gratification of id impulses within the limits of reality. It employs secondary process, or rational thinking, in the pursuit of gratification in place of the id's primary process, which is more immediate and irrational. In *The Problem of Anxiety* (1926/1959) Freud went on to give the ego even more prominence by stating that it was capable on its own of mounting a defense against id impulses when these were too threatening.

Nevertheless, it was left up to other psychoanalytic theorists to study the role of the ego in its own right, apart from the id, as a conflict-free aspect of personality beyond Freud's more restricted, conflict-oriented understanding of the ego. The history of psychoanalysis since Freud's death has been dominated by the study of the ego to the point that contemporary psychoanalysis is often called ego psychology. This has contributed greatly to an understanding of ego defenses (repression, denial, rationalization), ego functions (perception, reality testing, relationships), how the ego develops from birth through relationship, and how to treat patients with severe ego defects in their ability to test reality, relate to others, or moderate self-esteem.

References

Freud, S. (1975). The ego and the id. In J. Strachey (Ed. and trans.), *The standard edition of the complete psychological works of Sigmund Freud* (Vol. 19). London: Hogarth. (Original work published 1923)

Freud, S. (1959). The problem of anxiety. In J. Strachey (Ed. and trans.), *The standard edition of the complete psychological works of Sigmund Freud* (Vol. 20). London: Hogarth. (Original work published 1926)

W. L. EDKINS

See PSYCHOANALYTIC PSYCHOLOGY.

Ego Dystonic. An urge, symptom, or personality trait that is rejected by the ego as unacceptable. These may include obsessions or compulsions that are viewed as undesirable and are prevented from reaching the ego for behavioral consideration. Some common examples of ego dystonic impulses include homosexual urges, oedipal and incestual arousal, and criminal tendencies associated with intense anger or provocation. The term *ego alien* is often used synonymously with ego dystonic, and both terms describe the opposite of ego syntonic.

Ego Ideal. In psychoanalytic theory, the part of the ego that represents the sum of positive identifications with caring or reassuring parents or parent substitutes (such as God) from which consciously held standards of excellence and goodness originate. In contrast to the punitive and forbidding conscience of the superego, the ego ideal provides ideal standards for which to strive.

See CONSCIENCE; PSYCHOANALYTIC PSYCHOLOGY; SELF; IDENTITY.

Ego Psychology. Ego psychology refers to the development of psychoanalytic theory in terms of the impact of early relationships on the adaptive aspects of personality. As Sigmund Freud began his career in psychiatry and neurology, he observed the crucial role sexual instinct, or libido, played in the etiology of his patients' symptomatology as well as in normal infancy (Freud, 1905/1975). At a time when the rest of psychology was mostly concerned with how consciousness functions, Freud devoted the next two decades to understanding and treating the instinctual, unconscious aspects of personality. During these years he sought to bypass the more conscious functioning of his patients by using hypnosis and free association so that he could treat the more hidden unconscious material and conflict areas.

At this point Freud viewed the ego as this more conscious domain of personality that stood in the way of reaching the unconscious. However, as he continued to work with his patients, he noted that the resistance evoked by each patient's ego to the psychoanalytic process of exploring the unconscious was for the most part unconscious. However, if the ego is synonymous with consciousness, ego defense mechanisms should also be conscious. Freud also observed the ego's role in symptom formation. He noted that symptoms were really unconscious compromises between a forbidden impulse and the ego. For example, hysterical blindness might express a compromise between the impulse to view parental intercourse and the attempt to control the impulse by the experience of blindness.

From these experiences Freud concluded that the ego, as well as the instinctual aspect of personality, the id, had an unconscious aspect to it and that this also had to be dealt with in the course of psychoanalysis. In 1923 he proposed a model of the psyche that consisted of the id, ego, and another structure, the superego, which develops out of the ego by the child's identifying with the moralistic aspects of the parental figures. This model emphasized the unconscious ego and its role in symptom formation and in treatment. It also placed the ego in a prominent position in psychoanalysis and gave birth to ego psychology.

Freud's daughter, Anna Freud, carried her father's work on ego psychology even further. She was primarily interested in the way people master their conflicts by means of ego defense mechanisms such as rationalization, repression, and denial. She believed that instead of viewing these defenses as being hindrances to treatment, they should be seen as a means of getting to the unconscious by giving a clue to the analyst that an unconscious conflict was emerging. She found that as the defense itself was analyzed as to its origin and history, the ego would be strengthened and the person would feel strong enough to allow the unconscious material to emerge. Thus she changed the focus of analytic treatment from the id to the ego.

Hartmann, an influential and innovative psychoanalytic theorist, made the next major contribution to ego psychology. In his major work, *Ego Psychology and the Problem of Adaptation* (1939/1958), he proposed that the earlier psychoanalytic emphasis on unconscious conflict and the id gave psychoanalysis a slanted picture. It was like trying to understand a country by observing it only during a wartime economy. According to Hartmann, psychoanalysis also needed to observe the more regular and normal ego functions in personality. He thus expanded psychoanalysis to become more of a general psychology concerned with perception, thinking, development of relationships, and human coping processes. Also, he saw the ego as being as basic to human development as the id. Instead of the ego arising later in development out of the id, as Freud had posited, Hartmann saw certain necessary ego functions being present from birth.

Close to the time of publication of Anna Freud's (1936/1946) and Hartmann's (1939/1958) major works, Sigmund Freud died in 1939. This threw psychoanalysis into a crisis. There was no longer a central person to orchestrate the development of psychoanalysis, and there was question whether the theory would continue to develop within the boundaries of orthodoxy. At this same time World War II was breaking out in Europe, and there was an influx of European psychoanalysts into Great Britain and the United States. These countries became hotbeds of theoretical controversy. In England psychoanalysts such as Melanie Klein and Fairbairn proposed sweeping revisions of psychoanalysis with their object relations theories. Harry Stack Sullivan, Karen Horney, and Erich Fromm in the United States rejected traditional theory for more interpersonal and cultural dimensions.

As a result of the war Anna Freud fled to England and Hartmann immigrated to the United States. Hartmann, along with other influential analysts who had immigrated, founded the New York Psychoanalytic Society and Institute. The work of the New York group and Anna Freud was distinct in that these theorists continued to expand Sigmund Freud's ego psychology while maintaining orthodox emphases on instincts, psychosexual stages, and the structural model of personality. They also stressed the role of interpersonal, or object, relations, but they did this in the context of Freud's ego psychology; hence the name for this school, ego psychology.

The next major contribution to ego psychology came through the work of a colleague of Hartmann at the New York Psychoanalytic Society, Spitz. He undertook the task of observing infants to establish the validity of ego psychology's theory of development. He found (Spitz, 1965) that the role of mothering object, or person, is crucial to the development of instincts, language, perception, and affects. He noted that disturbances in the mother-infant relationship even resulted in various physiological diseases. Under extreme circumstances such disturbances could even lead to the death of the infant.

This emphasis on the role of relationship has prevailed in ego psychology. Jacobson pursued the process of how the actual, external mother becomes represented as an object, or image, within the infant's mind and how the ability to function depends on the healthiness of this representation. Margaret Mahler also conducted observational research of infants with their mothers. She found that infants go through definite stages in their psychological birth as persons. Infants start off life in an unattached, autistic mode. By approximately two months of age they progress to an intensely close, symbiotic dependence on their mother. From six months through the third year they then are involved in separating from their mothers and establishing a basic sense of their own identity.

These discoveries about early object relations and ego development have enabled ego psychologists to make great gains in the ability of psychoanalysis to treat more severe psychological disturbances. Freud saw his treatment as primarily geared to oedipal issues—that is, conflicts the child had over his or her sexual desires for the opposite-sex parent. Ego psychologists now are able to treat conflicts that have their etiology during the first years of life, such as certain forms of severe depression (Jacobson, 1971), borderline schizophrenic personalities (Kernberg, 1975), and narcissistic personalities (Kohut, 1971).

Despite its adherence to a common theoretical base of psychoanalysis and general agreement on most major issues, ego psychology is plagued by terminological confusion and points of conflict between theorists. The conflicts even involve very crucial treatment implications, as seen in Kohut's (1971) and Kernberg's (1975) different suggestions for the treatment of narcissistic personalities.

The theory has certain points of conflict with biblical theology. It does not hold to the existence of moral absolutes, and its emphasis on ego mastery and coping could become counter to a healthy dependence on God. However, there are many places where theology and ego psychology can be integrated, such as the teachings of both disciplines on relationship, the process of internalization, pride and narcissism, and maturity.

References

Freud, A. (1946). *The ego and the mechanisms of defense.* New York: International Universities Press. (Original work published 1936)

Freud, S. (1975). Three essays on the theory of sexuality. In J. Strachey (Ed. and trans.), *The standard edition of the complete psychological works of Sigmund Freud* (Vol. 7). London: Hogarth. (Original work published 1905)

Freud, S. (1975). Ego and the id. In J. Strachey (Ed. and trans.), *The standard edition of the complete psychological works of Sigmund Freud* (Vol. 19). London: Hogarth. (Original work published 1923)

Hartmann, H. (1958). *Ego psychology and the problem of adaptation.* (D. Rapaport, Trans.). New York: International Universities Press. (Original work published 1939)

Jacobson, E. (1971). *Depression.* New York: International Universities Press.

Kernberg, O. F. (1975). *Borderline conditions and pathological narcissism.* New York: Aronson.

Kohut, H. (1971). *The analysis of the self.* New York: International Universities Press.

Spitz, R. A. (1965). *The first year of life.* New York: International Universities Press.

Additional Readings

Blanck, G., & Blanck, R. (1974). *Ego psychology: Theory and practice.* New York: Columbia University Press.

Blanck, G., & Blanck, R. (1979). *Ego psychology II: Psychoanalytic developmental psychology.* New York: Columbia University Press.

Mahler, M., Pine, F., & Bergmann, A. (1975). *The psychological birth of the human infant.* New York: Basic.

Rapaport, D. (1959). A historical survey of psychoanalytic ego psychology. *Psychological issues, 1* (1), 5–17.

W. L. Edkins

See Psychoanalytic Psychology.

Ego Strength. A term commonly used by psychodynamically oriented psychotherapists to describe the level of effectiveness with which the ego accomplishes its various functions. The ego is the part of the personality that establishes a relationship with the world in which we live.

The group of functions that we metaphorically refer to as the ego deals with the environment by means of conscious perception, thought, feeling, and action. It contains the evaluating, judging, solution-forming, compromising, and defense-creating aspects of the personality that form the basis for reality testing, intermediary synthesizing, and the executive functions of the personality. The ego must mediate between the blind, instinctual drives of the id and the sometimes rigid demands and aspirations of the superego, all within the context of the reality principle. According to Sigmund Freud (1962), the ego seeks to channel the instinctual drives of the id into patterns of thought and behavior that will bring lasting satisfaction and fulfillment.

Good ego strength is present when the ego is able to accomplish these goals in a flexible, adaptive manner, without becoming restricted by inflexible, repetitive defenses that limit the personality's ability to cope with stress. Good ego strength allows for the presence of extra energy that can be channeled into creative, satisfying tasks and interests, while poor ego strength requires that all energy be rigidly channeled into basic survival. Where there is poor ego strength, the ego is likely to be underdeveloped, dominated by unconscious factors, prone to regression or even disintegration, and overwhelmed by mounting repression. This typically leads to symptom development and marked distress.

In psychodynamically oriented psychotherapy, ego strength typically becomes a focus. First, there must be sufficient ego strength present to withstand and adapt to increasing stress as the therapy uncovers and dismantles ineffective, restrictive defenses. Thus assessing ego strength becomes a focus for determining suitability for insight-oriented psychotherapy (Paolino, 1981). Second, some forms of therapy specifically focus on strengthening the ego, increasing its flexibility, and improving its useful defenses. This is especially true when it is determined that ego strength is poor and more classical psychoanalysis is inappropriate.

Where ego strength is good, the personality will be capable of exhibiting such traits as commitment, responsibility, loyalty, perseverance, integrity, empathy, likability, humor, playfulness, flexibility, curiosity, dedication, and courage. Through the course of psychotherapy, as rigid and restrictive defenses are surrendered to free up energy for other purposes, it is common to see the emergence of such traits almost spontaneously, without direction from the therapist.

References

Freud, S. (1962). *The ego and the id.* New York: Norton.
Paolino, T. J. (1981). *Psychoanalytic psychotherapy.* New York: Brunner/Mazel.

J. D. Guy, Jr.

See Ego Psychology.

Ego Syntonic. Personality traits, impulses, or urges deemed acceptable to an individual are known as ego syntonic (literally invigorating with or together). This compatibility with the ego is the opposite of ego dystonic.

Ego-State Therapy. Ego-state theory and therapy were created and developed by a husband-and-wife team, John and Helen Watkins (Watkins & Watkins, 1979; Watkins & Johnson, 1982). The basic tenet of this approach is that one's personality is not unified but consists of a variety of parts within the self that they call ego states. These internal subentitites are made up of psychological elements of behavior and experience held together by boundaries that are more or less permeable. Within and between individuals one may find varying levels of dissociative permeability. Minimal levels of dissociation are revealed in relatively normal mood changes, this reflecting easy movement between ego states. More extreme levels of dissociation are manifest in multiple personalities, which reflect less permeable boundaries between ego states. The primary theme of this theory is that one's personality is something of a family of the self and can be worked with as such using techniques adapted from group and family therapies within a primarily hypnotic modality.

Some historical background to this approach is helpful. The splitting off of semiautonomous parts of the self has traditionally been considered only in reference to hysterical dissociation and has been viewed by most clinicians as something of a rarity. The Watkinses appeal to some of the notions of Federn (Berne's psychoanalyst), who spoke of the ego as having organized subpatterns (Federn, 1952). Berne furthered these ideas with his development of transactional analysis. Other writers, such as Kohut and Hartmann, have recognized the existence of such entities but have attributed to them only minor significance. The Watkinses' work differs in that they attribute major significance to this organization of the self and do not limit the entities to preformed categories such as parent, adult, and child. Instead the therapist is free to explore all those parts within the client that are relevant to the current symptomatic picture. Conflicts between any one of an individual's ego states and others extant within the self may result in a broad range of symptoms, including various neuroses, psychoses, multiple personality trends, phobias, anxiety reactions, and habit control disorders.

The practice of ego-state therapy is a test of one's ingenuity and flexibility. The therapist typically will employ a type of internal shuttle diplomacy between conflictual ego states while using a variety of systemic, suggestive, supportive, confrontive, desensitizing, abreactive, and interpretative techniques. These techniques are best utilized within a hypnotic modality. Nonhypnotic techniques that utilize a relaxed state (e.g., free association) are also useful but appear to be less potent (Watkins & Watkins, 1979).

When these ego states are activated, each refers to itself in the first person and the rest of the self in third person. The ego state that is being addressed at the moment is said to be executive. Once a particular ego state has been activated the therapist must be careful not to contaminate the client's internal organization of self through the inadvertent use of hypnotic suggestion. The Watkinses hold that one may minimize this influence by working as carefully and objectively as possible to elicit information regarding an ego state's origin, content, function, and goals. The ego state will also inform the therapist of its name and sexual identity to the degree these attributes have been defined.

The therapist's goal is not to fuse the various ego states, since each jealously guards its own identity and existence. The goal is rather to increase cognitive cooperation and consonance among the parts of the self so they become better integrated. This is true even for that part of the self that seems malevolent or self-destructive; in this situation one strives to positively rechannel its activities and functions. As a result of this approach one finds that the client typically moves toward the less dissociated end of the continuum, where greater permeability exists among the various ego states. Clients reaching successful termination of therapy still possess covert, autonomous ego states that can be elicited hypnotically. One typically finds these functioning as cooperative subparts of a normal personality.

Ego-state therapy remains in its infancy. Its applications have thus far not been extensive, and research on its effectiveness is virtually nonexistent. However, as a creative, primarily brief therapy its clinical potential seems great. Furthermore, its theoretical contributions to the understanding of disorders such as multiple personality and Fugue states as well as the defense mechanism of dissociation seem promising.

References

Federn, P. (1952). In E. Weiss (Ed.), *Ego psychology and the psychoses*. New York: Basic.

Watkins, J., & Johnson, R. J. (1982). *We, the divided self*. New York: Irvington.

Watkins, J., & Watkins, H. (1979). In H. Grayson (Ed.), *Short term approaches to psychotherapy*. New York: Human Sciences.

V. L. SHEPPERSON

See HYPNOTHERAPY; DISSOCIATIVE IDENTITY DISORDER.

Elderly. *See* GERONTOLOGY.

Elective Mutism in Childhood. *See* SELECTIVE MUTISM IN CHILDHOOD OR ADOLESCENCE.

Electroconvulsive Therapy. The idea of using electricity to cure disease can be traced back to the ancient Romans who used shocks from eels. In the 1920s and 1930s European psychiatrists experimented with drug-induced convulsions as a treatment for schizophrenia. In 1938 Cerletti and Bini developed an apparatus that used electricity to induce convulsions. Although it proved to be of limited benefit for schizophrenia, electroconvulsive therapy (ECT) achieved remarkable success in rapid alleviation of depression.

In the decade after its discovery, the use of ECT was widespread and indiscriminate, perhaps excessive. This was undoubtedly due to the fact that it was highly effective, easy to administer, and frequently the only treatment available. Since the advances of psychiatric medications in the 1950s, the use of ECT has declined. Since the 1970s the political strength of patient rights organizations have resulted in legal barriers to ECT. Few American psychiatrists regularly perform ECT.

How ECT Works. Patients are prepared for ECT in several ways. Psychiatric medication may be discontinued. No food is given during the four hours prior to treatment. The bladder must be voided. The team administering the treatment usually includes a psychiatrist, an anesthesiologist, and a nurse. Patients are given injections of muscle relaxants in order to reduce physical expressions of the convulsion and to prevent fractures of the vertebra. General anesthesia is given and supplemented with forced respiration of pure oxygen. In order to protect the teeth and tongue, a plastic protective block is inserted prior to turning on the current.

The standard procedure for ECT is to apply the electrodes to the forehead. Skin resistance is reduced by a jelly. The voltage is usually between 70 and 130 but is applied only for a fraction of a second. Convulsions then occur and may last up to a minute. Oxygen is given until the patient resumes normal breathing. The patient regains consciousness in a few minutes but may not be fully alert and able to leave the treatment area for an hour. During this recovery period the patient has a clouded consciousness and may experience a headache.

What is not precisely known is the mechanism that accounts for ECT's efficacy. No single theory is comprehensive enough or has led to hypotheses that have been validated by appropriate research. Various psychological explanations have been advanced: that patients needed punishment to alleviate guilt complexes, that ECT is a technique for breaking through psychic defenses, that ECT serves to destroy painful memories. Such psychological theories are at best speculative and should not be used to select patients for the procedure. Most psychiatrists believe that ECT works because it succeeds in altering the functioning of the brain, in some way serving as a diencephalic stimulation via increased catecholamines.

Indications. ECT is reserved for serious cases of depression and catatonia. While the efficacy of ECT for schizophrenia and mania may be questioned, there is little debate about its impact on depression. Five to ten treatments, administered over a period of two weeks, will secure a dramatic remission of symptoms in almost 90% of depressives. With almost 60 years of studies behind it, ECT remains psychiatry's most researched treatment.

Patients who pose an immediate suicidal risk are important candidates for ECT. The dramatic drop in suicide rates, especially among noninstitutionalized patients, after 1940 must be attributed to ECT. Even after the introduction of tricyclic and monoamine oxidase inhibiting (MAOI) medication in the 1950s, ECT remained the treatment of choice for suicidal patients: ECT was more likely to be effective and was much quicker compared to medications, which could take up to a month. The great lethality of the (intentional, suicidal) tricyclic overdose has influenced many psychiatrists to go straight to ECT.

Even the side effects of antidepressant medication at prescribed dosage can be an argument for ECT. Cardiovascular conditions may make the use of tricyclics or MAOIs risky. Liver or kidney problems may preclude the use of lithium. These factors often made ECT look better than medication, especially in geriatric patients. However, the newer generations of low-side-effect antidepressants (e.g., Prozac, Zoloft, Wellbutrin, Paxil, Effexor) may further reduce the need for ECT.

Several studies have attempted to correlate response to ECT with background and personality factors. Sudden onset, weight loss, low salivation, and low galvanic skin response have been correlated with subsequent favorable response to ECT. However, these correlations are too low to serve as valid and reliable predictors. If a serious depression cannot be treated by other means or if suicidal risk is substantial, ECT is indicated.

Problems and Controversy. ECT is not the dangerous procedure that the layperson might imagine. Spontaneous seizures occurring after the completion of treatment have an incidence of 1 in 500 cases. Deaths occur in fewer than 4 in 100,000 cases, roughly equivalent to the death rate for general anesthesia without ECT. Conditions that are considered to be general contraindications are brain tumor and postpartum depression. Age, cardiovascular problems, and pregnancy are not generally regarded as contraindications, but child psychiatrists may question the use of ECT with pre-adolescents.

One limitation is that ECT is not a permanent cure. There is always the danger that the patient might become depressed again. While this is true of other psychiatric treatments (short of lobotomy), the relapse rates seem to be higher for ECT, perhaps because ECT is tried only on the most serious cases. One suggested way of handling the problem of relapses would be to give an ECT every few months as a maintenance therapy.

The most frequently reported side effect of ECT is memory loss, both in the form of retrograde amnesia (especially for what happened just before ECT) and anterograde amnesia. Almost half of all ECT patients complain of memory impairments right after treatments, but this is temporary. Although objective tests rarely document permanent memory impairments, some patients subjectively perceive such problems. The idea that ECT results in permanent brain damage is largely unsupported. In one autopsy of an 89-year-old woman who had received more than one thousand ECT treatments over her lifetime, no brain abnormalities were attributable to the treatment.

In an attempt to reduce memory disruption, several modified procedures have been developed. One is to use unilateral ECT (electrodes placed only on the right side of the head) to reduce memory loss without reducing ECT effectiveness. Another technique is the use of multiple monitored microseizures.

The greatest problem with ECT is not that it is cruel or barbaric but that the general public and many patients regard it as such. (Although the patient experiences no pain in the procedure, the clouded consciousness of the recovery period is not pleasant.) A few states have reacted by putting obstacles in the path of ECT. Many community, private, and even teaching hospitals do not perform ECT.

Additional Readings

Abrams, R. (1992). *Electroconvulsive therapy* (2nd ed.). New York: Oxford University Press.

Guttmacher, L. B. (1991). *A concise guide to psychopharmacology and electroconvulsive therapy*. Washington, DC: American Psychiatric Association.

T. L. Brink

Electroencephalography. The discovery of spontaneous electrical activity on the surface of the brain was made in 1875 by Richard Caton working in Liverpool. It was not until 1929, however, that the first recorded electroencephalogram was published by Hans Berger. The work of these two researchers, among others, laid the foundation for human electroencephalography, the recording of gross electrical activity across the cerebral cortex.

The electroencephalogram (EEG) is obtained by using scalp electrodes to record the electrical activity. These electrodes are placed directly on the scalp with glue or are embedded into a cap that is placed over the scalp. The EEG is a record of the changes in voltage taking place between two electrodes across time. These voltage changes drive galvanometers that move pens up and down, reflecting on paper the changes in brain activity. Output from the electrodes can also be stored on tape or disk for later computer analysis.

Electrical activity of the brain is defined in terms of its frequency in cycles per second, or the more conventional expression, Hz. Several distinct, rhythmical patterns of brain activity are recognized. The most obvious is alpha activity (8–12 Hz), which dominates the EEG when a person is awake but relaxed, typically with eyes closed. The other basic rhythm during wakefulness is beta activity (13–15 Hz), which is seen when a person is alert and aroused; for example, while performing an arithmetic problem or when a sudden stimulus is perceived. Additional rhythms are theta (4–7 Hz), delta (0.5–3.5 Hz), and lambda (single, low-amplitude spikes).

EEG activity varies in a predictable, cyclical pattern during sleep. At the onset of sleep, the EEG reveals alpha activity alternating with irregular fast activity; as sleep continues, brain waves become systematically lower in frequency with a preponderance of delta rhythm. During dreaming, however, the EEG shows brain activity typical of a person who is awake and alert, revealing an active brain. This cycle of rhythmical activity is repeated several times during a night's sleep (*see* Sleep and Dreaming).

EEGs are used clinically to diagnose Epilepsy and to aid in the localization of brain tumors or other neural irregularities. Because the EEG provides a record of gross brain activity, however, the precise localization of these anomalies requires the use of more advanced imaging techniques.

K. S. Seybold

See Brain and Human Behavior; Neuropsychology.

Ellis, Albert (1913–). American psychologist who developed Rational-Emotive Therapy (RET), recently renamed Rational Emotive Behavior Therapy (REBT). Born in Pittsburgh but reared in New York City, he had a difficult childhood. As he put it in his autobiography (Ellis, 1972), much responsibility for his brother and sister helped him become a "stubborn and pronounced problem solver." At the age of 12 he became "an unregenerate atheist." In junior high school he decided to become a renowned writer; he resolved first to make a fortune in business so he could retire and write what he pleased, without having to worry about book sales.

Ellis received a degree in business administration from the City College of New York in 1934. By the time he was 28 he had 20 unpublished full-length manuscripts in his files. He decided to abandon fiction, to use nonfiction to propound his revolutionary views, and to devote much of his life to furthering the sex-family revolution. While he was gathering material for a manuscript he called *The Case for Sexual Liberty*, his friends started coming to him for information and advice. He then realized he could be more than a "sex writer and revolutionist." He could be a "sex-love-marriage counselor."

Believing that psychoanalysis is the most effective therapy, he entered analysis himself. In 1943 he received an M.A. and in 1947 a Ph.D. from Columbia University. During the late 1940s and the early 1950s he taught at Rutgers University and at New York University. He also was a clinical psychologist at Greystone Park State Hospital, the New Jersey Diagnostic Center, and the New Jersey Department of Institutions and Agencies while he maintained a private practice. However, Ellis's faith in psychoanalysis was crumbling. Patients he saw only once a week or every other week did as well as those he saw daily. He began to take a more active role in therapy, and by 1955 he had given up psychoanalysis entirely and originated RET. By 1957 he had published a book on this therapy, and in 1959 he organized the Institute for Rational Living, where he held workshops to teach his principles to others. In 1968 he founded the Institute for Advanced Study in Rational Psychotherapy.

Ellis made two major contributions to psychology, both of which led to conflict with Christianity. First, he encouraged many kinds of sexual experimentation, both premarital and extramarital, as evidenced by some of his book titles: *The Case for Sexual Liberty* and *The Art of Erotic Seduction*. At first he was labeled a sensationalist and a sexual radical, but many of his views are now accepted by a large part of society. Second, he developed RET, in which he essentially placed humans at the center of the universe, listed "some supernatural power on which to rely" as an irrational belief, and advocated the use of strong language during therapy to loosen up the client or give the client an emotive jolt or shock.

From the 1950s through the 1970s Ellis's writings were uniformly hostile toward all kinds of religiousness. However, since that time he has divided religious people into those with devout religiosity and those with mild religiousness. Although he maintains that devout people uniformly show pathology, he believes that mildly religious people can be reactively free of pathology. By the 1990s he was characterizing the Bible as a self-help book that has helped many people make behavioral and personality changes.

An increasing number of Christians began overlooking Ellis's negative comments about religion and his strong language; they began using RET and integrating it with Christianity. This culminated with a special issue of the *Journal of Psychology and Christianity* (winter, 1994) devoted to RET.

Although Ellis remains a probabilistic atheist (i.e., one who thinks it is highly improbable that there is a God), he admits that Christianity has a healthy notion of grace and many other good ideas. He notes that the Bible is the most read self-help book in the world, and it includes some healthy ideas—as well as much self-damnation. He maintains that Christianity also gives people an absorbing interest and offers distraction from problems and a social view. He concludes that he is not against religion per se but an absolute, devout belief in anything. Dogmatic, authoritarian belief itself is what is harmful to people.

Although Christians do not accept his agnostic worldview (he realized that he himself was being dogmatic in his atheism), since all truth is God's truth, many of his methods are effective for use in therapy. Ellis has written hundreds of books and articles and continues to be productive and influential.

Reference

Ellis, A. (1972). Psychotherapy without tears. In A. Burton (Ed.), *Twelve therapists*. San Francisco: Jossey-Bass.

R. L. KOTESKEY

See RATIONAL-EMOTIVE THERAPY.

Ellis, Henry Havelock (1859–1939). Pioneer in the study of human sexuality. He was born in Croydon, Surrey, England, the son of a sea captain, and educated at private schools in South London. In 1875 he went to Australia on his father's ship and taught school there until 1879, when he returned to England. In 1881 he began the study of medicine at St. Thomas Hospital, London, living on a small legacy.

Ellis received his M.D. degree in 1889 but did not practice medicine. While studying, he met George Bernard Shaw and Arthur Symons at meetings of the Fellowship of New Life. He conceived and was editor (1887–1889) of the Mermaid Series, a collection of works by lesser-known Elizabethan dramatists. He held no academic or official medical position but supported himself through his writings and editorial jobs. In 1890 he published a study of Ibsen, Whitman, and Tolstoy, *The New Spirit*. From 1889 to 1914 he was editor of the Contemporary Science Series. During this same time he was working on his most influential contribution, *Studies in the Psychology of Sex*, which appeared in seven volumes between 1897 and 1928.

Although Ellis could be described as an essayist, editor, physician, or literary critic, it was his study of sexual behavior that made him famous. And while he worked in areas studied by Sigmund Freud, he drew his material from medical, anthropological, and historical data as well as interviews and questionnaires. Krafft-Ebing had dealt with sexual abnormality or perversion, but Ellis dealt with normal sexual behavior in both humans and animals.

The first volume in *Studies in the Psychology of Sex* was *Sexual Inversion* (1897), in essence an apology for homosexuality. It was a part of his lifelong effort to broaden the spectrum of acceptable sexual behavior. In the second volume, *Auto-Eroticism* (1899), he sought to do for masturbation what he had for homosexuality. In later volumes he treated topics ranging from sadism and masochism to erotic symbols, perfumes, and dream imagery. He opposed censorship in regard to public discussion and literary treatment of sexual practices.

A legal dispute over the first volume resulted in the judge calling Ellis's claims for the scientific value of the book "a pretense, adopted for the purpose of selling a filthy publication." The remaining volumes were published in the United States and were available only to those in the medical profession until 1936, when publishing rights were taken over by Random House.

R. L. KOTESKEY

See SEXUALITY.

Emotion. The word is derived from the Latin *emovare*, meaning to move. Affect, passion, and mood are other words that describe some aspect of the same phenomenon. In common usage emotion refers primarily to perceived feelings, while affect includes the drives that are presumed to generate both conscious and unconscious feelings. Passion is intense emotion, and mood is emotion of long duration.

Psychology of Emotion. James (1890) was correct when he stated that emotions are reflexes. They arise as a result of stimuli that have symbolic meaning to the individual. They usually are elicited by extrapsychic events that occur in the environment, either activities of other living organisms or natural phenomena that threaten the individual's control of his or her environment. The stimuli that arise as a result of the behavior of other people have both cognitive and emotional qualities. The display of an emotion by one person may elicit the same emotion in the observer. This process is called empathy. If it elicits sorrow, it is called sympathy.

Autopsychic stimuli also elicit emotions. Past events may arouse emotions when they are recalled in memory. The recall may be spontaneous or elicited by events in the environment that are similar to the emotionally significant memory. The process whereby emotional responses are attached to and stored with memories is called cathexis.

Because emotions are compound reflexes, they normally possess the properties of reflexes. They can be facilitated or occluded. They summate, are graded in intensity, and are subject to fatigue. Early in life they are likely to dramatically display the properties of irradiation and generalization, which become more limited as stimulus specificity develops. They do not, however, lose these properties with maturation.

Emotions are composed of sensory, skeletal, motor, autonomic, and cognitive components. The early theorists focused on the autonomic and skeletal motor phenomena because they were observable. McLean added the cognitive aspect. Recent work strongly suggests that the feeling of the emotion, the sensory component, may be reflexively elicited at the rhinencephalic level. The observation that certain experiences (e.g., chills running up and down one's spine or the sensation of one's hair standing on end) are not associated with observable autonomic change lends credence to this idea.

Many autonomic motor and sensory phenomena are common to several specific emotions. One may tear with sorrow, anger, pain, awe, joy, or love. In a like manner, epigastric tightness, a sensory phenomenon, may be experienced in anger, fear, jealousy, and sorrow. Motor responses are more variable, but almost all unpleasant emotions are associated with increased muscular tension in all or some muscles, whereas pleasant emotions are associated with decreased tension in all or some muscles. It would appear then that emotions are synthesized from a number of autonomic, sensory, and motor responses to provide their specificity. It is believed by most authorities in the field that the cognition of the specific emotion is concomitant with the autonomic, sensory, and motor responses.

The Varieties of Emotions. Lindsley (1951) in his discussion of emotion linked the drives for sleep, sex, nutrition, and psychomotor activity to emotion. He did so because of their relationship to the reticular activating system. Psychopathological observations would support this linkage. Emotional states that are prolonged almost always result in aberrations in the intensity of these biological functions. These functions or drives give rise to behaviors that are specific for the drive. Thus they can be considered tonic emotions, since they move the organism to specific behaviors.

James emphasized that nothing is immutable about an emotion and that emotions are not to be described and classified rigidly. Although there is truth in his statement, most persons who have studied emotion have attempted to develop a taxonomy. Twelve fundamental emotions have been repeatedly mentioned in the natural philosophical literature. These are divided into nine unpleasant and three pleasant emotions. The unpleasant ones are sorrow, fear, anger, jealousy, shame, disgust, pain, confusion, and emptiness. The pleasant ones are love, joy, and awe. Other terms, however, are used to describe these same emotions. These terms further indicate differences in intensity or duration or refer to the stimulus that elicited the emotion. An example of some words that refer to anger but also indicate intensity are irritation, fury, and rage. One that includes duration is hate. Examples of words that relate to the stimulus are jealousy and envy, the former being elicited by desire to have or maintain a relationship with other beings and the latter relating to the desire to have or maintain possession of material things.

Included in the list of emotions are three that are not usually encountered—disgust, emptiness, and pain. The first two have been emphasized by existentialists, who consider them to be the most common emotional responses to the predicament of being. Pain is not usually included because of the specificity of its exciting stimulus. It is nevertheless a real emotion, since the sensation of pain elicits specific behaviors that are recognized by observers as symbolizing the pain state and elicit empathy or sympathy in the observer.

Human beings have always desired rationality; however, they generally do not behave rationally but are driven by emotions. Ideas are of no value until emotions are attached to them, since the emotion provides the force for action. It is imperative, then, that as one accumulates a body of knowledge, appropriate emotions be cathected to ideas in order that they may have value. Values are ideas with cathected emotions that make a favorable difference in life.

Learning is a conditioning process that involves the cathexis of emotion. Operant conditioning occurs when a behavior is elicited and is rewarded by the eliciting of a pleasant emotion or the satiation of an appetite (*see* Conditioning, Operant). Love or joy is primary in operant conditioning. Avoidance conditioning occurs when a behavior elicits an unpleasant emotion or fails to produce satiation of an appetite. Fear and pain are commonly elicited emotions that produce avoidance, but anger may also serve to produce avoidance.

The capacity for emotion is inherent. Some emotions may be recognized at birth. The Perez reflex elicited by rapidly stroking the spine of a newborn child with a gloved finger will produce fear, which is immediately followed by anger. Evidences of joy are revealed in the smiles of the infant before three months of age. Jealousy has been observed as early as nine months, and shame within the first year. Love is probably present as a diffuse feeling tone at birth but can be recognized as a specific emotion by six months. The entire human emotional repertoire is recognizable by two years of age.

As the child develops, the process of cognitive and emotional training begins. The exercise of volition is manifest early. It becomes more channeled as the infant develops intellectual and motor functions. Discipline is directed toward achieving an appropriate channeling of children's spirit by their knowledge and its cathected emotions. Their emotions vector their spirit by facilitating or inhibiting its direction. It is imperative that children be taught emotional control. This is begun in the first year by the conditioning process. Neither pleasant nor unpleasant emotions should be expressed unrestrainedly, nor should they be overly inhibited. Inappropriate expressions of emotions profoundly handicap a person in relating to the environment and other people. Personality is built on a foundation of emotional expression.

Neurophysiological Theories. Because they produce sensations of bodily change as well as behaviors, emotions have always been thought to have their genesis in some biological process. The humors of the ancient Greeks were presumably chemical. When the means to study the physiology of the brain became available, behavioral scientists focused on the neurophysiology of emotion while at the same time they continued to investigate the neurohumoral mechanisms. The neurohumors that have been implicated are epinephrine, norepinephrine, acetylcholine, gamma aminobutyric acid (GABA), serotonin, and enkephlins.

Neurophysiological theories were first proposed by James and Lange, who believed that emotions are reflexes and that emotional feeling is the perception of changes in the activity of the viscera and skeletal muscles. They believed that emotion or feeling is the result of rather than the cause of the reflex response. According to this view, our body reacts first and we feel the emotion later. Developed independently by James and by Lange, this theory came to be known as the James-Lange theory. It is most clearly presented in James's *Principles of Psychology* (1890).

One problem with this theory is the observation that animals seem capable of experiencing emotion even when they are deprived of sensory input. As a result of this seeming inadequacy of the James-Lange theory, William Bradford Cannon proposed that a tonic force in the brain stem is released from cortical inhibition by signals from the thalamus. This process adds to the perception in the peculiar quality of emotion while at the same time adding in motor response. Bard elaborated the theory to make it a corticothalamic process. In what came to be known as the Cannon-Bard theory, the thalamus acts as a relay station transmitting impulses to the cortex (which are the feeling of the emotion) and to the visceral organs (the response pattern of emotion).

Subsequently the work of Hess brought about a further modification of the theory, moving the emphasis from the thalamus to the hypothalamus.

More recently the discovery of the significance of the ascending reticular system in the integration of cerebral activity led Lindsley to include it as an important part of the system that elaborates emotion. Papez proposed a theory of emotion that makes the limbic system of prime importance. McLean built upon this view, arguing that the limbic system (part of the "old brain") serves to interpret emotion in terms of feeling, while the neopallium ("new brain") gives it symbolic meaning.

Most recently Gellhorn (1963) has elaborated these theories even further. Although his work has not been widely accepted, recent neurophysiological research has added increasing evidence to support his theory. To Gellhorn emotions are reflexes that are mediated and controlled through two systems that balance one another. There is an activating system composed of part of the hypothalamus, the mesencephalic reticular system, the thalmic reticular system, and the paleocortex. Opposing this system is an inhibitory system composed of part of the hypothalamus, the head of the candate nucleus, the globus pallidus, and the neocortex. The balance between these two systems is a tonic one, but it is unbalanced by sensory stimuli. Once the balance in this system has been shifted, the rhinencephalic mechanisms elaborate the pleasant or unpleasant response to provide the feeling while neopallial mechanisms provide the symbolic or cognitive aspect. One can see that Gellhorn's approach is an integration and extension of the earlier theories. (See Wilson & Nashold, 1972, for a more detailed discussion of these theories.)

Psychopathology and Emotion. Thinking and feeling are inextricably linked. Thus it is not surprising that all mental disorder is characterized by disturbances of both. Many view psychopathology as etiologically consisting of two distinct classes of problems: those that are learned and those that are a result of dysfunction of the brain. In the former category are the personality disorders and neuroses. In the latter are the major mental disorders, including depressive illnesses, schizophrenia, and those diseases that are due to anatomical or physiological disease of the brain.

The personality disorders represent dysfunctional exaggerations of normal personality attributes. Only when personality traits are inflexible and maladaptive and cause either significant impairment in social or occupational functioning or subjective distress do they constitute personality disorder. When persons with such disorders become dissatisfied with their inability to function effectively, some may become depressed or suffer considerable anxiety. Others have emotional disturbances that are symptoms of the disorder. Anger is often expressed intensely or inappropriately by persons who have a histrionic, narcissistic, antisocial, or borderline personality disorder. Persons with paranoid disorders may display pathological jealousy, while those with histrionic, narcissistic, and borderline disorders may suffer exaggerated shame.

The neuroses are no longer considered diagnostically as a group but have been subdivided under various headings such as affective disorders, anxiety disorders, somatoform disorders, and dissociative disorders. These disorders, which have as their etiology disturbed learning in early life, all have marked disturbances of affect. The dysthymic disorder is characterized by pervasive depression accompanied by irritability (anger) and changes in biological function. The anxiety disorders are all characterized by intermittent or continuous severe anxiety. The term *anxiety*, defined here as fear without an object, is often used as a synonym for fear. Although fear is the predominant affect in these disorders, depression is also a concomitant. Somatization disorder, conversion disorder, psychogenic pain disorder, and hypochondriasis are characterized by the emotions of fear, depression, and pain. A lack of emotion (Belle indifference) in conversion disorder accompanies the ideational distortions that lead persons to believe that they have a physical disease. The dissociative disorders are characterized primarily by disturbances of memory function. As these disorders defend the person from overwhelming fear, they are characterized by a lack of emotion.

Of the major mental disorders, major affective disorder is the one most characterized by a gross disturbance of affect. This illness, which usually has a well-defined onset, involves a pervasive alteration of mood that is either pleasant or unpleasant. The most frequent unpleasant emotion is sorrow; the most frequent pleasant emotion is joy. That this tonic disturbance of affect may be expressed in other terms is undeniable; anger, fear, confusion, pain, shame, or emptiness can occur as the primary expression of the pathologically unpleasant affective tonus. In those disorders in which the exaggerated tonus is abnormally pleasant, love and awe as well as joy can be the primary expressions.

Although most major affective disorders are characterized by a continuing presence of unpleasant or pleasant emotion, some may have sudden shifts from one emotion to another. It is not uncommon to find sorrow and either shame, anger, fear, or emptiness occurring intermittently in the illness. One may similarly observe intense expressions of love and awe in the patients who have joy as their primary emotion. In bipolar disorder there may be longer or shorter periods of depression followed by a period of elation. The transition from one to the other may be abrupt or gradual, or it may be punctuated by periods of euthymia. In some instances one of the two states may be brief and/or mild in its severity.

Schizophrenic disorders disturb every aspect of mental functioning and are characterized by a splitting of thinking from emotion. Two major disturbances of emotion are seen. One is a loss of emotional tonus; the other is a concomitant loss of emotional responsiveness or an inappropriateness of emotional expression. The loss of emotional tonus usually manifests itself in a loss of will. The person cannot be motivated into activity. The loss of emotional responsivity gives rise to what is called emotional flatness. In the schizophrenic patient there is usually a loss of both emotional tonus and responsivity, whereas in the major affective disorder of the depressed type there is no loss of emotional tonus. In schizophrenia the emotional inappropriateness is manifest in the expression of the wrong emotion in response to a stimulus, in the partial expression of an emotion, or in the simultaneous expression of parts of two emotions. This last phenomenon is called emotional ambivalence.

In organic brain disease disturbances in intensity, duration, and appropriateness of emotion can occur. Patients with delirium may be extremely fearful, angry, sorrowful, or joyful. It is not uncommon to see patients with delirium frightened or angered to the point of defending themselves by their hallucinations or delusions, or they may be quite amused by the conversations or behavior of hallucinated persons or animals. In dementia there may be a blunting of emotional expression or its replacement by jocularity. Depression and anxiety sometimes occur early in the course of dementing diseases, especially if the person is aware of the loss of mental capacity. In other patients an inability to modulate emotions may result in sudden outbursts of anger, progressing to rage or exaggerated expressions of fear, sorrow, or joy. Some persons who have had encephalitis between the ages of 5 and 15 are particularly susceptible to outbursts of rage to the point of becoming homicidal. This may occur occasionally in persons with dementia.

Epileptics are believed to be unusually susceptible to emotional dyscontrol (*see* Epilepsy). There is, however, no scientific evidence to support this contention.

Finally, it is important to recognize that all persons can be stressed to the point of developing transitory emotional disorders. Life's problems cause anxiety that may temporarily interfere with living. Grief is a normal response to the loss of a loved one, whether it be by divorce or death. If one accumulates enough stress within a limited period of time, symptoms will develop. Symptoms that occur with any specific stress are dependent on the significance of the stress to the individual and the coping mechanisms for the specific stress. It is true that some individuals have low thresholds for stress and thus respond to seemingly minor problems, whereas others have high thresholds and manage overwhelming problems without Decompensation.

Christianity and Emotion. In contrast to the Stoics, who viewed emotion as irrational, and Epicureans, who acquiesced to the inevitability of emotion, Jesus realistically faced the role of emotion in human life and provided guidelines to control negative and facilitate positive emotion. The remarkable message in his teaching is that love is the most powerful positive emotion and anger the most powerful negative emotion. He understood that love draws people together in harmony and that anger drives them apart in strife. He further understood that these two emotions are antithetical and that the existence of one precludes the occurrence of the other. He taught, therefore, that we are to love God, our neighbor, and one another. He knew that we would have an inherent love for our children and spouse and used them as an example of how we should love other persons.

The language of the Bible describes how love is an installation of persons in one another. A psychospiritual union occurs in love that creates various degrees of oneness—the greatest being the total union of God's Spirit with our spirit and the total union that is to occur in marriage as man and woman become one. To emphasize this union Jesus said that he and the Father would come and live in us if we live in him. The same language was used to describe the indwelling Holy Spirit received at Pentecost. As God is considered to be love, persons are given an emotional tonus of love when they receive Christ into their lives.

The Bible has many instructions that help persons to cognitively structure their emotional life. It was noted earlier that emotion does not exist by itself but is always attached to ideas. Therefore, the command to love becomes significant if ideas have love cathected to them. The commands to not be angry or hate also become effective if love is cathected to them. But people cannot avoid being angry, for they are human, and so a derivative of God's love was given so that persons could decathect anger from ideas and replace it with love. This derivative is forgiveness (John 20:23). As God is the final judge, only he can forgive; so it is that true forgiveness is possessed only by those in whom God lives.

Unpleasant emotions are also addressed. Sorrow is to be overcome by the promise of eternal life; fear by the knowledge that God attends to our every need and watches over and protects us; emptiness by his glory and the wonder of his love; shame by the acceptance of our inadequacy and the forgiveness of our sin. Jealousy is destroyed by the trust that we have for others when we love them rightly. Other less frequently experienced unpleasant emotions are also dealt with in the teaching of Jesus.

Our Lord also recognized the need to control the biological drives with their behavioral concomitants, which we have described as emotions. To control them he provided attitudinal guidelines that call forth suitable inhibiting emotions to prevent inappropriate expression and suitable exciting emotions to facilitate appropriate expression.

Paul addressed emotional life with equal vigor. He taught that the control of biological drives as well as the more specific emotions is accomplished only by the office of the indwelling Holy Spirit, who provides power to effectuate right values. Paul provided practical guidelines for avoiding or controlling unpleasant emotional expression as well as direction on how to resolve the consequences of its expression. Finally, he emphasized the role of forgiveness in the resolution of damaging emotional interactions.

Only in Christianity is humans' emotional life given such a place of prominence. God certainly recognized that love, joy, and awe have to be the predominant emotions if persons are to have happiness, so he gave us himself that this might be accomplished.

References

Gellhorn, E., & Loofbourrow, G. N. (1963). *Emotions and emotional disorders: A neurophysiological study.* New York: Harper & Row.

James, W. (1890). *The principles of psychology* (2 vols.). New York: Holt.

Lindsley, D. B. (1951). Emotion. In S. S. Stevens (Ed.), *Handbook of experimental psychology.* New York: Wiley-Interscience.

Wilson, W. P., & Nashold, B. S. (1972). The neurophysiology of affect. *Diseases of the Nervous System, 33,* 13–19.

Additional Reading

Eccles, J. C. (1980). *The human psyche.* New York: Springer International.

W. P. WILSON

See PERSONALITY; AFFECT.

Emotion, Cultural Variations. While some researchers view emotions as predominantly caused by physiological mechanisms, others consider emotions the result of cultural processes. Most see both physiological and cultural factors as significant and seek to understand how both influence the experience and expression of emotion.

Ekman and Friesen (1975) performed several studies investigating the similarity of emotional expressions across cultures. Ekman showed photographs of facial expressions representing various emotions and found that people in different cultures similarly categorized emotions such as anger, fear, sadness, and happiness. These studies were replicated several times with both literate and preliterate cultures. Other studies indicate that people across cultures display similar emotional nonverbal behaviors: grimacing when angry, crying when sad, and smiling when happy. Blind children, having never seen a face, show similar facial expressions when they experience certain primary emotions such as anger, sadness, and happiness.

While evidence supports similarities in emotions across cultures, there is evidence also indicating significant differences. Several studies indicate cultural differences in the ways emotions are expressed. Although anger is experienced across all cultures, the expressions of anger may differ widely. Some cultures encourage open expression of anger, while other cultures encourage inhibition or hiding of anger. In general emotional expressions are intense and prolonged in people from countries that encourage individuality (e.g., in Western Europe and North America). People from Asian countries, which encourage interdependence, tend to express more social emotions such as shame or sympathy rather than personal emotions such as pride or sadness.

Cultural differences in emotional expression should be expected, for emotions connect individuals to their social and relational world. Studies have shown that cultural differences in emotional expression exist within American ethnic groups in addition to the differences observed between countries. Furthermore, studies indicate both age and gender differences in the tendency to express or inhibit emotions.

Research on cultural variations of emotions is fraught with difficulties. Until recently research in the United States has focused on basic or primary emotions such as anger, sadness, fear, happiness, and surprise in attempts to find cross-cultural similarities. However, relatively few emotions can be linked to recognizable facial expressions. Thus the methodology of showing pictures to people from other cultures in an attempt to find emotion similarities is self-limiting.

A second research difficulty is the differing number of words used to categorize emotional experiences in different cultures. Russell (1991) cites research that uncovered over 2,000 words in the English language for categorizing emotions, while other research reported only 58 words in Ifalukian to categorize emotion. Thus even the words used to describe emotional experience vary greatly between cultures.

Mesquita and Frijda (1992) provide a comprehensive review of the research on cultural variations in emotions, arguing strongly for viewing cultural similarities and differences at specific rather than general levels of description. They describe cross-cultural emotional similarities and differences at the following specific levels: antecedent events, event coding, appraisal, physiological reaction patterns, action readiness, emotional behavior, and regulation. From this review they found universal similarities in emotional reaction modes (facial expressions, voice intonations, physiological responses), event episodes linked to issues of emotional concern (death of a loved one, rejection from a group), and event appraisals (the event evaluated as relevant to one's well-being). Cultural differences were found in emotional regulation (rules about displaying or expressing emotions), significance of event types (if a serious illness is perceived as a curse from God, then it arouses strong emotions), appraisal of blame for an event (attribution of intent to another), and emotional behavior patterns (e.g., falling asleep rather than running when afraid, both of which are avoidance behaviors).

Although physiological and genetic factors provide humans with certain emotional capacities, culture clearly plays a large role in shaping the personal and social meaning of emotional events. In particular culture seems to influence when, where, how, with whom, and with what intensity emotions are displayed. The social context of emotional displays cannot be ignored in determining the meaning and significance of emotions.

It is essential that counselors or pastors recognize that the cultural and ethnic background of clients is significant when attempting to understand the meaning of their emotional expressions. Assuming that a Japanese person is not sad or angry because there are no tears or clenched fists may be a wrong assumption. We are more likely to impose our own cultural views and values on others when we are not aware of how culture shapes their emotional expression. In doing so we devalue others and may misinterpret behaviors.

Cultural factors are particularly important in determining how and when emotions are expressed. Furthermore, the meaning of emotional communication is largely determined by the cultural or social context of the person expressing the emotion.

References

Ekman, P., & Friesen, W. V. (1975). *Unmasking the face: A guide to recognizing emotions from facial clues.* Englewood Cliffs, NJ: Prentice-Hall.

Mesquita, B., & Frijda, N. H. (1992). Cultural variations in emotions: A review. *Psychological Bulletin, 112,* 179–204.

Russell, J. A. (1991). Culture and the categorization of emotions. *Psychological Bulletin, 110,* 426–450.

C. D. CAMPBELL

See CULTURE AND COGNITION; CULTURE AND PSYCHOPATHOLOGY; CROSS-CULTURAL PSYCHOLOGY.

Emotional Insulation. An unconscious process in which the ego seeks to avoid tensions through reduced emotional involvement. When a situation is perceived as threatening pain, disappointment, or extreme anxiety, the individual responds by withdrawal into a protective passivity. This may be seen in the concentration camp prisoner who loses all conscious hope, becoming resigned and apathetic. He becomes a passive recipient of any treatment or punishment given him, rather than endure the emotional pain of continual frustration and debasement.

See DEFENSE MECHANISMS.

Empathy. Empathy is generally understood to mean sharing in another person's emotional experience in a particular situation. To be empathic we must have the ability to step outside ourselves and into another's private world. We can experience empathy at different times, in various places, and in many forms: when we get teary during a sad movie; when we feel elated or disappointed with the fortunes of our favorite team; when we enter fully into the meaning of a work of art; and when we imagine the deep hurt of another's loss of a loved one.

The term *empathy* has a long philosophical and psychological history. Some social and moral philosophers give this term preeminence as the basis of all human emotion. Buber (1958) maintained that the self develops primarily in empathic relationships, in which there is always a "thou," never only a "me." Empathy is irreducibly other-regarding or other-directed; whereas there is such a thing as self-pity or self-love, there is no self-empathy. Vetlesen (1994) argued that empathy (the English rendering of the German *Einfuhlung*) is humankind's basic emotional faculty and lies at the bottom of all feelings for others.

Empathy is related to sympathy by the same Greek root, *pathos*, and the terms are often confused. Sympathy connotes feeling compassionate and perhaps feeling compelled to aid the other due to feelings of pity. Empathy includes capacity for participation in another's feeling and also involves an imaginative reconstruction of the situation's meaning for the other person based on the empathizer's experience of similar situations. The empathizer experiences the other's frame of reference intellectually and emotionally. Empathizers feel *with* while sympathizers feel *for*.

Psychiatry and clinical psychology have continued to develop the concept. Although psychoanalytic therapists such as Sigmund Freud, Otto Rank, White, Cameron, and Greenson discuss empathy, Carl Rogers was the first to make it a major therapeutic construct. Along with unconditional positive regard and genuineness, empathy became known as the therapeutic triad, conditions that Rogers believed were both necessary and sufficient for personal change and growth.

Rogers details his client-centered therapy as a philosophical orientation of the therapist toward the client. "We have come to recognize that if we can provide understanding of the way the client seems to himself at this moment, he can do the rest" (Rogers, 1951, p. 30). Thus the goal is an empathic identification in which the therapist is perceiving the hopes and fears of the client through immersion in an empathic process but without directly experiencing those hopes and fears. Rogers refers to this as the "as if" quality of human relations: we imagine another's pain or joy as if it were ours to experience but knowing that it is not.

Several of Rogers's students carried forward his work. Truax and Carkhuff (1967) detailed more clearly the therapeutic conditions for growth, developing the Accurate Empathy Scale and Relationship Questionnaire. Truax used the term *accurate empathy*, which involves both sensitivity to current feelings and facility to communicate this understanding in language attuned to the other's current feelings. Learning these verbal and nonverbal empathy skills has become standard practice in the initial phases of clinical psychology, counselor education, and pastoral care training programs.

When someone deeply understands and accepts us as we are, we lose our need to be defensive and we become accepting of others' shortcomings. As Roberts (1985) pointed out, such deep understanding looks like Christian love. God "reconciled us to himself through Christ and gave us the ministry of reconciliation" (2 Cor. 5:18, NIV). "We love because he first loved us" (1 John 4:19, NIV). The therapist becomes a type of savior, first loving us, then setting us free from our bondage and self-deception—freeing us to love others.

The biblical parallel leads some to construe empathy as equivalent to Christian love. But Rogerian empathy does not begin to compare to the sacrificial love that Jesus evidenced in his death for our salvation. Christian love is not merely a set of techniques to learn. Christians whose love is formed by Christ give themselves up for each other.

Jones and Butman (1991) more fully develop this theme in their critique of Rogers's therapy. They conclude that it is a serious error to mistake Christian love for empathy or the therapeutic triad in general. But Christians can learn much more about deeply understanding and affirming those around us. Rogerians "have taught us much about what it means to deeply care for (and be cared for by) others. . . . [W]e can certainly be grateful that Rogers and his followers have deeply sensitized us to what it means to listen to someone" (p. 274). Although Christian love and interpersonal empathy have much in common, they should not be confused or interchanged, but both should be practiced.

References

Buber, M. (1958). *I and thou*. New York: Charles Scribner's Sons.

Jones, S., & Butman, R. (1991). *Modern psychotherapies: A comprehensive Christian appraisal*. Downers Grove, IL: InterVarsity Press.

Roberts, R. C. (1985, November 8). Therapy for the saints: Does "empathy" equal Christian love? *Christianity Today, 29*, 25–28.

Rogers, C. R. (1951). *Client-centered therapy*. Boston: Houghton Mifflin.

Truax, C., & Carkhuff, R. (1967). *Toward effective counseling and psychotherapy: Training and practice*. Chicago: Aldine.

Vetlesen, A. J. (1994). *Perception, empathy, and judgment: An inquiry into the preconditions of moral performance*. University Park: Pennsylvania State University Press.

D. H. Stevenson

See Person-Centered Therapy; Attachment Theory and Disorders.

Empiricism. A philosophical commitment to sensory experience as the true source of knowledge. This perspective, particularly in the guise of those nineteenth- and twentieth-century movements that have variously been labeled positivisms, has probably had more influence on contemporary psychology than has any other philosophy. The advocates of psychology as science have from the beginning held a conception of science that is deeply influenced by empiricism, a fact that is evident in the high value academic psychology places on experimental research.

Historical Development. Although there were empiricists in ancient times and although there is a sense of the term in which Aristotle and his followers must be regarded as empiricists, the most influential stream of empiricism must be traced to the British philosophers John Locke, George Berkeley, David Hume, and John Stuart Mill.

Locke (1632/1704), in his famous *Essay Concerning Human Understanding*, mounted a strong attack on the claim that human beings possess innate ideas or knowledge. In contrast to the rationalist tradition, which held that some truths could be known in an a priori fashion, Locke argued that at birth the mind is like a blank tablet and that experience is the source of all human ideas. He held that sensory experience is the source of simple ideas, which could be combined in various ways by the mind to form complex ideas. Locke believed that our ideas of primary qualities (which included such quantifiable aspects as mass, velocity, size, and shape) correspond to real qualities in the physical world, while secondary qualities (such as smell and color) are subjective qualities produced by physical bodies when they impact our sensory organs.

Berkeley (1685–1753), an Anglican bishop, extended Locke's ideas in a consistent if sometimes counterintuitive manner. Berkeley argued that not only do all our ideas come from experience; we only have knowledge of experience. The idea of a material or physical world that exists independently of perception is a useless and even meaningless notion. Berkeley's limitation of knowledge to what is directly experienced contains the seeds of the later positivist suspicion of theoretical, unobservable entities and the demand for operational definitions of terms—though not many have followed Berkeley's mentalistic view of the material world.

Hume (1711–1776) extended Berkeley's skepticism about material substances to the mental realm. He challenged the idea that humans experience themselves as a unified soul or ego and claimed that he was only aware of himself as a "bundle of perceptions." Hume also divided all human knowledge into two areas: relations of ideas and matters of fact. Relations of ideas, such as all bachelors are unmarried males and 2 + 2 = 4 can be known with intuitive or deductive certainty because they only concern our own conceptions. All knowledge dealing with matters of fact (i.e., the earth is round) is grounded in experience and can never be absolutely certain. This distinction clearly underlies the common twentieth-century distinction between analytic or conceptual truths, which are grounded in conventional definitions, and empirical or synthetic truths, which are grounded in experience.

One of Hume's most influential doctrines was his empiricist interpretation of cause and effect. Hume denied that we have knowledge of any real connections between events that are regarded as causally linked. Rather, our knowledge of causality is a knowledge of constant conjunctions, or natural regularities. To know that A causes B is simply to know that A regularly precedes B in our experience. Causal knowledge therefore reduces to knowledge of empirical regularities that must be discovered experimentally.

James Mill (1773–1836) and his more famous son, John Stuart Mill (1806–1873), built on their empiricist predecessors to develop what is called associationist psychology, which was an attempt to develop empirical laws explaining all mental phenomena as the result of the association of basic mental elements. The associationists clearly foreshadowed the dominant view of learning in twentieth-century psychology.

Logical Positivism and Behaviorism. In the twentieth century, empiricist thought has been most strongly represented by the philosophy of logical positivism. Positivism arose in the nineteenth century from such thinkers as Auguste Comte, who developed a view of science that is expressed in his law of three stages. According to Comte all human sciences pass through an early theological stage, through a metaphysical stage, to a final stage of positive science, which consists of knowledge of natural regularities known by experience. Comte's view of the history of science is still influential and can be clearly seen in Skinner (1971).

Twentieth-century logical positivists differed from their nineteenth-century predecessors chiefly in the greater appreciation they had for formal logical techniques. Originating in a group of philosophers who met in Vienna for discussion, the logical positivists put forward the verifiability theory of meaning. In this theory all statements that are not intended as analytic statements (which hold because of definitions) must be empirically verifiable (Ayer, 1936). Their slogan was, The meaning of a sentence is its method of verification. This led to a program of giving operational definitions of scientific terms and to a suspicion of unobservable, theoretical entities.

Although logical positivism was not the only influence on behavioral psychology, its period of dominance in philosophy coincided with the development of behaviorism in psychology, and the two movements clearly supported each other. The influence of positivism is very clear in the work of psychologists such as Clark Leonard Hull, whose conception of science closely follows the hypothetico-deductive method developed by such positivists as Schlick. In this view a genuine scientific theory is one from which testable consequences can be deduced. The general behaviorist emphasis on measurability and on the notion of a purely factual database also reflects clear empiricist influences. The major nonempiricist influence on behaviorism that accounts for some of the major differences between behaviorism and associationist psychology is the behaviorist acceptance of physicalism.

At least three major tendencies in contemporary psychology, particularly in its behaviorist forms, can be traced to empiricism. These include a rejection of a priori theorizing and suspicion of all theories not experimentally testable; an emphasis on the passivity of the human organism, not in the sense that humans do not operate on their environment but in the more basic sense that they are ultimately shaped by their environment; an atomistic tendency to explain what is complex in terms of what is simple and what is later in terms of what is earlier. Allport (1955) discusses some of these tendencies and traces them to Locke.

Critical Evaluation. Empiricism, especially in its positivist forms, has suffered much criticism in the latter part of the twentieth century. Much of this criticism is directed to the empiricist view of science and much of it is relevant to psychology.

One area of criticism pertains to the aims of science. The positivist sees science as aiming at predictive power, which centers on the discovery of testable regularities. However, philosophers such as Toulmin (1961) have argued convincingly that science aims at understanding and theoretical intelligibility, not just predictive power. If this is correct, then theorizing has a greater and different role in science than positivists have allowed.

A second area of concern pertains to the nature of experience and observation itself. Many empiricists have spoken of experience as if it involves a simple registering of bare, uninterpreted facts. However, philosophers of science such as Hanson (1958) have stressed that scientific observations are "theory-laden" and that "all seeing is seeing something *as* something." If this is correct, then theory and interpretation cannot simply be derived from experience because they are involved in experience.

Many of these points have come to focus in Kuhn's influential book, *The Structure of Scientific Revolutions* (1970), which stresses the way in which scientific activity presupposes a shared framework of assumptions, which Kuhn calls a "paradigm." Philosophers who have accepted these ideas, even in modified form, have concluded that scientific theories are holistic systems that make contact with experience selectively and as a whole, and thus it is harmful to demand that all scientific concepts be operationally defined. With the recognition of the historical character of science and the theory-laden and interpretive character of observation, they have also been forced to recognize the problematic character of verification and falsification, understood as straightforward testing of isolated elements of theory.

References

Allport, G. (1955). *Becoming*. New Haven, CT: Yale University Press.

Ayer, A. J. (1936). *Language, truth, and logic*. New York: Oxford University Press.

Hanson, N. R. (1958). *Patterns of discovery*. Cambridge: Cambridge University Press.

Kuhn, T. S. (1970). *The structure of scientific revolutions* (2nd ed.). Chicago: University of Chicago Press.

Skinner, B. F. (1971). *Beyond freedom and dignity*. New York: Knopf.

Toulmin, S. (1961). *Foresight and understanding*. Bloomington: Indiana University Press.

C. S. Evans

See Psychology, Methods of; Psychology, History of.

Encopresis. Functional encopresis is usually defined as incontinence of feces that is not due to organic defect or illness (Carson & Butcher, 1992). *DSM–IV* gives three diagnostic criteria: repeated voluntary or involuntary passage of feces into places not appropriate for that purpose in the individual's sociocultural setting; at least one such event a month for three months after the age of four; and not due to a physical disorder. In this manner functional encopresis is distinguished from encopresis resulting from organic or medical causes, such as an anal fissure, Hirschprung's disease, rectal defect, neurological impairment, illness, or an aganglionic megacolon (Kolb, 1973).

Functional encopresis is further subdivided into primary and secondary encopresis. It is thought to be primary when a child who has not achieved fecal continence for at least one year reaches the age of four. Secondary encopresis involves cases in which the incontinence has been preceded by at least one continuous year of fecal continence. Thus by definition primary encopresis begins by age four, while secondary encopresis usually occurs between the ages of four and eight. Further differentiation is made between encopresis with and without constipation and overflow incontinence.

It is thought that primary and secondary encopresis generally occur with about the same frequency, although some report that primary encopresis may occur more frequently in the lower socioeconomic classes. Encopresis is more common among males. The overall incidence is estimated to be about 1% of all five-year-olds. Thus it is rather rare, and its presence is often disturbing to parent and child alike. On the part of the parent there may be anger, disgust, and acrid recrimination often aimed at the child. The child may experience shame, embarrassment, and anxiety. Attempts may be made to hide the problem, causing the child to dispose of the soiled clothing or to hide it in his bedroom. However, when the incontinence is deliberate, more serious psychopathology is suggested.

The etiology of encopresis is unclear. Some believe that primary encopresis is due to inadequate or inconsistent toilet training, while secondary encopresis may be the result of psychosocial stress that encourages regressive behavior. Examples of such stressors might be the birth of a sibling, sickness or death in the immediate family, the onset of school, or the separation or divorce of the parents.

While psychoanalytic treatment has had at least minimal success, the most popular treatment utilizes behavioral techniques such as positive reinforcement, modeling, and structured bathroom times. This may be combined with the use of mineral oil or a very mild laxative in the case of an impacted rectum. Before treatment is initiated, it is important that the child receive a thorough physical examination in order to rule out possible organic etiology. If the condition persists, formal psychological treatment should be considered in collaboration with good medical care.

References

Carson, R. C., & Butcher, J. (1992). *Abnormal psychology and modern life*. New York: HarperCollins.

Kolb, L. C. (1973). *Modern clinical psychiatry* (8th ed.). Philadelphia: Saunders.

J. D. GUY, JR.

See ENURESIS.

Endomorph. In Sheldon's system of constitutional types the endomorph is a person whose body is soft, round, and flabby in appearance. This body type, comparable to Kretschmer's pyknic type, is contrasted to the ectomorph and mesomorph types. Sheldon's research suggested that endomorphs tend to be warm and affectionate.

See CONSTITUTIONAL PERSONALITY THEORY.

Endorphins. Endorphins and enkephalins are endogenous neuropeptides that act as neurotransmitters in the nervous system and as hormones. The endorphins are similar in structure and effect to the opiate morphine, hence the term (*endorphin*: endogenous + morphine). Both types of neuropeptides interact with opiate receptors in the brain. Although they are classed as neurotransmitters, endorphins and enkephalins differ from the classical amino acid (i.e., norepinephrine) and monoamine (i.e., dopamine) neurotransmitters in two ways. Classical neurotransmitters are usually synthesized in the axon endings, close to their site of release. Neuropeptides are synthesized only in the cell body or dendrite and then are transported down the length of the axon for subsequent release. This may mean that neuropeptide transmitters are unable to repeatedly influence adjacent neurons over a short time. The other difference has to do with the effect of the transmitter substance on the receiving neuron. Classical neurotransmitters either depolarize or hyperpolarize the receiving membrane, thus making that neuron more or less likely to fire its own action potential. Neuropeptide transmitters act by making the receiving neuron less responsive to other inputs. They keep excitatory neurotransmitters from having a depolarizing effect and inhibitory neurotransmitters from having a hyperpolarizing effect. This inhibition has been referred to as disenabling.

A primary effect of endorphin release is modulating pain perception. The analgesic effect of enkephalins is of shorter duration and weaker. The endorphins also appear to modulate mood. Stress, both physical (e.g., pain) and psychological (e.g., conditioned fear), appears to stimulate endorphin release. Endorphins have also been linked to thermoregulation, appetite, memory, lipolysis, reproduction, pleasure experiences, fat breakdown, antidiuresis, depression of the ventilatory response to carbon dioxide, and inhibition of thyrotropin and gonadotropin.

Aerobic exercise stimulates endorphin release and is probably responsible for "runner's high" and exercise addiction. Plasma endorphin levels usually return to baseline within 30 minutes of the completion of exercise. Some athletes report lessened sensitivity to painful injuries while performing, an effect possibly due to endorphin release. There is some evidence that exercise therapy is beneficial in treating mildly depressed individuals by altering endorphin levels. Endorphins may also be responsible for some of the pain relief in acupuncture and the placebo effect.

Almost all drugs used in psychiatry and neurology act by blocking or enhancing the effects of the classical neurotransmitters. However, there are often multiple receptor types for the same neurotransmitter, effecting changes in different bodily functions. A drug, while producing its intended effect on one system, sometimes produces unwanted side effects by altering activity at other receptor sites. By regulating endorphin and enkephalin activity new, more specific-acting drugs may be developed for alleviating emotional and neurologic disorders.

W. D. NORMAN

See BRAIN AND HUMAN BEHAVIOR.

Enuresis. Involuntary discharge of urine, most commonly during sleep. According to *DSM–IV*, in order to receive a formal diagnosis of functional enuresis, the following diagnostic criteria must be met: repeated voiding of urine, whether voluntary or involuntary, into bed or clothes; at least two such events per week for three consecutive months or the presence of significant distress or impairment in functioning as a result; at least five years of age; and the disorder cannot be due to a physical disorder, such as diabetes or a seizure disorder.

Functional enuresis is subdivided into primary enuresis, in which there has not been a preceding period of urinary continence of at least one continuous year, and secondary enuresis, in which there has been at least one year of urinary continence preceding its onset. Enuresis is most often nocturnal (occurring during sleep), although a child may evidence diurnal enuresis (occurring during waking hours), or both nocturnal and diurnal enuresis. Estimated prevalence is as follows: at age 5, 7% for boys and 3% for girls; at age 10, 3% for boys and 2% for girls;

at age 18, 1% for boys and less for girls. By definition the onset of primary enuresis is age 5, while most cases of secondary enuresis occur between the ages of 5 and 8. Most children with this disorder become continent by adolescence, although some rare cases have continued into adulthood.

It is typically believed that primary enuresis results from inadequate, delayed, or inconsistent toilet training, delayed development of bladder musculature, or impaired bladder ability to adapt to urinary filling. Secondary enuresis is thought to result from a variety of psychosocial stressors, including the birth of a sibling, sickness or death in the immediate family, marital discord and/or divorce, the onset of school, and hospitalization prior to age four. A large body of psychoanalytic literature attributes functional enuresis to a variety of early factors, such as the oedipal conflict, lack of proper identification with the same-sex parent, and sibling rivalry (Kolb, 1973).

In many cases of nocturnal enuresis, the most common form, the urination occurs during the first third of the night, during non-REM sleep. The child may awake with no memory of having urinated and with no memory of a dream. At other times the child may recall a dream that involved urinating. In more unusual cases it has been found that the urination occurs during non-REM sleep typical of later phases of deep sleep, preceded by marked electroencephalographic arousal (Ritvo, 1970).

Enuresis is often the cause of shame, humiliation, embarrassment, and social isolation. Such children may avoid overnight visits to friends, camping trips, and so forth. The individual's self-esteem may suffer as a direct result of social ostracism by peers and anger, punishment, and rejection by parents. Treatment interventions have been developed that have been quite successful (Carson & Butcher, 1992). Behavioral techniques utilizing classical conditioning paradigms, such as the bell and pad apparatus available in some department stores, have been especially successful. With this device urination completes an electrical circuit that results in the sounding of a buzzer or alarm, awakening the child, who then immediately stops urinating, arises, and goes to the bathroom to finish voiding. It is thought that the feeling of fullness in the bladder immediately preceding urination is then paired with arousal and appropriate voiding, causing the child to eventually awaken prior to urinating. Other useful techniques have included the use of low doses of Tofranil, an antidepressive drug whose anticholinergic side effects often reduce the likelihood of nocturnal enuresis. Finally, more traditional psychodynamic forms of psychotherapy have been somewhat successful over extended periods of treatment. If the condition persists into early adolescence, professional psychological treatment should be sought.

References

Carson, R. C., & Butcher, J. (1992). *Abnormal psychology & modern life*. New York: HarperCollins.

Kolb, L. C. (1973). *Modern clinical psychiatry* (8th ed.). Philadelphia: Saunders.

Ritvo, E. R. (1970). Contributions of sleep research to understanding and treatment of enuresis. *International Psychiatric Clinician, 7* (2), 117–122.

J. D. GUY, JR.

See ENCOPRESIS.

Environmental Psychology. A subfield of social psychology associated with the study of the ways in which people are affected by their environments. For example, environmental psychologists are interested in the portable, invisible bubble we all carry around with us called personal space. They have demonstrated that the size and shape of this space vary as functions of the culture, sex, and personality of the individual. By keeping people at a distance we are able to control and express the level of intimacy of a relationship.

Environmental psychologists are also interested in the psychological impact of such natural phenomena as weather. Admissions to mental hospitals (north of the equator) peak during summer and spring. Sunshine often makes people more helpful, but a long hot summer facilitates aggression. And there is evidence that, despite the term *lunacy* and the many portrayals found in the media, the lunar cycle is not linked to emotional disorders.

Our manmade environment can also affect us psychologically. The architectural design of some low-cost housing projects has made them virtually uninhabitable. The colors blue and green do have a calming effect. And the arrangement of a room can profoundly affect the extent to which we feel crowded.

It is important to note that throughout these findings and environmental psychology in general there runs a common thread: the distinction between subjective and objective reality. Perhaps this distinction is clearest in the area of crowding. Research results have forced investigators to distinguish between physical density and the perception of crowding. Having a large number of people in a room does not guarantee feelings of being crowded. A well-attended party may lead to a sense of anticipation and success rather than discomfort and a desire to withdraw. Environmental psychologists, therefore, explicitly or implicitly emphasize subjective experience. Further, research has demonstrated that of all subjective experiences, perhaps the most debilitating is the perception of loss of control. Feelings of helplessness have been linked to everything from feeling crowded to dying (Seligman, 1975).

Reference

Seligman, M. E. P. (1975). *Helplessness*. San Francisco: W. H. Freeman.

R. L. BASSETT

See SOCIAL PSYCHOLOGY.

Envy. A bad feeling stirred up because of the presence of something good in another person but lacking in oneself. This emotion has received considerable attention from the authors of Scripture, theologians, and psychologists. A surprising degree of unanimity characterizes both the secular and sacred views of envy; namely, envy is universal in its occurrence, is destructive in its impact on the human personality, and can become a dominant, invasive emotion if left unchecked. While not a part of the well-known pantheon of vices such as greed, wrath, or jealousy, envy is a powerful emotion that deserves more attention than it usually receives.

Envy has several components. First, at least two persons are involved: the envier and the person being envied. The presence of envy can be completely unknown by those around the envier, since no verbal communication regarding the envy must occur in order for it to be present. Second, the envier must be aware of some feature or facet of another's life that he or she regards as good and that the envier feels is missing in his or her own life. Envy can occur only when a person perceives himself or herself in a position inferior to another. Hence the issue of self-esteem is related to the problem of envy. Third, the envier experiences a sadness that the missing feature is not present in his or her own life. When envy is a major feature of one's own personality, life becomes a constant, dreary calculation of how others are better, and the self is saddened because of it.

Emulation is the positive counterpart of envy (Davidson, 1908). Emulation similarly involves at least two people and a sense of inferiority or lack on the part of one of the two. But the component of sadness is replaced by a desire to obtain the missing feature of life by achievement or growth. Emulation sees the other person as a friend; envy sees the other as a rival. Envy is selfish; emulation is constructive and geared toward change. Envy often wishes harm to the other or rejoices if bad fortune befalls the envied person; emulation has a positive force.

Authors disagree on the precise difference between envy and jealousy. Although they are related emotions, jealousy often involves three persons, is based in fear, and includes the strong desire to possess exclusively the item or person of desire. Jealousy is wanting to hold on to what one already has, and envy is a sadness regarding what one does not have (Walker, 1939).

In the Old Testament envy is described as a powerful enemy (Prov. 27:4) and a destructive force (Job 5:2; Prov. 14:30). The insidious emotion of envy was powerful in the life of Saul (1 Sam. 18:9), Rachel (Gen. 30:1), and the brothers of Joseph (Gen. 37:11). (Many versions substitute "jealousy" for "envy" in these passages.) In the New Testament the verb form for envy occurs one time, in Galatians 5:26, where the exhortation to avoid envy is strongly given. Envy appears in lists of the acts of a sinful nature (Gal. 5:21; Rom. 1:29; 1 Tim. 6:4; Titus 3:3; 1 Peter 2:1). Christian ministry can be prompted by envy (Phil. 1:15), and envy was a driving emotion behind the actions of those who called for the death of Jesus (Mark 15:10).

Roman Catholic theologians have regarded envy as a capital (deadly or cardinal) sin because it leads a person to other sins (Meagher, O'Brien, & Aherne, 1979). Because it was regarded as a cardinal sin it was treated extensively by Dante and Chaucer. Envy is described as a sin because it is opposed to benevolence, an essential ingredient in charity (Herbst, 1967).

In psychology the theoreticians who have had the greatest interest in the emotion of envy are those of psychoanalytic persuasion. Envy was early recognized as a harmful and detrimental emotion by psychoanalysts. Sigmund Freud gave extensive treatment to the concept of envy in his theory of penis envy as a factor in the development of the female personality, a concept that many recent authors dispute extensively. Freud also saw envy as a powerful factor in the sociopsychological development of a sense of community. More recent analysts such as Melanie Klein (1957) postulate a very early developmental origin for the emotion. Klein feels that an infant receives a supply of mother's milk with either a sense of gratitude (necessary for the later task of love) or with a sense of envy (the base for later pathology).

VanKaam (1972) has aptly integrated the destructiveness of envy in a moral sense (as described in Scripture) with the psychologically harmful impact of envy as documented by the analysts.

References

Davidson, W. L. (1908). Envy and emulation. In J. Hastings (Ed.), *Encyclopedia of religion and ethics*. New York: Scribner's.

Herbst, W. (1967). Envy. In Editorial Staff at Catholic University of America (Eds.), *New Catholic encyclopedia*. New York: McGraw-Hill.

Klein, M. (1957). *Envy and gratitude: A study of unconscious sources*. New York: Basic.

Meagher, P. K., O'Brien, T. C., & Aherne, C. M. (Eds.). (1979). *Encyclopedic dictionary of religion*. Philadelphia: Sisters of St. Joseph of Philadelphia.

VanKaam, A. (1972). *Envy and originality*. Garden City, NY: Doubleday.

Walker, W. L. (1939). Envy. In J. Orr (Ed.), *The international standard Bible encyclopedia* (Rev. ed.). Grand Rapids, MI: Eerdmans.

J. R. BECK

See EMOTION; GREED AND GENEROSITY.

Epigenesis. The organismic principle that grounds the concepts of developmental theorists in many of the social sciences, especially prominent in the work of Erik Erikson. It is borrowed from embryology and has been helpful in understanding the relativity governing human phenomena and organismic growth. It may also be a useful tool in envisioning stage models.

In embryology, development is thought of as step-by-step growth of the fetal organs and organ systems. Each organ has a time of origin. If it does not arise at its time, its development may be completely interrupted, thus endangering the whole hierarchy of organs. If it arises too early, equally dire consequences to the organ and to the system would be felt.

The thrust of the embryo's development focuses on particular organs in their time. This is sometimes referred to as the period of dominance or supremacy of organ development. If that timing is lost the particular organ will not come into dominance again. Thus the whole of physical development is thwarted.

E. S. GIBBS

Epilepsy. The Greeks were the first to use the word *epilepsy* to describe a person who is under the control, or seized, by outside forces, although epilepsy was known and described in literature since antiquity. In about 400 B.C., Hippocrates wrote the first book on the subject; it was not until John Hughlings Jackson in the nineteenth century, however, that a more contemporary and accurate understanding of epilepsy was postulated.

Epilepsy is a common neurological disorder that affects over two million people in the United States, and it is defined as a condition in which a person has multiple seizures of any type at a time that are not due to an acute illness (e.g., fever). The prevalence rate of epilepsy is about 1 in 200; however, 1 person in 20 will have at least one seizure in his or her lifetime.

Current views regarding epileptogenesis focus on the neurophysiological mechanisms involved. During a seizure the electroencephalogram (EEG) shows abnormal and excessive discharging of brain cells due to alterations in membrane conductances or deficiencies in inhibitory neurotransmission. The abnormal discharging of the neurons is reflected in a spiking of the EEG wave. The causes of the altered conductances and neurotransmission remain to be elucidated; however, genetic factors, congenital abnormalities, perinatal injury, head trauma, infections, and tumors remain potential agents leading to the disorder.

Clinical features of epilepsy include an aura (a warning in the form of a sensation or feeling) of impending attack, loss of consciousness (either complete collapse or a brief staring off into space) and amnesia of the seizure, and a motor component of some sort such as shaking or automatic movements. The time interval between seizures varies from a few minutes to several months or years.

A variety of factors lead to seizures in susceptible individuals. Some of the principal inducing factors include sleep deprivation, hyperventilation, various sensory stimuli (e.g., flashing lights, reading, music, and laughing), hormonal changes (e.g., puberty and menses), emotional stress, and drugs (e.g., alcohol).

Several types of seizures have been identified and organized into a classification scheme. Partial seizures originate locally and spread to include large brain areas. Simple partial seizures consist of some sensory, motor, or autonomic alteration. Complex partial seizures typically arise in the temporal or frontal lobes and are characterized by variations in mood, hallucinations, automatic movements, and postural changes. Generalized seizures are bilaterally symmetrical but lack a local point of origin. Included in the generalized seizure category are absence (petit mal) attacks, tonic-clonic (grand mal) attacks, and drop (akinetic) attacks. Petit mal seizures involve a loss of awareness during which there is a lack of motor behavior with the possible exception of eye blinking and head turning. Grand mal seizures are also characterized by a loss of consciousness; however, there is motor activity during the attack that generally involves a tonic stage in which the body becomes rigid followed by a clonic stage distinguished by rhythmic shaking. Akinetic seizures typically occur in children, are often of short duration, and involve a sudden collapse.

Anticonvulsant drugs are the treatment of choice for epilepsy. A variety of anticonvulsants are available, but the choice of drug is usually based on seizure classification because these drugs have optimal effectiveness on a specific type of seizure. Drugs used to control partial and generalized tonic-clonic seizures include phenytoin (Dilantin), carbamazepine (Tegretol), and primidone (Mysoline). These drugs reduce neuronal firing by direct action on the cell membrane.

Drugs such as clonazepam (Rivotril) and ethosuximide (Zarontin) enhance levels of the inhibitory neurotransmitter gamma-aminobutyric acid (GABA) and are effective in controlling petit mal attacks. Valproic acid (Depakene and Depakote) seems to have its effect by both enhancing GABA levels and by action on the neuronal membrane. As such it is effective for both tonic-clonic and petit mal seizures.

Most individuals diagnosed with epilepsy and treated with anticonvulsants will be on these medications for life. Some will be seizure-free following cessation of drug therapy, but there is at present no way to predict successful medication withdrawal. If seizures do reoccur following drug withdrawal, reinitiation of anticonvulsant therapy is the primary treatment choice. The decision to end anticonvulsant therapy is generally based upon individual considerations such as the need for driving privileges as well as clinical factors such as drug side effects. Cognitive impairments such as memory problems and reduced attention are often seen with the use of anticonvulsants. The extent to which these impairments are due to the anticonvulsants per se or to a combination of the drug and structural brain damage due to the epilepsy is uncertain. Some drugs (e.g., valproic acid and carbamazepine) are known to be less deleterious to cognitive function when compared to other anticonvulsants.

An additional method of treating epilepsy is through surgery, which dates back to the nineteenth century and the work of Horsley, who was one of the first to remove portions of the cerebral cortex in an attempt to relieve seizures. Surgery, typically in the temporal lobe region, is considered if the epilepsy is intractable (i.e., no remission of seizures after two or more years of pharmacological treatment). A minimal area of brain in excess of what is abnormal is removed during the surgery, and excellent results are reported. Success rates (defined as total elimination or significantly reduced seizure frequency) are between 60% to 80% when patients are rigorously chosen.

Patients treated surgically for epilepsy form an important population for study by psychologists. The exact brain area removed during surgery can be identified, and the result of its removal can be correlated with both the pre- and postoperative behavior of the patient, thus yielding critical information about brain-behavior relations.

Additional Readings

Bennett, T. L. (1992). *The neuropsychology of epilepsy.* New York: Plenum.

Hopkins, A. (1987). *Epilepsy.* New York: Demos.

Kolb, B., & Whishaw, I. Q. (1995). *Fundamentals of human neuropsychology* (4th ed.). New York: Freeman.

K. S. SEYBOLD

See BRAIN AND HUMAN BEHAVIOR; NEUROPSYCHOLOGY.

Erickson, Milton Hyland (1901–1980). Erickson was born with a number of congenital sensory-perceptual difficulties that led him to perceive reality in a rather different fashion from most children. In addition to struggling with these difficulties he also was called upon to manage the painful effects of polio, which struck him at ages 17 and 51. These effects left him without clear speech, in much pain, and unable to walk.

It was probably this combination of liabilities in conjunction with an iron determination to rehabilitate himself that led Erickson to become one of the pioneers in hypnosis as well as the field now known as neurolinguistic programming. Over a span of more than 50 years Erickson published literally hundreds of scientific articles and co-authored a variety of books. (See Rossi, 1980, for a collection of many of his works.) He became something of a guru because of his innovative, intuitive, and authoritative uses of language in the area of hypnotherapy. He took particular pride in being able to subtly and indirectly intervene in the lives of individuals considered too resistant to work well in psychotherapy. Hence his approach to therapy has often been described as utilizing indirect applications of hypnosis. Erickson's careful and colorful use of language wove metaphors, created double binds, and presented other paradoxical interventions that puzzled the conscious mind and allowed other parts of the client's person to become therapeutically mobilized.

During his amazingly productive professional life, Erickson founded and edited *The American Journal of Clinical Hypnosis;* was president of the American Society of Clinical Hypnosis; and was life fellow of the American Psychiatric Association and American Psychopathological Association.

Reference

Rossi, E. L. (Ed.). (1980). *The collected papers of Milton H. Erickson on hypnosis* (4 vols.). New York: Irvington.

V. L. SHEPPERSON

See HYPNOTHERAPY.

Erikson, Erik Homburger (1902–1994). Psychoanalyst Erik Erikson, born in Germany, was educated in the traditional manner of the child of a middle-class family. An important part of his early experience was traveling throughout Europe during his adolescence, a period in his life he later described as his moratorium. His developmental theory was to include moratorium as an important aspect of the adolescent stage.

Before committing himself to a career, Erikson spent much time painting. Because he had obvious talent, he gained a minor reputation as a promising artist. Portraits of children became his specialty. A key point in his life came when he was commissioned to paint the portrait of the child of an Austrian doctor, Sigmund Freud. This work allowed him time for lengthy, informal discussions with Freud. Within a few weeks Freud invited Erikson to join the Psychoanalytic Institute of Vienna. He did so and focused on the analysis of children, under the direction of Anna Freud. His moratorium had come to an end.

Following the completion of his training in Vienna in 1933, Erikson emigrated to the United States. He began a private practice in Boston as that city's first child psychoanalyst. He also held positions at Massachusetts General Hospital and Harvard Medical School. He served from 1936 to 1939 as a research associate in psychiatry at Yale, and during this time he also worked with Henry Alexander Murray at Harvard. He then moved to positions at the University of California and to the Austen Riggs Clinic in Massachusetts, where at the same time he held an appointment as visiting professor with the University of Pittsburgh School of Medicine.

Soon after studying children on a Sioux reservation in South Dakota and on a Yurok reservation in California, Erikson published *Childhood and Society,* an influential book that helped establish him as a writer of literary as well as scientific ability. In 1958 he wrote *Young Man Luther.* This book made an important contribution to both psychohistory and psychobiography. In 1960 he wrote *Gandhi's Truth,* for which he received the Pulitzer Prize, the Melcher Award, and the National Book Award. In *The Life Cycle Completed* (1982), he reviewed, with modest revision, his whole developmental outline. His last book was *Vital Involvement in Old Age* (1986).

Three key concepts identified with Erikson are epigenesis, referring to growth and development; the life cycle, with eight stages of human life; and the search for identity, heightened during adolescence. Every stage in the life cycle presents the individual with potential hazards and potential for renewed growth, with a central focus for each. Erikson's insight has been that while persons are shaped by environmental and historical events, each one contributes to the environment and to the course of history.

Erikson's career came full circle when he returned to Harvard University as a professor of psychology, achieving emeritus status in 1970. In 1972 he became a senior consultant in psychiatry at Mt. Zion Hospital in San Francisco. It should be noted that he had an exemplary career in psychology and psychiatry without the benefit of any earned college degree.

Erikson was awarded many honorary degrees from such institutions as Harvard, Yale, and the University of Chicago. His many prizes included the Foneme in Milan, the Aldrich from the American Academy of Pediatrics, and the Montessori medal. He was a fellow of the American Academy of Arts and Sciences and of the Division of Developmental Psychology of the American Psychological Association and a life member of the American Psychoanalytic Association.

E. S. Gibbs

See Psychosocial Development.

Erotomania. A delusional state occurring almost exclusively in females wherein the woman is convinced that some man is deeply in love with her. The man is usually older and of higher status than the woman. The delusion is usually seen as a defense against a narcissistic injury that has made the patient feel unloved or unlovable. The term is also sometimes used to refer to excessive sexual desire.

See Delusional Disorder; Sexual Desire Disorders.

ESP. *See* Parapsychology.

Ethics, Professional. *See* Counseling and Psychotherapy: Overview; Moral and Ethical Issues in Treatment.

Ethnic Identity Development. Initial interest in the study of ethnic identity development originated in the field of cross-cultural counseling. Counselors began to address issues related to conflicts over perceptions of self and their cultural or racial heritage. Within this context, acculturation was viewed as a series of changes of "intrapsychic mechanisms" such as changes in perception, attitudes, and cognitive processes of the individual (cited in Olmedo, 1979).

Theoretical Roots. Most of the earlier work done in this field originated out of the research of African-American scholars (Cross, 1971, 1978; Jackson, 1975; Vontress, 1971, cited in Atkinson, Morten, & Sue, 1993). Two major views have directed the study of this concept throughout the years. The first view conceptualizes ethnic identity in the form of topologies. Within this framework, minority groups are organized in smaller subcategories or types ranging from ambivalent to militant in their orientation toward the dominant group (Atkinson, Morten, & Sue, 1993). Vontress (1971), for instance, pointed out the existence of three subgroups within African-Americans: Colored, Negro, and Black. These types indicated diminishing levels of dependence on white/Eurocentric sources for self-definition and -worth (cited in Atkinson, Morten, & Sue, 1993). This view, however, has been heavily criticized by scholars who argue for the need to recognize the "movement of individuals across categories or stages." Among them, Helms (1985) has argued that the earlier topology models have failed to recognize that stages are not linear or static but dynamic and evolving in their formation (cited in Atkinson, Morten, & Sue, 1993).

The second view follows the arguments raised by Helms (1985), defining ethnic identity as the product of the individual's transition through stages where attitudes and behaviors are not fixed but subject to change. Cross (1971, 1978) provides an example of this view. In his model, African-Americans move through four stages: pre-encounter, encounter, immersion/emmersion, and internalization. According to Cross, the individual begins this process with a view of the world that is nonblack or even antiblack. With time the person becomes aware of what it means to be black and gradually begins to identify with his or her ethnic and racial heritage. This level of identification will eventually lead the individual to reject all "nonblack" values as the person immerses in the culture. Finally, the individual reaches a sense of inner security that allows him or her to be open to other values and ideas (cited in Atkinson, Morten, & Sue, 1993).

Evaluation. In recent years, many models have emerged. The majority of them point to the development of ethnic identity among specific groups ranging from cultural groups such as Chinese (e.g., Sue & Sue, 1971), Latino (e.g., Ruiz, 1990), and White (e.g., Helms, 1984, 1990; Ponterotto, 1988) to gender (e.g., Downing & Roush, 1985) and sexual orientation (e.g., Cass, 1979; Troiden, 1989) (cited in Atkinson, Morten, & Sue, 1993). In light of all these models, would a more comprehensive model of ethnic identity formation be more helpful for counselors working in multicultural environments? The work by Atkinson, Morten, and Sue (1993) seems to support this position. In their Minority Identity Development Model, they argue that it is possible to conceptualize ethnic identity development from a more inclusive perspective because of a shared experience of oppression in areas of physical, economic, and social discrimination. The model is composed of five stages: conformity, dissonance, resistance/immersion, introspection, and synergistic articulation. The individual moves through a series of transitions in which the person grows in his or her identification with his or her culture of origin. The person often begins the process at a point of cultural ambivalence or conformity toward the dominant culture. Then the individual moves through periods of inner conflict and resistance to a point of total cultural identification. Toward the end of the process, the individual begins to abandon some of the rigidly held views adopted during the immersion stage and gradually moves to a period of openness and self-fulfillment (Atkinson, Morten, & Sue, 1993).

One of the difficulties, however, with these models is that they assume that changes in perception of ethnic identity take place in the same direction of conformity, crisis, introspection, and acceptance. These models seems to be tailored more toward individuals who are unaware of their ethnicity or searching for its meaning. Such is the case of minority adolescents in the U.S. However, for immigrant parents who come into this country with a well-established sense of their cultural identity, their experience may be one of transition or adjustment rather than formation or self-awareness. Counselors should be advised to make a distinction between these two processes. Finally, issues regarding immigration history, level of education, and social class may be critical components in understanding variations in the process of cultural adaptation.

References

Atkinson, D. R., Morten, G., & Sue, D. W. (1993). *Counseling American minorities: A cross-cultural perspective* (4th ed.). Dubuque, IA: Brown & Benchmark.

Cass, V. C. (1979). Homosexual identity formation: A theoretical model. *Journal of Homosexuality, 4,* 219–235.

Cross, W. E. (1971). The Negro to Black conversion experience: Toward a psychology of Black liberation. *Black World, 20,* 13–27.

Cross, W. E. (1978). The Cross and Thomas models of psychological Nigrescence. *Journal of Black Psychology, 5,* 13–19.

Downing, N. E., & Roush, K. L. (1985). From passive acceptance to active commitment: A model of feminist identity development for women. *The Counseling Psychologist, 13,* 695–709.

Helms, J. E. (1984). Toward a theoretical explanation of the effects of race on counseling: A Black and White model. *The Counseling Psychologist, 12,* 153–165.

Helms, J. E. (1985). Cultural identity in the treatment process. In P. Pedersen (Ed.), *Handbook of cross-cultural counseling and therapy.* Westport, CT: Greenwood.

Helms, J. E. (1990). *Black and white racial identity: Theory, research, and practice.* Westport, CT: Greenwood.

Jackson, B. (1975). Black identity development. *MEFORM: Journal of Educational Diversity and Innovation, 2,* 19–25.

Olmedo, E. L. (1979). Acculturation: A psychometric perspective. *American Psychologist, 34,* 1061–1070.

Ponterotto, J. G. (1988). Racial consciousness development among White trainees: A stage model. *Journal of Multicultural Counseling and Development, 16,* 146–156.

Ruiz, A. S. (1990). Ethnic identity: Crisis and resolution. *Journal of Multicultural Counseling and Development, 18,* 29–40.

Sue, S., & Sue, D. W. (1971). Chinese-American personality and mental health. *Amerasian Journal, 1,* 36–49.

Troiden, R. R. (1989). The formation of homosexual identities. *Journal of Homosexuality, 17,* 43–73.

Vontress, C. E. (1971). Racial differences: Impediments to rapport. *Journal of Counseling Psychology, 18,* 7–13.

J. R. REYES

See ACCULTURATION; BLACK ISSUES IN PSYCHOLOGY AND PASTORAL CARE.

Etiology. A division of medical science dealing with the systematic study of the causes of mental and physical diseases. It is concerned with both the physiological response of tissues to the disease and the psychological reaction of the individual to the results of the disease. In psychopathology theories of etiology are much more speculative. Seldom are they built on sufficiently uncontestable data so as to be universally accepted by clinicians or psychopathology theorists.

Evil, Psychology of. The psychological study of evil has been much needed but greatly neglected. Its neglect has been primarily due to psychology's infatuation with scientism and the myth of value-free scientific inquiry. As the philosophical foundations of this myth continue to erode, many behavioral scientists are increasingly willing to acknowledge the reality of evil without fear that scientific objectivity is being betrayed.

Peck (1983) has pointed out that scientific inquiry cannot presume to eliminate all of the mysteries of evil but that questions can be posed that are of a size manageable for psychological investigation. Thus a robust examination of the many facets of evil requires a healthy tolerance for ambiguity and mystery. Such examination is best served by avoidance of simplistic, reductionistic assumptions that attempt to explain human evil as nothing but the sum total of the psychological, social, and biological causes under investigation.

Evil can be examined in terms of its specific manifestations as well as its general or universal aspects. The theological description of the universality of evil is known as the doctrine of original sin. Freud (1962) was an unabashed proponent of a secularized version of this doctrine. He believed strongly in the inborn human inclination to aggressiveness, destructiveness, and cruelty. All persons, he held, are subject to the temptation to sexually exploit, steal from, humiliate, and cause pain to others. In language reminiscent of Augustine or Calvin he confessed his belief in "the evil in the constitution of human beings."

The psychoanalytic school is not alone in its pessimistic depiction of human nature. Wright (1994), arguing from the standpoint of evolutionary psychology, holds that there is "a force devoted to enticing us into various pleasures that are (or once were) in our genetic interests but do not bring long-term happiness to us and may bring great suffering to others. . . . If it will help to actually use the word evil, there's no reason not to" (p. 368).

Numerous social psychology studies have supported the notion that human beings are extremely skillful and creative in demonstrating their propensity for aggression, deceit, and selfishness. Myers (1980) cites many experimental studies demonstrating what is termed the self-serving bias. When their actions result in a positive outcome, persons will attribute the success to ability, but if the actions turn out poorly, they tend to blame external factors. Other research indicates that persons will often overestimate the accuracy of their opinions and judgments.

The inherent tendency toward aggression can be stimulated and sustained by social forces. Sherif, Harvey, White, Hood, and Sherif (1961), in a now-classic experiment, created conditions at a summer camp for 12-year-old boys that they theorized would generate hostility and conflict in the two competing groups formed by the researchers. The experiment succeeded all too well, with the boys eventually engaging in name calling, food throwing, and finally a full-scale riot.

In another well-known study, Zimbardo (1971) created a simulated prison at Stanford University. Normal, well-adjusted young men were randomly assigned to role play either the guards or prisoners. For six days they lived out these roles with excruciating realism. During that time the "guards" began to treat the "prisoners" like animals, concocting humiliating, sadistic routines. The prisoners became robotic, submissive individuals who developed an intense hatred for their captors. The experiment was abruptly suspended because, as the chief researcher noted, "human values were suspended . . . and the ugliest, most base, pathological side of human nature surfaced" (p. 3).

Penetrating insights into the dynamics of human evil in vivo have come from studying Holocaust perpetrators. Lifton (1986) probed the horrific paradox of the Nazi doctors who utilized their medical skills to experiment on and exterminate thousands of concentration camp prisoners.

In his study Lifton delineated the psychological processes enabling these physicians to do the unthinkable. Psychic numbing, for example, involved the interruption of the symbolizing and cognitive processes of the mind, leading to a diminished capacity to feel. Derealization allowed the perpetrators to separate themselves from the reality of their actions while still being aware that they were participating in the final solution.

Any psychological investigation of human evil must of necessity confront the enigma of the antisocial personality. These types of persons are often sensationalized in the entertainment media (e.g., Dr. Hannibal Lecter, the cannibalistic, serial killer in *The Silence of the Lambs*). Hollywood's lurid depictions of antisocial personalities often pale in comparison to the reality of a Jeffrey Dahmer, Ted Bundy, or John Wayne Gacy.

Antisocial personalities are not all serial killers, but most wreak havoc on human relationships with their egocentricity, lack of ability to feel remorse, manipulativeness, and facile deceitfulness. According to Hare (1993), they make up a significant proportion of swindlers, spouse abusers, child abusers, terrorists, and white-collar criminals. Their actions are not the product of insanity but stem from "a cold, calculating rationality combined with a chilling inability to treat others as thinking, feeling, human beings" (p. 5).

Researchers such as Hare are attempting to make some sense of these morally incomprehensible people. However, more work needs to be done from both a psychological and theological perspective in grappling with the questions surrounding this particularly distressing manifestation of human evil.

Unspeakable horrors from across the nation and the world are routinely beamed into living rooms via satellite transmission. It is now commonplace to electronically witness firsthand genocidal murders, bombings, and assassinations. Despite this constant and unrelenting exposure to human malevolence, it is becoming increasingly clear that the United States is swiftly losing its sense of the absolute reality of evil (Delbanco, 1995).

A psychology of evil, it is hoped, will open windows into the mysteries and ambiguities of evil without falling prey to naive reductionism. In so doing such a psychology may then aid culture in seeing again evil qua evil. But to do so it must answer the question asked in the novel *Silence of the Lambs* (Harris, 1988) as Hannibal Lecter confronts his police interrogator: "You can't reduce me to a set of influences. You've given up good and evil for behaviorism, Officer Starling. . . . Nothing is ever anybody's fault. Look at me, Officer Starling. Can you stand to say I'm evil?" (p. 21).

References

Delbanco, A. (1995). *The death of Satan: How Americans have lost the sense of evil*. New York: Farrar, Straus, & Giroux.

Freud, S. (1962). In J. Strachey (Ed. and trans.), *The standard edition of the complete psychological works of Sigmund Freud* (Vol. 21). London: Hogarth.

Hare, R. (1993). *Without conscience*. New York: Pocket.

Harris, T. (1988). *The silence of the lambs*. New York: St. Martin's.

Lifton, R. J. (1986). *The Nazi doctors*. New York: Basic.

Myers, D. (1980). *The inflated self*. New York: Seabury.

Peck, M. S. (1983). *People of the lie*. New York: Simon & Schuster.

Sherif, M., Harvey, O., White, T., Hood, W., & Sherif, C. (1961). *Intergroup conflict and cooperation: The robbers cave experiment*. Norman, OK: University of Oklahoma Institute of Intergroup Relations.

Zimbardo, P. (1971). *The psychological power and pathology of imprisonment*. A statement prepared for the U.S. House of Representatives Committee on the Judiciary, Subcommittee No. 3: Hearings on Prison Reform, San Francisco, CA.

W. G. Bixler

See Narcissism; Demonic Influence, Sin, and Psychopathology.

Exceptional Children. *See* Gifted Children.

Excessive Sexual Desire. In contrast to a lack of interest in sex or an inability to function adequately sexually, excessive sexual desire is not generally recognized as a psychological disorder. The great difficulty in dealing with the concept lies in determining how much sexual desire is excessive and to whom it is excessive. Tremendous variations exist within the boundaries of normal sexual desire. Some persons desire sexual intercourse only a few times per year, while others desire sexual intercourse several times per day. While both these variations are unusual, they are not necessarily pathological or sinful. Surveys have shown that most married couples engage in sexual intercourse between two and three times per week. The frequency is higher among younger couples and decreases as age increases. Neither the Scriptures nor contemporary psychologists prescribe an optimal amount of desire.

Often a person's sexual desire is labeled excessive by one's spouse, who does not wish to engage in sexual intercourse as frequently and who may feel pressured by the partner's desires. In this situation it is the couple's responsibility to communicate with each other about their feelings and beliefs and to work out a compromise that will be fair to each. Scripture makes it clear that the sexual relationship between spouses is very important and is of mutual concern, since both spouses are one flesh. Decisions about the frequency of sexual intercourse must not be made unilaterally (1 Cor. 7).

Sexual desires are a normal and healthy part of life. Human sexual desire can and should be used to image and glorify God through cementing the marriage relationship and procreation. If a person believes one's own sexual desire is excessive, a psychologist or a physician should be consulted for information on normal sexual desire. Ignorance of normal human sexual desire sometimes results in a person feeling as though one's own sexual desire is excessive, when in fact it is healthy and normal.

If one has learned about human sexual desire, consulted a professional, and still believes one's sexual desire to be excessive, one may decide to decrease it. It can be changed. While the foundation of sexual desire is hormonal, many aspects of it have been learned and therefore can be modified. Sexual desire depends on both stimulation and inhibition. Excessive sexual desire may be decreased by either avoiding stimulators or increasing inhibitors. Many forms of psychological therapy are currently available to change sexual desire.

Scriptural directives must be followed to avoid the degeneration of sexual desire into an action that dishonors God. Scripture commands that Christians put off the old nature and put on the new nature through a transformation of their thoughts. God promises to help individuals overcome unhealthy sexual temptations. In addition to depending on God for strength and the renewing of their minds, Christians are commanded to flee fornication and to avoid making provisions for fulfilling sexual lusts that displease God.

Excessive sexual desire in females traditionally was called nymphomania, in males satyriasis (nymphs and satyrs are mythological creatures known for their sexual appetites). Persons with nymphomania or satyriasis possess a constant, compulsive, and uncontrolled desire to engage in sexual intercourse with many partners. In spite of this high level of sexual activity they invariably find little or no satisfaction in the sexual act. Genuine personal and emotional relationships between the nymphomaniac or satyriac and the sexual partner are nonexistent. These persons feel unhappy, dissatisfied, and out of control, yet they are unable to stop. They are perceived by others to be exploitive and self-centered yet self-destructive.

Although excessive sexual desire has not been specifically included as a disorder in the *DSM-IV*, there have been some suggestions for labeling it as an addiction and including it under the title *sexual addiction*. This is still controversial because other professionals perceive excessive sexual desire as a compulsive behavior and a symptom or subtype of obsessive-compulsive behavior. Still others perceive it as an impulse control problem. Hypersexuality may also be symptomatic of affective disorders such as the hypomanic or manic phases of bipolar disorder.

Because excessive sexual desire is not a recognized disorder and there are so many theoretical approaches, there is no consensus on treatment approaches. Professionals in the recovery movement have been treating such behavior with an addiction paradigm and 12-step programs, which often emphasize spiritual bondage and freedom. Those who consider it to be a form of obsessive-compulsive disorder are more likely to treat it with cognitive and behavioral therapies as well as antidepressant medication. When excessive sexual desire is viewed as a symptom of hypomania, the bipolar disorder is first addressed through medication.

C. D. Dolph

See SEXUALITY; SEXUAL DESIRE DISORDERS.

Excuse Making. The commonality of making excuses demonstrates the power and importance of what researchers suggest is their driving force: the individual's attempt to maintain a positive self-image. Self-image is threatened when the individual is responsible for a negative performance. Often excuses are made to manage the impressions one wishes to make on others (*see* Impression Formation and Management). The most developed theoretical model for understanding why people make excuses has been offered by Snyder (1985; Snyder & Higgins, 1988).

Favorable Conditions for Excuses. To understand when we are particularly vulnerable to excuse making, it is important to identify the criteria people use to determine negative performance and those issues that help determine individual responsibility. Snyder (1985) suggests that performance will be judged more negatively when the standards for the performance are exceedingly clear, the activity is important to the individual performer, the behavior is intended rather than accidental, and the behavior is public, particularly when the external critic is of high expertise or status. Failure in an activity that meets all these criteria will be viewed as especially negative. An example in which all the criteria are met would be the professional golfer's missed three-foot putt that would have won the tournament.

The negative performance itself will not threaten the self-image unless the individual accepts a sense of responsibility for that performance. Snyder (1985) identifies three considerations by the performer that will help determine whether he or she should accept responsibility for the poor performance. These are not reflective or deliberate considerations as much as they are quick judgments that may or may not be accurate. Accuracy is less important as a determining factor than simple perception.

The first consideration is the extent to which other people would do just as poorly in the same situation (consensus). The golfer who missed the tournament-winning putt might consider whether others would have trouble with the same putt. Thus lower consensus implies more personal responsibility. The second consideration is whether this poor performance is consistent with the actor's other performances in the same or similar situations (consistency). The individual who has won many golf tournaments before, often by sinking important putts, is likely to see this failed performance as inconsistent with his or her norm. Higher consistency suggests more personal responsibility. The final consideration is whether the negative performance occurs differently from performances in other situations (distinctiveness). A less distinct poor performance hints at individual responsibility. If the golfer concludes that pressure affects all parts of his or her game rather than just the one weakness of putting, then individual responsibility is more likely to be assumed. Thus a pattern of low consensus, high consistency, and low distinctiveness will lead to greater perceived responsibility for the negative performance and will heighten the individual's need to make an excuse.

Excuse-Making Strategies. Snyder (1985) also points out several typical methods for making excuses. One way to make an excuse is to weaken any apparent responsibility for the poor performance. One may try to blame others (this may be common in group situations) or deny having anything to do with the bad performance. This strategy may be difficult to employ if the behavior was obviously performed, especially in public.

A second strategy may be to reframe the poor performance. One prominent reframing method is to reconceptualize the standards for bad performance. For example, the professional golfer may wish to point out that he or she is still better than virtually everyone else simply by making the professional tour. Another reframing method is to maintain that one did not realize just how negative the performance was. The child abuser may appeal to a lack of awareness of what he or she was doing. Yet another reframing technique, often used in excusing inhumane behavior ranging from the Holocaust to sexual offenses to the treatment of subordinates in a job setting, is victim derogation—that the victim deserves what he or she received and therefore the treatment is justified.

A third strategy is to derogate the sources of negative feedback. A student may claim that the teacher did not have a fair exam, that the teacher did not test what the student knows, that the teacher does not know the subject matter, or that the teacher likes girls (or boys), or people sitting in the front (or in the back), or musicians (or athletes).

Finally, one may try to lessen the responsibility for the poor performance by trying to alter any combination of the individual responsibility factors. Thus an individual may be self-convincing that the task was so difficult that anyone would have trouble doing it (consensus raising), that sufficient effort was not expended on the one occasion of the poor performance (consistency lowering), or that the negative performance is unusual compared to one's behavior in other domains (distinctiveness raising).

References

Snyder, C. R. (1985). The excuse: An amazing grace? In B. R. Schlenker (Ed.), *The self and social life*. New York: McGraw-Hill.

Snyder, C. R., & Higgins, R. L. (1988). Excuses: Their effective role in the negotiation of reality. *Psychological Bulletin, 104*, 23–35.

P. C. HILL

See SELF-HANDICAPPING.

Exhibitionism. A self-display of the genitals without the consent of others. It is prevalent in that one-third of all sexual offenses are for indecent exposure (MacDonald, 1973). Cox and McMahon (1978) further report that one-third of the female college students surveyed have come in contact with an exhibitionist. Almost all exhibitionists are male. The onset is in puberty, and the peak incidents are between the ages of 15 and 30. Exposures usually are to a single adult female. The few reported cases of female exhibitionism were performed by women diagnosed as retarded or psychotic.

Exhibitionists do not usually desire sexual involvement with the audience but use the exposure to elicit a particular reaction such as flight, fear, abuse, indignation, or pleasure. Most exhibitionists do not undress completely, and almost one-half of the exposures are performed in cars. The most common times for exposure are between 8 A.M. and 9 A.M. and between 3 P.M. and 5 P.M. The exposures are mainly during the months of May to September and are usually in the middle of the week (MacDonald, 1973).

Most exhibitionists feel urged to exhibit in conjunction with conflicts regarding females in their personal life. In adolescence it is conflicts with the mother, while in adulthood it involves the fiancée or wife. Exhibitionism is also precipitated by interpersonal stress or by a period of intense conflict over some problem involving authority figures that causes a person to feel inadequate.

The exhibitionist is usually a loner at school and therefore isolated from other children. He has few friends and has difficulty handling aggression. Many times he is bullied by others or is involved in fights. Exhibitionists' intelligence scores are lower than those of the general population and higher than that of other sexual offenders (Ellis & Brancale, 1956). Their educational achievement is poor even though they are usually hard workers and conscientious.

The family background of the exhibitionist usually involves an emotionally distant father who is often industrious, passive, ineffective, and meek. His mother is usually either an aggressive and masculine woman or a "clinging vine" (Rickols, 1950). The mother forms a strong bond with the child and rejects her husband. The dynamics in the home often result in divorce, more than 50% of all exhibitionists coming from broken homes. Many exhibitionists are reared in homes with a strict sexual moral code and where modesty is stressed. The child gains acceptance only if he is well-behaved and passive. He grows up to be a very insecure and sexually immature individual.

Most exhibitionists are married. Even so, their major form of sexual release, along with exposure, is masturbation. Masturbation may or may not precede, accompany, or follow the act of exposure.

Most exhibitionists do not graduate to more severe sexual offenses. Their recidivism rate of 20% (Mohr, Turner, & Jerry, 1964) is the highest among sexual offenders. There is some thought that the reason exhibitionists are apprehended and continue to get caught is a feeling of guilt and a need to be punished (see Punishment).

It should be noted that other forms of exhibitionism may or may not be considered psychological deviance. Some examples would be nudist camps, female striptease acts, streaking (running naked as a prank), or mooning (exposing one's posterior). The motivation for these acts is important as well as the intended reaction from the viewer. In the case of the streaker or mooner, it is usually part of youthful thrill seeking, while striptease dancers exhibit for monetary consideration. In the case of nudists, the viewers are willing, and therefore exposure does not bring individuals into conflict with the law.

There is a double standard between male and female exposure. Society passively condones a woman going braless with a see-through blouse or wearing microscopic beachwear, while similar behavior involving men's genitals would be promptly reported as exhibitionism. Perhaps the reason there are not very many female exhibitionists is because society passively condones their behavior and provides outlets such as go-go dancing and striptease work for those females so inclined.

Comprehensive treatment for exhibitionism includes insight therapy, group therapy, and behavioral treatment. The insight therapy is directed to help the individual gain insight into the causes of his maladaptive behavior. Group therapy should provide effective sex education, as well as help the individual develop more assertive or typical heterosexual behavior patterns.

The behavioral component of treatment includes aversion therapy and systematic desensitization. Aversion therapy usually involves presenting the exhibitionist with slides or pictures that call up images of heterosexual behavior or exhibitionist activities. The slides with exhibitionist material are accompanied with electric shock. When the subject changes to a slide describing normal sexual response, the shock is stopped. Aversive conditioning attempts to condition the patient away from exhibitionism by making it unpleasant.

Desensitization to the stress that precipitates the indecent exposure is another type of behavioral treatment. The patient builds a hierarchy of stress situations and then is helped by the therapist to become less sensitive to the stress-producing stimulus. Exhibitionists who receive treatment have a good chance of recovery. Cox and Daitzman (1975) found that if the exhibitionist behavior is stopped for 18 months after treatment, it is unlikely that it will recur.

References

Cox, D. J., & Daitzman, R. J. (1975). Behavior therapy, research and treatment of male exhibitionists. In I. M. Hersen, R. Eisler, & R. Miller (Eds.), *Progress in behavior modification* (Vol. 7). New York: Academic.

Cox, D. J., & McMahon, B. (1978). Incidents of male exhibitionism in the United States as reported by victimized female college students. *International Journal of Law and Psychiatry, 1*, 453–457.

Ellis, A., & Brancale, R. (1956). *The psychology of sex offenders.* Springfield, IL: Thomas.

MacDonald, J. M. (1973). *Indecent exposure.* Springfield, IL: Thomas.

Mohr, J. W., Turner, R. E., & Jerry, M. B. (1964). *Pedophilia and exhibitionism.* Toronto: University of Toronto Press.

Rickols, N. K. (1950). *Exhibitionism.* Philadelphia: Lippincott.

M. A. CAMPION

See SEXUALITY.

Existential Psychology and Psychotherapy. The word *existential* comes from the Latin *ex sistere,* meaning literally to emerge or to stand out. True to this emphasis, existential psychologists seek to understand human beings as not static but always in the process of becoming or emerging.

The beginnings of existential philosophy are usually identified with the Danish philosopher and theologian Søren Kierkegaard. Kierkegaard argued that knowledge can be discovered only via existence, and existence is incapable of further reduction. His major protagonist was Hegel, who identified abstract truth with reality. Against this Kierkegaard argued that truth cannot be found in abstract theory but only in existence. In contrast to René Descartes's dictum, "I think, therefore I am," Kierkegaard answered, "I exist, therefore I think." Existence precedes essence.

Defining Characteristics. As a system of psychology the existential tradition stands in opposition to those approaches that view persons reductionistically. Scientific psychology is viewed as treating people as objects rather than as human beings. Existential psychology rejects this subject-object cleavage. Rather than deal with human essence, the abstraction that has become the focus of traditional scientific psychology, existential psychology focuses on human existence. One's essence is one's existence.

In 1963 James Bugenthal, then president of the American Association of Humanistic Psychology, delineated five basic points that summarize the existential position. 1) People supersede the sum of their parts and cannot be understood from a scientific study of part-functions. 2) People have their being in a human context and cannot be understood by part-functions that ignore interpersonal experience. 3) People are aware and cannot be understood by a psychology that fails to recognize their continuous, many-layered self-awareness. 4) People have choice and are not bystanders to their existence. 5) People are intentional; they have purpose, values, and meaning. This understanding of human nature, or ontology, puts a completely new light on psychotherapy. The goal is not to communicate with the other in terms of presuppositions and expectations but rather to set aside our world and enter into the other's world as he or she lets us in. The therapist's concern and attention are focused on the phenomena themselves. In this way therapists do not abstract themselves or become objective about what is going on but are very much involved in the process. Disclaiming the protective veneer of objectivity, therapists are continually in the mainstream of the other's search for meaning and values. This might be described as a double-mirrored relationship. The therapist must be in quest of his or her destiny to better understand the process of searching.

Although existentialism is related to phenomenological psychology, most existentialists feel that the two traditions are separate. The Swiss psychiatrist Ludwig Binswanger notes that while the existential therapist enters into the phenomena present before and with him or her, existentialism does not confine itself to states of witness. It includes the existence of the whole being. Binswanger likewise points to the conflicting worlds in which the individual lives as opposed to the phenomenologist's notion of the unity of the individual's inner world of experiences. Again, while phenomenology limits itself to the immediate subjective worlds of experience, existentialism takes in the whole existence of the individual. This is where the individual's history comes into play.

View of Persons. In order to better comprehend the whole person, Binswanger (1958) divided his concerns around three aspects of a person's existence, one's mode of being in the world. He saw three worlds in which human beings live. These he termed *Umwelt, Mitwelt,* and *Eigenwelt.* By *Umwelt* he meant the biological world, including one's own body, the animal world, and the entire physical existence. *Mitwelt* includes a person in relation to other persons and emphasizes the more than biological interplay between persons. The aspect he termed *Eigenwelt* deals with persons in relation to themselves—the self relating itself to its self and thus becoming a self. This is what Kierkegaard termed *spirit.*

In this understanding of persons several important factors stand out. Since persons are seen as being, the implication is that they are moving toward becoming. This implies that persons are creatures who are going in a certain direction to fulfill their destiny. On this journey they encounter certain distractions and diversions that attempt to mislead them in their questing. While their chosen strategies for dealing with the obstacles are rooted in their history, their ontology informs them, via anxiety, of their waywardness. This reminds persons of their responsibility to be themselves in truth and to fulfill their destiny. This realization in turn implies that they have the freedom to choose. If they do not choose their destiny, they experience guilt. Boss (1956) points out that guilt is not for things done or not done but for who we refuse to be. Nor, says Boss, is guilt responsive to any other form of relief. Resolution of guilt comes about as the result of a change of direction in our lives toward the fulfillment of our destiny. In this view of personality symptoms are viewed as roadblocks that humans throw up to avoid and evade their destiny.

Psychopathology is a means of communicating. It is the purpose of the therapist to understand the language of the symptoms-symbols because symptoms are symbolic communications of what ails man.

Existential Psychodynamics. In *Existential Psychotherapy* Yalom points to death, freedom, isolation, and meaninglessness as the corpus of existential psychodynamics. He suggests these are the givens of existence and may be discovered by a "method of deep reflection. The conditions are simple: solitude, silence, time and freedom from the everyday distractions with which each of us fills his or her experiential world" (1980, p. 8).

Heidegger's (1962) discussion of death suggests that humans live on two levels: a state of forgetfulness of being and a state of mindfulness of being. To live in the former state is to live in continual distraction and diversion, in a preoccupation with things, abstractions, and impersonal concerns. Self-awareness is a very low priority in this existence. In the latter state one is continually aware of being. This awareness keeps one in touch with one's existence and the world of being. Living in awareness of one's being produces authenticity but is also fraught with anxiety. Anxiety increases when one who is aware of being is confronted with the reality of nonbeing, or death. An extraordinary sense of accountability is initiated with the realization of one's death. This limitation of time also urges one on to greater fulfillment or authenticity. Any experience that suggests a lessening of our individuality or a loss of our unique identity is in many ways reminiscent of our death, and this becomes a challenge to a fuller, more authentic existence.

The second major existential psychodynamic is freedom and its corollary, responsibility. The awareness of being has two dimensions, the awareness of our objective ego and the awareness of a transcending ego. This ability to transcend self not only reminds persons of their possibilities and their freedom but also places on them the necessity to accept that responsibility. To be fully aware of this is what Kierkegaard describes as dizziness. Failure to accept and discharge our responsibility leads to guilt and a sense of groundlessness.

A third concern of the existentialist is isolation. This may be likened to a schizoid state—a condition in which a fundamental separation portrays the nonrelational character of the existent. Carl Rogers describes this condition as the separation from one's own real wishes or desires. I am so unaware of who or what I am that I do not know who I am or what I want. All that confronts me is a sense of nothingness. People are urged to discover their identity, their destiny. But this is the most awful calling of being separate and alone. On these twin possibilities people spend their entire life. Yalom (1980) describes this as the oscillation between life anxiety, the fear of self-affirmation and authenticity, and death anxiety, the fear of loss of autonomy.

The fourth major concern of the existentialist is meaning. This dimension opens up the whole world of values. Questions such as What is life all about? Why do we exist? What meaning in my life makes existence worthwhile? are singularly and significantly relevant to existentialists. These are likewise most pertinent questions in therapy.

The elements of faith and commitment are both integral to the existentialist's notion of meaning. The question is, Faith in what or whom? The existentialist answer is that we begin with commitment to ourselves and our being, and only then do we find meaning. This is what is understood by reaching toward our destiny.

Yalom draws on Abraham Maslow when he speaks of the self-actualization process involving a person striving toward what most people would call good values—that is, toward kindness, honesty, love, unselfishness, and goodness. These values, according to Maslow, are "built into the human organism and . . . if one only trusts one's organismic wisdom, one will discover them intuitively" (Yalom, 1980, p. 438). Thus values and meaning are both seen to be rooted in existence.

Psychotherapy. While there is no single theory or approach to existential psychotherapy, May (1959) has summarized the major common elements in all existential approaches to treatment. He first points out that to look to existential psychology textbooks for techniques will be disappointing. The techniques used by existential psychotherapists are much like those used by other therapists. They are not, however, emphasized in existentialists' discussions of therapy. This is in reaction to the overemphasis on techniques in Western culture, which is viewed as objectifying persons.

According to May, the essential task of existential therapy is to "seek to understand the patient as a being and as being-in-his-world" (p. 77). Understanding a person is contrasted to analyzing an object. To understand a person means to relate to him or her as a person. The relationship of the therapist and patient is taken as a real one, not merely a professional role. Within this relationship the therapist attempts to help the patient experience existence as real. The quintessence of existential therapy is to enable the person to become more fully aware of his or her existence. Involved in this is helping the patient develop an orientation to commitment. The patient must be brought to a decisive attitude toward existence. "The points of commitment and decision are those where the dichotomy between being subject and object is overcome in the unity of readiness for action" (May, 1959, p. 88).

Christian Existential Psychology. This section explores a Christian alternative to existential psychology and, as such, constitutes a critique of that psychology from a Christian perspective.

Existential psychology has largely abandoned any concern for an ultimate reference point for the spirit or self. Adopting a relativism that virtually rejects any unifying purpose or meaning to existence, modern existentialism has cut itself off from the vital taproot of which Kierkegaard spoke when he asserted that spirit must be grounded in Spirit. Christian existential psychology returns to this basic theme in Kierkegaard as its central tenet.

As a distinct system Christian existential psychology has been developed in numerous articles and books over the past quarter century by Finch (1980b, 1982). These writings represent the meeting ground between his religious experience and his psychological awareness—a search that led him first into the pastorate and later into clinical psychology. Finch's approach represents an intentional integration of existential depth psychology and the Christian faith. The focal point for this integration lies in the Christian existential view of the nature of man.

Personality and Psychopathology. In concert with other existentialists, Finch affirms that humans are essentially what Kierkegaard called spirit. That is, a person is not mere machine, as Freud and others proposed, but rather has a definite potential and the freedom and responsibility to actualize that potential. But what is this potential? In Kierkegaard's terms it is the "absolute of all that a man can be." The secular existentialist speaks of one's destiny. But to what do these terms refer? The Christian, in contrast to the logical positivist or pure scientist, is free to respond in absolute terms: the self, the absolute of all that one can be, is defined by the *imago Dei*, the image of God in a person.

Although they are made in God's image, humans have allowed that likeness to be obscured by a network of defenses that, while purporting to protect the self, suffocates it. Enveloping the true, authentic self like a shroud, this false self prevents the spirit from coming to expression. The false self develops as a result of sin. Sin may be characterized as both a defense and a sickness, a sickness created by our egocentric tendency to assert that we are the captains of our fate, the masters of our souls. This act of pride cuts us off from the very Source of all life.

A person's spirit cannot be grounded or find meaning in itself but only in the Spirit who created it. Freedom, responsibility, and the transcendent quality of the self have meaning only as they relate to God. This relation is the core of Christian existential psychology, and in the life, death, and resurrection of Christ this relation is elaborated most fully. It is therefore in the choice to invest oneself in the way modeled by Christ that one truly undertakes the task of becoming oneself. Finch recognizes that placing Christ at the center of psychology is a philosophical assumption. But he claims that his experience as well as that of innumerable others throughout the ages validates the assumption.

Finch asserts that following Christ is the supreme corrective to psychological disturbance. Insofar as one was created to be one with God, any deviation from this path creates an intolerable inner tension, for one is then at war with one's own being. This con-flict must inevitably be expressed in physical and emotional distress. When one sets about becoming like Christ, one becomes aligned with one's ontology, the tension is eliminated, and the entire being—body, mind, and spirit—is once again integrated. This leads to another central theme in Finch's approach: the concept of anxiety.

Like other existential psychologists Finch sees anxiety in all its forms as demonstrating one's alienation from one's own being. Finch, however, puts the case even more unequivocally in his characterization of all anxiety as good. He sees anxiety as an inherent, positive, "creative directive to be oneself in truth, relentlessly" (Finch, 1980b, p. 154). When one makes life choices that are aligned with one's being as a child of God, anxiety is maintained at a creative level. However, when one violates one's nature, one blocks that creative flow and, like the waters of a dammed river, the pressure of anxiety intensifies and overflows into physical and psychological symptoms. By interpreting these symptoms and their causes biologically rather than ontologically or spiritually, we misconceive anxiety and increase it.

At the heart of anxiety we find the conscience. Anxiety is "a nebulous power that activates and drives the being to fulfillment" (Finch, 1980b, p. 162); conscience is the focal point, the "eye of anxiety." Conscience may be defined as the spirit's potential for urging in one's consciousness its authoritative actualization in relation to spirit. Conscience is ontological. That is, it is vital to one's being rather than contingent. It is not to be confused with the Freudian superego, which is the result of parental introjects and therefore potentially alien to one's ontology (consider the inner parental voice that may urge a woman "never to trust a man"), or with cultural norms or environmental influence, all of which conscience mediates and filters.

Failing to heed the call of conscience involves one in guilt. Viewed existentially, guilt consists not in what one has done or not done but rather in one's failure to fulfill one's possibilities in the moment—that is, in one's refusal to be. Virtually all physical and mental or emotional disorders have their genesis in our attempts to avoid the reality of our guilt. The only way to dissipate guilt is to choose to be. This choice is the essence of repentance and forgiveness. When we choose to be authentic, "the whole order of things cooperates with us to annul the past which has produced the guilt, and to affirm the present." Here we are in the realm of grace—that divine, patient, loving "acceptance which both pulls and pushes our development, using every condition of existence to facilitate the emergence of the self" (Finch, 1980a, p. 249).

Human Development. Christian existential psychology views human development in terms of the struggle between the true and false selves. In the womb the fetus begins to react to parental anxieties by assuming a defensive posture. This defense eventually takes the form of an egocentric mistrust of and withdrawal from the milieu and an inner commitment to use everything and everyone for one's own ends—in short, a commitment to make the world good on one's own terms. This response is inevitable. It is one's foremost developmental task (and therefore also the work of therapy) to shed these defenses in order to be revealed as one is. It is only in the extremity of this openness and vulnerability that one relates genuinely to God.

Finch conceives the developmental process in terms of four stages. Progression through the stages is a lifelong journey marked by frequent setbacks.

The first stage is that of dependence, the authentic or natural state of the neonate and infant. As natural growth processes carry the self farther from the security of the womb, the dizzying freedom and responsibility of one's increasing abilities and possibilities create an anxiety from which the self tries to escape by contorting itself and distorting reality. All such tactics constitute an attempt to recreate the security of the womb by enticing (e.g., placation) or by coercing (e.g., tantrums) from the environment the nurturance one either does not trust to come freely or does not wish to procure in an honest fashion.

The second stage, that of independence, is a variation of the first stage. In it one seeks the privileges of freedom without the attendant responsibilities. Characterized by the bullying, pouting, blackmail, and other tactics typically associated with the adolescent's masquerade of selfhood ("I'm old enough to drive, but you'd better pay for the gas"), independence is actually a way of spreading anxiety to the environment so that it will allow one to be dependent.

After an intense struggle one comes to the painful discovery that one's attempts to remain dependent only increase anxiety. As the self acts on this realization and gives up its viselike grip on the defensive strategies by which it has imprisoned itself, the self is born in true freedom and responsibility. This is the stage of self-dependence, in which the self becomes self-caring, self-creating, self-affirming, and self-supporting.

Self-dependence is not to be confused with the idea of needing nothing. As Finch notes, we all need blood to survive. Self-dependence is analogous to producing one's own blood, while dependency is like receiving an endless series of blood transfusions because an organism has lost the ability to produce its own. Nor is self-dependence to be confused with a schizoid withdrawal from or inability to depend on others. Rather, one functions in such harmony with oneself and the milieu that one is able to recycle and draw sustenance from what is offered rather than insisting on having things one's own way. Being in such spiritual harmony one is able to find meaning and value in even the harshest of life circumstances, even in the pain of a crucifixion or the irritations of an uncooperative spouse. This selflessness is possible because the self-dependent person is rooted both within and outside himself or herself in God.

Finally, when two selves are able to relate to each other with "a mutuality and sharing that assumes full responsibility for oneself but no less responsibility

for the other" (Finch, 1980b, p. 172), we reach the stage of interdependence or interrelation. In this stage anxiety is manifest in concern, and the source of motivation is a quiet inner serenity rather than a desire for satisfaction of one's needs at the other's expense.

One observes, then, that spiritual growth is marked by adoption of a mature *Weltanschauung*, or philosophy of life. This philosophy is not merely cognitive but is rather inclusive of one's whole existence. The highest value of philosophy of life, asserts Finch, is expressed in the concept of *nishkamakarma*. Literally translated as desireless action, this Sanskrit word conveys the idea of "doing one's duty with faith in God, without attachment to the fruit of the action" (Finch, 1982, p. 45). This stance of nonattachment (which is not to be confused with uncaring detachment) allows one to focus on the requirements of spirit rather than being pulled and pushed by the vagaries of time and circumstance.

Therapy. The fundamental task of Christian existential therapy is to facilitate spirit's encounter with Spirit. To this end the therapist seeks to dismantle, through loving confrontation, the strategies of the false self. The therapist guides the person into his or her anxiety rather than away from it, appeals to the individual's sense of responsibility, unclutters the conscience, and encourages a healthy perspective on guilt. The therapist's own values invariably become part of the therapeutic process as the therapist enters deeply into the person's struggles. Because the relationship with the therapist becomes the vehicle by which the person experiences grace and a more mature *Weltanschauung*, it is critical that the therapist be actively engaged in his or her own search for authentic existence.

As the person's facade disintegrates and the props of dependency are removed, the individual experiences the dread associated with what has been called the abyss. This is a radical and ineffable confrontation with one's own being that becomes at the same instant an experience of the infinite love of God. For, having abandoned one's feeble attempts to constitute one's own universe and thus ensure one's own security, one finds that he or she is and always has been held. One does not fall, as one fears, out of existence but rather into it.

Such a journey requires the most focused concentration. Integral, therefore, to Christian existential therapy is the ages-old concept of the monastic retreat for the purpose of spiritual direction. This retreat takes the form of a three-week intensive therapy, in which one lives alone and seeks oneself under God, with the therapist's direction. Writing and talking in absentia to one's significant others is one aspect of this process, which often resembles the primal therapies in its emotional intensity.

While existential psychology is not incompatible with a Christian worldview, Christian existentialism asserts that it falls short of a complete understanding of humanity by virtue of its lack of a reference point for the human spirit. In bringing a theologically informed perspective to bear on this problem, Christian existential psychology finds this reference point in Spirit—that is, in God. And, giving fresh meaning to the doctrines of sin, guilt, grace, and forgiveness, an existentially informed Christianity offers new promise for healing in depth.

References

Binswanger, L. (1958). The existential analysis school of thought. In R. May, E. Angel, & H. Ellenberger (Eds.), *Existence.* New York: Basic.

Boss, M. (1956). "Daseinsanalysis" and psychotherapy. In J. H. Masserman & J. L. Moreno (Eds.), *Progress in psychotherapy.* New York: Grune & Stratton.

Finch, J. G. (1980a). Guilt and the nature of the self. In H. N. Malony (Ed.), *A Christian existential psychology: The contributions of John G. Finch.* Washington, DC: University Press.

Finch, J. G. (1980b). The message of anxiety. In H. N. Malony (Ed.), *A Christian existential psychology: The contributions of John G. Finch.* Washington, DC: University Press.

Finch, J. G. (1982). *Nishkamakarma.* Pasadena, CA: Integration.

Heidegger, M. (1962). *Being and time.* (J. Macquarrie & E. Robinson, Eds.). New York: Harper & Row.

May, R. (1959). The existential approach. In S. Arieti (Ed.), *American handbook of psychiatry.* New York: Basic.

Yalom, I. D. (1980). *Existential psychotherapy.* New York: Basic.

J. G. FINCH AND B. VAN DRAGT

Exorcism. A ritual for delivering persons from satanic or demonic domination. It somewhat parallels deprogramming, popularized in the 1970s to free individuals from cult influences. Within the Roman Catholic tradition exorcism ("solemn exorcism") is restricted to priests with specialized training and commissioning; it is normally used for those who are possessed or dominated by demons. Deliverance ("simple exorcism") is for persons troubled by demonic influence in some area of their lives who earnestly desire to be freed. Deliverance requires only a simple prayer, such as "In the name of Jesus Christ, unholy spirit, I command you to depart from this creature of God" (Green, 1981), and may be practiced by all.

Demonic influence and mental illness have been considered opposing explanations for the same phenomena. With the rise of modern psychology and psychiatry, exorcism as an alternative to mental health treatment largely disappeared. The emergence in the late 1980s of dissociative identity disorder (formerly multiple personality disorder) as a common mental disorder sometimes associated with satanic ritual abuse renewed the controversy (Friesen, 1991) and strengthened the reemergence of exorcism in the United States.

While much discussion has emphasized the similarities in symptoms, mental illness and demonic influence are distinct phenomena that may occur separately or together (Bufford, 1988). Satanic/demonic influence varies from minimal influence (e.g., Satan's temptations of Jesus, Matt. 4:1–11) through increasing control (e.g., Satan's influence on Ananias and Sapphira) to total domination (e.g., the Gadarene demoniac). Sometimes associated in Scripture with bizarre behavior, demonic influence more commonly accompanies positions of power and social influence such as among the magicians of Egypt, the astrologers and Chaldeans of Babylon, and the Pharisees of Jesus' day (John 8:44). Contemporary counterparts might include witchdoctors in Third-World countries and persons in government, education, and industry.

While some Christian professionals encourage exorcism, others are more cautious. Christian professionals must consider legal and ethical issues as well as practical issues of how best to aid persons afflicted with satanic/demonic influence. First, informed consent may be impossible for persons totally under demonic domination. Second, third-party payers probably will oppose exorcism as a religious rite. Third, most mental health professionals view exorcism as outside their disciplines and unethical or irresponsible. Referral to the religious community for exorcism is preferred. However, deliverance in the form of discreet silent prayer seems appropriate for mental health counseling.

At a practical level exorcism or deliverance alone is rarely adequate. Filling with the Holy Spirit and practicing godly disciplines are required to remain free from demonic influence (see Matt. 12:43–45). Personal commitment is essential (Anderson, 1991). Emotional or psychological healing, detoxification of traumatic experiences, and development of new patterns of living are normally needed.

To understand exorcism one must consider the classic evil triumvirate: the world, the flesh, and the devil. The world is the fallen created order, including godless society and culture (cf. 1 John 2:15). The flesh includes fallen human impulses, bent toward evil (see Rom. 7). The devil is a personal agent of evil who, together with demons, uses the world and the flesh to involve humans in rebellion against God. Exorcism alone focuses too narrowly on the activity of the devil. Lasting change requires addressing the world and the flesh as well. Spiritual counsel and disciplines, along with mental health counseling, can aid in these areas. This may occur in conjunction with exorcism but more commonly with deliverance and perhaps apart from these. Exorcism seems overemphasized by some. Prayers of deliverance are often neglected; perhaps these should be normative among Christian counselors.

References

Anderson, N. (1991). *The bondage breaker.* Eugene, OR: Harvest House.

Bufford, R. K. (1988). *Counseling and the demonic.* Dallas: Word.

Friesen, J. G. (1991). *Uncovering the mystery of MPD.* San Bernadino, CA: Here's Life.

Green, M. (1981). *I believe in Satan's downfall.* Grand Rapids, MI: Eerdmans.

R. K. Bufford

See Demonic Influence, Sin, and Psychopathology.

Experiential Focusing. Developed by Gendlin in the 1960s, experiential focusing is a technique for introspection and change. Gendlin, a professor of psychology at the University of Chicago and past editor of *Psychotherapy: Theory, Research, and Practice,* discovered that patients who would succeed in therapy could be quickly identified by how they talked about their experiencing. That internal process is called focusing. The focus is a concrete, "felt sense" that Gendlin describes as a preconceptual experiencing that can be symbolized in many ways. For example, the name of a friend may release rich inner associations, the whole of which is one's felt sense about that person. Gendlin has investigated how focusing can be taught to a wide range of people for use in various therapies and in everyday situations when alone or with another.

Focusing proceeds through six movements (Gendlin, 1978). After pausing quietly, one first asks, How do I feel? One lists the problems mentally and steps back from them. Second, one asks, Which problem feels the worst right now? and attends to the whole felt sense of it. Third, one finds the crux of it by asking, What is the worst of it? and refraining from deliberately answering. Fourth, one lets words or images come from the feeling and labels it. Fifth, one checks these words against the feeling until a match occurs that is experienced as a felt shift, a pleasant, physical release. After pausing with this felt sense, one may begin the sixth movement by repeating this process to unlock the body message under the felt sense just experienced.

The Bible asserts both the importance of one's inner impressions and the limitations of relying on them (e.g., Prov. 4:23; 28:26; Rom. 7:22–23). Accordingly, focusing can be most useful when balanced with objective orientations.

Reference

Gendlin, E. T. (1978). *Focusing.* New York: Everest House.

T. J. Runkel

Experimental Group. Those subjects in an experiment who receive the experimental treatment. They are then compared to the control group, which consists of matched subjects who did not receive the treatment.

See Psychology, Methods of; Control Group.

Experimental Neurosis. *See* Neurosis, Experimental.

Experimental Psychology. The application of the experimental method to the study of behavior and mental processes. Although experimental psychologists initially studied only a few subject areas, they are currently identified not so much by what they study as by how they study it. They receive special training in research design, methodology, and the logic of the scientific approach. Experimental psychology is on the borderline between the physical sciences and the behavioral sciences. It is the most self-consciously scientific area of psychology, sharing much methodology with an area such as physics.

Although psychologists can make observations or do demonstrations on only one group, the experimental method logically demands comparing at least two groups. In some instances these two groups may be different groups of individuals that are treated the same in every respect except one, a between-subject design. In other instances experimenters use the same group of subjects but test them under different conditions, a within-subject design. In either case the different conditions must be compared.

Experimental psychology emerged from structuralism, functionalism, behaviorism, and Gestalt psychology during the latter part of the nineteenth and first half of the twentieth centuries. Since behaviorism became the dominant school of psychology in the United States during the first half of the twentieth century, experimental psychology came to be identified with behaviorism. The subject area of learning came to be the dominant one studied, with a major emphasis on classical conditioning and operant learning. Other traditional subject areas studied were psychophysics, sensation and perception, memory, thinking, motivation, and emotion. These subject areas are reflected in the four parts of the *Journal of Experimental Psychology.* Published as separate issues of this journal are *Human Learning and Memory, Human Perception and Performance, Animal Behavior Processes,* and *General.*

Experimental psychologists frequently work with animals as well as with humans. Although rats and pigeons are the most common, at one time or another almost every kind of animal has been subjected to behavioral study. Animals are used because they are simpler and because some types of experiments cannot be done on humans (*see* Animal Experimentation). Furthermore, animals are inexpensive, have a short life span (thus allowing for experiments of relatively short duration), and can be kept in a completely controlled environment. Variables such as brain operations and breeding experiments, which cannot be studied in humans for ethical reasons, can be manipulated with animals.

Although some Christian psychologists tend to reject animal research and other aspects of experimental psychology, it can contribute to Christian psychology. Since humans, like animals, are created beings, there are many similarities between humans and animals, especially in terms of their physiology, their sensations, their learning, and their biological motives. Phenomena found in animals in these areas frequently but not always have been generalized to humans. The experimental method is one of the best ways of investigating creation, so Christians should not reject it but remember that it is only one way to knowledge about creation. Some experimental psychologists unfortunately imply that it is the only way leading to valid knowledge.

Experimental psychology has traditionally been defined as the study of the relatively restricted set of subject areas mentioned above. However, since the 1950s the trend has been to define it as study involving scientific methodology, especially the experimental method. Experimental psychologists are no longer confined to a few areas but conduct research in almost the whole of psychology. One can easily find material on experimental child psychology, experimental social psychology, experimental clinical psychology, and many other such areas. The most widely accepted model for clinical psychology training programs is the scientist-professional one. In addition to their professional training, clinical and counseling psychologists receive training in statistics, research design, and methodology. Although the membership in the Division of Experimental Psychology of the American Psychological Association is relatively small, most psychologists have training in this branch of psychology.

Finally, experimental psychology should not be thought of as opposed to theoretical psychology. Experimental psychologists usually place great emphasis on theory as well as the experimental method. While the results of their experiments are scientific facts, such facts cannot be left in isolation. Theory serves two functions. First, theory serves to integrate the results of past experiments, to show how the facts are related. Theories are not opposed to facts but serve to summarize facts. Second, theories serve the function of generating hypotheses to be tested by experiments. They guide the experimenter in predicting what new facts may be found. Although some research is the "I wonder what would happen if . . ." type, most of it is tied to theory in some way.

Additional Readings

Elmes, D. G., Kantowitz, B. H., & Roediger, H. L. (1981). *Methods in experimental psychology.* Boston: Houghton Mifflin.

Kantowitz, B. H., & Roediger, H. L. (1978). *Experimental psychology.* Chicago: Rand McNally College Publishing.

Sheridan, C. L. (1976). *Fundamentals of experimental psychology* (2nd ed.). New York: Holt, Rinehart, & Winston.

R. L. Koteskey

See Psychology, Methods of.

Experimenter Bias. Experimental research in psychology is subject to bias. As Aronson, Ellsworth, Carl-

smith, and Gonzales (1990) state: "In performing experimental operations, we humans are imperfectly standardized; in estimating their effects, we are imperfectly calibrated. More seriously, human errors are often nonrandom; that is, they tend to bias the results in a particular direction, thus casting doubt on the validity of the experiment" (p. 292). One form of bias in conducting experimental research is due to the experimenter's unintentional effect on the subjects.

An impressive array of research suggests that the experimenter can be an unwanted influence on the research setting. The most convincing evidence demonstrating experimenter effects is the work of Rosenthal in a series of studies during the 1960s. Rosenthal's basic method was to present contradictory hypotheses to two separate groups of experimenters. For example, in probably the best-known of Rosenthal's studies (Rosenthal & Fode, 1963), some experimenters, who were the subjects for Rosenthal's purposes, were told that their rats were specially bred to be bright and should learn a maze rather quickly, while others were told that their rats were bred to be dull and should have difficulty learning a maze. In reality the rats were randomly assigned to the experimenters, and no differences should have been found. However, Rosenthal found that the data from the subjects clearly were in the direction of the hypothesis given to the experimenter. That is, the supposedly bright rats learned the maze more quickly than the supposedly dull rats. Rosenthal (1966) presents evidence of such experimenter bias in studies on a variety of phenomenon, including person perception, inkblot tests, reaction time, human and animal learning, and psychophysical judgment.

Rosenthal's studies have been criticized in that they do not represent the experimental methodology of most psychological studies (Aronson et al., 1990). Rosenthal's studies were set up to invite bias by creating experimenter expectations and by having experimenters run subjects in only one condition (i.e., experimenters usually run subjects in all conditions, such as both "bright" and "dull" rats). Nevertheless, Rosenthal's research suggests that experimenters are an active influence on the research they are conducting, contrary to the popular perception of the experimenter as a value-free, unobtrusive, and passive administrator of instructions.

The role of experimenter expectations is clearly a key factor in understanding experimenter bias, whether those expectations are explicitly induced from something external (as in Rosenthal's studies) or more implicitly carried by the experimenter. Thus any effort to reduce experimenter bias must counter the powerful role that expectations play in experimental research. Techniques that minimize the effects of experimenter bias recommend by Aronson et al. (1990) include:

1. Keep the experimenter unaware of the hypothesis. Aronson et al. (1990) question the effec-

tiveness of this technique because experimenters, like subjects, will often naturally engage in an active search for a hypothesis, and the search itself may foster experimenter bias.

2. Keep the experimenter blind to the subject's condition (often referred to as a "double-blind" experiment in which both the subject and experimenter are unaware of the subject's condition). In this situation the experimenter is aware of the hypothesis but is unaware of the specific condition that the individual subject is in (e.g., is unaware of whether this is a "bright" or "dull" rat). This method is not always useful in that the assignment of subjects to conditions is often obvious and cannot be hidden from the experimenter (such as when the experimenter provides instructions to create various conditions).

3. Use automated instructions such as video/audiotape, computerized instructions, written instructions, or even oral instructions that are read without deviation by the experimenter. Aronson et al. (1900) point out, however, that while this technique minimizes experimenter bias, it often reduces the impact of the treatment and negates the advantages of a live experimenter (such as answering questions).

4. Run all conditions simultaneously. Though not always possible, this technique may be available when conditions are assigned by instructions or feedback handed out on paper.

References

Aronson, E., Ellsworth, P. C., Carlsmith, J. M., & Gonzales, M. H. (1990). *Methods of research in social psychology* (2nd ed.). New York: McGraw-Hill.

Rosenthal, R. (1966). *Experimenter effects in behavioral research.* New York: Appleton-Century-Crofts.

Rosenthal, R., & Fode, K. L. (1963). The effect of experimenter bias on the performance of the albino rat. *Behavioral Science, 8,* 183–189.

P. C. HILL

See PSYCHOLOGY, METHODS OF; PSYCHOLOGY, PRESUPPOSITIONS OF.

Explanatory Style. A cognitive personality characteristic of how one habitually explains the causes of bad events involving the self. Of particular interest to psychologists is the depressogenic explanatory (or attributional) style. Many researchers are convinced that the depressogenic explanatory style, also known as a helpless or pessimistic explanatory style, is a key in understanding disruptions in motivation, cognition, and emotion, especially following an experience with an uncontrollable event (*see* Learned Helplessness).

When people experience negative events, they are likely to ask why the events occurred as they did. Their answer to this question, their explanatory style, will influence not only how they react to the event but also their expectations for future behavior in relation to the event.

Explanatory style involving the self appears to be a function of three important dimensions. The first issue is the stability factor. To what extent is the causal explanation reflecting a long-lasting or stable self-characteristic and to what extent is the characteristic unstable, suggesting a transient cause? The second important dimension in the search for causality is the global factor. A causal explanation can be global in that it can influence many outcomes, or it can be specific by influencing only the outcome currently under focus. The third consideration is the locus factor, ranging from an internal to eternal focus. The causal explanation may involve something about the individual (the internal explanation) or about something external to the individual.

The person burdened with a depressogenic explanatory style scores high on stability, globality, and internality in reaction to a negative event. Research suggests that people who demonstrate a depressogenic style in reaction to negative events do not employ the same style when good things happen to them. In relation only to negative (especially uncontrollable) events, the person who thinks "it's me, it happens every time, it appears in everything I get involved in" is the pessimist who may demonstrate learned helplessness.

The Attributional Style Questionnaire (see Peterson, 1991; Peterson, Maier, & Seligman, 1993) is the primary instrument developed to measure explanatory style. It consists of 12 scenarios, 6 positive and 6 negative, to which respondents are asked to rate the events described in each scenario along the stable, global, and locus dimensions.

References

Peterson, C. (1991). The meaning and measurement of explanatory style. *Psychological Inquiry, 2,* 1–10.

Peterson, C., Maier, S. F., & Seligman, M. E. P. (1993). *Learned helplessness: A theory for the age of personal control.* New York: Oxford University Press.

P. C. HILL

See PSYCHOLOGY, METHODS OF.

Explosive Disorder. *See* INTERMITTENT EXPLOSIVE DISORDER.

Expressive Therapy. A combination of action-oriented therapies used in mental health inpatient and partial hospitalization programs. Often misunderstood as mere time-structuring efforts, activity therapy is a potent treatment method that is effective in providing therapeutic experiences for persons of all ages.

Several types of activity therapies have emerged. Occupational therapy, therapeutic recreation, and art, dance, and music therapies became the leading innovations in what was called adjunctive therapy, meaning therapy that is additional to individual and group psychotherapy. The term *adjunctive* has more often been replaced by *activity*, reflecting the importance activity therapy has achieved as a therapeutic modality.

The therapeutic impact of each type of activity therapy is heightened by its collective use. Many activity therapists use combinations of dance, art, music, recreation, and occupational therapy to provide a well-rounded, highly personalized approach to treatment. Activity suggests action, and action is a major characteristic of the many therapies included within this approach. The patient is engaged in doing. The hands manipulate the brush, the clay, or the musical instrument. Larger muscles move the body in sports activities, dance, or creative movement. In addition to action is interaction. Many of the activity therapies involve interaction with another person or a group. In activities such as art and dance two or more individuals may co-create. Thus interaction develops into an even higher level of functioning, co-action.

Activity therapists generally use a here-and-now orientation in their work. Some attention is given to the patient's past experiences, but these are generally integrated with what is happening in the present. Emphasis is on what the patient is experiencing at the moment. What is he or she learning during the activity? How does the activity compare with other life situations in which similar feelings are experienced? How does what the patient experiences now relate to future situations? These are questions that the activity therapist considers.

The goals of activity therapy obviously differ for each patient. However, the following are some of the general changes often seen: enhanced creativity, better use of leisure time, improved physical and interpersonal skills, and increased self-esteem. It is also often helpful as a diagnostic aid in determining the patient's strengths, weaknesses, and interests.

Activity therapists work as members of a treatment team in conjunction with other mental health professionals. Some are employed in private practice. They are certified through national organizations in the major specialty areas—occupational, recreation, art, dance, and music therapy. Each provides a unique contribution to the overall holistic treatment of the patient.

Occupational Therapy. This was the first well-developed activity therapy and was the forerunner of modern activity therapy. In this form of treatment media that can be manipulated with the hands are used to assist patients in their recovery from emotional disabilities and psychosocial dysfunction. In nonpsychiatric settings such as general hospitals and schools it is used primarily as a treatment for physical rehabilitation and sensory motor development.

Traditionally occupational therapy has been associated with leather, art, metal craft, ceramics, sewing, woodworking, personal hygiene, and instruction in everyday living skills. Classes in remotivation are offered to patients who need moderately stimulating experiences in reality orientation. Some of the creative arts are helpful in increasing attention span while reducing anxiety.

Although some attention is given to the finished product, the focal point is the treatment process, that is, the experience of the patient in the activity. Psychodynamic activities are developed to deal with the patient's unconscious conflicts. Conflict themes center around issues such as aggression, self-image, and social relationships. The activity is a catalytic agent toward the development of meaningful relationships and helpful intrapsychic learning experiences.

In addition to the activity, the personality of the occupational therapist is an important part of the therapy. Occupational therapists have extensive training in treatment approaches, evaluative methods, and group dynamics and have been leaders in developing state licensing programs.

Recreation Therapy. This professional service provides recreational activities appropriate to the therapeutic needs of specific groups of people. These services are prevalent in psychiatric hospitals, day care agencies, homes for the aged, and penal institutions. The process of therapeutic recreation is directed toward a positive change in the individual.

The therapeutic recreation professional begins by assessing the patient's level of dysfunction. With the assistance of the treatment team, goals are established and specific recreational activities selected as interventions. The recreation therapist provides services on three levels—rehabilitation, leisure education, and independent recreation participation. As the patient moves up through these levels, the therapist becomes less directive and more facilitative. This therapeutic strategy promotes autonomy and independence in the patient.

The image and function of the recreation therapist have evolved considerably. Initially the job required organizing parties and recreational events. This was an outgrowth of programs provided for American armed service personnel in stateside military bases during World Wars I and II. In most settings for the mentally ill and handicapped, therapeutic recreationists now occupy an important place in the overall treatment program. Instead of helping the patient pass time by playing games, the therapist focuses on ways the individual can change and creatively designs the experiences that will facilitate this.

An important part of treatment receiving recent attention is the opportunity to provide patients with aftercare experiences in recreation activities. Such an emphasis requires active leadership on the part of therapeutic and municipal recreation professionals, who must combine efforts to provide meaningful activities for these special groups. Leisure counseling is also becoming an important skill of the therapeutic recreation professional.

Art Therapy. This is a human service profession that assists individuals in dealing with personal problems and conflicts through the medium of art. Art therapy programs are often included as one of the activity therapies in psychiatric centers, schools, prisons, and other mental health-oriented settings.

The art therapist uses the visual arts as a means to assist integration or reintegration of personality. Art is seen as a form of symbolic speech promoting the direct expression of fantasies and dreams. From a psychoanalytic point of view spontaneous art expression releases unconscious forces and attitudes that may be interpreted initially by the therapist and eventually by the patient.

In addition to the evaluative use of art therapy it also provides healing through the creative process. In the creative act conflict is reexperienced, resolved, and integrated. The atmosphere in the art therapy session is supportive and caring. The patient is invited to share thoughts and feelings activated by the experiences. The goal is to serve the total personality by developing a fusion between reality and fantasy, unconscious and conscious; to discover both the self and the world and thereby establish a rational relationship between the two. Through the creative processes these inner and outer realities are fused in a new entity.

Art therapists are trained in a combination of art and the psychodynamics of individuals and groups. Although many are skilled artisans, their major focus is not on the finished product but rather is aimed toward a healing experience for the patient.

Dance Therapy. Dance, or movement, therapy involves the therapeutic utilization of movement in order to help an individual integrate his physical and emotional aspects. Dance therapists view the body as a manifestation of the personality. Thoughts and emotions are closely connected to physical movement, and therefore the healing process uses the body as the instrument for its own restoration.

The particular goals of the dance therapist often determine the nature of the movement experience. An initial broad objective is an increase in body awareness. New movements expand the body's repertoire of actions. Tensions are recognized and relieved. The body is recognized as a potential source of joy. Another goal is the catharsis elicited through movement. Dance therapists believe that the expression of feelings through shaking, kicking, or pounding provides a purging and therefore results in renewal. They strongly encourage the verbal identification of feelings so that a more complete integration is achieved.

The results of successful dance therapy go far beyond improved dancing skills. Much more significant are the frequent gains in interpersonal communication, both verbal and nonverbal. Dance and other group movement activities bring people together in relaxed positive contact so that natural social interactions develop.

Music Therapy. Here music is employed as the major treatment medium. The music therapist adapts sound and rhythm to create an environment in which the patient will respond by developing healthy attitudes and responsible decision making. The patient is drawn to others and experiences structure and organization as well as self-confidence and mind-body stimulation.

Music has therapeutic benefits because it is a nonthreatening medium through which the patient may express feelings, develop creativity, increase self-esteem, learn to work with and trust others, and express himself or herself nonverbally. Learning how to play an instrument is a practical side benefit.

The therapy experience is a combination of music listening for reflective relaxation and music participation for the experience of learning and growing. The relaxing qualities of listening to music are therapeutic for all ages of people who experience the high stress levels of everyday living.

The major therapeutic goal is positive behavior change and insight into one's self. The therapist places most attention on the experience of the patient during the music therapy session. As in the other activity therapies, music therapy seeks to develop not great musicians but whole people.

Additional Readings

Bonny, H. L., & Savary, L. M. (1973). *Music and your mind.* New York: Harper & Row.

Feder, E., & Feder, B. (1981). *The expressive art therapies.* Englewood Cliffs, N.J.: Prentice-Hall.

Mosey, A. C. (1973). *Activity therapy.* New York: Raven.

O'Morrow, G. S. (1980). *Therapeutic recreation.* Reston, VA: Reston Publishing.

Ulman, E. [*Art therapy*] (1975). (E. Ulman & P. Dachinger, Eds.). New York: Schocken.

J. H. Vander May

Extinction. Any of three experimental operations or the corresponding behavioral changes produced by these operations. The three types of extinction are extinction occurring in classical conditioning, extinction occurring in operant conditioning, and vicarious extinction. The changes usually involve weakening some behavior, but in some circumstances the target behavior does not change or even increases in strength. Extinction is relevant only to previously conditioned or learned responses; the concept has no meaning in terms of original learning.

In classical conditioning a previously neutral stimulus (such as a bell) is consistently followed by an unconditioned stimulus (such as a squirt of food powder in the mouth). Prior to conditioning the bell cannot produce salivation, but the food powder can. The bell is the conditioned stimulus and salivation is the conditioned response. Following many pairings of the bell and food powder, presentation of the bell alone will elicit salivation; however, continuous presentation of the conditioned stimulus (bell) without the unconditioned stimulus (food powder) constitutes the operation of extinction. This operation will normally result in a weakening and eventual disappearance of the conditioned response (*see* Conditioning, Classical).

Emotional behavior seems to follow the principles of classical conditioning. Since emotional reactions can be classically conditioned, they can be weakened via extinction processes. An infinite variety of environmental events can function as conditioned stimuli. If the effective stimulus for a given emotional reaction can be identified and presented in the absence of the relevant unconditioned stimulus, the power of the conditioned stimulus can be extinguished. Such a conceptual analysis is consistent with treatment effects achieved through clinical procedures such as systematic desensitization and flooding.

Operant conditioning deals with emitted behaviors that are controlled by their consequences. Consequences can consist of producing a positive stimulus (positive reinforcement), removing an aversive stimulus (negative reinforcement), producing an aversive stimulus (punishment type I), or removing a positive stimulus (punishment type II). When an action has produced one of the consequences but now does not do so, the behavior is in extinction. What will happen to response rate during extinction will depend on what consequence had followed the action prior to the extinction phase. Previously reinforced behaviors will tend to be weakened during extinction, but previously punished behaviors will tend to be strengthened during extinction (see Conditioning, Operant).

For extinction to work, all positive reinforcers for the target behavior must be removed. Since carrying out such a prescription in the natural environment is usually difficult, programmed extinction is used sparingly in treatment programs. When parents are encouraged to ignore their children's misbehavior, the consultant probably is assuming that the parents' attention has been serving as the positive reinforcer for the misbehavior. Having parents ignore the tantrums of their toddler is a common example of extinction applied to an everyday problem.

Intermittent schedules of reinforcement or punishment constitute the most common approach to training for resistance to extinction.

Human observers may exhibit extinction effects of both a classical and operant variety without being directly exposed to the extinction conditions. Social models may produce extinction vicariously, just as classical or operant conditioning may occur through observational learning.

P. W. CLEMENT

See LEARNING.

Extrasensory Perception. See PARAPSYCHOLOGY.

Extraversion-Introversion. See INTROVERSION-EXTRAVERSION.

Extrinsic Religious Orientation. See RELIGIOUS ORIENTATION.

Eysenck, Hans Jurgen (1916–1997). Psychologist noted for his introversion-extraversion theory of personality. Eysenck was born in Germany but has spent his professional life in England. Although he received his early education in Germany, both his B.S. degree (1938) and his Ph.D. degree (1940) are from the University of London.

During World War II Eysenck served as psychologist at the Mill Hill Emergency Hospital. Following the war he was appointed reader in psychology at the University of London and director of the psychological department at the Institute of Psychiatry there. The institute includes Maudsley and Bethlehem Royal Hospitals, with which he has been affiliated since 1945 and 1948 respectively and where much of his research has been carried out. His entire professional life has been spent at the University of London, where he set up the first psychology department in England offering training in clinical psychology.

Eysenck has been a persistent critic of all types of psychotherapy, especially psychoanalysis. He has characterized such therapy as an art form and has questioned whether it does any good. While accusing other personality theorists of being subjective storytellers with theories based on conjecture and unfounded assumptions, he has attempted to develop a theory based on empirical data and experimental procedures. He has obviously been a controversial figure.

He has searched for the basic dimensions or traits of personality and has found two major ones. His introversion versus extraversion dimension, like Carl Gustav Jung's, refers to the degree to which a person is passive and quiet or outgoing and active. Neuroticism, which has anxious restlessness, can be contrasted with emotional stability, which has carefree calmness. More recently Eysenck has investigated a psychotic versus nonpsychotic dimension in which the psychotic is unable to distinguish between reality and fantasy.

Eysenck has developed a research method, criterion analysis, which is like factor analysis but more deductive. In criterion analysis one begins with a hypothesis about underlying variables and does the statistical analysis to test the hypothesis rather than letting the factors appear by themselves in the statistical analysis. Since Eysenck has advocated the use of behavior therapy, his approach bridges the gap between trait and learning approaches to personality.

He has written many books, ranging from scientific volumes to popular bestsellers. His most important are *Dimensions of Personality* (1947), *The Scientific Study of Personality* (1952), *The Causes and Cures of Neurosis* (1965, with Stanley Rachman), and *Uses and Abuses of Psychology* (1953). He was also editor of the comprehensive *Handbook of Abnormal Psychology* (1961).

R. L. KOTESKEY

See FACTOR THEORIES OF PERSONALITY.

Factitious Disorders. Factitious, or factitial, disorders refer to a category of behavior involving various physical and psychological complaints or symptoms that an observer would suspect to be simulated and subject to voluntary control. Thus the term has become a synonym for self-induced diseases. Although they are voluntarily controlled and produced with the conscious awareness of the individual, the repeated use of these behaviors has a compulsive quality, suggesting that they have been adopted involuntarily and maintained to serve the personal dynamics of the individual.

Moral and social disapproval of these illnesses has always existed despite the existence of systems within society to compensate and even encourage their development and maintenance. These self-induced diseases also evoke frequent negative emotion and reaction from physicians.

Factitious disorders may encompass practically the entire range of medical nosology. Dermatological concerns might involve the excoriation of skin and insertion of parasites. Surgical issues include bleeding from various orifices. Medical problems include metabolic and hematological disturbances, such as diabetics tampering with their diets and insulin regimen. Many times these feigned illnesses do considerable and often irreparable damage to health.

The discrimination of these symptoms from those associated with the real disorders that they masquerade is a judgment of the outside observer. The conclusion that the behavior simulates illness is determined through assessing the intellectual abilities of the patient to know the appropriate signs, the timing or process of the symptoms, and the lack of any positive gain through the behavior. The production of the symptoms, while concealing the voluntary control, requires an appreciable level of intellect and judgment. Simulation requires not only the production of appropriate signs but also the sequencing of these to be consistent with the real disorder. Further, the identification of any environmental gain such as avoiding work or getting insurance payments would indicate malingering, while the lack of such gain supports the diagnosis of factitious disorder.

Frequently less specific disorders are masqueraded so that concealment can be more easily maintained. Chemicals or drugs are ingested occasionally to produce supportive symptoms or test results for the simulated physical disorders. The simulation of nonorganic mental disorders (e.g., Ganser syndrome) may also be facilitated by stimulants, hallucinogenics, and hypnosis. Approximate or vague answers also can serve to protect from discovery.

The lack of environmental or secondary gain suggests that factious behavior is a maladaptive response in which the assumption of the patient role somehow serves the dynamics of the individual. The limited literature available suggests that these patients are generally dependent and demanding. Frequently they are single women with poor psychosexual adjustment and numerous hysterical traits. Fras (1978) characterizes these patients as immature, with persistent, primitive oral and tactile needs. They were very dependent on their mothers but generally had their dependency need unfulfilled due to its intensity and extent. Frequently their fathers were sick or in some other way unable to provide the needed emotional gratification. Furthermore, such patients usually possess poor verbal communication skills, thus rendering illness behavior suitable as a mode of communicating needs.

Due to the real risk to health, therapy must initially be cautious and involve support and establishment of the relationship. Confrontation of the characteristic denial must be postponed generally, with the exception of immediate intervention and interpretation in crisis situations. Occasionally these patients need to be hospitalized to prevent further damage. Only after a secure rapport is achieved can traditional psychotherapy be commenced. Even then it must be with the awareness of the existence of a brittle ego with weak defenses. The therapist can often be caught between a frustrating patient with few health responses and a frustrated, impatient medical profession lacking in understanding.

Such a role calls for a mature, secure, and patient therapist.

Reference

Fras, I. (1978). Factitial disease: An update. *Psychosomatics, 19,* 119–122.

Additional Readings

Berney, T. P. (1973). A review of simulated illness. *South African Medical Journal, 47,* 1429–1434.
Crabtree, L. H., Jr. (1967). A psychotherapeutic encounter with a self-mutilating patient. *Psychiatry, 30,* 91–100.
Fras, I., & Coughlin, B. F. (1971). The treatment of factitial disease. *Psychosomatics, 12,* 117–122.

G. MATHESON

See MALINGERING.

Factor Theories of Personality. Because the concept of personality is based on subjective insights, many theories of personality exist side by side, and while the merits and shortcomings of each approach can be analyzed, psychology cannot come to just one consensus position. Factor analysis is an attempt to give psychological concepts a more objective basis. Human behavior could be compared to a jungle. The psychologist is the hunter. How does the hunter decide whether the dark blobs he sees are two rotting logs or a single alligator (Cattell, 1965, p. 56)? Movement will tell: if the blobs move together, a single structure can be inferred.

Factor analysis is a mathematically sophisticated technique using John Stuart Mill's principle of concomitant variation in order to reduce a large number of behavioral data to a smaller number of factors. One might start, for example, by gathering 50 test results for each individual in a group and observe that tests 1, 3, 5, 23, and 49 are highly intercorrelated (*see* Correlation). Performance on any one of these tests is a good predictor of performance on any of the other tests. Hence these tests could be grouped into one factor. Naming and interpreting that factor however, is a more subjective process, the result of analyzing the similarities between tasks involved and linking them through the use of a theoretical label such as imagination or ego strength.

Early Applications. The use of factor analysis in psychology started with Charles Edward Spearman in 1904, in relation to his work on the nature of intelligence. Spearman taught at London University, where both Raymond Bernard Cattell and Hans Jurgan Eysenck, two major contributors to the factorial analysis of personality traits, did their doctoral work. Eysenck later taught at London University, while Cattell spent the major part of his professional life in the United States, at the University of Illinois.

In the United States, the first psychologist to apply factorial analysis to the study of personality was Guilford, in a 1934 study on the Jungian concept of introversion and extroversion. Guilford's main contribution to the field of personality is the Guilford-Zimmerman Temperament Survey, first developed in 1949 and revised in 1976, in which ten personality traits were identified: general activity, restraint, ascendance, emotional stability, sociability, objectivity, friendliness, thoughtfulness, personal relations, and masculinity-femininity. A second-order analysis of these personality traits shows that these ten traits may be reduced to two or three secondary traits similar to Eysenck's extroversion, neuroticism, and psychoticism. This is a subject, however, still of some controversy (Eysenck & Eysenck, 1985, p. 133).

Cattell. While Guilford deserves credit for being first in the field, the distinction for the most voluminous output of research belongs to Cattell, who by 1964 had written 257 chapters and articles and 22 books (Cattell, 1964, p. ix) and wrote for many years after that. Cattell's best known achievement is a widely used personality questionnaire named the Sixteen Personality Factor Questionnaire 16PF, in its fifth edition in 1993.

The Sixteen Personality Factor Questionnaire was constructed (Cattell, Saunders, & Stice, 1950) as the result of a long process that started with a study of the language we use to describe temperamental traits. In 1936 Allport and Odbert had compiled a list of 4,500 descriptive adjectives, which Cattell, by eliminating synonyms and intercorrelated traits reduced to 46 surface traits (Cattell & Kline, 1977, p. 31). Real-life data, questionnaire data, and test data analyzed on the basis of these traits, and then intercorrelated yielded 16 temperament source traits, the basis for his test.

The names Cattell chose for his factors reflect his fondness for neologism. They are sizia (reserve) versus affectia (outgoingness), intelligence, ego strength (emotional stability), submissiveness versus dominance, desurgency (taciturn) versus surgency (enthusiastic), superego strength (expedient versus conscientious), threctia (shy) versus parmia (venturesome), harria (toughminded) versus premsia (tender-minded), alaxia (trusting) versus protension (suspicious), praxernia (practical) versus autia (imaginative), alertness (forthright) versus shrewdness, guilt proneness (self-assured versus insecure), conservatism versus radicalism, group-adherence versus self-sufficiency, strength of self-sentiment (careless of social rules vs. controlled), ergic tension (relaxed versus tense) (Cattell & Kline, 1977, pp. 342–343).

Cattell's personality factors are not independent; some are even fairly highly correlated. Hence a second level of analysis into higher or secondary factors is possible. Some of the more interesting factors, which a number of other researchers have found are exvia versus invia (extroversion), adjustment versus anxiety (neuroticism), and what Cattell identified as a "real superego" factor, a factor that Eysenck thinks resembles his own "psychoticism" factor (Eysenck & Eysenck, 1985, p. 124).

The development of traits across the life span and their application to particular situations occur within a complex network of drives, attitudes, and sentiments: the dynamic lattice. Pathways within the lattice change over time as the result of learning, especially through rewards or favorable consequences (instrumental conditioning).

The breadth of Cattell's work is impressive. He tested and incorporated insights from sources as diverse as Sigmund Freud, Guilford, Eysenck, B. F. Skinner, Henry Alexander, Murray, and William McDougall. His theory is more complex than what was presented here and involves also the study of personality states, abnormal behavior traits, and genetic or environmental components of behaviors.

Eysenck. While Cattell's theory is remarkable for its scope, incisiveness is the hallmark of Eysenck's approach, which is grounded in observation and leads to experimentally verifiable predictions, some of which are based on possible biological mechanisms. Eysenck started his research career in a military psychiatric facility, the Mill Hill Emergency Hospital. There he became interested in Carl Gustav Jung's idea that intraversion and extroversion lead to different types of mental illness and decided to explore this idea empirically. He thus selected 700 patients, analyzed their intake forms and treatment histories according to 39 categories, intercorrelated the results, and discovered that they could be explained in terms of two independent factors: the introversion-extroversion factor, describing the individual's temperament, and the neuroticism factor, reflecting the degree of mental maladjustment. Jung had been right: introverts high on the neuroticism scale showed symptoms associated with high anxiety, whereas neurotic extroverts evidenced bodily symptoms without organic basis, lacked energy, and experienced sexual difficulties (all characteristics of a hysteria-like condition) (Eysenck, 1967, pp. 36ff.).

Eysenck sees a correspondence between his two factors and Galen's classical temperament categories. The choleric temperament characterizes the neurotic extrovert, while the neurotic introvert is melancholic. The former is more apt to acquire a criminal record, the latter a psychiatric one (Eysenck, 1967). Stable introverts are of the phlegmatic type, which is often encountered in successful industrial managers. Stable extroverts correspond to the sanguine type, frequently found in the armed forces (Eysenck, 1970, pp. 427–430).

Eysenck ascribes the introversion-extraversion dimension to the ascending reticular system (ARAS) in the brain, which functions like a central switchboard with a double function—activating the cortex and inhibiting it. Introverts are sensitive to incoming stimulation, extroverts less so. Extroverts also are more likely to tune out irrelevant or repeated stimulation because of their stronger inhibition functions. This understanding of introversion and extraversion leads to interesting practical applications. Introverted students are more alert in the morning than are their underaroused extrovert counterparts, who also fall asleep in quiet libraries at any time and study better in the humdrum of a cafeteria corner. It may take little of a stimulant drug to arouse introverts, but it will take quite a bit of a depressant to calm them. The individual who falls asleep easily after several cups of coffee is probably an extrovert (Eysenck, 1967). Extroverted children need firm parents who clearly enforce rules. Introverted children, who easily pick up the cues and social rules that govern behavior and are prone to anxiety, need a softer approach.

Both introverts and extroverts may be either neurotic or stable. For Eysenck, neuroticism is a matter of overly strong emotionality. Emotions are associated to the visceral brain (VB), comprising the brain's hypothalamic and limbic structures and connected to the activation of the autonomic (involuntary) nervous system. Thus, for example, we flush when we are embarrassed, tremble when we are frightened, as our heart beats faster. In mild emotional states, emotions affect the VB alone. In the case of strong emotions, the VB also bombards the ARAS with stimulation, and cortical arousal occurs also. Neuroticism thus is characterized by an overarousal of the VB, which chronically spills over into cortical arousal, thus impeding rational thinking. This may affect introverts and extroverts differently at various levels of stress (Eysenck, 1970, p. 437)

In 1975 the Eysenck Personality Questionnaire added psychoticism as a third dimension of personality, completing the PEN (psychoticism, extroversion, neuroticism) paradigm. Eysenck defines the psychoticism dimension as "unspecific vulnerability" (Eysenck & Eysenck, 1985, p. 64). It may be a blend of nonplanning impulsivity, boredom susceptibility, and experience seeking (p. 71). Persons of unusual ability may also be high P scorers. Some biological correlates have been found, such as the effect of LSD on the P factor and the higher levels of a human leukocyte antigen (HLA B–27) in schizophrenics scoring high on the P factor (p. 67). Although evidence for the P factor seems solid, its theoretical interpretation is not yet fully unified. Eysenck's theory moves beyond trait classification to the level of verifiable theoretical prediction and more precise diagnostic and treatment applications. It is therefore surprising to see that currently the field seems to be returning to a more descriptive stance.

The Big Five. Goldberg, McCrae, and Costa, and others (Goldberg, 1993), returning to a Cattell-like study of the language used to describe personality, reached, with some excitement, a consensus that there should be five personality factors rather than three. They are: surgency (or extroversion), agreeableness, conscientiousness, emotional stability (versus neuroticism), and openness to experience (also called intellect or culture). This is an ongoing debate. Eysenck disagrees and holds to his three PEN factors, while Cattell judges that five is too small a number. This is theory in the making.

References

Allport, G. W., & Odbert, H. S. (1936). Trait names: A psycholexical study. *Psychological Monographs, 47,* 63–171.

Cattell, R. B. (1964). *Personality and social psychology.* San Diego, CA: Knapp.

Cattell, R. B. (1965). *The scientific analysis of personality.* Baltimore: Penguin.

Cattell, R. B., & Kline, P. (1977). *The scientific analysis of personality and motivation.* New York: Academic.

Cattell, R. B., Saunders, D. R., & Stice, G. F. (1950). *The Sixteen Personality Factor Questionnaire.* Champaign, IL: Institute for Personality and Ability Testing.

Eysenck, H. J. (1967). *The biological basis of personality.* Springfield, IL.: Thomas.

Eysenck, H. J. (1970). *The structure of human personality.* London: Methuen.

Eysenck, H. J., & Eysenck M. W. (1985). *Personality and individual differences: A natural science approach.* New York: Plenum.

Goldberg, L. R. (1993). The structure of phenotypic personality traits. *American Psychologist, 48* (1), 26–34.

L. R. JOHNSON

See PERSONALITY; PERSONALITY ASSESSMENT; INTROVERSION-EXTRAVERSION.

Faculty Psychology. Within philosophy a number of theories have been put forward to account for various mental activities. Many of these have taken the form of faculty psychologies. A faculty psychology is a philosophical doctrine that ascribes a number of powers to the mind. These powers, or faculties, are the method by which the mind exercises its influence. They represent not so much substructures as forces for implementing mental activity. It is assumed that the mind normally is unitary but accomplishes its ends through multiple faculties. Originally faculties were descriptions of mental activity; later they became explanations. The existence of the faculties was deduced from observations of behavior that resembled the assumed underlying faculty.

A primitive faculty psychology is found in Plato's *Republic.* The mind is tripartite and its powers prioritized. Of highest value is intellect, located in the head, desired in rulers. Volition (spirit) is housed in the chest and is the source of courage for warriors. The lowest faculty, appetite, is located in the abdomen and is found in largest measure in artisans, tradesmen, and slaves. The relative development of faculties and the resulting division of labor ordered society (Heidbreder, 1933). The intellect strove for understanding, the spirit motivated one toward success, and the appetite sought bodily pleasure (Watson, 1978). These faculties were revised by Augustine as reason, memory, and will. Imagination is a lesser faculty that mediates between memory and reason.

Aristotle suggested the psychic functions are nutrition, sensation, and reason. Like expanding sets of rings, growth defines living nature, sensation highlights animal nature, and reason defines human nature. Thomas Aquinas, in the Aristotelian tradition, held that the soul exercises its powers through the faculties of reason, sensing, and appetite. The senses are divided into the five exterior senses and the four interior senses of common sense, estimation and cogitation, imagination, and memory.

In the work of René Descartes the mind retains its unity, but the faculties are reduced to two. Volition is unlimited; it provides for freedom of choice and is a means to account for error. Understanding is limited; it is aided by imagination, memory, and the senses.

Faculty psychologies reached their highest influence in the eighteenth century in "the systematization of mental science" (Kantor, 1969, p. 134). The German Christian von Wolff and the Scottish school of Thomas Reid, Dugald Stewart, Thomas Brown, and William Hamilton reacted to the atomizing and naturalizing of the mind advocated by British associationists David Hume and David Hartley. The mental scientists abhorred the fragmentation of mind into a collection of associations and maintained rather the unity of mind (soul). Further, they attempted to incorporate classical theological dogma into the new psychology and adjust theological accounts to fit the newly acquired scientific data regarding the mind.

The soul, according to Wolff, is the entity that makes one aware of self and outside events. Activities of the soul are accomplished through the faculties of cognition (which includes sensing, perceiving, apperceiving, attending, imagining, and remembering) and volition (which includes affections, appetites, and aversions). What marked cognition as distinct from volition is the former's clarity (cf. Descartes's analysis).

Reid extended the system by defining the mind as that which thinks, remembers, reasons, and wills. The body has certain properties, but the mind has its operations. "*Faculty* is most properly applied to those powers of the mind which are original and natural, and which make a part of the constitution of the mind" (Reid, cited by Kantor, 1969, p. 150). This stood in direct opposition to the British associationists' empiricism. The mind's faculties are listed as consciousness, sensation, perception, attention, association, memory, reason, feelings, passions, instinct, and will. In Reid's return to mentalism even bodily forces are faculties of the mind.

Hamilton represents an eclecticism of Scottish faculty psychology and British associationism. Each of the five mental faculties has one or more processes. The presentative faculty is evidenced in sensation and perception. Attention and memory constitute the processes of the conservative faculty. Association is the basis for the reproductive faculty, while imagination is instrumental in the elaborative faculty. The regulative faculty subsumes the processes of abstraction, classification, and conditioning.

As more came to be known about mental capacities and the structure of the brain, the number of faculties multiplied. In the phrenology of Franz Joseph Gall (1758–1828) and Johann Kaspar Spurzheim (1776–1832), the brain is envisioned as the secretory organ for mental processes. Highly developed mental processes depend on localized mental function and specialized brain structure. Cortical structures are the sites for some 37 mental faculties. The charlantanlike activities of Gall and Spurzheim and the multiplicity of faculties made phrenology the last faculty psychology. In spite of onerous reputations, faculty psychology and phrenology contributed to the development of modern neuroscience.

References

Heidbreder, E. (1933). *Seven psychologies*. New York: Appleton-Century-Crofts.

Kantor, J. R. (1969). *The scientific evolution of psychology* (Vol. 2). Chicago: Principia.

Watson, R. I. (1978). *The great psychologists* (4th ed.). Philadelphia: Lippincott.

R. L. TIMPE

See PSYCHOLOGY, HISTORY OF.

Failure, Fear of. *See* LEVEL OF ASPIRATION.

Fair Fight Training. *See* ASSERTIVENESS TRAINING; CREATIVE AGGRESSION THERAPY.

Faith. Faith is the inner posture of the psyche oriented in trust toward a proximate or an ultimate source of meaning and security. A proximate source may be a person who is trusted in a relationship or a truth proposition or statement that persuades or convinces one. Thus *faith* is a term that is also used to identify a religious system or worldview. It results in action appropriate to the posture of the faith. Our wills (*see* Will) are free within the constraints of that upon which our hearts are set. That to which our hearts are devoted is the object of our faith, and that devotion is the faith that shapes our worldviews. Some writers speak of faith as an ethereal assurance of that which cannot be known with certainty (Heb. 11). John Calvin thought that faith is the sure knowledge of God and of God's promises and the certain confidence that God directs all things to their appointed ends. The epistle of James counsels that faith cannot be separated from action or vice versa. The epistle to the Hebrews lists illustrations of faith in action, all of which depict heroic risk taking to keep one's worldview and life consonant with the posture of one's psyche toward God.

The Oxford English Dictionary defines faith as a confidence, reliance, and trust, describing it as a belief proceeding from reliance on testimony or authority. This emphasizes the crucial characteristic of the biblical-theological concept of faith as the trust and assurance we have on the good authority of experience, namely, that of the prophets and apostles in their testimony to their experience with God, that of the believing community in its scriptural witness to its experience of the mighty acts of God, and that of the historic church in its creedal confessions regarding its experience of the grace and providence of God in history. This trust, based upon warrantable and authoritative witness to empirical experience in history, is embedded in the Latin *credo* and is the original denotation of the English word *believe*. To believe is to set one's heart upon an object of warrantable worth. The inner disposition and the externalized active component are both present in this expression, implying the entrustment that is inherent to the Greek *pistis*, the common New Testament term for faith.

Psychological Contributions. Delacroix, an early-twentieth-century psychologist of religion, emphasized that faith tends to create cultural and institutional religious systems. He termed this authoritative faith and distinguished it from reasoning faith (belief) and trusting faith (action). This dimension provides for a person's need to identify with a given religious tradition as *the* faith for that person. Religious institutions in a culture provide this dimension with their creeds, rituals, and traditions. Delacroix's differentiation provided a basis for understanding people who identify themselves as members of the Christian faith, Judaism, or Islam, for example, as distinct from each other and other traditions. He suggested that adjustment and conformity are the dynamic processes operating in this dimension of the function of faith, just as reason, emotion, and empirical experience with God are inherent in the other dimensions.

Most psychological understandings of faith have depended heavily on the proposal of the psychotheologian Schleiermacher, who early in the nineteenth century suggested faith is "a feeling of dependence" in which the individual has an intense experience of powerlessness coupled with an absolute reliance on the strength of a transcendent reality, God. Søren Kierkegaard continued this emphasis with his depiction of faith as based on a "sickness unto death" that propels a person to make the "leap of faith" into the absolute assurances of the grace of God.

In this century Leuba built on the ideas of Schleiermacher and Kierkegaard and detailed the components of what he termed the "faith state." Faith is always preceded by a period of self-dissatisfaction and a yearning for enlightenment. Leuba compared this prefaith period to that of symptoms in a disease in which a person fears a breakdown and seeks resolution or relief. The higher state is envisioned but seems out of reach. The resolution of this turmoil becomes the dominant preoccupation of the individual's mental life. Leuba suggested that when faith arrives, it is characterized by two inner experiences. First, the person feels that nothing else matters now that faith has come. Second, the intensity of joy and peace that results from surrendering to God is greater than any before experienced. Leuba believed that faith is primarily an emotion and that these faith feelings provide the certainty with which people assert the truthfulness of their beliefs.

Leuba's ideas are similar to the "shift of energy" theory proposed by William James as an explanation for religious experience. This has been identified with faith by many theorists. James suggested that in religion the mind focuses its energy on the faith experience and excludes much else that might be distracting or troubling it. This theory provides the basis for his assertion that religious experience can integrate a person and provide a central purpose for life.

The most recent theorizing about faith has been done by a developmental psychologist and theologian, Fowler, who has defined faith as the "making and maintaining of meaning in life" (1981). He follows H. R. Niebuhr and Tillich in asserting that faith is a universal human concern in that one of the unique aspects of being human is a need to find meaning. Thus faith is the experience of becoming "ultimately concerned" in the sense that faith is that which ties life together finally or ultimately.

Stages of Faith Development. Fowler has been concerned primarily with delineating the developmental stages by which faith unfolds in human lives. In this endeavor he has relied heavily on the thinking of three scholars: Erik Erikson, a neoanalytic ego psychologist who has written about the several stages of identity formation and social development; Jean Piaget, a cognitive psychologist who has written about the cognitive development of mental structures that make thinking possible; and Lawrence Kohlberg, a philosophical psychologist who has applied Piaget's theory and models to moral development.

Fowler proposes six stages of faith after infancy, which he describes as an "undifferentiated faith" period. He suggests that the theorists noted above contributed to his understanding of these stages by their emphasis on how people know what they know (epistemology); the structure rather than the content, of faith; and the interactional, as contrasted with the behavioral or the maturational, dimensions of development. As contrasted with these theorists, Fowler emphasizes a spiraling as opposed to a hierarchical or a linear model of development and perceives faith as dealing primarily with the logic of conviction as opposed to the logic of rational certainty (Aden, Benner, & Ellens, 1992).

Following Erikson, Fowler sees infancy as a prefaith stage in which basic trust is the chief quest and the crucial result of good parent–child interaction. The mutuality, hope, and love that emerge from such experience provide the basis for faith in the later stages and can be distorted either by

overindulgence, which leads to narcissism, or negligence, which leads to isolation and distrust.

Stage 1 typically occurs from ages 3 to 7 and is termed intuitive-projective faith, in that the need for meaning is fashioned by fantasy-filled, imitative interactions with the overt faith of the primary adults in the child's life. Self-awareness comes into being during this time, and the child becomes aware for the first time of death, sex, and taboos that are central to cultural faith. The emergent strength of this stage is imagination, while the danger is that the child's mind will be filled with terror.

Stage 2 typically occurs at about 10 years of age and is termed mythic-literal faith, in that the need for meaning is fashioned by the child affirming for himself or herself the stories, beliefs, and observances that indicate belonging to the community of faith with which he or she is soon to identify. The imagination of the previous stage is curbed and channeled into an almost literal acceptance of the symbols of the faith culture in which the child lives. The emergent strength of this stage is the ability to live through story and drama, which give coherence to experience, while there is danger in the overliteral acceptance of the factual truth of the stories.

Stage 3 is typical of the adolescent years and is termed synthetic-conventional faith, in that the need for meaning is fashioned by identification with others beyond the family and an affirmation of the interpersonal dimension of the faith experience. The literalness of the previous stage is replaced with the vitality of present experiences with others. The emergent strength of this stage is that the individual begins to form a personal story of faith identity, while the dangers lie in a possible overconformity to others' wishes and a too-intense reliance on other persons who may betray such trust.

Stage 4 is typical of the adult years (20 to 30) and is termed individuative-reflective faith, in that the need for meaning is fashioned by the assumption of responsibility for fashioning one's own commitments, lifestyle, beliefs, and attitudes. Although many persons remain at stage 3, those who move to stage 4 have to face the tension of individuality and the reality of personal feelings that may have been suppressed. The emergent strength of this stage lies in the critical capacity to reflect on identity (self) and on outlook (ideology), while there is the danger of becoming overconfident in one's ability to critically examine one's faith.

Stage 5 is typical of middle adulthood and is termed conjunctive faith, in that the need for meaning is fashioned by acquisition of the ability to do both/and rather than either/or thinking. In this stage, when it occurs, the individual becomes able both to trust others and the traditions they represent and to reflect in a critical manner on any and all conventions. Fowler calls this dialogical knowing. It involves a new reworking of one's past and an integration of convictions and feelings in a new unity. The emergent strength of this stage is the acquisition of ironic imagination in which one can be in, but not of, one's surroundings, while the danger is the possibility that one will become passive and inactive due to this newfound insight.

Stage 6, which does not usually appear before late adulthood, if it appears at all, is termed universalizing faith, in that the need for meaning is fashioned by an overcoming of the paradoxes of stage 5 and an active involvement in the imperatives of love and justice as an expression of faith. The emergent strength of this stage is the perception of the truths beneath the creeds of traditional religion and the willingness to become involved in bringing about the order to which these religions point (e.g., the kingdom of God). The danger of this stage is possible disillusionment that may result when success does not come.

In all of the stages there is the implicit assumption that faith is a universal necessity and that it can be more or less mature, depending upon the individual. Fuller (1988), in his lifecycle approach to faith development, has demonstrated definitively how crucial faith is to enabling and empowering the human potential for making the transition from one stage to the next in life's unfolding. He has pointed out that our capacity to believe in transcendent hope and the ultimate coherence of the universe in God makes it possible for us to expand our paradigms with a sense of security at each stage's boundary, namely, the location at which the model of the earlier stage no longer adequately contains or meaningfully manages the expanding data of our experience and thought. Later studies of faith development have both supported and raised serious questions about Fowler's theory and model. A lifecycle approach to faith development adds a necessary dimension to Fowler's structural-cognitive approach (Aden, Benner, & Ellens, 1992).

References

Aden, L., Benner, D. G., & Ellens, J. H. (1992). *Christian perspectives on human development*. Grand Rapids, MI: Baker.

Fowler, J. W. (1981). *Stages of faith*. San Francisco: Harper and Row.

Fuller, R. C. (1988). *Religion and the life cycle*. Philadelphia: Fortress.

Additional Reading

Dykstra, C. R., & Parks, S. (Eds.). (1986). *Faith development and Fowler*. Birmingham, AL: Religious Education Press.

J. H. ELLENS AND H. N. MALONY

See DOUBT; RELIGIOUS DEVELOPMENT; CHRISTIAN GROWTH.

Faith Healing. In the United States faith healing is most commonly associated with miracles and religion. One imagines an emotionally charged gathering in which an enthusiastic, charismatic preacher exhorts members of the audience to trust in God, throw down their crutches, and claim their cure. The miracle services led by Kathryn Kuhlman followed this pattern. Healing obtained in such a setting is usually attributed by the participants to a divine intervention that sets aside the natural laws governing the course of physical illness. The sufferer's belief or faith in God is seen as the key to this miraculous event.

In the popular and scientific literature the term *faith healing* is used in a variety of contexts. Psychic healing, chiropractic, folk medicine, and shamanism, as well as religious or sacramental healing, have all been referred to as faith healing. Some authors seem to use the term interchangeably with nonmedical treatment. Others use it in a pejorative fashion to connote quackery or primitive or unscientific technique.

Faith healing has long been one of the more controversial topics in both the medical and religious communities. Nor has the debate over the validity of the phenomenon raged solely between the two camps, for each has been divided within its own ranks. The lines of argument have often been drawn absolutely, leading to incredible claims for the healing efficacy of religious faith on the one hand and to blind rejection of genuine extramedical healing phenomena on the other.

The resolution of at least some of this conflict has come in the research on psychosomatic relationships, which has made the concept of faith healing acceptable to the religious and scientific-minded alike. Studies in such areas as biofeedback and meditation have demonstrated the mind's ability to influence bodily function. Among others, Simonton's cancer research suggests that visual imagery and positive changes in attitude can alter the course of illness, even to the point of total remission of cancer symptoms (Simonton, Matthews-Simonton, & Creighton, 1978). There is by now a host of research findings correlating changes in attitude, feeling, or belief with changes in the body, thus providing an empirical base for what has been observed phenomenologically for millennia; namely, that faith healing often "works."

However, what is known of psychosomatics fails to account for the rare but well-documented cases of instantaneous and total cure of diseases otherwise thought to be incurable and the rejuvenation of organ systems thought to be beyond repair (cf. Clapp, 1983).

Two concepts of faith healing will be addressed here. First, the term *faith healing* often refers to any process whereby positive physical change correlates with and is apparently caused or mediated by changes in the individual's values, attitudes, or beliefs. While virtually every healing is probably affected by the person's disposition toward it, faith healing in this first sense refers to healing in which the primary cause or mediating influence appears to be faith, understood psychologically.

Note that this is a psychological rather than a religious or theological understanding of faith healing and that the content of one's beliefs may or may not relate to the divine. Faith healing in the psychological sense is differentiated from medical or surgical healing, in which the presumed cause is chemical or physical, and from psychic healing, in which the presumed cause is some power transmitted from or through the healer.

This first concept of faith healing is further differentiated from a second common usage, in which the term relates to miraculous healing, or healing occurring in contradiction to what is considered possible through medical/surgical or psychological intervention. Within the Christian religious community the presumed cause of such faith healing is God.

History. Healing by faith is an old tradition. In antiquity it often centered around religious ritual. The Greeks, for instance, believed that disease was the work of the gods and that cures required the intervention of other gods, such as Asclepius. Accordingly, people would journey far to one of his temples, there to sleep and, they hoped, to receive a healing vision of the god. Testimonial plaques left by some pilgrims attest to cures of blindness, lameness, paralysis, baldness, and a multitude of other ailments. Old Testament Hebrews also placed healing within the province of religion, believing that sickness was a result of sin, and therefore healing was a task reserved for the Levites and other religious figures.

Healing was an integral part of Jesus' ministry, and he also taught his followers to heal. Faith seems to have been a critical ingredient in at least some of these healings, in that Jesus often used the phrase, "Your faith has made you whole" (Mark 10:52). By contrast, on other occasions the utter disbelief of his audience apparently prevented healing from occurring (Mark 6:5–6).

Since the time of Christ there have been groups and individuals within the Christian church who have continued Jesus' emphasis on healing through faith. For example, since the mid-nineteenth century thousands of pilgrims yearly have journeyed to a shrine in Lourdes, France, in search of healing at the spring there. The shrine was constructed at the site of a young girl's vision of a woman calling herself the Immaculate Conception. The Roman Catholic church has since carefully documented numerous cures (actually a very small fraction of the cures sought) obtained there that defy medical explanation.

Until recently, however, the church as a whole had largely departed from the ministry of healing. Kelsey (1973) traces this official departure to about the tenth century, when the service of unction for healing was gradually transformed into extreme unction, a rite of passage for the dying. Subsequently a whole theology arose to show why the "gift of healing" disappeared and is no longer a proper concern of Christianity. As Kelsey demonstrates, however, more recent theology and practice have reinstated healing by faith into the fabric of the church. Today it is practiced widely across the Christian denominations.

Psychological Approaches to Faith Healing. Psychological studies of faith healing have approached it from many directions, including the interpersonal, situational, psychophysiological, and intrapersonal dimensions of the phenomenon.

Social factors have been shown to have a powerful influence on healing, as is clearly demonstrated in research on the placebo effect in medicine. Placebo medications (usually saline or lactose), which have no specific chemical activity for the condition being treated, bring symptom relief in about a third of the cases in which they are used (Beecher, 1955). The active ingredient appears to be the patient's belief in the medication, which is affected in turn by the doctor-patient relationship (Shapiro, 1964). In general the doctor who is warm, empathic, friendly, reassuring, and not conflicted about the patient or the treatment elicits positive placebo reactions, whereas the doctor who is angry, rejecting of the patient, or preoccupied with personal problems is more likely to elicit negative placebo reactions. Presumably any interpersonal variables affecting the doctor's ability to persuade the patient (cf. Frank, 1961) would be relevant. The doctor's own belief in the medication's efficacy also affects the patient's response, since the placebo effect increases if the doctor is told that the agent is active and not a placebo.

Patient variables thought to influence faith, and thereby healing, have often been studied under the rubric of suggestibility or susceptibility to interpersonal influence (Calestro, 1972). One broad area of research has tested hypotheses linking suggestibility to personality traits, various neurotic disorders, or other patient variables such as sex and age (Shapiro, 1964). Another line of research has studied the elements of communication that enhance attitude change. Compatibility of the patient's assumptive world or system of belief with that of the doctor or healer is one important factor.

Still another relevant area of study is that of psychosomatic research, which addresses the broad question, Under what conditions will what thoughts, feelings, beliefs, or attitudes produce what sorts of physiological changes and by what psychophysical mechanisms or pathways? For example, placebos have been hypothesized to act via the cerebral cortex, which activates elements of the endocrine system, thereby producing specific chemical changes in the body that promote healing.

Still, understanding the factors that enhance faith or the pathways by which it operates does not necessarily bring one to an understanding of faith itself.

Phenomenologically we observe that one has faith that something is the case when it does not occur to one to doubt it. A nearly parallel expression is that faith is the lack of resistance to that which one hopes to receive. These expressions imply two things. First, faith has cognitive content. That is, some situation or event is anticipated, based on a specific set of beliefs about the way things are—beliefs that may or may not have religious content. Second, faith involves an openness or a positive expectation that this event or situation will occur or is already occurring.

At this point existential psychology further illuminates our understanding of faith. To the existentialist faith is more appropriately conceived as faithing, that is, an act that one undertakes with the totality of one's being. Faith may be seen as the decision on the part of the self to open itself to the possibility of completion or growth. Such an act is the response of the person to life itself. It is the will to live—one's willingness to be. This act of opening oneself may be the key that unlocks the body's own healing resources. Faith healing is often seen simply as a facilitator of spontaneous remission.

A Transpersonal Approach to Faith Healing. There is possibly another aspect to faith healing; namely, a transpersonal dimension. One is forced into considering such a possibility by those cases of miraculous or instantaneous healing that apparently go beyond psychosomatics.

Viewed in this fashion faith is understood as that internal state of being "in which alone God can get near enough to man to do *his* work. The power of faith is, in one sense, nil. It is the state of personality in which God can exert *his* power" (Weatherhead, 1951, p. 431). In this religious concept of faith a person may be conceived as essentially spirit and healing as resulting from his or her faithing response to and joining with Spirit, or God. Faith then is an existential openness, a "thirst and a desire that moves man toward the Absolute" (Panikkar, 1971, p. 223).

This view of faith does not supplant psychological approaches to faith healing, since the transpersonal dimension of faith is seen either as orthogonal to its psychosomatic dimension or as prior to it in the sense of being an ultimate cause, with the psychosomatic relationship being the proximate cause of the healing.

A Christian Critique. Misunderstanding of the nature and purpose of faith in healing has led to serious distortions within the church. While there is a relationship between health (conceived holistically rather than purely physically) and holiness (conceived as right relationship with God), some Christians believe that failure to be healed implies some fault on the sufferer's part (namely, a lack of religious faith) and consequently stigmatize those who are not cured. Others will die refusing medical or other physical assistance, believing that sickness is sent from God to punish sin and must therefore be endured unless and until one can please God with appropriate faith.

Yet the concept of healing by faith is clearly rooted in the teachings of Jesus. Faith, whether considered in its psychological or religious aspect, is integral to healing. A balanced perspective on faith and healing would accept the help that psychology and medicine can afford, while at the same time being open to the possibility of miracles.

Whether such anomalous healing is the result of an unknown psychophysical mechanism, the direct intervention of the Deity, or something akin to the inner shift of which *A Course in Miracles* (Foundation for Inner Peace, 1975) speaks is yet unknown. The research problems inherent in any attempt to answer this question are enormous and probably insurmountable, although one may venture to discover the answer experientially.

References

Beecher, H. K. (1955). The powerful placebo. *Journal of the American Medical Association, 159,* 1602–1606.

Calestro, K. M. (1972). Psychotherapy, faith healing, and suggestion. *International Journal of Psychiatry, 10* (2), 83–113.

Clapp, R. (1983). Faith healing: A look at what's happening. *Christianity Today, 27* (19), 12–17.

Foundation for Inner Peace (1975). *A course in miracles* (3 vols.). Tiburon, CA: Author.

Frank, J. D. (1961). *Persuasion and healing: A comparative study of psychotherapy.* Baltimore: Johns Hopkins University Press.

Kelsey, M. T. (1973). *Healing and Christianity.* New York: Harper & Row.

Panikkar, R. (1971). Faith—A constitutive dimension of man. *Journal of Ecumenical Studies, 8* (2), 223–254.

Shapiro, A. K. (1964). Factors contributing to the placebo effect. *American Journal of Psychotherapy, 18* (Supplement No. 1), 73–88.

Simonton, O. C., Matthews-Simonton, S., & Creighton, J. (1978). *Getting well again.* Los Angeles: Tarcher.

Weatherhead, L. D. (1951). *Psychology, religion, and healing.* Nashville: Abingdon.

Additional Reading

Frazier, C. A. (Ed.). (1973). *Faith healing: Finger of God or scientific curiosity?* Nashville: Nelson.

B. Van Dragt

See Transpersonal Psychology.

False Memory Syndrome. A pattern of memory or memories, usually traumatic, for events that did not occur but that are regarded by the person as real. The content of these alleged false memories most often centers on childhood sexual or ritual abuse. The existence of such an unofficial syndrome is highly debatable and is the subject of a great deal of public, legal, and professional discussion.

Proponents of the existence of such a syndrome are well represented by the False Memory Syndrome Foundation of Philadelphia. The FMSF, founded in 1992, has on its scientific and professional advisory board many highly respected mental health professionals (False Memory Syndrome Foundation, 1995). The FMSF includes many parents who claim they have been falsely accused by their adult children of childhood abuse. These adult children often uncovered long-hidden and forgotten memories of tragic abuse while in psychotherapy. Proponents of the false memory syndrome assert that the retrieval of these memories is induced by therapists who have a vested interest in manipulating their clients into retrieving such memories.

Opponents who seriously doubt the existence of a false memory syndrome likewise include an impressive array of psychological and psychiatric professionals. They assert that an organization such as the FMSF can become a haven for guilty parties who are strongly motivated to continue hiding and/or denying their guilt. "In a psychotherapeutically inspired double-bind typical of our times, denial itself is evidence of . . . *denial*, the pathological indicator that makes declarations of innocence virtual proof of guilt" (Wylie, 1993, p. 20).

The public debate among professionals over this issue has intensified in the light of two major developments in the legal field. First, many states have substantially altered laws regarding statutes of limitation. Now the time limit for pressing charges regarding childhood crimes is calculated from the time the memory of a crime or tort resurfaces or in some cases after recovery from the retrieval of such memories rather than from the time the crime or tort was committed. Thus it is possible for victims to pursue justice in legal and civil courts long after it would be otherwise be possible. Second, highly publicized court decisions in favor of those alleging the creation of false memories by unscrupulous psychotherapists have substantially increased the almost palpable tension surrounding this controversial issue.

In many ways this issue revolves around extended families that are significantly disrupted by false or true allegations of abuse. The founding of the FMSF itself represents just such an unresolved family dispute. Prominent among the founders are Pamela Freyd and her husband, who was accused of substantial childhood sexual abuse by their daughter, Jennifer J. Freyd, a professor of psychology at the University of Oregon (Freyd, 1993).

Observers of this highly charged debate note that verification of childhood abuse memories is difficult given the private nature of these crimes. Arguments advanced by either side in this debate are quickly countered by the other side. Both sides are quick to impugn the motives of their opponents. Professionals aligned in support of the syndrome tend to represent the research side of the discipline, and professionals who question the widespread occurrence of this syndrome tend to come from the clinical side of the mental health field.

Arguments in Favor. Those who feel that most if not all of recovered memories of childhood abuse are false point out that therapists often suggest hidden abuse before the client is aware of any such history. The suggestion then shapes emerging material until the client uncovers what had previously been repressed or otherwise hidden in the mind. Strident charges against therapists who specialize in working with adult abuse victims associate them with the child abuse industry. The media has reported instances of pseudoclients who seek psychotherapy services from therapists who are known for treating large numbers of childhood abuse victims. These pseudoclients report intense pressure from these therapists to acknowledge that the best explanation for their presenting problem is that they were abused as children.

Proponents of the existence of the syndrome also point out the unreliable nature of human memory. An emerging body of scientific literature demonstrates that under laboratory conditions memories can indeed be induced; that memory retrieval can be partial, confabulated, and unreliable; and that when and if traumatic amnesia does occur it usually reflects one large block of time rather than a selective amnesia for discrete episodes separated by time (Loftus, 1993). Researchers assert that evidence is lacking to support the recovery of memories as widely reported by supposed victims. It is important to note that empirical foundations are lacking for many other, nondisputed features of psychotherapy.

FMSF members are quick to admit that child abuse does occur and that it is a major travesty in our times. But they maintain that abuse does not occur at the rates suggested by the current epidemic of reports. Proponents of the syndrome insist that such a terrible background could not possibly characterize these accused parents who are so reputable in every other way, although appearance and status are not necessarily reliable guides to one's innocence of secret, sexual crimes. The controversy is all the more complicated by people who have recanted their earlier accusations of parental misconduct. Yet their recantings do not fully settle the matter either, since we cannot definitively establish when these persons are misguided: when they could not remember anything, when they remembered, or when they recanted?

Arguments Against. Arrayed against the preceding arguments is a set of propositions almost equally convincing. Clinicians who argue vigorously in favor of the veracity of recovered memories question the use of laboratory findings regarding memory encoding and retrieval as relevant evidence regarding traumatic memories. The trauma of childhood sexual abuse is so profound, these authors argue, that the child develops an adaptive, dissociated part of self that remains cut off from other conscious experience until later in life. This process is poorly understood, is different from classic repression in a psychoanalytic sense, yet is nonetheless real. Laboratory experiments regarding memory are thus interesting but not germane to the question at hand because this research is not linked to trauma.

Clinicians insist that the clinical evidence in favor of the truthfulness of these recovered memories is overwhelming and cannot be dismissed. The emotional agony with which these memories surface and the reluctance of clients to face them both speak to the reality of the recovered memories. Therapists insist that these memories surface for victimized clients even when the therapist has no known bias toward their recovery.

In response to the insistence voiced by proponents of the false memory syndrome that therapists must investigate any such emerging memories before proceeding with therapy, therapists insist that they cannot provide forensic or investigative services for these clients. The therapeutic role is much more circumscribed than that and does not allow therapists to become private investigators.

Opponents of the false memory syndrome as an explanation for all the clinical data that have emerged in the 1980s and 1990s are quick to admit that some incompetent therapists may indeed have been guilty of inappropriate therapeutic intervention with disturbed people who later came to believe that they were victims of childhood sexual abuse. Nonetheless, they insist, the vast majority of cases of recovered memory stem from the work of competent, careful therapists who have not led or swayed their clients in any way.

Conclusions. "Concerning the issue of a recovered versus a pseudomemory, like many questions in science, the final answer is yet to be known" (American Psychological Association, 1995, p. 1). Meanwhile, what do we know? We know that some abuse reports based on recovered memories have been confirmed by the perpetrators. We know that some reported beliefs based on recovered memories defy rational belief and most likely did not occur. We know that a minority of therapists are incompetent and some of them may well have overzealously coached clients in their retrieval process. We know the therapist's role as client advocate may at times make it difficult for the therapist to be as objective as an outsider would be. We know that memory encoding and retrieval are minimally understood by researchers. And we know that sometimes a time lag occurs between the time when clinical work uncovers some new, undiscovered feature of human reality and when empirical science can confidently confirm or disconfirm those findings. All of these certainties do not allow us, however, to settle completely the controversies surrounding the issue of recovered memories and their exact implications.

References

American Psychological Association (1995). *Questions and answers about memories of childhood abuse* [Pamphlet]. Washington, DC: Author.

False Memory Syndrome Foundation (1995). *Frequently asked questions*. [Pamphlet]. Philadelphia: Author.

Freyd, J. J. (1993). Personal perspectives on the delayed memory debate. *Treating Abuse Today, 3* (5), 13–20.

Loftus, E. F. (1993). The reality of repressed memories. *American Psychologist, 48* (5), 518–537.

Wylie, M. S. (1993). The shadow of a doubt. *The Family Therapy Newtworker, 17* (5), 19–29, 70, 73.

J. R. Beck

See Memory; Abuse and Neglect; Hypnosis; Hypnotherapy.

False Pregnancy. *See* Pseudocyesis.

Family Choreography. A variation of the family therapy technique known as sculpting. The method involves asking family members to physically arrange themselves in various positions to create a picture of how they perceive themselves as a group. Individuals are requested to place themselves in the family tableau and to assume postures and expressions that describe their feelings about being in the family (Papp, 1976).

An angry, domineering father, for example, might stand on a chair angrily pointing at a rebellious son below. The son is facing the door as if he were about to leave the family. The mother has hold of the back of his shirt while she gives the father a pleading look.

Choreography is ordinarily used at the beginning of therapy as a diagnostic aid. The family can also be choreographed according to the ideal of each of its members. Choreographing the family as it is and as it would like to be helps to identify relationship changes needed within the family.

Reference

Papp, P. (1976). Family choreography. In P. J. Guerin, Jr. (Ed.), *Family therapy: Theory and practice*. New York: Gardner.

J. A. Larsen

See Family Sculpture Technique; Family Therapy: Overview.

Family Communications Theory. Family communications theory involves the study of communication processes within the context of the family. It is based on that premise that communication is an integral part of every relationship and that I cannot *not* communicate since everything I say or do participates in the communication that is already happening. Every communication has multiple meanings and occurs on both a conscious and unconscious, verbal and nonverbal, level. Family communication theory focuses on the patterns of interaction and communication in a relationship rather than on the individual psyche because beliefs and behaviors are seen as inextricably intertwined with their interpersonal context. The family is viewed as a system of mutual and interdependent relationships in which the behavior of an individual member has meaning only when viewed within that context.

Family Communications Theory

Key Concepts. Communication involves both the sending and receiving of information and the process of creating and sharing meanings in a relationship. Every communication includes both a report component that conveys information and a command component that includes a metamessage about the relationship itself. The report component provides the information necessary for daily functioning and problem solving in the relationship. The metamessage is an editorial comment about the relationship that can confirm the worth of the individuals sending the message or disconfirm it by casting doubt on their reliability or undermining their definition of reality.

When there is an incongruency between the reporting or informational and the command or metamessage aspects of a communication, the receiver of the message may be put in a double bind. This occurs when the overt meaning of the message is contradicted by a metamessage (perhaps at the level of tone of voice or context) and the receiver is not allowed to comment on the contradiction. For example, a parent's warning that "If you do that, I will severely punish you" may be accompanied by the nonverbal metamessage "Do not think of me as a punishing person or I will punish you." The child may experience a double bind because the parent's informational message and actions contradict both the parent's metacommunication and the child's own perception of the situation. Seemingly aberrant behavior may ensue when the child is not able to resolve these incongruencies, comment on the contradictions, or withdraw from the conflict.

Communication theorists analyze the informational and metamessages using a systems model of communication. All communication is seen as involving a source or a sender who encodes a message that travels through a channel and is then received and decoded by a receiver. The receiver responds or provides feedback to the original sender's message and initiates a new cycle of communication in which he or she becomes the message source or sender. The clarity of the communication is influenced by factors such as the amount of noise or interference in the communication channel, the context of the communication interchange, and the interpretive frameworks or codebooks whereby both sender and receiver match verbal and nonverbal symbols with meanings. In analyzing the communication, theorists focus on the sequence or pattern of interactions in the ongoing dialogue rather than on a single communication exchange.

Jenkins (1995) outlines four theoretical perspectives of the communication process: mechanistic, psychological, interactional, and pragmatic or systemic. The mechanistic approach views the process of family interaction process as a communication machine that can be reduced to its component parts (e.g., message, channel, sender and receiver, encoding and decoding) and the barriers and breakdowns in communication corrected. The psycho-logical perspective enhances the mechanistic approach by also paying attention to the internal conceptual filters (e.g., attitudes, beliefs, drives, cognitions, self-concepts) that influence how individuals respond to their external stimulus field or informational environment. The interactional orientation is based on symbolic-interaction theory and focuses on the symbolic nature of communication and the processes whereby people create, interpret, and act upon shared meanings through social interaction. The pragmatic approach views verbal and nonverbal acts or behaviors as the primary unit of communication and analysis.

Communication is the process whereby families negotiate shared meanings and establish and maintain their form, structure, and interpersonal relationships. In family communication theory, the family unit is viewed as a system in which the whole is greater than the sum of its parts. The continuous exchange and flow of information within the family system and between the family system and its external environment is the lifeblood that enables the family to maintain itself and adapt and respond to challenges and problems. Family communication theory draws upon the working assumptions shared by family therapy theories, namely, that families are a principal source of mental health and psychopathology, family interaction patterns influence the health and character of the family (and these patterns often repeat across generations), an individual's symptoms frequently have meaning within the context of the family's interaction patterns or worldview, family flexibility is the core trait that prevents dysfunction, and family health requires a balance of connection and individuation (Doherty & Baptiste, 1993).

Communication in Families of Schizophrenics. The development of family communications theory was strongly influenced by research and clinical work with the families of schizophrenics. Schizophrenic individuals display communication disorders such as disjointed and tangential conversation and abrupt transitions from abstract and overly metaphorical language to overly concrete and literal speech. Their moods or affects are also contradictory and difficult to understand, and the hallucinations and delusions they experience may be conceptualized as difficulties in discriminating between the self and the outside world. The schizophrenic's unclear communication and difficulty in establishing boundaries between the self and the world led researchers to the primary arena (i.e., the family) in which children learn to communicate and develop a sense of themselves as separate from the world.

In studying the interactional patterns in families of schizophrenics, researchers have focused on communication clarity (e.g., incongruence between verbal content and nonverbal cues, double-bind messages), the ability of the family to exchange factual information for the purpose of problem solving, interfamilial metamessages of confirmation, support and validation, the family's level of conflict and tension, the quality of expressed emotion, and the distribution and structure of power within the family. The conclusion of this research (e.g., Jacob, 1987) appears to be that families of schizophrenics show a deficit in their ability to share a focus of attention, take the perspective of another, and communicate clearly, and that these families are characterized by high expressed emotion and a negative affective style (e.g., criticism, hostility, guilt induction, intrusiveness). However, critics have also suggested that these characteristics may not be precursors or causes of schizophrenia but rather reflect the family's response to the emergence of the disease and its accompanying stigma, burden, and social isolation.

Therapeutic Applications. Several practical therapeutic applications have emerged from family communications theory and research. The double-bind theory led to the development of the paradoxical intervention, which involves encouraging clients to continue with the very behavior they desire to stop. The double-bind theory suggests that pathological or symptomatic behavior is prompted because it is the only spontaneous action persons see as possible when their feelings are caught in a double bind. When the therapist prescribes the very symptom that is causing difficulties, the behavioral response is brought into conscious awareness and the person can no longer do it spontaneously or unconsciously. The patient either follows the therapist's counsel or refrains from engaging in the problem behavior. The result is a new paradoxical but therapeutic double bind: the client is "blessed if you do, and blessed if you don't."

Satir (1983) is the foremost family therapist to utilize communication theory in her work. In her approach, a patient's symptoms are seen as illustrative of a deeper problem within the family and serve the function of maintaining stability, or homeostasis, within the existing family structure. An individual's problem symptoms are also one way of communicating a family's request for help in a nonverbal way. Families can experience problems when their members have not learned to communicate properly, deliver or receive conflicting messages, experience difficulty adapting their interpretations to the present context, or are unable to check out their perceptions or interpretations. Family communication is also closely linked to the self-worth of its members because, at the highest level of abstraction, every message includes a metamessage that either validates or disconfirms the individual. Satir identifies four unhealthy communication styles that often emerge in family situations: the blamer, who identifies problems and who caused them; the placater, who seeks to please at all costs; the analyzer, who denies his or her own feelings and seeks to explain how others feel and interact; and the distractor, who offers many communicational messages but manages to keep the conversation away from the real issues and resists solving the underlying problem. Family communication patterns provide the therapist with insight into the source of the family's problems, and therapy seeks to correct discrepancies in communication patterns, teach communication skills, and help family members find ways of realizing and accomplishing mutually beneficial outcomes.

In working with Christian families, the concept that communication involves the decoding or translation of a message can be useful in helping individuals recognize that their understanding of what the Bible says (e.g., regarding husband-wife or parent-child relationships) includes an interpretative element shaped by their own expectations, values, experiences, and personality. The concept of metacommunication is also useful in guiding clients to recognize the need for congruency between their attitudes and nonverbal communication and the messages or values they are attempting to communicate. The Gospels highlight numerous instances where Christ expressed a scathing condemnation of the Pharisees because their lifestyle and actions were incongruent with their espoused beliefs and communication. James also argues that faith without works is dead (James 2:17) and emphasizes how it important it is that verbal affirmations are accompanied by consistent and congruent metacommunicative actions.

Critique. Family communications theory provides a valuable set of concepts and techniques for understanding and analyzing the communication patterns that characterize family interactions. The theory emphasizes the interpersonal nature of psychopathology and the importance of close family relationships and patterns of communication in understanding and responding to the symptomatic behavior of individual family members. Using communication as a primary variable also allows researchers to focus attention on one category of behavior across many levels of analysis. However, the belief that careful attention to the communication processes in families is all that is required to adequately describe and understand family interactions and the assumption that pathological behavior can be adequately described solely in terms of family communication patterns is limiting. The neglect of individual psychological factors and social influences such as ethnicity, race, gender, religion, and sociocultural and political environment also disregards important influences that shape belief and behavior.

From a Christian perspective, communication is at the heart of the gospel message. John describes Christ as the manifested Word of life that we "have seen and bear witness [to] and proclaim to you" (1 John 1:2, NASB). Christ as God incarnated communicates both the metamessage of God's love and compassion for us and the words of life that bring us into relationship with God. As Christians committed to sharing this good news, our communication is enhanced as we both embody the spirit and share the letter of God's message. Within the family of God, healthy communication and ongoing dialogue are essential components in the task of building, maintaining, or healing the relationships between family members—whether at the congregational, denominational, or corporate level. Ongoing communication and dialogue are also essential in calling or recalling all who are created in the image of God, but outside the family of God, to a redemptive experience and a restored relationship within the family of God.

References

Doherty, W. J., & Baptiste, D. A., Jr. (1993). Communication theory and the family. In P. G. Boss, W. J. Doherty, R. LaRossa, W. R. Schumm, & S. K. Steinmetz (Eds.), *Sourcebook of family theories and methods: A contextual approach.* City: Publisher.

Jacob, T. (Ed.). (1987). *Family interaction and psychopathology: Theories, methods, and findings.* New York: Plenum.

Jenkins, K. W. (1995). Communication in families. In R. D. Day, K. R. Gilbert, B. H. Settles, & W. R. Burr, *Research and theory in family science.* Pacific Grove, CA: Brooks/Cole.

Satir, V. (1983). *Conjoint family therapy.* Palo Alto, CA: Science and Behavior Books.

N. Giesbrecht

See Conjoint Family Therapy; Family Systems Theory.

Family Diagram. *See* Genogram.

Family Group Therapy. While most other approaches to family therapy are clinically derived, Bell developed family group therapy based on group dynamics theory. Using social psychology research on small group interaction, he found several parallels between small group interaction and family dynamics, particularly the process of problem solving as a group task. Unlike persons in group therapy, the family members are involved in a long-term relationship both prior to and following completion of psychotherapy. Between sessions there is continuous interaction that relates directly to the family's problem-solving skills. The family is in the best position to identify and solve the family problems, and family group therapy is an approach designed to help them do that (Bell, 1970).

Instead of focusing on communication problems and content analysis, Bell stresses functional analysis. This is an emphasis on the family's use of "purposes or motivations, evaluations, resolutions and decisions, interpersonal adjustments, rehearsals, and other elements of the total action process" (Bell, 1976, p. 131).

Bell identified seven stages of family group therapy. First, therapy is initiated by some family concern or an external recommendation for the family to get help. The family seeks out the therapist and the terms of their relationship are discussed. At the first session the family members discuss expectations for themselves and the therapist, as well as who will attend the sessions. The second stage involves the family testing the firmness and flexibility of the therapy rules. This often involves expression of intense feelings as well as challenges for control of the session.

The third stage involves a more explicit struggle for power. This challenges the therapist's ability to work with the family without being drawn into their difficulties. The therapist must maintain a position of process leader in order for the family to pursue its priorities. This means that the selection of a common task, the fourth stage, agreed upon by all family members, becomes the focus of the sessions. The family becomes a group, focusing on a common task that utilizes the resources of each family member.

The fifth stage, struggling for task completion, necessitates family members developing creative ways to utilize each other's strengths in order to work out their problems. Intrusions, interruptions, and other events that slow or impede work on the common task become opportunities for family members to practice new ways of working with each other. The common task provides a continuous focus throughout the difficulties of learning to work together effectively. Task completion, the sixth stage, is reached when the family members agree that they do not need any further work on the common task. Each family member gives evidence of his or her satisfaction with the results through personal insights, support of other members, or other means. The final stage, separation, is usually accompanied by the strengthening of the familial bond. The desire to function without the therapist may be stated clearly, or the family may try to push the therapist away by strong negative statements. The therapist likewise must separate from the family and support their move toward independence (Bell, 1976).

Bell describes healthy and efficient families as those that have mutual satisfaction of their members, complementary aims and support of the family as a group, and flexibility to adapt to individual demands of the group. The healthy family also has a variety of patterns to deal with conflict and can evaluate "the consequences of its achievements of accommodations" (Bell, 1971, pp. 869–870).

The therapist's purposes play a pivotal role in the family group therapy process. Not only is the therapist a leader, but also the direction of leadership must be clear. The family is encouraged to be as autonomous as possible. Keeping the family on target with its agreed-upon task minimizes diversion into low-priority concerns. The hope is that the family will experience successful problem solving during the sessions and will be able to generalize these experiences and techniques to other family situations.

The therapist must remain free of emotional entanglements with the family in order that the family will learn to maximize its resources and to rely on each other to assist in problem solving. Because each family is different, each must work out its own problem-solving methods, with the therapist guiding family members through this process.

According to Bell, it is important that the therapist have no relationship with family members other than during the sessions. There are no private sessions with family members and no conjoint sessions. It is strictly a group process, and this must be adhered to throughout work with the family.

It is the therapist's role to attempt to bridge gaps between family members, model effective listening, affirm the value of each family member, and work with the family at a pace that facilitates development of its boundaries as well as its autonomy. Families are encouraged to experiment, to try different ways of working on problems in order to increase flexibility and awareness of the resources within the family system (Bell, 1976).

Family group therapy addresses many different aspects of family functioning and in general seems to balance the significance of individual growth and learning with working together effectively as a group. Its utilization of small group processes and dynamics is an interesting alternative to clinically derived family therapy approaches.

References

Bell, J. E. (1970). A theoretical position for family group therapy. In N. W. Ackerman (Ed.), *Family process*. New York: Basic.

Bell, J. E. (1971). Recent advances in family group therapy. In J. G. Howells (Ed.), *Theory and practice of family psychiatry*. New York: Brunner/Mazel.

Bell, J. E. (1976). A theoretical framework for family group therapy. In P. J. Guerin (Ed.), *Family therapy*. New York: Gardner.

T. M. JOHNSON

See FAMILY THERAPY: OVERVIEW.

Family Life Cycle. The family life cycle is a description of normative stages of development in family life. Families progress through predictable stages that can be understood in terms of the development of individual family members and of the family unit. Each stage presents circumscribed tasks to be accomplished. Mastery of these tasks occurs with the successful resolution of previous tasks and prepares for subsequent stages. The biological requirements (e.g., safety) and personal aspirations (e.g., autonomy) of each family member and the cultural imperatives (e.g., value transmission) for the family as a unit are themes throughout the cycle.

Despite general uniformity in these stages, cultural and socioeconomic groups can differ in aspects of this sequence (Carter & McGoldrick, 1988). Alterations in the family life cycle occur because of life experience (e.g., family moves, parental employment status), alteration in family structure (e.g., divorce, adoption, single parent status), and biologic events (e.g., illness, early death). Therefore, the following description should be seen as a general, not absolute, statement of normal family development.

The family view of the life cycle was first formally approached by Hill and Duvall in 1948 and culminated in Duvall's (1977) landmark work, which delineated eight stages of the family life cycle. The following description of the stages of the family life cycle is adapted primarily from Carter and McGoldrick's (1988) more recent work, with input from other sources (Nichols & Everett, 1986), and reflects contemporary American families. This sequential description emphasizes that the underlying process being negotiated is the expansion, contraction, and realignment of the system to support the healthy entry, exit, and development of family members.

Leaving Home. The new family life cycle begins as the unattached young adult becomes an independent self and formulates personal life goals. During this stage the individual achieves some measure of emotional and financial independence from the family of origin.

Joining Through Marriage (Formation). Individuals attempt to replace attachment patterns within the family of origin with fulfillment in an adult, heterosexual relationship. The stage begins with informal courtship; a formal commitment to the new system through marriage and realignment of relationships with extended families and friends is required. Married couples with no children can nurture each other and increase emotional and sexual intimacy during this period.

Families with Children (Expansion). During this stage the family must adjust by accepting children into the system, joining in child-rearing tasks, defining grandparenting roles, and introducing the child to institutions outside of the family. As the divorce rate is highest during this stage, negotiation of this stage also requires attention to maintaining a strong marital relationship. Depending on the spacing of children, the next stage begins to dominate the family experience as the oldest child reaches 14 to 16 years old.

Families with Adolescents (Beginning Contraction). The key task is increasing the flexibility of family boundaries. The family must adjust by shifting relationships to permit the adolescent to move gradually toward mature interdependence and the parents to refocus on marriage and career. Peers have increasing influence in the moral and cognitive development of children, a fact that can challenge the family's value system.

Launching Children (Continuing Contraction). The family is confronted with multiple exits from and entries into the system. The couple must work through feelings of loss and detach sufficiently from the departing children, allowing reinvestment of energy into the marriage and other pursuits while also developing relationships with their adult children. As their children begin their own families, in-laws and grandchildren force additional realignment of relationships. Finally, aging parents may require a shift in the family toward caring for the older generation. This stage begins as the first child leaves home and continues until the last child has left.

Families in Later Life. Losses of parents, spouses, peers, and one's own abilities are major concerns in this stage. The older generation is confronted with maintaining its own functioning while supporting the more central role of the middle generation. The middle generation must find a place in the system for their parents' wisdom and experience, supporting the older generation without overfunctioning for them.

Any discussion of normative family function raises the question of values and purpose in family life. A biblical model of family development is consistent with the life cycle and provides a model for healthy family functioning: children leaving parents and committing to each other (Gen. 2:24; Mark 10:7–9); spouses forsaking others (Exod. 20:14, 17) and reproducing children (Gen. 1:28) who respect and obey parents (Exod. 20:12; Prov. 6:20–21) while being guided and nurtured by them (Prov. 22:6; 29:17; Eph. 6:4). Contemporary psychological science merely amplifies and provides empirical support for this model.

The family life cycle is useful in identifying healthy and unhealthy aspects of family function. It also provides a template for clinical interventions through which effective family functioning can be established, often the most critical element of an individual's mental health.

References

Carter, B., & McGoldrick, M. (1988). *The changing family life cycle: A framework for family therapy* (2nd ed.). New York: Gardner.

Duvall, E. M. (1977). *Marriage and family development* (5th ed.). Philadelphia: Lippincott.

Nichols, W. C., & Everett, C. A. (1986). *Systemic family therapy.* New York: Guilford.

F. J. MONCHER AND A. JOSEPHSON

See MARITAL HEALTH AND PATHOLOGY.

Family Network Therapy. *See* SOCIAL NETWORK INTERVENTION.

Family Psychology. Family psychology is an emerging discipline within psychology. Based on systems theory, family psychology posits an inclusive model of psychology that incorporates intraindividual factors, interpersonal dynamics, and environmental issues. Family psychology is increasing in strength as it gains recognition in professional organizations and graduate psychology programs.

Systems theory advocates that living organisms, including human beings, exist in complex ecosystems. To adequately understand humans, systems theory suggests, it is necessary to pay attention to the variety of factors that influence life in an ecosystem and the manner in which these factors interact with each other.

In adopting a systemic orientation, family psychology critiques those theories of psychology that isolate the individual from the system of which they are a part. Family psychology suggests that it is not enough to look only within the individual. Family psychology also argues that the approach of family therapy has been inadequate when it suggests that psychology need not look inside the individual but only at the family or social system (Nichols, 1987). Environmental factors have also often been overlooked or understood as the domain of a separate discipline, such as sociology or social work. Family psychology assumes that it is necessary to recognize the reciprocal interaction between the multiplicity of factors that are involved in life if we are to truly understand human behavior.

In terms of individual factors, this means that family psychology recognizes the salience of such areas of study as psychobiology, neuropsychology, cognitive development, individual development, and personality theory. However, these disciplines have sometimes studied the individual in fragmented fashion; that is, from their particular perspective alone or without recognition of the interaction between their discipline and other diverse disciplines. For instance, family psychology would support the importance of examining individual development in the context of the social and environmental world of the individual. Development in context (Moen, Elder, & Luscher, 1995) hypothesizes a genuine reciprocity between developing individuals and their ecological contexts. Even fields such as neuropsychology are beginning to examine social and environmental factors in the etiology and treatment of neurological disorders. Family psychology creates an umbrella perspective capable of incorporating many psychological theories relative to the individual.

Interpersonal dynamics are the second major focus of family psychology. Parent-child relations, marital relations, and social network relationships interact with individual experience. Family development and the family life cycle theories provide an awareness of the family as the immediate context of individual development. In family psychology it is impossible to see only individual process; family process interacts with individual function and each influences the other (Mikesell, Lusterman, & McDaniel, 1995). For instance, family psychology indicates that it is inappropriate to examine the adolescent experience apart from an understanding that adolescence occurs within an interpersonal context that includes the family of the adolescent (in which parents may well be experiencing midlife adjustment), the extended family (in which grandparents may be experiencing physical and economic decline), and peers, as well as the geographic community and the economic and sociocultural environment. The particular experiences of individual adolescents may be very different due to these factors, and family psychology encourages the inclusion of this material in understanding and treating adolescents.

The third major focus of family psychology is on the environmental factors that interact with individual and interpersonal behaviors. These influences include culture (both individual cultural values and the dominant cultural values within which minority cultures exist), socioeconomic status, the physical environment in which one lives (crime-ridden or relatively safe, crowded or spacious, urban or rural), employment conditions, educational opportunities, community organizations (availability of social services), religious organizations, and recreational opportunities. Again, the individual experience will vary significantly, depending upon the idiographic combination of environmental factors experienced. To understand the individual, family psychology includes recognition of these factors. Successful psychological treatment of individuals may well require some address of environmental dynamics.

As this systemic orientation to psychology has grown, it has received recognition and status within organized psychology. The American Psychological Association (APA) now has a Division of Family Psychology (Division 43), which publishes a bulletin, *The Family Psychologist*, and a journal, *The Journal of Family Psychology*. These publications continue to refine the discipline and extend its scope of influence. APA recently moved to create policy for the recognition of specialties within psychology, and Division 43 is proceeding to apply for certification of family psychology as a specialty. The American Board of Professional Psychology (ABPP), a national postdoctoral specialty certification board, has created the diplomate in family psychology for individuals who satisfy education, training, and examination requirements in family psychology. It is increasingly common for graduate programs in psychology to offer courses or tracks in family psychology. A limited number of schools are shifting to offer full emphases in family psychology. Since APA currently recognizes for accreditation only programs in clinical psychology, counseling psychology, and educational psychology, these tracks or emphases continue to fall under the umbrella of one of these disciplines. There is some hope that family psychology will one day be recognized by APA as a parallel discipline to the existing three. Current debate in the field centers around whether specialties, such as family psychology, should be developed at the doctoral or postdoctoral level.

The field of family psychology has been welcomed in the Christian academic community. The key tenets of the orientation are compatible with the biblical emphasis on the family. An ecological systems approach to understanding the complex nature of interactive forces that shape human behavior accords well with the Old and New Testament recognition of humans as part of a living creation. Finally, the role of the church, as part of the environmental context of life, is conceptualized as a resource for healthy living within the family psychology paradigm.

References

Mikesell, R., Lusterman, D., & McDaniel, S. (Eds.). (1995). *Integrating family therapy: Handbook of family psychology and systems theory.* Washington, DC: American Psychological Association.

Moen, P., Elder, G., & Luscher, K. (Eds.). (1995). *Examining lives in context: Perspectives on the ecology of human development.* Washington, DC: American Psychological Association.

Nichols, M. (1987). *The self in the system.* New York: Brunner/Mazel.

M. STANTON

Family Scapegoating. Also described as the family projection process, this is a process whereby an individual is unconsciously selected to carry the symptoms of a disturbed family. While some scapegoating occurs naturally in most families without serious symptomatology, in more troubled situations the scapegoated member develops a behavioral and/or emotional disorder. In family therapy this person is commonly referred to as the identified patient.

Scapegoating takes various forms, but the process essentially involves one or both parents projecting their emotional problems onto a child. Unable to protect themselves against parental pathology, these children eventually accept the role and try to make the most of it.

The willingness of scapegoats to accept the symptom-bearing role is surprising to those who do not see the reinforcement involved. Parents, for example, often focus on and express overconcern about the child's problems. In some cases attention is negative, but it is nevertheless attention. The scapegoat also enjoys considerable power in that family stability depends on his or her staying in the role. To break out is to give up attention and power and to run the risk of producing considerable disruption within the family.

Scapegoats play a sacrificial role in troubled families. They do this by absorbing stress so that others may function with less tension and conflict. Also, locating the problem in one person distracts from the dysfunctions of other members, thus allowing them to appear normal at the expense of the scapegoat.

Because the benefits derived from the scapegoat role often outweigh the emotional stress that accompanies it, getting out can be a formidable task. Intrapsychic factors along with family pressure combine to keep the scapegoat locked in. Family therapy is ordinarily required if one's symptoms are a function of family scapegoating.

J. A. LARSEN

See FAMILY COMMUNICATIONS THEORY; FAMILY SYSTEMS THEORY.

Family Sculpture Technique. A body of action-oriented methods and strategies that help members of human systems to live out spatially the meanings, images, and metaphors they hold about their interpersonal relationships within the system. Sculpting taps these internal images or metaphorical maps to make them externally visible to everyone who participates in or observes the system. Thus the private conceptualizations of interpersonal patterns become accessible to all members of the family or system. Sculpture seeks to provide experientially and nonverbally the behaviors previously represented by word descriptions or verbal metaphors. For example, sculpture would map spatially and actively a wife's language metaphor of "My husband and I are not close at all." The sculpture process would use real physical distance to symbolize the perceived emotional distance.

Family sculpture has its historical and methodological roots in the work of Jacob Moreno, the founder of psychodrama. Other mental health professionals with interests in human relations and family therapy—for example, Kantor and Satir (1972)—have built on the efforts of Moreno.

The sculpting procedure involves four different roles that parallel those observed in the enactment of a psychodrama. First, the sculptor (protagonist or client) is the one who volunteers to disclose his or her private view of the family or system. Second, the monitor (director or therapist) is the professional who assists the sculptor in carrying out the sculpture. Third, the actors (other members of family or group) are those individuals who make themselves available to portray members of the sculptor's family as the sculptor perceives them. Finally, the audience (the same term used in psychodrama) consists of members of other families or the group who observe and give feedback to the sculptor at the appropriate time in the sculpting process.

Similar to psychodrama, three developmental stages are required for a complete sculpturing process. The initial phase focuses on the sculptor's establishing the specific situation or family event he or she desires to explore. This includes mapping out the physical space and the sculptor's associating kinesic and sensory experiences to this space. The first stage is concerned with topography and atmosphere. The second stage involves the sculpting, in which the therapist has the sculptor bring the actors on stage to fill out the family space. The sculptor, without talking, places the actors bodily in the family space to give external reality to his or her private experiences of familial relationships. The final stage involves processing, discussing, and giving feedback. All participants in the sculpture, including members of the audience, become active in the feedback and processing of experiences.

Sculpture can be used with individual clients, couples, entire families, family subsystems; extended families or kinship networks, multiple families, groups, and even corporations or organizations. When sculpture is used with an individual client, it is necessary for the therapist either to assume also the roles of family members or to substitute objects such as chairs. Dyadic or boundary sculpture is particularly useful in working with couples to help them clarify the issues of territoriality, kinesics, and proxemics. Each person is required to become aware of both his or her own personal space and that of the other person, including the rules and laws that govern the control of that space. This negotiating of space can be extended to a variety of relationships. Family or group sculpture is an extension of dyadic and relationship sculpture that involves a larger number of people in a more complicated system.

A sculpture can be linear or a matrix. Linear sculpture lends itself to both unipolar representations (members of a system placing themselves on a continuum assessing some theme, e.g., frequency of initiating conversation) and bipolar situations (e.g., introverted versus extraverted or passive versus aggressive). Matrix sculpture allows for the simultaneous sculpting of the relationship between two variables. For example, on one line or dimension the frequency of intimate behaviors can be portrayed, while on a second line or dimension, perpendicular to the first line, the importance of intimacy can be featured.

Sculpture has unusual potential for both diagnosis or evaluation and therapeutic intervention. It allows room for therapists to be resourceful, using their individuality and creativity in fitting a sculpting style to their personality and values. It also provides an opportunity for the client to deal with life situations and relationships as they are and to experiment with them as he or she would like them to be.

Additional Readings

Constantine, L. L. (1981). Family sculpture and relationship mapping techniques. In G. D. Erickson & T. P. Hogan (Eds.), *Family therapy* (2nd ed.). Monterey, CA: Brooks/Cole.

Duhl, F. J., Kantor, D., & Duhl, B. S. (1973). Learning, space, and action in family therapy: A primer of sculpture. In D. A. Bloch (Ed.), *Techniques of family psychotherapy*. New York: Grune & Stratton.

Satir, V. (1972). *People making*. Palo Alto, CA: Science and Behavior.

D. SMITH

See PSYCHODRAMA.

Family Stress Theory. Family stress theory provides a framework for understanding the manner in which families deal with the demands of life. The model focuses on the types of stressors families face and the elements families use to remain healthy and strong. The family stress model is helpful to professionals interested in assisting families because it identifies factors that may be addressed to enhance family functioning.

The modern study of family stress began in the 1930s, when researchers examined the adaptation of families to the sudden loss of income during the Depression. Subsequent researchers focused on separation and reunion stresses during World War II. The findings of these studies resulted in the seminal ABC-X Model of Family Stress (Hill, 1949). This model identified three variables that lead to an outcome (X) of stress or adaptation: A, the event or stressor; B, the strengths or resources of the family at the time of the stressor; and C, the meaning that the family attaches to the event. These variables became the foundation of family stress theory, and current models (e.g., the T-Double ABC-X model of McCubbin & McCubbin, 1987, or the Systems Model of Family Stress by Burr & Klein, 1994) build on them to understand the complex manner in which families adapt to stressors.

Stressors are not equivalent to stress in family stress theory. Some stressors are considered positive events by families, such as moving into a new home or having a baby. The basic notion is that stressors are events or circumstances that are capable of producing change in the family system. As such, stressors put a demand on the family to adapt to the new situation. To avoid the pejorative connotation of the term *stressor*, some theorists refer to these events as life challenges. Some challenges are normative or predictable, such as progressing through stages of the individual or family life cycle. Other challenges are nonnormative or unpredictable, in that they do not occur in all families, such as major illness, job loss, or employment promotion.

Some challenges have to do with how a family relates to its environment, as when the family home is in an unsafe location or medical services are not readily available. Even the mundane challenges of daily life, termed hassles in the literature, can add to the sense of challenge for families (consider the family with three children on soccer teams on a Saturday). Taken together these challenges accumulate in the process termed pile-up to present families with the need to change the status quo and find new ways of handling the demands of life. For the professional, assessing the number and intensity of life challenges that a family is currently facing can be an important part of providing assistance to that family. Interventions to assist families may range from preventive measures, such as seminars to prepare families for predictable events like a life cycle transition (e.g., preparing for your first child or preparing for adolescence), to measures to enable families to reduce their current challenges, to insight regarding the postponement of elective changes until the family handles its current stressors.

Research has indicated that all families face about the same number of challenges. However, some families are able to address these demands as they arise and continue life on a relatively steady course. Other families have a harder time and are more likely to transition into a crisis state due to life challenges. Recent research has focused more on the B (resources/strengths) and C (appraisal/meaning) factors to understand the differences between families (Boss, 1987).

Resources and strengths are often divided between external sources of support and internal family characteristics that may enhance the family's ability to deal with challenges. Internal strengths are the assets the family possesses when they encounter challenges. These include psychological health, physical health, personality traits, intelligence, education and training, problem solving and coping skills, belief systems, marital dynamics, and economic resources. External supports include the family's network of social relations, the social support received from that network, and the positive transactions with their environmental context (e.g., good schools or day care readily available, safe neighborhood). Religious faith and involvement in a religious community may be part of the resources a family may call upon when facing challenges. For the professional, it is important to note if a family is deficient in strengths and resources, since these families are considered most vulnerable to family stress. Aiding a family to develop its internal strengths (e.g., teach coping or problem-solving skills, provide psychotherapy for personality traits that are problematic, conduct marital therapy to strengthen that relationship) or assisting them in developing and utilizing their social network during times of difficulty may help them transition back on course. The encouragement of religious disciplines, such as prayer and worship, and involvement in the Christian community may provide much needed support when the family feels overwhelmed.

The family's appraisal of the meaning of life challenges is the third major factor. It has been noted that when facing a life challenge family members will interact and dialogue concerning the experience to construct a collaborative meaning of that event (Patterson & Garwick, 1994). Over time these shared interpretations of life evolve to form a complex set of assumptions about life and life events. Different families develop different sets of shared assumptions that come to characterize them and to distinguish one family from another. In family stress theory this concept helps to explain why some families see themselves as capable of managing life challenges, while other families feel vulnerable and unable to handle life challenges effectively. Each time a new challenge is faced, it is faced in light of this historically developed set of assumptions about who we are as a family and our ability to handle challenges. For the professional, understanding the nature of the evolved set of assumptions utilized by a family may help to explain their response to life challenges and provide an opportunity for intervention. Therapeutic insight, seminars, or sermons that promote an enhanced sense of family efficacy may help families to interpret life events differently and promote more effective functioning.

A systemic model of family stress suggests that it is inappropriate to hypothesize a linear, cause-effect relationship between stressors, appraisal, and resources. Instead, each family handles life challenges in a complex, interactive process that leads either to healthy adaptation to the challenges or in a dysfunctional direction to family stress and crisis in the face of the challenges. An effective professional may utilize family stress theory to help families enhance their process.

References

Boss, P. (1987). Family stress. In M. B. Sussman & S. Steinmetz (Eds.), *Handbook of marriage and the family*. New York: Plenum.

Burr, W. R., & Klein, S. (1994). *Reexamining family stress.* Thousand Oaks, CA: Sage.

Hill, R. (1949). *Families under stress.* New York: Harper.

McCubbin, M. A., & McCubbin, H. I. (1987). Family stress theory and assessment. In H. I. McCubbin & A. Thompson (Eds.), *Family assessment inventories*. Madison: University of Wisconsin-Madison.

Patterson, J., & Garwick, A. (1994). Levels of meaning in family stress theory. *Family Process, 33,* 287–304.

M. STANTON

Family Systems Theory. Three influences affected the development of family systems theory in the late 1940s and early 1950s. First, Bertalanffy (1968), a prominent biologist, applied laws pertaining to biological organisms to many areas from the human mind to the ecosphere in what he called general systems theory. This theory concerned itself with understanding the structural and functional rules considered valid for describing all systems. Although he had no extended contact with the pioneers of family therapy, he anticipated many conceptual issues that later shaped family systems and therapy.

A second influence was established by Norbert Weiner, who recognized that communication and self-regulation through communication are essential for the operation of systems. This process, by which results of past performances are reinserted into the system, using self-corrective feedback to influence future behavior, he labeled cybernetics. Bertalanffy distinguished cybernetics from systems theory in that he considered it only one way to meet the needs of a general systems theory.

Gregory Bateson, an anthropologist, had contact with cybernetic thinking during the 1950s and saw relevance in applying both general systems theory and cybernetics to human interaction to better understand communication. He was attracted to the idea that one could account for both uniformity and variability of human behavior by assuming they were rule-governed systems. He began a paradigm shift that moved away from focusing on the content of a relationship system to the pattern, process, and communication that described and explained it.

Bateson founded the Palo Alto group to focus on communication processes. Joining him were Jay Haley, who continued his own study of communication in families of schizophrenics, and John Weakland, another anthropologist. The group noted that communication could be divided between verbal and nonverbal types. To understand the dynamic beyond internal and linear motivation, the team realized the communication in a family was part of a context or relational system. Through the group's work, the cybernetic concept of self-governing systems became part of family systems thinking.

The family systems perspective then would have us see each member in relation to the other. Ultimately a family system is the parts of the whole family plus the way members interact, process being the way the family system functions. The processes in families, or transactional patterns, are seen as central to shaping individual behavior and personality. Family rules organize interaction and function to maintain a stable system by allowing and limiting members' behaviors. These relationship rules, both explicit and implicit, provide expectations about roles, behaving, and consequences of family life.

Interrelated Systems Concepts. Family systems theorists conceptualize the family as an open system that functions in a broader sociocultural context over the life cycle. Components of family functioning include systemic patterns, communication and problem solving, lifecycle development, and belief systems.

Systemically, family being viewed as a whole being greater than the sum of its parts is called nonsummativity. Members are interrelated in such a way that a change in one person affects change in others, impacting the whole system so that causality is seen as circular rather than linear. Cause and effect do not provide adequate understanding of a system. Ongoing reciprocity in relationships develops into predictable and observable patterns. Equifinality is the ability to observe the patterns of communication and relationship at any time. These patterns are influenced from within, where homeostasis (the balance of the system) is maintained, as well as from outside the system. The family is required to be open to allow input from its environment and other systems. Entropy is the lack of information or energy in a family system. In that a family must be open and closed at various times, it must have feedback to survive. Negative feedback loops are messages (verbal, nonverbal, and contextual) that the output by another has reached predetermined levels and indicates need to cut off or reduce inputs. Positive feedback loops signal to allow more input into the system.

The ultimate goals of the family system is to maintain homeostasis over time, requiring stability (morphostasis) and flexibility (morphogenesis). Systems thinkers realize the family must maintain its own values and consistent behavior while adapting to the family lifecycle development tasks (newly married, newborn, school age, teenagers, young adult, midlife, aging). A systems model of human development places the individual life cycle in the context of the family and culture. Reiss (1981) described the "family paradigm" as an enduring structure of shared beliefs, conceptions, and assumptions about the social world that are shared by family experiences. Culture, ethnicity, and religion are other basic contributions to family belief systems (McGoldrick, Pearce, & Giordano, 1982).

Major Approaches to Family Therapy. Although various schools of family therapy have a theoretical commitment to working with the process of family interaction, they are distinguished by conceptual positions. The approaches can be divided into problem-solving (structural, strategic, systemic, behavioral, solution-focused, psychoeducational) or intergenerational approaches (psychodynamic, Bowenian, experiential), which are more exploratory or growth oriented.

Structural family therapy, developed by Minuchin (1974) and his colleagues at Philadelphia Child Guidance, emphasizes family organization for the functioning of the family system and the well-being of its members. Problems are seen as an imbalance in the family's organization, especially in unclear parent and child subsystem boundaries. The symptoms commonly are found in dysfunctional patterns of transactions. The goal of therapy is to reorganize the family structure with more clear and flexible subsystems and boundaries and provide more adaptive coping so the symptom, which is often the presenting problem, is no longer needed.

The strategic approach was developed by Haley (1976) and Madanes (1981) while the Milan team (Selvini-Palazzoli et al., 1978) developed the systemic model. The focus for both is the immediate social situation of the identified patient, and the goal of therapy is limited to resolving the particular problem presented. The symptom is considered a communicative act that is part of a repetitious sequence of behaviors. While strategic therapists and systemic therapists share in communication theory, the strategic therapist uses indirect influence, interruption of sequences, and a more remote style that is highly intellectual. The Milan team utilizes circular questioning of members to tease out the problem, reframe it, and change the sequence of interaction. The most recent development in problem solving is the solution-focused therapy (de Shazer, 1988; O'Hanlon & Weiner-Davis, 1989), in which the symptoms are ignored and treatment moves toward solution by focusing on exceptions (times when the problem was not present) and utilizing strengths of family members.

The behavioral approach resulted from behavioral modifications and social learning theory in clinical psychology. It emphasizes family rules and communications processes. Symptoms in this model are reinforced by the family, causing failure in relationships. The therapist analyzes communication processes, both content and relational components, and builds skills in negotiation and problem solving.

The psychoeducational model has been the most promising family systems approach to chronic mental illness. Behavioral and structural family therapy elements are utilized while focusing on family education about the illness, offering concrete guidelines for crisis management, problem solving, and stress reduction. The family members are involved as collaborators in the treatment process.

Psychodynamic family therapists relate symptoms to shared family projections arising from past unresolved conflicts or losses in the family of origin. A symptomatic member may be a scapegoat as a result. Extended family members may be invited to sessions, or individuals may work at changing relationships outside the sessions. Resolution results in eliminating projections, relationship reconstruction and reunion, and individual and family growth.

The Bowen family systems model was created by Bowen (1978). He believed impaired functioning results from poorly differentiated patterns among family members who carry high anxiety and emotional reactivity. The goal of treatment is a process whereby clients are coached to change relationships within their families of origin in order to achieve a higher level of differentiation (increased freedom from emotional family reactivity) and reduce anxiety within the family.

Experiential family therapy was developed by Satir (1972) and Whitaker (Neill & Kniskern, 1982). Satir combined communication theory with a humanistic frame of reference, while Whitaker called his model symbolic-experiential family therapy. For both, current problems are viewed as a natural result of life experiences. The general goal of treatment is to achieve a fuller awareness and appreciation of self as family members are guided to communicate feelings and differences. Treatment, therefore, focuses on the here and now, and spontaneity is encouraged.

Family systems theory has sought to understand individuals in the context of the family. It is concerned not only with the identity of an individual but also with how one belongs within the family system. This belonging has been understood both from a systems perspective and also from a theological perspective. Anderson and Guernsey (1985) have combined both perspectives by utilizing a systems orientation and the concept of covenant. Belonging is not simply a matter of choice but a God-given assumption that is affirmed to members in a family over time. The relational systems of family members is the subject of both family systems and theology. As much as the biblical concept of covenant explains why we belong in families, a family systems approach provides the framework through which we better understand how we belong.

References

Anderson, R. S., & Guernsey, D. B. (1985). *On being family.* Grand Rapids, MI: Eerdmans.

Bertalanffy, L. V. (1968). *General system theory.* New York: Braziller.

Bowen, M. (1978). *Family therapy in clinical practice.* New York: Aronson.

de Shazer, S. (1988). *Clues: investigating solutions in brief therapy.* New York: Norton.

Haley, J. (1976). *Problem-solving therapy.* San Francisco: Jossey-Bass.

Madanes, C. (1981). *Strategic family therapy.* San Francisco: Jossey-Bass.

McGoldrick, M., Pearce, J. K., & Giordano, J. (Eds.). (1982). *Ethnicity and family therapy.* New York: Guilford.

Minuchin, S. (1974). *Families and family therapy.* Cambridge, MA: Harvard University Press.

Neill, J. R., & Kniskern, D. P. (Eds.). (1982). *From psych to system: The evolving therapy of Carl Whitaker.* New York: Guilford.

O'Hanlon, W. H., & Weiner-Davis, M. (1989). *In search of solutions: a new direction in psychotherapy.* New York: Norton.

Reiss, D. (1981). *The family's construction of reality.* Cambridge, MA: Harvard University Press.

Satir, V. (1972). *Peoplemaking.* Palo Alto, CA: Science and Behavior.

Selvini-Palazzoli, M., Boscolo, L., Cecchin, G., et al. (1978). *Paradox and counterparadox.* New York: Aronson.

R. W. MOSLENER

See FAMILY COMMUNICATIONS THEORY.

Family Systems Therapy. Family systems therapy may be applied to a variety of models of family therapy because these treatments incorporate an understanding of the family as a system (Mikesell, Lusterman, & McDaniel, 1995). The work of Bowen (1978; Kerr & Bowen, 1988) with families has been predominantly associated with what is specifically known as family systems therapy.

In the late 1940s Bowen began studying families as a unit of analysis that requires observation of the interaction and interdependence between its individual members. He has developed both a theory of the family emotional system and a method of therapy.

Bowen has made a unique contribution to therapy and understanding families by seeking to define normality in terms of freedom from emotional symptoms or behavior in the normal range. This approach is a striking departure from traditional theorists who attempted to first understand pathology and then interpret what might be normal. For Bowen the variability in functioning in families could be attributed to the degree of anxiety and the degree of differentiation in a family. The concept

of differentiation of self (emotional separation or autonomy while still experiencing intimacy) is not directly tied to symptoms. Even well-differentiated people can be stressed into dysfunction, but they have a flexibility of coping mechanisms and recover rapidly. When anxiety is low, most families or systems can appear normal. As anxiety increases, the dysfunctional or impaired family experiences increased tensions among relationships, interfering with differentiation and resulting in more problems. Thus there is a continuum from the most impaired to optimally functioning families. All families and individuals have stressors; however, they differ in their ability to implement healthy coping strategies.

The characteristic of self-differentiation is a product of emotional development and at any time a continuum. The continuum can be understood by the degree of fusion between emotional and intellectual functioning. At early stages of development and at the low extreme of the continuum are people dominated by automatic emotional processes and reactivity. These people are easily stressed into dysfunction and have difficulty recovering. At the high end intellectual functioning remains autonomous under stress. These people are more adaptable, flexible, and independent of surrounding emotionality. They cope better with life stresses. An example of the low person would be Judas after betraying Christ. He is so consumed by his failure and betrayal that suicide is his only option; he can only react. Christ represents the highest state of development and function. He can say, "Not my will, but thy will." He is confident in his relationship with his Father, experiences the pain and sorrow of his trial, and meets his future with peace. He can forgive those who persecute him.

Most people fall in the moderate range of self-differentiation, with variable intellectual and emotional balance. Their overt feelings are intense, and their relationship orientations make them reactive to others out of needs for closeness and approval. Problems and anxiety symptoms arise when the emotional system is unbalanced. The reactivity of Peter from the garden of Gethsemane to meeting the risen Christ would be an example of the middle group. He uses denial, aggression, fleeing, and blame to cope with the loss of closeness to Christ.

In family systems theory Bowen believed that each family has its own average level of differentiation around which members fluctuate. To further interpret family function, several factors are regulatory.

Fusion. This concept refers to the emotional "stuck togetherness" of a family. The degree of emotional fusion is related to the level of self-differentiation. Emotional fusion is primarily observed in marital conflict, dysfunction in a spouse, and in projection to one or more of the children.

Nuclear Family Emotional System. This refers to the pattern of emotional functioning between spouses and between parents and children, which replicates patterns of past generations. The level of functioning depends chiefly on the degree of differentiation of each spouse from the family of origin. Individuals marry others of equal level of differentiation of self. A common myth suggests that an individual will marry his or her "mother"; however, it is more likely that we marry people who reflect the level of emotional functioning of our parents.

Triangle. A three-person configuration in an emotional system is formed when a two-person system, overloaded and anxious under stress, involves a vulnerable third person. The focus of tension becomes the third person and prevents resolution in the dyad. Thus a child may be referred for treatment of dysfunction when unresolved parent conflicts are the primary issues.

Family Projection Process. Parental dysfunction or anxiety often focuses on one or more of the triangulated children. In almost every family, one child is more triangled than others with poorer life adjustment. This scapegoating serves to protect the parental relationship from recognizing its own dysfunction.

Emotional Cutoff. Children or family members may separate through withdrawal, isolation, running away, or denial of the importance of the parental family. The avoidance of the family pain through this strategy is functional but may restrict the adjustment of the individual in the life process.

Stress on the family system caused by life transitions, such as leaving home, marriage, or death, tends to decrease differentiation and heighten emotional reactivity. Anxiety commonly results in triangulation or cutoffs of highly charged relationships. Underfunctioning, or symptoms, may be linked with and reinforced by overfunctioning in other parts of the system in a compensatory manner. An example of this might be a father who spends more time at work and a mother who invests herself in church activities while their adolescent children are unsupervised. These parents might be low in differentiation and dominated by their emotions, thus allowing them to override painful, intellectual modes of thought. Perhaps they also do not want to face why they have no time for each other.

The Bowen model of therapy is growth-oriented, with a mandate for exploration and change beyond symptom reduction toward increased self-differentiation. Current marital, family, or child problems will be resolved with increased differentiation of the spouses/parents from each other and from their extended families. The goal of therapy is to assist both individuals to modify their relationships with their family of origin, achieving less emotional reactivity and fusion and greater cognitive control of feelings, autonomy, and reduced anxiety. The therapist assumes the role of coach or consultant, guiding each individual through carefully planned steps of intervention. The process might involve redeveloping personal relationships with key family members, repairing cutoffs, detriangling from conflicts, and changing the part played in emotionally reactive vicious cycles. The therapist may encourage "I" statements, a clear assertion of one's own feelings and thoughts. Humor may be used to detoxify emotionally charged situations and provide the family opportunity to reflect on its own dysfunctional behavior. In this approach it is important that the therapist maintain autonomy and not become emotionally engaged. Finally, the family or individuals may continue to work with the therapist over time as transitions or stressors induce regression to lower levels of self-differentiation.

References

Bowen, M. (1978). *Family therapy in clinical practice.* New York: Aronson.

Kerr, M., & Bowen, M. (1988). *Family evaluation.* New York: Norton.

Mikesell, R., Lusterman, D., & McDaniel, S. (Eds.). (1995). *Integrating family therapy.* Washington, DC: American Psychological Association.

F. B. WICHERN, SR.

See FAMILY THERAPY: OVERVIEW.

Family Therapy: Overview. In the 1950s a number of clinicians departed from the prevailing individual, intrapsychic models of therapy and came to believe that individual functioning could be better understood in terms of family functioning and that a family could best be understood as a system. Credit for the theoretical foundation for this move is given to the biologist von Bertalanffy (1945) in his introduction of general system theory. The theory was further developed by Bateson (1972, 1979), an anthropologist, with the introduction of cybernetic concepts. Accordingly, a family is viewed as an organism within an environment, an open system, which means it receives energy by interacting with the environment. This energy is used for the purposes of daily tasks and structure building among other things.

From the beginning, family therapists were interested in issues of metatheory—that is, the basic assumptions about reality that guide our theoretical thinking—and were often critical of the prevailing metatheories in individual models of therapy. Family therapists often challenged basic assumptions regarding ontology (the nature of reality) and epistemology (how we know). More recently family therapists have shown a decided interest in social constructionism (Berger & Luckman, 1967) and the manner in which a family constructs its own reality. One result of this awareness is the development of narrative family therapy (Zimmerman & Dickerson, 1994). The central idea is that how a family defines itself, its narrative, contributes to the problem the family is experiencing. Therefore, to change the narrative is to change the family.

There are several schools of family therapy. Among them are the psychodynamic, experiential/humanistic, extended family, structural, strategic, communication, and behavioral schools. Each school will be reviewed in terms of the major theoretical foundations and the founding theorists, view of family dysfunction, and the therapeutic change agent or agents.

Psychodynamic Family Systems. Major Theoretical Foundations and Founding Theorists. It is useful to make a distinction between the psychoanalytic and the psychodynamic theories. Psychodynamic theory is the broader term and encompasses all models that adhere basically to the psychoanalytic framework, but it includes those that differ in some major point as well. Analytical psychology (Carl Gustav Jung) is the most well known of these. Psychoanalytic theory, the narrower term, includes classical psychoanalysis, ego psychology, object relations, and psychoanalytic self psychology. A naive mistake concerning psychoanalysis is to equate Sigmund Freud with psychoanalysis and ignore the fifty years of development the theory has undergone since. Ackerman (1958, 1966) and Dicks (1967) are considered by many to be the first to apply psychodynamic theory to family treatment. Ackerman's frame would be considered more classical, while Dicks makes use of a more contemporary object relations frame. Contemporary authors Framo (1992), Skynner (1976), Scharff and Scharff (1987, 1991; Scharff, 1989), Slipp (1984, 1988), and Lachkar (1992) have led the field in applying object relations theory to family treatment, while Solomon (1989, 1994) is one of the pioneers in applying psychoanalytic self psychology to marital therapy.

View of Family Dysfunction. The focus of treatment in psychoanalytic family therapy is the effect that early childhood experiences have on the present. It is believed that early experiences form a template or structure through which all later experiences are filtered. Thus in some way a child who was abandoned early will have difficulty with trust in adult life. Classical models view family dysfunction as the result of unconscious intrapsychic conflicts, usually from the parents, that are acted out via projection or other defensive operations as some sort of repetition of past trauma in the present. The developmental model formulated by Freud and Abraham (oral, anal, phallic) informs the therapist, although most pathology is viewed in oedipal terms. Contemporary models hold to a similar form of dysfunction with the replacement of the Freud-Abraham developmental model with either Mahler, Pine, and Bergman's (1975) separation-individuation model or Stern's (1985) model of the development of the self. In both classical and contemporary models there is an emphasis on the interlocking nature of pathologies in relationships.

Psychodynamic models of the personality are based upon the impact the unconscious has upon consciousness. While conceptions of how the unconscious is formed and what its contents are have changed dramatically since Freud, the basic commitment to the power of the unconscious in affecting the present remains unchanged. For theorists in the more classical psychoanalytic tradition the unconscious is the reservoir of unacceptable impulses. In the more contemporary models, the unconscious is equated more with unawareness and usually refers to the patterns of ordering and structuring interactions that operate out of conscious awareness. In all psychodynamic models the dictum of making conscious the unconscious continues to be a central notion.

Therapeutic Change Agent(s). This area constitutes the largest change between the classical and contemporary models. Classical models emphasize insight, while contemporary models emphasize the relationship of the therapist and the therapeutic environment to the family as the primary carrier of therapeutic change. The therapist's primary tool is his or her own sensitive unconscious attuned to the nuances of the client's experience. Classical models used this technique, interpreting the countertransference as well, but contemporary models have reinterpreted and extended its emphasis.

Experiential/Humanistic Family Systems. Major Theoretical Foundations and Founding Theorists. Existential philosophy, particularly the systems of Søren Kierkegaard, Sartre, and Heidegger, along with phenomenology, forms the foundation for this school. Whitaker (Napier & Whitaker, 1978; Whitaker, 1981) is the most popular theorist in this group. What characterizes this group is its deemphasis on the role of theory in the change process. The practitioners of this approach insist that the experiences offered to the family by the therapist are primary in promoting health and growth, not the theory. Experiential family systems draws heavily on Gestalt psychology (Kempler, 1973, 1981) and Carl Rogers's thinking as well.

View of Family Dysfunction. The present interaction from the client's immediate experience is the focus of treatment. Dysfunctional families are not able to accept all of their experiences and must partition certain parts of their experience, resulting in a family myth that is designed to cover the unacceptable aspects. Family secrets function to keep members of the family unaware of the real nature of the family. Members' interactions are guided by roles rather than authenticity. Therefore, communication is restricted and the development of fully functioning human beings is limited.

Experiential theorists generally will acknowledge the existence of unconscious aspects of human social functioning but nonetheless will focus on the present. For Whitaker the unconscious means the symbolic interactional system the family has developed, whereas for Kempler the unconscious is seen more in Gestalt terms of wholeness. Both Whitaker's and Kempler's use of the term stand in contradistinction to the psychoanalytic use of the term. In practical terms, if exploration of the unconscious leads away from the here and now, it will be discouraged. If exploration of the unconscious enhances the focus on the present and will facilitate experience, it will be encouraged.

Therapeutic Change Agent(s). Experience is the change agent. Emotionally cathartic experiences are sought (*see* Catharsis). In this model the therapist's use of his or her own person is vital. Since pathology is viewed as the family's constriction of its experience, the therapist's own authenticity—that is, the degree of openness to all aspects of his or her own experience—is the primary tool. The therapist's authenticity acts as a catalyst for the family members to open themselves to their own experience.

Extended Family Systems. *Major Theoretical Foundations and Founding Theorists.* This model is largely associated with the works of Bowen (1978), though he did not use the term. He was the first to use the term *family systems* but soon changed it to natural systems theory, emphasizing his desire to build theory on the role of evolutionary process and biology.

View of Family Dysfunction. The focus of treatment is largely the present, but family-of-origin issues play an important role also. Pathology is viewed as arising from an undifferentiated family ego mass, a condition in which personal boundaries are diffused and the family is described as fused or enmeshed. The fused condition is usually a result of a typical pattern the family has developed for handling anxiety. Bowen discusses other pathological family structures, but a common structure is characterized by triangulation—that is, two members of the family bring in another member to stabilize an unstable dyad. This process is aided by the family projection process, wherein certain parental conflicts, anxieties, or experiences are projected upon certain others or family members. In this structure the parents fight out their conflicts through the child, a scapegoat, who is often the focus of parental concern (*see* Scapegoating). A child thus caught will resort to emotional cutoffs in an attempt to detriangulate himself or herself. The process of enmeshed and disengaged modes of coping is often transmitted generationally in families. Guerin, Fay, Burden, and Kautto (1994) present a diagnostic scheme for placing families in levels of functioning based upon levels of differentiation. This scheme then dictates which kinds of interventions are useful for families in each of the levels.

Therapeutic Change Agent(s). The therapist assumes the role of a coach, an active expert who assists the team members in achieving differentiation. The therapist often coaches the family in alternative ways of responding to the triangles as well. The approach is educative, cognitive, and controlled. Emotionally cathartic experiences are avoided. Although the therapist is direct, he or she usually avoids confronting the family; at all cost the therapist will avoid becoming triangulated in the family's projective process. Change is wrought by a rational recognition of the family's undifferentiated ego mass in combination with new alternate experiences in therapy brought on by the coaching of the therapist.

Structural Family Systems. *Major Theoretical Foundations and Founding Theorists.* Structural family therapy is primarily the work of Minuchin and his colleagues (Minuchin, 1974; Minuchin & Fishman, 1981) and Madanes (1981). Minuchin and his colleagues developed this model while working with families of lower socioeconomic status in Philadelphia. This was the first model to offer a clear and concise framework for understanding and intervention. As a result structural family therapy is probably the most popular model in terms of number of adherents claimed.

View of Family Dysfunction. Structural family therapy holds that the family is more than the sum of its parts of individual members. It is a system, indivisible as such. Family structure in general and inflexible structure in particular is the agent of pathology. All families have an implicit structure that governs how the members relate to each other. Pathology results from unclear boundaries between subsystems: that is, parental and child subsystems. The resulting families are either enmeshed or disengaged. Rigid, inflexible family structures are not able to change and flow with the growing and changing demands of the environment or the demands of the subsystems. For Minuchin boundaries have to do with the manner in which a family communicates rules, and therefore boundaries can be changed by how the family defines its problems.

Therapeutic Change Agent(s). Intervention is made at the family level; individual intervention is avoided. The unconscious is not acknowledged and exploration of it is avoided. Structural family therapists will rearrange the manner in which a family seats itself in the therapy room, facilitating boundaries between parents and children, for example. They may rearrange the way in which a family communicates. For example, they may refuse to let the children talk when the parents should be talking to each other or vice versa. Structural family therapists first join the family system and develop a therapeutic bond with the family, often copying the family's style of communication, affect, and modes of expression. Then an evaluation of the family's boundaries and structure is made to guide the treatment plan. Enactment, or the deliberate (almost overdone) recreating of a family's structure and interaction, emphasizes the dysfunction. Homework, often of a paradoxical nature, moves the family toward restructuring (*see* Homework in Psychotherapy). Restructuring a family's boundaries forces different family interactions and is the final agent of change.

References

Ackerman, N. (1958). *The psychodynamics of family life.* New York: Basic.

Ackerman, N. (1966). *Treating the troubled family.* New York: Basic.

Bateson, G. (1972). *Steps to an ecology of mind.* New York: Ballantine.

Bateson, G. (1979). *Mind and nature: A necessary unity.* New York: Bantam.

Berger, P., & Luckman, T. (1967). *The social construction of reality.* New York: Doubleday.

Bowen, M. (1978). *Family therapy in clinical practice.* New York: Aronson.

Dicks, H. (1967). *Marital tensions: Clinical studies towards a psychoanalytic theory of interaction.* London: Routledge & Kegan Paul.

Framo, J. (1992). *Family-of-origin therapy: An intergenerational approach.* New York: Brunner/Mazel.

Guerin, P., Fay, L., Burden, S., & Kautto, J. (1994). *The evaluation and treatment of marital conflict.* New York: Gardner.

Kempler, W. (1973). *Principles of gestalt family therapy.* Salt Lake City, UT: Deseret.

Kempler, W. (1981). *Experiential psychotherapy with families.* New York: Brunner/Mazel.

Lachkar, J. (1992). *The narcissistic/borderline couple: A psychoanalytic perspective on marital treatment.* New York: Brunner/Mazel.

Madanes, C. (1981). *Strategic family therapy.* San Francisco: Jossey-Bass.

Mahler, M., Pine, F., & Bergman, A. (1975). *The psychological birth of the human infant: Symbiosis and individuation.* New York: Basic.

Minuchin, S. (1974). *Families and family therapy.* Cambridge, MA: Harvard University Press.

Minuchin, S., & Fishman, H. (1981). *Family therapy techniques.* Cambridge, MA: Harvard University Press.

Napier, A., & Whitaker, C. (1978). *The family crucible.* New York: Harper & Row.

Scharf, D., & Scharf, J. (1987). *Object relations family therapy.* Northvale, NJ: Aronson.

Scharf, D. & Scharf, J. (1991). *Object relations couple therapy.* Northvale, NJ: Aronson.

Scharf, J. (Ed.). (1989). *Foundations of object relations family therapy.* Northvale, NJ: Aronson.

Skynner, R. (1976). *One flesh: Separate persons.* London: Constable.

Slipp, S. (1984). *Object relations: A dynamic bridge between individual and family treatment.* Northvale, NJ: Aronson.

Slipp, S. (1988). *The technique of object relations family therapy.* Northvale, NJ: Aronson.

Solomon, M. (1989). *Narcissism and intimacy: Love and marriage in an age of confusion.* New York: Norton.

Solomon, M. (1994). *Lean on me: The power of positive dependency in intimate relationships.* New York: Simon & Schuster.

Stern, D. (1985). *The interpersonal world of the infant.* New York: Basic.

von Bertalanffy, L. (1945). *General systems theory.* New York: Basic.

Whitaker, C. (1981). Symbolic-experiential family therapy. In A. S. Gurman & D. P. Kniskern (Eds.), *Handbook of family therapy.* New York: Brunner/Mazel.

Zimmerman, J., & Dickerson, V. (1994, September). Using a narrative metaphor: Implications for theory and clinical practice. *Family Process, 33* (3), 233–245.

D. W. Peters

Family Types. Family researchers and therapists have classified families according to at least five variables. These variables identify different significant features of families; consideration of each contributes to a fuller understanding and diagnosis of the family. The following typologies include both functional and dysfunctional family types. Distribution and use of power is a critical variable in family styles. Jackson and Kramer have each proposed a typology of families based on power dynamics. Each suggests three types: the symmetrical, the complementary, and the parallel (Jackson & Lederer, 1968); the overadequate-underadequate, the united front, and the conflictual (Kramer, 1980).

The symmetrical family "is one in which the spouses continually need to state to each other behaviorally, 'I am as good as you are'" (Jackson & Lederer, 1968, p. 161). These spouses are status strugglers. Each seeks at least equal control, equal power. Spouses are competitive, not collaborative. This pattern is close to what Kramer calls the conflictual family, in which continual conflict and disagreement occur. Avoidance of intimacy is usually one objective of the constant conflict, even though each spouse may verbally express a desire to be closer. Parents in these families may often involve the children by choosing favorites. Some parents will pick on a child because that child is more like the disliked spouse (scapegoating the child). Children in intensely conflictual families frequently manifest significant problems.

The complementary relationship is "one in which one spouse is in charge and the other obeys" (Jackson & Lederer, 1968, p. 161). This complementarity may be divided according to the areas of competence or responsibility, or it may characterize the majority of spousal interactions. Kramer describes this type as the overadequate-underadequate family. The overadequate spouse appears efficient, superresponsible, and totally capable, while the underadequate spouse seems to be always demonstrating incompetence. Children in these families often seek to identify with the apparently more competent parent and/or sympathize with the underadequate parent. Occasionally the underadequate parent uses this to wield significant power in getting sympathy and help. When the underadequate spouse begins to grow and to display greater adequacy, the overadequate spouse often falls apart and suddenly appears underadequate. This often occurs in the traditional family when the wife begins to work after the children are reared.

The third type for Jackson is the parallel family, in which the parents alternate between symmetrical and complementary relationships in response to the demands of different situations. Flexibility in the use of power characterizes these families.

For Kramer the third type is the united-front family, in which parents and often also children use their power to present a unified picture of the marriage or the family to the outside world. Often the children experience significant problems either emotionally or physically as a result of the hidden conflicts. The parents are usually resistant to seeing the children's problems as related to the marital dynamics.

A second system of classification proposed by Jackson is based on the two variables of spousal satisfaction and stability of the marriage. Four combinations are possible: the stable-satisfactory, the unstable-satisfactory, the unstable-unsatisfactory, and the stable-unsatisfactory. In the rarely observed stable-satisfactory marriage differences are considered variations of "tastes and values, not as symbols of a hostile relationship" (Jackson & Lederer, 1968, p. 131). In the unstable-satisfactory relationship, which describes most marriages that last more than 10 years, the spouses believe they have a comfortable relationship, but their disappointments on occasion are obvious. There may be periodic outbursts of aggression, but both spouses see sufficient positives to want to remain married.

In the stable-unsatisfactory marriage conflict is ever present but always avoided, and no one is really happy with the situation. "In a quiet socially respectable manner the people in this group suffer more pain, hate more profoundly, and cause more discomfort to others than to the members of the other three groups" (Jackson & Lederer, 1968, p. 153). This is the type most often seen in therapy. The final type is the unstable-unsatisfactory relationship—the infamous "I can't live with you, I can't live without you" relationship. Tremendous hostility is observed by others, but the family members are often unaware of it. In the last two types the children often experience emotional or physical problems.

A fourth variable used for classification is the intimacy level of the family. Glick and Kessler (1980) suggest five levels of intimacy: the conflict-habituated marriage, in which both spouses stay together because of fear of alternatives; the devitalized marriage, in which extrinsic reasons such as children or moral or legal principles keep the spouses together while each lives a fairly separate life; the passive-congenial marriage, in which interests are shared and life is pleasant, but interactions lack intensity; the vital marriage, in which one major area is intensely satisfying to both spouses; and finally the total marriage, in which many areas are intensely satisfying to both spouses.

The fifth variable is the amount of individuation permitted in the family. Bowen (1978) describes the schizophrenogenic family as characterized by an undifferentiated ego mass. The boundaries between individuals are unclear, and children do not develop a clear sense of themselves in distinction from other family members, especially parents. Families can thus be classified according to the amount of individuation present.

Additional variables suggested as bases for typing families include the personality style (Glick & Kessler, 1980) and the developmental stage of the family (McGoldrick & Carter, 1980).

References

Bowen, M. (1978). *Family therapy in clinical practice*. New York: Aronson.

Glick, I. D., & Kessler, D. (1980). *Marital and family therapy*. New York: Grune & Stratton.

Jackson, D. D., & Lederer, W. (1968). *The mirages of marriage*. New York: Norton.

Kramer, C. H. (1980). *Becoming a family therapist*. New York: Human Science.

McGoldrick, M., & Carter, E. (1980). *The family life cycle: A framework for family therapy*. New York: Gardner.

A. D. COMPAAN

See MARITAL TYPES; FAMILY SYSTEMS THEORY.

Family Violence. *See* DOMESTIC VIOLENCE.

Fantasy. Fantasy is a primarily mental activity in which the original stimulus is internal. It is a form of stimulus-independent thought and covert ideation (Klinger, 1971). While cognitive psychology examines fantasy processes in creativity and problem solving, the early theoretical work came from psychotherapists' insights into mental processes.

Freudian and its derivative psychodynamic psychologies gave special consideration to the individual's imaginative and fantasy life. In strict Freudian formulations, mental and imaginative activities occur at all levels of consciousness. In the primitive and instinctual operation of the id, symbols and actions are unified into narrative story plots. The narratives may be expressed in the form of primary process dreamwork in sleep or in daydreams during lapses of attention in waking hours. In such forms instinctual motives are envisioned in themes of wish fulfillment. If the content of the dreamwork is too controversial or provocative and hence threatens the stability of personality operation, the ego performs defensive maneuvers to facilitate a more acceptable symbolism. This defensive distortion embraces secondary processes in which symbol hides another truth. Yet fantasies are not relegated solely to id and ego. During both dreamwork and in daydreaming, the moral agenda of the superego can provide the story plot and symbolism. In Freudian theory, the occurrences of these fantasy types are not necessarily delusive or pathological. Thus the traditional conception defines fantasy as combining imaginative symbols into a unified story. Fantasy and imagination are often considered synonymous.

Disguising latent meanings and motives into symbols provides the occasion for assessing personality operations and dynamics through projective techniques. Projective techniques, such as the Rorschach inkblots and the Thematic Apperception Test (TAT), in the hands of skilled clinicians unmask the personality. The projective techniques require a person to interject personal elements to form a picture or plot in the absence of distinct external stimuli. In this form of storytelling, the intellect organizes the story elements; however, the emotions energize and fuel the plot. The result is that less conscious and less structured personality elements come to assert themselves in the ambiguity of external stimuli (Henry, 1956).

The play of children often embraces fantasy and imagination. The fantasy in play constitutes a mechanism in which the child solves problems. The original solutions exist only in idea and imagination but soon are tested through the action of toys. In the socialization of many adults, the lack of correlation between ideas and reality is censured and discouraged. In terms of attention, fantasy is less concerted and volitional than more deliberate cognitions and focused problem solving. Play then has the element of spontaneity.

Historically the church has been skeptical about fantasy, since fantasy and fiction stand opposed to fact and reality. Fantasy elements also are associated with the sins of lust, pride, and covetousness. When fantasy elements go unchecked and out of control, they constitute the essence of obsessions. Fantasy has fared no better in general and experimental psychology than it has in the church. Klinger noted that "theories of fantasy have, with rare exception, remained insulated from general psychology" (1971, p. vii).

The creative process often utilizes fantasy and imagery tools to assist in creative production. Brainstorming is a productive stage in problem solving. But the items developed from the brainstorming activities need to be evaluated subsequently against the operative contingencies and realities. Fantasy as a creative tool is powerful and productive, yet if the fantasy becomes an end in itself or if the individual engaging in fantasy games loses the ability to terminate the fantastic ideation, fantasy constitutes maladaptive irresponsibility and irreality. The preoccupation with the fantasy life, as seen in players of *Dungeons and Dragons* and video/computer fantasy games, illustrates the concerns of church, schools, and parents.

References

Henry W. E. (1956). *The analysis of fantasy: The Thematic Apperception Technique in the study of personality.* New York: Wiley.

Klinger, E. (1971). *Structure and functions of fantasy.* New York: Wiley-Interscience.

R. L. Timpe

See Imagery, Therapeutic Use of; Creativity.

Fantasy in Therapy. *See* Imagery, Therapeutic Use of.

Fasting. The voluntary abstinence from food. Fasting has been advocated as a means for weight loss, a religious exercise, and a way to prevent bodily diseases. It has also been implicated as a symptom of anorexia nervosa. For whatever reason, fasting has been the focal point of a great deal of controversy and deserves serious attention.

Fasting is often criticized for being a crash diet that may produce quick initial weight loss with equally rapid rebound gain. It is not a sound program of self-management that requires a long-term commitment and emphasizes gradual weight loss. Effective weight loss, researchers argue (Williams & Long, 1983), requires one to change one's style of eating permanently. This is accomplished through the development of weight management skills. Fasting, although it may achieve quick and dramatic weight loss, fails to teach these skills.

Fasting is not without possible physical risks. Berland (1974), after an extensive review of the literature, concludes that there are potential hazards with fasting that necessitate continuous medical supervision. Agreeing with the U.S. Public Health Service, he argues that a fasting diet should never be self-administered. Fasting for more than a day, even for religious or meditative reasons, can be dangerous to one's health.

Any discussion of fasting must mention the life-threatening eating disorder anorexia nervosa, in which fasting (self-starvation) leads to serious weight loss and is coupled with an intense fear of becoming obese and a refusal to eat sufficiently to gain or maintain body weight. Effective intervention includes individual and family therapy, together with biological and behavioral interventions to reestablish normal eating patterns.

Claims for the use of fasting as a means to prevent bodily disease have been numerous, but they are generally not substantiated by carefully controlled research.

An excellent example of a nondogmatic and biblically balanced treatment of fasting as a spiritual discipline can be found in Foster (1978). He contends that fasting has developed a bad reputation both inside and outside the church because of the excessive ascetic practices of the Middle Ages and the constant propaganda that implies that unless we eat three large meals a day, with snacks in between, we are on the verge of starvation. We make the mistaken assumption that the hunger urge must be satisfied.

Foster goes on to state that the Bible has much to say about fasting, and that if it is done correctly, one can fast with beneficial physical effects for up to 40 days. All major religions, he contends, see the value of fasting as a spiritual discipline.

Many Christians wonder if fasting is a commandment. Foster argues that Jesus expected his disciples to fast after he was gone, although in the strictest sense he did not command fasting. But it is obvious that Jesus "proceeded on the principle that the children of the kingdom of God would fast" (Foster, 1978, p. 47). Giving money has long been recognized as an element in Christian devotion, but fasting has been widely disputed. Strange indeed, says Foster, since fasting has far more of a biblical basis than does giving. Perhaps it is indicative of which is the larger sacrifice for contemporary Christians.

Foster concludes his discussion with suggestions about the practice of fasting. He is careful to warn diabetics, expectant mothers, and heart patients not to attempt to fast. To this list should be added growing children, adolescents, and persons who are described as well-behaved, conscientious, and perfectionistic (i.e., at high risk for developing anorexia nervosa).

References

Berland, T. (Ed.). (1974). *Rating the diets*. Chicago: Rand McNally.

Foster, R. (1978). *Celebration of discipline*. San Francisco: Harper & Row.

Williams, R., & Long, J. (1983). *Towards a self-managed life style* (3rd ed.). Boston: Houghton Mifflin.

R. E. BUTMAN

Fear. This most constricting emotion contrasts with other intense negative states: anger, anxiety, phobia. Anger incites attack against a threatening object; fear incites withdrawal. Fear relates to an identifiable object or event; anxiety is interpreted as free-floating apprehension and probably incorporates other emotions with fear. Normal fear addresses a realistic danger, phobia a relatively persistent and irrational fear.

Fear ranges from uneasiness to abject insecurity, with threats to one's physical and/or psychological self. Intense fear constricts perception, thinking, and motor processes. The frightened person simultaneously wants to investigate and escape from the threat; this conflict may cause one to freeze or panic. Compared to anger, fear is more strongly associated with increases in respiration rate, skin conductance, and peaks in muscle tension. These signs relate to the hormone epinephrine (adrenalin) and sympathetic nervous system arousal.

Physiological characteristics of different emotions vary widely among individuals and receive less study than in earlier years. Facial expressions are more reliable and display fear with relatively straight, raised eyebrows; inner corners of brows drawn together; horizontal wrinkles covering most of the forehead. Eyes are wide, lower eyelids tensed and upper lids slightly raised; the mouth is open, lips tense and drawn back tightly.

Much recent research has studied the overprediction of fear. Overpredicting how much fear one might experience in a given situation has implications for phobias and panic attacks but also occurs in the context of relatively normal levels of fear. Such overprediction may be adaptive (e.g., to avoid target situations) in the short run but dysfunctional in the long term (Rachman & Bichard, 1988).

Clinicians should know normal developmental trends in fear, to distinguish normal from abnormal fears (anxieties, phobias). Fear typically differentiates from generalized distress in the child's sixth month as an innate response to sudden, intense stimuli. In the first year children come to fear loud noises and threats of bodily harm. By one year a child fears strange or unexpected stimuli, especially of objects that differ strikingly from a familiar object—for example, the father in an unaccustomed hat. Such fears are not learned per se but are maturational (i.e., based on prior internalized precepts).

In the second year children fear their mother's departure. They gain many fears in the third year—mostly auditory but also large objects, rain, wind, animals, and the dark (a fear that often lasts until age six). Visual fears predominate in the fourth year, auditory fears in the fifth. Five-year-olds show less fear, but the end of the sixth year may bring more fears—sleeping alone and auditory stimuli.

Some of the numerous fears at age six may be learned: fears of ghosts, witches, large wild animals, loud weather, bodily injury. At seven fears become more personal: wars, new situations, being late for school, burglars. By eight children increasingly cope with fears and have fewer but more variable fears, especially school failure and self-esteem threats (Ilg & Ames, 1955).

Children learn fears several ways, including identification with adults or peers who model fears of objects or events. By classical conditioning, fear of an originally neutral stimulus may develop when the latter is associated with a fear-producing stimulus (*see* Conditioning, Classical). However, some neutral stimuli are more prone to formulation of conditioned fear responses than others. Some individual differences in intensity and number of fears depend on temperament and proneness to emotional conditioning.

Fear occurs naturally in all neocortical animal species and serves adaptive functions. A fearless animal is likely to become a predator's dinner or roadkill. In people, moderate fear is adaptive; patients with intermediate levels of presurgery fears respond to the surgery better than those with either little or great fear. Fear keeps social mammals in protective groups and bonds infant primates more tightly to their mothers. Maternal bonds paradoxically provide a security that allows infants more readily to explore their world. However, extreme fear produces exaggerated bonds that interfere with formation of other social relations (Suomi & Harlow, 1976).

Some parents try to control children's behavior by recourse to fear of the bogeyman, the devil, or "your father." Adult versions of socialization by fear (e.g., slowing your car when you see a patrolman) usually mix guilt, shame, or other emotions with fear. Instead of provoking fear, parents who tolerate fear may teach children to accept and master irrational fears. A further step encourages positive action in the face of fear—facing the dentist courageously despite apprehension. Excessive fear may be controlled cognitively by reinterpretation of supposed threats, assurances of security, and strengthening of incompatible behaviors: "Do not fear, for

I am with you" (Isa. 41:10, NIV); "perfect love drives out fear" (1 John 4:18, NIV).

References

Ilg, F. L., & Ames, L. B. (1955). *Child behavior.* New York: Harper.

Rachman, S., & Bichard, S. (1988). The overprediction of fear. *Clinical Psychology Review, 8,* 303–312.

Suomi, S. J., & Harlow, H. F. (1976). The facts and functions of fear. In M. Zuckerman & C. D. Spielberger (Eds.), *Emotions and anxiety.* Hillsdale, NJ: Erlbaum.

R. D. KAHOE

See ANXIETY; PHOBIC DISORDERS.

Fechner, Gustav Theodor (1801–1887). Founder of psychophysics. He was born in Gross-Särchen in southeastern Germany, where his father had followed his grandfather as the Lutheran pastor in the village. Since his father died when Fechner was only 5 years old, he, his mother, and his brother spent the next nine years with his uncle, who was also a preacher. He started medical school at Leipzig at the age of 16 and received his degree in medicine in 1822.

Rather than practicing medicine, Fechner began translating French handbooks of physics and chemistry into German. In 1824 he began lecturing in physics at Leipzig and received the prestigious appointment of professor in 1833. Following great intellectual activity and overwork, he had a severe breakdown in 1839. He was extremely depressed, could not sleep, could not digest food, and was oversensitive to light. For three years he spent most of his time in a darkened room, listening while his mother read to him through a narrow opening in the door. His neurosis lasted until 1851. In 1844 Fechner was given a small pension from the university and thus was officially established as an invalid. However, every one of the remaining years of his life resulted in a serious scholarly contribution, and his health was good until his death.

During his illness Fechner became deeply religious, spending many hours in meditation and reflection. Concerned with the problem of the soul, he set out to investigate the relationship between the mind and the body. On the morning of 22 October 1850 it occurred to him that the solution was to be found in a statement of the quantitative relationship between mental sensation and material stimulus. This was the beginning of psychophysics, the relationship between the mind and the material world. He believed that the mind quality or sensation (S) is equal to a constant (K) times the logarithm of the stimulus (R). Thus Fechner's law is S=KlogR. His psychophysical methods of average error, constant stimuli, and limits are still used.

Fechner wrote widely in many fields, but his most important work in psychology was *Elements of Psychophysics* (1860). His interest in religion is reflected in the title of another work, *Zend-Avesta,*

or The Things of Heaven and the Hereafter (1851). Fechner was a physiologist for 7 years, a physicist for 15, an invalid for 12, a psychophysicist for 14, an experimental estheticist for 11, and a philosopher for a least 40 of those years.

R. L. KOTESKEY

See PSYCHOPHYSICS.

Fees for Psychotherapy. One important aspect of the delivery of psychological services that has received relatively little attention is the setting of fees for service. For the most part individuals or institutions have established fees based on subjective judgments of the worth of the service relative to that provided by others. For individual psychotherapists this usually reflects training, years of experience, and competency. However, in the absence of guidelines and standards this involves to a large extent abiding by prevailing rates or a judgment of what the market will bear.

Although there has been a considerable amount of clinical folklore regarding the setting and handling of psychotherapy fees, relatively little research has been conducted on the issue.

Clinical Considerations. One guiding notion in the history of fee assessment has been the assumption that psychotherapy must involve a sacrifice for the patient if it is to be maximally effective. First expressed by Sigmund Freud, this view has been a cornerstone of psychoanalytic thought since then. Dewald (1969) argues that if the fee is set too low, the patient may depreciate the therapy and not take it seriously. The patient may also have to feel grateful to the therapist for the low fee, which in turn makes the expression of anger toward the therapist difficult. The acceptance of a reduced fee may also lead the patient to feelings of guilt and the feeling of having gotten something unfairly.

Setting too high a fee may also produce complications in therapy. In an effort to please the therapist patients may agree to an unrealistically high fee that may jeopardize their financial resources and place them under a significant additional burden. In such situations patients may be more prone to expectations of a magical cure or to transference reactions related to their perception of specialness to the therapist by virtue of their paying more than other patients.

From the standpoint of the therapist the fee will also have a variety of meanings. Too low a fee may be set by a therapist wishing to be liked or seen as kind and beneficent. However, this may later lead to feelings of resentment and other negative countertransferential responses. Such a therapist may also feel the patient should be appreciative and may therefore have a more difficult time handling negative transference reactions in the patient. Setting too high a fee will also have consequences for the therapist. Often this produces a feeling of guilt or a sense of pressure to do an extra good job, either of these reactions being counterproductive to good therapeutic work.

These considerations led Langs (1973) to advise that therapists should carefully set a fair fee for their services and communicate this directly to patients. Patients should then be allowed time to react. If they feel they cannot afford the stated fee, therapists should be ready to either offer a lower one, indicating that this is an acceptable fee to them, or offer to refer the patient to someone else who will accept a lower fee. Langs also feels that it is the therapist's responsibility to be as certain as possible that the agreed-upon fee is realistic for the patient. Therapists should also ensure that it will be acceptable to themselves for the duration of treatment. Langs believes that raising a fee during therapy always produces seriously undesirable complications.

One final clinical issue related to the fee is that of insurance. Some psychoanalysts refuse to accept insurance payments out of concern for the loss of confidentiality involved in such arrangements or the feeling that such coverage removes the necessary financial sacrifice from the patient. However, accepting insurance payments is standard practice for most therapists. The availability of insurance should not influence the therapist to charge a larger than usual fee. Therapists similarly must be careful never to participate in any of the devious fee arrangements that patients sometimes suggest in conjunction with insurance coverage. (See Langs, 1973, for a nonmoralistic discussion of why therapists must avoid such arrangements.)

Research. Research on fees in therapy has been limited to a small number of studies that have investigated the relationship between fees and outcome. Evidence reported by Rosenbaum, Friedlander, and Kaplan (1956) indicated that fee-paying clients improved significantly more than nonpaying clients. Goodman (1960) found a similar relationship. Several more recent studies have, however, contradicted this finding. Dightman (1970) found no relationship between fee and improvement, appointment-keeping behavior, or length of treatment.

Pope, Geller, and Wilkinson (1975) reviewed the records of 434 psychotherapy cases, distinguishing four fee arrangements: no payment, welfare, scaled payment, and full fee. They also controlled for two potentially confounding variables: socioeconomics status and diagnosis. Their results showed fee arrangement to be unrelated to outcome, session attendance, and length of therapy. Balch, Ireland, and Lewis (1977) report the same conclusion.

These studies suggest that fee payment may not serve as the source of motivation that clinical thought has suggested. Their limited number, as well as some methodological problems, suggest caution in drawing any conclusions until further research is carried out.

Christian Perspective. Principle 6 (Welfare of the Consumer) of the *Ethical Principles of Psychol-*ogists (American Psychological Association, 1981) indicates that psychologists should "contribute a portion of their services to work for which they receive little or no financial return" (p. 6). This public service ideal is easily ignored or forgotten. However, for the Christian it is ignored at the expense of the fundamental Christian virtue of charity, or self-sacrificing love and service of others with special concern for the poor.

Danco (1982) develops a Christian perspective on fee practices in psychotherapy, suggesting that churches should assist Christian professionals in providing psychological services to lower socio-economic clientele. They could do this by providing office space and support staff and by underwriting therapy costs. Christian therapists involved in such an arrangement would usually need to accept less total income than could be generated by traditional private practice. This would be one way, however, of demonstrating Christian charity and a way of involving the church in providing psychological services. Regardless of how it is done, the Christian psychotherapist should demonstrate concern for those needing but unable to afford his or her services. Fees will be set, therefore, with this in mind.

References

American Psychological Association. (1981). *Ethical principles of psychologists.* Washington, DC: Author.

Balch, P., Ireland, J. F., & Lewis, S. B. (1977). Fees and therapy: Relation of source of payment to course of therapy at a community mental health center. *Journal of Consulting and Clinical Psychology, 45,* 504.

Danco, J. C. (1982). The ethics of fee practices: An analysis of presuppositions and accountability. *Journal of Psychology and Theology, 10,* 13–21.

Dewald, P. A. (1969). *Psychotherapy: A dynamic approach* (2nd ed.). New York: Basic.

Dightman, C. R. (1970). Fees and mental health services: Attitudes of the professional. *Mental Hygiene, 54,* 401–406.

Goodman, N. (1960). Are there differences between fee and non-fee cases? *Social Work, 5,* 46–52.

Langs, R. (1973). *The technique of psychoanalytic psychotherapy* (Vol. 1). New York: Aronson.

Pope, K. S., Geller, J. D., & Wilkinson, L. (1975). Fee assessment and outpatient psychotherapy. *Journal of Consulting and Clinical Psychology, 43,* 835–841.

Rosenbaum, M., Friedlander, J., & Kaplan, S. M. (1956). Evaluation of results of psychotherapy. *Psychosomatic Medicine, 18,* 113–132.

D. G. Benner

See Counseling and Psychotherapy: Overview.

Feminism and Pastoral Care. Feminism is a diverse and complex social movement. It has neither a single methodology nor a single theoretical perspective. What most unites the diverse range of feminists is the concern that women's experience be a valid source of insight within modern cultures. As such, feminism is often a reaction against an unwarranted male dominance that is perceived to pervade all culture. Both theology and social science are seen by many feminists to have been tools of oppression consciously or unconsciously directed by males against females. Thus feminist spokespersons have tended to focus upon broad-scale cultural criticism, including both systems of knowledge and social practices that follow from them. A major focus of criticism has been existing theologies and the sources from which they derive, including the Bible. Insofar as pastoral care is biblically based, feminists have tended to attack it as furthering the exploitation of women rather than providing a legitimate avenue for their care in times of crisis.

At the theological level, feminist theologians such as Ruether (1982) have created explicit feminist theologies. Their assumption is that existing theologies, even when they are explicitly biblically based, have been interpreted in ways that exploit women. Assuming that all theologies support a community of believers who derive from initial revelatory experiences accepted by a formative group, Ruether criticizes the evangelical and fundamentalist Christian traditions for their patriarchal bias and argues that "many aspects of the Bible are to be frankly set aside and rejected" (1982, p. 23). Her theology, like many feminist theologies, utilizes sources other than the Bible as valid insights into constructing a variety of feminist theologies. Since pastoral care is always defined within a given theological context, the reliance upon nonbiblically based theologies creates alternative views of pastoral care. Many of these are hostile to traditional Christianity.

Insofar as pastoral care is not based simply upon secular social scientific theories, it must take sacred texts seriously as diagnostic and normative guides. An appropriate understanding of sacred texts and interventions appropriately based upon this understanding make pastoral care unique within the helping profession. This approach assures that pastoral care can be neither theoretically nor morally neutral (Stone, 1996). Thus feminist theologies that reject traditional biblical understandings do not support pastoral care within evangelical and fundamentalist contexts. They are more likely to provide "atrocity tales" of the purported harm done to women under such patriarchal and authoritarian systems and to urge women to reject pastoral care provided within these contexts (Ritter & O'Neill, 1996).

To the extent that feminist theologies rely heavily upon nonbiblical understandings of divinity, their vision of pastoral care is radically altered from mainstream Christian models of care. The greater they are from normative biblical beliefs or the further removed other traditions are from revealed Christianity, the greater their rejection of pastoral care models developed within an evangelical or a fundamentalist understanding of Scripture.

Feminists rely heavily upon unique interpretations of social scientific theories that have classically been associated with severe biblical criticisms, if not outright rejection of Christian Scripture. Marxism, liberalism, and psychoanalysis dominate feminist discourse (Neitz, 1995, p. 521). Each of these theories places biblical understanding of pastoral care in a radically new light.

Feminists tend to reject what they see as a dominant male narrative and understanding of religious experience. The work of Gilligan (1982) suggests that female development and thought are seen to occur in a context in which relations are crucial. In female development individual autonomy is seen as sacrificed for the care and concern for others, often in a context of submission to male authority. This contrasts with male development, in which autonomy is achieved in opposition to relational considerations. In a religious crisis normal male autonomy is sacrificed for submission to a higher authority. This typical male model of spiritual development—autonomy, then surrender—forms the basis of much of biblically based understandings of religious experience and guides much of pastoral care. As such, feminists see it as "androcentric" and not helpful to women (Neitz, 1995, pp. 524–530). Women, who are socialized into a submission in their relational concern for others, must achieve their own autonomy before it can be sacrificed in a willing submission to God. Thus the achievement of autonomy or empowerment is perceived to be a goal common to both feminist theology and a pastoral care that genuinely serves women's needs.

If feminism tends toward a liberal perspective, it is important to note that there is not a single feminism but many feminisms centering on appreciation and concern for women's life experiences. More traditional religions have also begun to develop their own feminist concerns within a biblical perspective. Models of pastoral care based upon Scripture are being developed in which women can maintain their evangelical and even fundamentalist religious beliefs, yet seek and provide pastoral care that is genuinely sensitive to their needs as women (Tan, 1991). More sensitive understandings of women within the biblical tradition support a proper autonomy for women. Both women and men are seen as autonomous beings within a biblical context that requires that both submit to God's will. Such understandings of Scripture assure that the largely hostile stance of feminists toward more conservative religious traditions will be but a phase in a larger movement to assure that all persons are given proper care by those who shepherd on God's behalf. Rather than a rejection of Scripture, there is likely to be a deeper appreciation of the complexities of God's Word as it applies to crisis situations for which males and females may be differently but fairly treated in the context of pastoral care that is genuinely biblically based.

References

Gilligan, C. (1982). *In a different voice*. Cambridge, MA: Harvard University Press.

Neitz, M. J. (1995). Feminist theory and religious experience. In R. W. Hood, Jr. (Ed.). *Handbook of religious experience*. Birmingham, AL: Religious Education Press.

Ritter, K. Y., & O'Neill, C. W. (1996). *Righteous religion: Unmasking the illusions of fundamentalism and authoritarian Catholicism*. New York: Haworth.

Ruether, R. R. (1983). *Sexism and God-talk: Toward a feminist theology*. Boston: Beacon.

Stone, H. W. (1996). *Theological context for pastoral caregiving*. New York: Haworth.

Tan, S-Y. (1991). *Lay counseling: Equipping Christians for a helping ministry*. Grand Rapids, MI: Zondervan.

R. W. Hood

See WOMEN, PSYCHOLOGY OF.

Feminist Psychology. Feminist psychologists focus on how beliefs about gender affect the study and application of psychology. They reveal and challenge the masculine bias that currently dictates the content, methods, and interpretation of psychological research and practice. They address the absence of women in psychology, both as researchers and as research participants, and argue that the discipline and by extension society have been negatively affected by this neglect. More recently feminist psychologists have also addressed issues such as race and class, both independently and in combination with gender. Not all women in psychology are feminists, and some men are. There is also considerable diversity of perspective within feminist psychology, reflecting the diversity and development in the broader feminist movement.

Feminist psychologists have challenged the content of psychology. While psychology purports to be the study of human thought and behavior, research participants have been predominantly male (and white, middle-class, university students); male thought and behavior have been used as the norm against which female thought and behavior are compared, with differences between males and females interpreted as female deficiencies; most researchers have been male and have uncritically generalized their experience of and assumptions about the world to females.

One way to redress this masculine bias in psychology is to focus on women and women's experiences. In 1973 the American Psychological Association approved the formation of a new division on the Psychology of Women. There is some controversy among feminists about the suitability of this approach. Some fear that a separate psychology of women serves to further marginalize women. Others argue for the need to focus exclusively on women for a time, so that women's experiences are highlighted rather than lost or ignored.

Focusing directly on women has borne fruit. For example, in 1982 Gilligan published her research on moral development in women. Her intent was to counter the prevailing view that women are generally less morally mature than men, a view that emerged from the work of her colleague, Lawrence Kohlberg. Gilligan argued that women's apparent moral immaturity is an artifact of the assumption that there is a single, masculine way to conceive of human moral development. She demonstrated that women make moral decisions on the basis of different criteria than do men, emphasizing relationships and mutual responsibility where men emphasize abstract moral principles and individual rights. Therefore the gender difference in moral reasoning is not quantitative, with women lesser than men, but qualitative, with women different from men.

The question of whether men and women are qualitatively different kinds of people or are basically the same, barring some minor reproductive differences, is an important one in feminist research. Gilligan's (1982) work fits in the former category, which is known as an essentialist approach because it purports to describe the essence or true nature of each gender. Essentialists take the position that men and women are different but equal, although some feminists view supposedly uniquely female qualities as superior. Because the essentialist approach looks for enduring differences that characterize the genders across culture, class, and race, it fits well with current mainstream psychological thought, which emphasizes immutable and biologically based traits and behaviors. However, the existence of qualitative gender differences does not of necessity mean that those differences are innate; they could be the result of systematically different socialization experiences for each gender.

The view that men and women are basically the same but become different as a result of culture and socialization practices is called social constructivism. An example of research from this perspective is that of Maccoby and Jacklin (1974), who have shown how research on sex differences is used to validate culturally created stereotypes about men and women. Their careful meta-analyses of hundreds of studies have shown that few reported sex differences stand up to scrutiny; most are small average differences that are swamped by much larger within-gender diversity. They also point out that when sociocultural conditions change, the magnitude and direction of sex differences sometimes change also. Yet usually only those studies that do find sex differences, however small, are published by psychological journals and are reported in the popular media. Thus social constructivists emphasize how our culture shapes our views and expectations of men and women, our gender identities, and gender roles. Some go as far as arguing that gender is an entirely constructed concept with no objective reality.

While some feminists have worked within the methods of mainstream psychology, critiquing and challenging current theories and models by pointing out methodological errors and using those methods to demonstrate the truth of their alternative claims, other feminists have challenged the methods themselves. They argue, along with sociologists and philosophers of science, that scientists are not detached observers of an objective and orderly natural and social reality; that science is a value-laden enterprise that occurs in particular historical, cultural, and political contexts that the scientist cannot escape. Psychology is an inherently reflexive science; that is, it involves the observation of human beings by human beings. Therefore it is particularly important that psychologists become aware of the ways in which their personal and cultural beliefs affect their research and practice.

Feminist psychology explicitly acknowledges the influence of context (culture, values, beliefs, power relations) on which methods are accepted as a means to valid knowledge and on the interpretation of observed behaviors. Feminists are developing alternative methods that take context seriously in examining human thought and behavior, methods that acknowledge, use, and value the subjectivity of the researcher as well as the participants (Nielsen, 1990).

Feminist psychology also has a distinctly political character. Not content with description, prediction, and control of behavior, feminist psychologists hope to change personal attitudes, government policies, and society. Their dream is to contribute to a safe world in which women can be liberated to take their place as equally valued participants in human culture and in which men and women share power and responsibility and develop their full potential. For example, feminist psychologists not only have shown that fathers can be as nurturing as mothers but also have challenged men to become active and responsible partners in parenting. Feminist psychologists might examine the sources of oppression by asking questions such as precisely how unequal power and status are maintained in the culture by both the powerful and the powerless and the relationships among power, gender, and violence.

There is much in the feminist approach to psychology with which Christians can resonate. There is biblical warrant for treating women as equally valued image bearers of God, and the feminist challenge to men to take on their share of the responsibility for nurturing healthy marriages and families is beginning to be echoed by Christian leaders (Van Leeuwen, 1984). The position that all of reality is a human social construction, however, goes against the belief that there is a meaning and purpose to creation beyond those we create for ourselves.

References

Gilligan, C. (1982). *In a different voice: Psychological theory and women's development.* Cambridge, MA: Harvard University Press.

Maccoby, E. E., & Jacklin, C. (1974). *The psychology of sex differences.* Stanford, CA: Stanford University Press.

Nielsen, J. M. (Ed.). (1990). *Feminist research methods: Exemplary readings in the social sciences.* Boulder, CO: Westview.

Van Leeuwen, M. S. (1984). The female reconstructs psychology. *Journal of Psychology and Christianity, 3,* 20–32.

H. Looy

See WOMEN, PSYCHOLOGY OF.

Feminist Psychotherapy. Feminist psychotherapy is a combination of feminist philosophy and the theory and research on the psychology of women and gender. As there are many forms of feminism and numerous schools of thought on the psychology of women, feminist psychotherapy takes many forms. Common to many of these variations, however, are some basic assumptions. The first assumption is that all persons should be valued equally. The second assumption is that the goal of psychotherapy with women should be to give voice to the unique experience of women and empower them to define their own lives in the midst of ever-changing roles and culture.

Another assumption is that most forms of psychotherapy are based on biased psychological theory. Much of psychotherapy is based on the work of early theorists, such as Sigmund Freud, who saw women as inferior to men. Through the late 1960s and early 1970s, feminist psychology began with the critique that traditional models of psychotherapy based mental health goals and techniques on male experience. Women's experience and subsequent psychological structures were ignored or considered irrelevant for psychology theory. Women's experience and personality structures were frequently discussed as pathological by traditional psychology. Broverman, Broverman, Clarkson, Rosenkrantz, and Vogel (1970), in a now-classic study, found that their sample of psychotherapists equated "healthy male traits" with healthy person traits. Traits considered female (e.g., passive) were unhealthy. The paradox was that if women were stereotypically feminine they would be unhealthy adults; if they exhibited healthy adult traits they would be violating traditional female role norms. Along these lines, Chesler (1972) examined the cultural bias inherent in diagnoses commonly given to women. More recently Brown and Ballou (1992) examined psychotherapeutic orientations for embedded bias.

Another line of critique focused on developmental theory. For example, women's lives rarely match the traditional developmental progression offered by Erik Erikson. For example, although women have children in early adulthood, Erikson considers generativity to be a midlife task. Erikson also separates identity formation from intimacy. Most women's psychology theorists believe the two are intertwined for women (Gilligan, 1982; Jordan, Kaplan, Baker-Miller, Stiver, & Surrey, 1991). While Erikson (1974) wrote that he based his theory on male experience and that it does not apply to women, most psychology texts present his theory as universal to men and women. As developmental theory is basic to most theories of psychotherapy, a relevant theory of women's development was called for. Jordan et al. offer a developmental schema based on women's relationships instead of Erikson's theme of individuation.

Growing dissatisfaction with inadequate approaches to women in therapy and the realization that the majority of clients are women being treated by male therapists led to some attitudinal changes within the profession. The American Psychological Association (APA) recognized the underlying sexism in much of psychology theory and practice. The APA Task Force on Sex Bias and Sex Role Stereotyping in Psychotherapeutic Practice (1978) published a set of guidelines for therapy with women that mirrored the concerns of the newly formed field of feminist psychology. The guidelines begin to address the devaluing behaviors of psychologists toward women clients, the sex bias in many theories of psychotherapy, the effects of bias on clients, the negative effects of client-therapist power differences, and the effects of sexual violence on clients.

Dambrot and Reep (1993) write that while the APA's guidelines are vital, feminist guidelines need to also incorporate the following assumptions. Pathology is not purely intrapsychic but is also social, political, and environmental, and the therapeutic relationship must be egalitarian. The client's familial and cultural environment contribute more to her mental health status than medical model diagnostic schemas recognize. Most diagnostic categories are seen as blaming women for environmentally caused stressors. (For example, depression in a married woman can be seen as an intrapsychic process or as the result of a conflicted marital relationship.) Feminist psychotherapy also recognizes the prolonged negative effects of oppression and bias on the functioning of individuals (Worell & Remer, 1992).

Power differentials between client and therapist are seen as countertherapeutic by feminist psychologists because they inhibit a client's self-discovery and self-creation. One goal of feminist psychotherapy is to demystify the therapeutic process. This gives control or power back to the client for her own healing process. By instituting egalitarian practices in psychotherapy, the therapist models skills that the client can use in the community to identify and change oppressive environments. Beyond the therapist's office, feminist psychotherapy also calls the therapist to be politically active in one's community and calls for commitment to low-income or disenfranchised women (Butler, 1985).

While there are many forms of feminist therapy, some common techniques can be identified. Through basic listening techniques feminist psychotherapy tries to give voice to a woman's self-experience and empower her to make decisions and changes in her life that are healthy. Worell and Remer (1992) list other techniques: for example, sex-role analysis to increase awareness of cultural pressures, power analysis, assertiveness training, bibliotherapy, and reframing intrapersonal problems as also being interpersonal problems. One major type of therapy involves work with women who have been abused. The authors stress the importance of reframing the abuse so the client is not blamed for what occurred and so the client's symptoms are interpreted as normal reactions to trauma rather than as personality deficits.

Feminist psychotherapists have specialized in areas of research, theory, and treatment that have been neglected by other groups or are disorders of high prevalence for women. These areas include stress associated with reproductive difficulty, intimate violence, body image, eating disorders, breast cancer, discrimination and sexual harassment, incest, motherhood, family stress, dependency, and anger. Treatment strategies have been developed specifically for women for a wide range of difficulties unique to women's lives. Feminist psychologists also have challenged traditional understandings of disorders such as borderline personality disorder. Instead of being viewed as a personality disorder, the symptoms can be seen as posttraumatic stress (Brown & Ballou, 1992).

Basing their comments on the general philosophies of feminist psychology, Rave and Larsen (1995) offer ethical guidelines for providing treatment to women that take into account that women are not a heterogeneous group. Psychotherapy should take into account a women's cultural background, socioeconomic background, developmental level, and sexual preference. This and work by Brown and Root (1990) and Comas-Diaz and Greene (1994) address the common criticism that feminist psychology has been too focused on white middle-class women, ignoring other cultural groups. Many of the feminist psychology theorists are suggesting that therapists become multiculturally appropriate by examining personal cultural bias, working to provide access to therapy to culturally diverse persons, and working within the community to empower multicultural persons.

Along these lines, feminist psychologists are also addressing spirituality (under the guise of diversity) as an important element of healing. Feminist psychology encourages the integration of faith into the psychotherapeutic practices of the therapist. While at this time a Christian feminist psychology is undeveloped, the Christian feminist writings of Van Leeuwen (1994) offer a foundation for such a theory.

Ongoing debates within feminist psychology include the discussion over who should be qualified to do feminist psychotherapy. Dambrot and Reep (1993) ask: Should men practice feminist psychotherapy? What qualifies women to be identified as a feminist psychologist? Should formal training and educational requirements exist for the designation? How should we train feminist psychologists? (Feminist training programs are being developed currently to address this issue.)

There is little agreement on the answers to these questions because the term *feminist psychotherapy* covers such a broad range of theory, research, and treatment. However, the underlying goal of feminist psychology is the valuing of women and their experience. Feminist psychologists have expanded our understanding of women and the relationship between women and the world.

References

American Psychological Association Task Force on Sex Bias and Sex Role Stereotyping in Psychotherapeutic Practice (1978). Guidelines for Therapy with Women. *American Psychologist, 41,* 1122–1123.

Broverman, I. K., Broverman, D. M., Clarkson, F. E., Rosenkrantz, P. S., & Vogel, S. R. (1970). Sex role stereotypes and clinical judgments of mental health. *Journal of Consulting and Clinical Psychology, 34* (1), 1–7.

Brown, L. S., & Ballou, M. (1992). *Personality and psychopathology.* New York: Guilford.

Brown, L. S., & Root, M. P. P. (Eds.). (1990). *Diversity and complexity in feminist therapy.* New York: Haworth.

Butler, M. (1985). Guidelines for feminist therapy. In L. B. Rosewater & L. E. A. Walker (Eds.), *Handbook for feminist therapy: Women's issues in psychotherapy.* New York: Springer.

Chesler, P. (1972). *Women and madness.* Garden City, NY: Doubleday.

Comas-Diaz, L., & Greene, B. (Eds.). (1994). *Women of color: Integrating ethnic and gender identities in psychotherapy.* New York: Guilford.

Dambrot, F., & Reep, D. C. (1993). Overview of feminist therapy: A treatment choice for contemporary women. *Journal of Training & Practice in Professional Psychology, 7* (1), 10–25.

Erikson, E. H. (1974). Womanhood and the inner space (1968). In J. Strouse (Ed.) *Woman and analysis.* New York: Laurel Editions.

Gilligan, C. (1982). *In a different voice: Psychological theory and women's development.* Cambridge, MA: Harvard University Press.

Jordan, J. V., Kaplan, A. G., Baker-Miller, J., Stiver, I. P., & Surrey, J. L. (1991). *Women's growth in connection: Writings from the Stone Center.* New York: Guilford.

Rave, E. J., & Larsen, C. C. (1995). *Ethical decision making in therapy: Feminist perspectives.* New York: Guilford.

Van Leeuwen, M. S. (Ed.) (1994). *After Eden: Facing the challenge of gender reconciliation.* Grand Rapids, MI: Eerdmans.

Worell, J., & Remer, P. (1992). *Feminist perspectives in therapy: An empowerment model for women.* New York: Wiley.

M.L. Dykstra

See Feminist Psychology; Women, Psychology of.

Festinger, Leon (1919–1989). Social psychologist whose major contribution was in the study of cognitive dissonance. Born in New York City, he earned his B.S. degree from the City College of New York and his M.A. and Ph.D. from the State University of Iowa.

Festinger taught and conducted research at many universities during the early years of his career. He was at Iowa until 1943, Rochester until 1945, the Massachusetts Institute of Technology until 1948, Michigan until 1951, and Minnesota until 1955. He taught at Stanford from 1955 to 1968 and then went to the New School for Social Research in New York City, where he remained until his death.

Festinger viewed humans as essentially thinking beings who try to bring order and coherence into their lives. He usually formulated problems as oppositions of tendencies, believing that people are motivated to resolve them. His early work on level of aspiration pitted performance against expectation. His social comparison theory pitted opinions and abilities against the need to know the truth about themselves. If no objective standards are available, persons will judge themselves by comparing themselves with other appropriate people. Even in his more recent work on vision he pitted visual against kinesthetic sensation.

Although Festinger conducted research in various areas of social psychology, no recent concept in that field has stimulated more research than his theory of cognitive dissonance. In *A Theory of Cognitive Dissonance* (1957) he stated that two cognitive elements (beliefs, opinions, understandings) "are in a dissonant relation if, considering these two alone, the obverse of one would follow from the other." For example, assuming that they want to live a long, healthy life, cigarette smokers experience cognitive dissonance when they know that they smoke and enjoy doing so and that smoking is hazardous to their health. Festinger himself was a chain smoker.

Cognitive dissonance is regarded as being an uncomfortable state that people are motivated to reduce or eliminate. Such dissonance can be reduced in several ways. Smokers can quit smoking, avoid information reminding them of the dangers of smoking, emphasize the pleasures that smoking brings, reinterpret the information about health hazards so that the risk seems small, and so forth.

Festinger applied cognitive dissonance theory to situations ranging from a cultist group waiting for the end of the world (*When Prophecy Fails,* 1956) to rats running in a maze getting partial reinforcement (*Deterrents and Reinforcement,* 1962). So great was his contribution to social psychology that in his obituary, Zajonc (1990) said that Festinger is to social psychology what Sigmund Freud is to clinical psychology and Jean Piaget is to developmental psychology.

Reference

Zajonc, R. B. (1990). Leon Festinger (1919–1989). *American Psychologist, 45* (5), 661.

R. L. Koteskey

See Cognitive Dissonance.

Fetishism. Sexual fetishism is the use of nonliving objects to obtain erotic arousal. The object must be used repeatedly, and it must be the exclusive or preferred method of achieving sexual excitement. Objects usually include women's underclothing, boots, shoes, or sometimes unrelated items such as plastic bags, automobile tailpipes, or baby carriages. Occasionally the fetish involves parts of the body such as hair or fingernails.

The fetish is usually fondled, kissed, smelled, or tasted to achieve sexual excitement. This may accomplish orgasm in itself, but it is usually accompanied by masturbation. Sexual fetishism most commonly involves males.

Fetishism is usually part of a larger pattern of maladjustment. The individual may have doubts about his masculinity and potency. He may fear humiliation or rejection by the opposite sex. The mastery over inanimate objects compensates for his feelings of inferiority and failure at mastery in relationships.

The mere involvement of objects in the process of sexual excitement is not necessarily fetishistic. The smell of perfume or viewing attractive articles of clothing for the purpose of stimulating sexual arousal is not considered a fetish unless the article becomes a sexual end in itself and precludes normal male-female sexual relationships.

The individual engaging in fetishism sometimes comes in conflict with the law in the pursuit of the desired object. This situation is illustrated by a man who had a fetish for large plastic bags. He was arrested by the police while coming out of a dry cleaning store carrying two rolls of plastic bags he had just stolen. Most referrals for treatment of fetishism come through such contact with the law.

The age of onset of fetishism is childhood. However, the object begins to be a trigger for erotic excitement during adolescence. The original conditioning process may be accidental, but it becomes paired with sexual excitement and orgasm over time.

The effects of the overall environment on the child and adolescent must not be excluded when the conditioning process is considered. A maladaptive environment often blocks the child from progressing normally through exploration and experimentation as he develops toward sexual maturity and appropriate behavior.

The treatment of sexual fetishism is difficult because of the chronic nature of the sexual deviation and the reluctance of the individual to seek treatment. Even after they are apprehended and referred by the court, such individuals usually deny the fetish and its sexual connotations. Behavior therapy is often effective. Aversive conditioning (*see* Aversion Therapy) is utilized to decondition the client by pairing unpleasant stimuli such as an electric shock with the fetish. The patient receives a mild shock while viewing slides of the fetish object, the theory being that the unpleasant stimulus will be paired with the sexual object, thus decreasing its attractiveness. Systematic desensitization can also be employed to lessen the fears associated with heterosexual relationships.

M. A. Campion

Fictional Goals. Hans Vaihinger was a turn-of-the-century philosopher who developed the concept of fictions. He contended that there are two spheres of reality: a world of motion and a world of consciousness. Human behavior can be comprehended only in the world of consciousness. Things in themselves do not explain behavior as causes. Behavior can be understood only when psychologists comprehend the way in which people find meaning and relevance in things (Vaihinger, 1935).

Fictions do not exist in the world of things. Fictions are abstractions that consciousness finds meaningful or relevant. In mathematics the concepts of zero, empty space, negative numbers, and infinity are all fictions. In science theories that cannot be conclusively proved (e.g., atomic structure) are fictions. People use fictions as if they were accurate representations of things in themselves. For example, when Britain was on a metallic money standard, people accepted pound notes and counted them as if they were pounds of sterling.

The natural world is discovered by observation. Machines and instruments are invented by human creativity. Fictions are mental instruments, and as such they are created, not discovered. Hypotheses about the natural world are verifiable (provable by observation). Fictions are not verifiable, and indeed they are known to be false. However, fictions are proved by means of vindication (justification). Justifiable fictions are those that are useful, that are means to an end. They are errors, but they are retained and acted upon because they are fruitful errors. Fictions that do not justify themselves (i.e., cannot be proved useful or necessary) should be eliminated.

Notions of categories and causes are not observable aspects of the natural world. We retain these notions because they have utility, giving order and facilitating communication. The idea of free will is an extremely important fiction. It allows us to act as if our actions were the product of independent reason and allows us to treat others as if they were responsible for their actions. Even though we shall never have the evidence to verify free will, the fiction is vindicated by its value.

Adler (1956) read Vaihinger in 1911 and was greatly influenced by the concept of fictions. This concept enabled Adler to clarify some of his basic differences with Sigmund Freud. Adler accepted the idea that human behavior is determined by fictions, not by mechanistic forces. He then modified Vaihinger's theory in several ways. First, he emphasized that human behavior is determined by goals rather then reactions to events. Goals are fictions because they do not exist, yet individuals behave as if the goal is the most important factor in behavior. Second, he suggested that each person is unique and has his or her own set of fictions for guidance. What is vindicable for one person is not necessarily vindicable for another. Third, the purpose of the fiction is to preserve self-esteem against inferiority feeling. Fourth, most fictions are unconscious. The individual will not admit that they are fictional. Fifth, when the individual adheres rigidly to a fiction, there is a danger that lack of relevant contact with reality and other people will result in a neurosis.

Psychotherapy along the lines of individual psychology focuses on understanding the patient's fictional goals, helping the patient to achieve these insights and assisting the patient to change those fictions that are dysfunctional.

References

Adler, A. (1956). *The individual psychology of Alfred Adler.* New York: Basic.

Vaihinger, H. (1935). *The philosophy of as if: A system of the theoretical, practical, and religious fictions of mankind* (2nd ed.). New York: Barnes & Noble.

T. L. BRINK

See ADLER, ALFRED; INDIVIDUAL PSYCHOLOGY.

Field Theory. *See* LEWIN, KURT.

Figure-Drawing Tests. Tests often used by psychologists to assess emotional maturity or the presence of psychopathology in children, adolescents, and adults. In one form of the test procedure the examinee is asked to draw a person (Draw-A-Person or Draw-A-Man Tests) or to draw a house, tree, and person (House-Tree-Person Test). The examiner observes as the figures are drawn and notes how the subject executes the task. After the drawings are complete, the examiner will often interview the subject to obtain verbal information about the drawings. Later the drawings are evaluated as to their content, quality, and overall characteristics.

Interest in using drawings as a guide to assess a person's psychological nature began in the nineteenth century with evaluations of art by persons labeled insane. Early in the twentieth century Goodenough (1926) developed a version of the human figure-drawing test to assess intelligence in children. Later researchers (e.g., Koppitz, 1968) expanded the assessment of children's drawings to encompass other psychological dimensions. Buck (1966) has expanded the technique so that the test can be administered to adults.

Figure-drawing tests are projective in nature. That is, the drawings are assumed to contain some inner elements of a person's psyche that are projected into the drawing task. Drawings are said to have value because they give the examiner a look at what otherwise might be a private, unrevealed world. Figure-drawing tests are valuable because they do not require verbalization and because their purpose is somewhat obtuse to the examinee. Faking good or bad behaviors may thus be minimized, since what constitutes a good or bad response is usually unknown to the examinee. However, the figure-drawing test does require a cooperative attitude from the subject.

The interpretation of figure drawings is predicated on the assumption that "normals" will include all the essential components of the figure, will add only a few nonessential details, and will not exaggerate or overelaborate any one element of the drawing. For example, Buck (1966) defines the essential elements of a human figure drawing as a head, a trunk, two legs, and two arms. Essential facial details are two eyes, a nose, a mouth, and two ears. The absence of one or more essential elements in a figure drawing is considered serious.

Extensive guides help the examiner score the test. Various researchers have agreed on the meaning of certain features. For example, in an adult's drawing an outlined human figure that is not filled in suggests serious problems. Drawing internal organs on the trunk of a human figure is indicative of psychotic functioning (Ogdon, 1967). Other details are not uniformly interpreted. Heavy shading of human hair has been seen as indicative of anger, anxiety, sensuality, or concern with sexual excitement (Ogdon, 1967).

Such ambiguity of interpretation is a central criticism of the tests. If advocates of the tests cannot agree on interpretation, critics argue, how can such tests be valid? Roback (1968) cites other weaknesses of the assessment procedure: a paucity of solid research substantiating the procedure, reliability problems, and other concerns regarding validity. Even the staunchest advocates of the tests warn that conclusions regarding a person's functioning should never be drawn solely from figure drawings but rather from data gathered from all measurement tools in the assessment battery.

References

Buck, J. N. (1966). *The house-tree-person technique: A revised manual.* Beverly Hills, CA: Western Psychological Services.

Goodenough, F. L. (1926). *Measurement of intelligence by drawings.* Yonkers-on-Hudson, NY: World Book.

Koppitz, E. M. (1968). *Psychological evaluation of human figure drawings.* New York: Grune & Stratton.

Ogdon, D. P. (1967). *Psychodiagnosis and personality assessment.* Beverly Hills, CA: Western Psychological Services.

Roback, H. B. (1968). Human figure drawings: Their utility in the clinical psychologist's armamentarium for personality assessment. *Psychological Bulletin, 70* (1), 1–19.

Additional Readings

DiLeo, J. H. (1973). *Children's drawings as diagnostic aids.* New York: Brunner/Mazel.

Schildkrout, M. S., Shenker, J. R., & Sonnenblick, M. (1972). *Human figure drawings in adolescence.* New York: Brunner/Mazel.

J. R. BECK

See PSYCHOLOGICAL MEASUREMENT; PERSONALITY ASSESSMENT.

Figure-Ground Relationship. A perceptual phenomenon in which one part of a perception stands out as a unified object (figure) while the rest is relegated to background (ground). This phenomenon is most clearly manifest in the visual sense but occurs in all senses. It was an important object of study in the early stages of Gestalt psychology.

See GESTALT PSYCHOLOGY.

Financial Counseling. Financial counseling means getting professional or semiprofessional help with personal and family financial matters such as budgeting, tax planning, investment management, planning for future goals such as the purchase of a home, college education, retirement, and estate distributions. It may also mean getting help with the financial aspects of a crisis or change in circumstances such as divorce, loss of a job, death of a major earner, bankruptcy, debt management, and medical needs.

Professional financial counseling is done by financial planners, accountants, stockbrokers, insurance agents, bankers, and attorneys. Some financial planners work strictly on a fee-for-service basis; others do not charge fees but sell financial products and services. Licensing, educational, and experience requirements will differ with the type of professional. Some professionals may be selective in accepting clients, so referrals are useful.

Limited semiprofessional financial counseling is offered by some local churches and community agencies; for example, the Salvation Army offers tax preparation services and Roman Catholic social services and Jewish family services offer help in personal and family financial affairs. Many Christian denominations, missions, colleges, and other organizations offer written material and sometimes the services of a professional adviser in will preparation, estate planning, and use of charitable gifts as part of a tax strategy. They generally do not charge for their services but hope for a charitable gift or bequest. Many churches, especially large ones, have business managers and other staff who do financial counseling, usually without charge.

Few therapists and pastors are prepared to offer financial counseling, so it is often advisable for people to use a combination of financial professionals, church representatives, and therapists to learn how to handle financial matters and the accompanying difficult family dynamics and feelings. There are also self-help financial books and computer software programs that have extensive financial planning and budgeting functions.

Additional Resources

Blue, R. (1993). *Mastering your money workbook.* Nashville: Nelson.

Quicken Deluxe, Version 5 for Windows. Menlo Park, CA: Intuit.

W. M. GOLDSMITH AND J. B. GOLDSMITH

See GREED AND GENEROSITY; GAMBLING, PATHOLOGICAL; COUNSELING AND PSYCHOTHERAPY: OVERVIEW.

Fitness to Stand Trial. *See* FORENSIC PSYCHIATRY.

Fixation. In psychoanalytic thought fixation refers to the arrested personality development associated with the persistence of strong energy attachments (cathexes) to memories and experiences in an earlier stage of development. Fixation generally implies psychopathology, as it assumes that the energy left behind at the earlier developmental level results in a weakening of the ego. It is therefore closely related to the concept of regression, which suggests that, when facing a serious trauma or stress in the present, the individual will tend to regress to the point where energy, or ego resources, were left behind.

In both normal and abnormal functioning earlier levels of personality development persist alongside each other. Thus the mere presence of some residual aspects of infantile functioning is not in itself sufficient to indicate the presence of fixation. When fixation is present, the energy retained at the earlier levels of development exceeds that seen in more normally functioning individuals and therefore is thought to be indicative of a weak spot in the psychic structure. This weakness may manifest itself either as a neurosis or as a character trait.

Predisposing factors relative to the formation of fixations include hereditary and constitutional factors, excessive gratification, excessive frustration, or some combination of these factors. Fixations most commonly seem to develop as a result of a traumatic experience of early childhood.

Sometimes the concept of fixation is used in a less technical manner to describe an aberration of affection in which an individual experiences exaggerated attachment to someone else (e.g., a father fixation).

D. G. BENNER

See PSYCHOANALYTIC PSYCHOLOGY.

Fletcher, Joseph F. (1905–1991). Social radical, pastoral educator, and ethicist. While he was enrolled at the University of West Virginia, Fletcher's socialist sympathies and advocacy for the United Mine Workers of America led the university to withhold his degree. Fletcher attended Berkeley Divinity School and was jailed for assisting the Sacco-Vanzetti Defense Committee. He studied economics at London University-Kenyon College and economic history at Yale University. These activities culminated in the publication of *The Church and Industry* (with Spencer Miller, 1930) and *Christianity and Property* (1947).

Fletcher's position as curate of St. Peter's, Regent Square, a London slum church, inspired his theology of social justice, which reflected the social gospel of Walter Rauschenbusch, the Christian sociology of the League for the Kingdom of God (he was a contributing editor to *Christendom*), and the social theology of William Temple (analyzed in *William Temple: Twentieth-Century Christian*, 1963). Fletcher spent three years as teacher and chaplain at St. Mary's College in Raleigh, a position jeopardized by his continued activity in labor relations. In 1935 he became Dean of the Graduate School of Applied Religion (GSAR) in Cincinnati and Dean of the Cathedral of the Episcopal Church (to 1939). In 1944 he moved to the Episcopal Theological School (ETS) in Cambridge as professor of pastoral theology and Christian ethics, taking with him the GSAR. He was an associate editor for *Pastoral Psychology* and a trustee of the Institute for Pastoral Care.

Fletcher's allegiance gradually shifted from Christianity to humanism. Rejecting legalism, antinomianism, pietism, and moralism, Fletcher systematized situation ethics, a controversial position derived from pragmatism, relativism, theological positivism, and personalism. Situational ethics acknowledges "that the claim of the person who stands in the concrete situation, either as recipient or dispenser of neighbor-love, is greater than the claim of any abstract conception of the right" (Long, 1968, p. 108). His interest in medical, social, and sexual ethics led to his appointments as Robert Treat Paine Professor of Social Ethics at ETS and as professor of medical ethics at the School of Medicine of the University of Virginia. His work is assessed in Cox (1968), and a complete bibliography is included in Fletcher (1993).

References

Cox, H. (Ed.). (1968). *The situation ethics debate.* Philadelphia: Westminster.

Long, E. L. (1968). The history and literature of "the new morality." In H. Cox (Ed.), *The situation ethics debate.* Philadelphia: Westminster.

Fletcher, J. (1993). *Memoir of an ex-radical: Reminiscence and reappraisal* (Ed. K. Vaux). Louisville, KY: Westminster/John Knox.

Additional Reading

Fletcher, J. (1966). *Situation ethics: The new morality.* Philadelphia: Westminster.

H. Vande Kemp

Flight into Health. A psychoanalytic concept referring to apparent improvement in psychological functioning that is a defense against further therapeutic exploration. Because the improvement is not based on a resolution of the neurosis, it is not seen as a real cure. In many cases such rapid improvement is based on the patient's passive-dependent relationship to the therapist, who is idealized and endowed with omnipotence. For this reason it is often also called a transference cure.

Flight of Ideas. A disturbance of thinking characterized by a continuous flow of rapid speech jumping abruptly from topic to topic. Although there is no common theme or continuity of thought, each idea is superficially related to the former idea, usually through common word sounds or play-on-word associations. In severe cases the speech is elated and incoherent, and the person is unable to retain any logical train of thought. Although it is most frequently observed in manic episodes (*see* Mania), flight of ideas may also be seen in organic mental disorders, schizophrenia, and psychotic disorders.

Flooding. A behavioral approach used in elimination of unwanted fears or phobias. In flooding the client either is directly exposed to or imagines highly frightening events in a protected setting. Presumably the fear-inducing stimuli will lose their influence once the individual is fully exposed to them and discovers that no harm occurs. Following a discussion of the person's fears, the person is then asked to imagine the most feared situation. The therapist describes the salient fearful elements to enhance visualization. Thus an individual who is fearful of elevators is asked to imagine boarding a glass-enclosed high-speed elevator, then watching through the glass as the elevator rapidly rises from the ground level to the twentieth floor.

Scenes are presented for extended periods, often several minutes at a time so that the individual experiences the full fear response and it begins to abate. For extinction of the fearful response to occur, it is important that the scene not be terminated until the anxiety abates. Terminating too soon may strengthen rather than alleviate the fearful response. It is sometimes difficult to judge this, and facial and body cues must be carefully observed. Although there are widespread individual differences in the timing, it is typical that the client shows an initial increase in anxiety response and then a gradual abatement of anxiety.

Flooding is based on two-factor learning theory. This theory postulates that individuals learn to escape from situations in which they are presented with unpleasant stimuli. When a warning stimulus reliably predicts the unpleasant event, the individual gradually learns to escape when the warning stimulus is presented, thus avoiding the unpleasant event. If Dad beats Johnny when he comes home drunk, Johnny leaves the house whenever Dad comes in, thus avoiding beatings.

According to two-factor theory, the warning stimulus, through pairing with the unpleasant stimulus, comes to produce anxiety responses in anticipation of the unpleasant event. Escape from the warning stimulus eliminates these anxiety responses and hence is negatively reinforced. Research has shown that avoidance behaviors learned in this way are extremely resistant to extinction, evidently because the person is so effective in avoiding the unpleasant stimulus. This normally is an adaptive response, as when the sight of fire comes to produce caution appropriate to the capacity of fire to cause painful burns. Not infrequently, however, through a variety of unfortunate experiences, persons learn to be anxious or fearful in the presence of relatively harmless stimuli. According to behavior theory, this is how phobic responses are initiated (*see* Phobic Disorders).

In animal studies of two-factor learning theory, one effective method for eliminating fear responses to conditioned aversive stimuli when they are no longer followed by the unpleasant stimulus is preventing the animal from escaping the warning stimulus. Prolonged exposure to the warning stimulus without opportunity to escape weakens the escape response. Flooding is analogous to this procedure since the person is exposed to the unpleasant phobic stimulus without opportunity to escape. However, the mechanism of change remains unclear. Wolpe (1995) discounts extinction, exposure, and cognition as adequate explanations for the changes; his hypothesis is that an emotional response to the presence of the therapist plays a vital role through reciprocal inhibition.

Systematic desensitization and implosion share similar treatment goals with flooding but use different approaches. In systematic desensitization the individual is first taught to relax; treatment then begins with minimally anxiety-inducing stimuli, presents them briefly, and progresses gradually to more threatening stimuli, maintaining relaxation throughout. In this way anxiety is minimized throughout treatment. The elevator scene might serve as the final step in systematic desensitization, whereas it is the beginning point in flooding.

Some theorists use the terms *flooding* and *implosion* interchangeably. There are similarities in the two procedures, but important methodological and theoretical distinctions suggest that this confusion is unfortunate. Implosion, as developed by Stampfl, draws heavily on psychoanalytic theory. It is assumed that the basis for phobias is unresolved conflicts involving rejection, dependence, orality, anality, sexuality, loss of impulse control, and guilt stemming from the childhood stages of psychosexual development. Thus the imagery used in implosion focuses on these underlying conflicts rather than concentrating on the identified phobic stimulus. In addition, in implosion it is common to dramatize the scenes to make them as traumatic as possible even though the individual may have never experienced such events. The individual may be asked to imagine climbing into bed with hundreds of snakes, feeling the snakes crawling over his or her body, squeezing and biting the snakes, and so on.

The results of experimental studies of flooding are mixed. Barlow (1988) found efficacy "equivocal"; Ost (1989) found highly favorable outcomes for specific phobias, such as animal phobias, in two-hour sessions. The procedures are not standardized; thus procedural variations may account for inconsistencies in results. Flooding may be more effective with mild than with intense fears. Early comparative studies found systematic desensitization probably is as effective as flooding; recent investigations generally conclude that in vivo exposure is the preferred approach (Emmelkamp, 1994).

Because of the need to present the fear stimulus in its full intensity, flooding is generally unpleasant. This contributes to premature termination of treatment. Thus most practitioners prefer systematic or in vivo desensitization. Flooding is mostly of historical significance.

References

Barlow, D. H. (1988). *Anxiety and its disorders*. New York: Guilford.

Emmelkamp, P. M. G. (1994). Behavior therapy with adults. In A. E. Bergin and S. L. Garfield (Eds.), *Handbook of psychotherapy and behavior change* (4th ed.). New York: Wiley.

Ost, L. G. (1989). One session treatment for phobias. *Behavior Research and Therapy, 27*, 1.

Wolpe, J. (1995). Reciprocal inhibition: Major agent of behavior change. In W. O'Donohue & L. Krasner (Eds.), *Theories of behavior therapy*. Washington, DC: American Psychological Association.

R. K. BUFFORD

See BEHAVIOR THERAPY; SYSTEMATIC DESENSITIZATION; ANXIETY.

Folie à Deux. First described by Lasèque and Falret in 1877, folie à deux, or insanity of two, is a relatively rare condition in which two persons share the same mental disorder. Usually having a paranoid psychosis of a persecutory type, they believe the same reality distortion to the extent that even delusions are held in common.

The persons usually belong to the same family and have been closely related for years. They live rather socially isolated, excluding others and having few outside interests. Women are more susceptible than are men. Two sisters or a mother-daughter combination are most frequent, but occasionally a husband and wife share the disorder.

One of the pair usually dominates and may be paranoid regardless of the relationship. The other person follows in a dependent, submissive, and suggestible manner. The follower's identity is so intertwined with that of the dominant person that reality distortions are accepted uncritically. If the relationship ends, the follower's adherence to the delusions and faulty beliefs will usually decrease. Terminating the relationship is usually sufficient treatment for the follower. The more dominant person requires treatment similar to that given for paranoid psychosis.

M. R. NELSON

See DELUSION; PSYCHOTIC DISORDERS.

Forensic Psychiatry. Forensic psychiatry is a branch of forensic medicine, the science that deals with the application of medical facts to legal problems. The term *medico-legal* refers to a contrasting distinction, a branch of law that deals with the application of legal principles to medical and psychiatric problems. Forensic psychiatry and medico-legal psychiatry are used interchangeably and while "forensic psychiatry" has a specific meaning, it is generically used to denote the interface shared by psychiatry and the law. Psychiatric input into legal issues, such as criminal responsibility, is not new, whereas legal involvement in the practice of psychiatry, such as civil commitment, is a distinctly twentieth-century phenomenon.

Psychiatric Issues in Legal Practice. *Criminal Responsibility.* Society considers individuals responsible for their behavior. In the criminal justice system, individuals may present a defense against the charges against them based upon their mental condition. The often misunderstood "insanity defense" is necessary because of the widespread belief that certain individuals should not bear the label of criminal because of their psychological or neurological condition.

Over the last several centuries, several specific legal rules and standards have further clarified the concept of criminal responsibility, with all psychiatric evidence measured against these rules. The first widely used standard for the insanity defense is that which resulted from the proceedings against Daniel M'Naghten, who was acquitted in the attempt to assassinate the Prime Minister of England in 1843. The M'Naghten rule emphasizes that "at the same time of committing of the criminal act, the party accused was laboring under such a defect of reason from disease of the mind, as not to know the nature and quality of the act he was doing, or if he did know it, that he did not know that what he was doing was wrong" (Guthiel, 1995, p. 2764). The subsequent irresistible impulse rule covers crimes of passion and implies that an individual who succumbs to an impulse leading to an alleged act is not responsible for that act.

In 1955 a group of legal scholars at the American Law Institute described a model penal code that holds that "an individual is not responsible for an alleged act if by reason of mental disease or defect, that person lacks substantial capacity to appreciate the wrongfulness of the act or lack substantial capacity to behave according to the requirements of the law" (Guthiel, 1995, p. 2764). This standard was deemed an improvement because it addresses the issue of understanding and the nature of behavioral action, and it gives the court latitude in weighing the quantitative importance of the evidence through the utilization of the term substantial capacity. Modifications continue but have not substantially changed these perspectives. "Guilty but mentally ill," a recent variation of this theme, has the advantage of identifying guilt yet allowing for treatment in a psychiatric setting.

The unpopularity of the insanity defense derives from two misperceptions. One is that hardened criminals use this defense to escape conviction when in reality the insanity defense is rarely used. A corollary to this view is that psychiatrists' "get criminals off" by justifying their evil actions.

Competency to Stand Trial. Competence is rooted in the societal expectation of fairness. Simply put, defendants must understand the nature of the charges against them and have an ability to consult with their lawyer with a reasonable degree of understanding. The defendant does not need to know all specific details of the legal process but should have an average awareness of the legal situation and the pitfalls of being a defendant. Psychiatrists do not determine competency but merely offer facts relevant to its decision. A judge determines who is competent and who is not, based on the information the psychiatrist provides.

Child and Adolescent Issues. Delinquent acts by young persons are viewed as the result of psychological and neurological deficits which, when combined with age, mitigate personal responsibility. In this context children are seen not as criminal but disturbed. The category of status offense is used to determine behaviors and acts that would be crimes if the young person was the age of majority (typically 18 years). A careful psychiatric assessment presented to a juvenile court may lead to the accused being held accountable for his or her behavior while at the same time pointing to mitigating factors that lead to a corrective, treatment approach. Particularly heinous crimes tend to counteract these developmental factors, and adolescents are increasingly being tried as adults.

The increasing rate of divorce has correspondingly increased child custody disputes. The psychiatrist's role is to assess the child's developmental needs, clinical symptomatology, and parental strengths and problems. This assessment is utilized by the court to determine appropriate custody and visitation arrangements, emphasizing what is in the best interest of the child. The ideal situation is for a child custody arrangement to be agreed upon by parents without court or psychiatric involvement. When this is not possible, most clinicians prefer that their assessment is requested by the court rather than each parent procuring an assessment for adversarial purposes.

Today every state has a statute allowing a child to be removed from the parental home if there is evidence of physical abuse or neglect (*see* Abuse Neglect; Child Abuse). Children who have been subjected to such parenting practices may demonstrate psychiatric disorders. Parents often have emotional problems that predispose them to abusive behavior. In both of these instances, psychiatrists are often asked for assessments of the needs of children and the psychopathology of parents and for recommendations for treatment. It is not uncommon for children who are physically at risk to be placed in foster homes, in institutions, or with other family members. Psychiatric reassessment is conducted before reunification occurs.

Legal Issues in Psychiatric Practice. *Civil Commitments.* The tension between individual rights and societal needs is most acute in the area of civil commitment. The legal justification for involuntary commitment stems from two principles. *Parens patriae*, a term from English law, means that the state has a parental responsibility for its citizens who are unable to care for themselves and provides mechanisms by which these citizens are protected. Civil commitment serves this purpose and in most states can occur only when individuals are mentally disordered and are dangerous to either themselves or others, or are unable to care for themselves or others, or need hospitalization and treatment.

The second principle justifying civil commitment is that of police powers, a term designating the state's responsibility for maintaining control and order among its citizenry. Guthiel (1995) has summarized that *parens patriae* refers to the state as a protector of psychiatric patients from their inability to survive unaided while the police powers principle casts the state as protector of other citizens from such patients.

Civil commitment can be classified as emergency commitment usually initiated by law enforcement officers or clinicians, temporary or observational commitment initiated by relatives, physicians, and hospitals, and indeterminate commitment authorized by the court. Controversies about civil commitment continue. One misconception is that psychiatrists commit patients. Psychiatrists may initiate the first step in the process (typically an emergency commitment), but direct judicial actions such as hearings and counsel complete the process.

Malpractice and Liability. Litigation, the most anxiety-provoking involvement of law in medicine, is increasing in all medical specialties, although it occurs less often in psychiatry. An individual's clinical work may not be mainstream but it cannot be termed malpractice unless the four elements of malpractice are present. These elements Guthiel (1995) has mnemonically summarized as the four ds of malpractice: "*d*ereliction (negligence) of a *d*uty *d*irectly causing *d*amages" (p. 2756). The commonest types of malpractice claims in psychiatric practice are those related to suicide, misdiagnosis, negligent treatment, false imprisonment, and sexual relations with patients.

The Right to Treatment. The most familiar context for the right to adequate treatment is the case of involuntary retention, in which it is held that to retain a patient without implicitly promising treatment is wrong. Right to treatment decisions have arisen from the realization that many patients have been hospitalized with inferior care being offered.

In defining treatment as a right, the courts can address the quality of care in institutions and exert pressure on government to increase funding for such care.

The Right to Refuse Treatment. This complicated area relates solely to involuntarily committed patients because voluntary patients are assumed to have the right to refuse treatment. Historically, involuntary committed patients were not considered to be able to make rational treatment decisions and had to take whatever professionals prescribed for them. In the late 1970s and 1980s, a great number of cases altered this position. The controversy in this area comes from the irony of having the ability to involuntarily admit patients to a hospital but not be able to treat them in the most appropriate manner.

The Assessment of Dangerousness. The psychiatrist's ability to predict dangerousness is controversial. Patient advocates have attempted to ensure that patients are not inappropriately committed involuntarily by pointing out how difficult it is to predict a behavior that has a low frequency. However, the Supreme Court has strongly supported the notion that clinicians can reliably predict dangerousness.

The current standard is that the psychiatrist is not expected to prevent every patient from committing dangerous acts to himself or herself or others, but the psychiatrist is expected to exercise reasonable caution. A landmark ruling in 1976, the Tarasoff decision, set the ground work for psychiatrists' obligation to inform third parties about their patient's dangerousness. In this case, Ms. Tarasoff was killed by a psychiatric patient who had admitted his homicidal intent to his therapist. The court decreed that a clinician must use reasonable care to protect an intended victim against danger posed by his or her patient, usually by informing the person at risk. With respect to the issue of breach of confidentiality, the court determined that "the protective privilege ends when the public peril begins."

Confidentiality. Confidentiality is the obligation of the psychiatrist to keep in confidence whatever information is shared by the patient, absent specific permission. Privilege is defined as the right of patients to exclude from judicial settings testimony about material that has been revealed within a professional relationship. Confidentiality covers the professional's obligation while privilege denotes the patient's right. Confidentiality applies to a variety of clinical contexts and privilege applies to legal and judicial ones. Breach of confidentiality remains a liability issue and it remains a reasonably common reason for malpractice claims.

The Role of the Clinician. The increased involvement of the law in psychiatric practice has led some psychiatrists to shift from a clinical frame of reference to a legal one. The tendency to forget the healer role and adopt a legal, adversarial mindset can impair the clinical alliance with a patient and result in the psychiatrist practicing defensive medicine. A balanced view recognizes that the law needs the data of psychiatry to mete out justice and, similarly, legal interventions can be used for the betterment of patients. It behooves all clinicians to become familiar with legal aspects as they relate to patient care.

There are three roles in which the psychiatrist, as expert witness, interacts with the legal system. Psychiatrists may be asked to evaluate patients and present their findings. Second, a patient under a psychiatrist's treatment may become involved in a legal conflict (e.g., custody dispute) and treatment findings are relevant to the legal decision. Finally psychiatrists, by virtue of their experience in research or clinical practice, may be asked to comment upon scientific aspects of a case without evaluating a patient.

It is important for the evaluating psychiatrist to inform the patient that the information disclosed will be shared with the court and that the patient understands this condition. It is more problematic when the clinical information the court desires is derived from a course of treatment that, at its outset, did not involve a legal problem. It is often in the patient's best interest for the psychiatrist to testify on his or her behalf although this could be reasonably resisted by a patient who believes the information to be privileged. Psychiatrists must recognize the role of expert witness does not involve decision making but solely that of providing clinical data to the court. Relatedly, it is important for the clinician to avoid investment in a particular legal outcome.

Theological Implications. Psychiatry has attempted to explain deviant behavior through the ages and, thus the relationship of theology to forensic psychiatry is unavoidable. With respect to criminal responsibility, one can ask: Was the individual unable or unwilling to conform his or her behavior to acceptable moral and legal precepts? Current data suggest that both concepts—a determined inability to chose good and a freely chosen unwillingness to do good—must be considered in determining matters of personal responsibility. In certain conditions an individual's behavior may largely be determined by biologic and psychosocial vulnerabilities which increase the likelihood they will commit a crime. It is also clear that in the last several decades there has been a cultural erosion of the concept of personal responsibility and, as a corollary, the notion of individuals as moral agents. Questionable court decisions that have absolved defendants from criminal responsibility, due to substances they have eaten or experiences in their past, illustrate this erosion.

A balanced perspective including psychobiologic influence and moral choice is possible. This means that individuals are more or less predetermined to commit crimes but should be still held responsible for them except in the rarest instances, such as the insanity defense. The vulnerabilities that may predispose to criminal behavior can be factored in as a circumstance that mitigates the severity of sentencing. Psychiatric treatment is devoted to eliminating the factors that made it difficult for the individual to choose to do good. Even so, there is still room for the Christian concept of conscious choice of wrongdoing, or sin, to explain the unwillingness to do good.

A theology that expects an individual's conformity to God's laws but does not incorporate the notion of a fallen world and the mental disorders that are part of that fallen world is a shallow theology. A psychiatry that attempts to explain psychopathology, but does not incorporate the notion of personal responsibility for mental health and behavior change is a shallow psychiatry.

Finally, many of the medico-legal themes in forensic psychiatry also reflect a relationship to Christian theology. The attempt to provide humane treatment to the mentally disordered and to respect their rights is often motivated by the belief in the ultimate worth of individuals, a worth rooted in the love of a redemptive creator.

Reference

Guthiel, T. (1995). Forensic psychiatry. In H. I. Kaplan & B. J. Sadock (Eds.), *Comprehensive textbook of psychiatry* (6th ed.). Baltimore: Williams & Wilkins.

A. M. JOSEPHSON

See MALPRACTICE; CRIME AND MENTAL DISORDER.

Forensic Psychology. A branch of psychology that deals with legal issues pertaining to mental health. This may include courtroom testimony, treatment, consultation, and research.

The late 1800s marked the beginning of psychologists in the courtroom. The first psychologist to enter the witness stand is believed to be Karl Marburg of Germany (Farrington, Hawkins, & Lloyd-Bostock, 1979). Hugo Munsterberg was the first, however, to draw attention to the psychologist in the courtroom with his research concerning the problems of witnesses' perceptions. His work, published in 1899, on the time interval between two gunshots is still used and was of theoretical value in the double-bullet controversy in the assassination of John F. Kennedy.

Yet forensic psychology has been slow to gain acceptance from the courts of the United States. This is not true in Great Britain and some other countries where, after World War II, psychologists have been accepted without question as experts in the courtroom.

There are efforts to develop board certification in forensic medicine. The American College of Forensic Examiners offers various levels of certification from associate to fellow, depending on the member's experience, training, and professional standing.

Most specialized training comes after the Ph.D. or Psy.D. in psychology has been earned and a license to practice psychology has been granted. The training includes attending seminars, reading relevant literature, and adapting previous training and experience to the courtroom. Some universities offer courses in forensic psychology, and students can take them on an elective basis.

Roles and Functions. The role and function of a psychologist in a court setting can involve pretrial, trial, and posttrial tasks. The pretrial question of competency of the defendant to cooperate with the attorney and understand the charges is usually determined by a combination of clinical interviews and tests such as intelligence tests, projective tests, and tests for literacy.

The psychologist may also be asked to determine the state of the defendant's mind at the time of the crime. This is a rather controversial aspect of the competency evaluation because the psychologist is asked to determine the defendant's mental state not at the time of evaluation but at some previous time. Questions to be determined are, Was the defendant's act at the time of the crime the product of mental illness, and can he or she therefore be held responsible for his behavior? Did the defendant know right from wrong, or was his or her behavior the result of an irresistible impulse that precluded an ability to control his or her behavior at the time of the alleged crime?

The defendant may be diverted into treatment in lieu of a trial and will not stand trial for the alleged crime if the treatment is successful. However, if the person does not cooperate with the therapy process, he or she may be returned to stand trial.

Forensic psychologists also are called upon to determine the risk potential of the defendant before possible commitment decisions are made. A very dangerous defendant may be committed to a mental hospital, possibly against his or her will. Psychologists may also be asked to recommend other appropriate treatment measures to be taken.

The potential for rehabilitation of a first offender or repeater is another question the courts ask the psychologist to address. This also includes recommendations for specific treatment or treatment programs. Whether the individual would profit from the treatment is particularly pertinent for persons accused of alcohol or drug abuse or if injury to family members has occurred.

Child custody cases demand much of the forensic psychologist's clinical time. Attorneys and judges are asking for information to help decide which parent should have custody of the child. Through the clinical interview, home study, and projective techniques, the psychologist is able to make the necessary recommendation in custody cases.

In juvenile cases involving serious crimes, the psychologist may be asked to help the judge in determining whether the defendant should be tried as a juvenile or as an adult. This is determined after considering the circumstances of the crime and the emotional factors contributing to the alleged criminal act. In juvenile cases, the psychologist would also offer opinions as to the possibility of rehabilitation.

Attorneys occasionally ask the forensic psychologist to assist in jury selection. The attorney and psychologist together determine the most appropriate jury members to weigh testimony in behalf of their client.

Pretrial assistance to the court also includes inpatient or outpatient treatment of persons accused of a crime if competency to stand trial is in question. The goal of the treatment is to restore the person to competency in order to allow him or her to stand trial.

During the trial forensic psychologists testify as expert witnesses. The testimony is based on their evaluation of the defendant through testing and clinical interview. The opinion is given in the context of accepted psychological principles and within the mainstream of psychological research. Testimony may include such topics as "perception, sensation, confessions, eye-witness identification, mental state; or about the results of their clinical evaluation of the defendant on such topics as motivation or mental status at the time of the alleged offense, or at the time of the trial" (Fersch, 1979).

During the trial the psychologist may consult with the attorney concerning the testimony of the opposing side's psychological or psychiatric expert witness. There may be questions as to the appropriateness of the research cited, the psychologist's or psychiatrist's credibility as an expert, or the appropriateness of the testimony presented from the tests and individual interview of the defendant.

The psychologist's work might not be finished when the trial is completed. Posttrial professional duties may involve treatment of the offender as part of probation or as a condition of a suspended sentence. The treatment is usually stipulated by the court for a period of time or until marked improvement is noted. The psychologist is usually asked to report to the judge or probation officer as to the progress toward rehabilitation.

Forensic psychologists also conduct research in legal mental health areas; offer training to probation officers, counselors, and social workers; and provide consultation to lawyers and judges in order to help clarify mental health issues.

Ethical Issues. The opinion for hire is a constant problem among forensic psychologists. The temptation is great to bias the testimony to assure continued use of a psychologist's expertise by a particularly generous law firm.

The American Psychological Association (APA) Code of Ethics (American Psychological Association, 1992) Principle 7 defines the professional ethical limits of forensic activities. The psychologist must comply with all APA ethics codes, as well as additional areas such as forensic assessment, role clarification, truthfulness and candor, prior relationship and compliance with laws and rules. Forensic psychologists must "base their forensic work on appropriate knowledge of and competence in the areas underlying such work including specialized knowledge concerning special populations" (7.01).

Another ethical issue for the forensic psychologist is set forth in Principle 5.01 of the Ethical Principles of Psychologists, which states that the psychologist is responsible for informing the client of the limits of confidentiality. If the psychologist has been appointed by the court, the psychologist has an ethical responsibility to inform the defendant that some or all of the psychological evaluation may be presented in open court as testimony. It is important to inform the defendant that he or she is waiving confidentiality as a result of a court-ordered examination.

The Future. The future job market for forensic psychology appears to be rather optimistic. The courts appear to be using expert psychological testimony with greater frequency due to a greater awareness of emotional and mental health issues regarding the individual's criminal behavior.

The courts also are more concerned with rehabilitation than with punishment. Therefore, they are more willing to use psychologists to help determine the best course of action to take in the rehabilitation process. With more divorces occurring, there is more opportunity to testify in child custody cases.

There are increasing challenges to the accuracy of forensic psychologists and psychiatrists. Some studies suggest professionals often fail to reach reliable or valid conclusions and that their judgment does not surpass that of a layperson (Faust & Ziskin, 1988).

With the greater use of forensic psychologists, greater controls will be placed on them. In the future degrees may be granted in forensic psychology, and licensing and certification will be part of the requirement to practice this specialty in psychology.

References

American Psychological Association. (1992, reprint). Standards for providers of psychological services. *American Psychologist, 47,* 1597–1628.

Farrington, D. P., Hawkins, K., & Lloyd-Bostock, S. M. (Eds.). (1979). *Psychology, law and legal processes.* Atlantic Highlands, NJ: Humanities.

Faust, D., & Ziskin, J. The expert witness in psychology and psychiatry. *Science, 241,* 31–35.

Fersch, E. A. (1979). *Law, psychology and the courts.* Springfield, IL: Thomas.

Additional Readings

Cooke, G. (Ed.). (1980). *Role of the forensic psychologist.* Springfield, IL: Thomas.

Fersch, E. A. (1980). *Psychology and psychiatry in courts and corrections: Controversy and change.* New York: Wiley.

For Further Information

American College of Forensic Examiners. 1658 South Cobblestone Court, Springfield, MO 16809.

M. A. CAMPION

See CHILD CUSTODY; MALPRACTICE; CRIME AND MENTAL DISORDER.

Forgiveness. Forgiveness as an interface concept among the disciplines of psychology, theology, and spiritual growth has blossomed in the 1990s. Many practitioners from various perspectives now explicitly point to forgiveness as a useful clinical concept in both psychotherapy and religious counseling. Conceptual clarification has made great strides. This has led to operational definitions and interventions, and a beginning has been made in collecting empirical data. The pragmatics of using the concept clinically have been much clarified thanks to the myriad of perspectives. This article will proceed from the conceptual to the scientific, then to the pragmatic and clinical.

The explosion of published literature on interpersonal forgiveness includes more than 70 books and many articles. A brief historical and philosophical analysis of the term as used in the past and present has been presented by Enright, Eastin, Golden, Sarinopoulos, and Freedman (1992) and provides an excellent conceptual foundation. A working definition can be stated thus: Forgiveness is overcoming of negative thoughts, feelings, and behaviors not by denying the offense or the right to be hurt or angry but by viewing the offender with acceptance (if not compassion) so that the forgiver can be healed.

To clarify further the boundaries we turn to what the concept is not. Forgiveness is not denial or indifference, pardon, reconciliation, condoning, excusing, passive forgetting, weakness, or an interpersonal game (for definition and expansion see Enright et al., 1991). Forgiveness in no way cancels the crime, but it works to take care of the distortions caused by the unhealthy aspects of anger and resentment so that the person may achieve peace of mind and body.

Models and theories of forgiveness have been derived in four different ways (McCullough & Worthington, 1994a): from extant psychological theories; tasks and processes; moral development stages; and descriptive typologies.

Psychological Theories. Psychological theories make use of general psychodynamics, particularly from the therapeutic situation, to conceptualize the process of forgiving. A pastoral example is provided by Patton (1985) in terms of shame, anger, power, and their various defensive unfoldings. He warns against clients using forgiveness for self-righteousness and further argues that forgiveness cannot be an act or an attitude but rather something that is realized by the patient after sufficient time has elapsed. During this time other therapeutic experiences have indirectly provided the necessary stance, healing, and higher cognitive ego skills to allow forgiveness. The following is a partial list of the cognitive processing capacities involved in forgiveness:

1. The ability to empathize and give up one's egocentric position. This involves a discovery of likeness or similarity and respect for the personhood of the other.

2. Appreciation for the self and growth of the self structure apart from the other.
3. A theory of motives.
4. Discrimination of boundaries between parties.
5. An understanding of vulnerabilities in both parties.
6. Awareness of reexperiencing of certain developmentally difficult emotions.
7. Ability to tolerate and clarify emotional contradictions, (i.e., ambivalence, confusion, logical contradictions).
8. The acceptance of limitations of self and other.

The growth of these ego skills requires a therapeutic relationship, insight, and time for effective working through. Examples of other psychodynamic models include Lapsley (1966), Smith (1981), and Brandsma (1982).

Tasks and Processes. Enright and his colleagues have identified 20 subprocesses involved in interpersonal forgiveness (Gassin & Enright, 1995). Theirs is the most differentiated example of an iteration of tasks and processes (see table 1). They emphasize that this is not a lock-step model but can be generally sequential, one from which various individuals will take different starting points and parts, depending on their particular issues. The first steps must be some variation of the following:

1. An awareness of emotional pain.
2. A decision to forgive understood as a process.
3. A commitment to work on thoughts, feelings, and behaviors as appropriate.

An individualized concatenation of the various tasks and processes follows until one experiences a release of most if not all of the negative emotion and thought directed at the offender. Particularly mentioned by most theorists is the operation of empathy and altruism as a process underlying forgiveness.

Moral Development Stages. The third type of model is analogous to that of moral development, usually based on Lawrence Kohlberg's six-stage model of cognitive justice strategies (Kohlberg, 1976; Enright et al., 1991; McCullough & Worthington, 1994b). Also taken from this area of inquiry is the gender difference between masculine and feminine values (i.e., forgiveness is seen as being feminine and merciful, emphasizing sacrificial love and relationship restoration rather than masculine self-interest or an "eye for an eye" fairness). These models emphasize the cognitive development of the person's ability to apprehend and use higher moral strategies. Persons' ability to forgive will be conditioned by their level of development in terms of how they process moral dilemmas and the cognitive principles that they have previously assimilated. In this literature interventions and expectations ideally are made at the level of the client's current stage of development or slightly ahead.

Otherwise the person is hypothesized to be unable to assimilate the intervention. Yet given the distortions possible with forgiveness, many think that true forgiveness cannot be obtained until the person has reached maturity; that is, to have some understanding of Kohlberg's stage 6 concepts (Enright et al., 1991; McCullough and Worthington, 1994b). Further, the best results will likely obtain when both therapist and client highly value forgiveness.

Descriptive Typologies. Typologies of forgiveness categorize phenomena based on critical descriptive features that differentiate them. Their concepts are usually not anchored in a theory and have little predictive or explanatory value but may be useful in the counseling setting. Some of the typologies proposed and receiving support are role expedient as contrasted with role expected and later intrinsic (Trainer, 1981); another discriminating by degree is detached as contrasted with limited and full forgiveness (Nelson, 1992).

In their review of the scientific literature on forgiveness, McCullough and Worthington (1994) found a smattering of studies supporting positive benefits from forgiving in the areas of chronic pain, cardiovascular problems, reduction in violent behavior, and a general positive relation to physical health. They listed several variables that are important in considering whether a client will be able to forgive and to what extent, such as mental disorder, age, moral development, religiosity, severity of hurt, defensive style, personality disorder, and dissociative disorder. They propose five elements provided by the therapist that underlie all therapeutic interventions concerning forgiveness:

1. Fostering unconditional positive regard to explore hurt and feelings.
2. Refocusing attention away from negative emotions by reframing or viewing from a larger context or different perspective.
3. Enabling empathy for offender.
4. Focusing on self-forgiveness.
5. Discussing reconciliation.

The growth of conceptual and scientific literature has added much to the pragmatics of counseling and psychotherapy. Notable now in this interface are the differences that arise between those who practice religiously based therapies versus those who practice secularly based therapies. Table 2 shows some of the philosophical and technical differences that inhere in a Christian approach when compared to a secular orientation. Much could be written about these distinctions, including their degree of separateness and utility. Suffice it to note that various authors in the field take different if implicit positions on these distinctions.

Secular therapists' degree of personal religiosity has minimal influence on the use of forgiveness content in therapy (DiBlasio & Benda, 1991), probably because they were not taught such in their training programs. In contrast, 6% to 23% of the sessions in explicitly Christian therapy involve forgiveness content (Worthington, DuPont, Berry, & Duncan, 1988).

There are many clinical pitfalls in using the concept of forgiveness. The clinical questions remain: how explicitly should a therapist encourage clients to forgive, and if so in what forms and at what time? Consensus is that where there is severe hurt, forgiveness should not be encouraged early. This is because of the pain that it stirs, the tendency to minimize brutality, and the lack of ego resources; forgiveness thus may inadvertently exacerbate feelings of low self-worth. A trauma must be resolved and the ego strengthened before forgiveness can be considered, or it will be used defensively (self-righteously) or take a pseudo form. Likewise, forgiveness out of a sense of duty or fear of retaliation later leads to increased negative emotions. Counselors must be sensitive to being persuasive instead of cajoling clients to forgive. In many ways a plant analogy would seem indicated as a strategy: the therapist plants the seed, waters and fertilizes at irregular intervals while attending to other issues, and then is pleasantly surprised by the new flowers that bloom when forgiveness is encountered. This analogy does not hold, however, in frankly psychoeducational interventions in which various aspects of forgiveness are engaged explicitly in each of several, time-limited, structured sessions. Differences between these approaches require further study in terms of outcomes.

Much conceptual work remains to be done. Some primary issues involve better linking of models with techniques, identifying pseudo forms of forgiveness, correlating the intrapsychic and interpersonal aspects, and developing a richer understanding of what it means (and how) to forgive one's self. Personality diagnosis may also be crucial; that is, forgiveness may be meaningless with antisocial personalities and may be counterproductive with dependent personalities who need to learn to express their anger and not comply with their therapists' prescriptions.

The explosion of literature and interest on the topic of forgiveness has been gratifying and productive. More needs to be done on several fronts. However, this is a propaedeutic, instructional concept, a model for others to follow, and one that may show robust superiority of an explicitly Christian orientation in both concept and therapeutics.

Table 1
Processes Involved in Interpersonal Forgiveness (from Gassin & Enright, 1995)

1. Examination of psychological defenses.
2. Confrontation of anger in order to release, not harbor, it.

3. Admittance of shame, when this is appropriate.
4. Awareness of cathexis.
5. Awareness of cognitive rehearsal of the offense.
6. Realization that self may be permanently and negatively changed by the injury.
7. Insight that the injured party may be comparing self with the injurer.
8. Insight into a possibly altered "just world" view.
9. A change of heart/conversion/new insights that old resolution strategies are not working.
10. A willingness to explore forgiveness as an option.
11. Commitment to forgive the offender.
12. Reframing (through role taking) the wrongdoer by viewing him or her in context.
13. Empathy toward the offender.
14. Awareness of compassion toward the offender.
15. Realization that self has needed others' forgiveness in the past.
16. Acceptance or absorption of the pain.
17. Finding meaning in the suffering and in the forgiveness process.
18. Realization that self may have new purpose because of what happened.
19. Awareness of decreased negative affect and, perhaps, increased positive affect toward the injurer.
20. Awareness of internal, emotional release.

Table 2
Secular versus Spiritual Emphasis in Forgiveness

Secular	Concept	Spiritual
Psychological phenomena from scientific psychology theory based on empirical data	Definition of concept	Spiritual phenomena from religious philosophy based on revelation
Defined by offended party	Offense definition	Defined by moral law
Offense because of ignorance	Offense motivation	Offense because of sin
Help self	Motivation to forgive	Follow imperative and model of God
		Advance the kingdom
		Emulate Christ
		A conduit for communing with God
		A mechanism of salvation, i.e., removing a hindrance to God's activity
Humans are	View of	Humans are

470

pleasure oriented, no deficiency	humanity	spiritual creatures, flawed, with a dark side
Individual	Foci	Make community, interconnectedness, unity again possible
Emotional neutrality	Goal	Reconciliation, agape
Meaning variable —a lesson, find a new purpose	Suffering	Suffering is meaningful—strengthens faith, discipline, increases benefits to others
Deal with emotional pain pragmatically	Pain	Absorbs the pain—a gift of self-sacrifice
Personal courage strength, and integrity	Necessary	Grace and faith needed
Problem solving strategy with many techniques	Treatment technique	Technique necessary but have meta meanings, part of a greater purpose oriented toward religious virtue
		Use of religious symbols encouraged
Difficult psychological processes	Frame	Spiritual warfare
Expression of love as an attitudinal value		
Psychopathology	Offender	Fellow sinner
Acceptance	Affect outcome	Compassion
Personal relationships, intrapsychic processes, somatization	Effects	Ultimately in relationship to God

References

Brandsma, J. M. (1982). Forgiveness: A dynamic, theological, and therapeutic analysis. *Pastoral Psychology, 31*, 41–50.

DiBlasio, F. A., & Benda, B. B. (1991). Practitioners, religion, and the use of forgiveness in the clinical setting. *Journal of Psychology and Christianity, 10*, 166–172.

Enright, R. D., Eastin, D. L., Golden, S., Sarinopoulos, S., & Freedman, S. (1992). Interpersonal forgiveness within the helping professions: An attempt to resolve differences of opinions. *Counseling and Values, 36*, 84–103.

Enright, R. D., & The Human Development Study Group. (1991). The moral development of forgiveness. In W. Kurtines and J. Gwirtz (Eds.), *Handbook of moral behavior and development* (Vol. 1). Hillsdale, NJ: Erlbaum.

Gassin, E. A., & Enright, R. D. (1995). The will to meaning and the process of forgiveness. *Journal of Psychology and Christianity, 14*, 38–49.

Kohlberg, L. (1976). Moral stages and moralization: The cognitive-developmental approach. In T. Likona (Ed.), *Moral development and behavior: Theory, research and social issues*. New York: Holt.

Lapsley, J. N. (1966). Reconciliation, forgiveness, lost contracts. *Theology Today, 22*, 44–59.

McCullough, M. E., & Worthington, E. L. (1994a). Encouraging clients to forgive people who have hurt them: Review, critique, and research perspective. *Journal of Psychology and Theology, 22*, 3–20.

McCullough, M. E., & Worthington, E. L. (1994b). Models in interpersonal forgiveness and their applications to counseling: Review and critique. *Counseling and Values, 39*, 2–14.

Nelson, M. K. (1992). *A new theory of forgiveness*. Unpublished doctoral dissertation, West Lafayette, IN: Purdue University.

Patton, J. (1985). *Is human forgiveness possible?* Nashville: Abingdon.

Smith, M. (1981). The psychology of forgiveness. *Month, 14*, 301–307.

Trainer, M. F. (1981). *Forgiveness: Intrinsic, role expected, expedient, in the context of divorce*. Unpublished doctoral dissertation, Boston: Boston University.

Worthington, E. L., DuPont, P. D., Berry, J. T., & Duncan, L. A. (1988). Christian counselors' and clients' perceptions of religious psychotherapy in private and agency settings. *Journal of Psychology and Theology, 16*, 282–293.

J. M. Brandsma

See Spiritual and Religious Issues in Psychotherapy; Religious Resources in Psychotherapy.

Foster Children. The care of needy children in out-of-home placement has a long history within the United States and has received substantial support from the community of faith. In 1727 French Roman Catholic nuns founded the first orphanage in the United States in New Orleans. By the mid-nineteenth century orphanages could be found in almost any major city, and a movement (called orphan trains) developed to transfer children from large dormitories in cities to suburban or rural family homes. Many of the largest child welfare agencies trace their roots to Roman Catholic, Protestant, and Jewish religious concerns.

By the turn of the twentieth century the welfare of children became a government responsibility. The sectarian interests of various religious groups became problematic and states began enacting laws to protect the religious preferences of families. Each state now has child protective services responsible for ensuring the safety and welfare of all children. When children live in abusive conditions, they are removed from their families by state child welfare agencies and are placed with relatives or in foster care. In 1990 it was estimated that approximately

2,500,000 million children in the United States were victims of abuse and that approximately 500,000 were removed from their homes by child protective agencies.

Children in foster care are at greater risk of underachieving in school, suffer poor physical health, and manifest a greater degree of problem behaviors. Most of these conditions are attributed to the living conditions that warranted removal from their biological parents as opposed to consequences of being in the child welfare system. Furthermore, these children show negative outcomes as adults: unemployment, welfare dependence, homelessness, marital dissatisfaction, and poor quality of life.

Foster families are recruited by either public or private nonprofit agencies to care for children in their own homes. These families receive a small subsidy for the support of the child in addition to the state and federally funded Medicaid program. Foster parents frequently come from large families and became involved through friends and relatives who also provide foster care. Research has shown that the most important trait is flexibility. The child's experience of victimization leads to a desire for nurturing support but also a fearful distrust of adults. Because children come with a unique combination of experiences and coping responses, they require sensitivity, commitment, and a broad range of adult caring responses.

Foster children have some unique problems that require special consideration by foster parents and community caregivers. The trauma of prolonged separation from parents gives rise to emotional conflicts such as distrust of adults, aggressive or withdrawn behavior, mood swings, irritability, and poor concentration. In some instances large sibling groups must be separated because foster parents cannot receive two or more children. Isolation from siblings who may have provided significant support and comfort may emotionally overwhelm a child's available coping responses.

Foster parents are sometimes not prepared for the challenges of foster children, and this leads to a placement breakdown. Multiple placements of foster children with difficult behavioral problems is a major concern of child welfare agencies. New programs called treatment foster care are being developed to meet the needs of these children. These foster parents are professionally trained, financially compensated, and provided more extensive services so that a child can be maintained within their home. Some institutions provide care in group homes, a setting in which a team of adults supervises six or more children. Group homes are utilized to end a cycle of moving a child from one foster family to another. Large institutions, formerly known as orphanages, may provide care for several hundred children, such as Boys Town in Omaha, Nebraska.

Children with physical disabilities, neurological disorders, or severe emotional problems require specialized foster parents, such as those who can use sign language or whose homes are wheelchair-accessible. A large number of these children remain in the foster care system for extended periods of time because the biological parents are unable to gather the resources they need to resume care.

Most states stipulate a time limit, typically 18 to 24 months, for parents to receive treatment and resume custody of their children. Many foster children move into adoptive placements, or legal guardianship is sought for them by their foster families. Many emancipate from the foster care system at age 18. Anyone in the Christian community coming into contact with foster children or their foster parents can help by being aware of the special needs of both child and caregivers.

W. T. AOKI

See PARENTING; BLENDED FAMILY.

Frankl, Victor Emil (1905–1997). Existentialist psychiatrist and the founder of logotherapy. He was born in Vienna, receiving his M.D. (1930) and Ph.D. (1949) from the University of Vienna. He is professor of psychiatry and neurology at the University of Vienna, professor of logotherapy at the United States International University, and visiting clinical professor of psychiatry at Stanford University. His system of therapy, logotherapy, is often referred to as the third Viennese school of psychotherapy (Freud's being the first and Adler's the second).

Although it is generally believed that logotherapy began with Frankl's own experience of imprisonment during the Holocaust of World War II, his experiences in the concentration camps were actually the proving grounds of his evolving existential theory. Frankl developed the fundamental concepts of logotherapy as a medical student and as a physician in Vienna. The exact birthday of logotherapy could be identified as an evening in 1909 when Frankl thought while falling asleep, "One day, I too will die. I will no longer be alive. What, then, is the meaning of my living?" It is around the pursuit of the answer to this question that both Frankl's life and the development of logotherapy revolve.

At the age of 14 Frankl wrote a school paper entitled "We and the World Process." At 15, while in high school, he attended adult education classes in applied and experimental psychology. At 17 he lectured in a philosophy seminar in the adult education classes on the meaning of life. He delineated the two main concepts that later developed into logotherapy: life does not answer our questions about the meaning of life but rather puts those questions to us, leaving it for us to find the answers by deciding what we find meaningful; the ultimate meaning of life is beyond the grasp of our intellect but is something we can live by without ever being able to describe it cognitively. Frankl's high school graduation paper, "About the Psychology of Philosophical Thinking," came about as the result of his correspondence with Sigmund Freud and reflected his interest in psychoanalysis as well as in the individual psychology of Alfred Adler.

Frankl is the author of 27 books, including the best seller, *Man's Search for Meaning*, in which he describes his brutal experience in four Nazi concentration camps and in which he outlines the basic concepts of logotherapy. He considers his death-camp experiences a validation of the concepts on which logotherapy is based. He has remarked that he is the product of the school of medicine, the school of philosophy, and the school of life.

J. B. DILLEY

See EXISTENTIAL PSYCHOLOGY AND PSYCHOTHERAPY.

Free Association. Introduced by Sigmund Freud after he became disillusioned with the results of hypnosis, the technique of free association was used to help discover—rather, uncover—subconscious or repressed thoughts, ideas, and complexes. Although the occurrence of association has been observed and described by writers of psychologically related thought since ancient times, Francis Galton was the first to experimentally investigate the phenomenon in 1879.

When free association is used as a therapeutic technique, the patient is typically asked to respond with the first thing that comes to mind and to continue to describe aloud any and every thought that is associated with it. Further, the patient is encouraged not to censor or edit the material but to flow with the streams of thought that spontaneously arise. Frequently the patient is instructed to lie on a couch, facing away from the therapist so as to minimize likely visual or interpersonal interruption of this flow. The analyst then takes this fundamental psychic information and synthesizes it into an analytic interpretation, later feeding it back to the patient in order to enhance insight. In psychoanalysis it is assumed that the accumulation of such insight will eventually lead to a healthier or more well-adjusted personality.

Although one might assume that most associations occur at random and that basing a theory of one's personality on such randomness is artificial, evidence indicates that one's associations are determined by previous experience and are idiosyncratic or very personal. Free association, therefore, has become the basic tool of classic psychoanalysis. Carl Gustav Jung used a related tool, the word association test, as a quick means of detecting complexes; that is, the more peculiar the word content as well as the longer the subject took to give a response to a stimulus word, the more likely that the stimulus-response word pair suggests a related psychological conflict.

J. B. DILLEY

See PSYCHOANALYSIS: TECHNIQUE; PSYCHOANALYTIC PSYCHOTHERAPY.

Free Will and Determinism. *See* DETERMINISM AND FREE WILL.

Freud, Sigmund (1856–1939). The founder of psychoanalysis. Freud was born to Jewish parents in Frieberg, Moravia. In 1859 the family moved to Leipzig and a year later to Vienna, where Freud later attended medical school. Possessing a broad liberal education, with special interests in philosophy, the classics, and antiquity, as a university student Freud nevertheless soon opted for the physiological research that occupied him for much of early adulthood. In the laboratory of the great physiologist Ernst von Brücke he imbibed the mechanistic tenets of German materialistic science that held him to some degree for the rest of his life.

The Early Years. In 1882, reluctantly acknowledging the financial nonfeasibility of a research career, Freud became a resident in the General Hospital of Vienna. There he studied internal medicine, neurology, and psychiatry, while continuing to pursue neuroanatomical studies. In the fall of 1885 he completed his residency, was given the academic title *Privatdozent* (on the strength of his histological publications), and journeyed to Paris to study with the eminent neurologist Jean-Martin Charcot. There he was introduced to the fascinating world of hysteria and hypnosis. Also in the early 1880s Freud had heard the internist Josef Breuer speak several times on his psychotherapeutic treatment of Anna O., the now famous hysteric. Breuer and his patient discovered that when she recollected and related the affects and events surrounding each symptom's initial appearance, it would disappear.

Upon returning to Vienna in 1886, Freud married Martha Bernays (who became his lifelong helpmate), opened his private practice, published some important papers on neuroanatomy and the classic monograph *On Aphasia* (1891), and concerned himself for a while with research into the therapeutic properties of cocaine. During this time, it must be remembered, psychiatrists confined themselves to the universities and hospitals, and outpatient psychiatric treatment was primarily in the hands of neurologists like Freud. Consequently much of Freud's practice consisted of hysterical symptoms masking as neurological disease. Like most other neurologists of the day, Freud initially interpreted hysteria as the epiphenomenon of underlying neurological disorder or degeneration. Freud's treatments of this condition also were generally somatic—tonics, electrotherapy, massage, and diet.

Nevertheless, through his work with Charcot and his conversations with Breuer, Freud had become convinced that hysterical symptoms, whatever their etiology, could be approached psychotherapeutically. This, coupled with the poor results from somatic therapies, led Freud to hypnotic suggestion in 1887. In 1889 he returned to

France to improve his hypnotic technique under the tutelage of Liébault and Bernheim.

From 1889 to 1895, Freud's psychotherapeutic technique gradually evolved from hypnotic suggestion through hypnotic catharsis to free association in waking consciousness. From his clinical work and collaborations with Breuer, Freud concluded that the etiology of hysteria is a psychical one—the repression or strangulation of painful, disagreeable memories and affects associated with traumatic experiences. The treatment consisted of undoing the repression of the unconscious memories and affects through the free association method.

Psychoanalytic Psychology. In *Studies on Hysteria* (1895) Freud clearly recognized the role of repressed sexuality in the etiology of neurosis. From 1895 to 1900, through his clinical work and self-analysis, he would become more and more convinced of the importance of sexual factors. The turning point occurred in 1897, when Freud discovered that his hysterics' accounts of seduction, which he had hitherto believed to be literally true, were fantasies. This awoke him to the importance of psychical reality. He also uncovered, in his patients and himself, the oedipus complex—an unconscious constellation of sexual longing for the parent of the opposite sex and rivalrous hatred toward the one of the same sex.

The year 1899, when *The Interpretation of Dreams* was published, is generally considered the birthdate of psychoanalysis. In this work Freud introduced the topographic theory of the mind (the conscious, preconscious, and unconscious), the concept of primary and secondary process mentation, of dreams as the disguised fulfillment of unconscious wishes, and of dreams and neurotic symptoms as compromise formations. Soon afterward Freud advocated the significance of transference—the patient's repetition of historically determined patterns of behavior in the present. The interpretation of the historical roots of the patient's transferential behaviors came to be viewed as the cornerstone of psychoanalytic treatment.

From 1900 to 1926 Freud's ideas underwent considerable development and modification. However, he seldom totally discarded his earlier conceptions but usually incorporated them into or allowed them to lie alongside his later ones. Freud's growing appreciation of the defensive operations of the psyche, as they manifest themselves to the therapist in the form of the resistance, led him to lay the foundations of ego psychology from 1920 to 1926. *Group Psychology and the Analysis of the Ego* (1921) and *The Ego and the Id* (1923) flesh out the structural theory of the psychic apparatus—id, ego, and superego. Along with this came the understanding that defensive maneuvers and moral ideals and prohibitions can be quite as unconscious as the impulses that they oppose. *Inhibitions, Symptoms, and Anxiety* (1926) presented the seminal theory of the relationship between unconscious intrapsychic conflict, anxiety, and symptom formation. In conflict an unconscious affect-laden fantasy (id impulsion), disagreeable to the demands of the superego or society, threatens to rise into consciousness, raising the possibility it might then be translated into action. The unconscious ego experiences this as an imminent danger situation. In order to prevent the feared response from superego or society, the ego generates anxiety. This signal anxiety, as it is termed, is unpleasurable. Since the psyche moves toward pleasure and away from pain (in accordance with the pleasure principle), the ego blocks the offending impulse from awareness and removes the need for signal anxiety. When the defense mechanism fails, a symptom results. A symptom is therefore a compromise between the unconscious fantasy striving for expression and the defense against it.

In tandem with these conceptual innovations Freud's therapeutic writings take increasing cognizance of the importance of analyzing the resistance (*see* Resistance in Psychotherapy). In other words, it becomes just as important to know why a patient is withholding a fantasy or a feeling (i.e., to discern the fear that motivates the resistance) as it is to uncover the unconscious feeling or fantasy itself.

Sociocultural and Religious Writings. After 1926, though Freud continued to write on psychoanalytic psychology, the bulk of his original thinking shifted to culture. Among the most important contributions of his sociocultural work are his ideas on social cohesion. He came to view the bonds that unite the members of society as aim-inhibited (or sublimated) libido and the mutual identification of individuals with one another through their incorporation of a similar set of ideals. Repression of aspects of both sensuality and aggression was viewed as vital to maintaining group cohesion.

Foremost among these cultural concerns is religion, a subject with which Freud was ambivalently preoccupied his entire life. Freud used the psychological mechanisms he had encountered in his work with patients to elucidate religious behaviors. In *The Psychopathology of Everyday Life* (1901) he introduced his conceptualization of religion as a projective system. He understood God, Satan, and the spirit world as personifications of humans' projected unconscious fears and fantasies.

In "Obsessive Actions and Religious Practices" (1907), Freud explained religious ritual on the model of obsessive-compulsive symptomatology. The religionist's rituals, like the obsessional's symptoms, were viewed as compromise formations between the repressed impulse and the repressing forces, as simultaneous defenses against unconscious strivings and disguised gratifications of them.

The omnipotence of thoughts, a mechanism particularly favored by obsessive-compulsives, was recruited in *Totem and Taboo* (1913) to explain animism and religion. The omnipotence of thoughts is the unconscious presupposition that the wish is equivalent to the deed and that wishing can effect, independently of any action, changes in one's environment. Freud believed that in the animistic-magical stage people ascribe omnipotence to themselves, while in the religious stage they transfer it to a deity and yet retain the idea that they can influence that deity through prayer and ritual according to their wishes.

Freud believed that one's attitude toward God derives from one's childhood attitude toward one's father; that one's attitude toward the Deity is a displacement of one's stance toward the parent. The heavenly Father is conceptualized as an exalted version of the earthly one. Not being content to account for this with ontogenetic factors alone, Freud introduced phylogenetic ones as well. In the dawn of humanity, people were said to have lived in a horde, dominated by a tyrannical "primal father" who maintained jealous possession of the women and excluded the sons to a life of celibacy and impotence. One day the young men, overcome with dissatisfaction, united and slew and ate the primal father. This was no sooner accomplished than remorse and longing for the father set in. The unconscious memory of and guilt over this deed, genetically transmitted, were then posited to determine each subsequent religion, including Christianity. Religious rituals as diverse as the totem meal and the eucharist were explained as simultaneous reenactments of the eating of the primal father and expressions of remorse over it.

In *The Future of an Illusion* (1928) Freud developed his thesis of religion as infantile dependency and illusion or wish fulfillment: "When the growing individual finds that he is destined to remain a child forever, that he can never do without protection against strange superior powers, he lends those powers the features belonging to the figure of his father; he creates for himself the gods whom he dreads, whom he seeks to propitiate, and whom he nevertheless entrusts with his own protection. Thus, his longing for a father is identical with his need for protection against the consequences of human weakness" (p. 24).

Elsewhere Freud emphasized the role of primary process in myth and religion, comparing them to dreams. He conceptualized religious behaviors as sublimations of sexual and aggressive drives. Religious mysticism was explained as a reactivation of the infant's experience of oceanic oneness with its mother's breast.

Wallace (1983a, 1983b) has criticized Freud's work on religion on several grounds. First, there is a good deal of personal bias implicit in his characterizations of religion as infantile dependency and in his many comparisons of it to psychopathology. References to religion as "neurotic relics," "mass delusions," and "blissful hallucinatory confusion" evidence the presence of hidden moral judgments. Second, Freud's treatment of religion ignores questions of history and sociocultural context. Third, it makes no distinction between the concept

of the individual and that of the institution, presupposes the existence of a mass mind, relies on an exaggerated concept of psychic unity, and gives insufficient attention to the conscious aspects and phenomenology of religious behavior and experience. Fourth, Freud pays insufficient attention to adaptiveness as a point of differentiation between psychopathology and religious behavior. Fifth, in his work on religion Freud failed to use his most powerful tool—the clinical method of psychoanalysis. His concepts of religion were derived not from clinical work with religionists themselves but from a speculative transfer of psychoanalytic ideas to groups of people and whole cultures whom he had never analyzed. Finally, Freud presumes to give scientific answers to metaphysical questions.

Nevertheless, to conclude from the speculative excesses and methodological weaknesses in Freud's work on religion and culture that he makes no contribution to the psychology of religion would be disastrous. However, it is in his psychological writings rather than those specifically addressed to religious issues that we find the greatest contribution.

Freud's psychoanalysis can contribute a great deal to the elucidation of religious phenomena. It can clarify the relationship between one's religious belief and the rest of one's psychical structure, including the quality of the integration with the rest of one's personality. It can disclose conflicts for which religious convictions and practices serve as the vehicle of expression or defense or in which they contribute force to one side or the other. It can uncover the history of each individual's religious beliefs, the childhood object cathexes and identifications that are associated with these beliefs and that help determine their final form. It can comment on the role of one's religion in one's overall adaptation or maladaptation to the internal and external environments. Finally, it can contribute to the ethical sphere of religion. Broadened awareness of one's motivations and enhanced ego strength can lead to a broadened sense of responsibility, avoidance of easy rationalizations, and a more subtle form of self-control.

Psychoanalysis is on most solid ground when it investigates the psychological meaning of the religious beliefs of an individual. Only from the cumulative results of such laborious, clinically based studies can psychoanalysis make meaningful statements about religion and religionists in general. What Freudian psychology can never do is determine whether, after all the psychodynamic factors are removed, there is a transcendental justification for religious faith; such a question remains forever beyond the range of a theoretical and empirical psychology.

References

Wallace, E. R. (1983a). Freud and religion: A history and reappraisal. In L. Boyer, W. Muensterberger, and S. Grolnick (Eds.), *The psychoanalytic study of society* (Vol. 10). Hillsdale, NJ: Erlbaum.

Wallace, E. R. (1983b). Reflections on the relationship between psychoanalysis and Christianity. *Pastoral Psychology, 31*, 215–243.

E. R. WALLACE IV

See PSYCHOANALYTIC PSYCHOLOGY.

Friendship. The relation of being allied with a person whom one knows, likes, and trusts. Friendship is characterized by a mutual and reciprocal desire to be together. The degree to which two acquaintances make their plans, decisions, and activities dependent upon one another is the degree to which they are friends. But this criterion is only the beginning, since thieves and cons make their plans dependent on the activity of their pigeons, and they are not friends. Caring, showing an interest and concern about another's welfare, is also a critical criterion for friendship.

Psychologists have studied friendship because of accumulating evidence that social support (which includes relationships with one's friends) is associated with better physical and psychological well-being. This evidence suggests that social support has this beneficial effect for two different reasons: as Durkheim was the first to note, being integrated into a social network is a good thing, independent of how hard one's life is in other ways (Durkheim, 1897/1951); and friendship buffers one against a wide variety of stressors that intrude on one's life (Cohen & Wills, 1985). Friendship helps overcome loneliness, develops personal confidence, and assists with crucial socialization tasks.

Friendships develop in great part due to self-disclosure, in which a person reveals private aspects of the self to another person. These private aspects include experiences, desires, fears, and fantasies. A substantial body of research indicates that people lacking friendships are also people who fail to disclose themselves to other people.

Self-disclosure plays an important role in the formation of friendship, but proximity is perhaps the most fundamental requirement. Proximity kindles liking. Although it may seem trivial to those pondering the origins of friendship, sociologists have found that most people befriend someone who lives in the same neighborhood, works at the same job, or sits in the same class. Perhaps the most convincing evidence regarding proximity comes from a classic study of friendships in housing for married graduate students at the Massachusetts Institute of Technology (Festinger, Schachter, & Back, 1950). Since students were randomly assigned apartments as they became available, researchers could assess the importance of proximity. When wives were asked to name their three closest friends within the entire complex of buildings, two-thirds of those named lived in the same building, and two-thirds of these lived on the same floor. The person who was most frequently chosen lived next door.

Another important factor in the formation of friendship is noted in contradictory clichés: Opposites attract but birds of a feather flock together. Research has supported the idea that similarity promotes friendship, but little evidence has been found for the idea that people who are very different from each other are likely to end up as friends. Nevertheless, according to one review of the literature (Berscheid & Walster, 1978, p. 80), the notion of complementary needs "sounds so reasonable" that psychologists are reluctant to abandon the hypothesis. Perhaps future research will demonstrate that under some conditions, opposites do attract. There is little doubt that similarity of attitudes and values is a far more potent factor in the formation of friendship.

Proximity, self-disclosure, and attraction combine to enable people through interaction to discover commonalities and develop friendships. The understanding and acceptance experienced in friendship may sometimes be viewed by a religious person as a means of divine grace, evidence of God's healing power in human creation.

References

Berscheid, E., & Walster, E. H. (1978). *Interpersonal attraction* (2nd ed.). Reading, MA: Addison-Wesley.

Cohen, S., & Wills, T. A. (1985). Stress, social support and the buffering hypothesis. *Psychological Bulletin, 98*, 310–357.

Durkheim, E. (1951). *Suicide*. New York: Free Press. (Original work published 1897)

Festinger, L., Schachter, S., & Back, K. (1950). *Social pressures in informal groups: A study of human factors in housing.* New York: Harper & Bros.

L. PARROTT III

See LONELINESS; LOVE.

Frigidity. *See* SEXUAL AROUSAL DISORDERS.

Fromm, Erich (1900–1980). Along with Erik Erikson, Karen Horney, and Harry Stack Sullivan, Fromm introduced into orthodox psychoanalytic thought careful and detailed considerations of social processes. Of the four, he was the most concerned with large-scale social forces.

Trained as a psychologist (Ph.D. from Heidelberg in 1922), Fromm was an avowed Marxist. He denounced all extant forms of government, including capitalism and communism, as incapable of fulfilling human needs. At the same time he staunchly believed that an adequate social organization could be achieved, and much of his writing is laced with utopian hopes and ideals.

For Fromm it was society that perverted human behavior. His proposal of five basic character types (receptive, exploitative, hoarding, marketing, and productive) also reflects his socioeconomic orientation. Only the last of these types is healthy, according to Fromm. However, there can be combinations of the five. Thus a particular individual might be productive-exploitative. Such a person might be an opportunistic building contractor who constructs houses and creates jobs.

Escape from Freedom (1941) is perhaps Fromm's most famous book, written as the Nazis controlled his native Germany and World War II was accelerating. Writing from the United States, Fromm saw the German people embracing fascism because it seemed to offer security. Freedom and the alienation and isolation that come with it is aversive. Social structures that offer people a sense of belongingness can be powerfully appealing, regardless of how heinous they may be.

Rootedness, relatedness, and identity are three of the five needs that Fromm argues are fundamental to the human condition. The others are the need for transcendence (to rise above one's animal nature and to create) and the need for a frame of orientation or reference (a way of making sense of the world and of one's experience in it). These uniquely human needs stem from the fact that we are part of nature yet separate from it. We are animals, but we have reason, imagination, and the capacity to self-reflect.

Fromm, who called himself a dialectic humanist and who promoted a form of government he termed humanistic communitarian socialism, was a learned and articulate writer. Over the span of his career he acquired a considerable following, perhaps more among the liberally oriented literati than among the ranks of behavioral scientists. His thought bears a resemblance to that of Rosseau and other proponents of noble savage ideology. Despite what may have been Fromm's blindness to personal evil and to evil's diabolical quality, he was the first well-known psychological writer to draw attention to the relationship between societal structure and personality.

From the vantage point of Christian theology Fromm is to be commended for his honest admission that he was engaging in philosophical speculation. He did not try to hide behind the authority of physical science. Moreover, he clearly saw that people are more than animals. However, there is a hopeless circularity to Fromm's ideas on mental health and morality: that which is healthy is good and vice versa. Ultimately, what is healthy *and* good must be taken to be what Fromm thinks they are. Christians appeal to revelation as the solution to such circularity.

C. W. McLemore

Frotteurism. Frotteurism is a paraphilia that involves rubbing against another person without the victim's consent or knowledge in order to become sexually aroused. Frottage is most likely to occur in crowded public areas such as stores, busy sidewalks, subways, or public transportation waiting areas where the victim may perceive the contact as unintentional and where the perpetrator (usually male) can escape without easy identification or pursuit. The perpetrator may rub his genitals against the victim's thighs or buttocks or may manually fondle genitals or breasts while fantasizing that the victim is in love with the perpetrator. Preoccupation with frotteurism develops in adolescence and begins to decline in frequency when young adult males are in their mid-twenties, because the perpetrators either adopt more intense sexually offending behaviors or learn to meet their intimacy needs in more reciprocal, appropriate relationships.

Incarcerated sexual offenders report that their own offending histories began with deviant sexual fantasies in their early teens. Often these deviant arousal patterns included frotteurism and other paraphilias such as voyeurism, exhibitionism, fetishism, and sexualized behaviors such as obscene telephone calls, sadomasochistic practices, sexual acts with animals, and preoccupation with X-rated films or pornography. These behaviors escalated over time and with practice into more intrusive, more intense sexual offenses such as child molestation or sexual assaults.

Effective intervention requires the early identification and treatment of children who are developing deviant sexual arousal patterns and sexualized behaviors. Sexual overstimulation in children results from early or prolonged exposure to sexually explicit or sexually violent material, primarily through television, advertising, and pornography. Once juvenile offenders have been identified, treatment must focus on breaking the offender's denial of responsibility for sexually manipulative or coercive behaviors. Only timely sex-offender specific treatment will prevent the continued escalation into more dangerous and more frequent sexual assault. Personal and systemic confrontation of all sexually abusive behaviors must occur in every forum possible, especially in our church communities, in order to prevent our society's tolerance of sexual violence.

H. Bray-Garretson

See Sexual Dysfunctions.

Frustration-Aggression Hypothesis. Proposed in 1939 by Dollard and his colleagues at Yale University, the frustration-aggression hypothesis has provided one of the most popular explanations of human aggression (Dollard, Miller, Doob, Mowrer, & Sears, 1939). In its original form the hypothesis stated that the occurrence of aggressive behavior always presupposes the existence of frustration and that the existence of frustration always leads to some form of aggression. In other words, aggression is always the result of frustration, and frustration always leads to aggression. Frustration is defined as the blocking of goal-directed behavior, and aggression is considered to be action intended to cause injury to another. Although aggression might be directed at its source, the authors maintained that fear of punishment may result in a displacement in which attack is directed toward a substitute, safer target.

The suggestion that frustration always leads to aggression was quickly challenged, and the authors of the hypothesis clarified the point by postulating that frustration creates the instigation to aggression. Whether it finds expression depends on the relative strength of the instigation and inhibitions. Research indicates that frustration does not always produce aggressive behavior. For example, some people become depressed and inactive in response to frustration. The nature of frustration also seems to be important in understanding how people respond. When it is severe, deliberate, or arbitrary, people are more likely to respond with aggression. When it is accidental or understandable, a hostile response is less likely. Frustration is not the same as deprivation. Frustration arises from the gap between expectations and attainments (Myers, 1996).

Berkowitz (1989) proposed an important reformulation of the original frustration-aggression hypothesis. According to Berkowitz, frustrations are aversive events and, like physical pain, fear, and crowding (*see* Crowding, Effects of), can produce negative feelings that create a readiness for aggression. Unpleasant events do not always lead to attack, however. For example, some animals prefer to flee, and the likelihood of aggression varies with prior learning, the presence of a suitable target, and the availability of alternative responses. Berkowitz (1978) has also suggested that a frustrated person is especially likely to respond with hostile behavior in the presence of aggressive cues. One such aggressive cue is a weapon, and the sight of a gun may provide the stimulation for aggression to occur or amplify its expression.

A variety of biological, social, and personal factors contribute to aggression. The frustration-aggression hypothesis seems most applicable to understanding hostile aggression, which springs from anger. Instrumental aggression, which also aims to hurt but as a means to some other end, is more likely shaped through rewards and by observing others.

References

Berkowitz, L. (1989). Frustration-aggression hypothesis: Examination and reformulation. *Psychological Bulletin, 106,* 59–73.

Berkowitz, L. (1978). Whatever happened to the frustration-aggression hypothesis? *Behavioral Scientist, 21,* 691–798.

Dollard, J., Miller, N. E., Doob, L. W., Mowrer, O. H., & Sears, R. R. (1939). *Frustration and aggression.* New Haven, CT: Yale University Press.

Myers, D. G. (1996). *Social psychology* (5th ed.). New York: McGraw-Hill.

M. BOLT

See AGGRESSION.

Fugue. *See* DISSOCIATIVE FUGUE.

Functional Autonomy. As defined by Allport (1961), the originator of this concept, functional autonomy refers to any acquired system of motivation in which the tensions involved are not of the same kind as the antecedent tensions from which the acquired system developed. In other words, in functionally autonomous behavior the motives for present behavior are independent (autonomous) of the conditions that first caused the behavior.

This initial conceptualization was later developed into two levels of functional autonomy. The more primitive level was perseverative functional autonomy. This referred to acts or behaviors that are repeated even though they have lost their original function. For example, an adolescent female may, due to rebelliousness, begin to smoke cigarettes because she knows it will irritate her parents. As the girl matures and becomes an adult, she may continue to smoke. This primitive level included activities such as compulsions, addictions to drugs and alcohol, and ritualistic behavior.

The second level of autonomy is what Allport called propriate functional autonomy. This referred to acquired interests, values, dispositions, sentiments, and lifestyles. Allport contended these and other adult life choices exist because a self-image, gradually formed, demanded this particular motivational focus.

Allport's conceptualization of motivation provided an alternative to the psychoanalytic paradigm (i.e., being motivated primarily by conflicts rooted in childhood) and the radical behaviorist explanation (i.e., a strict stimulus-response model).

Reference

Allport, G. W. (1961). *Pattern and growth in personality.* New York: Holt, Rinehart, & Winston.

M. L. MARVIN

See MOTIVATION; PERSONALITY.

Functional Family Therapy. This therapy has been used chiefly in the treatment of families with an adolescent delinquent member. The model focuses on the specific relationships (intimacy and distance) that family members want from each other. Adaptive behaviors are substituted for inefficient, problematic ones to achieve the same relational goals. For instance, adolescents seeking independence (relational distance) are encouraged to negotiate with their parents for this outcome rather than to engage in delinquent behavior to gain it.

This approach combines systems theory with a behavioristic approach. From a systems perspective, behavior is viewed as meaningful in the ways it is linked to the behavior of all the other family members, rather than individual response patterns. Emphasizing behavior, individual actions are rewarded by producing desired relationships with others in the family. Specifically, each person in the family routinely chooses behaviors that are reinforced for him or her by relational distance or intimacy.

Functional family therapy differs from traditional orientations, which regard individuals as responsible for their actions and behavior as good, bad, or healthy. Instead, the model makes the assumption that all behavior is adaptive in terms of what it accomplishes relationally. This means that behavior is not inherently good or bad, or even healthy or sick. Behavior is a communication vehicle for producing and maintaining specific outcomes from interpersonal relationships. These outcomes are conceptualized as distance, intimacy, or a moderated combination of both. To illustrate, an adolescent's running away is an inefficient, rather than an unhealthy, method to achieve distance in a relationship.

Maladaptive processes in delinquent families are altered to correspond more closely with the adaptive, problem-solving capacities of nondelinquent families. As the latter have been shown to communicate with more reciprocal supportiveness and less reciprocal defensiveness, have less silence, more equal talk time, and more constructive interruptions for feedback and clarification (Alexander, 1973), these are the targeted behaviors.

A complete assessment, consisting of three levels of analysis, is considered essential for successful treatment: what are the relationships among family members that result in regular, ritualized sequences of behavior; what are the functional payoffs (distance or intimacy) that each member receives in the behavioral sequence; and what are individual strengths, weaknesses, and behavioral styles? "Functional family therapists must understand how the behavior change of an individual must be embedded within the powerful processes of family relationships, and how these behaviors or other changes will consistently meet each family member's outcomes or functions" (Barton & Alexander, 1981, p. 417).

Intervention consists of therapy and education. Therapy prepares the family members for behavioral change by redefining the negative views that they hold toward each other. The therapist accomplishes this reattribution by addressing each person (rather than focusing on the identified patient), speaking nonjudgmentally, and helping the family understand how their actions are interdependent. Another use for reattribution is relabeling objectionable behavior, putting it in a more acceptable framework. For example, a truant teenager may be described as seeking his own way to be independent, and a possessive mother may be recast as an involved parent. Framing the behavior in a more well-intentioned, benign way decreases the tendency toward blaming, so toxic in these families. Morris, Alexander, and Turner (1991) placed college students in an experimental family situation designed to elicit blaming communication. Positive reframing of the behaviors lowered hostility and defensiveness. The authors suggest that blaming may be an automatic response in a repeating brain circuit and that reattribution interrupts this automatic circuit. This perspective reflects current trends in information processing theory.

Education implements the behavior change strategies. The therapist selects behavioral techniques consistent with the family's interpersonal and individual styles and teaches them to use these. The new behavior modality must fit the relational outcomes that individuals were previously seeking (i.e., the outcomes stay the same but the means of achieving them change) and the reattributions of the therapy phase. For instance, an independence-seeking adolescent would be better served by the flexibility of negotiating a behavioral contract with his parents than having behavioral demands closely monitored by them.

Research data (Alexander, Barton, Schiavo, & Parsons, 1976) have shown that a key factor in family change is the therapist's interpersonal skills. Therefore, the functional family therapist must possess relationship and structuring skills. Relationship skills include the ability to link the feelings of family members with their behaviors, the use of nonblaming language, interpersonal warmth and humor, and self-disclosure. Structuring skills, necessary to implement change, include directiveness (coaching and modeling effective communication), self-confidence, and clarity.

The functional family model has been shown to be particularly effective with families of delinquent adolescents. Compared to individual or no treatment, delinquent teens treated with their families in this approach showed improvement in family communication processes (Alexander & Barton, 1980). Sibling delinquency rates also are lower in families receiving this therapy. These results suggest encouraging implications for helping families with teenagers prevent affiliation with gangs and other deviant behaviors.

This model of family therapy diverges from Christian thought in that individuals are not considered responsible for their behaviors, since behavior is a message about relationships rather than being good or bad; and "the therapy process in the functional family model is admittedly very manipulative and does not reflect 'reality' or 'truth'" (Barton & Alexander, 1981, p. 423). Both these positions provide a relativistic view of behavior and personal responsibility. However, the intent of this approach seems to be to give persons an acceptable perception of themselves in order to help them attain goals they have chosen as important to them. This intent is congruent with the Christian faith's respect for the integrity of the person.

References

Alexander, J. F. (1973). Defensive and supportive communication in normal and deviant families. *Journal of Consulting and Clinical Psychology, 40,* 223–231.

Alexander, J. F., & Barton, C. (1980). Intervention with delinquents and their families: Clinical, methodological, and conceptual issues. In J. P. Vincent (Ed.), *Advances in family intervention, assessment, and theory.* Greenwich, CT: JAI.

Alexander, J. F., Barton, C., Schiavo, R. S., & Parsons, B. V. (1976). Systems-behavioral intervention with families of delinquents: Therapist characteristics, family behavior, and outcome. *Journal of Consulting and Clinical Psychology, 44,* 656–664.

Barton, C., & Alexander, J. F. (1981). Functional family therapy. In A. S. Gurman & D. P. Kniskern (Eds.), *Handbook of Family Therapy.* New York: Brunner/Mazel.

Morris, S. B., Alexander, J. F., & Turner, C. W. (1991). Do reattributions of delinquent behavior reduce blame? *Journal of Family Psychology, 5,* 192–203.

C. J. BRUUN

See FAMILY THERAPY: OVERVIEW.

Functionalism. Chronologically functionalism was the first of the major schools of psychology reacting against structuralism. It focused its critique on the structuralist's definition of the subject matter of psychology as the structure of the mind. Functionalism was unique primarily in its stress on function or usefulness of mental processes. Thus it served as a transitional movement between structuralism and behaviorism, and its pragmatic emphasis continues to characterize contemporary American psychology.

In its broadest sense any psychology may be described as functional if its main objective is the study of mental processes, operations, or functions. Thus early American psychologists used the term *function* in several ways: to denote a mental activity such as perceiving or calculating or imagining; a use for some end; or the dependency relationship between antecedents and consequents or stimuli and responses, using the term in its mathematical sense. A focus on any of these characterizes functional psychology in its broader sense. In a narrower sense functionalism refers to the psychological school emerging at the University of Chicago in the late nineteenth century under the influence of John Dewey and James R. Angell.

The roots of functionalism may be traced to several British sources. The Darwinian focus on the observation of animal behavior and morphology and a hypothesized continuity between human beings and animals became the justification for the extended study of animals, strongly identified with the work of George John Romanes and C. Lloyd Morgan. The evolutionary emphasis on adaptation to the environment was regarded as perhaps the most significant function of human behavior. Francis Galton's studies of hereditary genius became the impetus for both the American emphasis on individual differences and the mental testing movement.

Other roots are found in some American predecessors. The leading functionalist antecedent was William James, a vehement critic of the mind-stuff theory of structuralism. James argued for pragmatism as a criterion for the validity of knowledge: knowledge must be judged in terms of its consequences, values, and utility. Human beings must be considered in terms of their adaptation and readaptation to the environment, and psychologists must explore the conditions and purpose of consciousness. The functionalist agenda, with its evolutionary, genetic, and psychometric emphases, was also implicit in the works of George T. Ladd, Edward W. Scripture, James Mark Baldwin, Edward Lee Thorndike, James McKeen Cattell, and Granville Stanley Hall.

Functionalism was officially launched in 1896, when Dewey published an article on the reflex arc concept in psychology in the *Psychological Review.* Dewey protested against the reductionism and elementism implicit in breaking the reflex or any other behavioral act into sensory, motor, and associative components or into other units such as stimulus and response or sensation and movement. Dewey, whose attention turned toward education and philosophy, left it to Angell to crystallize the functionalist psychology. Angell addressed the American Psychological Association on "The Province of Functionalism" in 1906, stating its three primary assertions: the subject matter of psychology is mental operations and their ends; the mind is a means of mediating between the needs of the organism and its environment; psychology must be psychophysical, taking both mind and body seriously.

Several other characteristics of functionalism can be stated. The method of introspection, involving the subject's own report of his or her experience, was only gradually replaced by observation and other objective methods. A biological orientation directed the functionalist to the theory of evolution; an interest in the nature-nurture controversy; the concept of the person as organism; the study of animal behavior; and genetic, comparative, and psychophysiological studies. Practical applications encouraged the study of differential and social psychology and psychometric theory.

Harvey A. Carr succeeded Angell at Chicago and introduced an emphasis on motivating factors, thus adding a component of dynamic psychology to functionalism. C. H. Judd, also at Chicago, authored the most systematic textbook version of functionalism. Columbia University was also a stronghold of functionalism under the leadership of Cattell, Thorndike, and Robert Sessions Woodworth. Columbia emphasized the importance "of curves of distribution, of individual differences, of the measurement of intelligence and other human capacities, of experimental procedures and statistical devices, of the undercurrent of physiological thought" (Heidbreder, 1933, pp. 291–292). At Columbia functionalism also became foundational to educational psychology, as it freed the psychologist to study what was helpful to both the individual and society.

Criticisms of functionalism focused on its multiple definitions, its utilitarian motives, its theoretical and methodological eclecticism, and its teleological emphasis. Teleological explanations, which explain behavior by appealing to its ultimate consequences or final causes, have characteristically been criticized by twentieth-century psychology. Christian theology has consistently been teleological in its orientation, and thus a functional component may be regarded as a necessary aspect of any adequate psychology.

Reference

Heidbreder, E. (1933). *Seven psychologies.* New York: Appleton-Century-Crofts.

H. Vande Kemp

See Psychology, History of.

Fundamentalism. Although to describe someone as a fundamentalist implies a coherent pattern of religious devotion and practice for both lay and professional constituencies, experts disagree about the reliability and focus of the term *fundamentalism.* Definitions seem to fall along a continuum anchored at one end by zealous regard for a somewhat narrow evangelical perspective (e.g., Ammerman, 1991) and at the other by single-minded, even violent commitment to any conservative religious cause (cf. Dees, 1996; Hoffer, 1951). Whether or not fundamentalism denotes either a conceptually unified description for a set of beliefs or a consistent profile for religious behavior has come under increasing scrutiny (Hood, 1983). Differences even exist concerning the historical origins of the designation. Some give Curtis Lee Laws priority for coining the label in the 1920s while editor of the *Watchman-Examiner* (Riesebrodt, 1993); others cite the 1910 publication of "The Fundamentals," a position paper intended to stem the tide of "modernity" within evangelical Protestantism in America (Hill, 1995). Nonetheless, many contemporary classifications of significant theological and psychological motifs continue to include fundamentalism as a legitimate, unique category (e.g., Marty & Appleby, 1995).

Despite these differences of opinion, fundamentalism provides an adequate theoretical context for discussing certain features of religious movements and how these characteristics seem to influence their adherents. However, at least one dichotomy seems to be usefully preserved: Whether fundamentalism specifies acceptance of a particular set of doctrinal beliefs, or whether the term defines a particular behavioral complex in the expression of religious faith and practice, regardless of belief content. Historically the term derives from certain doctrinal positions, espoused to counter perceived tendencies toward secularism within Protestant Christianity, but contemporary analyses seem to adopt the latter "process" view of the concept. In order fully to capture the intended meaning of fundamentalism, perhaps this distinction should remain unresolved.

Characteristics of Fundamentalism.

Accepting for the moment that fundamentalism signifies a particular set of beliefs, at least four can be readily identified: biblical literalism, a position that typically goes beyond the traditional principle of biblical inerrancy that is accepted by most evangelical communities and embraces verbal inspiration or scriptural infallibility; prophetic interpretation based on premillennialism, which implies adequate historical explanations for the symbols in apocalyptic literature prior to the millennium of Revelation 20 and a literal second coming of Christ; the responsibility of proselytizing; the gospel commission is seen less as divine foresight and more as a task given to all believers; and separatism from the world, implying personal and moral isolation from the apostasy that characterizes the larger society of unbelievers.

Behavioral manifestations of these four guiding principles could be that since the Bible is infallible, veridical propositional truth can be derived from it to determine decisively any possible doctrinal issue; furthermore, this scriptural authority extends to all human beings on earth, regardless of their current personal awareness or understanding.

If the Bible contains a faithful record of future events as well as an accurate historical account, then no room for doubt remains; believers can have supreme confidence in religious leaders who understand the symbols and thus interpret the past or predict the future.

The whole world must hear of the gospel message before Christ can return, and so believers not only participate in hastening Christ's second advent but also must fulfill this responsibility before Christ's imminent return. Acceptance of this monumental task typically imbues fundamentalist doctrinal clarity with a certain urgency: Not only am I right, but surely everyone must be so convinced.

Finally, separatism serves to reinforce the attitudes of doctrinal purity through mutual interaction among believers, insulated from the scrutiny of the larger society. Whether such a behavioral profile applies consistently to all those adhering to fundamentalist doctrines and whether these response biases psychologically lead to a tendency toward violence remain open issues.

Psychological Implications of Fundamentalism.

Although many counseling professionals tend to describe fundamentalism with a certain disdainful detachment, it would be a mistake to characterize it as consistently negative from a psychological perspective. Perhaps certain personalities or dispositions more easily adopt a fundamentalist outlook than others; definitive conclusions in this regard await further research. However, several general advantages seem to accompany a fundamentalist commitment. For example, the assurance of veridical divine truth and understanding concerning ultimate reality most likely enables the experience of inner peace (*see* Peace, Inner) and repose more efficiently than its alternatives. In addition, even though fundamentalism's isolationist stance may attenuate this benefit, accepting responsibility to convince others of truth ensures unequivocal involvement and interest in one's community. Human contact of any kind is generally preferable psychologically to complete isolation.

However, several general disadvantages of the fundamentalist outlook can also be enumerated. The arbitrary authority and infallibility of Scripture as the ultimate source of truth across all cultures can lead to a strong in-group/out-group bias: "Those who believe as I do are superior—not only doctrinally, but in many other ways—to those who do not." Insulation from disagreement or critique can lead to an inflated sense of accuracy and precision regarding one's belief system. Furthermore, this unquestioning commitment to authority may generalize to extrareligious roles, such as one's role as a parent. Since adherence to fundamentalism requires belief not only in absolute truth but also in one's understanding of this truth, disagreement and dissension can readily be labeled as error and thus cannot be tolerated. Such intolerance becomes justified as the means for the ultimate salvation of those who disagree. Since the healthy individuation of children within a family environment typically requires open questioning of the belief system of parents, fundamentalism can provide the motivation for strict, authoritarian discipline, perhaps even violence (cf. Claussen & Crittenden, 1991).

Among investigators of the psychology of fundamentalism, distinctions between fundamentalism and religious orthodoxy or evangelicalism broadly defined must be preserved. Both orthodoxy and mainstream evangelicalism undoubtedly share some doctrinal positions with fundamentalism (e.g., the authority of Scripture; the divinity of Christ). However, the unquestioning adherence to these positions and the arbitrary, sometimes even militant imposition of them on others who do not share a compatible perspective, in addition to the isolationism required by doctrinal superiority, all serve to distinguish fundamentalism as it is generally conceived from orthodoxy and evangelicalism, although these latter terms convey the same urgent convictions regarding spiritual reality and its contemporary meaningfulness. Beyond this important distinction, whether fundamentalism as a sociological or psychological descriptor can apply equally well to the militantly committed minority of believers within non-Christian traditions such as Islam does not yet enjoy a consensus among behavioral and social scientists.

Possible Counseling Applications. Awareness of the central characteristics of fundamentalism not only provides caring professionals with the ability to identify these dynamics within their clients or congregations; this information also provides grounds for affirmation as well as guidance. The assurance

of salvation, the certainty of Christ's personal interest in individual lives and the future of this earth, and unswerving confidence in the Bible as a source of truth all represent admirable qualities, from a Christian perspective, inherent in fundamentalism. The influence of these views can provide succor through life's inevitable complexities and disappointments. On the contrary, the inflexibility typical of fundamentalism can sometimes prove impotent when adherents face overwhelming grief or inexplicable horror. Nonetheless, Paul's audacious assertions that "I am not ashamed of the gospel of Christ, for it is the power of God unto salvation" and "All Scripture is given by inspiration of God" remind us of truths contained within fundamentalism.

However, the in-group/out-group tendencies that frequently derive from the isolationist emphasis in fundamentalism represent a potential problem area. Christ's ready acceptance of the centurion, the Samaritan woman at the well, and the Phoenician woman could all be used to illustrate the inclusiveness that should characterize all of his followers, who seek to emulate his ministry on behalf of the world. Paul's admonitions in Colossians 3:11, Galatians 6:3, and 1 Corinthians 13 serve to corroborate Christ's example of acceptance, tolerance, and love. After all, Christ reserved the right to judge for himself in Matthew 7 and elsewhere. Although we are admonished to rightly divide the word of truth, arbitrary divisions among human beings for whom Christ has died, if such divisions imply differences in worthiness or acceptability, cannot easily be defended from sound, biblical exegesis.

Conclusions. Fundamentalism can be traced to a conservative reaction to perceptions of increasing secularization within American Protestantism occurring early in the twentieth century, although it has more recently been applied quite generally to many conservative religious movements. As a doctrinal position, fundamentalism espouses commitments to scriptural literalism, premillennial eschatology, the responsibility to win converts to fundamentalist tenets, and moral and social separation from the larger society. Behavioral manifestations of fundamentalism may include overconfidence in particular understandings of truth; arbitrary, authoritarian rigidity toward dissension; a strict, clear-cut view of biblical interpretation; a strong tendency toward an in-group/out-group bias supporting feelings of moral superiority and even violent responses toward presumed insurrection.

While the assurance of truth and confidence in supernatural reality represent advantages of fundamentalism, its rigidity can prove unsympathetic and empty when disaster strikes. Additionally, the arbitrary distinctions made by fundamentalism between its adherents and detractors may result in a divisiveness that precludes our Christian responsibility to emulate the love of Christ in our families and communities. Such harsh criticism of unbelievers might better be replaced with unconditional positive regard for those for whom God paid an infinite price (John 3:16).

References

Ammerman, N. T. (1991). North American Protestant fundamentalism. In M. E. Marty & R. S. Appleby (Eds.), *Fundamentalism observed*. Chicago: University of Chicago Press.

Claussen, A., & Crittenden, P. (1991). Physical and psychological maltreatment: Relations among types of maltreatment. *Child Abuse and Neglect, 15,* 5–17.

Dees, M. (1996). *The gathering storm*. New York: Harper-Collins.

Hill, P. C. (1995). *Fundamentalism and Christianity: A psychological perspective*. Paper presented to the annual meeting of the American Psychological Association, New York City.

Hoffer, E. (1951). *The true believer*. New York: Harper & Row.

Hood, R. W., Jr. (1983). Social psychology and religious fundamentalism. In A. W. Childs & G. B. Melton (Eds.), *Rural psychology*. New York: Plenum.

Marty, M., & Appleby, R. (1995). *Fundamentalism comprehended*. Chicago: University of Chicago Press.

Riesebrodt, M. (1993). *Pious passion*. London: University of California Press.

Additional Readings

Crabb, L. J., Jr. (1975). *Basic principles of biblical counseling*. Grand Rapids, MI: Zondervan.

Dudley, R. L., & Gillespie, V. B. (1992). *Valuegenesis: Faith in the balance*. Riverside, CA: La Sierra University Press.

Peck, M. S. (1978). *The road less traveled: A new psychology of love, traditional values and spiritual growth*. New York: Simon & Schuster.

Rice, R. (1991). *Reason and the contours of faith*. Riverside, CA: La Sierra University Press.

Thompson, A. (1991). *Inspiration: Hard questions, honest answers*. Hagerstown, MD: Review & Herald.

J. L. BRAND

See SPIRITUAL AND RELIGIOUS ISSUES IN PSYCHOHERAPY.

Galton, Francis (1822–1911). Few characters in the history of psychology can match the color and creativity of Sir Francis Galton. His scientific contributions range across geography, meteorology, criminology, biological statistics, behavioral genetics, and psychology. His intellectual brilliance and intense curiosity were apparent at an early age. By the age of 2 ½ years he could read and write, and by 5 he could read any English book. Such accomplishments led Terman (1917) to estimate Galton's Intelligence Quotient (IQ) at around 200.

Galton's contributions to psychology sprang largely from four key questions: What are the major psychological differences among individuals? How can these differences be accurately measured? How are these differences related to each other? To what extent are such differences attributable to hereditary and/or environmental factors? Galton is often called the father of differential psychology, a discipline that is still directed at these basic questions.

Galton's interest in individual differences was stimulated by the work of his cousin, Charles Darwin. When Darwin proposed that such differences fueled the process of natural selection, Galton was quick to recognize that these characteristics must be identified, measured, and understood, if not merely for the sake of science, for the sake of determining the future direction of the human race. His concern for humanity's future and the role of genetics in that future led him to found the controversial field that later became known as eugenics, which examines ways of moving human evolution along a more desirable path through selective breeding of individuals.

The foundations of differential psychology were established primarily in four of Galton's books: *Hereditary Genius* (1869), *English Men of Science: Their Nature and Nurture* (1874), *Inquiries into Human Faculty and Development* (1883), and *Natural Inheritance* (1889). Throughout these works we see almost religious commitment to the notion that critical human differences are largely attributable to heritable factors. In *Hereditary Genius*, Galton tried to substantiate this hypothesis by showing that eminence ran in families. When critics argued that

persons from eminent families may have benefited from similar enriched environments as well as similar genes, Galton developed a self-report questionnaire designed to trace the environmental and hereditary roots of two hundred English scientists. Thus the questionnaire method, so widely used in psychology today, was born.

Galton pursued the problem of measuring individual differences in his 1883 book. Here he describes the development and use of the Galton whistle for measuring auditory acuity; instruments measuring simple reaction time, breathing power, and color sense; and the first tests of mental imagery and word association. Many of these instruments and tests were put to use in his anthropometric laboratory, which attracted many subjects and spectators at London's International Health Exhibition of 1884.

Perhaps Galton's two most important contributions to psychology were methodological in nature. Through keen observation Galton identified two types of twins, which later became known as monozygotic (MZ) and dizygotic (DZ) twins. By looking at the relative similarity of MZ and DZ twins on various psychological characteristics, Galton was able to estimate the contributions of hereditary and environmental factors to these traits. The twin-study method is now a cornerstone of modern behavior genetics.

Prior to Galton psychologists and biologists struggled with the problem of mathematically summarizing the association of variables that tend to go together. Working with data from his measures of individual differences, Galton developed bivariate scatter plots, noted the "regression to the mean" phenomenon, and observed that the "slope" of the regression line corresponded to the degree of association between the variables. From there, Karl Pearson developed Pearson's *r* coefficient, the *r* referring to Galton's regression phenomenon. The fundamental ideas underlying this important statistical tool are attributable to Galton.

Although the fruits of Galton's efforts can be found throughout most contemporary psychology, they are most clearly seen in areas in which the measurement of individual differences is important—for example, personnel psychology, behavior genetics, clinical assessment, and educational psychology.

Reference

Terman, L. M. (1917). The intelligence quotient of Francis Galton in childhood. *American Journal of Psychology, 28*, 208–215.

D. D. MCKENNA

See PERSONALITY ASSESSMENT; HEREDITY AND ENVIRONMENT IN HUMAN DEVELOPMENT.

Gambling, Pathological. Gambling in the United States has been used to finance government projects since 1612, when the Virginia Company was authorized by King James I of England to finance a large portion of the Jamestown settlement. A lottery was authorized by the Continental Congress in 1776 to help finance the Revolutionary War. Lotteries have been used as voluntary taxes, although they are a form of regressive tax. Other forms of legalized gambling include casinos, parimutuel betting, riverboat VLTs (video lottery), and flourishing casinos located on reservations. People in the United States spend more than $40,000,000,000 a year gambling.

Gambling is legal in 48 states and has become a political issue. Proponents attempt to convince voters that gambling will bring jobs and money that will expand the local economy and provide tax money to increase funding for desirable projects such as education.

Opponents of legalized gambling point out that gambling hurts the economy. A pathological gambler, for example, has a conservative cost to the community of between $15,000 and $33,500 (crime, direct regulatory costs, and loss of productivity). There are also political problems from influence buying and associated political corruption. The loss of productive work is a social cost. Unproductive profitseeking is another less recognizable social cost. In unproductive profitseeking, the gambler neither produces anything of value nor enjoys the activity.

There are approximately 1.4% (2,600,000) addicted gamblers in the United States. Gambling has also become a problem for teenagers in America as they spend approximately $1,000,000,000 each year on gambling. Teenagers are about two times as likely as adults to become addicted.

The *DSM-IV* (American Psychiatric Association, 1994) defines pathological gambling as maladaptive behavior that includes at least five of the following ten behaviors: a preoccupation with gambling; an increasing amount of money needed to achieve the desired excitement; repeated unsuccessful efforts to control or stop gambling; restlessness when attempting to cut down or stop gambling; using gambling as a way of escaping or relieving feelings of depression; chasing lost money by trying to break even; hiding or trying to conceal the extent of gambling losses; jeopardizing relationships and opportunities in life; soliciting help from others to deal with financial problems as a result of gambling; and committing illegal acts to finance gambling.

What are the causes of pathological gambling? Gambling may be a learned behavior. The repeated exposure to gambling through family or social pressures may result in a learned response. Gambling also is theorized to be a chase after an endorphin high that comes from winning. Even though the person is losing, he or she is trying to capture that high felt while winning. Gambling may be an attempt to reduce the stress of loneliness, anger, or depression. It may be an attempt to impress others or to cope with the death or loss of a loved one. Pathological gambling is, therefore, the excess of the reasons why people gamble.

Pathological gambling may also be a desire to lose in order to punish oneself. That is why individuals keep gambling until they are losing. Pathological gambling is an example of the self-destructive nature of sin that is inherent in individuals and society. Sin can easily potentiate one's weakness such as in gambling and create a psychological bondage to a certain behavior.

The Bible warns of covetousness in the tenth commandment (Exod. 20:17) and of being on guard against greed (Luke 12:15). The Bible admonishes people to work for what they earn and not to seek financial gain without the commensurate honest labor (Prov. 21:25–26).

Pathological gamblers should be confronted with compassion when one has concern about their gambling behavior. They should be told exactly what the concerns are and that someone cares. They should be encouraged to talk about their problem and when appropriate to pray for release from the addiction of gambling. They can also be referred to Gamblers Anonymous.

Reference

American Psychiatric Association. (1994). *Diagnostic and statistical manual of mental disorders* (4th ed.). Washington, DC: Author.

Additional Readings

Campion, M. (1995). Riverboat casinos in Allegheny County. Unpublished master's thesis, Robertson School of Government, Regent University, Virginia Beach, VA.

Rosenthal, R. J. (1992). Pathological gambling. *Psychiatric Annuals, 22*, 72–78.

For Further Information

Gamblers Anonymous. P.O. Box 17173, Los Angeles, CA 90017. (213) 386-8789.

GAM-ANON. P.O. Box 157, White Stone, NY 11357. (718) 352-1671.

M. A. CAMPION

See MONEY, PSYCHOLOGY OF.

Game Analysis. One of the major techniques of transactional analysis. Games are a set of ulterior interactions (having double motives) between persons that lead to predictable bad results. Game analysis initially involves noting repetitive interactions in the life of the client. Usually these appear to be rational, straightforward behaviors (i.e., complementary transactions). The task of the therapist is to intuit the concealed or hidden motive beneath the surface. Games are usually played to confirm feelings of low self-esteem.

A game begins with the con (the invitation to play) and the gimmick (the response of the other indicating he or she is hooked into playing). This leads to a response (a series of interactions), followed by a switch (changes in ego states indicating the hidden message has been sent and received), and a crossup (confusion as to what happened). The result is a pay-off (bad feelings).

H. N. MALONY

See TRANSACTIONAL ANALYSIS.

Gender and Psychopathology. While *sex* refers to the biological expression of maleness and femaleness, *gender* indicates the social aspects of being a male or a female. However, these two terms are often interchanged without any implications for their original biological or social implications. Thus gender (sex) role represents social expectations about how males and females should behave.

How gender role may affect the diagnosis and the rates of mental illness may be illustrated by the tendency of women to talk about their symptoms and seek psychiatric help more than men do. Women report more illness than men do because it is more culturally acceptable for them to be ill. In contrast, men are expected to bear pain and avoid the public display of emotional behavior. Thus women are more likely than men to seek treatment for depression, while men deal with their depression by turning to drugs and alcohol or by committing suicide. However, seeking help from a physician or a therapist may increase women's dependency and helplessness, reduce their self-esteem, and explain their predominance among drug abusers. The effects of gender role may also be seen in the relationship between marital status and mental illness. Mental illness is higher among married women than among married men, but this trend is reversed among single men and women. The role of a married woman seems to be less advantageous than that of a married man.

Pattern of Psychopathology. There are gender differences in the prevalence of specific forms of mental illness. Boys are consistently higher than girls in the various types of psychoses, including childhood schizophrenia. Other disorders that are higher among boys than girls are infantile autism (M to F ratio, 3:1), attention deficit disorder with hyperactivity (M to F ratio, 10:1), conduct disorders (M to F ratio, 4:1 to 12:1), chronic motor tic disorder (M to F ratio, 3:1), and mental retardation (M to F ratio, 2:1). An excep-

tion to the advantage of girls over boys is epidemic hysteria, which is more frequent among adolescent girls who live in a closed community such as a boarding school or hospital and who may respond to group anxiety related to pregnancies, sexual activities, work stress, or death of a compatriot. Similarly, anorexia nervosa afflicts mainly females in late adolescence and early adulthood. Depression is equally common among boys and girls, in contrast to its predominance among females in adult life. In adulthood women are more likely than men to suffer from depression, phobias, and anxiety neuroses. Men are more likely to suffer from personality disorders, alcohol and drug addiction, and schizophrenia. Gender-differentiated patterns of psychopathology may be partly the result of gender roles that predispose men and women to express their distress differently.

Depression. Women are twice as likely to be depressed as men. They are also more likely to be afflicted with more severe clinical depression. Among married, divorced, and separated people, women tend to be more depressed than men; among the single and the widowed, men tend to be more depressed. Gender differences in depression seem to be eliminated in the employment setting when factors such as salary, age, education, and job classification had been taken into consideration.

Several theories have been proposed to explain depression in women. One explanation is that the feminine role predisposes women to depression because it encourages them to be helpless and to expect their efforts to be ineffective. Another likely explanation is that women's lives are more stressful than are those of men. Although the evidence on sex differences in stress is not conclusive, it is possible that the lower socioeconomic status of women and their exposure to chronic stressful life conditions (e.g., poor housing, low-status jobs, sexual harassment) may make them vulnerable to depression.

Depression in women is also explained in terms of their sensitivity to the disruption of personal relationships; for example, the loss of an important relationship is more likely to result in depression in women than it is in men. The biological explanation of higher depression among women attempts to link depression to hormonal changes related to reproductive processes such as menstruation, the postpartum period, and menopause. However, there is no evidence to demonstrate a hormonal basis for the link between menstruation, postpartum, or the menopause and depression. Finally, sex differences in depression may be explained by the way women and men respond to depression. Men tend to carry out activities to distract them from their depressive feelings, while women tend to react by reflecting on it and being concerned with its causes and implications.

Schizophrenia. The evidence on sex differences in schizophrenia is inconsistent but tends to favor higher rates for males. However, there is a sex-age pattern of the onset of schizophrenia, with males afflicted with the illness earlier than are females.

It has been suggested that the age of schizophrenic breakdown in the adult years may coincide with specific stresses related to the gender roles of men and women. Schizophrenia strikes men in their early twenties because of conflicts related to occupational choice. In contrast, women have their breakdown in their late twenties or early thirties because of stresses related to marital and family life.

Clinical observation of schizophrenic patients in hospital wards and in psychotherapy indicates that schizophrenic men tend to be more passive and withdrawn, whereas schizophrenic women tend to be active and aggressive. This observation has stimulated theory and research that conceived the illness as a manifestation of gender role reversal (i.e., men behaving like women and vice versa). Such behavioral differences between the sexes are also compatible with the finding that women tend to develop less severe types of schizophrenia than men do and remain more in touch with the social environment. Women also tend to show better prognosis as well as better social and occupational functioning after being discharged from the hospital.

Alcoholism. Men are more likely to drink or abuse alcohol. The heavier the drinking level reported, the greater the difference between males and females. General population surveys indicate that in North America about 120 men drink for every 100 women who do. There are three men who are problem drinkers for every woman; and the gender ratios are a little higher (M to F, about 4:1) when statistics are based on clinically defined alcoholics, such as alcohol-related death and alcohol psychosis. Such gender differences hold even though the same amount of alcohol intake results in more intoxication (i.e., higher blood concentration) in women than in men. Alcohol impairs women more than men because of their smaller average body size, higher proportion of body fat (alcohol is not absorbed by the body fat and therefore the concentration is higher in body water, which predominates in the blood and brain), and less of the stomach enzyme that breaks down alcohol. Biological factors resulting in more impairment of women than men from alcohol have been used to explain the lower rate of female drinking across cultures. An alternative sociocultural explanation is that gender differences may be the result of the negative response of society to female heavy drinking.

Phobias. Phobias, which are characterized by irrational fears and the tendency to avoid specific objects, situations, or activities, are more prevalent among women than they are among men. Gender differences are particularly evident in the case of animal phobia and agoraphobia. Although they are rare in adults, animal phobias tend to appear predominantly in women. Agoraphobia, which is the most frequently reported phobia among adult patients, tends to be consistently higher among females (F to M, 3:1). Agoraphobia has been often referred to as the housewife's disorder due to its high incidence among young, married women. Its onset is in the mid-twenties, a few years after marriage, and is characterized by fear of going out in the street, fear of visiting the supermarket or the beauty salon, and fear of harming one's own children.

Although the causes of gender differences in phobias are unknown, the most popular explanation is that conformity to the traditional female gender role such as being a housewife tends to increase the rates of phobias. Phobic stimuli may trigger a previously learned avoidance-dependent pattern of behavior that is compatible with gender stereotypes and the early training of women. It has been observed that boys and girls are similar in their fears until adolescence, when females begin to admit more fears than males. During socialization boys are encouraged to face and master their fears; girls are reinforced to respond in a helpless and dependent manner.

Additional Readings

Brannon, L. (1996). *Gender: Psychological perspectives.* Boston: Allyn & Bacon.

Lips, H. M. (1993). *Sex and gender: An introduction* (2nd ed.). Mountain View, CA: Mayfield.

I. AL-ISSA

See GENDER IDENTITY.

Gender Identity. The concept of identity popularized by Erikson (1959) is a description of eight stages of the life cycle during which we experience and express different styles of being a person. Identity combines the senses of who I am, what I do, and how I do it. The sense of identity may be inchoate, affective, and inarticulate in the young child, while the introspective adult may articulate precise descriptions of his or her identity. Gender identity is only a part of the whole sense of identity, yet at the same time it is a core component around which nongender aspects of identity are crystallized. Failure to achieve precise gender identity may impair the development of mature, complex adult identity, whereas the mature normal adult accepts gender identity as a given quality and elaborates other identity attributes.

Experience and Identity. Several aspects of personal experience must be identified and separated: the "me" experience, the "I" experience, and the "self" experience. Each is a part of the sense of identity but not necessarily gender-linked. The "me" experience refers to the sense of being alive, of possessing what happens to myself. Such experience is present probably in early infancy, later cognated upon, and then verbalized as the sense of me. The experience of me precedes and is distinct from the acquisition of sense of gender. The experience of "I" is the conscious appreciation of ego operations such as cognition, affect, and perception. That is, one experiences the sense of I am thinking, seeing, doing, feeling, deciding, acting. Again, the sense of I precedes and is distinct from the acquisition of sense of gender.

The term *ego* shall be construed operationally to describe mental operations—that is, cognition, perception, affect systems. Ego operations are experienced and directed. But ego operations are impersonal. We acquire different styles of ego operation that may become part of our identity formation, for example, "I am a fuzzy-thinking person" versus "I am a clear-thinking person." Ego styles are gender-linked. In a given culture males and females are differentially socialized in different styles of ego operations. We may say, for example, "You think like a woman" and thereby make an accurate observation of cultural influence on gender-linked ego style (Spence & Helmreich, 1978).

Self is the image of Who am I? It is a complex mental construction, including my ideal self or what I ought to be (the combined psychoanalytic ego ideal and superego), my desired self (a consciously constructed self-model), and my actual self (the observation of my person in action). Self-identity is neither innate nor epigenetic, as is true of me and I experiences. Rather, self-identity is learned, constructed, formulated, modified, and elaborated on throughout life (Gergen, 1971). Gender plays a major role in the development of self-identity. One can experience me, I, and ego operations apart from a sense of gender, but one does not experience self apart from a sense of gender.

It is obvious that sexual impulse, desire, and behavior are entwined with gender identity. Sigmund Freud interpreted sexuality as a basic determinant of identity. However, a century of research has demonstrated that sexuality is a reflection of gender identity rather than a determinant. That is, sexuality is acted out in terms of impulse, arousal, desire, and action on the basis of one's gender-identity formation (Stoller, 1968).

Anatomy and Destiny. A major question is raised by the obvious differences between male and female appearance, behavior, and role functions. Is this biological determinism or cultural artifact? It is appealing to assume that innate biological instincts account for male-female differences. In animal species we observe highly complex social behavior that is gender-linked. However, the biologic determinants of behavior shift with animal complexity; basic instincts are the same in human, monkey, pigeon, or worm. These generate drives, which become less directive as we ascend the phylogenic ladder, so that when we reach the level of humans, instinctual drive stimuli no longer determine specific behavioral complexes.

An example of this is the sexual instinct. The amoeba reproduces asexually at a predictable rate of fission. The earthworm has both male and female sex organs and copulates with another earthworm by matching male and female genitalia in random fashion. Frogs and birds mate only during a mating season, with gender-linked stereotyped courtship behavior and with a partner for the season. Higher mammals, such as the gorilla, form generational families, choose specific mates, mate during estrous seasons, and care for the young within the family structure. Young monkeys who are reared apart from the mother do not successfully copulate or care for their own young. In the human sexuality may never be expressed, in that celibate persons may live a normal and psychologically healthy life without significant sexual experience. Or persons may use sexual behavior to quell loneliness, anxiety, or conflict without experiencing any sexual pleasure. At the same time human sexual behavior is not necessarily linked to reproductive mating.

To conclude, in terms of biologic principles we cannot appeal to differences in male and female instincts to account for male-female variations in behavior per se.

The influence of genetic variation and hormonal influences on behavior must be considered. Persons with abnormal gender chromosomal patterns may exhibit genetic defects of deformations of skeleton or muscle formation. But their behavior may not differ from that of persons with normal gender chromosomes. If we administer sex hormones to a person, what will happen? In the average person, nothing. However, in some experiments, if one administers hormones to homosexual persons, they increase their homosexual activity level. That is, sex hormones increase the drive stimuli but do not change the sexual orientation of the person. Clearly then, gender behavior, including sexual behavior, cannot be accounted for primarily on biological grounds (Money & Musaph, 1977).

Facets of Gender Identity. The development of identity is biopsychosocial. We can truly speak of psychosexual identity, but more accurately we should speak of psychogender identity, since sexuality is an expression of gender sense. Eight variables contribute to psychogender identity (Money & Ehrhardt, 1972).

Variable 1: Chromosomal Gender. In the normal pattern the female has an XX sex chromosome pattern, the male an XY. In genetic abnormalities there may be five to six sex chromosome gene patterns, each giving rise to different clinical syndromes and involving different hormonal, musculoskeletal, and genital patterns and different levels of sexual potency. Yet a person with a female chromosome pattern may be born with male-appearing genitalia, be reared as male, and behave as male, and vice versa. The sex chromosome pattern obviously does not determine gender behavior.

Variable 2: Gonadal Gender. This refers to the presence of either testes or ovaries. In the embryo the human is bisexual, and under hormonal influence one set withers and the other grows. Yet in some cases of aberrant chromosomal and/or hormonal influence, the external genitalia may develop of one gender while the gonads are of opposite gender. Thus an infant may be born with female-looking genitals along with well-developed undescended testicles, or vice versa. Again, the primary gonads do not determine gender orientation or behavior.

Variable 3: Hormonal Gender. Males and females do have distinctive hormonal systems, produced by both the gonads and other body organs. Malfunction or disequilibrium in the hormonal systems may influence the male-female balance of hormones. In turn this may result in masculinization or feminization of body traits, such as voice, hair pattern, breast development, fat deposition, skeletal growth, and development of external genitalia in embryo. In children this may result in a chromosomal and gonadal male with a female hormone balance that causes feminization of body structure, or vice versa. Nonetheless, the person will act male or female in accord with that person's rearing, regardless of the hormonal balance or body habitus.

Variable 4: Internal Genitalia. This refers to the vagina and uterus in the female and prostate in the male. These internal organs develop in accord with embryonic hormonal patterns.

Variable 5: External Genitalia. These organs are the most visible evidence upon which we first assign gender. Yet they may be misleading. As noted, variations in chromosomal, gonadal, and hormonal variables may produce external genitalia that appear of one gender yet are opposite to all other previous gender variables. A male may not develop closure of the bilateral pubic genital tissues and appear to have a vulva. A female may have overdevelopment of the clitoris that looks like a penis. But the external genitalia do not determine gender identity.

In the case of transsexualism the person has the identity of one gender (I experience my identity as female) while having all the normal body attributes of the other gender (I live in a male body). In this instance the distinction between gender body attributes (biological) and gender identity (psychological) is clearly seen.

Variable 6: Gender of Assignment and Rearing. This refers to the label the parent gives the child as either male or female. Boys and girls are handled differently as infants by their parents. They are treated differently long before they can talk or cognate on their own gender identity. The child is socialized into a basic gender identity long before language acquisition. Such gender acquisition precedes language. The threshold for fixation of gender identity is about 18 months, while the point of no return for change in gender reassignment is about 30 months. After 4 years of age it is almost impossible to change gender assignment without severe psychological conflict in the child.

Variable 7: Core Gender Identity. This is the first basic sense of identity that is crystallized via cognition as part of self-identity. The child cognitively is able to state, I am a boy or girl. This appears to be organized as a cognitive construct between ages three or four. In contrast, the gender assignment has already been well established. It appears that when parents assign the child one gender (male) and treat the child as the other gender (female), the psychological conditions for transsexualism are created (I have been labeled a male but am treated as and expected to be a female). In psychotic regressive states we can observe similar confusion about core gender identity in patients who demonstrate no gender confusion in normal states. Persons with primitive character disorders similarly demonstrate gender identity confusion.

Variable 8: Gender Role Identity. This refers to the social patterns of appearance, behavior, and role performance associated with the sociocultural definitions of masculinity or femininity. There is probably some degree of psychological linkage between the sense of maleness or femaleness and behavior in masculine or feminine roles as defined by the culture. For example, in cultures with weak male roles the males demonstrate a higher incidence of identification with women, as in couvade (male pregnancy fantasies). One can experience a strong sense of maleness or femaleness, however, and not behave in traditional or expected gender-linked roles. For example, a feminine woman can be a police officer; a masculine man can knit doilies (Munroe & Munroe, 1977).

In the area of social gender roles there has been much confusion about the difference between gender identity and gender roles. The concept of androgyny has been promoted to do away with gender distinctions. This misses the point that gender identity is ineluctably a part of personal identity but that many social roles and behaviors need not be gender-linked (Sargent, 1977). The mature person with a secure gender identity is free to elaborate a wide variety of social role behaviors that become part of personal identity apart from gender.

Gender and Self-Identity. Although self-identity need not be tied to gender in many aspects, in another sense self-identity is always linked to gender. There are eight stages of psychological development of identity, according to Bemporad (1980). Each stage is not left behind but is incorporated into the next developmental level. Thus in the mature adult we continue to see reflections of each stage of identity.

Stage 1. In what is called an oral incorporative mode the newborn engulfs everything encountered. This style of relating to the world is to take it in and make it part of himself. The young infant does not differentiate between self and other. The lack of body boundaries, the timeless sense of fusion with the other, the experience of engulfing and being engulfed is reexperienced in adult life in sexual orgasm. The theme of incorporative identity is reflected in love play with nibbling or biting and in courtship with the primordial declaration: "I love you so much I could eat you up!"

Stage 2. Between 15 and 36 months the young child identifies the body as part of self, and body image becomes a major nidus of self-identity. Possession of body is possession of identity. The same motif is seen in adults who experience a sense of loss of identity when accident, surgery, or illness results in loss or immobilization of body parts. Where body is still a major source of self-identity and sexualized, the loss of genitalia (gonads, breasts) or sexual function may be experienced as a major loss of identity. The statement "I don't feel like a man or a woman anymore" reflects a sexualized fixation on body as a source of identity and of gender identity.

A bit later the child extends the body boundaries to objects, clothes, or playthings as body extensions. My things are my body, are part of me. Again, in adults we see identity rooted in possessions as a source of identity or gender identity reinforced through possessions: "I have a gun, ergo I am a male!" or "I have a house, ergo I am a woman!"

Stage 3. Between 3 and 5 the child differentiates self from other objects. There is generic identification with children of the same gender. Boys and girls reinforce gender identity by modeling and emulating behavior and social roles of the same-gender parent. Play helps the child to learn how to be an adult person. Identity is related to how one looks, acts, behaves. Playing house is modeling behavior that reinforces gender identity. Identity is developed in terms of social custom that differentiates men and women. Little girls cook, bake, and sew. Little boys pound nails and mow grass. This need not and should not be preparatory role behavior for adulthood, but some gender-linked role modeling is necessary to reinforce the sense of "I am becoming a man or a woman." This is identity through same-gender comparison.

Stage 4. Ages 5 to 7 is the oedipal period, in which identity development occurs through opposite-gender comparison. The child elaborates gender identity by modeling behavior of the same-gender parent with the opposite. The boy tries to behave with mother like father does. The girl treats father like mother does. Children will naturally emulate erotic and seductive behavior of the parent. Children act this way not because of infantile sexual strivings, as Freud suggested, but rather because they are modeling the sexy behavior of their parents. At this stage children need affirmation from both parents that these early strivings toward adult behavior are not bad and that in adulthood they will find mates to replicate the behavior of mother and father. Disapproval of either parent, fear of either parent, or failure to successfully identify with the parent of the same gender all lead to failure at this stage of identity development. In the view of some theorists, parents have, therefore, the potential to contribute to the development of a homosexual orientation. In such a view, homosexuality is not a problem of sexuality but a failure in maturation of identity development at the oedipal stage (Stoller, 1968).

Stage 5. In Latency, 7 to 12 years, the child elaborates personal identity via doing things. Skill acquisition enables the child to define personal abilities and ego coping style unique to him or her. Again, skill acquisition is in part linked to gender: learning male skills and female skills. But at this stage it is possible to also offer children androgynous skill acquisition not linked to gender but instead adding to development of unique individual skills and identity.

Stage 6. In adolescence the sense of self is heightened. Sexual drive stimuli are increased, and attraction to the opposite gender occurs. But what is the nature of the attraction? It is an exchange of mutual ideal images. The teenager falls in love with a projected image of an ideal, which is reciprocated. When the ideal image is tarnished by harsh reality, the puppy love dissolves. The attraction is reciprocated appreciation of an ideal self. When this is then eroticized, one feels a sexual attraction. Sexual interaction becomes a vehicle for reinforcement of self-identity.

Stage 7. In young adulthood a major transmutation of identity must occur from "what I do gives me identity" to "who I am gives meaning to what I do." That is, external attributes have given value to self-identity. Now the young adult must invest in internal attributes, an internal constructed sense of self, and identity apart from external exigencies. Failure to accomplish this task results in persons who seek others, sexually or not, to reinforce their own identity, self-esteem, value, and self-worth. So-called identity crises may occur in adults who lean on external definitions of identity and therefore lose their sense of self when those externalities diminish or disappear.

Stage 8. Mature adulthood involves the capacity to share one's identity with another. Mature love involves the capacity to retain one's own autonomy and identity but also acquire a shared identity with a partner. Marriage and sexuality can occur without sharing the intimacy of identity. Mature love involves "growing together" (Curtin, 1973). Here gender identity merges into a joint male-female identity of a marital pair.

The biblical observations that "male and female created he them" and "the two shall become one" represent the journey of psychogender development. The child begins with genderless fusion, acquires a gender identity, and moves on to an autonomous unique personal identity. But the mature adult shares gender identity with a mate of the opposite-gender identity in a new fusion that is a gender and sexual union, two unique self-identities, and a conjoint mutual marital identity. Thus there is the sense of paradox, in that identity is on the one hand profoundly rooted in a distinct sexual gender and on the other hand unites and transcends gender.

References

Bemporad, J. R. (Ed.). (1980). *Child development in normality and psychopathology.* New York: Brunner/Mazel.

Curtin, M. E. (Ed.). (1973). *Symposium on love.* New York: Behavioral Publications.

Erikson, E. H. (1959). *Identity and the life cycle.* New York: International Universities Press.

Gergen, J. J. (1971). *The concept of self.* New York: Holt, Rinehart, & Winston.

Money, J., & Ehrhardt, A. A. (1972). *Man and woman, boy and girl.* Baltimore: Johns Hopkins University Press.

Money, J., & Musaph, H. (Eds.). (1977). *Handbook of sexology.* New York: Excerpta Medica.

Munroe, R. J., & Munroe, R. H. (1977). *Cross-cultural human development.* New York: Aronson.

Sargent, A. G. (1977). *Beyond sex roles.* St. Paul, MN: West.

Spence, J. T., & Helmreich, R. J. (1978). *Masculinity and femininity.* Austin: University of Texas Press.

Stoller, R. J. (1968). *Sex and gender.* London: Hogarth.

E. M. PATTISON

See SEXUALITY; PERSONHOOD; SELF.

Gender Identity Disorder. People with a strong and persistent identification with the opposite sex may have gender identity disorder. Children and adults with this disorder express in words and actions symptoms of gender dysphoria: a strong desire to be a member of the opposite sex. They may say that they belong to the other gender, although they do not believe it. Rather, they feel that they have been assigned to the wrong sex.

Children with gender identity disorder prefer to dress, wear their hair, and play as the opposite sex. Girls reject attempts to dress them in sex-appropriate clothing. Both girls and boys may prefer the urinary posture of the opposite sex. They express disgust about sexually maturing in their assigned sex. They dream and fantasize that they will mature as a member of the opposite sex.

Adults with gender identity disorder attempt to a significant degree to appear and behave as a member of the opposite sex. Both in private and in public they commonly will cross-dress. Many adults with this disorder will try to look more like the opposite sex through hormonal treatments, binding or enhancing undergarments, and—for men—removal of body and facial hair. About three times as many men as women will seek to surgically alter their sexual anatomy, a behavior known as transsexuality.

People with this disorder may have poor relationships with others. Children, especially boys, are frequently teased and rejected by same-sex peers. Adolescents and adults may find that their preoccupation with behaving as a member of the opposite sex interferes with all relationships.

According to *DSM-IV* (American Psychiatric Association, 1994), gender identity disorder is diagnosed when a person's cross-gender identification is strong and persistent, appearing in both statements and behaviors. In addition, the assigned sex or gender role must cause persistent discomfort or a sense of inappropriateness. Gender identity disorder is not diagnosed if genetic or hormonal disorders have produced ambiguous or mixed sexual anatomy, a condition known as intersex.

Gender identity disorder does not describe people who simply do not conform to traditional sex roles or who admire or share the interests and attitudes culturally associated with members of the opposite sex. Neither is it the same as a homosexual or bisexual orientation, nor engaging in cross-dressing for sexual arousal (Transvestic Fetishism).

Neither the causes nor the frequency of gender identity disorder are known. Some European studies suggest that it affects about 1 in 30,000 men and 1 in 100,000 women.

Since symptoms of the disorder appear in children as young as two years, and since symptoms are usually gone by late adolescence, perhaps hormonal effects on the child prior to birth produce the early symptoms. Some of the hormonally induced intersex syndromes are accompanied by cross-gender behavior patterns.

In all very young children gender identity is not strongly formed and is tied to external features such as clothing, toys, and hairstyle. As children mature, they learn that gender is fixed and that it does not vary with external changes. Most children with the disorder gradually stop cross-gender behaviors as parents and peers react negatively. Perhaps they are slow to learn gender roles and thus show symptoms of the disorder until they correct their gender concept with experience. Some clinical studies have shown that parents and other adults have encouraged cross-gender behaviors in their children, even to the point of teaching sons how to apply makeup.

Most children diagnosed with gender identity disorder no longer meet the criteria by late adolescence, even without treatment. Time, parental response, and peer reactions apparently are sufficient to eliminate the symptoms. However, *DSM-IV* reports that 75% of males who had a history of the disorder in childhood are either homosexual or bisexual in orientation.

Treatment for adolescents and adults with gender identity disorder takes two routes: changing bodies, through sex-reassignment surgery; or changing gender identity. In the United States about 30% of adults with the disorder have had sex-reassignment surgery. Long-term follow-up studies are inconclusive, but they suggest that satisfaction with surgery is highest in people who have undergone skillful surgery, have a homosexual orientation, were previously female, and had gender identity disorder in childhood. Some less satisfied people who are not in these categories may consider the surgery a mistake.

Therapy to change gender identity to conform to biological sex has been recently developed. After analyzing the specific components of a client's cross-gender behavior, such as voice, gesture, emotional expression, and fantasy, therapists use education, demonstration, practice, and videotape to train sex-appropriate actions. While there is no controlled research on the effectiveness of this approach, case study reports claim success through a five-year follow-up.

Reference

American Psychiatric Association (1994). *Diagnostic and statistical manual of mental disorders* (4th ed.). Washington, DC: Author.

P. D. YOUNG

General Adaptation Syndrome. The general adaptation syndrome (*GAS*), so named by Hans Selye, describes the body's stepwise, progressive attempt to cope with stress. It consists of three phases: alarm, resistance, and exhaustion.

The initial phase, alarm, describes the body's physiological fight-or-flight reaction to a stressor. These responses include an increase in pulse rate, respiration, perspiration, and pupil size. Less visible signs include enlargement of the bronchial tubes within the lungs, constriction of the capillaries near the surface of the skin, cessation of the stomach's normal digestive processes, and slowing of the immune system. All of these responses are attempts by the body to prepare itself to deal with the threatening situation.

If the stressor is not removed, however, the second phase of the GAS, resistance, is set into motion. In this stage the body tries to cope with the stressor, be it a flat tire, a prolonged strike on the job, or a gunman. Whichever it may be, the body responds in a predictable way and continues its resistance until the stressor is removed. The body's prolonged efforts at resistance will possibly take their toll as the body tries to cope with everyday challenges as well as these additional adjustments. These effects may take the form of ulcers, high blood pressure, heart disease, or other physical ailments.

The final stage of the GAS is exhaustion or, potentially, death. The body begins to show its failure at adaptation through various psychophysiological breakdowns. The body systems are becoming exhausted, leaving them depleted and vulnerable to infection and disease. If the stressor remains, the eventual outcome of the exhaustion phase is death. Although this outcome is rare, it is foretold by the physical failures that begin permeating the body.

It is important to note that the body's response is nondirectional. It is set in motion following the individual's assessment of stress. The physiological response does not discriminate, however, among stressful life events such as catastrophes or significant life changes and physical threats or trauma. Once they are set in motion, the phases follow their course. Therefore, the process of managing stress may best be handled early in the process. Therapists may recommend training their clients to label the stressor as either a nonstressor or at least a manageable one as quickly and positively as possible, allowing the physiological response to be short-circuited via cognitive control.

J. W. LUND

See STRESS.

General Paresis. The brain syndrome associated with syphilitic meningoencephalitis, a disorder produced by progressive degeneration of brain tissue. Clinically general paresis is a comprehensive but variable syndrome characterized by a variety of neu-

rological and mental disturbances that increase in severity, leading to death when left untreated. Prior to 1920 about 8% to 10% of the patients committed to public hospitals in the United States were suffering from general paresis (Kolb & Brodie, 1982). In contrast, today less than 1% of all first-time admissions are due to this syndrome. Paresis has occurred four times more frequently in men than in women, although the probable ratio of initial infection has been thought to be about 2 to 1. The reasons for this gender-related difference in susceptibility are unknown.

The microorganism involved in general paresis is one of the few that can penetrate the bloodbrain barrier with relative ease. The actual infection is transmitted during sexual contact. The basic pathology of paresis involves two components: inflammation and eventual degeneration. The process of progressive degeneration typically begins in the frontal region and usually spreads to other areas, such as the cortex and cerebellum. Although it is not known whether the destruction of brain tissue is due to the action of the spirochetes or their toxic products, the damage can be widespread and severe. Following initial infection, general paresis develops after an incubation period of 5 to 30 or more years. In about half the cases the incubation period is from 10 to 20 years, with an additional 25% of cases involving less than a 10-year incubation period and the remaining cases incubating for more than 20 years. The peak curve of incidence occurs between the ages of 35 and 45 (Kolb & Brodie, 1982).

The personality changes associated with general paresis are typically the first identifiable signs of the illness. These initially may involve only an exaggeration of previously existing personality traits, so they are insidious and hard to identify. They may involve irritability, difficulty in concentration, depression, periods of confusion, impairment in judgment, and impulsivity. In more advanced stages psychoticlike symptoms may appear, such as delusional thinking and grandiose and expansive behavior (Buss, 1966; Sue, Sue, & Sue, 1994). The eventual dementia may be characterized by impairment in memory, logical reasoning, and learning. Physical symptoms often include fatigue, drowsiness, headaches, body aches, various somatic complaints, and general lethargy. Disturbances in eye movement or reflexes often occur, as well as retinitis or ocular atrophy. A progressive weakness and incoordination of voluntary muscles typically result from advanced stages of the syndrome. Enunciation, facial movements, and handwriting may also evidence deterioration. Three-quarters of all cases suffer from convulsions at some time.

Diagnosis is done primarily through the use of clinical analysis of spinal fluid, using the Wassermann test and the colloidal gold test (Kolb & Brodie, 1982). Although early identification of suspected cases may result from the slow, pervasive degeneration that is brought to the attention of mental health professionals or physicians, the ultimate diagnosis will almost certainly be based on the results of these serologic tests. Because of the constellation of certain symptoms, a diagnosis of general paresis may include a reference to the particular associated mood, affect, and behavior, leading to the identification of four subtypes: simple, expansive, depressed, and circular.

Penicillin is the treatment of choice for syphilitic meningoencephalitis. In the absence of treatment death usually occurs from two to five years after the onset of identifiable symptoms. The prognosis in treated patients depends on the promptness and thoroughness of treatment. If proper treatment is begun before symptoms appear, further deterioration is arrested in 85% of the cases. If treatment is begun during the early stages of identifiable symptoms, improvement or stabilization occurs in about 60% of the cases. Among all hospitalized cases, the number actually recovering is less than 30%, the death rate is 20% to 30%, and further deterioration is arrested in only 30% to 50%.

The drop in incidence, due to marked improvements in early identification and treatment, makes it unlikely that the typical clinician will be confronted with a case of general paresis. If such a client does appear for outpatient psychotherapy or counseling, a focus on providing a supportive, structuring treatment that enlists all available environmental resources will likely be the most helpful, in conjunction with penicillin treatment managed by a physician.

References

Buss, A. H. (1966). *Psychopathology*. New York: Wiley.

Kolb, L. C., & Brodie, H. K. (1982). *Modern clinical psychiatry* (10th ed.). Philadelphia: Saunders.

Sue, D., Sue, D., & Sue, S. (1994). *Understanding abnormal behavior*. Boston: Houghton Mifflin.

J. D. GUY, JR.

Generalization. The process of spreading or transferring the effects of education, training, or treatment from the circumstances under which learning initially took place to other settings. Generalization is the opposite process to that of discrimination. Whereas generalization expands responding, discrimination restricts or limits the range of responding along one or more dimensions.

Types. There are many types of generalization, but the best known is stimulus generalization, also known as setting generalization. In stimulus generalization cues that were not used during prior learning experiences become effective cues for signaling the acquired response. For example, a brown terrier bit four-year-old Bobby. Prior to being bitten, Bobby showed no signs of fearing the terrier or other dogs. One week after the biting incident Bobby manifested much distress and avoidance behavior when any dog was nearby.

Response generalization is the second-best-known form. This is the process in which a single stimulus comes to control more responses than those targeted during prior teaching, training, or treatment. For example, a mother has used the oral command "Stop!" under three circumstances in the past: when her toddler ran toward the street, when she reached toward the hot stove, and when she reached to touch a bee sitting on a flower. In each instance the mother shook her child by the shoulders. Subsequent observations demonstrated that the mother's saying "Stop!" would inhibit climbing, jumping, and throwing hard objects, even though she had not provided negative consequences for these actions in the past.

Temporal generalization is a third type, in which a subject makes a particular response in the training setting even though the response no longer produces a consequence. Temporal generalization occurs under extinction conditions. When a subject manifests resistance to extinction, this third form of generalization is present. Although they probably do not think about the technical issues involved, parents often seek to produce temporal generalization in their children. For example, Proverbs 22:6 (NIV) speaks to temporal generalization by admonishing, "Train a child in the way he should go, and when he is old he will not turn from it."

A fourth important category is subject generalization, in which treatment, training, or correction is applied to one subject who acquires the desired response, but untreated subjects also acquire the response. When untreated subjects change as though they had been treated, the concept of subject generalization is applicable. For example, in talking to teachers about their misbehaving children, some parents have said, "Don't yell at my kid when he acts up. Reprimand the student who sits next to him, and my son will shape up." Such parents are predicting that their children will manifest subject generalization.

These four types of generalization may be combined to produce more complex forms, but relatively little research has been done on these complex forms of generalization.

Methods of Producing Generalization. One approach is to teach only those behaviors that the person's natural environment is likely to reinforce after the treatment or formal lesson ends. Teaching a shy child how to make social greetings and to enter play with other children would be an example, because the other children are likely to reinforce the shy child's friendly gestures. If the subject identifies which behaviors he or she wants to strengthen and asks family, friends, or others to provide appropriate reinforcers for the occurrence of those behaviors, the change will be even greater.

Second, generalization itself can be treated as a response. The trainer can reinforce the learner for generalizations as they occur. Doing so will promote more rapid generalization.

Third, training or treatment settings should contain many of the stimuli that will be present in those settings to which generalization is desired. On the average, the amount of generalization increases as the number of stimuli common to the training and generalization settings increases.

Fourth, although initial learning may be most rapid under tightly controlled training conditions, generalization is promoted by loosening the training conditions—for example, by using a variety of cues, responses, and consequences.

A fifth method for promoting generalization is to train the learner in strategies for solving a particular type of problem. Presenting diverse examples of the type of problem to be mastered and approaches to solving the problem facilitates generalization.

Sixth, procedures that blur the differences between training and generalization settings also help. For example, gradually thinning the frequency of reinforcement promotes resistance to extinction (i.e., temporal generalization). Delayed reinforcement may have similar positive effects.

A final useful approach to promoting generalization is to employ self-regulation procedures by having the learner serve as his or her own teacher through self-observation, self-recording, self-evaluation, self-reinforcement, self-prompting, or self-modeling.

During most of the history of modern psychology theorists have viewed generalization as involving passive, automatic processes. More recently many psychologists have asserted that generalization is just as active a process as discrimination. This assumption has produced an emphasis on developing revised conceptual models of generalization and a methodology for producing the process. On a practical level parents, teachers, and therapists cannot assume that generalization will automatically follow initial learning. They must carefully engineer into the learning situation those conditions that will promote generalization.

P. W. CLEMENT

See LEARNING.

Generalized Anxiety Disorder. One particularly pernicious form of anxiety is that described in the *DSM-IV* as generalized anxiety disorder. Persons suffering from this disorder experience excessive anxiety and worry about a variety of events and activities. That is, the intensity, duration, and frequency of the worry are out of proportion to the likelihood or impact of the feared event. The worry is virtually impossible to control and as a result there is significant distress that interferes with normal activities and routine.

In order to be diagnosed as having generalized anxiety disorder persons must have been experiencing the excessive worry and anxiety more days than not for a minimum of six months. Also, at least three of the following six symptoms must have been occurring more days than not during the same time period. These symptoms are restlessness or feeling keyed up or on edge; being easily fatigued; difficulty concentrating or mind going blank; irritability; muscle tension; sleep disturbance (American Psychiatric Association, 1994).

Generalized anxiety disorder, as the term implies, involves worry that is not restricted to one specific event or situation. Rather, the worries are many, varied, and usually unrelated to each other. This contrasts with other Axis I disorders in which the worries are situation-specific, such as the fear of having a panic attack (panic disorder), fear of being contaminated or of intrusive thoughts (obsessive-compulsive disorder), and fear of gaining weight (anorexia nervosa). In addition, the anxiety associated with posttraumatic stress disorder (PTSD) is caused by a person's exposure to a severely traumatic stressor and continues to occur as a direct result of that specific stressor.

It has been suggested that the fundamental psychophysiological processes underlying generalized anxiety disorder represent the core processes in all anxiety disorders. The foundational character of this malady has prompted some to call it the basic anxiety disorder.

The core process, termed "anxious apprehension" (Barlow, 1988), is a future-directed mood state in which upcoming, negative events are anticipated in preparation to adequately cope with them. This state is accompanied by acute tension, vigilance, and a sense of uncontrollability.

There is evidence that the anxious apprehension process may be characterological in nature, possibly stemming from early life experiences and thus presenting as a highly significant factor in emotional disorders developing later in life. For example, many patients diagnosed with generalized anxiety disorder report that they cannot recall a time when they did not have the disorder or that they recall very early onset. This disorder also has been found to be one of the most frequent additional diagnoses assigned to patients with a primary anxiety or mood disorder (Sanderson, Beck, & Beck, 1990). As a result certain behavioral scientists are exploring the possibility that generalized anxiety disorder would best be understood in the context of a personality disorder (Sanderson & Wetzler, 1991).

Different systems of therapy advocate differing strategies for dealing with this type of debilitating anxiety. A psychodynamic understanding would hold that the intense anxiety is caused by inner conflicts such as fear of death, hostility, or separation. These fears are unconscious and can be triggered by threatening external events such as death in the family, illness, catastrophe, or major life change. Given this understanding of the disorder, the treatment of choice would be an uncovering therapy utilizing the transference relationship, making interpretations, and developing insight on the part of the client into the unconscious determinants of the anxiety.

A cognitive perspective would hold that a severe defect in the regulatory function of the cognitive system causes the indiscriminate interpretation of various life events as unnecessarily threatening or dangerous. These distorted, unrealistic interpretations then activate the autonomic nervous system, and pathological anxiety is experienced (Beck & Emery, 1985).

This understanding of the origin and maintenance of anxiety has spawned several sophisticated cognitive-behavior therapy approaches that incorporate a wide variety of treatment interventions. An example of this is the protocol designed by Brown, O'Leary, and Barlow (1993).

In order to address the varied cognitive, behavioral, and physiological aspects of generalized anxiety disorder, a treatment program has been devised consisting of six different components: cognitive therapy—teaching clients to identify, evaluate, and alter distorted cognitions such as catastrophic thinking and probability overestimation; worry exposure—identifying mental images of catastrophic worries with subsequent substitution of realistic, anxiety-reducing scenes; relaxation training—learning to relax muscle groups and slow diaphragmatic breathing; worry behavior prevention—teaching the extinction of behaviors functionally related to worry (e.g., frequent calls to loved ones to check on their safety); time management—training in the areas of assertiveness, delegating responsibility, and adhering to agendas; and problem solving—teaching clients to break problems into manageable size and then brainstorm their way to a solution.

The most widely used medicines for treating generalized anxiety disorder are the benzodiazepines such as Valium, Ativan, and Xanax. They are quite effective in quickly reducing anxiety symptoms in many patients; however, it is common for the symptoms to recur soon after the medicine has been discontinued. Thus in no sense can these drugs be considered a cure for this disorder.

Great caution must be used when considering the possibility of using the benzodiazepines long-term since they can be physiologically addicting. It is generally agreed upon that benzodiazepine treatment of generalized anxiety disorder should be with the lowest possible dose for the shortest possible time (Janicak, David, Preskorn, & Ayd, 1993).

An alternative medicine for this disorder, Buspar, has been shown to reduce rumination and worry with no sedation or potential for drug dependence. However, it must be taken regularly for one to two weeks before a therapeutic effect is noted.

There is also some clinical evidence that certain selective serotonin reuptake inhibitor (SSRI) antidepressants such as Zoloft may be effective as antianxiety agents. Antianxiety medications provide only temporary relief and thus should always be considered adjunctive to some other method of treating this disorder.

References

American Psychiatric Association (1994). *Diagnostic and statistical manual of mental disorders* (4th ed.). Washington, DC: Author.

Barlow, D. (1988). *Anxiety and its disorders*. New York: Guilford.

Beck, A. T., & Emery, G. (1985). *Anxiety disorders & phobias: A cognitive perspective*. New York: Basic.

Brown, T., O'Leary, T., & Barlow, D. (1993). Generalized anxiety disorder. In D. Barlow (Ed.), *Clinical handbook of psychological disorders* (2nd ed.). New York: Guilford.

Janicak, P., Davis, J., Preskorn, S., & Ayd, F. (1993). *Principles and practice of psychopharmacotherapy*. Baltimore: Williams & Wilkins.

Sanderson, W., Beck, A. T., & Beck, J. (1990). Syndrome comorbidity in patients with major depression or dysthymia: Prevalence and temporal relationships. *American Journal of Psychiatry, 147,* 1025–1028.

Sanderson, W., & Wetzler, S. (1991). Chronic anxiety and generalized anxiety disorder: Issues in comorbidity. In R. M. Rapee & D. Barlow (Eds.). *Chronic anxiety: Generalized anxiety disorder and mixed anxiety-depression*. New York: Guilford.

W. G. BIXLER

See ANXIETY; PANIC ATTACK; PHOBIC DISORDERS.

Genetic and Biochemical Factors in Psychopathology. Since the mid-1980s several advances have been made in understanding the etiologies of various psychopathologies; much of this progress has centered around the elucidation of genetic and biochemical contributions to these disorders. Six such disorders will be reviewed: schizophrenia, a mood disorder (depression), a substance-related disorder (alcoholism), and the neurological disorders of Alzheimer's, Huntington's, and Parkinson's diseases.

Schizophrenia. Affecting approximately 1% of the world's population, schizophrenia is a prevalent disorder, primarily characterized as a disorder of thinking. The disorder also typically includes impairments of perception, motor behavior, social function, and emotion. The presentation of schizophrenia can be divided into positive and negative symptoms. The positive symptoms (an excess of normal function) include delusions, hallucinations, motor dysfunction, and disordered language; the negative symptoms (a restricted range or intensity of function) include flattened affect and social withdrawal. The essential features must be present for most of a one-month period, and some signs of the disorder must be present for at least six months for a diagnosis of schizophrenia to be made (American Psychiatric Association, 1994). Onset is typically in late adolescence to early adulthood, and the course of the disorder is variable.

Family and twin research indicates a genetic contribution to schizophrenia, and some twin studies suggest genetic anticipation. (Anticipation is the phenomenon in which the symptoms of a disorder become increasingly severe and occur earlier in life across succeeding generations within a given family.) However, prenatal and/or postnatal environmental traumas are also more likely in schizophrenia. Birth complications, low birth weight, and brain/spinal cord stress are all more common in schizophrenics than in nonschizophrenics. Schizophrenics also are more likely to be born during winter and early spring months, and rates of schizophrenia are higher in offspring of mothers exposed to influenza during the second trimester of pregnancy, suggesting that exposure to maternal viruses during prenatal development might increase susceptibility to the disorder. These findings led some researchers to propose an interactive diathesis-stress model whereby a vulnerability to certain prenatal insults is genetically transmitted. In conjunction with later postnatal environmental factors, this vulnerability leads to the expression of the disorder, sometime during late adolescence or early adulthood (Stabenau & Pollin, 1993).

Numerous neurotransmitters are implicated in schizophrenia, with the primary transmitter being dopamine. Years of research indicate abnormal functioning within the dopaminergic system. Supporting the role of dopamine in schizophrenia is the fact that many antipsychotic medications have their effects at dopamine receptor sites. More recent evidence points to serotonin involvement in the production of schizophrenic symptoms, and the relatively new antipsychotic drug, clozapine, has its effects on both dopamine and serotonin receptors (Breier, 1995). Other transmitters implicated in schizophrenia are glutamate, gamma-aminobutyric acid (GABA), and norepinephrine.

The variety of symptoms and the inconclusiveness of much of the research in schizophrenia suggest a heterogeneous disorder with a complex etiology. Investigations into the neuropathology of schizophrenia support such a proposal. Abnormalities within many brain regions have been noted in schizophrenics (Chua & McKenna, 1995), but the differences typically are subtle and inconsistent from one study to the next. The most consistent observation is enlargement of the lateral ventricles, a finding of postmortem, computerized tomography (CT) and brain imaging (e.g., MRI) studies. Other brain structures often affected in schizophrenia include the frontal and temporal lobes, amygdala, and hippocampus. While many studies find neuropathologies, the results are mixed and inconsistent.

An attempt to integrate these neuropathological, genetic, and biochemical findings suggests schizophrenia is a disorder of neuronal development during the second trimester, a time of vulnerability to the effects of biological, environmental, and psychological influences. According to this account (Bunney, Potkin, & Bunney, 1995), exposure to insults during this period of development interferes with the normal process of neuronal development and migration, creating a compromised brain. Later stressors, whether physiological or psychological, during adolescence or early adulthood act on the compromised nervous system, triggering symptoms of the disorder. While additional research needs to be conducted, this view of schizophrenia is receiving much attention in the literature.

Depression. Depression is a mood disorder that means that the predominant feature is a disturbance of affect. Other symptoms of depression as given in *DSM-IV* include diminished interest and pleasure in most activities, weight loss or gain, increases or decreases in appetite, sleep disturbances, fatigue or loss of energy, feelings of worthlessness or guilt, impaired capacity to think and concentrate, and recurrent thoughts of death or suicide (American Psychiatric Association, 1994). The lifetime prevalence rate for depression ranges from 7% to 17%, making this disorder perhaps the most common form of mental illness. Risk factors for depression include gender (females are at greater risk than are males), lower socioeconomic status, stressful life events, and a family history of mood disorders.

Various family, twin, and adoption studies suggest a genetic role in unipolar depression. For example, twin studies estimate the concordance rate of depression for monozygotic twins to be as high as 69% compared to a concordance rate for dizygotic twins of 13%. These data suggest a genetic role in the disorder; however, no specific gene locus has been identified. Some evidence indicates that a variation on chromosome 11 is responsible for this inheritance risk, but subsequent research has been inconclusive on this point.

Research is clearer on biochemical factors in depression. Early treatment for depression involved the use of monoamine oxidase (MAO) inhibitors, which reduced the effectiveness of MAO in deactivating norepinephrine and serotonin from the synaptic cleft. Other early treatments inhibited the reuptake of these neurotransmitters from the synaptic cleft, thereby promoting the effectiveness of norepinephrine and serotonin in neural communication. Modern drug therapy also acts to enhance serotonergic and catecholinergic activity (e.g., Prozac is a selective serotonin reuptake inhibitor [SSRI]). The mechanism of drug therapy for depression suggests that mood is associated with regulation of these neurotransmitters; too little activity in serotonergic and catecholinergic pathways leads to depression. However, this relatively simple explanation has its problems. One problem is the finding that while these antidepressant drugs exercise their physiological effects on synaptic transmission quickly, their clinical effects take several weeks to develop. In addition, cocaine, which also increases norepinephrine at the synapse, has no antidepressant effect. It is thought that antidepressants act by promoting some type of long-term adaptive change in norepinephrine and serotonin receptors. Indeed, many antidepressant treatments, including electroconvulsive therapy (ECT), affect the sensitivity of these receptors.

Depression is also related to other physiological or biological activity in the body. The hypothalamic-pituitary-adrenal (HPA) axis (especially the release of corticotropin-releasing factor [crf], a substance implicated in the body's response to stress) seems to be involved in an increased risk of depression. Abnormalities in this axis are found in severely depressed individuals, and it is known through animal studies that early trauma (e.g., abuse and neglect) can produce alterations within the HPA axis. Supporting these findings is the observation that cortisol (the hormone ultimately released in response to crf) levels can rise during depression and are reduced by antidepressant drugs and electroconvulsive shock. These results suggest that neurophysiology is affected by early trauma and can influence one's risk of depression, given the proper stressful circumstances later in life.

Alcoholism. Alcohol dependence has become grouped with other psychoactive substance disorders. The clinical presentation of alcohol dependence includes various cognitive, behavioral, and physiological symptoms such as repeated self-administration, tolerance, withdrawal, and compulsive drug-taking (American Psychiatric Association, 1994).

The effects of alcohol are no longer understood as being a result of a nonspecific action on the neural membrane. Alcohol seems to have its effects through the modulation of a variety of neurotransmitters and receptors. Involvement of the neurotransmitter dopamine has been known for years. Like other drugs such as cocaine, amphetamine, and nicotine, alcohol's reinforcing effect comes from its activation of the mesolimbic dopamine system, a dopaminergic pathway whose origin is in the midbrain and which projects to various forebrain areas. Administration of ethanol increases both the firing of neurons and the release of dopamine in this pathway.

More recently the role of the neurotransmitters gamma-aminobutyric acid (GABA) and glutamate has been clarified in the depressant effect of ethanol. GABA is a primary inhibitory neurotransmitter in the central nervous system. Research suggests that ethanol enhances the inhibitory function of GABA via a specific effect on a GABA receptor. A few of the behavioral effects of ethanol at the GABA receptor are sleep disturbances, aggression, and withdrawal-associated anxiety.

A major excitatory transmitter in the brain is glutamate. As is the case with most transmitters, there are several different receptor sites for glutamate. One such site is the N-methyl-D-aspartate (NMDA) receptor, and ethanol inhibits function of this receptor, resulting in decreased NMDA release and decreased NMDA synaptic transmission. Behavioral effects of ethanol at the NMDA receptor include tolerance, physical dependence, intoxication, withdrawal seizures, and cognitive disruptions.

Prolonged ethanol consumption can produce an interaction between GABA and NMDA activity (Grant & Lovinger, 1995). Chronic enhancement of GABA produces downregulation of the system, and chronic inhibition of the NMDA receptor can lead to a compensatory increase in NMDA sensitivity. Some of the effects of alcohol withdrawal (e.g., seizures) might be understood by reference to this interaction in that increased NMDA activity resulting from this enhanced sensitivity can lead to a cascade of cellular changes producing hyperexcitability of the cell (seizures) and even cell death. Consistent with this proposal is the observation that following chronic ethanol use, some neuropathological changes are noted in both rats and humans, including cell loss in hippocampus, cortex, and cerebellum.

In addition to advances in the understanding of neurotransmitter actions involved in alcohol dependence, recent research has investigated the part genetics play in alcoholism. For years family, twin, and adoptive studies have suggested a role for genetics, environment, and choice in alcohol abuse. More recent twin studies have strengthened genetic involvement in the vulnerability to alcoholism. Alcohol dehydrogenase and aldehyde dehydrogenase are enzymes involved in the metabolism of ethanol in the body. Variants in genes responsible for these enzymes are associated with increased risk of alcoholism. In addition, genes involved in the synthesis and activity of the neurotransmitters serotonin and dopamine are thought to be associated with impulsive behavior and alcohol abuse. (Research suggests that impulsivity and alcoholism tend to occur together and run in families.) The data generated from genetic studies of alcoholism are equivocal at best; while suggestive, the precise effect these gene variants have on alcohol dependency is unknown.

Rats have been selectively bred for ethanol preference, and these animal models of alcohol dependence are used to clarify the genetic nature of behaviors associated with alcohol abuse and to study the biological mechanisms involved. For example, some animal models show that high alcohol preference is correlated with deficiency in the neurotransmitter serotonin. Data from these models also suggest that dopaminergic activity in the mesolimbic pathway is decreased in rats bred for an alcohol preference. This same pathway, however, seems to be more sensitive to the effects of ethanol in these rats.

GABA and endorphin (a naturally produced opiatelike substance that acts as a transmitter) activity are also abnormal in rats bred for alcohol preference. This last result supports other findings coming from these animal models suggesting that the rewarding effect of ethanol is due in part to endorphin activity. Naltrexone, an opiate antagonist, inhibits ethanol intake in animals and the craving for alcohol in humans, presumably because naltrexone blocks opiate receptors involved in reinforcement. Results such as these suggest that the use of naltrexone can be an effective new therapy in the treatment of alcoholism.

Neurological Disorders. *Alzheimer's disease* (AD). Several disorders of the central nervous system have genetic risk factors associated with them. The first of these disorders is Alzheimer's disease, which is the most common cause of senile dementia affecting between 3 and 4% of the population over 65 years of age (approximately 20 million people worldwide). The modern definition of AD comes from a case study by the physician Alois Alzheimer in 1906. The early symptoms of AD involve memory impairment, but the disease progresses over seven or more years to affect other cognitive abilities as well as personality, language, motor behavior, and social functioning. The progression of AD leads to death.

Several risk factors are associated with AD, the most important being age. AD is an age-related condition that rarely develops before the age of 55 and typically affects a person in the seventh or eighth decade of life. Some areas of the brain (e.g., hippocampus) are sites for degenerative changes associated with both normal aging and AD, leading some investigators to speculate that similar physiological mechanisms are involved in both processes but at a more exaggerated level in the disease state of Alzheimer's.

A second risk factor for AD is gender. Females are at a higher risk of AD (perhaps 2:1) than are males. This increased risk remains even when controls for the greater proportion of women in the older population and corrections for the increased probability of cardiovascular disease among men (a condition that can make diagnosis of AD problematic) are made. While the reason for this heightened risk is unknown, some investigators have speculated that it might be due to differential environmental or hormonal effects or to some gene on the X chromosome.

Another risk factor is genetics. Clearly there is a genetic contribution to the development of AD. A family history of AD, Parkinson's disease, Down's syndrome, or dementia poses an increase in an individual's risk of developing AD. Several chromosomes are implicated in AD (St. George-Hyslop, 1993). Early on chromosome 21 was considered a possible carrier of AD genes because of the association between Down's syndrome and AD. Most individuals with Down's syndrome (trisomy 21) develop AD in adulthood. Also, the amyloid precursor protein (APP) gene is located on chromosome 21. This protein, which when improperly metabolized in the brain produces a build up of beta-amyloid, is strongly implicated in the genesis of AD neuropathology; and variations of the APP gene are a leading contributor to AD. A version of the protein apolipoprotein E (ApoE), a protein that aids in the transport of cholesterol, is also thought to be involved in the genesis of AD pathology and is located on chromosome 19. Chromosomes 14 and 1 are also implicated in AD etiology and are under extensive investigation as molecular geneticists attempt to unravel the genetic factors in AD development.

Other risk factors of AD include head trauma and environmental toxins. Traumas to the head can produce neuropathological features of AD; however, the evidence for a role of environmental toxins in AD is poor. Some research suggests a causal effect of aluminum exposure for AD, but as a whole the research is contradictory and unconvincing.

While recent neurological and clinical tests make a diagnosis of AD more certain than in the past, neuropathological evidence is the surest way to diagnosis AD. Amyloid or senile plaques are necessary for a diagnosis of AD and are thought to play a central role in the pathogenesis of the disease. Senile plaques are areas of degenerating brain tissue surrounding a core of beta-amyloid. Neurofibrillary tangles (neuron cell bodies filled with paired helical filaments) and cell loss are also hallmark features of AD. Brain areas most affected by these neuroanatomical characteristics are hippocampus, cortex, and nucleus basalis (a basal forebrain structure).

Evidence exists for the involvement of several neurotransmitters in AD. The best evidence is for the loss of cholinergic cells, particularly in the nucleus basalis, septum, and reticular activating system. Postmortems indicate that more than 80% of cholinergic cells in these areas can be lost in AD. The early signs of AD, such as memory impairment, are probably linked to this diminished cholinergic activity in the brain. Noradrenergic and serotonergic deficits have also been found. One transmitter that is thought to be enhanced in AD is glutamate. As with other neurological conditions (e.g., Parkinson's disease), excessive activity at the NMDA glutamate receptor is a candidate mechanism whereby cell death in AD is accomplished.

Parkinson's disease (PD). Described by James Parkinson in 1817, Parkinson's disease is the second neurodegenerative disorder thought to have genetic risk factors associated with it, although the contribution of heredity to PD is undefined. PD is a progressive neurological illness with presenting symptoms of resting tremor, muscular rigidity, slowness of voluntary movements, disorder of gait, and impaired postural reflexes. Dementia and depression are also common symptoms. The rate of progression varies among individuals; however, 10 to 20 years typically elapse before the symptoms become disabling.

PD, which affects between 0.1% and 1.0% of the population, involves a relatively selective degeneration of dopaminergic neurons in the substantia nigra. These cells project to basal ganglia structures (especially the putamen and caudate nucleus) forming the nigrostriatal pathway. More than 80% of the cells in the nigrostriatal pathway must be lost before symptoms of PD appear. Replacement of dopamine and the restoration of normal basal ganglia function via the dopamine precursor levodopa is a major pharmacological therapy strategy. Other pharmacological therapies, compensatory therapies, aim at correcting the imbalance between dopamine and other neurotransmitters such as acetylcholine. Pharmacotherapy, especially replacement therapy, is limited in that responsiveness to levodopa diminishes after five to ten years of treatment, dyskinesia can develop as a result of levodopa treatment, and replacement therapy does not stop the progression of the disease.

While the cause of the degeneration seen in PD is unknown, there is little evidence to support an environmental etiology of PD. Recent research points instead to a role of the excitatory neurotransmitter glutamate and its interaction with dopamine in the degeneration of brain cells. Disturbances in glutamatergic synaptic transmission, particularly at the N-methyl-D-aspartate (NMDA) receptor site, seem to be involved in the development of PD symptoms. Hyperactivity of NMDA receptors in the substantia nigra and basal ganglia results in an increase in calcium influx into the cells, setting off a cascade of cellular changes that can lead to the death of cells in these brain areas. If this scenario is accurate, then blockade of this calcium influx should prevent or at least retard cell loss. Some experiments testing this hypothesis have found supportive results. Use of a NMDA antagonist has anti-Parkinson effects in various animal models of PD. Results such as these suggest that there is not only a dopamine-cholinergic imbalance in PD, an imbalance that has been known for some time, but also a dopamine-glutamatergic imbalance in basal ganglia and related structures. These results also suggest additional pharmacological therapies that might be tried in PD, therapies that do not have the limitations of levodopa.

Surgical treatments have also been developed in an attempt to relieve the symptoms of PD. Pallidotomy, surgical interruption of output pathways from the globus pallidus, a basal ganglia structure, has brought relief of tremor in Parkinson's patients. Other surgical interventions include transplantation of adrenal medullary cells into the basal ganglia and transplantation of fetal mesencephalic cells into PD patients. The former technique has met with limited success; the latter has ethical questions surrounding it.

Huntington's disease (HD). The third neurological disorder with clear genetic risk factors is Huntington's disease, which was first described by George Huntington in 1872 and consists of movement, personality, and cognitive impairments. Both involuntary and voluntary movements are affected with movement in the limbs becoming jerky and uncoordinated. Impairments in facial muscles can produce vocal, chewing, and swallowing difficulties. Depression, dementia, and poor impulse control characterize HD; impairments in attention, learning, and memory are also typically observed. The disease is fatal.

The prevalence of HD is 5–10 per 100,000 and affects males and females equally. One of the more insidious characteristics of HD is that the age of onset is usually 35 to 40 years of age, well after the onset of reproduction. Because there is a 50/50 chance a child of one parent with HD will inherit the predisposition to HD and eventually the disease itself, parents can unknowingly pass this genetic predisposition to their children.

While neuron loss is sometimes found in the brainstem, cerebellum, and spinal cord, the major neuropathological feature of HD is cell loss in the structures of the basal ganglia. To a lesser extent subthalamic nuclei, hippocampus, and neocortex are also affected. Recent research links the inhibitory neurotransmitter GABA to HD. Deficiencies in GABA have been found, suggesting a role of this substance in the presentation of the disease. As is the case with Parkinson's disease, the excitatory transmitter glutamate has been hypothesized as a mechanism, via excitotoxicity, in the cell loss seen in HD.

The fact that HD is genetically transmitted as an autosomal dominant trait has been known for years, and the search for the HD gene has recently brought success. A gene is made of DNA, which is comprised of nucleotides. Each gene can contain hundreds of thousands of nucleotides, all neatly arranged on a chromosome in a particular order or sequence. In HD the abnormal gene is found near the beginning of chromosome 4. In individuals without HD, there is a three-nucleotide sequence (the nucleotides cytosine, adenine, and guanine) at this site that is repeated no more than 34 times. In people with HD this cytosine-adenine-guanine sequence is repeated 42 to 100 times; the more the sequence is repeated the earlier the onset and the more severe the effects of HD (The Huntington's Disease Collaborative Research Group, 1993). It is now possible to positively identify individuals carrying this HD gene; such information can be used by an individual in deciding whether to have children.

The ability to identify carriers of the gene for HD or for any other disorder raises important medical and ethical questions. For example, what is the desirability of being tested for the gene when there is no treatment for HD? A positive test for the gene gives the person tested what amounts to a death sentence. A genetic test for HD in a fetus is also an indirect test of the parents and grandparents. A positive result of such a test raises questions about the use of such information. As is often the case, medical technology has advanced beyond our ethics, and more questions of this type will be raised as additional information regarding the genetic and biochemical factors involved in psychopathology is discovered.

References

American Psychiatric Association. (1994). *Diagnostic and statistical manual of mental disorders* (4th ed.). Washington, DC: Author.

Breier, A. (1995). Serotonin, schizophrenia and antipsychotic drug action. *Schizophrenia Research, 14*, 187–202.

Bunney, B. G., Potkin, S. G., & Bunney, W. E., Jr. (1995). New morphological and neuropathological findings in schizophrenia: A neurodevelopmental perspective. *Clinical Neuroscience, 3*, 81–88.

Chua, S. E., & McKenna, P. J. (1995). Schizophrenia—a brain disease? A critical review of structural and functional cerebral abnormality in the disorder. *British Journal of Psychiatry, 166*, 563–582.

Grant, K. A., & Lovinger, D. M. (1995). Cellular and behavioral neurobiology of alcohol: Receptor-mediated neuronal processes. *Clinical Neuroscience, 3,* 155–164.

The Huntington's Disease Collaborative Research Group. (1993). A novel gene containing a trinucleotide repeat that is expanded and unstable on Huntington's disease chromosomes. *Cell, 72,* 971–983.

St. George-Hyslop, P. H. (1993). Recent advances in the molecular genetics of Alzheimer's disease. *Clinical Neuroscience, 1,* 171–175.

Stabenau, J. R., & Pollin, W. (1993). Heredity and environment in schizophrenia, revisited. The contribution of twin and high-risk studies. *The Journal of Nervous and Mental Disease, 181,* 290–297.

Additional Readings

Blass, J. P. (1993). Pathophysiology of the Alzheimer's syndrome. *Neurology, 43* (supplement 4), S25–S38.

Carlson, N. R. (1994). *Physiology of behavior* (5th ed.). Boston: Allyn & Bacon.

Kolb, B., & Whishaw, I. Q. (1995). *Fundamentals of human neuropsychology* (4th ed.). New York: Freeman.

Markham, C. H., & Diamond, S. G. (1993). Clinical overview of Parkinson's disease. *Clinical Neuroscience, 1,* 5–11.

National Institute of Mental Health. (1993). *Special report: Schizophrenia 1993.* Rockville, MD: U.S. Department of Health and Human Services.

Purdon, S. E., Mohr, E., Ilivitsky, V., & Jones, B. D. W. (1994). Huntington's disease: Pathogenesis, diagnosis and treatment. *Journal of Psychiatry & Neuroscience, 19,* 359–367.

K. S. SEYBOLD

See BRAIN AND HUMAN BEHAVIOR; PHYSIOLOGICAL PSYCHOLOGY.

Genetic Counseling. Genetic counseling is a service for prospective or expectant parents that determines the probability that their children will be born with a hereditary defect. Genetic counselors are trained in genetics and counseling and may be geneticists, medical researchers, or doctors. Genetic counseling is available to any couple, although it is strongly encouraged if there is a family history of children with genetic defects or if the couple has already borne a child with a genetic defect. Genetic counselors can frequently do more than just provide probabilities; they can determine if the unborn child has the genetic defect. More than two hundred different disorders can be detected prenatally.

Prospective parents should realize that even though they do not have a particular disorder, they may carry the gene for it; consequently, a genetic counselor will obtain a complete family history from both parents. Whether relatives had certain disorders, how relatives died, and whether relatives had difficulty bearing children would be important to know. If one prospective parent's family history reveals several instances of a disorder, then there is the chance that this parent carries the recessive gene for the disorder. A counselor will inform this prospec-

tive parent that the likelihood of a child developing the disorder is very low unless the disorder has also occurred in the spouse's family. For many disorders, such as sickle-cell anemia, hemophilia, phenylketonuria, or Tay-Sachs disease, a simple blood test can detect the harmful gene (Edwards, 1993).

Although the tests exist to determine the presence of a chromosomal abnormality, would everyone at risk for a disorder want to be tested? Consider a person in his or her twenties or thirties whose mother or father died of Huntington's disease, a disorder caused by a dominant gene and characterized by a deterioration of the nervous system during middle age. This person can be tested to determine the likelihood of passing this gene (and therefore the disorder) to his or her children (there is a 50/50 chance). If this person will pass on the defective gene to his or her children, that also means the person will develop Huntington's disease in middle age. Not all persons at risk decide to be tested; they fear the prospect of learning that they have an incurable genetic disease. If this person did not take the test and did not have the defective gene but decided not to have children because of the potential risk, then taking the test would have eliminated any worries (Wiggins et al., 1992).

Genetic counselors may inform parents that although there is a risk of transmitting a genetic defect to a child, tests can be done before the child is born to determine whether the child has developed the genetic disorder.

One method of prenatal diagnosis of a genetic defect is amniocentesis, which can detect more than one hundred genetic disorders, including Down's syndrome, Tay-Sachs disease, cystic fibrosis, and sickle-cell anemia. Amniocentesis is usually performed during the fourteenth to sixteenth week after conception (when amniotic fluid is plentiful); whether the results of amniocentesis are reliable when the unborn child is younger is currently being debated (Hanson, Tennant, Hume, & Brookhuyser, 1992). The procedure involves extracting a small amount of amniotic fluid through a syringe inserted in the wall of the mother's abdomen. Cells shed from the unborn child are separated from the fluid by centrifuge and are analyzed to determine their chromosomal composition. The tests take two to three weeks. Mothers who are older than 35, who have previously miscarried, who already have a child with a genetic defect, or who have relatives with a genetic defect are likely to be advised to have amniocentesis. Risk to the unborn child is low, although the likelihood of infection and spontaneous abortion is increased slightly (Pergament & Fine, 1993).

In chorionic villus sampling (CVS), chorionic cells from the unborn child are collected, usually between the eighth and twelfth weeks after conception, and then analyzed. The chorion is the outer wall of the membrane in which the embryo develops, and the cells collected are small hairlike projections (villi). Because this procedure can be used at an earlier age, it is sometimes favored over amniocentesis; however, CVS is more difficult to perform and is linked to an increased risk of miscarriage and, in rare instances, birth defects (Burton, Schulz, & Burd, 1992). CVS is currently used only when the parents are at a particularly high risk of conceiving a child with a genetic defect (Pergament & Fine, 1993).

Another technique is ultrasonography (ultrasound), a method of scanning the womb with sound waves that allows the doctor to monitor the development of the unborn child, looking for potential abnormalities. Disorders like microcephaly, cardiac malformations, neural tube defects, and cleft palate can be revealed. Because ultrasonography is safe, it is used routinely in many parts of the world to determine the unborn child's age as well as to assist in lifesaving in-utero operations.

Parents obviously prefer to hear from a genetic counselor that their unborn child does not have a genetic defect, but if the defect is found, counselors can help the parents understand the situation, cope with the information, and make decisions for the future. Critics of genetic counseling argue that the information parents receive from their genetic counselor might prompt them to abort the unborn child if a defect is detected. However, parents who know their unborn child has a genetic disorder or is at risk for one do not necessarily automatically consider abortion; many parents who abhor abortion may appreciate knowing so they can be better prepared and equipped once the baby is born. Supporters also contend that genetic counseling can potentially reassure parents that their child will be born healthy, thereby reducing maternal stress during the pregnancy.

The popularity of genetic counseling has raised several significant legal and ethical questions. For example, should families with a history of hereditary disorders be required to obtain genetic counseling? Should test results be given to parents who are considering aborting an unborn child with a disorder? Are the counseling services sufficient to help someone cope with the news that they carry a genetic disorder and that their children might have the disorder? Do insurance companies or prospective employers have the right to know if someone has or is a carrier of a genetic disorder? Genetic counseling will be controversial for years to come (Bukatko & Daehler, 1995).

References

Bukatko, D., & Daehler, M. W. (1995). *Child development: A thematic approach* (2nd ed.). Boston: Houghton Mifflin.

Burton, B. K., Schulz, C. J., & Burd, L. I. (1992). Limb anomalies associated with chorionic villus sampling. *Obstetrics and Gynecology, 79,* 726–730.

Edwards, R. G. (1993). *Preconception and preimplantation diagnosis of human genetic disease.* Cambridge: Cambridge University Press.

Hanson, F. W., Tennant, F., Hume, S., & Brookhuyser, K. (1992). Early amniocentesis: Outcome risks and technical problems at 12.8 weeks. *American Journal of Obstetrics and Gynecology, 166,* 1707–1711.

Pergament, E., & Fine, B. (1993). The current status of chorionic villus sampling. In R. G. Edwards (Ed.), *Preconception and preimplantation diagnosis of human genetic disease.* Cambridge: Cambridge University Press.

Wiggins, S., et al. (1992). The psychological consequences of predictive testing for Huntington's disease. *New England Journal of Medicine, 327,* 1401–1405.

Additional Reading

National Genetics Foundation. (1987). *Clinical genetics handbook.* Oradell, NJ: Medical Economic Books.

D. Needham

See Moral and Ethical Issues in Treatment.

Genetic Factors in Personality Development. See Heredity and Environment in Human Development.

Genius. Historically the term *genius* has denoted individuals who possess exceptionally high levels of intellectual or creative ability, often manifested in new approaches to long-standing problems in science, art, philosophy, and other fields. Although the concept has a long history, only within the last hundred years or so have ideas and opinions regarding genius, its identification, and speculations about how it occurs been subjected to empirical study.

The modern phase of empirical study has radically altered or replaced several features of the earlier concept of genius. One assumption was that genius is an intrinsic quality or trait that an individual possesses that is relatively unaffected by education or nurture. A second assumption was that genius has a disruptive influence on society much like that associated with insanity. Common to both of these assumptions is the notion that the appearance of a genius is more or less inexplicable and unpredictable. During the Middle Ages this notion was even associated with the belief that the genius was possessed by supernatural agencies.

An important impetus to the modern study of genius was the work of Francis Galton, who pioneered in the field of mental measurement by elaborating on the assumption that mental traits, like physical traits, could be measured. Through the work of Alfred Binet and Terman in developing practical measures of intelligence, genius came to be understood in terms of measurable intellectual abilities. These abilities, in combination with particular personality traits (e.g., drive or persistence), led to real-life achievements and recognition. Speculative opinions about the nature of genius gave way to studies of exceptional, or gifted, children and adults, and the term *genius* was often restricted to anchoring the extreme end of the intelligence quotient (IQ) scale. Terman's longitudinal studies of a large group of intellectually gifted children demonstrated that exceptional abilities can be fruitfully studied and measured and that they continue to be manifested in individual achievements across the life span.

Another influence on the study of genius came from intensive investigations of the biographies and current psychological functioning of living individuals who have made outstanding and creative achievements in their respective fields. These studies generally showed that the emergence of those who will become eminent contributors can be illuminated, if not precisely predicted, by obtaining a knowledge of both their intellectual abilities and the dynamics of their development. For example, Roe (1961) found that eminent scientists were characterized by high intelligence as traditionally measured but also by a confluence of personal and family circumstances that fostered hard work, achievement, and independence. Studies of this type have revealed the importance of early development, which can foster the thinking styles, commitment, and social adjustments required, along with high ability, for significant achievement in various fields. Another factor frequently identified is the availability of role models in a field that is congruent with these abilities and dispositions.

The study of genius has generally proceeded away from the assumption that intrinsic and unpredictable characteristics can account for the achievements that have brought recognition to these individuals. This assumption is unfruitful because it merely labels the phenomenon and then invokes the label as an explanation, begging the question of how and under what circumstances exceptional achievement occurs. Greatest progress toward understanding genius seems to come from a focus on the study of eminent individuals.

Defining genius in terms of eminence or influence upon a field capitalizes on the fact that there has always been remarkable consensus as to which persons can be called geniuses. This approach has given rise to a program of research whereby the conditions for the occurrence of genius are better understood. It also has the important consequence that the genius must be viewed not merely as an unusual individual but also as one who has achieved widespread influence on those whose recognition counts toward success in his or her field. Productivity within a field proves to be a key to genius, seen as eminence, since eminent contributors are almost invariably individuals who entered their fields early in life and were prolific in their contributions over a long span of time. There is evidence that productivity is a cause and not merely a consequence of genius as intrinsic ability. Again, the genius must have high abilities but also must demonstrate extraordinary persistence in order to stay productive, overcome barriers to acceptance of his or her ideas, and eventually win status and recognition.

Ever since Galton's work it has been known that geniuses often appear in the same family. However, the notion that genius is an inherited trait has generally been discredited. The Christian's acknowledgment of a sovereign Creator does not require that an individual's gifts and talents be either inherited or bestowed suddenly. On the contrary, God's sovereignty is shown through his supervision of the family and other environmental circumstances that contribute to exceptional talent. The Christian's response in making these talents available for God's purposes is in part an acknowledgment that God was intimately involved in their formation.

Reference

Roe, A. (1961). The psychology of the scientist. *Science, 134,* 456–459.

D. R. Ridley

See Intelligence; Intellectual Assessment.

Genogram. A psychological family tree in which recurring behavior patterns of three or more generations are graphically displayed and examined. The founder of Bowen Family Systems Therapy, Murray Bowen, introduced the genogram concept in the late 1970s as a relatively nonthreatening tool for analyzing family structures (Marlin, 1989).

Genogram construction is relatively simple. Symbols are used to represent people and relationships (i.e., a circle for female and a square for male). Demographic information includes ages, dates of birth and death, geographic locations, occupations, and educational levels. Functional information includes data on the medical, legal, emotional, and behavioral functioning of different family members. Major illnesses, life transitions, and personality characteristics would be included here. Critical family events include important transitions (i.e., major move), relationship changes (i.e., divorce), losses (i.e., miscarriage), and successes (i.e., family births, promotions).

The clinician and client(s) together graphically map out relevant information and use it to form hypotheses about how a problem may have developed over time within the family context. The rationale is that what happens in one generation will often repeat itself in the next. For example, a couple may come to therapy on the brink of divorce because the husband is a workaholic. A genogram might reveal how achievement is the means by which men are shown love in a family. His problem then becomes an extension of many old family patterns, which is potentially less threatening to him, and places him and his current family in a better position to deal with it. The genogram allows both the clinician and the client(s) to see the bigger picture and to evaluate their strengths and vulnerabilities in light of this information.

Reference

Marlin, E. (1989). *Genograms: The new tool for exploring the personality, career, and love patterns you inherit.* Chicago: Contemporary.

K. R. Meek

See Family Therapy: Overview.

Geriatric Psychotherapy. The first term refers to the treatment of problems associated with later life; the second, with a specific form of treatment emphasizing communication with the patient. Psychopathologies such as depression and organic brain syndromes (delirium and dementia) can occur at any time but are especially prevalent in persons in the last third of the life cycle. A mental health professional specializing in geriatrics has expertise in dealing with dementia and depression or the biopsychosocial crises commonly encountered in later life (e.g., retirement, widowhood, declining health).

Many psychologists and psychiatrists have unfavorable attitudes toward working with older clients, often preferring not to work in the field of geriatrics. Many are of the opinion that the prognosis, especially for depression, is less favorable with aged clients. They often view geriatric patients as set in their ways and unable to change. These prejudicial views are not substantiated by the data. Elder clients tend to be more reliable when it comes to keeping appointments and following homework instructions (*see* Homework in Psychotherapy). Most of them have had a lifetime of successful coping experiences and just need a little professional assistance to help them cope with the special stresses of later life.

The great American pioneer in geriatric psychotherapy was Lillien J. Martin, a retired university professor. In 1929 she founded the San Francisco Old Age Counseling Center. The Martin method involved a series of five or six structured interviews emphasizing a directive approach of specific suggestions and motivating slogans. The counselor examined the client's daily routine and goals during the sessions and then worked behind the scenes to help the client find housing, employment, social services, and interpersonal networks. Although the Martin clinic appeared to be successful, Martin's influence in geriatrics never extended into the mainstream of social work or psychotherapy. However, both her basic strategy and many specific techniques have been rediscovered by other psychotherapists.

General Treatment Approach. The psychoanalytic movement has not been very interested in or optimistic about geriatric psychotherapy. Sigmund Freud did not have clinical experience in the field but believed that persons over 50 were too rigid to profit from psychoanalysis. Several of Freud's followers who took on older clients agreed that classical psychoanalytic treatment seemed inappropriate. However, instead of declaring the patient to be beyond help, they decided to modify the psychotherapeutic techniques: eliminating the sofa, making the therapist more active and directive, limiting the goals to specific problems, focusing on the present, and providing flexible scheduling. Such modified therapy was quite effective.

In order to comprehend the strategy of geriatric psychotherapy, it is necessary to abandon much of classical psychoanalytical (Freud) and person-centered (Carl Rogers) approaches. The goal in working with older clients is not to facilitate the creation of a growing Personality or to resolve a 70-year-old Oedipus complex. The starting assumption is that the client's underlying personality is healthy and that the purpose of intervention is to help overcome the particular stressful life events that have temporarily exceeded the client's coping capacities. The therapist will be able to uncover many behaviors that border on the pathological and many long-standing intrapsychic conflicts. The wise geriatric psychotherapist exercises a great deal of restraint and avoids intervention in most of these areas, concentrating the therapeutic efforts on those specific points at which the client's responses to the present environment are ineffective and painful.

While most counseling with the aged centers on highly selective intervention geared to concrete problem solving in a brief time frame, a minority of the patients have highly dependent personalities and will require a long-term supportive therapeutic relationship. Having a confidant is a key to maintaining mental health in later life. Usually the confidant is a friend or a grown child (particularly a daughter) to whom the elder can debrief daily routine and receive some degree of empathy. All elders can benefit from such a relationship, and most are able to sustain one on their own. Some individuals have an extreme need for a confidant and yet have difficulty in getting one. With passive-dependent individuals the resources for short-term problem solving may be lacking, and what the patient really needs is someone to lean on in a long-term relationship. Some therapists fit this role well, but they are not necessarily the same therapists who motivate elders to solve their own problems.

Whether the thrust of the therapy is supportive or problem solving, a team approach is essential in geriatrics. The causes of the elder's mental health problems are physical, social, and economic, and the therapist cannot ignore these fronts. Yet face-to-face discussion by itself will do little to improve these aspects. There are numerous resources for elders in the United States—specialized physicians, dentists, opticians, physical therapists, pharmacists, nutritionists, and lawyers. A therapist who is able to put the client in touch with such resources can effect much more both in terms of problem solving and emotional support. A therapist who is part of a team of multidisciplinary services can work within a coordinated approach to providing the elder with what is needed.

Transference and Countertransference. Transference is part of the dynamics of every psychotherapeutic relationship. The maintenance of a problem-solving orientation diminishes the likelihood of transference dynamics. It is difficult to predict what kind of transference will arise in psychotherapy with an elder. The patient might unconsciously relate to the therapist as if the latter were a parent, child, spouse, or peer. Countertransference, with the therapist unconsciously relating to the client as if the latter were a parent or a grandparent, can be countertherapeutic if it leads the therapist to falsely ascribe characteristics to the client. While transference issues can be largely ignored unless a major problem arises, therapists must continuously monitor their own countertransference pattern with a new client.

One of the best ways to avoid problems with either transference or countertransference is the therapist's maintenance of an aura of authority. Many elders are not used to dealing with a counselor on a first-name basis. The counseling paradigms with which they are most familiar and most comfortable are the physician and the clergy, who come into the relationship with a special title, knowledge, and authority. Physicians and clergy will find this easier than will secular, nonmedical counselors.

There is yet another reason why physicians and clergy may be the therapists of choice with elders who lack the psychological sophistication of the younger generation. Many older people may conceive of their mental problems in spiritual or medical terms and seek out the family physician, priest, minister, or rabbi. Some elders hold nineteenth-century views of mental health and believe that only insane people would go to a psychologist.

Techniques and Strategies. Over the 1980s and 1990s, cognitive therapy has become ascendant in the treatment of depression. This has definitely become the rule in geriatric psychotherapy.

The first session of therapy should involve the establishment of the therapist's authority, combined with a mutual respect for the client's dignity. The client and therapist should be addressed by the appropriate title (e.g., Colonel, Doctor) unless the client indicates a preference for informality. The therapist should exercise authority by controlling the time of the session, asking specific questions (about both background and the present situation), and interrupting politely yet firmly when the elder strays too far from the topic. Above all the therapist must not allow the client to wallow in self-pity, recriminations, or other negativisms. The first session should include an opportunity for both parties to express their expectations for counseling, specific goals, and commitments.

Elders tend to be rigid, and this may result in resistance to the therapist (*see* Resistance in Psychotherapy). When it does arise, it needs to be shown some respect. Admit that the patient has a strong will and praise it as a positive force: strength of character. Concede that nothing in your professional bag of tricks is strong enough to overcome the client's will. This approach increases the client's self-esteem, preserves the strong will as a future motivator, and wins the elder's trust in you.

The content of the sessions should focus on current problems and realistic solutions. Homework assignments are especially appropriate for this. Certain distressing symptoms might be removed by direct suggestion or behavior modification. For example, although guilt complexes are not the driving force behind most depression in later life, they can be found in some elders. Absolution by a sacerdotal figure can do more toward the elimination of a guilt complex than can hours of attempting to reason it away.

One popular technique is the use of life review, also known as reminiscence. Cataloging and reliving the past is useful if it serves the function of convincing the client that "I have been through some pretty tough times before, and although things look bad now, I am tough and resilient enough to see it through." If the patient uses the life review as an escape from the present, it will not serve the goals of therapy. If the client's past is a series of failures and pain, the life review could intensify the depression. Some Holocaust survivors prefer to relive their experience as a testimony that honors those who perished (and an admonition to future generations), while others prefer to ignore the painful details. Both approaches should be accommodated by therapists.

Dreamwork is another possible technique. Even though the aged dream less and are less likely to recall their dreams, it is possible to motivate them to bring dreams to the therapy session. Patients with distressing dreams need to be calmed by an authoritative explanation of dream mechanisms and symbols (*see* Dreams, Therapeutic Use of). Dreams can also be used as monitors and rehearsals of coping and can be combined with a psychodrama in which the client reenacts the dream and changes the ending by substituting more effective behavior.

Group therapy offers many potentials in geriatrics, primarily in the area of supportive networks. The basic strategy of grouping is homogeneity: put early-stage dementia patients in one group, put retired nuns in a group, put World War II vets in a group. Mixing a group by cognitive level, background, or current problem makes it difficult for the group to become cohesive or remain focused. The only geriatric patients who may not respond well to groups are those with a communication disorder (e.g., deaf, aphasic) or an overt hostility. Free-flowing groups left to their own internal dynamics may not succeed with this age group. Clear-cut leadership, structure, and language should be provided by the authority figure.

Suicidal comments and signs cannot be ignored. When an elder suffers from depression or physical pain, directly initiate the discussion of death and suicide. Most elders believe that suicide is wrong, but they find themselves caught up in racing thoughts of pessimism. Reassuring the patient of your confidence in the outcome of therapy is the first step. Next, help the patient monitor and control suicidal ideation. Prayer is one of the best ways of doing this. If the risk of suicide becomes high, institutionalization may become necessary. One of the best ways to assess suicidal risk is the elder's refusal to promise not to kill himself or herself before the next scheduled therapy session.

Scheduling must be flexible with elder patients. In general two or three sessions a week for a month or two should be sufficient. Most of the sessions should be brief, under an hour, and become shorter and less frequent, and become more of ongoing progress reports. Rather than an abrupt termination, sessions should be phased out as the client regains the capacity to self-direct coping operations. The therapist informs the client that the counseling relationship can be reinstated at a point in the future, should the client deem it necessary.

The families of elders can become involved in therapy in different ways. One way is conjoint therapy for the elder and significant family members: spouse or adult children. The entire family must adjust to the elder's physical and mental changes, and the elder's task is to adjust to the changing family system. Another way to involve the family is to form a group for caregivers of dependent aged. They benefit by the discussion of specific alternatives and resources and also receive emotional consolation from those in a similar situation.

One of the major trends in mental health care delivery since the mid-1980s has been an increasing willingness of general practice physicians to diagnose depression and prescribe antidepressant medication. Before that time the vast majority of cases of geriatric depression went undiagnosed. This trend has not alleviated the need for geriatric psychotherapy, but it does increase the need for the nonmedical therapist to play his or her part on the team by encouraging the patient to seek appropriate medical attention, take medications, and monitor for side effects.

Additional Readings

Brink, T. L. (1979). *Geriatric psychotherapy*. New York: Human Sciences.

Brink, T. L. (Ed.). (1986). *Clinical gerontology: A guide to assessment and intervention*. New York: Haworth.

Brink, T. L. (Ed.). (1987). *The elderly uncooperative patient*. New York: Haworth.

Brink, T. L. (Ed.). (1990). *Mental health in the nursing home*. New York: Haworth.

Brink, T. L. (Ed.). (1994). *Holocaust survivors' mental health*. New York: Haworth.

T. L. BRINK

See GERONTOLOGY.

Gerontology. The study of aging, a study that has become an increasingly multidisciplinary endeavor. Biologists, psychologists, sociologists, economists, and political scientists are doing research in this field.

There are two basic research designs in gerontological research. Cross sectional designs compare today's old people to today's young people. A cohort is a population of individuals who are born during the same historical period (e.g., 1910–1920). Cross sectional research ends up comparing two different cohorts, so that a study of 40-year olds versus 80-year olds results in the comparison of people born in the 1950s versus those born in the 1910s. If such research establishes that the latter group is higher in religiosity, we cannot infer whether this is due to a historical trend or a developmental feature intrinsic to the aging process.

Longitudinal research avoids this problem by studying only one cohort over time: measuring them as young adults and again as elders. Longitudinal studies of aging are rare for two reasons. One is that most researchers do not want to wait 40 years for publishable results. The other problem is that it is often difficult to locate the original participants after so long. Many of them have died, and it is questionable if the survivors are representative of the original sample. Usually there is differential attrition: the survivors tend to be the healthier, wealthier, more intelligent members of the original sample. So, both methods of gerontological research have their drawbacks.

The age of 65 has often been taken as a cutoff point to define old age, but this is arbitrary. Some people in their forties are undergoing some of the problems usually associated with later life, while some in their late seventies have avoided or postponed some of the crises of aging. If we use 65 and older as a definition of old age, we see that the percentage of elders in the United States has risen from 4% in 1900, to 8% at mid-century, to more than 12% near the end of the twentieth century. The figure should surpass 15% by the year 2015, when the bulk of the baby boomer cohort arrives at that age.

Two factors are responsible for this growing percentage. One is the declining birthrate. In a country like Mexico, with a higher birthrate, the median age of the population is about 16, and elders account for less than 5% of the population; but the percentage of elderly is growing higher as family planning becomes the norm. Another factor is the lengthening of life expectancy: the average age to which a child born today can expect to live. The current life expectancy in most industrialized countries is well over 70, with females and whites in the United States enjoying a slightly higher figure. This figure could be pushed up another 10 years with the conquest of cancer, control of hypertension, better automobile safety, or becoming a smoke-free society. However, do not use life expectancy to estimate how many more years of life a given elder can expect. Those who have already made it to 65 are likely to make it to 80.

Biopsychosocial Crises. Most of the problems that the aged experience are due to a failure to adapt to life changes. The greatest and most pervasive problem is physical decline. Long life does not always mean better life but rather suffering longer with chronic disabilities. While old age itself is not a disease, many disorders are more common in the aged: strokes, arthritis, deafness, cataracts, and sexual dysfunctions. Elders now account for over a third of the health care bill in the United States. Even cosmetic changes (e.g., wrinkles) can detract from elders' self-esteem and sense of well-being.

Compared to other age groups, elders, though on average closer to death, are less bothered by death anxiety. They worry more about physical suffering and being a burden to others than they do about death. Those in poor health or in nursing homes may look forward to death. An excessive fear of death may be associated with an underlying personality disorder, anxiety, or excessive feelings of guilt or failure.

Bereavement following the deaths of significant others (spouses, siblings, children, friends, even pets) is a far more serious threat to mental health. Two-thirds of aged females are widowed. The more dependent they were on the spouse, the greater the difficulty in adjustment. Even if the marriage was a stormy one, widowhood can be difficult due to the loss of a sparring partner or unresolved sense of guilt ("I should have been better to him when he was alive"). The widows who were caregivers for the terminally ill often go through an anticipatory grief, so death may come as a relief. Otherwise the first year of widowhood is the most difficult, with the incidence of depression and physical complaints rising. Along with time itself and bereavement rituals, widow support groups can be helpful.

Retirement is a difficult transition for some but not most. Teachers and professionals who can taper off active employment seem to fare best, as do those who can remain active in an absorbing hobby or community service. Those who fare worst are those who have no activities or social contacts apart from the job. Another problem is if the spouse comes to resent the increased frequency of contact after retirement.

The greatest fear that most urban elders have is crime. Some fear may be an overreaction to news reports of street crime. However, elders are the prime targets of fraud and confidence artists.

"Ageism" refers to any prejudiced or negative stereotypical attitude toward elders. While Western society is clearly ageist, there is no evidence that this in and of itself presents a problem for older people. If prejudiced views lead to discriminatory behavior against the aged, there obviously is harm. However, the stereotype of the feeble elder helps most aged believe that they are exceptionally spry for their age.

Various socioeconomic developments make aging more difficult than it was in previous centuries. The extended family has lost its importance. Industrialization has made the factory and office, rather than the home and farm, the centers of production. Education and the mass media, not old storytellers, are the custodians of culture. It is harder for the aged to participate in and have an impact upon society.

Institutionalization is the fate of one million elders in the United States. By age 85 almost 15% live in long-term care facilities. The percentage has increased fivefold since the mid-twentieth century. Most institutionalized elders are widowed or single and have grave physical problems (e.g., less than half can walk). The majority are seriously confused. The development of alternate levels and forms of care (e.g., day care, home care, respite care) can reduce institutionalization.

Mental Changes. Existing psychological theories about aging can be summed up in one word: inadequate. Erik Erikson and Carl Gustav Jung had virtually no clinical experience with older clients, yet they presented speculative, highly romanticized pictures of later life that were virtually useless in dealing with some of the more common psychopathologies. There are data to indicate that mental disorder in later life often occurs in people who were normal adults but who have now experienced a reaction to the stress occasioned by specific biopsychosocial crises. While broad theories about aging have been poorly substantiated, a great deal of survey, experimental, and clinical data exist on several points.

IQ scores decline with age. The difference is slight with longitudinal research, since the more intelligent subjects live longer and are easier to locate for the follow-up study. The difference is pronounced with cross sectional studies, perhaps indicating some cohort effect. The decline is greater for those subtests involving abstract or creative abilities. Declining IQ could be attributable to many factors: lack of familiarity with test-taking procedures, declining sensory acuity, slower reaction time, depression, lack of intellectual stimulation, or dementia.

Rigidity is a psychological construct that refers to measures of dogmatism, impulse control, cautiousness, and resistance to persuasion. Rigidity correlates positively with age, even when variables such as education, IQ, and social class are controlled. There is also a negative correlation between mental health and rigidity, but clinical experience suggests that rigidity is the result of neurosis rather than its cause. Indeed, rigidity may be the only way that many elders with limited mental resources can cope with crises that would otherwise overwhelm them.

Introversion, a shift of attention away from the external world, has been investigated by projective tests. The data indicate that old people become more introverted. Introversion, like rigidity, may be a defensive response to environmental stress.

Inferiority feeling, rather than guilt, seems to be the major factor eroding self-esteem in later life. In addition to the inferiority feeling generated by physical disabilities and the loss of productive roles, elders must cope with a society that is both youth-oriented and moving away from some of the traditions they cherish.

Senility is a popular term describing general mental decline, especially confusion and disorientation. The causes can be organic brain syndromes (*see* Delirium; Dementia) or depression.

Depression has a higher incidence in old age than in any other part of the life cycle. Although biochemical changes can be a predisposing factor, most geriatric depressions are reactions to the stress of widowhood and physical disability. Many depressed elders do not recognize that they are depressed, and many physicians who examine them fail to diagnose the mood disorder. Untreated depression is one reason why the geriatric suicide rate is higher than that of any other age group. If discovered and treated, however, geriatric depression is usually reversible.

Schizophrenia, mania, and personality disorders rarely have onset in later life. Delusion disorders, such as hypochondriasis and paranoia, are easy to observe but difficult to treat. Geriatric hypochondriasis is not fundamentally different from that observed in younger patients, except that the older hypochondriac probably has some real physical problems along with the imagined ones. Geriatric paranoia is different from the delusions of persecution found in young schizophrenics. Diminishing sensory and memory capacity leads to inability to account for various changes, especially lost objects. The delusion that a neighbor or relative is stealing or exchanging the patient's property is one way to account for these gaps. Many paranoids do a good job meeting their environmental demands in other ways, so that the disorder is largely a problem only for the people who have to listen to the patient's complaints.

Religion in Later Life. Older people have more traditional religious beliefs, including scriptural literalism and obedience to the commandments. However, the aged are less superstitious than the general population. The percentage of adults who affirm a belief of God rises steadily with age. Elders are more likely to describe themselves as religious, moral, conservative, and fundamentalist.

Aged are more likely than other age groups to pray, read the Bible, and listen to religious broadcasts. Attendance at religious services is higher for older Roman Catholics, Episcopalians, and Eastern Orthodox Christians but lower for Protestant and Jewish denominations. There is a tapering off of leadership roles. It remains unclear whether these figures are influenced more by historical trends (cohort factors) or developmental trends.

Most measures of adjustment correlate positively with most measures of religious activity. (The only exception to this trend is found in the fringe sects, in which the level of doctrinal acceptance and participation is slightly inversely correlated with adjustment.) For the mainline denominations, the happiest and healthiest elders attend church most often, and poor adjustment is found in those with low or declining attendance. What is not clear is to what extent this correlation means that healthy elders can keep active in religion, or whether the religious participation keeps them healthy and happy.

Additional Readings

Journal of Religious Gerontology.

Koenig, H. (1994). *Aging and God: Spiritual pathways to mental health in midlife and later years.* New York: Haworth.

Levin, J. S. (1994). *Religion in aging and health: Theoretical foundations and methodological frontiers.* Newbury Park, CA: Sage.

Thomas, L. E., & Eisenhandler, S. A. (1994). *Aging and the religious dimension.* Westport, CT: Auburn House.

T. L. BRINK

See LIFE SPAN DEVELOPMENT; GERIATRIC PSYCHOTHERAPY.

Gesell, Arnold Lucius (1890–1961). Pioneer in child psychology. He was born in Alma, Wisconsin, and spent two years at the University of Wisconsin. He then studied psychology at Clark University, where he received his Ph.D. in 1906. After teaching psychology for several years, he became convinced that medical training was necessary for the proper study of child development. He studied medicine at Yale while teaching there and received his M.D. in 1915.

After receiving his Ph.D. Gesell taught psychology at Los Angeles State Normal School. In 1911 he was appointed professor of education at Yale, where he founded the Yale Clinic of Child Development. He remained director of the clinic until 1948, when he became director of the Gesell Institute of Child Development, continuing the work begun by the Yale clinic. He was active as a research consultant until 1958.

Gesell initially was concerned with retardation but concluded that an understanding of normal infant and child development is necessary for an understanding of abnormality. By 1919 he was studying mainly the development of normal infant mentality, developing methods of observing and measuring behavior. After 1926 the movie camera became his principal tool, and he filmed about 12,000 children of all ages and levels of development through a one-way screen.

The results of Gesell's studies are in the form of minute descriptions of the films and other records, comparing the results with findings on other normal subjects. Rather than attempting to formulate a theory of mental development or analyze the factors influencing it, Gesell remained purely descriptive. He concluded that mental development proceeds in a predictable and measurable sequence, although the timing is not identical in all children. He believed that the emerging behavior patterns have as much structure as the growing physical organism, that the behavioral patterns are basically determined by internal forces rather than environmental ones. His emphasis on maturation was not widely accepted in psychology because it was proposed when behaviorism was dominant and psychology was taking an extremely environmentalistic position.

Gesell published more than four hundred papers and books. His most important books are *The Mental*

Growth of the Preschool Child (1925) and *Infancy and Human Growth* (1928). In these he presented his developmental schedules, containing items to evaluate child development during the first five years of life. Later he turned his attention to older children, publishing *The Child from Five to Ten* (1946) and *Youth: The Years from Ten to Sixteen* (1956).

R. L. Koteskey

See Life Span Development.

Gestalt Psychology. The movement that sprang up in Frankfurt and Berlin as a protest against the analysis of consciousness into elements and the exclusion of values from the data of consciousness. It is most closely associated with the founding triumvirate of Max Wertheimer, Wolfgang Köhler, and Kurt Koffka but is also strongly rooted in the Act Psychology of the Austrian school. Other roots lie in the phenomenological movement, the holistic psychologies, the revolt against positivism, and the more general tension between the *Naturwissenschaften* and *Geisteswissenschaften*. The Gestalt psychologists sought a system that permitted both understanding and scientific explanation.

The Austrian school contributed to the Gestalt movement both its name and the major problem of perception. The elementism of structuralism and associationism regarded perception as a composite of sensations, and even Wilhelm Wundt's famous experiments in fusion and complication did not resolve the complexity of space and time perception. Ernst Mach first addressed these issues in 1886 by positing "sensations of time-form" and "sensations of space-form," with *form* an experience or sensation independent of quality. Mach's ideas were systematized in 1890 by Christian von Ehrenfels, who spoke of "form quality," which he regarded as a new or secondary quality rather than a combination of primary qualities.

Alexius Meinong added the Gestalt production theory, which was later rejected by Gestaltists. This theory perception is a two-step process, the first leading from stimuli to sensations, the second from sensations to a whole perception in an act of production. Hans Cornelius regarded the form quality as a founded attribute rather than an act of production. Thus he claimed that the attributes are disestablished by analysis, while initial experience tends to be of wholes: attention to the parts destroys these wholes and their founded attributes. Within this tradition Vittorio Benussi was the first experimentalist, testing Meinong's act of production through the study of ambiguous figures.

While Gestalt psychology was one among many holistic psychologies, it proposed the radical view that the whole is psychologically, logically, epistemologically, and ontologically prior to its parts. The wholes were emergent qualities that inhered in no single element. Adequate knowledge of the whole could come only from observing the whole itself and must never be inferred from the parts and their relations. The most striking example of such an emergent whole was Wertheimer's phi phenomenon—that is, the illusion of movement produced when stationary stimuli are presented in rapid succession in slightly different positions.

In contrast to the structuralists the Gestaltists felt that the distinction between description and inference could not be clearly made and that all objects that are perceived immediately, without an inferential process, should be regarded as phenomena. Thus they adopted the phenomenological method, involving a free description of immediate experience rather than introspection. Their arguments were more often based on the *experimentum crucis*, a convincing single demonstration or illustration of a phenomenon, than on statistical analyses. Familiar illustrations of this sort are the ambiguous figures used to demonstrate the shifting nature of figure and ground and the lines and dots often used to illustrate the laws of form or principles of organization (which include nearness, quality, closure, common destiny, good continuation, and symmetry, simplicity, and order).

Wertheimer, who was the leader of the Gestalt group, contributed primarily to the psychology of perceived motion. He was also the epistemologist of the group, being the first to challenge Meinong's production theory and also challenging Benussi's interest in ambiguity (as opposed to the compelling stimuli that could be regarded in only one way).

Köhler, who was a physicist and an animal psychologist, contributed the most experimental research. On the basis of his experiments with anthropoid apes on the island of Tenerife, he challenged trial-and-error learning and concluded that the perception of relations distinguished Intelligence, terming the sudden perception of useful or proper relations *insight*. Köhler also articulated the principle of transposition, asserting that when parts change while their relations remain the same, the form or object remains constant. Thus we recognize a melody when it is transposed into a new key. Köhler also formulated the principle of isomorphism, postulating a structural correspondence between the external perceptual field and the internal, physiological field of the brain and nervous system. This extension of the physical dynamic concept of field theory into psychology became the foundation for Kurt Lewin's topological field theory, extending Gestalt psychology into the fields of personality theory and motivation, thus placing it in the realm of dynamic psychology.

Koffka, whose interests lay primarily in developmental and educational psychology, became the systematizer for the school (*see also* Developmental Psychology). His books and articles made Gestalt theory clear especially to American psychologists. With Köhler he founded *Psychologische Forschung* (Psychological Inquiry), the Gestalt journal that circulated from 1921 to 1938. Serving as co-editors of the journal were Hans Gruhle and Kurt Goldstein, whose major contributions were in the area of psychopathology and neurology.

Others associated with Gestalt psychology include several phenomenologists. Erich Jaensch made contributions in the areas of visual acuity, depth perception, and eidetic imagery. David Katz demonstrated the interrelationship between space and color perception and discriminated among surface, volumic, and film colors. Edgar Rubin extended Benussi's studies of figure-ground perception. His studies of ambiguous figures emphasized the fact that these involved phenomenal change rather than retinal changes induced by neurological factors. Gestalt principles also found their way into Edward Chace Tolman's sign-gestalt theory of learning.

Gestalt psychology, especially after the publication of Koffka's *Principles of Gestalt Psychology* in 1935, constituted a comprehensive system deeply rooted in philosophy. While it was originally founded to combat the traditional psychology of the structuralists, it soon found an even stronger challenge in behaviorism, to which it was diametrically opposed. The Gestaltists asserted that organisms do not merely respond to the environment but have transactions with it. And the environment itself is an outcome of the interaction between physical objects and perceptual dispositions of organisms, so that stimuli are transformed in the perceptual process.

Of considerable interest for the Christian is the Gestalt psychologists' interest in values. Meinong and his associates debated whether the experience of value was based on will or desire or should be reduced to feeling. This led to research on the theory of value and validity. In this area of values Köhler's William James Lectures, published as *The Place of Value in a World of Facts* (1938), have become classic. Gestalt psychology was also heavily influenced by twentieth-century religious history. Nearly every major theorist was Jewish, and the Nazi persecution (and American sympathy for the Jews) was responsible for its Americanization. The Gestalt therapy of Fritz Perls, while borrowing its language, "has *no* substantive relation to scientific Gestalt psychology" (Henle, 1978, p. 31).

Reference

Henle, M. (1978). Gestalt psychology and Gestalt therapy. *Journal of the History of the Behavioral Sciences, 14,* 23–32.

H. VANDE KEMP

See PSYCHOLOGY, HISTORY OF; GESTALT THERAPY.

Gestalt Techniques. The Gestalt approach to counseling and psychotherapy offers techniques that emphasize the here and now, the immediacy of experience, and both verbal and nonverbal expressiveness. Gestalt therapy is characteristically experiential in nature and is concerned more with being and doing than with thinking and talking. These experience-oriented strategies are used by the therapist to assist the client in making better contact with both self and the environment, to focus attention on particular situations that emerge within the organism-environment field, to integrate attention and awareness, and to restore organismic control and balance. Core Gestalt techniques are discussed under three categories: communication strategies, experiments, and dreamwork.

Communication Strategies. *Here and Now.* Communication in the present tense is encouraged in order to promote awareness and immediacy of experiencing. This mode of communicating helps also to integrate past material into the personality of the client. The historical moment is relived in the existential now.

I and Thou. Authentic communication and interpersonal experiencing involve the *I* of the sender making direct, personal contact with the *thou* of the receiver. This intersubjectivity facilitates better social contact and a keener sense of self.

I Language. Clients who refer to their body and behaviors in objective, second- and third-person language are asked to substitute *I* for *you* and *it.* This facilitates the individual's perception of self as an active, dynamic agent rather than a passive, acted-on object. *I* expressions also help the client to assume personal responsibility, involvement, and control regarding his or her total behavior.

What and How of Behavior. The therapist instructs clients to focus on the what and how of behavior in order to guide individuals in making good contact with their sensorimotor self and away from the interpretive why of behavior. The why tends to lead to intellectualizations, explanations, and defensiveness.

Gossip Is Forbidden. Often in group therapy a member will "gossip" or talk about another member rather than address the member directly. Usually gossip serves to protect the gossiper from strong feelings provoked by the other person. The therapist uses the no-gossiping principle to facilitate direct confrontation of the client's feelings.

Statements versus Questions. Rather than serving as helpful and supportive measures, questions frequently represent passivity, laziness, lack of personal involvement, manipulation, cajoling, and/or indirect advice giving. The therapist asks the client to change inappropriate questions into statements in order to personalize and optimize communication effectiveness.

Experiments. *Dialogue.* Individuals typically experience discordant polarization in their personality functioning at one time or another. These splits or dualisms include situations such as masculine versus feminine, aggressive versus passive, or commanding versus resisting. When the therapist detects the discordant poles in the experience of a client, one strategy to effect integrated functioning of the fragmented parts is to have the client engage the two disagreeing components in actual dialogue. The discordant parts confront and encounter each other until the two elements merge into a new, balanced realization. For example, the outcome of a dialogue between aggression and passivity is assertiveness. Two popular modes of dialogue are the use of two empty chairs or the two hands. One chair or hand can represent one pole, while the other chair or hand represents the opposing side. The client takes turns in speaking for the two sides of the polar conflict. The dialogue may be between two differing psychological attitudes or feelings, two parts of the body, or between the personality of the client and some significant other person who is in some type of unresolved conflict with the client.

Completing Unfinished Business. Clients bring unfinished business or unresolved feelings such as hurt, anger, guilt, or resentment to the therapy setting. When unfinished business surfaces in the therapy process, the client is asked to complete the task by living it out in the here and now. Role playing, psychodrama, pillow therapy (expressing attitudes and feelings regarding some other person by using a pillow or cushion as a substitute for the other person—verbal statements are addressed to the pillow and physical contact is made), and dialogue are some of the specific techniques used to resolve unresolved feelings.

Playing the Projection. Quite often what is understood by the client to be a perception is a projection. That is, a trait, attitude, feeling, or a mode of behavior that belongs to the client's personality is attributed to another person and then experienced as directed toward the client by the other person. Whenever clients express a projection disguised as a perception, they are encouraged to play the role of the personification involved in the projection to discover their own conflict in this area. For example, a client who says to the counselor, "You don't really care about me," may be asked to play the role of a noncaring person. Following the role playing the client could be asked to determine whether this is a disowned trait that he or she possesses.

Reversals. The reversal technique is used to help the client realize that manifest behavior often represents the opposite of the underlying impulse. For example, the client who fears being rejected by other people might be asked to play the role of a hermit or a recluse who does not care about other people and how others perceive and accept him or her.

Exaggeration. When clients make a significant gesture or statement in a casual, feeble, or underdeveloped manner, indicating a lack of awareness of its importance, they are invited to repeat it again and again with amplified movement, loudness, and/or emphasis. This facilitates the client's achieving better contact with self and putting more of himself or herself into integrated communication and experiencing.

May I Feed You a Sentence? Clients frequently will present significant messages that are implied but might not be in their full awareness. The therapist proposes a sentence for the client to try for size and fit and to amplify if desirable. Although interpretation is present, the primary objective is to enable the client to experience more of self through active participation. A spontaneous development of the sentence should follow if the statement proves to be an accurately relevant one.

Stay with It. Sooner or later in the therapy process the client will hit on a feeling, mood, or state of mind that is unpleasant and will prefer to run from rather than encounter it. Instead of making it easy for the client to avoid the unpleasant situation, the therapist encourages him or her to stay with it. If the client is able to confront the painful moment, he or she will advance in the maturation process. Both healing and growing are bedfellows in human existence with pain and suffering.

Guided Fantasy. An excellent opportunity for clients to explore, clarify, and come to grips with feelings and themes in their life situations is provided by fantasy journeys. Clients may project themselves into numerous fantasy situations, such as becoming an acorn and going through all the developmental processes from being planted to growing into a mature tree, or hiking in the mountains to visit a wise old man in a cabin who has the gifts and insights into life to share with his visitors. Rather than being mere fantasies, these experiences become genuine expressions of an individual's existence, what he or she is really concerned about or values. The fantasy trip is best done with the eyes closed while the client is deeply relaxed. The fantasy journey can be guided either by the therapist or by clients themselves after some basic instructions regarding the procedure.

Dreamwork. Gestalt theory considers the dream to be an existential-phenomenological self-revelation of the person. In a real sense the individual is his or her dream. But from another perspective, every image in a dream represents an alienated, disowned, discordant, and projected part of the self of the dreamer. Therefore, as Fritz Perls has observed, the dream is the "royal road to awareness and integration."

In Gestalt dreamwork an experiential rather than an analytical approach is followed. Clients first tell their dream and then play the part of the various images, be they persons, animals, or objects. By reexperiencing and enacting the dream in the present tense from the vantage point of each image, the client can begin to reclaim and integrate the alienated parts of the personality. Interpretation of the dream is left to the client. The therapist assists by suggesting the order in which the images are played, usually from the less to the more vivid ones, helping the client deal with avoidance and resistance in playing the disowned parts of self; and suggesting when the client might relate the images and feelings of the dream to his or her current situation. Dialogue and other techniques can be used in dreamwork to facilitate the integration of the discordant elements of the personality revealed in the dream.

Additional Readings

Fagan, J., & Shepherd, I. L. (Eds.). (1970). *Gestalt therapy now*. Palo Alto, CA: Science and Behavior Books.

Passons, W. R. (1975). *Gestalt approaches in counseling*. New York: Holt, Rinehart, & Winston.

Zinker, J. (1977). *Creative process in Gestalt therapy*. New York: Brunner/Mazel.

D. Smith

Gestalt Therapy. Developed by Fritz Perls in the 1940s, Gestalt therapy has rapidly evolved into an important and popular form of treatment. It attracts many because it represents a genuine alternative to more traditional insight-oriented approaches.

The major goal in Gestalt therapy is to teach the client to be more aware of what is happening both within and without. Perls thought that problems develop because people fail to maintain this awareness. Therapy attempts to restore awareness by focusing primarily on the here and now and by avoiding the twin traps of what Perls referred to as "obsessive remembering of the past" and "anxious anticipation of the future."

Theoretical Roots. Generally viewed as an existential-humanistic form of therapy, the approach has come to be considered a mainstream within humanistic psychology. Its roots reach beyond this orientation, however, and include three major systems: psychoanalytic psychology, Gestalt psychology, and existentialism.

Perls's training and early practice was as a psychoanalyst, and this system exercised considerable influence on his subsequent development. Though psychoanalytic roots are clearer in his early writings, they continue to show in his use of such concepts as superego, repression, introjection, and projection. While he believed he had completely abandoned his psychoanalytic heritage, classifying Gestalt therapy as an existential therapy, some still classify it as a form of psychoanalytic therapy.

As for the influence of Gestalt psychology, Perls initially intended to use the basic concepts of this movement as a foundation for a comprehensive system of personality, psychopathology, and psychotherapy (Perls, Hefferline, & Goodman, 1951). This ambitious goal went largely unfulfilled. He did borrow some of the basic concepts (most notably that of the figure-ground relationship) and the essential spirit of the movement (the desire to understand behavior and experience without analytic dissection), but he failed to do more than marry these to the other major concepts borrowed from psychoanalytic psychology and existentialism.

The third and perhaps most important influence was the existential movement in philosophy and psychology. Gestalt therapy's stress on such concepts as the expansion of awareness, freedom, the immediacy of experience, and the here and now all demonstrate its close relation to existentialism. Nowhere is this more clear than in the so-called Gestalt prayer:

"I do my thing and you do your thing. I am not in this world to live up to your expectations and you are not in this world to live up to mine. You are you and I am I and if by chance we find each other, it's beautiful. If not, it can't be helped" (Perls, 1969, p. 4).

Basic Assumptions and Therapeutic Task. Proponents of Gestalt therapy begin with the humanistic assumption that individuals have within themselves all they need to achieve personal wholeness and live effectively. The essential ingredient missing from most people's lives is courage, the courage to become aware of their feelings and of the ways they characteristically avoid experiencing the present in its fullness.

Living fully in the present is most difficult. It demands choice and therefore responsibility. Human beings tend to avoid choice by limiting awareness and consequently limiting freedom. This results in anxiety and a suspension of personal growth.

The heart of the therapeutic task lies in increasing one's awareness. Gestalt therapy assumes that awareness mobilizes energy within persons and enables them to act. Until a person becomes aware that he is hungry, he does not seek food. The awareness of hunger leads naturally to action. Similarly, if a person is unaware of being angry, she takes no action. Awareness of anger makes action possible.

Acting on an awareness is described as finishing an experience. This produces a Gestalt, or a completed experience. Unfinished business results from failing to act on an important past awareness. These experiences generally involve unexpressed feelings of anger, pain, guilt, and other negative emotions. Because they remain unexpressed, they linger on, continuously pressing for expression. Increasing awareness in the present not only stops the accumulation of unfinished experiences but also allows the individual to act on those of the past that are the most pressing.

Gestalt therapy does not suggest, as some critics have alleged, that it is either possible or desirable to act on every awareness. Perls recognized that in any moment the individual is confronted with thousands of possibilities for awareness, only a small number of which can be followed by action. Selective awareness operates constantly.

Perls also recognized that action is sometimes inappropriate. Not every feeling of anger should be expressed, both to preserve social order and to achieve personal mental health. He assumed, however, that most people err on the side of too little awareness and consequently too little expression of feelings. He noted that we fail to be aware of those things within us that we wish were not there. Only after we become fully aware of them can they be changed.

This pursuit of heightened awareness requires the Gestalt therapist to function in an active manner, continuously calling attention to present experience. The therapist does this primarily through the use of *what* questions (e.g., What are you aware of now?) and *how* questions (e.g., How do you experience your fear?). Therapists never employ *why* questions because they lead to rationalizations and intellectual rumination.

The goal is neither analysis nor understanding; it is integration. Lost parts of self are found when channels of awareness are reopened. Perls's dictum, "lose your mind and come to your senses," captures well this sensory focus of Gestalt therapy. He believed clients must once again learn to use their senses fully if they are to grow.

Related to this is the emphasis on action rather than mere talk. Therapy techniques often require the behavioral involvement of the client. Sometimes the client will reenact an important past situation during which he failed to take the necessary action (e.g., crying at a parent's funeral). Other times she may portray a dream or fantasy in a role play. This emphasis on action is reflected in the designation of many therapy techniques as games. The most common of these include the game of dialogue, the rehearsal game, and the exaggeration game.

Gestalt therapy usually follows a group format. The therapist customarily works with one group member at a time, with individuals volunteering to take the "hot seat" and work on some issue. In the pure form of Gestalt therapy spontaneous interaction among group members is minimal. Members observe the therapist's work with one member and contribute only after completion of the therapeutic work. Other styles of Gestalt groups allow more spontaneous interaction. While the group has emerged as a favored medium and probably represents Gestalt's most potent context, individual therapy is also appropriate and commonly practiced.

Evaluation. Because of the paucity of research on Gestalt therapy, gauging its overall effectiveness is difficult. The few studies that have been done have been generally encouraging. Foulds and Hannigan (1976) have shown Gestalt therapy to be effective in decreasing introversion and neuroticism; Nichols and Fine (1980), in increasing self-concept. These and most other existing studies, however, are therapy analogues conducted with student experimental subjects rather than clients seeking help.

Because Gestalt therapy has most frequently been applied to individuals who function relatively normally, little is known about its usefulness with more typical clinical populations. Most Gestalt therapists seem to agree with Shepherd that it is "most effective with overly socialized, restrained, constricted individuals—often described as neurotic, phobic, perfectionistic, ineffective, depressed, etc.—whose functioning is limited or inconsistent, primarily due to their internal restrictions" (1970, p. 235). She cautions against its use with psychotic or more severely disturbed individuals, and this caution seems sensible in the light of the degree of frustration and confrontation normally inherent in Gestalt therapy.

The most common criticism of Gestalt therapy is that it lacks a theoretical foundation. Initially Perls set out to develop an overall theory of personality, both normal and abnormal. He soon abandoned this pursuit, however, asserting that theoretical speculation interfered with creative clinical work. The theory that was developed consists of little more than a few hypotheses about psychopathology attached to one concept of normal personality development—the concept of awareness. The absence of a unifying theory reduces Gestalt therapy to an assorted collection of techniques with an overall philosophy of life. This theoretical deficiency constitutes a major weakness.

Related to this is the system's anti-intellectual bias. The mistrust of thinking, together with the consequent deemphasis on the cognitive factors in the therapy process, confines the therapist. It also conflicts with the biblical view that a person's thinking is an expression of one's heart or core (Prov. 23:7). Christian theology has historically understood rationality as one aspect of the image of God in which humankind was created. This suggests that a therapy system ought to take seriously the cognitive aspects of human functioning.

The biblical view of persons also stands in contrast to the strikingly independent person depicted as the healthy ideal of Gestalt therapy. The philosophy that "I do my thing and you do your thing" reflects an inadequate notion of our interdependence on each other. At least as described by Perls, Gestalt therapy denies our responsibility to others, and this fails to square with the Christian understanding of human relatedness to others and to God. The emphasis on personal responsibility and the refusal to accept helplessness as an excuse for not changing do reflect the Christian understanding of human nature. The emphasis on one's responsibility for oneself must also be joined, however, by an emphasis on responsibility to others.

References

Foulds, M. L., & Hannigan, P. S. (1976). A Gestalt marathon workshop: Effects on extraversion and neuroticism. *Journal of College Student Personnel, 17* (1), 50–54.

Nichols, R. C., & Fine, H. J. (1980). Gestalt therapy: Some aspects of self support, independence and responsibility. *Psychotherapy: Theory, Research and Practice, 17* (2), 124–135.

Perls, F. (1969). *Gestalt therapy verbatim.* Lafayette, CA: Real People.

Perls, F., Hefferline, R. F., & Goodman, P. (1951). *Gestalt therapy: Excitement and growth in human personality.* New York: Julian.

Shepherd, I. L. (1970). Limitations and cautions in the Gestalt approach. In J. Fagan & I. L. Shepherd (Eds.), *Gestalt therapy now.* Palo Alto, CA: Science and Behavior.

Additional Readings

Hatcher, C., & Himelstein, P. (Eds.). (1976). *The handbook of Gestalt therapy.* New York: Aronson.

Perls, F. (1969). *In and out of the garbage pail.* Lafayette, CA: Real People.

Polster, E., & Polster, M. (1973). *Gestalt therapy integrated.* New York: Brunner/Mazel.

D. G. Benner

See Gestalt Techniques.

Gifted Children. The term *gifted* is used to describe children who have exceptionally high intelligence quotients (IQs); children who display unusual abilities in artistic, creative, physical, or niche areas; and children who are outstanding in both dimensions. Using the Wechsler or Stanford-Binet intelligence tests, children who score 130 or above—about 2% to 3% of the population—are labeled gifted.

However, because children with special gifts do not always achieve this IQ score, other assessment measures are also used to identify a broader range of special talents. Gifted children may score a year or more above their age or grade level on tests of academic achievement in language arts or math. Children with exceptional creativity may be identified by behavioral checklists evaluating innovative problem-solving skills, initiative in developing concepts, and even boredom with school routine. Children with outstanding musical, artistic, or physical competencies can be identified by teachers, tutors, or coaches. Children with unusual niche-fitting skills are often found through special activities in which they show gifted abilities in diverse areas such as leadership, computers, or practical mechanics. This broadened definition of giftedness emphasizes the contributions of both genetic inheritance of competencies and environmental influences of identifying, developing, and training these inherited potentials. Casting a broad net allows gifted children who are hard to identify—those with fewer environmental advantages, with physical handicaps, with cultural differences, or with underachieving barriers—to achieve their God-given potential.

It remains true that intellectual assessment through IQ and achievement tests provides more standardized results and more reliable prediction of success in educational endeavors. The question of appropriate schooling for gifted children is always under debate. Educators with a philosophy of heterogeneity maintain that keeping gifted children in classes with children of all other ability levels benefits both groups of children; this approach appeals to democratic as well as economic concerns in some school districts. Other educators argue the necessity of a separate school program with classes of only gifted children; curriculum can then be consistently ahead of grade level and there is freedom for the whole class to do challenging special projects to draw out creativity often associated with giftedness. In many cases gifted children are moved up to the next grade level with good academic results, but many parents raise concerns about age differences in psychosocial and physical development. In between the extremes, various enrichment programs seek to help gifted children reach their potential while still attending classes with peers of the same age and different abilities.

Teachers of identified gifted children describe their students as intellectually curious, lively in generating ideas and questions in discussion classes, exercising initiative to learn, and unusually self-motivated in areas of gift. Gifted children with supportive learning environments may be recognized in various areas of talent by their large oral and written vocabulary; ability to perceive and organize visual/spatial relationships; broad range of information and ability to store and recall the data quickly; capacity to generalize, conceptualize, and deduce; intensity of concentration; elaborate and clever responses; and persistence of effort.

Research in giftedness addresses questions of cognition and culture. There are four approaches to the study of how humans learn. The stimulus-response approach emphasizes learning by rote association. The widely utilized Piagetian approach stresses stages of biological and cognitive development, from the infant's simple taking in data by the senses to the teen's or adult's highest order abstract and theoretical reasoning capability. The psychometric approaches seek to quantify and measure intelligence from two theoretical views: tests of general intelligence—Charles Edward Spearman's "g," a general mental energy or unitary underlying ability thought to exist in gifted persons; or tests of specific intelligence—multifactoral domains of ability, interconnected but distinct, such as spatial or comprehension abilities. The information processing approach seeks to understand the actual cognitive workings of the brain. Other theorists argue more attention should be paid to the outcomes of giftedness: do individuals apply their abilities not only to help solve social problems but also to identify significant new problems needing solutions? Giftedness, some theorists argue, must include development at the highest moral as well as intellectual levels. The values of the culture influence definitions of giftedness, these theoreticians maintain, and some children are thus not identified and given opportunities. Acknowledging the need for multiple tests of giftedness, proponents of intelligence testing still maintain considerable research shows no systematic or significant bias in IQ measurements and that IQ tests provide a fair and useful measure for identifying gifted individuals.

Additional Readings

Horowitz, F. D., & O'Brien, M. (Eds.). (1985). *The gifted and talented: Developmental perspectives.* Washington, DC: American Psychological Association.

Sattler, J. M. (1992). *Assessment of children* (3rd ed.). San Diego, CA: Jerome M. Sattler, Publisher.

K. M. Lattea

See Creativity; Intelligence; Intellectual Assessment.

Glossolalia. An unintelligible conglomeration of sounds that simulates normal speech in that the utterances contain distinctions of words, sentences, and even paragraphs. It is most often seen in states of religious ecstasy, although it sometimes is also present in schizophrenic speech.

See Ecstatic Religious Experiences.

Gluttony. During recorded history, church officials attempted on several occasions to develop a taxonomy of sins to classify human evils. The most notable one was developed by Pope Gregory the Great in the sixth century. Pope Gregory asserted that all sins can be categorized into the perfect taxonomy. These came to be known as the seven deadly sins and stood in prominent stead in moral theology. The seven include pride, anger, envy, impurity, gluttony, slothfulness, and avarice (Graham, 1955). Gluttony as insatiable desire produces an unbalanced pattern of living; it defiles the body as the temple of the Holy Spirit with excess consumption.

The central concept is the overindulgence of human appetites for the sake of immediate pleasures. The excessive appetites involve a cult of comfort that manifests a philosophy of materialism in explicitly physical form. Gluttony is overindulgent gratification and uncontrollable addiction. Even the phrases "glutton for punishment" and "glutton for work" acknowledge an unhealthy and destructive pattern of extreme and excess. In all this there is no self-restraint in engorgement. Lyman (1989, p. 212) captured the essential definition: "Gluttony, thus, is excessive and greedy absorption in the immediate appetitive pleasures of the self."

While the behaviors that Pope Gregory and other church leaders noted as gluttonous still present themselves in contemporary culture, the language used to describe them has taken on less onerous phrases. Instead of labeling them as sin, less offensive and more politically correct phraseology notes them as errors, negative actions, or diverse patterns of consumption. Menninger (1973) lamented the disuse of "sin" terminology and noted that the deadly sins became crimes. Gluttony is often portrayed as a victimless crime in that excesses of food and drink, apart from driving while intoxicated, hurt no one except the one who consumes. Little attention is directed toward the social, economic, and health care costs of gluttony. Social scientists rarely recognize gluttony as a social problem, acknowledging it is at worst a private sin.

The classical formulations lay substantial involvement of volition in the deadly sins. Volition as an important consideration has been removed from most contemporary analyses of psychiatric disorders and maladaptive behavior patterns. The *DSM-IV* (American Psychiatric Association, 1994) presents no major classification codes paralleling gluttony. The binge and purge symptoms of bulimia are held to be uncontrollable. Binge eating outside bulimia is relegated to an appendix in *DSM-IV*.

References

American Psychiatric Association (1994). *Diagnostic and statistical manual of mental disorders* (4th ed.). Washington, DC: Author.

Graham, W. F. (1955). *The seven deadly sins.* Grand Rapids, MI: Zondervan.

Lyman, S. M. (1989.) *The seven deadly sins: Society and evil* (Rev. ed.). Dix Hills, NY: General Hall.

Menninger, K. (1973). *Whatever became of sin?* New York: Bantam.

R. L. Timpe

See Obesity.

God, Concept of. The term *God concept* generally refers to an individual's private or personal view of God. The terms *God image* and *God representation* are also used in connection with the term *God concept.* Many authors follow Rizzuto (1979) in using the terms *God image* and *God representation* to refer to unconscious and preconscious experiential views of God and *God concept* to refer to more conscious, intellectual views of God. It should be noted, however, that many authors use these terms interchangeably. The term *God concept* will be used broadly throughout this article for the sake of consistency. The preceding distinction, however, points to the fact that regardless of the term used, there are multiple layers to the God concept, including the unconscious, preconscious, and conscious layers.

The unconscious and preconscious layers are generally viewed as more emotionally laden representations of God. These layers of the God concept refer to a person's experiential God and are formed from many factors. Tozer (1961) articulated these layers of the God concept well when he stated, "Our real idea of God may lie buried under the rubbish of conventional religious notions and may require an intelligent and vigorous search before it is finally unearthed and exposed for what it is. Only after an ordeal of painful self-probing are we likely to discover what we actually believe about God" (p. 2). In contrast, the conscious layer of the God concept generally refers to a more intellectual view of God based on a person's theological understanding and religious tradition.

Sigmund Freud initiated much of the theoretical discussion on the God concept. He was concerned with explaining the emergence of the idea of God from a purely psychological perspective. He theorized that people's ideas of God are formed from an internal representation of an exalted father created as a defense against their helplessness and mortality. Although Freud's motivation for studying this area was his atheism, some of his observations on the God concept have proven to be essentially accurate and have led to further fruitful exploration.

Many other authors began theorizing about and researching different aspects of the God concept from a variety of theoretical perspectives as far back as 1892. However, Rizzuto (1979) was the first to develop a comprehensive theory of the God concept. She did this by building on Freud's work and using object relations theory as a framework from which to consider the notion of God concept. Three major areas of the God concept are reviewed, followed by a brief summary of the research on God concept.

First, what is a God concept? According to Rizzuto, the experiential God concept is a particular type of object representation. An object representation refers to a relatively enduring schema or image of another person based on an organization of all experiences in relation to that person. The relationship with another person is psychologically taken in, or internalized, and becomes a permanent though malleable part of the psyche. Each God representation is connected to a particular sense of self by associated emotions at any given time. The experiential God concept is a relatively enduring organization or cognitive schema of God bound to a particular sense of self by feelings that were experienced in relation to him.

The experiential God concept as such functions as a type of template that determines to some extent one's feelings, beliefs, expectations, wishes, and fears in relationship with God. It is important to note that the experiential God concept is not a precise replica of actual experiences with God because it is initially formed at a very young age when cognitive abilities are limited. Rather, it is a mixture of actual experiences and perceptions of God and is also formed out of representations of parents and other significant figures.

Second, how is the God concept formed? The God concept is a representation of God based on experiences of relating to him. From a Christian perspective, relational experiences with God are clearly part of the process of how the God concept is formed, although little theorizing or research has addressed this aspect of God concept formation. There are two other basic sources from which the God representation is formed, according to Rizzuto. The first is the child's representations of emotionally significant authority figures such as parents or grandparents. The child's early interpersonal experiences with parents and other significant figures is half of the "stuff" from which the God concept is formed. For example, if one's parents are experienced as accepting and emotionally available, an aspect of the God concept will likewise be accepting and emotionally available. The other half of the "stuff" of which the God concept is made is the child's capacity to "create" a God according to his or her psychological needs. Thus individuals' experiential God concepts tend to be similar to their experiences of relationships with their parents and other emotionally significant figures, although they are also integrated with psychological needs.

Although Rizzuto examined predominantly unconscious and preconscious layers of the God concept, there is a conscious layer of the God concept that is based more on an intellectual view of God. This aspect of the God concept is formed from rational thought processes and is based on one's theological sensitivity and religious tradition. Although this is an important aspect of God concept, some authors argue that it does not contribute to the experiential God concept and thus plays a minimal role in one's relationship with God at an experiential level.

Third, what psychic functions does the God concept serve? The God concept is always available for further acceptance or further rejection, depending on the psychological needs of the individual (Rizzuto, 1979). It is always there to be loved, hated, feared, idealized, or whatever else is needed by a person at a particular time. The God concept serves the psychological function of protecting a minimum amount of relatedness with emotionally significant people while simultaneously balancing this with a minimally tolerable and stable sense of self. For example, if parents are experienced as emotionally unavailable, a child will "create" an aspect of his or her God concept to be attentive, involved, and emotionally available. In order to maintain its psychological usefulness, the God concept must be continuously reelaborated and reworked throughout development. This process follows developmental laws as well as dynamic laws such as defense mechanisms, adaptation, synthesis, and the need for meaningful relationships with oneself and others.

Research on God concept can be grouped into five major categories: developmental, God concept and parental images, self-esteem, interpersonal relations, and psychopathology. Although an exhaustive discussion is beyond the scope of this article, a brief summary of each area is offered.

The developmental research on God concept suggests that the development of the God concept corresponds to Jean Piaget's cognitive developmental stages. Several studies have found that as children move from concrete operational thinking to formal operational thinking, their concepts of God tend to shift from a more concrete, objective, and anthropomorphic one to a more abstract, subjective concept of God as Spirit (Babin, 1965; Baker & Koppe, 1959). The research regarding God concept and parental images generally indicates that representations of both father and mother are important in the formation of the God concept. When one parent is preferred or idealized, however, that parental image tends to be more important in the formation of the God concept. Regarding God concept and self-esteem, the literature generally points to a positive relationship between self-esteem and a loving God concept. Research on interpersonal relations suggests that the experience of God as close and loving is related to interpersonal styles that demonstrate empathy, influence others, include others in activities, make decisions independently, and demonstrate affection and acceptance toward others (Edwards, Goldberg, Hargrove, & Linamen, 1979). Finally, psychopathology appears to be inversely related to a positive concept of God as close, loving, and kind (see Brokaw & Edwards, 1994, for a more thorough review of the research).

References

Babin, P. (1965). The idea of God: Its evolution between the ages of 11 and 19. In A. Godin (Ed.), *From religious experience to religious attitude*. Chicago: Loyola University Press.

Baker, W. G., & Koppe, W. A. (1959). *Children's religious concepts*. Schenectady, NY: Union College Character Research Report.

Brokaw, B. F., & Edwards, K. J. (1994). The relationship of God image to level of object relations development. *Journal of Psychology and Theology, 22* (4), 352–371.

Edwards, K., Goldberg, G., Hargrove, J., & Linamen, C. (1979). *Religious experience as a function of self-concept and interpersonal behavior*. Unpublished manuscript, Rosemead School of Psychology, Biola University, La Mirada, CA.

Rizzuto, A. M. (1979). *The birth of the living God*. Chicago: University of Chicago Press.

Tozer, A. W. (1961). *The knowledge of the holy*. San Francisco: Harper & Row.

T. W. Hall

See Psychology of Religion; Religious Experience; Religious Orientation.

Godin, André (1915–1997). Born in Gembloux, Belgium, Godin joined the Society of Jesus in 1933 and was ordained to the priesthood in 1946. In 1942 he earned his Ph.D. (with an emphasis on criminology) from the University of Brussels, and in 1947 he was awarded the Licentiate in Sacred Theology at the University of Louvain. From 1948 to 1954 Godin taught psychology at the Gregorian University in Rome. He earned an M.A. in experimental psychology from Fordham University in 1951. Godin returned to Brussels in 1955, taking positions at the Higher Institute for the Training of Counseling Psychologists and the International Center for Religious Education. He completed postdoctoral studies at the Centre de Consultations Médico-psychologiques in Brussels and in 1957 joined the Belgian Psychoanalytic Association. He was assistant editor of *Lumen Vitae* from 1961 to 1975 and edited the series *Studies in Religious Psychology* (1957–1972). In 1960 he became secretary of the International Commission for the Scientific Study of Religion.

Godin's writing has covered the topics of religious development, religion and personality, pastoral psychology, and psychological factors in religious education. His special interests include psychology of religion, psychotherapy, psychoanalysis, and group dynamics in pastoral psychology. Godin organized the first international conference of Jesuit psychologists in 1951, and in 1966 he was the first Roman Catholic honored by the journal *Pastoral Psychology* as a "Man of the Month" (Bier, 1966, p. 66). In 1979 he was presented the William James Award, for conceptual and theoretical contributions to the psychology of religion, by Division 36 (Psychologists Interested in Religious Issues) of the American Psychological Association.

Reference

Bier, W. C. (1966, April). The man of the month: André Godin, S.J. *Pastoral Psychology, 17* (4), 4, 66.

Additional Readings

Godin, A. (Ed.). (1959). *Research in religious psychology: Speculative and positive*. Brussels: Lumen Vitae.

Godin, A. (Ed.). (1961). *Child and adult before God*. Chicago: Loyola University Press.

Godin, A. (1961). Studies in religious psychology. *Lumen Vitae, 16*, 187–388.

Godin, A. (1965). *The pastor as counselor* (B. Phillips, Trans.). New York: Holt, Rinehart, & Winston.

Godin, A. (Ed.). (1965). *From religious experience to a religious attitude*. Chicago: Loyola University Press. (Original work published 1964)

Godin, A. (Ed.). (1968). *From cry to word: Contributions toward a psychology of prayer*. Brussels: Lumen Vitae.

Godin, A. (Ed.). (1972). *Death and presence: The psychology of death and the after-life*. Brussels: Lumen Vitae.

Godin, A. (1985). *The psychological dynamics of religious experience* (M. Turton, Trans.). Birmingham, AL: Religious Education.

H. Vande Kemp

Goldstein, Kurt (1878–1965). Originator of organismic theory. Born in Kattowitz, Germany, he received his M.D. degree at the University of Breslau in 1903. In 1933 he came to the United States, where he held academic and clinical positions in a variety of institutions in addition to maintaining a private neuropsychiatry and psychotherapy practice in New York City for many years. Goldstein's work on brain-injured soldiers during the First World War made him famous and enabled him to develop much of his organismic theory.

Organismic theory emphasizes the unity, integration, and consistency of the normal personality. The organism (person) is viewed as an organized system. The person behaves as a unified whole and not as a series of differentiated parts. Rather than being motivated by a number of drives, the individual is motivated by the one sovereign drive of self-actualization. The inherent potentialities of the organism for growth is a prominent point in Goldstein's theorizing. Intense study of the individual rather than group studies accounted for many of his views.

Goldstein's major works were *The Organism* (1939), *Human Nature in the Light of Psychopathology* (1940), *After-effects of Brain Injuries in War*

(1942), and *Language and Language Disturbances* (1948).

S. N. BALLARD

See ORGANISMIC THEORY.

Gonorrhea. *See* SEXUALLY TRANSMITTED DISEASES.

Grace and Pastoral Care. Grace is a theological term that refers to the disposition of God toward humankind. According to both the Old and New Testaments, this disposition is one of unconditional goodwill despite human failure, radical acceptance despite human alienation, and universal reconciliation despite human indifference (Ellens, 1982; see Mic. 7:18–20, Luke 15:11–32). It is a translation of the Greek word *charis* and is used in Christian circles to point to God's loving and undeserved favor toward sinful persons. In the New Testament, especially in Paul's epistles, grace is a way of life that stands over against any human endeavor to win or to earn God's mercy. Moreover, Paul asserts that ultimately nothing can obstruct that grace to humans (Rom. 8) or subvert God's reconciling intervention on our behalf (1 Cor. 15:20–28). In the end, every eye shall see God (Rev. 1:7), every knee shall bow to God, and every tongue shall confess God, to the glory of God (Rom. 14:11; Phil. 2:10–11).

Roman Catholicism tends to see grace as an infused power that enables the person to live a more sanctified, God-pleasing life. In other words, it emphasizes the sanctifying effect of grace. Protestantism tends to see grace in relational terms, emphasizing God's initiative in healing the breach between the divine and the human. It emphasizes the justifying effect of grace. Reinhold Niebuhr shows us that we must consider both perspectives when he sees grace as pardon and as power. In either case it is considered a gift from God and not a quality or virtue that belongs to human beings (see Moffat, 1984; Parker, 1960; Smith, 1984; Williams, 1984).

For Christians, God's grace is manifested primarily in and through Jesus Christ. Christ's life, specifically his birth, death, and resurrection, is a preeminent expression of God's grace and the primary means by which it is made real and concrete. The believer grasps this grace by faith in Christ. Faith in this sense is a fruit of God's initiative, since it is not possible for one who does not believe to begin to believe without God's help. God's initiative here is sometimes called prevenient grace.

Protestant pastoral care and counseling have been more or less attentive to the operation of grace. In the 1960s, when Carl Rogers was a normative influence on pastoral counseling, his concept of unconditional positive regard was interpreted as a correlate of, if not a substitute expression for, divine grace. Unconditional positive regard means that the therapist is to accept the client unconditionally, that the therapist is "to prize and hold in valued esteem the other person as a unique and significant human being, above and beyond any external evaluations which one might place on his (or her) specific experiences" (Aden, 1969). While this therapeutic stance has some affinity with the theological concept of grace, it may reflect an excessively optimistic evaluation of human goodness that is in tension with the anthropological assumptions undergirding the biblical notion of human need for divine grace. Scripture makes it clear that divine grace is given in spite of the recipient's unacceptability, not because of his or her assumed goodness. In the practice of therapy, a reality like grace can be experienced by the client, whether or not the therapist's conceptual system articulates it. In fact, any genuine acceptance of the client is an instance of grace. In this regard Rogers's notion is not excessively optimistic. Such instances of grace witness to a structure of acceptance that transcends the concrete relationship in which it is enfleshed by the therapist for the client and points to the ultimate source of grace, namely, God (*see* Counseling and Psychotherapy: Theological Themes).

If grace becomes a basic assumption of pastoral care, it brings about several fundamental changes in the caring process. First, it means that clients are free from the need to prove their own worth or acceptability. Many clients come into therapy with feelings of guilt or with low self-esteem. They are caught in a feverish, though largely unconscious, attempt to make themselves acceptable. They may actually spend a good part of therapy trying to find out how to become more acceptable. Grace as the declaration of acceptance in spite of unacceptableness frees individuals from this endeavor (*see* Counseling and Psychotherapy: Theological Themes). It enables them to accept themselves as they are, basing their self-esteem not on what they accomplish but on what they receive. God's love and the certification implied in his unconditional acceptance of them in spite of themselves becomes the source of their self-respect and self-confidence. They are freed to see themselves as God's persons, God's co-laborers in this world, God's compatriots in building God's kingdom in the earth, God's companions in worship and work (*see* Work and Play). They are freed to see that this status holds in spite of themselves, just because God declares them to be his people. This status is rooted and grounded in the quality of God's character of love and faithfulness and not in the quality of the human person's character or behavior.

Second, if grace is basic to pastoral care it means that an increase of faith and not an endless analysis of the self is the final concern of pastoral care. Increase in faith means increased ability to cast one's self unreservedly into the arms of God's grace: to unconditionally accept God's unconditional acceptance of us. This is not to dismiss the importance of self-analysis, but it helps to put it in proper perspective. Self-analysis increases the accuracy and depth of self-knowledge and thereby releases the individual from self-inflicted repressions, but it does not remove certain stubborn givens, like finitude, infirmities, and death. It reframes and reinterprets them, giving them new and growth-inducing meaning. The individual is helped to live with these realities and to affirm life in spite of them; indeed, to celebrate their role in the whole spiritual pilgrimage. Faith in a loving and forgiving God can give a person necessary hope and courage. It can help that person to live with the assurance that there is a gracious person of power beyond the hazards of life.

Grace is not a single component of pastoral care but the heart of the pastoral relationship. It is the source of the church's pastoral caring. It is the endpoint of the church's pastoral endeavors. It is God's gracious disposition toward humankind made manifest in a relationship between the one who cares and the one for whom care is given.

References

Aden, L. (1969). Rogerian therapy and optimal pastoral counseling. In W. B. Oglesby, Jr. (Ed.), *The new shape of pastoral theology*. New York: Abingdon.

Ellens, J. H. (1982). *God's grace and human health*. Nashville, TN: Abingdon.

Moffat, J. (1984). Grace in the New Testament. In W. A. Elwell (Ed.), *The evangelical dictionary of theology*. Grand Rapids, MI: Baker.

Parker, T. H. L. (1960). Grace. In E. F. Harrison (Ed.), *Baker's dictionary of theology*. Grand Rapids, MI: Baker.

Smith, C. R. (1984). The biblical doctrine of grace. In W. A. Elwell (Ed.), *The evangelical dictionary of theology*. Grand Rapids, MI: Baker.

Williams, M. P. (1984). The grace of God. In W. A. Elwell (Ed.), *The evangelical dictionary of theology*. Grand Rapids, MI: Baker.

L. ADEN AND J. H. ELLENS

See PASTORAL CARE; SPIRITUAL AND RELIGIOUS ISSUES IN PSYCHOTHERAPY; RELIGIOUS RESOURCES.

Graphology. The study of handwriting as an expression of the writer's character and personality, also known as the psychology of handwriting.

The primitive interpretation of handwriting dates back to the second century, with the first real systematic approach linked to an Italian doctor, C. Baldi, in 1622. The term *graphology* was first coined in the 1800s by the French priest Jean-Hippolyte Michon. Early theories of graphology were based on an intuitive approach to dissecting and interpreting individual pieces of writing, such as the location of letters, size of loops, connections between letters, size, consistency, and other minute differences. These variables were then correlated with specific character traits or states of emotion, such as frustration, anger, insecurity, and joy. A chemist, L. Klages (1872–1956), was influential in broadening the base to look not just at individual parts of writing but at the whole, which he called form level. He also recognized the

limitations and cautions involved in handwriting analysis and viewed the procedure with more balance than many of its most ardent advocates.

Although many psychologists would be prepared to accept the general assumption that one's handwriting probably contains a good deal of information about one's personality, few view graphology as a serious clinical tool. The reason for this has been the inability to discover a valid method of analyzing handwriting. Although numerous systems have been proposed, none has yet been validated. It should be noted that the general pessimism of psychologists in the United States regarding the usefulness of graphology has not been shared by Europeans, who accept it more commonly and use it rather widely in personnel selection.

D. L. SCHUURMAN

See PERSONALITY ASSESSMENT.

Gratitude. In his research on the stress syndrome, Selye (1976) found that physical and emotional stress is reduced most effectively not by success, pleasure, or even love; stress is best reduced when we feel grateful. To be truly grateful is to have a heartfelt awareness that something good has happened to us and that we genuinely appreciate it (Rottschafer, 1992). Feelings of gratitude may be quietly held within or expressed in ways ranging from perfunctory acknowledgment to ecstatic celebration.

True gratitude calms the mind and body for several reasons. First, gratitude is an admission to ourselves that indeed we have received something. Our feelings confirm we have made contact with the object of our search and that some sense of fulfillment has occurred. We therefore feel more relaxed.

Second, genuine gratitude promotes happiness. When we are truly grateful we rejoice, and we do so spontaneously from our inner depths. The celebration relieves stress and makes us feel better because we let our guard down and deeply feel the relief or the joy for whatever has pleased us. Part of the happiness usually includes an awareness that we did not achieve our goals by pure chance but by the help of others or the guidance of God. We are even more joyous when we sense others care enough about us to help us. Gratitude confirms we are not alone in our efforts. Those who cannot genuinely say thank you are unwilling to accept the fact that someone has given to them.

A third benefit of gratitude is that it assures us that we are effective. When we celebrate our achievements we are admitting we had a direct hand in our own success. Exaggerated expressions of humility that disown any claim to personal excellence or diligent labor are unrealistic and rarely sound genuine. The fact that good fortune has come to us or that we were in the right place at the right time is insufficient reason to celebrate. However, we need to give ourselves credit for seizing the moment, for making something good happen from the opportunities fortuitously bestowed upon us. As we appreciate our victories we must appreciate also our own skill in obtaining them. This does not ignore being grateful to God for success but adds the affirmation of self that will encourage us to reciprocate to others.

References

Rottschafer, R. H. (1992). *The search for satisfaction.* Grand Rapids, MI: Baker.

Selye, H. (1976). *The stress of life.* New York: McGraw-Hill.

R. H. ROTTSCHAFER

See VIRTUE, CONCEPT OF.

Greed and Generosity. The most commonly used Hebrew word for greed, בֶּצַע (בָּאסֹהבָּאב), appears 23 times in 20 verses in the Old Testament. It is often translated "covetousness," "dishonest gain," "evil gain," "unjust gain," or "gain." Etymologically the word is claimed to have been a technical term used by weavers to designate the action of cutting a finished piece of cloth from the loom, thereby profiting (Harris, Archer, & Waltke, 1980). In the New Testament πλεονεξια occurs 10 times in 10 verses, twice in the Gospels. It is alternatively rendered "coveting," "covetousness," "avarice," and "insatiableness" while conveying the literal meaning "a desire to have more" (Bauer, Arndt, & Gingrich, 1979, p. 667).

The theorist who has the most to say about greed is Melanie Klein of the object relations school. She sees the development of greed occurring very early in the development of the child. According to this school, the child from earliest days experiences the world as good and bad. The child is busily about the business of taking in the good and bad objects. This taking in of the good and bad and the consequent manner of dealing with each becomes the foundation of personality formation.

According to the object relations school, the child is absolutely and completely dependent on others for its very survival. According to Klein, the infant becomes aware at a noncognitive level that what she or he desperately needs resides in an outside other, under the other's control. This is the basic anxiety of the infant, and its pathological development results in envy. For Klein, envy is an unavoidable process for the infant, the cornerstone of all personality development and later psychopathology. The infant envies the good other as well as the bad other, primarily because it is good and secondarily because it exists outside of the infant's control, and responds to this situation with aggression. Aggression is in the service of building up a store of good objects. When all goes well the infant's aggression is healthily developed and integrated into the personality structure.

However, when frustration thwarts the process of building up good objects, Anxiety increases and the infant becomes envious. In the face of these anxieties, the internalized good object becomes fragile and unstable. This, according to Klein, results in greed, a voracious appetite to take in the good objects so as to protect them from harm and to insure oneself a constant supply of good objects. "Greed aims at the possession of all the goodness that can be extracted from the object, regardless of consequences; this may result in the destruction of the object and the spoiling of its goodness" (Segal, 1974, p. 40). The possible destruction of the object reawakens anxieties, the very anxieties greed was employed to mitigate, which is responded to with redoubled greed. The result is a cycle of greed and anxiety that drives the infant to ever more aggressively seek and devour ever more good objects.

Analyzing the usage of words translated "generous" is a bit more difficult task. In the Old Testament the word is often linked to נָתַן (נבָאהבָאא, to give; more than two thousand occurrences) and is often rendered "give generously." Interestingly, נֶפֶשׁ בְּרָכָה הסבהֹפבן (הבאכבארבב) appears, although infrequently, to establish a link between generosity and blessing. In the New Testament a similar state of affairs exists. In Matthew 20:15 Jesus uses αγαθος (literally, good) to describe the actions of the generous landowner, and in 2 Corinthians 9:6 Paul uses ευλογια (good words) in a similar manner. In Acts 10:2 ελεημοσυνη (charitable giving) is used to describe Cornelius. Throughout the Bible generosity is seen as liberal giving without holding back. Generosity is the recognition that I will survive even in the face of unmet needs, that my heavenly Father looks after me even as he does the sparrows. Generosity recognizes that gathering more things can never fill the void that only God can fill. Generosity recognizes that doing goodness to others less fortunate is the way of the kingdom.

References

Bauer, W., Arndt, W., & Gingrich, F. W. (1979). *A Greek-English lexicon of the New Testament and other early Christian literature.* (2nd ed.). Chicago: University of Chicago Press.

Harris, R. L., Archer, G. L., & Waltke, B. K. (1980). *Theological wordbook of the Old Testament.* Chicago: Moody.

Segal, H. (1974). *Introduction to the work of Melanie Klein.* New York: Basic.

D. W. PETERS

See MONEY, PSYCHOLOGY OF.

Grief. The cognitive and emotional process of working through a significant loss. The removal of anyone or anything that has emotional value to an individual will precipitate a grief reaction.

Grieving is to the emotional system following a loss what healing is to the physical system after surgery. Just as an operation traumatizes the body, a loss jolts the emotional system, producing disruption and upheaval. While grieving is painful, it is to be viewed as a healthy response, for without it a complete emotional recovery is not possible.

The most salient symptom of grief is acute psychological pain. Emotional turmoil; wide fluctuations in mood; and feelings of hurt, guilt, depression, help-lessness, anger, sadness, love, rage, Loneliness, re-sentment, and hopelessness are commonly re-ported. A frequent perception of the normal grief-stricken individual is, "I'm losing my mind." This fear of disorganization threatens one's self-confidence and is perhaps the most debilitating aspect of grief.

Secondary symptoms may also emerge, though frequently their causes are wrongly attributed to factors other than loss. Eating, sleeping, and sexual disturbances, for example, may accompany grief. Somatic complaints—headaches, low energy level, ulcers, dizziness, colitis—may be present. The inevitable heightening of an individual's stress disturbs family relationships, which may become more distant or laden with conflict.

Stages of Grief. The notion that grief progresses in definable stages has gained wide popularity through the writings of Kübler-Ross (1969). On the basis of studies with dying patients she postulated five stages of grief: denial and isolation, anger, bargaining, depression, and acceptance. The survivor's grief, according to Kübler-Ross, generally parallels that of the dying patient.

While the vague outlines of stages can be seen in the experiences of many, grieving is hardly an orderly, sequential process. More typically it is chaotic, with feelings coming and disappearing only to reappear later. Some feelings are specific, others vague.

The course of grief varies considerably from person to person, depending on several factors. Cause of death, for example, will affect the survivor's reactions. A sudden, accidental death brings on an acute grief reaction, whereas a gradual demise through lingering illness allows for anticipatory grieving to occur.

Other factors that influence the course of grief include the individual's emotional stability, the social support system, age of the deceased person, and the degree to which he or she was at peace with self, God, and family. Because troubled relationships are more unfinished at the point of separation than positive ones, they are especially difficult to get over. Hence, contrary to popular opinion, loss of a good relationship is more easily grieved (with fewer complications) than a conflicted one.

Abnormal Grieving. Under normal circumstances grief is time limited. It is a self-limiting emotional process that runs its course and is completed after several months. Growing evidence suggests, however, that certain losses such as suicides are never completely resolved. While the survivor's pain might diminish over time, it is never completely eliminated as it normally is with other types of death.

Abnormal grief reactions may occur immediately following a loss, as in the case of the person who becomes psychotic and is totally unable to cope. The opposite extreme is to completely disown the pain and proceed with a business-as-usual attitude. Neither reaction is a healthy coping response.

Sometimes signs of abnormal grief are not evident until months after the loss. Enshrinement is a good example. This refers to the practice of leaving the deceased person's room and possessions untouched long after he or she is gone. Creation of a shrine becomes symbolic of the survivor's inability to let go of the loved one.

For others, abnormal grief is evidenced by persistent physical symptoms, angry withdrawal, intense loneliness, obsessing over the loved one, and lingering depression. If after 12 to 18 months following a loss grief continues to interfere with one's overall functioning, professional help is indicated.

Christians and Grief. The Christian's spiritual experience is not unaffected by grief, especially when a tragic loss is involved. Some will react defensively with an overdevotion to God and the church, to the neglect of all else. Others will accuse God of being distant and will eventually leave the church. None of these individuals effectively mobilizes faith resources in coping, because of a deep and unconscious anger toward God. So long as God-directed anger is unnamed, denied, and contained, spiritual paralysis is inevitable. In the healthy Christian response all the pain typical of grief is present, and anger at God is recognized, accepted, and appropriately released.

Because death is not an ultimate tragedy for Christians, their grief is without the sting experienced by those who have no hope. Yet this same belief can support an unhealthy denial of the real emotional pain brought on by the death of a loved one. Christian faith, with its emphasis on eternal life, in no way exempts one from the normal, human process of grieving.

Some Christians are in need of having their experience normalized by others who can give reassurance of the right to grieve. Those who feel pressure to be strong and a good and cheerful witness are especially in need of such support to prevent their grief and God-directed anger from being contained and allowed to fester inside. Biblical models like Job can be helpful in this regard.

The principal challenge for those dealing with loss is to release their grief. This involves respecting, specifying, and expressing painful thoughts and feelings associated with the loss. To get beyond grief one must go through it, not around it. Nor are there any painless shortcuts.

Good models for handling grief, a strong faith, an understanding of what is involved in mourning, and a caring support system can facilitate working through a difficult loss. Because grief is a social event, it cannot be resolved in isolation. Those who grieve must be willing to risk sharing their pain, and those who minister must be willing to risk the discomfort of being with the persons in their pain.

Reference

Kübler-Ross, E. (1969). *On death and dying.* New York: Macmillan.

J. A. LARSEN

See GRIEF THERAPY; LOSS AND SEPARATION; DEATH AND DYING.

Grief Therapy. A specialized type of treatment for bereaved individuals who experience significant loss and separation. Different types of losses cause different grief reactions and therefore require certain types of interventions. Losses can be major or minor, personal or material, tangible or symbolic, gradual or sudden. Dealing with normal grief reactions over a minor loss is usually less intense than dealing with grief over a major and significant loss.

Counseling with people who suffer multiple losses is rather delicate and demanding, yet, at the same time rewarding. Frequently, the survivor exhibits symptoms of anxiety and depression and is unable to move beyond the initial stage of shock and disbelief. The bereaved person becomes deeply affected and unable to completely resume normal functioning, although he or she tries to outwardly maintain a natural profile. Other intense emotions may be constantly present underneath like profound emptiness, self-blame and guilt, deep sorrow and sadness, poor concentration, high irritation, strong desire to be alone, unexpected anger, soul aching, and consuming fears.

Grief typically comes in waves, engulfing the whole personality and overwhelming the entire mind. After a tragic or sudden loss, the survivors basically refuse to accept what happened and how it happened. They utilize strong defenses and coping strategies and therefore remain unaware of their unfinished grief. Others may enter into unending mental bargaining hoping to change the painful reality of loss and restore the missed person, object, function, or dream.

Some theorists conceptualize the grieving process as moving into "stages" or "phases." Other grief specialists suggest terms like "tasks," "procedures," "mediators," or "steps" of mourning the bereaved must take and work through in order to reach resolution and closure. These stages or tasks do not happen automatically and, in most cases, outside assistance is certainly needed.

The goal of grief therapy is to help the bereaved progressively accommodate the loss and move through the mourning process at his or her own pace. The therapist gently guides the client through the process starting where grief was interrupted and bereavement had stopped. Grief work may require few sessions or long and extended hours of intense treatment depending on the freshness of grief, the client's readiness and motivation, and his or her current response to interventions.

A successful grieving process consists of the following:

1. Admitting that the loss has taken place and it is final. This will undo the coping mechanism of "denial." To accept the finality of loss or death is the most difficult task facing any bereaved individual or family. Although most survivors try to accept the facts on a cognitive level, they are unable or unwilling to accept them on an affective level. Through helping them face the reality of loss, they will gradually soften their resistance and begin accepting the new painful world, that is, life without the lost object or loved person.

2. Experiencing and expressing all range of emotions and deep thoughts, both pleasant and unpleasant, as related to the loss. This will eventually reverse the mechanism of "suppression." This is usually accomplished by recreating vivid images of the lost object or person, reliving many important scenes or special moments, recalling warm memories, and reflecting on the emotional involvement before, during, and after the death or loss.

3. Releasing the lost or deceased, letting go, setting free, and saying good-bye. This will undo the dynamic of "clinging." After focusing for a good while on what the client "misses" about the deceased or lost object or function, grief counseling should gradually introduce the other polarity, namely, "what do you not miss about '. . .' ?" That certainly will force the bereaved to face full reality, correct attitudes, clear perspectives, de-idealize the loss, and reconcile opposite feelings, especially if the pre-existing relationship was conflictual. Preparing clients to say "good-bye for now" after each focused session is essential, until they are ready to say "good-bye for good."

4. Reinvesting the psychological energy, consumed earlier in unsuccessful resolution of grief, in new endeavors, relationships, projects, and people. Helping clients develop new interests, set new goals, cultivate fresh dreams and aspirations, and engage in creative and productive activities. This will reverse the condition of "stagnation."

The therapist should explain these procedures or tasks and ask the clients where and at what point they find themselves in regard to each of their losses. Most individuals with unfinished grief find themselves at the beginning of step one, or between steps one and two. It is natural for bereaved people to move back and forth among these procedures and steps each time they are hit by a new wave of grief. Eventually with time, grief waves begin diminishing both in frequency and intensity.

Effective therapy techniques include combination of insight oriented and action oriented approaches. Utilizing experiential activities like psychodrama and empty chair techniques are essential and very powerful. However, some of these require special training. Therapy must be practical and creative. In an attempt to undo stuckness, reverse defenses, and remove internal blockages, the therapist might focus on sensitive details, ask penetrating questions, suggest innovative ideas, and introduce difficult terminology bereaved people normally avoid (e.g., "when your husband died . . ."; "now, as a widow . . ."). Assigning homework, bringing pictures, writing letters, playing or recording tapes, going through rituals, reading materials, visiting special sites (with therapist at times), and establishing memorials are essential for facilitating the mourning process and completing the grief work. All therapeutic activities are conducted with serious involvement of the counselor, who becomes partner in the bereavement process.

The most powerful phase of treatment is when the therapist suggests a visit with the deceased person or lost object. Some bereaved people are reluctant to engage in such activities because they are afraid of becoming overwhelmed. Others quickly engage because they are looking forward to the missed connection. They have so much on their minds they eagerly want to tell the lost or deceased. However, clients need the therapist's constant assurance that they are not alone in this experience. One way to encourage them is by saying, "let's imagine that we can invite '. . .' to come and be with us here right now." In order to make the scene more vivid, ask the client to describe the person or object. "Could you describe '. . .' to me?" (more details the better). Then offer a seat or chair and let client place a picture, a pillow, or a special reminder he or she brought into the session. Some prefer to leave the chair empty. "If '. . .' is here with us, what would you like to tell '. . .' today?" Some individuals immediately engage in one-way conversation and keep expressing themselves for a long time. Others need help to start. Feeding sentences and modeling are necessary at many points in the process.

One sign that indicates that the client has reached a good measure of resolution and closure is when he or she is able to freely talk about the lost object or person, see pictures, remember special events, go difficult places, and touch precious items related to the loss without being deeply moved or greatly overwhelmed. The open wound slowly becomes a scar. However, a small residual grief will remain in the form of a non-threatening shadow. After the majority of grief work is completed, the bereaved will experience an obvious sense of relief and release. Both clients and therapists will clearly notice this transformation. As much as grief work appears, at first, to be hard and painful the results are indeed marvelous. In the case of multiple losses, attention should be given first to the most pressing ones. Crying and sobbing should be encouraged and repeatedly facilitated. Tears of grief are truly cleansing and genuinely restoring of the harmony and peace within the anguished soul.

Occasionally, the therapist's own unfinished grief can be triggered while helping others, especially if the timing, nature, and circumstances of the client's loss are similar to his or her own. In this case, it is appropriate to openly and honestly share with the client how tender and sensitive is the impact of such work and suggest waiting for a while or referring the client to a colleague. The therapist's own intense emotions may be easily stirred, interfering with therapy, and crippling his or her ability to concentrate on the client's mourning. However, for the counselor to experience brief waves of deep sorrow and sadness, during and outside the sessions, is quite natural. The grief counselor should not be alarmed by them. In fact, sharing tears and grieving together can be highly therapeutic.

Grief therapy is highly focused. To be effective, this type of counseling must be intentional, direct, frequent, and goal oriented. Fresh grief is easily detected. With experience, the therapist will begin to differentiate between normal and complicated grief reactions and between tears of mourning and tears of hopelessness, despair, and clinical depression.

Similar to acute stress disorder and post traumatic stress disorder, major or sudden loss can become problematic and create severe symptomatology. Basic counseling skills may be sufficient to facilitate normal grief reactions. However, indepth therapy and advanced clinical skills are necessary for complicated grief reactions. The therapist should be able to understand the complexity of bereavement, detect the severity of losses, assess the degree of impact on the individual or family group, and plan interventions accordingly. Unresolved and unfinished grief could develop into masked, chronic, exaggerated, or complicated bereavement depending on the magnitude of loss and the psychological well-being or emotional stability of the survivors. This can lead to increased behavioral disturbances, abnormal conditions, and pathological reactions. Chronic or clinical depression and severe anxiety disorders are very common in complicated bereavement. Unless evaluated and diagnosed as such, both patients and therapists may completely overlook chronic grief and totally miss the severe impact of major losses. Many adults have suffered multiple and significant losses since childhood, yet they never had the opportunity to adequately grieve any of them.

When children are involved, counseling should focus on play, drawing, music, coloring, modeling, story telling, and the like. Children are not able to grieve intensely like adults. They mourn intermittently while playing funeral, coloring sad emotions, or talking briefly about their loss, confusion, and fears. Numerous recent works provide valuable information and guidance on how to effectively help bereaved children and identify those who are especially at risk.

It is essential for grief counselors to acquaint themselves with the prominent literature in the field and prepare lists of activities, projects, and reading materials for their clients. It is also crucial to check on major losses during the intake or initial evaluation and also during later encounters. The therapist should inquire about past and recent losses, major and minor losses, and anticipated future losses as well. For example, "Have you had any significant losses lately?" "What are some of the major losses you have suffered in your life?" "Were you able to grieve enough any of them?" "Which ones do you feel are still unresolved?" "Are you expecting any major separation, loss, or death in the near future?" People often can not reveal all their significant losses at once because they want to avoid any sudden flooding of emotions or because they have no immediate access to this material which had been pushed out of awareness and deeply buried for so long. Such assessment will truly reveal the root causes of several apparent psychological problems.

Unresolved grief can cause serious emotional, mental, physical, spiritual, and social disruptions. The bereaved person becomes highly sensitized to any possible or potential loss, real or imaginary, while he or she tries to continue functioning on the surface. Therefore, missing grief precipitators will cause counseling to merely focus on other related matters. Such interventions, including psychiatric medications, succeed temporarily in alleviating the severe bereavement symptoms only to discover that they will reoccur again.

The following are examples of common misconceptions about grieving and should be corrected or defused early in the therapy process: "Shut down your feelings and don't think or talk about them." "Quickly replace the loss! Find a substitute." "Get busy! Increase your activities and responsibilities." "Mourn alone in complete privacy! Don't share your grief! No one can understand you." "Allow yourself some time and you will be alright." "Change location! Leave town! Move away from all reminders."

The duration of normal grief reactions may range from a few months to few years, usually six to twenty months. However, complicated bereavement may not be resolved alone unless the person seeks help and begins serious indepth counseling. The resolution of grief generally depends on the circumstances of loss or death, the emotional and mental conditions of the survivors, the availability of support, the social norms and customs, and the religious or spiritual faith. Some cultures discourage and rather inhibit grieving. Other cultures openly encourage periods of extended bereavement as members of the community join the survivors in public mourning. In the Bible, we have vivid examples of great leaders and family groups who bravely faced their own loss, grief, and sorrows and took enough time to properly mourn, both publicly and privately, until their grief was adequately finished and completed.

Suggested Readings

Rando, T. (1993). *Treatment of complicated mourning.* Champaign, IL: Research Press.

Worden, J. W. (1991). *Grief counseling and grief therapy: A handbook for the mental health practitioner* (2nd ed.). New York: Springer.

N. ABI-HASHEM

See DEATH AND DYING; DYING, PASTORAL CARE OF; GRIEF; LOSS AND SEPARATION; LOSS OF FUNCTION.

Group Dynamics. People join groups for a variety of reasons. They may be attracted to the members of a group; the factors that influence interpersonal attraction have been studied more extensively than have any other determinant of group formation. People may also be drawn to a group's activities. For this reason they join discussion groups, social clubs, and athletic teams. Perhaps most importantly individuals form and join groups to attain a goal they could not achieve by themselves. They organize political groups to protest injustice, labor unions to improve working conditions, and neighborhood associations to combat crime. In certain cases people perceive group membership as the means to a goal that lies outside the group. For example, a person may join a church because such membership will be good for business. Finally, some psychologists maintain that people have a basic need to affiliate that is satisfied only in the context of the group.

When people join together to form a group their first task is to organize. The group establishes norms (shared rules of conduct) that serve to maintain behavioral consistency. These norms guide each individual's actions and also help each group member to anticipate the behavior of others. Associated with each place or position in the group may be a role, a set of norms that defines how a person occupying that position ought to behave. Psychologists have noted how role performance often comes to shape one's attitudes and values. Zimbardo (1972) found that role playing influenced both behavior and identity when he randomly assigned male college students to be inmates or guards in a simulated prison. Within six days the prisoners became servile, dehumanized robots while the guards became brutal and tyrannical. Status, another important element in group structure, refers to the respect or prestige that is accorded a person occupying a particular position. Those positions that contribute most to the achievement of the group's goal are typically granted the highest status.

Group Leadership. Researchers in group dynamics have been particularly interested in understanding the nature and influence of group leaders. The trait approach assumes that all leaders have certain personal characteristics that distinguish them from other group members. Although empirical support for this theory has generally been weak, the search continues with some recent findings ironically suggesting that flexibility of personality may be a trait shared by people who consistently emerge as leaders. This fits the finding that the specific abilities and skills for effective leadership depend largely on the context in which group interaction occurs. Thus various situations call for different leaders, and presumably anyone could become a leader in the right situation. A limitation of both trait and situational theories is that they assume leadership is unidirectional and fail to recognize that leaders are also influenced by their followers. Contemporary theories of leadership maintain that effective leadership is a complex interplay involving the characteristics of the leader, of other group members, and of the situation.

Fiedler's (1964) contingency theory has provided one of the most influential models of leadership effectiveness. Fiedler suggests that in most cases persons adopt one of two leadership styles. Some leaders are task-oriented; that is, they are primarily concerned with getting the job done. Other leaders are relationship-oriented, focusing first on the social-emotional climate of the group. The style that is more effective depends on the situation. A directive, task-oriented approach presumably produces better results when the situational conditions are either very favorable or unfavorable to the leader. In contrast, a relationship-oriented style is more effective when the conditions are moderately favorable. According to Fiedler, three factors determine the favorability of the situation: the leader's authority, the degree to which the group's task is well specified, and the quality of the leader's personal relationships with other group members. Some recent studies suggest that the most effective supervisors are high in both task and social leadership. They are actively involved in achieving goals and sensitive to the needs of their subordinates.

Communication and Cohesion. Group interaction involves communication among members. In the late 1940s and early 1950s several investigators examined the effect of communication networks on group dynamics. The degree to which communication flows freely through a group can influence morale, productivity, and various aspects of group structure. A decentralized or open communication network in which group members may converse freely with each other is associated with greater member satisfaction and with improved efficiency in the solution of complex problems. In contrast, a centralized network in which all communication must be directed to one person, and thus one in which members are unable to converse with each other, may be more efficient for solving simple problems. Organizational development, including the emergence of a leader, also occurs more rapidly in a centralized network.

Cohesiveness, the degree to which members are motivated to remain in the group, has been one of the most researched variables of group dynamics. Assigning individuals to different groups typically produces some degree of group loyalty. Cohesiveness may be further increased if the members are placed in intergroup competition or are exposed to an external threat. Highly cohesive groups exert greater influence over their members and often are more effective in achieving their goals than are less cohesive groups. People in highly cohesive groups communicate more, tend to be friendlier and more cooperative, and also feel more secure than members of less cohesive groups. However, cohesiveness may also have negative effects. People may spend more time socializing than working on the group task. And since people in highly cohesive groups are particularly responsive to each other's influence, norms that regulate productivity may occasionally lead some individuals to reduce their output.

Group Performance. The experimental investigation of group phenomena can be traced back to Triplett's (1898) studies of how the mere presence of others may influence an individual's performance.

He reported that children wound string faster when they worked with others than when they performed alone. Other investigators also found this social facilitation effect when people solved simple multiplication problems, crossed out designated letters, or performed simple motor tasks.

However, some studies failed to obtain this positive effect. The presence of others hindered people's performance in learning nonsense syllables, in completing a maze, and in solving complex multiplication problems. Zajonc (1965) reconciled these contradictory findings with a well-known principle from experimental psychology: Arousal enhances whatever response tendency is dominant. Since other research indicates that the presence of others arouses us, it follows that observers or co-actors should improve the performance of easy tasks, for which the correct response is dominant, but hinder performance of difficult tasks, for which an incorrect response is dominant. Subsequent research has supported this hypothesis.

Improved performance in the presence of others may occur when people work toward their own goals and when their efforts can be individually evaluated. However, when people pool their efforts toward a common goal and when individual contributions cannot be monitored, psychologists have often found social loafing. In one study people who worked alone or in groups were asked to pull as hard as they could on a rope attached to a meter that measured the strength of their pulls. Contrary to the common notion that in unity there is strength, results indicated that as group size increased, the amount of effort exerted by each person dropped. More recent experiments have also indicated that group members often work less hard when performing additive tasks. One explanation for this finding has been provided by social impact theory, which states that the effect of any external force on a group is divided among its members. Thus, according to this theory, the pressure to work hard is divided among all group members so that as group size increases, each person exerts less effort. Research suggest that people loaf less when the task is challenging, appealing, or involving.

Group Processes. While decisions by groups are often thought to be more cautious than those of individuals, research has shown that group discussion often enhances risk taking. This finding, which has been successfully replicated in dozens of studies, is known as the risky shift phenomenon. However, the risky shift is not universal. In some cases people became more cautious after group discussion. Analysis of these apparently contradictory findings led investigators to postulate the group polarization hypothesis: Discussion generally strengthens the average inclination of group members before discussion (Myers, 1996). Thus if the average inclination is toward risk, group discussion will enhance risk taking. If the inclination of individuals is toward caution, group discussion will strengthen that tendency. Research has shown more generally that the initial average position of individuals is enhanced through group discussion. In short, groups intensify the opinions of like-minded people.

At least two social influences account for group polarization. Through group discussion individuals become aware of more arguments favoring the viewpoint they are already inclined to support. Second, individuals discover that others are more supportive of the socially preferred tendency than they expected, and in order to be perceived favorably by others they themselves express stronger opinions.

Often two heads are better than one, and thus group decision making may be superior to that of individuals. Laughlin, VanderStoep, and Hollingshead (1991) have shown that with various intellectual tasks group discussion enables members to answer questions they are unable to answer alone. Moreover, several people critiquing each other may help a group avoid some forms of cognitive bias and thus produce some high-quality solutions. However, contrary to the conventional wisdom, researchers have repeatedly found that people working alone generate more creative ideas than do the same people brainstorming in small groups.

In analyzing the decisions that led to several political fiascoes, Janis (1982) concluded that a group's desire for harmony may sometimes lead to the loss of critical judgment, a phenomenon he called groupthink. He argued that the conditions that breed groupthink include high cohesiveness, isolation of the group from outside contact, and a directive leader. Janis also identified the major symptoms of groupthink: the group's illusion of invulnerability, an unquestioned belief in its own morality, direct pressure on dissenters to conform, an illusion of unanimity, collective rationalization, a stereotyping of outgroups, the presence of self-appointed mind guards, and individual self-censorship.

To prevent groupthink Janis recommends that group leaders remain impartial during group deliberation, that they encourage group members to express their reservations, that they assign one or more members to the role of devil's advocate, and that after the group reaches a preliminary decision they call a second-chance meeting at which each member is asked to express any remaining doubts. Janis further suggests that on occasion independent groups be assigned the same problem. After each has reached a decision, they should come together to air any differences. All these procedures, Janis argues, will serve to stimulate critical thinking and prevent groupthink.

Deindividuation. Psychologists have long observed that persons in large groups frequently display behaviors they would not exhibit if they were acting alone. Looting by rioters and the violence of the lynch mob provide two examples. Persons in groups may experience both loss of self-awareness and evaluation apprehension, a process called deindividuation. The individual's submergence in the group leads to a decrease in his or her inhibitions

about performing certain behaviors. The lessening of inner restraints allows individuals to seek satisfaction for certain needs or impulses that they could not otherwise satisfy. Group situations that produce anonymity and draw attention away from each person seem most likely to foster the deindividuation process.

References

Fiedler, F. E. (1964). A contingency model of leadership effectiveness. In L. Berkowitz (Ed.), *Advances in experimental social psychology* (Vol. 1). New York: Academic.

Janis, I. L. (1982). *Groupthink: Psychological studies of policy decisions and fiascos*. Boston: Houghton Mifflin.

Laughlin, P. R., VanderStoep, S. W., & Hollingshead, A. B. (1991). Collective versus individual induction: Recognition of truth, rejection of error, and collective information processing. *Journal of Personality and Social Psychology, 61*, 50–67.

Myers, D. G. (1996). *Social psychology* (5th ed.). New York: McGraw-Hill.

Triplett, N. (1898). The dynamogenic factors in peacemaking and competition. *American Journal of Psychology, 9*, 507–533.

Zajonc, R. B. (1965). Social facilitation. *Science, 149*, 269–274.

Zimbardo, P. G. (1972). Pathology of imprisonment. *Transaction/Society, 9 (6)*, 4–8.

M. Bolt

See Leadership; Decision Making, Group; Decision Making; Group Psychotherapy.

Group Homes. The history of group homes is embedded in the history of child welfare, which in turn is very much related to the social, economic, and educational philosophy espoused in Western culture. In antiquity there was no room for any child outside the kinship system. There is no term in the biblical or classical literature for foster homes or institutions. The early Christian church did attempt to care for abandoned children and adults who were sick or aged. During the Middle Ages monasteries and convents accepted abandoned children. During the Elizabethan period the Poor Laws came into effect. These regulated the care of abandoned children, placing them into two categories: those who were given out for indenture and those placed in almshouses. Indenture was the early beginning of the foster home, and the almshouse was the early beginning of the children's institution.

In the United States two figures are particularly well known for their work with unwanted children: Charles Loren Brate in New York and Charles Birtwell in Boston. During the 1800s these two men greatly encouraged the development of foster home care and were in large part responsible for the transformation of the old-fashioned almshouses. The controversy between foster homes and institutions grew to an alarming proportion and culminated in the 1909

White House Conference on Children. The conference decided that the child's own home was the best place for the child to be. This became the early beginning of the deinstitutionalization of dependent children.

Group homes are distinguished from foster homes in that foster homes tend to have one or more children living in an already established home, and a group home tends to be one in which a group of unrelated children live together in one house with a couple or some single people acting as houseparents. Further, the group home usually has more of a treatment focus.

The development of the group home accelerated in the 1940s when Jacob Kepecs of the Jewish Children's Bureau in Chicago set up a chain of group homes to take children who were moved out of institutions and foster homes. Since that time the number of group homes has increased tremendously all over the country—so much so that, according to Gula, a new group home is probably established each day somewhere in the nation (Gula, 1973). Although there has been a general decline in the total number of children in care, due to the decline in the number of children generally as well as other related factors, the group home movement has continued.

Group homes are generally divided into family group homes, peer group homes, and group residences. Family group homes are usually homes in which group home parents, with or without their own children, take care of from 4 to 6 other children. These group home parents are usually the employees of an agency, or they may do their work on a service fee basis. A peer group home is usually a home that is rented or owned by an agency and in which a child care staff supervises the living arrangements of 5 to 10 children. The child care workers are usually younger persons. A group residence is usually owned or rented by an agency, and a child care staff looks after approximately 10 to 15 children. A group residence is distinguished from an institution in that it is integrated into the community and the children attend school in the community.

The purpose of a group home is to provide treatment while keeping the children in an environment that is as close to a normal family environment as possible. The children therefore usually attend schools in the neighborhood and are involved in other community activities such as church or clubs. It is imperative that the children are healthy enough to live in a normal community. Much damage has been done to the concept of group homes because overly aggressive and disturbed children were placed in a group home that was not capable of controlling the child.

The staff of group homes are either trained child care workers or mature, dependable married persons who are interested in helping children. Owing to the difficult nature of the work and the frustrations involved, there is need for careful supervision as well as in-service training. Without this kind of service support, staff members tend to burn out quickly. In many group homes the average length of stay for staff is as low as six months.

Halfway houses are also called group homes.

Reference

Gula, M. (1973). Community services and residential institutions for children. In Y. Bakal (Ed.), *Closing correctional institutions*. Lexington, MA: Lexington.

Additional Reading

Mayer, M. F., Richman, L. H., & Balcerzak, E. A. (1977). *Group care of children*. New York: Child Welfare League of America.

S. SKARSTEN

See COMMUNITY MENTAL HEALTH; COMMUNITY PSYCHOLOGY.

Group Psychotherapy. The practice of persons forming into groups for purposes of mutual protection, support, and understanding is as old as humanity itself. However, the scientific investigation and utilization of the healing powers of groups is less than a hundred years old.

The beginning of modern group therapy can be traced back to 1905, when Joseph Pratt, a Boston internist, set up special classes for tuberculosis patients. These classes not only involved instruction to the patients about the treatment of their common malady but also provided them opportunity for interpersonal support and encouragement. As Pratt increased his work with these patient groups, he came to realize the psychological benefits that resulted from them.

Pratt's work became known to psychiatrists, including Edward Lazell and L. C. Marsh, who in the 1920s and 1930s adapted the group method for use with psychotic patients. Although they were methodologically unsophisticated, these men helped awaken the mental health professions to the therapeutic value of working with the psychologically disturbed in group settings.

The first group therapists were psychoanalytic in theory and technique. However, they were soon challenged by nonanalytic clinicians who saw this particular treatment modality fitting well with their own psychotherapy theories and methodologies. Thus the models of group therapy began to proliferate, with many, such as psychodrama and Gestalt group therapy, moving far afield from the psychoanalytic approach to groups.

The proliferation of group therapy models became a veritable explosion in the late 1960s and 1970s, with a new form of group therapy seeming to spring up almost daily. Despite the faddishness often associated with such groups, many persons experienced emotional and psychological healing by participating in therapy groups.

This same period saw the emergence of the encounter group movement, which emphasized the use of groups for enhancing the emotional growth of psychologically healthy people. Groups were no longer considered useful only to mentally ill persons; they could be used to teach principles of group dynamics, increase interpersonal intimacy, or help persons get in touch with their emotions. While encounter, or growth, groups have many adherents and are often used in businesses and industry, group therapy remains the primary focus for most mental health professionals who work with the psychologically disturbed.

It is somewhat of a misnomer to speak of group therapy in the singular, given the vast number of models in existence. These models often differ markedly in their methodology, theory, and understanding of human nature. Despite these differences, almost every type of group therapy can be defined at its most basic level as treatment of "several emotionally disturbed people who meet with the therapist as a group for the purpose of helping find a more comfortable and effective adaptation" (Halleck, 1978, p. 387).

Major Models of Group Therapy. *Psychoanalytic.* That the first group therapists were psychoanalytic in orientation may seem paradoxical, given Sigmund Freud's emphasis on understanding and treating the individual psyche. However, pioneering therapists such as Burrow, Wender, and Schilder recognized that many of Freud's concepts were applicable not only to individuals being treated by classical psychoanalysis but also to persons in therapeutic groups.

Psychoanalytic group therapy uses traditional Freudian concepts and treatment techniques, modifying them for use in a group context. Therapists engaging in this form of treatment see their patients as suffering from psychological problems due to conflicts experienced at various developmental stages. Not only are these conflicts unconscious, but also the patient resists their emergence into awareness.

The group therapist asks the members to comment on any and all things said and done in the group, similar to the technique of free association in individual analysis. During this process the therapist attempts to help the various members understand their resistance to unveiling internal conflicts. This is accomplished by the therapist's pointing out to the member the defense mechanisms he or she uses as these are manifested in interactions with other group members and with the therapist.

The relationship between an individual group member and the therapist leads to transference. This transference of feelings from a parental figure to the therapist is not only permitted but also encouraged by the therapist, based on the assumption that insight into the historical reasons for transference will free a person from its grip. Often a group member will also manifest transference toward other members. This multiple transference provides more opportunities for interpreting the transference to the patient than would be the case in individual analysis. Also, the numerous interactions between

members will highlight the defense mechanisms habitually used by each participant.

While not ignoring group dynamics, psychoanalytic group therapy focuses primarily on the unconscious intrapsychic experience of individuals within the group. It moves from the level of interpersonal interaction to that of investigating unconscious motivation. Because of this individual focus Wolf and Schwartz (1962) prefer to call it "psychoanalysis in groups" rather than psychoanalytic group therapy. (*See* Psychoanalytic Group Therapy for a discussion of this approach.)

Group Dynamic. Group dynamic theorists do not deny the validity of psychoanalytic theory when it is applied to individuals. However, they argue that an individualistic perspective is not adequate to understand what occurs in a therapy group. Thus they look to social psychologists, such as Kurt Lewin, to help explain precisely what happens when patients meet together for therapy. Lewin held that all elements in a social field, or environment, whether persons, motivations, or drives, could not be fully comprehensible apart from their context.

Thus from the standpoint of group dynamic theory the individual words and actions of each group member are no longer conceptualized as being independent of the group process. Rather, all behavior in the group is seen as embedded in the context of the group, with the group viewed and treated as if it were an organism with its own peculiar traits and characteristics.

A representative example of a group dynamic model of therapy is that of Whitaker and Lieberman (1964). They hold that seemingly independent and unrelated behaviors of group members actually refer to an implicit here-and-now concern. There is thus an underlying coherence to members' verbalizations that is unconscious even to the members.

The covert concern or theme of the group is conceptualized by Whitaker and Lieberman as always taking the form of a conflict, termed the focal conflict. This is usually a conflict between a wish motive and a fear motive. For example, one group's focal conflict may be between a shared wish to gain the attention and approval of the therapist and a fear that gaining the attention would result in feelings of rejection by other group members (Yalom, 1975).

The group will experience tension when confronted with the focal conflict. They will then work toward a group solution that will allay the fear while allowing for partial satisfaction of the wish. In the example cited, the group might share their desire for approval from the therapist with each other while supporting those in the group who are most fearful of rejection.

The group therapist has the task of dissipating unrealistic fears of members of the group that they will be rejected by him or her. Another responsibility is to increase the group's sense of psychological safety while helping them to circumvent restrictive solutions to the focal conflicts.

Each group member becomes increasingly involved in the group as more of the group's focal conflicts touch on his or her own unresolved emotions. Although the conflicts are frightening, a certain amount of security is provided as consensually arrived-at solutions emerge that promise to keep anxiety and conflict at manageable levels (Shaffer & Galinsky, 1974).

Existential. Existential psychology blends the thinking of philosophers such as Sartre, Heidegger, and Søren Kierkegaard with the therapeutic approaches of men such as Ludwig Binswanger and Boss. The first sympathetic presentation in the United States of existentialism as a movement relevant to the mental health professions came in 1958 with the publication of *Existence,* edited by Rollo May, Angel, and Ellenberger. The aim of existential psychology is to understand persons in their total existential reality, which includes their subjective relationship to themselves, to their fellow humans, and to the world (Misiak & Sexton, 1973).

The subjective, phenomenological experiences of each member of an existential therapy group are held in the highest regard and are generally not viewed as needing to be interpreted or analyzed for deeper, hidden meanings. The explicit denial of psychic and biological determinism carries with it an emphasis on the ultimate responsibility of each person for his or her own meaning in life. Life has no inherent meaning; humans are free and responsible to make choices; thus meaning must be chosen and created by each person.

Psychopathology is viewed as stemming from inauthentic modes of being. Inauthenticity may come from fear of responsibility and from not acting, even in the face of the ultimate absurdity of one's finiteness and eventual death.

Existential group therapy provides its members with many and frequent opportunities for I-thou encounters, relationships that reflect authenticity and beingness. Group therapists are to live the therapy rather than do it; that is, they are to be themselves without role or façade. Group members are treated as subjects to be experienced rather than as objects to be analyzed. There is no attempt on the part of the therapist to force his or her own world view on the group, for this would be treating the members as objects to control, change, or manipulate. The group provides support for its members as they struggle to relate to one another more authentically, to create their own sense of meaning in the universe, and to take absolute responsibility for their own actions.

Nondirective. Nondirective, or group-centered, group therapy takes its theory and methodology from the work of Carl Rogers, who asserts that a therapist must manifest nonpossessive genuineness and empathy to provide the proper therapeutic environment for change on the part of the patient or client.

In the same way a nondirective group provides an atmosphere of acceptance, openness, and empathy for its members so that they can then mobilize their own inner resources to help them change. Since each member enters the group with anxiety due to an inability to relate effectively with others, the proper group atmosphere will lessen the anxiety and accompanying defensiveness.

The group provides opportunity for self-discovery and self-disclosure. More positive and satisfying ways of relating to others are highlighted as each member becomes increasingly free and adept at self-examination, with assurances that the group will not condemn or reject. Persons who are blind to positive aspects of themselves gain clarity of self-perception, and with it an increase in the sense of self-worth.

The therapist models genuineness, empathy, and warmth for the group with no attempt to coerce or persuade members to change their value system. Members are exposed to values other than their own as they interact in the group; however, they are responsible for themselves in choosing and changing their values or beliefs. Thus the therapist, while maintaining a nondirective role, is nevertheless quite active as he or she responds to group members in a way that will help them to become increasingly aware of their deep feelings. The group usually deals with whatever problems come up in a session; there is no particular agenda or attempt to analyze beyond the level of emotional expression.

Here-and-Now/Process. This model is not associated with any one method of individual psychotherapy, as is the case with psychoanalytic and nondirective group therapy. Despite the handicap of not having a parent therapy, it is one of the most widely used models of group therapy. It is presented by Yalom in his widely read text, *The Theory and Practice of Group Psychotherapy* (1975).

Yalom argues that the therapeutic power of a group resides in two symbiotic tiers, here-and-now activation and process illumination. In the first tier the group members must focus their attention on their feelings toward one another, the therapist, and the group as a whole. The immediate events in the session thus take precedence over events both in the distant past and in the current outside life of the members. This here-and-now focus enhances the development and emergence of each member's social microcosm; it also facilitates feedback, catharsis, meaningful self-disclosure, and the acquisition of socializing skills. The vitality of the group is greatly intensified, and each member becomes deeply involved in the session.

However, the second step, process illumination, is necessary for any real therapeutic gain. The group must recognize, examine, and understand process—that is, it must understand itself, study its own transactions, transcend pure experience, and apply itself to the integration of that experience.

The group lives in the here and now and then doubles back on itself in order to examine the here-and-now behaviors that just occurred. The therapist steers the group into the here and now while guiding the self-reflecting process. The group can assist the therapist in focusing on the here and now, but the self-reflection, or process commentary, remains the responsibility of the therapist (Yalom, 1975).

Psychodrama. Psychodrama is one of the oldest models of group therapy extant. Jacob Moreno, credited with coining the term *group therapy,* began to develop this treatment modality in the 1920s. Despite its long history psychodrama has not been as widely accepted and utilized as its creator hoped it would be. However, many of the techniques used in psychodrama, such as the empty chair technique and role reversal, have been adopted by individual and group therapists of diverse theoretical orientations.

Psychodrama emphasizes action or behavior rather than mere verbalization. Instead of talking about life problems, group members are asked to act them out in spontaneous dramatization. The dramatization, or psychodrama proper, takes place on a stage in front of an audience consisting of group members and assistants to the therapist, who is called the director.

In order to emotionally prepare the audience to benefit from the psychodrama, the director engages in preliminary warm-up exercises to decrease the various levels of anxiety and defensiveness found in the members. Once the group is warmed up, a group member is chosen to be the protagonist, the central character in the psychodrama. The director helps the protagonist determine the problem to be dramatized; as much information as possible is obtained in order to get an accurate picture of the problem and of the significant persons in the protagonist's life who are part of the problem. Auxiliary egos are chosen from the other group members or from the director's assistants to play the significant persons in the protagonist's life, to play intrapsychic elements of his or her psyche, or to play the protagonist.

The purposes of the spontaneous dramatization are to help the protagonist achieve an emotional catharsis or total emotional release, to break down emotional blockages due to repression and suppression, to desensitize the protagonist to intense expression of affect, and to help the protagonist become comfortable with new ways of responding behaviorally to old conflictual situations.

The session often ends with a wrap-up time in which the audience is provided opportunity to be supportive to the protagonist while also sharing how they benefited via identification with the various characters in the psychodrama.

Gestalt. Gestalt therapy, created by Fritz Perls, became an exceedingly popular form of group therapy in the late 1960s and early 1970s. Like psychodrama it emphasizes action rather than words. Gestalt group therapy may take two forms. In the first, therapeutic work is done between the therapist and one participant within the group setting. The other group members are encouraged to observe and experience what is going on without interaction until the work is over. After the work is complete, they are free to interact and share what they experienced during the one-to-one work. The second method involves all participants interacting within the group.

The methods and techniques of Gestalt group therapy find their source in the philosophy and psychology of its founder. The major focus is on the enhancement of awareness of the group members. Being in touch with one's flow of awareness is considered an essential aspect of a Gestalt therapy group. However, the object of this awareness is not facts or cognitions but sensory data, feelings, and emotions. Talking about the past, asking questions, or making psychological interpretations are all considered futile exercises that cannot help persons change their behavior.

Numerous techniques are used to enhance awareness and decrease intellectualizations. For example, group members are asked to turn questions into first-person statements, to talk to persons directly rather than talking about them, and to eschew discussion of their personal histories (*see* Gestalt Techniques).

The Gestalt group therapist holds that each person is solely responsible for his or her own behavior and that behavior is only in the here and now. Each group member has the potential for greater self-reliance and for therapeutic change if the blockages to self-awareness, such as intellectualizing, can be removed (Greenwald, 1975).

Encounter Groups. The term *encounter group* is a generic label for a wide variety of experiential, humanistically oriented groups. T-groups, sensitivity groups, personal growth groups, marathon groups, truth labs, and human relations groups are all considered encounter groups (Yalom, 1975).

The encounter group movement began in the 1950s with the human relations training established by the National Training Laboratory. The basic skill training groups, or T-groups, were created to teach persons about interpersonal behavior, to explore group dynamics, and to discuss group members' problems in their home organization. The emphasis gradually moved away from group dynamics to group work for the sake of self-fulfillment and self-realization. Encounter groups became in essence group therapy for normals.

Goals within encounter groups are often vague and ill-defined but are usually shaped by a belief that even psychologically healthy people experience a certain degree of isolation and alienation from others and from themselves. Thus these groups will strive for goals such as increased emotional intensity, heightened sensory awareness, increased self-disclosure, and a reexamination of one's basic life values.

There are a number of important differences between encounter groups and therapy groups. Encounter group members are generally psychologically healthier than are group therapy members. They are able to communicate better, learn more quickly, and apply what they have learned to life situations. Group therapy members are usually fearful, suffer low self-esteem, are pessimistic about their ability to change, and desire safety rather than growth as a primary goal.

The encounter group leader is perceived as a guide or facilitator for the group. The group usually does not hold the leader in awe, tending to see him or her as a peer. Group therapy members, however, deal with the distortions in relationships that are symptomatic of psychological disorder. Transference reactions toward the group therapist are unavoidable. For better or worse, the therapist is most often seen as a healer, someone to be looked up to for guidance, insight, and safety.

Lastly, the atmosphere of encounter groups is usually less tense and disquieting than is that of therapy groups. Encounter group members look forward to learning more about themselves and others in the group; they eagerly anticipate getting more "in touch with themselves." Group therapy members often fear and loathe the idea of getting to know themselves better; they may be suspicious of other group members and resistant to change.

Research. Yalom (1975) has done a considerable amount of research attempting to identify the therapeutic aspects or elements common to all the group therapies regardless of their theoretical or methodological differences. He has divided these common elements or "curative factors" into 11 primary categories:

1. Instillation of hope—the creation of a sense of optimism and positive expectation.
2. Universality—decreasing each group member's sense of being alone in misery and psychopathology.
3. Imparting information about mental health and illness.
4. Altruism—the creation of a group climate of helpfulness, concern, support, and sharing.
5. Corrective recapitulation of the primary family group—helping group members to see that their interactions in the group recapitulate their interactions with primary family members.
6. Development of socializing techniques—increasing group members' ability to relate to one another in positive and mature ways.
7. Imitative behavior—helping group members to change via observation of functional, mature behavior on the part of the therapist and other group members.
8. Interpersonal learning—utilizing transference, corrective emotional experiences, and insight to assist members in changing themselves.
9. Cohesiveness—the sense of togetherness that causes a group to see itself holistically rather than as a collection of individuals.
10. Catharsis—the open expression of affect within the group process.

11. Existential factors—dealing with such issues as personal responsibility, contingency, basic isolation, and mortality.

The curative factors of group therapy are not static or autonomous but can be influenced by a variety of forces. Different types of groups may emphasize different clusters of curative factors, depending on the methodology of the group and the leadership style of the therapist. Also, various factors may be more salient at one stage of therapy than at another. For example, instillation of hope and universality may be more important in the early stages, whereas catharsis and the corrective recapitulation of the primary family group may be much more therapeutically valuable in the later stages of treatment.

Orlinsky and Howard's (1978) comprehensive review of research comparing the efficacy of group therapy versus individual therapy found that a majority of studies showed no significant difference in outcome between the two modalities. A few studies found group to be more effective than individual treatment, while other research found the combination of both types of treatment to be superior to individual therapy alone. Two studies indicated that persons in individual therapy sometimes had better outcomes than those who had only group therapy. However, group treatments have been shown often to be effective in helping people achieve more healthy, positive evaluations of themselves and others, as evidenced by instruments measuring self-concept assessment, attitude change, and positive personality development (Bednar & Kaul, 1978).

The available research data do not strongly support the notion of differential effects or superiority of any one type of group therapy. This lack of confirmation does not eliminate the possibility that some types of groups are more effective. The problem may lie with the research tools and methodologies, which may not be precise enough to separate out differential effects. Further research may discover that significant differential effects do exist.

Biblical/Theological Perspectives. A critique of group therapy per se will not be found in Scripture, since the Bible was not written as a psychotherapy textbook. However, the assumptions and goals of the group therapies need to be critically examined from a biblical perspective.

One of the basic working assumptions of all group therapies is that human relationships are not only important but essential for healthy functioning. This assumption is shared by Scripture; in Genesis it is the impetus for the creation of Eve. Adam's isolation was declared "not good," implying the goodness of the husband-wife relationship and by extension all human relationships. The goodness of relationships is confirmed throughout Scripture, from the story of David and Jonathan to Paul's plaintive lament that "no one came to my support, but everyone deserted me" (2 Tim. 4:16, NIV).

Further, the doctrine of common grace would support the notion that psychological healing can occur via group therapy as a function of God's general care and concern for all humanity. God, who causes rain to fall on the just and the unjust (Matt. 5:45), may also send penultimate healing via group therapy relationships, without diminishing the ultimate healing that is effected by faith in Christ.

Still it is necessary to critique and reject unbiblical assumptions and goals that are associated with certain therapies. A Christian worldview stands in opposition to the existential notion that humans create their own meaning in a meaningless universe. The psychodrama goal of achieving godlike autonomy is likewise antithetical to a biblical understanding of people as dependent on the Creator. Also, the Freudian notion that religious beliefs are nothing more than neurotic projections must be summarily rejected.

Despite these criticisms, the emphases of group therapies on honesty, empathy, individual responsibility, mutual support, and personal integrity cannot be gainsaid. While group therapy is not a substitute for Christian fellowship, many fearful, anxious, insecure Christians may benefit greatly from it.

References

Bednar, R. L., & Kaul, T. J. (1978). Experiential group research. In S. L. Garfield & A. E. Bergin (Eds.), *Handbook of psychotherapy and behavior change* (2nd ed.). New York: Wiley.

Greenwald, J. A. (1975). The ground rules in Gestalt therapy. In F. D. Stephenson (Ed.), *Gestalt therapy primer*. New York: Aronson.

Halleck, S. L. (1978). *The treatment of emotional disorders.* New York: Aronson.

Misiak, H., & Sexton, V. S. (1973). *Phenomenological, existential, and humanistic psychologies: A historical survey.* New York: Grune & Stratton.

Orlinsky, D. E., & Howard, K. I. (1978). The relation of process to outcome in psychotherapy. In S. Garfield & A. E. Bergin (Eds.), *Handbook of psychotherapy and behavior change* (2nd ed.). New York: Wiley.

Shaffer, J. B. P., & Galinsky, M. D. (1974). *Models of group therapy and sensitivity training.* Englewood Cliffs, NJ: Prentice-Hall.

Whitaker, D., & Lieberman, M. (1964). *Psychotherapy through the group process.* New York: Atherton.

Wolf, A., & Schwartz, E. K. (1962). *Psychoanalysis in groups.* New York: Grune & Stratton.

Yalom, I. (1975). *The theory and practice of group psychotherapy* (2nd ed.). New York: Basic.

Additional Readings

Kaplan, H. I., & Sadock, B. J. (1971). *Comprehensive group psychotherapy.* Baltimore: Williams & Wilkins.

Naar, R. (1982). *A primer of group psychotherapy.* New York: Human Sciences.

W. G. Bixler

See Group Dynamics.

Growth Counseling. An approach to counseling developed by Howard J. Clinebell. As a model for therapy, growth counseling focuses on a person's positive potentials rather than on his or her failures or weaknesses (Clinebell, 1979). As such, it can be seen as one of several approaches typically grouped together as part of the human potential movement of the late 1960s and early 1970s.

Clinebell has obviously been greatly influenced by the works of Carl Rogers, Abraham Maslow, Rollo May, and Erich Fromm; as a result growth counseling incorporates the optimistic, humanistic orientation of their thinking. As Clinebell states, "Growth counseling is a human-potentials approach to the helping process that defines the goal as that of facilitating the maximum development of a person's potentialities, at each life stage, in ways that contribute to the growth of others as well as to the development of a society in which all persons will have an opportunity to use their full potentials" (pp. 17–18).

As part of this process growth occurs in six major areas: the mind, the body, relationships with others, the biosphere or environment, relationship to groups and institutions with which one is associated, and the spiritual dimension. Growth counseling further focuses on facilitating and accelerating potentializing, the ongoing process of actualizing one's inner potential. This potentializing is enhanced by incorporating the "dynamic power of hope," encouraging "intentionality," and focusing on caring and confrontation within the therapeutic relationship (pp. 42–73).

The counselor seeks to communicate this hope-growth perspective in a supportive, largely nondirective manner. Clinebell maintains that helping the client to focus on his or her need for spiritual growth and transcendence is the key to enhancing true, lasting growth. This spiritual growth focuses on reestablishing communion with God, which provides a meaningful philosophy of life, socially responsible values, a sense of transcendence to one's higher self, a love for all of nature, a sense of unity with the universe, self-esteem, a sense of celebration, and movement away from the destructive alienation of guilt. This helps one to overcome the existential anxiety that Clinebell feels is characteristic of our age. For Clinebell the Bible is full of uplifting messages of hope, growth, freedom, and transcendence that can be usefully incorporated into the process of growth counseling. Growth counseling may appear to be best suited for individual therapy, although Clinebell asserts that it can be used with couples, families, and groups.

In evaluating Clinebell's growth counseling approach, one is initially struck by its obvious similarity to the nondirective, client-centered (person-centered) approach developed by Rogers, whom Clinebell mentions only once in passing. Thus it is difficult to view this approach as uniquely different from others that incorporate an optimistic, humanistic, self-actualizing philosophy into a therapy model. This leaves

Clinebell open to the same criticisms that have resulted in movement away from such approaches. Critics question the human potential for growth, wholeness, self-direction, and tranquility on historical, sociological, and theological grounds. Some scholars consider this optimistic view of human nature as idealistic and unrealistic.

Beyond disagreements concerning this philosophical foundation, some critics may take exception to Clinebell's portrayal of spiritual growth as "an integrating, energizing, growing relationship with that loving Spirit that religions call God" (p. 107). The absence of such concepts as rebellion, judgment, repentance, and true redemption in Clinebell's view of the relationship between God and humankind reduces spiritual growth to a concept of little meaning or biblical relevance in which God becomes nothing more than a mirror of human wholeness and potential.

Reference

Clinebell, H. J. (1979). *Growth counseling: Hope-centered methods of actualizing human wholeness*. Nashville: Abingdon.

J. D. Guy, Jr.

See Pastoral Counseling; Pastoral Care.

Guidance. A form of supportive psychotherapy in which the client is provided active help through advice and direction. Such help is given in employment (*see* Vocational Counseling), religion (*see* Pastoral Counseling), education, and a number of other areas.

While giving advice has a place in psychotherapy, a reliance on this mode of relating makes the relationship much more like that of friends or acquaintances. Because similar advice has frequently been given by others and found to be of minimal use, many people resent receiving advice from a psychotherapist. Others, however, are always willing to be told what to do and sometimes seem able to constructively use such advice.

Properly used, guidance is a supportive technique that can help people adjust and grow. In many cases it is the only type of intervention to which an individual will respond. However, it should not be expected to produce deep changes in underlying conflict or basic personality organization.

D. G. Benner

See Supportive Psychotherapy.

Guidance, Divine. Divine guidance presupposes what has been traditionally called the will of God. Being guided implies a destination, tangible or intangible, and divine guidance implies the revelation of some part of the divine intention. To state specifically how divine guidance works would be presumptuous of any psychologist. However, discussion of some of the psychological complications associated with divine guidance is appropriate, as it represents an aspect of religious life open to psychological examination.

The concept of divine guidance is biblically based. Many passages of Scripture support this—for example, "I will instruct you and teach you in the way you should go; I will counsel you and watch over you" (Ps. 32:8, NIV). Once we acknowledge that divine guidance exists, we must face the problematic questions of when and why this guidance is sought and how it is recognized as divine guidance. This is a move toward the psychological realm.

Such guidance shows itself in Scripture, but what of problems such as vocational and marital choice? Many persons engage in prayer, in listening for a divinely inspired thought or feeling, or in looking for a sign—some event that is interpreted as having a special meaning. As one listens to inner thoughts and feelings, how can one single out a God-given directive? Packer (1973) warns Christians against a reliance on inner promptings and advocates depending on Scripture. Nevertheless, inner promptings still influence how we interpret Scripture, and many personal questions are not directly answered biblically.

Misattribution of Inner Promptings. It is important to realize that the mind is full of many promptings that come from different sources. Christian tradition has often dichotomized inner voices into the voice of the flesh and the voice of the spirit. Oversimplifying the problem in this manner may lead to worse confusion. If these two voices, also seen as God versus the devil, are believed to be the only ones, then all voices that are not in some obvious way fleshly may be presumed to be of God.

An example would be the young person who prays for guidance about vocational choice and subsequently has the idea of becoming a missionary. This idea may be accepted uncritically as divine guidance, without giving consideration to the fact that the person's parents are missionaries and that they are hoping their child will make the same choice. The importance of internalized parental voices often is ignored or even unrecognized, since such voices may sound similar to how we imagine divine guidance might sound.

Until internalized parental voices can be recognized as such and separated from the individual's self, the analyzing and observing ego, there is always doubt as to the true source of what is attributed to divine guidance. Until this separation is accomplished, divine leading toward almost anything not thought correct by the parents' convention would be assumed incorrect or even a demonic temptation. Thus in this situation one is not truly open to God's leading. This separation is an aspect of being born again, as it dethrones the parents as gods (or as devils) and allows God to now be Father.

Parental internalizations constitute the superego. This includes the ego ideal, that which we strive to be, and the conscience, the internal threat of punishment for not acting in accord with the ego ideal.

Parental voices may often be identified as divine directives because they often carry this threat with them. It is a "do this or else" thought. However, if it is God guiding, the feeling should be one of peace. Although the recognition of possible negative consequences for not following through may be present, fear should soon be quelled. In Scripture, particularly in the opening chapters of the Gospel of Luke, when the Spirit of God reveals something the receiver is initially afraid but is told not to fear. The anxiety then subsides.

Personality Types and Their Vulnerabilities. When and why does one seek divine guidance? Since any action is influenced by a variety of motives, it is not productive to ask if we seek divine guidance to serve God or to satisfy ourselves. It is likely that in seeking divine guidance we are motivated both to serve God and to fulfill certain psychological needs. Some of these needs, such as wanting to see ourselves as good people, may be relatively benign. However, other needs reflect more pathological personality traits that can contaminate the whole process of seeking divine guidance.

In such situations the needs of the individual so predominate that what is thought to be a desire for guidance is often a wish to indulge a hidden pathological need. In the extreme, such needs are associated with personality disorders. However, most people have tendencies in the direction of at least one of these disorders. Therefore, each person should identify his or her own tendencies or vulnerabilities in the hope that knowing the self better will allow for a more mature discernment of divine guidance. Otherwise one risks confusing one's own wishes with divine guidance.

Histrionic Personality. The histrionic personality is characterized by overly intense, reactive behavior. Such persons are prone to exaggeration and often act out a role, such as the victim, without being aware of it. They crave stimulation and excitement and tend to be impressionable and easily influenced. Being suggestible, they show an initial positive response to any strong authority figure who might be able to provide a magical solution to their problems. The individual with a significant histrionic tendency might search for divine guidance in the hopes of avoiding the normal frustrations encountered in life and would use the search for guidance or its results to gain attention. Any search for divine guidance that seems to draw attention to the self must therefore be carefully examined to see whether it reflects underlying histrionic qualities rather than a search for God's will.

Narcissistic Personality. The traits of the narcissistic personality can also negatively influence the search for divine guidance in that grandiosity, preoccupation with attention and admiration, and characteristic responses to threats to self-esteem may result in utilizing a relationship with God to feel more important than others. When narcissism predominates, the person feels an inflated sense of self-esteem. This is due to an identification with God to the point that one might see the self as merged with God and above the human experience. The power, strength, and goodness of God are wished for by a self that senses a lack of these qualities. Since everyone has some narcissism, one must suspect the temptation to interpret divine guidance in a way that makes one more special or important than others.

Dependent Personality. The excessively dependent person allows others to assume responsibility for major areas of his or her life. Such persons lack self-confidence and the ability to function independently. They leave major decisions to others. Overly dependent persons may want God to decide daily minutia for them (e.g., what to wear that day). Overly dependent persons hope that divine guidance will enable them to avoid being thinking, responsible adults with the option of choice regarding their actions. It is hard to believe that God would not have us accept responsibility for utilizing our own judgment at times. Perhaps God even sometimes withholds guidance in order to encourage appropriate self-confidence, independence, and adult growth.

Compulsive Personality. Traits of the compulsive personality include excessive perfectionism, the insistence that things be done in his or her own way, and indecisiveness. In seeking divine guidance a person with compulsive traits might insist on guidance that conforms to a human notion of perfection, which may well not be identical to God's perfection. The compulsive would also be inclined to conclude that a leading in one direction must mean no subsequent changes. This definition of divine guidance is narrow and not necessarily God's view, but the compulsive clings to it out of fear of losing control of the situation.

The issue of indecisiveness is related to the importance of knowing the various voices of the mind. The more compulsive one is, the more doubting, obsessing, and ruminating there will be as to whether a prompting is indeed divine guidance. There will be a reluctance to follow a leading without some proof that this course will lead to good things. God has never promised to show all aspects of a path, but the compulsive person resists taking the first step without being able to see the whole path. Obviously such persons greatly limit the divine guidance they might receive by maintaining such stringent requirements.

Faith and Wisdom. Thus the paradox emerges that we are to ultimately follow God's leading on faith without guarantees or proofs, while at the same time we must attempt to discern which of the voices we hear is the divine voice guiding us. It is essential that we know ourselves, the instruments through which divine guidance is received, well enough to have confidence that what we interpret as divine guidance comes from outside the personality itself. Recognizing internalized parental voices and being aware of various motives of the personality for seeking divine guidance help us identify and interpret divine guidance more accurately.

Reference

Packer, J. I. (1973). *Knowing God.* Downers Grove, IL: InterVarsity Press.

J. E. TALLEY

See ATTRIBUTION THEORY; RELIGION AND PERSONALITY; RELIGIOUS DEVELOPMENT; CHRISTIAN GROWTH; FAITH.

Guided Imagery Technique. *See* IMAGERY, THERAPEUTIC USE OF.

Guilt. Guilt can be used as a judicial term referring to violation of a law or to designate an emotion that follows judging oneself in violation of a standard. The first usage refers to an objective state or condition. When individuals break a civil law, they are objectively guilty whether they feel guilty or not. The second usage refers to a subjective experience. People may feel guilty even though they are not legally guilty.

Objective guilt, in general, refers to one's condition in relation to either a human law/relationship or to God. With reference to God, all persons have been judged guilty (Rom. 3:23; Isa. 53:6), whereas only some people are guilty before human law. Moreover, there are two components to objective guilt. First, a state wherein an individual is objectively a violator of some standard or relationship ("basic criminality"). Second, a condition of external threat whereby the guilty individual must pay the requirements of justice (a "debt to punishment").

Subjective guilt involves three elements: shame, self-punishment and self-rejection, or fears of rejection. Shame is rooted in a more global sense of being inadequate, falling short, or being seen as small, inept, or bad in others' eyes. Self-punishment is an internal process whereby we inflict emotional or physical pain on ourselves in order to placate the demands of conscience. It is generally triggered by violating a prohibition. Self-rejection consists of the belief that one is essentially unlovable. Each of these components of the guilt emotions can trigger anxiety in the presence of another person. Anxiety relates to the perception of an external threat as a result of being guilty or falling short and deserving punishment, rejection, or shaming.

Subjective guilt can be further divided into self-condemning emotions called neurotic guilt (false guilt, punitive guilt, or simply guilt feelings) and love-based corrective feelings variously called true guilt, ego guilt, existential guilt, or constructive sorrow. Both emotions may involve either an awareness of one's objective guilt or a distorted perception of one's guilt, but they are experienced in radically different ways. Neurotic guilt is self-punitive and atoning in nature whereas constructive sorrow is love and forgiveness based.

Much confusion has been created by the failure to make these subtle distinctions concerning objective/subjective guilt and neurotic guilt/constructive sorrow. For example, theologians have sometimes been alarmed by psychologists' efforts to eliminate neurotic guilt feelings because they were not aware that psychologists wanted to replace these punitive feelings with healthy, love-based moral motivations. Similarly, some psychologists have mistakenly viewed Christianity as a neurotic, guilt-inducing religion because of its stress on humanity's guilt before God. Rejecting the notion of true objective guilt before God, psychologists often understand guilt feelings in a completely naturalist, reductionistic sense and fail to recognize our true moral natures. Moreover, some Christians have unfortunately failed to differentiate between neurotic guilt feelings and godly sorrow and have assumed that all feelings of guilt are Holy Spirit induced when, in fact, they may be the result of failed human relationships and false internalized standards.

Guilt and Neurosis. An understanding of guilt feelings is central to the understanding of psychological maladjustment. Guilt (along with anxiety) are some of the major emotions that set in motion the various psychological defense mechanisms. Because anxiety and guilt feelings are painful emotions, people attempt to repress the wishes and experiences surrounding them. This repression is one of the first steps in the formation of neurotic symptoms. It is also the main reason why many therapists promote a value-free approach to therapy in which they attempt to make no moral judgments of their clients. They believe any moral judgments in therapy will create further guilt feelings, motivate greater repression and rigidity, and move the client further into neurosis.

Development of Guilt Feelings. Punitive neurotic guilt emotions are usually referred to by psychologists simply as guilt. These feelings, based on attitudes of self-punishment, self-rejection, and low self-esteem, develop over a period of years within the context of the child's relationships with parents and significant others. Four dynamics appear to be central in their development: 1) the child's innate capacity for self-observation and judgment, 2) the taking in of the standards and expectations of others, 3) the taking in of the punishments and corrective attitudes of others, and 4) the child's anger over the frustration of his or her needs and wishes.

Although theorists vary in their understanding of the development of guilt feelings and other aspects of moral functioning, all agree that the child's innate potential for cognitive development is central to the process. Without the unfolding of these cognitive abilities, children would be unable to accurately evaluate their actions and the consequences of them or to profit from the socialization process. It is this process that sets humanity's sense of right and wrong on a totally different level from animals. Animals have the capacity for some simple learning of right and wrong through rewards and punishments but not the capacity for self-observation that can result in true moral judgments.

Although most psychologists view the human potential for mature morality as simply the ability of an amoral individual to profit from socializing influences of parents and others, the scriptural assertion that we are created in God's image suggests that we are born with more than simply the capacity to profit from experience. It suggests that every person has at least some ability (or potential ability) to know whether his deeds are good or evil apart from (or in addition to) what he is taught. The New Testament asserts that the unbeliever's awareness of God's existence in natural revelation is repressed insofar as there is knowledge in conscience that sin will be punished by death, resulting in a sense of impending threat, hence, anxiety (Rom. 1:18–32). This suggests we are not born morally neutral but have some inherent sense of right and wrong, a sense of what is in harmony or not with our nature as God-image bearers.

The second factor in the development of guilt feelings is the child's taking in of the standards of parents and significant others. This process, called internalization, takes place as children begin to adopt parental and societal values. Since children admire and look up to their parents and because they fear punishment, rejection, or shaming for disobedience, they gradually adopt their parents' standards. These standards, when merged with the child's inherent moral capacity, and own wishes and desires, form the core standards of conscience, or the child's ego ideal or ideal self. This set of ideals becomes the criterion by which the child judges his or her own level of morality and accomplishment. After it is well established it will operate much as an internal law, and the child will tend to feel guilty any time its standards are violated.

At the same time children are taking in their parents' ideals and standards they also take in corrective attitudes and actions. Consequently, if parental punishment is severely punitive or rejecting, children soon adopt these attitudes toward themselves and begin to mentally inflict similar punishments on themselves when they fall short of their ideals. These punitive and self-rejecting emotions form the core of neurotic guilt feelings.

Another contributor to the development of guilt feelings is the child's anger. When children become angry at parents and others, they naturally assume their parents are angry with them in return. Consequently, when parents punish children, children tend to see the parents as angrier than they really are. As children take in their parents' punitive attitudes, they take in these attitudes as they perceive them rather than as they are in reality. Thus, the strength of the child's punitive feelings of guilt is not simply a reflection of the punitiveness of parental discipline. Rather, it is actually as strong as the combination of the parent's anger and the child's own projected anger. This is one reason why many persons with loving parents still have serious problems with neurotic guilt feelings.

Guilt in the Bible. The Bible clearly addresses both objective and subjective guilt before God. All persons are objectively guilty before God: they have violated God's will and their potential for relationship and, by so doing, have a debt to punishment on account of God's justice. Moreover, it is clear that persons are immersed in their own neurotic guilt feelings both on account of impaired relations with God and others. These guilt feelings are evident in the account of the first sin (Gen. 3) where sin and objective guilt was immediately accompanied by shame (uncomfortableness with human nakedness) and fear of punishment or rejection by God (as evidenced by their hiding from His presence).

Christ's work on the cross, the indwelling Holy Spirit, and loving, forgiving relationships with others in the church are the solution to humanity's objective guilt before God and their subjective guilt feelings. First, the doctrine of justification by faith asserts that the believer is no longer a criminal before God with a debt to punishment (Rom 5:8–10). Objective guilt is satisfied in the substitutionary atonement of Christ. However, this forensic act does not of itself necessarily relieve the believer of guilt feelings. The dynamics of the heart can be dealt with only by an experiential application of the love of the indwelling Spirit and members of the Christian community to the heart of the believer (Rom. 8:14–17; John 13:34). The reality behind the doctrines of regeneration, filling and illumination of the Spirit, and the Christian community enable the believer by faith to experience the love of God as opposed to His wrath. Increased freedom from guilt feelings comes with increased awareness of what Christ has done on the cross to pay for all of our sins and a greater openness to the indwelling Spirit and members of the body of Christ who model non-punitive, loving, corrective attitudes instead of condemnation.

Even though Christians are no longer criminals under God's wrath because Christ has already paid for all of their sins, they still continue to sin against Him and neighbor. That is, they are in fact guilty of sinning. Nevertheless, their relationship with God is no longer as a guilty person but as a child of God, already forgiven and under His loving discipline. Consequently, there in no objective reason for the believer to experience guilt feelings. Because the believer's sins have been paid for by Christ, any further self-punishment is actually a form of self-atonement, which is ultimately based on a rejection of the efficacy of Christ's atoning death. From this perspective, any efforts to satisfy the demands of conscience apart from Christ only result in unnecessary guilt feelings based upon a standard of works-righteousness. This perspective is supported not only by biblical teachings on justification and forgiveness but also by John's explicit statement that "we shall know by this that we are of the truth, and shall assure our heart before him, in whatever our heart condemns us, for God is greater than our heart . . ." (1 John 3:19–20).

This scriptural teaching on the atonement has led some (Bonhoeffer, 1955; Narramore, 1984; Thielicke, 1966) to conclude that guilt feelings are not a divinely ordained type of motivation. Rather, motivation for change is based upon an awareness of one's sin *as a forgiven child of God* in the context of the love of the indwelling Spirit and the body which enables the gradual lowering of defenses and begins the transformation of inclinations toward self-atoning guilt feelings into confession of sin. This confession of sin accompanies the beginnings of Godly sorrow, a love-based corrective feeling, a constructive sorrow motivated by love. Thus, the believer's awareness of sin is a precondition for an increased awareness of one's relationship with God, not an occasion for self-punishment and self-atonement.

The Alternative to Guilt. While psychologists from a variety of theoretical perspectives point out the harm caused by punitive guilt emotions, most also see the need for an alternative form of motivation. We can distinguish what has been called true guilt (Tournier, 1962), existential guilt (Pattison, 1969), or constructive sorrow (Narramore, 1984) from this type of motivation based upon punitive guilt feelings in several ways. Whereas punitive guilt feelings are a self-centered form of punishment designed to atone for one's failures, constructive sorrow focuses on the damage done to others and desires to make things right. Feelings of guilt are focused more on past failures, whereas constructive sorrow is oriented toward future changes. And feelings of guilt are based on anger and self-rejection, whereas constructive sorrow is motivated by love. Paul wrote of this type of motivation when he spoke of the sorrow that is according to the will of God "that produces repentance without regret in contrast to the sorrow of the world that produces death" (2 Cor. 7:8–10). It must be stressed, however, that the movement from guilt feelings to godly sorrow is not possible on the basis of mere intellectual assent but is a work of faith as love is applied to the heart of the believer. In fact, a believer may be largely unable to experience godly sorrow on account of past hurts, expectations, and resistance to God's love and forgiveness. Numerous interventions involving the loving community and the spiritual disciplines may be required over time to remedy this situation.

From a developmental sense, as punitive guilt feelings develop out of the interaction of the child's innate capacity for moral functioning and internalized parental punitiveness, similarly feelings of constructive sorrow grow out of one's innate moral capacities and the internalizing of loving parental corrections. When parents and significant others correct children with firm but loving and respectful discipline, children learn to respond to their failures not with punitive self-rejection but with a healthy recognition of their shortcomings along with a genuine desire to do better based on a concern for others and a desire for personal integrity. Analogously, God's love in the Spirit applied to the heart of the believer and modeled by the Church makes possible confession of our objective guilt as children which forms the basis of constructive sorrow (or true guilt). Before Paul wrote of a godly or constructive sorrow in 2 Corinthians 7:8–10, he reminded the Corinthians of a number of God's Old Testament promises (2 Cor. 6:16–18) and then wrote, "Therefore, having these promises, beloved, let us cleanse ourselves from all defilement of flesh and spirit, perfecting holiness in the fear of God" (2 Cor. 7:1). His appeal was not to avoid the pain of guilty condemnation, since that issue was already settled. Instead it was to respond in love to the truth of ourselves in the context of the loving work of God on our behalf. This positive motivation is the biblical alternative to guilt feelings.

References

Bonhoeffer, D. (1955). *Ethics*. New York: Macmillan.

Hodge, (1977). *Systematic theology* (3 Vols.). Grand Rapids, MI: Eerdmans.

Narramore, B. (1984). *No condemnation: Rethinking guilt and motivation*. Grand Rapids, MI: Zondervan.

Pattison, E. (1969). Morality, guilt, and forgiveness in psychology. In E. Pattison (Ed.) *Clinical psychiatry and religion*. Boston: Little, Brown.

Thielicke, H. (1966). *Theological ethics* (2 Vols.). Philadelphia: Fortress.

Tournier, P. (1962). *Guilt and grace*. New York: Harper & Row.

S. B. Narramore and J. H. Coe

See Superego; Shame; Emotion; Religion and Personality; Religious Health and Pathology; Conscience.

Hair Pulling. This behavior, called trichotillomania, is typically associated with severe psychopathology in childhood, although it is occasionally found in adolescence and adulthood. The hair is usually pulled from the head in a compulsive, violent fashion that removes clumps, even fistfuls, of hair from the patient. In some cases, hair from other parts of the body (e.g., eyebrows) may be pulled (Sue, Sue, & Sue, 1994). At times there is a ritualistic, repetitive quality to the behavior. This has led psychodynamic theorists to view it as a masturbatory substitute or a denial of castration, particularly when the hair is pulled from the pubic area. Others have considered such behavior to be an expression of aggressive or exhibitionistic impulses.

Hair pulling in children often suggests a pervasive developmental disorder, such as infantile autism or childhood schizophrenia. In such cases hair pulling may appear at an early age, between ages 3 and 12. It is often associated with other self-destructive or self-mutilative behaviors, such as head banging, biting or hitting parts of the body, or eye gouging.

Behavioral techniques have often proven effective in the treatment of trichotillomania. An incompatible behavior such as finger painting is positively reinforced while the hair pulling is followed by an aversive consequence such as a mild electric shock or a time out. If the child does not respond to contingencies such as these, he or she is fitted with a helmet that prevents this behavior.

Reference

Sue, D., Sue, D., & Sue, S. (1994). *Understanding abnormal behavior*. New York: Houghton Mifflin.

J. D. Guy, Jr.

See Trichotillomania.

Hall, Granville Stanley (1844–1924). Pioneer psychologist who founded America's first psychology laboratory, the American Psychological Association (APA), the classic American Psychology of Religion, and four journals. Nurtured in New England Congregationalism, he evolved a humanistic theology that scandalized the orthodoxy of his time.

A descendant of Puritans John Alden and William Brewster, Hall grew up on the Massachusetts farm where he was born. After graduating Phi Beta Kappa from Williams College in 1867, he followed his mother's influence toward the ministry and attended Union Theological Seminary. There he soon found himself in lessening sympathy with religious orthodoxy. After Hall preached his first sermon at Union, his professor, despairing of mere criticism, knelt to pray for the skeptic.

Hall studied philosophy in Germany (1868–1870) and finished his Union divinity degree in 1871. While he was teaching at Antioch College (1872–1876), Wilhelm Wundt's psychology text captivated him. En route to Germany to study psychology, Hall detoured to Harvard, where he tutored English and in 1878 took America's first psychology Ph.D., under William James. He became Wundt's first American student during another two years abroad.

Back at Harvard in 1881 Hall gave a popular series of Saturday lectures on education that led to a professorship at Johns Hopkins University. There he founded the first American psychology laboratory (1883) and started the country's first psychology journal, *American Journal of Psychology* (1887).

Hall spent most of his career as president of Clark University, Worcester, Massachusetts, beginning in 1889. Although the university's benefactor, Jonas Clark, frustrated Hall's expectations for financial support, Hall kept his position until his retirement at 76.

Stanley Hall knew personal tragedy. In 1890 his wife and eight-year-old daughter were asphyxiated by a gas lamp that was turned on but failed to light. His second wife, within months after their marriage, developed a mental disorder that required Hall to maintain her in a nursing home until her death.

Hall's fertile mind leapfrogged from interest to interest, stimulating students and leaving new enterprises at each stop. He brought what he called his "child-study craze" from Johns Hopkins to Clark, founded the *Pedagogical Seminary* (now *Journal of Genetic Psychology*) in 1891, and produced his monumental two-volume *Adolescence: Its Psychology and Its Relations to Physiology, Anthropology, Sociology, Sex, Crime, Religion and Education* (1904). His interest in the psychology of religion overlapped the developmental studies and in 1904 spawned the *Journal of Religious Psychology,* which lapsed after a decade of irregular publication. Hall founded the *Journal of Applied Psychology* in 1915. He was the first president of the American Psychological Association, organized in his home in 1882.

Hall's earliest journals published his and his students' pioneering questionnaire studies of religious phenomena. Chapter 14 of *Adolescence*—"The Adolescent Psychology of Conversion"—forms his major early work on psychology of religion. The 82 pages range over and beyond the growth of conversion theology in New England, ages at conversion for 5,524 cases, conversion in literature, and comparisons of Christianity with "alien faiths." Hall's psychology of religion obviously transcended the recitation of numerical questionnaire data. Some followers were less creative, and by 1920 psychology of religion was waning, weakened within and attacked by psychoanalysis and behaviorism.

Hall retained his Puritan mysticism while abandoning orthodoxy and the institutional church. He believed the insights of other major religions reflected different stages of psychological development, but Christianity, with its emphasis on love and service, formed the highest revelation. He considered the Bible the greatest textbook in psychology, reflecting the needs of human souls.

Hall's late infatuation with psychoanalysis led to *Jesus, the Christ, in the Light of Psychology* (1917), his final major statement of his psychology of religion and personal theology. He believed that literal belief in Christ's miracles is a necessary early stage of faith but that they ultimately possess higher spiritual truths. Christ's supreme sacrifice produced the resurrection—not a literal fact, but a firmly held belief that motivated humanity to the highest spiritual levels. Hall was keenly disappointed that the book received damnation from the orthodox and scant attention from scholars.

After retirement Hall scrutinized his latest life stage in *Senescence* (1922). Elected to the presidency of the American Psychological Association a second time (an honor shared only with James), he died before the term expired.

Additional Reading

Pruette, L. (1970). *G. Stanley Hall: A biography of a mind.* Freeport, NY: Books for Libraries Press. (Original work published 1926)

R. D. Kahoe

See Psychology, History of.

Hallucination. A sensory experience such as seeing persons or objects, hearing voices, and smelling odors in the absence of environmental stimuli. Although hallucinations are usually associated with schizophrenia, they are also manifested in other psychiatric disorders as well as under conditions of drug intoxication, hypnotic trance, and stimulus deprivation. Moreover, surveys reveal that 10 to 25% of the general population have had certain hallucinatory experiences. Hearing voices (auditory hallucinations) is most frequently reported by schizophrenic patients, with seeing (visual hallucinations), smelling (olfactory hallucinations), touch (tactile hallucinations), and tasting (gustatory hallucinations) appearing in the most deteriorated patients (Al-Issa, 1995).

Although hallucinations are common in the general population and in other psychiatric groups, schizophrenic hallucinations tend to be qualitatively different from other hallucinations. Schneider (1959) suggested that certain hallucinations are important in the diagnosis of schizophrenia: audible thinking, in which the voice repeats almost all the patient's goal-directed thinking; voices arguing about the patient; and voices commenting on the patient.

In differentiating between hallucinations and other products of fantasy and imagination, much importance seems to have been assigned by psychiatrists and psychologists to the situations, conditions, and circumstances in which hallucinations are reported. When the precipitating conditions in which or the processes by which the individual comes to have hallucinations are unknown, the hallucinations are considered to be an indication of functional psychosis and/or schizophrenic disorder. Hallucinations with a known physical basis, such as acute brain syndrome and intoxication or fever, are considered to be a manifestation of organic psychosis. Whether dreams are differentiated or confused with visual hallucinations depends on whether these visions were experienced in a state of wakefulness or sleep (*see* Sleep and Dreaming).

In Western culture, which makes a rigid distinction between reality and fantasy, hallucinations are considered negatively, as they are expected to interfere with daily activity and interaction with the physical environment. Such negative attitudes toward hallucinations make individuals less familiar with their fantasy and imagination by discouraging people from exploring them. In this situation the sudden appearance of imagery may result in anxiety and denial of responsibility for them and the tendency to attribute them to outside sources.

In non-Western societies, where the distinction between reality and fantasy is more flexible, hallucinations are not anxiety-arousing or disturbing to the individual. In these societies the experience is sought, and a variety of methods (lack of sleep, fasting, prolonged physical pain, social isolation, drugs, special exercises) are used to achieve it. Sociocultural conditions in these cultures seem to be conducive to positive attitudes toward hallucinations and other imagery. These positive attitudes, which enable members of the group to familiarize themselves with their imagery and hallucinations, tend to facilitate the public report and the social control of these experiences by reinforcing commonly shared hallucinations and extinguishing those that are individual and idiosyncratic. Thus there is a high frequency of only culturally sanctioned hallucinatory experiences. In a village in the Philippines, for example, where imaginary noises, smells, and other images are reinforced, people saw and heard fairylike spirits in nearly every tree.

The frequency of hallucinations among ethnic and religious groups in the United States may also reflect different attitudes toward these experiences. Studies reveal that African-Americans have higher rates of hallucinations than whites among patients and normal populations (Adebimpe, Klein, & Fried, 1981). Among religious groups, black Baptists, black Methodists, and Church of God members had the highest number of hallucinations while Lutherans, Presbyterians, white Methodists, and Jews had the lowest. These subcultural differences raise the question whether some cults and religious sects that have relatively positive attitudes toward hallucinations could play a therapeutic role in helping psychotic patients to adapt to their hallucinations.

Patients may adapt to their hallucinations by using different strategies to cope with them. They may use distraction (taking a shower, jogging), ignoring the voices, selective listening (select the positive aspects from the voices), and setting limits (making a deal with the voices to be expressed only at a certain time) (Romme, Honig, Noorthoorn, & Escher, 1992). Schizophrenic patients may cherish their hallucinations and thus refuse to take medications because the drugs diminish or eliminate the strength of the hallucinations.

References

Adebimpe, V. R., Klein, H. E., & Fried, J. (1981). Hallucinations and delusions in black psychiatric patients. *Journal of the National Medical Association, 73*, 517–520.

Al-Issa, I. (1995). The illusion of reality or the reality of illusion: Hallucinations and culture. *British Journal of Psychiatry, 166*, 368–373.

Romme, M. A. J., Honig, A., Noorthoorn, E. O., & Escher, A. D. M. A. (1992). Coping with hearing voices: An emancipatory approach. *British Journal of Psychiatry, 161*, 99–103.

Schneider, K. (1959). *Clinical psychopathology*. New York: Grune & Stratton.

I. AL-ISSA

See SCHIZOPHRENIA.

Handedness. The term *handedness* refers to a clear preference of the left or right hand in certain activities. Overall handedness, however, is not in strict left/right terms—an individual's handedness lies along a spectrum of preference from extreme right-handedness in all activities to universal left-hand use. Left-handers, historically and presently, constitute a small percentage (10–15%) of the population. Some of the first historical references to handedness are biblical: Judges 3:15; 20:12–18; and 1 Chronicles 12:2 mention left-handedness or ambidexterity.

What causes hand preferences? Social pressures may influence handedness, encouraging left-handers to use the right hand for activities. Biological research, however, suggests prenatal hand preference. Ultrasounds of fetuses demonstrate an apparent hand preference before birth. Experimentally, the manipulation of animal embryo cells can yield a reversal of handedness. The current, dominant theory of handedness states that left-handedness results from slight prenatal trauma or brain damage that prevents the brain from naturally developing a right-handed preference.

Does research support common attributions assigned to left- or right-handers? Correlational studies have linked handedness with a number of traits. Remember, however, that correlational studies do not prove causality (e.g., handedness does not necessarily cause a correlated trait) and that the results of correlational studies on handedness are often contradictory.

If left-handedness results from slight prenatal brain trauma, are left-handers somewhat psychologically deficient? Some psychological disorders (such as alcoholism, aggression, and delinquency) have been weakly correlated with left-handedness. Some studies link homosexuality weakly with left-handedness; other studies deny this conclusion. There are small correlations between left-handedness and psychological disorders such as anxiety and schizophrenia.

As for mental and professional proficiency, no significant differences in verbal ability exist between left- and right-handers. Left-handedness is not positively linked with stellar mathematical ability; however, strong right-handedness has been weakly linked with mathematical deficiencies. The distribution of left- and right-handers in professions seems to match handedness distribution in the general population. Some studies have demonstrated a higher percentage of left-handers among architects and lawyers, though other results disagree.

Are left-handers innately clumsier than right-handers? Consistent right-handers (right hand use for virtually all handed activities) are slightly more coordinated than inconsistent right-handers and left-handers. With regard to sports, some studies have shown that left-handers enjoy heightened proficiency in confrontational sports but have no advantage or known disadvantage in other sports.

One interesting and controversial correlation regarding handedness suggests a link between handedness and health risks. Studies in this area are numerous; their results often contradictory. Some suggest that left-handers are underrepresented in the oldest age groups, leading researchers to assume decreased life span of left-handers. Surveys and research demonstrate that left-handers are more likely to report injury requiring medical attention (left-handed children are nearly twice as likely to be injured than their right-handed peers) and that left-handers are involved in more fatal accidents, especially automobile accidents, than right-handers.

Despite some weak correlations between left-handedness and negative traits, parents of a left-handed child should not try to switch that child's preference. The confusion and coordinational difficulties facing a child forced to switch handedness may cause greater danger than does left-handedness itself.

T. E. BASALLA

See BRAIN AND HUMAN BEHAVIOR.

Handwriting Analysis. *See* GRAPHOLOGY.

Happiness. The state and experience of well-being or maturity. Historically the term has been analyzed in objective and subjective terms. Subjective happiness has to do with person's experiences or reports of well-being, which typically reference pleasant emotions and circumstances as well as general reflections on characterological development. Objective accounts of happiness attempt to provide explanations and criteria for determining whether a person is happy; these accounts are not solely based upon private reports.

The controversy involved in understanding happiness has little to do with subjective happiness insofar as this depends only upon a person's accurate representation of present mental states. The issue of contention revolves around whether it is possible to get beyond a subjective or relativistic understanding of happiness to a universal, objective account. Numerous views have been presented on the nature of happiness, some arguing that it is pleasure alone, some virtue or the realization of one's character, some self-interest, and some experience of union with God.

Formal Notion of Happiness. Despite differences over the content of happiness, several formal ideas about happiness are acceptable to many people. First, whatever happiness means, it is at least possible to be happy in degrees insofar as one can be said to be happier than another person, or more in this year than the last. Second, a state of happiness can change so that one is less happy or more happy from time to time. Third, there must be some association between happiness and pleasure, whether it is one of identity or as a result of or as an element of a certain virtuous state. That is, a life utterly void of any pleasure or some zest in living cannot be said to be truly happy. Fourth, many have thought that something more deeply is implied in happiness than merely what is expressed by terms such as "comfortable," "amused," or "enjoyment." While these terms may refer to psychological states associated with happiness, in themselves they are considered more fleeting than the condition of happiness.

Fifth, at least a superficial account of pleasure does not seem to capture all that we might want to include in happiness. That is, many would accept that a person may experience many pleasant hours of sensuous pleasure without being truly happy. Likewise, a person could reasonably be called happy even in the moment when he or she is not presently experiencing pleasure. For example, a person may be happy even when the dentist is drilling or in other various difficult or painful experiences.

Sixth, many have thought of happiness as being both a state and an activity. That is, we call one happy because there is some history of a qualitative way of experiencing life so that now a state, disposition, or condition exists. We do not think of one as being happy just for a day and never again. However, we would not think that a person is happy if this was never actually borne out in experience, within activities of daily life. Seventh, though happiness is not entirely conditioned by external circumstances, it is not entirely independent from them. We can imagine one who is happy in bad times, though we are hard pressed to think of one happy whose circumstance (in this life and the next) are only utter and unending tragedy.

Aristotle on Happiness. The ancient Greek philosophers addressed the issue of happiness in great depth, and their ideas influenced thinkers for centuries. In particular Aristotle argued that happiness (Gk. *eudaimonia*) is the chief good and aim of all human activities consisting in the active exercise of a person's powers in accordance with reason and true human nature. In general, it is an ideal rather than an actuality; it is not attainable merely by chronological age, process, conscious choice or concern. It is a state or disposition whereby the individual has developed a certain character that issues forth in actions or activities informed by virtue, a habituated character with a healthy concern and accompanied pleasantness. The pleasure associated with happiness is understood as a "zest" component contained in the activity that gives vitality to the behavior and life in general. Of course, not all virtuous actions are accompanied with this zest element or to the same degree (such as in the case of fortitude), though if pleasure is altogether absent in the individual, we would not consider this a happy life.

Thus Aristotle distinguishes the virtuous life from other possible lives as follows: the vicious person thinks the good is pleasure and desires, chooses, and acts on this at all costs to his demise; the incontinent person knows the good, desires it (in part), chooses it, but fails to act on it; the continent person knows the good, desires it (in part), chooses it, and does it, but with no joy; and the virtuous person knows the good, desires it, chooses it, and does it with pleasure or joy.

Modern Philosophy and Psychology on Happiness. While philosophers and theologians through the medieval period into the Renaissance and the Reformation were absorbed with the issue of objective happiness, modern thinkers have been less interested in the subject. In part this was due to the their general rejection of any objective account of happiness, insisting that happiness is more a question of personal choice, taste, and pleasure. Interestingly, this tendency is evident in the first century of modern psychology as well which, according to Myers (1993), did not only leave unanswered the question of what happiness consists in but also left the whole question unasked. Part of the explanation for this oversight may be modern psychology's insistence (with modern science) that it is not possible to derive prescriptions for living or an objective account of the good life on the basis of a purely descriptive and objective science (what comes to be known as the "naturalistic fallacy").

Furthermore, according to Myers and Diener (1996), discussions in modern psychology have typically focused upon psychopathology while largely ignoring psychological health. They note that in the *Psychological Abstracts* between 1967 and 1994, 5,099 abstracts mention anger, 36,851 mention anxiety, 46,380 mention depression, yet only 2,389 mention happiness, 2,340 mention life satisfaction, and 405 mention joy. In this 27-year span, there exists a 17 to 1 ratio of articles addressing psychopathology and negative emotions over health and positive emotions.

Nevertheless, Myers and Diener (1996) note evidence of a change in this trend by the emergence of a new interest in a scientific approach to happiness. The concern is with how to quantify happiness given contemporary ways in which science can count crimes, measure memories, or assess intelligence. In general, social scientists have tended to neglect the more thorny problems involved in accounts of objective happiness and have concerned themselves with people's reports of happiness and unhappiness (subjective happiness). The emphasis is on studying and developing accurate instruments by which to measure subjective happiness.

As a result, contemporary discussions of happiness are typically couched in modern psychological language. Thus happiness is often discussed in terms of individuals having a realistic appraisal of oneself, others and the world; an ability to enjoy the actual world and not merely the possible or imaginary one; a strong sense of identity with others, which enables one to relate with others; an ability to spontaneously experience joy and sorrow without fear of humiliation or losing control; a sense of one's independence without being withdrawn; being creative; being humorous; able to experience intimacy with others without loss of personal boundaries; an ability to accept alternative courses of action when required; tolerant of misfortunes.

The New Testament on Happiness. The New Testament discusses happiness in the manner of neither the ancients nor the moderns. The New Tes-

tament writers fail to even use the term popularized by the ancients, *eudaimonia*, though it was still extant in the Greek world. Rather, the New Testament employs various forms of *makairos*, a term with an ancient pedigree going back to Homer and Hesiod, used chiefly of the gods and the departed dead, which carries with it the idea of one who is blessed, happy, or to be congratulated.

Jesus provides in the Sermon on the Mount a radical new vision of happiness for his followers: blessed (*makarioi*) or to be congratulated are the poor in spirit, the sad, the poor, the hungry, the persecuted for the sake of Christ (Matt. 5; see also Luke 6). Conversely, woe, doom, and misery are pronounced upon those who laugh, the well fed, those who are friends of the world, for they have their reward. The distinguishing factor between the blessed and the cursed has to do with allegiances: those who find difficulties in this age "for the sake of the Son of man" are blessed among the living; those who flourish apart from God and have their reward "now" shall be the cursed. By these striking words Jesus sets forth the Christian inversion of natural values that anticipates the church community in conflict with the kingdom of this age known as the world, an invisible network of human and demonic agency raised up against the knowledge of God. This conflict is also indicative of the psychological tension within believers between our life in the Spirit who opens to us new horizons of possible growth in love and our preconversion habits of sin that alienate us from God, neighbor, and ourselves.

Consequently the New Testament does not understand happiness or psychological well-being in terms of social functioning, feeling good, or the standard natural virtues attainable in common grace and discussed by the ancient philosophers. Rather, conversion becomes the interpretive metaphor for understanding human growth, which involves humility and repentance, virtues little referenced by the ancients or moderns. The solely natural, spontaneous movements of nature (life of autonomy) are understood relationally in Christian theology as pride, which must be mortified or transformed to make way for a new sphere of life of dependence upon the Spirit. This union with God transforms by love the growth of common grace into humility before God and neighbor.

This explains why the term *happiness* is less fundamental to biblical ethics than are the metaphors of life and death, understood relationally as the harmony and order which result from dependence upon God in the Spirit and disharmony or chaos that results from autonomy from God. Nature is not denied in the gospel, only transformed by Spirit-filled living in dependence upon God. In that sense, the natural virtues are according to nature as far as a non Christian can live but are still the life of sin insofar as they are not experienced or done in the love of God. Thus Jesus is the archetype example of health in this age who went out in the power of the Spirit to do the will of the Father. It should be clear, then, that if Jesus is our model of health in this age, true flourishing will not always look like what we can imagine it to be in the fullness of the kingdom of God where one day all the people of God shall experience full freedom from grief, struggle, and the characterological sins that beset us. Nevertheless, the path of letting go of our need of autonomy from God the way to freedom and experiencing fullness of life in this age.

References

Myers, D. G. (1993). *The pursuit of happiness.* New York: Avon.

Myers, D. G., & Diener, E. (1996). The pursuit of happiness: *Scientific American, 174* (5), 70–72.

Additional Readings

Aristotle. (1985). *Nicomachean ethics.* (Irwin, T. trans.). Indianapolis, IN: Hackett.

Diener, E. (1994). Assessing subjective well-being: Progress and opportunities. *Social Indicators Research, 31,* 103–157.

Diener, E., & Larsen, R. J. (1993). The experience of emotional well-being. In M. Lewis & J. M. Haviland (Eds.), *Handbook of emotions.* New York: Guilford.

Headey, B., & Wearing, A. (1990). Subjective well-being: a stocks and flows framework. In F. Strack, M. Argyle, & N. Schware (Eds.), *Subjective well-being.* Oxford: Oxford University Press.

Inglehart, R. (1990). *Culture shift in advanced industrial society.* Princeton, NJ: Princeton University Press.

J. H. Coe

See Emotion; Affect.

Headache. Headache pain is a condition that affects people of all ages. Although they are not usually life-threatening, headaches are a significant health problem when considered epidemiologically. Rasmussen, Jensen, Schroll, & Olesen (1991) estimated that the lifetime prevalence rate for all types of headaches is 93% for males and 99% for females in the general population. Furthermore, they note that while most headache pain is usually mild or infrequent, more severe or frequent forms of headache can cause considerable suffering. Headache pain can negatively impact personal relationships, social lifestyle, and vocational ability and can result in depression and emotional anguish.

The current headache classification system was developed in 1988 by the Headache Classification Committee of the International Headache Society (IHS). The IHS system consists of 13 major headache categories with more than 100 subcategories and includes operational diagnostic criteria for all types of headaches. Three primary headache categories are migraine, tension-type, and cluster.

Migraine with aura and migraine without aura have replaced the terms *classic migraine* and *common migraine* in the current IHS classification system. The prevalence of migraine has been especially well documented in the epidemiological literature. Data from the American Migraine Study (Lipton & Stewart, 1993), which used a nationally representative sample of the United States population, indicated that 6% of males and 17.6% of females suffer from migraine headaches. According to IHS classification, migraine headaches are attacks lasting 4 to 72 hours. Typical characteristics of the headache are unilateral location, pulsating or throbbing pain quality, moderate to severe pain intensity, aggravation by routine physical activities (e.g., lifting, bending, walking), and associated nausea or vomiting and photo- and phonophobia.

Four phases of migraine have been identified and can occur alone or in any combination with any other phase: prodrome, aura, headache, and postdrome (Saper, Silberstein, Gordon, & Hamel, 1993). The prodrome is comprised of premonitory phenomena and can precede the headache by hours or days. Premonitory symptoms can be emotional or psychological, neurological or physiological. The aura is a constellation of neurological signs that typically develop in the 5 to 30 minutes that precede the headache pain and usually last less than 60 minutes. Visual disturbances constitute the most common type of aura symptom and include scotoma, photopsia, and fortification spectra. Nonvisual aura symptoms occur less frequently and include paresthesia, olfactory disturbances, and auditory disturbances. Fifteen to 20% of migraine sufferers experience migraine with aura. The final phase of migraine is the postdrome, in which the individual may feel tired or irritable or have impaired concentration. Status migrainosus is a subclassification of migraine whereby the headache phase lasts longer than 72 hours despite treatment efforts.

Tension-type headache has replaced tension headache, muscle-contraction headache, and psychogenic headache in the new IHS classification system. The estimated lifetime prevalence rate for tension-type headaches is 69% for males and 88% for females (Stevens, 1993). According to IHS classification, tension-type headaches are recurrent episodes of headache lasting minutes to days. The pain is typically pressing or tightening in quality, mild to moderate in intensity, bilaterally located, and not aggravated by routine physical activity. Nausea or vomiting is absent, although photophobia or phonophobia may be present. This headache category is further subdivided into episodic tension-type headache and chronic tension-type headache. Tension-type headaches are episodic if they occur fewer than 15 days per month and chronic if they occur more than 15 days per month.

Cluster headache, although excruciatingly painful, occurs in approximately 1% of the population experiencing headache pain. Unlike migraine and tension-type headaches, cluster headache is predominantly a male disorder with a sex ratio (male:female) of greater than 5:1 (Blanchard & Andrasik, 1985).

According to IHS classification, cluster headaches are attacks of severe, strictly unilateral pain located orbitally, supraorbitally, and/or temporally, lasting from 15 to 180 minutes and occurring from once every other day to eight times a day. Associated characteristics include conjunctival injection, lacrimation, nasal congestion, rhinorrhea, forehead and facial sweating, miosis, ptosis, and eyelid edema.

Although the pathogenesis of headache remains unclear, various pharmacological and nonpharmacological treatments have proven successful in treating problematic headaches. Pharmacological treatments can be either symptomatic (to reverse or control the headache and related symptoms once the attack has begun) or preventive (to minimize the frequency of expected attacks). Symptomatic treatment choices include analgesics, nonsteroidal anti-inflammatory drugs, and ergotamine derivatives (vasoactive medications). Preventive treatment choices include beta-blockers and calcium channel blockers (both are vasoactive medications), antidepressants (for increased availability of certain neurotransmitters), anticonvulsants, and lithium.

Nonpharmacological treatment strategies can be classified into three major groups: relaxation training, biofeedback training, and cognitive-behavioral techniques. Relaxation training (e.g., progressive muscle relaxation) is intended to target the stress and tension that may precipitate and aggravate both tension-type headaches and migraines. The biofeedback training most commonly used for headache reduction is either electromyographic (EMG) biofeedback or thermal biofeedback. EMG biofeedback is typically used in the treatment of tension-type headaches whereby an individual receives audio or visual feedback (via surface sensors) of electrical information about the functioning of various muscles that seem to be involved in headaches. Thermal biofeedback is typically used in the treatment of migraines whereby an individual receives audio or visual feedback (via a thermistor) of finger temperature, an indirect measure of vasoconstriction that seems to be a mechanism involved in migraine. Cognitive-behavioral techniques are intended to provide an individual with problem-solving or coping skills that can be applied to a wide range of situations or stressors that can precipitate a headache.

References

Blanchard, E. B., & Andrasik, F. (1985). Cluster headache. In A. P. Goldstein, L. Krasner, & S. L. Garfield (Eds.), *Management of chronic headaches: A psychological approach* (pp. 174–178). Elmsford, NY: Pergamon.

Lipton, R. B., & Stewart, W. F. (1993). Migraine in the United States: A review of epidemiology and health care use. *Neurology, 43* (Supplement 3), S6–S10.

Rasmussen, B. K., Jensen, R., Schroll, M., & Olesen, J. (1991). Epidemiology of headache in a general population—a prevalence study. *Journal of Clinical Epidemiology, 44* (11), 1147–1157.

Saper, J. R., Silberstein, S., Gordon, C. D., & Hamel, R. L. (1993). In J. W. Pine (Ed.), *Handbook of headache management: A practical guide to diagnosis and treatment of head, neck, and facial pain*. Baltimore: Williams & Wilkens.

Stevens, M. D. (1993). Tension-type headaches. *American Family Physician, 47* (4), 499–805.

R. KORCHYNSKY

See HEALTH PSYCHOLOGY.

Healing. *See* FAITH HEALING; INNER HEALING; PSYCHIC HEALING; RELIGIOUS RESOURCES IN PSYCHOTHERAPY.

Healing of Memories. *See* INNER HEALING.

Health Maintenance Organization. A health maintenance organization (HMO) is a managed care organization that provides health care to subscribers for a fixed monthly payment. Most HMOs use networks of contracted physicians, hospitals, and other health and mental health care professionals to deliver the services. Individuals join an HMO either by direct enrollment or through a health plan offered by an employer. To receive care at preferred rates, members then must use the services of the health care providers who are in the HMO network. Often HMOs use a gatekeeper model to monitor the provision of services. HMOs using the gatekeeper model require patients to see their primary care physician before reimbursing for visits to a medical or psychological specialist. In this way, the HMO approach promises to limit unnecessary medical services and thereby reduce overall health care costs.

HMOs can be organized in a variety of ways. The four most common models are the staff model, group model, independent practice association, and mixed model HMOs. The staff model requires physicians and other health care professionals to be salaried employees of the HMO. Facilities and clinics usually are also owned by the HMO.

In a group model, the HMO contacts with independent groups of physicians and providers. These physician groups are not salaried but rather receive a negotiated rate for the care provided. From this rate of reimbursement, the physician groups are responsible for paying for hospital and specialist care.

An independent practice association is an association of solo private practice physicians who are paid a fee or a pre-set amount per patient to provide care to the HMO members. A mixed model involves one or more types of HMO structure within a single HMO.

A form of payment associated with HMOs is capitation. Capitation is means of paying for health care services on a per-person (capita) basis rather than a per-procedure basis. For instance, an HMO will often reimburse physicians by paying a fixed amount per month based on the number of HMO members.

The physician gets the same rate regardless of the number of actual patients treated or procedures performed.

HMOs were originated in the 1930s to provide fixed income to the hospitals and physicians who were struggling for income during the great depression. The federal government gave a great boost to the formation of HMOs in 1973 with the passage of the HMO Act. The legislation required most employers to offer the option of enrolling in an HMO where a federally qualified one was available (Health Insurance Association of America, 1996). By the end of 1994, there were 574 HMOs with a total enrollment of 51.2 million members, or nearly 20% of the population of the United States.

Reference

Health Insurance Association of America. (1996). *Source book of health insurance data: 1995*. Washington, DC: Author.

E. W. THROCKMORTON

See INSURANCE: HEALTH AND MENTAL HEALTH; MANAGED CARE.

Health Psychology. "Do not be wise in your own eyes; fear the Lord and depart from evil. It will be health to your flesh, and strength to your bones" (Prov. 3:7–8, NKJV).

The concern of God for health as revealed in the Bible is multifaceted. God characterizes the benefits of joy (Prov. 17:22) and warns of the harmful effects of emotional states such as envy (Prov. 14:30). God provides guidelines for handling property and persons with disease (Lev. 13–14). Moreover, the church is given specific instruction for the care of the sick (James 5:14). Obedience to God's commands is linked to overall good health and long life (Deut. 6:1–12; Eph. 6:1–3).

Historical Development. The modern experimental field of health psychology is a stepchild of an academic and clinical area generally labeled psychosomatic medicine. Articles and books concerning behavioral medicine, behavioral health, health psychology, and medical psychology overlap in many ways. However, terms such as *psychosomatic medicine* and *behavioral medicine* clearly relate to a medical area; that is, a clear pathophysiological disease state. Thus studies correlating internalized anger and cardiovascular disease are clearly psychosomatic studies.

Matarazzo (1982, p. 4) defined health psychology as "the aggregate of the specific educational, scientific, and professional contributions of the discipline of psychology to the promotion and maintenance of health, the prevention and treatment of illness, and the identification of etiologic and diagnostic correlates of health, illness and related dysfunction, and to the analysis and improvement of the health care system and health policy forma-tion." Therefore, personality-cardiovascular disease projects may be described as both health psychology and psychosomatic research. However, work that focuses on such areas as the role of prompting to encourage consistent aerobic exercise or the effects of a particular type of health insurance coverage on the frequency of annual physical exams would be health psychology research or practice. Division 38 (Health Psychology) of the American Psychological Association was founded in 1979, and in 1982 its journal, *Health Psychology*, was published. Whether the stepchild of health psychology grows to be larger than its parent is unknown, since the field has been in existence only since the mid-1970s.

Importance. The potential importance of health psychology becomes evident when one considers the current known causes of disease and health. As detailed by Snyder (1989), paradigm changes from health models that focused on purely physiological factors to those that include biosocial variables have significantly influenced the field's growth. In 1900 the top five leading causes of death were influenza, tuberculosis, gastroenteritis, heart disease, and cerebrovascular disease. By the 1980s and 1990s, infectious diseases have been eliminated as major killers and have been replaced by heart disease, cerebrovascular disease, and obstructive lung disease. Almost all primary causes of death are now either affected by lifestyle factors such as diet, exercise, and smoking or are purely behavioral problems (i.e., accidents, suicide).

Behavioral factors are widely accepted as important in health maintenance and prevention of disease. Moderate exercise is encouraged to establish good cardiovascular fitness. Smokers are encouraged to stop smoking to prevent lung cancer, strokes, and other associated diseases. Newspaper and magazine articles detail stress reduction strategies and the importance of regular physical exams for early detection of hypertension or breast cancer.

General Fields. No encyclopedia description of areas covered by health psychology would be exhaustive. The clinical research, practice, and service delivery aspects of health psychology are rapidly expanding. However, the following sections highlight some major subdivisions and sample relevant work.

Prevention. The shift in causes of death from infectious diseases to those involving lifestyle habits has encouraged many psychologists to enter the health promotion/disease prevention arena. Improving social competence in children, using media to encourage healthy diet habits, educating students not to start smoking, and prompting seat belt use are all examples of preventive health psychology. The organized church functions in a preventive role when it encourages believers to avoid sinful or harmful living habits (e.g., drunkenness) and to treat the body as a "temple of the Holy Spirit" (1 Cor. 6:19, NKJV).

Lifestyle Modification. Assessing and modifying existing unhealthy lifestyle habits are a major endeavor for clinically oriented health psychologists. For example, cigarette smoking is a major harmful factor in many medical problems (e.g., lung cancer, strokes, heart attacks, healing of orthopedic fractures). Health psychologists have investigated the effectiveness of physicians' distribution of materials about smoking, the effectiveness of various programs designed to stop smoking, and specific program procedures. Work has also focused on modifying alcohol use, type-A behavior pattern, illegal or excessive drug use, and social skills to eliminate or reduce disease-promoted behavior and increase health-enhancing behavior.

Medical Adherence. Medical adherence refers to continuing prescribed treatment, rehabilitation, or maintenance programs. Some disorders may have no early signs, such as subjective pain or discomfort, that encourage a patient to take medication. Individuals with no acute stress may be less likely to continue a rehabilitation program. Health psychologists would examine such factors as complexity, length, or cost of treatment, health care setting, health beliefs, prompts or reminders, self-monitoring, and contingency contracts in an effort to improve medical adherence.

Symptom Intervention. Some symptoms of disorders or side effects of treatments are uncomfortable. For example, tension headaches or pain secondary to surgery may be treated with interpersonal counseling, relaxation training, biofeedback treatment, or assertiveness training. Nausea associated with chemotherapy for cancer may be the focus of counter conditioning or cognitive-behavioral interventions. Health psychologists study which procedures are effective for which individuals under what conditions.

Neuropsychological Assessment. All clinical health psychologists engage in some form of assessment that is typically tied to treatment (e.g., biofeedback muscle levels, tension headache frequency). Neuropsychologists focus on the functional assessment of brain disorder. Neuropsychological assessments may aid in differential diagnosis of actual versus pseudodementia or in the monitoring of treatment improvement or failure of stroke patients. Neuropsychological assessments focus on functional abilities and generally supplement medical structural brain studies (e.g., computerized axial tomography).

Psychological Status and Medical Conditions. Much work has examined the extent to which different stress coping styles or personality patterns are related to disease states. Thus cynical anger is associated with higher incidence of cardiovascular disease. Social isolation increases the likelihood of developing cardiovascular disease. Extreme cardiovascular reactivity to stress as a young adult may predict hypertension or other cardiovascular disorders. (*See* Psychosomatic Factors in Health and Illness.)

Consultations. Physicians and others who refer to health psychologists sometimes need assistance. Health psychology is a new area, and some excellent clinicians have had limited exposure to it. Some issues are general ones, such as the differences in practice between psychologists and psychiatrists. Others may be more clearly related to health psychology (e.g., specifications of pain type in biofeedback clinic consultation). Increased specification helps clinicians determine both the appropriateness of the referral and the best means of answering the consultation question.

Religion and Health. David Larson declared in a major medical journal, "Spirituality and religion have important health benefits and some detailed studies using more accurate measures of this are warranted. The question today is not whether there are health benefits, it is how these benefits can be obtained. We can no longer afford to neglect this important clinical variable" (Marwick, 1995, p. 1562). Christians in health psychology have a unique opportunity to relate in an experimental manner faith and health in several areas (see Hill & Butter, 1995).

Church Attendance and Importance. Larson et al. (1989) found that the importance of religion and church attendance indirectly correlated with blood pressure. As these indices increased, blood pressure decreased. A few years later Oxman, Freeman, and Manheimer (1995) found that similar variables related to death after cardiac surgery. Patients who did not report strength and comfort from religion were more than three times more likely to die after elective open-heart surgery than those that did. Those who do not attend church and who attach little importance to faith activities (in violation of Heb. 10:25) may also be at risk for other health-related disorders, an area awaiting further exploration.

Prayer. As the 450 prophets of Baal found to their grief (1 Kings 18), prayers to a false god are not effectual. However, an active, righteous prayer life and intervention may be significant in promoting health and decreasing the effects of illness (James 5:15–16). Byrd (1988) found that intercessory prayer improved the health of coronary care unit patients relative to a control group. Patients who were prayed for by born-again Christians active in their churches were less likely to need ventilatory assistance, antibiotics, and diuretics than the others. No comparison has been made between Christian and non-Christian prayer groups on health indices.

Denominational Factors. Different denominations may be correlated with different levels or types of illnesses. Dwyer, Clarke, and Miller (1990) found that conservative or moderate Protestants and Mormons had significantly lower cancer rates than liberal Protestants, Roman Catholics, and Jewish communicants, even when demographic, environmental, and regional factors related to cancer were statistically controlled. Effects of specific theological beliefs (e.g., covenantal versus dispensational theology) have yet to be explored in health psychology research.

Stress Coping. Serious health problems inevitably tax the ability to cope effectively. Chronic conditions are particularly known to be associated with depression. Pressman, Lyons, Larson, & Strain (1990) found that religious belief was associated with lower levels of depressive symptoms and better ambulation states in elderly women recovering from broken hips.

Ethical Issues. The broad field of health psychology encompasses many clinical and social psychological ethical questions (cf. Payne, 1985). For example, some diseases (e.g., AIDS, lung cancer) are clearly related to behavior in the majority of patients. Should a Christian counselor continue to assist a patient who refuses to change sinful, unhealthy habits without at least informing the patient that the counselor is Christian? Is it appropriate to tax some people for the expensive treatment of others? Scripture helps answer these ethical problems with authority not available to unbelievers.

Causal Factors. Specific causal factors relating health to spiritual factors have been reviewed by others (Hill & Butter, 1995; Martin & Carlson, 1988). Healthy lifestyle habits, optimism, and explanatory style found in faith, specific denominational practices, and the personality correlates of sincere, mature believers have all been suggested as important. In addition Levin and Vanderpool (1989) have detailed various superempirical and supernatural influences outside the realm of experimental health psychology.

Much remains to be done. Some practitioners may see research in various health psychology areas as an effective means of encouraging unbelievers to consider the gospel of Christ.

References

Byrd, R. C. (1988). Positive therapeutic effects of intercessory prayer in a coronary care unit population. *Southern Medical Journal, 81,* 826–829.

Dwyer, J. W., Clarke, L. L., & Miller, M. K. (1990). The effect of religious concentration and affiliation on county cancer mortality rates. *Journal of Health and Social Behavior, 31,* 185–202.

Hill, P. C., & Butter, E. M. (1995). The role of religion in promoting physical health. *Journal of Psychology and Christianity, 14,* 141–155.

Larson, D. B., Koenig, H. G., Kaplan, B. H., Greenberg, R. S., Logue, E., & Tyroler, H. A. (1989). The impact of religion on men's blood pressure. *Journal of Religion and Health, 28,* 265–278.

Levin, J. S., Vanderpool, H. Y. (1989). Is religion therapeutically significant for hypertension? *Social Science and Medicine, 29,* 69–78.

Martin, J. E., & Carlson, C. R. (1988). Spiritual dimensions of health psychology. In W. R. Miller & J. E. Martin (Eds.), *Behavior therapy and religion: Integrating spiritual and behavioral approaches to changes.* Newbury Park, CA: Sage.

Marwick, C. (1995). Should physicians prescribe prayer for health? Spiritual aspects of well-being considered. *Journal of the American Medical Association, 273,* 1561–1562.

Matarazzo, J. D. (1982). Behavioral health's challenge to academic, scientific and professional psychology. *American Psychologist, 37,* 1–14.

Oxman, T. E., Freeman, D. H., & Manheimer, E. D. (1995). Lack of social participation or religious strength and comfort as risk factors for death after cardiac surgery in the elderly. *Psychosomatic Medicine, 57,* 5–15.

Payne, F. E. (1985). *Biblical/medical ethics.* Milford, MI: Mott Media.

Pressman, P., Lyons, J. S., Larson, D. R., & Strain, J. J. (1990). Religious belief, depression, and ambulation status in elderly women with broken hips. *American Journal of Psychiatry, 147,* 758–760.

Snyder, J. J. (1989). *Health psychology and behavioral medicine.* Englewood Cliffs, NJ: Prentice-Hall.

J. K. Neumann

See Stress.

Health Service Providers in Psychology. The Council for the National Register of Health Service Providers in Psychology was established in 1974 after a request by the American Psychological Association. The first edition of the *National Register of Health Service Providers in Psychology* was published in 1975 with 6,877 registrants. The most recent (13th) edition was published in 1995 with 16,000 psychologists.

Applicants for listing must meet the following current criteria: valid license/certification/registration to independently practice psychology (*see* Licensure), completion of a doctoral degree in psychology from a regionally accredited institution, and completion of at least 1,500 hours in an organized predoctoral direct service internship or training program and at least 1,500 hours of supervised postdoctoral health service experience in psychology. The *Register* provides a resource describing highly qualified psychologists to service recipients, governmental agencies, insurance companies, licensing boards, and others interested in psychological health care. Registrants may list phone number; address; licensing, internship, or educational data; employment setting; theoretical orientation; areas of expertise; ages or groups targeted for service; languages spoken; and hospital staff membership. No means exist to specify religious faith.

The *Register* is published annually. To maintain an annual listing, registrants must have valid licenses, certifications, or registrations, submit a renewal form with fees, and complete ethical attestation forms. Individual listings are deleted for those who do not satisfy these three requirements or who are sanctioned for professional misconduct, have been convicted of a serious crime or malpractice, or have become professionally incapacitated.

For Further Information

Council for the National Register of Health Service Providers in Psychology, 1120 G Street NW, Suite 330, Washington, DC 20005, (202) 783-7663.

J. K. NEUMANN

Healthy Personality. Most psychologies that describe human personality focus a great deal of their efforts on identifying the pathological aspect of personality. The diagnosis and classification of mental illness as well as the development and practice of psychotherapy constitute a major emphasis of clinical psychology, although some personality theorists have attempted to describe the positive potential of human nature or the high characteristics of human functioning. During the 1950s and 1960s there was an attempt to describe the nonpathological development of the human personality. This nonpathological description does not refer to the normal or average person, but rather the attempt has been to describe the highest characteristics of human functioning. Recently there has been a growing recognition of the social, relational, and interpersonal contexts of human development and functioning, as evidenced by the explosion of social psychology, Family Systems Theory (*see* Family Therapy: Overview), and the relational perspective in Psychoanalysis (Mitchell, 1988).

Family Functioning. Skynner and Cleese (1995) discuss three kinds of families in terms of quality of functioning: unhealthy, mid-range, and healthy. In their discussion of healthy families they list seven qualities: a positive and friendly attitude that is more spontaneous than feigned; a degree of emotional interdependence that allows for both intimacy and separateness and a flexible flow between the two; a family structure in which the boundaries between the parental dyad and the children subsystem are clear; authoritative parents who are in control but consult the children on decisions; a free and open communication style in which it is understood that family members will often have conflicting feelings about most things, including each other; an accurate perception of the world, including one's own feelings, without the need to project those feelings onto others; and the ability to meet the changing demands of life with a flexible, adaptable attitude because they sense strong emotional support from each other.

In an extensive study of family functioning at all levels, Scarf (1995) describes the qualities of optimal families, those at the highest level of functioning, as "where boundaries are clear, conflicts are resolvable," and "a trust that good things will happen in human encounters" (p. 36). Studies of healthy families by Walsh (1982), Lewis (1989), Lewis, Beavers, Gossett, & Phillips (1976), Housden and Goodchild (1992), and Beavers (1990) are worth consulting.

The Psychological Perspective. Most psychologists use the term *maturity* rather than healthy personality to describe their version of the nonpathological personality. Terms often used are self-actualized, transcendent, or authentic. Since these terms are approximately equivalent, the more frequently used concept of maturity or the mature personality will be used throughout this article.

Psychologists are not the only ones to speak of maturity. The New Testament repeatedly uses the concept to describe the character of Christian experience. The Greek word used most often is *teleios*, occurring 20 times in 17 verses throughout the New Testament and translated as "having attained the end or purpose, complete, perfect" (Bauer, Arndt, & Gingrich, 1979, p. 809) or "mature" in contemporary translations. The first occurrence is in Matthew 5:48 (NIV), where Jesus says "Be perfect, therefore, as your heavenly Father is perfect." In Matthew 19:21 (NIV) Jesus answers the seeker of eternal life, "If you want to be perfect, go, sell your possessions and give to the poor, and you will have treasure in heaven. Then come, follow me." In Romans 12:2 *teleios* is used to describe God's will for us, and in 1 Corinthians 2:6 and 14:20 it is used to describe mature believers.

Rogers (1961) lists 10 characteristics of "the self that truly is"; Maslow (1954) names 14 characteristic of self-actualizers; and Allport (1961) cites 6 aspects of the mature person. Despite the differences in the lists, terminology, and descriptions, these and other psychologists substantially agree on the nature of maturity. The differences are over the degree of detail and emphasis each author wishes to address. Therefore maturity will be described in terms of five basic dimensions: having a realistic view of oneself and others; accepting oneself and others; living in the present but being informed by the past and future; having guiding values; and developing one's abilities and interests so as to cope with the task of living. Although this list could be extended or elaborated upon, these dimensions cover the basic assumptions of maturity.

Realistic View of Self and Others. This dimension involves having an accurate, objective evaluation of oneself and others. Maslow (1954) lists this dimension first in describing self-actualizing people. Allport (1961) calls it self-objectification: the ability to know and understand oneself, to recognize how one's present behavior and actions are influenced by similar experiences in the past. This dimension also represents the whole development of the ego in Freudian thinking (Freud, 1927).

A realistic view of the self may be obtained by asking oneself such questions as, What kind of things can I do best? What are my strengths and weaknesses? At the same time it is necessary to ask, Would others agree, and have I had any success in my area of strength? It is important to remember that people have more than one real talent and a host of lesser abilities. In addition, one's talents and abilities are often related to one's interests (Allport, 1961). Often a person finds that he or she is good at things one likes to do or can learn to do them more quickly than someone who does not share his or her same interests. The variety of interests an individual has is related to the variety of his or her abilities. In gaining a realistic view of the self, an examination of one's interests may be helpful in discovering one's abilities and potential.

Immature persons often make one of two errors in gaining a realistic view of the self. The first is to assume that one is more talented in one or more areas than he or she really is. Coupled with this error is to assume that others have no real ability, having achieved their status by coincidence. This first error is often observed in children and particularly in adolescents who seem convinced that they can do things better than just about anyone. The second error is the reverse of the first. This person says that he or she is untalented and cannot do anything very well. The person says that almost anyone can do almost better than he or she can.

Persons with realistic self-perception avoid both errors. They know their strengths and weaknesses and do not over- or underestimate either. Just as there is a correlation between one's view of one's self and others in both errors of immaturity, so there is a close relationship in a realistic view of the self and a realistic view of others. When a person can perceive his or her own strengths as well as weaknesses, abilities, and talents accurately, the individual is more able to perceive others in a similar fashion.

Accepting Self and Others. This second dimension of maturity is closely related to the first. Rogers (1961) so stresses the importance of this dimension that he divides it into components and discusses each separately. Alfred Adler (Ansbacher & Ansbacher, 1956) repeatedly stressed the acceptance of others, calling it social interest and social feeling—a feeling of brotherliness toward one's fellows. To Sullivan (1953) relating to others in a healthy way and mutually meeting each other's needs is the very nature of personality. This trend, positing the primary significance of quality of relationships, is the direction the field has moved recently.

Accepting the self means allowing, believing, or recognizing that something is true or real in another person's experience. It does not imply that whatever is accepted is good, valuable, or right. It means acknowledging that it exists. It also means that the self or other selves are approved as persons apart from their many imperfections. The immature individual often confuses some specific habit, attitude, or action with the total person and rejects the person, rather than making a finer discrimination.

Living in the Present. The third dimension of maturity is living in the present but having long-range goals. For Adler (Ansbacher & Ansbacher, 1956), maturity means living in the world of others and finding meaningful work. The productive orientation described by Fromm (1947), which touches on several dimensions, includes meaningful work for the person and for the common good. Rogers (1961) calls the multitude of feelings that are related to the network of interaction patterns involved in living "being complexity," that is, one is involved in many relationships, both in the home and occupationally, with both positive and negative feelings; he or she is a complex being in the present.

Living in the present means facing and coping with one's present circumstances and situations. This involves dealing with and acknowledging the importance of one's self, job, church, friends, and family. Each and all of these situations could be described as "where I am." Each has some positive and negative qualities; it meets some needs but not others. The mature person is aware of these qualities and his or her needs. The individual is able to see both the good and the bad as well as what can and cannot be changed in each situation and takes personal responsibility for what is his or hers. In each the mature person has some goals that he or she would like to see accomplished and is aware of the progress toward those goals. The immature person tends to live with the "if only" or the "when" attitude. In either case there is little or no acceptance of the present situation and little personal responsibility. Immature people tend to blame others for their plight.

In addition, the mature person is aware that the present situation is not all it could be or all that he or she would like it to be. Consequently the mature person develops goals toward which he or she directs the course of his or her life and activity. Maslow (1954) refers to this quality in mature people being characterized by a high degree of autonomy, that is, the ability to set their own goals. White (1959) describes a related aspect of goal setting as competence, the learned ability to cope with tasks and to establish one's goals in the situation. The goals are usually spread over several areas of life such as familial, vocational, economic, and personal. The goals vary as to clarity, permanence, and desirability. As he or she moves toward them, the mature person assesses his or her progress and directs or redirects energies as needed. He or she may even change goals. The mature person remains the master of his or her goals and remains flexible. The immature person tends to be mastered by goals, becoming rigid and rejecting others or himself or herself for not making satisfactory progress toward his or her goals.

Having Values. At first this may not appear to be a psychological concept, but most psychologists recognize at least implicitly the necessity of having guiding values. Frankl (1963) claims that having values is having "the will to meaning," which organizes all of one's life. Allport (1961) speaks of mature people having a unifying philosophy of life, while Maslow (1954) says the mature have a strong ethical sense and are able to resist cultural pressures to conform. May (1953) speaks of values in terms of choice and the courage to decide how one is going to live. According to the psychologist, therefore, values must be self-chosen. They are not values one accepts because he or she is coerced by society or religion. Rather they are chosen by the mature person and integrated into the person's self-concept and behavior. Thus they are not external but internal values. Internalization and integration of values in the person imply harmony within the personality, a purposefulness of plan and action, and a sense of freedom from coercion because the values are self-chosen. An immature person thinks he or she can operate without values. This is a delusion because there is no such thing as a valueless position.

Developing One's Abilities. Developing one's abilities and interests and coping with the problems of living is the final characteristic of maturity. The first characteristic focuses more on the necessity of having an accurate self-perception, while this characteristic focuses on developing one's potential and skills and then utilizing them to create, make, and do things, both for necessity and for pleasure. This characteristic has a certain global and integrative quality that Freud would call reality orientation. In general Rogers and Maslow call it self-actualization. More specifically Maslow (1954) refers to mature people as problem-centered. Mature people are interested in their job, home, family, community, and themselves as well. Their degree of interest may vary from area to area, but they are not rigidly focused in a narrow set of areas. Not only are they capable of purposeful creative action but also they like to do things. They have a high degree of ability to concentrate on the task at hand but also the ability to leave it when necessary. The immature person seems to have more dislikes than likes and has not developed his creative abilities or interests to cope with life's daily problems.

Coleman (1960) summarizes this final aspect of maturity as a task-oriented approach to life versus a defensive orientation. The immature person spends most of his or her energy in defensive operations, trying to protect himself or herself from pain and disappointment, while the mature person is able to withstand the pain and disappointments in life because he or she has developed an ability to cope with the good as well as the bad aspects of life.

The Biblical Perspective. *Relational Context.* In Scripture the relational context of human nature is so universal that it may be overlooked directly by the authors of the text, since it is assumed or implied and therefore is not formally addressed. This can be seen, for example, when humanity was created in God's image (Gen. 1:27). Since God is a trinity the image must have a relational character. In the Old Testament persons are described in interpersonal contexts, and in the New Testament they are described as a part of the church or community. The New Testament also repeatedly stresses the importance of fellowship *(koinonia)* and of quality relating (loving, caring for, and not grieving one another). With this in mind, the biblical parallel to the psychological perspective becomes evident. The Bible asks people to have a realistic or objective view of themselves and others. The basic requirement is to perceive self, others, and the world from the divine perspective. God views each and every person as fallen and in need of a Savior (Rom. 3:23). Once a person recognizes his and her need for a Savior and responds, he or she becomes a new creature, with a new relationship to God, others, and the world (2 Cor. 5:17). Another aspect of the realistic biblical view of self and others is the recognition of natural traits and abilities as well as one's spiritual gifts (1 Cor. 12:14–25) and one's place in the spiritual body (1 Cor. 12:14; Eph. 4:4). A realistic perception of the need of others, both believers (Gal. 6:2) and unbelievers (Matt. 25:34–40), is the biblical expectation as well as the divine view of social order (Rom. 13:1–3).

Accepting Oneself and Others. A second part of biblical maturity involves accepting oneself and others. Perhaps the clearest statement of this principle is given by Jesus: "Love your neighbor as yourself" (Matt. 22:39, NIV). It is important to note that the love of neighbor depends in quality and amount on love of self in the sense of acceptance. Acceptance means allowing the biblical view of sinfulness and fallenness to be true or real in one's inner experience both before and after becoming a Christian. Sinfulness and fallenness are not eliminated by being saved. Righteousness always belongs to Christ and is legally attributed to the person by God. It does not become a personal quality so the person can boast (Phil. 3:9) either before God or others. A corresponding view of others is also characteristic of the spiritually mature.

In accepting both self and others one must recognize that both self and others are sinful and fallen. Each person is created in God's image (Gen. 1:27) and is also fallen (Rom. 5:12); each is redeemed or in need of redemption. God loves everyone whom God created, which means that everyone is worthwhile as a person. Hence everyone should be accepted as a person. Acceptance does not imply approval of behavior or motives. However, the Bible calls the mature believer to a very high level of love for other believers (1 John 3:16), to a deep sensitivity to their weaknesses (Heb. 12:12), and to the whole body as brothers and sisters in Christ (1 Cor. 12:25–26). The biblical words *agape, philia,* and *koinonia* call for a greater depth of warmth and maturity in a relationship than perhaps any psychologist emphasizes, other than Carl Rogers, who came from a Christian home (Rogers, 1961).

Living in the Present. Living in the present with long-term goals is basic to the Scriptures. Now is the day of salvation, for believers as well as unbelievers. Salvation has an eternally present aspect. While the Bible describes the future life with God, there is a heavy emphasis on present actions and attitudes. Believers are to manifest the fruit of the Spirit in all their life. Christ makes an observable difference in the believer's ongoing action. It is the carnal or immature person who does not show change. Believers are warned not to long to leave this world but to live in it now (1 Cor. 5:9–10). The writers of the New Testament urge their readers to "abide" and "grow up in Christ"; this language emphasizes the current, ongoing focus of Christians. However, the Christian life is also described as a race with a prize (Phil. 3:14). Most clearly Paul makes the third aspect of maturity the model of the mature Christian life. He describes his previous life in Judaism (Phil. 3:4–6), which he then gives up for Christ (Phil. 3:8), but the process does not end at that point. In verse 10 Paul goes on describing the model: "I want to know Christ and the power of his resurrection and the fellowship of sharing in his sufferings, becoming like him in his death." This last verb is a present participle and is the strongest possible way of stressing ongoing action: the focus is the present. However, Paul elaborates the model by saying, "Not as though I am already perfect [mature] but . . . I press on toward the goal to win the prize for which God has called me heavenward in Jesus Christ" (Phil. 3:14, NIV). Thus the model of Christian maturity has a present focus with long-term goals.

Having Goals. A fourth characteristic of Christian maturity is seen in having goals that are self-chosen. In the process of conquering and possessing the land Joshua appeals to the Israelites: "Choose for yourselves this day whom you will serve" (Josh. 24:15, NIV). Values are a package plan because they involve an integrated set of motives and actions, not just something one says he or she thinks is right. The values are clearly indicated in the description of the flesh and the works of the Spirit. Paul describes a complete rethinking of values, and accompanying actions are reinterpreted and reversed (Phil. 3:8). However, the reassessment is an ongoing process: "I do not consider myself yet to have taken hold of it. But one thing I do: Forgetting what is behind, I press on toward the goal" (Phil. 3:13–14, NIV). Thus the process of reassessing is an ongoing process that merges with the realistic evaluation of the self and focuses on the present but is pulled forward and clarified by the long-range goal of the high calling of God. It is the commitment of the self to a set of values that reorganizes the person and gives him or her an identity. For the Christian this is union with Christ, which is so characteristically described by Paul with the phrase "in Christ." The final characteristic of a mature Christian is developing one's abilities and interests in everyday living. The development and use of one's talents and gifts (Eph. 4:7) is a necessary part of Christian maturity, since the gifts are given to the church for the work of the ministry (Eph. 4:12). Timothy is encouraged to rekindle the gift of God within him (2 Tim. 1:6). The encouragement of growth toward Christian maturity seems to be the purpose of the gifts and the goal of the ministry (Eph. 4:15–16). Interest in everyday living involves working to support oneself (1 Tim 5:8). The daily tasks are not to be neglected or done grudgingly (Eph. 6:6; Col. 3:22). Thus developing one's

abilities, talents, and gifts begins to merge with Christian values and a biblically appropriate perception of oneself and others. This merger produces congruence in the mature Christian of all that he or she says and does (James 2:26; 1 John 3:18).

Perhaps this is best illustrated in the First Epistle of John, where the apostle describes three criteria of mature Christian faith: believing the truth (Jesus is the Christ), loving other Christians, and practicing righteousness. These three criteria are repeated three times in the epistle. They tend to focus on three different aspects of the person. Believing the truth has a strong cognitive component, while practicing righteousness has a strong behavioral focus and loving others involves the emotional-motivational aspects.

These joint criteria thus emphasize the unified or integrated aspect of Christian maturity in the personality. Mature Christians' behavior, beliefs, and emotions are thus organized in a consistent, congruent, and unified pattern. They are interested in daily life because this is where God has placed them (Phil. 4:11; Heb. 13:5; 1 Cor. 7:20) and thus persons act as unto the Lord (Eph. 6:8). Every task or sphere of activities is infused with spiritual meaning and interest. They recognize that every good thing in life is from God (James 1:17) and that much is worthy of attention and enjoyment in this life (Phil. 4:8). Furthermore, the mature believer is aware that the mandate to subdue the earth (Gen. 1:28) has never been revoked. Immature Christians, by contrast, are torn by conflict because they are pulled in two or more directions (James 1:8; 4:8). Because they are unclear about their identity as new persons, they try to operate as old creatures, which they are not.

Scripture grounds Christian maturity in two process dimensions: actualization and congruence. Actualization has two aspects. The first aspect is the process of salvation, including being sanctified, glorified, and made like Christ. The second aspect is found in Scripture's use of the word *teleois* (perfect, mature, complete) to describe maturity. The process of salvation focuses on something God causes to happen to the believer, while *teleois* seems to focus on the believer's choice or will (Phil. 3:14–15). Hence the mature Christian becomes what he or she is—a child being renewed after the image—and becomes what he or she chooses, pressing toward the high mark of the high calling of God.

The second process of Christian maturity is congruence, which can also be understood as integrity or consistency. The mature believer is characterized by the fruit of the Spirit. His or her actions and words flow consistently out of an inner thought and emotional life that has been committed to Christ. Since the mature believer lets the mind of Christ dwell within the person, his or her actions follow congruently (Phil. 2:5–8); that is, they are both Christlike and congruent.

Christian Maturity and Actualization. As each of the aspects of maturity has a psychological and biblical parallel, so the processes of self-actualization and congruence have parallels. Psychologically, actualization means developing one's body, mind, and emotions into a fully functioning person. Biblically, the process is parallel but the content is different. The non-Christian may actualize his or her full potential as a person made in God's image but fallen. The fall limits the potential and direction of self-actualization. It does not prevent the person from becoming good, healthy, kind, and a developed person, since the image is more fundamental than the fall. The fall mars the image of God in people (Berkhof, 1941). Some Christians seem almost to reverse the pattern, emphasizing the fall so much that it appears that fallen people are only tainted by the image. Counts (1973) calls this latter view "worm theology."

Many non-Christians show varying degrees of behavior and attitudes strikingly similar to the fruits of the Spirit. An individual may develop his or her humanity (the God-given divine image) by utilizing the principles of psychology and mental health, with or without the aid of a therapist, to become a more mature, healthy, self-actualized person. However, the most fully functioning non-Christian will not be characterized by a relationship to Christ or the body of believers, nor will he or she be motivated by *agape* love, and his or her self-perception and perception of the cosmos will not be Christlike in character.

Christians, however, actualize their potential as created, fallen, and redeemed. In Christians the image is being renewed (Eph. 4:24; Col. 3:10). Christ becomes the model or the ideal of Christians and the Scriptures function as their guidelines. Since Christians are related to the God of the universe, they become more in harmony (if they are growing and maturing) with the divine purpose and pattern in both themselves and the world. This is the meaning of the renewing of the image; but note that it is a process—the removal of the effects of the fall on the image. Christian self-actualization moves toward perfection after Christ (Phil. 3:10–14). The non-Christian can become complete as a created and fallen person, while the Christian becomes complete (or rather perfected) as created, fallen, and redeemed.

The image is of the Greek long-distance runner moving through the race to the finish line. The runner forgets what is behind him or her and does not consider himself or herself to have arrived but continues to press forward toward the goal. This is similar to the growth process of self-actualization. The past becomes irrelevant because the person is moving forward, realizing his or her goals are not yet achieved. Thus there is an awareness of one's progress without a sense of either failure or arrival. The focus of Christian maturity is the present but with the knowledge that one is currently moving toward the goal. This goal is self-chosen. The mature believer wills or chooses to follow Christ, and

Christ becomes his or her choice. Thus the biblical concept of salvation in its various facets parallels the psychological process of self-actualization described by Rogers (1959), Gendlin (1964), and Jung (1970).

Christian Maturity and Congruence. The dimension of congruence, consistency, or balance is also a biblical principle, and it is related to salvation and Christian maturity. While the Bible does not use the language of personality theory, it does describe human congruent functioning in its own terms. The congruence emphasized in Scripture usually involves a consistency between cognitive, affective, and/or motivational behavior. For example, "Faith without deeds is dead" (James 2:26, NIV); "Let us love not with words or tongue but with actions and in truth" (1 John 3:18, NIV); "Out of the overflow of the heart the mouth speaks" (Matt. 12:34, NIV). In each of these examples congruence between inner aspects of the person and outer aspects of the person is either described or encouraged as a part of Christian living. Furthermore, congruence in the Christian life is described by some concepts as fruit of the Spirit (Gal. 5:22–23) and the new creature (Eph. 4:24; Col. 3:10). In each case a consistent pattern of behavior, attitudes, traits, and/or motives is described. Each is also contrasted with an antithetical pattern of the works of the flesh or the old creature. In addition there is strong biblical exhortation and encouragement to try to live congruently. Regular incongruent living is biblically described as carnal (1 Cor. 3:3) or double-minded (James 1:8; 4:8). Finally, congruence is one of the major themes of the First Epistle of John, while this theme is certainly present in the prophets. More evidence could be cited, but enough has been given to indicate that Scripture represents the mature Christian as living a congruent or consistent life in which his or her thoughts and beliefs, motives, feelings, attitudes, and behaviors are consistent with each other and the Scripture.

Summary. By way of summary, five aspects or dimensions of maturity have been outlined. The parallel between the biblical and psychological views has been developed and illustrated. However, when all five aspects of maturity are taken together, two new higher dimensions emerge: actualization and congruence. In discussing the five aspects a certain degree of overlap was evident. The overlap occurs because a mature person in either a psychological or biblical sense is integrated, has a purposeful or goal directed quality about his or her life, and is open to oneself and others; the immature person is disorganized, having either conflicting or no goals, and is unaware and unaccepting of the various aspects of oneself and others.

References

Allport, G. W. (1961). *The pattern of growth and personality*. New York: Holt, Rinehart, & Winston.

Ansbacher, H. I., & Ansbacher, R. R. (Eds.). (1956). *The individual psychology of Alfred Adler*. New York: Basic.

Bauer, W., Arndt, W., & Gingrich, F. (1979). *A Greek-English lexicon of the New Testament and other early Christian literature.* Chicago: University of Chicago Press.

Beavers, R. (1990). *Successful families.* New York: Norton.

Berkhof, L. (1941). *Systematic theology* (2nd rev. ed.). Grand Rapids, MI: Eerdmans.

Coleman, J. C. (1960). *Personality dynamics and effective behavior.* Chicago: Scott, Foresman.

Counts, W. M. (1973). The nature of man and the Christian's self-esteem. *Journal of Psychology and Theology, 1,* 38–44.

Frankl, V. (1963). *Man's search for meaning.* Boston: Beacon.

Freud, S. (1927). *The ego and the id.* London: Hogarth.

Fromm, E. (1947). *Man for himself.* New York: Holt, Rinehart, & Winston.

Gendlin, E. T. (1964). A theory of personality change. In P. Worchel & D. Byrne (Eds.), *Personality change.* New York: Wiley.

Housden, R., & Goodchild, C. (1992). *We two.* Wellingborough, England: Aquarian.

Jung, C. G. (1970). The structure and dynamics of the psyche. *The collected works* (2nd ed.). (Vol. 8). Princeton, NJ: Princeton University Press.

Lewis, J. (1989). *The birth of the family.* New York: Brunner/Mazel.

Lewis, J., Beavers, W., Gossett, J., & Phillips, V. (1976). *No single thread: Psychological health in family systems.* New York: Brunner/Mazel.

Maslow, A. H. (1954). *Motivation and personality.* New York: Harper & Row.

May, R. (1953). *Man's search for himself.* New York: Norton.

Mitchell. (1988).

Rogers, C. (1959). A theory of therapy, personality and interpersonal relationship, as developed in the client-centered framework. In S. Koch (Ed.), *Psychology: The study of science.* (Vol. 3). New York: McGraw-Hill.

Rogers, C. (1961). *On becoming a person.* Boston: Houghton Mifflin.

Scarf, M. (1995). *Intimate worlds: Life inside the family.* New York: Random House.

Skynner, R., & Cleese, J. (1995). *Life and how to survive it.* New York: Norton.

Sullivan, H. S. (1953). *The interpersonal theory of psychiatry.* New York: Norton.

Walsh, F. (1982). *Normal family process.* New York: Guilford.

White, R. W. (1959). Motivation reconsidered: The concept of competence. *Psychological Reports, 66,* 297–333.

D. W. Peters and J. D. Carter

See Personality; Religion and Personality.

Heart Disease. *See* Coronary Heart Disease.

Hebb, Donald O. (1904–1985). Canadian psychologist best known for his theory of neural cell assemblies. Hebb was born in Chester, Nova Scotia, and studied English at Dalhousie University, receiving the A.B. degree in 1925. His introduction to psychology was the works of Sigmund Freud. In 1929 he enrolled as a part-time student in the psychology department of McGill University in Montreal. His master's thesis, written while he was confined to bed with a tubercular hip, attempted to explain spinal reflexes as a result of Pavlovian conditioning in the fetus. He continued part-time at McGill under the supervision of Leonid Andreyev and Boris B. Babkin, who had themselves been trained by Ivan Pavlov.

In 1934 Hebb began doctoral studies in Chicago under Karl S. Lashley, who kindled his interest in physiology. When Lashley moved to Harvard University, Hebb accompanied him, eventually receiving his Ph.D. from Harvard for work on the effects of early experience on the development of size and brightness discrimination in rats. He stayed on as a research assistant for a year and then took a position as fellow under Wilder Penfield at the Montreal Neurological Institute. There Hebb examined changes in intellectual functioning of patients following removal of cortical tissue. Hebb then moved to a faculty position at Queen's University in Ontario, where he collaborated with his student Kenneth Williams to develop an animal analogue of the intelligence test—the Hebb-Williams variable-path rat maze.

Hebb conducted research with Lashley again at the Yerkes Laboratories of Primate Biology for five years, beginning in 1942. The intended research project was to examine the effects of brain lesions on personality and emotional characteristics. However, it was Lashley's interest in the brain's translation of perceptions into knowledge that had the long-lasting effect on Hebb. From this he developed his ideas on the cell assembly, an internal, neural representation of an external stimulus. The concept was inspired by Lorento de Nó's work on reverberating neural circuits. Hebb came back to Montreal as chair of psychology at McGill and continued his work on cell assemblies. His book, *The Organization of Behavior: A Neuropsychological Theory,* was published in 1949.

Hebb returned to Nova Scotia in 1977 and was appointed an honorary professor of psychology at Dalhousie, where he remained active until his death. His second major book, *Essay on Mind,* was published during this period.

During his career Hebb was elected president of the American Psychological Association, a member of the U.S. National Academy of Sciences, and a member of the Royal Society of London.

W. D. Norman

Helmholtz, Hermann Ludwig Ferdinand von (1821–1894). One of the preeminent figures of intellectual history, whose career blurred the distinction between vocation and avocation. Helmholtz was born in Potsdam, Germany. From childhood he was interested in mathematics and physics, but his capacities were not recognized in the gymnasium, which emphasized training in classical literature. With an undistinguished academic record he entered the Royal Friedrich-Wilhelm Institute of Medicine and Surgery because he could train to be an army surgeon without paying tuition. Upon graduation he used his position as a surgeon to do research in physiology and write about physics, mathematics, and philosophy. These works earned him a position in physiology and anatomy at Königsberg. In 1871 he achieved his childhood dream when he was named professor of physics at the University of Berlin, a position he held until his death.

Helmholtz was not an advocate of a separate science of psychology, but his three editions of the *Handbuch der physiologisches Optik* with its pioneering research on vision and hearing would by themselves place him with Wilhelm Wundt and Gustav Fechner as a contributor to the establishment of experimental psychology. Yet according to Boring (1950), Helmholtz's contributions to psychology rank third behind his contributions to physics and physiology. Helmholtz published more than two hundred books and articles; a partial listing of his accomplishments includes the invention of the opthalmoscope, measurement of the speed of the neural impulse, mathematical formulation of the principle of the conservation of energy, preliminary statements of the Faraday-Maxwell conception of electrical phenomena, and pioneering papers on non-Euclidean geometry.

Helmholtz's impact on religion was unintentional but not inconsequential. He argued in favor of empiricism and against metaphysics. More importantly, he was an active opponent of vitalism, the doctrine that life can be explained only by postulating a supernatural vital entity that animates the physical bodies of living beings. In 1845 he entered into a pact with three other young scientists (Emil duBois-Reymond, Carl Ludwig, and Ernst Brucke), who pledged themselves to the promulgation of this statement: "No other forces than the common physical chemical ones are active within the organism" (Boring, 1950, p. 708). The success of these men has had an indirect impact on religion by contributing to the advance of secularism and by supporting a mechanistic, materialistic view of human behavior. Both these trends are seen in the work of one of Brucke's students—Sigmund Freud.

Reference

Boring, E. G. (1950). *A history of experimental psychology* (2nd ed.). New York: Appleton-Century-Crofts.

L. S. SHAFFER

See PSYCHOLOGY, HISTORY OF.

Helping Behavior. Helping or prosocial behavior is an activity that assists in solving problems of other people. Sometimes the term *altruism* is used synonymously with helping behavior. However, the motivation behind the helping behavior may be either altruistic (i.e., concern for the other person), egoistic (i.e., concern for the self), or both. Batson (1987) proposes an empathy-altruism hypothesis, suggesting that both self-serving and selfless considerations are involved in helping behavior. Helping behavior may result from an egoistic motivation to reduce one's own distress for another's plight or from an altruistic motivation to reduce the other's distress. The key, according to Batson, is the extent to which empathy for the individual is generated.

Philosophers and psychologists have long debated whether helping behavior can be of pure altruistic motivation. The empathy for another in dire circumstances may also lead to sadness, guilt, or certain other personally distressing emotions, and relief of such distress may be the real motivation behind helping (Schaller & Cialdini, 1988). Suggestive evidence supporting both sides of the argument is available; but the issue is difficult to determine conclusively since even the helper may find it a challenge to validly assess the degree to which a behavior is truly absent of any self-serving motive.

A wide range of helping behaviors has been studied in experimental research, including picking up spilled groceries, donating money, mailing letters that have supposedly been lost, helping a researcher distribute questionnaires, donating blood, and making a phone call for a stranger. Foss (1986) is critical, however, that most of these helping behaviors are fairly routine or trivial and involve little sacrifical effort or inconvenience. Drawing from a 1980 review of the literature review, he reports that only about 15% of the studies involve serious situations or fairly costly forms of helping. What has been ignored are studies of more significant and often more impressive but just as real helping behavior, such as donating significant amounts of time or money following natural disasters, or even placing one's life in jeopardy, such as the volunteer firefighter, to help another. Also, the type of helping behavior that may require long-term sacrificial care has been neglected by researchers. Thus what appears to be creative research involving a wide variety of situations may represent only a limited type of helping behavior.

Gender Differences. Limitations regarding the type of helping behavior studied by psychologists may have led to the premature conclusion that males are more likely than females to help. Research on altruism suggests that if the person in need is a stranger or if the helping behavior is potentially dangerous, males are more likely to help. (Women, however, are more likely to be the recipients of such help.) Yet, as Eagly and Crowley (1986) have pointed out, in safer situations or in situations in which the helping behavior may appear less magnanimous (such as serving as a subject in a psychological experiment), women are somewhat more likely to help.

Deciding to Help. Latane and Darley (1970) propose a sequence of decisions, all of which must be answered affirmatively if helping behavior is to occur. Once an event is noticed, does the bystander interpret the event as an emergency, assume personal responsibility, and feel capable to render aid? How these questions are answered involve a number of situational and personal factors. But even if the bystander's answer is yes to each question, there is still no guarantee that the person will help. Helping behavior itself also depends on additional personal and situational characteristics; it depends on being the right person in the right place and at the right time.

Situational Factors. Some rather definitive conclusions regarding the probability of offering aid center around aspects of the situation. The factors listed here, though not exhaustive, represent some of the clearest findings.

Degree of Need. All things being equal, the greater the need for help, the greater the likelihood that help will be provided. Exceptions to this rule may involve the costs associated with helping, since the need for help may require greater sacrifice by the potential helper.

Ambiguity. If the need for help is clear and unambiguous, help will more likely be provided. The clarity of the situation is often influenced by the nature of the need (e.g., a physical need may be more noticeable than a psychological need), surrounding conditions, and social influence from others. Ambiguous situations may generate questions about the appropriateness of providing help or concern about looking foolish if the person really is not in need.

Costs. What is demanded in terms of risk, effort, time, money, or other resources? The lesser such costs, whether direct or indirect, the more help can be expected.

Presence of Others. Bystanders around the person in need of help must assume responsibility for helping behavior to occur. One of the primary determinants of whether a person will assume responsibility is the number of potential helpers present, or what researchers have dubbed the bystander effect. If there are many potential helpers, the individual may be less inclined to assume responsibility and, should everyone present assume the same posture, the individual is less likely to receive help from anyone. Such diffusion of responsibility has been well-established in social-psychological investigations.

Social Acceptability. If the situation requires action that violates a moral, ethical, or legal code, helping behavior is less likely to occur. If the type of required action is socially acceptable and admired, helping behavior is more likely to occur.

Personal Factors. Not all people are equally likely to provide aid, even under those circumstances that clearly call for help. In addition to gender differences, researchers have uncovered a number of personal factors that help determine prosocial behavior.

Perceived Ability. People are more likely to help if they think they can (Brehm & Self, 1989). Thus behavior viewed as callous may really be a decision about one's inability to help.

Personality Traits. What personality traits are unique about the Mother Teresas of the world? Though few traits have been conclusively tied to helping behavior, and situational factors rather than personal characteristics seem to determine whether or not one may help, psychologists are beginning to uncover a number of important personality factors. Two traits stand out as clearly associated with helping behavior: empathy and self-efficacy (Batson, 1987). That is, those who naturally and frequently feel what others must be feeling as well as those who exercise control over their own functioning and environmental circumstances are more likely to lend a helping hand. Also, people who have a higher need for social approval or who are high self-monitoring individuals are also more likely to help, especially if that help is noticed by others (a situational factor). It is increasingly apparent that personality traits often interact with situational factors in determining the likelihood of helping behavior. For example, the self-efficacy of a medical professional such as a doctor or nurse may be unusually heightened during a medical emergency.

Personal Norms. Sometimes people help because they think they ought to help. One such norm is the sense of social responsibility—the expectation that people should be willing to help those who are less fortunate. Yet another norm is reciprocity—the expectation that people should help those who have helped them, though the extent of one's obligation may vary depending upon the degree of favor already received. Often an underlying assumption of the reciprocity norm is that in the long run we expect a balance in help given and help received.

Mood and Other Transient States. Though one may expect that bad mood inhibits helping behavior, the relationship between mood and prosocial activity is quite complex. For example, people are actually more likely to help if they are in a negative mood due to guilt or sadness, presumably because helping behavior is also self-gratifying (Cialdini, Kenrick, & Baumann, 1981). If, however, the negative mood is due to depression, anger, or grief, helping others is less likely to occur (Myers, 1990).

Religion. The parable of the Good Samaritan (Luke 10:30–35) suggests that religious people may not always adhere to religious teaching. Darley and Batson (1973) found that Princeton seminarians were remarkably similar to everyone else, even when they had to provide a talk on the good Samaritan. When they were rushed to get across campus to give a speech on the Good Samaritan, the seminarians were less likely to help an individual in need than when they were not rushed. Situational influences had a greater effect on their behavior than did religious thoughts.

Research in helping behavior has particular value for the Christian community, since the evidence appears to indicate that at best Christians are no more likely to be helpful than others. Rokeach (1969) maintains that people who place a high value on salvation are generally more indifferent to the plight of disadvantaged groups. Ignoring the church's recent history of social action (e.g., antislavery, prohibition), some twentieth-century Christians have argued that the church should not be involved in social concerns, fearing a degeneration into an unacceptable social gospel. These attitudes and behaviors contrast sharply with Christ's clear model of self-sacrificial giving. Further, the Scriptures command Christians to help those in need and connect helping behavior directly with personal salvation (Matt. 25:31–46). Knowledge of the factors facilitating and inhibiting helping can show individuals seeking a biblical lifestyle how to be more responsive to the needs of others.

References

Batson, C. D. (1987). Prosocial motivation: Is it ever truly altruistic? In L. Berkowitz (Ed.), *Advances in experimental social psychology* (Vol. 20). San Diego: Academic Press.

Brehm, J. W., & Self, E. (1989). The intensity of motivation. In M. R. Rosenzweig & L. W. Porter (Eds.), *Annual review of psychology*. Palo Alto, CA: Annual Reviews, Inc.

Cialdini, R. B., Kenrick, D. T., & Baumann, D. J. (1981). Effects of mood on prosocial behavior in children and adults. In N. Eisenberg-Berg (Ed.), *The development of prosocial behavior*. New York: Academic Press.

Darley, J. M., & Batson, C. D. (1973). From Jerusalem to Jericho: A study of situational and dispositional variables in helping behavior. *Journal of Personality and Social Psychology, 27,* 100–108.

Eagly, A. H., & Crowley, M. (1986). Gender and helping behavior: A meta-analytic review of the social psychological literature. *Psychological Bulletin, 100,* 309–330.

Foss, R. D. (1986). Using social psychology to increase altruistic behavior: Will it help? In M. J. Saks & L. Saxe (Eds.), *Advances in applied social psychology*. Hillsdale, NJ: Erlbaum.

Latane, B., & Darley, J. M. (1970). *The unresponsive bystander: Why doesn't he help?* New York: Appleton-Century-Crofts.

Myers, D. G. (1990). *Social psychology* (3rd ed.). New York: McGraw-Hill.

Rokeach, M. (1969). The H. Paul Douglass Lectures for 1969 (Part 2): Religious values and social compassion, *Review of Religious Research, 2* (1), 24–39.

Schaller, M., & Cialdini, R. B. (1988). The economics of empathic helping: Support for a mood management motive. *Journal of Experimental Social Psychology, 24,* 163–181.

P. C. Hill

Helping Relationships. *See* Human Relations Training.

Hemispheric Specialization. When the left hemisphere (LH) and the right (RH) hemisphere of the brain each exhibits processing capabilities not found on the opposite side, those functions are said to be lateralized. Cerebral asymmetries may be observed in anatomical structures, physiological processes, or metabolic activity. A major area of interest in psychology has been the extent of hemisphere specialization of high-level functions such as language, attention, or emotional processes. The evidence supporting such specializations comes from several sources: clinical observations of patients with LH or RH damage; specialized testing of commissurotomy or split-brain patients; lateralized presentation of stimuli to neurologically normal subjects and correlating variations in anatomical or physiological measures of the brain with variations in performance on behavioral tests. Each of these approaches has its own strengths and weaknesses for inferring hemisphere specialization. The conclusions drawn from one approach do not always coincide with those from others.

Much of the early evidence came from the clinic. In the 1860s and 1870s Paul Broca and Karl Wernicke identified regions of the frontal and temporal lobes of the LH involved in speech production and comprehension. Patients with damage in these areas displayed profound speech disorders; patients with damage to comparable areas of the RH did not. In the 1960s and 1970s investigators discovered that split-brain patients could respond verbally to information directed to the LH but not the RH. For these reasons primary language functions are believed to reside in the LH of most right-handers and the majority of left-handers. Additional observations from laboratory and clinic suggested that the RH is specialized for visuospatial processing. Since the mid-1970s numerous left-right processing dichotomies have been proposed, from the mundane (LH = analytic processing, RH = wholistic processing) to the exotic (LH = Western, rational thought, RH = Eastern, intuitive thought). It is generally agreed that all such dichotomies fail to capture the complexities of cerebral hemisphere involvement in processing information.

Current theories have moved away from models of unilateral specialization to models emphasizing the interactions between specialized modules in both hemispheres. One hemisphere does not perform all the processing for a complex task such as reading. Instead, highly specialized subprocessing units are distributed in both hemispheres, and the demands of a given task will require recruitment of an ensemble to perform that task. Coordination of modular processing is as important as the modular activity itself. The hemisphere interaction models do not discount hemisphere specialization but focus on coordination of lower-level rather than global aspects of information processing.

Of considerable interest is the question whether hemisphere specialization varies as a function of other factors such as gender, handedness, age, or neurologic, psychiatric or psychological disorders.

Women, it was claimed, have more functionally symmetric brains, a claim also made for left-handers. Support is generally weak for claims of gender differences in hemisphere specialization. However, observations of male patients with lateralized damage indicates that left and right lesions affect Weschler Adult Intelligence Scale (WAIS) verbal and performance measures, respectively. For females, left-sided lesions depressed both IQ scores, but right-sided damage failed to influence either score. As with all studies examining gender differences in hemisphere specialization, these results must be viewed cautiously, since they may represent differences in preferred cognitive style.

Apparent differences in specialization between left- and right-handers should also be accepted tentatively. Few individuals use only one hand for all tasks. Measures of degree of handedness vary, making comparisons across studies difficult. There also is a relationship between handedness and the hemisphere more highly specialized for speech representation. It may be that where speech is represented is a causal factor in handedness, not the other way around.

Research on the ontogeny of hemisphere specialization has led many theorists to conclude that some degree of specialization exists at birth. According to one theory, each hemisphere contains the blueprint for its own basic functions as a primary plan of development and those of the other hemisphere as a secondary plan. Under normal conditions each hemisphere will develop its primary plan while inhibiting the secondary plan. If there is damage to a hemisphere such inhibition would not occur, and the damaged function would develop according to the secondary plan of the other hemisphere. There is also evidence of a developmental trend in interactions between the hemispheres. The interhemispheric connections change in number and functional efficiency during the first 10 to 15 years. These changes are believed to influence the ability to share information and to shield processing in the hemispheres from possible mutual interference.

A wide variety of clinical disorders have been associated with LH or RH damage or with dysfunctional interhemispheric processing. aphasias are more likely following LH damage, as are kinetic and ideomotor apraxias. Constructional apraxias occur following left or right damage but with different symptoms. Contralateral neglect syndrome occurs with RH damage. Catastrophic or dysphoric emotional reaction follows LH damage, while euphoric emotional reaction follows RH damage. One model postulates that the LH subserves positive emotions and the RH negative emotions. LH dysfunction has been implicated in autism and schizophrenia. However, this overly simplistic interpretation is being incorporated with evidence suggesting problems of interhemispheric communication.

W. D. NORMAN

See BRAIN AND HUMAN BEHAVIOR.

Heredity and Environment in Human Development. According to attribution theorists, humans are universally interested in the causes of human behavior. This motive is evident within modern psychology in the study and debate of the causal roles of heredity and the environment in human development. Throughout the twentieth century psychologists in the United States especially have sought to explain human development as the result of genetic or environmental causes or an interaction of the two, called the nature-nurture debate since early in the century. Because of the implications of either locus, the debate has generated much research and dissension within psychology and without. A genetic explanation has seemed to some to foster the belief that humans are ordained to a fixed fate (Lewontin, Rose, & Kamin, 1984). At times it has been used to further ethnocentric prejudice, for example, in the eugenics movement prior to World War II. Some writers believe that a strict environmental explanation contributes to a sentimentalism that cannot acknowledge the genuine limitations that some people are born with (Jensen, 1973). Those who emphasize environmental influence typically also advocate large-scale cultural interventions through education, training, and welfare. A recent manifestation of this debate has been the publication of *The Bell Curve* (Herrnstein & Murray, 1994) and the vociferous response to it. Nevertheless, virtually every developmentalist today assumes that heredity and the environment both play an important role in human development. A primary question that remains is the extent to which a particular human characteristic is shaped by either one.

The Role of Heredity. Human development on earth is rooted in biological processes that are structured by genetics; all body systems are ultimately controlled by the patterns of DNA found in every cell. DNA is composed of various sequences of four molecules that form a biochemical code; this code provides the blueprints for cell function, body form, and the sequence of development. Genes are units of DNA responsible for particular traits that can be passed on to the next generation. Some characteristics are shaped by a single gene. However, many traits are influenced by more than one gene, a process called polygenic inheritance. Multifactorial traits are those that are influenced by two or more genes and by one or more environmental influences. A person's entire genetic endowment is called the genotype, while the manifestation of a person's genotype is called the phenotype.

Behavior genetics is a field that explores the relative contribution of genes and the environment to human behavioral traits through studies of similarities between twins, families, and other kinship relations and the use of structural modeling statistical methods (Loehlin, 1994). Studying relationship similarities with such methods has allowed researchers to better tease apart the influence of genetics and the environment. Kinship studies compare the similarity of members of extended families: aunts and uncles, grandparents, and nuclear family members. Adoption studies compare the similarities of biological parents and their children when reared by those parents and when adopted out, as well as those of adoptive parents and their nonbiological children. Twin studies compare the similarities of identical or monozygotic (MZ) twins with those of fraternal or dizygotic (DZ) twins. (MZ twins share 100% of their genes and DZ only about 50% [like any two biological siblings.]) Twin adoption studies examine the differences between twins reared together (rt) and those separated shortly after birth and subsequently reared apart (ra). All these relationships are measured using correlation as a measure of similarity. A correlation of .00 means there is no similarity; a correlation of .99 would mean virtually perfect similarity.

Each type of study has strengths as well as limitations, but together they provide the clearest picture available of the relative influence of genetics and the environment and permit behavior geneticists to test models of the respective contribution of genetics and the environment to a trait's phenotype. Many traits vary along a continuum of low to high (e.g., IQ). By comparing sets of relatives who have different degrees of genetic and environmental similarity, researchers can estimate the percentage of trait differences between a group of people that is due to genes or the environment. The following is a standard behavior genetic formula: A Trait's Phenotypic Variability = Genetic Variability + Environmental Variability + Gene-Environment Interaction + Measurement Error (Kimble, 1993). The total genetic variability in the formula is termed heritability, the percentage of trait differences in a group of people due solely to genetic influence, or the ratio of genetic variation to phenotypic variation (Rowe, 1994). Some traits appear to have more heritability than others. Height, for example, appears to have about 90% heritability; that is, 90% of the differences of height among people in the United States seems to be due solely to genetic factors. Summarizing studies of many psychological traits, Kimble estimates that genetics accounts for about 35% of human psychological variability; more for cognitive abilities and less for personality traits.

Estimating heritability percentages is an important aim of behavior genetics research. However, the concept is not beyond criticism. Lerner (1986) has argued that because of the difficulty of measuring gene-environment interactions, conclusions that one can draw about heritability estimates will always be compromised. Moreover, Lerner points out that if a group of people were all to have identical experiences (e.g., being raised in a pickle barrel!), their IQ differences would be due almost solely to heredity, resulting in a high heritability value, though the environment's impact on phenotypic outcome is obviously considerable. Bronfenbrenner and Ceci (1993) believe that heritability is not a pure measure of genetic causal factors but is actually an estimate of the amount of phenotypic differences attributable to the actualized genetic potential that has been realized through environmental experiences.

Nevertheless, no one disputes that genetic influences contribute to the formation of psychological structures. Complex psychological systems like reasoning, abstract concept formation, aesthetic appreciation, volition, and language are made possible through human genes. Organisms lacking the necessary genetic potential will never be able to realize these psychological achievements regardless of training.

The Role of the Environment. However, genetic potential cannot be realized apart from environmental conditions. Countless studies with humans have documented the impact of environmental experiences on the human condition. Though extreme behaviorists like Watson (1924) and Skinner (1971) overestimated the causal role of the environment, the results of behavioral research have repeatedly demonstrated that stimuli in the environment can lead to changes in an organism's behavior. Cognitive-behaviorists also showed that human behavior is shaped by observation of others (Bandura, 1971) as well as through beliefs humans form as a result of interacting with the environment (Mischel, 1979). Other researchers have documented the devastating impact that environmental deprivation has on the future mental and emotional development of children; for example, orphanages that provide little stimulation (Grusec & Lytton, 1988). Research in other domains has likewise underscored the role of the environment on subsequent development, including such areas as parenting style, differences in socioeconomic status, day care, parental employment, divorce, media effects, and urban versus rural differences (Bronfenbrenner, 1986).

Behavior genetics research on twins supports this notion. For example, on all traits the correlations between MZra (reared apart) are less than 1.00 and are less than MZrt. This shows that though MZra have identical genotypes, the phenotypes are not identical, and most researchers believe these differences are due to environmental variability. As a result of such findings, behavior geneticists have incorporated environmental influences into their models. However, they distinguish shared and nonshared environmental influences. Shared influences include all the experiences that family members have in common within the family, including parents' education level, family warmth or hostility, or common experiences in day care. Nonshared includes all environmental experiences a family member has that no one else has, including accidents and the peer environments the child selects. Dunn and Plomin (1990) note that biological siblings rt are much less alike than we might suspect given that they share about 50% of their genes and the same environment. They conclude that nonshared environmental influences impact siblings much more than shared influences, with the former contributing 35% and the latter no more than 5% of the variability in phenotypic differences in adult intelligence quotient (IQ) and most personality differences. Consequently behavior geneticists argue that shared family experiences are not nearly as important to future development as has been believed throughout most of the twentieth century (though these assertions too have been challenged on scientific grounds: Bronfenbrenner, 1977; 1986; Lerner, 1986; Wachs, 1993).

So then virtually all researchers agree that genetics and the environment are both important in human development. Nevertheless, genetics appears to have a logical priority. No amount of schooling will substantially increase the IQ of a rabbit. The same point is illustrated in adoption studies, in which the IQ of adopted children has been found to be more highly correlated with their biological parents than with their adoptive parents. Enriched adoptive environments, however, are known to lead to significantly higher IQ scores. Putting such findings together suggests that placing adoptive children in enriched environments will positively impact their IQs but will not affect their relative rank order (which is determined by their genotypes; Scarr & McCartney, 1983). Environmental influences are largely facilitative; that is, they provide the situational context within which one's genetic endowment can be realized and expressed. Conceding the logical priority of genetics should not, however, lead to a radical separation of nature and nurture, for both are completely involved in human development.

The Interaction of Heredity and the Environment. Earlier attempts to understand the causes of development tended to be either hereditarian or environmental. A more sophisticated approach (that of modern behavior geneticists) is to attempt to find out how much of each is needed in the development of a particular trait. Anastasi (1958) argued against this because it assumes that each is independent and additive. To say that the heredity or the environment contributes 20% of trait variability misleadingly implies that it does so apart from the influence of the other. She argues instead for an interactive relationship in which the specific contribution of genetics to a trait depends upon the precise environmental experiences of the organism and vice versa. The importance of gene-environment interactions is revealed in kinship and twin studies. Children who are biologically unrelated but who are reared together have IQs that are somewhat similar. The IQs of children who are biologically related but who are reared apart are more similar, while the IQs of biologically related children reared together are the most similar (Bouchard & McGue,

1981). Such results suggest that IQ phenotype is an interaction of both genes and environment.

Types of Interaction. Three types of gene-environment interactions have been identified (Plomin, DeFries, & Loehlin, 1977): passive, evocative, and active. Passive interactions involve the influence of the parents' genotype on the child by contributing to the child's genotype but also by helping to shape the environment of the child. For example, a parent's intelligence level is contributing to the child's as they read, talk, work, and solve problems together.

Evocative interactions are due to the response of the environment to the child's genotype. For example, babies who smile a lot and rarely cry are more likely to receive positive feedback and support from their environment than babies who are frequently distressed and difficult to comfort.

The active type of interaction involves children's selection of environments that best match their genotypic orientation (called niche-picking, Scarr & McCartney, 1983). Extroverted people, for example, naturally seek out environments in which they can be outgoing. Behavior geneticists see this type of interaction as the most direct way genes contribute to one's experiences (Scarr & McCartney, 1983; Rowe, 1994).

Active interaction highlights the importance of the person in the developmental process, a subject to be taken up further. However, this leads to the recognition that one's beliefs about oneself and one's environment, beliefs shaped by genotype and experiences, in turn shape future experiences (Bandura, 1986). Cognition is the intersection of genes and the environment, while it also contributes to further gene-environment interaction. Yet the precise causal role of cognition on overall human development has been little explored.

Interaction Concepts. In addition to the foregoing, a number of developmental concepts have been used that further help us understand how heredity and environment interact. Some developmentalists have suggested that one's genotype provides a certain "range of potential outcomes" (Lerner, 1986) that is conditioned by a person's environmental experiences. Scarr-Salapatek (1975) asserted that a genotype establishes a range of about 25 IQ points, depending on the environment provided by typical American families. At the other extreme are children who were reared in extraordinarily neglectful situations (*see* Abuse and Neglect). Such individuals are phenotypically at the lowest range of their genetic potential for intelligence. However, who is to say that everyone is not to some extent falling short of one's absolute potential? There is probably always going to be some gap between one's genotypic potential and one's phenotype, a gap that is minimized by enriching experiences and an active pursuit of trait-realization by the individual. Moreover, humans have multiple potentials with limited time and experiences. No one, therefore, can fully realize all of his or her genetic potential in all possible domains of human ability.

Traits also vary in the extent to which their genetic potential depends upon the environment. Eye color is impacted little by the environment, whereas cognitive abilities are decisively affected. This is referred to as a trait's "plasticity" (Lerner, 1986). Some traits have more plasticity than others; that is, they are more malleable and susceptible to environmental influence. Researchers also have identified critical periods in human development in which children seem to be especially susceptible. Studies of wild children (e.g., Curtiss, 1977) have shown that certain cognitive and linguistic deficits cannot be remediated if the child is beyond a certain age when the basic skills need to be mastered (though some improvement can occur; e.g., vocabulary can increase). The brain seems to lose its earlier plasticity and becomes fixed at an immature level.

The Influence of Heredity and Environment on Particular Traits. *Intelligence.* More research has been done on the causes of intelligence than any other human characteristic. Bouchard and McGue (1981; updated by Plomin, 1994) reviewed the best kinship, adoption, and twin studies of IQ and obtained the following results: MZrt = .86; MZra = .72; DZrt = .60; biologically related siblings rt = .47; biologically unrelated siblings rt = .32; parent and parent-reared offspring = .385; parent and offspring separated = .22; and adoptive parent-adoptee = .18. These differences reveal much about the causes of IQ development. Comparing MZ twins shows that the combination of similar environment and 100% identical genotype in MZrt leads to the greatest similarity in intelligence. Yet the fact that MZra are so highly correlated, though having completely different environments, demonstrates that intelligence is greatly influenced by genetics. The same point is made by the weak but significant correlation between parents and offspring separated. The small correlation obtained for adoptive parents and their adopted children shows that the environment provided by parents must also contribute to children's intelligence. Similarly the low-moderate correlation between unrelated siblings rt points to the importance of shared environment. In addition, since the pairs of DZrt and siblings rt share about the same percentage of genes (50%), the difference between their correlations suggests that similarity in the experiences of DZ contributes to their phenotypic similarity.

Using the Bouchard and McGue review, Loehlin (1989) conducted a model-fitting analysis and concluded that the heritability for intelligence is around 50% with a confidence level of 20% (resulting in an interval estimate of between 30% and 70%). Fifty percent heritability means that around 50% of the differences in IQ scores (in these studies) was due to genetic influences. Plomin (1994) estimates that shared environmental influences contributed to about 33% of the differences, a sizable influence. However, the twin studies reviewed by Bouchard and McGue assessed twin IQ when the twins were young, and some research has called into question

long-term shared environment influences. For example, a recent longitudinal study (Loehlin, Horn, & Willerman, 1989) of the IQ of adopted siblings found significant correlations between them only while they were younger but no correlation by the time they were 18 years old. This suggests that shared environmental influences may be temporary, lasting only as long as the shared environment.

Lerner (1986), however, questions the extent to which we can be confident about hereditarian conclusions drawn from Bouchard and McGue (1981). First, Lerner notes there is great variability in the correlations between each study. This may indicate that environment moderates genotype effects. Lerner also cites Farber (1981), who found that in studies of MZ twins, they tended to be recruited on the basis of their similarity, which would falsely increase the contribution of genetics. Lerner also notes, as we saw, that when adopted children are reared in similar environments the heritability estimates are inflated. Nevertheless, while the conclusions of the behavior geneticists should be interpreted cautiously, the results suggest that genetics contribute substantially to intelligence but that the environment also makes a sizable contribution.

Personality. Reviewing adoption and kinship studies regarding the "big five" traits (extraversion, emotional stability, agreeableness, conscientiousness, and intellectual openness), Loehlin and Rowe (1992) obtained the following correlations for extraversion: MZrt = .55; MZra = .38; DZrt = .11; siblings rt = .20; unrelated siblings rt = −.06; and biological parent-child = .16. These results show less similarity for genetically related persons for extraversion than for intelligence but still demonstrate a considerable genetic component. Depending on one's formula for heritability, Rowe (1994) estimates that heritability for the big five is between 31% and 43%. However, Rowe also notes that the largest component of trait variation is due to unshared environmental differences, revealing the importance of unique child experiences on personality formation. Shared differences accounted for no more than about 2 to 9% of the variability, suggesting that similar family experiences do not have much impact. This is supported by results of the Texas adoption study, which found median Minnesota Multiphasic Personality Inventory (MMPI) correlations for birth mother-adoptee to be .18, while adoptive mother-adoptee were .00 (Rowe, 1994). Agreeableness seems to be the major exception, showing 21% of its variability due to shared environment. Similarly the Minnesota twin study found heritabilities of more than 40% for a number of personality traits including leadership/mastery, traditionalism (tendency to follow rules and respect authority), stress reaction, absorption (tendency to become engrossed in sensory experiences), alienation, well-being, and aggressiveness (Tellegen et al., 1988).

Nevertheless, there is evidence of environmental influence on personality. For example, Kagan,

Arcus, and Snidman (1993) found a significant interaction between temperament and home environment on later child fearful behavior. Low limit setting and greater maternal holding were related to higher fearful scores among children who were high-reactive infants. This shows that temperament can be differentially affected by family experiences.

Psychopathology. Repeated studies have found a genetic component for schizophrenia. Gottesman (1991) reports that MZ have been found to be 48% concordant (both twins had schizophrenia), with DZ found to be 17% concordant. Rowe (1994) cites a Finnish adoption study that found 9% of children adopted away from mothers with schizophrenia developed schizophrenia, versus 1% in controls. These results reveal a genetic causality for schizophrenia. Gottesman (1991) estimates that heritability for schizophrenia varies between 42 and 64%. However, most researchers acknowledge that environmental factors also are implicated. The previously mentioned Finnish study found that severely disturbed adoptive parents were more likely to have their adoptees (from mothers with schizophrenia) develop schizophrenia than those adopted by mentally healthy adoptive families (62% versus 3.5%).

Research has also found considerable genetic influence on mood disorders. For example, Loehlin, Willerman, and Horn (1988) report that 5.2% of biological relatives of adoptees with depression were depressed, versus 2.3% of biological relatives of controls. Bipolar disorder appears to have a larger component of genetic influence than major depression. Research, however, also shows a considerable influence of rearing on depression (Rowe, 1994).

Criminality and juvenile delinquency have also been traced to genetics. For example, MZ concordance rates for adult criminality are 69% versus 33% for DZ (Plomin, 1989). However, a significant portion of the differences in criminality appear to be due to shared environment (Rowe, 1994).

There also is evidence of a genetic component for alcoholism (*see* Alcohol Abuse and Dependence). McGue (1993) estimates a heritability of about 60% in males (much less in females). Cummings (1994) reported that sons adopted by alcoholic men show a rate of alcoholism more like that of their biological father. Gender differences in alcoholism may be genetic but are surely shaped by social or environmental influences. Moreover, rates of alcoholism are known to differ among ethnic groups, across cohorts, over the life span, and as a function of religious views, providing strong evidence of an environmental component.

Some studies have found a genetic link to homosexuality (Cummings, 1994; LeVay & Hamer, 1994). Cummings reports heritabilities somewhere around 50%. However, he adds that homosexuality is likely a multifactorial trait involving both genetic and environmental influences.

In addition to these areas, evidence for genetic influence has also been found for such diverse characteristics as memory abilities, attitudes, religiosity, verbal fluency, divergent thinking, academic achievement, and creativity (Plomin, 1989; Loehlin, 1994; Rowe, 1994). For most of the twentieth century psychologists have assumed that one's environment, particularly one's early upbringing, is the chief determinant in the formation of human abilities and dispositions. Recent research has found that many important characteristics have a moderate to strong genetic influence. Consequently there has been a swing back to a stronger hereditarian position, although this swing may have gone too far. Critics point to various ways that the influence of the environment may have been underestimated. Regardless, most developmentalists agree that genetics determines the potential that is realized through the environment, both of which interact to form phenotypic outcome. But is there more involved in human development than mainstream psychologists have acknowledged?

The Person in Human Development. Modern developmental psychology is dominated by naturalism, determinism, and neopositivism. These assumptions have limited considerations of the influences on human development to naturalistic causal forces that impact all organisms (genes and environment). As a result they reinforce the notion that human behavior is determined by causes that lie beyond personal control. The closest that behavior geneticists come to personal control is their insight regarding active gene-environment interaction, that humans select the environments that conform to their genotype. However, this concept still assumes that the selection is controlled by genes. For most researchers in the field, human development is solely a product of heredity and the environment. However, a Christian view of persons suggests that humans are more than simply determined.

Some psychologists have begun moving in the direction of recognizing a stronger role for the individual. Bandura's (1986; Bandura & Schunk, 1981) research on self-efficacy beliefs has found that beliefs that we have that we are competent in a task influence our task performance. At the least Bandura argues that a belief in our ability to carry out a task impacts behavior. Beliefs are surely shaped by our environment as well as our genotype. However, self-efficacy beliefs are beliefs about oneself that involve a personal, depth commitment to one's potential that can lead people to attempt novel behaviors, activities, and thinking that are to some extent intrinsically unpredictable.

Humanistic psychologists have argued against strict determinism for years. Yet their relative lack of rigor limited the persuasive power of their arguments for mainstream psychologists. However, in recent decades philosophers have returned to topics such as action, the will, and human freedom at least in part to distinguish the unique features of human behavior and experience that cannot be grasped with deterministic models of science (Frankfurt, 1971/1991; Langford, 1971; Taylor, 1964, 1985). Moreover, recent psychological research and theorizing on action and agency have begun to describe the volitional dimension of human behavior (Gollwitzer & Bargh, 1996; Harre, 1984; Heckhausen, 1991; Kuhl & Beckmann, 1985). Though most issues in these fields are far from settled, this interest reveals a growing recognition among some psychologists that human actions cannot be completely predicted because they are incompletely determined by hereditary and environmental causes and that volition exercises a causal role in human behavior that can be analyzed rationally and empirically.

Research on heredity and the environment itself reveals a possible opening for volition. All behavior genetics models acknowledge a certain percentage of differences in phenotype that cannot be explained by either genetics or environment. This is usually attributed to measurement error. The models available are unable to disentangle this error from the role that the environment plays. If one assumes that human volition exists and that its influence is not completely determined by genes or the environment, then its role would be found in the error term of the behavior genetics models. Volitional influences may also help to explain why developmental behavior genetics has found that in some cases, shared environment influences disappear in adulthood. Perhaps that is because humans start to make their own decisions. If so, the fact that shared influence diminishes does not mean that genetics is the only explanation. Perhaps a new one develops: the human will. Future longitudinal studies of change should explore this possible causal force, in spite of the methodological difficulties that attend its study.

To add volition as a consideration in human development is also legitimate from a common-sense perspective. Humans nearly universally attribute to themselves causal power to decide on a course of action, decisions that they typically take responsibility for. Moreover, jurisprudence, literature, morality, and religion all assume this reality. Only the naturalistic assumptions of determinism and neopositivism have limited its recognition within modern psychology.

Nevertheless, given research to date, it would be absurd to argue for a radical view of volition that attributes to the person all responsibility for one's characteristics (e.g., Sartre, 1956). It is possible to maintain a belief in free agency that is consonant with a belief that human action is also largely determined. This is a variant of libertarianism (Evans, 1989). One can also recognize that some characteristics are more determined than others; for example, cognitive abilities seem to be more determined than religious attitudes.

From a developmental perspective, volition itself should be seen as an emergent trait, a personability that arises out of hereditary and environmental influences. Infants have little sense of themselves as the author of their own actions (Stern, 1985). Grad-

ually, through heredity and facilitative environmental experiences, children develop a greater autonomy and self-directedness that matures into adult forms of agency. Through such volitional influences, which are themselves influenced by genes and the environment, humans come to shape their own development, a shaping for which they are held responsible. Such a recognition is basic to a Christian view of human nature (Evans, 1989).

Supernatural Influences on Human Development. A Christian psychology also includes supernaturalism among its assumptions. Most fundamentally the Scriptures posit that God is the one who has orchestrated whatsoever comes to pass (Lam. 3:37–38; Dan. 4:35; Eph. 1:11). As a result some Christians would see God as the ultimate causal force, working through genes, the environment, and volition to bring about his plan (e.g., Berkouwer, 1952). However, all Christians agree that God directly intervenes in human development through conversion when, through the Holy Spirit, God brings about changes in one's life that the Christian attributes to God (John 15:5; Phil. 2:12–13; Heb. 13:20–21). In addition, although scriptural and empirical evidence is scanty, there is evidence of malevolent spiritual forces that also may impact human behavior; this evidence needs to be taken into account for a comprehensive view of human development. It is not clear how supernatural and volitional influences interact with hereditary and environmental influences. Much research and reflection in this area is needed. Nevertheless, a Christian approach is of necessity multidimensional, incorporating natural (genetic and environment), personal, and supernatural dimensions of human development that interact in the formation of a mature human being.

References

Anastasi, A. (1958). Heredity, environment, and the question "how?" *Psychological Review, 65,* 197–208.

Bandura, A. (1971). *Social learning theory.* Morristown, NJ: General Learning.

Bandura, A. (1986). *Social foundations of thought and action: A social cognitive theory.* Englewood Cliffs, NJ: Prentice-Hall.

Bandura, A., & Schunk, D. H. (1981). Cultivating competence, self-efficacy, and intrinsic interest through proximal self-motivation. *Journal of Personality and Social Psychology, 41,* 586–598.

Berkouwer, G. C. (1952). *The providence of God* (L. B. Smedes, Trans.). Grand Rapids, MI: Eerdmans.

Bouchard, T. J., Jr., & McGue, M. (1981). Familial studies of intelligence: A review. *Science, 212,* 1055–1059.

Bronfenbrenner, U. (1977). Toward an experimental ecology of human development. *American Psychologist, 32,* 513–531.

Bronfenbrenner, U. (1986). Ecology of the family as a context for human development: Research perspectives. *Developmental Psychology, 22,* 723–742.

Bronfenbrenner, U., & Ceci, S. J. (1993). Heredity, environment, and the question 'how?'—A first approximation. In R. Plomin & G. E. McClearn (Eds.), *Nature, nurture, and psychology*. Washington, DC: American Psychological Association.

Cummings, M. R. (1994). *Human heredity* (3rd ed.). St. Paul, MN: West.

Curtiss, S. (1977). *Genie: A psychological study of a modern-day wild child*. New York: Academic.

Dunn, J., & Plomin, R. (1990). *Separate lives: Why siblings are so different*. New York: Basic.

Evans, C. S. (1989). *Wisdom and humanness in psychology: Prospects for a Christian approach*. Grand Rapids, MI: Baker.

Farber, S. L. (1981). *Identical twins reared apart: A reanalysis*. New York: Basic.

Frankfurt, H. G. (1991). Freedom of the will and the concept of a person. In D. M. Rosenthal (Ed.), *The nature of mind*. New York: Oxford University Press. (Original work published 1971)

Gollwitzer, P. M., & Bargh, J. A. (Eds.). (1996). *The psychology of action*. New York: Guilford.

Gottesman, I. I. (1991). *Schizophrenia genesis: The origins of madness*. New York: Freeman.

Grusec, J. E., & Lytton, H. (1988). *Social development: History, theory, and research*. New York: Springer-Verlag.

Harre, R. (1984). *Personal being: A theory for individual psychology*. Cambridge, MA: Harvard University Press.

Heckhausen, H. (1991). *Motivation and action*. (P. K. Lappmann, Trans.). New York: Springer-Verlag.

Herrnstein, R. J., & Murray, S. A. (1994). *The bell curve: Intelligence and class structure in American life*. New York: Free Press.

Jensen, A. R. (1973). *Educability and group differences*. New York: Harper & Row.

Kagan, J., Arcus, D., & Snidman, N. (1993). The idea of temperament: Where do we go from here? In R. Plomin & G. E. McClearn (Eds.), *Nature, nurture, and psychology*. Washington, DC: American Psychological Association.

Kimble, G. A. (1993). Evolution of the nature-nurture issue in the history of psychology. In R. Plomin & G. E. McClearn (Eds.), *Nature, nurture, and psychology*. Washington, DC: American Psychological Association.

Kuhl, J., & Beckmann, J. (Eds.). (1985). *Action control: From cognition to behavior*. Berlin: Springer-Verlag.

Langford, G. (1971). *Human action*. Garden City, NY: Doubleday.

Lerner, R. M. (1986). *Concepts and theories of human development* (2nd ed.). New York: Random House.

LeVay, S., & Hamer, D. H. (1994). Evidence for a biological influence in male homosexuality. *Scientific American, 270*, (5) 44–55.

Lewontin, R. C., Rose, S., & Kamin, L. J. (1984). *Biology, ideology, and human nature: Not in our genes*. New York: Pantheon.

Loehlin, J. C. (1989). Partitioning environmental and genetic contributions to behavioral development. *American Psychologist, 44*, 1285–1292.

Loehlin, J. C. (1994). Behavior genetics. In R. J. Sternberg (Ed.), *Encyclopedia of human intelligence*. (Vol. 1). New York: Macmillan.

Loehlin, J. C., & Rowe, R. D. (1992).

Loehlin, J. C., Horn, J. M., & Willerman, L. (1989). Modeling IQ change: Evidence from the Texas Adoption Project. *Child Development, 60*, 993–1004.

Loehlin, J. C., Willerman, L., & Horn, J. M. (1988). Human behavior genetics. *Annual Review of Psychology, 38*, 101–133.

McGue, M. (1993). From proteins to cognitions: The behavior genetics of alcoholism. In R. Plomin & G. E. McClearn (Eds.), *Nature, nurture, and psychology*. Washington, DC: American Psychological Association.

Mischel, W. (1979). On the interface of cognition and personality: Beyond the person-situation debate. *American Psychologist, 34*, 740–754.

Plomin, R. (1989). Environment and genes: Determinants of behavior. *American Psychologist, 44*, 105–111.

Plomin, R. (1994). Nature, nurture, and development. In R. J. Sternberg (Ed.), *Encyclopedia of human intelligence*. (Vol. 2). New York: Macmillan.

Plomin, R., DeFries, J. C., & Loehlin, J. C. (1977). Genotype-environment interaction and correlation in the analysis of human behavior. *Psychological Bulletin, 84*, 309–322.

Rowe, D. C. (1994). *The limits of family influence: Genes, experience, and behavior*. New York: Guilford.

Sartre, J. (1956). *Being and nothingness: An essay on phenomenological ontology* (H. E. Barnes, Trans.). New York: Philosophical Library.

Scarr-Salapatek, S. (1975). Genetics and the development of intelligence. In F. D. Horowitz (Ed.), *Review of child development research*. (Vol. 4). Chicago: University of Chicago Press.

Scarr, S., & McCartney, K. (1983). How people make their own environments: A theory of genotype-environment effects. *Child Development, 54*, 424–435.

Skinner, B. F. (1971). *Beyond freedom and dignity*. New York: Knopf.

Stern, D. N. (1985). *The interpersonal world of the infant*. New York: Basic.

Taylor, C. (1964). *The explanation of behavior*. London: Routledge & Kegan Paul.

Taylor, C. (1985). *Human agency and language*. Cambridge: Cambridge University Press.

Tellegen, A., Lykken, D. J., Bouchard, T. M., Jr., Wilcox, K. J., Segal, N. L., & Rich, S. (1988). Personality similarity in twins reared apart and together. *Journal of Personality and Social Psychology, 54*, 1031–1039.

Wachs, T. D. (1993). The nature-nurture gap: What we have here is a failure to collaborate. In R. Plomin & G. E. McClearn (Eds.), *Nature, nurture, and psychology*. Washington, DC: American Psychological Association.

Watson, J. B. (1924). *Behaviorism*. New York: Norton.

E. L. JOHNSON

See PERSONALITY; LIFE SPAN DEVELOPMENT.

Hermaphroditism and Pseudohermaphroditism. A hermaphrodite is a person who possesses both male and female sex glands. The hermaphrodite may have an ovary and a testicle or a modified sex gland that contains both ovarian and testicular tissue. The cells of most hermaphrodites manifest the typical XX female chromosome pattern. Some hermaphrodites' bodies contain some cells with female chromosomes (XX) and other cells with male chromosomes (XY).

Most hermaphrodites manifest developed breasts and a penis above a vaginal opening. Both the penis and vagina are likely to be rudimentary and incompletely developed. Reproductive organs are usually only partially developed and nonfunctional. Hermaphrodites are characterized by an unusual mixture of sex glands, hormones, organs, and genitals.

True hermaphrodites are extremely rare: Fewer than one hundred cases have been documented in modern times. A similar hormonal disorder that occurs more frequently than true hermaphroditism is known as pseudohermaphroditism. Pseudohermaphrodites, like hermaphrodites, may have a combination of male and female genitals and reproductive organs. Unlike true hermaphrodites, pseudohermaphrodites do not have both male and female sex glands or both testicular tissue and ovarian tissue. Pseudohermaphroditism is also very rare.

Most instances of pseudohermaphroditism are caused by hormonal abnormalities during prenatal development. If the infant developing within the womb is a chromosomal female (XX), an excess of male sex hormones (androgens) can disrupt her normal sexual development. Too much androgen will result in the enlargement of the clitoris so that it resembles a penis and in the fusion of the labia to resemble a scrotum. In spite of the fact that the infant may have internal female organs, her genitals may resemble a male's more than a female's. As a result many of these children have been reared as males even though they are females.

At least three causes exist for excessive androgen levels during prenatal development. The first is genetic. In advenogenital syndrome a recessive gene stimulates the child's adrenal glands to produce excessive androgen. (All persons produce both male and female sex hormones.) Since this genetic defect is present throughout life, the masculinizing effect continues after birth. A second cause for excessive androgen during pregnancy is traceable to the ingestion of progestin, a synthetic form of the hormone progesterone, a female hormone secreted by the ovaries that may stimulate androgen. Progestin was prescribed to some women in order to minimize the risk of miscarriage. This practice has since been discontinued. A third androgen-related cause for pseudohermaphroditism in females is a maternal tumor that stimulates androgen secretion.

If the fetal child is a genetic male (XY), he may become pseudohermaphroditic through a failure to secrete androgens, or if these are secreted, a failure of the body tissue to respond to them. Testicular feminization is an example of this condition. Ample supplies of male sex hormones are produced, but due to a genetic anomaly the receptor sites are blocked. As a result prenatal development follows a feminine course and the infant's genitals look more female than male. These persons usually have a fairly typical feminine physique with developed breasts, undescended testes, a closed-ended vagina but no uterus, and sparse body hair. Most of these persons have been reared as women.

The psychological impact of hermaphroditism and pseudohermaphroditism on the patient and his or her parents is tremendous. The prospects for successful adjustment are much greater today than previously for several reasons. Physicians are able to make a rapid diagnosis and determine the genetic sex of the infant. Previously parents and physicians could only guess at whether they should rear the child as a male or female, and sometimes they guessed wrong. Second, surgery can be performed at a very early age to reconstruct the child's genitals. This can be done before gender identity is established, thus minimizing the trauma. Hormone therapy can be initiated to enable the child to develop more normally, especially through puberty. Finally, counseling can be provided to help the parents assign the proper gender and cope with the shock and guilt. Supportive developmental counseling of the child can also be of great benefit.

Money, who has done extensive research on these disorders, has indicated their value in demonstrating that a person's sex is actually based on six characteristics: chromosomal gender, gonadal gender, hormonal gender, internal accessory organs, external genital appearance, and assigned gender (Money, 1980). The life histories of hermaphrodites and pseudohermaphrodites make this clear. Most of the persons studied conformed to the sex role to which they were assigned and in which they were reared. While the contribution of social environment factors to gender identity is significant, the degree to which they interact with the person's biological state is still undetermined.

Reference

Money, J. (1980). The future of sex and gender. *Journal of Clinical Child Psychology, 9* (2), 132–133.

Additional Reading

Overzier, C. (Ed.).(1963). *Intersexuality.* New York: Academic.

C. D. DOLPH

See SEXUALITY; GENDER IDENTITY; GENDER IDENTITY DISORDER.

Heterostasis. *See* HOMEOSTASIS.

Hiltner, Seward. Seward Hiltner (1909–1984) was an American Presbyterian minister who lived his life and worked out his ministry and scholarship at the point of the interface between psychology and theology. He believed that the two disciplines are vital to each other and that together they should be a decisive force in shaping pastoral care and counseling. He elaborated his thought in numerous books and articles. The titles of his major works indicate the breadth and depth of his thought: *Pastoral Counseling* (1949), *Ferment in Ministry* (1969), *Preface to Pastoral Theology* (1958), and *Theological Dynamics* (1972).

Born in Tyrone, Pennsylvania, Hiltner received his A.B. in psychology in 1931 from Lafayette College and his Ph.D. in theological ethics in 1952 from the University of Chicago's Divinity School. Between 1935 and 1950 he served as executive secretary for the Council for the Clinical Training of Theological Students, and subsequently as executive secretary for the Federal Council of the Churches of Christ in America. In 1950 he was appointed associate professor of pastoral theology at the Divinity School of the University of Chicago and from 1961 until his retirement he served as professor of theology and personality at Princeton Theological Seminary.

The root metaphor underlying Hiltner's thought is what he called field theory. The simplest illustration of the model is an electromagnetic field. The model allowed Hiltner to avoid categorical thinking and, more positively, to see the world in general and psychological dynamics, theological dynamics, and interdisciplinary dynamics in particular, as a fluid interaction of focal and field forces. Concretely this means that while the gospel may be the focus of the pastor's ultimate concern, any truth, even the most "secular" truth, may be related to it and may contribute to our understanding of it. Thus no knowledge, least of all psychological knowledge, should be categorically excluded from the pastor's consideration.

Hiltner was especially attentive to Carl Rogers's theory of therapy. He used Rogers to develop what he called an educative approach to pastoral counseling. An educative approach eschews any attempt to impose solutions on the troubled parishioner and seeks to draw out answers that are within the individual or that are potentially available to the individual. The pastor is not to serve as a coercive guide, let alone as a moralistic judge, but is to try to make contact with the internal world of the parishioner and to help the parishioner find his or her own solution.

Hiltner's major contribution to the theoretical understanding of the pastoral task is found in his *Preface to Pastoral Theology*. In that book, he recasts the traditional functions of ministry like preaching, teaching, counseling, and guidance into three perspectives: communicating, organizing, and shepherding. This approach moved him beyond a ministry of compartmentalized activities and allowed him to see ministry as a fluid and contextual response to the situation at hand. Related to the shepherding perspective, which was Hiltner's primary concern, the approach means that pastoral care is a dimension of every ministerial activity and that in certain situations it is the dominant concern of the pastor. With one move, Hiltner had retained the distinctiveness of pastoral care and carved out a legitimate niche for it without devaluing the other functions of ministry. He then added to the clarity of the shepherding perspective by breaking it down into three functions that he called healing, sustaining, and guiding.

During his formative years, Hiltner was part of a discussion group in New York City that included giants like Paul Tillich, Erich Fromm, David E. Roberts, Rollo May, Harry Bone, and others. Throughout his career, he was in forthright dialogue with leaders in various disciplines. Nevertheless, he saw himself as a pastor and urged his students to keep sturdily to their role and identity as pastors with self-conscious authenticity. He enjoyed working with psychiatrists, especially with therapists at the Menninger Clinic in Kansas, where he served as a theological consultant, but he spent much of his life communicating with parish pastors and helping them to become more effective pastoral caregivers and pastoral theologians. He founded a journal, *Pastoral Psychology*, and served as both a contributor and a consultant to it for many years. He stood with the parish pastor but served as a standard-bearer and the definer of modern pastoral care and counseling.

L. ADEN

See PASTORAL CARE; PASTORAL COUNSELING.

History of Psychology. *See* PSYCHOLOGY, HISTORY OF.

Histrionic Personality Disorder. This term describes an immature, overdramatic person with intense, fluctuating feelings and seriously disturbed interpersonal relationships. Although the disorder is considered rare, many people think they know at least one histrionic person. In social situations they are often charming and flamboyant. Relationships begin passionately but deteriorate rapidly under the assault of childish, unpredictable self-centeredness. They are characteristically brought to therapy in an intense emotional storm, a crisis set off by a trivial injury.

As a discrete personality disorder this is relatively new, but it has a long and interesting history. The notion of a hypochondriacal, shallow, excitable woman who suffers from a "wandering womb" dates from Hippocrates. In common language "hysterical" describes an emotional reaction gone wild. Technically it was first applied to the seductive but frigid woman who has many sexual problems. But this impression has not held up under the scrutiny of statistical analysis (Slavney & McHugh, 1974).

Psychoanalytic Theories. In the nineteenth century psychologists focused on the conversion phenomena often seen in the hysteric, such as sensory losses and mutism. Sigmund Freud constructed much of his earliest theory of the unconscious in an effort to explain such symptoms. Later he related hysteria to "the erotic libidinal type," an early phallic (genital) organization. Freud never used the term *hysterical character* but others soon did.

An early study of the hysteric as a character disorder was that of Wittels (1930). He clearly linked the symptoms to character organization. Though he considered the fixation as oral, an earlier and more primitive phase than the genital, Wittels described these people as infantile and hyperfeminine. Other psychologists amplified this idea, noting that although the conversion symptoms might be easily resolved, the underlying character disorder was not.

The structural dynamics of the hysteric remained unclear until the work of Kernberg (1976) located the source of pathology even earlier in object relation development (*see* Object Relations Theory). Since then hysteria has been more usefully considered a personality disorder. Theoretical work has attempted to distinguish this from the narcissist (*see* Narcissism) on one side and the borderline on the other (*see* Borderline Personality Disorder). Clarity seems to be in the offing, since the disorder has been renamed the histrionic personality, or one who organizes reality around a drama (Slavney & McHugh, 1974).

Diagnosis. The most discriminating characteristic of the histrionic personality remains the individual's dramatic distortions. External reality is organized primarily as a story. Dramatic role determines the identity of both self and important others and everything shifts between scenes. When one scene ends, backstage confusion reigns and the histrionic seems a lost child until the curtain opens on the next. Appearance and style is everything, and reality itself is as flat, impressionistic, and changeable as stage scenery, designed to appear real from a distance.

The explosive anxiety of all personality disorders is here triggered when the action stops. The histrionic feels stasis as dull meaninglessness at a narcissistic level and aching, deathly emptiness at the borderline level. To avoid such pain a scene predictably explodes, which gets the action going with a new script.

The interpersonal difficulties of the histrionic usually begin with astonishingly effective charm, drawing the other close. When the desired other falls in love, there is a moment of exhilaration as the profound loneliness is relieved. But love inevitably means losing control, a terrifying feeling, and only a fight can reestablish control. Relationships then follow a course of warmth closely followed by unexpected hostility. Even though these people might be very effective sexually and be considered socially a good wife or a good husband, this inconstancy destroys the very loving relationship that alone could dispel their loneliness.

Cultural Observations. This most ancient of disorders still fascinates professionals and lay people alike. Perhaps this is because the compulsive Western culture casts these passionate people as our heroines in novels and films. The bright youthfulness, the sparkle and excitement of a succession of Scarlett O'Haras, relieves us from the dullness of our lives. Many people have noticed how often a compulsive man is drawn to a histrionic woman in stories or in life or how often good women fall in love with con men.

Histrionic personality disorder was thought originally to be a disorder of women or gay, effeminate men. But more recently histrionic men have been described who live in drama, though with more diverse scripts: explorers, soldiers of fortune, or actors.

Perhaps because the dramatic or narrative quality of life itself has been almost obliterated in the industrial age, the gift of the histrionic personality without a disorder is often overlooked. They teach that whatever else life is it is also a great story. In the past, odes, sagas, and Bible stories were vital ways in which life was informed and enriched. Relating history gave present experience a setting in time, a connection with the past. The great contemporary interest in the end times, in narrative theology, and in defining identity as story, and the lively rebirth of storytelling, affirm this. Since psychotherapists are generally compulsive, their insight into a therapy session might be more perceptive and interpretations more on target if they could cast what the patient is telling them in a dramatic sequence.

Treatment. In general the histrionic personality should be approached as the narcissist or borderline, depending on the level of pathology, dealing with the severe arousals and the splitting. The unique splitting of the histrionic personality seeks to defend against the intense anxiety and cognitive distortions that result when the person's inner world switches from a good one that is going according to script to the bad world of disillusionment. Cognitive therapy focuses on these distortions and these persons' peculiar reality testing. It is often helpful to affirm the legitimacy of their dramatic perspective both to them and those about them yet confront their tendency to interpret legitimate structure or relationship as drama.

The individual therapist must be alert to the special positive transference distortions common in dealing with these people. Much of their life and energy has been devoted to charming others, and the inattentive therapist can soon become another scalp on their belt. The dramatic, flighty woman and the con man obviously can be difficult for groups also, but the charm and anger they provoke does not influence everyone. When all group members are aware of the specific problems of histrionics, a group can help them more than individual therapy.

References

Kernberg, O. (1976). *Object-relations and clinical psychoanalysis.* New York: Aronson.

Slavney, P. R., & McHugh, P. R. (1974). The hysterical personality: a controlled study. *Archives of General Psychiatry, 30,* 325-329.

Wittels, F. (1930). The hysterical character. *Medical Review of Reviews, 36,* 186–190.

Additional Reading

Chodoff, P., & Lyons, H. (1958). Hysteria, the hysterical personality and "hysterical" conversion. *American Journal of Psychiatry, 114,* 734–740.

C. M. BERRY

See PERSONALITY DISORDERS.

HIV. *See* AIDS.

Holiday Depression. Holidays suggest a picture of festive celebration and family gatherings, expectations of joyful exuberance. Self-worth, acceptance by others, and popularity are often read into holiday festivity and rituals. Holiday depression, and emotional reaction to holiday events and rituals, may involve pessimism, sadness, internalized anger, indecisiveness, lingering unpleasant tension, anxiety and insecurity, melancholic rumination, and in the extreme, suicidal gestures and suicide. With the felt dejection and rejection, self-blame and guilt may be evident. Somatic problems, gastrointestinal disturbances, fatigue, insomnia, loss or increase of appetite, and moodiness may be experienced. Alcohol or drug abuse may add to the difficulties.

Pastoral guidance for persons experiencing holiday depression needs to focus on the true meaning and significance of the holiday rather than personal assessment of individuals' faults and shortcomings or attractiveness and charm. Planning the celebration of holidays on several alternative levels will help to ease the pressure—social, psychological, and physical—that individuals sometimes put themselves through at holiday times. When people place too-high expectations on themselves and on the holiday events to help them prove how worthy they are, the effort most often fails and feeds disappointment, anger, and depression.

C. A. RAYBURN

See DEPRESSION.

Holistic Health and Therapy. The holistic health movement is based on a philosophy of treatment that utilizes a broad array of therapeutic techniques to help persons attain and maintain health. It has become popular since the mid-1970s because it provides an alternative to more traditional models of health care, particularly the medical model.

The medical model has come under considerable criticism for a variety of reasons. It has often been criticized for being too molecular and impersonal. Health care providers have frequently treated the body but neglected the whole person. The role of psychological, environmental, social, lifestyle, and spiritual factors and their contributions to health problems or recovery have often been ignored because the physical condition received exclusive attention. In addition to being impersonal and limited in scope, traditional health care has been illness-oriented rather than health-oriented. The focus has been more on remediation than prevention. More is known about disease than health.

The medical model of health care has also been criticized for implicitly encouraging patients to take passive roles in maintaining their health. Medical treatment has been perceived as a unilateral effort on the part of the physician, who takes responsibility for restoring the patient to health, rather than a mutual effort in which the patients have primary responsibility for their own well-being and work with the health care provider. To some degree this imbalance in responsibility and roles has been due to physicians' extensive use of medications and surgery. These interventions are things that are done to patients; they are largely nonparticipative treatments. Since physical problems are almost the sole focus of physicians' attention and are treated by medication or surgery administered by experts, patients passively take their bodies to doctors to be fixed much as they take their automobiles to mechanics to be repaired.

The holistic health movement may be more clearly understood against the medical model. The central feature of this movement is holism, the belief that persons must be viewed in their entirety as complex and integrated beings who exist in an environment. Any attempts at understanding, diagnosing, or treating persons must be based on a macroscopic perspective that recognizes the significance of all aspects of personhood, not just physical symptomatology in isolation. Therapists must consider persons' psychological, social, environmental, and spiritual aspects as well as their physical status because they are all related. They influence one another. A change in one component will result in changes in the others. The holistic approach to personhood is a systems approach. According to the holists, the goal of the organism is health.

The holistic health movement views health as a dynamic process of development that includes all aspects of the person, not just the body. Pelletier states that "health is not the absence of disease but a state of optimum functioning about which we have very little information" (1979, p. 5). He makes the point that persons are not healthy by default (the lack of a discernible disease), but rather they are healthy when they are functioning up to their potential, experiencing inner harmony, and interacting effectively with their environment. Holistic health requires effective functioning physically, psychologically, socially, and spiritually plus the successful integration of all these components.

Holistic health requires continuing, conscious awareness and effort. It is best accomplished by developing a healthy lifestyle. The primary responsibility is upon the individual, not the medical establishment. The person must learn methods of self-control such as relaxation techniques, incorporate healthful habits such as regular exercise, and avoid destructive behaviors such as smoking and overeating. A heavy emphasis is placed on preventive medicine, especially through health education. Teaching lay persons about their bodies and how they function is an attempt to get persons more actively involved in assuming responsibility for attaining and maintaining their own health. The hope is that teaching will supersede the need for treatment.

The holistic health movement has gained momentum from research on stress and psychosomatic disorders that clearly demonstrates the effect of the mind (used in its broadest sense to include cognitive, emotional, volitional, and spiritual components) on physical health, especially on persons' vulnerability to disease. Human beings' unique possession, their minds, can be their undoing physically because it enables them to experience stress beyond their physical capability to endure it. Excessive stress leads to psychosomatic diseases that are caused or aggravated by stress. Pelletier (1977) estimates that 50 to 80% of all diseases are psychosomatic or stress-related. But the power of the mind can be used for good as well as for ill if properly harnessed. As surely as the mind can slay, it can also heal.

Since optimal health depends on the harmonious integration of many components of life (mind, body, and environment), it follows that most health problems will be relatively complex because they involve several of those components. For example, a spiritual problem such as a sense of meaninglessness may lead to a psychological problem such as anxiety, which may have physical concomitants such as an ulcer. These problems may require complex or multileveled solutions. The spiritual, psychological, and physical problems may all need attention simultaneously. To treat the ulcer medically without addressing the other aspects of the problem would be a shortsighted and most likely ineffective approach. A holistic view of the person would lead to a comprehensive, multidimensional treatment approach.

The holistic health movement has cautioned the public to be careful about submitting to potentially dangerous therapies such as surgery and medication, which may themselves cause a variety of problems. Holistic health advocates have instead championed a host of more participative and preventive therapies that are aimed at helping persons cope better, regulate themselves more effectively, and change maladaptive lifestyles. The goal is to use the mind to foster health rather than illness. Through the optimal development of persons' cognitive, emotional, spiritual, and social resources stress can be significantly reduced and better managed, and resistance to psychosomatic diseases can be significantly enhanced.

Holistic therapists vary widely in their training and their therapeutic methods. A partial listing of techniques used or suggested in the holistic health movement includes nutritional therapy, vitamin therapy, massage, acupressure, aerobics, exercise, biofeedback, meditation (of various types), autogenic training, assertiveness training, self-hypnosis, values clarification, imagery therapy, and support groups. The two that have probably received the most attention are nutrition and biofeedback. Note that all these techniques are programs that require active participation on the part of the persons receiving the treatment and that all the treatments involve some sort of education and self-regulation.

While holistic health practitioners do reject the medical model, most do not totally eschew conventional medical or psychological treatment. Many recommend psychological therapy to resolve marital, familial, or relational discord. Psychotherapy is often viewed as an important mind-expanding tool in changing personality and helping persons to change a stress-prone personality type and find their optimal style of living. Psychological and medical technology have proven helpful in developing stress profiles, which identify individuals' characteristic physiological and psychological responses to stress. Through analysis, individuals' particular vulnerabilities can be determined and individually tailored health maintenance programs can be developed. The holistic health movement has reacted mainly to the limited views and abuses of the medical establishment.

From a Christian perspective the strengths of the holistic health movement include its rich and holistic view of persons, its openness to spiritual concerns, its acknowledgment of the importance of a world-life view in health, and its emphasis on prevention, health, and personal responsibility. These values are consistent with Scripture.

However, several Christian authors (Reisser, Reisser, & Weldon, 1983) have pointed out that in spite of these more superficial compatibilities with Christianity the "new consciousness" worldview behind most of the writings in holistic health makes it necessary for Christians to examine this movement critically. These authors identify the roots of the movement in "a loose synthesis of various elements of mysticism, occultism, spiritism and animism" (Reisser et al., 1983, p. 12). They note, however, that not all writers or organizations promoting health for whole persons are based on a new consciousness worldview. The writings of Westberg (1979) and the network of Wholistic Health Centers founded by him are explicitly grounded in Christianity.

Since the holistic health movement is neither a discipline nor a professional association, its weaknesses reside in the lack of ethical and minimum training standards. Holistic health therapists, while sharing some common assumptions, vary widely in their education, competence, therapeutic approaches, and views on spiritual issues.

In conclusion, the holistic health movement has highlighted some valuable concepts, but its practitioners and their methods must be carefully evaluated on an individual basis in light of Scripture.

References

Pelletier, K. R. (1977). *Mind as healer, mind as slayer.* New York: Delacorte/S. Lawrence.

Pelletier, K. R. (1979). *Holistic medicine.* New York: Delacorte /S. Lawrence.

Reisser, P., Reisser, T. K., & Weldon, J. (1983). *The holistic healers.* Downers Grove, IL: InterVarsity Press.

Westberg, G. R. (Ed.). (1979). *Theological roots of wholistic health care.* Hinsdale, IL: Wholistic Health Centers.

Additional Reading

Allen, D. F., Bird, L. P., & Herrmann, R. (Eds.). (1980). *Whole-person medicine.* Downers Grove, IL: InterVarsity Press.

C. D. DOLPH

See TRANSPERSONAL PSYCHOLOGY; FAITH HEALING; INNER HEALING; PSYCHIC HEALING.

Holy Spirit, Role in Counseling. Christian counseling or people helping can be defined as counseling done by a Christian who is Christ-centered, biblically based, and Spirit-filled (Tan, 1992). The role of the Holy Spirit in Christian counseling is therefore crucial and central.

At least three persons are involved in every counseling situation: the counselor, the client or counselee, and the Holy Spirit (Adams, 1973). Two volumes have been published specifically on the Holy Spirit and counseling (Gilbert & Brock, 1985, 1988; also see Vining, 1995a, 1995b; Vining & Decker, 1996). In Scripture the Holy Spirit is called the Counselor or Comforter (John 14:16–17). The Holy Spirit's presence in every counseling situation needs to be acknowledged and the Spirit's healing power received with deep humility and gratitude by every Christian counselor, lay or professional, so that the most fruitful and effective counseling can be provided to counselees. The role of the Holy Spirit in counseling can be described in three major ways: power (and gifts), truth, and fruit.

The Spirit's Power. The power of the Holy Spirit is needed for Christian life and ministry, especially in witnessing and evangelism (Acts 1:8; cf. Eph. 5:18). The Holy Spirit empowers us as we yield daily and allow the Spirit to fill us, under the lordship of Christ. The Holy Spirit also enables or empowers us for different ministries, including counseling, by imparting spiritual gifts to us, according to God's sovereign will (see 1 Cor. 12; Rom. 12; Eph. 4; 1 Peter 4). The following spiritual gifts are especially relevant for an effective counseling ministry that is Spirit-led (see Tan, 1990b): exhortation or encouragement (Rom. 12:8), healing (1 Cor. 12:9, 28), wisdom (1 Cor. 12:8), knowledge (1 Cor. 12:8), discerning of spirits (1 Cor. 12:10), and mercy (Rom. 12:8). Other spiritual gifts considered to be important for counseling include prophecy, teaching, faith, miracles, tongues, and intercession. Wagner (1994) has provided helpful definitions of 27 spiritual gifts as well as a spiritual gifts questionnaire (Wagner—modified Houts Questionnaire) that can be used by Christians in the process of discovering their spiritual gifts.

The Spirit's Truth. The Holy Spirit is the Spirit of truth and will teach and guide us into all truth (John 14:26; 16:13). The Holy Spirit's ministry and work in counseling and other contexts will therefore never contradict the truth of God's word or the Bible. The Holy Spirit will always uphold the veracity and eternal validity of God's Word.

The Spirit's Fruit. The Holy Spirit also produces spiritual fruit in Christians and counselors yielded to his control. Such fruit that reflects mature Christlikeness (Rom. 8:29) includes love, joy, peace, patience, kindness, goodness, faithfulness, gentleness, and self-control (Gal. 5:22–23). It can be summed up in one word: *agape,* or love.

It is important to emphasize all three dimensions of the Spirit's work and ministry. Power without truth can lead to heresy. Power without love can lead to abuse. Power based on truth and manifested in love can bring about renewal and revival as well as deep and significant healing of broken persons.

The Holy Spirit in Counseling. During a counseling session the Holy Spirit can work in a number of ways. First, the Holy Spirit can lead the Christian counselor with specific words of knowledge or wisdom to get more quickly to the core or root problems that the counselee is struggling with. Swindoll has called these the "inner promptings" or nudges of the Spirit within a counselor as he or she remains prayerful and sensitive to the Spirit's leading during sessions with counselees (see Swindoll, 1994).

Second, the Spirit can provide guidance or spiritual direction to both counselor and counselee regarding God's will when they engage in more explicit forms of integration during counseling sessions; for example, by engaging in prayer together, using Scripture where appropriate, and discussing spiritual issues openly (Tan, 1990a; also see Tan, 1996).

Third, the Holy Spirit can release his healing power directly during a counseling session and touch and transform the counselee in deep ways so that greater wholeness and healing of symptoms take place. This can happen any time under God's sovereignty and grace. However, prayer can be particularly helpful in this regard. A specific type of prayer that calls upon the Holy Spirit to minister directly to the counselee is inner healing prayer or healing of memories (see Seamands, 1985; Tan & Ortberg, 1995).

Fourth, the Holy Spirit can enable the counselor to discern the presence of the demonic if demonization is present in the counselee's life. The Spirit can also empower the counselor to pray powerful and effective prayers of deliverance or exorcism if that is appropriate and if informed consent has first been obtained from the counselee. Otherwise it may be more appropriate or ethical to refer the counselee to a pastor or prayer ministry team in his or her own church (*see* Demon Possession).

Finally, the Spirit's presence and power can be more readily accessed or experienced if the counselor practices the spiritual disciplines on a regular basis (Tan, 1987). The spiritual disciplines such as prayer, meditation, fasting, study, simplicity, solitude, submission, service, confession, worship, guidance, and celebration (Foster, 1988; see also Willard, 1988), are power connectors to the Spirit so that the counselor can be transformed into a more Christlike person (Tan & Gregg, 1997). The counselor led by the Spirit can also encourage the counselee, when this is appropriate, to practice the spiritual disciplines so that the counselee can receive more of the Spirit's power to enable him or her to heal and grow as a person.

The role of the Holy Spirit in counseling is therefore a crucial one. He is the ultimate source of all true healing and wholeness. All true Christian counseling needs to be done in the Spirit, by the Spirit's power, truth, and love, under the lordship of Christ, and to the glory of God. Training and competence in counseling or therapy skills are still needed, but such skills are used in dependence on the Holy Spirit.

References

Adams, J. E. (1973). *The Christian counselor's manual.* Grand Rapids, MI: Baker.

Foster, R. J. (1988). *Celebration of discipline* (Rev. ed.). San Francisco: Harper & Row.

Gilbert, M. G., & Brock, R. T. (Eds.). (1985). *The Holy Spirit and counseling: Vol. 1. Theology and theory.* Peabody, MA: Hendrickson.

Gilbert, M. G., & Brock, R. T. (Eds.). (1988). *The Holy Spirit and counseling: Vol. 2. Principles and practice.* Peabody, MA: Hendrickson.

Seamands, D. (1985). *Healing of memories.* Wheaton, IL: Victor.

Swindoll, C. R. (1994). Helping and the Holy Spirit. *Christian Counseling Today, 2* (1), 16–19.

Tan, S.-Y. (1987). Intrapersonal integration: The servant's spirituality. *Journal of Psychology and Christianity, 6,* 34–39.

Tan, S.-Y. (1990a). Explicit integration in Christian counseling. *The Christian Journal of Psychology and Counseling, 5* (2), 7–13.

Tan, S.-Y. (1990b). Lay Christian counseling: The next decade. *Journal of Psychology and Christianity, 9,* 59–65.

Tan, S.-Y. (1992). The Holy Spirit and counseling ministries. *The Christian Journal of Psychology and Counseling, 7* (3), 8–11.

Tan, S.-Y. (1996). Religion in clinical practice: Implicit and explicit integration. In E. Shafranske (Ed.), *Religion and the clinical practice of psychology.* Washington, DC: American Psychological Association.

Tan, S.-Y., & Gregg, D. (1997). *Disciplines of the Holy Spirit.* Grand Rapids, MI: Zondervan.

Tan, S.-Y., & Ortberg, J., Jr. (1995). *Understanding depression.* Grand Rapids, MI: Baker.

Vining, J. K. (1995a). *Pentecostal caregivers: Anointed to heal.* East Rockaway, NY: Cummings and Hathaway.

Vining, J. K. (1995b). *Spirit-centered counseling: A pneumascriptive approach.* East Rockaway, NY: Cummings and Hathaway.

Vining, J. K., & Decker, E. E. (Eds.). (1996). *Soul care: A Pentecostal-Charismatic perspective.* East Rockaway, NY: Cummings and Hathaway.

Wagner, C. P. (1994). *Your spiritual gifts can help your church grow* (Rev. ed.). Ventura, CA: Regal.

Willard, D. (1988). *The Spirit of the disciplines.* San Francisco: Harper & Row.

S.-Y. TAN

See RELIGIOUS RESOURCES IN PSYCHOTHERAPY; SPIRITUAL AND RELIGIOUS ISSUES IN PSYCHOTHERAPY; DEMONIC INFLUENCE, SIN, AND PSYCHOPATHOLOGY.

Homelessness. Many people who live in or near major cities have seen homeless individuals who walk the streets during the day and shelter in doorways, cardboard boxes, or tent cities at night. Although 45% of homeless people are single men and 14% are single women (Clarke, 1995, p. 11), the homeless population on any given night also includes two-parent families in transition, single mothers with children, and runaway and "throwaway" teenagers and younger children. Many homeless individuals and families may be staying in shelters, sleeping in their cars, or doubling up with relatives while they seek permanent housing.

Scope of Homelessness. Estimates of the scope of homelessness vary widely. Some differences in estimates may be politically motivated; others may be due to the use of different definitions of the term *homeless.* A Columbia University study found that "at least 5.7 million Americans were homeless for some periods of time" between 1985 and 1990 (Mesler, 1995, p. 18). Government Accounting Office annual estimates of the size of the homeless population range from 250,000 to 3,000,000 (Barbieri & Fricke, 1989, p. 123). The National Alliance to End Homelessness (NAEH) estimates that "some 2,000,000 people are homeless in any given year, 736,000 on any given night" (1995b, p. 1).

Since "5.1 million U.S. home households . . . are [low-income] renters . . . who spend more than 50% of their income on housing," many of these people become part of the homeless population during brief or extended periods of transition (Clarke, 1995, p. 12). In 22 cities surveyed by the United States Conference of Mayors (USCM), it was found that low-income renters in transition were homeless for periods of between 1 month (St. Paul, MN) and 24 months (Los Angeles, CA), depending on the existing supply and cost of housing (United States Conference of Mayors, 1995, p. 38).

The Homeless Population. The homeless population in 1994–1995 was made up of single men (46%), single women (14%), two-parent families with children (10%), single-parent families with children (26.5%), and unaccompanied minors (3.5%). Half of the single-parent families were fleeing abuse (United States Conference of Mayors, 1995, p. 40; Clarke, 1995, pp. 11–16).

The homeless population was made up of African-Americans (56%), whites (29%), Hispanics (12%), Native Americans (2%), and Asians (1%). One-fifth were employed and 21% were veterans (United States Conference of Mayors, 1995, p. 40).

Causes of Homelessness. The two chronic causes of homelessness are alcohol and drug abuse (about 33%) and deinstitutionalization of the mentally ill (about 27%). The remaining 40% of homelessness is caused by unemployment, lack of sufficient income, an inadequate supply of low-cost housing, domestic violence, and other family crises (National Alliance to End Homelessness, 1995a, pp. 1, 9; United States Conference of Mayors, 1995, p. 2).

Services to the Homeless. Cities that systematically address homelessness attempt to organize a continuum of care similar to that used in the city of Chicago. Care consists of a partnership among government, secular nonprofit agencies, and religious providers and includes five key components: outreach and assessment, emergency shelter, transitional housing, low-cost permanent housing, and necessary supportive services to homeless persons with various problems. However, in many cities such as Denver, Colorado, there is still a large gap between transitional and permanent housing (United States Conference of Mayors, 1995, p. 64).

The operating money for homeless services during 1994–1995 came from five main sources: charitable funds and local government (28%), state funding (18%), federal McKinney Act funding (38%), community development block grants (12%), community services block grants (1%). Other sources contributed 3% (United States Conference of Mayors, 1995, p. 51).

A Multimodal Approach. Michael Teague of the Los Angeles Rescue Mission states, "[When I began], I thought all you needed was Jesus Christ and the Bible." Later he experimented with a service program "that was almost apologetic about our Christian faith; that one didn't succeed much better." Teague now directs efforts that incorporate a strong faith element into a comprehensive retraining and substance abuse recovery program (Clarke, 1995, p. 14).

An excellent beginning resource for pastors, churches, and individuals who wish to help the homeless is *What You Can Do to Help the Homeless*, developed by the National Alliance to End Homelessness (1991).

References

Barbieri, R. A., & Fricke, D. W. (1989, spring). The crisis in affordable housing. *GAO Journal*, 28–33.

Clarke, L. (1995, January/February). Are we winning the fight against homelessness? *Salt of the Earth*, 11–16.

Mesler, B. (1995, May/June). The homeless learn to hit back. *Third Force*, 18–25.

National Alliance to End Homelessness. (1991). *What you can do to help the homeless*. New York: Simon & Schuster.

National Alliance to End Homelessness. (1995a). *Annual report 1995*. Washington, DC: Author.

National Alliance to End Homelessness. (1995b). *The face of homelessness*. Washington, DC: Author.

United States Conference of Mayors. (1995). *A status report on hunger and homelessness in America's cities: 1995*. Washington, DC: Author.

J. R. CHEYDLEUR

See COMMUNITY MENTAL HEALTH; COMMUNITY PSYCHOLOGY.

Homeostasis. A physiological regulatory mechanism that maintains a constant and stable internal environment relative to a variable external environment. Though the American physiologist Walter Bradford Cannon coined the term *homeostasis*, the French physiologist Claude Bernard was the first to introduce the concept of *milieu interieur* (internal environment) in the late 1800s. Bernard maintained that the biological organism ensures its unity and independence from a changing external environment by developing an internal environment held stable through its own adjustments. For example, one's body temperature remains constant despite changes in the outside temperature.

The regulatory mechanism contains four essential components. First is the characteristic itself, or the system variable, to be regulated. Second is the optimal value, or the set point, of the system variable. This is the detector that monitors the system variable's current value. The final component is the correctional mechanism that restores the system variable to its set point. A clear example involving all four features is the room heater governed by a thermostat. Room temperature, the system variable, is maintained at a comfortable level, the set point, by presetting the thermostat. If the room temperature falls below the set point, a detector (closure of a switch's contacts) then turns on the correctional mechanism (the heater's coils). This regulatory system allows room temperature (the internal environment) to be relatively constant compared to the variability of the outside weather (the external environment).

Cannon's notion of homeostasis involves a complex relationship of not only the principles just described but also the nature of the self-regulating system. Cannon suggested, for example, that complex living beings, in contrast to machines, are open systems in that the internal environment is constantly open to the disturbing conditions of its surroundings. Therefore, internal adjustments are necessarily continuous (because the external environment varies) and systemic (because all parts of the regulatory mechanism must work in concert). On a philosophical level the concept of the open system has challenged conventional views of linear causality of human behavior.

The principle of homeostasis has also been used to help understand family interaction patterns and personality dynamics. For example, some personality theorists maintain that individuals, as self-regulatory systems, are fundamentally motivated to reduce tension and maintain an internal state of equilibrium.

P. C. HILL

See PERSONALITY; FAMILY SYSTEMS THEORY.

Homework in Psychotherapy. Many therapies utilize task assignments. Those who consider counseling and psychotherapy to be primarily educational, skill-building endeavors write most extensively and helpfully about this tool. Therapy based on homework became a conceptual model with the work of Shelton and Ackerman (1974) and later of Shelton (1979). In his recent writings Shelton refers to his approach as instigation therapy, which he sees to be a close ally of behavior therapy.

Homework in therapy is defined as "assignments given to the client which are carried on outside the therapy hour" (Shelton & Ackerman, 1974). Various theoretical positions use homework differently. Some offer occasional, nondirected, and/or open-ended tasks; others, consistent, well-defined, and systematic tasks. The systematic, consistent use of homework tasks is a part of therapy throughout the intervention in most behavioral models (Wells, 1981). In some longer-term therapies the desire and need to write often emerge as an expressive and creative act (e.g., keeping a diary or journal of one's thoughts and dreams).

The primary intention of this adjunctive therapy tool is to extend the work of the therapy hour. Therapy hours are not enough time for growth. Homework tasks are one way to reach beyond the session time to assure the impact of the therapy.

The homework assignment format includes one or more of the following five instructions: a do statement (e.g., read, say, observe); a quantity statement (e.g., talk three times about or give five compliments); a record statement (e.g., count and record the number of compliments or mark on a chart each time . . .); a bring statement (e.g., bring your chart, observations, child . . . to your next appointment); a contingency statement (e.g., call for your next appointment after you have done . . .) (Shelton & Ackerman, 1974). Toward the end of the therapy hour the reason for and nature of the homework assignment is explained to the client. Summarized homework instructions are usually written down, with both client and therapist keeping a copy.

Successful homework is a result of well-planned treatment. The client's cooperation in carrying out homework tasks is emphasized at the time of the assignment. Contingency statements, rewards, and other reinforcements act to ensure completion of the task. If clients fail to carry out their assignments, the therapist should take this seriously and never overlook the issue. If the task has been given simply and clearly and has been acknowledged, the therapist should never take responsibility for its unsuccessful completion; instead the responsibility should firmly and kindly be placed on the client's shoulders.

Not all clients can benefit from task assignments. Clients with magical expectations, individuals who refuse to accept any personal responsibility, clients who need time to ventilate in an accepting environment, and clients coming under external duress do not work well in this modality.

References

Shelton, J. L. (1979). Instigation therapy: Using therapeutic homework to promote treatment gains. In A. P. Goldstein & F. H. Kanfer (Eds.), *Maximizing treatment gains.* New York: Academic.

Shelton, J. L., & Ackerman, J. N. (1974). *Homework in counseling and psychotherapy.* Springfield, IL: Thomas.

Wells, R. A. (1981). *Planned short-term treatment.* New York: Free Press.

B. J. SHEPPERSON

See BIBLIOTHERAPY.

Homosexuality. "Homosexuality" means "same or like sexuality" and derives from the Greek word *homoitas* (likeness, similarity, or agreement). Sexuality is the God-given drive in every person toward wholeness and includes emotional, cognitive, psychological, and spiritual dimensions. This drive is expressed in adult human beings emotionally through intimate communications, physically through touching, and genitally through foreplay and the act of sexual intercourse. Sexuality and spirituality are interrelated in complex and multifaceted ways.

A homosexual orientation is to be distinguished from a homosexual act. A homosexual act is any sexual activity between two individuals of the same gender. A homosexual orientation describes an individual whose sexual drive is directed toward an individual of the same gender. Thus a homosexual orientation involves emotional attractions toward the same gender and may or may not involve homosexual acts. Most sociologists agree that the concept of homosexual orientation was not present in the culture of biblical times (Greenberg, 1988). Most evangelical psychologists believe that most individuals who own a homosexual orientation have not made an initial choice to direct their sexuality toward their own gender.

Homosexual and heterosexual orientations are not mutually exclusive categories. Since the landmark study by Kinsey, Pomeroy, and Martin (1948), psychologists commonly refer to the Kinsey scale to describe a person's sexual orientation, which can range from zero (0) for exclusively heterosexual behavior (behavior is defined to include dreams and fantasies) to six (6) for exclusively homosexual behavior. Any individual rated at different times in life may demonstrate a shift in orientation. More recently the Kinsey Institute has amplified this finding by describing sexual orientation as multidimensional, situational, and contextual.

Although as many as 40% of males and 20% of females may have had some homosexual experience after puberty, estimates of those claiming a primary or exclusive homosexual orientation range from 1 to 13% for males and 1 to 5% of females. Various surveys disagree on percentages and on methods of defining and measuring homosexuality, but all surveys agree that there are fewer female homosexuals than male homosexuals.

Diagnostic Criteria. Homosexuality traditionally was considered by Western medicine to be pathological and therefore a diagnosable mental disorder. However, in 1973 the American Psychiatric Association voted to remove the general category of "homosexuality" from the *Diagnostic and Statistical Manual of Mental Disorders*. In the *DSM-III* (American Psychiatric Association, 1980), the category of "ego-dystonic homosexuality" was introduced subsequently as a still diagnosable mental disorder. An ego-dystonic homosexual is one who has consistent and marked distress about having a homosexual orientation. Therefore, according to *DSM-III*, individuals who are ego-syntonic (those who accept the homosexual orientation with minimum distress) are not mentally disordered.

In describing ego-dystonic homosexuality, *DSM-III* notes that the individual often has made unsuccessful attempts at heterosexual relationships. Associated features are loneliness, guilt, shame, anxiety and depression. Dysthymia (a chronic, low-grade depression) is often a complicating factor. Given negative cultural attitudes about homosexuality, anxiety, shame, and depression would be expected responses. There is usually mild or no impairment in the ego-dystonic homosexual person occupationally or socially. The primary impairment is interpersonal and sexual.

Researchers are divided over whether homosexuals as a group (both ego-syntonic and ego-dystonic) are more or less mentally healthy when compared with like heterosexual populations. For example, the landmark study conducted by Hooker (1957) that found no difference in mental health between heterosexuals and homosexuals has since been challenged on a number of points: her subjects apparently were not randomly selected and represented only high-functioning homosexuals (Goldberg, 1992), and the raw data reanalyzed did reveal differences that Hooker regarded as surface only (Fine, 1990). However, other contemporary researchers have shown that homosexuals are not more mentally disordered on average than are heterosexuals (Ross, Paulsen, & Stalstrom, 1988).

In 1987 another shift occurred in the diagnostic criteria of *DSM III-R* when the diagnosis of ego-dystonic homosexuality (302.00) was removed. Instead, under the category of "Other Sexual Disorders Not Otherwise Specified" (302.90), one type of this kind of NOS sexual disorder is listed as "persistent and marked distress about one's sexual orientation" (American Psychiatric Association, 1987, p. 296). Through another revision of the *DSM*, this definition or placement has not been markedly changed.

The *International Classification of Diseases* (U.S. Department of Health and Human Services, 1992), after defining homosexuality, instructs "record homosexuality as a diagnosis whether or not it is considered a mental disorder" (p. 383).

Evangelical Christians have shown and expressed strong disapproval of the APA decision to remove homosexuality from the category of mental disorders. (Note that homosexuality can still be diagnosed if the person shows marked distress about his or her orientation.) However, many homosexuals are able to function successfully socially, mentally, and occupationally while their dysfunction may be interpersonal, marital, sexual, and possibly spiritual. While moral, ethical, and mental wrongs do at times overlap, they are also distinct categories, depending upon the issues. For example, a person who commits adultery may be morally and ethically at fault but not mentally disordered. Therefore, the evangelical community may do well to address homosexuality not as a mental disorder but as primarily a spiritual and sexual issue that Christians may have tools and power to treat through God's Holy Spirit.

Etiology of Homosexuality. Research and theory on etiology can be organized into two broad and overlapping categories: biological and environmental.

Biological Theories. In recent years a surge of research has revealed biological factors that are correlated with homosexuality and may contribute to its development. While it is incomplete, controversial, and subject to alternative interpretations, converging evidence strongly suggests that a homosexual orientation is reflected in a person's physical being.

Research has shown to be incorrect the theory that homosexual men have abnormally low levels of androgens (e.g., testosterone) in their blood, while the levels are abnormally high in homosexual women. However, some patterns of hormone response in homosexual men led to the theory that the brain, and particularly the hypothalamus, a structure in the brain that regulates hormone secretion and is involved in sexual behavior, functions differently in homosexuals than it does in heterosexuals. Such alterations in brain function are known as organizational effects because they are relatively permanent.

During fetal development, hormones influence brain organization. In nonhuman mammals, hormone manipulations at particular stages of brain development can produce inverted sexual behavior (males behave sexually like females and vice versa). For example, injecting a newborn female rat with androgens leads to male-typical sexual behavior in adulthood. To extrapolate to humans from these animal studies is difficult, because sexual behavior is less stereotyped and hormonally determined in humans and because sexual orientation cannot necessarily be inferred from sexual behavior. Studies with humans show that congenital and drug-induced hormone abnormalities that parallel the hormone manipulations that induce sexual inversions in animals are sometimes, but not always, associated with increased likelihood of a homosexual orientation. Confounding the interpretation of these clinical cases are gender identity confusions and contradictions between genetic and physical sex that are not present in the majority of homosexuals. There is only a weak predictive relationship between hormonal abnormalities during fetal development and adult homosexuality.

Direct examination of the hypothalamus in the human brain has revealed two areas—the suprachiasmatic nucleus and the third interstitial nucleus of the anterior hypothalamus—that differ in average size between heterosexual and homosexual men (LeVay, 1991). While these results have not yet been replicated, they are moderately convincing evidence for a biological aspect to homosexuality. However, although the brain's basic structure is organized during fetal development, there is a degree of flexibility and plasticity for many years after birth. Therefore, whether brain differences associated with sexual orientation are present at birth, are produced from particular environmental circumstances, are the result of feeling, thinking, or acting as a homosexual person, or are some combination of these, is not yet clear.

Other studies have focused on brain function by comparing the performance of homosexual and heterosexual people on a variety of cognitive tasks. This rather implausibly assumes that differences in sexual orientation are associated with more general differences in mental ability. The results are inconclusive.

There have been recent reports of an inherited component to homosexuality, primarily through studies of twins. Identical twins have identical sets of genes. Fraternal twins have 50% of their genes in common as do any siblings. These studies often assume, rather questionably, that each member of a twin pair experiences the same environment, whether the twins are identical or fraternal. Given that assumption, if identical twins are more likely to share a trait, such as a homosexual orientation, than fraternal twins, this is evidence that the trait is at least partly genetic. When twins share a trait, this is known as concordance. Studies show concordance for homosexuality in identical twins ranging from 20% to 52%. Concordance among fraternal twins ranges from 20% to 22%. Similar results have been reported for males and females.

Such results suggest a moderately strong genetic component to homosexuality. However, this conclusion should be made with caution. First, the highest concordance rate is 52% for identical twins. This means that when one twin is homosexual, there is a 52% chance that his or her co-twin will also be homosexual. But there is also a 48% chance that the co-twin will be heterosexual. Obviously genes are not playing a completely deterministic role. Second, the fact that one study reported a concordance of 11% for adopted brothers of homosexual men, who have no genetic relationship, when the population rate of homosexuality is less than 5%, further supports the possibility that environmental, especially familial, factors influence the development of sexual orientation.

Direct examination of genes in one study showed that brothers who are both homosexual had a greater than chance likelihood of sharing a particular region of the X-chromosome (Hamer, Hu, Magnuson, Hu, & Pattatucci, 1993). However, since this study has yet to be replicated and since the researchers did not include heterosexual brothers in their comparison, how this finding fits into our understanding of homosexuality is difficult to ascertain.

Biological research has revealed some intriguing correlates to a homosexual orientation, but an understanding of any causal relationship between biological factors and sexual orientation is still primarily speculative. Nevertheless sexual orientation appears to be reflected in, if not caused by, our biology.

Environmental Theories. In theory, environmental factors that could influence homosexuality include everything from diet, climate, and environmental toxins to culture, parenting, and personal values. In practice, environmental theories and research on homosexuality has focused on the latter group.

Operant conditioning theorists proposed that homosexuality results from the reinforcement received from pleasurable homoerotic experiences, particularly if they precede pleasurable heteroerotic experiences or if heteroerotic experiences are unpleasant (for example, in cases of incest or sexual abuse).

Another learning explanation for homosexuality involves classical conditioning principles. Early-maturing males become sexually awakened at a time when they interact primarily with other males, thus pairing sexual readiness with males rather than females and leading to homosexuality. Later-maturing males (presumably the majority) become sexually awakened at a time when these desires are paired with females.

Such learning theories for homosexuality have been largely discounted. The assumption that homosexuals mature earlier than heterosexuals has not been substantiated. Pleasurable homoerotic experiences can occur in the absence of the other sex (ships, armies, prisons, camps) without leading to an adult homosexual orientation. The Sambia of the New Guinea highlands have institutionalized exclusive homoerotic activity for all males from ages 7 to about 22, yet once they are married, 95% of these men become exclusively heterosexual in behavior and orientation (Stoller & Herdt, 1985). This occurs despite both the reinforcement of presumably pleasurable homoerotic experiences and pairing sexual awakening with males rather than females.

Sigmund Freud argued that male homosexuality reflects prematurely arrested psychosexual development, caused by a domineering mother and/or a weak or absent father, possibly also with an abnormally close mother-son relationship. This theory influenced the direction of research on homosexuality for many years. Later researchers explored female homosexuality and broadened the scope of factors that could arrest psychosexual development to include a variety of negatively stressful events, such as poor parenting, abusive parenting, broken homes, or inadequate role models. These can prevent children from resolving power and dependency needs and leaves them with a sense of personal inadequacy and dissatisfaction. In many of these theories, an element of confusion during a critical period of gender role learning, caused by poor relations with the same-sex parent, sexual abuse, early homosexual seduction and/or self-labeling as homosexual, or by a feeling of inadequacy in one's expected gender role, predisposes a person to homosexuality.

The difficulty with much of the evidence on which these theories are based is that the homosexuals examined were those who had sought psychoanalytic counseling. Homosexual persons who seek psychoanalysis are not necessarily representative of all homosexuals, most of whom do not. As well, much psychoanalytic research is based on retrospection, adults remembering and reflecting on their childhood experiences. Such memories are constructed and interpreted in light of current circumstances, and while the process can have therapeutic value, it is not a reliable method of collecting data to support theories about the etiology of a homosexual orientation.

A major study out of the Kinsey Institute (Bell, Weinberg, & Hammersmith, 1981) used a large, nonclinical sample of homosexual persons. While again these data were retrospective, the researchers tried to overcome some of the inherent problems by approaching questions by several different routes. Homosexuals and heterosexuals of both genders were asked about the personalities of their parents, parent-child, parent-parent, and sibling relationships, gender conformity, peer relationships, early sexual experiences, self-esteem, and childhood, adolescent, and adult sexuality.

Perhaps the most significant finding of this study was the lack of support it provides for many of the traditional psychosocial theories of homosexuality. For example, the researchers found no significant differences between homosexuals and heterosexuals in personality of and relationship with their mothers or in the personality of their fathers. There were few differences between the groups in type and amount of early sexual experiences. Subsequent investigations by other researchers have provided mixed support for these findings.

Differences that did emerge, such as homosexual males having poorer childhood peer relationships with their fathers, who tended to be relatively cold and detached, were not large. Nevertheless, several other studies have confirmed this observation. Some investigators conclude that colder, rejecting fathers play a causal role in the development of homosexuality in males; Bell, Weinberg, and Hammersmith (1981) argue that innate childhood behavioral and personality differences in homosexual males cause fathers to respond negatively to their sons. By far the largest difference between homosexuals and heterosexuals was gender nonconformity. That is, homosexual persons were from their earliest recollections consistently less interested in the activities that others of their sex enjoyed, and they perceived themselves as being less masculine (males) or feminine (females) than did their same-sex peers. All the other factors examined were relatively unimportant in comparison with the strong and persistent gender nonconformity of the homosexual participants.

This gender nonconformity among homosexuals from early childhood has supported by several other studies, both retrospective and prospective. This does not mean that all homosexuals behaved in gender-atypical ways during childhood or that all heterosexuals conformed. It also does not imply that male homosexuals would prefer to be female and vice versa. In fact, homosexuals have a gender identity consistent with their physical sex. Nevertheless, the consistency of this observation has led several researchers to argue that sexual orientation and gender identity are loosely linked and that there is an inborn tendency toward a particular sexual orientation that manifests itself in childhood as gender-atypical behavior.

The research on gender nonconformity should be interpreted carefully. There is the potential to reinforce demonstrably false stereotypes of homosexual men as effeminate and homosexual women as butch. As well, if gender nonconformity is seen as a causal factor in homosexuality rather than a predictive one, pressure from those who fear homosexuality may inappropriately force children into rigid gender roles. Gender-typical behavior is culturally defined, an acknowledgment that researchers themselves generally fail to make.

At present, researchers have not found any environmental factors that consistently predict and possibly cause homosexuality. The link between gender nonconformity and homosexuality, although it is difficult to interpret, does suggest the value of cautiously exploring the relationship among gender identity, gender role, and sexual orientation.

Evaluation of Etiologic Theories and Research. The biological research on homosexuality has had slightly better success in finding links to homosexuality than has the environmental research. This may reflect the fact that biological researchers have physical substances to observe and measure, whereas environmental researchers face the added challenge of measuring and comparing complex concepts such as parent-child relationships and quality of sexual experiences.

Both classes of research should be evaluated in light of several concerns and assumptions, some specific to one class, some true for both. The biological research in particular is reductionist, viewing human sexuality as a mechanical, biological phenomenon. It is also individualist and does not meaningfully incorporate relationships and cultural context. The media interpretations of this research are particularly guilty of treating biology as basic and not subject to influence by environmental factors.

Behind both types of research usually lurks the assumption that homosexuality is abnormal in more than a statistical sense. Even if we take for granted that a homosexual orientation is abnormal in some sense, explorations into the etiology of abnormal conditions are most legitimately done based on a good understanding of the normal, healthy condition. Yet we do not have such an understanding of the development of a heterosexual orientation. This is a significant weakness in etiological research.

Biological and environmental researchers often carry the assumption that theories that apply to males also apply to females, or they ignore female homosexuality. Also ignored is the possibility that different people might become homosexual for different reasons or by different processes. Finally, interpreters of the research tend to assume that people are more easily able to overcome through therapy traits that are environmentally caused than those that are caused by biological factors.

Homosexuality most likely results from a combination of biological and environmental factors. Certainly the two cannot be meaningfully separated. The environment alters our biology, changing available nutrients, altering brain connections, neurochemistry, hormones, and so on. People perceive and interact with the environment through their bodies. That researchers find biological correlates to homosexuality is not surprising. That environmental correlates have not been as easy to find is more surprising, but as mentioned this may be due to the relative complexity of these factors.

Treatment Approaches. Based on the theory that homosexual males suffer a hormonal imbalance, researchers have tried injecting homosexual males with the male hormone testosterone. This treatment increases sex drive, but orientation remains stable. Thus hormonal treatments so far have consistently failed.

Using behavioristic principles of reward and punishment, researchers have tried administering shocks to males for sexual responses to same-sex pictures. This kind of experimental treatment has also failed to have any permanent effect on orientation.

One noted behaviorist documented one case of a homosexual male changing orientation to heterosexual over time (Wolpe, 1969). The goal of therapy was to enhance assertiveness and independence; the resulting change in orientation (stable after a four-year follow-up) was unplanned and surprised the psychotherapist.

Traditional psychoanalysts have and continue to treat homosexuals with the goal of developing a heterosexual orientation. This treatment approach is based on the theory that the same-sex parent of the homosexual person failed to nurture and to bond appropriately with the child. This failure causes the child to then grow up with a sense of personal inadequacy and unresolved dependency and power needs. A primary mechanism for healing is a relationship with a same-gender therapist that over time compensates partially for the lack of adequate same-sex parenting. The therapist also teaches and models for the client appropriate boundaries, assertive skills, and self-care skills. Critical for successful treatment is working with a same-sex therapist and keeping the relationship nonerotic. Reparative therapy began in theory with the observations of Freud and continues to be amplified today by such theorist-practitioners as Nicolosi (1991) and Moberly (1988).

Practitioners of psychoanalysis have done extensive research and follow-up studies to determine the success of reparative therapy. For example, MacIntosh (1994) surveyed 285 psychoanalysts who analyzed 1,215 homosexual patients. The change rate was reported at 23%, with the rest not experiencing change but reporting that the therapy was significantly helpful to them in other ways. A similar change rate (27%) is reported in Bieber (1962). In follow-up studies, the change rate does drop but not drastically. Thus approximately 25% of those entering reparative therapy emerge with a stable reorientation. Possibly some of these 25% also still suffer from homosexual yearnings or urges.

In the last fifteen years, another promising treatment approach is being developed by Christians; some are formerly homosexual (Comisky, 1989; Foster, 1995) while others specialize in healing prayer (Payne, 1988). This approach has similarities to the psychoanalytic treatment previously discussed, with an additional focus on the healing power of God and the Holy Spirit as the primary mechanisms for change.

Like the psychoanalysts, these Christian reparative therapists believe that homosexuality began when dysfunction (sin) of the individual's parents affected the child's ability to grow into health. A breach in relationship with the same-sex parent (abuse, neglect, abandonment [*see* Abuse and Neglect]) may cause the child to "defensively detach" from that parent, thus hindering proper gender identification. Similar problems in the opposite-sex parent, the unhealthy marriage of the parents, prebirth traumatic events, and/or abusive peers are also viewed as potential sources of wounds that may cause homosexuality to develop.

This treatment approach involves an in-depth study of God's creation, the purpose of God for the world, the sacrifice of Jesus Christ and his love for all persons, and a study of the character of God and the person of Jesus Christ. It also includes understanding the events of childhood that caused the homosexual orientation to develop, forgiving the persons who perpetrated the wounds, and seeking God's healing for the events or ongoing circumstances that caused woundedness. Events that are repressed (forgotten) are brought to light by the Holy Spirit in God's timing. Healing prayer from Christians who are friends or pastors and psychotherapy with a Christian therapist are both recommended to bring about the desired change in sexual orientation.

Proponents of the Christian reparative approach report that the success of this treatment varies according to the depth and type of homosexual involvement experienced, the kind of Christian social support system that is available, the age of the individual, and his or her level of social skills. Much of the information available about the success of this treatment is anecdotal in nature. However, many people report that over time, even after a substantial amount of healing has occurred, that homosexual urges will persist. Most believe that despite this problem, they have a high degree of life satisfaction because their lives include marriage, children, and a heterosexual relationship.

Other major schools of psychotherapy (Rogerian, Gestalt, family-systems, cognitive, strategic) do not offer specific treatment programs to change homosexuality. However, their principles can be used in the context of reparative therapy (psychoanalytic or Christian) in that understanding the client thoroughly (Rogers), accepting his or her feelings as real and purposeful (Gestalt), examining the influences of the family system (system therapy), correcting faulty cognitions (cognitive therapy), and changing the environment to facilitate change (strategic and behavioral) can all be helpful therapeutic responses in helping the homosexual client.

Biblical Considerations. Most theologians agree that God's intention for healthy human sexuality is heterosexuality. This can be argued both from the design of the male and female genitals and from the creation account (Gen. 1:27–28; 2:18–25). God created Eve as a helpmate to Adam and commanded them to procreate. When man and woman are joined into one they become more like God since each kind of sexuality (male and female) reflects the image of the Creator. This link is perhaps the reason for the intricate connection between sexuality and spirituality.

If God did intend for humans to be heterosexual, does this mean that homosexuality and/or homosexual acts are sinful? Most theologians agree that homosexual acts committed by heterosexuals are wrong and that all heterosexual and homosexual acts that are promiscuous are wrong. However, because in the last 150 years the concept of a homosexual orientation has emerged, a concept that apparently did not exist in biblical times, some theologians posit that homosexuality as expressed between two homosexuals who are committed partners (therefore, not promiscuous) are not sinning when they joining themselves emotionally, sexually, and spiritually.

Five other biblical texts are often cited as God's condemnation of homosexuality: Genesis 19:1–26, the story of the destruction of Sodom; Leviticus 20:13, a part of the Holiness Code to maintain the people of Israel as separate from pagan cultures; Romans 1:24–32, Paul's description of Greco-Roman pagans; and 1 Corinthians 6:9–11 and 1 Timothy 1:8–11, both texts in which the apostle Paul lists various sins that are incompatible with living the Christian life.

On the basis of other biblical texts, the sins of the Sodomites have been interpreted as arrogance, greed, indifference to the poor, hypocrisy, social injustice, and sexual immorality. The Sodomites threatened to rape the strangers. Any kind of rape—homosexual or heterosexual—is clearly sinful and clearly violates a person's emotional, physical, and sexual boundaries. One can clearly argue that the sin of the Sodomites was wanton violence and violation of the hospitality law to strangers and is likely not speaking about persons who claim homosexual orientation.

Similarly the Leviticus Holiness Code also notes that having sex with a woman who is menstruating is likewise "an abomination," and therefore applying such a text to those who claim homosexual orientation also seems misdirected. The Holiness Code was likely written to keep the Hebrews from copying Egyptian or Canaanite practices that may have involved child sacrifice, idolatry, sexual perversion, and other social injustices.

The homosexual activities described in Romans 1 are likewise not those within loving committed partnerships. Rather, Paul is describing pagan, Gentile practices, same-sex religious rites to the goddess Aphrodite that were perverse and sadomasochistic and that sometimes involved frenzied public castration and human sacrifice. Understanding this background, it is easy to see Paul's strong condemnation of this kind of homosexual act.

The other two Pauline texts, from analysis of the Greek words *malakoi* and *arsenokoitai*, seem to refer to prostitution by and corruption of young men, a practice known as pederasty. For a detailed explanation of this practice of pederasty in the classical world see Boswell (1980). To combine these two words and to translate them as homosexual as has been done in some translations is inappropriate.

After the exegesis of these passages that reference homosexuality, note that the only evidence suggesting a homosexual orientation within a committed relationship is sinful would be the inference from the passage in Genesis. Jesus never spoke to the issue of homosexual acts, and he did not address the issue of homosexual orientation.

Some people argue that homosexuality is not sinful because it occurs in nature. However, whatever is a part of natural creation is not therefore automatically good; for example, cannibalism occurs in humans and in a variety of animal species, but we do not therefore declare cannibalism to be good. Nature does not teach us about good versus evil.

The term *homophobia* refers to fear of homosexuality. That fear can take many forms: fear that homosexuals will destroy society and families, fear of being perceived as homosexual, fear of sexual arousal to homoerotic stimuli, fear that one's children will be influenced to choose a homosexual lifestyle, fear that homosexuality is somehow contagious (Scanzoni & Mollenkott, 1978). Homophobia is widespread in North America; it is often manifested in intense hostility, even violence, toward homosexuals and any who appear to be sympathetic with them. In this context it is perhaps not surprising that people are often deeply dismayed, depressed, or fearful when they discover their homosexual orientation. Self-loathing and suicide occur at much higher rates among homosexuals than among the general population.

Homophobia is not the same as the belief that homosexual behavior is morally wrong. The former is an emotional response that manifests itself in un-Christian acts of denial, rejection, discrimination, contempt, hostility, or violence toward homosexuals. The latter can be a principled position based on one's faith or religious doctrine and does not prevent relating to homosexuals in loving, supportive ways.

Given the complexity of the issue of homosexual orientation and given biblical considerations, the evangelical Christian community will do well to exemplify a Christlike response to homosexuals. To offer hope for healing and acceptance of brokenness that is not to be healed on this earth is the most Christian response. Contributing to the polarization between the homosexual community and the Christian faith will be counterproductive. Listening to the experiences of homosexual persons, engaging homosexual persons in dialogue, and presenting the gospel as good news with love and hope are Christlike responses to this issue and to individuals who wrestle with or desire to accept their homosexual orientations.

References

American Psychiatric Association. (1980). *Diagnostic and statistical manual of mental disorders (DSM-III).* Washington, DC: Author.

American Psychiatric Association. (1987). *Diagnostic and statistical manual of mental disorders (DSM-III-R).* Washington, DC: Author.

Bell, A. P., Weinberg, M. S., & Hammersmith, S. K. (1981). *Sexual preference: Its development in men and women.* Bloomington: Indiana University Press.

Bieber, I. (1962). *Homosexuality: A psychoanalytic study of male homosexuals.* New York: Basic Books.

Boswell, J. (1980). *Christianity, social tolerance and homosexuality.* Chicago: University of Chicago Press.

Comisky, A. (1989). *Pursuing sexual wholeness.* Santa Monica, CA: Creation House.

Fine, R. (1990). *Love and work: The value system of psychoanalysis.* New York: Crossroad.

Foster, D. (1995). *Sexual healing: God's plan for the sanctification of our lives.* Nashville, TN: Mastering Life Ministries.

Goldberg, S. (1992). *When wish replaces thought: Why so much of what you believe is false.* Buffalo, NY: Prometheus.

Greenburg, D. F. (1988). *The construction of homosexuality.* Chicago: University of Chicago Press.

Hamer, D. H., Hu, S., Magnuson, V. L., Hu, N., & Pattatucci, A. M. (1993). A linkage between DNA markers on the X chromosome and male sexual orientation. *Science, 261,* 321–327.

Hooker, E. (1957). The adjustment of the male overt homosexual. *Journal of Projective Techniques, 21,* 17–31.

Kinsey, A. C., Pomeroy, W. B., & Martin, C. E. (1948). *Sexual behavior in the human male.* Philadelphia: Saunders.

LeVay, S. (1991). A difference in hypothalamic structure between heterosexual and homosexual men. *Science, 253,* 1034–1037.

MacIntosh, H. (1994). The attitudes and experiences of psychoanalysts in analyzing homosexual patients. *Journal of the American Psychoanalytic Association, 42,* 1183–1207.

Moberly, E. R. (1988). *Homosexuality: A new Christian ethic.* Cambridge: Guernsey Press.

Nicolosi, J. (1991). *Reparative therapy of male homosexuality: A new clinical approach.* New York: Aronson.

Payne, L. (1988). *The broken image: Restoring personal wholeness through healing prayer.* Westchester, IL: Crossway.

Ross, M., Paulsen, J., & Stalstrom, O. (1988). Homosexuality and mental health. *Journal of Homosexuality, 15,* 131–152.

Scanzoni, L., & Mollenkott, V. R. (1978). *Is the homosexual my neighbor?* San Francisco: Harper & Row.

Stoller, R. J., & Herdt, G. H. (1985). Theories of origins of male homosexuality. *Archives of General Psychiatry, 42,* 399–404.

U.S. Department of Health and Human Services. (1992). *ICD-9-CM: Code book of physician payment.* Alexandria, VA: St. Anthony.

Wolpe, J. (1969). *The practice of behavioral therapy.* New York: Pergamon.

For Further Information

Evangelicals Concerned, Inc.
311 E. 72nd St.
New York, NY 10021

Evangelicals Concerned is a national organization dedicated to assisting homosexuals and churches to better understand homosexuality and the good news of God's grace and peace. Supporting responsible, monogamous homosexual partnership for gay and lesbian Christians, this organization offers help through meetings and publications. A quarterly literature review on religion and homosexuality is free upon request.

Exodus International
P.O. Box 2121
San Rafael, CA 94912

Exodus International is clearinghouse for smaller, local, nonprofit ministries to persons who desire Christian support and help in their efforts to change their homosexual orientation. The organization provides information on support groups as well as resource and reference materials. It also sponsors a yearly week-long conference to equip and encourage those individuals who minister to homosexuals.

Homosexuals Anonymous
P.O. Box 7881
Reading, PA 19603

Patterned after Alcoholics Anonymous and the 12-step program toward recovery, Homosexuals Anonymous is a national clearinghouse of support groups for those struggling with the issue of homosexual orientation. It incorporates Christian belief but is marked by a more general style of spirituality.

National Association for Research and Treatment of Homosexuality
16542 Ventura Boulevard, Suite 416
Encino, CA 91436

NARTH consists largely of psychoanalytically oriented therapists who view homosexuality as pathological for psychological reasons. Currently the association is actively working to counter the movement among psychiatric and psychological organizations to make the practice of reparative therapy for homosexuals unethical.

C. ROSENAK AND H. LOOY

See SEXUALITY.

Hope. A desire accompanied by the expectation that the desire will be obtained. It is partly cognitive (it is a thought), partly emotional (it involves anticipation and other positive affects), and partly volitional (it contains belief). Hope has traditionally had spiritual or religious connotations. For this reason hope has not been a major focus of psychological study in spite of its obvious emotional components. It has, however, been present in literature and is a prominent concept in the Bible.

In Scripture hope is a major theme in both Testaments. The psalmist often spoke of hope as a major resource for coping with defeat, discouragement, and danger (e.g., Pss. 119:116; 146:5). The hope of the Old Testament was but a foreshadow of the hope found in Jesus Christ (1 Tim. 1:1; Col. 1:27). Hope is prominent in Acts and the epistles and is described as a central element of the Christian's resources.

Hope serves the function theologically of linking the believer to the future promised by Christ. As the follower of Christ experiences a new spiritual life, there is a keen awareness that the earthly enjoyments of faith in Christ are incomplete. What has begun on earth will continue into eternity. Hope links the believer's present with a glorious future.

Biblical anthropology does not give an exhaustive commentary on the psychological value of hope to men and women. Psalm 22:9 (KJV) reads, "Thou didst make me hope when I was upon my mother's breasts." At first glance the verse appears to suggest that hope is innate or is a part of human experience reaching back into infancy. More recent translations suggest that the more probable interpretation is that the Lord caused the psalmist to trust as an infant, thus referring to the mother-child bonding phenomenon. However, the Bible emphasizes the strategic role of hope in the human personality. Faith seems to answer to the human need for spiritual meaning, love relates to the intrapersonal and interpersonal needs of humans to relate to self and others, and hope reflects the motivational needs of humans to find meaning and purpose in the future. Hope is clearly portrayed as a significant motivator of human endeavor (Titus 2:11–14; 1 John 3:3). Hope longs for the resurrection body (Jeeves, 1976).

Psychology has indirectly studied the concept of hope from three different vantage points: the role of hope in human motivation theory; the importance of hope in human personality (as inferred from the absence of hope in certain pathologies); and the curative power of hope in the recovery of severely disturbed persons.

Several important personality theories emphasize the significance of purpose as an ingredient in the human system. Hall and Lindzey (1957) describe purposive or teleological qualities as those which are goal seeking and future oriented. The classical analytic theories of Sigmund Freud, Carl Gustav Jung, and Alfred Adler all emphasize purpose, as do those of Erich Fromm and Harry Stack Sullivan. So many contemporary theorists emphasize the purposive side of human personality that Hall and Lindzey suggest this aspect of personality is almost taken for granted and is no longer an issue of debate in psychology, as it was in the early twentieth century. Purpose is related to hope in that both are future oriented and both assume the attainment of some longed-for desires.

Hopelessness, or the lack of hope, is a prominent feature of the various depressive syndromes and of suicidal persons. Beck (1967) notes that hopelessness is a clinical feature of moderate and severe depressions and is present in about one-half of mild cases. Furthermore, Beck states, "In our studies we found that suicidal wishes had a higher correlation with hopelessness than with any other symptom of depression" (p. 58). It seems reasonable to conclude that if hopelessness is so highly associated with the desire to kill oneself, then the presence of hope in the human psyche must be vitalizing and central to survival.

The final avenue of psychological investigation into hope, exemplified by Stotland (1969), confirms the preceding deduction. Stotland views hope as a mediating variable that helps explain data regarding the recovery of hospitalized schizophrenics and depressives. When optimism and hopefulness are conveyed by the staff and the milieu, he concludes, people recover.

References

Beck, A. T. (1967). *Depression: Causes and treatment.* Philadelphia: University of Pennsylvania Press.

Hall, C. S., & Lindzey, G. (1957). *Theories of personality.* New York: Wiley.

Jeeves, M. A. (1976). *Psychology and Christianity: The view both ways.* Downers Grove, IL: InterVarsity Press.

Stotland, E. (1969). *The psychology of hope.* San Francisco: Jossey-Bass.

J. R. BECK

See FAITH.

Hopelessness. Hopelessness, a sense of helplessness and pessimism, can be characterized as a perception that the individual has no reason to try. Hopeless people see no relationship between their actions and outcomes. They do not believe there is a causal relationship between their actions and the positive or negative effects that may follow. They believe they can do nothing to affect the future and in turn they become less optimistic about it. If people believe they are in control and are competent to meet the demands of life, however, they tend to cope with life more successfully, optimistic about their chances of success.

The effects of these attributions affect the emotional, cognitive, and behavioral domains of the individual. That is, hopelessness may spiral downward with the victim feeling more helpless with each additional failure. These feelings of failures may continue in large part due to the self-defeating thought pattern that leads to a lowered level of motivation and commitment to working toward the goal. It is not hard to imagine why a person would fail in a given task when that person believes success is unlikely, feels frustrated and disappointed in previous attempts, and begins to exert less and less effort in what is seen as a hopeless case.

One popular explanation for the development of hopelessness speaks of options available to people when attributing cause to their failures. These choices include global versus specific, stable versus temporal, and internal versus external. More specific details may prove to be helpful.

One conscious choice to be made about personal failure is whether the specific failure is seen as either an isolated scenario with no connection to related events in life (specific) or as a snapshot that is representative of the larger flow of life (global). If the failure is seen as a sign or symbol of the whole, hinting of other mistakes and shortcomings, the failure is seen as global, creating a less hopeful or optimistic perspective.

A second decision to be made revolves around the issue of consistency across time. Is this a new experience (temporal) or has failure like this been around for a long time and will it be present in the future as well (stable)? If the latter is seen to be true, the impression would serve to discourage and defeat that person, leaving a state of depression and hopelessness because the failure will persist; it is stable.

The final attribution to be made is whether the failure is the result of either internal or external causes. Are circumstances (external) or personal dispositions (internal) to blame for the error or mistake? If people consistently consider themselves to blame for all of their troubles, they may become depressed and helpless, no longer trying to improve their lives. A note of caution must be sounded in this area because too often psychologists have allowed people to minimize their personal responsibility by excusing themselves and holding others accountable for their own woes. Balance is critical.

Hopeless people usually describe failures as global, stable, and internal. They believe that the failures that plague them are representative of their entire existence. These specific weaknesses and others will last forever because they are irresistible, internal variables that the persons carry with them. They do not attribute the shortcomings to the circumstances that surround them. Rather, they blame their circumstances on their personal inability to make life any better. They fail to see any way that they can solve the problem and brighten their future. Failure is not due to bad luck or difficult challenges. Their failures are due to a lack of intelligence, or beauty, or another personal flaw.

The options chosen by hopeless people are not the typical ones made by the average individual. Most people have a tendency to avoid making these depressing attributions. Rather, people typically tend to attribute successes as a result of personal, dispositional strengths, and failures are alternately explained as a function of situational pressures. However, the individual who has been a victim of repeated failures or a particularly traumatic event may opt for the hopeless explanatory style, spiraling downward as its victim. Efforts to assist the hopeless could focus on the reevaluation of the explanatory labels for their behaviors, moving them to a more realistic and optimistic option, namely, specific, temporal, and external. Therapists need to place the clients' focus on powers (e.g., God, a sense of self-efficacy) available to them to help meet their needs.

J. W. LUND

SEE LEARNED HELPLESSNESS; DEPRESSION; HOPE.

Hormones and Behavior. Hormones are released by endocrine glands directly into the circulatory system, where they travel to a target site: body tissues or another endocrine gland, for example. Neurohormones influence activity in the nervous system. Of great interest to psychologists is the relationship between hormones and sex. Two areas have been extensively investigated: the development of anatomical structures, physiological processes, and behavioral characteristics that distinguish males and females; and the activation of reproduction-related behaviors in adults.

The gonadal hormones are androgens and estrogens, testosterone being the most common of the former and estradiol the most common of the latter. The testes and ovaries release both types, with estrogen release higher from the ovaries and testosterone greater from the testes. The anterior pituitary gland releases tropic hormones (those that influence the release of hormones from other glands). Gonadotropin-releasing hormone from the hypothalamus stimulates the anterior pituitary to secrete gonadotropins, follicle stimulating hormone, and luteinizing hormone. Both positive and negative feedback loops influence subsequent release of hormones at the level of anterior pituitary, hypothalamus, and brain circuits.

Large minute-to-minute fluctuations in circulating hormonal levels result from the fact that many hormones are released in pulses. In addition, female gonadal hormonal levels fluctuate according to the menstrual cycle of approximately 28 days. Male gonadal hormone levels vary little on a day-to-day basis.

The general principle accepted by most researchers is that in humans pre- and perinatal development will proceed according to a female plan unless this is overruled by masculinizing factors. As one researcher has stated, the female pattern is the default value.

Sexual differentiation of the gonads, internal reproductive ducts, and external reproductive organs occur during fetal development. In genetic males the Y chromosome triggers the development of testes instead of ovaries, and testosterone from the testes must be present for further development of male reproductive ducts and external organs. Shortly after birth, if testicular testosterone is present male brain characteristics develop; if not, female characteristics develop. This process is complex, with masculinization resulting from estradiol that has been converted from perinatal testosterone. The normally circulating estrogens of a mother do not masculinize female fetuses because they can-not pass the placental barrier. However, synthetic estrogens such as diethylstilbestrol (DES) do cross the barrier and may produce a variety of male characteristics in female fetuses. Animal research has shown that perinatal testosterone also influences subsequent copulatory behaviors, levels of aggressiveness, maternal behavior, and social play.

Hormones continue to influence development at puberty. Growth hormone stimulates muscle, tissue, and bone growth. Gonadotropic and adrenocorticotropic hormones cause further development of the genitals and secondary sex characteristics. Under normal circumstances androgen levels are higher than estrogen levels in males, leading to masculinization. The reverse is true for the feminization of females.

Problems may occur when hormones fail to properly guide sexual development. In androgenic insensitivity syndrome, a genetic male releases normal amounts of androgens, but the body does not respond to them. Therefore, development proceeds along the default, female program. At puberty the testes release sufficient estrogens that in the context of androgen insensitivity feminize the body. Such apparent females will lack a menstrual cycle and have a shortened vagina and underdeveloped uterus. If they are reared as females their play, fantasies, sexual behavior, and maternal tendencies (i.e., with adopted children) are in line with cultural norms for females.

Genetic females suffering from adrenogenital syndrome have had deficient release of cortisol from the adrenal corticies. This produces adrenal hyperactivity and excess adrenal androgens. These individuals are born with an enlarged clitoris and partially fused labia. Menstruation may be delayed, along with dating and marriage in many cases. Sexual interests appear normal. Without cortisone treatment it is hard to predict whether masculinization by adrenal androgens or feminization by ovarian estrogens will predominate at puberty.

Orchidectomy (i.e., the removal of the testes) is accompanied by a reduction in sexual interest and behavior. The rate and degree of the reduction varies across individuals. Mild feminizing body changes, such as reduction of facial and body hair, may occur. Testosterone replacement injections are therapeutically effective in reversing these symptoms. However, sex drive is not related to the amount of circulating testosterone in normal men. Unlike nonhuman mammalian species, a woman's sexual motivation, behavior, and feminine appearance are not directly related to hormonal changes during her menstrual cycle. Nor does ovariectomy have much effect except for a reduction in vaginal lubrication, which can be treated with estrogen replacement therapy. Sex drive in women appears to be influenced by androgens released by the adrenal glands.

Recent research has examined the influence of perinatal hormone levels on sexual preference in adults. Animal research indicates that perinatal castration in males or testosterone treatment in females induces same-sex preferences. In one quasi-experimental study women who were exposed to DES during their fetal development were more likely to report same-sex attraction than those in a control group. In another study the third interstitial nucleus of the anterior hypothalamus was found to be more than twice as large in heterosexual men than in either women or homosexual men.

Hormones are implicated in other adult behaviors. High doses of anabolic steroids increase strength. They also reduce gonadotropin release, which results in testicular atrophy and sterility, breast growth in men, cessation of menstruation in women, muscle spasms, and episodes of depression and anger. Disruption in the timing of hormone release has been examined in some depressive disorders. For example, depressed individuals show no daily variation in cortisol levels, whereas in nondepressed people secretions of cortisol are lowest at night and highest in early morning and afternoon.

W. D. NORMAN

See BRAIN AND HUMAN BEHAVIOR; PSYSIOLOGICAL PSYCHOLOGY.

Horney, Karen (1885–1952). Widely influential American psychoanalyst, born in Hamburg, Germany. Her father was a devoted Christian, but her mother was a freethinker and ridiculed his Bible reading. Dominated by her mother, Horney followed her in eventually renouncing her Christian beliefs during adolescence. She trained in medicine and psychoanalysis in Berlin, where she not only studied and interacted with many famous pioneers of psychoanalysis but also supervised, analyzed, and taught at the Berlin Institute.

Primarily an interpersonal theorist, Horney has played a crucial role in establishing the importance of interpsychic as well as intrapsychic forces in the personality. Because of her interpersonal orientation she has been criticized for not dealing with the depth of the psyche, a criticism that probably has some justification. Early on she criticized Sigmund Freud's biological emphasis not only for its negative implications for women but also for its inadequacy as a base for personality structure.

Neurotic Needs and Personality Types. First presented in 1942 in *Self Analysis*, Horney's list of ten basic neurotic needs has been her best-known contribution. The development of these needs begins with the child being subjected to a stressful environment, which produces anxiety. The child responds to this by developing a strategy to cope with the stress. Because the strategy reduces anxiety, it becomes highly significant for the individual. It becomes a need. Horney feels these needs become so strong that they determine the person's basic orientation toward others and his or her environment

and thus determine a person's personality. In *Our Inner Conflicts* (1945) Horney classified the ten neurotic needs according to three basic interpersonal styles with which they are associated: moving toward, against, or away from people. She described these as the major solutions to the problem of basic anxiety.

Moving Toward. Overt or covert rejection leads the child to feel that he or she does not belong and produces neurotic or exaggerated belongingness needs. There are two such needs: the neurotic need for affection and the neurotic need for a partner who will take over one's life. The neurotic need for affection and approval involves an indiscriminate need to please others and to be liked and approved by everyone. Pleasing others is seen as the way to win the desperately needed love. The neurotic need for a partner to take over one's life involves the individual looking to one person, often a spouse, to fulfill all expectations and needs. The successful manipulation of this person becomes the predominant life task.

These two needs combine to produce what Horney calls the moving toward, or self-effacing, personality. Such individuals feel compelled to be loving and lovable, self-sacrificing, sympathetic, and dependent. They hope that these virtues will produce the sought-for intimacy and sense of belonging. Their basic life slogan is, If you love me, you won't hurt me.

Horney lists three attitudes held by this personality type: the feeling that he or she is weak and helpless, a tendency to subordinate self to others, and a general dependence upon others. This dependence includes clinging to others not just to meet nurturance needs but also to try to achieve a sense of identity. The identity comes from being an appendage to the partner or stronger person.

Moving Against. The second basic personality style is that of moving against people. Associated with this personality type are the neurotic or exaggerated self-esteem needs. There are five such needs: the need for power, for exploitation, for recognition, for admiration, and for achievement.

The neurotic need for power involves the person craving power for the purpose of dominating others, keeping them in a subordinate position. Power and strength are glorified and weakness is despised. This need takes two forms: control of others through reason and foresight and control through omnipotence of the will.

The second need is the neurotic need to get the better of other people. This person uses others for his or her own gain and dominates them by exploitation. The third need is the neurotic need for social recognition or prestige. For this person all things are judged by their competitive value.

The fourth neurotic need is the need for personal admiration. As these individuals maintain an inflated picture of themselves or their idealized image, they need to have this image admired. Their self-evaluation depends on adequate admiration of their image by others. Finally, the neurotic need for personal achievement is reflected in the drive to surpass others in all activities. Such individuals must be the best in all pursuits.

These five needs combine to form the moving against, or expansive, personality type. This person takes it for granted that everyone is hostile and refuses to be convinced otherwise. His or her slogan is, If I have power, no one can hurt me. The person must therefore dominate and control others while maintaining an inner sense of self-glorification. While this personality may present manipulative façades and use all the right words, he or she is exploiting in order to control. Affection, sympathy, and trust are seen as weakness to be shunned. The person is afraid to admit to error, imperfection, or even illness, for these represent limitations. Other people are mistrusted and seen as competitors.

Moving Away. The third personality type is that of the person moving away from other people. Three needs are associated with this type: the need for self-sufficiency, the need for perfection, and the need to restrict one's life within narrow borders.

In the neurotic need for self-sufficiency and independence, distance and separateness are seen as the only source of security. Such an individual can never need anybody, yield to any influence, or be close to anyone. The neurotic need for perfection and unassailability involves a relentless driving for superiority. The resulting feeling of being superior gives one a sense of being infallible. Finally, the neurotic need to restrict one's life within narrow borders involves being undemanding and contented with little. The need is to be ultraconservative and retire to the background.

These needs form the moving away from, or resigned, personality. Such people strive to be free of all emotional feelings. Therefore, both the first two basic orientations must be repressed as the person moves away from others as well as from his or her own feelings. Such a person's slogan is, If I withdraw, nothing can hurt me.

The moving away style can be visualized as a person building an emotional fort in which he or she lives alone. Retreating behind huge emotional walls which shut all others out, this person can communicate only by yelling over the walls of the fort, since he or she can never be coaxed to come out of its safety and security. Life in the fort, though lonely, feels unassailable and invulnerable. In order to maintain such an attitude this person needs to feel superior and strong compared with others. Detachment allows feelings of being stronger or better to go unchallenged, thus reinforcing a sense of safety and security.

This need for detachment means that close ties with others are impossible. The attitude toward oneself is one of objective interest and numbness. The moving away can take one of three forms: the person who is persistently resigned, with an aver-

sion to activity; the rebellious person whose passive resistance becomes active and is directed against environmental factors or inner restrictions; and the person whose shallow living causes emptiness and despair, driving him or her to avoid the pain of loneliness through sex, constant activity, or other escapes.

The Idealized Image. In order to deal with feelings of anxiety and insecurity people also develop what Horney calls an idealized image. This corresponds closely to Freud's ego ideal and Alfred Adler's striving for superiority. However, Horney's idealized image is more clearly and completely expounded, and here lies what may be her most valuable contribution to the understanding of abnormal psychology.

The idealized image is a false self that is developed when living with one's actual self becomes too painful. If the actual self is hated or despised, a flight into fantasy can relieve the awfulness of living with it. The idealized image initially is conscious, as in the case of a child who envisions herself as a beautiful princess living in a huge castle with a handsome prince. Later the image becomes more and more inclusive of the total personality, until the individual so identifies with his or her idealized image that it becomes the glorified self. This identification with the idealized image is, for Horney, narcissism. The individual is driven to keep this image actualized because it relieves anxiety, satisfies his or her exaggerated needs, and transforms the despised qualities of the actual self into the glorious ones of the idealized image.

In the moving toward person, compliance and submission become goodness, love, saintliness, and service. The moving against person transforms his or her aggressiveness into strength, heroism, leadership, and power. The moving away person transforms aloofness into wisdom, self-suffering, and independence.

Horney felt that the idealized self represents the perfect person and as such is never attainable. Because of this she called the image "a devouring monster." In *Neurosis and Human Growth* (1950) she laments the abandonment of the actual self for the idealized image. Surveying the ravaging forces unleashed by the idealized self, she stated that "we cannot help but see in it a great tragedy, perhaps the greatest of the human mind. Man in reaching out for the Infinite and Absolute also starts destroying himself. When he makes a pact with the devil, who promises him glory, he has to go to hell—to the hell within himself" (p. 154). She points to Christ's successful resistance to Satan's promise to give him the kingdoms of the world as an example of not abandoning one's actual self (who Jesus really was) in favor of the idealized image (ruling over the kingdoms of the world). She comments that it is a testimony of true greatness when one person can resist such temptation. Identification with one's idealized image constitutes what she calls the devil's pact, since it costs the individual so dearly in the alienation from who he or she really is.

It is interesting to note that we have here an excellent picture of the Pharisees whom Jesus so vehemently denounced because of their false standards of righteousness. Indeed, the whole thrust of the Sermon on the Mount is Christ's attempt to get the religious leaders of the day to see their real selves below their idealized selves, which consisted of a righteousness based on ritual, rules, and regulations. Jesus' dispute was with their distortion of the teachings of Moses by presenting them as a means of appearance and office rather than as a way to God. They held up the idealized image of righteousness both to God and to other people. Jesus' message was that one must acknowledge one's real self because it is genuine and acceptable to God. But, he says, God will never accept the false self with its pride, hypocrisy, and alienation of self and God.

Implications for Therapy. Horney's insights can inform the task of counseling or psychotherapy. First, the counselor must ascertain which movement a troubled person is using in attempting to cope with his or her insecurities, anxieties, and depressions. Second, the counselor must see what kind of form the idealized image is taking. This, as has been seen, will be based primarily on the interpersonal style. The idealized image causes the person to be alienated from his or her real self and to live under a standard of perfection with its systems of oughts and shoulds. It also causes the person to utilize externalization. Through this defense mechanism one betrays the alienation from the actual self by blaming failures on outside forces. This not only shifts the responsibility toward some other object but leads the individual to feel that all these things take place outside of self.

In dealing with a person's idealized image a counselor must gradually show that it is a search for glory that drains away one's whole life. Horney compares it to the creation of Frankenstein's monster, which in time usurped the creator's best energies. It eventually strangles the drive to grow. All energy is directed toward actualizing the idealized self. "It entails not only the compulsive drive for worldly glory through success, power and triumph but also the tyrannical inner system by which he tries to mold himself into a godlike being; it entails neurotic claims and the development of neurotic pride" (Horney, 1950, pp. 367–368).

The idealized image also demonstrates a basic self-hatred and nonacceptance of self. The reconciliation of the idealized image and the actual self must occur so that the real self can emerge. This is the ultimate goal of counseling for the Christian. If the actual self is in Christ, nothing about it should be avoided or denied. In principle the Christian should have no need for the idealized image, nor should he or she use one. Such a use betrays an inward rejection of his or her real being. Based on Christ's death and unconditional acceptance, the Christian can face self without the use of pharisaism and its futile flight from truth.

As reconciliation with the real self takes place, the particular interpersonal style, whether it is toward, against, or away, will also be diminished in intensity and strength. Since these movements are rooted in the despised and hated actual self, they serve their weak and cowardly master by attempting to protect. If the actual self is reconciled, its acting-out methods will gradually diminish and be eroded.

References

Horney, K. (1942). *Self analysis.* New York: Norton.
Horney, K. (1945). *Our inner conflicts.* New York: Norton.
Horney, K. (1950). *Neurosis and human growth.* New York: Norton.

W. T. Kirwan

See Neurosis; Interpersonal Psychology; Psychoanalytic Psychology.

Hull, Clark Leonard (1884–1952). American psychologist best known for his attempt to construct a general theory of behavior. Hull was born near Akron, New York. Several years later his family moved to a farm in Michigan, where he grew up and received his education at Alma College and the University of Michigan. Since his family had little income, he had to drop out of school several times to work. He was also plagued with illnesses, crippled from polio at the age of 24, and had poor eyesight. He finally received his Ph.D. degree from the University of Wisconsin in 1918 at 34 years of age.

Hull remained at the University of Wisconsin until he became a professor in the newly founded Institute of Human Relations at Yale in 1929. He remained at Yale until his death. His famous open seminar attracted many students who performed the experimental work necessary to test his theory.

Hull did research in concept formation, the effects of tobacco smoking, hypnosis, suggestibility, and aptitude testing. He began to develop his theory of behavior while still in graduate school but worked on it in earnest from 1929 until his death. He wanted to develop a hypothetico-deductive theory in which he could begin with a small set of postulates and corollaries and then logically deduce the behaviors that would occur when a given stimulus was presented.

Hull's theory was a mechanistic, reductionistic, objective behaviorism. It was essentially a theory of learning inspired by Ivan Pavlov's work but extended to all behavior of all species, including humans. This approach dominated the psychological conceptions of learning for nearly 30 years, and it continues to be influential.

Although Hull's books on hypnosis and aptitude testing were well received, those works developing his theory of behavior have had a lasting impact.

Principles of Behavior (1943) was his major contribution, first setting forth his overall theory. He revised his theory in *Essentials of Behavior* (1951) and *A Behavior System* (1952), but neither of these had the impact of the 1943 book. His contribution to psychological theory building in general is much more than his own theory. Although many parts of his theory are questioned, many psychologists respect and admire the methods he used to develop it. It is to his credit that his theory is stated specifically enough to be shown incorrect. Although well known in the psychology of learning, he is almost unknown to the general public.

R. L. KOTESKEY

See BEHAVIORAL PSYCHOLOGY.

Human Relations Training. Systematic human relations training is a program of learning experiences designed to teach lay people to relate to others more helpfully. As most commonly used the term refers to the approach developed by Carkhuff (1969). This approach grew out of his association with Carl Rogers and his subsequent identification of core dimensions of a helping relationship. He then placed these dimensions, or helper characteristics, within an overall model of the helping relationship and developed training procedures and assessment devices for the development of the core skills.

Carkhuff outlined three goals of helping relationships. The first is to encourage the person's self-exploration. The helper listens as the one seeking help talks and explores the problem areas. This leads to the second goal, self-understanding. The third goal is action or problem resolution. This is not a natural consequence of understanding but must be planned for and actively pursued. It is important to note that not all helping interactions lead through all these steps and achieve the desired outcome of problem solution; often the helper is just one link in the chain of life of a person.

The Core Dimension. The first phase of the helping process as conceived by Carkhuff is directed toward establishing a sound caring relationship with the person seeking help. Before any action dimensions are employed in the helping process, the helper utilizes the safe, less threatening facilitative dimensions that are deemed necessary to prepare the person to accept and thus benefit from the more threatening action dimensions.

The helper begins building the base by responding with empathy, respect, and warmth. Empathy is judged to be the most important dimension in the helping process. Empathy involves the helper's understanding of both content (the facts of the situation) and affect (how the person feels about it). Persons are never quite able to put into words all that they feel; no word is so powerful that its meaning is completely clear. Thus the helper's initial responses should reflect to the person the information and feeling the helper perceives (e.g., "You sound angry because your husband doesn't seem to care about your problem at work").

Respect is another facilitative dimension. Respect involves faith in the person's ability to solve the problem. Hastily given advice communicates disrespect for his or her intelligence. Warmth, or caring, is closely related to empathy and respect. People tend to love or have concern for those whom they understand (empathy) and in whom they believe (respect). Warmth is communicated primarily through nonverbal means, such as eye contact, posture, or gestures.

These first three dimensions are a restatement of Rogers's necessary and sufficient conditions for therapy. Carkhuff views their role as facilitating establishment of a therapeutic relationship that will then involve other dimensions.

The facilitative dimensions encourage the person to self-explore. With repeated empathic reflection of content and feeling a point will eventually be reached where no new feelings or information will be forthcoming. At this point the helper needs to encourage the person to risk more self-exploration. Thus the dimensions of concreteness, genuineness, and self-disclosure are added. These three dimensions are action-oriented as well as facilitative.

To achieve concreteness the helper must encourage discussion of specific feelings and experiences. Generalities and vague discussions are avoided. Genuineness refers to the helper's honesty in the relationship. Genuineness does not mean brutal honesty but rather honesty timed so that it can be of assistance to the other person. It also means not being dishonest in what is communicated. Self-disclosure of the helper can also enhance the relationship if the disclosure is appropriate. When helper self-disclosure is premature or irrelevant to the other's problem, it may confuse him or her or shift the focus to the helper.

Human relations trainers view the action phase as the goal, since in this stage some type of problem resolution is reached. Action dimensions are confrontation and immediacy.

Confrontation refers to dealing with a discrepancy between what the person has been saying and what he or she has been doing. One should use confrontation only when that right has been earned through empathic responses. Immediacy is closely related to confrontation. It refers to the helper commenting on important aspects of what is happening in the relationship. The timing of immediacy is critical if it is to be used beneficially by the helper.

There are many courses of action for problem solution or achievement of goals. The important thing is to identify possible courses and consider the consequences and their ramifications. Then the chosen course of action can be broken down into steps to allow for intermediate success experiences that offer encouragement and reinforcement along the way to problem resolution.

Evaluation. Extensive research has been done on the effects of systematic human relations training. Aspy and Hadlock (1967) found that during one school year students with teachers possessing the highest levels of warmth, empathy, and genuineness gained an average of 2 ½ academic years, while students with the lowest level teachers gained only an average of 6 academic months. Further, the association between marital communication and adolescent self-esteem suggests that unfacilitative communication affects all relationships in the family (Matteson, 1974). In a study by Carkhuff and Banks (1970) systematic human relations training was effective in shaping more facilitative levels of communication and understanding among people of different races. A study conducted to evaluate the effects of human relations training on members of church groups revealed significant improvement in both perceiving and responding skills (McCurdy, 1976).

Polls have indicated that the influence of the church on society may be diminishing. As Christians live in the home, school, and business arena, as they live in every relationship of life, they are the church in the world. If the church's influence is decreasing, it would appear that there must be some deficit in the personal relationships within the church and the world. Ellens (1973) emphasizes that worship is essentially a horizontal experience of communication with other people about the facts of grace shared and lived. In order to facilitate worship, then, and to sensitively minister to people in need, it seems appropriate for the church to train people in human relations as a major response to God's call to serve our neighbors.

References

Aspy, D. N., & Hadlock, W. (1967). The effects of high and low functioning teachers upon student performance. In R. R. Carkhuff & B. G. Berenson (Eds.), *Beyond counseling and therapy.* New York: Holt, Rinehart, & Winston.

Carkhuff, R. R. (1969). *Helping and human relations* (Vols. 1 & 2). New York: Holt, Rinehart, & Winston.

Carkhuff, R. R., & Banks, G. (1970). Training as a preferred mode of facilitating relations between races and generations. *Journal of Counseling Psychology, 17,* 413–418.

Ellens, J. H. (1973). Psychological dynamics in Christian worship: A beginning inquiry. *Journal of Psychology and Theology, 1* (4), 10–19.

Matteson, R. (1974). Adolescent self-esteem, family communication, and marital satisfaction. *Journal of Psychology, 85,* 35–47.

McCurdy, M. E. (1976). Human relations training with a church related population. *Journal of Psychology and Theology, 4,* 291–299.

M. E. McCurdy

See Applied Psychology.

Human Resource Training and Development.

The development of people who serve within the local church has always been an important part of Christian development. One could argue that in order to carry out the teaching of Jesus Christ, his disciples had to be trained and developed. Furthermore, the Bible is filled with stories about people such as Timothy, Priscilla and Aquila, and Philip, who were all trained and developed for their work with God's people. As the Christian church approaches the twenty-first century, successful and competent human resources training and development (HRTD) is vital and critical to the mission and function of the church. As Christian congregations increasingly become more knowledgeable of and influenced by world and current affairs, Christian leaders will need to prepare church members for entrance into an information-based, technologically sophisticated, international, and intercultural world as never before. HRTD is one avenue available to clergy, Christian counselors, and pastoral counselors. Furthermore, these persons typically will be the individuals who will be challenged to provide this type of training and development.

HRTD Definitions. Human resource development is defined by Nadler (1984) as organized learning experiences directed toward increasing and improving job performance and growth in people. Human resource training and development, therefore, can be considered coaching employees to higher performance levels. Three other key HRTD terms are important to know and understand. First is training, which Nadler (1984) defined as learning related to one's present job. Thus training enables an individual or team to function more effectively and more efficiently in current ministries. For example, providing a training session would help adult Sunday school teachers apply adult learning principles in their classrooms.

Another important term is education. Education is learning that prepares the individual for a different but identified job (Nadler, 1984). For instance, education is necessary if a church is developing a new ministry for members of the congregation and community who are age 55 and older. This staff would have to learn life span developmental issues as well as physical, emotional, social, and other systemic issues that influence successful ministry with this age group.

Third, the term development is also important in the HRTD function. Development is defined as learning for the growth of the individual but not related to a specific present or future job. An example would be a class on stress management to help parishioners know principles of stress reduction and relaxation. This training may provide personal development for an individual, but it is not offered to prepare members for any particular function in the church.

The HRTD Function and the Church. The church is an assembly of local Christian believers who are associated with one another by Christian covenant, faith, fellowship, service, discipleship, and worship. The church is a body of Christian believers who must make known and engage in the purposeful redemptive plan of God. As the church of God goes about doing the work of the Lord, the need for training, education, and personal and organizational development is critical.

Most churches embrace the mission of doing the work of the Lord, and most churches readily provide education and fellowship to their members for the purpose of fostering spiritual growth and development. Certainly spiritual growth and development play a critical role in the life of the church. However, what is often overlooked is the need for church members, especially paid staff, to participate in learning opportunities to increase their effectiveness from a training and development point of view. Many members of congregations serve in lay leadership positions in which they are called upon to speak in public, prepare presentations, facilitate meetings, resolve conflict, lead a group to consensus, analyze problems, build teams, assess needs, and manage budgets. Through the HRTD function the church can be more involved in helping its parishioners learn these critical skills in order that they may be utilized in the church. Some people may argue that training and development of this nature is beyond the scope of the church. However, providing training and development opportunities on these subjects, along with an undergirding of Christian principles, could be a powerful way to foster personal, professional, and spiritual growth.

Process Questions. When HRTD growth opportunities are offered, they should be based on the needs as identified by the members. There are three primary questions to identify HRTD needs in a congregation: What are ministries and people doing that they should not be doing (Laird, 1985)? What aren't they doing that they should be doing (Laird, 1985)? What training could be provided that will help you to become better skilled and knowledgeable to serve the church in your current position?

References

Nadler, L. (Ed.). (1984). *The handbook of human resources development.* New York: Wiley.

Laird, D. (1985). *Approaches to training and development.* Reading, MA: Addison-Wesley.

Additional Readings

Forbess-Greene, S. (1983). *The encyclopedia of icebreakers.* San Diego, CA: University Associates.

Tracey, W. R. (Ed.). (1985). *Human resources management and development handbook.* New York: American Management Associations.

J. E. M. McCreary and M. L. McCreary

See Industrial/Organizational Psychology; Applied Psychology.

Humanistic Psychology. Broadly conceived, humanistic psychology is a movement within psychology that in its theorizing and research emphasizes what it perceives to be the distinctly human characteristics of humanity.

Though not devoid of a number of articulate theories or a respectable body of knowledge, humanistic psychology is characterized less by its theoretical stance or research orientation than by its attitude toward human beings. Its emphasis is on spontaneity, internal locus of control, uniqueness, wholeness, personality, and capacity for self-actualization. Thus it seeks to humanize what is a predominantly mechanomorphic psychology and to replace it with a psychology based on a concept of persons as creative, self-transcending beings, controlled not by outside or unconscious forces but by their own values and choices alone.

The movement counts a large number of prominent psychologists as its adherents. Among them are Buhler, Erich Fromm, Rollo May, Victor Frankl, Henry A. Murray, Gordon Allport, Carl Rogers, and Abraham Maslow. These by no means agree with each other on every point. In the broadest sense humanistic psychology includes theorists and practitioners who operate from a phenomenological and existentialistic tradition as well as those who work from a predominantly holistic, pragmatistic, and Darwinian tradition. What unites all of these into one movement is their opposition to the mechanistic, deterministic view of humanity, positivism in philosophy, and behaviorism in psychology.

In the literature phenomenology and existentialism are frequently described separately as systems of philosophy and psychology, next to humanistic psychology. Thus it is perhaps more accurate to characterize humanistic psychology in the broadest sense as a humanistic movement in psychology and philosophy. This allows us to reserve the name *humanistic psychology* in the strictest sense for that branch of psychology proper of which Maslow and Rogers are the chief proponents.

History and Development. Humanistic psychology has had great impact on psychology as a whole. It is an American product that has incorporated many of the typically European phenomenological and existentialistic themes. But in doing so it has nevertheless remained firmly rooted in the American individualistic and evolutionistic tradition.

The origin of humanistic psychology as a school dates back to 1954, when Maslow described its adherents as "people who are interested in the scientific study of creativity, love, higher values, autonomy, growth, self-actualization, need gratification, etc." (Misiak, 1973, p. 127). In subsequent years there followed a series of publications by various authors, each taking humanistic psychology as a point of departure. In 1961 the *Journal of Humanistic Psychology* was founded by Anthony Sutich. One year later the American Association for Humanistic Psychology was established. In 1970 the American Psychology Association approved the establishment of a Division of Humanistic Psychology (Division 32). During that same year the First International Conference on Humanistic Psychology was held in Amsterdam, with Buhler as its president, and from then on the movement was off and running.

The movement has generated a veritable troupe of second-generation adherents, all of them busily applying humanistic psychology principles in therapy, education, family life, business, interpersonal, and international relations. Through the use of encounter groups the movement currently offers a smorgasbord of growth-enhancing workshops that is so diverse that it makes one wonder whether anything short of behaviorism cannot be included under its banner. The ability to incorporate whatever is new and creative is one of the hallmarks of this school of psychology.

Philosophical Roots. Humanistic psychology has several philosophical roots. This accounts to a large degree for the inner tensions that the movement is experiencing.

Phenomenological-Existentialistic Tradition. The first root lies in what may loosely be called the phenomenological-existentialistic tradition. Its history goes back to Franz Brentano (1838–1917), who is the acknowledged father of both Husserl's philosophical phenomenology and Stumpf's empirical phenomenology.

Brentano's chief contribution was his notion of intentionality. This notion implies that consciousness is not a matter of contents impressed upon our minds by an external reality but it can be understood only with reference to the subjective activity of human intentions. Conscious content is what human subjects intend there to be. At the same time intentionality also implies that consciousness is always consciousness of something. Intentionality is always directed toward and stands in relation to some intended object. When he or she forms, intends, or intuits the object, the human subject must therefore always be guided by the nature or the essence of the object.

This makes the intended object simultaneously the product of the intentional act of the human subject and the object toward which that act is directed. From that intentional vantage point investigation can go one of two ways. It can go in the direction of Husserl's philosophical phenomenology, which investigates the intentional act of the human subject that constitutes consciousness. It can also go in the direction of Stumpf's empirical phenomenology, which investigates the relation of human intentionality to the intended object. In either case, however, phenomenology consists of the investigation of psychic acts rather than psychic contents.

Via Stumpf's empirical phenomenology Brentano became the grandfather of Gestalt psychology in general and of Kurt Lewin's field theory in particular. His influence is evident in the Gestalt notion of perception. It manifests the ambivalence of phe-

nomenology in that perceiving is clearly viewed as a constructive act but nonetheless an act that is governed by the laws of perception inherent in the perceptual object or percept. Similarly, the self in Lewin's field theory functions as the subject pole of every perceptual act that constitutes the phenomenal field. But also as perceived object in the phenomenal field it regulates if not determines the nature of the perceptual acts of the self as subject.

Humanistic psychology borrows from Brentano and Husserl the notion that the human subject (i.e., the organism) is active in the sense that it organizes the world that surrounds it. The organism responds only to an environment that it itself has perceived (Rogers, 1961). But the human subject also finds its organizing purpose or direction in the phenomenal field. It incites the organism to perform its perceptual activity. Experience (here understood as experiential field) has meaning, and the organism must let experience tell it its own meaning (Rogers, 1961). The organism must be open to and receptive of the phenomenal field. More than that, it must seek to enhance the phenomenal field, particularly that part of it that constitutes the self.

Thus a number of the basic notions of humanistic psychology such as the self, experience, perception, the phenomenal field—all of which it views as distinctly human characteristics—are directly derived from the phenomenological-existentialistic tradition.

Pragmatism. But humanistic psychology is also rooted in the pragmatism of William James and even more firmly in that of John Dewey. Dewey's main importance for humanistic psychology was that he served as the conduit for the influence of Darwinism on the movement. Darwinian thought held that reality is dynamic, that living things develop in adaptive interaction with their environment.

Following Darwin, Dewey too saw change rather than stasis as the primary characteristic of reality. This dynamic notion allowed him to conceive of the order of the different kingdoms in reality (i.e., rocks, plants, and animals) as one of different levels of interactive complexity. For Dewey reality originally consisted of an infinite number of interactions. Things emerged or came into being when series of these interactions grouped themselves into organized wholes. When these wholes began to interact with other wholes, they made it possible for even more complex wholes to emerge.

For Dewey this ongoing process is characteristic of all that exists in nature. No organized interactive whole or thing is ever complete in itself. Its meaning lies perpetually in the consequences it engenders in subsequent, more complex interactive wholes. Things are always in the process of becoming integrated into more complex things. Reality is thus perpetually (re)ordered or (re)constructed in a process that runs from lower to higher differentiation and integration. This dynamic order of ongoing, naturally occurring differentiation and integration is what Dewey called growth.

Humanistic psychology owes a great deal to Dewey's pragmatism and, via Dewey, to Darwin's theory of evolution. Notions such as becoming, growth, actualization, organism, and the hierarchical structure of human activity are all derived from this philosophical root.

However, on one significant point humanistic psychology parts company with Dewey. This concerns the formative influence of human subjects on the process of growth. Dewey held that on the human level of interaction the innovative activity of the human subject can shape the process of growth and redirect it to its own human ends. Thus at that level of interaction the naturally occurring growth process becomes a historically formative process, governed by changes that have their purpose in a source outside the growth process itself. Simply put, Dewey held that people can form growth.

While humanistic psychology certainly recognizes the existence of subjects, it denies that they exist external to the process of growth, and thus it also denies that subjects can form growth to their own human ends. On the contrary, the growth process itself has formative power, and it naturally shapes the human subject rather than the reverse.

Humanistic psychology holds that everything that exists, including human beings, is taken up in this total evolutionary process of becoming. This becoming or growth process has its own ends in view and its own organizational principle within itself. It has morphological properties. It forms itself dynamically. Individuals, as microcosms of this total process, each uniquely have the capacity to form themselves or to actualize their potentials. But they have this capacity only insofar as they are open to and receptive of this evolutionary process of becoming, thus only insofar as they function as the organisms that they are.

This morphological principle hails back to Aristotle's doctrine of entelechy. He defined it as the impulse of an organized body or organism to become what it is. Driesch defended this principle as late as the beginning of the twentieth century against the predominantly mechanistic view of mainstream biology.

The problem with the entelechy doctrine is that it implies a teleology—that is, it implies that the growth process is directed by goals. And once these goals are fulfilled, they can conceivably stop the growth process, thus endangering its status as a total, perpetually ongoing process of becoming. To avoid such negative consequences humanistic psychology rejected the notion of entelechy and opted for the notion of directionality.

This notion, originating with Kurt Goldstein, is derived from a biological version of holism developed by the South African philosopher-biologist Jan Smuts. Andras Angyal, following Smuts, has suggested that the goal does not "define the direction of an activity, but rather the intrinsic pattern of a direction of behavior determines what object is a suitable goal" (Angyal, 1958, pp. 53–55). This notion of directionality safeguards the dynamic self-motivation and self-direction of the growth process at every level of differentiation and integration.

Essential Characteristics. Humanistic psychology is often called the third force in psychology because it pits itself against the deterministic picture of persons evident in both psychoanalysis and behaviorism. Thus it presents itself as an alternative to both these systems of psychology. It rejects the pessimistic view of psychoanalysis, which holds that one's actions are wholly driven by the libidinal energy of an unconscious, irrational id. It also rejects the behavioristic view that human behavior is wholly determined by environmental forces. Thus it rejects the internal determinism of psychoanalysis as well as the external determinism of behaviorism because both reduce persons to something lower than human (*see* Determinism and Free Will).

Over against the position of traditional psychology that people are nothing but animals or machines it posits the view that people are human. Over against the view that behavior is nothing but a response to a stimulus it states that human behavior is purposive. Over against the view that culture is nothing but a sublimated, covert attempt at gratifying dark sexual urges it emphasizes the view that culture is the expression of humanity's higher aspirations. Over against the elementarism of Wilhelm Wundt and John B. Watson alike it argues that a person is a totality. Over against the determinism of mainline psychology it stresses human freedom, creativity, spontaneity, and playfulness. Over against a preoccupation with needs and drives that drag people down to the level of animals it talks about goals that draw people up to the height of the gods. Over against mechanism, which depicts human behavior as randomly governed by perilous chance, it steadfastly maintains the orderly, organized character of human acts. Over against a depth psychology it proposes a psychology of heights. In short, it states that human beings are always more than the reduced picture that traditional psychology has given of them.

Humanistic psychology is a "more than" psychology; more than is its basic paradigm. Traditional psychologies are viewed as all being reductionisms. But humanistic psychology, with its emphasis on all things human, is a thoroughgoing, dynamic transcendentalism in which one's reach must exceed one's grasp. It is a celebration of human potentiality and possibility. Its motto is *semper excelsior* and its key is transcendence. Moreover, to guarantee the perpetuity of this process of transcendence or growth and to avoid the stultifying effects of finalism it stresses that the direction of the process is primary and its goals secondary.

Basic Themes and Their Implications. *Growth.* Humanistic psychology is primarily a growth psychology as opposed to a depth psychology or a stimulus-response psychology. This emphasis on growth and actualization represents its first and major theme. It characterizes its view of human reality as dynamic, with its constant emphasis on novelty. The picture of people in humanistic psychology is that of *homo novus*.

Personhood. A second theme stresses the importance of such notions as person, autonomy, uniqueness, self, experience, and (inter) subjectivity. This theme states that humans are unique. This not only means that as a species they are distinctly human as opposed to other creatures, but more importantly it means that it is in the nature of people to be unique. Every human being alive is first and foremost universally unique, thus wholly unlike his or her fellows (Rogers, 1961).

Second, it stresses that every human being, without exception, is a person. This means that every person is the initiator, the director, and the evaluator of his or her own development. Personal growth, actualization, and enhancement are not externally controlled but occur internal to the human person. Everyone is in that sense autonomous—that is, a law unto himself or herself.

Third, it stresses that every person is uniquely the subject pole of his or her own experience, perception, awareness, and reality. This means that no one's experience, perception, or reality is identical to that of any other. A reality that holds for every person does not exist. There are as many realities as there are persons. Quite literally all that exists or occurs in the world exists or occurs within the internal frame of reference of persons.

Fourth, it stresses that people are aware of themselves as persons. This self-awareness makes that part of a person's experience that constitutes one's own being (i.e., the self) the most important element in one's entire experiential field. The self functions as the reference point to which all other parts of the field are centrally and directly related.

Finally, every person meets with others in his or her experience. These others are also unique, thus principally unlike himself or herself. These others are persons who are the master of their own destiny, who have their own experience and their own world. It behooves all of us, therefore, in the spirit of the best of empiricism, not to treat others as extensions of ourselves. Rather than manipulate them or explain them as objects in our experience, we must be open to them, receive them, and understand them as autonomous subjects. The other can never be counted, measured, or manipulated as our object, because he or she is a subject. For this reason there is no such thing as objectivity among people. Human fellowship is always a fellowship of subjects, an intersubjectivity.

Taking these two themes together we can state that each person is a unique principle of self-actualization or self-transcendence. This formulation characterizes humanistic psychology both in its depth and in its breadth. This formulation further implies that the only viable stance anyone can ever take toward one's fellows is to be receptive and even reverent of their capacity to grow, to transcend themselves. We must always be open to their newness and, what is more, allow ourselves to be changed by their dynamic uniqueness.

While this ultraempiricism has its good points, it results in such particularization of experience that one loses sight of the woods for all the trees. In the field of personal growth this has resulted in a burgeoning of all kinds of growth-promoting methods and approaches. However, it is a diversity, where the point of unity that connects each of them to the other is lacking. Humanistic psychology is thus faced with the problem of finding unity in its diversity. It needs a common denominator. This brings us to its third theme, which stresses wholeness, universality, and being.

Wholeness and Universality. Under the guidance of Ockham's principle of parsimony traditional psychology had found its point of unity in science, and it realized this unity in science by reducing all created activity, including human activity, to nothing but physical states of affairs. Thus it achieved wholeness and universality by insisting that at bottom everything is matter—physical being. This door is closed to humanistic psychology because it commits itself to a dynamic view of reality (everything is in a state of becoming). It rejects the static view of matter as being in favor of potentiality and becoming. Thus it can locate its point of unity only in the human subject and in the growth process. In its view, therefore, persons are whole insofar as they remain true to themselves *and* continue to evolve.

While this formulation satisfies the need for wholeness, it does nothing for universality. The assertion that everyone is universally unique, far from solving the problem, propagated the bewildering particularism and individualism that characterizes humanistic psychology.

Maslow was the first to recognize this problem and began to stress his concept of "B-(eing) cognition." Persons who have transcended to a kind of superconsciousness are said by him to be capable of B-cognition. It involves a person in rising to ecstatic peak experiences of cosmic wholeness, where one can stoically contemplate and stand in awe of the colorful particularity "below." That level of cognition is universal, unified wholeness personified. It exists above and beyond the lower dichotomies, such as those of good and evil. Similarly Rogers, the lifelong champion of persons, has in his later years begun to stress the need for persons to dissolve themselves into the universal stream of life as a further step in their actualization process (Van Belle, 1980).

This latest development seems to suggest that humanistic psychology is drifting toward the universalism, mysticism, and spiritualism of transpersonal psychology. In the first issue of the *Journal of transpersonal psychology,* Sutich, who is also the founder of the *Journal of Humanistic Psychology,* calls transpersonal psychology the fourth force in psychology. Its adherents are described as people who are interested in studies of ultimate human capacities and potentialities. Sources for these studies are Eastern religions, parapsychological phenomena, and phenomena typically studied by humanistic psychology.

The term *fourth force* is apt, for it is likely that humanistic psychology as the unique champion of persons will be superseded if it persists in its movement toward transpersonal psychology. Yet, given its dynamic, transcendental character, one may wonder whether it can do anything but exchange its personalism for a transpersonalism. In doing so it will lose its ability to fruitfully engage in cultural formation, since mysticism and universalism of any kind have always thrived on withdrawal from the rip and tear of concrete culture and society into the ethereal realm of pseudoreligious spirituality (Roszak, 1975).

Humanistic psychology has always had a particularly seductive pull for Christians. It has loosened the antispiritual, materialistic, and reductionistic grip of psychoanalysis and behaviorism on psychology. In doing so it has made talk of persons, purpose, values, and spirituality, all topics dear to Christians, once more respectable. But its transcendentalism seems to lead to a subjectivistic, pantheistic and world-denying spiritualism in which wholeness is the highest good to be attained. Moreover, if one sees that the path to this wholeness implies that good and evil, as commonly understood, must be seen as structural parts of creation rather than its postfall continuum of direction, then one wonders whether humanistic psychology is not more Christianity's bane than its boon.

References

Angyal, A. (1958). *Foundations for a science of personality* (2nd ed.). Cambridge, MA: Harvard University Press.

Misiak, H. (1973). *Phenomenological, existential, and humanistic psychologies.* New York: Grune & Stratton.

Rogers, C. R. (1961). *On becoming a person.* Boston: Houghton Mifflin.

Roszak, T. (1975). *The unfinished animal.* New York: Harper & Row.

Van Belle, H. A. (1980). *Basic intent and therapeutic approach of Carl R. Rogers.* Toronto: Wedge Publishing Foundation.

Additional Readings

Dagenais, J. (1972). *Models of man.* The Hague: Nijhoff.

Maslow, A. H. (1943). Theory of human motivation. *Psychological Review, 50,* 370–396.

Maslow, A. H. (1959). Cognition of being in the peak experience. *Journal of Genetic Psychology, 94,* 43–66.

Maslow, A. H. (1971). *The farther reaches of human nature.* New York: Viking.

Rogers, C. R. (1977). *Carl Rogers on personal power.* New York: Delacorte.

Tart, C. T. (1975). *Trans-personal psychologies.* New York: Harper & Row.

H. A. VAN BELLE

See PERSON-CENTERED THERAPY; TRANSPERSONAL PSYCHOLOGY.

Hume, David (1705–1757). Scotland's greatest philosopher and a distinguished historian. Hume advocated a science of mental life in which humans are considered a part of the natural world (pneumatic philosophy) and are to be studied using the same methods. As in natural science, Hume believed, it is possible to determine the basic laws that govern the function of the mind. This position helped pave the way for the development of the science of psychology. Hume's major works include *A Treatise of Human Nature* (1739) and *An Enquiry Concerning Human Understanding* (1748).

Like George Berkeley, Hume believed the material world did not exist unless it was perceived. Taking this belief a step further, Hume believed the mind too existed only when perceived. In Hume's conception of the mind there are two key contents: impressions and ideas. Impressions are either the result of what we would call sensation or the result of reflection. Ideas are faint copies of impressions (actual experience). For example, when you taste something you have a distinct impression of the experience, but later your memory of the taste is a representation of the original impression and often is less vivid.

The contents of the mind can be described as either simple or complex. A simple idea is one that could not be broken down into separate ideas. For example, the idea of "red" cannot be reduced to more basic ideas. Complex ideas are made up of many ideas and can be reduced. The idea of "American flag," could be reduced to red, white, blue, stars, and stripes.

Complex contents are explained through the process of association, which is governed by two laws: resemblance (similarity) and contiguity. Ideas that resemble one another are more likely to be associated (resemblance), as are ideas that occur together in time and space (contiguity). Hume's third law of association, cause and effect, was eventually reduced to contiguity plus a feeling of necessity.

Hume's preference for impressions over ideas, which were less trustworthy copies, identifies him as a positivist who believes all ideas should be traced to the observable. Because of Hume's efforts to expunge theology of ideas that have no empirical base, many scholars identify (1947) Hume as a religious skeptic.

References

Hume, D. (1739). *A treatise of human nature.* London: Noon.

Hume, D. (1748). *A enquiry concerning human understanding.* London: Dent.

Hume, D. (1947). *Dialogues concerning natural religion.* New York: Bobbs-Merrill.

J. D. FOSTER

See EMPIRICISM.

Humility. To persons attempting to integrate their personal faith with psychology, humility is an issue of great concern. Christians frequently ask, How can I avoid pride, as the Bible commands, and still feel good about myself? How can I be truly humble and assertive at the same time? Isn't it more biblical for me to feel bad about myself than to be proud? Humility is a spiritual virtue that appears to be at odds with much of the emphasis in modern psychology.

Most modern English dictionaries list a two-pronged definition of humility, including an attitude, quality, or state of being free from pride or arrogance, and having a low opinion of one's importance or the attitude that others are superior. The second part of the definition is more frequently referred to as inferiority feelings or an inferiority complex by modern authors. The first part is most often seen by Christians as a positive Christian value highly commended in Scripture.

This dichotomous view of humility has its roots not in Scripture but in developments subsequent to the close of the canon. Christian mystics, in their zeal for purity of spirit and heart, viewed humility as an active process of debasing self in order to glorify God. For example, Bernard of Clairvaux wrote in *The Steps of Humility* that humility is an important monastic virtue that helps Christians see their own miserableness. The Benedictine Rule gives 12 steps of humility: fear of the Lord, ignoring desire, submission to superiors, perfect obedience, complete confession, admission of inferiority, belief in one's inferiority, conventionality, silence, gravity, restrained speech, and downcast eyes. The monastic or mystical view of humility incorporated selflessness, a sense of inferiority, and a docile physiognomy.

The New Testament presents a much different picture of humility. Two central passages unfold a simple definition of this important Christian grace. The first, Matthew 11:28–30, is a self-description of our Lord: "I am meek and lowly in heart" (Matt. 11:29, KJV). As with all biblical virtues, humility is seen most clearly in the life of Christ, who was fully aware of his dependence on God. There is no painful introspection or self-debasement seen in Christ, only a single vision to serve God. In Augustinian thought humility is a complete bowing of the sinner and creature before God.

The second major passage is Philippians 2:1–11 (KJV), a Pauline description of Christ. "Let this mind be in you, which was also in Christ Jesus: who . . . made himself of no reputation, and took upon him the form of a servant, and . . . he humbled himself, and became obedient unto death, even the death of the cross." Jesus is the prime scriptural figure of humility, and Jesus' servant heart was nowhere seen more clearly than in his washing of the disciples' feet (John 13). "The feeling of obligation for all one is or has, and of shortcoming in the use of those gifts which we cannot even praise ourselves for having well employed, is a mark of humility" (McClintock & Strong, 1867, p. 403). "To be humble means to put the interests and needs of others before your own, and to put yourself at others' disposal as a servant" (Kinzer, 1980, p. 69). The practical difficulty of living as a servant for others is evident to all, even to the fictitious Screwtape and his trainee Wormwood (see Lewis, 1942, pp. 62–63).

Humility, however, does not loom large as a topic of investigation for modern psychology. Sigmund Freud used the word *humility* nine times among his millions of words (Guttman, Jones, & Parrish, 1980). In most of the nine occurrences the word itself was not the topic of consideration. *Humility* is rarely found in abstracts of research, in indices for journals, or in personality textbooks. The Christian concept of humility is indirectly measured by certain personality inventories but never under the label of humility. For example, certain features of the deference scale ("to accept the leadership of others") and the nurturance scale ("to treat others with kindness and sympathy") on the Edwards Personal Preference Schedule are components of humility (Edwards, 1959). Likewise some scales on the California Psychological Inventory (Gough, 1969) touch on the Christian virtue of humility. But for the most part humility is seen as a spiritual or religious concept and not a worthy topic for psychological investigation.

Humility may indeed represent a feature of personality that runs counter to the spirit of twentieth-century thought with its emphasis on individuality, assertiveness, independence, and introspection. For the Christian, however, the example of Christ's footwashing on the night before his death and the obedience of his death itself make humility an obligatory goal and a worthy aim.

References

Edwards, A. L. (1959). *Edwards personal preference schedule manual.* New York: Psychological Corporation.

Gough, H. G. (1969). *Manual for the California psychological inventory.* Palo Alto, CA: Consulting Psychologists Press.

Guttman, S. A., Jones, R. L., & Parrish, S. M. (Eds.). (1980). *The concordance to the standard edition of the complete psychological works of Sigmund Freud* (Vol. 3). Boston: Hall.

Kinzer, M. (1980). *The self-image of a Christian: Humility and self-esteem.* Ann Arbor, MI: Servant.

Lewis, C. S. (1942). *The Screwtape letters.* London: G. Bles, Centenary.

McClintock, J., & Strong, J. (1867). *Cyclopedia of biblical, theological and ecclesiastical literature* (Vol. 4). New York: Harper & Bros.

J. R. BECK

See SELF-ESTEEM; NARCISSISM.

Humor. The concept of humor is as old as human nature. It is an integral part of every community life. Its function varies among the cultures. Since recorded history, individuals and cultural groups have always been fascinated by the phenomenon of humor and laughter.

Humor is a habitual or constitutional disposition which affects the human character and temperament. It is fundamentally a complex behavior. Humor is a temporary state of mind with a beautiful combination of cognition and affect. It can manifest itself in a sudden, unpredictable, and unreasonable response or in a delightful inclination of mood and passions. It can be full of wild fantasies, sharp commentaries, or colorful reactions around the ordinary details of life.

The use of humor requires a natural ability for a wide imagination and free expression. It is the "mental faculty of discovering, expressing, or appreciating ludicrous or absurdly incongruous elements in ideas, situations, happenings, or acts" (Webster's, 1993, p. 1102).

The humorist is a person who has some peculiarity about his or her character and is highly playful and amusing. He or she can display whimsical and dramatic behaviors and indulge in somewhat incongruent, odd, or comic ways for personal pleasure and the enjoyment of others (Webster's, 1993). On the other hand, the humorless individual is someone who is clearly lacking any wit, light heartedness, or comical quickness. Most probably, he or she is rigid, slow-reacting, very methodological, and deadly serious.

Humor and Psychology. Humor can be thought of in terms of certain theories of temperaments and is recently used to refer to, (a) a dynamic personal trait manifested in a bright mood and a cheerful attitude toward life, and (b) a generic term for graphic behavior or verbal expression designed to provoke laughter and mirth, known as a sense of humor.

Humor is an indirect form of communication. A distinction is usually made between two aspects of humor. The first is personal, informal, or affective, and the second is impersonal, formal, or cognitive. Humor enhances learning, stimulates alertness and creativity, and strengthens the social bond. In addition, humor and laughter diffuse tension, clarify perspective, increase self-confidence, boost energy, build cohesiveness, and promotes flexibility.

Some thinkers, like Plato and Freud, saw the origin of humor as based in suppressed aggression. To them excessive humor could be a sign of psycho-logical disturbance. However, appropriate humor is regarded as supreme coping device. Poland (1990) affirmed that clinical analytic change often brings with it a maturing of the patient's sense of humor, leading to an internalized capacity to acknowledge pain and frustration while soothing oneself with wit.

The use of humor is encouraged in demanding or difficult relationships and promoted in highly stressful places. It can serve as a surviving strategy and healthy defense mechanism. However, if a person heavily relies on inappropriate humor to mask undesirable realities, a shift of balance or splitting usually takes place within his or her core self on the intrapsychic level.

Humor and Physiology. In Medieval physiology, *neurohumor* was considered one of four fluids entering into the constitution of the body and determining their relative proportions for personal health and temperament (Webster's, 1993). Current studies have shown that humor enhances immunity (Labott, et al., 1990) and generates wellness (Strickland, 1993). Humor and laughter produce positive changes in the body, releasing excessive energy and reducing stress, worry, and frustration. Evidently, there is an interplay between the physiological and psychological aspects of the human functioning during the adaptive processes, like stress management. Research projects in the area of psychoneuroimmunology are awakening health care professionals to the importance of positive and pleasant emotions during the process of healing, recovery, and restoration (Macaluso, 1993).

Humor and Culture. Humor is a universal behavior. It is found in every culture and is an integral part of all communities. Humor varies in form and content among the societies. In many cultures, humor plays an important role in controlling conflict and aggression. However, what is appropriate in one culture may be totally inappropriate in another. While some forms of humor and laughter are amusing, constructive, and quite entertaining, other forms are destructive, sharp, and very damaging—like ridiculing and stereotyping. In certain sub-cultures, these are well accepted and easily tolerated. Psychosocial explanations of the nature and function of humor are derived from the assumption that humor virtually meets certain basic human needs and is used to maintain group solidarity.

Humor and Spirituality. Throughout history, laughter as well as weeping have been parts of many religious practices. Humor and laughter can be considered as a natural manifestation of an authentic spiritual joy. Humor can be described as "la joie de vivre." One of the blessings of the Christian faith is the occasional exuberant feeling of gladness and laughter (Psalm 126:2–3; Job 8:20–21). Perhaps it is safe to assume that Christ Himself had a well balanced sense of humor.

Humor is an attempt to appeal to the Spirit rather than to the letter and to dwell on the positive rather than the negative. Humor is the quality of being laughable. It is the ability to appreciate the beautiful and aesthetic and, at the same time, tease the rigid and painful.

According to Cousins (1979), like faith and hope, laughter may eventually reverse illnesses and other serious physiological maladies. Obviously, there is an intimate relationship between faith and humor. Both reflect one's capacity for self-transcendence and represent an attempt to directly resolve the incongruities of our human existence which threaten the very meaning and purpose of our life (Niebuhr, 1946).

Humor and Therapy. Humor is becoming an important component of modern treatment and patient care. It is a meaningful factor in regard to the client's well-being and to the therapeutic relationship between the health care professional and patients (Astedt-Kurki & Liukkonen, 1994). A well developed sense of humor furnishes the organism with beneficial ingredients and increases the individual's adaptive capabilities. Perhaps there is a correlation between having a good sense of humor and an optimistic view of life. Healthy humor ought to be encouraged in counseling with people who struggle with depression, anxiety, compulsive behaviors, or perfectionism, and those who operate under heavily stressful and oppressive conditions.

Laughing, joking, and utilizing wit can be done in a healthy or unhealthy way. People at times smile, laugh, mock, become cynical, make fun of, or dismiss an idea or person in order to protect themselves from unpleasant feelings or undesirable situations. Humor can be used to brush off intensity as a way of hiding from or avoiding painful matters. It is the role of the therapist to point out these patterns and heighten the clients' awareness of their unconscious habits. It is essential to teach clients self-monitoring techniques so that they are able to pay attention to themselves, gradually change their unhealthy patterns, and better face the tough issues of life.

For some psychotherapists, humor is a major goal of treatment. Humor and laughter can be employed in therapy to facilitate integration of the different aspects of personality and restore the interrupted flow of emotions. Humor can be taught or modeled by the counselor not as a measure of defensiveness but as a mechanism of coping, transforming difficulties, and cultivating hope. Furthermore, it can serve as a means to acquire existential skills for transcending and enjoying the passing moments of life.

References

Astedt-Kurki, P., & Liukkonen, A. (1994). Humor in nursing care. *Journal of Advanced Nursing, 20,* 183–188.

Cousins, N. (1979). *Anatomy of an illness.* New York: Norton.

Labott, S. M., Ahleman, S., Wolever, M. E., & Martin, R. B. (1990). The physiological and psychological effects of the expression and inhibition of emotion. *Behavioral Medicine, 16,* 182–189.

Macaluso, M. C. (1993). Humor, health and healing. *American Nephrology Nurses' Association Journal, 20,* 14–16.

Niebuhr, R. (1946). Humor and faith. *Discerning the signs of times: Sermons for today and tomorrow.* New York: C. Scribner's.

Poland, W. S. (1990). The gift of laughter: On the development of a sense of humor in clinical analysis. *Psychoanalytic Quarterly, 59,* 197–225.

Strickland, D. (1993). Seriously, laughter matters. *Today's OR Nurse, 15,* 19–24.

Webster's third new international dictionary of the English language. (1993). Springfield, MA: Merriam-Webster.

Additional Reading

Chapman, A., & Foot, H. (Eds.). (1977). *It's a funny thing, humor.* Oxford: Pergamon.

McGhee, P. E. (1979). *Humor: Its origin and development.* San Francisco, CA: W. H. Freeman.

Trueblood, E. (1964). *The humor of Christ.* New York: Harper and Row.

NAJI ABI-HASHEM

See CREATIVITY; PERSONALITY.

Hydrocephaly. The increase in the volume of cerebrospinal fluid in the skull, usually associated with an increase in pressure. Hydrocephaly may result from an injury or an obstruction to the flow of fluid within the system or a decrease in absorption of the fluid. In children the size of the head frequently increases, but in adults this enlargement is rare. Neurological and mental symptoms develop, sometimes leading to severe mental retardation, convulsions, or loss of sight and hearing. Drainage operations to relieve the volume of fluid in the skull are possible.

See MENTAL RETARDATION.

Hyperactivity. *See* ATTENTION DEFICIT/HYPERACTIVITY DISORDER.

Hypertension. Blood pressure is expressed as two components, with a larger top number (systolic pressure) and a smaller bottom figure (diastolic pressure). These readings are measured in millimeters of mercury. The systolic pressure reflects the heart's contraction as blood is forced out of the heart; the diastolic measure reflects the pressure during the heart's resting stage when its chambers are filling with blood in preparation for the next contraction. Normal blood pressure depends on age and other variables but is usually considered high if it is above 140/90 for extended time periods.

Hypertension is an elevation of systolic and/or diastolic blood pressure. There are two types: primary (essential) and secondary. The cause of primary hypertension is unknown. Heredity probably predisposes individuals to hypertension, but the condition is usually attributed to a complex of physiological, genetic, and emotional factors. Approximately 95% of all high blood pressure is diagnosed as essential hypertension. Secondary hypertension is associated with such medical conditions as kidney disorders, toxemia of pregnancy, adrenal tumors, or ovarian tumors. Blood pressure usually returns to normal once the underlying medical condition is treated.

Hypertension affects approximately 15% of the adult population in the United States. If untreated, it can cause serious and irreversible damage to the brain, heart, kidneys, eyes, and blood vessels. It can even prove fatal by causing strokes, heart attacks, or kidney failure. High blood pressure is a particularly difficult medical problem to deal with because people often have no symptoms and may not even know they have the condition.

It is mandatory that high blood pressure be medically treated. The person with hypertension can be treated with several types of antihypertensive medications. One type, called beta blockers, reduces the contractility of the heart and the output of blood. A diuretic may be administered to remove some of the sodium and water from the body and thus decrease the total volume of blood. Sympathetic nerve inhibitors keep the sympathetic nerves from causing arteries to constrict. Vasodilators reduce tension in the blood vessel walls and let them dilate. Newer types of drugs inhibit the body's production of angiotensin, a chemical which causes arteries to constrict. Calcium antagonists can help relax blood vessels and decrease the heart rate. Salt restriction is usually prescribed, in addition to medication; dietary changes can be equally as important as taking medication. Medication used to treat hypertension can be expensive and can cause unpleasant side effects such as lethargy, weakness, sexual impotency, depression, dry mouth, and sleep disturbance. However, the long-term problems resulting from hypertension are much worse than the side effects of medication.

Many people use relaxation techniques, including biofeedback training and meditation, in conjunction with their antihypertensive medication and salt restriction. Weight loss may help return blood pressure to normal; increased physical exercise can help reduce blood pressure, and alcohol use should be restricted since more than two ounces daily raises blood pressure in some people. Lifestyle changes and the practice of relaxation methods are important adjuncts to medication. They can help reduce the dosage levels of medication required, and in some cases medication can be discontinued completely. This must always be monitored by a medical doctor since high blood pressure frequently has no symptoms. Ongoing medical supervision is required for adequate treatment of this dangerous and potentially life-threatening condition.

Research has shown that people who attend church regularly tend to have lower incidence of hypertension than does the general population. Regular churchgoers perhaps have lower levels of anxiety and anger, both of which activate the nervous system and increase blood pressure.

Because high blood pressure does not produce noticeable symptoms, it has been termed the silent killer. It is extremely important to have one's blood pressure checked at least once each year and more frequently if high readings have ever been obtained. If hypertension is diagnosed, working closely with a physician and following the doctor's treatment prescriptions will minimize the effects of this condition. If hypertension is detected early and treated, the hypertensive can live a long and productive life.

M. A. NORFLEET

See HEALTH PSYCHOLOGY.

Hypnosis. *Definition.* Hypnosis is an altered state of consciousness that may be induced by the subject, by a guide or facilitator, or by another physical phenomenon. In this altered state the subject may experience changes in attention and memory, become more open to suggestion (*see* Suggestibility), and accept new ways of thinking and interpreting data that might otherwise remain unexplored. Depending on the particular use of hypnosis, it may produce such characteristics as paralysis, anesthesia, rigid muscles, fluctuations in blood vessels, or increased concentration.

The therapeutic use of hypnosis, as opposed to its use in stage entertainment, is widely accepted by reputable experts in medicine and psychotherapy. In the hands of a highly trained physician or therapist, hypnosis can be a valuable tool in the treatment of both physical and mental problems (*see* Hypnotherapy).

Mythology, Folklore, and Entertainment. Much of the current misunderstanding and skepticism about hypnosis stems from its historical ties to pagan worship and folklore and its exploitation for entertainment value. In ancient Egypt, people suffering from various ailments could go to sleep temples, where pagan priests made suggestions to their patients to generate healing. This practice spread to the Greeks and Romans, who adapted it to their own religious beliefs. The Greek god Asclepius purportedly visited the sleep temples and gave advice to patients in their dreams. This healing ritual was known as incubation, or temple sleep. Inscriptions in Epidauras, an ancient Greek town, record that cures did take place—and modern scholars speculate that hypnotic suggestion may have helped produce these positive results.

Because of its original ties to pagan and occultic rituals, many people still refute and even refuse to consider the genuine value of hypnosis as a natural phenomenon in medical and therapeutic treatment. Many people falsely believe that hypnotized subjects fall under the control of the hypnotist, who may then direct them to perform unnatural or evil behaviors.

Exploiting hypnosis as a means to entertain or manipulate emotions has also contributed to the misunderstanding of its genuine nature. As a stage performance hypnosis is often perceived as a method to force people to bark like dogs, strip off their clothes, and perform similarly undignified acts to amuse an audience. Rather than exert some sort of control over the subjects, however, the hypnotist more likely chooses and facilitates the actions of people who give signs that they want to make a public exhibition of themselves.

History of Hypnosis in Medicine. Interest in ancient healing practices resurged in the dawn of the European Renaissance (late fourteenth century). Pioneers in medicine and science examined old cultic practices and superstitions and then combined their findings with subsequent discoveries of nature to foster new explorations of hypnosis. This article will highlight only a few key links in the chain of exploration.

Mesmerism. During the eighteenth century, when many medical practitioners still linked science with mysticism and folklore, a number of Europeans claimed that lodestones and magnets had special curative powers. Franz Anton Mesmer (1734–1815), an Austrian physician who founded the Magnetic Institute in 1778, adapted this theory to coin the term *animal magnetism*, which he defined as an invisible fluid that flowed from the sun, moon, stars, animals, and humans, as well as from iron. Mesmer believed that disease results from a person's magnetic imbalance. His treatment consisted of using iron rods and magnetic wands to direct curative magnetic fluid into his patients. During this process his patients would often go into a deep trance.

Although word of Mesmer's cures heightened his patient load, more traditional medical practitioners accused him of being a magician and charlatan. In 1784 the king of France appointed a commission of notable scientists and physicians to investigate Mesmer's procedures. After observing his healing sessions, the commission concluded that magnetic fluids did not exist and that any reported effects were due only to suggestion and imagination.

Though they were seriously flawed, Mesmer's theories and practices opened doors to further examination of the nature and effect of trances. The Marquis de Puysegur, a former student of Mesmer, developed the practice of artificial somnambulism (inducing a deep hypnotic trance) and made many claims of miraculous powers and cures. His painstaking work revealed that the facilitator's control over the subject is limited by the subject's judgment and will. If the subject was prompted to commit an act he or she considered immoral or wrong, the trance abruptly ended.

Abbé Jose di Faria, a Portuguese monk who studied with Puysegur, rejected the idea of animal magnetism and defined a trance as a state of lucid sleep brought about by facilitated concentration. He also discovered that patients in a trance could be desensitized to the agonizing pain of surgery—a phenomenon that many physicians incorporated with some success. The subsequent discovery and use of chloroform, ether, and other chemical anesthetics eventually lessened the use of hypnosis in medicine.

As many of Mesmer's ideas were redefined and modified, nineteenth-century British researcher James Braid dropped the term *magnetism* and introduced *hypnosis,* from the Greek word *hypnos* (to sleep). He proposed that a state of somnambulism or trance derived from changes in the body's nervous system, not an invisible fluid.

Traditional medical practitioners continued to debate the therapeutic value of hypnosis. Jean-Martin Charcot, a French neurologist, likened it to hysterical disorders with no underlying physical causes. He claimed that hypnosis is an artificially induced neurosis to be encountered only in "hypersensitive, weak-minded and ill-balanced people." On the other side, Ambroise-Auguste Liebeault and Hippolyte Bernheim, both of the University of Nancy in France, argued that the power of suggestion on the human mind is very strong and influences not only weak patients but normal people as well.

Despite the ongoing debate, the use of hypnosis continued, with some notable successes. Phineas Quimby, credited as the father of the New Thought movement (a religious, metaphysical healing cult), used hypnosis to cure the founder of Christian Science, Mary Baker Eddy, of hysterical paralysis in 1862. Hypnosis also reportedly cured Rachmaninoff's three-year creative block after his First Symphony failed miserably in 1897. After receiving treatment by hypnosis in 1901, the composer produced 22 major works during the next 15 years.

Josef Breuer successfully used the posthypnotic suggestion developed by Charcot. In 1882, using hypnosis, he conceived the talking cure (free association) and other concepts that won the attention of Sigmund Freud.

The Twentieth Century. Freud's initial attraction to hypnosis apparently diminished after he tried to use it to remove physical symptoms or disturbing thoughts or memories. He grew extremely impatient when some of his subjects were resistant to hypnosis and thus not under the hypnotist's control. After several failures he concluded that certain hypnotic effects were tricks. Nevertheless, his experience with hypnosis led him in part to create a new field of therapy, psychoanalysis, which soon became the new rage.

Pierre Janet, who in the previous century adamantly opposed hypnotism, later became one of its greatest advocates. He noted the beneficial effects of relaxation in the healing process.

World War I produced hundreds of cases of battle neurosis. James McDougall treated many of these patients and was one of the first psychotherapists to use hypnosis for exploring psychopathology. Subsequently hypnosis became a commonplace clinical tool for both physicians and psychiatrists. In 1956 the American Medical Association stated that hypnosis is "valuable as a therapeutic adjunct." The American Society of Clinical Hypnosis was formed in 1957.

With this growing acceptance of hypnosis, the debate no longer focused on if it works, but on what it is. Traditionalists believed that the hypnotic state is a state of consciousness different from the waking and sleeping states. They further believed there are levels of hypnosis: the deeper the level, the more responsive a subject would be to types of suggestions.

Others rejected the special state view of hypnosis. They proposed that the subject's actions are influenced by the desire or pressure to fulfill the hypnotist's expectations.

In the 1950s Barber (1969) began an extensive course of study to show there is no special state that "a subject enters, goes deeper into, and comes out of as a result of suggestion." Barber, along with Spanos and Chaves (1989), pointed out that hypnotized people have normal EEGs and can remember what happens during hypnosis unless they are given the suggestion not to remember.

Barber (1969) conducted and reviewed many scientific studies of the medical and psychiatric use of hypnosis. One study he examined was conducted by the Japanese team Ikemi and Nakagawa, who experimented with people who had allergic reactions to a certain kind of tree leaf. The experimenters used one group who were hypnotized and a control group of people who were not. They rubbed one arm of each subject with what they said was a harmless leaf and the other arm with an allergy-producing leaf. However, unknown to the subjects, the experimenters switched the leaves. Many subjects from both groups developed symptoms of allergy from the harmless leaf or did not develop symptoms when their arms were rubbed with the allergy-producing leaf. From this Barber concluded that the hypnotic trance is not needed to induce a reaction to a suggestion that a leaf is harmful or not harmful.

Barber and his fellow opponents of the special state viewpoint were considered "skeptics" by Hilgard (1970). Based on extensive hypnotic research from 1957 until 1979, Hilgard regarded hypnosis as an altered state of awareness or consciousness that could have physiological connections. Thus a suggestion to the mind that one's arm is tingling could indeed send a message through the nervous system to create a genuine tingling sensation.

The Hilgards (1975) also concluded that different people have different levels of hypnotic susceptibility, which can be measured by using such methods as the Stanford Scale. The Hilgards are also recognized for their work on "imaginative involvement" (inducing altered awareness through such "right-brain" behaviors as visualization) and "dissociation" (a simulated out-of-body experience in which subjects seem to watch themselves from a distance, as on a movie screen).

Orne, Whitehouse, Dinges, and Orne (1988) raised important concerns about the accuracy of information recalled under hypnosis. Orne defined, for example, a "social demand characteristic," suggesting that the desire to meet the hypnotist's expectations may cause the subject to recall or provide inaccurate or untrue memories. Orne, perhaps more than any other person in the medical field, influenced the U.S. courts' rejection of legal evidence obtained through hypnosis because of the uncertainty of suggestibility.

The issue of suggestibility raises an important caution in the use of hypnosis, particularly in memory recall or interpretation. How a facilitator talks to the subject can influence how the person remembers a particular experience. For example, suppose the facilitator suggests that certain symptoms, such as depression or an eating disorder, indicate past sexual abuse. The individual could then begin to imagine or reinterpret experiences to fit that suggestion. Since the mind becomes increasingly receptive to new ideas under hypnosis, it is imperative that a subject select a facilitator who is well-trained and certified in hypnotic technique.

Milton H. Erickson is considered the founder of modern clinical hypnosis. He worked with more than 30,000 patients and developed a series of special clinical techniques, including indirect suggestion (see Hypnotherapy).

Hypnosis in the 1990s. The successful methods used by hypnotists in the past continue to be examined in light of new information about human behavior and the workings of the brain. In the future we can expect that these ongoing studies and discoveries will help create new and more effective clinical uses of hypnosis in the treatment of physical disease and mental disorders.

Christian Implications. Reputable scientific studies have diffused many false beliefs and suspicions about hypnosis and its ties to the occult. This altered state of consciousness apparently is not evidence of demonic influence or possession. Hypnosis does not involve evil spiritual entities, nor does the subject lose the individual right to choose. Rather, hypnosis is presently understood as a function of the nervous system, which, when used by a trained and trusted facilitator, can be a legitimate and safe therapeutic tool.

Our minds are often deceived and dimmed by misperceptions, misinterpretations, and misinformation. These distorted thoughts warp our understanding not only of ourselves and our environment but also of God and God's Word.

In Psalm 51:6 (NASB) David proclaims to God: "Behold, Thou dost desire truth in the innermost being, and in the hidden part Thou wilt make me know wisdom." We should not ignore our unconscious minds, where repressed or hidden memories and misinterpretations continue to shape our beliefs and behaviors and hamper our movement toward spiritual maturity. The informed use of hypnosis, through suggestion or a shift in consciousness, can help a Christian expose and shed false and damaging beliefs in order to become more open and receptive to the true and redemptive Word of God. Hypnosis can be a valuable tool in heeding Paul's admonition to "be transformed by the renewing of your mind, that you may prove what the will of God is, that which is good and acceptable and perfect" (Rom. 12:2, NASB).

Genesis reveals how the deceptive suggestions of the evil serpent induced Eve to misinterpret God's commands and doubt his goodness—with tragic consequences (Gen. 3). The question is not, Do we have the capacity to be vulnerable to suggestion? Experience and Scripture confirm that we do. God created us with the capacity to experience shifts in consciousness. The major concern is to whom will we entrust our vulnerability? In the hands of an ethical professional, hypnosis can be used to discern truth in our innermost beings and become more Christlike.

References

Barber, T. X. (1969). *Hypnosis: A scientific approach.* New York: Dover.

Hilgard, J. R. (1970). *Personality and hypnosis: A study of imaginative involvement.* Chicago: University of Chicago Press.

Hilgard, E. R., & Hilgard, J. R. (1975). *Hypnosis in the relief of pain.* Los Altos, CA: William Kaufmann.

Orne, M. T., Whitehouse, W. G., Dinges, D. F., & Orne, E. C. (1988). Reconstructing memory through hypnosis. In H. M. Pettinati (Ed.), *Hypnosis and memory.* New York: Guilford.

Spanos, N. P., & Chaves, J. F. (1989). *Hypnosis: The cognitive-behavioral perspective.* Buffalo, NY: Prometheus.

Additional Readings

Edmonston, W. D., Jr. (1981). *Hypnosis and relaxation: Modern verification of an old equation.* New York: Wiley.

Gauld, A. (1995). *A history of hypnotism.* New York: Press Syndicate of the University of Cambridge.

Ross, I. L. (1986). *The psychobiology of mind-body healing: New concepts of therapeutic hypnosis.* New York: Norton.

D. H. DECKER

Hypnotherapy. *Historical Development.* Hypnotherapy, the use of hypnosis in treating mental and physical ailments, originated in some form as long as three thousand years ago. Born from a mix of mysticism and science, hypnotherapy has survived the rigors of scientific analysis, exposed charlatans, refined its principles and practices, and matured into a respected, legitimate therapeutic process. In the last half of the twentieth century, as science has excelled in understanding the complexity of the nervous system, hypnotherapy has gained wide acceptance from both the medical and psychological communities (*see* Hypnosis).

Hypnosis is commonly viewed as something that is done to a person as a therapy. But as Spiegel and Spiegel (1978) note, hypnosis is not itself a therapy; rather it greatly facilitates a therapeutic strategy. It is not something done to a person; it is a capacity for a certain type of concentration that can be adduced alone or in others' presence.

How Hypnotherapy Works. Milton H. Erickson was the reputed genius in using hypnotherapy in clinical work. His work is so well respected that it generated a special framework of hypnotherapeutic tools and techniques.

According to Ericksonian principles, the patient already has the resources to solve his or her problem; hypnotherapy is a process to help the patient discover those resources. The therapist functions as a facilitator, not a controller. Erickson emphasized the necessity for the therapist to work in the patient's model of the world.

First the therapist needs to accurately assess the person's internal map or model of the external environment as it relates to the problem. This means determining what the person feels and thinks about the sensory data he or she has absorbed through seeing, smelling, tasting, touching, and hearing. These thoughts and feelings form the internal representation of the sensory data and become a filter through which the person evaluates similar data in the future. When something in this filter is distorted or painful, the person may repeatedly react to similar data (events, situations, relationships) in ways that are irrational, unnecessarily restrictive, and ultimately harmful. To break this negative cycle, the therapist needs to interrupt the subject's thinking process and have the patient generate a positive alternative.

An Illustration. Imagine a young woman named Susan who is terrified of public speaking. Her hands sweat, her stomach turns to knots, her voice shakes—a painful physiological experience. She seeks the help of a professional to get rid of this fear.

Through the therapist's use of hypnotherapy, Susan recalls a time when she was chosen to give a speech at a junior high school assembly. Proud and excited, she worked hard on her speech. On the day of the assembly, Susan was midway through her speech when she lost her place in her notes. Suddenly she tensed up and stumbled badly through the rest of the speech. As other students snickered, Susan felt ashamed, stupid, and worthless. Ever since then, even the thought of speaking to groups of people has triggered the same painful feelings. Fear keeps her from expressing her views aloud.

The counselor's role is to encourage Susan to think differently about the event at school, which in turn will reshape her view of herself in that situation. This can provide an alternative, positive structure for reacting to similar situations in the future.

Methods of Inducing Hypnotic States. In Susan's case, a therapist could use hypnosis to focus her concentration and facilitate a shift or alteration in her consciousness. The therapist may choose from a variety of ways to induce a hypnotic state (or trance), depending on the subject's characteristics and openness to suggestion.

The use of direct suggestion (e.g., "Go to sleep") may work effectively with patients who are open to the hypnotic process. For others indirect induction methods (e.g., "You may want to think about going to sleep soon") may be more effective. Other techniques include truisms (e.g., "You learned to walk and talk; you can learn a lot of things"), binds (e.g., "Do you want me to talk first, or do you want to talk first?"), and double binds (e.g., "Do you want me to go first and then you? Or do you want to go first and then me?"). These methods enable the therapist to understand and help modify how the subject's mind and body respond.

Another effective Ericksonian method is the use of metaphors, stories, or parables that encourage the patient to identify with the subject matter and discover alternative choices in behavior.

Additional hypnotic phenomena include dissociation (letting go or looking at oneself from a distance); age regression (in which the patient is asked to act out experiences at an earlier age or time); automatic writing or drawing (done with the non-dominant hand, usually to help the subject recover information); and visualization.

Physiological Effects. Because of the relationship between the brain and the rest of the nervous system, hypnotherapy can be used effectively to control pain, asthma, allergies, and pruritus (itching). It has been used as an anesthetic in Cesarean sections and other surgical procedures in which chemical anesthetics may be risky. Hypnotherapists have successfully treated facial tics, bruxism (grinding teeth), and urinary problems.

Psychological Effects. Hypnotherapy has been applied to problems of dependency (smoking, eating disorders, drug or alcohol abuse), anxiety, problems with concentration, and insomnia. It has been used to treat fear (phobias, performance anxiety), depression, and manic behavior. Both adults and children respond effectively to hypnotherapy.

New Directions. In 1972 John Grinder and Richard Bandler developed a model called Neuro-Linguistic Programming (NLP). They claimed NLP can induce effective communication, personal change, accelerated learning, and "greater enjoyment of life" (O'Connor & Seymour, 1993, p. 2). This model derived from three ideas: All behavior stems from neurological processes (i.e., the five senses); we use language to order our thoughts and behavior and to communicate; we use programming to choose the way we organize our ideas and actions to produce results.

By observing specific body language and eye movements, the hypnotherapist can pick up many clues as to how a patient conceptualizes or expresses information. This knowledge enables the hypnotherapist to use a variety of approaches to establish better communication and better choices for treatment.

In a new field called psychoneuroimmunology (PNI), scientists are exploring how the relationship between the mind and body affects health. States of mind have an impact on the nervous system and the neuromodulators, which regulate the immune system. Recent popular writers such as Norman Cousins, Bernie Siegel, Bill Moyers, and Depak Chopra have raised society's awareness of the mind-body relationship and how suggestion, imagery, and states of mind affect the body's physiological responses.

Imagery and relaxation involving hypnosis are being used in the treatment process of life-threatening illnesses such as cancer, heart disease, diabetes, and immune deficiencies such as HIV. Hypnosis also helps relieve hyperactive immune responses that result in allergic reactions.

Christian Implications. Scripture clearly acknowledges the relationship between the mind and behavior—and the need for right thinking. Romans 12:2 (NASB) urges Christians to "be transformed by the renewing of your mind, that you may prove what the will of God is."

Ephesians 4:22–23 (NASB) commands that "in reference to your former manner of life, you lay aside the old self, which is being corrupted in accordance with the lusts of deceit, and that you be renewed in the spirit of your mind."

Before our minds can be renewed or altered, our false and darkened ways of thinking need to be exposed. This is not always easy, for, as Jeremiah 17:9 (NASB) says, "the heart is more deceitful than all else and is desperately sick; who can understand it?"

God understands our hearts and minds fully, even those areas that we often repress, misinterpret, or deny. That is why David cried out in Psalm 139:23–24 (NASB): "Search me, O God, and know my heart.... See if there be any hurtful way in me, and lead me in the everlasting way."

With the help of an ethical, well-trained hypnotherapist, Christians who are stuck in deceptive ways of thinking may open themselves more fully to God's examination and exposure. This will enable them to experience a truly godly sorrow over their sin, a deeper gratitude for God's forgiveness, and a genuine joy in following God and God's Word.

References

O'Connor, J., & Seymour, J. (1993). *Introducing neuro-linguistic programming: Psychological skills for understanding and influencing people* (Rev. ed.). London: Aquarian.

Spiegel, H., & Spiegel, D. (1978). *Trance and treatment: Clinical uses of hypnosis.* Washington, DC: American Psychiatric Press.

Additional Readings

Chopra, D. (1990). *Perfect health: The complete mind-body guide.* New York: Harmony.

Cousins, N. (1989). *Head first: The biology of hope*. New York: Dutton.

Dilts, R. (1983). *Applications of neuro-linguistic programming*. Cupertino, CA: Meta.

Fisher, S. (1991). *Discovering the power of self-hypnosis: A new approach for enabling change and promoting healing*. New York: HarperCollins.

Gilligan, S. G. (1987). *Therapeutic trances: The cooperation principle in Ericksonian hypnotherapy*. New York: Brunner/Mazel.

D. H. DECKER

Hypoactive Sexual Desire. *See* SEXUAL DESIRE DISORDERS.

Hypoactivity. A state of depression characterized by hopelessness and helplessness. It is frequently the result of a loss of self-esteem or ego depletion and involves a nonreactive and passive lack of activity.

Hypochondriasis. A technical medical term that describes the behavior of the hypochondriac: exaggerated, morbid preoccupation with health and the false belief that one is suffering from physical disease. (However, *DSM-IV* removed the requirement that such beliefs be of delusional intensity.) These patients frequently consult physicians and vigorously complain about their bodies. Although no bodily function is lost or impaired, the patient is convinced that there is a dire illness that previous examinations have been unable to detect. In some cases there is a verifiable physical problem, but the patient's level of complaint and concern is out of proportion to the actual disorder.

The complaints may involve any part of the body and are usually as vague as they are urgent, and the site or nature of the complaint may shift. When extensive medical investigations reveal no organic pathology, the patient refuses to accept a verdict of health but insists on more testing or even treatment. If the physician refuses, the hypochondriac will probably look for another clinic. Eventually such patients become chronic attenders at several clinics, perhaps simultaneously. Hypochondriacs can also fall prey to quacks.

Whether hypochondriasis constitutes a primary psychiatric disorder, as opposed to a medical condition or personality disorder, remains a debated topic. The hypochondriac usually has another psychiatric disorder to which the hypochondriasis may be viewed as secondary. Estimates have been made that four out of five hypochondriacs have an underlying depression. About a third of depressions in later life have the classic mood symptoms masked by somatic concerns. Hypochondriasis can be seen as a somewhat effective defense against a deepening depression. Patients may prefer to reinterpret their dismal interpersonal situation as a set of physical problems, which also gives them an excuse for their personal failures and sins.

The diagnosis of depression is largely the outcome of extensive medical testing, negative findings, and the patient's continuing refusal to accept reassurances of health. There is a hypochondriasis scale on the Minnesota Multiphasic Personality Inventory ([MMPI] scale 1, abbreviated Hs), but it is largely a symptom checklist. Its validity is suspect, especially with hospital and nursing home patients, who have many real physical symptoms. The hypochondriasis scale (institutional geriatric) measures health attitudes rather than specific physical complaints.

Hypochondriasis is easily distinguished from other psychological disorders involving physical complaints. In psychophysiologic (psychosomatic) illness, the cause is also mental, but the physical symptoms (e.g., ulcer, migraine) are real and can be treated medically. In conversion reactions (e.g., hysterical blindness or paralysis), the cause is an unconscious defense against anxiety or a stressful environment, but the physical symptoms are limited to the loss of an active function. In malingering (factitious disorder) the patient consciously feigns a particular physical disorder in hopes of escaping from some undesirable situation or cashing in on an insurance policy or personal injury suit.

There are several theories regarding the origin of hypochondriasis. Harry Stack Sullivan contended that hypochondriacs unconsciously focus on physical explanations as a way of avoiding their interpersonal problems. Alfred Adler saw hypochondriasis as a result of the patient's pampered childhood: what the patient really seeks is to have the medical staff give the kind of elaborate attention that the patient enjoyed as a child. The behaviorists have a similar explanation: sickly behavior has been rewarded with special attention (positive reinforcement) and release from normal obligations, such as not having to go to school or work (escape conditioning).

Research on the epidemiology of hypochondriasis has not been conclusive. The disorder is equally common among males and females. It may be more prevalent among the aged, the poor, and recent immigrants. Hypochondriasis may be predisposed by a personality that is apprehensive, unstable, dependent, and timid. It is also more likely to occur among individuals who are lonely and lack effective social functioning. Such behavior may also be triggered by an environment that is stressful.

The treatment of hypochondriasis is difficult because the patient steadfastly believes that the condition is physical and therefore rejects psychiatric treatment as inappropriate. Many clinics speak of managing such patients rather than curing them. Effective management involves firm policies and limit setting enforced by the entire staff, starting with the receptionist. The goal is to prevent the hypochondriac's demands from overtaxing the staff or disrupting the operations of the clinic.

One approach to treatment is to attempt to alleviate the underlying depression. Placebos rarely achieve the desired results with hypochondriacs, since placebos rely upon the patient trusting the physician and having confidence that health can be attained. Of all the tricyclic antidepressants, doxepin seems to be the best tolerated, giving the patient less opportunity to complain of side effects. Clomipramine, which has anti-obsessional qualities, may also be appropriate. Fluoxetine (Prozac) and other selective serotonin reuptake inhibitors (SSRIs) have also achieved favorable results. Sulpiride, an antidelusional compound, may also be effective. Although electroconvulsive therapy (ECT) is highly effective in most cases of severe depression, this is generally not the case with hypochondriasis, because the patient is looking for a cure that is not overtly psychiatric.

Few hypochondriacs accept counseling or psychotherapy with someone designated as a mental health professional. The most appropriate therapist is the primary care physician with whom the patient has already established a relationship. The physician must be willing to listen to the patient's description of symptoms without offering excessive sympathy or offering to perform surgery. The physician should not directly confront the patient with the position that the symptoms are merely imaginary. What the physician must do is to resist the temptation to refer the patient but schedule a follow-up appointment in the medical setting. The physician remains a benevolent authority who uses a directive yet patient approach. These regular visits are brief (10 to 20 minutes) and the patient's complaints gradually shift from the somatic to the psychosocial.

The role of pastoral care in hypochondriasis is unclear. The patient is seeking help in a medical context, not a spiritual or psychological context. While cases of conversion reaction may respond to faith healing, this is not the case for the hypochondriac. Perhaps the best thing the psychologist or pastoral counselor can do for a hypochondriac is to make a referral to a physician who is willing to establish the firm, caring, listening relationship that the patient needs.

Additional Readings

Baur, S. (1988). *Hypochondria: Woeful imaginings.* Berkeley: University of California Press.

Brink, T. L. (1982). Geriatric depression and hypochondriasis: Incidence, interaction, assessment and treatment. *Psychotherapy: Theory, research, practice, 19,* 506–511.

Brink, T. L., Belanger, J., Bryant, J., Capri, D., Janakes, C., Jasculca, S., & Oliveira, C. (1978). Hypochondriasis in an institutional geriatric population: Construction of the HSIG. *Journal of the American Geriatrics Society, 26,* 557–559.

Brink T. L., & Yesavage, J. A. (1982). Delusional illness: Hypochondriacal and somatoform disorders. *Postgraduate Medicine, 72,* 189–198.

Ehrlich, R. (1980). *The healthy hypochondriac: Recognizing, understanding and living with anxieties about our health.* Philadelphia: Saunders.

Ford, C. V. (1983). *The somatizing disorders: Illness as a way of life.* New York: Elsevier.

Kellner, R. (1986). *Somatization and hypochondriasis.* New York: Praeger.

T. L. BRINK

See SOMATOFORM DISORDERS; ANXIETY.

Hypoglycemic States. Since the 1960s several authors have linked hypoglycemia with various behavioral disorders (panic attacks, depression, aggression, and hyperactivity) and more transient symptoms (nervousness, trembling, irritability, and impaired concentration) in popular articles and books. Most of these reports were based on anecdotal case reports or correlational studies and did not employ adequate controls, so some have been misleading. Controlled studies have shown that some of these relationships are valid while others probably are not.

Hypoglycemia is a physical state in which blood glucose levels drop below normal, causing subsequent neurological and physiological symptoms. (Blood glucose levels are critical because the brain depends upon a consistent, moment-by-moment supply of glucose for fuel. Neurons that are deprived for even a few seconds cannot function normally.) Mild hypoglycemia may be accompanied by transient weakness, faintness, nervousness, excessive sweating, hunger, or heart palpitations. These symptoms are typically responses to low or falling glucose levels and can be alleviated by consuming carbohydrates (which rapidly break down to glucose.) More severe hypoglycemia (less than 80 mg of glucose per minute reaching the brain) can result in impaired concentration and problem solving, confusion, headaches, ataxia, visual disturbances, muscle weakness, hallucinations, and bizarre behavior. If this state persists, it can cause extensive and permanent neurological damage, coma, and death.

Reactive hypoglycemia, defined as low blood glucose in a nonfasting state that is provoked by the ingestion of drugs or carbohydrates, typically produces symptoms two to four hours after a meal and may be caused by a delayed insulin response in people with mild, adult-onset diabetes, the administration of too much insulin in diabetics, or consumption of alcohol or other drugs. (Alcohol can cause hypoglycemia in susceptible individuals because it suppresses the liver's production of glucose.) Spontaneous hypoglycemia occurs in the fasting state (five or more hours after a meal) and may be due to excessive glucose utilization or deficient glucose production. Persons with reactive or spontaneous symptoms should seek medical advice.

Blood glucose levels are usually measured with the five-hour glucose tolerance test (GTT). After an overnight fast and a preliminary blood sample to determine fasting glucose levels, patients are asked to consume 75 to 100 grams of glucose dissolved in

300 ml of water. Blood glucose levels are then assessed from samples drawn every 30 to 60 minutes. Under these conditions blood glucose levels typically rise 50% above fasting levels in the first hour, approach the fasting level in the second hour, and then drop below the fasting level to approximately 65 mg/dL of blood in the third and fourth hours.

Even though this test is straightforward, researchers have found that they cannot diagnose hypoglycemia simply on the basis of GTT scores. Individuals vary a great deal in fasting glucose levels, and levels that produce transient hypoglycemic symptoms in some people fail to produce them in others (Johnson, Dorr, Swenson, & Service, 1980). Quite a few healthy people have minimum fasting glucose levels that are lower than the standard cutoff points on the GTT (65 mg/dL) without concomitant hypoglycemic symptoms. Consequently diagnosis is usually based upon very low glucose levels (less than 50 mg/dL) plus concomitant hypoglycemic symptoms.

Well-controlled studies on the possible relationships between hypoglycemia and psychopathology are sparse. In an updated, comprehensive review of the literature, Messer, Morris, and Gross (1990) concluded that there is evidence for a relationship between low and/or rapidly declining blood glucose levels and the transient symptoms listed. However, the evidence for a relationship between hypoglycemia and psychopathology is either negative or inconclusive. Hypoglycemia does not appear related to panic disorder because inducing hypoglycemia in panic patients fails to bring forth true panic attacks. Blood glucose levels may be related to major depression; however, depressed patients often have elevated rather than decreased blood glucose levels relative to controls. So far there is insufficient support for a link between hypoglycemia and aggression. Hypoglycemic patients do tend to have higher than average scores on certain Minnesota Multiphasic Personality Inventory (MMPI) scales (i.e., those that reflect varied somatic complaints). However, this does not necessarily imply psychopathology. Such patients may be reporting real physical symptoms that are related to their medical condition.

References

Johnson, D. D., Dorr, K. E., Swenson, W. M., & Service, F. J. (1980). Reactive hypoglycemia. *Journal of the American Medical Association, 243* (11), 1151–1156.

Messer, S. C., Morris, T. L., & Gross, A. M. (1990). Hypoglycemia and psychopathology: A methodological review. *Clinical Psychology Review, 10,* 631–648.

E. L. HILLSTROM

See DEPRESSION.

Hypothesis, Testing and Development. *See* PSYCHOLOGY, METHODS OF.

Hysteria. *See* CONVERSION DISORDER; SOMATIZATION DISORDER.

Hysterical Personality. *See* HISTRIONIC PERSONALITY DISORDER.

Ii

I and Thou. *I and Thou* is a term made popular through a book of the same title by Martin Buber (1878–1965), a Jewish existentialist philosopher who is also known for his revival of Hasidism. Two translations of *I and Thou* are available in English. The Smith translation retains the poetry and majesty of Buber's work by translating the German *du* as *Thou*, whereas the Kaufmann translation, which translates *du* as *you*, contains critical footnotes and other useful information. Buber's model has been called a philosophical anthropology. His basic insight is that we can relate to the world of people, things, and God in one of two ways: *I-It* or *I-Thou*, emphasizing their inseparability by the use of the hyphen. *I-It* is knowledge about, from the outside. *I-It* is relating to someone or something as a thing, an object of study. This mode of relating lends itself to classifying objects by finding commonalties or differences. It acknowledges the object only as it impinges upon my being. *I-Thou* is a relationship focused on the between, the dialog. It centers the relationship in the other, not in the I. The quality of relationship is entirely different between the two modes, and the difference is due to the I that is doing the relating. "The I of the basic word I-You is different from that of the basic word I-It. The I of the basic word I-It appears as an ego and becomes conscious of itself as subject (of experience and use). The I of the basic word I-You appears as person and becomes conscious of itself as subjectivity (without any dependent genitive). Egos appear by setting themselves apart from other egos. Persons appear by entering into relations with other persons" (Buber, 1922/1970, p. 111).

Buber's main thesis is that the universe is relational; the *I* can never be separated from the *It* or the *Thou*. He claims that both modes of relating are necessary but that to restrict oneself to *I-It* relations narrows the self and denies the fundamental reality of mutual relationship. *I-It* calls forth people as manipulators, while *I-Thou* calls forth people as relaters. As human beings our personhood is not defined by a set of states or traits belonging to or residing within the individual, separated from God and others, but by the quality of our relationships. There is no personality outside of relationship because there is no person outside of relationship. Personhood is defined by relationship. In this idea Buber's work foreshadows the insights of the systems, object relations, and interpersonal theorists.

There exists a school of therapy, known as dialogical therapy, based upon Buber's work. One of his disciples, Maurice Freedman (1960, 1985), founded The Institute for Dialogical Psychotherapy in San Diego, California. According to Heard (1993), there are eleven principles of dialogical psychotherapy: the between, the dialogical, distancing and relating, healing through meeting, personal direction, the unconscious, inclusion, the problematic of mutuality, confirmation, existential guilt, and touchstones. In examining this list of principles, one can see that this school bears a striking resemblance to the humanistic/existential and Gestalt schools of psychotherapy.

References

Buber, M. (1922/1958). *I and thou*. (R. G. Smith, Trans.). New York: Collier. (Original work published 1922)
Buber, M. (1922/1970). *I and thou*. (W. Kaufmann, Trans.). New York: Scribners. (Original work published 1922)
Friedman, M. S. (1960). *Martin Buber: The life of dialog*. (3rd rev. ed.). Chicago: University Press of Chicago.
Friedman, M. S. (1985). *The healing dialog in psychotherapy*. New York: Aronson.
Heard, W. G. (1993). *The healing between: A clinical guide to dialogical psychotherapy*. San Francisco: Jossey-Bass.

D. W. PETERS

See EXISTENTIAL PSYCHOLOGY AND PSYCHOTHERAPY.

Iatrogenic Psychopathology. An iatrogenic disorder is one that is inadvertently induced by a doctor. Thus iatrogenic psychopathology is psychopathology induced by a psychotherapist. This concept has been explored mainly within the psychoanalytic tradition, in which a number of theorists have argued that the therapist's involvement in the life of a patient can be for good or for bad.

Langs (1980) has been the major spokesman for this position, pointing out that the unresolved neurotic problems of the therapist readily lead to a contamination of the therapeutic relationship. This not only blocks therapeutic progress but also, according to Langs, can lead to the patient introjecting aspects of the therapist's psychopathology. This leads to Langs's focus on the interactions, conscious and unconscious, between therapist and patient. His approach is therefore often identified as an interactional one in that it emphasizes not just the one-way transmission of healing from therapist to patient but rather the two-way conscious and unconscious interchange of health and pathology.

Reference

Langs, R. (1980). *Interactions*. New York: Aronson.

A. F. X. CALABRESE

See ABNORMAL PSYCHOLOGY.

Id. A concept from psychoanalysis representing a realm of the mind that functions in terms of instinctual drives. Sigmund Freud postulated that the mind could be described by three functional realms: the id, the ego, and the superego. This postulation, called the structural hypothesis, views these realms or structures not as concrete entities but as metaphorical representations.

The id is best understood as a container of instinctual drives or energy (libido) seeking discharge. It is wholly part of the unconscious and hence can be defined only in relationship to its opposite structure, the ego, which is conscious and knowable. An independent description of the id was attempted by Freud (1933), but he only talked in terms of images. He pictured the id as a "cauldron of seething excitement" that somehow connects with one's biological substratum and is there filled with instinctual energy and a corresponding impulse to obtain satisfaction for those instinctual needs. This is all directed by what he called the pleasure principle. Freud felt that the id is innate, the other mental structures (ego and superego) developing in the first few years after birth.

The human mental state at birth is described in terms surprisingly reminiscent of those used by some theologians to describe the native state of humanity. The mental makeup of the young child, composed solely of the id, is described by Freudians as amoral, not knowing good from evil, seeking only selfish gratifications. These childlike demands for gratification of the drives are never outgrown. The mind continues throughout life to seek immediate discharge (cathexis) of id impulses. These operations of the id are labeled the primary process. This process ultimately brings a person into conflict with the environment. These conflicts further stimulate the id to supply its own energy to the development of the other mental structures as well as to the development of their corresponding mental maneuvers that serve to provide either neurotic or healthy means of id impulse discharge.

The id is commonly thought of as representing a person's darker side. For Freudians this darker or unknown aspect of one's being is a major factor in explaining pathology. Today id psychology has been replaced to a large part by ego psychology, which focuses on people's knowable ego in the formation of theories of psychopathology. Although this contemporary relative deemphasizing of the id is viewed with concern by some psychoanalysts, ego psychology does probably represent a more balanced total psychology in that it more adequately addresses all three basic mental structures.

Reference

Freud, S. (1933). *New introductory lectures on psychoanalysis*. New York: Norton.

D. S. McCULLOCH

See EGO; SUPEREGO; PSYCHOANALYTIC PSYCHOLOGY.

Idea of Reference. The notion that conversations or actions of people relate to oneself. Such a belief is held less firmly than is the case in a delusion.

See DELUSION.

Idealization. An ego defense mechanism whereby another person or love object is idealized, elevated, and overvalued in the mind of the individual. Perhaps a common example would be the young man who sees in his newfound companion the perfect lover. In this state of idealization she seems to fill all that he lacks, and the faults that others see in her are to him merely endearing facets of her engaging but flawless personality. Such romantic idealization is, according to Sigmund Freud, the root of the human experience of being in love.

Idealization is often preliminary to identification. Both play a vital role in superego development and in character formation. As a defense mechanism, idealization often is a response to dissatisfaction with one's self through the transfer of libidinal attachment to the new ideal. Therefore, it is also used in the aid of denial. Finally, it may be used to replace a lost love object, facilitating the emotional rebound to a new love object.

R. LARKIN

See DEFENSE MECHANISMS.

Identification. A generally unconscious defense mechanism in which the person identifies with some object, person, or institution, seeking to think, feel, and behave in a manner consistent with his or her incorporated mental picture of that object. The purpose of this process is to protect the individual from threatened self-devaluation and to increase feelings of self-worth.

Identification is seen in psychoanalytic thought as one of the most primitive methods of recognizing external reality. It begins with the infant's identification of the mother's breast as part of his or her own body, transforming what is external and potentially uncontrollable or threatening into something internal, safe, and familiar. Identification also operates during the oedipal phase of development, when identification with the father serves to resolve fear of the father as the omnipotent rival for the mother's affections. An example in adulthood might be seen in the generally ineffectual person who draws feelings of self-worth from identification with the powerful, prestigious multinational corporation for which he or she works.

R. LARKIN

See DEFENSE MECHANISMS.

Identity. In the most general terms *identity* refers to one's answer to the question, Who am I? Erik Erikson, the most well-known thinker in this area, proposed that identity involves a sense of personal uniqueness and self-continuity and an identification with group ideals. Erikson (1968) described the identity development process, maintaining that it "employs a process of simultaneous reflection and observation, a process taking place on all levels of mental functioning, by which the individual judges himself in the light of what he perceives to be the way in which others judge him in comparison to themselves and to a typology significant to them; while he judges their way of judging him in the light of how he perceives himself in comparison to them and to types that have become relevant to him. . . . Furthermore, the process described is always changing and developing: at its best it is a process of increasing differentiation, and it becomes ever more inclusive as the individual grows aware of a widening circle of others significant to him, from the maternal person to 'mankind'" (pp. 22–23). In theory one's relationships and capacity to take others' perspectives are critical to identity development. Research empirically substantiates some of this process (e.g., Enright, Ganiere, Buss, Lapsley, & Olson, 1983).

Erikson claimed that the identity struggle is especially important for adolescents. According to theory, society offers teenagers a moratorium, or time relatively free of adult responsibilities, during which they are expected to explore social roles and personality styles, make decisions about important issues (sexuality, occupation), and integrate new choices, personal history, and goals into a coherent sense of self. Erikson maintained that an ideological commitment is a crucial aspect of the identity crisis, as adopting a life philosophy provides a framework for making all other decisions (p. 27). (This has obvious implications for spiritual growth: after committing to a Christian worldview, other life choices are theoretically easier to make.) The resolution of the adolescent identity crisis depends in part on the resolution of previous developmental crises and in turn lays a foundation for the resolution of future conflicts. Those who do not adequately resolve the identity crisis will experience identity confusion and isolate themselves, draw their identity from a peer group, and/or engage in delinquent behaviors (Erikson, 1968; Santrock, 1995).

Marcia (1966) expanded on Erikson's ideas by identifying where individuals are in their search for a personal identity. Marcia classified individuals according to their experience of "crisis" (or exploration) and commitment. Individuals who demonstrated no exploration or commitment were called diffused, while those who made commitments without exploration were foreclosed. People who were in the process of exploration but had not yet made commitments were considered to be in moratorium, and those who had made identity commitments after a period of exploration were called achieved. Although some scholars have cogently criticized this model (e.g., Cote & Levine, 1988), Marcia's classification system has proven useful in studying individual differences. Often those who are identity achieved (and to a lesser extent, moratorium) display more healthy social and psychological traits (e.g., Orlofsky, Marcia, & Lesser, 1973; Rowe & Marcia, 1980).

Recently the notion of ethnic identity has received attention in the psychological literature. Work in this area, pioneered by William Cross, suggest that individuals go through four stages as they develop a sense of themselves as a minority ethnic group member: pre-encounter (preferring dominant culture values), encounter (realizing one will never fully be part of the dominant culture), immersion/emersion (completely immersing oneself in minority culture and then feeling uncomfortable with the exclusion and rigid views associated with such an experience), and internalization and commitment (integrating personal and cultural identity and experiencing comfort while interacting with members of different backgrounds) (Cobb, 1995; Santrock, 1995). Similar models have been used to describe the development of a feminist identity (e.g., Bargad & Hyde, 1991) and, given the position of Christianity in secular society, may have some implications for religious identity development as well.

References

Bargad, A., & Hyde, J. S. (1991). A study of feminist identity development in women. *Psychology of Women Quarterly, 15,* 181–201.

Cobb, N. J. (1995). *Adolescence: Continuity, change, and diversity* (2nd ed.). Mountain View, CA: Mayfield.

Cote, J. E., & Levine, C. (1988). A critical examination of the ego identity status paradigm. *Developmental Review, 8,* 147–184.

Enright, R. D., Ganiere, D. M., Buss, R. R., Lapsley, D. K., & Olson, L. M. (1983). Promoting identity development in adolescents. *Journal of Early Adolescence, 3,* 247–255.

Erikson, E. H. (1968). *Identity: Youth and crisis.* New York: Norton.

Marcia, J. E. (1966). Development and validation of ego identity status. *Journal of Personality and Social Psychology, 3,* 551–558.

Orlofsky, J. L., Marcia, J. E., & Lesser, I. M. (1973). Ego identity status and the intimacy versus isolation crisis of young adulthood. *Journal of Personality and Social Psychology, 27,* 211–219.

Rowe, I., & Marcia, J. E. (1980). Ego identity status, formal operations, and moral development. *Journal of Youth and Adolescence, 9,* 87–99.

Santrock, J. W. (1995). *Adolescence: An introduction* (5th ed.). Madison, WI: Brown & Benchmark.

E. A. GASSIN

See SELF; PERSONHOOD.

Identity Disorder. *See* DISSOCIATIVE IDENTITY DISORDER; GENDER IDENTITY DISORDER.

Identity Disorder of Childhood and Adolescence. Developing a sense of personal identity is seen as a normal developmental milestone for adolescents. For this reason the American Psychiatric Association (APA) removed identity disorder from its classification of major psychiatric/psychological disorders. However, APA has maintained a diagnosis of identity problem for when the focus of "clinical attention is uncertainty about multiple issues relating to identity such as long-term goals, career choice, friendship patterns, sexual orientation and behavior, moral values, and group loyalties" (1994, p. 685).

Erikson (1968) is credited with formulating the notion of identity crisis as an active process of self-exploration and definition that is an appropriate aspect of healthy personality development. Adolescence is seen as a stage of life that allows individuals to experiment with different roles, values, and beliefs. It is a period of questioning, self-doubt, and self-discovery. The identity crisis is a period of time when adolescents must confront any incongruent conceptualizations of the world offered by competing interests of peers, teachers, religious leaders, and family members. When this task becomes overwhelming for any number of reasons then an identity problem may develop. This period of time is meant to culminate in an integration of values and beliefs so that as a young adult, individuals have achieved an identity in terms of sexual orientation, vocational goals, and clearly articulated presuppositions about the world.

Other researchers have extended Erikson's theory to separate out four different resolutions of the identity crisis (Marcia, 1966, 1980). Adolescents may reach identity achievement, which involves actively questioning and exploring an identity and coming to a self-definition. Adolescents may foreclose, meaning they have committed to an identity without ever questioning the ideology of their family. They have become clones of their parents without ever having an identity crisis. Some adolescents may maintain a state of moratorium, where they continue to question and search for self-definition. Other adolescents may remain confused and possess identity diffusion. These individuals may or may not have had an identity crisis but nevertheless have not formed an integrated self-concept.

One of the complex tasks facing an adolescent are doubts and questions about the religion they were taught by their parents. As adolescence proceeds, individuals come into contact with peers who have grown up in different religions or with no religious teaching in their background. Some may actively question and pursue religions other than the one of their parents while others may begin to separate completely from religious ideology. Adolescents who show a pattern of foreclosure are most likely to continue ongoing attendance at their family's church without ever questioning those beliefs. Some psychologists view this type of religious foreclosure as "unhealthy religion" (Batson & Ventis, 1982). The struggle to define his or her religious beliefs becomes an identity problem for an adolescent only when that struggle is a source of continued, intense conflict and anxiety.

References

American Psychiatric Association. (1994). *Diagnostic and statistical manual* (4th ed.). Washington, DC: Author.

Batson, C. D., & Ventis, W. L. (1982). *The religious experience: A social psychological perspective.* New York: Oxford University Press.

Erikson, E. H. (1968). *Identity: Youth and crisis.* New York: Norton.

Marcia, J. E. (1966). Development and validation of ego identity status. *Journal of Personality and Social Psychology, 3,* 551–558.

Marcia, J. E. (1980). Identity in adolescence. In J. Adelson (Ed.), *Handbook of adolescent psychology.* New York: Wiley.

E. M. BUTTER

Idiot Savant. An individual diagnosed as mentally retarded who performs unusual, often incredible mental feats, frequently involving complicated puzzle solving or calculations based on numbers or calendar dates. The term *idiot* originally referred to a mentally retarded individual whose mental age is less than 3 years. *Savant* is the term for a person of exceptional learning. Thus the name *idiot savant* was applied to a person of low mental age who could perform an unusual mental feat.

Such unusual abilities among the retarded are rare. In occasional cases, however, seriously retarded persons may show a high level of skill in some specific aspect of behavior that does not depend on abstract reasoning. Cases have been reported in which an individual was able to remember the serial number on every dollar bill he was shown or had ever seen. Another was able to instantly name the day of the week for any date for any year without the use of pencil and paper. A musical prodigy with a diagnosed IQ of 54 could play 11 different musical instruments by ear. A famous

Japanese painter had an assessed IQ of 47. One woman could recall the birthdates of any person whose birthday she had ever been told.

The classic example of the idiot savant was the "Genius of Earlswood Asylum." Admitted to the asylum at age 15 with personality and speech defects, this mildly retarded man constructed model ships of masterpiece quality. In one ten-foot model, he used more than a million tiny wooden pins and pegs. He wore a navy uniform, and when his models were admired by visitors to the institution, he would express his pleasure by patting his head and repeating "very clever, very clever."

L. N. FERGUSON

See MENTAL RETARDATION.

Illusion. A distorted perception that misrepresents external stimuli. Illusions always involve the perceptual distortion of stimulus patterns, unlike hallucinations, which are false perceptions, and delusions, which are mistaken beliefs.

There are illusions of apparent movement, such as the phi phenomenon, in which apparent movement is generated by two spatially separated flashing lights. There are illusions that misrepresent spatial figures, such as the Müller-Lyer illusion. In the Müller-Lyer illusion a line that is bounded by two arrowheads pointing outward appears shorter than a line of equal length bounded by two arrowheads pointing inward. Other familiar illusions include reversible figures, such as the Peter-Paul goblet and the staircase illusion. There are also illusions of smell, taste, temperature, time, and touch. A solid representation of the Müller-Lyer illusion, for example, works for the sense of touch.

According to the Gestalt theory illusions are the result of innate processes of organization in the brain. However, learning and experience must play some role in illusions, since people of different cultures vary in their susceptibility to specific illusions. Attitudes, instructions, and repeated exposure will also affect one's experience of an illusion.

Most geometric illusions appear to be due in part to certain expectations that people have governing relationships among perspective, distance, shape, and size. In the familiar distorted-room illusion people in a room with distorted dimensions appear distorted in size because viewers expect walls, ceilings, and floors to meet at right angles. In the moon illusion the moon looks considerably larger at the horizon than when it is up in the sky. The main reason is that the horizon looks farther away than the overhead sky. Since the perceptual system compensates for perceived distance, the horizon moon is seen as larger.

The study of illusions supports the viewpoint that the behavioristic, stimulus-response view of the person cannot be entirely correct. This was the emphasis of Max Wertheimer, the founder of the Gestalt school of psychology and a contemporary of John B. Wat-

son, the founder of behaviorism. Illusions demonstrate that perception (and ultimately personhood) is not just a passive product of sensory input but that a person's attention, motivation, expectation, memory, and perceptual processes actively filter and alter sensory input. This Gestalt view is in agreement with the Christian view of the person, which describes the person as more than a collection of behavioristic, stimulus-response connections.

M. P. COSGROVE

See PERCEPTUAL DEVELOPMENT.

Imagery, Therapeutic Use of. The term *imagery* here refers to a seeing with the mind's eye, or the formation of mental pictures. Such mental pictures may appear in a variety of forms. Dreams, daydreams, paintings that remain vividly in the memory, and hallucinations are all images. Certain images, especially if they occur repeatedly, may indicate strivings or conflicts that are important.

Further, imagery may be thought of as a type of information processing that begins during infancy and functions as a form of language in the preverbal child by giving pictorial representations of objects and events. The preverbal child "thinks" with images (Singer, 1974, p. 281). Verbal language and logic are controlled primarily by the brain's left hemisphere, whereas imagery, particularly when it is creative, is dominated by the brain's right hemisphere. Since emotions also appear to be controlled primarily by the right hemisphere, Singer (1974, p. 218) suggests the possibility that working with imagery increases accessibility to affect.

Access to affect and to early experience via imagery are compelling points favoring the use of imagery in all forms of psychotherapy. Moreover, an image permits the simultaneous assimilation of many aspects of a situation into a whole experience, thus allowing an intellectual and emotional reaction to the big picture. This all might happen in the same amount of time a patient could verbalize one small aspect of what heretofore had been viewed as a host of separate problems.

In Leuner's (1969) guided affective imagery, the therapist suggests the general situation and it is understood that what the patient constructs is a symbolic projection. Leuner's approach begins with relaxation training. This is followed by asking the patient to imagine a series of ten scenes that the therapist suggests in general and the patient is to give a verbal detailed description of the imagery and the associated feelings.

The first scene that the therapist asks the patient to imagine is of a meadow, any meadow that comes to mind. The next scene is of a landscape while climbing a mountain and then of a view from the top. In the third scene the image is of a brook upstream to its source or down to the ocean. The subsequent scenes are of a house (including the inside details), a close relative and the associated affect, situations designed to evoke sexual feeling, a lion, a fantasy of the ego ideal, looking into a dark forest or the opening of a cave, and finally a figure emerging from a swamp.

During this process the therapist should discover the qualities of the different themes, factors inhibiting progress, the presence of seemingly contradictory situations, and the nature of the emerging symbolic figures as well as their behavior. For more understanding the patient may be encouraged to free associate (*see* Free Association) verbally and with images to the situations.

Leuner suggests six methods to alter therapeutically the images and the unconscious material they represent. The methods consist of feeding the hostile symbolic figures, calling on an "inner psychic peacemaker" to govern the direction and speed of treatment, confronting hostile figures by holding ground while attempting to suppress anxiety (avoiding running or struggling), reconciling with the hostile figures (including making friends with them and perhaps physically touching them), exhausting a hostile figure by exercise and killing it, and finally utilizing "magic fluids" for fatigue or pain. Treatment times vary from 1 to 160 hours with an average length of 40 hours.

Autogenic therapy (Schultz & Luthe, 1969) and contemporary American methods such as transactional analysis, Gestalt therapy, psychodrama, and Shorr's (1974) psychoimagination therapy use imagery in which a specific act may be acted out as it comes to mind.

Shorr's use of imagery in psychotherapy varies with each patient, while Leuner employs the same basic procedure with everyone. Shorr believes that problems result from an individual being falsely defined by others and that the patient must find a more independent definition of self. In psychoimagination therapy the therapist attempts to identify the patient's major conflicts by asking the patient to complete such sentences as, "I feel . . . ," "The best adjective to describe me is . . . ," "I wish . . . ," imagine and describe certain scenes, such as "What do you hear yourself saying if you imagine whispering in your father's ear?" and "What do you see, feel, and do if you imagine dancing with your mother?" It may appear that Shorr focuses on images more for diagnosis than for treatment; however, when the therapist discovers a significant conflict, it will be worked with via imagery. If the patient experiences intense conflict between thoughts and emotions, the therapist might suggest that the patient, with eyes closed, imagine an animal coming out from the head and another from the stomach or heart. Then the patient is to describe what happens as the two animals walk down the road together.

All but certain behavioral approaches appear to be descendants of Carl Gustav Jung's active-imagination technique. Jung assumed that all images represent some part of the personality and that the integration of these parts into an organized and balanced unity would reduce the intensity of inner conflict (Singer, 1972). Jung considered patients' associations to dominant images that represented these parts to be important working material. Jung might suggest that the patient imagine a dialogue between the primary self and a representation of a specific part of the personality or a dialogue between two such parts. The objective of establishing a comfortable relationship between the various parts is similar to Leuner's idea of reconciliation.

In 1543 Ignatius of Loyola constructed a series of spiritual exercises utilizing imagery. In his colloquies Ignatius would speak to the Christ he pictured before him and go through a ritual of confession, repeating of certain prayers, and listening for God's direction. Psychosynthesis and inner healing also utilize imagery in psychospiritual approaches.

An example of the power of imagery to capture a complex problem is evident in the case of a male graduate student who came for therapy because he frequently had been told that his aggressive bravado was offensive. In the third session the therapist asked him to close his eyes, take a few deep breaths, and see if he could form a mental picture to represent, perhaps symbolically, his current situation. He described the image of a huge armored warrior fighting his way forward with a large sword, challenging the world. However, a frightened crying infant was on the warrior's back, holding the warrior around the neck, and as the warrior pushed forward the frightened infant would attempt to hold him back with a chokehold. Simultaneously the warrior was trying to kill the infant on his back with the sword so that he would be free of the burden it imposed. The student realized that the infant represented his feelings of dependency and helplessness that he was hoping to mask with bravado.

A therapist might follow the sequence just described, asking the patient to take some time to access an image in the mind's eye of a kind and wise inner guide and to hear in the imagination what the inner guide would say that might lead to change or progress for the better. After this ideal image a third image depicting the obstacles impeding movement from the current situation to the desired situation might be repeated. Finally a mental image of the resources and personal qualities that would enable these obstacles to be overcome might be elicited. This would include an image of how the next state might be and a symbol or other image depicting how this change might come about.

Imagery may be incorporated as part of psychotherapy in a number of ways, depending on the type of therapy. Nevertheless, imagery is always only one aspect of the psychotherapeutic process.

References

Ignatius of Loyola. (1963). *The spiritual exercise of St. Ignatius.* New York: P. J. Kennedy. (Original work published 1543)

Leuner, H. (1969). Guided affective imagery. *American Journal of Psychotherapy, 23,* 4–22.

Schultz, J., & Luthe, W. (1969). *Autogenic therapy.* New York: Grune & Stratton.

Shorr, J. (1974). *Psychotherapy through imagery.* New York: Intercontinental Medical Books.

Singer, J. (1974). *Imagery and daydream methods in psychotherapy and behavior modification.* New York: Academic.

Singer, J. (1972). *Boundaries of the soul.* Garden City, NY: Doubleday.

J. E. TALLEY

See DREAMS, THERAPEUTIC USE OF.

Imaginary Friends. Imaginary friends are fictional persons or characters created by children typically during their preschool years. Between 15% and 30% of preschool children develop imaginary friends, and boys and girls are equally likely to have them. An imaginary friend may be another person (child or adult), an animal, or some other creature. The personality of the imaginary friend is not necessarily related to that of the child; in other words, an imaginary friend may have a personality that is very similar to or very different from that of the child who created it.

Taylor, Cartwright, and Carlson (1993) reported that children have no difficulty talking about or describing their imaginary friends to adults, and they openly play with them in front of adults. Imaginary friends age with the children; as the child gets older, so too does the imaginary friend. When a child outgrows the imaginary friend, he or she may tell an adult the friend "has died."

A boy's imaginary friend is usually more competent than the child; boys create larger-than-life or superhero imaginary friends. A girl's imaginary friend is usually less competent than the child; girls create imaginary friends who play house and who need to be nurtured (Harter & Chao, 1992).

Harter and Chao (1992) asked parents and preschool teachers to rate the physical competence, social competence, and cognitive competence of preschool children with imaginary friends and preschool children without imaginary friends. In cognitive competence, children with imaginary friends did not differ from children without them. However, children with imaginary friends were rated as less socially and physically competent than children without them.

Psychologists believe that imaginary friends serve several functions. When there are no other playmates around, imaginary friends are constant companions. They can become confidants in whom the children can confide matters of great importance. If a child has few friends, having an imaginary friend can bolster self-confidence. Imaginary friends can also be scapegoats; a child may blame the imaginary friend for some wrongdoing rather than accept the responsibility.

Although many parents are concerned when their children invent imaginary friends, psychologists advise them not to worry, noting that they are signs of creativity and imagination and that they may enhance social development. Psychologists tell parents that their child is going through a stage and will probably outgrow the friend. There is cause for concern when having an imaginary friend interferes with the child's ability to make real friends and when the imaginary friend persists beyond the preschool years. Extreme stress and unhappiness or overdiscipline are reasons children over the age of six continue to have imaginary friends.

References

Harter, S., & Chao, C. (1992). The role of competence in children's creation of imaginary friends. *Merrill-Palmer Quarterly, 38* (3), 350–362.

Taylor, M., Cartwright, B., & Carlson, S. (1993). A developmental investigation of children's imaginary companions. *Developmental Psychology, 29* (2), 276–285.

D. NEEDHAM

See FANTASY; DISSOCIATIVE IDENTITY DISORDER.

Imagination. *See* FANTASY.

The *Imago Dei* in Personality Theory. *Definitions and Basic Parameters.* The *imago Dei* as applied to God's creation of humankind is multidimensional and many-faceted even in the most economical attempts at definition. Henry (1960) defines the evangelical view of the created image of God in humankind as existing "formally in man's personality (moral responsibility and intelligence) and materially in his knowledge of God and his will for man" (p. 341). Implicit in Henry's definition but not central in his presentation is the relational aspect of being made in God's image as highlighted by a number of integrative Christian psychology authors in reference to marital therapy (Guernsey, 1994), object relations theory (Jensma, 1993; White, 1983), and psychotherapy (Vanderploeg, 1981a, 1981b). In addition to moral, agency, intellectual, teleological, and relational dimensions, ontological and contextual concerns are included by Young (1962), who points out that the image of God in humankind is a derived likeness resulting from creation. "On the one hand, there is the fundamental distinction between man and the animals, but on the other hand it is demonstrated that man has not the same status as God, but is dependent on him and exists only because of the will of God" (Young, 1962, p. 556). Finally, there are process and developmental concerns that include such issues as the universal creation image of God in all persons that was sullied but not eradicated in the fall and the redemption image unique to Christians that is being reconformed to God's image in Christ through salvation and sanctification.

Aiken (1993) defines personality as "the organized totality of the qualities, traits, and behaviors that characterize a person's individuality and by which, together with his or her physical attributes, the person is recognized as unique" (p. xi). It is noteworthy that Aiken includes the physical dimension. Many theorists have traditionally deemphasized or neglected the role of genetic and biological factors, but this position has become increasingly less tenable as twin studies, cognitive research, clinical psychopharmacology, and other lines of psychological inquiry have demonstrated the importance of biological factors in psychological functioning.

In terms of the self, central in many conceptualizations of personality theory is the etymology of the Latin term *persona*, which originally referred to a theatrical mask worn while playing a role in a staged drama. Timpe (1985) observes that some theorists have overemphasized the presentation or social stimulus value aspect of personality since "behind each of the actor's masks stood a person, an individual with individual thoughts and feelings beyond those demanded by the role" (p. 815). Timpe further comments that the actor's personal thoughts and feelings can affect how the role is played. Thus Timpe describes a foundational characteristic of personality; namely, that it includes both inner and outer aspects and results partly from the interaction of the two. Millon (1990) refers to developmental processes in describing his evolutionary approach to personality (or his descriptive term, personology) and its development in both individuals and the human race.

Seven Basic Questions. In personality theorizing at least seven essential areas will be addressed, either explicitly or implicitly: ontology; teleology; psychopathology; relationships; prevention and intervention; epistemology; and integration. Some personality theories may include positions in all seven areas, while others may be more limited in scope and directly cover only two or three areas in any detail. All personality theories will be stronger in some areas than others, but they all include assumptions about each of the seven areas that can be deduced to some extent from the stated theory.

Ontology. Ontological concerns, or questions of being, in personality theory reflect questions of what humankind is, or the nature of man and woman. Freudian theory characterizes humanity as being evolved from lower animals and therefore instinct-driven from animal groups through the primal horde to the present, with a thin but potentially earthly salvific intellectual veneer. Radical and cognitive behaviorism both come from the same general evolutionary perspective, viewing humankind as essentially animals on an unbroken continuum with all animal life, albeit comparatively highly complex and sophisticated animals. Humanistic personality theorists have argued for the uniqueness of humanity but without rigorous definitions or standard sets of assumptions regarding what the criteria are for distinctive human status.

The biblical doctrine of humankind's creation in the *imago Dei* influences at least three areas in reference to the ontological question. First, human beings are a product of the direct actions of a Creator, reflecting certain of his aspects and responsible to him. Second, humans are eternal beings, with considerations extending beyond their physical birth and death. Third, humankind has moral and spiritual dimensions that make human beings qualitatively different from lower animals, no matter what other features they may share.

Teleology. Teleology in personality theory can be summarized as the functional aspects of persons and/or systems, as well as the ideal qualities and behaviors toward which growth may be aimed. In all secular personality systems, the goals and directions that may be preferable for pursuit generally flow directly from the predilections of the various theorists, usually predetermined mostly by the sociocultural and family environments of origin, as well as the confirmatory and challenging experiences of the theorists during various developmental stages and crises. The concept of the *imago Dei* universalizes certain thoughts, behaviors, and goals as coming from humanity's common Creator who transcends yet understands all cultures. Properly understood, the concept of creation in the *imago Dei* recognizes the essential purposes of humankind to be marshaled toward the restoration of God's image in all cooperating persons as demonstrated in Christ, therefore completing the fallen creation image in the redemptive image.

Psychopathology. The pathological question is most fully addressed by personality theory systems that include psychotherapy as a central concern. Questions of pathology revolve around what barriers, hindrances, or processes destructive to actualization of maximum psychological health and potential can be identified, studied, and treated. Some intrapsychic pathological features related to the *imago Dei* would include such dynamics as the defensive activities needed to avoid direct, traumatic confrontation with one's own sin and appropriate responsibility for it. This defensive distortion can go in opposite pathological directions, either taking the immature, personality-disordered path of minimizing personal responsibility or the more neurotic, anxious, and/or depressed overemphasis on personal responsibility. A similar polarizing split can be observed in self-esteem, which can be pitched too high (failing to properly evaluate "creature" status in relation to the God in whose image we are created) or too low (feeling human beings are worthless and can be killed, abused, or cursed, in direct contradiction to scriptural passages mentioning our status as cast in God's image and relevant behavioral constraints). Existential anxiety (resulting from awareness of responsibility to act, but without God's guidance) and guilt that cripple psychologically but do not constitute the "godly sorrow" that leads to repentance (Narramore, 1978, p. 143) are two of the many other intrapsychic tolls resulting from the ultimate source of all pathology, sin.

It is further possible that genetic and biological predispositions, passed down intergenerationally and combined with social and environmental learning experiences, may produce pathological diathesis-stress (person-environment) interactions that could ultimately be traced to a complex matrix of original, individual, and corporate sin. Humanity's dominion over the earth, another aspect of the *imago Dei*, is radically changed as a result of sin, possibly reflected in the attributions regarding environmentally generated pathology made by some of the classical and operant behaviorists.

Relationships. The relational question concerns the role of interpersonal factors in personality development, as well as what types of relational elements reflect and/or influence healthy versus unhealthy personality features. Social learning theorists have forged numerous original concepts to account for the relational aspects of personality development. Prime examples include such formulations as the expectancy, reinforcement value, and locus of control concepts of Julian Rotter; the vicarious learning of Albert Bandura; and the person/situation interaction research of Walter Mischel. Humanistic and existential theorists have spanned an incredible range in relational observation, including focus on relationships with deity, other human beings, and intrapsychic self-relations.

The *imago Dei*, almost no matter who the commentator, includes a central theme of humanity in relationship with God. Some scholars have observed that humans, made in the image of a triune God, have available to them a model of communication that includes at one level the three persons or personalities (subsistences) of the Godhead interacting with each other, as well as another internal level where God, taken in terms of his entire essence, communicates internally with himself. Authority issues and even potential disagreement are evident as Jesus questions the Father, and both Jesus and the Holy Spirit clearly speak with, and submit to, the Father.

Prevention and Intervention. These questions are clearly interrelated and revolve around the genesis and early disposing factors impinging on the development of psychological health and psychopathology in terms of personality features and habits, as well as change or improvement related to perceived need for such change. It is important to note that the causal attributions made for psychopathology are critical in determining the prevention and/or intervention strategy. Prevention and intervention research in psychology generally has ignored the spiritual realm, including being made in God's image but having his image tarnished by sin. In terms of the application of the *imago Dei* concept, it is vital to remember that some of the ripple effects of sin and related cycles of psychopathology such as addiction and abuse may be preventable, while some of the other effects of original sin (need for salvation, alienation from God) are not preventable but only remediable. Humankind, made to be in relationship with God but now pathologically separated and alienated from the Creator and fellow human beings, is in need of remedial interventions ranging from basic evangelism to interdisciplinary treatment teams designing sophisticated multidimensional strategies aimed at the confluence of spiritual, psychological, social, biological, and environmental factors that shape and maintain personality development and change. Christian psychotherapy can thus be conceived as located at every point on a continuum from remediation of the most severe psychopathology to augmenting the maximum potential spiritual development of the most productive and exemplary individuals as part of the restoration of the *imago Dei.*

Epistemology. Questions about the nature of knowledge and the knower have always been implicit in personality theory but have become much more obvious as the postmodern critiques have unfolded with championing voices such as Kenneth Gergen in scientific psychology and Barbara Held in clinical practice. Quickly surfacing in such accounts are fundamental and difficult questions regarding issues such as guidelines for authority, acceptability of evidence, and even the nature of reality itself. These questions and related issues have always been significant but are currently receiving much more attention.

Integration. Beyond the scope of this article but worth mentioning in closing is the question of integration. How do all the various systems and dimensions impacting on personality development interact and influence each other? The *imago Dei* is clearly a central characteristic of humans with impact in and beyond all the above-mentioned areas, a major aspect that has been neglected far too long in personality theorizing.

References

Aiken, L. R. (1993). *Personality: Theories, research, and applications.* Englewood Cliffs, NJ: Prentice-Hall.

Guernsey, D. B. (1994). Christian marriage counseling. *Journal of Psychology and Christianity, 13* (2), 117–126.

Henry, C. F. H. (1960). Man. In E. F. Harrison, G. W. Bromiley, & C. F. H. Henry (Eds.), *Baker's dictionary of theology.* Grand Rapids, MI: Baker.

Jensma, J. L. (1993). Kohut's tragic man and the *imago Dei:* Human relational needs. *Journal of Psychology and Theology, 21* (4), 288–296.

Millon, T. (1990). *Toward a new personology: An evolutionary model.* New York: Wiley.

Narramore, S. B. (1978). *You're someone special.* Grand Rapids, MI: Zondervan.

Timpe, R. L. (1985). Personality. In D. G. Benner (Ed.), *Baker encyclopedia of psychology.* Grand Rapids, MI: Baker.

Vanderploeg, R. D. (1981a). *Imago Dei,* creation as election: Foundations for psychotherapy. *Journal of Psychology and Theology, 9* (3), 209–215.

Vanderploeg, R. D. (1981b). *Imago Dei* as foundational to psychotherapy: Integration versus segregation. *Journal of Psychology and Theology, 9* (4), 299–304.

White, S. A. (1983). *Imago Dei* and object relations theory: Implications for a model of human development. *Journal of Psychology and Theology, 12* (4), 286–293.

Young, E. J. (1962). Image. In J. D. Douglas, F. F. Bruce, R. V. G. Tasker, J. I. Packer, & D. J. Wiseman (Eds.), *The new Bible dictionary*. Grand Rapids, MI: Eerdmans.

J. A. INGRAM

See BIBLICAL ANTHROPOLOGY; PERSONALITY.

Immediacy. As defined by Carkhuff (1969) and used in his approach to human relations training, the term *immediacy* refers to a person's ability to perceive what is happening in a present interpersonal interaction. In therapy immediacy provides the link between empathy and confrontation. Until a good working alliance is established, the interaction should be focused on the client and his or her experience rather than on the therapeutic relationship (Gazda et al., 1973). However, once the therapist has established an empathetic, understanding relationship, the use of immediacy is necessary in order to provide a full growth experience.

Immediacy means perceiving and interpreting in the moment what is transpiring between the client and therapist. Carkhuff argues that in responding immediately to his experience of the relationship with the client, the therapist not only allows the client "to have the intense experience of two persons in interaction but also provides a model of a person who understands and acts upon his experience of both his own impact upon the other and the other's impact on him" (1969, p. 192). Individuals who communicate with immediacy share of themselves openly, honestly, in the moment. Thus for Carkhuff one of the ultimate goals of a helping relationship is to model such full communication between persons.

It is the therapist's utilization of both positive and negative experiences of the relationship that provides for maximal understanding and growth. Frequently when the client is experiencing difficulty in communicating, this resistance is due to feelings about the therapist or the relationship, feelings that the therapist must identify through immediacy if the therapeutic process is to continue profitably. The therapist will often find that it is most effective in interpreting immediacy to employ the frustrating, directionless moments of therapy to search the question of immediacy. Sensitivity is required in order to discriminate when such interpretation will enhance a meaningful experience and when it will interfere with the communication at hand.

The term *immediacy* has not been widely used in the literature of psychotherapy, although the concept is obviously crucial. The narrower concept of transference has been more commonly employed.

References

Carkhuff, R. R. (1969). *Helping and human relations* (Vol. 1). New York: Holt, Rinehart, & Winston.

Gazda, G. M., Asbury, F. R., Balzer, F. J., Childers, W. C., Desselle, R. E., & Walters, R. P. (1973). *Human relations training: A manual for educators*. Boston: Allyn & Bacon.

M. E. McCURDY

See HUMAN RELATIONS TRAINING.

Implosion Therapy. *See* FLOODING.

Impotence. *See* SEXUAL AROUSAL DISORDERS.

Impression Formation and Management. In attempting to understand other people we carefully note their physical appearance, style of dress, manner of speech, and behavior. From these cues we typically begin to form judgments about their qualities or traits. The process through which we combine this diverse information into a unified picture or impression of another has received considerable attention from social psychologists.

Our first step in forming an impression is to interpret the cues themselves (Smith & Mackie, 1995). While sometimes their meaning may be clear (e.g., winning a decathlon connotes the trait of athleticism), other times the links are ambiguous. Associations we have learned through experience as well as our expectations, motives, and moods may all influence our interpretations of another's appearance and behavior. Research indicates that we quickly make correspondent inferences; that is, we characterize others as having traits that correspond to their observed behaviors. We make correspondent inferences even when situational causes account for behaviors, a pattern that social psychologists refer to as correspondence bias.

Asch, one of the first psychologists to study impression formation, suggested that our perception of another is not simply a collection of specific pieces of information but an organized, integrated conception of that individual's personality. In a highly influential study, Asch (1946) presented college students with a list of seven traits that characterized a hypothetical individual. He asked the students to write a general description of the individual as well as to select other traits they felt would characterize that person. For one group of students the individual was described as "intelligent, skillful, industrious, warm, determined, practical, and cautious." For a second group the list was the same, except that the trait "cold" was substituted for "warm." Two major findings of the study were that students experienced little difficulty in integrating the various traits into a coherent whole and that manipulation of the warm-cold variable produced a striking difference in the overall impression formed. Asch concluded that certain traits such as warm and cold may be central organizing traits, while others, such as polite and blunt, may be of secondary importance.

While Asch's conclusions have been questioned, his research fostered the development of implicit personality theories. Presumably through experience we develop intuitive notions about what traits are associated with each other in personality. Thus knowing that a person is intelligent may lead us to conclude that he or she is also industrious. Another example of this process is the halo effect, in which knowing something favorable about a person typically leads us to infer other desirable qualities. For example, a large number of studies have indicated that physically attractive persons are perceived as being more sensitive, kind, strong, poised, and sociable than those less attractive.

Studies indicate that not all information is equally important in our judgments of others. A primacy effect often occurs in which greater weight is given to information that is obtained first. This demonstrates that first impressions are indeed important and also explains why impressions may be hard to alter once they are formed. We also seem to assign greater weight to negative than to positive traits.

Clearly many people strive to influence the images others form of them. One of the basic assumptions of impression management theory is that individuals may present different sides of themselves to different people in different situations. High self-monitoring persons (Snyder, 1987) are particularly likely to exercise control over their self-presentations and to tailor them to fit the circumstances confronting them. They may present themselves as conformists or as independent, depending on the demands of the situation. High self-monitoring persons are effective not only at practicing impression management but also at detecting such attempts by others.

Research indicates that impression management may include false modesty or self-disparagement. Such a strategy readily elicits support and reassurances from others. Praising an opponent's abilities before competitive contests while disparaging one's own not only conveys good sportsmanship but sets the stage for a favorable evaluation regardless of outcome. Research has indicated that people privately will credit their opponents with much less ability as well as assume greater personal credit for their own successes.

Sometimes people may even sabotage their own performance to provide a ready excuse for failure. For example, fearing failure, they may handicap themselves by reducing their preparation for an important test or competitive event. If they fail while working under a handicap, they can cling to a sense of competence. Success under these circumstances gives an even greater boost to their public image.

References

Asch, S. E. (1946). Forming impressions of personality. *Journal of Abnormal and Social Psychology, 41*, 258–230.

Smith, E. R., & Mackie, D. M. (1995). *Social psychology*. New York: Worth.

Snyder, M. (1987). *Public appearances/private realities: The psychology of self-monitoring*. New York: Freeman.

M. BOLT

See ATTRIBUTION THEORY; INTERPERSONAL ATTRACTION; SELF-DISCLOSURE.

Imprinting. The phenomenon where the newly born offspring forms an attachment relationship to the caregiver (usually the mother). It was initially identified by Lorenz around 1935 in his observation of the attachment process of the female greylag goose and her offspring. Lorenz observed that as each gosling hatched, the mother engaged in an obviously patterned series of dance steps, wing movements, and calls. The fruition of all this behavior was a gaggle of goslings following and imitating their mother in walking, swimming, and eating behavior. Lorenz became more interested in this phenomenon after he observed the same imprinting phenomenon in an abandoned duckling reared by an adult female chicken.

This experience led Lorenz to consider other mother-absent imprinting conditions (Lorenz, 1961). In the experiment for which he is most famous, Lorenz incubated geese eggs, and while the eggs were hatching, he danced dramatically so that each newborn had an opportunity to observe him. Lorenz recorded that each of the newly hatched goslings imprinted on him. They followed him wherever he went and, perhaps most surprisingly, later refused to accept an adult female goose as a substitute. As a result of these observations, Lorenz concluded that this imprinting phenomenon is genetically based, ensuring that as a result of the attachment to the caregiver the newborn gosling received protection, food, and training in the ways of being a goose. It had survival value for the species. Lorenz and others have found imprinting in other species (e.g., fish, guinea pigs, deer, and some farm animals) and have suggested that the emotional bonding between a human mother and her child is the human equivalent of the phenomenon first reported in the greylag geese. Although serious debate has resulted from this contention, Lorenz's observations have forced psychologists to consider the possible impact of genetic factors in the attachment relationship.

Reference

Lorenz, K. Z. (1961). Imprinting. In R. C. Birney & R. C. Teevan (Eds.), *Instinct: An enduring problem is psychology*. Princeton, NJ: Van Nostrand.

K. A. HOLSTEIN

See SENSITIVE PERIOD; ATTACHMENT THEORY AND DISORDERS.

Impulse Control Disorders. A general category of disorders whose essential feature is the inability to resist an impulse or temptation to perform an act that is harmful to others or to the self. The act is usually preceded by a sense of tension or arousal and followed by a sense of gratification or pleasure. *DSM-IV* identifies the following disorders as impulse control disorders: intermittent explosive disorder, kleptomania, pyromania, pathological gambling, and trichotillomania.

P. C. HILL

Incest. Any sexually arousing contact within a family except that between husband and wife, whether members are blood related or not, has traditionally been called incest. Often referred to as intrafamily child sexual abuse, it is a universally prohibited behavior. Incest has been recognized and reported in almost every civilized society. Leviticus 18:6–18 cites 16 prohibited intrafamily sexual involvements. The most common forms of incest are father/daughter, stepfather/stepdaughter, uncle/niece, and brother/sister. Incest may also be homosexual.

The frequency of incest is difficult to assess and varies from study to study. Studies seem to indicate, however, that between 3 and 6% of all females have experienced some type of sexual molestation. Some research suggests as many as 25% of college-age females engaged in sexual activity with family members during childhood or adolescence. Incest crosses cultural, economic, geographic, racial, and religious lines.

Studies of families in which incest occurs suggest complicated interaction patterns and may include at least five causal factors. One factor is the family dynamic. Poor communication patterns, unhealthy alliances, inadequate methods of handling conflict, and dependency are seen. A second factor is the inability to deal with sexual issues and intimacy. In many cases the strongly religious homes have more difficulty talking about sexuality. Needs or urges are not discussed. Behaviors begin subtly and remain hidden. A third factor is a strong authoritarian milieu as found in many religious homes. The men in the families believe they own their women. The fourth factor is the unconscious dynamic of unresolved hostilities or wishes toward parents. Coming from a family in which incest occurred, either as a victim or a witness, may predispose the person to unhealthy interaction patterns with a spouse or children that reflect anger, fear, or distrust. A fifth factor is the emotional immaturity and poor impulse control often noted in the men who commit incest. Sexual addictions and intense angry episodes are frequently seen. Patterns of avoidance and denial are common.

Incestuous fathers present a mixed picture as good provider; religious; actively involved in church; dependent on the family for emotional needs; lacking intimacy in life; having a poor self-concept; having an unsatisfying marriage; often abused or emotionally neglected as a child. The daughter, or victim, may be attractive; well-developed; affectionate; the eldest daughter; an obedient girl; one who takes responsibility for household chores. The mother may be a passive, dependent person, incapable of protecting her children from a domineering husband; she may have been a victim herself as a child; or she may be absent from the home frequently due to work or illness.

The development of incest generally is subtle and slow. When pathology is already present within the father, the behavior may occur sooner. But often the complicated nature of causal factors finds incest beginning innocently. There may be tickling, wrestling, and friendly play. Then these acts become more exploratory and frequently coercive. Incest may begin with fondling and proceed to masturbation or intercourse. Once begun, the acts tend to continue and become more involved. The father frequently approaches the girl when he thinks she is asleep. The girl, confused and scared, feigns sleep. She may then pretend to waken, at which time the father may leave.

In other more involved cases the father rapes or has intercourse with the daughter, bribing or threatening her to prevent disclosure. The father may have a pattern he follows when the mother is away or sleeping. The girl generally dreads these times but feels powerless to do anything. Fear of family disruption, rejection, punishment, and even guilt may enter in. She may believe she is at fault and the cause of this. Who would believe her anyway?

If the girl finally tells someone, the consequences are multiple. Disbelief on the mother's part, denial from the father, and relief from the daughter are seen. The daughter sometimes retracts her accusation because the family disruption may include jail for the father, divorce, or foster home placement. If the girl is already rebellious, reporting incest could be viewed as a weapon, which then backfires when the family is separated.

Treatment must begin with prevention. Marital communication and positive, intimate relationships are critical. Understanding one's own sexual feelings, processing those feelings without guilt, and focusing sexuality to the spouse are vital. Intimacy and affection toward the children must be nonsexual, treating the children as persons, not objects. Training families in appropriate means of expressing intimacy and affection and in building strong marital ties is one step churches could take to strengthen the family. Individuals who were abused as children should seek treatment or talk it out with the spouse to reduce the potential of behaving the same way.

In many states reporting incest results in the father's going to jail or the daughter's placement in a foster home. Treatment must include therapy for each individual as well as for the family. The family treatment issues are often complex in that incestuous families typically show many maladaptive patterns, poor conflict resolution, or a long history of marital discord. The alliances that developed between mother/daughter or father/daughter must be treated. The daughter needs support to believe that she was not at fault. Fear, guilt, and anger must be handled. Even if there was a hint of seductiveness by the daughter, it was the father's responsibility to avoid incest.

Fathers give many reasons for incest. Sex education, preventing promiscuity, the daughter's seductiveness, and frigidity of the wife must all be seen as rationalizations. These excuses must be challenged and personal responsibility admitted for healing to take place.

Most states require mental health professionals and pastoral counselors to report to the appropriate authorities, in writing and by phone, any case of incest that is identified in therapy or treatment.

Additional Readings

Meiselman, K. C. (1978). *Incest.* San Francisco: Jossey-Bass.
Mrazek, P. B., & Kempe, C. H. (1981). *Sexually abused children and their families.* New York: Pergamon.

L. N. FERGUSON

See ABUSE AND NEGLECT.

Incongruence. *See* CONGRUENCE.

Incorporation. The instinctual aim toward swallowing or taking in and making part of the ego external objects that are desirable or pleasurable. It is an ego defense mechanism. Though occurring symbolically in later years, the process has its roots in the oral phase of infancy, in which the attempt to ingest pleasurable external objects is quite literal. This is viewed in psychoanalytic theory as the original form of instinctual satisfaction, from which all sexual expressions are derived. An example may be seen in a man who seeks to envelop his spouse, incorporating her to the extent that he sees her largely as an extension of his own life and ego.

See DEFENSE MECHANISMS.

Independent Variable. The predictor variable in an empirical experiment that is some aspect of the environment, usually representing an abstract concept or hypothetical construct, investigated for the purpose of determining its influence on behavior (the dependent variable). The value assumed by the dependent, or predicted, variable is hypothesized to be dependent upon the value of the independent variable. Thus a change in the independent variable is expected to produce a resulting change in the dependent variable. Other variables besides the independent variable may influence the dependent variable and therefore control procedures should be implemented.

P. C. HILL

See PSYCHOLOGY, METHODS OF.

Individual Psychology. The theory of personality and method of diagnosis and treatment formulated by Alfred Adler. The term itself has a dual implication; *individual* refers both to the fact that each person has a unique personality and to the fact that the personality is an indivisible unit that cannot be separated into mental structures (e.g., drives, habits, or traits) that have an existence apart from the whole. Therefore, individual psychology is a personality theory that is both humanistic and holistic.

Historical Development. Individual psychology arose out of Adler's clinical practice and represented a synthesis of five basic intellectual roots. These influencing systems and persons provided Adler with many of his basic concepts. Pierre Janet spoke of inferiority feeling as the cause of neurosis. Nietzsche emphasized both the importance of the individual and the striving for perfection as a universal goal. Vaihinger contended that people are motivated by fictions (goals and interpretations) rather than reality. Marx identified social forces as the prime determinants of human behavior and urged reforms promoting equal opportunity regardless of birth or gender.

By far the greatest impact on individual psychology was that of Sigmund Freud, with whom Adler collaborated for almost a decade. Freud's emphasis on the importance of early childhood and parental factors was adopted by Adler. One psychoanalytic perspective on determinism, that all behavior results from and reflects the underlying personality, was never doubted by Adler. However, he did dispute the claim that neither hereditary nor environmental forces could completely determine an individual's personality.

Adler's initial theoretical formulation came in 1907, after ten years of general medical practice and five years of association with Freud. Adler sought the secret of the mind in the morphological and functional tendencies of the body. Specifically he was impressed by the fact that if heredity, disease, or injury produces inferiority or damage to any organ or organ system, the body's health-oriented forces go to work to compensate either by rebuilding that organ or by increasing the organism's functional capacity in some other way. If a bone is broken, it heals in such a way that it is stronger at that point than it was before the break. Adler believed that this process of compensation is achieved because the organic inferiority becomes a stimulus to the central nervous system, which in turn stimulates the rebuilding of the affected organ and results in the kind of training that helps the organism meet the environment's needs despite the organic deficiency.

Because the central nervous system has a central role in this process, the dynamics of inferiority and compensation are bound to have an impact on the personality. The central psychological problem in humans is *Minderwertigkeitsgefühl*, inferiority feeling. Everything that a person does, thinks, and feels reflects that person's efforts to overcome inferiority feeling. Adler was a great optimist and firmly believed that although inferiority feeling is universal, all persons can successfully compensate and find happiness.

In 1908 Adler attempted to reduce compensation to a drive for power or aggression. He discarded the theory of the universality of this drive soon afterward but kept the idea that all people strive for perfection. Later he termed this drive *masculine protest* and contended that only maladjusted people seek compensation via aggression, power over others, or blind rebellion.

Adler gradually increased his emphasis on social and interpersonal factors, such as the need for affection. By 1911 his view of humans as social rather than sexual beings led to a rift with Freud. Although Adler conceded that sexual components exist in most neuroses, he viewed them as being more symptomatic than casual. The oedipus complex, for example, was to be found only in little boys who felt inadequate to the challenges of the external world and therefore clung closely to their mothers. Any sexual attachment to the parent is secondary and the result of this clinging.

In 1911 Adler also discovered the writings of Vaihinger and soon adapted the latter's concept of fictional goals to individual psychology. Each person has a private logic through which objective reality becomes phenomenal reality. We cannot understand behavior in terms of causes but only in terms of goals and strivings. It is not the fact that someone has an organic inferiority or a traumatic experience in the past but the individual's interpretation (which is idiosyncratic or even unconscious) of the fact that determines behavior. The individual's general pattern of interpretation is a style of life, a guiding whole to which specific judgments and behaviors are subordinate. The tenacity with which an individual clings to a given behavior or thought reflects its centrality to the style of life or the degree to which it enables private logic to assuage feelings of inferiority. In general the greater the feeling of inferiority, the more one holds to fictional goals. The small country has great passport formalities, reflecting the fictional belief that ceremony bespeaks or compensates for the lack of greatness.

Adler's later works developed the concept of *Gemeinschaftsgefühl*, which is usually translated as social interest. This is the degree to which the individual overcomes self-boundedness *(Ichgebundenheit)* and the hold of private logic and compensates for inferiority feeling via cooperative and constructive interaction with others. Social interest is the barometer of mental health and is manifested in three areas: friendship, family, and career. Having friends helps one overcome inferiority feeling because friendship allows one to be important to someone else. The interpersonal exchange between friends establishes objective, consensually validated reality that supplants some of the more rigid and dysfunctional aspects of private logic.

Marriage is intended to supply the affection and approval that everyone needs to avoid serious inferiority feeling and also an opportunity to overcome self-boundedness by focusing on the needs of the spouse and offspring. Career is the opportunity to overcome inferiority feeling with a sense of accomplishment and contribution.

Before Adler's death in 1937 individual psychology had become an international movement with local societies in three dozen nations. Most of Adler's followers have been practitioners. Few have had any interest in revising his major precepts. Unlike the Freudians and Jungians, the Adlerians have not sought interaction with other disciplines, nor have they attracted historians, anthropologists, or literary critics into their fold.

Brachfeld (1951) carried individual psychology to Hungary and Spanish-speaking countries. He focused on inferiority feeling and reformulated it as auto-estimative instability, which is found to vary from one individual to another and even from situation to situation, being determined by the interaction of environmental demands and maturity.

Dreikurs (1950) was the chief apostle of individual psychology in the United States and Brazil. Most of his innovations and improvements were in the area of clinical practice, but several of his insights had theoretical import as well. Many of the parental mistakes in child rearing are due to the parents' own private logic. Dreikurs emphasized the principle of an impersonal order, rather than interpersonal power struggles, in discipline.

Low (1950) was closely associated with individual psychology in Vienna but went his own way in the United States. He developed a peer group therapy that has grown into a self-help movement known as recovery. The basic principle is training in self-monitoring and will power.

One of the more creative offshoots of individual psychology was the "we" psychology of Kunkel (Kunkel & Dickerson, 1940). His attempt to synthesize individual psychology (Adler) and analytical psychology (Carl Gustav Jung) was appreciated by neither Adler nor Jung. Kunkel deemphasized the organic basis for compensation. The newborn child lives in the world of the "primal we." This is disrupted by a breach-of-the-we experience in which the parent becomes seen as an other imposing demands upon the child: a white giant (fostering dependency) or a black giant (punishing). Everything in the child's personality that the parents reject becomes rejected by the child also and forms the basis for inferiority feeling (the shadow). The solution is the we-experience and anything that serves the developing we-group.

Clinical Applications. *Psychopathology.* Neurotics are to be understood as persons who have not managed to achieve compensation through social interest. They do not continue on the path of social interest because they have lost courage. The neurosis is not a mere reversion to an infantile form. It can be a creative attempt to find a sham superiority. Obsessive thoughts and compulsive behaviors are attempts to defend the private logic from the encroachments of reality. Other neurotics (e.g., depressives) love to wallow in inferiority feelings because it renders them pitiable and occasionally provides the sympathy that meets their need for affection.

Psychotics handle the conflict between reality and fiction by severing contact with reality. In their delusional world paranoids are the most important person on earth, for how else could they be the target of international and interstellar conspiracies? Some schizophrenics believe that they are famous persons or have special creativity. All these delusions serve to provide the feeling of superiority not given by social interaction.

Psychosomatic, hypochondriacal, and conversion reactions illustrate what Adler called organ dialect. These physical disorders, real or imagined, bespeak the individual's improper lifestyle. Physical disorder can serve as an excuse for failure and a plea for sympathy. Sexual dysfunctions fall into this category and manifest a failure in overcoming self-boundedness—that is, a lack of social interest.

Personality disorders, delinquency, and crime spring from masculine protest, the attempt to overcome inferiority feeling through rebellion and violence instead of participation and production. Prostitution and addictive behavior are due to strong and unresolved inferiority feeling coupled with an ambivalent approach to dependency.

Diagnostic Techniques. Adler and Dreikurs developed several methods of discovering the patient's style of life. Early childhood recollections were elicited by the question, What is the farthest back that your memory can go? The patient's response may be inaccurate, but that is not important. The technique is essentially projective. The patient unconsciously distorts the situation recalled in order to have it reflect chosen life goals.

Dreams are another projective technique, but focus more on the current situation and short-range goals. The dream is a rehearsal for coping in real life. The dream content reflects the present challenges in the environment. The dreamer's behavior in the dream is the key to coping strategies. Adler contended that successful coping in waking life removed the need for rehearsal; he mistakenly believed that mentally healthy people do not dream.

Another technique for understanding the style of life is a thorough history of the patient's childhood. Adler believed that the style of life is fairly fixed by age 6 and that such factors as parental relations, sibling relations, and physical diseases have an impact. The Adlerian psychologist asks about childhood illnesses and the family constellation. Of special interest is birth order and any evidence of pampering or neglect by the parents.

Because all behavior is determined by fictional goals, Adlerians are also interested in body language—firmness of handshake, eye contact, slouch-ing. Adler once said that one could observe a patient as one would a mime, ignoring all the patient's words, and render an accurate diagnosis. Even current physical disorders are a tipoff. Adler would ask his patients something like this: "If you were cured of this disorder, what would happen to you?" The answer reveals what the disease is a defense against.

Treatment. Both Adler and Freud probed the patient's childhood, trying to understand central conflicts and to convey this insight to the patient. Adlerian psychotherapy differs from psychoanalysis in several basic respects. The client sits in a chair and faces the therapist. Progress should be apparent in weeks, and treatment should be completed in less than a year. The therapist does not attempt to get the client to have an abreaction but to build the capacity for self-control.

Adler was a precursor of Carl Rogers in advocating that the psychotherapist accept the patient as a human being, without conditions or restrictions. (Giving this gift freely models social interest.) Adler analogized the therapist's role to the maternal function: providing emotional support and encouragement but moving the patient along to an eventual independence. However, he cautioned therapists to be on guard against giving a patient sympathy that would provide reinforcement for being inferior. Furthermore, therapists must try to prevent the development of any transference relationship that would prolong childish dependency. Finally, the therapist must be optimistic and concerned and yet not express too much personal interest in the recovery of patients, lest they be tempted to demonstrate their (fictive) power by proving that they can still decide to fail despite the therapist's best efforts on their behalf.

Adler was a master at developing insight in patients by responding with the unexpected. When one patient called at three in the morning, desiring his attention over a trivial matter, she apologized for awakening him. Adler replied that he had been sitting at his phone for half an hour waiting for her call. She gained the insight that she was behaving like a pampered child. A syphilophobe saw Adler and explained that every other physician in Vienna had failed to diagnose the dreaded disease, but the patient was certain that he had it. Without any further examination Adler agreed with the patient, who immediately began arguing with Adler, citing the prior medical tests as evidence.

Dreikurs had a technique called antisuggestion. If a patient told Dreikurs about an uncontrollable urge that the patient was attempting to hold in check, the suggestion was to practice that which the patient was making an effort against. Another technique would be to concede that if the therapist had the same goal and private logic that the patient had, the former would have the latter's problems as well.

The first phase of therapy is devoted to developing empathy and insight. The cultivation of the patient's social interest is the subsequent phase. If the foundations of empathy and insights about self-boundedness have been established, the social interest develops easily. Many therapists find that it is helpful to assist the clients with specific opportunities for the expression of social interest.

Child Rearing. Because the style of life is harder to change after age five, the process of child rearing has a great impact on mental health. Adler viewed child rearing as the process of directing the emerging strivings for superiority into social interest channels. Adler's great optimism was due to the fact that he believed parents could be educated in the proper techniques of cultivating social interest in their children.

When the child's inferiority feeling is great, it becomes difficult to promote proper guidance. All children start off with some degree of inferiority feeling due to the fact that they are born into an adult world. They are smaller, weaker, and lacking in learned skills and adult privileges. This is why children pretend to be adults. Children who are also inferior compared to other children due to handicaps, athletic inability, appearance, or lower intelligence have their inferiority feelings intensified.

Another factor that can intensify these feelings is a faulty parent-child relationship. Children are good observers but poor interpreters. Harshly treated or neglected children wonder why their parents mistreat them and conclude that the fault lies within themselves. Parents who are too demanding make the child feel inferior to what is expected. At the other extreme overprotective parents convey to the child their belief that the child is too weak to fend for himself. Parents who spoil the child convey the message that the child is entitled to receive without giving, and this makes true social interest harder to cultivate.

Adler also emphasized the importance of birth order and sibling relations in the development of personality. Oldest children were prone to have overly demanding parenting. Later borns usually compared themselves unfavorably with older siblings. If a later born actually surpassed an older sibling in something, the effect on the older sibling was devastating. Youngest and only children ran a high risk of being pampered. Whenever one child receives more attention than the others, an unfortunate rivalry can be the result.

The best atmosphere is one that is supportive and encourages the child to develop independence. Discipline is a necessary aspect, but it is best accomplished by an all-embracing impersonal order to which everyone, including parents, is subject. This begins with regular feeding schedules. Misbehavior is due to an attempt to gain attention, demonstrate defiance of overly dominating parents, or seek revenge. Adlerians do not favor corporal punishment because it reconfirms the belief that children are powerless and all others are against them. Nagging and scolding are likewise counterproductive. Identify the problem behavior, but never ridicule or prophesy a bad end for the child.

Aging. Many of the adjustment problems at the other end of the life cycle can also be comprehended from the perspective of individual psychology. The increasing physical disability brought about by chronic diseases coupled with changing appearance can yield an intensified feeling of inferiority. This is compounded by a youth-oriented society that no longer respects the knowledge of the elders. The reduced income of the aged adds a financial dimension of inferiority.

Many changes in later life reduce the opportunities for healthy compensation through family, friends, and career. Old friends die, move away to institutions, or become deaf. The elder's mobility becomes reduced, and there is less chance to see friends. Children grow up, leave the nest, and move away. The loss of a spouse is the greatest blow to the family. Retirement brings an end to the productive participation in one's career. The opportunities for finding new friends, family, or productive endeavors are quite limited in later life.

Many elders, for financial and/or physical reasons, become dependent on their adult offspring or on institutions. Dysfunctional relationships can arise from this. In certain institutions the staff discourages independent behavior on the part of the patients; they are overprotected though not pampered. More frequently the elders' needs are neglected, and sometimes older people are harshly treated by those charged with their care.

The intensified inferiority feelings, reduced opportunities for compensation, and dysfunctional relationships distort guiding fictions, resulting in excessive rigidity and even senile behavior. The way to prevent many geriatric problems is to make sure that elders have adequate opportunity to express their social interest.

Religious Implications. Adler regarded the idea of God as a fiction that embodies the ideals of perfection, power, superiority, and social interest. Hall (1971) described Adler as rejecting the God of the prophets and the God of the philosophers and substituting a synthesis of being and value, a final goal that can serve as a transcendent basis for the ideal community. Adler criticized atheists for trying to bolster their own sense of superiority by conquering God.

Adler's view of the social aspect of religion was positive, insofar as it is a technique of increasing social interest. Unlike Freud, Adler did not analogize religion to a neurosis, but he was critical of the way in which neurotic individuals perverted religion to serve their faulty styles of life. Anyone who claims a private pipeline to heaven is seeking a sham superiority. This is also the case with highly moralistic people who are eager to note sinfulness in others.

Yet individual psychology offers a framework within which we may gain new insights about Christian theology. The fall is the realization of inferiority feeling, especially the knowledge that one lacks immortality. The fall is necessary for salvation in that it is our defects that spur compensation. The law brings a guiding fiction against which people are measured. Those who live under the law feel either inferior because they cannot live up to it or proud because, like the Pharisees, they believe they have fulfilled it, and claim a sham superiority. But the motivating factor under the law is self-boundedness: individuals attempt to protect themselves from God's wrath or win a place in heaven. Life under works is the piecemeal attempt to deny inferiority. The essence of Christianity is a call for individuals to transcend their self-boundedness and develop a wholesome social interest, manifested in love and charity. The inferiority feeling does not condemn one who lives under grace. Life in the Spirit is the realistic evaluation of one's shortcomings and a commitment to their improvement.

Critique. There are several bases for the evaluation of any school of psychology. Internal consistency in individual psychology is adequate, but some of the interrelations of the internal mechanisms are not clear. Does inferiority feeling counteract social interest or vice versa? Does the adherence to an inappropriate fiction cause inferiority feeling or vice versa? Adlerians seem to argue it both ways, depending on the situation.

A further test of any theory is its ability to comprehend phenomena. Individual psychology, like psychoanalysis, is a remarkably flexible system that can be used to understand the dynamics of almost all clinical material, child development, aging, art forms, religion, and social and political phenomena. Adler's critics contend that his capacity to facilitate understanding is broad but not very deep, and the resulting level of understanding is little more than common sense or naïveté (Ewen, 1980). Adler (Dreikurs, 1950) has responded that people are misled by the apparent simplicity of individual psychology and that most people who dismiss it as common sense do not fully comprehend it. Szasz (1973) lauded the direct, common-sense approach in individual psychology and lamented the fact that people have an innate tendency to follow the mystification employed by would-be leaders.

The fact that a theory can generate empirically verifiable predictions is often taken as a touchstone for the scientific status of that theory. Prediction is not the strength of individual psychology. Adler's theory does not enable us to make any prediction about how a person will behave as an adult if he or she is treated a certain way as a child. An inferiority feeling makes some people excessively shy and others boastful and aggressive. Adult neuroses could be due to pampering or to neglect. Clinicians are not able to use early recollections or dreams to predict what the patient will do next. Indeed, there is scant evidence on the reliability and validity of those procedures. On the positive side, Adler's theory of the impact of birth order has received a great deal

of confirmation from correlational studies (Altus, 1966). Adler's basic assumptions about humans' evolutionary history are endorsed by other disciplines (Montague, 1970).

Perhaps the greatest testimonial to Adler's theories has been the extent to which other theorists have accepted them, although in slightly altered form. Freud's ideas have been the best remembered, but Adler's have been the most rediscovered. Jung (1953) agreed that the inferiority complex is a major factor in introverts and admitted that he used Adlerian techniques in treating younger patients. The existentialists have emphasized the importance of uniqueness and fictions. Abraham Maslow's self-actualizers have gotten over the need to defend against inferiority feeling. The Adlerian duty of making a contribution to the whole parallels Erich Fromm's idea of the productive character. Rogers's emphasis on empathy is an outgrowth of one aspect of Adlerian therapy. Beck's (1976) cognitive therapy is a development of another. Wilder (1959) commented that the question is no longer whether one is an Adlerian but how much of an Adlerian one is.

References

Altus, W. D. (1966). Birth order and its sequelae. *Science, 151,* 44–49.

Beck, A. T. (1976). *Cognitive therapy and the emotional disorders.* New York: International Universities Press.

Brachfeld, O. (1951). *Inferiority feelings.* New York: Grune & Stratton.

Dreikurs, R. (1950). *Fundamentals of Adlerian psychology.* New York: Greenberg.

Ewen, R. B. (1980). *An introduction to theories of personality.* New York: Academic.

Hall, R. W. (1971). Alfred Adler's concept of God. *Journal of Individual Psychology, 27,* 10–18.

Jung, C. G. (1953). [*Psychological reflections: An anthology from the writings of C. G. Jung*] (J. Jacobi, Ed.). New York: Pantheon.

Kunkel, F., & Dickerson, R. (1940). *How character develops: A psychological interpretation.* New York: Scribner's.

Low, A. (1950). *Mental health through will-training.* Boston: Christopher.

Montague, A. (1970). Social interest and aggression as potentialities. *Journal of Individual Psychology, 26,* 17–31.

Szasz, T. (1973). *The second sin.* Garden City, NY: Anchor.

Wilder, J. (1959). Alfred Adler's influence. In K. Adler & D. Deutsch (Eds.), *Essays in individual psychology.* New York: Grove.

Additional Readings

Adler, A. (1956). *The individual psychology of Alfred Adler.* New York: Basic.

Adler, A. (1964). *Superiority and social interest.* Evanston, IL: Northwestern University Press.

Brink, T. L. (1977). Adlerian theory and pastoral care. *Journal of Psychology and Theology, 5,* 143–149.

Mosak, H. H., & Mosak, B. (1975). *A bibliography for Adlerian psychology.* Washington, DC: Hemisphere.

T. L. Brink

See Adler, Alfred; Adlerian Psychotherapy.

Individuation. A Jungian concept that denotes the process by which a person becomes a psychological individual; that is, an indivisible unity or whole. This process of self-realization involves differentiating a totality called the self from all the components of the personality. Thus individuation is a synthetic process of integrating the various components of personality to the point that the parts, especially the conscious and the unconscious, begin to complement rather than oppose one another. The result is a self that is supraordinate even to the conscious ego.

According to Carl Gustav Jung, the process of individuation takes place typically during the last half of life. Throughout the first half of one's life the concern is with developing the distinct personifications such as ego, persona, shadow, conscious, unconscious, and anima or animus. These separate subpersonalities are oppositional to each other. For example, the conscious opposes the unconscious, and the ego opposes the shadow. The data of one component of personality are often threatened by the data of its counterpart. Individuation means breaking up these separate components, transcending their oppositional forces, and coming to unique selfhood.

The mechanism for transforming a network of subpersonifications into a unified person is a dialectical encounter between and among the various partial personalities. The conscious can be seen as the thesis; the unconscious, the antithesis; and the new self as the resulting synthesis. When individuation is complete, the components no longer suppress, oppose, and injure one another; instead, the dynamic forces of personality are harmonized, balanced, and centered. The person has become a true self and experiences wholeness and inner peace and quiet. Jung's concept of individuation should not be confused with Margaret Mahler's concept of separation-individuation, which refers to a much earlier developmental process occurring in the mother-child relationship.

Additional Readings

Jung, C. G. (1959). Conscious, unconscious, and individuation. In C. G. Jung, *The archetypes and the collective unconscious.* New York: Pantheon.

Jung, C. G. (1954–1991). *The collected works of C. G. Jung.* (22 Vols.). Princeton, NJ: Princeton University Press.

D. SMITH

See ANALYTICAL PSYCHOLOGY.

Indoctrination. *See* CULTS.

Industrial/Organizational Psychology. The field of industrial/organizational (I/O) psychology largely overlaps the field of organizational behavior. The latter discipline is usually taught in a business school and tends to place greater emphasis on practice and applications. The former, while not ignoring applications, tends to put greater emphasis on theory and research. The field relies on applied research rather than basic research, often drawing from and developing social psychological principles. The primary psychology journal in this field is the *Journal of Applied Psychology.*

The field began around the turn of the twentieth century. A major force in the early years was that of scientific management. This strategy sought to minimize wasted effort and hence improve individual productivity. One of the leaders of this concept was Frank Gilbreth, whose principles were popularized in *Cheaper by the Dozen.* After the field made significant contributions during both world wars, I/O psychology rose to greater prominence due to the work of Kurt Lewin.

Areas of specialization within I/O psychology include personnel (industrial) psychology (selection and hiring, training, and performance appraisal), organizational psychology (satisfaction, motivation, leadership, and communication), engineering psychology (the interface between people and machines), vocational and career counseling, organizational development (organizational culture and organizational change), and industrial relations.

Because personnel psychology deals with hiring, firing, and promoting, I/O psychology has been greatly affected by the civil rights movement and governmental regulation. Hence one focus of the discipline is on the development and use of screening and testing instruments that are valid and nondiscriminatory.

I/O psychology seeks to understand the organization as a system, rather than focusing on the individuals within that system. For example, when employees struggle with too much stress on the job, the usual tendency has been to look for individual emotional and coping problems within the employees. Hence counseling services might be provided. I/O psychology, although not ruling out the possibility of individual intervention, will consider whether the workplace needs to be changed. When employees experience difficulty with stress, it may be that they are experiencing an inordinate and unreasonable amount of stress. Hence the I/O psychologist will consider ways to adjust the organizational setting to reduce the stressors involved.

Another focus of I/O psychology is the concept of systemic change. Because the organization is seen as an organism, it is believed that any change within the organization will potentially cause changes throughout the system. Thus, when a change is proposed to impact problem A, one must also consider how this change will impact the rest of the system.

I/O psychology tends to value participative decision making. It is assumed that the individuals closest to the problem have important information that cannot be ignored. When decisions are made from the top of the organization, without such participation, they are usually ineffective. This implies not that all decisions can be made at a low level but that rarely should a decision be made without some input from those who will be most affected.

I/O psychologists are sometimes employees of a company, working as internal change agents. Other times they work under contract as external change consultants. This will depend on the size of the company and the extent of the problem.

One area that has received a great deal of research attention is that of leadership. In the early studies researchers asked, What kinds of people make good leaders? This question was not very productive, however. Researchers found only a few obvious personal characteristics that had only a small relationship with effective leadership. The research question was then altered: What kinds of things do successful leaders do? The general answer is that successful leaders demonstrate both a concern for their people and a concern for productivity. The third question was, Under what situations are certain behaviors most critical? Research looked at the differences between experienced and inexperienced employees and the differences between a favorable and unfavorable work environment. The results were various contingency theories of leadership. More recently the research question has been, How do leaders and followers enable each other to achieve their particular goals?

Although this field concentrates on employment settings, many of the concepts have implications for other types of organizations, such as churches. Topics such as leadership, conflict, change, motivation, and communication relate to most of the difficult human problems that develop within the church.

Additional Readings

Dunnette, M. D., Hough, L. M., & Triandis, H. (Eds.). (1994). *Handbook of industrial and organizational psychology* (Vol. 4). Palo Alto, CA: Consulting Psychologists Press.

Wilpert, B. (1995). Organizational behavior. *Annual Review of Psychology, 46,* 59–90.

G. L. Welton

See Applied Psychology; Human Resource Training and Development.

Inferiority Complex. The idea that every person feels inferior and that this complex underlies all human behavior forms the core of Alfred Adler's system of individual psychology. However, the idea of the inferiority complex did not begin or end with Adler. Similar concepts can be found in literary and philosophical sources: Montaigne, Shakespeare, Hobbes, Rousseau, Mandeville, Stendahl. Several authors, including the Swiss theologian Haberlin, have attempted to classify inferiority feelings.

Psychologists have speculated about the relationship between internal and external factors in the inferiority complex. William James spoke of an innate craving to be appreciated and attributed mental anguish to the feeling that one is insignificant or unworthy of appreciation. Pierre Janet spoke of an obsessional impulse of self-shame. Adler initially believed inferiority feeling to be due to myelodysplasia (organ inferiority) but later broadened the concept of inferiority to include social factors, especially interpersonal relations in early childhood. Sigmund Freud reduced the inferiority complex to the girl's penis envy and the boy's feeling of inadequate genitals after a comparison with his father. Carl Gustav Jung believed that inferiority feelings are especially characteristic in introverts and result in dissociation of the personality via repression and projection of everything dark and culpable (the shadow).

The empirical study of inferiority feelings has been hampered by problems with operational meaning. Several self-esteem scales exist, but both validity and reliability are questionable. Murray (1938), after using a comprehensive battery of tests to examine 50 normal, young male adults, concluded that 68% had suffered from inferiority feelings. Numerous factors have been correlated with low self-esteem: physical defects (handicaps, obesity, ugliness, stature, weakness, or poor coordination); parental factors (pampering, neglect, ridicule, contrasts with other children, favoritism); teasing; defeat or failure (academic, athletic, sexual, social); poverty; lack of group acceptance. The correlations are far from perfect because inferiority feeling is a negative emotional reaction, not an objective evaluation of a deficiency. The degree of inferiority feeling is heavily determined by subjective factors and standards of comparison. A man who earns $50,000 a year has a comfortable income but may feel inferior to an entrepreneurial sibling who has amassed a fortune. No one, as Eleanor Roosevelt said, makes us feel inferior without our consent.

Inferiority feelings may induce different kinds of behavior in different persons. One response (the true inferiority complex) is resignation, conscious acceptance of the inferior role, and the attempt to use it to gain sympathy and avoid responsibility. One alcoholic who had not worked for 25 years told everyone about his condition, blaming war injuries from the Korean conflict. Another reaction is to deprecate others, especially those persons who make us feel inferior. Employees who are passed over are quick to accuse the promoted co-worker of being a toady.

Another response is to attempt to overcome the factor responsible for the inferiority feeling, and in so doing many persons overcompensate and become superior. Glenn Cunningham, whose legs were badly burned as a child, ran in order to rehabilitate his limbs and became a champion distance runner. Theodore Roosevelt, a nearsighted and sickly child, learned boxing and horseback riding in order to toughen himself. Able-bodied motorists have an accident rate almost 20 times that of handicapped drivers. Ray (1957) contends that people do not succeed in spite of an inferiority complex but because of one. She gives many heartwarming and inspiring examples of how inferiority feelings spur people on to success through overcompensations. The treatment of an inferiority complex is generally best accomplished by the techniques of individual psychology, in which the emphasis is on encouraging compensation through useful contributions to others (social interest).

Inferiority feeling can be a useful tool in explaining many social phenomena. An advertisement states that sophisticated people use a certain product and then relies on the audience's inferiority feeling to generate sales. Various authors have contended that ethnic stereotypes have a kernel of truth and describe characteristic behaviors that developed in societies and subcultures as a response to inferiority feeling. The drive for wealth in the United States is an attempt to respond to a feeling of inferiority about Europe's culture. The Mexicans' machismo is a response to feeling inferior to Europe's culture and America's wealth (Ramos, 1962). Many strikes (especially the violent ones) are largely unnecessary for economic gains, yet they give workers a feeling of power to compensate for their normal feelings of inferiority with respect to management.

Inferiority feeling can be seen theologically as the result of pride and refusal to accept the status of creature. Humans are inferior to the Creator; but once humans accept that role and realize that all other humans are mere creatures they need feel inferior to no one else.

References

Murray, H. A. (1983). *Explorations in personality.* New York: Oxford University Press.

Ramos, S. (1962). *Profile of man and culture in Mexico.* Austin: University of Texas Press.

Ray, M. B. (1957). *The importance of feeling inferior.* New York: Harper & Row.

Additional Reading

Brachfeld, O. (1951). *Inferiority feelings.* New York: Grune & Stratton.

T. L. BRINK

See INDIVIDUAL PSYCHOLOGY.

Infertility Counseling. Infertility is a medical, psychological, and social experience that can cause psychological distress severe enough to warrant counseling. Despite the failure of researchers to establish infertility as a crisis, many professionals consider it to be a personal crisis based on a conflict between an ideal self as a mother or a father and the real person. Research can find no common emotional reaction.

Advances in medical technology have overcome infertility in some cases. In vitro fertilization counseling helps patients to cope with the anxiety and distress associated with this common medical treatment. The reaction to infertility of their spouse by

men is characterized by support and organization, while the woman experiences emotions of longing and distress. The counseling helps lower the anxiety of the treatment and improve communication between the spouses.

Psychological distress can be affected by the perceived view of the spouse's care, control, support, and disregard for the infertile partner. The degree to which the infertile patient expresses emotions can also affect the experience of distress. Infertility can be very stressful for the patient. While men and women alike suffer from distress, women are more likely to seek counseling. Men usually experience embarrassment, as opposed to women's guilt and depression. Coping mechanisms can become destructive, exhibiting self-blame and avoidance patterns. Counseling intervention for emotional problems seeks to reduce anxiety and depressive symptoms and change destructive coping patterns. Anger, guilt, grief, and depression are all emotions experienced with infertility.

Infertility can reverberate through social networks, going beyond the partner to family and friends. A loss of self-affirmation and affirmation in relationships with others can be a result of infertility. The reestablishment of empathic connections with self and others helps the patient to regain coping mechanisms and self-affirming processes. Increased psychosocial functioning utilizes self-help and support groups and team approaches with the spouse.

Treatment can be successful using varied approaches. The alleviation of psychological distress through professionally led support groups is shown to be successful by lower scores on distress and depression evaluation tests. Psychotherapy emphasizes the establishment of emphatic connections in therapy. Family therapists view the problem not as an individual one but as one faced by the couple.

The goal of counseling is to reinforce the infertility experience as an opportunity for personal and marital growth. Therapy helps clients to negotiate the grieving process, relinquish and accept control, heal relationships, reassess the motivation and desire for parenting, and make decisions regarding future parenting options.

C. R. STITES

Inhibited Orgasm. *See* ORGASMIC DISORDERS.

Inhibited Sexual Arousal. *See* SEXUAL AROUSAL DISORDERS.

Inhibited Sexual Desire. *See* SEXUAL DESIRE DISORDERS.

Inner Healing. The concept of healing refers to the restoration of health and elimination of illness. In recent years, the movement for emotional well-being has indeed flourished. It emphasized a balanced lifestyle and inner freedom. However, the concept of spiritual healing is as old as human nature. Throughout history, all religious traditions have practiced *prayer* for the liberation of mind, body, or soul. People who suffered from diseases fervently interceded with their gods and their religious leaders. Priests, elders, magicians, gurus, and spiritual healers conducted interventions, prayer rituals, and ceremonies on behalf of the sick and mentally ill, at many times, including the whole family, tribe, or community. The Old and New Testament Scriptures have emphasized strongly both personal sanity and public health. Christ was a remarkable healer and his ministry was extremely cleansing. One of the basic functions of the church today is to be a community of renewal, healing, and nurture.

Christian healing is based on the existential aspects of sickness, the psychological aspects of pathology, and the theological doctrine of sin. Redemptive healing was associated with the sacraments and liturgy of the early church. To the monastic and desert fathers, healing was central to the Christian faith. They perceived healing as the doorway to the true knowledge of God and the manifestation of the indwelling Christ in the believers. The incarnation of Christ has brought healing and reconciliation to the dichotomy of spirit and matter, mind and body, and sickness and health. Spiritual healing resulted in wellness, inner harmony, and restoration of the soul (cf. Brooke, 1991).

Within the Christian communities, *inner healing* is currently known as a new form of healing and a new approach to recovery. It is a therapeutic process where two or more people are involved and wherein God's Spirit is allowed to touch the root cause of disturbances, hurts, and agonies and to restore health in the deepest core of the person's being. At times, this process is very intense, highly experiential, and remarkably profound.

Inner healing is a method of prayer by which Christ is invited to address the hurts of the past and repair their damaging effects and negative results. Basically, it involves a twofold-procedure in which a) the power of darkness and evil is broken as the believer's heritage of wholeness is reclaimed, and b) the painful memories and unresolved issues from the past are healed through the therapeutic power of prayer.

Flynn and Gregg (1993) try to define what inner healing *is* by listing the following: It is release, correction, reframing of the past, exchange, process more than event, application of forgiveness, healing of memories, set of dynamics and procedures, and a means of grace (pp. 15–20). According to Flynn and Gregg, inner healing *is not* positive thinking, psychiatry, meditation, escapism, group therapy, grief work, 12-step recovery program, salvation, panacea, or New Age spirituality (pp. 20–21).

Forms of Healing. There are several leading figures in the "inner healing" movement. Among them are Anges Sanford, Francis McNutt (1974), Betty and Ed Tapscott (1975), and Ruth Carter Stapleton (1976).

McNutt (1974) considers inner healing as one of four types of healings which is directed primarily toward the healing of memories. McNutt believes there are three major forms of sickness: sickness of the spirit, caused by personal sin and transgressions; sickness of the emotions, caused by psychological hurts from the past; and sickness of the body, caused by diseases and physical accidents. Prayer of repentance seeks forgiveness for sin. Prayer of healing seeks restoration of bodily functions. Prayer of inner healing seeks alteration of the negative effects of painful memories. And finally, prayer of deliverance or exorcism seeks break from demonic oppression and release from possession.

Betty and Ed Tapscott (1975), agree with McNutt's model but do not include exorcism as one of the primary forms of healing. They suggest that "breaking the power of Satan" is the first step in any healing but they felt this is accomplished through spiritual healing, which means coming to know Jesus Christ as personal Savior. This involves confession of sin, renunciation of occult power, willingness to forgive, honesty, and humility. To them, spiritual healing is the foundation of inner healing and any other type of healings, like mental and physical restoration. The other side of breaking the power of Satan is reclaiming one's Christian inheritance by reaffirming what was true both in creation and in salvation. God wants people to be whole and has given them many spiritual riches if they only claim these blessings. The acts of renouncing evil and reaffirming faith in God's goodness become the basis for inner healing from harmful memories.

Of special interest is some inner healers' attitude toward secular healers (professional caregivers) such as physicians, counselors, and psychologists. After noting that millions of dollars are spent each year going to physicians and psychiatrists, one healing minister suggested that divine healing is ultimately the best. The old adage, "Doctors treat but Jesus heals," is offered as an unquestioned truth. Removing symptoms (which doctors do) is not the same as healing the cause (which Jesus does). One writer praised God for Christian psychologists but concluded that "inner healing is psychotherapy, plus God!" Another writer (Stapleton, 1976) put it thus, "Psychiatrists bring a degree of healing by probing into the past and bringing understanding of our weak and vulnerable spots and our angry and fearful reactions, but only the Holy Spirit can move into these areas and remove the scars" (p. x). Some of those who practice "inner healing" acknowledge the role of and try to coordinate the treatment with other professionals. Some others prefer to work alone believing that the prayer for the healing of memories is often the treatment of choice.

Techniques and Interventions. Focusing on the memories is the core of inner healing. Memories are the residues of earlier experiences. Almost anyone has memories from which he or she needs release, even if these are only minor hurts or child-like fears. Others have memories of being unwanted or neglected, or of unexpected accidents or evil deeds, sudden losses, crises, or traumas, or events that happened while they were still in their mothers' wombs. Breaking the power of oppressive memories is a prime factor of inner healing ministry.

This premise is the foundation and major diagnostic model for healing prayers that release persons from the tyranny of the past. It is presumed that the fears, guilts, lethargies, anxieties, and depressions which result from oppressive memories are against the will of God and, as such, are susceptible to being remedied by him if the person is open and willing. Of particular interest to inner healers has been the book, *Your Inner Child of the Past*, by Hugh Missildine (1963). They feel they have sound psychology, because many models of psychopathology put similar emphasis on early developmental experiences. Therefore, they see themselves as legitimate, yet they insist they are not (nor pretend to be) psychotherapists.

Although there are basic similarities in approach among those figures who practice inner healing, there are some distinctions and variations as well. The specific approaches of three prominent practitioners—the Tapscotts, Francis McNutt, and Ruth Carter Stapleton—will be examined here.

The Tapscotts. The Tapscotts feel that memories can be healed by the individual himself as well as by the ministrations of another who has the power of healing. They encourage the person to begin with a prayer for the forgiveness of sins and reaffirmation of Jesus as personal Savior. Next, they suggest the person ask the Holy Spirit to reveal all the forces of evil that have become part of his or her life and renounce them by faith. At this point, the person is to trust the Holy Spirit to bring to mind the images and memories that are emotionally crippling. Even though no release or healing is apparent up to that point, the person is to vocally renounce the power of these memories and images. Then visualizing Jesus walking hand in hand with him or her through every moment of that particular situation, redeeming the painful memories, protecting from harm, and repairing the damage. As the person begins to thank the Lord in advance for the healing and freedom, the Holy Spirit will lift up the unpleasant memories and fill the void with peace, contentment, joy, and love.

The Tapscotts provide written prayers for every stage of the process. They would like to believe that healing is a once-for-all event. However, they recognize the possibility that the release from such experiences might fade and some residuals may periodically surface later on. For that, they prescribed a set of activities to maintain the healing. They include daily prayers, Bible reading, conscious praise, regular commitment to God, standing firm against Satan, dedication of one's home to the Lord, becoming part of a spirit-filled fellowship, finding a prayer partner, and constantly forgiving others.

Francis McNutt. McNutt begins with the assumption that the basic need of life is for love; if we are ever denied love at any time in our lives, our ability to trust others may be seriously hindered. The wounds resulting from a loss of love fester and handicap us. Whenever people become aware of anxieties, fears, resentments, hates, or inhibitions, then it is time to seek inner healing. Christ first heals the injuries by draining the poison of past hurts, and second fills the empty space with love and tenderness.

Before the prayer of healing is offered, two questions are usually explored with the person. When did you first feel this way? And, what was happening at the time? If the person cannot remember the incident, then in prayer, God is asked to reveal it. After the time and place of the hurt has been identified, the prayer for healing is offered. In an as imaginative and childlike manner as possible, the minister prays that Christ will go back into those experiences and touch the open wounds. McNutt (1974) states, "Jesus, as Lord of time, is able to do what we cannot . . . The most I was ever able to do as a counselor was to help the person bring to the foreground of consciousness the things that were buried in the past, so that he could consciously cope with them in the present. Now I am discovering that the Lord can heal these wounds . . . and can bring the counseling process to its completion in a deep healing" (p. 187).

Because of the basic need for love, full healing cannot occur until the person is given what he or she has been missing, namely, love. To McNutt, this part of inner healing is often more difficult than the release of the unpleasant memories themselves. Since the person is so accustomed to being without love, he or she does not normally know how to receive it. Normally, the nature of wounds is known to the minister who earnestly prays to the Lord to provide the very specific kind of love the struggling person needs.

Ruth Carter Stapleton. Of note is Stapleton's emphasis on inner healing as a process, not a one-time event. Her accounts are replete with long-term relationships in which the person frequently returns to the healing minister. In only a few cases does she report immediate and final results. Furthermore, she stressed that inner healing is more than insights into traumatic events or even sound doctrines. She noticed that most people act as though they need help when, in fact, they really do not want to change.

Stapleton suggests that an "inner child" lives in most of us and has an insatiable need for approval and love. This inner child needs to be revealed and healed. Although she agrees with other inner healing practitioners that there are real past traumas and injuries, yet, in many cases, these are fantasized hurts grounded in the child within. Thus, she seems to have an implicit model of evil which must be faced or revealed in the healing process. Finally, she emphasizes group experiences of inner healing much more than did others. Group members often gave constructive feedback, gained insights, and role played each others' situations.

Stapleton uses the term *faith imagination therapy* to describe the healing process. She recommends that people visualize, as vividly as possible, Jesus coming into their past experiences and taking charge over the seriously troubled and disturbing situation. In this process of faith imagination, with Jesus at the center, deep healing inside the person occurs. She contends that forgiveness lies at the center of all healings and encourages people to use every opportunity to forgive and let go. As Jesus dominates the visualization, persons are guided to experience freedom and allow themselves to become whole again. The final step of this process, which may be prolonged, happens when the individual ceases to be too self-deprecatory or too proud and begins some kind of ministry service to others.

Comparison with Guided Imagery. The therapy technique most similar to the procedures of inner healing is guided imagery (Leuner, 1969). Stapleton, for example, is in accord with many therapists in asserting that faith imagination is a way of inducing positive changes deep within the mind. According to Leuner, guided imagery attempts to replace regressive and defensive patterns with more mature, healthy, and adaptive functioning. The core method in both approaches is that of *suggestion*. Several aspects of these procedures should be noted.

First, the role of the therapist or healing practitioner is definitely an active role. Although many inner healers listen long and empathize well, when they begin to intervene they become active. They are not client centered in their approach or presumptions. However, they act on a great deal of intuition and assertively lead the person in a fantasy toward healing. Although there are some similarities with hypnosis, neither of these two types of fantasies are hypnotic suggestions. Unlike hypnosis, the individual is encouraged to imagine the action and provide the basic details of the situation.

Second, both inner healing and guided imagery use archetypal personages in their fantasies. Guided imagery, as a psychotherapeutic technique, usually relies on Jungian conceptualization of psychic structure and dream analysis. For example, roads are life lines, mountains are ambitions or problems, crossroads are decision points, caves are suppressed memories or fears, witches are denied impulses, and old men are inner wisdoms. Inner healers confine themselves to two figures in the Trinity—the Holy Spirit and Jesus Christ. They encourage the individual to allow the Holy Spirit to reveal the incidents that provoked trauma and to allow "Jesus" to be present in the reliving and healing of those events.

Third, the person of "Jesus" is somewhat similar to the "old man" of guided imagery, yet with a radical difference. Guided imagery considers the old man as the source of inner wisdom which was

there all along but has been suppressed. Inner healing makes a different assumption. It relies heavily on reclaiming the inheritance of the image of God at the time of creation. It emphasizes the gift of salvation which has been made available through Christ's redemption on the cross. The living Jesus is not inner wisdom or denied power but a transcendent personal authority. He exists outside the struggling individual and brings insight and healing that were previously unavailable. What is needed is the presence of Christ who heals the hurtful memories and empowers the person to live anew, something the person could not do for himself or herself.

Fourth, there is a common presumption among inner healers and guided imagists that something more than insight is needed for the healing to begin. Both approaches are action oriented in the sense that they promote reexperiencing, reliving, or reenactment as the prime means of release and change. They resemble experiential and phenomenological therapies (like Gestalt therapy) although their presumptions of the dynamic processes are somewhat different.

General Evaluation. Trying to explain what inner healing is and what it is not, Flynn and Gregg (1993) indicated that inner healing, among other definitions or properties, is "a set of dynamics and procedures," yet "it is not psychiatry" (p. 20). Inner healing's approach clearly overlaps with psychiatric and psychological principles, interventions, and methodologies. Its practitioners use basic counseling skills, therapeutic techniques, psychological common sense, and spiritual discernment, yet they try to distance themselves from conventional counseling and psychotherapy similar to what some new spiritual movements distance themselves from "organized religion" and mainstream Christianity.

Most probably, inner healing could be considered as a counseling orientation and could be classified as a specialized treatment approach since it has many of the basic necessary elements (even in preliminary form) of a counseling modality (like conceptualization, theory, methodology, techniques, and interventions). Several critiques of inner healing have been written. For example, Alsdurf and Malony (1980) have analyzed the assumptions underlying especially the work of Stapleton. Although inner healers' work differs in many ways, Alsdurf-Malony's critique, in general, seems to apply to all of them.

Like Stapleton, many other healing practitioners denied the fact that they were engaged in a simplified psychotherapy. They claimed that their approach is not counseling or clinical in the sense of the word as used among mental health professionals. Yet, when one closely examines this approach, it becomes obvious that it is indeed a form of treatment. The structure, format, and frequency of sessions (for individuals and groups) and the dynamics of the counseling relationship, types of interventions, and experiential activities practiced all give evidence to that fact.

While Stapleton's basic presumption that "Jesus" can heal quickly and deeply allowed her to expect miracles, she used many standard psychotherapeutic methods without acknowledging them. Furthermore, she seemed naively free from the caution that most psychotherapists have in approaching some problems optimistically, while recognizing great inherent difficulties in others. Again, her too easy acceptance of one model (Missildine's) caused her to assume an almost photographic memory of the past while almost reifying a psychic structure (the inner child) that most theorists would find problematic.

Perhaps the basic problem is that while inner healing practitioners provided, at times, fairly intensive psychotherapies, they did not seem to acknowledge the manner in which professionals who observed human behaviors and studied psychopathologies are trying to help hurting and struggling people. To deny this reality is to remain free from self-criticism while evoking the discount of those who know better. This is not to say that the inner healers' basic belief in the authority and power of Jesus Christ needs to be subjected to psychological analysis by secular theorists. Rather, this tradition of healing could be much strengthened if the caregivers and healing ministers would be better informed about human nature, mental structure, personality function, and emotional stability and the many causes of psychological illness and health.

Another issue of importance, which may apply to some leading figures in the healing movement who prescribe to global spirituality, is their lack of a thorough doctrine of sin and salvation. It seems that they are willing to identify their approach, often too simplistically, with holistic healers who may be operating from Eastern philosophy and consciousness worldview. Thus, while using Christian terminology, they may be implicitly using other non-Christian assumptions and generic spirituality. Facing the power of evil and seeking God's redemption, grace, and sanctification is absolutely essential for any authentic healing in the core of the person's mind and being.

Inner healing can be considered as a unique form of treatment and a powerful type of healing. It is currently held with respect in many Christian circles. Therapists, counselors, physicians, psychologists, and other helping professionals should take this approach seriously. They ought to explore its great resources, learn from its major techniques, and try to incorporate some of its bold interventions into their counseling ministry and human and clinical services.

References

Alsdurf, J. M., & Malony, H. N. (1980). A critique of Ruth Carter Stapleton's ministry of "inner healing." *Journal of Psychology and Theology, 8,* 173–184.

Brooke, A. (1991). Christian healing in history. *Weavings: A journal of the Christian spiritual life, 6,* 6–19.

Flynn, M., & Gregg, D. (1993). *Inner healing: A handbook for helping yourself and others.* Downers Grove, IL: InterVarsity.

Leuner, H. (1969). Guided affective imagery. *American Journal of Psychotherapy, 23,* 4–22.

McNutt, F. (1974). *Healing.* Notre Dame, IN: Ave Maria.

Missildine, W. H. (1963). *Your inner child of the past.* New York: Simon & Schuster.

Stapleton, R. C. (1976). *The gift of inner healing.* Waco, TX: Word.

Tapscott, B., & Tapscott, E. (1975). *Inner healing through healing of memories.* Houston, TX: Tapscott.

Additional Readings

Alsdurf, J. M. (1989). Personality theory or spiritual discernment. *Journal of Psychology and Theology, 17,* 245–249.

Chirban, J. T. (1991). *Healing and spirituality.* Brookline, MA: Holy Cross Greek Orthodox School of Theology. *Journal of Psychology and Theology,* (1980), *8,* 185–210.

Kraft, C. H. (1994). *Deep wounds, deep healing: The vital link between spiritual warfare and inner healing.* Ann Harbor, MI: Vine.

McNutt, J. C. (1991). How I discovered inner healing. *Weavings: A journal of the Christian spiritual life, 6,* 20–27.

Sanford, J., & Sanford, P. (1982). *The transformation of the inner man.* Tulsa, OK: Victory.

Wagner, P. C. (1988). *How to have a healing ministry without making your church sick.* Ventura, CA: Regal.

Wimber, J. (1987). *Power healing.* San Francisco, CA: Harper & Row.

N. ABI-HASHEM AND H. N. MALONY

See IMAGERY, THERAPEUTIC USE OF; RELIGIOUS RESOURCES IN PSYCHOTHERAPY.

Insight in Learning. In the study of problem solving insight refers to the act of apprehending the principles involved in a task or the relationships involved in a puzzle. The result is a solution to the problem primarily arrived at by cognitive, as opposed to trial-and-error, means. Although this type of problem solving is usually associated with human beings, it was first systematically studied in apes by the Gestalt psychologist Wolfgang Köhler and reported in *The Mentality of Apes* in 1927.

In the most famous experiment Köhler's brightest ape, Sultan, was able to discover how to use objects like sticks and boxes to extend his reach and obtain food that was outside the cage or suspended above the cage floor. After he failed to reach the food by repeated efforts of stretching and jumping, the solution to the problem came to the ape following a period of exploration of the cage and a long pause in which the ape appeared to be thinking about the elements of his problem. Köhler's interpretation was that the ape did not solve the problem until he grasped it as a whole (or Gestalt) and considered using the objects in the cage as implements to extend his efforts.

When the ape solved the problem, his actions were immediate, purposeful, direct, and effective; he seized the implement and used it without hesitation to extend his reach by dragging food toward the cage with a stick or by climbing on a box to stretch high enough to reach food suspended from the ceiling. In contrast to trial-and-error learning, Köhler found, once the ape had solved the problem he could readily repeat the solution effectively. That is, where trial-and-error learning is gradual, insight seemed to be instantaneous. Further, the insight seemed to be transferable; that is, the ape was able to apply the same approach to solving new but similar problems.

Insight in human beings seems descriptively similar to Köhler's account in apes. The process by which insight occurs seems to be mental transformation of the setting and elements of a problem until the elements are set in a relationship to one another that permits the solution to be recognized. But while this general description is widely accepted, more detailed understanding of the factors that promote insight has not been forthcoming. This is because insight has not been an active topic of research since the 1960s in American psychology. Rather, the results of the earlier study of insight served to lessen the emphasis on repetitive forms of learning (e.g., rote memorization), which had been encouraged by the study of trial and error, and to assert the importance of understanding, especially in formal education. Insight is primarily a descriptive term, and the investigation of the ability to solve perceptual and linguistic problems has shifted to cognitive psychology.

L. S. SHAFFER

See LEARNING.

Insight in Psychotherapy. As applied to psychotherapy the term *insight* is found most frequently in the psychoanalytic literature. Within this context it can be defined as "a state of knowledge about one's own conscious and unconscious thoughts, feelings, or psychic processes that is the result of deeper genetic understanding of one's behavior and a constructively altered self-perception in which new facts about oneself are learned and some old facts are perceived more beneficially" (Paolino, 1981, p. 146). Insight also refers to the general extent to which the patient is aware that he or she is emotionally troubled, recognizes the nature and extent of the problem, and understands the special underlying factors that have helped to produce this psychological disturbance. Finally, insight refers to the patient's ability to observe himself or herself reflect retrospectively on feelings and experiences, and understand how the past interferes with present functioning.

Insight-oriented psychotherapy, such as psychoanalysis, emphasizes the central importance of insight in the overall therapeutic process. The main goal of insight-oriented psychotherapy is that the patient be helped to gain sufficient insight into the unconscious roots of his or her problems that changes in the dynamic structure of the personality will result. This becomes the main focus of the psychotherapy, with all the therapist's interpretations directed at increasing the patient's insight. It is generally believed that such insight alone will not cure underlying psychopathology unless it is applied by the patient. However, it is also generally felt that true insight inevitably results in profound changes in how patients regard themselves, followed by almost irresistible applications of this newfound understanding, resulting in personality change.

The use of insight is not limited to psychoanalytic psychotherapy. Many psychotherapists representing a wide variety of psychotherapeutic modalities seek to improve the level of insight of their patients. While they may not seek to alter unconscious dynamics and conflicts, they usually hope that a patient's insight into the underlying causes of psychological symptoms will result in conscious changes and willful decisions to think, feel, or behave differently in the future.

There are several means of determining patients' capacity for insight during the early stages of therapy. Patients are asked their reasons for seeking treatment, their thoughts concerning the causes of present symptoms, and their assessment of the possible patterns related to the difficulty. The more patients are able to reflect upon their thoughts, feelings, and behavior and demonstrate some understanding of possible underlying causes and related patterns, the more likely will be their capacity for insight. Where such ability for insight is demonstrated to be present, patients can be encouraged to examine their psychological functioning closely, both within and without the therapy session, to determine possible underlying causes. This helps patients to feel more in control of their behavior, and their thoughts and feelings become less mysterious and more easily understood. If patients demonstrate a marked lack of insight or even an inability for such insight to develop, it may be preferable for therapy to be conducted in a more directive and/or behavioral manner.

The use of insight has some important limitations. Perhaps most important is the point that insight alone is not always enough to produce desired change. In chronic behavior problems, character disorders, and addictive behaviors, a patient's insight may not be sufficient to bring about a cure. In such cases other therapeutic techniques, such as behavior modification, may be necessary to help patients apply insight and retrain automatic responses. Another limitation is that patients may have intellectualized rationalizations for their behavior that may be mistakenly regarded as true psychological insight. In such cases these intellectualizations hinder attempts at increasing true insight. Rather than resulting from true change-producing understanding, these rationalizations are more often excuses for behavior typically given to release the person from responsibility and confuse the therapist, thereby hindering attempts at confronting the patient's true problems.

When it is used properly, insight can be a powerful therapeutic tool for producing personality change in a patient capable of such self-understanding.

Reference

Paolino, T. J. (1981). *Psychoanalytic psychotherapy*. New York: Brunner/Mazel.

J. D. GUY, JR.

See PSYCHOANALYTIC PSYCHOTHERAPY; PSYCHOANALYSIS: TECHNIQUE.

Insomnia. *See* SLEEP DISORDERS.

Instinct. An unlearned, species-specific behavior that appears fully developed at a certain point in the growth of an organism. Some examples include nest building in birds, web spinning in spiders, and mating patterns in rats and other lower animals. Sigmund Freud used the term *instinct* in a different way to mean an inborn primitive force or drive such as hunger, thirst, or sex. He also described thanatos, the death instinct, and eros, the life instinct, as important factors behind human motivation.

William James expressed his belief in human instincts, but the psychologist most famous for espousal of the instinct concept in humans was William McDougall. He felt that human instincts are related to the emotions and saw fear, repulsion, curiosity, self-assertion, and gregariousness as examples of instincts. However, use of the term *instinct* nearly reached absurd levels early in the twentieth century with most types of behavior claimed as instinctively motivated.

The belief in human instincts by psychologists declined after this time because the work of the behaviorists left little doubt that human behavior is not primarily the result of instincts. The view of a human instinct as an innate, hereditary response not modifiable by environmental factors had to yield to the evidence in favor of learned behavior. By 1919 John B. Watson argued that one may safely disregard virtually all innate factors in accounting for individual differences in the behavior of adults.

The concept of instinct began again to influence American psychology in the 1960s through the field of ethology and its nominal founder, Lorenz. The strict definition of instinct, however, was dropped in favor of the concept of biological predisposition. Such a predisposition represents an inherited tendency toward a certain behavior. To psychologists this meant that no behavior would develop independently of the organism's hereditary predisposition. Research showed that species differed with regard to the range and kind of stimuli to which they were particularly sensitive and with regard to the range and kind of responses they were capable of making.

While the concept of instinct is not a major theme in psychology, psychologists do recognize inborn propensities without at the same time feeling obliged to accept the proposition that there is a class of behaviors completely directed by heredity and entirely immune to environmental factors.

M. P. COSGROVE

See DRIVE; MOTIVATION.

Instructional Psychology. A relatively new subfield of educational psychology, concerned with the application of learning theory to human problems. It considers clients in their roles as learners, and therefore intervention is viewed primarily as some form of teaching. It differs from educational psychology by its inquiry into the vast wealth and diversity of human interaction considered as teaching-learning processes. Its scope of contribution thereby lies well beyond the boundaries of schooling. Indeed, the broad range of therapeutic interaction may also be analyzed in terms of learning and teaching, which are thus a legitimate part of the domain of the instructional psychologist.

P. C. HILL

See EDUCATIONAL PSYCHOLOGY.

Insurance: Health and Mental Health. Insurance is a method to provide protection from financial loss. An insurance policy is "a private contractual arrangement allocating the burden of individual losses to members of a selected group who are exposed to similar losses" (Mehr & Cammack, 1976, p. 5). Insurance allows the sharing of risk among an insured population.

Insurance companies or insurers administrate contractual arrangements, and insurance agents market and sell the plans to consumers. Consumers of health insurance most often are employers who purchase a plan for use of their employees, although self-employed individuals can purchase coverage for themselves or their families. The cost of insurance is generally proportional to the probability and severity of loss. Premiums will elevate as the likelihood and severity of a loss increase.

As applied to health, insurance is a guard against financial loss due to accident or sickness (Mehr & Cammack, 1976). Thus disability, specific disease insurance (e.g., cancer insurance), hospitalization, and medical expense insurance are all forms of health insurance.

Patients and health professionals often think of health insurance as a means to finance optimal health. This notion does not fit the traditional concept of insurance. While the use of health insurance benefits may enhance health, the product is an arrangement to prevent financial loss due to illness or injury. This mismatch of perceptions is often at the root of controversy among health care providers, patients, and insurers.

A Brief History of Health Insurance. The growth and development of health insurance seems to correspond to the fragmentation of close-knit communities and families (Eilers, 1963; Faulkner, 1960). As Western societies became more industrialized, with increased hazards and potential for injuries, insurance allowed for the pooling of risks to protect families with increasingly loose ties to kinship systems. Changing economic and political conditions also spurred the development of health insurance.

Since approximately the thirteenth century, seamen in Scandinavian and British societies were provided coverage for sickness expenses. By the 1700s, Britain passed laws requiring sickness insurance for seamen and railway workers. These workers had great need for financial resources in the event of illness or injury.

In 1847, the first insurer to issue sickness insurance in the United States was the Massachusetts Health Insurance Company of Boston. Later that same year, the Franklin Health Assurance Company of Massachusetts was organized to provide accident insurance.

Due to the hazards of traveling in the mid-nineteenth century, the concept of accident insurance became popular. One of the first accident policies written by the Travelers Insurance Company of Hartford, Connecticut, in 1864 was to cover a man walking two blocks from his home to the Hartford post office (Mehr & Cammack, 1976). The policy cost two cents, and no benefits were paid since the individual covered the distance without peril.

The business of insurance grew in the early 1900s. In 1910 Montgomery Ward adopted the forerunner of the group health plan. However, the Depression was difficult for the insurance industry. Hard times led many policyholders to seek benefits for feigned illnesses (Mehr & Cammack, 1976). In response many insurers either eliminated or cut back on underwriting of new policies.

The Depression era also affected the development of the insurance industry in two ways that have ramifications for today's market. In 1929 the forerunner of Blue Cross/Blue Shield plans was developed. A group of Texas school teachers arranged for the Baylor University Hospital to provide hospitalization services for a monthly prepayment. This arrangement provided coverage for the subscriber and needed income for the hospital. Also in 1929, the Ross-Loos Clinic was established in Los Angeles as the first health maintenance organization (HMO). A decade later, the Kaiser-Permanente HMO was developed for Kaiser Aluminum construction workers (Dorken, 1983).

However, to offset this risk insurers began to restrict coverage to a hospital setting. Insurers came to believe that moral hazard (the insured exaggerating or faking a loss and profiting thereby) could be minimized by requiring a hospital setting since

"few would accept hospitalization unless it was necessary" (Hall, 1974, p. 1079). While Germany was the first Western country to legislate national health insurance in 1883, the Depression era brought many calls for national health insurance in the United States (Numbers, 1984). Many industrializing nations in Europe followed Germany's lead. However, in the U.S., the prospects of socialized health care spurred the rapid development of alternative systems of heath care delivery and financing. In 1937 the Health Service Plan Commission was established to oversee the new Blue Cross plans that were developing. The first Blue Shield plan was formed in 1939. Called the California Physician's Service, the plan was formed in part to oppose health insurance legislation (Eilers, 1963). The American Medical Association, although wary of prepayment plans, endorsed the plan as long as the doctor-patient relationship is not compromised. With AMA blessing, great expansion of Blue Cross/Blue Shield plans occurred after 1940.

The success of the Blues, along with emergence from the Great Depression and the advent of World War II, spurred phenomenal growth in the health insurance industry. Between 1946 and 1956, the total number of persons covered by insurance rose from 42 million to 116 million with 53 million being Blue Cross/Blue Shield subscribers (Eilers, 1963). Commercial insurers were eager to be in the market since Blue Cross/Blue Shield plans demonstrated that group health risks could be predicted and underwritten profitably. Also prompting premium growth during this era was the freeze on employees' wages during World War II. Unions and other employee groups found that collective bargaining to improve health benefits allowed an expansion of real earnings without raising wages (Baker & Dahl, 1945). This development helped to establish the association between employment and the possession of health insurance.

The period from the mid-1950s to the mid-1960s saw expansion of certain benefits, such as vision and prescriptions in certain plans (Health Insurance Association of America, 1995). In the 1960s, the expansion of the Great Society saw the federal government become a major force in the provision of health benefits. Social Security, first enacted in 1935, was expanded to include hospital insurance for disabled and elderly (Medicare) and indigent (Medicaid) persons.

In the 1970s, the Health Maintenance Organization Act gave support to the development of HMOs. The Nixon administration predicted that by 1980, 90% of the population would have access to an HMO (Fein, 1986). In 1974 the Employee Retirement Income Security Act (ERISA) was enacted with provisions that exempted certain employee benefits from taxation and regulation (Health Insurance Association of America, 1995). This statute generally is credited with supporting the trend into self-insurance.

The 1970s also saw another sustained debate over the enactment of national health insurance. Although the major outcome of this debate was a number of statutes refining the Medicaid and Medicare programs (Health Insurance Association of America, 1995), mental health professionals began positioning for inclusion in the coming system. For instance, psychologists debated the appropriateness of inclusion of mental health benefits in a national health care plan (Dorken, 1975).

Current Developments. Rising costs and change describe the present health care scene. Between 1986 and 1993, the costs of employer-purchased health care plans grew 3.5 times more rapidly than the rate of inflation. Spending for employee mental health care doubled between 1987 and 1992 (Yenney, 1994).

Insurers have responded to these rising costs by attempting to avoid state mandates requiring coverage of mental health services, limiting mental health benefits, decreasing yearly and lifetime caps on benefits, increasing coinsurance (costs paid by the subscriber), and limiting the choice of health care providers. More positively, insurers have also developed alternative means of delivering and financing health care. Since most individuals think of these methods as health insurance, we will consider them below.

Self-Insurance. Employers who assume responsibility for employees' health care instead of purchasing insurance are referred to as self-insured. Employers may choose to be completely at risk for all health claims, or they may opt to purchase stop-loss insurance (i.e., insurance against catastrophic claims that might be more than the employer can handle). Such coverage can be either for large claims generated by individual employees or significant health costs accrued by an entire group, often 125% of annual group health costs (Cowans, 1995a).

Employers often choose to self-fund to avoid taxes on health care premiums, to provide a consistent health benefits plan in multistate operations, and to avoid state mandates (Schachner, 1995). ERISA (PL 93–406) preempts state laws that relate to employee benefits plans, including health insurance. Employers who self-insure are not subject to state-mandated laws that require insurers to reimburse for mental health benefits or the services of certain providers.

Self-insured companies often use the services of third-party administrators (TPA). A TPA is a company that administrates the claims for self-insuring companies. Sometimes called administrative services only (ASO), this arrangement is often confusing to providers. Since insurance companies also provide the administration services, providers and clients often believe they are dealing with an indemnity insurance plan.

The market impact of self-insurance is significant. In 1994, 77% of employers with between 1,000 and 4,999 employees self-funded their health plans, while an estimated 84 to 89% of companies with more than 5,000 employees self-insured (Schachner, 1995). In 1994, 69% of companies with 500 to 999 workers self-funded, while only 18% of smaller companies (100 to 499 employees) did so (Cowans, 1995b).

Blue Cross/Blue Shield. Blue Cross and Blue Shield (BC/BS) are independent, nonprofit membership organizations providing health insurance by arranging for the care to be provided by participating providers within a specified geographic area (Health Insurance Association of America, 1995). Often called a hospital service association in state legislation, Blue Cross typically covers the hospital services with Blue Shield (medical service association) responsible for the services of health care practitioners. BC/BS plans sell only health coverage and are service arrangements whereby employers purchase access to a group of participating providers for their employees. Covered employees seeing nonparticipating providers will often face higher costs or denied claims.

Both BC/BS are trademarks controlled by the Blue Cross/Blue Shield Association (BCBSA) (Eilers, 1963). Each BC/BS plan is independent with the national organization providing research support and coordination of benefits and lobbying support services (G. Babcock, personal communication, March 1991). As of 1994, there were 69 BC/BS plans operating nationally (Woolsey, 1994). Enrollment in all private plans is an estimated 66 million lives with an additional 34 million enrolled in plans underwritten by the government (P. Kelch, personal communication, 8 March 1995).

Managed Care. Managed care is a term for a wide-ranging set of activities that are designed to provide oversight to the delivery of health services. Managed care has been described as a "system that integrates the financing and delivery of appropriate health care services to covered individuals" (Health Insurance Association of America, 1995, p. 19). A managed care organization (MCO) may provide some or all of the following elements: networks of selected providers to furnish a preselected group of health care services, explicit standards for the selection of health care providers, formal programs of quality assurance and utilization review, and financial incentives for clients to use the network of providers (Harden, 1994).

The spread of managed mental health care has been nothing short of breathtaking. According to Sipkoff and Oss (1995), 102 million people are enrolled in managed care plans, representing approximately 46% of the 222 million insured individuals in the U.S. Employers using a managed care arrangement for group health coverage jumped from 52% in 1993 to 63% in 1994. Employers attribute recent declines in per employee costs for health coverage (1.1% nationwide from 1993 to 1994) to this large shift of employers away from indemnity health insurance plans and into managed care plans (Geisel, 1995).

Insurance: Health and Mental Health

Health insurance is one means of sheltering the financial resources of individuals and families. Through an interaction of insurers, health and mental health professionals, and patients, a variety of methods to provide and pay for health care have been developed. Americans will continue to wrestle with finding means to provide comprehensive care at a cost that society can afford.

References

Baker, H., & Dahl, D. (1945). *Group health insurance and sickness benefit plans in collective bargaining.* Princeton, NJ: Princeton University Press.

Cowans, D. S. (1995a, February 6). An explanation of stop-loss insurance. *Business Insurance*, 19.

Cowans, D. S. (1995b, February 6). Insurers eager to stop loss of business. *Business Insurance*, 18–19.

Dorken, H. (1975). National health insurance: Prospect for profound change. *American Psychologist, 30,* 1156.

Dorken, H. (1983). Health insurance and third-party reimbursement. In B. D. Sales (Ed.), *Professional psychologists' handbook.* New York: Plenum.

Eilers, R. D. (1963). *Regulation of Blue Cross and Blue Shield plans.* Homewood, IL: Richard D. Irwin.

Faulkner, E. J. (1960). *Health insurance.* New York: McGraw-Hill.

Fein, R. (1986). *Medical care, medical costs: The search for a health insurance policy.* Cambridge, MA: Harvard University Press.

Geisel, J. (February 13, 1995). Health market changes spur 1% drop in costs. *Business Insurance*, 1, 10.

Hall, C. (1974). Financing mental health services through insurance. *The American Journal of Psychiatry, 131,* 1079–1088.

Harden, S. L. (1994). *What legislators need to know about managed care.* Denver, CO: National Conference of State Legislatures.

Health Insurance Association of America (1995). *Sourcebook of health insurance data: 1994.* Washington, DC: Author.

Mehr, R. I., & Cammack, E. (1976). *Principles of insurance* (6th ed.). Homewood, IL: Richard D. Irwin.

Numbers, A. (1984). *Compulsory health insurance.* New York: Basic Books.

Schachner, M. (1995, February 6). Self-insurers rally to defend favored benefit funding tool. *Business Insurance*, 3–4.

Sipkoff, M. Z., & Oss, M. E. (1995, January). I need to sign a managed care contract: Who are these people anyway? *Behavioral Health Practice Advisor*, 4–5.

Woolsey, C. (1994, August 15). Blues switching to managed care to be competitive. *Business Insurance*, 1, 25.

Yenney, S. (1994). *Business strategies for a caring profession: A practitioner's guidebook.* Washington, DC: American Psychological Association Practice Directorate.

E. W. Throckmorton

See Health Maintenance Organization; Managed Care.

Integration of Psychology and Christianity. *See* Christian Counseling and Psychotherapy; Christian Psychology.

Integrity Therapy. A moral approach to psychotherapy that places a critical emphasis on the interrelationship between mental health and behaviors concerned with honesty, responsibility, and involvement with others. Its fundamental principles were formulated by Mowrer, who is best known for behavioristic research on learning theory. He proposed that emotional disturbance is a symptom of concealed guilt, which in turn emerges from violations of the individual's conscience. In Mowrer's view a return to psychological well-being requires confession of one's moral failures to significant others and subsequent acts of restitution. This approach is distinguished from more orthodox deterministic therapies by its insistence on the individual's personal responsibility for his or her psychopathology.

Integrity therapy is an innovative synthesis of diverse clinical and philosophical traditions. Its principal roots include Harry Stack Sullivan's interpersonal psychiatry, the Judeo-Christian religions, and behavioral psychology.

Mowrer's core assumption is that "human personality is primarily a *social* phenomenon" (1972, p. 22). Since we are social creatures by nature, our moral and psychological integrity depends on community with other persons. Mowrer holds, as do the interpersonalists, that psychopathology and mental health are intimately related to the quality of one's relationships with others.

A second major root is found in the Judeo-Christian tradition. Mowrer finds in the early Christian church an excellent model of healing; in it he identifies precedents for the form, process, and goal of integrity therapy. In terms of form, Mowrer's group format is modeled after the intimate house churches of early Christianity. The therapeutic process involves Mowrer's accommodations of spiritual disciplines such as confession of sin and penance (restitution). As for the goal, group members are called to strive toward moral ideals compatible with the Judeo-Christian ethic.

Behavioral psychology makes up a third root of integrity therapy. Paraphrasing an E. Stanley Jones aphorism, Mowrer endorses the behavioral principle that "it is easier to *act* yourself into a new way of feeling than to *feel* yourself into a new way of acting" (Drakeford, 1967, p. 116). Mowrer's theory of neurosis, attributing emotional disturbance to specific transgressions of social norms, draws heavily from learning theory (London, 1964). His technique of cure (i.e., prescribing acts of restitution) clearly involves the learning and reinforcement of new behaviors, leading some to describe the integrity approach as an action therapy.

The integrity philosophy of neurosis and treatment may be contrasted with psychoanalytic theory. Freudians maintain that anxiety is partially a result of an overly strict conscience, termed the superego. Treatment is thus directed toward reforming the superego along less punitive lines. Mowrer, however, posits that anxiety reflects the moral dis-ease of an appropriately guilty conscience, driven by fear of community reprisal. From his perspective treatment must facilitate personal growth, such that the individual behaves more responsibly vis-à-vis the reality demands of conscience and society.

Mowrer further postulates that neurotics are alienated from others as a consequence of breaking societal rules. He insists that treatment must therefore facilitate the individual's return to community. This process occurs within the context of a subcommunity or therapy group. Such groups offer the added advantage of holding individuals responsible for their misbehavior and rewarding more mature life choices.

Integrity therapy specifies a clearly delineated technique of cure involving two primary client activities: confession and restitution. The former requires the client to accept personal responsibility for wrongdoing and is distinguished from complaining or blaming. Confession is directed toward the significant others who have been wronged.

The technique of restitution follows from Mowrer's contention that symptoms reflect the punishment of a guilty conscience. Integrity therapists insist that guilt must be resolved through restorative actions. This action principle includes giving up one's current misbehavior, rectifying past injustices, and serving others. Mowrer emphasizes that confession without restitution is cheap grace and is ineffective for dealing with real guilt.

In addition to confession and restitution Mowrer encourages emotional honesty. This involves activities such as verbalizing feelings or physically touching other group members. Such practices serve to facilitate emotional release and to promote greater interpersonal involvement.

Due to the scarcity of research on the results of integrity therapy, its benefits are difficult to assess. Practitioner observations suggest that integrity techniques are applicable to a wide variety of psychological problems, including marital conflict, anxiety, and depression. Three groups in particular, however, appear nonamenable to this approach: antisocial (psychopathic) personalities, paranoid personalities, and persons whose emotional difficulties are due to physical causes.

Apart from the issue of treatment efficacy, integrity therapy may be assessed in terms of its compatibility with biblical principles. Despite Mowrer's frequent use of religious terminology his approach to persons is clearly nontheistic. For example, words such as *sin, confession,* and *forgiveness* have no transcendent referent: these terms refer exclusively to the horizontal dimension—that is, what persons do to one another. Mowrer clarifies his humanistic emphasis: "Our assumption is that our first obligation is to be good human beings . . . and that in pursuing that end we cannot be displeasing whatever Higher Power or Divine Intelligence one may or may not believe to exist" (1972, p. 11). Although Mowrer rightly points out the individual's responsibilities to other persons, his perspective ignores biblical teachings that individuals are ultimately

responsible to God; moral failures involve transgressions of divine standards; and forgiveness comes from God through Christ.

Many concepts and principles of integrity therapy appear compatible with Christian thought: the importance of community (Heb. 10:25), confession (James 5:16), honesty (Exod. 20:16), and restitution (Lev. 5:16). Mowrer's emphasis on acting out moral behaviors is not inconsistent with the exhortation in James 2 that believers demonstrate faith through good actions. Integrity theory is also consonant with Christianity in advocating some crucial Judeo-Christian standards of right and wrong. Because of these areas of convergence, this approach may be accommodated to a biblically based therapy approach (cf. Drakeford, 1967).

References

Drakeford, J. W. (1967). *Integrity therapy.* Nashville: Broadman.

London, P. (1964). *The modes and morals of psychotherapy.* New York: Holt, Rinehart, & Winston.

Mowrer, O. H. (1972). Integrity groups: Principles and procedures. *The Counseling Psychologist, 3* (2), 7–33.

Additional Readings

Mowrer, O. H. (1961). *The crisis in psychiatry and religion.* Princeton, NJ: Van Nostrand.

Mowrer, O. H. (1964). *The new group therapy.* Princeton, NJ: Van Nostrand.

D. W. Brokaw

See Mowrer, Orval Hobart.

Intellectual Assessment. An important aspect of assessing individual differences is the evaluation of general cognitive ability or intellectual capacity, particularly for the purpose of predicting a child's potential for school achievement or an adult's capacity to respond to treatment.

Intellectual assessment is typically defined as the measurement of general ability by an Intelligence Quotient (IQ) and a series of cognitive abilities such as verbal and nonverbal reasoning, problem solving, spatial and visualization abilities, memory, and the speed of information processing. The definition and nature of intelligence should be the foundation for such a listing of cognitive abilities, but the exact nature of intelligence has been debated for decades. Because of this debate, the published test batteries designed to measure intellectual ability have varied in the types of abilities assessed. Hence it is widely recognized that comprehensive assessment should involve an array of information on each client, including background factors and direct observations (Kaufman, 1990) to supplement standardized test results.

For these reasons, one should not assume that intellectual ability is only the skills measured by an IQ test. For example, the widely used Wechsler intelligence tests each include more than 10 separate subtests measuring verbal, nonverbal, and memory aspects of intellectual functioning. In contrast, the Stanford-Binet Intelligence Scale (Thorndike, Hagen, & Sattler, 1986), includes more memory subtests and a different collection of verbal and nonverbal subtests. Batteries such as the various Kaufman scales (see Kaufman, 1994), the Differential Ability Scales (Elliott, 1990), or the Woodcock-Johnson Psychoeducational Battery (Woodcock & Johnson, 1989) include a wide array of both cognitive and achievement subtests. For a comprehensive listing of available measures and their contents, the reader is referred to the standard textbooks in intellectual assessment such as Sattler (1988), Kamphaus (1993), or Kaufman (1990), to name only three.

The IQ Score. Although IQ was originally developed as the ratio of mental age to chronological age, all reputable IQ measures used in the last several decades have been normative standard scores. The ideal IQ measure consists of a battery of highly reliable standardized tests that have been normed on a nationally representative sample. Sums of raw scores (or technically sums of subtest standard scores) are converted to normalized standard scores for each of several age groups, typically with a mean of 100 and a standard deviation of either 15 or 16. Thus the typical cutoff scores for evidence of gifted status are above 130 (two standard deviation above the national average for an age group), and cutoff scores evidencing cognitive delay are typically below 70 (two SD below the mean). Appropriate psychometric practice also includes the use of confidence intervals surrounding the IQ score to indicate to all consumers of test results that global scores are inherently error-prone and are an estimate of hypothetical true scores that exist within an interval of potential error.

Comprehensive Assessment. Matarazzo (1990) has made an important distinction between psychological measurement and comprehensive assessment. Psychological measurement is the systematic study of human responses for purposes of assigning scaled values or categorical descriptors to human attributes such as attitudes, traits, skills, and personality factors. Assessment, according to Matarazzo, is the total process of evaluation by a trained professional who considers a wide range of test and nontest data concerning a client for purposes of making a comprehensive description or diagnosis. Thus intellectual assessment should be intelligent enough (Kaufman, 1994) to include the flexible, hypothesis-generating functions of a detective whose aim is to uncover the reasons for the test results, not simply the numbers obtained from scoring the protocol.

Common examples of the importance of comprehensive assessment are the cases of non-English-speaking individuals who show poor verbal abilities on standard, English-language intellectual batteries. In interpreting results of standardized intelligence testing, the professional must take into account the language background but also the socioeconomic, educational, and medical background before making conclusions about the client's general cognitive capacity (Kaufman, 1994).

Nonverbal Assessment. A new generation of nonverbal intelligence measures have recently been developed to meet the needs of non-English-speaking, speech-impaired, and other individuals with sensory or motor disabilities. Nonverbal batteries include the Comprehensive Test of Nonverbal Intelligence (CTONI) (Hammill, Pearson, & Wiederholt, 1996), the modernized and restandardized Leiter-R (Roid & Miller, 1995), and the anticipated Universal Nonverbal Intelligence Test by Bracken and McCallum (in press). These collections of multiple subtests will provide more diagnostic profile information than currently provided by briefer tests such as the Test of Nonverbal Intelligence (TONI-2), the Ravens Progressive Matrices, the Matrix Analogies Test, or Cattell's Culture Fair Scales, which have been used as supplemental assessments for years. Nonverbal assessments of intellectual abilities can be particularly effective when they emphasize fluid reasoning (e.g., as measured by pictorial or geometric matrix analogies items), which research (Carroll, 1993) has shown to be highly correlated with global intellectual ability or "g." Although school achievement and employment success in North American culture certainly require verbal ability, the promise of nonverbal assessment is to provide an accurate estimate of global cognitive potential for individuals who are in a temporary life phase of non-English proficiency or reversible disability.

Assessment of Global Ability or "g." A frequently unspoken assumption in intellectual assessment is the goal of evaluating the global or general cognitive ability, labeled "g" in Charles Edward Spearman's pioneering research on intelligence. Although many theorists and researchers continue to disagree on the existence of a unitary "g" (*see* Intelligence), Carroll (1993) has convincingly demonstrated the existence of "g" among collections of cognitive tests. Carroll examined more than 460 intercorrelational studies of cognitive tests (e.g., correlations within and among most of the widely used intelligence batteries) and applied his own hierarchical factor analysis to these data. He identified a psychometric "g" factor in most instances, resulting in his proposal of a three-stratum theory of intelligence having "g" at the apex, several broad factors such as fluid and crystallized ability, visualization, memory, auditory perception, and processing speed at a second level, followed by more than 70 specific factors at the third level. Carroll's monumental study provides strong evidence for the existence of "g" that is often the focus of intellectual assessment efforts. Psychometric "g" was defined by Elliott (1990) as "the general ability of an individual to perform complex mental processing that involves conceptualization and the transformation of information." Thus the intention of users of full-scale IQ measures appears to be to assess global "g" by using total scores such as those obtained from the Weschler Intelligence Tests, the Stanford-Binet, the Kaufman K-ABC, the Woodcock-Johnson, Elliott's (1990) DAS, or numerous other summative scores from alternative intelligence tests or batteries. Kaufman (1990) has summarized the compelling evidence that global "g" predicts important societal criteria such as academic achievement, educational level, and occupational status.

Multiple-Ability Approaches. Alternatively, many clinicians prefer to examine a profile of cognitive test scores to supplement the evaluation of an overall "g" level. Some clinicians, researchers, and test developers, however, disagree completely with the concept of global "g" and, instead, examine only the profile of multiple cognitive skills, in the tradition of Louis Leon Thurstone's work on primary mental abilities, Guilford's structure-of-intellect, the Cattell-Horn fluid versus crystallized models as implemented in Woodcock and Johnson (1989), Sternberg's triarchic theory, the Das-Naglieri (in press) model of planning-attention sequential-simultaneous (PASS) processes, or Gardner's theory of multiple-intelligences (see Sattler, 1988, for references to these models). Two of the prominent multiple-factor models have not yet spawned standardized assessment devices (Sternberg and Gardner models). An eclectic position on multiple abilities can be taken by using an available test battery, such as the Wechsler Intelligence Tests, and interpreting verbal and performance factors and other composite indexes using profile analysis. Rigorous profile analysis involves the examination of statistically significant differences between scores (e.g., V-P differences) and the relative frequency with which such differences occur in the normative population. Most prominent test manuals provide statistical tables of the significance and frequency of subfactor differences to promote informed clinical profile analysis. Also, computerized scoring programs typically include such computations (see Kaufman, 1994).

Learning Potential Assessment. In recent years a model of intellectual assessment pioneered by Feuerstein (1979) has emerged as a controversial alternative to conventional assessment. The learning potential approach uses a test-teach-retest design to instruct low-functioning examinees in the cognitive strategies needed to solve problems that occur on intelligence tests (e.g., matrix reasoning tasks from the Raven's matrices). The theory of this dynamic approach is that cognitive skills are modifiable in different degrees with different clients, and the task of the examiner is to test the limits of learning potential for each client. Critics of the method point to the limitations of teaching to the test or coaching and the problems of reliability when evaluating difference (change) scores between test and retest. More controlled experimentation is needed to establish the scientific validity of the learning potential approach.

Future Trends. As the driving force behind the trend toward nonverbal assessment of intellectual functioning, the increasing multicultural nature of society will continue to demand improvements in assessment methods and improvements in examiners' sensitivity to background characteristics of examinees. The influence of cognitive psychology, as explained by Carroll (1993), calls for more fine-grained analysis of multiple elements and stages of cognitive processing. The microassessment of multiple cognitive processes is complex and time-consuming and requires extensive training in cognitive theory, making a detailed approach unwieldy and impractical for many practicing clinicians. More research, development, and, perhaps, sophisticated computerization will be needed to achieve new levels of specificity in intellectual assessment.

References

Bracken, B. A., & McCallum, R. S. (in press). *Universal nonverbal intelligence test.* Chicago: Riverside.

Carroll, J. B. (1993). *Human cognitive abilities.* New York: Cambridge.

Das, J. P., & Naglieri, J. A. (in press). *Das-Naglieri cognitive assessment system.* Chicago: Riverside.

Elliott, C. D. (1990). *Differential ability scales handbook.* San Antonio, TX: Psychological Corporation.

Feuerstein, R. (1979). *The dynamic assessment of retarded performers: The learning potential assessment device.* Baltimore: University Park.

Hammill, D. D., Pearson, N. A., & Wiederholt, J. L. (1996). *Comprehensive test of nonverbal intelligence.* Austin, TX: Pro-Ed.

Kamphaus, R. (1993). *Clinical assessment of children's intelligence.* Boston: Allyn & Bacon.

Kaufman, A. S. (1990). *Assessing adolescent and adult intelligence.* Boston: Allyn & Bacon.

Kaufman, A. S. (1994). *Intelligent testing with the WISC-III.* New York: Wiley.

Matarazzo, J. D. (1990). Psychological assessment versus psychological testing. *American Psychologist, 45,* 999–1017.

Roid, G. H., & Miller, L. J. (1995). *Leiter International Performance Scale—Revised (Standardization Ed.).* Chicago: Stoelting.

Sattler, J. (1988). *Assessment of children* (3rd ed.), San Diego, CA: Author. (Supplement on WISC-III and WPPSI-R, 1992)

Thorndike, R. M., Hagen, E. P., & Sattler, J. M. (1986). *Technical manual for the Stanford-Binet Intelligence Scale—Fourth Edition.* Chicago: Riverside.

Woodcock, R. W., & Johnson, M. B. (1989). *Woodcock-Johnson tests of cognitive ability.* Chicago: Riverside.

G. H. Roid

See Psychological Measurement.

Intellectualization. A defense mechanism whereby the ego attempts to achieve insulation from emotional pain or undesirable impulses through blocking or distorting the emotions normally associated with some thought or event. Also known as brooding, this process involves escaping one's emotions through a focus on intellectual concepts, abstract and insignificant details, or rational explanation devoid of personal significance. This may be seen in the example of the person who, having suffered a major career setback, discusses with apparent detachment all the ways the debacle could have been more devastating. This defense mechanism is closely related to both emotional insulation and rationalization and is common in obsessive-compulsive disorder.

R. LARKIN

See DEFENSE MECHANISMS.

Intelligence. Intelligence is a frequently used concept whose connotations include problem-solving ability, test-taking skill, environmental adaptation, academic success, and mental quickness. Despite this widespread everyday familiarity with the word *intelligence*, psychologists generally concede that one of the most difficult tasks in dealing with the subject of intelligence is providing an acceptable definition.

Definitions and Theories. Spearman (1927) proposed an understanding of intelligence that included a general factor ("g") and factors specific to various tasks ("s"). Since the theoretical entity which is symbolized by "g" reflects an individual's overall mental ability, a score on a test measuring "g" reflects that individual's core of intelligence. The "s" factors reflect specific abilities that are revealed on tests requiring a diverse range of intelligence capacities (e.g., vocabulary, mathematical skills, reasoning). Comparison of individuals will show diversity in overall ability "g" and an even larger set of differences for a varied smorgasbord of specific abilities "s."

Alfred Binet, generally credited with being a founding father of modern intelligence testing, proposed a definition that focused on problem solving and adaptability. He believed that reasoning and comprehension, when combined with initiative, common sense, and adaptation to circumstances, are the marks of an individual with high intelligence. Binet's view reflects the concept of generalized intelligence and his intelligence tests were a smorgasbord of items requiring a diversity of mental abilities. The performance on such a varied test was believed to reflect an individual's overall level of intelligence. Binet's most famous measurement efforts were those commissioned by the Paris school system. The expressed purpose of the testing program was to identify students who were not likely to benefit from a regular classroom experience.

The primary place given to "g" by Charles Edward Spearman and Binet was subsequently challenged by a number of well-known psychologists. Thurstone (1938), building on complex statistical analysis of numerous test results, believed intelligence is best expressed as a function of primary mental abilities such as verbal comprehension, inductive reasoning, perceptual speed, number facility, spatial relations, memory, and verbal fluency. Careful analysis of much data, however, led Leon Louis Thurstone to acknowledge that his primary abilities were not statistically independent. As a result Thurstone recognized that "g" is a necessary component of an understanding of intelligence, but he continued to believe that a more complete understanding of the structure of intelligence comes with the inclusion of a primary abilities perspective.

More recently Guilford (1967) has proposed an even more extensive multidimensional view. Guilford proposed a "structure-of-intellect" model involving five types of mental operations (cognition, memory, divergent thinking, convergent thinking, evaluation), four content categories (verbal, figural, symbolic, behavioral), and six products (units, classes, relations, systems, transformations, implications). The combination of these components yields a total of 120 distinct intellectual abilities. Guilford argues that the 120 factors are not correlated (a fact many critics dispute) and this statistical independence conflicts with a definition of intelligence that focuses on "g."

In the tradition of Thurstone and Guilford, Gardner (1983) has formulated a theory of multiple intelligences. According to this theory, an intelligence includes not only the capacities needed to solve real problems, but also the ability to create appropriate questions as a method of knowledge acquisition. Gardner outlines eight specific criteria that an intelligence must meet. These include a core operation, the existence of individuals who are exceptional in one way or another, support from experimental psychology, and evidence based on psychometric research. Gardner identifies seven intelligences that meet his criteria: linguistic, musical, logical-mathematical, spatial, body-kinesthetic, interpersonal, and intrapersonal. Each individual has a unique profile reflecting his or her degree of ability and competence in these areas.

Sternberg (1988), in a complex theory he refers to as triarchic, argues that intelligence is most directly linked to an individual's ability to shape and adapt to the environments of everyday life. The theory itself is comprised of three parts. First, a part that links intelligence to the internal states of the individual. Second, a component that is experiential and connects intelligence to both internal states and external context. Third, a part that relates intelligence to the external environment. These three components of the theory are interactive and are under the direction of a set of executive metacomponents that guide knowledge acquisition and relevant performances. Sternberg's emphasis on the close links between intelligence and living have led to increased emphasis on how individuals use intelligence and its benefits and to less emphasis on how much measured intelligence capacity one might possess.

Measurement. Disputes concerning definitions and theories as well as practical and applied concerns led psychologists to a desire for empirical data. For nearly a century the intelligence test has served as the research tool that generates both numbers and controversy. The best known of these tests are the Stanford-Binet (a modification of the Binet test by Stanford University psychologist Lewis Terman), the Wechsler Intelligence Scale for Children (WISC), and the Wechsler Adult Intelligence Scale (WAIS) (both named after a prominent intelligence theorist and measurement expert).

These intelligence tests and a large number of lesser known tests employ a wide variety of verbal and nonverbal tasks (most of which are timed) that rigorous test construction has shown to measure the intelligence construct. Among the tasks may be recall of common facts, mental rotation of complex figures, reasoning from facts to a conclusion, arrangement of blocks or parts of an object, matching of objects and their characteristics, numerical computations, vocabulary tests, and picture completions. This diversity reflects the lack of agreement on a common definition of intelligence as was discussed.

Intelligence tests have fulfilled their intended purpose. They have provided enormous quantities of data. However, this large amount of data has not only failed to resolve issues of definition and theory but it has fueled sometimes bitter disagreements concerning the origins of intelligence and group differences in intelligence.

Origins of Intelligence. All psychologists agree that intelligence is a product of a genetic heritage (nature) and a developmental environment (nurture). However, there is spirited disagreement over how much nature and how much nurture contributes to an individual's adult level of intelligence. Some psychologists believe that intelligence is largely inherited, while others believe that social and psychological factors are much more important than chemistry and biology in determining intelligence.

Identical twins, both those raised together and those separated at birth and reared apart, have provided crucial data for partisans in the origins debated. Since identical twins are genetically alike, any differences in their measured intelligence must be due to environmental factors. If identical twins reared in varied environments show similar levels of intelligence, that similarity must be due to genetic factors. Numerous and varied twin studies have led psychologists such as Burt and Jensen to make a case for a large (70% or more) effect of heredity on intelligence (Jensen, 1969, 1980).

Although their data are tantalizing and persuasive, those researchers who believe that intelligence is largely a product of genetics have encountered considerable resistance from psychologists who favor environmental variables (Fraser, 1995; Kamin, 1974; Scarr & Carter-Saltzman, 1982). Those who favor the nurture position believe that uncontrolled environ-

mental variables undermine hereditarian arguments based on twin data. Some environmentalists also feel that the nature position has been weakened by the actions of a British psychologist. Burt, one of the pioneers and primary proponents of the genetic view, has been the target of numerous accusations of scientific misconduct and fraud (Dorfman, 1978; Hearnshaw, 1979; Kamin, 1974, but see also Fletcher, 1991; Joynson, 1989). It now seems clear that Burt made a number of errors in judgment concerning the publication of his twin studies, and as a result the hereditarian position has been tarnished by the whiff of scandal. Regardless, to date no definitive answer is available on the origins of intelligence question.

Issues of Race and Culture. The differences among psychologists concerning definitions and origins of intelligence lead directly to the debate over the meaning and implications of group differences in measured intelligence. If those who argue that intelligence is largely inherited are correct, racial differences reflect genetic advantages or deficits about which little can be done. If those who espouse social and developmental factors as the basis for the development of intelligence are correct, group differences reflect significantly dissimilar social environments. If so, alteration of crucial social factors could result in an increase in measured mental ability.

Kamin (1974) has provided an intriguing, if controversial (Fletcher, 1991; Joynson, 1989), account of the trail of racism, ethnocentrism, and bigotry that have troubled the history of intelligence theory and testing. He notes that Henry Goddard used the Binet test when evaluating immigrants at Ellis Island in New York harbor and reported that more than 83% of Jews and Russians and about 80% of Hungarians and Italians were "feeble-minded" (Kamin, 1974). Kamin also cites Lewis Terman, the Stanford University psychologist who Americanized the intelligence test, as writing that borderline intelligence is commonly found among those of Spanish-Indian, Mexican, and African ancestry.

The evidence linking ethnic groups with low intelligence, coupled with the assumption that low intelligence predicts a life of marginal productivity, led to many controversial positions (Herrnstein & Murray, 1994). Some, like Terman, argued that the "feeble-minded" not be allowed to reproduce, while others advocated laws restricting immigration from countries believed populated by those of low intelligence (although this latter issue is controversial, see Kamin, 1974; Samuelson, 1975; Snyderman & Herrnstein, 1983). Still others, such as Jensen (1969), argue that there is little we can do to childhood environments to boost intelligence and achievement; thus programs such as Head Start are futile.

As might be expected, the fact that intelligence test data have shown significant mean differences between members of various racial groups has led to passionate charges and countercharges. Those arguing for the validity of the data feel they are doing what science should do (Herrnstein & Murray, 1994): pursuing significant issues whatever the consequences. Others scholars argue that data on group differences are at best of little value and at worst constitute a cover for ethnocentrism and racism.

Issues of Gender. The available research supports the conclusion that the measured differences between men and women are quite small (Jensen, 1980; Maccoby & Jacklin, 1974). The more contentious issue is whether one or the other gender excels at particular types of intelligent activity. The most vigorously debated issue has been the gender difference in spatial and mathematical ability. In their early comprehensive review, Maccoby and Jacklin (1974) found males to be better than females at both visual-spatial and mathematical abilities. Recent work by Benbow and her associates (Benbow, 1988; Lubinski & Benbow, 1992) seems to confirm this male/female difference, especially at the high end of the ability curve.

Other recent reviews and critiques downplay the magnitude of the gender difference for math and spatial ability for a variety of reasons. For example, Sharps, Welton, and Price (1993) report that the format of the instructions affects performance, with the difference between males and females becoming very small when nonspatial instructions are given. A recent comprehensive review of 100 studies (Hyde, Fennema, & Lamon, 1990) concluded that the magnitude of the male/female difference in mathematics performance is quite "small."

A second debated cognitive difference is the commonly accepted female advantage in verbal intelligence. Maccoby and Jacklin (1974) found that females are superior to males in verbal ability, although the difference is only about one-quarter of a standard deviation. However, recent work downplays even this small male/female difference. After a meticulous review of 165 studies, Hyde and Linn (1988) conclude that the hypothesized male/female differences in verbal ability "no longer exist."

The Christian and Intelligence. The Bible does not provide much guidance in helping Christian psychologists define intelligence, formulate a comprehensive theory of intelligence, or debate the genetics versus environment issue as it pertains to the source of intelligence. There are, however, a number of intelligence issues with direct links to Christian principles.

It must be acknowledged that there is much that seems unfair about intelligence. Why should some people be intellectually impaired while others are gifted and bear the label genius? The reason for such differences may be of importance to scientists but should have no effect on the value we attribute to people. One principle seems especially important to Christians. The worth or value of a human individual is not correlated with his or her score on an intelligence test. Indeed, Christians should likely be particularly sensitive to the inclusion and affirmation of those at the lower end of the intelligence distribution.

As North American society moves into a more technological phase, intelligence seems increasingly predictive of professional, economic, and social success (Herrnstein & Murray, 1994). The intelligence test may thus be construed as measuring an important human variable. Intelligence test scores can be used to place and track, guiding individuals to their appropriate social and professional position. While Christians affirm the importance of identifying and using individual gifts (1 Cor. 12), they may wish to join with those who question the place of importance given to intelligence tests.

The study of intelligence has confirmed that there are individual and group differences among the human family in measured intelligence. However, any use of intelligence theory or testing that reinforces ethnocentric or racist ideology must surely be opposed by Christians. Rather, believers must find ways to rejoice in the diversity designed by the Creator, including the diversity of intellectual gifts.

References

Benbow, C. (1988). Sex differences in mathematical reasoning ability in intellectually talented pre-adolescents: Their nature, effects, and possible causes. *Behavioral and Brain Sciences, 11,* 169–183, 217–232.

Dorfman, D. (1978). The Cyril Burt question: New findings. *Science, 201,* 1177–1186.

Fletcher, R. (1991). *Science, ideology, and the media*: The Cyril Burt scandal. New Brunswick, NJ: Transaction.

Fraser, S. (Ed.). (1995). *The bell curve wars.* New York: Basic.

Gardner, H. (1983). *Frames of mind*: The theory of multiple intelligences. New York: Basic.

Guilford, J. (1967). *The nature of human intelligence.* New York: McGraw-Hill.

Hearnshaw, L. (1979). *Cyril Burt, psychologist.* Ithaca, NY: Cornell University Press.

Herrnstein, R. J., & Murray, C. A. (1994). *The bell curve*: Intelligence and class structure in life. New York: Free Press.

Hyde, J., Fennema, E., & Lamon, S. (1990). Gender differences in mathematics performance: A meta-analysis. *Psychological Bulletin, 107,* 139–155.

Hyde, J., & Linn, M. (1988). Gender differences in verbal ability: A meta-analysis. *Psychological Bulletin, 104,* 53–69.

Jensen, A. (1969). How much can we boost I.Q. and scholastic achievement? *Harvard Educational Review, 39,* 1–123.

Jensen, A. (1980). *Bias in mental testing.* New York: Free Press.

Joynson, R. (1989). *The Burt affair.* London: Routledge.

Kamin, L. (1974). *The science and politics of IQ.* New York: Wiley.

Lubinski, D., & Benbow, C. (1992). Gender differences in abilities and preferences among the gifted: Implications for the math-science pipeline. *Current Directions in Psychological Science, 1,* 61–66.

Maccoby, E., & Jacklin, C. (1974). *The psychology of sex differences.* Stanford, CA: Stanford University Press.

Samuelson, F. (1975). On the science and politics of IQ. *Social Research, 42,* 467–488.

Scarr, S., & Carter-Saltzman, L. (1982). Genetics and intelligence. In R. Sternberg (Ed.), *Handbook of human intelligence*. Cambridge: Cambridge University Press.

Sharps, M., Welton, A., & Price, J. (1993). Gender and task in the determination of spatial cognitive performance. *Psychology of Women Quarterly, 17*, 71–83.

Snyderman, M., & Herrnstein, R. J. (1983). Intelligence tests and the immigration act of 1924. *American Psychologist, 38*, 986–995.

Spearman, C. (1927). *The abilities of man*. New York: Macmillan.

Sternberg, R. (1988). *The triarchic mind*: A new theory of human intelligence. New York: Viking.

Thurstone, L. (1938). Primary mental abilities. *Psychometric Monographs*, No. 1. Chicago: University of Chicago Press.

D. KAUFFMANN

See INTELLECTUAL ASSESSMENT; INTELLIGENCE QUOTIENT.

Intelligence, Artificial. Artificial intelligence (AI) is a subdiscipline in the cognitive sciences with two major concerns: understanding the human mind as a computational and information-processing system and engineering artificial systems capable of exhibiting intelligent behavior. Research in one area ultimately influences the other. Some researchers in the field of AI take the view that machines will be intelligent not just when they act intelligently but when the processing underlying their actions is functionally equivalent to that of humans. Others assert that human information processing is but one means by which a system might display intelligent behavior. The results, they argue, not the manner in which processing occurs, is important.

Research in AI has had both practical and theoretical orientations. These include building machines that recognize human faces for security purposes or navigate ocean floors to repair undersea cables. At the same time researchers have used what we know about human intelligence to build more intelligent systems and then employed them as models to theorize about human information processing. The underlying assumption in both cases is that intelligent action is constructed from computational processes that can be modeled in a formal manner.

History. The history of AI can be traced back to Hobbes, who claimed that "reasoning is but reckoning," and Rene Descartes, who taught that the human body apart from the soul (mind) is a mechanism. Although Descartes would have objected, materialists after him sought to bring the mind too into a deterministic and mechanistic framework. The next steps were supplied by the associationism of the British empiricists (*see* Empiricism) and by Leibnitz's proposal for a universal precise symbolic system that could be used to express all truths and their relationships. In the early 1800s George Boole employed a binary system of mathematics to express elementary logical functions such as "OR" and "AND" that could then be used to combine and manipulate propositions. Charles Babbage used these ideas in the 1820s and 1830s to design a "difference engine," which was never completed, and an "analytic engine," which was never built during Babbage's lifetime, to perform logical and mathematical operations (Dreyfuss, 1979). The first electronic computers were built in Germany, the United Kingdom, and the United States around 1940. The most famous of the early computers, ENIAC, was constructed in 1946.

At a 1956 conference attended by scientists including Allen Newell, John McCarthy, Marvin Minsky, Oliver Selfridge, and Herbert Simon, the term *artificial intelligence* was coined. Early work by Frank Rosenblatt in 1959 attempted to simulate limited aspects of the brain's neural networks using perceptrons. Technical problems stalled these efforts, and the publication of an article titled "Perceptrons" by Minsky and Papert in 1969 effectively killed research in this area; coincidentally, in the same year movie audiences were introduced to Hal in Stanley Kubrick's *2001: A Space Odyssey*. The 1980s and 1990s have witnessed renewed interest in neural networks, especially following the work of John Hopfield.

Newell, Simon, and Shaw developed their "logical theorist" around 1960 in which knowledge was expressed as rules and relationships among rules instead of numbers and logical operators. The 1950s and 1960s also saw computer programs that could play checkers at the championship level, prove geometry theorems, solve analogy problems, and develop a winning strategy for playing poker. Later programs were developed for interpreting simple visual scenes, recognizing human speech and handwriting and, by the 1990s, playing chess at the grand master level. The Japanese Fifth Generation Project for developing intelligent computers was announced with fanfare in 1981 and ended in 1992.

One development with possible long-term impact has been knowledge-based expert systems. The first such system, Dendral, written in 1967, predicted the structures of unknown chemical compounds. Mycin, a later development, uses rules to deduce disease diagnoses from a list of symptoms. The major challenge to developing expert systems is determining how to represent knowledge in a computer. Similar questions have intrigued cognitive neuropsychologists concerning human knowledge acquisition and storage. The dominant model proposes that declarative knowledge (facts and logical rules) can be represented separately from procedural knowledge (decision-making algorithms). However, some researchers believe that human intelligence works quite differently from current expert systems instantiations. Knowledge, they say, results from millions of genetically and experientially programmed details enabling us to anticipate specific challenges and deal with them effectively. With such a hypothesis in mind, Doug Lenat began the CYC (from enCYClopedia) project in 1984. Tens of millions of common-sense facts, along with 20 to 40 million rules, are being programmed into a system that, according to Lenat, will understand and speak ordinary language and detect violations of common sense.

A generally accepted model of AI assumes that truly intelligent artificial systems will be able to receive input, determine appropriate actions, and respond. Many researchers assumed that the second of these processes, the decision-making stage, would be the most difficult to implement and so most research efforts were directed there. It may be, however, that we overestimated the complexities and importance of the second stage while underestimating the difficulties of speech comprehension and generation, vision, and motor activity control. We know that input and output cannot be easily separated from the interpretive, reasoning, and planning processes. Human vision, for example, does not work like a video recorder, storing up images of the external world. Perception is an active process in which there is constant interplay between the data in the visual field and interpretations of that data based on past experience, expectations, intentions, and more. Breaking a visual scene down into its constituent lines, angles, and shadows, as most early computer vision mechanisms did, is not seeing. Similar arguments could be made for speech perception and on the output side for speech production and motor activity. This is not to say that such processes are beyond the grasp of machines. However, it points out the complexity of input/output processes and argues that they cannot be easily segmented from mental processing.

Computers as Thinking Machines. Many people have two key questions concerning AI. Can machines think, and can a machine be conscious? To understand how a computer can be viewed as a thinking machine it is essential to understand the notion of a formal system. A formal system is a type of game in which particular tokens can be changed from one position or state to another according to a system of rules. The rules specify what positions tokens can and cannot be in and how they can or must change. In the game of checkers, for example, red pieces can be placed on only squares of one color; black go on the other color. There are specific starting positions for the pieces, and the game progresses as the players take turns making only legitimate moves.

Logic and mathematics are also formal systems, but in them we often attach meaning to the numbers, symbols, and logical connectives. A digital computer can be thought of as an automated formal system, in this case a system that plays the game by itself (Haugeland, 1981). The game the computer plays is a binary form of mathematics, physically realized in the machine by electrical circuits in either the on or off position. Using Boole's logical algebra, the game can be played with propositions (i.e., all dogs are animals) as tokens. The digital computer has been called a uni-

versal machine, since it can be used to mimic any formal game (Turing, 1950). Critics of AI argue that computers will never be as intelligent as humans because computers cannot perform a specific set of activities, such as play chess or plan financial investments. AI proponents accept such challenges and seek to translate these activities into a formal set of rules that can be implemented on the computer. Past successes have led some to the hope that computers are capable of any intelligent activity. Dreyfuss (1979) disagrees, arguing that most significant human activity is made possible by a "tacit understanding" that is possessed in a bodily, visceral manner. Human understanding is contextual and holistic and cannot be stated in a finite set of formal rules.

One problem in deciding whether machines can think has to do with our definition of thinking. For too long we have equated thinking with mental processes that are rational and logical. When those processes fail to meet such criteria we say they are influenced by feelings. However, a strong neuropsychological argument can be made against straining emotions out of thinking processes (see Damasio, 1994). Intuitively we question the normalcy of psychopaths who rationally understand their actions yet fail to experience any emotional involvement. We must be careful about attributing thinking to a machine because it is able to reason inductively and deductively. Programming logical reasoning may be the easy part of building a truly thinking machine.

Computers as Conscious Systems. Questions about machine consciousness have sometimes been clouded by how high or low we rate their thinking capacity. We may assume that more complex rational processing implies a greater likelihood of consciousness. Perhaps this follows from the fact that we judge other people to be conscious from what they say and do. When machines appear to behave similarly we make similar attributions. But if consciousness means awareness or even self-awareness then it is possible to have a thinking machine that is not conscious.

Several avenues might provide for consciousness in machines. First, it may be possible to formalize what we mean by consciousness. Having done so, one would proceed to program consciousness as one does other processes. Second, consciousness might be endowed with the addition of analogue components to a digital system that instead of the digital either-or fashion would respond in a continuous manner to physical qualities. It remains to be shown how such an approach would capture what we call emotions. Finally, it might be argued that consciousness is not something one puts into a computer but what emerges from the interactions of components that have reached a critical mass of complexity.

It has been argued that, even if the emergent properties model is correct, machines will never reach the necessary level of complexity. Another criticism states that although it might act conscious, a digital computer can never be so because the formal system by which it operates has meaning only because we, the human users, endow it with such (Haugeland, 1981). The computer plays its internal game according to specified syntactic rules, devoid of semantic content.

Interest in machine thinking and consciousness is important because of the questions raised about human nature. If silicon chips can yield thought and consciousness, then why assume humans to be more than "meat machines," to use Marvin Minsky's phrase? But scientists like MacKay (1988) and philosophers like Searle (1984) have argued the opposite. Producing a truly thinking, even conscious, machine would show that events at the level of mind are independent of any single physical instantiation (silicon versus flesh and blood). MacKay argues that rule following by itself is inadequate to endow a machine with consciousness. Current developments in information science and the neurosciences suggest avenues for future research. It is an empirical question whether machines will ever think or be conscious and an open question how we will respond to such entities.

References

Damasio, A. R. (1994). *Descartes' error: Emotion, reason, and the human brain.* New York: Grosset/Putnam.

Dreyfuss, H. (1979). *What computers can't do* (Rev. ed.). New York: Harper & Row.

Haugeland, J. (1981). Semantic engines: An introduction to mind design. In J. Haugeland (Ed.), *Mind design.* Cambridge, MA: Bradford.

MacKay, D. M. (1988). Artificial intelligence?—A Christian appraisal. In M. Tinker (Ed.), *The open mind and other essays—Donald M. MacKay.* Leicester: Inter-Varsity.

Searle, J. (1984). *Minds, brains, and science.* Cambridge, MA: Harvard University Press.

Turing, A. M. (1950). Computing machinery and intelligence. *Mind, 59,* 433–460.

W. D. NORMAN

See INTELLIGENCE.

Intelligence Quotient. A number that expresses an individual's overall mental ability. The conventional method for determining an individual's intelligence quotient (IQ) is to divide the individual's mental age by the appropriate chronological age and multiply the result by 100. Chronological age is the individual's age expressed as the number of years and months since the day of birth. The mental age of intelligence test items is determined after a lengthy process of test construction during which it is ascertained how individuals of various ages perform on specific test questions. An intelligence test consists of a large number of items of varying difficulty, with each item linked to a particular age. The individual who takes an intelligence test is assigned a mental age based on performance on the various age-rated questions.

In response to conceptual limitations, a deviation method of establishing IQ has replaced the traditional ratio formula. The deviation procedure compares an individual's test performance to that of an average individual of the same age. This comparison is made using a table of performance data provided in the test manual and allows a psychologist to determine the appropriate IQ score (sometimes called standard age score).

An IQ of 100 indicates intelligence that is average. For the traditional method, the person who has a mental age (e.g., age 8) equivalent to his or her chronological age (e.g., age 8) is defined to be average (i.e., dividing mental age by chronological age yields 1.0, which multiplied by 100 gives an IQ of 100). For the deviation method, consulting the appropriate age table in the test manual will yield an IQ of 100 for an individual whose test performance exceeds that of 50% of those of the same age who took the test. For both methods, those with intelligence ability above average will have IQs above 100, the greater the number beyond 100, the greater the individual's mental ability. Numbers less than 100 show below-average mental capability; the lower the IQ below 100, the lower the measured intellectual capacity. Approximately 68% of the population scores between 85 and 115 (one standard deviation in either direction from 100). The following ranges have traditionally been used to classify IQ scores:

Range	IQ
Very superior	130 and above
Superior	120–129
High average	110–119
Average	90–109
Low average	80–89
Borderline	70–79
Intellectually deficient	69 and below

Some psychologists have expressed considerable skepticism about the value of the IQ. Among the most serious limitations are the following. First, the links between age and performance are critically dependent on the adequacy of test construction and standardization. Procedural shortcuts and/or flawed methodology can generate misleading norms for IQ test items. Second, the use of IQ tests with groups not properly represented in the test development process can be highly misleading. Interpretation of gender and ethnic group differences often revolve around this point of controversy. Third, intelligence tests employ items that are focused primarily on reasoning and memory. To the extent that intelligence is more than reasoning and memory, the IQ fails to adequately reflect the entire set of abilities and capacities that constitute intelligence. Fourth, using IQ scores for decision-making has sparked controversy and legal action. In the best known case, a California judge ruled that intelligence tests could not be used to identify those to be placed in special classes for remedial purposes. Fifth, IQ scores have often been the basis for labeling. Persons whose IQ is below 70 are labeled as mentally disadvantaged or intellectually deficient (sometimes demeaning labels such as "moron" and "imbecile" are used), while those with IQs above 130 are called gifted or genius. The accuracy and consequences of IQ-based labels are much debated.

Most psychologists and educators, while recognizing the limitations of the IQ, believe that it is a useful measure of intellectual ability. If they are misused, psychologists agree, IQ scores can be the source of pejorative labels, denigration of groups, and misleading decisions concerning an individual's cognitive potential.

Additional Reading

Snyderman, M., & Rothman, S. (1988). *The IQ controversy, the media and public policy.* New Brunswick, NJ: Transaction.

D. KAUFFMANN

See INTELLECTUAL ASSESSMENT; INTELLIGENCE.

Interest Measurement. Some individuals need a great deal of assistance in deciding which career is best for them. Because of the importance and difficulty of this decision, it is helpful to have a tool to provide guidance in the career selection process. Interest inventories can be precisely the tool required for assistance in this matter.

Interest measurements evaluate one's likes and dislikes. An interest is considered anything that one likes or an activity in which one enjoys participating. Those who devise interest tests often take hobbies, choices of entertainment, or preferred reading materials into consideration. Personal values, because they affect every part of life, may also be included in an evaluation. These tools not only help individuals find the best-fitting career but also may help employers to find the right people to fill available positions in the most efficient way. Therefore businesses use interest tests as well. Individuals have been using interest tests for some time: the first interest measurement, the Carnegie Interest Inventory, was used in 1921 (Kaplan & Saccuzzo, 1997, p. 370).

All interest tests are not created to evaluate the same things. Many tests, such as the Strong Vocational Interest Bank (SVIB), which with changes became the Strong-Campbell Interest Inventory (SCII), compare the interests of the test taker with the interests of individuals who are content and established in their professions. Researchers have found that people in the same occupations do have similar interests. The Campbell Interest Skill Survey examines much the same thing as the SCII, because its roots

are in the Strong. The Strong is one of the most widely used tests in a research or practice setting. Other tests that compare interests are Kuder Occupational Interest Survey (one of the most widely used interest tests), The Minnesota Vocational Interest Inventory, and the Career Assessment Inventory. Earlier criticism about lack of theory inspired makers of the SCII to utilize Holland's theory concerning vocational choice (Kaplan & Saccuzzo, 1997, p. 371). There are generally six classification categories: realistic, investigative, artistic, social, enterprising, and conventional. Another criticism of the SVIB is gender bias, addressed by a change from separate male and female tests to male and female keys in the same form.

Some tests focus on personal characteristics, which may include personality, abilities, interests, and personal values. Because these things may change in youth, it is generally suggested that vocational tests be given at age 17 or later. Osipow's Vocational Dimensions take information from many tests to find clusters of traits that are attributed to those in a particular occupation. The California Occupational Preference Survey, and The Vocational Maturity Inventory, which evolved into The Career Maturity Inventory, are some tests that measure personal characteristics. There is much speculation whether traits predict behavior in work situations. Also, critics say the tests do not assess the individual's ability to work in a particular environment.

Some tests use work environment as the main determiner of which job is best for whom. There are several methods of measuring the influence of situations that occur in the work setting and defining it. One way is through social ecology, a study of behavioral settings. There are often unwritten rules in behavioral environments. Members of an environment may look down upon those who break these rules. Therefore, employers should hire people who will function best in the work setting and with the other individuals. However, interest tests do not promise to measure the chance people have in succeeding in the suggested careers. Aptitude tests may help in predicting career success.

Reference

Kaplan, R. M., & Saccuzzo, D. P. (1997). *Psychological testing.* Pacific Grove, CA: Brooks/Cole.

R. A. SHEAFFER

See PSYCHOLOGICAL MEASUREMENT.

Interfaith Marriage Counseling. All couples deal with differences in their faith. Even couples who attend the same church have differing beliefs and religious values. However, as each spouse's faith becomes more divergent, increasing numbers of issues arise. Interfaith marriages range in diversity from interdenominational to interreligious marriages. A couple that is Presbyterian-Methodist and a couple that is Catholic-Hindu would both be considered interfaith. Clearly the degree of difference in religion or denomination is an important factor in trying to understand interfaith marriages. One thing appears to be certain: interfaith issues become more salient as the differences in religion increase and as each spouse's personal devotion to his or her faith increases.

Trends show that interfaith marriages are on the rise with younger couples having higher rates of intermarriage (Ellman, 1987). Based on this data, marriage counselors can expect to see increasing numbers of interdenominational and interreligious marriages in the future. Meanwhile, interreligious marriages appear to have higher divorce rates than intrareligious marriages (Mayer, 1985). These researchers believe that the high divorce rate is due to additional stressors that tend to act as a wedge in interreligious marriages.

Theories and research in healing interfaith marriages are scarce. Priests, ministers, and rabbis are most likely to offer marriage counseling and often advise against interfaith marriage and are reluctant or refuse to marry interfaith couples. Marriage counselors face difficult issues, such as different worldviews and different values, with interfaith couples. Effective assessment and treatment of interfaith couples requires addressing several pertinent issues.

Issues that should be considered when assessing for importance of religion in interfaith marriages include devoutness of each spouse, religion of each spouse's family of origin, parents' opposition to the marriage, religious training and schooling, premarital versus postmarital conversions, and cultural and ethnic differences (Eaton, 1994; Packard, 1993; Shortz, 1995). Knox and Schacht (1991) propose that as spouses become more devout, religious issues in marital therapy become more salient. Similarly, as increasing differences and stressors occur, interfaith couples are more likely to experience marital difficulties and dissolution.

Several authors suggest that interfaith couples face specific stressors in their marriage. Shortz (1995) proposes that the sources of stress that interfaith couples face can be divided into three categories: personal, external, and random. Personal stresses include cultural differences, differences in religions, and normal conflict that evokes larger reactions due to personal differences. Common external stressors include family of origin, child rearing, and wedding ceremonies. Other random stressors include spouses changing religious affiliations and change in referent group status. These stressors are specific to interfaith couples and could be addressed in counseling interfaith marriages. Other issues that often become points of contention in interfaith couples are issues such as celebrating religious holidays, sharing personal religious experiences, different values, and celebrating different religions in the home (Packard, 1993).

Learning to value differences and becoming more open to compromise appear to be the key to resolutions with interfaith couples. Eaton (1994) suggests that couples face trouble in their marriage because they lack understanding of the cultural context and the meaning of personal differences. Cowan and Cowan (1987) believe that difficulties begin to arise when weddings and rearing children become issues. When there is a lack of understanding, couples tend to polarize and focus on their differences rather than their similarities and the value of each spouse. If couples can begin to value the differences between themselves they can begin to come to appreciate each other and eventually find suitable compromises to unavoidable issues.

References

Cowan G. A., & Cowan, R. (1987). *Mixed blessings: Overcoming stumbling blocks in an interfaith marriage*. New York: Penguin.

Eaton, S. C. (1994). Marriage between Jews and non-Jews: Counseling implications. *Journal of Multicultural Counseling and Development, 22,* 210–214.

Ellman, Y. (1987). Intermarriage in the United States: A comparative study of Jews and other ethnic and religious groups. *Jewish Social Studies, 49,* 1–26.

Knox, D., & Schacht, C. (1991). *Choices in relationships*. St. Paul, MN: West.

Mayer, E. (1985). *Love and tradition: Marriage between Jews and Christians*. New York: Plenum.

Packard, G. (1993). *Coping in an interfaith family*. New York: Rosen Publishing Group.

Shortz, J. A. (1995). *Interfaith relationship development: A proposed model*. Unpublished doctoral dissertation, Virginia Commonwealth University, Richmond.

J. S. RIPLEY

See MARRIAGE COUNSELING; MARITAL COMPATIBILITY; MARITAL TYPES.

Intergroup Dynamics. *See* GROUP DYNAMICS.

Intermittent Explosive Disorder. Intermittent explosive disorder is classified as an impulse-control disorder in *DSM-IV* (American Psychiatric Association, 1994). The primary feature of impulse-control disorder is the failure to resist an impulse, a drive, or a temptation to perform an act that is harmful to the individual or to others. For most disorders of this type, the individual feels an intensifying sense of tension or arousal before committing the act and then experiences pleasure, gratification, or relief at the time of carrying out the act.

Diagnostic Criteria. According to *DSM-IV* (American Psychiatric Association, 1994), there are three diagnostic criteria for intermittent explosive disorder. The first criterion is the occurrence of several discrete episodes of failure to resist aggressive impulses that result in serious assaultive acts or destruction of property. Second, the degree of aggressiveness expressed during an episode is grossly out of proportion to any provocation or precipitating psychosocial stressor. Third, the diagnosis of intermittent explosive disorder is made only after other mental disorders that might account for episodes of aggressive behavior have been ruled out. Mental disorders that should be ruled out include antisocial personality disorder, borderline personality disorder, psychotic disorders, a manic episode, conduct disorders, or attention deficit/hyperactivity disorder (ADHD). Moreover, the diagnosis requires that the aggressive episodes are not due to the direct physiological effects of a substance or a general medical condition. The individual may feel an increased sense of tension or arousal preceding the explosive behavior and may then experience a sense of gratification or relief immediately ensuing the aggressive episode. Later the individual may feel disturbed, remorseful, or embarrassed about the aggressive behavior.

Etiology and Onset. Laboratory investigations suggest that individuals with the disorder may produce nonspecific electroencephalography (EEG) findings. Additionally, signs of altered serotonin metabolism have been discovered in the cerebrospinal fluid of some impulsive and temper-prone individuals, but the exact relationship of these findings to intermittent explosive disorder remains unclear.

Research utilizing physical examinations has shown that there may be nonspecific or soft findings on neurological examinations such as reflex asymmetries or mirror movements. Developmental difficulties indicative of cerebral dysfunction such as delayed speech or poor coordination may be present. A history of neurological conditions such as head injury, episodes of unconsciousness, or febrile seizures in childhood may also be present.

Although limited data are available, the age at onset of intermittent explosive disorder appears to be from late adolescence to the thirties. Intermittent explosive disorder is apparently rare, although reliable information regarding prevalence is lacking.

Reference

American Psychiatric Association. (1994). *Diagnostic and statistical manual of mental disorders* (4th ed.). Washington, DC: Author.

J. M. SMITH IV

Interpersonal Attraction. Considerable attention has been given to the study of factors that influence our liking others. Psychologists have most often utilized reinforcement theory to explain interpersonal attraction. That is, we like those who are in some way rewarding to us, and we will continue relationships that offer more rewards than costs. Some theorists further argue that while we are governed by self-interest in our interpersonal relationships, we have learned that rewards are maximized only if we follow the principle of equity in which each receives benefits from a relationship in proportion to what he or she has contributed to it.

One of the best predictors of whether two people will be attracted to each other is their proximity, and more specifically, how often their paths cross. Numerous studies indicate that people are most likely to be attracted to and even marry those who live in the same neighborhood, who work in the same office, or who sit nearby in class. Not only does proximity enable people to discover commonalities and exchange rewards; research also indicates that mere exposure to any unfamiliar stimulus boosts liking of it.

Another factor that influences our initial attraction to another is physical appearance. While most people seem to believe that physical attractiveness plays an insignificant role in their evaluation of others, research indicates otherwise. Walster, Aronson, Abrahams, and Rottman (1966) found that the one determinant of whether college students who were randomly matched for blind dates liked each other and repeated the date was their physical attractiveness. Several studies have indicated that people tend to select friends and especially to marry those who are a good match in their level of attractiveness. Research also suggests the presence of a physical attractiveness stereotype in which what is beautiful is assumed to be good. The stereotype is evident not only in the judgments dating partners make but also in the evaluations members of the same sex make of each other, in adults' evaluations of children, and in children's liking for one another.

Studies also indicate that the more similar two people are in any of a variety of attributes, including beliefs, attitudes, and values, the more likely they will form a friendship. The "likeness leads to liking" principle holds true for children, college students, the elderly, people of various occupations, and persons in different countries. Research suggests that the greater the similarity between husband and wife, the happier they are and the less likely they are to divorce. Agreement may promote attraction because those who share our opinions provide us with social validation of our beliefs. Research is much less supportive of the notion that opposites attract or that we are likely to form close relationships with those whose needs and personalities complement our own.

Another important determinant of whether we will like another person is whether that person likes us. This is particularly true if we are experiencing self-doubt or if our self-esteem has been temporarily lowered. We are especially attracted to those whose attitude has reversed from disliking to liking. Curtis and Miller (1986) report that when we believe people like us, we respond to them more warmly, which leads them to like us even more.

References

Curtis, R. C., & Miller, K. (1986). Believing another likes or dislikes you: Behaviors making the beliefs come true. *Journal of Personality and Social Psychology, 51*, 284–290.

Walster, E., Aronson, V., Abrahams, D., & Rottman, L. (1966). Importance of physical attractiveness in dating behavior. *Journal of Personality and Social Psychology, 4*, 508–516.

M. BOLT

See LOVE.

Interpersonal Diagnosis. The classification of psychological disorders in terms of observable social behaviors. To the interpersonal diagnostician, the most important aspect of any nonorganic psychological dysfunction is the way an individual acts in relation to other people. For example, to what extent is the client dominant or submissive? Friendly or hostile? Dependent or independent?

Traditional psychiatric diagnosis suffers from a number of defects. Some of these are an emphasis on symptoms, which tend at times to be dramatic, rather than on basic personality characteristics; a bias toward viewing psychological disorders as "diseases," which most clearly they are not; an overreliance on the clinician's subjective impressions; little if anything in the way of prescriptions for treatment (which, after all, is the most important function of any diagnostic system); and the near total neglect of social-psychological variables.

It has been suggested that there are at least six interacting psychological "systems," any one or combination of which could be used for diagnosis. These systems are motoric, perceptual, biological, cognitive, emotional, and social. Behaviorists, for example, diagnose largely in terms of the motoric system, while organically oriented clinicians stress the biological system. Interpersonal diagnosticians emphasize the importance of the social system but not to the point of ignoring the other five. It is so-cial *behavior*, after all, that the interpersonalist attempts to classify, along with socially relevant cognitions, perceptions, emotions, and perceptions.

It is important to note that mental events can also be interpersonal. For example, probably all of us carry on, inside our own minds, conversations with others. Significant others from the past populate our psyches.

To arrive at an interpersonal diagnosis the clinician needs some kind of diagnostic scheme, some framework into which to fit the patient's data. Several such frameworks have been advanced, the two most notable of which are Leary's (1957) interpersonal circle and Benjamin's (1974) structure of social behavior.

Leary's pioneering work was of sufficient merit to earn him an appointment to the Harvard faculty. His involvement with psychedelic chemicals began later and should not be allowed to obscure the sheer brilliance of his earlier work on interpersonal assessment. The Leary circle, as it is informally called, is constructed around two axes at right angles to each other: love-hate and dominance-submission.

To arrive at a diagnosis on the basis of the Leary circle, the clinician needs first to specify carefully the level of personality from which any particular bit of information has been obtained. Leary articulated five levels: 1) the patient's impact on another, that is, how others respond to him or her; 2) conscious self-report, that is, how the patient conceives of and perhaps describes himself, even on such psychological tests as the Minnesota Multiphasic Personality Inventory; 3) symbolic or thematic material, for example, what might be revealed through the Thematic Apperception Test or the Rorschach inkblots; 4) the unexpressed or avoided, that is, those interpersonal themes that are conspicuously absent from the other levels; and 5) values. Leary's own research and most contemporary diagnosis based on it deal only with levels 1, 2, and 3.

Benjamin's system is somewhat more complicated than Leary's and is constructed around three axes: affiliation (similar to Leary's love-hate), interdependence (autonomy versus dominance and submission, both forms of high interdependence), and focus (either on oneself or on the other person). One advantage of Benjamin's model is its versatility. It can be used globally—in terms of such general categories as "invokes hostile autonomy." It can be used molecularly—in terms of such highly specific points as "uncaringly lets go." Or it can be used in a fashion intermediate between the global categories and the molecular behaviors—in terms of such behavior clusters as "ignores and neglects."

Interest in interpersonal diagnosis, either as a supplement to traditional diagnosis or even as its replacement, seems to be mounting. From the point of view of Christian theology the interpersonal orientation has much to recommend it. For one thing, it emphasizes the importance of relationality to human personality, and it is a basic tenet of most Christian theologies that people were created for the express purpose of relating to God and to each other.

References

Benjamin, L. S. (1974). Structural analysis of social behavior. *Psychological Review, 81*, 392–425.

Leary, T. F. (1957). *Interpersonal diagnosis of personality.* New York: Ronald Press.

Additional Reading

McLemore, C. W., & Benjamin, L. S. (1979). Whatever happened to interpersonal diagnosis? A psychosocial alternative to DSM-III *American Psychologist, 34*, 17–34.

C. W. McLemore

See CLASSIFICATION OF MENTAL DISORDERS.

Interpersonal Psychology. An approach to basic and applied behavioral science that rests on the foundational assumption that one's personality is best defined by how one characteristically behaves toward other people. Harry Stack Sullivan, who was renowned for his work as both a theoretician and a teacher of psychotherapeutic practice, was the force behind the crystallization of interpersonalism. He went as far as to suggest that apart from one's typical interactions with others the word *personality* has no meaning. Sullivan was famous for saying, "It takes people to make people sick and it takes people to make people better."

To the interpersonally oriented psychologist the most clinically significant observation about people is how they structure their relationships. Are they dominant or submissive, loving or hateful, controlling or freeing? Interpersonal therapists pay careful attention to what their clients attempt to do in relation to them as the therapy session unfolds. They also want to know everything they can about how the client interacts with people outside the consulting room. How has the patient done with others? Did the patient have a close friend during childhood? Has he or she ever been in love and, if so, at what age(s)? What about occupational history or relationships with parents and siblings?

Psychoanalysis and Behaviorism. Interpersonal psychology stands between the mentalism of psychoanalysis and the positivism of behaviorism, and in this sense it functions for many psychologists as a unifying theoretical framework (see Wachtel, 1977). Although behaviorists have become increasingly receptive to the significance of internal events, what they call covert behaviors, the traditional behaviorist stance has been to eschew anything with a subjective cast to it. Thus the concept of mind has enjoyed very little status among classical behaviorists, who still tend to view the new cognitive behaviorism with suspicion.

Psychoanalysts have often been criticized for neglecting concrete behavior in favor of the study and alteration of psychodynamics. It is not uncommon to find analysts so immersed in the dynamics of the analysand's psychic life that they neglect what they might be doing to perpetuate those problems that brought the person into treatment. Interpersonalists want to retain the richness of psychodynamic study without sacrificing the rigor of methodological behaviorism—in other words, of careful behavioral science.

Intrapsychic Interpersonal Transactions. The interpersonal psychologist believes that even a person on a desert island has interpersonal relationships so long as that person had previous experience with people. Memories of these people populate the islander's mind, just as we all carry around inside mental personifications of significant people from our past. Sigmund Freud referred to these personifications as introjects. When in the privacy of our own minds we hear our mother or father say "Well done," it is our mental representations of them who are silently speaking. Alternatively we may hear someone, sounding perhaps like our grade school teacher, decry us for being "dumb."

We carry around inside of us not only other people's voices but also our stored perceptions of and reactions to them. Consequently, when we encounter someone we have never seen before, we rarely if ever respond to them in anything like a pristine way. Almost always how we perceive them and by implication how we react to them is conditioned by our previous experiences with persons of whom they may remind us.

Anxiety, Avoidance, and Self-Defeating Cycles. Interpersonal psychologists, like many other students of human behavior and its dysfunction, are explicitly concerned with sources of anxiety. Who or what triggers insecurity? How are these stimuli prompting the person to behave in ways that may be self-defeating? Efforts to avoid anxiety are precisely what get people into psychological trouble. What a person says or does or perhaps fails to say or do evokes in other people negative responses, which in turn perpetuate dysfunctional behaviors. For example, someone who whines a great deal is likely to prompt others to respond with persecution. A person who is persecuted will more often than not respond by whining. Much abnormal human behavior is maintained by cycles such as these, in which what Person A does both prompts and maintains what Person B does and vice versa.

As a concrete clinical illustration of how behavioral circularity works, suppose Mary comes to therapy complaining that her husband, Jim, continually messes up their finances. Their bills are months in arrears and the collection agencies are beginning to harass them. She is so distraught by all this that she is seriously contemplating divorce.

Upon careful inspection it becomes evident that Jim and Mary have gone through the same behavioral cycle many times before. Like most neurotic behavior, such interactions tend to repeat themselves even though they do not work. The cycle in this case may be that Jim neglects paying the bills for several months until the notices of default begin to pour in. Mary ignores them in the hope that Jim will finally take responsibility and straighten out their money problems. Eventually the bill collectors call her at work. When she gets home that evening, she blows up at him and takes the checkbook, telling him that if he cannot manage it, she will have to. She then handles the money for the next few months and during this time manages to restore order to their fiscal situation. However, after some time she again asks Jim if he would not like to take back control of the bills. He consents, and the cycle begins again.

The interpersonally attuned clinician will want to know what is in Mary's mind when she tries to get Jim to do their finances, what is going on inside Jim when he fails to do them adequately, and so on. Breaking this kind of dysfunctional cycle is no easy task and requires a solid understanding of what the payoffs are for each person involved. It may be that Mary wants a traditional home in which the man takes care of the money. Her need for this, which in turn may be motivated by a desire to gain her parents' approval of her marriage, may override the clear implication of her experience, which is that Jim is not going to manage their finances effectively.

Jim may feel inadequate to handle the finances, and this leads to procrastination. As he delays dealing with their bills, they pile up, he forgets exactly what he owes and thus overspends, and they are again in the clutches of the collection agency. Moreover, he may also employ a passive-aggressive strategy of lousing things up as a way to irritate his wife. Perhaps he bears a grudge that in his passivity he has not expressed to her.

Even this analysis may not be the whole story, and obviously any attempt to make sense of such complex interpersonal behavior is dangerous. The clinician can spin out endless "psychomythologies" that do not correspond to reality. Or the clinician may underestimate the complexity of what is going on, and his or her therapeutic efforts will fail when he or she makes too superficial an intervention.

Models of Interpersonal Behavior. Interpersonal psychologists attempt to make systematic sense of how people act in relation to one another, believing that social behavior has a certain degree of regularity and is therefore to some extent rule governed. Persons who do not say hello when someone greets them, for example, are behaving in an unusual manner. It may be that they have poor hearing, or they may be distracted at the moment. But a person who routinely does not respond to a simple social overture is acting in a way that is sure to impair his or her intimacy with others. The interpersonal researcher wants to know what behaviors in Person A lead to what behaviors in Person B. For example, what has been the interpersonal experience of a person who refuses to respond to an ordinary social greeting? How are others likely to respond to this refusal? How will different responses affect the probability of future refusals?

Addressing such questions has led interpersonal researchers to develop and validate models of interpersonal behavior. While Sullivan was the progenitor of the interpersonal orientation, he did little to develop a scientific formulation of exactly which behaviors lead to which other behaviors during the course of social transactions. Nor did he come up with much in the way of a scheme for describing what has come to be known as a person's interpersonal style.

Leary (1957) was the first researcher to systematize interpersonal behavior. For nearly ten years he and his colleagues worked at the Kaiser Hospital in Oakland. The fruit of their work was published in *Interpersonal Diagnosis of Personality,* which remains a classic and which obtained Leary's appointment to the Harvard faculty. Leary's model of social behavior is such that, as one proceeds through the range of the behaviors it portrays, one eventually returns to the place from which one began. The Leary interpersonal circle is constructed around two axes: dominance-submission and love-hate.

Another important model was developed by Benjamin (1974), a mathematical psychologist at the University of Wisconsin Psychiatric Center. While Benjamin's model, like Leary's, has love-hate (affiliation) as one of its primary axes, it treats both dominance and submission as two kinds of highly interdependent behavior. Two further axes are therefore included in the system. On the second (interdependence) are behaviors reflecting either the giving or taking of autonomy. The polarities on this axis are autonomy versus dominance or submission, either of the latter two reflecting high interdependence. The third axis (focus) reflects the extent to which the individual's focus is on self or on others. The Benjamin model for observable behavior is portrayed on two diamonds, each of which is composed of many individual chart points. Each of these points corresponds to a particular kind of interpersonal action. Benjamin has also provided a third diamond to account for interpersonal behavior with oneself as the object.

Both Leary and Benjamin specify rules of human social behavior. For example, both refer to complementarity—behaviors that tend to evoke each other. Within the Leary framework, for example, "guide, advise, teach" tends to prompt others to "respect, admire, conform." Both theorists also specify ways to counteract social behaviors. From the vantage point of Leary's model, the way to stop "punitive, sarcastic or unkind" action is to "support, sympathize, treat gently" or even to "pity, dote on, treat soft-heartedly." Benjamin refers to such counteractions as "antidotes." Within her model the antidote to "whine, defend, justify," for example, is "friendly listen."

Evaluation. The great strength of interpersonal psychology is its ability to accommodate both behavioral and psychodynamic concepts and findings. Benjamin's structural analysis of social behavior model, for example, allows one to encode both observable social interactions and introjected psychological processes (those in which one's own self is the object). Some interpersonalists would argue that an even greater asset of their approach is that it explicitly focuses attention on that which lies at the heart of almost all functional psychological disturbances: what goes on or has gone on between people.

However, interpersonal conceptions have always been a minority voice within psychology, and only recently has the interpersonal perspective received visibility through journal articles and books. This relative neglect of the interpersonal view seems to stem from fears by behaviorists that an interpersonal orientation is insufficiently operationalized and excessively mentalistic and fears by psychodynamists and phenomenologists that an interpersonal framework is insufficiently sophisticated with respect to mental events and excessively behavioristic.

Works such as Anchin and Kiesler (1982) have served to make clinicians more alert to the importance of relationships to mental health. McLemore and Benjamin (1979) have argued that therapists can no longer afford to ignore a client's social context. This emphasis on relationships seems to be an important component of the biblical perspective on persons and is, therefore, an important movement in contemporary psychology.

References

Anchin, J. C., & Kiesler, D. J. (Eds.). (1982). *Handbook of interpersonal psychotherapy.* New York: Pergamon.

Benjamin, L. S. (1974). Structural analysis of social behavior. *Psychological Review, 81,* 392–425.

Leary, T. F. (1957). *Interpersonal diagnosis of personality.* New York: Ronald.

McLemore, C. W., & Benjamin, L. S. (1979). Whatever happened to interpersonal diagnosis? A psychosocial alternative to *DSM-III. American Psychologist, 34,* 17–34.

Wachtel, P. C. (1977). *Psychoanalysis and behavior therapy: Toward an integration.* New York: Basic Books.

Additional Reading

Carson, R. C. (1969). *Interaction concepts of personality.* Chicago: Aldine.

C. W. McLemore

See Interpersonal Diagnosis.

Interpretation. The process whereby the psychotherapist presents to the patient an understanding of behavior, events, dreams, or other psychological material in the pursuit of the resolution of the patient's psychological distress.

The psychotherapeutic use of interpretation was initiated primarily by Sigmund Freud (1913). Freud wished to provide the patient an understanding of the event or dream, an interpretation of the symbolic material present therein, an understanding of the psychic conflicts that are represented in the symbols, and finally a resolution of the patient's internal primitive desires and frustrations. Freud was principally interested in four phenomena requiring interpretation: the transference relationship between therapist and patient, somatic ailments arising from anxieties and unresolved desires, parapraxes (slips of the tongue and accidents), and most importantly dreams.

In his work Freud endeavored to establish a safe relationship with patients in which patients could regress to their infantile feelings and allow themselves to feel like a child in the presence of the therapist. Patients would then transfer their feelings from their parents to the therapist, albeit in symbolic form. The task of interpretation was to help patients understand that the feelings they were having were the same feelings they had as an infant or young child. This interpretation then would serve as the beginning of the resolution of the patient's early unfulfilled primitive longings.

Somatic complaints and symptoms would be interpreted by Freud and his followers as representations of displaced drives. Parapraxes likewise are

seen and interpreted as substitute or displaced drive gratification, inasmuch as all slips or accidents are viewed as being caused by unconscious desires.

Beyond the interpretation of the transference experience, Freud's most intense interest in interpretation came regarding patients' dreams. Freud worked toward understanding the dream by interpreting otherwise unintelligible content as symbolic. The unconscious would encode its processes in dreams as a way of hiding this material from the conscious, and the person would dream as a means of relieving the anxiety caused by repressed feelings and strivings. Most of Freud's interpretations were highly sexual in content. Thus buildings represented men (or male genitals) and landscapes represented women. A death in a dream represented a death wish, and being naked was the fear of the unconscious being discovered.

The psychoanalytic writers who have elaborated on Freud's method of interpretation offer some additional elements. Giovacchini (1979) asserts that all nontransference interpretations are not only nonessential but usually harmful. He asserts that patients always feel depreciated when their behavior and feelings are interpreted outside of the transference relationship.

Spotnitz (1976) points out the importance of uncovering resistance before other interpretative work is begun. Spotnitz adds that the interpretation process should be consistently maturational and that one should offer an interpretation only when the patient asks for it. Interpretation is ineffective unless the content of the therapy warrants it; thus to interpret external behavior or make a judgment about a patient may be premature and harmful. Spotnitz favors having the focus of interpretation on the feelings and thoughts that encompass the therapeutic relationship. Having fun, anger, grief, or joy in a therapeutic hour can and should be interpreted.

Jacobson (1971) asserts that depressive patients have extreme reactions to therapeutic interpretations and will alternatively perceive them as seductive promises, severe rejection, lack of understanding, or sadistic punishments. Like Spotnitz, Jacobson suggests the appropriate response of the therapist is his or her honest one: anger, grief, joy, or whatever, followed by still another interpretation. Obsessional patients will have a detached, overly logical acceptance of interpretations while perhaps not really digesting them. Dependent patients might accept all interpretations without digesting them. Patients with character disorders may reject all of them.

The interpretive process is seen by analysts as a splitting of the ego into an observing and an experiencing part so that the former can judge the irrational character of the latter. Timing of interpretations is therefore critically important. If it is premature, an interpretation can strengthen resistance. No interpretations should be given until a good therapeutic alliance exists. Finally, all writers agree that the correctness and value of an interpretation should be the change that occurs in a patient's life, not merely his or her acceptance or rejection of it.

Psychoanalysts are not the only therapists who utilize interpretation as a therapeutic technique. Therapists of other traditions also regularly engage in meaning attribution. Behavior therapists may identify reinforcement value in symptoms, and Gestalt therapists might suggest the meaning of nonverbal behavior to be in repressed parts of self or experience. Yet the literature on interpretation is dominated by psychoanalytic thought, and it is hard to avoid recognizing the accuracy of the observations lying behind many of the analytic interpretations.

References

Freud, S. (1913). *Interpretation of dreams.* New York: Macmillan.

Giovacchini, P. L. (1979). *Treatment of primitive mental states.* New York: Aronson.

Jacobson, E. (1971). *Depression: Comparative studies of normal, neurotic and psychotic conditions.* New York: International Universities Press.

Spotnitz, H. (1976). *Psychotherapy of preoedipal conditions.* New York: Aronson.

R. B. JOHNSON

See PSYCHOANALYTIC PSYCHOTHERAPY; PSYCHOANALYSIS: TECHNIQUE.

Interracial Marriage Counseling. In general the greater the difference in background between spouses, the more difficulty they will have in marriage. Assessment of whether or not conflicts originate from within a cultural context is one of the major tasks a counselor faces when working with interracial couples. If cultural context is not at the root of the marital problem, the counselor can rely on conventional marriage counseling strategies. However, if cultural context is determined to be at the root of the marital problem, then the couple will need assistance in understanding each other's behavior in relation to the larger context. Couples often exhibit a dramatic shift in their responsiveness to each other when they can interpret each other's behavior in terms of culture rather than as a personal attack.

First, a counselor needs to understand that each culture has distinct rules regarding marital choice (intermarriage is often prohibited either due to the threat it poses to the survival of a particular group or due to feelings of prejudice or ethnic superiority) and method of mate selection (arranged marriages versus love marriages). When these rules are violated, opposition to the relationship from family and/or society can create a tremendous amount of stress on a relationship. It is not uncommon for one or both partners in an interracial marriage to have suffered rejection from their families and/or peers (and in the case of prejudice and discrimination, from society). Not only do some couples have to live without the approval or support of loved ones, but also they have to contend with attempts to intentionally interfere and create marital strife. It is helpful for couples in these circumstances to understand the external sources of their stress and frustration so that those feelings are not displaced onto each other.

Cultural norms also dictate relational expectations between a couple and their family members or in-laws. The consequences for not meeting those expectations can be both tangible (e.g., loss of financial or emotional support) and intangible (e.g., feelings of shame or guilt). Some examples of these cultural norms include choice of postmarital residence, participation in family rituals, definitions of nuclear versus extended family and their boundaries of influence or intrusion, and familial caretaking responsibilities. When there is conflict in this area, couples need assistance in identifying and verbalizing the cultural expectations and the anticipated or felt consequences of not meeting those expectations.

Family structure is another area in which cultural norms may have an impact. Examples of these norms include gender roles (e.g., allocation of household tasks, child care and discipline), family authority and power (patriarchal versus matriarchal versus egalitarian), and child-bearing and child-rearing practices (e.g., the importance of children, the role of grandparents, the role of discipline). When conflict is in this area, couples once again need assistance in identifying and verbalizing the cultural norms filtering their definitions of appropriate and inappropriate family structure.

Finally, cultural norms bear heavily on communication styles. Some of the commonly misinterpreted differences include volume of speech (soft versus loud), rate of speech (slow versus fast), maintenance of eye contact (indirect versus direct), use of pauses or silence (long versus short), and expression of affect (reserved versus open). Not only does misinterpretation in this area cause conflict, but also it can exacerbate conflict. For example, during a disagreement, a spouse whose cultural norm is to avoid eye contact out of deference or respect may be interpreted as being avoidant or deceptive. However, a spouse whose cultural norm is to maintain direct eye contact may be interpreted by the other as threatening or challenging. It is helpful for a counselor to point out to the couple the potential for misinterpretation due to the influence of cultural norms.

K. H. WIBBERLY

See MARITAL COMPATIBILITY; MARITAL TYPES; MARRIAGE COUNSELING.

Interview. A method sometimes used in marketing and social science research in which questions are asked verbally and respondents' answers are recorded. General rules for interviewing include a similar appearance and demeanor to the people being interviewed, a thorough familiarity with the questionnaire, question wording must be followed exactly, responses must be recorded exactly, and preestablished rules for probing must be adhered to. As in all types of research, the interviewer must be as neutral as possible and should avoid leading the respondent in one direction or another. The same general rules and procedures also apply to conducting clinical interviews.

See PSYCHOLOGY, METHODS OF.

Intimacy. A process in which an individual expresses personal feelings and information to another and as a result of the other's response comes to feel known, validated, and cared for. Most theorists use the term to refer to a process that incorporates affection, warmth, self-disclosure, closeness, and interdependence. Distance, in stark contrast to intimacy, is associated with anger, resentment, criticism, insensitivity, and inattention.

When people know they are loved and liked, they naturally become more willing to risk exposing their ideas and feelings. That is not as easy as it sounds, for people are often more timid than one might think. Even a hint of rejection seems to inhibit self-disclosure, and people rarely confide in others who are uncaring or disinterested.

Some people are more motivated to experience intimacy than others. Researches have found that people who are so motivated are more loving and affectionate, warmer, more egalitarian, and less self-centered and dominant. They spend more time thinking about people and relationships, more time talking and writing to others; they are more tactful and less outspoken. Not surprisingly, others like them too (McAdams, 1992).

People long for intimacy in and of itself, but intimacy has some positive side benefits too. A number of studies document that intimacy and psychological health seem to go hand in hand. Intimacy has long been associated with happiness, contentment, and a sense of well-being. In early adulthood, intimate relationships foster creativity, productivity, and emotional integration. A number of medical researchers have also confirmed that intimacy and physical well-being are connected. Intimate relationships apparently buffer the impact of stress. If persons have a chance to disclose emotionally upsetting material to someone who cares, they exhibit improved mental and physical health in follow-up physical examinations (Pennebaker, 1990).

Intimacy takes time. As couples get better acquainted, they begin to disclose more, increasing the breadth of topics they touch on in conversation. Later, as they come to feel closer to one another, they increase the depth of their revelations. There is no such thing as instant intimacy. As intimacy slowly progresses in a relationship, however, intimates feel more and more comfortable in physical proximity. They sneak little looks at their mates to convey shared understandings and they gaze at one another.

Schaefer and Olson (1981) have identified five types of intimacy: emotional intimacy, which involves experiencing closeness of feelings; social intimacy, involving the experience of having common friends, similarities in social networks, and so on; intellectual intimacy, involving the experience of sharing ideas; sexual intimacy, involving the experience of sharing general affection and/or sexual activity; and recreational intimacy, involving the sharing of interests in hobbies, mutual participation in a sporting event, and so forth.

As the meaning of marriage has changed from dutifully obeying one's family or tribe to that of a free choice of mate, the kinds of intimacy expected within marriage have increased. There is little hint of psychological intimacy between husbands and wives in the Old Testament and similarly little if any in the times of the New Testament. But modern marriage is idealized as providing a structure of all kinds of intimacy; that is, the perfect marriage is to feature spouses who enjoy emotional, social, intellectual, sexual, and recreational intimacy.

When they are asked to recall their most intimate moments with someone they cared about, it is interesting to note that college men and women seemed to mean something slightly different by intimacy (Helgeson, Shaver, & Dyer, 1987). Women tended to focus primarily on love and affection and the expression of warm feelings when reliving their most intimate moments. They rarely mentioned sexual intimacy. For men, however, a key feature of intimacy was sex and physical closeness.

People differ both in how interested they are in intimate relationships and even more in how capable they are of maintaining them. McAdams (1992) found that young men and women who have problems getting close to others or who are too dependent find it difficult to establish deeply intimate relationships. The goal of most people, therefore, is to maintain their own identity and integrity while yet engaging in deeply intimate relationships with others. Intimacy and independence are not opposite personality traits but interlocking skills. The risk of losing oneself in another through intimacy is overcome when this fact is realized.

References

Helgeson, V. S., Shaver, P., & Dyer, M. (1987). Prototypes of intimacy and distance in same-sex and opposite-sex relationships. *Journal of Social and Personal Relationships, 4*, 195–233.

McAdams, D. P. (1992). *Intimacy: The need to be close.* Garden City, NY: Doubleday.

Pennebaker, J. W. (1990). *Opening up: The healing power of confiding in others.* New York: Morrow.

Schaefer, M. T., & Olson, D. H. (1981). Assessing intimacy: The PAIR inventory. *Journal of Marital and Family Therapy, 7* (1), 47–60.

L. PARROTT III

Intrinsic Religious Orientation. *See* RELIGIOUS ORIENTATION.

Introjection. This process involves the incorporation into the ego of a mental picture of an external object, animate or inanimate, transferring psychic energy from the real object to the mental image. The individual then tends to identify with the qualities and values of the introjected object even though these may be inconsistent with previously embraced perspectives. Events affecting the external object may sometimes affect the person's internal experience with the introjected image.

One example of introjection would be the junior executive who, after a drastic change in top management and company policy, takes on values, perspectives, and beliefs he previously opposed in an unconsciously motivated attempt to protect himself. As described in this example, introjection has been referred to in psychological literature as identification with the aggressor. Another example would be that of the widow who continues to direct her thoughts, conversation, and feelings toward the mental image she holds of her late husband, as if that internal picture were really he.

R. LARKIN

See DEFENSE MECHANISMS.

Introspection. Introspection is the oldest research technique in psychology: the researchers reflect upon their own thoughts and feelings and come to certain conclusions about the human mind. This remained the primary research technique of those pioneers who founded the first psychology laboratories: William James and Wilhelm Wundt. The former said, "Introspective observation is what we have to rely on, first, foremost and always" (1981, p. 185). Many of the theories of Sigmund Freud, Alfred Adler and Carl Gustav Jung began in reflection upon their own dreams and childhoods rather than those of their patients. The last of these great depth psychologists, Jung, bemoaned Western civilization's lack of introspection and hoped that psychotherapy would be able to reestablish such self-reflection.

It will be helpful to distinguish three kinds and two levels of introspection. The kinds include sensory (What sense experiences am I having?), affective (What feelings or emotions am I having?) and cognitive (What thoughts am I having?). The two levels of introspection are simple (a direct report of sensations, feelings, and/or thoughts) and reflective (What is my reaction, cognitive and affective, to what I am experiencing and reporting?). The first level of (simple) introspection can be criticized as being unreliable data, but the second level (reflective) remains an inescapable and necessary part of good research in the social sciences, necessary to overcome the danger that researchers will project their own theories into the vagueness of their data.

The greatest attack on introspection has come from the behaviorists. John B. Watson (mis)understood all introspection to be of the simple variety, and no substitute for the objectivity of observing a caged animal. "'Introspection' is nothing but another name for talking about obscure bodily reactions that are taking place" (1930, p. 39). B. F. Skinner, rather than continuing the behaviorist attack on introspection, assumed that the battle had been won and merely dismissed the value of the technique. Perhaps inadvertently Skinner shifted the focus of introspection to the reflective. For examples of introspection he chose Eastern meditation and Western psychoanalysis, admitting that they produced a highly introverted individual with self-knowledge of covert behavior.

There remain two unavoidable objections to the use of introspection in the behavioral sciences. The first is the distinction, both practical and philosophical, between the observation of an experience and the report of that observation. Titchener (1909) appreciated this distinction and recommended holding off breaking the stream of consciousness as long as it was coming, preferring to rely on retrospection to reconstruct the key elements of the mental experience for the report.

The second criticism is that introspection is intrinsically subjective: the observer is the observed. What is introspectively obvious to an investigator merely reflects what is going on in the mind of that investigator, not what is necessarily true of external reality. The solution to the problem is an objectivity in the practice of introspection: facing data as they come, not trying to fit them into a specific theory (Titchener, 1909) and realizing that introspection merely suggests certain hypotheses, which should then be tested by other methods (e.g., experimentation).

Since the 1950s several reviews of the role of introspection in psychology have given it a firm niche, though one that is clearly small and subordinate. McKellar (1962) concluded that introspection is inferior in many ways to the more objective techniques of research, and although it is clearly no longer one of the main tools of the psychologist, it could still yield valuable information in a number of cases. Therefore, introspection should not be rejected or used only in a grudging or apologetic way. Radford (1974) concluded that it gave information about experience, data otherwise inaccessible.

Although most academic psychology has followed the lead of the behaviorists (e.g., most university departments do not teach psychological researchers how to self-reflect), such introspection remains unavoidable and unnecessary. Even the objective research of an archival survey or laboratory experiment bears the subjective imprint of the design and the interpretation of the researcher's assumptions about human nature. The questionnaire is an even more obvious example. Perhaps Sigmund Freud's greatest limitation as a researcher was not that he introspected too often but that he did not introspect deeply enough and realize that he could have been infusing his own unconscious conflicts into his interpretations of what his patients were telling him.

References

James, W. (1981). *Principles of psychology.* Cambridge, MA: Harvard University Press.

McKellar, P. (1962). The method of introspection. In J. M. Scher (Ed.), *Theories of the mind.* London: Macmillan.

Radford, J. (1974). Reflections on introspection. *American Psychologist, 29,* 245–250.

Titchener, E. B. (1909). *A text-book of psychology.* New York: Macmillan.

Watson, J. B. (1930). *Behaviorism* (2nd ed.). Chicago: University of Chicago Press.

Further Reading

Brink, T. L. (1985). *The middle class credo: 1,000 all-American beliefs?* New York: Fawcett Gold Medal.

T. L. BRINK

Introversion-Extraversion. In the early part of the twentieth century, Carl Gustav Jung first developed the concepts of introversion and extraversion in his theory of personality. Since then both psychological theories and everyday conversations have used these terms to describe personality. Many of the personality tests also measure the degrees of introverted and extraverted orientations. These concepts have become widely researched and utilized over the last century.

In his theory, Jung suggested that each individual develops either an introverted or an extraverted orientation or attitude toward the world. The first orientation, introversion, describes the direction of interest inward, rather than outward to the external world. Introverts are interested in their own thoughts and feelings and generally tend to be quiet, cautious, sensitive, imaginative, and more interested in ideas than people and things. The second orientation, extraversion, describes the direction of interest outward to nature and other people rather than inward to the thoughts and feelings of the self. Typically the extravert is described as sociable, friendly, outgoing, and talkative. In Jung's own words, "The first attitude [introversion] is normally characterized by a hesitant, reflective, retiring nature that keeps itself to itself, shrinks from objects, is always slightly on the defensive and prefers to hide behind mistrustful scrutiny. The second [extraversion] is normally characterized by an outgoing, candid, and accommodating nature that adapts easily to a given situation, quickly forms attachments, and, setting aside any possible misgivings, will often venture forth with careless confidence into unknown situations" (Jung, 1953, p. 44).

Jung avoided a simplistic division of the numerous personality traits into one of these two categories.

Instead he emphasized the differing degrees of introversion and extraversion in each person. Jung also explained that a tendency toward a particular orientation does not mean that under certain circumstances the opposite orientation characteristics never come through. For example, introverts may become more interested in the objective outside world when the world affects the inner self. The extravert may turn inward, becoming more subjective and moody, when frustrations arise with the outside world. Furthermore, Jung's eightfold typology included different types of introverts and extraverts. He divided both introverted and extraverted orientations into thinking, feeling, sensing, and intuitive types. Thus to simply categorize someone as introverted or extraverted is often misleading.

Jung also emphasized that neither orientation is particularly better than the other. In fact, the functioning of any community of people may perhaps be best when there is a combination of both introverts and extraverts. However, problems can arise when individuals develop extreme personality patterns. Jung hypothesized that the extreme introvert may be characterized by intense anxiety, chronic fatigue, and irritability due to the individual's concentrated emphasis on subjective and internal feelings. The extreme extravert, who is strongly influenced by social surroundings, values, and opinions, may develop pathological dependencies on people and things.

Recent research shows that occupational interests among college students are often related to Jungian typology. For example, introverts have strong interests in mathematics, computer programming, library science, chemistry, and engineering, whereas extraverts have more interest in sales, public relations, acting, and restaurant and hotel management.

The first personality inventory developed by Jungian analysts was called the Gray-Wheelwright. It has since been replaced by the more popular Myers-Briggs Type Indicator (MBTI). The MBTI has been used to identify extraverts and introverts as well as the subtypes of thinking, sensing, feeling, and intuitive.

Other personality theorists have followed Jung's lead and have further researched the concepts of introversion and extraversion. British psychologists Hans Eysenck and Sybil Eysenck theorized that various individual variations can be reduced to two genetically influenced dimensions, one being extraversion-introversion. They developed the Eysenck Personality Questionnaire to measure in part the degree of extraversion and introversion in individuals. Through the use of this questionnaire and much research, these psychologists have found that introverts have sensitive and easily aroused central nervous systems, while extraverts have less sensitive, less highly aroused, and more inhibitory brain processes. While giving some credit to early environmental factors, the Eysencks believe these orientations to be biologically rooted.

Other psychologists have expanded on the work done by Eysenck and Eysenck, developing and assessing what they consider the "big five" personality factors. Extraversion is included as one of these five factors. A widely used test that includes an introversion-extraversion scale is the Minnesota Multiphasic Personality Inventory (MMPI). Although other personality inventories, such as the California Personality Inventory (CP) and the Taylor-Johnson Temperament Analysis, do not have specific introversion-extraversion scales, they include other scales that appear to measure introversive and extraversive qualities.

Reference

Jung, C. G. (1953). Two essays on analytical psychology. In H. Read, M. Fordham, & G. Adler (Eds.), *The collected works of C. G. Jung* (Vol. 7). Princeton, NJ: Pantheon.

A. E. KING

See PERSONALITY; PSYCHOLOGICAL TYPES; JUNG'S VIEW; JUNG, CARL GUSTAV; ANALYTICAL PSYCHOLOGY.

Intuition. Of the three main lines of thought regarding intuition, one maintains that there is a magical or spiritual knowing one can have by dipping into his or her soul. This can be the so-called female intuition and should not be ruled out as completely unscientific. Some psychologists believe that women have an ability, learned or inherited, that allows them to know what is happening with someone else. In this same line there is much clinical experience to indicate that schizophrenics not only may have a similar ability but also may be able occasionally to know what will happen in the future, sometimes by means of predictive dreams. All these phenomena, however, are poorly researched and must be considered speculative.

The second area of intuition is that used by people in their interactions with one another. This is based on observations one makes of another person in conversation. Kohut (1977) believes intuitions are observation conclusions that occur very quickly at an unconscious level. This means they are based on identifiable, if subtle, data collection.

Jung (1971) renders a unique and functional use of the term *intuition*. He identifies intuition as one-half of the polarity of sensing versus intuition, one of three such polarities that he uses to identify psychological types. This sensing-intuition polarity indicates how people perceive the world, how they gather information. Sensing types perceive the world in concrete and factual terms, while intuitive types perceive what is more abstract. Sensing is an external function, while Jung's intuition is internal.

Intuitive types in Jung's definition are imaginative, inquisitive, internal, creative, speculative, and perfectionistic. These people are interested in understanding the present in light of the past, function on hunches rather than visible facts, and are inspired by the possibilities of life rather than the present facts. Intuition of this type causes people to be interested in relationships rather than individual elements of a system. Thus intuitives focus on job, marriage, and friendship relationships.

The strength of intuition is that one can sometimes make brilliant observations of the world by looking inward. Such a person can avoid the distractions of external stimulation. The weakness of a dependence on intuition is that one who looks only inward is inclined to be stubborn about his or her observations, neglecting contradictory visible facts. When one looks inward for insight, one also sees sin, so an intuitive type is often inclined toward undue self-criticism.

References

Jung, C. G. (1971). *Psychological types*. Princeton, NJ: Princeton University Press.
Kohut, H. (1977). *The restoration of the self*. New York: International Universities Press.

R. B. JOHNSON

See PSYCHOLOGICAL TYPES: JUNG'S VIEW.

IQ. *See* INTELLIGENCE QUOTIENT.

Isolation. An ego defense mechanism wherein thoughts, ideas, or memories are separated from the emotional charge with which they are normally associated. This unconscious process serves to protect the individual from the pain or conflict threatened by that association. The result is thoughts or memories that, despite their real significance in the life of the individual, are experienced as lifeless and free of emotional charge. An example would be the parent who can recount every act of child abuse entirely without conscious awareness of feeling.

R. LARKIN

See DEFENSE MECHANISMS.

Jj

James, William (1842–1910). An important figure in the intellectual history of the United States whose contributions defy simple categorization. He has been called America's first great psychologist, although he preferred not to be called a psychologist at all. James's contributions to modern thought encompass three major disciplines: philosophy, psychology, and religion.

James was born in New York City, and much has been written about the eminence of his immediate family, especially his brother, Henry, the novelist. But of greater relevance is the influence of his father, whose writings include both philosophy and theology. Henry James, Sr., studied at Princeton Theological Seminary but turned against what he considered the formality of "professional religion." He found a congenial form of spirituality in the writings of Emanuel Swedenborg, whose writings centered on attempts to synthesize science, philosophy, and biblical doctrine. Until his matriculation at Harvard, William James never had long periods of sustained formal schooling; rather, his family was the locus of his education. Although James's mature thought bears little resemblance to the particulars of his father's views, his ultimate areas of interest clearly seem to have been influenced by his father's interests. His sympathetic attitude toward religious phenomena in a time when secularism was more fashionable also seems traceable to his father.

After periods of study of foreign languages and the arts in Europe, James enrolled at Harvard in 1861. However, he was unable to settle on a career path, studying chemistry, biology, and then medicine. He finally completed a medical degree at Cambridge in 1869 and returned to Harvard as a faculty member in 1872. James stayed at Harvard until his retirement in 1907.

One field of James's contribution is philosophy. He purposely avoided a systematic philosophy; to him the value of asking the right questions was of greater value than any answers. Like his father he eschewed even the appearance of dogmatism. He had also picked up the European custom of writing for popular rather than professional audiences. These twin qualities of being unsystematic and popular are best expressed by Ralph Barton Perry, who called James "an explorer, not a map maker."

James's most famous philosophical work is *Pragmatism: A New Name for Some Old Ways of Thinking* (1907). As an epistemological idea, pragmatism is a position on the character of truth: a statement is true if it leads to correct uses of the world or correct predictions of what will happen when one acts experimentally. In its popular form an idea is true if it works when tried in a natural setting. Pragmatism was James's contribution to the founding of the functionalist school of psychology, which asserts that the important study of behavior is how an organism adapts itself for survival.

Another important doctrine is James's concept of radical empiricism. In a 1904 essay entitled "Does Consciousness Exist?" James asserted that consciousness, considered as a principle of explanation of behavior, had come to be reified and treated as a thing for philosophers and psychologists to discover, describe, and explain. This error represented an intellectual blind alley; James did not deny that individuals have thoughts, but all that could meaningfully be said is that thoughts have the function of knowing. Radical empiricism argued that the old distinction between a knower (subject) and the known (object) was a useless dualism; the elements of the world are pure experience, and knowing refers merely to one possible relationship between two episodes in an individual's experience. This doctrine affected later students of epistemology, including Bertrand Russell, and it also affected psychology by reinforcing the conviction that the discipline was wrongly conceived by those who defined it as a study of the mind.

A second field to which James contributed is psychology. The single work to be considered is *Principles of Psychology* (1890). Twelve years in the writing and more than a thousand pages in length, the *Principles* was immediately recognized as a milestone achievement for the new discipline of psychology and was widely adopted as a textbook in

Europe as well as the United States. James thought of the book as a description of the current state of affairs in psychology, which revealed the discipline to be young, incomplete, and not yet amenable to a global theory. But it might also be said that the book mirrors the years when James was publicly, albeit reluctantly, identified as a psychologist. The *Principles* contains the sum of the physiological psychology that James studied in Europe during his days as a medical student and offered as the first psychology course taught at Harvard in 1875. The *Principles* also contains a summary and critique of the experimental psychology of perception advocated by Wilhelm Wundt and his students. However, even though James established the first American psychology laboratory at Harvard, he professed no great enthusiasm for the results or the methods of the experimental approach to psychology.

The chapter in *Principles of Psychology* entitled "The Stream of Thought" has affected literature as well as philosophy and psychology. Opposing a mental chemistry that divided consciousness into discrete atoms such as images, ideas, or feelings, James described consciousness as having continuity like a stream, which exhibits both identifiable substantive parts and transitive parts in which boundaries are blurred and distinctions are made only imprecisely. When his chapters on emotion (propounding what is now called the James-Lange theory), habit, and the multiplicity of the self are added to the list of novel ideas and fruitful reformulations of older ideas, it is clear that the *Principles* is not only James's most important work but also one of the most influential works in the history of psychology.

Santayana (1920) once remarked that while James's *Principles* represented his best work, he would be destined to be remembered for three lesser works: *Pragmatism, The Will to Believe* (1897), and *The Varieties of Religious Experience* (1902)—the two latter books containing the substance of his thoughts on religion. James, like his father, fled from religious orthodoxy but for different reasons. The application of pragmatism to religion specified that beliefs cannot be held to be true on a priori grounds but must prove themselves by pragmatic test. On that score, belief in God is justifiable to James if holding that belief leads an individual to better behavior than if that individual had acted from unbelief. Indeed, by objecting to the doctrine or justifying religious beliefs on historical or rationalistic grounds, James opened the door for people to expand the range of their beliefs. One can reasonably choose to believe something if one is willing to believe it conditionally and discard the belief if it fails to work experimentally.

It is no surprise that James actively entertained many nonstandard beliefs, including everything from animistic metaphysics to parapsychological phenomena. The most valuable product of those interests is the *Varieties*, in which James uses historical sources and personal documents as raw materials for a psychology of religion. In addition to discussing the phenomena of conversion, mysticism, and saintliness, James makes two central points. First, the value of religious sentiments and activities cannot be assessed by discussing the rationality of their origins. True to the spirit of pragmatism, James showed that healthy activity occurs even in people moved by questionable doctrine, and he argued that religion's function as a way of knowing life is vitally important to humanity. Second, James sought to demonstrate that one could plausibly explain religious experience by applying psychological knowledge.

Reference

Santayana, G. (1920). *Character and opinion in the United States*. New York: Scribner's.

L. S. SHAFFER

See PSYCHOLOGY OF RELIGION.

Janet, Pierre Marie Félix (1859–1947). French neurologist who sought to integrate academic psychology and the clinical treatment of mental illness. In 1882 Janet's report of an unusual case of hypnosis and clairvoyance enabled him to become a student of Jean-Martin Charcot. Janet received his Ph.D. from the University of Paris in 1889 with a thesis on the psychology of automatic ideas. At Charcot's invitation he then became director of the psychological clinic at the Salpêtrière Hospital, where he completed his M.D. degree in 1892 with a thesis on the mental state of hysterics. He became lecturer in psychology at the Sorbonne in 1895 and professor at the College de France in 1902 while remaining a practicing physician specializing in nervous and mental disorders.

Janet was interested in both therapy and theory. He believed that academic psychology and clinical psychology could enrich each other. He thought that the level of psychic energy and the particular mental level are causes of some neurotic reactions. Janet saw neurotics as having low mental tension, without enough energy to meet life's needs. Both heredity and environment influenced the amount of energy available. Fatigue, malnutrition, disease, and even inadequate education could lead to lowered energy.

Janet proposed that persons have both conscious and unconscious mental levels. Ideas that would normally be under conscious control could split off and develop their own system. A lack of integration could result in a splitting of the personality into alternating personalities unaware of each other. He claimed that Sigmund Freud's psychoanalysis was based on his work and that of Charcot, a claim which led to a strained relationship with Freud. Although Janet used the term *unconscious,* he was using it in a descriptive rather than a dynamic sense. He never attributed psychiatric symptoms to unconscious forces, as Freud did.

Although he was the spokesman for French psychology during the first third of the twentieth century, Janet left few followers either in France or elsewhere. He wrote many articles and 16 books, but only *The Major Symptoms of Hysteria* (1907), *Principles of Psychotherapy* (1924), and *Psychological Healing* (1925) were translated into English. He is best known for his study of hysteria. His system of psychology and psychopathology was promoted primarily by Morton Prince, a disciple of his who lived in the United States.

R. L. KOTESKEY

See HYPNOSIS; CHARCOT, JEAN-MARTIN; PSYCHOANALYTIC PSYCHOLOGY.

Jealousy. Variously described as a sin, an emotion, an anxiety state, or a trait, depending on the perspective of the definer, jealousy is almost as old as the human race (Gen. 4). Perhaps it is because jealousy is such a pervasive ingredient in the human experience that it is so difficult to define. Scripture describes jealousy as unyielding (Song of Sol. 8:6), angry (Prov. 6:34), and cruel (Prov. 27:4), but does not directly label jealousy as a sin. Most biblical references to jealousy center around God as a jealous God. God's name is jealous (Exod. 34:14); idolatry is banned on the basis of God's jealousy (Exod. 20:5); God views the church with godly jealousy (2 Cor. 11:2); we can provoke God to jealousy through idolatrous behavior (1 Cor. 10:22). These figures of speech point to the intensity of God's affection, fervency, and sincere love for his own (Harris, Archer, & Waltke, 1980).

Jealousy always involves three persons: self, a loved one, and a rival. Feelings of fear arise in the self when there is a threatened (real or imagined) loss of the affection of the loved one. "Jealousy is never wholly rational" (Cameron, 1963, p. 490). Fear can be accompanied by hostility toward the rival, and both are often intense emotions because the threatened loss strikes at one's self-esteem and narcissism. Opinions vary as to whether there is a cohesive continuum connecting "normal" jealousy with the extreme instance of morbid or delusional jealousy. Some theories posit similar dynamics for both, while others see them as different.

Jealousy is usually encountered in one or more of five different settings. The first setting occurs in the context of sibling rivalry. An only child of preschool age will often exhibit signs of jealousy when a sibling is brought home for the first time to join the family. The young child is suddenly dethroned from exclusive access to parental affection to a position in which all the good emotional supplies in the family must be shared, and with a newcomer at that. Regressive behavior (soiling, thumb sucking, baby talk) may occur, or the displaced child may exhibit aggressive behavior toward the new infant (Anthony, 1970). Sibling rivalry can persist throughout childhood and into the adult years (cf.

Jacob and Esau). The second setting for jealousy is in the peer relationships that children establish in schools and neighborhoods as their social skills develop. The success or failure children experience as these friendships develop can have a powerful impact on their adult social behavior.

Love and romance provide the third major setting for jealousy. Insecure persons who are enjoying the affections of a loved one can become obsessed with losing that affection to another. Jealousy in this context can become insidious, since it preys on the unknowable aspect of a relationship and can grow into monstrous proportions. Jealousy will eventually destroy a relationship, sometimes even creating what it mistakenly suspected initially. In the Old Testament a special provision was made for the jealous husband: the offering of jealousy and the waters of jealousy (Num. 5:11–31). If a husband suspected his wife of adultery and she denied it, they were to go to a priest and present an offering. The wife would drink water mixed with soil, which would produce health in her if she were innocent and would cause her death if guilty.

The fourth occurrence of jealousy is rare but indicative of the destructive quality of jealousy: the morbidly jealous murderer. Mowat (1966) found that morbid jealousy accounted for 12% of insane male murderers incarcerated at Broadmoor in England. The crime was most frequently committed by bludgeoning or strangulation. Most morbidly jealous murderers are male; most victims are wives or mistresses. On the average these murderers had been married ten years and had been delusional for half that time.

Finally, jealousy is a frequent symptom among the paranoid. Jealousy operates under the defense mechanisms of denial and projection and thrives in personalities with narcissistic wounds and fragile self-esteem structures. Suspicion and mistrust abound in the jealous person (Meissner, 1978), and false judgments, illogical deductions, and misinterpreted trivia feed it. While not the most important symptom of the paranoid person, jealousy is a significant one and one that greatly impairs the quality of life.

References

Anthony, E. J. (1970). The behavior disorders of children. In P. H. Mussen (Ed.), *Carmichael's manual of child psychology.* New York: Wiley.

Cameron, N. (1963). *Personality development and psychopathology.* Boston: Houghton Mifflin.

Harris, R. L., Archer, G. L., & Waltke, B. K. (1980). *Theological wordbook of the Old Testament.* Chicago: Moody.

Meissner, W. W. (1978). *The paranoid process.* New York: Aronson.

Mowat, R. R. (1966). *Morbid jealousy and murder: A psychiatric study of morbidly jealous murderers at Broadmoor.* London: Tavistock.

J. R. BECK

See PARANOIA; EMOTION.

Jesus Christ. Although he wrote no books on psychology or any other subject, Jesus Christ must be counted among the eminent contributors to psychology, through his life and teaching. Whatever one may believe about Jesus, it is safe to say that no one, upon a serious reading of the Gospels, can fail to acknowledge his role as a profound teacher. Jesus' role as a teacher derived its power and authority in part from the fact that he lived what he taught. He was his teaching. Those who were convinced of the truth of his teaching were grasped by his presence and by the fact that his teaching was a verbal expression of the truth manifested by his presence. He not only spoke of love, he was loving. He not only spoke of forgiveness, he was forgiving.

Since Jesus' teachings were congruent with the truth of his being, it can be said that they had ontological validity. With respect to human nature, if a statement has ontological validity it expresses a truth about the essence of human nature. As Christians we affirm that as Jesus expressed the truth of his being in his life and teaching, he also manifested what is true for us. Jesus said, "I am the way and the truth and the life. No one comes to the Father except through me" (John 14:6, NIV). His truth is our truth. For us to know God means that we have to grapple with the meaning and relevance of Jesus' truth for ourselves.

If we believe that Jesus' teachings are ontologically valid, then we also imply their psychological validity. This is to say that Jesus teaches a way of life that facilitates mental and emotional health and brings about wholeness within. Jesus calls each one to align with a way of being that brings one inwardly in touch with the deepest possibilities within the self. If psychology ignores this way and its potential for those who have mentally and emotionally lost their way, it does so to its own detriment. One might even argue that Jesus' teachings set the agenda for psychology, for he addressed those concerns that are most fundamental to human nature. It is on these concerns that psychology needs to focus in order to contribute to the development of wholeness within persons.

What did Jesus emphasize about human nature that has implications for psychology? What really is the good news? Jesus proclaimed that one is not bound by or limited by that which one's senses would tell one is reality. The world perceived by the senses is not the real world. The view that sees persons as constituted essentially of matter, as beginning with the birth of their bodies and ending with the death of their bodies, is not only inaccurate but terribly limiting. Jesus asserted repeatedly in many different ways that there exists an inner dimension to people that is incorporeal. He called this dimension the spirit, and it is in the spirit that the real source of one's personhood and the truth of one's being reside. This is the light within that must shine rather than stay hidden. The light within is a much more reliable guide to illuminate one's way than a code of expectations that comes from without, such as human traditions and laws.

This inwardness, the realm of spirit, is the kingdom of God; it is there for persons to inherit if they but seek it. At the time of Jesus the Jews were looking for a messiah who would restore the kingdom of Israel and reign as God's representative on earth. The Jews anticipated an earthly kingdom with a political leader sent by God. Jesus turned this anticipation inward. The kingdom of God is not external and will not come as a political institution. Rather, it is within. Persons' connection with God is that of spirit to Spirit.

Since the kingdom of God is within, we are not separated from each other, as our three-dimensional frame of reference suggests, but at the level of being we are one. We are united and together with each other in God. Separation then becomes an illusion, a transitory phenomenon. The truth is that we are in union in spirit though we persist in our illusion of separation. Jesus directed his teachings toward enabling one to discover the nature of being, union at the level of being with others and with God, and the nature of illusions.

From a psychological standpoint the inheritance of the kingdom of God may be viewed as the process of self-discovery. If self and spirit are the same, then the therapeutic process of self-discovery becomes a spiritual quest. The nature of each person's quest is different because each person is unique, but since each is essentially spirit, there are challenges or tasks that each quest shares.

Jesus' teachings are most relevant for psychology because he addressed those challenges that are common to everyone's quest. For example, the process of self-discovery has to involve severing dependency ties to parents. Jesus addressed this challenge when he said: "Do not suppose that I have come to bring peace to the earth. I did not come to bring peace, but a sword. For I have come to turn a man against his father, a daughter against her mother, a daughter-in-law against her mother-in-law—a man's enemies will be the members of his own household. Anyone who loves father or mother more than me is not worthy of me; anyone who loves his son or daughter more than me is not worthy of me" (Matt. 10:34–37, NIV). Jesus did not mean that he had come to foster domestic strife but rather that the process of following him, the quest for the discovery of the truth of one's own being, inevitably involves a revision of the nature of one's parental relationships. This can cause strife, but strife is certainly not the primary goal.

What is it that Jesus taught that is most germane to the tasks we all face in the process of self-discovery? Jesus said that the two most important commandments are "Love the Lord your God with all your heart and with all your soul and with all your mind. . . . And . . . Love your neighbor as yourself" (Matt. 22:37–39, NIV). These commandments put the challenge to be loving at the heart of self-discovery. A close look at the first commandment suggests it can be taken as an exhortation and as a statement of fact. As an exhortation it is a directive. As a statement of fact the first commandment contains the truth that what one has as one's central concern one will love with all one's heart, soul, and mind. "Where your treasure is, there your heart will be also" (Matt. 6:21, NIV) is another way of saying this. If the pursuit of money has become one's central concern, then that is what will grasp one totally. If another person has become one's central concern, then that relational involvement will grasp one totally. This fact underlines how important it is that one's central concern allow for the fullest and most meaningful growth of oneself. To love anything short of that which calls forth the fullest expression of one's being only violates one's being. Love of God is the only central concern that does not violate one's being.

Too often love of God implies an objectification of God, as though God is out there somewhere and it is one's duty to love him and worship him. Once God is objectified, what becomes emphasized is one's separation from him. As long as one believes there is a separation that must be bridged, one precludes the bridgement. One's belief sustains the separation. To love God without objectifying God is to commit oneself to love. For "God is love." To love God is to love loving. To love loving is to make loving God one's central concern.

To take on the challenge to be loving does not violate one's being. It draws the fullest possible expression of one's being out of oneself. To be loving also requires one to love one's own being. One cannot reject or hate oneself and love another, for since persons relate through self to another and since self is the channel for love, self-rejection sabotages one's efforts to love. A person cannot relate around self to another. One relates through one's self-hate and projects this on the other in such a way that the other comes to be seen as an attacker.

The relationship between love of self and love of another leads to the second commandment, "You shall love your neighbor as yourself." This can also be seen as a statement of fact as well as an exhortation. As an exhortation it is a directive. As a statement of fact it asserts that you will love your neighbor as yourself. If you love yourself, you will love your neighbor. If you do not love yourself, you cannot love your neighbor. So love of self becomes the basis for love of neighbor.

This may sound egocentric. However, egocentricity and self-love are antithetical. Egocentricity is self-protectiveness, not self-love. Egocentricity seeks to resolve feelings of insecurity with the erection of defenses around the self. Then these defenses come to be taken for the self and one loses sight of the true self.

Self-love is self-affirming and seeks the nondefensive expression of being. Self-love emerges in the struggle to be loving, for in this effort one has to cull away the inner obstacles to self-love. As one lovingly engages in this culling process, one is brought closer and closer to the beauty of one's own being. This is a gradual and lengthy process and requires an ongoing, rigorous self-examination to bring to awareness the nature of one's defenses and the myriad ways one substitutes a reliance on them for being true to oneself.

How does one learn to love? This is not a question that can be addressed prescriptively. One cannot tell another how to love but can only suggest that a person go and try it. Jesus did show what it means to love by loving those around him. How did Jesus love? He remained consistently true to himself in all his interactions with others. He insisted on his freedom to be true to his own being and granted others the freedom to be true to their being. He shared his vision of himself unreservedly and so awoke those around him to their own beings.

Forgiveness as a manifestation of love is crucial to the process of self-discovery. In the struggle to forgive one discovers self, because in forgiveness the person shifts focus from blaming another to self. In blame one can only see another's fault. One loses sight of self in the challenge to be oneself in truth. In blame one says, "I cannot be until you acknowledge the wrong you did to me." As Finch asserts: "How little do we appreciate the fact that what gets the focus of our attention, gets us. The feat of holding some grudge actually has the effect of the grudge holding us. Being unwilling to let go of yesterday retards us. The self becomes stifled in a mode of existence that does not exist" (Malony, 1980, pp. 253–254).

Forgiveness is particularly relevant in working through the blame one holds toward one's parents. As long as one blames one's parents for their failures to care, one continues to hold one's parents responsible for one's being. It is as if one says to one's parents, "You have been bad parents, and until you become good parents on my terms I cannot be myself." If one cannot be oneself, one cannot love oneself. So the blame one sustains toward one's parents impedes one's self-discovery. Forgiveness is the only antidote. In forgiveness one releases any claim one has on the other to be good on one's own terms.

Forgiveness is not simply an intellectual process. It may necessitate that one experience intense rage in order to allow one to existentially discover the basis for one's blame. Forgiveness, if it is genuine, is a process of working through one's feelings to a release of a grudge one is holding against the other. The challenge to forgive is ongoing. Any time one turns away from forgiveness, one locks oneself into a grudge and imprisons oneself therein.

The effort to be loving in all love's manifestations facilitates the emergence of authentic selfhood. To live in this effort is to take Jesus' teachings seriously. If psychology ignores what Jesus taught by way of modeling and by way of instructing, it ignores what is crucial to accomplishing the clinical task—that of facilitating the development of personhood.

Reference

Malony, H. N. (Ed.). (1980). *A Christian existential psychology: The contributions of John G. Finch.* Washington, DC: University Press of America.

W. T. WEYERHAEUSER

See HEALTHY PERSONALITY; CHARCOT, JEAN-MARTIN; PSYCHOANALYTIC PSYCHOLOGY.

Jung, Carl Gustav (1875–1961). Swiss psychotherapist, founder of analytical psychology. Eight of Jung's uncles were clergymen; his father was a Lutheran pastor who inwardly struggled with the validity of his faith throughout his life. Jung began to perceive that the religion of his father and of most Christians seemed to consist of theological doctrine—knowledge about God at the expense of the experience of God. He advocated primary knowledge of God. Shortly before his death, when he was asked directly whether he believed there is a God, he responded, "No, I do not believe, I know."

Life's opposites fascinated Jung; his parents exemplified what he later saw as the inevitable nature of things. His mother was earthy, while his father was spiritually removed. His early observations laid the foundation for later theories about introversion-extroversion.

Jung studied at the University of Basel and the University of Zurich. Though he pursued a degree in medicine, he also studied philosophy and theology. Between the ages of 16 and 25 he read widely in theology and philosophy, moving from Plato to Kant and Hegel, to the mystic Meister Eckhardt, and to Nietzsche. It was while reading the *Textbook of Insanity* by Krafft-Ebing that he felt his calling. Here was the blending of the spiritual and the biological. Psychiatry was not a respected vocation in the early twentieth century, however, and Jung went against the advice of teachers and friends when he became Eugen Bleuler's assistant at the Burgholzli mental hospital in 1900.

Jung was quickly promoted to senior staff physician, and in 1902 he went to Paris to study psychopathology with Pierre Janet. His fascination with the occult led him to research a young medium's work. His doctoral thesis "On the Psychology and Pathology of So-called Occult Phenomena" included themes that would later be incorporated into his theories. He saw the personalities the medium assumed during her trances as manifestation of the parts of herself buried in her unconscious.

In these initial years Jung produced the thesis that behind all psychosis and its strange manifestations is a story. Therapy, in Jung's perspective, began only after the investigation of that whole story. At the center of that story was a secret that wanted to be revealed. His next experiments were in word association. This work led to his definition of complexes, influential linked ideas or collections of associations that determine behavior.

After being appointed lecturer at the University of Zurich in 1905, Jung published *Psychology of Dementia Praecox,* a pioneering work on schizophrenia, in 1907. He theorized that delusions and hallucinations could have psychological origins; Jung was one of the first to attempt psychoanalytic treatment of these cases. After Sigmund Freud read the book he asked to meet Jung in Vienna. This was the beginning of Jung's seven years of close association with the psychoanalytic movement. A schism developed when Jung published *Psychology of the Unconscious,* in which he proposed that the son's incestuous desire for his mother lay in spiritual roots. Indeed, Jung's growing interest in the unconscious and its relationship to a person's general and religious history diverged from Freud's emphasis on infantile sexuality. These and other differences led to Jung's inevitable break with the psychoanalytical school in 1913. Meanwhile, Jung was busy in intense studies of his own unconscious. Preceding and during World War I he was troubled by dreams of Europe drowning in blood. He recorded these dreams and even painted them, as an artistic expression of his unconscious drives. During this period Jung formulated important life concepts; namely, that one must be aware of and harness both the conscious and the unconscious aspects of the psyche.

Though Jung maintained his practice at his house at Kusnacht on Lake Zurich, he traveled extensively to lecture and received many honorary awards. Though his first lecture tour of the United States was with Freud, he later went back on his own. In 1924 he studied the Pueblo Indians in New Mexico. Looking for lost aspects of the human myth, he also studied a variety of cultures in Europe and Africa. In India he was impressed with the Buddhists' ability to assimilate the nature of opposites more effectively than was evidenced in Western culture.

Jung's lifetime of study, travel, and introspection substantially advanced the study of psychology. His major areas of contribution include definitions and development of personality types (extraversion/introversion, intuiting/sensing, feeling/thinking), the collective unconscious, archetypes, the self, the nature of dreams, word association, the value of myths, individuation, and the psyche's drive toward wholeness.

Jung's emphasis on the reality of the soul and his incorporation of this reality into his analytical psychology enables one to see numerous connections between analytical psychology and religion. Jung had a deep and abiding respect for the Bible and saw it as a book that speaks of the meaning of life, the meaning of death, and of the mysteries of evil and suffering as well as the mysteries of love and healing. It deals with the psychic fact of sin and guilt and the liberation that comes with forgiveness. Above all it deals with the holy, with the realities that are beyond words and simple formulations. Much of the power of the Bible for Jung was in its stories, figures, and symbols.

In 1952 Jung published an essay entitled *Answers to Job,* which touched on the psychological understanding of Scripture. He made some significant connections. He postulated that all religious statements are rooted in the soul, or psyche, and are forms of confessions of the soul. He felt the purpose of religious statements is the tutelage of souls. Jung also saw religious statements as being rooted in the experience of the transcendent. For Jung the psyche/soul is the place where the divine and the human intersect. He understood that Christ was the divine model of that intersection. He also affirmed that the cross is the most appropriate symbol of that intersection between the vertical and the horizontal and that it represents the need for the ego to die so that the soul can come to life.

Jung proved to be one of the most prolific writers in the field of psychology and religion. He left a legacy of material, most importantly *Symbols of Transformation; Psychological Types; Two Essays on Analytical Psychology; The Archetypes and the Collective Unconscious; Psychology and Religion: East and West; Memories, Dreams and Reflections; Man and His Symbols;* and *Modern Man in Search of a Soul.*

D. J. FRENCHAK

See ANALYTICAL PSYCHOLOGY; JUNGIAN ANALYSIS; PSYCHOLOGICAL TYPES: JUNG'S VIEW; ARCHETYPES.

Jungian Analysis. At the turn of the twentieth century Carl Gustav Jung and Sigmund Freud independently developed their ideas about the reality and importance of the unconscious. Freud, the older man, was the first to publish some of his findings, and Jung was greatly impressed by Freud's work. The two met and enjoyed a close working relationship and friendship from about 1906 to 1913, when personal and theoretical differences drove them apart.

After he left Freud, Jung worked alone and developed his own depth psychology, which he called analytical psychology to distinguish it from Freud's psychoanalysis. Jung agreed with Freud on the idea of libido or psychic energy, on the existence of the unconscious part of the mind, on repression, and on the importance of dreams. However, Jung believed the unconscious contained not only repressed or forgotten memories and emotions that were personal to an individual but also typical patterns of energy and behavior that are common to everyone. These patterns Jung called archetypes. He called the latter strata of the unconscious the collective unconscious or objective psyche to distinguish it from the personal unconscious.

Jung also observed in people an innate urge toward wholeness. He distinguished between the ego and the self. The ego he regarded as the center of consciousness, while the self is the center of a total personality that embraces both the conscious and the unconscious. He believed the self to be the whole personality that exists from the beginning as a potentiality and strives to be realized through a developmental life process in which the ego must participate. Jung called this process individuation. In this process the center of the personality shifts from ego to self, and as the ego becomes more conscious of the self, the range of consciousness greatly expands.

Process and Style. The cornerstone of Jungian analysis is the individuation process. The Jungian analyst tries to help this process take place in clients in the belief that as persons individuate they become more whole and therefore find healing and creative solutions for their difficulties.

Jung did not prescribe any set treatment methodology. For one thing, he perceived that people are psychologically different. Some are extraverts (more oriented to outer reality), and some are introverts (more oriented toward inner reality). In addition, there are four psychological functions: thinking, feeling, sensation, and intuition. Each person uses one of these functions as his or her main function, and this determines one's particular approach to life. For this reason a therapist of one personality type may work differently than a therapist of another type. A therapist may also work one way with a client who is an introverted thinking type and a different way with a client who is an extraverted feeling type.

In addition, Jungian psychology as it is practiced is not a monochromatic system. Some Jungian analysts tend to pattern their therapy after Jung's own approach. Others are more eclectic in their approach and may combine Jungian methods with methodologies from other schools of psychology. Still others have altered Jung's original ideas so much that they refer to their psychology as archetypal psychology to distinguish it from Jung's analytical psychology. Jungian analysts come from varied professional backgrounds, and this also may influence how they work as therapists.

Techniques. Nevertheless, there are certain typical methods and procedures widely used in Jungian analysis. While Jungian analysts can and do function as marriage counselors, family counselors, and group therapists, the main thrust of Jungian analysis is individual therapy. Because all Jungian analysts are trained first as psychotherapists, generally accepted psychotherapeutic procedures are usually followed. However, in addition there is an attempt to work with unconscious material as it emerges in dreams, fantasies, or slips of the tongue. It is the use of unconscious material that distinguishes analysis from therapy or counseling. Viewed in this way all analysis is a form of therapy, but not all therapy is analysis, since a great deal of therapy deals only with the ego.

Dreams are frequently especially important in Jungian analysis. Dreams are seen as manifestations of the unconscious that tend to compensate inadequate or one-sided ego attitudes. They are regarded as emanating from the self, and for this reason they tend to illuminate and heal when they are recognized, contemplated, and (when possible) understood. The language of dreams is symbolic. This means that they use something known and familiar in the everyday world of consciousness to represent something that is unconscious and therefore not yet known. In this way unconscious contents can approach consciousness and thus enlarge and creatively alter a person's conscious viewpoint.

Dreams are pertinent to particular people at specific times in their lives. For this reason no single theory of the meaning of dreams is always applicable. Jung rejected Freud's narrow interpretation of dreams as always symbolic of repressed sexual urges. Instead of imposing a meaning on the dream from a theoretical structure, the Jungian analyst tries to listen carefully to the structure and symbolism of the dream to see what the dream itself is expressing.

Because dreams are, like a tailor-made suit of clothes, so highly individual, one needs to know who the dreamer is and what that person's life circumstances are before a dream can be understood. When a client presents a dream, he or she is often encouraged to express his or her associations to the various dream symbols and images. Sometimes the analyst may also amplify the dream by pointing to similar archetypal motifs in myths and fairy tales. It is as important to explore the dream as a living experience as it is to interpret the dream along the lines of psychological theory.

Dream images and other manifestations of the unconscious may be further developed by the process of active imagination. In this process a person who is fully awake and alert interacts with images that have arisen from the unconscious. For instance, a figure who appeared in a dream may be brought back to consciousness and a dialogue with that figure may develop. By concentrating on dream figures and images they may begin to have a life of their own, and the ego can then interact with the enlivened psychic image. Sometimes a whole story may develop, the dream or fantasy being continued in this way and allowed to evolve. This method allows consciousness and the unconscious to approach each other, and permits the self, as a function of the psyche transcending and uniting them both, to bring about a process of inner unification. Because active imagination requires a certain amount of psychological maturity and development, it is not a recommended procedure with everyone and often is utilized only in later stages of analysis.

Jungian analysis also regards creative expressions of the psyche as important for the healing process. Dancing, painting, sculpting, and writing are often found to be helpful ways to express and integrate the unconscious. When these methods are used, the point is not to become a good dancer or artist but to use nonintellectual ways of contacting the vital energy of the self. It is also often recommended that a client keep an informal notebook called a journal in which he or she can record and contain dreams, fantasies, thoughts, creative inspirations—anything that crosses the screen of consciousness.

The Analytic Relationship. Jung regarded the relationship between therapist and client as especially important. It was his belief that in the process of therapy the personality of the therapist could beneficially affect the personality of the client. If this is to happen, the therapist must be a relatively conscious, mature, and ethical person. Because Jung felt the relationship of therapist and client is so important, he rejected Freud's idea that the client should lie on a couch and the therapist sit behind him or her. Instead he worked with his clients face to face so there could be a direct and equal interaction.

The relationship between therapist and client is called the transference. The transference may be a relatively simple matter of rapport, a warm relationship in which the concerns of the client can be talked over in a friendly and understanding atmosphere. The transference also includes the hopes and expectations that the client brings into the relationship plus the interest in the client that the therapist brings. But sometimes the transference may include the transferring to the therapist of reactions that come from childhood. For example, the client may unconsciously see in the therapist the figure of the mother or father and repeat patterns of relating that were learned in childhood. The transference may also include the projection onto the therapist of unconscious archetypal images. For instance, the savior archetype or the archetype of the anima or animus (the contrasexual side of a man or woman) may be projected onto the therapist.

Projection is an unconscious mechanism that results in vital aspects of one person being seen in the other person. When projections occur in the transference, it is helpful and often necessary to analyze them in order to make conscious the projected images. In this way the client can withdraw his projections and thereby enlarge the scope of his personality.

It may also work the other way around, and the therapist may project contents of her own onto the client. This is called the countertransference. It is expected that with the help of her extensive personal analysis the therapist will be aware of this when it happens and will integrate what is taking place within herself.

One reason for the importance of the relationship between the therapist and the client is that it provides a container for the client's personality. Their relationship has been likened to an alchemical vessel in which the various components of the client's psyche can be contained and gradually transformed: projections can be recognized and withdrawn, dreams can be remembered and reexperienced, emotions can be freely expressed and integrated, all within the closed vessel of the analytical relationship.

Training. Since so much in the process of Jungian analysis depends on the personality of the therapist, Jungian training programs place a heavy emphasis on the therapist's individuation. The wholeness, consciousness, and integrity of the therapist are thought to be as important as the acquisition of techniques of therapy. For this reason the cornerstone of training to be a Jungian analyst is the continuing analysis of the therapist, although many other things are also involved.

Training is undergone at Jungian Institutes in major cities throughout the United States and Europe. Although requirements for admission to training programs vary from one institute to another, all require that a person is or will soon be a licensed psychotherapist and have a considerable amount of personal Jungian analysis. Psychiatrists, psychologists, marriage and family counselors, specially licensed social workers, and sometimes clergy may all be eligible for training programs that lead to certification as a Jungian analyst.

Jungian Analysis and Other Traditions. Jungian analysis can be compared to other psychological approaches to Christianity. As indicated, Jung agreed with many of Freud's ideas but saw the psyche in a much broader light than Freud and never insisted upon a specific treatment methodology. Like Carl Rogers, Jung believed the psyche is self-healing and that the true doctor is in the patient; unlike Rogers, Jung emphasized the importance of integrating unconscious material. Jungian psychology sees the emphasis transactional analysis places upon the interaction of parent-child-adult as the exploration of an important archetype (that is why it is so universally applicable) but understands that personality includes many other archetypes in addition to this one. Where Gestalt psychology has little personality theory, Jungian analysis rests on an extensive theory of personality. Gestalt therapy also frequently utilizes an extraverted group approach, whereas Jungian work usually is individual and frequently more introverted.

The concepts of analytical psychology can both enrich and challenge the Christian viewpoint. For instance, Jung's theory of the collective unconscious can be viewed as giving a scientific basis for the biblical view of the objective existence and reality of a spiritual world. Likewise, Jung's idea of individuation corroborates and vitalizes the Christian premise that the life of the individual has a meaning. Jung's idea that Christ is a symbolic representation of the self may enrich the Christian doctrine of Christ as the Son of God, but it also challenges the Christian idea of a unique revelation in Christ, since Jung saw the self represented in many different religious traditions. Finally, Jung's treatment of the nature of evil and its relationship to the self and to individuation may also prove problematical to the Christian.

Yet some of the methods frequently used in Jungian analysis can be helpful to the Christian counselor or spiritual director. Jung's emphasis on the importance of dreams, for instance, finds ample support in the view of the Bible and early church, where dreams were universally regarded as an important way in which God spoke to people. Jung's symbolic approach to the unconscious also finds a fruitful parallel in the parables of Jesus, for Jesus also taught in the "as if" language of symbols. The Bible also contains several excellent instances of active imagination—Ezekiel's vision of the dry bones and Isaiah's vision of Yahweh.

J. A. SANFORD

See ANALYTICAL PSYCHOLOGY.

Jungian Psychology. *See* ANALYTICAL PSYCHOLOGY.

Justice. *See* MORAL DEVELOPMENT.

Juvenile Delinquency. A distinct category within the study of criminology. Its scope includes particular definitions of certain behavior, a body of theoretical explanations of the activity, and approaches to treatment and prevention.

Definitions and Trends. Delinquency involves behavior that violates the law, although there is a wide range in the severity of such acts. On one end of the continuum are status offenses, such as truancy or possession of alcohol. Status offenses would not violate the law if they were committed by an adult. At the other end of the continuum are index offenses, such as murder, rape, assault, or robbery. Some states reserve the term *delinquency* for index offenses.

Most juveniles arrested in the United States for index offenses are charged with property crimes, particularly burglary and larceny. Most states set the age limit for delinquency between 16 and 18. Violations of law by those over the designated age are defined as adult crimes and treated accordingly. Serious violent behavior may be treated as an adult crime and the juvenile may be tried as an adult.

Based on the doctrine of *parens patriae* (wherein the state may legally intervene to provide assistance to persons in need of care), separate courts were created to remove children from the criminal process. In 1899 Illinois became the first state to establish a juvenile court. Reformers of the late nineteenth century mounted the "save the child" movement and emphasized the distinction between adult and juvenile courts.

The typical case in juvenile court begins with a referral made by police, school, public or private social service agencies, or parents. The referral is handled by an intake officer, who evaluates the case and responds by rejecting the case; placing the youth on informal probation or referring to a child care agency; or filing a petition in juvenile court if the offense is serious or guilt is not admitted. A petition is the juvenile equivalent of an adult indictment. Juveniles are then given a hearing and adjudication. A juvenile court hearing results in a finding and a disposition. The disposition may be a dismissal of the case, a referral to adult court, probation, placement in foster care, or commitment to a residential facility of public or private operation. If a child is sent to a residential facility, a probation officer will usually be assigned upon release to provide supervision.

Violent crime among juveniles has risen during the 1980s and 1990s, and juvenile arrests for violent crime rose 47% between 1988 and 1992 (Federal Bureau of Investigation, 1993). An important change in youth violence involves the availability of firearms, as the number of juveniles killed by firearms rose by 144% between 1986 and 1992 (Federal Bureau of Investigation, 1993).

Correlates of Delinquency. Research has suggested numerous factors correlated with juvenile delinquency (Henggeler & Borduin, 1990; Yoshikawa, 1994). Delinquent adolescents demonstrate lower levels of moral reasoning than nondelinquent youth. Many delinquent adolescents appear to be motivated by immediate gratification of needs and display deficits in social skills. There is also a consistent link between lower cognitive ability or intelligence and delinquency (Yoshikawa, 1994). Cognitive deficits may combine with other factors, such as impulsivity, and lead to poor problem solving.

Family factors also appear to influence delinquent behavior. Inconsistent parental discipline and monitoring, an absence of positive communication and nurturance, child maltreatment or neglect, marital conflict, and maternal stress and depression are associated with the families of delinquent youth (Yoshikawa, 1994). Parents of delinquent youth also tend to have less social support than parents of nondelinquent youth. Social support includes ties to people or organizations (family, friends, churches, agencies) that provide information, resources, or emotional support.

Association with delinquent peers appears to be the strongest influence on adolescent delinquency (Henggeler & Borduin, 1990). Low socioeconomic status is consistently related to juvenile delinquency. Finally, dozens of studies have found an inverse relationship between religiosity and delinquency (Cochran, Wood, & Arneklev, 1994), especially in the nonviolent areas of substance use and sexual behavior.

Explanations of Delinquent Behavior. Jensen and Rojek (1992) suggest four general sociological theories of juvenile delinquency, which include social control, structural strain, normative conflict, and labeling theories.

Social control theories focus on the strength of social bonds of an individual or family to conventional institutions, goals, and values. Bonds to social institutions (family, school, church) control or prevent delinquency by reinforcing norms of behavior.

Cochran, Wood, and Arneklev (1994) suggested that the research on religiosity and delinquency indicates religion serves a social control influence that inhibits deviance.

A variation of social control ideas is drift theory (Matza, 1964), which suggests delinquency arises from a lack of motivation for conventional behavior. Youth with little investment in conformity may drift toward criminal behavior. Delinquency is a lack of commitment to prosocial behavior and organizations.

Structural strain theories focus on cultural definitions of success and limits within the social structure for some groups to achieve that success. According to Merton (1957), when people learn that they should strive for certain goals and there is not an equal opportunity to achieve those goals, some people will be frustrated. This frustration prompts some people toward means of achieving those goals in the form of crime and delinquency. A youth who desires expensive tennis shoes as a symbol of success but does not have the means to buy them may resort to stealing. Delinquency is thus explained by studying the ways in which means are blocked for various groups within the social order.

Cohen (1955) presents a variation of Merton's strain theory. According to Cohen, youth at the bottom of the social ladder may create delinquent gangs in response to status frustration. Gangs could be considered collective efforts to cope with such frustration by turning middle-class norms upside down to create a new set of contracultural norms. Instead of viewing delinquents as drifters, structural strain theorists view delinquent youth as problem solvers.

Cloward and Ohlin (1960) provide an elaboration of structural strain theory. They argue that problems in social status are also influenced by opportunities for organized criminal activity and identify three distinct delinquent subcultures: criminalistic-theft-oriented groups, which serve to introduce youth to adult organized crime; conflict-oriented groups, which focus on violence with other gangs; and retreatist groups, which are made up of individuals ill-equipped for organized criminal activity and who withdraw from society through drug use. If status problems exist in a context with organized criminal opportunities, then involvement with a criminal subculture is likely. If no such well-organized opportunities exist, then gang life involves fighting or drug use.

Normative conflict theories suggest delinquency is a result of diverse cultural norms of right and wrong. Rather than viewing delinquency as an intentional rebellion against the dominant culture, normative conflict theorists see deviance as conformity to the norms of a particular subculture. Gang membership then involves successful socialization into lower-class cultural values. Conflicting views of morality among subcultures are considered a normal aspect of culture in the United States, with minority subcultures judged delinquent.

Labeling theory focuses on the way legislation defines the categories of delinquency. Labeling theorists suggest that the label *delinquent* may be adopted by the individual as a self-concept and thereby influence future behavior. The labeling process also includes the expectations of others, who relate to delinquent youth differently than other youth labeled normal. A child labeled delinquent may perform in ways consistent with the expectations of others.

Treatment. Juvenile law has historically operated with the goal of rehabilitating youthful offenders rather than simply punishing them. In the late 1970s several major reviews of research on the treatment of juvenile offenders suggested most treatments were ineffective. Modest support has been reported for the efficacy of behavioral parent training, cognitive problem-solving skills training, and family therapy in reducing recidivism (Kazdin, 1995). Most of this research involved relatively mild cases of antisocial behavior. Deterrence programs involving encounters between adolescents and hardcore prisoners were associated with higher recidivism rates for participants.

One of the few promising approaches to treatment of serious juvenile offenders with demonstrated effectiveness is multisystemic therapy (MST; Henggeler & Borduin, 1990). MST is based on the assumption that behavior is determined by various environmental influences that make up a social ecology. An ecology consists of multiple interconnected systems, such as family, peer group, school, neighborhood, parental workplace, and culture. These systems interact to influence behavior.

Henggeler and Borduin (1990) suggest that other approaches to treatment may not have been effective with serious juvenile offenders for two major reasons. First, many approaches are too narrow and intervene at only one causal factor of delinquency. MST is derived from research that indicates antisocial behavior is determined by multiple causes, so MST interventions target multiple factors. Second, many treatment approaches are too removed from natural environment of a youth (e.g., residential setting). MST service delivery usually occurs in the home of delinquent youth and involves the entire family. Therapists also engage teachers, peers, and other individuals within the ecology of the family.

MST is flexible in drawing on interventions from cognitive behavioral therapies, parent training, and family therapy. Research on MST has demonstrated positive long-term effects on recidivism and family functioning with serious juvenile offenders across several studies (Henggeler, Schoenwald, & Pickrel, 1995). Two of the most common targets of intervention in MST include empowering effective parenting and promoting the adolescent's disengagement from deviant peers to build stronger ties to prosocial groups. Parenting can be improved through parent training (e.g., teaching discipline strategies) and establishing parental social support (e.g., church or extended family). Youth can be disengaged from deviant peers by monitoring peer involvement and encouraging prosocial interests.

Prevention. Several programs aimed at preventing juvenile delinquency have shown promising results (Yoshikawa, 1994). Successful programs involve strengthening the two broad categories of family support and education. The common elements of successful programs include affecting multiple risk factors; engaging multiple settings (home, school); targeting urban, low-income populations; lasting at least two years; and intervening during the first five years of life.

References

Cloward, R. A., & Ohlin, L. E. (1960). *Delinquency and opportunity.* New York: Free Press.

Cochran, J. K., Wood, P. B., & Arneklev, B. J. (1994). Is the religiosity-delinquency relationship spurious? A test of arousal and social control theories. *Journal of Research in Crime and Delinquency, 31,* 92–123.

Cohen, A. K. (1955). *Delinquent boys: The culture of the gang.* Glencoe, IL: Free Press.

Federal Bureau of Investigation. (1993). *Uniform crime reports 1992.* Washington, DC: U.S. Government Printing Office.

Henggeler, S. W., & Borduin, C. M. (1990). *Family therapy and beyond: A multisystemic approach to treating the behavior problems of children and adolescents.* Pacific Grove, CA: Brooks/Cole.

Henggeler, S. W., Schoenwald, S. K., & Pickrel, S. G. (1995). Multisystemic therapy: Bridging the gap between university- and community-based treatment. *Journal of Consulting and Clinical Psychology, 63,* 709–717.

Jensen, G. F., & Rojek, D. G. (1992). *Delinquency and youth crime* (2nd ed.). Prospect Heights, IL: Waveland.

Kazdin, A. E. (1995). *Conduct disorder in childhood and adolescence* (2nd ed.). Thousand Oaks, CA: Sage.

Matza, D. (1964). *Delinquency and drift.* New York: Wiley.

Merton, R. K. (1957). *Social theory and social structure.* New York: Free Press.

Yoshikawa, H. (1994). Prevention as cumulative protection: Effects of early family support and education on chronic delinquency and its risks. *Psychological Bulletin, 115,* 28–54.

S. J. Sandage

See Community Psychology.

Kk

Kelly, George Alexander (1905–1967). Developer of the personal constructs theory, a cognitive model of human personality that suggests that the critical dimension of human personality is the way in which the individual views, experiences, and experiments with the world. Frequently using the concept of person as scientist, Kelly stated that the fundamental motivation of human life is to understand, predict, and control events. To meet this need people learn distinctive ways of looking at the world that are pragmatically useful. Human distress occurs when one's personal constructs, one's way of viewing the world, cease to work well.

Born in Kansas, Kelly received his undergraduate education at Friends University in Kansas and Park College in Missouri. He pursued graduate training at the University of Kansas, the University of Minnesota, the University of Edinburgh, and the State University of Iowa, where he completed his Ph.D. in 1931. He directed a traveling rural psychological clinic in his early career, was an aviation psychologist during World War II, and later succeeded Carl Rogers as director of the Psychology Clinic at Ohio State University, where he was also professor of psychology.

It was at Ohio State that Kelly developed and wrote his most famous work, *The Psychology of Personal Constructs* (1955), a carefully written formal exposition of his theory of personality. Kelly's theory was a rather radical departure from the three major forces in psychology at the time of its writing (behavioral, psychoanalytic, and nondirective theories). Kelly himself was a man whose career reflected great breadth and willingness to experiment.

Kelly published relatively few works (two books and 12 articles); his greatest influence was through his graduate students at Ohio State. For example, the work of his student Walter Mischel, the social learning personality theorist, continues to show the profound influence of Kelly's cognitive view. Toward the end of his career Kelly engaged in a wide variety of activities that furthered the development of psychology as a profession; these activities included serving as a member of numerous federal and professional commissions. For the last two years of his life he served as a professor at Brandeis University.

S. L. JONES

See PERSONAL CONSTRUCT THEORY.

Kierkegaard, Søren Aabye (1813–1855). Danish Christian author whose writings continually cross the parochial boundaries that separate psychology, literature, philosophy, theology, and devotional writings. His literary career began with a series of pseudonymous works that were initially prompted by a failed love affair and ended with a series of pamphlets and newspaper articles in which he attacked the state church in an attempt to "reintroduce Christianity into Christendom." These writings were accompanied by a steady stream of devotional works, which became explicitly Christian in his later years.

Kierkegaard struggled all his life with what he termed his melancholy, the result no doubt of an upbringing that he himself described as crazy. The dominant figure in his life, besides his disappointed fiancée, was his father, a man whose stern religious exterior apparently shrouded an interior life of guilt and anxiety. However, Kierkegaard's acute analytical mind and literary gifts enabled him to wrest insights from his own suffering that have universal power and validity. Much of his struggle revolved around his attempt to actualize a Christian faith in his own life, so his writings have a particular depth and interest to Christians.

Kierkegaard was concerned with an effort to help his reader develop the inward personal concern, or subjectivity, that he saw as the essential precondition for becoming a true Christian. Kierkegaard saw human beings as spirit. This does not mean they are immaterial but rather that each human being is intended to be a self. To be a self is to be a self-conscious, responsible agent who becomes what one is and is what one becomes. Kierkegaard presents many withering critiques of the "mass man" who loses his self in the crowd, being content to be a self like all the others. Selfhood is an achievement, not a birthright; a self is acquired only through free, responsible choice.

There are many different ways of attempting to become a self. The structure of the human self is such that its destiny—an eternal happiness—can be realized only by using its freedom to relate to God. However, Kierkegaard believed that there are different kinds and levels of God relationships. The Christian view, as he saw it, demands a recognition that humans are incapable of truly choosing God because of sin. Christians are the ones who recognize their inability to truly become the self they are destined to be and who recognize their selfhood as a gift made possible by faith in Christ, a gift that is realized by the believer's willingness to die to self with Christ. Thus the Christian view is paradoxical: only the one who is willing to lose life can save it.

Three major themes in Kierkegaard's writings are of particular interest to psychologists: a developmental theory of selfhood, an implicit therapeutic methodological ideal, and a descriptive analysis of certain passions and moods. A brief account of his contributions in these three areas follows.

The Stages on Life's Way. Kierkegaard believed there are three major answers to the question, How should I exist? These three answers make up what he termed the three spheres of existence, or "stages on life's way." These are the aesthetic stage, the ethical stage, and the religious stage. The aesthetic sphere is characterized by living for the moment and attempting to enjoy life by cultivating one's natural inclinations. The ethical sphere is marked by a dutiful commitment to ideals that are seen as having eternal validity. The religious sphere, from which the Christian way of existence is demarcated as a special case, is noted by the struggle to relate properly to God through suffering and repentance.

Although Kierkegaard saw these three stages as a natural progression, in the sense that everyone begins with the aesthetic stage and ideally should progress to the religious, he insisted that this development is far from automatic or even normal. Since human beings are spiritual creatures, this growth toward selfhood is rooted in freedom. Hence each stage can be and often is a way of existence that the individual never surpasses. For this reason Kierkegaard termed them spheres of existence as well as stages.

The Maieutic Ideal. Although Kierkegaard hoped to help his contemporaries achieve moral and spiritual growth, he believed that this ultimately depends on the individual's freedom. Hence he did not think it possible to directly help another person. Rather, he attempted to help his readers indirectly by creating a situation in which they might possibly grasp the truth for themselves and choose to actualize it in their lives. To this end he regarded himself, like Socrates, as a midwife who would help others give birth; this is the maieutic ideal. According to Kierkegaard, even God acts maieutically. When God appears to humans, he appears as a humble servant, which makes it possible for human beings to reject God's help and creates the possibility of offense.

Kierkegaard personally attempted to follow the maieutic ideal in a variety of ways. Rather than simply telling his readers about the three stages of existence, he created fictional characters, pseudonyms, who write books representing and embodying these three spheres. In this way he attempts to withdraw from the reader, forcing readers to think about the books in relation to their own lives. These pseudonymous books are permeated by humor and irony, and since their content is supposed to be attributable to their pseudonymous authors, they have often misled unwary interpreters of Kierkegaard.

Passions and Moods. Kierkegaard gave detailed analyses of crucial human moods and passions. Certain moods, particularly anxiety (sometimes translated as dread) and despair, have a decisive significance as revelations of the nature and condition of the self. Anxiety is seen as a necessary accompaniment of human freedom. In anxiety the self confronts its own possibilities and recognizes the possibility of its own nothingness. *The Concept of Anxiety* (1844) explains how anxiety plays a crucial role in the psychological explanation of the possibility of sin.

Despair is the mood in which the lack of selfhood reveals itself. *The Sickness unto Death* (1849) chronicles and analyzes the many forms of despair. Kierkegaard views despair as a universal human condition, though most people are not conscious of this despair. From a Christian viewpoint despair is sin, a failure to ground one's self in God, and the only cure is the passion of faith.

From Kierkegaard's view the achievement of selfhood involves a synthesis of contrasting elements: temporality and eternity, soul and body, necessity and freedom. This synthesis is made possible by the passions. Genuine passions are not transitory emotions that happen to a person but enduring caring concerns around which the whole personality coalesces. Kierkegaard's *Works of Love* (1847) contrasts the Christian passion of neighbor love with various natural loves such as erotic love and friendship. The supreme passion from a Christian perspective is faith, which is not mere intellectual assent but a condition in which the whole person is totally rooted in God.

Additional Reading

Kierkegaard, S. (1967–1978). [*Kierkegaard's journals and papers* (7 vols.)] (H. V. Hong, and E. H. Hong, Eds. and Trans.). Bloomington: Indiana University Press.

C. S. EVANS

See PHILOSOPHICAL PSYCHOLOGY; EXISTENTIAL PSYCHOLOGY AND PSYCHOTHERAPY.

Kinsey, Alfred Charles (1894–1956). A pioneer in the contemporary study of sexual behavior. Born in Hoboken, New Jersey, Kinsey suffered from rheumatic fever and rickets in high school and was known as the boy who never had a girl. Although he was reared in a strict Methodist home, Kinsey began to lose his faith as a college student (B.S. Bowdoin, 1916; D.Sc. Harvard, 1920). In 1920, at age 26, he began teaching at Indiana University as an instructor in the zoology department. That year he met the first girl he ever dated and married her the next. He never attended church after 1921, expressing indignation about what he felt the Judeo-Christian tradition had done to Western culture. He also felt that Christianity is full of inaccuracies and paranoia.

Possibly because as a zoology instructor he was reportedly always discussing sex with students, Kinsey was chosen in 1938 to coordinate a marriage course at Indiana University. He began by taking sexual histories from students. In 1940, under fire from the religious community, he was pressured to resign teaching the course but was permitted to continue his sex research.

The research that started with his student interviews in 1938 expanded with funding from the Rockefeller Foundation in 1941. These reports, and the others written by Kinsey and his associates, were based on surveys of 5,300 white males and 5,490 white females conducted over a period of 15 years. All were sponsored by the Institute for Sex Research at Indiana University, of which Kinsey was the director until his death. Kinsey's work on sexuality culminated in *Sexual Behavior in the Human Male* (1948) and *Sexual Behavior in the Human Female* (1953).

The Institute for Sex Research has since its inception featured an unusual degree of secretiveness about what was inquired into and from whom. To date a complete list of the questions asked has never been published, and the samples employed are known only in scant outline. As more has become known, serious methodological problems have become apparent, some of which cast doubt on Kinsey's major conclusions.

The most serious of these problems concerns the method of sampling. Kinsey reported being surprised at the high incidence of deviant sexual practice, since he claimed that "no preconception of what is rare or what is common, what is moral or socially significant, or what is normal and what is abnormal . . . entered into the choice of histories" (Kinsey, Pomeroy, & Martin, 1948, p. 7). However, scrutiny suggests that Kinsey's sampling methods unquestionably skewed his figures toward high incidence of all forms of sexually unusual behavior. Kinsey was interested in sampling not those whose sex lives were dull but rather those whose were bizarre. Pomeroy relates how he and Kinsey traveled thousands of miles by car to interview one man about whose sexual exploits they had heard (Pomeroy, 1972, p. 122). Known homosexual communities were included in population samples selected each year but the first of the 15-year project. All these bizarre histories were added together to give the estimates for the general population.

These and other methodological and statistical problems (Cochran, Mosteller, & Tukey, 1953) give reason to seriously question the Kinsey data as a description of normal sexual behavior, which is how they are presented. Kinsey's major contribution, therefore, should be seen to lie in the fact that his work opened a new phase in empirical studies of human sexual behavior.

References

Cochran, W. G., Mosteller, F., & Tukey, J. W. (1953). Statistical problems of the Kinsey report. *Journal of the American Statistical Association, 48,* 673–716.

Kinsey, A. C., Pomeroy, W. B., & Martin, C. E. (1948). *Sexual behavior in the human male.* Philadelphia: Saunders.

Kinsey, A. C., Pomeroy, W. B., Martin, C. E., & Gebhard, P. H. (1953). *Sexual behavior in the human female.* Philadelphia: Saunders.

Pomeroy, W. B. (1972). *Dr. Kinsey and the Institute for Sex Research.* New York: Harper & Row.

P. CAMERON

See SEXUALITY.

Klein, Melanie (1882–1960). Born in Vienna, Klein came across Sigmund Freud's *Interpretation of Dreams* about the time of World War I. This so impressed her that she entered psychoanalytic training and personal analysis under Sandor Ferenczi. Later she pursued further personal analysis with Karl Abraham in Berlin. Her interest in child development and her clinical work with children led to development of a psychoanalytic treatment approach for children that brought her prominence. In 1925 she was invited to lecture in England and later, because of political instability on the Continent, she settled there permanently.

Klein's work has always been creative but controversial in psychoanalytic circles. She is one of the first psychoanalytic theorists to seriously develop Freud's theory of object relations. She is considered an object relations theorist because she addresses early human experience by focusing on the development of internal images, or objects, that the infant forms as internal representations of external people.

Klein identifies two positions from which infants relate to objects: paranoid-schizoid (birth to approximately 6 months) and the depressive (6 to 12 months). Technically these are not stages that one goes through and completes. According to Klein, no one is ever completely finished with aspects of these ways of relating; thus her use of positions instead of stages.

Paranoid-Schizoid Position. Klein completely accepts Freud's concept of two instinctual drives that are basic to all human motivation: libido, which has to do with the biological need for gratification, and the death instinct, which involves self-destruction and aggression. According to Klein, both instincts create fantasies in regard to the infant's first human contact, the mother's breast. The death instinct first becomes manifested in cannibalistic fantasies involving devouring the breast. The infant then perceives frustration or delay while nursing as the breast's intentionally withholding nurturance. The infant responds with envy and greed, wishing to spoil this bad breast. Libido, however, attaches to the image of a gratifying breast. This gives rise to the experience of gratitude in the infant for the good breast. Klein identifies the good and bad breasts as part objects in that the infant as yet is incapable of relating to his mother as a whole person or object.

This instinctual situation gives rise to the most extreme conflict and terror for infants. Because of their envy and greed they are faced with the possibility of destroying their internal good breast on which they are dependent and annihilating themselves along with it.

Klein posits the presence from birth of an ego that intervenes by dissociating the good and bad objects from each other in order to protect the good object. This splitting of the infant's internal world into good and bad is the schizoid aspect of this position. The paranoid aspect emerges as the ego projects in fantasy the death instinct and its object, the bad breast, outside the ego by a process called projective identification. However, in creating a bad object that they consider outside themselves, infants then view the source of danger from their bad object as originating outside themselves. Klein calls this persecutory anxiety. Thus instead of fearing that they will devour the good breast, infants fear an external persecutor that can devour them and their good object.

Depressive Position. In spite of the turmoil in the infant's internal world, in normal development the ego develops through gratifying experiences. These experiences stimulate gratitude in the infant, which begins to outweigh aggression and persecutory anxiety. With this change in the balance of the infant's inner world comes the decreasing necessity for the ego to split itself. Typically, according to Klein, this starts to occur around three to four months of age. Because of a more integrated ego the infant goes from fantasizing in terms of part objects to perceiving his or her mothering object as a whole person.

With the commencing of these ego developments comes the depressive position. In using the earlier defenses of splitting and projective identification the infant did not feel personal responsibility for the object. The source of attack against the ideal object was seen as coming from outside the self. However, in the depressive position infants come to realize that they have been hating the same object they love. Now the infant's anxiety changes from persecutory anxiety to depressive anxiety and guilt.

Normal working through of depressive anxiety involves attempts, sometimes lifelong, at reparation of the perceived injured love object through genuine concern and empathy for others. Pathological ways that infants or adults utilize in an attempt to escape from the pain of hurting the very one whom they love involve either regression to more primitive split relationships or a frantic display of hyperactivity to avoid awareness of feeling.

Critique. Klein's theory continues to be controversial. She is considered to be outside the mainstream of psychoanalytic thought because she posits far too complex mental fantasies for the first six months of life, emphasizes instinctual fantasies to the neglect of environmental factors, and bases too much on the concept of an inborn death instinct. However, her emphasis on how internal needs and conflicts color memory of relationships and experiences is invaluable to understanding the human condition. The importance of early object relations, aggression in early development, and projection identification and splitting have all been accepted into psychoanalysis.

The theory is rich in its potential to interface with theology. Its emphasis on relationship and interpersonal contact parallels the heart of the Old Testament's focus on an intimate knowledge of God and of New Testament theology of body of Christ interrelatedness. By identifying the part that the child plays in coloring his or her experiences she illustrates the role of responsibility in psychoanalytic theory.

Additional Readings

Klein, M. (1975). *Love, guilt and reparation and other works* (Vol. 3). New York: Delacorte.

Klein, M. (1975). *Envy and gratitude and other works* (Vol. 4). New York: Delacorte.

W. L. Edkins

See Object Relations Theory.

Kleptomania. A disorder of impulse control, the failure to resist impulses to steal objects. The material stolen is not necessarily taken because the person wants its use or because it is valuable. In fact the objects may be given away, secretively returned, or stored. Most kleptomaniacs steal alone and do not plan their thefts. In concert with other disorders of impulse control (pathological gambling, pyromania, and the explosive disorders), kleptomania features a gradual increase of inner turmoil before the impulse appears. After the act of stealing the kleptomaniac often reports some gratification or release of tension. The pathology of this disorder is even more apparent in the fact that the person stealing the objects usually has the money to pay for them. The motivation for stealing involves the thrill of doing something illegal without being caught.

Most kleptomaniacs show limited insight into the consequences of their behavior. Law enforcement personnel are often the first professionals to encounter the kleptomaniac. Stealing occurs in the context of other disorders (schizophrenias, conduct disorders, antisocial disorders, and manic episodes) without the central features of kleptomania. Most incidents of shoplifting are not examples of kleptomania because shoplifting is often planned, unresisted, and for immediate use or gain. King Victor of Sardinia and King Henry IV of France are some of history's more notable kleptomaniacs.

Statistics regarding the incidence of true kleptomania and its sex ratio are scarce; the best evidence suggests it is a rare disorder. Sometimes thieves will attempt to feign kleptomania as a defensive legal maneuver. Differential diagnosis must center on whether there was a resistance to the impulse to steal and whether the objects were of value and for personal use. The disorder sometimes first appears in childhood or adolescence.

Psychoanalytic theorists have given considerable attention to this relatively rare condition. Most suggestions by the analysts link the impulse to a desire to replace lost objects of esteem. For example, Fenichel (1945) writes, "Cleptomania means in principle to take possession of things which give the strength or the power to fight supposed dangers, especially . . . dangers of loss of self-esteem or affection" (p. 370).

Reference

Fenichel, O. (1945). *The psychoanalytic theory of neurosis*. New York: Norton.

J. R. BECK

Koffka, Kurt (1886–1941). One of the three founders of Gestalt psychology, the only one born in Germany. Although he came from a long line of lawyers, Koffka developed an interest in science and philosophy. With the exception of one year in Edinburgh he was educated entirely in Berlin, receiving his Ph.D. from the University of Berlin in 1909.

Koffka took a number of research positions, meeting Max Wertheimer and Wolfgang Köhler in Frankfurt in 1910. In 1911 he went to the University of Geissen and remained there until 1924, when he came to the United States. After holding visiting professorships at Cornell and Wisconsin, he was appointed research professor at Smith College. With no pressure on him to publish or teach, he did many experiments in the field of visual perception. He remained at Smith College until his death.

After World War I, psychologists in the United States were only vaguely aware of the new psychology developing in Germany. Koffka wrote "Perception: An Introduction to Gestalt-Theorie" for the *Psychological Bulletin* in 1922. This article was the first formal presentation of the Gestalt approach available to American psychologists. The title gave rise to the misunderstanding that Gestalt psychology deals only with perception.

While Wertheimer was the originator and leader of the movement and Köhler was the physiologist

and representative to the general public, Koffka was the most productive of the three Gestalt founders. He was the most complete systematizer and organizer of the theory, the selector and integrator of all the experimental evidence. Although he wrote more than either of the other two, he showed less originality. He was an organizer rather than an originator of knowledge.

Koffka first became widely known through his book on developmental child psychology, *The Growth of the Mind* (1921). While he was recuperating from a fever caught while on an expedition to study the people of central Asia, he began work on a book intended for lay readers. However, *Principles of Gestalt Psychology* (1935) developed into a book very difficult to read and never became the definitive treatment of Gestalt psychology he intended. Koffka was always the most vocal proponent of the Gestalt position. When Americans were wondering if this was just another German philosophy, Koffka's vivid personality and good-tempered debating tactics effectively presented the mass of ingenious and challenging experiments generated by the theory. Soon everyone realized that Gestalt psychology could not be ignored.

(1927–1987) R. L. KOTESKEY

See GESTALT PSYCHOLOGY; PSYCHOLOGY, HISTORY OF.

Kohlberg, Lawrence (1927–1987). Premier scholar in the field of moral education and known for his cognitive-developmental theory of moral reasoning. Kohlberg was born of a Jewish father and a Christian mother. His affinity appeared to be with his father, not so much in terms of religion as with a sense of belonging to the Jewish people.

In 1945, while he was still in his teens, Kohlberg joined the merchant marine, then volunteered as an unpaid engineer to bring a ship of Jewish refugees illegally through the British blockade and land them in Palestine. The ship with its two thousand occupants was rammed by the British navy, tear gas was used, and several children died. This experience caused him to wonder when human life takes precedence over the laws of a country.

Kohlberg received both the B.A. and the Ph.D. from the University of Chicago. In graduate school he studied psychoanalysis under Bruno Bettelheim, humanism with Carl Rogers, and Behaviorism with Jacob Gewirtz. He felt none of these psychologies dealt adequately with the moral problems people face. By studying the writings of such philosophers as Locke, John Stuart Mill, and John Dewey and by reading Jean Piaget's work, in which moral development is viewed as inherent within the person as reasoning processes mature, he came to see that the basic principle of morality is to treat every person as an end in himself or herself, not as a means to some other good. His six-stage sequence of moral judgment places respect for every human being at the pinnacle of moral understanding. The rules of the society are in a midposition on the hierarchy, with self-interest at the lowest level.

Kohlberg held appointments at Yale University and the University of Chicago, where he instituted the Child Psychology Training Program, and Harvard University's Graduate School of Education, where he established the Center for Moral Development and Education. He applied his ideas to the classroom by advocating the use of moral dilemma stories and by encouraging the creation of Just Community Schools in which students as well as teachers decide on issues of fairness and justice.

His two major works are *The Philosophy of Moral Development* (1981) and *The Psychology of Moral Development* (1984). The third volume of the trilogy, *Education and Moral Development,* was never published due to his untimely death at the age of 59.

B. CLOUSE

See MORAL DEVELOPMENT.

Köhler, Wolfgang (1887–1967). One of the founders of Gestalt psychology. He was born in Reval, Estonia, but his family moved to Germany when he was five. He studied at Tübingen, Bonn, and finally Berlin, where he received his Ph.D. in 1909. He then went to Frankfurt as an assistant in psychology, arriving shortly before Max Wertheimer.

Köhler remained in Frankfurt until 1913, when he was invited to study chimpanzees on Tenerife, the largest of the Canary Islands. Six months after he arrived, World War I broke out, and he had to remain because he could not get home to Germany. He returned to Germany in 1920, and in 1922 became professor at the University of Berlin, the chief post at Germany's most important university. He left Germany in 1935 because of his continual conflicts with the Nazis and came to the United States. He served as professor of psychology at Swarthmore College until his retirement in 1953.

Köhler took the responsibility of presenting the Gestalt position to the general public. He wrote less than Kurt Koffka did, but his books were more readable, so they have became the authoritative word on Gestalt psychology. Although it is difficult to separate the contributions of the leaders of Gestalt psychology, Köhler is probably most responsible for the concepts of insight and isomorphism.

It is fortunate for psychology that Köhler was marooned on Tenerife, because while there he did what he called "intelligence tests on anthropoid apes." This work led to the concept of insight as opposed to trial-and-error learning. Insight is a sudden solution to a problem, a reorganization of the total field so that new relationships are seen. The chimpanzees showed this insight in solving various problems, so that once a given problem was solved, they could repeatedly solve it without error.

Köhler was the physiologist and physicist of the movement and thus most responsible for the concept of isomorphism. Isomorphism says that form and order in perceptual experience correspond to form and order in the physical world and in the physiological processes. Perceptions represent the real world but are not copies of it.

The Mentality of Apes (1917) reports Köhler's work on Tenerife and introduces the concept of insight. *Static and Stationary Gestalts* (1920) was a very scholarly work and never completely translated into English. *Gestalt Psychology* (1929) was published in English and is the most comprehensive argument for Gestalt psychology.

R. L. KOTESKEY

See INSIGHT IN LEARNING.

Korsakoff's Syndrome. Korsakoff's syndrome is an inability to form new memories, although old memories remain intact. Most often found in people who have chronically abused alcohol, Korsakoff's syndrome is a result of thiamine deficiency. Thiamine is necessary for the metabolism of fats, carbohydrates, and amino acids; without thiamine, the metabolite pyruvate damages the brain. People who consume alcohol heavily lack thiamine for two reasons: their diet is usually poor, and alcohol interferes with intestinal absorption of thiamine.

DSM-IV (American Psychiatric Association, 1994) calls Korsakoff's syndrome alcohol-induced persisting amnestic disorder. Neurological signs of confusion, movement difficulty, and odd eye movements comprise Wernicke's encephalopathy, an acute condition often preceding Korsakoff's syndrome. Thiamine treatment of Wernicke's encephalopathy sometimes forestalls development of Korsakoff's syndrome.

Korsakoff's syndrome typically develops after age 40, following many years of heavy alcohol consumption. Inability to form new memories usually occurs suddenly, and the symptoms are chronic, even if the victim abstains from alcohol. However, abstinence helps prevent further brain damage. Treatment then develops strategies to assist memory.

Symptoms of Korsakoff's syndrome are found in some patients who have brain damage from surgery or a gunshot wound, affecting the same structures in the brain as Korsakoff's.

Reference

American Psychiatric Association. (1994). *Diagnostic and statistical manual of mental disorders* (4th ed.). Washington, DC: Author.

P. D. YOUNG

See ALCOHOL-INDUCED DISORDERS.

Kraepelin, Emil (1856–1926). German psychiatrist who undertook the systematic classification of mental disorders. Born in Neustrelitz, Germany, a village near the Baltic Sea, he received his M.D. degree at the University of Würzburg in 1878. After that he studied neuroanatomy in Munich for four years and then neuropathology in Leipzig, where he worked with Wilhelm Wundt, under whom he had studied one summer while in medical school.

Although Kraepelin almost made a career of neurophysiological research, Wundt and others encouraged him to return to clinical psychiatry. He began teaching at the University of Dorpat in 1885, went to the University of Heidelberg in 1891, and was appointed professor of clinical psychiatry at Munich in 1903. In 1922 he retired from teaching to become head of the Research Institute of Psychiatry in Munich, where he remained until his death.

Kraepelin made contributions to early experimental psychology by investigating sleep, expectation, work, fatigue, and the effect of drugs on mental processes. However, his major contribution was his systematic classification of psychoses. He was determined to make psychiatry strictly scientific and to make it follow the methods of the biological sciences. He studied thousands of case histories, traveling to India, Java, Mexico, and the United States in search of material. He wanted to look not only at symptoms but also at the full course of the disorder, from its obscure origins to its recurrence, if there was one.

Although he did not originate the ideas, he brought order to classification, recognizing two major types of psychosis. Dementia Praecox (now called Schizophrenia) was seen as including several types of cases, such as catatonic, hebephrenic, or mixed. He regarded it as being caused by internal factors, with a tendency toward progressive deterioration and permanent disability. Although he admitted that 13% of such cases recovered, he concluded that either a wrong diagnosis originally had been made or that the patient would suffer a relapse.

The other major psychiatric category was the manic-depressive (now called bipolar disorder), characterized by swings of mood from elation to depression. He considered manic-depressives curable, and many of them did recover. His *Textbook of Psychiatry* was first published in 1883 and soon became the standard text. He was revising a ninth edition of it at the time of his death 43 years later. His classification system became the basis for the current ones, as reflected in the recent diagnostic and statistical manual of mental disorders of the American Psychiatric Association *(DSM-IV)*.

R. L. KOTESKEY

See CLASSIFICATION OF MENTAL DISORDERS.

Kunkel, Fritz (1889–1956). Psychotherapist who developed the concept of we-psychology. Born in Germany, Kunkel studied medicine at the University of Munich, but his broad range of interests also involved him with drama, poetry, and the arts. In World War I he was a battalion surgeon; while tending the wounded at the Battle of Verdun he was hit by shrapnel and eventually lost his left arm. He was profoundly influenced by the war and the suffering it brought, and from this experience emerged his decision to be a psychotherapist.

After the war Kunkel studied Freudian psychology and became a close friend of Alfred Adler. However, he was most influenced by Carl Gustav Jung and Jung's ideas of the collective unconscious, individuation, and the self as the center of the whole personality. Kunkel published the first of his many books in 1928, and during the next decade he became a well-known psychologist, author, and lecturer in his native Germany.

Kunkel was greatly disturbed by the rise of national socialism. When he was invited to lecture in the United States in 1936, he accepted, and in 1939 he returned and became an American citizen. He practiced psychotherapy in Los Angeles and was beginning to be as well-known in this country as he had been in Germany when he died on Easter Day, 1956, of a ruptured aorta.

Kunkel developed his own synthesis of Sigmund Freud, Adler, and Jung, and out of this emerged a distinct theory of personality that he called the we-psychology. The cornerstone of his thought is the distinction between the sterile life of the egocentric ego and the creative life of what he called the real self. Kunkel believed that because of childhood injuries the ego emerges into adult life as egocentric—that is, concerned with its own defense and the furtherance of its own ambitions. However, life eventually brings about a crisis that, if a person goes through it honestly and courageously, leads to the destruction of egocentric patterns and the emergence of a new center in the self. His masterful description of egocentricity and how it defeats the process of growth fills a gap in Jungian psychology, while his dynamic idea of the self takes him beyond the boundaries of Freud's thought.

Kunkel's books in English include his psychological commentary on the Gospel of Matthew, *Creation Continues*, and his two most important books, *How Character Develops* and *In Search of Maturity* (recently reprinted under the title *Fritz Kunkel: Selected Writings*). Although Kunkel was not a member of any particular denomination, he was a deeply religious person whose ideas have marked parallels in Christian concepts of humanity.

J. A. SANFORD

See CHRISTIAN PSYCHOLOGY; BIBLICAL ANTHROPOLOGY.

Ll

Lacunae, Superego. Defects frequently found in the superego of individuals diagnosed as having antisocial personality disorder. Conduct disorder children sometimes show the same holes or gaps in their system of morality. Such individuals are often colloquially described as having a Swiss cheese superego. The psychoanalytic assumption is that the superego defects originate from similar defects in the parents and that the child is thus unconsciously acting out the wishes of the parents. An example would be a 14-year-old boy charged with numerous counts of fire setting. All other aspects of this boy's superego functioning seemed intact. However, in this one area he experienced no guilt and saw nothing wrong with his behavior. Close examination of the family dynamics showed that in spite of his overt condemnation of the fire setting the boy's father was experiencing a good deal of vicarious excitement through his son's behavior.

D. G. BENNER

See SUPEREGO; CONSCIENCE.

Language Development. Language may be defined as a means of communicating thoughts and feelings by the use of vocalized symbols. Sounds (phonemes) are combined to produce meanings (morphemes), which are spoken in accordance with the rules of grammar (syntax). Words representing objects or events are combined with other meaningful sounds (e.g., prefixes, plurals) in a variety of ways so as to convey a message. Oral language is the primary means by which people relate to one another, thereby sharing ideas and experiences. No other species has the vocal apparatus or the intellectual capacity to develop speech as we know it, thus giving the human race an advantage over all other forms of life.

Language has its origins in the cry of the newborn and the babbling of the infant and proceeds to the first meaningful words of the one-year-old, the two-word phrases of the toddler, and the adultlike sentences of the child of four years of age. Such rapid progress in oral communication remains a mystery, baffling the mind of the scholar and delighting the heart of the parent. Jean Piaget, a careful observer of young children, noted that infants will make the same sound over and over and then will experiment by varying the sound slightly. Babies as young as two months of age respond to their own vocalizations by repeating an utterance again and again and then modifying it by changing the position of the tongue in the mouth or by increasing the volume (Flavell, 1963). Infants also learn by listening to others, so that by the time they are a year old they have restricted their speech sounds to those that correspond to their native tongue.

Repetition with variation continues with the pivot words of the toddler, the chanting of nonsense syllables by the preschooler, and the rhymes accompanying games and activities (e.g., jump rope) of the school-age child. Although they are monotonous to adults and at times exasperating to teachers and parents, such repetitions appear to be closely linked with learning a language. Pivot words are used by the small child to apply to a range of situations. For example, "allgone" may be a pivot word. When father leaves for work, the child will say "Daddy allgone." When the dog cannot be found, it is "Doggie allgone." When Mother washes the child's face after lunch, it is "Sticky allgone." Sameness with variation enables the child to learn how words are put together to express a thought. Similarly the chants, jingles, and rhymes of the older child provide a link between the familiar and the novel as clauses are repeated again and again with only a small portion of the cadence being changed with each repetition.

Although individual differences are apparent, the average 12-month-old has a vocabulary of about three words, which increases to 25 words by the age of 18 months. The number of words rises dramatically to several hundred by age 2 and several thousand by age 6. Children understand more than they verbalize, and it may be years before they pronounce some words correctly. Nouns are acquired first (e.g., baby) and then are linked with modifiers (pretty baby) and verbs (baby cry), followed by more complex sentence structures (Why is the baby crying?). Language continues to develop after the child begins school but at a slower pace. Girls have a slight advantage over boys, learning to talk sooner, articulating better, and having fewer speech defects.

There are two basic views as to how language is acquired. The first comes from social learning and reinforcement psychology with its emphasis on principles of modeling and conditioning, the second from cognitive and humanistic psychology with its stress on the potential of the human infant. The first looks to the environment as the teacher, the second to the capabilities inherent within the human organism. The learning position is that children imitate the speech sounds of parents and other models and in this way acquire the native language with its idioms, accents, and intonation. The meaning of words is learned by pairing a word with its concrete referent (e.g., the word *ball* with the object ball), and the pronunciation of words is acquired by being reinforced with parental attention for closer and closer approximations to the correct way of saying a word (e.g., "bah" becomes "ball"). Cognitive psychologists, by contrast, hold that children are able to discover for themselves the rules needed to communicate with others on a verbal level. Children will try various forms of expression, keeping those that correspond to the language around them and eliminating those not recognized by others. It is the inborn capacity of the child to make sense of the environment, not the environment itself, that results in language acquisition. Language is a symbolic representation of events the child experiences in the real world.

Language is closely related to many other areas of a person's life. It enables each of us to store information, plan our day, read a book, or write a letter. By its use we express not only our thoughts but our feelings as we communicate with others and with the God who created us.

Reference

Flavell, J. H. (1963). *The developmental psychology of Jean Piaget.* Princeton, NJ: Van Nostrand.

B. Clouse

See Communication Disorders; Cognitive Development; Life Span Development.

Lashley, Karl Spencer (1890–1958). American psychologist noted for a wide range of research. Lashley was born in Davis, West Virginia. He became interested in zoology at the University of West Virginia, from which he graduated in 1910. He continued study in zoology, receiving an M.A. from the University of Pittsburgh in 1911 and a Ph.D. in 1915 from Johns Hopkins University, where he became acquainted with John B. Watson.

Lashley held teaching and research positions at the University of Minnesota (1917–1926), the University of Chicago (1929–1935), and Harvard, from 1935 until his death. While under appointment at Harvard he worked for many years at the Yerkes Laboratory of Primate Biology.

Scientists then regarded the brain as a switchboard for making connections between stimuli and responses. Lashley set out to find these specific pathways and connections, looking for definite points of localization in the brain. However, rather than supporting the reflex arc as an element of behavior, his work challenged Watsonian behaviorism. Lashley systematically destroyed different parts and different amounts of the cerebral cortex of rats, studying the effect of such destruction on learning and memory. He found that it generally made no difference what parts of the brain were destroyed, only how much was destroyed. He discovered as well that the effect was greater when rats faced complex problems rather than simple ones.

Lashley proposed two concepts about brain function to account for his findings. The concept of mass action says that in any fairly complex learning situation the whole cortex or at least a large area of it is involved. The more cortical tissue available, the faster and more accurate the learning. The concept of equipotentiality says that one part of the cortex is essentially equal to another in tasks like maze learning. If one part is destroyed, another part can assume its functions. Most of Lashley's work was published in journals, but he summarized his findings in *Brain Mechanisms and Intelligence* (1929), which is now a classic.

R. L. Koteskey

See Brain and Human Behavior.

Latency Period. In psychoanalysis the latency period is one of the stages of psychosexual development. Its onset is the resolution of the oedipal crisis and its termination is at puberty. It is thus normally thought to begin at age 5 or 6 and to end at approximately age 12.

Sigmund Freud assumed that people experience a period of relative quiescence or inactivity of sexuality during these years. We now know that sexual interest still exists, but it is no longer at central stage, as is the case during the earlier years of oedipal struggle. The latency period is a time of consolidating and integrating previous attainments in psychosexual development. The most important of these attainments are gender identity and sex roles. Latency years are therefore characterized by a predominance of same-sex relationships that serve to solidify gender identity and basic sex roles.

D. G. Benner

See Psychosexual Development; Psychoanalytic Psychology; Gender Identity.

Law and Psychological Practice. The involvement of psychiatry and psychology with the practice of law can be traced to Daniel M'Naghten's case in England. On 20 January 1843, at the parish of Saint Martin in the Fields, County of Middlesex, M'Naghten murdered Edward Drummond, the secretary of the British prime minister. He was actually aiming at the prime minister but missed him and mortally wounded the secretary. In court M'Naghten pleaded not guilty by reason of insanity. This was perhaps the first time that medical/psychiatric evidence on the mental status of a defendant was considered in an English court The original decision hinged on the defendant's capacity, due to mental impairment, to distinguish between right and wrong and to conform his actions to the mandates of the law. To this day the M'Naghten standard, with minor variations, is the rule in most U.S. states.

Forensic psychologists credit Hugo Munsterberg as being the father of forensic practice for psychologists. Munsterberg was chair of psychology at Harvard University in 1908 when he published *On the Witness Stand* advocating for the use of psychological expertise by courts in rulings on the guilt or innocence of defendants. Controversy arose in both psychology and law as to the appropriateness of psychological testimony in court. In 1931, Lewis M. Terman, then professor of psychology at Stanford University, spoke before the Los Angeles Bar Association and emphasized the value of experimental psychology for clarifying the value of testimony in court (cited by Blau, 1984). But until the landmark case of *Jenkins v. United States* (1962), psychologists were not given equal credibility with the medical professions in court testimony.

The field of forensic psychology is now well established and respected as a specialty within clinical psychology. The American Board of Professional Psychology (ABPP) has a division of forensic psychology and offers examinations for diplomate status in the specialty. Other certifying boards also have been developed, such as the American College of Forensic Examiners and the American Board of Professional Disability Consultants; these boards recognize psychologists as expert witnesses in courts of law and offer diplomate examinations that are respected and accepted.

Traditional roles for psychologists in law have been examinations for competence to stand trial and insanity pleadings in criminal courts. Roles in the criminal justice system have expanded to include testimonies regarding dangerousness and potential for treatment in sentencing and parole hearings, as well as providing psychological services in prisons and drug rehabilitation centers.

In probate courts psychologists are recognized as expert witnesses in hearings regarding persons' ability to manage their financial and civil affairs. In civil courts psychologists testify in cases or personal injuries, workers' compensation and equal opportunity issues, product liability and wrongful death. In family courts psychologists are recognized as experts in matters of child custody and divorce settlements.

An emerging role for psychologists at present is in litigation involving the credibility of witnesses in cases of so-called recovered memory syndromes. In these cases psychologists are called in to present research data on memory, hypnosis, and related issues.

Perhaps the fastest growing specialty in clinical psychology is the field of neuropsychology. That is the subspecialty that deals with the relationship between brain and behavior. A combination of neuroscience and psychometrics has resulted in the development of specific testing instruments that can document deviations from normal functioning in cases of head injuries, strokes, invasive brain tumors, cardiovascular deficiencies, and the effects upon the brain of diseases that attack the immune system such as multiple sclerosis, HIV infections, and AIDS.

Joint degree programs in clinical psychology and law have been created at such universities as the University of Arizona, Hahnemann University with Villanova University School of Law, and the University of Nebraska-Lincoln, to name a few. Professional schools of psychology are continually adding forensic psychology courses to their curricula, and some have begun to offer a major track in the field, such as the California School of Professional Psychology-Fresno.

Another developing area is the field of police psychology, which involves not only the selection, promotion, and counseling of peace officers but also the profiling of criminal personalities to aid in detective work for tracking down murderers and serial killers. Forensic psychologists also participate in debriefings and the prevention and treatment of post traumatic stress disorder (PSTD) among victims and witnesses of both natural disasters and those that are the result of criminal activities. Hostage negotiations are often conducted either by forensic psychologists or by law enforcement personnel who have been trained by psychologists.

References

Blau, T. H. (1984). *The psychologist as expert witness.* New York: John Wiley.

Munsterberg, H. (1908). *On the witness stand.* New York: Doubleday.

L. M. Marmol

See MORAL AND ETHICAL ISSUES IN TREATMENT; MALPRACTICE.

Lay Counseling. Lay counseling refers to people helping done by lay counselors who lack the training, education, experience, or credentials to be professional therapists but who nonetheless are involved in helping people cope with personal problems (Collins, 1986). The use of such nonprofessional or paraprofessional counselors has grown considerably in recent years (Tan, 1991, 1992). Lay counseling has become a significant part of both the contemporary mental health scene (Tan, 1997) as well as Christian ministry, particularly in local churches. It is anticipated that lay caring and counseling services will take on even greater prominence in the near future as managed health care grows in the United States, with more limited coverage for mental health services and fewer people being able to afford long-term psychotherapy conducted by mental health professionals. More people will therefore turn to lay counselors, especially in local churches and parachurch organizations, which usually provide counseling services free of charge.

While there is some controversy in the literature on the relative effectiveness of lay counselors versus professional therapists (e.g., see Beutler & Kendall, 1995; Stein & Lambert, 1995), the majority of comparative studies done so far seem to favor the conclusion that lay counselors are generally as effective as professional therapists (Berman & Norton, 1985; Christensen & Jacobson, 1994). The Christian research literature is more sparse, but the few studies available also tend to support the effectiveness of lay Christian counseling (see Tan, 1991, 1992; Toh & Tan, 1997; Toh, Tan, Osburn, & Faber, 1994). More research is needed to investigate further the specific skills, deficiencies, and limitations of lay Christian counselors.

Models of Lay Counseling Ministry. Three major models of lay counseling ministry have been described (Tan, 1991). The first is the informal, spontaneous model in which lay counseling takes place in natural settings such as homes, classrooms, restaurants, neighborhoods, businesses, and churches. The lay counselors may or may not receive some basic training in helping skills, but no formal organization or direction of the lay counseling is provided and there is no ongoing supervision of the lay counselors. The second is the informal, organized model, in which the lay counselors are carefully selected, trained, and supervised regularly as they provide lay counseling services in informal and natural settings. The third model is the formal, organized model in which lay counseling is provided in settings such as a church counseling center, a community clinic or agency, or even a hospital. The lay counselors in this third model are also carefully selected, trained, and supervised regularly. Evaluation of the effectiveness of the lay counseling provided, as well as client satisfaction, may also be periodically conducted.

Starting a Lay Counseling Ministry. At least five steps are required in starting a lay counseling ministry (Tan, 1991, 1995). First, an appropriate model of lay counseling should be selected. Some churches, especially ethnic minority churches, may prefer the informal, organized model, since there may be too much stigma attached to seeking help formally, even from lay counselors. Larger churches or parachurch organizations may decide to use both the informal, organized model and the formal, organized model to more adequately meet the diverse needs of that constituency or community.

Second, in a local church, the full support of the pastor or pastoral staff and the church board should be obtained for the idea of lay counseling and the model(s) selected. Pastoral and church leaders should fully support the ministry of lay counseling as an extension of pastoral care and counseling in the church and as an essential part of the priesthood of all believers (1 Peter 2:5, 9).

Third, lay counselors need to be carefully selected using a number of helpful criteria such as spiritual maturity; psychological and emotional stability; love for and interest in people, with empathy, genuineness, and warmth or respect for them; appropriate spiritual gifts relevant to counseling (e.g., the gift of encouragement [Rom. 12:8]); some life experience (unless one is developing a peer counseling ministry in youth groups or among teens); previous training or experience in people helping (helpful but not necessary); age, gender, socioeconomic, and ethnic or cultural background relevant to the needs of the people being served; availability; teachability; and ability to maintain confidentiality. Potential lay counselors should be interviewed. The process of selection can be closed (e.g., based on nominations by pastors or church leaders) or open (anyone can apply for possible selection as a lay counselor).

Fourth, an adequate training program should be provided for the lay counselors. Many good training programs are available. Length of training varies from 24 to 50 or more hours, usually spread over several weeks to several months and covering basic listening and helping skills. Collins (1980) has recommended that the following content areas be covered: basic Bible knowledge, especially that which is relevant to counseling ministries; knowledge of counseling skills, with opportunities for practice, for example, through role playing; understanding of common problems such as anxiety, depression, stress, and spiritual dryness; awareness of ethics and dangers in counseling; and knowledge of the importance and techniques of referral, including awareness of the limits and limitations of lay counselors. Professional therapists can be involved in the training and subsequent supervision of lay counselors. A number of training manuals are available, including peer counselor training in youth groups (see Sturkie & Tan, 1992, 1993), which can be adapted for use in training adult lay counselors as well.

Finally, programs should be developed in which the trained lay counselors can be used to provide helping services to people in need of them. Ongoing regular supervision is essential for the lay counselors, and so is further training for them as they begin their counseling ministries. Such supervision is usually conducted by a licensed mental health professional or at least by a pastor or church leader with some experience and training in people helping, often in small groups of lay counselors, meeting weekly or biweekly.

If a formal, organized model is chosen and a lay counseling center needs to be set up, the following guidelines may be helpful (adapted from Partridge, 1983): determine clear objectives for the center; establish the ethos or distinctive character of the center by giving it an appropriate name; carefully select, train, and supervise the lay counselors; arrange for appropriate facilities and office space for the center; establish the operating hours of the center; set up a structure for the functioning of the center, including having a director and a board of reference or advisors; publicize the center and its services; decide on what services the center will offer and *not* offer; carefully consider the finances needed and include that amount in the annual budget of the church or organization; determine the affiliation of the center to the church or organization.

It is also important to seek legal advice regarding whether malpractice insurance is needed for the lay counselors and what is the appropriate term to use for them. In some states "lay counselors" and "lay counseling" may not be appropriate terms to use because of licensing laws for professional counselors that limit the use of the term *counselor* to those who are licensed (*see* Licensure). "Lay helpers" or "lay caregivers" may therefore be more acceptable terms to use in place of "lay counselors."

Lay counseling has continued to grow in recent years. As it develops even more, a distinctively Christian, biblical approach to lay counseling will focus on the following areas: healing and deliverance ministries; evangelism and discipleship training; missions; small group ministry; peer counseling; and cross-cultural counseling (Tan, 1994). The Lord Jesus has called us to reach out to one another with his agape love (John 13:34–35) and hence to carry each other's burdens (Gal. 6:2). The ministry of lay counseling is crucial in this context, having both biblical and research support.

References

Berman, J. S., & Norton, N. C. (1985). Does professional training make a therapist more effective? *Psychological Bulletin, 98*, 401–407.

Beutler, L. E., & Kendall, P. C. (1995). Introduction to the special section: The case for training in the provision of psychological therapy. *Journal of Consulting and Clinical Psychology, 63*, 179–181.

Christensen, A., & Jacobson, N. S. (1994). Who (or what) can do psychotherapy: The status and challenge of nonprofessional therapies. *Psychological Science, 5*, 8–14.

Collins, G. R. (1980). Lay counseling within the local church. *Leadership, 7* (4), 78–86.

Collins, G. R. (1986). *Innovative approaches to counseling.* Waco, TX: Word.

Partridge, T. J. (1983). Ten considerations in establishing a Christian counseling center. *The Christian Counselor's Journal, 4* (4), 31–33.

Stein, D. M., & Lambert, M. J. (1995). Graduate training in psychotherapy: Are therapy outcomes enhanced? *Journal of Consulting and Clinical Psychology, 63*, 182–196.

Sturkie, J., & Tan, S.-Y. (1992). *Peer counseling in youth groups.* Grand Rapids, MI: Zondervan.

Sturkie, J., & Tan, S.-Y. (1993). *Advanced peer counseling in youth groups.* Grand Rapids, MI: Zondervan.

Tan, S.-Y. (1991). *Lay counseling: Equipping Christians for a helping ministry.* Grand Rapids, MI: Zondervan.

Tan, S.-Y. (1992). Development and supervision of paraprofessional counselors. In L. Vande Creek, S. Knapp, & T. L. Jackson (Eds.), *Innovations in clinical practice: A sourcebook* (Vol. 11). Sarasota, FL: Professional Resource Press.

Tan, S.-Y. (1994). Lay counseling: A Christian approach. *Journal of Psychology and Christianity, 13*, 264–269.

Tan, S.-Y. (1995). Starting a lay counseling ministry. *Christian Counseling Today, 3* (1), 56–57.

Tan, S.-Y. (1997). The role of the psychologist in paraprofessional helping. *Professional Psychology: Research and Practice, 28*, 368–372.

Toh, Y. M., & Tan, S.-Y. (1997). The effectiveness of church-based lay counselors: A controlled outcome study. *Journal of Psychology and Christianity, 16*, 260–267.

Toh, Y. M., Tan, S.-Y., Osburn, C. D., & Faber, D. E. (1994). The evaluation of a church-based lay counseling program: Some preliminary data. *Journal of Psychology and Christianity, 13*, 270–275.

S.-Y. TAN

See PARAPROFESSIONAL THERAPY; SUPPORTIVE PSYCHOTHERAPY; COUNSELING AND PSYCHOTHERAPY: OVERVIEW.

Laziness. Laziness can be described as a general lack of motivation, especially for work or other tasks that are necessary though not intrinsically pleasant. Perhaps the best way to view laziness is in this greater context of motivation for work. Laziness considered by itself can be viewed as a personality trait of the subject being described or as an attribution that the subject makes about another person.

If laziness is to be considered a trait, that assumes it is a semipermanent or enduring characteristic of an individual, persisting through different situations. For example, Friedman's Type B individual would be lazier than the hard-driving Type A. Managers who hold to MacGregor's Theory X assume that most workers are inherently lazy and must therefore be motivated by fear and greed if management can expect to get any work out of them.

The idea that an inherited temperament can account for laziness would be consistent with Hippocrates' notion of bodily fluids determining personality. The phlegmatic (with an excess of the slow and sticky phlegm) would be the laziest of the four classic types. In the nineteenth century laziness was seen as a symptom of neurasthenia, a disease attributed to the nervous system depletion caused by excessive mental labor. In the latter part of the twentieth century chronic fatigue syndrome is cited as a culprit. Glandular malfunctions (e.g., hypothyroidism) can result in laziness, but most lazy individuals would not be able to use that excuse.

Environmental and cognitive factors conducive to the development of the lazy personality were suggested by Alfred Adler. Some people respond to inferiority feeling with an attitude of "Why try? I would only fail and look worse." Adler also noted laziness as a trait of the spoiled child, who has been insufficiently encouraged to develop social interest. From a purely behavioral perspective, the lazy person may have experienced insufficient positive reinforcement for previous efforts, and striving behavior may have extinguished. Laziness can be seen as a kind of learned helplessness: "My efforts don't matter, so why try?"

Against this assumption of laziness as a fixed trait is the view that the motivation for a specific task varies according to the nature of the task and does not reflect an underlying and pervasive low level of motivation. "I am a workaholic on my computer but a slow-moving slacker when it comes to yard work: different tasks, different responses, same individual."

Laziness should be considered an internal attribution that a person makes disparagingly about someone else: a disapproving label hung on another person who is usually despised or condemned by the person making the attribution. There is a comprehensive stereotype behind this label. The lazy other is seen as irresponsible, selfish, and inconsiderate as well as undermotivated. The reason for these attributions is that it helps the private logic of propping up one's own self-esteem with an easy comparison: "I am better than those other (lazy) people."

In a fat-phobic society the obese are assumed to be lazy and are correspondingly victims of job discrimination. In the United States, working people look down upon the poor, especially the homeless and welfare recipients, and label them as lazy. In Third-World countries without a social welfare system, the poor look down upon the rich as idle consumers, so lazy as to be unable to do their own cooking and cleaning. In Europe, many countries view their neighbors as lazy. Gypsies are frequently labeled lazy. In Australia, the Aborigines may be perceived as lazy. In the United States, Mexicans are sometimes stereotyped as lazy: taking long siestas and having an attitude of *mañana*. In Mexico, it is the North Americans who are stereotyped as too lazy to work as maids, gardeners, and fruit pickers.

Carl Gustav Jung's theory of the shadow may unite the inner and interpersonal worlds and explain how they interact on the concept of laziness. The shadow is that part of ourselves of which we are most ashamed. We push these traits into the personal unconscious, but if we remain unaware of it, we always end up projecting it onto others. Anytime we find ourselves making an internal attribution about someone else's laziness, we need to look within and explore our self-dissatisfactions.

T. L. BRINK

See MOTIVATION.

Leadership. Study of leadership and its development has flourished in both corporate and Christian arenas in recent years. Ample education is available for those seeking to improve their leadership effectiveness by studying Jesus' model, looking at both secular and Christian research, evaluating issues of leadership style and fit, and examining literature from Christian leadership experts.

Jesus' Model. A leader can be defined as one who influences followers. The ultimate example of powerful, effective, and beneficial leadership is Jesus. Ford (1991) describes Jesus' ability to create vision, shape values, and empower change as transforming leadership. Jesus' leadership was both modeled and taught, culturally relevant and transcultural, enabling and empowering and enduring. Ford's thesis is that Christian leaders in any arena of influence must allow Jesus to lead through them. Ford develops his theme by examining Jesus, the leader, as son, strategist, seer, servant, shepherd maker, spokesperson, struggler, and sustainer. Lessons of use of power, entrusting one's mission to others, and calling forth passionate commitment in followers who are changed and trained are relevant for leaders seeking to follow Jesus' model. Thus leaders must be identified with Jesus and with their followers as he was. While leaders may learn from secular leadership models, they must be cautious in their application.

Research Findings. Research in leadership has largely been applied to corporate or organizational settings. Griffin (1985) summarized studies of trait, situation, style, and interactional approaches to leadership research. Trait studies sought to isolate personality qualities essential to leadership, but findings provided minimal predictive success. Situational studies reveal cases in which circumstances call forth leaders, but prediction is also low here due to novelty of situations. Style approaches are helpful in identifying how different leaders express their different personality styles. Finally, the interactional approach examines how different styles of leaders lead different followers. For example, the autocratic or "tells" leader works best with group members of lower maturity; the "sells" leader persuades members as they mature; a democratic or "joins" leader gives encouragement to members of greater maturity; and a "laissez faire" leader intervenes little with a highly motivated group. Debate rages as to whether different style leaders must succeed each other as member qualities and needs change or whether an adaptive leader can adjust styles to changing environments.

A recognized pioneer in the area of leadership, Covey (1989, 1990) has combined lessons of organizational psychology (*see* Industrial/Organizational Psychology) and business management with a spiritual concept of objective and eternal principles. He stresses integrity of character and adherence to higher-order natural laws of right and wrong as the means for achieving personal and organizational goals. Self-examination and motivation for personal growth are prerequisites to becoming a highly effective leader. Covey enumerates seven leadership habits: being proactive, beginning with the end in mind, putting first things first, thinking win/win, seeking to understand others, using synergy, and staying personally renewed. Thus a "win/win or no deal" approach to negotiation calls for a leader to show consideration of others' views while manifesting courage to state his or her own nonnegotiable values. In a team approach to goals, a principle-centered leader creates synergy by empowering group members to freely contribute their particular strengths. Covey's leadership paradigm demands personal resolutions to show self-discipline and self-denial, character and competence, and service in a noble purpose. Allusions to a spiritual foundation are evident.

Christian Writings. Christian writers also focus on character, service, and goals beyond profit. Smith (1986) sees leaders as bringing out the best in people. Having a title or doing the best work does not define a leader; leadership is the ability to get followers to do the work better than the leader can. Leaders serve and are rewarded by God first, and they can inspire others to sacrifice for the shared cause of Christ as this goal is clearly articulated and lived out by the leader. Time management is important to the leader, but self-management is crucial; discipline of thought, action, acquisition, and recognition must be honed. A good leader must be a motivator; establishing a healthy atmosphere, enjoying and understanding people's strengths and weaknesses, keeping an upfront agenda, complimenting often and openly, and giving people a reputation to uphold are some of Smith's techniques. Smith also stresses the centrality of good communication, both interpersonal and before all members of the team.

Maxwell (1993, 1994), specializing in training pastors in leadership, says "Everything rises and falls on leadership." He maintains that men and women with little exposure to leaders or leadership training can utilize a strong desire for leadership and develop an effective ministry. Leaders know that everyone influences someone, and they set about becoming influential in Christlike ways. Leaders know how to leverage proper priorities into multiplied results. Leaders have integrity because their deeds match their words, and this quality maximizes influence. Leaders create positive change even in the face of natural disinclinations in followers. Leaders solve problems in both people and production areas. Leaders cast a vision and develop other leaders who will own and help achieve it. Leaders, as Maxwell repeatedly evidences in his writings, have an understanding of human nature. Leaders have patience with people who are seeking to grow, coupled with a willingness to withstand criticism from people who are not on the team. Personal costs of leadership are consciously paid for the sake of kingdom goals.

This issue of costs and requirements of leadership brings up the question of the personality many pastors bring to their calling. Pastors often have a high desire for approval—a drive to achieve combined with a motivation to nurture a group. These qualities make certain pastor's tasks difficult in the local church: confrontation, absorbing criticism, and plotting a course against a tide of complacency. Seminaries will serve their students well by addressing the potential gap between the necessary skills a leader must show and the gentler shepherding natures of many persons who are called to the ministry.

A related question, particularly relevant to pastors studying church growth, is whether certain leadership qualities are reliably related to church success regardless of changes over time and in society. Patterns of pastoral leadership have shown changes. A consensus style, waiting for general agreement of the group before making a leadership decision, has given way to a more active pastoral role in defining the particular mission of the specific church. Churches showing greatest growth, across denominations, have pastoral leadership that values insights of congregants while casting the vision for their body of Christ in their community. The growth in leadership training programs for pastors is a response to these findings as experienced pastors teach younger leaders how to hone their gifts.

Nevertheless, caution in defining church success is wise, and a balance must be struck between use of corporate strategies and humble servant leadership. Maxwell (1995) addresses the differences between secular and spiritual leadership, identifying eight critical points for Christian leaders to ponder. Secular leaders fill a role; Christian leaders form a relationship. Secular leaders gain increasing rights; Christian leaders gain greater responsibility. Secular leaders wield authority to overcome competition; Christian leaders empower others to live out greater obedience to God. Secular leaders achieve position, are self-confident, and focus on temporal gains; Christian leaders seek the right disposition, are God-confident, and seek eternal gains. Finally, secular leaders focus on how they lead best; Christian leaders must concern themselves with how they live, to have a witness worth imitating. Christian leadership must be about equipping others to advance the kingdom of Christ.

References

Covey, S. R. (1989). *The seven habits of highly effective people*. New York: Simon & Schuster.

Covey, S. R. (1990). *Principle-centered leadership*. New York: Summit.

Ford, L. (1991). *Transforming leadership*. Downers Grove, IL: InterVarsity Press.

Griffin, E. (1985). Leadership. In D. G. Benner (Ed.), *Baker encyclopedia of psychology*. Grand Rapids, MI: Baker.

Maxwell, J. C. (1993). *Developing the leader within you*. Nashville: Nelson.

Maxwell, J. C. (1994, May). Personal communication, Leadership Training Institute, Maryland.

Maxwell, J. C. (1995, May/June). Secular vs. spiritual leadership. *New Man*, 78–80+.

Smith, F. (1986) *Learning to lead*. Waco, TX: Word.

K. M. Lattea

See Group Dynamics.

Learned Helplessness. During the late 1960s and early 1970s Martin Seligman and his colleagues conducted an extensive program of research documenting the debilitating effects on several animal species of inescapable, noncontingent Trauma; that is, trauma (usually shock) that could not be controlled by the animal because its responses could have no influence on the termination of the trauma. They found that animals exposed to trauma that could be controlled typically experienced no ill effects from it. Animals that received the same pattern of trauma but whose responses were unrelated to the termination of the trauma demonstrated extreme disruption in their subsequent performance. They were noted to be less motivated to perform tasks, took longer to learn subsequent tasks, and seemed generally despondent and passive. This phenomenon of disrupted responding was labeled learned helplessness. It was subsequently demonstrated that the helplessness effect could be alleviated by forcing the animals to respond under conditions in which their responses were effective in controlling their environment. Animals could be immunized against the helplessness effect by previous success in controlling traumatic events.

To explain this phenomenon Seligman (1975) and his colleagues argued that the animal, based on the experiences with noncontingent trauma, formed a global expectation of learned helplessness—an expectation that its responses would have no effect in controlling outcomes. They proposed that this expectation led to the observed behavioral manifestations.

During the 1970s helplessness researchers, impressed by the perceived parallels between the behavior of helpless animal subjects and depressed humans, proposed that the expectation of helplessness might be a major factor in human depression. They initiated a series of studies with humans using unsolvable problems as the noncontingent traumatic event. These studies generally showed that a subject's performances on tasks following exposure to unsolvable problems were disrupted and that normal subjects exposed to a helplessness induction performed much like depressed persons without such an induction. The conclusion of the researchers that these and other experimental studies supported a helplessness model of depression has been hotly debated (Depue & Monroe, 1978). Without question, the theory in its early form was much too simplistic to be of much value.

In 1978 Abramson, Seligman, and Teasdale (1978) reformulated the theory to suggest that the expectation of helplessness is much more complex than previously thought. The foundational process of belief in noncontingency between response and outcome remained from the old model, but in the reformulated model this belief was qualified by the person's judgments of the location of the cause of uncontrollability (within the person or outside in the situation?), the permanence of the state of un-

controllability (enduring or temporary?), and the extensiveness of the uncontrollability (global or specific to a limited set of behavior?).

Subsequent research using the reformulated helplessness model has been very complex, focusing on the causal judgments and other cognitive processes of depressed persons. The research support for the reformulated model had been mixed. As the research has continued, it has moved farther away from the basic concept behind the whole theory of helplessness—the concept of noncontingency.

Learned helplessness theory is no longer very influential in the study of depression. Seligman (1991) has proceeded to focus on learned optimism as a predictor of persistence and productivity. Cognitive approaches to depression have subsumed the essence of the original helplessness theory. The concept is still used in a popular or casual way to refer to any experience of performance decrement, loss of Motivation, or despondency that occurs after a person experiences a salient inability to influence an outcome or escape an aversive experience.

References

Abramson, L. Y., Seligman, M. E. P., & Teasdale, J. D. (1978). Learned helplessness in humans: Critique and reformulation. *Journal of Abnormal Psychology, 87,* 49–74.

Depue, R. A., & Monroe, S. M. (1978). Learned helplessness in the perspective of the depressive disorders: Conceptional and definitional issues. *Journal of Abnormal Psychology, 87,* 3–20.

Seligman, M. E. P. (1975). *Helplessness: On depression, development, and death.* San Francisco: Freeman.

Seligman, M. E. P. (1991). *Learned optimism.* New York: Random House.

S. L. JONES

See CODEPENDENCY; DEPRESSION.

Learning. A branch of psychology with a rich history, learning is principally concerned with the acquisition of knowledge. As such its influences, like those of psychology itself, include both philosophy (i.e., epistemology) and science. A definition of learning often used by psychologists working in this area is that learning is a more or less permanent change in behavior resulting from experience. Behavior (generally defined) is always the dependent variable in psychology, and to demonstrate that learning has taken place it is necessary to show that a change in behavior has occurred. Learning, however, cannot be equated with performance. As any student knows, performance on a task might be poor for several reasons (e.g., motivation, uncertainty regarding instructions, distractions); therefore, inferior performance on a task does not necessarily mean that learning has not occurred. This change in behavior must also be more or less permanent in that the behavioral change cannot be due to a temporary condition such as fatigue or a drug-induced state. Finally, the change in behavior must be due to experience. Some behavioral changes occur because of native response tendencies or physiological maturation (e.g., flying, walking), but these phenomena are not typically classified as learning.

Philosophical Foundations. The major philosophical influences on learning come from the epistemologies of empiricism and rationalism. Empiricism is the view that all knowledge comes from experience, with special emphasis placed on sensory experience. Ideas are either direct copies of sensory impressions (simple ideas) or are combinations of several simple ideas (complex ideas). John Locke, James Mill and John Stuart Mill, David Hume, and George Berkeley are a few philosophers who made significant contributions to empiricism. The epistemology of empiricism also includes other features such as reductionism, the position that all complex ideas or behaviors can be reduced to simple ideas or behaviors; associationism, the thesis that ideas or behaviors that are contiguous in time become connected; and mechanism, the belief that the mind is like or is a machine.

Rationalism, a position held by René Descartes, Leibnitz, and Kant, among others, is the epistemological position that knowledge is derived through reason rather than sensory experience. For the rationalists sense data provide the raw material that the rational mind interprets according to certain innate principles.

Both empiricism and rationalism provide the philosophical groundwork for theories of learning. Empiricism is the foundation of most learning theories, including those of Edward Lee Thorndike, Ivan Pavlov, Clark Leonard Hull, and B. F. Skinner. Gestalt theory and the cognitive theories (e.g., information processing and the learning theory of Edward Chace Tolman), while certainly not without influences from empiricism, are more in keeping with rationalistic assumptions.

Historical Theories. A brief review of a few major learning theories in psychology's history is warranted. The first theory to have a significant impact on the psychology of learning in the United States was that of Thorndike. Thorndike proposed that learning is incremental due to trial and error, not insightful (as was supposed at the time), and that an association or connection between a stimulus (S) and a response (R) is strengthened when the response is followed by a "satisfying state of affairs." This principle, known as the law of effect, was the basis for later behaviorist notions of reinforcement.

A second theorist to make a major contribution to the psychology of learning was Pavlov, a Russian physiologist. Known for his discovery of classical conditioning, Pavlov's work was the harbinger of years of research investigating the phenomenon of conditioned reflexes. By making an unconditioned stimulus (a stimulus that reflexively elicits an unlearned or unconditioned response) contingent upon the presentation of a neutral stimulus (the conditioned stimulus), Pavlov found that a new response (the conditioned response) could be acquired by the subject. Classical conditioning remains a central paradigm for investigating learning processes as well as an approach to the treatment of certain types of psychopathological disorders.

From the 1930s to the early 1960s Hull's learning theory was the most ambitious and influential in psychology. Hull sought to develop a theory of learning that consisted of a systematic and logical structure of postulates and theorems. In his effort to develop such a theory, Hull made use of intervening variables, or theoretical constructs, such as habit strength, drive, and inhibition. Hull believed that by knowing the value of each of these variables (as well as other variables that are included in his system) the likelihood of a learned response being made at a given moment, known as reaction potential, could be calculated. Reinforcement, according to Hull, is accomplished through drive reduction. A response that reduces the drive state will be strengthened, more likely to occur in future similar situations. The importance of Hull's theory of learning is the basic approach it takes; that is, the assumption that behavior is determined and mechanistic and that it is thoroughly knowable in a systematic and scientific manner. Although Hull's theory did not reach its lofty goal, the contributions of Hull, both through his own work and that of his followers such as Kenneth Spence, Neal Miller, and Orval Hobart Mowrer, are numerous and significant.

Tolman represents a blending of behavioral and cognitive approaches in his introduction of the concept of expectancy to learning theory. Hull and Tolman were contemporaries, but their theories were vastly different. While Hull was thoroughly mechanistic in his theory, Tolman denied that behavior is automatic. Behavior to Tolman was purposeful; his brand of learning was known as purposive behaviorism because it attempted to explain behavior in terms of goals. Tolman, however, remained a behaviorist in that he studied what every other behaviorist studied: observable stimuli and observable responses.

One of Tolman's important theoretical concepts is latent learning, learning that is not demonstrated through the performance of the subject. According to Tolman, we know much more about our environment than our behavior indicates; in other words, we act upon only a small part of the information we have available. We act upon information only when we need to do so. This distinction between learning and performance remains an important consideration in learning.

Another concept of Tolman's was the cognitive map. According to Tolman, an organism does not simply learn S-R relationships; an organism essentially learns that certain events lead to other events, or that one sign leads to another sign. For example, an animal running through a maze develops a picture or cognitive map of the environment and accesses that map in order to navigate through the maze. Thus the behavior of an animal is more advanced and cognitive than other behaviorists believed. Tolman, therefore, adumbrated the movement toward cognitivism that took place in the 1960s and 1970s.

No other individual in psychology had greater impact within the discipline or without than Skinner. Upon Skinner's death, psychology lost perhaps its last larger-than-life personality, its last celebrated figure that commanded the attention of both psychologists and the general public alike. One of the ironies of psychology is that for most nonpsychologists, and perhaps for most psychologists as well, Skinner is the quintessence of behaviorism; the model from which all other behaviorists follow. While Skinner was a behaviorist, his brand of behaviorism was unlike that of Tolman's or even Hull's. The kind of learning theory that Skinner proposed was so different from what most behaviorists were discussing during the 1930s to the 1950s that it was known as radical behaviorism.

Skinner differed from other theorists mentioned in that he believed that any discussion of theoretical constructs (e.g., drive, habit, cognitive maps) hampers a scientific understanding of the controls of behavior. Skinner was interested in a functional, or experimental, analysis of behavior; by this he meant an analysis of behavior only in terms of specific environmental determinants of specific behaviors. A behavior is explained in Skinner's behaviorism when all of the antecedent factors, or independent variables, acting on that behavior are identified. Only then can a psychologist predict the occurrence of the response and also influence its occurrence by manipulating the independent variables.

Skinner was consistent in insisting that a true functional analysis of behavior had never been tried in psychology. All other behaviorisms were, according to Skinner, too mentalistic in their use of intervening variables, variables not located within the peripheral environment.

While Skinner's behaviorism was a minority view in psychology, his popular writings such as *Walden Two* and *Beyond Freedom and Dignity* made him a center of controversy for the public. In his novel *Walden Two*, Skinner tried to apply his learning principles to the shaping of a model society, and in *Beyond Freedom and Dignity* Skinner discusses cultural engineering. Both books brought Skinner's ideas of psychology's role in society to the public's awareness and fostered in many a distrust and even fear of psychology, a distrust that remains to this day.

Beginning in the 1950s, different views, known as mathematical (or statistical) models of learning, were proposed by various theorists. An example of such a theorist is William Estes (b. 1919). According to these statistical approaches, the learning process is not entirely predictable; it is random in certain ways that can be described statistically. Rather than attempt to predict the behavior of a single individual on a single learning trial (as Hull, for example, sought to do), statistical learning theorists attempt to predict the average behavior of a single individual over many trials or the average behavior of many individuals on a single learning trial. The development of these types of mathematical theories further prepared the psychology of learning for its current state.

Contemporary Learning Theory. While learning theories during the first 70 years of the twentieth century attempted to provide comprehensive global theories of the learning process, contemporary learning theory is more limited in scope, often proposing different mechanisms for different behaviors. Some of the reasons for this change in perspective are data that do not fit neatly into the traditional view of learning; that is, learning due to classical conditioning, operant conditioning, or some combination of the two.

For example, contrary to the theory of Thorndike, animals do seem to have a certain degree of insight. Not all animal learning is by trial and error. Contrary to the traditional view of classical conditioning, not all stimuli can be presented contiguously to produce a conditioned response. There are biological constraints that allow only certain kinds of associations to be made. Research in conditioned toxicosis (or learned flavor aversions) clearly shows that organisms are biologically prepared to learn associations between internal CSs (e.g., taste) and internal USs (e.g., a substance that makes an animal temporarily ill), but not between external CSs (e.g., lights) and internal USs. Finally, the phenomenon of instinctive drift (an organism's drift toward instinctive behaviors to the detriment or even preclusion of conditioning) challenges the traditionally accepted views of instrumental conditioning.

The contemporary state of learning can be illustrated through a brief description of two developments, the current view of classical conditioning and recent advancements in the neurophysiology of learning. The traditional view of classical conditioning is that it is a simple process based on the contiguous pairing of two stimuli (the CS and the US). However, it is now known that contiguity is not sufficient to produce learning. In addition to the problem of preparedness, the current view of classical conditioning is that it is a much more complex and cognitive learning process. The subject in classical conditioning is now seen as an active information seeker using logical relations among events to create a representation of the world. Conditioning is based on a contingency (or predictiveness) between the CS and the US, and it is this information that the subject acquires during learning.

Neuroscience has brought tremendous changes to our understanding of learning. The brain changes both physiologically and structurally as a result of experience. Learning, therefore, can be thought of as represented by these physical changes in the neural network. When learning occurs, the connections between brain cells are modified, a process known as synaptic plasticity. New connections are made and old connections can be lost or changed in strength. This synaptic plasticity is the subject of the new connectionism, or network theory. Using techniques from biology and other natural sciences, psychologists investigating learning from a neuroscience perspective can literally see changes in the brain following a learning trail. A putative mechanism for synaptic plasticity is long-term potentiation (LTP), an artificial way of inducing changes in brain that are similar to the changes naturally seen during learning. By studying LTP, psychologists have gained valuable insight into the biochemistry and physiology of learning.

A specific example of neuroscience's contribution to learning is in classical conditioning. It is now known that classical conditioning is accomplished in the cerebellum. Destruction of certain cells in the cerebellum precludes classical conditioning or abolishes the performance of the conditioned response if the cerebellar damage occurs after conditioning has taken place. Evidence such as this suggests that the traditional attempt to find the engram might have found success in the case of classical conditioning and opens up other opportunities to study where in the brain learning takes place in other learning situations.

Contemporary learning is very physiological in nature. While many learning experiments take place that are not directly physiological in scope, the generally accepted view is that learning is intimately linked to the brain. At the end of the twentieth century researchers are attempting to elucidate what these more or less permanent changes in the neural network that result from experience are, what the mechanisms behind the changes might be, and if those mechanisms can be modified to facilitate the learning process.

Additional Readings

Bower, G. H., & Hilgard, E. R. (1981). *Theories of learning* (5th ed.). Englewood Cliffs, NJ: Prentice-Hall.

Carlson, N. R. (1994). *Physiology of behavior* (5th ed.). Boston: Allyn & Bacon.

Hergenhahn, B. R., & Olson, M. H. (1992). *An introduction to theories of learning* (4th ed.). Englewood Cliffs, NJ: Prentice-Hall.

Hill, W. F. (1990). *Learning: A survey of psychological interpretations* (5th ed.). New York: Harper & Row.

Klein, S. B., & Mowrer, R. R. (1989). *Contemporary learning theories: Pavlovian conditioning and the status of traditional learning theory.* Hillsdale, NJ: Erlbaum.

Klein, S. B., & Mowrer, R. R. (1989). *Contemporary learning theories: Instrumental conditioning theory and the impact of biological constraints on learning.* Hillsdale, NJ: Erlbaum.

Rescorla, R. A. (1988). Pavlovian conditioning: It's not what you think it is. *American Psychologist, 43,* 151–160.

Schwartz, B., & Robbins, S. J. (1995). *Psychology of learning and behavior* (4th ed.). New York: Norton.

K. S. SEYBOLD

See COGNITIVE DEVELOPMENT; BEHAVIORAL PSYCHOLOGY; CONDITIONING, CLASSICAL; CONDITIONING, OPERANT.

Learning, Discrimination. The process whereby different responses are made to different stimulus situations. It is opposite behaviorally from the process of generalization, in which the same response is made to different stimulus situations. Discriminations can be made between two or more stimuli (stimulus discrimination) as well as between two forms of the same response (response discrimination).

The basic operation for the formation of a stimulus discrimination involves differential reinforcement of the same response under different conditions. Whenever one stimulus is present, the response leads to a positive consequence. Whenever another stimulus is present, the response either fails to produce a positive consequence or it is punished. Over repeated exposure to this situation the response comes to be made only to the appropriate stimulus. For example, a stimulus discrimination has been learned when an infant's generalized response of "da-da," initially given to all men, comes to be given only to the child's father. The formation of response discriminations involves, essentially the same process; that is, the form of the response, such as its intensity, amplitude, or latency, is altered by different consequences (reinforcement). Familiar forms of response discriminations are those associated with learning to ride a bicycle or to steer an automobile.

Both humans and animals are capable of making remarkably complex discriminations. In general, discriminations are more easily learned when the difference to be learned is large rather than small, the consequences of responding are consistent, and correct responses are frequently reinforced.

S. R. OSBORNE

See LEARNING.

Learning, Escape. A response made in order to escape an aversive stimulus. The removal of an aversive stimulus following a response reinforces that response and makes it more likely to occur in the future. In escape learning the punishing stimulus continues to be experienced until the appropriate escape response is made. Therefore, escape learning often is a precursor of avoidance learning, in which punishment is avoided rather than escaped.

For example, a dog will readily learn to jump over a hurdle to escape an electric shock delivered through the floor of its cage. After a number of trials the escape response becomes an avoidance response; that is, the dog learns to jump over the hurdle at the start of the trial before it is shocked. If the dog is prevented from escaping and is repeatedly shocked, it may subsequently fail to try to escape in future situations even when escape is possible. This phenomenon, termed learned helplessness, may have a counterpart in human learning inasmuch as people who repeatedly fail to escape from aversive situations sometimes adopt a defeatist attitude that prevents them from learning appropriate escape or avoidance behavior when the opportunities for such learning arise.

In the laboratory the aversive stimulus in escape learning usually is painful electric shock. However, escape and avoidance responses are learned for a broad variety of aversive situations.

S. R. OSBORNE

See LEARNING; LEARNED HELPLESSNESS.

Learning, Latent. Learning that occurs without any apparent reward but is not revealed in performance until sufficient motivation is present.

In early latent learning experiments (e.g., Tolman & Honzik, 1930) two groups of food-deprived rats were allowed to negotiate a maze. The rats in one group found food in the goal box of the maze, and over successive trials their time to run the maze and the number of entries into blind alleys decreased. Rats in the other group found no food in the goal box, and their performance showed no evidence of learning. The rats in this group then were placed in the goal box and given food there for the first time. Then the performance of both groups was tested again. This time the rats that previously negotiated the maze without food in the goal box began to run as fast and with as few errors as the rats who had found food in the goal box in all the previous trials.

The results of latent learning experiments were significant from a theoretical perspective because they challenged some of the basic tenets of early reinforcement theories. For example, law of effect theories (e.g., Edward Lee Thorndike) presumed that reinforcement works directly upon response strength so that all that is learned will be revealed in performance. However, latent learning suggests that learning can occur and be available without being used until motivational or reward conditions make it profitable.

Edward Chace Tolman, one of the early behaviorists who studied latent learning, emphasized the cognitive nature of learning and described an animal's behavior in terms of its motives, cognitions, expectations, intentions, and purposes. He argued that the nonreward situation was a good one for learning the spatial relations of the maze but that there was no reason for the rat to show what it had learned. However, when food was placed at the end of the maze, the rat used its previously learned cognitive map to find its way through the maze to the goal box.

Reinforcement theorists argued, however, that food in the goal box was not the only possible reward for the rat's running of the maze. Consequently

any learning that had taken place was still due to reinforced responses and not to cognitive learning that occurred without reward.

A number of experiments on latent learning were conducted during the 1940s and 1950s to resolve this controversy over the nature of learning. Despite this effort the issue was never resolved; different latent learning experiments led to different results. However, of 48 studies reviewed by MacCorquodale and Meehl (1954), 30 reported positive findings relative to latent learning, whereas only 18 showed negative findings.

The lasting importance of latent learning research has been threefold. First, it influenced the development of subsequent learning theories. Second, it provided some empirical support for learning theories that suggest that cognitive structure, in addition to responses, is learned. Third, it emphasized the importance of distinguishing between learning and performance. This last point is especially important because it reminds us that learning will be revealed only under appropriate motivational conditions.

References

MacCorquodale, K., & Meehl, P. E. (1954). In W. K. Estes, S. Koch, K. MacCorquodale, P. E. Meehl, C. G. Mueller, W. Schoenfeld, & W. S. Verplanck (Eds.), *Modern learning theory.* New York: Appleton-Century-Crofts.

Tolman, E. C., & Honzik, C. H. (1930). Introduction and removal of reward, and maze performance in rats. *University of California Publication in Psychology, 4,* 257–275.

S. R. OSBORNE

See LEARNING.

Learning, Social. *See* SOCIAL LEARNING THEORY.

Learning Disability. Approximately 5% of school-age children are identified as having a learning disability, although the incidence may be twice this figure. The difference in number is due to varying opinions as to which problems must be evident, how many problems must be present, and how severe the problem or problems must be before the diagnosis is made. The term does not apply to children whose difficulties in learning stem primarily from visual or auditory impairment, physical injury, mental retardation, emotional disturbance, or lack of environmental opportunity. The designation is reserved for those children who, although they are normal in appearance and possess average or above-average intelligence, are unable to learn commensurate with their abilities. In all cases there is a marked discrepancy between expected and actual achievement in one or more areas.

The learning-disabled child is more apt to have allergies and a history of ear infections before the age of six, when language development is crucial (Smith, 1994). As a toddler the child may display frequent temper tantrums, poor motor coordination, and slow or irregular speech patterns. Some children are unable to complete a task, running from one activity to another, and destroy toys and household furnishings. The child does not seem to profit from experience or from usual methods of discipline. The reaction of parents is one of frustration, often accompanied by hostile feelings toward the child. "He won't listen," "She doesn't mind," "He's a bad boy" are common complaints.

Learning disability takes a different course with each child. Some children experience problems in many areas; others have difficulty in only one or a few. The disability may be so severe as to cripple the child socially and academically or so slight as to be undetected. More than 100 forms of learning disability have been described in the literature and at least 50 names have been given to them, the most common being attention deficit disorder, minimal brain dysfunction, perceptually handicapped, dyslexia, dyscalcula, psychoneurological learning disorder, and hyperkinetic behavior syndrome.

The principal abnormalities are hyperactivity, in which the child is incessantly in motion and lacking self-control; attention deficit, in which the child is easily distracted and unable to concentrate on appropriate tasks; motor awkwardness, visible in a lack of coordination of large and small muscles; orientation defects, seen when the child cannot memorize the route to school or is unable to differentiate left and right; emotional instability, witnessed by bouts of excessive excitement and times of sadness; unsatisfactory interpersonal relationships, demonstrated by a resistance to social demands and a tendency to be demanding; and dyslexia, the inability to store word images in the brain, making it difficult to recognize words and thus affecting the child's ability to read, write, and spell.

Parents may take heart that such well-known figures as Leonardo da Vinci, Thomas Edison, Woodrow Wilson, Albert Einstein, and Nelson Rockefeller were learning disabled. But the usual pattern is not fame. Instead the learning-disabled child becomes the learning-disabled adolescent who continues to do poorly in school and is three times more apt to become delinquent than peers of similar age, social class, and race (Rubenstein, 1982). Whether the propensity toward wrongdoing is because of such personality attributes as impulsivity, inability to learn from experience, and poor reception of social cues or whether it is a reaction to the negative attitude of parents and teachers and being labeled and grouped with other problem children is not known. Learning-disabled adults also have adjustment difficulties, although some manage to cope quite well.

The etiology of learning disability is not known, although many theories have been offered. These range from improper child-rearing techniques to poor diet, from inner-ear infection to genetic predisposition, from slow neurological development to cerebral brain damage. Each view has studies to support it.

It is true that children may be confused by parental expectations, but this does not explain why other children in the family reared in the same way are not learning disabled. Eliminating artificial flavors and dyes in foods and reducing carbohydrates has helped some children, especially those who are hyperactive. Learning disability tends to run in families, with boys being affected four times (Bender, 1995) to eight times (Holley, 1994) as often as girls. Identical twins are three times as apt to share the disorder as fraternal twins (Smith, 1994). The most commonly held view is that of neurological impairment, with a developmental lag in one or both halves of the brain or injury to brain cells before or during the birth process being cited as the probable cause. A single gene on chromosome 6 is now thought to underlie at least some cases of dyslexia (Nash, 1996).

Remedial procedures vary, depending on the nature of the difficulty and the orientation of the educator or therapist. The use of stimulants, such as ritalin or coffee, combined with behavior modification exercises, have helped some children with attention deficit/hyperactivity disorder. Physical education and the building of models may improve motor coordination. Computer games have enabled some preschool children to differentiate fine differences in sounds, thereby preparing the child for reading (Nash, 1996).

Early intervention is more effective than later mediation. Some schools screen all children before they enter kindergarten. Public Law 94–142 guarantees equal educational opportunity to all handicapped children, including those diagnosed as having a learning disability. But economic constraints mean that the number must be limited and some children who should qualify may not receive the needed attention.

Parents find that neither the hard approach of punishing the child for not doing better nor the soft approach of trying to protect the child is effective. Telling the child to try harder only makes matters worse. "Requiring a child with attention deficit disorder or dyslexia to compete academically is like forcing a child with cerebral palsy to run the 100–yard dash. Imagine a mother and father standing disapprovingly at the end of the track, berating their handicapped child as he hobbles across the finish line in last place" (Dobson, 1994, p. 5). Meeting with other parents who have children with the same problem, lobbying for educational programs within the schools, and being familiar with research methods that may be duplicated in the home provide some relief. It is important that parents not blame themselves for having a learning-disabled child. Nor should they blame the child. Neither parent nor child is at fault.

The extent to which learning disability touches the lives of people within the Christian community is greater than realized. Pastors, teachers, and counselors should become familiar with the characteristics of learning-disabled children and endeavor to help them rather than seeing them as trouble-makers. Letting children act out Bible stories and encouraging individual talents and interests are but two of the ways found to be effective (Rowan, 1977).

References

Bender, W. N. (1995). *Learning disabilities: Characteristics, identification, and teaching strategies.* Needham Heights, MA: Allyn & Bacon.

Dobson, J. C. (1994, October). Dr. Dobson answers your questions. *Focus on the Family, 18,* 5.

Holley, S. (1994). *A practical parent's handbook on teaching children with learning disabilities.* Springfield, IL: Thomas.

Nash, J. M. (1996, January 29). Zooming in on dyslexia. *Time, 147,* 62–64.

Rowan, R. D. (1977). *Helping children with learning disabilities: In the home, school, church and community.* Nashville: Abingdon.

Rubenstein, C. (1982). Oops—learning disabilities do get boys in trouble. *Psychology Today, 16* (5), 74–75.

Smith, C. R. (1994). *Learning disabilities: The interaction of learner, task, and setting.* Boston: Allyn & Bacon.

B. CLOUSE

See ATTENTION DEFICIT/HYPERACTIVITY DISOR-DER; DYSLEXIA; LEARNING; SCHOOL PSYCHOLOGY; COG-NITIVE DEVELOPMENT; EDUCATIONAL PSYCHOLOGY.

Legal Issues in Counseling. *See* LAW AND PSYCHO-LOGICAL PRACTICE; MORAL AND ETHICAL ISSUES IN TREATMENT.

Legal Psychology. *See* FORENSIC PSYCHIATRY; FOREN-SIC PSYCHOLOGY.

Legalism. An approach to living in which a person attempts to conform to a particular standard or set of standards to achieve a desired status or goal. In Jewish and Christian traditions, the term *legalism* has most frequently referred to attempts to con-form behavior, attitudes, and/or thoughts to the Mosaic law as contained in the Pentateuch (the first five books of the Old Testament), as well as com-patible extensions of such principles found in the Old Testament, New Testament, or related docu-ments and communities. Among Christians, the proper role of the Mosaic law is to serve as a guide or a mentor to lead us to faith in Christ, as is clearly stated in Galatians 3:24. Legalism, with its emphasis on self-sufficiency and acceptability based on per-formance compared to a standard, tends to lead people away from dependence on Christ.

The most common perversions of the proper use of the law include the polarities of legalism and li-cense. Legalism falls short of understanding the proper role of the law by stopping with conformity to standards as a means of pleasing God in itself, rather than placing the law in its appropriate per-spective as a steppingstone toward faith in Christ. In the Old Testament, the realization that no per-son or group of people could ever fully obey God's laws was designed to lead to temporary sacrificial rituals that ultimately pointed to redemption through the Messiah. Legalism is often confusing in this re-spect because the purpose of the law is paradoxi-cal. Instead of providing a direct path to God, the law's purpose (and our efforts to abide by it) is to reveal and even magnify our inability to obey the law in its entirety until the process runs its pre-dictable course to ultimate failure, at which time we must either throw ourselves on God's mercy in Christ through confession, faith, and repentance or eject from the system.

In contrast to the correct responses of confes-sion, faith, and repentance, license is another way of attempting to address failure to successfully obey the law and is usually described as an approach to life in which the person attempts to live without ref-erence to any external standards or guidelines, some-times arising directly out of frustration from failed attempts to obey the law. In its extreme form license not only can include living apart from the law but also may be characterized by breaking the law (and even any related standards and principles) as much as possible. Some theologians see this rebellious ex-treme of license as having a mirrored similarity to legalism, since in both approaches the person's life is controlled by improper reactions to the law and decisions are constantly made in reaction to it.

Although the prototypical stimulus for legalism has been the Mosaic law, a legalistic approach to living can become attached to almost any standard, rule, guideline, or set of the same. Legalism always includes at least two basic elements for its activa-tion: an external standard (sometimes internalized over time) and a perspective in which a conforming response to the standard is seen as making the per-son better than a nonconforming response. When Martin Luther commented that all humans strug-gle with a Jewish element within, he was not mak-ing a racist comment; rather, he was describing a universal principle of law responsivity within all people that he felt must be addressed in some way by everyone, regardless of race, creed, or ethnic ori-gin. Jewish and Christian communities, however, were seen by Luther as being particularly sensitive to legalistic spiritual issues because of their con-cern for living in proper relationship to God and his laws. Legalism, or the concept of making one-self better in God's valuation through adherence to such standards, is one common but errant way of responding to this internal law principle.

The ultimate issue in legalism, sometimes called works righteousness or works, is whether confor-mity to the law makes one acceptable in God's sight. It is clear from many sources in the biblical text that no human being has the capacity to perform "works of the law" to God's requirement, which is 100%. Thus, no one can do such works in sufficient degree and number to satisfy God's criterion. Even in light of this knowledge, legalism is often still tempting to and is even practiced by many people who know better, since its emphasis on performance or merited favor is reflected in so many earthly families, systems, and situations. The contrasting biblical solution of receiving God's favor through faith in Christ's performance as a gift applied to us, the unmerited favor of grace, requires greater spiritual maturity than legalism for its consistent practice and application as a governing system for living.

J. A. INGRAM

See RELIGIOUS HEALTH AND PATHOLOGY; RELIGIOUS ORIENTATION; DOGMATISM; AMBIGUITY, INTOLERANCE OF; PERFECTIONISM.

Lesbianism. See GENDER IDENTITY; HOMOSEXUALITY; SEXUALITY.

Leuba, James Henry (1867–1946). One of the earliest experimental psychologists in the United States, best remembered for his extensive empirical research on the psychology of religion. He was born in Neuchâtel in 1867, living there until he took the B.S. degree from the University of Neuchâtel. He moved to the United States to study with Granville Stanley Hall at Clark University, completing his Ph.D. in 1896. He then took an academic position at Bryn Mawr, where he remained until his retirement in 1933.

Among Leuba's first actions at Bryn Mawr was the establishment of one of America's first psychological laboratories in 1898. His interests in experimental psychology included animal learning (particularly the relationship of instincts to learned behaviors) and motivation. In addition to his experimental interests, Leuba could be classified as one of the early dynamic psychologists. He was favorably impressed by the work of Pierre Janet and William McDougall, but he had little respect for Sigmund Freud or the other psychoanalysts.

Leuba's interest in dynamics was clearly reflected in his work on the psychology of religion, which began with his doctoral dissertation, published as *Studies in the Psychology of Religious Phenomena: The Religious Motives, Conversion, Facts, and Doctrine* (1896). Leuba continued to be an active writer in this area until his retirement. By the reckoning of editor James McKeen Cattell, Leuba was one of the top 50 eminent psychologists listed in *American Men of Science.*

Leuba's work on the psychology of religion was at once influential and controversial. McBride (1947) characterized Leuba as a reformer whose work was opposed by press and church alike because it questioned, albeit on an empirical basis, traditional religious beliefs. Ironically, his work was used by secular writers and religious fundamentalists alike to buttress their own beliefs. Leuba thought of his research as developing a firm scientific basis to "show man how to mitigate his moral and intellectual perfections," yet his *Belief in God and Immortality* (1916) helped persuade William Jennings Bryan to launch

his crusade against the teaching of evolution. Leuba used questionnaires to study the traditional religious beliefs of college students and showed statistically that students' acceptance of these beliefs declined with exposure to college course work, findings that confirmed Bryan's impressions of the matter.

In addition to particular beliefs Leuba also studied other elements of Christianity, including sin and morality, faith, and the conversion experience. Adopting the nonsectarian stance of comparative religion, Leuba argued that "sin" refers to a general religious sentiment of current moral imperfection and the aspiration for the feeling of personal wholesomeness and peace. His study of conversion led to the conclusion that particular doctrinal beliefs are not crucial to having a conversion experience. Rather, the prior condition of the convert is the feeling of helplessness coupled with a desire for a higher form of help. Such doctrineless conversions occur when the convert feels the presence of such help as a "joyous conviction" that all will be well in one's life. Perhaps most controversial was Leuba's observation that most worshipers are neither concerned about the nature of their deities nor loyal to them but rather come to use them to meet their intellectual and emotional needs.

Reference

McBride, K. E. (1947). James Henry Leuba 1867–1946. *American Journal of Psychology, 60,* 645–646.

L. S. SHAFFER

See PSYCHOLOGY OF RELIGION.

Level of Aspiration. In the 1930s Henry Alexander Murray developed a theory of personality in which need for achievement is a major motive. Need for achievement (see Achievement, Need for) subsequently became a major research and theory domain in personality and social psychology. One of the first areas examined in achievement research was level of aspiration.

In the typical level of aspiration experiment the experimenter manipulated the outcome of a game, unknown to the participant. After each round the participant was asked to predict the score in the next round. The usual pattern of results indicated that when a person had a high score (i.e., good performance), the participant predicted better performance in the next round. When the score was lower than expected, the participant reduced the prediction for the next round. The level of aspiration was adjusted with the history of success or failure.

Level of aspiration came to be defined as the level of performance the individual expected to achieve. Level of aspiration operates as a criterion by which the individual evaluates whether performance is a success or failure. The level of aspiration for future events reflects one's achievement history, with the level modified upward after a series of successes and downward after failures. One's aspiration level serves as the level of performance considered acceptable within one's self-image. Persons with high need for achievement normally exhibit a higher level of aspiration than those less motivated by achievement. Higher performance is expected by those participants scoring higher in measures of internal locus of control.

Level of aspiration then became a major component in a broad theory of achievement. Atkinson (1964) developed an expectancy-value model of achievement in which the individual's motivation to engage in achievement behaviors is a multiplicative function of the success motive, the probability of success, and the incentive value of success. When the probability of success is low, incentive is high, and vice versa. Atkinson predicted that persons with high need for achievement would choose medium-risk tasks, as this would maximize the tendency to success. This is exactly what was observed, such individuals choosing tasks of moderate difficulty associated with moderate incentives.

In the same way the tendency to avoid failure is a product of fear of failure, its probability, and its incentive value. The tendency to avoid failure is highest with tasks of moderate probability of failure and moderate incentive, which implies that individuals with high fear of failure would choose either extremely easy tasks (guaranteed success) or extremely difficult ones (no blame for failure). This prediction has also received experimental support.

Atypical shifts in level of aspiration have been shown in persons with a high fear of failure. In these individuals level of aspiration is raised after failure and lowered after success. Atkinson suggested the individual confronts damaging information about self in moderately difficult tasks. By this strategy the individual avoids information that directly reflects one's ability.

Level of aspiration is a subjective expectancy of an individual about anticipated performance. It operates as a standard below which the individual finds performance unacceptable. In persons with a high need for achievement the level of aspiration is realistically adjusted upward or downward, depending on previous success or failure. For persons motivated to avoid failure, tasks that enable the person to realistically evaluate skills and performance are avoided.

Reference

Atkinson, J. W. (1964). *An introduction to motivation.* Princeton, NJ: Van Nostrand.

R. L. Timpe

See Motivation; Personality.

Lewin, Kurt (1890–1947). Seldom do the ideas of one man alter the course of an entire discipline, but Lewin had just such an impact upon social psy-

chology. Its emphases on rigorous experimentation, cognitive and motivational processes, and the importance of perceived situational factors in the explanation of social behavior can be traced back to Lewin's seminal work in the 1930s and 1940s (see Festinger, 1980). It is for this reason that Lewin is appropriately called the father of experimental social psychology.

Born in Mogilno, Germany, Lewin earned his Ph.D. in psychology in 1914 at the University of Berlin. At the university Lewin became interested in the work of the Gestalt psychologists Max Wertheimer and Kurt Koffka. Through their influence and his own experimental research, Lewin became convinced of the limitations of simple stimulus-response explanations of human behavior and began to develop his field theory as an alternative.

Field theory provides a view of persons that differs sharply from behavioristic accounts. First, the theory has a distinct phenomenological flavor. Perceptions and interpretations of stimuli prompt action, not the objective stimuli themselves. Lewin attempted to capture this perspective with his concept of life space. The life space is a dynamic composition of all the perceptions and cognitions—real or unreal; past, present, or future—capable of influencing an individual's current behavior.

Opposing the elementalism of the behaviorists, Lewin also held to the Gestalt notion that the whole is not the sum of its parts but rather the relations between them. The life space is a Gestalt in the sense that it is composed of interconnected psychical regions to which and through which the individual could possibly move. Locomotion, or movement through the life space, is not determined by a single stimulus but by the complex, changing pattern of psychical regions and their relations. Lewin thought that this view fit the complexity of natural behavior settings better than the stimulus-response approaches, which insisted on isolating the effects of one stimulus at a time.

Field theory also contrasts the environmental determinism of behavioral accounts with an emphasis on the intentionality and goal-directedness of behavior. Lewin believed that, once formed, our intentions and goals take on the character of quasi-needs. These self-created needs have no necessary linkage to basic biological needs but nevertheless cause tension in the life space that the individual seeks to reduce or satisfy through goal attainment. Lewin considered these quasi-needs as more fundamental than biological needs to an understanding of most human behavior. Indeed, most of us know the very real tension that comes from work deadlines or the desire for a new car or to spend time with a friend, none of which may affect our survival but which seem essential to understanding our day-to-day motivations.

While he was at the University of Berlin, Lewin and his students conducted experiments on a wide variety of hypotheses derived from the basic ideas of field theory. Perhaps most famous were Zeigarnik's studies of recall for completed versus interrupted tasks. Her finding that people remember interrupted tasks better than completed ones has come to be known as the Zeigarnik Effect. Other studies examined tendencies to resume interrupted tasks, the effects of substitute activities on tension systems, and the relationship of level of aspiration to experiences of success and failure.

By 1932 Lewin's work was well known, even in the United States, and he decided to spend a six-month leave as a visiting professor at Stanford. In 1933 the Nazi threat prompted him to leave Germany permanently, and he spent two years at Cornell before moving to the Child Welfare Station at the University of Iowa. Although Lewin continued to explore field theory in his research, Festinger (1980) reports that by the time Festinger arrived at Iowa to work as a graduate student, Lewin's interests were firmly in the area of social psychology. "He wanted to understand the behavior of groups" (Festinger 1980, p. 237).

A classic study of groups operating under autocratic and democratic climates (Lewin, Lippett, & White, 1939) was among those that began to change the face of social psychology. First, this research demonstrated that complex social interactions could be fruitfully examined in the laboratory. Second, it showed that social psychological interventions can have large, practical results and that these interventions have potential for use in the real world. Both these consequences flow from Lewin's conviction that theory, research, and the real world must come together in the form of action research—research directed at the goal of positive social change. During World War II his studies comparing group decisions versus lectures as methods for convincing housewives to buy glandular meats are classic examples of such action research, contributing both to the war effort and to our understanding of group dynamics and behavior change.

In 1945 Lewin and a number of his colleagues and students left Iowa for M.I.T., where they established the Research Center for Group Dynamics. Work at the center ranged from designing interventions to increase worker productivity to the founding of the National Training Laboratories at Bethel, Maine, where the T-group approach to interpersonal skills training was born. Lewin's sudden death in 1947 left the research center without a prestigious leader, and it was subsequently moved to the University of Michigan, where it was joined with the Survey Research Center to become the Institute for Social Research.

Lewin's critics typically focus on the formal properties of field theory, arguing that many of its central constructs (e.g., life space, tension systems) are loosely defined and difficult to test. Although this is true, Lewin's work must be credited with tremendous heuristic value, having stimulated a whole generation of social psychological research. Furthermore, Lewin's emphasis on the importance of reciprocal interaction between theory, data, and social problems is a legacy that should never be forgotten.

References

Festinger, L. (Ed.). (1980). *Retrospectives on social psychology.* New York: Oxford University Press.

Lewin, K., Lippett, R., & White, R. K. (1939). Patterns of aggressive behavior in experimentally created "social climates." *Journal of Social Psychology, 10,* 271–299.

Additional Reading

Lewin, K. (1935). *A dynamic theory of personality.* New York: McGraw-Hill.

D. D. McKenna

See Group Dynamics.

Liberation Theology. Liberation theology arose in Latin America in the 1960s, but its roots may be traced to the work of Walter Rauschenbusch in the 1920s in North America. Liberation theology is an endeavor to interpret the message of the Christian gospel primarily in terms of social revolution in solidarity with the poor or oppressed people of society. At its center is the claim that the salvation the gospel reveals is that of deliverance of humankind from every form of institutionalized disadvantage that prevents the full actualization in every person of all those potentials for creativity, meaning, self-realization, freedom, and community with which God has endowed us in making us in his image (Gen. 1).

Liberation theology urges that the task of the church in the world is to implement sociopolitical liberation of the poor, oppressed, and disadvantaged from those political, social, legal, or economic forces that reserve the power in society for the established power structures and prevent the needy from participating in shaping their own destinies. This puts the church on the side of the unempowered and against the established institutions of society. In Latin America this sociopolitical and economic mission of liberation theology frequently identified the church with Marxist revolution and made it the object of anti-Marxist policies of various nations, including the United States.

The general community of Christian theologians around the world tended to divide over the relevance and significance of liberation theology, some seeing it as the most important theological movement in the world and others wondering how Jesus' call to inner renewal and its outer reformative consequences could be reduced to a Marxistlike social revolution in politics and economics. The response of the liberation theologians to this problem tended to take the form of the contention that God has a preferential option for the poor. This seemed reductionistic to most Christians worldwide because it raises the question of whether God is not as passionate about the up-and-out as God is about the down-and-out. Few Christians were persuaded by the argument that the up-and-out have institutionalized power on their side and therefore are not so centrally the object of God's passion and compassion. To many Christians it seemed readily obvious upon the slightest reflection that spiritual quandary, psychological pain, routine deprivation and loss, and the omnipresence of sickness and death crowd and terrorize the life of the wealthy as well as those of the poor, of the empowered as much as of the unempowered. No one gets away from abject suffering in life. The gospel story seems as impassioned about Zacchaeus as about blind Bartimaeus and is clearly more about reformation than revolution.

Liberation theology has receded from the center of theological and ecclesiastical interest since the end of the 1980s. There are undoubtedly two reasons. First, its reductionism was never quite believable in terms of the claims of the gospel, despite the fact that much of what the liberation theologians wished for Latin American society evoked the best Christian sympathies worldwide. Second, its quasi-identification with Marxist revolution in Latin America weakened its credibility when Marxism failed worldwide, particularly in its primary centers: the Soviet Union, where it collapsed, and China, where it metamorphosed into a controlled market economy.

Additional Readings

Boff, L., & Boff, C. (1986). *Liberation theology, from confrontation to dialogue.* San Francisco: Harper.

Gutierrez, G. (1973). *A theology of liberation.* Maryknoll, NY: Orbis.

Hanks, T. D. (1983). *God so loved the third world: The Bible, the reformation, and liberation theologies.* Maryknoll, NY: Orbis.

Hodgson, P. C. (1989). *God in history, shapes of freedom.* Nashville, TN: Abingdon.

Mainwaring, S., & Wilde, A. (Eds.). (1989). *The progressive church in Latin America.* Notre Dame, IN: Notre Dame University Press.

Moltmann, J. (1983). *The power of the powerless, the word of liberation for today.* San Francisco: Harper.

Rauschenbusch, W. (1991). *Christianity and the social crisis.* Louisville, KY: Westminster/John Knox. (New York: Macmillan, 1907).

Rauschenbusch, W. (1945). *A theology for the social gospel.* Nashville, TN: Abingdon. (Nathanael W. Taylor Foundation Lectures at Yale School of Religion, 1917).

J. H. ELLENS

See PASTORAL CARE; PASTORAL COUNSELING.

Libido. Defined in Sigmund Freud's earliest formulations as the energy of the sexual drive. However, the term often is used more generally to refer to both sexual and aggressive energy. According to psychoanalytic thought libido can be changed from its original sexual or aggressive nature through a process of neutralization. It is then available for use by the ego, energizing such diverse ego functions as thinking, creative and artistic expressions, and motor activity. Libido is thus the energy source for all human psychic and behavioral activity.

D. G. BENNER

See PSYCHOSEXUAL DEVELOPMENT; PSYCHOANALYTIC PSYCHOLOGY.

Licensure. Licensure is one form of state regulation of occupations. In contrast to certification by a professional association, licensure is a function of state governments. Physicians were among the first professions required by the state to be licensed to practice. In mental health, state regulation of the disciplines has increased considerably in the last quarter of the twentieth century.

Licensing is often a catch-all term for various forms of state regulation. Licensing in the technical sense means a person must possess a license in order to practice a profession. Certification allows a state to verify minimum qualifications of a health care professional without requiring that a person be certified in order to practice in the state. For instance, a state may require a person to be regulated by the state in order to use the title "psychologist" but would not require a person to be licensed in order to do work of a psychological nature. Registration is the listing of professionals who voluntarily submit their credentials to a state agency. The variability of state regulation among mental health professionals makes it important for consumers to take care in choosing a mental health professional.

The requirements for licensure vary considerably among the mental health professions. Psychiatrists are generally licensed as physicians and then specialize in psychiatry. Many psychiatrists attain a certification in psychiatry from the American Board of Psychiatry and Neurology, a nongovernmental professional certifying body.

Nearly every state requires an applicant to possess a doctoral degree in psychology or a related field to be licensed as a psychologist. In addition, all states require two years' experience, one of which must follow the awarding of the doctorate. Licensees must also pass at least a written examination; some states also require an oral examination.

For the professions of marriage and family therapy, mental health counseling, and social work, applicants can be licensed with a masters degree in their respective discipline. Requirements vary concerning the licensing examination and post-master's experience, although most states require an examination and the demonstration of post-master's experience. Not all states license these professionals, and the state department of professional or occupational regulation can give the interested consumer information concerning mental health disciplines regulated by a given jurisdiction. Psychiatric nurses are generally required to become registered nurses and then qualify for certification as an advanced practice nurse in psychiatric nursing.

Because the public often has difficulty identifying qualified mental health professionals, states require professionals to possess minimum educational and experience requirements in order to practice. In many states, mental health professionals must be licensed in order to hold themselves out to the public using a title conveying expertise in mental health care. The rationale often given in support of licensing occupations is to protect the consuming public from unscrupulous or ill-trained persons. However, licensing does not mean that the provider is endorsed by state government. Consumers choosing a mental health professional should also examine the credentials and experience of a potential mental health care provider prior to the initiation of services.

E. W. THROCKMORTON

See COUNSELING AND PSYCHOTHERAPY: OVERVIEW.

Lie Detection. The procedure involves the use of a device, often called a polygraph, to measure several physiological responses that are under autonomic control and accompany strong emotions. These include heart rate, blood pressure, respiration, skin resistance (galvanic skin response), and electrical activity of the brain (EEG). The word *polygraph,* meaning literally *many writings,* comes from the use of several pens in a polygraph device to record the autonomic responses. Lie detectors are used by many police departments to question suspects and by some employers in interviewing applicants for particularly sensitive jobs.

The theory behind a lie detector is that if a person is anxious about a lie, his or her breathing, heart rate, and other autonomic responses will increase. The lie detector is thus more accurately a nervousness detector.

The usual procedure in operating a polygraph is to make a recording while the subject is relaxed, and this recording serves as a baseline for evaluating subsequent responses. The examiner then asks questions that can be answered yes or no. These include neutral questions interspersed with questions critical to the investigation at hand. Sufficient time is allowed between each question for the measures to return to normal. Presumably the suspect's lie is indicated by the increased physiological responses to the critical questions. Since the inflated blood pressure cuff used for the cardiovascular measure may become uncomfortable, the examination is often limited to several minutes and about a dozen questions.

Another type of lie detector has recently been developed to measure changes in a person's voice that are undetectable to the human ear. All muscles, including those controlling the vocal cords, vibrate slightly when in use. The muscle vibration, which is transmitted to the vocal cords, is suppressed by the activity of the autonomic nervous system when a speaker is under stress. When a tape recording of a person's voice is played through a device called a voice stress analyzer, a speaker under stress can be detected. Like the polygraph, the voice stress analyzer indicates only that an individual is anxious, not necessarily that he or she is lying. The voice stress analyzer has an advantage over the polygraph in that the subject does not have to be attached to any equipment. Since the voice analyzer can work from the telephone, radio, television, or tape-recorded messages, there is concern over its ethical use.

No lie-detecting device is foolproof. A subject who is telling the truth may be tense and react emotionally to the content of the questions and thus appear to be lying. Attempts to defeat the lie detector usually fail. It is extremely difficult to suppress or augment the autonomic responses by, for example, thinking emotional thoughts or clenching one's teeth or sphincter muscle. The purpose of such behavior would be to increase one's responses to neutral questions, thus creating a baseline comparable to reactions to the critical questions.

It is possible for pathological liars not to realize that they are lying or not to care and thus show little abnormal response to questioning. It is also clear that tranquilizers can be used to reduce the physiological responses to the polygraph test. Kleinmuntz and Szucko (1984) show that with the use of lie detectors one-third of innocent people are likely to appear guilty and one-fourth of guilty people are likely to appear innocent. Since physiological responses are much the same from one emotion to another, the polygraph has difficulty distinguishing between anxiety and guilt responses (Lykken, 1983). Because of these problems most courts do not admit lie-detector results as evidence, although such tests are used in preliminary criminal investigations. In what is known as the guilty knowledge test criminals will autonomically react to details of a crime presumably known only by the police and the guilty person.

Research suggests that the context of both the lie and the detection of the lie must be considered. The accuracy of the polygraph can be affected by such variables as attentiveness, personality, drugs, and the interaction between examiner and subject (Waid & Orne, 1982). Subjects' beliefs in the accuracy of the test can also affect their physiological responses. If the examiner gives subjects feedback about their failure to fool the machine, their next lies are even more easily detected. In spite of these limitations lie-detecting techniques are somewhat effective, and thus their use is likely to continue.

References

Kleinmuntz, B., & Szucko, J. (1984). A field study of the fallibility of polygraph lie detection. *Nature, 308,* 449–450.

Lykken, D. (1983, April). Polygraph prejudice. *APA Monitor,* 4.

Waid, W., & Orne, M. (1982). The physiological detection of deception. *American Scientist, 70,* 402–409.

Additional Reading

Holden, C. (1986). Days may be numbered for polygraphs in the private sector. *Science, 232,* 705.

M. P. COSGROVE

Life Script. The term used in transactional analysis to refer to the personal plan for life (Steiner, 1974). Out of their interaction with parents, children adopt one of the basic life positions (I'm OK—You're Not OK; I'm Not OK—You're OK; I'm Not OK—You're Not OK; I'm OK—You're OK). Scripts are the themes for life that stem from one of these positions and dictate how the child will survive.

Berne described several types of scripts, such as never scripts—never getting what one wants; always scripts—doing the same thing over and over; until scripts—waiting before a reward is given; and after scripts—having ominous things occur at certain times.

Scripts can be winner's scripts (outcomes are mostly positive), loser's scripts (outcomes are mostly negative), and tragic scripts (outcomes are mostly disastrous). Often scripts can be understood through the themes of fairy tales.

Reference

Steiner, C. (1974). *Scripts people live.* New York: Grove Press.

H. N. MALONY

See TRANSACTIONAL ANALYSIS.

Life Skills Counseling. Life skills counseling refers to a counseling approach developed by Adkins in the middle 1960s (Adkins, 1970; Adkins & Wynne, 1966). The background for this approach was the belief at that time that traditional counseling methods had been shown to be ineffective with clients from disadvantaged backgrounds. This failure seemed to be especially pronounced when the counseling method employed focused on discussing the clients' feelings in an unstructured, ambiguous relationship between counselor and client. Adkins had experience in a vocational training program, where a structured format was used to help disadvantaged adolescents and adults learn skills related to employment, interpersonal adjustment, and citizenship. Adkins used this experience as a basis for designing a structured counseling approach with three goals. First, it should be centered on problems related to living and working in an urban environment. Second, skills that clients brought to counseling should serve as the foundation for learning new skills. Third, the program should allow for both group interactions and personal attention.

Adkins worked with counselors to formulate a task analysis of the skill requirements for successful relationships in work, family, and community settings. On the basis of this analysis, he developed a list of 50 common life problems that were then grouped into five areas: developing oneself and relating to others; managing a career; managing home and family responsibilities; managing leisure time; and exercising community rights and responsibilities. Each of these areas, which are titled curriculum tracks in the program, was divided into smaller units (Adkins, 1973). For example, representative units of managing a career are completing interviews, tests, and application blanks; relating to one's supervisor; and understanding paycheck deductions.

Adkins also developed a four-stage process for teaching these skills that was targeted to the needs of his audience. The first stage was the stimulus stage, in which the counselor presents a problem using a tape recording, a movie segment, or an interview, and thus stimulates the group's interest in the topic. Once the group begins to discuss the problem, the counselor moves to the *evocation stage* where the counselor's objective is to draw from each group member what he or she knows about the topic. The group's ideas are written on the blackboard or newsprint, the ideas are categorized, and questions are developed. The third stage, objective inquiry, has the group members locate answers to the questions using prepared multimedia kits to direct their information-seeking activities inside and outside of the classroom. Once the information has been obtained and presented to the group, the group selects one or several aspects of the problem to work out during the application stage. In this stage, the development and application of new skills are completed.

Adkins meant the life skills approach to be flexible in its use. Thus a counselor might focus on one area (e.g., employment) and spend several sessions going through the final stages. Or a counselor might choose to cover every curriculum track at a less specific level of involvement. Another advantage is that the emphasis on life problems and skills translates counseling goals into specific behavioral objectives rather than insight-oriented affective and cognitive outcomes. Transfer of learning from life skills counseling to real-life problems is therefore heightened. Maintenance of change is also likely as the newly learned skills are incorporated and used successfully after the counseling has ended. Finally, the learning process is learner-centered rather than teacher-oriented. Thus motivation for learning is high.

This particular approach to life skills training is emblematic of a broader definition of the use of structured groups. Drum and Knott (1977) define a structured group as "a delimited learning situation with a predetermined goal, and a planned design to enable each group member to reach this identified goal with minimum frustration and maximum ability to transfer the new learning to a wide range of life events" (p. 14). They discussed three types of structured groups. First are life skills groups, where the term is broadly used to denote training in skills that will enhance success in a variety of life domains; examples are assertiveness training, parenting skills, and conflict management. Second are life theme groups, in which the group focuses on personal issues such as clarifying values. Last are life transition groups, in which all the participants are experiencing similar life transitions such as divorce, marriage, and parenthood.

Drum and Knott (1977) argued that these types of structured groups provide a high level of value for both consumers and providers. First, the groups are relatively nonthreatening and allow participants to approach difficult topics as they are personally able. Second, the groups offer a high likelihood of change for a motivated participant. Third, the groups are limited to the topic at hand, thus reducing the possibility of off-task work. Fourth, within the group setting, the participants will realize that others experience concerns and problems similar to theirs, thus fostering a sense of universality (i.e., I'm not alone in this). Fifth, there may be the belief on the part of the participants that there is less stigma in an educational group than in a traditional psychotherapy treatment. Sixth, the group allows participants the chance to try new skills on each other in a nonthreatening and supportive environment. Last, using a group with one or two counselors is an economical use of professionals' time and allows each participant to have both professional and peer contact.

Life skills approaches, in general, offer a Christian counselor an excellent template for fostering changes among clients. Although life skills training as conceptualized by Adkins is remedial in nature, later approaches have focused on prevention as well, teaching clients skills that will increase their success in new endeavors. In addition, although research has typically been conducted on specific types of life skills training approaches, this research base has been supportive of the benefits of such programs.

References

Adkins, W. R. (1970). Structured counseling for the disadvantaged. *Personnel and Guidance Journal, 49,* 108–116.

Adkins, W. R. (1973). Life skills education for adult learners. *Adult Leadership, 22,* 55–58, 82–84.

Adkins, W. R., & Wynne, J. D. (1966). *Final report of the YMCA youth and work project.* Contract 24-64, Department of Labor. New York: YMCA of Greater New York.

Drum, D., & Knott, J. E. (1977). *Structured groups for facilitating development.* New York: Human Sciences.

E. M. Altmaier

See Coping Skills Therapies; Counseling Psychology.

Life Span Development. *Content in Life Span Development.* Life span development is the multidisciplinary study of how people change over time. Life span development involves the multidisciplinary study of physical, cognitive, social, and emotional changes. Historically the study of human develop-

ment focused on the changes in individuals during infancy, childhood, and adolescence; however, since the 1960s theorists and researchers have broadened their interest to include the entire life span, from conception to old age.

Issues in Development. As theorists attempt to describe life span development issues they must deal with several such issues before they can begin to codify their constructs and categorize their observations. These issues are pretheoretical assumptions that theorists make about development. These issues are often presented as dichotomies, but readers should realize that this reflects the convention of describing extreme points on a continuum. Most theorists adopt more moderate positions. Theorists' positions on these issues are considered assumptions because no data clearly support one position more than another; often both positions find ample support in the data. And so, each theorist's position is a reflection of his or her assumptions about how development occurs.

Development versus Change. Theorists must decide whether there is or is not an ultimate goal or accomplishment to which the life span is focused. The developmental position assumes a goal, and a change position assumes that there is no end state or goal. Currently most lifespan theorists take the developmental position, and their definition of the goal of development describes the domain their theories seek to explain (e.g., personality development, cognitive development, or social development).

When developmental psychology focused on children and adolescents, developmental change was assumed to be synonymous with increasing competence and complexity. Now that developmental psychology has expanded to include adult development, developmental change can refer to either gain or loss.

Nature versus Nurture. This is the question of whether nature or nurture exerts a greater influence on the development of one's domain of interest. Readers may be aware of many synonyms for nature, such as genetics, biology, innate abilities, and maturation, and the synonyms for nurture, such as learning, experience, environment and social or cultural context. At different times in the history of developmental psychology it has been more popular to endorse a nature emphasis, and at other times a nurture position was more popular. Currently, theorists acknowledge both of these influences and neither position is clearly the more popular. Although both nature and nurture affect development, nature has its greatest influence at the beginning and the end of the life span, while nurture's effects seem to be cumulative and increase over the course of the lifespan.

Continuity versus Discontinuity. This is the question of whether the qualities of a phenomenon remain consistent throughout development (a continuity position) or whether those qualities change (a discontinuity position). Continuity theorists suggest that the qualities of developmental processes are the same throughout the life span and that development involves a change in the amount or speed of those qualities or processes (e.g., as we get older we can remember more, but the process we use to remember stays the same). Stage theorists adopt the discontinuity position and suggest that each stage is focused on a different set of tasks, abilities, or defining issues. Some stage theorists might suggest that stages are sequential (occur in a specified order), or are age-linked, or are cumulative (earlier stages lay the foundations for later stages). Currently stage theories dominate developmental psychology.

Universal versus Culture-Specific. Theorists differ in the extent to which they believe that all people develop in the same way regardless of experiences or cultural differences. Most new theories of development restrict their predictions to specific cultures, but the best known developmental theories were proposed when the popular belief was that universal statements could be made.

Sources of Change Revisited. Baltes, Reese, and Lipsitt (1980) categorize sources of developmental change in a slightly different way than do the traditional nature and nurture positions. They describe three sources of change, all of which have both nature and nurture components within them. The first, non-normative events, are unique to the individual and are the greatest source of individual differences. Death of a child, experiencing an automobile accident, and receiving an inheritance are all examples of non-normative events. Research shows that the timing of a non-normative event is important for predicting how stressful the experience will be, as unexpected events will be more stressful than anticipated events (Neugarten, 1979).

The second, normative age-graded changes, are linked to chronological age and are shared by most people. They include biologically influenced events (puberty) and culturally influenced events (legal voting age). Normative age-graded changes make 20-year-olds alike whether they were born in 1950 or 1980. Normative age-graded changes can be explained using universal theories.

The third type of influence, normative history-graded changes, reflect how development differs from one generation, or cohort, to another. A cohort is a group of people who were born at approximately the same time and share cultural and historical experiences. Normative history-graded changes can be biologically based (such as the AIDS epidemic or the fact that the onset of puberty has occurred at younger ages over successive generations), or they can be culturally based (such as wars or economic trends). Normative history-graded events make one generation of 20-year-olds different from another, and the effects of these changes are better explained by culture-specific theories than by universal theories of development.

Theories of Development. *Erikson's Theory of Psychosocial Development.* Erik Erikson focused on personality and emotional developments, especially the development of identity and ego. He proposed eight stages that span the entire life. Movement through the stages comes primarily from maturation. Each stage is characterized by a conflict between internal (maturational) impulses and social norms. The eight stages (each named for the characteristic crisis) are trust versus mistrust, autonomy versus doubt, initiative versus shame, industry versus inferiority, identity formation versus identity confusion, intimacy versus isolation, generativity versus stagnation, and ego integrity versus despair. Successful resolution of each crisis yields an ego strength. Earlier stages provide strengths that make crisis-resolution in the later stages easier.

Behaviorism and Social Learning Theory. These theories are nonstage change theories. There is no particular goal toward which development points. These theorists, among them B. F. Skinner and Albert Bandura, are more interested in describing the mechanism of change. That mechanism is reinforcement history (rewards and punishments) and, in the case of social-learning theories, cognitively mediated modeling and imitation. The mechanisms of change are the same throughout the life span. These theories emphasize contributions of the environment to change.

Piaget's theory of cognitive development. Jean Piaget focused on the development of cognitive structures called schemes. He proposed four stages (sensorimotor, preoperational, concrete operational, and formal operation), each of which is dominated by a different scheme. Movement through the stages is driven by maturation. Cognitive development models have been applied to explain moral development, self-concept, and problem solving.

Ecological Systems Theory. Systems theories are nonstage change theories. There is no particular goal toward which development points. These theorists, like Bronfenbrenner, are more interested in describing the interactions of the individual (the microsystem), their immediate environment (the mesosystem), and their culture (the macrosystem). These theories typically discuss both nature and nurture contributions to change, and they acknowledge that their descriptions of change are not universal.

The Process of Life Span Development. This section will be a brief description of normative age-graded change from conception to death. Each age will be describe in terms of the physical, cognitive, and psychosocial growth that characterizes it. No single theoretical framework will be implied. It should be noted that these descriptions best describe cohorts of the recent past and present and are likely to change as culture changes.

Prenatal Period. The goal of prenatal development is for the developing child to become physically mature enough to be able to live independently. The embryonic period, from 2 to 8 weeks postconception, is the time when basic organ systems are established, as are the membranous structures, such as the placenta. During the fetal period, from 8 to 40 weeks postconception, the organ systems grow and mature enough to sustain the child's life independently. Little is known about the cognitive or psychosocial development during the prenatal period. We do know that the unborn child can hear during the last trimester of the pregnancy and can remember what was heard. Thus the foundations of language learning are laid in the prenatal period.

Birth is a stressful transition to independent life. The child's body must breath, regulate temperature, ingest and process nutrients, and eliminate wastes, among other processes; all these functions were previously performed solely by or with the aid of the mother's body. In the psychosocial domain, it was once thought that the time soon after birth was a sensitive period for developing a bond with the mother and father, but this understanding is not supported by current research. Current research also suggests that, barring physical damage, the conditions of birth do not have a long-lasting effect on the child's cognitive or personality development.

Newborn Period. The newborn period extends for the first month after birth. The transition to independent body functioning continues as homeostatic functions—those body functions that maintain life—stabilize. Newborns spend 90% of the day in sleep, and of their sleep time, half is spent in Rapid Eye Movement (REM) sleep. REM sleep is the sleep stage when adults dream, but it is not known whether newborns experience dreams as older children or adults do. When newborns are awake they are capable of coordinated reflexive and some limited voluntary movement. The coordination of reflexes has been used as a way to assess brain damage. Newborns can hear and see, although they do not rely on these senses as older children and adults do. Newborns rely on smell, taste, and touch more than on sight and sound. Newborns can learn and remember. For example, they recognize mother at 3 days old, based on mother's smell. Visual memories are also formed, but those memories are more transitory.

Infancy. The period of infancy extends from the second month to the age of 2 years. During infancy rapid physical, cognitive, and emotional growth takes place. In the physical domain, infancy is one of the three times during the life span of very rapid growth (the other two being the fetal period and puberty). Birth length doubles by 40 months. Gross motor skills such as rolling over and standing and walking, which all require coordination of the large muscle groups, develop and are refined. Fine motor skills, such as grasping, which require coordination of the small muscles of the hand, are also developing. Physical development during infancy is characterized by a transition from reflex-controlled to voluntarily controlled movement. The transition happens earliest for the muscles closer to the head and latest for those near the feet (a cephalo-caudal progression) and earlier for the muscles close to the body trunk and later for those near the extremities (a proximo-distal progression).

In the cognitive domain, infants must complete two major tasks. First, they must develop the realization that objects have a separate existence from the infant and that objects continue to exist even when they are out of the infant's sight. Second, the infant must learn language. Language skills differ over the first year from crying to cooing (stringing together vowel sounds) to babbling (combining vowels and consonants) to the use of holographic, single-word sentences. In the second year, utterances expand from one-word sentences to two-word and later three-word sentences as vocabulary and understanding of sentence structure continue to increase.

In the social-emotional domain, the major task of infancy is to develop an emotional attachment with a consistent caregiver, usually the mother or the father. Secure attachments allow infants to see themselves as lovable and their care givers and the world as worthy of trust (Bowlby, 1969). Infants who have consistent care that is appropriate to their temperament and their needs develop secure attachments and are more likely to have healthy relationships in childhood and in adulthood (Main, Kaplan, & Cassidy, 1985).

Childhood. Childhood extends from years 2 to 12. In the physical domain, children grow at a slower rate than they did in infancy. Children continue to develop and refine gross and fine motor skills. In the cognitive domain, childhood is a period of rapid acquisition of skills and knowledge. Refined information processing and problem solving skills allow children to manage the newly acquired information and develop more complex thoughts and patterns of interaction. Childhood is also a period of rapid acquisition and increasing complexity in the socioemotional domain. Children learn about social roles, especially gender-specific roles, cooperation and conflict, and social norms. As their social environment expands beyond the family to include the adults and children in the classroom and later in the school or church, children see more models of social behavior and have more opportunities to practice social skills.

Adolescence. This is the period between childhood and adulthood. The beginning of adolescence is typically set at 13 years old. However, identifying the end of adolescence is more difficult because there are no physical, cognitive, or social milestones that are consistently associated with the transition to adulthood. The ability to take on the status of a productive adult is most often identified as the end of the adolescent period. In the physical domain, adolescence is the third period in the life span when there is a rapid rate of growth. This period is marked by a growth spurt, the development of secondary sexual characteristics, and reproductive maturity. Whether an individual is early or late maturing in the physical domain interacts with development in the social domain. Early-maturing boys have a social advantage and are more likely to take on or be given leadership roles than are late-maturing boys. Early-maturing girls have a social disadvantage because they tend to be shorter and stockier in physical build than are late-maturing girls.

Cognitive and socioemotional development is focused on identity formation—a sense of self. The ability to engage in abstract reasoning emerges at this time. Abstract reasoning involves the ability to go beyond the actual and experienced to the possible and imagined. Facility with abstract concepts takes years to develop, and may develop first in those areas in which the individual possesses expertise and special facility. Before abstract reasoning skills are fully developed, adolescents show a naive optimism in which they reject the actual failures of the world (the concrete) and embrace the possibilities (the abstract). Another implication of abstract thought is that adolescents are developing a future time orientation. Erikson notes that socially and emotionally adolescence is focused on development of identity, the self-concept that can include values and morals, occupational choice, and ethnic self-concept among other components. The development of identity also often involves religious questioning, which can lead to a movement from an inherited set of beliefs to a personal faith.

Early Adulthood. This period extends from the end of adolescence to the mid-thirties. Early adulthood is the time of peak physical abilities (e.g., strength, speed, agility, fertility). Illnesses during this period are usually acute and not chronic. However, substance abuse, especially of alcohol, is at the highest rate in this period. Homicides and AIDS are the leading causes of death for this age group.

In the cognitive domain, early adulthood is a time of acquiring and mastering new skills and roles. Perry (1970) suggests that young adults transition from dualistic (black-and-white) thinking to acknowledging that relativism exists and finally to making a commitment to personal beliefs while accepting that others may come to a different conclusion.

Most theorists agree that in the social and emotion domain, young adulthood is a period characterized by increased independence from the family of origin, a search for emotional intimacy (through friendships and especially through a mating relationship), and an increase in new roles (e.g., worker, spouse, parent). The increased number of roles and the potential for conflicts among those roles makes young adulthood an age with the potential for high levels of stress and distress. For example, the conflict between the motivation to leave home to go to work and the motivation to stay home to be with a spouse or a child can cause stress. High levels of stress and low levels of life satisfaction are especially notable in the early years of parenting, when new roles are being learned, old roles are often being renegotiated, and role conflict is most common.

Middle Adulthood. This period extends from the mid-thirties to the mid-fifties. In the physical domain, middle adulthood is a time when the first evidence of physical limitations may become apparent. Researchers make a distinction between primary aging, age-related physical changes that are unavoidable, and secondary aging, physical changes that are due to abuse or disease and are avoidable. For example, some amount of thinning and wrinkling of the skin is a primary aging effect that is caused by a loss of collagen, but extensive wrinkling is a secondary aging effect that can be caused by overexposure to the sun. Most secondary aging represents the accumulated effects of abuse and disease and, researchers suggest, the effects can be avoided and even reversed by following a healthy lifestyle that includes a balanced diet and regular exercise.

Cognitively, middle adulthood is a time of adjustment to primary aging effects in the nervous system. Reduced sensitivity to visual and auditory information and slower neural processing are thought, at this time, to be primary aging effects and can mean that middle-aged adults have slower reactions. However, if the adult is able to adapt, functionally middle-aged adults can be more effective in managing information and learning than are young adults. This increased efficiency reflects a subtle shift in cognitive strategy from the young adult strategy of learning and remembering large amounts of information to the middle-aged adult strategy of first assessing what needs to be learned and then learning and applying that information effectively.

Socially and emotionally, middle adulthood is a time characterized by responsibility. Middle-aged adults are at the peak of their earning power and occupational responsibility. They may become more active in the community and church than they were when they were young adults. And within the family, they are typically parenting adolescents. Some researchers suggest that in the future, an increasing number of middle-aged adults may become responsible for helping their elderly parents although currently this is true for less than 20% of them. Interaction with aging parents, and especially the death of a parent, can change the perception of time and mortality for middle-aged adults from one of believing that most of life is ahead of them to the belief that most of life is behind them. Levinson (1986) coined the term *midlife crisis* to reflect his belief that most middle-aged adults experienced great distress however, surveys show that only about 20% of middle-aged adults report experiencing such a crisis.

Late Adulthood. This period extends from the sixties until death. If adults survived to the age of 60, then the average longevity is 74 years for men and 77 years for women. Many researchers have begun to distinguish between the "young-old" and "old-old" to reflect the fact that for most adults, the early years of this period are a time of good health in which physical changes, both primary and secondary, follow the same trajectory as they did during middle adulthood. The "young-old" contradict the popular stereotypes of the elderly as less intelligent, sexless, disabled, and isolated.

Cognitively, primary aging effects continue. This means that tasks requiring speed, selective attention, and short-term memory may be more difficult than they are for younger adults. Adults who continue to use their cognitive abilities in late adulthood retain more of those abilities. Cognitive strategy in late adulthood involves acknowledging the complexities of most situations, tolerating ambiguity, and holding paradoxes in tension.

Socially, late adulthood is characterized by a reduction in the number and intensity of roles and responsibilities. Occupational responsibilities are reduced; retirement is a normative age-graded event that most experience around the age of 65. Most older adults live independently in the community. They have contact with children (an average of twice a month) and with siblings, especially sisters. Older adults have more close friends than they did in middle adulthood, perhaps because they have more time due to reduced role responsibilities. Older adults who have good health, financial security, and social support report greater life satisfaction.

Death. Death, is preceded by a precipitous drop in functioning in many of the body systems simultaneously. This is called tertiary aging and can involve declines in cognitive performance and reduced personality organization. Among individuals who are aware of their own imminent death, common responses include denial, anger, depression, and acceptance. These responses do not reflect stages.

References

Baltes, P. B., Reese, H. W., & Lipsitt, L. P. (1980). The life-span perspective in developmental psychology. In M. R. Rosenzweig & L. W. Porter (Eds.), *Annual review of psychology* (pp. 65–110). Palo Alto, CA: Annual Reviews Inc.

Bowlby, J. (1969). *Attachment and loss:* Vol. 1, *Attachment.* New York: Basic.

Levinson, D. J. (1986). A conception of adult development. *American Psychologist, 41,* 3–13.

Main, M., Kaplan, N., & Cassidy, J. (1985). Security in infancy, childhood, and adulthood: A move to the level of representation. Monographs of the Society for Research in Child Development, 50 (serial No. 209), 66–104.

Neugarten, B. L. (1979). Time, age, and the life cycle. *American Journal of Psychiatry,* 136, 887–894.

Perry, W. (1970). *Forms of intellectual and ethical development in the college years.* New York: Holt.

K. A. GATHERCOAL

See COGNITIVE DEVELOPMENT; ADOLESCENCE; PSYCHOSOCIAL DEVELOPMENT; GERONTOLOGY; MATURITY.

Life Style. See STYLE OF LIFE.

Limit Setting in Psychotherapy. This term usually refers to therapeutic interventions aimed at protecting patients from their own destructive or self-destructive acting out. The basic concept is that for a variety of reasons patients can enact internal, psychic catastrophes in their external lives in severely damaging ways instead of expressing them in a workable manner. In extreme cases the only recourse a therapist might have is to intervene to prevent a patient from dying or to keep treatment from becoming compromised beyond repair. Examples of this would be a mandatory hospitalization of an actively suicidal patient or requiring a patient to enter a drug detoxification program before psychological assessment and treatment occur.

Possible reasons for a patient's acting out in a way that requires limit setting are so numerous that all of them cannot be mentioned. A major reason involves ego immaturity or ego deterioration. For instance, a child in play therapy who has not yet mastered aggressive impulses would need clear boundaries as to not hitting the therapist, or a depressed patient who has lost the ability for self-care would require hospitalization. Another reason could be a determination to gratify destructive aggressive or libidinal impulses instead of facing them. The patient might want to use a session solely for the pleasure of berating and mistreating the therapist or for some kind of seduction. Needing the experience of the therapist stopping them in a way patients have not been able to stop themselves is another possible source of this kind of acting out. For example, a patient might be so identified with a mean and critical parent that he or she cannot deal with the flood of accusations experienced in his or her own mind. By abusing the therapist in some hypercritical way that requires limit setting from the therapist, the patient might be unconsciously seeking someone outside who can stop the internalized parents. Another reason can be the need to test the limits of the therapist to know where are the boundaries on which to rely.

There is a continuum of limit-setting interventions, going from the most concrete management of the patient to much more complex relational and mental interventions. On the concrete end are the more blatant interventions the therapist makes to impose boundaries on destructive acting out. The therapist might need to function as an auxiliary ego for the patient, insisting on certain behaviors, contracts, or commitments from the patient in order to save the patient's life (Eissler, 1953; Kernberg, 1984).

Moving toward the middle of the continuum involves the limit setting provided by the structure of the treatment situation. Fees are charged, a specific appointment time is set, participation of the patient is expected and defined, policies regarding length of session and missed sessions are discussed. Bleger (1967) has compared these therapeutic provisions to the analogy of a picture and frame. The frame is obviously not the main feature. However, the importance of the frame is that it defines the space for the presentation of the picture. Langs (1973) has elaborated this idea of the frame of psychotherapy and applied it to numerous ground rules of treatment. Regardless of one's treatment approach, the structure of it provides limit-setting functions such as keeping the treatment on course, delineating therapeutic expectations of the patient's and therapist's roles, and communicating a sense of personal responsibility to the patient. Maintaining the ground rules usually is extremely important to the patient. For example, the patient who cancelled an appointment at the last minute because someone demanded time might be acting out a pattern of not considering his or her own needs. The therapist's holding to a ground rule of charging for missed sessions might motivate the patient to explore reasons for the cancellation. The patient could also experience the therapist placing a limit around the pattern of maladaptive self-denial instead of the therapist colluding with the pattern.

Toward the other end of the continuum would be the limit-setting qualities of less concrete and more mental interventions. The therapist's understanding and empathy for the acting-out behavior and its causes usually is a sufficient and powerful limit. In the preceding example, if the patient can be helped to truly face neurotic guilt, he or she might be greatly helped in stopping the pattern. In regard to this kind of limit setting Bion (1967) has talked about the therapist's understanding and mental functioning as a container for the most primitive, intense, nonverbal, and painful experiences of the patient. A lifetime of being doomed to repeat these experiences can be helped and limited by the therapist's willingness to experience and survive the patient's unbearable anxieties or pain. The containment comes through the therapist's ability to offer the patient empathetic understanding of what has previously been too dreadful to remember or realize.

The dangers in limit setting lie all along the continuum. Not providing necessary limits, whether they be concrete, ground rules, or empathetic, can be disastrous. However, the therapist could err in acting too concretely and overlook the patient's ability for self-limitation if given the containment necessary. Finally, there is the danger of intervening from the therapist's superego instead of providing a missing ego function for the patient. This intervention could stem from unresolved needs in the therapist to control or change the patient or self according to a legalistic standard.

References

Bion, W. R. (1967). *Second thoughts*. New York: Aronson.
Bleger, J. (1967). Psychoanalysis of the psychoanalytic frame. *International Journal of Psycho-Analysis 48*, 511–519.
Eissler, K. R. (1953). The effect of the structure of the ego on psychoanalytic technique. *Journal of the American Psychoanalytic Association, 1*, 104–143.
Kernberg, O. F. (1984). *Severe personality disorders*. New Haven, CT: Yale University Press.
Langs, R. (1973). *The technique of psychoanalytic psychotherapy*. New York: Aronson.

W. L. Edkins

See Counseling and Psychotherapy: Overview.

Listening Skills. *See* Empathy; Human Relations Training.

Lithium Therapy. Lithium, a naturally occurring salt, was the first agent in psychiatry to be specifically effective against a major psychotic disorder. Given orally in tablet form, it usually calms psychotic manic states within 5 to 10 days. When it is taken on a maintenance schedule it has been shown to prevent the recurrence of manic highs. Once they are stabilized on lithium, even persons with severe cases of manic disorder can be treated on an outpatient basis. Although its mechanism of action is still unknown, it appears that lithium may interfere with sodium retention within brain cells.

See Psychopharmacology.

Lobotomy. A surgical procedure consisting of the ablation of the prefrontal area of the frontal lobe of the cortex. Because of the drastic nature of the treatment and undesirable side effects that are often present, prefrontal lobotomies, as with all psychosurgical approaches, are ordinarily resorted to only after all other methods have failed. At such a point the operation may be considered as treatment for severe and chronic states of affective disorder as well as paranoid and catatonic schizophrenia.

See Brain and Human Behavior.

Locke, John (1632–1704). Born in Somerset, England, Locke studied philosophy, medicine, and science. He is best known for his contributions to empiricism and associationism. His major psychological work was *Essay Concerning Human Understanding*. Two other works, *Two Treatises on Government* and *A Letter Concerning Toleration*, both had a profound effect on the United States Constitution. He also wrote several books on Christianity, the best known being *An Appeal for a Rational Interpretation of the Gospels* and *Reasonableness of Christianity*.

See Empiricism; Associationism.

Locus of Control. Locus of control refers to the belief that one can or cannot influence the directions and outcomes of life. When people believe their outcomes are contingent upon their behavior, they are said to have an internal locus of control. When people believe their outcomes are the result of forces beyond their control, they are said to have an external locus of control (Levenson, 1981). This construct emphasizes expectations rather than motivations. Hence it is based on a cognitive model and reflects the shift from psychodynamic approaches to cognitive ones. Locus of control largely overlaps with some other concepts, such as perceived control, self-efficacy, learned helplessness, and causal attributions (Lefcourt, 1992). These concepts share a concern for the manner in which individuals experience their personal situations and whether they perceive themselves to be capable of coping with them (Lefcourt & Davidson-Katz, 1991).

The concept of external control has been differentiated into two types (Levenson, 1981). A chance locus of control refers to a belief in the basic unordered and random nature of the world; a powerful other locus of control refers to the expectation that powerful other people are in control.

The concept of locus of control has received extensive attention. The *Social Sciences Index* lists 958 citations over the last 13 years. Lefcourt's (1966) article has become a citation classic, being 1 of the 10 most often cited in the *Psychological Bulletin*. It was one of only three nonmethodological papers to make the list and has had more than 500 citations (see Lefcourt, 1992). The recent edition of the *Measures of Personality and Social Psychological Attitudes* reviews 18 different locus of control scales, including measures relating to marital satisfaction, parenting, children, the elderly, weight issues, drinking problems, and general health (see Lefcourt, 1991).

Much of the research has assessed the impact of locus of control on health. The general finding has been that an internal locus of control is predictive of health and well-being. People with an internal locus of control have many advantages. They are better information seekers and more effective learners about wellness and disease. They practice more preventive and precautionary health measures. For example, they are more likely to follow prescribed diets and to become involved in vocational rehabilitation. They are also less likely to smoke. They are less likely to feel threatened by difficult situations and hence experience less stress. As a result they tend to have a stronger immunological system. They use more problem-solving coping strategies and employ fewer emotion-directed coping strategies. After heart attacks, they have a lower peak temperature and remain in intensive care and in the hospital a shorter time. In a related finding, nursing home residents who were given more control over their environments were more active, happier, more alert, and lived longer. As a result of these various factors, internals retain their health longer than externals (see Lefcourt & Davidson-Katz, 1991).

Nevertheless, research has concluded that being external is not always bad (Levenson, 1981). Sometimes outcomes are under the control of powerful other people, and a recognition of this is not necessarily problematic. For example, both cancer research and alcoholism research have supported the notion that one type of external control, the chance locus of control, is problematic. Both internals and powerful others seem to recover from and cope with these problems more successfully (Lefcourt & Davidson-Katz, 1991).

The concept of control has obvious relationships to Christian thought. Although there are significant differences within the church in the interpretation of divine sovereignty and providence, there is universal belief in the general notion of God's control. For some people this may be control through active manipulation by God. For others, it may be control through active exchange or interaction with God (Pargament, Kennell, Hathaway, Grevengoed, Newman, & Jones, 1988). How should we understand the theological notion of God control along with the psychological construct of locus of control? Does God control operate in a manner similar to external control, or does God operate in a manner more similar to internal control?

Research by Welton, Adkins, Ingle, and Dixon (1996) addresses these questions. We developed a measure of God control and combined it with Levenson's (1981) multidimensional measure of control. We also measured health habits and coping styles. In both cases we found that individuals who had either an internal locus of control or a high God control demonstrated positive health habits and coping styles. This research points to the conclusion that God control operates in a manner more similar to internal control. Given this research, and the previous research indicating that a powerful other's control is sometimes associated with health and well-being, it seems that health is associated with a positive expectation about the future, which results from a belief in a benevolent control, whether that is a belief in oneself, in powerful others, or in God.

References

Lefcourt, H. M. (1966). Internal versus external control of reinforcement: A review. *Psychological Bulletin, 65,* 206–220.

Lefcourt, H. M. (1991). Locus of control. In J. P. Robinson, P. R. Shaver, & L. S. Wrightsman (Eds.), *Measures of personality and social psychological attitudes* (2nd ed.). San Diego, CA: Academic.

Lefcourt, H. M. (1992). Durability and impact of the locus of control construct. *Psychological Bulletin, 112,* 411–414.

Lefcourt, H. M., & Davidson-Katz, K. (1991). Locus of control and health. In C. R. Snyder & D. R. Forsyth (Eds.), *Handbook of social and clinical psychology.* New York: Pergamon.

Levenson, H. (1981). Differentiating among internality, powerful others, and chance. In H. M. Lefcourt (Ed.), *Research with the locus of control construct* (Vol. 1). New York: Academic.

Pargament, K. I., Kennell, J., Hathaway, W., Grevengoed, N., Newman, J., & Jones, W. (1988). Religion and the problem-solving process: Three styles of coping. *Journal for the Scientific Study of Religion, 27,* 90–104.

Welton, G. L., Adkins, A. G., Ingle, S. L., & Dixon, W. A. (1996). God control: The fourth dimension. *Journal of Psychology and Theology, 24* (1), 13.

G. L. Welton

See Social Learning Theory; Self-Efficacy.

Logical Positivism. *See* Empiricism; Psychology, Methods of.

Logorrhea. Excessive, rapid, and uncontrollable speech, often incoherent. It is commonly observed in the manic phase of bipolar disorder. Logorrhea is also known as tachylogia, verbomania, logomania, hyperlogia, and hyperphrasia.

See Bipolar Disorder.

Logotherapy. A theoretical approach to psychotherapy developed by Victor Frankl (1962, 1969, 1978, 1967/1985). The term is derived from two Greek words, *logos* (word or meaning) and *therapeia* (healing). Logotherapy is providing or experiencing healing through meaning. Logotherapy can be subsumed under existential psychiatry and psychology. Frankl at one time referred to his approach as *Existenzanalysis* but has subsequently preferred logotherapy in order to distinguish his work from that of Boss and Ludwig Binswanger, who have also created existential analytic approaches. Logotherapy views the individual as being free, responsible, unique, and holistic. In the therapy process the client is challenged to become decisive in using his or her freedom in order to discover meaning in life.

Frankl views the individual as a self-determining and self-actualizing person. Thus a human being possesses the innate capacity to transcend environmental factors, be they biological, psychological, or sociological. The transcendent ability is possible because of spiritual freedom that characterizes human beings and distinguishes them uniquely from animals. This spiritual freedom is not so much freedom from oppressive forces as it is the potential for discovering, deciding, and actualizing one's existence. Such freedom cannot be taken from the individual, and this dimension makes life meaningful and purposeful.

Human personality is a unity composed of three intermeshing realities: the somatic (physical), the mental (psychological), and the spiritual (noölogical). The combined interaction of the physical and psychological components forms what might be called the psychophysicum. Each dimension of the personality is indispensable, but the spiritual dimension gives meaning. The primary motivation in human behavior is the will to meaning. This is in contrast to Sigmund Freud's idea of the pleasure principle and Alfred Adler's concept of will to power or superiority. This will to meaning involves a set of ideals and values that pulls rather than pushes an individual in life. It is a fulfillment of spiritual needs in the process of choosing and deciding.

Like Adler, Frankl thinks it is necessary for an individual to first solve some basic life tasks before finding meaning and purpose in life and thus being fully actualized. These tasks include discovering the meaning of love, the meaning of work and mission, and the meaning of death and suffering. Only then can the meaning of life itself be found.

Problems in living can be discussed under three classifications: neuroses, noögenic neuroses, and psychoses. The neuroses are psychogenic and are experienced either as a type of anticipatory anxiety or an obsessional disturbance. The noögenic neuroses have a spiritually based etiology and are manifested as existential boredom and frustration, a vacuum existence, and a loss of meaning and purpose in life. The psychoses are organic or physically based. A diagnosis always seeks to differentiate these three basic types of problems. Most problems, however, tend to be mixed in nature, and seldom does one problem have a single causation and unitary symptomatology. Accurate differential diagnosis work indicates the appropriate form of therapy. A neurosis is treated with psychotherapy, a psychosis with physical medicine, and a noögenic neurosis with logotherapy.

The relationship between the logotherapist and the client is characterized by warmth and closeness with a consistent concern for scientific objectivity. An ultimate goal of logotherapy is to help individuals accept responsibility for themselves through using spiritual freedom to make personal choices and decisions in the discovery of meaning in and to life.

A variety of methods and strategies is used in the practice of logotherapy. Logotherapy in the purest sense consists of Socraticlike dialogue. Another mode of intervention is logodrama, in which clients are guided in narrating and experiencing the events and meaning of their life. A third strategy is paradoxical intention. This involves asking clients to intend that which they fear. The technique is designed to help individuals overcome anticipatory anxiety or hyperintention. The final major strategy is dereflection. This counteracts obsessive ideation or hyperreflection by helping clients stop thinking about the problem. Both paradoxical intention and dereflection are based on the individual's capacity to detach himself or herself from absorption with personal problems. Both methods have a cognitive behavior emphasis but were developed before cognitive behavior approaches existed.

Logotherapy is the most systematic of all the existential approaches to counseling and psychotherapy. It offers a clear perspective on the nature of the human being, a useful theory of personality, a multidimensional answer to the nature and cause of problems in living, a well-articulated set of procedures and processes to follow in therapy, and a body of clearly defined techniques. Much of Frankl's thinking is compatible with historical Judeo-Christian theology (Tweedie, 1961).

References

Frankl, V. E. (1962). *Man's search for meaning.* Boston: Beacon.

Frankl, V. E. (1969). *The will to meaning.* New York: World.

Frankl, V. E. (1978). *The unheard cry for meaning.* New York: Simon & Schuster.

Frankl, V. E. (1985). *Psychotherapy and existentialism.* New York: Washington Square Press. (Original work published 1967)

Tweedie, D. F. (1961). *Logotherapy: An evaluation of Frankl's existential approach to psychotherapy.* Grand Rapids, MI: Baker.

D. SMITH

See EXISTENTIAL PSYCHOLOGY AND PSYCHOTHE-RAPY; FRANKL, VICTOR EMIL.

Loneliness. Loneliness is a generally episodic yet common universal human experience with diverse features and causes, whose biblical origins can be traced to the fall of humanity (Gen. 3). As a result, loneliness has both emotional and spiritual features in people. It is distinguished from solitude, a healthy form of aloneness, both of which are frequently overlooked by the counselor involved in attempting to help people.

Psychological Considerations. Loneliness, as a clinical syndrome, is marked by painful feelings of sadness and longing and almost always by the absence of, yet felt desire for, relationship with others. Moreover, symptoms can include experiences of isolation and abandonment marked by anger, irritability, crying, agitation, negative ruminative thoughts, and potentially unhealthy behaviors set forth to compensate for these feelings and symptoms. Loneliness can serve as a primary source of clinical depression, and in more severe cases it can be a precursor to suicidal feelings.

Loneliness can be self-inflicted and/or the result of others' actions. Some people can appear to regularly make themselves lonely (often due to poor interpersonal relational skills), while others experience loneliness for reasons having little to do with their efforts (e.g., bereavement). It is important to note that despite these differing origins, loneliness is not bound by time. Some people can experience loneliness as a transitory phenomenon (i.e., situational loneliness), while others can be arrested in its grasp for years (i.e., existential or character loneliness). Regardless of its source, loneliness involves both a quantitative and qualitative appraisal of relationships with others. One can appear to be highly involved in relationships yet simultaneously experience great loneliness. For example, it is commonly heard in counseling sessions with married couples how they experience great periods of loneliness and alienation in the midst of marital discord. Davies (1996) supports the view that it is not merely the quantity but the quality of relationships that influences a person's sense of loneliness.

As previously mentioned, loneliness can have either a situational source or a more existential cause. That is, people can experience the painful feelings of loneliness due to a specific and more or less clearly articulated loss, or they may be unable to address the source of their loneliness. The latter can be seen as existential loneliness, a kind of loneliness that is without direct cause. May (1991) refers to this type of loneliness as a kind of rootlessness, a lack of personal history, attributable in the United States to our constant transitions. This kind of loneliness is unique in that it tends to course deeper in human experience and is perhaps more common to the human condition.

Solitude. Solitude is different from loneliness in that the latter is marked by the all-important component of anxious desire for relationship. There is such a thing as healthy loneliness in that people occasionally need a respite from active relationships in order to gain perspective in life. Storr (1988) supports this concept by suggesting that solitude can represent a retreat from daily habits that can lead to greater self-understanding and contact with one's deeper being. However, even solitude, which presumes the absence of human contact, has some aspect of relationship embedded within the experience. This can take the form of a retreat in which individuals might attempt to clarify and enhance their relationship with God or to attempt to gain greater self-understanding. Davies (1996) notes that throughout history clergy would retreat into monasteries to spend focused time upon God. History is filled with the accounts of Christian mystics (e.g., Francis of Assisi, Teresa of Avila) and other historically famous individuals (e.g., Admiral Byrd, William Keats) who reported regular benefits from solitude. Solitude may be represented by the physical absence of a human relationship, but oftentimes a mental or a spiritual relationship is highly present. Western culture tends to discourage the practice of solitude due to such intrusive elements as the cellular telephone, which we can now take with us into even the remotest parts of the world and still be in touch. Noise tend to be ever-present in our Western culture, the skies filled with the sounds of jets passing by or automobiles on the highways. Storr (1988) offers that this kind of intrusiveness is so present that people can feel uncomfortable with the absence of it. Nevertheless many benefits can be derived from engaging in solitary reflection that can nourish one and serve as a wellspring for such things as greater spirituality and creativity.

Biblical Considerations. Both loneliness and solitude are regularly found throughout Scripture. In the Book of Genesis, one can observe the preliminary presence of loneliness, evidenced in Genesis 2:18, when God observes that man is better off with earthly relationships. In stark contrast, however, loneliness soon takes on a particularly painful quality when, in Genesis 3, Adam and Eve succumb to temptation and as a result experience profound loneliness in the form of alienation from God, from each other, and from the self. It is suggested that when they realize their nakedness (Gen. 3:7), they are becoming aware of their extreme alienation from God, each other, and themselves. The immediate outcome of this is the onset of blaming, Fear, and self-deception in humanity (see Gen. 3:10–12), all of which are common characteristics of loneliness.

A further example of loneliness can be painfully yet gratefully seen in the crucifixion of Christ on Calvary. Clearly he experiences the greatest loneliness of all—the brief but all-critical abandonment of the Father set forth in Matthew 27:46 (NIV): "My God, my God, why have you forsaken me?" For our sake, he suffered the epitome of loneliness, the taking on of sin for our eternal benefit.

There are also many examples of the practice of solitude within God's Word. In Matthew 4, we see the temptation of Jesus occurring during a period of solitude that was "led by the Spirit" (Matt. 4:1, NIV). He is tempted by Satan in the desert and in the mountains, both desolate, solitary locales. On numerous occasions Jesus himself retreated into solitude, presumably for prayer and reflection. Upon hearing of the tragic death of John the Baptist, Jesus "withdrew by boat privately to a solitary place" (Matt. 14:13, NIV). Further evidence of the practice of solitude is found in Jesus' activities in Gethsemane, where he retreats with his disciples and then further retreats into brief solitude for prayer, asking the Father to release him from his burdens (Matt. 26:36–39).

The Bible is replete with examples of both loneliness and solitude and furthermore offers some positive examples of the benefits and purpose of the practice of solitude for Christians.

Counseling Considerations. While loneliness is a component present in most people seeking counseling, it can require of the counselor some special considerations. First of all, the counselor must be sensitive to the source of a person's complaint of loneliness and whether there may be possible benefit to the loneliness. That is, many people seeking counseling are too quick to escape from their difficulties and fail to reap the growth possibilities from them. This is commonly seen in grief counseling. Furthermore, people seeking counseling for loneliness may benefit from being introduced to the practice of solitude as a means of gaining insight and perspective into their relationships with God and his people. Additionally, those experiencing loneliness may lack adequate social skills, frequently running afoul of others in their attempts to be relational. These people would benefit from social skills counseling. As a final note, much can be done by professionals to prevent the damaging effects of loneliness by educating people as to the causes and symptoms. Moreover, Collins (1988) suggests that churches can address this same issue by offering rich and welcoming communities for people to join and develop lasting relationships in Christ.

References

Collins, G. R. (1988). *Christian counseling.* Dallas: Word.
Davies, M. G. (1996). Solitude and loneliness: An integrative model. *Journal of Psychology and Theology, 24,* (1), 3–12.
May, R. (1991). *The cry for myth.* New York: Norton.
Storr, A. (1988). *Solitude.* New York: Free Press.

S. A. Cappa

See Friendship; Love.

Loosening of Associations. A thought disorder characterized by speech that abruptly shifts from topic to topic in a completely unrelated manner. No affective awareness of the unconnected statements is evidenced by the speaker. Phrases may shift totally from one frame of reference to another or be juxtaposed so that no comprehensive meaning can be formulated. For example, in reply to the question, "When did your father die?" the person may start talking about skiing, shift to a movie he or she has seen, and comment on recent trends in the weather. When the disorder is severe, speech may be incoherent, particularly in manic episodes, schizophrenia, and other psychotic disorders.

D. L. Schuurman

See Psychotic Disorders.

Loss and Separation. Inextricably entwined with change, separation and loss are universal phenomena. The many kinds of separation can be classified into two general types: developmental and situational. Developmental separations are an inherent part of the maturational stages a human being experiences from birth to death.

Separation in the ever-changing stages of the life span inevitably involves a constant series of attachments and detachments; closeness and distance; togetherness and separateness; losses and gains. The struggle to maintain an equilibrium between these polarities is particularly accented at certain transitional points of life, such as the passage periods from one psychosocial stage to another (Erikson, 1968). A newborn, for example, experiences the loss of the security of intrauterine life but gains the possibility of a more exciting, autonomous life. The mother at the same time loses a physical part of herself to gain the fulfillment of raising a child. The adolescent gives up the primary security of depending upon parents in order to consolidate his or her identity. Parents simultaneously lose the satisfactions of the more intense dependency of their children to eventually gain the pleasures of grandchildren, of new interests, of deeper peer companionship. The maturational separations with their concomitant losses and gains are a predictable part of human development and growth wherein old sources of gratifications are replaced with new modes of need fulfillment and self-perception.

Separations and losses that result from the less predictable and therefore often more traumatic situational circumstances are seemingly infinite in number. An accident, a rape, the birth of a deformed child, a young person's cardiofracture, a job change, a natural disaster, a geographic move are all examples. They could involve such deeply felt separations and losses as valuable possessions, relationships, aspirations, sense of integrity, body parts, functioning levels, and coping skills. Even separation from a hope, an interest, or a physical symptom can be a traumatic loss.

Universal Reactions. A plethora of research reveals that separation with its inevitable losses can be a stressor event eliciting the emergence of a syndrome of reactions that follow a defined pattern. As early as 1872 Darwin perceived that the reactions to separation from a loved one are innate when he observed similar body movements in grieving individuals regardless of their cultural background.

In *Mourning and Melancholia* (1917/1950) Sigmund Freud describes reactions to separation caused by death of a loved one as being dejection, disinterest in the environment, and a detached air toward others. He explains mourning as a period of the gradual withdrawal of libido from the now missing loved object. According to Freud, adjustment to the loss must be a process over time to prevent an out-of-control libido with no structuring of direction. He sees the process as self-limiting; the effects of the loss end when the libido completes its withdrawal from the loved object. Investment of the libido in an alternative object or an internal representation of the lost object ideally happens concurrently.

Bowlby (1969) saw what he believed to be a universal specific syndrome of reactions to separation and loss in his studies on the separation of children from their parents. He further observed other kinds of separations and concluded that a similar process goes on in any loss. He identifies (1973) the three stages—protest, despair, and detachment—as essentially the same for all separation.

Since separation and loss are generators of stress, field studies of stress, particularly those done in settings of disaster (e.g., war, earthquakes, fires), reveal common reactions to the changes that these circumstances generate. Lindemann (1944), a psychoanalyst and social psychologist, did a classic field study in which he concluded that reactions to loss fall into a syndrome that contains both psychological and somatic symptomatology; the syndrome may start immediately upon a loss, may have a delayed reaction, may be exaggerated, or may be absent; the syndrome may follow the typical course or distorted courses that represent a particular aspect of the grief syndrome; with appropriate interventions the distorted pictures can be directed into normal grief reactions with ultimate resolution.

Lindemann's study gave impetus to other researchers to investigate the effects of loss in situational crises that did not involve death. For example, Grayson (1970) found some of the same reactions to the loss of unfulfilled hopes. He points out that abreaction and catharsis help the individual more realistically to admit the agonized feelings and relinquish the hope. Burgess and Holmstrom (1974) found that rape victims who had lost a sense of trust also underwent a similar process, as do adults who lost limbs (Parkes, 1972).

Kübler-Ross (1969) popularized the grief syndrome that occurs when one faces death in her delineation of the stages of denial, anger, bargaining, depression, and acceptance. Other important studies on bereavement are summarized by Parkes (1972). All the studies reveal a pattern of reaction that can be called the separation or loss syndrome.

Separation Syndrome. In its healthiest form the separation syndrome is a self-limiting process of fairly well-defined stages through which an individual passes over a broadly defined time span. The first reaction in the syndrome is a sense of injury and a groping to hold on to the lost object. Particularly if the separation is unanticipated, there can be such unfocused grief responses as a cry of alarm, panic, protestation, or hyperactivity.

Within a relatively short time the task of the first stage, cognitive reorganization, begins. It is characterized initially by disbelief, denial, or numbness, during which a full awareness of the loss is not permitted. This avoidance of reality serves the purpose of enabling the individual to mitigate the pain of the loss by maintaining a degree of distance from it. The individual can then deal slowly with its cognitive aspects as he or she starts to work through it. A pervading lack of interest in establishing an attachment to a new object is evident. There is an attempt to regain what has been lost. This is particularly obvious when the individual, cognitively starting to grasp the reality of the loss, tends to oscillate between conscious and unconscious avoidance of facing it while alternately being flooded by emotionally laden intrusive-repetitive thought representations of the loss. The representations take many forms, including sleep disturbances, hallucinations, ruminations, preoccupations, and disorganizations, which may be accompanied by pangs of fear, guilt, rage, sorrow, and hypervigilance.

Once the individual acquires some cognitive realization of the loss, the affective response to the separation becomes more pronounced. This second stage is often indicated by a general aura of depression or a sense of despair. Since all relationships include some degree of ambivalence, the gradual resolution of the separation process also provokes feelings of anger and guilt that surface particularly during this stage. The emotions permit a gradual reexperiencing of the loss, in increasingly tolerable degrees. When the affect has been sufficiently diffused, the individual enters the next stage, that of identification with the lost object. This involves internalizing the characteristics of the lost object that are most important to the griever. It means that for the healthy individual "grief works itself out through a process of reformulation rather than substitution. Confidence in the original commitment is restored by extracting its essential meaning and grafting it upon the present" (Marris, 1974, p. 91).

This opens the door to the final phase, the acceptance of the loss. It frees the individual to benefit from the new gains in identity, cognitions, and affects by reaching out to form new relationships.

Movement through the stages is not a clearly defined process. There can be as many variations within the general pattern as there are differences among individuals. The stages may vary in their sequential order, length, and intensity. They may overlap, repeat themselves, or be skipped. Episodic changes may occur within a stage. Often such events as birthdays, anniversaries, and holidays stimulate a repeat of some aspect of the cycle.

Resolution of the separation process is occurring when intervals between stages are longer, reactions within stages are less intense and of shorter duration, and there is an apparent response to new objects. The healthy individual experiences the pain inherent in the separation process and ultimately comes to grips with the loss and restitution with no undue interruption in his or her daily life. The ability to integrate the loss is considered a mark of maturity.

For some individuals, a more pathological reaction results from a significant separation. Indications can be an expansive sense of overactivity that denies any significant loss or need for reintegration; maintenance of most aspects of the behavior before the separation without any considerable modification; a psychosomatic reaction; a prolonged change in patterns of interaction that may manifest itself in inappropriate hostility, withdrawal, or impatience; a display of self-punitive behavior, possibly in the form of depression, insomnia, self-accusations, suicidal threats or attempts; a morbid preoccupation with the lost object that may take the form of clinging to symbolic objects; a marked appearance of the traits of the object in the behavior of the griever; attributing magical powers to the lost object.

The continual flow of circumstances involving some nuance of separation, loss, and therefore withdrawal and eventual reinvestment of energy is ubiquitous. Each individual should therefore routinely confront the task of restoring an equilibrium between former and present meanings lest he or she be stagnated in growth. There are identified variables that determine whether a separation with its concomitant losses will be a growth-producing or a growth-constricting experience.

Determiners of Separation Reactions. The determiners of an individual's reactions to separation and loss can be grouped under three main headings: the nature of the person experiencing the separation; the nature or quality and quantity of the loss involved in the separation; the nature of the milieu in which the separation occurs.

Nature of the Individual. The quality of an individual's experiences during the separation-individuation developmental phase is the most basic variable in determining responses to life's recurring separations (Mahler, Pine, & Bergman, 1975). This separation process refers to the steps in a child's movement from infant fusion with the mother. Individuation refers to the developmental stages children go through to perceive themselves as a separate entity from the mother. This requires the development of object constancy, whereby the child realizes that the object still exists even when it is out of sight. Although it is an ongoing process with reverberations throughout the life cycle, the basic determining foundation for future separation is laid from about the age of 4 months to 36 months. If children succeed in this initial differentiation of their internal self-representation from that of the mother figure, they will be able to perceive their ever-expanding world as independent from themselves and develop a growing sense of self-identity. In subsequent separations they would then have the inner structure to identify with the important elements of the meaningful object while emotionally relinquishing what is necessary, albeit with appropriate grief, in order to make new attachments. To the degree that an individual remains unhealthily attached to the mother, he or she is vulnerable to neurotic and even psychotic reactions to separation and loss.

Each developmental transitional period—puberty, marriage, and parenthood—offers individuals the potential to strengthen, enrich, and even modify their individuation experiences as they terminate their present life structure to initiate a new one. At the same time how they have experienced individuation in past transitions conditions their reactions to the new phase.

The second determining factor of separation reactions is the quality of an individual's attachment to a significant object. Bowlby (1969) sees the need to attach to someone as a normal innate propensity of every human being. When this bond with a significant other is threatened or ruptured, separation anxiety in the form of attachment behavior results. In the small child it takes the form of crying, clinging, following, and calling. Although in normal individuals the manifestations become more sophisticated with age and are directed to new attachment figures appropriate to the developmental period, some form of separation anxiety is apparent throughout the life span. It is especially activated when separation with its accompanying threat of loss has or is about to occur. Since there is a continuous stream of experiences in life that involve loss of some kind, all individuals are forever susceptible to separation anxiety. During separation, gratification of this attachment need seems to sustain self-esteem and reduce hostility, making possible the expression and tolerance of painful tension and minimizing abnormal forms of avoiding reality (Hansburg, 1972).

Individuals who are anxiously attached manifest neurotic symptoms in the face of separation. Anxious attachment is the result of an insufficient relationship with a mothering figure because of death, illness, threats of or actual abandonment, parental discord, insufficient attention, and the like (Bowlby, 1969). These experiences can cause a child, an adolescent, or an adult to live in constant anxiety lest he or she lose the attachment figure.

701

Separation reactions tend to be atypically manifested. There is often intense anger, self-reproach, or depression that tends to last longer than normal. Other people manifest anxious attachment through compulsive self-reliance. Even so, some strain and irritability tend to be present and episodic depressions may occur. However, the causal connection is generally not recognized and the resolution could be postponed for months or years (Bowlby, 1977).

The quality of an individual's cognitive development is a third vital internal variable in the separation process. The two cognitive aspects that play the most crucial role in resolving separation experiences are the development of abstract cognitions and thinking modes that permit adaptation to change (Piaget & Inhelder, 1969). The former makes possible object constancy. It means the individual can identify with the object even in its absence. The latter provides the cognitive sophistication whereby the individual can internalize the significant qualities of the object by extracting its essential meanings and integrating them with the new situation into which the separation has thrust him or her. Since this process demands the use of abstract thinking, an ability that does not develop to its fullest until adulthood, it is imperative that a child have a real object substitute.

A fourth determiner of separation reactions is the quality of parental attitudes, particularly in the child's early years. Individuals whose parents give out messages that are perceived as confidence in their ability to grow and eventually become autonomous will confront life's separations more successfully. Those individuals whose parents convey a lack of confidence in them often find separations more traumatic. The quality of the expectations an individual picks up from his or her parents depends on the parent's ability to provide the environment that develops basic trust; promote an appropriate comfortable expression of feelings, including such ambivalent ones as guilt and anger; communicate a deep security in their love that fosters an age-appropriate independence; maintain an open congruent communication pattern that leads to closer and more secure interpersonal relations.

How healthily parents transmit positive messages about separation is conditioned by how they separated from their own parents. Those who had traumatic or poor experiences in breaking from parents tend to pass the conflict of their unfinished issues on to their own children. They therefore interfere with their child's separation through an often unidentified parental expectation conveyed to the child, which militates against his or her potential for autonomy.

The quality of an individual's previous life experiences is a fifth influencing factor. The individual who experienced comfortable separations in the past tends to be better prepared for successive ones. The child who has had good school experiences, enjoys spending time with friends, has fun at camp, makes a good transition to the first grade and then to high school, will probably be less anxious in life's new transitions. Children who have experienced traumatic separations with deeply felt losses in their early years tend to be more prone to separation anxiety. This is particularly true when the separation occurred during the initial individuation separation developmental period.

Individuals who have undergone multiple separations from persons, places, things, or ideas might tend to protect themselves from the pain of separations by avoiding new in-depth attachments to other objects. Again, a significant factor is the presence of a consistent nurturing attachment figure in the midst of such changes.

A sixth element in the nature of the individual is the quality of life philosophy. Individuals' beliefs about life have a far-reaching impact on how they perceive a separation from a meaningful object. It affects how they view themselves, others, and life events. A deep inner sense of God's sovereignty at work in not only the overall pattern but also the details of life gives a meaning even to loss through death.

Nature of the Loss. Inherent in the loss itself are factors that affect reactions. The timeliness of loss, particularly when it comes through a maturational separation such as marriage, empty nest, or even a death, often gives it a more appropriate feeling, thereby making it easier to resolve. Although separation through death may never seem timely, the death of an older person is often easier to accept than that of a child. A child's death diminishes the survivor's confidence in the future.

Maturational separations can be anticipated, and therefore a gradual adaptation to the losses involved is possible. Unanticipated losses are often followed by longer and more intense stages of denial than are anticipated ones. It is possible that this longer stage of denial allows the individual to go through some of the emotional preparation that takes place when an anticipatory period exists (Hamburg & Adams, 1967). Janis (1958) substantiated this in his studies on patients' previous preparation for surgery. He found that the patients who experienced reasonable stress before surgery had the least amount of distress after surgery. Those persons who showed the most distress after surgery denied anticipatory fear or were extremely preoccupied previous to the surgery. He concluded that moderate fear motivates an anticipatory stage of cognitive processing. This affective and cognitive processing has adaptational effects.

The death of a loved one from a chronic disease also permits the family to do some of the work of mourning before the actual death. In other potential life events such as retirement, a geographic move, or a career change, individuals are able to plan ahead and share their expectations, possibly in seminars. This has been found to greatly ease the intensity of the moment when the event arrives.

The expected duration of the loss also affects adjustment. A temporary separation, even when it is painful, is easier to support than a permanent one. In a prolonged separation individuals discover that they need more time to readapt to people, places, and such, but the processing is not as complicated as in a brief separation. If elements of the loss are continually revived, such as in the case of a handicapped child, the process is complicated by the fact that there is a forced openendedness, since new problems constantly arise as the child develops.

Some losses have the potential to trigger a chain reaction of additional losses. For example, a stroke victim not only loses health but also has to face alteration in such areas as job satisfaction, economic security, status, mobility, freedom, and body image. The effect of the changes is exacerbated when the separation has both developmental and situational components. If a father's stroke occurs at the midlife transitional point with its usual changes such as children leaving home, the adjustment period could become longer, more complicated, and more intense. Separation from each former state must be worked through until the many-faceted implications can be handled in tolerable measure.

The extent of the significance of a loss also plays a role. Significant losses imply deep emotional investment. Significance might be centered in more abstract areas such as the investment of time. The parents whose children leave home and the person who loses a job must work through the loss of a habitual time schedule and discover how to use the new time at their disposal. The loss of irreplaceable items such as family photographs or a family heirloom could be more deeply felt than a large monetary loss. Cultural attitudes contribute to the significance of a loss. In a culture that emphasizes youth, sexuality, and attractiveness, the loss of a breast could be traumatic and the severity of the reaction can be increased. Such an experience demands not only present adaptation but also future changes.

The extent of the changes involved plays a large role in completing a separation syndrome. If considerable differences exist in the new situation, the stages could be prolonged and felt more deeply. A geographic move from the city to a mountain village calls for more adjustment than a change from one city to another. A move to a country where customs, language, and places are entirely different would probably require a longer adjustment period than a move from the United States to Canada.

The Milieu in Which the Loss Occurs. Reactions to losses are also conditioned by environmental and social factors.

Expectations of society play a large role. For example, adolescents, who are expected to start detaching from parents and turning to peers to complete the developmental tasks of this period, have society's approval of their many changes. A divorced person in a community that frowns on this type of separation may experience additional struggles going through the syndrome.

A second environmental factor is the rate at which change takes place. A case in point is the increasing lack of a sense of continuity in the values from one generation to another. This too is evidenced among adolescents, who consequently could find their struggle with individuation a more pronounced experience.

The more clearly defined the separation process, the easier the transition. The growing-up process is often more difficult for a young person in a culture in which initiation points are not clear-cut. For example, in Western culture college students often see themselves as fairly independent, while the parents who support them might perceive them as quite dependent.

The support system within the environment can maximize or minimize the effects of change. Persons involved in closer, more supportive groups conceivably have less difficulty. The very stress of separation elicits the attachment behavior described earlier. In adulthood it is likely to be present when one is depressed, ill, or afraid, and leads to seeking the contact and comfort of an attachment figure. This behavior is adaptive and contributes to the successful resolution of a separation syndrome. The attachment source can be in the form of a church group, a school, a work group, or another organization that gives the security needed at this time. The role of the body of Christ has tremendous implications in a society where change is rampant and natural support structures often are not present.

Treatment Implications. The majority of separation and loss reactions follow the normal course through the syndrome, with the stages varying in intensity according to the significance of the loss. In some instances there is hardly an awareness of any adjustment. In other cases, however, individuals seek help because of a lack of understanding of their reactions or because of the inordinate amount of pain they are suffering.

The goal of treatment is to help the person work through the stages to a completion of the process. Therapy is usually supportive, with the specific techniques varying to fit the therapist's orientation. The criterion for choosing a therapy should be its efficacy to promote a fairly progressive movement through the stages. The therapy is generally short-term, from one encounter to a series of sessions up to about 6 months.

An educative approach can be helpful to those relatively healthy individuals who are confused over reactions that are normal for their situation. It can likewise benefit those who face a disproportionate share of separations, such as missionaries. Whether therapy is individual or group, the goals in such an approach would be to help these persons understand the normalcy of the separation process, identify and understand their own reactions as well as those of the persons from whom they are separating, and learn how to diffuse the effects of leave taking for themselves and significant others. A comprehension of the total process can be particularly helpful to missionaries parting from their native country, to new missionaries going through the throes of culture shock, to children and their parents as children go off to school, and missionaries who are going through departure in reverse.

The factors that determine the reactions to separation play a decisive role in the time required to resolve the issues successfully. The intradynamic factors have a particularly high potential to stir up latent conflict stemming from previously unintegrated separation experiences. Where a short-term approach is used, these neurotic conflicts are linked to their role in the current separation struggle. However, if deeply rooted core conflicts, particularly those with their genesis in the early separation individuation developmental stage, seem to be preventing a healthy resolution, a long-term therapeutic approach that deals more concentratedly with the area of conflict may be indicated.

Mann (1973) has developed a time-limited dynamic approach that can provide a corrective emotional experience for individuals who are conflicted about the recurring life crises of separation and individuation and therefore suffer a painful amount of separation anxiety in the face of loss. These individuals tend to hold on emotionally to relationships beyond the appropriate developmental time and are therefore hindered in facing the mature demands of adulthood. The goal of therapy is to enable patients to master their anxiety about separation. The method is an empathic acceptance of the patients' feelings with a focused emphasis on the termination date. The patients' ambivalence about fusion and separation is thereby stirred up. Their comments often oscillate between the magical fantasies of permanence and the harsh realities of separation. With the therapist's consistent empathy patients continue to experience feelings of closeness in spite of the inevitable impending separation. This allows patients to internalize the therapist "as a replacement or a substitute for the earlier ambivalent object. This time the internalization will be more positive, . . . less anger laden, and less guilt laden, thereby making separation a genuine maturational event" (Mann, 1973, p. 36).

Although this approach is effective in cases of unresolved or delayed grief, Mann also sees it as tailor-made for adolescents who are painfully conflicted about separating from their parents.

Whatever the therapeutic approach, the termination phase can play a significant role in the healing of separation anxiety. Termination of therapy provokes many ambivalent feelings connected with previous separation issues in both the patient and the therapist. The resulting reaction can be the impetus to promote a corrective emotional experience with its implication for growth for both the patient and the therapist to the degree that the feelings are dealt with rather than ignored (Edelson, 1963).

Successful resolution of separation and loss, with or without professional help, is indispensable to growth. The most potent benefit is its assault on self-centeredness. The person is forced to relinquish degrees of his or her infantile delusions of immortality and omnipotence, which can lead to the realization that he or she functions within a greater whole. This is a motivating factor to lead one to come to grips with the larger meaning of life. The depths of emotions are experienced as they might be in no other way. A deeper level of empathy is often developed. A new confidence in facing life's upheavals may result as old coping mechanisms are strengthened and new ones are developed. As a result overall functioning may well be at a higher, richer level. Therefore, while inevitable separation and loss upset the present, the experience of integrating the old into the new permits individuals to go on to fuller lives.

References

Bowlby, J. (1969). *Attachment and loss* (Vol. 1). New York: Basic.

Bowlby, J. (1973). *Attachment and loss* (Vol. 2). New York: Basic.

Bowlby, J. (1977). The making and breaking of affectional bonds: 1. Aetiology and psychopathology in the light of attachment theory. *British Journal of Psychiatry, 130,* 201–210.

Burgess, A. W., & Holmstrom, L. L. (1974). Rape trauma syndrome. *American Journal of Psychiatry, 131,* 981–986.

Edelson, M. (1963). Termination of intensive psychotherapy. In C. C. Thomas (Ed.), *American lectures in psychiatry.* Washington, DC: American Psychiatric Association.

Erikson, E. H. (1968). *Identity, youth, and crisis.* New York: Norton.

Freud, S. (1950). Mourning and melancholia. In J. Riviere (Ed.), *Collected papers* (Vol. 4). London: Hogarth. (Original work published 1917)

Grayson, H. (1970). Grief reactions to the relinquishing of unfulfilled wishes. *American Journal of Psychotherapy, 25,* 287–295.

Hamburg, D. A., & Adams, J. E. (1967). A perspective on coping behavior: Seeking and utilizing information in major transitions. *Archives of General Psychiatry, 17,* 277–284.

Hansburg, H. (1972). *Adolescent separation anxiety.* Springfield, IL: Thomas.

Janis, I. (1958). *Psychological stress: Psychoanalytic and behavioral studies of surgical patients.* New York: Wiley.

Kübler-Ross, E. (1969). *On death and dying.* New York: Macmillan.

Lindemann, E. (1944). Symptomatology and management of acute grief. *American Journal of Psychiatry, 101,* 141–148.

Mahler, M. S., Pine, F., & Bergman, A. (1975). *The psychological birth of the human infant.* New York: Basic.

Mann, J. (1973). *Time-limited psychotherapy.* Cambridge, MA: Harvard University Press.

Marris, P. (1974). *Loss and change.* New York: Pantheon.

Parkes, C. M. (1972). *Bereavement: Studies of grief in adult life.* New York: International Universities Press.

Piaget, J., & Inhelder, B. (1969). *The psychology of the child.* New York: Basic.

Additional Readings

Bowlby, J. (1980). *Attachment and loss* (Vol. 3). New York: Basics.

Schoenberg, B., Gerber, I., Wiener, A., Kutscher, A., Peretz, D., & Carr, A. (1975). *Bereavement: Its psychosocial aspects*. New York: Columbia University Press.

F. J. WHITE

See ATTACHMENT THEORY AND DISORDERS; GRIEF; DIVORCE; DEATH AND DYING.

Loss of Function. The human life is a series of attachments and losses. Some individuals and families adapt to separation and loss better than others. Certain losses are inherently very devastating. People usually struggle to manage the impact of loss, to adjust, and to resume thereafter their normal living. Major as well as minor losses can be very significant and may substantially disturb the person's psychological functioning.

There are different types of losses. Loss can be personal or material, tangible or symbolic, sudden or gradual. We may lose a close person, an important object, or a vital function. Loss occurs in various degrees, shapes, and forms and at different times in life. This is also true for losing a particular function. It can be a mental faculty, a part of health, a major role, a financial asset, or a specific dream essential for survival and striving in life.

Losing a main role can be very personal. It can happen due to life's unpredictable events, various transitions, or just the passage of time, like losing the role of a mother, a father, a mentor, a grandparent, a sponsor, a significant other, or an intimate friend. The empty nest, graduation, marriage, illness, moving away, or even widowhood are vivid examples of inevitable changes which may cause deep sorrow, maladjustment, and pain.

The loss of a function could also mean losing one's career or job, professional identity, cherished position, and social status. This type of loss is usually caused by either natural development, like retirement, or by unexpected economic forces like unemployment and layoffs. Similarly, the loss of a physical ability, an essential mental faculty, or a part of health function could happen because of the process of aging, traumatic accidents, hazardous diseases, or natural disasters. It can be the loss of memory, vital skill, concentration, performance, speech, writing, driving, walking, etc. . . .

Normally, there are several factors that determine the intensity of a person's reactions to a particular loss, called "grief reactions." Among them, 1) the importance of the function or role in one's life, 2) the degree of attachment to or dependence on that function, 3) the emotional stability of the person who suffered the loss, 4) the experience in handling previous losses, and 5) the availability of support during and after the loss.

When suffering a loss, either major or minor, it is essential for the bereaved person to adequately grieve, work through the mourning process, and begin to adjust to regular activities and normal living without the lost function. If the person alone is not able to reach some resolution or achieve a degree of closure after a year or two, it is highly recommended that he or she seek professional help specifically for grief counseling.

The bereaved individual usually faces mental battles on two fronts. The first is internal—struggling with shock, confusion, disbelief, fear, guilt, shame, anger, loneliness, sadness, hurt, anxiety, intense feelings of loss, and depression. In addition, he or she may very well experience a mixture of feelings toward what has been lost. Ambivalence is a very common emotion or attitude in times like these, and perhaps it is the most experienced feeling throughout our human lifespan.

The second front is external. Most probably, the bereaved individual or family may receive more *sympathy* (feeling sorry for the hurt) rather than genuine *empathy* (feeling deeply with the hurt) from others. The one who has suffered the loss of a precious function may be questioned, challenged, blamed, or even ridiculed by others. This may be especially true when the loss has crippled the person physically, mentally, emotionally, financially, or in any other obvious or visible way.

Frequently, bereaved people become angry with God for allowing such loss to happen. When counseling with them, it is very important for the therapist to let the existential crisis and emotional agony take their course rather than jumping quickly to correct the clients' theological misconceptions. Eventually, bereaved individuals will discover on their own that God was grieving and suffering with them rather than the one who caused their loss and pain. And they will be able to identify with the beatitude of Christ, "Blessed are those who mourn for they will be comforted" (Matt. 5:4).

Additional Reading

Wright, H. N. (1991). *Recovering from the losses of life*. Grand Rapids, MI: Revell.

N. ABI-HASHEM

Love. The word *love* is used broadly and has such variety of meanings that the concept, although familiar, is difficult to define. It helps to define love by specifying the context in which it is used. When a person says to an intimate friend, "I love you," there is quite a difference from the meaning of the word in the sentence "I love your outfit."

Love has specific, contextual meanings. However, in the widest usage it generally refers to a strong attraction toward an object—a desire to reduce the distance between that object and oneself. For example, if one loves either a person or a thing, one exhibits more of a yearning for that person or object, a desire to clasp it excitedly or fondly, than if the object were merely attractive or of some interest. To love always implies personal investment in the object of love; where there is no evidence of such personal caring, one may question whether love exists for the object.

Kinds of Love. The ancients specified four kinds of love, a classification that is still widely used. The most general form is *philia*, love for one's fellow humans, including care, respect, and some compassion for the plight of others. The most common form is friendship. A second kind of love, *agape*, is seen in our love for God, a reverence for and deep acknowledgment of the divine being of God, including his commandments for humanity. Third is erotic love *(eros)*, an affectionate, tender hungering for union with the loved one; a passionate yearning for full relationship may include genital stirrings but does not have to do so. Eros was made a god (May, 1969). Both the Romans and the Greeks had different words for love and sex. The fourth kind of love is libido, sexual love, physical and emotional need that ends in the physical release of tensions in the act of sexual intercourse. Erotic love grows on and on; libidinal love builds up and is released.

In modern usage the word *love* most commonly connotes deep feelings between a man and a woman. There is a differentiation between the state of love and the feelings of love. The state of love implies a sense of committed caring and responsibility whereby there is concern and action taken for the well-being of the loved one. This state does not necessarily have to include feelings within a person toward the love object. When one allows himself or herself to feel love, however, there is an inner awareness of affect, of involvement from the heart rather than from habit or obligation. A state of love without corresponding feelings within leaves the persons involved somewhat distant and colorless. Many people suspect that such love is not genuine. Whether that is true or not, when one does not feel something within, this may reflect the person's inability to do so. Some persons are not emotionally mature enough to feel the inner stirrings of love.

How We Learn to Love. The study of early mother-child interactions has made clear that infants need a symbiotic acceptance by the mother that conveys adequate nurturance both physically and emotionally. The infant, and later the child, grows best in a climate of unconditional love in which the mother's patient responsiveness clearly demonstrates that she is here to take care of the baby, not vice versa. Love grows best when there is no fear of driving the mother away or consuming her with one's neediness.

The purpose of reliable, trustworthy parental love is to provide security and hence maximize the child's growth. It also teaches the baby how to love as he or she imitates the parents. The parents' ultimate purpose is to have the child internalize the love messages so the child believes he or she is lovable. This belief becomes the inner confidence and self-esteem that not only promotes exploration, learning, and growth, but also becomes the grounds for loving others in turn.

As the person grows through the various stages and cycles of life, he or she experiences different needs, and hence differing forms of love are sought (Orlinsky, 1972). Thus the infant seeks nurturance, the child responsiveness, the preadolescent a close friend, the teen a lover, and the adult a spouse. Personal love relationships foster psychological growth. There is a cyclical rhythm to these relationships all through the life cycle; closeness provides the inner fuel to separate and individuate and hence climb to a new level where one again develops a new communion before pushing on again. In communion there is cooperation and mutual sharing to satisfy each other's needs. In individuation the love of self is stressed by assertiveness and contest. Love must include mutuality and individuality, other and self. In Judeo-Christian thinking this same theme characterizes the relationship between God and persons.

One of the most difficult aspects of love relationships is to maintain a rich sense of self within the context of loving the other person. Many personal-emotional problems seen in psychotherapy relate to a fear of love based on the loss of self in the relationship (Branden, 1980).

Degrees of Love. There are different degrees to which one shows love; that is, various depths of loving interpersonally. Perhaps the most shallow form of love is fearful clinging, in which the person's immaturity includes an overwhelming dependency that bonds lover to loved one out of fear of loss. Up the scale one step from clinging is love by obligation, in which one feels stuck with the so-called loved one and thus cares out of duty. This is seen especially in marriages where the mates feel little personal emotional commitment but stay together for the children's sake. Both these forms of love are noteworthy for their lack of genuine mutuality and the creative joy that love should bring.

Progressing upward in terms of levels of loving, we find unrequited love; despite the inequality of feelings, one person loves another who does not return the love. Often there is frustration for the person not receiving love, but he or she may still choose to demonstrate a genuine loving care for the love object. This may be seen in parental care for seriously retarded children or in a marriage where one mate does all the loving and is relatively satisfied.

Further upward toward full mutual love are relationships that are reasonably stable, partially gratifying, but less than one or both partners would like to have. Whether through carelessness or lack of sophistication the partners are friendly, helpful, and generally affectionate but do not dare risk the deeper revelations of self and the explorations of the full range of emotions. Perhaps most married couples settle for or degenerate into this kind of reasonable if not entirely satisfying kind of love.

The quality of love in relationships between persons need not necessarily be impugned because there are problems or troubles. All human relationships have difficulties, hurts, disappointments, and problems. These can bind persons closer together as they seek to solve those issues. The worst one can expect is that the problems will erode the rapport between partners.

Mature Love. In a full sense of mutual human love we should expect several elements to exist. First is the willingness of each partner to be involved in the relationship as deeply as possible in four distinct ways: physically, intellectually, emotionally, and spiritually.

Second, full love involves both a giving and a receiving of love by each partner. That means that each person is responsible for giving to as well as getting from the other. Serious problems in the relationship can result when either partner is not giving or getting enough out of the relationship. Love is not giving, as popularly thought; it includes both giving and getting (Rottschafer, 1980). There has to be a daily monitoring of the balance between these two plus the willingness to correct the inequalities. The ratio of how much one gives to how much one gets (whether by taking or by receiving) may vary from day to day, but over time the health of the relationship depends on a balance between these two.

Third, mature love includes as full an experiencing of the broad range of human emotions as is possible. Therefore, in full love the partners open themselves to both joy and sorrow, agony and ecstasy, always keeping in mind the needs of both self and other as the experiences and feelings of life are shared. Love is an art that needs to be learned and practiced throughout one's entire lifetime (Fromm, 1956).

Last, full love must include a willingness to commit to one's loved object, whether country, home, family, child, mate, or friend. Commitment involves promise, deliberate intention to take the bad with the good, and a willingness to share one's life with the loved one. Commitment brings mutual trust for quality care in the now, plus predictable, responsible, mutual involvement in the future. Many current social, emotional, and physical ills can be seen as directly related to an absence of these qualities of love.

References

Branden, N. (1980). *The psychology of romantic love.* Los Angeles: Tarcher.

Fromm, E. (1956). *The art of loving.* New York: Harper & Row.

May, R. (1969). *Love and will.* New York: Norton.

Orlinsky, D. E. (1972). Love relationships in the life cycle: A developmental interpersonal perspective. In H. Otto (Ed.), *Love today.* New York: Association.

Rottschafer, R. H. (1980). Giving and getting, a clinical and spiritual evaluation. *The Bulletin of the Christian Association for Psychological Studies, 6* (2), 23–28.

R. H. ROTTSCHAFER

See INTERPERSONAL ATTRACTION.

LSD. *See* PSYCHEDELIC THERAPY.

Lying. A normal process during childhood development. It usually peaks between the ages of five to six and eight to nine with boys lying more than girls. During the maturation process children first learn not to lie because punishment usually follows, but they later learn to internalize reasons for not lying. Children's lies are often make-believe lies (A teddy bear flew in my window) or lies of confusion, although they develop into a moral understanding through lies of selfishness (I don't have the toy) and fear of punishment (I didn't break the lamp).

Pathological lying, however, is characterized by excessive lying that is frequent, vague, and often appears purposeless in that the liar has nothing obvious to gain from the lies. It is a reaction characteristic of people who have failed more than they have succeeded, and these persons often are antisocial or psychopathic personalities. Lying then sometimes becomes a character trait, and the person may use lies to bolster his or her ego or as a way of resolving a conflict. Often he or she lies to get praise, to react against psychic pain, or to deceive himself or herself. Compulsive lying is sometimes usefully viewed as a kind of wish fulfillment in that the compulsive liar may half-believe his or her own lies and often forgets former lies.

D. L. SCHUURMAN

See DENIAL; LIFE SPAN DEVELOPMENT.

Macrocephaly. A rare congenital defect that produces an abnormally large head. The cause of the disease is unknown, but physiologically it is due to an abnormal growth of the supporting tissue of the brain, resulting in moderate or severe retardation. There is no known treatment.

See MENTAL RETARDATION.

Magical Thinking. Magical thinking is present when a person views an internal thought as having external significance and power. A thought, although private and unobservable, becomes a substitute for action. The logic of magical thinking says that thoughts are powerful, and therefore thinking certain thoughts will cause various consequences to occur in the outside world. Magical thinking is not confined by normal barriers between thought and actions, between private thinking and public knowledge, between what is internal and what is external. Nor is it limited by the logical connections that normal thinking posits between ideas. The best-known example of magical thinking is the young child who, when angry, will close his or her eyes with the thought of making the disciplining parent disappear. The logic in this childish behavior is: If I can't see, I can't be seen.

Magical thinking is common and considered normal in young children. Developmental psychologists have isolated several stages in the development of cognitive processes, including a phase from 18 to 24 months when mental representations are organized (Greenspan, Lourie, & Nover, 1979). The organization is primitive and incomplete. Ideas, feelings, and perceptions can be "combined or distorted according to need or drive state" (p. 161); hence thinking at this level is magical. Magical thinking is considered pathological when it persists beyond the age of its normal occurrence. In older children it can occur in school phobics, anorexics, or psychotic children.

Psychoanalytic thought views the childish magical thought patterns as part of primary process thinking (concretistic, diffuse, pictorial, magical), which later gives way to secondary process thinking (abstract, focused, verbal, logical) (Fenichel, 1945). The prior, primary patterns of thought can again predominate under the influence of alcohol, sleep (dreams), or extreme stress such as in psychosis and schizophrenia (Weiner, 1966). Primary process thought patterns, including magical thinking, are thought to dominate the unconscious thought of neurotics (Brenner, 1973). Magical thinking is an associated feature of schizophrenia and can also be found in schizotypal personality disorders and in schizophreniform disorders.

Obsessive-compulsives also indulge in magical thinking when they feel that their thoughts can cause harm to others. The defense mechanism of undoing is predicated on magical thoughts, since wishing something makes it so (Brenner, 1973). For example, the child who first hits an adult and then kisses the same person is convinced that the second behavior will undo the first; hence it is magical thinking.

Evolutionary theorists often describe magical thinking as archaic or paleological, a remnant of preverbal and prelogical humanity. Primitive cultures are sometimes described as being permeated by magical thinking. Antireligionists whose worldview does not allow for the existence of a supernatural being use the concept of magical thinking to explain belief in God, prayer, and the miraculous.

References

Brenner, C. (1973). *An elementary textbook of psychoanalysis* (Rev. ed.). New York: International Universities Press.

Fenichel, O. (1945). *The psychoanalytic theory of neurosis.* New York: Norton.

Greenspan, S. I., Lourie, R. S., & Nover, R. A. (1979). A developmental approach to the classification of psychopathology in infancy and early childhood. In J. D. Noshpitz (Ed.), *Basic handbook of child psychiatry.* New York: Basic.

Weiner, I. B. (1966). *Psychodiagnosis in schizophrenia.* New York: Wiley.

J. R. BECK

See SUPERSTITION.

Mahler, Margaret (1897–1985). Born on the border of Austria and Hungary, Mahler received her training in medicine, pediatrics, and psychoanalysis in Vienna. In 1941 she migrated by way of England to New York, a refugee from the Nazi Holocaust. Her early professional interests in well-baby development, psychotic disorders in infants, the association between the tic syndrome and early parental separation, and the psychoanalysis of children with other kinds of difficulty resulted in formulation of a process in which the child moves from a symbiotic attachment with the mother toward a distinct individual identity. This process begins at approximately 6 months and proceeds normally for another 18 months. The process has come to be referred to as the psychological birth of the infant. Its description, as well as the identification of its relationship to many adult psychopathologies, is Mahler's most important professional contribution.

Drawing from the work of Melanie Klein, Spitz, Jean Piaget, Donald Winnicott, Bowlby, and others, Mahler described this process as consisting of three rather ordered subphases: differentiation, practicing, and rapprochement. Differentiation begins at five or six months and continues for about the same time. It is marked by the first behaviors of interaction with the mother, such as a smile preferential to the mother, pulling her hair, attempting to feed her, and pulling the body away from the mother to see her better. Bodily dependence on the mother decreases during this subphase as awareness of the outside world increases. Exploration of this world expands with the development of sensory capacities and locomotor skills.

This is followed by the second subphase, practicing. From about 10 to 16 months of age the infant tentatively experiments with both psychological and physical separation from the mother. The child progressively becomes more interested in people and objects, and with the ability to walk explores the world more actively. During this subphase these movements take place in proximity to the mother. Intrapsychically there is a parallel increase in the sense of a separate self, or individuation.

The third subphase, rapprochement, coincides with the beginnings of symbolic play and more complex speech, eventuating normally in the toddler's awareness of separateness and of the mother's love. This stage begins zestfully, with cautious awareness—of the dangers of the world and the child's need to cope with them on his or her own—growing over time.

These three subphases culminate in a consolidation period, in which there are firm foundations for the development of a lifelong concept of individuality and object constancy. This latter is understood by Mahler to include not only the ability to maintain an internal representation of an absent love object but also to bring together the good and bad part objects into a realistic whole.

The labor pains of this psychological birth are increasing anxiety over fusion, or symbiosis, with the mother. The process moves against a gradually decreasing anxiety over the loss of this primitive security. In Mahler's terminology, separation anxiety is not simply a fear of being apart from the physical presence of the mother but more a signal anxiety relating to the loss of attachment to the intrapsychic mother-object, occurring at the time when this inner representation has become clearly enough separate and distinct to be meaningful.

Disorders occur primarily as the residuals of symbiosis, or incomplete separation, and are manifested by recurrences of the primitive anxiety and depression as well as splitting of the good and bad objects, both of which Mahler feels occur normally during these phases of development. The focus of the psychoanalytic exploration that Mahler recommends for resolving these difficulties are these primary object relations. She sees the distortions causing pathology as resulting from inadequate or retarded development rather than primary conflicts.

While it appears that the usefulness of this model is considerable, there seems to be pressure for major revisions to accommodate insights coming from two more recently developing fields of research. The first of these is direct observation of the normal infant during these early months, which now seems to encourage the notion that an infant's perceptual world might be much better organized than the fragmentary sea of unrelated sensory and affective experiences conceptualized by the object relations theorists. This is suggested by the relative peace and contentment of many infants, as well as relatively sophisticated interactions with others that demonstrate clear separation and even individuation.

Another difficulty is the concept held by Mahler that maturity is manifested by completely separate and distinct individuals. Social psychologists, anthropologists, and the biblical model of one body with many members all suggest that mature identity is expressed in a profound unity with significant others that is not symbiosis or fusion but is a new union that respects and even enhances individuality. Unhealthiness then could take the form of either residual fusion or excessive isolation.

Whatever the outcome of future explorations into early human psychosocial development, the pioneering work and thought of Mahler will long be appreciated.

Additional Readings

Mahler, M. S., (1979). *The selected papers of Margaret S. Mahler* (2 vols.). New York: Norton.

Mahler, M S., Pine, F., & Bergman, A. (1975). *The psychological birth of the human infant*. New York: Basic.

Kaplan, L. J. (1978). *Oneness and separateness: From infant to individual*. New York: Simon & Schuster.

C. M. BERRY

See ATTACHMENT THEORY AND DISORDERS; OBJECT RELATIONS THEORY.

Mainstreaming. *See* MENTAL RETARDATION; NORMALIZATION IN HUMAN SERVICES.

Malingering. The conscious and intentional production or maintenance of symptoms in order to feign a disease that is either medical or psychological so that environmental benefits can be obtained and enjoyed. It is to be distinguished from factitious disorders, in which the patient simulates or produces illness for no other reason than the desire to be a patient. In malingering the voluntary production of symptoms is associated with a goal that is obviously recognizable with an understanding of the individual's circumstances.

In some cases malingering is the extension of an earlier existing but now improved illness, while in others it is the initial production of symptoms in order to achieve the benefits of illness. The feigned disease may be either medical in nature, such as pain syndromes (e.g., headache, low back pain), or gastrointestinal (e.g., flu symptoms, gastric distress), or psychological (e.g., a psychotic disorder with delusions and hallucinations or a depressive disorder).

Malingering is dependent on a basic intellectual ability to know the suitable symptoms and on apparent environmental gain either through the avoidance of an unpleasant event (e.g., hospital discharge for a lonely or poor patient) or the attainment of economic or social gain (e.g., disability insurance, welfare housing). Treatment intervention often takes the form of social and environmental manipulation directed toward making the gains previously produced by the illness available independent of the illness. An alternate strategy is to attempt to reduce the comfort or gain produced by the illness, thus removing the payoff for malingering. Psychotherapy can also be addressed initially toward support and later, after a relationship is established, toward confrontational approaches directed toward the patient effecting his or her own changes.

G. MATHESON

See FACTITIOUS DISORDERS.

Malpractice. Litigation against mental health professionals is increasing. Contrary to popular opinion, however, it is not always easy for the person bringing the complaint to prevail in a malpractice suit. Yet large monetary awards have focused a great deal of attention on the whole issue of professional incompetence.

The relationship between law and ethics is complex. Nearly all illegal actions that are relevant to professional functioning are unethical, and would be judged so by established professional societies. On the other hand, many things that are unethical are not specifically illegal. Thus, the range of unethical behavior is much larger than that of professionally illegal behavior. To put it another way, professionals can behave unethically without necessarily violating the law.

Malpractice litigation, however, usually has little to do with whether the practitioner has transgressed the laws of the land, that is, behaved criminally. Malpractice suits fall within the province of civil litigation rather than criminal prosecution. It should be noted that some actions can put the practitioner in the position of being liable both to criminal prosecution and to civil suit.

For a plaintiff to prevail in a malpractice suit, he or she has to demonstrate to the court's satisfaction a number of key elements. Before the suit can even be lodged, the plaintiff must have what attorneys call a "standing to sue." This means that the person bringing the action must have some kind of legally recognized basis for doing so. It is not possible for someone merely reading about a professional's bad treatment in the newspaper to sue that professional. This principle parallels the fact that you cannot take out a life insurance policy on someone with whom you have no recognized close and legitimate relationship.

It must first be demonstrated that the practitioner owed the client the duty to behave according to the standard of care prevalent in the community in which the services were rendered. Ordinarily it is not difficult to establish that the practitioner owed such a duty, but the establishment of exactly what constitutes the relevant standard of care can be more difficult. Expert testimony is often employed. Other professionals are brought in to present their views of what would have been the ordinary prudent actions of any reasonable practitioner under the given circumstances. We should note that judgment errors, of themselves, are theoretically an insufficient basis for winning a malpractice suit. Professionals are allowed to make errors—we are all human—so long as the error was one that could *reasonably* have been expected in the situation at issue.

The next thing that has to be established is that the duty was breached. It has to be demonstrated that the practitioner failed, either by omission or commission, to do what he or she should have done.

Next, the plaintiff must prove that the client was in fact injured in some way. When the injury concerns something as tangible as loss of employment, it is not hard to quantify the severity of the loss by translating it into dollars. On the other hand, it is more difficult to assign dollar values to such ambiguous injuries as mental anguish. Finally, it must be proved that the professional who is being sued was the legal (proximate) cause of the injury. This is where many malpractice suits falter and ultimately fail. It is not as easy as one might think to demonstrate causation when it comes to complex human behavior.

In criminal law conviction rests on guilt having been demonstrated "beyond a reasonable doubt." In civil law, however, liability has to be demonstrated only by a "preponderance of the evidence." It is therefore easier in theory for a plaintiff to prevail in a malpractice litigation than it is for the state to secure a conviction in a criminal proceeding.

In order to reduce the risk of a malpractice suit, mental health professionals (and clergy) should ensure that their dealings with clients are benevolent. Stated differently, malpractice suits typically signify a breakdown in the relationship between a service provider and a consumer of services. Beyond maintaining good relationships it is important for providers of services to confer frequently with colleagues in order to keep abreast of legal and ethical principles that bear on what they do and, in general, to make sure that they behave in a responsible manner.

A person who feels that he or she has been mistreated by a professional has a number of options. The most humane and biblical of these is to express the grievance directly to the professional. If satisfaction is not obtained, the individual can then appeal to such sanctioning professional organizations as the American Psychological Association. Beyond this, courts of law are available for seeking legal redress. Naturally, when Christians are aggrieved by other Christians, it is a good idea for them to settle their disputes out of court. The Christian Legal Society is an exceedingly good way to do this. Attorneys who are involved in this organization are committed to informal resolutions of differences between Christians and serve more or less as arbitration boards.

Additional Reading

Cohen, R. J. *Malpractice: A guide for mental health professionals.* New York: Free Press, 1979.

C. W. McLemore

See LAW AND PSYCHOLOGICAL PRACTICE; MORAL AND ETHICAL ISSUES IN TREATMENT.

Managed Care. Managed care is a term for a wide-ranging set of activities that are designed to provide oversight to the delivery and financing of health care services. To varying degrees, managed health care plans coordinate the health care of covered individuals and authorize payment for only those services approved by plan administrators. A managed care organization (MCO) may provide some or all of the following elements: networks of selected providers to furnish health care services, standards for the selection of health care providers, methods to determine whether quality services are being delivered, and lower co-payments and deductibles as incentives for members of the managed care plan to use the network of approved providers (Harden, 1994).

Familiar forms of managed care include health maintenance organizations (HMOs), preferred provider organization (PPOs), exclusive provider organizations (EPOs), and hybrid organizations of each form (Harden, 1994). An HMO is a system of doctors, health care providers, and hospitals that delivers health care services to a group of subscribers. In some HMOs, the doctors and other health care providers are employees of the HMO; in others they are contracted for a set fee per member, a practice referred to as capitation. Subscribers pay an annual fee to the HMO in advance for all health services rather than paying for each procedure. Those who use many services do not pay more than those who do not, which is the rationale for HMOs often seeking healthier individuals.

A PPO is an independent organization that assembles a group of professionals to deliver health care services. PPOs service employee health care plans with the network of providers. Employers often save money because the PPOs negotiate reduced rates from the network providers in exchange for a steady stream of referrals. Members can go to other providers but are usually penalized by higher deductibles and co-payments (Harden, 1994). An EPO is a more exclusive form of PPO. With some exceptions for emergency care, EPO contracts provide health benefits only if services are secured from network providers (Coopers & Lybrand, 1990).

During the 1990s, the growth of managed care was quite remarkable. For instance, by 1995, 102 million people were enrolled in some form of managed care plan, representing approximately 46% of the 222 million insured individuals in the United States.

Why the dramatic move to managed care arrangements? Employers responsible for providing health care to employees have looked to managed care arrangements to help control the use and cost of health care. From 1970 to 1990, health care costs went from 7.4% to 12.2% as a percentage of the gross national product. Between 1986 and 1993, the costs of employer purchased health care plans grew 3.5 times more rapidly than the rate of inflation (Health Insurance Association of America, 1996). Such cost concerns have motivated employers and policy makers to consider change in the delivery and financing of health care.

Such sweeping changes in health care have not come without controversy. Proponents credit the movement to managed care plans for decreases in growth of health care costs in the mid-1990s (Geisel, 1995). Others suggest that health care is improved due to the increased coordination of care. An example in mental health care involves the matching of Christian clients to Christian counselors, a practice common in many managed behavioral health care plans.

Detractors of managed care suggest that large managed care organizations put profits ahead of patient care. Since managed care companies make more profits if fewer procedures are authorized, opponents assert that many of these organizations deny authorization for needed care. Concerning the cost savings impact, a 1993 General Accounting Office report found little empirical evidence that managed care has reduced health care costs (General Accounting Office, 1993).

Congress has considered proposals to create incentives for Medicaid and Medicare recipients to move into managed care plans. Given the ongoing need to control the costs of providing health care, some form of managed care principles is likely to be a part of any future health system.

References

Coopers & Lybrand. (1990). *Managed health care: A reference guide*. Chicago: Author.

Geisel, J. (February 13, 1995). Health market changes spur 1% drop in costs. *Business Insurance*, 1, 10.

General Accounting Office. (1993, October). Report delivered to the House Ways and Means Committee. (Tech. Rep. No. GAO/HRD–94–3, B–254303). Washington, DC: Author.

Harden, S. L. (1994). *What legislators need to know about managed care*. Denver, CO: National Conference of State Legislatures.

Health Insurance Association of America. (1996). *Source book of health insurance data: 1995*. Washington, DC: Author.

E. W. Throckmorton

See Health Maintenance Organization; Insurance: Health and Mental Health.

Management Theory. Although some managers contend that leadership is a combination of intuition and experience, the behavioral sciences have contributed much to the theories and practice of management this century. One perspective has been descriptive. Early studies examined the organization of French industries and government offices, emphasizing the themes of division of labor, unity of command, and responsibility. A more recent descriptive approach has been to focus on the characteristics of the individual manager's role: planning, decision making, delegating, supervising, coordinating, motivating, communicating, representing, staffing, disciplining, negotiating, mediating, investigating, evaluating, and gathering, interpreting, and disseminating information.

The behavioral sciences usually go beyond description and give a diagnosis of problems and prescription for optimal strategies. This tradition began with the work of Taylor and other students of time and motion: how to get the most output from the fewest workers, hours, and materials. The biggest problem in these efficiency expert programs was not the prior ignorance of these methods, but worker resistance to them. Taylor recommended financial incentives as a motivator.

The Humanistic Approach. The period of 1930 to 1960 saw management theory emphasize the human element, especially the need for participation. The roots of this emphasis go back to Owen, who early in the nineteenth century contended that improvements in production required improvements in the condition of workers, on and off the job. The scientific impetus for humanistic management came from Mayo's (1933) interpretation of the Hawthorne studies. Although there had been economic incentives for workers, Mayo observed the high levels of production resulting from these experiments and credited them to such factors as group participation and the special attention given to the research subjects by the experimenters.

Much of the research of this period emphasized sociograms, morale, and the human qualities of managers. Case studies, surveys, and experiments generally indicated that there were positive correlations between background variables such as managerial consideration and participation in decision making and the outcome variables of morale and productivity. The correlation between productivity and the closeness of supervision was negative. Likert (1961) hoped that the bulk of firms in the United States were slowly moving through the phases of exploitive-authoritative, benevolent-authoritative, consultative, and participative management. In the 1960s and 1970s a process known as organizational development was popular: This used a participative group experience to redesign managerial structures and processes. In the 1980s and 1990s these efforts have continued under an ever-changing barrage of buzzwords: the quest for excellence, reengineering, high-tech, and high touch.

Another aspect of this humanistic approach has been a consideration of the noneconomic needs of workers. Abraham Maslow's theory of the higher levels of needs has been widely although perhaps uncritically accepted by managerial theorists. Schein (1969) constructed a typology of workers: rational-economic (motivated by material gain), social (motivated by affiliative needs), and self-actualizing (motivated by the need to be autonomous and creative). Schein suggested a historical shift among workers in the United States away from the rational-economic and toward the self-actualizing. Herzberg (1968) presented a two-factor theory. He suggested that job satisfaction and dissatisfaction are two separate variables rather than polar extremes on the same variable. Job dissatisfaction is due to hygiene factors (e.g., company policies, working conditions, salary, status, interpersonal relations), but true satisfaction can only come from content factors (e.g., achievement, recognition, growth, intrinsic enjoyment of the work). These kinds of theories have led managers to experiment with job enrichment; that is, intentionally giving workers more responsibility and task variety in order to increase the sense of challenge. Although this has been successful with better educated employees, it has not always been well received by unionized, blue-collar workers.

MacGregor (1960) divided managers into two types: those who accept Theory X (workers are lazy and need to be closely supervised, even intimidated, in order to get them to produce) and those managers who accept Theory Y (workers want to do a good job and only need to be supported and encouraged). MacGregor made a case for Theory Y as being the better set of assumptions. The 1980s saw the arrival of Theory Z (also known as Theory J), which was seen as the Japanese way: collective decision making, lifetime employment, long-term evaluation, nonspecialized career paths, and concern with the overall quality of work life.

Researchers and executives in the 1960s and 1970s championed management by objectives. Drucker (1967) and Odiorne (1965) recommended that superior and subordinate discuss the goals of the latter's unit and mutually agree on the objectives that the latter would strive for, with the support of the former. It is hoped that the process will focus both superior and subordinate on participative decision making and teamwork. Then the former must measure the latter's progress in attaining the objectives, give appropriate rewards (if the subordinate is successful), and diagnose underlying problems (if the subordinate is not successful). When this is done well, management by objectives is an excellent tool for both research and practice. However, many tasks do not lend themselves to clear statements about measurable objectives. What frequently happened, as in performance objectives in education, was that what ends up being stated as the objective is what is easiest to measure, not what is most worth striving for, thereby distorting the long-term goals of the organization.

Interaction of Factors. The simplistic assumptions of both the efficiency experts and the participative pollsters have become apparent. There was a tendency to make a mile of inference from inches of data on the Hawthorne studies or the Japanese postwar industrial expansion. No one technique achieves all of a firm's objectives. Different methods of designing work and compensating employees achieve different objectives in different organizations with different employees. The chief trend since 1970 has been an appreciation of the complexity of the interaction of personalities and different environments.

Indeed, several humanistic theorists were pointing in this direction. Maslow conceded that only a small percentage of people are capable of sustained functioning at the self-actualizing level and noted the impact of the environment in determining an individual's most pressing needs. Schein (1969) concluded that rational-economic, social, and self-actualizing are not distinct and mutually exclusive types but traits that can be stronger or weaker in given individuals, companies, societies, or eras, depending upon socialization and other environmental factors.

The idea of identifying several types of situations that call for different managerial approaches has been advocated by many writers. Blake and Mouton (1964) devised a managerial grid that looks at concern for people and concern for production not as polar opposites but as two different dimensions, suggesting that different supervisory styles may be appropriate in different contexts. Fiedler (1967) considered the interaction of the variables of leader-member relations, task structure, and leader power position, estimating to what degree a task-oriented management style or relationship-oriented style would be effective. Vroom (1964) developed a series of seven branching questions to help a manager decide which combination of five styles would be most appropriate for a situation.

Even the idea that all business organizations should strive to develop and maintain the same structure has been questioned. Mintzberg (1979) developed a theory of five types of organizational structures and attempted to describe environments in which each is most appropriate. Brink (1991) suggested four very different corporate cultures that embraced different rules for selecting, promoting, and motivating employees, and entirely different roles for managers. Background variables such as the age and size of the company, level of management, and external economic conditions may determine which managerial goals and tactics are more appropriate.

Tom Peters and other popular writers of the 1980s and 1990s have followed up on an idea introduced by Drucker: the customer is the business. A recent trend in management theory is that every level of management in every department (indeed, that every employee) is part of the marketing department. Each level of management must have contact with the customer base and have the authority to change company policy in order to meet that customer's needs.

References

Blake, R. R., & Mouton, J. S. (1964). *The managerial grid.* Houston: Gulf Publishing.

Brink, T. L. (1991). Color coding corporate cultures. *Business Horizons, 35* (5), 39–44.

Drucker, P. (1967). *The effective executive.* New York: Harper & Row.

Fiedler, F. E. (1967). *A theory of leadership effectiveness.* New York: McGraw-Hill.

Herzberg, F. (1968). One more time: How do you motivate employees? *Harvard Business Review, 46* (1), 59–62.

Likert, R. (1961). *New patterns of management.* New York: McGraw-Hill.

MacGregor, D. (1960). *The human side of management.* New York: McGraw-Hill.

Mayo, E. (1933). *The human problems of industrial civilization.* New York: Macmillan.

Mintzberg, H. (1979). *The structuring of organizations.* Englewood Cliffs, NJ: Prentice-Hall.

Odiorne, G. (1965). *Management by objectives.* New York: Putnam.

Schein, E. H. (1969). *Process consultation.* Reading, MA: Addison-Wesley.

Vroom, V. (1964). *Work and motivation.* New York: Wiley.

Additional Readings

Aamodt, M. G. (1996). *Applied industrial organizational psychology* (2nd ed.). Pacific Grove, CA: Brooks/Cole.

Auerbach, A. (1996). *The world of work: An introduction to industrial/organizational psychology.* Madison, WI: Brown & Benchmark.

T. L. BRINK

See INDUSTRIAL/ORGANIZATIONAL PSYCHOLOGY.

Mania. A distinct period of at least one week (unless a person is hospitalized) involving an abnormally and persistently elevated or irritable mood (*see* Mood Disorders). The mood is usually euphoric to the point that it is recognized as excessive by others, the person is often easily distracted by irrelevant external events, self-esteem is typically inflated, there is a decreased need for sleep, thoughts may race, and speech is frequently rapid and loud.

See Bipolar Disorder.

Manic-Depressive Psychosis. *See* Bipolar Disorder.

Marital Communication. *See* Communication; Communication Skills Training; Marriage Enrichment.

Marital Compatibility. This term describes the character of the relationship fit of the two spouses. In the highly compatible marriage both spouses act, think, and feel in such a way that their needs and expectations are being met and few blockages exist to interfere in the relationship. In the highly incompatible marriage significant blockages are present that prevent one or both spouses from obtaining satisfaction of their needs and expectations. Most marriages exist between these extremes and have areas of both compatibility and incompatibility.

The general evaluation of marital compatibility involves an assessment of the specific areas of compatibility and incompatibility as well as an assessment of the relative importance of each area. Significant marital incompatibility may exist when many areas of incompatibility exist or when a few highly important areas of incompatibility exist. If a person highly values religious life and experiences considerable need or expectation frustration in this area, the marriage may be threatened. For a person who does not value this highly, it may have little consequence for the overall marital compatibility.

Happiness and satisfaction are the subjectively experienced consequences of marital compatibility. When both spouses experience need and expectation satisfaction to a significant degree in the marriage, they report marital satisfaction. The assessment of marital satisfaction has focused on the evaluation of several areas of needs, including affective communication, problem-solving communication, time together, financial disagreements, sexual dissatisfaction, role orientation, family history, and child-rearing practices (Snyder, 1979). Research points to a strong relationship between marital compatibility and sexual attitude and behavior. A positive affective sexual attitude correlates with marital satisfaction and compatibility (Smith, Becker, & Byrne, 1993). A high frequency of intercourse correlates with marital satisfaction (Pietropento, 1986). Personality compatibility appears in research to be a large factor and the best predictor of marital compatibility (Wiggins, Moody, & Lederer, 1983).

Marital compatibility changes over the life cycle of the relationship. Personality traits that were unimportant at one stage may be very important at a later stage of marital life. Being an enjoyable playmate is highly desirable in the early 20s, but by the age of 35 and after two children, being a responsible wage earner and parent will be more highly valued. Thus compatibility may change as a result of lack of adjustment to the changing needs of the marital relationship. The occurrence of an affair often is an indication of needs and expectations no longer being filled in the marital relationship, even though earlier the marriage was considered a compatible one. This suggests that the maintenance of compatibility, and hence marital satisfaction, involves continued adjustment and work throughout the marriage. Most couples experience some kind of incompatibility at major transition times in the marriage; for example, at the birth of the first child, as the nest empties, at retirement. McGoldrick and Carter (1980) consider most marital crises to be precipitated by a difficulty in adjusting to the requirements of the new stage of marital life. Marital therapy then becomes a resource to use in adjusting to the needs of the new phase of life.

Mate selection studies have also suggested that the choice of a spouse depends upon the compatibility of the interpersonal needs. Specifically, Murstein (1980) suggests that attraction relates to the initial stimulus factors, similarity of values, and agreement on individual role functions. The theory advanced by Centers (1975) even more clearly suggests that spousal attraction depends upon maximum gratification and minimum deprivation of personal needs.

References

Centers, R. (1975). *Sexual attraction and love: An instrumental theory.* Springfield, IL: Thomas.

McGoldrick, M., & Carter, E. (1980). *The family life cycle: A framework for family therapy.* New York: Gardner.

Murstein. B. I. (1980). Mate selection in the 1970s. *Journal of Marriage and the Family, 42,* 777–792.

Pietropinto, A. (1986). Inhibited sexual desire. *Medical Aspects of Human Sexuality, 20,* 46–49.

Smith, E. R., Becker, M., & Byrne, D. (1993). Sexual attitudes of males and females as predictors of interpersonal attraction and marital compatibility. *Journal of Applied Social Psychology, 23,* 1011–1034.

Snyder, D. K. (1979). Multidimensional assessment of marital satisfaction. *Journal of Marriage and the Family, 41,* 813–823.

Wiggins, J., Moody, D., & Lederer, D. (1983). Personality typologies related to marital satisfaction. *American Mental Health Counselors Association Journal, 5,* 169–178.

A. D. Compaan

See Marital Types; Mate Choice; Conflict; Conflict Management.

Marital Contract Therapy. Developed by Sager, a psychoanalytically trained psychiatrist, marital contract therapy is a therapeutic approach to marital dysfunction based upon the concept of contracts (Sager, 1976; *see* Contracts, Therapeutic Use of). According to this approach, each spouse has an individual, unwritten contract for the marriage. It is the set of expectations and promises, conscious and unconscious, he or she has for the relationship. A third contract, the marital contract, develops as a consequence of the marital interaction. It is the operational, interactional contract created by the marital system and the unconscious and conscious ways the two spouses seek to fulfill their individual contracts.

Sager groups the various individual contracts into seven different types: equal, romantic, parental, childlike, rational, companionate, and parallel. The combinations of the individual contracts become the 48 different marital contracts, or marital types, he describes. Marital discord results from contractual disappointments when the expectations of one spouse are not being met by the other. Most often these expectations have not been clearly expressed and may be largely unconscious.

Therapy primarily seeks to clarify the terms of the two individual contracts and those of their interactional contract. This begins with helping each spouse explain the expectations they have but have not clearly verbalized. It also involves helping each to become more aware of the unconscious expectations they have for the marriage. This process of making conscious what is unconscious requires considerable clinical skill. Finally, once clarification of the contract has been obtained, agreement on its terms must be reached in order for marital satisfaction to continue.

The identification of individual contracts, the diagnostic phase of therapy, is made by collecting information from three categories. First is the expectations each spouse has for the marriage (e.g., my mate will be loyal and devoted, or marriage will be a respectable cover for the expression of my aggressive drive). Second is the intrapsychic and biological drives of each spouse. Sager identifies 13 basic parameters useful in evaluating each spouse (e.g., independence-dependence, closeness-distance, and dominance-submission). The reciprocal nature of contracts is particularly operative in this area: "I want so-and-so and in exchange I am willing to give such and such." The third source of information is the external manifestations of marital problems, the problems often presented as the reasons for seeking therapy (e.g., poor communication, sexual dysfunction). These symptoms, according to Sager, are secondary manifestations of problem areas originating in the other two areas.

In examining each of these three sources of information, three levels of awareness must be considered. The first is the conscious and verbalized level. These are the expectations and needs that both spouses have talked about in their marriage. The second level is conscious but not verbalized. This includes expectations and needs that the spouses know they have but for a variety of reasons have been unwilling to tell each other. The third level is the needs and expectations that are present and that influence behavior but are beyond the awareness of both spouses.

The interactional contract is the behaviors followed by each spouse in trying to fulfill his or her individual contract. According to Sager, "much of therapy consists of making the interactional contract and the partners' behavior in it more conscious, and of using the consciousness to work toward a new single contract that provides the basis for healthier interactions" (p. 29).

Contract therapy incorporates many methods proposed and utilized by other therapists. What is distinctive is the focus on expectations and the relationship of these expectations to underlying biological and psychological needs. The implications for assessment and diagnosis of mental dynamics are also a significant contribution (*see* Marital Types).

Marital contract therapy is psychoanalytic in its emphasis on the levels of awareness and intrapsychic needs. However, systems theory has influenced the concept of interactional contracts and expectations of marriage. Learning theory has also influenced the approach in its use of behavioral observation in order to identify the interactional contracts of the marriage. In the absence of research, it would appear that the approach may be useful for persons with good ego strength, observational abilities, and verbal abilities. It also provides many helpful concepts and techniques that would fit within virtually any other approach to marital therapy.

Marital contract therapy has some basic similarities to the Old Testament concept of the covenant in that it focuses on promises and expectations in the relationship between two contracting or covenanting parties. Problems in the relationship of God to man and woman result from the breaking of covenant, just as marital discord results from unmet contracts. Sager makes clear that such making and breaking of contracts in marriage (as in our relationship to God) occurs significantly at unconscious and unverbalized levels in the relationship.

Reference

Sager, C. J. (1976). *Marriage contracts and couple therapy.* New York: Brunner/Mazel.

A. D. COMPAAN

See MARRIAGE COUNSELING.

Marital Health and Pathology. Married life is a mixture of health and pathology, of both life-enhancing and life-destroying behaviors. The message of grace in the Christian gospel frees marriage partners to recognize the pathology in their relationships while releasing a Spirit-filled pull toward change. When spouses acknowledge and receive this grace, they then can more easily face the realistic strengths and weaknesses of their marital relationship. Seven areas of marital life involve dynamics important in assessing the health of a marriage: ideals, commitment, communication, intimacy, dependency, sexuality, and power.

Ideals. The first area for assessment is the relationship between the images of an ideal marriage relationship and the reality of the relationship. All attitudes, feelings, and behaviors in marriage are affected by the ideal image of marriage that the spouses have. These ideal images are shaped by individual experiences in the family of origin, by cultural and religious teaching, and by other life experiences. The greater the disparity between the husband's ideal and the wife's ideal, and between each of their ideals and the reality of their relationship, the greater is the distress in the marriage. Marital life is enhanced when both spouses accept the realities of their marriage and are able then to agree on a mutually accepted ideal and collaborate in working toward it.

While the Bible has a great deal to say about married life, it does not set forth a single ideal marital relationship that can be called the Christian marriage. If only one ideal model for marriage is set forth as the Christian model, the diversity of human behavior and the uniqueness of each marriage are denied. Making room for personal differences within the marriage is a necessary part of a healthy marriage. Whitaker (1988) says, "The capacity to deal with differences is one development that greatly stabilizes and enhances the quality of the marriage" (p. 204).

The creative effort of both spouses is necessary to lead marriage toward this goal. Spouses will sometimes equate their personal ideal for marriage with a supposed biblical ideal in order to lend credibility and power to their preference. As a power play by one spouse this usually works against the creative work necessary for achieving a mutually acceptable ideal. Since it is inevitable that each spouse will have an ideal, it is important to recognize that many different options are acceptable and can meet the requirements of a Christian life. Health is fostered when both spouses can agree on the basics of an ideal marriage while making room for differences.

Commitment. Christian marriage is a covenantal relationship in which fidelity for life is pledged by each spouse. Fidelity is a commitment to place the other's good above self-interest. Smedes (1976) defines fidelity in partnership as "commitment to an ongoing, dynamic, changing, sensitive facing off of two people bent on the total well-being of each other. And each is faithful to the extent that he is dedicated to the constant growth, healing and regrowth of the other person" (p. 178). Every spouse fails frequently at meeting this high ideal. As Whitaker (1988) says, "All healthy marriages experience literally dozens of emotional divorces over

the course of the years" (p. 204). The ability to reconcile and heal the wounds of broken fidelity is more essential than whether and how fidelity is broken. Commitment is not only to be together but also to seek resolution for all conflicts and healing for all of the inevitable wounding that will occur in the marriage.

Covenant keeping in marriage, as in our relationship with God, reaches its intended height only as it becomes an ethical commitment or choice of the individual. Persons forced to remain together by circumstances (e.g., a pregnancy), by parents, by social or communal pressure, or by personal developmental deficits have not thereby met the biblical goals for marriage. The dynamics of such marriages are often very destructive. Anger and resentment over being forced to be together may be expressed destructively toward the spouse and often also toward the children.

Communication. Fulfilling the marital vow of placing the interests and needs of the other above one's own self-interest and needs requires communication. Understanding of another person's needs comes only as these are communicated. However, the natural tendency is to hide rather than disclose feelings, thoughts, and desires.

One way to hide is to blame the spouse for something and thus avoid personal responsibility and honest self-disclosure. This communication dysfunction is described as far back as Adam and Eve (Gen. 3). Adam blamed Eve and Eve blamed the serpent, both hoping to direct attention away from their own failures. Such a pattern of blame blocks the communication of one's real thoughts and feelings. This in turn makes it difficult for the spouse to relate in such a way that needs can be met. Satir sees communication to be at the heart of marital pathology, and treatment for marital problems involves improvement in communication skills (Satir, 1983).

Intimacy. A fourth important area of marriage is intimacy. The Bible sees intimacy as both becoming one and maintaining individuality. The one-flesh union presented as an ideal for marriage requires that both husband and wife first become individuals distinct from their families of origin (Gen. 2:24; Matt. 19:5). Marital health is marked by an ability to be intimate with one's spouse without losing one's distinctive and separate self and without destroying the other distinct and separate self.

A pathological marital relationship that sometimes is equated with this biblical description of marriage is a relationship in which ego boundaries of each spouse have been blurred or fused with each other. Each spouse becomes unable to distinguish his or her partial self from the common self. Bowen (1985) describes this situation as the "undifferentiated family ego mass." He feels that the level of differentiation of the self of each spouse determines the degree of emotional fusion in the relationship.

The way the spouses handle this fusion governs the areas in which the undifferentiation will be absorbed and the areas in which symptoms will be expressed under stress. According to Bowen, the most common symptomatic expressions of this lack of differentiation are marital conflict, dysfunction in a spouse, and dysfunction in one or more of the children. The lower the level of differentiation of each spouse, the greater is the difficulty in responding to stress without manifesting symptoms in one of these areas. The achievement and maintenance of intimacy is made easier by greater differentiation of self both from the family of origin and within the nuclear family.

Often the family of origin will work to keep the person tied into the family and thus unable to separate and begin a new family. Symptoms of such a situation may include financial ties, entangled living arrangements, and parental judgments of decisions made by the daughter-in-law or son-in-law. All of these work against the achievement of intimacy.

Intimacy must be distinguished from fusion. Intimacy does not have to do with sameness but with self-disclosure and empathy. It comes as each spouse acknowledges, respects, and empathizes with the joys, successes, failures, and struggles disclosed by the other spouse.

Dependency. Both communication and intimacy are closely connected to a fifth dynamic, managing dependency in marriage. While marriage involves giving to the other and placing the other as more important than self, it also necessarily involves seeking the other for self. No marriage can sustain itself without each spouse both giving and taking. Total self-giving, as altruistic as it may seem, is destructive in a marriage. It saps a partner of the creative independence he or she needs in order to contribute to the other person. Thus one condition of self-giving is self-assertion (Smedes, 1976). Often the greatest gift in marriage is to fully and joyfully receive, just as the greatest gift we can return to God is to fully and joyfully receive God's gift in Christ.

Pathology exhibits itself when both spouses are unable to ask for or clearly receive the gifts of the other spouse. Bowen (1985) describes one typical marital fusion where "one [spouse] denies the immaturity and functions with a facade of overadequacy. The other accentuates the immaturity and functions with a facade of inadequacy" (p. 19). Health in marriage requires the ability of both spouses to acknowledge their needs as well as to joyfully receive the meeting of their needs.

Where dependency is not acceptable to a spouse (e.g., to a male who sees dependency as feminine or an indication of personal inadequacy), he or she is likely to use covert or manipulative behavior in order to obtain satisfaction for these needs. Such manipulation usually generates anger and resistance in the other spouse, who then may not want to give anything. Accepting dependence as a normal, God-created human situation frees the individual to ask and to receive.

Sexuality. A sixth crucial dynamic of marriage is sexuality. The Christian church has consistently viewed the sexual relationship of marriage to be of the highest significance, even though it has often erred in favor of an unbiblical Greek dualistic split of body and soul and an equally unbiblical dichotomy of sex roles (Nelson, 1978). Sexuality in marriage involves the expression of both *eros* and *agape*, seeking and giving love, and thus is crucially related to the spiritual search for God and the spiritual response of loving God and neighbor. The sexual relationship in marriage can thus be seen as a barometer of many of the other dynamics as well as a barometer of a person's spiritual relationship to God.

Healthy sexual relationships involve a delicate combination of desiring and giving. The communication of what is physically pleasurable and satisfying in the sexual experience is a key part of both experiencing fulfillment in the sexual relationship and of assisting the spouse to give unselfishly (Masters & Johnson, 1966). Sexual inadequacies frequently involve difficulties in both giving and receiving. Healthy sexuality thus requires health in all dynamics of marriage and is in many ways the expression of a healthy marital relationship. Sexual dysfunctions, however, are not necessarily a sign of marital problems, since they sometimes result from nothing more serious than erroneous information or expectations.

Power. Christians are sometimes reluctant to see marriage in terms of the use and abuse of power, often considering any use of power to be unacceptable. However, God clearly gave both Adam and Eve considerable power. They were to subdue nature and rule over it (Gen. 1:26–31). Furthermore, they were so powerful that each could act in ways counter both to God's desires and to their own best interests. As a result of the abuse of power in eating the forbidden fruit, man and woman became repeated abusers of that power. Man began to dominate woman, and woman began to use her power manipulatively toward her husband (Gen. 3:16). Thus the ideal of jointly exercising their power in dominion over the rest of creation was lost as they exercised their power over each other.

In marriage spouses often engage in elaborate power struggles. These struggles take a wide variety of forms, and to varying degrees they may destroy the life of the marriage. The therapeutic task is to help the spouses get out of the power struggle and begin to use power constructively.

Paradoxically, most often both spouses experience or feel themselves to be powerless in the marriage relationship even while they use extremely powerful methods in the destructive conflict. Spouses need to recognize that feeling helpless is a warning sign indicating that conditions are ripe for the expression of abusive power. When spouses get into power struggles both are disowning the God-given power that is theirs while using that power in maritally destructive ways. When the struggle between spouses is a win-lose battle, the relationship will always lose. Assisting each to recognize that he or she is very powerful helps each to become more responsible in the use of that power.

The healthy marriage is one in which both spouses can recognize and accept the unhealthy or problematic areas of the marriage. Each spouse's knowing how he or she routinely and repeatedly fails in the relationship is immensely relieving to the spouse and prepares the situation for healing and reconciliation.

References

Bowen, M. (1985). *Family therapy in clinical practice.* New York: Aronson.

Masters, W. H., & Johnson, V. E. (1966). *Human sexual response.* Boston: Little, Brown.

Nelson, J. (1978). *Embodiment.* Minneapolis: Augsburg.

Satir, V. (1983). *Conjoint family therapy.* Palo Alto, CA: Science and Behavior.

Smedes, L. (1976). *Sex for Christians.* Grand Rapids, MI: Eerdmans.

Whitaker, C. (1988). *Dancing with the family.* New York: Brunner/Mazel.

Additional Readings

Clinebell, H. J. (1970). *The intimate marriage.* New York: Harper & Row.

Goldenberg, I., & Goldenberg, H. (1996). *Family therapy: An overview.* Pacific Grove, CA: Brooks/Cole.

A. D. COMPAAN

See COMMUNICATION; COMMUNICATION SKILLS TRAINING.

Marital Stages. *See* FAMILY LIFE CYCLE; MARITAL TYPES.

Marital Types. The grouping of marital systems on the basis of their similarities. A number of typologies have been suggested but none has been widely accepted (Glick & Kessler, 1980; Kramer, 1980; Lederer & Jackson, 1968; Sager, 1976). The most extensively elaborated and most helpful typology is that of Sager.

Sager proposes 48 possible marital types, each based on the combination of two of seven identified individual behavioral profiles. Each profile is based on the observations of individual responses in 12 areas of needs and expectations (e.g., independence-dependence, active-passive, closeness-distance). The seven individual profiles are the equal, romantic, parental, childlike, rational, companionate, and parallel partners.

Basic Behavioral Profiles. The equal partner seeks a relationship in which both partners have the same rights, privileges, and obligations. The equal partner is independent and self-activating; capable of close sustained intimacy midway between submissive and dominant; and disowns possession of or being possessed by the spouse.

Romantic partners find the elements and symbols of love paramount in the relationship. Security and fulfillment come in the presence of the beloved, and the need for assurance of being loved is insatiable. The romantic wishes to be the sole object of adoration and support, is dependent, seeks emotional closeness, fears abandonment to the extent that it determines behavior, and is possessive and controlling.

The parental partner is a controlling parent who enjoys caretaking and governing. A specific and frequently found subtype is the rescuer, who enjoys saving the helpless child-spouse. The parental partner tends to appear independent as long as the spouse remains dependent. This partner is active, needs to use power to dominate, is competitive, is afraid of the loss of the mate, and needs to possess and control the mate.

The childlike partner desires to be cared for and protected. This partner may appear to be the helpless slave, but often he or she is the wielder of immense power. The "save me" partner is a subtype who seeks a parental (rescuer) partner. The childlike partner tends to be dependent and passive, appears to submit but may use the power of helplessness to dominate, is motivated strongly by fears of abandonment, and submits to being controlled and possessed.

The rational partner seeks a logical and well-ordered relationship. Duties and responsibilities are primary concerns. The rational partner may appear to have little emotion but in crisis can express it freely. The rational partner is pragmatic, down-to-earth, and loyal, appears powerful and in charge, and is active in practical matters. This type of person is also usually quite dependent, although he or she hides this through immersion in the practical administration of the relationship.

The companionate partner acts to ward off aloneness. Thoughtfulness and kindness, not necessarily love, are adequate for a satisfying relationship. These persons want someone with whom to share life and see marriage as a realistic arrangement between adults. The companionate partner tends to mix dependence and independence and to be more active than passive, avoids extremes of closeness and distance, and uses power but not to extremes.

The parallel partner seeks to avoid intimacy and desires a spouse who respects emotional distance and independence. He or she wants all the advantages of marriage without emotional intimacy. Parallel partners usually fear loss of integrity and being controlled; they appear cool and guarded though charming. Their behavior is often a reaction formation to great dependency needs that cannot be admitted. Hence they appear independent, are active and distant, are in charge of self and life, show no fear of abandonment, and have no desire to possess or be possessed as long as rules for distance are observed.

Partnership Combinations. These seven partner profiles combine to make 48 partnership combinations, each of which has a characteristic style.

The most gratifying and durable relationship is the one in which both spouses accept each other as they currently are and where some compatibility of styles exists. The following more frequently encountered styles describe both the normal and the mildly to moderately pathological marriages.

The equal-equal combination, although it is idealized by many, is achieved by few. It is the most difficult to maintain, since the spouses stay together "because they want to be together, not because either is afraid not to be" (Sager, 1976, p. 137). No outside forces such as social institutions or children keep them together. Often partners have differing ideas of what is equality, and considerable discussion is required before agreement is reached. In the 1990s this is the dominant marital ideal in the United States.

The equal-romantic combination often makes for a good relationship. The equal partner usually respects the individuality of the romantic in his or her desire for closeness, communication, and dependence. When the romantic can recognize the equal partner's need for distance, a quid pro quo balance is struck. Problems arise when one is unwilling to accept the other's needs and begins to demand changes.

The equal-rational partnership often emerges out of an equal-equal combination in which one spouse's anxiety leads toward stronger rational attempts to control the relationship in order to reduce the anxiety. The equal partner soon responds negatively, and a confusing struggle may follow. The combination may be fairly stable because the rational mate is often trying to be an equal partner.

The romantic-romantic combination is the best combination for the romantic partner. The early stages of this relationship are marked by passion, openness, intimacy, and pervasive interdependence. The inevitable reduction of this intensity is often regarded as the loss of love, bringing a crisis in the relationship. The spouse most aware of the change may seek a new romantic partnership in an affair, which may devastate the other, unsuspecting partner. The element of needing the partner to bring completion to oneself is an essential element in this combination.

The romantic-rational combination often does not work well because the romantic partner feels the rational partner is not close enough, is too logical, and does not express feelings.

The parental-childlike combination is the most frequently found and most enduring combination for both the partners. The parental partner desires someone to whom he or she can feel superior; the childlike partner seeks a powerful protector and caretaker. The parental partner stance may mask the more severe pathology that becomes apparent when the childlike partner ceases to function as the needy, helpless one. Successful therapeutic alteration of this combination depends on significant motivation in both partners. Attempting to alter the system when only one partner expresses a desire to change may lead to rapid decompensation by the other spouse. The rescuer-save-me partnership, a specific subtype of the parental-childlike combination, is frequently found if one spouse is a substance abuser.

The childlike-childlike combination is found in a relationship characterized by fun and play with little concern for responsibility. Usually it is only a matter of time before each partner experiences frustration over not being able to get the other to function as a parent. If they are able to each accept some parental roles toward the other, a complementary relationship can be successfully maintained.

The rational partner often seeks a spouse who will supply the emotion and spontaneity of which he or she is afraid. A romantic or childlike partner often is chosen; sometimes an equal or companionate partner works out well. The romantic seeks and expresses great emotions and the childlike partner has fun and free play. The rational partner may appreciate both as long as little pressure is exerted for change.

The companionate-companionate combination is the most common and satisfying for the companionate partner. The contract is to respect and take care of each other. Kindness and consideration are expected, but not love.

The large number of partner combinations possible in this typology suggests clearly the rich diversity of marital systems that can be fulfilling, satisfying, and problematic for spouses. The variety of partner profiles and partner combinations is consistent with a biblical view of the uniqueness and differences of each person. The application of a Christian ethic of love requires that this diversity be taken seriously so that the partners' differences can be respected while a meaningful marital relationship is worked out. Sager's view that a combination is more workable when spouses can accept the basics of their own and their spouse's profile is consistent with a biblical view of self-love and other love (Matt. 22:37, 39).

References

Glick, I. D., & Kessler, D. R. (1980). *Marital and family therapy* (2nd ed.). New York: Grune & Stratton.

Kramer, C. H. (1980). *Becoming a family therapist*. New York: Human Science.

Lederer, W. J., & Jackson, D. D. (1968). *The mirages of marriage*. New York: Norton.

Sager, C. J. (1976). *Marriage contracts and couple therapy*. New York: Brunner/Mazel.

A. D. COMPAAN

See FAMILY LIFE CYCLE.

Marriage Counseling. Marital counseling or marital therapy (which are treated synonymously) is treatment aimed at improving a troubled marriage of a partner or a couple who have sought help for that purpose. Marital therapy aims at improving a troubled relationship, not at the individual fulfillment, satisfaction, or happiness of either partner. In marital therapy the client is the relationship. Individuals may have to make some sacrifices to achieve the goal they agreed to when they entered marital therapy (i.e., bettering the troubled marriage). In marital therapy partners are counseled to give up destructive patterns of interaction and replace them with more constructive patterns of interaction. In successful marital therapy, such behavior change occurs and attitudes toward marriage become more positive, love is rekindled, hope and faith are restored, and effort to maintain and improve the relationship is renewed. Marital therapy can be conducted with an individual, if the clear focus of treatment is on the marriage and not the individual.

Marital therapy is not marriage enrichment, which aims to help already well-functioning relationships. In marital therapy partners acknowledge their need of treatment. In marital enrichment some couples may have troubled marriages but couples do not acknowledge that they need treatment.

Marital therapy is not two-person group therapy. Group therapy is conducted with a group that has neither history nor future outside of the purpose of the ad hoc group. In group therapy individual goals are pursued. Group members are usually cautioned not to interact with each other outside of the group. Marital therapies assume ongoing interaction between partners.

Marital therapy is not family therapy. Since the rise of family systems theory in the 1960s, the field has been known as marital and family therapy, suggesting a kinship. Until recently most theories of marital therapy have been derived from family therapies. For example, Jacobson and Gurman (1985) summarized marital systems therapies, marital therapy a la Bowen, structural marital therapy, and strategic marital therapy, each derived from a family therapy. Only one exception, behavioral marital therapy, was not derived from family therapy. Numerous approaches to marital therapy are independent of family therapy. For instance, in Jacobson and Gurman's (1995) textbook, chapters by Greenberg and Johnson (emotionally focused marital therapy), Wile (ego-analytic marital therapy), Scharff (psychoanalytic marital therapy), Baucom, Epstein, and Rankin (cognitive-behavioral marital therapy), and Christenson, Jacobson, and Babcock (integrative behavioral couple therapy) show little influence of family therapies, while only two (Bowen; problem and solution-focused) therapies have significant ties to family therapy. Systems theory—weakened by postmodern, noncausal philosophy and by the attacks of angry family members who feel blamed when a child's psychopathology is attributed to the family system—has largely fallen into disuse among marital therapists. Marital and family therapies have separated and divorce is near (Alexander, Holtzworth-Munroe, & Jameson, 1994).

Marital therapy is not couple therapy. Jacobson and Gurman (1995) reconceptualized the field from marital to couple therapy because the diversity of marriagelike relationships includes cohabiting, divorcing, remarrying, and homosexual couples. Marital therapy is a distinct subcategory of couple therapy. Married partners (including those who are considering divorce and those who are remarried) have a legal commitment to each other, a commitment to vows taken before God, and a special, biblically approved status as being a metaphor for the Christian's faithful and committed relationship with God and Christ's commitment to the church (Eph. 5:27–29). Cohabiting and homosexual couples do not meet all of those criteria.

Christian marital counselors recently have published articles and books describing theory. Theories of Christian marital therapy have been heavily cognitive-behavioral. Wright (1981, 1994), Friesen and Friesen (1994), Harley (1994), Stanley and Trathen (1994), and Worthington (1994) all show heavy influences of cognitive-behavioral or behavioral marital therapies, although all are somewhat eclectic. Other approaches to marital counseling have been advocated: pastoral approaches (Joy, 1994; Worthington & McMurry, 1994), psychoanalytically informed approaches (Guernsey, 1994), communication-based approaches (Oliver & Miller, 1994), adaptation of Bowen's systems theory (Parrott & Parrott, 1996), and sex therapy (Penner & Penner, 1990).

Most writing about marriage and marital therapy with Christians occurs in mass-market books aimed at the general population. Although those books influence ideas among lay people and thus are an invaluable ministry, they do not lead to rapid advances in Christian marital therapy. Christian marital therapy will continue to progress, but it will be a weak stepsister of secular marital therapy as long as Christian professionals do not exchange ideas and research at the professional level.

Modern modifications of marital therapy include the following three considerations. Therapies will become briefer. Marital therapies may become reimbursable by third-party payers. Marital therapy traditionally has not been considered a health problem and has thus not been reimbursable by third-party payers. But marital troubles affect people's productivity at work, and with the increase in involvement of businesses and managed mental health care companies, the door is open for reimbursement under some managed health care agreements with employers. The popularity of brief therapies will affect not only professional but also pastoral and lay counselors. Many couples will not receive the help they need in brief marital therapy. Many couples may seek help from pastors. Already overworked, pastors will probably create more congregational programs to help marriages—premarital, neomarital, marriage enrichment, lay marital counseling, and marriage mentorship programs.

As those programs develop, they will inevitably affect marital therapy as practiced by pastors and counselors, either sending more couples to marital counselors or siphoning potential clients from marital therapy because the laity is performing counseling that is currently done by professionals.

Marital counseling continues to be the most requested mental health treatment (Benner, 1992). With changes in divorce rate, social mores (such as acceptance of cohabitation), financial arrangements for counseling, demands for brief treatments with demonstrated effectiveness, the landscape is changing. Marital therapists must adapt or the specialty will perish.

References

Alexander, J. F., Holtzworth-Munroe, A., & Jameson, P. B. (1994). The process and outcome of marital and family therapy: Research review and evaluation. In A. E. Bergin & S. L. Garfield (Eds.), *Handbook of psychotherapy and behavior change* (4th ed.). New York: Wiley.

Benner, D. G. (1992). *Strategic pastoral counseling: A short-term structured model.* Grand Rapids, MI: Baker.

Friesen, D. D., & Friesen, R. M. (1994). Our approach to marriage counseling. *Journal of Psychology and Christianity, 13,* 109–116.

Guernsey, D. B. (1994). Christian marriage counseling. *Journal of Psychology and Christianity, 13,* 117–124.

Harley, W. F., Jr. (1994). My approach to marriage counseling. *Journal of Psychology and Christianity, 13,* 125–132.

Jacobson, N. S., & Gurman, A. S. (Eds.). (1985). *Clinical handbook of marital therapy.* New York: Guilford.

Jacobson, N. S., & Gurman, A. S. (Eds.). (1995). *Clinical handbook of couple therapy.* New York: Guilford.

Joy, D. M. (1994). Marriage counseling. *Journal of Psychology and Christianity, 13,* 143–150.

Oliver, G. J., & Miller, S. (1994). Couple communication. *Journal of Psychology and Christianity, 13,* 151–157.

Parrott, L. III, & Parrott, L. (1996). Relationship development. In E. L. Worthington, Jr. (Ed.), *Christian marital counseling: Eight approaches to understanding and helping couples with problems.* Grand Rapids, MI: Baker.

Penner, J. J., & Penner, C. L. (1990). *Counseling for sexual disorders.* Dallas: Word.

Stanley, S. M., & Trathen, D. W. (1994). Christian PREP: An empirically based model for marital and premarital intervention. *Journal of Psychology and Christianity, 13,* 158–165.

Worthington, E. L., Jr. (1994). Marriage counseling: A Christian approach. *Journal of Psychology and Christianity, 13,* 166–173.

Worthington, E. L., Jr., & McMurry, D. (1994). *Marriage conflicts.* Grand Rapids, MI: Baker.

Wright, H. N. (1981). *Marital counseling: A biblical, behavioral, cognitive approach.* San Francisco: Harper & Row.

Wright, H. N. (1994). Marital counseling. *Journal of Psychology and Christianity, 13,* 174–181.

E. L. Worthington, Jr.

See Marital Contract Therapy; Family Types.

Marriage Enrichment. It is ironic that in the United States, a country known to promote the pursuit of excellence, many couples often settle for mediocre or poor marriages. If half of the schools or Fortune 500 companies failed, the country would be in a panic. But when more than half of all first marriages end in divorce, too many people are willing to passively accept it as the price we must pay for personal success and fulfillment.

We live in a day of increased stress and rapid social change. Many of the values and social influences that used to keep couples together have deteriorated or no longer exist. The culture glamorizes courtship and the wedding ceremony but after that the main question is, How long will it last?

Marital disharmony continues to be a major social and spiritual problem. Troubled marriages often appear to be the rule, not the exception. For many years the primary source of help for couples was to be found at the office of the pastor or marriage counselor, and most of the time help was sought only after the problems had grown to the point of threatening the relationship.

Only a generation ago most people did not know about marriage enrichment, let alone why it might be important. Marriage enrichment is far from the fad that many thought would soon disappear. For example, since 1977, Family Life, a ministry of Campus Crusade for Christ, has had close to a half million people attend their marriage conferences.

Since the 1970s marriage enrichment has become a major attempt to solve the problem of failing marriages and stagnant relationships. Although marriage counseling can be helpful and will continue to be a necessary option, a growing number of people are committed to strengthening their marriages.

Historical Development. Since 1962 marriage enrichment has grown from a few scattered attempts to strengthen marriages to a national movement that has led to a new mindset as to the nature and importance of the marriage relationship. While the roots of marriage enrichment are varied, the first programs were church-related. Some of the earliest structured activity that could be called marriage enrichment can be traced to the pioneer work of David and Vera Mace, begun in 1962 with the Society of Friends (Quakers). In 1964 Leon Smith began the Marriage Communication Labs through the United Methodist Church.

In 1967 Catholic Marriage Encounter was brought to the United States from Spain, where it had been started in 1962 by Father Gabriel Calvo. The Association of Couples for Marriage Enrichment (ACME) was founded in 1973 by the Maces to provide weekend retreats; offer local, statewide, and national meetings; and publish a monthly newsletter.

Several factors have contributed to the sustained growth of the marriage enrichment movement. These include the high divorce rate; the knowledge that many marriages could have been saved if couples had been given insights and skills before the problems grew out of control; the realization that more than remedial counseling is needed; the fact that many stable and surviving marriages are not happy ones; and the growing shift in society's view of marriage from that of a static institution to that of a dynamic, growing relationship that needs to be nurtured and cherished if it is to grow.

Hundreds of preventive programs involving millions of couples can be grouped under the heading of marriage enrichment. There are national organizations whose sole purpose is to provide marriage enrichment programs, and there are thousands of resources that individual couples can use on their own to strengthen and enrich their relationship.

What Is Marriage Enrichment? Marriage enrichment is a term that covers a wide variety of activities. This makes a concise definition difficult. A functional definition of marriage enrichment might be any formal or informal program, exercise, or activity designed to build and strengthen marriage relationships. Marriage enrichment can be a program in which couples participate, an activity in which a couple engages, a perspective a couple adopts, and a commitment a couple makes.

It is important to distinguish marriage enrichment from marriage counseling. While marriage counseling has more of a remedial and reconstructive emphasis, enrichment emphasizes primary prevention, promoting growth, and maximizing relational potential. Marriage enrichment is based on the belief that all relationships are functioning at a fraction of their relational potential and that every relationship has potential for growth. Enrichment goes beyond mere maintenance and emphasizes the growth concept of how to develop new, more satisfying behaviors and increase mutual understanding.

Most enrichment programs are for couples who perceive their marriage as functioning fairly well and who wish to go beyond the status quo to make their relationship the best it can be. Marriage enrichment means refusing to settle for less than a warm, loving, creative relationship. It involves a proactive commitment and determination on the part of both partners to appropriate all the potential they possess and to build together the kind of shared life they want.

Does Marriage Enrichment Work? For years critics asked, Does marriage enrichment work? Considerable research has been conducted on the effectiveness of various aspects of different programs, and more than 100 doctoral dissertations focus on researching the effectiveness of marriage enrichment.

A review of the literature (Alexander, Holtzworth-Munroe, & Jameson, 1994) on marital enrichment and prevention programs cites several studies demonstrating that enrichment and prevention programs do have positive effects on relationships that do not seem to be attributable to placebo factors.

Are all enrichment experiences positive? Given the growing number of nonprofessional programs, some of which are led by charismatic leaders who may encourage an emotionally intense pressure for disclosure and conformity, it should be no surprise that some marriage enrichment programs can have negative effects (Doherty, Lester, & Leigh, 1986). However, a meta-analysis of 85 studies of premarital, marital, and family enrichment representing 3,886 couples or families showed that on average marriage enrichment programs led to significant improvements and that these gains often were sustained for many months (Giblin, Sprenkle, & Sheehan, 1985).

In their decade review of marital and family enrichment research, Guerney and Maxson (1990) conclude that "there is no doubt that, on the whole, enrichment programs work and the field is an entirely legitimate one. No more research or interpretive energy needs to be devoted to that basic concern."

Forms of Marriage Enrichment. One of the many positive aspects of marriage enrichment is the wide variety of ways in which it can be experienced. The various kinds of experiences can be grouped into two general categories: formal programs and informal activities and exercises.

Formal Programs. The most common form of marriage enrichment involves structured programs, seminars, and workshops offered on a weekend or over several weeks. The process usually involves a group of couples meeting together and listening to presentations and participating in exercises under the direction of trained leaders. Although the majority are presented live, an increasing number of programs are available on film and videocassettes.

These formal programs vary along such dimensions as time format (weekend or several weeks); the number, training, and style of leaders; the composition of participants (by age, socioeconomic status, denominational affiliation, or stages of marriage); degree of structure; content emphasis (love, communication, conflict resolution, sexual fulfillment, intimacy, expectations, differences, roles, decision making, goals, and values); teaching methods used (lecture or group techniques); and kinds of follow-up, if any. Three of the most successful programs that illustrate many of these variables are the Marriage Enrichment Retreat, Marriage Encounter, and Couple Communication.

The Marriage Enrichment Retreat was developed by the Maces and is offered through the Association of Couples for Marriage Enrichment. The leaders of a retreat are a couple whose role is to serve as facilitators. Each retreat is different, depending on the couples involved. The structure is flexible. Participants are told to design the program on the basis of their needs and concerns. At the beginning of the retreat couples are given three ground rules: no confrontation, share experiences rather than opinions, and try not to analyze others. From this point the couples collectively make a list of concerns that will become the agenda for the weekend. A sample list might include making decisions together, lack of intimacy, sexual fulfillment, expressing negative emotions, roles of husband and wife, and showing appreciation. After a weekend retreat couples are encouraged to participate in monthly follow-up groups.

Probably the best known form of marriage enrichment is the Marriage Encounter. Initially introduced by the Roman Catholic church, it now includes Baptist, Lutheran, Episcopal, and other expressions of Encounter. The format continues to be the same. The leaders of an Encounter are several couples who give 10 to 12 lectures over the course of the weekend. Each presentation introduces the 20 to 30 participating couples to a basic part of the weekend, the dialogue technique. At the end of each presentation each person is instructed to go somewhere alone and, after a time of personal reflection, to write his or her feelings in a notebook. Spouses then exchange notebooks and read what the other has written. This is followed by the spouses' verbal communication of their feelings to each other in greater depth.

The Couple Communication program is one of the most widely researched and effective of the formal programs available. The four highly structured three-hour sessions are conducted over several weeks. The content is communication. The trained leaders direct an average of seven couples through lecture, video examples, role play, and group interaction while they work through the text *Talking and Listening Together* (Miller, Miller, Nunnally, & Wackman, 1991). Couples are given simple yet effective homework so that they can practice the skills they have just learned. The program emphasizes insights and practical skills to help spouses develop more effective ways of talking and listening, better understanding of self and partner, more enjoyment of one another, new ways of being intimate, and improved parent-child communication.

In addition to these three programs a wide variety of other formal programs and a range of resources can be offered by both professionals and nonprofessionals to groups of couples.

Informal Activities and Resources. These programs differ from formal programs in that they involve individual couples pursuing enrichment on their own. A few couples may meet together in a home or a group sponsored by a local church or community organization. The content usually involves resources such as books, videotapes, and magazines.

Books such as *Communication: Key to Your Marriage* (Wright, 1974, Regal), *Building Your Mate's Self-Esteem* (Rainey & Rainey, 1986, Here's Life), and *How to Change Your Spouse (Without Ruining Your Marriage)* (Wright & Oliver, 1994, Servant) provide couples with insights and specific exercises they can do on their own.

In the 1980s and 1990s videotapes have become an especially popular tool for marriage enrichment. Tape series such as *The Marriage Renewal Series* (Gospel Light) by H. Norman Wright and *Hidden Keys to Loving Relationships* (Gary Smalley Seminars, Inc.) by Gary Smalley can be watched by individuals or groups and then discussed at a convenient time. Magazines such as *Marriage Partnership* and *Christian Parenting Today* give readers encouraging stories and practical tips for building strong relationships and equipping the Christian home.

Conclusion. Aldrich (1981) has written that "the two greatest forces in evangelism are a healthy church and a healthy marriage. The two are interdependent. You can't have one without the other. It is the healthy marriage, however, which is the 'front lines weapon.' The Christian family in a community is the ultimate evangelistic tool, assuming the home circle is an open one in which the beauty of the Gospel is readily available. It's the old story: when love is seen, the message is heard" (p. 20).

Marriage enrichment is a maturing movement that continues to have an increasingly significant impact in millions of marriages. Many church leaders have come to understand the significant implications of marriage enrichment to help accomplish what God designed marriage to be. Marriage enrichment not only helps to save and strengthen many marriages; it also helps to build strong families and strong churches and provides a powerful witness to the reality of the difference that Jesus Christ can make in a marriage relationship.

References

Aldrich, J. (1981). *Life-style evangelism.* Portland, OR: Multnomah.

Alexander, J. F., Holtzworth-Munroe, A., & Jameson, P. B. (1994). The process and outcome of marital and family therapy: Research review and evaluation. In A. E. Bergin & S. L. Garfield (Eds.), *Handbook of psychotherapy and behavior change* (4th ed.). New York: Wiley.

Doherty, W. J., Lester, M. E., & Leigh, G. (1986). Marriage encounter weekends: Couples who win and couples who lose. *Journal of Marital and Family Therapy, 12,* 49–61.

Giblin, P., Sprenkel, D. H., & Sheehan, R. (1985). Enrichment outcome research: A meta-analysis of premarital, marital and family interventions. *Journal of Marital and Family Therapy, 11,* 257–280.

Guerney, B., & Maxson, P. (1990). Marital and family enrichment research: A decade review and look ahead. *Journal of Marriage & the Family, 52,* 1127–1135.

Lambert, M. J., & Bergin, A. E. (1994). The effectiveness of psychotherapy. In A. E. Bergin & S. L. Garfield (Eds.), *Handbook of psychotherapy and behavior change* (4th ed.). New York: Wiley.

Miller, S., Miller, P., Nunnally, E. W., & Wackman, D. (1991). *Couple communication I: Talking and listening together.* Littleton, CO: Interpersonal Communication Programs, Inc.

G. J. Oliver

See Marital Health and Pathology; Family Therapy: Overview.

Marriage Preparation. *See* Premarital Counseling.

Maslow, Abraham Harold (1908–1970). Influential humanistic psychologist, founder of the American Association for Humanistic Psychology, known now as the Association for Humanistic Psychology. Maslow obtained the Ph.D. degree at the University of Wisconsin, was departmental chairman at Brandeis University, and in 1967 served as president of the American Psychological Association. He authored some 150 publications over a 38-year period of productivity, culminating in his final work, *The Farther Reaches of Human Nature* (1971).

Maslow sought a theory of human nature beyond the interpretation of psychoanalysis and behaviorism. In 1961 he founded, with Anthony Sutich, the *Journal of Humanistic Psychology*. The humanistic movement within psychology was termed third force psychology, and following the lead provided by Maslow has been concerned with such topics as love, creativity, self-actualization, meaning, responsibility, and values.

Maslow's perspective has been variously described as holistic-integrative (Bischof, 1964), holistic-dynamic (Hall & Lindzey, 1978), organismic (Misiak & Sexton, 1966), and self-actualization theory (Cofer & Appley, 1964). His classical article, "A Theory of Human Motivation" (1943), was subsequently reprinted in 22 works by other authors. A complete bibliography of Maslow's works is contained in Appendix E of *The Farther Reaches of Human Nature*.

Basic Theories. Maslow claims his motivational theory fuses the functional tradition of William James and John Dewey with the holism of Max Wertheimer, Kurt Goldstein and Gestalt psychology, as well as the dynamism of Sigmund Freud, Erich Fromm, Karen Horney, Reich, Carl Gustav Jung, and Alfred Adler (Maslow, 1970, p. 35). He believes there are seven broad classes of basic, instinctual needs, hierarchically arranged in that a person proceeds up the ladder to higher needs once lower needs have been met. At the bottom of the hierarchy are the physiological needs, homeostatic in nature (e.g., hunger and thirst). Next come safety needs, concerned with security, safety, protection, freedom from fear and chaos, as well as the need for structure, order, and law. Next come belongingness and love needs, followed by the esteem needs, the requirement of achievement, confidence, independence, recognition. This is followed by the need for self-actualization and the desire to know and understand. Finally, at the top of the hierarchy, are found the aesthetic needs, the craving to experience beauty (Maslow, 1970).

Convinced that human values can be found within human nature with no need to appeal to external sources, Maslow concluded that a study of supposedly fully actualized people would provide direction for those less self-actualized. He therefore compiled a list of such individuals and studied their character traits. Maslow believed that the negative criterion of self-actualization is the absence of neurosis, psychopathic personality, psychosis, or strong tendencies in those directions, and the positive criterion is the full utilization of talents, capacities, and potentialities (Maslow, 1970).

Analysis of the group of self-actualized people identified by these criteria yielded such characteristics as more efficient perception of reality; acceptance of self and others; having a mission in life; autonomy and independence of cultural thinking; aesthetic appreciation of people and of nature; compassion for and empathy with humanity; strong moral and ethical convictions; creativeness, originality, and inventiveness; and frequent enjoyment of peak experiences. In a later work Maslow (1971) distinguished between two kinds of self-actualizers: transcendent and nontranscendent. Nontranscendent actualizers are pragmatically oriented, whereas transcendent actualizers have higher, mystical, contemplative insights.

In contrasting healthy with unhealthy growth Maslow used the terms *Being-cognition* and *Deficiency-cognition*, and the correlative concepts of B-love and D-love. In B-love, characteristic of self-actualizing people, there are qualities of openness and nondefensiveness, fusion of sex and love, care and responsibility, greater perceptiveness of the one loved, and a nonpossessive, unselfish admiration of the one loved. Peak experiences, common with self-actualizing people, include aesthetic, creative, love, insight, and mystic experiences (Maslow, 1968).

A test of Maslow's self-actualization concept has been devised (Shostrom, 1963), and his theory has been applied to education theory, industrial management, and social reform (Goble, 1970). Maslow himself envisioned a psychological utopia in which all basic human needs would be met, a Taoist, loving society that he called *Eupsychia* (Maslow, 1970).

Critique. From a Christian perspective Maslow's views of human nature, needs, and motivation suffer from several limitations. First, his philosophical position is that of atheistic, naturalistic humanism. Maslow rejects any source of information concerning human purpose that lies outside human endeavor. He dismisses divine revelation, stating that the scientist pays "as little attention" to theological norms as to any other (Maslow, 1970, p. 267). He believes human nature to be intrinsically good, invariably and spontaneously directed to the good; evil results from the frustration of this nature, and such frustration is largely due to society (Maslow, 1968).

Maslow overlooks the question of why supposedly good people who make up society frustrate others. He wrestles with the question of whether destructive and evil behavior is instinctual, concluding that we do not know enough, or the research data are insufficient, to reach a conclusion (1970). For the Christian these difficulties are resolved through divine revelation, wherein the origin of evil is explained as consequent to humankind's rebellion against God (Hammes, 1978).

Maslow's rejection of fallen human nature leads him to believe there is no opposition between head and heart, reason and instinct; the rule to follow is, "Be healthy and then you may trust your impulses" (1970, p. 179). The Christian, to the contrary, recognizes the struggle between the tendency toward good and the inclination toward evil, a continuing battle between the law of the spirit and the law of the flesh (Rom. 7:14–25), a contest that can be won not through natural means but rather through the supernatural strength of life in Christ.

This difference in perception is related also to self-actualization. Maslow endorses growth on the natural plane, whereas the Christian recognizes self-actualization to be necessary and even more important on the supernatural level. For Christians self-actualization means to become more Christlike, to the point of proclaiming that no longer they, but rather Christ, lives in them (Gal. 2:20; 3:27). The concept of love, too, is given greater depth and dimension in Christian thinking, going beyond Maslow's admirable treatise on the natural level to the supernatural height of loving to the point of death and loving one's enemies as well (John 15:13; Matt. 5:44; Luke 6:27–28).

A further contrast lies in the treatment of humanity's basic needs. To Maslow's seven the Christian would add an eighth, the need for a personal Absolute, the source and embodiment of ultimate truth, beauty, and goodness, in whose image human beings were made and whom they must eventually love if they are to attain complete and perfect self-actualization.

These observations do not demean Maslow, who has carried naturalistic humanism as far as it can be developed, but rather show that Christian humanism more adequately presents the human condition and its solution. Only through him who is the way, the truth, and the life (John 14:6), as well as the light of the world (John 8:12; 9:5), can humankind attain its perfection on earth and its eternal destiny hereafter.

References

Bischof, L. J. (1964). *Interpreting personality theories*. New York: Harper & Row.

Cofer, C. N., & Appley, M. H. (1964). *Motivation: Theory and research*. New York: Wiley.

Goble, F. G. (1970). *The third force*. New York: Grossman.

Hall, C. S., & Lindzey, G. (1978). *Theories of personality* (3rd ed.). New York: Wiley.

Hammes, J. A. (1978). *Human destiny: Exploring today's value systems*. Huntington, IN: Our Sunday Visitor.

Maslow, A. H. (1943). A theory of human motivation. *Psychological Review, 50,* 370–396.

Maslow, A. H. (1968). *Toward a psychology of being* (2nd ed.). Princeton, NJ: Van Nostrand.

Maslow, A. H. (1970). *Motivation and personality* (2nd ed.). New York: Harper & Row.

Maslow, A. H. (1971). *The farther reaches of human nature*. New York: Viking.

Misiak, H., & Sexton, V. S. (1966). *History of psychology.* New York: Grune & Stratton.

Shostrom, E. L. (1963). *Personal orientation inventory.* San Diego, CA: Educational & Industrial Testing Service.

J. A. HAMMES

See HUMANISTIC PSYCHOLOGY; TRANSPERSONAL PSYCHOLOGY; SELF-ACTUALIZATION.

Masochism. *See* SEXUAL MASOCHISM.

Mass Evangelism. The use of communications media to convey the gospel of Jesus Christ to large numbers of people in efforts to persuade them to become Christians. The media include television, radio, movies, and newspapers. Mass evangelism is comparatively indiscriminate in its targeting, although selective viewing and the advent of public television have resulted in some narrowing of the audience.

Although there have been some positive results from the use of mass communications, the failure of the church to understand the strengths and weaknesses of these approaches often results in haphazard evangelism strategy that is costly and relatively ineffective.

In general, mass communication rarely brings about major attitude change (Klapper, 1967). People are most likely to expose themselves to presentations with which they agree and to avoid those messages that challenge their beliefs. This is especially true for those attitudes that are central to a person's identity and are expressive of his or her fundamental values. Changing a central belief has change repercussions throughout a person's belief system. Such changes create uncertainty and anxiety until the implications of a new set of core beliefs can be perceived and worked through in the self-image, decisions, and behaviors of the person. As a result, people usually ignore, distort, or forget messages that threaten a centrally important belief.

The implications of this for mass evangelism are significant. The likelihood that those who are uninterested in Christianity, for whatever reason, will choose to be exposed to evangelistic messages is minimal. Second, the probability of causing a major change in the core values of the viewer is small. Those who are not antagonistic to Christianity in general but do not wish to respond positively to appeals for fundamental change will tend to avoid evangelistic programs that are highly persuasion oriented. If their lack of response is due to ego-defensive reasons, some research suggests a boomerang effect may occur in response to persuasive attempts (Katz, 1960). If a communicator is unaware of the recipient's attitudinal base, he or she may unwittingly stimulate resistance to subsequent presentation of the gospel. Further, the fact that emotional arousal is normally crucial for radical change to occur militates against mass conversions. These factors suggest that the format and content of mass evangelistic appeals need to include channels of persuasion beyond the purely cognitive and that the content needs to be focused primarily toward those who are interested in Christianity and open to the possibility of change.

The increased use of music and drama as means of connection with the emotional roots of religious belief increases the likelihood that viewers will listen and the possibility that conversion will occur among the interested. The development of content designed to identify with the life context of typical viewers who are interested in Christianity and showing how commitment to Christianity helps meet their needs would be more effective than appeals for change that are abstract and theological. Since mass communication is relatively unsuccessful in effecting a major change in the unsaved person's attitudinal core, it would be better to direct the bulk of mass communication efforts to building bridges of relevancy and aiming toward modification of existing attitudes. Such modification would soften a person's attitude for future conversion.

This is not to say that people cannot be converted through mass evangelistic appeals. However, awareness of the fact that spiritual decision making is a process (Engel, 1975) and that those most likely to be saved normally have at least a positive attitude toward the gospel is important for effective programming strategy. Regarding those who are more neutral or uninterested in Christianity, attitude modification and exposure to basic, positive aspects of the Judeo-Christian faith should be the goal.

In cultures where the masses are relatively unaware of the basics of Christianity and have no opinion about it, research suggests mass communication can be used successfully to bring about radical conversions. This is due to the fact that mass communication has been found to be highly effective in creating attitudes about topics on which a person had no previous opinion (Klapper, 1967). Although the potential for foreign missions may be significant, the response of a person to persuasion attempts will depend upon his or her felt need, the extent to which the message addresses that need, whether the change required is seen as antagonistic to other cultural mores, and whether the mode of communication connects with the person's primary channel of receptivity (abstract versus concrete thinking; emotion versus cognition; aural versus visual). While making certain that biblical principles are not compromised, missionaries should make every effort to adapt the message of Christ to those values and beliefs that are prevalent in a particular culture.

The fact that mass communication serves as an agent of reinforcement for the attitudes, opinions, and behavioral tendencies that viewers already possess further suggests an important role for mass communications in evangelism follow-up. Programs designed to identify with and nurture the spiritual development of new believers could be highly effective.

References

Engel, J. F. (1975). World evangelization: A myth, a dream, or a reality? *Spectrum, 1,* 4–6.

Katz, D. (1960). The functional approach to the study of attitudes. *Public Opinion Quarterly, 24,* 163–204.

Klapper, J. T. (1967). Mass communication, attitude stability, and change. In C. W. Sherif & M. Sherif (Eds.), *Attitude, ego-involvement, and change.* New York: Wiley.

C. W. ELLISON

See COMMUNICATION; COMMUNICATION, NONVERBAL; GROUP DYNAMICS.

Masturbation. Also called autoeroticism, masturbation is any type of self-stimulation that produces erotic arousal. It is a sexual behavior that is frequently discussed (with opinions ranging from unqualified condemnation to total acceptance as a gift from God) and practiced commonly from infancy through senescence (Oraker, 1980). Further, masturbation may be one of the most important ways individuals learn about their own sexuality. Still, it would be fair to say that masturbation evokes ambivalent and confusing feelings for many Christians (see Jones & Jones, 1993).

Under certain circumstances masturbation should clearly be considered a maladaptive behavior. In some forms of psychosis, mental retardation, and serious childhood disorders, masturbation can become a stereotyped part of a limited behavioral repertoire. It potentially leads to extreme withdrawal and disengagement, factors that can certainly contribute to the maintenance of psychopathology. For less disturbed individuals it can become obsessive (preoccupation with sexual fantasies), compulsive (one's masturbatory habits become highly ritualized), or guilt-producing (fear that one has violated an important standard of behavior). Such psychological consequences can become deeply disturbing on a personal level and cause much distress and discomfort or even despair. For other people, masturbation can become a problem when it is utilized as the sole method for sexual fulfillment when other opportunities are unavailable (i.e., a marital partner). Other authors contend that suppression of the natural tendency to masturbate is far more likely to lead to an emotional or sexual problem (McCary, 1978).

The history of popular and professional opinion about masturbation has often been one of ignorance, pseudoscience, and hysteria. The most frequently cited arguments against masturbation are that only the immature person masturbates; it is condemned in Scripture; masturbation is unsociable or antisocial; it violates the divinely intended purpose of sex; it causes fatigue and physical debilitation; it is a manifestation of low self-control; the fantasies associated with masturbation are emotionally unhealthy; it is sexually frustrating and not as satisfying as sex relations with a marital partner; it is an indication of selfishness; and it leads to undesirable feelings (guilt, anxiety, fear, depression). These arguments have been carefully critiqued by a number of Christian authors (Johnson, 1982; Jones & Jones, 1993; Sanford, 1994). Most arguments against masturbation appear to be oversimplified or false. Jones and Jones conclude that "we can neither regard it is an unquestionably and intrinsically evil act, nor as a blessing from God which we were meant to enjoy with clear consciences" (p. 195).

Those persons familiar with the treatment literature on the psychosexual dysfunctions realize masturbatory techniques are often used to increase awareness about one's own sexuality (Bird & Bird, 1976; Kaplan, 1974). Persons who because of a lifetime of sexual taboos and restrictions are not able to respond freely or completely to sexual stimulation are encouraged to explore and experiment with their own bodies in order to discover that which gives them pleasure. The assumption is that this awareness will improve marital communication, increase arousal and responsiveness prior to genital intercourse, and lead to greater sexual satisfaction for both partners. For those not yet married but intending to marry, such self-exploration can help develop physical sensitivities and potentially contribute to improved body images and self-concepts. For many people such acceptance of masturbation is often slow to develop. Although there may be intellectual understanding that autoeroticism may be acceptable in certain situations, they may continue to feel that it is unhealthy or morally wrong. The transition to the marital relationship may be more challenging and difficult for these individuals in terms of their psychosexual functioning.

Moral concern about masturbation ought to focus on its role in the person's total development toward a wholesome heterosexual life (Smedes, 1976). Adolescence and the transition into adulthood are highly significant stages in personal identity development, especially for the coalescence of personal integrity and the consolidation of sexual identity (Kennedy, 1977). Healthy attitudes about masturbation may contribute to the transition from narcissism to relationships with others in a mature, egalitarian, and intimate manner. As Jones and Jones (1993) observe, "[t]here is probably more suffering caused in Christian circles by overreactions to masturbation than there is by the practice itself" (p. 196).

For this reason Kennedy (1977) argues that sensitive counseling is extremely significant; overgeneralized advice or ill-conceived stands for or against masturbation may not foster development in the long run. Further, since the Bible says nothing directly about masturbation, it is difficult to take a dogmatic stand (Johnson, 1982). However, since masturbation is usually a solitary activity, it would be seen by many to fall short of the sexual expression intended by God (Sanford, 1994). The Bible has a high view of sexuality as part of a relationship, and excessive masturbation could certainly distract one from the wholeness of relationships.

Masturbation must therefore be seen within the developmental context of the person's drive toward intimate communion, where one has the other person's interests and fulfillment in mind. Counselors must be prepared to respond to persons across the life span who share conflicts, misgivings, or uncertainties associated with masturbation. In order to do this effectively, the counselor must clarify personal feelings about personal sexuality, including masturbation, and respond with understanding and compassion. A calm ability to let persons investigate their conflicts and their own shame and anxiety is extremely healing for persons of whatever age or situation. The greatest service that can be done for the person who struggles with concerns about masturbation is to listen without embarrassment or the need to judge. Such a response can help those persons rebuild their self-esteem and potentially propel them into more meaningful and satisfying interpersonal relationships. The counselor should model the assurance of God's grace, confident that it is total and unconditional.

References

Bird, J., & Bird, L. (1976). *Sexual loving.* Garden City, NY: Doubleday.

Johnson, J. R. (1982). Towards a biblical approach to masturbation. *Journal of Psychology and Theology, 10* (2), 1237–146.

Jones, S., & Jones, B. (1993). *How and when to tell your kids about sex.* Colorado Springs, CO: NavPress.

Kaplan, H. S. (1974). *The new sex therapy.* New York: Brunner/Mazel.

Kennedy, E. (1977). *Sexual counseling.* New York: Seabury.

McCary, J. L. (1978). *McCary's human sexuality* (3rd ed.). New York: Van Nostrand.

Oraker, J. R. (1980). *Almost grown.* San Francisco: Harper & Row.

Sanford, K. (1994). Towards a masturbatory ethic. *Journal of Psychology and Theology, 22* (1) 21–28.

Smedes, L. (1976). *Sex for Christians.* Grand Rapids, MI: Eerdmans.

R. E. BUTMAN

See SEXUALITY.

Mate Choice. The choice of a spouse has become a matter of extreme importance to young adults. With soaring divorce rates and broken families now common, the possibility of marrying the wrong person creates anxiety, well founded or not, among those contemplating marriage.

The terms *mating* and *mating behavior* are often used for the sexual rituals of animals, and one may find some literature on human behavior in which mate selection refers to the choice of casual sexual partners. But most literature and research on mate choice among humans has to do with how and why persons select particular partners for marriage and the enduring commitment traditionally expected.

Cultural differences are striking. It is well known to anthropologists and to Western missionaries in other cultures that many mates are chosen not by one another but by their families. In some Eastern societies it is done traditionally by parents; it is possible that bride and groom never meet one another before the marriage ceremony. In these arranged marriages there is often bargaining over what each party shall take (Windemiller, 1976). Marriage brokers may be used—professional matchmakers who know the histories of families, what spouse characteristics are most important, and what is likely to bring the best exchange (bride price, groom price, or dowry). Taking into account these cultural differences, it is less difficult to understand mate choice in biblical narratives (e.g., the story of Jacob, Rachel, and Laban in Genesis 29).

Some Amish living in the United States also reflect a very different mate choice pattern from that of their surrounding society. Dating activities common to most Americans are forbidden (movie going, dancing, athletics), as are drinking and automobiles. Mates may choose each other only from within the Amish community and only with parental permission. Change in mate selection becomes more apparent in most ethnic groups. For example, first-generation Italians coming to America experienced only arranged or tightly controlled courtship, mate choice, and marriage. In the second generation young adults began choosing their own mates, with parental approval. Third-generation young, while still close and proud of their heritage, have adopted American courting patterns, including selection of non-Italian mates (Kephart, 1981).

In some religious groups only God is to select marriage partners. Anxiety is generated among adolescents who hear that "God has one special person for you." The testimonies of Christian couples regarding their stable marriages may heighten this anxiety: "We know that God made us for one another" may be honest in retrospect, but for those facing mate choice there may be no such confidence. Even if there were scriptural support for divine selection of specific mates, pastoral problems with the teaching are immense. Many marriageable persons do not know how to be sure, nor is there adequate help in the process of discovering the divine choice. They conclude, understandably, that it would be a grave mistake or sin to marry anyone not designated by God. Another problem arises when parents insist that one person is the mate of divine choice, while the daughter or son insists that it is another.

In a society where the partners choose one another, courtship is the process; it may include dating, going steady, and engagement. Falling in love is usually the basis for selecting a mate. Falling in love is difficult to define, though there are stages of romantic attraction. While it may have tremendous immediate emotional force, the state of being madly in love seldom endures. It also may produce anxieties at the time of mate choice (Is this *real* love, or just a feeling? I have fallen in love so many times, how will I ever know whom to marry?).

Where choice is most free and love is the criterion, one might expect random mating—anyone selecting anyone. But in fact falling in love respects limits (Kephart, 1981; Windemiller, 1976). The field of eligibles excludes members of one's immediate family. People tend to marry in their own age range. Although interracial marriages are increasing, they are a small minority; we tend to marry persons of the same race. Religion is a selective factor; Catholic and Jewish intermarriage rates are increasing, but there is still substantial opposition in both groups. Protestants intermarry more. Social class (including such factors as intelligence, occupation, income, and education) is very important; most persons marry within their own social class. Geographical propinquity is also highly significant: "The 'one-and-only' may have better than a 50–50 chance of living within walking distance!" (Kephart, 1981, p. 241).

There is a variety of theories about factors in mate choice. Genetic and cultural factors may interact from generation to generation, as Eckland (1968) points out. He divides theories of mate choice into individualistic (Carl Gustav Jung's unconscious archetype; parent image of psychoanalysis: like attracts like; complementary needs) and sociocultural (including such factors as propinquity and values).

Winch (1958, 1967) is largely responsible for the popular theory that needs interact in mate selection. Do likes or opposites attract? As noted, falling in love takes place between persons who are alike in social and cultural ways. Winch urges a concept of complementary needs: each person, in choosing a mate, seeks one who may best meet his or her needs. Pairs of needs such as dominance-submissiveness and nurturance-receptivity are some of those on which spouses may differ but be complementary. It is not so much that opposites attract but that different needs make it possible for individuals to complete one another in the intimacy of marriage (*see* Marital Types).

One final theory of mate choice grows out of the British approach known as object relations theory and is most fully presented by Dicks (1967). Dicks argues that while mate choice often appears to be based in need complementarity, a deeper dynamic is to unconsciously choose a mate and relate to that person on the basis of the relationship between unconscious introjected representations of parents. According to this view, love is the response of recognition of someone who will serve as a good container for the person's projections and who therefore affords the possibility of working through unresolved unconscious conflicts. Because the mate is chosen as a symbol for a lost part of one's own personality, when this part is recognized in another person it leads to attraction. However, these same initially attractive qualities often later become the source of irritation as they represent and tend to resurrect parts of self that are frightening or for some other reason unacceptable. This rather complex theory emphasizes unconscious factors in mate choice but does not eliminate conscious factors suggested by other theories.

References

Dicks, H. V. (1967). *Marital tensions.* New York: Basic.
Eckland, B. K. (1968). Theories of mate selection. *Eugenics Quarterly, 15* (2), 71–84.
Kephart, W. M. (1981). *The family, society, and the individual* (5th ed.). Boston: Houghton Mifflin.
Winch, R. F. (1958). *Mate selection: A study of complementary needs.* New York: Harper & Row.
Winch, R. F. (1967). Another look at the theory of complementary needs in mate selection. *Journal of Marriage and the Family, 29,* 756–762.
Windemiller, D. (1976). *Sexuality, pairing, and family forms.* Cambridge, MA: Winthrop.

H. KLINGBERG, JR.

See MARITAL COMPATIBILITY; MARITAL TYPES; MARITAL HEALTH AND PATHOLOGY.

Maternal Deprivation. Maternal deprivation refers to the absence or impairment of the mother's care between the time of the child's birth to two years of age. Of all environmental stimuli, that provided by the mother is among the most critical to survival and growth. However, there is little recent research on maternal deprivation, possibly due to political and social ramifications.

Despite the possible implications, the idea that the mother is essential to a child's development is one that has long interested us. *The Anglo-Saxon Chronicle* (A.D. 891–924) documents how Emperor Frederick's curiosity led to an experiment. A group of infants were isolated from human speech in order to see what language, if any, they would develop. Wet nurses cared for the infants by performing the bare minimal care necessary while remaining mute. Even though all of the children's physical needs were met, every infant died (Loomis, 1985).

Spitz (1945), a pioneer in psychoanalytic developmental psychology, reported similar findings. He described a syndrome found in institutionalized children that he dubbed hospitalism. Infants were weaned from their mothers at approximately four months of age, kept in sanitary cribs with the sides draped with sheets to avoid drafts, fed and changed by nurses, and visited daily by doctors. They saw no one else. They had no toys and an obviously unstimulating environment. Within only one month, the infants became unresponsive and withdrawn. They showed a progressive decline in intelligence from an average IQ level of 100 at the onset of their

isolation to 76 one year later and 46 two years later (Loomis, 1985).

These children's behavior ranged from extreme anxiety and bizarre stereotyped movements to apathy or profound stupor. Their play was limited to their own fingers and toes. Their physical development was remarkably delayed, as were locomotion and speech. As in Emperor Frederick's experiment, despite daily care, death occurred in about one-fourth of the children. This is significant when compared with no deaths in a parallel nursery group with mothers present and less than one-half percent in the community at large (Loomis, 1985; Spitz, 1945). In the parallel nursery group, the mothers were active with their children, spending a great deal of time with them cuddling, playing, and talking.

Spitz researched another infant syndrome. Infants who had been close to their mothers and were abruptly cut off from them between the sixth and eighth month experienced marked distress. Many of the infants became weepy and then withdrawn, lying in their cribs face down and refusing to acknowledge their surroundings. If the mother did not return or was not replaced by a new maternal figure after about three months, frozen rigidity of expression replaced the withdrawal. These children were much more prone to infections. Spitz called this anaclitic depression. Since not all the children separated from their mothers developed anaclitic depression, Spitz deemed maternal separation to be a necessary but not sufficient cause for its development (Loomis, 1985; Spitz, 1946).

Spitz concluded that children under one year of age receive their capacity to appreciate both inanimate and animate objects and their differentiation from each other through the interaction with their mothers. While the institutionalized children he studied were isolated from almost all visual experiences through solitary confinement in their cribs, Spitz did not judge the critical deprivation to be general perceptual stimulation. Rather, he believed they suffered because they were deprived of human contact (Loomis, 1985; Spitz, 1945).

Children susceptible to maternal deprivation may also include those who see parents work out of the home excessively or whose mothers lack parenting skills and neglect or abuse their children (*see* Abuse and Neglect; Parenting). As in the case of physical separation from the mother, the child's reaction to the deprivation depends on whether the deprivation is continuous or intermittent and the age at which the child is deprived (Breslin, 1984).

Inadequate mothering often occurs when the mother is very young or is from a poor parenting background or when the mother does not want the child. It can also occur when the mother is ill or when there is abnormal interference by circumstances or by other family members. Occasionally maternal deprivation may be due to the inability of the infant to accept the available mothering due to inborn impairment. Also, the problem may be perpetuated by the child's failing to meet maternal expectations, therefore evoking less response from the mother or inviting less spontaneity or initiative otherwise appropriate to normal mothering. Any of these factors can lead to deficiencies in the way a child is fed, held, or cared for. Children from this type of background are more prone to allergies, emotional distress, and poor motor or intellectual development. Most of today's failure-to-thrive infants come from situations such as these. They fail to gain weight or grow at a normal rate, yet they have no known biological problems (Breslin, 1984).

One solution to maternal deprivation found in many cultures is having several caregivers. Foster children are examples of children receiving this treatment. The success of multiple caregivers depends on the specific patterns of interaction between the child and the maternal figures and the type of social structure present. The major differences between the child in a single maternal caregiver situation and a multiple maternal caregiver one are generally within the realm of personality (Breslin, 1984).

The role of the father cannot be ignored. He can be a primary factor in multiple mothering. The concept of paternal leave, granting leave to the father when a new child joins the family, is one that should be encouraged. The two-parent family is beneficial in that each parent can make up for what the other parent may lack.

It is important to note that every child is different. Children react differently to comparable maternal deprivation experiences (Rutter, 1980). What may cause much distress to one child may not create any problems in another. Furthermore, researchers have found that the harmful effects of deprivation are sometimes reversible, depending on the extent of the child's resistance to the stress (Brofenbrenner, 1979). Therefore, we should prevent maternal deprivation at the onset. However, if the child has been maternally deprived, there is hope for recovery.

References

Breslin, F. D. (1984). Maternal deprivation. In R. J. Corsini (Ed.), *Encyclopedia of psychology, 2.* New York: Wiley.

Brofenbrenner, U. (1979). *The ecology of human development.* Cambridge, MA: Harvard University Press.

Loomis, E. A., Jr. (1985). Maternal deprivation. In D. G. Benner (Ed.), *Baker encyclopedia of psychology.* Grand Rapids, MI: Baker.

Rutter, M. (1980). Maternal deprivation, 1972–1978: New findings, new concepts, new approaches. In S. Chess & A. Thomas (Eds.), *Annual progress in child psychiatry and child development.* New York: Brunner/Mazel.

Spitz, R. A. (1945). Hospitalism: An inquiry into the genesis of a psychiatric condition in early childhood. *Psychoanalytic Study of the Child, 1,* 153–172.

Spitz, R. A. (1946). Hospitalism: A follow-up report on the investigation described in volume 1, 1945. *Psychoanalytic Study of the Child, 2,* 113–117.

K. J. Hetrick

See Abuse and Neglect; Parenting.

Mathematical Psychology. The use of mathematical methods to investigate psychological problems. It is not defined in terms of content, such as learning, perception, or motivation. Rather, it is characterized by a style of investigation. This style is not uniform; mathematical psychologists use a variety of methods to investigate different content areas.

The use of mathematical methods dates back to the middle of the nineteenth century, to the work of Gustav Fechner, who looked for the mathematical relation between the mind and the body. During the first half of the twentieth century mathematical methods were used in the measurement of intelligence by Charles Edward Spearman, in the representation of learning by Clark Leonard Hull, and in social psychology by Kurt Lewin. However, it was not until the 1950s that many individuals became involved. In 1963 Luce, Bush, and Galanter edited the *Handbook of Mathematical Psychology.* The *Journal of Mathematical Psychology* began publication in 1964.

The use of mathematics involves selecting a phenomenon to observe, finding a mathematical system to represent it, and establishing the relationship between the two. Some models are algebraic, others are geometric, and still others are probabilistic. Some are stated as computer programs, others as systems of equations, and others in axiomatic form. The advantage of using mathematics is that it increases precision and deductive power. Theories can be stated in a form that is both general and precise. Theorists are forced to state all their assumptions explicitly and derive the consequences of their assumptions logically.

Nearly every area of psychology has been touched by mathematics, but some have been more affected than others. The areas of psychological measurement and scaling are obviously affected by mathematics, as are many learning theories, which are often stated as mathematical models. Theories of sensory processes have been formulated in terms of signal detection theory and cognitive theories are often stated in terms of information processing, both models also strongly reflecting mathematical influence.

R. L. Koteskey

Maturity. In order to better understand the concept of maturity, it would be helpful to define, not only what maturity is, but also, what it is not. Maturity is a process, not a destination. It is a journey, not an arrival point. Maturity is completion and not perfection. Maturity is not the absence of needs or struggles. Essentially, it is a state of completeness blended with a good degree of personhood and wholeness.

To be mature means to be fully developed in mind, body, and soul and fully seasoned in personality as a whole. Maturing is unfolding the inherent talents and abilities, especially what has been latent, dormant, or underdeveloped. It is fulfilling one's potential, attaining a good measure of height, and maintaining the established growth over time. Maturing reflects stability, depth, refinement of character, inner security, and integrity. In other words, it is the process of advancing toward completion and becoming ripe in form and substance.

Some aspects of maturity are time related (like physical maturation). Other aspects are experience related (like emotional maturity). Similar to the global human personality, there are many facets to maturity: intellectual-mental, interpersonal-relational, affective-emotional, spiritual-existential, social-cultural, physiological-physical, adaptive-behavioral, and financial-material. Maturity is a simple concept and a complex phenomenon at once. Most often, people mature in one or two areas faster (or slower) than the others. It all depends on the individual's degree of exposure, influence of others, self-discipline, tolerance of pain, personal worldview, and general life experience. It is worth noting here that maturity can take place, not only on an individual level, but also on familial, communal, and cultural levels as well, though the process may involve different dynamics and broader dimensions.

Spiritual maturity is a process as well. It is not an outcome of one time event. In fact, maturity is not a state of sinlessness but a healthy awareness of one's humanness. Our humanity includes not only the strengths, accomplishments, positive qualities, and bright sides of ourselves but also the weaknesses, limitations, failures, negative qualities, and dark sides (the shadow). Maturity is completion or, more accurately, it is the process of being completed. This principle is well conveyed in 1 Corinthians 1:10 ". . . you be made complete [or united]," and in Philippians 1:6 "For I am confident of this very thing, that He who began a good work in you shall completed it until the day of Christ Jesus."

Progress, not perfection, should be the goal of maturity. It is learning to keep the flow of progress alive and maintain the achievement of growth. Maturity is the ability to transform schooling into learning, knowledge into wisdom, incidents into insights, and casual encounters into rich experiences. It is the virtue of learning from one's own mistakes and failures, having the courage to apologize and ask for forgiveness, and remaining human and humble in the midst of successes and great accomplishments.

The following are some characteristics of a healthy self, signs of an ego strengths, and marks of a mature person:

- Being in touch with self and knowing one's own deep passions, needs, emotions, desires, unresolved issues, impulses, and reactions.
- Ability to delay gratification.
- Accepting one's limitations and admitting one's weaknesses.

- Learning to grieve well the losses of life.
- Tolerating ambiguity; not always having answers or knowing all.
- Displaying healthy lifestyle habits, coping strategies, and reality testing.
- Achieving a healthy balance between giving and receiving.
- Having clear personal boundaries.
- Ability to assess and view oneself and the world realistically (neither overestimating or underestimating).
- Able to be transparent (open, honest, and accountable) and capable of intimacy and closeness.
- Projecting a sense of integration and harmony rather than fragmentation and splitting.
- Being at ease with self; being comfortable and content when alone or when with others.
- Mastering the skills of self examination, self-discovery, and self-awareness.
- Able to share deeply and make a good contribution in the life of others.

N. ABI-HASHEM

See CODEPENDECY; CONGRUENCE; DOMINANCE; EGO STRENGTH; EMPATHY; HEALTHY PERSONALITY; INNER HEALING; LIFE SPAN DEVELOPMENT; MATURATION; PERFECTIONISM; PERSONALITY, CHRISTIAN THEORIES OF; SANCTIFICATION; SELF; SELF-ACTUALIZATION; SELF-DISCLOSURE; SELF-ESTEEM; VIRTUE, CONCEPT OF.

May, Rollo Reese (1909–1994). Born in Ada, Ohio, May spent his formative years in Marine City, Michigan. In 1930 he received the A.B. degree from Oberlin College.

As a youth May developed a strong interest in art. After college he went to Eastern Europe with a group of artists, where he painted scenes of country life and simple people. He spent three years in Europe traveling and teaching at the American College at Salonika, Greece. During this time he became acquainted with Alfred Adler and his work. He greatly admired Adler but later felt that he was guilty of oversimplification in his theorization.

When he returned to the United States in 1934, May served as a student adviser at Michigan State College. In 1936 he enrolled at Union Theological Seminary in New York, and in 1938 he graduated with the B.D. degree. His goal was to seek answers to the questions of human life, not to become a preacher (Harris, 1969). At Union, May was exposed for the first time to existential thought through the influence of Paul Tillich and was especially impressed with the thinking of Søren Kierkegaard and Heidegger. He became acquainted at this time with Kurt Goldstein, whose theoretical understanding of self-actualization and anxiety was especially important to him. May was later able to use Goldstein's neurological work as supporting data for his own psychological and philosophical insights.

In the year he graduated from seminary, May married and began pastoring a congregation in Montclair, New Jersey. During the summers of 1937 and 1938 he delivered lectures on counseling and personality adjustment to Methodist student workers. In 1939 those lectures, in expanded form, were published as *The Art of Counseling*. The next year May linked his view of the healthy personality to his general liberal perspective on Christian beliefs. The book in which this linkage appeared, *The Springs of Creative Living: A Study of Human Nature and God*, became one of May's least favorite, and he has not allowed it to reappear (Reeves, 1977). In *The Art of Counseling* he defined religion as "a basic attitude as man confronts his existence" rather than as sectarian dogma (p. 217). "This broad approach to creative or healthy personality development as inalienable from affirmation of meaning and purpose in life as a whole . . . remains characteristic of May's work as a whole. In *The Springs of Creative Living . . .* May seems to assure a close link between such affirmation and the Judeo-Christian God (even proposing a conception of Christ as 'therapist for humanity' and of religion as 'the stream of meaning')" (Reeves, 1977, p. 255).

During 1943–1944 May worked as a counselor at the College of the City of New York and studied psychoanalysis at the William Alanson White Institute of Psychiatry, Psychoanalysis, and Psychology. In 1946 he began a private practice in psychotherapy. He became a member of the faculty of the White Institute in 1948 and a fellow in 1952. He completed his doctoral degree at Columbia University in 1949, the school's first Ph.D. in clinical psychology. His dissertation was on anxiety, and the following year he published it as *The Meaning of Anxiety*. May followed Kierkegaard in seeing anxiety as the threat of becoming nothing. In 1953 he published *Man's Search for Himself*, which seems to have been part of his continuing attempt to clarify for himself the quest for maturity in personality and self-realization.

May taught at the New School of Social Research in New York between 1955 and 1960. In 1958 he co-edited *Existence: A New Dimension in Psychiatry and Psychology* with Angel and Ellenberger. In 1959 he became a training analyst at the White Institute and an adjunct professor of psychology in the Graduate School of New York University. *Symbolism in Religion and Literature* (1960) and *Existential Psychology* (1961) both appeared under his editorship during the next two years. His next two books, *Psychology and the Human Dilemma* and *Existential Psychotherapy*, both appeared in 1967. These were followed by *Dreams and Symbols* (co-authored with Caligor) in 1968, *Love and Will* (1969), and *Power and Innocence* (1972).

While May sees himself as a neo-Freudian of the interpersonal school, he believes that people can-

not be understood fully without consideration of the nature of persons. Intellectually he has made a significant impact on both the fine arts and the liberal arts. He has worked with existential ideas apart from their applications in European psychiatry and can thus be seen as having developed his own approaches to existential psychology. In this he has helped to support basic spiritual considerations somewhat lacking in contemporary American psychological thinking.

References

Harris, T. G. (1969, August). The devil and Rollo May. *Psychology Today*, 13–16.

May, R. (1939). *The art of counseling*. Nashville: Cokesbury.

Reeves, C. (1977). *The psychology of Rollo May*. San Francisco: Jossey-Bass.

E. S. GIBBS

See EXISTENTIAL PSYCHOLOGY AND PSYCHOTHERAPY.

McDougall, William (1871–1938). Pioneer in the instinctivist approach to behavior. Born in Lancashire, England, he entered the University of Manchester at the age of 15 and graduated with honors in 1890. He then studied physiology, anatomy, and anthropology for four years at Cambridge, graduating with highest honors. He received a scholarship for medical studies at St. Thomas Hospital in London and earned his degree in medicine because he believed it was a desirable part of a thorough education.

To further broaden his basis for the study of persons, McDougall joined the Cambridge Anthropological Expedition to the Torres Straits. He then spent a year studying at Göttingen under Müller. When he returned to London in 1900, he taught experimental psychology at University College. From 1904 to 1920 he taught mental philosophy at Oxford, then moved to Harvard. His final move was to Duke University in 1927, where he was professor and chairman of the psychology department until his death.

McDougall developed what he called a hormic psychology (from the Greek word meaning an "urge"). The basic proposition of this psychology is that all behavior is purposive or goal-seeking. Behind this striving to reach an end is an instinctive energy force striving for some sort of goal. McDougall developed various lists of instincts throughout his career and associated an emotion with each instinct. Any emotion could develop into a sentiment, an organization of feelings and attitudes that causes the person to react to an object.

McDougall wrote 24 books and well over 100 articles. The most important of his books are *Introduction to Social Psychology* (1908), *Body and Mind* (1911), *The Group Mind* (1920), *Outline of Psychology* (1923), and *Outline of Abnormal Psychology*

(1926). His *Introduction to Social Psychology* appeared in 23 editions and has been reprinted 30 times. He was the champion of many unpopular causes. He spoke of the soul and had an antimechanistic attitude when behaviorism was gaining strength. He supported psychic research and a teleological psychology and attempted to prove the Lamarkian theory of inheritance of acquired characteristics. All these causes lost ground during his lifetime, but he did not give up on them.

R. L. KOTESKEY

See PSYCHOLOGY, HISTORY OF.

Media Psychology. Media psychology is a division of psychology concerned with the use of print, electronic, and broadcast media to communicate with the public. Media psychologists study the impact of media on behavior, they investigate the use of media to disseminate information, and they explore the use of media for educational and instructional purposes. Media psychologists are represented in the American Psychological Association (APA) by Division 46, Media Psychology. Membership includes both scientists studying media effects and practitioners employing media in their professional endeavors.

Media psychology includes all media content within its province. However, of particular interest to media psychologists is the communication of psychological information, especially expert advice, through the media. Thus, the term *media psychology* often refers to the use of electronic and print media by mental health professionals to provide psychological services on a large scale. The increasing stress and isolation felt in modern society, the relatively small number of professional therapists, and the high cost of individual treatment have combined to make the public media an attractive alternative for the delivery of psychological expertise. Consequently the presence of psychology in the mass media continues to grow.

Initially opposed to the dissemination of psychological services through impersonal public media, the APA (American Psychological Association, 1971) gradually adopted ethical guidelines within which such services could be delivered (American Psychological Association, 1981, 1995). Under these guidelines, the statements the psychologists make must be consistent with the code of professional ethics published by the APA, the psychologists must be careful that their statements are based on appropriate psychological literature and practice, and they must try to ensure that individuals who receive the psychologist's information are not encouraged to believe that the psychologist has established a personal relationship with them. In sum, the services provided via public media must meet recognized standards for services provided in the context of a professional relationship.

In addition to the possible therapeutic value of this form of media psychology, it also serves to educate a broad audience in the content and value of psychology itself. In this way media psychology has helped to correct a long-standing problem of a lack of public understanding of psychology. With the expansion of new technologies for mass communications, such as the Internet, continued growth in the study and practice of media psychology appears inevitable.

References

American Psychological Association. (1971). *Ethical principles for psychologists*. Washington, DC: Author.
American Psychological Association. (1981). *Ethical principles for psychologists*. Washington, DC: Author.
American Psychological Association. (1991). *Ethical principles for psychologists*. Washington, DC: Author.

R. PHILIPCHALK

See COMMUNITY MENTAL HEALTH; COMMUNITY PSYCHOLOGY.

Mediation/Conciliation. Mediation is a strategy for conflict management in which a neutral third party facilitates the problem solving of the conflicting parties (Duffy, 1991). This method has been employed with conflicting individuals, small groups, organizations, and nations. The goals of the neutral mediator are generally threefold: to assist in developing reasonable and feasible solutions to the problems, to provide a role model of effective conflict management behavior, and to expand alternatives to courtroom litigation, thereby enhancing the effectiveness of the judicial system (Carnevale, Putnam, Conlon, & O'Connor, 1991).

Theory and research on mediation (see Wall & Lynn, 1993, for a review) has been interdisciplinary, with contributions from psychology, economics, political science, sociology, anthropology, communications, industrial relations, law, and organizational behavior. It has been employed in diverse cases, such as neighborhood feuds, civil and criminal litigation, police intervention, family disputes, divorce, public disputes, environmental planning, and organizational decision making (Carnevale & Pruitt, 1992).

Community mediation programs have become a popular alternative to courtroom litigation since the mid-1970s. Although mediation is an ancient form, and community mediation has long been institutionalized in China, it is only recently that such programs have become popular in the United States. In the mid-1970s there were fewer than 12 community mediation centers in the U.S. By the mid-1980s, there were as many as 400 (Duffy, 1991). The current movement received impetus from the Mennonite Central Committee. Mennonites have a long-standing interest in noncoercive conflict resolution, which is consistent with their historic position on nonviolence. As a result, Mennonites supported a number of private mediation centers in the 1970s to provide such services (Woolpert, 1991). Church-sponsored mediation programs are supported by the apostle Paul, who instructed the church members to settle their own disputes rather than proceeding to the state system (1 Cor. 6).

At the same time there was a growing dissatisfaction with the function, effectiveness, and costs of the judicial system. Crime was seen as an act against the state, and criminal conflicts were taken away from the parties directly involved. As a result of these factors, states began to experiment with mediation programs. In 1981 California mandated that parents participate in a mediation program before a custody or visitation hearing could be scheduled. The State of New York began an initiative that established a local community mediation center in every county (Duffy, 1991).

Community mediation programs are generally used for a limited type of case (Welton, 1991). The typical case involves minor harassment and assault. If money is involved it is generally less than $2,000, often much less. The cases usually involve a long-term relationship between the parties, for these are the relationships that have the most to gain from the mediation approach. Mediation is seen as most appropriate when the parties come to the table with approximately equal power. It is difficult to develop a mutually agreeable alternative when one side holds the balance of power.

The typical community mediation hearing begins as the parties in turn tell their perspective on the problem. This part of the hearing tends to focus on the past and is characterized by contentiousness and hostility. The mediator then tries to assist the parties to focus on their future relationship and ways to address the problem so it can be managed more effectively. The mediator will assist the parties in their attempts to problem solve but will not take control from the parties. When the parties have reached a decision, the mediator will write it down in the form of a binding contract. If the case has been referred through the court system, the agreement may also have the weight of a legal decision, depending on state law and local practices.

Research evidence indicates that community mediation programs have been very well received (Duffy, 1991). Between 80 and 90% of participants typically report high satisfaction with their experience. Parties are able to reach agreement in about 90% of cases. Mediation programs, however, report that many individuals choose not to participate. One study found that only 56% of cases actually went to a hearing. Hence it seems that mediation fails most often because parties refuse to use the process. This may become less of a problem as the programs become more institutionalized into American life.

Research has also investigated when mediation is most likely to be effective. Results indicated that effectiveness rates are highest when the conflict is of moderate intensity rather than high intensity, when parties have a high motivation to settle, when the disputes do not revolve around principles, and when the parties have a minimal power difference (Carnevale & Pruitt, 1992). Research has also found that long-term satisfaction with the mediation process is primarily a function of perceived fairness. When parties indicated that fair procedures were used in the hearing and when parties felt that their case had been heard and understood, the likelihood of compliance and improvement in the relationship was the strongest (McGillicuddy, Pruitt, Welton, Zubek, & Peirce, 1991).

Some mediation programs have been expanded to include more serious crimes. Victim Offender Reconciliation Programs have been developed to enable the victim and the accused to meet each other as a means of enabling reconciliation and restoration. Victims indicate that their primary motivation for participating in such programs are to recover losses, to help offenders, to learn more about crime, and to participate in a meaningful way in the criminal justice process. Experimental research has found that such programs are more likely to result in improved behavior of defendants and reduced anger by the victims (Woolpert, 1991).

References

Carnevale, P. J., & Pruitt, D. G. (1992). Negotiation and mediation. *Annual Review of Psychology, 43,* 531–582.

Carnevale, P. J., Putnam, L. L., Conlon, D. E., & O'Connor, K. M. (1991). Mediator behavior and effectiveness in community mediation. In K. G. Duffy, J. W. Grosch, & P. V. Olczak (Eds.), *Community mediation: A handbook for practitioners and researchers.* New York: Guilford.

Duffy, K. G. (1991). Introduction to community mediation programs: Past, present, and future. In K. G. Duffy, J. W. Grosch, & P. V. Olczak (Eds.), *Community mediation: A handbook for practitioners and researchers.* New York: Guilford.

McGillicuddy, N. B., Pruitt, D. G., Welton, G. L., Zubek, J. M., & Peirce, R. S. (1991). Factors affecting the outcome of mediation: Third-party and disputant behavior. In K. G. Duffy, J. W. Grosch, & P. V. Olczak (Eds.), *Community mediation: A handbook for practitioners and researchers.* New York: Guilford.

Wall, J. A., & Lynn, A. (1993). Mediation: A current review. *Journal of Conflict Resolution, 37,* 160–194.

Welton, G. L. (1991). Parties in conflict: Their characteristics and perceptions. In K. G. Duffy, J. W. Grosch, & P. V. Olczak (Eds.), *Community mediation: A handbook for practitioners and researchers.* New York: Guilford.

Woolpert, S. (1991). Victim-offender reconciliation programs. In K. G. Duffy, J. W. Grosch, & P. V. Olczak (Eds.), *Community mediation: A handbook for practitioners and researchers.* New York: Guilford.

G. L. WELTON

See CONFLICT; CONFLICT MANAGEMENT.

Medical Model of Psychopathology. *See* MENTAL ILLNESS, MODELS OF.

Medication. *See* PSYCHOPHARMACOLOGY.

Meditation. This practice can include a variety of efforts to produce an altered state of consciousness. Meditation has become popular in recent years in the Western world with the introduction of Eastern meditative practices such as Zen Buddhism, yoga, and similar disciplines. The reason for this increased interest in meditation has been the growing search for inner peace and spiritual truth.

While there are many Eastern meditative techniques, all seem to share the common view that human beings live their lives at a low level of conscious experience and that true enlightenment and peace will only come as conscious experience is elevated. A variety of techniques can be used to accomplish this end, including sensory deprivation, biofeedback, and hallucinogenic drugs, but the technique preferred by many is some sort of meditative exercise.

The exact methods in such mind-altering mediation can involve a wide variety of practices, including bizarre dancing, gazing at an object, focusing on one's breathing, or concentrating on a meaningless phrase. The knowledge gained in such meditation is intuitive and experiential rather than rational.

Transcendental Meditation. A clearer picture of meditation can be gained by examining more closely one particular type: Transcendental Meditation (TM). TM is a commercialized form of meditation taught in the United States by Maharishi Mahesh Yogi. It is also called the Science of Creative Intelligence. TM became popular in the United States in the 1970s when the Maharishi discovered that Americans would seek to learn his techniques if they were taught devoid of spiritual and religious ideas.

In Transcendental Meditation a mantra, or a sound repeated continuously, is used to increase a person's deep relaxation and refined specialized awareness. The Maharishi's theory behind the choice of a mantra for a person is that each person meditates best with a sound that fits the vibrations that constitute his or her personality. After a mantra is chosen, the recommended steps in meditation include sitting quietly in a comfortable position; closing the eyes; relaxing all the body's muscles; concentrating on the act of breathing or on the mantra and banishing all other thinking; and practicing these steps twice daily.

Meditators practicing these steps report feelings of peace, well-being, and a deep sense of relaxation. Experienced transcendental meditators learn to experience both a loss of sense of self and a union with things around them. This oneness experience is the goal of the meditation experience. Psychotherapists who use meditation in therapy seek to produce these same results in their clients. They hope that regular meditation will bring a calming peace to the emotionally troubled person and that the oneness feeling will allow people to better understand and relate to self, others, and the world.

The mind-altering experiences in this type of meditation seem to relate to the sensory reduction practices used. With the eyes closed and attention focused on a mantra, the meditator seeks to decrease the amount of incoming sensory information. Eastern meditators have argued that the human brain as a sensory reducer screens out valuable information about the greater realities of the universe. According to this view, what a person of normal consciousness experiences is only a fraction of the total picture of reality. According to the Eastern meditator's worldview of panpsychism (all things are one mind or force), the ordinary person has an erroneous experience of physical reality and personal identity. The person who does not meditate, they feel, is not in touch with the greater reality of the immaterial essence of the universe and a nonpersonal identification with all things. The meditative techniques of closing the eyes and narrowing concentration and experience to a single sound or feeling serve to allow the greater nonpersonal, nonrational reality to be experienced.

Physiological Research. In a study of the physiological changes during meditation it was found that heart rate slows, respiration is reduced, less oxygen is consumed, and the meditator's brain waves show a marked increase in alpha frequencies (West, 1987). These bodily changes are the opposite of what occurs in the body when a person is subjected to stress. Therefore, it is possible that meditative techniques such as Transcendental Meditation can be a useful means of dealing with the stresses of modern life. The brain-wave changes in meditation are similar to what occurs in the technique of biofeedback, which is also used to ease some of the symptoms of stress. In biofeedback training people learn to control brain waves and autonomic responses by receiving feedback on these states. Therefore, it seems likely that the experienced meditator is learning to tune in to internal bodily states and brain waves in order to control them.

A challenge to the claims of Eastern meditators is that the physical benefits of meditation are similar no matter what is used for a mantra. It may be that meditation produces a relaxation response in the body, a response that counters the body's autonomic stress response. Other research has challenged the spiritual enlightenment claims of Eastern meditation by showing that meditation does not reduce arousal more than does simple rest. It is found that the biochemical states of meditators are highly similar to control data from subjects who merely rest. Therefore, it may be summarized that Eastern forms of meditation may produce a sense of peace and relaxation if they are practiced regularly, but there is little evidence to support claims for spiritual enlightenment.

Christian Meditation. Meditation can also be practiced as a part of the Christian life of worship, but it is only remotely similar to Eastern meditation. Christian mystics, most of whom regularly experienced meditative states, have adorned church history down to current times. Some of these include Augustine, Theresa, Francis of Assisi, George Fox, John Wesley, and Brother Lawrence.

These Christian mystics understood that human life is meant to be a personal relationship with a personal God and that Christ is the only way into spiritual knowledge and life. The meditative experience in this context is the act of listening to God, communing with him, and experiencing a love relationship with him. When Christians have a blissful, peaceful experience in the act of meditation, they are not experiencing a cosmic consciousness so much as they are learning to shut out the chatter of a noisy world that can interfere with focusing attention on God. This is not to say that the mystic is more Christian than one who has not had this experience. All Christians experience a relationship with God to a greater or lesser degree and are therefore mystical. The differences in the depth of that experience are probably related more to psychological temperament and God's calling than to a person's degree of commitment to God.

The Christian mystic may practice some of the same techniques as the Eastern mystic in order to further closeness to God. These techniques could involve fasting or focusing one's attention on an attribute of God or a Bible verse. However, the experience gained from these meditative exercises is not the central facet of Christian meditation.

The Eastern meditator seeks to shatter the feelings of self and personhood and to merge with the cosmic consciousness of the universe. The Christian meditator sees personhood as a creation of God and not an erroneous experience. A Christian seeks to lose not self but self-centeredness. The Christian meditator's goal is not to annihilate human nature but to master it with Christ's help. The Eastern mystic seeks to become one with the universe because all of the universe is god. The Christian understands that God is a person and humans have become estranged from him. The Christian may seek to draw closer to God while in this life on earth through meditative worship.

The Eastern mystic seeks to become detached from the world and shuns both its pleasures and its evils. In Eastern mysticism there is a longing to be released from the burdens and pains of this life and to enter into the effortless, blissful state of nirvana. The Christian meditator may also shun some of the pleasures of life and will certainly shun its sins but for a different reason. The Eastern mystic uses virtue as a tool to achieve a higher cosmic consciousness. The Christian, knowing that unconfessed sins estrange people from both God and other persons, has as a goal to live in obedience to God. The Christian believes that a practical asceticism may aid in withdrawing from the confusion of life that often dampens the contemplation of spiritual matters. Christians may detach themselves from some of the things of this life but only as a method of redirecting life toward

a richer attachment to God and to other human beings. Christian meditation, therefore, represents an expansion of the human personality toward the experience of a relationship with God (Foster, 1983).

References

Foster, R. (1983). *Meditative prayer.* Downers Grove, IL: InterVarsity Press.
West, M. (Ed.). (1987). *The psychology of meditation.* New York: Oxford University Press.

M. P. COSGROVE

See CONSCIOUSNESS; PRIMAL THERAPY; STRESS; IMAGERY, THERAPEUTIC USE OF; MYSTICISM.

Meehl, Paul Everett (1920–). American psychologist whose career has spanned a remarkable breadth of interests and accomplishments. Meehl completed his A.B. (1941) and Ph.D. (1945) degrees at the University of Minnesota and has spent his entire career at his alma mater, rising through the ranks to become chairman of the department of psychology (1951–1958) and Regents' Professor of Psychology. He is also professor in the medical school's department of psychiatry, in the Minnesota Center for the Philosophy of Science, and in the department of philosophy. He is a diplomate in clinical psychology (American Board of Examiners in Professional Psychology) and a fellow of the Institute for Advanced Study in Rational Psychotherapy. He is a member of a large number of professional and academic societies in psychology, science, philosophy, and law. In 1958 he received the award for Distinguished Scientific Contributions from the American Psychological Association.

Meehl has made significant contributions in a large number of professional areas. Early in his career he was active in research in learning theory, co-authoring the influential text *Modern Learning Theory* (1954) along with many empirical and conceptual articles in this area. He was also active in research in psychological assessment and had particular influence in the development and widespread acceptance of actuarial assessment, wherein text scores are interpreted by standard quantitative rules rather than by more subjective clinical judgment. These procedures eventually gave rise to the computerized interpretation of psychological tests. His writings in philosophy of science and the methodology of the social sciences in particular have contributed substantially to the discipline of psychology. He has continued to contribute numerous articles in the areas of psychoanalysis and of clinical psychology as a professional discipline. Most recently his major area of interest has been the development of new methodologies for the investigation of taxometrics (the assigning of objects to their most appropriate classes), particularly the accurate assignment of individuals into meaningful diagnostic categories.

Finally, Meehl, formerly a Lutheran layman, was an early contributor to the literature relating behavioral science and Christian faith. His co-authored *What, Then, Is Man?* (1958) has continued to be an important monograph, although he did not stay active in this area after the mid-1960s. Meehl's impact on the field of psychology has been broad, significant, and positive.

S. L. JONES

Megalomania. A type of delusion in which an individual feels that he or she has great superiority. Common delusions include the belief that one is Christ, God, or Napoleon. The person may believe he or she is everything and everyone, omnipotent and omniscient. Those ideations are called delusions of grandeur. The term *megalomania* may be misleading in that it implies a presence of mania, which is not the case in the delusion.

Melancholy. *See* DEPRESSION; DEPRESSIONOGENIC ATTRIBUTION STYLE.

Memory. The study of memory is one of the most fascinating areas of neuroscience and neuropsychology. This ability to recall events, ideas, and feelings from one's past is one of the distinguishing characteristics of humans. The loss of memory, either through trauma or deteriorating disease, is among the most devastating and dehumanizing things that can happen to a person. It was Hermann Ebbinghaus, at the turn of the century, who began for the first time in the history of psychology to pay attention to the mechanisms of memory (Ebbinghaus, 1913). His experiments with the memorization of nonsense syllables developed the first attempts to establish learning curves for retention and loss of memories.

The pioneering work of Wilder Penfield in Canada, presented at the 1956 Vanuxem Lectures at Princeton University and published as *Speech and Brain Mechanisms* in 1959, sparked the idea that all events in a person's life are encoded in memory somewhat in the way a tape recording keeps sounds indefinitely. By stimulating points in the cortex of a patient whose skull had been cut open, Penfield and his associates elicited both auditory and visual "recollections" that allegedly the patient did not consciously admit remembering. Subsequent research has challenged whether these responses were true memories or new reactions to the electrical stimulation.

From that time there has been a proliferation of language to speak of memory. These terms have become confusing to the casual reader due to the overlapping concepts used and the different emphases and outcome measures employed. One reads about sensory, primary, secondary and tertiary memory and also about short-term versus long-term memory. The stages of encoding, storage and retrieval are often noted in the literature. Discussions of memory mechanisms are at times, complicated by looking at the loss of memory or amnesia. The effects of aging on memory occupy a large portion of the field of gerontology.

Another consideration in the discussion of memory has to include the effects of psychological states upon memory. Of special note is the effect of depression on memory. Depression plays an important role in the number of memory complaints that come into the clinics. In these cases memory performance does not correlate with the complaints presented by patients. One of the differential diagnoses that has to be made in every evaluation is the differentiation between truly organic deficits and the patients' subjective impression of their ability to perform. The truly neurologically impaired patient is unable to perform the normal tasks of the assessment instruments, while the depressed patient will be able to perform once he or she is motivated and his or her attention is engaged. Popkin Gallagher, Thompson, and Moore (1982) and Kahn Larit, Hilbert, and Niederehe (1975) found increased levels of depression among elderly patients complaining of memory loss. Other researchers have found that the complaints of memory loss increase and decrease as the levels of depression fluctuate (Zarit, Gallagher, & Kramer, 1981).

The neuroanatomy of memory focuses on the study of the limbic system, the structure of the brain located below the cortex and involving the hippocampus, the amygdala, the hypothalamus, and the cingulate gyrus. Contemporary theories of memory differ chiefly on the emphasis they place on the roles of each of these structures in the mechanisms of memory. One important point of discussion among these is the role played by emotions in the perception and storage of memories. The most prominent models of the neuroanatomy of memory at this time are those of Mishkin and Appenzeller (1987) and of Squire and Zola-Morgan (1991). Mishkin and associates place the most important role in the amygdala; Squire and Zola-Morgan do not.

For the purpose of understanding the types of memory that we all possess, the classifications suggested by Reeves and Wedding (1994) are most useful. The first division is between declarative and procedural memory. This distinction is important in that only one type is impaired by amnesia.

Declarative memory can be described as "knowing that" while procedural is "knowing how." Declarative memory is directly accessible to consciousness. It deals with facts and data. It is all that we can "declare" when needed. It can be episodic—events and time, and semantic—general knowledge, and linguistic. Amnesia impairs the ability to acquire the information that comes from facts or events. However, amnesia spares the capacity for skill learning—procedural memory. The latter involves the memory necessary to remember the steps of skills learned before and even after the onset of amnesia. Amnestic persons will remember skills learned but will not remember the events of having been taught the skill. Amnestic persons are able to drive a car safely. For example, amnestic persons can also learn by simple classical conditioning (*see* Conditioning, Classical) and will respond consistently to the appropriate cues without remembering having learned the behavior.

The crucial differentiation in evaluating loss of memory rests with the location of the damaged structure in the brain. Amnesia stemming from damage to the hippocampus will affect declarative memory while sparing procedural memory. Conversely, Parkinson's disease, which affects the basal ganglia will affect learning ability but will leave conscious and long-term memory intact.

Ongoing research by Squire and his colleagues at the University of California at San Diego and by UCLA psychologist Barbara J. Knowlton in collaboration with Toronto psychologist Jennifer Mangels suggests that there are four separate memory systems. They theorize that one is located in the basal ganglia and deals with the memories of learned skills. In the hippocampus resides the conscious memory of facts and events. A third location of memories is in the cerebellum, where associative learning takes place, a la Pavlovian conditioning paradigm. A fourth location, and perhaps psychologically the most important, is in the amygdala, where emotional memories are stored.

One of the more controversial topics in psychology is the issue of so-called recovered memories. Such memories involve the total repression of traumatic events in the lives of persons, chiefly during childhood, which appear to pop into consciousness during therapeutic anamnesis or hypnotic trances and which are believed to be recollections of historic events. It is interesting to note that the Squire and Zola-Morgan school, which has downplayed the role of the amygdala in memory, are now suggesting an increased role in that structure for emotional memories. More research is needed before establishing the role of emotional filtering in the accuracy of so-called repressed memories.

The assessment of memory is one of the most developed and researched areas in neuropsychology. Reeves and Wedding (1994) review as many as 21 different published instruments that are now in the market and in use by neuropsychologists and clinical psychologists to test people's memory skills or the lack thereof. Current standards of practice in neuropsychology dictate that no neuropsychological evaluation is complete without the administration of several measures of memory. New instruments are constantly being researched and developed.

The improvement of memory is another topic for research both in rehabilitation centers and in pharmaceutical laboratories. A recent report in the *Los Angeles Times* related experiments being conducted by Gary Lynch at the University of Califor-

nia at Irvine of a new class of biochemicals called ampakines which are expected to improve the memory skills of patients with Alzheimer's disease. Preliminary tests with standardized memory tests offer hope of developing a drug that could eventually be licensed by the Food and Drug Administration for use with Alzheimer's patients.

We now know that while there is some decline in memory functions with aging, what used to be called senility is not a normal part of aging. When serious memory deficits occur, especially in conjunction with diminishing cognitive capacities, a degenerating disease process or the presence of an invasive growth somewhere in the brain should be suspected. Neuropsychological evaluation and neurologic follow-up should be sought for the person in question.

References

Ebbinghaus, H. (1913). *Memory: A contribution to experimental psychology* (H. A. Roger & C. E. Bussenius, Trans.). New York: Teachers College, Columbia University.

Kahn, R. L., Zarit, S. H., Hilbert, N. M., & Niederehe, G. A. (1975). Memory complaint and impairment in the aged: The effect of depression and altered brain function. *Archives of General Psychiatry, 32,* 1560–1573.

Penfield, W., & Roberts, L. (1959). *Speech and brain-mechanisms.* Princeton, NJ: Princeton University Press.

Popkin, S. J., Gallagher, D., Thompson, L. W., & Moore, M. (1982). Memory complaint and performance in normal and depressed older adults. *Experimental Aging Research, 8,* 141–145.

Mishkin, M., & Appenzeller, T. (1987). The anatomy of memory. *Scientific American, 256,* 80–91.

Reeves, D., & Wedding, D. (1994). *The clinical assessment of memory.* New York: Springer.

Squire, L. R., & Zola-Morgan, S. (1991). The medial temporal lobe memory system. *Science, 253,* 1380–1386.

Zarit, S. H., Gallagher, D., & Kramer, N. (1981). Memory training in the community aged: Effects of depression, memory complaint, and memory performance. *Educational Gerontology, 6,* 11–27.

L. M. Marmol

See False Memory Syndrome; Cognitive Psychology.

Memory Disorders. *See* Amnestic Disorders.

Men, Psychology of. Significant interest in the psychology of men surged from about the mid-1970s, after the feminist movement. Early "masculist" authors included Goldberg (1976) and Farrell (1975), whose original suggestions fell in line with the psychology of the times, namely, that men should be more sensitive and less aggressive. Their later works (e.g., Farrell, 1986) were reconstructions of these early manifestations of North American culture's interest in gender differences. The mid-1980s saw a new turn in the interest of male psychology with the development of the men's movement. This movement is headed by two predominant forces only loosely aligned: the mythopoetic leaders exemplified by poet laureate Robert Bly (1990) and his colleagues Michael Meade and Robert Moore (Moore & Gillette, 1992), and the International Men's Conference, a loose confederation of men generating out of the San Antonio, Texas, area who gathered together in "wild men" retreats. Joining the foray into the men's movement was Jungian analyst James Hillman, who brought the only solidly psychological perspective to the understanding of maleness. The men's movement of the 1980s was short-lived, however, as were the publications and meetings it fostered. Taking the place of the secular men's movement has been the increasingly popular Promise Keepers' meetings, the brainchild of former Colorado football coach Bill McCartney, which draw tens of thousands of Christian men annually for revival of the male spirit from a distinctively evangelical Christian perspective.

During the course of the now largely dormant feminist movement and in the wake of the seemingly dead secular men's movement, there has been a small amount of research into masculinity and an even smaller amount of biblical and theological research into what it means to be male. Nothing in the biblical-theological literature matches the immensely valuable work by Trible (1978), which examined femininity as well as the nature of God from a biblical perspective. That which has been written from a Christian perspective, aside from an occasional journal article (Johnson, 1988), has been universally from a conservative and limited perspective (Neuer, 1991; Piper & Grudem, 1991). A plethora of books written by contemporarily popular authors (Crabb, 1990; Dobson, 1991) have kept the matter of masculinity in front of the Christian audience. From the secular side of psychology a few important examinations of gender differences in general have helped in our understanding of maleness (Gilligan, 1982; Gray, 1992; Tannen, 1990), but little has substantiated an understanding of what it means to be male. Many authors examining gender differences follow early, somewhat strident feminist theory suggesting that most gender differences are social roles (VanLeeuwen, 1990). Thus we are left with much more theory than fact, and it is expected that the next few years will greatly increase our understanding of gender differences in general and masculinity in particular.

What we know about maleness comes from several quarters: extant biological research, primarily regarding the effect of hormones, genes, brain differences, musculature, and physical illness; sociological and behavioral research; study of child development as it relates to gender differences; gender-specific biblical and theological directives; and theoretical formulations. Biological research has identified the predominance of testosterone in the male body, which seemingly has a strong causative effect on males' tendency to be physically aggressive more than females. The lack of normative testosterone levels in males is highly correlated with evident passiveness in behavior. Some research shows that larger amounts of testosterone lead to overly aggressive or criminal activity. Evidence of gender differences due to hormone levels is also tangentially related to brain differences in males and females because the hypothalamus of the brain regulates hormonal functions as well as motivation and at least some emotion. More important brain differences are that male brains are lateralized, or one-sided; female brains are more bilateral. The lateralized male brain does not allow for as rapid a shift from left to right brain functions as occurs in women, hence making men less able to create and produce simultaneously, think and feel simultaneously, and talk and listen simultaneously. Possibly related to these factors is that men are found to be better at seeing the environment while women are found to be better listeners.

While testosterone and other genetic factors lead to the male body converting caloric intake more to musculature than fat storage, it appears that this physical superiority also leads to the profound inferiority of males in being much more susceptible to almost all physical diseases, such as cancer, heart, and lung disease. Related to some hard evidence of physical differences between the sexes is the fact that not only are men more inclined to most physical illnesses, but also they are highly inclined to accidents, criminality, and suicide. Males of all ages are approximately twice as likely as females to have auto accidents, falls, drowning, and most other accidents. Ninety-five percent of current prison inmates are men, and the men who are incarcerated have committed more serious and more frequent crimes than have the incarcerated women. For reasons that are not entirely clear but that relate to their tendency toward criminality, even the youngest of boys tend to be more inclined to some kind of dishonesty than girls.

Rates of suicide gestures and suicides reveal that 10 times more gestures are made by women, who are also more inclined to complain of depression, but 10 times more suicides are committed by men, who tend to become depressed much more seriously and later in life. In their drinking patterns men tend to drink earlier, more often, and in greater quantity, and have more serious complications of their drinking (see Alcohol Abuse and Dependency).

In their day-to-day activities males are found to be superior in mathematical functions, mechanical functions, and spatial relations compared to females' superiority in language-based functions of life, such as reading and speaking. Activity levels of males of all ages, but particularly of neonates, are found to be higher than those of females, but males are found to be much less compliant and group-minded than females. One research study found that in groups of children there was always fighting when the groups were male-only, never fighting when the groups were female-only, and usually fighting when there were mixed-sex groups, with the fighting always being initiated by the boys. The fact that boys are more active relates to their being more exploratory of their environment and theoretically may lead to their tendency to be more exploratory and scientific in their adult lives. If boys and men are attuned to the physical possibilities of the real world, girls and women are more attuned to the emotional and relational aspects as evidenced by their compliance, tendency to seek agreement rather than argument, and what some researchers call communality (i.e., seeking emotional connectedness with other people). The question as to how much of female communality and male directedness is socially determined is open to debate. The probable truth is that the tendencies stem from nature, nurture, and the interaction of those two ingredients of human behavior. Additional study has found that a relatively stable phenomenon among males across age levels is that they value independence, competitiveness, play, and individualism; females tend to value social intimacy.

The sparse amount of solid theological literature regarding gender differences, let alone the nature of maleness, allows for only marginal considerations of spiritual differences between men and women. The Old Testament presentation of women as being responsive and sometimes seductive may be an artifact of the apparent patriarchy of the time or a reflection of something basic to gender difference. Eve's creation as helper, not so much assistant to the male, can be perceived as a reflection of a basic ingredient of femaleness being to complement or perhaps to correct maleness. Conservatives and many evangelicals would point to Paul's suggestion that the man is the head as Christ is the head of the church as evidence of male superiority in the household, but such a view seems to be inadequate to understand unmarried persons and may be too concretized an understanding of maleness.

Following Paul's suggestion that sin is anything to excess, hence idolatrous, it has been suggested that female sin may be the inclination to help to a fault (hence criticize) as well as speak to a fault (utilizing her verbal superiority). Male sin may be inclined toward being dominant, aggressive, or anger-based, whether at home, at work, or with friends.

Paul's suggestion (1 Thess. 2:11–12, NIV) that fathers are to be "encouraging, comforting, and urging" may be the Scripture's best description of what it means to be a Christian male. Other scholars have suggested that Paul similarly exhorts men to love their wives because spousal loving comes less naturally to men than to women and requires more effort. Following this line of thought, it has been suggested that after the fall women retain the pre-fall understanding of human connectedness and communality (hence the curse to seek after the man), while men retain the pre-fall understanding of the value of work and production (hence the curse of toiling with sweat). An extension of this theology is that the communality of women is complemented by the directedness of men, thus giving females a better understanding of our unified existence and need for each other and males a better grasp of our ultimate individual natures and separateness.

Other Bible students have remarked on the frequency of male-to-male intimacy, such as that seen between Joseph and his brothers, Jonathan and David, Jesus and his disciples, and Paul and his many students, noting that such intimacy seems to be lacking in North American culture. The fact that 65% of church attendees are female, 80% of therapy patients are female, and 90% of same-sex intimate relationships are female-to-female would seem to suggest that the present culture does not support or reward male-to-male intimacy.

The theoretical formulations of maleness come out of this broad array of research in biology, psychology, and theology. Our present understanding leads us to believe that the relevant distinctive qualities of maleness include being significantly less fluent and effective verbally (although men actually talk more than women); being physically superior and more aggressive and inclined to physical excesses, such as in work, play, and criminality; possessing the spiritual quality of leadership that generates from physical superiority and a feeling of separateness in the world; needing female connectedness and help through correction; and usually lacking in intimate male friendship, which seems contrary to many biblical examples.

References

Bly, R. (1990). *Iron John: A book about men.* New York: Random House.

Crabb, L. (1990). *Men and woman: Enjoying the difference.* Grand Rapids, MI: Zondervan.

Dobson, J. C. (1991). *Straight talk.* Dallas: Word.

Farrell, W. (1975). *The liberated man.* New York: Random House.

Farrell, W. (1986). *Why men are the way they are.* New York: McGraw-Hill.

Gilligan, C. (1982). *In a different voice.* Cambridge, MA: Harvard University Press.

Goldberg, H. (1976). *The hazards of being male.* New York: Signet Classics.

Gray, J. (1992). *Men are from Mars, women are from Venus.* New York: HarperCollins.

Johnson, R. (1988). The theology of gender. *Journal of Psychology and Christianity, 7* (4), 39–49.

Moore, R., & Gillette, D. (1990). *King, warrior, magician, lover.* New York: HarperCollins.

Neuer, W. (1991). *Man and woman in Christian perspective.* Wheaton, IL: Crossway.

Piper, J., & Grudem, W. (Eds.). (1991). *Recovering biblical manhood and womanhood: A response to evangelical feminism.* Wheaton, IL: Crossway.

Tannen, D. (1990). *You just don't understand.* New York: Morrow.

Trible, P. (1978). *God and the rhetoric of sexuality.* Philadelphia: Fortress.

VanLeeuwen, M. S. (1990). *Gender and grace.* Downers Grove, IL: InterVarsity Press.

R. B. JOHNSON

See WOMEN, PSYCHOLOGY OF.

Menopause. Menopause is the culmination of a woman's climacteric. The climacteric is a period of several years, usually beginning in the forties, during which ovulation and menstruation become irregular as the ovaries produce less estrogen. Menopause is reached when menstruation completely stops, usually by age 55 but sometimes by age 40. Commonly called the change of life, menopause involves physical and psychological changes that vary in their extent and in the effects they have on women. Although many symptoms have been blamed on menopause, only a few are direct consequences of declining estrogen, including hot flashes, vaginal changes, weakening of muscles controlling urination, and loss of bone density (osteoporosis).

Hot flashes are reported by as many as 75% of women in the year surrounding the actual menopause. The flashes or flushes are feelings of warmth and sometimes cause profuse perspiration. They last for a few minutes to an hour.

Vaginal changes include lack of lubrication and thinning of the vaginal walls, which may produce pain and bleeding during intercourse. Weakening of the urethral muscles may cause women to leak urine under the stress of sneezing, coughing, or laughing.

Lowered estrogen causes loss of bone density in about 25% of white, Asian, and Hispanic women. African-American women are at low risk for this effect, while smokers and thin women are at higher risk. Bone density loss increases the risk of fractures and the deformed vertebrae of dowager's hump.

An obvious consequence of menopause is infertility. However, during the climacteric but before final cessation of ovulation, women are still fertile and may have an increased likelihood of conceiving a child if they stop using contraceptive practices. A simple blood test can determine when a woman has become infertile.

Menopause is normal; it is neither a physical nor a psychological disorder. The meaning that menopause has for a woman may lead to worries and even depression, however. For some women, especially in the United States, menopause means declining femininity and sexual attractiveness. For others, loss of fertility signals uselessness and old age. These and other psychological reactions may combine with hormonal changes to produce additional signs associated with menopause, such as headache, nervousness and anxiety, weight gain, and memory problems.

Some women lose interest in sexual activity due to a combination of vaginal changes and concerns about femininity and attractiveness. Some women believe that sexual activity ought to cease after menopause, but that idea is not supported by medical research.

Many women welcome menopause as liberation from dealing with menstruation and contraception, and they may become more interested in sexual activity. In many Asian and African cultures, in which older women are respected sources of advice and wisdom, menopause is more likely to be welcomed than it is in cultures that eulogize youth and ignore the aged.

Treatments are readily available if the physical signs of menopause are distressing. Hormone replacement therapy, which supplies the missing estrogen by pill, vaginal cream, or patch, is the most effective treatment. It is also the treatment of choice for osteoporosis. There has been considerable controversy over the advisability of estrogen replacement for symptoms of menopause, since estrogen is associated with increased risk of cancer of the breast or endometrium (lining of the uterus). Taking progestin for part of a monthly cycle appears to prevent endometrial cancer, but it reestablishes menstruation. Women with none of the risk factors for breast cancer can probably take estrogen safely, especially if they take it for less than five years. Most physicians believe that estrogen reduces the risk of heart disease more than enough to offset any increased risk of breast cancer.

Other ways to manage signs of menopause are satisfactory for many women. Osteoporosis may be offset by exercise and calcium supplements. Exercise and a low-fat diet help to control the cholesterol elevation that is associated with higher risks of heart disease after menopause. Kegel exercises (repeated contraction of the muscles that stop the flow of urine) maintain and improve bladder control.

Many women find practical remedies effective. A drink of ice water may end a hot flash, or removing a sweater may make it less troublesome. Thirty minutes of exercise may relieve insomnia, and pain during intercourse may be eliminated by spending more time in foreplay for arousal before attempting penetration. Using a water-soluble lubricating jelly in the vagina may make intercourse more enjoyable for both partners.

Husbands and other family members play a significant role in a woman's feelings of usefulness and desirability. The church may also play a beneficial role by providing opportunities for service that draw on her accumulated wisdom and experience. In addition, church leaders should reinforce Christian teachings of respect for the aging process, opposing the contrary cultural stereotypes that produce negative reactions to menopause.

P. D. Young

See Women, Psychology of.

Mental Age. An individual's mental age is an expression of the level of mental development. It is determined by comparing the individual's ability with the ability of others of the same age. The concept was first systematically developed by Alfred Binet and is based on the assumption that intellectual ability can be measured and that it increases progressively with age.

See INTELLIGENCE; INTELLECTUAL ASSESSMENT.

Mental Disorders, Classification of. See CLASSIFICATION OF MENTAL DISORDERS.

Mental Health. See COMMUNITY MENTAL HEALTH; HEALTHY PERSONALITY; PREVENTION OF PSYCHOLOGICAL DISORDERS; RELIGION AND PERSONALITY.

Mental Illness, Models of. Although the concept of mental illness is central to the field of mental health and the practice of counseling, there is continuing disagreement about its definition. Several views are widely held. Each has important implications for understanding mental illness, determining which conditions are disorders and who has them, and choosing appropriate approaches to treatment. This controversy involves several important issues.

In a recent review, Wakefield (1992) presents a summary of the different approaches to defining mental illness. They include the views that mental disorder is a myth, purely a value concept, whatever professionals treat, statistical deviance, disadvantage, unexpectable distress or disability, or harmful dysfunction. Wakefield prefers the harmful dysfunction approach, which he believes is essentially identical with common conceptions of physical illness. Several of Wakefield's major points are summarized.

Psychiatrist Thomas Szasz contends that mental illness is a myth. Central to the illness model is the notion that biological lesions and disorders go together. However, physical lesions are possible without constituting a disorder (e.g., albinism, webbed toes), and disorders may occur without a known lesion (e.g., trigeminal neuralgia, senile pruritus). Szasz believes a few mental disorders are based on biological causes. The rest, he contends, are merely evaluative labels that legitimize social sanctions and change efforts directed at persons who do not behave in socially approved ways. Examples include labeling homosexuals, runaway slaves (drapetomania), and social dissidents mentally disordered. Demonstrating abuses, however, does not establish that mental disorder is a myth. Evidence that schizophrenia occurs widely across cultures strains the claim that mental disorder is purely a value concept.

Limiting mental disorder to that which professionals treat also has problems. It implies that without treatment one does not have a disorder. Conversely, seeking treatment only to discover that one is normal becomes impossible under this criterion.

Statistical deviance likewise fails. One can be deviant in both positive and negative ways, yet the statistical approach treats these as equally disordered. Also, some disorders, such as high blood pressure,

are statistically common. Statistical rareness is thus inadequate. Defining disorder as negative deviation helps—but it introduces values. Further, crimes, discourtesy, and moral transgressions, while undesirable, are not considered disorders.

Biological disadvantage, an evolutionary concept, labels as disorders those conditions that impair fertility or speed mortality, thus threatening species survival. However, many disorders appear to have neither of these consequences.

The American Psychiatric Association's *Diagnostic and Statistical Manual of Mental Disorders* (American Psychiatric Association, 1994), or *DSM-IV*, is based on the notion of unexpectable distress or disability. Although harmful dysfunction provides the conceptual foundation, the criteria for specific disorders are based on distress or disability and statistical infrequency. The problem is twofold, Wakefield points out. First, normal reactions that are statistically rare are defined by *DSM-IV* as disordered. Second, such unexpected conditions as extreme misfortune and ignorance can cause distress and disability yet are excluded as mental disorders; *DSM-IV* describes some of these conditions under the V codes.

Wakefield (1992) concludes that harmful dysfunction is the best definition of mental disorder. Harmful dysfunction is a hybrid definition: "disorder must include a factual component . . . (and) disorder requires harm, which involves values" (p. 381). For Wakefield the factual-scientific component of disorder is based on evolutionary biology; that is, disorder involves a failure of a human biological system to perform its intended function in preserving the organism. Wakefield infers intended function from the effects of the system; it need not imply active agency such as that of a creator God. He concludes "an evolutionary approach . . . is central to an understanding of psychopathology. Dysfunction is thus a purely factual scientific concept" (p. 383). In addition, "only dysfunctions that are socially disvalued are disorders" (p. 384). A key factor is that "it is the nature of the cause of the symptoms, and not the nature of the symptoms themselves, that determines whether a disorder is mental" (p. 384).

Central to the concept of mental illness is the notion that behavioral disturbances are in some sense diseases. Although it is clearly no longer the sole model, the disease model, or harmful dysfunction, remains the most widely accepted view. The difficulty one faces in attempting to refer to these phenomena without using terms connoting illness reflects the pervasiveness of the disease/mental illness model.

Historical Perspective. From antiquity until the late nineteenth century persons with deviant behavior were considered to be malingerers, a moral concern, or to be possessed by spirits, a religious concern. Exorcism and torture were used in an effort to remove the influence of evil spirits. Special favor was given to benevolent spirits.

Treatment of the mentally ill changed markedly during the period from the late eighteenth century through the time of Sigmund Freud. The humanitarian reforms under Phillipe Pinel, Tuke, and Dorothea Lynde Dix resulted in modification of asylums. Greisinger and Morel advanced the disease hypothesis. John Gray, editor of the *American Journal of Insanity* from 1855 to 1885, insisted that physical lesions produced insanity and led in the transformation of mental asylums into treatment facilities. The work of Jean-Martin Charcot, Pierre Janet, Bernheim, and Freud led to a conceptual shift; persons who had previously been considered malingerers were subsequently diagnosed as hysterics. Thus the disease model was extended to persons outside the institutional care setting.

Further credence was given to the disease model by the dramatic discovery that advanced syphilitic infection causes general paresis, a psychotic disorder. This hypothesis was first suggested in 1857; positive identification of syphilitic infection as the causative agent was provided in 1913. Together these movements culminated in a major paradigm shift in which the disease notion replaced moral-religious explanations.

The view that mental disorders are diseases has been widely accepted in the twentieth century. However, there is considerable conceptual ambiguity regarding the nature of the disease or medical model. Blaney (1975) suggests four versions: mental disorders are physiologically based diseases; evidences of disorder are manifestations of an underlying condition (not necessarily organic); the individual has no responsibility for his or her behavior; psychiatric symptoms can be best understood by ordering them into syndromes.

Alternative Models. A number of alternative models have been advanced to replace the medical model. Most widely accepted are the various sociopsychological or behavioral models. Sociopsychological models postulate that there is no radical discontinuity between normal and disturbed behavior. The underlying mechanisms of behavior are the processes of learning and behavior control. Diagnosis is focused on identifying the frequencies, topographies, and social or environmental conditions controlling problem behaviors (Kazdin, 1989).

The systems model locates the problem within family and social systems rather than in the individual. For example, many contemporary family therapists view parent-child problems as problems of the system. Neither the parent nor the child is identified as a patient who has the problem. Rather, the problem arises from the interaction between parent and child and may be significantly affected by interactions with other family members or circumstances as well.

Culture and Mental Disorder. DSM-IV contains an appendix that examines culture-related syndromes. Anorexia nervosa and chronic fatigue syndrome, disorders that are largely found in the United States and Europe, remain in the main body of the *DSM*, while *ataques de nervois,* a Latin American disorder similar to hysteria, and *tajin kyofusho,* a Japanese disorder similar to social phobia, are relegated to the appendix on culture-related disorders. A study of Hopi culture reveals five conditions that overlap with the *DSM-IV* criteria for depression, although none fully fit: two conditions are translated worry sickness, others include unhappiness, heartbrokenness, and drunkenlike craziness with or without alcohol.

Two conclusions may be drawn. First, mental disorders occur across cultural boundaries. Second, the precise form of disorders varies across cultures, with some disorders being very different and others fairly similar in varied cultures. Stix concludes "although some diseases, such as schizophrenia, do appear in all cultures, a number of others do not. Moreover, the variants of an illness—and the course they take—in different cultural settings may diverge so dramatically that a physician may as well be treating separate diseases" (Stix, 1996, p. 16).

In a recent discussion of culture and mental disorders, Dana noted that there is a tendency to treat cultural differences as pathology. He proposed that cultural information is essential to reduce egregious misclassification. Dana went on to say, "DSM is a very dangerous instrument, and it really is used for social control. . . . It lumps together disease (medical model) and cultural model etiologies" (Dana, 1996).

Christian Perspective. Since a Christian approach is particularly concerned with ethical and moral issues, the differences between a medical and a sociopsychological conceptualization of mental illness have profound implications for a Christian perspective. In a medical conceptualization the alcoholic, the depressive, the psychopathic, the retarded, and other disordered individuals are seen primarily as victims of processes outside their control. If the problem is viewed as a behavioral disorder, the individual's personal responsibility for his or her present condition becomes a prominent issue with clear moral implications. In reality the issues may be even more complex, since contemporary research increasingly shows that personal-social lifestyle is a major contributing factor in contracting various physical diseases.

For many Christians, Wakefield's (1992) appeal to evolutionary biology in explaining dysfunction is objectionable. However, failure to perform a God-intended function is a plausible alternative. The claim that dysfunction is purely factual fails, since science is not possible without making prescientific assumptions, and any interpretation of scientific data inevitably mingles observations and assumptions. In the words of Bevan and Kessel (1994), "most often implicit, ideologies are complex, not easily broken into elements . . . they are like sand at a picnic: they get into everything . . . to talk of scholarship and science as separate from the life experience, the intentions, the values, the world-view, and social life of the people who create it is to deny its fundamental character as a human activity" (p. 506).

While articulate presentations that are sensitive to complex issues remain rare, the ramifications of these models have not escaped Christian writers. At one extreme Adams (1970) emphatically proclaims that all problems reflect either organic disorder or sin. Other writers recognize that sin and organic disorders are only two of many potential causes of psychological problems. Some causes include response to existential issues, maladaptive use of defense mechanisms, demonic influence, and learning (Cosgrove & Mallory, 1977).

All mental disorders—indeed, all problems in our world—may ultimately be traced to the entry of sin into the world and the subsequent disruption of the created order (cf. Rom. 8:19–22). Thus at one level it is accurate to say that the cause of psychological problems is sin. However, viewing the problem solely as personal sin is too simplistic. The effects of sin are manifested in mental disorders on at least three different levels: the effects of personal sin leading to guilt or anxiety; the effects of sin in the world, resulting in various biological disorders such as genetic disorders, endocrinological malfunctions, disease, and traumas; the effects of the sin of others, such as retardation due to neglect or abuse by a parent and anxiety or depression following an assault. In addition, we see interactions among these factors, such as when a person's abuse of alcohol or drugs results in brain damage.

Ethical and moral issues have often been viewed as largely irrelevant within the medical model of mental illness. However, it is becoming increasingly clear that moral issues are significant. The medical model suggests that individuals should not be held responsible for their diseases. But increasing evidence that personal habits are a major factor in illness underscores the role of personal responsibility for disease. Such habits as use of alcohol, tobacco, and drugs; diet; exercise; sleep patterns; and sexual promiscuity contribute significantly to risk of disease. In addition, compliance with treatment has become an increasing source of professional concern and research. All of this suggests that the distinctions between medical and psychosocial viewpoints may not be as clear-cut as the foregoing discussion might imply.

Analogies can be drawn between the various effects of sin in psychopathology and models of psychopathology. The presence of sin in the world is most clearly reflected in the disease model, which focuses on the physical basis for disorders. The effects of personal sin and to some extent the sins of others seem consistent with the sociopsychological model. Finally, the systems model emphasizes phenomena most consistent with problems stemming from the sinfulness of others.

Conclusions. The medical model has been helpful in some respects and has created problems in others. However, the complexity and diversity of phenomena included in *DSM-IV* require acknowledgment of multiple causal factors in mental disorders, and therefore the medical model alone is inadequate. A comprehensive model of mental functioning must include the following components: biological factors, including genetic, anatomical, and biochemical causes and infectious diseases; psychological factors, including personal, developmental, and family history, and relationships to others; social factors such as societal and cultural norms and standards; spiritual factors, including personal sin, ethical and moral responsibilities, relationship to God, and spiritual growth and development. It is doubtful that any existing model is able to fully encompass this diversity.

Medical considerations are essential to a full understanding of mental disorders, and further advances will likely be made through the medical approach. However, the medical model does not encompass all of the phenomena included under mental illness, and hence other models are required as well. Perhaps an integrative model that brings together elements from several of the present models will emerge. Alternatively, a comprehensive new system may eventually develop. Such a model should reflect the biopsychosocial and spiritual complexity of human functioning.

References

Adams, J. E. (1970). *Competent to counsel.* Grand Rapids, MI: Baker.

American Psychiatric Association (1994). *Diagnostic and statistical manual of mental disorders (*4th ed.). Washington, DC: Author.

Bevan, W., & Kessel, F. (1994). Plain truths and home cooking: Thoughts on the making and remaking of psychology. *American Psychologist, 49,* 505–509.

Blaney, P. H. (1975). Implications of the medical model and its alternatives. *American Journal of Psychiatry, 132,* 911–914.

Cosgrove, M. P., & Mallory, J. D. (1977). *Mental health: A Christian approach.* Grand Rapids, MI: Zondervan.

Dana, R. H. (February, 1996). *Multicultural assessment.* Newberg, OR: George Fox College.

Kazdin, A. E. (1989). *Behavior modification in applied settings* (4th ed.). Pacific Grove, CA: Brooks/Cole.

Wakefield, J. C. (1992). The concept of mental disorder: On the boundary between biological facts and social values. *American Psychologist, 47,* 373–388.

R. K. Bufford

See Abnormal Psychology.

Mental Mechanisms. *See* Defense Mechanisms.

Mental Retardation. A condition affecting about 6.5 million people in the United States, in which the individual's general intellectual functioning is significantly subaverage, adaptive behavior is impaired, and the condition is present at birth or begins before age 18. The *DSM-IV* (American Psychiatric Association, 1994), in line with the American Association on Mental Deficiency, set these criteria to indicate that the deficiency interferes with the person's ability to adjust to the demands of life and manifests itself in poor learning, inadequate social adjustment, and delayed achievement.

Assessment. Psychological assessment of intellectual functioning and a social assessment of adaptive behavior are both necessary when retardation is suspected. When an individual is low in one area but normal in the other, the conclusion would likely be that an emotional problem or specific brain damage accounts for the deficits. Both intelligence and adaptive behavior must be low for mental retardation to be diagnosed.

Psychological Assessment. Normal intelligence is placed at an IQ of 100. Persons scoring below 70 IQ, two standard deviations below the mean, are considered to be mentally retarded. Psychological assessment, which can be done at any age, is designed to assess the intellectual and social adaptation of an individual. Below the age of 2 the Kuhlman-Binet test will assess developmental behaviors that occur at more or less specific ages. A normal newborn infant should give a startled response to a loud noise, carry the hand to the mouth, and respond to a light with eye movement. At the age of 1 a child should be able to stand, imitate sounds and movements, and make marks with a pencil. By 2 a child should be able to copy a circle, obey simple commands, and point out objects in a picture.

Between the ages of 2 years and 6 years, the Gesell Developmental Schedules and the Bayley Scales of Infant Development are commonly used. These tests employ the same approach as the Kuhlman-Binet. Motor skills, adaptive skills, personal-social skills, and language skills are assessed. Again, all these skills are based on what a normal child at a particular age can perform.

Above the age of 6 tests focus more heavily on the verbal component of intelligence. The Stanford-Binet, Wechsler Preschool and Primary Scale of Intelligence (Revised), the Illinois Test of Psycholinguistic Abilities, and the Wechsler Intelligence Scale for Children (third edition) are the most frequently used. If problems such as deafness, blindness, or the inability to use one's arms or hands exist, special tests are available. The Peabody Picture Vocabulary Test, the Columbia Mental Maturity Test, and the Leiter International Performance Scale were designed to allow for these handicaps. They allow pointing, are often untimed, and can be used in quite severe situations.

The assessment of brain damage may be done with the Reitan Battery or the Luria. The Bender-Gestalt and the Benton Visual Retention tests are commonly used as an initial screening of brain damage. The Bender-Gestalt requires an individual to reproduce several geometric figures. Noting the type of distortion or difficulty in drawing can indicate the presence of brain dysfunction.

The psychological evaluation must also include assessment of motivational, emotional, and interpersonal factors. The combination of intellectual ability and the emotional aspects will give a fairly clear picture of the person's capabilities and current functioning.

Social Adaptiveness Assessment. Adaptive behavior refers to how well an individual is able to cope with life expectations. Independent functioning, personal responsibility, and social responsibility are the three major facets of adaptive behavior. By assessing what behaviors a person is able to perform and by comparing these to what is developmentally and socially expected, a social maturity score is obtained. Retardation occurs when the person's score is at least two years below expectation. The Vineland Adaptive Behavior Scales is a frequently used rating scale.

Classification. Mental retardation may be classified according to the severity of the symptoms, by etiology, or according to the symptom constellation.

Prior to 1954 retardation was generally classified by severity of symptoms. Idiot, imbecile, and moron were used to denote abilities roughly equivalent to the IQ ranges of 1 to 30, 30 to 50, and 50 to 70, respectively. Since then these terms have been replaced with less offensive ones. Classification by severity now is based on the American Association of Mental Deficiency system (Grossman, 1973) of using the standard score obtained by the individual on a reliable test of intelligence. The terms applied to scores that are more than 2, 3, 4, and 5 standard deviations below the mean of 100 IQ are labeled mild, moderate, severe, and profound, respectively. They are roughly equivalent to an IQ rating of 55–69, 40–54, 25–39, and under 25.

An etiological classification looks for the factor causing retardation. Pathological conditions such as disease, injury, chromosomal aberration, or a discrete genetic disorder may be used to classify retardation. Whether the cause was exogenous or endogenous may be considered. Locating exogenous factors such as injury or infection, however, is sometimes as difficult as finding endogenous causes such as chromosome or genetic involvement.

Classification by symptom constellation uses syndromes that bear strong resemblance to one another. This is sometimes useful when the cause is elusive. For example, microcephaly, characterized by a small brain and skull, may be caused by heredity, environmental factors, or an unknown factor.

Whether an etiological or a symptom cluster classification is used to describe the retardation, it is still the intellectual level that must be assessed to determine retardation. Therefore, classification by level of intellectual functioning is probably the preferred system, and this method is endorsed by both the American Association of Mental Deficiency and by the American Psychiatric Association *(DSM-IV).*

Causes. There are three major causes of retardation: genetic and hereditary, physical, and psychosocial.

Genetic and Hereditary. In some cases retardation can be directly traced to a chromosomal defect, to heredity, or to another genetic deficiency. Each individual is born with 23 pairs of chromosomes, on which the physical build and appearance of the person is coded. Each parent provides 23 chromosomes. These match up at conception, and the parents' features are passed on to the children. Sometimes an extra chromosome is accidentally present. Other times dominant or recessive traits are passed on to the child. Sometimes there are disorders in the way the body functions, which develop from unknown genetic involvement but which suggest deficiencies in genetic makeup.

Down's syndrome occurs when an extra chromosome in the twenty-first pair is found. While there is no known reason why this occurs, and either parent may contribute the extra chromosome, it is known that the chance of giving birth to a Down's child increases with the age of the mother. Down's syndrome results in a moderate to severe level of retardation. It is characterized by slanting eyes, a flattened and wide nose, and small ears, tongue, and mouth.

Four other chromosome defects produce recognizable syndromes. The cat-cry syndrome results from a missing part of the fifth chromosome. Due to vocal chord abnormalities the infant gives a characteristic cat cry. Severe retardation and numerous other physical complications are present. Trisomy 13, occurring once in 5,000 births, refers to an extra chromosome in the thirteenth pair. It is characterized by low-set ears, cleft palate, cleft lip, sloping forehead, extra fingers, retardation, and often minor seizures. Of these children only 18% survive the first year; poor growth is evidenced. Trisomy 18, with an extra chromosome in pair 18, occurs about once in 3,000 births. Around 80% are females and only 10% survive the first year. Many die before birth. Low birth weight, incomplete development of skeletal muscle, cardiac defects, severe retardation, and numerous other abnormalities are seen. Trisomy 22 is rare and is characterized by retardation, small head, slanted eyes, slow and delayed growth, and heart defects.

Several syndromes are related to abnormalities in the chromosomes determining the sex of the child. These chromosomes, called X and Y, produce a female when the pair is XX and a male when the pair is XY. If only one X occurs rather than a pair, a girl is born with Turner's syndrome. She is short of stature, has no sexual organs, and lacks sexual development. While 95 to 98% of the fetuses with Turner's syndrome fail to survive to birth, some girls may not be diagnosed until adolescence, when the failure to develop sexually is noted. Mild retardation may be present, but more notable is a defect in space-form perception.

Klinefelter's syndrome is found in males when the sex chromosome consists of XXY. Retardation is not usually characteristic, although 25 to 50% of reported cases had subnormal intelligence. In some cases as many as five X chromosomes have been found with a Y. The male with more than two X chromosomes has a higher risk of significant mental retardation.

The XYY male appears to be prevalent in the population with only slight intellectual retardation noted. At one point it was thought that this chromosome combination is associated with criminality, since reports of numerous XYY men in prisons were published. Later studies failed to verify this, but some lowered language ability was found.

Many syndromes are inherited in simple Mendelian fashion. When one parent passes on a dominant gene to the child, the trait carried by the gene will always occur. Recessive traits require a similar gene from both parents before the trait occurs. While they are rare and isolated, several syndromes resulting in mental retardation have been associated with dominant and recessive genes.

Most dominant gene syndromes that lead to severe retardation produce death before birth. Four syndromes are related to dominant gene transmission.

Tuberous sclerosis is a disease manifested by severe mental retardation, seizures, and a peculiar skin condition characterized by butterfly-shaped reddish-yellow tumors, usually on the cheeks alongside the nose. These tumors are nonmalignant and later may be found in the brain or other organs of the body. They may not be observable, and the disease may not be recognized until the child develops seizures around age 3 or facial skin tumors around age 5.

Neurofibromatosis is a condition characterized by light brown patches on the skin, the color of milky coffee (café-au-lait spots), and by tumors on the nerves and in the skin. The tumors may be tiny or grotesque overgrowths. At least six such spots must be present before a diagnosis is made, since normal people may have one or a few spots. Mental retardation and epilepsy occur in about 10% of cases, possibly due to tumors in the brain.

Sturge-Weber syndrome displays a growth the color of port wine formed by blood vessels on the face, usually in the area of the trigeminal nerve on the cheek or forehead. Similar malformations of the blood vessels within the meninges covering of the brain can give rise to mental retardation and seizures.

Myotonic dystrophy affects the whole body. Cataracts, testicular atrophy, frontal baldness, muscle spasms, and muscle wasting are evident. Considerable behavioral abnormality is seen in adults, and retardation may be present. In most cases the child has received the dominant gene from the mother. This suggests that a combination of an abnormal gene and an abnormal prenatal environment is necessary for very early onset.

There are thousands of recessive genes, many of which are harmless, such as the one producing blue eyes. Others are serious, such as the one producing cystic fibrosis. Many recessive disorders that involve retardation produce specific metabolic deficiencies. Metabolism refers to the ability of the body to break down and use particular foods or release energy for use. Some of the more common metabolic disorders are discussed according to the type of deficiency affected. Several nonmetabolic disorders related to recessive genes will also be covered.

Disorders of protein and amino acid metabolism include the much researched phenylketonuria (PKU). PKU is the inability of the body to oxidize the amino acid phenylalanine to tyrosine. As a result, untreated individuals are severely retarded and often are unable to walk or talk. Besides being bedridden, PKU persons are often restless, jerky, and fearful. They may be shy, restless, and anxious, or destructive with noisy psychotic episodes, irritable, and have uncontrollable temper tantrums. Since the 1930s considerable research has demonstrated that most of the severe symptoms can be prevented with a diet that restricts phenylalanine. Prompt diagnosis is essential, including identifying the parent carrier and screening newborn infants. Dietary control can reverse biochemical abnormalities, but structural defects and brain damage cannot be reversed.

Menkes disease, or the maple syrup disease, refers to the inability to metabolize the amino acid leucine. The disease gets its name from the distinct maple syrup odor of the urine. Dietary control prevents many severe symptoms. If it is untreated, the disease is usually fatal by age 2.

Histidinemia is a block in the metabolism of histidine. Abnormal speech patterns or retardation in language development are seen. Dietary control is used. There is some question in the literature about the relationship of this deficiency to retardation.

Disorders of carbohydrate metabolism, represented chiefly by galactosemia, involve the inability to break down sugars into usable parts. When lactose, the primary sugar in milk, is converted into glucose and galactose, the body must convert galactose into a glucose substance. If the child's body is unable to do this, life-threatening symptoms develop from a milk diet. Jaundice, vomiting, cataracts, malnutrition, and potentially fatal susceptibility to infection occur. Strict dietary control and prompt identification are necessary to prevent severe damage and death.

When the complex carbohydrate substances are not properly broken down, and the resultant mucopolysaccarides are stored, severe physical and mental retardation occurs. Hurler syndrome children are dwarfed, deaf, have clouded corneas, widely spaced teeth, short neck, a large and bulging head, and several internal problems with liver, spleen, and hernias. These children tend to be friendly and affectionate. Hunter syndrome is less severe but includes gargoyle appearance, stiff joints, dwarfing, and enlarged liver and spleen. These children are characteristically hyperactive and hard to manage.

Several disorders have been identified related to the inability of the body to metabolize complex fats and lipids. The most common of these disorders is Tay-Sachs disease, named after a British ophthalmologist, Warren Tay, and an American neurologist, Bernard Sachs, who described cases of this disease in the 1880s. This recessive trait is frequent among Ashkenazic Jews, of whom 1 in 30 is a carrier. In all other groups 1 in 300 is a carrier. The presence of this disease can be detected with blood tests or amniocentesis. It usually begins insidiously by 6 months, with listlessness, weakness, hypersensitivity to sounds, and visual difficulties developing. Blindness occurs and death is frequent by 3 years. A partial deficiency of the same enzyme has been reported with less severe effects.

A final recessive disorder is microcephaly, or a small head. The skull is unusually tiny. Severe retardation and blindness are prominent.

Physical. During the normal development of the individual from conception to maturation, interruptions may occur that result in retardation. These exogenous causes will be discussed according to when they occur—prenatal, perinatal, or postnatal.

The primary prenatal physical causes of retardation are infections and trauma. During the nine months of pregnancy the fetus develops from one cell to a fully functioning body with a brain and all organs in proper order. An interruption of this normal development affects the part of the body that is growing at the time. Most infections are prevented from reaching the fetus by the placenta. Rubella, or German measles, is the only acute infection commonly acquired during pregnancy that is not blocked by the placenta. This acute infection disrupts the normal development and results in severe damage and deformity. In one study of 153 children whose mothers contracted rubella during pregnancy, one-half evidenced borderline to severe mental retardation. Deafness, blindness, and heart defects are common.

Trauma includes drugs; maternal undernutrition; radiation; Rh blood incompatibility; chronic maternal infections such as certain viruses, bacteria, and protozoa; and various disorders such as maternal anemia, high blood pressure, and diabetes. Treatment during pregnancy and at birth may reduce the severity of effects in many of these cases.

Perinatal problems, those occurring during the birth process, include prematurity, anoxemia, and direct injury to the head. Premature infants are those born weighing less than 5 ½ pounds. Babies weighing about 3 pounds at birth stand a greater chance of developing more slowly and evidencing lower intellectual abilities. Anoxemia, or oxygen deprivation, occurs when the placenta is blocked at birth or spontaneous breathing does not occur. In several studies with rhesus monkeys deprived of oxygen at birth, up to 7 minutes of deprivation had no noticeable effect on later functioning. The breech or transverse birth may increase the possibility of suffocation, but the physician is usually able to turn the baby properly. Direct trauma to the head may arise from a quick birth through a narrow cervical opening. Evidence is scanty for mechanical damage to the head using forceps. It has been suggested that poorly adjusted mothers tend to blame the child's problems on the birth process rather than seeing them as a response to her or the family's tensions.

Postnatal hazards include head injury, asphyxiation, poisons, malnutrition, infections, and brain tumors. Automobile accidents and child abuse are the two most common causes of severe head injury in young children. Meningitis, a viral inflammation of the brain's lining membrane, and high, persistent fever may affect the brain. These are treatable, and it is usually in severe cases that lingering effects will be noted. Asphyxiation may result in brain damage, depending on the length of time of oxygen deprivation.

Psychosocial. Some individuals show retardation even though no known genetic, hereditary, or physical cause can be found to account for it. Two clusters of characteristics that have proven to be convenient descriptive categories, and which are related to the underlying cause of retardation, are psychosocial disadvantage and emotional disturbance. Some children obviously fit one category, while others have characteristics of both. In all cases the children evidence signs of retardation, slow learning, and poor academic performance.

Psychosocial disadvantage is diagnosed when four criteria are present. First, the person must function at a retarded level. Second, there must be retardation within the immediate family. Third, no clear evidence of brain damage is present. Fourth, the family background must include impoverished living, care, and nutrition. This kind of retardation will probably not show up until the child enters school, at which time the academic and social learning are seen to be slow and below that of the other children.

Numerous studies have tried to show the relationship of low socioeconomic status to poor learning abilities. In a home environment lacking adequate heating, water, or safety precautions, physical health care may be minimal. Lack of exposure to intellectually stimulating opportunities and poor child-rearing practices may reduce the child's ability to respond to learning experiences. Family tensions and pressures may create numerous obstacles to adequate interpersonal relationships.

Emotional disturbance can interfere with educational performance. The child may be withdrawn or excessively active. The more severe the problem, the more likely that the normal processes of school attendance, homework, and socialization will be disrupted. Retardation in this case may be clearly due to emotional factors but is often difficult to assess.

Treatment and Education. *Historical.* Early records tell of Spartan parents exposing their handicapped offspring to the elements to perish. Few other accounts are available, but by the Middle Ages the retarded were exploited as fools or jesters. The Protestant Reformation found the retarded suspected of being possessed with the devil. The common treatment was "to beat the devil out of them."

Despite the poor treatment afforded the retarded, the churches of Europe from the thirteenth century on began to systematically provide asylums for the less fortunate members of society. No treatment or education was provided, but sanctuary was available from the cruel and competitive society.

Prior to 1800 the prevalent belief was that retardation was inherited and consequently not treatable. In 1800 Jean Itard, a French physician, began working with the "wild boy of Aveyron." This boy, captured in the forests of Aveyron, was diagnosed as severely retarded. Itard believed that training and practice could reverse some of the effects of retardation. His efforts produced marked changes in the boy's behavior. While the boy never achieved the ability to talk or live independently, this was the beginning of treatment and education for retarded persons.

In 1850 Edward Seguin, a student of Itard, arrived in the United States. Having expanded Itard's work, Seguin opened residential schools for the retarded. His complex, systematic sequence of training made him recognized as an international leader in the field. By 1900 residential schools were established throughout the country. These schools were intended as training schools, dedicated to curing mental retardation. But cure did not occur, and the nature of these schools has radically changed. Rather than attempting a cure, they now emphasize the enhancement of social competence, personal adequacy, and occupational skills.

In 1912 Maria Montessori, a student of Seguin, opened her schools for training the retarded. She developed a system of self-teaching that trains through the senses. In 1914 Charles Scott Berry began a teacher training program in Lapeer, Michigan. Soon after, the first college course on mental retardation was offered at what is now Eastern Michigan University.

Current Trends. The movement from viewing retardation as purely hereditary to purely environmental has led to a contemporary position that views it as usually the result of the interaction of both these factors. Treatment focuses on training in personal skills to help an individual reach the highest possible level attainable for the deficiency.

One important trend in recent work with the retarded has related to the concept of normalization or mainstreaming. This refers to the right of retarded individuals to participate in normal activities. Such activities include privacy, dignity, liberty, the right to engage in loving relationships, and marriage. Special classrooms, although designed to provide homogeneous groupings to enhance manageable training, specialized curricula that would be in line with the interest of the group, and special training needs for teachers, have often been seen as dumping grounds and discriminatory.

In 1965 the passage of the Elementary and Secondary Education Act provided special programs of assistance to disadvantaged and handicapped children in the United States. In 1969, 14 regional instructional materials centers were developed to provide ready access to valid materials and information.

The provision of free public education for all mentally retarded citizens within the context of as natural an environment as feasible was mandated by passage of Public Law 94–142 and Section 502 of the Rehabilitation Act of 1973. The presumption is that society is obligated to support efforts to integrate retarded individuals into the fabric of the community. Mainstreaming attempts to reduce the discriminatory aspect of being retarded.

The implications of these laws for education are drastic. Free education is provided, even if it means special schooling. The least restrictive environment allows a retarded person to study in regular schools if possible. It is necessary for public schools to make allowances for handicaps, with facilities for wheelchairs or other devices. These requirements have given retarded persons an opportunity for normal education and interaction in society. Special education is provided for the more severe cases where participation in regular classrooms is not possible. In both cases yearly plans specify what is to be taught. This reduces the possibility of ignoring the children and reverting to minimal training.

Likewise, more adequate living situations are provided. Rather than dumping children into institutions, it is mandated that more normal housing be provided. While institutionalization is necessary for some retarded persons, due to the severity of retardation or specific problems involved, these persons are to receive normal treatment as much as possible. Otherwise, group homes, foster homes, nursing homes, even support in one's own home are provided. Residential facilities are designed to be as colorful, warm, and friendly as a typical home.

Where possible, vocational training is given. Providing a means of earning an income gives retarded persons a sense of achievement and worth. It enhances self-esteem to be in a work situation and accomplish a task.

Regular psychological assessments are also required. These occur naturally in normal schools, where academic advance is a primary means of assessment. Since retarded persons learn slower, more regular assessments are needed to verify the strengths, determine if there are other underlying problems, and provide direction for educational plans.

Prevention. Primary Prevention. Any preventive approach must begin with public education. The public must be taught that mental retardation is a handicap that can be studied, treated, and helped. People must know that retarded persons have feelings and emotions and the need for belonging, like the rest of us.

Socioeconomic standards must improve. Malnutrition, prematurity, and other conditions that seem related to the disadvantaged and that give rise to retardation must be changed. Raising of living standards, vocational training, and education are all necessary.

Medical measures, such as detection of Rh and other blood incompatibilities, restricting the number of pregnancies in adolescence and after the age of 40 to reduce chromosomal aberrations, and control of diet would reduce the number of reproductive casualties. Preventive measures in obstetrics and pediatrics would further reduce retardation associated with birth and neonatal difficulties.

Genetic counseling to reduce the possibility of recessive traits is needed. Although this is a complicated procedure, the known facts and uncertainties must be presented to the parents. They must know the chances and decide what to do in the presence of any particular set of odds. Amniocentesis, the study of the amniotic fluid during pregnancy, can reveal genetic defects. Therapeutic abortions have gained wide acceptance based on these findings.

Secondary Prevention. At this level there must be early identification and treatment of hereditary disorders. In some of the metabolic disorders, such as PKU, early identification and dietary control are crucial to prevent severe retardation. Medical and surgical treatment of other conditions is needed. Reduction of the effects of hydrocephaly is but one example. Immunizations and prompt medical treatment can reduce effects of various diseases or traumas that might lead to retardation.

Identifying the mentally retarded child and building positive home situations to reduce emotional and behavioral disturbances, handicapping situations, and cultural deprivation are important. Enhancing a retarded child's self-image and providing help for the parents would reduce the possibilities of stigma.

Tertiary Prevention. Direct treatment of the retarded individual is indicated. Treatment of the behavioral and personality difficulties through therapy, schooling, or institutionalization is required. Behavior modification has proven effective in many cases. Counseling the parents in both management and acceptance can reduce much guilt and anxiety. Vocational and physical rehabilitation combined with special education can meet the direct needs of the retarded individuals for self-sufficiency and self-respect.

References

American Psychiatric Association. (1994). *Diagnostic and statistical manual of mental disorders* (4th ed.). Washington, DC: American Psychiatric Association.

Grossman, H. (Ed.). (1973). *Manual on terminology and classification in mental retardation, 1973 revision.* Washington, DC: American Association of Mental Deficiency.

L. N. FERGUSON

See INTELLIGENCE; INTELLECTUAL ASSESSMENT; MAINSTREAMING.

Mental Status Examination. *See* PSYCHIATRIC ASSESSMENT.

Mesmer, Franz Anton (1734–1815). Born in Iznang, Austria, Mesmer studied philosophy at a Jesuit university in Bavaria and medicine and theology at the University of Vienna. He wrote his doctoral thesis on the magnetic effects of the planets on the human body. Mesmer's thinking was greatly influenced by the Renaissance physician Paracelsus and Flemish chemist Jan Baptista van Helmont. Both these men believed that the human body is inherently polarized into positive and negative and that if this polarity could be connected with the Universal Spirit, the power resulting from the union would cure any illness. Mesmer believed that the celestial forces could be attracted and applied through the use of magnets. One of his first cases was that of a woman suffering from attacks of neuralgia, convulsions, and agitation. His treatment was to place magnets over her stomach and legs. With a successful outcome in this case he continued his treatment with other patients, believing that the magnets captured magnetic fluids from the atmosphere and rejuvenated the nervous system.

Mesmer began to adopt many of the mannerisms of a showman when treating his patients, and he made many claims about his perfect process of healing. The Faculty of Medicine in Vienna denounced his cures as products of imagination, and he was expelled from the medical profession.

Mesmer left for Paris, where he constructed a baquet, a large tub filled with magnetized water and with metal rods protruding from all sides. Patients were required to sit around the tub with hands clasped while the rods were placed on their ailing body parts. His technique became popular, but he was challenged by two scientific committees that discredited his claims as being unscientific. His apparent cures were attributed to imagination, whereby a person could be influenced by the power of suggestion and the interpersonal relationship between doctor and patient.

Mesmer withdrew from public view and died in obscurity in Switzerland. Other physicians such as Puységur, and later Elliotson and Esdaile, continued to experiment with mesmerism in their practice but without any supernatural connotations. The practice of mesmerism later developed into hypnosis.

G. A. JOHNSTON

See HYPNOSIS; HYPNOTHERAPY.

Mesomorph. In Sheldon's system of constitutional types the mesomorph is a person with a hard, muscular body. This body type, comparable to Krestchmer's athletic type, is contrasted to the ectomorph and endomorph types. Sheldon's research suggested that mesomorphs tend to be aggressive, adventurous, and courageous.

See CONSTITUTIONAL PERSONALITY THEORY.

Metacognition. Psychologists define metacognition as persons' knowledge and awareness of their own cognitive system and cognitive processes. Metacognition involves using cognitive processes to determine how well memory and other cognitive processes are functioning. Among other things, metacognitive awareness and knowledge inform people that items must be rehearsed to be remembered; allow learners to determine how much and how well information is understood; and provide strategies that can be implemented to improve performance. Researchers believe that "metacognition plays an important role in oral communication of information, oral persuasion, oral comprehension, reading comprehension, writing, language acquisition, attention, memory, problem solving, social cognition, and various types of self-control and self-instruction; there are also clear indications that ideas about metacognition are beginning to make contact with similar ideas in the areas of social learning theory, cognitive behavior modification, personality development, and education" (Flavell, 1979, p. 906).

Adults possess a good deal of metacognitive knowledge and awareness. They know what influences their cognitive processes (for example, motivation to learn, type of material, and time of day). Adults also know the contents of their knowledge, they know how their cognitive abilities compare with those of others, and they know the tasks they do easily and those they find difficult.

Research examining metacognitive judgments requires people to make ease-of-learning (EOL) estimates for certain material or "feeling-of-knowing" (FOK) judgments about unretrievable information. A person makes an EOL judgment before studying the to-be-learned item; it refers to persons' estimates of their difficulty of learning each item. EOL judgments differ with the type of the to-be-learned material. EOL judgments are related to the amount of study time allocated to each item and accurately predict the rate of learning.

Persons who have not recalled the correct answer to a general-knowledge question may be asked to make an "FOK" estimate; that is, they estimate the likelihood that they could later recognize the currently nonrecallable item. Comparisons of the predictions and subsequent performance show that with general-knowledge information, the accuracy of FOK judgments is well above chance, although far from perfect. There is no relationship between FOK judgments and performance on problem-solving tasks.

When people are confident that they do know the item that they cannot remember, cognitive psychologists say they are in the tip-of-the-tongue state. Their confidence is well-justified because, although they cannot remember the exact item, they can usually give the item's first letter, the number of syllables in the item, and a word that sounds similar to the item, all at levels far greater than chance.

Adults' metacognitive abilities are not perfect, however. They often use a less than optimal strategy to solve a problem. For example, if they are asked to learn new vocabulary words, adults will initially prefer a simple rehearsal method to learn the information and switch to a more effective associative method only after the inadequacy of the rehearsal method becomes apparent.

Perhaps one of the most inaccurate metacognitions is that memory is poor. People frequently lament over their poor memories and forgetfulness. Yet research suggests that people's memories are better than they think. People underestimate their memory because they do not realize that memory's storehouses can accommodate vast amounts of information; or they may underestimate their memory because they evaluate it based on recall performance. When people cannot recall something, they say that they have forgotten the information; however, they can often recognize the information, suggesting that it is not truly forgotten but only temporarily inaccessible. Research with university students suggests that memory for information from a psychology course is far more memorable a decade later than the students had predicted while enrolled in the course.

In contrast to adults, children frequently behave as if they have little or no knowledge of their cognitive system. For example, young children seem oblivious to the importance of rehearsal. They greatly overestimate their memory, and when they are confronted with their poor performance, they seem perplexed. Flavell, Friedrichs, and Hoyt (1970) asked children to study a list of items until they were confident that they had learned them perfectly. When the older children said they were ready, they usually were, giving perfect recall. When the younger children said they were ready, they usually were not. In another study (Markman, 1977), children were asked to determine how understandable some instructions were. Although the instructions were incomprehensible, with important points omitted and others stated obscurely, the younger children claimed they could be understood. They incorrectly believed that they had understood and could follow the instructions. Results like these suggest that children are limited in their metacognition and do little monitoring of their own memory, comprehension, and other cognitive processes.

References

Flavell, J. H. (1979). Metacognition and cognitive monitoring: A new area of cognitive-developmental inquiry. *American Psychologist, 34*, 906–911.

Flavell, J. H., Friedrichs, A. G., & Hoyt, J. D. (1970). Developmental changes in memorization processes. *Cognitive Psychology, 1*, 324–340.

Markman, E. M. (1977). Realizing that you don't understand: A preliminary investigation. *Child Development, 48*, 986–992.

Additional Reading

Nelson, T. O. (Ed.). (1992). *Metacognition: Core readings.* Boston: Allyn & Bacon.

D. Needham

Methods of Psychology. *See* Psychology, Methods of.

Meyer, Adolf (1866–1950). Born in Niederwenigen, Switzerland, Meyer received his M.D. from the University of Zurich and did further study in pathology, neurology, and psychiatry in Vienna, Paris, London, Berlin, and Edinburgh before coming to the United States in 1892. He was a pathologist at the Illinois Eastern Hospital for the Insane until 1895, at the Worcester State Hospital until 1902, and at the Pathological Institute of the New York State Hospital Service until 1910. He was also professor of psychiatry at the Cornell University Medical College (1904–1909) and at Johns Hopkins University (1910–1941), where he became director of its Henry Phipps Psychiatric Clinic in 1914.

Meyer was disturbed by the claim of psychologists that their interest is only in the mental life of the person and by the attitude of psychiatrists whose interest was in the physical or organic condition of the patient. He believed that this led to two dead ends, pointing out that humans are wholes and that they respond to social, psychological, and biological influences. He called his approach psychobiology because he wanted to take all these factors into account. Meyer held the common-sense view that mental illness is a matter of maladaptive habits and that psychotherapy is a process of reeducation, replacing maladaptive patterns with effective ones.

He encouraged psychiatrists to take case histories and to study the patient's life situations. The psychiatric interview developed from his work. He encouraged his students to look at both the behavioral life history and the present condition of their patients. He also emphasized prevention and became a dominant force in the mental hygiene movement. He encouraged Clifford Whittingham Beers to publish *The Mind That Found Itself* and was instrumental in establishing the National Committee for Mental Hygiene.

As he realized that social factors were important in mental illness, Meyer and his wife began visiting the homes of mental patients. Her interviews in 1904 are considered to be the beginnings of psychiatric social work and established closer ties between psychiatry and the social sciences.

Although Meyer is called the dean of American psychiatry, he did not produce an appreciable amount of literature, not even a simple textbook. A selection of 52 of his papers was edited by Albert Lief and published as *Commonsense Psychiatry* (1948). His influence was primarily a personal one on the many students who studied under him at Johns Hopkins.

R. L. KOTESKEY

Microcephaly. Literally small-headedness, microcephaly is a skull deformation characterized by defective development of the brain and premature ossification of the skull. The impaired functioning of the central nervous system usually includes profound or severe mental deficiencies. Approximately 5% of the mentally retarded population suffers from microcephaly. The head is elongated with a receding forehead and chin. The disease may be caused by a single recessive gene or by various prenatal infectious diseases such as rubella or toxoplasmosis. There is no known treatment.

See MENTAL RETARDATION.

Midlife Crisis. Midlife, or middle age, refers to the time after young adulthood until the onset of old age (roughly ages 30 to 70). In these years there is not merely one problem confronting people; they face several crises. A myth promulgated by books of the 1970s (e.g., Sheehy, 1976; Levinson, 1978) is that midlife is a predictable series of crises. This does not hold true because of the great variability between individuals: in the kinds of problems confronted, when those problems are confronted, and how well the individual can cope with those problems.

Age norms are important determinants of who we are, especially in terms of the obligations and privileges attached to our social roles. This is definitely true for the child, somewhat true for the elder, but minimally the case at midlife. The key factor defining one's place in society during midlife is not age but variables such as gender, career, family, and socioeconomic status.

Marital Dissolution. Midlife is possibly the worst time for a woman to be widowed. The grief reaction can be intense at any age, but the 25-year-old widow can remarry and make a new life, and the 75-year-old widow of the Alzheimer's patient has done most of her grieving in the last year of her husband's illness. The worst-case scenario is a woman in her forties, a homemaker, relying upon her husband to both earn and manage the family's finances, and then there is a sudden and unanticipated death (e.g., heart attack, car accident). Midlife widowerhood is hardest for men who still have small children, particularly daughters.

A growing problem has been midlife divorce. An old rule was that most divorces occurred in the first seven years of marriage: if a couple could make those early adjustments, they would be able to negotiate other adjustments. The exceptions occurred primarily at the upper end of the socioeconomic spectrum and were male-initiated: the 50-year-old business executive leaves his wife of 25 years to marry a trophy wife half his age.

In recent years divorce in midlife has become more of a female-initiated phenomenon. Part of this is the healthy development of women's refusal to stay in abusive or codependent relationships. Another dynamic is that some women react to or foresee an empty nest with the children growing up, and they may want to return to college or the labor force. When the husband resists the idea as a threat to his power or comes to resent her expanding horizons, he may retreat to primitive power strategies that drive the wife further out of the home and end in divorce.

Extramarital affairs in midlife are not as prevalent as fiction and fantasy would have them. It is not so much that males have significantly lowered sex drive or that they are more virtuous at 45 compared to 25; they have other priorities. Many professional and executive men lack the time to develop an ongoing extramarital affair. Many lower-level white collar workers also lack the financial resources. Men who have been accumulating assets (e.g., home, stock portfolio, retirement plan) over 20 years of marriage must also think about how expensive a divorce can become. (Only the very rich and the very poor can afford such a divorce.)

Parenting. Most of the children of adults in their forties and fifties are in adolescence or young adulthood. The challenge is to provide guidance when it seems to be increasingly resisted by the offspring, making this the least satisfying stage of parenthood. The empty nest (when children leave the household) is seen not with fear but with relief. A greater fear might be "when will the kids move out" and/or "when will the kids become financially independent."

One of the greatest frustrations for parenting in midlife has been the rising phenomenon of "boomerang kids": the son who left the nest to go to college or the military, or the daughter who left to get married. The son now has a degree but cannot find a job, and the daughter just got divorced. These children return, frequently with emotional scars from their first foray into the world, and sometimes they bring grandchildren. Not only are there more people cramped into the living space, but also there are conflicts. Who makes the rules: the head of the household or the biological parent of the young child?

Another confusing parenting situation that has developed in the last half of the twentieth century is the rise of the blended family. Most midlife marriages involve some children from previous relationships. This not only brings financial pressures but also raises issues of authority and obligations of time.

One issue arising primarily in new marriages is that of childbearing. Some women over 40, even if they have children from previous relationships, may desire to bear another child. While any baby at any time of the parents' life cycle is a source of stress, there are special issues for older parents. One conflict may arise with teenage and young adult half-siblings who now question their place in the parent's heart.

Aging Parents. When the crises of old age (e.g., poor adjustment to retirement, declining physical health, senile confusion) hit individuals over age 65, it is also their midlife children who suffer. Many 35-year-old women spend most of their afternoons driving their children to soccer games and ballet lessons. A decade later these women may spend their afternoons bringing their 75-year-old mothers to the doctor, the Social Security office, or the grocery store. As the elder's health, mental status, or finances fail, the midlife generation will have to make decisions about paying the bills and institutionalization. The elders may react to unavoidable decisions with resentment. Brothers and sisters in their forties and fifties may have gotten along well for decades, but decisions about aging parents can create charges of "you left us all the dirty work" or "you didn't consult us."

The greatest challenge of midlife is to provide in-home care for a cognitively impaired parent. Dementia is usually punctuated by angry outbursts as well as a profound inability to follow instructions. Paranoia also develops in many cases. Institutionalization will become necessary, and even then there will be feelings of guilt: "I could have done more; I should have stood it a little longer."

Financial Issues. In the United States, people at midlife are in the "sandwich generation": they give their time and financial resources to support their own children in high school and college, then weddings, and then buying a first home; and there is the problem of caregiving for a declining, aging parent and paying for the nursing home.

Forty- and fifty-year-olds know that Social Security will not be there for them. They must provide for their own retirement but, given declining middle-class real incomes, cannot begin to save. The financial situation of Americans at midlife has never been so precarious since the Great Depression. An uncovered illness, unemployment, or a legal suit can undo 20 years of accumulation of assets.

Stage Theory. Developmental psychologists (e.g., Piaget, Freud) have always had a penchant for stage theories that view each stage as a step on the stairs of life: one must go through each stage at a particular time, and there is no chance of skipping over a stage or of doing them in a different order. Such models are frequently useful in understanding early life because there is a synchronization of physical change, intellectual abilities, and social roles.

Erikson (1950) took the psychoanalytic model, added three adult stages, and toned down the sexual in favor of interpersonal dynamics, coming up with an eight-stage model of life-span development.

Midlife was his longest stage (stage 7) stretching roughly between ages 30 and 60. He defined the central conflict during this stage as one of generativity versus stagnation. The central task of this stage of life is to build something beyond one's own narrow interests, something that is a genuine contribution to others and will outlive one (e.g., career achievement and raising children). *Gandhi's Truth* (Erikson, 1967) represents a great man overcoming his stagnating legal career to reinvent himself as the spiritual and political leader of the people of India. The best examples of male stagnation in midlife are characters in television comedies: They hate their jobs, do not understand their wives, and are endlessly frustrated by their children. Their lives revolve around food, beer, and television.

Decisions and Roles. My objection to Erikson's formulation is that it ignores the variability of individuals. The developmental challenges of childhood are predictable and inevitable, but those of midlife are the result of the individual's decisions and conflicting roles. There is not one big problem that we must all face in midlife, because we have made different decisions earlier in life. The childless spinster, the welfare mother, the recently divorced 45-year-old are women who have made different decisions earlier in life and have a different set of issues before them. The same can be said for 45-year-old men. Many problems at midlife are due not to one particular unwise or immoral decision but rather to the wake of many decisions undertaken in life (even though most of those decisions may have been the best possible decision when it was made).

One midlife problem pattern is that of rapid role transition. For example, a 45-year-old homemaker goes back to work to help her two children who are entering the university. This strains the marriage, and she divorces her husband. The family home is sold in the settlement, and she moves into an apartment.

Another situation is role overload. For example, a 50-year-old man has a white-collar job requiring 50 or 60 hours of work per week, but then an older child gets a divorce and moves back in, bringing grandparenting responsibilities, and then an aging mother needs more care.

Another midlife problem pattern is role deficiency. For example, a 50-year-old homemaker's children have been launched into successful careers but have not yet settled down on their own. Her parents have passed away, and then she is suddenly widowed. She not only suffers from the grief of multiple deaths of significant others but also may not have any immediate role in which she feels needed.

Support Groups. Intervention with midlife clients should avoid two pitfalls. One is that the solution to midlife's problems lies in the emotional catharsis of life's previous hurts. Such an approach might be useful with women who were sexually abused as children or men who have lingering posttraumatic stress disorder from wartime experiences in Vietnam, but most people at midlife need cognitive-behavioral therapy. The groups need to be focused on the problems currently faced by the clients. The support groups cannot undo the lifetime of decisions that have brought about the current problems but can only find better ways of coping with current problems and avoiding future ones.

Another flawed assumption is that homogeneity of age is the best predictor of group success. A group of men who have nothing more in common other than that they are in their forties will not be very supportive. Groups need to be formed on the basis of homogeneity of problems. For example, have a group of caregivers of parents suffering from dementia, another for grandparents with custody of small children, another for those coping with boomerang children, another for the recently widowed, another for those reentering the workforce. Groups that are issue centered will provide emotional support and concrete advice for the specific problems confronted by the members.

References

Erikson, E. H. (1950). *Childhood and society.* New York: Norton.
Erikson, E. H. (1967). *Gandhi's truth.* New York: Norton.
Levinson, D. J. (1978). *Season's of a man's life.* New York: Knopf.
Sheehy, G. (1976). *Passages: Predictable crises of adult life.* New York: Dutton.

T. L. Brink

See Life Span Development.

Milieu Therapy. A form of psychological treatment based on the modification of the patient's environment. Also sometimes called sociotherapy, the approach is closely related to the concept of therapeutic community, which is the label applied to a treatment program that utilizes milieu therapy. In such a program the entire environment, including not just the physical environment but much more importantly the interpersonal environment, is shaped to make life within it a continuous program of treatment.

One important noninstitutional example of milieu therapy is the Belgian community of Gheel. Since the seventh century residents of this town have taken mental patients into their homes, allowing them to live with normal, healthy families for as long as needed in order to return to healthy psychological functioning. The systematic application of the principles of milieu therapy to psychiatric treatment did not develop until the 1930s and 1940s.

D. G. Benner

See Therapeutic Community.

Mill, John Stuart (1806–1873). The son of Scottish philosopher James Mill, he is generally regarded as the most influential philosopher in the English-speaking world during the nineteenth century. Educated by his father and never having attended school, Mill built upon the foundation of earlier empiricist philosophers and did much to contribute to the development of associationism.

See Empiricism.

Mind-Brain Relationship. For millennia people have recognized two things about themselves. First, we are physical beings, affected by disease, hunger, and a host of physical inputs. Ultimately we wear out or are damaged beyond repair and cease functioning. Second, we also know that we are physical beings. We feel sorrow over the death of loved ones. We may believe that someday we will be reunited with them in our resurrected bodies. Something physical and also something mental about our nature and various systems have been proposed to explain this mental-physical or mind-body relationship. More recently, on the basis of research in the neurosciences, the relationship has been rephrased as one between mind and brain.

In examining the ways in which thinkers have attempted to make sense of this relationship it is important to recognize two separate questions in this context: 1) Does the common distinction between mental and physical events support a further distinction between mental and physical substances? and 2) What is the nature of the relationship between mental and physical events and/or substances in human existence? Answers to these questions are important for understanding our own nature and in formulating positions on such issues as determinism in human actions, bioethical matters (e.g., when a person should be pronounced clinically dead), and spirituality.

Major Relationship Theories. A key to understanding theories of mind-brain relationships can be found in looking at how we conceptualize mind. Three major positions have been proposed: mind as material, mind as immaterial, and mind and body as neither material nor immaterial.

Theories of mind as material have been held since the sixth century B.C. (Thales of Miletus). On the assumption that only physical matter and physical energy exist, mental events such as perceptions, emotions, thoughts, beliefs, and desires can be handled in one of several ways. Eliminative materialists deny the existence of mental events. Talk of thoughts or desires might be considered as meaningless. Or reference to mental events may be seen as part of a prescientific, outmoded language. Still other eliminative materialists may admit that talk of mental events is meaningful, not in describing any true state of affairs but in prescribing or evaluating human action. Reductive materialists acknowledge the existence of such events as perceptions and emotions but redefine them by reducing them from their status as mental events to physical events. Fear is not a mental state but a set of physiological reactions and bodily actions or potential actions. One form of reductive materialism, logical behaviorism, views mental events as referring to behavioral events. Another form, central-state theory (or the identity thesis), sees mental states as brain states. To experience joy means that the central nervous system displays a particular pattern of activity.

There is no mind-body problem for materialists to solve since there is no mind. Mental events are either dismissed as meaningless fantasies or translated into a physical form (behavior or brain activity). It is difficult to imagine how such approaches could be acceptable within a Christian framework. Why stop once one has purged the world of immaterial mental events? Any entity outside of nature, including God, should also be eliminated or reduced to nature. However, when materialists dismiss mental events we feel cheated. Our mental life operates as a given for us. Our hopes and fears are as real to us as the materialist who denies them. To be told otherwise does not match our most basic experience. The reductive materialist's concession that we may retain mental event language is hardly consoling. If our intentions are no more than behavioral potentials and our beliefs no more than interacting patterns of cortical and subcortical activity, then we are no more than complex physiochemical machines. As B. F. Skinner argued, we should discard high-sounding concepts like freedom, dignity, and responsibility. There is no truth, only utility (though few would be willing to concede that such applies to the statement that we are only machines).

Two additional problems for the identity thesis are the implicit notions that every mental event is identical with a certain neurophysiological state and that all mental events must be neurophysiological states. The theory of functionalism has been proposed to address these problems. Functionalists assert that when neurophysiological brain states and other types of states, such as specific computer operations, result in the same behavioral outcome they should be viewed as functionally equivalent mental states. Thus the person and the computer making the same chess move both exhibit functionally equivalent mental states. Like the central-state theorist, the functionalist believes that each human mental event is a brain state. Unlike the central-state theorist, the functionalist emphasizes not the brain state (in computer terms, the hardware) but the functional or causal nature of the operations performed (the software). Mental states in humans are neurophysiological in nature, but two people experiencing the memory of a specific picture may not be experiencing the identical brain state. What matters is that the result, in this case the memory, is the same. A further implication is the functionalist's willingness to attribute mentality to nonhuman animals and to machines designed to exhibit artificial intelligence (*see* Intelligence, Artificial). Although functionalism appears to be an improvement on central-state theory by avoiding reductionism it shares with that theory the problem of how one gets from a purely mechanical event to a self-conscious awareness of a mental event. The functionalist's recognition that a computer can solve an algebraic equation as well as a human is not equivalent to proving that the computer experiences a conscious awareness of the act as a human does.

Theories of mind as immaterial have an equally long and distinguished heritage, with none other than Plato as an initial proponent. Whereas for the materialist mind dissolves into nothingness, behavior, or brain activity, here mind is accorded status as a substance, albeit a nonmaterial one. The rational aspects of mind usually have been emphasized in this approach. As materialist theories deny mind, so one form of the immaterialist approach denies physical matter. However, neither absolute idealism (the view that reality is composed of one all-encompassing mind) nor subjective idealism (reality consists of a plurality of minds) have captured the attention of psychologists as adequate explanations for the mind-brain relationship. Instead, most immaterialists have been of the dualist variety. Two kinds of substance are said to exist, immaterial substance, including mind, and material substance, including body and particularly brain. The pressing issue for dualists is to explain how such different substances are related to each other. Interactionists propose that mind and brain may causally influence each other. For René Descartes in the seventeenth century such interactions took place in the pineal gland located deep within the brain. In the twentieth century the neurophysiologist Sir John Eccles has placed that interface in the processing modules of the left hemisphere's cerebral cortex. In a major work with Popper (1981), Eccles argues the case for interactive dualism. The interface between mind and body is found in the language-controlling (usually left) cerebral hemisphere. Citing neuroanatomical and neurophysiological evidence, Eccles points out the modular arrangement of the cortex. It is here, he argues, that mind is able to influence neuronal processing and from there brain processing on a larger scale. In turn the mind can read the everchanging pattern of cortical activation in the modules and thus have a readout of brain activity.

In contrast to dualism, epiphenomenalism is the view that while brain activity influences mental events, mental events cannot affect brain activity. Mental events are byproducts of the brain's processing, like the steam rising from a cup of coffee or the shadow of a tree. In this sense mental events exist, but just that. Taking the final step in this immaterialist progression, psychophysical parallelism avoids any causal interaction between mind and brain. There is correlation but not causation between what happens in our minds and what happens in our brains.

Immaterialist conceptions attempt to solve the mind-body problem in various ways, each with its own accompanying difficulties. Neither absolute nor subjective idealism appears to be a hospitable framework for research in the neurosciences, which are committed to the search for brain mechanisms underlying our thinking, feeling, and acting. And given the advances in the neurosciences in understanding and treating problems with cognitive or mental components, it would appear that such research will continue and will need to be taken seriously. Psychophysical parallelism leaves us wondering how to explain the multitude of instances in which brain events and mental events appear to influence each other. What explanation can be offered for the high correlation between mental and brain activities? The epiphenomenalist tells us that we are wrong to believe that mental events have any causal force over physical events. Suppose that while working you think about your spouse and decide to phone to see how he or she is doing. The epiphenomenalist would argue that brain processes, under the influence of environmental stimuli such as a picture of your spouse on the desk, cause both the mental event of a conscious thought about your spouse and the behavioral event of making the phone call.

Outside professional psychology and philosophy circles interactive dualism has been the most popular option for explaining mind-body relationships. The influence of Plato, filtered through Plotinus, led to an adoption of mind-body and soul-body dualisms by many thinkers during the early patristic period. That legacy is evident in the folk psychologies of the West. Some people have rejected interactive dualism because of its failure to provide convincing evidence for an interface whereby material and immaterial substances might interact. Others, on more philosophical grounds, reject any picture of the nature of persons that includes dualistic language. The debate concerning what the Judeo-Christian Scriptures tell us about mind-body relations is complex. Interested readers are referred to the works by Cooper (1983). The amalgamation of neo-Platonist theology and received neuropsychological wisdom along with good common sense have led many Christians to assume a dualist view.

A recent variant on interactive dualism and epiphenomenalism is Sperry's (1988) emergentism. Emergentism proposes that the physical and mental are distinct but that the mental is fundamentally dependent upon (in the sense of emerging from) the physical; in this case, the brain. Hasker (1983) uses the analogies of a magnet and its magnetic field and the earth and its gravitational field to provide some understanding. In both cases these fields are real and distinct phenomena that nevertheless cannot exist apart from the physical entity from which they arise. The emergentist further believes that mental events can cause physical events. Sperry (1988) suggests that the mental properties supersede the neurophysiological events on which they are based. The mind emerges from the brain's functioning to become a distinct, separate, and causally efficacious agency. Sperry has also conducted research with patients who for medical reasons have had the major connections severed between the two cerebral hemispheres. This has led him to conclude that a separate stream of consciousness emerges from each hemisphere. The two normally are interconnected and their functioning is coordinated, but our dual mental life is revealed by special testing of these patients. One might conclude that rather than resolving the mind-brain problem, Sperry has expanded it to the two minds-two brains problem.

The third major category, the neutral theories, view mind (and body) as neither material nor immaterial. The things of the world are not physical or mental but some other substance. In the seventeenth century Spinoza proposed one underlying substance, God or Nature, which had both mental and material attributes. Peter Strawson, of Oxford's "ordinary language" school, argues for many, not one, underlying substance. Some substances are physical; others, like persons, have both physical and mental qualities. For other neutral theorists different kinds of language distinguish the mental and physical. For Christians the best-known proponent of this view is the late Donald MacKay (1991). According to MacKay, one may describe the events surrounding human action in two ways. When reporting my own experience I tell my I-story. This is my personal view and rightly includes my intentions, wishes, and beliefs. A neuroscientist might at the same time tell the brain-story of that same experience, which includes reference to changing levels of electrical activity or cerebral blood flow in various parts of my brain but not my mental states. These are two ways of describing the same underlying reality. They complement each other. As MacKay often wrote, it is people, not brains, who think. Yet thinking is not possible without a properly functioning brain.

The disadvantage of the neutral theories is their ambiguity in describing the mind-brain context in terms that make sense to us. It must be admitted, however, that this may be due to the fact that we are prone to operate out of either a dualist or materialist framework and find it difficult to conceive of categories of substance other than physical and mental.

It is impossible to advocate the Christian stance on mind-brain relations. Committed Christians such as Eccles and MacKay stand far apart on key elements of this problem. Yet in both views mental events are taken seriously. They cannot be reduced to nothing but physical events and they have a causal role to play in human action. Whether further research in the cognitive and neurosciences will enable us to decide between these views or to propose another remains to be seen. In the meantime we need to have an open and active mind on this matter.

References

Cooper, J. W. (1983). *Body, soul and life everlasting: Biblical anthropology and the monism-dualism debate.* Grand Rapids, MI: Eerdmans.

Eccles, J. C., & Popper, K. R. (1981). *The self and its brain.* New York: Springer International.

Hasker, W. (1983). *Metaphysics: Constructing a world view.* Downers Grove, IL: InterVarsity Press.

McKay, D. M. (1991). *Behind the eye.* Oxford: Basil Blackwell.

Sperry, R. W. (1988). Psychology's mentalist paradigm and the religion/science tension. *American Psychologist,* 607–613.

Additional Reading

Jeeves, M. A. (1995). *Mind fields: Reflections on the science of mind and brain.* Grand Rapids, MI: Baker.

W. D. NORMAN

See BRAIN AND HUMAN BEHAVIOR; CONSCIOUSNESS; SELF; PERSONHOOD.

Minnesota Multiphasic Personality Inventory. The Minnesota Multiphasic Personality Inventory (MMPI) has been the most widely used measure of personality in the United States. Results from this instrument can provide information about someone's coping abilities, self-esteem, degree of contact with reality, energy level, and interpersonal style. Created in 1943 by Starke Hathaway and J. Charnley McKinley, the MMPI was designed originally to assist clinicians in making psychological diagnoses. The items of the MMPI were selected because they effectively differentiated "normals" from psychiatric patients. In 1989 the instrument was revised and its successor, the MMPI-II, is likely to be used even more than the original.

The MMPI-II is a paper and pencil self-report instrument, which requires between 60 and 90 minutes to complete its 567 true/false statements. This inventory is designed for adults (age 18 and older) and requires a person to function at a minimum eighth-grade reading level. Young people, ages 13 to 17, with a minimum sixth-grade reading level, are eligible to complete the Minnesota Multiphasic Personality Inventory-Adolescent.

Although additional instruments are typically used in conjunction with the MMPI-II during psychological evaluations, clinicians tend to value the MMPI-II because of its breadth in providing information about people's internal processes. As an objective measure of personality functioning, the MMPI-II produces scores on 10 primary scales: *Hypochondriasis*—the tendency to dwell on physical/medical symptoms and resist psychological explanations of behavior; *Depression*—the experience of sadness, withdrawal, and pessimism about the future; *Hysteria*—the tendency to lack insight into personal behavior and to be psychologically immature; *Psychopathic Deviant*—the degree of conformity to social standards and antisocial behavior; *Masculinity/Femininity*—the degree of conformity to gender stereotypes; *Paranoia*—the experience of suspiciousness; *Psychasthenia*—the endurance of anxiety and psychological turmoil; *Schizophrenia*—the experience of psychotic and bizarre thinking; *Hypomania*—the tendency to act impulsively, to become excitable, to experience an increase in motor activity, and to become grandiose; and *Social Introversion*—the degree of introversion and experience of social comfort.

Because motives may vary when people complete personality tests, the authors developed validity scales to detect test-taking attitudes. People who respond to the test items with a negative bias, a positive bias, or an unusual perspective can be detected, as can persons who provide all-true answers, all-false answers, or random responses.

When they analyze test results, clinicians avoid interpreting any scale in isolation but instead view the scales collectively. This broad perspective enables clinicians to integrate the test results with background information, which serves as a framework for interpreting the MMPI-II.

Many subscales also are available to provide more detailed information. For example, some scales provide specific information on various components of depression such as subjective feelings, psychomotor retardation, physical malfunctioning, mental dullness, and brooding. Scores on the schizophrenia scale can be further analyzed to distinguish between a person who is feeling alienated from others and a person who is experiencing psychotic symptoms. Other supplemental scales measure domains such as repression, anxiety, substance abuse, ego strength, dominance, and posttraumatic stress disorder (PTSD).

T. J. AYCOCK

See PSYCHOLOGICAL MEASUREMENT; PERSONALITY ASSESSMENT.

Missionaries, Care of. When individuals or families are accepted as missionaries and sent to a foreign country, they are immersed in a new and different culture. What they are used to as clues to get through the day are not present. Consequently, stress, confusion, and discomfort increase. Although this is normal and to be expected, it is possible to care for these workers in ways to minimize the negative effects of this differentness. Member care, as this is often called, refers to those activities designed to provide emotional, physical, spiritual, and intellectual support to missionaries.

Member care usually focuses on the emotional and spiritual aspects of care. The physical and intellectual components are often built into the system. Many agencies require regular health checkups for their missionaries. Further education is negotiated by the missionary and has been seen as appropriate. However, the emotional needs of the missionary, including the spouse and children, have often been neglected. Five levels of care are usually provided.

First is preparation and training. The selection of candidates is a process that includes proper education, fund raising, and determining the suitability of the candidates. Psychological testing and interviewing may occur. Once missionaries are selected, orientation is given. This may include the basics of operation for the agency or an in-depth exposure to linguistics and culture. The focus in part is on giving the candidates a frame of reference from which to move into a new culture as an outsider and gain language and cultural proficiency in order to be an acceptable insider. Some training programs place the missionaries in a setting that simulates their intended destination. Jungle camp is such an exposure, where the missionaries learn to live in environments similar to where they will be working.

Second is on-field support. Living in a foreign setting increases the risk of crises, whether political, criminal, or natural. Care in these cases assists the missionaries in processing the event and recuperating from the threat or danger. Removing the missionary family from the setting may be important, but there are times when staying in the setting is more feasible. In those cases maintenance interventions are useful. Counseling, talking, having someone listen to the experience and offer understanding to the whole family is valuable. One does not need a crisis, though, to be offered a listening ear, a wise word of counsel, or practical advice. Many mission agencies are using counselors, pastors, or a psychologist on the field to help families with practical concerns from child rearing to marital, from organizational to interpersonal.

Third is the issue of returning. When missionaries return home on furlough or leave the field, the reentry and reverse culture shock can be extensive. Offering a reentry or debriefing time allows the families to evaluate what they learned and experienced. In some ways these people have changed and are now out of step with their home culture. Any change is a loss in some way. Different people handle the grief of loss in different ways, and this is true within a family too. Reentry is a time to think through the missionary experience and allow the changes to be assimilated. Debriefing is often more focused on events but allows persons the chance to express feelings and observations that impacted them.

Fourth is spiritual care. Spiritual warfare is a reality. The clash of Western, scientific thought with animistic or spirit systems must be addressed. Providing prayer, spiritual support, and biblical reminders of this fact are part of missionary care. Since none of us are perfect, our own guilt and failures can be addressed. While not every uncomfortable event is necessarily spiritual in nature, Scripture is clear that we are in a spiritual battle (Eph. 6:12). Giving attention to the spiritual well-being of missionaries is critical.

Fifth is restoration and personal growth. Sometimes personal or family crises require a time of healing and renewal. Whether physical or emotional, there are psychological aspects of guilt, failure, or inadequacy that confront the missionary. The whole family may be affected by one problem, but not all are affected in the same way. Caring for these emotional needs in a healing setting helps restore the missionary to health.

To support all these endeavors of missionary care, research is ongoing that focuses on understanding how best to select, train, and predict the success of missionaries. Flexibility, resilience, a sense of adventure, and family happiness are some areas found to be important in the success of people working overseas. Psychological hardiness is another term used to describe those who have a sense of personal control, commitment, and an openness to change.

Missionary care is an effort to provide emotional and spiritual support to those on the field. Meeting these needs prefield, on the field, and postfield is a healthy way to care for those who labor as missionaries.

L. N. FERGUSON

MMPI. *See* MINNESOTA MULTIPHASIC PERSONALITY INVENTORY.

Modeling. The process of observing and imitating another person's behavior is referred to as social modeling. In the past it was thought that operant and classical conditioning were the only two significant ways by which an organism could acquire new responses. However, more recent research clearly indicates that observational learning should be included in this list. Modeling phenomena have been differentiated, and much time has been spent in debate over the criteria used in these arbitrary classifications. Among the diverse terms applied to matching behavior are imitation, modeling, observational learning, social facilitation, role-taking, identification, internalization, introjection, and contagion.

Learning through the processes of observation and imitation is distinct from both classical and operant conditioning. In modeling, neither conditioned reflexes nor conditioned stimuli are vital to the acquisition of specific behavior, and learning can occur without reinforcement or practice.

Imitative learning seems to occur naturally in primates, but whether nonprimate species can acquire new behavior patterns via observation remains a controversial issue. Animals and birds can learn new patterns of behavior observationally, and modeling stimuli can acquire the capacity to evoke existing matching responses even though the organism was not performing them beforehand (Bandura, 1974).

Despite the fact that several experiments dealing with the question of whether lower animals can acquire behaviors through imitation have been largely inconclusive, the majority of investigations purport that higher-level organization of the central nervous system is essential. Historically the modeling phenomenon has been viewed as an innate propensity even in nonprimates (Bandura, 1974). Therefore, each individual of this species has an inherent tendency to model others.

Four theorists have established the foundation on which the vast majority of subsequent research has been based. Sigmund Freud's research concluded that modeling involved an extensive identification process. Freud realized that ideas, attitudes, values, and behavior all affect the modeling process; thus he was a pioneer in this field of research. Freud's work was further developed by Holt, who proposed an understanding of modeling based on the importance of typical parent-child interactions. A parent would provide the model for the appropriate behavior, and then the parent and the child would engage in spontaneous mutual imitations. After many parent-child imitations, the child could perform the behavior without prompting cues by the parent (Holt, 1931).

Skinner's research stressed the importance of three sequential processes for modeling to occur. First, the proper stimulus had to be provided. Second, an observer had to imitate that specific behavior. Finally, reinforcement had to immediately follow emulation. If reinforcement did not occur, learning was not considered to have taken place (Skinner, 1953). One of the more recently proposed conceptualizations of social learning has been provided by Albert Bandura. His theory suggests the existence of four cognitive-mediational subprocesses. Bandura referred to the first of these subprocesses as attention, which is defined as the observer seeing the modeled behavior. The second subprocess, retention, requires that the observer be able to recall what was seen either through symbolic coding or imagery. The third subprocess, motor reproduction, involves the observer's ability to physically produce the modeled behavior. The fourth subprocess, termed the incentive-motivational function of reinforcement, hypothesizes that reinforcement is a facilitative but unnecessary condition for observational learning. Thus Bandura concluded that an individual can observe a model, covertly learn the new behavior, and decide whether or not to exhibit the behavior depending on the consequences associated with that behavior (Bandura, 1974).

Bandura, Ross, and Ross (1963) produced one of the most convincing and most often cited modeling studies. The study investigated the effect of aggressive models on the behavior of nursery school children. Four different groups were used in the experiment. The first group observed a model who was positively reinforced for acts of physical and verbal aggression. The second group viewed this same model being punished for the same behavior. The third group witnessed a nonaggressive model. The fourth group, the control group, saw no model at all. Bandura and his colleagues concluded that children who observed the model being rewarded for aggressive behavior tended to imitate this behavior themselves. Children who observed the model being punished and children who viewed no model at all showed less aggression than their counterparts in the first group. Moreover, this landmark study demonstrated both the powerful influence of models and the proclivity of children toward aggression.

The acquisition of imitative learning depends largely on the characteristics of the model displaying the desired behavior. In other words, people have a tendency to model those who exhibit characteristics that are highly desirable to the individual and society. Culture, race, geographical location, and peers may also play a role in modeling behavior.

Imitation learning is generally considered to have three distinctly different possible outcomes on behavior. Each effect produces a separate set of variables. First, an individual observing a model may acquire a novel response. This effect is manifested when an observer produces a previously unexhibited behavior in a form essentially equal to the model's behavior. Often a simple opportunity to observe a novel response will cause the observer to acquire it, although performance of the response may be postponed for a brief period.

Another common effect of imitation learning is the inhibition and disinhibition of a previously established response through the observation of a model. This is dependent upon the outcome of the model's behavior. The observer will be disinhibited and the probability of engaging in a behavior increases if one is rewarded for a behavior that is normally inhibited (e. g., stealing candy from a store, fibbing). Hence, when the observer sees that the model's behavior leads to a negative outcome, the opposite effect will take place.

Yet another significant product of observational learning is the facilitation of previously learned responses, which differs from its other effects in two important ways. First, the behavior being displayed is not commonly inhibited. Second, the facilitation is caused by the observation of the behavior and inevitably the outcome of the model's behavior. An additional facilitative effect may be caused by highly positive outcomes, but the critical cause is the observation of the model's behavior.

Recent research expanding the understanding of modeling from the classic studies has been extensive. The study of Werts, Caldwell, and Wolery (1996) examined peer modeling of response chains. Classmates without disabilities were used as peer models. These students were proficient in performing a task and completed one response chain each day and described the steps they performed while their classmates with disabilities observed. Three students with disabilities participated, and their performance of the response chains was assessed immediately prior to and following the peer modeling each day. The results indicated that the peer models performed the response chains precisely and rapidly, and the students with disabilities attained the response chains.

Across the study, participation in classroom activities was high, social interactions were low, and neither was affected by peer modeling intervention. Given the findings of the study, observational learning should be implemented systematically, peer models should describe the steps as they perform them, and the performance of the students with disabilities should be assessed regularly.

Another area furthering the understanding of modeling is the study of infants' verbal imitation and lexical development. The study of Masur (1995) examined early verbal imitation and later lexical development of infants longitudinally at ages 10, 13, 17, and 21 months. Infant lexicons were determined from maternal interviews. Actions, vocalizations, and words either outside or within infants' current capabilities were introduced at ages 10 and 13 months. Nevertheless, 13-month-olds who were more verbally advanced imitated more words within their capabilities, but replication of words outside their current lexicons solely predicted their future lexical development. The study traced the relationship between infants' early verbal imitation, when the ability to copy behavior never before produced first emerges, and their lexical development during their second year of life. The early imitators in this study have demonstrated that they are capable of implementing a strategy effective for future lexical development.

A sufficient understanding of the concept of modeling must include a biblical perspective. "For you yourselves know how you ought to follow our example. We were not idle . . . not because we do not have the right to such help, but in order to make ourselves a model for you to follow" (2 Thess. 3:7, 9, NIV). Paul states even more explicitly, "Follow my example, as I follow the example of Christ" (1 Cor. 11:1, NIV). Perhaps the most powerful statement exemplifying the importance of modeling is Jesus' statement. "Now that I, your Lord and Teacher, have washed your feet, you also should wash one another's feet. I have set you an example that you should do as I have done for you" (John 13:14–15, NIV). These biblical passages provide the basic tenets of social model learning. Obviously, people model others throughout life, and one's characteristics do influence the degree to which modeling takes place (Marvin, 1980).

References

Bandura, A. (1974). *Psychological modeling: Conflicting theories.* New York: Lieber-Atherton.

Bandura, A., Ross, D., & Ross, S. A. (1963). Vicarious reinforcement and imitative learning. *Journal of Abnormal and Social Psychology, 67,* 601–607.

Holt, E. B. (1931). *Animal drive and the learning process.* New York: Holt.

Marvin, M. L. (1980). Social modeling: A psychological-theological perspective. *Journal of Psychology and Theology, 8,* 211–221.

Masur, E. F. (1995). Infants' early verbal imitation and their later lexical development. *Merrill-Palmer Quarterly, 41,* 286–304.

Skinner, B. F. (1953). *Science and human behavior.* New York: Macmillan.

Werts, M. G., Caldwell, N. K., & Wolery, M. (1996). Peer modeling of response chains: Observational learning by students with disabilities. *Journal of Applied Behavior Analysis, 29,* 53–66.

Additional Readings

Bandura, A. (1959). *Adolescent aggression: A study of the influence of child-training practices and family interrelationships.* New York: Ronald Press.

Bandura, A. (1973). *Aggression: A social learning analysis.* Englewood Cliffs, NJ: Prentice-Hall.

Pettijohn, T. F. (1991). *The encyclopedic dictionary of psychology* (4th ed.). New York: Dushkin.

J. M. SMITH IV, P. N. SHULTZ, AND E. P. PITTS

See LEARNING; SOCIAL LEARNING THEORY.

Money, Attitude toward. *See* GREED AND GENEROSITY.

Money, Psychology of. Given the obvious importance of money, it is somewhat surprising that relatively little attention has been paid to the topic by psychologists. That which has been done has been associated with two subspecialties, clinical psychology and social psychology.

The majority of the work on the psychology of money has been done by clinical psychologists and psychiatrists, often working from a psychoanalytic perspective. The bulk of this research has focused on pathological aspects of monetary behavior. Compulsive gambling (*see* Gambling, Pathological), spending, saving, and giving money away have all been studied from this perspective and theories offered regarding the unconscious roots of these patterns of behavior (see, for example, Goldberg & Lewis, 1978). The ways in which money becomes connected to psychological needs such as love, security, power, or intimacy have also been investigated by psychoanalytic psychologists and psychiatrists (see, for example, Wiseman, 1974).

Psychoanalysts suggest that a psychology of money must begin with an understanding of the unconscious associations people have to money. Sigmund Freud identified a frequent unconscious symbolic equation of money and feces. Building on this, Ferenczi provided a detailed description of the transition of anal pleasuring into an interest in money, suggesting that this process begins during toilet training, when the child learns to be proud of his or her "deposits" while at the same time learning the pleasure of "savings" (Ferenczi, 1952). Such behaviors as miserliness and compulsive spending are suggested as examples of anality in money relations. Other psychoanalytic theorists have suggested unconscious associations of money to food and comfort objects (i.e., security blankets or soothers).

The limitation of this psychoanalytic work has been its focus on the pathological and unconscious aspects of money attitudes and behavior. While the clinical psychology of money forms a valuable core of what we currently know about money, a more wholistic psychological understanding requires that nonpathological aspects of money management also be studied directly.

The second major group of psychologists who have studied money behavior are social psychologists. Much of the social psychological research on money has involved laboratory experiments that focused on such things as the use of money as an incentive or a reward for behavior and the relationship between wealth or poverty and status. Illustrative of such experimental research is work done on the role of perceived wealth in the creation of first impressions of a stranger. Interestingly, both rich and poor hold almost identical stereotypes. Both perceive wealthy people to be more intelligent, responsible, hard-working, attractive, educated, and in control of their life and environment than are poor people, who are perceived generally to be lazy, unmotivated, and lacking in ability but warmer, friendlier, and more self-expressive (Dittmar, 1992).

Social psychologists have also begun recently to observe people in the context of their regular life, studying such things as how attitudes toward money affect and are affected by such behaviors as spending, saving, investing, and financial decision making. They also are beginning to study the attitudes and beliefs about money associated with poverty, unemployment, work, taxation and tax avoidance, and some attention has also been paid to the questions of how children develop their understanding of money and how males and females differ in their money management and attitudes.

The following findings are illustrative of the results of this line of direct observational research. Compared with those who do not save, those who regularly do save money feel more in control of their finances and less fatalistic about their lives, are more likely to discuss their personal finances with others, tend not to buy on impulse, and use fixed rather than flexible budgeting strategies. They also tend to be older and middle-aged and to have higher incomes (Lunt & Livingstone, 1992). Similarly, when employed and nonemployed women are compared to each other, those who work outside the home and who combine this with the responsibilities of raising a family are generally happier than those involved only in rearing a family (Baruch, Barnett, & Rivers, 1983). The only exception to this is those women with low-paying, monotonous jobs.

Because money has as much to do with values as with value, a biblical perspective is relevant to an adequate and comprehensive understanding of money relations. Thus, for example, Jesus' warning about the dangers of the excessive love of money points out the importance of money being seen and used as a means, not an end. When this is combined with the ample instruction about the responsibility of Christians for the care of others, particularly the oppressed and disenfranchised, the importance of using money for the well-being of others, not only oneself, is also clearly seen to be a foundational part of a Christian view of money.

References

Baruch, G., Barnett, R., & Rivers, C. (1983). *Lifeprints: New patterns of love and work for today's women.* New York: McGraw-Hill.

Dittmar, H. (1992). Perceived material wealth and first impressions. *British Journal of Social Psychology, 31,* 379–391.

Ferenczi, S. (1952). The ontogenesis of the interest in money. *First contributions to psycho-analysis.* New York: Brunner/Mazel.

Goldberg, H., & Lewis, R. (1978). *Money madness: The psychology of saving, spending, loving, and hating money.* New York: Morrow.

Lunt, P., & Livingstone, S. (1992). *Mass consumption and personal identity: Everyday economic experience.* Birmingham, AL: Open University Press.

Wiseman, T. (1974). *The money motive.* New York: Random House.

Additional Reading

Benner, D. G. (1996). *Money madness and financial freedom.* Calgary: Detselig Enterprises.

D. G. BENNER

Mongolism. *See* DOWN'S SYNDROME.

Monoideism. An obsession or fixation on a single idea and an inability to think about anything other than that one idea. It is frequently observed in schizophrenia and senile personalities.

Mood. A pervasive emotion of sustained duration in which the internal quality of feeling affects the person's perception of himself or herself and the surroundings. Although it is not necessarily pathological in and of itself, a mood may persist over a length of time and require professional help. The feelings may be unpleasant (such as depression, anger, or anxiety) or pleasant (such as elation or an exaggerated sense of well-being).

See AFFECT.

Mood Disorders. *DSM-IV* defines mood as "a pervasive and sustained emotion that colors the perception of the world" (American Psychiatric Association, 1994, p. 768). Common examples of moods include fear, anger, happiness, or depression. In contrast to affect, which refers to more transitory, fluctuating changes in emotional weather, mood refers to the more pervasive and sustained emotional climate.

Mood disorders are those disorders that have a disturbance of mood as the predominant feature.

The most current diagnostic classification system includes major depressive disorder (*see* Depression), bipolar disorder, dysthymic disorder, and several categories for atypical depressions and bipolar disorders.

Reference

American Psychiatric Association. (1994). *Diagnostic and statistical manual of mental disorder* (4th ed.). Washington, DC: American Psychiatric Association.

D. G. BENNER

Moral and Ethical Issues in Treatment. Psychological treatments are inextricably connected with moral and ethical issues. Virtually all forms of verbal psychotherapy, for example, embody some conception of the good life or of how one ought ideally to think, feel, and act. Moreover, Frank (1961) has argued with considerable force that psychotherapy is, at root, persuasion. The client comes in demoralized, and the therapist assists her or him to a new way of viewing life and of assessing what is and is not desirable. Szasz (1961) argues that even defining mental health is a subjective if not arbitrary enterprise.

London (1964) also emphasizes the great extent to which therapy is a metascientific undertaking, at best an art grounded in bits and pieces of science. The bulk of what therapists do might be best viewed as "clinical philosophy." While attorneys specialize in the use of logic to enhance clients' concrete advantages, most therapists seem to use some combination of metaphysics and ethics to enhance clients' psychological sense of well-being.

The Nature of Ethics. It is important to understand that moral-ethical questions cannot, in principle, be answered by science. Such questions are by nature speculative, meaning that there are no universally accepted standards, no laboratory observations that will certify which answers are correct. Science cannot address such questions as, "Should I put my mother in a nursing home?" or, "Should I leave my husband?" However, such questions are frequently encountered in psychotherapy, and the therapist must realize that at these points he or she leaves the realm of science and enters what is here being called the realm of clinical philosophy.

One might argue that the Bible tells us what is right and wrong, and therefore that its prescriptions and proscriptions are scientific. Such an argument amounts to little more than an expression of one's confidence in the Bible itself, since the word *scientific* is being used here in an unconventional way. Whatever else it may mean in this context, *scientific* cannot mean demonstrable or provable, as is required by the canons of twentieth-century physical science.

Questions of ethics and personal morality are by nature philosophical. If one is a Christian, much of one's philosophy is conditioned by one's understanding of, and level of commitment to, Christ. Thus, for the Christian most if not all of the philosophical questions that touch on ethical issues are also in some way theological questions; they concern the nature of God and the cosmos, including his ways with us and his desires regarding our ways with each other.

The Nature of Psychological Treatment. Almost everything that positively affects human thoughts, feelings, or actions can be held to be a psychological treatment. Drugs, biofeedback, hypnosis, hospitalization, conditioning, talking, reading, and even ordinary education may be included. Note that within this framework of understanding, the defining characteristic of a treatment is its psychological effects.

It is possible, however, to turn this conceptualization around and to define as psychological treatment only those things which, via alterations of thought, feeling, or action, alter something else, whether physical (e.g., level of adrenalin) or psychological (other thoughts, feelings, or actions). Within this framework the defining characteristic of a treatment is the psychological nature of its mode of action.

One important ethical issue in any psychological treatment relates to the presence of coercion. Seldom is coercion as overt as a threat of harm for noncompliance. However, in a great many subtle but powerful ways therapists can act coercively. When, if ever, is such coercive action ethical? Who decides that coercion is appropriate? When should the client be required to provide informed consent? How much comprehension of risks and benefits must the consenter have in order for the content to be valid? When, if ever, ought society override the will of the individual to obtain or refuse a treatment? These are only a few of the complex ethical questions involved.

To the degree that a treatment is not coercive, a partially overlapping set of issues emerges. There are still the complexities of informed consent. A more important issue, however, involves the kinds of potentially persuasive "advices" that a therapist ought and ought not to give, as well as the manner in which such advice should be given. Therapists seem to have more than an ordinary amount of influence over their clients. How is this power to be used?

Finally, it should be noted that the issue of coercion in treatment is not synonymous with that of the voluntary or involuntary status of the client. Voluntary clients may be persuaded to undergo a certain treatment without full awareness of the alternatives or the advantages and disadvantages of this particular treatment. Many of these ethical issues are examined and standards provided in *Ethical Principles of Psychologists* (APA, 1981). Similar standards exist for other mental health professionals. Ethical standards in involuntary treatment are usually established by legislation (see Schwitzgebel & Schwitzgebel, 1980).

The Interpenetration of the Moral and the Psychological. God, we believe, desires that we do the right. God, if he is who we believe he is, also desires that we be psychologically healthy. If the cosmos is both orderly and benevolent, it seems reasonable to conclude that all of the Creator's intentions are interlocking—that there is, therefore, an intimate connection between goodness and health. God's laws cannot be arbitrary unless we are the victims of a cruel joke. Whatever he commands must on the whole be in our best interests. Striving to live morally must have positive psychological consequences. And striving for true psychological well-being has to lead us in the direction of a higher morality.

However, sometimes what seems to promote our health flies in the face of Christian teaching. Similarly, obeying God's will as we understand it sometimes appears to hurt us psychologically. Just as there is "pleasure in sin for a season," there seems at times to be health in sin for at least a while.

Few human experiences bring these issues and ambiguities into such sharp relief as the psychotherapeutic encounter. When persons come for psychological help, they are typically in turmoil and pain. "Should I get a divorce?" "Should I have an affair?" "Why am I so discouraged?" "What does life mean?" "Why did my 14-year-old son die in that awful car accident?" These are the sorts of questions that bring people to therapists, and not one of them is devoid of theological and therefore moral implications.

On the other side of the health-morality connection there is also a complex and often subtle interpenetration of sin and sickness. While it is possible to be seriously disturbed without being particularly bad morally, and while it seems possible to be immoral without being psychologically disordered in any conventional sense, psychopathology and baseness are sometimes closely related. Thus, a therapist who attempts to ameliorate psychological disorder sometimes seems to end up affecting the moral character of the person as well.

Law and Ethics. As noted earlier, standards of practice relating to many of these ethical areas exist both within each of the mental health professions and within state legislation. Within the professions serious ethical violations result, at worst, in peer censure, expulsion from an association, and loss of one's license or state registration. However, violation of state criminal or civil law can result in prosecution by government attorneys and conviction by the courts, which may impose fines or imprisonment. Harm to clients may result in their lodging a civil suit against the practitioner, who may be ordered to compensate the aggrieved party.

Many things are unethical that are not illegal, but illegal acts that relate to a practitioner's performance of professional duties are routinely unethical. The range of unethical behavior, therefore, is wider than that of illegal behavior.

Conflicts of interest frequently underlie ethical infractions, and in civil proceedings such conflicts as are relevant to the "cause of action" typically cast the practitioner in an unfavorable light. Courts tend to assume that practitioners cannot properly perform their duties when they have an interest in potential conflict with these duties. Accepting stock market tips from clients, engaging in sexual activities with clients, and serving as a therapist to one's students are examples of unacceptable practices. In each case the practitioner's singleness of purpose and, by implication, clarity of judgment fall under suspicion.

Malpractice suits are civil proceedings. Some malpractice actions are brought on the basis of alleged breach of contract. The plaintiff may argue, for example, that the practitioner did not perform what, for a fee, he or she promised. Most malpractice suits are filed on the basis of an alleged wrong—some for malice (deliberate injury) but the vast majority for negligence. Typically the plaintiff will hold that the practitioner did not adhere to the standard of care prevalent in the community in the way that a reasonable person (practitioner) of ordinary prudence would have, thus failing to fulfill a duty that he or she owed the client and thereby causing injury. Taking negligent action (e.g., administering a harmful treatment) or negligently failing to take appropriate action (e.g., not responding to clear signs of suicidal intent immediately prior to a self-destructive act) are grounds for legal action.

Some professional behavior can be grounds for both a civil suit and a criminal prosecution. For example, a psychotherapist who injures a client with a physically damaging treatment may be brought to trial for assault and battery by the district attorney as well as named in a civil suit by the client.

Religion and Cultural Values. The issues surrounding the question of religious concerns in therapy are complex and are dealt with separately (*see* Spiritual and Religious Issues in Therapy). When religion (in general, or of a particular sort) is in disfavor in a society, practitioners who offend their clients with religious material are likely to be viewed as negligent or even fraudulent. Since one's professional peers are routinely called upon to render opinions in malpractice actions, a negative disposition toward religion by society at large or by particular professional segments could adversely affect the fate of a religiously oriented practitioner facing a malpractice suit. On the other hand, during times of religious fervor there may be a negative bias toward any practitioner who cares even to question the possible neurotic nature of a religious behavior.

We seem to be at a point in history when esoteric religions (e.g., cults or Eastern religions) or quasi-religions (e.g., astrology) may enjoy more favor than traditional ones. Although there have been a number of important church-state clashes, the place of Christianity in psychological services has yet to receive major legal attention; neither has the place, if any, of religious dissuasion in psychotherapy. (See McLemore & Court, 1977, for further discussion of this latter issue.)

Strongly held ethical principles tend to get reflected in laws, which are society's rules for conduct. These rules and the principles from which they derive have more than a casual connection with cultural values—in particular, with what society views as desirable and healthy behavior. Since the specification of desirable and healthy behavior is fundamentally a philosophical—and, in the opinion of Christians, a theological—activity, laws and ethics are heavily informed by speculative ideas. Christian ideas ought therefore to be injected into the shaping of societal standards (codes of ethics and systems of legislation). Because of the intimate relationship between psychological procedures and ideals of health, which in turn relate directly to morals and thus to theology, ethical and legal issues bearing on psychological treatments are of more than trivial significance to Christians.

References

American Psychological Association. (1981). *Ethical principles of psychologists*. Washington, DC: Author.

Frank, J. D. (1961). *Persuasion and healing*. Baltimore: Johns Hopkins Press.

London, P. (1964). *The modes and morals of psychotherapy*. New York: Holt, Rinehart, Winston.

McLemore, C. W., & Court, J. H. (1977). Religion and psychotherapy: Ethics, civil liberties, and clinical savvy: A critique. *Journal of Consulting and Clinical Psychology, 45*, 1172–1175.

Schwitzgebel, R. L., & Schwitzgebel, R. K. (1980). *Law and psychological practice*. New York: Wiley.

Szasz, T. S. (1961). *The myth of mental illness*. New York: Hoebel-Harper.

Additional Readings

McLemore, C. W. (1982). *The scandal of psychotherapy: A guide to resolving the tensions between faith and counseling*. Wheaton, IL: Tyndale House.

Sharkey, P. W. (Ed.). (1982). *Philosophy, religion and psychotherapy: Essays in the philosophical foundations of psychotherapy*. Washington, DC: University Press of America.

C. W. McLemore

See Counseling and Psychotherapy: Overview.

Moral Development. The process whereby the amoral infant knowing neither good nor bad, becomes the moral adult who knows the good, desires the good, and does the good. Moral knowing, moral feeling, and moral behavior—what Lickona (1991) calls "habits of the mind, habits of the heart, and habits of action" (p. 51)—are interrelated and all are necessary for moral maturity.

Each of the major psychologies emphasizes a different expression of morality, begins with a different assumption as to the nature of the amoral infant, and employs a different method for enhancing moral growth (Clouse, 1993). Cognitive psychology, as exemplified in Jean Piaget and Lawrence Kohlberg, stresses moral knowing, sees the child as born with the ability to construct his or her own experiences and understanding of the good, and makes use of moral dilemma stories to encourage moral reasoning. Humanistic psychology, as seen in the writings of Sidney Simon and Howard Kirschenbaum emphasizes moral feeling, sees the amoral infant as having the potential for moral self-actualization, and favors the encouragement of the child's natural propensity to be moral by the use of values clarification strategies. Psychoanalytic psychology, with its founder Sigmund Freud, also emphasizes moral feeling but views the child as basically depraved and maintains that moral conflict brought about by the advent of the ego and the superego is the natural way for conscience development to take place. Learning psychology with its spokespersons B. F. Skinner and Albert Bandura stresses moral behavior, says that the child is born neither good nor bad, and advocates a control of the environment in order to produce responses that benefit the society.

Moral Knowing. Piaget (1932) saw moral development as proceeding from heteronomy, or the constraint of an external authority, to autonomy, or self-rule. Heteronomy occurs in early childhood when the child is under the domination of the parent. Goodness lies in respecting those in authority, in obeying their commands, and in accepting whatever rewards and punishments are given. "Right is to obey the will of the adult. Wrong is to have a will of one's own" (p. 193). Autonomy occurs in middle childhood, when the child moves from a morality that is imposed from without to one that is guided from within, from one that is based on authority to one that is based on equality and fairness. Concern for the rights and welfare of others develops naturally through interaction with peers.

Kohlberg's (1984) research focused on the moral understanding of adolescents and young adults. By studying people at a higher level of cognition, he was able to expand Piaget's two-process system to a six-stage sequence that extends from early childhood through adulthood. A key term used by Kohlberg is conventional, which means that right and wrong are determined on the basis of convention or what society expects of its members. The conventional level is at the midpoint of moral development and includes the two middle stages (stages 3 and 4) in the hierarchy of moral reasoning. The person at stage 3 equates good behavior with whatever pleases or helps others and wishes to conform to stereotypical ideas of how the majority of people in the group behave. Being a good boy or a nice girl or a good neighbor comes at this stage. Stage 4 reasoning holds that right behavior consists of doing one's duty, showing respect for authority, and maintaining the given social order for its own sake. Obeying the laws of the land assures that all citizens are held to the same standard of conduct and all must receive equal treatment under the law. Most adults in the United States make statements at the conventional level.

A child at Kohlberg's earlier preconventional level (stages 1 and 2) interprets right and wrong on the basis of the physical consequences to the self. The child is unable to see the purpose or plan behind the rules; attention is focused on the end result. What is rewarded must be good; what is punished must be bad. The first stage parallels Piaget's heteronomy. Avoidance of punishment and unquestioning deference to power are valued in their own right. The second stage is the beginning of Piaget's autonomy in that social interaction is possible; however, the person at stage 2 believes that right action consists of doing to others what they do to you. What could be more fair than to hurt someone, or help someone depending on how that person has treated you? One is obligated only to those who are in a position to return the favor.

Those who advance to the postconventional level (stages 5 and 6) reason according to moral principles that have validity apart from the authority of groups to which the individuals belong. The stage 5 person is like an impartial spectator judging the social system in terms of community welfare and endeavoring to change those laws that are not fair to all, minority as well as majority. People were not made for the law, but the law was made for people. Moral reasoning at stage 6 considers that all human life is sacred and that individuals are ends in themselves rather than means for some other good. The postconventional level allows for judging right and wrong, good and bad, not in terms of one's own interests (preconventional) or in terms of what is best for one's group (conventional) but rather by what is best for all humankind. Few reach this highest level, but those who do have progressed in moral reasoning from seeing only the consequences of behavior (stages 1 and 2) or what society says is right (stages 3 and 4) to self-directed, socially responsive and responsible persons who have an integrated set of values that apply to the whole human race (stages 5 and 6).

Moral Feeling. Awareness of self, sensitivity to others, appreciation of the potential within humankind, and the ability to express and analyze feelings are traits stressed by humanists. Morality may take the form of joyful and creative emotions such as openness, spontaneity, exhilaration, prizing, and love. It finds its greatest meaning in identifying with other people, in having strong feelings of sympathy with and affection for them. Values clarification exercises (Raths, Harmin, & Simon, 1966; Kirschenbaum, 1992) in the home or the school will encourage the child's natural propensity to develop morally. Seven criteria must be met to choose a value. A person must be able to choose freely without restriction; consider alternatives; choose only after thoughtfully considering the consequences of each alternative; be happy with the choice; affirm the choice publicly; act upon it; and incorporate the behavior into one's life pattern. Children develop morally by expressing their feelings and ideas and listening to the feelings and ideas of others.

Psychoanalytic psychology also emphasizes the affective realm of the human condition. As proposed by its founder, Freud (1920/1949), the child is born as an id or "it" with irrational passions and instincts and oriented to gratification and pleasure. In time the ego or "I" emerges, which is oriented to a real world, and later a superego or "conscience" develops, which is oriented to matters of right and wrong. Development from infancy to adulthood is seen as bringing about a more goodly or moral individual, goodly in the sense of the person being able to live in a society with others and also in the sense of a developing conscience that monitors attitudes and behaviors. Moral development takes place when the young child incorporates within the self societal expectations of behavior and attitude as interpreted by the parents.

Moral Behavior. What a person does affects others more than what a person knows or how a person feels, and all psychologies are concerned with moral behavior. We may say that what we do stems from our own reasoning of right and wrong (cognitive) or from our identification with parents (psychoanalytic) or from our naturally wanting to be good persons (humanistic), but learning psychology says that morality is what morality does. Morality is the development of good habits that comes by reinforcing socially desirable behaviors and punishing socially undesirable behaviors (Skinner, 1983) and by following the example of those who act morally (Bandura, 1986). Consistent and extensive training in good behavior while one is young will result in good habits that persist for a lifetime.

References

Bandura, A. (1986). *Social foundations of thought and action*. Englewood Cliffs, NJ: Prentice-Hall.

Clouse, B. (1993). *Teaching for moral growth: A guide for the Christian community*. Wheaton, IL: Victor.

Freud, S. (1949). *A general introduction to psychoanalysis* (J. Riviere, Trans.). New York: Perma Giants. (Original work published 1920)

Kirschenbaum, H. (1992). A comprehensive model for values education and moral education. *Phi Delta Kappan, 73*, 771–776.

Kohlberg, L. (1984). *Essays on moral development: The psychology of moral development* (Vol. 2). New York: Harper & Row.

Lickona, T. (1991). *Educating for character: How our schools can teach respect and responsibility*. New York: Bantam.

Piaget, J. (1932). *The moral judgment of the child* (M. Gabain, Trans.). London: Kegan Paul, Trench, Trubner, & Co.

Raths, L. E., Harmin, M., & Simon, S. B. (1966). *Values and teaching: Working with values in the classroom*. Columbus, OH: Merrill.

Skinner, B. F. (1983). *A matter of consequences*. New York: Knopf.

B. CLOUSE

See COGNITIVE DEVELOPMENT; KOHLBERG, LAWRENCE.

Moral Therapy. An approach to the treatment of the mentally ill that had its development and focus in late-eighteenth-century France. The term *moral* was understood as something closer to morale in that it carried the connotations of zeal and hope. The approach was a movement toward a more humane treatment of the insane. It included such reforms as the removing of chains and shackles from patients and the first attempts to train staff in therapeutic care.

In France this movement is primarily associated with Phillippe Pinel, who is usually credited with being the first to remove chains from the insane. This credit should go to Jean-Baptiste Pussin, a tanner by trade, who was the governor of mental patients at a major Paris psychiatric hospital. In the United States, Benjamin Rush (1745–1813) was a major figure in the moral therapy era. His initiatives were responsible for the abolition of mechanical restraints and the betterment of physical care in numerous American hospitals.

In many ways moral therapy was the first psychological treatment for mental illness. It assumed mental illness is primarily an emotional disturbance, which is therefore curable. Furthermore, mental patients were felt to be not fully responsible for their actions. These combined assumptions led to a treatment that was primarily psychological. This accounts for the important place moral therapy plays in the history of abnormal psychology.

The period of moral therapy is the historical antecedent of therapeutic community and milieu therapy. It differed from milieu therapy in its assumption of curability. However, most of the basic thrusts of the movement have remained and are now well entrenched in mental health care.

Additional Reading

Bockoven, J. S. (1972). *Moral treatment in community mental health.* New York: Springer.

D. G. BENNER

See ABNORMAL PSYCHOLOGY; THERAPEUTIC COMMUNITY.

Mother-Infant Bonding. Bonding is the establishment of the close emotional tie that flows from parent to child, whereas attachment is the tie that flows from child to parent. Both terms derive conceptually from the phenomenon of psychological imprinting (a process by which a gosling, during the sensitive period found only immediately after birth, becomes attached for life to the first animal with which it has contact).

Influenced by the psychological imprinting phenomenon, the notion of bonding as a single event occurring immediately after birth was unwittingly propagated. Needless guilt was consequently imparted upon mothers who either failed to fall in love instantaneously with their newborns or who,

due to hospital regulations or medical reasons, were temporarily separated from their newborns.

The existence of an absolute critical period of cementing the mother-infant relationship is recognized to be a myth. Bonding between mother and infant is not a single event but a process that can be stimulated and fostered through a variety of interventions beginning at conception and extending into the early weeks and even months of life. Fully 40% of mothers take a week or longer after birth to feel that the baby is truly theirs.

K. H. WIBBERLY

See ATTACHMENT THEORY AND DISORDERS; MAHLER, MARGARET.

Motivation. Many psychologists have sought to answer why people behave as they do through the study of underlying motives. The term *motivation* is used to refer to factors that energize and direct behavior. It addresses why behavior is initiated, continues, and stops, as well as what choices are made (Weiner, 1992).

Instinct theory provided one of the earliest psychological perspectives on motivation and was heavily influenced by Darwin's evolutionary theory. An instinct is a genetically programmed behavior that has a fixed pattern throughout a species. In the early part of the twentieth century it was common to classify virtually any behavior as an instinct. Many prominent psychologists, including Sigmund Freud, adopted some version of the instinct doctrine. In scanning the literature one sociologist found references to almost six thousand supposed human instincts (Myers, 1995). As it became clear that instinct theorists were merely naming behaviors, not explaining them, their influence waned.

Clearly, however, the notion that genes predispose species-specific behavior remains as strong as ever. Evolutionary psychology, which began to take form in the 1960s, explores how natural selection predisposes psychological traits and social behavior. Presumably all organisms, including humans, have the basic motivation of perpetuating their own genetic pool. This is accomplished by surviving, reproducing, and aiding in the survival of others related to oneself. Wright (1994) argues that "essentially everything about the human mind should be intelligible in these terms." Evolutionary psychologists have specifically attempted to show how evolution influences our attraction to certain other people, our helping behaviors, and our gender differences, especially in sexual behavior.

One of the most influential views of motivation to appear in this century was Hull's (1943) drive reduction theory. According to Hull, a drive is an aroused state that is produced by a biological need such as a need for food, water, air, or the avoidance of injury. Basic to drive theory is the concept of homeostasis, which refers to the body's tendency to maintain a constant internal environment. Many physiological states (e.g., body temperature, concentration of blood sugar, level of oxygen) must be maintained at a constant level. According to drive theory, a need is any physiological imbalance or departure from this state of equilibrium. Needs initiate behavior that will restore balance and reduce tension. While drives energize behavior, previously established stimulus-response associations, or habits, provide the direction for action. Hull is perhaps best known for the equation stating that drive and habit relate multiplicatively in producing behavior. To account for behaviors that occur in the absence of any actual physiological imbalance, he distinguished between primary and secondary, or learned, sources of drive. Fear, for example, may be a learned drive, as is evident when a stimulus previously associated with shock comes to produce avoidance behavior in animals.

A number of objections were raised to the theory and contributed to its declining influence. First, considerable research indicates that both animals and people often strive to increase rather than reduce stimulation. Sensory deprivation studies, in which the subject lies alone in a room wearing translucent goggles and receives very limited stimulation, indicate that people need new and changing sensory input. On the basis of this evidence Hebb (1955) hypothesized that organisms are motivated to maintain an optimal level of stimulation. Too intense or too great a change in stimulation may motivate a person to reduce tension, but too little sensory input or variation will move the individual to increase stimulation.

Another objection to drive theory was that it overlooked the importance of external stimuli in arousing behavior. Goal-directed behavior may occur when an organism is not in a drive state at all. The presentation of delicious food may arouse the hunger drive in people who would not otherwise be hungry. Thus while an internal drive may push an organism to act, external stimuli called incentives may pull an organism into action. It has become clear that motivation is better understood as an interaction between stimuli in the environment and the physiological state of the organism.

Perhaps the major reason drive theory lost influence is that it neglected cognitive or mental processes and assumed that people are merely complicated machines. One popular cognitive approach to motivation is expectancy-value theory. According to this perspective, behavior is jointly determined by the strength of a person's expectation that certain actions will lead to goal attainment and by the value that the goal has for the person. Thus goal-directed behavior is strongest when a goal is highly valued and there is also a high expectation that certain actions will result in achieving the goal.

According to Rotter's (1954) social learning theory, expectancy is shaped by one's prior reinforcement history; that is, by the previous outcomes of the same situation and by experiences in similar situations. The value of a goal is closely linked to the specific needs of an individual and, according to Rotter, most needs are learned. While expectancy and value are viewed as independent constructs, their interrelationships greatly influence personal adjustment. For example, a low expectancy of success in the presence of a highly valued goal may result in serious behavioral problems.

One of the interesting issues raised by the cognitive perspective concerns the distinction between intrinsic and extrinsic motivation. When an action is performed for the sake of a reward, it is extrinsically motivated. When it is undertaken for its own sake, because the task itself is interesting and challenging, it is said to be intrinsically motivated. One cognitive theory states that when people receive extrinsic rewards for behaviors that were intrinsically motivated, intrinsic motivation may be undermined. A shift in attitude may occur in which the activity is no longer engaged in because it is liked but because it produces rewards. Research indicates that rewarding children for performing an initially interesting and freely chosen activity reduces the time the children later spend in the task on their own. Rewards may have hidden costs.

The intrinsic-extrinsic distinction has been important in the psychology of religion as well. Gordon Allport distinguished between extrinsic and intrinsic religious orientations (*see* Religious Orientation). Presumably extrinsics use religion to gain social status, business contacts, or relief from feelings of failure. According to Allport, they turn to God but not away from themselves. For intrinsics religious faith becomes the master motive in life, with other needs being subordinated to it. Allport and Ross (1966) developed a scale to measure religious orientations, and research indicates that intrinsics tend to be lower in racial prejudice and significantly more consistent in church attendance than are extrinsics.

While most theories of motivation have subscribed to the pleasure-pain principle, in which organisms are viewed as maximizing pleasurable stimulation and minimizing pain, recent cognitive approaches have emphasized humans as information seekers who are attempting to understand themselves and their environment. This position is most clearly seen in the work of attribution theorists. Kelley (1967), one of the leading proponents of this perspective, states that humans are motivated to "attain a cognitive mastery of the causal structure of the environment" (p. 193). People desire an understanding of why events occur; humans are not merely driven by hedonic concerns but are seeking meaning in their world. Attribution theorists are particularly concerned with the perception of causality; that is, the perceived reasons for an event's occurrence. Fritz Heider, the originator of attribution theory, concluded that we tend to attribute behavior to internal causes (dispositions) or external causes (situations). Although our attributions are often rational, we are vulnerable to predictable error. For example, observers are prone to underestimate situational influences and overestimate dispositional influences upon others' behavior. Studies also indicate that people readily accept credit for their own success but attribute failure to external factors.

Humanistic theorists such as Maslow (1954) have emphasized the person's struggle toward self-actualization, which is the tendency to maximize one's inborn potentialities. Maslow distinguished between deficiency needs, which are concerned with physical and social survival, and growth needs, which motivate one to develop his or her full potential. Presumably in order for the growth needs to manifest themselves, deficiency needs must first be met. Maslow proposed a needs hierarchy in which physiological and safety needs appear and must be satisfied before love and esteem needs become evident. These are followed by the higher aesthetic and cognitive needs, with the highest of all human needs being self-actualization.

References

Allport, G. W., & Ross, J. M. (1966). Personal religious orientation and prejudice. *Journal of Personality and Social Psychology, 5,* 432–443.

Hebb, D. O. (1955). Drives and the CNS. *Psychological Review, 62,* 243–254.

Hull, C. L. (1943). *Principles of behavior.* New York: Appleton-Century-Crofts.

Kelley, H. H. (1967). Attribution theory in social psychology. In D. Levine (Ed.), *Nebraska symposium on motivation* (Vol. 15). Lincoln: University of Nebraska Press.

Maslow, A. H. (1954). *Motivation and personality.* New York: Harper & Row.

Myers, D. G. (1995). *Psychology* (4th ed.). New York: Worth.

Rotter, J. B. (1954). *Social learning and clinical psychology.* Englewood Cliffs, NJ: Prentice-Hall.

Weiner, B. (1992). *Human motivation: Metaphors, theories, and research.* Newbury Park, CA: Sage.

Wright, R. (1994). *The moral animal.* New York: Pantheon.

M. BOLT

See PERSONALITY.

Motor Development. Motor development is concerned with the origins of and changes in motor behavior across the life span. The biological and environmental influences on human movement are usually studied in stages: infancy, childhood, adolescence, and adulthood. Both gross movements, involving large muscles of the body (e.g., sports skills), and fine movements, comprising precise movements of limited parts of the body (e.g., writing and typing), are considered by researchers interested in the development of motor control.

At birth, movement is largely limited to involuntary sequences of behavior such as the sucking, rooting, startle, grasp, and stepping reflexes. These reflexes reveal innate patterns of organization in the nervous system, patterns that will undergo extensive modification during infancy (birth–2 years). Two well-established principles describe the developmental process. The first is the cephalocaudal principle, which states that development proceeds from top to bottom (i.e., from the head to the feet). For example, a newborn has little or no coordinated movement of the chest or arms. However, by the fourth month an infant can hold up its chest and reach for objects placed in plain view. By month 5 an infant can sit up with support, and by month 13 a typical infant can pull itself up in a standing position and walk unassisted. The second developmental principle is the proximodistal, which states that motor control progresses from the center of the body to the extremities. For example, control of the trunk is accomplished prior to control of the hands and fingers.

During this period the brain is undergoing extensive change. Brain cells, called neurons, are growing in size, establishing new connections with other neurons, and undergoing the process of myelination. Myelin is a lipid substance that acts as a type of insulation around the neuron and also speeds the transmission of electrical messages from one part of the neuron to another. Myelination results in a more efficient processing of information by the brain and is reflected in part in the increasing coordination of movement by the infant.

The developmental sequence is not entirely biologically based; environmental factors also influence the course of motor development. A relatively poor sensory-motor environment can delay the normal development of coordinated motor behavior. For example, visual feedback regarding the location of the hand and the effect certain movements have on hand location facilitate coordinated control of that extremity in visual guided behavior (e.g., a reaching response). While the brain undergoes dramatic changes during infancy, these changes require an adequate amount of environmental stimulation to occur.

Motor development during childhood (2–11 years) does not evidence the dramatic change seen in infancy. There are, however, important improvements in the control of motor behavior that are accomplished during this developmental period. Much of the development in fine and gross motor skills comes through active play in children; it is through play that a child learns about his or her body and its movement capabilities. Gross motor abilities in particular develop rapidly. Running, for example, becomes a favorite means of movement, indicating improvements in gross motor skill. Fine motor ability is also developing, and during early childhood (preschool years) a child typically becomes proficient at dressing, although help might still be needed with fastening certain articles of clothing. By later childhood (elementary school years), most fundamental movement abilities are established; however, activities involving perceptual-motor coordination (e.g., hitting a baseball or spiking a volleyball) require much practice.

As with many forms of development, the sequencing of the pattern of motor development is the same from one child to the next. Based upon both environmental and hereditary factors, however, the rate of progression will vary between children. In addition, a given child will vary in his or her rate of progression. For example, a child may advance rapidly in some motor skills and more gradually in others, depending in part on environmental factors such as amount of play and instruction.

During adulthood, motor performance is of concern because it forms the basis of such vital behaviors as walking, eating, dressing, and working. The maintenance of good motor performance can mean the difference between independent living and assisted or total care for older adults. The expected pattern of motor development across the adult years is for motor ability and performance to peak during early adulthood (19–40 years) and then decline through middle (40–65 years) and late (+65 years) adulthood. However, the individual variation seen during infancy and childhood continues during adulthood; the interaction of biology and environment increases the interindividual differences in motor development in adulthood. Although there is a general trend toward decreased muscular strength and a loss of some fine and gross motor control with age, an abundance of research indicates that both neural and muscular plasticity in older adults is such that this decline can be abated with physical activity of sufficient intensity and duration during the adult years.

K. S. SEYBOLD

See LIFE SPAN DEVELOPMENT.

Mourning. *See* GRIEF; LOSS AND SEPARATION.

Mowrer, Orval Hobart (1907–1982). The formulator of integrity therapy, Mowrer had a long and distinguished career in American psychology. He completed his undergraduate work at the University of Missouri (1929) and obtained his Ph.D. from Johns Hopkins University. Further training at Northwestern University and Princeton prepared him for a position at Yale (1934–1940), followed by an assistant and later an associate professorship in education at Harvard (1940–1948). In 1948 he became a research professor in psychology at the University of Illinois, Urbana, where he worked until his retirement in 1975. His specialties included learning theory, language, and personality. He held diplomate (clinical) status from the American Board of Professional Psychology.

Mowrer served as president of the American Psychological Association in 1954 and was the recipient of numerous awards and citations. He authored 12 volumes spanning the years 1939 to1980. His early work was on learning theory, and he began his career as a behaviorist. Later he moved toward integrating concepts such as fear and hope into his theory of the second signal system, a filtering structure bridging the individual with the surrounding world (Mowrer, 1980). This shift toward incorporating softer concepts into the hard data of learning theory was later followed by the addition of a major new area to Mowrer's professional interests: therapy and psychopathology. Meanwhile he wrote or edited four major texts on learning theory.

Mowrer's integrity therapy urges neurotics and others to confess past misdeeds as a necessary step toward health. His approach to therapy was developed as part of his attempts to heal himself of severe, periodic episodes of depression. By his own assessment, analysis by three of the nation's best analysts failed him. His self-treatment program of confession and restitution helped him greatly, and his theories have found fertile footing.

Mowrer's writings have been of great interest to Christians because of his emphasis on sin and confession. However, although he uses such terms as sin, grace, and confession, he uses them in an ethical rather than a theological sense. "What I hope for eventually, is some sort of synthesis: a continuation of the ethical concern of traditional religionists with the thoroughgoing naturalism of science" (Mowrer, 1966, p. 25).

Mowrer is unmistakably anti-Freudian. He suggests that during the Freudian era (1920–1955) personality disturbance was seen to arise from the excesses and rigidity of conscience. Remediation came from a loosening of standards and from permissiveness. "It is now widely recognized that psychotherapy based on this 'diagnosis' has been conspicuously unsuccessful" (Johnson, Dokecki, & Mowrer, 1972, p. 38). He views conscience and morality as a necessary and normally helpful part of the human personality. "The main reason 'mental illness' has been such a mystery in our time is that we have so assiduously separated it from the realm of personal morality and immorality" (Mowrer, 1967, p. vii).

According to Mowrer, the neuroses develop because of undersocialization and faulty interpersonal relationships (as opposed to Sigmund Freud's oversocialized superego) and the failure of repression to continue to cover up past misdeeds. The neurotic suffers from guilt that is real (as opposed to Freud's guilt feelings). "The condition which we currently refer to as neurosis or psychosis is the same which an earlier era knew as a state of sin or disgrace; and the defining characteristic of both is the presence in one's life of shameful secrets" (Mowrer, 1961, p. 148).

Obsessive-compulsives are driven and tortured people energized by displaced guilt that is terribly real. Paranoids project their own outraged conscience onto others and then perceive the others as after or against them. Anxiety comes "not from acts which the individual would commit but dares not, but from acts which he has committed and wishes he had not" (Mowrer, 1950, p. 597). Depression is self-inflicted suffering. "A depression looks very much like an act of 'serving time,' comparable to what happens in those other places of penance [penitentiary]. . . . The question of whether an individual will have one or more later depressions . . . depends upon whether he has really 'connected' crime and punishment" (Mowrer, 1961, p. 100).

Integrity therapy involves acts of confession and restitution so that the troubled conscience can rest and allow normal functioning to begin again. Peace and relief are the benefits of forgiveness and treating the past with integrity.

Observers of the American psychology scene credit Mowrer with opening the discipline for more favorable consideration of values, religion, and morality. He has had considerable influence on such divergent writers as Adams (1970), Glasser (1965), and Menninger (1973). In an edited volume Mowrer (1967) reprinted works that sustained him in times of discouragement. Included are writings of Fulton Sheen, C. S. Lewis, William Glasser, Thomas Szasz, and Anton Boisen.

References

Adams, J. E. (1970). *Competent to counsel.* Philadelphia: Presbyterian and Reformed.

Glasser, W. (1965). *Reality therapy: A new approach to psychiatry.* New York: Harper & Row.

Johnson, R. C., Dokecki, P. R., & Mowrer, O. H. (Eds.). (1972). *Conscience, contract, and social reality: Theory and research in behavioral science.* New York: Holt, Rinehart, & Winston.

Menninger, K. A. (1973). *Whatever became of sin?* New York: Hawthorn.

Mowrer, O. H. (1950). *Learning theory and personality dynamics: Selected papers.* New York: Ronald.

Mowrer, O. H. (1961). *The crisis in psychiatry and religion.* Princeton, NJ: Van Nostrand.

Mowrer, O. H. (1966). *Abnormal reactions or actions?* Dubuque, IA: Brown.

Mowrer, O. H. (Ed.). (1967). *Morality and mental health.* Chicago: Rand McNally.

Mowrer, O. H. (Ed.). (1980). *Psychology of language and learning.* New York: Plenum.

J. R. BECK

Multigenerational Transmission Process. The notion of a multigenerational transmission process is embedded in the old covenant, when God proclaims "I the LORD thy God am a jealous God, visiting the iniquity of the fathers upon the children unto the third and fourth generation of them that hate me; and showing mercy unto thousands of them that love me, and keep my commandments" (Exod. 20:5–6, KJV). Bowen (1978) defines the multigenerational transmission process as a "pattern that develops over multiple generations as children emerge from the parental family with higher, equal, or lower basic levels of differentiation [i.e., mental health] than the parents" (p. 477). Bowen assumes that people marry at similar levels of differentiation. As architects of the family system, the couple in their role as parents function in ways that "de-termine each child's degree of emotional separation (emotional autonomy or differentiation) from the family" (Kerr & Bowen, 1988, p. 225). Bowen first introduced the multigenerational transmission process in 1960, describing it as a "speculative three-generation" process leading to schizophrenia (see Bowen, 1978, pp. 45–69); by 1976 he surmised that the process might take as long as "eight to ten generations" (Bowen, 1978, p. 384). Whitaker (1978) framed a similar etiological hypothesis when he spoke of "the schizophrenic offspring of a socially adapted family: a three-generation story" (p. 157). Kerr and Bowen (1988) later prefer the phrase "multigenerational emotional process" to denote this process "anchored in the emotional system" and including "emotions, feelings, and subjectively determined attitudes, values, and beliefs that are transmitted from one generation to the next" (p. 224). Over multiple generations "every family eventually produces members who are at most points on the scale of differentiation" (p. 228). Each person "plays a part in creating the basic levels of differentiation of people in future generations of his or her family" (p. 228). Friedman (1985) extends this process to the life of the church and other religious institutions.

References

Bowen, M. (1978). *Family therapy in clinical practice.* New York: Aronson.

Friedman, E. H. (1985). *Generation to generation: Family process in church and synagogue.* New York: Guilford.

Kerr, M. E., & Bowen, M. (1988). *Family evaluation: An approach based on Bowen theory.* New York: Norton.

Whitaker, C. A. (1978). Co-therapy of chronic schizophrenia. In M. M. Berger (Ed.), *Beyond the double bind: Communication and family systems, theories, and techniques with schizophrenia.* New York: Brunner/Mazel.

H. VANDE KEMP

See FAMILY SYSTEMS THEORY; FAMILY SYSTEMS THERAPY.

Multimodal Therapy. An eclectic approach to psychotherapy developed and popularized by Lazarus (1976, 1981, 1989). It is not identified with any particular school of psychological thought but has achieved recognition as a reputable orientation to psychotherapy among current systems of counseling and psychotherapy (Lazarus, 1995). Multimodal therapy is integrative, systematic, and comprehensive in providing a workable paradigm for conducting thorough assessment and diagnosis and making carefully selected modes of intervention. It is pragmatic and holds to a scientific empiricism without following a reductionistic style of reasoning. More concern is given to the technical dimensions than to the theoretical. Lazarus has referred to multimodal therapy as a technical eclecticism.

Although multimodal therapy remains technically eclectic, apart from identification with any specific theoretical orientation, it draws strongly from social learning theory, cognitive theory, and behavioral theory and to a smaller degree from general systems theory and communications theory. Its roots lie substantially in behavior therapy (Lazarus, 1971). The initial label assigned by Lazarus to his therapeutic approach was multimodal behavior therapy (1976).

Assessment and treatment focus on the person's BASIC I.D. or seven distinct modalities of human activity. Information about an individual's salient *b*ehaviors, *a*ffective processes, *s*ensory reactions, *i*magery, *c*ognitions, *i*nterpersonal relations, and biological functions (*d*rugs) must be included in the comprehensive multimodal assessment. All these modalities are interdependent and interactive. The diagnosis results in a modality profile that indicates deficits and excesses across each modality. The tendency of clients to favor particular modalities as their reactor styles can be assessed by using special rating scales to obtain structural profiles. Multimodal therapy works on the assumption that patients are disturbed by a multitude of interactive problems and stresses and that effective psychotherapy consists of making the types of interventions proposed by an accurate assessment of the presenting problems.

Following a thorough diagnosis, multimodal therapy encompasses three major areas of concern: the specification of goals and problems; the identification of treatment techniques to achieve the stated goals and remedy the problems; and the systematic measurement of the relative success or effectiveness of the techniques used in the therapy process. In the therapist-client relationship, multimodal therapists prefer to relate on a continuum in keeping with patients' needs and expectations. Therapist behavior can range from formal and businesslike to gentle, warm, and nurturing as indicated by the individuality of the client. They are preferably nonmechanistic, flexible, empathic, and genuinely concerned for the total welfare of their clients. Two therapeutic procedures, bridging and tracking, are especially important to multimodal therapists. Bridging denotes the therapist's deliberate effort to focus on the individual's preferred modality of reacting before exploring other experiential dimensions. Tracking describes the observation of the "firing order" characteristic of a particular client. For example, a client with a CISB firing order has a *c*ognitive-*i*magery-*s*ensory-*b*ehavior sequence of experiencing.

Multimodal therapy offers a storehouse of therapeutic methods drawn from numerous approaches. However, in order to remain theoretically consistent, all these methods and strategies have some connection with the principles of social learning theory. Examples of techniques that make up this technical eclecticism are assertiveness training, sensate focusing, empty chair dialogue, modeling, relaxation training, Gestalt dreamwork, hypnosis, cog-

nitive restructuring, rational-emotive interventions, and behavioral rehearsal. More than 36 major procedures make up the body of central techniques.

A survey of trends in counseling and psychotherapy (Smith, 1982) indicated that multimodal therapy is an umbrella term descriptive of the approach of an increasingly large percentage of therapists. This approach has a much stronger research base at this time, and the voices of Lazarus and others predict that multimodal therapy will continue to grow in popularity and could become the therapeutic *Zeitgeist* well into the twenty-first century (Lazarus, Beutler, & Norcross, 1992; Lazarus & Beutler, 1993).

References

Lazarus, A. A. (1971). *Behavior therapy and beyond.* New York: McGraw-Hill.

Lazarus, A. A. (Ed.). (1976). *Multimodal behavior therapy.* New York: Springer.

Lazarus, A. A. (1981). *The practice of multimodal therapy.* New York: McGraw-Hill.

Lazarus, A. A. (1989). *The practice of multimodal therapy.* (Updated ed.). Baltimore: Johns Hopkins University Press.

Lazarus, A. A., Beutler, L. E., & Norcross, J. C. (1992). The future of technical eclecticism. *Psychotherapy, 29,* 11–20.

Lazarus, A. A., & Beutler, L. E. (1993). On technical eclecticism. *Journal of Counseling and Development, 71,* 381–385.

Lazarus, A. A. (1995). Multimodal therapy. In R. J. Corsini & D. Wedding (Eds.), *Current psychotherapies* (5th ed.). Itasca, IL: Peacock.

Smith, D. (1982). Trends in counseling and psychotherapy. *American Psychologist, 37,* 802–809.

D. SMITH

See ECLECTICISM IN PSYCHOTHERAPY; BEHAVIOR THERAPY.

Multiple Family Therapy. A natural outgrowth of two parallel developments in the history of psychotherapy that emerged in the 1950s: group therapy and family therapy. A basic tenet of group therapy is that persons best learn about themselves through interaction in a group where they can risk self-disclosure and receive feedback from other group members about the impact of their communication style. Family therapy arose out of dissatisfaction with the limitation of individual therapy that involves contact between one client and one therapist. It also emphasizes the importance of group interaction, specifically within the most intimate of groups, the nuclear family.

Multiple family therapy brings these two streams together. Families are dealt with in a group setting. Thus the individual member of the group is itself a subgroup, the nuclear family. The acknowledged founder and only true theorist of this form of therapy is Laqueur, a psychiatrist who began experimenting with this approach with schizophrenic patients and their families at Creedmoor State Mental

Hospital in New York in 1950 (Laqueur, La Burt, & Morong, 1964). He found that patients experiencing such therapy with their families had a lower readmission rate to hospitals than do those who were not given the benefit of the experience. Since that time the approach has been widely adopted not only in inpatient psychiatric settings but in schools, clinics, and growth centers as well. It has become a relatively commonplace adjunct to individual and group therapy in many psychiatric hospitals.

When it is used in a hospital setting, the approach follows a typical pattern. Usually on a weekly basis, families of 10 to 12 patients meet to discuss therapy themes each family is currently working on with its individual therapist. The length of such a session runs to two hours or more and is often combined with social activities such as eating together before or after the session. The experience initially serves a new family by helping them through the "why did this happen to us" crisis. Family members see that other families entered the hospital with the same fear and shame they did. Often an immediate sense of relief and support develops.

As the family becomes more trustful of the group, it often begins to share the themes of therapy it is working on individually. Families begin to see patterns of communication causing other families difficulty that they then recognize as similar to their own. As is the case in group therapy, an individual is usually able to spot quickly the pathology in others that he or she is blinded to in himself or herself. Families that are able to grow into such an awareness often find multiple family therapy critical to the healing that takes place for them and the identified patient of their family in the hospital setting. Families that entered the hospital in deeply disturbed conditions often find themselves eventually encouraging other families going through the same difficult times.

There is no set limit to the number of people who can be effectively helped in one multiple family therapy session. Many ongoing groups can contain 30 or 40 members and three or four cotherapists. Often not only spouses, parents, children, or siblings attend, but also members of the extended family. Friends and neighbors sometimes participate, especially if they have an important role in the posthospital adjustment of the individual patient and his family.

Techniques used in this approach vary as much as they do in group or family therapy. Common group techniques such as role playing and psychodrama are popular. Transference often takes place in multiple family therapy. For example, a teenager who cannot bring himself to confront his own father may be able to express his anger at the father of a fellow patient. Most therapists attempt to keep the families focused on the here-and-now relationships that are developing between family members rather than allowing each family to report solely on what has happened to them separately. Therapists help families to learn by the examples of others—healthier families modeling for those who are still more pathological. This approach is especially helpful to broken, one-parent families in dealing with the loss of a significant member; for instance, they may find in the group a father figure who is able to deal with some of the experiences of a fatherless home.

Implications of this approach for the Christian community are significant. There are typically few opportunities available to members of a Christian congregation to share openly their struggles with each other in a safe, supportive, accepting atmosphere. We tend to want to hide the reality of our family problems, out of embarrassment or fear of judgment that such things are not to occur in a Christian family. Such isolation flies in the face of clear biblical models that seem consistent with the opportunity for self-disclosure and feedback that multiple family therapy offers. Paul's description of the body of Christ in 1 Corinthians 12 includes the provision "so it happens that if one member suffers, all the other members suffer with it. If one member is honored, all the members share a common joy." Paul seems to be saying that if a Christian individual or family suffers or rejoices alone, if the experience of elation or pain is totally private, the body of Christ—the Christian community—fails itself and him. The success of multiple family therapy in secular settings bears unfortunate witness to the lack of community in the experience of many Christians.

The church as community has become accepted as a vital part of its function. Local congregations have experimented, often with great success, in structured activities—usually under the leadership of a trained professional—that allow Christian families to share with each other the struggles and joys of their lives (Cassens, 1973). Prayer groups and house church experiences provide this outlet for some, but for many other Christian families suffering and pain are borne in isolation and a false sense of shame.

All families, Christian or not, have to deal with parent-child relations, marital conflicts, expression of feelings, privacy, and individuality. Multiple family therapy has successfully enabled families to learn from others, and to gain a sense of kinship and belonging to a larger community as a result. This model would seem to ideally fit a basic calling of the Christian church.

References

Cassens, J. (1973). *The catalytic community*. River Forest, IL: Lutheran Education Association.

Laqueur, H. P., La Burt, H. A., & Morong, E. (1964). Multiple family therapy. In S. H. Masserman (Ed.), *Current psychiatric therapies* (Vol. 4). New York: Grune & Stratton.

Additional Readings

Raasock, J. W., H. Peter Laqueur—A reflection. (1980). In L. R. Wolberg & M. L. Aronson (Eds.), *Group and family therapy*. New York: Brunner/Mazel.

Strelnick, A. H. (1977). Multiple family group therapy: A review of the literature. *Family Process, 16* (3), 307–325.

J. F. CASSENS

See FAMILY THERAPY: OVERVIEW.

Multiple Impact Therapy. An intensive short-term family evaluation process based on the premise that when a family is in distress and desiring change, they are most responsive to treatment. It is an interdisciplinary approach using a team of mental health professionals to work simultaneously with the family members for a period of 2 ½ days.

Considerable planning with the referral source is done prior to the beginning of multiple impact therapy. The referral source is usually involved in preliminary evaluations of the problems, which often concern an adolescent who is the identified patient. The family members' attitudes are crucial to this process, so considerable time is directed to promoting the process with family members.

Sessions usually begin on Monday and are completed Wednesday near noon. Prior to the family's arrival on Monday team members meet to discuss the data concerning the family and assign team members to see particular family members. Following this, the team meets with the whole family. At the initial conference early interaction focuses on getting the family to make a clear statement about the reason for coming. Usually the response is strained and unclear. A team member then breaks the ice by stating a blunt observation that reflects what he or she has assimilated from the preliminary data. An example of such a statement might be, "Obviously this boy has to stay childish in that setting. Only by extending childhood could he help mother justify her excessive attention to him" (MacGregor, 1971, p. 893). This usually results in extensive interaction that demonstrates the family's defective communication.

Team members freely discuss family members with each other and with other members of the family. The interaction is open, and all are encouraged to participate. Team members may openly discuss strategy changes that were originally developed in the briefing session. Following this each family member goes to a team member's office. The individual session gives each parent an opportunity to clarify his or her perception of the family and develop a support relationship with a team member. This is termed a pressured ventilation. Later, that team member may meet with the other spouse in order to hear another perception and achieve cross-ventilation of the family problems.

Meanwhile the teenager has been in an individual session describing his or her perception of himself or herself and the family. This session usually lasts about half an hour and is followed by diagnostic testing. This adolescent's team member may then join a parental session for an overlapping session—the team member assigned to the parent describes the session to the adolescent's team member, giving the parent opportunity to clarify and elaborate on the interaction. The youth's team member describes the session with the youth and tries to fit together the parental and youth descriptions of the family.

The following lunch break gives family members a chance to discuss their experiences as well as a chance for the team to confer and plan the afternoon individual and overlapping sessions. After lunch the team members switch family members and explore the family difficulties with their added information. Overlapping interviews with two family members and two team members may continue to occur as well as cross-ventilations. Frequent use is made of overlapping sessions. The task is to clarify perceptions and validate what family members are saying as well as what team members are observing. A team-family conference is held at the end of the first day. Impressions and observations are again expressed to confirm family members' experiences or shed new light on problems. Team members may have experienced the same communication problems family members have complained about with each other. This conference adds more information to the team's expanding experience of the family and is designed to increase communication between family members.

The second day begins with a brief team-family conference to discuss what happened during the evening. Presumably the family members have discussed the previous day's events. If a family member has an urgent need to discuss a personal concern, this morning briefing session is omitted. More individual, overlapping, and cross-ventilation sessions continue through the second day. The second afternoon the focus changes to rehearsals and applications directly related to the problem that initiated the family's coming. Parental and marital relationships are discussed, with the focus on problem solving. Information gained from the numerous sessions is directed toward responsible ways of solving problems: "You came here feeling that your son was being deprived of your participation. Why not start by inviting him to prepare those reports to his probation officer with you?" (MacGregor, 1971, p. 897).

The third day's sessions are directed toward a final team-family conference. Specific plans concerning the youth are discussed such as returning to the same school. The youth may be dismissed from part of the session so that the marital relationship may be focused upon.

This intense therapeutic approach exposes family problems rapidly by using a number of mental health professionals. The overlapping and cross-ventilation conferences clarify perceptions and attitudes and facilitate improved communication and the use of problem-solving techniques. Although research on the approach is limited, it does seem to hold considerable promise as a creative alternative to or supplement to more traditional ongoing family therapy.

Reference

MacGregor, R. (1971). Multiple impact therapy with families. In J. G. Howels (Ed.), *The theory and practice of family psychiatry*. New York: Brunner/Mazel.

T. M. JOHNSON

See FAMILY THERAPY: OVERVIEW.

Multiple Personality Disorder. *See* DISSOCIATIVE IDENTITY DISORDER.

Murphy, Gardner (1895–1979). An extraordinary psychologist whose career spanned 40 years. In a study conducted in 1957 Murphy was cited more frequently in the psychological literature than anyone except Sigmund Freud, making him among the most influential psychologists in the twentieth century. Murphy wielded a command of the breadth of psychology that made him outstanding.

Murphy's parents were an Episcopal minister and a high school teacher. They were exemplars of curiosity, intellectual acumen, and humanitarian interests—qualities manifest in Gardner. They lobbied for greater educational opportunities for blacks and whites, child labor reforms, and improved racial relations.

Murphy attended Yale, Harvard, and Columbia universities and held faculty appointments at Harvard, Columbia, and the City College of New York. He was director of research at the Menninger Foundation and a visiting professor at George Washington University. He was elected to the presidency of the American Psychological Association in 1944. In 1926 he married Lois Barclay, who became a renowned child therapist. She provided intellectual support by reading and critiquing his works and collaborated with him on others.

Murphy preferred to call himself a social psychologist, although by many standards he is more noted for his contribution to a systematic personality theory. His work is innovative and comprehensive in that he attempted to integrate biological and social perspectives. His biosocial theory of personality sought to incorporate various data bases in psychology. This integration was courageous, as it strived to be comprehensive at a time when the mainstream of psychology was becoming increasingly specialized, narrow, and provincial. He wrote *Experimental Social Psychology* (1931) before social psychology existed, and he also wrote one of the first histories of psychology (*Historical Introduction to Modern Psychology*, 1929). His biosocial theory is articulated in *Personality: A Biosocial Approach to Origins and Structures* (1949) and *Human Potentialities* (1958). Other professional interests included parapsychology and Asian psychology.

Murphy is remembered by students and colleagues as an unusually generous man and an advocate of human dignity and world peace.

R. L. TIMPE

See BIOSOCIAL THEORY; PERSONALITY.

Murray, Henry Alexander (1893–1988). One of the most fertile and wide-ranging minds that American psychology has seen. His thinking has been shaped by early training in medicine, by an avid involvement in the arts and humanities, and by the works of Sigmund Freud, Carl Gustav Jung, Alfred Adler, and Otto Rank as well as the academic psychologists Kurt Lewin and William McDougall. Murray's writings range from his seminal work, *Explorations in Personality* (1938), which presented his initial formulations of personality theory, to a psychological assessment of Herman Melville's self-destructiveness. Murray's creativity in the area of psychological assessment engendered the Thematic Apperception Test (TAT), which draws on an individual's response to a series of ambiguous pictures to assess his or her motives and the major environmental forces impinging on him or her.

Murray was a product of private schools, attending Groton and Harvard, where he received a B.A. in history in 1915. He earned an M.A. in biology from the Columbia College of Physicians and Surgeons. Murray then spent two years in a surgical internship at Presbyterian Hospital in New York, followed by two years on the staff of the Rockefeller Institute for Medical Research, where he conducted embryological research. He received his Ph.D. in biochemistry in 1927 from Cambridge.

While Murray was apparently on his way to a career in medical research, he also demonstrated periodic interest in psychology. A number of influences, most significantly reading and later meeting Jung, prepared him to accept an invitation to join the fledgling Harvard Psychological Clinic in 1927 as an instructor. In 1928 he was appointed an assistant professor and director of the clinic. With this appointment began his consuming affair with the study of personality. Murray remained at the clinic until 1943, when he enlisted in the Army Medical Corps. During the remainder of the war he spearheaded an effort to develop techniques to test the qualifications of recruits for the Office of Strategic Services. Out of this experience he wrote *Assessment of Men* (1948).

Murray returned to Harvard after the war and in 1949 established the Psychological Clinic Annex. He was appointed professor of clinical psychology in 1950 and continued his research until his retirement in 1962. Since then he has devoted his energies to the study of Melville's works and has sought to awaken concern for the current challenges to human survival. In 1979 the Henry A. Murray Research Center for the Study of Lives was founded at Radcliffe College.

In his study of personality Murray shunned the prevailing behavioristic paradigm as too limited. He sought to develop research approaches and a theoretical perspective that took into account persons' inner world, the world of conscious and unconscious needs, as well as the external world. It is difficult to appreciate the radical departure that both Murray's willingness to embrace the inner world and his case study approach to research were from the established tenets of academic psychology (*see* Case Study Method).

Murray's investigations focused on the study of motivation or need. The concept of need is fundamental to Murray's personality theory. According to Murray, a need is a hypothetical construct. That is, it is assumed to have a physiological basis in brain activity, and its operation is inferred from behavioral observation and subjective reports. A need represents "an organic potentiality or readiness to respond in a certain way under given conditions" (Murray, 1981, p. 42). Needs may be evoked by internal events, such as fantasies, as well as by environmental stimuli. Needs arouse the organism and direct behavior until need satisfaction occurs. The development of a taxonomy of needs and the investigation of the manifold ways needs are manifested in behavior have preoccupied Murray.

Murray has not been unmindful of the impact of the environment on the individual. As a correlative to his need theory he developed his notion of environmental press. Press refers to "a property or attribute of an environmental object or person, which facilitates or impedes the efforts of the individual to reach a given goal" (Lindzey, 1957, p. 178). The concept of press classifies a situation as to whether it is beneficial, harmful, or neutral for the individual on the basis of how the individual interprets the situation in relation to his or her strivings. In addition to need and press Murray developed a host of concepts in his effort to describe the dynamics of personality and the influence of the environment on the development and manifestation of personality. He strongly advocated longitudinal studies of individuals, as he firmly believed that "the history of the personality is the personality."

Certain of Murray's contributions, such as the Thematic Apperception Test, continue to enjoy an impact. But his influence lies more in the perspective he brought to his study of personality and in the students he inspired. His appreciation of the complexity and the uniqueness of the individual, his unwillingness to disregard this complexity to simplify the research task, his appreciation for the workings of the unconscious, and the creativity he brought to the development of assessment techniques provided his colleagues and students a corrective for the oversimplifications and reductionistic tendency of behaviorism. Murray substantially broadened psychology's vision of the nature of its subject matter.

References

Lindzey, G. (1957). Murray's personology. In C. S. Hall & G. Lindzey (Eds.), *Theories of personality*. New York: Wiley.

Murray, H. A. (1981). Proposals for a theory of personality. In E. S. Schneidman (Ed.), *Endeavors in psychology: Selections from the personology of Henry A. Murray*. New York: Harper & Row.

W. T. WEYERHAEUSER

See PERSONOLOGY THEORY; PERSONALITY ASSESSMENT; THEMATIC APPERCEPTION TEST.

Muscular Armor. A concept introduced by Wilhelm Reich, the originator of body psychotherapy. It refers to a pattern of chronically tense and inflexible muscles that represent at an unconscious level the expression of certain personality and character formations.

Reich believed that the structure of the body is not fixed and immutable. In the course of human development the body of an individual is subject to external influences from the family and society that act upon and modify the body's features, expression, and flexibility. These social forces of conditioning result in admonitions and permissions that the developing child learns to accept and follow. Learning how to act or how not to react is a process in the developing child of gaining muscular control and coordination. In time these controls become automatic and result in a fixed pattern of neuromuscular expression.

An example of this might be the child who has become frightened of harsh reprimands and develops a muscular tendency toward slouching, restricted and limited breathing, a hushed vocal pattern, and a tendency toward avoiding direct eye contact. These neuromuscular expressions may also be accompanied by feelings of lack of self-worth that would also be expressed in deep body muscular tension. This pattern would represent a muscular armoring for the individual.

Muscular armoring develops gradually over a long period of time and is therefore an unconscious reaction. It is accompanied by fixed patterns of attitude and behavior regarding self and others. These fixed patterns represent the development of character in that the individual's personality is strongly shaped by the muscular tensions that have formed during life development. These muscular tensions continue to limit the individual's perception of reality, both within and without, due to the unconscious nature of the unnatural muscular tension.

According to Reich, muscular armoring is a defense developed by the socialized ego against the external environment and the dangerous impulses that come from within. Personality that is based on muscular armor rather than the free recognition and expression of the internal life of the body is limited in its resourcefulness for healthy and meaningful expression.

C. E. Barshinger and L. E. LaRowe

See Bioenergetic Analysis.

Music Therapy. See Expressive Therapy.

Mutism. See Selective Mutism in Childhood or Adolescence.

Mutual Help Groups. Mutual aid or self-help groups have been in existence since the 1940s and represent a growing and popular resource for helping people both inside and outside the church. With their focus on peer support, education, and minimal professional involvement, they are likely to fill an expanding role in the provision of mental health services in the era of managed care and cost containment.

As defined by the Surgeon General's report (U. S. Department of Health and Human Services, 1987), self-help groups have members who are self-governing, share a common concern, give each other emotional support and material aid, charge either no or a low fee, place a high value on experiential knowledge, and provide members with information and education.

Mutual aid or self-help groups differ from traditional therapy groups because of their peer leadership, belief that group support is the key to personal change, and valuing of mutual support and assistance over professional leadership. Other characteristics include being voluntary, the sharing of similar problems, interests, or purposes, and providing peer-organized clearinghouses of information.

Group meetings are characterized by attitudes of hope, compassion, and acceptance. Meetings are informal, open to the community, and scheduled for members' convenience. Members support each other by sharing their common needs and experiences while providing support for struggling with the social, emotional, and existential dimensions of their problems. Although groups usually begin with a more exclusive and internal focus, they often seek the involvement of family and friends. With further evolution, groups frequently become involved in supporting research and changing government policies related to their cause.

Research has consistently supported the effectiveness of mutual aid or self-help groups. In research reviewed by Gould and Clum (1993) self-help approaches were generally as effective as psychotherapy alone; the most effective treatment for many disorders was a combination of both psychotherapy and mutual help groups. The research also suggested that self-help approaches, like traditional therapies, have their lowest success in changing habit behaviors such as drinking, smoking, eating, and exercise. Gottlieb (1982) and others indicate that the most important factor contributing to the effectiveness of these groups is experiencing community and being committed to a common cause with shared beliefs. For many people the group is the first place where they overcome the isolation of coping with their situation. The sharing of seasoned group members such as AA sponsors also supports change by teaching newer group members how to cope and producing a feeling of togetherness in facing their common problems. Other important therapeutic elements included being able to help others while receiving help, receiving inspiration and hope to carry on, and developing social support networks. A final contribution is the provision of information and education, which allows group members to become better at self-care and as consumers of traditional medical and psychotherapies.

There have been many attempts to understand and categorize self-help or mutual support groups. Defining groups based on the types of problems addressed, Katz and Bender (1976) identified five categories. They defined groups as focused on self-fulfillment and personal growth, advocating to decrease social stigma and change governmental policies, supporting alternative lifestyles, creating a sense of community among society's outcasts, and groups with a mixed focus. Looking at the group's mission and approach, Powell (1990) also developed five categories. He defined them as habit disturbance groups, such as the various 12 step/anonymous groups; general purpose organizations, such as anxiety, depression, and bereavement groups; lifestyle organizations, such as divorce recovery or adoptive parents' groups; significant other organizations, such as Alanon/Alateen and The Alliance for the Mentally Ill (AMI); and physical handicap organizations. Finally, Schubert and Borkman (1991) identified five types of groups by organizational structure. They defined groups as unaffiliated, which are one-group organizations with no organizational affiliation; federated, which are affiliated with state, regional, or national organizations; affiliated, which are subordinate to and must conform to the guidelines and procedures of the main headquarters; managed, which are under the direction and monitoring of professionals; and hybrid, which are a mixture of affiliated and managed groups.

Historical origins of mutual support groups are often related to religious, humanitarian, and economic values. The New Testament repeatedly emphasizes the need to encourage, support, pray for, teach, comfort, care for, and otherwise support one another. Early Wesleyanism had a dynamic small group/mutual support emphasis. Judeo-Christian beliefs were important to the founders of AA, and spiritual life is inherent in the 12 steps. Other origins relate to humanitarian and economic forces in eighteenth-century England and twentieth-century America. The concept of self or mutual help has been part of American culture and encouraged by its general distrust of institutions.

Although mutual aid or self-help groups have a demonstrated effectiveness, there are potential problems and limitations. These groups produce greater gains in attitude change than in behavioral improvement; thus they often work best in conjunction with traditional therapy. Care must also be given to avoid simplistic assumptions, unrealistic expectations, group-imposed self-condemnation, and a rejection of professional help that can predominate in some groups and self-help writings. A final concern expressed within the Christian community is that self-help groups may foster a self-centered orientation that leaves no room for dependence on God. As with all interventions, awareness of potential limitations can insure that this powerful and effective means for helping people inside and outside the church can be used constructively.

References

Gottlieb, B. H. (1982). Mutual-help groups: Members' views of their benefits and of roles for professionals. In L. D. Borman, L. E. Borck, R. Hess, & F. P. Pasquale (Eds.), *Helping people to help themselves: Self-help and prevention.* New York: Haworth.

Gould, R. A., & Clum, G. A. (1993). A meta-analysis of self-help treatment approaches. *Clinical Psychology Review, 13,* 169–186.

Katz, A. H., & Bender, E. I. (1976). *The strength in us: Self-help groups in the modern world.* New York: New Viewpoints.

Powell, T. J. (Ed.). (1990). *Working with self-help.* Silver Spring, MD: National Association of Social Workers.

Schubert. M. A., & Borkman, T. J. (1991). An organizational typology for self-help groups. *American Journal of Community Psychology, 19,* 769–787.

U. S. Department of Health and Human Services. (1987). *Surgeon General's workshop on self-help and public health.* Washington, DC: U.S. Government Printing Office.

B. E. ECK

See GROUP DYNAMICS; COMMUNITY MENTAL HEALTH; GROUP PSYCHOTHERAPY.

Mutual Storytelling Technique. A method of child psychotherapy developed by Gardner (1971). Although it has been a time-honored practice in child therapy to elicit stories, Gardner's technique suggests a more systematic method of utilizing these stories therapeutically.

The technique consists of first asking the child to make up a story. After it is told, the child is then asked to tell the moral or lesson that the story teaches. The therapist listens to this story and, in the light of everything else known about the child, makes a surmise of its psychodynamic meaning. The therapist then tells a story containing the same characters in a similar setting but introducing healthier adaptations and resolutions of the conflicts exhibited in the child's story. The therapist then tells the moral of his or her story. By speaking in the child's own language the therapist is more likely to be heard by the child. Furthermore, the child is not burdened by alien interpretations.

Mutual storytelling is not a therapy per se but rather a technique that is useful in combination with other techniques. Gardner suggests that it is most useful in the latency period, when the products of the child's imagination are too difficult to access. It has been utilized with a wide variety of childhood disorders, the only limit on its usefulness being the creative capacity of the therapist for prompt formulations and improvisation of stories.

Reference

Gardner, R. A. (1971). *Therapeutic communication with children.* New York: Science House.

D. G. BENNER

See CHILD THERAPY.

Myers-Briggs Type Indicator. The Myers-Briggs Type Indicator (MBTI) is an instrument developed by Isabel Briggs Myers, a student of psychoanalyst Carl Gustav Jung, and her daughter, Katherine Myers, in the late 1940s, but it was not ready for popular use until the first edition of the MBTI in 1962. The MBTI became used by the psychological community in the late 1970s, but during the next 10 years it became popular particularly among educators and business management trainers, with whom it has remained popular. It is much less popular with psychologists, who tend to view the instrument as too simplistic and contrary to most tests available.

The Association for Personality Type (APT), which is based singularly on the use of the MBTI, as well as the Center for Application of Type (CAPT), militate strongly against the definition of the instrument as a psychological test, preferring that the nomenclature *indicator* be used. This follows Jung's and Myers' theory that the MBTI is a instrument examining one's inclination toward a particular personality type that indicates one's preference. The focus of APT and others using the MBTI is on human differences rather than on human problems. Since the 1980s the APT has grown rapidly; also, great numbers of trainers use the MBTI, and many other people believe that the indicator is the best way to understand human functioning.

The attractiveness of the MBTI comes primarily from its lack of pejorative language, psychopathology, and problem orientation in its assessment of personality. Although certain other psychological instruments tend to avoid pathology-laden categories, such as the Taylor-Johnson Temperament Analysis, the Adjective Check List, and the newest entry to the market, the NEO-PI, even these tests retain negative-sounding components such as neuroticism, which the MBTI scrupulously avoids in its assessment categories.

Following Jungian thought, the MBTI constructs a personality type profile utilizing four dimensions of personality. The first three of these dimensions are distinctly Jungian: a dimension of energy, extraversion or introversion. The next two dimensions are those that Jung called functions, namely, the perceptive, or information-gathering, function, and the judging, or information-assessment, function. The perceptive function is scaled across a spectrum from sensing to intuitive. Sensing and intuitive, as distinctly Jungian terms, should be understood roughly to be concrete and abstract; that is, representing persons who gather information in a concrete, down-to-earth way, or persons who gather information in an abstract, theoretical way. The third MBTI function, the judging function, is scaled across a spectrum from thinking to feeling. Jung understood humans to be inclined to judging, or evaluating, primarily from one of these dimensions, the former being rational, factual, and based on objective assessment processes, the later being a subjective means of assessment based on intuition and inner feeling. The last dimension of the MBTI, the judging versus perceptive function, was the particularly unique contribution of Myers and represents a person's attitude toward the world but perhaps is better understood as one's approach to the world. Persons who are judgers, which should not be confused with being judgmental, are those who plan and order their lives, prefer boundaries, and focus on the future, whereas perceivers, focusing on the present, tend to be spontaneous and resist boundaries.

While Myers constructed the MBTI as an essentially Jungian instrument, it quantifies and concretizes Jungian theory of personality far more than Jung intended and thus truly represents a marked change from the analyst's original intention. The unique scoring and scaling procedure of the MBTI allows for a four-part assessment of one's personality as represented by the letters assigned to the four dimensions, E or I, S or N, T or F, and J or P, and these letters are then combined into an MBTI type, such as ENFP or any other of the 16 possible combinations of these elements of personality. Individuals and trainers who regularly use the MBTI find great favor in identifying themselves and others by this means of typing persons and personality, but there is great resistance to such typing in most of the psychological community, including true Jungians who view this kind of personality assessment as intrinsically limiting.

A large body of research is being developed on the MBTI, primarily from its users, but comparisons and correlations with other tests as well as examinations of validity of the instrument are not readily available. Additional concerns include validity of the scoring procedure of the MBTI, the feeling-laden language of the instrument, the apparent correlation of the F scale with gender role, and the lack of clarity as to persons who score midline between the four polarities.

Additional Readings

Jung, C. J. (1971): *Psychological types*. Princeton, NJ: Princeton University Press. (Original work published 1921)

Kiersey, D., & Bates, M. (1978). *Please understand me*. Del Mar, CA: Prometheus.

Myers, I. B. (1980). *Gifts differing*. Palo Alto, CA: Consulting Psychologists Press.

Myers, I. B., & McCaulley, M. H. (1985). *Manual: A guide to the development and use of the Myers-Briggs Type Indicator*. Palo Alto, CA: Consulting Psychologists Press.

R. B. JOHNSON

See PERSONALITY ASSESSMENT; PSYCHOLOGICAL MEASUREMENT; PSYCHOLOGICAL TYPES: JUNG'S VIEW.

Mysticism. Mysticism classically refers to unmediated, direct, and intuitive experience of the Ultimate Reality, of God. The experience does not come from reasoning or an emotional high and is not based on what others have said about the object of experience. Mystical teachings are often secret, given only to those who can understand them correctly.

The word *mystical* entered the Christianity lexicon through a Syrian monk, Pseudo-Dionysius, who wrote a classical treatise on mysticism. He said mysticism refers to the closeted secrecy of a mind that has experienced God (1987).

Misconceptions. Many people have peculiar ideas about mysticism. They think the word refers to a mysterious event. Some people use the word pejoratively. Calling something mystical does not mean that it is spooky, unreal, abstract, or vague. It does not refer to such parapsychological phenomena as extrasensory perception (ESP) or hunches, although some mystics also experience these. Mysticism is not poetic imagination, New Age spirituality, superstition, or the occult, as popularly understood. Finally, it does not refer to heresy or unwholesome Greek influences in Christianity.

Some common religious experiences that may be inspiring and helpful are excluded. Feelings of religious commitment or of being saved are not usually mystical, nor are warm feelings, deep fervor, or positive emotions associated with prayer and religious ritual. Such charismatic experiences as ecstasy (*see* Ecstatic Religious Experience), glossolalia, or trance dancing are not mysticism.

Criteria of Mysticism. Mystical experiences usually last only a short time and often produce a great sense of paradox. Although meditation makes such experiences more likely, they seem more something that happens to one than something that one can make happen. Psychologist William James, in his classic *Psychology of Religion*, named four main mystical characteristics: ineffability, noetic quality, transience, and passivity (1902, chaps. 16, 17). Other mystics and scholars have other criteria.

Unity. The sense of self as separate disappears in mystical experience. Christian mystic Meister Eckhart wrote: "Go completely out of yourself for God's love, and God comes completely out of himself for love of you. And when these two have gone out, what remains there is a simplified One" (1981, p. 184).

Ineffability. Mystical experiences are ineffable. They do not translate well into words; understanding lies only in the experience itself. References to "a dazzling darkness," "the formless Form," or "the cloud of unknowing" "show the inadequacy of language to express the experience" (Johnson, 1953/1971, pp. 329–330).

Reality. Mystics insist strongly that their experiences are real, infinitely more real than the material world. Mystics may well say that they no longer believe but now know. Pascal wrote: "Fire! God of Abraham, God of Isaac, God of Jacob, not of the philosophers and the wise. Security, security. Feeling, joy, peace. Joy, Joy, Joy, tears of joy" (1670/1889, p. 2).

Transcendence of Time and Space. Mystics lose their sense of time and space. St. John of the Cross said that people may "remain in deep oblivion and afterward will not realize where they were, or what occurred, or how the time passed" (1991, p. 195).

Noetic Quality. Mysticism gives infused knowledge, knowing that does not come by sense or thinking. From Teresa of Avila: "The intellect does not work, but . . . it understands because God desires that it understand" (1976, p. 74).

Joy and Love. We already heard of Pascal's joy. Although mystical experience transcends emotion, mystics later are usually flooded with highly positive emotion. Intense love for everything typically follows.

Types of Mysticism. *Theism, Monism, and Nature.* Theistic mysticism is experience of union with a personal God. Wisdom traditions, like Hinduism and Buddhism, commonly produce a monistic perspective; experiencers see the ultimate oneness of all phenomena. In nature mysticism one experiences unity with nature or sees the underlying meaning of nature.

Apophatic-Kataphatic. Kataphatic mystics work with images or forms to rise to higher understandings until they finally touch that to which the forms point. This is the way of many who practice devotional religion. Apophatic mystics eschew forms or symbols, penetrating the darkness of emptiness to come to full light. Many wisdom traditions walk this path, and some high Christian mystics have been apophatic.

Sacred-Secular. Although mysticism is traditionally a sacred endeavor, Abraham Maslow introduced the notion of secular mysticism or peak experiences. He agreed that "the universal nucleus of every known high religion . . . has been the private, lonely, personal illumination, revelation, ecstasy of some acutely sensitive prophet or seer" (Maslow 1964, p. 19). He also felt that any sufficiently worthy experience, attended to with sufficient attention, can trigger a peak. Peakers, he said, experience the same values that religious people refer to God.

Effects of Mystical Experience. Eastern and Western mysticism describe mystical development similarly (Meadow & Culligan, 1987; Underhill, 1911/1974).

Mysticism profoundly transforms and heals. "The mystic is [one] who has fallen in love with God . . . the happy victim of an experience that is at once total, shattering and transforming" (O'Donoghue, 1979, p. 148). Maslow said peaks produce "a true integration of the person at all levels" (1968, pp. 92, 96).

This personality change usually requires persevering spiritual practice. Mystics eventually come to a state of egolessness or dying to self. Underhill said mysticism is something the whole self does with "wholly transcendental and spiritual" aims. It "is obtained neither from an intellectual realization of its delights, nor from acute emotional longings. . . . It is arrived at by an arduous psychological and spiritual process" (1911/1974, p. 81).

Mysticism sometimes has one unfortunate effect. Intense, direct experience of God tends to confirm the belief and ritual systems with which the mystic entered the experience. Such belief is narrowing when it excludes the possibility that other traditions contain truth. Having intense mystical experience in more than one tradition cures this limitedness; many people, however, are not open to such experimentation.

References

Eckhart, M. (1981). *Meister Eckhart: The essential sermons, commentaries, treatises, and defense.* New York: Paulist.

James, W. (1902). *The varieties of religious experience.* New York: McKay.

John of the Cross. (1991). *The collected works of St. John of the Cross* (Rev. ed.) (K. Kavanaugh & O. Rodriguez, Trans.). Washington, DC: Institute of Carmelite Studies.

Johnson, R. C. (1971). *The imprisoned splendour.* Wheaton, IL: The Theosophical Publishing House. (Original work published 1953)

Maslow, A. H. (1964). *Religions, values, and peak experiences.* Columbus: Ohio State University Press.

Maslow, A. H. (1968). *Toward a psychology of being* (2nd ed.). Princeton, NJ: Van Nostrand.

Meadow, M. J., & Culligan, K. (1987). Congruent spiritual paths: Christian Carmelite and Theravadan Buddhist Vipassana. *The Journal of Transpersonal Psychology, 19,* 181–196.

O'Donoghue, N. (1979). *Heaven in ordinaire.* Edinburgh: Clarke.

Pascal, B. (1889). *Thoughts of Blaise Pascal* (C. K. Paul, Trans.). London: George Bell & Sons. (Original work published 1670)

Pseudo-Dionysius. (1987). *Pseudo-Dionysius: The complete works* (C. Luibheid, Trans.). New York: Paulist.

Teresa of Avila. (1976). *The collected works of St. Teresa of Avila* (Vol. 1) (K. Kavanaugh & O. Rodriguez, Trans.). Washington, DC: Institute of Carmelite Studies.

Underhill, E. (1974). *Mysticism.* New York: New American Library. (Original work published 1911)

M. J. MEADOW

See SPIRITUALITY, PSYCHOLOGY OF; RELIGIOUS EXPERIENCE; CONSCIOUSNESS; MEDITATION.

Nn

Nail Biting. Also known as onychophagia, this is a common behavioral disturbance, occurring mainly in children and occasionally persisting into adulthood, particularly when the individual is under severe psychological stress. One-fifth of all adolescents bite their nails, and the most widely accepted reason is that it reduces tension and relieves anxiety. Psychoanalytic interpretation views nail biting as a fixation at the oral stage of libido development. The American Psychological Association classifies it as a special symptom reaction under personality disorders. Two other theories view nail biting as a substitute for masturbation or an outlet for hostile impulses. Male nail biters outnumber female nail biters at later ages.

D. L. SCHUURMAN

Narcissism. An ancient myth tells of a handsome youth, Narcissus, the offspring of the river god Cephesus and the nymph Liriope, who fell passionately in love with his own image reflected in a woodland pool. He was loved by Echo, who for problems of her own from previous brushes with the gods, was prohibited from speaking on her own and limited to mirroring the words of others. When he said, "I love you" to his own image, she replied unheard, "I love you, I love you." Narcissus pined away and died, leaving behind the flower that thrives when it is bent over cool streams. The infatuation with self, a tragic, unrequited hunger for the ideal lover, and difficulty in communication with a love are so much a part of human experience that the myth lives on, and *narcissism* has become a dynamic term in contemporary psychology (Spotnitz & Resinkoff, 1954).

The term *narcissism* refers to a vain preoccupation with self or a preening self-centeredness. In the earliest usage by psychologists it was applied to autoeroticism as a perversion (Ellis, 1927). Later the term described a triad of vanity, exhibitionism, and arrogant ingratitude. The late twentieth century has been called The Age of Narcissism or an intensely individualistic, self-centered, and hedonistic culture devoted to the quest of a peak experience (Lasch, 1978). Our motto might be, Since you only go around once, make it with gusto! Just as hysteria was the disorder around which psychological formulations developed in Europe at the turn of the twentieth century, narcissism seems to be the problem serving this function at its end.

Yet there is an appealing adolescent quality to many narcissists. Their lives are passionate and exciting but are thin in the solid relationships and quieter satisfactions of normal maturity. Narcissus's boyishness and aching need for love attracts to his descendants a series of Echoes who step in to fill this need only to discover they must struggle to distract their love from a mirrored self-image.

Definitions and Dynamics. Contemporary psychologists have difficulty in arriving at any consensus or precision in the term *narcissism*. Psychoanalysts usually follow Sigmund Freud's formulation of it as a disorder of drive. A normal, grandiose, self-centered phase of development is postulated in which the infant glories in libido primarily invested in the self. This period is pre-oedipal and becomes pathological in later life as a fixation or regression to this stage. In contemporary psychoanalysis this developmental period is seen less in dynamic, libidinal terms and more as a disorder of object relations. At the narcissistic phase of development the infant is forming distinct and coherent forms, images, models, or concepts of self and significant others. Narcissism now often refers to disorders of these objects and the way in which they relate.

The picture most widely held of this internal world in the early months of life has been developed by a number of thinkers. Melanie Klein (Segal, 1979) and Margaret Mahler (1968) describe primary experiences that are both good and bad. Originally separate, these begin to coalesce, forming fragmentary, part objects of self and others. These would have four configurations initially: good self, bad self, good other, and bad other. Effective (or "good enough") mothering normally will encourage these part objects to merge into distinct and realistic objects, or images of self and others that are distinct and include both good and bad. This process is referred to as separation and individuation. There is much less consensus on the details of how this proceeds or what, from early mothering, encourages healthy maturation and what kinds of trauma or deprivation cause it to fail.

Much current object relations thinking centers on grandiosity. Who can deny the charming self-centeredness and omnipotence often seen in a child? An analyst tells of a small boy who leans out of his window on the night before his mother's surgery, shakes his fist, and shouts, "Listen! If you mess this one up, you'll have *me* to deal with!"

We laugh, but when we consider ourselves the center of the universe, is it not just as absurd? Perhaps in the naked boldness of narcissistic grandiosity we face a bad photograph of ourselves, alien yet undeniably familiar. We all mourn our banishment from Eden. And, if we allow ourselves, the vision of these perfections will lure us across our reserve into passionate and destructive quests.

Contemporary psychologists have more difficulty in arriving at consensus or precision in the term *narcissism*. Bromberg (1983) describes this task as "somewhat like trying to chill fine Russian Vodka by adding ice cubes." We may partially accomplish our purpose, but in doing it we dilute the experience. The experience seems larger than our words; certainly it is a good deal more than an esoteric mental disorder. As the books and articles about narcissism proliferate, one begins to realize that in this narcissistic world of object relations gone sour are clearly seen caricatures of things fundamentally human. One horn of the great paradoxes of love of self and love of neighbor, of vulnerability and risk, of awesome, individual responsibility in an apparently impersonal universe, seems to be played out by the narcissist with reckless abandon. The more prosaic of us struggle to work through these ambiguities. Adding sharp poignancy to this struggle is the backdrop of the inspiring ideal, alluring us with fragmented godlikeness, yet at the same time judging, punishing us, and leaving our yearning unsatisfied. In narcissists also we see mirrored our own struggle with self-centeredness, with grandiose potential and with our failure. We cannot completely disown them.

People who are undeniably narcissistic play powerful roles in our world. These are the Type-A personalities, the driving business leaders, the charismatic screen personalities, the compelling athletes and renegades of the evening news, the people who set off vibrations when they enter the room. Scarlett O'Hara and Rhett Butler could never keep us up all night without their reckless narcissism.

Even if we were successful in restoring normality to these people, life would lose a measure of its sparkle and wonder. If we are wise, we accept these persons, love them for what they are, and appreciate the often considerable contributions to life they do make.

Still, we must remember that their own lives are not as happy as they seem. They are often empty and frustrated, filled with unfulfilled longings. The lives of those who love the narcissist are also painful and are frustrating should they hope for them to change for the better.

One may also sense on a spiritual level a very special gift in these people. Many of our religious leaders, pastors, evangelists, and teachers suffer from more than a normal share of narcissism. Something in the ecstasy and agony of these leaders that endows them with a godlike aura yet also speaks to us of Adam.

Still, however, the sparks fly. The vain exhibitionist, the selfish ingrate who attacks life with passionate hedonism is ill, and this illness is discussed in Narcissistic Personality Disorder.

References

Bromberg, P. M. (1983). The mirror and the mask. *Contemporary Psychoanalysis, 19,* 359–387.

Ellis, H. (1927). The conception of narcissism. *Psychoanalytic Review, 14,* 129–153.

Lasch, C. (1978). *The culture of narcissism.* New York: Norton.

Mahler, M. S. (1968). *On human symbiosis and the vicissitudes of individuation.* New York: International Universities Press.

Segal, H. (1979). *Melanie Klein.* New York: Viking.

Spotnitz, H., & Resnikoff, P. (1954). The myths of Narcissus. *Psycho-analytic Review, 41,* 173–181.

Additional Readings

Kernberg, O. (1975). *Borderline conditions and pathological narcissism.* New York: Aronson.

Kohut, H. (1971). *The analysis of the self.* New York: International Universities Press.

C. M. Berry

See Self; Self Psychology.

Narcissistic Personality Disorder. This category was added to the *DSM-III* in response to a host of articles that dominated the literature during the 1970s and early 1980s. This disorder has been extensively studied statistically in an effort to discriminate it from affective disorders and from other personality disorders, particularly the borderline. These conclusions remain far from compelling. Perhaps this is because the symptoms selected include some that fairly well delineate it from all other personality disorders and others, sometimes called core characteristics, that are phenomena of all personality disorders. Those most discriminating cluster around vanity, exhibitionism, and an enhanced sense of self-importance. Core features, such as emotional instability, self-centeredness, grandiosity, and difficulty in making relationships, describe personality disorders in general or that large group of people that inflicts an incredible amount of suffering in families, in the workplace, and in the community. If the reader will stop and identify a person or two within his or her own family who seems much more commonly part of the problem than part of the solution, this person is probably a narcissist.

Since understanding these people is helpful to those around them and to themselves, this discussion will focus on these core characteristics. The distinguishing qualities, such as vanity and exhibitionism, help us less. Consider the following: narcissists are self-centered to the point of being astonishingly inconsiderate of those close to them, even when they might be otherwise good people. They repeatedly injure those they love to the point of childish dependency. The narcissist is extremely sensitive, and can be unbelievably injured by insults most other people would shrug off; hence others instinctively walk on eggshells around them. To defend against this sensitivity they are often very controlling. Finally, they and the world around them are inconstant to an astonishing degree. Their reality shifts abruptly and completely with no explanation. At one time a loved one or close friend seems wonderful; later the same person has become their abuser. Life can be wonderful, delightful, and vivacious; at another time all becomes miserable. This is disconcerting for those people with this disorder who think of themselves, of others they know well, and of the world in general, as reasonably constant.

Should we get to know them better, we find that they are profoundly lonely, perhaps stemming from their insurmountable difficulty in making a truly loving, mutually nourishing relationship with anyone. We are also often surprised to find how insecure they are beneath their thin veneer of pride and boastfulness, how poorly they evaluate their own accomplishments and gifts, and how concerned they are with self-esteem. We are surprised to discover how inflexible they are, how often what skills and achievements they have result from stylized approaches to their tasks.

Even when we identify such a pattern, we want to understand what causes it and what is going on inside the person who lives so damagingly and unpredictably. The psychoanalysts who have studied this pattern extensively will give us some important clues.

Psychoanalytic Theories. Most of the current thinking by psychiatrists in narcissism and its impact on personality is based on psychoanalytic theory. Two theorists, Kernberg (1975) and Kohut (1971), have dominated the literature. They both start with Sigmund Freud's (1914/1958) description of a normal stage of primary narcissism, or of grandiosity and self-centeredness. Since this occurs sometime between six months and two years, fixations and regressions manifested in the adult have a very primitive quality. Beyond this developmental base, Kernberg and Kohut move in rather different directions.

Kernberg pictures the infantile experience of the narcissist as turbulent, violent, and ambivalent, marked by intense envy and rage. These affective surges of anxiety and depression disperse widely through the psyche of the infant, demanding primitive defensiveness and leaving in its wake a residue of bitter hostility and resentment. The defenses of the narcissist are similar to those of the borderline, depending primarily on splitting and projection. Kernberg would distinguish the two conditions by the nature of the self-object as it emerges in the transference. In the narcissist the grandiose self, though still highly pathological, is more coherent and integrated than in the borderline (Kernberg, 1966). Kernberg's diagnosis depends upon interpreting the transference, and his approach to therapy is essentially traditional Freudian analysis, directed toward primary conflicts, though he modifies his technique somewhat.

Kohut sees narcissism as a failure in normal development of the earliest internal images or objects of self and significant others. Good and grandiose part objects should mature into whole objects that are realistic, stable, and reasonably predictable. Such internal structures then encourage healthy self-esteem and the capacity to enjoy and appreciate others as distinct from self. Successful treatment provides a reparative mothering experience that partially restores the healthy nurturing that these patients are thought to have missed (Kohut, 1977).

Other writers organize their understanding of narcissism around one or another of its clinical features: masochism (Gear, Hill, & Liedo, 1981); perfectionism (Rothstein, 1980); self-love (Lavelle, 1973); existential anxiety (Lichtenstein, 1977); and splitting (Volcan, 1976). To date no one has made a convincing enough case to win broad consensus, though the formulations of Kohut seem to come the closest to doing so.

A Symptomatic Approach. The disorder may be profitably understood by nonanalysts by approaching its clinical symptoms in already familiar ways. Behind the inconstancy of their views of themselves and those close to them, people with this disorder are seen to have a sense of self and others that is split into good and bad. When they are injured everything is bad. When the sun is shining they all are good, grand in fact, those close to them are wonderful, and the world is a wonderful place. In these abrupt shifts any constancy and validity goes, replaced by a disabling confusion.

Behind this splitting is a pathological sensitivity. Narcissistic persons universally feel their emotions more intensely than is normal. Fears, threats, and any precipitous arousal of emotions have an explosive quality, ballooning up and spilling over into the rest of their lives. This storm of feeling is so violent and painful that reality testing of all kinds is distorted, sometimes for a few moments, often for days at a time. Self and other objects first merge, then split between objects that are all good or all bad.

Over time these painful waves of affect produce an anticipatory dread, and emotions become alarming, even dangerous. It is not long before intimacy itself is feared as a source of pain and the characteristic narcissistic ambivalence evolves, in which the beloved is both drawn in and driven away. It is as if the narcissist is saying, "If you're going to abandon me, let me face it now before I really love you and the loss becomes unbearable." A peculiar pattern is often seen in which a mate finds the narcissist particularly warm after a brutal fight and yet becomes abusive right after a particularly warm, loving episode. Analysts see this phenomenon as a manifestation of masochism. It is more understandable when we realize that a fight dispels momentarily a profound loneliness, whereas warmth quickly brings the fear of losing control. The abuse reestablishes control.

These volatile swings in the narcissistic affect, from ecstasy to deep despair, end as fear, guilt, and depression. Midrange feelings are blotted out, leaving a life devoid of tenderness, mild pleasures, and modulations of warming and distancing toward loved ones. Since these gentler sensitivities fine-tune intimacy, the narcissist learns to relate more intentionally, learning rigid cognitive systems that make people more understandable and predictable. This stylized approach to others may work away from home, but closer to the heart it fails miserably.

The internal model of others is totally determined by the patient's own needs and desires. Any failure or refusal of the other to respond to this constant demand for gratification and affirmation threatens to set off another affective explosion, an event commonly called a narcissistic injury.

Treatment. There is at present no consensus as to what effectively treats this condition. Insight-oriented and experiential therapies have probably been used most extensively, since they are usually the most agreeable to the patient. Intelligent narcissists learn and appreciate these insights. However, insight alone does not address the explosive emotions and the cognitive distortions that destroy reality testing.

An ideal treatment plan that would address the central problems of narcissism directly might begin with learning to control the affective storms by a cognitive-behavioral approach, reinforced by medications. The antidepressants have been the most effective, though the minor tranquilizers and occasionally small doses of major tranquilizers can be helpful in individual patients. Only when these storms are controlled can the patient begin to repair object relations and come to appreciate a more stable, predictable experiential world.

After the destructive affects are tamed, therapeutic attention can be focused on the specific feelings themselves, verbalizing them and making them clear. In this task the persons close to the patient can also be helpful by clearly expressing their own emotional responses in situations that are shared with the narcissist. In both cases it is important to explicitly define feelings as opposed to cognitions. Even though most of what the narcissist says is cog-

nitive, what disorders him or her is affective. The narcissistic splitting and projections that are so destructive to primary relationships are corrected only by naming the feelings. Supportive therapy, such as teaching the patient simple relational and living skills that have been lost over time, are helpful. Groups that are sharply focused on arousals, on feelings, and on distorted cognitions are necessary to maintain the gains of therapy. A simple, direct support group of this nature is offered by Alcoholics Anonymous along with its 12-step program.

These people highlight the way in which all intense feelings, fears, humiliations, shames, and even moments of ecstasy tend to distort reality. They can be the seasoning that bring vitality to life, but they can also lead to empty, frustrating lives filled with failure and unfulfilled longings. Anyone subjected to particularly intense feeling states should teach the rest of us that these touches of the transcendent are to be turned over to the Lord for their meaning and fulfillment. We, like Adam, are destroyed when we grasp our passions and run with them, or like Cain, try to pacify our rage with our own hands.

References

Freud, S. (1958). On narcissism. In J. Strachey (Ed. and Trans.), *The Standard Edition of the complete psychological works of Sigmund Freud.* (Vol. 14). London: Hogarth. (Original work published 1914)

Gear, M. G., Hill, M. A., & Liedo, E. C. (1981). *Working through narcissism.* New York: Aronson.

Kernberg, O. (1966). Structural derivatives of object relationships. *International Journal of Psycho-Analysis, 47,* 236–253.

Kernberg, O. (1975). *Borderline conditions and pathological narcissism.* New York: Aronson.

Kohut, H. (1971). *The analysis of the self.* New York: International Universities Press.

Kohut, H. (1977). *The restoration of the self.* New York: International Universities Press.

Lavelle, L. (1973). *The dilemma of Narcissus.* New York: Humanities.

Lichtenstein, H. (1977). *The dilemma of human perfection.* New York: Aronson.

Rothstein, A. (1980). *The narcissistic pursuit of perfection.* New York: International Universities Press.

Volcan, V. D. (1976). *Primitive internalized object relations.* New York: International Universities Press.

C. M. Berry

See Narcissism; Personality Disorders.

Narcotherapy. A specialized form of psychotherapy during which a physician introduces drugs intravenously in order to create an altered state of consciousness. The therapy is based on the assumption that diagnostic clarifications and therapeutic gains are thus facilitated in a willing subject at the hands of an experienced clinician. Present-day narcotherapy has developed from a confluence of observations that a narcotized person may be more self-disclosing and expansive and the widely accepted idea that exploration of preconscious and unconscious memories and feelings is of therapeutic benefit.

Many agents have been used in an attempt to relax patients or to gain access to repressed experiences: opium, alcohol, ether, nitrous oxide, and LSD are a few. Various side effects and undesirable alterations in consciousness have consequently led to their disuse. Since 1930, when it was first used in psychiatric interviewing, sodium amytal (sodium amobarbital) has been widely accepted as the preferred agent. Amytal is a moderately long-acting barbiturate with a moderately rapid induction time.

The procedure is relatively free of hazard, the medical contraindications being those physiological conditions prohibiting the use of barbiturates. Its use in children is medically inadvisable. Postpubescent adolescents and adults have reportedly benefited from the procedure.

Most psychiatrists employ amytal for selected diagnostic and therapeutic indications. The major impetus to its use in psychiatric emergencies came during World War II in the treatment of acute war neuroses. Other acute traumatic psychiatric disorders soon responded to narcotherapy. Two American physicians, Roy Grinker and John Spiegel, expanded the European use of narcotherapy. They went beyond suggestion as a tool under an amytal-induced state of consciousness into what they termed *narcosynthesis*. Abreaction or catharsis of the painful wartime experiences repeatedly allowed discharge of the painful feelings, or affects, until they could be accepted by the person. On occasion acute hysterical or traumatic psychiatric disorders are still successfully treated in this fashion.

Like most treatment modalities, narcotherapy then was applied to a variety of resistant disorders. This slowly led to a working consensus of indications for the use of this treatment. Acute panic states following rape, disaster, or traumatic loss are amenable. Temporary complete amnesia, in which the patient is incapable of recall despite conscious effort, may respond to psychotherapeutic exploration during an amytal-induced state.

Diagnostic explorations suitable for amytal interviewing include the differential diagnosis of organic brain disease from functional (emotionally induced) disorders. In the latent brain-diseased person neurological symptoms such as disorientation, memory defects, and confabulation appear in an apparently organically intact individual. Diagnostic interviewing under amytal may uncover previously undetected or even unsuspected suicide potential, paranoid ideation, or schizophrenia. There are times in the course of extended psychotherapy when severe repression blocks progress. At these times an amytal interview may enable the cooperative patient to uncover repressed material and thereby make a fresh psychotherapeutic endeavor.

The distinction between a stuporous mute catatonic condition and a stuporous depressive state is often most difficult to make. Under an amytal interview the depressed patient will tend to withdraw further; the catatonic will verbalize in a remarkable and revealing manner. In this lucid period psychodynamic information useful for future therapy may be captured.

The implications of such therapy for the Christian must take into account the ethics behind this procedure. Patients' rights must be respected even if the patient may choose to his or her detriment. Ethical medical practice calls for clear, detailed interpretation of the nature of the procedure, any hazards for that patient, and the possible benefits to the patient. In this fashion informed consent may be obtained. A common misconception needs to be cleared up. There is no truth serum, and the function of the amytal interview is not to gain a confession or to probe purposes outside the patients' desire. Usually the patient is asked to prepare an agenda of areas of self-inquiry about which he or she wishes to know more. Often a spouse or other family member is present during the procedure and the entire process is tape recorded, the tape becoming property of the patient. This is especially useful when partial amnesia blocks some important data. The recording may thus be used as reference material in subsequent therapy.

A Christian view of humanity is based on biblical sources for understanding people's spiritual nature and sojourn. Christians are also open to truth from many other sources in their search for understanding themselves. The existence of unconscious and preconscious parts of our mental and emotional apparatus seems indisputable. Similarly our motivations and experiences are influenced not only by what we know consciously but also by those unresolved, painful experiences we thought we left behind because we could forget them. A Christian view would encompass these complexities in the search for truth and the resolution of individual problems.

The amytal interview is one technique for gaining partial access to such unconscious and preconscious material. If one accepts the validity of the existence of an unconscious world and that benefit can accrue from its being explored, then narcotherapy is a possible source of aid.

One last consideration remains: the quality of trust between the doctor and the patient. This trust must be based on common assumptions and mutual openness so that the patient finds his or her answers self-convincing and resolving. The benefits of narcotherapy, like any therapy, will be derived from the truth and insights gained.

Additional Readings

Sharoff, R. L. (1967). Narcotherapy. In A. M. Freedman & H. I. Kaplan (Eds.), *Comprehensive textbook of psychiatry.* Baltimore: Williams & Wilkins.

Naples, M., & Hackett, T. P. (1978). The amytal interview: History and current uses. *Psychosomatics, 19* (2), 98–105.

T. G. Esau

See Consciousness; Hypnosis; Hypnotherapy; Psychopharmacology.

Nature-Nurture Controversy. *See* Heredity and Environment in Human Development.

Near-Death Experiences. Most modern psychologists would probably reject the notion that the human personality survives bodily death and would likewise reject the idea that a spirit world exists. Even if some of these thinkers should acknowledge such possibilities among their personal beliefs, they would most likely rule the study of the psyche after death as out of bounds for psychology because such phenomena are considered to be nonobservable. However, since the mid-1970s this whole set of assumptions is being questioned seriously by a group of investigators of the near-death experience (NDE).

The NDE is a series of phenomena experienced by individuals who were clinically dead for short periods of time (perhaps ten minutes, though sometimes longer). These near-death survivors report extraordinary experiences that, although somewhat variable, are remarkably homogeneous considering the diversity of the individuals studied. The classic description of the NDE is outlined by Moody (1975a). First, the person sometimes reports hearing himself or herself pronounced dead by a doctor. The patient then hears a loud ringing or buzzing and feels like he or she is moving through a dark tunnel. The individual may then suddenly find the sense of self to be outside the physical body and may see his or her own body as if a spectator, watching as resuscitation attempts are made.

If the NDE progresses further, the individual may find others coming to help. The individual may see spirits of deceased relatives and friends and what many have described as a "warm loving spirit" of a kind never encountered before. This spirit asks the individual nonverbally to evaluate his or her life and helps by showing a panoramic, instantaneous playback of the person's life. A later stage of the NDE may involve approaching some kind of barrier, which apparently represents the limit between earthly life and the life beyond. The NDE person finds that it is not time for death and is told to return to earth. Often the person does not wish to return because of the overwhelming and intense feelings of joy, love, and peace (Moody, 1975a).

The basic elements making up the NDE were found by researchers independently of Moody (Grof & Grof, 1980; Rawlings, 1978; Sabom, 1982). This research is the subject of much controversy. The first controversy involves the explanation of the NDE itself. Some researchers have attempted to explain it as resulting from psychological defense mechanisms (Siegel, 1980). Such an explanation would argue that the dying person wishes to deny his or her imminent death and becomes psychologically detached from it. The ensuing experiences are then interpreted as resulting from depersonalization and denial. Another set of interpretations involves physiological rather than psychological factors. These include possible effects presumed to result from anesthetics or other drugs. However, many NDE survivors did not have any anesthetic or other drugs at the time, and those who did have drugs tended to report less intense NDEs (Ring, 1980). Noyes and Kletti (1972) have offered an explanation of the panoramic playback of one's past as resulting from a seizurelike neural firing pattern in the temporal lobe. However, Moody (1975a) observes that such temporal lobe firing does not usually result in memory images played back in an orderly fashion, nor are such flashbacks seen at once in a unifying vision. Also, seizure victims typically do not remember their flashbacks after regaining consciousness.

Cerebral anoxia involving visual and auditory hallucinatory phenomena is another physiological occurrence that has given rise to several explanatory hypotheses. However, some individuals have NDEs in which no apparent clinical death took place, yet their NDEs are essentially the same as those who were clinically dead (Moody, 1975b). It is also hypothesized that the body's release of large amounts of endorphins during an emergency explains release from physical pain and the experience of feelings of peace and even euphoria.

The reductionistic hypotheses of Blackmore and others have been addressed by Ring (Ring & Lawrence, 1993), who maintains that even the most sophisticated psychophysiological theories cannot account for paranormal factual knowledge obtained by NDE survivors, which is subsequently corroborated to be accurate by independent and reliable witnesses. For example, patients who were blind reported seeing and describing persons and things in their environment that they could not have described prior to or subsequent to their NDE. Their descriptions were independently corroborated by eyewitnesses. Also, Moody (1988) reports the case of a patient who, during her NDE, observed a shoe sitting on a ledge many stories above where her physical body remained. Returning to consciousness, she described this shoe to a staff member of the hospital, who then retrieved the shoe. The shoe was real, not a hallucination or the figment of anyone's imagination.

Other controversies that have been generated by NDE research include the relative frequency of unpleasant or "hellish" NDEs (Atwater, 1994; Rawlings, 1993) and the aftereffects on the lives of NDE survivors (Atwater, 1994; McDonagh, 1982; Morse, 1994; Ring, 1980). Many of these and other related issues are discussed in the *Journal of Near Death Studies*.

Investigators of the NDE are careful to point out that their research does not prove in any strict scientific or philosophical sense the existence of an afterlife, nor does it specify indisputably the nature of an afterlife. However, even with this qualification it does seem to represent an important development. The survival of the human personality after death is being taken by some scientists as a possibility and has at least gained the status of a plausible scientific hypothesis—something that probably would have been dismissed out of hand in academic circles only a generation ago.

References

Atwater, P. M. H. (1994). *Beyond the light*. New York: Avon.

Grof, S., & Grof, C. (1980). *Beyond death*. New York: Thomas & Hudson.

McDonagh, J. (1982). *Christian psychology: Towards a new syntheses*. New York: Crossroad.

Moody, R. (1975a). *Life after life*. Atlanta: Mockingbird.

Moody, R. (1975b). *Reflections on "life after life."* Carmel, NY: Guideposts.

Moody, R. (1988). *The light beyond*. New York: Bantam.

Morse, M. (1994). *Parting visions*. New York: Villard.

Noyes, R., & Kletti, R. (1972). The experience of dying from falls. *Omega 3*, 45–52.

Rawlings, M. (1978). *Beyond death's door*. Nashville: Nelson.

Rawlings, M. (1993). *To hell and back*. Nashville: Thos. Nelson.

Ring, K. (1980). *Life at death*. New York: Coward, McCann & Geoghegan.

Ring, K., & Lawrence, M. (1993). Further evidence for veridical perception during near-death experiences. *Journal of Near Death Studies, 11*, 223–229.

Sabom, M. B. (1982). *Recollections of death: A medical investigation*. New York: Simon & Schuster.

Siegel, R. K. (1980). The psychology of life after death. *American Psychologist, 35*, 911–931.

J. M. McDonagh

See Death and Dying.

Necrophilia. A rare morbid sexual perversion in which an individual gains satisfaction from performing sexual acts on a dead body or parts of it. The perversion seems to be confined to men, and it is claimed by some researchers that morticians form a high percentage of subjects with necrophilia. In some cases the necrophiliac will mutilate the body. In most recorded instances he has murdered a woman in order to gratify his psychotic desire. This severe disturbance may be related to a fear of failure in sexual relations. By performing sexual acts on a dead body, the humiliation and rejection so feared by the individual are impossible. Necrophilia is said to be the rarest sexual behavior in men.

D. L. Schuurman

See Sexuality.

Needs. Hypothetical constructs prominent in several theories of motivation. Needs represent generally internally or externally aroused forces accompanied by subjective emotions that serve as an impetus for behavior. Needs are characterized by two motivational properties: a tendency to energize behavior if the strength is greater than its threshold; and a tendency to activate cognitive processes such as imagining, wish-fulfilling fantasies, and long-range planning. The cognitive processes serve to channel bodily arousal toward need gratification.

Many theorists identified two categories of physiological needs: deficiency and excess needs. Both refer to products related to survival. Need is an intervening variable between deprivation or excess on the antecedent side and health or survival on the consequent side.

Some theories consider need to be equivalent to drive, while others distinguish between them. In the latter view an excess or deficiency need elicits tension within a physiological system. This tension evokes a drive (i.e., energy mobilization) toward satisfying the need state. This need-drive-incentive pattern "asserts that physiological needs are created by deprivation, that these give rise to drives which stir to, and may guide, activity until a related goal object (incentive) is attained, and that the response to the goal object (consummatory response) reduces the drive" (English & English, 1958, p. 339).

In experimental studies need is operationally defined as length of deprivation or extent of excess (e.g., hyperoxygenation). Tissue deficiency is assumed to be directly related to the degree of deprivation or excess.

Personality theories have made extensive use of need, especially acquired needs. Kurt Lewin was one of the first psychologists to adopt the need construct. He offered it as a replacement for the instinct suggestion by William McDougall. Lewin held that need provides arousal without completely prescribing a uniform behavior sequence. He defined need as any motivated state that may have been evoked by a physiological event, a desire for an object, or a will to achieve. Disequilibrium and tensions accompany needs. Disequilibrium exists when there is an uneven distribution of tension. Behavior achieves equilibrium through release of tension. Tensions are dispelled as needs are satisfied (Chaplin & Krawiec, 1974).

The strength and direction of needs were described by Lewin in vector terms. Vectors are either positive, satisfying or attractive to the organism, or negative, threatening or repelling the organism. When vectors are opposite in direction and equal in valence, a conflict is said to exist. Lewin defined three types of conflict: approach-approach, avoidance-avoidance, and approach-avoidance.

The most highly developed need theory is that of Murray, who defined need as a "construct . . . which stands for . . . a force which organized perception, apperception, intellection, conation and action in such a way as to transform in a certain direction an existing, unsatisfying situation" (Murray, 1938, pp. 123–124). He distinguished between viscerogenic and psychogenic needs. Viscerogenic needs are the physiological ones related to survival. The psychogenic needs are those acquired in the process of socialization. The psychogenic needs and the proceedings to satisfy those needs form the basis of personality. Psychogenic needs are categorized as latent or manifest, proactive or reactive, and modal or effect. The relative strength of the personality needs identified by Murray are measured by the Thematic Apperception Test (TAT) or the Edwards Personal Preference Schedule. The former measures latent needs, while the latter assesses manifest needs.

Needs that represent repressed or inhibited drives are latent, while manifest needs are more freely expressed and consciously recognized. Murray classified needs as to their origins. Needs originating within the organism are proactive, while reactive needs respond to environmental stimulation. Modal needs concern the process of need satisfaction, while effect needs lead to the achievement of a goal. For example, a pianist who strives to play well would exhibit a modal need, while one who plays well to win a prize is responding to an effect need.

Murray believed that needs are organized within personality. When needs are functionally interconnected or fused so they can be satisfied simultaneously, it is termed subsidiation. At other times the degree of organization may be less adequate and one need might be in conflict with another.

Other personality theorists have also employed need concepts. The motivational theory of Abraham Maslow conceived personality as a hierarchy of needs. Needs that have the greatest potency at the time demand satisfaction and drive behavior. Once a need has been satisfied, other needs that are less potent manifest themselves. The hierarchy, which includes both physiological and social needs, in order of priority is physiological, safety, love and belongingness, esteem, and self-actualization needs. Maslow differentiated between deficiency needs (e.g., physiological and safety) and growth needs. Growth needs are derived from the motive of self-actualization when all deficiency needs have been satisfied.

In her study of neurotic personality Horney enumerated ten neurotic needs. If an individual's security is disturbed, Anxiety is experienced, in response to which the individual develops strategies of adjustment. Adjustment patterns may assume the character of needs or drives in personality. Needs may become neurotic if they are irrational solutions to the problems of insecurity. Neurotic needs include the need for affection and approval, for a partner to take over one's life, to restrict one's life within narrow borders, for power, to exploit others, for prestige, for personal admiration, for personal achievement, for self-sufficiency and independence, and for perfection and unassailability. In these neurotic needs the more the person has, the more the person wants (Horney, 1942).

In recent years considerable work has been done by personality and social psychologists on three needs: the need for achievement (*see* Achievement, Need for), the need for affiliation, and the need for power.

References

Chaplin, J. P., & Krawiec, T. S. (1974). *Systems and theories of psychology* (3rd ed.). New York: Holt, Rinehart, & Winston.

English, H. B., & English, A. (1958). *A comprehensive dictionary of psychological and psychoanalytical terms.* New York: Longmans, Green.

Horney, K. *Self-analysis.* (1942). New York: Norton.

Murray, H. A. *Explorations in personality.* (1938). New York: Oxford University Press.

R. L. Timpe

See Motivation; Personality; Murray, Henry Alexander.

Needs Met by Religion. *See* Psychological Roots of Religion.

Negative Effects in Therapy. *See* Iatrogenic Psychopathology.

Neologism. A word created by an individual who attaches his or her own meaning to it. Such words are often condensations of other words and carry a private significance. Overuse of neologisms is often indicative of a schizophrenic disorder.

See Schizophrenia.

Nervous Breakdown. A euphemism for acute psychopathologies that require immediate treatment. It does not refer to any particular disorder or clinical entity. It seems intended to imply that the individual has been under strain and has collapsed under the pressure. Since the problem is then seen to be wholly or largely physical, the individual generally escapes the stigma often attached to problems that are recognized to be more of an emotional nature. Usually, however, this inaccurate term has little or no correspondence to the etiology of the psychological problem being described.

See Abnormal Psychology; Anxiety.

Network Therapy. *See* Social Network Intervention.

Neurasthenia. *See* Depression; Depressionogenic Attribution Style; Dysthymic Disorder.

Neurolinguistic Programming. Bandler and Grinder (1975, 1976) studied particularly successful psychotherapists, especially Satir, Fritz Perls, and Milton H. Erickson. Based on their findings, they developed a model of psychotherapy and successful communication that focuses on how individuals process information and on how to utilize their internal strategy for producing desired changes.

Representational Systems. Fundamental to this model are three representational systems: auditory, visual, and kinesthetic. The dominant system employed by an individual is indicated by both eye patterns, called accessing clues, and linguistic patterns. Bandler and Grinder report that as you face other people, their eyes will look up and left when they are accessing remembered images visually, up and right when they are visually constructing their images, down and right when they are accessing feelings and other kinesthetic sensations, down and left when they are listening to internal auditory sounds such as internal dialogue, level left for remembered auditory sound, and level right for constructed auditory sounds or imagined conversations.

For example, if you were to ask a person with a visual representational system when she last saw a movie, her eyes would move up and left as she searches for a visual representation of herself the last time she attended a movie. If you were to ask a person with an auditory representational system when he last heard Handel's *Messiah*, his eyes would go level and left as he searches for the memory of that experience auditorily. If you ask a person with a kinesthetic representational system when he last felt angry, he would look down and to the right to access that feeling and retrieve that memory kinesthetically.

The other way of determining persons' representational system is through the linguistic patterns they use. For example, persons with a visual representational system tend to use words that are visual (e.g., picture, vague, bright, flash, perspective). Persons with an auditory representational system use words that are auditory (e.g., scream, screech, hear, amplify, harmonize). Individuals with a kinesthetic representational system use words that are kinesthetically oriented (e.g., handle, feel, grasp, warm, tight, rough).

Knowledge of an individual's representational system makes it possible to establish rapport with the individual. For example, if an individual is looking up while talking and using visual linguistic patterns, responding to that person with visual linguistic patterns and also looking up can put the individual at ease. Rapport is increased by mirroring nonverbal communications, sitting in the same position, using the same voice volume and tone, and employing the same gestures as the client.

Techniques. Having established rapport, the therapist is ready to use the techniques for intervention. One technique is overlapping, the process of connecting a representational system that is ordinarily not used by the client with one that is regularly used. The result is that the clients gradually are enabled to use the new representational system to expand their effectiveness in any situation.

Another technique is anchoring. Based on the principles of classical conditioning (*see* Conditioning, Classical), anchoring is a process whereby a positive, powerful behavior is connected to a fearful, negative experience for the client. For example, while a client is remembering a powerful, confident moment in the past, the therapist may lean over and lightly touch the client on the hand. In the future the therapist can bring the resources of that memory into the client's awareness by touching the client in exactly the same way. Anchoring can be used to change negative memories and to create a better feeling about any situation.

Reframing is based on the principle that every behavior, both internal and external, has some useful and meaningful purpose. Reframing aims to make the client aware of the positive intention of a behavior or situation previously perceived as negative. Perceiving the positive intention of the problem situation allows the individual to find more constructive ways of fulfilling this intention. Reframing can also refer to looking at the problem in a new way and thereby accepting it with more ease.

Neurolinguistic programming makes significant use of metaphor. The value of metaphor is that the telling of a parallel story to the problem situation of the client allows the person to change without trying. People's conscious efforts to change often interfere with their ability to change. The use of metaphor allows a hidden example to become available to them so they can follow the lead of the metaphor and resolve their problems without consciously trying so hard.

Two other important concepts of neurolinguistic programming are meta model and strategies. The meta model deals primarily with linguistic patterns that frame or distort external reality in such a way that healthy adjustments are difficult. The meta model consists of questions aimed at clarifying hidden limitations individuals place on themselves.

Strategies are individual, unique patterns for processing experience. For example, when a client is asked why he cannot study, a person might habitually look quickly up and to the left (visual recall) and then, looking down and right, say, "I just can't feel confident." The client might be unaware of the visual picture from the past that flashes before the feeling of discouragement. This strategy can be improved by bringing the picture from the past into the client's awareness and thereby counteracting some of its negative impact.

Critique. Neurolinguistic programming is a useful and effective collection of therapeutic strategies and techniques. It is criticized for its absence of an overall theory of personality or psychotherapy. It is sometimes criticized as a manipulative tool to accomplish what the practitioner thinks is best for the client, especially since NLP has entered the field of business and sales. Christian practitioners can utilize the techniques while maintaining their Christian values and ethics as a safeguard against manipulation.

References

Bandler, R., & Grinder, J. (1975). *The structure of magic.* Palo Alto, CA: Science and Behavior Books.

Bandler, R., & Grinder, J. (1976). *The structure of magic II.* Palo Alto, CA: Science and Behavior Books.

Additional Readings

Bandler, R., Grinder, J., & Satir, V. (1976). *Changing with families.* Palo Alto, CA: Science and Behavior Books.

Lankton, S. R. (1980). *Practical magical: Translation of basic neurolinguistic programming into clinical psychotherapy.* Cupertino, CA: Meta Publications.

Cameron-Bandler, L. (1980). *They lived happily ever after.* Cupertino, CA: Meta Publications.

C. E. BARSHINGER AND L. E. LaROWE

Neuropsychological Assessment. Clinical neuropsychology is primarily concerned with how expressions of behavior are affected by brain dysfunction (Lezak, 1995). A neuropsychological assessment consists of a series of systematic clinical diagnostic procedures used to determine the extent of behavioral or cognitive deficits after a person sustains brain injury or damage (*see* Brain Injuries). It initially involves a clinical interview in which detailed information about the patient's history, premorbid functioning, and factors surrounding the precipitation of the dysfunction or damage are gathered. Often a mental status examination is then performed, in which a brief assessment is made of appearance and behavior, speech and communication processes, thought content, cognitive and memory functions, emotional functioning, insight and judgment, and orientation (Gregory, 1996).

Depending on the reason for the referral of the patient, the next step includes the administration of various neuropsychological tests that tap into the specific concerns of the patient. These procedures vary from a few specific standardized tests to a full-length battery; it depends on the questions that need to be answered about the patient's functioning as well as the particular approach of the neuropsychologist. The patient-centered or flexible approach uses an individualized test battery based upon the patient's presenting problems, reason for referral, and initial assessment (Gregory, 1996). The fixed battery approach uses a battery of tests that measure neurocognitive functioning in a variety of areas: attention and concentration, learning and memory, receptive and expressive language, executive functions (logical analysis, planning ability, reasoning ability, conceptualization, and flexibility of thinking), visuospatial and visuoconstructional abilities, sensory-perceptual abilities, and psychomotor speed and strength.

Often intelligence and personality tests are also administered to determine general intellectual functioning and personality style and mood. An example of a fixed battery is the Halstead-Reitan Neuropsychological Test Battery. The Halstead-Reitan consists of five measures: the category test, the tactile performance test, the speech sounds perception test, the rhythm test, and the finger tapping test. Other tests usually included in the battery, which takes about six to eight hours to administer, include trail making A and B, grip strength, tactile form recognition, the sensory-perceptual examination, the aphasia screening test, the Wechsler Adult Intelligence Scale (WAIS), and the Minnesota Multiphasic Personality Inventory–2 (MMPI–2) (Lezak, 1995; Reitan & Wolfson, 1985). A Halstead-Reitan Neuropsychological Test Battery has also been developed to assess brain dysfunction in older children between 9 and 14 years of age (Reitan & Wolfson, 1992).

Some neuropsychologists prefer the process approach to neuropsychological assessment in comparison with the fixed or flexible battery approaches because less emphasis is placed on the correctness of responses (achievement) and the focus is on the observation and monitoring of the step-by-step procedure the patient carries out in order to achieve the solution (process). The standardized and experimental tests are not scored in the standardized fashion and in some cases are not administered in the standardized manner. The quality of the patient's performance is also captured by his or her problem-solving behavior (Kaplan, 1988). Lezak (1995) noted that prerequisites to doing a thorough job in the neuropsychological assessment are excellent clinical skills; knowledge of psychometrics; knowledge of neuroanatomy; and knowledge of neuropathologies and their behavioral expressions.

A neuropsychological assessment may be prompted by four different purposes: diagnosis; patient care; treatment; and research. In terms of diagnosis, a neuropsychological assessment can distinguish psychiatric and neurological symptoms, identify possible neurological disorders in a patient without psychiatric problems, differentiate various neurological conditions, and provide behavioral information in order to determine the site of a lesion (Lezak, 1995). However, it must be noted that accurate diagnosis, which includes the specific site of the lesion, must include examination by a neurologist and by neurologic AIDS such as a computer tomography (CT) scan, positron emission tomography (PET), or magnetic resonance imaging (MRI). In some cases, such as patients with dementia or mild head trauma, neuropsychological assessments have proven to be crucial diagnostically.

In terms of patient care and planning, a neuropsychological assessment is often useful in providing detailed information about the cognitive functioning and personality characteristics of patients that helps caregivers to understand how the neurological problems are affecting the patient's behavior. The assessment provides information about the patient's capabilities and limitations, the various psychological changes they are experiencing, and the impact of these changes on their behavior and self-concept. Findings from the neuropsychological assessment also provide information about the patients' capacity to care for themselves, to follow through on treatment recommendations, and to handle various emergency situations and money, comprehension of the patients' responses to their deficits and how compensation can occur, and the development of a rehabilitation program. Periodic neuropsychological assessments also assist in monitoring the course of neurological diseases (Lezak, 1995).

Neuropsychological assessments are especially useful in the evaluation of rehabilitation and treatment, in that they provide valuable information that is shared by professionals from the various disciplines who work with the patients. In terms of research, neurological assessment has been used in the study of the organization of brain activity and its relationship to behavior and the workings of various brain disorders and behavioral problems (Lezak, 1995).

Neuropsychological assessments have proven to be useful with individuals who have experienced a head injury, epilepsy, stroke, or dementia. They are also helpful in the diagnosis of AIDS dementia complex (*see* AIDS). In educational settings, neuropsychological evaluations can identify various developmental and learning disabilities and assist in designing educational programs to assist with remediation. A formal written report of the evaluation is usually sent to the referring professional, and oral feedback is given to the patient and/or family.

References

Gregory, R. J. (1996). *Psychological testing: History, principles and applications.* Boston: Allyn & Bacon.

Kaplan, E. (1988). A process approach to neurological assessment. In T. Boll & B. K. Bryant (Eds.), *Clinical neuropsychology and brain function: Research, measurement, and practice.* Washington, DC: American Psychological Association.

Lezak, M. D. (1995). *Neuropsychological assessment* (3rd ed.). New York: Oxford University Press.

Reitan, R. M., & Wolfson, D. (1985). *The Halstead-Reitan neuropsychological test battery.* Tucson, AZ: Neuropsychology Press.

Reitan, R. M., & Wolfson, D. (1992). *Neuropsychological evaluation of older children.* Tucson, AZ: Neuropsychology Press.

W. Seegobin

See Psychological Measurement; Personality Assessment; Neuropsychology.

Neuropsychology. Neuropsychology is the study of brain-behavior relations and draws its information from a variety of fields, including psychology, biology, physiology, pharmacology, and ethology. Although the field itself is relatively new, one of the first uses of the term *neuropsychology* was by Donald O. Hebb in the subtitle of his influential book, *The Organization of Behavior: A Neuropsychological Theory* (1949). The foundation of the discipline is grounded in the traditional hypothesis that the brain is the origin of behavior.

The idea that the brain is the source of all behavior and mental processes is traced to Alcmaeon of Croton (ca. 500 B.C.) and is contrasted with the belief that the heart is the location of behavior and thinking, an idea postulated by Empedocles of Acragas (ca. 450 B.C.). Both hypotheses had supporters. Aristotle (384–322 B.C.) believed that the heart is the source of thought, while Plato (428–348 B.C.) and physicians such as Hippocrates (460–370 B.C.) and Galen (A.D. 130–200) argued for the brain hypothesis. Evidence provided by Galen (e.g., the observation that nerves travel from the sense organs to the brain, not the heart) helped lead to the eventual triumph of the brain hypothesis.

The acceptance of the brain as the source of behavior and thought led to the attempt to localize certain functions in specific brain regions. Localization of function means that certain functions are distributed among various areas of the cortex. The beginning of work toward localization began with the phrenologists. Franz Gall (1758–1828) and Johann Spurzheim (1776–1832) developed an early physiological psychology known as phrenology, which held three fundamental positions: the exterior conformation of the skull corresponds to the interior (brain); mind is analyzable into a number of functions (e.g., combativeness, hope, acquisitiveness, cautiousness, and secretiveness); and the functions of mind are differentially localized in the brain, and an excess in any function is correlated with an enlargement of the corresponding place in the brain.

Phrenology had a certain popular appeal; people thought personality could be determined by feeling an individual's skull. However, phrenology was never accepted by scientists because its methodology was largely anecdotal. Although scientists disputed the theory of phrenology, the theory did further scientific thought and research in localization of brain function.

The research of Pierre Flourens (1794–1867) was conducted, in large part to refute the phrenologists. Flourens accepted certain separate units of the brain (e.g., the cerebellum and spinal cord) but insisted that they are interconnected. Flourens also doubted that functions such as secretiveness could be localized to a specific region of the brain. Using the brain lesioning technique that he developed, Flourens believed he had demonstrated that intellectual functions are distributed throughout the cerebrum. The extent of the lesion, according to Flourens, not the location, was crucial in determining loss of function.

Flourens's notion of an uncommitted cortex was challenged by Gustav Fritsch (1838–1929) and Eduard Hitzig (1838–1907), who demonstrated that the cortex is excitable electrically, that the cortex is involved in motor movement, and that function is localized. Paul Broca (1824–1880) also supported the idea of localization of function. In 1861 Broca performed an autopsy on the body of a man who had been unable to speak and found a lesion in the left anterior lobe. By 1863 Broca had examined the brains of eight other individuals who had lost the ability to speak and confirmed his original finding: each of the eight had a lesion in the left anterior lobe. These findings helped support the idea of language as a localized function.

The localization suggested by the work of Broca and Carl Wernicke (1848–1904), who also identified an area of brain involved in language, was not a strict localization (i.e., behaviors such as language can have several dedicated brain sites, and these sites interact not only with each other but also with additional, widely distributed brain areas). The concept of interaction led John Hughlings Jackson (1835–1911) to propose a hierarchical organization within the brain such that various areas of cortex must work together for a function, such as language, to operate properly. For example, language might be a left hemisphere function and spatial organization a right hemisphere function in most people; but if the right hemisphere is damaged, language will also be affected because spatial concepts are necessary for efficient processing of language.

Despite the understanding of brain-behavior relations acquired during the nineteenth century, neuropsychology did not become a distinct discipline until the middle of the twentieth century and the development of neurosurgery. While brain surgery has been used since prehistoric times, modern neurosurgery techniques provide possible solutions to brain abnormalities such as epilepsy and Parkinson's disease. Before surgery is performed the surrounding tissue is mapped according to its function. As a result of these mapping procedures, a greater understanding of brain-behavior relations is obtained. The behavioral change resulting from the surgery is also assessed to determine what role certain brain tissue plays in the behavior of the individual.

Other advances that have promoted neuropsychology include imaging techniques and psychometric assessment. Modern functional imaging techniques, among them magnetic resonance imaging (MRI) and positron emission tomography (PET), allow for a detailed picture of the brain at work. As a result brain activity during mental processing can clearly be seen and studied. Psychometrics is an attempt to statistically evaluate an individual's performance on various intellectual tasks. This form of mental testing, although it is criticized in some settings, is considered appropriate in neuropsychology in identifying people with possible brain damage.

Neuropsychologists study and help treat a variety of behavioral and mental disabilities, including aphasia, alexia, agnosia, neglect syndrome, schizophrenia, amnesic disorders, and dementia. Together these disorders represent major mental health concerns and social problems. Using the information learned and the techniques developed in neuropsychology, specialists in this field are looking for possible solutions to these problems.

Additional Readings

Heilman, K. M., & Valenstein, E. (1993). *Clinical neuropsychology* (3rd ed.). New York: Oxford University Press.

Kolb, B., & Whishaw, I. Q. (1995). *Fundamentals of human neuropsychology* (4th ed.). New York: Freeman.

K. S. Seybold

See Neurolinguistic Programming; Brain and Human Behavior.

Neurosis. In psychoanalytic thought a neurosis is the emotional disturbance resulting from unconscious conflict. The term was introduced by William Cullen in the 1770s but was not systematically defined or extensively used until Sigmund Freud. It quickly became standard terminology, representing a broad class of nonpsychotic psychopathologies. The current classification of mental disorders, *DSM-IV*, has abandoned the term, preferring others more descriptive and less theory-laden. In spite of this the term *neurosis* is still used extensively, although with a variety of meanings.

Freud originally divided the neuroses into two categories: actual neuroses and psychoneuroses. The actual neuroses, which included neurasthenia, anxiety neurosis, and hypochondria, were thought to be caused by a holding back of sexual excitation. They are the result not of unconscious conflict but of current sexual behavior. Later Freud abandoned the concept of the actual neurosis, as have most contemporary psychoanalysts.

In this article the term *neuroses* refers to the psychoneuroses. These have their basis in an unconscious conflict between instinctual forces striving for gratification and counterinstinctual defenses seeking to block both gratification and conscious awareness of the instinctual strivings. This conflict, called a neurotic conflict, results in a damming up of tension and leads eventually to the formation of the neurotic symptom. This symptom is a partial, involuntary, and indirect discharge of the tension. It is a compromise between the instinctual and counterinstinctual forces in that it simultaneously affords some gratification and at the same time further reinforces the defense against direct gratification of the instinct.

This process can be illustrated by looking at a neurotic symptom such as obsessive thinking. An individual may describe the thought of killing his wife as a recurrent and persistent idea that does not seem to be under his control or in any way reflective of his real feelings for his wife. Such a symptom would be viewed psychodynamically as the result of unconscious conflict related to aggression. More specifically the obsessive thought would be seen as providing partial and indirect gratification of the aggressive impulses (through thinking about killing) while providing further defense against such impulses (through emotional isolation and denial: "I don't really feel that way about my wife").

Behavior is viewed as neurotic when it is based on an unconscious conflict between the id (instinctual forces) and the ego (counterinstinctual defenses) that results in a damming up of tension and finally an involuntary partial discharge of this tension through the behavior. Such behavior is experienced subjectively as irrational and beyond voluntary control. It also interferes with the individual's capacity for love and productive work.

This understanding of the development of neurotic behavior is far from universally accepted. A cogent alternative explanation based on learning theory exists within behavioral psychology. The decision to eliminate the term from recent editions of the *Diagnostic and Statistical Manual of Mental Disorders* was in large part due to the lack of consensus regarding the etiology of the disorder. Disorders previously classified as neuroses are now therefore officially classified as mood, anxiety, somatoform, dissociative, and psychosexual disorders.

D. G. BENNER

See PSYCHOANALYTIC PSYCHOLOGY.

Neurosis, Experimental. The disturbed and disorganized behavior patterns that can be induced in animals in experimental settings through the use of specialized techniques. It has been suggested that the responses of these animals closely parallel several forms of human neurotic disturbances and that therefore hypotheses about the development of neurotic behavior in humans, as well as principles of treatment, can be extrapolated from the study of these phenomena (Wolpe, 1958).

The first demonstration of experimental neurosis occurred in Ivan Pavlov's laboratory (Pavlov, 1927). Dogs were presented with illuminated circles (a conditioned stimulus), which were followed by feeding (an unconditioned stimulus); subsequently the presentation of a circle elicited salivation in the dog. Flattened ellipses were also presented followed by no feeding and thus came to elicit no response from the dog. Slowly ellipses that more and more closely approached the shape of a circle were presented to the dog. At a point where the ellipse was very close to the circle the dog's performance began to degenerate rapidly, with the dog even losing the ability to make discriminations that had been easy before that point. The dog's behavior changed in other ways also, most notably in showing obvious agitation and fear when the animal was placed in the experimental chamber. It was this type of behavior that was termed experimental neurosis.

Similar behavior has been produced through other experimental paradigms and with other species. Difficult discriminations in other sense modalities have produced similar effects. Pavlov also found that if the time lag between presentation of a conditioned stimulus and the unconditioned stimulus (food) was gradually lengthened, some animals would become "quite crazy, . . . howling, barking, and squeaking intolerably" (p. 294). Cats shocked as they were feeding, or with air blown into their ears, developed behavior patterns of yowling, crouching, and clawing in the experimental chamber. In addition they uniformly refused to eat in the experimental chamber. Learned helplessness with animals is a contemporary example of experimental neurosis.

The generally accepted explanation of this phenomenon is the classical conditioning explanation of Wolpe (1958): experimental neurosis represents the acquisition of a generalized conditioned response of anxiety (*see* CONDITIONING, CLASSICAL). In explaining Pavlov's original studies it is asserted that anxiety and fear are the unconditioned responses to impossible discriminations and other aversive experiences. Upon the occurrence of such a response the experimental setting comes to serve as a stimulus to which the response of fear is conditioned. Hence, subsequent exposures to the experimental chambers lead to agitated, "neurotic" behavior. It is assumed that neurotic behavior in humans represents similar instances of anxiety reactions, conditioned to certain stimuli.

Fenichel (1945) offered a psychoanalytic interpretation of these phenomena. He suggested that the neurotic behavior occurs when previously gratifying stimuli are associated with aversive stimuli. This leads to the confluence of two conflicting motives: to obtain gratification and to escape. The conflict between the impulses leads to a buildup of tension that is discharged through neurotic behavior.

Wolpe's (1958) studies of persistent experimental neurosis in cats culminated in his development of procedures to alleviate the reaction. He gradually increased exposure to the feared stimuli while the animal was engaged in behavior incompatible with fear (e.g., eating). This process, termed reciprocal inhibition of fear, became the basis for the development of systematic desensitization and assertiveness training in behavior therapy.

References

Fenichel, O. (1945). *The psychoanalytic theory of neurosis.* New York: Norton.

Pavlov, I. (1927). *Conditioned reflexes.* Oxford: Oxford University Press.

Wolpe, J. (1958). *Psychotherapy by reciprocal inhibition.* Palo Alto, CA: Stanford University Press.

S. L. JONES

New Age Movement. The New Age movement (NAM) is a recent collection of loosely related religious and spiritual movements. There have been several critiques of NAM from a Christian perspective (e.g., Groothius, 1988; Pacwa, 1992); however, the present article evaluates NAM primarily from social and psychological perspectives (e.g., Vitz, 1994).

Proponents of New Age spirituality present it as a radically new worldview and reject old paradigms based upon science, secular philosophy, and traditional religion, all of which they see as having failed. They believe themselves to be empowered to initiate a "millennium of light" (Ferguson, 1980) that will redeem society from its present ills. They aim to change every sphere of society through extensive networks that have been or will be established throughout the world.

The basic tenets of New Age thought (Groothuis, 1988) are that

1. All is one. Dichotomies do not exist; even boundaries are viewed with hostility. Such a view is

incompatible with Christianity, which argues for distinctive realities created by God, realities that are different from each other and from God.

2. All is God; this is a standard pantheistic position.

3. All humanity (in particular) is God. New Agers criticize the Judeo-Christian understanding of a God who is superior to human beings. New Agers see themselves as being free from the servile bondage of Christians to God—free to develop their own divinity.

4. A change of consciousness is needed. Ignorance keeps us from recognizing our divinity, but New Age techniques and methods (Forum, A Course in Miracles, Lifespring, Eckankan, Scientology) promise to awaken our dozing divinity. Different names for this transforming experience are cosmic consciousness, God-realization, enlightenment, *nirvana* (Buddhist), *satori* (Zen), *satchitananada* (Hindu).

5. All religions are one and basically the same.

6. Evolutionary optimism is needed. Humanity, through its newfound God-consciousness, is close to a great transformation that will usher in an era of peace, unity, and bliss.

The relative clarity of these general principles masks an ambiguous hodgepodge of particulars. NAM includes elements from all the major religions, plus a good many other things. The blend of elements from Eastern religions would offend serious practitioners of any of them. This smorgasbord approach seems to be peculiarly American and is supported by the social, ethnic, and religious pluralism of society in the United States. Another source for NAM is primitive religion: shamanism, witchcraft, druidism, earth motherhood, and the cult of Isis. Satanic cults are also part of the penumbra of the New Age and are an expression of the ecumenical devotion to the spirit world. Despite the emphasis on the positive within NAM, the abandonment of dichotomy makes it open to the dark side of spirituality.

Various cultural factors have given rise to NAM. For example, the decline of liberal Christianity has left a spiritual emptiness that is often filled by the apparent sophistication and novelty of New Age messages.

Support has also come from rootlessness, in particular the collapse of historical and cultural traditions since the 1960s. Nowhere has this rootlessness been more prevalent than in California, the center and source of NAM, home of everything from the Esalen Institute to Shirley MacLaine to Matthew Fox and his creation spirituality. As links to the past withered, New Age filled the cultural vacuum for many people.

Psychology also has helped to bring NAM into prominence. Carl Gustav Jung's psychology of archetypes, with its interpretations of myths and symbols and its interest in religion and spirituality, has been a major influence on New Age thought.

Further support came from humanistic psychology, in particular Abraham Maslow's central concept of self-actualization, capped by a transcendent peak experience of wholeness and unity with the cosmos. For Maslow this is a natural, not a supernatural, phenomenon. He proposed that in the past religious figures often reached peak experience but interpreted it wrongly in terms of the religion of their culture (Maslow, 1964).

In 1969 Maslow was among the founders of *The Journal of Transpersonal Psychology (JTP)*, which focuses on the implications of transcendent experience for personal life and growth. Thus *JTP* entered a realm of intellectual discourse very different from that of traditional psychology. But humanistic psychology was the launch pad. Explicit links between transpersonal psychology and NAM are clear: in 1978 *JTP* held a conference on "Consciousness and the Cosmos" that included Capra (1975) and other important New Age figures.

A few writers have pointed out the similarities between New Age systems and Gnosticism, which arose in the Hellenistic period; by the time of early Christianity there were many Gnostic sects. As the word *gnostic* (knower) implies, these systems proposed knowledge as the key to the meaning of life: salvation comes through knowledge. The knowledge in question was philosophical or spiritual, and esoteric (secret). These sects combined various ingredients taken from a wide assortment of ancient religions and philosophical sources.

The social conditions of the ancient Greco-Roman world, especially in the eastern Mediterranean, are similar to those in which NAM flourishes. Los Angeles is a new Alexandria: rich, pleasure-loving, a crossroad of cultures and religious traditions. The conditions in California are increasingly found on a smaller scale throughout the world, suggesting that NAM has a growing future.

A number of psychologists have argued that humanistic psychology, despite some positive features, is fundamentally narcissistic and individualistic, with its emphasis on the autonomous self. Ethical egoism (equivalent in many ways to narcissism) is the central moral principle found in all self theories. Narcissism in this context does not mean the seriously disturbed narcissistic personality but rather a general, social narcissism and extreme individualism.

The popularity of humanistic psychology and its derivatives in the United States in the 1950s and 1960s led to large-scale disappointments with the promises made. Psychology may have helped, but life remained painful and difficult. People still sought true happiness, inner peace, or an internal positive state and turned to a spiritual understanding of their condition. Large numbers, however, did not turn to traditional religions in part because of the moral and theological restraints that are fundamental to every major religion. The freedom to have one's own way is central to the appeal of New Age spirituality, which appears to be the transformation of psychological narcissism into spiritual narcissism.

We have gone from self-actualization, supported by an individualistic consumer economy, to New Age consumer spirituality and self-worship. A popular NAM advocate, Shirley MacLaine, sums it up: "Each soul is its own god. You must never worship anyone or anything other than self. For *you* are God. To love self is to love God" (1985, p. 358).

References

Capra, F. (1975). *The tao of physics*. Suffolk, England: Chaucer.

Ferguson, M. (1980). *The Aquarian conspiracy*. Los Angeles: Tarcher.

Groothius, D. (1988). *Confronting the new age*. Downers Grove, IL: InterVarsity Press.

MacLaine, S. (1985). *Dancing in the light*. Toronto and New York: Bantam.

Maslow, A. (1964). *Religions, values and peak experiences*. Columbus: Ohio State University Press.

Pacwa, M. (1992). *Catholics and the new age*. Ann Arbor, MI: Servant.

Vitz, P. (1994). *Psychology as religion: The cult of self-worship* (2nd ed.). Grand Rapids, MI: Eerdmans.

P. C. Vitz

See Religious Experience; Psychology of Religion.

Nightmare. Both nightmares and night tremors involve a person awaking from sleep in a state of fear and anxiety. A nightmare is usually associated upon awakening with a particular dream. Nightmares occur during the REM stage of sleep and are most frequently experienced by children seven to ten years old. The best initial treatment for a nightmare is calm reassurance that there is nothing to be afraid of.

Night tremors, technically known as *pavor nocturnus*, are more dramatic than nightmares, resembling panic attacks. They are not associated with a dream and upon waking are not typically remembered to have occurred. Research has shown that night tremors are a disorder of the slow wave deep sleep stage and do not occur during the REM dream stage. Night tremors are most frequent in children aged three to five years.

The occurrence of nightmares and night tremors should not be interpreted as being of great psychological significance unless they become chronic. Chronic problems may be a reaction to emotional stress or may indicate a physiological-biological defect.

D. S. McCulloch

See Sleep and Dreaming; Sleep Disorders.

Nondirective Therapy. *See* Person-Centered Therapy.

Nonprofessionals as Therapists. *See* Lay Counseling; Paraprofessional Therapy.

Noogenic Neurosis. According to Victor Emil Frankl, a noogenic neurosis is the result of moral conflicts or conflict among values. This is in contrast to the psychoneurosis, which Frankl views, in orthodox psychoanalytic fashion, as the result of conflicts between drives and instincts.

Since the noogenic neuroses reflect what Frankl calls a spiritual problem, he argues that what is needed is not psychotherapy in general but logotherapy, a therapy that he developed to specifically address spiritual and existential dimensions of existence. It should be noted, however, "that within the frame of reference of logotherapy, 'spiritual' does not have a primarily religious connotation but refers to the specifically human dimension" (Frankl, 1963, p. 102).

Reference

Frankl, V. E. (1963). *Man's search for meaning*. Boston: Beacon.

D. G. Benner

See Logotherapy; Frankl, Victor Emil.

Normality. Many psychologists consider normality and abnormality together, since abnormality is deviance from normality. Normality represents the lack of abnormality or the other anchor of a continuum. Professional consensus suggests several conditions that define personality as abnormal: self-proclaimed deviance, antisocial action or intent, antisurvival elements, irrationality, subjective distress, social deviance, or psychological handicap.

Allport (1977) offered a more theoretical and systematic definition. Normality is conforming to a given norm, an authoritative standard, while abnormality is deviance from that standard. But Allport noted there are two competing traditions for defining the norm.

The statistical tradition assumes human traits vary along a continuum on which the relative frequencies approximate the normal curve. The norm is the usual value and is expressed by a central tendency measure (e.g., mean, median, or mode). The degree of deviance from the group's central tendency determines the individual's degree of abnormality. The genius is as abnormal as the retardate. The orientation of this tradition is toward objectivity and value neutrality. It seeks to measure accurately the isness of human nature.

In the second tradition, an ethical one, the norm is defined as something valued, an oughtness of human nature. Frequently the usual is not the desired. As a values-invested approach this tradition may reflect a moral perspective. In reference to some value theory (e.g., the Bible) the norm is morality, while the abnorm is that which is immoral. In describing the normal personality Christ may be held as the norm for human conduct.

The medical perspective provides a second ethical position. Health is to be desired; health is the absence of illness. The norm is that individuals live lives free from the effects of illness, disease, and dysfunction. The current emphasis on holistic health states this norm.

A third value position is naturalistically derived and suggests that humans should maximize the ways in which they differ from animals (Allport, 1977). Human uniqueness stems from the propositional use of symbols and protracted childhood. These combine as a substratum for responsibility, social interest, ideals, self-control, and guilt. An alternative naturalistic approach specifies the minimum conditions for survival as growth and cohesion. To fall below those levels is to experience the abnorm and tend toward death and destruction.

A fourth position resembles the naturalistic. In the humanistic perspective normality is the attainment of freedom, self-actualization, personal growth, and intimacy. The abnorm is whatever is excessively repressive or demanding and violates the principles of freedom and cohesion.

In summary, there are two competing traditions for defining normality. The statistical one focuses on the isness of the individual by referring to a known distribution of traits and is reflected in the use of norm-referenced test scores. The ethical tradition defines normality by what is desired or ought to be. These value statements may be generated from several sources. The statistical approach describes what is usual, while the ethical one prescribes what is desired.

Reference

Allport, G. W. (1977). Personality: Normal and abnormal. In H. Chiang & A. H. Maslow (Eds.), *The healthy personality: Readings* (2nd ed.). New York: Van Nostrand.

R. L. TIMPE

See PERSONALITY; ABNORMAL PSYCHOLOGY.

Normalization in Human Services. The principle of normalization is a basis for planning, providing, and evaluating services to persons who have disabilities such as mental retardation, quadriplegia, cerebral palsy, mental illness, or alcoholism (*see* Alcohol Abuse and Dependence; Disability).

The historical roots of normalization can be traced to 1959, when Denmark became the first nation to pass legislation establishing an agency concerned with the health, education, and welfare of people with special needs and particularly designed to help them experience life as normally as possible. In 1967–1968 Sweden passed a similar law establishing an agency to unite resources for retarded people based on the normalization principle. In the United States, Wolfensberger, Menolascino, and a few co-

workers subsequently labored for several years to establish normalization in service systems for the mentally retarded. This culminated in *The Principles of Normalization in Human Services* (Wolfensberger, Nirje, Olshansky, Perske, & Roos, 1972), which summarized the historical background and formulated the philosophical and practical aspects of normalization. Wolfensberger's approach has been expanded to include persons with all kinds of disabilities rather than focusing only on the mentally retarded.

Definition. Normalization can be described as a system for increasing the probability that over time handicapped people will more and more live in society as valued neighbors rather than as devalued objects of pity or derision. This could be stated another way: "And as ye would that men should do to you, do ye also to them likewise" (Luke 6:31, KJV).

Wolfensberger (1980a) defines normalization as the "use of culturally normative means (familiar, valued techniques, tools, methods) . . . to [improve] persons' life conditions (income, housing, health services, etc.) . . . and to . . . enhance or support their behavior (skills, competencies, etc.), appearances (clothes, grooming, etc.), experiences (adjustment, feelings, etc.), and status and reputation (labels, attitudes of others, etc.)" (p. 25). Services designed on this concept of normalization are likely to result in increasing competence and social participation for individuals with disabilities and in increasing social acceptance of them as a group.

Applications. Implementation of the normalization principle requires that people and service systems avoid devaluing responses to persons who have any type of disability. Three frequent responses that are most harmful are isolation (segregating people with handicaps); dehumanization (treating people with handicaps as if they are less than fully human); and age inappropriateness (treating people with disabilities as if they are and always will be children). Understanding each of these patterns of devaluation helps define positive practices to ensure that people with handicaps experience as much participation in the life of the community as possible.

In the past many residential services for handicapped people were founded and grew when isolation was considered the treatment of choice. For a time the belief that people with disabilities needed protection from community life justified isolation. This eventually turned to a belief that the community needs protection from the costs and dangers allegedly posed by people with handicaps. Therefore, many service systems have moved these people away from their age peers; others move them away from their home communities; and some isolate people from friends, relatives, and immediate family members.

According to advocates of the normalization concept such practices deprive these individuals of a wide variety of learning experiences, the support of valued peer models, many opportunities to exercise choice, the chance to become a part of a natural social network, and the challenge of contributing to community life.

If persons with handicaps are to learn to meet their needs in the least restrictive possible relationship to their community, proponents of normalization believe they must experience that community individually as an essential part of their learning. They assert that a person needs to experience two dimensions of community life: the physical world of places and things, and the social world of people and typical human groups. The isolation of handicapped people from community life breeds suspicion, fear, and rejection. If individuals are to develop and mature as normally as possible, a significant number of community members must support their development in natural communities by getting to know them on a one-to-one basis, inviting them to their homes, taking them to church, taking them to ballgames, and the like. As long as isolation persists, social acceptance cannot develop.

Advocates of normalization allege that dehumanization is fostered through settings that do not allow for personal space and privacy. Examples of such conditions include sleeping arrangements that permit no choice regarding whether one will share a room and with whom, lack of privacy in toileting and bathing, food preparation with few choices of menu or option to cook for oneself, and lack of space for personal possessions.

Further, normalization proponents contend that persons are treated as subhuman when people regard them as one of a group rather than as individuals. This is apparent when persons are grouped according to disability and/or functioning level for leisure activities rather than on the basis of individual performance. This is also observed when persons are not included in decisions about their own lives. Dehumanization can also be signaled by language that fails to promote the integrity of a person (i.e., labels).

The absence of dehumanizing conditions, however, does not automatically guarantee persons dignity and respect. In order to develop a sense of worth as an individual, a person needs opportunities for self-expression and time apart from a group. It is believed that persons have the right to privacy and personal space wherever they live. Living space should be comfortable and attractive. Special equipment to aid posture or mobility should be comfortable, well fitting, and designed to minimize stigmatizing appearances. All facilities should be physically accessible to people with mobility limitations. Individuals also deserve some choice regarding activities and the people with whom they spend their leisure time. Community members can provide these opportunities for choice as they relate on a one-to-one basis with these persons.

In order to participate in life fully, each person deserves the opportunity to participate in the decisions affecting his or her life. Individuals with handicaps, especially those who have been insti-tutionalized for extensive periods, often need systematic training to develop their ability to choose. Nevertheless, issues affecting a group of people, even when they have disabilities, should be decided by that group when possible. When this is not feasible, decisions should be made only after input from the group has been obtained.

Persons need to be allowed to take appropriate risks. They have the opportunity to realize success only when they also have the opportunity for failure. People have the right to be systematically taught to understand their legal and personal rights and the means of protecting them. Decision making and citizenship training ought to be available.

Positive interactions are also crucial to enhancing the dignity and individual respect of persons with disabilities. People should not be treated condescendingly, regardless of their disability. Communication needs to be warm and personal, with people genuinely sharing their lives and personal time with disabled individuals. Handicapped adults have the right to experience personal relationships with friends, including those of the opposite sex.

Another area of concern is age-inappropriate practices that treat handicapped people as if they are and always will be children. Consciousness of age appropriateness is seen as critical in the selection of learning activities and materials. Activities that are designed to teach skills should be selected according to age-appropriate processes and carried out at appropriate times. For example, a person who needs training in self-care skills should ideally receive it individually at the appropriate times (upon waking or before bed) in his or her own bedroom or bathroom. Training materials should be selected that are appropriate to a person's chronological age. An adult may need to learn how to pour. If this is taught in a sandbox with pails and shovels, it loudly signals devaluation for the integrity of that individual. The same skill could be appropriately taught through cooking or potting plants.

It is considered important that the rhythms of the day, week, and year be the same for persons labeled disabled as for those labeled normal. Children ought to attend school; adults should go to a place of work, earn money, experience personal leisure time, and so on. Promoters of normalization contend that a disproportionate amount of time is often spent in recreational and leisure activities. There is often little concern for the quality of performance; the expectation is, It's enough for them just to try. This disregards the status a person can earn by excellence in at least one area of activity. Acceptance of shoddy work by a handicapped person (or anyone else) communicates a lack of respect for the person's abilities. Such practices and expectations are demeaning and hinder individual development.

Critique and Evaluation. One of the most common criticisms of normalization is that people with disabilities cannot be made normal. Defenders of normalization would tend to agree on this point. Some individuals, when they are provided optimal opportunities for growth and development of personal worth, may achieve a nonhandicapped and/or nondevalued functioning and status. Such, however, is not the essence of the concept. Proponents feel that all handicapped individuals have a right to as normal an environment as they can utilize, regardless of prognosis for future change.

Another criticism develops when those who do not fully understand normalization philosophy place handicapped individuals in normal situations where they have many problems or fail. Mentally retarded persons, blind individuals, or persons possessing certain other disabilities should not be put in an apartment by themselves, for example, without first identifying the needs such a person would have and developing strategies to meet those needs.

Research on the normalization principle has been difficult because of the vast number of components, corollaries, and action implications that fall into a hierarchy of levels in the normalization process. Not all have the same amount or quality of research support. One way of studying these issues has been to look at the ratings provided by the tool called Program Analysis of Service Systems (Wolfensberger & Glenn, 1975). This instrument is a systematic method of evaluation that breaks services down into 48 areas relating to the quality of services provided to handicapped persons. Wolfensberger (1980b) summarizes some of this research as well as other studies conducted with regard to role expectancies, and role demands. These provide encouraging support for the application of the normalization principle.

The Bible is filled with pertinent directions about the responsibility persons share for their neighbors and the quality of their lives. Moreover, a church is called to be a model community that will enhance persons. Certainly, therefore, it seems appropriate for Christians to be actively committed to and give leadership in efforts to respond to all persons with valuing and respect.

References

Wolfensberger, W. Research, empiricism, and the principle of normalization. (1980a). In R. J. Flynn & K. E. Nitsch (Eds.), *Normalization, social integration, and community services*. Baltimore: University Park Press.

Wolfensberger, W. The definition of normalization. (1980b). In R. J. Flynn & K. E. Nitsch (Eds.), *Normalization, social integration, and community services*. Baltimore: University Park Press.

Wolfensberger, W., & Glenn, L. (1975). *Program analysis of service systems: A method for the qualitative evaluation of human services* (Vols. 1 & 2) (3rd ed.). Toronto: National Institute on Mental Retardation.

Wolfensberger, W., Nirje, B., Olshansky, S., Perske, R., & Roos, P. (1972). *The principles of normalization in human services*. Toronto: National Institute on Mental Retardation.

M. E. McCurdy

See COMMUNITY PSYCHOLOGY; COMMUNITY MENTAL HEALTH.

Nosology. A branch of medicine concerned with the study and classification of diseases. Discovery of symptoms and consequent grouping into syndromes is the main area of concern. The delineation and definition of diseases perform four major functions in the medical field: classification of terminology, the categorizing of names and codes within each classification, the establishing of reliable and specific procedures for collecting information, and the operationalizing of rules for making classifications. The three main purposes or uses of information gathered by nosology are to serve as a guide to selection of treatment, to make prognoses, and to function as administrative devices for hospital admissions, insurance purposes, and similar medical or legal requirements.

D. L. SCHUURMAN

Nouthetic Counseling. A counseling theory formulated by Jay Adams and based on the New Testament Greek verb *noutheteō*. Adams's most systematic work on counseling appeared as *The Christian Counselor's Manual* (1973) and *More Than Redemption* (1979), in which he develops a theology of counseling. Since then he has written several books and numerous articles. Seminary trained, Adams has a doctorate in speech. After serving in a pastorate and after teaching speech for three years, he became professor of practical theology at Westminster Seminary. The Christian Counseling and Educational Foundation (CCEF) and the Biblical Counseling Foundation (BCF) base their approach on Adams's theory. Counselors who operate within this theory call themselves biblical counselors, although others who do not share Adams's view use this name as well.

Personality Theory. Nouthetic counseling can be described in terms of its theory of human nature, view of pathology, and model and process of counseling. With respect to personality theory, nouthetic counseling stresses the overt aspects of human nature. Adams maintains that God describes love in attitudinal and behavioral terms by defining it as commandment keeping (John 14:15). Hence nouthetic counseling focuses less on how clients feel and more on how they behave. Adams sees voluntary changes in behavior as a function of intelligent decisions, and the emotions are affected as a result. "People feel bad because of bad behavior: feelings flow from actions" (Adams, 1970, p. 93).

To Adams the sequence is clear: God's commands deal with behavior and attitudes. Behavior is defined as responsible conduct. An attitude is a habitual pattern of thought that strongly influences actions. Attitudes may be changed more easily than feelings, which Adams defines as the perception of a bodily state, either pleasant or unpleasant. He views other emotional responses, both good and bad, of the body as "responses to judgments made about the environment and oneself" (Adams, 1973, p. 112). The individual chooses to behave consistently or inconsistently with God's commands, and good or bad feelings flow accordingly. The result is communicated to the whole person, but Adams does not define the whole person.

Adams's psychological theory is that behavior is central and has fundamental significance. Attitudes are second and interior, but as habitual thought patterns they have an external thought focus. Feelings are the most internal and therefore the least accessible. They follow or are caused by behavior. Adams maintains this sequence is clearly the biblical ideal (1973, p. 135).

Adams holds a dichotomous view of humanity, maintaining that *soul* and *spirit* are used interchangeably in the Bible. The image of God in humans is of more central importance in nouthetic theory than is soul or spirit. This image is moral and cognitive. In the fall the image became a "reflection of the father of lies" (Adams, 1970, p. 128). The Christian is described as restoring the image by eliminating confusion and disorder (1973, p. 342). The fall, Adams says, was "a fall into loss of control over the environment, and God calls the Christian to master his environment. In this way he may once again reflect the image of God by subduing and ruling the environment around him" (Adams, 1970, p. 129). The focus for the Christian is on behaviorally confronting the environment. The cognitive aspect of the image would appear to be related to the attitudinal or judgment process that mediates feelings, although Adams does not integrate his psychological and theological description of persons.

View of Psychopathology. Adams maintains then that the key problem with which Christian counselors must grapple is sin. In his analysis of the fall (Gen. 3) Adams views the basic temptation as the satisfaction of desire rather than obedience to God. The same choice, according to Adams, exists today.

According to Adams, the choice is between two ways of living: "the feeling-motivated life of sin oriented toward self" or the "commandment-oriented life oriented toward God" (Adams, 1973, p. 118). The choice is reduced to love or lust, God's commandments or the clients' desires. In nouthetic counseling feelings arise from desire, and desire is tied to sinful actions (Adams, 1973, p. 120). Hence feelings are not to be attended to or trusted. Nouthetic counseling maintains that feelings do not necessarily lead to sinful actions, since commandment living is called for in spite of feelings. In addition to sin as a cause of psychopathology, organic disease and demon possession are possible causes, although the latter is not possible for the believer. According to Adams, there is no such thing as an emotional disorder.

Three levels of problems exist: presenting problems (I'm depressed), performance problems (I

haven't been much of a husband), and preconditioning problems (I avoid responsibility when the going gets tough). Presentation problems are often presented as a cause when they are an effect. Performance problems are often presented as an effect when they are a cause. Preconditioning problems are presented as an effect when they are the underlying cause (Adams, 1970, p. 148). Adams goes on to say the preconditioning problem is a habitual response that, as the root problem, often clarifies the relationship between the other two problems.

Counseling Process. The model of nouthetic counseling is based on the Greek verb *noutheteō*, which occurs eight times in eight verses in the New Testament. The verb is often translated "warn, admonish or instruct" (Bauer, Arndt, & Gingrich, 1979). The verb is translated "warn" four times and "admonish" three times in the New International Version. Adams drew the title for his first book, *Competent to Counsel*, from Romans 15:14 (NIV). "I myself am convinced, my brothers, that you yourselves are full of goodness, complete in knowledge and competent to instruct one another." Adams admits that there is no exact English equivalent, so he uses the phrase *nouthetic confrontation* to describe his model of counseling.

The model has four basic characteristics. First, confrontation in counseling is viewed as inseparable from pastoral authority. Second, the goals of nouthetic counseling are stated to be the same as those of the Scripture: "Nouthetic confrontation is in short, confrontation with the principles and practices of the Scripture" (Adams, 1970, p. 51). Third, nouthetic counseling was originally conceived as team counseling, a practice that was later abandoned. Fourth, nouthetic counseling has a strong similarity to legal counseling: it is directive, gives advice, and imparts information. The process of counseling that unfolds from this model is grounded in Adams's basic assumption that people need meaning or hope in their lives. He thinks that one way to raise hope is by confronting people with the Scripture when they are in sin.

In addition to this general approach Adams uses the Personal Data Inventory, as presented in the appendix of *The Christian Counselor's Manual*, to gather history and assess problems. Early sessions may be information-gathering sessions; however, by the sixth session the major issues should be clear. By the eighth to tenth session the problem should be well on the way toward solution (Adams, 1973, pp. 233–234). Adams does not specify the length of therapy, but it appears to be rather short.

The main focus in nouthetic counseling is on what, not why. The counselor directs attention to the presenting, performance, and preconditioning levels of the problem. The counselor imparts information, gives advice, and confronts. Homework assignments are a normal part of nouthetic counseling. A frequent technique is restructuring all areas of the client's life and pressing for change in each area so as to prevent relapse.

According to Adams, the Holy Spirit is the real counselor. "Ignoring the Holy Spirit or avoiding the use of Scripture in counseling is tantamount to an autonomous act of rebellion" (1973, pp. 6–7). Counseling is truly nouthetic only when the counselee is a Christian. If a non-Christian seeks nouthetic counseling the counselor must do precounseling, which is designed to lead the client to Christ. After the client has become a Christian, then counseling can begin. Adams maintains that every Christian is called to be a counselor, but counseling is the special calling of the pastor. Accordingly, there is no need for psychologists, psychiatrists, or other mental health professionals to treat mental disorders. Adams maintains that a good seminary education is more appropriate for preparing counselors than is medical school or clinical psychology training.

Finally, the nouthetic counselor cannot listen to or accept the client's sinful attitudes or ventilations, since the "acceptance of sin is sin" (1970, p. 102). Acceptance or support is passive; hence it is wrong for three reasons: the counselor must never support sinful behavior; support is harmful because it approves of the client's handling of his or her problems; and there is no biblical basis for passively "being" but not "doing" or "saying" (1973, p. 154). There is no room for empathy that is not problem-oriented. Admonishing is the evidence of love, since love, for Adams, is concerned primarily with responsible behavior (1970, p. 55).

Evaluation. Four areas of criticism are useful with respect to Adams's theory. First, Adams seems to be not fully knowledgeable regarding theories he criticizes. At one point he attributes the concept of transference to "Rogers and other Freudians" (1970, p. 101). This is a serious misunderstanding of both Carl Rogers and Sigmund Freud. No serious analysis has ever viewed them as similar with regard to transference. Rogers never discusses transference or makes it a part of his therapy. Also, Adams (1970) has consistently criticized Freud for promoting irresponsibility. In addition to other statements, Adams says, "The Freudian viewpoint boils down to this, that God is to blame for the misery and ruin of man" (p. 214) and "All that can be said of Freud is that his views have encouraged irresponsible people to persist in and expand their irresponsibility" (1970, p. 17). These comments seem in stark contrast to what Freud wrote: "To believe that psychoanalysis seeks a cure for the neurotic disorders by giving free rein to sexuality is a serious misunderstanding which can only be excused by ignorance. The making conscious of sexual desires in analysis makes it possible, on the contrary, to obtain a mastery over them which the previous repression has been unable to achieve" (Freud, 1923, p. 252). Again, he states that the analyst is in "a perpetual struggle with his patient to keep in the psychical sphere all the impulses which the patient would like to direct into the motor sphere" (Freud, 1914, p. 153).

Second, Adams fails to demonstrate why *noutheō* is to be chosen as foundational for counseling theory. An argument could be made as well from Scripture that *parakelō*, translated comfort, console, or exhort, is a much more appropriate choice, since it is a gift to the church as well (Rom. 12:8). Likewise, Adams fails to take into account Scriptures that conflict with his viewpoint. First Thessalonians 5:14 (NIV) says, "And we urge you, brothers, warn those who are idle, encourage the timid, help the weak, be patient with everyone." Paul describes three kinds of counseling relationships; admonish *(noutheteō)* the unruly, encourage *(paramutheō)* the fainthearted, and help *(antexō)* the weak. Yet Adams urges a single way of thinking. For example, Adams's foundational point that sin is the problem is at variance with the theme of the Book of Job. While Adams (1979) recognizes that Job's problems do not result from sin, one must ask how Adams would counsel Job. Would he also be one of the "miserable comforters" (Job 16:2, NIV)?

Third, in terms of presuppositions Adams seems to have adopted a particular view vis-à-vis general revelation and special revelation. Adams wants special revelation to have priority over general revelation in building counseling theory because, according to Adams, special revelation exists for such a purpose while general revelation can be valid only when it is affirmed by special revelation. Special revelation is, according to Adams, given to help us know how to love God and our neighbor, which he sees as having direct impact on counseling theory (Adams, 1979). He does not see anywhere in the Scripture the admonition to study general revelation for the purposes of deriving principles for living and loving. Nouthetic counselors, following Adams, believe the Bible to be completely adequate to build a counseling theory and have consistently opposed those who believe differently, implying they are unbiblical. Adams's view is roughly equivalent to that of Van Til (1974). Adams's followers repeat the same theme: "Nouthetic counseling was founded in the confidence that God has spoken comprehensively about and to human beings. His Word teaches truth. The Holy Spirit enables effective, loving ministry. Our positive call has been to pursue and then promote biblical truth and methods in counseling. As a secondary application of this positive call, nouthetic counselors have consistently opposed the 'integration' movement" (Powlinson, 1993).

At issue is the manner in which errors in understanding of the data from either special or general revelation are to be corrected. If biblical truth can be arrived at only by interpretation of scriptural data, and we must also interpret data from general revelation, how can one interpretation be given a position of higher authority over the other? If either interpretation is given authority, one must ask, how is one to resolve conflicts such as that between the church and Copernicus? The insight that the sun does not revolve around the earth did not come from a study of special revelation. Adams seems to suggest that when one misunderstands special revelation, then others, arguing from those same presuppositions, will correct the error.

Adams's desire to put interpretations developed from the study of Scripture on a plane above interpretations derived from the study of nature seems to give God his rightful position of authority. But upon closer inspection, what is given authority is not God or the Bible but what an interpreter thinks God is saying.

Fourth, most biblical counselors are strident critics of what they see as secularism in psychology. They argue that psychology has replaced God, his centrality, and the authority of the Bible with the centrality of the self and the authority of psychology. They see a part of the larger whole, the larger development since the Enlightenment, of the secularization of society and the trivialization of God, the Bible, and faith. They are zealous to return God and the Bible to positions of authority in the hearts and lives of people. This desire is to be commended. In keeping with this desire they are on record as strongly opposed to the integration of psychology and theology. In their criticisms, however, there is a failure to make appropriate distinctions, lumping together all manner of people with varied and disparate views under the "big umbrella of integration" (Powlinson, 1993, p. 2). While their heartfelt criticisms of psychology in general and integrative psychology in particular have some validity, they fail to see that these issues are on the hearts and minds of many integrationists who are likewise working toward the same goals. With nouthetic counselors there is a fail-ure to see validity in alternative approaches. The attitude of nouthetic counselors is stated well by Powlinson (1993, p. 1), "We nouthetic counselors have many failings. But I believe that by the grace of God we are fundamentally right and occasionally wrong, foolish and blind. . . . But integrationists are fundamentally wrong and, by the grace of God, occasionally right, wise and perceptive" and "Let's wield the evangelistic sword effectively."

References

Adams, J. (1970). *Competent to counsel*. Philadelphia: Presbyterian & Reformed.

Adams, J. (1973). *The Christian counselor's manual*. Grand Rapids, MI: Baker.

Adams, J. (1979). *More than redemption*. Phillipsburg, NJ: Presbyterian & Reformed.

Bauer, W., Arndt, W. F., & Gingrich, F. W. (1979). *A Greek-English lexicon of the New Testament and other early Christian literature* (2d ed.). Chicago: University of Chicago Press.

Freud, S. (1914). On the history of the psychoanalytic movement. *The standard edition of the complete psychological works of Sigmund Freud*. London: Hogarth.

Freud, S. (1923). The ego and the id. *The standard edition of the complete psychological works of Sigmund Freud*. London: Hogarth.

Powlinson, D. (1993, spring). Critiquing modern integrationists. *The Journal of Biblical Counseling, 11*, 3.

Van Til, C. (1974). My credo. In E. R. Geeham (Ed.), *Jerusalem and Athens*. Nutley, NJ: Presbyterian & Reformed.

D. W. PETERS AND J. D. CARTER

See CHRISTIAN COUNSELING AND PSYCHOTHERAPY; PASTORAL COUNSELING; BIBLICAL COUNSELING.

Oates, Wayne Edward (1917–). Oates was born in Greenville, South Carolina, into a family of textile-mill workers. He wrote about his childhood of poverty in *The Struggle to Be Free* (1983). Much of his outlook on life seems to be due to his early experiences.

Oates's teachers noticed his curiosity and gave him encouragement. He loved learning but saw no way to avoid leaving school after the eighth grade to support his family. Later Oates could see God's providence was at work when he was selected by Senator Ellison D. Smith to be a page in Congress. Oates worked in the Senate and went to school at night.

Oates had almost no religious instruction during childhood. As a teen in Washington he began to attend church and eventually prayed to receive Christ. Oates returned to Greenville to finish high school. He worked for a time in the textile mills, educating himself in the Bible and taking classes at the local YMCA. Through the Y he was introduced to the president of Mars Hill College, a Baptist junior college near Ashville, South Carolina. With $125 savings and the assurance of grants, he entered Mars Hill, where he had a spiritual renewal experience. After Mars Hill, he went to Wake Forest College. Soon after beginning Wake Forest he acknowledged God's call to the ministry. Quickly he conceived of his ministry focus to individuals and families who were conflict-ridden, poor, and hopeless. However, this put him under some pressure, since the accepted mode for Baptist ministers was of revival evangelist. Oates wanted to minister to the whole person. He eventually graduated from Southern Seminary with a Th.D. degree, writing the dissertation "The Significance of the Work of Sigmund Freud for the Christian Faith."

Oates conceived of the work of pastoral counseling in relation to the life of the Spirit, the life of the church, and the hope of the kingdom of God. He saw his work in pastoral care counseling as eclectic, with a phenomenological learning theory and favoring a developmental method.

In 1948 Oates joined the faculty of Southern Baptist Seminary and helped work out its first full curriculum in pastoral care and counseling. In 1969 he received the Distinguished Service Award of the American Association of Pastoral Counselors. In 1974 he become professor of psychiatry and behavioral sciences at the University of Louisville School of Medicine and director of program in ethics and pastoral counseling at Louisville General Hospital.

Oates has published more than 40 books and numerous articles in the areas of pastoring, grief, religious care of psychiatric patients, counseling, and human suffering. He is the editor of the 12-volume *Christian Care* and author of the *Pastor's Handbook* (Vols. 1 and 2).

Reference

Oates, W. E. (1983). *The struggle to be free.*

E. S. GIBBS

See PASTORAL COUNSELING.

Obedience. In studying conformity and obedience to social influence, psychologists found it occurring at three levels. The deepest level involves the personality and value structures of the individual utilizing conformity as a dominant adjustment mode. The internalized conformity becomes a way of meeting personal needs. Conforming personalities have lower self-esteem, greater authoritarian tendencies, and more unquestioning respect for convention than nonconformists.

A second level concerns attitudes privately held and publicly expressed. If an individual finds a certain group attractive and desirable, he or she may change important attitudes to match those of the group. The individual conforms to group opinion through identification (e.g., dress and musical preferences of teens).

Conformity also exists at more surface and behavioral levels. Groups exert pressure on individuals to exhibit a particular behavior. The group's power to change individual behavior lies in its ability to provide rewards for conformity and punishments for nonconformity. Social psychologists define behavioral conformity as compliance when the internal group pressures of equal peers produce the conformity. However, if someone in a leadership role is viewed as an authority or is in a power position to administer rewards and punishments, then compliance is considered obedience.

Milgram (1973) studied destructive obedience, the ability of an authority figure to induce subordinates to damage property or harm others. Destructive obedience underlies such historical occurrences as the Spanish Inquisition, the Nazi persecution of European Jews, the My Lai massacre in Vietnam, and tragedies in Iraq, Rwanda, and Bosnia. In each case a leader (ecclesiastical, governmental, or military) ordered followers to torture or kill. The followers obeyed.

Milgram's experiments followed a common format. He advertised for volunteers to help him conduct an experiment in learning. Those who volunteered were cast in the experimental role of teacher. The teacher's task was to punish the learner whenever he or she failed to learn by administering an electric shock. The shock apparatus was labeled for each shock level (e.g., 15 volts, slight shock; 100 volts, severe shock; 450 volts, danger!). The researcher, who stood in the room with the teacher, required the teacher to administer progressively stronger shocks each time there was a failure to learn. Unknown to the teacher, the learner was the researcher's accomplice who was programmed to fail in the learning tasks. The learner was not actually shocked but staged more violent reactions as the shocks became more intense. If the teacher tried to quit the experiment, the researcher demanded that teacher continue in the name of science. The actual variable that was measured was the level of shock the teacher was willing to administer.

Milgram originally predicted few teachers would administer extreme shocks. He sampled psychiatrists, college students, and middle-class adults, who concurred with his predictions. However, in the experiment he found that no teacher administered less than 300 volts, and 65% gave the most severe shock possible. In the experimental setting the teacher could neither see nor hear the learner (i.e., the remote condition). Interviews with the teachers did reveal that many experienced anxiety from giving extreme shocks.

Milgram conducted other experiments to determine what variables might influence the obedience level. He manipulated the amount of contact between the teacher and learner. When the teacher could hear the learner (i.e., voice-feedback condition) 62.5% administered maximum shocks. When the teacher and learner were located in the same room (i.e., proximity condition), 40% administered maximum shock. If the teacher and learner were seated at the same table (i.e., touch-proximity condition), 30% of the teachers administered the maximum level. Obedience decreased as the distance and contact between the teacher and learner decreased.

Milgram also examined the legitimacy of the authority. When the research was conducted at Yale University, there was a higher rate of obedience than when the research was conducted at a private commercial research firm housed in a rundown office building in Bridgeport, Connecticut. In the latter setting 48% delivered maximum shocks as opposed to the 62% at Yale. Nevertheless, there was considerable obedience even when the authority was not particularly reputable. Bickman (1974) reported greater obedience when the authority was legitimized by a uniform.

When the researcher stood closer to the teacher and when there was more than one researcher present, there was greater obedience. When there were multiple teachers, obedience levels decreased. Milgram noted that certain individuals were more likely to be obedient: police and military personnel, individuals who believed the learners deserved and were responsible for their punishment, persons with stronger authoritarian characteristics (*see* Authoritarian Personality), and individuals who had less advanced levels of moral development.

Subsequent to Milgram's original experiments, additional studies found that the destructive level of obedience is lessened if there is greater emotional closeness between the one ordered to obey and the victim. Personalizing the victim lessens the likelihood of harm, while conditions that depersonalize the victim increases the likelihood of inflicting harm. Any conditions that link the experimenter and teacher (e.g., physical proximity, return of a favor, light touch on the arm) strengthen the obedience to authority. Conditions which legitimize and institutionalize the authority also strengthen obedience, while increasing the size of the group of teachers decreases obedience.

These studies, however distressing and depressing they are, provide pointed evidence that individuals' behavior is often more affected by external situations than by inner attitudes and dispositions, in spite of the commonly held belief that inner forces are more potent than situational or environmental influences. This tendency to overly ascribe causality to inner conditions is what social psychologists term the fundamental attribution error.

References

Bickman, L. (1974). Social roles and uniforms: Clothes make the person. *Psychology Today, 7,* 48–51.
Milgram, S. (1973). *Obedience to authority.* New York: Harper & Row.

R. L. Timpe

See Conformity; Compliance.

Obesity. In view of the current emphasis on physical health and slim appearance, it is not surprising that few physical conditions carry the social disapproval that accompanies obesity. In the past the media as well as the health care professions have gone so far as to single out obesity as a matter of "national disgrace" (Bruch, 1978). In recent years there has been a softening of the rhetoric and greater understanding of this issue. Nonetheless, there continues to be a subtle prejudice against those regarded as obese. To effectively assist such individuals it is important to understand the etiology, psychological features, and treatment methods associated with obesity.

Although there is little agreement regarding the precise definition and measurement of obesity, general consensus is to define it as a weight that exceeds the ideal weight by 20%. More precise but less popular is a method of calibrating excess body fat (Seltzer & Mayer, 1965). National statistics on the prevalence of obesity in the United States estimate that between 20 and 30% of the adult population falls within this category. While some studies suggest that a greater number of boys than girls are overweight, others have disputed this conclusion. While some maintain that middle-aged women have a greater tendency to be obese than men, differences between the sexes disappear by age 60; both sexes tend to decrease in weight after that age (Stuart & Davis, 1972).

Research has revealed several etiological factors that may lead to obesity. Such biologically related factors as genetic predisposition, endocrine and biochemical disorders, abnormal neuroregulatory mechanisms, and early adipose tissue development may contribute to the onset of obesity (Bruch, 1978). Most basic is the thermodynamic model, which attributes obesity to caloric intake that exceeds energy burned (Mayer, 1968). However, such biologically related factors are not the only causes of obesity. Psychological factors such as an inability to identify hunger or distinguish it from other bodily needs or emotional arousal may also contribute to its development. Other related psychological factors include dysfunctional families, disturbances in size awareness, misperception of bodily functions, misperception of sexual role, issues concerning ownership of one's body and its control, and the use of food and eating as a pseudosolution for a variety of personality problems (Bruch, 1978). Recent studies have suggested that serious overeating may result in response to nonspecific emotional tensions, chronic frustration, emotional disturbance such as depression, and psychological addiction to food. It may also occur in reaction to specific traumatic events.

Reasons for an apparent higher frequency of obesity in middle-age females than males have been sought. Schachter's (1971) research has demonstrated that many individuals tend to eat in response to external environmental cues rather than internal physiological states. Thus it is thought that a woman's typical involvement in menu planning, shopping, preparing and storing food as well as other related tasks may increase the risk of obesity for the predisposed homemaker (Hall & Havassy, 1981). It has also

been suggested that lack of exercise, subtle role expectations, and societal pressure to be extremely slim have differentially influenced the development of obesity among females in contrast to males.

A wide variety of treatment techniques has been developed during the past two decades. Biologically related interventions include special diets, exercise programs, medication, surgery, and intensive hospital programs (Bruch, 1978). Psychotherapeutic approaches include behavior modification (Kingsley & Wilson, 1977), family therapy (Bruch, 1978), group therapy (Wollersheim, 1970), and approaches based on Schachter's externality hypothesis (Weiss, 1977) and on a psychoanalytic model (Orbach, 1978). Recent cognitive-behavioral techniques, which focus on correcting false beliefs, show great promise (Carson & Butcher, 1992).

Several special factors must be considered when developing a treatment strategy for such individuals. First, some clinicians question the assumption that a definite height-weight relationship and specific fat-lean tissue ratio are normal for all people because they are found among the majority (Bruch, 1978). It may be more useful to determine, in consultation with the client and his or her physician, the preferred weight at which the person feels most comfortable. It is also important to avoid being influenced by the gross bias found in current literature, both popular and medical, which abounds with generalized statements about the possible health hazards of being overweight and its ugliness, social handicaps, and psychological damage. Such stereotypical beliefs often lack scientific support and can be destructive when they are allowed to influence treatment goals and methods.

Goals for weight loss must be realistic and conservative, in view of the low success rate typically reported (Carson & Butcher, 1992; Hall & Havassy, 1981). A comprehensive treatment plan must be formulated that directly confronts the possible role expectations and conflicts that may have led to the initial development of the overweight condition. Finally, the psychological symptoms associated with the obesity must be addressed in a way that seeks to relieve distress as well as provide insight into the relationship between the psychological and the physical well-being of the individual. It is only when the obese client is treated with respect, dignity, and understanding, free of subtle prejudice, that treatment has the optimum chance for success.

References

Bruch, H. (1978). *Eating disorders.* Cambridge, MA: Harvard University Press.

Carson, R. C., & Butcher, J. (1992). *Abnormal psychology & modern life.* New York: HarperCollins.

Hall, S. M., & Havassy, B. (1981). The obese woman: Causes, correlates, and treatment. *Professional Psychology, 12,* 163–170.

Kingsley, R. C., & Wilson, G. T. (1977). Behavior therapy for obesity: A comparative investigation for long-term efficacy. *Journal of Consulting and Clinical Psychology, 45,* 288–298.

Mayer, J. (1968). *Overweight*. Englewood Cliffs, NJ: Prentice-Hall.

Orbach, S. (1978). *Fat is a feminist issue*. New York: Paddington.

Schachter, S. (1971). *Emotion, obesity, and crime*. New York: Academic.

Seltzer, C. C., & Mayer, J. (1965). A simple criterion of obesity. *Post-Graduate Medicine, 38* (2), A-101–A-107.

Stuart, R. B., & Davis, B. (1972). *Slim chances in a fat world*. Champaign, IL: Research.

Weiss, A. R. (1977). A behavioral approach to the treatment of adolescent obesity. *Behavior Therapy, 8,* 720–726.

Wollersheim, J. P. (1970). Effectiveness of group therapy based upon learning principles in the treatment of overweight women. *Journal of Abnormal Psychology, 76,* 462–474.

J. D. GUY, JR.

See HEALTH PSYCHOLOGY.

Object Relations Theory. A development in psychoanalytic thought based on the role of early relationships and how these relationships then continue as objects, or images, within the mind.

The roots of object relations theory are found in classical Freudian psychoanalysis. Sigmund Freud first used the term *object* in his *Three Essays on Sexuality* (1905). In this work a person in the external environment who is the focus of instinctual interest is termed an object. Freud developed the meaning of object further in *On Narcissism* (1914). In this work he discovered that a person's own ego could become an internal object for libidinal attachment. Thus the narcissistic person experiences love objects as aspects of himself or herself, so that the external object is seen as a self-object. In *Mourning and Melancholia* (1917) Freud expanded the understanding of object relations by identifying the role of internal objects in mourning and depression. He concluded that mourning involves holding on to the lost love object by internalizing certain of its aspects. In depression, anger that is against a perceived lost love object is turned inward against an internal representation of the lost object. Freud demonstrated how clinical phenomena like depression could be thought about from an object relations perspective.

British Approaches. From these roots psychoanalytic theorists have expanded Freud's overall theory of personality largely by exploring the role played by object relations, both internal and external. Some of the most significant developments in object relations theory have taken place in Great Britain. These developments are frequently identified as the British school of object relations. Melanie Klein, a child analyst who emigrated to England just before World War II, produced a comprehensive elaboration of Freud's discoveries about object relations (Klein, 1975). Like Freud, she saw the tie between instinct and object. However, Klein identified the connection as primarily internal in that libido

and the other basic motivating drive, the death instinct, have the capability of representing themselves mentally by creating internal images, or objects in fantasy.

Klein posited that in the first six months of life objects are only part objects because the infant cannot yet comprehend that experiences of frustration and gratification come from the same person. This condition, of having split good and bad part objects, Klein labels the paranoid-schizoid position. The second half of the first year of life involves the beginning of unification of the infant's experience and objects. The frustrating bad-object images and the gratifying good-object images come together. This results in the depressive position, because the infant starts to grasp that the object he or she has hated and attacked in fantasy is actually the same object he or she loves and needs. Klein's elaboration of Freud was extremely controversial. She was considered by Freud's daughter, Anna, to be outside the mainstream of psychoanalysis. Klein was criticized for neglecting the significance of actual external relationships, attributing improbable cognitive capabilities to the infant, and her emphasis on the death instinct.

W. R. D. Fairbairn, another British psychoanalyst, was greatly influenced by Klein. As Fairbairn developed his theory, he gradually discarded Freud's and Klein's focus on instincts and reinterpreted most of their theories in terms of relationships. For instance, he proposed that libido is a drive for object relationship rather than an instinct for merely gratification (Fairbairn, 1952). Fairbairn also revised Freud's structure of the psyche in terms of object relations. Instead of the impersonal mental processes of id, ego, and superego being the primary explanation for psychological functioning, Fairbairn proposed internal images or objects as the basic structures of the mind. According to Fairbairn it is the perception one has of one's significant others and how they relate to one's self that most accurately accounts for a person's emotions, reactions, and behavior. Fairbairn's student and analysand, Harry Guntrip, used Fairbairn's object relations theory to understand schizoid phenomena, which pertain to the split off, neglected, infantile parts of the personality needing rebirth (Guntrip, 1968).

Two other major theorists in Great Britain who have made significant contributions to object relations theory are Donald Winnicott and Wilfred Bion. Winnicott, a pediatrician, was influenced by Klein's emphasis on the first months of life. However, where Klein focused on the role of the infant's internal fantasy in early object relations, Winnicott stressed the significance of the actual mothering provided and the impact of early failures in mothering on the development of the self. For Winnicott (1965), it is the mother being able to provide a holding environment (a safe, nonintrusive experience of human contact) that allows the infant to begin to experience his or her own pristine sense of self. When this kind of relationship is disturbed by a mother who continuously impinges on the infant, the true self is hidden and a false, as if self is erected.

Bion moved to England from India. He underwent classical analysis, later became interested in Kleinian theory, and went into analysis with Klein. He is best known for his object relations theory of the development of thought and his application of psychoanalysis to psychotics and groups (Bion, 1967). Both Winnicott and Bion made enormous clinical contributions that involved the application of their understanding of mothering and psychic development to the role the analyst plays with infantile aspects of patients.

American Approaches. There was also much being done in the United States to elaborate on and expand psychoanalytic thought. However, the concern for orthodoxy in terms of classical psychoanalysis tended to dominate. Hartmann, an immigrant from Europe, probably set the direction for how psychoanalytic thought would develop in the United States. Hartmann (1958) challenged psychoanalysis to become a general psychology by addressing individuals not only in conflict but also in their normal capacities and ego functions such as perception, memory, and object relations.

Hartmann's work opened the door for other psychoanalytic theorists to address the important ego function of object relations. Spitz, a psychoanalytic pediatrician and a colleague of Hartmann, undertook observational studies of the first year of life to examine the role of object relations. He found that many disorders of infancy are due to problems in the mother-infant relationship (Spitz, 1965). He also found that internal representations or objects are crucial to the development of language, to psychological growth in terms of the differentiation of emotions and the neutralization of intense instinctual drives, and to cognitive development. If infants are deprived of adequate object relations, he found, death results in spite of otherwise adequate care.

Margaret Mahler is another psychoanalytic theorist who conducted observational research concerned with object relations. Her research emerged out of her interest in childhood schizophrenia and autism. She observed infants going through stages of nonattachment, or autism, to intense attachment, or symbiosis, followed by a process of emotional hatching out of the intense union with the mother. This was followed by an internalization of the mother with the ability to tolerate separation from the maternal object (Mahler, Pine, & Bergmann, 1975).

Many other psychologists in the United States expanded on Freud's initial theories of object relations while following Hartmann's ego psychology. Jacobson (1964) worked out a comprehensive object relations theory by tracing not only the process of how relationships become represented in the internal world but also how the self comes to be represented. Kernberg (1976) has contributed to object relations theory by tracing the development of object and self representations and then demonstrating the relationship between the earliest states of object relations and the more primitive disorders of schizophrenia and the borderline and narcissistic personalities. Kohut (1971) has written from the perspective of the development of healthy and pathological self-representation. Even though he saw himself as distinct from object relation's theory, he has added to an understanding of narcissistic object relations and the place of a self-object, which Freud had alluded to decades ago.

Summary and Evaluation. Object relations theory has its roots in Freud's theory. Object relations theory has taken two major paths. One path follows the developments in Great Britain by such theorists as Klein, Fairbairn, Guntrip, Bion, and Winnicott. These theorists have reinterpreted classical psychoanalytic concepts and are sometimes considered to be unorthodox. The second path follows the work of Hartmann in the United States and stays within the boundaries of classical psychoanalysis.

There are some major points of contention between these two paths as well as among theorists within each approach: how well the theories of such early mental representations fit with what is known of the infant's limited cognitive capacities; the etiology and treatment of some of the primitive disorders (especially narcissism); and the lack of consensus on the meaning of key terms. There is also a lack of empirical data to clarify some of these crucial questions. Nevertheless, taken as a whole, object relations literature and research have contributed greatly to psychology's understanding of early human development and relationships; the relationship between internal objects and cognitive and affective processes; and the etiology and treatment of the more primitive disorders (schizophrenia, borderline, and narcissistic personalities). It has led to the demise of many of the mechanistic and impersonal aspects of Freud's theory.

It is noteworthy that object relations theory, possibly more than any other psychological theory, addresses many of the same aspects of human existence as does Scripture. Its emphasis on relationship, dependency and independence, internalization, and narcissism have obvious parallels in Scripture. Object relations theory coincides with Scripture by following a depth or dynamic model of motivation; the sins that defile a person come from within. It also allows for and explains the effects of sin and the fall being passed down from generation to generation in less than optimal parenting while not negating the place of personal responsibility and the individual's own sin in distorting parental discipline and relationship.

References

Bion, W. R. (1967). *Second thoughts.* London: Heinemann Medical.

Fairbairn, W. R. D. (1952). *An object relations theory of personality.* New York: Basic.

Guntrip, H. J. S. (1968). *Schizoid phenomena, object relations and the self.* London: Hogarth.

Hartmann, H. (1958). *Ego psychology and the problem of adaptation.* New York: International Universities Press.

Jacobson, E. (1964). *The self and the object world.* New York: International Universities Press.

Kernberg, O. F. (1976). *Object relations theory and clinical psychoanalysis.* New York: Aronson.

Klein, M. (1975). *Envy and gratitude and other works* (Vol. 4). New York: Delacorte.

Kohut, H. (1971). *The analysis of the self.* New York: International Universities Press.

Mahler, M., Pine, F., & Bergmann, A. (1975). *The psychological birth of the human infant.* New York: Basic.

Spitz, R. A. (1965). *The first year of life.* New York: International Universities Press.

Winnicott, D. W. (1965). *The maturational processes and the facilitating environment.* New York: International Universities Press.

W. L. EDKINS

See PSYCHOANALYTIC PSYCHOLOGY.

Object Relations Therapy. *See* OBJECT RELATIONS THEORY; PSYCHOANALYSIS: TECHNIQUE; PSYCHOANALYTIC PSYCHOTHERAPY.

Observational Learning. *See* MODELING.

Obsession. A persistently recurring thought or feeling that is egodystonic; that is, it is not experienced as voluntarily produced but rather as something that invades consciousness. Psychoanalytic thinkers consider it to be the result of denying certain unconscious wishes or fears. While one obsession derived from a fear may restrict action, another obsession may tempt one to act out a certain impulse, and still another may take the form of an all-consuming preoccupation with a particular philosophical question.

An obsession is pathological to the extent that it impairs productive work and loving relationships. When an individual experiences sufficient distress due to obsessions, psychotherapy is recommended in order to uncover the basis of the obsession and reduce its frequency, duration, and intensity. Obsessions are characteristic of obsessive-compulsive disorder and may also be seen in schizophrenia.

J. E. TALLEY

See COMPULSION.

Obsessive-Compulsive Disorder. Obsessions are repetitive, persistent ideas, thoughts, and images that are not experienced as subject to the will but intrude unwanted into consciousness. In many ways they are like phobias in that once they are experienced intensely, they become repetitive. They are interesting in that the imagery of these intrusions is typically the dark underside of what the person might think voluntarily. Ideas of dirt strike the cleanly, of sin the righteous, of violence the kindly, of sex the socially proper. Though they are involuntary they can provoke great guilt or anxiety.

Further, obsessions often insistently demand action. In response compulsions seem appropriate, or behaviors that directly or symbolically protect against the implications of the obsessive thoughts. Perhaps for this reason many compulsions are meticulous and ritualistic. Patients do not find this behavior pleasant or even soothing, as are other repetitive, neurological behaviors, but they promise relief from the painful tension that mounts when the compulsives are blocked. The relief is only momentary, however, and the behavior is repeated endlessly.

Obsessions and compulsions range from mild to so severe they dominate the life of the patient. They begin in childhood or adolescence and occur as frequently in females as males. The incidence is about 1% in population samples, and only 20% of these come to treatment. Drinking, gambling, overeating, or sexual disorders are sometimes called obsessive, but since these are fueled by rushes of intense pleasure, they are more profitably considered addictions. But true obsessions and compulsions such as pathological checking, doubting, or procrastination are distinctly unpleasant, like phobias (*see* Phobic Disorders).

History. Since these demanding voices are so ego-alien and unexpected, the earliest explanations considered them demonic, the product of witches or spells. In the nineteenth century the unconscious offered a more scientific rationale for the mysterious quality, the hostile, dirty, sexual aspects of obsessions and compulsions. Psychoanalysts hypothesized that their origins lay in various intrapsychic conflicts of infancy and childhood (Salzman & Thaler, 1981). As colorful and ingenious as these explanations were, they are now seldom discussed.

In *DSM-III* obsessive-compulsive disorder was reclassified under the anxiety disorders, and this decision has proven both wise and fruitful. This paradigm shift probably represents the failure of psychoanalysis as effective treatment. Also, in analysis the introspective, obsessive intellectualizing of the patient floods free association with distracting, irrelevant data. These problems have also dogged insight-oriented and relational therapy. Since compulsive patients also fall easily into hopeless Pessimism and guilt, they defend strongly against any confrontation.

Therapy. As often happens, a new, unexpectedly successful treatment strategy opens new insight into the cause of a psychological disorder. Wolpe (1958) began to apply systematic desensitization to obsessions and compulsions. The success of behavior therapy of all kinds, particularly when it is reinforced by cognitive approaches, has radically changed fundamental concepts. The initial success rate of around 50% has remained constant, though virtually all workers report dramatic results in a few difficult patients. Marks (1981) reviews the literature to that date and summarizes the most effective strategies.

Medication. During the late 1960s therapists found that some obsessive patients responded dramatically to antidepressants. Soon the monoamine oxidase inhibitors (MAOI) proved more consistently effectively than the tricyclics, and currently the specific serotonin uptake inhibitors (SSRI; e.g., Prozac) have been even more helpful. Since such medications are developing rapidly there has not been an opportunity to review a large experience, but antidepressants are at least as effective as behavioral therapy, though in a slightly different group of patients. Hence a combination of medication and a cognitive-behavioral regimen seems to be the treatment of choice.

Neuroanatomy. Many hints of a neuroanatomical or neurochemical etiology have also surfaced: the success of medications; a high incidence of neurological soft signs among compulsives; the abrupt onset of similar pathology in some head-injured patients, and the occasional success of psychosurgery in severely disabled patients. Consequently, obsessive-compulsive patients have been widely studied using the newer imaging techniques for visualizing both the anatomy and function of the brain in a living person. Insel (1992) gives a recent review of the findings from all of these sources. His conclusions strongly point to a neural circuit of three involved areas of the brain: the orbitofrontal cortex, the cingulate cortex, and, to a lesser extent, the head of the caudate nucleus. A dense concentration of serotonin receptors in these same areas reinforces this hypothesis.

Any attempt to correlate these findings with symptoms must be considered tentative, but a picture seems to be developing in which a lack of dampening or inhibition permits a repetitive cycle of remembered, cognitive-affective stimuli to develop with each cycle intensified, much like feedback howl in a public address system. This repetitive pattern might begin, as phobias often do, in hypnogognic seizures that strike cognitive as well as affective centers. These, like dreams, accrue meaning appropriate to past experience and day residue (see Lesse, 1972).

In a typical clinical situation a slightly drowsy grandmother is sewing, watching her beloved grandchild play on the floor, when she suddenly is shocked by an explosive feeling of horror. Her brain handles this much like a dream: her usual devotion is completely reversed, the scissors in her lap is added, and a scenario that makes sense out of these develops; that is, she is about to stab the child! She then becomes both phobic (of babysitting, perhaps) and obsessive, fending off anxiety with a compulsive ritual until an antidepressant causes these symptoms to subside, allowing her therapist to explain her disorder as a neuroanatomical incident, not an unconscious wish to kill the child.

Neuroanatomy. A combination of medication, reassurance, and what cognitive-behavioral therapy has indicated to control the arousal itself (along with any residual obsessions and compulsions remaining) is the optimal management for such a patient. When symptoms have subsided, the patient can be reevaluated for any need of insight or relational therapy. Many times, however, distinct symptoms of personality disorders and other anxiety disorders that surfaced in the obsessiveness will subside when the primary symptoms are treated.

References

Insel, T. R. (1992). Toward a neuroanatomy of obsessive-compulsive disorder. *Archives of General Psychiatry, 49,* 739–744.

Lesse, S. (1972). Anxiety—Its relationship to the development and amelioration of obsessive-compulsive disorders. *American Journal of Psychotherapy, 26,* 330–337.

Marks, I. M. (1981). Review of behavioral psychotherapy, I: Obsessive-compulsive disorders. *American Journal of Psychiatry, 138,* 584–592.

Salzman, L., & Thayler, F. H. (1981). Obsessive-compulsive disorders: A review of the literature. *American Journal of Psychiatry, 138,* 286–296.

Wolpe, J. (1958). *Psychotherapy by reciprocal inhibition.* Palo Alto, CA: Stanford University Press.

Additional Readings

Baraban, J. M., Worley, P. F., & Snyder, S. H. (1989). Second messenger systems and psychoactive drug action: Focus on the phosphoinositide system and lithium. *American Journal of Psychiatry, 146,* 1251–1260.

Kandel, E. R. (1983). From metapsychology to molecular biology: Explorations into the nature of anxiety. *American Journal of Psychiatry, 140,* 1277–1293.

C. M. BERRY

See PERSONALITY DISORDERS.

Obsessive-Compulsive Personality Disorder. Persons with obsessive-compulsive personality disorder are held captive by their unwavering devotion to three life-governing principles—order, perfection, and control. These principles have the force of moral absolutes and are obeyed at the expense of spontaneity, flexibility, and authenticity. Such persons are driven by these principles to an often soulless life of work-obsession, criticalness, and miserliness rivaling that of Ebenezer Scrooge, the archetypal sufferer of this disorder.

The need for order will manifest itself in a variety of ways. These individuals can be rigidly deferential to authority figures while being exceedingly demanding and critical of their own subordinates. Obsessed with work, they gain esteem primarily from performance. To be ordered is to be fact-oriented, problem-solving, and goal-driven. Emotions are usually seen as hindrances to functioning effectively in an orderly world.

These persons want a place for everything and everything in its place. Although they do not have the contamination phobia of persons with obsessive-compulsive disorder, they find dirt and clutter to be emotionally aversive. Often they are slaves to time, operating rigidly by lists and schedules and placing great stress on punctuality. Paradoxically, time is often poorly allocated with procrastination being a major problem.

Perfectionism is the second value holding these persons captive. Horney (1950) described perfectionists as suffering from the "tyranny of the should." Their lives are spent appeasing a demanding, unrelenting conscience that readily resorts to generating intense feelings of shame and guilt when the perfectionistic standards are not met.

This merciless conscience goads such persons into painful self-criticalness, bordering on self-hatred. Often seen as overly conscientious and rigid moralists, their ethical perspective emphasizes duty, obligation, and responsibility. Compassion, mercy, and grace are usually given short shrift. Their attitudes toward others are usually characterized by intolerance and judgmentalism.

The need to be perfect includes the need to be right. This leads to dogmatic insistence that things be done the right way, that is, their way. At the same time such persons are often psychologically paralyzed when faced with a major decision for fear of choosing wrongly.

Salzman (1980) believes that the third operative principle, the attempt to gain control over self and the environment, is the primary dynamism of this disorder. Emotions in particular are subject to severe control and censorship. Strong negative affects such as anger and hostility are forbidden expression through suppression or repression.

These persons will try to dictate how, when, and where things are to be done. It is common for them to eschew psychiatric medication, fearing loss of control over their own mental functioning. Hoarding and saving used items illustrates the need to control for unpredictable circumstances when such items might be needed. To be prepared is to be in control.

Freud (1908/1963) described obsessive-compulsive personality disorder with the term *anal character* to emphasize his belief that the traits in question originated in conflicts between the child and parents centering on toilet-training behavior (*see* Anal Stage).

Sullivan (1956), taking an interpersonal perspective, held that such persons were reared in a home in which anger and hate were extensive but were camouflaged by superficial expressions of care and warmth. This caused them to learn "verbal magic," whereby the actual experience of things is disguised or excused by use of words. This forces these individuals to depend on rules and words to direct their behavior.

Millon (1981) theorized that this disorder stems from overcontrolling parents who show "care" by keeping the child in line, putting a premium on compliance and obedience. Harsh punishment is meted out for inadequate compliance, while praise is rare and based on performance.

Empirical research has found scant support for the Freudian notion that toilet-training issues are central to the formation of this disorder (Pollack, 1979). However, factor analytic research (Sandler & Hazari, 1960) did find that obsessional character traits do cluster in a manner consistent with traditional psychoanalytic formulations. A study of obsessional children (Adams, 1973) found their parents possessed traits such as overconforming, unempathetic, strictness, control, and disapproving of spontaneous emotional expression.

Persons in the Christian community with obsessive-compulsive personality disorder often have their faith perspectives shaped and molded by the disorder. They are prone to a legalistic interpretation of the gospel (*see* Religious Legalism) with greater emphasis on prohibitions and obligations than on joy and freedom.

Their obsession with the intellectual and doctrinal content of faith does nothing to relieve them of what Oates (1987) calls an "unnecessary conscience." Perfection is required according to their compulsive-based theology; perpetual anxiety is the price that is paid for being finite, fallible, and unable to completely overcome their innate sinfulness. The punitive conscience is equated with spiritual conviction, while God, via projection, is conceived as being hypercritical, perfectionistic, harsh, and controlling.

Treatment of these persons requires a multifocused approach. The cognitive distortions of these clients as described by Beck (1990) can be easily altered to accurately reflect the unhealthy religious beliefs held by Christians. The goal then is to transform these distortions into psychologically and spiritually healthy beliefs.

The client needs to experience a sense of permission in regard to the expression of negative emotion, the goal being to identify the actual sources of anger and rage, which are usually found in the family of origin. The client needs to be continually encouraged to approach God apart from the demands of the conscience for performance and perfection. This can be attempted through a variety of means such as imagery, reframing, and bibliotherapy.

References

Adams, P. (1973). *Obsessional children: A sociopsychiatric study.* New York: Brunner/Mazel.

Beck, A. T. (1990). *Cognitive therapy of personality disorders.* New York: Guilford.

Freud, S. (1963). Character and anal eroticism. In P. Reiff (Ed.), *Collected papers of Sigmund Freud* (Vol. 10). New York: Collier. (Original work published 1908)

Horney, K. (1950). *Neurosis and human growth.* New York: Norton.

Millon, T. (1981). *Disorders of personality.* New York: Wiley.

Oates, W. (1987). *Behind the masks: Personality disorders in religious behavior.* Philadelphia: Westminster.

Pollack, J. M. (1979). Obsessive-compulsive personality: A review. *Psychological Bulletin, 86,* 225–241.

Salzman, L. (1980). *Treatment of the obsessive personality.* New York: Aronson.

Sandler, J., & Hazari, A. (1960). The obsessional: On the psychological classification of obsessional character traits and symptoms. *British Journal of Medical Psychology, 33,* 113–122.

Sullivan, H. S. (1956). *Clinical studies in psychiatry.* New York: Norton.

W. G. BIXLER

Occupational Therapy. *See* REHABILITATION.

Oceanic Feeling. A general term signifying a large range of personal experiences in which one feels a profound sense of unity with God and/or his creation. It has been called mystical experience, cosmic consciousness, unity experience, and peak experience, in addition to a variety of specifically religious terms such as *nirvana, satori,* and communion with Christ.

Most typically oceanic feeling is accompanied by a deep sense of peace, reverence, and joy; an intense conviction of realness coupled with a feeling of incommunicability; a transcendence of the normal senses and corresponding unusual sensations and percepts; the transcendence of subject-object duality; and the feeling of unlimited omnipotence. Thus the core experience of oceanic feeling is similar for different people, but its interpretation depends upon one's worldview and religious orientation.

There are two different explanations for the phenomenon. First, the psychoanalytic approach views this experience of oneness as a regression to the primary narcissistic stage in which the child's sense of self has not yet differentiated from his or her environment, a period when the ego believes itself to be omnipotent. Second, the oceanic experience could be due to any phenomenon that disturbs the usual processes of perception that limit, select, organize, and interpret stimuli. Therefore, the truthfulness of what one perceives while in this altered state of consciousness depends upon one's beliefs about the nature of reality and the function of the perceptual processes. The question is whether this different way of perceiving is more likely to open up aspects of God and his creation that are under more normal circumstances unknowable or whether the altered state is more likely to make one more susceptible to deception.

W. C. DREW

See MEDITATION; CONSCIOUSNESS; TRANSPERSONAL PSYCHOLOGY.

Oedipus Complex. The behavior and feeling in childhood that indicate that the child is erotically and emotionally attached to the opposite-sex parent.

The idea that infants have sexual feelings was first developed by Sigmund Freud, who proposed that a young child is attracted to the opposite-sex parent in the natural course of infantile development (approximately between the ages of three and six). He coined the phrase *oedipus complex* after the Greek tragic hero who, through a fated chain of events, unknowingly had sexual contact with his mother. This phenomenon has become a central theme in psychoanalytic theory.

Psychoanalysts have suggested that most neurotic symptoms have their origins in the oedipus complex. If in infancy a child represses his or her sexuality, these desires and the associated conflicts will surface in later-life neuroses.

On the positive side of this theorized experience the infant can develop, through the oedipal experience, a sense of his or her sexual identity, can feel the security of physical love, and can see the need for another in his or her life. Psychoanalytic theorists suggest that this sexual energy can be sublimated toward such positive activities as work and creative endeavor. The theory holds that the oedipus complex is resolved by the development of the superego, or the natural restriction of primitive impulses. This makes an uncontrolled aggressive infant into a creative and productive adult.

R. B. JOHNSON

See PSYCHOSEXUAL DEVELOPMENT; PSYCHOANALYTIC PSYCHOLOGY; CASTRATION COMPLEX.

Oligophrenia. Literally "small mentality," this term indicates a mental deficiency characterized by inherited biochemical alterations in the body.

See MENTAL RETARDATION.

Omnipotence, Feelings of. Usually symptomatic of either paranoid or manic states, feelings of omnipotence can range from inflated feelings of power, control, and importance to delusions about possessing special communication and authority from God. Occasionally a person might believe he or she is Christ or God. Such thoughts and feelings betray a fantasy world that is more acceptable to the person than his or her actual state in life.

Many clinicians find that Narcissism, excessive emotional investment in oneself, and an injured self-concept are at root of feelings of omnipotence. The defense mechanisms of identification and denial protect the person from the injured self-concept and support the narcissism. The person cannot tolerate any personal weakness or failure. Therefore, he or she denies the inadequacy and takes on the identity or qualities of someone ideal, powerful, or good.

If other areas of personality remain intact, such a person sometimes misleads others. He or she may misuse Christianity or occasionally may start a cult. Churches have been exploited by some of these self-proclaimed healers, prophets, and zealots. Since they view themselves as God's special agents, it is very difficult to reason with them, and sometimes they can be dangerous.

M. R. NELSON

See NARCISSISM.

Only Child. Families with only one child have increased in number from 1 in 20 a generation earlier to 1 in 5 in 1980, and the trend toward smaller households continues. The rising cost of rearing children, women waiting until their thirties to have their first child, and a high divorce rate have contributed to fewer children being born. Other reasons for having a single child include more freedom for the parents, less family tension, more time to devote to the well-being of the child, and more time for self and spouse. Increasing numbers of women are entering the labor market, and there is concern as to how they can contribute financially to their households and establish their careers while experiencing the joys and responsibilities of motherhood. For many women having a sole offspring is the answer.

The long-standing prejudice against the only child has lessened somewhat, although onlies still have the reputation of being selfish, egotistic, socially maladjusted, and lonely. Parents of the single child also have been criticized for not providing a brother or sister who will give companionship to the child and with whom the child can learn to share. The research, however, does not support the negative stereotype of the only child. When single children are compared with their peers who have siblings, the picture tends to favor the single child (Falbo & Polit, 1986; Mellor, 1990). Onlies as a group are confident and resourceful, have a heightened sense of responsibility, are more at ease with adults, and are popular with classmates. Furthermore, they possess superior language development, have higher IQs, make higher grades, go further in school, and have a higher occupational status as adults. The greater degree of parent-child interaction and the higher socioeconomic status enjoyed by the only child appear to be related to these positive characteristics. Polit, Nuttall, and Nuttall (1980) state: "The data thus do not support the notion that only children are emotionally or personally handicapped by their lack of siblings" (p. 99).

To be sure, there are problems faced by the single child and the parents that are unique to a three-person household. A power structure of two against one may occur in which the child or one of the parents may feel estranged and there is no one in the family to turn to for support. Adult onlies have the sole responsibility for providing companionship and assistance to their parents and may feel overwhelmed when they alone must make decisions regarding the care of aging parents. The parents may express reservations about having only one child. They have less basis for knowing what to expect of the child at each age level; they may fear for the child's safety, realizing that if something happens they will be left childless. They also may feel that having more children would increase the chances of at least one child bringing them joy and being a credit to the family name.

Only Child International has been founded to provide a forum for people who never had brothers or sisters to discuss their situation and find answers to common problems. Members of the group do not consider that being an only child is a big social problem, but they do feel they can profit by sharing their experiences (Greene, 1983). Parents of the only child should enjoy the child without feeling guilty for having a sole offspring. Any loss to the child or the parents for not having more children in the family appears to be compensated for in other ways.

Research on the only child is being conducted in China, where the one-child family is mandated and tens of millions of children are being reared without siblings. The resulting social changes will add to our knowledge of the effects of one-child families when practiced on a massive scale.

References

Falbo, T., & Polit, D. (1986). Quantitative review of the only child literature: Research evidence and theory development. *Psychological Bulletin, 100,* 176–189.
Greene, B. (1983, November 29). An only child shares his life with others. *Chicago Tribune,* Section 5, p. 1.
Mellor, S. (1990). How do only children differ from other children? *Journal of Genetic Psychology, 151,* 221–230.
Polit, D. F., Nuttall, R. L., & Nuttall, E. V. (1980). The only child grows up: A look at some characteristics of adult only children. *Family Relations, 29,* 99–106.

B. CLOUSE

See BIRTH ORDER.

Operant Conditioning. *See* CONDITIONING, OPERANT.

Oppositional Behavior. *See* DISRUPTIVE BEHAVIOR DISORDERS.

Optimism. Optimism is the general expectation that outcomes will be positive. Researchers (Scheier & Carver, 1985) have shown that optimism is a stable personality trait and that individuals who are optimistic enjoy better physical and psychological health. For example, in one study optimists recovered from coronary artery bypass surgery faster than pessimistic patients and reported better quality of life six months after discharge from the hospital. Similar effects have been found with other medical patients, including individuals receiving bone marrow transplants.

One of the reasons that optimists are healthier than pessimists is that optimists cope more effectively. Optimists are more likely than pessimists to use problem-focused coping (which is aimed as addressing the source of the stress), to seek social support, and to emphasize the positive aspects of a situation. Pessimists tend to cope by using denial, focusing on their stressful feelings, or becoming disinterested in the goal they were pursuing.

Hope is a psychological construct similar to optimism. Snyder, Irving, and Anderson (1991) define hope as a way of thinking about the world that is based on both a sense of agency, or goal-directed determination, and pathways, which refers to ways to meet goals. Individuals high on hope are goal-directed and believe that ways exist to meet their goals. High levels of hope are associated with better physical and psychological adjustment. For example, adults with spinal cord injuries who had high levels of hope were less depressed than adults with lower hope levels. In a study of children and adolescents with sickle cell disease, hope was related to lower anxiety.

A key question concerning psychologists is how optimism or hope develops. Most theorists agree that feelings of optimism or hope develop during childhood and have the capacity to stay with an individual throughout life. Further, parents are thought to have one of the strongest influences on the development of hope. Erik Erikson has posited that during infancy the first psychosocial crisis children face is basic trust versus mistrust. Children who successfully resolve this crisis emerge with a sense of hope and a belief that the world can be trusted. According to Erikson, a sense of hope is fostered by sensitive, responsive, consistent parenting behavior. Seligman (1991) has also emphasized the role of parents in shaping children's optimistic orientation toward life. Seligman has suggested that an optimistic or pessimistic orientation toward life is associated with three factors in childhood: mother's level of optimism, adult criticism, and children's life crises. Seligman believes that adult criticism is a particularly important contributor to children's beliefs about themselves. If children receive critical explanations for their behavior that characterize the causes as permanent and pervasive, this becomes part of their theory of themselves. Causes explained as being temporary and specific can lead to problems being viewed as solvable and local.

Biblical perspectives on hope are founded on the belief that we can look to the future expectantly because Christ has promised peace in this life and beyond, and he is trustworthy. Psychological views of the development of hope are not inconsistent with the Bible. However, a biblical perspective suggests that an individual's degree of hopefulness or optimism can be changed by Christ. Individuals who choose to follow Christ become new creatures. Old things pass away, including negative patterns of thinking.

References

Scheier, M. F., & Carver, C. S. (1985). Optimism, coping, and health: Assessment and implications of generalized outcome expectancies. *Health Psychology, 4,* 219–247.

Seligman, M. E. P. (1991). *Learned optimism.* New York: Knopf.

Snyder, C. R., Irving, L. M., & Anderson, J. R. (1991). Hope and health: Measuring the will and the ways. In C. R. Snyder & D. R. Forsyth (Eds.), *The handbook of social and clinical psychology: The health perspective.* Elmsford, NY: Pergamon.

W. KLIEWER

See PESSIMISM.

Oral Stage. According to Sigmund Freud, this is the first stage of a child's psychological development. It encompasses approximately the first 18 months after birth.

See PSYCHOSEXUAL DEVELOPMENT.

Organismic Theory. The aim of organismic theory is to put the mind and body back together and to treat the organism (person) as a unified, organized whole. It rejects René Descartes's seventeenth-century split of the individual into two separate yet interacting entities, body and mind.

Within recent years this organismic emphasis has also been known as the holistic viewpoint. In psychology, organismic theory has been emphasized by Gardner Murphy and Carl Rogers. Other thinkers whose concepts are compatible with the organismic stance are John Dewey, Aristotle, Spinoza, and William James. The Gestalt movement of Max Wertheimer, Kurt Koffka, and Wolfgang Köhler is also closely related to the organismic position. However, since Gestalt psychology said very little concerning the organism or personality as a whole, organismic psychology may be treated as an extension of Gestalt principles (Hall & Lindzey, 1978).

The primary advocate of organismic theory was Kurt Goldstein, and this article emphasizes his concepts. For Goldstein the organism always is a single entity, behaving as a unified whole and not as a series of differentiated parts (Goldstein, 1939).

The central theme in Goldstein's personality theory is self-actualization, which is defined as fulfilling of one's capacities or potentialities in the best possible way under a given condition. All Goldstein's dynamic concepts and types of behavior are to be viewed as having the ultimate purpose of self-actualization. Self-actualization occurs in the process of coming to terms with the environment. The individual tries to find a workable position between his or her potentialities and the demands of the outer world.

In normal functioning all parts of the organism work as a unified whole as each task presented by the environment is mastered, thus enhancing self-actualization. On occasions, however, the environment contains obstructions and pressures that hinder self-actualization. These properties of the environment tend to upset the average state of tension in the organism. Following its actualization tendencies, the organism uses its organic and psychological processes to return to the average state of tension prior to the stimulus (environmental event) that changed the tension level. This return to an average state is brought about by the equalization process. The equalization process is vitally related to Goldstein's master motif of self-actualization and accounts for the consistency, coherence, and orderliness of behavior in spite of disturbances.

Psychopathology comes about when the equalization process is thwarted by strong disturbances in the environment that are too arduous for the individual (Goldstein, 1940). The person will then develop reactions inconsistent with the principle of self-actualization. These inconsistent reactions provide the conditions for the development of pathological states.

Therapy is aimed at helping the person to master the environment and thus achieve self-actualization. If this is not possible, the goal of therapy is to help the person adjust to the difficulties and realities of the external world.

In the last few years a number of Christian psychologists and theologians have been investigating the biblical emphasis on anthropological holism. Being familiar with the comprehensive principles of organismic theory would be of benefit in pursuing this theme, as Goldstein's emphasis on humans as unified wholes seems consistent with the biblical emphasis. However, his position conflicts with Christian theology in its emphasis that there is nothing inherently bad in the organism; it is made bad by an inadequate environment.

References

Goldstein, K. (1939). *The organism*. New York: American Book Company.
Goldstein, K. (1940). *Human nature in the light of psychopathology*. Cambridge: Harvard University Press.
Hall, C. S., & Lindzey, G. (1978). *Theories of personality* (3rd ed.). New York: Wiley.

S. N. BALLARD

See SELF-ACTUALIZATION; PERSONALITY; HEALTHY PERSONALITY; HOLISTIC HEALTH AND THERAPY.

Organizational Psychology. *See* INDUSTRIAL/ORGANIZATIONAL PSYCHOLOGY.

Orgasmic Disorder, Female. Female orgasmic disorder, formerly known as inhibited female orgasm, is diagnosed in women who experience normal sexual desire and excitement but are persistently unable to climax within a reasonable period of time during sexual activity. Since women vary in the duration of sexual activity needed for orgasm, the clinician must interpret a "reasonable period of time" in the context of the client's age, sexual experience, and quality of stimulation. Female orgasmic disorder is diagnosed only if the symptoms significantly upset the woman or her relationship.

Female orgasmic disorder is the most common complaint of women seeking clinical help for a sexual problem. For most the problem has been present since the woman first began sexual activity. A small but significant proportion of women, fewer than 10%, have never experienced orgasm. Since most women more readily experience orgasm as they mature, younger women may be more likely to have orgasmic disorder.

The disorder may be generalized to all situations and types of stimulation, or it may be restricted to particular settings, times, or partners. It is not associated with personality types or mental disorder, although it may impair body image and self-esteem.

Cultural factors may influence the condition. Some cultures emphasize the importance of sexual satisfaction for women; others do not. Some Christian writers have asserted that orgasm is not important for women, and a rigidly religious background is associated with female orgasmic disorder. Although survey research suggests that evangelical women may be the group most satisfied with their level of sexual expression, some Christian women have been taught that sex is sinful or that sexual enjoyment is wrong. If a woman has been taught since childhood that sexual activity is appropriate only for conceiving children, and if she has no models of women who enjoy sexual activity, she may be totally unaware of her potential for orgasm. If during sexual intercourse she approaches orgasm, the feelings may trigger fear rather than anticipation.

Many women have to learn to have orgasms. They have to learn sexual anatomy, the types of stimulation they find pleasurable, and how to communicate their desires to their partners. Communication may be especially difficult for Christian women. Even if they have positive attitudes toward sexual activity and clearly desire to experience orgasm, they may be reluctant to express this desire lest they appear excessively sensual, selfish, or unromantic.

Since most women take longer to reach orgasm than men, the man's loss of an erection and possible loss of interest in sexual activity following orgasm interferes with the woman's continuing sexual excitement. Some men may be unwilling or unable to stimulate their wives except through sexual intercourse, and a significant proportion of women are unable to reach orgasm without additional stimulation. Other men, eager to please their partners, may stimulate too aggressively or roughly, causing fear, discomfort, or pain instead of sexual arousal.

Some women fear losing control at orgasm. Fatigue, long-term stress, and anger may impair orgasm, but they will typically impair sexual desire and arousal as well. Paradoxically, excessive desire to please the partner may inhibit orgasm in some women. In one study of 750 women, desire to please their husbands led 58% to fake orgasm. A man's desire to please his wife may focus on bringing her to climax, and she may resent questions about his effectiveness either during or shortly after sexual activity.

Treatment of female orgasmic disorder focuses on the presumed causes. Education of both partners, particularly about female sexual anatomy and responsiveness, plays a significant role. Negative attitudes toward sexual enjoyment may be countered by clear communication about sexuality, modeled by the therapist and taught to the couple. Learning that most women, including married Christian women, enjoy orgasm can help counter inhibitions based in prior religious teaching.

Most therapists will provide clients with printed material to help teach both sexual information and communication skills, especially about sexual values. Some will also use videotapes or audiotapes to explain or guide the couple through sexual techniques that help treat the disorder. Christian therapists will vary in their willingness to use some of the available materials. For couples with significant sexual anxiety, reading, discussing, and seeing sexually explicit material may have a beneficial desensitizing effect.

Some therapists use directed masturbation as a tool to teach women to have orgasms. Those who object to masturbation on religious or other grounds may accept similar stimulation performed by the husband and guided by the wife.

Finally, those who counsel people with marital difficulties should remember that they may not admit to any difficulty with orgasms, especially at first. In many couples, sexual difficulties are enmeshed in other relationship problems and may be overlooked. It is likely to take time for the couple to trust the counselor enough to mention such an intimate topic.

P. D. YOUNG

See ORGASMIC DISORDERS; SEXUAL DYSFUNCTIONS.

Orgasmic Disorder, Male. Some men are able to achieve sexual arousal and engage in sexual intercourse but are unable to climax and ejaculate or are able to do so only after an unreasonable and often frustrating delay. Most of these men, however, are able to have an orgasm through other forms of sexual activity, including stimulation by a partner, masturbation, and erotic dreams.

If the delay or absence of orgasms is upsetting to the man or if relationships are harmed, then he may be diagnosed with male orgasmic disorder, formerly known as inhibited male orgasm. However, many happily married couples rarely experience orgasm, so the simple absence of climax is not a sufficient basis for diagnosis. The diagnosis is appropriate only if he does not have another nonsexual mental disorder or a medical condition that directly causes the lack of orgasm. Although the disorder refers specifically to orgasm, it is diagnosed only if both orgasm and ejaculation are missing or delayed.

Clinicians should diagnose with caution if the client has been taking a drug, since alcohol, antidepressants, some blood pressure medication, and various drugs of abuse may contribute to the disorder. Occasional problems with orgasm should not be diagnosed.

Male orgasmic disorder may be present from the first experience of sexual intercourse, or it may be acquired after previously normal functioning. It may be generalized to all situations or it may be restricted to particular settings, times, or activities.

Men with this disorder typically enjoy beginning intercourse. As orgasm is delayed, however, the pleasure diminishes and continued sexual activity becomes hard work. Some men will persist, for 40 minutes or more, until they finally ejaculate; others will give up. Some couples will seek medical help for infertility when the man with orgasmic disorder has pretended to climax during intercourse. One-third of men in one study reported faking orgasm. Orgasmic disorder may place a strain on a marriage, although sexual problems are more often a consequence of marital strife than a cause.

While medical conditions and drug use may contribute to orgasmic disorder in a minority of cases, theorists usually point to psychological factors. Fatigue and stress may reduce the stamina necessary for sustained sexual intercourse. Since older men typically take longer and require more stimulation to reach orgasm, middle age may bring an increased likelihood of orgasmic disorder.

Since men must maintain sexual arousal in order to climax, anything that distracts a man's attention may prevent orgasm: worries, hostility, interruptions, or paying too close attention to sexual performance. Men who are spectators of their own sexual activity may become anxious about the quality of their performance and thus lose arousal and delay orgasm.

Since a woman may take much longer to arrive at a climax, she may see her husband's delayed orgasm as beneficial. Some marriage manuals have recommended that men delay ejaculation to coincide with the wife's orgasm, and some Christian couples believe that sharing in such a way is ideal. Similar attitudes may contribute to orgasmic disorder or to premature ejaculation.

Internal conflicts may also contribute. For example, some men believe that if they do not ejaculate, they have not really engaged in sexual intercourse or masturbation. Consequently, men who feel guilty about coitus or masturbation may deal with the internal conflict by withholding orgasm. Others may inhibit ejaculation because they fear conceiving a child.

In the cognitive-behavioral approach, treatment begins by focusing on the couple's relationship and attitudes toward each other. Therapists attempt to build open communication, especially about sexual matters. Then, to deal with the specific problem, the woman learns to stimulate the man's penis, asking him for directions to maximize pleasure. Once he is stimulated to orgasm—which may take several sessions—they then progressively move to intercourse:

first by penetrating when he signals that he is near climax, and then earlier in the process of sexual arousal until the man is able to function normally.

Couples therapy and psychodynamic techniques focus more exclusively on the meaning the problem has for the couple and the individual. For example, if a wife is anxious about her ability to satisfy her husband's sexual desires, his orgasmic problem may mean that she is relieved of responsibility. Couples therapy confronts such mixed motivation and attempts to treat orgasmic disorder by improving the relationship. In practice, couples therapy and psychodynamic techniques are routinely combined with a cognitive-behavioral approach.

When the disorder is a result of strongly held attitudes about sexual expression, treatment may be very difficult. If the troubling attitudes are consistently and gently countered by information from sources who share the client's ideology or religious perspective, the attitudes may gradually change. Thus Christians may be especially effective helpers for other Christians.

P. D. Young

See Orgasmic Disorders; Premature Ejaculation; Sexual Dysfunctions.

Orgasmic Disorders. Orgasm is the rush of pleasurable sensations occurring at the climax of the sexual act. It normally varies in intensity and subjective quality. If it is persistently or frequently delayed or missing after sufficient sexual stimulation, clinicians may diagnose an orgasmic disorder but not if lack of orgasm is due to disease or drugs.

In orgasmic disorder, levels of sexual desire and arousal are normal. Sexual functioning is adequate; only orgasm is delayed or missing. However, orgasmic disorder may accompany another sexual dysfunction.

In women lack of sexual knowledge or experience, an inattentive or selfish partner, and exclusive dependence on intercourse for sexual stimulation also contribute. Some fear losing control or believe that orgasm is unseemly.

Men with orgasmic disorder may fear losing control or that their partner will become pregnant. Some theorists have suggested that anger or withholding love cause the disorder.

People who feel guilty about engaging in sexual intercourse may fail to have orgasms to deny that they have completed the sexual act or to cope with guilt-induced anxiety.

Especially for women, orgasmic disorder is likely to have a long history. Nonetheless, education and communication training are particularly effective in the hands of a competent counselor who, while providing instruction about sexual anatomy and behavior, demonstrates that it is appropriate to discuss sexual matters and to explain to a partner what is and is not pleasurable.

P. D. Young

Overcompensation. A term used by Alfred Adler to describe a process by which an individual overcomes a weakness of the body, usually located in a particular organ. He proposed that since some people are born with damaged limbs, poor eyesight, or malfunctioning hearts, their physiological system, in an effort to maintain the appropriate equilibrium, would strive to correct the defect. Later Adler theorized that overcompensation occurs psychologically as well as phsyiologically. That is, one overcompensates for feelings of inferiority generated by parental neglect, sibling rivalry, peer rejection, and for legitimate bodily impairment.

Overcompensation is typically conceptualized as a direct attack on the situation responsible for the inferiority. It is an exaggerated effort to go beyond achieving a balance or removing a defect. Therefore, overcompensation may turn the defect into a strength. However, it may also become negative in the sense that one could be overreacting or denying reality. In this case it would be considered excessive and harmful. Overcompensation is differentiated from compensation in that compensation is more of an indirect attack on the situation. In compensation one seeks to lessen the deficit feelings of inferiority rather than excessively overreacting.

A number of noteworthy individuals have overcompensated, either physically or psychologically, in the course of their lives. One famous example is Demosthenes, who stuttered as a child but became one of the world's greatest orators. Another example is Theodore Roosevelt. A weakling in youth, through exercise he developed himself into a physically fit and sturdy individual.

M. L. Marvin

See Inferiority Complex; Individual Psychology; Personality.

Overcorrection. Like extinction, response cost contingency, and time out, overcorrection is a behavioral procedure used to decrease the frequency of an undesired behavior. Overcorrection involves an exaggerated form of making amends or restoring the damages caused by misbehavior. Schreibman, Charlop, and Kurtz (1992) describe overcorrection as a weak or "mild but effective form of punishment [requiring] effortful behavior contingent on the occurrence of inappropriate behavior" (p. 339). For example, a child who runs in the hall may be required to return to the point of the offense and repeatedly walk from there to the desired destination; one who left the milk out may be required to take out the milk and then replace it in the refrigerator several times. In some applications the person is manually guided in the corrective activity if it is not voluntarily performed. Overcorrection makes behavioral requirements of the person, whereas time out and most common forms of punishment do not.

Overcorrection has been most commonly used with institutionalized retarded individuals. Overcorrection may be used instead of electric shock in eliminating self-stimulatory and self-injurious behaviors and for aggressive and antisocial behaviors where timeout procedures are not effective, but it is also suited to a variety of behaviors in normal home and school settings.

Olendick (1986) reports overcorrection is highly effective. As with other punishment procedures, overcorrection is most effective when it is used in conjunction with contingent reinforcement for desired behaviors.

The basic ethical concern is the appropriateness of inflicting pain and causing emotional distress. Some psychologists view overcorrection or punishment as cruel and inhumane. Bufford (1981, 1982) argues that when it is appropriately used, punishment procedures are both effective and consistent with Christian beliefs.

Overcorrection that involves manually guided training in an alternative behavior is coercive. This raises ethical problems. There are also practical problems with this form of overcorrection, since it may produce counteraggression. Offering overcorrection as an alternative that the individual could choose in preference to contingent punishment is one way to minimize these problems. Offering community service as an alternative to fines or jail time for violations such as vandalism and littering is a common practice similar to overcorrection.

Overcorrection is a mild punishment procedure involving an exaggerated form of restitution or restoring of the harm done. It is effective, especially when it is used with contingent reinforcement for desired responses, and it can be implemented in ways consistent with Christian beliefs about punishment.

References

Bufford, R. K. (1981). *The human reflex: Behavioral psychology in biblical perspective*. San Francisco: Harper & Row.

Bufford, R. K. (1982). Behavioral views of punishment: A critique. *Journal of the American Scientific Affiliation, 34*, 135–144.

Olendick, T. H. (1986). Childhood and adolescent behavior therapy. In S. L. Garfield & A. E. Bergin (Eds.), *Handbook of psychotherapy and behavior change* (3rd ed.). New York: Wiley.

Schreibman, L., Charlop, M. H., & Kurtz, P. F. (1992). Behavioral treatment of children with autism. In S. M. Turner, K. M. Calhoun, & H. E. Adams (Eds.), *Handbook of clinical behavior therapy*. New York: Wiley.

R. K. Bufford

See Behavior Therapy.

Overprotection. While everybody is aware that a child is damaged by neglect (*see* Abuse and Ne-

glect), few realize how many negative consequences can result from overprotection.

One of the major causes of overprotection is a premature birth or extensive physical illness in the child, either of which requires special care in the first years of life. This often sets a pattern that parents have trouble altering. Such parents often remain anxious about their parenting responsibilities and perceive their child as more disabled than he or she is. The loss of previous children can also produce fear in parents and lead to overconcern with their children's wellbeing. Overprotection may also reflect reaction formation, through which the parents exaggerate, out of guilt, the care for a child whom they resent. Single parents or parents having poor relationships with their spouses may also overinvest in a child as a compensation for marital disappointments.

Some of the symptoms that may indicate overprotection are a tendency to do things for the child that he or she could do; interfering with children's relationships and fighting their fights even when there is no threat of serious consequences; sheltering children from experiences that are good learning opportunities with a low or no price to pay; parental overinvolvement, beyond the necessary supervision and guidance, in all of the child's activities (school, play, relationships, hobbies). It may also be evidenced by a general watchfulness, control, or overchecking.

Overprotection can have many undesirable consequences on children's development. Through lack of experience the sheltered child's growth is stifled. Furthermore, such children remain unprepared to handle demanding situations. Not having been taught to deal with frustrations and lacking assertiveness, they may become overly submissive and accommodating to whoever promises protection and provides structure and leadership. Or they may be resentful for not getting the service they feel everybody owes them. They may display an inclination to be self-centered, inconsiderate, and lacking empathy, qualities creating difficulties in relationships with others. They may also become fearful and insecure, with a demanding, rebellious, or paranoid attitude toward life.

Several remedial measures can be taken to prevent or reduce the damages produced by overprotection. For best results both parents and children should be involved in therapy. The parents can be helped by being treated for anxiety and obsessions, if these are present. A dynamic exploration of the causes of this attitude can be of help in most situations. An analysis of their lifestyle may reveal areas of conflict and help eliminate the power struggle between parents that may result in one of them turning excessively toward the child. Parenting education (*see* Parent Training Programs) is of great value in that it helps parents understand the consequences of overprotection and makes them more secure in dealing with children.

For Christian parents an important part of therapy can be helping them understand that God himself does not overprotect his children; he lets them grow and learn by facing the consequences of their behavior and choices. He guides, teaches, supports; he intervenes when the demands of the situation surpass our resources; and yet he allows us to make choices and educates us by entrusting us to do part of his work.

The children are helped by communication and assertiveness training, involvement with peers (through group therapy or church or community organizations), by being given responsibilities, and by being offered the minimal support needed. It is important to help them build autonomy and confidence in themselves. It is necessary, therefore, to assess their natural abilities and encourage their development.

Additional Reading

Parker, G. (1983). *Parental overprotection: A risk factor to psychosocial development*. New York: Grune & Stratton.

D. MOTET

See PARENTING.

Pain. The International Association for the Study of Pain describes pain as "an unpleasant, sensory and emotional experience associated with actual or potential tissue damage or described in terms of such damage" (International Association for the Study of Pain, 1979). Pain is therefore not just a physical sensation; it is a subjective experience and hence a psychological phenomenon, although it is usually described in terms of a local stimulus.

Acute pain refers to pain of limited duration, and chronic pain to that of at least several months' duration. Pain threshold refers to the point at which one first perceives a stimulus as painful, and pain tolerance to the point at which one is not willing to accept stimulation of a higher magnitude or to continue to endure stimulation at a given level. In general threshold is related more to physiological conditions and tolerance to emotional or psychological variables.

Theories of Pain. Traditional theories of pain view it as a specific sensation with intensity proportional to the extent of tissue damage. Specificity theory proposes that a specific pain system carries messages from receptors in the skin to a center in the brain. However, contemporary conceptualizations of pain challenge such specificity views (see Melzack & Wall, 1988).

Gate-control theory (Melzack & Wall, 1965) emphasizes that pain perception and response are complex phenomena resulting from the interaction of cognitive-evaluative and motivational-affective as well as sensory-discriminative components. The gate-control theory also proposes that information resulting from noxious stimulation is modified as it passes from peripheral nerve fibers to those in the spinal cord by a specialized gating mechanism in the region of the dorsal horns of the cord—in particular the substantia gelatinosa. In simple terms, information reaches the brain only if the gate is open. Whether the gate is relatively open or closed depends on the balance of activity in large and small afferent fibers (large fibers tend to open it) and in fibers descending from the higher centers of the brain.

Recently there has been more emphasis on higher levels of pain control, or gating mechanisms in the brain itself (Melzack & Wall, 1988). Although some of the more speculative aspects of the gate-control theory have been challenged, it nevertheless has proved heuristic, inspiring both basic research and clinical applications.

Physiology and Psychology of Pain. Research on the biochemistry of pain has suggested that neurokinins, or proteins that increase in concentration as a result of pain, tend to further lower the pain threshold. More recently natural pain-suppressing substances called endorphins have been discovered in some parts of the brain and seem to act in ways similar to powerful drugs like morphine or narcotics. Some researchers believe that a common biochemical or physiological mechanism operating in a number of pain-reducing interventions (e.g., morphine and some kinds of electrical stimulation) involves enkephalin, one type of endorphin (see Feuerstein & Skjei, 1979).

Whatever the physiological or biochemical bases of pain may be, it is clear that psychological and social factors play a significant role in pain perception and response (see Sternbach, 1978). These factors include ethnic background, socioeconomic status, family size, birth order, present circumstances, meaning of the situation or the pain itself, anxiety and uncertainty, expectation, depression or hopelessness, and stress. Anxiety, for example, may exacerbate or even produce pain. In general moderate arousal tends to increase pain, whereas extreme arousal or less intensive experiences tend to reduce pain. Pain is therefore a perceptual experience that is influenced by the unique history of the individual, by one's state of mind at the moment, and by the meaning one attaches to the pain-producing situation (Melzack & Wall, 1988).

Treatment. A number of pain treatments are available. Some have been developed as a result of the gate-control theory, which suggests that pain can be attenuated by psychological methods (e.g., see Gatchel & Turk, 1996) or by stimulation interventions to close the pain gate. Traditional pain treatments include medications, neurosurgery, and nerve blocks aimed at reducing noxious afferent input to the brain. However, these have often not been successful, and debilitating side effects do occur. Other pain treatments include transcutaneous electrical nerve stimulation, physical therapy, chiropractic care, exercise, diet, acupuncture, hypnosis, biofeedback training, relaxation training, behavior modification, marital and family therapy, psychotherapy, multifaceted or multiple convergent therapy, and the use of spiritual resources such as prayer, Scripture, and the support of small groups (Tan, 1996). Several recent applications of cognitive-behavioral interventions such as stress-inoculation training, relaxation strategies, distraction, imagery techniques, and calming self-talk have also been reported (see Hanson & Gerber, 1990; Tan, 1982; Turk, Meichenbaum, & Genest, 1983). Cognitive behavior therapy for chronic pain (Keefe, Dunsmore, & Burnett, 1992) has recently been listed as one of 25 empirically validated psychological treatments available for different disorders (Sanderson, 1995; also see Tan & Leucht, 1997).

Pain assessment has included a number of self-report measures such as the use of verbal or visual analogue scales of pain intensity and the well-known McGill Pain Questionnaire (Melzack, 1975); behavioral measures such as ratings of actual pain behavior or amount of analgesic medication used; experimental pain tests using a number of noxious stimuli including heat, pressure, ice water, electric shock, and muscle ischemia; and physiological measures such as evoked potentials (see Turk & Melzack, 1992).

A biblical perspective on suffering or pain can provide meaning, facilitate psychological and spiritual growth, and help an individual better cope with pain. Prayer for healing may at times bring about complete remission of certain medical conditions and the associated pain (Tan, 1996; also see Brand & Yancey, 1993).

References

Brand, P., & Yancey, P. (1993). *Pain: The gift nobody wants.* Grand Rapids, MI: Zondervan.

Feuerstein, M., & Skjei, E. (1979). *Mastering pain.* New York: Bantam.

Gatchel, R. J., & Turk, D. C. (Eds.). (1996). *Psychological approaches to pain management: A practitioner's handbook.* New York: Guilford.

Hanson, R. W., & Gerber, K. (1990). *Coping with chronic pain: A guide to patient self-management.* New York: Guilford.

International Association for the Study of Pain. (1979). Pain terms: A list of definitions and notes on usage. *Pain, 6,* 249–252.

Keefe, F. J., Dunsmore, J., & Burnett, R. (1992). Behavioral and cognitive-behavioral approaches to chronic pain: Recent advances and future directions. *Journal of Consulting and Clinical Psychology, 60,* 528–536.

Melzack, R. (1975). The McGill Pain Questionnaire: Major properties and scoring methods. *Pain, 1,* 277–299.

Melzack, R., & Wall, P. D. (1965). Pain mechanisms: A new theory. *Science, 150,* 971–979.

Melzack, R., & Wall, P. D. (1988). *The challenge of pain* (Rev. ed.). New York: Penguin.

Sanderson, W. C. (1995). Which therapies are proven effective? *APA Monitor, 26* (3), 4.

Sternbach, R. A. (Ed.). (1978). *The psychology of pain.* New York: Raven.

Tan, S.-Y. (1982). Cognitive and cognitive-behavioral methods for pain control: A selective review. *Pain, 12,* 201–228.

Tan, S.-Y. (1996). *Managing chronic pain.* Downers Grove, IL: InterVarsity Press.

Tan, S.-Y., & Leucht, C. A. (1997). Cognitive-behavioral therapy for clinical pain control: A 15-year update and its relationship to hypnosis. *International Journal of Clinical and Experimental Hypnosis, 45,* 396–416.

Turk, D., Meichenbaum, D., & Genest, M. (1983). *Pain and behavioral medicine: A cognitive-behavioral perspective.* New York: Guilford.

Turk, D., & Melzack, R. (Eds.). (1992). *Handbook of pain assessment.* New York: Guilford.

S.-Y. TAN

Panic Attack. A panic attack is a psychological problem in which people are overwhelmed with intense anxiety for a brief but discrete episode. Typical symptoms include pounding heart, sweating, trembling, shortness of breath, chest discomfort, nausea, dizziness, lightheadedness, depersonalization, numbness, tingling, chills or hot flashes (American Psychiatric Association, 1994). Panic attacks are such powerful and frightening experiences that first-time sufferers often believe that they are having a heart attack or are going crazy. Some people report a strange sense of unreality during the attack.

The *DSM-IV* (American Psychiatric Association, 1994) describes three types of panic attacks. The first is unexpected panic attacks in which there is no apparent trigger for the attack. This may include nocturnal panic attacks that occur in delta wave sleep, the deepest stage of sleep. The second type of panic attack is a situationally bound or cued panic attack, which means it usually occurs immediately in the presence or in anticipation of the feared situation. The third type of panic attack is called situationally predisposed panic attacks, in which the panic will likely but not invariably occur immediately after the presentation of the situational trigger. Since panic attacks may be symptomatic of several different anxiety disorders, these categories of panic attacks are useful in establishing differential diagnoses.

People who experience an anxiety attack are usually so frightened that they search for reasons for the attack. Unexpected and nocturnal panic attacks are especially distressing because there seems to be no reason for them. Therefore sufferers will often seek medical help. It is important that medical causes of paniclike symptoms be ruled out. Some medical conditions that may produce such symptoms include hypoglycemia, hyperthyroidism, heart valve and arrhythmia problems, and drug and medication reactions.

If medical conditions are not contributory, people begin to search their environment for possible causes for their panic. They may begin to avoid any situation that they think could trigger a panic attack. This leads to superstitious behaviors (e.g., "I was at a movie during my last panic attack. Movies cause me to panic.") and strong avoidance patterns that can rapidly generalize and significantly restrict people's lives. When people avoid public places or situations from which they could not easily escape should they have panic symptoms, they are experiencing agoraphobia. Agoraphobics may avoid not only geographic situations but also activities like exercise that provoke symptoms such as sweating or rapid heart rate, which remind them of panic attacks.

People are diagnosed with panic disorder when they have recurrent unexpected panic attacks, are preoccupied with the possibility and implications of having more attacks, or significantly change their behavior due to panic attacks. People with panic disorder may or may not be agoraphobic. Panic disorder is a condition that represents the union of panic attacks and anxiety. The individual has had unexpected panic attacks and is subsequently dominated by anxiety over having more. Panic attacks may occur in many other disorders such as specific phobia, social phobia, obsessive-compulsive disorder, and posttraumatic stress disorder (PTSD), but in each case panic attacks and anxiety over the panic are not the central issues.

Clear causes for panic attacks and panic disorder have not yet been discovered. Some people seem to inherit biological overreactivity that makes them more vulnerable to anxiety. Such people seem to be prone to panic. They are high self-monitors who are especially sensitive to their anxiety and distressed by it. Neurotransmitters in the brain are certainly involved, although there is controversy as to which neurotransmitters are most crucial. Some researchers think that panic may be linked to the activation of particular brain circuits. Psychological explanations emphasizing childhood perceptions of control, conditioning, and cognitive interpretations of situations are widely used as a basis for psychological interventions for panic sufferers. Whatever the combination of causes, women are two to three times more likely than are men to experience panic attacks, panic disorder, and agoraphobia. Panic disorder is most prevalent in early adulthood.

Treatment for panic attacks and panic disorder is usually quite effective. The majority of sufferers receive relief from their panic rapidly. Treatment usually consists of medication, cognitive-behavioral psychotherapy, or both. The most common medications are benzodiazepines, especially alprazolam and the newer antidepressants. Barlow and Durand (1995, p. 175) report an effective psychological treatment for panic attacks called panic control treatments. In this approach therapists in the context of cognitive therapy create mini panic attacks in the office. The therapists help clients to recognize and modify their basic attitudes and perceptions toward these harmless but feared situations. This is one example of exposure-based cognitive-behavioral therapies in which people are exposed to real anxiety-provoking situations so that they can gain experiential as well as intellectual mastery of the situation they avoided due to panic.

Spiritual resources must not be overlooked when counseling people with panic. The Bible urges Christians not to panic but to pray. The Bible is filled with promises for strength and the ability to overcome fearsome and difficult circumstances. A sense of self-efficacy based on one's relationship to God provides a solid foundation for overcoming a host of psychological problems. Panic may also serve spiritual ends when it forces people to face difficult situations they need to confront and recognize their need for God.

References

American Psychiatric Association. (1994). *Diagnostic and statistical manual of mental disorders* (4th ed.). Washington, DC: Author.

Barlow, D., & Durand, V. (1995). *Abnormal psychology: An integrative approach.* Pacific Grove, CA: Brooks/Cole.

C. D. DOLPH

See ANXIETY.

Paradoxical Intervention. A group of therapeutic techniques that rely on asking clients to continue symptomatic behavior and assume that persons can change by being asked to "behave as he is already behaving" (Watzlawick, Beavin, & Jackson, 1967, p. 237). Paradoxical interventions in both historical and contemporary practice reflect a wide diversity of approaches. Their complex history begins with Knight Dunlap, who in the 1920s first used the technique of negative practice, instructing patients "to practice the symptom under prescribed conditions with the expectation of losing the habit" (Weeks & L'Abate, 1982, p. 9).

Adler (1956) also utilized such common paradoxical strategies as "(1) giving the client permission to have a symptom, (2) encouraging the client to exaggerate the symptom, (3) refining and improving the symptom through practice, and (4) redefining the symptom so that it could be cast in a positive rather than a negative light" (Smith & Berg, 1990, pp. 20–21).

Frankl in the 1920s developed the technique of paradoxical intention, inviting phobic patients "to intend, even if only for a moment, precisely that which" they feared (Frankl, 1946/1965, p. 223), thereby enabling patients "to develop a sense of detachment toward [their] neurosis by laughing at it" (p. 225).

Rosen (1953) developed the procedure of reenacting an aspect of the psychosis, directing the patient "to act out the psychotic episode in its most florid state" (Weeks & L'Abate, 1982, p. 13). Jackson (1963) routinely encouraged his paranoid patients to be more suspicious, thus underlining the absurdity of their position. These pioneers applied paradoxical interventions to individual therapy.

In contemporary practice, paradoxical interventions are used primarily by strategic family therapists. The early work at the Mental Research Institute (MRI) assumed that therapists could construct a therapeutic double bind (a paradoxical injunction) that would be a mirror image structurally to a pathogenic double bind but with a critical difference: "In a pathogenic double bind the patient is 'damned if he does and damned if he doesn't,' in a therapeutic double bind he is 'changed if he does and changed if he doesn't'" (Watzlawick, Beavin, & Jackson, 1967, p. 241). Haley's problemsolving therapy reflects both the MRI model and Milton Erickson's hypnotic techniques: Haley incorporates the paradoxes inherent in all therapy (Haley, 1963) and regards paradoxical intervention (prescribing the symptom) as a way to "gracefully disqualify the current authority on the problem" (Haley, 1976, p. 73). Haley's (1984) unique contribution is the therapeutic ordeal.

The Milan Group (Selvini Palazzoli, Cecchin, Prata, & Boscolo, 1978) constructs a counterparadox to the family's pathology-inducing paradox, thereby breaking the "homeostatic tendency" and activating "the capacity for transformation by changing the rules which perpetuate dysfunctional transactional patterns" (Massey, 1986, p. 26). The Ackerman Brief Therapy Group works in the Milan tradition: when a family problem involves double binds, "paradoxical interventions that prescribe both the symptom (positively connoted) and the system served are constructed in the language of the family to break the 'homeostatic cycle'" (Hoffman, 1981, p. 29). In addition, "whenever the family shows signs of changing, the therapist must retrain them" (Papp, 1983, p. 37). Madanes "designs paradoxes eliciting not resistance, but play and pretending" (Massey, 1986, p. 29).

Paradoxical interventions are often troubling to Christians, who regard reframing of symptoms and paradoxical prescriptions as forms of lying. Most practitioners who use paradoxical interventions insist that these "interventions should be implemented only when straightforward methods have failed" (Massey, 1986, p. 36). Doherty and Boss (1991) review this debate and outline an ethical test to determine when deception might be appropriate.

These ethical problems disappear when it is understood that paradoxical prescriptions work only when they in fact constitute a true and empathic statement about the ambiguities inherent in the family's reality (Papp, 1983).

References

Adler, A. (1956). *The individual psychology of Alfred Adler* (H. L. & R. Ansbacher, Eds.). New York: Basic Books.

Doherty, W. J., & Boss, P. G (1991). Values and ethics in family therapy. In A. Gurman & D. Kniskern (Eds.), *Handbook of family therapy, vol. II*. New York: Brunner/Mazel.

Frankl, V. (1965). *The doctor and the soul* (2nd ed.). (R. Winston & C. Winston, Trans.). New York: Knopf. (Original work published 1946)

Haley, J. (1963). *Strategies of psychotherapy*. New York: Grune & Stratton.

Haley, J. (1976). *Problem-solving therapy*. San Francisco: Jossey-Bass.

Haley, J. (1984). *Ordeal therapy*. San Francisco: Jossey-Bass.

Hoffman, L. (1981). *Foundations of family therapy*. New York: Basic Books.

Jackson, D. D. (1963). A suggestion for the technical handling of paranoid patients. *Psychiatry, 26*, 306–307.

Massey, R. F. (1986). Paradox, double binding, and counterparadox: A transactional analysis perspective (A response to Price). *Transactional Analysis Journal, 16*, 24–26.

Papp, P. (1983). *The process of change*. New York: Guilford.

Rosen, J. (1953). *Direct psychoanalysis*. New York: Grune & Stratton.

Selvini Palazzoli, M., Cecchin, G., Prata, G., & Boscolo, L. (1978). *Paradox and counterparadox*. (E. V. Burt, Trans.). New York: Aronson.

Smith, K. K., & Berg, D. N. (1990). *Paradoxes of group life*. San Francisco: Jossey-Bass.

Watzlawick, P., Beavin, J. H., & Jackson, D. C. (1967). *Pragmatics of human communication*. New York: Norton.

Weeks, G. R., & L'Abate, L. (1982). *Paradoxical psychotherapy*. New York: Brunner/Mazel.

H. Vande Kemp

See Provocative Therapy; Family Communications Theory; Strategic Therapy.

Paranoia. Paranoia is a common term referring to a tendency for everyday offenses and frictions to become overloaded with implications of hostility or persecution. It is probably more commonly used by people under 50 because paranoid delusions are common in toxic reactions to drugs of abuse. The word may refer to persecutory states, persons, or various delusions.

History. A technical definition, though, is more muddled. Lewis's masterful review (1970) of the history of the concept begins with its use in ancient Greek literature to mean what we would call crazy, initially referring to the organic delirium of high fever and later including dementia. A revival of the term in the eighteenth century defined it as impaired judgment without fever, hallucinations, or "erroneous appetites." Again it was retired for some 40 years, then revived, launching it on the troubled course that has continued to this day. The history of the term *paranoia* recapitulates most of the problems of nomenclature and conceptualization of all abnormal psychology.

All this time paranoia has been considered an illness of the mind, occasionally of the personality, including brief or long-term psychosis. Generally it has been thought a cognitive, not an affective, disorder primarily distorting perspective as opposed to thinking. It has been accepted that the disorder is associated with a particular personality. It often presents as delusions, occasionally hallucinations, which are inaccessible to influence. The systematic, internally consistent, logically coherent, single focus of the delusions, particularly in reference to the relationship between the self and the outer world, were almost universally observed. Hot debates have erupted over whether its etiology is psychogenic or somatic. Although it was always thought an illness, it is a deviation of something natural. Everyone has under pressure or isolation assembled suspicious bits of evidence into an evil plot.

Many names were introduced to make paranoia more precise, prompting Lewis to say, "It might be a good thing for psychiatry if coining names for diseases were made as serious an offense as coining money without authority." Kraepelin (1912) questioned whether, considering its shabby history, paranoia should not be dropped completely. With the same reasoning, *DSM-III-R* relegated it to brackets among the acute delusional disorders.

The most precise meaning of paranoia today is of a self-referential, grandiose delusional state, usually persecutory or erotic. It occurs on a scale extending from a personality disorder, to a delusional state particularly subject to hystericlike distortions, to full-blown delusions or psychosis. If history means anything, paranoia is much too common and distinct to bury between brackets.

Psychopathology. Freud's (1911/1958) analysis of the Schreber case determined later analytic thinking of paranoia. He said the fundamental pathology derives from desperate efforts of the ego to avoid the conflicts of homosexual desire. More recently analysts have moved away from this position, freeing up new thinking. In an insightful paper Salzman (1960) emphasized the messianic presumptions of the paranoid, seeing it as grandiosity.

Although Salzman's insights have not been enlarged upon in the professional literature, they can have a special meaning for the therapist working with paranoid religious individuals. Consider the paranoid personality's perspective as that of the we community, the inside group versus the they community, the alien. This is certainly valid. Although the Bible usually addresses Christians as fellow members of humankind at large, they are also a family, a called-out and blessed community, the body of Christ. This body is embedded in "this present age" whose spirit is hostile, alien to what binds us together, and we are admonished to shield ourselves from its influences. The paranoid is one who is unusually sensitive to this adversarial position, this spiritual-secular warfare, of the church.

People gifted with this sensitivity serve us as monitors of error that can so easily creep into our thinking from the world and destroy our integrity. Such warnings are vital to the spiritual health of others who are primarily more sensitive to relationship, law, story, or any other biblical perspectives.

As this community-sensitive person becomes disordered, he or she becomes a heresy hunter seeing a liberal or a modernist, a New Age or an existential thinker behind every rock. Paranoids tend to be rigid, suspicious, and litigious. As the disorder deepens, primary relationships are destroyed; "coming out from among them" sometimes means an endless quest for a new, purer church.

The disordering proceeds much like any other personality disorder, beginning with an abnormal sensitivity, a tendency to become intensely aroused, in this case by any hint of error. With the arousal we, or the church, becomes defensive, in a state of war, behind protective walls. The calling of a watchman is to be vigilant, alert, always aware of enemy strategy. Those who are oblivious to the small fissures in our doctrinal defenses incite the paranoid to uncover any sign of heresy and sound the alarm.

The transition from normal to disorder can be best understood in the light of a dream. Most dreams begin with a burst of emotion, one demanding an explanation, a story to explain its rationale. Paranoid people characteristically organize such stories as conflict between the good guys and the bad. As in most dramatic novels, the bad are part of organized systems such as the Mafia, Nazis, or Communists, which make the paranoid state not only reasonable but essential. Most heroes of such stories are loners, and isolation, like drug trips, can incline anyone to paranoia. Add to this matrix a congenital weakness for delusions or schizophrenia, and each of these take on a distinct paranoid form.

Management. The normal personality variant requires no treatment; when a body functions well, this watchman is heard and appreciated. They alert those who are blithely unaware of the warfare of the faith life. When others belittle or fail to hear this warning, the paranoid's arousal becomes more intense, his or her tone more strident.

For the paranoid, people are sharply divided, either inside or outside. The insiders are good but must be watched; the outsiders are invariably hostile. As fewer and fewer listen, the alarm becomes more intense and the life of the paranoid deteriorates.

Considering the awesome responsibility of such a messianic burden, it is little wonder that the paranoid personality resists treatment. Treatment usually becomes possible only when the pain of anxiety presses or important relationships flounder. It would reasonably begin with a therapist who hears the message and gratefully acknowledges it, even explaining it to others. Then treatment can focus on the anxiety itself, controlling the arousal process by behavioral techniques, and gradually approaching the distortions that are part of the aroused thinking.

Much of the literature of treatment discusses the therapist's difficulty in maintaining the trust of the patient, in this case, remaining among the we inside the fortress. Hearing the message of the patient as opposed to belittling or ignoring it is the most reassuring thing we can do to maintain this trust. Moving from there to the inner pain and loss of efficiency (even as a watchman) caused by the anxiety can often be done without losing trust and cooperation. Once the anxiety abates, the distortions, even those that have become delusional, can be confronted.

Paranoia vera (true paranoia) is a rare condition in which a particular delusion becomes fixed and inalterable within a mind that is otherwise rational. It is unusually inaccessible to medication or psychotherapy. Such patients, however, can often live reasonably effective lives with help like that already suggested. The delusions themselves that do not respond to medication might be bypassed by the reduction of anxiety and supportive therapy. Sometimes they disappear spontaneously with a valid experience of community and inner peace (*see* Peace, Inner); sometimes they persist but are no longer a problem. Though paranoid schizophrenia will require other measures, this is an excellent psychotherapeutic approach to their support.

References

Freud, S. (1958). Psycho-analytic notes upon an autobiographical account of a case of paranoia (dementia paranoides). *The standard edition of the complete psychological works of Sigmund Freud* (Vol. 12, pp. 3–82). London: Hogarth. (Original work published 1911)

Kraepelin, E. (1912). Uber paranoide. Erkrankungen. *Zemtrlblaatt für die gesamte neurologie und psychiatrie, 11,* 617–638.

Lewis, A. (1970). Paranoia and paranoid: A historical perspective. *Psychological Medicine, I,* 2–12.

Salzman, L. (1960). Paranoid state—Theory and therapy. *Archives of General Psychiatry, 2,* 679–693.

Additional Readings

Cameron, N. (1974). Paranoid conditions and paranoia. In S. Arieti (Ed), *American handbook of psychiatry* (Vol. 3). New York: Basic.

Will, O., Jr. (1961). Paranoid development and the concept of self: Psychotherapeutic intervention. *Psychiatry, 24,* 74–86.

C. M. Berry

See Psychotic Disorders.

Paranoid Personality Disorder. The core feature of a paranoid personality disorder (PPD) is a longstanding, pervasive pattern of mistrust in the motives of others. Persons with this disorder assume that others have malevolent intentions to harm, exploit, or deceive them, even when no objective evidence exists. They ruminate over unfounded suspicions that their family and friends are disloyal and will scrutinize these relationships for evidence of untrustworthiness. In particular they are prone to pathological jealousy of their spouse or lover.

They are often reluctant to confide in others out of fear that anything they say will be used against them. This makes them appear interpersonally cold and aloof. They also tend to distort benign remarks into hidden meanings that are threatening and insulting. For example, they might respond to an offer for help with, "So you think I'm incapable of doing it myself!" People with this disorder often stubbornly refuse to forgive others for insults or injuries that they think they have received. They are swift to counterattack with hostility for such imagined offenses. In order to meet the criteria for a diagnosis of PPD, these symptoms must not occur as part of a psychotic disorder and must not be directly caused by a medical illness. PPD begins by early adulthood and typically endures for life.

It is widely believed that PPD is caused by an experience of severe rejection by one's parents very early in life. As a result the young child internalizes a belief that she is profoundly inadequate. Such a belief raises intolerable anxiety, which is defended against with a paranoid projection that one's self is worthy but that the world is hostile and critical.

Treatment of PPD is particularly difficult for several reasons. First, the lack of subjective distress felt by such persons does not motivate them to seek relief in treatment. Second, they may experience a therapy office as an inquisition chamber or as a laboratory for scrutinizing them as if they were rats in a maze. The most effective treatment of PPD begins with supportive therapy aimed at gaining the person's trust. The therapist must refrain from challenging the paranoid beliefs while at the same time refraining from seeming too sympathetic. Confronting the paranoia before a therapeutic alliance is forged will usually backfire and provoke the patient to strengthen her defenses. Too much kindness and intimacy extended by the therapist will likely backfire as well, causing the patient to feel invaded or frightful of symbiotic merger. The best approach to take with such patients is one of professionalism, in which the therapist interacts in a reserved and straightforward manner.

Therapy at this early stage should focus on empathic reflection of the person's experience of the world as a threatening place. As the therapist validates the patient's feelings of hostility and vigilance, gradually the patient may feel safe enough to access more vulnerable underlying feelings such as fear, rejection, and loneliness. If supportive therapy successfully uncovers such feelings, the patient may be ready to tolerate the anxiety of deeper reparative treatments such as cognitive retraining or insight-oriented psychotherapy. Unlike supportive therapy, which has a goal of symptom relief, these two treatments aim at personality reconstruction and healing the root causes of the disorder.

Cognitive retraining seeks to alter the faulty beliefs that underlie the patient's suspiciousness. The therapist helps the patient to label and challenge such logical errors as overgeneralization (e.g., "A motorist cut me off on the freeway today. It only goes to show that all motorists are out to get me.") and drawing incorrect inferences (e.g., to point out to the patient that the motorist may have been late for work and not maliciously "out to get her").

Psychodynamic (insight-oriented) therapy focuses on helping the patient to uncover deeply repressed feelings of parental rejection early in life. Such therapy is like a tunnel, in which the only way out is through. For the patient, this means allowing herself to remember and work through excruciating feelings of inadequacy and depression. As the early parental losses are grieved, the patient finds that she is able to regain some of the lost parental nurturance through a corrective emotional experience with the empathic therapist. Finally, she discovers that she can become a nurturing parent to herself and function as a whole, autonomous person.

For the Christian therapist, treatment of PPD carries a redemptive metaphor. The therapist serves as an ambassador of Christ and gradually helps the patient to view herself as Christ views her. Her critical and unforgiving response to the world is but a mirror of her unconscious conviction that she herself is unlovable and unforgivable. Therapeutic healing comes as she grows to internalize the therapist's model of Christ's acceptance of her.

N. S. THURSTON

See PERSONALITY.

Paraphilia. A group of sexual perversions in which sexual arousal is persistently achieved by stimulated or real suffering or by the use of nonhuman objects, children, or other nonconsenting partners. This must occur over a period of at least six months. Some of the more common paraphilias include sexual sadism (inflicting suffering and humiliation), sexual masochism (receiving humiliation and suffering), pedophilia (using prepubescent children as sex objects), exhibitionism (exposing genitals in view of an unwilling audience), zoophilia (sexual activity with animals), telephone scatologia (obscene phone calls), fetishism (sexual arousal from nonliving objects), transvestic fetishism (cross dressing), voyeurism (exaggerated interest in viewing sexual activity), and frotteurism (rubbing against or touching a nonconsenting person).

Paraphilias cause impairment of social and sexual relationships. Individuals with sexual deviations have difficulty receiving or giving affection and are usually emotionally immature. Males constitute almost all reported cases of paraphilia. Paraphilias are often triggered by stress in the individual's life. Even though he is married, the person's sexual needs are not met, and to fulfill sexual desires the perverted sexual behavior must be acted out.

The origins of paraphilia are based in learning and pleasurable reinforcement, fueled by humankind's sinful nature. At birth the child is open to a variety of sexual patterns that can be developed. Through environmental conditioning children and adolescents begin to develop what is pleasurable and erotic. These sexual patterns become well developed as they mature into adulthood.

Additional Reading

Levine-Stephin, B., Risen-Candice, B., & Althof-Stanley, E. (1990). Essay on the diagnosis and nature of paraphilia. *Journal of Sex and Marital Therapy, 1* (2), 89–102.

M. A. CAMPION

See SEXUALITY.

Parapraxis. Sigmund Freud used this term to refer to misactions such as slips of the tongue or mislaying of objects, actions that he assumed reveal something of underlying unconscious dynamics. Thus the person who says "sex" instead of "six" or who suddenly forgets the name of the best friend with whom he or she had a fight should not be seen as engaging in accidental behavior but rather in behavior that betrays the true state of the unconscious. Because of this assumption psychoanalysts treat parapraxes as important pieces of behavior for analysis.

See PSYCHOANALYTIC PSYCHOLOGY.

Paraprofessional Therapy. Fewer than one-third of those who experience difficulty coping with life's stresses receive the help they need. In many parts of the country, especially in certain economically disadvantaged, rural, and ethnically diverse areas, trained professionals are in short supply. The upsurge in paraprofessional therapy is a welcomed response.

More popular now than at any other time in modern history, paraprofessional therapy may be defined as therapy led by someone who has no graduate-level training in mental health. Some such therapists are paid for their work, while many others volunteer their time. Paraprofessional therapists engage in a variety of tasks, including work with older adults, substance abusers, children with learning disabilities, prison inmates, the homebound, the recently divorced, abused and battered spouses, new parents, and those in crisis. Some work in health care facilities, others via hotlines, and others still may do much of their work in churches or persons' homes. The use of paraprofessional therapists is a popular response to unmet mental health needs.

What makes paraprofessional therapy so attractive? Perhaps, most obviously, is the overall shortage of low-cost professional counseling. Working for low or no pay, paraprofessional therapists often perform much-needed services where resources are limited. They also offer service to those who are reluctant, for cultural or other reasons, to see a professional therapist. And many paraprofessional therapists may be sought for their religious values when the available professionals are not perceived to be religiously sensitive.

Is paraprofessional therapy effective? A meta-analytic review of some 35 therapy outcome studies investigating the effectiveness of graduate-level preparation in psychotherapy found only modest benefits for advanced training (Stein & Lambert, 1995). Research looking at the question of client satisfaction suggests that, given a structured, easily implemented therapy format such as that used in cognitive-behavioral therapy, paraprofessionals may be as effective with many types of problems as their professional counterparts. Counseling "that is given away (or at least sold much less expensively) through paraprofessional, self-administered and mutual-support group treatment may be as effective for some problems as the professional psychology that is sold" (Christensen & Jacobson, 1994, p. 13).

While paraprofessional therapists may not in every instance or with every problem perform as effectively as professionals with graduate-level training, paraprofessional therapy is nonetheless effective in a variety of situations and is especially appropriate when working with persons with less complex difficulties. Professional training, though helpful, does not appear necessary for establishing a helping relationship.

What does appear necessary, however, is emotional maturity. Persons needing assistance will seldom progress beyond the level at which their therapist resides. This means that a mature high-school student may be able to effectively counsel a peer in need but may not be able to effectively assist a middle-aged adult.

Other attributes also appear necessary for establishing a helping relationship. First, most persons need to feel safe before they will talk with someone about their problems. Establishing a safe environment requires that one be relatively comfortable around those who are expressing painful emotions.

The ability to listen to another person's pain and to then accurately communicate one's understanding of the other's experience is also essential. Those who are hurting need to know that someone understands, and it is the paraprofessional therapist's responsibility to effectively communicate this understanding.

Finally, an effective paraprofessional therapist must truly care. Along with providing a safe place to talk and communicating accurately one's understanding of the other's experience, paraprofessional therapists must show those in pain the love they may be unable to show themselves.

Some limitations of paraprofessional therapy, however, should also be noted. One of the challenges facing helping agencies is that of providing the training and supervision necessary to produce competent paraprofessional counselors. Where resources are already limited, securing sufficient funding for even minimal training and supervision for paraprofessionals may be difficult.

The perception of paraprofessionals as lacking competence is another limitation of paraprofessional therapy. Although guidelines for establishing competence have been proposed (Scanish & McMinn, 1996), and the research suggests that paraprofessional therapists have demonstrated their effectiveness in a variety of situations, the public perception of paraprofessional competence has not followed. Since a trusting therapeutic alliance is based on the assumption that the counselor is competent, paraprofessional therapists must speak to this misperception of incompetence before those who need assistance will engage paraprofessional services with confidence.

References

Christensen, A., & Jacobson, N. S. (1994). Who (or what) can do psychotherapy: The status and challenge of nonprofessional therapies. *Psychological Science, 5,* 8–14.

Scanish, J. D., & McMinn, M. R. (1996). The competent lay Christian counselor. *Journal of Psychology and Christianity, 15* (1), 29.

Stein, D. M., & Lambert, M. J. (1995). Graduate training in psychotherapy: Are therapy outcomes enhanced? *Journal of Consulting and Clinical Psychology, 63,* 182–196.

J. D. Scanish

See Lay Counseling; Community Mental Health; Community Psychology.

Parapsychology. The study of all psychic phenomena, *psychic* referring to either the events or the persons who seem to possess inexplicable abilities to perceive or influence events. *Psi* refers to hypothetical energy forces assumed to mediate psychic phenomena. The subject of parapsychology elicits responses ranging from fervent belief to rabid rejection, from laypersons, religious believers, psychologists, and other scientists alike.

The Scope of Study. In formal study parapsychology encompasses three varieties of extrasensory perception (ESP) and psychokinesis (PK). Telepathy is the ability to read another's thoughts; clairvoyance implies knowledge of inanimate objects or events without use of the known senses; and precognition is knowledge of events before they occur. Psychokinesis is the ability to move or otherwise control an inanimate object or event without known physical energies.

These presumed phenomena are defined negatively: they cannot be explained by scientific laws, principles, or energies. The knowledge, perceptions, or behavior also must not be a product of unconscious mental (brain) processes, employing sensory cues, past or present, however subtle. Parapsychology assumes that the mind is an unextended substance, not merely a product of the brain, and therefore involves energy separable from the physical body.

Reports and Research. Parapsychology arose from common situations. Countless stories tell of uncanny premonitions, precognitive dreams, hauntings, and fortune telling that defy explanation. Around this kind of observation many belief systems have developed—spiritualist churches, palmistry, astrology, I Ching, out-of-body experiences (OBEs), and near-death visions. Poltergeists (noisy spirits) break dishes and furniture or propel objects through the air or off shelves. Mystics claim to levitate—rise bodily into the air—by purely mental powers. Healers perform psychic surgery, removing apparently malignant tissue from a patient with bare hands, leaving no incision. Dowsers witch for water or minerals; performers inexplicably bend keys or spoons; Kirlian photography reveals unearthly auras around human fingertips and other objects.

Such reports are widely critiqued by scientists (Hansel, 1966), magicians (Christopher, 1970), and other skeptics. Careful investigation of reports usually reveals critical errors of fact. Poltergeists are usually associated with youths playing tricks on gullible adults. Fortune tellers vary from outright frauds to astute observers who lead their clients to reveal what they want to hear. Astrological and other predictions, when carefully checked and tabulated, have negligible validity. Psychic surgeons and metal benders do not withstand the scrutiny of trained magicians. Even prominent parapsychologists see Kirlian photographs as chemoelectrical artifacts. Not every case is discredited, and some must be counted as coincidences. But even a few unexplained reports encourage many people to believe that psi exists.

Some surveys of psychic phenomena include what might better be called pseudopsychic events—phenomena without clearly mechanistic explanations, including possession, automatic writing and other automatisms, fire walking, faith healing, hypnosis, and biofeedback. The latter two have been accepted into psychology's domain of fact, and but for its association with religion, faith healing would probably hold such status. The first three phenomena can be explained by suggestion, learning, and unconscious processes (*see* Ecstatic Religious Experiences).

Formal investigation of parapsychology began with the founding of the Society for Psychical Research at Cambridge University, England, in 1882 and a similar society a few years later in the United States. In 1920 psychologist William McDougall, then president of the British Society for Psychical Research, went to Harvard University and began a study of psychic phenomena. Botanist Joseph B. Rhine joined McDougall as a research assistant in 1926 and followed him to Duke University the next year. Rhine and his wife, Louisa E. Rhine, founded the Duke Parapsychology Laboratory, which has conducted the most consistent psychical research. During an initial period of disappointing work psychologist K. E. Zener designed ESP (or Zener) cards that were used in many later studies. A deck of the famous cards included five sets of five bold symbols: plus sign, three parallel wavy lines, and outlines of circle, square, and star. The telepathy procedure usually involved one sender, who thought of five Zener symbols in a run, with the subject or receiver making five guesses.

More encouraging results began appearing in the winter of 1931–1932 and were published in 1934 and 1935. Statistical probabilities against the Rhines's results being mere chance are astronomical, and most parapsychologists consider the experimental controls to have been tight. However, Hansel (1966) identified a number of weaknesses, including evidence for recognizing the ESP cards from their backs and/or edges. Rhine's best subject, Hubert Pearce, no longer showed clairvoyance when the deck of cards was moved 8 to 12 feet away. When ESP card guesses were typically checked after every five cards, subjects could rationally infer the last five cards in the deck. Rhine himself was aware of this problem, noting high scores on the last trials with this procedure.

More recent studies control for the Rhines's apparent defects, but they still draw frequent, damaging criticisms. Contemporary research includes use of sophisticated electronic gadgets and new ventures outside the laboratory. From early psychokinesis research with hand-thrown dice the Rhines progressed to dice mechanically thrown down a corrugated, incline plane. Instead of affecting the throw of dice a subject may now attempt to alter the outcome of an electronic random number generator. Another psychokinesis subject reportedly was able to raise or lower temperatures on a highly accurate thermister on a random schedule. Some psychics are said to impress photographic film with images that have no known physical source.

In the Ganzfeld procedure a telepathy subject relaxes in a soundproof room, eyes covered with split table tennis balls. Meanwhile a sender, some distance away, looks at a picture or series of color transparencies and mentally transmits the images to the sensory-deprived receiver. Astonishing claims have been made for this procedure. In remote viewing telepathy a psychic (supervised in a laboratory) describes the journey taken by experimenters who leave the laboratory, randomly select a route or destination, and drive for a half-hour or so. Independent judges attempt to match the psychic's report with descriptions or pictures of the route driven. Brain waves of some psychics have been monitored to study optimum mental conditions for the expression of psi. Animals and plants have also been studied for evidence of psi. Even convinced parapsychologists admit that no current research procedure consistently yields positive results.

Research Conclusions. After more than 50 years of research, what facts, laws, or principles of parapsychology have been established? Not many, and none assuredly. Most research merely demonstrates that something can occur beyond statistical odds. One review (Bowles & Hynds, 1978) concluded that everybody potentially has psychic abilities, although some people are exceptionally sensitive. Nothing can be affirmed about the relation of psi to intelligence or personality. Some studies relate success in psychic tasks to friendly, outgoing personalities, good visual imagery, and the subject's belief in psi. Some find that hypnosis, dreaming, relaxation, and meditation enhance psychic abilities. Partners with good rapport frequently make better telepathy subjects. Telepathic communication with animals is equivocal, and plant psi has not been replicated beyond a few spectacular reports.

What can psi communicate? If all reports are accepted, practically anything. All sorts of symbols, perceptions, and knowledge have supposedly been received by the various forms of extrasensory perception, and an almost endless list of events have reportedly been affected by psychokinesis. When does the supposed psi force operate? Time presents no barriers. In some Ganzfeld trials the receiver begins to describe pictures before the sender has looked at any. If the pictures match, precognition rather than telepathy has occurred. Many other situations cannot unambiguously be identified among the four prime forms of parapsychology. If the experimenter knows a fact before a clairvoyant subject does, a correct explanation might be telepathy. When the experimenter or a machine selects items to be guessed in telepathy or clairvoyance, the subject might have exercised psychokinesis over the choices. Such ambiguities early led Rhine to disregard the separate categories of extrasensory perception.

Where can psi occur? Again, anywhere: in life and in laboratories and across virtually any distance. If psi were an as yet unknown energy, it would violate the scientifically established inverse square law for the propagation of energy (Reber, 1982). The apparent limitlessness of psi may impress the believer as pervasiveness, but it rouses doubts among skeptics. All natural phenomena are affected or limited by definable parameters; without such limits scientifically oriented observers tend to dismiss parapsychology as illusory or to investigate the source of the illusions.

Parapsychology critics continue to attack methodologies and reporting of psychic demonstrations. A typical, widely reported case involves platform psychic Uri Geller. A secondary source tells: "Geller was asked to guess which face of a die was up in an opaque box shaken by the experimenter. Geller, who was not permitted to touch the box, was told he could decline to choose when he felt uncertain. The die was shaken ten times, and Geller chose to respond eight of those times. Each time that he chose to respond he was correct, giving a result at odds of 17,500,000 to 1" (Bowles & Hynds, 1978, p. 66). The original report cited the statistical odds as about 1,000,000 to 1. Gardner reports that one of the experimenters said Geller "was allowed to place his hands on the box in 'dowsing fashion'" (1982, p. 34). Further inquiry revealed that the tests took place over a three- to seven-day period; records reportedly were kept but were not provided when Gardner requested them. A film was made of one of the trials (on which Geller chose not to guess), and reports of videotapes were never confirmed by film documents. One magician thought cheating could have occurred in several ways, but without seeing the records or films he could not confirm his suspicions.

Contradictory reporting, methodological looseness, and withholding of primary experimental records are typical of much parapsychology research. Defenders of the psychic realm accurately retort that few other research areas attract this kind of critical analysis. No known data could convince most skeptics of the existence of psi, nor is any critique of the work sufficiently cogent to persuade a believer that it is all artifact.

Psychologist Reber (1982) cites three canons of science that parapsychology violates, thus prejudicing scientists against the field. Whereas nature is reliable, psychic phenomena are elusive, frequently disappearing under the closest controls. While science is coherent, psi violates the inverse square law for transmission of energy, and precognition itself violates at least three scientific laws: the principle that cause precedes effect, the linearity of time, and the first law of thermodynamics (that anything without substance can have no impact on a material substance). Scientific explanations are mechanistic, but parapsychology has not proposed any mechanism whereby psi might operate without violating other scientific canons. Science is admittedly conservative with regard to new facts and systems, but it has accepted biofeedback principles, and it is prone to accept acupuncture as a physiological reality.

Since parapsychology meets none of the three canons, it is not accepted by most scientists. Some phenomena now classed with parapsychology probably will find acceptance within psychology. The regularity of near-death experiences points toward unconsciousness and/or brain mechanisms as an explanation; out-of-body experiences may engage similar mechanisms. Some mind reading by stage magicians avowedly employs such keen sensitivity to cues from the audience as almost to constitute an altered state of consciousness. Heightened psychic powers associated with hypnosis, relaxation, and meditation may result from sensitization to physical and/or social cues that have eluded experimental control. The unconscious mind and subtle neurological structures hold unplumbed secrets that probably operate in many parapsychology experiments.

Belief and Christian Faith. The psychology of belief offers a different explanation for parapsychology. Adherents tend also to accept unlikely, extrascientific phenomena such as the Bigfoot legends, the Loch Ness monster, UFOs, and Bermuda triangle mysteries. Little research has studied the functions and causes of such belief systems, but many people seem strongly inclined to believe in the psychic. Psychologists arranged for a magic demonstration in several California university classes, explicitly warning students that the performer "does not really have psychic abilities, and what you'll be seeing are really only tricks" (Benassi, Singer, & Reynolds, 1980, p. 338). When they were questioned about the performance, 58% of the students called it psychic, and only 33% considered it mere magic.

Religious believers tend to believe the nonmaterial claims of parapsychology also, sometimes even citing them as objective evidence for God and the spiritual realm. Rhine left ministerial study because psychology provided no basis for free will (*see* Determinism and Free Will); he hoped parapsychology would give evidence for a transcendent aspect of human nature. Some Christians, however, reject the psychic realm as blasphemy (Bowles & Hynds, 1978). The Jewish prophetic tradition had roots in the clairvoyant seer (1 Sam. 9:6–9). However, the practice of sorcery—seeking answers or affecting events by psychic means—was condemned in the Old and New Testaments (Lev. 20:6; Deut. 18:10–11; Acts 19:18–19).

Pursuit of the psychic poses dangers for Christians. Although psychic evidences may reinforce belief in the nonmaterial, actively seeking a sign implies that religious faith needs outside support. Parapsychology claims a degree of technology and truth held by science itself. If psychic claims are eventually falsified by empirical research, religious faith that depends on them will be unnecessarily undermined. If nonmaterial psi were accorded scientific status, religion might be reduced to technology, not a matter of faith. More significantly, focus on the psychic, whether miracle or illusion, courts triviality in religion. When people revel in the marvelous, they may abandon "the search for truth by other more orthodox and more strenuous and more profitable means, calling for a measure of self-discipline" (Moore, 1977, p. 116).

Even though we may remain skeptical about psi, Christians might be humbly open to the claims of parapsychology. Our relationship with God implies direct knowledge through nonsensory means; our claim for prayer power implies faith in spiritual effects on the real world (the first law of thermodynamics notwithstanding). However, attempts to prove the nonmaterial or resting our faith on statistical experiments is a poor substitute for faith in God through Christ Jesus.

References

Benassi, V. A., Singer, B., & Reynolds, C. B. (1980). Occult belief: Seeing is believing. *Journal for the Scientific Study of Religion, 19*, 337–349.

Bowles, N., & Hynds, F. (1978). *Psi search*. San Francisco: Harper & Row.

Christopher, M. (1970). *ESP, seers & psychics*. New York: Crowell.

Gardner, M. (1982–83, winter). How not to test a psychic: The great SRI die mystery. *The Skeptical Inquirer, 7* (2), 33–39.

Hansel, C. E. M. (1966). *ESP: A scientific evaluation*. New York: Scribner's.

Moore, E. G. (1977). *Try the spirits: Christianity and psychical research*. New York: Oxford University Press.

Reber, A. S. (1982–83, winter). On the paranormal: In defense of skepticism. *The Skeptical Inquirer, 7* (2), 55–64.

R. D. KAHOE

Parataxic Distortion. A concept introduced by Harry Stack Sullivan to refer to distortion in interpersonal perception that is based on an identification of a person with someone from one's past. Although it is roughly equivalent to Sigmund Freud's concept of transference, it is a slightly broader term. Sullivan did not agree with Freud that we are bound to repeat our reactions to early significant people by transferring these attitudes to others. Rather, he felt that one develops ways of coping with those people and then tends to apply these same ways in later relationships. Sullivan felt, however, that this results in distortions in our perception of later significant people. The way we learn what is true and what is parataxic in our thinking about others is to compare our evaluations with those of others. Sullivan referred to this process of consensual validation as the syntaxic mode of communication. He regarded it as a mature mode of relating and contrasted it to the more immature parataxic mode.

D. G. BENNER

See TRANSFERENCE.

Parent Training Programs. For the simplest jobs people receive training, yet too many people become parents without any training. The child tends to be reared the way the parents were, even when they did not like it. Many people try to improve upon the model provided by their own parents by reading the available books, which range from excellent to outright damaging. Others, more cautious, hire a qualified person as consultant or join a parent training program. There are hundreds of such programs. Some of them have gained a broad acceptance among parents, educators, and professionals.

Representative Examples. The Parent Involvement Program is based on Glasser's (1965) views. The parents are urged to become more involved with the children in an honest, warm, and personal relationship, mainly through conversation and mutual interests. The children are considered responsible for their behaviors because they can make choices. Feelings are not ignored, yet the main focus is on behavior. The children are asked to look at themselves and see whether their behaviors are constructive; then they are helped to establish realistic goals for responsible behaviors and to make a commitment. Excuses for failing to fulfill the plan are not accepted, but the children can revise the plan or try it again following a commitment renewal. Parents are urged to be nonjudgmental and nonpunitive. Logical consequences can be applied, but the main focus is on praise for success.

Responsive Parent Training (Willis, Crowder, & Willis, 1976) instructs parents in the behavioristic methods of recording the children's behaviors and establishing a base line. Desired behaviors are reinforced and undesirable ones are extinguished by ignoring them, using deprivation of reinforcers or through overcorrection (e.g., repairing the damage the misbehavior has produced). The program strongly recommends the use of reinforcement over punishment. Even when punishment is used, it has to be paired with reinforcement as soon as the positive behavior occurs.

Parent Effectiveness Training (Gordon, 1970) stems from a humanistic philosophy and focuses mainly on communication. It teaches parents how to interact with children at a feeling level and keep the communication flowing. Roadblocks to communication such as advising, blaming, or shaming are avoided. Parents are trained to detect who owns the problem and act accordingly. If the parents own the problem (even though the children may have caused it), an I-message has the best chance of bringing about changes in the problem-causing behavior. The I-message is a nonblaming message describing the feeling of the sender, the behavior that produced it, and the causal relationship between behavior and feeling. By not arousing defensiveness, anger, and resentment, such a message keeps the communication open and stimulates children to do something about the situation.

When the children own the problem, parents reflect back what they suspect to be the children's feelings. Being correct is not essential. Important is that in this way the parents communicate interest and care.

When both parents and children own the problem, there is a conflict. The no-lose method of conflict resolution is then recommended. There are several steps in this method. The conflict is defined; as many solutions as possible are generated in a nonevaluative way; the solution that seems the closest to satisfying both sides' needs is chosen; decisions are made about implementation, including consequences for failure to adhere to the decision; the outcome is evaluated and, if needed, a new solution is chosen and implemented. When the no-lose method fails, there may be a value conflict. While Parent Effectiveness Training accepts value teaching, it is against imposing the parental values on children. The children may keep their values, yet they may not act them out in a way that creates problems for parents.

The Adlerian parent training programs (Dreikurs & Soltz, 1964; Corsini & Painter, 1975; Dinkmeyer & McKay, 1976) are applied in the parent conferences in schools that adhere to Adlerian principles, in many Adlerian family education centers, and in the Systematic Training for Effective Parenting training centers.

A misbehaving child is considered to be a discouraged child. The misbehavior has four possible goals: to get attention, to win a power struggle, to revenge, or to express inadequacy. The parents should encourage more constructive behaviors by working toward the development of the 4Rs: responsibility, respect, responsiveness, and resourcefulness. For this the children must be encouraged by being trusted with responsibilities and realistic expectations and being allowed to make decisions. Weekly family councils, democratically run, are convened to discuss the problems and make decisions. Misbehaviors are corrected by allowing natural consequences to occur. When there are no such consequences or when they are dangerous, logical consequences can be set.

An important part of the Adlerian programs are the parents' study groups. These provide a deeper understanding of the child-rearing principles and a prolonged contact for exchange of information and for encouragement.

Summary and Evaluation. All of these four representative parent training programs are from a Christian point of view useful tools. They can be easily complemented with the teaching of Christian spirituality, values, and ethics based on love and respect for God and neighbor.

The Parent Involvement Program, by emphasizing warm relationships and responsibility, sets itself within the scriptural framework. Although it is broader than the behavioristic program, it still falls short of approaching children as whole persons.

The Responsive Parent Training program agrees with the Bible in the use of reward and punishment. However, the view that the affective and cognitive aspects are products of conditioning is unnecessarily reductionistic. It also eliminates or reduces the child's responsibility in this area. The program works best with very young children, but even there it benefits from being supplemented for a more holistic approach.

Parent Effectiveness Training is an excellent program in the area of establishing communication and improving relationships—important areas for Christians. Issue may be taken with the reluctance to teach values. However, the approach has been successfully used in churches, and the Lutheran church's Concordia Press has published an edition of Gordon's *Parent Effectiveness Training* with biblical quotations added.

The Adlerian parent training programs are complex and flexible, and they teach parents to prepare children to face real life. Responsibility, respect, resourcefulness, and responsiveness are highly valued by Christianity. The Corsini (1977) article on individual education has been adopted in several

Christian schools, and clergymen are frequently involved in Systematic Training for Effective Parenting programs and in family education centers.

References

Corsini, R. J. (1977). Individual education. *Journal of Individual Psychology, 33* (2a), 292–418.

Corsini, R. J., & Painter, G. (1975). *The practical parent.* New York: Harper & Row.

Dinkmeyer, D., & McKay, G. (1976). *Systematic training for effective parenting (STEP).* Circle Pines, MN: American Guidance Service.

Dreikurs, R., & Soltz, V. (1964). *Children: The challenge.* New York: Hawthorn.

Glasser, W. (1965). *Reality therapy.* New York: Harper & Row.

Gordon, T. (1970). *Parent effectiveness training.* New York: Wyden.

Willis, J. W., Crowder, J., & Willis, J. (1976). *Guiding the psychological and educational growth of children.* Springfield, IL: Thomas.

D. Motet

See Parenting.

Parentification. The term used by family therapists to refer to the phenomenon in some pathogenic families of parents who reverse roles with one or more of their children. In such cases the parent is usually uncomfortable with the dependence of the child, and the child not only is treated as an adult but also is expected to care for the infantile parent. Sometimes such parents attempt to justify their abdication of parental responsibilities under the guise of permissiveness or being democratic or nonauthoritarian.

Parentification may be direct and obviously pathological, as when one of the parents is explicitly allied with a child against the mate or when the parents turn to a child to settle their arguments. Such blurring or denial of generational boundaries always has negative consequences on the psychological development of the child. However, the phenomenon is more and more manifest when one parent deserts the family, forcing a child to fill the parent role. The consequences of this sort of situation are not necessarily pathological. They are, however, always present and need to be more clearly understood.

D. G. Benner

See Structural Family Therapy; Family Systems Theory.

Parenting. The range of behaviors involved in the primary caretaking of children. Salient features of parenting have been summarized in the form of six fundamental, functional categories: bonding, discipline, education and guidance, general protection and welfare, responsivity to specific needs, and the display of sensitivity (Mowder, Harvey, Moy, & Pedro, 1995). The effects of these parental functions on children will be discussed, as well as how parenting behaviors are influenced by a number of powerful factors.

The Effects of Parenting on Children. One important perspective on parenting was initiated by Baumrind's (1966) analysis of parenting styles. Expanded upon by others, this line of investigation categorizes parenting behaviors into four distinct styles based on the degree to which two fundamental dimensions of behavior are exhibited: responsiveness and demandingness. Parents who are highly responsive to their children as well as providing high levels of demands in the way of supervision and strictness are deemed authoritative. In contrast, highly responsive parents with low levels of demands are considered indulgent. Authoritarian parents show the inverse combination of attributes: they provide a high degree of supervision and strictness but little warmth and involvement. Finally, neglectful parents show low levels of both these dimensions of parenting behavior.

Researchers have developed ways to assess parental styles and have examined the relationship between these four types and children's psychological, social, and academic functioning. Authoritative parenting has been positively associated with children's coping strategies (Hardy, Power & Jaedicke, 1993), maturity and independence, and adolescents' adjustment and competence (Steinberg, Lamborn, Darling, Mounts, & Dornbush, 1994) and self-esteem (Parish & McCluskey, 1994). Authoritative parenting has also been linked with children's cooperation with peers and adults, in contrast to the fearful, timid, and compliant behavior observed in some groups of children experiencing authoritarian parenting. Finally, evidence has been presented linking authoritative parenting with children's academic success in white, middle-class families. (It is worth noting that studies outside the parenting style tradition have identified the following parental behaviors as contributors to positive academic outcomes: belief in the child's ability to succeed, high but attainable expectations for achievement, and high levels of verbal interactions with children in the course of daily family life.)

While the relationships between parenting behaviors and child outcomes is intriguing, it is far from deterministic. Almost everyone can identify at least one example of a highly responsive, highly structuring parent who struggled for years with a child's significant behavior problems or emotional disturbance. Likewise, a fascinating group of resilient children exist who, despite absent, less than optimum, or abusive parenting appear to flourish.

Beyond the perspective of more global parenting styles is the somewhat controversial literature investigating distinctions in mothers' and fathers' parenting. Although parenting may be and is carried out by individuals other than mothers and fathers (e.g., grandparents), mother and father behaviors have been most widely investigated and will be reported.

Mothers' and fathers' parenting behaviors, as well as their effects on children, have been shown to vary along a number of important dimensions. Contemporary research continues to support the long-held importance of mothers on the well-being of children. Regardless of family structure, maternal supportiveness is strongly related to positive child development. Children also appear to do better when their mothers feel more positively about themselves, report high levels of enjoyable interactions with their children, show low levels of aggression toward them, and help children conform to culturally prescribed norms (Acock & Demo, 1994).

Despite an increase during the 1980s and 1990s, the role of fathers has received significantly less attention in the professional literature. What attention has been given has often been from a deficit perspective such as the rather extensive line of studies investigating the effects of father absence on children. A consistent finding is that both residential and nonresidential fathers tend to spend less time interacting with their children than do mothers, but this time and the quality of it have been found to be extremely important. For example, the amount of enjoyable time versus negative interactions fathers have with their children has been associated with children's social development, overall sense of well-being, and academic achievement (Acock & Demo, 1994).

The literature on parents' involvement in play highlights some additional contributions made to children by fathers. While both mothers and fathers spend time playing with their infants, studies show that by the time the child is two years old parental roles tend to shift in a significant way. Mothers' interactions with children become characterized more exclusively by caretaking functions while fathers retain significant proportions of their time with their children playing. The apparent emphasis on play by fathers is important given the value of play in intellectual and social development. In particular rough-and-tumble play, a form typically though not exclusively associated with fathers and other male play partners, has been strongly linked with social success in children.

Finally, investigations of the relationship between family structure and child outcomes contribute to our understanding of the influence of parenting on children's development. A thorough review of this extensive area is not possible. To illustrate this complex literature, however, a recent study found that while children and adolescents in first-married families measured slightly higher in global well-being and academic performance than did those in divorced and stepfamily constellations, psychological adjustment varied more widely within family types than between them (Acock & Demo, 1994).

One rather consistent finding is the apparent importance of a supportive versus undermining relationship between parents, regardless of family structure. High levels of conflict between married parents has been found to be predictive of both later child behavior problems and divorce. Children of divorced parents appear to cope best when the level of conflict between parents is low and cooperation in child rearing is high (Belsky, Crnic, & Gable, 1995).

Influences on Parenting Behaviors. There is evidence, however, that parenting behavior is more complex and contextually influenced than neat categories of parenting styles, mother/father roles, or family composition can explain. For example, parental disciplinary practices have been shown to vary according to the nature of the child's infraction and the situation in which it occurs. A parent may be likely to use a power-assertive strategy like an unexplained command for infractions involving noncompliance. In contrast, inconsiderate behaviors like lateness may be more responded to with a more cognitive approach such as reasoning (Smetana, 1994).

Other powerful influences on parenting relate to specific child characteristics. In the past parents were often assigned complete blame for fussy babies and difficult child behaviors. Most contemporary developmental psychologists, however, include the influence of child temperament on parental behaviors in a transactional model explaining the behaviors of both child and parent.

The nature, proportion, and importance of various parental functions are also modified by developmental processes. This dynamism is obvious in the area of basic caretaking functions such as the evolution from feeding and changing the infant to the homework assistance and chauffeuring characteristic of parenting older children.

Other functional changes coincide with the developing child's changing orientation to significant others, such as the increasing salience of peer relationships. The proportion of time spent in social activity with peers increases over time from toddlerhood through adolescence and provides a context for social development distinct from adult interactions in which power is more obviously and unalterably distributed.

Still, parents exert direct and indirect influences on the nature and quality of peer relationships. Indirectly the quality of the parent-child relationship may provide a basic social orientation out of which other relationships are formed. Direct influences encompass the variety of ways in which parents act as managers of children's peer relations. These range from parents' choice of neighborhood and school, which influences which peers will be available to the child, to parental involvement in arranging visits between friends or direct coaching of child-child interactions.

Direct parental influence on peer relationships appears to remain important in adolescence, where effective monitoring of youngsters' whereabouts and social contacts has been linked to lower levels of delinquent behavior. In addition significant evidence supports the enduring influence of parental values on adolescents' choices in social contexts such as choice of friends and sexual conduct.

A final set of influences on parenting behaviors include ethnicity, culture, and socioeconomic status. The literature on parenting styles has inadequately included persons of color in the groups of families studied. Some evidence exists that suggest important differences in what constitutes effective parenting for children of varying ethnic identities. For example, authoritarian parenting has been associated with assertiveness among African-American girls in contrast with its association with timidity in Euro-American youth. And while authoritative parenting has been linked to academic success, this style appears least effective in enhancing the achievement of Asian-American and African-American adolescents. Differences in socioeconomic status appear to influence the values parents seek to instill, as well as the occupational models and other resources parents may offer their children. Continued investigation is needed to enhance our understanding of the distinct aspects of adaptive parenting across cultures and classes.

References

Acock, H. C., & Demo, D. H. (1994). *Family diversity and well-being*. Thousand Oaks, CA: Sage.

Baumrind, D. (1966). Effects of authoritative parental control on child behavior. *Child Development, 37,* 887–907.

Belsky, J., Crnic, K., & Gable, S. (1995). The determinants of cooperating in families with toddler boys: Spousal differences and daily hassles. *Child Development, 66,* 629–642.

Hardy, D. F., Power, T. G., & Jaedicke, S. (1993). Examining the relation of parenting to children's coping with everyday stress. *Child Development, 64,* 1829–1841.

Mowder, B. A., Harvey, V. S., Moy, L., & Pedro, M. (1995). Parent role characteristics: Parent views and their implications for school psychologists. *Psychology in the Schools, 32,* 27–37.

Parish, T. S., & McCluskey, J. J. (1994). The relationship between parenting styles and young adults' self-concepts and evaluations of parents. *Family Therapy, 21* (3), 223–226.

Smetana, J. G. (1994). Parenting styles and beliefs about parental authority. In W. Damon (Series Ed.) & J. G. Smetana (Vol. Ed.), *New directions for child development: No. 66. Beliefs about parenting: Origins and developmental implications*. San Francisco: Jossey-Bass.

Steinberg, L., Lamborn, S. D., Darling, N., Mounts, N. S., & Dornbush, S. M. (1994). Over-time changes in adjustment and competence among adolescents from authoritative, authoritarian, indulgent, and neglectful families. *Child Development, 65,* 754–770.

S. S. Canning

See Life Span Development.

Parkinson's Disease. Parkinson's disease primarily affects voluntary movement. A muscle tremor is particularly obvious in the hands and feet when they are at rest. Muscles are rigid and starting movements are slow and difficult. Walking and grooming are especially affected, and patients often lose balance while walking. Symptoms usually appear after age 60 and progress slowly over as much as 20 years.

As the disease develops it affects fine movements, and the patient must pay close attention even to write. Between 20 and 60% of patients find that advanced Parkinson's disease slows their thinking, makes decisions difficult, and impairs access to memory. These cognitive problems are collectively known as dementia. To compound the problem, patients often become depressed as they notice loss of cognitive skills, and they may require psychological treatment.

Parkinson's disease can usually be readily distinguished from other neurological disorders, such as Alzheimer's disease, by the prominent motor symptoms and the slow progression of any dementia. Any dementia that does develop with Parkinson's disease is less severe (thinking is slowed rather than disrupted) than it is with Alzheimer's disease.

The tremors of the hands and feet may affect one side of the body more than the other, and patients can suppress them for a short time with conscious effort.

Evidence strongly indicates that Parkinson's disease is due to deterioration and death of dopamine-secreting cells in the substantia nigra, a structure in the middle of the brainstem. Neural pathways connect the substantia nigra to many parts of the brain, including the caudate nucleus in the interior of the cerebral hemispheres. The caudate nucleus normally energizes voluntary movement, and the dopamine from a functioning substantia nigra normally serves to moderate and smooth out muscle action. In Parkinson's disease, the deteriorating substantia nigra no longer governs the caudate nucleus, resulting in tremors and other problems of movement.

Treatment enables the remaining neural cells in the substantia nigra to produce more dopamine, typically by oral administration of the drug levodopa, which the brain converts to dopamine. Other drugs may be given in combination with levodopa to reduce its side effects.

Knowledge of Parkinson's disease has helped us understand schizophrenia. Early in the history of drug treatment of schizophrenia, therapists observed that among the side effects of drugs like chlorpromazine and haloperidol were symptoms very much like those of Parkinson's disease. Later researchers theorized that the antischizophrenia drugs somehow interfered with the action of dopamine (producing Parkinsonlike symptoms), and consequently, that schizophrenia must involve excessive activity in dopamine systems of the brain.

Whatever causes the death of cells in the substantia nigra is currently not known. Interesting possibilities were raised, however, by a tragedy in northern California in 1982. People in their twenties went to hospitals and clinics with symptoms of Parkinson's disease. They were found to have taken an illicit drug that was contaminated with MPTP. A natural enzyme in the brain, MAO, converts MPTP to MPP+, which is lethal to substantia nigra cells and produces Parkinson's disease. Since MPP+ is chemically similar to many environmental toxins, including certain pesticides, some researchers have suggested that elderly patients may have inadvertently consumed compounds over a lifetime that were converted into something like the destructive MPP+ by natural MAO.

This hypothesis led to a new treatment for Parkinson's disease. The drug deprenyl had been used for some years to treat high blood pressure by inhibiting MAO. In Parkinson's patients deprenyl blocks the production of MPP+; used in combination with levodopa, it is the first compound that has been shown to slow the course of a degenerative brain disorder.

P. D. YOUNG

See DEMENTIA.

Pastoral Care. Pastoral care may be broadly defined as spiritual care and guidance or the shepherding of human souls. Pastoral care historically included the collective duties of the clergy aimed at healing, guiding, and sustaining a congregation. The term is often used more narrowly to describe the solicitous care offered to an individual or a group that specifically addresses a life dilemma or crisis. To designate care as pastoral is to identify both the provider and context of care and distinguish it from other helping acts. Pastoral care is provided by ordained or acknowledged religious leaders who bring the perspective, resources, and authority of the faith community to bear on the multidimensional challenges of life. Pastoral care may also be provided by representatives of the religious community who are authorized and trained to offer care that reflects the shared values and commitments of the group.

In historical perspective pastoral care is in the "cure of souls" tradition but finds its theological grounding in the New Testament metaphor of the *poimen,* or shepherd. Although the metaphor shares richly symbolic Jewish roots, its operative definition has been principally hammered out in Christian experience. The historic ministry of pastoral care springs from the conviction that Jesus modeled and established the pastoral office for the care and guidance of the church (John 10:11–14; 21:16–17) and continues to call and gift women and men to that ministry. The history of the shepherding of souls illuminates the concerns and compassions of pastors through the ages, much of which continues to offer the modern pastor a classic tradition by which his or her ministry may be enriched.

While the faithful of the church often maintained an inward well-being through their participation in corporate worship, there have always been individuals who required private pastoral assistance. As far back as Cyprian's episcopate (A.D. 247–258), for example, exhortations to faithfulness for individual Christians suffering persecution mingled freely with words of Christian comfort. Cyprian's letters of consolation reminded the persecuted of the crown of life to come and of the advantages of leaving this world. Letters expressing consolation and sympathy upon death were also penned by Gregory of Nazianzus, Ambrose, and Jerome (among others) offering pastoral care to the grieving.

Augustine outlined a list of pastoral duties, reflecting the inclusiveness of the shepherding task as well as its tone, saying, "Disturbers are to be rebuked, the low-spirited to be encouraged, the infirm to be supported, objectors confuted, the treacherous guarded against, the unskilled taught, the lazy aroused . . . and all are to be loved" (McNeill, 1951, p. 100). Gregory the Great penned the *Book of Pastoral Rule* in which he adapts his pastoral advice to individual cases and personality types, noting the frailty and temptations of each. Gregory taught that pastoral authority should be exercised with humility by one who acts as a compassionate neighbor. His book was to guide priests for centuries thereafter. The two most significant modes of the care and cure of souls in the patristic period, however, remained the celebration of the mass and penance.

The Reformation itself was deeply rooted in pastoral concerns and ignited in Germany by Martin Luther's response to the sale of indulgences. Luther, whose personal correspondence radiates a deep pastoral sensitivity, was deeply aroused against indulgences, for he viewed them as an offense against the people and contrary to Scripture. Not less than in Germany, the Swiss Reformation was concerned with abuses of the pastoral office. Huldrych Zwingli (1484–1531) wrote the earliest Protestant design for the guidance of pastors. In *Der Hirt* the Swiss Reformer stresses faithful preaching of repentance which is followed by devoted service to people. "The shepherd must be alert to prevent the sheep that is healed from falling again into sickness . . . so God has provided pastors to stand on guard for his people" (McNeill, 1951, pp. 192–193).

"The office of a true and faithful minister is not only publicly to teach the people over whom he is ordained pastor, but as far as may be, to admonish, exhort, rebuke and console each one in particular." So wrote John Calvin, the Geneva Reformer, whose correspondence abounds with the element of personal guidance. During the persecutions by Henry II of France, Calvin wrote frequently to prisoners soon to die as martyrs. Consoling five young men imprisoned at Chambery (5 September 1555), he tenderly writes to acknowledge that worldly means to deliver them may fail, "But God urges us to look higher" (McNeill, 1951, p. 205).

A variety of Protestant theological traditions emerged from the Reformation and found expression in early America. Each of the four main patterns of Christian pastoral care (Roman Catholic, Lutheran, Anglican, Reformed) reflects a distinctive theological heritage while sharing some common assumptions. In all four traditions the clerical counselors envisioned the cure of souls primarily as a remedy for sin. It is not to be suggested, however, that the history of pastoral care corresponded to changing theological conceptions, for as Holifield (1983) notes, it is the interweaving of theology with other fields of learning, such as psychology and ethics, and the interconnection of pastoral activity with changes in culture and society that reveal the complexity of the cure of souls in the mainstream United States churches (Holifield, 1983).

This complexity was evident in the Great Awakening (1740s), described as a time when multitudes were seriously, soberly, and solemnly out of their wits. Pastors in New England were kept busy by parishioners seeking council in understanding "deep soul concerns" aroused by the revivals. Jonathan Edwards responded by writing on the inner workings of the faculties, employing at least in part the new psychology of John Locke as well as considerable use of the older Reformed divines. *A Treatise Concerning Religious Affections* (1746) was Edwards's pastoral response to the pressing question of the relationship of the will to the understanding and affections, all of which related to the topic of greatest significance during the revival, the salvation of souls.

The most significant influence on pastoral care in the twentieth century was the emergence of the psychological sciences. Influenced by the provocative work of Anton Boisen in 1925 with "living human documents," pastoral theologians began reinterpreting pastoral ministry and human nature in the light of psychological theory. Of particular significance was Carl Rogers's client-centered therapy, in which he described the human organism as marked by an "inherent tendency toward self-actualization" and in which he proposed that an atmosphere of thoroughgoing acceptance in counseling permitted a person to achieve insight and self-acceptance leading to "growth." Seward Hiltner also borrowed in large part from Rogers. This is apparent in a distinctive feature of his shepherding theory. He requires responsibility of the parishioner in the pastor-parishioner relationship, so that "the pastor facilitates the caring process in various ways but does not control or coerce it" (Aden & Ellens, 1990, p. 63). Few pastors would have disagreed with Hiltner's noncoercive shepherding theory, but enthusiasm for its Rogerian underpinnings had waned by the mid-1960s. In 1965 Howard Clinebell of the Claremont School of Theology announced that Rogers's client-centered approach had dominated pastoral counseling literature for too long, and Paul Johnson, one of the most enthusiastic of early proponents of Rogerian methods, characterized Rogerian notions of self-actualization as "a sterile and introvert narcissism of I for Me by Myself" (Holifield, 1983, p. 320).

Tillich (1952) seemed to strike the needed balance between therapeutic wisdom and theological insight and was considered as one who provided the pastoral psychologist with a theological method for translating the power of the gospel into the idiom of twentieth-century thought, namely, a psychological way of thinking. Tillich's student, Wayne Oates (1962), warned, however, against the tendency of pastoral counselors to seek a borrowed identity derived from psychotherapy, a concern shared by others to this day.

The contemporary practice of pastoral care retains the historic commitment and compassion for persons that has characterized its tradition. It has been increasingly criticized, however, for its uncritical and sometimes wholesale accommodation to current psychological and psychotherapeutic trends (Pruyser, 1976). Theologians as well as psychologists, such as Karl Menninger, Paul W. Pruyser, and Orval Hobart Mowrer, among others, have urged pastors and chaplains to recover their historic identity in order to best serve those who seek their perspective. As Christian pastoral care continues to forge its identity, its significant challenge will be to integrate its clinical accomplishments and the resources of contemporary psychotherapy into its practice without losing sight of its theological and classical moorings.

References

Aden, L., & Ellens, J. H. (Eds.). (1990). *Turning points in pastoral care*. Grand Rapids, MI: Baker.

Holifield, E. B. (1983). *A history of pastoral care in America from salvation to self-realization*. Nashville: Abingdon.

McNeill, J. T. (1951). *A history of the cure of souls*. New York: Harper & Brothers.

Oates, W. E. (1962). *Protestant pastoral counseling*. Philadelphia: Westminster.

Pruyser, P. W. (1976). *The minister as diagnostician*. Philadelphia: Westminster.

Tillich, P. (1952). *The courage to be*. New Haven, CT: Yale University Press.

B. N. MITCHELL

See PASTORAL COUNSELING.

Pastoral Care and Counseling, Role Conflicts in.

Pastoral care and counseling are a special component to the myriad of duties commonly found in the pastorate. While the two terms are increasingly being merged into that of pastoral counseling (Patton, 1990), both generally involve the support and care of people from a ministerial perspective. The pastoral counselor recognizes the physical, spiritual, emotional, and intellectual dimensions of people in his or her efforts to help (Davis, 1985).

People seek pastoral care and counseling because they desire understanding within a spiritual context—to be seen as whole persons (Miller & Jackson, 1995). By definition pastoral care and counseling imply a connection to some kind of religious community that authorizes that pastor to perform specific duties. These duties include preaching and teaching, visitation, performing marriages and funerals, and counseling. It is possible that role conflicts can occur in all the various duties of the pastorate, but it is primarily within counseling that this can occur. This may be due to the unique characteristics of counseling, including the sharing and exploration of deep personal issues such as intimacy and loneliness coupled with the private, confidential setting of the pastor's office.

Role conflicts within the pastoral setting might best be understood by borrowing from the arena of secular counseling, which has long discussed the notion of dual-role relationships as contrary to effective helping. Dual-role relationships are those relationships in which a pastor provides formal counseling to someone while also maintaining a different relationship with that same person. Helping people, especially within the counseling setting, involves the presence of a power differential that the pastoral counselor holds over the counselee. The pastoral counselor, by virtue of offering help to someone, occupies a position of trust and power. It is assumed that the person is seeking help, and how this power is respected can be crucial to a positive outcome.

When this power differential is ignored or diminished, especially if this leads to a loss of objectivity and clear judgment within the pastor, harm can come to the counselee (Keith-Spiegel & Koocher, 1985). This is an inherent problem for pastors since their profession demands a multiplicity of roles. It is common for people within a church setting to seek counseling from the pastor with whom they already have some kind of relationship. This leads to potentially confusing and conflicting roles. For example, people who attend church services and who have had counseling with the preacher may mistakenly perceive a message from the pulpit as making direct reference to them (Miller & Jackson, 1995). The result might be great offense at the perceived error leading to great hurt and even withdrawal from the church. All of this may occur completely independent of the pastor's knowledge. This may also occur in reverse when, for example, the pastor has intimate knowledge of a person through counseling and who may be considered for a leadership position within the church. Should the pastor divulge this information to those considering the person for the position, or should the pastor remain silent in the interest of the person's privacy? These and other issues reflect classical ethical questions regarding one's pastoral roles.

While this creates a great tension that can lead to great harm and stress for a pastor and for those being ministered to, much can be done to prevent these kinds of conflicts. A few simple considerations are

in order. One of the most important considerations is that of the pastor being clear when counseling is occurring and when it is not. That is, counseling is best performed in a formal setting, within an office and at specific times, and this must be communicated to the counselees prior to initiating the service. Additionally, it is important for pastors to know their own limitations in helping people. Well-meaning pastors often overextend themselves with people's issues that are far in excess of their expertise, leading to more harm than good. These limitations can best be addressed through such things as peer supervision or professional supervision within the helping community. It is also important that pastors have the foresight to predict possible role conflicts to their counselees, discussing such things as future contact in noncounseling settings and how that might be handled. This, too, should be discussed prior to the initiation of formal counseling.

While role conflicts cannot be entirely avoided, much can be done to reduce their occurrence. Being aware of one's power as a pastor, being aware of limitations in helping, and finally, being able to predict possible conflicts can greatly enhance the effectiveness and well-being of both the pastor and those who come for help.

References

Davis, C. (1980). Pastoral counseling. In D. G. Benner, (Ed.), *Baker encyclopedia of psychology*. Grand Rapids, MI: Baker.

Keith-Spiegel, P., & Koocher, G. (1985). *Ethics in psychology*. New York: Random House.

Miller, W., & Jackson, K. (1995). *Practical psychology for pastors*. Englewood Cliffs, NJ: Prentice-Hall.

Patton, J. (1980). *Dictionary of pastoral care and counseling*. Nashville: Abingdon.

Additional Readings

Collins, G. L. (1988). *Christian counseling, A comprehensive guide*. Dallas: Word.

Corey, G. (1996). *Theory and practice of counseling and psychotherapy* (5th Ed.). New York: Brooks/Cole.

S. A. CAPPA

See PASTORAL CARE; PASTORAL COUNSELING.

Pastoral Counseling. Pastoral counseling can refer to one of two major forms of Christian ministry. First, pastoral counseling describes a major function of the pastor who provides counseling for parishioners as one of many services offered to them. In this sense pastoral counseling is a type of pastoral care that has become a mandatory component of every pastor's task list. Second, pastoral counseling can refer to a specialized form of ministry dedicated solely to the counseling of persons. This meaning of the term describes a type of pastoral vocation that has emerged in the last half of the twentieth century in which the pastoral counselor focuses almost exclusively on counseling.

A Pastoral Function. Christian pastors in all times and in all places have ministered to the pressing personal problems of their parishioners. We have not always labeled this important pastoral function as counseling, but this function has always existed as a vital expression of ministry for undershepherds caring for their sheep in the name of the great Shepherd. Under the influence of the rise of a new discipline called psychology (in the last 100 years) and the rise of a clinical expression of that discipline called counseling (in the last 50 years), we have grown accustomed to counseling as an expected component of ministerial vocation.

Most observers classify the counseling done by pastors as a type of the broader category of ministerial service called pastoral care. Pastoral care involves crisis ministry, serving the needy, caring for the helpless, assisting parishioners through the normal grieving process, attending to their specific spiritual needs, and counseling. Counseling conducted by pastors is generally modeled in structure after its secular analog: one or more sessions, appointments, goals, and several different phases ending in termination. The substance of pastoral counseling, however, varies a great deal from secular counseling by its inclusion of a theological and biblical perspective on the presenting problem, by its use of spiritual resources (the Bible and prayer, for example), and its context within the church.

Surveys continue to show that people in distress often turn first to a pastor for help in spite of the proliferation of Christian counseling services. People often express that they want trustworthy help from someone who genuinely cares about them, both qualities of care that pastors can easily provide. Distressed and hurting people come to pastors for help with marital difficulties, child rearing, the challenges of blended families, emotional struggles, addictions, and chronic mental problems. The increase in availability of counseling services in our society has not tempered the demand on pastors; if anything, the more counseling that is available, the more parishioners expect their pastors to provide counseling for them. Pastors generally report that the demand for pastoral counseling far exceeds their expectations upon first entering the ministry.

Several practical questions have emerged. How much counseling should the busy pastor attempt to do? What is the best model of counseling for the pastor to use? How safe legally is pastoral counseling?

Pastors find that the many demands on their time can render them ineffective unless some strategizing provides basic regulation for their calendars. Counseling, like many other components of the pastor's job description, can consume so much time and energy that it squeezes out other necessary tasks. Most pastors have come to the conclusion that they must control the number of hours per week that are set aside for counseling. In this way they can regulate how much of their ministerial service is dedicated exclusively to counseling. Most pastors develop extensive knowledge of competent counseling services available in the church's vicinity so that referrals can be made when the needs of a parishioner exceed what the pastor can easily handle within the confines of a busy parish ministry.

The literature available to pastors regarding pastoral counseling is extensive. Suggestions for the pastor range from rather elementary procedures such as structured problem-solving techniques to more complex approaches such as object-relations therapeutic interventions. Benner (1992) has developed what probably is the wisest type of model for the pastor to use. Called strategic pastoral counseling, Benner's approach is a time-limited (five sessions) plan that deals with the cognitive, affective, and behavioral components of the client's problem, all from a spiritual perspective. Most seminaries now provide some courses for ministerial candidates in pastoral counseling.

An unnerving trend is illustrated in the rising number of lawsuits against churches and pastors related to the counseling function. The best defense against such a prospect is for churches and pastors to provide quality and competent counseling services. At one point in the 1980s it appeared that some courts were anxious to hold pastors and churches accountable for providing the same standards of care to their pastoral counseling clients that exist in the wider profession of counseling. If such a decision were to be enforced, pastors would have to obtain a far higher level of training in order to do any counseling as a part of their ministry. To date, such an imposition by the courts has not occurred. However, some churches feel it is wise for them to relabel any counseling that they provide as spiritual care or pastoral care so as to minimize legal exposure and risk.

A Pastoral Vocation. Another important use of the term *pastoral counseling* refers to a specialized vocation for pastors who engage full time or nearly full time in the specific ministry of counseling. "A pastoral counselor is a person with commitment to and education for religious ministry who is functioning in an appropriate setting for ministry and accountable to a recognized religious community" (Patton, 1990, p. 849). The pastoral counseling movement has thus given us a new category of Christian mental health worker. It has grown out of general parish ministry and is now represented by its own journals (the *Journal of Pastoral Counseling* and *Pastoral Psychology*), a major dictionary (Hunter, 1990), and its own credentialing organization (the American Association of Pastoral Counselors). The pastoral counseling movement is primarily active in mainline Protestant circles, although some Jewish and Roman Catholic counselors participate.

History. Some authors (Clebsch & Jaekle, 1983; Oden, 1984) have documented the ancient roots of pastoral counseling. Throughout church history pastors have counseled distressed parishioners as part of the tradition of the care and cure of souls. But it is only in the twentieth century that pastoral counseling has become the discrete and definable vocation for pastors that it now is.

The modern pastoral counseling movement traces its roots to Anton Boisen. Boisen experienced a lifelong struggle with alternating periods of emotional stability and instability. When he was hospitalized during three of his five psychotic episodes, Boisen experienced the trauma of emotional dislocation, the value of understanding and compassionate pastoral care, and the strength he could derive from spiritual themes as he recovered from these disquieting struggles. He learned much about the emerging psychiatric and psychological disciplines, about how hospital chaplains could best serve patients, about various psychiatric syndromes, and about the value of learning about one's own internal world when trying to be of help to others.

Boisen's major autobiographical statement (1936) was self-described as an extensive exploration of his inner world. Dittes (1990), however, maintains that Boisen's self-insight was remarkably inadequate and shallow. "The point of view from which he writes never transcends his afflictions; the story is not understood other than in terms of the fear and fantasies which are part of his pathology" (p. 231). "So, indeed, is the autobiography itself, a descriptive marvel, charting, one after another, each event—once over all lightly— but without shading or nuance or interpretation or thematic connection" (p. 230).

In spite of these limitations, Boisen's work clearly set the tone for two movements that were to develop subsequent to his work: clinical pastoral education (CPE) and the pastoral counseling movement. Boisen's influence on these movements is seen in the emphasis on knowing oneself psychologically; the value of discovering about one's weaknesses in the midst of helping other people through crisis and trauma; and a preference for depth psychological theory as seen in the multiple references Boisen made to Sigmund Freud, Carl Gustav Jung, and other early psychoanalytic writers.

Bonnell, whose *Pastoral Psychiatry* (1938) proved to be a seminal work for the emerging field of pastoral counseling, grew up in the home of a physician who worked in a mental institution. Bonnell's interest in the hospitalized mentally ill and how to minister to them was typical of the beginning years of the pastoral counseling movement. "In more recent years . . . students at theological seminaries have put in an internship of from three to six months in mental and general hospitals as a part of their training for the ministry, in an endeavor to acquaint themselves with the problems of human life which, afterwards in one form or another, they will meet in their parishes" (Bonnell, 1938, p. 23).

Numerous authors who followed in Bonnell's train sought to make a clear distinction between what pastoral counseling ought to be (genuine psy-

chotherapy) and what counseling by pastors often was and had been (advice giving and educative instruction). Hence the movement soon took on a sophistication that placed it on a level similar to that of other mental health vocations. The literature of pastoral counseling is rich and varied. Pastoral counseling authors have provided their readers with integrative treatments of the major schools of psychology and psychotherapy as well as giving readers psychological reflections on the major schools of theology.

Credentialing. As the pastoral counseling movement began to gain momentum, the need soon arose for credentialing procedures that would provide quality control and accountability for clergy who wished to specialize in counseling. The first response to this need for standardization was the CPE movement. CPE generally consists of an internship at a hospital. Each student participates in a small group with other students under the close supervision of an experienced supervisor. The main goal of the program is to provide the student with the opportunity to learn about oneself in more profound and meaningful ways than has previously been possible. Many seminaries now require students to complete a basic unit of CPE work as part of the M.Div. curriculum. Many chaplaincy positions also require that applicants have had CPE training as part of their preparation for service. CPE or its equivalent is also required of all members of the second major credentialing organization to develop in the pastoral counseling movement, the American Association of Pastoral Counselors (AAPC).

AAPC was established in 1963. Its purpose is to promote pastoral counseling, a form of ministry dedicated to the "exploration, clarification and guidance of human life, both individual and corporate, at the experiential and behavioral levels through a theological perspective" (American Association of Pastoral Counselors, 1986, p. I–1). The association credentials pastoral counselors at four levels: pastoral counselor in training, member, fellow, and diplomate. Requirements at these four levels progressively increase until a person reaches the diplomate level, which is primarily structured around the functions of supervision and training. The organization is noted for its emphasis on requiring self-knowledge gained through formal psychotherapy experience and on accountability to peers and supervisors regarding the quality of work performed as a pastoral counselor. In addition to its credentialing program for individual pastoral counselors, AAPC also sets standards for the operation of pastoral counseling training centers. These standards involve accreditation procedures and policies that attempt to provide quality assurance for those persons who receive therapy and/or training in these centers.

Distinctives. The pastoral counseling movement brings to the general cluster of Christian mental health disciplines several important and noteworthy distinctives. First, the pastoral movement vigorously pursues the clinical application of its theological base. Members are required to reflect on their personal theological convictions and to work out in detail how those convictions inform their work with clients. At the highest level of AAPC membership, applicants must produce their own substantial model for counseling that addresses issues of human suffering, effective interventions, ethical matters, and how one's ministerial and counseling vocation reflects one's own faith tradition. Many of the models thus produced for AAPC diplomate status have become fine books published by major book houses. The particular theological perspective adopted by AAPC members will vary across the theological landscape, although the majority of them would reflect liberal Protestant understandings of Scripture.

Second, AAPC and the surrounding pastoral counseling movement require significant education in the behavioral sciences (especially at the fellow and diplomate levels of AAPC membership) and in the theological disciplines (at all levels of AAPC membership). Training requirements in the theological arena are primarily supplemented by clinical experience, whereas the reverse is true in the behavioral science training requirements, especially at the lower levels of training. As a result, the therapy training preparation of pastoral counselors often parallels more closely the psychiatric training model (clinical experience predominating) rather than the psychological model (academic preparation followed by clinical experience).

Third, the pastoral counseling movement requires ordination of its members. Thus the organization is focused on the clergy rather than on the laity. This distinctive is reflective of the origins of the movement, which were in the parish ministry. AAPC has attempted to interpret this ordination requirement consistently while making allowances for pastoral leaders who work in denominational settings that do not ordain their leadership and for women, who sometimes are excluded from the ranks of the ordained because of their gender.

Another way of looking at the distinctives of the pastoral counseling movement is to compare it more specifically to the Christian counseling or Christian psychology movements. Patton (1990) maintains that the factor of accountability pastoral counselors maintain to their ordaining body is a major distinctive between pastoral counselors and other "so-called religious counselors, 'Christian psychologist,' et al." (p. 850). This focused accountability is designed to provide professional competence as well as disciplined commitment to theological reflection. However commendable the intent may be, the outworking of this distinctive loses some of its intensity in the light of two facts. First, many Christian counselors and Christian psychologists are ordained individuals who likewise are accountable to their ordaining organizations, or they are lay persons who work in other settings that require them to reflect deeply and intently on the theological implications of their work with people. Second, those pastoral counselors who work outside the setting of a church function practically as if they were in private practice with only occasional contact with the ordaining body. In reality Patton's distinctive between the two types of Christian ministry may not be as sharp as intended.

The Christian counseling and Christian psychology movements tend to involve both lay and ordained persons in their ranks as opposed to only ordained pastors. Also, Christian counseling is a stronger movement among evangelicals than among mainline denominations, a situation quite reversed for pastoral counseling. Finally, the Christian psychology and counseling movements have traditionally placed a far greater emphasis on licensure with state governmental bodies than is true for pastoral counseling.

Models. The pastoral counseling movement has advanced the use of several theoretical models. A major unifying theme among pastoral counselors, especially in the early years of the movement, was an advocacy of Rogerian relating styles. Even when theorists moved on to other emphases, the basic Rogerian attitudes toward clients have prevailed.

Clinebell (1966) identified many forms of pastoral counseling then in use among his colleagues: informal, short-term counseling; role-relationship marital counseling; family group therapy; transactional analysis; supportive and educative pastoral counseling; crisis, group, and confrontational counseling; and depth pastoral counseling. Wicks, Parsons, and Capps (1985) discuss yet other models that are used in prison settings, industrial and corporate venues, primary and secondary schools, community service centers, and the military. They also describe pastoral counseling interventions that are used with minority populations, women, the handicapped, aging segments of society, and addicted populations. Capps (1981) addresses the biblical side of pastoral counseling by reviewing the use of the Bible, especially the psalms, proverbs, and metaphors of Scripture, in pastoral counseling. Hunsinger (1995) provides us with a recent model for pastoral counselors that utilizes Jungian concepts with Barthian theological categories and methods. Augsburger (1986) addresses pastoral counseling as it works across cultural boundaries in dealing with the demonic, with liberation, and with diversity. The pastoral counseling movement is very diverse in theory and approach as it seeks to work with many varied populations in a wide variety of settings. This feature of the pastoral counseling movement parallels the scope of Christian psychology, Christian counseling, and the Christian social work movements.

Delivery Systems. Pastoral counselors work within parish church settings, in nonprofit agencies organized around a distinctive pastoral emphasis, in prisons and other institutions, and in various denominational organizations. A recent trend has been for pastoral counselors to work in private practice or quasi-private practice settings.

References

American Association of Pastoral Counselors. (1986). *The AAPC handbook* (Rev.). Fairfax, VA: Author.

Augsburger, D. (1986). *Pastoral counseling across cultures*. Philadelphia: Westminster.

Benner, D. G. (1992). *Strategic pastoral counseling*. Grand Rapids, MI: Baker.

Boisen, A. T. (1936). *The exploration of the inner world: A study of mental disorder and religious experience*. Chicago: Willett, Clark & Company.

Bonnell, J. S. (1938). *Pastoral psychiatry*. New York: Harper & Brothers.

Capps, D. (1981). *Biblical approaches to pastoral counseling*. Philadelphia: Westminster.

Clebsch, W. A., & Jaekle, C. R. (1983). *Pastoral care in historical perspective*. Northvale, NJ: Aronson.

Clinebell, H. J. (1966). *Basic types of pastoral counseling*. Nashville: Abingdon.

Dittes, J. E. (1990). Boisen as autobiographer. In L. Aden and J. H. Ellens (Eds.), *Turning points in pastoral care: The legacy of Anton Boisen and Seward Hiltner*. Grand Rapids, MI: Baker.

Hunter, R. J. (Ed.). (1990). *Dictionary of pastoral care and counseling*. Nashville: Abingdon.

Hunsinger, D. (1995). *Theology and pastoral counseling: A new interdisciplinary approach*. Grand Rapids, MI: Eerdmans.

Oden, T. (1984). *Care of souls in the classic tradition*. Philadelphia: Fortress.

Patton, J. (1990). Pastoral counseling. In R. J. Hunter (Ed.), *Dictionary of pastoral care and counseling*. Nashville: Abingdon.

Wicks, R. J., Parsons, R. D., & Capps, D. E. (Eds.). (1985). *Clinical handbook of pastoral counseling*. New York: Paulist.

J. R. BECK

See PASTORAL CARE; SPIRITUAL AND RELIGIOUS ISSUES IN PSYCHOTHERAPY; RELIGIOUS RESOURCES IN PSYCHOTHERAPY.

Pathogenesis. A term used to describe the origin and development of diseases and disorders. Other terms used interchangeably include *pathogenesy*, *pathogeny*, and *nosogenesis*.

Patience. Patience belongs in a class that could be called the virtues of resistance or of will power. Other members of this class of valuable traits are courage, forbearance, perseverance, and self-control. These traits enable their possessors to resist improper inclinations, whether they be emotions, desires, urges, habits, or a combination of these. Thus courage is the ability to act properly despite fear; forbearance enables its possessor to tolerate annoyances and irritations by people it is important to get along with; self-control is applied to a range of emotions such as anger and envy as well as appetites for food and sex; and by perseverance one resists the urge to give up or slack off in important tasks.

Three New Testament words tend to be translated "patience." *Hypomone* is also often translated "endurance," "steadfastness," "longsuffering," or "perseverance" and tends to have the sense of faithful, patient enduring of persecution and other difficulties for the sake of the gospel and the kingdom of God. Job is said to have had patience in this sense (James 5:11b). *Makrothumia* is sometimes translated "forbearance" and tends to be used of putting up with wrongs committed by others or perhaps annoyances caused by them. Peter speaks of the time "when God waited patiently in the days of Noah" (1 Peter 3:20, NIV). *Anoche (anechomai)* is translated "forbearance," "bearing with," and "enduring," as well as "patience," and can be used both of putting up with others and of enduring trials and persecutions. Paul exhorts the Ephesians "with all lowliness and meekness, with longsuffering *(makrothumia)*, forbearing *(anechomai)* one another in love" (4:2, KJV).

Patience, like the other virtues of resistance, seems to require the cultivation of a certain psychological self-criticism and self-management. The value of the virtue presupposes that trials are unpleasant and that we have a natural tendency to avoid them and/or give in to them by giving up our faith or acting unlovingly. The value of forbearance presupposes that others will offend and annoy us in ways that will make it difficult for us to love them; we may have the urge to write them off or avoid their company or do things that undermine them and ourselves and our community. The person of patience then is one who does not live in the immediacy of natural impulses but rather is able to take a critical distance from his or her emotions and desires, to assess them as to whether they are healthy and worthy of the Christian. This is part of patience, but in addition to this power of self-criticism the patient person will also have the ability to resist or modify the impulse so that it or at least his or her behavior conforms better to the standards of the Christian life. This ability is probably best thought of as a self-management skill that can be developed by practice and by the encouragement of one's moral community.

Patience can be a distinctively Christian virtue, but traits that go by the name of patience and similar names may also belong to other outlooks and psychologies. Christian patience is distinctive in at least two important ways. First, the goal is distinctive. When the Christian exercises patience in the most characteristically Christian way, he or she does so for the sake of Christ and his kingdom, for the nurturing of the kind of love and fellowship that characterizes that kingdom, and for the sake of the neighbor (in case patience is being exercised in the mode of forbearance). One can imagine an outlook in which a person controls impulses not for these purposes but for material profit and personal power.

That might be patience, but it would not be Christian patience.

Second, the criteria of self-assessment and the means of self-management are distinctive. When a Christian assesses his or her impulses, one's criteria are does this impulse glorify God? does it promote God's kingdom? does it express love of neighbor? Another outlook might use a different criterion, such as does this impulse express my inner child? is this impulse going to lead to glory and profit or the reverse? And the means of self-management are distinctive. When the Christian exercises patience, the individual may do so by reminding the self of saints he or she has heard of or knows or by seeking encouragement from spiritual friends. The individual may forbear the faults of others by remembering that Christ died for them, just as Christ died for him or her.

Virtues like patience in their distinctively Christian versions are dimensions of mental and relational health. They are not merely matters of ethics, but also matters of psychology. Christian psychologists, both theoreticians and counselors, would do well to pay close attention to the New Testament virtues both as displaying the nature of personality in a properly Christian view and as the mental health goals to which psychotherapy should be directed.

Additional Reading

Roberts, R. C. (1984). *The strengths of a Christian.* Philadelphia: Westminster.

R. C. ROBERTS

See PERSONALITY; HEALTHY PERSONALITY.

Pavlov, Ivan Petrovich (1849–1936). Russian physiologist who developed the concept of the conditioned reflex. Most students become familiar with his work through introductory courses in psychology or learning. However, Pavlov, the son of a poor parish priest, was by training a physiologist, not a psychologist. He is known primarily for his work on the physiology and pathophysiology of the higher parts of the brain. In 1904 he became the first Russian to receive the Nobel Prize for his classical experiments on the regulation of the digestive glands by conditioned reflexes of the nervous system.

After graduating from the University of St. Petersburg, Pavlov spent four years at the Military Medical Academy, where he received his medical degree in 1879. He then spent two years studying with such leading scientists as Emil DuBois-Reymond in France and Johannes Müller, Carl Ludwig, and Hermann von Helmholtz in Germany. For ten years he worked in S. P. Botkin's physiology laboratory, where he devoted full time to experimental research. He subsequently was appointed professor of pharmacology at the Military Medical Academy of St. Petersburg. In 1891 he was given the responsibility to organize and direct the department of physiology in the new Institute of Experimental Medicine, and he held this position until his death.

An important phase of Pavlov's work grew out of his investigations of digestion. He found that saliva and gastric juices were secreted by dogs not only when food was introduced into their mouths but also when a variety of stimuli appeared. Pavlov initially ignored these effects, but through systematic study he discovered that nearly any stimulus—sound, sight, or scent—could act as a signal for the same response as did the presence of the object being signaled. As he collected additional data and made generalizations, a new science of higher nervous activity took shape. The basis of that science was the division of reflexes into two categories: unconditioned and conditioned. Unconditioned reflexes are inborn responses that are necessary for minimal survival (e.g., reflexes related to nutrition, defense, or reproduction). Conditioned reflexes are the result of experience and enable an animal to adapt to environmental changes throughout the course of its life.

Pavlov further believed that the higher nervous system sorted out signals from the surrounding environment on the basis of reinforcement. If a signal is important to the survival of the organism, it will be reinforced by unconditioned reflex activity.

One outgrowth of Pavlov's work was that scientists began to accept the view that the behavior of an organism could be understood and described in terms of observable and measurable reflexes. Pavlov's work had a significant impact on the development of American behaviorism, which saw the conditioned reflex as the basic building block of behavior. To Pavlov we also owe much of our current vocabulary in the field of learning and the formal beginning of the learning methodology known as classical conditioning. This methodology has become the dominant approach in cerebral physiology and pathophysiology as well as in psychiatry and psychotherapy in the Soviet Union and other socialist countries. Classical conditioning also continues to be a familiar research topic in the psychology of learning.

S. R. OSBORNE

See CONDITIONING, CLASSICAL; LEARNING.

Peace, Inner. To study the phenomenon of inner peace one needs first to consider *peace* as a concept. Peace is a word with rich and diverse meanings. Historically, it meant the basic absence of conflict or war. In the Hebrew tradition, *shalom* was used as a courteous greeting and a genuine wish for health and prosperity. The Old Testament usage of this word generally implied soundness, completeness, and total well-being. It had several tangible aspects referring to personal safety from danger, length of days, and a quiet and easy death. It was used to describe good relations among individuals, communities, and nations. Peace was often associated with true friendship, righteousness, and sound judgment. Most important, peace implied tranquility, contentment, serenity, and wholeness. In the Greek literature, *eirene* meant an underlying principle, a harmonious state of mind, and a tranquility that could exist regardless of external circumstances.

Peace has also a theological dimension. It reaches its full meaning in the context of a personal relationship with God. Ultimately, God is the author and giver of peace; therefore, an authentic peace cannot be experienced or attained in isolation from God. In the Scriptures, there is an obvious correlation between being in the kingdom, that is, being part of the covenant, and having peace with God.

Most of the church fathers deeply acknowledged the idea and eagerly pursued inner peace. For Thomas Aquinas, inner peace is tranquility both within and without. It is the harmony of desires when the human soul is directed by charity. That is only possible when our will and intellect guide our passions. However, partial peace is attainable in this lifetime.

Some thinkers and philosophers equate inner peace with solitude. Although there is a natural connection between the two, experiencing inner peace is not limited to solitude or to creative aloneness. And the question that poses itself today is how can a state of inner peace be achieved in this industrial and technological age? To answer this, we need to consider the different aspects of our functioning and various faculties of our personality. Maintaining a balanced lifestyle and exercising healthy habits on multiple levels will eventually result in a state of inner harmony and lead to an experience of peace within.

On the emotional level, experiencing inner peace may include striving to discover our basic emotional needs, facing unresolved issues and incomplete matters, seeking healing for our remaining open wounds or hurtful memories, continuing personal growth, fortifying our internal resiliency, maintaining emotional stability, giving and receiving nurture, and building meaningful relationships. On the mental level, the experience of peace within may involve watching our inner anxieties, correcting our faulty thinking, negative automatic statements, disruptive ideas, and irrational beliefs, refining our coping strategy, basic attitude, and approach to life, practicing mental alertness and stimulation, and sharing in the joy of learning.

On the physical level, the pursuit of inner peace may include getting enough rest, eating properly and healthy, exercising regularly, decreasing or limiting the sources of stress, balancing work and play, remaining in touch with nature, and enjoying the beauty of creation. On the spiritual level, such pursuit may involve practicing closeness and intimacy with God, enjoying meaningful worship experiences both corporate and personal, memorizing Scriptures, singing and listening to Christian music, engaging in a particular incarnational ministry, and cultivating purity of passion and transparency of soul.

N. ABI-HASHEM

See RELIGIOUS EXPERIENCE.

Peak Experiences. Personal moments of great happiness and joy, a concept developed by Maslow. In the 1950s and 1960s Maslow set forth his idea that the study of exceptionally healthy and mature individuals would give psychologists a more complete understanding of human nature. Behaviorism's penchant for reductionism and the Freudian stress on psychopathology resulted in a view of human beings that tended to neglect their positive and higher aspects. Maslow and other humanistic psychologists studied examples of psychologically healthy people, those rare self-actualized individuals who make full use of their potential and who are most wholly and fully human (*see* Self-Actualization). It was found that these exceptional people typically were creative, spontaneous, independent, and accepting of themselves and others and that most of them had at some time experienced egotranscendent or mystical experiences.

Maslow (1968) defined these personal occasions as "peak" experiences. This broad definition allowed for a wide range of experiences. However, through analyzing a number of personal reports Maslow was able to list 19 characteristics of peak experiences. This led him to conclude that peak experiences comprise a special type of cognition that he called cognition of being, or "B-cognition." Furthermore, he felt that B-cognition is a manifestation of "Being-love," which is a nonpossessive love for the other that is undistorted by the lover's own needs and deficiencies. Thus for Maslow a peak experience is an intense transitory experience of Being-love in which one suddenly transcends the usual limits of one's identity to perceive the world as it truly is: an integrated and unified whole, full of truth, goodness, and beauty.

This experience typically involves feelings of ecstasy, awe, and a loss of fear, anxiety, and inhibition. During peak experiences individuals may lose track of time and place as they are caught up in the rapture of the immediate present. Their attitude is one of passive and receptive attention rather than active and forced vigilance. While in this mode of complete absorption a person is able to give full attention to an object, and one's perceptual experiencing is much the richer for it. The peak experience is felt as self-validating and self-justifying. It is an end in itself, and many people state that attempts to justify it take away from its dignity and worth. During the peak experience dichotomies, polarities, and conflicts are often viewed from a radically different vantage point that enables them to be transcended or resolved. However, many individuals find great difficulty in describing their peak experiences, as language seems too inadequate a vehicle for such a powerfully profound and personal event.

Maslow and others describe the aftereffects of peak experiences as therapeutically beneficial. They believe that once a person is exposed to the beauty, goodness, and truth inherent in a peak experience, he or she will feel more positive about life as a whole. Some research has shown that peak experiences do result in a better self-concept and a greater capacity for creativity, spontaneity, and expressiveness. Moreover, Maslow notes that in some cases neurotic symptoms have been cured in the wake of a peak experience.

At first Maslow thought that peak experiences were the province of only a chosen few. However, as his research developed, he and his colleagues agreed that many people have peak episodes but are reluctant to acknowledge them. Part of the difficulty in studying peak experiences is in choosing the terms in which to describe them meaningfully. Maslow himself says that his concept of peak experiences is similar to what are commonly known as religious or mystical experiences. In *The Varieties of Religious Experience* William James noted four characteristics of mystical experience—a sense of profound understanding, ineffability, transiency, and passivity—that are also common to peak experiences. Maurice Bucke's term *cosmic consciousness* is descriptive of peak experiences, and Carl Rogers's concept of "fully functioning" in a therapeutic context includes the characteristics of peak experiences that Maslow listed. Even Sigmund Freud, who was an atheist, acknowledged these religious experiences, but he described them as oceanic feeling in which one regresses to a period when the ego believed itself to be omnipotent.

Thus it can be clearly seen that Maslow's peak experience lies at the interface of the disciplines of psychology and theology and is subject to many of the debates between the two fields of inquiry. A major issue is the perennial philosophical argument over the validity of mystical experience in finding truth about God and his creation. Faith seems to have both rational and nonrational components, and history has shown that personal subjective experience must be tempered by a more objective form of revelation, especially as this is found in church tradition and God's Word. For example, many Christians would not accept as ultimate truth the idealized picture of the world that so often results from peak experiences, a world that is never seen as evil or chaotic.

Another important point is whether peak experiences are beneficial both psychologically and spiritually. While these experiences may be the hallmark of a healthy and self-actualized person, it does not necessarily follow that the forced production of peak experiences will bring about psychological health to those in need. In 1962 Maslow stated that the peak experience happens to people and cannot be generated on command. However, Maslow (1970) later felt compelled to warn that the trend toward a compulsive searching for triggers to peak experiences could result in a selfish and evil attitude toward others and a vicious circle of subjectivity that could further lead to superstition and involvement in the occult. Maslow's concept of peak experiences has, however, helped to reacquaint psychology with realms of personal subjective experience that could be empirically studied.

References

Maslow, A. (1968). *Toward a psychology of being* (2nd ed.). Princeton, NJ: Van Nostrand.
Maslow, A. (1970). *Religions, values, and peak-experiences.* New York: Viking.

W. C. DREW

See CONSCIOUSNESS; HUMANISTIC PSYCHOLOGY; MASLOW, ABRAHAM HAROLD.

Pedophilia. Sexual activity, actual or fantasized, with prepubescent children, usually 13 years or younger. The offender must be at least 16 years old and 5 years older than the child. This does not include a person in late adolescence who is sexually involved in an ongoing relationship with a 12- or 13-year old. The pedophiliac's preferred or exclusive method of achieving sexual arousal is with children. Most incidents are initiated by adult males who are known to the child.

In general the younger the victim, the more profound the pedophiliac tendencies in the adult and the more the offender fits the diagnosis of pedophiliac. The *DSM-IV* (American Psychiatric Association, 1994) appears to minimize the dysfunctional nature of pedophilia when compared to the *DSM-III-R*, published in 1987. The more recent edition suggests that pedophilia is a problem if it causes significant distress or impairment. The performance of the sex act itself does not appear to be as significant. This may suggest an effort toward normalizing pedophilia.

The heterosexually oriented pedophiliac tends to prefer 8- to 10-year old girls. Sexual acts involve fondling and exhibiting genitals. Orgasm is sought by only 6% of the offenders. The homosexual pedophiliac more often tries to attain orgasm with the child through masturbation, fellatio, or anal intercourse. Orgasm is sought by 50% of the homosexual pedophiliacs who prefer slightly older children. The condition in the homosexual pedophiliac tends to be chronic. The recidivism rate is second only to that for exhibitionism and ranges from 13% to 28%.

Pedophilia occurs over the entire age range of adulthood, with the peak in middle age. The younger pedophiliac is usually psychosexually and socially immature. The middle-aged pedophiliac tends to be maladjusted and has severe marital problems. He tends to abuse alcohol and generally exhibits repressive behavior. The older pedophiliac (mid- to late fifties) is usually a lonely, impotent man. In general the pedophiliac's sexual deviancy is triggered by psychological stress such as loss of an important relationship, marital discord, or extreme loneliness.

The person is not diagnosed as a pedophiliac if the sexual acts with the child are an isolated occurrence. A single incident with a child may, for example, have occurred as a result of an impulsive act after alcohol intoxication and is not the consistent method of achieving sexual arousal.

The pedophiliac is unable to cope with normal adult stress and may use children as a means of releasing tension. He has feelings of masculine inadequacy and feels sexually comfortable only with children. The pedophiliac usually was reared in a home where the father was distant and impersonal and the mother overprotective or rather cold. Pedophiliacs usually come from broken and unhappy homes.

The four major treatment modalities for treating pedophiliacs are psychotherapy, behavior therapy, surgery (castration), and punishment. There is some research effort to use medroxy progesterone acetate (MPA) to lower testosterone levels in pedophiliacs (Berlin & Krout, 1986). In most states pedophiliacs are punished by imprisonment or committed to a mental hospital. This usually does not change behavior, but it does protect society. The Christian viewpoint would consider sex with children as a disease of the soul, as well as pathological. A distinct part in the cure would involve repentance and acceptance of the claims of Jesus Christ.

Reference

American Psychiatric Association. (1994). *Diagnostic and statistical manual of mental disorders* (4th ed.). Washington, DC: Author.
Berlin, F., & Krout, E. (1986). Pedophilia diagnostic concepts treatment and ethical considerations. *American Journal of Forensic Psychiatry, 7*, 13–30.

Additional Readings

Freund, K., Watson, R., & Dickey, R. (1950). Does sexual abuse in children cause pedophilia: An exploratory study. *Archives of Sexual Behavior, 19*, 557–568.
Jester, D. (1975). *Unusual sexual behavior.* Springfield, IL: Thomas.

M. A. CAMPION

See ABUSE AND NEGLECT.

Penis Envy. According to Sigmund Freud, penis envy is a girl's reaction in the early genital stage to the discovery of the anatomical difference between the sexes. Not only does the girl wish she had a pe-

nis, but also she blames her mother for her deficiency. This is responsible for the loosening of her relationship with her mother and the movement toward the father. In this way Freud viewed penis envy as responsible for the onset of the oedipal crisis in the female.

See OEDIPUS COMPLEX; PSYCHOSEXUAL DEVELOPMENT.

Perception. *See* SENSATION AND PERCEPTION.

Perceptual Deprivation. *See* SENSORY DEPRIVATION.

Perceptual Development. Although the essential neural mechanisms for sensation begin to appear early in prenatal life, the neuromuscular mechanisms for sensation and perception are not yet perfected when an infant is born. However, the infant develops a mature perceptual system by the end of the second year of life.

Fantz (1958) developed the "infant looking chamber" to aid in the study of perception in young infants. With this apparatus the experimenter peers through a small hole in the screen and observes the reflected image on the surface of the infant's eyeball. The technique makes it possible to accurately record the amount of time infants look at different patterns.

At birth the infant is able to see light, dark, and color and has reasonably good visual acuity. Infant visual acuity is estimated by measuring the optokinetic nystagmus, which is a rapid sideways snap of the eye followed by a slower return to normal fixation. Nystagmus occurs in response to the eye following a moving object. By measuring the response of newborn babies to alternate black and white stripes presented at different speeds psychologists estimate that the neonate acuity is between 20/150 and 20/350. The neonate seems to have a fixed focus at about eight inches from its eyes, which limits its visual acuity. Convergence (the rotation of the eyes inward toward a target) and accommodation (changes in the curvature of the lens of the eye in response to a change in distance) are absent at birth but are developed after four to eight weeks.

The newborn is able to respond to the movement of stimuli and to different intensities of light. The infant also reacts to contrast created by brightness contours by focusing more on a contour than other parts of a visual field. At two or three months of age infants show clear visual preferences. They will gaze longer at a bull's-eye than at a striped pattern. They are also more attracted to an accurate but simple representation of the human face. They will gaze at a smiling face whose features are in the proper places more than at a jumbled version of the same photograph (i.e., mouth upside down on the forehead, an eye in the chin). This early attraction to faces and the existence of face recognition areas in the human brain suggest the early preparation of the infant for personal interaction.

From 4 to 12 months attention to jumbled stimulus patterns decreases, but it increases toward the end of the second year. Psychologists hypothesize that the 12-month-old has been exposed to more stimuli than has the 4-month-old, and so the jumbled stimuli are not as interesting. Two-year-olds, however, have acquired some language that helps them to analyze what they are looking at. Some ask, "What happened to the man's face? Did someone hit him?"

Visual habituation appears at almost 10 weeks of age, suggesting that the cerebral cortex takes a long time to mature to the point where the infant can remember visual patterns. Up to that time infants do not seem to get bored with the same stimulus.

Since the human infant is not able to crawl or focus its eyes efficiently until it is several months old, it is impossible to find out about its depth perception before it has acquired a backlog of experiences. Visual cliff experiments suggest that children are born with a capacity to appreciate depth (Gibson & Walk, 1960). The visual cliff is a center runway that has a sheet of strong glass extending outward on two sides. On one side a textured pattern is placed far below the glass, thus giving the impression of depth. Both six-month-olds and land animals avoid the side that appears to have the drop-off. Even children who cannot crawl shows a marked decrease in heart rate, indicating attention, when they are placed on the deep side.

Less research has been done on the development of the senses other than vision. Research indicates that even the unborn fetus has a sense of taste, and newborns will show taste preferences by frowning or refusing to swallow (Sullivan et al., 1991). The newborn is capable of hearing at birth and is sensitive to the location of sound as well as to frequency. The newborn is also capable of responding to odors, turning the head away from unpleasant smells. There is little systematic information on pain sensitivity in infants, but it seems that sensitivity to pain is present to some degree at birth and becomes sharper during the first few days of life.

References

Fantz, R. (1958). Pattern vision in young infants. *The Psychological Record, 8*, 43–47.

Gibson, E., & Walk, R. (1960). The "visual cliff." *Scientific American, 202* (4), 64–71.

Sullivan, R., Taborsky-Barba, S., Mendoza, R., Itano, A., Leon, M., Cotman, C., Payne, T., & Lott, I. (1991). Olfactory classical conditioning in neonates. *Pediatrics, 87*, 511–518.

M. P. Cosgrove

See Sensation and Perception.

Perfectionism. One of those profound paradoxes that constitute human experience is a deeply embossed image of the perfect, which rubs against constant reminders that life is imperfect. Everyone is aware of the completely pure, true, and beautiful without ever having such experiences. Denial of the perfect is a denial of something profoundly human, yet anyone claiming to be perfect is clearly deluded.

At best this ideal serves Don Quixote as a noble friend and sure motivator, the goal of life's quest. At other times it torments him as the anvil upon which his conscience hammers him into feelings of paralyzing guilt and worthlessness.

Religion offers solutions to the guilt of sin but insists on a good and powerful God who yet allows pain and rebellion to run their courses. Where does the ideal fit into human experience? Wesley (1821) associates it with love, Flew (1934) with the charismatic. But these merely describe the problem; the dilemma persists.

Patients, too, seek relief from this conflict. The richest psychological insights into the origin and function of this flame that both inspires and punishes come from psychoanalysis. Freud identified the inspiring component with the ego ideal, a standard that "finds itself possessed of every perfection that is of value," and the punishing component with the superego, the "faculty that incessantly watches, criticizes and compares" (1920/1963, p. 428). He uses the term *superego* for both and sees it as having two roots in infantile and childhood experience. The earliest is the primary narcissistic bliss of the infant who is thoroughly loved and entirely cared for. The other is a complex internalization of moral standards from powerful parents. In the conflict of the oedipal triangle an overtone of anxious danger is added to this idealized parental imago as the child becomes aware that powerful libidinal forces will bring down the judgment of a puritanical society.

Analytic data obtained from personality-disordered patients center around turbulent inner experiences of early childhood in which real or imagined injuries are experienced in the violent images of absolute good and evil. Personality distortions often originate in homes that do indeed inflict injuries but also in personalities that react excessively, probably for biological reasons. Good experiences are also intense, creating overwhelming yearning for unadulterated love and approval. More recent analytic thinkers conceptualize this violent polarity in terms of a failure in separation and individuation from mother. Part objects of self, other, good, and bad fail to fuse into realistic and distinct self and others that are capable of both good and evil. In this failure lies the roots of the splitting and the profound lack of self-esteem seen in disordered adult personalities.

Anyone treating personality disorders soon discovers that whatever the origins, any healing requires confronting and resolving the perplexing fluctuations between soaring grandiosity and dreadful guilt and shame. After an interpersonal injury, an unrealistically worthless self is recalled and the pain of this fall can apparently be healed only by superimposing an equally unrealistic grandiose self that is completely good, worthy, and also all-powerful. In this split a secure experience of "I'm just plain me, and that's OK," is lost (*see* Narcissistic and Borderline Personality Disorders).

The Christian therapist offers another insight into this human dilemma. The ideal can be seen as an internal structure designed by God to maintain a constant awareness of God in our life. It serves to remind us of our failures and our need of a Savior. It also nourishes our hope and confidence in these promises: The course of the believer is destined to be perfect. While it never will be complete in the here and now, the end is certain—we will be perfected. For now, our perfection and our hope lies in Christ, not ourselves. forgiveness is graciously offered for our sins; the guilt of our imperfection can be put behind us. The work of therapists, pastors, and friends is to encourage our brothers and sisters to repent of true sin, to seek and receive forgiveness, and to encourage healing, growth, and unity within the body of Christ (Eph. 4:7, 16).

References

Flew, R. N. (1934). *The idea of perfection in Christian theology.* London: Oxford University Press.

Freud, S. (1963). Introductory lectures on psycho-analysis. In J. Strachey (Ed. and Trans.), *The standard edition of the complete psychological works of Sigmund Freud* (Vols. 15 & 16). London: Hogarth. (Original work published 1920)

Wesley, J. (1821). *A plain account of Christian perfection.* New York: Harper.

Additional Readings

Kohut, H. (1971). *The analysis of the self.* New York: International Universities Press.

Warfield, B. B. (1931). *Perfectionism.* New York: Oxford University Press.

C. M. Berry

See Superego; Psychoanalytic Psychology; Legalism.

Performance Appraisal. One of a supervisor's most difficult tasks. Latham and Wexley (1981) suggest that performance appraisal systems are much like seat belts; most people believe they are necessary, but they do not like to use them. Supervisors and subordinates both recognize that appraisals are often based on vague or poorly communicated performance standards, infrequent or haphazard observation of the worker on the job, and personal likes or dislikes. When such ratings are linked to important decisions about pay, promotion, training, and termination, resistance to performance appraisal becomes understandable. As a result performance appraisal is often treated as a necessary evil, and its potential for motivating and develop-ing employees is lost. Although there is no perfect performance appraisal system, appraisal practice can be improved by evaluating the type of performance measures used and the manner in which performance feedback is given to the employee.

Latham and Wesley (1981) define performance appraisal as "any personnel decision that affects the status of employees regarding promotion, termination, demotion, transfer, salary increase or decrease" (p. 4). This includes not just formal performance evaluations but also informal day-to-day decisions affecting worker status. All organizations practice performance appraisal in one form or another.

Performance appraisal measures can be broken down into three major types: trait, outcome, and behavior. Trait measures are by far the most popular. These measures ask the supervisor to rate the worker on a number of presumably job-relevant characteristics such as cooperation, dependability, initiative, and communication. Trait measures are popular because they appear to measure important aspects of job performance and they are relatively easy to develop.

Trait measures have a key weakness: Each trait can be interpreted in many different ways. For example, Bass and Barrett (1972) cite a study in which 47 executives produced 75 different definitions of dependability. Lacking clear reference to specific things the worker does on the job, trait ratings may be based on the supervisor's impressions of the worker's personality rather than on his or her work. Another problem with trait measures is that they do not tell the worker how to improve a low rating. For example, an unsatisfactory rating on cooperation tells the worker that he or she is not cooperating. It does not tell the worker specifically what to do to improve his or her future performance (e.g., volunteer to work extra hours when the office is busy).

Outcome measures are grounded in job goals and objectives. They are concerned with the results of work rather than the process. Batting averages, production rates, and sales volume are all examples of such measures. While one cannot deny the importance of bottom-line figures, they are often influenced by factors beyond the worker's control (e.g., lack of resources, poor economy, inept coworkers). When this is true, decisions based on outcome measures may be perceived as unfair and may undermine worker motivation.

Behavior measures focus specifically on what the employee does on the job that makes him or her effective. They are based on the assumption that good results do not come about by chance, that someone must do something to create them. Behavior measures differ from trait measures in that they communicate performance expectations specifically. Two examples are "involves subordinates in planning and forecasting" and "generates new ways of tackling new or ongoing problems." Because they are less subjective than trait measures and more under the control of the employee than are outcome measures, behavior measures appear to be the wave of the future in performance appraisal. Latham and Wexley (1981) provide straightforward guidelines for the development of these measures.

Beyond the question of which type of performance measure to use lie many other important issues. One is the question of how frequently to conduct formal performance appraisals. Most experts recommend three to four performance appraisal meetings per year between supervisor and subordinate. Good supervision, however, requires day-to-day performance appraisal, with both positive and negative feedback given as instances of good and poor job performance arise. With this kind of frequent, informal communication between supervisor and subordinate there should be none of the surprises or bombshells that can make these sessions so tense and difficult for both parties.

In their research Burke, Weitzel, and Weir (1978) have identified several factors that affect the quality of formal performance appraisal interviews. Supervisors would be well advised to put these suggestions into immediate practice. Allow the subordinate to voice his or her opinions. Assure the subordinate that you want to help him or her succeed on the job. Set specific goals for the next performance period. Focus the discussion on problems and work toward solutions. Minimize the number of criticisms.

Finally, supervisors should also be aware that performance appraisal practices are increasingly coming before the courts in cases involving various forms of alleged job discrimination. No organization is immune to this costly kind of litigation, and all should carefully review their appraisal practices, consulting with a qualified professional if necessary.

References

Bass, B. M., & Barrett, G. U. (1972). *Man, work and organizations*. Boston: Allyn & Bacon.

Burke, R. J., Weitzel, W., & Weir, T. (1978). Characteristics of effective employee performance review and development interviews: Replication and extension. *Personnel Psychology, 31*, 903–919.

Latham, G. P., & Wesley, K. N. (1981). *Increasing productivity through performance appraisal*. Reading, MA: Addison-Wesley.

Additional Reading

Lindquist, S. E. (Ed.). (1983). Assessment of missionary and minister effectiveness [Special issue]. *Journal of Psychology and Christianity, 2* (4).

D. D. McKenna

See Industrial/Organizational Psychology.

Perls, Frederick Salomon (Fritz) (1893–1970). Originator of Gestalt therapy. He was born and reared in a Jewish family in Berlin and was educated in Germany, obtaining the M.D. degree with specialization in psychology. He also studied at the Vienna and Berlin Institutes of Psychoanalysis. His work reflects the influence of his Jewishness, his unhappy childhood, two world wars, Nazism, his own genius, his psychoanalytic training, an unhappy and competitive marriage, the opportunities of the freedoms in the United States, and his ever-present integrity of searching for truth and reality.

Perls's parents were often bitterly unhappy with each other, apparently caught in upward social mobility. One of his two sisters died in a concentration camp. Fritz was unruly at home and in school, although he did well academically. He finished medical school just in time to join the German army and serve as a medic.

After World War I, Perls returned to Berlin and began psychoanalytic training. He worked with Karen Horney, Clara Happel, and other analysts in Berlin and Frankfurt. Sensing the onset of anti-Semitism in Germany, he emigrated to South Africa in 1933 and established the South African Institute for Psychoanalysis in 1935. As director of this institute he lived and worked in South Africa as a somewhat traditional analyst for about ten years.

Perls began to challenge traditional psychoanalytic theory as early as 1936, but his alternative, Gestalt therapy, was not put forward until his emigration to the United States in 1946. Together with his wife, who has developed her own approach to Gestalt therapy, he founded the New York Institute for Gestalt Therapy. He was associated subsequently with the Gestalt Therapy Institute in Cleveland and was instrumental in the development of the Esalen Institute in Big Sur, California. For the last ten years of his life his work was mostly conducted in an experimental workshop format at Esalen and other cities. When he died, he was living in Vancouver, British Columbia, where he had recently established another Gestalt therapy institute.

Perls's books include *Ego, Hunger, and Aggression* (1947), *Gestalt Therapy* (with Hefferline & Goodman, 1965), *Gestalt Therapy Verbatim* (1969), and *In and Out of the Garbage Pail* (1969). His earlier works were more theoretical, something he explicitly rejected in his later experiential writings.

Perls's influence on psychotherapy has been substantial. Gestalt therapy has come to be a major experiential therapy, providing a provocative challenge to other theoretical approaches, particularly psychoanalytic approaches.

R. B. Johnson

See Gestalt Therapy; Gestalt Techniques.

Perseveration. A term first used by psychiatrist F. S. Niesser to denote the involuntary persistence or repetition of the same thought or activity, usually expressed verbally. The person's attention seems to be fixated on a subject, so that no matter what other topics are brought up, his or her comments remain on this subject. Perseveration occurs most frequently in cases of brain damage but is also found in schizophrenia. It is sometimes defined by experimental psychologists as the general inability to shift from one activity to another.

Person Perception. Person perception involves the processes of identifying, organizing, and interpreting the characteristics of others. This appraisal of others is highly personal and subjective. The accuracy of our perceptions and judgments does not seem to be the primary objective when we try to understand or predict another person's behavior. Speed and simplicity are considered to be much more important than accuracy. It is as if we could not have made a mistake, so why consider it?

One important source of subjective influence, our underlying assumptions and beliefs about ourselves and others, appears particularly potent when situations are vague or ambiguous. When concrete, visible explanations do not readily appear, we are tempted to opt for quick, self-generated explanations based on our preconceived notions and biases. In doing so we create people according to our desires and expectations rather than their behavior and intent.

Errors in Perception. As a result of this preference for velocity over veracity, our perceptual process involves a number of inaccuracies and misinterpretations. One common mistake we make, called the self-enhancing bias, is our apparently unconscious effort to make ourselves look good or at least better than the other person, even if it is only in our own eyes. In this process of social comparison, our self-image influences our perceptions and interpretations of others. Illustrations of this affinity abound in life. For example, when we are asked about some desirable yet subjective quality about ourselves, we often tend to rate ourselves above average in comparison to others of similar background and training. But can we all be above average? We also tend to overrate the importance of our personal, positive qualities as those toward which others should strive rather than differences that are neither necessary nor even attractive to or for others.

Another example is found in our recollection of the past. It is rather selective, lending support to the perspective that "What makes the good ol' days the good ol' days is nothing more than a poor memory." Even our understanding of God's view of humankind plays a significant role in our picture of others. If a person, for example, holds a self-concept of people as "worthless worms" lacking any significant personal value as opposed to one emphasizing "being created in the image of God," the perceived value of others' intentions would be altered significantly.

A second type of error often occurring in person perception involves the consistently different attributions we make for our behavior versus that same behavior performed by others. This actor-observer bias may stem from the restriction common to all:

we are limited to a single perspective . . . our own! Remembering again that accuracy is all too often forfeited in favor of speed and simplicity, we look for obvious cues as to the cause of another's actions. Since the actor is the one to whom our attention is drawn at the outset, we tend to attribute internal, dispositional causes more often than situational ones to others' actions. The opposite would be true when we are trying to understand ourselves because we are aware of our surroundings, not our physical self. When this fact is considered along with the self-enhancing bias, some interesting effects can be seen. For example, when Bill fails he typically searches for external variables that can provide some rationale for his failure (self-enhancing). However, when he succeeds he tends to identify personal strengths that played a significant role in his success (self-enhancing). In contrast, when Bill sees Jerry fail at a similar if not identical task, Bill tends to attribute the failure to some personal inadequacy of Jerry (actor-observer bias). This results in raising Bill's self-image, but it occurs at the cost of his opinion of Jerry.

Models of Attribution. In attempting to answer the most fundamental question in person perception, Why? Heider (1958) hypothesized that the options were simple. We choose either an internal or external cause as an explanation of other people's behaviors. Internal causes may include dispositions, personality characteristics, intelligence, or moods, and external attributions would consist of environmental conditions such as an easy task, no competition, or luck. What is important to remember is that the judgment made is a subjective one. The result is that the individual is seen as being more responsible for actions driven by internal rather than external causes and vice versa.

Based on this simple beginning, major attributional models have developed including the two described here: Kelley's (1973) Covariation Model and Jones and Davis's (1965) Correspondent Inference Model. It may be helpful to consider these in this order based on the assumption that the first decision one makes is whether the behavior is considered to be internally or externally motivated, and Kelley describes this sequence well.

Kelley (1973) identifies three possible causes for behavior: the actor (the performer of the target behavior), the entity (the target of the actor's behavior), and the circumstances (the environmental setting, lighting). In order to ascertain which of the three possibilities is the primary or sole cause, three types of information are gathered. First, the question of consensus must be answered: Do others do this behavior also? Secondly, the consistency of the actor's actions is determined by asking, Does the actor always act this way toward the entity? Finally, the perceiver must determine how distinctive the action is: Does the actor act this way toward everybody or in response to the particular entity in question? The answers to these three questions help the perceiver form a best guess as to why the actor acted that way. The actor is given responsibility for the action when it is believed that others do not do it (low consensus), and the actor always acts that way not only toward this entity (high consistency) but also toward everybody else (low distinctiveness). This illustrates how we assess and assign responsibility for behavior with other possible combinations resulting in contrasting conclusions. For example, an attribution of high consensus, high consistency, and high distinctiveness would place responsibility for the action on the entity, that is, the target.

If we cannot answer all three of these questions, we must rely upon some shorthand techniques based on personal notions about people in general. These shortcuts subject the judgment to even more prejudice. As a result we need to admit that we are often inaccurate in the identification of others' motives. Nonetheless, if we conclude that a person is acting out of a personal motive, a second step is taken: Determine what trait the actor has and how confident we can be in making that attribution. Jones and Davis (1965) prove helpful in this regard.

Working from the fundamental assumption that behaviors are reflections of intentions that are grounded in personal dispositions, Jones and Davis (1965) identify several variables that help in ascertaining the degree of confidence we can have in describing the dispositions of another person. Jones and Davis conclude that others' actions that result in either unpleasant or unusual effects for the actor are informative; they indicate something unique about the actor. In this regard Jones and Davis assume that we are not motivated by painful consequences but rather pleasant ones.

Additional helpful cues occur when we are given the opportunity to watch a person perform a series of behaviors. The possible rationales that are common to the series probably indicate an important motivational attribute of the actor. For example, if a person's behavior in several situations can be explained in a variety of different ways but a common motive of generosity is found throughout, it may be considered a reasonable cause for all of the incidents: the common effect that *could* describe the actor's motives.

However, when the behavior is one chosen in light of known alternatives, effects that are atypical (noncommon) are considered informative. We usually conclude that the noncommon effects probably motivated the individual's choice. Choosing one model of car over its competitors, for instance, cannot be explained by what they share in common but rather by a unique quality of that particular vehicle.

Finally, actions that affect the perceiver personally (hedonically relevant) and are considered to be intentional (personalism) are also highly informative. We believe we know a person very well when we are convinced that his or her actions are intentionally directed at us. For example, many of us pay little attention to the commercials warning us against drunk driving until a family member or close friend is killed in just such an accident at the hands of a repeat offender. At that point the issue becomes more personal; the action more premeditated; and our opinion more strongly held. There is no guarantee that our new perspective is any more accurate than the previous one!

It appears that person perception is more of an art that can be polished rather than a science with an objective, replicable strategy. Our own humanity is revealed in an inclination toward quick, clean answers, all too often sacrificing accuracy for ease. God calls us to be slow to speak and by implication slow to label as well. Therefore, we must be cautious in how we evaluate and classify others' intentions. These designations can become self-perpetuating and dangerous weapons threatening our relationships with these people. We must remember to be humble, open-minded, and willing to reconsider and correct our misperceptions of others.

References

Heider, F. (1958). *The psychology of interpersonal relations.* New York: Wiley.
Jones, E. E., & Davis, K. E. (1965). From acts to dispositions: The attribution process in person perception. In L. Berkowitz (Ed.), *Advances in experimental social psychology* (Vol. 2). New York: Academic.
Kelley, H. H. (1973). The process of causal attribution. *American Psychologist, 28,* 107–128.

J. W. LUND

See IMPRESSION FORMATION AND MANAGEMENT.

Person-Centered Therapy. Developed by Rogers in the 1940s, person-centered therapy (originally called client-centered therapy) is probably the first typically American system of therapy ever formulated. Like all other forms of therapy it is historically dependent on psychoanalysis; thus it is not free from imported European influences in its constitutive parts. But the distinguishing characteristic of this approach to therapy as a whole is that it is made in America for Americans.

Philosophical Roots. More than any other form of therapy, person-centered therapy embodies the early American faith in the primacy of the individual. Early American culture held that if individuals are left to themselves, they will naturally exercise their capacity to realize their fullest potential. It insisted on the necessity of allowing individuals the freedom to choose their own course of action. Person-centered therapy reiterates this theme in therapeutic language when Rogers states that the therapist should rely on the client for the direction of movement in the therapeutic process (Rogers, 1959). Rogers's adherence to this cultural notion of the primacy of the individual is responsible for the individualistic stamp of person-centered therapy as well as for the typically nondirective character of its earliest formulation. It represents the influence of Rogers's view of human beings on his approach to therapy.

Rogers is often seen as a spokesperson for that theoretical orientation in psychology called third force or humanistic psychology. For that reason person-centered therapy is frequently characterized as a phenomenological approach to therapy; that is, an approach that shows unqualified respect for the client's perception of reality. While this characterization has some validity, it is one-sided and superficial because it neglects the other, much deeper dimension of Rogers's thought: his emphasis on growth. Rogers's reverence for growth is ultimately deeper than his respect for individuals. For that reason also it is more correct to call his person-centered therapy a growth therapy rather than a phenomenological therapy.

This emphasis on growth in person-centered therapy is due to the fact that for its theoretical-philosophical roots it hails back to a typically American philosophy rather than to a European import. Pragmatism rather than phenomenology or existentialism forms the philosophical backdrop of this approach. There exists a particularly close affinity between Rogers's person-centered therapy and John Dewey's pragmatism. Dewey elevated the notion of change and growth to the central characteristic of living existence. Person-centered therapy does the same. Structure is always dependent on process in Dewey's pragmatism. This holds for person-centered therapy as well.

To be sure, there is also a difference between Dewey and Rogers at the human level of functioning reality. For Dewey change requires human forming, or experimentally guided (re)construction, to become growth. For Rogers change is growth. If allowed, growth occurs naturally and has its own formative power. We can obstruct it or surrender ourselves to it, but we can never induce it or (re)form it. Dewey takes a culturally formative attitude to growth. Rogers takes an actively receptive attitude toward it. This makes Dewey the father of all eclectic forms of therapy and Rogers the father of all nondirective, person-centered forms of therapy. However, both forms of therapy are united in their common emphasis on change and growth.

Evolution of Theory. Because of this dynamic emphasis it is difficult to give a systematic description of person-centered therapy. Those systematic descriptions that do exist tend to describe it in terms of one of the stages of its development. For example, strictly speaking it is incorrect to characterize the approach to therapy developed by Rogers as person-centered therapy. Person-centeredness is only one of its formulations. At least two other formulations can be distinguished. In order to do justice to the developing character of Rogers's views on therapy, as well as to the dynamic character of his thought, we need to understand person-centered therapy systematically in its de-velopment. The central theme running through this developmental description is a movement from fixity to fluidity.

First Formulation. Rogers's first formulation of therapy is nondirective (Rogers, 1942). It states in essence that therapy is an autonomous process in the sense that it occurs entirely within the client. The therapist can either facilitate its release or obstruct the occurrence but can never cause or induce it. For that reason Rogers repeatedly warns the therapist against interfering with the life of the client. Such intervention would be therapeutically counterproductive.

Instead, Rogers enjoins the therapist to free the process by creating a warm relationship that is maximally permissive of the expression of feeling. By focusing on the feelings of the client, the therapist brings to open expression all the conflicting feelings that clients have regarding themselves and their situation. This yields a process of catharsis, or emotional release, in which these feelings are resolved.

The inevitable and spontaneous result of catharsis is the achievement of insight on the part of the client. Again, this second movement of the process cannot be given to the client by any form of direction or education. It is the inevitable and spontaneous consequence of the first, cathartic movement because it is entirely brought about by the growth forces inherent in the client. To be genuine, such insight must be a working insight. It necessarily involves a process of choice and action on the part of the client. For that reason also the client must earn or achieve this insight. It cannot be given to him or her by the therapist.

Since the therapeutic process is autonomous and thus driven entirely by the growth forces within the client, the only stance that the therapist can possibly take is a nondirective, nonauthoritarian, permissive one. The main aim of therapy in this conception is to avoid obstructing the growth process.

Second Formulation. In his second formulation of therapy Rogers moves from nondirectiveness to person-centeredness (Rogers, 1951). In doing so he also gives a richer description of the therapeutic process. The fundamental attitude of the person-centered therapist is one of active trust in the client's capacity for self-help. This attitude of trust must be unconditional because it itself forms the condition for therapy. It makes therapy therapeutic. It must also be pervasive. It cannot be a technique that one tries on the client and modifies or discards depending on the client's response. Herein lies the essential difference between eclectic and person-centered therapy. The attitude of the eclectic therapist changes depending on the effect of techniques on the client. But the active trust that characterizes the whole of the person-centered therapist's attitude lasts for the duration of therapy, irrespective of the changes that occur in the client. To be sure, techniques are not without their usefulness for the person-centered therapist. They serve to communicate an attitude of trust to the client. But this also exhausts their function. As a result of this person-centered attitude in therapy the client gradually becomes more and more aware of the potential for helping himself or herself. Thus it leads the client toward a sense of personal autonomy.

The process that elicits this awareness is essentially that of disorganization and reorganization of the client's self-concept. The self-concept of a person who has no need for therapy is internally consistent with what he or she daily experiences and perceives. Yet even such a person is occasionally bound to have experiences that are incongruent with his or her self, and these experiences tend to threaten the internal consistency of the self. However, a congruent person normally defends his or her self against these experiences by denying them access to his or her awareness. When these incongruent experiences become so powerful or numerous that he or she can no longer keep them from awareness, the person enters therapy.

As clients begin to explore themselves in therapy, they are likely to discover even more attitudes, feelings, and experiences that are incongruent with their self-concept. This tends to further threaten the self until clients move into the amorphous state of no longer having an organized self-concept. This disorganization process tends to be extremely disturbing emotionally for clients. With every new discovery they are forced to ask themselves anxiously what this will do to the basis of their life. The actively and unconditionally trustful attitude of the therapist allows clients to continue their self-exploration process in spite of their emotional upheaval. The therapist demonstrates unconditional and pervasive trust in clients by actively following them, without fear, in any direction and toward any outcome that they may determine. If clients are supported by the therapist, this process of self-disorganization will inevitably result in the growth of an enlarged and reorganized self. This self now can much more comfortably include all those experiences that were previously denied.

The sense of growth further forms the backdrop for the despair that clients experience in therapy, thus making it possible for them to continue the process to its completion. The outcome of this therapeutic process is a reorganized self-concept that now is much more congruent with their experience. As the process of reorganization occurs, clients begin to feel themselves more and more in action. In effect they discover that by relinquishing their hold on experience, they have gained more control over experience. Once again, however, the force driving this therapeutic process is not the structuring or interpreting efforts of the therapist but the forward-moving growth forces of life inherent in the clients. Once they are released in therapy, these forces make clients aware that they are not mere products of outside influences but in some real sense the makers of themselves, their own products.

Third Formulation. While Rogers's first and second formulations of therapy deal with the attitude and action of the therapist, his third and final formulation focuses almost exclusively on the therapeutic process. In this conception therapy is that process through which the client becomes a fully functioning person (Rogers, 1961). In therapeutic terms to become a fully functioning person means to become the therapeutic process which, as a result of therapy, is released in the client. This third formulation differs from Rogers's person-centered description in that the outcome of therapy is now no longer an enlarged, reorganized self but rather the process of therapy itself. The result of therapy is no longer openness to and congruence with experience but rather an identification with the dynamic living experience that a person is.

This process entails first of all that clients lose all control over their experience. They must surrender themselves to their organism (which Rogers largely identifies with experience). Rather than impose meaning upon their experiential organism, clients must let it tell them the meaning that it has. This will happen only if they become nondirective and receptive toward their own organic experience. The self as thinker about experience must diminish in order for the growth forces of the experiential organism to bear fruit. When this occurs, the client's self is no longer the watchman over experience but an inhabitant in living dynamic experience.

From the point of view of Rogers's third and most mature formulation, therapy is a process that moves the client from fixity to changingness. Since the organism is a perpetual process of change or actualization, dynamic changingness is the inevitable result of becoming one's experiential organism. For Rogers this dynamic changingness is the hallmark of a mentally healthy person. It means that the client's self is at its best when it functions as a fluid Gestalt that changes with the experience of the moment. As a result of this therapeutic movement the client begins to live existentially, literally changing from moment to moment, ever and anew transcending himself or herself. Finally, instead of having a set of values he or she becomes a valuing process.

This dynamic changingness is not random movement, however. It is constructive movement in a positive direction. It is also realistic because it is open to all the client's impulses and experiences. Thus the client has access to a maximally possible amount of information. For that reason clients are in a position to make the best possible choices for themselves so that they can live as fully as possible. The change for the better that clients obtain according to this conception of therapy is that they become experiential organismic processes and therefore also more fully functioning persons.

Evaluation. For the neurotic client who is torn apart by conflicting feelings and internal inconsistencies, person-centered therapy offers a sense of emotional relief and a renewed sense of personal wholeness and competence. It helps clients become themselves more comfortably, and it helps them change themselves more freely.

But this enhanced sense of personal autonomy is not without its costs, because it condemns clients to a life of perpetual change, with no chance of anchoring themselves to abiding structures either outside or inside themselves. The picture of the fully functioning person that emerges at the end of therapy is that of a person who is thrown back upon himself or herself for the task of maintaining personal integrity and who is driven by a compulsion to grow. It evokes a sense of intense restlessness about human life. The fully functioning person cannot find rest in this dependence on his or her fellows or on the Person who is the source of his or her being, nor on the created structures in terms of which he or she lives and moves and has dynamic being. To do so would be a violation of personal autonomy and of the internal growth principle that, according to this conception of humanity, forms the essence of a person's being.

This state of being is the direct result of Rogers's fixation on growth, as exemplified by his lifelong simultaneous preoccupation with the autonomy of persons and the centrality of dynamic growthful experience in human life. The following statement illustrates Rogers's basic intent: "Experience is, for me, the highest authority. The touchstone of validity is my own experience. No other person's ideas and none of my own ideas are as authoritative as my experience. It is to experience that I must return again and again; to discover a closer approximation to truth as it is in the process of becoming in me. Neither the Bible nor the prophets—neither Freud nor research—neither the revelations of God nor man—can take precedence over my own direct experience" (Rogers, 1961, p. 23).

The central thrust of Rogers's view of therapy is decidedly anti-Christian. At the same time his system of therapy contains many valuable insights that Christians can gratefully use in their own approach to therapy. Such notions as the respect and care for persons together with an emphasis on human freedom are reflections of important biblical themes, albeit that because of their secularized character they are pale reflections. However, in utilizing these moments of truth we do well to carefully reform them in order to make them conform to the revealed will of the Lord.

References

Rogers, C. R. (1942). *Counseling and psychotherapy.* Boston: Houghton Mifflin.
Rogers, C. R. (1951). *Client-centered therapy.* Boston: Houghton Mifflin.
Rogers, C. R. (1959). A theory of therapy, personality, and interpersonal relationships, as developed in the client-centered framework. In S. Koch (Ed.), *Psychology* (Vol. 3). New York: McGraw-Hill.
Rogers, C. R. (1961). *On becoming a person.* Boston: Houghton Mifflin.

Additional Readings

Kirschenbaum, H. (1979). *On becoming Carl Rogers.* New York: Delacorte.
Van Belle, H. A. (1980). *Basic intent and therapeutic approach of Carl R. Rogers.* Toronto: Wedge Publishing Foundation.

H. A. VAN BELLE

See ROGERS, CARL RANSOM; SELF THEORY; HUMANISTIC PSYCHOLOGY.

Persona. The term used by Carl Gustav Jung to refer to the external or social aspects of a person's self. The word is taken from the Latin *persona*, which means an actor's mask. Tournier (1957) has written of the same concept but prefers the term *personage*. With Jung he views the choice of social presentations of self to be crucial in that it must be more than a response to the expectations of others. The persona must be a good medium for the expression of the unique and personal aspects of oneself. This concept is Tournier's major contribution to personality theory.

Reference

Tournier, P. (1957). *The meaning of persons.* New York: Harper & Row.

D. G. BENNER

See ANALYTICAL PSYCHOLOGY.

Personal Construct Theory. Personal construct theory was developed by the American psychologist George A. Kelly (1905–1967). He conceived of the human person as an inquisitive, theorizing creature who views the world through a set of individually devised theories. These individual theories, or personal constructs, are formed whether the person involved is aware of the process or not or whether the theory construction process has used good or poor rules. The individual constructs within any given person may be well-integrated and cohesive or independent and unrelated.

The theory was highly abstract when it was first described by its originator, but it has been applied to several practical issues such as therapy (Winter, 1992) and education (Fransella, 1978). Kelly conceived his system as a comprehensive psychology (Kelly, 1955), although most descriptions of his work categorize it as a theory of personality.

A personal construct is an individual's view as to how two things are alike and different from a third thing. The system of internally held constructs determines how one views and evaluates people, places, and things. These internal predictions we make about our world then form the basis for our actions and behavior. A person can revise or replace these constructs as needed (constructive alternativism). The theory predicts that we can understand individuals better if we can elicit and graph their internal theories about the world. Kelly described his theory by developing 11 corollaries that deal with construction, individuality, organization, dichotomy, choice, range, experience, modulation, fragmentation, commonality, and sociality. His view of the human person was generally positive and hopeful.

Kelly and his followers developed a test designed to help map out a person's set of personal constructs. The Role Construct Repertory Test, also known as the Rep Test, can be administered in several different ways. A typical administration would be as follows: The subject is asked to name several acquaintances in various roles such as friend, mother, and others with whom the subject interacts on a frequent basis. The subject then considers any three of these acquaintances as to how two of them are similar and how the same two are different from the third person in the triad. Each time such an operation is performed by the subject, a personal construct emerges. In this manner a person's internal theories are exposed for observation and analysis. Kelly theorized that these personal constructs are fundamental to the way the individual anticipates events and shapes his or her behavior. The test requires extensive scoring techniques. Computer analysis of the Rep Test is possible.

Kelly proposed that his personal construct theory could be applied to therapy (Maher, 1969). Personal construct therapy is a science, and both therapist and client are scientists. The goal is not to produce certain types of behavior but to observe the behavior of the client as a way of uncovering constructs and of testing their validity. The task of therapy is to devise new and better constructs as inadequate or deficient constructs are found. Therapy is an ongoing process, and clients are urged to make this scientific discovery technique a way of life. Kelly wrote, "What, hopefully, the therapy has demonstrated is a way of getting on with one's life, not an answer to the question of 'How shall I behave?'" (Maher, 1969, p. 220).

Personal construct therapy uses a variety of techniques, such as urging a client to reverse his or her position on a construct, helping a client make preverbal constructs verbal, or expanding the applicability of existing constructs. Personal construct therapists also use palliative, elaborative, tightening, or loosening techniques. Fixed role therapy is the technique most closely connected with Kelly's theory. The therapist devises a fixed role for the client that is in some important ways significantly different from the client's existing construct set. After a period of in vivo experimentation with the new fixed role, the therapist and client explore the implications of this experiment for future situations.

Kelly's theory is phenomenological and in the individual psychology tradition of Gordon Allport. In spite of its similarities to other cognitive theories, Kelly's work is distinct from most cognitive methodologies because he used clinical material more extensively than he used empirical research. The theory is respected for its simplicity as well as for its testability. In recent years there has been a revival of interest in Kelly's work, especially in Great Britain.

References

Fransella, F. (Ed.). (1978). *Personal construct psychology.* New York: Academic.

Kelly, G. A. (1955). *The psychology of personal constructs* (2 vols.). New York: Norton.

Maher, B. (Ed.). (1969). *Clinical psychology and personality: The selected papers of George Kelley.* New York: Wiley.

Winter, D. A. (1992). *Personal construct psychology in clinical practice: Theory, research and applications.* London: Routledge.

J. R. BECK

See KELLY, GEORGE ALEXANDER; PERSONALITY; PERSON PERCEPTION.

Personal Unconscious. In Jungian or analytical psychology the psyche is understood to consist of two broad regions: conscious and unconscious. Both these major components are subdivided into several personifications. The two principal subdivisions of the unconscious are the collective unconscious and the personal unconscious.

The personal unconscious owes its existence to personal experience and is a personal acquisition, in contrast to the collective unconscious, which is accounted for by heredity. The contents of the personal unconscious were at some time conscious but have disappeared from the conscious either through repression or forgetting. A characterizing feature of the personal unconscious is that it is made up of complexes (feeling-toned trains of thought or emotion-ladened ideas), whereas the collective unconscious is composed of archetypes.

A central aspect of the personal unconscious is the shadow, which represents the negative side of personality, the sum of all the unpleasant qualities or traits an individual wishes to hide. Along with those characteristics that the person refuses to acknowledge are insufficiently developed functions.

The personal unconscious is thought to lie less deeply in the realm of psychic unconscious than does the collective unconscious. Therefore the contents can be brought into consciousness more easily than can the primordial messages contained in the archetypes. Projection is the chief vehicle for tapping the shadow. Since the data of the shadow are uniquely personal in nature, the projections will reflect themes that represent the person.

Although the contents of the personal unconscious, particularly the shadow, are considered to be negative by the individual, this body of knowledge about the person is invaluable. It is only after these parts of personality are integrated with the more positive qualities that the individual can become a whole person.

Additional Reading

Jung, C. G. (1956). *Two essays on analytical psychology. Collected works* (Vol. 17). Princeton, NJ: Princeton University Press. (Original work published 1935)

D. SMITH

See ANALYTICAL PSYCHOLOGY.

Personality. Personality is one of the more fascinating concepts in contemporary psychology. The term's etymological origins lie in the English word *person* and in the Latin infinitive *personare.* The Latin phrase was a drama term that originally referred to the mouthpiece or hole in a mask through which an actor spoke. Later it denoted the mask itself that the actor wore. The meaning eventually spanned a continuum ranging from surface externals to the individual's deepest identity. The English term *personality* spans the same range (Allport, 1937).

Implicit in persona is a tension that also exists in various definitions of personality. When a play was performed, it was common practice for one actor to play several parts, each designated by a different mask. Switching masks indicated the switching of roles. Thus persona took on the idea of presenting a facade, of acting a role that may belie one's true thoughts or feelings, of a falsehood taken for convenience.

Several personality theories adopted this external metaphor. Carl Gustav Jung's analytic theory distinguished between ego and persona. The ego is the center of consciousness composed of perceptions, feelings, thoughts, and memories. The ego constitutes the basis for the individual's identity and continuity. Persona is a mask adopted as a reaction to social convention. It reflects public behavior expected by society and roles demanded in society. Persona presents humans as social animals. If ego identified too strongly with persona, one's true feelings or inner nature became a mere reflection of society instead of an autonomous identity. Sociological approaches to personality often take this view whereby personality represents an individual's "social-stimulus value."

Yet behind each mask stood a person, an individual with unique thoughts and feelings beyond role expectations. It was possible that the actor's personal thoughts and feelings might affect how the role was played. This belief developed into an approach that viewed personality as something internal, underlying, or latent to actual behavior. The observer of the drama might question whether the words expressed by the actor and the mode of expression indicated the external role or the actor's true, inner inclinations. This mode of thought remains a source of variation in the definition of personality (Stagner, 1974).

Psychological and theological approaches often conceive of personality as the locus of personal causality, involving cognition and choice. Personality (i.e., latent structure) causes behavior (i.e., manifest evidence). Personality is not directly observable, but its existence is established by inference from variation in an individual's behavior. Personality (Allport's *proprium*) is that which gives a person consistency from situation to situation and from time to time. Personality is that which makes it possible to predict behavior before it occurs and explain it after it occurs.

In this view personality incorporates the individual's unique social, emotional, and motivational attributes. It does not generally include the physical or the intellectual, although personality may tangentially affect them. Personality as an inner structure is that which gives personhood to person; it makes individuals distinct from one another. Personality also differentiates persons from other animals. Personality transcends one's biological framework to emphasize the spiritual or mental uniqueness of the human race. In this sense personality ties with religiosity and values. It is in this tradition that Allport defined "personality [as] the dynamic organization within the individual of those psychophysical systems determine his unique adjustments of his environment" (Allport, 1937, p. 48).

This tension between true self and outer manifestations is present in classical theological analyses of the Trinity. There is one true God (persona as selfhood) who accomplishes his plans by means of one of three persons (persona as roles). Father, Son, and Holy Spirit are external manifestations of an inward unity and identity.

Maddi (1968) integrated these internal-external dimensions into a unifying framework. The core of personality is that which is common to all humans but not present in subhumans. This core does not change much during the course of living. As assumed inherent attributes the core has a pervasive causal effect on behavior by providing direction, continuity, and purpose to life. The periphery of personality is the generally learned attributes that make individuals unique. These concrete differences are more readily observable than are core elements. Traits and types illustrate this peripheral view of personality. Maddi assumed that all individuals share the common core, but variations in developmental experience contribute to the peripheral differences among individuals. A similar view was advocated by Allport (1961) in his distinction between central traits as common elements and personal dispositions as peculiar to the individual. Allport also distinguished between nomothetic approaches to the study of personality, which focus on the lawful central core, and the idiographic study of individual differences.

Personality as an abstract concept refers to those internal qualities that define personhood and those external characteristics that make individual differences evident. The study of personality in the first half of the twentieth century was dominated by comprehensive theories often derived from the insights of clinical practice. Toward the end of the century, the macrotheories have given way to microtheories. In this switch clinical insights have given way to systematic research and assessment (Phares, 1984).

References

Allport, G. W. (1937). *Personality: A psychological interpretation.* New York: Holt.

Allport, G. W. (1961). *Pattern and growth in personality.* New York: Holt, Rinehart, & Winston.

Maddi, S. R. (1968). *Personality theories: A comparative analysis.* Homewood, IL: Dorsey.

Phares, E. J. (1984). *Introduction to personality.* Columbus, OH: Merrill.

Stagner, R. (1974). *Psychology of personality* (4th ed.). New York: McGraw-Hill.

R. L. TIMPE

Personality, Christian Theories of. Some Christian psychologists have proposed key biblical concepts regarding the nature of humanity that could form the presuppositions for a comprehensive Christian theory of personality. Among these psychologists are Cheydleur (1988), Collins (1993), Crabb (1977), Koteskey (1980), and Nielsen (1983). Other Christian authors have synthesized their own personality models by "combining . . . major [secular] theories of personality with each other and Christian doctrine [to provide] a foundation for a Christian theory of personality" (Meier, Minirth, Wichern, & Ratcliff, 1991, p. 227).

This review encompasses key biblical concepts for understanding and evaluating Christian theories of personality, representative Christian authors, and a variety of Christian personality approaches. Authors' citations of supporting Scripture are included for reference and evaluation.

Key Biblical Concepts. Biblical personality issues begin with a recognition of our continuing grief and loss due to separation from God, stemming from the fall of Adam and Eve. Barr (1981) describes this as creating our need to regain a three-dimensional existence: body, soul, and spirit (p. 18), while Meier, Minirth, Wichern, and Ratcliff (1991) remind us of Augustine's statement: "a God vacuum . . . exists in every person, an emptiness only God can fill" (p. 246). Tournier (1962) underlines the value of conversion in therapy: "to seek above all other things . . . a living and personal relationship with God" (p. 166).

Writing about normal and abnormal human development, Nielsen (1983) reminds us of God's interest in allowing children to be children: "When I was a child, I spoke as a child, I understood as a child, I thought as a child; but when I became a man, I put away childish things" (1 Cor. 13:11, NKJV). Nielsen emphasizes that the biblical pattern of development that has as its goal the value of transcending and dying to self (Luke 18:29–30) should first include a period of healthy identity formation and the age of positive personal relationships.

Edwards and Kimball (1992) stress a relational basis for maintaining mental health in the postconversion personality. "We are His workmanship, created . . . for good works" (Eph. 2:10 [NASB]); "[therefore] God has not created us to wallow in dejection, self pity or feelings of worthlessness." Once a person is a new creation in Christ (2 Cor. 5:17), he or she is a son or daughter of God (2 Cor. 6:18), the "salt of the earth" (Matt. 5:13 [NIV]), "coheirs with Christ" (Rom. 8:17 [NIV]), and is "crowned . . . with glory and honor" (Ps. 8:5). A Christian has the privilege to have his or her thoughts disciplined and reformatted by studying the Word of God, "tak[ing] captive every thought to make it obedient to Christ" (2 Cor. 10:5 [NIV]). A sense of being forgiven is a necessary psychological and spiritual dynamic for maintaining self-esteem: "If we confess our sins, he is faithful and just and will forgive us our sins and purify us from all unrighteousness" (1 John 1:9 [NIV]) (p. 116).

A significant biblical personality concept, based on Jeremiah 1:5, is the idea that God knows each of us from the point of our conception, before any other biological, family, or cultural influences act upon us. Since there is a unique core to each of us, says Narramore, "God is intensely interested in the individual" (1979, p. 12).

Collins (1993) points out that the first psychological clue to human personality is the biblical claim that we are created in the image of God. Therefore, our personalities are designed to reflect the image and characteristics of God. What are God's characteristics? Buswell (1962) answers: "God is a spirit, infinite, eternal and unchangeable, in His being, wisdom, power, holiness, justice, goodness and truth." God has both natural and moral characteristics. Natural characteristics are those such as aseity, infinity, eternity, immensity, and immutability. Moral characteristics are qualities of God's character such as justice, mercy, love, goodness, and truth (Wiley & Culbertson, 1964).

Which of these characteristics of God can be reflected in humans? Some are restricted to God, because God is infinite. As finite creatures we cannot be self-creating, infinite, eternal, or unlimited. However, as Koteskey (1980) points out, we can reflect some characteristics of God, although imperfectly, due to sin. These reflected traits form the basis of a biblical approach to understanding human personality. God's character of immutability suggests that a measure of stability or faithfulness can be reflected as a human trait. God's characteristics of mercy and love can be reflected in the human trait of emotion. The characteristics of goodness and knowledge can also be reflected as a human truth trait. Even power as a human trait is a reflection of God when it is combined with goodness and truth to promote justice (Cheydleur, 1988).

Payne (1989) suggests that there are biblically documented personality drives, such as the need to sense God's favor on what we do (Ps. 90:17) and the need to become people who transmit blessing to others (1 Peter 2:5) (pp. 64–65). A healthy relationship with God affirms us as communicating creatures. Our creation by God as male and female affirms our intimacy in the act of marriage. God's injunction for us to have dominion over the earth (Gen. 1:26–28) establishes our moral responsibility (Collins, 1993).

Representative Christian Authors. Clark (1958) attributes the beginning of Christian psychology in the United States to Anton Boisen, a clergyman hospitalized for a nervous breakdown, who had a religious experience and became well in the hospital. He later founded the Council for Clinical Pastoral Training (*see* Clinical Pastoral Education) and developed a theory of schizophrenia as a type of interrupted spiritual journey that requires a religious cure.

A rationalistic approach, representing many Christian clinical psychologists, is that of Frame (1961), who believes that all psychological problems are "ultimately" due to the status of humans as fallen creatures. But Frame believes that "a theological study of psychological mechanisms and personality development [is not] likely to give an understanding of the difficulties in the lives of individual people" (pp. 58–59).

Tournier (1962), a Christian psychiatrist, along with other early Christian therapists, saw a biblical value in secular psychoanalysis: "Honesty with one's self, as laid down by psychoanalysis, is the condition of man in which revelation touches him, in which the sense of guilt, the very mainspring of morality, matures" (pp. 132–133) (Rom. 3:10–12). However, Mowrer (1961), a past president of the American Psychological Association, announces: "today we can say . . . that psychoanalysis has not been a success, . . . and the only way [we] can understand the situation . . . [is] in terms of the absurdity of the Reformation doctrine of human guilt and divine grace" (p. 175).

Like many contemporary Christian psychologists who specialize in counseling adults suffering from childhood emotional, physical, or sexual abuse, Wilson (1993) teaches victims to recognize the sins of others and to say, "It was not my fault." Her perspective differs from the biblical behaviorism of Adams (1970) and others who believe, "Blame shifting leads to the idea that man is not responsible for what he is or does . . . the important thing is how you handle these wrongs. . . . God will hold you responsible for the way you respond" (p. 214).

Christian Personality Approaches. Secular personality research focuses on the person's subjective internal world (Kurt Lewin or Carl Rogers), on cognitive development or moral development or on self-actualization (Lawrence Kohlberg or Abraham Maslow), or on matching personality traits and types to various situations. Vocational tests and premarital inventories such as the Strong Vocational Interest Blank and the Taylor Johnson Temperament Analysis are based on questionnaires measuring personal traits (elements of the personality) or types (broader personality descriptions). Christian personality research has similar interests.

Personality Trait Theory. In 1966 LaHaye introduced Christians to a four-trait approach to understanding healthy human personality differences, an approach that was originally proposed by Hippocrates. Hippocrates listed four temperaments that were named in relation to body fluids, or humors. This theory was later disproved, but the second-century Greek physician Galen retained Hippocrates' names for the human behavioral traits that he observed: choleric (hot, quick, active), sanguine (warm, buoyant, lively), melancholy (analytical, self-sacrificing), and phlegmatic (calm, slow, easygoing). LaHaye's contribution to the four-temperament theory is the addition of a Christian conversionist perspective, which details how each of these traits is altered yet retains its own uniqueness when the Spirit of Christ is allowed to take control.

Keating (1987) states that satisfying worship styles are linked to matching personality traits. Using the Myers-Briggs Type Indicator (MBTI) as a base, Keating offers specific guidance for prayer, reflection, spiritual dialogue, need for religious framework, spiritual exercises, sharing, reason, feeling, spiritual commitment, and Christian growth. This approach suggests that specific congregational worship styles, devotional aids, and spiritual disciplines are more growth-producing for individuals with particular personality traits and/or types.

Personality Type Theory. During the 1980s Bill Gothard, the director of the Institute in Basic Youth Conflicts, began to teach a model of seven motivational gifts (personality types) that utilizes a classification scheme creatively developed from the differences chronicled in Romans 12:6: "prophecy, ministry, teaching, exhortation, giving, leading, and showing mercy." Gothard elaborates these labels into a comprehensive personality type system similar in some respects to the secular six-value system developed by Allport (1960). Owen (1983, pp. 11–12) presents the system of seven motivational personality gifts to help parents understand the different ways they approach parenting tasks and to show them how their styles can be modified when parenting children who have different personality gifts.

Wagner (1979) describes 27 spiritual gifts that are found in the body of Christ. The first 7 gifts in his series are the same as the personality types used as the basis for Gothard's and Owen's approach to personality styles. Wagner makes the vocational assessment that "a person's *call* and his or her spiritual gifts are very closely associated," and he also affirms, "There is no substitute for finding your gift-mix and knowing for sure you are doing just what God designed you to do" (Wagner, 1979, pp. 40–47, 259–261).

Personality Development Theory. Captain (1984) presents eight stages of Christian growth, paralleling Erikson (1968) in overall outline but with careful attention to biblical, moral, and spiritual issues at each stage of development. He titles his stages innocence, nurturance, obedience, behavior, motive, meaning, love, and fruit.

Colston and Johnson (1972) also extensively review the eight stages of human development, including the secular theories and research of Sigmund Freud, Lidz, Erik Erikson, Jean Piaget, and Harry Stack Sullivan. However, while the authors clearly believe in a Christian worldview, they do not offer a biblical perspective on spiritual or moral development. Sandford and Sandford (1985) define nine biblically derived functions of the mature human spirit: corporate worship, interactive private devotions, ability to hear God, inspiration and creativity, hope beyond the present situation, communication with others, the glory of marital sexual union, good health and resilience when disease strikes, and an adult conscience that keeps us out of trouble (pp. 109–121).

Trait and Type Theory. Littauer (1983) further develops the LaHaye model when she enumerates six frequent combinations (personality types) of the four temperaments (personality traits). Littauer's six common trait combinations (types) are choleric/sanguine, *motivational leadership;* sanguine/phlegmatic, *caring relationships;* melancholy/phlegmatic, *educator,* choleric/melancholy, *business,* choleric/phlegmatic, *money oriented,* and sanguine/melancholy, *moral voice* (pp. 141–145).

Bustanoby (1976) presents a trait theory with two axes: dominant/submissive and hostile/affectionate. From these two dimensions he creates four combinations of behavior: hostile-dominance, affectionate-dominance, hostile-submissive, and affectionate-submissive. Placed on this trait grid are eight personalities (types). These are *blunt/aggressive* and *competitive/exploitative* (in the hostile-dominant quadrant), *managerial/autocratic* and *responsible/overgenerous* (in the affectionate-dominant quadrant), *cooperative/overemotional* and *docile/dependent* (in the affectionate-submissive quadrant) and *skeptical/distrustful* and *modest/self-effacing* (in the hostile-submissive quadrant). Bustanoby's system can be compared with the Shostrom (1967) and the Allport (1960) secular models. Like Shostrom, Bustanoby uses two words for each of his personality types to indicate both an adaptive and maladaptive version. This may have implications for personality alterations as a result of Christian conversion.

Trait-Type-Developmental Approaches. The Personality Development Portrait, as presented by Cheydleur (1988), is a system based on four human personality traits and is designed to reflect the attributes of God according to Jewish and Christian theology. The four traits in this system are power, emotion, faithfulness, and truth. The traits are measured in a forced-choice instrument with factors balanced for social desirability. These traits are then combined into seven personality types, similar to those of Owen (1983). Three stages of adult development are described for each type, corresponding to the three adult stages of the Erikson (1968) model: identity, intimacy, and generativity.

Another comprehensive Christian trait-type-developmental approach, using the Myers-Briggs personality system as a base, has been developed by Grant, Thompson, and Clarke (1983). Presenting a developmental model combining both psychological maturity and spiritual sanctification, they have constructed sixteen patterns of development for the MBTI combinations (types), predicting anticipated changes in traits for each personality type due to personality growth during four stages of development: ages 6 to 12 years, 12 to 20 years, 20 to 35 years, and 35 to 50 years. In this system the ultimate developmental goal is "fullness of love" in Jesus Christ.

Discussion. Authors who attempt the challenging task of constructing Christian theories of personality are dependent on both Scripture and their own cultural, educational, and religious backgrounds. An increasing amount of creative work in this field is being conducted; however, authors often seem to be unaware of each other's efforts, and most of the theories presented appear to have been subjected to testing and development only by their primary authors. Significantly more empirical research and critical interaction between theorists is necessary.

References

Adams, J. E. (1970). *Competent to counsel.* Phillipsburg, NJ: Presbyterian & Reformed.

Allport, G. W. (1960). *Personality and social encounter.* Boston: Beacon.

Barr, W. D. (Ed.). (1981). *Counseling with confidence.* Plainfield, NJ: Logos International.

Bustanoby, A. (1976). *You can change your personality: Make it a spiritual asset.* Grand Rapids, MI: Zondervan.

Buswell, J. O. (1962). *A systematic theology of the Christian religion* (Vol. 1). Grand Rapids, MI: Zondervan.

Captain, P. A. (1984). *Eight stages of Christian growth.* Englewood Cliffs, NJ: Prentice-Hall.

Clark, W. H. (1958). *The psychology of religion.* Toronto: Macmillan.

Cheydleur, J. R. (1988). *How to find and be yourself.* Anaheim, CA: Living Publications.

Collins, G. R. (1993). *The biblical basis of Christian counseling for people helpers.* Colorado Springs, CO: NavPress.

Colston, L. G., & Johnson, P. E. (1972). *Personality and Christian faith.* Nashville: Abingdon.

Crabb, L. J. (1977). *Effective biblical counseling.* Grand Rapids, MI: Zondervan.

Edwards, T. D., & Kimball, W. R. (1992). *Common care counseling handbook.* South Lake Tahoe, CA: Christian Equippers International.

Erikson, E. H. (1968). *Identity, youth and crisis.* New York: Norton.

Frame, J. D. (1961). *Personality development in the Christian life.* Chicago: Moody.

Grant, W. H., Thompson, M. M., & Clarke, T. E. (1983). *From image to likeness.* Ramsey, NJ: Paulist.

Keating, C. J. (1987). *Who we are is how we pray: Matching personality and spirituality.* Mystic, CT: Twenty-Third Publications.

Koteskey, R. L. (1980). *Psychology from a Christian approach*. Nashville: Abingdon.

LaHaye, T. (1966). *Spirit-controlled temperament*. Wheaton, IL: Tyndale House.

Littauer, F. (1983). *Personality plus*. Old Tappan, NJ: Revell.

Meier, P. D., Minirth, F. B., Wichern, F. B., & Ratcliff, D. E. (1991). *Introduction to psychology and counseling: Christian perspectives and applications* (2nd ed.). Grand Rapids, MI: Baker.

Mowrer, O. H. (1961). *The crisis in psychiatry and religion*. New York: Van Nostrand.

Narramore, C. M. (1979). *The psychology of counseling*. Grand Rapids, MI: Zondervan.

Nielsen, L. E. (1983). *The liberation of the soul: An introduction to biblical psychology*. Anaheim, CA: California Christian Institute.

Owen, P. H. (1983). *Seven styles of parenting*. Wheaton, IL: Tyndale House.

Payne, L. (1989). *The healing presence*. Westchester, IL: Crossway.

Sandford, J., & Sandford, P. (1985). *Healing the wounded spirit*. South Plainfield, NJ: Bridge.

Shostrom, E. L. (1967). *Man the manipulator*. Nashville: Abingdon.

Tournier, P. (1962). *Guilt and grace*. New York: Harper & Row.

Wagner, C. P. (1979). *Your spiritual gifts can help your church grow*. Ventura, CA: Gospel Light/Regal.

Wiley, H. O., & Culbertson, P. T. (1964). *Instruction in Christian theology*. Kansas City, MO: Beacon Hill.

Wilson, S. D. (1993). *Hurt people hurt people*. Nashville: Nelson.

J. R. CHEYDLEUR

See BIBLICAL ANTHROPOLOGY; CHRISTIAN PSYCHOLOGY.

Personality Assessment. Personality assessment provides systematic ways to compare global characteristics of people and to examine unique features of specific persons. As one of the major fields of psychological measurement, personality testing deals with motives, attitudes, emotions, interpersonal relations, beliefs, psychological adjustment, values, and temperament. Research into these topics is often aimed at developing scientific personality theories based on technologically sophisticated tests. Broader facets of assessment procedures become especially conspicuous in applied settings where the focus is on making important decisions in people's lives. For instance, the legal situations addressed by forensic assessment highlight possible conflicts between the interests of different parties involved in the proceedings. Personality assessment in organizations and educational settings accentuates the interpersonal and cultural dimensions of testing. And clinical assessment emphasizes interpretation and evaluation in the judgments of practitioners about their clients. Although systematic assessment has been practiced in some manner for many centuries across many different cultures, contemporary forms of assessment have taken shape almost entirely within the twentieth century.

Personality assessment is usually distinguished by questions that have no correct answer. (This feature contrasts with ability testing, which scores correct responses.) Although many different procedures are employed, the most common approaches are projective tests and self-report questionnaires.

In projective techniques people are asked to give open-ended reactions to ambiguous items such as pictures or inkblots. Projection refers to the influence of one's motives, needs, or attitudes on the responses. Recurring patterns in such unstructured responses are taken to reflect basic features of personal motivation and personality structure of the test taker. Scoring such complex responses typically relies on elaborate coding procedures. The projective techniques currently in use include word association, sentence completion, and drawings of human figures. One of the most widely used projectives, the Thematic Apperception Test (TAT), asks the respondent to tell a story about ambiguous pictures. The Rorschach and other inkblot tests ask people to describe what they see in the symmetric patterns on the cards.

Objective personality tests usually take the form of a questionnaire or checklist. These tests are objective in that the response options are limited to structured formats such as yes/no or ratings on a scale from 1 to 7. With items structured in these ways, a person's responses can be easily scored and combined with scores on other items. The overall scores on a questionnaire are then interpreted by comparing them to norms (usually a group of others' responses on the same set of questions). Most often questionnaires ask for self-descriptions from the person taking the test. However, some checklists are filled out by family members or others who know the subject well. For example, teachers can fill out checklists on the behavior of students in their classroom. Global inventories like the Personality Research Form measure a number of different traits or dimensions at the same time. Other questionnaires are single scales that measure one or a few traits at a time.

Psychologists have directed a great deal of attention to the discrimination of adequate testing procedures from poor ones (*see* Psychological Measurement). In personality assessment the evaluation of testing procedures becomes controversial once one recognizes that the definitions of validity, reliability, and utility of tests are inseparable from the theoretical and practical contexts in which tests are developed and used. For instance, debates over the value of the Rorschach inkblot test reflect a number of issues, including differing priorities for practitioners and researchers and debates over what observations count as evidence for validity.

Another longstanding contrast exists between nomothetic and idiographic norms for the scoring, standardization, and interpretation of assessment results. Nomothetic norms base comparisons on group scores derived from representative samples of specific populations, while idiographic norms involve comparisons with other responses from the person being tested.

Some valuable advances have been made in synthesizing both kinds of norms, but these efforts have achieved only limited recognition in the field. Growing sophistication in test theory and ethical reflection help sort out many of the complexities in the evaluation of personality assessment, but some issues involve fundamental values commitments and so will not be resolved by professional developments alone. There is no consensus on the appropriateness of different ways to integrate traditional requirements of formal test theory with the practical demands inherent in applied decision making. The responsible evaluation of assessment practices has been advanced recently by the growing awareness of crucial historical background to the field. This awareness is even beginning to shape textbooks in fundamental ways (e.g., Rogers, 1995).

The most striking recent development in objective personality assessment is an emerging consensus on the five-factor model as a general framework for the domain of personality traits (see McCrae & John, 1992). These five dimensions are often designated as emotional instability (or neuroticism), extraversion, openness to experience, interpersonal agreeableness, and conscientiousness. The theoretical significance of the model is still an open question, but it does provide an orienting framework in much the same way the four cardinal directions of the compass can orient us geographically. For specific applications, the broad five-factor framework usually requires supplementation with more narrowly focused assessment tools. The implications of this unification are being actively explored by researchers. Moreover, efforts to extend the model to practical applications are underway.

Another major development with wide-ranging implications for personality assessment is the flourishing of narrative psychology. The fundamental place of story and human discourse in shaping human lives has long been recognized outside of psychology, but psychological approaches to these issues have long been scattered across a wide range of subdisciplines, institutions, and literatures (see Polkinghorne, 1988). In applied psychology narratives are assessed in psychotherapy, health psychology, organizational development, and community psychology. In personality research the traditions of projective assessment and psychobiography have combined with quantitative research to ground recent work on motivation, identity, and the self (e.g., McAdams, 1993). Moreover, converging contributions are springing up from cognitive assessment, developmental psychology, social psychology, psychology of religion, neuropsychology, and cross-cultural psychology. The unique challenges of evaluating the adequacy of narrative assessment require advances in both scientific research methods and applications of personality assessment (see Harré & Gillett, 1994).

Perhaps no recent development in testing has received as much attention as has computerization. Computer technology has shown improvements for virtually every phase of test construction, standardization, scoring, and interpretation. Some professionals remain cautious, however, about the viability of automated testing procedures. First, current professional standards for computerization require full professional competence by the users of automated services to prevent misuses of the technology. But the implementation of those standards is not without difficulty. Second, the very successes of automated procedures may encourage professionals to forego an important source of observations for personality assessment: interaction of test administrator with the test taker. The overall value of technologically guided developments like computerization depend directly on the ways that the procedures are implemented. In this area, as elsewhere, responsibility for the adequacy of personality assessment extends beyond professionals to the larger community.

Personality assessment is a thriving endeavor, continuing to expand in depth and scope. Advancements in test theory and related technical domains show no sign of abating. Practitioners continually develop creative means of shaping assessment to serve the needs of clients. Professional associations are actively institutionalizing responsibility in elaborate professional codes. Intellectual and ethical vitality is evident across the entire breadth of the field in a host of debates pursued with vigor and sensitivity. Yet there is no place for complacency. The continuing concerns of many critics are no mere illusions. Abuses still arise both within and outside of existing professional frameworks. A key challenge for Christian communities in these contexts is to sustain the full resources for proactive integration between psychology and theology in the largest sense.

References

Harré, R., & Gillett, G. (1994). *The discursive mind.* Thousand Oaks, CA: Sage.

McAdams, D. P. (1993). *The stories we live by: Personal myths and the making of the self.* New York: Morrow.

McCrae, R. R., & John, O. P. (1992). An introduction to the five-factor model and its applications. *Journal of Personality, 60,* 175–215.

Polkinghorne, D. (1988). *Narrative knowing and the human sciences.* Albany: State University of New York Press.

Rogers, T. B. (1995). *The psychological testing enterprise.* Pacific Grove, CA: Brooks/Cole.

Additional Readings

American Psychological Association PsychNET URL: http://www.apa.org/

Canadian Psychological Association URL: http://www.cycor.ca/Psych/home.html

Personality Assessment

ERIC Clearinghouse on Assessment and Evaluation URL: http://www.cua.edu/www/eric_ai/

Kline, P. (1993). *The handbook of psychological testing.* New York: Routledge.

Revelle, W. (1995). Personality processes. *Annual Review of Psychology, 46,* 295–328.

M. J. McDonald

See Psychological Measurement; Myers-Briggs Type Indicator; Sixteen Personality Factor Questionnaire.

Personality Disorders. The category of personality disorders traditionally defines a group of disturbances that are distinguishable from the neuroses, being more fixed and inflexible, and from the psychoses in that they do not include persistent distortions of thought and perception. Each of these three categories presents its own clinical problems. In the neuroses, such as depression and anxiety, problems are quite troublesome to the patient (or are ego dystonic), thereby enhancing the therapeutic working relationship. Psychoses are less accessible to words and often present in chaotic crises, both of which complicate the therapeutic working relationship. Personality-disordered patients are less troubled by their internal problems (are ego syntonic), feeling whatever problems they have are caused by others (are alloplastic). From their perspective, all would be well if those close to them and the world in general were changed to their specifications. This combination makes the personality disorders among the most difficult of all disorders to treat.

Most people encountered in everyday life who continually make problems for those around them are probably best understood as suffering from personality disorders. Even when they apparently function well, closer acquaintance indicates that they are seriously disturbed. Should we really get close, these people, even though they are often attractive and appealing, brutally wound us, infuriate us, or at best astonish us when they disclose their inner world and thinking. A review of the history of the personality disorders concept will lay a foundation for understanding this disturbance and provide a context for contemporary thinking.

Classification. Individuals differ, and attempts to define these differences date back before the Christian era. Phillipe Pinel technically defined the disorders of personality in 1801 with his description of *manie sans délire*, or irrational behavior with intact intellect. Since then many systems have been proposed, based on such variables as emotional instability, morality, or genetic inferiority, each following the thinking of its day about what most influences human behavior.

Two tracks thus formed, one considering normal personality types and the other the disordered personality. These have mostly remained separate, perhaps because psychiatrists treated the ill, while psychologists sought to understand the normal.

Recent changes in the health care system require all mental health professionals to work together more closely. Also, the government with other third-party payers require providers to describe precisely what they are doing. Both require a classification system understandable to laypeople that all can work with comfortably.

In the United States the *Diagnostic and Statistical Manual of Mental Disorders (DSM),* a descriptive system based on signs and symptoms, responds to this need. In Europe the *International Classification of Diseases (ICD)* parallels this. Both are in a process of refining and reducing ambiguities as well as overlap. In its personality disorder section *DSM* has generally followed analytic leadership, while the *ICD* considers constitution and environment more influential. Recent revisions based on clinical signs and symptoms have brought them closer together, resulting, one hopes, in a single truly international system in the future.

The same shifts in the care system toward disorders tilt the discussion toward the medical model, with each disease a distinct entity. This approach begins with a syndrome, then presents a distinct pattern of symptoms, and ends with a cause or etiology. To describe the cause of a specific personality disorder we need some idea of its essential flaw or flaws and how such flaws create the symptoms. This perspective reflects psychoanalytic thought, and the mass of observations and creative insights that psychoanalysts have accumulated must be our starting point.

Perhaps due to this divergence of paths between understanding normal personality types and specific disorders, it has been difficult for laypeople to understand how the normal person becomes disordered. Both psychologists and common sense tells us that normal people vary in personality. It is an undeniable observation that personality differences are both a bane and a blessing. At best our differences are complementary, each supplying to the whole something less well developed in others. Differences tend to produce conflict, especially when we do not understand each other. At this writing many books are appearing, each with its own personality categories, each encouraging understanding of self and important others in order to highlight this complementarity.

Type. The discussions of personality disorders in this volume will begin with a definition of those personality types, or perhaps temperaments, that, when they are disordered, present a *DSM* personality disorder. The types are defined largely by the peculiar perspective, or how this particular person organizes the complexity of experience. For example, the histrionic personality disorder is discussed as a disordering of a person who tends to organize the complexity of reality around a dramatic sequence or story. When normal, this person appreciates the legitimate drama of life. Yet life fully understood involves not only drama but many other perspectives as well. In the hysteric, other perspectives such as relationships, structures of right and wrong, true or false, and reality itself are bent to fit a script within the drama.

Disorder. What happens to the normal personality type that afflicts it, converting it into a disorder? In general it becomes extremely sensitive to insult, self-centered and controlling (either passively or aggressively), and blindly insensitive to others. Intimate relationships flounder, life loses meaning as passions rule, and injury is defended against at all costs. The patient experiences this as explosive anxiety, depression, and chaos. The symptoms of a particular personality disorder result from both aggressive and defensive responses to this inner turbulence.

But what initiates this widespread breakdown of personality structure and function? Psychoanalysts, studying from an intrapsychic perspective, have described the impact of primitive conflicts and deprivations in early infancy and childhood. As these are described in analysis, words like rage, terror, and hopeless abandonment seem too feeble for the intense feelings these injuries inflict. In adult life conflicts, injuries, and deprivations that others would consider trivial repeat this primitive experience and revive the same intense feelings.

The patients described by analysts seem to have had more than their just share of injury and deprivation in childhood. They also have tended to respond more explosively than does a normal sibling who shares the same parents. This explosive arousal is indeed a characteristic of personality disorders. In milder arousals, patients describe internal images of those injuring them much like the reality and object distortions of narcissism. Those more explosively aroused eloquently describe the quasipsychotic distortions of reality and objects of the borderline personality disorder. The typical intense and shifting affect and twisted cognitions of the disordered personality are direct expressions of these overwhelming arousals. In the narcissist these distortions largely right themselves between arousals, though the defenses persist. In the borderline they tend to become part of normal perception and hence are much harder to correct.

Such descriptions appeared first in psychoanalytic writing about all personality disorders, but later they concentrated on narcissistic and more recently on borderline personality disorder. Although these two are listed as distinct disorders in both *DSM-IV* and *ICD*-10, it is becoming apparent from the overlap between the narcissistic and the borderline (and the concentration of conceptual thinking on them) that they are more usefully considered degrees of disordering that occur in all personality types. The discussions in this volume of the traditional personality disorders will begin by describing how this personality type perceives complex reality or in some cases the particular temperament of this type. Then there will be a description of how a disorder of the personality type emerges under the impact of intense arousal, at a narcissistic level when milder to borderline when more severe.

Diagnostically a given patient can be placed on a graph, one axis of which is the personality type and the other is the degree of disorder, ranging from normal to narcissistic to borderline. The clinical picture will be most strongly influenced by the degree of disorder but colored by the personality type.

Treatment will be directed at understanding first the pathological arousal process with its feelings and cognitions and second the unique qualities of the particular personality type. Along with this understanding, a behavioral program designed to modify the arousal process itself is combined with a cognitive restructuring of the powerful distortions that fuel the arousal and hamper dealing more effectively with the legitimate injuries and deprivations that are part of life.

Any discussion of personality disorders that covers only their intrapsychic and interpersonal impact is inadequate. Socially and culturally almost all the great achievers of our world are narcissistic or borderline personalities. Perhaps the power they exert over individuals and the world around them lies in their intensity, their single-mindedness, their capacity to hold on a single course without being diverted by relationships or consequences. If we approach our patients without an appreciation of the great debt we owe to men and women like them we miss a vital dynamic of reality and an important first step of empathy.

When treatment is proposed, many patients fear that they will lose their identity and the sharp edge of their effectiveness. Becoming healthier psychologically does not hinder these gifts and can enhance them.

C. M. BERRY

See ABNORMAL PSYCHOLOGY; CLASSIFICATION OF MENTAL DISORDERS.

Personality Psychology. Personality psychology describes individual differences in human cognition, emotion, motivation, and behavior. The general approach examines systematically how people vary in reactions. This individual differences approach (idiographic orientation) has been more prominent than approaches designed to formulate general laws about all individuals (nomothetic orientation). Clinical theories have been more numerous than experimental theories. As a result of psychotherapists' attempts to address human need, they have directed more effort to understand one individual in depth than to generate laws about aggregate individuals. Experimental theories are more geared to the latter goal than to the former. These differences as well as questions on the locus of control of behavior remain issues in personality theory and research (Pervin, 1984).

Mischel (1971) identified the subfields within personality psychology as theory, assessment, development, and deviance and change. Controversy exists among personality theorists' views. This owes in part to variant definitions of personality, to diverse assumptions about human nature, and to different convictions about the locus and cause of behavior. Most early theories (ca. 1900 through 1950) focused on intraorganismic factors as primary causes of individual differences. Ekehammar (1974) termed this approach personologism. But during the 1950s and 1960s a rival viewpoint emerged that focused on situational or environmental causes. This was termed situationism. Personality theory in the 1970s developed a more integrated approach that considered how person and situation interact to produce behavior. The study of person x situation interaction (i.e., interactionism) combined the strengths of clinical observation of individual differences with the experimental study of situational variables while overcoming the limitations of each.

To make a theory testable and thus more than speculation, accurate data are essential. The methods available are as numerous as theories. Some measurement approaches rely on the subjective insight of the clinician (e.g., clinical observation, interviewing, diagnosis through projective tests), while others use objective tests and behavioral samples.

Most theories of personality recognize that children are not miniature adults in thoughts and feelings. As a result the question of how the child comes to be a socialized adult is addressed through a search for developmental and maturational processes. The source of developmental influence is variously placed in stages (e.g., psychosexual and psychosocial), in infant-parent interactions (e.g., object relations), and in imitation of adults (e.g., modeling). Maturational theories may rely on instincts, genetic predispositions, and body types.

Many personality theories developed within clinical practice where therapeutic intervention focused for therapist-client interaction as a prototype for other relationships. Personality theories, relying on assessment and diagnostic techniques, strive to define and describe personality deviance or disorder, so that effective therapeutic change can be effected. Therapy becomes an application of personality theory.

For many persons personality study is one of the most fascinating facets of psychological inquiry because of potential self-insight and the desire to help others.

References

Ekehammar, B. (1974). Interactionism in personality from a historical perspective. *Psychological Bulletin, 81,* 1026–1048.

Endler, N., & Magnusson, D. (Eds.). (1976). *Interactional psychology and personality.* New York: Halsted.

Mischel, W. (1971). *Introduction to personality.* New York: Holt, Rinehart, & Winston.

Pervin, L. A. (1984). *Current controversies and issues in personality* (2nd ed.). New York: Wiley.

R. L. TIMPE

See PERSONALITY; PERSONALITY, CHRISTIAN THEORIES OF.

Personality Research Form. A tool developed by Jackson for the purpose of measuring personality traits of broad relevance for research in personality and applications in academic, clinical, and organizational settings. Twenty-two dimensions of personality are measured in the five versions of the test. Twenty of these were drawn from the work of Murray (1938).

The Personality Research Form's distinctive lies in the psychometrically sophisticated manner in which it was developed. Jackson followed four steps in the construction of each scale. First, each construct (e.g., need for achievement) was explicitly defined according to Murray's work and more recent studies. Then scale items were written in conformity with these definitions. Second, items were empirically selected from these item pools to maximize each scale's homogeneity. Third, response biases, such as desirability, were controlled at the item selection stage by eliminating items showing high correlations with a separate social desirability scale. Finally, item selection and scale development attempted to maximize convergent (consistency of response within scales) and discriminate (discrimination of response between scales) validity. The result of this involved procedure is, as one reviewer put it, a paragon of technical sophistication.

The care with which the Personality Research Form was developed is reflected in the psychometric quality of its scales. Internal consistency reliabilities for the 20 content scales are among the highest in the personality assessment literature. Test-retest stability is also excellent for short-time intervals. Validational evidence for the Personality Research Form comes largely from studies in which peers are asked to describe the test taker in terms of adjectives relevant to each of the test's content scales. Correlations produced by this method suggest strong convergent validity. Similar findings were obtained with self-ratings. (See Jackson, 1967, for further discussion of the test's psychometric properties.)

The Personality Research Form can be used with persons ranging from seventh grade to adult. Normative data, however, are based almost entirely on samples of college students. Thus the user must exercise caution in interpreting standard scores derived from these norms where characteristics of the respondents differ significantly from those of college students. The test is designed to be group administered and takes from 30 to 70 minutes, depending on the form being used. It can be easily scored by hand, or machine-scorable answer sheets are available. Interpretive descriptions for each scale are given in the manual, but no empirical evidence is offered in their support.

Although the Personality Research Form represents the best in objective personality testing, it is not without its critics. Chief among the criticisms is that the test has not been shown to predict behavior in real settings. At this point, then, further applied research is necessary to show whether the test's psychometric sophistication will result in practical payoffs. One must certainly conclude, however, that the test represents a promising major contribution to the field of personality testing.

References

Jackson, D. N. (1967). *Personality research form manual.* Goshen, NY: Research Psychologists Press.
Murray, H. A. (1938). *Explorations in personality.* New York: Wiley.

D. D. McKenna

See Personality Assessment.

Personhood. Both in ordinary and philosophical usage persons are usually contrasted with mere things. Thus to say of a human being that she is a person is to emphasize the differences between the human and subhuman orders, and to inquire about the nature of personhood is to inquire about the nature of those differences.

It was probably Kant who most shaped the meaning of the word *person* with his insistence that persons and only persons are ends in themselves, who should never be treated solely as means. Thus to speak of human beings as persons is among other things to speak of them as morally significant beings, the potential bearers of rights and obligations. This moral sense of personhood must be distinguished from the related legal sense in which infants may not be considered full persons while corporations are. The term *self* often does much of the same work as the term *person,* and some philosophical discussions use the terms interchangeably.

Although there is general rough agreement on the characteristics that distinguish human persons from nonpersons, different thinkers have at various times regarded different characteristics as being most fundamental. Medieval thinkers emphasized rationality as the essential characteristic of persons, following Boethius, who defined a person as an individual substance of a rational nature. In the modern classical period John Locke, while not ignoring rationality, emphasized the quality of self-awareness over time as decisive for personhood, including particularly memory. More recent thinkers have tended to emphasize activity, seeing persons as responsible agents whose decisions reflect values or caring concerns (Macmurray, 1957). These different views should be regarded as complementary perspectives rather than as rivals, since all these characteristics are significant elements of personhood.

Although the term *person* is usually employed to differentiate human persons from the subpersonal order, some thinkers have attempted to reduce or eliminate these differences. The view that human persons are not unique or qualitatively different from the rest of the natural order is generally called reductionism, since the aim is to eliminate the special status human persons seem to enjoy by reducing them to the status of other animals. Early behaviorism, as developed by John B. Watson (1930), was an avowedly reductionistic program. B. F. Skinner's (1971) radical behaviorism continues this reductionistic program, as is evidenced by the title of his popular book, *Beyond Freedom and Dignity.* More recent social behaviorists have, however, modified behaviorism considerably in a nonreductionistic direction.

Most thinkers who have defended historically the uniqueness of the person have been dualists who have held that the self or soul is not a material entity and must be distinguished from the body. Not surprisingly, therefore, most reductionists have been materialists who have identified the person with the body.

Not all materialists are reductionists, however. Some recent thinkers have attempted to avoid both dualism and reductionism. Strawson (1959) developed a view of the person as a unique kind of entity that must be described in two different ways. To properly describe human persons we must employ both material predicates and personal predicates. Since personal predicates are not reducible to material predicates, Strawson's view should not be regarded as reductionistic.

Most contemporary discussions of personhood have been problem-oriented and have tended to focus on one of three areas: the problem of consciousness, or the relationship of mind to body; the problem of the identity of the person over time; and the nature of personal actions. The last area encompasses the traditional debate over freedom and determinism (*see* Determinism and Free Will).

The Mind-Body Problem. Two facts about human persons seem obvious. First, persons have bodies. Second, persons are conscious. The mind-body problem concerns the relationship of these two facts and their relative significance for answering the question as to what kind of entity human persons are.

Classical positions on the mind-body problem fall naturally into two groups: monistic positions and dualistic positions. Dualistic views regard the mind or soul (roughly equivalent terms), the seat of consciousness, as a distinct nonphysical substance. In this view a human person is a composite of this nonmaterial substance and the body. Some dualists prefer to identify the person exclusively with the soul. Not all dualists agree on the relationship between the soul and body. Most, like René Descartes, have been interactionists who hold that body and soul can reciprocally control and influence each other. Thus dualism is compatible with the obvious ways in which consciousness is affected by and even dependent on the brain and central nervous system. Other dualists have been parallelists, who have denied interaction between soul and body because of the difficulty in explaining interaction between two radically different substances.

Monistic views, which deny that a human person is or has two distinct substances, are an even more varied lot. Idealists or panpsychists believe that the person is a purely spiritual entity, interpreting the body as being in some sense spiritual. Materialists reject the existence of any nonphysical substance; on this view a person is identical with his or her body. Neutral monists teach that a person is one substance that has both mental and physical characteristics.

Epiphenomenalism is a special case that does not fit easily into any other category. The epiphenomenalist views consciousness as a byproduct of the body. Thus the mind is distinct from the body, as dualists affirm, but completely a function of the body, as materialists affirm.

Materialists differ among themselves as to how to describe and explain the mental aspects of persons. Metaphysical or philosophical behaviorism (to be distinguished from methodological behaviorism) holds that the mind consists of certain types of behavior as well as tendencies to engage in behaviors. Central state materialism, or the mind-brain identity theory, holds that conscious events are not just conditioned by but are strictly identical with neurophysiological events in the brain and central nervous system. Eliminative materialism boldly denies that mind or consciousness exists. On this view a scientific description of the workings of the brain and central nervous system could in principle if not in practice replace our mentalistic language altogether.

Christians do not all hold to the same position on the mind-body problem. Most Christians traditionally have been dualists, and many still are. Some contemporary Christian thinkers have attempted to develop dualistic views that do justice to the unity of the person and body and do not devalue the body in Platonic fashion. In general anyone who believes in an intermediate state after death, in which a person continues to exist prior to the resurrection, is committed to dualism. Other Christians are more drawn to forms of neutral monism or nonreductionistic materialism, which make life after death depend completely on a bodily resurrection (Reichenbach, 1978).

Personal Identity over Time. Over the course of a lifetime persons change enormously, both intellectually and physically. In what sense, then, can a person be said to be the *same* person at one point in time that he or she was at some earlier point in time? Unless a good answer to this question can be given, it would seem wrong to punish or reward a person for some past action. Surely one is not generally responsible for actions performed by a dif-

ferent person. The choice of criteria for personal identity also has a crucial bearing on the possibility of life after death, for these criteria express our beliefs about how much and in what ways a person can change and still remain the same person. For example, could a person leave his or her body and still remain the same person? Could he or she receive a new body?

Several different views of personal identity have been defended. One of the most prominent is the memory theory, which was put forward by Locke. In this view a person is identical with a past person if he or she has memories of that person's actions and experiences. One major difficulty with this theory is that to remember myself doing some past action presupposes that I am identical with that person rather than accounts for that identity. A second theory proposes bodily continuity as the criterion of personal identity. This position obviously rules out any possibility of life after the death of the body.

Dualists who believe that the self is a conscious soul that, though embodied, is not identical with its body handle this issue differently. From the dualistic perspective, since the self is a metaphysical reality, a resurrected person can be the same person, even though the body is new, so long as the new body is possessed by the same self or soul. Christians who are nondualists must argue that bodily similarities and memory experiences would be sufficient to regard a resurrected person as the same individual.

Theory of Action. Correlated with the distinction between persons and mere things is the distinction between actions and mere events. If a rock rolls down a hillside and crushes a car, it makes sense to ask what caused the event. However, if a person pushes a rock down a hillside onto a car, it makes sense to ask who did it and to inquire about the meaning of the action. In the case of the action it is not obvious that the action is caused in the way in which mere events are caused, for most human beings believe that at least some of their actions are freely chosen. Making sense of this distinction between actions and mere events has generated a great deal of discussion, which is still largely unresolved. Among the most debated issues is the relation between reasons for action and causes. Unlike most cases of causal explanation, giving a reason for an act does not seem to render the act inevitable but rather to make the act intelligible. One can know the reason for an act without knowing any relevant causal law. Reasons also serve to justify as well as explain actions in a way that ordinary causal explanations do not. Despite these differences between reasons and ordinary causes, reasons do seem to serve as motives, and it is widely held that they must therefore serve as causes in some sense.

Closely related to this dispute about action is the traditional debate over freedom and determinism. Three classical positions on this issue continue to have adherents. The determinist insists that all human actions have antecedent conditions that necessitate their occurrence and that freedom of the will is an illusion grounded in ignorance of the casual factors. The libertarian, or advocate of free will, claims that at least some human actions, usually those involving rational reflection or moral effort, are not completely determined by their antecedent conditions. This position is easily caricatured. The libertarian admits that not all human behavior is free and that even free choices are limited by the past but insists, however mysterious it may seem, that human persons are not completely a product of their past.

The compatibilist believes that freedom and determinism must both be accepted. This is possible if freedom is defined as acting in accordance with one's own wants or preferences, yet those preferences are seen as causally determined. On this view a free action is one that is shaped by the person's internal wants and is not compelled or coerced by an external factor. Libertarians object to this on the grounds that the compatibilist view reduces to determinism. Libertarians claim that since the compatibilist admits that our wants are ultimately caused by external factors, this implies that even in the case of uncoerced acts the ultimate responsibility for an action always rests outside the individual. To the libertarian a person can be held morally responsible for an action only if he could have done otherwise, even given his or her history.

The debates about personhood have a particular significance to Christians. Not only do Christians believe that human beings have an eternal destiny, but also they believe that God himself, the ultimate reality and ground of everything else real, is a person. Many twentieth-century theists have termed their whole philosophy personalism. For the theist, to explore the nature of personhood is to plumb the depths of the whole of reality, and the unique characteristics that demarcate human persons from other creatures must be seen as forming the image of God in people, an image that has been defaced but not obliterated.

References

Macmurray, J. (1957). *The self as agent.* New York: Harper & Row.
Reichenbach, B. (1978). *Is man the phoenix?* Grand Rapids, MI: Christian University Press.
Skinner, B. F. (1971). *Beyond freedom and dignity.* New York: Knopf.
Strawson, P. F. (1959). *Individuals: An essay in descriptive metaphysics.* London: Methuen.
Watson, J. B. (1930). *Behaviorism* (3rd ed.). Chicago: University of Chicago Press.

Additional Readings

Allport, G. W. (1955). *Becoming.* New Haven, CT: Yale University Press.
Berofsky, B. (Ed.). (1966). *Free will and determinism.* New York: Harper and Row.
Bertocci, P. A. (1970). *The person God is.* New York: Humanities.

Borst, C. V. (Ed.). (1970). *The mind-brain identity theory.* New York: St. Martin's.
Evans, C. S. (1977). *Preserving the person.* Downers Grove, IL: InterVarsity.
Penelhum, T. (1967). Personal identity. In P. Edwards (Ed.), *The encyclopedia of philosophy.* New York: Macmillan.
Ryle, G. (1949). *The concept of mind.* New York: Hutchinson's University Library.
Shaffer, J. (1968). *Philosophy of mind.* Englewood Cliffs, NJ: Prentice-Hall.

C. S. Evans

See SELF.

Personology Theory. A distinct tradition in the field of personality concerned with the study of whole persons rather than with more molecular aspects or views of personality. It is associated with Henry Alexander Murray and to a lesser degree Gordon Allport. For Murray personology is "the branch of psychology which principally concerns itself with the study of human lives and the factors that influence their course, which investigates individual differences and types of personality; . . . the science of men, taken as gross units" (Murray, 1938, p. 4). History and biology play major roles.

The personological approach examines the life history of the individual, including traits, needs, and situations. In its approach personology is a field theory that takes into account the interaction of person and environment as a determinant of behavior. The focus is on a comprehensive understanding of an individual.

Murray's personology was a prototype taxonomy of organismic and environmental influences on behavior. These organismic and environmental factors defined Murray's theory as a motivational one. Behavior is motivated by viscerogenic (primary) and psychogenic (secondary) needs. The former represent the impact of organismic survival tendencies, most of which are innate (e.g., need for air, water, food). Murray also included some less familiar survival needs such as "noxavoidance," the need to rid oneself of noxious stimulation by withdrawing or vomiting, and "sentience," the desire for sensuous gratifications as exemplified in thumb sucking and carrying one's security blanket (Murray, 1938, p. 78). The focus of viscerogenic needs is restoring homeostasis to the organism.

The psychogenic needs represent the social survival motives. They may reflect social habits or rituals of interaction. Murray listed 28 psychogenic needs, including the need for abasement, achievement (*see* Achievement, Need for), affiliation, aggression, autonomy, defendance, deference, dominance, exhibition, nurturance, order, play, rejection, and succorance.

Influenced by Sigmund Freud, Murray conceived of psychogenic needs as being latent (i.e., unconscious underlying determinants) or manifest (i.e., evidences in overt behavior). Murray (1943) developed the Thematic Apperception Test (TAT) to assess latent motives, while the Edwards Personal Preference Schedule (EPPS) measures manifest motives (Edwards, 1959).

Press was Murray's term for the impact of environment on the individual. "The press of an object is what it can *do to the subject* or *for the subject*—the power that it has to affect the well-being of the subject in one way or another" (Murray, 1938, p. 121). A press then is an environmental stimulus that motivates behavior. Press can be categorized as a fact of objective reality or a subjective, phenomenological interpretation. In the former case it is termed an alpha press; the latter is designed a beta press. When a wide divergence occurs between a specific alpha press and its beta correspondent, a delusion is said to exist. Press may take on various forms (e.g., danger or misfortune, lack or loss, rejection, birth of a sibling). Often a need emerges as a reaction to a press.

Temporal units are employed in the analysis of person-situation interactions. A single need-press unit constitutes a thema. When a particular thema occurs with great frequency or intensity, especially in infancy, an underlying pattern or habit develops that gives consistency to behavior; this unity thema serves as a central trait as in risk taking or shyness.

Murray's personology was influenced by Gestalt psychology (i.e., field theory) in its use of molar units. Patterns of themas combine to form larger behavioral sequences known as serials. Serials constitute the basic datum of the personologist in analyzing personality. Proceedings are sequences of serials leading to the achievement of goals, similar to scenes and acts in drama.

Murray's view of personality built on the depth psychology of Freud and Alfred Adler. Murray conceived of the id as a repository of primitive instincts and unacceptable impulses but thought it also possesses socially acceptable impulses. The ego inhibits and represses the negative impulses but facilitates the positive ones. The superego develops from cultural conditioning and serves as an internalized regulation system. Closely associated with the superego is the ego ideal, which represents personal ambitions and aspirations.

Prenatal and early childhood experiences contribute substantially to personality. When an early experience makes a clear and marked effect on later behavior, those experiences constitute a complex. The claustral complex embodies a wish to return to prebirth conditions, to seek protection and nurturance. The fear of insupport complex is seen in fear of open places, loss of family, or falling. Behavior designed to escape to fresh air and open places, to avoid suffocation, emanates from the egression complex.

Murray's study of personality was devoted to the whole person, including the individual's history and biology (Kluckhorn, Murray, & Schneider, 1953). The brain is the site of personality, because to Murray personality is not possible if the individual lacks a brain. Brain activity is a regnant process prerequisite for personality functioning. His personology anticipated recent research that has linked personal motives with situational demands (i.e., interactionism).

References

Edwards, A. L. (1959). *Manual for Edwards Personal Preference Schedule* (Rev. ed.). New York: Psychological Corporation.

Kluckhorn, C., Murray, H. A., & Schneider, D. M. (1953). *Personality in nature, society, and culture* (2nd ed.). New York: Knopf.

Murray, H. A. (1938). *Exploration in personality.* New York: Wiley.

Murray, H. A. (1943). *Thematic Apperception Test manual.* Cambridge, MA: Harvard University Press.

R. L. TIMPE

See NEEDS.

Persuasion. *See* BRAINWASHING; COMPLIANCE.

Pervasive Developmental Disorders. The global term *pervasive developmental disorders* refers to a cluster of autisticlike diagnoses marked by severe impairments evident in the first years of life. Particularly incapacitating are abnormalities in language and communication skills, disinterest in social interaction, and preference for repetitive behaviors. These children experience significant deficits in cognitive development, typically presenting with various levels of mental retardation. Although the exact mechanisms have yet to be clearly identified, these disorders are likely caused by significant central nervous system damage. Alternatively these disorders have at times been seen as variants of schizophrenia, in which the early onset of psychotic symptoms preclude the development of ego functioning and adaptive skills.

The *DSM-IV* category of pervasive developmental disorders includes autistic disorder, along with less well-known syndromes that have been identified with distinctive symptoms and clinical courses. Rett's disorder is marked by deceleration of head growth and loss of purposeful hand skills sometime after the age of five months, even though all developmental indices have been within normal limits up until that time. Rett's disorder has been diagnosed thus far only in females and progresses into difficulties with coordination of trunk and gait, along with severe or profound mental retardation. Childhood disintegrative disorder, also referred to as Heller's syndrome, dementia infantilis, or disintegrative psychosis, is marked by a severe regression in all skills following a period of at least two years of normal development. Impaired social functioning and repetitive behavioral patterns are evident in Aspberger's disorder but without clinically significant delays in language acquisition or cognitive development. The terms *atypical autism* or *pervasive developmental disorder NOS* (not otherwise specified) are used when children do not fully meet diagnostic criteria by virtue of age of onset, atypical symptomatology, or subthreshold symptoms. These disorders are lifelong in duration and individuals with any of the pervasive developmental disorders require extensive care and support services throughout their lives.

H. Bray-Garretson

Pessimism. A negative cognitive mindset about life's outcomes. Though it is heavily influenced by particular situational factors, researchers maintain that pessimism is also a general state reflecting an underlying disposition across time and situations. There are two general approaches to defining and measuring pessimism.

The first approach to defining and measuring pessimism is to view it as a dispositional quality (Scheier & Carver, 1985). This approach, although it is represented in the literature more through pessimism's counterpart, optimism, suggests that a dispositional sense of pessimism is based on a person's generalized outcome expectancy. That is, a broad range of outcomes should be influenced by a general expectation that is related to more than one behavioral domain. Thus, when they are confronted with a behavioral task, pessimists approach the task influenced by a general assumption that bad things can and will happen. Scheier and Carver (1985) have developed the Life Orientation Test that measures both a general optimistic and pessimistic orientation.

The second approach to defining and measuring pessimism suggests that pessimism is an appraisal pattern of the causes of events, especially negative events, in one's life (Peterson, 1991; Peterson, Seligman, & Vaillant, 1988). This approach suggests that some people maintain a pessimistic explanatory style by attributing bad events in one's life to stable, global, and internal personal characteristics (also *see* Learned Helplessness). The Attributional Style Questionnaire measures how people respond to both positive and negative hypothetical events by asking respondents to postulate a primary cause for the events and then to rate the cause in terms of the three underlying dimensions (stability, globality, and internality).

Research (Peterson, Seligman, & Vaillant, 1988) shows that a pessimistic explanatory style is related to physical illness. Introductory students who saw negative personal experiences as stable and global were more likely to have more colds and sore throats a year later. In contrast, an optimistic outlook on life is associated with less physical illness and faster recovery from coronary bypass surgery (Sheier & Carver, 1987).

Are religious people more or less pessimistic than their less religious counterparts? There is not a conclusive answer to this question, although most intrinsically religious individuals (*see* Religious Orientation) see God as highly active, working through multiple channels, and working with or through natural causes, including one's own behavior. Hill (1995) suggests that this different attributional logic, by providing a sense of hope especially when one faces adversity, may prevent an overwhelming sense of pessimism.

References

Hill, P. C. (1995). Affective theory and religious experience. In R. W. Hood, Jr. (Ed.), *Handbook of religious experience*. Birmingham, AL: Religious Education Press.

Peterson, C. (1991). The meaning and measurement of explanatory style. *Psychological Inquiry, 2,* 1–10.

Peterson, C., Seligman, M. E. P., & Vaillant, G. E. (1988). Pessimistic explanatory style is a risk factor for physical illness: A thirty-five-year longitudinal study. *Journal of Personality and Social Psychology, 55,* 23–27.

Scheier, M. F., & Carver, C. S. (1985). Optimism, coping and health: Assessment and implications of generalized outcome expectancies. *Health Psychology, 4,* 219–247.

Scheier, M. F., & Carver, C. S. (1987). Dispositional optimism and physical well-being: The influence of generalized outcome expectancies on health. *Journal of Personality, 55,* 169–210.

P. C. Hill

See Optimism; Depression.

Pfister, Oskar Robert (1873–1956). Protestant minister and pioneer Freudian psychoanalyst. He was cofounder of the Swiss Society for Psychoanalysis and remained a loyal follower of Sigmund Freud even during the interim in which the group disbanded (1914–1919) and the others turned to Carl Gustav Jung.

Pfister's father, a liberal Swiss Protestant minister, died while attending medical school, preparing himself for a medical ministry to the parish poor. From an early age Oskar identified with the poor in spirit, the troubled and abused, particularly children who were victimized by the neurotic behavior and rigid regimentation of their schoolmasters. He integrated his perceptions of divine and human love with a grasp of personality development derived from psychoanalysis. From this integration he devised his technique of "psychoanalytic paedegogik," a method of psychoanalytic education for children. Testimony to its importance is its impetus and foundation for Anna Freud's child and adolescent psychoanalysis.

Pfister also turned his attention to the "hygiene of religion," by which he meant a two-way interaction between religion and mental hygiene. His approach emphasized the healing force of religion in human development and life as well as the cleansing and clarifying power of psychoanalytic insight in ridding religion of soul-scarring aberrations. He took pains to correct what he deemed to be misinterpretations of the gospel and to scourge the theologies and moralisms of the church fathers, the

Roman Catholic church, and the Reformers. He was particularly hard on Calvin, gentler with Luther.

Pfister found that graduate studies in the academic psychology of his time offered little help in pastoral work and the cure of souls. Least of all did it assist him with the children in his parish. For him the newly developed psychoanalysis became the answer to his quest for a means through which to express the love of Christ actively. It became not only a technique in fulfilling his Christian aspirations for his ministry but also a way of life for him. Praising Pfister's 1917 publication of *The Psychoanalytic Method,* Freud wrote that such a book "will . . . be able to count on the gratitude of later generations" (Zulliger, 1966, p. 175). Meng, a Swiss psychoanalytic colleague, commented further: "The new psychology awakened in him the clarity of thought and sensitivity of empathy which enabled him to learn the language of demons and gods in the unconscious, and which simultaneously made possible to bring to life the meaning and language of the Bible, without dogma and in the service of pastoral care" (Zulliger, 1966, pp. 175–176).

Pfister managed to conduct his psychoanalytic, theological, and educational explorations while fulfilling duties as preacher, pastor, and administrator of the Prediger Church (Zwinglian) in Zurich. Having met Freud in Vienna in 1909, he maintained a lifelong friendship through visits and correspondence (134 letters exchanged between 1908 and 1937). Some 300 of Pfister's journal entries testify to the fruitfulness of the interaction between these two minds.

Reference

Zulliger, H. (1966). Oskar Pfister: Psychoanalysis and faith. In F. Alexander, S. Eisenstein, & M. Grotjahn (Eds.), *Psychoanalytic pioneers.* New York: Basic.

Additional Readings

Brown, S. H. (1981). A look at Oskar Pfister and his relationship to Sigmund Freud. *The Journal of Pastoral Care, 35,* 220–233.

Meng, H., & Freud, F. (Eds.). (1963). *Psychoanalysis and faith: The letters of Sigmund Freud and Oskar Pfister.* New York: Basic.

Pfister, O. R. (1948). *Christianity and fear: A study in history and in the psychology and hygiene of religion.* New York: Macmillan.

E. A. Loomis, Jr.

See Psychoanalytic Psychology; Psychology of Religion.

Phallic Stage. According to Sigmund Freud, the third major stage of a child's psychological development. It lasts from approximately 30 months to 7 years.

See Psychosexual Development.

Phantom Response. A delusional perception of the presence of any body part subsequent to its removal or loss. The most common and best described and understood of the phantom phenomena is that of an amputated limb or digit. Less frequently the loss of nose, eyes, teeth, breasts, penis, or other body parts can result in a phantom percept. Not only is this response common, it is also considered to be healthy and appropriate as an immediate reaction to such a sudden loss. However, it can proceed to pathological proportions and has been reported to persist as long as 20 years after the surgery.

A phantom limb or digit is a generally universal response to amputation and is estimated to occur in as many as 98% of such surgical cases. This phantom is generally painless and exists for a period of time in one's perception of body image before fading. In proportionately few cases the phantom may be experienced as painful and necessitate various therapeutic interventions. Breast phantoms, usually in response to mastectomies for breast cancer, are less frequent, occurring in 22% to 64% of the cases (Simmel, 1966).

The phantom delusion usually involves an initial awareness being on the distal (or outerly) part such as foot or hand. The sensory impression of the phantom generally consists of three general types: mild tingling; momentary, more pronounced pins and needles, often triggered by touching the stump; and unpleasant sensations of burning, twisting, itching, or a variety of other disturbing feelings. The phantom percept is generally intermittent, and the associated sensations are ties to this awareness, being felt only when the phantom is experienced.

The phantom is initially experienced as a whole, but this perception is generally modified by experience through time. It gradually becomes more faintly perceived and the awareness fades away, first proximally (closest to the body), then toward the distal. Thus there can be a period of confused body image when the percept neither matches the original state nor mirrors the true altered state. The distal part sometimes feels as if it were directly attached to the body, as in hand to shoulder, and sometimes as if a space exists between the body and the part. This collapsing in subjective perception over time is called telescoping and generally occurs in the natural course of the phantom response.

Supportive therapy focused toward the larger issue of loss is generally sufficient for the natural adaptation to occur. However, psychological resistance to this process, frequently related to anger and strong resentment, may necessitate more active psychotherapy. The occurrence of painful phantom phenomena often warrants various approaches, including direct intromission of anesthetic locally to the stump, hypnosis for analgesia, or more extensive psychotherapies.

Reference

Simmel, M. L. (1966). A study of phantoms after amputation of the breast. *Neuropsychology, 4,* 337–350.

G. Matheson

Phenomenological Psychology. An attitude and an approach; an attitude of respect for the dignity and integrity of each person's experience and an approach or a methodology for studying the personal meanings of experience. The context for such study is collaboration and trust rather than manipulation and deception. The results of a psychological investigation utilizing a phenomenological method are qualitative descriptions of the personal meanings of particular experiences. These differ significantly in content as well as form from the results of more traditional psychological research—quantitative analyses of impersonal measurements of behavior.

Phenomenological psychology can be viewed as primarily a critique of the more established schools of psychology, a corrective to some of the emphases and methods of contemporary psychology, or an alternative psychological methodology in and of itself. This article presents a concise discussion of each view, preceded by a brief look at the historical development of phenomenological psychology and some of its central concepts

Historical Development. The dominant figure in the early development of the phenomenological movement was the philosopher Edmund Husserl, during the first third of the twentieth century. The term *phenomenology*, however, was coined much earlier, in the middle of the eighteenth century, and has since been applied in a variety of directions. The direction that Husserl chose was heavily influenced by another European, Franz Brentano, generally regarded as the main forerunner of the phenomenological movement. The most thorough and competent review of the predominantly European and philosophical side of the phenomenological movement is the two-volume work of Spiegelberg (1969).

A clear distinction must be made between phenomenological psychology and phenomenological philosophy, even though they have many similarities and common inheritances. Misiak and Sexton (1973) have compiled an excellent survey of the development of the psychological side of the phenomenological movement, as has Spiegelberg (1972). Of particular note are the first contribution of a systematic phenomenological psychology to the American psychological literature (Snygg & Combs, 1949) and the first major American symposium on phenomenological psychology, with such notable participants as Sigmund Koch, Robert MacLeod, Carl Rogers, and B. F. Skinner (Wann, 1964).

Also of importance are the highly original and significant works of the French scholar Maurice Merleau-Ponty, especially in the area of perception, and the development of the psychology department of Duquesne University in Pittsburgh, Pennsylvania. Psychologists at Duquesne and several of their graduates have made diverse and substantial contributions to the ever-developing literature. In 1971 they founded the successful *Journal of Phenomenological Psychology*. The journal's stated policy characterizes well the emphasis of contemporary phenomenological psychology: "This journal is dedicated to the aim of approaching psychology in such a way that the entire range of experience and behavior of man as a human person may be properly studied. The priority is placed on the fidelity to the phenomenon of man as a whole and all aspects that are studied must be mindful of their human relatedness. The challenge facing us is to invent methods and other types of analyses that will unveil significant aspects of man's relatedness to himself, others and the world."

Central Concepts. There have been several attempts to list the central concepts of phenomenological psychology. Among the clearest are the works of Merleau-Ponty (1969) and Giorgi (1976). A complete listing would have to include at least the following.

Description. A phenomenological study aims to describe rather than explain, to understand how rather than why. The goal is to provide reliable guideposts for others to be able to understand their own similar experience. Applied in a Christian context, personal testimonies, for example, would provide guideposts to help others better understand their own experience of God.

Bracketing. In order for a description to be faithful to what someone has experienced instead of what he or she perhaps should have experienced, one needs temporarily to leave aside (bracket) questions of reality, truth, and cause and any other personal biases. This does not involve valueless tolerance, but it does involve tolerance of ambiguity. That is, can I stand not knowing something for sure or not letting someone else know that I know for sure? Can I temporarily leave aside what I know will impede the revelation of experience?

Meaning. A phenomenological description is a detailed account of what a particular experience means to someone. It portrays the significance or value of the experience plus the details of what it was like or how it was for that person. Applied to interpersonal communication, for example, to share with you how I value our interaction—what you are like for me, how I feel about you—is to tell you what you mean to me.

Experience. It can be said that meaning is to experience as measurement is to behavior. This highlights the difference between experience, the focus of phenomenological psychology, and behavior, the focus of behavioristic psychology. Whereas a phenomenological description relies on verbal and nonverbal behavior, the importance of the behavior is that it represents the underlying experience. Behavior can in varying degrees represent or misrepresent the experience—what the person really means—so the job of phenomenological psychology is to devise methods to facilitate the accurate representation of experience by self-report behavior.

Phenomenal Worlds. Experience is composed phenomenologically of phenomenal worlds and intentionality. Phenomenal worlds are the reflective organization or structure, the rationality, the individualized perceptions, feelings, and meanings that people refer to as reality, or at least reality as they see it. This is consciousness, which is often spoken of as the object of the phenomenologist's study.

Intentionality. The prereflective, nonrational part of experience is called intentionality. This is the preverbal tending or orienting toward something that we then become consciously aware of. It is our spontaneous, bodily involvement in a situation before we have words for it. For example, one may break out in a cold sweat while talking with a friend and not have any idea why. Or one may be prayerful without uttering words. This is the realm of the unconscious and is an integral part of human experience. As such it is crucial for understanding what a person means and what a person knows. The apostle Paul may not have been able adequately to put it into words, but he knew the love of Christ (Eph. 3:19) and knew the peace of God (Phil. 4:7) that passed his mental understanding.

Phenomenological Psychology as Critique. Perhaps the greatest impact of phenomenological psychology to date has been its critique of mainline psychology. Central to the critique is calling into question the professionally orthodox belief in emotionless, uninvolved abstraction from detached observation—the belief that third-person information is more accurate, more objective, than first-person information. This could be called the myth of immaculate perception. Maslow (1966) calls it "spectator knowledge," or peeping at people through keyholes rather than being in their worlds.

To be truly objective one must participate with the other person. One must be sufficiently involved to be in contact with how the specific individual (object) qualities of the other person present themselves and with the feeling and drama of the situation. This will of necessity involve dialogue rather than deception and help build trust rather than mistrust.

The basic issue is whether psychology is exclusively a natural science founded on an unbending belief in detached observation, experimental manipulation, and statistical analysis and the assumption that the subject is merely a passive respondent. Or is it also a human science, founded on belief in participant observation, experiential collaboration, and description of personal meanings, and the assumption that the coinvestigator is an active participant in the research process (see Giorgi, 1970)?

The pressing need for the development of psychology as a human science is indicated by the continuing treatment of persons as objects and personal feelings and meanings as error. Human persons are being assigned "to the same ontological status as weather, stars, minerals, or lower forms of animal life" (Jourard, 1972, p. 7). Psychologists are making molehills out of mountains, making the

person over into the image of their childhood erector sets (May, 1967).

Phenomenological Psychology as Corrective. The consequence of having a choice between psychology as a natural science and a human science is that there is an unavoidable trade-off between rigor on the one hand and relevance on the other. To avoid having precision at the expense of significance some psychologists have utilized a phenomenological method as a preliminary step in generating hypotheses to be tested later experimentally. MacLeod in particular championed this approach. Others have developed phenomenologically oriented procedures as correctives to the experiment itself.

The most radical corrective is to take the entire psychological study out of the laboratory—removing manipulation from the methodology—as a supplementary field test for the laboratory findings. This is a type of naturalistic observation (Willems & Rausch, 1969).

Two important correctives deal with the persistent findings that the personality of the scientist can be a biasing factor in the experiment and that the subject often responds more to personal agenda and environmental distractions in the experimental situations than to the verbatim instructions. Bakan (1967), for example, points out that the personality type of the experimenter can determine the choice of the statistical test of significance and thereby bias the results. In addition Rosenthal (1966) warns of experimenter bias, or the unintended communication to subjects by supposedly neutral, uninvolved experimenters of expectations regarding the outcome of the experiment. In both cases awareness of the potential problem can serve in and of itself as a corrective, although Rosenthal also proposes detailed solutions to the expectancy problem.

Concerning the not-so-passive subject, several studies have revealed a wide variety of role enactments determined by the subjects' preconceptions, motives, and suspicions (Weber & Cook, 1972). Orne (1970) has also discovered the pervasive effects of demand characteristics, or the environmental cues that create compelling expectations and demands on the subject. Orne's double corrective of the preexperimental inquiry and postexperimental interview helps with the problem of role enactments as well as that of demand characteristics.

Phenomenological Psychology as Alternative. As a complete methodology in and of itself phenomenological psychology does not try to control but rather utilizes the effects of the personality of the experimenter and the active participation of the subject. The process is called a coinvestigation and is based on dialogue.

A phenomenological study ideally begins in silence with an attitude of wonder, of quiet, inquisitive respect. It proceeds inductively from dialogue between the coinvestigators to facilitate the self-report of an experience, to extraction of related meaning—themes—from the self-report data, back to dialogue for a check on the accuracy of the themes, to an exhaustive description that combines the relevant themes into a concise statement, and finally back to a dialogue for an evaluation of how well the description represents the original self-report and any modification that may be needed. The product is a rich description of experience as it is lived.

Representative studies would begin with van Kaam's (1966) study of the experience of feeling understood and include Stevick's (1971) investigation of the experience of anger, Keen's (1975) study of a five-year-old changing her mind, and Colaizzi's (1977) research into the process of existential change occasioned by reading. Although these four studies adequately portray the diversity of methods within phenomenological psychology, each is significantly less than ideal in fully incorporating dialogue into its methodology.

The phenomenological approach should also prove useful in helping us understand religious experience by inquiring directly into the experience itself rather than checking the Bible to see if it is legitimate (Farnsworth, 1981). In terms of attitude, respecting how people present themselves has definite application to the Christian life. It means being nonjudgmental: "Does our law condemn anyone without first hearing him to find out what he is doing?" (John 7:51, NIV); "Everyone should be quick to listen, slow to speak" (James 1:19, NIV); "He who answers before listening—that is his folly and his shame" (Prov. 18:13, NIV).

References

Bakan, D. (1967). *On method: Toward a reconstruction of psychological investigation.* San Francisco: Jossey-Bass.

Colaizzi, P. F. (1977). *Psychological research as the phenomenologist views it.* In R. S. Valle & M. King (Eds.), *Existential-phenomenological alternatives for psychology.* Baltimore: Williams & Wilkins.

Farnsworth, K. E. (1981). *Integrating psychology and theology: Elbows together but hearts apart.* Washington, DC: University Press of America.

Giorgi, A. (1970). *Psychology as a human science: A phenomenologically based approach.* New York: Harper & Row.

Giorgi, A. (1976). Phenomenology and the foundations of psychology. In J. K. Cole & W. J. Arnold (Eds.), *Nebraska symposium on motivation* (Vol. 23). Lincoln: University of Nebraska Press.

Jourard, S. M. (1972). A humanistic revolution in psychology. In A. G. Miller (Ed.), *The social psychology of psychological research.* New York: Free Press.

Keen, E. (1975). *A primer in phenomenological psychology.* New York: Holt, Rinehart, & Winston.

Maslow, A. H. (1966). *The psychology of science: A reconnaissance.* New York: Harper & Row.

May, R. (1967). *Psychology and the human dilemma.* Princeton, NJ: Van Nostrand.

Merleau-Ponty, M. (1969). What is phenomenology? In J. D. Bettis (Ed.), *Phenomenology of religion: Eight modern descriptions of the essence of religion.* New York: Harper & Row.

Misiak, H., & Sexton, V. S. (1973). *Phenomenological, existential, and humanistic psychologies: A historical survey.* New York: Grune & Stratton.

Orne, M. T. (1970). Hypnosis, motivation, and the ecological validity of the psychological experiment. In W. J. Arnold & M. M. Page (Eds.), *Nebraska symposium on motivation* (Vol. 18). Lincoln: University of Nebraska Press.

Rosenthal, R. (1966). *Experimenter effects in behavioral research.* New York: Appleton-Century-Crofts.

Snygg, D., & Combs, A. W. (1949). *Individual behavior: A new frame of reference for psychology.* New York: Harper & Row.

Spiegelberg, H. (1969). *The phenomenological movement: A historical introduction* (2 vols.). (2nd ed.). The Hague: Nijhoff.

Spiegelberg, H. (1972). *Phenomenology in psychology and psychiatry.* Evanston, IL: Northwestern University Press.

Stevick, E. L. (1971). An empirical investigation of the experience of anger. In A. Giorgi, W. F. Fischer, & R. Von Eckartsberg (Eds.), *Duquesne studies in phenomenological psychology* (Vol. 1). Pittsburgh, PA: Duquesne University Press.

van Kaam, A. (1966). *Existential foundations of psychology.* Pittsburgh, PA: Duquesne University Press.

Wann, T. W. (Ed.). (1964). *Behaviorism and phenomenology: Contrasting bases for modern psychology.* Chicago: University of Chicago Press.

Weber, S. J., & Cook, T. D. (1972). Subject effects in laboratory research: An examination of subject roles, demand characteristics, and valid inference. *Psychological Bulletin, 77,* 273–295.

Willems, E. P., & Rausch, H. L. (Eds.). (1969). *Naturalistic viewpoints in psychological research.* New York: Holt, Rinehart, & Winston.

K. E. FARNSWORTH

Phenomenological Therapy. A form of therapy emphasizing description rather than explanation. Psychotherapies are most often constructed around what each one regards as the essential explanation of the therapeutic process. Such explanations, however, typically reduce the phenomenon of psychotherapy to theoretical abstractions that are something less than or at least different from the therapeutic process as it is experienced by its participants. For the behavior therapist, for example, therapy works because of the application of selective reinforcement. For the person-centered or client-centered therapist the key explanation is unconditional positive regard. For the psychoanalyst it is transference.

The phenomenological therapist asks how, not why. An attempt is made to understand how the client experiences his or her body, self, space, time, and relationships (Keen, 1976). Phenomenological therapy is as much an attitude as it is a method (*see* Phenomenological Psychology). It is an attitude of respect for the client's experience and of distrust of theoretical conclusions about that experience. It is a suspension of clinical judgment until after the experience, however abnormal it may be, has thoroughly presented itself (Van den Berg, 1955).

Phenomenological Therapy

Phenomenological therapy historically had no distinct beginning, because as part of the more general phenomenological movement it has usually been an applied afterthought of the phenomenological research process. From a new depth of understanding of the human condition has come a new desire to help people experiencing psychological pain. Consequently, there is no such thing as phenomenological therapy as in the sense of a complete set of techniques and procedures.

Rather, there are many therapies that either implicitly or explicitly rely on the phenomenological attitude in the client-therapist encounter, interpersonal strategies that can be applied from phenomenological research (van Kaam, 1966; Zinker, 1977), and/or phenomenologically derived conclusions regarding human psychopathology (Fischer, 1970; Keen, 1970). Thus, it is useful to show, as Spiegelberg (1972) has done, the degree to which such therapists as Rollo May (existential therapy), Carl Rogers (person-centered therapy), Victor Frankl (Logotherapy), Boss (Daseinsanalysis), and Fritz Perls (Gestalt Therapy) are or were phenomenological. In order to do so, one must draw on appropriate historical figures in the phenomenological movement, such as Karl Jaspers, Ludwig Binswanger, F. J. J. Buytendijk, Kurt Goldstein, and Paul Schilder.

A completely phenomenological therapy would have to align itself with the work of historical and contemporary phenomenologists to prevent inauthentic detours. Rogers, for example, assumes that the job of the therapist is to provide an atmosphere for and not interfere with the natural unfolding of the "organismic self" of the client; this is based on the further assumption that feelings are most important in human functioning. He then assumes that the therapeutic process can be studied by means of pre- and posttherapy tests and measurement by outside observers of the in-therapy behaviors of client and therapist. This is clearly at odds with the consensus of phenomenological understanding that suspends such beliefs as the existence of an organismic self that naturally unfolds in a world awash in feelings (Barton, 1974) and calls for direct interrogation of the experience of both therapist and client rather than relying on extratherapy tests and the judgments of external observers (Smith, 1971).

Rogers does, however, bring a significant phenomenological emphasis to his therapy. Barton (1974) argues that the task of the phenomenological therapist is to express as faithfully as possible only those meanings, feelings, sensings, and interpretations that are given by the client. "Within client-centered practice, this dwelling on the face-presentation, of not leaping to the theoretical, explanatory, or high-level interpretive ideas, is lived out in a faithful, plodding dwelling within what the client says" (p. 266).

Gendlin (1966), an early follower of Rogers, takes this even further when he states that the therapeutic change "occurs not from more exact revelation of how the patient is and came to be as he is, not from more and more fully showing him that he must be as he is. . . . It comes from making this now ongoing relationship into a new and different concrete life experience for him, a kind of experiencing he could not be, and was not, until now" (p. 213).

Phenomenological therapy offers exciting possibilities for the Christian. An attitude of respectful and nonjudgmental listening combined with shared experiences, such as praying together (Farnsworth, 1975), representing a faithful living out of the client's expressed needs, can be tremendously freeing.

References

Barton, A. (1974). *Three worlds of therapy: An existential-phenomenological study of the therapies of Freud, Jung, and Rogers.* Palo Alto, CA: National Press Books.

Farnsworth, K. E. (1975). Despair that restores. *Psychotherapy: Theory, Research and Practice, 12,* 44–47.

Fischer, W. F. (1970). *Theories of anxiety.* New York: Harper & Row.

Gendlin, E. T. (1966). Existentialism and experiential psychotherapy. In C. Moustakas (Ed.), *The child's discovery of himself.* New York: Ballantine.

Keen, E. (1970). *Three faces of being: Toward an existential clinical psychology.* New York: Appleton-Century-Crofts.

Keen, E. (1976). Confrontation and support: On the world of psychotherapy. *Psychotherapy: Theory, Research and Practice, 13,* 308–315.

Smith, D. L. (1971). Phenomenological psychotherapy: A why and a how. In A. Giori, R. Knowles, & D. L. Smith (Eds.), *Duquesne studies in phenomenological psychology* (Vol. 3). Pittsburgh, PA: Duquesne University Press.

Spiegelberg, H. (1972). *Phenomenology in psychology and psychiatry.* Evanston, IL: Northwestern University Press.

Van den Berg, J. H. (1955). *The phenomenological approach to psychiatry.* Springfield, IL: Thomas.

van Kaam, A. (1966). *The art of existential counseling.* Wilkes-Barre, PA: Dimension.

Zinker, J. (1977). *Creative process in Gestalt therapy.* New York: Brunner/Mazel.

K. E. FARNSWORTH

See COUNSELING AND PSYCHOTHERAPY: OVERVIEW.

Phenylketonuria. A congenital metabolic disorder, phenylketonuria (PKU) results from the inability of the body to convert phenylalanine, an essential amino acid. Ten to 25 times the normal amount of phenylalanine is found in the blood and urine, causing severe mental deficiency. The average victim has an intelligence quotient below 20. The disorder appears in infancy and is transmitted by a recessive gene in 1 in 10,000 births. One-third of the cases have eczema and convulsions. The majority are undersized and light complexioned, with coarse features and small heads. The typical PKU child is hyperactive and unpredictable and may be incapable of verbal and nonverbal communication. The disorder was discovered in 1934 by Folling, and research in the 1950s found an early diagnosis (prior to six months of age) and treatment with a low phenylalanine diet could result in significant improvements for the PKU infant.

D. L. SCHUURMAN

See MENTAL RETARDATION.

Philosophical Psychology. A point of view that cuts across all schools of psychology. Its importance is to be seen in the fact that one of the divisions of the American Psychological Association is expressly dedicated to philosophical psychology.

While most psychologists define themselves as scientists, practitioners, or both, much of what psychologists actually do is philosophical in nature. Their work has to do, in one way or another, with questions that are not answerable by scientific methods. Questions about the ultimate nature of reality, how the universe is fitted together and, by implication, how people fit into it, what is ethically or morally good and bad, the nature of knowledge and consciousness, the nature of beauty, and the logical consistency of conceptual systems will never be answered in the laboratory. It is impossible to perform an objective experiment and thereby come up with definitive answers to such speculative questions. One could only discover through psychological surveys what various people *think* about these questions themselves through scientific means.

Clinical services are particularly fraught with philosophical issues. For example, many clients come to psychotherapists for philosophic guidance. A person suffering from serious depression might very well be interested in the results of scientific studies that elucidate the effectiveness of various antidepressant drugs, but he or she would usually also be concerned with questions about life's meaning, whether it is worth living, and so on.

Psychotherapists who are centrally interested in these sorts of questions frequently call themselves existential therapists or existential analysts. In so doing, they acknowledge that their services are not only open to, but purposely centered upon, the philosophical concerns of their clients. Moreover, psychologists who adopt a phenomenological point of view are also often candid in admitting the philosophical nature of their clinical activities.

Great confusion has been spawned by the sloppiness with which both psychologists and lay persons have approached the definition of psychology. Many persons confuse behavioral science (research psychology) with speculative psychology (philosophical psychology), and much of what gets passed off on the public as psychology is essentially philosophy. There are, in fact, very strong and inescapable links among philosophy, theology, and psychology. Philosophical psychologists make these links their points of study—issues such as determinism and free will, personhood, self, and the mind-brain relationship.

C. W. MCLEMORE

See PSYCHOLOGY, PRESUPPOSITIONS OF; DETERMINISM AND FREE WILL.

Phobic Disorders. A phobia is an irrational fear of presumably harmless objects or situations. A phobia also occurs when the perceived danger of an object or a situation is out of proportion to the real danger. Phobic reactions vary from a moderate degree of anxiety or feeling of unpleasantness to panic levels of anxiety with accompanying physical manifestations. Particularly common but nonetheless distressing are physical symptoms, which may include palpitations and missed heartbeats; sweating, dizziness, and feeling of collapse; difficulty in breathing and expanding the chest; and difficulty in swallowing. Often psychological and emotional problems accompany these physical symptoms. These may include indecision, loss of confidence, feelings of unreality, obsessive worrying, feeling that one is "going crazy," depression, and low self-esteem.

A phobic condition so restricts an individual's life that he or she is unable to go places or do things that the person would otherwise like to do. Such a person becomes a prisoner of his or her own imaginary fortress. This provides a false sense of security in that as long as the person avoids the potentially fearful or anxiety-producing situations, anxiety will be reduced. The reduction in anxiety reinforces the avoidant behavior. The individual's futile attempt to resolve the problem by avoiding the phobic situation thus becomes the means of perpetuating the phobic condition.

In the past specific phobias derived their names from the Greek word that represented the feared object. Those ranged from acrophobia (dread of high places) to zoophobia (fear of animals). The most recent revision of the *Diagnostic and Statistical Manual of Mental Disorders (DSM-IV)* (American Psychiatric Association, 1994) has placed all phobic disorders under the general classification of anxiety disorders, which is a fairly broad umbrella of those conditions with the primary symptom of anxiety or panic. Within this broad anxiety disorder classification, phobic disorders have been separated into three categories: agoraphobia (with or without a history of panic), social phobia, and specific, formerly known as simple, phobia.

Agoraphobia is the fear of open places. However, this phobic condition may manifest itself as panic attacks (severe anxiety with accompanying physical manifestations) when one is alone, when away from home, left alone, going into stores, or any other situation where immediate help is not readily available. Some agoraphobic patients may become so terrified when confronted with such a situation that they faint.

A social phobia is the experience of intense anxiety when an individual is presented with a social situation that is perceived as potentially embarrassing or awkward. The intensity may be so great that the person shuns even family activities and reunions with relatives. The anxiety does not have to be associated with the individual's fear of doing something humiliating but may consist of a general uneasiness or awkwardness when around others. Treatment approaches with socially phobic individuals typically include training in assertiveness and social skills (*see* Assertiveness Training).

Specific phobias, in contrast to agoraphobia and social phobias, are typically monosymptomatic, meaning that the phobic condition consists of a single, fairly circumscribed object or activity. The specificity of specific phobias simplifies their treatment. The treatment of choice for simple phobias has been systematic desensitization.

The two most prominent explanations for phobic disorders have been advanced by the psychoanalytic and learning theorists. According to psychoanalytic clinicians, the phobic object or situation symbolizes an underlying unconscious conflict. The situation or object to which one is phobic is in some way associated with or represents this underlying conflict. Classical psychoanalytic thinking viewed conflicts of phobic individuals as sexual in nature, resulting from disturbances during the phallic stage of psychosexual development. Treatment entailed uncovering and confronting the unconscious conflict rather than dealing directly with the phobic object or situation.

Learning theory views phobic behavior as a result of a conditioned fear response. Such a response results when intense anxiety becomes associated with a neutral object or situation. This neutral object, which is now paired with anxiety, becomes the phobic object. Wolpe (1958) developed a procedure originally known as reciprocal inhibition, in which either relaxation, assertiveness, or sexual excitement were counterconditioned to the anxiety-producing situation. Reciprocal inhibition allows the extinction of fear to take place by preventing it from occurring in the presence of the feared object. Now known as systematic desensitization, this technique has come to be the treatment of choice for most clinicians working with simple phobias.

Multiple phobias (agoraphobias and social phobias), due to their behavior, emotional, and cognitive effects, are usually too amorphous to be eradicated solely by desensitization procedures. It may be that in multiple phobias it is not the particular external event that is feared but rather an internal state. This feared internal state may range from the thought of fainting to the thought of having a heart attack. The feared internal state then becomes generalized to many different situations. For the individual this creates a hypersensitivity and hyperarousal to be on guard and vigilant for anxiety-producing situations. This hypervigilance increases the level of anxiety, making the possibility of a panic attack greater and culminating in a vicious, self-defeating cycle.

The first step in a cognitive behavioral treatment of multiple phobias should deal specifically with decreasing or eliminating anticipatory fears. During this phase of the treatment a patient may be asked to develop a short phrase that will enable better acceptance of the symptoms. These statements are helpful in shutting off negative thought patterns and decreasing the amount of one's anxiety. The second step involves the use of relaxation to circumvent or decrease the patient's general level of anxiety. Two approaches may be used: somatic and cognitive. The somatic approach relies on deep muscle training and biofeedback in order to teach the difference between tense and relaxed states. The cognitive relaxation approach relies on having the patient visualize a calm and serene scene in his or her mind, thereby eliminating negative or fearful thoughts. This may be followed with instruction in positive self-statements and coping imagery. Such statements and images should include confronting the phobic situation and coping with the phobic reaction. The final step is the gradual approach of the phobic situation. This step involves each of the three previous steps.

References

American Psychiatric Association. (1994). *Diagnostic and statistical manual of mental disorders* (4th ed.). Washington, DC: Author.

Wolpe, J. (1958). *Psychotherapy by reciprocal inhibition.* Stanford, CA: Stanford University Press.

K. R. KRACKE

See ANXIETY; ANXIETY DISORDERS.

Phrenology. A psychologist theory originated in the early 1800s by Franz Josef Gall and based on the idea that certain mental faculties are related to specific areas of the brain. A contemporary, Johann Kaspar Spurzheim, coined the term *phrenology,* meaning literally the science of the mind. The theory asserted that personality and character traits could be judged by the location and size of bumps on the skull.

More than a superficial character-reading technique, phrenology proposed the idea that anatomy directly influences mental behavior. Some 37 localized areas of the brain were specified to contain independent and inherited regions relating to such character traits as self-esteem, conscientiousness, and spirituality. Three general character types—mental, motive, and vital—facilitated grouping of personalities. Phrenology maps were drawn to indicate the locations of particular faculties and were then used to analyze the corresponding bumps on the skull of a client.

This practice was popular in the first half of the nineteenth century and greatly influenced the treatment of mental illness. Diagnosis consisted of finding the region of the brain responsible for the illness and treating it as a physical problem, with techniques such as laxatives, exercise, rest, good food, and cutting off the blood supply. This view of mental illness as a brain disease was contrary to the popularly held belief that mental illness was a result of demon possession, and it changed such common practices in mental hospitals as exorcisms, beatings, starvation, and solitary confinement. While phrenology was later proven to be scientifically unverifiable, the theory may be credited with introducing the idea that mental phenomena can be approached scientifically and objectively.

D. L. Schuurman

See Psychology, History of.

Physical Contact in Therapy. Physical contact is among the earliest forms of communication known to humans. It also is the first meaningful interaction between mother and child. Touch conveys warmth, caring, and acceptance; it soothes and heals when it is intended as such and is accepted by the recipient.

Since human physical contact has a curative, restorative quality of its own, there is potential for use in psychotherapeutic treatment. This is especially true if therapy can in part be understood as a corrective emotional experience in which various pains from the process of maturation are relived, better understood, and integrated into the person's ego. Since touch, whether by its absence or presence, is an important part of that developmental interaction between parent and child, so too in psychotherapy physical contact is used to facilitate growth and to convey acceptance.

Historical Context. Mythology, art, tribal medicine, and historic religions have all described the importance of touch as a powerful interpersonal communication (Mintz, 1969). With mysticism and magic contaminating the rigorous demands of nineteenth-century science, Sigmund Freud perhaps had no choice but to deliberately distance his emerging theories from touch. There is evidence to suggest that Freud was uncomfortable with physical contact, as seen in his posture behind the therapeutic couch. Psychoanalytic technique historically has maintained neutrality in the therapeutic hour so that the patient's transference will develop in as uncontaminated an atmosphere as possible.

Prior to the 1970s little was written about touch in therapy (whether as an erotic or nonerotic experience) except the early writings of Ferenczi and Reich. Both broke from Freud's touch taboo and advocated physical contact as a means of enhancing progress in treatment. Reich came into public and professional disrepute by also using sexual intercourse as a therapeutic technique.

Dahlberg (1970) found widespread evidence of both nonerotic and sexual contact in therapy, as did Masters and Johnson (1970). The American Psychological Association referred to the practice as the "new morality in psychotherapy." Kardner's survey of 450 physicians from five areas of specialization revealed that roughly two-thirds believed nonerotic contact may possibly be of some value. Only 20% believed sexual contact could be helpful, and only 5% admitted having such contact with their patients (Kardner, Fuller, & Mensh, 1973). Holroyd and Brodsky (1977) found approximately the same statistics for 500 male and 500 female Ph.D. psychologists. About 27% admitted to nonerotic contact (hugging, kissing, touching); 4% admitted to genital intercourse.

Since that time a large number of articles have appeared in the professional literature, most of which have encouraged prudent, conscientious efforts at facilitating treatment by including any form of direct physical touch, but almost all have strongly advised against sexual touching of patients. In his review of the literature Pope (1990) concludes that although "severe damage" can result from sexual contact with patients, "[t]here are no published data supporting the premise that therapists who engage in non-sexual physical contact with their patients are more likely to become sexually involved with their patients" (p. 484).

Both the American Psychological Association and the American Psychiatric Association have made ethical statements against intercourse or any form of sexual exploitation within the therapeutic relationship and remind their members that the highest number of malpractice suits have involved sexual exploitation of patients.

The Purpose of Touch. Touching patients should be done only when the therapist knows what he or she is doing. That is, by virtue of professional training and experience the therapist must assess what is going on within both the patient and the therapist before deciding to make physical contact. Touch is a service to be given; it is not something to be taken. It should spring from a desire to help, comfort, encourage, and reassure. Touching is used to share genuine joy and the enthusiasm of celebration. It reminds both parties of their humanness. Touching allows a parental kind of loving care to be displayed for both preverbal infantile needs and childlike needs for security, affection, and acceptance. The therapist becomes a substitute parent briefly to provide a healing acceptance of the hurt, angry child of long ago as if to facilitate growth toward maturity.

Brown (1973) refers to touch as conveying warmth, acceptance, and intuitive understanding. He calls touch an "essential healing influence." Brown recommends that physical touching should be discontinued after the patient's reflective, intuitive, contemplative skills are brought into therapeutic interaction.

Perhaps the most important use of touch is to enhance self-esteem. It could be argued that at the core of all neurotic symptoms may be the fear of becoming an autonomous, independent person. Most patients have a defective self-concept and are struggling with issues of security, love, and acceptance by others. They have not learned to love themselves and are guarded and evasive. At bottom is a need for but fear of becoming a person. If psychotherapy is done in an atmosphere of mutuality much akin to what ideally should have occurred between parent and child, then the therapist must include the willingness to be physical, much the same as a good parent is. In the nursing profession touch is recognized as healing, relaxing, encouraging, and giving hope (Krieger, 1979); why would it not do the same when expeditiously used in psychotherapy?

For many therapists touch is difficult because they prefer to remain safely intellectual and objective rather than to allow themselves to be lovingly human. For some therapists it threatens to remind them of their own childlike needs. For others it risks sexual urges that they cannot handle as clinicians. It is difficult to make oneself truly available to another person, body and soul, mind and heart. Yet, as Marmor (1974) points out, therapists too have needs and in fact respond better to those patients whom they like more and who satisfy some of their own needs. Touching then may also be construed as an act that helps heal the therapist in some way, much the same as parents need encouragement or love from their children.

Kernberg (1975) argues that these countertransference needs do not have to be seen as negative in treatment. He suggests that therapists view countertransference as "a total emotional reaction of a therapist to his patient . . . including the therapist's own reality needs as well as his neurotic needs" (p. 49). Robertiello (1974), a psychoanalyst, describes his use of touching and holding schizoid patients as one of the essentials in developing transference; it minimizes the risks of misinterpretation by the patient, he states.

Touching patients holds dangers even if the therapist's intentions are primarily to help. Spotnitz (1967) illustrates how touching can stimulate anxiety, arouse to violence, or promote feelings of fear, alienation, distrust, loss of control, and infantile craving. He asks, "If touching can have deleterious consequences, why employ it at all in psychotherapy?" His answer: "Because it is essential for human beings to have some natural, physical contact with one another, it strengthens one's sense of reality . . . and can have a strong maturational effect" (p. 457).

Therapists must guard against using their patients to satisfy their own needs for whatever reason—power, affection, or sexuality. Despite the opinions of some writers (Hammer, 1973; Shepard, 1971), there is little justification for sexual intercourse in psychotherapy, not only because of the questionable ethical and moral practice but also because it violates the incest taboo implicit in the therapist-patient relationship. There may be reported instances where intercourse has had positive effects (Taylor & Wagner, 1976), but such practices are highly questionable and give the profession a bad reputation (Rottschafer, 1979). Yet to refrain from any touch whatsoever because of risks of pa-

tient arousal or misinterpretation may be an unnecessary overreaction.

Most important is the intent of the therapist. Regardless of the patient's distortions or fear of human touch, if in the therapist's professional judgment contact of some appropriate form may be helpful, careful explanations should accompany the touch to minimize misinterpretation. The therapist's intention should be to use physical contact in service of the healing process.

Therapists need further instruction, discussion, and research to guide them in their effective use of this potentially important treatment modality.

References

Brown, M. (1973). The new body psychotherapies. *Psychotherapy: Theory, Research and Practice, 10*, 98–116.

Dahlberg, C. C. (1970). Sexual contact between patient and therapist. *Contemporary Psychoanalysis, 6*, 107–124.

Hammer, L. I. (1973). Activity—an immutable and indispensable element of the therapist's participation in human growth. In D. Milman & G. Goldman (Eds.), *The neurosis of our time: Acting out.* Springfield, IL: Thomas.

Holroyd, J. C., & Brodsky, A. M. (1977). Psychologists' attitudes and practices regarding erotic and non-erotic physical contact with patients. *American Psychologist, 32*, 843–849.

Kardner, S. H., Fuller, M., & Mensh, I. N. (1973). Survey of physicians' attitudes and practices regarding erotic and non-erotic contacts with patients. *American Journal of Psychiatry, 130*, 1077–1081.

Kernberg, O. (1975). *Borderline conditions and pathological narcissism.* New York: Aronson.

Krieger, D. (1979). *The therapeutic touch: How to use your hands to help or heal.* Englewood Cliffs, NJ: Prentice-Hall.

Marmor, J. (1974). *Psychiatry in transition.* New York: Brunner/Mazel.

Masters, W. H., & Johnson, V. E. (1970). *Human sexual inadequacy.* Boston: Little, Brown.

Mintz, E. E. (1969). Touch and the psychoanalytic tradition. *Psychoanalytic Review, 56*, 365–376.

Pope, K. S. (1990). Therapist-patient sexual involvement: A review of the research. *Clinical Psychology Review, 10*, 477–490.

Robertiello, R. C. (1974). Physical techniques with schizoid patients. *Journal of the American Academy of Psychoanalysis, 2*, 361–367.

Rottschafer, R. H. (1979). The healing touch: The uses and abuses of physical contact in psychotherapy. *The Bulletin, Publication of the Christian Association for Psychological Studies, 5*, 1–7.

Shepard, M. (1971). The love treatment. New York: Wyden.

Spotnitz, H. (1967). The toxoid response. In N. Greenwald (Ed.), *Active psychotherapy.* New York: Atherton.

Taylor, B. J., & Wagner, N. N. (1976). Sex between therapists and clients: A review and analysis. *Professional Psychology, 7*, 593–601.

R. H. ROTTSCHAFER

See MORAL AND ETHICAL ISSUES IN TREATMENT.

Physical Health and Religion. Researchers have generally found a positive relationship between religion and physical health. However, the relationship is complex and difficult to study, the research has been primarily correlational in nature (i.e., cause-and-effect relationships are not determined), the religion variable has been inconsistently and often poorly defined or measured, and underlying psychological mechanisms have only recently begun to be explored. Therefore, one must be cautious in making claims.

Empirical Findings. In the area of mental health, the results of the religion-health linkage are mixed. Gartner, Larson, and Allen (1991) scoured the research literature and found that religion is positively associated with mental health in depression, delinquency, drug and alcohol use, and a general sense of well-being. But they also found religion to be associated with psychopathology in such areas as dogmatism or rigidity as well as suggestibility or dependency. Finally, they discovered the relationship between religion and such mental health measures as anxiety, sexual disorders, psychosis, prejudice, and self-esteem to be ambiguous or complex.

In the area of physical health, the religion-health relationship is similarly mixed. Hill and Butter's (1995) review of the literature found that religion is negatively associated with health when the religion is practiced by extreme groups with fanatical beliefs and practices, including such behaviors as self-abuse as a purification exercise or refusing medical treatment. Although Hill and Butter also found some studies that report no relationship between religion and health, the majority of studies indicate a positive relationship between religion and physical health. For example, a large number of studies found evidence of a relationship between religion and longevity, although again these studies are primarily correlational in nature and the direction of causality cannot be assumed. Researchers also have found that some diseases (e.g., cardiovascular disease, gastrointestinal disorders, many forms of cancer, and hypertension) are more prevalent among nonreligious than religious individuals.

Explanatory Mechanisms. Although the correlation nature of the data is subject to other interpretations, there is good reason to believe that certain aspects of religious teaching or practice may promote physical health. Hill and Butter (1995) identified five such possible explanatory mechanisms.

First, religious teachings often promote a healthy lifestyle, frequently forbidding such behaviors as drug or alcohol abuse and illicit sexual behavior. Some research has documented better health among religious groups (e.g., Mormons, Seventh-Day Adventists, Old Order Amish, and some Orthodox Jewish groups) who practice dietary restrictions or who abstain from such substances as alcohol, tobacco, coffee, or tea than is found in the general population.

Second, Hill and Butter (1995) found that religion often provides social networks, and research has shown that people who are well-connected to others, particularly in a setting such as the church, where people demonstrate great care and concern for others, often have fewer health-related problems.

Third, research indicates that religion often emphasizes a health promotion-oriented philosophy. In Christian circles, for example, this may involve the teaching that the body is God's temple and should be cared for. The extent to which such teachings and beliefs are put into practice (*see* Attitude-Behavior Relationships) requires further research.

Fourth, two strands of research, one that indicates that optimism is related to health and the other that suggests religion is associated with optimism, point to optimism as an important mediating variable in the relationship between religion and health.

Fifth, there is a good deal of research (see Pargament, 1990) that religion is a useful resource in coping with stressful agents.

References

Gartner, J. W., Larson, D. B., & Allen, G. D. (1991). Religious commitment and mental health: A review of the empirical literature. *Journal of Psychology and Theology, 19,* (1), 6–25.

Hill, P. C., & Butter, E. M. (1995). The role of religion in promoting physical health. *Journal of Psychology and Christianity, 14* (2), 141–155.

Pargament, K. I. (1990). God help me: Toward a theoretical framework of coping for the psychology of religion. In M. L. Lynn & D. O. Moberg (Eds.), *Research in the social scientific study of religion* (Vol. 2). Greenwich, CT: JAI Press.

P. C. HILL

See RELIGION AND PERSONALITY; RELIGIOUS HEALTH AND PATHOLOGY.

Physiognomy. The attempt to read personality and individual traits from outward appearance, particularly facial features such as the shape of the jaw, the size and shape of the eyes, nose, forehead, and even eyebrows. Its origin as a theory of personality is traced back to Aristotle, the supposed author of *Physiognomica*, who suggested that people who resemble certain kinds of animals also possess their temperamental characteristics (*see* Temperament).

From the end of the nineteenth century to the first quarter of the twentieth century the theory was embellished by Ernest Hooten and Katherine Blackford, among others. Hooten related organic inferiority and primitivism to certain groups, races, and nationalities, while Blackford applied the theory to a method for personnel selection that was popular for some time. This typing was extended to social stereotypes, correlating attributes such as close-set eyes and a low forehead with criminal characteristics and has become a fertile field for quacks and charlatans. Many of the stereotypes are perpetuated by literature and the media, prejudice, and attempts to further understand human nature through rigid categorization. No significant correlations have been established to validate the theory of physiognomy, although it may be that the myth is often perpetuated because people live up to the expectations of others who have placed stereotypical demands on them.

D. L. SCHUURMAN

See PERSONALITY ASSESSMENT; CONSTITUTIONAL PERSONALITY THEORY.

Physiological Factors in Psychopathology. See GENETIC AND BIOCHEMICAL FACTORS IN PSYCHOPATHOLOGY.

Physiological Psychology. The study of the physiology of behavior, perception, memory, learning, motivation, emotion, language, and self-awareness. The importance of the brain to the human personality has been known for many years. René Descartes recognized that the brain is the organ that mediates certain behavioral functions such as sensation and body movements. However, he did not think the rational faculties were localized in the brain but interacted with the body in the pineal gland in the center of the brain.

Modern neuroscience dates from the work of Charles Bell in the early 1800s. Bell, along with François Magendi, discovered what has been called the Bell-Magendi law: that sensory and motor fibers enter and leave the spinal cord by separate roots. Bell was also one of the first to observe that different areas of the brain serve different functions. Several decades later Hermann von Helmholtz made important measurements of the neural impulse in a frog's nerve. In the 1860s Paul Broca, a French physician, provided support for the localization of function hypothesis, which said that specific areas of the brain controlled specific behavioral functions. He was able to relate a patient's inability to speak to a damaged portion of the brain, now called Broca's area, in the speech center of the left hemisphere.

The guiding assumptions of physiological psychology from this time were much closer to materialistic monism than to the interaction dualism of Descartes. This meant that the functions of mind and behavior were seen to be entirely a product of brain activity. Thus from its very beginnings physiological psychology has been searching for those brain areas producing all of what we call the person.

Great advances in physiological psychology have occurred because of the rapid development of sophisticated techniques to study the brain. Most important among these are stimulation and recording techniques in which even single cells of the brain can be electrically or chemically stimulated and their electrical activity recorded. More recent developments include computerized tomography (CT scan), positron emission tomography (PET scan), and magnetic resonance imaging (MRI).

The neuron has been identified as the primary functioning cell in the brain. Its electrical signal is passed between neurons via chemicals known as transmitters. Large collections of neurons on the surface of the brain (cortex) are responsible for vision, hearing, body senses, speech, and motor movement. Internal portions of the brain seem to be responsible for motivational and emotional functions. The hypothalamus in the interior portion of the brain seems to be involved in hunger, thirst, and sexual motivation. Lateral lesions, for example, in the hypothalamus produce hyperphagia or overeating in rats. Emotions such as aggression and rage have also been related to the hypothalamus as well as many areas of the limbic system of the brain. So-called pleasure centers have been isolated in the interior portions of the brain, and these may relate to both emotions and learning. In general the search for centers of specific function in the brain has given way to the search for circuits of activity. This view stresses the interaction of many brain areas in any behavior.

The search for the engram, or the physical basis for learning and memory, has produced a challenge to the localization of function theory. Support for specific storage locations for learning and memory was first provided by Donald O. Hebb's cell assembly model and later by Wilder Penfield, who found specific localized stores for certain sensory memories. However, Karl Lashley shifted physiological psychology to a more holistic model of learning with research showing that any learned material is stored everywhere in the brain rather than in a specific location. In this model some have compared brain activity to a hologram (a three-dimensional photograph).

The clinical research of physiological psychology has included Hans Selye's work on the effects of stress and the human defenses against stress called the General Adaptation Syndrome. Recent studies of Posttraumatic Stress Disorder (PTSD) suggest that severe emotional stress may damage neural connections between the frontal lobes and memory and emotional centers in the brain. Visceral learning studies related to biofeedback indicate that people and animals can learn to control their autonomic nervous system responses and the effects of stress. Biochemical research indicates that some mental and emotional problems seem to be related to abnormal levels of neural transmitters. Treatment emphasizes the use of drugs to increase or decrease the effectiveness of transmitters. One common treatment for depression is the use of the drug fenfluramine (Prozac).

The central concern of physiological psychology has always been the mind-brain problem (see Mind-Brain Relationship). In its attempt to demonstrate central state materialism, physiological psychology as a whole has believed that the mind is an epiphenomenon of the brain—that is, a direct product of brain activity. The research of Nobel Prize–winner Roger Sperry on the split brain has been interpreted to mean that dividing the brain produces two minds, each half of the brain producing its own epiphenominal mind. This interpretation seems to attack the Christian concept of the soul. However, not all physiological psychologists accept this materialistic view of the person. Nobel Prize–winner John Eccles (1994) believes that the physiological evidence points to the existence of a human mind that interacts with the brain. Physicist Roger Penrose (1994) also suggests that neurophysiologists ought to look for the human mind in the immaterial mysteries of quantum gravity. MacKay (1974) argues that the Christian view of the person remains valid even if brain activity could be shown to correlate perfectly with mental activity. Even with great progress in neurophysiological methods, the mind still remains a mystery.

References

Eccles, J. (1994). *How the self controls its brain*. New York: Springer-Verlag.
MacKay, D. (1974). *The clockwork image*. Downers Grove, IL: InterVarsity Press.
Penrose, R. (1994). *Shadows of the mind: A search for the missing science of consciousness*. Oxford: Oxford University Press.

M. P. Cosgrove

See Genetic and Biochemical Factors in Psychopathology; Brain and Human Behavior; Neuropsychology.

Physique and Temperament. *See* Constitutional Personality Theory.

Piaget, Jean (1896–1980). Swiss psychologist known for his study of the development of intelligence. Originally trained as a biologist, he developed an interest in psychology after his doctoral studies in the natural sciences at the University of Neuchâtel in 1917. He became interested in philosophy of science and in epistemology, which led him to the field of psychology in an attempt to find the connections between history and philosophy of science and epistemology.

His interest in psychology in turn led to study of the ideas and methodology of clinical psychologists. These studies took him to the Sorbonne in France. While in Paris he became involved at the Binet laboratory school, where he worked on standardized tests. As he worked on these tests, he noticed that there were patterns to the kinds of wrong answers children gave to the questions and that the wrong answers of younger children had a different pattern from that of older children.

Combining his training in biology, his interest in epistemology, and his interest in psychology, Piaget launched himself into a study that he called genetic epistemology. The primary focus of this field is the relationships between biological development and how a person thinks.

In 1929, at the age of 33, he became director of research at Jean-Jacque Rousseau Institute in Geneva. During the first part of his career in genetic epistemology he focused his attention on children's development of various concepts such as language, causality, and morality. He then turned to the intelligence of infants and young children. During the last part of his career he also gave some attention to the meanings of his theory for the enterprises of education. In 1955, with the help of the Rockefeller Foundation, Piaget developed the International Center of Genetic Epistemology at the University of Geneva. At the time of his death he was working on cross-cultural studies under the auspices of UNESCO, with which he had been affiliated since its inception.

Piaget's native language was French, and much of his work went unread by English-speaking psychologists and educators until the 1950s. Since then more attention has been given to his ideas, as most of his many writings have been translated in English. His major works include *The Origins of Intelligence* (1936), *The Psychology of Intelligence* (1947), *Six Psychological Studies* (1964), and *Genetic Epistemology* (1970).

R. B. McKean

See Cognitive Development.

Pica. The desire for and eating of nonnutritive substances. Pica occurs in humans or animals as a result of nutritional deficiencies or, in humans only, as a result of psychopathology. Pica is listed in *DSM-IV* as an eating disorder typically seen in children and adolescents. Criteria for diagnosing pica include the repeated eating of a nonnutritive substance for one month and the absence of other conditions in which pica may occur as a symptom, such as mental retardation, pervasive developmental disorder, or schizophrenia. Substances consumed by children suffering from this disorder include clay, hair, paint, plaster, starch, or cloth. Normal children may consume some of these items for a short period of time without being considered for the diagnosis.

Pica has been observed as a symptom among chronic schizophrenics, regressed senile patients, and various deprived groups. Pica is also used as a more general term to refer to unusual food cravings by pregnant women.

This disorder may be rooted in nutrient deficiencies or, according to analytic theory, in unmet oral needs. Pica may also have strong cultural roots, especially when the symptom is observed in adults. Geophagy, the ingestion of dirt, has been observed in Africa among starving peoples as a means of staving off hunger pains and among warriors who eat the soil of their homeland as preparation for battle in a faraway place. In the nineteenth century geophagy was also observed among Southern slaves.

In the Bible geophagy was part of Satan's curse in Genesis 3:14 (see also Isa. 65:25; Mic. 7:17). Licking dust off the feet of a conquering warrior is a frequent figure of speech depicting the humiliation of defeat (Ps. 72:9; Isa. 49:23).

J. R. BECK

Pinel, Phillipe (1745–1826). French physician who initiated human care of the mentally ill. The son of a physician, Pinel was first interested in philosophy and planned to enter the priesthood. Later he became interested in science and mathematics and decided to follow his father's profession. He received his medical degree from the University of Toulouse in 1773. After tutoring Latin, Greek, and natural history for two years, he went to Montpellier for further study in comparative anatomy.

Pinel arrived in Paris in 1778 but for 14 years remained obscure, impoverished, and studious. He tutored, translated books, and wrote papers on medicine, physics, and philosophy. His interest in insanity began in 1785. In 1792 he was appointed a municipal medical officer, and in 1793 he became head of the lunatic asylum, the Bicêtre. Two years later he was transferred to the Salpétrière asylum. He remained in Paris until his death.

Pinel's innovations at the two asylums became his greatest contribution. Finding the usual combination of squalor, cruelty, and neglect, he approached the president of the Commune for permission to remove the chains from the patients. Although his own sanity was questioned for wanting to do this, he was not forbidden. First he removed the chains from a few patients and eventually from all. Patients were given food and encouragement, were treated kindly, and were not beaten. They began to recover, and one even saved his life when a mob was about to lynch him.

Pinel believed that mental illness is a result of heredity, physiological damage, and excessive exposure to stress. He developed a simple and accurate description of mental illnesses in his *Philosophical Classification of Diseases* (1798), which became a standard text, going through many editions. He developed a psychologically oriented approach in his *Medico-Philosophical Treatise on Mental Alienation or Mania* (1801). His books were simply written and were understandable to intelligent laypeople. Rather than using bleeding, purging, and blistering, he advocated close and friendly contact with patients, discussion of personal difficulties, and purposeful activities.

Through Pinel's efforts France became a leading nation in the treatment of the mentally ill. His moral treatment became the model for similar movements in England and the United States. A succession of brilliant men, including Esquirol and Jean-Martin Charcot, followed him at Salpétrière

so that this hospital remained the psychiatric center of the world for nearly a century. Students of mental disorders flocked to it as experimental psychologists did to Leipzig.

R. L. KOTESKEY

See ABNORMAL PSYCHOLOGY.

Placebo Effects in Therapy. A placebo may be defined as any substance or procedure that, when it is used as a method of treatment, is incapable of producing any effect due to its inert, inactive composition. The placebo effect refers to the psychological and/or physiological changes brought about solely by the expectation that the administered substance or procedure will be effective.

Prior to the twentieth century virtually all medicines used by physicians and other healers were pharmacologically inert. The numerous cures supposedly wrought by these medicines often were due to the placebo effect. A medical historian, reflecting on this fact, notes that until recently the history of medical treatment is the history of the placebo effect (Shapiro, 1959).

Mechanisms of Action. Although it is believed that the placebo effect works via the arousal of expectation, the exact nature of that arousal remains unclear. Placebos do not work for everyone, nor do they always work for the same person in the same way. Sometimes they may precipitate negative effects if they are accompanied by negative expectations. In one such study patients were told the medicine they were taking (actually a placebo) might produce side effects. As a result they developed nausea, headaches, and vomiting (Pincus, 1966).

A review of research on the placebo effect (Shapiro & Morris, 1978) indicates that a number of factors have been investigated that might help explain how and why placebos work. The variables examined include suggestibility, dependency, psychopathology, introversion-extraversion, acquiescence, social desirability, treatment settings, treatment procedures, and patient and therapist attitudes. The arousal of expectations has also been examined in terms of concepts such as transference, role demand, guilt reduction, classical conditioning (*see* Conditioning, Classical), and cognitive dissonance. Very likely the placebo effect is a multifactored phenomenon in which any one element is dependent on a variety of other variables.

Implications for Psychotherapy. The use of a placebo in medical research assists in validating the efficacy of the pharmacological agent in question rather than any improvement due to the psychological effect of expectation. However, when the same placebo concept is applied to psychotherapy and psychotherapy research, a host of problems is generated.

The usual research design attempting to identify the effects of specific therapies utilizes three groups for the sake of comparison: a treatment group, a no-treatment group (often composed of those on a waiting list for treatment), and a placebo group. The last group is not given the therapeutic regimen that is administered to the treatment group. Instead a more general approach to the patients is prescribed such as the group leader being empathetic, or engaging in reflective listening, or providing moral support.

The use of such groups using psychological placebos has been justified on various grounds. Rosenthal and Frank (1956) argued that such placebos are theoretically inert. But this particular definition falls victim to theoretical short-sightedness. That is, theoretical concepts considered inert in one theory of therapy would be considered not only efficacious but essential from the standpoint of a different theory. Critelli and Neumann (1984, p. 33) have aptly noted that "virtually every currently established psychotherapy would be considered inert, and therefore a placebo, from the viewpoint of other established theories of cure."

The definition of psychological placebos as nonspecific factors has also been roundly criticized. Does a nonspecific factor once identified and labeled cease to become nonspecific and thus no longer a placebo? If a variable such as therapist warmth is not part of a specific technique and thus considered a placebo, how can it also be an effective and powerful factor in client change according to certain theories (Lambert & Bergin, 1994)?

Unlike medical/pharmacological research, in which the placebo helps to eliminate the psychological effects variable, placebos in psychotherapy research utilize those very effects. Wilkins (1984) has noted that "by using placebo groups, psychotherapy researchers have paradoxically searched for psychological causes with tactics that were specifically developed in chemotherapy research to rule out all psychological causes" (p. 571).

Critics of the placebo concept in psychology thus argue that it is too vague to be of any value in research and too general to assist in identifying the various psychological processes that are necessary and sufficient for change. Some of these critics have suggested that research dealing with the psychological placebo effect should be directed toward the efficacious factors common to most if not all therapies. These common factors have been shown to be vital in bringing about therapeutic change.

A meta-analysis of fifteen different psychotherapy research studies found that patients in the placebo control groups showed greater improvement than patients in the no-treatment group (Lambert, Weber, & Sykes, 1993). Although the therapeutic effects of the common factors placebo groups were less than the formal psychotherapy groups, this analysis suggests that common factors are potent ingredients in the change process.

The results of an elaborate National Institute of Mental Health (NIMH) study of the treatment of depression found that the placebo-attention group was as effective in alleviating depression in one particular subsample as were the two different formal psychotherapies (Elkin, 1994).

Hope—the expectation of help or healing—appears to be one of those common factors so vital in affecting therapeutic change. Freud (1953) acknowledged this, stating, "Expectation colored by hope and faith is an effective force with which we have to reckon . . . in all our attempts at treatment and cure" (p. 289).

A number of studies were reviewed (Frank, Hoehn-Saric, Imber, Liberman, & Stone, 1978) supporting the importance of positive expectations regarding the outcome of therapy. One such study found that the degree of symptomatic relief in psychiatric patients following a single contact with a therapist was related to the patients' expressed expectation that they would be helped. A similar study found a correlation between psychiatric outpatients' estimates of how well they expected to feel after six months of treatment and the degree of reported symptom relief after an initial evaluation interview.

It has been observed (Frank & Frank, 1991) that since patients often bring vague expectations into therapy initially they will likely profit from it only if their expectations are congruent with what occurs in the sessions. If the patient does not understand the process of therapy (i.e., how and why change will occur) then the expectation of help will be severely diminished.

A study on the importance of clarifying patients' expectations in therapy involved comparing two groups of psychiatric patients, each of whom received four months of therapy. Only one of the groups received a preparatory role induction interview designed to clarify the processes of treatment, assure the patients that treatment would be helpful, dispel unrealistic hopes (to guard against disillusionment), and help the patients behave in ways that accorded with the therapist's image of a good patient. The results indicated that as a group the patients receiving the role induction interview showed more appropriate behavior in therapy and had a better outcome than the controls (Hoehn-Saric et al., 1964).

Ethical Issues. The element of deception involved in medical placebo research and treatment raises serious ethical questions regarding the appropriateness of deliberately misleading a patient about the effectiveness of the placebo. However, the psychological placebo effect is a misnomer given that the effects, properly understood as common factors, are in no wise inert.

Thus it is not only ethical but also highly desirable that therapists recognize and utilize the common factors in the service of healing, regardless of which specific theory drives their clinical methodology. Whatever benefits might be derived from a specific methodology can only be enhanced by deliberate utilization of the common factors.

Placebos and Faith Healing. Attempts have been made to explain faith healings such as those performed by Christ in the New Testament solely in terms of the placebo effect. While the psychological effects that have gone by the term *placebo effect* may account for some of the cures wrought by present-day healers, objections must be raised to attributing all miraculous healings to the curative power of those effects. Such reductionistic efforts stem from a naturalistic bias that precludes the possibility that the cause-and-effect universe can be subject to supernatural intervention. This bias not only is patently unbiblical but also ignores the findings of quantum physics that suggest that the causal nexus is not inviolate.

Further, the placebo effect explanation does not square with the scriptural descriptions of a number of Christ's healings. It is recorded that on several occasions Jesus healed persons, including the centurion's servant (Matt. 8:5–13) and the official's son (John 4:46–54), without their knowledge and from a geographical distance. On other occasions Jesus is reported to have raised deceased persons to life, including Lazarus (John 11:1–44) and the widow's son (Luke 7:11–15). In none of these instances were the recipients of the healing capable of having their expectations aroused by Jesus. Thus the placebo effect, or more accurately the psychological effects, could not have been the curative force in these experiences.

By extrapolation one may conclude that the healings in which Jesus spoke directly to the ill were manifestations of the same supernatural power. Once supernaturalism is affirmed, the door opens to accepting the validity of many faith healings, past and present. At the same time we can recognize that the common factors, previously known as the placebo effect, may play a part in some but not necessarily all cures.

References

Critelli, J., & Neumann, K. (1984). The placebo: Conceptual analysis of a construct in transition. *American Psychologist, 39,* 32–39.

Elkin, I. (1994). The NIMH treatment of depression collaborative research program: Where we began and where we are. In A. Bergin & S. Garfield (Eds.), *Handbook of psychotherapy and behavior change* (4th ed.). New York: Wiley.

Frank, J. D., & Frank, J. B. (1991). *Persuasion and healing: A comparative study of psychotherapy.* Baltimore: Johns Hopkins University Press.

Frank, J. D., Hoehn-Saric, R., Imber, S., Liberman, B., & Stone, A. (1978). *Effective ingredients of successful psychotherapy.* New York: Brunner/Mazel.

Freud, S. (1953). From the history of an infantile neurosis. *The standard edition of the complete psychological works of Sigmund Freud* (Vol. 7). London: Hogarth.

Hoehn-Saric, R., Frank, J. D., Imber, S., Nash, E., Stone, A., & Battle, C. (1964). Systematic preparation of patients for psychotherapy: Effects of therapy behavior and outcome. *Journal of Psychiatric Research, 2,* 267–281.

Lambert, M., & Bergin, A. (1994). The effectiveness of psychotherapy. In A. Bergin & S. Garfield (Eds.), *Handbook of psychotherapy and behavior change* (4th ed.). New York: Wiley.

Lambert, M., Weber, D., & Sykes, J. (1993, April). *Psychotherapy versus placebo.* Paper presented at the annual meeting of the Western Psychological Association, Phoenix.

Pincus, G. (1966). Control of conception of hormonal steroids. *Science, 153,* 493–500.

Rosenthal, D., & Frank, J. D. (1956). Psychotherapy and the placebo effect. *Psychological Bulletin, 53,* 294–302.

Shapiro, A. (1959). The placebo effect in the history of medical treatment: Implications for psychiatry. *American Journal of Psychiatry, 116,* 298–304.

Shapiro, A., & Morris, L. (1978). The placebo effect in medical and psychological therapies. In S. Garfield & A. Bergin (Eds.), *Handbook of psychotherapy and behavior change* (2nd ed.). New York: Wiley.

Wilkins, W. (1984). Psychotherapy: The powerful placebo. *Journal of Consulting and Clinical Psychology, 52,* 570–573.

W. G. BIXLER

See COUNSELING AND PSYCHOTHERAPY: OVERVIEW.

Plato (ca. 427–347 B.C.). Probably the most influential philosopher in the history of Western thought. Alfred North Whitehead's famous comment that "the history of Western philosophy is a series of footnotes to Plato" is in many ways no exaggeration. Plato founded the Academy at Athens, the prototype of the Western university. Through such thinkers as Clement and Augustine he has also exercised an incalculable influence on Christian theology. His writings consist for the most part of dramatic dialogues written over a long period of time; hence it is not easy to derive a consistent system from Plato's writings.

Plato viewed human beings as a composite of an immaterial, immortal soul and a physical body. Although this idea is probably of religious origin and is certainly older than Plato, he was the first philosopher to develop and defend such a view. His attitude toward the body is somewhat positive in some dialogues, but he is most famous for the view presented in the *Phaedo* that the body is the "prisonhouse of the soul." The goal of the soul is to escape its embodiment and reach a pure spiritual existence, a goal that requires a disciplined, somewhat ascetic attitude toward the body and bodily desires.

The soul is seen by Plato as both preexistent and immortal, although he apparently believed in the possibility of multiple bodily incarnations. His most famous argument for the immortality of the soul is derived from his theory of knowledge. Plato saw the human soul as capable of knowing truth of an eternal character. Humans are capable of grasping absolute, timeless standards such as beauty, justice, equality, and the good. This is the famous theory of forms. Since the soul's function is to grasp these eternal truths, Plato reasoned that the soul must share their eternal character. Specifically he held that knowledge of the forms is innate and is best explained as recollection of truth known prior to birth. Christian Platonists replaced this recollection with a theory of divine illumination to explain such innate knowledge.

The functioning soul is described by Plato in the *Republic* as tripartite in character. The soul contains an appetitive part, the element of impulsive cravings and desires; a rational part, whose proper function is to rule or govern the person; and a spiritual element, which is capable of assisting reason by curbing the impulses. A truly virtuous person integrates these elements harmoniously. Much of Western psychology has been influenced by Plato's divisions, which are still reflected in such distinctions as that between the cognitive and affective dimensions of personality.

C. S. EVANS

See PHILOSOPHICAL PSYCHOLOGY.

Play, Adults'. *See* WORK AND PLAY.

Play, Children's. Play is spontaneous, voluntary activity, engaged in for no observable reason other than for pleasure. Play may include another person or an object or may be engaged in alone, and young children play more often than do older children and adults. Although most researchers agree on roughly this description, play has proved hard to define more specifically and to explain theoretically.

Play has traditionally been contrasted with exploratory behavior (Berlyne, 1960); that is, behavior elicited by curiosity and oriented toward finding out about an unfamiliar object. This distinction may be heuristically useful, but children move seamlessly between exploration and play, and exploratory behavior may best be seen as a kind of play.

Paradoxically, play is children's work. Cross-species observations indicate that play is necessary for development. In play children mimic reality without being bound by it. Play stimulates emotional, social, and cognitive development (see, e.g., Hellendoorn, van der Kooij, & Sutton-Smith, 1994), and can be used to stimulate faith development (see, e.g., Westerhoff, 1977).

Parents and teachers who would like to encourage faith development can choose experiences that reflect the child's developmental level, for example, preschool programs that encourage hands-on play with objects that depict images of faith (such as filling and emptying Noah's Ark, using play dough to explore building the tomb and rolling away the stone) or school-age programs that involve extended crafts projects depicting the theme in a series of lessons (such as constructing a biblical village).

Piaget (1951) believed play is primarily an indicator of cognitive development, and psychologists agree that play develops concurrently with cognitive skills. In the first year of life, children's play is primarily sensorimotor play, made up of exploring and manipulating objects. By age two, children are engaging in constructive play, combining or constructing such objects as block towers, clay objects, and puzzles. Pretend play begins at about the same age and first involves solitary activities such as drinking from an empty cup. Later, children pretend that one object, perhaps a pencil, serves as another, a comb or a spoon, or pretend to feed Mom imaginary food. Sociodramatic play, taking parts or roles, can begin in some two-year-olds but appears in the play of almost all four-year-olds. Piaget argued that play peaks in the later preschool years and begins to diminish after children start school because, he believed, children begin sports or other games with rules or engage in elaborate pretend play sequences. More recently definitions of play have been revised to include these as play. By these definitions play does not diminish markedly until adolescence.

For normally developing children, parents need not stimulate play. There is no evidence that the plethora of toys being sold with the promise that they maximize normal development produce high achievers. Parents can, however, facilitate children's play, providing unscheduled time for children to be playful and simple objects that encourage rather than limit creativity; for example, construction rather than remote-controlled toys, doll houses and buildings with unspecified open space rather than name-brand characters generally used in predictable ways. For developmentally challenged children, parents or therapists may wish to design activities that stimulate a more developmentally complex level of play (Hellendoorn, van der Kooij, & Sutton-Smith, 1994).

Children play with various elements in their world (Garvey, 1977): with motion (e.g., climbing every piece of furniture in reach, using and stretching their newfound abilities), with language (e.g., using words to create pretend scenes that can be changed into another scene with a turn of phrase or a quick laugh), with other people (play that begins as early as six weeks of age and becomes increasingly important during the preschool years), and with rules (e.g., as the four-year-old answers Dad's "we leave in two minutes" with a quick "three"). Playfulness with rules is sometimes hard to tolerate, but testing limits indicates children understand the rules and how parents respond can help children learn how to negotiate.

Television provides more limited play than computers. Although educational television programs have increased children's knowledge of letters and numbers, in general television is not interactive enough to enhance learning. Computers are interactive within limits and can enhance children's learning and creativity with age-appropriate programs, but the computer cannot take the place of play dough and popsicle sticks for stimulating construction and creativity in free-form play.

Play is not specifically mentioned in Scripture, but God does call Christians to become like little children (Matt. 19:13–15; Mark 9:36–37), and playfulness is a desirable quality of childhood to emulate. Christians are often too sober and proper to experience the sheer pleasure inherent in being with God. Many of the psalms (see, e.g., Ps. 33:1–5) express just such pleasure. Recognizing that playfulness is constrained by obedience, we should cultivate a playful spirit in the presence of God. We may then play with ideas of faith, images of God, or ways of being Christian and express ourselves creatively through whatever medium we feel led to choose.

References

Berlyne, D. E. (1960). *Conflict, arousal and curiosity*. New York: McGraw-Hill.

Garvey, C. (1977). *Play*. Cambridge, MA: Harvard University Press.

Hellendoorn, J., van der Kooij, R., & Sutton-Smith, B. (Eds.). (1994). *Play and intervention*. Albany: State University of New York Press.

Piaget, J. (1951). *Play, dreams and imitation in childhood*. New York: Norton.

Westerhoff, J. H. (1977). *Will our children have faith?* New York: Seabury.

K. V. Cook

See Cognitive Development.

Play Therapy. *See* Child Therapy.

Pleasure Principle. Sigmund Freud's hypothesized motivating force in the id, the original aspect of personality and the only part of the personality that is rooted in the biological make-up of the individual. The unconscious impulses of the id operate according to the pleasure principle: the immediate discharge of psychic energy that otherwise creates tension in the personality system. The immediate tension reduction that accompanies this discharge provides satisfaction and reduces discomfort. The maximization of pleasure and the minimization of pain become such powerful forces that the id blindly obeys, reflecting its irrationally impulsive and narcissistic character. As a result, the id is hopelessly ineffective in the real world and the pleasure principle must be tempered through the ego's reality principle.

P. C. Hill

See Psychoanalytic Psychology.

Poetry Therapy. *See* Expressive Therapy.

Political Correctness. Political correctness can be traced back to the early 1980s, when it was used to describe a position or belief associated with nontraditional viewpoints in the United States. Through the 1980s the term was infrequently used until the media grasped it and started to apply it to environmentalist and feminist viewpoints. Political correctness has evolved into a host of practices with a negative tone associated with groups that attempt to stifle the positions and speech of other groups.

With the progression of political correctness, multiculturalism has arisen. Multiculturalism is a paradigm that is furthered through the use of politically correct language. It is the realization of equal opportunity for minorities, the disabled, women, and others. The aim is inclusiveness of the broader cultural content.

Politically correct language is similar to social labeling. The meaning conveyed by words depends not only on the textual context under which the word is spoken but also on the context into which the words are launched. The listener's background and individual experience affect the interpretation of the word's meaning. Positive and progressive social labeling is associated with a positive self-image and greater flexibility.

Political correctness thrives from the debates between politically correct and anti-politically correct groups. This is necessary in order to keep the groups in check. Political correctness could stifle universities, murder the English language, and set one interest group against another if not kept in line by anti-politically correct groups. On the other side, anti-politically correct groups could breed intolerance and repress minorities.

The movement of political correctness has influenced many people to desert the idea of a common culture. Though we have many differences, there is still a common intellectual, artistic, and moral legacy that we hold.

The effects of political correctness are seen most in the world of academia. University campuses are where politically correct thinking is thought to have taken hold. The view of history has been progressively changing to include more viewpoints and descriptions from a multicultural view. University administrations have been forced to review policies concerning cultural discrimination. Policies have been developed in order to reduce sexism and racism. However, many people have seen political correctness as a violation of free speech. The word "diversity" has been used to enforce uniformity on campuses through the enactment of politically correct laws. The aim of political correctness is to reduce prejudice, but it has been ineffective in the context of real prejudice. The changing of a word or an image will not change the world.

C. R. Stites

Popular Psychology. Popular psychology is a term given to a certain group of psychological writings in order to differentiate them from academic psychological writings. Popular psychology writings cover the gamut of topics from improving marriage and relationships to interpreting dreams. Popular psychology writings are usually less rigorous, in that they demand less of their readers, than do their academic counterparts. Academic psychological writing often is based on research, case studies, or the application, refinement, and extension of an accepted theory. The purpose of academic writing is to communicate to a more narrowly defined audience, usually one's colleagues, to stimulate further research or dialog on a topic. The purpose of popular psychology writings is to get useful information into the hands of everyday people. Therefore, in contrast to academic psychology, popular psychology is almost completely concerned with applications to everyday problems that people face. Popular psychology requires of the reader less knowledge and mastery of the entire field of psychology in order for the reader to be able to benefit. Few popular writers write academic works; many academic writers, however, write in the popular genre. In selecting popular psychology books, one must ask what qualifications the author has to be able to speak authoritatively on the subject.

Two examples of authors who write solely for the popular audience are John Bradshaw and M. Scott Peck. Peck's works are based on his training and years of work as a psychiatrist and draw on the richness of his experiences. He is espousing a psychology of "Love, Traditional Values and Spiritual Growth" (Peck, 1978). Bradshaw's works do not rigorously adhere to a theory but draw from many theories, including family systems, contemporary psychodynamic theories, and addiction treatment models. He discusses the problems of dysfunctional families and the effect of addictions on child, family, and adult development. Bradshaw, it is claimed, "lived everything he writes about" (Bradshaw, 1990). He was born into an alcoholic family, was abandoned by his father, and was out of control as an adolescent. He studied for the Roman Catholic priesthood and completed three degrees from the University of Toronto.

An example of an author who writes for both audiences is John Gottman (1994). For two decades he has conducted sophisticated research on predicting divorce. His academic books are filled with research findings and require of readers a high level of competency in statistics and research design. His popular works are much more accessible, applicable, and therefore useful to laypersons. All three of these individuals are quite popular on the lecture circuit, though each appeals to different audiences.

References

Bradshaw, J. (1990). *Homecoming: Reclaiming and championing your inner child*. New York: Bantam.
Gottman, J. (1994). *Why marriages succeed or fail*. New York: Harper.
Peck, M. S. (1978). *The road less traveled*. New York: Touchstone.

D. W. PETERS

See APPLIED PSYCHOLOGY.

Pornography. Although pornography has existed for centuries, it is only with the recent growth of the mass media that it has significantly impacted the whole of society. The term comes from the Greek *pornographos*, meaning the writing of harlots, but that no longer provides an adequate definition. With strong pressure from publishers and others to give it First Amendment protection, it has changed in its styles and content so remarkably that definition has become crucial to any clear discussion of its significance.

The U.S. Presidential Commission on Obscenity and Pornography (1970) favored a very general interpretation of pornography as referring to any sexually explicit materials capable of arousing sexual passion. This approach proved confusingly ambiguous, since it covers an enormously wide range of materials, from medical texts to hard-core presentations of perverse sexuality.

A more precise definition was offered in the Longford Report: "That which exploits and dehumanizes sex, so that human beings are treated as things and women in particular as sex objects" (Longford, 1972). This approach enables one to discriminate between various types of material of greater or lesser explicitness, with attention paid more to the meaning of the materials and their effects on behavior than to subjective evaluations of either shock or approval.

The terms *pornography* and *obscenity* are often used interchangeably, but distinctions are necessary. In the United States obscenity has been defined by the Supreme Court as involving patent offensiveness, affronting community standards (as also in Canada), and lacking redeeming social value. It commonly but not necessarily refers to sexual obscenity, while in England it has been linked legally with the "deprave and corrupt" test laid down in 1868.

While pornography remains a difficult term to define, some helpful distinctions have emerged from a developing body of research. This offers distinctions among violent pornography, which treats sexual violence, especially against women, as normative; degrading pornography, which without overt violence nonetheless degrades, debases, or dehumanizes those whom they depict; and erotica, which represents nonviolent sexual expressions as normal, without debasing sexuality or people. Other sexually explicit materials include artistic presentations in which the beauty of sexuality is portrayed aesthetically and scientific presentations whose primary purpose is to inform.

The argument in defense of pornography, that it can be therapeutic for sexually disturbed persons, lacks support when these distinctions are made. While certain well-chosen sexually explicit materials (books and films) can educate and reduce fear in those with sexual dysfunctions, pornography has not been shown to have beneficial effects.

Just as research into most aspects of sexuality is of recent origin, so too investigation into the nature and effects of pornography was vestigial until the U.S. report of 1970. It was widely assumed that pornography is socially undesirable. Few users would publicly admit to an interest in it. After that report claimed to be unable to find convincing evidence of harm from its availability, pornographic books, magazines, and films multiplied rapidly, achieving greatly increased public visibility. Concurrently those findings were subject to heavy professional and political criticism, and the report was subsequently rejected overwhelmingly by the U.S. Senate.

Since that time the quality of research has improved and has become more focused and informative. First, the parameters have been more clearly defined. Whereas much earlier research failed to identify materials precisely, experimental and clinical studies have focused on precise components of pornography such as explicitness, type of sexual activity, inclusion of aggression, and degree of consent (Malamuth & Donnerstein, 1984).

Second, it has been possible to test competing theories of effects. The catharsis theory, which argued that wide availability of pornography would result in a reduced incidence of sexual crimes, has not found support. Widely publicized Danish evidence has been shown to be methodologically flawed (Court, 1980).

Studies on the dual themes of sexuality and aggression suggest that exposure to erotica can lead to a reduced probability of sexual aggression against others (Baron & Bell, 1977), but a whole range of negative effects related to how users perceive women has been identified (see Itzin, 1992). When high levels of arousal associated with violent or degrading pornography are used, there is an increased probability of sexual aggression. This evidence has been derived using normal and clinical populations (Malamuth & Donnerstein, 1984). The presentation of either explicit violence or explicit sex has the potential for breaking social taboos so that both aggressive and sexual behavioral expressions are increased, with reduced inhibitions.

The presentation of rape themes in pornography has been one expression of the sex and violence linkage and has led researchers to conclude that this results in increased acceptance of the rape myth, of rape fantasies, and of violence against women. Even where pornography is only implicitly hostile to women, without overt violence, a dehumanizing effect still is found. The expression of such exposure could be expected in increased reports of rape where pornography has become accepted, even though the relationship is complex and not simply causal. This is true in Scandinavia, in contrast to earlier optimistic predictions, as well as in the United States. It has been said of pornography that "one can only conclude that pornography is indeed the 'theory,' and battery, rape, molestation, and other increasing crimes of sexual violence are not so coincidentally the 'practice'" (Morgan, 1980).

It was widely argued that liberalization of pornography laws would result in reduced interest, with a consequent withering of the market: the forbidden fruit hypothesis. Evidence for this view has been found faulty, and in recent years the trade has escalated to an unprecedented degree. This development has been not only a matter of quantity. The type of material becoming available has changed constantly to meet changing demands. Current technology includes well-produced films and videos, while growing public concern is now expressed about unrestricted access to pornography via the Internet. Production has become more sophisticated, while the themes presented have become increasingly perverted. Sadomasochism and child pornography have emerged with support from the liberal orthodoxy that has pushed for First Amendment freedom by claiming there is no evidence of harm. This position was vigorously challenged by the Attorney General's Commission on Pornography, which produced the Meese Report, and argued for evidences of harm from several categories of material (Attorney General, 1986). The dangers from pornography are now widely established in the mainstream of the psychological literature, and legal restrictions on child pornography apply in many countries.

Public resistance to pornography has come from three directions. The feminist lobby has been increasingly vocal in its protest against the exploitation of women (Itzin, 1992). The feminist critique emphasizes the distortion of power relationships in pornography, seeing them as an extreme expression of a male-dominated society. This has led to special emphasis on themes of aggression and rape in pornography, with evidence of a corresponding growth of such behavior in society.

A philosophical critique of pornography emphasizes how dangerous pornography is to the fundamental meanings of human relationships. The acceptance of pornography implies an acceptance of debased values, impoverishment of cultural ideals, and a significant loss of meaning. This existential critique, highlighting the essential hate and underlying hostility of pornography, has been most fully developed by Holbrook (1972).

A moral reaction against pornography has developed with Christians rallying with many other religious groups to provide a critique (e.g., Minnery, 1986), while public protest has taken many forms, sometimes based on moral and theological presuppositions and at times based on personal revulsion or moral outrage.

From a Christian standpoint, pornography can be understood as epitomizing some essentially alien principles. While some sexually explicit materials can enrich, educate, and, in clinical situations, assist in overcoming irrational fears of sexuality, pornography by its nature debases sexuality. Sex is no longer seen as a God-given means of expressing mutuality and fulfillment in relationships. The Christian emphasis on monogamic, heterosexual relationships based on love and commitment is challenged in favor of hedonistic promiscuity. An inversion of values ensures that goodness and purity are ridiculed in favor of lust and immorality. The biblical taboos against incest, bestiality (*see* Zoophilia), and homosexual practices (Lev. 18; *see* Homosexuality) are rejected in favor of a moral relativism that goes well beyond secular humanistic values of consent and caring. Economic pressures of an expanded market have generated extreme expressions of sexuality combined with hate and aggression that attack the sensibilities of civilization. Pornography stands not so much as a cause of sexual immorality as a commentary on and symptom of contemporary decadence.

References

Attorney General. (1986). *Final Report of the Attorney-General's Commission on Pornography*. Nashville: Rutledge Hill Press.

Baron, R. A., & Bell, P. A. (1977). Sexual arousal and aggression by males: Effects of type of erotic stimuli and prior provocation. *Journal of Personality and Social Psychology, 35,* 79–87.

Court, J. H. (1980). *Pornography: A Christian critique.* Downers Grove, IL: InterVarsity Press.

Holbrook, D. (1972). *Sex and dehumanization.* London: Pitman.

Itzin, C. (Ed.). (1992). *Pornography: Women, violence and civil liberties.* Oxford: Oxford University Press.

Longford, L. (1972). *Pornography: The Longford report.* London: Coronet.

Malamuth, N. M., & Donnerstein, E. (Eds.). (1984). *Pornography and sexual aggression.* New York: Academic.

Minnery, T. (Ed.). (1986). *Pornography: A human tragedy.* Wheaton, IL: Tyndale House.

Morgan, R. (1980). Theory and practice of pornography and rape. In L. Lederer (Ed.), *Take back the night: Women on pornography.* New York: Morrow.

U.S. Presidential Commission Report on Obscenity and Pornography. (1970). New York: Bantam.

J. H. COURT

See SEXUALITY.

Positive Thinking. Positive thinking is an optimistic psychophilosophical worldview grounded in the conviction that life is embraced by God's unconditional grace, and therefore this is a win-win world. The positivists of the sixteenth through the nineteenth centuries wrote a profoundly significant chapter in the history of philosophy. Particular attention must be paid to the works of David Hume, René Descartes, and Auguste Comte in any appreciation of modern Western thought. It is tempting, therefore, to seek the roots of the contemporary religious positive thinking movement as represented by Norman Vincent Peale and Robert Schuller within the development of the philosophy of positivism. Such an attempt might suggest the link between the classic positivists and the contemporary religious positive thinkers to be the philosophy of John Dewey.

The difficulty with this thesis, however, is that the apparent similarity between modern religious positive thinkers and classic positivism masks a major philosophical or methodological difference. Classic positivism is rooted in the philosophical assumption that the world is coherent and empirically discernible. Truth, therefore, can be arrived at through formal Aristotelian method and its rational consequences (*see* Aristotle). The psychological posture of positivism is hopeful, optimistic, and confident. The positivist's certainty that rational-empirical method will disclose all truth is virtually absolute.

The philosophical assumption of the positive religious thinkers such as Peale and Schuller stands in sharp contrast to this. They begin with the assumption that the spiritual forces of death or deterioration can be overcome by the spiritual forces of life and growth, since the latter are more powerful. It is further assumed that divine revelation is the source of that information.

Philosophically, therefore, the positive thinkers in religion are virtually opposite from classic logical positivism. The contrast is precisely that of the rational empiricism of the positivists versus the romantic idealism of the religious positive thinkers. For the positivists the foundation for the search for truth is the claim that the Aristotelian scientific method discloses absolute truth because it corresponds in method to the coherent structure of the universe and its laws of existence and function. For the positive religious thinkers the foundation for the search for truth is divine revelation. It is evident, therefore, that the romantic idealism of the religious positive thinkers looks more like a form of Platonism than a form of Aristotelianism (*see* Plato).

Peale and Schuller are similar psychologically to the classic positivists in that they are imbued with an absolute form of hopefulness, optimism, and confidence. Their optimism is in and about their apprehension of divine truth and its redemptive applicability in human life. The optimism of the classic positivists is in the rational-empirical method of pursuing truth.

It is interesting to note that both Schuller and Peale stand within the Reformed theological tradition, Schuller developing within that tradition and Peale coming to it later. This fact is not unrelated to their positive thinking perspective, for at its best the positive thinking movement is the result of the Reformed tradition taken to its logical and psychological conclusion. In this tradition grace means an arbitrary divine disposition of unmerited goodwill toward unworthy humans, leading to an eternal hopefulness and unquenchable optimism for all who perceive and take seriously this truth.

Schuller (1981) and Ellens (1987) point out that the freedom for growth implied in God's grace invests everything, including our sin and tragedy as well as our health and holiness, with meaning and hope. Taking his cue from Peale, Schuller shapes his message and style in terms of that transcendent optimism. He contends that positive thinking has profound spiritual and psychological consequences. It incites meaning, infuses one with self-esteem (Schuller, 1985), mobilizes healing and growth, evaporates debilitating anxiety, constructively channels misdirected energy, affirms a durable security, and inspires legitimate comfort for life and eternity. For the positive thinkers all of that, and the faith in God's grace in Christ, is to be part of salvation—spiritual, psychological, and social (Ellens, 1982). Clinebell (1979) is an example of this same positive grace orientation applied to psychotherapeutic theory and practice.

Recent research in mind-body relationships in psychosomatic disorders (Gottschalk, 1978) as well as the insights of cognitive behavior therapists on the relationship between cognitions and affect states (Meichenbaum, 1977) suggest that the claims of the religious positive thinkers may have some basis. Persons who can be hopeful and grateful can mobilize physiological, psychological, and spiritual dynamics of health that are unavailable to the person who cannot be hopeful or grateful. The names we put on experiences determine in large part how they affect us (Meichenbaum, 1977). Humans can, by their thoughts and acts of will, considerably influence their feelings, health, and even their chemistry. This is the truth behind the effectiveness of positive thinking.

References

Clinebell, H. J. (1979). *Growth counseling: Hope-centered methods of actualizing human wholeness*. Nashville: Abingdon.

Ellens, J. H. (1982). *God's grace and human health*. Nashville: Abingdon.

Ellens, J. H. (1987). *Psychology: Key issues*. Pretoria: UNISA.

Gottschalk, L. A. (1978). Psychosomatic medicine today: An overview. *Psychosomatics, 19* (2), 89–93.

Meichenbaum, D. H. (1977). *Cognitive behavior modification: An integrative approach*. New York: Plenum.

Schuller, R. H. (1985). *Self-esteem*. New York: Berkley Jove.

Schuller, R. H. (1981). Why Bob Schuller smiles on television. *Leadership, 2* (1), 26–32.

Additional Readings

Meyer, D. (1980). *The positive thinkers: Religion as pop psychology*. New York: Pantheon.

Peale, N. V. (1952). *The power of positive thinking*. Englewood Cliffs, NJ: Prentice-Hall.

J. H. ELLENS

See MIND-BRAIN RELATIONSHIP.

Positivism. *See* EMPIRICISM; PSYCHOLOGY, METHODS OF.

Postabortion Counseling. Postabortion women (and, more recently, men) are seeking help from their pastors, physicians, and therapists in ever-increasing numbers, challenging the long-held assumption by the professional community that emotional problems following an abortion represent only temporary hormonal fluctuations.

The Impact of Abortion. The following scenario is a common experience shared by a large percentage of women who have chosen abortion. First, a quick or pragmatic solution to the fear and anxiety of a crisis pregnancy is sought. In the midst of this, a moral dilemma develops between the nurturing and parental bond of the woman with the child she carries in contrast to the felt pressure from circumstances and/or significant others. This tension is particularly acute in those whose moral code or sense of their feminine identity is contrary to the thought of having an abortion. Nevertheless, in many cases the need for an immediate and expedient solution wins, and the abortion is procured. The woman (couple) enters into a brief relief phase lasting anywhere from a few days to a few weeks, because, for better or worse, the crisis is finally over. The moral dilemma eventually resurfaces, and the decision to abort is now questioned. Often the answer is, "No, I violated my own moral code by destroying my child" (Zimmerman, 1987). Again, this is particularly true of those who have acted contrary to their own sense of moral identity.

At this stage the woman either talks about the pain she is beginning to experience or she employs coping strategies (Defense Mechanisms) and avoidance behaviors to protect against the pain. This pushing down of painful emotions and memories can be kept in place for years. Eventually, however, as normal life changes and stresses enter her life over the years, she may begin to re-experience the painful thoughts and emotions related to her abortion experience, whether she wants to or not. Dr. Julius Fogel, an obstetrician-gynecologist and psychiatrist who performed more than 20,000 abortions during his career, perhaps explained best the psychological situation confronting many women after an abortion. He states, "There is no question about the emotional grief and mourning following an abortion. It shows up in various forms. I've had patients who had abortions a year or two ago . . . but it still bothers them. . . . There is no question in my mind that we are disturbing a life process. . . . Often the trauma may sink into the unconscious and never surface in the woman's lifetime. . . . [But] a psychological price is paid. I can't say exactly what. It may be alienation, it may be a pushing away from human warmth, perhaps a hardening of the maternal instinct. Something happens on the deeper levels of a woman's consciousness when she destroys a pregnancy. I know that as a psychiatrist" (McCarthy, 1989).

A woman may be so psychologically influenced by this experience over time that, once in therapy, it is not uncommon for her to begin her first session with the confession, "My life is out of control— I think I'm on the verge of a complete breakdown."

Men and Abortion. Men are by law excluded from the abortion decision even if the woman carrying his child happens to be his wife. If his partner procured an abortion against his will, the potentially resulting feelings of rage and helplessness may assault the core of his masculinity and identity as one who needs to protect his offspring. Many men take the more passive approach of "I'll support you in whatever you decide to do, dear," having accepted the contemporary feminist position that abortion is solely a woman's choice. At a time when the pregnant woman may really want to hear the man's inner feelings and thoughts about her, the pregnancy, and his interpersonal commitment to work this out with her, his passivity or lack of responsibility is often a disappointing response. More often than not this results in a break in the relationship. Men who encouraged or even coerced an abortion decision due to pragmatic reasons are often consumed with guilt and remorse later in life, particularly if their moral identity was against abortion in general. These individuals will often need to work through areas of forgiveness and emotional healing.

Factors that Exacerbate the Impact of Abortion. The likelihood of a woman experiencing emotional problems after an abortion increases when the following factors accompany the abortion: coercion (Payne, Kravitz, Notman, & Anderson 1976; Reardon, 1987); ambivalence (Adler, 1975); rearing in a conservative religion (Congleton & Calhoun, 1993; Diehm & Diehm, 1991); poor relationship with or little support from parents and/or sex partner (Barnard, 1990); born into a "high risk" family in which parents, grandparents, or siblings have a history of emotional, physical, alcohol/drug abuse, financial, or legal problems (Deutsch; 1982); prior abortions, which applies to approximately 40% of postabortion women in the U.S. (Bradley, 1984); abortion for fetal anomalies or other medical problems (Kolker & Burke, 1993); late-term abortion (Kaltreider, Goldsmith, & Margolis, 1979); inadequate pre-abortion counseling (Reardon, 1987); having existing children at the time of the abortion (Reisser, 1989); prior emotional problems or significant amount of past trauma (Barnard, 1990; Belsey, Green, Lal, Lewis, & Beard, 1977), and younger (teen-aged) women (Lyons, Larson, Huckeba, & Mueller, 1988).

Psychological Healing from an Abortion. Healing from the emotional damage of a past abortion often involves successfully navigating a number of psychological tasks. First, with a trusted counselor one must work through any denial and allow past painful emotions to surface by remembering and relating the details and negative feelings surrounding the abortion experience. Second, one needs to deal appropriately with issues of guilt in relation to God and receiving forgiveness from him. This involves assuming responsibility for the decision, understanding the full meaning of repentance, correcting toxic views of who God is and how God

operates, and finally accepting a new view of God as the ultimate loving, forgiving parent. Third, one must identify and release the anger toward oneself and others involved in the abortion decision, which includes releasing any need for vengeance. Fourth, one must become open to grieving over the lost child, acknowledging the full personhood of the baby. This allows for the possibility to say good-bye to the child with the future hope of experiencing perfect reconciliation with the child in the kingdom of God.

References

Adler, N. E. (1975). Emotional responses of women following therapeutic abortion. *American Journal of Orthopsychiatry, 45,* 446–454.

Barnard, C. A. (1990). The long-term psychological effects of abortion. Portsmouth, NH: Institute for Abortion Recovery & Research.

Belsey, E. M., Green, H., Lal, S., Lewis, S., & Beard, R. W. (1977). Predictive factors in emotional response to abortion: King's termination study–IV. *Social Science and Medicine, 11,* 71–82.

Bradley, C. (1984). Abortion in subsequent pregnancy. *Canadian Journal of Psychiatry, 9,* 494–498.

Congleton, G. K., & Calhoun, L. G. (1993). Post-abortion perceptions: A comparison of self-identified distressed and nondistressed populations. *International Journal of Social Psychiatry, 39* (4), 255–265.

Deutsch, M. (1982). Personality factors, self-concept, and family variables related to first time and repeat abortion-seeking behavior in adolescent women. Unpublished doctoral dissertation, Washington, DC: American University.

Diehm, J. C., & Diehm, P. (1991). The long-term psychological effects of abortion on Christian women. Unpublished paper. Irvine, CA: 714-955-3224.

Kaltreider, N., Goldsmith, S., & Margolis, A. (1979). The impact of midtrimester abortion techniques on patients and staff. *Psychiatry and Medicine, 4,* 129–134.

Kolker, A., & Burke, M. (1993). Grieving the wanted child: Ramifications of abortion after prenatal diagnosis of abnormality. *Health Care for Women, International, 14* (6), 513–526.

Lyons, J., Larson, D., Huckeba, W., & Mueller, C. (1988). Research on the psychological impact of abortion: Systematic review of the literature 1966 to 1985. From an unpublished paper prepared for Family Research Council, Washington, DC.

McCarthy, C. (1989 February 5). The real anguish of abortion. *The Washington Post.*

Payne, R., Kravitz, A., Notman, M., & Anderson, J. (1976). Outcome following therapeutic abortion. *Archives of General Psychiatry, 33,* 725.

Reardon, D. C. (1987). *Aborted women: Silent no more.* Westchester, IL: Crossway.

Reisser, T. K. (1989). *Help for the post-abortion woman.* Lewiston, NY: Life Cycle Books.

Zimmerman, D. R. (1987, March 9). Abortion clinics' toughest cases. *Medical World News,* 55–61.

Additional Readings

Women in Ramah: A post-abortion Bible study. (Care Net, 109 Carpenter Dr. #100, Sterling, VA 20164).

Turning a father's heart. (Care Net, 109 Carpenter Dr. #100, Sterling, VA 20164).

Michels, N. (1988). *Helping women recover from abortion.* Minneapolis: Bethany House.

T. K. REISSER AND J. H. COE

See COUNSELING AND PSYCHOTHERAPY: OVERVIEW; MORAL AND ETHICAL ISSUES IN TREATMENT; MARRIAGE COUNSELING; PREMARITAL COUNSELING.

Postoperative Disorders. Surgery historically was used as a last resort in the treatment of life-threatening illnesses. However, since the development of safer anesthetics and procedures, it is no longer restricted to acute, critical illnesses. Surgery is done frequently on an elective basis or as a preventative procedure (e.g., tubal ligations to prevent future pregnancies). It is also used as a diagnostic technique (e.g., laparoscopy) and as a reparative or cosmetic procedure (e.g., plastic surgery).

The surgical event alone is not the only stressful aspect for the surgical patient. The prospective patient enters into a stressful environment the moment he or she leaves home to go to the hospital. Depending on his or her adaptive capacities to stressful situations, the patient will experience normal or disturbing emotional responses. These reactions, which may begin even as early as admission to the hospital, can affect the postsurgical recovery process.

The patient often is minimally knowledgeable about physiological functioning and about how the proposed procedure will affect the body. This lack of knowledge plus the lack of any foreknowledge of the postoperative course (particularly in the case of first surgical experiences) can lead to considerable preoperative anxiety, which may be shown in excessive questioning, irritability, or regression with demandingness and suspicion. Janis (1958) has shown that a moderate amount of anxiety is both appropriate and indicative of a good postoperative recovery in general. Other preoperative factors that enhance postoperative recovery are general emotional support from hospital staff and the availability of supportive family members or close friends.

The common postoperative experiences immediately after surgery are drowsiness, nausea and occasional vomiting, and a lack of appetite. These are the general effects of the systemic anesthetics and usually wear off in a day or two. Analgesics prescribed for pain often produce sleep and some amnesia or mild confusion. After several days, and particularly with nonambulatory patients or those in intensive care, a state of sensory deprivation can set in due to the monotony and the lack of variety in the environment. This may be evident in the form of fantasies, perceptual distortions, hallucinations, or even psychoticlike behavior. Consistent, concerned human contact and sensory stimulation in the form of pictures, tapes, or a radio can frequently alleviate this and speed recovery.

Certain surgical procedures can lead to specific postoperative issues. For example, the amputation of a limb can activate a sense of loss and body disintegration that may result in denial and the temporary sense of a phantom limb (*see* Phantom Response). Fisher and Cleveland (1968) have demonstrated that the occurrence of phantom limb phenomena is associated with the surgical removal of a limb rather than with the accidental loss of the body part.

The control of elimination is generally viewed as an indicator of developing maturity. Thus the loss of this control with colostomies and ileostomies often produces doubts about maturity, embarrassment and anxiety, and an impairment in self-confidence. Plastic surgery usually requires a number of stages separated over some length of time and may lead to postoperative depression. This necessitates support and the patient's understanding that the expected result is a product of numerous separate steps.

Postoperative complications in pediatric surgery are a product not only of the nature of the surgery but also of the developmental stage of the child at the time of the operation. This generally involves issues of separation and dependency. For instance, infants in the first few months generally respond with depressed functioning and apathy. After the sixth to eighth month, the separation produces crying and clinging to the mother. Later (years one through four) the hospitalization and surgery are often experienced as abandonment and may be presumed to be a form of punishment. This may result in regression. In years five to ten the child understands the reason for the surgery but fears mutilation. Finally, the adolescent who is asserting autonomy will experience any major surgery as traumatic to this independence. At each stage the crucial issues will come to the fore in the postoperative recovery and will need to be addressed or supported if recovery is to proceed smoothly.

The management of postoperative complications begins at the point of hospitalization. Adequate preparation of the patient both to what is going to happen during the surgery and what can be expected in the days immediately succeeding it is exceedingly important. Some preoperative anxiety is to be expected. The involvement of a well-prepared family and supportive hospital staff is also conducive to the avoidance or management of these postoperative effects.

References

Fisher, S., & Cleveland, S. E. (1968). *Body image and personality* (2nd ed.). New York: Dover.

Janis, I. L. (1958). *Psychological stress: Psychoanalytic and behavioral studies of surgical patients.* New York: Wiley.

Additional Readings

Furst, J. B. (1978, June). Emotional stress reactions to surgery. *New York State Journal of Medicine,* 1083–1085.

Matheson, G. (1979, February). Terror in the ICU: Exercise in hyperbole? *Forum on Medicine,* 102–104.

Thunberg, U. H., & Kemph, J. P. (1977). Common emotional reactions to surgical illness. *Psychiatric Annals,* 7 (1), 39–58.

G. MATHESON

Postpartum Depression. Postpartum depression, as it has traditionally been known, is now called major depressive disorder with postpartum onset. The postpartum onset specifier may also be applied to bipolar disorder (I or II) or brief psychotic disorder. Thus postpartum symptoms may appear as depression, mania, or psychosis.

The common feature is onset within four weeks of the birth of a child in women who do not have either cyclothymia or dysthymia. Postpartum mood episodes with delusions or hallucinations may be more common with a first birth, and 30% to 50% of women who have had one such episode have another with subsequent deliveries.

The symptoms of postpartum onset mood disorders and nonpostpartum mood disorders are the same. However, the course of the symptoms may vary more in postpartum depression, and the moods are frequently less stable. For a diagnosis of postpartum onset depression, a depressed mood or loss of pleasure or interest in nearly all activities must last for at least two weeks, accompanied by at least four other symptoms affecting appetite, sleep, activity level, self-concept, or thinking.

Mothers with a postpartum onset mood disorder may contemplate suicide and may be obsessed with thoughts of the new child being injured or killed. They may find it difficult to concentrate, and they may be physically agitated.

If delusions are present, as they are in as many as 1 in 500 births, they are usually about the baby. As the delusions may be that the baby is possessed by a demon or has special powers, a pastor or Christian therapist may be especially helpful. Christian counselors may be well prepared to assist women with postpartum depression who feel guilty about being depressed at a time when others are telling them that they should be happy.

New mothers who do not have a postpartum onset mood disorder may experience some of the same symptoms, but these so-called baby blues typically last for less than one week after the birth. Clinicians should consider a diagnosis of a postpartum onset mood disorder only if the symptoms (especially those of severe anxiety, repeated weeping, and lack of interest in the new baby) persist for more than one week. Lack of interest must be distinguished from lack of attention or awareness, which may indicate delirium during the postpartum period rather than depression.

Postpartum mood episodes may be severe. Especially if they are accompanied by delusions or hallucinations, they may interfere with developing a bonding relationship with the baby and may even lead the mother to attempt to kill her infant.

Many factors contribute to postpartum onset mood disorders. Physical exhaustion from the pregnancy and labor probably plays a role, as does the accompanying dehydration. Within a few days after delivery, the mother's hormone levels drop abruptly, and estrogen levels in particular have been linked to mood.

Psychological pressures on new mothers and fathers are significant. Both must cope with the physical demands of parenting, with sleep disruption increasing the difficulty. They must learn to communicate with the baby and in a new way with each other. They may be ambivalent about their new family status and roles, and the baby may bring financial and emotional pressures.

The most effective treatment appears to be postpartum counseling within a few days of the birth. Women who know that they should expect their emotions and attitudes to fluctuate for awhile can anticipate recovery in two to three weeks. Those who do not may need clinical treatment for a mood disorder.

P. D. YOUNG

See DEPRESSION.

Posttraumatic Stress Disorder. Posttraumatic stress disorder (PTSD) is a psychological disorder precipitated by exposure to a traumatic event or a series of events. This event is usually experienced by an individual. However, PTSD can also develop as a result of observing or hearing of a traumatic event occurring in someone else's life (such as a relative or a close friend). PTSD was introduced as a disorder in 1980 in the *DSM-III*. The *DSM-III-R's* condition for diagnosis was the experiencing of a traumatic event that was "outside the range of usual human experience." However, in *DSM-IV,* the focus is not so much on the nature of the event as it is on the individual's response to the event and his or her vulnerability to developing the characteristic symptoms.

Clinical Picture. Individuals with PTSD experience three categories of symptoms—intrusive recollections, avoidant-numbing symptoms, and hyperarousal. Reexperiencing the trauma through intrusive recollections such as flashbacks and nightmares, in which the individual involuntarily feels or acts as though the events were recurring, are considered the hallmark symptoms of PTSD (Calhoun & Resick, 1993). The nightmares are usually replications of the traumatic event, whereas flashbacks are evidenced by extreme physiological and emotional arousal in which the individual feels immobilized and becomes unaware of his or her surroundings. The intrusive recollections are triggered by specific events that resemble or symbolize some aspect of the trauma: an anniversary, the sound of a gunshot, weather conditions, a particular scent, clothing, or location. For instance, a woman who was raped in an elevator would breathe quickly and begin to sweat upon entering one.

Individuals also tend to avoid stimuli related to the trauma. Conscious efforts are made to avoid feelings, thoughts, and activities related to the traumatic events. Individuals also resist talking about the trauma because it brings up recollections of the events. The numbing behavior is usually evident through a lessened response to the outside world that occurs soon after the traumatic experience. Individuals no longer enjoy some of the activities they were previously interested in and maintain distance from others. They have difficulties labeling their feelings or trusting others, and they often feel that the future is meaningless. Individuals may also experience problems recalling important aspects of the event because of their tendency to avoid the anxiety aroused by memories of the events. For some individuals, dissociation may occur; they become amnestic about the feelings and memories of the trauma. They also feel anger toward those who were responsible for the events, ashamed of their feelings of helplessness, and guilty about what they did or failed to do. These feelings of anger, avoidance, guilt, and shame may cause them to feel isolated and demoralized (American Psychiatric Association, 1994; Long, 1996; Tomb, 1994).

These individuals also become easily startled or physically aroused, responses that were not present prior to the trauma. They experience symptoms of anxiety as evidenced by difficulties falling or staying asleep because of the nightmares they repeatedly experience. Individuals also tend to be hypervigilant about their environment. For instance, rape victims continually scan their environment watching for potential rapists. Other symptoms include irritable feelings, uncontrollable anger, and problems with concentrating and finishing tasks.

The symptoms usually take a different form with children. They experience nightmares about monsters rather than traumatic events. They reenact the events in compulsive play and daydreams and often complain of headaches and stomachaches. They also regress to more infantlike behaviors and forget toilet training. Separation anxiety, fear of strangers, and school phobias are not uncommon. Defiant, passive, or clinging behaviors also occur (American Psychiatric Association, 1994; Long, 1996; Tomb, 1994).

Etiology. Disagreement exists concerning the relationship between particular predispositions and the probability of developing PTSD. However, the likelihood that a stressor will produce PTSD is greater if the stress is sudden, severe, unexpected, prolonged, repetitive, life-threatening, humiliating, isolating, causes physical damage, and destroys one's community and social support system. Individuals seem to have a higher risk of developing PTSD if they have a previous psychiatric disorder, a family history of psychiatric illness, a personality style such as introversion, personality disorders, a history of trauma, inadequate coping skills, poor stress tolerance, and insufficient social supports (Tomb, 1994).

Diagnostic Criteria. In order to make a diagnosis of PTSD, the *DSM-IV* criteria require that the individual be exposed to or have a history of exposure to a "traumatic event" or events that involve actual or threatened death or serious injury or a threat to physical integrity. These events include military combat, natural or manmade disasters, accidents, violent assaults (sexual abuse, rape, kidnaping, torture), and diagnosis with a terminal disease. The immediate response to these events is fear, helplessness, or horror. Witnessing the events or learning about them occurring with family members or close friends rather than directly experiencing them is also included in the criteria. Other symptoms include persistent reexperiencing of the traumatic event, avoidance of stimuli that are related to the events and feelings of numbness, and increased arousal. These symptoms must occur for more than one month and cause severe impairment in social, occupational, and other areas of functioning. The diagnosis is "acute" when the symptoms have occurred for less than three months, "chronic" when the symptoms persist for three months or longer, and "with delayed onset" when the symptoms begin six months after the occurrence of the trauma. If the symptoms of anxiety occur within one month after being exposed to the traumatic event, the diagnosis is acute stress disorder (American Psychiatric Association, 1994).

Treatment. Treatment should occur immediately after the traumatic event occurs or as soon as possible after its occurrence. Three significant goals of therapy are to establish a safe, trusting environment so that the individual can talk about traumatic material; to explore traumatic material in sufficient depth so that the individual can gradually integrate intrusive recollections with avoidant symptoms; and to assist the individual in disconnecting from the trauma and working on reestablishment of relationships with family and friends (Friedman, 1996; Herman, 1992). The therapist's genuineness, warmth, and empathy aid the patient in this process by his or her confidence about the treatment and ability to understand the significance of the trauma. Various approaches to treatment are common. The psychodynamic approach focuses on altering destructive attributions and reinterpreting the experience and involves gradual confrontation of the patient's feeling of shame, helplessness, and vulnerability. The behavioral approach emphasizes how the patient can cope with present symptoms and problems through exposure, rather than uncovering the story of the trauma (Tomb, 1994). Eye Movement Desensitization and Reprocessing (EMDR), a relatively new and controversial treatment that uses rapid rhythmic eye movements, shows some promise (Shapiro, 1989). Many trauma victims also find group treatment helpful (Tomb, 1994).

References

American Psychiatric Association. (1994). *Diagnostic and statistical manual of mental disorders* (4th Ed.). Washington, DC: Author.

Calhoun, K. S., & Resick, P. A. (1993). Post-traumatic stress disorder. In D. H. Barlow (Ed.), *Clinical handbook of psychological disorders*. New York: Guilford.

Friedman, M. J. (1996). PTSD diagnosis and treatment for mental health clinicians. *Community Mental Health Journal, 32,* 173–189.

Herman, J. L. (1992). *Trauma and recovery.* New York: Basic Books.

Long, P. W. (1996, June). Post-traumatic stress disorder. *The Harvard Mental Health Letter.*

Shapiro, F. (1989). Eye movement desensitization: A new treatment for post-traumatic stress disorder. *Journal of Behavior Therapy and Experimental Psychiatry, 20,* 211–217.

Tomb, D. A. (Ed.). (1994). Post-traumatic stress disorder. *The Psychiatric Clinics of North America, 17* (2).

W. SEEGOBIN

See TRAUMA; STRESS.

Poverty, Psychological Effects and Counseling.

Low socioeconomic status has been consistently associated with a range of risk factors, including chronic stress, unemployment, and poor mental health. In an epidemiological study Bruce, Takeuchi, and Leaf (1991) demonstrated a causal link between mental disorder and poverty by examining the patterns of new disorders that developed over a six-month period. Significant proportions of new episodes of mental disorder could be attributed to poverty. This article will examine three areas in which poverty greatly compromises mental health and the delivery of mental health services.

Poverty and the Developmental Needs of Children. Profound effects of poverty have been discovered on the psychological development and mental health of children. Families living in poverty are less able to obtain adequate housing, health care, and educational and social services. They are more likely to experience the highest levels of stress and yet procure fewer social and community support services. The indirect consequences of poverty are also pernicious. These often invisible effects operate within the homes, challenging marital and parent-child relationships. Experiencing chronic stress can alter a parent's ability to nurture and parent responsibly. This easily leads to generational cycles of both poverty and distressed parenting. Each new generation, reared by parents facing debilitating circumstances and lacking a solid foundation for thoughtful parenting, in turn finds itself lacking the emotional and social tools necessary to nurture its own offspring. Many poor families are headed by single mothers, which not only adds to the financial problem but also requires one person to do the emotional and physical work of two. All of these stresses compromises adequate parenting.

Parental poverty is related to a host of behavioral and academic shortcomings in the children. Children from economically disadvantaged homes are disproportionally represented in special-education classes and experience more grade retention. Research indicates that poor families tend not to promote cognitive development in their homes. Lower socioeconomic mothers are more controlling and disapproving and give less attention to their children than do middle-class mothers. In problem-solving situations, lower-class mothers spent less time on a task than do middle-class mothers. Lower-class mothers were more likely to intrude physically and give negative feedback, while the middle-class mothers gave more nonspecific suggestions and used thought-provoking questions. Lower-class mothers are more likely to use commands and less likely to praise their children than are middle-class mothers. These style differences places the lower-class child at risk for academic achievement, which often leads to further behavioral and motivational problems.

Other studies have found that socioeconomic status significantly predicted mental ability (using Bayley Scales of Children's Abilities and Wechsler Preschool and Primary Scales of Intelligence). Several other academic areas studied with school-age children have discovered the following significant correlations: socioeconomic status and grade point average, socioeconomic status and reading and math achievement, socioeconomic status and mathematics achievement test scores, and socioeconomic status and academic achievement. The potential role of inherited mental ability in determining academic success has been recognized and many studies controlled for the effect of parental intelligence quotient (IQ) and education. These studies still find low-socioeconomic children performing more poorly than high-socioeconomic children even when they match on parental IQ and education. Poverty during the toddler/preschool years is a significant predictor of decline in academic achievement during elementary school. Academic failure is significantly related to teenage pregnancy and school drop-out, which limit future employment opportunities. "Poor children, then, may be doubly handicapped. If they live in inner cities, the schools to which they must go are likely to be deficient in resources and ineffective as learning institutions. But their home environments, too, are likely to be deficient in those qualities and resources that promote children's learning" (Neal, 1996, pp. 344–345).

Homelessness. Homelessness is defined as having no shelter, living in shelters or missions, living as transients in cheap hotels or rooming houses, or staying with family or friends on a temporary basis (Belcher, 1988). According to a recent National Institute of Mental Health (NIMH) report (Sargent, 1989), mental illness is quite high among homeless populations. Approximately one-third of those who are homeless are suffering from severe mental illness, including schizophrenia, bipolar disorder, or severe depression. The report also recounts that 35% to 40% of these homeless mentally ill individuals also suffer from an alcohol or other substance-abuse problem. In the research examining the issues of contemporary homelessness a consistent finding is that homeless individuals with alcohol, drug, and mental disorders represent one of the most disadvantaged and underserved subgroups among the homeless population.

The majority of the homeless are male, although women are overrepresented among the homeless mentally ill subcategory. The median age range of the homeless mentally ill extend from 29 to 38 years, and blacks and Hispanics are overrepresented. Most of the homeless have little education, only about half have graduated from high school, and a large number are veterans of the armed services. Approximately one-third receive public benefits such as Social Security, and most have poor physical health.

The homeless mentally ill and the chronically stressed poor family have presented the mental health field with new and often misunderstood needs that require different and varied types of services.

Mental Health Service Providers. Community mental health centers have come under attack for their lack of understanding of the unique needs of diverse populations, in particular the poor and homeless, thus rendering services inaccessible. Bigel (1984) has documented the extent to which mental health services are underutilized by the poor. Personal factors that lead to this underutilization include unwillingness or inability to ask for help; unwillingness to admit a problem exists; pressure from informal networks of family, friends, and coworkers not to seek professional help; pride; and a value difference in defining what a problem is. Some of the more structural factors are problems related to accessibility; auspices of services; sex and ethnicity of service providers; confidentiality; availability of services; fragmentation of services; and lack of accountability of services. Too often the community itself is not linked with the service delivery system and problems are defined by policymakers or grant agencies. This renders the service providers largely ineffective. More recently research is demonstrating that models of service delivery that build upon community strengths, involve community leaders in problem definition, and utilize the notion of empowerment are more likely to be utilized by residents.

There are counseling implications when one works with diversity, whether class or ethnicity. Many counselors unfortunately have not received adequate training in understanding multicultural values, both those that affect the client and those that govern the counselor; this lack of training subsequently influences the counseling process. Multicultural knowledge that is needed includes group values, expectancies, behavioral patterns, differences within groups, family structures and roles, socialization patterns, attitudes toward exceptionalities, and historically important themes (Esquivel & Keitel, 1990). Other factors also inhibit therapists from working effectively with the poor. Often the problems lie in the therapists' attitudes and lack of understanding of the unique needs of the poor person rather than treatability. Language and style of communication prevent both the client and the therapist from understanding meaningful information.

Fragmentation of services has been a frequent complaint whether the target population is the homeless mentally ill or poor and chronically stressed families. This fragmentation began when differing entitlement agendas encouraged specialized programs for narrowly defined subgroups. Eligibility criteria were regulated by the funding agency, an approach that resulted in a patchwork quilt of programs. More recent emphases have been on comprehensiveness, colocation of service components, blending resources from different programs, and the operational integration of services. This new interest for service integration emerged from the realization of the immense cost and bureaucracy of the entitlement programs and the increased desire for accountability regarding treatment effectiveness. An integrated system that collaborates with the target populations for problem definition, intervention plans and implementation, and outcome assessment has proven far more effective. This new emphasis on integrated systems of service delivery provides a rich arena for research, theory, and practice—strengths the field of psychology offers.

Conclusion. Whether one is a child or elderly, male or female, poverty wreaks havoc on mental health. Moreover, the effects are not equally distributed. More women than men, one-quarter of all children under age six, and a disproportionate number of minority groups live in poverty. Therefore, beyond economic disadvantage, poverty places families and ethnic minorities at increased risk for mental or emotional problems.

The Christian church must ultimately face the question: What is our responsibility for the poor? Jesus clearly calls us to respond empathically, materially, and spiritually. "Jesus said to him, 'If you wish to be perfect, go, sell you possessions, and give the money to the poor, and you will have treasure in heaven; then come, follow me'" (Matt. 19:21, NRSV; Mark 10:21); "But when you give a banquet, invite the poor, the crippled, the lame, and the blind. And you will be blessed, because they cannot repay you, for you will be repaid at the resurrection of the righteous" (Luke 14:13, NRSV). Finally, James articulates forcefully the sin of ignoring the poor: "Listen, my beloved brothers and sisters. Has not God chosen the poor in the world to be rich in faith and to be heirs of the kingdom that he has promised to those who love him? But you have dishonored the poor" (James 2:5–6); "If a brother or sister is naked and lacks daily food, and one of you says to them, 'Go in peace; keep warm and eat your fill,' and yet you do not supply their bodily needs, what is the good of that? So faith by itself, if it has no works, is dead" (James 2:15–17, NRSV). The poor, whether parents, children, or the homeless, need resources and skills, food and clothes. And yet they need far more; they need hope and support. Hope brings vision, a plan for the future, the belief that one can make it despite incredible barriers. Surely Christians have much to offer in the way of hope. The church needs to serve in an advocacy role and as a healing community to those suffering the adversities of poverty.

References

Belcher, J. (1988). Defining the service needs of homeless mentally ill persons. *Hospital and Community Psychiatry, 39* (11), 1203–1205.

Bigel, D. E. (1984). Help seeking and receiving in urban ethnic neighborhoods: Strategies for empowerment. *Prevention in Human Services, 3* (3), 119–143.

Bruce, M. L., Takeuchi, D. T., & Leaf, P. J. (1991). Poverty and psychiatric status: Longitudinal evidence from the New Haven epidemiologic catchment area study. *Archives of General Psychiatry, 48,* 470–474.

Esquivel, G. B., & Keitel, M. A. (1990). Counseling immigrant children in the schools. *Elementary School Guidance & Counseling, 24,* 213–221.

Neal, C. (1996). Family issues in welfare reform: Developmental pathways as a theoretical framework for understanding generational cycles of poverty. In S. W. Carlson-Thies & J. W. Skillen (Eds.), *Welfare in America: Christian perspectives on a policy in crisis.* Grand Rapids, MI: Eerdmans.

Sargent, M. (1989). Update on programs for the homeless mentally ill. *Hospital and Community Psychiatry, 40* (10), 1015–1016.

Additional Readings

Carlson-Thies, S. W., & Skillen, J. W. (Eds.). (1996). *Welfare in America: Christian perspectives on a policy in crisis.* Grand Rapids, MI: Eerdmans.

Ellwood, D. T. (1988). *Poor support: Poverty in the American family.* New York: Basic.

Polakow, V. (1993). *Lives on the edge: Single mothers and their children in the other America.* Chicago: University of Chicago Press.

C. J. NEAL

Poverty of Speech. A disorder characterized by a restriction in the amount of speech or conversation of an individual. Replies to questions are brief and unelaborated, and if the condition is severe, the person may speak only in monosyllables or grunts. Poverty of speech is common in schizophrenia, major depressive episodes, and organic mental disorders such as dementia.

Power. Having the authority, control, influence, or physical might over others; the ability to act or produce an effect; the right of ruling, governing, or determining; potency, might, force, strength; dominion, dominance, supremacy, sovereignty: these are power.

All power comes from God and belongs to God (Matt. 6:13; 26:64). Individuals take part in God's power, and they must choose between using this power in a giving way that benefits the world and other people or in service primarily to oneself. Responsibility must be exercised in the use of power, in deciding whether and how to use or not use it. Christ proclaimed the power of love to conquer not only death but also domination and oppression, particularly over the weak and needy.

However, although religious believers across many denominations throughout history rejected absolute use of power, the ecclesiastical institution enthusiastically accepted a position of authority and power over the laity and especially over females. The laity were to humbly obey the ecclesiastical ruling in all manner of affairs. Many people unquestioningly acquiesced to religious authority. Those most often held in submission by such authority, females and ethnic minorities, are questioning such use of power and demanding to share in the decision making as equals with males and nonminority group members.

Females have most likely been held in submission through direct or implied physical force by males, with perhaps a secondary reinforcement of accepted right of authority of the male patriarchy and traditional male society. Females were conditioned not to question the stronger sex or male dictates.

Ethnic minorities, who by definition are outnumbered by others in the population, have also been subjected to submission to the religious, economic, and political control of others. As disenfranchised and disempowered individuals and groups of individuals become increasingly aware of their desire to share in the power structure of various institutions and become more and more uncomfortable in being left out, they join with likeminded people to be heard. The current movement in ecclesia, for instance, is toward less top-heavy bureaucracy in religious authority and dictum and more democratic ruling by laity participating with clergy.

Power has been viewed from its personal, social-psychological aspects and its effects on others. Further, power has been analyzed both as a quality possessed by persons and as a process of interaction between individuals. An analysis developed by Rollo May can be used to study personal, social, and psychological power and its effects on people. The exercise of power may be seen as

1. Nutrient power: Power used for others' benefit, such as in parenting, healing, some ministering. The relationship is temporarily or permanently unequal.
2. Integrative power: Power with others, involving cooperative freedom and mutual influence.
3. Competitive power: Power against another, involving a contest among equals.
4. Manipulative power: Power gained over another, relying on psychological interaction in situations of domination and inequality.
5. Exploitative power: Power over others, involving force, inequality, and domination.

Ethical, spiritual, and religious individuals and groups have continued to struggle with the use of power and its perversions. For instance, nutrient power could be oppressive if the nurturing persons keep the nurtured individuals in a position of inequality and servitude. To be satisfying to both parties, the more powerful must permit the temporary inequality of the less powerful to be overcome. In nurturing relationships, the dependency may shift and be mutually felt but at different times. For instance, one spouse may parent or nurture the other spouse, and at another time this role reverses in the parent-child paradigm. In that way the relationship is more even and the balance of power is achieved.

When those in dominant positions see those in subordinate positions as not able to become equal to themselves, nutrient power is abused. Such plantation mentality is evidenced in relationships of slaveowners and slaves, men and women, dominant ethnic and nondominant ethnic groups, and younger and older adults. One of the most insidious and pervasive aspects of abusive power is the defining by the dominant persons as to who the nondominant group is and as to what attributes and values are to be considered positive, good, and worthy of possessing. Ethnic differences, such as skin color and other features, could be defined as belonging to subordinate groups of people and as attributes of those needing to be taken care of by the dominant group. Older adults may be seen as weaker physically than younger adults. The abled would define themselves as physically stronger than the disabled, looking at one handicap and defining that as the overall worth or power of disabled people instead of seeing the many attributes and skills as equal to or better than those of the abled persons. Perhaps, though, it is in the area of gender and ethnic-cultural differences that abuses of power are the most abhorrent and odious. In these two areas being different in some presumed ways is defined as inferiority by the dominant people.

The dominant group predefines itself, with all of its particular attributes, as superior and worthy forever of domination, leadership, and powerfulness. Traditions of institutions, such as ecclesia and social clubs and other organizations, may be used to further hold the outgroup in an inferior or subordinate position. This locks them in a prison and throws away the keys. Only banding together with others in such circumstances and taking on the cloak of protection and power granted by the Constitution or some other legal protection can the doors of opportunity be opened and the possibilities for true sharing of power be realized. In psychotherapy care is being taken to make roles of client and therapist more equal.

C. A. RAYBURN

See AUTHORITARIAN PERSONALITY.

Power Motive. See DOMINANCE.

Prayer, Psychological Effects of. Prayer is a complex activity. One person prays for healing from cancer while another prays for strength to live with the cancer. One person prays according to God's will, another person does not. One person prays an intercessory prayer, another person prays a prayer of confession. With so many different types of prayer and different motives for praying, it is understandable that the effects of prayer will be varied and research results contradictory. Most research on prayer is correlational, not causal, in nature because it is practically impossible for psychologists to control for all the variables that must be controlled in order to be able to say that prayer causes a specific effect. Therefore, the psychological effects of prayer must be considered with these caveats in mind.

Most psychologists view prayer as a coping technique. Prayer is often a response to overwhelming life situations in which people feel as though they are helpless and lack the resources to overcome. Physical illness and addictions are two good examples. Many prayers are offered for healing from physical disease. Prayer is also called for in the eleventh step of 12-step recovery programs such as Alcoholics Anonymous (AA), in which addicts pray for the knowledge and power to do God's will in order to overcome their addiction, over which they admitted they were powerless in step one.

By praying people begin to exert some control over their circumstances. They are doing something significant about their situation. They are communicating with God, and through God they believe that they can impact their circumstances and their lives. This increases people's sense of mastery and lowers stress. It promotes a sense of self-efficacy, which is associated with many positive psychological effects such as decreased anxiety and depression and increased success on a variety of tasks. Prayer gives people a sense of strength for overcoming their problems.

Humanistic critics have sometimes argued that praying contributes to an external locus of control, that is, it makes people feel inadequate in themselves and as though they need something outside themselves to cope with life. Thus they abdicate all responsibility to God and take a passive role. Recent research on the role of faith and prayer in life has not supported this criticism (Brown, 1994). Recent research has indicated that prayer is not incompatible with an internal locus of control or adaptive behavior such as seeking medical help. There is increasing evidence that having and practicing a strong faith has many physical and mental health benefits. There is some evidence that prayer may even enhance immunocompetence (McCullough, 1995).

Prayer serves important cognitive purposes. Praying is a means of controlling or ordering one's thoughts, which may in itself reduce anxiety that comes from racing thoughts and feeling out of control. Prayer may be a type of cognitive therapy in which people review their attributions, set their expectations, and rehearse their beliefs. A number of Christian psychotherapists prescribe prayer to help clients correct faulty irrational beliefs and internalize healthy biblical beliefs. Prayer may also be an important avenue of self-exploration and discovery as people grapple with their thoughts, feelings, and behaviors. Augustine suggested that since God already knows people's needs and wants, their prayers are the construction of their desires. People's prayers reveal their values.

Prayer serves important social functions. Being prayed for helps people to feel secure, valued, and part of a caring community. Patients often report wanting their physicians and counselors to pray with them and for them. Praying for others is a way that people bear one another's burdens and form bonds of empathy and identification. Christians are often told to pray for those toward whom they are bitter because prayer develops positive feelings toward them and leads to forgiveness and caring. Prayer also allows people to have an important part in the lives of people thousands of miles away, whom they may never have met. Prayers for others enhance both self-efficacy and a sense of community.

Prayer is not always healthy or beneficial. Prayer may be a form of avoidance, when people pray instead of facing psychological conflict or taking constructive action. In some studies prayer has been found to be associated with higher levels of pain, anxiety, and psychoticism. Prayer may be a form of obsessive-compulsive disorder in which people mechanically repeat prayers to stave off anxiety or guilt. Prayer may be a superstitious behavior or used as a magical charm. In such cases prayer fails and people's faith and lives are shattered.

Above all it must be remembered that prayer is a form of praise and worship to God. God commanded it, delights in it, and reveals himself to those who do it. Through the communication of prayer people are transformed into Christ's likeness.

References

Brown, L. B. (1994). *The human side of prayer: The psychology of prayer.* Atlanta: John Knox.

McCullough, M. E. (1995). Prayer and health. Conceptual issues, research review, and research agenda. *Journal of Psychology and Theology, 23,* 15–29.

C. D. DOLPH

See RELIGIOUS RESOURCES IN PSYCHOTHERAPY.

Prayer, Use of in Counseling. Prayer can be a life-changing experience and a key component in all forms of healing. It is about embracing God and ourselves in all our complexity and mystery. It is at the heart of our relationship with God. If God is the One in whom "we live, move, and have our being" (Acts 17:28, NIV), then prayer may be a legitimate activity in counseling a Christian believer.

People come to therapy with healthy beliefs about prayer.

Prayer generates hope. We hope that God, who is good, will always act in our best interests according to God's will and wisdom.

The inner workings of prayer are a mystery.

Prayer works and people are healed. Just how they are healed is a matter of degree and definition.

The focus in prayer is more on the giver (God) than the gift.

Prayer is not a monolithic experience. It ranges from silent meditation, to loud and joyful thanksgiving, to earnest requests for help, to confession of sin, to a worshipful prayer language (tongues).

The purpose of prayer is not asocial or antisocial. It is intended to make us a more compassionate, justice-loving, and mission-oriented people.

In psychotherapy the therapist seeks to enter as completely as possible the world of the patient. A therapeutic goal is then agreed upon, and all the resources of the art and science of psychotherapy are used to achieve that goal. The debate is whether one of the resources is prayer. It enters psychotherapy according to the beliefs and goals of both the patient and the therapist.

Therapists have a wide range of attitudes toward prayer in psychotherapy.

It should be avoided. The attitude is, That's the realm of the pastor. The rationale is that therapists should not impose their value systems on patients. Such a sacred/secular split ignores the fact that values play a part in the therapy process. It also ignores the powerful component of divinely inspired change that is accepted in the patient's frame of reference.

It should be universal. If prayer is a part of the patient's life and the patient requests prayer, then prayer should be used. This position ignores the fact that prayer may not be always therapeutic.

It should be therapeutic. If prayer is a natural part of the patient's life, the patient requests prayer, and the therapist deems it therapeutic, then it should be used in counseling.

A therapist should be cautious in using prayer in therapy when

- Prayer is an escape from responsibility and reality. Sometimes a patient uses prayer as a defense mechanism to tranquilize unpleasant feelings.

- Prayer represents an unhealthy dependency. For example, the patient, afraid of intimacy, prays, "God, meet my love needs." The therapist needs to help the patient find healthy forms of intimacy and find better ways to deal with rejection.

- Prayer reinforces a personality disorder (e.g., the narcissistic patient who expects everything from God on his or her own terms).

- Prayer reinforces a childish belief in magic. God is seen as the magician who manipulates the world as the child anticipates.
- The patient's prayer life is part of a delusional system in a psychotic disorder. Here, as in all therapy, an accurate diagnosis is the first order of business in treatment.

Prayer can be a powerful therapeutic tool when

- The patient requests prayer at the beginning of treatment. In so doing a bond of trust or zone of safety is sought with the therapist. However, care must be taken not to focus on the therapist's faith but rather on the needs of the patient.
- It is a natural and healthy part of the patient's belief and practice. He or she sees therapy as a part of the journey of faith in which God has to be explicitly included through prayer.
- It is used to reinforce the meeting of basic needs of safety and acceptance. We all need a place of safety from which we take risks and make changes.
- Prayer can be a summary of the therapy session and used to invoke blessings on the patient's therapeutic homework assignments. It facilitates behavioral, emotional, and cognitive changes (e.g., "God give me courage to set boundaries with my abusing spouse").
- It serves the function of letting go of the past (e.g., a prayer of forgiveness that releases resentment).
- It helps the patient reframe suffering. God's goodness is not measured in terms of the outcome to a difficult situation. It is seen more in loving encounters with God through others.
- It generates the hope essential to the recovery process. The hope may be in God's care, the patient's capacity to make good decisions, or the remembrance of past incidents where God came through for the patient.
- It makes the patient less self-absorbed and more other or community conscious.

A change of focus can be the catalyst for a changed life. When prayer is used therapeutically it can be a powerful tool in redirecting broken, hurting, and confused lives. It is not a substitute for therapy but a way of being and practice that presupposes the power that comes from a personal relationship with God.

C. B. JOHNSON

See RELIGIOUS RESOURCES IN PSYCHOTHERAPY.

Preconscious. Sigmund Freud divided unconscious mental structures into two categories: the preconscious and the unconscious. The preconscious consists of those psychic elements readily available and accessible to the conscious mind with a minimal effort of thought. Any moment's conscious thought or memory can be brought from the preconscious and will go back to the preconscious before and after that moment. When one turns attention to a mathematical problem or recalls a favorite aunt's birthday, one is drawing on preconscious thoughts not always present in the conscious mind.

See CONSCIOUSNESS.

Prejudice. A prejudice is traditionally defined as a stereotype accompanied by emotions that predispose a person to react in a consistent way (usually negative) toward a class of persons. Prejudice is a negative attitude that expresses itself in unjustifiable negative behavior (discrimination) if social situations permit. Racism, sexism, and religious discrimination are evidences that prejudice and discrimination still exist in contemporary culture. These biases against individuals are made on the basis of group (e.g., ethnic, gender, or faith) characteristics and membership. When it is defined in this way, prejudice typifies a negative attitude.

The classic example of racism involves the actions of the priest and the Levite in the parable of the good Samaritan (Luke 10:20–37). Prejudice received little attention from psychologists until the racial atrocities of World War II came to light. Shortly afterward Adorno, Frenkel-Brunswik, Levinson, and Sanford (1950) published *The Authoritarian Personality*, giving specific correlates of the authoritarian personality, of which prejudice was one. They had developed the California F (Fascist) Scale as a measure of prejudice and ethnocentrism without reference to specific racial groups. Subsequently Allport (1954) published his classic work, *The Nature of Prejudice*.

The etymological roots of *prejudice* lie in the Latin noun *praejudicium*, which denoted a precedent or judgment based on previous experience. Later it denoted a judgment formed before facts were examined. It eventually took on the emotional connotations of an unsupported judgment based on inaccurate information. The emotional tone could be favorable or unfavorable, but much greater use is made of the latter. The work of most social psychologists supports this view and demonstrates that the emotional elements of prejudice change more slowly than cognitive components.

Allport (1954) suggested prejudgments become prejudices when two conditions occur: an overgeneralization produces an irreversible misconception. Overgeneralizing the underlying concept makes the judgment irreversible in that it prevents further evidence from changing the cognitive elements.

Attitudes normally serve individuals through two functions. They summarize experience and guide individuals in upcoming situations. They also filter selectively sensory experience and admit relevant portions to consciousness. The filtering is not random but systematically biased. The bias occurs in the direction of experience. In prejudice the extreme is taken. The individual overgeneralizes from experience, rigidly adhering to preconceptions, which renders those misconceptions functionally resistant. Prejudices screen contradictory evidence from awareness and prevent the individual from entering circumstances in which the misconceptions might be exposed.

Social psychologists have traditionally conceptualized attitudes as having three components: cognitive (belief), affective (emotional), and behavioral (action). In the case of racial prejudices the cognitive component is represented in an ethnic stereotype. The affective component is marked by the individual's desire to avoid, malign, express hostilities toward, or overcriticize others' mistakes. The behavioral component constitutes discrimination or other hostilities. Whether the behavioral component occurs depends on the intensity of the emotional component, dimensions of the situation (e.g., the proximity of the rival group, scarcity of resources important to both groups, degree of competition, degree of anonymity, intergroup cultural differences, degree of intimate contact) and certain personality traits (e.g., authoritarianism). Hostile action and discrimination occur when the social situation defines the situation as safe to express the underlying emotion (e.g., audience sympathies and size and ability to hide between a mask or screen).

The cognitive component of prejudice is a belief reflecting the individual's categorizing of events. This stereotype may contain a kernel of truth that permits the person's prejudgment. The process of categorizing and generalizing is normal. When one interacts with new persons or objects, the individual abstracts and sharpens essential features that distinguish the particular person or object. The abstraction is then applied to others that share the same features (generalization). Categories formed in this way enable the individual to respond to new objects. Thus the stereotype as "an exaggerated belief associated with a category" (Allport, 1954, p. 191) leads to stereotypic behavior toward the class. The individual is responded to as a member of the class rather than as a unique individual. These categories are formed on the basis on minimal information and tend to be discrete and dichotomous. Stereotypes in a given society tend to be associated with specific ethnic groups, are widely diffused throughout the society, and reflect a high degree of consensus in the society (Ehrlich, 1973). Stereotypes justify or rationalize behavior in relation to the category. Institutional policies often subordinate one group to another (e.g., females to males, blacks to whites) and serve to legitimize discrimination. The unequal status and power breed further discrimination.

Emotional associations direct, support, and strengthen the beliefs. Some theorists (e.g., those working within the cognitive consistency tradition) suggest that the cognitive aspects adapt to justify the emotional response. Disliking someone is verified in finding something to dislike. The actions also produce change in the victims of discrimination; the victims are apprehensive and act in ways to self-confirm the prejudice. As in other emotional responses, prejudices activate the autonomic arousal system. When physiological arousal is accompanied by appropriate cognitions and labeling of affective states, the individual is likely to engage in discrimination, provided the situation (conditions of anonymity or differential power) permits it. The emotional components, usually accompanied by feelings of mistrust, suspiciousness, and rejection of the object of prejudice, heighten the arousal.

Under certain conditions the negative stereotypes and feelings are manifested in negative action toward the objects of the prejudice. The negative action includes the maintenance of social distance, discrimination, and various forms of hostility and aggression.

The seminal work on social distance was conducted by Bogardus (1959), whose social distance scale measures the willingness of an individual to admit a member of an identified race to a category: close kinship by marriage, personal friend, neighbor, fellow in one's occupation, citizen of one's country, or a visitor to one's country. Social distance indicates the normative distance advocated by a group toward others, while personal distance is the behavioral intention of the individual. Just as stereotypes are shared in groups, groups display consensus about social distance norms. Ethnic groups that have different cultural heritages or are politically estranged are attributed more social distance than are other ethnic groups that are more similar (Bogardus, 1959). Other types of behavioral intentions are seen in ethnic jokes, ethnic slurs, racial hostilities, racial discrimination, rioting, and lynching.

Certain personality types are more prone to prejudice. Authoritarianism is a personality-attitude complex that "consists of interrelated antidemocratic sentiments including ethnic prejudice, political conservatism, and a moralistic rejection of the unconventional" (Byrne, 1974, p. 86). Adorno, Frenkel-Brunswik, Levinson, and Sanford (1950) postulated nine dimensions of authoritarianism: conventionalism, or rigid adherence to conventional middle-class values; authoritarian submission, or uncritical obedience to leaders; authoritarian aggression, or a tendency to reject and punish those who violate conventional values; destruction and cynicism, or generalized hostility; preoccupation with power and toughness; superstition and stereotypy, or magical beliefs about one's fate and thinking in rigid dichotomies; anti-intraception, or opposition to the subjective, imaginative, and artistic; projectivity, or outward projection of unconscious emotional impulses; and exaggerated concern for sexual events. Experimental evidence provides modest support for these interrelated dimensions.

Authoritarian parents typically adopt autocratic family structures wherein punishment is physical and harsh and relations are generally restrictive in nature. Autocratic family structures tend to produce authoritarian offspring. By way of contrast, equalitarian parents adopt more democratic family structures marked by love-oriented discipline, permissiveness, and absences of punitiveness. The result is equalitarian personalities in children.

Greater social distance had been observed in authoritarians as well as in those of lower intelligence. Rokeach (1960) argued that prejudice is more likely in individuals with closed minds. He further suggested that authoritarian and prejudiced personalities are drawn to the fundamentalist end of the religious spectrum, because fundamentalist religious dogmas legitimize that attitude and personality while providing definitive answers to critical questions. Intolerance of ambiguity and intolerance of deviance further characterize the prejudiced personality. Further, individuals who are most prone to conformity are also most prone to prejudice.

Many prejudices occur in the context of intergroup competition. Ingroup tension is projected outward in the form of outgroup aggression. The outgroup becomes the scapegoat for the social problems experienced by the ingroup. To maintain the ingroup's identity, to coalesce it into a group from a mob, leaders differentiate and diversify the groups and pressure members to conform to uniform feelings and cognitions within the group. In addition to providing a sense of group identity, these ingroup biases are self-serving and describe merit. Ingroup members attribute outgroup actions to personal traits rather than situational forces (e.g., fundamental attribution error; Pettigrew, 1979). Furthermore, the outgroup hostility is justified. The negative qualities of the outgroup deserve the negative action in a just world. While the transmission of prejudice from generation to generation involves the socialization of children by parents, teachers, and other societal agents as well as identifying with and conforming to one's own reference group, these mechanisms operate most when peculiar historical conditions and politicoeconomic structures sustain intergroup rivalries.

References

Adorno, T. W., Frenkel-Brunswik, E., Levinson, D. J., & Sanford, R. N. (1950). *The authoritarian personality*. New York: Harper & Row.

Allport, G. W. (1954). *The nature of prejudice*. Reading, MA: Addison-Wesley.

Bogardus, E. S. (1959). *Social distance*. Ann Arbor, MI: University Microfilms.

Byrne, D. (1974). *An introduction to personality: Research, theory, and application* (2nd ed.). Englewood Cliffs, NJ: Prentice-Hall.

Ehrlich, H. J. (1973). *The social psychology of prejudice*. New York: Wiley.

Pettigrew, T. F. (1979). The ultimate attribution error: Extending Allport's cognitive analysis of prejudice. *Personality and Social Psychology Bulletin, 55*, 461–476.

Rokeach, M. (1960). *The open and closed mind*. New York: Basic.

R. L. Timpe

See Attitude; Attitude-Behavior Relationships.

Premack Principle. A behavioral phenomenon observed by Premack (1959). He discovered that the behaviors performed most frequently by an individual who is given the opportunity to choose among various activities will function to reinforce behaviors performed less frequently. In his research Premack let children have free access to pinball games and candy, and he observed that playing pinball was the higher frequency behavior. By changing the contingencies so that playing pinball was allowed only after eating a certain amount of candy, he found he could increase the children's frequency of eating candy. This principle can be applied in personal behavior modification programs. For example, a high-frequency behavior such as television watching or socializing can be used to reinforce and thus increase a lower frequency behavior such as jogging or dieting.

Reference

Premack, D. (1959). Toward empirical behavior laws: Positive reinforcement. *Psychological Review, 66*, 219–233.

K. M. Lattea

See Learning.

Premarital Counseling. After reviewing the history of modern premarital counseling, Wright (1985) noted the lack of uniformity in approaches but nonetheless summarized common objectives:

- to arrange for the wedding
- to establish a relationship that might provide the basis for later marital counseling should it become necessary
- to provide information about each partner, marriage, and potential adjustments to marriage through directly teaching partners
- to provide correction of faulty information and inaccurate expectations about marriage so that the partners can approach marriage more realistically
- perhaps to restore relationships between partners and estranged parents
- to help couples make their final decision about whether to proceed with the marriage.

Wright reviewed several approaches to premarital counseling (conjoint or group counseling or their combination). He suggested that evaluation instruments were often employed, and counseling usually occurred in multiple sessions. Wright found research on the effectiveness of premarital counseling almost completely lacking, citing only his own research, which showed that attending more sessions was related to better results. Given Wright's description, we describe changes in premarital counseling through the mid-1990s.

Update on Objectives. Since 1985 other objectives for premarital counseling have become prominent.

Wright characterized premarital counseling as being designed to prevent marital problems and lower the probability of divorce. More recent approaches have sought to enhance premarital and marital relationships as well as to prevent marital discord and divorce.

More emphasis has been placed on behavioral training in communication and conflict resolution.

In recent years, nonmarital sexual activity and cohabitation have increased. Because the divorce rate for couples who have cohabited prior to marriage is about 1.5 times as high as for couples who have not cohabited and relationship quality is usually less (Brown & Booth, 1996), premarital counselors often need to tackle the issue of cohabitation.

The frequency of premarital counseling with previously married people has increased. Special preparation is needed for remarriage or to prepare a first-marrying partner for marriage to a formerly married partner.

Update on Approaches to Premarital Counseling. *Assessment.* Attention to assessment has remained high. Several assessment instruments have received considerable evaluation for use with premarital couples. Three assessment instruments are commonly used on premarital interventions (see Larson et al., 1995):

- PREPARE, with 125 items, takes 30 to 45 minutes to administer. Internal consistency is high. Larson and Olson (1989) have predicted marital dissolution and adjustment at three years with 80% accuracy utilizing only PREPARE.
- FOCCUS takes 45 minutes to administer and has a high internal consistency (Markey, Micheletto, & Becker, 1985).
- PREP-M takes 45 to 60 minutes to administer and also has high internal consistency (Holman, Busby, & Larson, 1989).

Each of these measures is reasonably priced.

Educational Approaches to Premarital Counseling. Many counselors educate couples about the risks and challenges of marriage. In these educational seminars or meetings, couples may benefit from learning about the research on marital risk factors. Factors that have predicted marital distress or dissolution include depression or alcoholism of

one partner, previous marriage, poverty, teenage marriage, extreme differences in educational or religious background, and individual psychopathology (Brody, Neubaum, & Forehand, 1988; Coyne et al., 1987).

Markman's research (Floyd, Markman, Kelly, Blumberg, & Stanley, 1995) has identified several relationship variables that place couples at risk. Markman proposes that the major risk factor for couples is difficulty resolving differences and managing conflict, notably a lack of problem-solving facilitation between partners, high levels of problem-solving inhibition, and emotional invalidation. Gottman (1994) found that physiological reactivity and withdrawal from the relationship during conflict predicts marital dissolution. Couples could benefit from exposure to the findings of Markman, Gottman, and others who have studied risk factors in marriage.

Teaching Communication Skills. Premarital programs have increasingly taught couples skills for communication and conflict resolution. The Christian Preparation and Relationship Enhancement Program (C-PREP; Stanley, Trathen, & McCain, 1996) teaches couples communication and conflict management using Christian themes. Research on the secular PREP model for engaged couples has been fruitful. Markman and Hahlweg (1993) found that PREP couples were less distressed and improved in their communication skills after a six-session PREP intervention compared with non-PREP couples. In a five-year follow-up Markman, Renick, Floyd, Stanley, and Clements (1993) found that couples who participated in PREP were more likely than control couples to remain married and to rate their relationship as satisfying. More generally Hahlweg and Markman (1988) found positive effects for 17 behaviorally based premarital counseling studies (see also Giblin, Sprenkle, & Sheehan, 1985).

Understanding the Influence of Families of Origin. Giblin (1994) described one approach to premarital counseling as the backwards glance. Marriage is a time of transition. Therefore many counselors, particularly those psychodynamically informed, focus on couples' families of origin in premarital counseling. The most common intervention is the genogram, which is similar to a family tree. Couples discuss family structure and how families of origin might affect the couple's forthcoming marriage. There are two goals of such intervention: to promote insight on the influence of families of origin and to promote the partners' differentiation from their families (see Lawson, 1985; Parrott & Parrott, 1996, for techniques).

Eclectic Approaches. Premarital interventions such as Marriage Encounter (Doherty, Lester, & Leigh, 1986) and Relationship Enhancement (Guerney, 1977) have incorporated education, behavioral training, and family-of-origin analysis in their interventions. Guerney's approach has been evaluated as the most effective approach that has been investigated empirically (Alexander, Holtzworth-Munroe, & Jameson, 1994). Research comparing eclectic interventions to other premarital interventions has yet to be published in peer-reviewed journals.

Formats for Intervention. Premarital interventions have taken a wide variety of formats. Many premarital counselors conduct group or couples premarital counseling or run weekend retreat-style workshops. Books and workbooks are also used as premarital intervention and as adjuncts to counseling. Parrott and Parrott (1996) encourage churches to put older marriage mentoring couples in frequent contact with engaged couples. Clergy in larger churches or diocese often have premarital classes that are usually informational rather than interactive.

Two studies have investigated what premarital couples prefer and expect of premarital counseling. Silliman and Schumm (1990) found that 150 college students preferred brief, high-quality, low-cost, voluntary programs led by clergy or mental health professionals. Females, students having more family support, and more religious students wanted longer, more expensive programs led by clergy.

Williams (1992) surveyed 170 engaged individuals about their top five preferences for premarital counseling, which were handling stress from work and marriage; understanding children's effect on marriage; how to keep romance alive; dealing with anger and silence; and resolving differences. Williams (1992) also found engaged participants wanted counseling from a minister, weekend retreats, small-group discussions, lecture and classes, and a workbook. Meeting with another married couple and receiving counseling from a therapist were the least preferred. However, religious individuals preferred meeting with a minister, while less religious people preferred meeting with a therapist.

Update on Research. Research on premarital counseling, although it is in a rudimentary state relative to research on psychotherapy, has accumulated quickly since 1985. Worthington summarized research on premarital counseling:

Premarital counseling programs . . . [are] thought to be effective to the extent that they (1) have clear goals, (2) last at least six to twelve weeks, (3) focus on communication and problem solving about issues the couple considers relevant, and (4) include information, interaction between partners (especially with feedback by video or by other people), and discussion. Purely information-oriented approaches and time-constrained conjoint sessions might be effective, but there is no research to support that method (Worthington, 1990, p. 2).

Those conclusions still seem valid, but three additional comments are needed. First, research has accumulated supporting the effectiveness of programs that train couples in communication and conflict management. Second, there is still an ab-

sence of published research on the effectiveness of information-oriented programs or family-of-origin programs. Third, no empirical investigations of specifically Christian programs have been published in peer-reviewed journals.

Conclusions. Effective premarital counseling can be important, influencing couples for years. The formats of premarital counseling are varied enough to allow for individual differences and needs in programs in local churches or counseling offices. However, there is a need for further understanding of premarital counseling and its effectiveness with couples, particularly as marriages change in society. This is especially true for explicitly Christian premarital counseling programs.

References

Alexander J. F., Holtzworth-Munroe, A., & Jameson, P. (1994), The process and outcome of marital and family therapy: Research review and evaluation. In A. E. Bergin & S. L. Garfield, (Eds.), *Handbook of psychotherapy and behavior change* (4th Ed.). New York: Wiley.

Brody, G. H., Neubaum, E., & Forehand, R. (1988). Serial marriage: A heuristic analysis of an emerging family form. *Psychological Bulletin, 103,* 211–222.

Brown, S. L., & Booth, A. (1996). Cohabitation versus marriage: A comparison of relationship quality. *Journal of Marriage and the Family, 58,* 668–678.

Coyne, J. C., Kessler, R. C., Tal, M., Turnbull, J., Wortman, C. B., & Greden, J. F. (1987). Living with a depressed person. *Journal of Consulting and Clinical Psychology, 55,* 347–352.

Doherty, W. J., Lester, M. E., & Leigh, G. K. (1986). Marriage Encounter weekends: Couples who win and couples who lose. *Journal of Marital and Family Therapy, 12,* 49–61.

Floyd, F. J., Markman, H. J., Kelly, S., Blumberg, S. L., & Stanley, S. M. (1995). Preventive intervention and relationship enhancement. In N. Jacobson & A. Gurman (Eds.), *Clinical handbook of couple therapy.* New York: Guilford.

Giblin, P. (1994). Premarital preparation: Three approaches. *Pastoral Psychology, 42,* 147–161.

Giblin, P., Sprenkle, D. H., & Sheehan, R. (1985), Enrichment outcome research: A meta-analysis of premarital, marital and family interventions. *Journal of Marital and Family Therapy, 11,* 257–271.

Gottman, J. M. (1994), *What predicts divorce?* Hillsdale, NJ: Erlbaum.

Guerney, B. G., Jr. (1977), *Relationship enhancement: Skill training program for therapy, problem prevention, and enrichment.* San Francisco: Jossey-Bass.

Hahlweg, K., & Markman, H. J. (1988). Effectiveness of behavioral marital therapy: Empirical status of behavioral techniques in preventing and alleviating marital distress. *Journal of Consulting and Clinical Psychology, 56,* 440–447.

Holman, T. B., Busby, D., & Larson, J. H. (1989), *PREParation for marriage.* Provo, UT: Brigham Young University, Marriage Study Consortium.

Larsen, A. S., & Olson, D. H. (1989). Predicting marital satisfaction using PREPARE: A replication study. *Journal of Marital and Family Therapy, 15,* 311–322.

Larson, J. H., Holman, T. B., Klein, D. M., Busby, D., Stahmann, R. F., & Peterson, D. (1985). A review of comprehensive questionnaires used in premarital education and counseling. *Family Relations, 44,* 245–252.

Lawson, D. M. (1985). Differentiation in premarital preparation. *Journal of Psychology and Christianity, 4,* 56–63.

Markey, B., Micheletto, M., & Becker, A. (1985), *Facilitating open couple communication, understanding and study (FOCCUS).* Omaha, NE: Archdiocese of Omaha.

Markman, H. J., & Hahlweg, K. (1993). The prediction and prevention of marital distress: An international perspective. *Clinical Psychology Review, 13,* 29–43.

Markman, H. J., Renick, M. J., Floyd, F. J., Stanley, S. M., & Clements, M. (1993). Preventing marital distress through communication and conflict management training: A 4- and 5-year follow-up. *Journal of Consulting and Clinical Psychology, 61,* 70–77.

Parrott, L., & Parrott, L. (1996). Relationship development. In E. L. Worthington, Jr., (Ed.), *Christian marital counseling: Eight approaches to helping couples.* Grand Rapids, MI: Baker.

Silliman, B., & Schumm, W. R. (1990). Client interests in premarital counseling: A further analysis. *Journal of Sex and Marital Therapy, 21,* 43–55.

Stanley, S. M., Trathen, D. W., & McCain, S. (1996). Christian PREP: An empirically based model for marital and premarital intervention. In E. L. Worthington, Jr., (Ed.), *Christian marital counseling: Eight approaches to helping couples.* Grand Rapids, MI: Baker.

Williams, L. M. (1992). Premarital counseling: A needs assessment among engaged individuals. *Contemporary Family Therapy, 14,* 505–518.

Worthington, E. L., Jr. (1990). *Counseling before marriage.* Dallas: Word.

Wright, H. N. (1985). Premarital counseling. In D. G. Benner (Ed.), *Psychotherapy in Christian perspective.* Grand Rapids, MI: Baker.

J. S. Ripley, E. L. Worthington, Jr.,
and D. G. Benner

See Marriage Enrichment.

Premature Ejaculation. Premature ejaculation is one of two orgasmic disorders found in men. It is diagnosed when men climax before they want to, either before, during, or shortly after entering the vagina. Occasional early ejaculation is common and does not indicate a disorder. *DSM-IV* requires that the problem be persistent or recurrent and that it cause significant distress or relationship problems.

Premature ejaculation affects more than 30% of men at some point in their lives and is the most common sexual problem in men seeking professional help. Young and sexually inexperienced males are particularly likely to experience the disorder, as most men learn to delay orgasm as a long-term relationship matures. However, premature ejaculation may reappear with a new partner or after a period of sexual abstinence.

Some men develop premature ejaculation after having difficulty obtaining an erection, for a man with an unreliable erection is less concerned about delaying orgasm. In other men premature ejaculation causes problems with erections. Therapists expect premature ejaculation to develop during cognitive-behavioral treatment of male orgasmic disorder.

As premature ejaculation may abbreviate the sexual encounter well before the woman is satisfied, marital tension is often the result. The woman is frustrated, and the man feels guilty and inadequate, resenting the demands of his wife. The majority of men who seek help for premature ejaculation do so because of the complaints of their wives. Some theorists have argued that premature ejaculation should be diagnosed if it occurs prior to the wife's climax more than half of the time, but the lack of synchronization may be due to many factors beyond the man's control. In addition, the 50% rule would diagnose about 90% of men with this disorder at some point in their lives. *DSM-IV* (American Psychiatric Association, 1994) does not use such a criterion.

Concerned about their ability to satisfy a sexual partner, many young men who ejaculate prematurely may avoid dating and forming intimate relationships, leading to social isolation. Most men in American culture are unwilling to admit to the problem, even with close friends.

Youth, sexual inexperience, a new partner, and periods of abstinence all contribute to premature ejaculation. Withdrawal from sedative drugs may precipitate the problem. Regular use of alcohol, a depressant drug, delays ejaculation, so drinkers do not learn other ways to control orgasm. Men who cease drinking may then develop premature ejaculation.

Cultural changes have also contributed to diagnoses of premature ejaculation. Fifty years ago, when Americans were less concerned about women's orgasms, early ejaculation was often considered to be a sign of health and vigor. Today, women are supposed to reach climax, and men whose early ejaculation frustrates their wives are considered to have a disorder.

Men who ejaculate prematurely show considerable anxiety about sexual expression. At first anxiety may be a consequence of the uncontrolled orgasm, but later it contributes to the problem. Anxiety is also a factor in men who learned to masturbate (*see* Masturbation) to orgasm as quickly as possible in order to avoid discovery and punishment.

When both partners are unhappy with early ejaculation, it is clearly premature. Since sexual intercourse within marriage is the sexual activity most widely endorsed in the church, Christian couples may stop intercourse after the husband ejaculates, so premature ejaculation prematurely ends intercourse.

One fairly effective treatment is to expand the couple's definition of sexual intimacy to include more than sexual intercourse. If other forms of sexual expression continue after the man's ejaculation, both partners have increased enjoyment and the wife may be brought to climax. Greater satisfaction with sexual activity then reduces anxiety, enabling the man to gain better control over ejaculation. In addition, continued sexual intimacy following one ejaculation may produce a second erection. Then he may resume intercourse and find that the second ejaculation is much easier to delay.

Some men drink alcohol to cope with premature ejaculation, but alcohol is a poor treatment, since it contributes to male erectile disorder.

Cognitive-behavioral therapy uses information and communication exercises to reduce anxiety and improve the relationship. Therapists then recommend the squeeze technique, developed in the 1950s and still the most effective treatment for premature ejaculation. The wife stimulates her husband's penis with her hands until he is near ejaculation, then uses her thumb and forefinger to squeeze it very tightly just below the glans until the urge to ejaculate passes. After 30 seconds, she repeats the procedure. When ejaculation is delayed for 15 to 20 minutes, she initiates intercourse. After several days of the squeeze technique, the man is able to control ejaculation during coitus.

Reference

American Psychiatric Association. (1994). *Diagnostic and statistical manual of mental disorders.* (4th ed.). Washington, DC: Author.

P. D. YOUNG

See SEXUAL DYSFUNCTIONS.

Prematurity. *See* PRETERM BIRTH.

Prenatal Development. Prenatal as well as some postnatal development is highly influenced by genetically controlled maturation. However, the environment does influence prenatal development as the effects of genes and environment interact.

Maturation. Prenatal development is described in terms of three periods of growth: the zygotic, the embryonic, and the fetal periods. These periods get their names from the scientific terms used to describe the developing child at different points in the pregnancy. The terms *first trimester, second trimester,* and *third trimester* are used often by the public to describe the periods of pregnancy; however, these terms are more descriptive of the changes experienced by a pregnant woman than they are of the changes in the developing child. The timing of developmental events during these periods is believed to be genetically determined.

The zygote period (conception to 2 weeks postconception) includes the important events of the establishment of a unique genotype, rapid cell division, the passive movement of the zygote from the fallopian tube, where fertilization takes place, to the uterus, where implantation occurs, and differentiation of two pools of cells that will develop into the child and the membranes that support the developing child.

The embryonic period (2 to 8 weeks postconception) is when the basic body form and organ systems are established and the membrane systems (e.g., the amnion, chorion, and placenta) that support the developing child are differentiated and become functional. During the third week postconception, three types of cells become differentiated in the body of the child. Endoderm will give rise to parts of the body such as hair, skin, and nervous system that come into contact with the external environment. Mesoderm gives rise to parts of the body such as muscle, bones, and the circulatory system, which give the body structure. The endoderm gives rise to internal organs such as lungs and digestive system. By the end of the embryonic period the developing child is only one inch long and weighs less than an ounce, but the child appears more human than it did in the zygote period.

During the fetal period (9 weeks postconception to birth) the body grows rapidly and organ systems are refined and continue to mature. By 25 weeks postconception (the age of viability), a child's organ systems function well enough that he or she has a chance to survive outside the uterus. Reflexes such as sucking and sensory abilities such as hearing, which are controlled by the child's developing brain, are added to the child's behavioral repertoire in the seventh and eighth months postconception. The average child is 20 inches long and weighs 7 pounds at birth (38 + 2 weeks postconception for a full-term birth).

Premature Birth. Normal length of gestation is 38 + 2 weeks postconception. When infants are born before 36 weeks postconception they are considered preterm or premature. Preterm infants have higher risk of mental retardation (10% of preterm infants have IQs below 70 compared with 3% in the general population). Even among nonretarded preterm infants, development of cognitive, social, and motor abilities may appear delayed when compared with the development of full-term peers. This is because the postnatal development of these abilities proceeds on a time line from conception, just as prenatal development did. Thus if the appearance of an ability is calculated in terms of the infant's age after conception rather than the age after birth, the behavior of the nonretarded preterm infant is not delayed. Most delays in development due to prematurity are no longer noticeable after age four.

Environment. Teratogens are substances that cause birth defects. Teratogens include drugs (e.g., exposure to alcohol is correlated with cognitive and motor impairment [Barr, Streissguth, Darby, & Sampson, 1990]), diseases (e.g., exposure to AIDS and other sexually transmitted diseases results in central nervous system damage and mental retardation [Schmitt, Seeger, Kreuz, Enenkel, & Jacobi, 1991]), and environmental hazards such as toxic chemicals (e.g., exposure to PCBs is associated with cognitive deficits [Jacobson, Jacobson, Padgett, Brumitt, & Billings, 1992]).

Maturation and environment interaction can be used to explain some of the specific effects of teratogens. The specific effects of a particular teratogen depends upon the genetic endowment of the exposed individual (some individuals are more susceptible to the effects of teratogens), the organ systems that are typically targeted by the teratogen (rubella tends to effect eyes, ears, and heart while thalidomide damages developing limbs), and the timing of teratogen exposure (the developing child is particularly vulnerable during the embryonic period). In general we can say that the part of the body that is undergoing the most rapid development at the time of teratogen exposure is the part of the body most likely to have a birth defect (Vorhees & Mollnow, 1987).

References

Barr, H. M., Streissguth, A. P., Darby, B. L., & Sampson, P. D. (1990). Prenatal exposure to alcohol, caffeine, tobacco, and aspirin: Effects on fine and gross motor performance in 4-year-old children. *Developmental Psychology, 26*, 339–348.

Jacobson, J. L., Jacobson, S. W., Padgett, R. J., Brumitt, G. A., & Billings, R. L. (1992). Effects of prenatal PCB exposure on cognitive processing efficiency and sustained attention. *Developmental Psychology, 28*, 297–306.

Schmitt, B., Seeger, J., Kreuz, W., Enenkel, S., & Jacobi, G. (1991). Central nervous system involvement of children with HIV infection. *Developmental Medicine and Child Neurology, 33*, 535–540.

Vorhees, C. V., & Mollnow, E. (1987). Behavior teratogenesis: Long-term influences on behavior. In J. D. Osofsky (Ed.), *Handbook of infant development* (2nd ed.). New York: Wiley.

K. A. GATHERCOAL

Pressure of Speech. A disorder characterized by accelerated and emphatic talking that is difficult or impossible to interrupt. The speech is frequently loud, and the speaker may talk without any stimulation or response from another. This increased speech is found most often in manic episodes but also in organic mental disorders, schizophrenia, and other psychotic disorders, and occasionally as an acute reaction to severe stress.

Preterm Birth. Despite many efforts made to improve health care, prematurity continues to be a condition that affects about 10% of the babies born in the United States. Approximately five billion dollars are spent each year helping preterm babies recover and grow in neonatal intensive care units (NICUs) (Gilbert & Harmon, 1993), representing one of the largest health care expenditures in this country. The rate of prematurity, despite innovative medical technology, has not decreased since the 1950s (American College of Obstetrics and Gynecology, 1995).

A preterm infant is one born after 20 and before 37 completed weeks of gestation, regardless of birthweight (Creasy, 1994). The cause of preterm births is not known; however, numerous maternal, fetal, and environmental risk factors have been identified.

During pregnancy, a woman's well-being must be maintained in order to carry the infant to term. If there are alterations in her physical health, such as diabetes, hypertension, infections, or placental deviations, she may be at risk for delivering prematurely. Uterine abnormalities or a history of preterm labor with another infant puts the mother at greater risk for delivering her infant before term. With an increased incidence of women having children later in life and using infertility drugs, the prevalence of multiple births is rising. When a woman is carrying more than one infant, the rate of preterm births is 51% (Simpson & Creehan, 1996).

Psychosocial risks are also linked to preterm deliveries. For example, women who are from a lower socioeconomic status often access prenatal care late in pregnancy, thus increasing the chances of preterm labor and delivery. In addition, stress as a result of poverty, inadequate nutrition, single parenting, domestic violence, and extremes of maternal age (young or old) are also associated with preterm births. Smoking cigarettes and the use of recreational chemicals such as marijuana, cocaine, and heroine, besides doing physical harm to the mother, increase the risk of a preterm delivery. Cocaine use in the third trimester, for example, can cause separation of the placenta, leading to a preterm birth; the infant may also suffer from neurobehavioral abnormalities that can lead to learning difficulties and school failure (Gilbert & Harmon, 1993).

Preterm infants can suffer from several conditions that result from the immaturity of major organs. For example, preterm infants might have neurological impairments affecting motor skills and the ability to maintain body temperature. Heart defects and visual and hearing impairments are also common. A preterm infant may have a weak or absent suck, poor swallow and gag reflex, and problems with metabolism affecting growth and development (Bobak & Jensen, 1993). Depending on the gestational age at birth, many preterm infants experience respiratory distress syndrome and chronic lung disease, which can necessitate monitoring once they arrive in the home. Also, because of the time needed for organs to mature, prolonged hospitalization and in-home care by health care providers is often required, which can disrupt the family unit.

A mother experiences many feelings and fears with the delivery of a preterm infant. She may endure feelings of grief because a normal, full-term infant was not born to her. She planned, often for years, for this infant, and it is lost to her, if only in her mind. She may have feelings of guilt and inadequacy as a mother because she did not carry her baby to term and deliver a healthy child, or she may wonder if something she did caused the preterm delivery (Johnson, 1986).

At the time a preterm infant is born, many things occur to the mother and baby that might interfere with the attachment or bond between the mother and her infant. If the baby is transported to a hospital for high-risk infants, perhaps several miles from the hospital where the delivery occurred, the only contact the mother might have with her baby is through stories by family members or a simple Polaroid picture.

When parents are separated from their preterm infant, the attachment process is disrupted, but there may also be the risk of failure to thrive and neglect in the future (Klaus & Kennell, 1982; *see* Abuse and Neglect). The incidence of physical and emotional abuse is three times greater toward a preterm infant who was separated from the mother for a time after birth (Fomufod, 1976).

When a mother is able to visit, her new baby might be attached to mechanical devices that assist in the maturation process, and she might be afraid she will harm the baby through touching or by disturbing vital tubes and monitors. In addition, she might fear that her child will die or will suffer from a chronic condition (Johnson, 1986).

Because of the amount of stress a preterm birth creates for the family, every effort must be made to promote a positive experience. The family may need assistance with care for the older children at home or someone to assist with transportation to the tertiary center for one of the parents. The parents need to be allowed to verbalize their fears and concerns about their infant. Because the preterm infant may spend weeks to months in an NICU, the family will need support as they go about the process of bringing home their new baby.

References

American College of Obstetrics and Gynecology. (1995). Preterm labor. *ACOG Technical Bulletin, 206*, 1–10.

Bobak, I. M., & Jensen, M. D. (1993). *Maternity and gynecologic care* (5th ed.). St. Louis: Mosby.

Creasy, R. K. (1994). Preterm labor and delivery. In R. K. Creasy & R. Resnick (Eds.)., *Maternal-fetal medicine: Principles and practice*. Philadelphia: Saunders.

Fomufod, A. K. (1976). Low birthweight and early neonatal separation as factors in child abuse. *Journal of the National Medical Association, 68*, 106.

Gilbert, E. S., & Harmon, J. S. (1993). *Manual of high risk pregnancy and delivery*. St. Louis: Mosby.

Johnson, S. H. (1986). *Nursing assessment and strategies for the family at risk: High risk parenting* (2nd ed.). Philadelphia: Lippincott.

Klaus, M. H., & Kennell, J. H. (1982). *Parent-infant bonding*. St. Louis: Mosby.

Simpson, K., & Creehan, P. A. (1996). *AWHONN's perinatal nursing*. Philadelphia: Lippincott-Raven.

K. S. Seybold

Prevention of Psychological Disorders. This subject has received significant attention in recent years. A large body of literature is now available, including a series of volumes based on the Vermont Conference on Primary Prevention of Psychopathology (e.g., see Kessler & Goldston, 1986; Kessler, Goldston, & Joffe, 1992) and several handbooks or textbooks on primary prevention (e.g., Bloom, 1981; Edelstein & Michelson, 1986; Felner, Jason, Moritsugo, & Farber, 1983; Price, Cowen, Lorion, & Ramos-McKay, 1988; Roberts & Peterson, 1984). This increased interest in prevention is understandable in light of the shortage of mental health professionals to meet the needs of the emotionally disturbed and the great cost of mental illness, estimated to be more than $40,000,000,000 annually (Hatch, 1982). Albee (1982) has pointed out that the mental health community sees only about one in five of the estimated 15% (32,000,000 to 34,000,000) of the American population who are seriously disturbed emotionally. A more recent study by the National Institute of Mental Health (NIMH) put this estimate closer to about 20% or 43,000,000 people. NIMH has also created an office of prevention and established a network of Preventive Intervention Research Centers (PIRC). Christian authors have begun to focus on the need for Christian counselors and churches to be more involved in preventive interventions.

Prevention of psychological disorders has usually been divided into three types: primary, secondary, and tertiary (see Zax & Cowan, 1976). Primary prevention involves preventing the development of psychological dysfunction and hence reducing the rate of occurrence of new cases of disorder (its incidence) in the general population. Secondary prevention refers to the reduction of the prevalence of the disorder by shortening its duration and negative consequences. It therefore seeks to stop mild disorders from becoming prolonged or acute and focuses on early identification and prompt, effective treatment of psychological dysfunction. Tertiary prevention aims at reducing the severity, discomfort, or disability associated with psychological disorder that is already well established.

A number of authors have suggested that the terms *secondary* and *tertiary* prevention be replaced by *treatment* and *rehabilitation*, respectively, in order to reduce confusion over terminology. The term *prevention* will therefore be used in this article to refer mainly to primary prevention aimed at reducing the incidence of new cases of psychological disorder, as well as enhancing psychological wellness, especially through competence building. Its two main strategies are systems-level (i.e., to reduce sources of stress and increase life opportunities for people) and person-centered (i.e., to develop interventions that enhance people's ability to deal with stress and adapt effectively) strategies (Cowen, 1986). Attempts at primary prevention by definition occur in a population that is free of the disorder being prevented.

Examples of Primary Prevention. There are many excellent examples of preventive intervention with a wide variety of populations. A particularly well-known and significant prevention program is the Primary Mental Health Project conducted by Cowen and his colleagues in Rochester (see

Cowen et al., 1975). This is a program for early detection and prevention of school adjustment problems in children. Cowen found that many of the children identified as high risk but who received no intervention continued to have problems or had worse difficulties during the later school years. His intervention involved the use of housewives as nonprofessional child aides who worked directly with high-risk children in the schools. The children were typically seen about twice a week, usually for the entire school year. The housewives provided an empathic and accepting relationship with the children on an individual basis. Research has shown that this preventive intervention has provided both immediate and long-term benefit to the children who received it and has significantly reduced later school adjustment problems. It is being used in some five hundred schools in two hundred school districts worldwide (Cowen, 1986).

Shure and Spivack (1980) reported that significantly fewer young children who were trained in interpersonal cognitive problem-solving skills showed signs of impulsivity or inhibition when compared to a control group of children a year after the intervention. They concluded that problem-solving training prevented the emergence of these behaviors as well as helped children who were already having difficulties. Their study was therefore only partly preventive in nature. Attempts by other investigators to duplicate these results with other age groups and settings have not been as successful.

Another example of a successful and systematic preventive program is the behavioral work done by Poser and his colleagues (see Poser & Hartman, 1979). In a series of studies they have shown the effectiveness of preexposure and symbolic-modeling strategies for the prevention of maladaptive fear responses in children in situations involving dental treatment and handling of snakes. Measures of psychological vulnerability and environmental adversity or press have also been validated and used to identify asymptomatic high school students who may be at risk for psychological disorder. Hartman (1979) found that students who received an eight-week group intervention of coping and social skills training improved significantly more than those who did not. There was a strong trend for these gains to be maintained at a three-month follow-up. However, longer-term follow-up is needed before more definitive conclusions can be made.

Another successful prevention program involved reducing child abuse and neglect (*see* Abuse and Neglect) with families identified to be at risk by using parent support groups, parent education, school system coordination, and the utilization of other agencies during prenatal, childbirth, and postpartum care (Turkington, 1983a, 1983b).

More recently effective and innovative primary prevention efforts have included the Brookline Early Education Project, the Colorado Separation and Divorce Program for newly separated persons, and the Stanford Heart Disease Prevention Program as an example of disease prevention in communities, all of which were reported in Price, Cowen, Lorion, and Ramos-McKay (1988). Promoting healthy behavior and preventing adolescent parenthood and AIDS are other recent attempts at prevention and lifestyle change (Levine, Toro, & Perkins, 1993; also see Heller, 1990). Gesten and Jason (1987) reviewed primary prevention in the areas of competence building, social support, empowerment, mutual help, and behavioral community psychology, as well as with diverse cultures and groups. The need for greater involvement in research and public policy arenas was also emphasized. Most recently successful prevention programs have included those aimed at preventing depression associated with job loss, conduct disorders in children, and adjustment problems in children coping with divorce (Burnette, 1996). However, it should be pointed out that not all efforts at prevention of psychological disorders have been successful. Examples of failure include attempts at preventing juvenile delinquency and crime (e.g., McCord, 1978) and immunizing children for speech anxiety (Cradock, Cotler, & Jason, 1978).

The Church and Prevention. Several authors have proposed that the prevention of mental disorders should be a concern of the church (Collins, 1980; Uomoto, 1982; also see Pargament, Maton, & Hess, 1992). Uomoto argues that the church is a potent mental health resource because of its proximity in the community, its independent financial set-up, its consistency in providing a stable social environment, and its mission to enhance the physical, emotional, and spiritual well-being of its members. He suggests three levels of preventive interventions as options for the church: individual interventions, social system interventions, and the provision of a healing community.

Individual interventions could include mental health education (i.e., educating church leaders on psychological principles, mental health resources, mental disorders, referral methods, skill training); skills and competence training (i.e., conducting problem-solving workshops, language skills training, and lay counselor training); and the facilitation of stress reduction and coping (i.e., teaching preventive stress inoculation techniques, relaxation training, and cognitive restructuring procedures). Social system interventions might include the development of social support groups for high-risk individuals such as divorcees, single parents, business executives, jobless people, families with disabled members, and former mental patients; regular visitations to peripheral members of a church; connecting people with specific needs to appropriate agencies or resources; establishing a telephone network; and working more closely with other community agencies. Finally, the overall goal would be the establishment of a healing climate in which all of the preceding interventions can be optimally undertaken. Uomoto suggests that such a climate can best be developed within a caring community of believers who are experiencing newness of life in Christ, living according to the law of love, and reaching out to the world.

Barriers to Prevention. Albee (1982) has argued that one-to-one psychotherapy is indefensible because of the unbridgeable gap between the large numbers in need and the small numbers of helpers. Furthermore, he argues that support for primary prevention as an alternative derives from the demonstrated role of poverty, meaningless work, unemployment, racism, and sexism in producing psychopathology and from the demonstrated effectiveness of programs promoting social competence, self-esteem, and social support networks in reducing psychopathology. He therefore asks why most mental health professionals continue to practice an individually oriented approach to treatment, ignoring the arguments for movement from treatment to prevention.

Bloom (1981) suggests several barriers to prevention: the personal tendency to avoid making immediate sacrifices in order to obtain remote goals in the future, which runs counter to what prevention often requires; the professional reluctance to shift one's focus of practice from traditional psychotherapy after having invested years in it; conceptual inadequacies and the lack of more sophisticated and systematic theory in prevention; the lack of data, especially long-term follow-up data, to support the efficacy of preventive interventions; the great costs of some preventive programs; and ethical objections to the invasion of privacy or the tampering with self-choice, especially among minority or disadvantaged groups. Albee (1982) adds to this list the challenge that prevention represents to the traditional defect model (or medical model) of psychopathology. Focusing on social and environmental factors, prevention efforts are grounded in more of a social learning model. Thus they are resisted by those trained in the more traditional model, who are predisposed to see preventive efforts as modifying human unhappiness and misery but not affecting mental illness.

Albee (1982) has also proposed a religious source of resistance to prevention, arguing that opposition to prevention comes as a result of Calvinistic theology. Believing that neither the individual nor society is perfectible because of the stigma of original sin, Calvinists oppose efforts to better society and the lot of the individual sinner, according to Albee. However, while it is true that Christians do not believe that individuals or society can be made perfect by purely humanistic efforts, it is not true that they therefore have to oppose prevention.

The biblical view of prevention is centered in the redemptive work of Christ, since ultimately only Jesus Christ can meet the deepest psychospiritual needs of human beings. However, this does not mean that psychological, social, and environmental changes are not helpful for healthy mental func-

tioning. While they are inadequate without the new birth in Christ, which alone can deal with the fundamental problem of sin, they are important and legitimate spheres of Christian service.

Bloom (1981) is of the opinion that barriers to prevention can be overcome by rigorous and systematic research. Albee (1982), however, argues that what is needed is something more like ideological reeducation for mental health professionals. He suggests that significant movement toward the prevention of psychopathology will come as more and more people line up with those who believe in "social change, in the effectiveness of consultation, in education, in the primary prevention of human physical and emotional misery, and in the maximization of individual competence" (p. 1050). Prevention of psychological disorders has indeed come a long way in recent years, but it still has a long road ahead.

References

Albee, G. W. (1982). Preventing psychopathology and promoting human potential. *American Psychologist, 37,* 1043–1050.

Bloom, M. (1981). *Primary prevention: The possible science.* Englewood Cliffs, NJ: Prentice-Hall.

Burnette, E. (1996). Researchers work to prevent social ills. *A.P.A. Monitor, 27* (1), 32.

Collins, G. R. (1980). The future of Christian counseling. In G. R. Collins (Ed.), *Helping people grow.* Santa Ana, CA: Vision House.

Cowen, E. L. (1986). Primary prevention in mental health: Ten years of retrospect and ten years of prospect. In M. Kessler & S. E. Goldston (Eds.), *A decade of progress in primary prevention.* Hanover, NH: University Press of New England.

Cowen, E. L., Trost, M. A., Dorr, D. A., Lorion, R. P., Izzo, L. D., & Isaacson, R. V. (1975). *New ways in school mental health: Early detection and prevention of school maladaptation.* New York: Human Sciences.

Cradock, C., Cotler, S., & Jason, L. A. (1978). Primary prevention: Immunization of children for speech anxiety. *Cognitive Therapy and Research, 2,* 389–396.

Edelstein, B. A., & Michelson, L. (Eds.). (1986). *Handbook of prevention.* New York: Plenum.

Felner, R. D., Jason, L. A., Moritsugu, J. N., & Farber, S. S. (Eds.). (1983). *Preventive psychology: Theory, research and practice.* New York: Pergamon.

Gesten, E. L., & Jason, L. A. (1987). Social and community interventions. *Annual Review of Psychology, 38,* 427–460.

Hartman, L. M. (1979). The preventive reduction of psychological risk in asymptomatic adolescents. *American Journal of Orthopsychiatry, 49,* 121–135.

Hatch, O. G. (1982). Psychology, society, and politics. *American Psychologist, 37,* 1031–1037.

Heller, K. (1990). Social and community interventions. *Annual Review of Psychology, 41,* 141–168.

Kessler, M., & Goldston, S. E. (Eds.). (1986). *A decade of progress in primary prevention.* Hanover, NH: University Press of New England.

Kessler, M., Goldston, S. E., & Joffe, J. M. (1992). *The present and future of prevention.* Newbury Park, CA: Sage.

Levine, M., Toro, P. A., & Perkins, D. V. (1993). Social and community interventions. *Annual Review of Psychology, 44,* 525–558.

McCord, J. (1978). A 30-year follow-up of treatment effects. *American Psychologist, 33,* 284–289.

Pargament, K. I., Maton, K. I., & Hess, R. E. (Eds.). (1992). *Religion and prevention in mental health: Research, vision, and action.* New York: Haworth.

Poser, E. G., & Hartman, L. M. (1979). Issues in behavioral prevention: Empirical findings. *Advances in Behavior Research and Therapy, 2,* 1–25.

Price, R. H., Cowen, E. L., Lorion, R. P., & Ramos-McKay, J. (Eds.). (1988). *14 ounces of prevention.* Washington DC: American Psychological Association.

Roberts, M. C., & Peterson, L. (Eds.). (1984). *Prevention of problems in childhood.* New York: Wiley.

Shure, M. B., & Spivack, G. (1980). A preventive mental health program for young "inner city" children: The second (kindergarten) year. In M. Bloom (Ed.), *Life span development.* New York: Macmillan.

Turkington, C. (1983a). At risk: Project helps hard-to-reach parents, kids. *A.P.A. Monitor, 14,* 6.

Turkington, C. (1983b). National center supports prevention efforts. *A.P.A. Monitor, 14,* 7.

Uomoto, J. M. (1982). Preventive intervention: A convergence of the church and community psychology. *Journal of Psychology and Christianity, 1,* 12–22.

Zax, M., & Cowen, E. L. (1976). *Abnormal psychology: Changing conceptions* (2nd ed.). New York: Holt, Rinehart, & Winston.

S.-Y. Tan

See Community Mental Health; Community Psychology.

Preventive Medicine. *See* Health Psychology.

Pride. Unreasonably high self-esteem. Pride is frequently alluded to in Scripture but is not a topic of great interest to contemporary psychology. Perhaps the reason for such neglect of a critical human fault is to be found in the late-twentieth-century Western mindset, which sees less wrong with pride than with inferiority complexes and less offensiveness in pride than in self-effacement. It is not uncommon to idolize the proud politician or music star and to ignore the humble. Pride has its roots deep in the human soul, however. Payne (1960) wrote what he terms a history of the human soul by studying pride in literature. "Was not pride the soul confronting itself in a mirror, overjoyed at the recognition?" (p. 1).

The Bible describes pride (self-regarding love and self-satisfaction with one's person, status, behavior, reputation, and traits) as sin. Pride goes before destruction (Prov. 16:18), puts one in an undesirable relationship with God (1 Peter 5:5; James 4:6), and will yield a regrettable end (Prov. 29:23). Nebuchadnezzar was judged for his proud spirit (Dan. 4), Haman was beset with pride (Esther 5), and Pharaoh fell because of it. God promises to humble the proud (Matt. 23:12).

Christian theologians have dealt with the concept of pride mainly in the tradition of Augustine, who viewed pride as the first sin and thus spent a considerable amount of his energy on discussing it. The keystone of his argument was a text in Ec-clesiasticus that reads, "pride is the beginning of sin." The verse has later been regarded as questionable in meaning. Nonetheless, on this basis Augustine proceeded to view the fall of Satan as portrayed in Ezekiel and Isaiah as principally motivated by pride. "Your heart became proud on account of your beauty" (Ezek. 28:17, NIV). What led Satan to his fall was likewise the downfall of the human race in the garden of Eden. Augustine felt that pride in its extreme is the unpardonable sin (Green, 1949). He wrote extensively about his own struggles with pride, describing it as his greatest temptation.

The study of pride has also been the subject of great interest to Christians in monastic traditions and later to the Pietists. Bernard of Clairvaux in *The Steps of Humility* said that people can take steps upward if they pursue humility; but if they pursue pride, their steps will lead downward, following the course of Satan. Bernard suggests that there are 12 steps that could lead one from the beginnings of pride—curiosity—to its most severe expression, habitual sin. The intervening steps are frivolity, foolish mirth, boastfulness, singularity (going to all ends to prove oneself superior), conceit, audacity, excusing of sins, hypocritical confession, defiance, and freedom to sin. The first step of pride (curiosity) is the last step of humility (downcast eyes). The last step of pride (habitual sin) should be the first step toward true humility (the fear of the Lord).

Bernard's outline is obviously sermonic in tone and designed as an instructive tool for aspiring monastics. But with all its medieval format, his description of pride rings true. Modern psychology does not have much to add to his outline. Pride elevates the self, seeks to have one's worth recognized by others, and is blind to obvious personal faults. The proud person has difficulty functioning interpersonally, since he or she does not receive or process feedback from others in a satisfactory manner. Nor does the proud person fare well in the task of being other-centered. Pride forms a key element in the psychological construct of narcissism.

Pride, psychologically considered, is defensive in nature. By definition pride is not a fair and true estimate of self; it is an overestimate. Hence the proud person is motivated to hide a subconscious feeling of inferiority or is motivated to overcompensate for actual inadequacies. Pride can be part of an ill-formed approach to social interaction; the proud person may genuinely feel his or her pride to be the best approach to dealing with self and others and may be unaware of flaws that preclude the pride. Pride thrives on deference and praise from others. It may have its roots in parental overindulgence or in a background that created deep personal insecurities for which the pride is compensating.

References

Green, W. M. (1949). *Augustine on pride as the first sin.* Berkeley: University of California Press.

Payne, R. (1960). *Hubris: A study of pride.* New York: Harper & Row.

J. R. BECK

See EMOTION; PERSONALITY.

Primal Therapy. Primal therapies embrace the traditional notion that psychological illnesses are the result of repressing, or removing from consciousness, the feelings surrounding traumatic life experiences. Healing involves reexperiencing and integrating these repressed feelings in as totally uninhibited a fashion as possible. The screaming that often accompanies the release of these powerful emotions has earned the primal therapies their reputation for being a radical treatment approach.

The primal therapies have a complex ancestry that can be traced to the cathartic method of Josef Breuer and Sigmund Freud (see Swartley, 1979, for primal therapy's family tree). In 1897 Freud first used the term *primal* or *primary* to denote psychological processes that ignore reality and attempt to gratify every wish either by simple motor activity (such as eating or sexual intercourse) or by identifying with the source of previous satisfaction (such as mother's breast). In contrast, secondary processes take external reality into account when seeking to satisfy a wish. Psychodynamic theorists now use the term *primal* (meaning first in time) for a memory or scene from early childhood that is apparently the first stage in the development of a neurosis.

Freud initially attempted to release and work with these primal experiences directly through free association and hypnosis, but he later abandoned this task as too difficult and as potentially damaging to both therapist and patient. Others, however, have resumed where Freud left off, and in 1972, under the leadership of William Swartley, the International Primal Association was formed. Among contemporary versions of primal-type therapy, Janov's primal therapy has drawn the most attention, both for the coherence and breadth of the theory and for its somewhat sensational presentation in *The Primal Scream* (1970).

After 17 years of practicing standard insight therapy as a psychiatric social worker and psychologist, Janov encountered a baffling clinical situation that forced him to change his theories of neurosis. During an otherwise ordinary group therapy session Janov invited a patient to call out, "Mommy! Daddy!" in imitation of a scene from a play that had fascinated the young man. The patient complied and was soon writhing on the floor in an agony that finally ended in a piercing, deathlike scream. This ordinarily withdrawn person was as puzzled as Janov about the experience and could only report, "I made it! I don't know what, but I can *feel!*" (Janov, 1970, p. 10). Analysis of this and similar clinical experiences led to Janov's theory and therapy, which would regard the young man's scream as a product of the primal pains that reside in all neurotic individuals at all times.

Janov believes that all neurotic behaviors and most physical symptoms derive from a single common source: the suppression of feeling. This suppression begins early in life when the child's basic needs go unmet for any length of time. The pain that results from this deprivation continues until the child either gets the parents to satisfy him or her or shuts off the pain by shutting off the conscious awareness of need.

The thousands of parent-child interactions that deny the child's needs make the child feel that there is no hope of love when he or she is being himself or herself. The child therefore begins to act in the expected manner rather than out of real needs and desires. The primal scene for Janov is the critical point at which the child shifts from being more real to being more unreal. At this juncture the child is said to be neurotic, and the unreal behavior soon becomes automatic. The real, feeling self is locked away behind layers of defense.

What is crucial is that the child does not eliminate the need by splitting off from it. When excessive pain causes needs to be buried, the body goes into a state of emergency alert, which is experienced as constant tension. Because one's real needs have been removed from consciousness, one must pursue the satisfaction of these needs symbolically. Thus an incessant smoker who was weaned too abruptly or too early may be symbolically expressing the need to suck the mother's breast. This, for Janov, is the essence of neurosis: the pursuit of symbolic satisfactions. And because the satisfaction is only symbolic, there is no end to the pursuit.

The goal in primal therapy is a tensionless, defense-free existence in which the individual experiences internal unity and is freely and deeply himself or herself. Janov believes that this state is impossible for the neurotic to achieve without eliminating (i.e., experiencing) primal pains. When one feels fully the pain of one's basic unmet needs, when one finally *wants* what one *needs*, the struggle for love is resolved and the unreal self is destroyed. The patient is then said to be normal.

The primal therapist's objective is therefore to dismantle the patient's defenses in order to destroy the barrier between thoughts and feelings. The therapeutic milieu is carefully contrived to facilitate this. For the first three weeks of treatment the patient is seen daily in individual sessions lasting as long as the person needs (usually two to three hours). For at least the first week the individual stays alone in a motel room. Isolation, sleeplessness, and elimination of tension-relieving activities weaken defenses and keep the patient focused on self.

During therapeutic sessions the patient lies spread-eagle on the couch. He or she is encouraged to relive early situations that evoke strong feelings. Defensive maneuvers such as intellectualization are confronted immediately and forbidden, so that one comes at last to experience one's feelings and pain—to "have a primal"—rather than to discuss these things. The therapist is thus "the dealer of Pain, no more, no less" (Janov, 1970, p. 247).

After the third week the person is placed in a post-primal group composed of people who have been through the treatment. The function of this group is to stimulate its members into new "primals." The patient usually stays in the group for 12 to 15 months.

Many primal therapists reject Janov's "busting" technique, preferring gentler methods such as massage or music to move the person into primal experiences. The role of pain in neurosis is also controversial. Some therapists observe that pleasure is sometimes more assiduously avoided.

The primal therapies usually last from one to two or more years, depending on the patient's readiness to allow his or her chaotic primal feelings into awareness. These therapies should not be used in their radical form with individuals who have fragile ego structures. The experience of primal hurts carries with it the potential for harmfully disrupting the psychotic or near-psychotic personality. Great skill is required of the therapist to avoid what Swartley calls the "insidious accumulation of side effects" (1979, p. 209) in either therapist or patient.

Though Janov has been criticized for going too far, perhaps the most salient critique from the Christian perspective is that he does not go far enough. For although Janov follows his patients into the primal experiences of birth and even intrauterine trauma, he stops short of the final abyss; his reductionistic view of persons as essentially biological entities forces him to consider neurotic those experiences that arise out of one's spirit dimension. For example, Janov sees the experience of "oneness with God" as irrational and interprets it as a "loss of reality" (1970, p. 222). For the Christian, however, such a transcending experience is the truest expression of the true self, for God is the ground of reality. Anxiety calls one to reckon not only with repressed childhood feelings but also with one's responsibilities and commitments, both immediate and ultimate. In the oft-quoted words of Augustine, "Thou hast made us for thyself, and our hearts are restless till they find their rest in thee."

Christian alternatives to Janov's primal therapy include Osborne's (1976) primal integration and Finch's Christian existential psychology (Malony, 1980). Though developed independently of Janov, primal integration uses essentially the same concepts, terminology, and techniques but in a context that is accepting of religious experiences and values.

Christian existential therapy uses many primal techniques, including a three-week intensive therapy that the patient spends in isolation. However, Finch's approach goes beyond emptying the well of childhood hurts to an exploration of what lies beneath the well itself, namely, God. Finch views persons as essentially spirit—created in God's image, by God, and for God. Until one comes to know God experientially, as he is revealed in Christ, one is not truly oneself. In such a context primal therapy finds a responsible, holistic, deeply Christian expression.

References

Janov, A. (1970). *The primal scream.* New York: Putnam.

Malony, H. N. (Ed.). (1980). *A Christian existential psychology: The contributions of John G. Finch.* Washington DC: University Press of America.

Osborne, C. G. (1976). *The art of learning to love yourself.* Grand Rapids, MI: Zondervan.

Swartley, W. (1979). The new primal therapies. In A. Hill (Ed.), *A visual encyclopedia of unconventional medicine.* New York: Crown.

B. Van Dragt

See Counseling and Psychotherapy: Overview.

Primary Gain. Sigmund Freud theorized that a patient accrues some gains from the formation of a neurotic symptom. The primary gain is obtained when the symptom allows partial instinctual gratification without the incapacitating guilt or anxiety accompanying direct instinctual discharge. The id impulse is kept unconscious while it is also partially indulged. Thus the patient complaining of disturbing thoughts of killing his wife can honestly claim no conscious desire to perform the act while simultaneously achieving discharge of aggressive instincts through his symptomatic obsessive thoughts.

See Secondary Gain.

Primary Process. A psychoanalytical term referring to the primitive mental activity of young children and some seriously disturbed adults. Sigmund Freud theorized that psychic functioning consists of two basic modes of operation, primary process and secondary process. Primary process refers to a type of thinking or a particular way of manipulating psychic energy. The id operates according to primary process throughout life, while the ego gradually gives up primary for secondary process during the first years of life. The two main traits of primary process functioning are drive toward immediate gratification of instincts and relatively easy shift from one object or method of gratification to another. The first is shown in the child's inability to delay pleasurable gratification, and the second is illustrated by the child's shift to sucking the thumb when the breast or bottle is unavailable (*see* Thumb Sucking). Other characteristics of the primary process mode are a generally illogical quality, thinking in allusion or analogy, visual over verbal representation, compatibility of mutually contradictory ideas, and absence of negatives or qualifying conditionals. Examples of primary process can also be found in normal adults in jokes or dreaming. Abnormality in adults exists only when psychic functioning is dominantly primary.

K. M. Lattea

See Psychoanalytic Psychology.

Primary Reinforcer. In the terminology of behavioral psychology a primary reinforcer (also called an unconditioned reinforcer) is a stimulus that functions naturally to increase the probability of the behavior preceding it. A primary reinforcer need not be previously associated with any other stimuli in order to have behavioral reinforcing qualities. For example, food, water, and air are primary reinforcers because an organism will work to receive them without prior conditioning or learning. A thirsty animal or person will perform required behaviors to receive the primary reinforcer of a drink of water.

See SECONDARY REINFORCER; LEARNING.

Prince, Morton Henry (1854–1929). One of the pioneers in psychopathology and abnormal psychology. Born in Boston, he received his M.D. degree from Harvard Medical School in 1879 and continued his studies in France, where he came into contact with the work of Jean-Martin Charcot and Pierre Janet. When he returned to the United States, he went into private practice, treating disorders of the nervous system. While practicing medicine he taught neurology at Harvard (1895–1898) and at Tufts (1902–1912).

In 1906 Prince founded the *Journal of Abnormal Psychology,* which became the *Journal of Abnormal and Social Psychology* in 1922. He edited it until his death. It was restored to its original name in 1965. In 1927 he founded the Harvard Psychological Clinic in an effort to bring normal and abnormal psychology into a closer relationship.

As a result of his studies in Paris Prince became interested in dissociation. He interpreted multiple personality in terms of unconscious conflicts that split one part of the personality from another. Although he was a disciple of Janet, his view was actually closer to Sigmund Freud's than to Janet's. His *Dissociation of a Personality* (1906) caused a stir because it read more like fiction than fact. Although his colleagues were advocating the rest cure, he insisted that psychiatry should gear its treatment to the inner dynamics of the disturbance.

Prince believed that the same principles involved in normal learning could be found in pathological behavior. He argued that when the association between ideas is useful, no one becomes concerned; but when it is harmful, then they think it needs treatment. He viewed neurosis as a perversion of memory, or an association neurosis. Prince thought that theoretically what was done by education could be undone the same way, and he found this to be true in practice. He concluded that psychotherapies were different forms of education, implying that people who were not physicians could treat functional disorders.

Prince was the author of more than one hundred articles as well as many books on psychological, neurological, and political issues. His best-known psychological works are *The Unconscious* (1913), and *Clinical and Experimental Studies in Personality* (1929). During the war he wrote *The Psychology of the Kaiser* (1915), which was used as a guide by the British to organize their propaganda campaign against Germany. Several Allied governments decorated him for his contribution.

R. L. KOTESKEY

See ABNORMAL PSYCHOLOGY; DISSOCIATIVE IDENTITY DISORDER.

Problem Solving. Knowing about a problem but being unable to solve it is a common difficulty addressed in professional counseling, especially pastoral counseling. Success in life calls for effective problem management. For many people who do not have a systematic set of problem-solving skills, the following five step model has proven effective. GRACE is the acronym for five tasks of problem management: *G*oals, *R*esources, *A*lternatives, *C*ommitment to action, and *E*valuation.

Goals change the focus from negative problems to positive solutions. They have seven key elements (Berg, 1991):

- Goals must be considered important by counselees.
- Goals should describe the desired behavior in concrete, measurable terms.
- Goals are best kept small (not "going to college and graduating" but "making a list and ranking five college majors").
- Goals need to be described as the infancy of a new vision for change. The counselor's intent may be to start counselees on the right track and then get out of their way. In a church setting, other ministries—worship, fellowship, service—may continue to support and encourage clients.
- Goals must be realistic and achievable within a short time.
- Goals should describe the presence of something other than the problem, not the absence of something.
- Goals involve considerable effort for counselees even though they may not seem difficult to helpers. Counselees need to expect to work hard at achieving them.

Taking inventory of resources, both internal and external, is the next step. Internal resources include inner strengths and skills, coping methods, and successful experiences with problem solving. For those who have had little or no past success, counselors can share their own experiences.

External resources are found in people's environments: church, family and friends, schools, money and assets, and so forth. These offer assistance, moral support, and gratification as people handle difficult situations. An inventory should include how the resources might be used and what difficulties they might present.

After establishing goals and assessing resources, the counselee and counselor can list all alternatives, no matter how unlikely, for reaching a solution. The counselor may need to illustrate how many courses of action are possible, but it is always better that most ideas come from the person with the problem.

The list then needs to be narrowed and inappropriate alternatives weeded out. Because several courses of action may achieve the same goal, it is necessary to consider other aims, especially a person's ethics and values. For example, counselees involved in child custody battles would reject kidnapping their children as an alternative, because it would violate their ethical standards.

After the initial elimination process, it is time to weigh the probable effectiveness of the remaining courses of action. Listing and selecting alternatives is a collaborative effort in which counselor and client together choose those that are most likely to be fruitful. The client should take as much initiative and responsibility as possible.

Commitment to action—a chosen course that may and often should be broken down into small, concrete, and easily attainable steps—follows when the list of alternatives is narrowed to a few or even one that appears to have a high chance of success. Taking action is essential in problem management, but it is the point at which people often resist moving forward. They may forget, become too busy, or fear the consequences of change. The minister needs to encourage them in any way possible to begin acting, because only then can they experience the benefits of positive change. If resistance persists at this point, referral may be in order.

Evaluation, or review and refinement, is an ongoing part of the problem management process but occurs more consciously once concrete initiatives are under way. When evaluation reveals progress, the counselee will be encouraged to continue. When the review discloses lack of progress, the goals or alternatives may need fresh scrutiny or change.

People learn problem management best while being guided through their own troubled times. In counseling, counselees not only work at managing their present problems through use of a systematic model like the GRACE model; they also learn a way of addressing future difficulties.

Reference

Berg, I. (1991). *Working with the problem drinker: A solution-focused approach.* Lecture presented at the meeting of Marriage and Family Therapists, Dallas, TX.

H. STONE

See DECISION MAKING.

Problem-Centered Family Systems Therapy. In this family therapy approach problems are seen as a disruption of the basic functions a family needs to provide for its members: providing survival needs (food, shelter, money); managing developmental stages; and giving emotional support in stressful situations.

Therapy Process. Emphasis is on current family problems. Treatment generally requires 6 to 12 sessions. Family members are enlisted as active collaborators in the problem-solving process. The family provides most of the momentum in the treatment process by identifying its own strengths and weaknesses and by devising means to solve its own problems. The therapist is the catalyst, clarifier, and facilitator.

The major intervention steps of this model are assessment, contracting, treatment, and closure. Each step begins with an orientation to explain that particular phase. At the end of each step the therapist summarizes the family's perspective and seeks a consensus with the family and their permission to proceed. This position shows respect for the family members and reduces resistance to therapeutic change.

Assessment is the most detailed step and includes all family members living at home. Using the Family Assessment Device (Keitner et al., 1990), six dimensions are investigated to give an overall picture of family functioning and the presenting problem: problem solving, communication, roles, emotional responsiveness, emotional involvement, and behavior control. Each of these dimensions is carefully explored to gain understanding of the family's strengths and weaknesses.

Problem solving concerns the family's ability to discuss difficulties and implement alternatives. Communication involves the family's ability to speak clearly and directly to each other. Roles are reliable patterns delegated to appropriate family members to provide material needs and nurturing. The family is assessed as to how well the roles are performed. Emotional expressiveness measures the degree to which the full range of human emotion is appropriately experienced in the family. Emotional involvement is the degree to which family members show interest and caring for each other, from the extremes of no involvement to overinvolvement. Behavior control concerns the ways the family monitors and sanctions its members' behavior, ranging from rigid to flexible.

Additional problems concerning individuals (physiological and psychological) are also assessed, as well as those concerning the family and wider social systems (school, church, extended family). The assessment stage is completed when both therapist and family agree on a list of family problems.

Contracting is the second major phase. The therapist helps the family decide whether they would like to work alone on their problems or continue in treatment. If the latter, the family specifies what changes they expect from each other and sets concrete goals. Then the family and therapist commit themselves to meeting these goals by signing a contract agreement.

The third step is treatment. The therapist provides initiative for action to the family by identifying problems and tasks that move toward meeting the goals. Tasks are distributed among the family members and progress toward goals is evaluated. If goals are met, further tasks are assigned. If a task is not completed or even attempted in three successive sessions, the therapist recommends outside consultation or termination.

Closure is the final step. Therapist and family summarize what they have learned in treatment, discuss how they can adapt these gains to future problems, establish long-term goals, and plan a follow-up session to monitor the family's progress.

Evaluation. This approach has recently focused on families with a depressed member (Keitner et al., 1990). The General Functioning and Problem Solving scores on the Family Assessment Device appear to differentiate families with a depressed and suicidal member. Helping the family to resolve its problems effectively and providing emotional support and acceptance are important interventions in dealing with depression as a family concern.

Epstein and Bishop (1981) explicitly state that the underlying value system of this approach is the Judeo-Christian ethic. The individuals in the family are respected for their capacity to generate productive, healthy solutions to their problems, and emphasis is given to the optimal development of each human being. The therapist is not considered all-knowing but a collaborator with the family. Regarding the family as the primary experts on themselves seems to restore the dignity the family may feel it has lost by revealing its problems and weaknesses. The humility of the therapist's stance and the belief in the worth of the individual are both consistent with the biblical perspective.

References

Epstein, N., & Bishop, D. (1981). Problem-centered systems therapy of the family. In A. S. Gurman & D. P. Kniskern (Eds.), *Handbook of family therapy.* New York: Brunner/Mazel.

Keitner, G. I., Ryan, C. E., Miller, I. W., Epstein, N. B., Bishop, D. S., & Norman, W. H. (1990). Family functioning, social adjustment, and recurrence of suicidality. *Psychiatry, 53,* 17–30.

C. V. BRUUN

See FAMILY THERAPY: OVERVIEW.

Problem-Solving Therapy. Assisting clients in solving their problems is a highly relevant topic for counselors, who frequently work with clients facing difficult issues and/or possessing inadequate problem-solving skills. In fact, D'Zurilla and Goldfried (1971) were among the first to note that "much of what we view clinically as 'abnormal behavior' or 'emotional disturbance' may be viewed as ineffective behavior and its consequences, in which the individual is unable to resolve certain situational problems in his life" (p. 107). The task for the counselor, then, is to assist the client in solving the presenting problem while also ensuring that the client has learned new skills for use in other problems, a process that can be termed as "counseling for effective decision making" (Horan, 1979).

Problem solving appears to be a unitary skill, and therefore one that should be easily acquired. However, effective problem solving consists of a series of interrelated stages, each with relevant skills. Heppner (1978) defined five such stages of problem solving, beginning with a general orientation or set. The optimal set toward problem solving is one in which the person acknowledges the existence of the problem and behaves as though an effective resolution is possible. An effective set also involves patience, for neither acting impulsively nor retreating from the problem is likely the best solution. The second stage is formulating an accurate description of the problem. For reasons that will be discussed, individuals can make inferential errors at this point that lessen the likelihood of successful resolution.

An accurate description of the problem is necessary for the third stage, in which alternative solutions or responses are generated. After contemplating these options, the person selects and implements a choice in the fourth stage. The fifth and last stage involves testing the choice against a predetermined standard and evaluating the process itself. The last stage is particularly important for the counselor to assist a client in completing, as from the vantage of hindsight many gains in problem solving skills can be achieved from analyzing how effective and ineffective choices were made.

Much of the problem-solving research has been conducted using laboratory problems. These were carefully defined and controlled by the researcher and involved such tasks as mazes, puzzles, and anagrams. However, recent research has turned to understanding how real-life problems can be complicated by errors that individuals make in thinking about their own situations. This research is conducted by scientists interested in human inference, how individuals gather and interpret information. This research is of great importance to counselors, for how both clients and counselors can fall prey to a number of biases in gathering information and in thinking about choices is a critical component for understanding effective problem solving.

Nisbett and Ross (1980) have discussed how people make errors in the ways in which they form inferences and make judgments. First, when people go about gathering information, they need to decide what information to gather, a process that can be influenced by preexisting information. A counselor might find that a client rejects a particular solution because of what he or she believes to be true without going through the necessary steps of getting the types of information needed to evaluate the solution. In a family counseling situation, for example, a counselor might suggest the use of family meetings. If a parent rejected that option by stating that the teens in the family would never agree without actually consulting them on their opinion, the parent is basing that inference on prior data that may or may not be relevant to the new situation.

A second bias can occur when individuals combine new information with information they already have. Research suggests that people may inappropriately weigh what they already know rather than give weight to new and apparently incompatible information. It is important for counselors to remember that they too are prone to biases in information seeking and processing. Counselors may find themselves rejecting in advance a particular approach with a particular client because "it just won't work with people like her." In that case, while there is relevant information from the counselor's experience, it may be given more weight than the new information about this particular client.

Spivack and colleagues (e.g., Spivack Platt, and Shure, 1976) have given attention to teaching real-life problem solving skills. Their system emphasizes means-ends thinking, which is spelling out the steps by which a resolution would be reached and determining the obstacles that must be overcome for the solution to work. A related skill is anticipating the consequences of one's own actions on others. Counselors and clients can encourage this type of thinking in both the third step and the fifth step of problem solving as defined by Heppner. More specifically, when clients think about possible solutions, they can also weigh obstacles to their success. And in evaluating the outcome of a solution, the contributions of others' reactions to its success or failure can be considered.

The importance of effective problem solving can be seen in research conducted by Heppner and Peterson (1982) with a problem solving inventory that measured three aspects of problem solving: personal confidence, approach-avoidance, and personal control. These researchers used this measure to study successful and unsuccessful problem solvers among college students and found that the successful problem solvers were less depressed, had more positive self-concepts, and used coping styles that were less blame-focused and more problem-focused in comparison to unsuccessful problem solvers.

Considerable research indicates that problem solving skills can be learned and that doing so improves adjustment. Many of the problem-solving programs described by Spivack Platt, and Shure (1976) include games and dialogues in which problem solving skills are gained in the context of everyday activities. For example, Shure (1981) discussed a training project in which parents and teachers were taught how to respond to typical children's problems in playing with other children: to

elicit the child's view of the problem, to determine how each child felt about the problem, to obtain descriptions of the problem and alternate solutions, and to select a solution. In the research, those children who learned this solution-oriented problem solving skill were rated as more adjusted both immediately after training and at later points in time than were nontrained children.

It is important to remember that each stage of problem solving is important. Thus it is equally valuable to spend time describing the problem as it is choosing the solution, and it is especially important to define as many alternative solutions as possible before a solution is chosen. Finally, the skill of evaluating the success or failure of a solution so that future problem solving is enhanced is critical. Enhancing the problem solving skills of clients is an important approach for the Christian counselor and is especially suited for focused problems of a developmental or transitional nature. In addition, teaching problem-solving skills would be an essential element for preventive interventions such as premarital counseling or parenting skills workshops.

References

D'Zurilla, T. J., & Goldfried, M. R. (1971). Problem solving and behavior modification. *Journal of Abnormal Psychology, 78,* 107–126.

Heppner, P. P. (1978). A review of the problem solving literature and its relationship to the counseling process. *Journal of Counseling Psychology, 25,* 366–375.

Heppner, P. P., & Peterson, C. H. (1982). The development and implications of a personal problem-solving inventory. *Journal of Counseling Psychology, 29,* 66–75.

Horan, J. J. (1979). *Counseling for effective decision making.* Belmont, CA: Wadsworth.

Nisbett, R. E., & Ross, L. (1980). *Human inference: Strategies and shortcomings of social judgment.* Englewood Cliffs, NJ: Prentice-Hall.

Spivack, G., Platt, J. J., & Shure, M. B. (1976). *The problem-solving approach to adjustment.* San Francisco: Jossey-Bass.

Shure, M. B. (1981). Social competence as a problem-solving skill. In J. D. Wine & M. D. Smye (Eds.), *Social competence.* New York: Guilford.

E. M. Altmaier

See Decision Making; Cognitive-Behavior Therapy.

Professional Schools of Psychology. The rapid rise and increasing popularity of professional schools of psychology, graduate programs in psychology that stress training in the practice of psychotherapy, has caused profound evaluation of approaches to advancing the field of psychology. Traditional psychology doctorate programs bestowing Ph.D. (Doctor of Philosophy in psychology) degrees claim that rigorous education in scholarly research promotes the theoretical underpinning of both psychology and psychologists. Psychologists trained in this scientist-practitioner model are well equipped for academic careers, but many graduates move into professional practice without strong therapy skills. Newer professional programs, largely offering the Psy.D. (Doctor of Psychology) degree state that the need for competent practitioners requires more training time spent in the practice of applied psychotherapy technique. State licensing boards have recognized the Psy.D. as adequate training for licensure as a psychologist, and the American Psychological Association has accreditation guidelines for professional schools of psychology.

Peterson (1991), an early promoter and founder of professional schools, identifies three historical phases of psychology in the United States. The preprofessional phase, comprising the first two-thirds of one hundred years of American psychology, consisted of research and testing work with no systematic training for professionals entering careers of applied psychology.

The second phase, after World War II, established basic conditions for educating professional psychologists as scientist-practitioners. Called the Boulder model, this approach dominated training in the field until the development of professional schools. It stresses graduating psychologists competent in experimental design, research methodology, and academic rigor.

In the 1960s, responding to a weakness in training in applied psychotherapy practice, professional schools began with the University of Illinois and the California School of Professional Psychology offering Psy.D. degrees. The National Council of Schools and Programs of Professional Psychology (NCSPP) now lists 47 member organizations, free-standing and university-affiliated, offering both Psy.D. and Ph.D. degrees in professional psychology. Standards for core curriculum have been developed, including course work and strong practicum experience in theoretical understandings of psychopathology, psychological assessment and testing, and techniques of treatment for different pathologies and populations. Several Christian professional Psy.D. programs have been established, notably Rosemead and Fuller schools in California, Wheaton College in Illinois, and George Fox College in Oregon.

Reference

Peterson, D. R. (1991). Connection and disconnection of research and practice in the education of professional psychologists. *American Psychologist, 46,* 422–429.

For Further Information

National Council of Schools and Programs of Professional Psychology. Philip D. Farber, School of Psychology, Florida Institute of Technology, 150 West University Blvd., Melbourne, FL 32901–6988. (407) 768-8000.

K. M. Lattea

Prognosis. A prognosis is a prediction about the probable course and outcome of a mental health disorder or a problem situation. Prognosis is somewhat difficult in the mental health field, given the array of variation in human interactions, life circumstances, and the environmental context. Certain disorders are more predictable than others; however, each disorder presents with a measure of uniqueness, making prognostication an inexact science. The problem is more complex when one considers that humans are involved in a wide variety of biological, psychological, social, and spiritual differences and that treatment approaches vary.

Often not considered in prognosis is the spiritual condition of clients. Christian therapists report a noticeable difference in recovery between unbelieving clients and clients who are biblically focused. When Christian clients submit themselves to God and seek the assistance of the Holy Spirit in solving their problem (especially if the symptom is a sinful behavior; see 1 Cor. 10:13) the prognostic picture can be quite different when compared to that of clients closed to supernatural intervention. From the Christian perspective miraculous healing is always a possibility.

Each disorder can be studied for its course and prognosis. The standard resources for this information can be found in the *DSM-IV* (American Psychiatric Association, 1994) and *Synopsis of Psychiatry* (Kaplan, Sadock & Grebb, 1994). Prognosis as it relates to schizophrenia, personality disorders, and major depression are briefly reviewed as examples.

Schizophrenia is a disorder that usually develops in late adolescence and has a lifelong pattern of psychotic episodes, frequent hospitalizations and downward drift into poverty and homelessness (*see* Poverty, Psychological Effects and Counseling). Recovery rates range from 10% to 60%; about 20% to 30% of schizophrenic individuals are able to live normal lives (Kaplan, Sadock, & Grebb, 1994). The majority of schizophrenic clients are affected for life with moderate to severe symptoms. The *DSM-IV* lists the following group of factors that are associated to better prognosis: good premorbid adjustment (before disorder), acute onset, later age at onset, being female, precipitating events, associated mood disturbance, brief duration of active-phase symptoms, good interepisode functioning, minimal residual symptoms, absence of structural brain abnormalities, normal neurological functioning, a family history of mood disorder, and no family history of schizophrenia.

Personality disorders involve longstanding, pervasive, and maladaptive personality traits that can be traced back to at least late adolescence (some personality disorders can be diagnosed in children). When clients are diagnosed with a personality disorder, it implies serious problems that are at the core of the personality structure. The prognosis generally is poor that such clients will ever be symptom-free. As people with personality disorders get older, usually starting at around 60 years of age, they begin to show less intense manifestations of the disorder. Although these findings are not yet validated by research, decreasing stress and increasing love and nurturance by others seem to reduce the severity of the symptoms.

A major depression is characterized by a major depressive episode that often includes dysphoria, loss of pleasure, and feelings of worthlessness. The symptoms cause significant distress and can sometimes lead to suicidal ideation or suicide attempts. The *DSM-IV* reports the following: about two-thirds of major depressive episodes improve completely. The remaining one-third either experience some partial relief or no relief at all. In the cases of partial remission, there is greater likelihood of developing additional full depressive episodes. The suicide rate is high (15%) among individuals with major depressive episodes.

Although the outcome research is far from developed, practitioners are using prognosis in marital and family situations. Recent research (Doherty & Simmons, 1996) indicates that 83% of clients report that the marriage and family therapy they received mostly or completely accomplished therapeutic goals. From their years of experience practitioners develop a prognostic opinion about the outcome of interpersonal problems and relationships.

Whether the presenting problem is a mental disorder or an interpersonal problem, a favorable prognosis can provide hope and encouragement that clients can become symptom-free. Under this motivation therapists and clients may take on positive attitudes and work diligently toward resolving presenting problems.

The reverse may be true in situations having a poor prognosis. In these cases therapists and clients may become discouraged and less motivated toward change. Sometimes the prognosis can become a self-fulfilling prophecy as clients and therapists may unknowingly move toward the predicted poor outcome. A realistic prognosis, however, may help family members to adjust to the problem and to set expectations commensurate with the disorder. Nurturance and support by family members improve, which in turn may influence a better outcome or may help to prevent deterioration. For example, when a previously well-functioning teen becomes schizophrenic, it is helpful to all concerned to accept the poor prognosis and not to unduly press the teen to become normal again.

References

American Psychiatric Association (1994). *Diagnostic and statistical manual* (4th ed.). Washington, DC: American Psychiatric Association.

Doherty, W. J., & Simmons, D. S. (1996). Clinical practice patterns of marriage and family therapists: A national survey of therapists and their clients. *Journal of Marital and Family Therapy, 22,* 9–12.

Kaplan, H. I., Sadock, B. J., & Grebb, J. A. (1994). *Synopsis of psychiatry* (7th ed.). Baltimore: Williams & Wilkins.

F. A. DIBLASIO

Projection. The unconscious process by which an individual attributes to another the desires, impulses, or ideas that one finds unacceptable in oneself. This ego defense mechanism allows the person to take whatever is internally threatening or conflictually undesirable, whether instincts or their derivatives, and make it part of an external object or person. The conflict over the projected issue can then be dealt with as an attack from without rather than as a more ego-threatening internal struggle.

This defense is employed in externalizing responsibility for one's failures or undesirable behavior (for example, a student may always find something unfair about any test he or she fails). It may also externalize responsibility for undesirable thoughts, feelings, or impulses. This is illustrated by the rigidly moral person who is sexually attracted to his married coworker and, unable to consciously admit to or cope with such feelings, claims that she is attempting to seduce him.

R. LARKIN

See DEFENSE MECHANISMS.

Projective Identification. A mental mechanism first described in the psychoanalytic writings of Melanie Klein. Its most comprehensive discussion is provided by Grotstein (1981), who defines it as a mechanism whereby "the self experiences the unconscious fantasy of translocating itself, or aspects of itself, into an object for exploratory or defensive purposes" (p. 123). If the purpose is defensive, the intent of this maneuver is believed to be the effort to rid the self of unwanted, split-off aspects while retaining some identification with the externalized contents. Its more positive and most sublimated form is involved in the experience of empathy.

A good deal of confusion exists in many of the discussions of this concept, with some authors distinguishing between projection and projective identification and other authors viewing them as identical. Still others reinterpret the concept, arguing that it should be called projective disidentification, since the intent seems to be projection of some part of self and the subsequent severing of any identification or ownership of this part. The point of consensus in these discussions is that it is one of the most primitive mental mechanisms (along with splitting) and that it therefore will most frequently be utilized by patients suffering from borderline and psychotic disorders.

In its most blatant forms projective identification is sometimes recognized in the fantasy that the individual can enter another person so as to (actively) control him or her or (passively) disappear and evade feelings of helplessness. In more subtle forms it is sometimes hypothesized to be present when the therapist becomes aware of personal inner emptiness or chaos, which is felt to have been disowned and projected by the patient onto the therapist. Implicit in this hypothesis is the belief that therapists can learn to identify the presence of projective identification by carefully monitoring subjective experience in order to differentiate countertransference or other personally idiosyncratic responses from the interactional influence of projective identification.

Reference

Grotstein, J. S. (1981). *Splitting and projective identification.* New York: Aronson.

D. G. BENNER

See DEFENSE MECHANISMS.

Projective Personality Tests. One of the two major groups of personality assessment instruments, the other being self-report inventories (objective tests). Whereas the self-report tests require the subject to describe himself or herself, the projective techniques require the subject to describe or interpret objects other than self. The underlying assumption is that an individual's responses to an unstructured stimulus are influenced by underlying needs, motives, and concerns. Thus the individual can be assumed to project something of himself or herself into the response to these tasks. The interpretation of the responses should therefore yield important information about a person's basic personality structure and motivations.

The two most commonly used projective techniques are the Rorschach inkblot test and the Thematic Apperception Test (TAT). In addition to those instruments, numerous sentence-completion tests, figure-drawing tests, storytelling methods, and other approaches exist. These differ tremendously in terms of normative samples, amount of reliability and validity data, and objectivity of scoring and interpretation. When they are used by someone with the necessary training and experience, they are extremely helpful and have come to be a standard part of the comprehensive psychological assessment.

D. G. BENNER

See PERSONALITY ASSESSMENT; PSYCHOLOGICAL MEASUREMENT.

Promiscuity. A form of sexual delinquency; the practice of transient sexual relations with a variety of partners chosen indiscriminately. It differs from prostitution in that it is not commercial, although it often leads to prostitution. It is considered a major factor in the spread of venereal disease (*see* Sexually Transmitted Diseases).

With the rapidly changing attitudes toward sexual practices the word *promiscuity* takes on different meanings to different people. There is a differentiation between casual sex, premarital and extramarital sex, and promiscuity, in that promiscuity is considered to be complete indiscrimination in the selection of sexual partners, which is not usually found in the other cases. Gagnon and Simon (1970) estimate that half of all married men and one-quarter of all married women will have sexual intercourse outside of marriage at some time. Under this definition of promiscuity more than 4,000,000 married people alone are promiscuous. However, complete indiscrimination regarding partners is extremely rare and nearly always is related to a severe disturbance of a nonsexual nature.

Sexual gratification is not generally considered a motivational factor, since the majority of girls involved in promiscuity are partially or wholly frigid. Factors believed to be involved include the longing to feel loved or wanted and an expression of revenge or defiance. Promiscuity is often a disguised plea for help. Young men may be motivated to prove they are sexually and socially adequate and may out of fear be avoiding a relationship with someone they know.

Causal factors may include a disturbed family life in which the child is neglected (*see* Abuse and Neglect), and often the mother is promiscuous. Many promiscuous young people have alcoholic fathers. Peer pressure from a group holding loose standards may cause the desire for belonging to push an adolescent into promiscuous behavior. The common fear that sexual knowledge leads to promiscuity is unfounded, according to most research. The promiscuous individual typically is fairly ignorant about sex and has learned through experience rather than training or education. It is the most common form of delinquency among mentally retarded girls.

Reference

Gagnon, J., & Simon, W. (1970). *The sexual scene.* Chicago: Transaction.

D. L. SCHUURMAN

See SEXUALITY.

Promises. A promise is a declaration made by one person to another assuring total intention to act upon the pledge in due time. It is the process of making a moral commitment to the other party.

The promise is an undertaking that something will certainly happen or will not happen in the future regarding what has been clearly mentioned or extended. It virtually becomes a right given to the other person, in the form of a claim or an oath, that performance will definitely follow. For example, a promissory note is a written document guaranteeing payment of a specific amount of money upon demand or at a fixed future date.

Through promising, people enter into a defined contract binding themselves with a specific pledge and imposing on themselves a moral obligation. When a person makes a promise, he or she indulges in a clear intent to fulfill a commitment, deliver a service, grant a wish, or perform a duty. Some promises are indefinite in nature. While they assure the recipient of the right intent and definite implementation of what has been agreed upon, they do not include specifics or details on how and when they will be fulfilled. Promises can be conditional or unconditional, mutual or unilateral, and they often manifest different degrees of solemnity.

Promises are different from future predictions, mere planning, or personal resolutions and vows. Promises must be communicated and clearly expressed to the other party involved, at times in written form, while predictions and planning are not binding and personal resolutions and vows may be kept private. On the other hand, threats do not qualify as promises because of the power and control the threatener has over the promisee. A true promise, however, binds the person with an obligation to act upon what has been pledged unless the recipient chooses to release the promiser from his or her commitment.

By promising, people extend themselves into the future. It is an existential position taken in the here and now motivated by a pressing need or demanding situation and shaped by a serious intention regarding the future. Promises can be voluntary, based on one's deep convictions and desire to help others, improve their conditions, and enrich their lives, or can be forced, based on a threat, fear, or humiliation.

Not all promises are made with a positive intent or under favorable conditions. Some promises may have negative intents, immoral motives, or hurtful consequences. This raises a philosophical question whether the parties involved in such a contract remain under the moral obligation to fulfill the promises. In other words, to what extent a person is under obligation to carry a promise when it becomes clearly evident that, if fulfilled, the act will take advantage of the recipient (utilitarian/immoral position) or will cause serious damage upon the promisee (abusive/antisocial position)?

Fortunately, several fundamental rules and moral principles guide the formulation and content of promises and subsequently limit their power. The nature and motive of a promise are as equally important as the moral commitment to fulfill it. There will obviously be serious ethical questions regarding any promise which lacks the elements of truth, fairness, and fidelity. Only when the intent of a promise is inherently destructive in nature, the person becomes free from the moral obligation to keep it. In this case, the moral imperative to preserve the human welfare and dignity, and ultimately the common good, will take higher priority. Thus the parties involved should renegotiate, adjust, or even cancel the agreement(s) according to the new understanding and demands of the situation.

Promises should be made cautiously. In making promises, individuals must avoid rash decisions and hasty impulses and yet, at the same time, conform to the highest ethical standards. There are some individuals who easily make multiple promises and repeatedly overcommit themselves, consciously or unconsciously, distorting the concepts of quality and rationality, and the virtues of honesty and integrity. On the other hand, there are those who are totally afraid of making any definite promise or binding themselves with any specific pledge involving future deadlines. These behaviors normally stem from deep psychological roots revealing internal struggles or disturbances like major insecurities, emotional injuries, perfectionistic tendencies, unmet basic needs, or certain personality types and characteriological symptomatology (e.g., narcissistic and schizoid traits).

Early developmental psychologists emphasized the importance of the element of "trust" in human interactions, especially in parent-child relationships. Adulthood promising takes into serious consideration the notions of time and accountability. Childhood promising is usually based on observational events and concrete realities and not on abstract measurements. However, both may contain a factor of risk taking and creativity without sacrificing the consequences. Parents should carefully formulate, communicate, and keep their promises in order for their children to develop a healthy level of "basic trust" and, therefore, exhibit a balanced mental and emotional functioning.

A promise is morally binding. Fidelity requires honesty, truthfulness, and conformity of actions to the spoken words. Historically, a spoken word was as powerful and as binding as a formal document or written treaty. Some modern social thinkers hold that promise-keeping is a major ingredient in the development of sound human characters and emotional maturity and a key moral aspect vital for family stability and healthy communal living (cf. the recent Christian movement of Promise Keepers).

According to biblical ethics, there is a moral obligation on the part of the initiator to keep his or her promise irrespective of the other party's intention or behaviors. Once made, the promise must be carried into completion provided that its content is not harmful. This is repeatedly modeled in the Old Testament when God initiated covenants, made promises, and took oaths; and God faithfully kept them. Several variations of God's promises appear in the Scriptures. These were, at times, kept unilaterally because of the honor, faithfulness, and integrity of the Lord's name.

God occasionally renews or reiterates the given promises in an effort to nurture the personal relationship with the genuine believers—God's own people—and to remind them of their privileges and responsibilities. "For by these He has granted to us His precious and magnificent promises, in order that by them you might become partakers of the divine nature . . ." (2 Peter 1:4). The fact that God grants, fulfills, and lives up to his promises gives the Christian journey a divine assurance, a solid ground for faith and hope, and a pattern for moral ethics and righteousness.

N. ABI-HASHEM

See VOWS.

Provocative Therapy. A type of psychotherapy developed by Frank Farrelly in the 1960s from his work with psychotics and severe character disorders. It has since been adopted successfully in many different settings with a wide variety of patients and clients. Carl Rogers had seminal impact, especially his concepts of empathy, genuineness, and congruence. At the same time Farrelly's experience in state mental hospitals with the mentally ill convinced him that they were in touch with certain system realities, were more responsible and robust than they were given credit for, and were experts in utilizing social systems for deviant but functional purposes.

A series of clinical experiences led Farrelly away from his initial Rogerian position. One of these involved work with a client who was part of Rogers's research on therapy with schizophrenics. After 91 traditional person-centered sessions Farrelly introjected something new: a humorous style of agreeing with the patient and taking a cynical, negative position that overtly encouraged deviancy and distress. This client's response (and that of most others since) was to take the complementary role, disagree with the therapist, and quickly improve his functioning. Thus this style has proved particularly adept at using the patient's resistance in service of prosocial goals as the patient is provoked into disagreeing in an assertive, constructive manner with the therapist who is taking the devil's advocate position.

Like several other systems of psychotherapy, provocative therapy emphasizes that people have more potential than they assume; that choice is crucial to all therapeutic changes; that current experience is at least as important as the past; and that the client's behavior in therapy is a relatively accurate reflection of his or her habitual coping strategies. Unlike most other therapeutic systems, provocative therapy assumes and emphasizes that people change and grow best in response to a challenge, whatever their degree of chronicity or the severity of the problem; that psychological fragility is vastly overrated; that nonverbal expression is crucial in the impact of many levels of therapeutic communication; and that a judicious expression of "therapeutic hate and joyful sadism" (in evaluating behaviors or as related to specific behaviors) can benefit people greatly (Farrelly & Brandsma, 1974).

Provocative therapy differs from most other forms of therapy in its style: a greater degree of directness and confrontation; the use of a paradoxical communicational style; the use of verbal and nonverbal cues; a high level of playfulness on the part of the therapist; and, perhaps most crucial, the deliberate use of humor in many forms. The basic working hypothesis is that if the therapist provokes a client humorously, perceptively, and paradoxically, the client will move away from his or her negative self-image and behavior toward increased health.

Five major goals for clients in provocative therapy are to learn to affirm self-worth both verbally and behaviorally; to learn appropriate assertion in work and relationships; to learn to defend oneself realistically; to learn necessary psychosocial discriminations in order to respond adaptively; and to learn how to take risks in relationships, especially those that communicate with immediacy both affection and vulnerability.

A wide range of freedom is afforded the provocative therapist in applying many different kinds of techniques. The thrust of this variety is to allow the therapist access to more of his or her experiences in order to increase empathic contact, to employ strategies that counter those destructive adaptations of the client at multiple levels and to enjoy the therapeutic encounter while dealing with some very difficult problems.

The basic technique is verbal communication of a provocative and paradoxical nature. Here the therapist amplifies and encourages self-defeating behaviors and attitudes. This is most often accompanied by nonverbal communication such as a twinkle in the eye, selective use of touch, type of intonation, and so on. These qualifiers are meant to convey the therapist's empathy and contact with the patient. Humorous techniques, including banter, exaggeration, reduction to absurdity, ridicule, sarcasm, irony, and relevant jokes, are also frequently employed. Confrontation and feedback, both in terms of social consequences and in terms of the therapist's immediate subjective perception of the client, are also frequently employed. Finally, dramatic techniques such as the therapist's role playing various fantasized scenarios, modeling the patient's negative behavior, and playing along with the client while suggesting ridiculous solutions are common techniques.

Some Christian therapists find it difficult to play the devil's advocate or to lampoon religious attitudes and beliefs, even if the purpose is to test or strengthen them. Also, the emotionally loaded and frequently coarse language often used in provocative therapy would offend many Christians. However, the complimentary intent and the goals of the therapy, properly understood, would not offer problems to Christians.

This type of therapy tends to inoculate against despair and to inculcate hope and responsibility. It affirms all of life, all one's capacities and experiences to be organized in service of living better internally not only but more importantly in relationships. The therapist strives for a balancing of cognition, feelings, and behavior through the use of humor. Humor is excellent at puncturing pretensions and at dealing with too low or too grandiose a view of the self.

Provocative therapists take evil seriously and make the awareness of it an integral part of therapy rather than attempting to sidestep it. The encounter helps one learn that evil cannot be avoided but must be transformed through choice, humor, and one's relationships. Love is communicated in an indirect way through intense honesty and caring for the individual and his or her autonomy and growth as a total person.

Reference

Farrelly, F., & Brandsma, J. M. (1974). *Provocative therapy*. Fort Collins, CO: Shields.

J. M. BRANDSMA

See PARADOXICAL INTERVENTION; HUMOR.

Pruyser, Paul W. (1916–1987). Paul W. Pruyser was born 29 May 1916 in Amsterdam, the Netherlands, and died 9 April 1987 in Topeka, Kansas. He completed graduate work in psychology at the University of Amsterdam and immigrated to the United States in 1948, earning his Ph.D. in clinical psychology at Boston University in 1953, with clinical training at Boston State Hospital, Boston Children's Hospital, and the National Veterans' Epilepsy Center at Framingham. He moved to Kansas in 1954, served two years as a senior psychologist at Topeka State Hospital, and joined the staff of the Menninger Foundation in 1956. From 1962 to 1971 he served as director of Menninger's Department of Education and from 1972 to 1985 was Henry March Pfeiffer Professor of Research and Education in Psychiatry.

Pruyser wrote five books, edited several anthologies, and authored more than 80 journal articles, obituaries, and historical essays, 27 book chapters, and dozens of book reviews in the areas of diagnosis (1976, 1979), education, epilepsy, mental retardation, pastoral counseling, personality theory and psychopathology, psychiatric treatment, psychology of religion (1968, 1974), philosophy, values, and art, literature, and creativity (1983). To all this work he brought an ego-psychological perspective with an object-relational emphasis. Pruyser was on the editorial boards of the *Journal for the Scientific Study of Religion* and the *International Forum for Psychoanalysis* and *Pastoral Psychology*, and was editor from 1978 until his death of the *Bulletin of the Menninger Clinic*.

Pruyser was a fellow of the American Psychological Association (APA) and the American Society for Psychopathology, and president of the Society for the Scientific Study of Religion (SSSR). He was honored with the William C. Menninger Award from the Menninger School of Psychiatry (1967), the Distinguished Contributions Award from the American Association of Pastoral Counselors (1978), the I. Arthur Marshallmar Distinguished Alumnus Award from the Menninger Alumni Association (1983), and the William C. Bier Award from Division 36 (Psychologists Interested in Religious Issues) of APA (1986).

References

Pruyser, P. W. (1968). *A dynamic psychology of religion*. New York: Harper & Row.

Pruyser, P. W. (1974). *Between belief and unbelief*. New York: Harper & Row.
Pruyser, P. W. (1976). *The minister as diagnostician*. Philadelphia: Westminster.
Pruyser, P. W. (1979). *The psychological examination: A guide for clinicians*. New York: International Universities Press.
Pruyser, P. W. (1983). *The play of the imagination: Toward a psychoanalysis of culture*. New York: International Universities Press.

Additional Readings

Allen, J. G. (Ed.). (1987). A tribute to Paul W. Pruyser. *Bulletin of the Menninger Clinic, 51*, 413–489.
Malony, H. N., & Spilka, B. (Eds.). (1991). *Religion in psychodynamic perspective: The contributions of Paul W. Pruyser*. New York: Oxford University Press.

H. VANDE KEMP

See PSYCHOLOGY OF RELIGION

Pseudocyesis. Pseudocyesis is a condition in which an individual believes herself or himself to be pregnant and develops objective pregnancy signs in the absence of an actual pregnancy. Although pseudocyesis usually occurs in women, there have been a few cases reported in men.

Several theories address the cause of pseudocyesis, and the following three theories are the most accepted. The first theory is the conflict theory, which states that a desire for a fear of pregnancy creates an internal conflict and causes endocrine changes. The endocrine changes are believed to cause the signs, symptoms, and laboratory findings that occur in patients with pseudocyesis. The second theory is the wish-fulfillment theory, which states that minor body changes initiate the false belief in pregnancy in susceptible individuals. The last theory is the depression theory. The depression theory states that pseudocyesis may be initiated by the neuroendocrine changes associated with a major depressive disorder (*see* Depression).

Evidence exists to support all of these theories. One or more of these theories may be simultaneously appropriate for some patients. Pseudocyesis is considered a heterogeneous disorder without a unifying cause.

Pseudocyesis occurs at a frequency of 1 to 6 cases per 22,000 births. However, many cases of pseudocyesis seem not to be reported. Between 1890 and 1910, 156 cases were reported in the English literature. Only 42 cases were reported between 1959 and 1979. Pseudocyesis has become uncommon in industrial societies, with the exception of a large number of cases reported in West and South Africa.

The age range of patients with pseudocyesis is 6 to 79 years of age (with the average age being 33 years). Eighty percent of individuals with pseudocyesis were married, 14.6% were unmarried, and 2.3% were widows. Pseudocyesis is more common in individuals who are in their second marriage.

Symptoms usually last about nine months but can last for a few months up to several years.

Almost every symptom and sign of pregnancy (except for true fetal heart tones, fetal parts seen by imaging techniques, and delivery of the fetus) have been documented in patients with pseudocyesis. Abdominal distension is the most common sign of pseudocyesis. It is thought to be due to excess fat, gaseous distension, and fecal and urinary retention. The abdominal distension often resolves under general anesthesia.

Pseudocyesis has been considered a conversion symptom that is exclusive of pseudopregnancy (a medical condition), simulated pregnancy (malingering), or hallucinatory pregnancy (psychosis). Pseudocyesis, therefore, is considered a paradigm of psychosomatic disorders.

Findings in patients with pseudocyesis show variable results. Estrogen and progesterone values can be high, low, or normal. Prolactin tends to be elevated. Follicle stimulating hormones (FSH) tend to be low. Positive pregnancy tests have been documented in patients with pseudocyesis. Elevated prolactin levels have been implicated as the cause for many of the signs of pseudocyesis. An abdominal ultrasound can confirm and document the absence of a fetus and placenta.

Pseudocyesis is a heterogeneous condition with no one unifying cause and no one universally accepted therapy. There is no clear demographic or sociocultural indicators for a population at risk. The most successful and least invasive form of therapy currently used seems to be revealing to the patient that he or she is not pregnant by using an abdominal imaging technique, counseling and educating the patient, and treating any underlying depression that may exist. Successful treatment has been defined as a six-month symptom-free period.

C. L. KELLY

See PSYCHOSOMATIC FACTORS IN HEALTH AND ILLNESS.

Pseudomutuality. The appearance of mutuality and a close relationship when in fact the marriage or family is characterized by great distance. It is most often seen in families that fear conflict. Pressure is applied to members to present a picture of harmony and intimacy even when conflict is present. Because individual differences are perceived as threatening to group stability, they are not allowed expression.

Christians who fear negative feelings are especially prone to relate in a pseudomutual manner. The polite wife and ingratiating husband are a classic example. A careful look at their relationship shows that the polite but emotionally distant wife is angry at her husband, whose apparent overconcern belies his frustration with her passive-aggressive style. While maintaining the appearance of intimacy, this couple avoids making contact at deeper

emotional levels. Moving from pseudomutuality to true mutuality involves accepting individual differences and acquiring conflict resolution skills. Genuine mutuality invariably involves a balance between individual and family group needs.

J. A. LARSEN

See FAMILY SYSTEMS THEORY.

Psychedelic Therapy. A therapeutic approach that uses a variety of psychedelic or mind-revealing substances to treat a wide array of psychological problems. Mescaline, psilocybin, LSD, MDA, MMDA, harmaline, ketamine, and other drugs have been used in a therapeutic context, although LSD is most commonly administered, and each has its own unique set of effects on human beings. Moreover, various techniques require different dosages of these substances, and therapists vary widely in the kind of setting in which their therapy takes place.

In 1943 Albert Hoffman discovered that LSD, which he had synthesized five years earlier, produced symptoms that at first seemed to model natural psychoses. This psycomimetic effect was the main topic of LSD research until the mid-1950s, when investigators began to discover the substance's therapeutic potential. Two major paths of interest then evolved. It was found that LSD often enabled individuals to experience more easily and fully the process of regression, transference, and insight that takes place in psychodynamic psychotherapy. Also, researchers were receiving reports of positive personality change in subjects who experienced a peak or mystical experience after taking LSD.

In the following years two types of therapy with LSD reflected these developments. Psycholytic, or mind-loosening, therapy, practiced mostly in Europe within a psychoanalytic context, consists of giving relatively small doses of LSD (150 micrograms) to a patient over a series of sessions. This allows the patient to gradually deal with and resolve those unconscious conflicts causing his or her psychopathological symptoms.

Psychedelic therapy in the more narrow use of the term is more popular in North America and strives for personality change through a profound transcendental experience. In psychedelic therapy the administration of a large dose of LSD (500 micrograms); the careful manipulation of the patient's surroundings; and the provision of a warm, sensitive, and supportive atmosphere all work together to facilitate the patient's reaching a deeply religious experience that can serve as a turning point in his or her life. Therapy with psychedelic drugs usually consists of a combination of psycholytic and psychedelic therapy in that both analytic and transcendental aspects are stressed according to each patient's unique personality and therapeutic goals.

Psychedelic therapy has been used in treating character disorders such as psychopathy and sociopathy; psychosomatic and neurotic disorders; alcoholism and other addictions; some types of psychoses and autism; and the psychological distress of the terminally ill. While initial studies on LSD's beneficial therapeutic effects looked promising, later research revealed many methodological shortcomings. LSD's promise as a therapeutic panacea was short-lived. The controversy over the dangers of LSD, the counterculture's predilection for using contaminated street drugs, the wild claims of a number of psychedelic proselytizers, and the polarization of society in the late 1960s have led to severe bureaucratic restrictions that have essentially killed research and practice of psychedelic therapy in the United States.

Even though many researchers believe that the psychedelics have great therapeutic promise and numerous studies have shown that these substances are relatively safe when used in a therapeutic or experimental context, few institutions or individuals have the resources and incentive to overcome the barriers to research with LSD. This is especially tragic because psychedelic therapy can serve as an outstanding vehicle for bringing together the disciplines of psychology, religion, and education to more fully understand human nature and to use this understanding to alleviate suffering.

Additional Readings

Grinspoon, L., & Bakalar, J. (1979). *Psychedelic drugs reconsidered.* New York: Basic.
Grof, S. (1975). *Realms of the human unconscious: Observations from LSD research.* New York: Viking.

W. C. DREW

See NARCOTHERAPY.

Psychiatric Assessment. The interview of a patient by the psychiatrist is not a random, casual meeting. The patient brings a set of expectations, apprehensions, and ambivalence. The patient's motivation is often limited or clouded by anxiety and other strong affects. The psychiatrist brings a unique background both as a person and as a professional with theoretical commitments. The psychiatrist's values and experiences need not prejudice clinical judgments but must yield to understanding tempered by professional awareness.

The fact that there is a variety of psychiatric orientations leads to the possibility of interview conclusions that are more influenced by the orientation than the realities of the patient's situation. The seasoned interviewer recognizes these dangers and listens to the patient while resisting any impulse to impose conclusions. The conclusions are consequently neither hasty nor routine. They go beyond description of behavior to the dynamic that encompasses the biological, social, intrapsychic, interpersonal, and value perspectives.

Many factors influence the interview. These include the setting, whether it be at the bedside in a general hospital, in the psychiatrist's office, or in a psychiatric unit. The psychiatrist will be careful to assure the pledge of confidentiality no matter where the interview takes place. These assurances are commonly verbalized during an initial exploration of why this meeting is taking place. Out of the impressions gained in this initial exploration the psychiatrist begins to formulate a plan for the interview. At the same time he or she must not lose sight of the necessity to observe and inquire about the standard information necessary for a complete evaluation.

Sufficient time is required for the many transactions in the initial interview. Issues such as note taking, placement of chairs, and presence of family are dealt with in a manner that affords the psychiatrist optimum opportunity to fulfill the task in his or her own manner without invasion of the patient's rights or sensitivities.

Psychiatric History. The two major components of a psychiatric assessment are the history taking and the mental status examination. The inclusion of a history presumes a developmental viewpoint. This does not prejudice the interviewer because all psychological theories view the course of illness in the context of earlier symptoms, experiences, and transactions. Psychiatric syndromes develop over time, with characteristic features at various phases of the illness.

The life cycle to date will need reviewing, as will the illness itself. In the main this history will be provided by the patient. However, because self-report includes distortions and selective recall, psychiatrists of interpersonal persuasion often seek consultation with the spouse or family. This is often conducted in the patient's presence and always with the patient's awareness and permission. For a child or an adolescent patient this involvement is essential. Psychiatrists have recently become more comfortable and flexible in seeing the patient in the context of his or her family.

Chief Complaint. The chief complaint traditionally is the patient's reason for seeking professional assistance. It is best recorded in the patient's words. But psychiatric illness being what it is, the patient often is resistant, reluctant, or confused. Consequently, the chief complaint may be a report of others about the patient's behavior, verbalizations, attitude or mood. Therefore the chief complaint may be as much the concern of others about the patient as the patient's own concern. Often there will be a brief description of the patient as part of the chief complaint.

The psychiatric history starts here because the chief complaint is the entrance to the psychiatric syndrome. The psychiatrist immediately searches for the clues that alert one to the natural history of the disorder.

Present Illness. One moves logically and readily into an exploration of the present illness. Adequate time is necessary to delineate the common complexities. Dynamically oriented observers need to exercise care to differentiate present illness from earlier developmental issues that serve as background to the present illness. As the patient unfolds these details, the psychiatrist will start to assess ego functioning, organizational ability, and distractibility, as well as memory, intelligence, and motivation. All aspects of the interview are appropriate resources for evaluation of the patient's mental status. There is a natural overlap between present illness and the mental status examination. Precipitating causes are an appropriate aspect. Sequences of events and temporal connections suggest possible causation of symptoms. Description of the present illness is more than a recitation of symptoms; it is the basis for the exploration of intrapsychic and interpersonal events.

Past Illnesses. Any medical history, psychiatric included, examines previous disorders throughout the life span of the patient. This needs to include reference to age of the patient at time of hospitalizations (if any) or other treatment intervention or forms of treatment, including medication usage. It is important that the exact drug and dosage be identified, as a history of successful response to a particular medication may lead to a treatment regimen with the same agent.

Developmental History. This is a personal history of the patient from birth to present, with a developmental perspective. The psychiatric patient often is unable to give detailed information because of the disability. Family members are then needed either as a primary resource or to supplement the patient's report. Psychiatric emergencies do not lend themselves to gaining this information immediately, so later interviews are needed to explore these details. The developmental history encompasses several facets of personality development, including motor, cognition, social, psychosexual, and school and work performances.

Prenatal and birth histories often contain invaluable clues for the diagnosis. Defects or injury evident at birth as well as maternal illness or drug or alcohol use during gestation bear significantly on infant development (*see* Prenatal Development). Maternal and paternal attitudes about the pregnancy set the stage for bonding, which develops at birth. Inquiry of the mother as to her feeling toward the patient at birth is an important ingredient of a family psychiatric history.

The first three years are perhaps the most important in personality development and interpersonal relatedness. The more that can be learned of the child's need fulfillment, the better. Not only gross maternal rejection but also maternal depression may significantly interfere with the child's bonding and trust. Early illnesses, eating disorders, sleep patterns, maturational milestones, and constancy of human care need exploration. The presence of splitting by bonding to multiple maternal objects should be noted. Experiences of separation anxiety as well as excessive symbiosis with the mother should also be explored. Power issues may become evident around toilet training history. Other expressions of excessive willfulness will be seen in temper tantrums. Regression at the birth of a sibling or loss of a significant object is also important.

Throughout these three years distinctive personality patterns and traits are emerging. These set the stage for subsequent capacity for self-control and socialization. In addition to information about gains in developmental tasks in all these areas psychopathological features can be ascertained by the history of the first three years. Diagnoses such as mental retardation, attention deficit/hyperactivity disorder, separation anxiety, and pervasive developmental disorders (including autism) can all become evident in these years.

Ages three through latency extend the issues of early childhood into growing intrapsychic and interpersonal spheres. Gender identification becomes apparent. Early peer relatedness develops. Intellectual capacity or learning disability surfaces. Patterns of aggression or passivity form rather substantially.

Preadolescent and adolescent development see the finalization of the development of adult personality. The adolescent must deal with intimacy-sexuality as well as independence-separation-individuation issues. Adolescence may be viewed as a resurrection and reprocessing of childhood struggles. The defensive structure of the child becomes the adult defenses through the kaleidoscope of adolescence. With the exception of infancy there is perhaps no other time when the child needs his or her family more than in adolescence. This is commonly the time when parents are all too ready to give their tasks away to community institutions or peers. Presently the despair of youth as well as their rejection of society's values are manifest in adolescent substance abuse. Superficially this is seen as a conduct disturbance having to do with authority conflict, whereas in reality it much more commonly reflects anguish about family patterns. Such a child is best helped through and in the family, whose usefulness is now greater than ever.

Adulthood has its own developmental tasks and issues, and passage through these should be reviewed for the adult patient. Advanced educational experiences, occupational history, sexuality, social relationships, marital history, children, and military experience constitute the most frequently questioned areas. Retirement history for older adults should also be explored.

As hereditary factors are becoming better understood in psychiatric illness, family history must include reference to possible genetic disorders. There is great value as well in a history of interrelationships between the patient and all significant others and in a careful exploration of family attitudes about the patient and the illness. This provides an early opportunity to influence their attitudes about therapy.

Religious-Value History. Historical divergence and conflict between religious and psychiatric thought have contributed to frequent avoidance by psychiatrists of religious and moral development. More recently mutual respect has grown between the fields, and now the psychiatric examiner will more often include this domain within the assessment. Value development usually goes beyond religious background and upbringing but has its roots in these experiences. To understand these complex interactions the psychiatrist needs a wide perspective and a respect for the patient's unique commitments and experiences. A wealth of data concerning motivation, self-perception, and guilt production can follow. The highly value-oriented patient responds with trust toward the therapist who respects his orientation.

Mental Status Examination. *Behavior and Appearance.* History taking very readily becomes clinical evaluation. The alert observer lets no occasion pass in gaining data to identify the patient's mental status. The earliest observations are descriptive in nature. These include the patient's appearance and behavior. Observations of gross behavior are possible even in the mute patient. These include various motor behaviors ranging from severe agitation to mute rigidity. The patient's attitudes about the examination should also be noted. These attitudes are best seen as responses to the examiner's own mood and attitudes. The psychiatrist should have a reasonable awareness of his or her own attitudes and how the patient responds to them and should, from the beginning of the interview, be watchful for manifestations of transference or countertransference.

Affect and Mood. Affect, or emotion, is the feeling experience of the patient. Sustained affect is considered a mood. The range of affect goes from flat (shallow or inadequate) to inappropriate (not corresponding to cognition or event), to labile (cycling or changeable). Affect may be vibrant, pleasurable, disagreeable, or any of the human emotions. The interviewer seeks to assess the predominant sustained emotion. To do this he or she observes and inquires into the patient's feelings about a wide variety of subject matter. Facial expression, verbal expression, and bodily movement suggest inner feelings.

Present mood is understood in the context of recent and present circumstances and also is viewed historically. Mood disturbances are of cyclical or recurrent nature and are usually expressive of early life experiences. Disturbances of mood manifest themselves in disturbances of relationships. The bonds of love and care require expressions and feelings of attachment. Mood disturbances interfere with these. The observer detects not only the mood but also its influence on or by significant others.

Thinking. In examining the form of thinking the psychiatrist explores the stream of thought. This is viewed as quantitative in expression; the amount of thinking and the pattern of its production are significant. Ideas may flow rapidly or with agonizing deliberateness or apparent paucity. In extreme, thinking may be so rapid it is termed a flight of ideas. The content may not be illogical, but interconnecting ideas are missed, leaving an impression of scattered associations. The continuity of thoughts suggests logical thinking. Illogical thinking is suggested by associations that are disconnected or that violate Aristotelian logic. Loose associations suggest schizophrenia, whereas flight of ideas suggests mania. Thinking may be described variously as circumstantial, tangential, perseverative, evasive, or blocked. Severe thought disorder may be manifest as incomprehensible speech with neologisms or word salad.

The content of thinking is also vital. It may be characterized by preoccupations of an obsessive, phobic, or some other nature. More specific disturbances of thought disorder include delusions. Here the psychiatrist attempts to ascertain the delusion's organization and meaning to the patient. The psychiatrist also evaluates the patient's ability for abstract thinking. Deviations may be in the direction of being overly concrete or too abstract. These may be tested by interpretation of proverbs or metaphors. More commonly the conversation in the interview suffices for conclusions regarding the capacity for abstract thinking.

The psychiatrist also learns about the patient's education and fund of information. Simple serial subtraction of 7s from 100 yields observations about concentration, cognitive abilities, and perceptual impairment.

Consciousness. Altered states of consciousness suggest brain impairment or dysfunction. Clouding of consciousness is a blunting of attentiveness resulting in inattention to stimuli and some disruption to goal-directed behavior. Disorientation in time, place, and person are usually evident only in organic brain disorder. Questions about the specifics of orientation are an essential component of a thorough mental status examination. Memory functions are usually observed in the course of the examination, including recent and remote memory as well as immediate retention and recall. If these are not observed in the natural flow of the interview, simple questioning will usually provide gross assessment of memory.

Ego Functioning. The voluntary mental capacities are viewed in their adequacy to self-preserve, control impulses, maintain a relationship to reality and to people, and to organize human functioning. As these are commonly impaired in psychiatric illness, they deserve special attention. The psychiatrist will examine the ego defenses, which are characteristically associated with coping mechanisms as well as psychiatric disorders. These defenses are not necessarily pathological.

Social judgment is required for effective human relationships. It involves a capacity to assess the outcome of one's behavior and attitudes. Impaired judgment is characteristic of psychotic disorders. Judgment is usually revealed by the patient's spontaneous report but can be assessed more directly if necessary through psychological testing or through asking what should be done in specific situations (e.g., fire in a crowded movie theater).

Insight refers to the patient's awareness of his or her psychiatric illness and also needs to be assessed. It may be intellectual only, limiting the ability to alter one's experiences. Emotional insight implies readiness to self-explore, looking for newer means of adaptation.

Psychiatric Assessment in Context. The psychiatrist is a physician by training and responsibility. The person and the brain are not clinically separable; the psychiatrist uses the latest mind-body understandings to distinguish organic disorders from those disorders that are thus far best understood in psychodynamic terms. Knowledge of bodily dysfunctions allows a comprehensive assessment and referral in cases of organic illness. A thorough psychiatric history and mental status examination bring the psychiatrist to diagnostic conclusions, fitting the patient's syndrome to a disorder classified under *DSM-IV.* This psychodynamic formulation represents the best notion of the development of the illness and its principal social, emotional, intrapsychic, and interpersonal components. Such a formulation suggests areas of deficit and also leads directly to a treatment plan.

The treatment plan encompasses whatever interventions are necessary to correct, if possible, the dysfunctions. It will consider the role of the significant others in the patient's life and how they may aid the recovery. It also should include the role of the therapist as well as the goals. The methods to reach these goals should also be identified.

Additional Reading

Kaplan, H. I., & Sacock, B. J. (1981). *Modern synopsis of comprehensive textbook of psychiatry III* (3rd ed.). Baltimore: Williams & Wilkins.

T. G. Esau

See Psychological Measurement; Personality Assessment.

Psychiatrist. A medical doctor who has received further specific training in the areas of mental health and disease. A psychiatrist has studied human thought, feeling, and behavior in its normal development and its aberrations. With training in both medicine and psychiatry, the psychiatrist stands ready to appreciate the emotional and physical connections within us in both health and disease.

The training for psychiatry includes a minimum of three years of premedical college, four years of medical school leading to an M.D., and four years of psychiatric residency. An approximation of a typical curriculum would include rotations through internal medicine and neurology during the first year or two. The early years usually concentrate on inpatient work with the more serious illnesses. The focus then shifts to outpatient treatment and later to special rotations, research, and pursuit of individual interests (administrative psychiatry, forensic psychiatry, community mental health centers).

Certification in psychiatry by the American Board of Psychiatry and Neurology is preferred but is not required in all situations. Teaching appointments in medical schools require certification, but many clinical positions do not. Certification requires completion of an approved four-year residency training program, two years of experience, and passing a comprehensive written and oral exam. The oral exam consists of three separate hours. One hour involves examination of a psychiatric patient with an examiner present, followed by questions from several oral examiners. The other two hours involve viewing videotapes of psychiatric and neurological patients and then being questioned by examiners. About 40% to 50% of the U.S. psychiatrists are currently certified. Certification in child, administrative, and forensic psychiatry is also currently available.

Child psychiatry is the most formal area of subspecialization. Other subspecialty areas are biological, geriatric, administrative, psychoanalysis, hospital, adolescent, and forensic psychiatry. Psychoanalysis involves further formal classroom training at a psychoanalytic institute, supervised analysis of one or two patients, and successful completion of one's own personal analysis by a training analyst.

One of the major current trends in psychiatry is the movement back toward general medicine, with increasing attention being paid to physical disease and mind-body relationships. Strong interest in biological and biochemical aspects of psychopathology is part of this movement. The discovery of endorphins and enkephalins and the apparent ability to consciously control their production in the brain have led to new insights into such areas as acupuncture, the placebo effect, the importance of touching, and the healing value of the laying on of hands. Issues involved in forensic psychiatry, particularly the insanity defense, are also increasingly prominent in the field. The specifics of treatment and detention are receiving a great deal of attention. Finally, preventive psychiatry is an increasingly important area of work. Unfortunately, however, it is usually limited by lack of public interest and therefore lack of funding.

Indications for referral to psychiatrists include the suspicion of the presence of organic physical disease, the possible need for hospitalization, and the need for prescription of psychotropic medication. Some physical diseases involve psychological complaints. Depression, for example, may be the only early complaint of a patient with carcinoma of the head or of the pancreas or with hypothyroidism. Depression may accompany a treatable dementia such as normal pressure hydrocephalus. Bizarre and impulsive behavior with unusual stereotyped thought patterns may be caused entirely by complex focal seizures. The psychiatrist will cooperate with other mental health professionals in the diagnosis and treatment of these various mind-body interfaces.

D. C. SCHUTZ

See AMERICAN PSYCHIATRIC ASSOCIATION.

Psychic Healing. One of the growing number of so-called paranormal phenomena that have recently come under organized scientific investigation. Falling outside of conventional medical models, psychic healing was once the sole province of the occult arts and the more esoteric branches of religion. Within the past century, however, researchers have, through controlled study and careful documentation, validated many of the healers' claims despite enormous methodological obstacles and prejudices within both the scientific and religious communities. Departments of psychology and parapsychology at several major universities in the United States and abroad have taken part in this research, as have many independent foundations.

Psychic healers may be found in virtually all cultures, from the primitive to the scientifically sophisticated. In Great Britain, for example, the practice is so widespread that regulatory bodies have formed (such as the National Federation of Spiritual Healers), and the government has sanctioned spiritual healing in more than 1,500 hospitals. In the United States, however, healers must generally operate within a religious context, where the recognized church function of laying on of hands circumvents laws prohibiting diagnosis and treatment by the nonmedically trained.

Psychic healing is a form of mental healing that can be traced back to prehistoric shamanism. Modern movements such as mesmerism, Christian Science, spiritualistic healing, and the psychic surgery of the Philippines continue this ancient tradition. Some healings reported in the Bible, effected simply by prayer or touch, bear some formal similarities to psychic healings.

Well-known psychic healers of this century (cf. Krippner & Villoldo, 1976) include Edgar Cayce, Rolling Thunder, Olga Worrall and Ambrose Worrall, and Jose P. de Freitas, all of whom have submitted their practices to careful scientific study.

Many healers dislike the term *psychic* because of the vaudevillian images it conjures up. Terms such as spiritual, natural, mental, religious, paranormal, or parapsychological are often preferred. Psychic healing is generally distinguished from faith healing in that the locus of activity is different. Healing by faith may be seen to result from an attitude adopted by the one healed, whereas in psychic healing the one healed is considered the more or less passive recipient of something done to him or her by the healer.

The Practice of Psychic Healing. The field of psychic healing comprises a broad spectrum of theories and therapeutic techniques. If one observes merely the healers' external practices, one would conclude that there are as many ways of doing psychic healing as there are healers themselves. However, most healers would agree that the essence of the process lies in the being of the healer and in the reality of a transcendent source rather than in the techniques. Whereas the surgeon's tool is the scalpel, the psychic healer's instrument is the self or spirit (conceived as the totality of one's being) in existential interaction both with the one being healed and with a power or Being beyond them both, in which both participate.

Viewed psychologically, psychic healing represents an ideal of human interrelationship. The moment of healing is the moment in which two selves become one in the sense of abandoning the egocentric pretense of separateness. In that moment there is a flow between the two that becomes rejuvenating for each.

Viewed phenomenologically, from the standpoint of the typical healer's experience, the process may be described as follows: While healing, the healer goes into an altered state of consciousness that is characterized by an inner stillness in which he unself-consciously centers on the task. The healer strives for inner balance and emotional calm, seeking freedom from emotional investment in the other. While healing, the healer experiences herself as being in vital and immediate relationship with some being or force beyond her ordinary self, from which or from whom she receives help and for which or for whom she is a channel or instrument. In this capacity the healer transmits something that flows toward the other and effects healing. The healer is not herself the source of the healing.

The transcendent reality for which the healer is a channel may be conceived as God, universal mind, electromagnetic force, one's own higher self, something else, or a combination of these, depending on the healer. From this transcendent reality the healer may receive pertinent information or power that enables healing to come about. The healer's emotional balance and attitudinal clarity are vital to contact with these transcendent sources.

In assessing the nature of the other's illness the healer may either ask questions or scan the condition of the person by extrasensory means. This process (called psychic reading) may include sensing the other's feelings and experiencing his or her nonphysical, or energy, body. The healer receives relevant extrasensory information both spontaneously and in response to questions that he asks of himself. This extrasensory input comes in various modes, depending on the healer and the situation. Interpretation of extrasensory information is usually based on the healer's own internal, experiential criteria. Extrasensory abilities are usually experienced intermittently rather than being totally at the healer's command.

During the phase of healing in which the healer is intervening, he focuses on and experiences an acceptance or love toward the other. In each instance the healer seeks to act in response to the other's need rather than according to the healer's own agenda. He may effect healing by being with the person in an unusually close or accepting way and allowing to happen for the other whatever is to happen. Or he may actively seek to bring about or alter specific conditions in the other, using techniques that vary with the healer and the situation.

Many of these techniques have to do with the transference of energy from the healer to the other. This energy often radiates from or through the healer's hands. During this process the healer may experience sensations relating to the flow of energy. Often she seeks to effect healing by actively visualizing some desired condition in the other's body or psyche, thereby bringing about change by the direct influence of thought. In working toward psychological healing the healer will often seek out the experiences in the other's past that are responsible for current maladies and work with the memories of these traumatic experiences to heal present disharmony. This process may revolve around verbal exchanges of information, extrasensory processing, or other techniques that vary with the healer and the context.

Healing may be effected with the healer either in the presence of or absent from the other. The healer experiences spatial distance as irrelevant to healing, and time seems also to have altered significance.

In psychic healing, then, the healer enters a reality in which he or she is continuous both with the other person and with a transcendent source that provides the effective power for creating wholeness and harmony in the other. The healer is an instrument or channel through which this transcendent power operates. The healer enters this reality by intending simply but unequivocally the good of the other.

Psychic healers view people's essential nature as contained not in the material body but in the energy body, which is said to occupy the same space as the physical body. This energy body is detected visually by some healers as a colorful aura surrounding the physical body. The aura reflects the person's immediate physical and emotional state. Aberrations in the flow or vibration level of this energy are believed to be the primary cause of physical and emotional maladies. Psychic healing is said to involve a flow of energy from the healer that raises the vibration of the other's energy to a level that is incompatible with disease.

Experimental Research. Much of the experimental research on healing centers around the hypothesized existence of these energies and the influence of thought upon them. One-to-one correlations have been established between the various colors that healers see in the aura and the specific frequencies of electrical activity measured on the surface of the skin (Ferguson, 1978). Other experiments have demonstrated, for example, the ability of some healers to alter the surface tension of water, to influence plant growth, to decrease the time required to heal wounds in mice, to increase blood hemoglobin levels in humans—all of this by laying on of hands (Rindge, 1977). All these experiments have controlled for random error and yield statistical results well within accepted confidence levels.

Whatever energies are involved in psychic healing, they are apparently unaffected by spatial distance. Experiments with the well-known healer Olga Worrall have demonstrated her ability to increase the rate of plant growth (on one occasion by 830%) by visualization or prayer from six hundred miles away. Worrall was also able to induce wave patterns in a cloud chamber from the same distance, again by visualization. In an extension of LeShan's (1974) work, Goodrich (1978) found that persons trained through meditation to enter a state of oneness with another were able to effect remote healing in medical patients. Most of these experiments clearly control for the often advanced alternative hypotheses of suggestion or placebo effect.

A Christian Response. Viewed phenomenologically, the ability to heal psychically is just another human capacity, on a par with sensation, locomotion, and thought. It is not, therefore, the paranormal phenomena themselves but rather the healer's philosophy that a Christian evaluation would address.

At the center of the gospel is an emphasis on the spiritual dimension of human beings as that which qualifies or defines them. Humans are spirit. Psychic healers accept this premise wholeheartedly but at times seem to equate spirit with a quantifiable energy rather than with the existential qualities of freedom, responsibility, and transcendence. While psychic healing may involve some form of measurable energy, it would be from a Christian viewpoint a reductionistic error and a new, subtler determinism to attempt to confine the numinous aspects of people in this way.

Both Christianity and psychic healing view human beings as related to a transcendent source, from which comes the power for healing. However, whereas a particular healer may equate this source with the personal God of the Bible, she may also see it as, among other things, a loving energy field or even some aspect of her own self. Although this may seem problematic theologically, from an experiential standpoint the process is the same for both the Christian and psychic healer. What is essential is that one surrender to some power higher than one's own ego or conscious self.

Finally, both Christianity and psychic healing posit that love (in the sense of an absolutely unequivocal intent for the other's good) is the essence of the healer's gift and the sine qua non for healing. At its best the process of psychic healing involves the healer in a radical personal commitment to *be* love to the other. This is also the heart of a commitment to Christ. It is in this emphasis on love that Christian and psychic healer are most in agreement.

References

Ferguson, M. (Ed.). (1978). Electronic evidence of auras, chakras in UCLA study. *Brain-Mind Bulletin, 3* (9), 1–2.

Goodrich, J. (1978). The psychic healing training and research project. In J. L. Fosshage & P. Olsen (Eds.), *Healing: Implications for psychotherapy.* New York: Human Sciences Press.

Krippner, S., & Villoldo, A. (1976). *The realms of healing.* Millbrae, CA: Celestial Arts.

LeShan, L. L. (1974). *The medium, the mystic, and the physicist.* New York: Viking.

Rindge, J. P. (1977). The use of non-human sensors. In G. W. Meek (Ed.), *Healers and the healing process.* Wheaton, IL: Theosophical Publishing House.

B. VAN DRAGT

See FAITH HEALING; TRANSPERSONAL PSYCHOLOGY; PARAPSYCHOLOGY.

Psychoanalysis: Technique. Developed by Sigmund Freud from the mid-1880s through the 1930s, psychoanalysis was the first truly psychological form of therapy for the treatment of mental and emotional maladjustments. It is considered the most in-depth approach to psychotherapy because of its frequency (four or five times weekly), its length (three to five years), and its focus on the reconstruction of early childhood experiences and mental functioning.

As a form of psychotherapy, psychoanalysis grows logically out of the psychoanalytic theory of personality development and psychopathology. This theory holds that maladjustments develop out of conflicts between biologically based drives such as sex and aggression, which arise from a group of processes known as the id, and the repressing forces of the personality, the ego defense mechanisms. Psychoanalysis is designed to identify these conflicts and overcome them. By becoming aware of previously hidden wishes and conflicts that were too threatening or anxiety-provoking to be faced, patients are enabled to confront them more maturely, give up inappropriate defense mechanisms, and develop a balanced functioning between their instincts (id), their reality-judging functions (ego), and their moral standards (superego). Since conflicts between impulses and defenses were developed in the context of intimate relationships with parents and siblings, psychoanalysis places a strong emphasis on the healing nature of the therapeutic relationship.

According to psychoanalytic theory, anxiety-provoking wishes and feelings have been repressed because the ego was too weak to face them. Awareness of them would generate excessive anxiety because of the fear they would get out of control or because key people in the environment would react to them with punishment, rejection, or disapproval. Because the child's ego was too weak to cope with these psychic realities, the person had to rely excessively on defense mechanisms such as repression and projection. Although these defenses help avoid painful or frightening wishes and memories, they also use up a great deal of emotional energy and result in a denial or avoidance of some aspects of reality. Pathological symptoms are a kind of compromise between the repressed wish and the defenses in which the wish is consciously avoided but finds a substitute expression through the symptom. Repression of one's anger, for example, may enable the person to avoid the conscious awareness of being an angry person. But the repressed anger may show up in disguised form as self-hatred and depression. Until these previously avoided conflicts can be found and faced, the person cannot develop the ego strength to face reality, be honest with his or her emotions, and function efficiently and congruently.

Both the quality of the therapeutic relationship and a number of specific techniques are utilized to bring these previously repressed conflicts to the surface so they can be analyzed, understood, and resolved.

The Role of the Analyst. The psychoanalyst's role can be roughly divided into two parts. The first is the offering of a sensitive, caring relationship in which patients feel free to explore the painful psychic material that is at the root of their personality disturbance. This real relationship is the context for all psychoanalytic work, but it lies somewhat in the background as a necessary but not sufficient cause of effective analytic work. It includes the analyst's ability to hear and understand the patient's struggles without anxiety or condemnation as well as the ability to comprehend the meaning of previously repressed material. This role is that of a deeply sensitive listener who hears both the conscious and unconscious mental processes of the patient.

The second part of the analyst's role consists of his or her technical procedures. These technical procedures are the analyst's actions or techniques. They comprise what analysts do as they listen empathically to their patients. These procedures center around encouraging the patient to free associate and interpreting the meaning of these associations. They also include the analyst's use of silence, dream interpretation, and the interpretation of resistances and transference.

Free Association. Since the psychoanalytic theory of pathology sees the roots of maladjustment in the conflict between the largely unconscious impulses and wishes of the id and the evaluative control functions of the ego, the techniques of psychoanalysis are aimed at resolving and reworking these conflicts. The basic rule of psychoanalysis is that the patient tells the analyst everything that comes to mind during the analytic hour. The purpose of this is to help patients go beyond their conscious, rational, ego-controlled thoughts in order to become aware of previously repressed wishes, thoughts, feelings, and experiences.

By saying everything that comes to mind, no matter how embarrassing, irrelevant, or painful it may seem, the psychoanalytic patient gives the analyst a full view of his or her psychological life. By listening carefully to the patient's free associations the analyst is able to sense painful areas, contradictions, or defenses patients are using to avoid facing aspects of their lives.

Resistance. Although patients seeking treatment consciously desire to change, psychoanalytic theory proposes that at an unconscious level they do not want to give up the defenses that hide painful or unacceptable feelings and wishes because they know of no other way of handling them. In psychoanalysis all the patient's efforts (both conscious and unconscious) to avoid these anxiety-provoking thoughts and feelings by continuing the defenses are called resistance (*see* Resistance in Psychotherapy). Resistance is the use of defense mechanisms during psychoanalytic treatment. Since the inappropriate use of defense mechanisms keeps patients from facing the conflicts that give rise to their maladjustments, the analysis of resistances is one of the major therapeutic activities of the psychoanalyst. Common resistances include not talking, censoring one's thoughts, talking in a highly intellectual manner that avoids feelings, missing appointments, talking only of present concerns (rather than both the past and the present), and acting out one's hidden conflicts in pathological or defensive behaviors.

Psychoanalysts begin to help patients overcome their resistances and become aware of hidden conflicts by pointing out and demonstrating how the patient is resisting. They may observe, "It is interesting that each time we talk about your father you miss your next appointment," or, "When you mention your brother's death you seem to pass over it very quickly and change the subject." Once patients become aware they are resisting, the analyst helps them explore what memories, feelings, or wishes are being pushed from awareness and why. In each case it is some painful emotion such as fear, guilt, shame, or anger.

As patients become aware of what and why they are resisting, the analyst helps them explore the sources of these conflicts. If the patient consistently avoids any semblance of angry feelings in talking about experiences that normally prompt anger responses, the analyst encourages the patient to explore his or her family dynamics in order to learn why the patient is so fearful of experiencing angry feelings. By repeatedly analyzing these resistances and helping patients face upsetting emotions and memories, the analyst hopes to open the patient to finding better ways of coping. As this is done, the patient's ego grows progressively stronger and able to cope, and his or her id impulses are more maturely integrated into the total personality.

Interpretation. The psychoanalyst's primary therapeutic activity is interpretation. Interpretation consists of making previously unconscious mental processes conscious. This is done in conjunction with the analysis of resistances, since the resistances keep these processes out of awareness during the analytic hour. Interpretations, however, go beyond analyzing resistances to explore in depth the meaning, cause, and dynamics of a psychological process or experience. In formulating interpretations that help patients understand their dynamics, analysts rely heavily on dreams and free associations to piece together a picture of the conflicts the patient has been avoiding.

For example, in the same or succeeding sessions a patient may discuss an aggressive colleague at work, a policeman he believes mistreated him, and a dream he had about his father. The analyst will see a pattern in which the patient is tending to view most of the significant men in his life as threatening to his masculinity. By asking the patient to give associations to these men, the reason for the fears will usually become apparent. In line with psychoanalytic theory, one hypothesis might be that the patient harbors competitive and resentful feelings toward male authority figures growing out of his childhood desire to replace his father as the object of his mother's love (the oedipus complex). By slowly uncovering resistances, making interpretations, and tying different bits of psychological experience together, analysts help patients gradually explore the roots of their current adjustment struggles and conflicts.

Transference. Another cornerstone of psychoanalytic technique is the process of transference. In transference patients experience (transfer) feelings or reactions toward a person in the present that are really a reliving of childhood reactions to other significant people. Although everyone transfers some reactions and feelings from childhood figures (such as parents and siblings) to adult social relations (such as spouses and employers), the psychoanalytic situation is set up to maximize this process so that the patient will relive and resolve earlier conflictual relationships. The frequency of sessions, the use of free association, the use of the couch (which prevents usual social interaction and encourages exploration of one's inner feelings), and the focus on dreams and past significant relationships are all designed to promote regression to earlier, more primitive psychological levels of functioning and transference. Within the transference patients experience their fears, guilt, sexual and aggressive wishes, and their defenses against these thoughts and feelings, much as they did in childhood. This time, however, they experience them with a person (the analyst) who is not threatened and who can help them understand and accept their wishes and feelings and handle them in mature ways.

Psychoanalytic theory holds that as patients react to their analysts, earlier maladaptive relationships are brought into focus and can be understood and altered. Along with free association and interpretation, then, the transference relationship is one of the major procedures for uncovering repressed feelings and experiences.

The transference relationship is also a key to keeping the analysis from serving as an intellectual excursion into the past. By actively experiencing transferred feelings with the analyst the patient is able to struggle with difficult emotions on a first-hand basis. In this way the analyst in part becomes a substitute parent who is able to help patients cope with difficult wishes and feelings they felt they could not handle with their real parents.

Summary. Although some critics claim that psychoanalysis encourages people to act out their sexual and aggressive drives, this is not the case. The issue for analysts is being aware of one's wishes and drives so that one can face them and make mature, conscious choices that take into account one's wishes, the demands of reality, and one's own moral valuations.

Since the 1950s a wide variety of therapeutic alternatives to psychoanalysis have been developed. Most of these are of shorter duration, less expensive, and more focused on specific symptoms. Psychoanalysis itself has also been evolving as analysts place greater stress on the importance of the child's very earliest interpersonal relationships (the first four years of life) and on the role of aggression in the development of maladjustment, and less emphasis on Freud's biological views of instincts. In spite of the variety of therapeutic approaches, however, psychoanalysis continues to be one of the few depth therapies that attempt to make fundamental alterations in the structure of the patient's personality.

Additional Readings

Freud, S. (1963). *Therapy and technique.* New York: Collier. (Papers originally published between 1888 and 1937)
Greenson, R. R. (1967). *The technique and practice of psychoanalysis.* New York: International Universities Press.
Menninger, K. (1958). *Theory of psychoanalytic technique.* New York: Harper & Row.

S. B. NARRAMORE

See PSYCHOANALYTIC PSYCHOLOGY; PSYCHOANALYTIC PSYCHOTHERAPY.

Psychoanalysis: Theory. *See* PSYCHOANALYTIC PSYCHOLOGY.

Psychoanalyst. Unlike most mental health practitioners who are identified by their particular disciplines (e.g., psychology, social work, psychiatry), psychoanalysts represent all the major mental health disciplines and have in common their commitment to the theory and practice of psychoanalysis. Psychoanalysts may operate from a variety of theoretical orientations (e.g., Freudian, Sullivanian, Kleinian), but all practice an intensive form of therapy that generally involves seeing patients four or five times weekly for between three and five years.

The prerequisite for training in psychoanalysis is a degree in medicine, clinical psychology, clinical social work, or a related field. After being licensed to practice in one of the fields, individuals desiring to practice psychoanalysis undergo a lengthy training program (typically four or more years) in a psychoanalytic institute. These institutes are run by local psychoanalytic associations rather than university medical schools or psychology departments, and the training is typically carried out on a part-time basis while students continue to practice in their respective professional fields. These psychoanalytic training programs consist of three components. The first is a set of courses in psychoanalytic theory and therapy. These cover the psychoanalytic theory of personality and psychopathology as well as the theory of psychoanalytic technique. The second part of the training consists of the control analyses. This involves receiving weekly individual supervision on at least three different psychoanalytic therapy cases over a period of years.

The third component of psychoanalytic training is the candidate's personal psychoanalysis. This experience is considered the central and unique aspect of psychoanalytic training, since only by becoming aware of one's own conflicts and mental dynamics can one be comfortable with and sensitive to the potentially confusing, frightening, or embarrassing thoughts and feelings one's psychoanalytic patients will be experiencing. The training analysis usually involves five sessions weekly for a minimum of three years.

After completing such a rigorous training program most psychoanalysts develop a full-time private practice of psychoanalysis or psychoanalytically oriented psychotherapy. Since psychoanalysis is demanding work, most analysts also engage in some clinical supervision, teaching, or consultation for the diversity and balance these provide in their professional lives.

S. B. NARRAMORE

See PSYCHOANALYSIS: TECHNIQUE.

Psychoanalytic Family Therapy. This approach assumes a reciprocal relationship between conflict among family members and conflict within the mind of any one member (Ackerman, 1966). There is a circular feedback loop between interpersonal conflict and intrapsychic conflict, but generally interpersonal conflict in the family group triggers the establishment of fixed patterns of intrapsychic conflict. When persistent and pathogenic patterns of family conflict are internalized, symptoms result that are reversible if the intrapsychic conflict can be treated in the family that precipitated it. The psychoanalytic family therapist is interested in historical family relationships as the basis for current interactional patterns, which are of interest only if they illuminate internalized patterns.

At the beginning of the family's life cycle unconscious factors influence mate selection. When two people marry they inevitably replicate parts of the relationship of their parents and recreate what is called the childhood emotional pattern (Saul, 1979). A mate is chosen who reduces one's anxiety and recreates the warmth of the original parent-child relationship. The dynamics of romantic love allow for the denial of the negative characteristics of the mate, which also mirror the patterns of the parents (see Friedman, 1980). In order to live with the tension of the partner's combined negative and positive characteristics, both spouses collude (Willi, 1982) in the denial of these aspects and attempt to make the partner into the person who will meet their innermost needs. When both partners are well-adjusted, these dynamics produce a healthy marriage. When the partners are poorly adjusted, the marriage will become symptomatic, creating problems for the children born into the family through the family projection process (Bowen, 1978). Mismatched partners will most likely divorce.

The process of inducing problems in the child as a result of marital distress is known as scapegoating, a concept borrowed directly from the Bible: the scapegoat carried the sins of Israel into the wilderness. This process requires the existence of a group (the family) whose members feel threatened by some hint of evil (an undesirable characteristic or personality trait) and who agree to use some other person (a family member) to personify that evil, which can ultimately be eliminated by destroying the scapegoat through a serious physical or emotional illness that takes the child away from the family. In treatment the scapegoat is not held personally responsible for the symptoms thus induced by the family, and therapy will focus on finding a way to take the person out of the scapegoat role (see Family Scapegoating).

Scapegoating and other family image-maintaining processes are often maintained by the formation of family myths (Bagarozzi & Anderson, 1988). These involve patterns of mutually agreed upon, distorted roles resulting from compromises between all family members so that each individual's self-identity and defenses are maintained through the myth. Collusion among family members allows the family to see itself as living up to its ideal image and avoiding other repudiated images (Byng-Hall, 1973). Children are recruited into the maintenance of family images first defined in the parents' unconscious marriage contract (Sager, 1976). When parents see in themselves characteristics contradicting the family myth, they delegate a child or an adolescent to resolve the issues, often reinforcing various kinds of undesirable behavior by which they themselves are unconsciously tempted. Such a child may then be expelled from the family in order to maintain its ideal image. Other children may be bound to the family, unable to leave because their loss would create an unbearable blank in the family's image (Stierlin, 1977).

The maintenance of the family myth also leads to the creation of family secrets, which may involve facts or events known by one family member and kept secret from others. They may also involve events or conditions known by all family members but not talked about. Such secrets constitute a taboo. Other secrets involve shared or individual fantasies that are not talked about. Bringing such secrets into the open and discussing their impact on the family may be an important focus of family therapy (Imber-Black, 1993).

Ghosts and skeletons in families are other unconsciously perpetuated dynamics. Skeletons are the facts that embarrass family members, parts of the family's darker side that often become secrets as well. Family ghosts are created when members of past generations continue to be psychologically present, a situation that occurs when unresolved familial issues reverberate throughout the system. Often ghosts result from unmourned deaths in the family. The mourning process is not an automatic one, and professional assistance may be needed to facilitate it (Paul & Paul, 1975). When the ghost is a living family member, family therapy may involve bringing this person into the therapy.

Psychoanalytic family therapy is often indicated for serious, long-standing emotional problems that have resisted treatment from a structural, functional, or strategic perspective. It tends to involve long-term rather than short-term treatment and generally requires the cooperation of several generations of family members.

References

Ackerman, N. W. (1966). *Treating the troubled family.* New York: Basic.

Bagarozzi, D. A., & Anderson, S. A. (1988). *Personal, marital, and family myths: Theoretical formulations and clinical strategies.* New York: Norton.

Bowen, M. (1978). *Family therapy in clinical practice.* New York: Aronson.

Byng-Hall, J. (1973). Family myths used as defenses in conjoint family therapy. *British Journal of Medical Psychology, 46,* 239–250.

Friedman, L. J. (1980). Integrating psychoanalytic object-relations understanding with family systems intervention in couples therapy. In J. K. Pearce & L. J. Friedman (Eds.), *Family therapy: Combining psychodynamic and family systems approaches.* New York: Grune & Stratton.

Imber-Black, E. (Ed.). (1993). *Secrets in families and family therapy.* New York: Norton.

Paul, N. L., & Paul, B. B. (1975). *A marital puzzle: Transgenerational analysis in marriage counseling.* New York: Norton.

Sager, C. (1976). *Marriage contracts and couple therapy: Hidden forces in intimate relationships.* New York: Brunner/Mazel.

Saul, L. J. (1979). *The childhood emotional pattern in marriage.* New York: Van Nostrand Reinhold.

Stierlin, H. (1977). *Psychoanalysis and family therapy: Selected papers*. New York: Aronson.

Willi, J. (1982). *Couples in collusion*. New York: Aronson.

H. VANDE KEMP

See FAMILY THERAPY: OVERVIEW.

Psychoanalytic Group Therapy. As a method of treating psychological disorders psychoanalysis focuses exclusively on the individual psyche. While Sigmund Freud recognized the importance of social groups such as tribes, clans, and especially the family, his approach was to look at these groups primarily in terms of their effect on the psychological growth and development of individuals making up the groups. Thus the notion of treating many persons simultaneously by group therapy was alien to the first psychoanalytic practitioners.

The extension of psychoanalytic personality theory and treatment procedures to group therapy began in the 1930s with the pioneering work of Trigant Burrows, Louis Wender, and Paul Schilder. Burrows referred to his group therapy as group analysis, Wender observed the phenomenon of transference in groups, and Schilder encouraged his group patients to say whatever came to their minds in an effort to model the technique of free association. Consolidators of the psychoanalytic group model included Samuel Slavson and Alexander Wolf; the former worked with groups of children while the latter treated adults in group sessions.

Although almost all types of group therapy utilize a number of psychoanalytic principles in their theory and technique, they differ significantly from psychoanalytic group therapy per se. Psychoanalytic group therapy by definition places primary emphasis on exploration of the latent, unconscious material of each group member. This does not mean that the observable behaviors of the group member are ignored or discounted as being unimportant. However, the psychoanalytic group therapist always attempts to move from the behaviors to the unconscious processes causing them. This approach contrasts with nonanalytic groups, which tend to emphasize the meaning and significance of whatever is occurring in the group at the moment.

Basic Concepts. To understand how psychoanalytic group therapy works it will be helpful to review briefly the assumptions underlying individual psychoanalytic treatment. Psychoanalytic theory postulates that conflicts derived from experiences in certain stages of development result in specific forms of neurotic behavior in later years. The patient is unaware of these conflicts and resists their emergence into consciousness. This resistance precludes conscious recognition of the forbidden impulses, feelings, and thoughts that underlie the conflicts. The task of the psychoanalyst is to penetrate these defenses in order to foster awareness and then resolution of the unconscious conflicts. The technique of free association was developed to implement the goals of uncovering and resolving these conflicts.

This basic understanding of the origin and treatment of psychological disorders is applied to patients in a group setting in the following way. Members of a psychoanalytic group are not specifically told to free associate, but they are asked to discuss whatever is on their minds at the moment, whether about themselves or other group members. This technique not only aids in unveiling unconscious material but also helps to establish an attitude of openness and noncondemnation that will encourage deeper levels of self-disclosure from the group members. It further gives the members opportunity to become aware of their various resistances—being silent, seductive, hostile, or intellectualizing. It is left up to the group therapist to interpret the meaning of the resistances and their relationship to childhood events, but the group members assist the therapist by pointing out resistances in one another (*see* Resistance in Psychotherapy).

A special form of resistance occurring in group therapy involves a collusion among group members. Two or more members team up unconsciously to divert the therapist and the group from looking at the teamed-up members' inner conflicts. Collusion may take many different forms, including romantic involvement, philosophical debating, and prolonged verbal conflicts. Collusion, as with any resistance, needs to be dealt with openly and forthrightly by the group and interpreted by the group therapist in a noncondemning manner.

Transference occurs when attitudes and behaviors toward significant figures in a person's past are projected onto the therapist. Psychoanalytic group therapy provides opportunity for transference not only between patient and therapist but also between patient and patient. Transference in the group provides a concrete example to patients of how their relationships with significant others in their past have colored their present thoughts, feelings, and relationships, especially those occurring in the group at the moment.

The therapist is not immune from the phenomenon of transference, since he or she will also react to patients at times as if they were persons from the past. This is called countertransference. Group therapy, due to the number of patients the therapist is working with, can compound the countertransference. While this can be especially stressful for the therapist, it can also strengthen him or her, provided there is a willingness and openness to deal with the countertransference feelings.

A one-time interpretation of a defense or uncovering of a conflict will almost never cause the patient to change permanently. Psychoanalytic theory asserts that a person's resistances must be pointed out numerous times before lasting change can occur. This accumulation of interpretations over time and the cumulative effects of those interpretations is called working through. Group therapy provides an ideal environment for working through, since the defenses and conflicts of the members are brought out repeatedly in each group session. For example, a person who intellectualizes as a primary defense will tend to intellectualize at every session, and as the group becomes comfortable with non-condemning confrontation, they will let the patient know that they see this defense in operation. After hearing this a number of times and possibly from a number of different group members, the intellectualizing patient will begin to recognize and discard this defense (see DEFENSE MECHANISMS).

Thus psychoanalytic group therapy, while adhering rather closely to Freud's individualistic theories of personality and treatment, offers advantages compared to individual analysis. The opportunities for the overt expression of unconscious material via transference, group free association, and working through are often more intense and more frequent than in individual psychoanalysis.

Christian Perspective. Psychoanalytic group therapy is open to the same criticisms from a Christian perspective as is Freudian theory in general. The antireligious reductionism of doctrinaire Freudianism discounts the reality of spiritual experiences. The emphasis on the curative power of insight gained by interpretation ignores or discounts the emotional, behavioral, and spiritual components of change, all of which are recognized by Scripture. Insight without these components may produce no change. This is not to say, however, that psychoanalytic group therapy is without value. It can be a powerful tool in assisting persons to understand the effect their past has on their present while helping them to alter destructive ways of dealing with themselves and others in the present.

Additional Readings

Abse, D. W. (1974). *Clinical notes on group-analytic psychotherapy.* Charlottesville: University Press of Virginia.
Slavson, S. R. (1964). *A textbook in analytic group psychotherapy.* New York: International Universities Press.
Wolf, A., & Schwartz, E. K. (1971). Psychoanalysis in groups. In H. Kaplan & B. Sadock (Eds.), *Comprehensive group psychotherapy.* Baltimore: Williams & Wilkins.

W. G. BIXLER

See GROUP PSYCHOTHERAPY.

Psychoanalytic Psychology. The branch of psychology founded by Freud in the 1890s. It has gone through a series of alterations and refinements, both during Freud's lifetime and after.

During his early career Freud was heavily involved in research. He wrote a highly regarded monograph on aphasia and carried out some careful histological studies on the eel. In 1884 he also published a review of the medical uses of cocaine. Freud's medical and scientific training was in the thoroughly physicalistic tradition popular in German universities during the last half of the nineteenth century; this tradition contended that all actions are the result of chemical and physical forces within the organism. Consequently, all mental disorders were assumed to have an organic basis, such as brain lesions or inadequate blood circulation, and psychiatric therapy consisted of physical treatments such as drugs, altered diet, and electrical stimulation.

Although Freud was thoroughly trained in this tradition, his clinical work soon led him to look beyond strictly physical explanations of behavior to psychological ones. He discovered that many of the thoughts and feelings that influence personality functioning operate outside of conscious awareness, and he proposed a complex theory of psychology to take this into account. Because of its stress on inner personality processes, psychoanalysis is considered the first dynamic or depth psychology. The fact that psychological factors lie at the root of many personal maladjustments is almost universally accepted, yet it was a radical departure from accepted psychiatric theory and practice in the last half of the nineteenth century. Therefore, Freud is seen as the father or grandfather of all later depth approaches to personality, even though many of those approaches reject some of the cornerstones of psychoanalytic theory. Whether one agrees with the specifics of psychoanalytic theory, there is no doubt that it has generated more study into the deeper dynamics of personality functioning than has any other single school of psychology.

Although psychoanalysis is often thought of as a theory of psychopathology or even more narrowly as a technique of psychotherapy, it is a general psychology of human behavior. The essential features of the psychoanalytic theory of behavior are based on six basic assumptions: unconscious mental processes exist; all human behavior is motivated and purposeful; past experiences influence current adjustments and reactions; personality functioning is inherently conflictual, and these conflicts can be understood on the basis of hypothetical mental structures such as id, ego, and superego; psychological processes involve various quantities of energy, strength, or force; and human behavior is influenced by interaction with the environment.

Over the course of the development of psychoanalysis these six basic assumptions have been formulated into six points of view or metapsychological assumptions. They are known respectively as the topographical, dynamic, genetic, structural, economic, and adaptive points of view. Psychoanalytic theory holds that to fully comprehend any human behavior we must understand it from each of these perspectives. These points of view function like sets of glasses or lenses that focus attention on different aspects of the same phenomenon in order to provide a complete picture.

The topographical point of view, for example, calls attention to the fact that the mental process in question has both conscious and unconscious aspects. The genetic view focuses on previous experiences and patterns that have influenced the behavior. And the adaptive point of view looks at the environmental influences on behavior or mental processes. Since all other aspects of psychoanalytic theory are formulated in terms of these six assumptions or points of view, an understanding of them is central to a comprehensive view of psychoanalytic psychology.

The Topographical Point of View. During Freud's early practice he treated a sizable number of hysterical personalities suffering from somatic symptoms. In looking into the onset and background of these symptoms he found that in each case the patients had undergone a painful or traumatic experience that they had forgotten. He also found that when they recalled their experiences through hypnosis or catharsis, the symptoms often disappeared. Since all of Freud's first patients reported being sexually abused by their father, he concluded that the traumatic events that led to repression and maladjustment were sexual experiences. He soon began to question the possibility of such widespread sexual abuse of children by their parents, however, and suggested that the forgotten experiences were often not real but fantasized (*see* Abuse and Neglect; Incest; False Memory Syndrome).

In time this concept evolved into his theory of drives, or motivation, and he concluded that the thoughts that prompted people to forget were sexual wishes growing out of a basic physiological drive. According to this view, all people have strong sexual drives that strive for expression but also create anxiety or guilt that causes them to be repressed. After the First World War, Freud broadened his theory of drives to include aggression as well as sexuality. He concluded that the destructiveness of war and much human behavior could not be explained unless some basic aggressive/destructive drive was postulated in addition to a sexual/loving one. Later analysts have further altered the psychoanalytic theory of motivation by including broader social goals and minimizing the concept of physical drives. Throughout the evolution of psychoanalytic theory, however, the concept of anxiety-producing wishes, experiences, and desires that are pushed from conscious awareness because of their unacceptability has remained constant.

Freud's observations on the role of unconscious thoughts in his neurotic patients was complemented by his study of dreams, hypnosis, slips of the tongue, and normal, momentary forgetting. He observed that in dreams, when normal censuring processes are relaxed, people often experience thoughts that are alien to their conscious wishes, thoughts, and feelings. He also realized that in posthypnotic suggestion people perform actions with no conscious awareness of why they are carrying them out (*see* Hypnosis). And in observing the everyday life of normal people he observed that many of us occasionally forget the name of a well-known acquaintance or accidentally slip and utter a word we had not intended to speak.

All these phenomena led Freud to conclude that there is a large area of mental life that operates outside conscious awareness. Some of this (e.g., our street address) is outside our immediate range of attention and can be easily recalled. Freud labeled these thoughts preconscious. Others can be recalled only with great effort, apparently because in some way the individual does not want to remember. These thoughts are labeled unconscious.

The Dynamic Point of View. At the same time Freud was developing his understanding of unconscious mental processes he was also formulating a dynamic view of personality. This viewpoint asserts that all human behavior is purposive and lawful. It is motivated, in other words, and directed toward certain goals. In the history of psychoanalysis various motivations have been proposed. As we have seen, Freud initially assumed the memory of traumatic sexual experiences motivated neurotic individuals to repress these memories and caused neurotic problems. Later this portion of his theory was discarded, and Freud postulated the sexual drive as the prime motivator of behavior. In his final theory of motivation Freud recognized two primary drives, sexual and aggressive.

Although the sexual and aggressive drives have received the greatest emphasis in psychoanalytic theories of motivation, they are by no means the only ones considered. Alfred Adler, for example, stressed the drive for power or mastery in order to overcome feelings of inferiority. Carl Gustav Jung, Karen Horney, and Harry Stack Sullivan all criticized Freud's original overemphasis on the sexual sources of maladjustment and proposed broader personal and social motivations. In spite of their varying theories of motivation, however, all psychoanalytic theorists stress the goal-directed nature of human functioning.

The Genetic Point of View. This point of view asserts that neither normal nor pathological mental processes can be fully understood apart from the life history of the individual. Psychoanalysts assume that an individual's current manner of functioning is the result of the interaction of constitutional givens (such as the strength of drives) and the environment. The way that a person has learned to fulfill his or her basic drives within the context of the environment, especially the family and immediate social network, is the way he or she will attempt to satisfy these drives in adulthood.

The genetic viewpoint helps explain the reappearance of infantile behavior during adulthood. If people become partially fixated at one level of development they may later regress to that level of psychic functioning. Freud initially worked out his concepts of fixation and regression in terms of sexual development. He theorized that the sexual drive passes through three basic stages on the way to adult functioning. In the first, the oral phase (from birth until approximately 18 months), pleasure is largely associated with the mouth and activities of sucking and eating. In the next, the anal phase, Freud hypothesized that the locus of pleasure is especially linked to stimulation of the anal membranes and bowel functioning. Between 3 and 4 years of age the genitals were viewed as becoming the primary source of pleasure. Freud called this the phallic phase (*see* Psychosexual Development).

Since Freud was desirous of linking his psychological theories to existing scientific beliefs, he theorized that the sexual drive (libido) had a certain quantity of physical energy. If some of this energy is fixated at an early stage of psychosexual development (e.g., the oral), Freud concluded people do not have that energy available to move on to more mature developmental levels. Consequently, under the impact of stress in later life they may return to the earlier stage. From this perspective persons suffering from depression or from alcoholism and other addictions are presumed to be fixated at the oral level, where feeding and oral gratifications are prominent. Obsessive-compulsive personalities (obsessed with orderliness, cleanliness, and guilt) are viewed as fixated at the anal level, where issues of messiness and cleanliness are prominent. And hysterical personalities (who frequently demonstrate exaggerated femininity) are seen as fixated at the phallic level rather than moving on to the mature adult genital phase of sexuality.

The Structural Point of View. Freud spelled out the structural viewpoint of psychoanalysis in *The Ego and the Id*. This book marked the official beginning of ego psychology and opened psychoanalysis up to become a full-fledged general psychology rather than a way of viewing unconscious processes and psychological maladjustments. Although Freud had long talked of drives, defenses, and other mental processes included in his new conceptualization, he had never integrated these concepts in a comprehensive manner. In *The Ego and the Id* he described three sets of mental processes, systems, or structures. The first, the id, consists of the individual's drives, wishes, and impulses. These processes are the seat of motivation and are largely unconscious. Since they are unconscious, they do not necessarily operate by the same logical processes that conscious ideas do. Consequently, conflicting wishes, ideas, and feelings (e.g., love and hate) can coexist in the unconscious.

The ego consists of processes such as perception, memory, judgment, and motor control that are essential in relating to the world. The ego serves to reconcile the demands of the id with the demands of the environment in order to satisfy the drives as fully as possible while still attending to reality, including the reality of others' potential reactions to one's attempts at unbridled gratification. The development of the structural theory with its emphasis on the ego was essential if psychoanalysis was to ever become a general theory of psychology; the topographical and dynamic views were not sufficient to understand such functions as perception and memory, which are essential to a comprehensive understanding of human functioning.

In *The Ego and the Id*, the superego, comprising personality's moral functions, was considered a special structure gradually developing out of the ego. Roughly equivalent to the conscience, the superego contains both one's goals and aspirations (the ego ideal) and the self-corrective functions. It develops from the child's relationship with his or her parents and functions to approve or disapprove one's actions and to pass out praise in the form of self-esteem or punishment in the form of guilt.

The Economic Point of View. Freud's clinical experience and his desire to build a theory of personality congruent with the materialistic science of his day led him to postulate the economic point of view. This assumes that there are quantitative factors involved in human behavior. To put it differently, Freud assumed that drives and affects and the individual's ways of handling them involved actual amounts (potentially quantifiable, at least in theory) of psychological energy. This concept and Freud's use of such terms as cathexis, which refers to the amount of energy attached to an idea, were based on the energy concepts of late-nineteenth-century physics.

Although the reality of such quantities of energy has often been questioned, most psychoanalysts feel the need for some type of hypothetical, quantifiable energy to explain human behavior. This hypothesis is used, for example, to account for the observation that some people's sexual and aggressive drives seem more powerful than those of others. It is also used to explain the phenomenon of resistance, in which a large amount of energy appears to be devoted to keeping ideas out of awareness during the process of psychotherapy. Psychoanalysts also use the concept of amount of energy to explain the process of displacement, in which an amount of affect is changed (displaced) from one experience to another almost like a stream is diverted from its original bed.

The Adaptive Point of View. This final point of view stresses the fact that there is a reciprocal relationship between the individual and the environment and that personality development and functioning cannot be understood apart from this mutual adaptiveness. Although Freud repeatedly discussed this interaction, the adaptive point of view was not clearly formulated and articulated until Rapaport and Gill (1959) published "The Points of View and Assumptions of Metapsychology."

The Psychoanalytic Theory of Neurosis. The psychoanalytic theory of psychopathology views all psychoneurosis as growing out of conflicts between the id and the ego. If the individual's drives (for orthodox psychoanalysts, sex and aggression) are potentially too strong or threatening, the individual turns to various ego defense mechanisms such as repression to control the impulses and reduce the anxiety or guilt associated with them. These defense mechanisms are not fully successful, however, since they require a substantial expenditure of emotional energy and involve some denial, distortion, or avoidance of reality. Since the impulses keep struggling for expression, the ego must continue these defensive processes. The neurotic symptom is a sort of compromise in which the initial drive is at least partially repressed or is disguised sufficiently to be acceptable to the ego. In depression, for example, the unacceptable anger (id impulse) is repressed but reappears as self-hatred. In paranoia the anger is repressed and projected onto another person so that the paranoid person becomes the innocent victim of others' anger instead of an angry person. The superego can enter into this struggle on the side of either the id or the ego, although its most obvious manifestations in the neuroses is as an ally of the ego. In these cases the ego and superego team up to try to control the unacceptable id impulses.

In this formulation the problem can be traced to excessively powerful instincts, a weak ego, or a too harsh superego. To understand any individual neurotic it is necessary to know what the conflicts are between the id and the superego, why the ego cannot handle the drives, the defenses the ego uses in attempting to cope with the drives, and how these processes ended up in the formation of the neurotic symptom or personality. Both constitutional and environmental factors are seen to be involved in this process, and neurotic problems are resolved when the ego becomes strong enough to manage the demands of the id and the three structures of the personality (id, ego, and superego) come into an appropriate balance. Health, in other words, involves a balance of fulfilling one's drives or needs in a nondestructive manner.

Psychotic pathologies are believed to develop in the same general way as the neuroses, but greater attention is given to basic ego defects arising out of experiences in the early years of infancy.

Psychoanalytic Psychology after Freud. In the years following Freud's death many modifications and developments have taken place in psychoanalytic thinking. The two major trends that encompass these are ego psychology and object relations theory. Although these two trends are intimately related and both flow from Freud's foundation, they have influenced psychoanalysis in slightly different ways. Psychoanalytic ego psychologists, such as Anna Freud, Heinz Hartmann, and Ernst Kris, placed increasing stress on the role of the ego in personality functioning and relatively less emphasis on id processes. Although drives and impulses are seen as no less important than they were in Freud's day, current psychoanalysts tend to see the health and ability of the ego to cope with internal and external threats as the critical factor in ad-

justment. They also suggest that the functions of the ego pass through normal developmental processes and that functions of the ego such as perception and memory cannot all be traced to the id and its conflicts with external reality. In focusing more on the ego these psychoanalysts also place a great deal of emphasis on the impact of early interpersonal relationships upon the development of the ego.

Object relations theory stresses the impact of interpersonal relationships on the development of the personality. Although Freud coined the phrase *object relation* and laid the groundwork for this emphasis, and while all analysts incorporate the concept of early interpersonal relationships into their theories, several British psychoanalysts (Melanie Klein, Harry Guntrip, and Donald Winnicott) have probed the importance of the dynamic relationship between infants and their primary provider in greater depth than other schools of psychoanalysis. Their research and writing suggest that the development of personality is strongly impacted by the infant's taking in, or internalization, of its perceptions of its parents in the first year or two of life.

Evaluation. Although many Christians have dismissed psychoanalytic theory because of Freud's emphasis on sexuality and the belief that psychoanalysis promotes acting out of sinful impulses, a closer evaluation indicates that at least some aspects of psychoanalytic theory are congruent with scriptural teachings and with careful observation of human functioning. From a biblical perspective it seems that many aspects of the broad structure of psychoanalytic theory are consistent with a biblical view of human nature, while much of the specific content is questionable or in conflict.

Freud's stress on the existence of unconscious mental processes (the topographical view), for example, is supported by phenomena such as dreams and hypnosis, which demonstrate the activity of thoughts we are not consciously aware of. It is also consistent with scriptural passages that speak of the human personality's complexity and tendency to self-deceit (e.g., Jer. 17:9). Psychoanalysis' understanding of the role of defense mechanisms in warding off unacceptable wishes and feelings goes beyond scriptural descriptions of how we avoid facing painful reality but is consistent with that scripturally described process.

The psychoanalytic assumption that all behavior is purposeful and motivated is consistent with a biblical view of human nature that sees individuals as intelligent, self-determining, social persons created in the image of God. So is the genetic point of view, which asserts the continuity of childhood and adult experiences. Parents, for example, are instructed to train children properly so the parents can have assurance that their children will follow that way in adulthood (Prov. 22:6). The psychoanalytic belief that there is a reciprocal relationship between the individual and his or her environment (the adaptive point of view) is also consistent with scriptural teaching on the role of both personal and societal responsibility.

The structural division of personality into the id, ego, and superego and the economic viewpoint have no apparent biblical parallel. As hypothetical constructs, concepts such as ego, id, and superego can be seen as biblically neutral, since they are shorthand ways of describing or conceptualizing certain personality processes. Their usefulness depends on the accuracy with which they allow us to describe the functioning of personality rather than on specific biblical witness to their accuracy. Freud's economic viewpoint, which postulates certain actual amounts of psychological energy, is another concept that needs to stand or fall on its utility rather than on an explicit scriptural teaching.

When we come to the specific content of Freud's theory, particularly his view of motivation, we encounter serious problems. Although Scripture has a great deal to say about human sexuality, it does not give it the prominent motivational role that psychoanalysis does. The Bible clearly describes humanity's drive to be autonomous and godlike as the major motivating force behind human maladjustment. Similarly Freud's theory of neurosis appears inadequate. Although the broad outline of conflicts that motivate defenses, which in turn produce neurotic symptoms, is widely accepted, most theorists question the central role Freud gave to the oedipus complex in this process. Broader social motivations and dynamics appear to be closer to both clinical observations and scriptural revelation.

Even given the compatibility of some of psychoanalytic theory with a Christian view of human nature, psychoanalysis leaves us with a truncated view of personality. Freud and his followers have provided a depth technique for exploring the dynamics of human personality. As such, psychoanalysis can provide a good deal of understanding of human functioning. However, it remains for Christians to thoroughly evaluate psychoanalytic theory in light of the biblical view of human nature, motivation, and growth. Even when that task is completed, psychoanalysis will not provide a full picture of human nature. Like all theories of personality, psychoanalysis gives only one perspective or way of looking at human personality. It is limited by the finitude of the theorist, the selection of methods of observation, and the complexities of the subject matter.

Reference

Rapaport, D., & Gill, M. (1959). The points of view and assumptions of metapsychology. *The International Journal of Psychoanalysis, 40,* 153–162.

Additional Readings

Brenner, C. (1955). *An elementary textbook of psychoanalysis.* New York: International Universities Press.

Fine, R. (1973). *The development of Freud's thought: From the beginnings (1886–1900) through id psychology (1900–1914) to ego psychology (1914–1939).* New York: Aronson.

Freud, S. (1933). *New introductory lectures in psychoanalysis.* New York: Norton.

S. B. NARRAMORE

See FREUD, SIGMUND.

Psychoanalytic Psychotherapy. An intensive method of therapy based on psychoanalytic personality theory but differing somewhat from the technique of classical psychoanalysis. It is sometimes called psychoanalytically oriented psychotherapy or psychodynamic psychotherapy, although the latter term actually includes a number of insight-oriented therapies other than psychoanalytic psychotherapy (e.g., Gestalt and Adlerian therapy). Psychoanalytic psychotherapy was developed as a modification of psychoanalysis due to the inability of some patients to handle the intensive self-exploration of analysis and because of the desire to find a shorter, less expensive treatment that could be utilized with a greater variety of individuals.

Like psychoanalysis, psychoanalytic psychotherapy assumes that adult personality maladjustments grow out of conflicts between one's wishes or drives and forces that cause repression. It sees the roots of adult maladjustments in childhood experiences, stresses the role of sexual and aggressive drives, and conceptualizes maladjustments in terms of conflicts between the id, ego, and superego. It also shares its major therapeutic techniques with psychoanalysis, as well as its terminology of resistance, defense, transference, and interpretation (*see* Defense Mechanisms; Resistance in Psychotherapy).

While the understanding of personality development and psychopathology held by psychoanalysts and psychoanalytic psychotherapists is identical, the therapeutic goals and the course of therapy are slightly different. Traditional psychoanalysis is generally carried out four or five times a week for three to five years. The goal of this extensive therapy is a major restructuring of the total personality. By contrast, psychoanalytic psychotherapy involves between one and three sessions weekly for a period of one to three years. It is oriented more to eliminating symptoms and solving problems than to a radical restructuring of the personality.

In psychoanalysis patients are encouraged to follow the fundamental rule of free association and to verbalize anything that comes to their minds during the analytic hour. Coupled with the analyst's nondirectiveness this promotes the exploration of every area of the patient's life, including those that at first seem irrelevant to the presenting problem. In contrast, psychoanalytic psychotherapy limits its focus more to issues surrounding the presenting problems and their development. In line with this more limited goal psychoanalytic psychotherapy does not rely as heavily on free association. While psychoanalytic psychotherapists do encourage patients to discuss everything that comes to mind, the psychotherapy is structured in a way that is frequently more focused and problem centered and does not result in true free association.

In psychoanalysis the therapist-patient relationship is the main focus of therapy. By encouraging the development of transference the psychoanalyst hopes to activate the main features of the patient's pathology within the patient's relationship to the analyst. In contrast, psychoanalytic psychotherapy does not focus as intensely on the transference, and the therapist endeavors to help the patient gain insight into conflicts, struggles, and problems without necessarily fully reliving them in the present relationship.

In both psychoanalysis and psychoanalytic psychotherapy the therapist's primary task is twofold: to provide an atmosphere or relationship that encourages self-exploration and to help patients become aware of previously unconscious wishes, feelings, conflicts, and experiences through the technique of interpretation. In psychoanalysis interpretation is usually seen as the only significant therapeutic technique. Analysts listen carefully to patients' dreams and free associations in order to identify the patients' resistances and the warded-off wishes, feelings, and experiences. Any technique that would hinder the process of free association and the interpretation of resistance is viewed as countertherapeutic. By contrast, psychoanalytic psychotherapists may occasionally make careful use of advice or guidance, and they may even encourage certain neurotic defenses if these will further the patient's adaptation to the environment. Such techniques are considered inappropriate in psychoanalysis because they encourage dependency and may reinforce repression, whereas in psychoanalytic psychotherapy they are viewed as appropriate if they will help the patient achieve a higher level of functioning.

A final distinction between psychoanalysis and psychoanalytic psychotherapy is the depth of the patient's regression to primitive levels of thought and feelings. In psychoanalysis the reclining position, frequent sessions, use of free association, and relative anonymity and nondirectiveness of the analyst encourage patients to reexperience their emotional conflicts with the analyst. This regression to primitive or infantile levels of functioning is encouraged in order to understand the sources of adult maladjustments and rework them. In psychoanalytic psychotherapy, by contrast, the less frequent sessions, the shorter length of treatment, and the greater focus on symptoms and present conflicts mean that patients do not typically undergo such a deep regression. This reexperiencing of infantile feelings and reactions is not always viewed as crucial in the more problem-oriented approach of psychoanalytic psychotherapy.

Although it is generally agreed that psychoanalytic psychotherapy is significantly different from psychoanalysis, those differences are not clear-cut, and these two forms of therapy are best seen as different points on the same continuum. Both therapies stress the uncovering of repressed memories, wishes, and feelings; and both utilize transference, interpretation, and dream analysis. The difference is more in degree than kind. The more frequent the sessions, the greater the use of interpretation, the more the focus on transference and dream interpretation, and the deeper the patient's regression, the more the therapy can be considered psychoanalysis. The less frequent the sessions, the greater the focus on presenting and environmental problems, and the greater the therapist's reliance on techniques other than interpretation, the more appropriate the label *psychoanalytic psychotherapy* becomes.

Additional Readings

Fromm-Reichman, F. (1950). *Principles of intensive psychotherapy.* Chicago: University of Chicago Press.
Langs, R. (1973). *The technique of psychoanalytic psychotherapy* (2 vols.). New York: Aronson.

S. B. Narramore

See Psychoanalysis: Technique.

Psychobiology. Prior to 1960 the term referred to the many-sided approach to personality developed by psychiatrist Adolf Meyer, who used the term to emphasize the importance of dealing with mental as well as physical factors in human psychological problems. Meyer's holistic view recognized that there are multiple determinants of behavior. He believed that since mental illness is the result of the interaction of many factors, there should be an interdisciplinary approach to the subject that coordinated the findings of psychology, biology, and sociology (Meyer, 1950).

After 1960 the term reemerged in common usage and came to mean the broad science concerned with the biological bases of behavior. Not a formal discipline in and of itself, it is a collective field drawing together the research in many disciplines, including ethology, genetics, psychology, neurology, neurophysiology, biochemistry, endocrinology, pharmacology, psychiatry, and anthropology. Psychobiology has developed rapidly during the 1980s and 1990s because of the growing recognition of the interdependence of behavioral and biological processes.

Psychobiology seeks to analyze behavior in terms of the biological factors that might play a role. It seeks to discover which anatomical structures and pathways and which physiological processes might be involved in the mediation of specific behaviors. Psychobiology is related to but is not identical with physiological psychology, which deals specifically with physiological mechanisms underlying behavior.

Psychobiology

The field of psychobiology represents the culmination of a trend in thinking about human nature that can be traced back to René Descartes. Philosophical and theological speculations prior to Descartes emphasized a dualism in human nature that stressed the effect of the mind on the body. Cartesian dualism stressed a two-way interaction that helped place mind within the domain of biology, a viewpoint that later became a foundation of psychology.

Research in psychobiology includes studies in the hormonal control of behavior, developmental psychobiology, physiological determinants of perception, and drugs and behavior. Comparative animal research in all areas is also much more common than in psychology proper. A central thrust of psychobiological research has been to produce a better understanding of the relationship between the brain and the human personality.

Psychobiological research exploring the biological foundations of the mind generally proceeds from assumptions that are materialistic and reductionistic. These assumptions state that mind is merely a product of brain activity. Psychobiologists thus seek to explain behavioral observations in terms of the neural substrates that are presumed to account for them. One of the most important principles of the psychobiology of the mind is that neural activity is the sole basis of mental activity and that psychological processes can be explained by neural ones. Furthermore, the interconnectivity of neurons is viewed to be the proper level of investigation of psychobiology. This means that modern monistic psychobiology in its most fundamental premises is in logical and conceptual conflict with religious doctrine concerning human nature.

The Christian view of human beings does not suggest that the human mind is not related to brain states but insists that the description of the human mind cannot be reduced to mere biology. MacKay (1974) argues that even the most complete description of the brain could not invalidate the Christian concepts of the mind and freedom.

Neurophysiological research itself does not clearly support the reductionistic, materialistic assumptions of psychobiology. There is the unanswered question of when and how the electrical firing of collections of neurons turns into mental experience. As yet there is no hint as to what properties of the sodium-potassium exchange that creates the electrical activity of neurons relate to one's experience of an emotion or a thought. Brain stimulation and recording experiments also have failed to reveal any portion of the brain that acts as a receiving area for combining elementary experiences into the holistic experience that composes the human mind. The question remains unanswered as to how a unified mental state arises out of the actions of huge numbers of individual neurons. Brain stimulation experiments have also repeatedly failed to produce thinking, willing, or complex emotional experiences in human subjects.

Studies in the psychobiology of the mind have relied very heavily on the establishment of correlations between brain activity and the activity of the mind. But such correlations by themselves do not suggest that neural activity alone gives rise to the experiences of mind. Nobel Prize–winner John Eccles (1994), for example, cites neurophysiological evidence that argues for the existence of a human mind that interacts with brain matter. In another discipline Penrose (1994), a physicist, also argues for the immaterial nature of consciousness that he sees as rooted in the indeterminacy of subatomic particles and quantum gravity.

In summary it can be said that the principles of psychobiology can serve to enrich the study of the human mind and behavior and their important connections to the physical structures of the brain. However, the more reductionistic and materialistic psychobiology becomes, the less likely it is that its themes and interpretations of data will be helpful in understanding the complexities of the human personality.

References

Eccles, J. (1994). *How the self controls its brain.* New York: Springer-Verlag.

MacKay, D. (1974). *The clockwork image.* Downers Grove, IL: InterVarsity Press.

Meyer, A. (1950). *Collected papers of Adolf Meyer.* (E. E. Winters, Ed.). Baltimore: Johns Hopkins University Press.

Penrose, R. (1994). *Shadows of the mind: A search for the missing science of consciousness.* Oxford: Oxford University Press.

Additional Reading

Penfield, W. (1975). *The mystery of the mind.* Princeton, NJ: Princeton University Press.

M. P. COSGROVE

See MIND-BRAIN RELATIONSHIP.

Psychodrama. A form of psychotherapy based on the philosophy and theoretical principles of Jacob Moreno. A client, or protagonist, acts out situations to creatively resolve conflicts in and with others. This is usually done in the context of a therapeutic or an educational group. Psychodrama is an action-oriented approach that restores the individual's lost spontaneity, or ability to live creatively and wholeheartedly, through the use of dramatic interactions.

Historical Development. Moreno was born in Bucharest, Rumania, in 1892. His early work in psychodrama was with children in the gardens of Vienna. He would assist them to act out their fantasies and problems. Moreno continued to develop his emerging theoretical system in work with Viennese prostitutes. It was in these brothels that the Moreno version of group psychotherapy was conceived. In 1921 he created the theater of spontaneity, a totally new version of theater in which professional actors took on roles from newspaper accounts and enacted the stories.

In 1925 Moreno came to the United States. He founded a private psychiatric hospital at Beacon, New York, in 1936. Psychodrama was the primary therapeutic method. Within the next 11 years Moreno, although ridiculed by his peers, developed a unique group treatment that continues to flourish. His ideas have permeated the encounter and human potential movements.

Basic Instruments of Psychodrama. Moreno (1978) describes psychodrama as having five instruments. The stage is the first. Many therapeutic stages are circular in design, modeled after Moreno's circular, three-tiered stage with overhanging balcony and lights. The top level of the stage represents the highest level of involvement, the area wherein one places the agonies and ecstasies of life. Lower levels represent the steps of warming up, the periphery or external aspects of existence. These intricate designs are not necessary for a productive psychodrama but are helpful.

The second basic instrument is the protagonist, the individual who receives primary focus in the psychodrama. The protagonist recreates situations from past, present, and future, portraying them with dramatic realism so that new behaviors may be learned and new cognitive patterns established. The protagonist acts as a representative of the group, often exploring a theme that the group has identified as meaningful to them.

A third instrument is the auxiliary ego. Auxiliary egos are representations of the protagonist's significant others. As the protagonist moves into action, he or she chooses group members to represent those individuals who are part of the scene being played. These roles are often parents, spouses, or parts of the self. The auxiliary becomes the other in the drama after having been given the necessary information to play the role.

Another type of auxiliary ego is the psychodramatic double. The double helps the protagonist to express thoughts and feelings that would otherwise remain suppressed. The double mimics the protagonist's bodily posture and mannerisms so that the highest level of identification may occur (*see* Double Technique).

The group is considered a fourth instrument. Although psychodrama may be conducted individually in an office, it is generally applied as a group treatment. The group is strategically involved in the selection of the protagonist so that the issues to be explored are relevant to the lives of group members. The group members assist through becoming auxiliary egos and in their sharing and support following the psychodrama.

The process is guided by the fifth instrument, the director. The director assists the group in the selection of a protagonist, directs role reversals and scene setting, and acts as the overall coordinator of the drama. The director challenges the protagonist to achieve new insights and new behaviors that lead to healthier living. The whole process of the initial group warm-up activities, the enactments of the protagonist, and the verbal closure are guided by the director.

Therapeutic Process. The process of the psychodramatic session is threefold. The initial warm-up phase serves to lessen the social tensions and offers group members an opportunity to identify their feelings and needs. The warm-up is often an activity suggested by the director. Activities range from group interaction exercises to verbal sharing of concerns.

A group theme often becomes the criterion for the selection of the protagonist. The action phase then not only becomes a psychodramatic portrayal of an individual's private concern but also represents the overall concern of the group. Common themes are returning to the community; handling anger, grief, marriage and family tension; and loss of self-esteem.

The protagonist, guided by the director, develops scenes that depict the conflict. Auxiliary egos are chosen to represent significant others in the scene, and role reversals are conducted to determine the characters of the significant others. The action, whether past, present, or future, is dramatized in the here and now. Once maximum insight and catharsis occur, the intensity diminishes and sharing begins.

The group becomes the central focus of the sharing-integration phase. They share their common humanity with the protagonist. They relate the scenes portrayed on the stage to their own lives and to significant others. A group healing occurs, one relating to the initial group concern.

Theoretical Principles. Moreno's basic principles are sociometry, social atom, tele, roles, and spontaneity. Sociometry is the measurement of one's feelings of attraction, repulsion, and indifference to others on the basis of a specific criterion. This is generally done in a therapeutic group or school classroom. A criterion could be, With what group members would you be willing to share a secret about yourself? The sociogram is the basic measuring instrument. Haskell (1967) suggests several examples of sociometric tests.

Moreno used the concept of the atom to illustrate the relationship of the individual to significant others. It represents the smallest social unit in which significant emotional relationships occur. The social atom usually is represented as an illustration placing the individual at the center with lines reaching out like spokes to significant people. The content of the relationship, such as attraction, repulsion, or indifference, is then measured through sociometric techniques.

Tele refers to a feeling that is transmitted from one individual to another. Tele, however, is based on the assumption that one sees others clearly and without transference. Transference is a one-way projection of feelings toward another individual (such as the husband who unconsciously transfers feelings about his mother onto his wife). Tele assumes reciprocity. Both individuals have positive feelings such as mutual empathy. It is a two-way process of attaining and maintaining realistic relationships. Tele is the substance of significant relationships, the glue that cements the social atom and encourages it to expand.

Roles and role playing are important aspects of Moreno's thinking. A role is the characteristic function and contribution of the individual as well as the expected behavior and position defined by the group for the individual. Conflicts occur between the individual and societal demands, as can be seen in the conflicting roles of women in North American culture. Role confusion is exhibited by adolescents who are developing and learning new roles. In these situations role training is a useful function of psychodrama. The individual explores role conflicts and develops new skills in these areas.

Spontaneity is a most important concept in psychodrama. Moreno considers spontaneity as self-initiating behavior, usually in response to some life situation. It requires novelty and adequacy. Without spontaneity the individual will display stereotypic robotlike behaviors. Pathological spontaneity occurs when the individual is being novel but demonstrates little competency or appropriateness in the situation. Such a response is psychosis.

The application of spontaneity to the psychodramatic enactment is very important. The protagonist is challenged to create novel roles and perceptions. Spontaneity for the passive individual could be the act of risking the expression of feelings or of developing more open and intimate relationships with others. For another who is extremely opinionated it may be a sincere attempt to listen to and respect the views of others. Spontaneity is seen by Moreno as basic to all forms of productive creative acts.

Applications. Psychodrama is applicable to three areas: therapy, training, and education. Most often group treatment lends itself well to this modality, especially in inpatient and partial hospitalization settings. Outpatient groups may also benefit. Another therapeutic use is known as psychodrama a deux, or the application of psychodrama techniques to individual therapy.

Psychodrama is usually conducted as sociodrama when it is introduced into the educational system. This form is more familiarly known as role playing. It employs the use of stories and situations acted out for the affective and attitudinal learning of the students. Several other agencies use psychodrama techniques for training. The Federal Bureau of Investigation trains its staff in hostage negotiation with psychodrama, as do several police departments. Medical students treat trained auxiliary egos playing roles of patients whom these future doctors will be treating.

View of the Cosmos. Moreno believes that the God of the Hebrews and the Christ of the New Testament are no longer suitable supreme beings in our society. His new focus is on the I-God, the infinitesimal part of the Universal Self that each person represents. "Every self is identical with the self of God. All have taken part in the creation of themselves and in creating others. Thus, we can become not only a part of the creation but a part of the creator as well. The world becomes our world, the world of our choice, the world of our creation" (Moreno, 1941, p. xv).

Even amid speculation that Moreno was poetically describing a psychodramatic God, there was an unexpected reaction by others who condemned him as a megalomaniac. However, it seems that his intent was to encourage and invite individuals to search the fullest dimension of themselves and others and to assume full responsibility for his own creating.

Moreno rates Christ as an extremely gifted psychodramatist. Christ is the Son of God only as we are all sons of a god. The Scriptures are viewed as a fallible record of events and not as a holy revelation of God.

It is important at this point to separate the invention from the inventor in this therapeutic modality. Psychodrama itself is neither Christian nor unchristian. It is an instrument, a psychotherapeutic scalpel that, in the hands of the Christian therapist, can assist in bringing about healing and integration for a client.

Many of the biblical guidelines for living are enhanced by psychodrama. Role reversal may produce a new understanding of one's relationship with another and therefore promote forgiving, healing, and loving. Role training assists the Christian in practicing more Christlike behaviors in simulated situations. Psychodrama as a therapeutic treatment or educational modality is compatible with a biblical Christian perspective.

References

Haskell, M. (1967). *An introduction to socioanalysis.* Long Beach: California Institute of Socioanalysis.

Moreno, J. L. (1941). *Words of the father.* New York: Beacon House.

Moreno, J. L. (1978). *Who shall survive?* (3rd ed.). New York: Beacon House.

Additional Readings

Moreno, J. L. (1964). *Psychodrama* (Vol. 1). (3rd ed.). New York: Beacon House.

Moreno, J. L., & Moreno, Z. T. (1969). *Psychodrama* (Vol. 3). (3rd ed.). New York: Beacon House.

Moreno, J. L. (1973). *The theatre of spontaneity* (2nd ed.). New York: Beacon House.

Starr, A. (1977). *Psychodrama: Rehearsal for living.* Chicago: Nelson.

J. H. Vander May

See Expressive Therapy.

Psychohistory. Psychological studies of historical figures have existed since at least the nineteenth century, when the German psychiatrist Möbius was writing "pathographies." At the turn of the twentieth century, the fledgling Vienna Psychoanalytic Society was the scene of numerous psychological dissections of the famous dead. Sigmund Freud produced one major psychobiographical work, *Leonardo da Vinci and a Memory of His Childhood* (1910/1975) and a psychological sketch of Dostoyevski. Freud's *Moses and Monotheism* (1938/1975) must be counted as largely psychohistorical as well. A psychobiography of Woodrow Wilson attributed to Freud seems to have been written by William Bullitt, with some collaboration with Freud. Early psychoanalysts such as Jones, Otto Rank, and Karl Abraham were soon publishing their own psychohistorical studies. Psychohistory has remained overwhelmingly psychoanalytic history; with few exceptions, other psychological and psychiatric schools have had little impact on history writing.

It was not long before professional historians and social scientists perceived the potential usefulness of psychoanalysis for their disciplines. In 1930 Harold Laswell's *Psychopathology and Politics* appeared. Prominent anthropologists were beginning to use psychoanalytic insights in their writing of culture histories. In his 1958 presidential address before the American Historical Association, William Langer called familiarizing oneself with psychoanalysis the historian's next assignment. Psychoanalytically informed studies of historical figures and movements by professional historians are by now legion. Psychoanalytic psychiatrists and psychologists, such as Erik Erikson, Eissler, and Lifton, have continued to pursue such work.

Although there are variations in the mode in which psychoanalysis has been applied to history, many psychohistories have followed along the lines of Freud's *Leonardo* and *Moses and Monotheism* and consequently bear the methodological weaknesses of these two famous works. In *Leonardo* Freud attempts to explain da Vinci's tension between art and science and his preference for certain artistic themes, as well as certain aspects of his character, with reference to his oedipus complex and latent homosexuality. Much of Freud's speculation is carried by the analysis of a putative childhood fantasy. In *Moses and Monotheism* three millennia of Jewish religious history are explained by the Jews' supposed murder of Moses and rejection of his doctrines, their subsequent collective repression of this event, and the eventual return of this recollection. This is an expression of Freud's penchant for explaining social and sometimes individual history with reference to a single, decisive archaic event—a *kairos.*

The difficulties with these works are obvious. In *Leonardo,* Freud had little access to reliable historical data about his subject. Some of the information from which he constructed his hypothesis was erroneous. No account was taken of cultural or intellectual historical factors in the life of the artist. Large segments of his intellectual and creative life were reductively explained as aspects of his psychopathology. And, most tellingly, da Vinci could not furnish Freud with any associations to his own fantasies or to the latter's interpretations. *Moses and Monotheism* harbors the same difficulties, with the added problematic assumption of a collective mind whose processes are identical to those in the individual psyche.

Erikson's *Young Man Luther* (1958), though in many respects wanting in scholarly and critical rigor, is a considerable advance on Freud's work. It elaborates the great man in history model in which the historical giant is seen not so much as imposing his idiosyncratic, psychopathologically determined will on his era, as acknowledging needs and tensions in himself that are present but only dimly appreciated by the members of society. By satisfying and resolving these needs and tensions in himself, the great individual thereby succeeds in satisfying and resolving them in others.

Lifton's (1975) "shared psychohistorical themes" is promising. He focuses upon themes, forms, and images that are shared among many individuals of a period or culture and attempts to correlate these patterns with specific types of experiences and preoccupations. Much of Lifton's work has focused on themes of death and survival, as exemplified in the survivors of overwhelming catastrophes such as Hiroshima and the Holocaust. A related theme is that of the individual's and society's attempt to attain some mode of immortality. His concept of Protean man as an individual characterized by a fluid identity and interminable experimentation and exploration (in reaction to society's dislocation from the nourishing symbols of its past and in response to his constant bombardment with novel and evanescent cultural stimuli) is another fruit of the shared themes approach.

Evaluation and Summary. The contributions of psychoanalysis to history are substantial but have often been obscured by the speculative excesses of Freud and certain other psychohistorians. These include analyzing whole cultures and epochs as if they were personalities, making deep interpretations about the motives of dead persons notoriously resistant to furnishing their associations, ignoring all factors but the psychological ones, and abandoning the evidential and critical canons to which any good historian cleaves. Many scholars gratefully take such excesses, which any college sophomore could recognize, as sufficient excuse to be done with psychoanalysis. However, there is room for a middle way.

One must appreciate that psychoanalysis is a clinical method, applicable to one situation alone—the ongoing interaction between therapist and patient in the consulting room. It is only here that one can listen to the train of associations; frame the questions, confrontations, and clarifications through which one garners so much information; observe the unfolding transference; and test one's clinical hypotheses against the patient's subsequent recollections and behavior. It is important to appreciate that when psychoanalysis is applied to history, what is transferred are insights about human nature originally arrived at by the psychoanalytic method but not the method itself. Such insights applied to history cannot be treated with the same assurance as the clinically based propositions of psychoanalytic therapy.

If, however, the historian recognizes this, there is no reason why he or she cannot use psychoanalytic theory to draw limited inferences about the personalities of subjects. When one uses economics and social science in one's work, it is generally their theory and insights that one is transplanting rather than their methods. The historian already has a rough and ready concept of individual motivation that can be considerably enriched by psychoanalytically informed systemization and appreciation of the role of unconscious motives, defensive processes, and intrapsychic conflicts in human affairs. However, psychoanalytically informed inferences can be used only with personages about whom one has a wealth of reliable information in the form of diaries, letters, reports of contemporaries, and perhaps even (as with Freud) accounts of their dreams. Their usage with whole cultures is much more problematic (Wallace, 1983). Psychodynamic factors must be placed within the context of all other factors. Because of this there is no justification for a subspecialty such as psychohistory; history is history and will make use of any insights at its disposal, psychoanalytic ones included.

Greater than the aforementioned, however, is the role psychoanalysis can play in historians' refining and monitoring of their best instrument—themselves. To the extent that one becomes cognizant of one's own historical conditioning, and the conscious and unconscious issues and affects deriving therefrom, then to that degree will one approach the unrealizable ideal of objectivity.

References

Erikson, E. (1958). *Young man Luther*. New York: Norton.

Freud, S. (1975). *Leonardo da Vinci and a memory of his childhood*. In J. Strachey (Ed. and Trans.), *The standard edition of the complete psychological works of Sigmund Freud* (Vol. 11). London: Hogarth. (Original work published 1910)

Freud, S. (1975). *Moses and monotheism*. In J. Strachey (Ed. and Trans.), *The standard edition of the complete psychological works of Sigmund Freud* (Vol. 23). London: Hogarth. (Original work published 1938)

Lifton, R. K. (Ed.). (1975). *Explorations in psychohistory*. New York: Simon & Schuster.

Wallace, E. R. (1983). *Dynamic psychiatry in theory and practice*. Philadelphia: Lea & Febiger.

E. R. WALLACE IV

Psycholinguistics. Psychologists interested in language have focused primarily on the issues of language development and the relationship between language and thought. Babies begin by making cooing and crying sounds, progress through babbling (consonant/vowel combinations), and typically utter their first word at about one year of age. By the end of the second year children are beginning to combine words into simple, two-word sentences. For the next year or so the child's speech seems to be telegraphic. It is as if the child has to pay for each word (much like a telegram), and thus only the essential words are spoken. There has been considerable controversy over the meaning behind these simple utterances. Some psychologists argue that two- to three-year-olds understand and mean much more than they say (the "rich" interpretation), while others are convinced that infants say what they mean and no more (the "poor" interpretation). In any case, by using words the young child has demonstrated a significant cognitive advance, the ability to use symbols to represent objects or events.

Perhaps the most important controversy in psycholinguistics historically has revolved around the issue of how children develop language. Those psychologists with a behavioral or environmental orientation have tended to stress the importance of imitation and parental reinforcement, while others have emphasized inborn abilities in children for understanding and generating the rules that govern language. Obviously this represents a modern variation of the age-old nature/nurture controversy (*see* Heredity and Environment in Human Development).

For some Christians, however, the most important issue in psycholinguistics has been the capacity for language in animals. Threatened by the evolutionary notion of the similarity between humans and animals, these individuals have struggled to identify something that makes humanity unique, that gives a human being a special kind of dignity and value. Several possibilities for uniqueness have been suggested (e.g., tool use, humor, self-reflection), but one of the most popular candidates has been language use.

Most scientists would agree that in the natural state, language in a narrow sense is a uniquely human attribute. The more complicated question is not the natural use of language but rather the capacity for language. Is it possible that given the right approach (e.g., sign language) apes and monkeys can learn to use language? Recent evidence suggests that the answer to that question may be at least a qualified yes. Therefore, if Christians want to argue that language makes us unique, then these Christians must argue for a significant qualitative difference in the trained language of nonhuman primates and human language.

But, from a Christian perspective, perhaps a more interesting question to ask of psycholinguistics is the role of language in shaping thought and character. Scripture often accepts the principle that out of human hearts flows human behavior. Perhaps part of that process is language. The words we use may shape our attitudes about people and our perceptions of the world. Out of those attitudes and perceptions may flow our actions. That may be why it is so dangerous to call someone "fool" (Matt. 5:22). Such words may create and/or enhance attitudes and perceptions that are "murderous." The Book of James indicates the tongue is a powerful force. Perhaps part of that power involves the capacity of speech to shape our own minds.

R. L. BASSETT

See LANGUAGE DEVELOPMENT.

Psychological Birth. See MAHLER, MARGARET.

Psychological Health. See HEALTHY PERSONALITY.

Psychological Measurement. Psychological measurement is the process of assigning numerical values or categorical descriptors to discernible levels or classes of attributes in which people differ. Ideal psychological measurement is developed from a rigorous program of research in which constructs (e.g., anxiety, verbal comprehension) are defined, operationalized, pilot tested, and refined through multiple stages of psychometric analysis. The word *test* is used quite broadly here to include many varieties of educational and psychological instruments (any testlike event or standardized stimulus presented to a subject for response). Tests technically refer to only those instruments that have correct answers, such as achievement, ability, aptitude, and intelligence tests. In contrast, the words *scale, questionnaire,* and *inventory* apply to personality, interest, and attitude measures in which the items have preferences rather than strictly correct answers.

After more than a century, following Sir Francis Galton's first test-battery application in 1884, the field of psychological measurement has emerged as a thoroughly research-based and foundational methodology in psychology, education, sociology, marketing, and many academic fields. Accompanying the development of the methodology has been the growth of an enormous testing industry throughout the developed nations of the world. Because of the resulting importance of testing in the lives of children and adults, the principles of psychological measurement and issues of ethical practice are routinely examined with critical attention by citizens, consumer advocates, government agencies, and professional reviewers. For these reasons the concepts of reliability, validity, potential test bias, and the consequences of test usage have become increasingly important in the professional training of psychologists. Technical standards for developers and users of tests also have become increasingly important (American Psychological Association, American Educational Research Association, and National Council on Measurement in Education [APA-AERA-NCME], 1985).

Domains of Psychological Measurement. Psychological measurement traditionally has been divided into content domains based on the types of individual differences measured. Domains have included such categories as achievement tests, aptitude tests, attitude assessment, behavioral assessment, intellectual assessment, interest measurement, neuropsychological assessment, personality assessment, projective personality tests, psychiatric assessment, and values assessment. Issues of test construction, reliability, validity, and usage are often dramatically different, depending on the domain of measurement. For example, intelligence, achievement, and aptitude domains involve tests that require analysis of item difficulty across age groups and item response theory (Lord, 1980) is often applied.

In contrast, personality, attitude, and interest measures require analysis of item endorsement frequency, internal consistency reliability and, often, factor analysis. Issues of test usage, test administration methods, score interpretation, and ethical concerns are often different between domains of measurement. For example, individually administered intelligence batteries (e.g., Stanford-Binet or Weschler Intelligence Tests [WISC-III]) require more advanced training in test administration and more subtle profile interpretation than do group-administered achievement or vocational-interest tests. Test usage and interpretation also are different for norm-referenced tests (those that compare raw scores to the percentile distribution of a normative sample) and criterion-referenced tests (those that define standards or criteria of performance in an absolute rather than normative fashion). A comprehensive treatment of criterion-referenced tests used in education, employment, and professional licensing is provided by Berk (1984). The reader is referred to textbooks such as Anastasi (1988), Gregory (1996), and Sattler (1988) for complete chapters describing each type of testing domain.

One domain of psychological measurement that is relatively new and of critical importance to religious clients is the spiritual domain. Accumulated research has demonstrated the importance of religiosity, faith, prayer, and other spiritual variables to the physical health, marital satisfaction, and general well-being of the general population (e.g., Spilka, Hood, & Gorsuch, 1985). Although many religious scholars are skeptical that spiritual matters can be subjected to psychological measurement, decades of research have been devoted to exploring the dimensions of our concept of God, religious orientation (intrinsic versus extrinsic, as measured by Gordon Allport's Religious Orientation Scale), and spiritual development (Spilka, Hood, & Gorsuch, 1985). A new program of research has been exploring the concept of spiritual well-being, including the effects of psychotherapy on such constructs. Bufford, Paloutzian, and Ellison (1991), for example, have provided useful norms for the Spiritual Well-Being Scale. Much research and development is still needed on such spiritual constructs because of the difficulty of measuring intangibles, the problem of skewed distributions (significant proportion of scores above the mean) in religious samples, and questions of construct validity and clinical usefulness.

Concepts of Reliability and Validity. The foundations of psychological measurement are the concepts of reliability and validity. Reliability refers to the consistency of measurement across items, test forms, testing occasions, scorers, or other facets. Reliability is a characteristic that can only be estimated by various procedures and statistical coefficients. Because reliability varies across samples, across levels of a scale, and across methods of estimation (e.g., test-retest, internal consistency, interscorer, parallel forms; see Anastasi, 1988 or Nunnally, 1978), there is typically no single reliability value for a given test. Like validity, reliability will vary across different uses or interpretations of tests. For example, using a measure of intelligence quotient (IQ) to identify gifted students (a dichotomous decision of gifted versus nongifted) ideally requires an estimate of decision consistency reliability using test-retest data (Berk, 1984). In contrast, using an IQ measure to provide intelligence scores for all the people in a research study would ideally require a generalized index such as the split-half internal-consistency estimate (Nunnally, 1978).

Validity evidence is accumulated over time and across many individual research studies to answer fundamental questions such as Does the test measure what it was intended to measure? and Is a certain use or interpretation of a test adequate, accurate or appropriate? (Messick, 1995). Validity technically is not a characteristic of a test but is an attribute of a specific usage or interpretation of a test. In other words, neither a single validity study nor a single index of validity will ever provide all the evidence needed to validate a test, because most tests have multiple uses and interpretations. For example, the use of Minnesota Multiphasic Personality Inventory (MMPI) to assist in the diagnosis of an antisocial disorder might require clinical research on the contrast between a control group, general psychiatric patients, and antisocial cases (identified independently of the MMPI). The use of the MMPI to predict antisocial or aggressive acts on an inpatient ward requires a longitudinal study of inpatients having a database of MMPI intake data and records of behavioral observations during their residency.

Evidence of validity is traditionally divided into categories such as content, criterion, and construct (APA-AERA-NCME, 1985). Content-related evidence of validity includes studies of expert ratings of the match between items and the construct being mea-sured, evidence of representative sampling of item content, and, often, internal consistency of items. Criterion-related evidence of validity includes studies such as the predictive power of test scores (e.g., use of GRE scores to predict graduate-school grades), the correlations among similar tests given concurrently, and the accuracy of a test score in identifying or diagnosing a certain condition (e.g., accuracy of IQ in identifying cognitive delay or mental retardation). Construct-related evidence of validity is more complex and requires a program of research aimed at showing that a measure of the targeted construct relates to other constructs in predictable ways. For example, a measure of reading comprehension must be correlated with other measures of reading such as vocabulary but also must show significant differences between children at different grade levels who have been given progressively advanced reading instruction. One of the most widely used methods of construct validation is the multitrait-multimethod matrix (see Gregory, 1996), which investigates the pattern of intercorrelations among instruments measuring two or more traits (e.g., depression and extraversion) by two or more different methods (self-report and peer ratings).

Recently Messick (1995) has emphasized the unified nature of validity, with construct validity being primary. He distinguishes between content, substantive, structural, generalizability, external, and consequential aspects of construct validity. For example, substantive aspects refer to the theoretical rationale or model underlying the measure. Structural aspects refer to dimensionality, often measured by factor analysis. An important aspect of test validation delineated by Messick (1995) is the study of intended and unintended consequences of test usage, including bias or fairness and justice. The next revision to the APA-AERA-NCME (1985) standards is also expected to emphasize that construct validation provides a unifying framework for all varieties of evidence of test-usage validity.

Methods of Test and Scale Construction. The development of high-quality measures is a research-based and multiple-stage endeavor. Many of the nationally standardized test batteries require five years or more of research and millions of dollars in development costs, with complex planning, pilot testing, tryout, and standardization phases before the final version is ready for publication. Even a brief personality scale used in research requires multiple stages of development to examine the content and dimensionality of the scale prior to its use in substantive studies. A typical sequence of scale construction would involve a literature review and drafting of items, examination of content-experts' ratings of item quality, and pilot testing to obtain internal-consistency reliability and factor analysis results. After these initial steps multiple research studies are conducted to establish different types of construct validity for the scale. Thus the development of a psychological test, scale, or inventory should be considered a program of research with multiple studies rather than a single development study.

Test development begins with a definition or theory about the psychological process being measured. A blueprint for the test is created by planning the number of items for each category or facet of a theory or organizational schema for the construct. For example, the construct of depression, according to Beck's (1987) theory, is composed of facets such as mood, pessimism, sense of failure, guilty feelings, self-accusations, somatic preoccupations, and fatigue. To develop a measure of depression requires representative sampling of such facets and drafting items of each type. Another decision is the form of measurement, such as self-report (true-false, Likert rating scale, forced-choice ipsative), peer ratings, objective test (multiple-choice, open-ended response, picture-easel approach with a pointing response), projective, or behavioral observation (see Anastasi, 1988 or Gregory, 1996 for definitions and examples). There is a technology of test-item development, especially in objective testing (e.g., Roid & Haladyna, 1982).

The second step in test development is usually content validation. There are both judgmental and empirical phases (Berk, 1984; Gregory, 1996; Roid & Haladyna, 1982). For example, expert panels review items and make judgments about the match between items and their intended content categories and judgments about the potential of item bias. Percentages of agreement among judges also can be tabulated, or item analyses such as item-total correlations and fit indexes from item response theory scaling (Lord, 1980) can be used to quantify content validity.

A third step in test development is usually pilot testing in which the initial draft of a measure is administered to a small but targeted sample representative of the ultimate population for the test. Item analysis studies such as internal consistency, item ambiguity (consistency across test-retest administration), factorial composition, and fit to a scaling model are often examined using a pilot sample of 50 to 200 subjects. Often, multiple steps in pilot testing are used before the test is ready for further experimentation. In the development of the WISC-III, for example, a new subtest was subjected to multiple rounds of pilot testing. Symbol Search was proposed as a measure of information-processing speed and consisted of figural symbols, letters, or numbers as targets, for which the children were to identify in a long list of search sets. Samples of 50 to 100 school children were given multiple versions of the subtest, some with 1 or 2 target symbols, letters, or numbers, and some with 3, 4, or 5 symbols, letters, or numbers in the search sets. It was determined that the best reliability and validity (factorial validity with the other WISC-III subtests) was obtained by using unique symbols, with simpler items for ages 6 to 7.

A fourth step in test development is a larger tryout of the measure and preliminary studies of validity. Continuing the example of WISC-III development, an initial tryout of the new battery was administered to about 200 children in age groups 6, 11, and 15. Items that did not show significant age trends, did not contribute to subtest reliability, or were otherwise flawed were revised or eliminated. Initial factor analyses were conducted to determine whether verbal and performance factors were present and whether new subtests such as symbol search loaded properly on the expected factor (performance scale, in this case, with the later finding that it loaded on its own processing speed factor with coding). An experimental subtest of rapid digit naming was dropped due to weak relationships with the other subtests and lower reliability compared to symbol search.

The final steps in test development are standardization, often with nationally representative samples using stratified random sampling, and final selection of the best items for the published edition. Further guidelines on test development can be obtained from Anastasi (1988), Berk (1984), Gregory (1996), or Nunnally (1978).

References

Anastasi, A. (1988). *Psychological testing* (6th ed.). New York: Macmillan.

APA-AERA-NCME (1985). *Standards for educational and psychological testing*. Washington, DC: American Psychological Association. (Revised Standards in press)

Beck, A. T. (1987). *Manual for the Beck Depression Inventory*. San Antonio, TX: Psychological Corporation.

Berk, R. A. (Ed.). (1984). *A guide to criterion-referenced test construction*. Baltimore: Johns Hopkins University Press.

Bufford, R. K., Paloutzian, R. F., & Ellison, C. W. (1991). Norms for the Spiritual Well-Being Scale. *Journal of Psychology and Theology, 11*, 56–70.

Gregory, R. J. (1996). *Psychological testing* (2nd ed.). Boston: Allyn & Bacon.

Lord, F. M. (1980). *Applications of item response theory to practical testing problems*. Hillsdale, NJ: Erlbaum.

Messick, S. (1995). Validity of psychological assessment. *American Psychologist, 50*, 741–749.

Nunnally, J. C. (1978). *Psychometric theory* (2nd ed.). New York: McGraw-Hill.

Roid, G. H., & Haladyna, T. M. (1982). *A technology for test-item writing*. Orlando, FL: Academic Press.

Sattler, J. (1988). *Assessment of children* (3rd ed.). San Diego, CA: Author. (Supplement on WISC-III and WPPSI-R, 1992)

Spilka, B., Hood, R. W., Jr., & Gorsuch, R. L. (1985). *The psychology of religion*. Englewood Cliffs, NJ: Prentice-Hall.

G. H. ROID

See PSYCHOLOGY, METHODS OF.

Psychological Reactance. The desire to restore and assert one's freedom, especially when that sense of freedom is threatened. We take for granted certain freedoms, especially when the freedom involves choice: what dress or tie to wear, what items we choose to eat or drink, who our friends will be, and our choice of a college major. Such freedoms may be restricted—we may not want to wear a tie or dress but feel compelled to because of the nature of the occasion. The phenomenon of reactance occurs when we feel that a justifiable freedom is threatened, especially when we are explicitly told we have to do something. The natural inclination is to reassert our freedom by doing the opposite.

Reactance theory (Brehm, 1966) attempts to describe the conditions under which the individual is likely to reestablish a threatened freedom. The theory identifies a number of variables that influence the course of reactance.

First is the issue of threat. Threats can range from being strong (the college administration's new antialcohol policy that will be enforced by academic suspension) to being weak (the suggestion that a menu item may not be available).

Second is the nature of the freedom. If students have assumed that the administration does not mind alcohol consumption, then the sense of freedom and the sense of reactance when the freedom is restricted may be strong. If, however, one feels no freedom in the first place, such as what the average taxpayer may feel when filing his or her income tax, then the sense of freedom and any subsequent reactance to the threat of freedom is relatively weak.

Third is the importance of the freedom. For the individual who does not consume alcohol, the administration's decision may be unimportant. Psychological reactance is most likely to be aroused under conditions in which there is a strong sense of threat, the sense of freedom is high, and the freedom is important. Under these conditions the individual is likely to try to reassert his or her freedom.

Psychological reactance has been long observed and has been commonly termed reverse psychology. The parent may restrict the child to get the child to engage in the desired behavior. Recognizing the importance of a sense of freedom, the astute teacher may give the students a choice between an objective or essay exam.

Reference

Brehm, J. W. (1966). *A theory of psychological reactance.* New York: Academic Press.

P. C. Hill

See Locus of Control; Compliance.

Psychological Roots of Religion. Religion refers to the culturally accepted practices, rituals, disciplines, and symbols that express the profoundly personal beliefs, enigmas, and paradoxes of human experience. There are individual, social, and cultural aspects of religion. Psychologists traditionally have emphasized individual aspects of religion over the social and cultural ones. The focus, therefore, is on the individual experience and expression of religion rather than the social and cultural influences on religious practice.

The individual, personal perspective on religion is seen in James's (1902) definition of religion as "the feelings, acts, and experiences of individual men in their solitude, so far as they apprehend themselves to stand in relation to whatever they may consider the divine" (p. 42). This perspective emphasizes one's experience of the divine and precludes a focus on the nature of God, which is seen as the focus of theology. One's belief in and experience of the divine forms the basis of religion. Four prominent traditions in clinical psychology address the psychological (personal experience) roots of religion: psychoanalytic, object relations, Jungian, and existential.

Freud (1961) was perhaps the most pointed in his statements about the origin of religious ideas (*see* Freud, Sigmund). He writes that religious ideas "are not precipitates of experience or end results of thinking: they are illusions, fulfillments of the oldest, strongest and most urgent wishes of mankind" (p. 30). Psychoanalytic theory conceptualizes the roots of religion as being found in the nature of one's relationship with his or her earthly father. Freud believed that religion and the concept of God develop from an unresolved oedipal conflict wherein the young boy both needs a benevolent caretaker and fears a powerful persecutor.

Within the oedipal situation the young boy has unconscious sexual desires for his mother but fears retaliation from his father if he acts on these desires. Through healthy resolution of this conflict the boy identifies with his father and learns to balance and control sexual and aggressive impulses. A poorly resolved conflict leads one to fantasize a god who is an exalted father figure containing the projections of one's needs and fears. From the psychoanalytic perspective God is only an exalted father figure. Freud (1961) writes, "God was the exalted father, and the longing for the father was the root of the need for religion" (p. 22).

The object relations perspective is based on the idea that we form images of self and others based on early relationships that we then bring forward into subsequent relationships. These images become powerful forces in shaping our thoughts, feelings, and actions. Unlike classic psychoanalysis, which emphasizes sexual and aggressive drives and the fulfillment or frustration of these drives as the basis of relationships, object relations theory emphasizes the internalized images of self and other as motivating one in relationships. These images are internalized through introjection and identification in early childhood relationships, particularly relationships with parents.

As a result of children's absolute dependence on parents to meet their needs, they create an idealized internal representation of parents that forms the god-image. Rizzuto's (1979) view is that children use this god-image as a transitional object image that facilitates healthy development from childlike dependence to the mature capacity to deal with the complexities of adult relationships. In her view God is similar to a psychic teddy bear or a blanket—objects that represent protective figures and provide security to the child. She writes, "Throughout life God remains a transitional object at the service of gaining leverage with oneself, with others, and with life itself. This is so, not because God is God, but because, like the teddy bear, he has obtained a good half of his stuffing from the primary objects the child has 'found' in his life. The other half of God's stuffing comes from the child's capacity to 'create' a God according to his needs" (p. 179). The roots of religion from this perspective are found in the transitional object images formed in early childhood.

Carl Gustav Jung wrote extensively about religion, and it played prominently in his personality theory and views on psychotherapy. Jung postulated a collective unconscious that all humans share. The collective unconscious is different from the personal unconscious, which contains forgotten or repressed experiences unique to the individual. The collective unconscious contains the archetypes, which are symbols, myths, rituals, dreams, or traditions that give meaning and organize our experience. These archetypes are cross-cultural but may manifest themselves in ways unique to particular cultures. Archetypes form conduits or molds through which our experiences flow and are given meaning.

Jung's theory holds that God is an archetype in the collective unconscious. Jung (1964) writes, "the idea of an all-powerful divine Being is present everywhere, unconsciously if not consciously, because it is an archetype" (p. 124). The God archetype gives meaning and order to our experiences and makes them more understandable. The roots of religion from the Jungian perspective are with the archetypes of the collective unconscious.

A fourth perspective within clinical psychology is the existential view of the roots of religion. Frankl (1969) asserted that there is a fundamental drive for meaning within persons that is equal to other basic drives such as sex, aggression, and hunger. This will to meaning is strong yet unique to each individual as he or she comes to terms with existential issues such as freedom, responsibility, isolation, and death (see Frankl, Victor Emil). The will to meaning is a personal spiritual quest that gives rise to religion for many people.

The existential perspective postulates that we are confronted with inescapable choices in life, which naturally lead to anxiety. We may accept the anxiety as a consequence of authentic living, or we may choose to protect ourselves from this threat by engaging in beliefs or behavioral patterns that are ultimately self-defeating. The belief that there is something or someone (God) that can ultimately rescue us from the anxiety of authentic living is seen as a common defense that keeps us from taking responsibility for ourselves. The roots of religion in this perspective have their basis in the will to meaning but lead to a defensive posture designed to reduce the anxiety of facing the existential issues of life.

All four of these psychological theories appear to endorse a presupposition that either God does not exist or, if he does, we cannot know that he does. Christians presuppose that God does exist, taking on faith the biblical account of God's existence and redemptive work in the world. Scripture reminds us that we encounter God through general and special revelation and that God creates faith in the individual. Psychological theories contribute to our understanding by indicating possible avenues through which God creates faith within individuals: through early relationships with parents and the resulting object images; through archetypal forms in the mind; and through existential encounters with our finiteness.

References

Frankl, V. E. (1969). *The will to meaning*. New York: New American Library.

Freud, S. (1961). *The future of an illusion*. New York: Norton.

James, W. (1902). *The varieties of religious experience*. New York: Macmillan.

Jung, C. (1964). *Man and his symbols*. New York: Dell.

Rizzuto, A. (1979). *The birth of the living God*. Chicago: University of Chicago Press.

C. D. CAMPBELL AND C. B. JOHNSON

See PSYCHOLOGY OF RELIGION.

Psychological Types: Jung's View. Carl Gustav Jung, an Austrian analyst and one of Sigmund Freud's principal students, developed a system of personality assessment in which he classified people into various types utilizing three polarities: extravert versus introvert, sensing versus intuitive, and thinking versus feeling (Jung, 1971). This system of personality types has been further developed by Isabelle Myers-Briggs, who added a fourth polarity, judging versus perceptive, and with her associates developed the Myers-Briggs Type Indicator (MBTI), a psychological test designed to assess personality in terms of these four polarities (Myers, 1962). In this system a person's type is some combination of these four polarities—for example, an extraverted-intuitive-feeling-judging type. There are 16 possible types in her system. Jung focused on only the 8 basic types associated with the first three polarities.

Extraversion versus Introversion. Jung suggested that a person has as a basic orientation in life either an external, outward, and thus extraverted style or an internal, inward, and thus introverted style. Jung saw himself as an introvert, along with most writers and other philosophers. He suggested, with reservation and without data, that one's inclination to be extraverted or introverted is inherited. An extravert is interested in and engages the visible world of reality; the introvert is interested in the universe within oneself. The extravert is interested in breadth; the introvert in depth. The extravert usually has more relationships but these tend to be less intense; the introvert seeks intimacy from one or two people. The extravert is public and flexible; the introvert is private and more inflexible.

It is in this polarity that Jung has made the most valuable addition to understanding personality, for he suggests that it is equally valuable and acceptable to be an introvert as an extravert, although North American society seems to value the latter. Myers suggests that only 25% of the population is introverted, the rest extraverted. The introvert enjoys and needs solitude and depth in relationships to be satisfied and productive in life; the extravert needs external stimulation and publicity. Thus the extravert is more dependent on approval, the introvert inclined toward melancholy.

Sensing versus Intuiting. What Jung called the irrational part of one's personality is the perceptive function, the part that gathers information. One can collect information primarily by using one's senses—by seeing and hearing. Likewise, one can collect information primarily by using intuition. An intuitive person uses hunches and imagination to observe the world. It is as if an intuitive person experiences a perfect mirror of the world inside and needs only to see more clearly that internal experience to properly understand the external world.

The sensing person is inclined to be concrete, fact-oriented, practical, and realistic, while the intuitive person is abstract, fantasy-oriented, creative, and imaginative. Sensing people understand the present in light of the past, while intuitives understand the present by speculating on the future. Intuitive persons think of possibilities and look for relationships between things or people; sensing people watch for facts and are more aware of the independent functions of individual elements in a system.

Thinking versus Feeling. By far the most difficult function to understand is the so-called rational function, whereby one evaluates the information collected. While Jung believed the extraverted or introverted approach to life to be inherited, he believed both the perceptive and evaluative functions to be learned. One could collect information by means of thinking (a rational, intellectual, objective, and impersonal way) or by feeling (an internal, emotional, subjective, and personal way). Thus a person who is primarily a thinker is analytical, while one primarily a feeler is synthetical. A thinker takes apart to find truth; a feeler puts together to find truth. Justice is important to a thinker, mercy to a feeler; thus principles are foremost to the former, values to the latter. The thinker would do what is clearly right regardless of personal feelings or those of others; the feeler would do what would least likely offend the

feelings of anyone. Feeling in Jung's terminology tends to be an internal function because it is not definable in objective terms, while thinking, as an objective function, is more external.

It is important to note that this polarity is emotional and that in a way thinking and feeling are means of displaying the emotion that lies under all decisions. Thus feeling people are not more emotional; thinkers are not emotionless. Feelers show their emotions; thinkers keep their emotions private.

The Shadow. Jung believed that the conscious part of one's personality is the visible personality type (e.g., extraverted-intuitive-feeling), while the unconscious part is the complement, or what he called the shadow of one's personality. The shadow is primitive and thus less developed and is also more volatile and uncontrolled. If it is unexplored, one's shadow can intrude into personality unexpectedly and harmfully, usually without compromise, as would typify an infantile expression. The purpose of life, in Jung's view, is to explore and develop one's shadow.

A person has all components of each of three Jungian polarities (or four Briggs polarities). When there is a strong visible trait, the unconscious opposite trait is equally strong and activates itself in some kind of neurotic form. For example, a very sensing person in a threatening or an unprotected moment may have exaggerated intuition and go with that intuition, defining it as a sensible observation.

The Combinations. Jung also described the general qualities of persons with each of the eight possible combinations of the three basic personality polarities.

The extraverted-thinking type is described as moral, rigid, objective, justice-oriented, and truth-oriented. He or she is less interested in religion than are other types but is visibly altruistic. However, the unconscious part of this type may lead the person to episodes of unexpected compromise because he or she is so exacting of self and is secretly self-seeking. The end justifies the means. He or she is usually visibly positive and productive, unconsciously negative and even lazy.

The extraverted-feeling type Jung sees as primarily a female phenomenon. It is distinguished sometimes by an abhorrence of thinking, a certain absolutist or opinionated orientation, and an interest in being allowed to be free. This type is often generous, and in Briggs's terms is sometimes a vendor of good works. There is sometimes a lack of depth to commitments and relationships because they are made so easily. This type needs to see things to believe them and is overly dependent on the object sometimes to the exclusion of the subject. Extraverted-feeling types are often hysterical when neurotic.

Jung indicates the extraverted-sensing type to be most interested in what is visibly real. Usually male, he is objective and practical, often to a fault. His aim is concrete enjoyment, and he is often loving and lovable, although deep love exchange is sometimes hard to maintain. He is physical in his orientation: he loves sexually, commits physically, and is often physically malaffected. On the negative side he is inclined to projections and criticism, as he sees only what is obvious.

The extraverted-intuitive type is easily committed to a cause or idea but is not always consistent. These persons trust their own intuitions at the risk of rational judgment. They are not always interested in others' welfare and can even exploit others unconsciously. They promote new things and inspire courage. They often do not stay around long enough to reap the benefits of their work. Their projections are even more severe than those of other extraverted types. In neurotic form they are compulsive.

The introverted-thinking type is by nature a philosopher, a thinker par excellence. Jung saw this type as valuing the so-called subject at the expense of the object. He may appear amiable but always seems distant, analytical, even superior. He is often calculating and can be a formidable opponent because the genesis of his ideas is internal while his expression reflects thinking rather than feeling. He is usually stubborn, headstrong, and unamenable to influence. He is relatively uninterested in social interaction and, although concerned by his frequent social offenses, he seldom changes his demeanor. Introverted-thinking types are usually male and have a vague fear of women.

The introverted-feeling type is dominated by internality in that both introversion and feeling are internal functions. This type has had a sort of vision which he or she seeks to discover or create in visible reality. As still waters run deep, so this type has depth. Expressions of feelings are infrequent, perhaps because they are so deeply felt. Consequently, these people are frequently misinterpreted as having no feeling. She (Jung's choice of pronoun) is often convinced of what other people think and is often unshakable in her opinion.

The first of the two introverted "irrational" types is introverted-sensing. This individual is guided by internal sensation, so that acquaintances often feel devalued in his presence. He is inclined toward fears and ambiguity, but he can also be especially responsible if he also possesses good judgment. Neurotic forms are compulsive.

The second is the introverted-intuitive. For him (usual gender) internal images are most important, and in severe cases revered. Thus he can be brilliant in perceiving symbols, possibilities, subjective experiences, and the indefinable. However, he is equally prone to visionary error. He professes but seldom debates. He rarely "believes"; rather, he "knows." Neurotic forms are subtle dependency and hypersensitivity.

Evaluation. Research on Jung's typology has been relatively sparse but generally supportive of his hypotheses. The majority of studies have employed the MBTI, which includes one additional polarity and eight additional personality types. This test is, however, a useful device for the measurement of the Jungian types in that it includes both attitudes and functions and has been well standardized.

Using the MBTI, Stricker and Ross (1963) showed that occupational interests among college students were related in many instances to the Jungian typology. Carlson (1980) has shown the kinds of significant differences in memories that introverted thinkers and extraverted feelers report, which are in accordance with the typology's hypotheses. Similarly Kilmann and Taylor (1974) obtained the predicted differences between introverts and extraverts with regard to the acceptance or rejection of a group learning experience. However, there is research that is inconsistent with Jung's view, and further research is needed.

Jung's system has stimulated interest in personality typology. When it is augmented by the Myers-Briggs additions, his work is a useful tool in understanding differences among people. One weakness of his analysis is the absence of a concerted effort to deal with psychogenesis of types. Likewise, his focus is largely negative, following all the early analysts. He does not present much of the adaptive aspects of the various types, nor does he deal with interactions among types. Nevertheless, no other system of personality assessment is so incisive, useful, and provocative.

References

Carlson, R. (1980). Studies on Jungian typology: II. Representations of the personal world. *Journal of Personality and Social Psychology, 38,* 801–810.

Jung, C. G. (1971). *Psychological types.* Princeton, NJ: Princeton University Press.

Kilmann, R. H., & Taylor, V. (1974). A contingency approach to laboratory learning: Psychological types versus experiential norms. *Human Relations, 27,* 891–909.

Myers, I. (1962). *The Myers-Briggs Type Indicator.* Princeton, NJ: Educational Testing Service.

Stricker, L. J., & Ross, J. (1963). Intercorrelations and reliability of the Myers-Briggs Type Indicator scales. *Psychological Reports, 12,* 287–293.

R. B. JOHNSON

See INTROVERSION-EXTRAVERSION; FACTOR THEORIES OF PERSONALITY, MYERS-BRIGGS TYPE INDICATOR.

Psychologist. Unlike the term *physician* or even *psychiatrist*, the word *psychologist* is laden with ambiguities. Almost everyone knows that a physician is someone who holds an accredited medical degree and is legally sanctioned to practice medicine. Many people also understand that a psychiatrist is a physician who specializes in the diagnosis and treatment of mental disorders. Few persons can define exactly what a psychologist is.

The title *psychologist* has been used in two general senses. One refers to someone who studies psychological processes and the other refers to someone who ameliorates psychological difficulties. What adds to the confusion is that almost everyone is in some sense an expert on his or her own psychological processes, and furthermore the legal regulation of the practice of psychology has been lax. Only since the 1970s have the majority of states instituted licensing or certification statutes that control who can and who cannot represent himself or herself to the public as a psychologist (*see* Licensure).

Perhaps the best definition of a psychologist is someone who is eligible for full membership in the American Psychological Association (APA). To achieve such eligibility one must earn a doctorate that is primarily psychological in nature from an accredited educational institution. Earning such a doctorate ordinarily implies that the candidate must complete a psychological dissertation that represents an original research contribution. While only about half the physicians in this country belong to the American Medical Association, nearly all legitimate psychologists hold membership in the American Psychological Association. Further, is should be noted that the Ph.D. is primarily a research degree. However, in the case of clinical and counseling psychologists a doctoral psychology program also includes substantial training and experience in applied areas. The same is true of some other areas of applied psychology (e.g., School Psychology, Industrial/Organizational Psychology), which also include internships within the doctoral program.

There are many different kinds of psychologists. Those most familiar are clinical psychologists, who ordinarily complete at least one full year of hospital internship work and a number of other preinternship clinical experiences (*see* Clinical Psychology). Their graduate training typically includes courses in such areas as psychopathology, clinical assessment, and psychotherapy. Many clinical psychologists have had considerably more training than this, and in some states it is necessary for the psychologist to complete an additional year of clinical training beyond the doctorate in order to be licensed for independent practice.

Most closely related to clinical psychologists are counseling psychologists. While there is much overlap in their training experiences, counseling psychologists are oriented somewhat more toward the normal while clinical psychologists are oriented somewhat toward the abnormal (*see* Abnormal Psychology).

The other kinds of psychologists described here ordinarily undertake little or no training in psychodiagnosis or psychotherapy and therefore should not be engaged in providing such services to the public. Some psychologists who first trained in other than clinical areas later became qualified as clinicians. The American Psychological Association, however, has fairly stringent criteria for such additional education to qualify someone as a clin-

ician. Completing a clinical internship is ordinarily not sufficient.

Social psychologists study how people influence one another (*see* Social Psychology). They are especially concerned with how normal people interact. Many social psychologists work in academic settings, and some work in industry, in the military, or in consulting firms. Social psychologists are experts in such areas as attitude formation and change; how we form impressions of other people; factors that contribute to effective group performance; and the nature of altruism, aggression, bargaining, negotiation, competition, and cooperation (*see* Cooperation and Competition). There is probably a close but largely unexplored connection between normal and abnormal behavior and therefore between what social and clinical psychologists study.

Social and personality psychologists are closely related (*see* Personality Psychology). The close relationship between the two domains is reflected in the fact that of the 15 or so journals published by the American Psychological Association a single publication *(Journal of Personality and Social Psychology)* is devoted to both areas. Yet while many social psychologists have what might be termed a sociological or social theory orientation, nearly all personality psychologists are concerned with the functioning of the individual. Personality psychologists nevertheless study such socially relevant phenomena as the development of moral behavior (*see* Moral Development), the nature of interpersonal anxiety, and the extent to which an individual's behavior is consistent in different situations. Personality psychologists also concern themselves with the nature-nurture (environment-heredity) controversy (*see* Heredity and Environment in Human Development); the relationships among thinking, feeling, and acting; and sex role differences.

Developmental psychologists are concerned with how personality comes to be what it is (*see* Developmental Psychology). While developmental specialists have shown increasing interest in the extent to which people change or remain the same throughout their lifetimes, developmental psychologists have traditionally focused their research on children. Again there is overlap across specialties. For example, developmental psychologists, like personality psychologists, are concerned with how people acquire the values they hold.

Physiological psychologists are experts in determining the psychological effects of physiological conditions. There is a technical difference between physiological psychology and psychophysiology. The former refers to the mental and behavioral effects of physical phenomena (e.g., how brain tumors impair problem solving), and the latter refers to physical phenomena as reflections of psychological states (e.g., how electrical skin conductance reflects stress). In practice, however, the line between the two blurs. Physiological psychologists conduct research into the location and functions of various brain centers, the electrical activity of the brain, and other such topics as how color vision works and the effects on personality of various chemical substances. Neuropsychologists are typically clinical psychologists with extra specialization in the functioning of the nervous system, although some neuropsychologists are physiological psychologists (*see* Neuropsychology).

Industrial/organizational psychologists often work for large companies, helping them to develop better work environments, construct personnel screening procedures, and troubleshoot business problems of a psychological nature. Most industrial/organizational psychologists are familiar with the complicated steps necessary to develop good aptitude and ability tests. Therefore they are often in charge of personnel testing programs.

Cognitive psychologists study how human beings think, usually with special attention to how people solve problems (*see* Cognitive Psychology). Often they are especially interested in human intelligence and its measurement. Most cognitive psychologists— social, personality, developmental, and physiological psychologists—work in educational institutions, usually colleges and universities. However, some work for think tanks such as Rand Corporation.

Mathematical psychologists are knowledgeable about statistical methodologies and research methods (*see* Mathematical Psychology). Since the 1940s highly sophisticated ways to analyze psychological data have emerged, and few research psychologists can hope to master all of these methods. Consequently, some psychologists devote all their professional time to the study of mathematical methods and to the development of mathematical models. Such models usually take the form of equations for predicting some kind of behavioral outcome—performance in school or voting behavior. While some mathematical psychologists also have a substantive area of research (e.g., attitude research), many quantitative psychologists are concerned only with statistical methods.

Experimental psychologists can specialize in almost anything, but usually they conduct laboratory research to investigate such processes as sensation and perception (*see* Experimental Psychology). They are ordinarily experts in the methods of psychophysics, which have to do with ways in which sensations and perceptions are related to physical phenomena. Like most of the other kinds of psychologists mentioned, including cognitive and mathematical specialists, experimental psychologists ordinarily work in academic settings. Virtually all university psychologists, however, conduct some kind of research.

In some states psychologists are licensed only if they offer clinical services to the public. In other states many kinds of psychologists are licensed—industrial psychologists who want to establish private consulting practices, for example. In still other states the license granted to a psychologist is a generic one, and thus all psychologists who offer their services to the public are given the same license, with exhortations not to practice beyond the limits of their training. Generic licensure is not always an effective way to regulate the conduct of psychological practice, and some psychologists continue to operate in areas beyond their competence.

The relationship between psychology and psychiatry has already been noted, and it may be useful to look at the roles of social workers and marriage counselors. While a Ph.D. ordinarily takes at least three years to earn, and in the case of a clinical or counseling psychologist four years or more, an individual can obtain a master's degree in social work within two years of continuous full-time study. There are many kinds of social workers. Only psychiatric social workers are trained to render psychotherapeutic services. Moreover, in many states a person may be employed as a social worker with only a bachelor's degree, but the job functionings of this person will entail little more than the dispensing of public assistance monies.

The practice of marriage counseling is poorly regulated in most states. Consequently, while many marriage therapists are well trained, many are not. Membership in the American Association of Marriage and Family Therapists is generally a good indication of competence in this specialty area.

Finally, there is a distinction between clinical counseling or psychotherapy and pastoral counseling. The functions of clinical and counseling psychologists are in many ways different from the functions of ministerial counselors.

Additional Readings

American Psychological Association. (1977). *Standards for providers of psychological services* (Rev. ed.). Washington, DC: Author.

American Psychological Association. (1979). *Psychology as a health care profession.* Washington, DC: Author.

American Psychological Association. (1980). *Careers in psychology.* Washington, DC: Author.

American Psychological Association. (1981). *Ethical principles of psychologists* (Rev. ed.). Washington, DC: Author.

C. W. McLemore

Psychologists of Religion. Psychologists of religion usually have their educational training in a traditional subfield of psychology such as clinical psychology, social psychology, or developmental psychology. Most psychologists of religion use their knowledge from these other specialties and apply insights to religious experience. Thus most see themselves as psychologists first, are frequently employed in psychology settings (in an academic setting, primarily in psychology or psychology-related departments), and are members of psychology-related organizations such as the American Psychological Association (APA). A smaller group of psychologists of religion are employed in divinity schools and seminaries.

Research and applied interests within the psychological study of religion vary greatly. Common theoretical frameworks for studying religion from the field of psychology include stage developmental theories in cognitive and moral reasoning (such as Jean Piaget or Lawrence Kohlberg), attribution theory, and several theories within the field of clinical psychology such as coping theory and object relations theory. Psychologists of religion also vary widely in their methodology. Some will study religious experience using only strict empirical methods, sometimes without much theory guidance, while others operate from theoretical frameworks (e.g., phenomenological, psychoanalytic) that utilize broader methodological approaches.

Although psychologists of religion are involved in such organizations as the Religious Research Association and the Society for the Scientific Study of Religion (SSSR), the largest association of strictly psychologists of religion is Division 36 of the American Psychological Association (APA), Psychology of Religion. This division, until 1993 known as Psychologists Interested in Religious Issues, was in 1994 the twenty-fourth largest division (of 49 divisions) of the APA with 1,263 members. Individuals may join Division 36 without membership in the APA. Information on joining Division 36 (with or without APA membership) may be obtained from the APA.

Members of Division 36 vary widely in terms of their own religious identities, ranging from evangelical Christian to atheist. Although individuals of other major world religions can be found within the division membership, a criticism of Division 36 and the field of study as a whole is that religions from other than the Judeo-Christian tradition are underrepresented, thereby limiting our total understanding of religious experience.

P. C. HILL

See PSYCHOLOGY OF RELIGION.

Psychology, History of. In 1907 Hermann Ebbinghaus penned the epigram, "Psychology has a long past but only a short history," a statement that in many respects remains true. Psychology's past goes back at least two thousand years into the early beginnings of philosophy. Its history goes back only to 1879, when Wilhelm Wundt founded the first psychology laboratory in Germany.

The Roots of Modern Psychology. Three disciplines played key roles in the growth and development of psychology: philosophy, physiology, and psychophysics. Most surveys of the history of psychology trace the philosophical beginnings at least as far back as Plato (ca. 427–347 B.C.) and Aristotle (384–323 B.C.). Plato's clear statement of the difference between mind and body gave philosophy and

psychology one of their most enduring problems. His teaching that persons profoundly influence one another engendered the seeds of an environmentalism that reached its peak in the behaviorism school founded by John B. Watson. Aristotle wrote extensively on such modern psychological topics as memory, sleep, thinking, intelligence, motivation, emotion, growth, and development. His concept of the mind as a blank wax tablet *(tabula rasa)* upon which experience writes resulted in the doctrine that all knowledge comes from experience. Aristotle's three primary laws of association—similarity, contrast, and contiguity—provided the basis for the school of associationism.

René Descartes (1596–1650) freed philosophy from the bonds of theological and traditional dogmas and helped to establish the dominance of a new force—empiricism, the search for knowledge by the observation of nature itself. British empiricism and associationism, as represented in the works of Thomas Hobbes (1588–1679), John Locke (1632–1704), George Berkeley (1685–1753), David Hume (1711–1776), David Hartley (1705–1757), James Mill (1773–1836), and others, provided the basic subject matter for the newly emerging science of psychology. However, in order to move beyond theory toward a natural science of human nature, psychology needed to be able to attack the subject matter experimentally. The means for this attack came from the new field of experimental physiology.

Physiology developed into an experimental discipline during the early part of the nineteenth century. A critical discovery occurred in 1850. Hermann von Helmholtz (1821–1894), a German physicist and physiologist and one of the greatest scientists of the nineteenth century, measured the speed of the neural impulse. Others had said that such a measurement was impossible. The nerve impulse traveled too quickly to be measured. Maybe it was even instantaneous. Helmholtz calculated the speed to be a relatively slow 50 to 100 meters per second. His discovery suggested the possibility of isolating and measuring psychological events. Perhaps the mind could be measured and understood scientifically. Other physiological research studies (e.g., the localization of psychological functions in particular parts of the brain, the study of sensation and perception) provided additional impetus for the development of the new science of psychology.

The third root of modern psychology, psychophysics, developed out of the efforts of Gustav Fechner (1801–1887) to make his philosophy an exact science. Fechner sought to establish in a quantitative way the relationship between mind and body or between the psychological world and the physical world. In 1860 he published *Elements of Psychophysics,* which contained his calculations of the quantitative relationship between stimulus intensity and sensation. Early in the nineteenth century Immanuel Kant, the German philosopher, had maintained that psychology could not become a science because it is impossible to measure or experiment upon psychological phenomena and processes (Schultz, 1981). Fechner's work, combined with Helmholtz's, helped to dispel the pessimism of Kant.

The Founding of Modern Psychology. In 1879 Wilhelm Wundt (1832–1920) established the first formal psychological laboratory in Leipzig, Germany. This marked the beginning of experimental psychology as an independent science. It took a man of great courage, with a solid background in experimental physiology and philosophy, to combine these two disciplines into a new science. Previously, in a handbook, *Principles of Physiological Psychology,* Wundt had outlined his goal of marking out a new domain of science. In 1881 he established a journal, *Philosophical Studies,* which was to be the official organ of his laboratory and the new science. With a handbook, a laboratory designed expressly for psychological research, and a scholarly journal, the new science of psychology was off to a good start.

Wundt's efforts attracted considerable attention. Students flocked to the Leipzig laboratory and to Wundt's lectures. At one time he had more than six hundred students in a class. Many of the students who came from the United States returned to found laboratories of their own. Granville Stanley Hall, James McKeen Cattell, and Edward Bradford Titchener are three of the many prominent pioneers of psychology who studied with Wundt.

Wundt believed that the subject matter of psychology is immediate experience. He wanted to analyze consciousness and experience into elemental components, in much the same way as the natural scientists were analyzing their subject matter. In a sense Wundt set out to produce a chemistry of the mind.

Since Wundt defined psychology as the science of experience, the method of psychology had to involve the observation of experience. Because experience is observable only by the person who has it, Wundt saw introspection or self-observation as his primary method. In order to maintain strict control he established explicit rules for the proper use of introspection in his laboratory. His trained observers acquired the necessary skills through a long period of apprenticeship and training. Observers in Wundt's reaction-time experiments performed about ten thousand introspective observations before he considered them to be skilled enough to provide valid data (Boring, 1953).

Many critics give Wundt credit for founding psychology but charge him with leading it in the wrong direction. Introspection receives the brunt of much of the criticism. However, in recent years many of Wundt's later writings have received some long-overdue attention. Modern researchers are often surprised at the relevance of many of his ideas to current thinking. Wundt's three-factor theory of feeling, his view of schizophrenia, his theory of lan-

guage, and his studies of apperception are being viewed with new interest.

The Early Schools of Psychology. Like other sciences in their early years, psychology experienced a period when groups of psychologists became associated with the ideas and interests of particular leaders. These schools of psychology, as they are called, usually worked on similar problems and shared the same theoretical and methodological orientation. These schools often experienced a period of competition, growth, and ascendancy, followed by decline and replacement by a newer school.

Associationism. Associationism represents a principle of psychology more than it does a school of psychology. The principle derives from such philosophical questions as, How do we know? and Where do complex ideas come from? To these questions the British empiricist philosophers gave the following answers: We know by means of the senses. Complex ideas such as patriotism, which cannot be directly sensed, must come from the association of simpler ideas.

The associationistic movement received substantial support from the work of three men: Ebbinghaus, Ivan Pavlov, and Edward Lee Thorndike.

Ebbinghaus (1850–1909) made his contribution only a few years after Wundt had declared that it was impossible to study the higher mental processes in an experimental way. Ebbinghaus examined the formation of associations by using nonsense syllables and showed that complex phenomena such as human learning and memory could be studied by carefully controlled research. Almost a century after publication many of his findings (e.g., his curve of forgetting) are still valid and cited by psychologists.

Pavlov (1849–1936), a Nobel Prize–winning physiologist, investigated the higher nervous centers of the brain using the technique of conditioning (*see* Conditioning, Classical). In his research Pavlov shifted the emphasis from the association of ideas to the association of stimulus-response connections. His use of precise and objective measures created a trend in psychology toward greater objectivity in subject matter and methodology. The school of behaviorism most readily reflects the influence of Pavlov.

Thorndike (1874–1949) developed the best example of an associationistic system in psychology. To him psychology was the study of stimulus-response connections or associations. While Thorndike began his career studying learning in laboratory animals, he soon shifted his interest to human learning and became the first educational psychologist in the United States.

Associationism survives as a methodological tool, if not as a systematic position. Most psychologists view the association of variables as a fundamental task of science.

Structuralism. Wundt's founding of experimental psychology marked the beginning of the structuralism school. During the first two or three decades of psychology, structural psychology was *the* psychology. Structural psychologists proposed to analyze the structure of the human mind by means of introspection.

For Wundt the task of psychology was threefold: to analyze conscious processes into basic elements; to discover how these elements become connected; and to determine the laws of connection.

Structuralism provided psychology with a strong scientific identity within the academic community. It also served as a ready target for the criticisms of the later schools—functionalism, behaviorism, and Gestalt psychology. These newer schools flourished as they organized their efforts against structuralism's strong orthodox position. Structuralism died of its own narrow dogmatism. It lacked the support that practical applications might have given. The contemporary role of structuralism is virtually nonexistent. Modern psychology accepts only the basic scientific attitude of structuralism.

Functionalism. Functionalism represents the first distinctly American school of psychology. It began in the psychology of William James (1842–1910) and shortly provided the bridge to Watson's behaviorism. The functionalists defined psychology as the study of the mind as it functions in adapting the organism to its environment. According to Woodworth and Sheehan (1964, p. 15), "a psychology that attempts to give an accurate and systematic answer to the question, 'What do men do?' and then goes on to the questions, 'How do they do it?' and 'Why do they do it?' is called a *functional psychology.*"

While James served as the pioneer of the functionalist movement, John Dewey (1859–1952), a respected philosopher, educator, and psychologist, wrote a paper in 1896 on the reflex arc, which marks the founding of functionalism. Other psychologists at the University of Chicago, especially James Angell (1869–1949) and Harvey Carr (1873–1954), molded and developed functionalism into a leading school of psychology.

By opposing the narrowness and restrictions of structuralism, functionalism performed an important service to American psychology. It expanded methodology beyond the technique of introspection by collecting data, using questionnaires, mental tests, physiological research, and objective descriptions of behavior. In addition functional psychologists pioneered in some of the most important areas of psychology: child psychology, animal and human learning, educational psychology, and psychopathology.

Functionalism no longer exists as a distinct school, even though psychology in the United States is largely functional in its orientation. Functionalism was such an overwhelming success that it was absorbed into contemporary psychology.

Behaviorism. At the age of 35 John B. Watson (1878–1958) led the revolt that produced the most influential and controversial school of American psychology. While the movement from structuralism to functionalism has been described as evolutionary, the movement to behaviorism was revolutionary. Watson declared the old order to be a failure. In a short time he succeeded in his efforts to destroy it.

Watson made the basic tenets of behaviorism simple and straightforward. He defined psychology as the scientific study of observable behavior. He wanted an objective science of behavior. Mentalistic concepts such as mind and consciousness, which had been carried over from philosophy, were to be discarded. The chief method of Watson's behaviorism was the conditioned reflex; however, he accepted and used other techniques for the observation of overt behavior. Introspection was relegated to the dust heap. An indication of Watson's rapid acceptance came with his election to the presidency of the American Psychological Association (APA) only two years after starting the revolt.

While Watson was the chief promoter and propagandist for behaviorism, four later psychologists expanded the horizons and developed subschools of behaviorism during the 1930s. Most of their influence has come through their theories of learning.

Edward Chace Tolman (1886–1959) rejected the strict stimulus-response theory of Watson in favor of a more eclectic viewpoint, often called purposive behaviorism. The molar aspects of behavior (i.e., the total response of the whole organism) rather than the elemental units studied by Watson received his attention. In this sense his theory combined the concepts of behaviorism and Gestalt psychology.

From his systematic study of learning Clark Leonard Hull (1884–1952) developed a complex hypothetico-deductive theory of behavior. Perhaps the most serious barrier to an understanding of Hull's theory is its intrinsic difficulty and complexity. Nevertheless, he exerted a great deal of influence on the study of learning and behavior.

Starting from a behavioristic orientation, Edwin Ray Guthrie (1886–1959) influenced psychology through the formulation of an extremely simple learning theory. He promoted a theory of learning that depended on one principle: contiguity. All learning occurred because of the contiguity of a stimulus and a response in one trial. Repetition and reinforcement played no essential role in his system.

B. F. Skinner (1904–1990) ranks as the most influential of the behaviorists. He developed a strictly descriptive form of behaviorism that is atheoretical. Intervening variables and physiological processes are not a part of his system, which is often called the empty-organism approach. Operant conditioning provides the focus of most of Skinner's work on learning and behavior (*see* Conditioning, Operant). Among his most notable research studies are those dealing with schedules of reinforcement, verbal behavior, and behavior modification. Teaching machines and programmed learning represent two areas in which his work has had a profound impact.

Of all the early schools of psychology in the United States behaviorism provoked the most criticism, attained the greatest popularity among psychologists, and exerted the most influence. It remains a powerful force in psychology today.

Gestalt Psychology. As Watson started his revolt in the United States against structuralism and functionalism, a new movement in Germany revolted against Wundt. This movement, Gestalt psychology, eventually took on behaviorism as well. It was a revolt against artificial analysis and elementism.

Max Wertheimer (1880–1943) founded Gestalt psychology, with assistance from Kurt Koffka (1886–1941) and Wolfgang Köhler (1887–1967). The perception of apparent movement provided Wertheimer with a chance to explain a phenomenon that the structuralists could not explain. His explanation was so simple and yet ingenious that it precipitated a new psychological school. According to Wertheimer, apparent movement existed as a real phenomenon, irreducible to simpler sensations or elements of any kind.

The Gestalt psychologists defined psychology as the study of the immediate experience of the whole organism. While most of the traditional subject areas of psychology (e.g., learning, memory, personality) were studied, perception received the most attention. Most of the data for Gestalt psychology came from immediate, unanalyzed experience obtained through introspection. However, behavioral data were used, especially in studies of learning and problem solving.

The basic principle of Gestalt psychology developed out of a concern for the whole-part relationship. To the Gestaltists the whole is not just greater than the sum of its parts, nor is it any simple function of the parts. The whole is different from the sum of its parts. The whole dominates the parts, determines their characteristics, and constitutes the basic datum of psychology. Psychology, according to the Gestaltists, should study the molar aspects of behavior and experience.

The Gestalt school created an interest in problems that had been previously ignored. The Gestaltists initiated the study of insight and problem solving in animals and humans. They outlined the principles according to which our perceptions are organized. And they took a fresh look at conscious experience. Contemporary interest in cognitive psychology and phenomenology is traceable to the Gestalt movement.

Psychoanalysis. None of the other schools of psychology or their leaders, with the possible exception of behaviorism during the heyday of Watson, has enjoyed the popular appeal of psychoanalysis and Sigmund Freud (1856–1939). It is not unusual for laypersons to consider *psychology* and *psychoanalysis* synonymous terms. However, psychoanalysis as a school developed differently from the other schools. It started outside of the university setting, expressed little interest in most of the traditional subject areas of psychology, and focused almost entirely on the etiology, development, and treatment of abnormal behavior. While psychoanalysis has never been received enthusiastically by academic psychology, it has exerted considerable influence on psychology as well as many other disciplines.

The publication of *Studies in Hysteria* by Freud and Josef Breuer in 1895 marks the beginning of the psychoanalytic school. Five years later Freud published *The Interpretation of Dreams,* which is now considered his most significant work. Shortly thereafter Freud's views began to attract attention. At first there was only a small and devoted coterie of followers. But gradually the following increased, and the movement became international in scope. In 1909 Freud accepted the invitation of Hall to speak at the twentieth anniversary celebration of Clark University. This was Freud's only visit to the United States. During the next decade the ranks of psychoanalysis were torn by disagreements and defections, but Freud's fame and influence continued to increase until his death.

Many of the basic ideas of psychoanalysis received initial exposure in *Studies in Hysteria.* Among these ideas were the importance of the unconscious in the development of the neuroses, the role of early traumatic sexual experiences, the importance of symbolism, and the relevance of transference. Freud's therapeutic techniques represent one of his most original contributions. After discarding hypnosis he developed the technique of free association, which consisted of instructing the patient to say whatever came to mind, without selection or rearrangement. Freud regarded dreams as "the royal road to the unconscious." By analyzing the symbolic content of dreams he believed he could gain greater access to the unconscious processes. Awareness of the unconscious forces, according to Freud, should enable patients to free themselves from those forces and lead a more rational and satisfying life.

Two early defectors from Freudian psychoanalysis, Carl Gustav Jung (1875–1961) and Alfred Adler (1870–1937), formulated their own theories. At one time Jung was the heir apparent of the psychoanalytic movement; Freud referred to him as the crown prince. Jung's defection resulted from his disagreement on two major points. First, he redefined libido as a generalized life energy as opposed to Freud's sexual energy. He also believed that a person is not primarily determined by childhood experiences. He stressed the importance of future goals and aspirations as well as the past. Many of Jung's ideas are novel and thought-provoking, such as his archetypes, which are a part of the collective unconscious. Jung's theory, which he called analytical psychology, offers a much more optimistic view of human nature than does Freud's deterministic view.

Adler's individual psychology developed out of his criticism of Freud's emphasis on sexual factors. In the theory Adler, like Jung, focused on the future rather than the past. Instead of dividing the personality into parts, such as id, ego, and superego, Adler stressed the unity of personality. He also emphasized the importance of social forces rather than biological forces in the shaping of human personality. According to Adler, the basic goal or motivation underlying human behavior is a striving for superiority. For him the unconscious was much less important than the conscious in the determination of behavior. Contemporary psychoanalysis incorporates many of Adler's ideas, and he has had a significant influence on the development of humanistic psychology.

Karen Horney (1885–1952), Erich Fromm (1900–1980), and Harry Stack Sullivan (1892–1949) represent some of the more recent developers of psychoanalytic theory. Each of them has stressed the societal and interpersonal origins of neurotic behavior and made important contributions to the development of neo-Freudian psychoanalysis.

While psychoanalysis has been criticized for deficient methodology and a lack of scientific rigor, it remains an important force in modern psychology. Boring (1950), the historian of experimental psychology, calls Freud "the greatest originator of all, the agent of the *Zeitgeist* who accomplished the invasion of psychology by the principle of the unconscious process" (p. 743). Among the contributions of psychoanalysis to psychology several deserve mention: it opened up new areas for research such as sex and the unconscious; it suggested the importance of childhood and genetic factors in personality development; it gave impetus to the study of motivation; and it presented evidence for a number of defense mechanisms. Despite its appeal and acceptance by the public, many academic psychologists consider psychoanalysis outside the mainstream of psychological thought.

The Postschool Era and Contemporary Developments. After the demise or assimilation of the earlier schools of psychology the later schools have demonstrated more staying power. There are still psychologists who identify their interests as Gestalt in orientation, and significant numbers of psychologists regard themselves to be in the behavioristic or psychoanalytic tradition. However, many splinter groups have developed since the days of Watson and Freud.

Within behaviorism one of the most significant recent developments is referred to as the cognitive revolution. All behaviorists do not regard words such as *mind, consciousness,* and *feeling* as taboo. Increasingly since the early 1960s there has been a return to the study of consciousness. While behaviorism continues as a dominant force in American psychology, it is a different brand of behaviorism than that promoted by Watson and Skinner during the first 50 years of the school.

The fragmentation within psychoanalysis has been more extensive than the divisions within behaviorism. All behaviorists agree that some form of behavior should be the primary focus of study, but all psychoanalysts do not agree on the importance of the unconscious or the relevance of sex and aggression as motivators of behavior. Recent developments within psychoanalysis include ego psychology, object relations theory, and self psychology, each marked by some major departures from classical Freudian thought.

The closest approximation to a new school of psychology is the movement called humanistic psychology or the third force in psychology. Beginning in the early 1950s humanistic psychologists emphasized several themes: the importance of conscious experience as the primary phenomenon in the study of human beings; an emphasis on such human qualities as creativity, choice, and self-realization; a concern for the dignity and worth of people; an emphasis on meaningfulness in psychological research; and an interest in the development of individual human potential. Many of these themes can be found in the writings of earlier psychologists, but the humanistic psychologists have molded them into a movement. Existential psychology and phenomenological psychology share many of the same themes with humanistic psychology.

Several early trends in psychology continue to be important in modern psychology. Empiricism and quantification receive widespread support and emphasis. The search for the physiological correlates of behavior remains a powerful force. But perhaps the most dramatic trend is the trend toward professionalism.

Lightner Witmer founded the first psychological clinic in 1896 at the University of Pennsylvania, and in the 1930s almost all psychologists were still in academic positions.

Twenty years later the majority of psychologists could be found working outside the academic setting. The First and Second World Wars created a sudden need for professional psychologists to do psychological testing and to treat psychological problems. The community mental health movement, along with state hospitals and veterans' hospitals, created additional positions for clinical psychologists. The demand for trained clinicians coming out of graduate school still seems to exceed the supply.

Industrial/organizational psychology represents another important growth area for professional psychology. Personnel psychology, human factors engineering, and consumer psychology are just three of the many areas of specialization. One of psychology's most pressing problems is the tension between the professional branch and the academic/scientific branch of psychology.

Conclusions. Modern twentieth-century psychology is a rapidly changing discipline. All aspects of human behavior provide subject matter for the study and application of psychology. The movement of psychology into such diverse fields as law, art, religion, and forensic medicine illustrates the breadth of the discipline. In the process the discipline of psychology shows signs of becoming more open, tolerant, and human.

References

Boring, E. G. (1950). *A history of experimental psychology* (2nd ed.). New York: Appleton.

Boring, E. G. (1953). A history of introspection. *Psychological Bulletin, 50*, 169–189.

Schultz, D. (1981). *A history of modern psychology* (3rd ed.). New York: Academic.

Woodworth, R. S., & Sheehan, M. R. (1964). *Contemporary schools of psychology* (3rd ed.). New York: Ronald.

C. E. HENRY

Psychology, Methods of. Since psychology is a science, the methods of psychology are the methods of science; however, the subject matter of a science determines the particular methods used. Because human behavior and mental processes are so varied, psychologists use many different methods. These have been developed to gain knowledge about the natural world, to study what Christians call natural, or general, revelation (Rom. 1:18–20). They are the most reliable means of learning about the created world, although they may lead to incorrect conclusions if they are not used properly.

In addition to this natural revelation God has given us his special revelation in Scripture. The study of the Bible leads us to a more complete knowledge of God and his creation. Since all truth is God's truth, these two revelations (natural and special) are complementary and not in conflict. When the two seem to be in conflict, it means that either the scientist has reached an incorrect conclusion or that the theologian has misinterpreted Scripture. Anyone who reads either science or theology knows that both errors occur.

Methods of Gathering Data. In general psychologists develop hypotheses, gather data to test them, and evaluate the data to decide whether their hypotheses were correct. This process is the basis on which psychological theories are developed and tested. The nature of the hypotheses influences the ways data are gathered and evaluated.

The Experimental Method. When they are using the experimental method psychologists control the presence, absence, or intensity of factors thought to influence the behavior while keeping all other factors constant. As a result experimenters can reach cause-effect conclusions, something they cannot do as well with other methods. The basic principle of this method is that one takes two groups of subjects and treats them both the same, except in one way. Then if the groups behave differently after the treatments, one concludes that the one different treatment caused the differences.

Although many scientists maintain that the experimental method is a creation of only the last 400 years, we find a good example of it recorded more than 2,500 years ago in the first chapter of the Book of Daniel. During their three years of education Daniel and his friends were to be fed rich food, which they did not believe would be good for them.

Daniel proposed that he and his friends eat only vegetables and water for 10 days, while the others ate the king's rich food. At the end of this time the teacher could compare how the two groups looked and decide which was the better diet. At the end of the 10 days those on vegetables and water looked healthier and better nourished, so they continued to eat such food.

In this experiment those eating the vegetables were the experimental group, and those eating the usual rich food were the control group. Both groups were treated the same. Metaphorically speaking, they went to classes together, slept in the same dormitories, did the same physical work, and so forth. These variables are called the controlled variables or the constants. Diet was one factor that was different for the two groups. This variable, manipulated by the experimenter to see whether it causes a change, is called the independent variable. Finally, the appearance of the students was measured to see if there was any difference between the groups. This variable is called the dependent variable because the experimenter wants to find out whether it depends on the independent variable.

Since the appearance of the Hebrews was better than that of the others, the experimenter concluded that the diet of vegetables caused the difference. This is a logical conclusion, since that was the only way the groups were treated differently. Although modern experimenters would insist on some refinements to eliminate other possible causes, the basic idea of the experimental method is found in this incident in the Old Testament. It can lead to false conclusions if other variables change at the same time as the dependent one. For example, one investigator thought he had caused neurosis in rats by giving them an unsolvable conflict. Other researchers showed that the odd behavior of the rats was caused by the high-pitched sound of his apparatus, not the conflict. Eliminating these confounding variables is a major task in designing an experiment.

The experimental method, preferred by many psychologists, sometimes cannot be used because it is impossible or unethical to manipulate the variables in question. Therefore, psychologists use a variety of other methods, descriptive methods that cannot show cause-effect relationships as easily, if at all.

Correlation Methods. When they use the simplest correlation methods, psychologists take measurements of two variables and determine whether the two are related in any way; that is, whether they are correlated. For example, a positive correlation shows up between scores on intelligence quotient (IQ) tests and grades in school. Students who score high on such tests tend to make high grades. A negative correlation exists between sociability and suspiciousness, so that persons who are suspicious are generally less sociable.

The correlation methods usually provide an index to tell the degree of relationship. A correlation of +1.00 indicates a perfect positive relationship, one of –1.00 indicates a perfect negative relationship, and one of 0.00 indicates no relationship. Perfect relationships are seldom found in life, but any degree of relationship is often helpful in predicting what persons will do. Although the relationships are not perfect, IQ scores can be used to predict how well an individual will do in school, high school grades to predict college grades, and so forth.

As with other descriptive methods, it is difficult to demonstrate cause-effect relationships with the correlation method. However, the method is useful in many instances where psychologists cannot experiment. For example, there is a high correlation between the intelligence quotient of parents and that of their children. We do not know how much of this is caused by heredity and how much by environment. For obvious ethical reasons we cannot arbitrarily breed persons with given IQs and then let some rear their own children while switching other parents and children. But we can use the correlation method and see what happens to the IQs of children who are reared by their natural parents and those reared by adoptive parents.

Observation Methods. Another descriptive method is naturalistic observation, in which the scientist observes and records behavior in its natural setting without attempting to intervene. This is the most basic method of science, because all of science begins with the observations of the scientists. Although one cannot prove cause-effect relationships with this method, it is a valuable source of hypotheses about causes of behavior. For example, we know that many children drop out of Sunday school during their junior high years, and through observing the classes we may develop ideas about why they do.

If subjects know they are being observed, such knowledge may influence behavior. An observer, standing and writing on a clipboard, may result in a Sunday school class being much better or much worse than usual. This problem can be avoided by having the observer join the group—the method of the participant observer. Others in the group do not know that they are being observed, so their behavior is unchanged.

Written and Oral Methods. Some behaviors or attitudes are very difficult to observe, so psychologists can gather data through the use of questionnaires or surveys in which people are asked to report their behaviors or opinions on a variety of subjects. We are all familiar with the results of the U.S. Census, the Gallup poll, the Harris poll, and surveys on everything from sexual behavior to religious attitudes. When such surveys are taken, it is essential that the sample be representative of the entire population from which it is drawn.

Another written method is the use of tests. Nearly everyone has taken an IQ test of one kind or another. Literally thousands of tests are available to measure achievement, aptitude, personality, val-ues, interests, and so forth. Tests are essentially a kind of short-cut, a relatively small sample of behavior used to obtain a standardized measurement of a person.

The clinical interview is another descriptive method used to gather data. As an individual undergoes psychotherapy, the interview may be recorded and later analyzed as to the ideas discussed, the words used, the pauses taken, and so forth. Psychologists can use such an analysis to find marked changes taking place over the course of therapy.

Finally, clinical psychologists often write case histories. Case histories are essentially scientific biographies of individuals in which the psychologist reconstructs the important events over many years of their lives in an effort to see how various behavior patterns emerged. These case histories may be constructed from remembered events in the persons' lives or from personal documents and records.

All these methods of gathering data are valid means of learning about the created world, but they are used in different situations. In general the experimental method is most appropriate for studying those aspects of humans that are most similar to animals and for situations in which variables can be controlled and in which subjects are reacting rather than initiating. The other methods are most appropriate for studying those aspects of humans that are most similar to God and for situations in which variables cannot be controlled and in which subjects are active and initiating.

Methods of Evaluating Data. After data have been collected, they must be interpreted in some way. Verbal data, such as interviews and case studies, are usually summarized in a written report. However, if the data are in the form of numbers, statistics are usually used to summarize them and draw implications from them.

Descriptive Statistics. Psychologists use some types of statistics for summarizing or describing large amounts of information. Sometimes the data are presented in a frequency distribution in which each score is represented. However, the scores frequently are summarized in just a few numbers. The most frequent types of such statistics are measures of central tendency and measures of variability.

Measures of central tendency, or averages, are used to represent the center of the frequency distribution. Although many measures exist, three appear most often: the mode is the score that occurs most frequently; the median is the middle score, with half the scores above it and half below; and the arithmetic mean is the sum of the scores divided by the number of scores (what most people call the average).

Measures of variability, or dispersion, describe how the scores are spread out around the measures of central tendency. The range is the difference between the highest and lowest scores. The variance and the standard deviation are more useful than the range. The variance is the average squared distance from the mean, and the standard deviation is the square root of the variance. About two-thirds of the scores fall within one standard deviation of the mean, and about 95% fall within two standard deviations.

Inferential Statistics. Other types of statistics are used for drawing inferences, for making statements about an entire population when only a sample has been measured. In most national surveys about 1,500 people are chosen as representative of the whole population; then those making the survey state how 200,000,000 people voted, what they think, what television shows they watch, and so forth. Statistics are also used to measure the size of the correlation, to tell whether or not there is a true correlation in the population, and to make predictions on the basis of the correlation.

Psychologists frequently conduct an experiment using several groups and want to know whether the differences between the groups are due to chance or if they indicate a real difference. By using standard techniques, such as the t-test or analysis of variance, they can find out how likely the differences are to have been caused by chance. If the probability of the results being produced by mere chance is less than 5%, the differences are said to be statistically significant. Some experimenters set this chance level at 1%, making an even more stringent criterion.

Ethical Principles. As psychologists have used these methods, a number of ethical problems have arisen. Although psychologists have wrestled with these problems and come to some conclusions, Christians should consider the problems again and see if they agree with the solutions.

Deception. The use of deception in psychological research and testing is a widely accepted practice. Psychologists argue that such deception is necessary in some types of research and that nothing is wrong with it as long as the subjects are told the truth before they leave the experiment. A similar situation is found in psychological testing. People do not know what they are revealing about themselves by their answers. As a result the public has become suspicious of psychologists and often tries to outwit them.

Invasion of Privacy. This is probably not an issue when one is openly observing in a natural setting. However, it becomes an issue when one is observed through a one-way glass or from hiding, or while engaged in sexual activity, and so forth. It may also be an invasion of privacy to ask certain questions on tests or in an interview.

Harm to Subjects. A basic principle is that psychologists should not do anything that will cause lasting harm to a research subject or patient. This is a valid principle, and we must be careful not to interpret it too loosely. If we imply to persons in an experiment that they are stupid, debriefing after the experiment may not remove the self-doubts that have been created. How is the subject to know if the experimenter was lying during the experiment or after it? A sexual question on a personality test may lead persons into temptation and sin rather than helping them. Therefore, psychologists must be careful to treat others with the respect and dignity due to individuals made in God's image.

Additional Readings

Agnew, N. M., & Pike, S. W. (1978). *The science game: An introduction to research in the behavioral sciences* (2nd ed.). Englewood Cliffs, NJ: Prentice-Hall.

Collins, G. R. (1977). *The rebuilding of psychology: An integration of psychology and Christianity.* Wheaton, IL: Tyndale House.

Koteskey, R. L. (1983). *General psychology for Christian counselors.* Nashville: Abingdon.

R. L. KOTESKEY

See PSYCHOLOGICAL MEASUREMENT.

Psychology, Presuppositions of. Presuppositions are assumptions about reality that have a major impact on all the sciences, including psychology. Presuppositions about the nature of the universe, cause and effect, human nature, and knowledge help guide science by giving it a framework from which to operate. Scientists, for example, may presuppose that the laws of matter operate similarly everywhere in the universe. By assuming some regularity in the universe they are able to investigate the problems in their sciences with more confidence in their theories and tools of investigation. Assumptions about the nature of human nature are likewise important for the psychologist in both research and clinical settings.

What the natural and social sciences have been slow to recognize is that presuppositions about reality and human nature affect the scientist's ability to be objective in the scientific process. Psychological research supports the notion that individuals resist interpretations of data that run counter to their expectations. This is certainly a possibility for psychology, which has many assumptions that run counter to the biblical picture of human nature.

Interest in the subjectivity of science was kindled by Kuhn's (1962) classic book, *The Structure of Scientific Revolutions.* It was Kuhn's contention that change in scientific ideas takes place as revolutions in whole paradigms, or sets of presuppositions about reality, because people's underlying beliefs about reality have to change before new contrasting ideas can be accepted. It has been suggested that in a scientific revolution people do not change their ideas. The scientists who hold the established views eventually die, and thus new ideas can become accepted.

Presuppositions in psychology serve as a framework within which research can be conducted and therapies can be developed. Assumptions also affect the psychologist's objectivity and can become rigid dogmas in the face of conflicting data. The importance of psychologists being aware of their presuppositions cannot be overemphasized, because all psychologists have assumptions that undergird and influence their work whether they are aware of them or not. In addition some of the subject matter of psychology is less accessible to experimental research and thus is more dependent on the psychologist's assumptions.

The presuppositions of psychologists can affect their work by limiting the subject matter they are willing to investigate, the methods of investigation, and the interpretations they place upon their data. Psychological research on the effects of persons' belief structure on their objectivity is substantial. Research areas such as cognitive dissonance, prejudice, and social aspects of perception illustrate the biasing potential of assumptions. The research process itself is also strongly affected by the psychologist's beliefs, as is illustrated by the phenomenon of experimenter expectancy (Barber, 1976) and the effect of subject beliefs on experimental results (Silverman, 1977).

The biasing effects of assumptions should not lead anyone to reject the search for truth as hopeless, but rather should challenge psychologists to recognize the presuppositions of their field as well as the benefits of Christian assumptions in the study of human nature.

Basic Assumptions. The presuppositions that provide the framework within which most psychology is practiced are summarized below. It is important to note that these assumptions may be held as convenient to the methodology of science without necessarily believing that they specify truth about the nature of the way things are. For example, a belief in determinism may be a belief in methodological determinism, which does not mean that a psychologist does not accept the concept of human freedom but that human behavior does seem to follow regular laws. Therefore, it may be useful to think of behavior as being determined.

Naturalism. This is an assumption at the core of secular science. It means that the universe can be explained completely by natural processes. This is a rejection of the idea of the God of the universe who ultimately provides the sustaining power of the universe and who can impact the universe in ways that according to our understanding go beyond natural law (e.g., miracles). For the psychologist naturalism means that the natural causes in the universe have to be the sole explanation for all that human beings are and can do.

Materialism. Related to naturalism is the belief in materialism, which says that everything that exists in the universe is composed of matter-energy. This means that human nature in its entirety (behavior, thinking, feeling) is ultimately reducible to material explanations. It usually means that brain activity is equated with personhood.

Reductionism. This assumption means that explanations about human behavior and personhood can be reduced to or equated with explanations in terms of physical-chemical processes that accompany human activity. MacKay (1974) calls this type of thinking "nothing buttery," since reductionistic psychologists try to describe human nature as nothing but neuronal or chemical activity.

Determinism. Following directly from the assumptions of materialism and reductionism is the assumption of determinism, which says that all human behavior is completely caused by natural processes. This means that human beings do not decide their own actions, regardless of their feelings of freedom.

Evolution. This assumption attempts to provide an explanation for the uniqueness and complexity of human nature in a naturalistic order. Evolutionary theory would say that all of human nature has evolved from simpler organisms. This includes the idea that the complex human mind is a product of the evolution of the brain.

Empiricism. This assumption is both a method of knowing and a theory about human nature. Empiricism means that one can know only through the senses and with whatever scientific instrumentation expands the senses. Empiricism may be more radically stated as whatever cannot be shown to register as sensory data, such as God or mind, does not exist. Obviously empiricism can be a benefit to careful, scientific observation and control, but it also sets limits on what can be observed about human nature.

Empiricism may also be defined as a theory of human nature. The person in the empirical sense is a product of sensory input. The mind, according to empiricist John Locke, is a *tabula rasa*, a blank slate on which sensory experience writes. British empiricism of the 1800s contributed much to the behavioristic model in psychology, in which behavior alone is seen as acceptable data in psychology and the person is seen as a product of environmental factors.

Relativism. This is the assumption that there are no absolute standards of right or value to guide psychological research, counseling, or behavioral engineering. In a naturalistic universe all things related to morality and value become arbitrary and related to the individual person. Consequently, there is much debate in psychology about the value and purpose of human life, values to guide counseling, and the moral structures by which society can be organized.

There are several counterassumptions in psychology that rebel against the rigid nature of these assumptions. Humanistic psychology, for example, assumes the freedom and personality of human nature. Transpersonal psychology emphasizes the immaterial essence of the universe and human nature; this assumption is labeled *pantheism* or *panpsychism*.

Biblical Presuppositions. Since beliefs are important to the development of psychology, Collins (1977) and Cosgrove (1979) suggest that Christian psychologists should build their psychology upon biblical presuppositions about reality and human nature. While the existence of God may not seem pertinent to psychology, it should be clear that all of psychology's assumptions depend heavily on the natural basis for the origin and operation of the universe. For this reason Christians need to state clearly their belief in the supernatural God of the universe. The assumption of a creator God gives psychology a source for the human person, a confidence in knowledge, additional revelation on human nature in the Bible, and a source of ethics and value. The immaterial essence of human nature gives a basis for human freedom and purpose and meaning in life. Christian beliefs about the fall of human nature and sanctification can expand the Christian's view of psychological problems and therapy. In general Christian assumptions support a needed balance in psychology. They can serve to correct psychology's limited view of human nature arising from its extreme positions on empiricism, materialism, determinism, and reductionism. At the same time Christian beliefs do not rule out the physical nature of the person, the laws of cause and effect, and the strong influences of nature and nurture on the human personality.

References

Barber, T. X. (1976). *Pitfalls in human research*. New York: Pergamon.

Collins, G. R. (1977). *The rebuilding of psychology*. Wheaton, IL: Tyndale House.

Cosgrove, M. P. (1979). *Psychology gone awry*. Grand Rapids, MI: Zondervan.

Kuhn, T. (1962). *The structure of scientific revolutions*. Chicago: University of Chicago Press.

MacKay, D. (1974). *The clockwork image*. Downers Grove, IL: InterVarsity Press.

Silverman, I. (1977). *The human subject in the psychological laboratory*. New York: Pergamon.

M. P. COSGROVE

See DETERMINISM AND FREE WILL; REDUCTIONISM.

Psychology and Religion. For the purpose of this overview of the relationship between psychology and religion, the two terms will be understood quite broadly. The term *religion* in particular will be used inclusively of other faiths and of more generic concepts of spirituality, although many comments specific to Christianity will be included. Nine nonexhaustive aspects of this relationship will be discussed. References for specific concepts or findings can typically be found either in Jones (1994) or Worthington et al.

Historical Roots: The Religious Psychologies.
Before it achieved its present status as an independent academic discipline and legally recognized professional specialization, the term *psychology* referred to any organized system for understanding the human person. Thus most of the major systems of thought had their own distinctive psychologies. The more inclusive histories of psychology such as Robinson (1995) or Peters (1962) discuss some of these ancient psychologies, explicitly recognizing, for instance, that the various Hellenic and Christian systems of thought (e.g., Platonic, Aristotelian, Augustinian, Thomistic) included developed and nuanced psychologies. These psychologies were primarily deductive in nature, but all were to some degree or another influenced by empirical observation of daily reality; for example, Oden (1984) presents a compelling picture of the manner in which the psychology of Pope Gregory the Great in the fifth century was shaped by acute observation of the influence of personality upon pastoral care methods.

Less commonly recognized is the continuation of this psychological work in Christian and other religious settings after natural philosophy became independent from theology in the West during the Enlightenment. Richard Baxter, Jonathan Edwards, and others continued to develop sophisticated analyses of the human condition and their implications for the care of souls. Edwards especially showed confident brilliance in developing Christian conceptions of the person while interacting with the secular learning of his day. This work of developing a distinctively biblical psychology continues in recent times. Some, such as Emil Brunner and Wolfhart Pannenberg, have tried to develop biblical psychologies in interaction with nontheological fields. For others there has been less willingness to engage secular learning, as the divorce between secular and sacred learning seems to necessitate confrontation with secular ways of understanding personhood. This resulted in the spate of biblical psychologies that emerged around the turn of the last century (such as Delitzsch, 1885) and the contemporary and putatively purely biblical psychology of the nouthetic counseling movement. The detachment of these latter works from contemporary secular psychology does not render them nonpsychological, even though they may not be recognized as psychology by the secular discipline.

Personal Religiosity of Psychologists. Religion is intrinsically personal, so we might expect that if personal life commitments shape scholarship or practice, then understanding the personal responses of psychologists to religion will inform our understanding of how the discipline relates to religion. A survey in the mid-1980s of religious preferences of academicians found that 50% of psychologists had no current religious preference, in stark contrast to the general population. Parallel findings have been reported regarding the religiosity of psychotherapists, who are typically less committed to traditional religion and its associated values than are the general population. Shafranske and Malony (1990) found that while a majority of a sample said religion was helpful to people and that spirituality is personally relevant to their lives, less than

20% described organized religion as the source of their spirituality. The data suggest that while a substantial percentage of psychologists (though less than the general population) are accepting of broad spirituality, they are significantly less committed to traditional religious faiths than are the general public. The lack of personal engagement with traditional religion may help explain the relative lack of attention to religion in textbooks of psychology, the inattentiveness of empirical researchers to religion as an important dimension of human diversity in studies of personality and psychopathology, and the infrequency with which management of client religious issues has been discussed in training programs and textbooks in applied psychology (though the latter two seem to be changing).

Psychology of Religion. The scientific study of religion by psychology is typically termed the psychology of religion. The definition of what constitutes scientific investigation has been fluid over time, spanning the highly speculative and clinical methods of Sigmund Freud or Carl Gustav Jung to the rigorously empirical methods of the experimentalists. Psychology of religion was one of the major areas of study in the field from the 1880s until the 1930s, as typified by the work of William James. After three decades of relative disinterest in the field, psychology of religion is in the 1990s receiving increased attention as evidenced by renewed publication of psychology of religion textbooks, by the viability of such journals as the *Journal for the Scientific Study of Religion* and the *International Journal for the Psychology of Religion*, and by the growth of the Psychology of Religion division of the American Psychological Association (APA). Psychologists of religion only constitute a tiny fraction of the field, however.

Many religious believers are discomforted by the idea of empirical study of religious experience. Some believers mistakenly believe that the psychology of religion is necessarily a nascent form of natural theology, an attempt to construct a new empirically validated religion on the basis of scientific study of religious experience. Others are concerned that such study is necessarily destructive of religion as the scientist relentlessly pursues the reductive explanation of living faith experience by the operation of personality variables, biologically grounded consciousness states, and the like. Such fears are not groundless, as such motives may be present for some researchers. But the universality of religious experience and the necessity of the contribution of some potentially explainable human element in even the most pure religious experience would suggest that there can be value in the rigorous empirical investigation of the human element of such religious experiences as conversion, glossolalia, or close community. Such empirical study might assume for methodological purposes that the religious experience under scrutiny is explainable in part according to measurable variables, without going the additional step of being radically reductionistic. Further, not all findings in this field have been hostile or damaging to religious faith. Much recent effort has gone into the examination of the relationship of religiosity and mental health, with rather consistent findings emerging that religiosity tends to be positively associated with improved mental health, especially when the religious faith is intrinsic in nature. The entire spectrum of research methods in the psychology of religion continue to show viability; empirical research continues apace, and there has been recent resurgence of clinical reflection on religious experience from a psychodynamic perspective.

One major topic in the psychology of religion is the discussion and study of religion as a variable influencing the process and outcome of psychotherapeutic intervention. This matter has received serious study in the 1980s and 1990s, as exemplified by forthcoming publications by Shafranske (in press) and Worthington et al. In this subfield religion is often viewed as a clinical phenomenon to be managed much like race or other person variables (this is not to say that religion is not treated with respect and competence). Worthington et al. reviewed all available empirical research on religion and counseling; the following are a sampling of the more well-validated conclusions of that research: that highly religious people prefer counselors who are a close match to their own values, that disclosure of the religious beliefs of the counselor has a differential effect on client behavior depending upon client religious values, that even highly religious clients do not typically prefer counseling to focus primarily upon religious issues, that value convergence tends to occur in successful therapy with client values moving toward those held by the therapist (even though religious values do not tend to change), and that a substantial percentage of religious counselors use religious techniques in their counseling, such as prayer with clients (*see* Prayer, Use of in Counseling) or implicitly instructing clients in scriptural principles, though the efficacy of such techniques has not been measured. It seems likely that vigorous attention will be paid to this kind of research in the near future.

Psychological Imperialism Against Religion. Each of the four major paradigms of twentieth-century psychology has been used to challenge, reinterpret, redefine, or dismiss established religious traditions. When the proponents of a psychological paradigm see their understanding of personhood not as a tentative hypothesis but as metaphysical truth that is exhaustive in its explanatory power, it is perhaps natural that confident pronouncements on the reform of traditional religious belief will be made.

Freud, founder of psychoanalysis, saw religion as a defensive and regressive life adjustment, one wherein religious persons project onto an ambiguous and meaningless universe their neurotic desires to be cared for by an omnipotent parent. Maturity obviously requires relinquishing such infantile projections (*see* Healthy Personality). B. F. Skinner, a staunch advocate of behaviorism and positivistic science, saw religion as a transitional explanatory fiction that is needed as long as the true (environmentalistic) causes of behavior are yet obscure, and also analyzed religion functionally as a system for the control of deviant behavior and the reward of adaptive behavior. Skinner argued that the development of behaviorism rendered religion irrelevant, as the true determinants of behavior were now obvious, and psychology could now scientifically manage deviant and adaptive behavior without the useful fictions of divine reward and punishment. Humanistic psychology, with its presumptions that the person is basically good and free, that our primary drive in life is toward self-actualization, that we are fundamentally self-sufficient, and that pathology is often the result of external impositions of expectations and standards, renders traditional religion irrelevant. The newest dominion paradigm in the field, cognitivism, has predictably followed suit. Sperry (1988), a Nobel laureate, recently argued that the success of cognitive psychology has direct implications for morality and religion. Sperry argued that the new mentalist paradigm, built upon his concept of emergentist mind, implies that religion should be based upon biospheric ethics (an ethic of preservation of the context for continued evolutionary development), with continued evolution of mind enshrined as the highest good. This revised religion would be devoid of supernatural beliefs. In short he argued that humanity, the highest known product of evolution, should view its minds as its ultimate concern. The reality that each of the major psychological systems have been put to such use would seem to justify religious caution about psychological theory.

Psychologizing of Pastoral Care. Secular applied psychology has been enthused to share its insights on the care of persons with pastoral care practitioners. Clerics in turn have looked to the mental health disciplines for insights to guide pastoral care throughout the last century. The result has been ever-increasing reliance by pastoral care professionals upon secular psychology for the self-definition of the field and its understanding of its mission and methods (Holifield, 1983). Almost every trend and movement in the mental health field has been mirrored in pastoral psychology, as even the most cursory review of pastoral care textbooks will show. Oden (1984) has shown that pastoral care texts prior to 1920 were dominated by references to the historical and theological roots of the pastoral care tradition, while after 1920 pastoral care texts came to be dominated by references to the major psychotherapy theoreticians. Perhaps the deepest problem is not that useful information is gleaned from secular psychology but rather that it is done uncritically and to the exclusion of the

historic theological and ecclesiastical roots of pastoral care. Some scholars, such as Oden (1994), are trying to restore pastoral care to its historic theological and ecclesiastical roots.

Spiritualizing of Psychological Intervention. There is considerable contemporary interest in the incorporation of the spiritual into psychological treatment techniques. There seem to be a higher number of sources for the impetus to move in this direction. One source is certainly the explosive spread of the 12-step movement from its humble beginnings in the Alcoholics Anonymous (AA) movement. The growth of the AA movement into an international phenomenon from the 1940s through the 1970s was staggering. The 12-step movement has not just spread through the growth of AA, however. It has spread also in the application to other supposedly addictive behaviors such as drug addiction, gambling, overeating, and sex.

A second source of the growth of interest in spirituality has been the psychology of Jung.

Third, the humanistic psychology of the 1950s and 1960s gave birth to the transpersonal psychology movement. Transpersonal psychology, with its panreligious conceptions of the connections of the individual ego to some sort of suprapersonal reality (e.g., Walsh & Vaughn, 1980), has encouraged greater attention to spiritual factors in healing and growth.

Fourth, the search for effective treatment methods for anxiety led early behavioral researchers to develop the technique of progressive muscle relaxation, which was partially based upon or inspired by Eastern meditation practices, which in turn fueled interest in those Eastern methods and the religious roots thereof.

Finally, psychology has been influenced by the general cultural discontent with utterly secular understandings of the person, as evidenced in the enthusiastic welcome of the writings of M. Scott Peck and others on life as a spiritual journey. This nonexhaustive list of factors encouraging greater interest in spiritual factors is indicative of the eclecticism of this movement; it bears little common ground with the concerns of orthodox Christianity. Only time will tell whether these developments portend greater acceptance of Christianity within psychological circles.

Christian Integration of Academic Psychology and Faith. Most psychologists conceive of the field as a science or at least as grounded in science, and thus the supposed incompatibility of science and religion has been cited as the reason that religion can have no part in psychology. It is common to think of religion and science as opposed to one another. Lindberg and Numbers (1986) provided conclusive evidence that this motif of conflict is mostly a byproduct of several polemical interpretive histories of the relationship of science and religion that were published at the end of the nineteenth century. Faith and science have been divorced at a cultural or individual level throughout most of Western history.

Christian scholars have never been content with their faith being ruled as irrelevant to their quest for understanding. As rationalistic and positivistic understandings of science have been increasingly discredited, Christian scholars have sought again to understand how faith might relate to the quest for knowledge in the sciences and social sciences. The two recent works that have been most influential in setting the framework for dialogue about the interrelationship of academic psychology and Christian faith are Evans (1977/1982) and Carter and Narramore (1979). Both discuss ways in which faith and psychology are often pitted against one another or used to explain the other away; are viewed as independent, complementary, and non-interactive ways of understanding the person; or are viewed as able to be integrated. Both argue in favor of the last view, wherein a foundational commitment to Christian faith and its doctrines shape the broad outlines of one's understanding of the field of psychology (*see* Christian Psychology).

What will this process look like in academic psychology? The influence of Christian belief on scholarship in psychology will vary depending on which aspect of psychology one has in mind. At the minimum Christian belief should always serve as the foundational cognitive framework out of which all study proceeds, including the study of psychology. It should ground our core assumptions of what sorts of beings humans are, what are their unique characteristics as God's special handiwork, and the appropriate philosophical assumptions for approaching the study of persons. As we move across the spectrum for neuroscience or animal learning to personality theory, the necessary role of some religiously grounded metaphysical beliefs and the proper role of distinctively Christian control beliefs in mediating understanding of the foci of study increase. One reason for this is that the irreducible complexity of the more molar phenomena of interest (a complexity that requires more reliance upon background metaphysical assumptions to impose order upon or see order in the complex phenomena being studied). Second, the lessened strict accountability of theory to specific empirical findings increases the role of metaphysical assumptions in adjudicating theory confirmation and disconfirmation. Also, as we move along that spectrum of psychological topics toward more molar and uniquely human phenomena such as personality psychology or abnormal psychology, we also move into arenas that are more obviously the preoccupation of biblical revelation (and of other religious thought systems as well) and that are more likely to engage and interact with the deepest life commitments of the scientist.

As our subject matter becomes more molar and irreducible, more uniquely human, more related to the distinct subject matter of divine revelation, and more central to our most basic human concerns, religious presuppositions will and should become more operative in a scientific understanding of the person (Jones, 1994). For all these reasons there will be no obvious Christian versions of specific laws of perception or of neuronal functioning, as such matters are not matters with which faith is preoccupied, although Christianity does have something to say about the presuppositions of the nature of mind and of the human person that might form the conceptual background of such basic psychophysical or neuropsychological research. At the other extreme of broad personality theory, Christian faith will speak volumes to us about the broad contours of a credible understanding of persons. For example, it will anchor our philosophical presuppositions on such issues as determinism or reductionism and will suggest unique human capacities and characteristics that a well-founded personality theory must explain. In the study of human development and of psychopathology, religious presuppositions will ground our vision of what constitutes normalcy or wholeness, the end goal of development and health (Browning, 1987).

Progress in the integration of academic psychology and Christian faith has been limited, in part because so many Christian psychologists are in clinical areas of the field. Also, prominent Christian integrators have been prone to publish for popular audiences, which is certainly helpful but does little to influence the broader field or to establish empirical justification for these views. Few Christian integrators have established progressive and productive research programs that can stand scrutiny by secular academicians. Integrated accounts of learning and of psychosocial development have been attempted, as well as topical examinations of such issues as guilt. These have been of uneven quality.

Christian Integration of Applied Psychology and Faith. Much of the Christian integration literature is of applied nature, written either to consumers of psychological services or to fellow practitioners of such services. Most applied psychological work is done in the context of personality theory, psychopathology, and change that shape the practitioner's understanding of the needs of clients and his or her role in addressing those needs. Thus Christian presuppositions should transform how we think about these theories in a manner identical to that regarding academic psychology. Much of the integration dialogue has been preoccupied with foundational questions about the compatibilities and incompatibilities between major psychotherapy theories and Christian doctrine; much of this literature is summarized by Jones and Butman (1991). A number of highly visible works of integration have been attempts to reconceptualize the whole of applied psychology from a Christian perspective; the early works of Lawrence J. Crabb are examples of this genre. None of these attempts has met with widespread acceptance among other Christian professionals.

The question of how Christian faith should transform the concrete realities of the practice of applied psychology has been another frequent topic in this literature. Christian professionals have debated the proper usage of uniquely Christian resources (e.g., prayer and Scripture teaching) in the context of counseling. Critical considerations in this literature have included the adequacy of preparation of the Christian mental health professional to use such practices, the role of the church in superintending such practices, the spiritual receptivity of the client, and the unique demands of the professional context within which the services are offered. This type of integration of faith and psychology is not a Christian phenomenon only; similar discussions are under way in Jewish, Muslim, and Buddhist contexts.

Finally, many published integration works have been directed toward a general readership, and many of these are written in the self-help genre of literature. These include Christian understandings of such topics as addictions, depression, marriage, guilt, and so forth. These works have varied widely in sophistication, quality of biblical exegesis and the theological reflection, and currency with the best literature in the broader discipline.

Psychology as Adversary. A final facet of the relationship of psychology and religion is the contemporary vilification of psychology in some conservative Christian contexts, where psychology is seen as an exemplar of secularism and humanism and the integration work of Christian psychologists as syncretism and heresy rooted in deficient trust in God and his Word. These warnings should not be treated cavalierly. Often embedded in these extreme statements are legitimate concerns about the fundamentally anti-Christian presuppositions of secular systems, the imperialistic attitudes of many secular psychologists toward traditional religion, the sloppy biblical underpinnings sketched by enthusiastic proponents of psychology in the church, and the drift of many toward a pragmatic and self-serving faith. Christian critics of integrative psychology, however, often underemphasize the doctrine of common grace, a confidence that truth is revealed inside and outside the household of faith, including the possibility that checking our hypotheses against human reason and empirical reality has the potential to add substantively to our legitimate knowledge base; that God's revelation in the Scriptures is authoritative but not exhaustive; and the belief that acquiring such knowledge is an enterprise that honors God.

References

Browning, D. (1987). *Religious thought and the modern psychologies*. Philadelphia: Fortress.

Carter, J., & Narramore, B. (1979). *The integration of psychology and theology*. Grand Rapids, MI: Zondervan.

Delitzsch, F. (1885). *A system of biblical psychology*. (Trans. R. Wallis). Edinburgh: Clark.

Evans, C. S. (1982). *Preserving the person: A look at the human sciences*. Grand Rapids, MI: Baker. (Original work published 1977)

Holifield, E. B. (1983). *A history of pastoral care in America: From salvation to self-realization*. Nashville: Abingdon.

Jones, S. L., (1994). A constructive relationship for religion with the science and profession of psychology: Perhaps the boldest model yet. *American Psychologist, 49* (3), 184–199.

Jones, S. L., & Butman, R.E. (1991). *Modern psychotherapies: A comprehensive Christian appraisal*. Downers Grove, IL: InterVarsity Press.

Lindberg, D. C., & Numbers, R. L. (1986). *God and nature: Historical essays on the encounter between Christianity and science*. London: University of California Press.

Oden, T. C. (1984). *The care of souls in the classic tradition*. Philadelphia: Fortress.

Oden, T. C. (1994). *Pastoral counsel*. Grand Rapids, MI: Baker.

Peters, R. (Ed.). (1962). *Brett's history of psychology*. New York: Macmillan.

Robinson, D. (1995). *An intellectual history of psychology* (3rd ed.). New York: Macmillan.

Shafranske, E. P., & Malony, H. N. (1990). Clinical psychologists' religious and spiritual orientations and their practice of psychotherapy. *Psychotherapy, 27,* 72–78.

Shafranske, E. P. (Ed.). (in press). *Religion and the clinical practice of psychology*. Washington, DC: American Psychological Association.

Sperry, R. (1988). Psychology's mentalist paradigm and the religion/science tension. *American Psychologist, 43,* 607–613.

Walsh, R. N., & Vaughan, F. (Eds.). (1980). *Beyond ego: Transpersonal dimensions in psychology*. Los Angeles: Tarcher.

Worthington, E. L., Kurusu, T. A., McCullough, M. E., & Sandage, S. J. Empirical research on religion and psychotherapeutic processes and outcomes: A ten-year review and research prospectus. *Psychological Bulletin, 9* (3), 448.

S. L. JONES

See RELIGIOUS HEALTH AND PATHOLOGY.

Psychology as Religion. The similarity to religion of modern psychological theories of mental pathology and psychotherapy was noticed from the time these approaches emerged early in the twentieth century. Each theory was a general interpretation of the meaning of personal existence, complete with an explanation of what facilitates and what blocks the development of a healthy or ideal personality. Since these theories were based on secular philosophy and values, they were explicitly or implicitly hostile to religion, especially Christianity (see Browning, 1987).

Modern psychologies initially functioned as alternative worldviews or secular religions primarily in the lives of the psychotherapists, most of whom were drawn to psychology because they were already alienated from traditional religion and were looking for a worldview that could be interpreted as scientific and as compatible with the increasingly secular society. Even those who started training in psychology with a religious commitment often abandoned their faith or greatly reduced its importance. This replacement of religion by psychology resulted from immersion in a secular framework that assumes that religion and religious experience are psychological phenomena and that the supernatural does not truly exist. Religion is interpreted as an illusion at best or as some kind of pathology at worst.

Psychology often came to serve the same religion-replacing function in the lives of the patients who entered therapy at a time of mental anguish actively looking for answers. It was common for the patient to accept the theoretical framework of the therapist—to be "converted" to psychology. Such change was facilitated by the frequency of therapy sessions and by the reinforcing effect of any cures or benefits caused by or attributed to the therapist. Negative experiences with religion that the patient might have had would also support the move to psychology.

A fundamental way in which psychotherapy functions as a religion is that at its best it heals. The healing aspect of psychotherapy is its primary justification. It is probably no accident that the secular psychotherapies first developed in a period when healing was much neglected in the major Christian churches, especially those that ministered to the educated and sophisticated.

An important characteristic of psychology has been the serious involvement with religion of many of its theorists and innovators. This was the case for the founders of psychotherapy, Sigmund Freud and Carl Gustav Jung, and for Alfred Adler, who converted to a somewhat liberal Protestantism from a Jewish background. The following psychologists either started with a serious religious concern, clearly expressed such in their professional life, or both: William James, Granville Stanley Hall, Carl Rogers, Erich Fromm, Rollo May, Karl Menninger, and Gardner Murphy. Such examples imply an affinity between the religious and the psychological mentality.

With the growth of psychotherapy and the increasing secularization of society, psychological ideas began to spread throughout the culture. Colleges and universities with their many psychology courses, plus such media phenomena as advice columns, contributed greatly to the disseminating of psychology. A consequence has been that the public discourse concerning people who are facing life crises is almost entirely dominated by secular psychology. The religious understanding of these issues is restricted to private life and is no longer even understood by many secularized Westerners. There has been a "triumph of the therapeutic" over the theological (Rieff, 1966; see also Becker, 1975; Lasch, 1978).

Psychoanalysis: Freud. The connections of Freud's thought and life with both Judaism and Christianity are deep and complex. Freud directly acknowledged the essential similarity between psychoanalytic therapy and religious counseling by describing psychoanalysis as "pastoral work in the best sense of the words" (1927/1959, p. 256). He recognized in psychoanalysis what is true of all secular psychotherapy and counseling; namely, that it is similar and indeed a rival to the long Christian tradition of confession and counseling.

There were also specific cultic characteristics of early psychoanalysis. Freud often functioned like the founder of a religion: he was surrounded by disciples who formed a kind of inner sanctum; the best and most loyal of these were given rings to designate their special status; a deep allegiance to Freud's ideas, especially the dogma of his sexual theories, was expected of any true follower. Freud likened himself to Moses and Jung (before the schism) to Joshua. The psychoanalytic establishment that emerged after Freud's death has often been compared to an orthodox religious organization that excommunicated deviants (see Roazen, 1975).

Freud was personally involved in religious issues all his life and he wrote frequently on them (*Totem and Taboo*, 1913; *The Future of an Illusion*, 1927; *Moses and Monotheism*, 1938). Partly this interest came from both religious and ethnic Jewish influence (Klein, 1981; Ostow, 1982), but much of it came out of his complex hostility and attraction to Christianity (Vitz, 1988).

Freudian psychoanalysis never developed a positive synthesis to provide a clear meaning to life. Freud always remained an analyst focused on exploring the unconscious. His attitude and that of psychoanalysis is pessimistic, stoical, and skeptical. He refused to provide a secular form of salvation, since he saw religion in any form as an illusion to be rejected. Thus Freudian theory, which is in important respects an antireligion, was never made into a positive alternative. Freud was very critical of Jung and Adler, who did make psychology into a kind of positive alternative to religion.

Analytical Psychology: Jung. Jung was also quite aware of the religious nature of psychotherapy, and the theological cast of much of his writing is apparent, for example, in *Answer to Job* (1954), an extensive exercise in scriptural interpretation. Jung's awareness of the religious issue is stated when he writes: "Patients force the psychotherapist into the role of priest, and expect and demand that he shall free them from distress. That is why we psychotherapists must occupy ourselves with problems which strictly speaking belong to the theologian" (Jung, 1933, p. 278).

Unlike Freud, Jung provided positive, synthetic concepts that could serve as a conscious goal not only for therapy but for life as a whole. Jung's answer to religious needs is summarized by Jacobi (1973), a prominent student of his: "Jungian psychotherapy is . . . a *Heilsweg*, in the twofold sense of the German word: a way of healing and a way of salvation. It has the power to cure. . . . In addition it knows the way and has the means to lead the individual to his 'salvation,' to the knowledge and fulfillment of his personality, which have always been the aim of spiritual striving. Jung's system of thought can be explained theoretically only up to a certain point; to understand it fully one must have experienced or better still, suffered its living action in oneself. Apart from its medical aspect, Jungian psychotherapy is thus a system of education and spiritual guidance" (p. 60). The process of Jungian movement on this path is, Jacobi continues, "both ethically and intellectually an extremely difficult task, which can be successfully performed only by the fortunate few, those elected and favored by grace" (p. 127). The last stage on the Jungian path of individuation—salvation—is called self-realization. This goal is essentially gnostic; the commandment Know (and express) thyself has replaced the Judeo-Christian Love God and others. In many respects modern psychology of whatever theoretical persuasion is a gnostic phenomenon because of its emphasis on specialized knowledge as the answer to life.

Much Jungian psychology is concerned with interpreting the patient's dream symbolism, the collective unconscious and the personal unconscious of the patient and archetypes: the anima (or animus) or shadow. Jung acknowledged the patient's basic religious concerns, and his psychology is directly applied to the archetypal expression of religious motives, for example, in dreams about the wise old man (God archetype) or dreams about rebirth. Jung's discovery of the psychology of religious symbols is important, but there is the danger of substituting the psychological experience of one's religious archetypes for the salvation that comes through the transcendent God who acts in history (see Hostie, 1957). Those who make this mistake have truly treated psychology as religion.

Self or Humanistic Psychology: Rogers, Maslow, and Others.

Another expression of psychology as religion is seen in the self psychologies. These place the self at the center of personality and make the growth or actualization of the self the primary goal of life in general and of psychotherapy and counseling in particular. Self psychologies share all or most of the following characteristics: an emphasis on the conscious self as an integrated or at least potentially integrated system; an emphasis on the true self as entirely good, not characterized by any natural tendency to aggression, self-indulgence, or narcissism. Such undesirable phenomena are attributed to the false self created by external factors such as family, traditional religion, society, or the economic system; and an emphasis on the true self as having almost unlimited capacity for change through freely made decisions. This process of choosing brings about self-actualization, the ideal way of being. Self-actualization is an ongoing process of change, not a finished state; an emphasis on personality prior to self-actualization, as primarily the result of learned

social roles. That is, the false self is the product of social learning of an essentially arbitrary kind; an emphasis on breaking with the past, especially with commitments to others, with tradition, with fixed moral codes. Morality is interpreted as personal, subjective, and relative; an emphasis on getting in touch with and expressing emotions and feelings. This promotes a presumed greater awareness of the true self and greater self-acceptance and trust in one's instincts; and an emphasis on short-term counseling of relatively normal adults.

Examples of self psychology theories are those proposed by Rogers (1951, 1961), Maslow (1970), and Fromm (1947). The writings of May (1953) and the Gestalt psychology of Perls (1969) are also closely related. Self psychology had much of its origin in Adler (1924), in Goldstein (1939), and in Jung's notion of self-realization. Most of the psychology that was immensely popular in the United States during the 1960s and 1970s was a form of self psychology; for example, transactional analysis (Berne, 1964). Other movements, such as Erhard Seminar Training (EST), combined self psychology with elements from Eastern religions.

This general framework served as a worldview that undermined or replaced Christianity. Some specific claims of the self psychologists make this clear. Rogers (1961) stated that the goal of psychotherapy is to help the client become self-directing, self-confident, self-expressive, creative, and autonomous to such a degree that he or she experiences unconditional positive self-regard. The client is increasingly to experience the self as the only locus or source of values.

Fromm devoted many pages in his books to interpreting and reinterpreting parts of both the Old and New Testaments. The titles of some of his books illustrate his religious agenda: *The Dogma of Christ* (1963) and *You Shall Be as Gods* (1966). Fromm (1947) explicitly stated that his psychology would be untenable if the doctrine of original sin were true. He believed that evil is in no way intrinsic to human nature, and self-theory follows from this basic assumption, for the self is to be perfectly trusted only if it is perfectly free of intrinsic evil. The Pelagian assumption of "I'm OK and you're OK," found throughout transactional analysis, is a popular expression of this position (Berne, 1964; Harris, 1967).

Some of the popular self-theory has gone so far as to claim that the self is God: "You are the Supreme Being. . . . Reality is a reflection of your notions. Totally, Perfectly" (Frederick, 1974; pp. 171, 177; Schultz, 1979, reached the same conclusion). Rogers's position, in which the self is the sole locus of values, comes close to the same position. The influence, often indirect, of Sartre and other existential thinkers on American self theorists has been substantial. Sartre stated that once we've rejected "God the Father," then "life has no meaning *a priori*. Before you come alive life is nothing; it's up to you to give it a meaning, and value is nothing else but the meaning that you choose"

(Sartre, 1947, p. 58). Since Sartre (1957) also argued that people's goal is to become God, self psychology often can be interpreted as a commercialized American packaging of much of European existentialism.

The widespread acceptance of self psychology (called selfism by Vitz, 1977/1994) has been due to various cultural and economic factors. Contemporary upper-middle-class Americans, wealthy, increasingly secular, and with time on their hands, were happy to find a rationale that encouraged an extremely self-centered way of living. Economic support for this kind of psychology came from the needs and pleasures of the consumer economy of the 1960s and 1970s. These self psychologies can be viewed as justifications and descriptions of the ideal consumer (Vitz, 1977/1994; Cushman, 1990; *see* Consumerism).

The single-minded glorification of the self is a kind of psychological self-worship and is at direct cross-purposes with the Christian injunction to lose the self. Certainly Jesus Christ neither lived nor advocated a life that would qualify as self-actualized. For the Christian, the self is the problem, not the potential paradise. Understanding this problem involves an awareness of sin, especially that of pride. Correcting this condition requires the practice of such unself-actualized states as contrition, humility, obedience, and trust in God—attitudes either neglected or explicitly despised by self theorists.

One of the first psychologists to identify the way in which such psychology with its emphasis on self-acceptance underminded the idea of both sin and personal responsibility was Mowrer (1961). The problem remained neglected until its analysis by Adams (1970) and Menninger (1974), both of whom noted the social and psychological benefits that follow from taking responsibility for one's actions, especially one's sinful behavior that has hurt others.

Myers (1980) has collected much evidence from social psychology and cognitive psychology demonstrating that the self is intrinsically biased in its own favor, thus documenting the natural human tendency to pride. He cites studies that show the following: people are much more likely to accept responsibility for success than for failure. If I win, I take the credit, but if I lose, then it was bad luck or someone else's fault; most people judge themselves as above average on most self-ratings; people have a natural but unrealistic tendency to think their own judgment and beliefs are especially accurate; and people tend to overestimate how morally they would act as compared with how they do act. For example, many more people say that they would help a stranger in need than actually do so when an opportunity arises. Such studies led Myers to conclude that low self-esteem is not the great problem it is often claimed to be.

Bergin (1980) has summarized the many value differences between a theistic and a humanistic or self-theory approach to psychotherapy. For example, humility and obedience are theistic virtues, while autonomy and rejection of obedience are humanistic virtues. Love, affection, and self-transcendence are primary for believers, while personal needs and self-satisfaction are primary in secular self theory. Commitment to marriage, emphasis on procreation and family life are theistic; open marriage or emphasis on recreational sex without long-term responsibility are humanistic. Forgiveness of others is theistic, whereas self-acceptance and expression of accusatory feelings are humanistic. Bergin's comparisons clearly show how self-oriented humanistic psychology has functioned as an alternative to religious values. Other important treatments of the religious aspects of psychotherapy are the criticisms of Bobgan and Bobgan (1979).

Yet another analysis of how self psychology functions as religion has been presented by Kilpatrick (1983), who focused on the way in which the psychological categories of self psychology replace religious categories. Slowly and subtly God disappears from our thoughts and concerns, and preoccupation with the self comes to dominate. This self-preoccupation has several pathological consequences, especially destructive ones being the growth of subjectivism (see Frankl, 1967) and the loss of contact with reality. A person quickly begins to perceive others only or primarily in terms of his or her own self-needs. This leads to serious misperceptions of others as well as to an inability to view oneself objectively. Our narcissistic desire for self-esteem gets in the way of objective self-awareness. Kilpatrick also points out how close self psychology is to such American traditions as the self-made man. In spite of its opposition to tradition, self psychology is an example of one of America's oldest social attitudes (see Bellah et al., 1985).

The overriding religious character of much of psychology is its tendency to replace God with the self. Intrinsic human pride and narcissism have found one of their more effective expressions in modern psychology, a discipline that substitutes for the ancient, exotic worship of the golden calf today's psychological worship of the golden self.

References

Adams, J. (1970). *Competent to counsel*. Philadelphia: Presbyterian & Reformed.

Adler, A. (1924). *The practice and theory of individual psychology*. New York: Harcourt, Brace.

Becker, E. (1975). *Escape from evil*. New York: Free Press.

Bellah, R. N., Madsen, R., Sullivan, W. M., Swidler, A., & Tipton, S. M. (1985). *Habits of the heart: Individualism and commitment in American life*. New York: Harper & Row.

Bergin, A. E. (1980). Psychotherapy and religious values. *Journal of Consulting and Clinical Psychology, 48*, 95–105.

Berne, E. (1964). *Games people play*. New York: Grove.

Bobgan, M., & Bobgan, D. (1979). *The psychological way/the spiritual way*. Minneapolis: Bethany Fellowship.

Browning, D. (1987). *Religious thought and the modern psychologies*. Philadelphia: Fortress.

Cushman, P. (1990). Why the self is empty: Toward a historically situated psychology. *American Psychologist, 45*, 599–611.

Frankl, V. (1967). *Existential psychology*. New York: Washington Square Press.

Frederick, C. (1974). *Est: Playing the game the new way*. New York: Delacorte.

Freud, S. (1959). Postscript to the question of lay analysis. In J. Strachey (Ed. & Trans.), *The standard edition of the complete psychological works of Sigmund Freud* (Vol. 20). London: Hogarth. (Original work published 1927)

Fromm, E. (1947). *Man for himself*. New York: Rinehart.

Fromm, E. (1963). *The dogma of Christ*. New York: Holt, Rinehart, & Winston.

Fromm, E. (1966). *You shall be as gods*. New York: Holt, Rinehart, & Winston.

Goldstein, K. (1939). *The organism*. New York: American Book.

Harris, T. A. (1967). *I'm ok—You're ok*. New York: Avon.

Hostie, R. (1957). *Religion and the psychology of Jung*. New York: Sheed & Ward.

Jacobi, J. (1973). *The psychology of C. G. Jung* (8th ed.). New Haven, CT: Yale University Press.

Jung, C. G. (1933). *Modern man in search of a soul*. New York: Harcourt, Brace.

Jung, C. G. (1954). *Answer to Job*. Cleveland: World.

Kilpatrick, W. K. (1983). *Psychological seduction*. Nashville: Nelson.

Klein, D. B. (1981). *Jewish origins of the psychoanalytic movement*. New York: Praeger.

Lasch, C. (1978). *The culture of narcissism*. New York: Norton.

Maslow, A. H. (1970). *Toward a psychology of being* (2nd ed.). New York: Harper & Row.

May, R. (1953). *Man's search for himself*. New York: Norton.

Menninger, K. (1974). *Whatever happened to sin?* New York: Hawthorn.

Mowrer, O. H. (1961). *The crisis in psychiatry and religion*. Princeton, NJ: Van Nostrand.

Myers, D. G. (1980). *The inflated self*. New York: Seabury.

Ostow, M. (Ed.). (1982). *Judaism and psychoanalysis*. New York: KTAV.

Perls, F. S. (1969). *Gestalt therapy verbatim*. Lafayette, CA: Real People Press.

Rieff, P. (1966). *The triumph of the therapeutic*. New York: Harper & Row.

Roazen, P. (1975). *Freud and his followers*. New York: Knopf.

Rogers, C. R. (1951). *Client-centered therapy*. Boston: Houghton Mifflin.

Rogers, C. R. (1961). *On becoming a person*. Boston: Houghton Mifflin.

Sartre, J.-P. (1947). *Existentialism*. New York: Philosophical Library.

Sartre, J.-P. (1957). *Existentialism and human emotions*. New York: Philosophical Library.

Schultz, W. (1979). *Profound simplicity*. New York: Bantam.

Vitz, P. C. (1994). *Psychology as religion: The cult of self worship*. Grand Rapids, MI: Eerdmans. (Original work published 1977)

Vitz, P. C. (1988). *Sigmund Freud's Christian unconscious*. New York: Guilford.

P. C. VITZ

Psychology of Religion. The study of religion by psychologists. This tautological definition distinguishes the psychology of religion from such concerns as religious psychology (*see* Christian Psychology) and psychology as religion. The psychology of religion refers to the psychological study of religious issues, just as there might be the psychological study of social or family or developmental issues. Therefore, the psychology of religion involves efforts to understand and predict the thoughts, words, feelings, and actions of individuals when they are acting religiously. A reasonably well-accepted definition of acting religiously is that offered by James (1902/1961) in his Gifford lectures: "Whatever men do in relation to that which they consider to be divine" (p. 42).

Historical Developments. The psychology of religion was a topic of major interest for psychologists at the turn of the twentieth century. After the first two decades of the century, however, religion became a taboo topic and was not revived as a legitimate area for investigation until the 1960s. The reasons for this demise and rebirth of interest are varied.

The Early Period: 1880–1920. Although the psychology of religion movement was given its major impetus by the publication in 1902 of James's classic *The Varieties of Religious Experience*, the last decade of the nineteenth century had seen not only the first published study of conversion (Leuba, 1896) but also the first textbook (Starbuck, 1899). The concern with conversion was to be a dominant theme for study. James, more a theoretician than an empirical researcher, depended heavily on Starbuck's surveys for material in *The Varieties of Religious Experience*.

The stability of the psychology of religion movement was due in no small part to the leadership of G. Stanley Hall. He had initially trained for the ministry but shifted to philosophy and psychology. His interest in religious issues remained strong, however, and as early as the 1880s he lectured to educators in Boston on the moral and religious training of children and adolescents. Although he is chiefly remembered for the encouragement and support he gave to others, Hall wrote *Adolescence* (1904) and *Jesus, the Christ, in the Light of Psychology* (1917). Both dealt with the motivations and psychodynamic rationale for religious conversion, a phenomenon thought to be characteristic of the teenage years.

Hall taught at, and subsequently became president of, Clark University. Here he gathered a group of students who engaged vigorously in a program of research in the psychology of religion. Out of this Clark school came many of the studies that made the psychology of religion a highly respected part of American psychology during the first two decades of the twentieth century. That Hall became the first president of the American Psychological Association no doubt added to the legitimacy the movement acquired. Both the *American Journal of Psychology* and the *Psychological Bulletin* printed many articles on the psychology of religion, and beginning in 1904 the *Bulletin* carried an annual review of the literature in the field. One of Hall's most important contributions, however, was the establishment of a journal devoted to the psychology of religion, the *American Journal of Religious Psychology and Education*. It continued periodic publication under the title *Journal of Religious Psychology* until 1915. Perhaps the irregular appearance of the journal plus its demise were omens of a declining interest as early as the second decade of the century.

Among the students of Hall, Leuba was the most prolific. As contrasted with Starbuck, who offered no rationale for religion beyond the storm and stress of the adolescent quest for meaning and identity, Leuba offered a physiological reductionistic alternative. He followed Sigmund Freud and others in explaining away the validity of supernatural objects of worship (i.e., gods) and suggested they are only physiological epiphenomena.

The tenor of much of this study was strictly positivistic in that it explicitly saw itself as engaged in applying scientific rigor to "the most complex, the most inaccessible and, of all, the most sacred domain—that of religion" (Starbuck, 1899, p. 1). However, the majority of the researchers were not antagonistic toward religion and, on the contrary, were concerned to contribute to the progress of religion. It was this applied concern that some have thought was partially instrumental in the loss of respect that the field was later to have in the wider psychological community.

The middle period: 1920–1960. There is little doubt that the 1920s saw a rapid demise of interest in the field. The annual reviews of the field in the *Psychological Bulletin* were not published between 1928 and 1932. They ceased altogether after a single review in 1933. This decline persisted until the 1960s, during which the Society for the Scientific Study of Religion (SSSB) and the Christian Association for Psychological Studies (CAPS) were founded. Also the Catholic Psychological Association began meeting along with the American Psychological Association, an event that eventually led to the establishment of a division for the psychology of religion in the national association in the mid-1970s.

The reasons for this hiatus of interest in the psychology of religion include concern over an overly close alliance with theology and philosophy and with the goals of religious institutions; the lack of an integrating theory around which to gather facts; the overuse of the questionnaire as a method of data collection; the rise of a behavioristic, positivistic world view that led to an avoidance of subjective introspection; the emphasis on psychoanalytic interpretations, which came to supersede empirical approaches; the lack of an impact on general psychology. Although the psychology of religion had defined itself as empirical and positivistic, subsequent advances in social psychology, for

example, did not incorporate interest in religion; thus the field became neglected in much of mainline psychology. Many of the issues of the psychology of religion were taken over by religious-education and pastoral-counseling movements, both of which began in the late 1920s.

One of the major influences on this change of interest may have been the lack of belief in the importance of religion by psychologists. In contrast to sociologists, who would understand religion to be one of the major institutions of society and a necessary field of study, many psychologists have been heavily influenced by scientism and consider religion to be a vestige of premodern times that is unhealthful and will be outgrown with the passing of the years. Therefore, those who study religion or are religious have been discounted by many general psychologists.

The Current Period: 1960–present. The contemporary revival of interest in the psychology of religion was due in no small part to a revival of interest in religion in the culture at large. The 1950s were the time of a religious revival in the United States. The first modern text in the field, Clark's *The Psychology of Religion: An Introduction to Religious Experience and Behavior* (1958), by its very title attests to a theme that has continued to occupy the interests of psychologists to the present; namely, the experience of being religious.

Scholarly journals with a special focus on the social scientific study of religion began to flourish early during this period. For example, the Society for the Study of Religion has published a journal since 1961 *(Journal for the Scientific Study of Religion)*, while the Religious Research Association has published its journal *(Review of Religious Research)* since 1959. Though neither journal focuses exclusively on the psychology of religion, both publish social scientific studies by psychologists. In 1991 a journal exclusively focused on the psychology of religion, the *International Journal for the Psychology of Religion*, was founded. Other journals have emphasized the psychology of religion within a particular religious tradition, sometimes emphasizing the goal of integrating the findings of psychological science with the claims of that particular tradition. Many readers of this volume may be aware of such journals as the *Journal of Psychology and Christianity* and the *Journal of Psychology and Theology*, but journals from other faith traditions also exist (e.g., *Journal of Psychology and Judaism*).

Functional and Substantive Approaches to Religion. Psychological studies of religion have historically approached religion from either a functional or substantive perspective. This distinction resembles somewhat the contrast made by James between roots and fruits. The functional approach to religion emphasizes the roots, or motivations, for religious behavior, while the substantive approach emphasizes the fruits, or the overt expressions, of such motivations. For example, Freud

(1928) dealt entirely with the way religion served to assuage the neurotic individual's longing for a protective father figure (a functional approach), while Starbuck (1899) focused on the age and occasion of conversion (a substantive approach).

The Functional Approach. Among the many broad traditions that have emphasized a functional approach to the study of religious experience, Hood, Spilka, Hunsberger, and Gorsuch (1996) maintain that two traditions seem to particularly emphasize strictly psychological motivations: the defensive/protective tradition and the growth/realization tradition. The defensive/protective tradition suggests that religion helps alleviate the many shortcomings, weaknesses, and deficiencies of being human such as when it helps an individual face a fear or handle anxiety under conditions where he or she may be unable to control a situation or fails to make sense out of what is happening. The growth/realization tradition, which has received less attention by psychologists of religion, emphasizes the self-enhancement benefits of religion, often drawing upon the tenets of creativity, growth, and progress stressed by humanistic and phenomenological psychologies.

The Substantive Approach. The substantive approach suggests that what a person believes (not just that a person believes) is important, and therefore research must emphasize the belief, doctrine, and practice of religion. This can be analyzed on both an individual (one's unique set of beliefs and awareness of the sacred) and social (assent to formal creeds, church rituals, church polity on social issues) level. Empirical research within this approach considers not only the substance of religion itself but also the fruits of that substance. The extent to which being religious results in greater (or lesser) mental health and personality integration would be an example of the type of question of interest to the researcher investigating religion's substance.

Major Content Areas. Research in the psychology of religion has characteristically focused on a limited number of content areas. What has resulted is a number of discrete topics within single theory of religious experience emerging. The topics discussed below, representing both functional and substantive topics, typify many of the more visible content areas.

Religious development. Psychologists have been primarily concerned with two issues regarding religious development: How does religion relate to the developmental needs of persons from childhood through old age? and How does religious experience and the content of religious beliefs change across the life span? Taking cues from Jean Piaget, Elkind (1970) proposed that the developing child's cognitive needs for conservation, representation, relations, and comprehension could be met through religion's offering of permanence in God, authority in Scripture, experience in worship, and meaning through providence. Building on contemporary humanistic psychology, Clippinger (1973) proposed

a model for personhood that includes a deep-seated religious need. Like Carl Gustav Jung's religious dynamism, this need must be met or personality is truncated and inadequately developed. Thus religion is presented as meeting an innate and instinctive urge in persons.

Change in religious belief and experience is the other developmental issue that has been frequently addressed in the literature. For example, Tamminen (1991) has conducted extensive research, both cross-sectionally and longitudinally, on the religious experience of Finnish children and adolescents. He found religious thinking and experience along a "developmental line from concrete, separate, and external to more abstract, general, and internalized. In addition, experiences in childhood were related almost exclusively to everyday situations—as was the case also with evening prayer—whereas at the age of puberty and in adolescence, they were more frequently related to congregational situations" (p. 82). Feldman's (1969) survey research on changes in religious belief and practice during the college years found, as expected, a trend toward liberalization and secularization in this age group. Fowler (1981), working within Lawrence Kohlberg's theories of moral development, has proposed a theory of faith development that involves the relating of cognitive structures, innate needs for meaning, and the interpretation of religious symbols.

Religious Orientation. As originally conceived by Allport and Ross (1967), religious orientation has been a major theme in the psychology of religion for three decades. Originally conceived by Allport to explain the relationship between religiosity and prejudice, religion that is oriented intrinsically (toward inner, personal, private meaning) and religion that is extrinsically oriented (toward fellowship, pragmatic satisfaction, external value) have been contrasted in numerous studies. While Allport and his students found intrinsically oriented religion to be more idealistic and less related to ethnic prejudice, subsequent theorists have found less clear relationships between these orientations and other behaviors.

Some researchers have noted that the concepts behind the terms *extrinsic* and especially *intrinsic* are value loaded in favor of conservative Christian theology and that the intrinsic orientation, as it is measured by Allport and Ross's religious orientation scale, is susceptible to socially desirable responses (Batson, Naifeh, & Pate, 1978). Others (e.g., Kirkpatrick & Hood, 1990) have concluded that the two orientations, especially intrinsic religion, are not as clear conceptually as might be hoped. Batson and his colleagues have proposed yet a third orientation, termed *quest,* which is "an approach that involves honestly facing existential questions in all their complexity, while at the same time resisting clear-cut, pat answers. An individual who approaches religion in this way recognizes that he or she does not know, and probably will never know, the final truth . . ." (Batson, Schoenrade, & Ventis, 1993, p. 166).

Pargament (1992) has offered a conceptual critique of the religious orientation construct by arguing that the intrinsic-extrinsic distinction is an artificial one; religiously mature people combine both functions in an integrated way such that they both live their religion intrinsically while still enjoying both personal and social benefits from their religion. Though psychologists of religion increasingly question its usefulness, religious orientation continues to be a dominant concept in empirical research.

Religion and Mental health. A major factor that renewed interest in the psychology of religion during the 1960s was the developing research agendas on mental health, with religion being a variable of potential significance (*see* Religious Health and Pathology). This was one of the concerns initiated by Freud's writings. The relationship between religion and mental health never fully disappeared even though much academic study of the psychology of religion did. Numerous writers in the field, beginning with Pfister and Anton Theophilus Boisen and continuing into the contemporary era with Erich Fromm, Menninger, and Albert Ellis, have kept these issues alive.

After reviewing three decades of research, Gartner, Larson and Allen (1991) concluded that the relationship between religion and mental health is complex. They found that religion often appears to be good for one's mental health, especially if the mental health index is behaviorally measured. That is, religion is positively associated with such measures of mental health as lower levels of drug and alcohol use, mortality, divorce, suicide, delinquency, and depression and higher levels of a general sense of well-being, marital satisfaction, and physical health. Religion is less likely to be positively associated with mental health if the mental health measure involves theoretical constructs, such as paper-and-pencil measures of personality characteristics. That is, religion appears also to be associated with such pathological tendencies as dogmatism, rigidity, authoritarianism, suggestibility and dependence, and lower levels of self-actualization. Finally, Gartner, Larson, and Allen found an ambiguous or complex relationship between religion and such mental health indicators as anxiety, sexual disorders, psychosis, prejudice, self-esteem, and intelligence/education.

Religious Dimensions. Since the 1960s increasing attention has been paid to describing the several dimensions of religiousness. This line of research has attempted to develop taxonomies of how religious persons differ from one another. While it has been obvious that there are variations in beliefs among religious persons (e.g., fundamentalist, conservative, mainline, liberal), it has been less apparent that religious persons differ in religious knowledge, the importance of religion, openness to doubt, and participation. In a study involving a national sample, King and Hunt (1975) isolated a number of dimensions, including belief, devotional practices, church attendance, church activity, financial support, religious knowledge, rated importance of religion, intrinsic/extrinsic orientation, and attitude toward despair. Currently attempts are being made to see if this pattern can be replicated among racial and ethnic groups, since the original research was conducted among whites.

Religion and Coping. People often use religious beliefs to help them cope with stressful life events (*see* Coping). Pargament et al. (1990) found that when experiencing significant negative life events, people use religion in a variety of ways, some potentially healthy (e.g., petitioning God for help, getting support from others, a generalized form emphasizing God as a source of strength) and some potentially unhealthy (e.g., avoiding a problem by turning it over to God, doubting God). The extent to which people use religion in helpful and harmful ways to adjust to the many demands of life appears to be a continuing interest of many psychologists of religion.

Religious Attributions. Attribution theory suggests that everyone attempts to make sense of the world, and this involves gaining knowledge of both one's self and others. In so doing, people must make causal inferences of what they observe in themselves and others. Suggesting that "causal explanation is a hallmark of religion" (p. 1), Spilka, Shaver, and Kirkpatrick (1985) contend that attribution theory provides a useful theoretical framework to study how people explain observed events through a religious meaning-belief system. During the 1990s, a number of studies have used attribution theory to study religious experience.

The Religion of Psychologists. One final aspect of research in psychology of religion should be noted; namely, studies of the religion of psychologists. This issue is important because, as Malony (1972) has pointed out, only the religious psychologist may know the appropriate questions to ask of religion in psychological research. Since research has indicated that psychologists are among the least religious of all scientists, it has become of interest to see how, if at all, this pattern is changing and what effect, if any, the religion of the psychologist has on the research that is done. Recent evidence indicates that while psychologists overall remain quite nonreligious, an increasing number of psychologists are actively religious ("Psychologists' faith in religion," 1996).

References

Allport, G. W., & Ross, J. M. (1967). Personal religious orientation and prejudice. *Journal of Personality and Social Psychology, 5,* 432–443.

Batson, C. D., Naifeh, S. J., & Pate, S. (1978). Social desirability, religious orientation, and racial prejudice. *Journal for the Scientific Study of Religion, 17,* 31–41.

Batson, C. D., Schoenrade, P., & Ventis, W. L. (1993). *Religion and the individual.* New York: Oxford University Press.

Clark, W. H. (1958). *The psychology of religion: An introduction to religious experience and behavior.* New York: Macmillan.

Clippinger, J. A. (1973). Toward a human psychology of personality. *Journal of Religion and Health, 12,* 241–258.

Elkind, D. (1970). The origins of religion in the child. *Review of Religious Research, 12,* 35–42.

Feldman, K. A. (1969). Change and stability of religious orientations during college. *Review of Religious Research, 11,* 40–60.

Fowler, J. W. (1981). *Stages of faith.* San Francisco: Harper & Row.

Freud, S. (1928), *The future of an illusion.* New York: Liveright.

Gartner, J., Larson, D. B., & Allen, G. D. (1991). Religious commitment and mental health: A review of the empirical literature. *Journal of Psychology and Theology, 19,* 6–25.

Hall, G. S. (1904). *Adolescence* (2 vols.). New York: Arno.

Hall, G. S. (1917). *Jesus, the Christ, in the light of psychology* (2 vols.). New York: Doubleday.

Hood, R. W. Jr., Spilka, B., Hunsberger, B., & Gorsuch, R. (1996). *The psychology of religion: An empirical approach* (2nd ed.). New York: Guilford.

James, W. (1961). *The varieties of religious experience.* New York: Modern Library. (Original work published 1902)

King, M. B., & Hunt, R. A. (1975). Measuring the religious variable: National replication. *Journal for the Scientific Study of Religion, 14,* 13–22.

Kirkpatrick, L. A., & Hood, R. W., Jr. (1990). Intrinsic-extrinsic orientations: Boon or bane? *Journal for the Scientific Study of Religion, 20,* 442–462.

Leuba, J. H. (1896). A study in the psychology of religious phenomena. *American Journal of Psychology, 5,* 309–385.

Malony, H. N. (1972). The psychologist-Christian. *Journal of the American Scientific Affiliation, 24,* 135–144.

Pargament, K. I. (1992). Of means and ends: Religion and the search for significance. *The International Journal for the Psychology of Religion, 2* (4), 201–229.

Pargament, K. I., Ensing, D. S., Falgout, K., Olsen, H., Reilly, B. Van Haitsma, K. & Warren, K. (1990). God help me: I. Coping efforts as predictors of the outcomes to significant negative life events. *American Journal of Community Psychology, 18,* 793–824.

Psychologists' faith in religion begins to grow. (1996, August). *APA Monitor,* 1.

Spilka, B., Shaver, P., & Kirkpatrick, L. A. (1985). A general attribution theory for the psychology of religion. *Journal for the Scientific Study of Religion, 14,* 317–330.

Starbuck, E. D. (1899). *Psychology of religion.* London: Walter Scott.

Tamminen, K. (1991). *Religious development in childhood and adolescence: An empirical study.* Helsinki: Suomalainen Tiedeakatemia.

P. C. HILL AND H. N. MALONY

See PSYCHOLOGISTS OF RELIGION; RELIGIOUS ORIENTATION; ALLPORT, GORDON WILLARD; JAMES, WILLIAM.

Psychoneuroimmunology. An interdisciplinary field of study concerned with the relationship among the immune, the nervous, and the endocrine systems. It incorporates neuroscience, immunology, psychosomatic medicine, emotions, cognition, and the psychology of behavior.

Basically, it is an effort to understand the interplay among the brain, the behavior, and the immune system. It is a recent attempt to address an old issue: the mind-body relationship. Psychoneuroimmunology (PNI) is a significant development in reframing the traditional ideas of mind and body. Though the term was coined by Ader (1981), Salk (1961) first introduced the concept when he included the immune system along with genetic, behavioral, and neurological functions in his interfactoral model of disease.

It has been hypothesized that the psychological-behavioral processes and the immunological functions mutually affect, modulate, or alter each other. For example, Maier, Watkins, and Fleshner (1994) emphasized the existence of bidirectional communication pathways between the brain and the immune system. Implications are that the behavioral-psychological processes ought to be capable of altering immune response and that some events which occur as part of the immune function ought to modulate behavior.

PNI attempts to determine the effects of cognition, emotions, attitudes, personality traits, stressors, and other psychosocial factors on the immune system. Traditionally, it was thought that the immune system is largely autonomous and unaffected by the Central Nervous System (CNS). Recently, however, psychological stress has been linked to alterations within specific immunologic functions.

A review of the research indicates that the immune system is integrated with other physiological functions and is sensitive to regulation/modulation by the brain. Eventually, the immune system stands as a potential mediator among a variety of psychophysiological effects. Ader (1983) reviewed the relation of immunoreactivity to developmental factors and to psychosocial factors. Ader found that (1) environmental stimulation during early postnatal life is capable of altering immune development, (2) stressful stimulation experienced by pregnant females can influence immunocompetence, and (3) prenatal maternal stress, plus a variety of postnatal environmental circumstances, are capable of influencing behavioral interactions between mother and young, and thus the immunologic interactions between them, thereby influencing a variety of psychobiologic outcomes or processes.

PNI is on the cutting edge of research and represents one of the new frontiers in the health sciences; yet, like any other new trend, it is controversial. It has been both praised and criticized. Skeptics question the methodologies, findings and outcomes, and applicability of the research studies in this field. Additionally, there are multiple approaches in the PNI literature, including those that attempt to address in some fashion the issue of situatedness of illness (Lyon, 1993).

PNI is an effort to integrate the different approaches to the study of the human nature and functioning rather than furthering the fragmentation of knowledge or compartmentalization of the human faculties. The advances within the field of psychoneuroimmunology affirm the marvelous design of God's creation which is manifested in the highly complex yet harmonious interplay among our various faculties. These testify to the truth that we are fearfully and wonderfully made (cf. Psalm 139).

From a Christian perspective, we can also assert that we have a spiritual dimension which transcends the activities of the brain, central nervous, endocrine, or immune systems. It is the principle which organizes our personality and integrates our various faculties. For "in Him we live and move and exist (have our being) . . ." (Acts 17:28). With our spirit and mind we are able to seek the Lord and relate to the divine Spirit. Therefore, God's good will and perfect design eventually lead us into health and harmonious living.

References

Ader, R. (1981). *Psychoneuroimmunology*. New York: Academic.

Ader, R. (1983). Developmental psychoneuroimmunology. *Developmental-Psychobiology, 16*, 251–267.

Lyon, M. L. (1993). Psychoneuroimmunology: The problem of the situatedness of illness and the conceptualization of healing. *Culture, Medicine, and Psychiatry, 17*, 77–97.

Maier, S. F., Watkins, L. R., & Fleshner, M. (1994). Psychoneuroimmunology: The interface between behavior, brain, and immunity. *American Psychologist, 49*, 1004–1017.

Salk, J. (1961). Biological basis of disease and behavior. *Perspectives in Biology and Medicine, 5*, 198–206.

N. ABI-HASHEM

See PSYCHOSOMATIC FACTORS IN HEALTH AND ILLNESS.

Psychopath. *See* ANTISOCIAL PERSONALITY DISORDER.

Psychopathology in Primitive Cultures. This discussion must begin with three caveats. First, there is no one, uniform primitive culture; primitive, or preliterate, cultures differ from one another as much as from Western society. Second, primitive is by no means to be equated with primeval or simple; primitive cultures have histories as long as those of Western societies and social structures that are often more, not less, complicated than Western ones. Third, one must beware of interpreting primitive behaviors as psychopathological merely because they differ from Western norms.

This last, particularly ethnocentric bias is especially hazardous and all too common in many psychiatric examinations of primitive behaviors; it must to some extent be laid at the feet of Sigmund Freud himself. Ackerknecht, a physician, historian, and ethnologist, has trenchantly argued against psychopathological reductionism of primitive institutionalized behaviors: "When [primitive] religion is but 'organized schizophrenia,' then there is left no room or necessity for history, anthropology, sociology, etc. God's earth was, and is, but a gigantic state hospital and pathography becomes the unique and universal science" (1971, p. 61).

Such psychopathologizing has been particularly evident in studies conceptualizing shamans, sorcerers, and witches as so many cases of mental disorder. Rosen (1968), Jackson and Jackson (1970), Hoch (1974), Hippler (1976), and others have demonstrated that witches are more likely to be socially deviant than mentally ill and that witch doctors and seers, while often exceptional individuals, usually show no more psychopathology by the standards of their culture than do their peers. In their study of the Mescalero Apache, Boyer, Klopper, Brauer, and Kawai (1964) proposed that shamans, if they are culturally deviant, are deviant in the direction of mental health. What all this points toward is a recognition of the cultural relativity of concepts such as normality and pathology. What is adjudged commonplace and adaptive in one culture may well be labeled pathological in another.

Specific Syndromes. Tseng and McDermott (1981) delineate five subtypes of culture-related specific psychiatric conditions: those given a cultural interpretation and remedy (e.g., *susto*); those resulting from specific culturally induced stressors (e.g., vodou death and *malgri*); those distinguished by well-defined psychiatric syndromes peculiar to the society (e.g., *latah*, amok); those influenced by multiple levels by cultural factors (e.g., *koro* and *windigo*, or *wiitiko*); and conditions possibly culture-related (e.g., the diffuse hysterical and depersonalization symptoms of Puerto Rican syndrome).

Susto occurs among Spanish-speaking persons in Latin America and the United States. Its symptoms of weakness, headache, diarrhea, fearfulness, anxiety, and tremulousness are precipitated by shocking or frightening experiences. The resultant syndrome is explained by the loss of one of several souls that are believed to reside in the body. Being culturally accepted, susto provides the sufferer with a valid reason to rest and recuperate and a socially ordained treatment—ritual recapture of the soul.

Malgri is a disorder manifesting anxiety and abdominal complaints found in many aboriginal Australian societies. It follows the breaking of a taboo and is believed to result from the invasion of the sufferer by the spirit he has offended. Vodou death, or thanatomania, is psychological and physical wasting away in response to the belief that the one has been victimized by malevolent magic.

Latah in Indonesia and *imu* among the Ainu of Japan are syndromes precipitated by startle reactions. The startled individual (usually a woman) may mimic the words or actions of the one who has startled her, may burst forth with obscenity and profanity, or may assume a guarded posture or strike out. Among Ainu women the most common occasion for such attacks seems to be seeing a snake. Some writers speculate that the symptoms of *latah* and *imu* serve to release otherwise repressed sensual and aggressive impulses. Amok, seen in southeastern Asia, is preceded by a period of brooding. Usually occurring in young males, it is precipitated by loss, rage, or shame and public insult. The individual seizes a dangerous weapon and indiscriminately smites all in his path until he is himself killed or apprehended. If he survives, the episode is followed by amnesia and exhaustion.

Windigo, or *wiitiko,* psychosis afflicts Ojibwa Indians in the United States and Algonquin-speaking Indians in Canada. The sufferer believes himself afflicted by the cannibalistic windigo demon. It is often precipitated by an unsuccessful hunt. Preceded by withdrawal and morbid depression, the syndrome progresses to murderous and cannibalistic behavior. This psychosis occurs in an environment of severe cold and frequent famine and in a culture where males are pushed toward independence at an early age and base their self-esteem on their ability to secure game. Tseng and McDermott (1981) interpret windigo as a pathological adjustment of the modal Ojibwa personality to severe pressures.

Koro, or impotence panic, is encountered among the Chinese. It is a state of severe anxiety brought on by the conviction that one's penis is receding into his abdomen. Masturbation is a common precipitant, and it is related to the Chinese folk belief that semen (equated with life force) lost through masturbation is not replenished, as it is in normal intercourse. Koro sufferers seem to come from households with physically or emotionally absent fathers and smothering mothers—classic aggravants of oedipal conflicts (*see* Oedipus Complex).

Interpretations. Theoretical interpretations of these and related syndromes vary widely. Many scholars view them as nothing more than cultural variations of universal disorders such as schizophrenia and hysteria. Others see them as primary psychiatric syndromes in their own right. There is even disagreement over whether many of these syndromes are truly culture-bound. Much empirical and epidemiological work remains to be done.

For many years it was believed that schizophrenia is relatively uncommon in primitive cultures. The evidence is equivocal, although it is becoming increasingly accepted that there are not significant differences in the prevalence of this psychosis in preliterate and Westernized societies. Moreover, the core symptoms are the same: hallucinations, delusions, thought disorder. Cultural factors seem to determine the content of delusions and hallucinations rather than affecting the underlying process of the disorder itself.

If certain primitive cultures appear to have indigenous syndromes, they also have their unique ways of treatment. While primitive psychopathology itself is far from elucidated, primitive psychotherapy is even less so (see Frank, 1973, and Torrey, 1972).

The investigation of preliterate psychopathology offers excellent opportunities to investigate the relationship between intrapsychic dynamics and social structure and to understand the ways in which cultural institutions function variously as stressors and coping mechanisms. It also serves as a check to facile extrapolations from Western character and psychopathology to humanity in general.

References

Ackerknecht, E. H. (1971). *Medicine and ethnology.* Baltimore: Johns Hopkins University Press.

Boyer, L. B., Klopper, B., Brauer, F., & Kawai, H. (1964). Comparisons of shamans and pseudoshamans of the Apache of the Mescalero Indian Reservation. *Journal of Projective Techniques and Personality Assessment, 28* (2), 173–180.

Frank, J. (1973). *Persuasion and healing* (Rev. ed.). Baltimore: Johns Hopkins University Press.

Hippler, A. C. (1976). Shamans, curers, and personality: Suggestions toward a theoretical model. In W. P. Lebra (Ed.), *Culture-bound syndromes, ethnopsychiatry, and alternate therapies.* Honolulu: University Press of Hawaii.

Hoch, E. C. (1974). Pir, faquir, and the psychotherapist. *Human Context, 6,* 668–677.

Jackson, S., & Jackson, J. (1970). Primitive medicine and the historiography of psychiatry. In G. Mora & J. Brand (Eds.), *Psychiatry and its history: Methodological problems in research.* Springfield, IL: Thomas.

Rosen, G. (1968). *Madness in society.* Chicago: University of Chicago Press.

Torrey, E. F. (1972). *The mind game: Witch doctors and psychiatrists.* New York: Emerson Hall.

Tseng, W., & McDermott, J. F. (1981). *Culture, mind, and therapy: An introduction to cultural psychiatry.* New York: Brunner/Mazel.

Additional Readings

Kardiner, A. (1939). *The individual and his society.* New York: Columbia University Press.

Levine, R. (1973). *Culture, behavior, and personality.* Chicago: Aldine.

E. R. WALLACE IV

See CULTURE AND PSYCHOPATHOLOGY.

Psychopharmacology. The study of the action of drugs on and the use of drugs to modify psychological functions and mental states. The two primary pharmacological actions consist of pharmacokinetic and pharmacodynamic interactions. Pharmacokinetics describes how the body handles a drug; pharmacodynamics describes how drugs affect the body.

The principal divisions of pharmacokinetics are absorption, distribution, metabolism, and excretion. The major pharmacodynamic considerations involve receptor mechanism, the dose-response curve, the therapeutic index, and the development of tolerance, dependence, and withdrawal phenomena. These principles are especially important to keep in mind when it comes to drug-drug interactions, polypharmacy, and drug-system interactions. Without an awareness of these interactions, patients can, as an example, experience toxicity on medications that at a certain dose (if they are given without other medications) would not cause such toxicity.

The primary classes of psychotropic medications include neuroleptics, mood stabilizers (antimanic agents), anxiolytics/antianxiety agents, antidepressants (ADs), hypnotics, psychostimulants, and "other" (examples in this category include off-label [not FDA-approved] but frequently used medication interventions, nonpsychotropics commonly used in psychological/psychiatric conditions, and investigational new drugs [INDs]).

Psychotropic Medication Classes. *Neuroleptics.* The common denominator underlying the efficacy of the neuroleptics (antipsychotics) is the blockade of central dopamine receptors. The principal types of antipsychotics, which are used primarily to treat thought disorders, include phenothiazines (e.g., Thorazine), thioxanthenes (e.g., Navane), dibenzoxazepines (e.g., Loxitane), butyrophenones (e.g., Haldol), dihydroindolenes (e.g., Moban), diphenylbutyrylpiperidines (e.g., Orap), and the dibenzodiazepines (e.g., Clozaril).

The two newest neuroleptics of interest to clinicians, clozapine (Clozaril) and risperidone (Risperdal), are novel, atypical neuroleptics in that they are less likely to induce parkinsonian symptoms, dystonic reactions, or tardive dyskinesia (TD). Clozaril has been demonstrated to be clinically effective in treatment-resistant patients with schizophrenia. Its use, however, has been limited by its propensity to induce agranulocytosis in 1% of patients. Risperdal is a 5-HT (serotonin)/D2 (dopamine) antagonist (SDA). It appears to have less risk of inducing agranulocytosis when compared to Clozaril. Because of their potential superior efficacy and improved side effect profile, these two agents have been increasingly used both as first-line agents and in treatment-resistant populations. Other (although not FDA-approved) uses that have been anecdotally reported to be of some value include use in agitation or aggression in mentally retarded populations, use in Tourette's disorder or tics, and ego-syntonic, severe, treatment-resistant Obsessive-Compulsive Disorder (OCD), or OCD with comorbid Axis II cluster A (odd-eccentric subtype [paranoid, schizoid, or schizotypal]).

Mood Stabilizers. This group of agents, otherwise known as antimanic or anticycling agents, consists of two approved agents: lithium and valproic acid (Depakote/Depakene). These are used primarily to treat bipolar disorder (Type I as well as Type II). Valproic acid was initially approved as an anticonvulsant and has only recently gotten formal approval (November 1995) as having an indication in bipolar disorder. Blood levels are consistently used when administering these medications to assist the clinical in assessing compliance, achieving maximum efficacy, and minimizing the likelihood of toxicity. With lithium, most prescribers prefer to have the blood plasma levels between 0.7 mEq/l (milliequivalents/liter) and 1.2 mEq/l. With valproic acid, most prescribers prefer to have the blood plasma levels between 50 and 120 g/ml (micrograms/milliliter).

A number of experimental antimanic agents are used, the most common being carbamazepine (Tegretol), which is currently approved only as an anticonvulsant. Two other agents less widely used but anecdotally reported to be of some use in some patients are the noradrenergic agent clonidine (Catapres) and the calcium channel blocker verapamil (Calan). Currently there are not enough double-blind, placebo-controlled trials using these agents in bipolar disorder to support their use other than in patients who have had clear nonresponse to all other anticycling strategies (i.e., adequate dose and adequate duration of treatment), including augmentation/potentiation strategies. The Lithium Information Center at the Dean Foundation in Madison, Wisconsin, is an excellent resource for literature and patient-oriented materials for those individuals and families battling this illness. It should also be noted that lithium is the most widely used agent in treatment-resistant recurrent unipolar major depressive episode (MDE) as a potentiating/augmentation agent. Of ongoing concern to psychopharmacologists is how to treat those who have a rapid-cycling form of bipolar disorder. Overall, however, the maintenance/prophylaxis with mood stabilizers favorably changes the longitudinal course of the illness.

Anxiolytics/Antianxiety Agents. The history of this class of agents has progressed from the use of alcohol, to the development of opiates, to the synthesis of bromides and barbituates. Because of a variety of serious side effects (high risk of dependence, lethality in overdose), the development of the benzodiazepines (BZ) was viewed as a breakthrough, and they have become widely prescribed. Although they are safer in terms of lethality in overdose, side effects, and in use with other drugs, concerns about abuse continue to be a concern. BZ receptors were identified in the brain in the late 1970s and were found to be related to gamma-aminobutyric acid (GABA), the inhibitory neurotransmitter system.

The primary BZ anxiolytics currently available include alprazolam (Xanax), chlordiazepoxide (Librium), clorazepate (Tranxene), diazepam (Valium), halazepam (Paxipam), lorazepam (Ativan), oxazepam (Serax), and prazepam (Centrax). The BZ anxiolytics are usually distinguished or differentiated by their elimination half-lives (short-acting [< 5 hours], short-to-intermediate acting [6 to12 hours], and long-acting [> 12 hours]). Side effects include behavioral disinhibition, psychomotor and cognitive impairment, and withdrawal symptoms. The rule followed by most prescribers is "lowest dose for shortest time." Most prescribers are using BZ anxiolytics only for acute, short-term situations, and even then often on a p.r.n. (as needed) basis only. The unique structure of the triazolo-BZ alprazolam

(Xanax) led it to be approved by the FDA for use in panic disorder. Since its approval for panic disorder, however, other nonapproved strategies have become more widely used because of concerns about habituation with this or any BZ anxiolytic.

A new group of non-BZ anxiolytics, known as the azapirones, has become of interest to clinicians. This group of agents, represented in the United States by buspirone (BuSpar) is not habituating, lacks sedative properties, and does not produce the cognitive and performance impairment seen with the BZ anxiolytics. In some ways it is more like an antidepressant in that its latency of onset of action is often 2 to 4 weeks. Patients used to or dependent on BZs will not likely tolerate (be willing to) a switch to buspirone. In addition, it is not useful in the treatment of panic disorder. Other European examples of azapirones include gepirone, tandospirone, and ipsapirone. Many clinicians use buspirone in situations of chronic anxiety if there has been no previous BZ use or in generalized anxiety disorder (GAD). Anecdotal reports also have cited buspirone as being useful in treatment-resistant OCD as an augmentation agent. For other anxiety disorders such as performance anxiety or simple phobia agents such as the betablockers have been reported to be useful. Propranolol (Inderal) has been most widely reported.

Antidepressants. The antidepressants (AD) can be divided into the following categories: tricyclic (TCA)/heterocyclic (HCA) agents (medications that were the first to be developed and have one, two, three, or four carbon rings in their chemical structure), select serotonin reuptake inhibitors (SSRIs; agents recently developed that selectively target the neurotransmitter serotonin [as opposed to norepinephrine or dopamine]), monoamine oxidase inhibitors (MAOIs; agents that have numerous dietary restrictions including foods, beverages, and even over-the-counter [OTC] preparations), and atypical or other agents (represented by the newer agents that are structurally dissimilar to the TCAs, SSRIs, and MAOIs but that have equal efficacy and a slightly different side effect profile).

The primary use of these agents is in unipolar major depressive episode (MDE). Similarities among all ADs revolve primarily around their efficacy and latency of onset of action. Differences among all ADs revolve primarily around their presumed mechanism of action and side effects. Since the introduction of fluoxetine (Prozac) in 1989 and the resultant flood of new, similar agents for the treatment of MDE, the use of the TCA/HCA agents has significantly diminished. These agents, except for a few instances, have fallen into relative disuse. The clear reason for this has been an improved side effect profile (less cardiotoxic, safer in overdose, less sedating, less anticholinergic).

Antidepressant Classes. *Tricyclic (TCA)/Heterocyclic (HCA).* The TCA/HCA class consists of the first-generation (oldest/earliest discovered) ADs imipramine (Tofranil) and amitripyline (Elavil) as two examples and the second-generation (next to be developed) ADs amoxapine (Loxitane), maprotiline (Ludiomil) [no longer available in the U.S.], trazodone (Desyrel), and norpramin (Desipramine). The second-generation ADs were developed in an attempt to have agents with a more favorable side effect profile. Elavil is frequently used by neurologists in pain syndromes while Tofranil, although it is less widely used as an AD, is still being used as an antipanic agent, as a treatment for enuresis (bedwetting), and in attention deficit/hyperactivity disorder (ADD/ADHD). Desyrel, because it is fairly sedating but not very anticholinergic (drying), is now very widely used as a popular hypnotic. Prescribers can use something that is not habit-forming, is not a central nervous system depressant (like all the approved hypnotics), and still offers something for sleep disturbance that rarely has any morning hangover effect. Desyrel is also being used in combination with the SSRIs when the SSRI that is given in the morning causes significant activation in the form of insomnia (*see* Sleep Disorders). Once the initial activating side effects wear off and sleep normalizes, the Desyrel can be discontinued.

Select Serotonin Reuptake Inhibitors (SSRIs). The SSRIs are represented by four agents: fluoxetine (Prozac), sertraline (Zoloft), paroxetine (Paxil), and fluvoxamine (Luvox). These four are listed in order of when they were introduced to the United States market.

Citalopram, an SSRI that is available in Europe, may become available in the United States. The SSRIs are more similar than they are different. Each of these four agents has a broad spectrum of efficacy in that they have antidepressant, antiobsessional (and possible anticompulsive), and anxiolytic efficacy. The following chart summarizes their current indications, indications that are consistent with their broad spectrum of efficacy.

Agent	Major Depressive Episode	Obsessive-Compulsive Disorder
Fluoxetine	X	X
Sertraline	X	
Paroxetine	X	(soon to be approved)
Fluvoxamine		X

The primary side effects that are usually experienced with this group of agents are headaches, gastrointestinal distress, activation (restlessness, agitation, and insomnia), and sexual dysfunction (decreased libido, delayed orgasm, or anorgasmia). These side effects are generally temporary and level off within the first week or two of treatment. The literature and clinical experience indicate that the majority of patients who get moderate to good efficacy, even in the face of unrelenting side effects, prefer to continue using the drug. Clinical experience, literature, and independent observers all point to the fact that these agents, fluoxetine in particular, do not cause patients to become suicidal and/or homicidal. Because of their broad spectrum of efficacy, a number of double-blind, placebo-controlled studies are underway to evaluate the efficacy of SSRIs in the treatment of panic disorder.

Monoamine Oxidase Inhibitors (MAOIs). There are two types of monoamine oxidase (A and B), which represent different proteins. The three MAOI's currently available in the United States are the hydrazine MAOIs phenelzine (Nardil) and isocarboxazid (Marplan) and the nonhydrazine MAOI tranylcypromine (Parnate). All three MAOIs are nonselective, irreversible MAOIs. This class of psychotropics have the most serious pharmacodynamic interactions of all the antidepressants. They potentiate the hypertensive effects of many sympathomimetic amines and tyramine. This is why patients on these agents must follow a very strict diet for products that have a high tyramine content (e.g., aged cheese, yeast products, pickled herring) and products containing caffeine or other stimulants. The diet is usually learned very quickly and patients have little problem with it.

Recently there has been an interest in the development of several selective and reversible MAOIs that have fewer complications (specifically fewer interactions with tyramine) than the currently available MAOIs. Some of the clinical trials in Europe have focused on the so-called RIMAs (reversible inhibitors of monoamine oxidase-type A), with specific emphasis on two agents, moclobemide and brofaromine. Because of a high placebo response rate, however, these agents have fallen out of favor after having received the initial interest. There were several studies showing the RIMAs to have some promise in the treatment of social phobia.

The most widely used MAOI is phenelzine (Nardil). Marplan is moving off the United States market because of lack of use. For the patients who are preferentially responsive to this MAOI there is approximately a two-year supply of the drug left, and it will likely be available on a compassionate-use basis only (personal communication with manufacturer).

MAOIs are not the first line choice for MDE because of the various dietary restrictions. Some studies suggest that atypical major depression (marked by reverse neurovegetative symptomatology [hypersomnia and hyperphagia]) may be a variant of MDE that is preferentially responsive to MAOIs.

The other use of MAOIs is in the treatment of treatment-refractory major depression. If someone has had an adequate trial of a first-line agent (defined primarily by adequate dose and adequate duration of dose), then an MAOI may be used. Given the drug-drug interactions between MAOIs and other ADs, it is important to observe a "washout" period between the discontinuation of the AD and the onset of the use of an MAOI. For most agents this is two weeks. With fluoxetine, however, the washout period is generally considered to be five weeks because of the long half-life of its metabolite norfluoxetine.

Hypnotics. There are currently five benzodiazepine hypnotics available in the United States. These are estazolam (ProSom), flurazepam (Dalmane), quazepam (Doral), temazepam (Restoril), and triazolam (Halcion).

These agents are typically used only for the relief of transient and short-term insomnia. Because they are BZs the major concern is habituation or dependence. The use of L-tryptophan is currently on hold because of its association with the development of ENS syndrome, something manufacturers are trying to work out, and that was felt to be related to a bad batch of the amino acid from an overseas manufacturer.

The hypnotic most widely used at this point is the non-BZ hypnotic zolpidem (Ambien). Another non-BZ hypnotic available in Europe is zopiclone. These agents are being used because of a lower side effect profile, specifically, not being habit-forming.

Within pharmacologic circles a current trend in treating sleep disturbance is to avoid hypnotic altogether and use the antidepressant trazodone (Desyrel) because of its sedating but not anticholinergic properties. Because it is an antidepressant, it has no habituation potential. Antihistamines such as dephenhydramine (Benadryl) may be effective over the short term and are available over the counter. Barbiturates and barbituratelike agents should rarely, if ever, be used.

Psychostimulants. These agents are typically used in the treatment of attention deficit disorder (ADD) and/or attention deficit/hyperactivity disorder (ADHD). There are currently three agents available: methylphenidate (Ritalin), pemoline (Cylert), and dextroamphetamine (Dexedrine).

Methylphenidate is both the most widely used and best studied. Insomnia and anorexia can be side effects. It is also available in a sustained-released (SR) formulation so as to have a longer effect between dosings. Dexedrine is the least widely used of the three because of its abuse potential. Growth stunting has been voiced as a concern, but the spurt in growth in adolescence is seen as something that compensates for this after psychostimulant discontinuation.

Currently there is a trend to use clonidine (Catapres) as an augmentating or potentiating agent in cases of treatment-resistant ADD/ADHD. The other uses of psychostimulants (typically Ritalin) include anecdotal reports of its effectiveness in treatment-resistant depression in the elderly and possibly in narcolepsy (a hypersomnia disorder characterized by irresistible sleep attacks and rapid onset of REM sleep).

Other. This category is reserved for examples of agents that are commonly used but are not FDA-approved at this time, investigational new drugs (INDs), and nonpsychotropics commonly used in psychological or psychiatric conditions. Examples in this category include the blockade of extrapyramidal side effects of neuroleptics with antiparkinsonian agents such as benztropine (Cogentin); the use of imipramine (Tofranil) in panic disorder, enuresis, and ADD; the use of SSRIs in the treatment of panic disorder; the use of T3 (thyroid) to augment an AD in treatment-resistant MDE; the rare use of selegilene (L-deprenyl/Eldepryl), an anticonvulsant that is an MAOI, in the treatment of depression; the anticipated release of several INDs in the treatment of major depression and psychosis/treatment-resistant schizophrenia (e.g., mirtazapine [Remeron] for depression and several novel neuroleptics such as sertindole, olanzapine [anzac], and seroquel.

New agents will continue to be developed that will improve efficacy, that will have fewer side effects, that will have a more rapid onset of action, and that will have fewer drug-drug interactions. Perhaps a biological marker will be discovered for the diagnosis of major depression so as to allow prescribers to pick the agent that is most likely to work quickly and accurately. Within their own profession and in battling psychiatry psychologists are in the process of deciding whether they should develop the knowledge and skill bases sufficient to obtain prescribing privileges. The brain, via the use of more and more sophisticated technology (CT scanning, MRI, PET scans, and SPECT), is being better viewed and understood. These advances may lead to more effective pharmacologic interventions. The whole field of psychopharmacology is expanding rapidly and is such that the Creator's work is so clear and strikingly affirms the beauty of the fact that we are "fearfully and wonderfully made" (Ps. 139:14).

D. EGLI

See BRAIN AND HUMAN BEHAVIOR.

Psychophysics. Psychophysics refers to a set of techniques used to study relationships between the physical stimuli of various types and the psychological experiences, or sensations, these stimuli produce. Two German scientists, Ernst Weber and Gustav Fechner, are credited with founding psychophysics. Both men were interested in sensory thresholds, for instance, what is the dimmest light, softest tone, or lightest touch that humans can detect. Weber, Fechner, and others who followed in their tradition assumed that humans have sharply defined sensory thresholds that divide sensing from not sensing.

In the 1840s Weber began studying difference thresholds, in essence asking what are the smallest differences in stimulus values that humans can detect. For instance, to determine difference thresholds for weight, Weber devised small discs that differed slightly in weight but were identical in size. Trained observers held a standard disc in one hand and a comparison disc in the other and had to judge whether the comparison disc was lighter, heavier, or the same as the standard disc. Observers carefully repeated this process many times with different standard and comparison discs to determine difference thresholds. Weber also studied difference thresholds for loudness and brightness. He discovered that as the magnitude of the standard stimulus is increased, the difference in magnitude between the standard and the comparison stimulus also has to be increased in order for observers to notice a difference. The ratio of the just-noticeable difference to the magnitude of the standard stimulus is constant over a large range of stimulus values (Weber's Law), and the constants are different for loudness, brightness, and perceived weight. The ratios for the different sense modalities are known as Weber fractions and can be used to predict how much stimulus change will be needed to be noticeable for different stimulus magnitudes.

In 1860 Fechner published a treatise, "Elements of Psychophysics," that formalized psychophysical methods and extended Weber's Law. His revised equation, known as Fechner's Law, states that sensation is a function of the logarithm of the stimulus magnitude multiplied by a constant. (As in Weber's Law, the constants are different for different sensory attributes.) Subsequent studies have shown that Weber's and Fechner's laws are fairly accurate except for extremely large or small stimulus values.

With time investigators began to question the assumption that humans have sharply defined sensory thresholds. Even Weber's trained observers varied in their ability to detect stimulus differences from trial to trial. Because of this variability, Weber found it necessary to run many sets of trials for each observer, defining the threshold as the midpoint of a whole range of values (called the interval of uncertainty) that could be detected on some trials but not on others. Weber believed that these fluctuations are due to random variations in testing conditions or in the observer but not in the threshold.

Those who questioned Weber's assumptions bolstered their objections with studies in which they presented the same near-threshold stimulus (for instance, a very brief soft tone or dim light) a number of times but only on randomly selected trials. (Observers were informed that the stimulus would be present on some trials but not on others.) Observers gave four types of responses. They correctly identified some stimuli (hits) and blank trials (correct rejections) but missed some stimuli (misses) and sometimes reported sensing stimuli when none were present (false alarms). Researchers also found that the percentages of hits and false alarms tended to vary together, depending upon several factors. For instance, an observer would score more hits and more false alarms if told that the stimulus would be present on 80% of the trials than if told the stimulus would be present on only 40% of the trials. Rewarding observers for hits versus penalizing them for false alarms had the same effect.

Results like these led Tanner and Swets (1954) to propose signal detection theory to account for threshold phenomena. According to this theory, threshold signals are always superimposed on a background of irrelevant noise in the brain (e.g., neural activity in the same modality that is unrelated to the stimulus) and the amount of neural activity produced either by the stimulus or by noise will vary from trial to trial. Observers presumably use a criterion (a particular level of sensory activity) to decide whether a stimulus is present. If stimulus effects plus background noise exceed this criterion, observers report the stimulus and score a hit; if the effects of stimulus plus noise fall below the criterion, observers report that no stimulus is present, thus missing the stimulus. When noise levels alone exceed the criterion, observers falsely report that a stimulus is present, and when noise falls below criterion they correctly discern that stimuli are absent.

According to the theory, observers shift their criteria, depending upon a number of variables (such as the observer's expectations, the rewards for hits, or penalties for false alarms), and this must be taken into account to correctly identify sensory thresholds. Some observers who seem less sensitive by standard psychophysical techniques might be using a more conservative criterion (to avoid false alarms) than those observers who appeared more sensitive. Signal detection techniques allow investigators to measure an observer's actual sensitivity, apart from changes in his or her criterion. (See Green and Swets, 1966, or Gescheider, 1976, for a more complete treatment of this topic.)

References

Gescheider, G. A. (1976). *Psychophysics method and theory.* Hillsdale, NJ: Erlbaum.

Green, D. M., & Swets, J. A. (1966). *Signal detection theory and psychophysics.* New York: Wiley.

Tanner, W. P., & Swets, J. A. (1954). A decision-making theory of visual detection. *Psychological Review, 61,* 401–409.

E. L. HILLSTROM

See SENSATION AND PERCEPTION.

Psychosexual Development. The psychological development of an individual is intricately involved with the development of his or her sexuality. While psychosexual development occurs throughout life, it is probably predominant in the first six years of life and has seeds in the infant's earliest human contact. One's love relationship with parents will determine future loving relationships with the opposite sex. Adequately developed sexuality will also contribute to adult achievement, success, and capacity to accept failure.

Psychoanalytic authors, depending heavily and expanding upon Sigmund Freud's ideas of infantile sexuality, dominate the literature on psychosexual development. Fenichel's (1945) remarkable summary work provides a review of the classical Freudian perspective. He begins with Freud and draws also upon Karl Abraham, Franz Alexander, Paul Federn, and Sandor Ferenczi. These authors suggest that there are various stages of psychosexual development during which certain aspects of sexuality and related psychology develop. Adequate parental love and proper adaptation lay the groundwork for good adult mental functioning, whereas inadequate adjustment during these periods is cause for fixations at one or more of these stages. Such psychosexual developmental fixations are at the root of the adult neurosis.

Freudian Developmental Stages. *Earliest Infantile Life (0–6 Weeks).* During this phase the infant has an uncomplicated psychic apparatus and responds only with excitation or relaxation. The newborn has no real ego and is driven by instinctual forces, primarily the life-sustaining drive of hunger. The infant alternates between hunger/dissatisfaction and sleep/satisfaction. Freud (1936) suggests that birth causes a flooding with excitation, called birth trauma, and the manner in which the infant copes with the first excitation determines much of his later adjustment.

This first stage of life where the infant has no real sense of anything separate from himself is called primary narcissism. In the absence of boundaries between self and others (particularly the mother) the infant conceives of himself as omnipotent and is entirely self-serving. If he is hungry, he projects his feelings of omnipotence onto the outside world and perhaps loses a sense of existence momentarily. When he is fed, he receives the omnipotence back.

While there may be some early sense of sexuality during this phase, sexual feelings are sufficiently merged with the hunger drive as to be indistinguishable. Even pleasure as such may not really exist.

Oral Stage (1 Week–18 Months). The age span in this and all other stages is approximate. However, in the first year and a half of life the primary narcissism of earliest infancy is gradually replaced by the passive-receptive activity of eating. Increasingly the infant masters his own excitation and relaxation by means of his mouth. The mouth is used both to eat and to scream as a means of getting fed. This orality is so dominant that most of the infant's activities in his first year of life are mouth-related.

Freud viewed these oral activities as also erotic. Infantile eroticism is not genital, as it is for later children and even more for adults; rather, it is a drive-related experience in which the infant seeks a reduction of libido (instinctual tension) by oral means. Some activities having infantile sexual overtones include thumb sucking, fondling of a comforter-blanket, and screaming. It appears that eating is often simultaneously a hunger-satisfying and an erotic pleasurable experience for infants.

Abraham (1927) suggests that there are two substages of orality: a preambivalent phase, in which the infant sucks and feeds for intrinsic pleasure, and the ambivalent phase, in which a sense of an external object feeding him has developed. In this second substage the infant both loves (feeds) and hates (bites) the feeding object. When the infant is feeding, he feels that he is not being fed a substance but that he is eating the mother in a kind of cannibalistic sense. This incorporation of the infant's first love object serves as the basis for later ways of relating to the world.

If one is fixated at the oral stage, whether by unknown personal factors or by inadequate parenting, he will retain in his psychological makeup evidence of orality and omnipotence. Earliest deprivations and fixations often result in schizophrenia or other psychotic disorders. Later fixations may lead to the development of a narcissistic or borderline personality disorder. Other oral fixations will show themselves in the symptoms of greed and unsatiable hunger in some form.

From a positive standpoint much adult sexuality relates to oral pleasure: kissing, sucking, and talking. However, drinking, smoking, and eating also retain a certain sexual quality in adult life, and oral deprivations in childhood are hypothesized to be involved in excesses in these areas.

Anal-Sadistic Stage (1–3 Years). The overlap of time among the stages of psychosexual development indicates that one stage begins before its precursor has elapsed. All previous stages continue to have effect on all more advanced stages. The anal-sadistic stage is roughly the terrible twos, during which time an infant struggles with limits and frequently responds with negativism.

In the oral phase of life the libidinal force of the id originates and predominates; in the second major phase of life the ego develops. With the development of the ego the toddler begins to perceive a clearer distinction between himself and his environment. Kohut (1971) suggests that a self exists originally in the infant. However, most other psychodynamicists agree with Freud that the self develops in the anal stage as a consequence of the toddler encountering boundaries. It appears that the ego begins to define itself as separate by integrating the frequent limits set by parents and other environmental influences.

Freud labeled this second and third year of life anal because it is during this time of life that the child finds pleasure of control in the sensations surrounding excretion. The sadistic part of this stage relates to what Freud and his followers suggest is the destructive tendencies of the child of this age. This destructive element can be seen in the gross motor activity and generally belligerent behavior of two-year-olds, but also more internally in the child's desire to harm his environment (usually his mother) through defecation. Abraham (1927) suggests that this sadistic-destructive element predominates in the first half of the anal stage, whereas later the child learns the pleasure of retention. Abraham sees in this second subphase the seeds of love.

Two further elements of the anal-sadistic stage are important. The first is that the infant, in feeling both destructive and pleasurable impulses, develops his first ambivalent feelings in life. Ambivalence will be a part of his psychic experience hereafter. Second, these anal-sadistic and related feelings are highly libidinally charged and serve to eroticize the infant. Again, this stage of sexuality is not genitally localized but is localized in anal functions.

Neurotic results of fixations in the anal stage include the specifically anal neuroses (constipation, colitis, hemorrhoids) and related conditions such as obsessive-compulsive neurosis, hoarding, and germophobia. Fenichel (1945) also suggests that paranoia originates here, perhaps related to the failure of the infantile environment to provide adequate and gentle control.

The positive results of this phase contribute to both specifically sexual as well as general personality development. General characteristics include the development of personal value, ability to control impulses, self-restraint, and early forms of love. Sexuality is enhanced by the infant broadening his sense of erotic pleasure beyond the area of his mouth and developing other skin-related sensations of pleasure.

Phallic Stage (3–7 Years). This stage of life begins in some form near the end of the anal phase and continues until age 6 or 7 in normal development. It is the central component in the Freudian conception of personality development, for it is here that the ego at first has free reign and later is subjected to control by the development of the third major component of the psychic apparatus: the superego.

This stage, often referred to as the genital phase, involves the localization of erotic pleasure in the genitals. Masturbation usually occurs and replaces previous sexual sublimations such as thumb sucking. In this stage the love object becomes more clearly sexual. Further, the self-love of the oral phase and the object-use of the anal now begin to be replaced by the rudiments of mutual love of self and object.

The dominant theme in boys during this time of life is what Freud called castration anxiety. The boy identifies his self with his penis, and his fear of punishment, harm, or annihilation results in the fear that he will lose his penis. Sometimes this fear is aggravated by adult comments and behavior, but largely the young boy seems to come by castration fear naturally because of his unduly high narcissistic self-evaluation.

In girls the complement to castration fear is penis envy. According to Freud, girls feel cheated, wish they were complete genitally, and envy the visible genitals of boys. This envy generalizes to wishing they were boys and can be the origin of female homosexuality.

Clearer distinctions are made between love and hate during this stage as one loves one parent more than the other. Tenderness develops as the result of striving to acquire and to admire external objects. Social feelings such as sympathy and antipathy develop, and the child begins to imitate and idealize his parents and others.

For both girls and boys the climax of infantile sexuality is the oedipus complex, the love and erotic affection for the opposite-sex parent. The complement of the love of one parent is the jealousy of the other and the death wish upon him or her. The oedipal feelings remain latent for several years and are only slowly replaced by adult sexuality. Siblings or other adult figures may substitute for absent or emotionally unavailable parents.

The genital stage is completed with the onset of the superego. In the simplest sense this psychic entity is that which says no to the instinctual demands of the id, which has had free reign in the oral and anal stages. The coming of the superego resolves and finishes the oedipus complex and ends infantile innocence. This means that the infant becomes somewhat aware that he cannot have the hetero-genital parent. Similarly he cannot have all the unlimited sexual and other things he presumably wants.

Deprivations during the genital phase of infantile sexuality are primarily parents who are emotionally unavailable for oedipal feelings. Fixations at this stage lead to hysteria in some form and to the symptoms of seductiveness, dependency, passiveness, jealousy of same-sex adults, and envy of the opposite sex. The positive results of this phase include the ability to love and experience genitally satisfying sexuality. Ideals, values, and the seeds of morality also germinate here.

Later Stages. Freud had little to say about the period of life from 6 to 12 years, which he called latency, because he felt explicit sexual development was dormant. At puberty the child reactivates old oedipal conflicts and begins to work them out in the form of early adult sexual experiences. Among others Sarnoff (1976) has suggested that latency is important in psychosexual development. He argues that the latent child experiences humiliation, confusion, and early heterosexual development. Moral development also seems centralized here, as is the related cognitive development.

Puberty, or the onset of adultlike sexual feelings and capabilities, is clearly a watershed for adequate adult psychosexual development. However, puberty is not strictly a developmental stage but rather a freeing and experimenting with previously established sexuality.

Critique and Evaluation. Although critics of Freud's theory of psychosexual development have come from both psychoanalytic and nonanalytic traditions, the most important critiques have come from the psychodynamic camp. It is said that Freud was remarkably correct in his overall analysis, given his limited access to thorough research. However, conclusions suggested by more recent research include the following: there is more overlap between the stages of infantile development; latency is a misnomer in that this period of life is actively sexual; adolescence is an additional and important stage in psychosexual development; object relationships are more central to ego development than Freud proposed; the development of the self has a separate place beyond the more basic ego functions of the ego, id, and superego; and some of Freud's basic conceptions of feminine psychology are inaccurate.

Bernstein and Warner (1981) summarize the evidence substantiating the overlap of the oral, anal, and phallic stages. Klein was perhaps the first to suggest that oedipal feelings develop in early infancy, not only in the genital stage. More recently Galenson and Roiphe (1976) have discovered that the genital stage may begin as early as 16 months, with observations of genital masturbation occurring even earlier.

Many contemporary psychoanalysts argue that the importance of object relationships in psychosexual development was deemphasized by Freud. Here again Klein (1975) was the first to propose an elaboration of the Freudian model, suggesting in 1921 that the infant first acquired object relationships with feces, then genitals, and finally the mother as he developed a capacity to love. Klein's conception has been challenged as too elaborate, but the importance of early and developing love objects in psychic development is of increasing significance to psychodynamicists.

Kohut (1971) has been the central figure in self psychology, although some of the pioneering work was done by Jacobson (1964). These theorists suggest that the ego-id-superego formulation is insufficient to comprehend the human psyche. There is, they say, a more basic and yet more comprehensive and lasting entity. The self, they argue, develops very early in infancy parallel to the rest of the psychic apparatus. It is here that one finds the real essence of identity, self-value, and eventually the capacity to love. Kohut's work represents a critique of Freud's psychosexual theory in that it suggests that Freud's failure to see the centrality of self in development marks his theory as incomplete.

Criticism of Freud's psychology of women came first from two of Freud's female students, Karen Horney and Helene Deutch. Horney (1926) described Freud's penis envy theory as an expression of male arrogance resulting from upbringing in a patriarchal society. Deutch (1944) posited that the mother did not favor the son, as Freud suggested, arguing that perhaps she favored her daughter because of easier identification.

Of major concern to these and other analysts is whether there exists a primary sex (male) and a secondary reaction to it (female), as Freud suggested, or whether each sex develops in parallel fashion. Stoller (1965) and Kleenan (1971) among others suggest the existence of a core gender identity in early infancy. Mixed gender identity is due to inadequate bonding with the mother, whereas adequate love from the mother will foster the separate but equal identities of male and female.

There is general agreement among all these writers that there is predominance of masochism, passivity, low self-esteem, and narcissism in women. When Freud found this phenomenon, he concluded it to be innate or reactionary in that the woman is incomplete. Other theorists have suggested that it might come from cultural factors or from inadequate mothering of the female infant. Few analysts would agree that the female is biologically or psychically deficient. However, a clear understanding of female psychosexual development awaits further research.

References

Abraham, K. (1927). *Selected papers of Karl Abraham*. London: L. & V. Woolf.

Bernstein, A. E., & Warner, G. M. (1981). *An introduction to contemporary psychoanalysis*. New York: Aronson.

Deutch, H. (1944). *The psychology of women* (Vol. 1). New York: Grune & Stratton.

Fenichel, O. (1945). *The psychoanalytic theory of neurosis*. New York: Norton.

Freud, S. (1936). *The problem of anxiety*. New York: Norton.

Galenson, E., & Roiphe, H. (1976). Some suggested revisions concerning early female development. *Journal of the American Psychoanalytic Association, 24,* 29–57.

Horney, K. (1926). The flight from womanhood: The masculinity-complex in women as viewed by men and by women. *International Journal of Psychoanalysis, 7,* 324–339.

Jacobson, E. (1964). *The self and the object world*. New York: International Universities Press.

Kleenan, J. (1971). The establishment of core gender identity in normal girls. *Archives of Sexual Behavior, 1,* 117–129.

Klein, M. (1975). *Love, guilt, and reparation*. New York: Delacorte.

Kohut, H. (1971). *The analysis of the self*. New York: International Universities Press.

Sarnoff, C. (1976). *Latency*. New York: Aronson.

Stoller, R. J. (1965). The sense of maleness. *Psychoanalytic Quarterly, 34,* 207–218.

R. B. JOHNSON

See SEXUALITY.

Psychosis. *See* PSYCHOTIC DISORDERS.

Psychosocial Development. This term is usually associated with the theoretical work of Erik Erikson, whose outlook was both neo-Freudian and functional. He was concerned about the content of development, rather than the how, which would be the concern of a structural theory. He put forth a plan that utilized an epigenetic depiction of human development through the life cycle. This was followed by a series of stages, one built upon the other and facilitating the next. Both positive and negative poles of an aspect of the psyche were believed to appear at an appointed time. The poles were in conflict toward ascendance. Erikson called the conflict a crisis. If the previous stage had been accomplished with the positive pole ascending above the negative, then the current stage had opportunity to engage in a normal crisis. The goal was for the positive to be superior but not to annihilate the negative.

Erikson proposed a psychosexual stage and mode, after Sigmund Freud, in parallel with the psychosocial crises. These were identified in terms of a radius of significant relations, a basic strength, and a core pathology:

This is an expansion over Freud, especially in genitality, which Erikson breaks into several stages of adulthood. Considering the entire lifespan rather than childhood and adolescence only was a major contribution to thinking about human development.

Thus persons advance through the stages as they grow older. In infancy, the psychosocial crisis involves trust. If the positive ascends, the person will become more trusting than mistrusting, and this has the potential to broaden with experience. If the negative ascends, the person will be more mistrustful than trusting. The positive outcome of the

Stage	Psycho-sexual	Psycho-social	Relations	Strength	Pathology
infancy	oral-respiratory-sensory	basic trust vs. mistrust	maternal	hope	withdrawal
early childhood	anal-urethral	autonomy vs. shame, doubt	parental	will	compulsion
play age	infantile-genital	initiative vs. guilt	basic family	purpose	inhibition
school age	"latency"	industry vs. inferiority	neighborhood school	competence	inertia
adolescence	puberty	identity vs. confusion	peer group	fidelity	repudiation
young adulthood	genitality	generativity vs. isolation	partners, friendships	love	exclusivity
adulthood	procreativity	generativity vs. stagnation	divided labor	care	rejectivity
old age	generalization of sensual modes	integrity vs. despair	"My Kind" "Human Kind"	wisdom	disdain

crisis aids in achieving a positive outcome in the next stages. A negative outcome tends to reappear in various forms through other stages until the person deals again with the crisis. This is by no means inevitable or in some cases even possible. The negative ascendancy at any stage makes normal development through other stages difficult.

The stages are to be thought of as stacks of blocks. The first stage contains one block. The second stage stack has two blocks; for example, trust and autonomy vs. shame. The final stage could be conceived as a stack of eight blocks. This is why aspects characteristic of earlier stages may reappear in some form at later stages. For example, trust, a first-stage aspect and most important at that stage, reappears in the form of faith in stage eight.

While individual differences produce broad variation in the accomplishing of the stages, one mechanism important to the process is interaction between nature and nurture; hence the *social* in psychosocial. The resolution of each stage is open rather than determined.

Another important feature of psychosocial theory has been adolescent identity crisis. Erikson claims to have coined the term during World War II. While working with patients who seemed to have lost any inner agency, he realized that often adolescents sense similar loss because they are in inner conflict with society and with themselves. The condition of the soldiers was called loss of ego identity; that of adolescents was called identity crisis. His theory sees this as a normative crisis consistent with the bipolar aspects of his stage theory. Erikson's theory in general and the adolescent and expanded adult stages in particular have helped produce useful research.

Erikson's psychosocial development is limited to Western societies. However, it contributes to seeing psychological development broadly from birth to old age. It is a definite departure from pure Freudianism, which Erikson believed placed too much emphasis on sexuality.

Additional Readings

Erikson, E. H. (1968). *Identity: Youth and crisis.* New York: Norton.
Erikson, E. H. (1982). *The life cycle completed: A review.* New York: Norton.

E. S. GIBBS

See LIFE SPAN DEVELOPMENT.

Psychosomatic Factors in Health and Illness.

"If you listen carefully to the voice of the LORD your God and do what is right in his eyes, if you pay attention to his commands and keep all his decrees, I will not bring on you any of the diseases I brought on the Egyptians, for I am the LORD, who heals you" (Exod. 15:26, NIV).

Historical Development. The relationship between mind and body, the psychosomatic relationship, has been revealed to believers for thousands of years. In general, faithful obedience to God's Word is blessed with good health while disobedience is cursed with sickness (Deut. 6:1–12; Prov. 3:7–8). At times God may allow poor health to continue (2 Cor. 12:7–10) or may cure by miraculous healing (John 9:1–12). These exceptions discussed in Scripture are usually allowed for the benefit of the believer or as a means of manifesting God's glory to unbelievers.

The Bible even reveals effects of specific emotions. For example, envy is unhealthy (Prov. 14:30), while an optimistic, merry outlook is linked with good health (Prov. 17:22). David laments that his sinfulness has resulted in God's wrath. David's depressed affect is paired with physical complaints, including feelings of heaviness, skin problems, wounds that do not heal quickly, inflammation, and lack of energy (Ps. 38:1–14).

More recently, in 1897 Sir William Osler described an association between aggressive behavior and coronary heart disease (Weiss, 1987). In the 1930s Franz Alexander hypothesized a specific personality pattern that could cause identifiable organ disease. By 1947 Helen Flanders Dunbar's publication of *Mind and Body: Psychosomatic Medicine* had clearly established the term *psychosomatic* in health care and research. Psychosomatic medicine investigates and treats the influence of psychological factors (e.g., stress, anger) on physiological processes relevant to physical disease. For psychologists, psychosomatic medicine is a subset of health psychology, a phrase that refers to the application of psychological principles or procedures to health issues (i.e., health promotion endeavors as well as disease-related studies).

Psychosomatic research moved from considerations of specific hypothesized personality patterns and disease states to the concept of stress as elucidated by Selye (1956) in the 1950s (*see* Selye, Hans). Stress is defined as a generalized physiological response (e.g., increased plasma cortisol, increased heart rate) that is nonspecific both in terms of causal stimuli (i.e., not a simple phobia) and effects (i.e., several body systems change). Selye discussed the positive effects of stress (e.g., increased mental focusing) but focused on its potential for production of disease. His General Adaptation Syndrome (GAS) conceptualized three stages of adjustment to physical or psychological stressors: alarm, resistance, and exhaustion levels. Exhaustion is associated with excess levels of catecholamines and cortisol, which are hypothesized to lead eventually to organ damage. Friedman, Rosenman, and Rosenman (1959) were the first to systematically assess and link a stressful behavioral syndrome, Type A Behavior Pattern, to statistically excessive coronary heart disease. Type A Behavior Pattern is characterized by such characteristics as verbal aggressiveness, internalized anger, restlessness, and facial tenseness.

Specific Medical Areas. The following summarizes specific associations found between psychological factors and physical health/illness found experimentally in recent years (cf. McDaniel, Moran, Levenson, & Stoudemire, 1994; Snyder, 1989).

Cancer. Depressed affect has frequently been associated with the onset and progression of cancer in some studies but not others. Likewise, a cooperative, unassertive, and repressive coping style (Type C Behavior Pattern) has been inconsistently related to cancer etiology. Psychosocial interventions with breast cancer and malignant melanoma patients have been successful. These treatments focus on relaxation training, interpersonal support, and stress/pain control. No systematic research has focused on the potential role of Christian faith in intervention strategies. Treated patients have less mood disturbance, higher vigor, longer life, and better immunological function than controls. Even if stress or personality factors play only a small part in the cause of cancers, psychological interventions seem clearly helpful in terms of improving the quality of life for many cancer patients and, perhaps, the quantity. Improvements in immunological parameters are generally thought to be the primary mechanisms for these positive effects.

Immunology. Acute and chronic stress have clearly affected immunological parameters, although the clinical significance is not always clear. Short-term stressors (e.g., hand in ice water) generally increase peripheral circulation of natural killer cells and T-cytotoxic/suppressor cells. These cells destroy pathogens. These cells are also involved in the action of B_2-adrenoceptors, which influence peripheral (i.e., arm, feet) vasoconstriction. Long-term work/caregiving stress, divorce, and depression have generally been associated with decreased immunological function both in terms of number of cells as well as functional ability of existing cells. In most studies macrophage activity, white blood cell count, antibody responses to antigen, T-cell responses to viruses, natural killer cell activity, and other parameters are suppressed with chronic stress and depression. Stress and depression are both associated with increased cortisol, which inhibits immune functions. Clinically stress and depression have been associated with increased frequency of infections. Psychosocial intervention (e.g., imagery techniques, support groups) appear promising but not well established.

Endocrinology. Speculation concerning the onset of diabetes mellitus and stress has existed since the seventeenth century but never has been demonstrated experimentally. Stress does more clearly negatively affect glucose control in diabetic patients. Stress management training has been helpful and allows more stable insulin usage, particularly in more severe or brittle diabetics. Grave's disease and Cushing's disease have also been thought to have psychosomatic aspects, but clear data supporting these hypotheses are lacking. No experimental research has investigated the role of religious factors in the etiology or psychosocial treatment of endocrinological problems.

Cardiology. The extensive research into the Type A Behavior Pattern in the late 1950s and 1960s was the forerunner of sophisticated psychosomatic experimental research. By far the majority of psychosomatic research to date has focused on cardiovascular disease or cardiovascular disease risk factors. Type A Behavior Pattern has now been examined and only certain elements appear predictive of cardiovascular disease such as myocardial infarction. Behavioral factors such as high levels of cardiovascular reactivity to stress, cynical anger, depression, and social isolation have been positively correlated with specific cardiovascular disease. For example, hypertension has particularly been related to inhibited anger expression, excessive anger expression, and stress reactivity. Myocardial infarction has been related to cynical anger, aggressive responding, depression, and lack of social support. Stress management, biofeedback training, and relaxation training have all been helpful in individual and group therapy formats. Counseling usually involves identification of coronary-prone behaviors, relaxation training, cognitive relabeling, and behavioral rehearsal. Anecdotal results indicate that discussion of life or religious values in counseling may be especially helpful, but experimental research backing this claim is lacking. Religious factors have been statistically related to the development of cardiovascular disorders.

Pulmonary. Early psychoanalytic notions concerning specific personality conflicts and asthma have lacked any research backing. Support does exist for the role of psychological factors in a multifactorial model of asthma in individuals constitutionally and genetically predisposed to asthma. Extreme inhibition and dependency seem associated with asthma. Psychosocial interventions are promising but are not firmly established. Further, psychosocial interventions have been helpful in alleviating the anxiety, depression, and family problems that often accompany chronic obstructive pulmonary disease as well as other chronic diseases (*see* Chronic Illness).

Gastroenterology. Peptic ulcer disease and irritable bowel syndrome have been related to anxiety, defensive coping styles, depression, and self-perceived significant stress. Duodenal ulcer has been clearly associated with a bacteria, *Helicobacter pylori*, for which no clear psychosomatic relationship has yet been established. Some research has suggested that irritable bowel syndrome clinic patients are significantly different (e.g., more anxious) from outpatients seen infrequently by physicians. Some psychosocial interventions related to assertion training or stress management skills have received some research support for their efficacy but have not been widely adopted in clinical practice. In addition, muscle biofeedback procedures have demonstrated an excellent ability to improve functional bowel and incontinence problems in community patients but have been employed clinically in only a limited fashion.

Dermatology. The well-known association of the normal range of emotions to flushing and sweating strongly point to potential psychosomatic relationships in dermatology. Dry skin (psoriasis) has been related to interpersonal anxiety and depressed affect. Dermatitis correlates positively with family stress. Several studies have related acne to poor self-efficacy and depressed affect. Psychosocial intervention research is limited or nonexistent for some conditions (e.g., rosacea).

Rheumatology. Rheumatoid arthritis had been considered a psychosomatic disease, although this viewpoint has largely been disproved. The depressed affect associated with arthritis and fibromyalgia syndrome seems more a function of chronic, disabling pain than personality factors of any etiological significance. Coping style research in this area as well as the role of psychological variables in various types of arthritis is lacking.

Other Problem Areas. Depression frequently occurs with end-stage renal disease and pain. Psychosocial interventions have been helpful in improving affect as well as compliance to medical procedures. Work has also been conducted in other areas (e.g., medication compliance training, pain management, smoking cessation) that cannot be reviewed in this space but are discussed by others (Snyder, 1989).

Religious Factors. High church attendance and high importance of religious variables have generally been associated with improved health. For example, Larson et al. (1989) found that committed believers had significantly lower diastolic blood pressure than others even after adjusting for age, socioeconomic status, smoking, and weight and height. Oxman, Freeman, and Manheimen (1995) declared that patients who received no religious strength or comfort were more than three times more likely to die within six months after open-heart surgery than were patients who reported receiving this strength and comfort.

The precise mechanisms by which religious factors may influence psychosomatic factors remains largely unexplored. King and Funkenstein (1957) reported that college students whose parents attended church regularly had a blood pressure/heart rate acute psychological stress reaction linked to expressing anger outwardly. Those subjects with infrequently attending parents had a pattern that reflected inwardly directed anger or anxiety (i.e., a coronary-prone personality).

Neumann and Chi (1995) reported preliminary data comparing subjects who rated their values as similar or dissimilar to their father's . Further, subjects also rated fathers' church attendance as frequent or infrequent. Differences at rest and in response to stress were found in several factors that influence cardiovascular health or reflect risk such as levels of heart rate, facial muscle levels, plasma protein, plasma cortisol, high density lipoprotein, nonesterified fatty acids, T-cell subsets/total percents, and natural killer cell percents. Generally "father similar" and "father frequently attend" groups had healthier stress response patterns to

the psychological stressor. Further, the "father attend frequently" and "father similar" group tended to be more active, less likely to smoke, less cynical, more forgiving, less generally angry, less anxious, and more task-oriented than the others.

Much remains to be investigated in the area of psychosomatic factors in health and illness. Some specific disease states have only loosely been related to psychological factors. Specific mechanisms for the effects are largely unexplored. The effects of specific religious factors on stress coping and psychosomatic health/illness remain to be elucidated by interested believers. God's Word has clearly suggested that mining this area will provide a God-honoring ore for his glory.

References

Friedman, M., Rosenman, L., & Rosenman, R. H. (1959). Association of specific overt behavior with blood and cardiovascular findings. *Journal of the American Medical Association, 169*, 1286–1269.

King, S. H., & Funkenstein, D. H. (1957). Religious practice and cardiovascular reactions during stress. *Journal of Abnormal and Social Psychology, 55*, 135–137.

Larson, D. B., Koenig, H. G., Kaplan, B. H., Greenberg, R. S., Logue, E., & Tyroler, H. A. (1989). The impact of religion on men's blood pressure. *Journal of Religion and Health, 28*, 265–278.

McDaniel, J. S., Moran, M. G., Levenson, J. L., & Stoudemire, A. (1994). Psychological factors affecting medical conditions. In Hales, Yodofsky, Talbot (Eds.), *Textbook of psychiatry.* Washington, DC: American Psychiatric Press.

Oxman, T. E., Freeman, D. H., & Manheimer, E. D. (1995). Lack of social participation or religious strength and comfort as risk factors for death after cardiac surgery in the elderly. *Psychosomatic Medicine, 57*, 5–15.

Neumann, J. K., & Chi, D. S. (1995, March 31). Physiological stress response and psychological differences as a function of parental value similarity and church attendance. Presented at Psychiatry Grand Rounds, James H. Quillen College of Medicine, Johnson City, TN.

Selye, H. (1956). *The stress of life.* New York: McGraw-Hill.

Snyder, J. J. (1989). *Health psychology and behavioral medicine.* Englewood Cliffs, NJ: Prentice-Hall.

J. K. NEUMANN

See RELAXATION TRAINING.

Psychosurgery. According to Valenstein (1986), psychosurgery involves the destruction of healthy brain tissue in order to alleviate severe and debilitating psychiatric disorders. This differs from neurosurgery, which is the removal of neural tissue known to be damaged or malfunctioning. Psychosurgery practitioners assume that by disrupting neural circuits or processing centers maladaptive behavior and thought patterns can be modified.

There is archaeological evidence from as early as 2000 B.C. of trepanning (i.e., drilling holes through the skull) in an effort to release evil spirits. However, the widespread use of psychosurgery on psychiatric patients did not begin until the mid-1930s. Valenstein has argued that psychosurgery must be understood within the broader context of somatic therapies to treat psychiatric illnesses. The somatic treatments and their proposed mechanisms varied tremendously. Injections of insulin to induce shock were used to treat schizophrenia. Hydrotherapy consisted of spraying or soaking patients. It was in this therapeutic climate that Portuguese neurologist Egas Moniz observed the calming effect of lesions of the frontal lobes in a chimpanzee. With neurosurgeon Almeida Lima he performed the first prefrontal lobotomy (or leucotomy) in 1935. The connecting fibers between frontal lobes and thalamus were severed. Walter Freeman, an American physician, later developed the transorbital lobotomy technique, in which access to the fibers in the frontal lobes was through the orbital plate of the eye. Because this technique could be used in an outpatient setting it precluded the need for a neurosurgeon, thus enabling Freeman to carry out many more operations.

Moniz and Freeman advocated the use of prefrontal lobotomies for patients with schizophrenia, depression, obsessive-compulsive disorders, anxiety, and phobias. Although they claimed a considerable success rate, more controlled studies later called into question the effectiveness of this treatment. Negative side effects were increasingly viewed as a liability.

The number of psychosurgeries declined after the introduction of antipsychotic drugs in the mid-1950s. These drugs provided an alternative for managing patients in psychiatric wards, even enabling some to function outside the wards. However, some patients failed to respond, and so psychosurgery continued. Psychosurgical procedures changed with the development of better neurosurgical equipment. In particular the stereotaxic device allowed for precise localization and destruction of deep brain structures. In the older, prefrontal lobotomy technique neural fibers running from the frontal lobes back to the thalamus were crudely sectioned. Often these blind procedures resulted in damage to adjacent tissue. With the stereotaxic device precise, localized lesions were possible using electrical or radio frequency stimulation. Operations currently are performed on more than a dozen targets in the frontal lobes, cingulum, amygadala, thalamus, and hypothalamus. A new term, *psychiatric surgery*, was coined partly as an attempt to dissociate the newer practices from the earlier, cruder methods. In addition, who receives the operations has also changed. Psychosurgeries are no longer used to treat schizophrenia and neuroses. The new, more localized procedures have been employed to treat rage disorders, phobias, obsessive-compulsive disorders, and severe depression and to relieve intense, intractable pain.

It was believed that patients experienced little change in intellectual functioning over the first few postoperative months. However, when measured over longer periods, prefrontal lobotomy is now believed to result in lowered intellectual functioning. In part this is due to lowered ability in tasks requiring sustained attention, abstraction, and planning. Lobotomy patients may also demonstrate increased self-esteem along with a lack of self-criticism. Difficult personality traits may become accentuated by lowering inhibitory controls with resultant facetious and tactless social behavior.

Psychosurgery is and always has been a controversial intervention. The original procedures were developed in the absence of sound theoretical understanding of the brain structures being destroyed. There was little animal research prior to the use of the techniques with human patients. Patient selection was not based on adequate screening procedures. Follow-up studies were poorly designed and often were conducted by the physicians who had an interest in positive outcomes. Finally, alternative treatments were in many cases ignored. Valenstein has argued that in spite of these problems psychosurgery was adopted and advocated in part because of the leading role taken by ambitious practitioners and also because it offered a way of coping with desperate patients, families, and staff in overcrowded psychiatric hospitals.

Current psychosurgical procedures address many of these problems. However, the controversy remains. Destruction of brain tissue is nonreversible. Physical interventions imply physical, rather than social, environmental, or experiential causes of the treated problem. The procedures may alter core personality traits of patients and are thus seen by some critics as a tool for manipulating someone's personhood. But always one must balance these concerns with a proposal of what will be done for suffering or dangerous individuals for whom no other intervention has worked. The documented success stories of modern psychosurgery require decisions to be made on a case-by-case basis.

Reference

Valenstein, E. S. (1986). *Great and desperate cures.* New York: Basic.

W. D. NORMAN

See BRAIN AND HUMAN BEHAVIOR.

Psychosynthesis. A therapeutic process developed by Assagioli, a psychiatrist. Its goal is the harmonious integration of elements of the psyche under the direction of a personal center of consciousness or will. Psychosynthesis has affinities with humanistic and existential psychologies (*see* Existential Psychology; Humanistic Psychology) and with Carl Gustav Jung's analytical psychology, although it goes beyond these, especially in its emphasis on will and the direct experience of self.

Psychosynthesis attempts to deal with what it sees as an apparent duality between the personal self and the true self of which the personal self is usually unaware. The duality results from the dominance of subordinate aspects of personality, which obscure the true self that needs to be firmly established as a center of unity. The goal is first to develop a more integrated personality and second to develop a spiritual mode of living (Assagioli, 1973). According to Assagioli, the lack of personal integration and the enslavement to inhibiting demands of subordinate aspects of personality can be overcome by the discovery of a higher level of the unconscious and a unifying transpersonal self to which one surrenders.

Assagioli (1965) distinguishes seven levels of the psyche. There are three levels of the unconscious: a lower unconscious composed of instincts, primitive drives toward self-preservation, complexes, deep dreams, and pathological manifestations; a middle unconscious composed of ordinary mental activities such as memory, ideas, and imagination accessible to consciousness; and a higher unconscious composed of higher drives that manifest themselves in aesthetic interest, intellectual curiosity, altruism, search for meaning, and similar intrinsically valuable pursuits. There are also three dimensions of consciousness: a field that includes whatever content is conscious at a given time; an organizing center within the field capable of exercising a directive will; and a higher transpersonal center, both related to the personal center and in touch with higher unconscious, which enables one to transcend ego concerns and bring into awareness an essential relatedness to the rest of reality. Surrounding and interacting with this multidimensional structure is the collective unconscious, by means of which there is a constant interchange with the general psychic environment.

Assagioli describes two forms of psychosynthesis. The first, personal psychosynthesis, which is relevant for the individual who seeks to reach the "normal state of the average man or woman," is directed toward eliminating repressions, inhibitions, inappropriate dependencies, and excessive self-centeredness. The goal of personal psychosynthesis is the reconstruction of the personality around a new authentic center. It involves a decision to formulate a plan of action or, for the more intuitive person, to be led by the spirit within. The means for attaining this goal include exploration of conscious and unconscious aspects of personality and the development of specific strengths and attitudes.

The second form of psychosynthesis, spiritual psychosynthesis, is relevant for individuals who have attained the ability to function normally without crippling inhibitions and conflicts. For these individuals the task is not the basic integration of personality but the proper assimilation of the inflowing superconscious energies from the higher levels of the unconscious, which lure them toward self-realization, and the integration of higher values and motives with preexisting aspects of the personality. For those who have attained a satisfactory degree of personal integration but fail to pursue a higher synthesis, normalcy itself may become a cause of neurosis. Further, spiritual psychosynthesis is illustrative of a general principle of interindividual and cosmic significance that affirms that individuals are not isolated but exist in intimate relation with all other individuals who are part of the spiritual superindividual reality.

Assagioli suggests a variety of techniques, exercises, and methods that therapists are to practice themselves before using them to help clients. The tools are such that eventually clients can use them independently as part of a lifelong development process. For personal psychosynthesis the therapist may use techniques of catharsis such as speaking, writing, and muscular discharge; exercises of disidentification and self-identification; exercises for training the will; and guiding imagery of ideal models or symbols to foster behavior more in keeping with an integrated personality. Techniques of spiritual psychosynthesis are directed toward releasing the energies of the spiritual self; they include the use of symbols to guide decisions, dialogue with an inner teacher or wise person, and exercises designed to develop intuition or specific states such as serenity.

Psychosynthesis appears to be compatible with some scriptural perspectives on the human personality, particularly in its emphasis on responsibility for one's decisions and behavior and on the capacity to develop the will to cooperate with higher spiritual principles. It tends, however, to give little attention to certain negative tendencies underlying human behavior and to concentrate heavily on individual development without giving much consideration to interpersonal dependence and responsibility.

References

Assagioli, R. (1965). *Psychosynthesis*. New York: Hobbs, Dorman.
Assagioli, R. (1973). *The act of will*. New York: Viking.

J. KOPAS

See COUNSELING AND PSYCHOTHERAPY: OVERVIEW.

Psychotherapeutic Eclecticism. *See* ECLECTICISM IN PSYCHOTHERAPY.

Psychotherapy. *See* COUNSELING AND PSYCHOTHERAPY: BIBLICAL THEMES; OVERVIEW; THEOLOGICAL THEMES; FAMILY THERAPY: OVERVIEW.

Psychotherapy, Effectiveness of. Outcome research examines the extent to which the process of psychotherapy is effective. Knowing empirically the consequences of their collaborative efforts with patients, psychotherapists can insure that they appropriately use the most effective treatment in the most cost-effective manner. In this quest researchers use appropriate research designs and experimental control groups to look at questions such as: Does therapy work? Is psychotherapy better than no treatment? Does the effect last? Finding out which therapeutic interventions are most effective is also an important research topic. Additionally the relationship of therapist and patient characteristics to outcome must be examined. Research on the effectiveness of psychotherapy is vital if psychotherapists are to insure the most effective treatment will be used appropriately in the most cost-efficient manner and to fulfill their moral responsibility to protect consumers from potentially harmful techniques.

Overall Effects. In 1952 Hans Jurgen Eysenck published an important paper challenging the effectiveness of psychotherapy in producing greater change than that brought about by naturally occurring experience alone. Eysenck based his findings on a review of insurance company files, which showed 72% of individuals diagnosed psychoneurotic improved within two years with or without professional intervention. This finding, contradicting what many well-known clinics were reporting at the time, spurred a flurry of studies to establish an empirical base for the effectiveness of psychotherapy. These studies employed traditional therapies: behavioral, cognitive, humanistic, and psychodynamic. They represented data on thousands of patients and hundreds of therapists from across the Western world as well as populations from mildly disturbed persons with specific, limited symptoms to severely impaired patients whose disorders were both personally intolerable and socially dysfunctional. The changes made by these patients were reflected in diverse and comprehensive measures of improvement that included the perspectives of patients, patients' families, therapists, and various measures of social role functioning. The results repeatedly showed, contrary to Eysenck's report, that psychotherapy produces substantial beneficial effects above those that occur in the natural healing process (Lambert & Bergin, 1994).

Smith, Glass, and Miller (1980) reported that the average client receiving therapy was better off than 80% of the people who did not. Positive effects hold true whether the goal of therapy is narrowly defined, such as a specific change in symptomatology for a particular disorder, or encompassed in broad areas, such as work and social functioning (Lambert & Bergin, 1994). Improvement has been shown even when the symptoms presented suggest serious psychopathology. Overall the research has conclusively demonstrated that those entering therapy can expect greater relief than time alone could provide.

Effect Permanency. An important question is whether the beneficial effects of psychotherapy last. Although there is no reason to believe that a single course in psychotherapy should permanently inoculate a person from psychological disturbance, reviews of the research show that many patients who undergo treatment achieve healthy adjustment for long periods of time (Nicholson & Berman, 1983). Several recent reviews have even suggested that some patients continue improvement after termination of treatment (Jorm, 1989). Lasting relief

occurs despite the fact that many patients have had a long history of recurrent problems. At the same time there is clear evidence that some patients do relapse. Problems that have shown to be particularly prone to reoccurrence include drug addictions, alcohol abuse, smoking, obesity, and possibly depression. The use of booster sessions, which attempt to maintain treatment gains with periodic therapy sessions after formal treatment is over, delays relapse but does not prevent it. A major factor in maintaining positive results seems to be the degree to which patients recognize changes are partially the result of their own effective effort (Lambert & Bergin, 1994).

Length of Therapy and Outcome. The rate of change in psychotherapy plays an important role in its effectiveness. Psychotherapy historically has been considered a long-term process, in many cases taking up to several years. In the current health care environment, where much of the payment for psychotherapy comes from third-party sources, there is an increasing emphasis on cost effectiveness. Brief therapies have developed and even become the standard form of therapy practiced. Research has shown that psychotherapy can bring about change quite rapidly. Howard, Kopta, Krause, and Orlinsky (1986) reported that approximately 50% of patients were measurably improved by the eighth session and 75% by the twenty-sixth (see also Kadera, Lambert, & Andrews, in press). Research has also supported the effectiveness of brief therapies for some problems and cast doubt on their value for others. Shapiro, Barkham, Hardy, and Rees (1995) found there was a significant relationship between severity of depression and duration of treatment. Clients with mild and moderate depression did as well with 8 as with 16 sessions; clients with severe depression improved more during 16 than during 8 sessions. Knowing which disorders require more or less treatment allows practitioners and payors to better allocate resources. The research suggests that mental health care cost-containment measures can be based on patient severity ratings rather than on arbitrarily set limits so that enough treatment is available for individual patients to benefit. Continued research on the rate of change in psychotherapy is important due to its practical, economic, and ethical consequences.

Psychotherapy versus Pharmacotherapy. While psychotherapy may have considerable effectiveness when compared to no treatment, it is not the only method of treatment available for most disorders. Psychotherapeutic medication prescribed by a psychiatrist is utilized as often as psychotherapy. When comparative effectiveness between pharmacological and psychological treatment has been studied, many researchers have found the effect of psychotherapy to be equal to or above that of medication (Lambert & Bergin, 1994). No study is more important than that of The National Institutes of Mental Health Collaborative Depression study conducted in the early 1980s. This multisite endeavor examined the comparative outcomes of a standard medical treatment for depression (imipramine, a commonly prescribed drug for depression, plus clinical management) with two psychotherapies (cognitive-behavioral therapy and interpersonal psychotherapy, a kind of dynamic and humanistic therapy). These three treatments were contrasted with a control group taking a drug placebo plus clinical management.

This study was important for several reasons. It was the first head-to-head comparison of two psychotherapies that had been shown in previous research to be specifically effective with depression. It also typified improving research strategies in studying ideal pure form therapy by using manuals and competency ratings rather than by examining therapy as usually practiced. The use of manuals that set guidelines and limit how a therapy is to be practiced is important because it enables researchers to standardize how a therapy is carried out by clearly defining and monitoring its implementation, including its goals, tasks, and the recommended sequence of procedures. This standardization enables easier and more accurate replication by future studies because the actual components of each therapy are clearly stated.

Findings from the NIMH depression study showed more than two-thirds of the patients were symptom-free at the end of treatment, and all patient groups improved. Little evidence was found for the superiority of the psychotherapies in contrast to the placebo plus clinical management group. When patients were dichotomized on their level of severity, however, interpersonal psychotherapy and medication appeared to be equally effective, and both appeared more effective than the placebo and cognitive-behavioral treatments (Elkin et al., 1989; Imber et al., 1990).

Other studies have found the effects of psychotherapy equal to or surpassing the effects of a variety of antidepressant medications. Since antidepressant medication is often considered the treatment of choice for depression, psychotherapies that produce comparable effects are significant (Robinson, Berman, & Neimeyer, 1990; Steinbrueck, Maxwell, & Howard, 1983). Reviews of the treatment of agoraphobia (fear of open places) and panic disorder show results similar to those on depression. The psychotherapies that have been tested with these disorders have been shown to be equal to or more effective than pharmacotherapeutic interventions, especially when follow-up data are considered because relapse rates are typically higher for medication-only treatment. Research on the comparative effectiveness of psychotherapies and pharmacotherapy for schizophrenia and similar disorders generally indicates the greater value of medication than of psychotherapy for alleviating symptoms.

Differences among Therapies. While it has been shown that psychotherapy can produce effects equal to or above that of medication, the success rates of one psychotherapy over another are still debatable. The variants of psychotherapy have proliferated to such a degree that one review made reference to more than four hundred kinds (Kazdin, 1986). This enormous variation is a serious obstacle to conclusive research. Most studies have focused on the major schools: behavioral, cognitive, humanistic, and psychodynamic. These reviews generally find little difference in success among these four approaches (Lambert & Bergin, 1994). When differences have been found, they often support cognitive and behavioral over humanistic and psychodynamic treatments. Behavioral and cognitive treatments have been shown to have significant success with a number of specific problems such as panic, phobias, health-related problems, and a wide variety of childhood disorders. The treatment of choice for panic, for example, seems to be a cognitive-behavioral therapy package including relaxation, breathing retraining, cognitive restructuring, and simulation of the sensations of panic within the session to practice coping (Barlow, 1988; Michelson & Marchione, 1991). Continued research on the most effective treatment for specific disorders will enhance the ability of practitioners to bring about beneficial outcomes in an efficient manner.

Common Factors across Treatments. The lack of consistent differences in the overall success rates of varied therapies and the growing trend toward an eclectic approach has spurred research on factors found to be common across all therapies. It has been argued that the common factors in therapies account for substantial degrees of improvement in psychotherapy patients (Lambert & Bergin, 1994). Common factors can be viewed as originating from three sources: therapist, therapy procedures, and client. Together these sources create a cooperative working endeavor. The patient's increased sense of trust, security, and safety, along with decreases in tension, threat, and anxiety, leads to changes in conceptualizing problems and ultimately in acting differently by refacing fears, taking risks, and working through problems in interpersonal relationships.

Among the common factors most frequently studied have been those identified by the humanist or client-centered school. They list empathy, positive regard, nonpossessive warmth, and genuineness as factors that are necessary for change. Reviewers are virtually unanimous in their opinion that the therapist-patient relationship is critical. Even for behavioral techniques aimed at helping problem drinkers control their alcohol intake, therapist empathy is highly related to beneficial outcomes (Miller, Taylor, & West, 1980). Less effective trainee therapists, a study has shown, have lower levels of empathic understanding (Lafferty, Beutler, & Crago, 1991). The authors state: "The present study supports the significance of the therapist's empathy in effective psychotherapy. Patients of less effective therapists felt less understood by their therapists than did patients of more effective therapists" (p. 79).

Psychodynamically oriented researchers have generated research on the importance of the therapeutic alliance, a measure of the degree to which patient and therapist are able to develop a collaborative relationship. Some components that are measured include the patient's affective relationship to the therapist, the patient's capacity to work purposefully in therapy, the therapist's empathic understanding and involvement, and patient-therapist agreement on the goals and tasks of therapy (Gaston, 1990). Although in some instances the therapeutic alliance fails to predict or has little association with outcome, a strong therapeutic alliance appears to be one of the common factors leading to a positive outcome.

Another approach to studying the common factors involved in outcomes has been the use of client checklists, which rate client perceptions of therapists in various areas. Clients who view their therapists as understanding and accepting also have higher self- and therapist-rated improvement (Lorr, 1965; Cooley & LaJoy, 1980). A study in which clients generated a list of curative factors found that talking to someone and receiving advice correlated most highly with good outcome. Patients frequently attribute their success in treatment to personal qualities of the therapist. These qualities bear a striking resemblance to each other across studies, which is evidence they are important in outcome. Lazarus (1971) listed some of these qualities as sensitivity, gentleness, and honesty. Patients also clearly believed that the personal qualities of the therapist are more important than specific technical aspects, about which there was little patient agreement. Some researchers have even questioned the value of separating specific techniques from common factors. Butler and Strupp (1986) concluded, "The complexity and subtlety of psychotherapeutic processes cannot be reduced to a set of disembodied techniques because techniques gain their meaning and, in turn, their effectiveness from the particular interaction of the individuals involved" (p. 33). Continued research on the common variables among diverse treatments promises to be helpful in clarifying the factors that help bring about positive change.

Effect of Training and Experience on Outcome.
The effects of psychotherapy offered by experienced clinicians have been contrasted with the effects of helping efforts on the part of lay therapists, paraprofessionals, and inexperienced clinicians. The research findings have been highly debated due to mixed results. Some research suggests that more experienced clinicians obtain outcomes superior to those obtained by less experienced clinicians (Stein & Lambert, 1995). Professionals appear to do better overall with varying age groups and with problems that stem from overcontrol such as shyness and phobias than do graduate students and paraprofessionals (Weisz, Weis, Alicke, & Klots, 1987).

Therapist level of training did not affect the outcome with undercontrol problems like aggression. One study even indicated that clients who seek help from paraprofessionals are more likely to achieve resolution of their problems than those who consult professionals (Hattie, Sharpley, & Rogers, 1984). However, several subcomparisons suggest that the most effective therapists were those who were currently undergoing training or had just completed it and that experienced paraprofessionals were superior to less experienced paraprofessionals. Other studies have noted that, while a failure to detect an overall difference between professionals and paraprofessionals might be unsettling, a more thoughtful consideration of the findings shows that in almost all studies, the paraprofessionals were selected, trained, and supervised by professionals in techniques designed by professionals (Weisz, Weis, Alicke, & Klots, 1987). Many of these studies, however, have been cited for conceptual problems, and improvements in patient morale seem to be the result of attention and support. If this is true, it reemphasizes the role of common factors such as attention and support in positive outcomes and establishes that they can be used effectively by paraprofessionals (see Paraprofessional Therapy).

Causes of Deterioration.
Some patients are worse as a result of psychotherapy. Understanding these cases is important for ethical as well as scientific reasons. In addition, the extent to which negative changes occur obviously subtracts from overall success rates. Negative effects are of course impossible to study in an experimentally induced setting because of the resulting harm it would cause patients. Researchers have looked instead at those studies that have reported negative outcomes. The worsening of some patients that occurs is not necessarily due to therapy itself. Some patients may be on a progressive decline that no therapeutic effort can stop. A causal link between negative outcomes and therapeutic activities, however, has been suggested, particularly with specific kinds of clients (Lambert, Bergin, & Collins, 1977; Mohr, 1995). More severely disturbed patients have been associated with negative outcomes. In addition, several diagnostic types, such as schizophrenia, have a disproportionate number of negative outcomes.

Therapist errors have also been identified with negative outcomes. Examples include failure to structure or focus the therapy time, failure to address a patient's negative attitudes toward either the therapist or the therapy, the passive acceptance of problematic aspects of the patient's behavior such as resistance or evasiveness, and the use of inappropriate or poorly timed interventions (Sachs, 1983). Value differences among therapists also correlate with poor outcome. Therapists who place emphasis on values such as "having a comfortable and exciting life" were not as effective as therapists who placed significantly more emphasis on intellectual values (Lafferty, Beutler, & Crago, 1991).

In group treatment a widely quoted study reported that variables such as low involvement in the group, low levels of self-esteem, and greater anticipation or need for fulfillment were positively related to deterioration (Lieberman, Yalom, & Miles, 1973). Examining types of group therapy in an inpatient setting, other researchers found that expressive-experientially focused therapy, which emphasized emotional expression, breaking down defenses, and emotional release, outscored two other therapies in the numbers of negative outcomes, which led the authors to express caution in using such treatments (Beutler, Frank, Schieber, Calvert, & Gaines, 1984). There has also been research reported on the growing number of nonprofessional programs that foster an emotionally intense pressure for disclosure and conformity. Doherty, Lester, and Leigh (1986) reported that one in eight couples who had undergone a Marriage Encounter weekend were strongly affected by the encounter. Of these, approximately 50% were helped and 50% were negatively affected. Similar rates of negative effects have been reported in other studies (Lambert & Bergin, 1994). Unrealistic expectations for help by some participants as well as coercive group norms for openness and intimacy should lead the professional clinician to avoid these techniques.

Conclusion. Many psychotherapies have been subjected to empirical study and shown to have meaningful positive effects. Psychotherapy both speeds up the natural healing process and often provides additional coping strategies and methods for dealing with future problems. Psychologists, psychiatrists, social workers, and marriage and family therapists, as well as patients, can be assured that a broad range of therapies, when they are offered by skillful, wise, and stable therapists, are likely to result in appreciable gains for the client. Research continues to provide information on the amount of time needed for meaningful changes to take place, suggesting brief therapies are effective for some problems but not for others. The effects of therapy tend to last over time, with some patients continuing to make appreciable gains after treatment has concluded.

Although there is little firm evidence for the superiority of one form of psychotherapy over another, behavioral and cognitive methods appear to be significantly more effective in treating certain specific problems. Psychotherapy also has effects that are equal to those of medication. Significant research supports the role of common factors, such as empathy and support, in creating a beneficial outcome. Helping people deal with depression, inadequacy, anxiety, and inner conflicts, as well as helping them form viable relationships and develop meaningful directions for their lives, can be greatly facilitated in a therapeutic relationship that is characterized by trust, warmth, acceptance, and human wisdom. Research suggests that clients would be wise to pick therapists on the basis of their ability to relate. However, recognition of the important role a therapist's relationship skills and related nontechnical skills play in producing positive change should not be construed as suggesting that technical proficiency has no unique contributions to make. The use of manuals to guide the practitioner in implementing psychotherapies is an important development that will enable more reliable research and practice to be carried out. Paraprofessionals, who in many cases are selected, trained, and supervised by professional therapists, are sometimes able to be as helpful as practicing clinicians. They are especially useful in providing social support and in offering structured treatment programs under supervision.

Although the foregoing statements about psychotherapy can be made with more confidence than ever before, it is important to point out that some patients do get worse. These outcomes are instructive and should not be dismissed lightly. Knowing empirically what kinds of treatments are appropriate for a particular patient is crucial. The practice of psychotherapy needs to be regulated by professional boards to ensure the correct implementation of the most effective treatments by knowledgeable and experienced caregivers in order to protect the patients' best interests.

References

Barlow, D. H. (1988). *Anxiety and its disorders: The nature and treatment of anxiety and panic.* New York: Guilford.

Beutler, L. E., Frank, M., Schieber, S. C., Calvert, S., & Gaines, J. (1984). Comparative effects of group psychotherapies in a short-term inpatient setting: An experience with deterioration effects. *Psychiatry, 47,* 66–76.

Butler, S. F., & Strupp, H. H. (1986). Specific and nonspecific factors in psychotherapy research. *Psychotherapy, 23,* 30–40.

Cooley, E. F., & LaJoy, R. (1980). Therapeutic relationship and improvement as perceived by clients and therapists. *Journal of Clinical Psychology, 36,* 562–570.

Doherty, W. J., Lester, M. E., & Leigh, G. K. (1986). Marriage encounter weekends: Couples who win and couples who lose. *Journal of Marital and Family Therapy, 12,* 49–61.

Elkin, I., Shea, M. T., Watkins, J. T., Imber, S. D., Sotksy, S. M., Collins, J. F., Glass, D. R., Pilkonis, P. A., Weber, W. R., Docherty, J. P., Fiester, S. J., & Parloff, M. B. (1989). NIMH Treatment of Depression Collaborative Research Program: General effectiveness of treatments. *Archives of General Psychiatry, 46,* 971–983.

Eysenck, H. J. (1952). The effects of psychotherapy: An evaluation. *Journal of Consulting Psychology, 16,* 319–324.

Gaston, L. (1990). The concept of the alliance and its role in psychotherapy: Theoretical and empirical considerations. *Psychotherapy, 27,* 143–153.

Hattie, J. A., Sharpley, C. F., & Rogers, H. F. (1984). Comparative effectiveness of professional and paraprofessional helpers. *Psychological Bulletin, 95,* 534–541.

Howard, K. I., Kopta, S. M., Krause, M. S., & Orlinsky, D. E. (1986). The dose-effect relationship in psychotherapy. [Special issue: Psychotherapy research.] *American Psychologist, 41,* 159–164.

Imber, S. D., Pilkonis, P. A., Sotsky, S. M., Elkin, I., Watkins, J. T., Collins, J. F., Shea, M. T., Leber, W. R., & Glass, D. R. (1990). Mode-specific effects among three treatments for depression. *Journal of Consulting and Clinical Psychology, 58,* 352–359.

Jorm, A. F. (1989). Modifiability of trait anxiety and neuroticism: A meta-analysis of the literature. *Australian and New Zealand Journal of Psychiatry, 23,* 21–29.

Kadera, S. W., Lambert, M. J., & Andrews, A. A. (In press). How much therapy is really enough: A session-by-session analysis of the psychotherapy dose-effect relationship. *Psychotherapy Research: Theory and Practice.*

Kazdin, A. E. (1986). Comparative outcome studies of psychotherapy: Methodological issues and strategies. *Journal of Consulting and Clinical Psychology, 54,* 95–105.

Lafferty, P., Beutler, L. E., & Crago, M. (1991). Differences between more and less effective psychotherapists: A study of select therapist variables. *Journal of Consulting and Clinical Psychology, 57,* 76–80.

Lambert, M. J., & Bergin, A. E. (1994). The effectiveness of psychotherapy. In S. L. Garfield & A. E. Bergin (Eds.), *Handbook of psychotherapy and behavior change* (4th ed.). New York: Wiley.

Lambert, M. J., Bergin, A. E., & Collins, J. L. (1977). Therapist-induced deterioration in psychotherapy. In A. S. Gurman & A. M. Razin (Eds.), *Effective psychotherapy: A handbook of research.* New York: Pergamon.

Lazarus, A. A. (1971). *Behavior therapy and beyond.* New York: McGraw-Hill.

Lieberman, M. A., Yalom, I. D., & Miles, M. B. (1973). *Encounter groups: First facts.* New York: Basic.

Lorr, M. (1965). Clients' perceptions of therapists. *Journal of Consulting Psychology, 29,* 146–149.

Michelson, L. K., & Marchione, K. (1991). Behavioral, cognitive and pharmacological treatment of panic disorder with agoraphobia: Critique and synthesis. *Journal of Consulting and Clinical Psychology, 59,* 100–114.

Miller, W. R., Taylor, C. A., & West, J. C. (1980). Focused versus broad-spectrum behavior therapy for problem drinkers. *Journal of Consulting and Clinical Psychology, 48,* 590–601.

Mohr, D. C. (1995). Negative outcome in psychotherapy: A critical review. *Clinical Psychology Science and Practice, 2,* 1–27.

Nicholson, R. A., & Berman, J. S. (1983). Is follow-up necessary in evaluating psychotherapy? *Psychological Bulletin, 93,* 261–278.

Robinson, L. A., Berman, J. S., & Neimeyer, R. S. (1990). Psychotherapy for the treatment of depression: A comprehensive review of controlled outcome research. *Psychological Bulletin, 100,* 30–49.

Sachs, J. S. (1983). Negative factors in brief psychotherapy: An empirical assessment. *Journal of Consulting and Clinical Psychology, 51,* 557–564.

Shapiro, D. A., Barkham, M., Hardy, G. E., & Rees, A. (1995). Effects of treatment duration and severity of depression on the maintenance of gains after cognitive-behavioral and psychodynamic-interpersonal psychotherapy. *Journal of Consulting and Clinical Psychology, 63,* 378–387.

Smith, M. L., Glass, G. V., & Miller, T. I. (1980). *The benefits of psychotherapy.* Baltimore: Johns Hopkins University Press.

Stein, D. M., & Lambert, M. J. (1995). Graduate training in psychotherapy: Are therapy outcomes enhanced? Special section: The case for training in the provision of psychological therapy. *Journal of Consulting and Clinical Psychology, 63,* 182–186.

Steinbrueck, S. M., Maxwell, S. E., & Howard, G. S. (1983). A meta-analysis of psychotherapy and drug therapy in the treatment of unipolar depression with adults. *Journal of Consulting and Clinical Psychology, 51,* 856–863.

Weisz, J. R., Weis, B., Alicke, M. D., & Klots, M. L. (1987). Effectiveness of psychotherapy with children and adolescents: A meta-analysis for clinicians. *Journal of Consulting and Clinical Psychology, 55,* 542–549.

M. J. LAMBERT AND M. J. DAVIS

See COUNSELING AND PSYCHOTHERAPY: OVERVIEW.

Psychotic Disorders. A broad class of disorders characterized by the presence of delusions or hallucinations in which the person may or may not be aware that their perceptions depart from reality. Psychotic disturbances can appear as complications of other problems such as a general medical condition, substance use, or an affective disorder, or they can occur on their own without having been activated by another disorder. The advent of improved brain-imaging techniques has demonstrated that many cases of primary psychosis that would once have been considered inorganic can now be traced to structural or chemical malfunction of the brain; however, psychoses that have no discernible biological basis are still common.

A number of general medical conditions can act to physiologically trigger hallucinations or delusions. Conditions that impact the endocrine system, the immune system, or the metabolism can affect the brain. Also, many neurological conditions such as Huntington's disease, epilepsy, and brain tumors can create temporary or permanent secondary psychoses.

Psychosis can also be caused by the presence of a variety of substances in the body, including not only illicit drugs but also medications and toxins. The *DSM-IV* (American Psychiatric Association, 1994) now recognizes that particular substances can cause characteristic patterns of hallucinations or delusions that can occur either during intoxication or withdrawal. Substances such as cocaine and amphetamines can cause psychotic symptoms to appear intermittently up to four weeks after use of the substance has ceased.

It is also common for psychotic disturbances to accompany severe affective disorders. For instance, persons suffering from major depression may have hallucinations or delusions that they are responsible for a catastrophe that occurred in another part of the world, or that their body is rotting away. Persons experiencing a manic episode may hear voices telling them they are a god or that they will win a million dollars that night in Las Vegas. Most commonly the psychotic content is congruent with the mood of the individual, but it is also possible to have psychotic experiences that are not related to one's mood, such as the delusion that others can hear one's thoughts.

Psychotic disturbances also frequently occur without having been caused by another physical or mental disorder. Primary psychoses that involve only hallucinations or delusions are often less severe. For instance, both delusional disorder and shared psychotic disorder (once known as folie à deux) are disorders in which delusions are present but do not seriously impair daily functioning in other areas.

The most notorious primary psychotic disorders, the schizophrenias, are often characterized by not only delusions and hallucinations but also disturbances of behavior, speech, affect, volition, motor skills, or ability to experience pleasure. People suffering from a schizophreniform disorder, such as schizophrenia, schizoaffective disorder, or brief psychotic disorder, may demonstrate diverse combinations of psychotic symptoms. One person might constantly hear a voice commenting on his or her life but might otherwise behave normally, while another person may sit rigidly in a contorted position for hours, unable to speak except to repeat what is said. These schizophrenic disorders may occur in a single episode and never recur, they may appear repeatedly but fully remit between episodes, or they may take a chronic course.

Psychotropic drugs are the primary method of treatment for the psychotic disorders, and though their efficacy varies widely across individuals, medications are now available that can influence a variety of neurological systems with fewer major side effects. Because of the changes in health care policy, many people suffering from psychosis are treated on an outpatient or day-treatment basis and are hospitalized only during times of acute distress.

Reference

American Psychiatric Association (1994). *Diagnostic and statistical manual of mental disorders* (4th ed.). Washington, DC: Author.

K. P. Rankin

Psychotropic Medication. *See* Psychopharmacology.

Pubescence. As the child moves into sexual maturity and reproductive potency, pubescence is the physiological vestibule. Puberty is sometimes used to denote the actual arrival at reproductive capacity, with pubescence being used to denote a two-year transition during which physiological changes of a secondary nature are preparing for the primary transformations. The words derive from the Latin *pubertas* (the age of manhood) and *pubescere* (to grow hairy).

Pubescence will be regarded as the span of months marked by the appearance of secondary sex characteristics and by the physiological maturing of the primary sex organs. In girls the observable phenomena include height growth spurt, breast buds, pubic hair, the first menstrual period, and axillary hair. In boys observable phenomena include height growth spurt, the enlargement of testicles and penis, pubic hair, voice change, the first ejaculation, facial hair, axillary hair, chest hair, and hair in ears.

In technological cultures pubescence corresponds with preadolescence or early adolescent years. But adolescence is a complex of psychosocial factors that are enmeshed in the fabric of early sexual maturity. Pubescence includes psychological dimensions but is primarily concerned with physiological phenomena. Except during the months between conception and age 15 months there is no other two-year period during which such major physiological changes occur in humans. In Stone Age cultures a rite of passage often follows closely on puberty to initiate the child into the adult world with its privileges and responsibilities.

While many of the physiological changes may be regarded as clues to emerging sexual maturity, McCandless (1970) found that adolescents themselves view first menstrual period and first ejaculation as major landmarks in their development. These landmarks indicate the onset of pubescence and are biologically triggered. It has not been established whether psychosocial factors may accelerate or delay their appearance, although in dairy breeding the constant presence of an adult male has been found to accelerate first estrus and consequent calving and first lactation. Average age for first menstruation for North American girls is now 12 years 2 months, down from 17 years 6 months in 1840 in Norway. Mean age of first ejaculation tends to run one year behind that of girls' first menstruation. The earlier pubescence has been thought to be a consequence of nutrition, heredity, better health, and even geographic location. Current attention is being given to light, both natural and synthetic, with focus on the production of melatonin in the pineal gland when the child is under conditions of total darkness. Melatonin circulates in the bloodstream and has a slowing effect on ovarian and testicular production and on the development of the primary sex organs in children. Light is being used to enhance fertility in animal husbandry and to regulate the waning cycles of menopausal women.

Among physiological changes at pubescence it is likely that hormonal brain chemistry is related to the dawning of reflective self-consciousness. Formal operational thought, essential for making complex moral choices, comes within reach at about the same time that concern for physical appearance drives the pubescent child to stand before the mirror asking the deep questions of life. These developments may be related to the last phases of meylinization of the nervous system with the high-speed transmitting sheath. The last nerves to be meylinized are the correlation fibers of the central cortex. The question remains open. Although Jean Piaget anticipated it, he lacked today's physiological research resources to push the question (*see* Cognitive Development).

Rites of passage at pubescence include religious rituals. In Christian tradition confirmation, first communion, and baptism often are timed for pubescence. In other traditions there are special membership vows for those leaving childhood. Given the cortical, sexual, and psychosocial changes of the pubescence years, these remain significant agenda issues for those who guide in matters of evangelism, nurture, and development.

Reference

McCandless, B. R. (1970). *Adolescents: Behavior and development.* Hinsdale, IL: Dryden.

Additional Readings

Koteskey, R. L. (1981). Growing up too late, too soon. *Christianity Today, 25* (5), 24–28.

Wyshak, G., & Frisch, R. E. (1980). Delayed menarche and amenorrhea in ballet dancers. *The New England Journal of Medicine, 303,* 17–19.

D. M. Joy

See Life Span Development.

Punishment. Behavioral consequences are classified as reinforcers and punishers. Reinforcers increase the frequency or likelihood of the responses that produce them, whereas punishers are stimuli or events that decrease response frequency or likelihood. A punisher may consist of an aversive stimulus, such as a painful electric shock, or it may be the removal of a positive reinforcer.

Punishment is one of the most common methods used to control behavior. Parents routinely spank their children for misbehavior; undesirable personal or social behavior often results in censure, snubbing, disapproval, or social banishment; and many legal systems are based on punishment such as fines, incarceration, and removal from society.

Despite its prevalence punishment remains a controversial topic. Several arguments often are given against the willful use of punishment to control the behavior of others. These arguments normally concern the possible undesirable behavioral side effects that may accompany punishment. Such concern is justified; however, many of the unfavorable outcomes associated with punishment are due to the faulty application of punishment procedures rather than to any inherent shortcoming in the concept of punishment. Much of human behavior is learned and closely regulated by natural aversive consequences without any serious ill effects.

One undesirable side effect is that severe punishment applied over a long period of time may have a general suppressive effect on behavior that is not being directly punished. Repeated harsh punishment, therefore, may not only eliminate troublesome behavior but also may stifle desirable behavior. This generalization effect of punishment is especially pronounced if the contingency between behavior and punishment is ambiguous and if punishment is applied to a wide range of responses in a variety of different settings.

Punishment also can result in chronic anxiety or other disruptive emotional states. The continual occurrence of potentially punishing stimuli (e.g., threats or stimuli that are associated with punishment) can result in persistent emotional conditioning. Such conditioning is more likely if punishment is applied inconsistently or unpredictably.

Sometimes patterns of behavior are punished even though they are not only permitted but also expected at some later period of life (e.g., sexual curiosity). Consequently, punishment may be effective in suppressing present behavior at the expense of later behavioral flexibility. If there is a genuine fear of suppressing behavior that may be required later in life, punishment should be replaced with a different behavioral control technique.

A frequent reaction to punishment is aggressive behavior. The person being punished may attack the punisher or displace aggressive reactions to an innocent third party. Negative modeling also may occur where the punished person models (imitates) the aggressive behavior of the person who applies the punishment.

Most of the undesirable side effects of punishment can be eliminated or minimized by adhering to the following rules: Undesirable behavior, and the conditions under which it will be punished, should be clearly defined. Punishment should be consistently applied. Each occurrence of the undesirable behavior should be punished. Occasional punishment may be ineffective and it may confuse desirable and undesirable patterns of behavior. Punishment procedures should be selected that minimize the elicitation of emotional responses. Punishment procedures should be combined with other behavioral control techniques (e.g., positive reinforcement); desirable behavior should result in consequences that are clearly different than those for undesirable behavior. The rejection or acceptance of punishment is directly related to the perceptions of the person being punished. Consequently, the person being punished should be made to perceive that punitive sanctions are being applied for his or her benefit and not only for the convenience of the punisher.

Undesirable behavior also may be suppressed or eliminated through the removal of positive reinforcers. This method of punishment consists of depriving people of rewards and privileges that are normally available, such as loss of television viewing privileges, exclusion from social activities, or monetary fines. Although removal of positive reinforcement has not been as widely investigated as the application of aversive consequences, it has nonetheless been demonstrated to be an effective punisher. As in other forms of aversive control the amount of behavioral suppression produced through removal of reinforcement depends upon, among other things, the relative value of the reinforcer being removed and the relative magnitude of the opposing consequences. In contrast to the use of physical punishment, the removal of reinforcement seems to generate much weaker emotional effects, and it tends to foster an orientation toward those who control the desired positive reinforcers. If return of the reinforcer is made dependent upon performance of behavior other than the one being punished, rapid behavioral changes may result.

All other considerations aside, punishment of a response normally reduces its occurrence. Several characteristics can make a punishing stimulus more effective. Aversive stimuli that have a sudden onset (e.g., a slap) are more effective than stimuli whose aversiveness grows gradually. A punishing stimulus is more effective if it is delivered immediately after the response has been made rather than after some delay, unless the delay is bridged cognitively (e.g., through verbal instruction) or with a conditioned stimulus. The suppressive properties of an aversive stimulus are related to its intensity; the greater the intensity, the greater the suppression. Continual punishment of an undesirable behavior is more effective than intermittent or occasional punishment. Punishment that is consistently applied is more effective than the haphazard or ambiguous application of aversive consequences.

There are several cases where punishment is ineffective in suppressing behavior regardless of how consistently it is applied. One case is when the punished response is the only way to obtain reinforcement. For example, if the performance of an undesirable behavior is the only way a child has of getting parental attention, then this behavior may persist despite the fact that it is punished. Another case is when the value of the reinforcement received by exhibiting the punished response exceeds the aversive properties of the punishing stimulus. In this case the value of the reinforcement is worth the punishment received. A third case where punishment is ineffective is when punishment itself becomes a stimulus signaling that positive reinforcement is forthcoming, or if the punishment signals a period of relief when further punishment will not be delivered. Under these conditions punishment may actually increase rather than suppress a response because punishment takes on the properties of a positive conditioned reinforcer. It has been argued

that masochism may result from this discriminative function of punishment.

When aversive consequences follow a response, they generally suppress or eliminate that behavior. However, when punishment is discontinued, the punished response may reappear. Even if the punished response does not return, punishment alone does not normally bring about desired changes in behavior. Punishment does, however, make possible the occurrence of other behaviors. If these behaviors are strengthened (e.g., through reinforcement), they may effectively replace the punished response. The degree to which other behavior is positively reinforced is one determinant of both the suppressive power of punishment and the extent to which punished responses are likely to return.

S. R. OSBORNE

See LEARNING; AVERSION THERAPY.

Pyromania. The compulsive urge to set fires, often accompanied by a desire to endanger the lives of others. The pyromaniac does not necessarily want to kill people with the fires he starts and often expresses surprise and shock when this happens. The disturbance is most often classified as an obsessive-compulsive reaction or the manifestation of an antisocial or psychopathic personality. Characteristically the individual cannot explain or justify his behavior and usually claims he cannot control it or does not know what he was doing.

Several theories have been proposed as to the motivation behind compulsive fire setting. These include the defiance of authority, an expression of hostility and aggression, and the attempt to resolve deep-seated sexual conflicts. The act may be directed at a specific person, family, or business, or it may be generalized anger directed at someone the pyromaniac does not know. This hostility often originates in rejection and deprivation during childhood and reflects a fear of relationships and feelings of inadequacy. In cases involving unresolved sexual conflict the pyromaniac may feel forced to watch the fire he starts; he is sexually excited to the point of orgasm but quickly feels guilt and may even attempt to help put out the fire he started.

D. L. SCHUURMAN

Qq

Qualitative Research Methods. These are research techniques that do not yield raw data in quantifiable form. Rather than yielding percents, means, standard deviations, correlation coefficients, and levels of confidence, the type of data coming from qualitative research is narrative: a verbal description of what the participant did or said. Synonyms for the qualitative approach would be phenomenological, humanist, antireductionist, holistic, ethnographic, contextual, grounded, interactionist, reflective, hermeneutic, subjective, or *verstehenist*. Reviews of and guides to qualitative methodology are provided by Strauss and Corbin (1990), Denzin and Lincoln (1993), Renzetti and Lee (1993), and Sarbin (1986).

Previous debates about qualitative research usually emphasized basic philosophical differences: quantitative versus qualitative research methods or positivistic versus phenomenological approaches. Other terms for the distinction between these methods have also been noted: reductionistic versus molar, social science versus humanistic, and testing specimens versus casting nets (Runkel, 1990). The debate between the qualitative and quantitative methodologists is reducible to preferences about the relative merits of richness (offered by the qualitative) versus precision (offered by the quantitative).

Qualitative research includes all of those approaches in which the emphasis is on describing the subject's experience in terms of subjective phenomena. Forms of introspection, field observation (participant and covert), case studies (*see* Case Study Method), life histories, interviews, and content analysis of dreams and art forms may qualify, as long as what is recorded is a narrative rather than numbers.

Most qualitative research is a type of case study, either of an individual (e.g., life history or clinical report) or an event, organization, or society (i.e., an ethnography). Anthropologists, sociologists, and journalists are generally more advanced than most laboratory or clinically trained psychologists when it comes to doing ethnographies. The researcher may be covert (as when Jane Goodall hid behind a bush to observe chimpanzee society) or may be a participant observation (the researcher becomes an actor in the event or member of the organization or society under study).

The next major category of qualitative research would be interviews. The kind of interviewing done by poll takers is more quantitative than qualitative: the goal of the interviewer is to get the interviewee's response onto a codable format that can be quantified into percentages or means. For interviewing to be qualitative, the questions and response format must permit and even encourage interviewees to respond with their own words, and the researcher must record these words as primary data. Interviews can be face to face or over the phone (or via e-mail or postal service). The interviews can be one on one or there can be a focus group specially assembled. One advantage of the focus group interview is that each participant's answer serves to encourage and support other participants to reflect and reveal a little more. Even more so than with surveys based upon quantifiable questionnaires, sampling is an issue: it is a self-selected sample of those who agreed to participate.

Some qualitative studies may use many separate bits of seemingly unrelated data (e.g., Brink, 1985), while others may involve a tightly reasoned central theme substantiated by standardized instruments; for example, the use of the Rorschach test in Fromm and Maccoby's (1970) study of social character in a Mexican village. When Tom Peters argues for management by wandering about rather than hiding in one's office and reading or writing reports, he is arguing for a qualitative approach. When we teach any social science class, we should be telling our students that they have unknowingly been doing qualitative research for most of their lives. The purpose of formal training is to have them do it better.

Qualitative research is the preferred technique when we are studying the decision-making process of the participants: why some pregnant teenagers get abortions while others become single mothers and others opt for adoption; or how consumers come to a decision about which type of computer to purchase; or whether a man on a one-night stand will use a condom. The important thing is that qualitative research gives some empathic evocativeness that allows readers to participate vicariously in the subject's experience so that they can understand in a more profound way why the behavior occurred.

But the strength of qualitative research for obtaining richness becomes its weakness for the attainment of precision. First, the subjects infuse their subjectivity into the data. The narrative response produced as subjects talk to the interviewer or psychotherapist or jot down the day's happenings in a journal are reflected justifications rather than direct experience, defense mechanisms, not feelings. Qualitative data are not facts in the sense of being precisely measured and objective: they are at most private, interpersonal, or social constructions of the subjects.

The personality of the researcher also penetrates every phase of the qualitative research process. All qualitative research necessarily depends on the insight of the researcher. These methods do not discover something external as much as they create something intersubjectively and then project it onto the externals. An example of this would be oral histories and life histories with the elderly or a case report of psychotherapy: what we have is the result of an interpersonal interaction, a mutual intersubjectivity that creates a dynamic social reality rather than merely observes a static impersonal reality.

The danger comes in the possibility of blurring data (what the researcher observes) and inference (how the researcher interprets those data, according to some theoretical perspective). Theory determines not only how we interpret the facts but which facts we select for interpretation. The problem is that the qualitative researcher who has already become committed to a given theory can perhaps unconsciously go looking only for those data that fit that theory. Riebel (1979) referred to this as the problem of the "self-sealing doctrine": data that do not fit the theory must be discarded because, since the theory is obviously true, those data that do not fit must be inaccurate.

Certainly this problem is seen in the excesses of classical psychoanalysis. Once Sigmund Freud was convinced of the universality of the oedipus complex, he looked for it in all patients, whether they admitted it or not. If Little Hans was afraid of horses, it must be because he has displaced the fear of castration anxiety from his father onto that animal. If Dora claims to have been propositioned by Herr K., it must be a mere fantasy of her unresolved Electra complex. If Wolfman has an ambiguous dream about wolves in a walnut tree outside his bedroom window, it must be because he witnessed his parents in copulation. Anyone who fails to agree with Freud's interpretation of these cases either lacks the special expertise of the initiated or else is repressing the obvious because of his or her own unresolved complexes.

This problem of confusion of theory with data cannot be eliminated from qualitative research, but these problems can be identified, controlled, and minimized. Strauss and Corbin (1990) have advocated that qualitative research should not necessarily substantiate a preestablished theory but should lead to a new theory arising from and truly grounded within the data. To accomplish this it is necessary for qualitative researchers to have a disciplined subjectivity.

More recently sociologists involved in participant observation and evaluation research have suggested more specific safeguards for the inherent vulnerabilities of qualitative methods. One of the greatest advances in qualitative research methods has been the application of computerized analysis of texts (Weitzman & Miles, 1995). This not only makes analysis of tens of thousands of words easier but also introduces more objectivity.

References

Brink, T. L. (1985). *The middle class credo.* New York: Fawcett.

Denzin, N. K., & Lincoln, Y. S. (Eds.). (1994). *Handbook of qualitative research.* Thousand Oaks, CA: Sage.

Fromm, E., & Maccoby, M. (1970). *Social character in a Mexican village: A socio-psychoanalytic view.* Englewood Cliffs, NJ: Prentice-Hall.

Renzetti, L., & Lee, R. (Eds.). (1993). *Researching sensitive topics.* Thousand Oaks, CA: Sage.

Riebel, L. (1979). Falsifiability, self-sealing doctrines and human psychology. *The Humanistic Psychology Institute Review, 2,* 41–60.

Runkel, P. J. (1990). *Casting nets and testing specimens.* New York: Praeger.

Sarbin, T. (1986). *Narrative psychology.* New York: Praeger.

Strauss, A., & Corbin, J. (1990). *Basics of qualitative research.* Beverly Hills, CA: Sage.

Weitzman, E. A., & Miles, M. (1995). *Computer programs for qualitative data analysis: A software sourcebook.* Thousand Oaks, CA: Sage.

T. L. BRINK

Quest Religious Orientation. *See* RELIGIOUS ORIENTATION.

Questionnaires. *See* PSYCHOLOGY, METHODS OF.

Quid pro Quo. An agreement, usually unconscious, between two or more family members. Literally meaning "something for something," *quid pro quo* describes the intricate exchanges and understandings that define particular family relationships.

An example of a positive agreement is seen in the understanding that if the child behaves, he or she will be appropriately rewarded by the parent. Countless other quid pro quos, both healthy and unhealthy, govern how parent and child relate. Together they make up the relationship contract.

Negative quid pro quos abound in troubled marriages and families. For instance, a husband agrees to withhold comment on his wife's obesity while she tacitly accepts his chronic absence from the family. A major task in marriage and family therapy is to uncover dysfunctional quid pro quos and replace them with more adaptive exchanges.

J. A. LARSEN

See FAMILY THERAPY: OVERVIEW.

Racism. *See* PREJUDICE.

Randomization. *See* PSYCHOLOGY, METHODS OF.

Rank, Otto (1884–1939). Recognized as one of the most important founders of psychoanalysis. Rank became a disciple and colleague of Sigmund Freud at age 21, when he was introduced to Freud by Alfred Adler. At Freud's encouragement Rank did not study medicine but took a general curriculum at the University of Vienna and earned the Ph.D. in 1912 before continuing with extensive study in psychoanalysis. During his doctoral studies he served as secretary to the Vienna Psychoanalytic Society. By the time he had completed his doctoral studies, he had become a trusted member of Freud's inner circle and served as co-editor of *Imago* and *Internationale Zeitschrift für Psychoanalyse.*

After his break with Carl Gustav Jung and Adler, Freud solicited the loyalty of his closest associates, asking them to be his praetorian guard. This Rank willingly did, and he spent a dozen productive years devoted to publications in the journals and beginning his own practice. But his own work ultimately led to a schism with Freud over his 1924 book, *The Trauma of Birth.* The idea of the birth trauma, the most famous of Rank's ideas, deviated from Freud's theory of the origins of anxiety by arguing that all anxiety originates from the child's separation from the mother. Ironically, Freud initially accepted the book as an important advance in psychoanalytic theory but later viewed it as abandoning the sexual theory of anxiety with which Freud had become identified. As his relationship with Freud cooled, Rank experienced profound disorientation and anxiety himself, and he tried to patch up their relationship even as he began to disengage himself with a move to Paris in 1926. He finally moved to the United States, where his work won a sympathetic response from social workers; the School of Social Work at the University of Pennsylvania was an influential center for dissemination of Rank's neopsychoanalytic views (*see* Social Work). He continued to write and to see clients until his death in 1939, less than a month after the death of his estranged mentor Freud.

Rank had a relatively small but faithful number of adherents until the 1970s, when he was rediscovered in connection with developments in ego psychology. He rejected biologically based drives and environmental events as determiners of behavior, arguing that will (his term for ego) is the cause of behavior. His view of neurosis employed a striking metaphor: the artist. In his 1932 book *Art and Artist,* Rank argued that the creativity of the artist is like the conflict of the neurotic. Artists must contend with guilt because the novelty of their work is antisocial, breaking down the consensus of social reality. But where most people express their will through conformity to group views and artists must oppose the views of the group, the neurotic is a "failed artist" who is incapable of successful independence or opposition. The result is guilt, and the neurotic's maladjustment is traced through guilt to failure of the will.

In his 1936 book, *Will Therapy,* Rank sketched his view of therapy, which by now differed radically from Freud's. Eschewing the belief that neurosis is illness, Rank developed three ideas that profoundly affected future forms of therapy: the use of the analytic session as an occasion to explore the present feelings of the patient, the elucidation of rights of the patient, and the radical step of planning to terminate therapy rather than allowing it to continue indefinitely. In *Psychology and the Soul* (1931) Rank extended his theories to religion, viewing deity as a personification of will and the religious concern for the soul as the will to personal omnipotence.

L. S. SHAFFER

See PSYCHOANALYTIC PSYCHOLOGY; WILL.

Rapaport, David (1911–1960). Born in Munkacs, Hungary, Rapaport was a leader in a politically radical Zionist youth movement. He studied mathematics and physics at the University of Budapest before his family joined their group's kibbutz in Palestine, where he worked as a surveyor. After two years the family returned to Hungary, where he entered psychoanalysis for personal reasons and changed his field of study to psychology.

Rapaport received his Ph.D. from the Royal Hungarian University in 1938, then fled to the United States to escape the Nazis. After a brief stay in New York City he went to Osawatomie State Hospital in Kansas, where he began research on Metrazol shock therapy. In 1940 he moved to the Menninger Clinic at Topeka, where he soon became chief psychologist, director of psychology training, and director of research. Finding that administration was taking too much of his energy when he really wanted to do scholarly work, he moved to the Austin Riggs Center in Stockbridge, Massachusetts, in 1948. It was at Riggs that Rapaport made his most lasting contributions.

Rapaport's goal was to understand the nature of human thought, and he believed that psychoanalysis is the most fruitful approach to such an understanding. He believed that Sigmund Freud's drive theory must be expanded by ego psychology into a general psychology. He thought that human thinking could be studied by a battery of diagnostic tests. Rapaport worked on systematizing psychological theory, especially its abstract level of theorizing, to explain its clinical theory. He was a theorist rather than a clinician and was not bound by the usual limits of psychoanalysis. Although he rejected behaviorism itself, he used concepts from Jean Piaget's developmental psychology and from animal and human experimental psychology.

Rapaport wrote much but is best known for three books. His *Diagnostic Psychological Testing* (1945), later revised and condensed by Holt, was a standard in the field for many years. In *Organization and Pathology of Thought* (1951) he presented his view of the psychoanalytic theory of thinking. Finally, he translated psychoanalysis into the idiom of contemporary psychology in *The Structure of Psychoanalytic Theory* (1959). His intricately and carefully reasoned writings must be carefully studied rather than simply read.

R. L. KOTESKEY

Rape. Rape is an act of violence in the sense of violation of the subject, usually with genital or sexual associations. It may be perpetrated by an adolescent or an adult male upon an adult male, female, or children of either gender; or by an adolescent or adult female upon an adult male, female, or children of either gender. It is primarily an act of assault and may not necessarily include penetration of the subject's body or be a genital act. If penetration occurs it may involve manual, oral, lingual, or instrument penetration. Rape is a complex crime that may encompass a wide range of violating behavior, usually of a sexual nature.

Recent reports indicate that date rape is prevalent in human society and involves the forcing or enticement of a subject into sexually vulnerable and apparently intimate behavior, which may initially be pleasant or desirable to the subject but which in the end the subject unsuccessfully endeavors to stop. North American society is becoming increasingly aware of the occurrence of marital rape, and legal recognition of this crime is now established. Marital rape is usually forced sexual intercourse within marriage and is usually perpetrated by husbands upon their wives as part of a generally abusive relationship. It is seldom reported to the authorities, probably because the subjects of the rape fear further retaliation from the perpetrators and because of some persistence of the notion that marriage authorizes sexual dominance of the male.

The definitive criterion for determining that a behavior is rape is that it is forced and against the will of the subject, even if there was some initial apparent complicity or desire for intimacy. It is now generally considered a standard that if the subject resists or says no at any point in the relationship, the process of sexual play or intimacy must stop. If the perpetrator persists thereafter, the process is violation, violence, and rape. Rape has historically been defined as a sexual act on the part of the offender. Today it is defined as an act of power or coercion. Research increasingly indicates that the offender views the interaction as a means of both intimidation and sexual gratification. Legal definitions vary from state to state in the United States. Pastors and counselors should be informed of pertinent statutes. Interventions should focus on the victim's perceptions of the event and subsequent emotional and behavioral responses. Attempted assaults may be as damaging as those that are legally defined as completed acts.

The incidence of rape is difficult to determine in any given population, since the rate of reporting probably lies somewhere between 1 in 5 to 1 in 10 or between 10% and 20% of actual incidences. Approximately 100,000 children are raped in the United States annually. Somewhat in excess of half that number of adult rapes are reported in the United States annually. It is thought that 1 woman in 6 will be subjected to an attempted rape during her lifetime, while 1 in 25 will be raped. Most professionals in the helping professions perceive that as many as 50% of all females experience some form of very invasive molestation during their lifetime. Such experiences should likely also be defined as rape, in which case the statistics change radically and are relatively meaningless by themselves. Though report rates are increasing, rape appears to be increasing at a rate beyond what can be accounted for by that increased reporting.

Victims' response patterns closely mirror those for other crises, passing through a series of stages that have been labeled the rape trauma syndrome. In each stage certain tasks must be mastered for the victim's restoration. Counseling interventions also vary in each of the succeeding stages. The rape trauma syndrome has much in common with the standard paradigm for posttraumatic stress disorder (PTSD), and similar therapeutic intervention is required.

In the first stage, acute reaction, attention should be directed to a medical examination to determine possible venereal disease and pregnancy. Notification of family may also be appropriate. The counselor's role will be to provide support and information and to assist the victim in making decisions regarding legal action. This stage is generally followed by a period of outward adjustment, wherein problems encountered in the first stage bring various coping strategies into effect: denial, suppression, rationalization, grief reaction, and the like. It is common for interest and conversation about the event to wane, and intervention is chiefly supportive as reactions run their course. If the counselor has not worked with family or close friends, it is wise to do so, paying attention to their anger, blame of subject of the rape, or sense that she or he is ruined or damaged goods. If counselor intervention is initiated during this stage, the victim may resist reopening the situation, and the assistance may be limited to clarification of issues in the first stage and anticipation of those in the third.

The third stage, the integration stage, often begins with a sense of depression and a desire to talk with someone. This may be triggered by some event associated with the attack. Two central issues should be dealt with: the victim's self-perception of being guilty, damaged, or ruined, and her or his perceptions about the perpetrator, that is, that he or she is a threat to the subject's security.

A correlation has been discerned between personality styles and client-counselor interactions. Dependent persons utilize the counselor as an ally whose strength can be vicariously appropriated. Extraverts tend to be open and free with their accounts of the victimization and do not require as intense a relationship with the counselor. Introverts will often avoid talking about the offense or subsequent responses with anyone and may even perceive the persistence of the counselor as in some sense a repetition of the rape process and its forced violation of the subject. This is a delicate issue to handle.

The most serious injury sustained by the subject of rape seems to be the damage it does to self-image. Persons who have experienced rape readily interpret it as meaning that they are permanent victims of this violation and the damage it has done. A crucial intervention by the therapist is to assist the subject to reinterpret or reframe the memory of the assault as an event that has happened to her or him, not an event that permanently defines him or her as victim. The subject of rape has been victimized but is not inherently and forever a victim by definition. Control and celebration of his or her ideal person, self, and destiny can be recovered by the subject of the rape event, despite the fact that in common parlance society tends to use the term *victim*.

Generally the counselor should attempt to establish early short-term rapport, urge extended therapy if possible, and assist the subject in defining accurate perceptions of the event, effective coping strategies, and organization of a social support system. Social agencies are often available to provide specialized assistance.

Additional Readings

Brackensiek, L. S., & Hunter, R. J. (1990). Rape and rape counseling. In R. J. Hunter (Ed.), *Dictionary of pastoral care and counseling*. Nashville: Abingdon.

Burgess, A. W., & Holmstrom, L. L. (1974). *Rape: Victims of crisis*. Bowie, MD: R. Brady.

Fox, S. S., & Scherl, D. J. (1972). Crisis intervention with victims of rape. *Social Work, 17* (1), 37–42.

Patton, J. (1985). *Is human forgiveness possible?* Nashville: Abingdon.

J. H. ELLENS AND A. R. DENTON

See VICTIMS OF VIOLENT CRIMES; ABUSE AND NEGLECT.

Rational Disputation. A treatment technique utilized in rational-emotive therapy and cognitive-behavior therapy. It is based on the theoretical rationale that the manner in which an individual construes the world essentially determines his or her affect and behavior and dysfunctional emotional reactions and behavior are mediated by distorted conceptualizations and the erroneous beliefs underlying these cognitions. The goal of rational disputation is the cessation of the client's maladaptive and faulty patterns of thinking and the development of adaptive and rational thought patterns. It endeavors to obtain this goal by evaluating the reasonableness of the client's specific misconceptions and underlying erroneous beliefs. Accordingly the client is taught to monitor negative, self-defeating cognitions; recognize the connections among cognition, affect, and behavior; logically examine the evidence for and against his or her distorted cognitions; substitute more reality-oriented interpretations for these faulty cognitions; and learn to identify, dispute, and alter the underlying irrational beliefs that predispose him or her to distort his or her experiences (cf. Eph. 4:22–25; Rom. 12:2). Cognitive-behavior therapy differs from rational-emotive therapy in the implementation of this treatment technique in that the latter approach is more didactic. The use of rational disputation enables clients to recognize, test, and change their mistaken beliefs. They learn not simply to think more realistically and adaptively but to think for themselves.

D. PECHEUR

See COGNITIVE-BEHAVIOR THERAPY.

Rational-Emotive Therapy. A therapy developed in the 1950s by Albert Ellis, who became disenchanted with the convoluted theory of and the passivity required in classical psychoanalysis. Ellis claims that his basic premise can be traced to the Greek stoic Epictetus and is stated most clearly by Marcus Aurelius: "If thou art pained by any external thing, it is not this thing that disturbs thee, but thy own judgment about it. And it is in thy power to wipe out this judgment now."

Ellis has had an extremely productive career and has done extensive work in the field of sexology. His major psychotherapeutic statement was *Reason and Emotion in Psychotherapy* (1962); since then his approach has been summarized in many different publications (e.g., Ellis & Harper, 1975). This approach has provided a broad and flexible framework for and was a forerunner and part of the cognitive-behavioral approach to psychotherapy that became very popular in the 1970s. It has had great impact on the whole field of psychotherapy and has produced many new applications and spin-offs (Wolfe & Brand, 1977). There can be a rational approach to any human problem, as its various proponents continue to demonstrate. Maultsby (1975), among others, has been an important popularizer by making this approach more concrete, specific, and behavioral. He has written several self-help books.

The Concept of Rationality. Rationality has a long history of meanings and definitions of which these present-day proponents, characterized by an ahistorical approach to behavior and philosophy, have little or no awareness. Ellis defines rationality in terms of four basic values: survival, maximizing pleasure (and avoiding all except internal, prosocial pain), being part of a social group, and attaining intimacy with a few of that group. Maultsby is more specific and sets up five criteria. Rational behavior and thinking are based on objective, consensual reality; are self-protective and life-enhancing; enable goal achievement; prevent significant conflict with others; and prevent significant personal, emotional conflict. To be rational one must fulfill the first two criteria and at least one of the latter three.

The ABC Theory of Emotions. In connection with their definition of rationality, rational therapists have a theory of how emotions work (Russell & Brandsma, 1974). The ABC theory is employed as a useful device to explain emotional response and distress. This theory postulates that all emotional responses are the result of cognitive processes, and the invariant sequence is (A) perceptual processes—situational determinants; (B) cognitive processes—thinking, evaluating, self-talk; (C) physiological responses—feelings. It is implied in this sequence that thinking, or self-talk, is crucial in creating and maintaining emotional responses, and the important cognitive processes can be verbalized (with some effort) in simple declarative sentences. Thus the talking to self that one does in evaluating complex stimuli is the root cause of emotional disorder. C responses can be produced by B alone. They can also become conditioned or habitualized to A stimuli with little or no intervening consciousness (B). The former is called a belief and the latter an attitude or "thought shorthand." These processes can be either adaptive and efficient or disordered, depending on how well they match up with the criteria for rationality.

Rational Psychotherapy. Therapy leads clients to ask four basic questions: What am I saying to myself? Is it true? What is the evidence for my belief? What is the worst that could happen if . . . ? Clients are taught, often by written homework assignments (Maultsby, 1971) or by persuasive argumentation, to separate As from Bs from Cs, facts from opinions, thoughts from feelings. An appropriate A section will pass the camera check; that is, all statements there can be verified by a camera with sound equipment. If they cannot pass the test, they belong in B. When all important beliefs have been identified and the person's feelings and behaviors are accounted for (B), patients are taught to identify their irrational ideas, their sane versus insane statements. Assuming a statement to be relevant to A, there are many kinds of irrational statements. The most common are positive and negative exaggeration, rationalization, catastrophizing, absolutistic statements, meaningless metaphors, lies, rhetorical questions, non sequiturs, denial-minimizations, and overgeneralizations.

After these statements are identified and labeled, the client is taught to apply the logicoempirical method to his or her personal statements and hypotheses (as in the previous four questions and criteria for rationality). This is the D, or disputation, part of the ABC theory. Some proponents add an E section to specify a desired outcome in terms of feelings and behavior. Ellis has identified 12 major irrational ideas, but by far the 4 most common ones, with their rational alternatives, are those in table 1. By argumentation and direct teaching the client is taught to challenge and replace his or her irrational thinking with rational alternatives. Then the client is given the homework assignment to visualize himself or herself thinking and acting on the basis of his or her new cognitions and the desired outcomes (*see* Homework in Psychotherapy). This is called rational-emotive imagery (REI) and is practiced several times each day, usually for specific problem situations. After this internal preparation behavioral techniques such as assertion training, role playing, and practicing are used to further imprint the new cognitions. Specific activities may be prescribed by the creative therapist to help the person test out experientially the irrationality of his or her position. Rational therapists differ in the extent to which they emphasize and apply various aspects of this process, but the preceding is a general outline of their approach.

Table 1

Irrational Idea	Rational Alternative
It upsets me.	Reality just is. I upset myself by how I think about it.
I have to . . .	I don't have to do anything. I will consider only my long-term best interests. "Musturbation" is self-abusive.
I should get what I want.	Everything is exactly as it should be. I may wish for, want, or desire what I want, but it is only unfortunate if I don't get it—not awful or a catastrophe!
My self-worth is defined by my behavior.	Behavior is only a small part of my total self. I can rate performances, in order to increase my efficiency, but it is illegitimate to even attempt to rate myself.

Critical Perspective. The ability to think, abstract, and make sense out of reality is one of the greatest blessings that human beings have. Rational therapy is excellent in helping people to separate classes of problem behavior and to evaluate their own thinking; thus to be more responsible, make better choices, and stop whining. The thrust toward critical thinking and autonomous functioning is commendable. However, the strength of this approach is also its weakness. The implied view of persons is rather mechanical, overly cognitive, and exceedingly individualistic. Rational therapists translate everything into cognitions, including motivation, and assume that all cognitive processes can be easily verbalized and are available to awareness. They do not emphasize the interpersonal nature of individuals or their enmeshment in various systems (e.g., family, cultural).

The view of reality taken by most rational therapists is quite limited from a Christian perspective because they make the mistake of assuming that scientific methodology and principles define the universe. They often slip into scientism by transmuting legitimate methodological naturalism into illegitimate methodological naturalism; that is, they confuse a useful method with the nature of reality. The therapists who most strenuously dispute the religion of Sigmund Freud, Carl Rogers, and any form of theism then proceed to set up their own religion based on empiricism and scientific method. It follows that ethics are always situational, since there are no absolutes except perhaps avoidance of social chaos and harm to others, and the attainment of one's personally defined goals, that is, the values of rationality.

Rational therapists (with only a few notable exceptions) tend to have a negative orientation toward feelings. Their interest is not in integration of feelings but rather in controlling or eliminating them. Rational therapists do not emphasize listening carefully or empathic understanding. They are interested in words and semantics, not experiences or meanings. Thus they tend toward premature attacks on language; they do not hear or understand deeper meanings or see and understand nonverbal communication. This system is an excellent example of the advantages and pitfalls of a philosophy of science taken from the first half of the twentieth century. Christians would do well to use many of its insights to discipline their own thinking and behavior but retain a critical posture toward several of the deficits in technique and its underlying assumptions and philosophical mistakes.

References

Ellis, A. (1962). *Reason and emotion in psychotherapy.* New York: Lyle Stewart.
Ellis, A., & Harper, R. (1975). A. *A new guide to rational living.* Englewood Cliffs, NJ: Prentice-Hall.
Maultsby, M. C. (1975). *Help yourself to happiness through rational self counseling.* Boston: Malborough House.
Maultsby, M. C. (1971). Systematic, written homework in psychotherapy. *Psychotherapy: Theory, Research, and Practice, 8,* 195–198.
Russell, P. L., & Brandsma, J. M. (1974). A theoretical and empirical integration of the rational-emotive and classical conditioning theories. *Journal of Consulting and Clinical Psychology, 42,* 389–397.
Wolfe, J. L., & Brand, E. (Eds.). (1977). *Twenty years of rational therapy.* New York: Institute for Rational Living.

J. M. BRANDSMA

See COGNITIVE-BEHAVIOR THERAPY; ELLIS, ALBERT.

Rationalization. A person's attempt to justify or present as reasonable his or her maladaptive behavior. An unconsciously motivated ego defense mechanism, rationalization generally employs faulty logic or falsely ascribed lofty motives in an effort to avoid conscious awareness of the irrational, maladaptive nature of the defended behavior. This process serves two major roles: it reduces the pain and disappointment associated with failure to attain goals, and it works toward justifying particular behaviors. Several behaviors that together may indicate the use of rationalization are the attempt to find justification or defensible reasons for one's actions or attitudes; anxiety or anger when those reasons are challenged; inability to consciously perceive inconsistencies in reasoning or contradictory evidence.

R. LARKIN

See DEFENSE MECHANISMS.

Reaction Formation. The development of socially or personally acceptable attitudes and behavior that are the opposite of repressed, unacceptable unconscious desires. This unconscious process provides reinforcement of the repression of those desires, helping to defend against their threatened intrusion into consciousness or overt expression.

Sustaining this double-level repression creates a serious drain on the individual's psychic energy. Yet it remains a fragile defense, under continual threat of a return of the repressed impulse to conscious awareness. Such a defensive structure often results in exaggerated fears and rigid belief systems that limit adaptability and promote severity in coping with the shortcomings of others. For example, this process may cover repressed hostility with an overwhelming show of kindness, unconscious desires for sexual promiscuity with celibacy or great moral restraint, or unconscious desires to commit some crime with strong demands that those particular criminals receive the severest punishment possible.

R. Larkin

See Defense Mechanisms.

Reactive Attachment Disorder. The essential feature of reactive attachment disorder (RAD) is markedly disturbed and developmentally inappropriate social relations in most contexts. To be diagnosed as RAD, the inappropriate behavior must begin before age five.

There are two subtypes of RAD, inhibited and disinhibited. The inhibited type is associated with a failure to initiate and to respond to a majority of social interactions in an appropriate way. A child diagnosed with the inhibited type of RAD may exhibit exceedingly inhibited, hypervigilant, or ambivalent responses. A child with the disinhibited type of RAD may exhibit a pattern of diffuse attachments, which may include indiscriminate sociability or a lack of selectivity in the choice of attachment figures.

Certain features are shared by a majority of the children who are diagnosed with RAD. These features include unusual patterns of language, poor attention and concentration, motor delays, failed acquisition of age-appropriate self-care behaviors, impulsiveness, and aggressiveness.

RAD is not accounted for exclusively by developmental delay. It also does not meet criteria for pervasive development disorders. RAD is associated with grossly pathological care. Pathological care is defined as persistent disregard of the child's basic emotional needs for comfort, stimulation, and affection. There is also an enduring disregard for basic physical needs, or there may have been several changes of the primary caregiver, a circumstance that prevents the formation of stable attachments.

The following is an example case of a child who would meet current criteria for RAD. Sam has experienced many changes of his primary caregiver during his early childhood. He moved often because his parents were assigned to several different military bases. Due to marital discord, the responsibility for caregiving changed often. After his parents divorced, Sam lived with his mother and stepfather until he was eight. His home life at that time seemed to be disordered, and abuse was suspected. After an investigation by child services, Sam was returned to his father and stepmother. Upon his return, Sam's father noticed that Sam's speech was disordered. He could not perform basic self-care activities, and he also displayed self-injurious behavior. Sam's social interactions were marked by gaze aversion, unprovoked aggression, and a strong dislike of being touched. He also experienced sleep disturbance and repeated nightmares.

Certain situations may lead to the development of pathological care and thereby the possible development of RAD. Some of these situations include prolonged hospitalization of the child, extreme poverty, and parental inexperience. However, it should be noted that grossly pathological care does not always lead to the development of RAD.

Laboratory findings that are consistent with malnutrition may be found in a child diagnosed with RAD. A physical examination may reveal general medical conditions that can be associated with difficulties in child care. Some of these conditions include growth delay or evidence of physical abuse (see Abuse and Neglect).

RAD appears to be uncommon. Prevalence rates that have been determined from maltreatment literature have been estimated at about 1%. The onset of RAD usually occurs within the first several years of life. The course of RAD seems to vary depending on the individual characteristics of the child and caregivers involved, the duration and severity of associated psychological deprivation, and the nature of intervention. Improvement or even remission may occur if a suitable environment can be provided for the child.

RAD must be differentiated from severe mental retardation, autistic disorder, pervasive developmental disorder, and attention deficit/hyperactivity disorder (ADHD). In mental retardation, appropriate attachments usually develop consistent with the child's general developmental level. However, some infants or children with severe mental retardation may present special problems to their caregivers and exhibit symptoms characteristic of RAD. RAD should be diagnosed only if the problems in attachment formation are not a result of the retardation.

RAD must also be differentiated from pervasive developmental disorder (PDD). PDD is characterized by either highly deviant attachments or the failure to establish attachment. Unlike RAD, PDD occurs in the presence of a relatively supportive and stable environment. Both autistic disorder and PDD are characterized by the presence of a qualitative impairment in communication and restricted patterns of behavior.

RAD, specifically the disinhibited type, must be differentiated from the impulsive and hyperactive behavior that is associated with attention deficit/hyperactivity disorder. One way to differentiate RAD from hyperactivity disorder is to search for evidence of grossly pathological care, which is a defining feature of RAD.

The diagnosis of RAD was carried over to the *DSM-IV* (American Psychiatric Association, 1994) from the *DSM-III-R* because it characterizes a pattern of disturbance that is not included with other diagnostic categories. Early diagnosis of the disorder is important because RAD is a condition that can potentially endure in the child.

Reference

American Psychiatric Association. (1994). *Diagnostic and statistical manual of mental disorders* (4th ed.). Washington, DC: Author.

C. L. KELLY

See EGO; ATTACHMENT THEORY AND DISORDERS.

Reading Disabilities. In the *DSM-IV* individuals with reading difficulties are diagnosed as having a reading disorder if their measured reading proficiency is significantly below what would be expected based on intelligence quotient (IQ), age, or grade expectancy. In addition the reading difficulty must severely impact the individual's educational functioning or life functioning and may not be attributable to a sensory deficit.

In a broad sense all reading disabilities can be placed under the umbrella of what is known as dyslexia. Dyslexia literally means difficulty *(dys)* with the written word *(lexia)*. The term *dyslexia* has come to describe a vast array of reading difficulties with little specification.

The reading disorder manifests itself when the child has significant difficulty in deciphering letters in a word and/or associating them with the sounds they represent. Frequently the child or adult may confuse or rotate letters and numbers that are similar; for example, *b* and *d*, *m* and *w*, *p* and *g*, *3* and *w*. Some individuals may have associated deficits in memory and in left-right orientation.

Many theories attempt to account for reading disabilities. Some experts have hypothesized visual and/or auditory perceptual deficits; others implicate a faulty short-term memory in assessing the relevant visual-aural information. Still others have emphasized deficient linguistic and temporal-spatial abilities. No theory as yet has proven conclusive.

Deficits in reading may also arise from emotional factors or a lag or delay in the maturational skills needed to read. Frequently emotional factors cause a child to be inept in developing or mastering the skills required to read. Four emotional factors commonly seen are lack of interest in academic endeavors, severe depression, low self-esteem, and low frustration tolerance. Each of these robs the child of the needed energy to give sustained attention to the frequently unsatisfying task of learning to read. However, these emotional characteristics may be secondary to either developmental dyslexia or delayed maturation in reading skills.

Some individuals have reading difficulties as a result of being at the low end of the bell-shaped curve of reading ability. For these individuals there is a maturation lag in acquiring reading skills. Typically these people are known as slow readers. Such individuals do not usually show the many associated characteristics of developmental dyslexia. However, they find reading so frustrating that they are at risk of early school failure.

K. R. KRACKE

See LEARNING DISABILITY.

Reality Principle. In psychoanalytic theory, the governing principle by which the ego operates. The ego is aware of the demands of the environment and meets those demands in a way that ultimately satisfies the instinctual needs of the individual. In this way the reality principle is a modifier of the pleasure principle.

See EGO; PSYCHOANALYTIC PSYCHOLOGY.

Reality Therapy. Glasser (1965) initiated reality therapy as a reaction against the prevailing medical model of pathology and therapy (*see* Mental Illness, Models of). At once innovative and eclectic, Glasser and his followers have continued to deepen and expand the system, with theoretical underpinnings in biological psychology and sundry applications.

Glasser's seminal work involved mental hospital and youth correctional settings, and he soon expanded it into elementary and secondary school administration and teaching. In William Powers's perception-based control theory, Glasser (1981) saw a behavioral (though explicitly not s-r) justification for the clinical approach he had intuitively and empirically developed. Subsequent reality therapists base their presentations and understandings of reality therapy on control theory (Glasser, 1986). Also during the 1980s Glasser incorporated Deming's (1982) management principles into reality therapy, having recognized essential commonalities between Deming's ideas and control theory and reality therapy. The amalgam of these complementary systems was then applied to counseling settings, management practices, and school organization and instruction. The umbrella organization that owns the development and practice reality therapy is now called "The Institute for Control Theory, Reality Therapy, and Quality Management." In addition to training and issuing credentials for reality therapists, the organization has long included the Educator Training Center (school applications) and sponsors the semi-annual *Journal of Reality Therapy* (Volume 14 in 1995).

A View of Humanity. Glasser consistently rejects the concept of mental illness and eschews psychiatric labels, preferring to view functional pathology as ineffective learned behaviors. From his original two sets of human needs, "the need to love and be loved and the need to feel that we are worthwhile to ourselves and to others" (1965, p. 9), Glasser now addresses five basic, innate human needs: love and belonging, power, freedom, fun, and survival. All human motivation comes from within, from internalized pictures of these needs. We act toward the environment so as to control the world in the satisfaction of one or more needs. Rejecting s-r views of elicited behavior (by either classical or instrumental conditioning), Glasser says we always act, never react. Environmental input constitutes information to which we may choose to respond, not stimuli to which we must react.

Whether in relation to our social lives, work, or school, we act to meet the needs as they have developed over our lifetimes, insofar as we perceive the environment as potentially meeting such needs. Suppose a child's need for love results in sulking and wailing so that the parents do not leave him or her alone with a babysitter. Over time the child learns that "choosing misery is a powerful, controlling choice and may sulk and depress as a major way to attempt to control people for the rest of his or her life" (Glasser, 1992, pp. 273–274). Or a student who has had minimal experience learning to read, for example, will not find reading class an opportunity for power, freedom, fun, or survival (and only if the teacher has developed a special relationship with that student might "love and belonging" be obtained from the process). Glasser says, "what we actually do is control . . . the total behaviors that we believe will best get us what we want from the world about us" (1992, p. 273).

In control/reality theory, behaviors combine some proportions of four components: acting, thinking, feeling, and the physiology that accompany the three others. Earlier presentations of reality therapy were criticized for ignoring feelings or emotions, so central to many other therapeutic systems. The contemporary version of control theory sees feelings and accompanying physiology as subordinate to the components we consciously control: acting and thinking. Thus reality therapy resembles rational-emotive and cognitive-behavior therapies, focusing on aspects of behavior that most people believe they control, assuming that the subjectively experienced feelings and visceral reactions will change accordingly.

The love and self-esteem needs originally posited in reality therapy have moral implications, and Glasser's system acknowledges moral realities. "The child knows the difference between right and wrong behavior and is frustrated because receiving love for behavior that he knows is wrong does not allow him to feel worthwhile" (Glasser, 1965, p. 10). Reality therapy recognizes standards of responsible behavior, as contrasted with psychoanalytic rejections of an overly strong superego, thus showing an affinity with the Judeo-Christian worldview. Glasser's emphasis on loving and belonging reflects "it is not good for the man to be alone" (Gen. 2:18, NIV) and "the greatest of these is love" (1 Cor. 13:13). Self-worth recalls that "he gave his one and only Son" (John 3:16) and we are made "a little lower than the heavenly beings" (Ps. 8:5). While reality therapy's explicit moral bases are more humanistic than theocentric, they reject ethical relativity and recognize some behaviors as inherently wrong.

The Reality Therapist. Reality therapy practitioners come from many professional backgrounds and function accordingly in sundry settings: social work, school administration, clinical psychology, guidance counseling, the ministry. Full-fledged clinical reality therapists are certified by Glasser's institute after a series of training experiences. Therapists are expected to internalize the principles of control theory. The process of adopting control theory to one's own life and relationships typically takes about two years.

Since reality therapy was initially influenced by a youth correctional facility, it has been applied in many settings with reluctant or resistant clients, including delinquent youth and chemical abusers. Glasser observes that treatment with such populations often involves more managing than traditional counseling. He defines managing as "the process of working with someone so that this person will accept and work hard at someone else's agenda" (1992, p. 271). Reality therapy, especially the theory and practice of control theory, may also be taught and practiced as a system for people who merely want to be able to lead a more effective life (1992). More frequently reality therapy is used in conventional clinical settings for problems ranging from existential neuroses to schizophrenia. The remainder of this article will focus on such clinical applications, despite Glasser's many applications in other settings.

Sometimes the principles of reality therapy have been oversimplified, suggesting that anyone can become a reality therapist from attending a workshop and/or reading a book or two. While the therapeutic process, especially in its beginnings, was systematically and succinctly stated, people who attempt to become reality therapists without careful training and supervision are usually led astray by one or another idea taken out of context.

The Therapeutic Process. Reality therapy teaches clients by model, exhortation, and practice to meet their individual and internal needs responsibly, respecting others' needs and rights. Techniques used to solve immediate problems are generalized to other situations so that clients become increasingly independent of the therapist. The teaching process may incorporate many direct and indirect tactics, often of great subtlety, so that teaching in reality therapy transcends a merely didactic process.

Glasser originally identified three therapeutic procedures: involvement, rejecting unrealistic behavior, and teaching better ways to fulfill the client's needs (1965, p. 21). Later (e.g., 1981, chap. 15) he identified and promoted eight steps of reality therapy, which became the hallmark of the system for many years and are summarized below. Presently he disavows the apparent lock-step system, although its elements continue to appear in series of more or fewer, often less concrete, steps.

Step one is to make friends, wherein the therapist comes to know the client's internal needs and long-term goals to be employed in further steps. The therapist also reveals her or his own values and becomes emotionally involved with and committed to the client.

Step two asks the client, What are you doing? This focus on behavior per se suggested an alliance of reality therapy with behavior therapies. It is still evident in an emphasis on action as a readily controllable component of total behavior.

Step three follows by asking, Is what you are doing helping you? The question focuses on longer-term, more fundamental needs. Step four involves helping the client to make a plan to do better, that is, to meet fundamental individual needs. Step five invokes a commitment to the plan, perhaps in the form of a written contract.

Steps six and seven involve following up on the plan: accepting no excuses and "neither punish[ing] nor interfer[ing] with natural consequences" of the client's lapse. Step eight is "never give up." The therapist maintains his or her initial commitment to the client as long as the client is willing to work on the presenting problem.

Glasser recently addressed two aspects of the reality therapy process: creating the counseling environment and the specific procedures that lead to change (1992). The former encompasses developing a friendly and safe relationship with the client, communicating that no psychological problem is unsolvable, and sticking with the client in the process of change.

Within control theory logic, "procedures leading to change" first convince clients that the behaviors they have been choosing will not get them what they want in the long run. They are confronted with the fact that the pain that brought them to therapy is the result of behaviors they have chosen. People tend to focus on the most recognizable component of behavior (e.g., on depressed feelings) and fail to see that their choices (acting and feeling) result in the painful affective and physiological components of behavior. Reality therapists may shift awareness of conscious control by changing the way they and their clients talk about the latter's behaviors from nouns to gerunds or infinitives. They do not suffer a depression, but "are depressing" or "choosing to depress." Or they say "people are anxieting, phobicking, obsessing, . . . choosing to compulse, be crazy, have a headache, or be sick" (Glasser, 1992, p. 272).

Clients are then led to adopt other total behaviors that are more likely to get them what they want. Therapists must be skillful enough in their teaching to get clients to see that their choices of acting or thinking determine their life outcomes. Reality therapy does not indulge in generalities but deals concretely with each client, identifying individual needs, internalized perceptions of the world, and discrete behaviors and thoughts that may more effectively meet that client's needs and ease the pain that brought her or him to therapy. Even when managing resistive clients, the therapist cannot coerce change, in part because such coercion runs counter to the client's basic need for power. Therapists must convince them that they would be better off following the therapist's agenda. Such a task depends crucially on the first step of classical reality therapy, making friends, or putting oneself into the client's brain as a "need-satisfying person"—given everyone's basic need for love and belonging.

Evaluation. Three decades of development by a cohesive group of therapists from diverse backgrounds have honed reality therapy into a coherent treatment that Glasser believes is effective for any psychological problem. That cohesion can perpetuate blind spots, even though Glasser has exposed reality therapy to mainstream psychotherapy (1992). Critics question some basic control theory assumptions. So many thoughts crowd our minds; how can all thinking be consciously controlled? Results of biofeedback, however, suggest that people may control physiological processes. Some therapists mistrust the focus on teaching, choosing instead to employ more experiential techniques in therapy (Jeffrey K. Zeig, in Glasser, 1992).

Reality therapy requires both clinical intuition and deep insight into dynamics of human behavior. Specific training in reality therapy should complement, not substitute for, graduate education in psychology or clinical pastoral training. However, its foundations in caring, authenticity, honesty, commitment, and responsibility commend it to greater acceptance in pastoral counseling and other Christian-oriented therapeutic endeavors.

Possibly reality therapy's continued ownership by Glasser's organizations most limits its wider use by ministers and other counselors. While control over orthodoxy of the system has merit, reality therapy's values might be more widely applied if they were taught in other counselor-training programs.

References

Deming, W. E. (1982). *Out of the crisis*. Cambridge, MA: Massachusetts Institute for Technology Press.

Glasser, W. (1965). *Reality therapy*. New York: Harper & Row.

Glasser, W. (1981). *Stations of the mind*. New York: Harper & Row.

Glasser, W. (1986). *Control theory in the classroom*. New York: Harper & Row.

Glasser, W. (1992). Reality therapy. In J. K. Zeig (Ed.), *The evolution of psychotherapy: The second conference.* New York: Brunner/Mazel.

R. D. KAHOE

See BEHAVIOR THERAPY; COUNSELING AND PSYCHOTHERAPY: OVERVIEW.

Rebellion, Adolescent. Adolescence has long been characterized as a time of stress, turmoil, and rebellion against parents and society. Granville Stanley Hall was one of the first to formulate a theory explaining adolescent behavior with the publication of *Adolescence* in 1904. Hall's work was heavily influenced by a biological point of view and the theory of evolution.

Hall postulated that individual development recapitulated the development of the species. The recapitulation thesis states that the storm and stress of this period of life replicated a time in human history when laws of the jungle gave way to laws of responsible society. Adolescence is the intermediary phase when both savagery and civility coexisted, with civility taking supremacy only after a significant conflict. On the positive side, love, altruism, and self-sacrifice are emerging traits that moved the human race from savagery to civility and will move youth from adolescence to adulthood. Herein lay opportunities for parental influence and by implication conflict, but the adolescent phase was primarily a biological development.

Whereas Hall postulated a general concept of biological forces, Anna Freud identified the emerging sexual drive as the force behind adolescent rebellion and turmoil. According to Freud, the maladjustments of adolescence are defenses against acknowledging the internal conflict between giving expression to sexual urges and the fear of parental reprisal. Like Hall, Freud believed that this struggle is a necessary preliminary stage to entering society.

Contemporary psychoanalytic thought diminishes the importance of the biologically based sexual drive and instead focuses on the developmental task of self-definition and redefining the former parent-child relationship. Rebellion in this context is not a phase but manifestations of the adolescent's uneven attempts at forming an identity. Furthermore, this identity, which is neither child nor adult, must redefine the parent-child relationship, which was characterized by the authority of the parent and the obedience of the child.

A large body of research suggests that the turmoil and rebellion of adolescence are not necessarily universal or even normative. Social learning theorists such as Albert Bandura think that the conflicts of adolescence, especially with parents, are overgeneralized from small samples of deviant youth, sensationalized by the mass media, and is part of a self-fulfilling cultural prophecy that adolescents ought to be rebellious. Anthropologist Margaret Mead and others have suggested that the transition from childhood to adult roles in a society are determined by cultural values and expectations. Furthermore, populations in many non-Western countries do not evidence adolescent rebellion.

Cross-cultural researchers also describe adolescent rebellion as a unique problem to the United States not as a difficulty of adolescence but as a broad social problem of violence. For example, among the 17 industrialized countries, the United States has the highest rate of homicide. Youth violence is perceived as modeling a general culture of violence. Adolescent drug abuse is another example where the problems for youth are a reflection of the broader social problems in our communities.

Adolescent surveys conducted during the 1970s and 1980s suggest that 70% to 80% of 14- to 18-year-olds transition through adolescence without significant difficulties with either parents, peers, school, or vocational choice. While 20% to 30% of adolescents surveyed show moderate to severe symptoms, this is the same rate of psychopathology observed in the adult population. These findings have led many behavioral scientists to challenge the early conceptualizations that adolescence is a difficult developmental stage of life.

Researchers and theorists studying family life believe that conflict is a part of all intimate relationships and the difficulties of adolescence are due to the transition of a family with two adults to a family with three adults. The rebellion of an adolescent is interpreted as an attempt to break free from a rigidly defined "obedient child" role imposed by parents. Rebellion is the demand to be recognized as an autonomous individual and challenges parents to renegotiate their relationship with the emerging adult in their child.

Adolescents need help in developing healthy ways of expressing themselves other than being antiparent. James Coleman, a researcher on youth culture, suggests that industrialized society's placement of children in schools for an extended period of time has led to the development of youth subcultures in which peer acceptance and popularity are the tokens of achievement. While still needing adult guidance, adolescents have increasingly less exposure to adult role models. Nevertheless, other researchers argue against Coleman, stating that adolescents generally accept the values of their parents and the differences are in degree and not content.

The church is one of the few community organizations that seeks to accommodate all ages. It is therefore a unique environment that exposes adolescents to adults who are not family and provides a comparison group by which adolescents can judge their own parents. The Christian community has the potential for offering alternatives to the adolescent need for autonomy. The church can provide outlets for altruism and opportunities to change society for a better tomorrow, an expressed ideal of many rebellious adolescents.

W. T. AOKI

See ADOLESCENCE; PARENTING.

Reconstructive Psychotherapy. Although there is no universally accepted classification of psychotherapies, reconstructive psychotherapy is generally distinguished from supportive psychotherapy and reeducative psychotherapy by its depth of exploration and breadth of goals. Wolberg (1967) suggests that this general category of therapies has as its distinctive quality the goal of insight into unconscious levels of conflict. In this regard symptom relief is only part of the goal of a reconstructive therapy; the broader goal also includes a promotion of emotional development through insight.

Reconstructive psychotherapy is closely associated with psychoanalysis in that most of the therapies that would be generally classified as reconstructive have their origins in the psychoanalytic tradition. In addition to the classical psychoanalytic technique, other therapies usually classified as reconstructive include psychoanalytic psychotherapy, Adlerian psychotherapy, Jungian analysis, the will therapy of Otto Rank, and the dynamic-cultural therapies of Karen Horney and Harry Stack Sullivan.

Reference

Wolberg, L. (1967). *The technique of psychotherapy* (Vol. 1) (2nd ed.). New York: Grune & Stratton.

D. G. BENNER

See PSYCHOANALYSIS: TECHNIQUE; PSYCHOANALYTIC PSYCHOLOGY.

Record Keeping. In the present litigious environment that pervades the nation, the issue of record keeping has become one of paramount importantce not only to mental health and medical professionals, but for ministers and pastoral counselors as well. In California, the mental health laws that apply to psychologists mandate that a document of "informed consent" be part of each patient's chart, as well as dates of service, type of treatment provided and some notation of the patient's status or progress. Because the Ethical Standards for Psychologists and Code of Conduct of the American Psychological Association (APA, 1992) require psychologists to obtain informed consent as well as adherence to state and local laws, failure to take notes or keep records, at least for psychologists, may be construed as a significant departure from standard care. Clinical social workers as well as marriage and family counselors are subject to similar laws in most states. Therapists' records must be kept for at least seven years after the last contact for adults. For children the "clock" starts counting when they reach their eighteenth birthday. However, some attorneys advise that records should never be destroyed at all. When destroying records, a shredder must be used. They cannot simply be put in the paper recycling bin or in the ordinary garbage can.

Most mental health and medical providers who have graduated from university or professional schools in the last ten years have received this information through classes specifically focused on legal and ethical issues. Guidelines for record keeping and how to document issues that may later prove useful in legal proceedings is now part of the curriculum of such courses.

However, pastors and pastoral counselors do not usually have specific guidance on these issues in their seminary training. The following are recommendations from the author that come from many years of teaching psychology students and serving in ethics committees of professional organizations.

Pastors and pastoral counselors need to keep basic records of consultations with parishioners or even casual visitors to their churches when the consultation involves personal matters that would fall into the general category of "counseling." Pastors in many states are included in the mandates regarding reporting of child and elder abuse and neglect, as well as the *Tarasoff* (1976) mandate regarding the duty to protect intended victims of bodily harm. In California, a law that went into effect January 1, 1997, specifically requires clergypersons to report child and elder abuse, except when the communication is covered by a "sacramental seal."

It is recommended that clergy counselors keep as a minimum the name, address and date of birth of the counselee, along with brief statements of the nature of the issues brought by the parishioner, and any recommendations made to the person. This latter information is crucial. Consider, for example, the case where the counselee appears to be suicidal and the pastor recommends that the person seek psychiatric care. If the person does not follow through and commits suicide, the family may want to sue the pastor for not protecting the person from him or herself. If the pastor made the recommendation and the person failed to follow through, the pastor must demonstrate in a form acceptable to the legal system that the recommendation was made. Clear documentation is necessary. In the forensic arena there is an unwritten law that "if it is not written down, it didn't happen." The word of the pastor that he or she made the recommendation is not enough defense in court. Another example of the need to document recommendations would be as follows. A pastor makes a referral to a specific professional and that therapist abuses or commits malpractice against that individual. The parishioner may include the referring pastor in the law suit as having exercised poor judgment in making the referral. It is better to always give two or three names and make a record of these. Then the choice of the counselee is her or his own and not following the specific recommendation of the pastor.

The pastor needs to keep these records locked and accessible only to him or herself. These records cannot be left behind in the church office when the pastor moves to a new call. He or she must keep these records for a recommended length of time usually determined by state law.

References

American Psychological Association. (1992). Ethical principles of psychologists and code of conduct. *American Psychologist, 47,* (12), 1597–1611.

Tarasoff v. Regents of the University of California, 13 Cal.3d 177, 529 P.2d 533 (1974), *vacated,* 17 Cal.3d 425, 551 P.2d 334 (1976).

L. M. Marmol

Reductionism. A fundamental scientific theory which states that one can explain a phenomenon of nature at one level of inquiry by showing how its mechanisms and processes arise out of a lower or more microscopic level. For example, the reductionism of science assumes that chemical reactions can be explained by appealing to the activity and properties of molecules and atoms and ultimately to the physical forces holding atoms together. Reductionism in psychology assumes that all behavioral and mental phenomena can be explained in terms of the physical world. Physiological explanations seem to be the preferred level of explanation in psychology.

Two forms of reductionism are found in the natural sciences and psychology. Methodological reductionism in psychology refers to the decision to confine the language of psychology to expressions that are in principle reducible to a science such as physiological psychology. This is similar to methodological behaviorism, in which mental and psychological phenomena are not denied. In the interest of developing a scientific psychology, the language of private data is avoided in favor of behavioral language that is anchored in public observation. Metaphysical reductionism asserts that for psychology questions of theory are to be resolved by physiological explanations. This compares with metaphysical behaviorism, which assumes that all sentences in the mental language are really translatable into sentences of physical language.

Most psychology is built on the foundation of reductionism, with metaphysical reductionism being frequently held by psychology's leading scientists. This means that much of scientific psychology takes the position that human nature can be described and explained entirely by reference to neurophysiology or conditioned responses and not to concepts such as mind or consciousness.

Metaphysical reductionism implies a belief in both materialism and determinism. This means that human beings have no immaterial essence but are entirely material and that there are physical explanations for every aspect of personality and consciousness. Reductionism does not agree with the philosophical idea of emergentism, which teaches that the organization of parts into a compound structure results in the emergence of new properties that could not have been predicted even from a full knowledge of the parts and their interactions. In other words, reductionism believes that the whole of a person's behavior is nothing more than the sum of its parts.

There are abundant examples of reductionism in psychology from its founding until the present. Adopting the assumptions of materialism and empiricism from the natural sciences, psychology began as a field prone to reductive explanations. The psychophysics of Wilhelm Wundt, the founding father of psychology, suggested this kind of analysis. The term *psychophysics* describes the relating of mind (psyche) to physical laws. John B. Watson's school of behaviorism, which created the central philosophical foundation for psychology as it grew, encouraged the development of a unique reductive language in terms of conditioned reflexes.

One of the strongest proponents of a metaphysical reductionism in psychology was B. F. Skinner, who believed that what have been labeled mental phenomena are the result of physiological responses to environmental stimuli and can be totally explained by the contingencies of reinforcement in a person's environment. It is probably true that most psychologists invariably come to think of neurophysiology as the ultimate level of explanation for all mental and personal phenomena. Carlson (1980), in a popular physiological psychology textbook, states, "Physiological psychologists believe that all natural phenomena (including human behavior) are subject to the laws of physics. Thus, the laws of behavior can be reduced to descriptions of physiological processes. No consideration has to be given to concepts such as free will" (p. 2).

Nowhere in science are the issues of reductionism and levels of explanation more debated than they are in psychology. The distance between psychology and any lower level of explanation is greater than between any other set of levels of explanation in science. Reducing genetics to biochemistry seems acceptable. But it is a much larger step to move from the human personality, with its thoughts, imaginations, and complex emotions, to the interaction of neurons in the brain.

It is precisely this metaphysical reductionism that is opposed to the Christian view of human nature. MacKay (1974), a neurophysiologist, argues that even the most detailed description of the human brain will not exhaust the mystery of the person. MacKay calls the thinking of reductionism "nothing buttery" because of its tendency to say the person is nothing but an assemblage of functioning neurons. When the complexities of the human brain are explained in this way, they are explained away. Explaining the human personality in terms of nothing-buttery allows the reductionist to deal with the complexities of human beings primarily by prior assumption. This is assuming there is nothing more to human nature than the physical; therefore, why look beyond physical explanations? The Christian has no problems with methodological reductionism but feels that the assumptions of metaphysical reductionism clearly pass judgment on the makeup of human nature, when science should be open to investigating all levels of the human personality.

Another problem with reductionism is its decision on the proper level of inquiry. How does the reductionist decide where to base the description of human nature? Why is the organizational level of neurons a better level of description of a human being that the biochemistry of neural firing? To choose any level short of the subatomic world of physics seems to be practicing only a partial reductionism. But to explain human nature entirely in terms of quantum physics results in the loss of the subject matter. It seems more reasonable to describe human nature on the levels of our ordinary experience, including spiritual, psychological, and physical levels. Descriptions at one level should never be considered complete nor be used to invalidate descriptions at other levels.

Neither neurophysiology nor Skinner's behaviorism should be considered sciences with sufficient maturity that one can immediately cancel all holistic explanations of human nature. Many schools of psychology have, in both theory and research, questioned the reductionism of behaviorism and neurophysiology. The ideas of Gestalt psychologists, rationalists such as Jean Piaget and Chomsky, and cognitive behaviorists such as Edward Chase Tolman and Albert Bandura, have rejected the reductionistic notion that detailed information about the physiological or behavioral components of a person produces a complete description of the person.

The limits of metaphysical reductionism do not rule out the advantages of a methodological reductionism to the Christian who is interested in a scientific psychology. In their work psychologists should use language as carefully and objectively as possible. Objective description of human behavior or neurophysiology may be a valuable starting point for psychology. Any psychological investigation that remains at these starting levels will be unable to deal with the complexities of the human personality. A reductionist's precise, objective investigation may be an appropriate place to start but never an appropriate place to stop.

References

Carlson, N. R. (1980). *Physiology and behavior* (2nd ed.). Boston: Allyn & Bacon.
MacKay, D. M. (1974). *The clockwork image.* Downers Grove, IL: InterVarsity Press.

Additional Readings

Collins, G. R. (1977). *The rebuilding of psychology.* Wheaton, IL: Tyndale House.

Turner, M. B. (1968). *Psychology and the philosophy of science.* New York: Appleton-Century-Crofts.

M. P. Cosgrove

See Psychology, Presuppositions of.

Reeducative Psychotherapy. The term Wolberg (1967) uses to describe a group of therapies falling between the two more usually recognized groups known as supportive psychotherapy and reconstructive psychotherapy. Wolberg views the goal of reeducative approaches as interpersonal and behavioral education. Whereas supportive therapy aims for a restoration of equilibrium and reconstructive therapy aims for something closer to a reorganization of personality, reeducative therapy aims for symptom removal through direct attack. Behavior therapy, strategic therapy, reality therapy, and many of the sex and family therapies are examples of reeducative approaches.

Reference

Wolberg, L. (1967). *The technique of psychotherapy* (Vol. 1) (2nd ed.). New York: Grune & Stratton.

D. G. Benner

See Counseling and Psychotherapy: Overview.

Referral. *See* Consultation and Referral.

Reflection of Feeling. *See* Empathy.

Reframing Technique. The therapeutic technique of positively restating or paraphrasing what is perceived by an individual as negative. Used primarily in marriage and family therapy, this intervention helps to get clients out of blaming postures and into more functional interactions. Reframing aims to change the perception of one's own behavior or that of another.

For example, a distancing husband is criticized by his wife for not wanting to be close. The therapist reframes the husband's behavior as his way of trying to get the appropriate space he needs to feel comfortable in the marriage. The therapist is stating indirectly that individuals differ with regard to their need for closeness and that these differences are normal. This understanding paves the way for a discussion of how the couple might achieve a workable compromise on this issue.

The terms *relabeling* and *positive connotation* are used interchangeably with reframing. The controlling behavior of a wife, for instance, is relabeled as her way of showing concern. When her motivation is given a positive connotation, the husband's attitude softens, and he can then proceed to propose alternative ways for her to express concern.

J. A. Larsen

See Family Therapy: Overview.

Regression. In psychoanalytic thought regression is viewed as a defense mechanism, operating outside awareness, wherein an individual retreats to an earlier and therefore more primitive level of psychological development. It is closely connected to the concept of fixation in that the assumption is that the ego is weakened by unresolved past conflicts and the energy remaining with these conflicts. The individual therefore has a tendency to revert to these points of fixation when he or she is faced with serious trauma or anxiety that cannot be managed by other means. Sigmund Freud's metaphor for regression was an army that has left some of its troops behind at sites of earlier battles and that in the face of a strong enemy (psychic conflict) retreats to previously established strongholds. Thus seen, the more serious the fixation, or the greater the number of points of fixation, the more prone the individual is to regression.

Although they are very closely related, regression may be viewed from the separate perspectives of the id, ego, or superego. From the perspective of the id regression is seen as a return to more primitive forms of instinctual expression. This is illustrated by the schizophrenic patient who might desire to be bottle fed or who may engage in childlike expressions of aggression. From the perspective of the ego regression appears as the loss of one or more of the ego functions. The mute psychotic, for example, has lost the ego function of speech. From the perspective of the superego regression may be seen as involving the return to an earlier developmental level of morality. Thus individuals in seriously regressed states sometimes show a return to a morality organized around exaggerated denial or reaction formation, both being typical of an earlier level of moral functioning. While regression may be seen as sometimes affecting one of these systems more than another, usually it is reflected in all three to one degree or another.

In classical psychoanalytic thought the psychopathologies are understood to result from a combination of fixation and regression. The diagnosis of regression requires the demonstration of more advanced levels of functioning being abandoned for more primitive levels. This is usually the case in the psychoses where impaired functioning has often been preceded by a period of much higher level functioning. The degree of the regression is assumed to be reflected in the severity of the psychopathology. Thus schizophrenia is assumed to be associated with a regression to the very earliest level of development, the oral stage.

Abraham's (1953) classification of psychopathologies identified paranoia with a regression to the early part of the anal period, the compulsion neuroses with the late anal period, and hysteria with the phallic period (see Psychosexual Development). While these specific points of regression have been much debated and alternatives presented and of-

ten more widely accepted (e.g., Kernberg, 1980), most psychoanalysts agree that the psychoses represent preoedipal points of fixation/regression, whereas the psychoneuroses represent fixation at an oedipal level, sometimes with the additional operation of regression, although more often without evidence of regression.

Some therapists view regression as normal or even healthy under certain circumstances. For example, regressions seem to occur regularly during puberty and are probably necessary in order to assist the psychic organization of that stage. Similarly some degree of regression following a serious loss (e.g., the death of a loved one) is quite normal and, provided it does not last too long, probably assists in the mourning process (see Grief; Loss and Separation). Sports and other play activities also contain an element of regression, frequently providing an outlet for controlled, socially acceptable aggression. Kris (1952) has described what he calls "regression in the service of the ego," wherein a controlled and partial regression allows for an enhancement of ego functions. This is particularly clear in artistic activities but can also be seen to be operative in humor, imagination, aesthetic expression, and much of our intellectual activity. Arieti (1976) also has provided a very helpful discussion of regression in creativity. In all of these situations the ego of the individual is not overwhelmed, as is the case in psychosis. Rather, it is opened up to previously closed-off levels of the personality, and both the methods and contents of these more primitive levels then serve to enrich the ego.

It should be noted that this controlled regression in the service of the ego is precisely what happens in many psychotherapies (see Regressive Therapy). In psychoanalysis and to a lesser extent in psychoanalytic therapy it is an indispensable component of the therapy process.

References

Abraham, K. (1953). *Selected papers on psycho-analysis.* New York: Basic.
Arieti, S. (1976). *Creativity.* New York: Basic.
Kernberg, O. (1980). *Internal world and external reality.* New York: Aronson.
Kris, E. (1952). *Psychoanalytic explorations on art.* New York: International Universities Press.

Additional Reading

Laughlin, M. C. (1979). *The ego and its defenses* (2nd ed.). New York: Aronson.

D. G. BENNER

See DEFENSE MECHANISMS; PSYCHOANALYTIC PSYCHOLOGY.

Regressive Therapy. The utilization of a regressive process in a fashion that fosters human growth and development. Regressive therapy was first described by Cox and Esau (1974). Similar therapeutic approaches are known by other terms and are often associated with the psychoanalytic movement.

This approach to therapy is used with those persons who have healthy elements of ego functioning but only at a regressed level. These elements are experienced as ego-syntonic despite terror, paranoia, or whatever pathological defenses have interfered. The purpose of the regressive therapeutic approach is to foster the exposure, experiencing, and sharing of these healthy elements in the context of as real a relationship as is available. The selection of the love object is made by the patient, preferably from natural family relationships. In the event no family member is available, because of death, mental illness, or incapacity to offer true love and caring, a surrogate object may be found in the therapist. This poses many problems, due to the limitations of a therapeutic relationship. Transference considerations may complicate such a process, as will the fact that the regressed patient seeks bonding to someone whom he or she experiences in a real, not just a fantasized, relationship.

In psychological and psychiatric literature regression is used in several ways. Some authors view it as a neurological phenomenon, brought about by various organic therapies such as electroconvulsive therapy (ECT) and insulin coma therapy. Hypnotherapy is used for regressive purposes to enable the individual to retrieve previously unconscious affects and memories. Narcoanalysis allows the person to regress to earlier levels of consciousness for retrieval of significant affective experiences. In psychoanalytic psychotherapy regression is defined as a return to earlier levels of ego development. It is viewed as an ego-coping mechanism in response to severe anxiety-provoking experiences. In particular the schizophrenic has been viewed as regressing into narcissism with a development of overt psychotic symptomatology. Regressive therapy views regression in a somewhat different manner. This therapy uses regression in the service of the ego.

Regression in the service of the ego is a part of everyday life. Vacations, recreation, and other overt or symbolic activities and affects that awaken the child in us are beneficial regressions used to restore and renew at the emotional level. In transactional terms, if the child is sacrificed for the development of the adult and/or parent, an imbalance of pathological proportions develops (*see* Transactional Analysis). This results in a pattern of interpersonal and intrapsychic problems. In the emotionally disturbed individual there may be regressions in order to grow and develop one's personality. Regression in the transference relationship has been widely noted (see Searles, 1965).

Regressive therapy utilizes those regressive impulses that can aid the individual in identifying and experiencing a profound level of trust from which healthy psychotherapeutic object relatedness and growth may occur. The thesis of psychoanalytic treatment is that the patient is to be allowed to regress to deeper levels and then to grow. The development of a dependency transference allows for the exploration of this regression (see Balint, 1968). The regressive process in regressive therapy focuses more on regression within a real relationship and is applicable to psychiatric maladies not traditionally treated by a classic psychoanalytic method. Whereas the psychoanalytic approach tends to encourage fantasy concerning the therapist, diminishing the expression of real feelings in the treatment hour, regressive therapy seeks the genuine sharing of real human expressions with the aim of bonding between the patient and love object. For obvious reasons it is best that such object be a family member if possible.

The goals of a regressive therapeutic process are the enhancement of those ego capacities that, although they are at a younger age of development, are healthier than the current pathological functions. This is most startlingly demonstrated in schizophrenia, but the principle remains the same elsewhere. The development of trust between a love object and those regressed and healthy parts of the ego allows for working out and abandoning pathological defenses that are based on paranoia and mistrust.

The manner in which these goals are achieved is best understood in object relations theory. The cathexes in the afflicted individual are complex. In many schizophrenic patients, and in others as well, there are those fragments or segments of personality in which trust still is desired and intimacy is preferred. As in a normal child growth and development trust is bonded in human relationships, especially parental ones. In a regressive therapeutic process the patient is given the opportunity to reexperience these hitherto covert but ego-syntonic desires in a new experience of trust. This has been done both in individual therapy, where the therapist becomes the object, and more commonly in a marital or family approach, where the original object is given opportunity to reestablish trust and thence promote a growth process in the family relationships.

For much of the twentieth century parents have been viewed as the cause of psychiatric illness. Wiser observations point to the frequency with which both the parents and the child are victims of circumstances, pressures, and relationships that they did not consciously choose and that they may have a common desire to undo. Efforts are made, therefore, within regressive therapy to reexperience the events of the early childhood traumas together in a family context. This will often result in regressive desires and actions by the patient. Under no circumstances are these regressive behaviors forced or demanded. Rather, they are a natural outgrowth of the reexperience.

The regression may be only in certain aspects of life and around key events. It does not necessarily involve a total regression of all of life. The patient does not become a small child again, although childish affects, desires, and relatedness develop. The preferred therapeutic approach is for the patient to experience the regressive process in relationship to the natural environment, those relationships in which the person grew and to which he or she still has a strong desire for bonding. When this is not possible and a strong regressive wish is evident in the psychotherapeutic process, a therapist may be such an object. There are, however, natural limits to this. The fantasy of the naïve could lead one into a major rescue effort without realizing that a therapist is a therapist, not a mother or a father. If the therapist takes on the function of parent, he or she not only steps outside a role established by society but may hurt those to whom he or she belongs. On some occasions the therapist as object is sufficient for those patients who have less need of a full regressive approach and where only segments and specific issues are involved. This approach is most appropriate for the seasoned therapist who has at his or her command a wide range of psychotherapeutic techniques and experiences.

This method of treatment is based on interpersonal theory and calls upon an object relations theoretical framework. It views estrangement and the resulting desire for restitution of the relationship as the strongest need. The establishment and maintenance of bonding are synonymous with health. Subsequent differentiation is based on healthy bonding. This view is seen to be readily compatible with and supported by the biblical view of humans as lost creatures. This is not the same, however, as saying that emotional problems are the result of conscious sin or that restoration from serious psychopathology comes by a simplistic application of the principles of Christian living. It would suggest that a common core of psychopathology has to do with the loss and distortion of relationships.

References

Balint, M. (1968). *The basic fault: Therapeutic aspects of regression.* London: Tavistock.

Cox, R. H., & Esau, T. G. (1974). *Regressive therapy.* New York: Brunner/Mazel.

Searles, H. F. (1965). *Collected papers on schizophrenia and related subjects.* New York: International Universities Press.

T. G. ESAU

See PSYCHOANALYSIS: TECHNIQUE; PSYCHOANALYTIC PSYCHOTHERAPY.

Rehabilitation. Rehabilitation is the process of assisting dysfunctional persons back to functionality in society. It therefore includes the endeavors to rehabilitate criminals, those persons who are physically handicapped, emotionally handicapped, socially handicapped, or mentally handicapped, persons with insufficient skills or ability to sustain themselves with useful work and are thus laid off or unemployable, persons with histories of addictions, persons who have sustained injuries resulting in their requiring assistance to return to normal or useful function, and persons who have experienced diseases that have impaired them in some manner. The industrial nations of the world have developed many private and public programs for rehabilitation of persons by providing education, training, physical therapy, psychotherapy, vocational therapy, occupational therapy, speech therapy, and the like.

The federally funded programs to help handicapped persons return to competitive employment are good examples of vocational rehabilitation in the United States. Guidelines and specifications of methods and goals are set by the federal government, and the programs are administered by the states with federal and matching funds. The motivation for all rehabilitation programs is both humane and economic: to reduce the degree of human suffering, dysfunction, and disadvantage in society and to increase the efficiency of the economy by returning people to the work force and tax rolls while removing them from public assistance. Two criteria control selection for rehabilitation, namely, a documented status of dysfunction such as imprisonment, injury, or loss of employability, and the potential for gaining genuine profit from the rehabilitation process.

Determination of eligibility for vocational rehabilitation, for example, is made by a vocational rehabilitation counselor who assesses medical records, psychological records, employment records, records of injury, vocational test results, response to counseling, and the like. Thereafter a referral is made to ensure that the client is provided the optimal rehabilitation experience, location, and outcome. The client and counselor devise the rehabilitation program together, and the services may include medical or psychological care, convalescence, prosthesis, transportation, personal needs, maintenance, clothing, and formal programs of training of all kinds. In vocational rehabilitation programs, specifically the services provided directly by the counselor include personal counseling, training in job-seeking skills, vocational education information, setting up on-the-job training programs, job placement assistance, and coordination of services from other agencies (Honour, 1990).

After the client has succeeded in reestablishing himself or herself in the work force the counselor undertakes a follow-up evaluation for a specified period of time, such as two or three months, to ensure that the client is appropriately employed, can effectively accomplish the work, remains motivated to succeed, and has developed short-range, medium-range, and long-term goals. Vocational rehabilitation has demonstrated a rather high level of effectiveness in the United States.

Rehabilitation of criminals or prison populations in the United States does not evidence such a positive level of efficiency or fruitful outcome. Even the statistical reports issued by the various levels of government do not present an optimistic picture of the effectiveness of such rehabilitation. Rehabilitation programs for juvenile delinquents, for example, rarely are effective, and restraint programs such as community supervision arrangements, tethers, incarceration early in criminal careers, and the like are now preferred (*see* Juvenile Delinquency). This protects society, but confinement to youth facilities and adult prisons has not achieved restoration of social function at satisfactory levels.

Some prison rehabilitation programs for felonious offenders are exceptions to the rule. Whereas child molesters have a high degree of recidivism if they are untreated and unsupervised, both the federal and state programs for their rehabilitation produce higher results than is average for the general prison rehabilitation system. The reason may be traced to three facts. First, the treatment program in the prisons themselves is intensive, psychologically sophisticated, medically supported when the client indicates requirements for psychotropic medications, aggressively confrontational, and designed to hold the client accountable for his or her reality.

Second, the follow-up program after release from incarceration includes intensive probation supervision and therapy designed to work with the client on accountability and preventive maintenance issues. These factors are heavily reinforced by the measures taken for raising the levels of community awareness which reinforce accountability.

Third, these programs have been afforded extraordinary financial and media support. An issue that has not been adequately addressed regarding prisoner rehabilitation is the potential link between criminal behavior and endogenous psychopathology, particularly those types that are rooted in biochemical deficits or inherited disorders of various kinds. It is increasingly apparent that a very high percentage of persons who appear for psychotherapy are suffering from genetically or biochemically induced conditions such as borderline personality disorder. This specific disorder manifests itself with a predictable array of symptoms, including a rather towering narcissism; some depression and anxiety, which may in some cases be bipolar disorder; a schizoid view of reality; significant paranoia; and a lack of socio-affective appropriateness. There is some reason to believe that significant percentages of prison populations may be suffering from this biochemically based disorder. Persons so afflicted have virtually no capacity to learn from training or from their own experience or pain unless they are medicated with such antipsychotic psychotropic drugs as Risperdal or Navane. If they are unmedicated, such persons have little capacity to respond constructively to rehabilitative training or assistance.

This hypothetical case raises two crucial questions in the entire matter of rehabilitation in all fields. It is first the theologicophilosophical question of genetic or biochemical determinism, which will require a great deal of careful attention in the coming millennium. Second is the ethical question. Are clients required to rehabilitate for their own good and for the well-being of society, or are they free to live out their lives in dysfunction at enormous cost to their families and the state? Are they required to undertake those steps that make them responsible contributors rather than liabilities to the commonweal? If the latter is the case, as most would agree, and the case is that they are unable to respond to rehabilitative programs unless they are medicated for biochemically induced or inherited disorders, who can take the responsibility to make that decision to medicate and enforce it? Does the medical profession have that prerogative and responsibility, does the judicial system, the prison system, the state, the family? This is a crucial problem that will come to the forefront of social concern in the forthcoming century and require careful and ingenious solutions (Ellens, 1997).

References

Ellens, J. H. (1997). The interface of psychology and theology. *Journal of Psychology and Christianity, 16* (1).

Honour, R. E. (1990). Vocational rehabilitation. In R. J. Hunter (Ed.), *Dictionary of pastoral care and counseling*. Nashville: Abingdon.

J. H. ELLENS

See BIOPSYCHOSOCIAL THERAPY.

Rehearsal, Obsessional. A sort of dress rehearsal of an anticipated event that helps a person plan how to carry out a compulsive ritual in as socially inconspicuous manner as possible. Persons who have well-developed compulsions are usually able to carry out their compulsive rituals with ease in private settings. However, when a compulsive person is obligated to participate in a setting that makes the performance of the ritualistic behavior difficult, a serious dilemma occurs. Obsessional rehearsal is one solution.

For example, a person whose compulsive rituals include washing his or her hands seven times before picking up the eating utensils is faced with a serious dilemma when he or she is invited to sit at the head table at a large banquet. The compulsive person may choose to visit the banquet hall, locate the restroom closest to the head table, recruit a friend who could accompany him or her to the restroom, and ask the friend to open all necessary doors between the restroom and the banquet hall. By means of such planning, or obsessional rehearsal, the compulsive person is able to participate in what otherwise would be an impossible event. Obsessional rehearsal obviously adds a great deal of complexity and inconvenience to the already cluttered life of a compulsive.

J. R. BECK

See OBSESSIVE-COMPULSIVE DISORDER.

Reinforcement. A substantial body of scientific evidence derived from operant conditioning research indicates that behavior is strongly influenced by its consequences. Consequences are classified according to the effect they have on behavior. Stimuli or events that increase the likelihood that a response will occur again are termed reinforcers, whereas stimuli or events that decrease the likelihood of response are termed punishers. Reinforcers are further distinguished according to whether their presentation or removal increases responding.

If the presentation of a reinforcer following a response increases the likelihood that the response will recur, then it is a positive reinforcer and the process is known as positive reinforcement. For example, giving a hungry animal a food pellet after a lever press response will increase the probability that the animal will press the lever again. In this case food serves as a positive reinforcer. Similarly if parental praise increases the frequency with which a child makes his or her bed, then praise is a positive reinforcer for bed making.

If the removal of a stimulus or an event increases the likelihood that the response will recur, then it is termed a negative reinforcer and the process is known as negative reinforcement. For example, if a response terminates or avoids a painful electric shock, then the response will be likely to occur again. In this case electric shock is a negative reinforcer. Escape and avoidance behaviors maintained by negative reinforcement are part of everyday life. People have ways of getting away when they are trapped in an unpleasant social situation, and they learn behaviors that enable them to avoid such unpleasant situations.

Types of Reinforcers and Their Results. Reinforcers also are classified as either primary or acquired. Primary reinforcers usually are related to the biological needs of the organism; acquired reinforcers are those resulting from the individual's experience with the environment. A primary reinforcer is a stimulus or event that innately affects behavior without any prior experience. Positive primary reinforcers may be things that are vital to survival, such as food and water, or they may be less obvious events such as sensory change or opportunities to explore a novel environment. Negative primary reinforcers may be such things as physically painful events, loud noises, bright lights, and noxious odors.

A conditioned (secondary) reinforcer is a stimulus that, because it is consistently accompanied by a primary reinforcer, acquires reinforcing properties itself. For example, if an animal that has learned to press a lever to obtain food pellets is placed in a separate box and is fed pellets each time a buzzer is sounded, the buzzer will become a conditioned reinforcer and will sustain lever presses in the absence of food pellets. Stimuli that reliably accompany negative reinforcers similarly acquire conditioned reinforcing properties, and their removal will reinforce behavior. For example, animals will perform a specified response to terminate a stimulus that is consistently followed by painful electric shock. However, conditioned reinforcers, both positive and negative, will lose their power if they are not accompanied by the primary reinforcer at least some of the time. By the proper use of conditioned reinforcement elaborate sequences of behavior can be trained and maintained with a single primary reinforcer that occurs at the end of the sequence.

A stimulus that has been associated with many types of primary as well as conditioned reinforcements may acquire the capacity to function as a generalized reinforcer. Money is an obvious illustration of a generalized reinforcer because it provides access to food, drink, shelter, or entertainment and thereby becomes a reinforcer for a variety of activities. Social reinforcers also are thought to represent a special class of generalized reinforcers.

The concept of conditioned and generalized reinforcers helps bridge the gap between simple laboratory procedures and complex human and animal learning. The range of human behavior attributable directly to primary reinforcers is small. Moreover, the development of social reinforcers is particularly critical because human behavior is frequently strengthened, sustained, and modified by praise, approval, encouragement, positive attention, and affection.

Although there is little dispute about the validity of the principle of reinforcement, numerous alternative explanations have been proposed for the manner in which reinforcement produces its effect. Some early theories argued that reinforcers are events that ultimately satisfy some vital need of the organism; others argued that the sensations involved in performing these acts are themselves innately reinforcing. However, no single theory adequately accounts for the full range of activities and stimuli that can be used to reinforce behavior. Therefore, many psychologists have turned to defining reinforcers operationally in terms of their effect on behavior without attempting to identify why a particular event serves as a reinforcer.

Although it may not be possible to specify why a particular event is reinforcing, a number of factors generally influence the effectiveness of a reinforcer. For example, the longer that rewards are delayed following responses, the less effective they tend to be unless the gap between response and reinforcement is bridged cognitively (e.g., through verbal instructions) or with a conditioned reinforcer. Primary positive reinforcers also are usually effective only if the organism has been deprived of them in the recent past; food is not likely to serve as reinforcer for an animal that is not hungry. Larger or higher quality reinforcers also are more effective than smaller or lower quality reinforcers. Schedules of reinforcement, which determine when appropriate responses will be reinforced, also are important. Schedules determine both the pattern of reinforced responding and how persistent responding will be if responses fail to produce reinforcement (extinction). Finally, the effectiveness of a given reinforcer is affected by the potency of other available reinforcers.

In addition to its ability to strengthen behavior, reinforcement can provide information concerning the appropriateness of behavior. New behavior can be shaped by selectively reinforcing bits of behavior that come successively closer to the desired behavior. Differential reinforcement can establish discriminations by reinforcing a response in the presence of one stimulus and withholding reinforcement in the presence of others.

Misunderstandings and Evaluation. The deliberate use of positive reinforcement to influence human behavior, especially in the form of tangible rewards, has given rise to ethical objections and concerns about the possible harmful effects that may result from such practices. A frequently expressed attitude is that desirable behavior should be intrinsically satisfying. One concern is that, if people are frequently rewarded, they will behave appropriately only when they are paid to do so. Some observers believe that reinforcing practices may interfere with the development of spontaneity, creativity, intrinsic motivational systems, and other highly valued self-determining personality characteristics. Others even consider the deliberate use of reinforcement as deceptive, manipulative, and an insult to the personal integrity of human beings. However, such negative attitudes often stem from basic misunderstandings and from the observed misapplication of reinforcement principles.

Much of the work on reinforcement principles has been conducted with animals in operant conditioning experiments. This has led to the erroneous belief that the use of reinforcement is somehow beneath human dignity. In addition, people tend to associate the use of reinforcement principles with behavioristic practitioners whose nonbiblical philosophies conflict with an acceptable Christian view of humans and human behavior. Finally, the use of reinforcement to bring about desirable behavior challenges beliefs that desirable behavior (e.g., learning) are themselves inherently rewarding. Yet, available evidence does not justify such beliefs; few behaviors are inherently rewarding for all people. Moreover, sometimes it is necessary to use external rewards to bring people into contact with the natural rewards associated with desirable behaviors.

The use of external rewards has led to the false impression that the total province of reinforcement theory lies in the manipulation of behavior through materialistic reinforcement. However, abundant evidence suggests that reinforcement procedures, if they are thoughtfully and skillfully implemented, can produce enduring changes in social behavior and facilitate the acquisition of self-monitoring reinforcement systems. If rewards are repeatedly and explicitly associated with cues that signify competency or correctness, then these stimuli have informative value, and qualitative differences in performance may acquire secondary reinforcing properties. At this higher level of development cues that indicate the adequacy of one's performance may be as reinforcing as monetary incentives. Once informative response feedback becomes a source of personal satisfaction, then maintenance of behavior is less dependent on external or material incentives. The highest level of autonomy is achieved when behavior generates self-evaluative and self-reinforcing consequences; that is, when a person sets standards of achievement and creates self-rewarding or self-punishing consequences depending on the quality of his or her behavior relative to his or her self-imposed standards. Self-reinforcement not only may maintain behavior without external support but also may override the influence of rewards that conflict with a person's own norms of acceptable behavior.

Reinforcement plays a vital role in the learning process. Its thoughtful application is instrumental in helping shape desirable behavior. The application of reinforcement principles, often referred to as behavior modification, has been shown to be a fruitful approach to some behavior problems. Its successful application has been demonstrated in teaching, psychotherapy, industry, prisons, and institutions for the mentally retarded and emotionally disturbed. At the same time, if reinforcement procedures are improperly applied and the incentives inappropriate to the individual's development, then the use of reinforcement may be insulting as well as ineffective.

Additional Readings

Bandura, A. (1969). *Principles of behavior modification*. New York: Holt, Rinehart, & Winston.

Reynolds, G. S. (1975). *A primer of operant conditioning* (Rev. ed.). Glenview, IL: Scott, Foresman.

S. R. Osborne

See Learning.

Reinforcement, Schedule of. A behavior rule that specifies under what conditions a response will produce reinforcement. For example, a schedule of continuous reinforcements means that every appropriate response produces reinforcement. However, in most cases reinforcers do not occur on schedules of continuous reinforcement. Instead they are obtained on schedules of intermittent reinforcement.

Simple intermittent schedules can be classified into two types: ratio and interval. Ratio schedules prescribe that a certain number of responses must be made to produce reinforcement. Interval schedules prescribe that a given interval of time must elapse before response can be reinforced. Under ratio schedules the amount of time taken to make the required number of responses is irrelevant as long as the required number of responses are made. Under the interval schedule the number of responses is irrelevant as long as the one response necessary for reinforcement occurs after the interval has elapsed.

Ratio and interval schedules are further classified into two types: fixed and variable. Under a variable schedule the number of responses or the amount of elapsed time required for one reinforcement varies from reinforcement to reinforcement in an irregular but usually repeating fashion. Under a fixed schedule the number of responses or the amount of elapsed time required for one reinforcement is always the same.

The value of a variable schedule is the average number of responses or time interval required for reinforcement. For example, a variable-ratio 70 (VR 70) schedule prescribes that on the average every seventieth response produces reinforcement even though the exact number for any given reinforcement may vary from numbers much below 70 to numbers much larger. Similarly a variable-interval schedule varies the amount of time that must elapse before a response can be reinforced. For example, a variable-interval one minute (VI 1-min) schedule prescribes that on the average after one minute has elapsed, a response produces reinforcement even though the exact interval of time may vary from times much longer than one minute to intervals much shorter.

The value of a fixed schedule is always the same. For example, a fixed-ratio 50 (FR 50) schedule prescribes that every fiftieth response produces reinforcement. Similarly, a fixed-interval one minute (FI 1-min) schedule prescribes that the first response that occurs after each one-minute interval produces reinforcement.

Each of these schedules of reinforcement produces a characteristic pattern of responding. Fixed-ratio schedules generate a rapid, continuous response rate following a pause after each reinforcement. Variable-ratio schedules also generate a fairly high, constant rate of responding. On fixed-interval schedules there is a pause after reinforcement; thereafter responding increases gradually and then accelerates as time to reinforcement decreases. Variable-interval schedules maintain a constant, uninterrupted rate of responding. Overall, response rates are determined by the average interreinforcement interval; that is, shorter average intervals or response ratios maintain higher response rates.

When responses are no longer reinforced, they decrease in frequency and eventually cease. This extinction process is different for the various schedules of reinforcement. In general the greater the difference between conditions prevailing during extinction and conditions when responses were reinforced, the more rapid the extinction. Behavior maintained by intermittent reinforcement is more resistant to extinction than behavior maintained by continuous reinforcement. A mother who occasionally reinforces her child's temper tantrums by comforting the child is building more persistent tantrums than the mother who always comforts an unhappy child.

There are many examples of schedules of reinforcement in everyday life. Behavior is reinforced on a fixed-ratio schedule when a factory pays a worker a certain amount each time a fixed number of items has been manufactured. Slot machines at gambling casinos pay off according to variable-ratio schedules of reinforcement. Bus drivers arrive at fixed intervals. An hour before a bus is due, no one looks to see if it is coming. But as the scheduled time nears, people tend to glance down the street more and more frequently. In contrast, dialing a telephone number after hearing a busy signal is an example of a variable-interval schedule.

Some psychologists study simple schedules of reinforcement because they believe that complex patterns of behavior are maintained by combinations and mixtures of simple schedules. Schedules of reinforcement also provide a convenient and stable set of procedures for laboratory investigations of learning.

S. R. Osborne

See Reinforcement.

Reinforcement, Self. The self-administration of positive reinforcers (rewarding events) or the self-removal of negative reinforcers (punishing events) contingent on a particular target behavior in the individual. In either case the intended purpose of self-reinforcement is to strengthen the target behavior. In contrast, self-punishment is defined as the self-removal of positive reinforcers or the self-administration of negative reinforcers.

To a great extent these concepts grew out of the research and theorizing of B. F. Skinner. His distinction between controlling and controlled responses was particularly important in stimulating research and writing on self-reinforcement. Controlling responses are the behaviors individuals use to modify a target behavior in themselves or in another person, whereas controlled responses are the changed behaviors. Human beings have the unique potential of being counselor and client, therapist and patient, experimenter and subject, or teacher and student within the same skin. This potential is based on the fact that persons can change themselves through the same operations they use to change others, and self-reinforcement is perhaps the most commonly used self-controlling operation.

Whereas positive self-reinforcement (the self-administration of rewards) is often used, negative self-reinforcement (the self-removal of punishers) has rarely been employed for clinical purposes. Positive self-reinforcement may involve the self-administration of tangible reinforcers such as candy or peanuts, token reinforcers such as points on a counter or checks on a sheet of paper, activity reinforcers such as taking a walk or reading a book, social reinforcers such as self-praise, and symbolic reinforcers such as self-evaluation or comparing one's own performance with a goal.

As normally practiced self-reinforcement consists of several operations: presenting an immediate cue for the target behavior; observing the target behavior when it occurs; recording the occurrence of the target behavior or its byproducts; comparing one's own response with a performance objective or with a criterion for reinforcement; and administering a positive reinforcer or removing a negative reinforcer. The common labels for these operations are self-cuing, self-observation, self-monitoring/self-recording, self-evaluation, and self-consequating, respectively.

The effects of self-reinforcement may be enhanced by self-administering an appropriate deprivation or satiation schedule, injesting certain drugs, noncontingently self-applying pleasant or aversive stimulation, providing oneself with choices, writing a performance contract, choosing back-up reinforcers before the intervention begins, or exposing oneself to a social model who is being reinforced for the same target behavior.

Self-reinforcement became an important treatment strategy during the 1970s. Because it developed out of basic research on learning and social influence processes, it first appeared in the clinical procedures of psychotherapists who used behavioral and social learning approaches to treatment. Self-reinforcement has allowed patients and clients first to assist the professional therapist and then to take control of their own treatment.

Among the issues treated by self-reinforcement have been academic achievement and work output, alcoholism, angry outbursts, attentional deficits, dating and heterosexual relations, compulsions, devotional life and spiritual development, drug abuse, impulse control, phobias, physical exercise, smoking, social skills, speech problems, and using bad language.

P. W. CLEMENT

See REINFORCEMENT.

Relabeling Technique. *See* REFRAMING TECHNIQUE.

Relaxation Training. A term commonly applied to a family of techniques that includes Jacobsonian progressive relaxation and its variants; autogenic training; alpha-wave, electromyography, and other forms of biofeedback targeted to relaxation; some forms of hypnotherapy; and meditation and yoga exercises more influenced by Eastern practices. Only Jacobsonian and related deep muscle relaxation procedures will be discussed here.

Jacobson, a physician, developed his technique of progressive relaxation for the treatment of anxious patients. Working from the Watsonian notion that emotions are peripheral in nature, Jacobson (1938) attempted to develop a procedure that would directly reduce the unpleasant experience of tension and anxiety. His procedures involved extensive exercises of tensing and relaxing all the muscle groups in the body.

Jacobson's work went largely unnoticed by mental health professionals until Wolpe began his pioneering work in developing systematic desensitization. Wolpe worked from the theory that to eliminate a conditioned anxiety response, the therapist must condition an antagonistic counterresponse. Wolpe used the relaxation produced by Jacobson's exercises as the suitable antagonistic response. In the treatment of phobias, for example, Wolpe had the person learn progressive relaxation; then he slowly exposed the person imaginally to the feared stimulus while that person was relaxed, so that relaxation rather than fear was increasingly associated with the phobic stimulus. In time it was shown that Wolpe's counterconditioning notions were untenable and that relaxation training is not essential to fear reduction. Nevertheless, many clients had received relaxation training with positive results, and the technique was increasingly being used as an integral part of many behavior therapy treatment approaches.

Wolpe condensed Jacobson's original procedures, and this shortened version is most commonly used today. Called Jacobsonian or progressive relaxation, the procedure in the initial stages calls for the client to progressively tense and relax major muscle groups (e.g., right hand, right forearm, right bicep, shoulders). It is thought that the tensing serves two major functions: highlighting the sensation of muscular tension, so that the person can better exercise conscious control to relax the musculature, and fatiguing the muscle, better allowing relaxation to occur. Each muscle group is tensed and relaxed separately, and the exercise closes with general bodily relaxation. In the early stages the exercises might take 30 to 40 minutes as each muscle group is tensed twice. As training progresses the tensing is reduced to once and then eliminated, thus shortening the time required to complete the exercises (see Goldfried & Davison, 1976).

The most commonly used variants of the basic progressive relaxation procedure are differential relaxation, wherein similar procedures are used, but only certain body parts (as opposed to a whole body focus) are targeted for relaxation; cue-controlled relaxation, where relaxation is paired with a cue word such as "calm," "relax," or "peace," so that subsequently concentrating on or saying that word may produce the experience of relaxation; and variants of any of the above that use the standard procedures but present them in novel formats such as group settings or on audiotape or combine the procedures with biofeedback, autosuggestion, or other techniques.

Progressive relaxation is still a part of standard systematic desensitization. In addition it is a valuable part of many stress-management and anxiety-control treatment approaches, where it is used more as a self-management technique (i.e., a way to moderate the experience of anxiety and stress) than as a way of directly eradicating the problem. It has been shown to be a helpful part of treatment for agoraphobia, social anxieties, alcohol abuse, and other problems. It is the treatment of choice for most forms of insomnia. It is a valuable component in the therapeutic management of chronic and acute pain. Lamaze childbirth procedures use a variant of relaxation procedures. Finally, it is widely used in the treatment of psychosomatic disorders such as migraine and tension headaches, essential hypertension, and a number of other disorders (Taylor, 1982). Some experts suggest that it is just as effective as many forms of biofeedback.

The mode of action of relaxation training is unclear. Some evidence suggests that peripheral (muscular) relaxation induces a reduction in central nervous system sympathetic activity. Numerous studies have documented physical changes produced by relaxation that support this hypothesis, though the evidence is by no means totally consistent (Taylor, 1982). It should be noted that physical relaxation is not equivalent to meditation and that there are many varieties of meditative practices. Care should be taken by the Christian that relaxation procedures used do not become infused with Eastern mystic practices.

References

Jacobson, E. (1938). *Progressive relaxation* (2nd ed.). Chicago: University of Chicago Press.

Goldfried, M., & Davison, G. (1976). *Clinical behavior therapy.* New York: Holt, Rinehart, & Winston.

Taylor, C. B. (1982). Adult medical disorders. In A. S. Bellack, M. Hersen, & A. E. Kazdin (Eds.), *International handbook of behavior modification and therapy.* New York: Plenum.

S. L. JONES

See BEHAVIOR THERAPY.

Reliability, Test. *See* PSYCHOLOGICAL MEASUREMENT.

Religion and Personality. Psychologists commonly use the term *personality* to denote the total of the individual's attitudinal, cognitive, and emotional predispositions. When viewed in this way, it is no surprise that the concepts of religion and personality have been closely associated in Western thought. The origin of the relationship is found in their etymologies. The Latin noun *persona* developed from the infinitive *per sonare,* which indicated the theatrical player projecting the voice through a mouth hole in the facial mask that designated a theatrical role. The English terms *person* and *personality* share *persona* as a point of origin. From that context persona indicated a mask or facade suggestive of a social role. Persona was a social facade adopted in interpersonal contexts.

However, over time persona took on a second, contrary connotation. The surface designation did not correspond with the second usage, which referred to the actor (and the accompanying thoughts, feelings, desires) behind the mask (Monte, 1980). The dual use of persona is an embodiment of the tension experienced when social roles and expectations lead the individual in directions that belie personal inclination, resulting in a disjointed or fragmented individual. Inner reality is divorced from outer requirements.

Religion is a binding force, uniting fragmented personality. The origin of *religion* lies in two Latin verbs. *Religio* denoted a binding or fastening together and came to indicate a reverence and fear of deity. The reverence and fear manifested themselves in an apprehensiveness to fulfill a covenant obligation. *Religio* denoted a restraining or holding back. While the former points to the reverential aspects of religion, the latter points to the ethical restraint role of religion's bridling of human motives and impulses. Hence religion is seen etymologically as a force that reconnects human disjointedness, restrains errant impulses, and gives uniqueness, identity, and integrity to the individual.

Psychological Analyses of Religion. The dimensions of reverence and restraint are incorporated into psychological analyses of religion. Sigmund Freud's view is developed in *Totem and Taboo, Civilization and Its Discontents, The Future of an Illusion,* and *Moses and Monotheism.* For him religion originated in the oedipus complex and its resolution. Respect and reverence for the father figure represent a displaced and sublimated hostility. Identification with the father figure occasions the introjection of values into the superego, the ethical/moral arm of personality, linking religion and personality.

The magnum opus of the psychological analyses of religious experience is James's *Varieties of Religious Experience.* James's definition of religion as "the feelings, acts, and experiences of individual men in their solitude, so far as they apprehend themselves to stand in relation to whatever they may consider the divine" (James, 1902, pp. 32–33) emphasized the reverential, emotional, and sentimental dimensions of religion. Consistent with his pragmatic philosophy, he was more attuned to the fruits of religion than its roots. As well as giving life a sense of hallowedness and sacredness, the fruits of religion regulate individual action through ethical seriousness.

James's approach is reflected in the work of Allport (1937, 1950). The psychological impact of religion on the person is twofold, as the individual seeks to find a personal niche in creation and to develop a frame of reference for life's meaning. The origin of one's religious quest lies in bodily needs, temperament and mental capacity, personal interests and values, the pursuit of rational explanations, and conformity to one's culture (Allport, 1950). Religion involves the whole individual, and the individual's preferences in cognitive, emotive, and social forms reveal themselves even in worship patterns.

Modern theories of personality may be secularized versions of older theological dogmas. Oates (1973) pointed out that recent holistic or self perspectives in personality parallel ancient Hebraic views of human nature. The Hebrews used *nephesh* to portray the unity or wholeness of the person when viewed from without. When wholeness was viewed from within, the term *leb* was used. These were translated *soul* and *heart*, respectively, in the King James (Authorized) Version.

Fromm (1955, 1973) suggested that the essence of human nature is to be found in five existential needs. According to Fromm, personality originated in the needs for orientation and devotion, for rootedness, for relatedness and unity, for identity, and for excitation and stimulation. Religion provides a meaningful frame of reference and an object of devotion. It ties humans to the natural world yet enables an individual to transcend the natural order. One's identity is contingent upon relationships with others of like orientation. Religious activities provide regular excitation and stimulation in the form of rituals, holidays, feasts, and celebrations.

Similar views are to be found in Buber's I-Thou relation and Abraham Maslow's hierarchy of needs. Allport (1950) suggested personality is operative in the formation of religious sentiments. Endogenous mechanisms of organic desire, temperament, psychogenic desires and spiritual values, and the pursuit of meaning are tempered, psychogenic desires and spiritual values, and the pursuit of meaning are tempered by exogenous conformity pressure of culture. Thus religion addresses the issues of individual identity as well as fostering a sense of community.

Religiousness and Personality. The relationship between religiousness and specific temperament or personality characteristics is complex (Sadler, 1970). Many theoretical predictions about religious individuals having different personalities stem from James (1902). James suggested individuals who are healthy experience gradual conversions (are "once born") but sudden converts ("twice born") individuals are sick of soul. In the latter case the experience of a divided self (ideal versus real self) is accentuated in evangelicalism, since it points to an incongruity of what is and what ought to be. Experienced as guilt and anxiety, the divided self motivates redemptive activities such as renunciation of the natural world. Thus an individual needs to be twice born to change a divided self (natural and physical versus spiritual) into a unity (Oates, 1973). For these reasons it has been asserted and reported that sudden converts have more manifest anxiety than do gradual converts or the unregenerate (Rokeach, 1960). Other research fails to confirm this idea (Johnson & Malony, 1982), but these studies made no attempt to distinguish between state and trait anxiety.

The foregoing analysis localizes anxiety in human fallenness. However, state or trait anxiety may also involve human frailty and finiteness. In these cases anxiety may not be resolved by conversion or repentance for sin. Anxiety may involve uncertainty or fear over economic needs, human finiteness, and the existential dread of death. Growth in grace is upheld as a solution to the various sources of anxiety (Grounds, 1976; Oates, 1955).

Others (e.g., Ferm, 1959) have suggested that conversion leads to personality changes. Conversion as a radical process eventually changes behavior. If behavior is changed, then its underlying cause (i.e., personality) must have been transformed. If conversion is radical, it must alter the inner dimensions of human nature. Research (Johnson & Malony, 1982) has failed to confirm such predictions, although it may be that traditional personality assessment instruments are insensitive to the nature of these personality changes.

While James did not do so, many theorists (e.g., Freud, Allport, Fromm) conceived of religiousness at two levels: the personal and the institutional. In the former the focus is on individual personality and how religion affects one's inner life. The institutional level is concerned with the external manifestations of religion, especially as group expectancies and conformity pressures influence the behavior of the individual. The question is then asked about the relative power of each level. Internal religion and institutional, external religion may countermand each other in the operation of personality.

In recent years social learning theorists (Phares, 1973; Rotter, 1966) have examined the situation-specific expectancy of the individual and its relation to belief and behavior. Individuals who expect to control their own outcomes, to dispense their own reinforcements, and to pursue self-control are described as having an internal locus of control. Individuals who expect to be influenced by the social situation, or chance, are termed external locus of control personalities. Rotter (1966) and others have developed assessment instruments to measure this internal-external dimension.

On the basis of the internal-external research one would predict that individuals who have intensely personal religious experiences would be internal in locus of control, while individuals whose religious experiences are of a more institutional, social nature would be external in expectancy and attribution. Such differences have indeed been found between various religions as well as within religious groups. Fundamentalist Protestants could be expected to have higher scores on an internal locus of control scale than liberal Protestants. Furnham (1982) found precisely those differences in clergy responding to an internal-external scale who were asked to describe their theological position, thus supporting other research literature.

Rokeach (1960, 1970, 1973) summarized his survey work as indicating that religious personalities are more authoritarian, more dogmatic, more closed-minded, and more ethnically prejudiced than are less religious and nonreligious individuals. His interest in values and their relationship to religion grew out of participation in authoritarianism research (Adorno, Frenkel-Brunswik, Levinson, & Sanford, 1950). His measure of religiousness was frequency of church attendance, which is more external. Mangis (1995) failed to find closed-mindedness and prejudice (against women) in individuals with religious belief.

Allport (1950) distinguished between intrinsic and extrinsic religious orientation and linked these to personality differences. The extrinsic orientation is pragmatic and self-serving, utilizing religion as means to personal ends. The intrinsic orientation embodies a basic trust of others and empathetic understanding of others. Allport contended that those of an intrinsic orientation are more open-minded and tolerant than the extrinsic. Rokeach agreed but contended that most religious individuals have an extrinsic orientation to religion.

Allport and Ross (1967) found prejudice to be curvilinearly related to religiousness, not linearly as Rokeach suggested. They differentiated between four religious orientations: intrinsic religious orientation, in which religious teachings are internalized to guide daily life; extrinsic religious orientation, in which religion is used to advance personal ambition; indiscriminately proreligious orientation, which uncritically endorses all religious ideas; and antireligious orientation, which rejects all religious teachings. They found the intrinsically religious individual to be the least prejudiced, the extrinsically oriented more prejudiced, and the proreligious the most prejudiced. Antireligious persons were slightly more prejudiced than the intrinsically religious. These findings bear some similarity to the internal-external research.

The locus of control literature suggests that intrinsic religious orientation may operate quite differently from external religious orientation. Several researchers (Donahue, 1985; Watson, Milliron, Morris, & Morris, 1995a, 1995b) report evidence that intrinsic religious orientation is associated with personal control and mental health, while extrinsic religious orientation is more problematic in health terms and relinquishes control from self to other forces. In addition parenting styles may affect the individual's development of a religious orientation. Giesbrecht (1995) found evidence that intrinsic orientation in adolescents is linked to authoritative and supporting parenting styles, while extrinsic religious orientation is associated with permissive parenting.

Psychologists with an antireligious bias often point out that religion generates guilt in its adherents. Supposing guilt to be a negative emotion and contrary to personal health, these have recommended avoiding guilt. However, Christian psychologists (e.g., Narramore, 1985) distinguish between constructive guilt that leads to confession, repentance, and eventual health from guilt that damages self-esteem by being focused only on self. In an interesting analog study, Meek, Albright, and McMinn (1995) found evidence the "intrinsically religious participants were more prone to guilt, but they were more likely to confess their wrongdoing and more likely to forgive themselves than extrinsically religious subjects" (p. 190). Thus for intrinsically religious individuals guilt has an instrumental function, while in extrinsically religious individuals it has a more terminal function.

For Christian psychologists and personality psychologists, personality's link to religion is complex and presents many riddles (Malony, 1977). The associations are complex and paradoxical. Religion has yet to fully actualize its potential in the ethical, healthy operation of personality. Standard personality assessment instruments, because of their ideological surround, fail to measure adequately significant religious concepts (Watson, Milliron, Morris, & Morris, 1995a). The relationship among faith, personality, and religion remains an active research concern in contemporary Christian psychology.

References

Adorno, T. W., Frenkel-Brunswik, E., Levinson, D. J., & Sanford, R. N. (1950). *The authoritarian personality.* New York: Harper & Row.

Allport, G. W. (1937). *Personality: A psychological interpretation.* New York: Holt.

Allport, G. W. (1950). *The individual and his religion.* New York: Macmillan.

Allport, G. W., & Ross, J. M. (1967). Personal religious orientation and prejudice. *Journal of Personality and Social Psychology, 5,* 432–443.

Donahue, M. J. (1985). Intrinsic and extrinsic religiousness: Review and meta-analysis. *Journal of Personality and Social Psychology, 48,* 400–419.

Ferm, R. (1959). *The psychology of Christian conversion.* Westwood, NJ: Revell.

Fromm, E. (1955). *The sane society.* New York: Holt, Rinehart, & Winston.

Fromm, E. (1973). *Anatomy of human destructiveness.* New York: Holt, Rinehart, & Winston.

Furnham, A. F. (1982). Locus of control and theological beliefs. *Journal of Psychology and Theology, 10,* 130–136.

Giesbrecht, N. (1995). Parenting style and adolescent religious commitment. *Journal of Psychology and Christianity, 14,* 228–238.

Grounds, V. C. (1976). *Emotional problems and the gospel.* Grand Rapids, MI: Zondervan.

James, W. (1902). *The varieties of religious experience.* New York: Longmans, Green.

Johnson, C. B., & Malony, H. N. (1982). *Christian conversion: Biblical and psychological perspectives.* Grand Rapids, MI: Zondervan.

Malony, H. N. (Ed.). (1977). *Current perspectives in the psychology of religion.* Grand Rapids, MI: Eerdmans.

Mangis, M. W. (1995). Religious beliefs, dogmatism, and attitudes toward women. *Journal of Psychology and Christianity, 14,* 13–25.

Meek, K. R., Albright, J. S., & McMinn, M. R. (1995). Religious orientation, guilt, confession, and forgiveness. *Journal of Psychology and Theology, 23,* 190–197.

Monte, C. (1980). *Beneath the mask* (2nd ed.). New York: Holt, Rinehart, & Winston.

Narramore, S. B. (1984). *No condemnation.* Grand Rapids, MI: Zondervan.

Oates, W. E. (1955). *Anxiety in Christian experience.* Philadelphia: Westminster.

Oates, W. E. (1973). *The psychology of religion.* Waco, TX: Word.

Phares, E. J. (1973). *Locus of control in personality.* Morristown, NJ: General Learning Press.

Rokeach, M. (1960). *The open and closed mind.* New York: Basic.

Rokeach, M. (1970). Faith, hope and bigotry. *Psychology Today, 3* (11), 33–37; 58.

Rokeach, M. (1973). *The nature of human values.* New York: Free Press.

Rotter, J. B. (1966). Generalized expectancies for internal versus external control of reinforcement. *Psychological Monographs, 80* (1), 1–28.

Sadler, W. A. (1970). *Personality and religion.* New York: Harper & Row.

Watson, P. J., Milliron, J. T., Morris, R. J., & Morris, R. W. (1995a). Locus of control within a religious ideological surround. *Journal of Psychology and Christianity, 14,* 239–249.

Watson, P. J., Milliron, J. T., Morris, R. J., & Morris, R. W. (1995b). Religion and the self as text: Toward a Christian translation of self-actualization. *Journal of Psychology and Theology, 23,* 180–189.

R. L. TIMPE

See PSYCHOLOGY OF RELIGION; PERSONALITY; RELIGIOUS HEALTH AND PATHOLOGY; DEMONIC INFLUENCE, SIN, AND PSYCHOPATHOLOGY; HOLY SPIRIT, ROLE IN COUNSELING.

Religious Development. In broad terms religious development deals with how the individual's relationship with God changes over the life span. In a narrower sense religious development in this article will be viewed in the biblical perspective of spiritual development. This entails the individual being born again (John 3:3) and then experiencing a progressive conformity to the image of God in Christ over the life span (2 Cor. 3:18; Eph. 4:13; Col. 3:10).

Spiritual Development and Developmental Theories. Developmental psychology investigates the process of cognitive, behavioral, affective, and moral change across the life span. It is assumed in this article that an understanding of general human development principles will enhance one's understanding of spiritual development and will afford insights into how spiritual development might be brought about.

The major theories of development that bear relationship to spiritual development are those of Jean Piaget, Lawrence Kohlberg, Erik Erikson, and James Fowler. Piaget suggests that a person's cognitive development proceeds through sequential stages that are progressively more mature and better defined. These stages are associated with particular chronological ages. What is learned at one stage of development can be learned only if there have been the necessary prerequisite learnings dur-ing earlier stages. Piaget's four stages of intellectual development are the sensorimotor stage (birth to about 2 years), the pre-operational stage (2 to 7 years), the concrete operations stage (7 to 12 years), and the formal operations stage (12 years and older). Specific Piagetian cognitive concepts in these stages that are related to spiritual development will be noted in the application section of this article.

Kohlberg's moral reasoning stages view moral reasoning as a specific kind of cognitive operation. Kohlberg researched the ways people think about moral situations (1981). From his research he developed three levels of moral reasoning. Each of the three levels is subdivided into two stages. Level 1 (preschool to early school years) is identified as preconventional morality. At this level the morality of self-interest dominates. The main objective is to avoid punishment or gain concrete rewards. Level 2 morality represents conventional morality (middle school years). This type of moral reasoning refers to the morality of law and social rules and is characterized by the gaining of approval or avoiding disapproval. In level 3 postconventional morality (may develop from adolescence on), moral reasoning sees laws as temporal and necessary guides to human institutions but tests the validity of any law or rule by the criteria of the common good and personal ethical principles.

Erikson's (1963) psychosocial theory outlines a set of developmental stages that extend from the first year of life through old age. Each of the stages is characterized by a central conflict or crisis. A positive resolution to these crises needs to occur for optimal development to proceed. Young children (1–5 years) deal with the issues of trust versus mistrust, autonomy versus shame and doubt, and initiative versus guilt. Elementary school children (6 years to puberty) face the crisis of competence versus inferiority. The adolescent (teen years into the twenties) undergoes the task of establishing a single identity or role confusion. The span of adulthood (twenties on up) revolves around the issues of intimacy versus isolation, generativity versus stagnation, and integrity versus despair.

Fowler's (1981) faith development theory is a sequential-stage approach to faith development. Fowler defines faith as a broad and comprehensive pattern in the way persons construe themselves and the world in relation to God (p. 95). Steele (1986) notes that Fowler's definition of faith is a way of knowing that may or may not make reference to a set of religious beliefs. Faith is a basic attitude that helps shape a person's life (p. 99). This basic attitude develops in the context of six stages. They are designated as intuitive-projective faith (stage 1: 1 year up to school age); mythic-literal faith (stage 2: beginning of school age); synthetic-conventional faith (stage 3: early adolescence); individuative-reflective faith (stage 4: beginning of young adult to about 20); conjunctive faith (stage 5: midlife—age 35 and beyond); and universalizing faith (stage 6: later adulthood).

Critique and Application of Theoretical Developmental Concepts to Life Span Spiritual Developmental. Before considering how aspects of the developmental theories might be applied to spiritual development in Christian life, a brief critique of the assumptive foundations of the theories is in order. Steele (1986) sees the theories of Piaget, Kohlberg, and Fowler as structural in nature. The emphases in a structural viewpoint is on how thinking is done and not on content or what is thought about (p. 97). A biblical approach to spiritual development would emphasize content (what is thought about) without neglecting structure (how thinking is done). Steele (1986) labels the approach of Erikson a functional theory (p. 97). In this perspective human development is related more to content of thought (what) than on structure (how). This emphasis on the importance of content in developmental progression correlates positively with Christian thinking. In Christian thought there is primary emphasis on biblical content as a prime determinant of acceptable spiritual growth. Some of Kohlberg's assumptions are problematic in view of biblical teaching. As Steele (1986) points out, Kohlberg does not link moral reasoning to behavior and does not take human sinfulness seriously. His definition of justice, treated only in terms of rewarding right and punishing wrong, is of serious concern for thinkers approaching spiritual development from a biblical perspective. Biblical treatment of justice would also include the concepts of grace, mercy, and love (p. 111). The primary philosophical difficulty with Fowler is his aforementioned definition of faith. As indicated by Steele (1986), Fowler defines faith as "a human universal that may or may not include a religious component" (p. 112). This definition does not square with biblical descriptions of faith. In biblical teaching faith is anchored in particular content pertaining to the personhood of God. In thinking about Erikson's approach to psychosocial development, one assumption might be questioned. Erikson relates one issue or crisis to one particular stage (e.g., trust versus mistrust to the infancy period, 0–2 years). It is possible that some of the issues highlighted by Erikson at one stage are equally important throughout life (all of the psychosocial stages).

Even though there is some reservation concerning some assumptions of these developmental theorists, helpful insights can be gained that relate to the fostering of spiritual development. Some of these insights will be considered as the life span is divided into infancy, early childhood, middle childhood, adolescence, and adulthood. Any insights gained from a particular theory would be of use to parents, teachers, pastors, and other spiritual mentors.

Infancy (0–2 Years). In infancy spiritual development is not empirically evident. Erikson, however, is instructive for this phase of development. The psychosocial issue dealt with during this period is trust versus mistrust. When parents develop a trust relationship with their children they are laying a solid foundation for any healthy spiritual development in the future. Childlike trust is characteristic of the biblical description as to how believers relate to God as heavenly Father. If young children do not develop trust in this crucial human relational period, it is possible that later on in life they may have some difficulty trusting God.

Early Childhood (2–7 Years). In early childhood more opportunities for enhancing spiritual development are available. As Piaget indicates, the child during this period (preoperational thinking) uses percepts and images, but thinking is fragmentary and discrete. Even though the child cannot reason objectively, the imagination and creativity characteristic of the child at this phase of development can be utilized for spiritual development. Spiritual content is important, but the methodology of content presentation is also important. Spiritual instruction must not rely solely on verbal explanation. Biblical material is to be related to the firsthand experiences of the child. Deuteronomy 6:1–9 is relevant at this point. This passage indicates that childhood spiritual education is to be comprehensive in scope, making all of life a school. God is to be seen in the totality of the child's experience. Spiritual content can be related to the child's experiences and spontaneous questions in direct fashion. Since children in this age group enjoy fantasy, play, and motor involvement, the utilization of story playing offers a great opportunity to teach specific biblical content. This type of activity ties into the imaginative and creative cognitive abilities that are operative at this particular stage. As Kohlberg points out in his preconventional moral stage, there is an emerging sense of morality at this time. Connecting moral connotations drawn from scriptural material to the developmental dimensions of this age span affords great opportunity for facilitating spiritual and moral development. At this time children can be encouraged to move about freely in their environment in order to initiate action and build relationships. Linking religious concepts with these efforts by the child affords great potential for spiritual growth. In Erikson's framework, such linkages may encourage self-reliance rather than doubt and shame and initiative rather than guilt.

Middle Childhood (7–12 Years). In middle childhood, Piaget discovered, new forms of thinking come about that make possible even greater gains in spiritual development. In this stage the child is becoming more able to put facts together, to generalize and classify experiences. Limitations, however, still accompany this period. When a child is asked to use verbal propositions rather than objects, only one statement at a time can be used in reasoning the proposition through. Even though the thinking involved in the generalizing cannot go beyond particular situations or examples, the child can carry on spiritual dialogue. In discussing spiritual content it is to be remembered that the child is concerned with concrete people, actions, and situations. Factual information pertaining to Jesus and to the sources and people of the Christian faith would be appropriate to stress at this time. In presenting these concepts the methodological emphasis would be upon reinforcing children's efforts to finding out, experimenting, and thinking creatively. In Erikson's thinking, this stage involves the crises of industry versus inferiority. For children to develop competency as opposed to inferiority at this stage, spiritual teaching would emphasize that the child's efforts in every aspect of life are known and appreciated by God.

Adolescence (12 to Adulthood). At this developmental time the individual is capable of mature conceptual thinking. Issues and problems can be approached in a systematic manner and potentially solved by using logical procedures that are expressed in abstract form. Piaget refers to this cognitive facility as the formal operations stage. In this stage this cognitive ability is used to deal with real-life experiences and needs (e.g., the opposite sex, problems of science, life ambitions, happiness, and the place of God in one's life). Fowler calls this period synthetic-conventional faith. Faith is designated as synthetic in that the person attempts to make sense out of the various authorities in his or her life. The adolescent tries to synthesize one's own self-reflection and the thinking of others in trying to make sense of his or her life. Fowler uses the term conventional because in his view adolescents become dependent upon authority figures for building and maintaining identity and faith. Kohlberg refers to this stage of moral reasoning as the conventional level. His view is somewhat similar to Fowler's in that the person making moral choices considers the perspective of others in their moral deliberations. In relating biblical content to the above-mentioned areas, it can be done in mature cognitive fashion. In so doing the relational importance of the individual to God and others in their moral decisions is emphasized. For Erikson the psychosocial crisis during this period deals with self-identity versus identity confusion. A source of values or beliefs that gives the person a sense of coherence or wholeness to life is crucial in answering the question Who am I? A sense of identity constructed on biblical themes is important in this phase of spiritual development. The Christian's identity found in God's purpose for the individual is to be greatly emphasized. This significant truth would in turn be related to the other life experiences indicative of this period.

Adulthood. The formal operational thought coming about in adolescence is widely used in conjunction with the content areas of life that come into being during this stage. In contradistinction to Kohlberg, biblically based content (not just how moral thinking is done) is brought to bear on the moral processing involved in confronting these content areas. Spiritual development in accordance with the application

of mature cognitive, moral reasoning based on Scripture, will help the individual to more successfully negotiate Erikson's final psychosocial crisis, that of integrity versus despair. If an older adult thinks about his or her entire life and comes only to a negative conclusion with regard to its successes and failures, a feeling of despair will ensue. Spiritual development informed by biblical truth, however, will lead to a judgment of integrity. Even in view of reversals, sinful disobedience, and spiritual developmental lapses, the persevering adult will feel that his or her life was meaningful and productive and will be more accepting of the end of temporal life.

Conclusion. Spiritual development may not proceed in the exact manner portrayed by the developmental theories described in this article. Four principles gained from the theories, however, are helpful in bringing about spiritual development in the Christian context. First, scriptural material is to be presented in a manner that is appropriate to the cognitive and moral development of the maturing person. Second, Bible-centered content must be methodologically presented in a way appropriate to the individual's developmental stage. Third, parents and other spiritual mentors are to model the Bible material they are attempting to inculcate into the lives of developing persons. Finally, that which is taught spiritually is to be related to the person's real world of needs and experiences.

References

Erikson, E. H. (1963). *Childhood and society.* New York: Norton.

Fowler, J. (1981). *Stages of faith: The psychology of human development and the quest for meaning.* San Francisco: Harper and Row.

Kohlberg, L. (1981). *The philosophy of moral development: Moral stages and the idea of justice.* San Francisco: Harper and Row.

Piaget, J. (1952). *Origins of intelligence in children.* New York: International Universities Press.

Steele, L. (1986). Developmental psychology and spiritual development. In S. Jones (Ed.), *Psychology and the Christian faith: An introductory reader.* Grand Rapids, MI: Baker.

S. N. BALLARD

See CHRISTIAN GROWTH; RELIGION AND PERSONALITY.

Religious Doubt. See DOUBT.

Religious Experience. The term *religious experience* can mean very different things in different contexts. For instance, in common usage it might refer to a sense of awe and mystery evoked by a beautiful sunset, a mountain scene, or the birth of a child. Within evangelical circles it might refer to a sense of assurance that God is guiding and leading, moments of clear insight into God's power and surpassing greatness during prayer or Bible study, or the feelings of wonder and praise these evoke. To Eastern meditators it might refer to ecstatic visions, involuntary physical manifestations (uncontrollable movements, trembling, shaking, laughing, crying, speaking in tongues, whistling, animal sounds), or suddenly "knowing" in a deep and profound way that physical reality is an illusion and that "all is one" (i.e., people and objects are composed of the same spiritual substance).

The perceived sources of these experiences vary considerably, ranging from human musings and emotion in the first case, to the work of the Holy Spirit in the second, to spiritual experiences provided through the agency of one's "Higher Self" in the third. (In New Age and Eastern systems, the Higher Self is the true, spiritual self, which reincarnates in different bodies from time to time and is privy to spiritual realities that lie beyond the physical plane of existence.)

In this article, I use "religious experience" to refer to events in which humans perceive that they have witnessed a supernatural event or have interacted with a spiritual/supernatural agent. In some cases, events of this type can be verified by other witnesses or by tangible evidence or aftereffects that are left behind. There are many events of this latter type in the Bible (Moses and the burning bush, the miracles accomplished through Moses in Pharaoh's court, God's interventions during the exodus from Egypt, God's visit to Abraham and Sarah, Jesus' miracles, Paul's encounter on the road to Damascus, Peter's escape from prison, etc.). Other religious experiences are private and authentication rests totally upon the experiencer's report and personal convictions as to what occurred. Religious experiences of this type have two components to consider: the perceived actions of the supernatural agent and the experiencers' responses to the event (their feelings, emotions, interpretations of what happened and why). Both components can be influenced by psychological factors like one's state of consciousness at the time of the incident and one's personal beliefs, expectations, and needs.

It is vital to be informed in this area because mysterious, faith-challenging experiences currently abound in popular books and in the media. These experiences include purported "paranormal" events (telepathy, prophetic dreams and visions, clairvoyance, healing), near-death and out-of-body experiences, and alleged contacts with spirits (e.g., deceased humans, "spirit guides," angels) and UFOs. Reports like these need to be evaluated carefully because many convey messages that contradict fundamental Christian doctrines, and some encourage practices (divination, mediumship, or spiritualism) that are expressly forbidden in the Bible (see Deut. 18:9–12; Lev. 19:26, 31; 20:6). In addition, virtually all of the current experiences are private so there is no way to verify that they are what they seem. There is also a lucrative market for such stories, so it is possible that some authors are exaggerating or even creating false accounts for financial gain (Hillstrom, 1995).

A fourth reason for exercising care when evaluating popular experiences is that many occur in altered states of consciousness (e.g., sleep, deep relaxation, hypnosis, trance states, states induced by Eastern-style meditation, drugs, or medications) that often alter brain function. Although the states produced by these agents do vary in significant ways, they also have commonalities that encourage or enhance mystical experiences. For instance, they can all impair thinking, memory, and the ability to distinguish between what is real and what is unreal. They exaggerate emotional responses and increase suggestibility, making it possible to believe all sorts of improbable things (as in hypnosis). They can also make events seem exceptionally real and spiritually significant although they obviously are not.

Researcher Arnold Ludwig (1969) illustrated this crucial point with one of his own experiences. Once while under the influence of LSD he entered a public restroom and there noticed a sign above the urinal that read, "Please Flush after Using." He was suddenly gripped with ecstatic feelings and a deep inner knowledge that these words conveyed a profound truth. Thrilled by this startling revelation he rushed back to a companion to share his discovery. As Ludwig relates it, "Unfortunately, being a mere mortal he could not understand the world-shaking import of my communication and responded by laughing." Although we, too, may laugh at this example, it does make the serious point that altered states have qualities that could make them a perfect tool for spiritual deception.

Alongside the current explosion in popular mystical experiences, there is also a widespread interest in spiritual growth and development, both in the culture at large and among Christians. Many spiritual seekers are rejecting Christianity, and are selecting beliefs and practices for their own journey from Eastern, New Age, tribal, or even occult traditions. Many nominal and liberal Christians appear to be following similar paths. More conservative Christians appear to be confining their search for deeper wisdom and spiritual development to the fathers and doctors of the church and ancient Catholic mystics like Bernard of Clairvaux, John of the Cross, and Teresa of Avila (Bloesch, 1991).

Some of the spiritual disciplines advocated by the Christian mystics are probably beneficial, but we should not just assume that this is so without exercising discernment. The early Christian mystics aspired to living a life that was as completely yielded to God as possible and to having direct experiences of or from God. They chose to go through extreme deprivation and hardship to mortify their fleshly appetites and achieve yieldedness, but it is not clear whether the primary motive for doing this was their intrinsic love for God or their desire to acquire firsthand experiences of his presence. In his book, *Knowing God*, J. I. Packer (1973) makes the very insightful observation that a real knowledge of God does not depend as much on our own efforts as upon God's willingness to make himself known to us. This raises the question of whether any technique, aside from a faithful and yielded obedience, which is rooted in love for God and a desire to please and serve him, will bring genuine encounters with God. It is also possible for the spiritual disciplines to become "works" that encourage self-absorption, or to become a subtle means of trying to coerce God into dispensing spiritual experiences.

The purpose of Christian mysticism was to achieve a direct experience of God. The methods for doing this relied heavily upon the renunciation of worldly possessions, passions, and appetites, and the use of a special type of disciplined meditation. The purpose of this meditation was to train meditators to concentrate so thoroughly that they could shut out all physical sensations, memories, or thoughts that might detract from communion with God. Mystics like St. John of the Cross (in *The Dark Night of the Soul*) argued that this was necessary because God does not usually communicate through the senses, since our physical faculties are ignorant of spiritual things. He and others also believed that Satan could introduce deceptive images and experiences through the physical senses or imagination.

One method of meditation called for the constant repetition of a single word or phrase from Scripture like, "Lord Jesus Christ, Son of God, have mercy on me, a sinner" (know as the "Prayer of the Heart"). Meditators were instructed to repeat this phrase over and over continually, aloud or silently, throughout the day, day after day, until it became as spontaneous and instinctive as breathing. This exercise was supposed to release meditators from passionate thoughts, words, or evil deeds and give them a surer knowledge of God. In another method, meditators worked through a graduated series of efforts to imagine holy scenes. The result might be an imaginary image of Christ that would fully occupy the mind. This method did help to shut out everything else, but was not considered an end in itself. John of the Cross argued that it was only a first step and should be abandoned as soon as possible because such images could be deceitful and influenced by Satan. John believed that meditators needed to move beyond these initial stages to contemplation, a passive state in which the mind is completely blank except for a loving attention to God. Any experiences that occurred in such states were presumably from God.

Meditative methods of this type brought forth many experiences, including visions, raptures, bliss, surpassing joy, deep experiences of God's greatness and love, and so on. According to John of the Cross, advanced meditators could also expect many physical weaknesses, digestive disturbances, spiritual fatigue, and periods of excruciating spiritual pain and loss in which God appeared to have abandoned them.

There are several potential problems with using these techniques to promote spirituality. One is the fact that such techniques and their results are not unique to Christianity. Similar forms of meditation are an essential feature of the Eastern religions (Hinduism and Buddhism) and appear in Jewish (Kabbalah) and Muslim (Sufism) mysticism (Goleman, 1988). (For instance, most traditions use the constant repetition of a word or mantra, or concentration on a simple image to shut out distractions and create a state of mental blankness). In all cases, the purpose of such techniques is to alter consciousness in a way that presumably allows for a clear apprehension of spiritual realities.

It is also noteworthy that the disciplined use of such techniques brings about some similar consequences. On the positive side, these include bliss, rapturous feelings, extraordinary visions, equanimity, and a deep sense of spiritual growth and self-control. On the negative side, they are also accompanied by digestive problems, headaches, insomnia, anxiety, confusion, and deep periods of darkness and doubt (Otis, 1984; Shapiro, 1992). (Meditation of this sort may also be difficult to discontinue. Leon Otis found that many long-term TM meditators were having negative side effects and wanted to quit, but found that the side effects became worse when they tried to do so.) There are some meditative techniques such as "mindfulness" meditation within Buddhism, which lead to specific religious experiences that only provide support for Buddhist beliefs. However, most of the effects are general enough to support Eastern, Jewish, Christian, or Muslim worldviews, depending upon the way individual meditators interpret them.

A final reason for questioning the use the meditative practices of Christian mystics is their potential for deception. They apparently create altered states of consciousness, and events that occur in such states can be very misleading. In addition, even those who have used such techniques extensively, like John of the Cross, warn repeatedly of the danger of satanic of self-deception for those who venture out on this path, especially if they do not have an experienced and knowledgeable teacher to guide them. In light of such warnings, and uncertain value of such practices, we are probably well advised to avoid them.

References

Bloesch, D. G. (1991, August 19). Lost in the mystical myths. *Christianity Today*, 22–24.

Goleman, D. (1988). *The meditative mind.* Los Angeles: Jeremy P. Tarcher.

Hillstrom, E. L. (1995). *Testing the spirits.* Downers Grove, IL: InterVarsity Press.

Ludwig, A. M. (1969). Altered states of consciousness. In C. T. Tart (Ed.), *Altered states of consciousness.* New York: John Wiley and Son.

Otis, L. S. (1984). Adverse effects of transcendental meditation. In D. H. Shapiro, Jr., and R. N. Walsh (Eds.), *Meditation: Classic and contemporary perspectives.* New York: Aldine.

Packer, J. I. (1974). *Knowing God.* Downers Grove, IL: InterVarsity Press.

Shapiro, E. H. (1992). Adverse effects of meditation: A preliminary investigation of long-term meditators. *International Journal of Psychosomatics, 39*, 62–66.

ELIZABETH L. HILLSTROM

See PSYCHOLOGY OF RELIGION.

Religious Health and Pathology. Students of religious experience have long recognized that religion manifests itself in both positive and negative ways. Bergin's (1983) analysis of the literature found that 23% of the studies reported a negative relationship between religious commitment and mental health, 47% found a positive relationship, and 30% reported no relationship between these two variables. What at first glance appear to be contradictory results may reflect an intricate interaction between two complex variables.

Though some psychologists see religion as strictly pathological (e.g., Albert Ellis) or fundamentally conducive to mental health (e.g., Carl Gustav Jung), others are more likely to distinguish between various forms of religious expression. For example, William James contrasted the religion of the "healthy-minded" with that of the "sick-souled," while Gordon Allport distinguished "mature" from "immature" religion through his conceptualization of intrinsic and extrinsic religious orientations. Even Sigmund Freud, though he concluded that religion is a universal obsessional neurosis and is thus devastatingly restrictive to the individual, admitted that religious teaching is necessary for society's survival by taming destructive instincts. Since the 1960s considerable research has generally confirmed what has been suspected all along: religion can be a potent health-inducing, health-maintaining influence, or can it can be an insidious health-depleting, health-preventing force in a person's life.

Mixed Results. In reviewing more than two hundred studies on religious commitment and mental health, Gartner, Larson, and Allen (1991) found mixed results. For example, they found that religion is positively associated with such measures of mental health as lower levels of drug and alcohol use, mortality, divorce, suicide, delinquency, and depression and higher levels of a general sense of well-being, marital satisfaction, and physical health. Yet religion appears also to be associated with such pathological tendencies as dogmatism and rigidity, authoritarianism, suggestibility and dependence, and lower levels of self-actualization. Furthermore, the authors found an ambiguous or complex relationship between religion and such mental health indicators as anxiety, sexual disorders, psychosis, prejudice, self-esteem, and intelligence/education.

The Gartner, Larson, and Allen (1991) study is especially useful because the authors categorized the studies according to whether the measures of mental health consisted of hard behavioral variables that can be directly and reliably observed and measured, or soft variables, that is, paper-and-pen-

cil tests designed to measure theoretical constructs (primarily in the area of personality characteristics). The studies that linked religious commitment with positive mental health tended to involve hard variables while those that have uncovered a relationship between religion and pathology used soft variables. Thus religion predicts a more positive mental health outcome if it is measured as a behavior rather than as a generalized assessment of a personality characteristic or internal state. Gartner, Larson, and Allen also concluded that low levels of religiousness are usually associated with disorders related to undercontrol of impulses, whereas high levels of religiousness are most often related to disorders of overcontrol.

Religious Orientation and Mental Health. How one appropriates religious beliefs will help distinguish between healthy and unhealthy religion. Allport's (1950) distinction between mature and immature religion is particularly useful. Mature religion, later conceptualized as an intrinsic religious orientation (Allport & Ross, 1967), serves a central integrative function in the personality that produces a consistent value-laden behavior pattern. Religiously mature people internalize religious values, making them an integral part of their whole being and way of life, yet they do so in a cognitively complex and flexible fashion that avoids a narrow-minded dogmatism, even at times to the point of tentativeness. In contrast, immature religion, later identified as an extrinsic religious orientation, is far less self-reflective and is associated with self-gratification.

Batson (1976), maintaining that the later Allport and Ross (1967) designation of intrinsic religion overlooked the mature religion attributes of cognitive complexity and open-mindedness, proposed three religious orientation categories: religion as a means to some other end (extrinsic religion), religion as an end in itself (intrinsic religion), and religion as a quest. Ventis (1995), using Batson's three-part religious typology, conducted an extensive review of the literature that links religious orientation to seven mental health criteria: absence of mental illness, appropriate social behavior, freedom from worry and guilt, personal competence and control, self-acceptance and self-actualization, unification and organization of personality, and open-mindedness and flexibility. Ventis found that *religion-as-means* is negatively associated with virtually all of the mental health measures, especially absence of illness (i.e., shows greater illness symptoms) and freedom from guilt and worry. He also found that *religion-as-end* is positively associated with absence of illness, appropriate social behavior, freedom from worry and guilt, personal competence and control, and personality unification and organization, but is not clearly related in either direction to self-acceptance and self-actualization, and open-mindedness and flexibility. *Religion-as-quest* has been far less frequently studied and, therefore, the findings are more tentative. A questing orientation appears positively associated with open-mindedness and flexibility, and tends toward a positive relationship with personal competence and control, and self-acceptance and self-actualization, but appears negatively associated with absence of illness, and freedom from worry and guilt. Ventis states that "the intellectual honesty and openness to religious questioning implied in this dimension may yield a sense of self-esteem and self-control, but at a possible price of personal unification and organization, and continuing encounter with existential anxiety, worry, and/or guilt" (p. 41).

Religion and Well-Being. As Ventis's (1995) research points out, the relationship between religion and mental health need not always employ psychiatric criteria. In fact, many studies have investigated such interrelated phenomena as purpose or meaning in life, life satisfaction, and subjective well-being, usually relying on self-assessment scales. A frequently used measure is Ellison and Paloutzian's (Ellison, 1983) Spiritual Well-Being Scale (SWBS), a general indicator of personality integration and resultant well-being. Spiritual well-being, as measured by this scale, consists of two subscales: existential well-being and religious well-being. In general, spiritual well-being is higher for self-identified born-again Christians than it is for non-Christians or those who identify themselves as ethical Christians. Ellison and Smith (1991) reviewed the extensive research literature using the SWBS and found that spiritual well-being is positively related to hope, self-esteem, general assertiveness, and self-confidence while negatively related to perceived stress, aggressiveness, dependency, and authoritarian parenting (for males only). Though the relationship between spiritual well-being and marital relationship is somewhat mixed, there appears to be an overall positive correlation between spiritual well-being and marital adjustment, especially for women.

Religion and Stressful Coping. The words of the apostle Paul (Phil. 4:6: "Be anxious for nothing") and Jesus (John 14:1: "Let not your hearts be troubled") set the stage for a question that begs research: Does religious faith influence the perception of a stressful threat or demand? An extensive body of literature documents the negative effects of stressful agents on both mental and physical health. What appears important in the stress-illness linkage is how the stressful agent is perceived. Research (see Kobasa, Maddi, & Kahn, 1982) suggests that when people become strongly committed to, for example, their work and its meaningfulness, perceive new tasks as challenging rather than threatening, and operate with a sense of control over their environment, they are less likely to experience symptoms associated with serious illness. Of interest is the parallel of these three conditions with the three important functions of religion identified by Spilka, Shaver, and Kirkpatrick (1985); namely, religion provides people with a sense of meaning and control and serves to enhance self-esteem. Precisely these three functions may make religion an invaluable coping resource.

Optimism and Explanatory Style. Several overlapping concepts such as self-efficacy, self-esteem, and an optimistic explanatory style (also see optimism) have been shown to be important determinants of mental health. What does this have to do with the religion-mental health connection? Sethi and Seligman (1993) reported that religion, especially more conservative or orthodox religion, encourages an optimistic explanation of personal events in that a sense of hope is often promoted by religious belief. In fact, religious conservatives may use a different attributional logic (*see* Attribution Theory) that fosters optimism. Research by Smith and Gorsuch (1989) has found that religious conservatives are more likely to attribute greater responsibility to God, view God's activity through multiple channels rather than a single modality, and see God working conjunctively with or through natural causes, including one's own abilities, interests, and personal characteristics. These two divergent lines of research (i.e., religion is related to optimism and optimism is related to mental health) suggest that optimism, in addition to being a mental health criterion itself, is an important mediating variable in the relationship between religion and mental health.

Characteristics of Healthy Religion. A major consideration for the Christian is that religious health in its fullest sense has its roots in the restoration of humanity's wholeness intended in the creation. What constitutes health is thus within the very nature of being human, marred by the fall but restored and empowered through a relationship with Jesus Christ. Drawing from White (1985), characteristics of healthy religion, particularly Christianity, are discussed in terms of the following five sets of polarities representing universal themes of human functioning that emanate from human nature created in God's image. In each case, it is argued that healthy religion involves a balance between the extremes, though the exact point of equilibrium may vary slightly from person to person, and such factors as age, personality type, spiritual maturity, and situational circumstances must be considered.

Dependency–Independency. Healthy religion fosters a harmonious balance between these two polarities in such a way that permits the development and maintenance of one's individual identity yet encourages the experience of a sense of oneness with others.

Control–Freedom. Healthy religion will encourage a spontaneity, creativity, and self-direction that is tempered by inner discipline and a sense of responsibility toward oneself and others. Overemphasizing one extreme or the other can lead to either a judgmental legalism and an unhealthy constriction of affect, cognitions, and behaviors or to a blurring of Christian distinctives and a lack of accountability to others.

Self-Denial–Self-Acceptance. Steering between the extremes involves recognizing the unconditional acceptance Christians have in Christ Jesus as the basis for self-worth without developing an exaggerated sense of self-importance and demands for one's rights at the expense of others.

Stability–Change. A healthy religious group, sensing the amount of change it can tolerate over a period of time, establishes an equilibrium between the constancy it maintains and the amount of change it encourages, thus permitting growth and avoiding stagnation while still appreciating the immutable truths of Scripture and religious practice.

Finiteness–Transcendence. Humans were created as finite creatures by a sovereign God, and human limitations are necessary to fulfill fully the purpose of glorifying God, even as human nature yearns to extend beyond itself to a superior Being. As evidenced by reactions to life's events, people with a healthy religious perspective realistically accept the normalcy of humanness (e.g., hurt, discouragement) while still manifesting in themselves and encouraging in others an underlying hope and sense of purpose in all happenings.

These dimensions are but key representatives of those characteristics that differentiate healthy from unhealthy religion. These dimensions are so intricately interrelated that an imbalance in one will create disturbance in others.

Conclusion. Is religion good or bad for one's mental health? Certainly to the extent that these ideal characteristics of healthy religion are realized, religious experience, particularly as it is involves the redemptive work of Jesus Christ, is potentially of great benefit to the individual's mental health. But research also clearly demonstrates that a distorted religion may deplete mental health, leaving some researchers to suggest that, religious people are neither more nor less mentally healthy than anyone else. In the words of Paloutzian (1996), "there are no general effects, only specialized ones. Religious persons, as far as personality and psychological adequacy are concerned, appear to be neither better off nor worse off than other persons. They are only different—slightly better off and worse off, each in specialized ways" (p. 260).

References

Allport, G. W. (1950). *The individual and his religion.* New York: Macmillan.

Allport, G. W., & Ross, J. M. (1967). Personal religious orientation and prejudice. *Journal of Personality and Social Psychology, 5,* 432–443.

Batson, C. D. (1976). Religion as prosocial: Agent or double agent? *Journal for the Scientific Study of Religion, 15,* 29–45.

Bergin, A. E. (1983). Religiosity and mental health: A critical reevaluation and meta-analysis. *Professional Psychology: Research and Practice, 14,* 170–184.

Ellison, C. W. (1983). Spiritual well-being: Conceptualization and measurement, *Journal of Psychology and Theology, 11,* 330–340.

Ellison, C. W., & Smith, J. (1991). Toward an integrative measure of health and well-being. *Journal of Psychology and Theology, 19,* 35–48.

Gartner, J., Larson, D. B., & Allen, G. D. (1991). Religious commitment and mental health: A review of the empirical literature. *Journal of Psychology and Theology, 19,* 6–25.

Kobasa, S. C., Maddi, S. R., & Kahn, S. (1982). Hardiness and health: A prospective study. *Journal of Personality and Social Psychology, 42,* 168–177.

Paloutzian, R. F. (1996). *Invitation to the psychology of religion* (2nd ed.). Boston: Allyn & Bacon.

Sethi, S., & Seligman, M. E. P. (1993). Optimism and fundamentalism. *Psychological Science, 4,* 256–259.

Smith, C. S., & Gorsuch, R. L. (1989). Sanctioning and causal attributions to God: A function of theological position and actors' characteristics. In M. L. Lynn & D. O. Moberg (Eds.), *Research in the social scientific study of religion,* Vol. 1. Greenwich, CT: JAI Press.

Spilka, B., Shaver, P., & Kirkpatrick, L. A. (1985). A general attribution theory for the psychology of religion. *Journal for the Scientific Study of Religion, 24,* 1–20.

Ventis, W. L. (1995). The relationships between religion and mental health. *Journal of Social Issues, 51* (2), 33–48.

White, F. J. (1985). Religious health and pathology. In D. G. Benner (Ed.), *Baker encyclopedia of psychology.* Grand Rapids, MI: Baker.

P. C. Hill

See RELIGION AND PERSONALITY; RELIGIOUS ORIENTATION.

Religious Issues in Therapy. See SPIRITUAL AND RELIGIOUS ISSUES IN PSYCHOTHERAPY.

Religious Legalism. The term refers to a complex set of attitudes and beliefs organized around the conviction that certain laws must be obeyed in order to establish and maintain a relationship with God. These laws are usually considered divine in origin and therefore immutable. They may encompass any area of life, with no aspect of human activity considered too insignificant or private to warrant possible exemption from regulation.

A belief in a moral code is not ipso facto religious legalism. However, legalism results from such a belief when strict obedience to the code is conceived as being the sole or primary means of gaining and keeping the favor of the deity. Legalism thrives on a distorted sense of obligation.

The theological roots of modern-day religious legalism may be traced to the intertestamental period, when a fundamental change occurred in the role of Old Testament law for the Jews. The concept of the covenant as the condition of membership in the people of God was replaced by that of obedience to the law. This obedience became the basis of God's verdict of pleasure or displeasure toward the individual. The sole mediator between God and humans became the torah, and all relationships between God and people, Israel, or the world became subordinated to the torah. Justification, righteousness, and life in the world to come were thought to be secured by obeying the law (Ladd, 1974).

This attitude was prevalent during the time of Christ and influenced the biblical precursors of twentieth-century legalism: Pharisaism, judaizing theology, and Gnosticism.

Pharisaism attempted to represent the true people of God by obeying the law and in doing so hoped to prepare the way for the Messiah. The Pharisees observed all the legal prescriptions of Scripture in fine detail; they also held to the authority of the halakah, the body of legal descriptions that interpreted the law. The regulations increased in number and complexity to the point of pedantry. For example, because food could not be cooked on the sabbath, a debate arose between two groups as to whether water alone or both water and cooked food could be placed on a previously heated stove without committing a violation (Muller, 1976). The regulations became so difficult to obey that they proved a stumbling block to those who could not keep them all and who thus felt they were outside the kingdom of God. Christ spoke to that tragic situation in his scathing denunciation of Pharisaical legalism (Matt. 23:4).

A variant of this form of legalism was introduced into the churches in Galatia, prompting Paul to write his famous letter on Christian liberty to the congregations in that province. The Judaizers, as they became known, infiltrated the churches, claiming that full salvation was impossible apart from observance of Jewish law and ritual. They were especially adamant that Gentile Christians be circumcised, since this was the symbol of membership in the new Israel. Paul's theological and emotional antipathy toward this form of legalism is quite evident in his sarcastic suggestion that those who argue for the necessity of circumcision should take the next logical step and castrate themselves (Gal. 5:12).

The apostle also had to combat legalism in the form of incipient Gnosticism at Colosse. This syncretistic heresy taught that the goal of life for gnostic adherents was to obtain true knowledge (gnosis), which would eventually allow them to leave the prison of the body and merge with the composite whole. A number of Colossian Christians apparently were seeking heavenly visions as part of their rite of passage into a knowledge of the divine mysteries. They were informed that such visions could come about only by a rigorous discipline of asceticism and self-denial. Abstinence from food and drink, observance of initiatory and purifactory rites, and possibly a life of celibacy and mortification of the human body (Col. 2:21, 23) were all prescribed as part of the regimen necessary to obtain fullness of life (Martin, 1978).

While each of these ancient forerunners of present-day legalism differed from the other in certain respects, all three attempted to legislate certain behavior as the primary means of obtaining "salvation," whether that was defined as hastening the advent of the Messiah, gaining membership in the new Israel, or seeking the eventual release of the soul from the confines of the body.

These forms of legalism did not die; they merely altered their appearance and continued to plague the church throughout the centuries. A study of church history suggests that too often religious legalism has been the norm rather than the exception. Evangelicalism in the United States continues to wrestle with legalistic tendencies within its ranks, partly due to its Puritan roots and fundamentalist legacy. The Puritans, for example, at one time decreed that one could dress a baby on the sabbath but not kiss it; they also allowed that a man could comb his hair on that day but not shave his beard (Brinsmead, 1981b). Fundamentalism, while it is usually not as extreme, continues in a similar legalistic framework with its absolutizing prohibitions that do not have sufficient scriptural warrant.

An examination of the phenomenon of religious legalism reveals some striking similarities to obsessive-compulsive disorder (which includes characteristics of both obsessional neurosis and obsessional personality disorder; the former is usually more dysfunctional).

Religious legalism often infects the practitioner with a sense of moral superiority and a concomitant critical, condemning attitude toward those who do not conform to the same standards of conduct. This type of attitude is graphically illustrated in the biblical story of the Pharisee who stood in the temple thanking God that he was not like the terrible sinners around him. Christ warns that this type of self-exaltation can prevent a person from being justified before God (Luke 18:10–14). Similarly the obsessive-compulsive individual claims moral superiority and will often show an air of condescension to those around him or her. The manifestation of moral superiority most often hides feelings of inferiority and self-hatred that are then projected onto those who are deemed inferior. Just as the legalist must obey all the laws perfectly, so too the obsessive-compulsive person strives for perfection, avoiding tasks that might cause him or her to fail. Failure for the obsessional is equivalent to breaking the law for the legalist. Absolute perfection is the minimum acceptable standard for both.

Both types of persons have great difficulty with the gray areas of life. The legalist wishes to legislate every area of life and thus tends to concentrate on behavioral and religious minutiae. The obsessive-compulsive is characterized by aversion to ambiguity and a tendency to put all of life into neat, black-and-white categories.

Anxiety and fear are primary motivators for both the legalist and the obsessive-compulsive. The practitioner of legalism is driven to obedience by an overwhelming fear that God will punish or reject those persons who do not obey perfectly. The person caught in obsessive-compulsiveness is driven to obey rules, obsessions, and compulsions by the unceasing threat of internal punishment meted out by the perfectionistic and hypercritical superego. Although the rules of conduct may differ for both types of person, they serve a similar function of assuring that catastrophe, whether spiritual or psychological, may be averted as long as the laws are obeyed or the compulsions followed.

Legalism is caused by biblical and doctrinal distortions and misunderstandings. Obsessive-compulsiveness can be traced in theory to a basic anxiety (Horney, 1950), defined as a feeling of profound insecurity, apprehensiveness, and helplessness in a world conceived as potentially hostile. Thus they are not the same phenomenon. However, the affinities between the two are such that they can exist closely with each other. The intertwining of legalism and obsessive-compulsiveness creates a hybrid that is resistant to alteration through counseling or psychotherapy.

Counseling of the legalist/obsessive-compulsive must be grounded in the therapeutic triad of empathy, genuineness, and unconditional acceptance on the part of the therapist. The importance of acceptance cannot be overstated. By accepting the client just as he or she is, the therapist models, although imperfectly, a loving, accepting Christ whose love is not contingent on one's being perfect, since he died for us while we were yet sinners (Rom. 5:8). At the same time this unconditional acceptance will help mitigate the destructiveness of the critical, perfectionistic superego.

An examination of the cognitive elements of the disorder will decrease their power over the person as he or she learns to look at the world, self, and God in a new light. Individuals with this type of problem usually have negative concepts of God stemming from doctrinal distortions and/or an equation of the heavenly Father with the person's punitive, rigid earthly father. Helping a person to gain insight into these aspects of the problem can prove both spiritually and emotionally liberating.

Lastly, the Reformation principle of *sola fide,* justification by faith alone apart from works or obedience to the law, can provide an antidote to the poison of legalism/obsessive-compulsiveness. Bruce (1977) notes that Paul's statement that Christ is the end of the law (Rom. 10:4) means that since Christ has come law has no place whatsoever in one's approach to God. "According to Paul," he adds, "the believer is *not* under the law as a rule of life—unless one thinks of the law of love, and that is a completely different kind of law, fulfilled not by obedience to a code but by the outworking of an inward power" (p. 192).

The New Testament does not make appeal for proper behavior on the basis of Old Testament rules. Christians' behavior throughout the New Testament is shaped and colored by what Christ has done. The law of Christ demands that believers forgive as they have been forgiven (Col. 3:13), accept one another as Christ has accepted them (Rom. 15:7), and place the same value on people that the blood of Christ places on them (Brinsmead, 1981a).

As Luther observed, no good work helps justify or save an unbeliever. Thus the person who wishes to do good works should begin not with the doing of works but with believing, which alone makes a person good; for nothing makes a person good except faith or evil except unbelief.

Only faith in Christ can liberate the legalist/obsessive-compulsive from the twin tyrannies of the law and the superego. As the person comes to experience the freedom and forgiveness in Jesus Christ, he or she begins to see that laws and compulsions are unnecessary and can be replaced by "works done out of spontaneous love in obedience to God" (Luther, 1943, p. 295).

References

Brinsmead, R. D. (1981a). Jesus and the law. *Verdict, 4* (4), 6–70.

Brinsmead, R. D. (1981b). Sabbatarianism re-examined. *Verdict, 4* (6), 5–30.

Bruce, F. F. (1977). *Paul, apostle of the heart set free.* Grand Rapids, MI: Eerdmans.

Horney, K. (1950). *Neurosis and human growth.* New York: Norton.

Ladd, G. E. (1974). *A theology of the New Testament.* Grand Rapids, MI: Eerdmans.

Luther, M. (1943). The freedom of a Christian. In M. Luther, *Three treatises.* Philadelphia: Muhlenberg.

Martin, R. P. (1978). *New Testament foundations: A guide for Christian students* (Vol. 2). Grand Rapids, MI: Eerdmans.

Muller, D. (1976). Pharisee. In C. Brown (Ed.), *Dictionary of New Testament theology* (Vol. 2). Grand Rapids, MI: Eerdmans.

Additional Readings

Salzman, L. (1980). *Treatment of the obsessive personality.* New York: Aronson.

Shapiro, D. (1965). *Neurotic styles.* New York: Basic.

W. G. Bixler

See Religious Health and Pathology; Dogmatism; Ambiguity, Intolerance of.

Religious Need. *See* Psychological Roots of Religion.

Religious Orientation. One's religious orientation demonstrates the impact of motivational and sentimental factors on one's religious expression (Malony, 1977). Religious persons differ considerably in the depth, sentiments, and expression of their religiosity. Religion may serve an instrumental function for those who use religion to pursue personal ends, an integral function for those who live religion, or an identity function for those who are their religious commitments. These functions illustrate the varieties of religious orientations in which personality and temperamental processes influence religious behavior. They also illustrate that one's mental health may be tied differentially to operative religious orientations.

Psychologists have long held that an individual's religiousness is founded on personality (e.g., Allport, 1937; Oates, 1973) and that underlying attitudes influence action. Sigmund Freud speculated that religion originated in the tribe's worship of a totem (an animal or a plant that was normally taboo to the clan). The taboo symbolized a prohibition against incest within the clan, the source of which lay in sexual cathexes of the oedipal complex. Fear and guilt initiated a ban on incest and on marriage within the clan. In a seasonal act of sublimation the totem was sacrificially or ritualistically eaten, as a symbolic substitution for the father's murder, the murder stemming from thwarted oedipal desires and hostility from the father's ban. Oedipal dynamics form the basis of organized religion; the doctrine of God develops from experiences with parents, especially the father (Freud, 1918; Gleason, 1975).

Similar psychological accounts of the individual's religion are found in James's (1902) *Varieties of Religious Experience* and Erikson's (1958) *Young Man Luther*. Allport's (1950) fivefold account of origins includes organic needs, temperament and mental capacity, psychogenic interests and values, a desire for rational explanation, and response to surrounding culture. It seems apparent that an individual's religion grows out of personal needs and motives, especially those having existential significance (Oates, 1973; Batson, Schoenrade, & Ventis, 1993).

Individuals express their religious commitments in a variety of styles (Smart, 1976). Ritual coordinates an outer expression with an inner intention. Mythologies embody the stories believed within the religion. As religious expression matures theologians formalize the mythical and symbolic elements into doctrine. In the process the ethical prescriptions that govern the individual's behavior are formalized and systematized. But the religiosity extends beyond the individual. The mythological, symbolic, and ethical elements reveal significant, underlying social commitments among the adherents. The ritualistic, mythological, doctrinal, ethical, and social aspects appear as the external evidences of religion that inform an individual's identity. The external elements tie the assembly, congregation, denomination, or diocese together. But behind the external religious elements lie an individual's significant, internal(ized), subjective sentiment. The subjective, internal, and invisible elements reveal themselves in the way a person communes, prays, and worships (*see* Prayer, Psychological Effects of; Worship). The varieties of religious expression mark a diversity of external identifications as well as internal existential and temperamental elements. Religious behaviors exhibit the interaction of social enculturation and restraint with personalities.

Psychologists have been intrigued with the interaction of sentimental and temperamental variables with religiosity. The literature on religious orientation originated from research findings that linked racial prejudice to religiosity. The first studies reported a simple linear relationship; racial prejudices increased as religiosity increased. But further investigation revealed a more complex relationship in which prejudice was a curvilinear function of religiosity (Allport & Ross, 1967). When religiousness was measured by a self-report of the frequency of church attendance (a standard measure of religiousness), individuals who reported attending church from once a month to once weekly were more prejudiced than individuals who did not attend at all. Those attending twice a month or more were less prejudiced than nonattenders. It was this consistent finding that Allport and Ross sought to explain. They hypothesized that the motivation of different religious orientations was operating. The two poles of the religious orientation concept are the extrinsically oriented individual, whose religion serves self, and the intrinsically motivated person, whose self serves religion (Allport, 1960). In the former religiosity performs an instrumental function, but in the latter religiosity takes on a intrinsic value.

Allport and Ross (1967) then noted the motivational differences in the type of religion. "Persons with [extrinsic] orientation may find religion useful in a variety of ways—to provide security and solace, sociability and distraction, status and self-justification. The embraced creed is lightly held or else selectively shaped to fit more primary needs. . . . Persons with [intrinsic] orientation find their master motive in religion. Other needs, strong as they may be, are regarded as of less ultimate significance, and they are, so far as possible, brought into harmony with the religious beliefs and prescriptions" (p. 436).

The research of Allport and Ross prompted additional investigation. Extrinsically oriented individuals who attended church only occasionally were the highly prejudiced. The very frequent attenders were more likely to be intrinsic and thus less racially prejudiced. In addition to consistently extrinsic and consistently intrinsic individuals, they found individuals who were indiscriminately proreligious and others who were indiscriminately antireligious. The indiscriminately proreligious individuals were found to be highly prejudiced, more so than even the extrinsically oriented.

Hunt and King (1971) reviewed the literature on the intrinsic-extrinsic concept. Rather than being bipolarities on a unidimensional continuum, they found a multidimensional construct as anticipated by Allport and Ross (1967). Item and factor analyses revealed two components in the extrinsic orientation: an instrumental one and a selfish one. Intrinsic religion is more personal and more relevant to all of life and is associated with such religious practice components as church attendance and reading religious literature. Allport and Ross (1967) anticipated that the extrinsic-intrinsic concept is a complex of personality and cognitive variables. Hunt and King (1971) explicitly evaluated the construct as a pervasive personality and motivational process that could explain secular behavior as well as religious action. It is not surprising that extrinsic orientation correlated with aspects of authoritarianism (Adorno, Frenkel-Brunswik, Levinson, & Sanford, 1950), prejudice (Allport, 1954), closed-mindedness (Rokeach, 1960), and external locus of control.

What evolved to become a personality variable began for Allport (1950, 1954) as two types of religion. Interiorized religion became the intrinsic orientation; institutionalized religion became the extrinsic orientation. Dittes (1971) suggested a similar concept in the church-sect typology. The sect typifies a primitive, pure state of religion initially independent of culture and society. But with growth and through time the culture imposes itself and compromises the purity of the sect. The church accommodates itself to culture, with increased insensitivity to social issues, by adopting the administrative structure and governance polity of secular institutions but with a greater eye toward social interaction and social norms. In doing so the religious body moves from an intrinsic commitment to communal purity to an extrinsic association serving other than purely religious purposes.

Batson, Schoenrade, and Ventis (1993) summarized the current line of research of the impact of religion upon the individual. They noted that sex, race, age, socioeconomic status, education level, town size, geographic region, family ethnic origin, parents' religion, political affiliation, and marital status affect the degree and type of religiosity displayed by the individual. Their research and that of others (Watson, Morris, & Hood, 1994; Watson, Milliron, Morris, & Hood, 1994) suggest that the relationship among religious, personality, social, and mental health variables are more complex than theorists (like Adorno, Albert Ellis, and Freud, who were antagonist toward religion) originally intimated.

The sociopsychological analysis of religious orientation posits the etiology of divergent religious lifestyles in underlying personality and motivational variations and considers the style of one's religious expression to be founded on the personality substratum. When considered alongside sociological and cultural processes, the religious orientation approach explains varieties in religious expression such as asceticism, monasticism, and mysticism, as well as the once-born versus the twice-born typology of James (1902). The need for inner assurance and solace and the need for participation in external rituals arise from fundamental differences in human personality.

References

Adorno, T. W., Frenkel-Brunswik, E., Levinson, D. J., & Sanford, R. N. (1950). *The authoritarian personality*. New York: Harper & Row.

Allport, G. W. (1937). *Personality: A psychological interpretation*. New York: Holt.

Allport, G. W. (1950). *The individual and his religion*. New York: Macmillan.

Allport, G. W. (1954). *The nature of prejudice*. Reading, MA: Addison-Wesley.

Allport, G. W. (1960). *Personality and social encounter*. Boston: Beacon.

Allport, G. W., & Ross, J. M. (1967). Personal religious orientation and prejudice. *Journal of Personality and Social Psychology, 5*, 432–443.

Batson, C. D., Schoenrade, P., & Ventis, W. L. (1993). *Religion and the individual*. New York: Oxford.

Dittes, J. E. (1971). Typing the typologies: Some parallels in the career of church-sect and extrinsic-intrinsic. *Journal for the Scientific Study of Religion, 10*, 375–383.

Erikson, E. H. (1958). *Young man Luther*. New York: Norton.

Freud, S. (1918). *Totem and taboo*. New York: Moffat, Yard.

Gleason, J. J. (1975). *Growing up to God*. Nashville: Abingdon.

James, W. (1902). *The varieties of religious experience*. New York: Longmans, Green.

Hunt, R. A., & King, M. B. (1971). The intrinsic-extrinsic concept: A review and evaluation. *Journal for the Scientific Study of Religion, 10*, 339–356.

Malony, H. N. (Ed.). (1977). *Current perspectives in the psychology of religion*. Grand Rapids, MI: Eerdmans.

Oates, W. E. (1973). *The psychology of religion*. Waco, TX: Word.

Rokeach, M. (1960). *The open and closed mind*. New York: Basic.

Smart, N. (1976). *The religious experience of mankind* (2nd ed.). New York: Scribner's.

Watson, P. J., Milliron, J. T., Morris, R. J., & Hood, R. W. (1994). Religion and rationality: II. Comparative analysis of rational-emotive and intrinsically religious irrationalities. *Journal of Psychology and Christianity, 13*, 373–384.

Watson, P. J., Morris, R. J., & Hood, R. W. (1994). Religion and rationality: I. Rational-emotive and religious understandings of perfectionism and other irrationalities. *Journal of Psychology and Christianity, 13*, 356–372.

R. L. TIMPE

See PSYCHOLOGY OF RELIGION; RELIGIOUS EXPERIENCE; ALLPORT, GORDON WILLARD.

Religious Research Association (RRA). The Religious Research Association is a nonprofit research organization incorporated within New York State. The organization's goal, as given on the inside cover of its official publication, the *Review of Religious Research (RRR)*, is to seek "to further the understanding of the role of religion in contemporary life." To this end the association not only publishes the *RRR* but also cosponsors an annual convention, usually during late October or early November, with its sister society, the Society for the Scientific Study of Religion.

Membership is open to anyone, regardless of religious identification, interested in the study of religion. Membership includes social scientists (sociologists, psychologists, anthropologists, and political scientists), church researchers and planners, theologians, teachers, clergy, and religious educators.

The *RRR* reports primarily sociological studies of religion and religious experience and is provided as a benefit of membership in the association. Both members and nonmembers of the association may publish in the journal. Instructions regarding submissions to the journal are located inside the front cover. Also inside the front cover of each issue is the address of the association's business office.

P. C. HILL

See PSYCHOLOGY OF RELIGION; PSYCHOLOGISTS OF RELIGION; SOCIETY FOR THE SCIENTIFIC STUDY OF RELIGION.

Religious Resources in Psychotherapy. The process of psychotherapy involves the relationship between a mental health or pastoral professional and a person seeking a solution to a problem in living. The therapist seeks to enter as completely as possible that person's world. The extent to which religious resources are included in the therapeutic process is a challenge to Christian therapists who wish to be clinically responsible and yet make full use of all the resources at their disposal.

The advent of Christian counseling in recent years leads patients to expect some faith orientation in the psychotherapy process. At the least there is the expectation that therapists will understand the Christian worldview.

To what degree should mental health professionals use religious resources in psychotherapy? The issue has to be decided on philosophical and professional grounds. A range of opinions exists.

Some therapists exclude religion from the practice of therapy. The patient's religion is viewed as a cultural issue where respect and understanding is indicated. However, is it possible to keep values out of therapy? Every therapeutic modality has some vestiges of a value system.

Some counselors encourage the consistent use of religious resources. The problem with such positions is that they sometimes may not be therapeutic. Can the therapist not better reflect the pain of the patient in nonbiblical language? What about the patient who has major problems with and resistance to the Scriptures? Religion may not be the best intervention resource.

Many patients profess a Christian faith and expect the resources of the faith to be used. The therapist, trained in the use of such resources, must decide whether they are clinically indicated.

Prayer. A broad definition of prayer includes the variety of human endeavors wherein people focus their attention on God. The process goes beyond talking with God to include other ways of experiencing the divine. In Christianity the experience is mediated through a personal faith relationship with Jesus Christ. Prayer is one dimension of therapy that can help a patient connect with the source of meaning in life and introduce the supernatural to the therapy process.

To what extent can this component of religious life be included in psychotherapy? And what are the theological and psychological dangers inherent to the use of prayer in therapy?

In seeking to enter the world of the patient the therapist needs to recognize that his or her own personal prayer practice may not be the same as that of the patient. For example, some patients may be at the developmental level of a child who sees God as the magician who does the seemingly impossible. Therefore, when a patient asks, "Will you pray for me?" the therapist needs to be discerning and therapeutic in the use of prayer.

A theological danger is for the therapist or patient to use prayer but to give it less value than its biblical importance. This may be done by employing prayer as a psychological technique until a better strategy is found. Prayer is not a technique but the way of life of the believer in relationship to God.

Religious practice includes the whole spectrum of prayer experience. A prayer of thanksgiving can help a patient reframe a painful experience and have hope for the future. The therapist who is not comfortable with praying with a patient can give an assurance, "I will be praying for you." The therapist models ultimate dependence on God and shows concern for the patient.

Prayer should not be used in therapy if it is an avoidance mechanism on the part of the patient. Painful issues may be avoided when the person suggests prayer rather than further exploration or talk. People sometimes seek to evade personal responsibility through an infantile desire that God will make everything better. Such expectations require the therapeutic skill of confrontation in a context of acceptance. Sometimes it is the therapist who is afraid and uses prayer as a distancing technique. For instance, the experience of the patient's sexuality or the severity of the problem may be so great that the therapist wishes to escape to the safety of prayer. Questions like How does my patient wish to *use* prayer? Am I as a therapist seeking to please this person with my prayers? and Is this prayer consistent with the patient's need or theological tradition? help the therapist avoid the improper use of prayer and yet remain open to its appropriate use.

Notwithstanding the dangers, the use of prayer in therapy can mobilize the patient's inner spiritual resources and provide help in dealing with problems. Hope, essential to change in psychotherapy, can be generated in prayer. The spoken prayer of the patient may also be a way of reaffirming before God old covenants like a marriage vow. The presence of the therapist stimulates accountability.

Inner healing has become a therapeutic modality used by some Christian therapists. Here prayer is applied to the patient's painful past experiences or present fears. Through the imagery of Jesus in the painful event the prayer is seen as a powerful agent of healing. Again this practice should not be seen as a type of psychological quick fix that promises more than it delivers. Christian therapists need to be careful that clinical practice does not outstrip theory building and research.

The Scriptures. The use of the Bible also has dangers and challenges as well as great potential. One problem with reading biblical passages to Christian patients is that they may be overfamiliar with the passages to the point of being unresponsive. To people who have problems with the authority of the Bible, simply because of a transference relationship with authority figures to whom they defer or against whom they rebel, the therapist will encounter great resistance. The naive therapist may seek either to browbeat the rebel or to shape the compliant person's behavior through prooftexting.

Another problem is that the therapist and patient may have different interpretations of Scripture. For example, the therapist may hold to a egalitarian view of the marriage relationship while the patient may have a hierarchical perspective. At this point the therapist needs to decide whether there will be an explicit or implicit challenge to the patient's values, termination of the relationship, or work within the personal values of the patient to redefine the issue. For instance, to the domineering husband who seeks the submission of his wife, the therapist may ask, "How can you love your wife like Christ loved the church and gave his life for it?" (Eph. 5:25). Such a question changes the therapeutic emphasis from a power struggle to a challenging of the patient's personal responsibility.

The assets of the use of the Bible in therapy must not be eclipsed by its dangers. Like prayer, it can refer the therapeutic endeavor to the divine dimension and point people to their God-given potential. The Bible also gives direction and content to personal growth and can lead a person to a deeper relationship with the Divine author. Here the patient is encouraged to read portions of Scripture and apply them to life problems and challenges. Therapists should not underestimate the power of the Holy Spirit in applying scriptural truth to the patient's change process. The feelings and thoughts generated by such an exercise may be fruitfully explored in subsequent sessions.

Other Church Resources. A wide range of spiritual and therapeutic resources exist within the context of the church. The patient may be given the therapeutic assignment of participating in selected activities. The guilty patient from a Roman Catholic tradition may be encouraged to go to confession with his or her priest. A class on divorce recovery at a church may be suggested for another patient.

Some religious resources like the sacraments are the unique domain of the church. It would be inappropriate for a therapist to give a patient holy communion, since it is meant to be received in the context of the gathered church. However, certain ordained therapists may administer the sacrament at the church and have their patients partake in that context. The redemptive power of the sacrament may be an issue to be explored at a later time in therapy.

The Question of Evangelism. One area of special concern is evangelism in therapy. The definition of evangelism is important. What exactly does it mean to lead someone to Christ? Evangelism is more than telling a person, "You are a sinner and need to be saved." Rather, conversion should be seen as a process of growing awareness of our need for a personal relationship with God. Evangelism, therapeutically practiced, may then be the process of divesting oneself of dysfunctional views of God based more on a hurtful psychohistory than biblical revelation. Healing in therapy leads to a more grace-oriented view of God.

Broader Questions. The debate over whether religious resources have a place in psychotherapy continues on a number of fronts. Some people may question whether reimbursement for religious therapies, billed as psychotherapy, is both appropriate and valid. The fact that therapists are being trained in professionally accredited programs that integrate faith with therapy lends credence to the validity of religious interventions. The demand of the consumer is another compelling reason to consider the use of these resources.

There continues to be a need for a cohesive personality theory that is consistent with the tenets of the Christian faith. Many Christian therapists baptize their existing theory with their religious worldview. They approach the use of religious resources in a pragmatic way ("If it works then pray"). This could make such resources an addendum rather than an integral part of therapy. There is also the need for outcome studies with prayer and psychotherapy.

The practical realities of the marketplace are relevant to the practice of Christian therapy. The drive is to solve current problems quickly and efficiently and not compromise therapeutic outcome. Therapy needs to be goal-oriented. Vague goals lead to vague therapy. The challenge is also for patients who need longer-term therapy. Patients with a higher level of acuity, who are socially isolated, and have chronic mental problems like schizophrenia need the support of therapeutic communities, training in practical skills, and public assistance. The church can take up the challenge of providing such care, especially for those on the margins of society such as the mentally ill homeless. Christian therapists can be on the cutting edge of such effort.

The process that produces change needs to be better understood in the light of faith issues. Research indicates both nonspecific and specific factors to be involved in the psychotherapy process. The nonspecific issues transcend theoretical approaches and have to do with the therapy relationship. The ideal relationship is one in which patient and therapist relate well, there is mutual respect, and trust and hope are generated. Here the therapist models the loving acceptance of God and positive aspects of faith. The nonspecific factors are not always curative in and of themselves. They represent more the climate of therapy. They are a necessary but not sufficient condition for therapeutic reversal.

Specific factors can be viewed as the science of psychotherapy. They involve goal setting and strategies that specifically reverse old and ineffective ways of responding to life. The art of therapy is seen in the wise selection of specific strategies at the right time. Religious resources must be coupled with these nonspecific and specific factors and remain in harmony with good therapeutic and theological principles. For example, change for the growing Christian includes the development of a biblical worldview (Rom. 12:2). Such a renewal requires a scriptural content, understanding of cognitive change, and a therapeutic context that relies on the Holy Spirit to facilitate deep personal change. Religious resources in the hands of an experienced, sensitive, and faith-oriented therapist can be the agents of change and growth.

C. B. Johnson

See Spiritual and Religious Issues in Psychotherapy; Prayer, Use of in Counseling.

Remembering. *See* Memory.

Repetition Compulsion. The more or less irresistible impulse to repeat earlier experiences regardless of the pain they may produce. This principle is more fundamental than the pleasure principle and in fact seems incompatible with it. Sigmund Freud described the repetition phenomenon but did not provide much of an explanation for it. Fairbairn (1954) views the behavior as an attempt to solve old conflicts and thereby attain healing of the ego splits that resulted from early childhood nonsatisfactory relationships. The goal in psychoanalysis or psychoanalytic psychotherapy is to replace repetition with remembering, thereby undoing the repetition compulsion.

Reference

Fairbairn, W. R. D. (1954). *An object relations theory of the personality*. New York: Basic.

D. G. Benner

See Psychoanalytic Psychology; Object Relations Theory.

Repressed Memory. *See* False Memory Syndrome.

Repression. The process by which anxiety-producing ideas or impulses are kept out of or removed from conscious awareness. It is recognized in a number of theoretical perspectives as the most basic of defense mechanisms and, according to Sigmund Freud, provides the foundation on which most other defenses are constructed. Although the person is not consciously aware of repressed material or of the process of repression, this material continues to influence behavior.

When an idea or group of ideas associated with strong feeling, or affect, threatens to seriously lower self-esteem, conflict with deeply instilled values, or provoke anxiety, the ego seeks to remove this threat from consciousness. This process may involve repression of the idea with associated affect, the idea alone, or the affect alone. However, repressed material may gain conscious expression in various disguises. If the affect alone is repressed, the idea remaining in consciousness may be tied to an acceptable affect. When repression involves only the idea, the affect may become associated with an idea or object possessing no conscious connection to the threatening idea. Should both idea and affect be repressed, they may return to consciousness in some form of symbolic expression.

For example, an adult may have suffered a terrible act of child abuse in early years. If anger over this toward the abusing parent is fully repressed, leaving no conscious memory of the event or feelings surrounding it, it may seek conscious expression symbolically through anger toward some authority or parentlike figure not consciously associated with the parent. If affect alone is repressed, the person may recall the event with no conscious awareness of anger, even claiming instead feelings of love and forgiveness. The unexpressed anger may resurface, directed toward an unconscious parent substitute. If only the idea is repressed, conscious anger may again find an unconsciously chosen parent substitute as its object.

R. Larkin

See Defense Mechanisms.

Resiliency. Resiliency refers to successful adaptation despite challenging and threatening circumstances. For example, some children who experience severe loss, abuse, or chronic conditions such as poverty, parental psychopathology, or serious caretaking deficits distinguish themselves in school, work, or with other achievements. Studies of resiliency examine development from a strengths model rather than from a problem-oriented approach.

Resiliency is a relatively new focus in developmental psychology and clinical psychology. In the mid-1950s Emmy Werner and her colleagues began following a community of children born on the island of Kauai. One-third of her sample was considered high risk because they were born into poverty and lived in troubled family environments. Yet, one-third of these high-risk children did not develop serious behavioral or mental health problems and instead became competent, caring adults. Werner and her colleagues focused on what made these children resilient. In the late 1970s and early 1980s other researchers such as Norman Garmezy, Michael Rutter, Ann Masten, and Emory Cowen similarly examined factors that predicted successful adaptation despite adverse living conditions.

Common to studies of resiliency is a focus on protective factors or mechanisms that reduce the likelihood that individuals will have adjustment problems in response to stressful situations or chronic adversity. A common core of these protective factors has now been identified that transcend ethnic and social-class boundaries. Individual, familial, and community factors are part of this common core.

Individual factors seen early in life that are associated with resiliency include a temperament that elicits positive responses from a wide range of caregivers and coping behaviors that combine autonomy with an ability to ask for help when needed. During childhood and adolescence, good communication and problem-solving skills, having a talent or hobby to be proud of, outgoing and autonomous behavior, nurturance and emotional sensitivity, intelligence, a belief in one's abilities, and high self-esteem have been identified as protective. It is important to note that resilient children are not necessarily the brightest children but those who have the capacity to elicit support from those around them.

Within the family, factors that protect children include having a close bond with at least one emotionally stable, competent adult. This adult could be one of the child's parents, a grandparent, or another relative. Care by a consistent, responsive, loving adult is important so that children develop a sense of trust and hope about the world. Resilient children are particularly skillful at recruiting surrogate parents when their own parents cannot give them the attention they need.

Religious beliefs that provide stability and meaning in times of adversity are also related to resiliency. The importance of finding meaning in the midst of stress is a key notion of Aaron Antonovsky's salutogenic model of health and illness. Antonovsky argues that a sense of coherence—which refers to a belief that life is comprehensible, manageable, and meaningful—is why people remain healthy despite stress.

During childhood and adolescence the familial factors that are associated with resilience in boys and girls differ. For boys the presence of structure and rules, encouragement of emotional expression, and having good male role models appear critical. For girls encouragement of risk taking and independence and having reliable support from a female caregiver appear to be the most important.

One of the most important community factors associated with resiliency is available social support to provide counsel and comfort. Teachers are particularly important in this regard. Having opportunities open up at major life transitions (grad-uation from school, for example) also is associated with resiliency.

Recent research with urban adolescents has suggested that resiliency in one life domain (e.g., school) may not translate into resiliency in other life domains (e.g., peer relations, mental health). It is particularly important, therefore, when working with adolescents that their functioning in all areas be assessed.

How can Christian families and communities foster resiliency in youth? First, it is important to believe that successful outcomes are possible. This requires a transactional view of development. As Christians we can hold a transactional view of development by believing that Christ has the power to change people at any point in their lives. Second, it is important to provide caregiving that fosters competence and self-esteem. Children need to have opportunities to engage in activities at which they can excel. Children also need an adequate balance of limit setting and autonomy. Third, children need support from adults both within and outside of their families. Christian communities can provide children contact with adults outside their family who offer additional support or compensate for inadequate parental care. This is particularly important for boys who lack adequate male role models in the home. Fourth, Christian communities, through shared religious commitments and beliefs, may provide meaning for youth struggling with challenges. Christian communities have both the capacity and the responsibility to facilitate resiliency in these ways.

W. Kliewer

Resistance in Psychotherapy. A client's efforts to obstruct the psychotherapeutic process and thwart the psychotherapist's efforts to help that client. All clients manifest resistance, although the degree to which they resist may vary from minimal to massive. Resistance is not a phenomenon limited to involuntary clients but is also characteristic of clients who come for therapy at their own initiative. Most psychotherapists believe that resistance is an important part of the psychotherapeutic process.

General Considerations. Why do clients resist the psychotherapy they have initiated? Why do they drag their feet in reaching psychotherapeutic goals that have been formulated specifically for their benefit? Cavanagh (1982) attributes client resistance to three factors. First, growth is painful. Clients may have to stop well-learned destructive behaviors such as making excuses, addictions, pretending, and being dependent. They may have to begin new and unfamiliar healthful behaviors such as becoming independent, assertive, responsible, and exerting self-control. Psychotherapy makes some healthful but difficult demands.

A second reason for resistance in psychotherapy is that maladaptive behavior meets a need or in some way gratifies the client. This is known as secondary gain. The client's symptoms may bring attention, disguise the real problem, provide an excuse for anger, or provide an unhealthy way of atoning for guilt through self-punishment. Third, persons may enter psychotherapy with the wrong motives or with limited commitment. They may go into psychotherapy in order to blame others, to get permission not to change, to validate a decision, to manipulate others, to satisfy others, to prove they are beyond help, or to defeat the counselor.

Cavanagh also lists some vivid examples of how clients resist. These include missing or being late to appointments, evading questions, intentionally boring the counselor, focusing on the therapist more than self, and trying to evoke certain responses such as shock or sympathy from the therapist. The client may claim to forget things, avoid sensitive content areas, dwell on irrelevant areas by repeatedly bringing up past experiences, or try to force the therapist into a no-win, paradoxical situation. All these common client behaviors may indicate resistance.

While Cavanagh provides a good overview of resistance, it should be noted that psychotherapists' perspectives on the specific nature and treatment of resistance vary according to their theoretical orientation. Anderson and Stewart (1983) have summarized psychoanalytic, behavioral, and family therapy approaches to resistance. These three approaches illustrate some of the similarities and differences in different therapists' perspectives on resistance.

Psychoanalytic Perspective. Psychoanalytically oriented therapists believe that resistance is largely unconscious and defensive. Since they also believe that most personality problems result from unresolved childhood conflicts, resistance is seen as an unconscious attempt on the part of the client to avoid disturbing those painful and frightening areas that have been sealed off in an attempt to minimize anxiety. As the transference relationship develops, the psychotherapist identifies and interprets the meaning of the client's resistances. As the client comes to understand and accept the psychotherapist's interpretations, he or she discovers what he or she has been avoiding and deals with it consciously in a more adaptive fashion. This is by no means a brief or easy process.

Resistance therefore is one of the primary concerns of psychoanalytically oriented psychotherapy. Resistance is considered to be inevitable, pervasive, and valuable. Anything that works against the progress of psychotherapy is considered to be resistance. The client's resistances guide the psychotherapeutic process because they reveal to the psychotherapist what the client is unconsciously hiding and what needs to be addressed. Working through resistance is the heart of psychoanalytic psychotherapy.

Behavioral Perspective. Behavior therapists' perspectives on resistance stand in bold contrast to psychoanalytic perspectives. Behavior therapists believe that resistance is an unnecessary annoyance that can be avoided by the therapist through a good relationship with the client, anticipation of flaws in the behavior change program, and giving careful instructions to the client. Instead of interpreting and working through resistance, behavior therapists attempt to avoid it.

Behavior therapists do not acknowledge unconscious motivation or related concepts such as defensiveness. They believe that behavior is controlled primarily by environmental contingencies and associations the client has learned throughout life. Behavior therapists believe their role is an informative and technical role whereby they help clients learn new behaviors by identifying reinforcers, by counterconditioning, and by shaping. Behavior therapists focus on behaviors, not on presumed underlying causes, and they are not very concerned with early childhood experiences or conflicts.

Resistance is a concept that does not fit well within the behavioral theoretical framework. Even the term *resistance* is seldom found in behavioral literature. When clients do not cooperate, behavior therapists do not believe that it is due to unconscious defensiveness. Instead they believe that resistance is due to a misunderstanding between therapist and client or the client's failure to see the relevance of the behavior change program for his or her problem. Sometimes the therapist prescribes increments in the plan that are too large, and the client is unable to perform the prescribed behaviors. Most frequently clients resist because their misbehavior results in secondary gains.

Minimizing resistance is the responsibility of the behavior therapist. In addition to building good rapport the behavior therapist carefully explains both rationale and prescriptions in specific and concrete terms, prepares the client for anticipated difficulties, and rehearses prescribed tasks to ensure that the client understands them and can perform them. Behavior therapists minimize resistance due to secondary gains by teaching clients more effective behaviors for achieving their goals.

Family Therapy Perspective. The emergence of family therapy as a significant treatment modality has rekindled interest in resistance and added a new complexity to the concept. Family therapists are concerned primarily with the relationships among family members, the family's relationship to its social environment, and the family's rules governing those two relationships. Resistance is not viewed as the sole possession of an individual family member; rather, it is a force in the relationship that emanates from the family's rules and common assumptions. These rules are usually assumed or implied and may operate at an essentially unconscious level.

Family rules prescribing roles and relationships are important to family functioning. They preserve the identity of the family and its members; they let members know where and how they fit in; they apportion the work of the family; and they provide guidance and organization for family members in times of stress and ambiguity. Family rules maintain balance, or homeostastis, within the family.

Families, however, face a series of developmental tasks that require change. Children are born and grow, income levels change, members age, parents die, members are added through birth or marriage, illnesses strike, and persons retire. While family rules help guide the family through these crises, the rules and structure must also change to accommodate some of these developments. Very often families break down and come for therapy when the rules are too resistant to change and the family cannot adapt to its environment or family members' needs. Family rules are very difficult to change because they are shared by several family members and are consensually validated. Family rules also span generations, having their roots in the parents' families of origin.

Families then come into therapy with rigid, maladaptive rules that have resulted in tensions between members and in the breakdown of at least one member, usually a child. The family usually wants the therapist to cure the symptomatic member but resists changes in the family rules and structure. The therapist resists treating only the symptomatic family member. Members' symptoms are seen as the result of family rules that are unhealthy or functionally autonomous, which means that at one point in development the rules were adaptive, but they became habitual and continued to operate long after they were helpful. The family therapist regards the family system, not the individual, as the client.

Therefore, family therapists face a great deal of resistance in their work. The resistance is shared in varying degrees by all persons, including the therapist, in the therapeutic process and may be directed toward differing targets. Resistance may be adaptive or maladaptive, and the therapist's goal is to adjust and direct the resistance, not necessarily eliminate it. Family therapists must recognize resistance and use it therapeutically to restructure the family system.

Regardless of the therapist's theoretical orientation, resistance is always difficult for the therapist to handle because it seems like an attack against the therapist's person and competence. The therapist's tendency is to respond defensively. The best preparation for handling resistance therapeutically includes thorough professional preparation, self-confidence, and understanding that all therapists encounter resistance.

References

Anderson, C., & Stewart, S. (1983). *Mastering resistance.* New York: Guilford.
Cavanagh, M. E. (1982). *The counseling experience.* Monterey, CA: Brooks/Cole.

Additional Readings

Freud, S. (1920). *A general introduction to psychoanalysis* (Lecture 19). New York: Boni & Liveright.
Langs, R. (1981). *Resistances and interventions.* New York: Aronson.
Marshall, R. J. (1982). *Resistant interactions.* New York: Human Sciences Press.

C. D. DOLPH

See COUNSELING AND PSYCHOTHERAPY: OVERVIEW.

Response Cost Contingency. The withdrawal or loss of material reinforcers contingent upon the occurrence of an undesirable response.

There are two major forms of punishment: positive punishment, in which an aversive consequence is presented to the organism after a response and results in the response becoming less likely to occur; and negative punishment, in which as a consequence of a response something is taken away from the organism, again resulting in the response becoming less probable. Response cost contingency is one of the most common forms of negative punishment (time out being the other most common form).

An example of response cost contingency might go as follows. A teacher develops a token economy in a classroom for noncompliant children. Positive reinforcement in the form of tokens is given for appropriate behavior; these tokens can be redeemed for material rewards. When inappropriate behavior occurs, such as yelling or striking a peer, the teacher chooses not to ignore the behavior but to impose a response cost of loss of previously earned tokens. A child might have worked to earn 15 tokens earlier in the day but incurs the loss of 5 tokens after yelling at the teacher. Response cost contingency is a technique widely used in token economies and behavior modification in general. It is used in more informal ways in child rearing (e.g., taking away a child's allowance or privileges as a result of disobedience) and in social policy (e.g., personal and corporate monetary fines for illegal behavior).

S. L. JONES

See PUNISHMENT.

Response Generalization. *See* GENERALIZATION.

Responsibility, Psychology of. Responsibility is a concept that intersects the philosophical, moral, legal, theological, and psychological domains. Traditionally the word has had constituent or etiological and obligatory aspects: the former referring to intentionality or casual agency and the latter to duty *(Oxford English Dictionary)*. The philosopher Kaufman (1967, pp. 183–184) suggests that a person is generally regarded "as morally responsible for some act or occurrence x if and only if he is believed (1) to have done x, or to have brought x about; and (2) to have done it or brought it about freely." But he then goes on to acknowledge the dissent and confusion over "what is meant by a human action;

what would count as bringing some outcome about; and, above all, in what sense the terms 'free,' 'freely,' or 'freedom,' are employed."

Psychology and psychiatry, like the social sciences generally, began to emerge from philosophy in the latter eighteenth and early nineteenth centuries. Befitting their origin, they continue to occupy themselves with issues central to theology and ethics—concepts of personhood and the good life, theories of motivation and behavior, notions of normality and deviance, and purviews on healing. Indeed, until the mid-nineteenth century the term *moral* customarily referred to what we now parse into the "mental" or "psychological" and the "moral" or "ethical."

The aspect of responsibility relating to persons' claims upon and duties toward others is philosophically less problematic than the aspect relating the agent to his or her deeds and their consequences—though ascertaining the former in principle and practice can be difficult enough (Hart & Honore, 1985). The Old Testament covenant spelled out God's claims upon the Hebrews and their corresponding duties or responsibilities. Mutual rights or claims and obligations among individuals, and between individuals and the state have been codified in a variety of secular (social contract) contexts, along with the consequences for abrogating them. Moral theorists have diverged over whether the right (deontologists, e.g., Kant) or the good (the teleologists or consequentialists, e.g., Mill) assumes ethical priority. Others, such as Niebuhr (1963, p. 63), have developed concepts mediating between them—responsibility as the situationally "fitting action" that is "alone conducive to the good and alone is right." Finally, although I am dealing primarily with the concept of personal responsibility in its immediate interpersonal context, it is important to note that our greatest moral thinkers (e.g., Kant) have dealt with the matter of national and international responsibly as well.

From the obligational facet of responsibility, we turn to the more complex issue of personal agency, interwoven as it is with the age-old debate over free will and determinism. Do we ever possess the capacity to do other than we actually do at any instant? Theologians from Augustine and Pelagius through Luther and Erasmus have differed over this nettle, as have philosophers and ethicists. Classical Freudians, behaviorists, and biological theorists and clinicians have favored determinism, whereas ego psychologists and humanistic and existential psychologists have allowed for some measure of contracausal freedom (see Wallace, 1986a, 1986b). Since we can never place a human agent back into precisely the same situation (which would mean that he or she would have to have precisely the same state of mind) to see if he or she actually could have acted otherwise, the debate seems purely metaphysical or empirically insoluble. Meanwhile, phenomenology suggests that (and moral discourse and psychotherapy proceed as if) the human con-

dition includes degrees of both bondage and possibility. If one possesses the capacity for optimal reality—testing, for appreciating what constitutes right and wrong, and for engaging in moral review of past behaviors and moral deliberation over future courses of action and their likely consequences—then one may be considered a responsible agent. Whether such responsibility and the action ensuing from it are in fact necessitated seems not only unascertainable but beside the point.

Since at least the Middle Ages, canon and civil law have considered that sufficiently severe mental derangement can mitigate the attribution of criminal responsibility, with the important exception of states of diminished responsibility (or even madness) that are occasioned by an individual's misuse of his or her freedom (e.g., vehicular homicide by a drunken driver). With the 1843 M'Naughten rule, psychiatry increasingly influenced judicial thinking about criminal responsibility. This culminated in the 1954 Durham test, by which a finding of diminished responsibility required only that the unlawful act was "a product of mental disease or defect." Since a host of states of mind (including antisocial personality disorders) were considered potentially diagnosable "diseases[s] or defect[s]," there was considerable public and legal backlash against what was viewed as psychiatric imperialism. Recall, in this context, the work of antipsychiatrists such as Szasz (1961) and Mowrer (1961).

Apart from influencing legal thinking and popular morality on conditions of diminished responsibility and on the importance of mental illness generally, psychiatrists and psychologists have formulated theories of moral development and notions of autonomous or mature and responsible personhood (e.g., Freud, Jung, Erikson, Piaget, Kohlberg, Allport, Maslow, and even Skinner). Ostensibly purely scientific, cosmology-free, and value-neutral, the most superficial scrutiny reveals a plethora of philosophical and ethical precommitments, some more compatible with traditional Judeo-Christian visions and values than others (see Browning, 1987; Wallace, 1990). In recent decades psychiatric taxonomies have become ever more expansive (e.g., the *DSM*s) and concepts of mental health have proliferated phenomenally (Wallace, 1995). If, as Rieff (1968) persuasively argues, psychotherapists have assumed the moral and salvific role of the church and clergy for many, then it behooves us to examine our hidden moral and metaphysical agendas. Thereby both we and our patients may become more responsible.

References

Browning, D. S. (1987). *Religious thought and the modern psychologies.* Philadelphia: Fortress.

Hart, H. L. A., and Honore, T. (1985). *Causation in the law.* Oxford: Oxford University Press.

Kaufman, A. S. (1967). Responsibility, moral and legal. In P. Edwards (Ed.), *The encyclopedia of philosophy* (Vol. 7). New York: Macmillan.

Mowrer, O. H. (1961). *The crisis in psychiatry and religion.* New York: Van Nostrand.

Niebuhr, H. R. (1963). *The responsible self: An essay in Christian moral philosophy.* New York: Harper & Row.

Rieff, P. (1968). *The triumph of the therapeutic: Uses of faith after Freud.* New York: Harper.

Szasz, T. (1961). *The myth of mental illness.* New York: Harper & Row.

Wallace, E. R. (1986a). Freud as ethicist. In P. Stepnausky (Ed.), *Freud: Appraisals and reappraisals.* Hillsdale, NJ: Analytic Press.

Wallace, E. R. (1986b). Determinism, possibility, and ethics. *Journal of the American Psychoanalytic Association 34,* 933–974.

Wallace, E. R. (1990). Psychiatry and religion: Toward a dialogue and public philosophy. In J. Smith & S. Haudelmem (Eds.), *Psychoanalysis and religion.* Baltimore: John Hopkins University Press.

Wallace, E. R. (1995). The meaning of mental health. In W. Reich (Ed.), *The encyclopedia of bioethics* (Vol. 3). New York: Macmillan.

E. R. WALLACE IV AND A. RAINWATER III

Retirement. Retirement is the stage of life following withdrawal from the labor force in which an individual receives a retirement pension. In American society, the status of retiree is considered a position of merit attained after many years of hard work. Currently, retirement is the primary reason middle-aged and older adults exit the workforce. However, this has not always been the case.

Prior to the twentieth century, retirement was virtually an unknown phenomenon. Persons worked until they were disabled or died. Factors leading to retirement as we understand it today include high productivity resulting from advanced industrial production systems, a large surplus of workers due to a decline in death rates, and an increase in the standard of living.

The Social Security system, established in the 1930s, made it financially feasible for persons to retire. Mandatory retirement at a specified age such as sixty-five or seventy soon followed. In 1986, Congress phased out mandatory retirement laws, which were overtly discriminatory to older workers, virtually ending the practice of forced retirement by 1987. However, the majority of American workers today still retire at about age sixty-five.

The next century holds further shifts in retirement trends. First, there will be an increase in the number of retirees due to the last of the baby boomers reaching retirement age, and there will be a decrease in the number of workers due to a decline in birthrates. Also, an increase in life expectancy creates the possibility of a person facing up to thirty years of life past full-time employment. These factors highlight the importance of understanding and meeting the needs of persons in this lengthy stage of the lifespan.

Phases of Retirement. Atchley (1991) has identified seven phases of retirement which are helpful in understanding the process of taking on the role of retiree, living this role out, and eventually giving it up. Several of the phases are optional and will be experienced by some but not all retirees. During pre-retirement, the period of time prior to retirement, persons begin to consider the implications of retirement and prepare for it. Persons who can accurately anticipate what their lives will be like after they stop working and plan ahead have the most positive adjustment to retirement. Health and income are reported to be concerns of persons during this stage rather than leaving the labor force.

Many new retirees experience the honeymoon phase of retirement. During this phase, a person often expresses feelings of excitement and an intense desire to do the many things that he or she has never done before. Travel and leisure activities take on an increasingly significant role. Possible reasons for not experiencing a honeymoon phase of retirement include lack of resources and a negative outlook on retirement in general.

In contrast to the fast-paced honeymoon phase of retirement, a person may go through a period of rest and relaxation. Many persons relish this time of low activity after many years of hard work. The rest and relaxation phase is usually temporary and is followed by an increase in activity.

Disenchantment is not a common response to retirement. This phase, which sometimes follows the honeymoon or rest and relaxation phase of retirement, is not experienced by the majority of retirees. Disenchantment may occur for various reasons, including unrealistic fantasies of what retirement will be like, poor health, or death of a spouse.

The reorientation phase of retirement sometimes follows disenchantment. During this phase, a person may be launched into reexamining his or her life after dissatisfaction with the current experience of retirement. Some persons go back to their previous mode of employment, while others begin careers in completely different fields. More and more retirees are going back to school to learn new skills. In the future, we will probably see persons with two or more consecutive careers.

Most persons establish retirement routines or predictable, orderly ways of doing things. Stability rather than unpredictability appears to be associated with life satisfaction during the retirement years. Many individuals move directly to this phase from the honeymoon phase.

Eventually termination of the retirement role will take place. Retirement is often halted by illness or loss of independence. More dependent roles may be taken on by the individual. For example, one may take on the sick role.

Adjustment to Retirement. The literature indicates that retirement is a positive experience for most individuals. A common misconception is that retirement itself has a negative effect on physical well-being and on mental health. Ekerdt, Bosse', and LoCastro (1983) actually found that retirement is associated with improved functional health among persons who retire due to poor health. Retirement can serve to reduce demands placed on individuals. Poor physical health prior to retirement is associated with feelings of depression rather than the act of retirement itself (Crowley, 1985).

Retirees exhibit much variability in their response to exiting from the working world. Some persons must find an outlet in which to carry their former work-related activities into their retirement years. For these persons, maintaining an occupational identity is important for adjustment. Other persons are thrilled with the idea that they may now pursue all the things that they have always wanted to do but never had the time for. For instance, a music teacher might turn composer after retirement. Some persons rest in solitude and isolation. For these individuals, freedom from work-related pressures and responsibilities is welcome.

Although retirement sometimes fits the common image of being a period of restful activity after years of hard work, it sometimes means the loss of familiar routines as well as boredom. Like any life transition, retirement demands that a person learn new and different ways of living while simultaneously unlearning patterns and routines of earlier life. A nearly equal transition is required of the nonworking wife or husband who must change routines to accommodate a spouse now spending more time in the home. Some women experience the presence of a retired husband in the home as a difficult adjustment. However, the majority of couples report new joys in spending time with each other (Macionis, 1991).

Atchley (1991) reports that there are several factors associated with positive adjustment to retirement, which include the following four sets of circumstances: retirement is voluntary rather than forced; the individual does not hold work as the most important area of his or her life; good health and adequate income allow the person to invest in leisure activities; and retirement has been prepared for and planned.

Working with the Retiree. For the concerned professional, family member, or friend, important issues in working with a retiree include helping the retiree to accept retirement as another positive phase of life, adjusting attitudes and roles, considering work for pay or volunteerism, and using free time creatively. There are several suggestions offered in the literature for increasing meaning and satisfaction in the retirement years.

First, retirement planning and education may facilitate the transition into this new and potentially satisfying time of life. Currently, many companies and community organizations offer programs for retirement planning in the area of financial security. Local churches may serve as a resource for the pre-retiree by launching special retirement programs that address leisure needs that will enhance feelings of purpose and connectedness in the future. Health and wellness are other important areas of education for the pre-retiree.

Second, it has been suggested that the pre-retiree actually rehearse his or her future role by taking part in new leisure activities, part-time work, volunteer work, or a new line of business. The option of part-time employment may serve as a transition from full-time employment and its attendant roles to full-time retirement. Also, it may give the person a continuing sense of contributing to society.

Third, creative ways of using free time range from taking part in a continuing education program at a community college or university to gardening to reading quietly in solitude. The important thing to note is the interests of the retired person. Finally, and perhaps most important, society as a whole must provide retired persons with new, different, and more meaningful roles to fill in the future.

References

Atchley, R. C. (1991). *Social forces and aging: An introduction to social gerontology* (6th Ed.). Belmont, CA: Wadsworth.

Crowley, J. E. (1985). Longitudinal effects of retirement on men's psychological and physical well-being. In Herbert S. Parnes (Ed.), *Retirement among American men.* Lexington, Mass.: Heath.

Ekerdt, D. J., Bosse', R., LoCastro, J. S. (1983). Claims that retirement improves health. *Journal of Gerontology, 38,* 231–236.

Macionis, J. J. (1991). *Sociology* (3rd Ed.). Englewood Cliffs, NJ: Prentice-Hall.

J. S. McGee

See Life Span Development.

Rett's Disorder. *Clinical Picture.* When Sandy was born to Robert and Carolyn, they felt like the happiest couple in the world. Sandy was a beautiful baby girl who was filled with life and promise. Robert and Carolyn were filled with hopes and plans for an exciting, fun-filled life. However, after about five months their hopes began turning into fears and their laughter into tears of concern.

Robert and Carolyn began to notice that Sandy not only seemed to be losing interest in playing with her toys but also had a hard time picking up and manipulating many of them. It seemed difficult for Sandy to hold anything in her hands regardless of the size of the object. She also seemed to involuntarily clasp and rub her hands together as if she were washing them. What was most alarming was how Sandy's body seemed to be growing faster than her head.

Robert and Carolyn found Sandy's illness difficult to comprehend because Carolyn had had no problems during her pregnancy. All prenatal tests were fine, and there seemed to be nothing wrong with Sandy at birth.

Diagnostic Criteria. Sandy's condition might be diagnosed as a pervasive developmental disorder called Rett's disorder. Rett's disorder was first described by Andreas Rett, a German neurologist who studied two mentally retarded female patients who were exhibiting similar hand-wringing movements and developmental histories (Braddock, Braddock, & Graham, 1993).

According to the American Psychiatric Association's *DSM-IV*, Rett's disorder involves a characteristic pattern of head growth deceleration, a loss of purposeful hand skills, impairments in the condition of the trunk movement or gait, a decrease of interest in the social environment, and severe impairment to expressive and receptive language. These developmental abnormalities occur after a period of normal prenatal and perinatal development, normal psychomotor development through the first five months after birth, and normal head circumference at birth. Moreover, Rett's disorder is observed only in females.

Hagberg and Witt-Engerstrom (1986) proposed a four-stage model to provide guidelines for stage patterns and profiles of girls with Rett's disorder from infancy through adolescence. Stage 1 (onset 6–18 months) suggests a deterioration or stagnation of motor development, deceleration of head growth, and disinterest in the surrounding environment. Stage 2 (onset 1–3 years) is characterized by the obvious loss of previously acquired skills, the development of stereotypic hand wringing, loss of expressive language, insomnia, self-abusive behaviors, increased irritability, and seizures. Stage 3 (onset 2–10 years) is reported to be more stable in that the tantrums, screaming, and sleep problems are generally no longer present. Thus stage 3 girls tend to enjoy physical contact and improved social interactions. However, there is a generally reported drop in intellectual functioning and loss of muscular coordination (ataxia), and inability to perform coordinated movements (apraxia) becomes prominent. Stage 4 (onset 10+ years) is characterized by progressive muscle wasting, scoliosis, spasticity, decreased mobility, and growth retardation. During this fourth stage of Rett's disorder, girls develop improved social interaction and attentiveness, and they experience fewer seizures.

Rett's disorder is often misdiagnosed as infantile autism. However, in contrast to autism, children with Rett's disorder appear to lose interest in toys completely, demonstrate progressive loss of purposeful hand movements, and develop stereotypic hand movements (Braddock, Braddock, & Graham, 1993; Van Acker, 1991).

Etiology. The cause of Rett's disorder is unknown (Braddock, Braddock, & Graham, 1993; Van Acker, 1991). However, the progressive deterioration in girls suggests a metabolic cause. The only agreement about the cause of Rett's disorder is that further study on larger samples of girls is necessary.

References

Braddock, S. R., Braddock, B. A., & Graham, J. M. (1993). Rett syndrome: An update and review for the primary pediatrician. *Clinical Pediatrics, 32,* 613–626.

Hagberg, B. A., & Witt-Engerstrom, I. (1986). Rett syndrome: A suggested staging system for describing impairment profile with increasing age towards adolescence. *American Journal of Medical Genetics, 24,* 47–59.

Van Acker, R. (1991). Rett syndrome: A review of current knowledge. *Journal of Autism and Developmental Disorders, 21,* 381–405.

Additional Reading

Perry, A. (1991). Rett syndrome: A comprehensive review of the literature. *American Journal on Mental Retardation, 96,* 275–290.

M. L. McCreary

See Pervasive Developmental Disorders.

Ritual. A pattern of repetitive behavior in an established routine, intended consciously or subconsciously for efficient achievement of personal fulfillment or anxiety reduction and for manipulative control with regard to some significant aspect of one's internal or external world. The objectives and the routine patterns designed to meet them may be physical, psychological, social, or spiritual. They may include several of these facets of human experience simultaneously (Taylor & Thompson, 1972). Ritual is readily evident in at least three spheres of human function: worship, relationships, and work. In each of these areas ritual may be either pathological or healthy.

Worship is the area of human behavior in which the role of ritual has been most obvious throughout human history (Westerhof & Willimon, 1980). This is probably due to the fact that humans universally experience relatively high levels of anxiety about spirituality, as we do about sexuality. Both are rooted in personality and character close to the center of our sense of identity. Both are forces driving toward relationship, which has its own inherent anxiety. Moreover, in religious and spiritual matters humans perceive themselves dealing with sacred, transcendent, divine relationship. The sense of the sacred historically has carried with it an understandable sense of awesome encounter with the world of the unknown and eternal. Such encounter has usually produced a sense of anxiety or even dread. Only in the Judeo-Christian religion of unconditional grace is our encounter with God a source of relief, assurance, joy, and health.

The high anxiety function of religion has caused humans to experience a high level of need to conduct religious matters with great care. That carefulness tends to lead to the creation of closely controlled procedures for religious behavior: orthodox theology, rigid codes of ethical-moral conduct, and ritualization of the worship process (MacGregor, 1974). These controlled systems function as anxiety-reducing mechanisms in religions in which the radical and redemptive nature of God's grace is not perceived or is not trusted. As such ritualized religion becomes more and more tightly controlled for the purpose of managing the ever increasing religious anxiety, and the rituals tend to become increasingly compulsive and ultimately obsessive (Loder, 1966).

Ritual can also play a constructive role in religion. It is helpful for Christians to adopt a generally agreed-upon perspective in theology, a functionally effective code of conduct, and a patterned worship process. Ritual in worship adds dignity and aesthetic quality to communal behavior and gives programmatic focus to the experiences of prayer, praise, and religious pronouncement.

There remains in all religion a tendency to cabalistic ritual in worship. Cabalistic worship is that in which the ritual has become an end in itself and has lost its rational connection between the procedure and the objective it was originally designed to achieve: personal fulfillment or anxiety reduction. Cabalistic ritual is always imbued with some significant degree of compulsivity. It is pathological in that it callouses both the soul and psyche by decreasing the sensitivity of the human spirit to the genuine meaning of worship. It has the same effect upon the psyche as a constant chafing has upon one's hand. It desensitizes that organ and creates a defensive and protective callous at the place where the rub is. True worship always moves through ritual to encounter with God in his grandeur.

Ritual also plays an important role in the patterning of human relationships. Emerson thought that politeness is the ritual of society as prayers and praises are the ritual of the worshiping church. Since effective interpersonal relationships depend essentially upon trust, friendship requires that the agenda of mutual expectations be clearly and openly shared. The number and variety of individual differences, therefore, tend to enhance the desirability of predictable patterns and styles of interpersonal behavior. Thus the rituals of friendship arise and make the processes of friendship gratifying, comfortable, and edifying. Friendships, like personalities, can get sick. When they do, the rituals, or predictable behavior patterning, become compulsively oriented toward manipulative control by one or both of the persons in the relationship. The objective in that case is anxiety reduction by excessive dominance of one by the other. When that compulsivity is challenged or its goal achievement frustrated, it tends toward obsessiveness unless the wholesome objective of mutual fulfillment and gratification for all participants in the relationship can be brought back into focus.

It is clear that ritual also plays an important role in work behavior. Routines can enhance efficiency, particularly in a mass-production society. However, they can also sometimes obstruct job efficiency and must then be seen as pathological. Obsessive checking and rechecking of one's work exemplifies this.

The psychopathology most closely associated with pathological ritual is the obsessive-compulsive disorder. Obsessiveness and compulsivity are always fueled by insecurity and driven by the need for anxiety reduction through certainty or control. So an obsessive-compulsive personality may be manifested in the need to check and recheck a door lock or gas jet or in the repeated ritual of washing one's hands. Since these rituals enacted to achieve certainty and control do not result in significant change in the original insecurity, they tend to increase in intensity and in obsessional quality and move toward the pseudoomnipotent dynamics of magic. The rational link between the cause of the original insecurity and the function of the ritual is then no longer discernible. The process becomes a self-reinfecting exaggeration of the insecurity; that is, the insecurity fuels the obsessive ritual, which does not increase security by anxiety reduction. Fear therefore increases, and the intensity of the ritual is heightened to compensate for the increased anxiety.

Ritualistic behavior of this sort is clearly pathological whether it appears in work, worship, or relationships. The criteria for pathological ritual would seem to be the presence of any of the following conditions: the relationship between the ritual and its objective is lost or nonfunctional; the behavior obstructs the functioning of the life of the person or community; or the enactment of the ritual increasingly fails in its objective of reducing anxiety and therefore escalates in frequency. In extreme cases only the self-limiting experiences of physical and psychic exhaustion or the limits of formal external constraint can control the infinite wildfire effect of the expansion of the self-defeating ritualistic behavior (Salzman, 1980).

It is evident, therefore, that ritual may be constructive or destructive, depending on its nature and function. All wholesome idealism requires routines to lead humanity to civilization and aesthetic self-actualization. Efficiency in productivity requires precision and its inherent patterning. Communal life requires coordination, schedule, and ritualization if it is to achieve success, mutual trust, comfort, and gratification. Instruction in the faith requires the routines of catechesis in the symbology of theology and praxis if it is to achieve its growth-enhancing objectives. All of these tend to institutionalize themselves in constructive ritual. All are impaired by pathological ritual.

References

Loder, J. E. (1966). *Religious pathology and Christian faith.* Philadelphia: Westminster.

MacGregor, G. (1974). *The rhythm of God.* New York: Seabury.

Salzman, L. (1980). *Treatment of the obsessive personality.* New York: Aronson.

Taylor, J. C., & Thompson, G. R. (1972). *Ritual, realism, and revolt.* New York: Scribner's.

Westerhof, J. H., & Willimon, W. H. (1980). *Liturgy and learning through the life cycle*. New York: Seabury.

J. H. ELLENS

See WORSHIP.

Rogerian Personality Theory. *See* SELF THEORY.

Rogers, Carl Ransom (1902–1987). The founder of person-centered (client-centered) or nondirective therapy. Rogers was born in Chicago, the middle child of a family of six in a fundamentalist Protestant home where the work ethic was revered. His family was loving but noncommunicative. During his youth he was a lonely child with few friends.

Early in his adult life Rogers turned from Christianity to liberalistic humanism, largely, it seems, in reaction to the rather harsh religious convictions of his mother. She was a strong person who insisted on a separation between persons on the basis of religious differences. With equally strong convictions she held that even at best a person is never good enough. In contrast to this, Rogers's adult life has been characterized by what he himself calls "an obsession" with communication between people regardless of religious or other differences. He is also a champion of the belief in the inherent goodness of people.

In 1919 Rogers entered the University of Wisconsin. Initially he studied agriculture, but in his sophomore year he switched to history in preparation for seminary training to become a "religious worker." Religious work was a program of the YMCA aimed at converting people to Protestantism through humanitarian services. In his junior year he took a six-month trip to China as one of the American student representatives to an international congress of the YMCA. During this trip he rapidly moved away from the childhood religion of his family. He experienced this change as a developmental liberation.

Upon graduation in 1924 Rogers married and entered Union Theological Seminary in New York. In the freewheeling intellectual climate of that institution he thought himself out of religious work. Humanitarian service had now become an end in itself for him. Accordingly, he left Union and enrolled in Teachers College, Columbia University, to study psychology.

At Teachers College Rogers became acquainted with John Dewey's pragmatism, and Dewey's influence on Rogers's thought has been considerable. For example, Rogers was trained clinically to become a dogmatic Freudian. For therapy this meant that clients would have to adapt themselves to the methods and interpretations of the therapist if they were to obtain emotional healing. Dewey's experimentalism allowed Rogers to adopt an eclectic approach to therapy in which both the therapist's methods and the client's input contributed to the outcome of therapy. This meant that he could transform existing therapeutic dogmas into techniques, retaining those that proved effective in therapy while discarding those that did not.

For 12 years following his graduation from Teachers College, Rogers worked for the Society for the Prevention of Cruelty to Children in Rochester. There he collected a large number of effective therapeutic techniques, which ultimately were published in 1939 in his first book: *The Clinical Treatment of the Problem Child*.

During these years Rogers also came to a definitive position on his own nondirective approach to therapy. In doing so he moved away from both the dogmatic Freudian and the eclectic pragmatistic approaches to therapy by insisting that the therapist should follow the lead of the client with regard to the direction, movement, and outcome of therapy. In subsequent years Rogers never wavered from this position.

From 1940 to 1944 Rogers taught at Ohio State University. During these years he wrote *Counseling and Psychotherapy* (1942), his first detailed description of nondirective therapy. The years from 1945 to 1957 were perhaps his most productive. During this time he taught at the University of Chicago and, with a sizable group of promising young therapists, did a great deal of important research in psychotherapy. He also completed his second major publication: *Client-Centered Therapy* (1951).

After a brief and personally disappointing stint at Wisconsin (1957–1963), Rogers moved to La-Jolla, California, to become a resident fellow at the Western Behavioral Science Institute. Later (1970) he became affiliated with the Center for Studies of the Person and remained there until his death. Both these institutions were loosely organized around the promotion of research in human learning and growth.

During these years Rogers's interests moved from psychotherapy to group therapy and encounter groups, with a concomitant stress on the interpersonal rather than the intrapersonal. His interests also switched from the narrow confines of therapy to other areas of life such as education, family relations, industrial relations, and international relations. Some of his most thought-provoking publications date from these years: *On Becoming a Person* (1961), *Freedom to Learn* (1969), *Carl Rogers on Encounter Groups* (1970), *Carl Rogers on Personal Power* (1977), and *A Way of Being* (1980).

During the last decade of his life and mainly because of his experiences in encounter groups, Rogers became more and more preoccupied with the parapsychological and transpersonal theme of universal wholeness rather than with individual wholeness. He came to believe that the well-being of individual persons depends largely on their willingness to dissolve themselves into a larger whole, such as the group, the life force, or cosmic consciousness. With this shift in Rogers's thinking, third force humanistic psychology became superseded by fourth force transpersonal psychology.

Additional Readings

Kirschenbaum, H. (1979). *On becoming Carl Rogers.* New York: Delacorte.

Van Belle, H. A. (1980). *Basic intent and therapeutic approach of Carl R. Rogers.* Toronto: Wedge Publishing Foundation.

Van Belle, H. A. (1990). Rogers' later move to mysticism: Implications for client-centered therapy. In G. Lietaer, J. Rombauts, & R. Van Balen (Eds.), *Client-centered and experiential psychotherapy in the nineties.* Leuven, Belgium: Leuven University Press.

H. A. VAN BELLE

See SELF THEORY; PERSON-CENTERED THERAPY; CONDITIONS OF WORTH.

Role Playing. The rehearsal or recapitulation of an event, real or imagined, with the goal of changing behavior, thinking, and/or feelings. As a therapeutic technique it is attributed to Moreno (1946), a psychiatrist who developed the American Society of Group Psychotherapy and Psychodrama and the journal *Group Psychotherapy.*

Role playing may be used by the counselor to serve several purposes: diagnosis, instruction and training, and as a catalyst for change in the client. On a diagnostic level the role-playing situation enables the counselor to better understand the client through watching him or her act out as a representation of real behavior. It may also serve to help demonstrate other alternatives and reactions and therefore fulfill an instructional purpose. Participation in role-playing experiences also gives the counselee the opportunity to relive, reenact, or imagine situations that may be causing psychological pain, with the goal of changing patterns of thinking, feeling, or behaving. Observers or other participants also profit vicariously from the experience. One further benefit of role playing is the creation of a comfort zone whereby the client can play out a problem in a safe situation, gaining skills, experiencing emotions, and obtaining information.

Role playing may be used effectively with individuals in a one-to-one counseling setting, in groups, and alone, as in practicing a speech or rehearsing possible responses to an upcoming situation. The person may role play himself or herself in a particular situation (real or fictional), may switch roles, or may observe others playing his or her role. The technique is generally applicable to most counseling situations and is particularly valuable with delinquents and criminals and for some marriage and relational problems. Because of the potential for change in behavioral, affective, and cognitive areas, role playing may be used as a tool with any therapeutic approach as a main technique or in combination with others. As a therapeutic tool it

may elicit strong, often deeply repressed emotions, and for that reason is potentially dangerous under the direction of untrained persons.

Reference

Moreno, J. L. (1946). *Psychodrama* (Vol. 1). New York: Beacon.

Additional Reading

Corsini, R. J. (1966). *Roleplaying in psychotherapy.* Chicago: Aldine.

D. L. SCHUURMAN

See PSYCHODRAMA.

Rolfing. *See* STRUCTURAL INTEGRATION.

Rorschach, Hermann (1884–1922). Swiss psychiatrist who developed the inkblot test that bears his name. Born in Zurich, he was nicknamed *Kleck* (inkblot) in school because he was interested in sketching and his father was an art teacher. He attended the universities of Neuchâtel, Zurich, Berlin, and Bern between 1904 and 1909 and received his M.D. from the University of Zurich in 1912. After a few months' work in Russia he returned to Switzerland to work in mental hospitals there. He advocated psychoanalysis and was elected vice president of the Swiss Psychoanalytic Society in 1919.

While he was in medical school Rorschach did some studies on how people react to inkblots, but he never published the results and abandoned the area to concentrate on psychoanalysis. In 1917 he came across the dissertation of a Polish student who had used an inkblot test of eight cards to study fantasy in normal people and psychotics. After reading this dissertation, he devoted all his energy to the creation of an inkblot test and the development of its rationale.

In 1918 Rorschach began experimenting with 15 inkblots, using his patients as subjects. At the same time he began work on his book, *Psychodiagnostik.* The manuscript and the inkblots were sent to seven publishers, all of whom rejected it. He finally found one to publish it but on the condition that only 10 rather than 15 cards be used. When the book appeared in 1921, the printer had reduced the cards in size, altered the colors, and introduced shading into the uniformly black areas on the cards.

Rorschach presented his test to the Swiss Psychiatric Society and the Swiss Psychoanalytic Society, but they showed little interest. The book was a failure. Most of the copies remained unsold in the basement of the publisher. When it was reviewed before the German Society of Experimental Psychology, William Stern denounced it as faulty, arbitrary, and showing no understanding of the human personality.

In spite of the initial poor reception of his ideas Rorschach's inkblot test has come to be an accepted and standard tool for clinical psychologists. It is the most commonly employed projective test in the United States and is second only to the Wechsler Adult Intelligence Scale in overall usage. This is a tribute to Rorschach, whose considerable creative abilities were unrecognized by his own generation.

R. L. KOTESKEY

Rorschach Inkblot Test. A projective measure of personality developed by Swiss psychiatrist Hermann Rorschach. The test consists of 10 reproductions of inkblots printed on cardboard. In his work in asylums and psychiatric clinics Rorschach observed that emotionally disturbed persons tended to perceive objects in their environment in a unique manner. To quantify these observations he began to record patient responses to nonspecific, accidental forms. Rorschach eventually developed a set of forms that he made by throwing ink on paper and folding the paper in half, thus allowing the ink to spread onto both halves. The designs were simple yet suggestive. Rorschach described his instrument as a psychiatric experiment (Rorschach, 1964).

Procedures of administering the test have been standardized. The cards are first shown one at a time to the subject. The examiner carefully records the associations made by the subject to the blots. The second phase of the test, the inquiry, consists of reviewing all responses to further clarify which feature of the card was the main determinant used by the subject in forming the percept. Some systems of the Rorschach advocate a third phase of the administration, testing the limits, in which the examiner attempts to discover whether the subject is able to visualize the most common or frequently given responses.

Scoring a Rorschach protocol is a complicated task requiring extensive experience and training (Goldfried, Stricker, & Weiner, 1971). Each response is scored for its location on the blot itself, the main characteristic of the blot used to determine the response (form, color, perceived movement, or shading), the content of the response (objects, humans, animals, landscapes) and the general quality of the response.

Over the years several schools of Rorschach interpretation have evolved. Beck, Hertz, Klopfer, Piotrowski, and David Rapaport and Schafer have all developed interpretive and scoring systems. While there is a great deal of similarity, there are also sufficient differences to breed confusion among researchers. Recently Exner (1974) has developed a comprehensive synthesis of previous Rorschach systems.

Critics argue that the test is more subjective than objective and that the Rorschach is essentially an interview rather than psychological test (Zubin, Eron, & Schumer, 1965). Advocates claim that insights into personality dynamics, defense mechanisms, and reality orientation can be gleaned from the Rorschach (Schafer, 1954). Published findings include general works on frequency of responses and specific works such as the Rorschach responses of Nazi leaders (Miale & Selzer, 1975).

References

Exner, J. E. (1974). *The Rorschach: A comprehensive system* (Vol. 1). New York: Wiley.

Goldfried, M. R., Stricker, G., & Weiner, I. B. (1971). *Rorschach handbook of clinical and research applications*. Englewood Cliffs, NJ: Prentice-Hall.

Miale, F. R., & Selzer, M. (1975). *The Nuremberg mind: The psychology of the Nazi leaders*. New York: Quadrangle.

Rorschach, H. (1964). *Psychodiagnostics* (6th ed.). Bern: Hans Huber.

Schafer, R. (1954). *Psychoanalytic interpretation in Rorschach testing: Theory and application*. New York: Grune & Stratton.

Zubin, J., Eron, L. D., & Schumer, F. (1965). *Experimental approach to projective techniques*. New York: Wiley.

J. R. BECK

See PERSONALITY ASSESSMENT; PSYCHOLOGICAL MEASUREMENT.

Rosenthal Effect. *See* SELF-FULFILLING PROPHECY.

Sacraments in Pastoral Care. A sacrament refers to a ceremony in which a common earthly element, like bread, is combined with the word of God to convey a divine blessing. Thus a sacrament is often referred to as an earthly sign with a heavenly meaning. The sacraments of the church rest on, but are to be distinguished from, something that is sacramental. Any historical event or natural object can have sacramental meaning in the sense that it becomes the temporary vehicle for the mediation of God's presence and promise. Observations of a sunset or participation in an intimate relationship can have sacramental significance for a particular person, but they are not accorded the status of sacraments by the Christian church.

Protestantism believes that there are two sacraments that have been instituted by Jesus Christ: baptism and the Lord's Supper. Roman Catholicism adds five more to the list, confirmation, penance, marriage, ordination, and extreme unction, even though they lack at least one of the three characteristics of a sacrament: an earthly element, a divine command, and the gift of grace. Sometimes the five are called "sacraments of the church" to distinguish them from the two that were instituted by Christ.

Sacraments have been a primary resource in the pastoral ministry of the church from its very early days and continue so until now. As concrete ritual manifestations of God's grace, they have fulfilled an essential role in the upbuilding and nurturing of believers in both an individual and communal sense. Each sacrament makes its own distinctive contribution to pastoral care.

Baptism is an initiation rite into God's kingdom. It represents God's acceptance of the person not just as a child of nature but as a child of God. Pastorally, it means that the individual who believes is accorded all the blessings of God, including the forgiveness of sins and unconditional acceptance by God in grace. Baptism can be especially comforting at the time of death, as St. Paul indicates. He maintains that those who are baptized into Christ are also baptized into his death and that just as Christ was raised from the dead by God, so too we will be raised. "If we have been united with (Christ) in a death like his, we shall certainly be united with him in a resurrection like his" (Rom. 6:5). In this sense, baptism provides pastoral assurance, not because it is a magical act that saves *ex opere operato* but because it is a concrete and definite instance when God acts to make us his own. This assurance can be very comforting, especially in situations where prolonged suffering has sorely tested and seemingly destroyed the faith of the deceased. We mourn with the assurance that God's grace, and not our loved one's faith, determines his or her status before God.

The Lord's Supper is a foretaste of the feast to come. It is a present assurance of God's grace and a concrete experience of the fellowship of believers, but it is also an anticipation of the consummation of God's reign over evil and death. The pastoral significance of the Eucharist is found in the promise of God that life will triumph over death, that forgiveness will cancel out condemnation, that fellowship will wipe away all loneliness. The pastoral power of the Eucharist is seen, for example, in the comatose patient who, upon receiving the bread and the wine, regains consciousness and manifests a genuine sense of peace.

The sacraments have been used in pastoral care more than in pastoral counseling. The rites of the confessional and of penance, however, are ideally suited to address a person with a tormented conscience. Taking the form of private confession, it provides for the personal acknowledgment of particular sins and the immediate assurance of God's absolution. For this reason Martin Luther, for example, wished to retain the confessional in the Reformation churches. In actual practice, though, the pastoral power of confession can be compromised. In the Roman Catholic church private confession can become perfunctory; in the Protestant church is it largely neglected and devalued.

Sacraments are vital to pastoral care. They are dramatic enactments of the gospel of grace. They are concrete vehicles of God's grace and as such they are invaluable resources in the church's ministry of helping and healing. Most churches tend to preserve the "sanctity" of the sacraments so assiduously that they conserve them exclusively for members or confessing Christians. This overlooks the remarkably valuable communication effectiveness of the sacramental drama as a proclamation of God's radical, unconditional, and universal grace to humankind. Therefore, the sacraments should likely be employed as dynamic instruments of evangelism ministries to those who are not yet part of the believing community but can be inspired by the sacramental drama to inquire after the faith.

Additional Readings

Cook, B. (1976). *Ministry to word and sacraments, history and theology.* Philadelphia: Fortress.

Davies, J. G. (Ed.). (1986). *The new Westminster dictionary of liturgy and worship.* Philadelphia: Westminster.

Haan, F. (1973). *The worship of the early church.* Philadelphia: Fortress.

Hoon, P. W. (1971). *The integrity of worship, ecumenical and pastoral studies in liturgical theology.* Nashville: Abingdon.

Saliers, D. E. (1984). *Worship and spirituality.* Philadelphia: Westminster.

Stafford, T. A. (1942). *Christian symbolism in the evangelical churches.* New York: Abingdon.

Thompson, B. (1965). *Liturgies of the western church.* New York: World Meridian Books.

Webber, R. E. (1986). *Celebrating our faith.* San Francisco: Harper.

White, J. F. (1971). *New forms of worship.* Nashville: Abingdon.

L. ADEN

See PASTORAL COUNSELING.

Sadism. *See* SEXUAL SADISM.

Sampling Techniques. *See* PSYCHOLOGY, METHODS OF.

Sanctification. Sanctification refers to the act or process by which humans become holy. The term is derived from the Latin *sanctus* (holy) and *facere* (to make) and is used to translate biblical terms related to holiness (Walters, 1962). Its most primitive meaning is to be set apart for or consecrated to God's service (Berkhof, 1939). This meaning is not absent from the New Testament (1 Cor. 1:2; Heb. 13:12), but there is a shift in emphasis to the ethical (Muller, 1988); that is, sanctification is primarily seen there as a function of holy human activity.

The Scriptures teach that God alone is essentially holy (Isa. 6; 43:3; 1 Peter 1:16) and the source of all human holiness. However, humans are by nature unholy (Rom. 3:10–18). Through his death and resurrection, Christ created a way by which God would sanctify people through union with God's Son (1 Cor. 1:30; Heb. 13:12; Rom. 6:1–11). This making holy occurs in two stages. The first stage, definitive sanctification (Murray, 1977), occurs when God regenerates believers and sets them apart spiritu-

ally through an inner renewal of heart, "so that the believer is no longer ruled or dominated by sin and no longer loves to sin" (Grudem, 1994, p. 747; cf. Rom. 6:6; 1 Cor. 6:11; Col. 2:11–12; 1 Peter 1:2; Heb. 8:10–11; 10:10, 14). This renewal initiates the process of spiritual and ethical growth known as progressive sanctification: the ongoing, gradual increase in holiness of heart and life. The final stage occurs at death, when the believer is glorified (Rom. 8:30; Murray, 1977), a state that could be termed final sanctification.

All sanctification should be seen as fundamentally God's work through the Holy Spirit (Hodge, 1872/1995; Packer, 1992; cf. Phil. 2:13; 1 Peter 1:2; 2 Thess. 2:13). However, progressive sanctification requires human participation grounded in God's grace and power (Phil. 2:12; Rom. 8:13; Heb. 12:14). All of salvation is through faith (Eph. 2:8; Heb. 10:38); so also sanctification. Spiritual growth cannot be self-generated; it occurs only through faithful abiding in the divine source of that growth (John 15:4–5). God's Spirit gives life; his law, apart from the Spirit, brings death (2 Cor. 3:6; Rom. 7:10; Gal. 3:2–14). Nevertheless, the standard for human sanctification remains God's law as revealed through Scriptures (Ps. 19:7–10; 2 Tim. 3:16; Packer, 1992), a standard that includes behavior (1 Cor. 6:9–11) as well as motives and desires (Matt. 5:28). The end of sanctification is character conformity to God (1 Peter 1:16), best summarized as love (Matt. 5:43–48; 22:37–38); a theme especially emphasized by theologians like Augustine, Aquinas, and Bernard (Muller, 1988).

The substance of sanctification has been commonly understood as having positive and negative dimensions (Hodge, 1872/1995). Positive sanctification is what Paul called "put[ting] on the new self" (Eph. 4:24, NIV) and involves developing new thoughts, desires, motives, and behaviors that flow from the Spirit's nature, the virtues or fruit of the Spirit (Gal. 5:22–23). Negative sanctification is what Paul called "put[ting] off the old self" and its practices (Eph. 4:22, NIV), or mortification (Rom. 8:13; Col. 3:5). This involves resisting the thoughts, impulses, desires, and behavior tendencies of the flesh (Gal. 5:16) and experientially reckoning them dead (i.e., powerless), as they are as a result of Christ's death and resurrection (Rom. 6:1–11).

Sanctification then is not mere external behavior; not a list of some traditional do's and don'ts of the Christian life; and not prayer and Bible study or evangelism per se. Such a focus flows from a legalistic orientation that inevitably results in anxiety or pride. Nevertheless, the so-called means of grace (worship, witnessing, fasting, Christian fellowship, self-discipline, prayer, Bible reading, and meditation) are necessary components of sanctification, testified to by Scripture and the church as activities that mediate grace as they are used by faith in dependence upon God's mercy (Packer, 1992; Grudem, 1994).

Over the centuries numerous schools have arisen within Christianity that view sanctification with differing emphases. At least six major approaches exist in our day: Lutheran, Reformed, Pentecostal, Wesleyan/Keswick, contemplative, and dispensational (Alexander, 1988; Dieter, Hoekema, Horton, McQuilkin, & Walvoord, 1987). One aspect of sanctification being debated in the present concerns its necessity. The Roman Catholic church has taught that justification and sanctification should be viewed as different aspects of the one work of salvation in which God helps the believer to become righteous. This led to the tendency to view one's imperfect life as the ground of one's eternal destiny. The Reformers, however, recognized the scriptural distinction between God's work for us (justification: a perfect, completed work of God that is the ground of one's salvation) and God's work in us (sanctification: an ongoing, imperfect activity of believers in dependence upon God) (Toon, 1983). At the other extreme has been a common error of churches influenced by the Reformation involving a radical disjunction between sanctification and justification, suggesting that one can receive eternal forgiveness by faith in Christ as Savior without any subsequent evidence of spiritual life working itself out in the individual's life. However, 1 John and James were written to make clear that God's salvation decisively affects the true believer's life. "Without [personal] holiness no one will see the Lord" (Heb. 12:14b, NIV, see context; cf. Matt. 7:17–20). While it provides no ultimate ground for our salvation (only Christ's work can do that), personal sanctification seems to be an inevitable component of true faith.

Some Implications for Christian Psychology and Counseling. Theologians have hitherto done the most important work on sanctification. Yet its relevance to psychology is obvious. Progressive sanctification is essentially a developmental/therapeutic concept. Therefore, a Christian approach to the study of the spiritual development or maturation of Christians requires a biblical understanding of sanctification. However, the Christian church would likely benefit in turn from a more in-depth, psychologically sophisticated study of the process of progressive sanctification than that provided by theology alone. Beyond the general recognition that sin must be mortified and holiness increased, specifics are needed concerning the influence of sanctification on such things as aggression, depression, object relations, doubt, psychotic experiences, mental retardation, sexual abuse experiences, sexual orientation, and so on, as well as their influence on progressive sanctification. More generally research is needed that addresses how biological, cognitive, personality, and psychosocial development interact with sanctification processes. Most of the work in the area of spiritual development thus far has been done from a liberal Christian standpoint (e.g., Fowler, 1981; Gillespie, 1991). Comparatively less work has been done that explicitly assumes an evangelical theological framework that recognizes the exclusivity of Christianity, the pre-

eminent authority of the Bible, and the role of the Holy Spirit in sanctification.

A general goal of therapy is to enhance the client's personal well-being. However, the substance of this goal will differ according to one's therapeutic system (Roberts, 1993). For the Christian, one's personal well-being is tied to God's glory (Rom. 5:2; 1 Cor. 10:31), a goal best realized in this life through personal sanctification (Murray, 1977). Moreover, Christian mental health would seem to be synonymous with the fruit of the Spirit. A life characterized by love, joy, peace, patience, and so on, is what most Christian clients seek. Therefore, counselors and therapists who work with Christians will want to work at enhancing the sanctification process in their clients as they assist them in tackling psychological issues. The means of grace, especially prayer, would seem to be essential to any attempt to further a process entirely dependent upon God's gracious activity; at the same time counselees must be helped to see their own responsibility (in dependence upon God) for maturational progress.

References

Alexander, D. L. (1988). *Christian spirituality: Five views of sanctification*. Downers Grove, IL: InterVarsity Press.

Berkhof, L. (1939). *Systematic theology*. Grand Rapids, MI: Eerdmans.

Dieter, M. D., Hoekema, A. A., Horton, S. M., McQuilkin, J. R., & Walvoord, J. F. (1987). *Five views on sanctification*. Grand Rapids, MI: Zondervan.

Fowler, J. W. (1981). *Stages of faith*. New York: Harper & Row.

Gillespie, V. B. (1991). *The dynamics of religious conversion: Identity and transformation*. Birmingham, AL: Religious Education Press.

Grudem, W. (1994). *Systematic theology: An introduction to biblical doctrine*. Grand Rapids, MI: Zondervan.

Hodge, C. (1995). *Systematic theology*. Grand Rapids, MI: Eerdmans. (Original work published 1872)

Muller, R. A. (1988). Sanctification. In *International standard Bible encyclopedia* (Vol. 4, pp. 321–331). Grand Rapids, MI: Eerdmans.

Murray, J. (1977). *Collected writings of John Murray* (Vol. 2). Edinburgh: Banner of Truth.

Packer, J. I. (1992). *Recovering holiness*. Ann Arbor, MI: Servant.

Roberts, R. (1993). *Taking the word to heart*. Grand Rapids, MI: Eerdmans.

Toon, P. (1983). *Justification and sanctification*. Westchester, IL: Crossway.

Walters, G. (1962). Sanctification. In *New Bible dictionary*. Grand Rapids, MI: Eerdmans.

E. L. JOHNSON

See CHRISTIAN GROWTH; RELIGIOUS DEVELOPMENT; HEALTHY PERSONALITY.

Sanity and Insanity. Sanity and insanity are legal terms for an individual's mental state. Originally, sane meant mentally normal, and insane meant abnormal. Two hundred years ago, abnormal individuals were committed to so-called insane asylums. Over the last one hundred years, however, the mental health profession has abandoned the sanity/insanity distinction, preferring the terms mentally ill, or disordered, to refer to disturbed individuals. Mental health terminology generally allows for levels of dysfunction, whereas sanity and insanity are considered discrete either/or categories. On the basis of expert testimony from psychiatrists and psychologists, courts must judge an individual sane or insane. (Note that it is the court and not the psychiatrist or psychologist that makes the decision.)

Western law has absolved an individual from responsibility if the individual did not know what he or she was doing. In 1724, for example, an English court argued that a man was not responsible for his behavior if "he doth not know what he is doing, no more than . . . a wild beast." In 1843 a precedent was established that became the basis for modern Western standards of legal responsibility. In that year, Scotsman Daniel M'Naghten attempted to assassinate the British prime minister, believing that he, M'Naghten, was being persecuted by the prime minister's Conservative Party. In attempting to kill the prime minister, M'Naghten mistakenly killed the prime minister's secretary.

M'Naghten was charged with murder, but his senseless ramblings convinced the court that he had not understood what he was doing. The court decided he was not guilty "on the grounds of insanity," and it sent him to an asylum where he remained until his death. The case established the M'Naghten rule. This rule states that a defendant may be found not guilty by reason of insanity if he was so severely disturbed at the time of his act that he did not know what he was doing, or if he did know what he was doing, he did not know that it was wrong.

The M'Naghten rule has been widely adopted as the basis for similar rulings in the laws of Canada, the United States, and other Western countries. Some jurisdictions have expanded it to absolve individuals acting on an "irresistible impulse." They reason that some mentally disturbed individuals may answer correctly when asked if an act is morally right or wrong, but these individuals may have been unable to control their behavior in the situation in question. Presumably a person's understanding may be adequate, but his or her will deficient, at least temporarily.

The insanity defense has led to not guilty verdicts in some highly publicized trials. For example, in an interesting parallel to the original M'Naghten case, John W. Hinckley, Jr., in attempting to assassinate President Ronald Reagan, shot three other men. He was found not guilty of attempted murder by reason of insanity.

The public has not always accepted such verdicts complacently. In fact, the Hinckley case triggered a public outcry. Many people felt that the law had gone too far, that criminals were using a legal loophole to escape punishment for serious crimes. Congress reacted by passing the Insanity Reform Act of 1984, making it more difficult to use the insanity defense successfully. For example, the burden of proof was shifted from the prosecution to the defense. Where previously the prosecution had to show beyond reasonable doubt that the defendant was sane, now the defense must prove, with "clear and convincing evidence," that the defendant was not sane. Other jurisdictions followed suit or went even further. The Canadian province of Ontario commissioned a complete review of the insanity plea, and the American states of Montana, Idaho, and Utah abolished the plea. Some states replaced the "not guilty by reason of insanity" plea with a new plea, "guilty but mentally ill." Others added the new plea but retained the old one as well.

It should be noted that individuals judged not guilty by reason of insanity are not set free. They are usually confined to mental hospitals, where they often remain for longer terms than they would have received had they been found guilty. The "guilty but mentally ill" verdict allows for a conviction where it is justified and yet ensures that the individual will receive treatment for the disorder. Following treatment the person is returned to prison to complete any portion of the original sentence that has not been served.

It should also be noted that, contrary to popular opinion, the insanity defense is not often used, and when it is attempted, it is not usually successful. The American Psychiatric Association (1996) reports that the insanity defense is used in fewer than 1% of cases, it is successful only one time in four, and in most of these the prosecution and defense agreed on the appropriateness of the plea before trial. Moreover, most insanity pleas are entered for crimes other than murder. In other words, the insanity defense does not appear to be a huge loophole through which large numbers of murderers escape by faking mental disorders.

These figures do not include those individuals judged not competent to stand trial. Competency is a separate issue from sanity and the insanity defense. Mentally disturbed individuals are sometimes judged not competent to stand trial because they lack sufficient ability to consult with their attorney with a reasonable degree of understanding or because they do not have a rational, factual, understanding of the legal proceedings. Competency questions can also arise at other points in the justice system, such as over an individual's competency to plead guilty or confess to a crime.

The insanity defense and its derivatives are motivated by humanitarian concern for persons with mental disorders. However, this category of defense raises complicated issues of responsibility and rehabilitation. For example, if an individual is judged insane and committed to a mental institution, how long should he or she remain there? How do we know when the "not guilty by reason of insanity" person or the "guilty but mentally ill" individual has been adequately rehabilitated to return to society or to prison to complete a sentence?

Reference

American Psychiatric Association. (1996). The insanity defense. *APA Online: Public Information.* Available: www.psych.org.

R. PHILIPCHALK

See FORENSIC PSYCHIATRY.

Satanic Ritual Abuse. Satanic ritual abuse (SRA) has been defined as a brutal form of abuse of children, adolescents, and adults, consisting of physical, sexual, and psychological abuse and involving the use of rituals. Ritual does not necessarily mean satanic. However, most survivors state that they were ritually abused as part of satanic worship for the purpose of indoctrinating them into satanic beliefs and practices. Ritual abuse rarely consists of a single episode. It usually involves repeated abuse over an extended time (Los Angeles County Commission for Women, 1991). Many professionals have pushed for the replacement of the spiritually charged word *satanic* to the less religiously emotive word *sadistic*, which is commonly used today and has been for several years by many professionals. The argument has been that the type of abuse reported by SRA victims is experienced by individuals outside satanic ritual. Thus SRA has become a more generalized category.

The most common reports of abuse given by those detailing SRA experiences are being locked in cages, threatened with death, buried in coffins, held under water, threatened with weapons, drugged and bled, tied upside down and burned, abused by people wearing robes and costumes, forced to participate in the staging of mock marriages, defecated and urinated upon, forced to observe the killing of animals, forced to witness torture and homicide, forced to pour or drink blood, taken to churches and cemeteries, and forced to watch and participate in pornographic photography (Young, Sachs, Braun, & Watkins, 1991). Although these reports experienced a noticeable resurgence among therapists and the media during the 1980s and early 1990s (Snow & Sorenson, 1990), they have been described by professionals, victims, and perpetrators both verbally and in writing since the 1400s (Bataille, 1991).

There are essentials of treatment to be considered regarding SRA. In many ways SRA may be one of the most complex and evolving treatment issues in psychological counseling in many years. Certainly there has not been a more hotly contested and debated issue in quite some time (Horn, 1993). Therefore, one must both seriously and thoroughly become educated with the issues surrounding SRA reports and treatment.

Because those who report SRA also report sexual, physical, mental, and spiritual abuse, one must have familiarity with treating those issues. It is not uncommon for SRA reports to be disclosed by an individual who has been in therapy for some time for symptoms that may have been manifestations of more deeply rooted problems. Common symptoms experienced by those who report SRA trauma are genital pain and numbness, eating disorders, self-mutilation, choking and vomiting, urinary disturbance, substance abuse, anxiety attacks, depression, amnesia of early childhood experiences, obsessive self-reproaches, and possible sexual inhibitions (Braun, 1992). A host of other behavioral manifestations result from these abuses; however, individuals displaying or reporting these symptoms do not necessarily have SRA backgrounds. When treating those reporting SRA it may be advisable and necessary to refer out for particular disorders associated with the SRA history. A treatment team may need to be established, a primary support person outside of the therapist enlisted, and a psychiatrist educated in SRA issues obtained for appropriate medication management.

The therapeutic relationship is both critical and foundational. It takes most SRA survivors quite some time before they are able to develop trust with others, as their ability to trust has been shattered through relationships that were both primary and formative. Because symptomatology is often out of the victim's control and suffered as a result of involuntary trauma, a strong therapeutic alliance must be maintained and undertaken throughout the treatment (Kluft, 1993). The boundaries of those reporting SRA have been greatly violated and therefore healthy, firm, and consistent boundaries must be established and maintained. The developmental process has taken place within an environment of inconsistency and double-bind situations. Consistency is essential from those individuals working with the victim. It is important to follow through and not to promise what one cannot reasonably fulfill.

One must take into consideration the many allegations of false memory that have been leveled against those treating SRA and those who are reporting it (Goldstein, 1992). Therefore precautions must be taken in the overall treatment frame. Uses of sodium amytal and other drugs to induce memories have been successfully litigated and should be avoided (Staff, 1994). Hypnosis should be considered a marginal approach, if it is used at all, in protracting memory.

Those reporting SRA often also have a *DSM-IV* diagnosis of dissociative identity disorder (DID) (Braun & Sachs, 1988). Many therapists might say this is more the case than not. However, there are yet no validated studies that provide hard data regarding these specific statistics. There is some probability that SRA victims will have dissociative features. The majority of abuse suffered during SRA trauma exceeds an individual's capacity to tolerate it, and it often is perpetrated on individuals at very young ages. Both factors are conducive to the development of a dissociative disorder as a psychological defense against the abuse (Kluft, 1984). If an individual who reports SRA shows signs of a dissociative disorder or of DID in particular, it is important to either be able to treat the dissociation as part of the overall treatment frame or to refer to someone specializing in dissociative treatment.

Inherent in those who have undergone SRA trauma is that the beliefs of Christianity and primarily of a biblical view of God have been greatly distorted, making it very difficult for clients to integrate Christian spirituality into therapy, although many greatly desire it. Facilitating a reconstruction of biblical Christianity at the victim's request can provide a much needed element in treatment. Spirituality within treatment is documented to have a positive effect toward healing (Matthews, Larson, & Berry, 1993). This can help lead the victim to a greater degree of inner healing and empowerment, moving the individual out of a victim's role in the past to that of a person of freedom. Primary spiritual issues with which SRA victims struggle are how they view Father God, the origin of good and evil, forgiveness, justice, belief that Satan is more powerful than God, and why God did not intervene to rescue them from their abuse and abusers (Power, 1992).

References

Bataille, G. (1991). *The trial of Gilles de Rais: Documents presented by George Bataille.* (Original work published in French in 1965)

Braun, B. G. (1992). *Multiplicity: Form, function & phenomena.* Chicago: Associated Mental Health Services.

Braun, B. G., & Sachs, R. G. (1988, October). *Recognition of possible cult involvement in MPD patients.* Paper presented at the Sixth International Conference on Multiple Personality & Dissociative States, Chicago, IL.

Bobgan, M., & Bobgan, D. (1981). *Hypnosis and the Christian.* Minneapolis: Bethany House.

Goldstein, E. (1992). *Confabulations: Creating false memories, destroying families.* Boca Raton, FL: SIRS Books.

Horn, M. (1993, November). Memories lost and found. *Science and Society,* 52–63.

Kluft, R. P. (1984). Treatment of multiple personality disorder: A study of 33 cases. *Psychiatric Clinics of North America, 7,* 9–29.

Kluft, R. P. (1993). Multiple personality disorder. In D. Spiegel (Ed.), *Dissociative disorders: A clinical review.* Lutherville, MD: Sidran Press.

Los Angeles County Commission for Women. (1991). *Ritual abuse: Definitions, glossary, the use of mind control* (Reports of the Ritual Abuse Task Force). Los Angeles: Author.

Matthews, D. A., Larson, D. B., & Barry, C. P. (1993, July). *The faith factor: An annotated bibliography of clinical research on spiritual subjects.* Bethesda, MD: National Institute for Healthcare Research.

Power, E. (1992). *Managing our selves: God in our midst.* Brentwood, TN: Power & Associates.

Snow, B., & Sorenson, T. (1990). Ritualistic child abuse in a neighborhood setting. *Journal of Interpersonal Violence, 5,* 474–487.

Staff. (1994, June). Ramona ruling narrows practice parameters even more. *The Psychotherapy Letter, 6* (6), 1–2.

Young, W. C., Sachs, R. G., Braun, B. G., & Watkins, R. T. (1991). Patients reporting ritual abuse in childhood: A clinical syndrome; Report of 37 cases. *Child Abuse and Neglect: The International Journal, 15,* 181–189.

B. A. Hanson

See Abuse and Neglect; Trauma.

Scapegoating. *Biblical Usage.* The Old Testament Book of Leviticus refers to Yom Kipper, the Jewish holiday or fast day on which no work is done and people atone for the sins of the past year. The goals of Yom Kipper are to cleanse the sanctuary of defiling pollution produced by the priests and people's wrongdoings and to cleanse the people from their sins. The sacrifices for the priest were a bull for purgation sacrifice and a ram for burnt offering. For the people two goats were used for a purgation sacrifice and a ram was sacrificed for a burnt offering. One goat was sacrificed and a second goat was allowed to escape. The escaping goat was selected by lot. Then the high priest placed both hands upon the head of the goat and confessed over it the iniquities, transgressions, and sins of the people. Through this act the wrongs of the people were symbolically transferred to the scapegoat and with the sin-laden goat were then driven into the wilderness.

Theoretical and Therapy Usage. When symptomatic behaviors are projected onto a family member family therapists called this projection scapegoating. Scapegoating as a clinical concept has been conceptualized differently by different fields of psychology. Classical psychoanalytic Freudian therapists identify sin or pathology within the individual. Neo-Freudian therapists and theorists shifted their emphasis from internal instincts within the individual to core problems that occur during childhood development. These therapists suggested that a child's relationships with parental objects, ability to form attachments, and ego development during the early years of life are the primary causes of pathology. Therefore, they suggested, as a result of problems in development people internally project anxiety-provoking aspects of themselves onto others. Sigmund Freud called the projection of anxiety-provoking behaviors and feelings onto others transference. Neo-Freudians called this projective identification.

For early family therapists the development of behavior disorders occurs in the interactions between people. They view symptoms as having meaning, functioning as meaning, having consequences, and controlling other family members. Vogel and Bell (1960) believe that emotionally disturbed children are singled out as objects of parental projection on the basis of traits that set them apart from other members of the family. They suggest the scapegoat is the member of the family who is the object of displaced conflict or criticism.

Many family therapists deny that symptoms themselves have either meaning or function. Behavioral and strategic therapists do not assume that symptoms are necessary to maintain family stability. Behavioral family therapists treat problems as the uncomplicated result of faulty efforts to change behavior and lack of skills. Strategic family therapists, for instance, believe it is best to keep the focus on the problem person and to use the focus as leverage to change the family situation. According to Haley (1988), therapy is more effective if the focus is kept on the symptom bearer and on the problem.

Systemic family therapists, however, suggest that the symptoms may serve a purpose but deny that it is necessary to consider that purpose when planning therapy. Instead of trying to figure out what function may be served by the symptom, they concentrate on understanding how the pieces of the system fit together in a coherent fashion. They take the position that if they can free the family from its symptoms, the family will take care of itself.

Some schools of family therapy continue to believe that symptoms signal deeper problems and that they function to maintain family stability. In families that cannot tolerate open conflict, a symptomatic member serves as a diversion. Thus a couple's inability to form an intimate bond may be ascribed to the fact that one or both partners are still being used to mediate the relationship between others. In this way symptomatic behavior is often projected onto a scapegoated family member who absorbs and detours the anxiety and stress and allows the family to avoid core issues. For example, if the parents' loyalty is to their families of origin and they need to avoid absolute rage felt toward their parents, one of their children must be sacrificed and must continue to sacrifice himself or herself so that such anger can find a place.

The Therapeutic Process. Most schools of family therapy suggest that the counselor address the issue of scapegoating by clearly defining the family's core problems, focusing treatment on the problem and on the symptom bearer, and competently working systemically with the family to resolve their core conflicts. Thus during the process of counseling the scapegoat or symptom bearer is promoted upward; the righteous family members or spouse is demoted. The counselor thus joins the family and directs them to a new light and a new positive and productive reality without the symptom(s).

Reference

Vogel, E. F., & Bell, N. W. (1960). The emotionally disturbed as the family scapegoat. In N. W. Bell & E. F. Vogel (Eds.), *The family.* Glencoe, IL: Free Press

M. L. McCreary

Schizoaffective Disorder. With the introduction of lithium in the 1970s, bipolar disorder became more sharply defined as distinct from schizophrenia. But between these two disorders patients present with both affective and schizophrenic symptoms, having an acute onset, functioning well premorbidly, and tending to remit completely. Unlike affective disease, the psychotic symptoms persist either before or after the peak of mania or depression, but otherwise the course is more like affective disorders. In a discussion on some of these patients, Kasanin (1933) added the observation of marked emotional turmoil and perceptive distortions, using the term *acute schizoaffective psychosis.* Other researchers later added depressive heredity, particularly intense emotional disorganization, and the presence of precipitating factors. These all predict accurately the complete remission of an acute episode.

Diagnosis. Under the pressure of the development of more specific treatments for both schizophrenia and the affective disorders, research focused on whether schizoaffective disorder is a variant of schizophrenia, an affective process, or a condition distinct from both. Their conclusions seem to affirm that schizoaffective illness is a heterogeneous mixture of disorders composed of mania, depression, and schizophrenia (Fowler, 1978).

Levitt and Tsuang (1988), after an excellent review, advocate subdividing schizoaffective disorder bimodally by symptom presentation, distinguishing those presenting with full mania (closer to affective disease) and those with full depression (closer to schizophrenia) with a bipolar group between. This construct has been helpful in treatment but leaves many questions open as nosology. It is hard to predict how this discussion will end, but it seems wisest to consider schizoaffective disorders as a heterogeneous group lying between the affective disorders and psychoses.

Treatment. Without uniformity in definition, treatment studies have not been able to give clear guidance. In individuals displaying mania, treating the manic symptoms with lithium (in conjunction with a major tranquilizer for acute mania) is the best approach. Both drugs have significant toxicity and some patients are more susceptible to lithium neurotoxicity, but fortunately each medication can moderate the side effects of the other.

Schizodepressed patients respond more often to major tranquilizers than antidepressants, though combinations of the two, even augmented by lithium, are occasionally effective. For this group also, electroconvulsive therapy (ECT) can have dramatic results. In larger studies ECT also has been shown to decrease mortality and suicide, both considerable risks in untreated patients.

Optimal treatment requires experience, skill, and patience. The newer neuroleptics and antidepressants show some promise, but as yet the management remains essentially empirical.

References

Fowler, R. C. (1978). Remitting schizophrenia as a variant of affective disorder. *Schizophrenic Bulletin, 4,* 68–77.
Kasanin, J. (1933). The acute schizoaffective psychoses. *American Journal of Psychiatry, 90,* 97–126.

Levitt, J. J., & Tsuang, M. T. (1988). The heterogenicity of schizoaffective disorder: Implications for treatment. *American Journal of Psychiatry, 145,* 926–936.

C. M. BERRY

See SCHIZOPHRENIA; MOOD DISORDERS.

Schizoid Personality Disorder. Schizoid personalities pathologically withdraw from social and intimate relationships. They seem indifferent to human connectedness, have no need for intimacy, rarely date or marry, and generally limit their confidants to first-degree relatives. They are often humorless, affectively dull, and react to emotional situations with detachment. Therapists, accustomed to working with empathy and anxiety, often think of such aloofness as autistic and quasi-psychotic.

A well-known example of the schizoid is Laura in Tennessee Williams's *The Glass Menagerie.* Like Laura, the schizoid is a loner whose inner world can be vivid and inhabited by odd, imaginary friends. These fantasies can appear psychotic and materialize only symbolically in real life.

With *DSM-III* the schizoid personality was distinguished from the schizotypal personality disorder. The latter more clearly mimics psychotic thought and behavior, and the condition appears genetically related to schizophrenia as well.

History. The schizoid has long interested psychoanalysts, since this pathology so obviously suggests disturbed early object relations. Analysts focus on the social withdrawal, the autistic thinking, the affective dullness, and the ambivalence toward aggression.

Wolff and Chick (1980) reviewed the history of the concept of the schizoid personality as it is used in Europe, especially in children's clinics. They describe a disorder, mostly of boys, that shares many characteristics with autistic children (*see* Autistic Disorder), is somewhat familial but seldom becomes schizophrenia. These are solitary, empathically impaired, emotionally detached, yet extremely sensitive children who communicate in odd styles. The pattern begins in early childhood and remains remarkably fixed through life. They often adjust to adulthood by becoming expert in a single endeavor.

Course. Most schizoids change little over time and ultimately find a niche in life where they can function. They say they are content with their isolation, but their obvious unhappiness and high suicide rate indicate otherwise.

More recently a group of patients with central borderline structural defects has been included in the schizoid category. These patients also are isolated and withdrawn, were shy as children, and become anxious when relationships deepen. Many have noted that these symptoms are clinically related to paranoid personality disorder.

Etiology. Research suggests that the usual schizoid has been reared in a cold, emotionally bleak home. Such children learn to expect aloofness in life and to be anxious of closeness. Since introversion has been shown to be genetic and since other members of the schizoid's family tend to be odd or themselves schizoid, the condition could also be genetic (Heston, 1970).

There is still much to learn because this disorder has only recently been sharply distinguished from the schizotypal on one side and the borderline on the other. It is hoped that as *DSM-IV* has improved diagnosis, the comprehensive studies needed to answer many such questions will follow.

Treatment. Therapy of the schizoid is difficult but not hopeless. Those individuals who demonstrate at least some emotional capacity respond about as favorably to psychotherapy as the paranoid personality, whatever approach is chosen. It would seem logical to assume that anxiety is aroused at the moment closeness becomes alarming, even if it is not apparent, and consider the cognitions associated with this arousal as defensive. Challenging the thinking distortions of each arousal gently with the techniques of cognitive therapy works better than harsh confrontation.

Establishing a warm therapeutic relationship with the schizoid is difficult but not impossible. Either all closeness feels dangerous, as with other borderlines, or they defend against warmth by denying any interest in an inner life that is not easily accessible. With patience, though, a relationship can often be established that is rewarding to the patient, although it might not seem so to the therapist. Such a healing experience can teach primary lessons in empathy and encourage schizoids to abandon their shyness and risk other friendships.

Groups often face a prolonged initial silence from the schizoid. Without patient understanding the group becomes quickly frustrated and aggressively confronts this silence. Given time and patience, involvement can take place and the group becomes a new and meaningful experience.

Course and Prognosis. As with all personality disorders the schizoid faces a lifelong struggle, and few improve. The more successful pour prodigious energy into a single pursuit to gain independence and reasonable satisfaction.

Having said all this, though, there is hope. The organic feel of these patients suggests that one day a medication will be identified that will significantly help them.

References

Heston, L. L. (1970). The genetics of schizophrenia and schizoid disease. *Science, 167,* 249–256.

Wolff, S., & Chick, J. (1980). Schizoid personality in childhood: A controlled study. *Psychological Medicine, 10,* 85–100.

C. M. BERRY

See PERSONALITY DISORDERS.

Schizophrenia. A clinical syndrome marked by severe, widespread disturbance in feeling, mood, and thought. The diagnosis is not made unless it lasts longer than six months and there is significant intrapsychic pain and a breakdown in effective work and relationships.

The most intense form of schizophrenia occurs during a psychotic break, or a complete disorganization of the personality. These occur suddenly, typically in young adults, often in response to what seems a trivial provocation. Delusions and hallucinations are usually present. Since this disorganization violates an innate sense of order and coherence, such an event is terrifying, creating chaos in both the sufferer and those around. Still, experienced observers sense elements that are fundamentally shared by all of us; in the words of Harry Stack Sullivan, it is a "human disease."

Even though schizophrenia is a common problem for mental health professionals and absorbs nearly one-half of public expenditures on mental health, a precise definition remains elusive and no consensus has emerged as to its cause. Though the symptoms can be described accurately, there is yet no clear idea of what has gone wrong within the mind of the patient. Several patterns are described that may represent variations of one disease or different diseases. But for the present, considering schizophrenia a single entity seems useful.

Because of the ominous, destructive nature of the condition, making the diagnosis stigmatizes the patient. Even so, the disease is so common, the suffering so widespread, that some term is needed to collect our experience and guide research toward better understanding and management.

The Acute Syndrome. When one becomes psychotic there is a drastic change in how the world is perceived. An abrupt perceptual switch changes the affect, thought, and behavior radically. The word *schizophrenia* means split mind, referring not to multiple personality but to a dissociation between thinking and feeling. The affect becomes inappropriate, blunted, or flat. Delusions intrude compellingly into the thinking and disturbing hallucinations into the sensorium. The patient becomes either excited or withdrawn. Behavior becomes violent or rigidly immobile. Though these changes seem irrational, from the primary process thinking of the psychotic, they become understandable.

By definition delusions are unquestioned, unprovoked convictions, implanted on the mind with little or no supportive evidence. While they are the defining phenomenon of classical schizophrenia, they are also its most puzzling symptom. Intense, usually carrying more assurance than even the strongest convictions of normal minds, they are impervious to either argument or evidence. They are characteristically symbolic, theological, transcendent notions, even in those who previously were not religious. Delusions characteristically are paranoid, of persecutions and harassments that carry the grandiose and fearful conviction that the patient is the focus of a widespread network of supernatural, even demonic hostility. This cosmic self-centeredness is a characteristic of schizophrenia called autism.

Delusions concerning changes in the nature of the body or its functions also occur. A patient might complain that bodily tissue is melting or turning to stone, or thoughts are being broadcast at large, or "others are putting thoughts into my head." A mechanic complained that "my brain is like a motor transmission that's broken down. The thoughts won't go through." Such delusions almost always indicate schizophrenia.

Hallucinations are distinct auditory sounds, usually human voices heard as though spoken from outside, often providing a running commentary on behavior or thoughts. They are often accusatory and usually disturbing, though they can be benign and may even keep an elderly recluse company on occasion. These delusions and hallucinations doggedly persist, but if the patient is asked, "Do you hear voices that are not there?" the patient will answer, "Yes," when in other situations the absurdity of such an exchange might be apparent.

Thinking itself is often illogical, as in the ambivalence of schizophrenia. Ambivalence technically means holding rationally opposite and mutually exclusive thoughts simultaneously, without explanation.

In loose associations speech is most confusing, since a logical connection is not given between one thought and the next. Speech also sometimes flows more rapidly, as though pressured, and sometimes more slowly and sparsely as though from a poverty of thought. On occasion meaningless, incoherent words gush out in what is called word salad. Since the schizophrenic often is sufficiently fused to think the hearer is party to his or her unuttered thoughts, the connections are unnecessary and such disordered speech is probably more rational than it sounds.

The Chronic Syndrome. After an acute break the schizophrenic is less excited, less wild, but rarely normal. Chronic schizophrenics are awkward and socially inept, as though unaware of the subtle, multileveled clues of ordinary social interchanges. Their shyness and disturbed perspective makes it difficult for them to fit comfortably into a group. This deficit is often concealed by stilted behavior or by stylized role playing within the group. Since the patient rarely understands the problem, life is blighted by repeated failures, and when the grandiose autism fades, self-esteem is devastated.

Occasionally one finds schizophrenics who seem to have few problems, but on closer scrutiny their ideas are so odd that their superstitiousness and paranoia deny them the very social interactions they desire with a primitive, yearning urgency. Many are convinced they can read others' thoughts or feel others' feelings, and most are convinced that others share their inner world. Many observers sense there is some eerie truth to these assumptions: the schizophrenic often seems to be almost clairvoyant.

Gainful employment is often impossible since the strangeness of the schizophrenic breeds fear and lack of trust, and insensitivity keeps them from working easily with others. Those who do find a job function far below their intelligence and skill level.

Pathogenesis. Experienced experts have no consensus on the cause of schizophrenia in a given individual. There are several schools of thought, each offering a rational explanation of the salient features and each with enthusiastic supporters. A mountain of research supports these theories without clearly establishing one or another. A few of these theories are briefly discussed here.

Psychoanalytic Theories. Analysts usually begin with Freud's (1892/1958) fundamental insights into defense neuropsychoses. The stress placed on the ego to mediate between powerful libidinal or aggressive drives and the more repressive demands of the social world produces enough pain to demand relief. Freud believed that the particular symptoms of any mental abnormality can best be understood as a defensive response to such psychic pain. Psychosis, or a complete mental breakdown, is the last maneuver available to the embattled ego.

In response to such stress the patient regresses to an oedipal fixation around an unresolved homosexual attachment to the father. The unbearable disgrace of being homosexual produces a generalized withdrawal of libidinal energy from outside objects. This concentration of libido within the ego is expressed in the autistic grandiosity of paranoia. This is then projected outwardly onto the environment, which retaliates with persecutory delusions.

A great deal of analytic thought has elaborated these fundamental insights since Freud's time. Klein (1949) laid the foundation for our contemporary understanding of object relations theory in her efforts to understand schizophrenia, seeing it as resulting from a failure of the mother to provide the very young infant with security and need satisfaction. The concept of a nurturing, or "good enough," maternal environment has been enlarged by Winnicott (1958) and the complex relationships between primary objects of self and other by Margaret Mahler (1968).

Stress. The social thinking of Adolf Meyer saw the stressors in social life as more destructive than intrapsychic conflicts. The break coming at life's transitions became more rational than to nonanalytic mental health workers.

Bonding and Communication Theories. Other thinkers, among them Sullivan (1953), thought the profoundly disordered interpersonal relationships of these patients and their failure to establish satisfying intimacy even in infancy were more damaging than more nebulous intrapsychic mechanisms proposed by other analysts.

Social thinking, following Sullivan, soon focused on the family unit. Lidz, Fleck, and Cornileson (1965) described parents of schizophrenics as fostering a parasitic relationship with the child. Bonding in such homes is distorted in two characteristic ways, making individuation difficult. In marital skew one partner so dominates the home that healthy relationships are never modeled. In marital schism the parents are so divided that they receive no nurture from each other and seek to satisfy their emotional needs from the child. In either case the child defensively retreats into autism, which in turn blocks emotional growth.

Bateson, Jackson, Haley, and Weakland (1956) identified a characteristic pattern of disturbed communication in the families of schizophrenics that they called the double bind. The term is often applied to the impact of any conflicting commands on the child, but technically it describes a powerful negative command opposed by another at a more abstract level. This bind is then intensified by a third injunction that prevents escape. The frustration of this dilemma leads directly to the thought disorder of the psychosis.

Wynne, Ryckoff, Day, and Hirsch (1958) alerted us to the destructiveness of a family that is excessively controlled by society's unspoken pressure to conform to role patterns and obey complex behavioral injunctions. In such rigidity the delightful diversity encouraged within the unity of a healthy family is replaced by patterns of false fusions called pseudomutuality. The child in such a home grows up not only devoid of warmth and nurture but also without an appreciation for his or her own individuality and soon takes on the seriously disturbed communication that is the only option at home. The growing fear that this complex and fragile system will disintegrate under such a mass of unmet needs implodes in a psychosis.

These formulations have not withstood the test of time, probably because such patterns are often also seen in disordered families without psychosis. Further, it is commonly observed that some children grow up surviving the most disordered families, apparently doing well. Still, these thinkers have added useful terms to the language of schizophrenia and psychology generally.

Biological Theories. Beginning in the early 1950s with the serendipitous discovery of the major tranquilizer Thorazine, a great deal of research has elaborated an understanding of the neurotransmitters of the brain in all mental disorders. Though this research has extended our understanding of the brain's function, it has become a veritable maze of biochemical processes with a thousand new leads as to etiology and more precise treatment. Yet no compelling evidence has pointed toward a precise neurochemical origin of schizophrenia, nor has it yet produced any medications much more effective than Thorazine.

More recently biological markers of various kinds have been identified as being associated with schizophrenia, along with many subtle changes seen by dramatic new imaging techniques of visualizing brain anatomy and function in the living subject. In all of these explorations there are many intriguing hints as to the psychopathology of psychosis.

Several findings, like a rise in incidence in winter births and an increased concordance in twins who share the same placenta, suggest a viral component as well. Perhaps viral disorders, maternal or infantile, could damage brains in a way that might produce a fairly typical disease, as does an occasional head injury, but whatever influence such injury might have seems minor.

Genetic Research. A clear familial incidence of schizophrenia has encouraged many researchers to seek a genetic explanation of the disease. Many twin studies, whether monozygotic or dizygotic twins, whether reared together or reared apart, indicate a strong familial influence. An expected incidence of schizophrenia in the general population of about 1% doubles among aunts and uncles, doubles again among parents, doubles still again among siblings, rises to about 12% among offspring of a patient, and to 40% among the children of two schizophrenic parents. There is 50% concordance among monozygotic twins and about 17% among dizygotic twins.

In recent years there has been a good deal of study of the genes themselves of schizophrenic subjects. Again these studies indicate a complex genetic influence with no single chromosome at fault.

Summarizing what we have learned from genetic investigations, schizophrenia has a major familial component, but it is also either a disorder with multiple causes or several heterogeneous disorders with disparate causes. None of these biological leads is yet convincing as to etiology, although among the experts there remains a conviction that a specific biological defect is involved. An excellent review of the current state of our understanding of schizophrenia, including the neurochemical, biological, and genetic influences, is found in the 1993 *Schizophrenic Bulletin* (Vol. 19, No. 3).

The Natural History. The acute schizophrenic break typically occurs under stress, yet unexpectedly. This crisis is often a loss, especially of someone upon whom the patient has become dependent. In other cases handling the normal demands of life becomes impossible with a mind that explosively changes. The stresses of late adolescence both to relate effectively with the opposite sex and the demands of being thrust into the working world in order to gain independence commonly are instrumental in psychotic breaks.

In retrospect, however, subtle precursors to the break are often identified. The preschizophrenic typically relates pathologically with peers and is painfully dependent. The yearning for social successes and independence from parents produces conflict at home and failure outside, with a profound loss of self-esteem. The grandiosity and excitement of the acute psychosis is ego-restorative to some degree, but then new insult strikes when the patient ends up in jail or a hospital with a degrading diagnosis.

A frequent associated crisis is sexual. The psychotic break causes sexual maturity to regress along the lines of adolescent development. When the patient loses the sharp focus of sexuality around genital, gender-specific objects, sexual desire becomes more diffuse. Also, the soft youthfulness of the dependent schizophrenic invites unwanted sexual advances. It then occurs to the patient, "I am becoming homosexual!" and the response is explosive, an event called homosexual panic.

In the acute form of schizophrenia, issues of family conflict, social failure, self-esteem, and homosexuality are almost universal. It is important to remember that when the mania subsides these issues are rarely significant.

Even when schizophrenia does not begin with a break, its onset may be associated with stress. Challenges like graduation from high school, finding and settling into a job, marriage, childbirth, menopause, a move, or even the general deterioration of old age, often so enthusiastically undertaken by the healthy, become insurmountable when one's mind is progressively deteriorating, haunted by perceptual distortions or bewildering early hallucinations and delusions. This explains why the disease often surfaces at these transitions of the life cycle.

The course any individual follows after the syndrome develops is unpredictable. Some will heal from the first break or two and go on to live a nearly normal life. Others will have a long course of repeated breaks with more or less normal intervals between. Still others retain many painful and disabling psychotic symptoms and gradually deteriorate. In the past these burned-out schizophrenics filled the back wards of the old mental hospitals. Such facilities grew and grew until they cared for thousands.

The radical new care systems introduced in most Western countries in the 1960s brought optimism that care at home might both be more humane and more therapeutic. This expectation of emptying the human warehouses has been realized partially. Home care and the introduction of neuroleptic medications have helped many schizophrenics. However, the expanding cost of a huge new bureaucracy, the general disillusionment of a society that now sees the disease on every corner even with huge public expenditures, has caused widespread disillusionment. A therapeutic lethargy among caretakers also has left many schizophrenics with poor care, choosing between the dangers of the street and a bleak bed in a rescue mission, suffering acute episodes from time to time, ending in a revolving door from an elaborate hospital to a cheap hotel. Even so, most patients prefer their freedom to find a niche that is reasonably comfortable in the city to being shut up, however safely and predictably, in the old hospital. How mental health professionals can help these unfortunate people to a more rewarding life is unquestionably today's greatest mental health challenge.

Outcome. The percentage of patients who can return to a normal life is variously estimated at from 10% to 25%. Probably 50% will have to struggle with a hobbled capacity to function in periods between recurrent acute breaks. The remainder include those who end up in back rooms at home, on the street, or in hospitals more or less permanently. Even though the overall fate of the schizophrenic sometimes seems little changed in recent years, there is no question that the level of function in the individual case has considerably improved with medication and home care.

When studies are done cross-culturally, the incidence of schizophrenia seems similar everywhere. However, the outcome is paradoxically better in less developed countries. This seems to happen when the patient is embraced by a local community that has integrity and ministers to its own. There is almost no such community in more advanced societies, and these same people transplanted as immigrants do poorly. This gives a strong hint that a close, supporting community that can administer love with a measure of discipline makes the most therapeutic milieu for patient care.

Management. Without such support, the management of the schizophrenic is a demanding task. Their lack of insight and tendency to project blame onto others often makes them resist those efforts that would most help them. For example, somewhere between 50% and 70% of patients who have been helped by medications in a hospital fail to take them after discharge. With patience and understanding on the part of caretakers, however, a measure of trust and later of insight ultimately develops, and patients can more fully cooperate with caretakers. Management may be expanded later to include teaching life skills and personal care.

A vital part of management that is often slighted is teaching the family and others around the patient the nature of the disease and recruiting them as a part of the treatment team. Whatever problems are created among these important others by the labeling of the patient as schizophrenic are balanced by the helpfulness of having a name for the bewildering complexity of the disease.

Medication. Care will inevitably include at least a trial of medication. In general positive symptoms such as hallucinations, delusions, and severely disordered thinking respond. The negative symptoms, such as social awkwardness and failure to function effectively in a working community, are less helped by medications. Still, many are protected by low ongoing doses of major tranquilizers from the inevitable breaks of the longer disease course.

But medications are unpleasant to take and not without risk. Much research is currently being invested to find effective medications with less troubling side effects. In general the physician who is experienced in the use of these agents and knows the patient well will achieve the greatest benefit at the least risk.

Psychotherapy. There is universal agreement that individual therapy is helpful in the management of the schizophrenic, whatever the modality. How much help comes from insight derived from therapy or how much from the relationship itself remains uncertain. Effective therapy invariably involves appreciating value in these people while providing a stable relationship that offers hope and love. These are not only helpful but are profoundly appreciated by the patient.

Bellack and Mueser (1993) described a wide-range psychosocial approach to treatment that requires little professional sophistication but makes common sense both to the therapist and to the patient. The bedrock of all care is support, which includes training the patient and the family in the nature of the illness, in basic living skills, and often acting as an ombudsman in the inevitable struggles of the patient with the larger community, particularly the bureaucracies that tyrannize the life of the chronic schizophrenic.

A second goal of therapy is understanding. Without help in understanding, each individual episode of psychosis is sealed over and nothing is learned. Such teaching requires ingenuity and is most effective when it is administered by the therapist the patient knows well and considers a friend.

Both theoretically and practically a supervised, loving community would be the optimal context for therapy. Occasionally this is found in a loving family, in group homes, in long-care missions that have a spiritual calling to serve these "little ones." Any such community will depend heavily on supporting professionals to make its ministry effective.

Employment. The schizophrenic, perhaps more than most other mentally ill patients, is acutely and painfully aware of our common human need to work, to carry one's own share of the labor of the world. Without employment, without the prestige of place and role, the patient soon loses confidence and a sense of value. Occasionally, with patience, a niche can be found for the chronic schizophrenic, but carrying a steady job is usually a herculean task. But without such a place, the overall management must be considered inadequate.

Most training programs in psychology and psychiatry require experience with the schizophrenic; it would also be most helpful for other psychotherapy training programs as well. Insight into these profoundly broken people probes deeply into an understanding of all human nature. There is universal agreement that caring for the schizophrenic changes the therapist and enriches life experience. Such people have no economic leverage but morally demand the best from us all. When the time comes that we more fully understand this disorder, we will know ourselves and our patients much more empathically and therapeutically.

References

Bateson, G., Jackson, D. D., Haley, J., & Weakland, J. (1956). Toward a theory of schizophrenia. *Behavioral Science, 1,* 251–264.

Bellack, A. S., & Mueser, K. T. (1993). Psychosocial treatment of schizophrenia. *Schizophrenic Bulletin, 19,* 317–336.

Freud, S. (1892/1958). The neuro-psychoses of defense. *The standard edition of the complete psychological works of Sigmund Freud.* (Vol. 3). London: Hogarth.

Klein, M. (1949). The significance of early anxiety situations in the development of the ego. In E. Jones (Ed.), *The psychoanalysis of children* (3rd ed.). London: Hogarth.

Lidz, T., Fleck, S., & Cornelison, A. R. (1965). *Schizophrenia and the family.* New York: International Universities Press.

Mahler, M. S. (1968). *On human symbiosis and the vicissitudes of individuation.* New York: International Universities Press.

Sullivan, H. S. (1953). *The interpersonal theory of psychiatry.* New York: Norton.

Winnicott, D. W. (1958). The observation of infants in a set situation. In D. W. Winnicott, *Collected papers.* London: Tavistock.

Wynne, L. C., Ryckoff, I. M., Day, J., & Hirsch, S. I. (1958). Pseudo-mutuality in family relations of schizophrenics. *Psychiatry, 21,* 205–220.

Additional Readings

Michaels, R. (Ed.). (1994). *Psychiatry.* Philadelphia: Lippincott (chapters 52–55).

Petronis, A., & Kennedy, J. L. (1995). Unstable genes—unstable mind? *American Journal of Psychiatry, 152,* 164–172.

C. M. BERRY

See PSYCHOTIC DISORDERS.

Schizophreniform Disorder. The historical concept of psychosis as a bimodal curve, with schizophrenia on one end and affective psychoses or bipolar disorder on the other end, left a number of patients stranded between them. This, plus a lingering suspicion that schizophrenia is not a single disorder, encouraged nosologists to attempt to define these other psychotic disorders.

Langfeld (1937) first applied the term *schizophreniform psychosis* to conditions of sudden onset, brief course, and complete recovery, emphasizing the psychosis mixed with affective symptoms. Since then this group of disorders with features of both psychosis and disturbed affect has been divided. The differentiation is largely around whether the affect, the psychosis, or the psychosocial stressor predominates. In the schizophreniform disorder the psychosis appears primarily with classical symptoms of schizophrenia but is distinguishable from it by a course that begins, runs, and ends within six months (Kendler, Gruenberg, & Tsuang, 1986). Should the affective symptoms predominate, consider schizophreniform disorder. Should the precipitating events be extraordinarily stressful and the duration very brief (less than two months), consider the brief reactive psychosis.

Definition. The schizophreniform disorder category has proven useful since the prognosis is hopeful and management less demanding than for schizophrenia. Since patients ordinarily present before the length of the course is known, research has been directed toward defining a subgroup with "good prognostic features" when first seen: these include an acute onset (within four weeks); confusion; disorientation and perplexity; good premorbid functioning; and lack of a flattened affect. More recently better rapport with the therapist has been added (Beiser, Fleming, Iacono, & Lin, 1988).

Etiology. Whether this condition originates as other affective disorders, or represents a peculiar vulnerability to psychosis, or begins within the mysterious headwaters of schizophrenia is not known. A good case could be made for any one. For the present it is probably best considered a heterogeneous group of illnesses.

Clinical Features. Schizophreniform disorder usually begins with emotional stress, often one that is part of normal life rather than excessive, as in the brief reactive psychoses. It is characterized by prominent schizophrenic signs and symptoms, including delusions and hallucinations. The delusions are ordinarily fairly straightforward but can be complex and bizarre. The hallucinations are usually not congruent with the predominant mood. Premorbid functioning generally is good with a recovery to this same level, even after several episodes.

Affective symptoms are often present and usually are limited to the peak of the psychosis, fading rapidly with recovery. But they would rarely warrant a mood disorder diagnosis. In the schizophreniform disorders, psychosis precedes and dominates the affective symptoms, whereas in the affective psychoses severe depression or mania are primary.

A number of medical, neurological, metabolic, and toxic conditions can present with similar psychotic symptoms. Such conditions are rare but occasionally dangerous enough to warrant a careful medical history and examination.

Treatment. Antipsychotic drugs are the treatment of choice for the schizophreniform disorder. They should be initiated early, and because the psychosis is often intense, they occasionally require megadoses. These should be tapered off and withdrawn rapidly when the patient calms down. Long-term administration to prevent relapses is rarely necessary. Several papers reporting good results with lithium, antidepressants, and anticonvulsants suggest that either these cases were misdiagnosed or there are occasional patients who respond more like affective disorders while appearing more psychotic.

Individual psychotherapy is recommended to help the patient and those around him or her understand the process and the prognosis. Both the severity of the acute course and the symbolism of the delusions and hallucinations often mean to the patient there are serious unconscious deficits. This is rarely true, but exploring this is still helpful to the patient.

References

Beiser, M., Fleming, J. A. E., Iacono, W. G., & Lin, T. (1988). Refining the diagnosis of schizophreniform disorder. *American Journal of Psychiatry, 145,* 695–700.

Kendler, K. S., Gruenberg, A. M., & Tsuang, M. T. (1986). A DSM-III family study of nonschizrenic psychotic disorders. *American Journal of Psychiatry, 143,* 1098–1105.

Langfeld, G. (1937). The prognosis in schizophrenia and the factors influencing the course of the disease. *Acta Psychiatrica et Neurologica (Suppl.) 13.*

Additional Reading

Vaillant, G. (1964). An historical review of the remitting schizophrenias. *Archives of General Psychiatry, 138,* 48–56.

C. M. BERRY

See PSYCHOTIC DISORDERS.

Schizotypal Personality Disorder. A diagnosis used to describe those individuals whose general personality functioning is characterized by highly idiosyncratic perceptions, thought processes, behavior, and speech. Although their condition is not severe enough to warrant a diagnosis of schizophrenia, such persons will appear to be quite odd and unusual to those around them. They are uncomfortable with close relationships, and there is often evidence of cognitive or perceptual problems and eccentric behavior.

The symptoms associated with this disorder include at least five of the following: magical thinking (e.g., superstitiousness, clairvoyance, telepathy, bizarre fantasies, or preoccupations); ideas of reference (the impression that the conversation or behavior of other persons has reference to oneself); social isolation or withdrawal; unusual perceptual experiences or recurrent illusions (e.g., sensing the presence of a person or force not actually present, depersonalization); odd thinking and speech that is digressive, vague, overelaborate, circumstantial, or metaphorical; lack of close friends or confidants; constricted or inappropriate affect that interferes with normal social interactions; paranoid ideation or marked suspiciousness; behavior or appearance that is odd or peculiar; and undue social anxiety or hypersensitivity to real or imagined criticism. Associated features may include varying mixtures of anxiety, depression, and other dysphoric moods, as well as occasional transient psychotic symptoms during times of unusual stress. Schizotypal personalities may also hold rather eccentric convictions, such as bigotry or fanatical religious beliefs.

Symptoms typically associated with the schizotypal disorder are usually of a chronic, long-term nature (Sue, Sue, & Sue, 1994). These symptoms often first appear during adolescence. What may initially seem to be isolated, unrelated traits later become inflexible and rigid maladaptive patterns as the individual approaches early adulthood (Buss, 1966). Thus the unusual thinking and behavior are not the result of a reaction to a particular stressful event. Instead this chronic maladaptive pattern markedly interferes with social and occupational functioning throughout most of the person's adult life (Gallatin, 1982). Such individuals rarely become truly schizophrenic, and most successfully avoid psychiatric hospitalization. The prevalence rate is estimated to be about 3% of the general population, according to *DSM–IV*.

Differential diagnosis is a rather difficult task. A history of an active phase of schizophrenia with psychotic symptoms differentiates this disorder from schizophrenia, residual type. The oddities of behavior, thinking, perception, and speech distinguish it from schizoid and avoidant personality disorders, as well as depersonalization disorder. People diagnosed as borderline personality disorder frequently also meet the criteria for schizotypal personality disorder, making it difficult to differentiate between the two. In such cases both diagnoses are sometimes used simultaneously.

The precise etiology of this personality disorder remains unknown. Many theories abound, attributing this pattern of behavior to everything from genetic to environmental factors. Perhaps the origin of the disorder can best be thought of as being the result of an arrested or deviated development of the personality. This is eventually associated with a failure to establish an identity with constructive and socially useful adaptations, poor impulse control, and inappropriate or inadequate interpersonal skills (Kolb & Brodie, 1982). Whether this is the result of a genetic or teratogenic fetal insult or the lack of proper parenting and nurturance remains to be determined.

Treatment of such individuals is a difficult undertaking. Their inability to form a working alliance with the therapist often frustrates attempts to conduct therapy in a more psychoanalytic or psychodynamic modality, with a few exceptions. Since they typically seek psychotherapy only during times of situational crisis or unusual stress, when their anxiety or depression becomes severe enough to cause noticeable distress, therapeutic approaches that are more short-term, behavioral, supportive, cognitive, directive, goal-oriented, symptom-focusing, and reality-oriented will most likely have the greatest potential for success. The adjunctive use of medications is typically not thought to be very helpful, other than possibly to decrease the severity of troubling dysphoric moods during unusually stressful times. Antipsychotic medications have been regarded as largely ineffective in eliminating the bizarre characteristics of speech, behavior, thinking, and perceptions typically present. Such individuals are likely to terminate psychotherapy prematurely, usually as soon as the crisis that precipitated the contact is resolved. Only in rare cases will they remain beyond this point and undertake a more long-term, reconstructive form of psychotherapy. To result in more permanent personality changes, such treatment may last several years.

It should be noted that the use of the term *schizotypal personality* is of rather recent origin. Before *DSM-III* and *DSM-IV* such individuals were typically diagnosed as simple schizophrenics or pseudoneurotic schizophrenics (Gallatin, 1982). The current nomenclature is perhaps more precise in that it draws attention to the chronic, nonpsychotic pattern that usually characterizes the entire adult life of such an individual.

References

Buss, A. H. (1966). *Psychopathology*. New York: Wiley.
Gallatin, J. E. (1982). *Abnormal psychology: Concepts, issues and trends*. New York: Macmillan.
Kolb, L. C., & Brodie, H. K. (1982). *Modern clinical psychiatry* (10th ed.). Philadelphia: Saunders.
Sue, D., Sue, D., & Sue, S. (1994). *Understanding abnormal behavior*. New York: Houghton Mifflin.

J. D. GUY, JR.

See PERSONALITY DISORDERS.

School Phobia. *See* ATTACHMENT THEORY AND DISORDERS; SEPARATION ANXIETY DISORDER.

School Psychology. School psychology appears to have began with the work of Lightner Witmer, the director of the first psychological clinic in the United States (Bergan, 1985). In the late 1800s he worked with a few students with learning problems and later suggested that a new profession be developed: psychologists who work in the school system. During the first half of the twentieth century, intelligence tests were developed of increasing sophistication, and various school systems began providing intelligence as well as academic skill assessment. Professionals were needed to administer and interpret these tests. In 1947 the American Psychology Association (APA) formed a division for school psychologists, Division 16. APA membership is limited to those with doctorates (and the APA now accredits doctoral programs in school psychology). However, most professionals in the field have no doctorate. The National Association of School Psychologists (NASP) was formed in 1969 to meet their needs. NASP suggests that two years of training beyond college be required. As a result education specialist (Ed.S.) degree programs in school psychology are available at many universities. Still, each state continues to have different standards for credentialing school psychologists. The field currently maintains three journals: *School Psychology Review, Journal of School Psychology,* and *Psychology in the Schools.*

The need for school psychologists has grown because of an increasing desire within American education to meet the educational needs of all its students, including those with various impairments. School psychologists are usually those in a school district charged with classifying eligible children for special education services (when the child's school difficulties are not due mostly to medical causes). Therefore, their primary tasks include the testing, educational assessment, and classification of children referred for evaluation.

In addition, school psychologists have also been viewed as psychoeducational clinicians (Bardon, 1982) who may assist the child more broadly through personality, classroom, and family assessment; child counseling; and the provision of behavioral, teaching, and learning interventions at home and school. Depending upon the school district, school psychologists may also work in such areas as school policy, advocacy, primary prevention, teacher training, evaluation of school programs, or research itself, as well as the dissemination of relevant psychological research to interested parties (Bergan, 1985; Fine, 1989). Because school psychology is a discipline at the intersection between education and psychology, school psychologists tend to be broadly knowledgeable about such topics as learning and cognition, teaching, special education, child development and abnormality, clinical psychology, measurement and assessment, and systems theory.

School psychologists have sought an expanded role in recent decades because of an increasing recognition that a child's learning problems are not caused solely by internal deficits that tests identify but are usually a result of an interaction of contextual factors, including the classroom environment, task demands, past skills training, the child's family background and prior history, present circumstances, and the larger culture, including the school district. (Christians might add the importance of student responsibility to this otherwise deterministic list.) Although school psychologists rarely deal directly with religious issues, they perform an essential service to lower-functioning students and those who work with them.

References

Bardon, J. I. (1982). The role and function of the school psychologist. In C. R. Reynolds & T. B. Gutkin (Eds.), *The handbook of school psychology*. New York: Wiley.
Bergan, J. R. (1985). *School psychology in contemporary society: An introduction*. Columbus, OH: Merrill.
Fine, M. J. (Ed.). (1989). *School psychology: Cutting edges in research and practice*. National Education Association and National Association of School Psychologists. Washington, DC: Author.

Additional Readings

Kratochwill, T. R., & Gettinger, M. (Eds.). (1982–1992). *Advances in school psychology*. Hillsdale, NJ: Erlbaum.
Reynolds. C. R., & Gutkin, T. B. (Eds.). (1982). *The handbook of school psychology*. New York: Wiley.

Thomas, A., & Grimes, J. (1995). *Best practices in school psychology III*. Washington, DC: National Association of School Psychologists.

E. L. JOHNSON

See EDUCATIONAL PSYCHOLOGY.

Schools of Professional Psychology. *See* PROFESSIONAL SCHOOLS OF PSYCHOLOGY.

Scream Therapy. The early 1960s saw the birth of a number of schools of psychotherapy that elicit screaming. Primal therapy was developed by Arthur Janov and quickly became the best known. Independently of Janov, another scream therapy called new identity process was developed by Casriel (1972). A few years later bio scream psychotherapy was developed by Saltzman (1980). The techniques and goals of these and other scream therapies are all quite similar. They share the foundational assumption that there is but one neurosis, an individual's response to unintegrated childhood pain. The technique of integration is screaming.

References

Casriel, D. (1972). *A scream away from happiness*. New York: Grosset & Dunlap.

Saltzman, N. (1980). Bio scream psychotherapy. In R. Herink (Ed.), *The psychotherapy handbook*. New York: New American Library.

D. G. BENNER

See PRIMAL THERAPY.

Screen Memory. In psychoanalytic terminology, a memory that is used as a shield to conceal another more important memory. Thus, for example, when a patient in psychoanalysis recalls playing in the bathroom at age three but does not remember the nature of the play, he or she is said to be providing a screen memory. The assumption is that the remainder of the memory is still unacceptable to consciousness, and the fragment is therefore offered as a substitute and a diversion.

See MEMORY; FALSE MEMORY SYNDROME.

Script Analysis. An attempt to facilitate understanding of the basic life theme underlying one's behavior. It is a technique of transactional analysis but goes beyond the analysis of single interpersonal interactions (transactions) or the analysis of a set of interactions (e.g., games) to an analysis of one's total life goal. Most persons are unaware of their script, and such understanding provides the freedom to redecide. This is based on the assumption that the decision for living out a given script was prematurely made by (not for) the individual in early childhood.

Steiner (1974) has given much attention to script analysis. He suggests that such analysis should begin by reflecting on the interactions the individual had with parents who either empowered or inhibited the individual through permissions or injunctions. This is called the script matrix. Next follows reflection on the decision whereby the person decided to live the life he or she is living. This involves reliving and reowning the process, coupled with giving up blame on one's parents.

Steiner mentions three basic scripts: depression—no love; madness—no mind; and addiction—no joy. Understanding these themes in one's life makes possible but not probable a change of life script to love, power, and happiness. Eric Berne, from whose ideas transactional analysis evolved, suggests that scripts are almost impossible to change.

Reference

Steiner, C. (1974). *Scripts people live*. New York: Grove.

H. N. MALONY

See TRANSACTIONAL ANALYSIS.

Sculpting. *See* FAMILY CHOREOGRAPHY; FAMILY SCULPTURE TECHNIQUE.

Seasonal Affect Disorder. Seasonal affect disorder (SAD) is listed as a type of major depressive disorder in the *DSM-IV*. This condition occurs for most individuals during the winter months when the number of daylight hours is reduced. A smaller subgroup experiences depression during the summer. The depression is accompanied by irritability and excessive sleeping and eating, especially of carbohydrates, and is more commonly observed in women in early to mid-adulthood. It is believed many people experience a less severe, nonclinical form of the disorder: seasonal depression. A study conducted at the National Institute of Mental Health (NIMH) on seasonal depression revealed that 92% of respondents indicated noticeable changes in seasonal behavior and mood patterns. Forty-three percent reported feeling worse in winter and 27% indicated this caused problems.

One possible mechanism for the disorder is an excess secretion of the hormone melatonin. Light information from the eyes influences pineal gland activity, which in turn regulates melatonin release. Melatonin is released under dark conditions, and in animals it regulates hibernation, activity levels, and sexual cycles. As the number of daylight hours decrease, melatonin levels increase, preparing the animal for lower-level winter activity. Some researchers believe humans respond in a similar manner and while most individuals adjust, some do not. Instead they experience symptoms consistent with animal hibernation plus depression. In the spring, as melatonin levels decrease, they may become overactive, even displaying a manic pattern.

Aside from moving to a more southerly latitude, exposure to extra amounts of light has proved to be the most effective treatment for seasonal affect disorder. Different treatment regimens have been proposed, with some researchers believing that only intense light levels (2,500 lux compared to the normal 250 lux) are effective. Others claim successful outcomes even with dim light. Some administer light therapy both in the morning and at night; others use only one daily session.

W. D. NORMAN

See DEPRESSION.

Secondary Gain. Sigmund Freud formulated the idea that neurotic symptoms may provide secondary gains, or indirect opportunities for gratification. A symptom, though disturbing, may become valuable to the patient because of side benefits it affords after its development. Thus the woman complaining of recurring dizziness may gain nurturing concern and attention while avoiding adult responsibilities. The patient may have a resulting unconscious desire to keep the neurosis, a possibility that must be addressed in treatment.

See PRIMARY GAIN; RESISTANCE IN PSYCHO-THERAPY.

Secondary Process. Sigmund Freud used this term to describe the mature ways of thinking that develop gradually and progressively during the first years of life. It is contrasted to primary process, which describes the primitive mental functioning characteristic of the young child whose ego is still immature. Secondary process thinking, according to psychoanalytic theory, is governed by the reality principle in that it is realistic, logical, and goal-oriented. In contrast, primary process thinking is described as following the pleasure principle, which leads to immediate gratification of needs or drives. While secondary process thinking should characterize adult mental life, the presence of some primary process activity is not in itself necessarily pathological or suggestive of immaturity.

D. G. BENNER

See PSYCHOANALYTIC PSYCHOLOGY.

Secondary Reinforcer. In behavioral psychology, a stimulus that acquires reinforcing properties through association with primary reinforcers (e.g., food, water, air). A stimulus has become a secondary reinforcer (also called a conditioned reinforcer) when it increases the probability of behaviors preceding it. Thus in animal studies a red light or a loud tone when paired with delivery of food may become a secondary reinforcer, and the animal will eventually perform specified behaviors when reinforced with presentation of the light or tone alone.

An example of a secondary reinforcer for humans is money. Money is not a primary reinforcer; that is, it cannot by itself meet primary needs for food, water, or air. But people learn the association of money with acquisition of primary needs, and they will then work to be reinforced through the presentation of cash alone.

K. M. LATTEA

See LEARNING.

Selective Mutism in Childhood and Adolescence. The American Psychiatric Association (APA) has defined selective mutism as a "consistent failure to speak in specific situations (in which there is an expectation for speaking, e.g. school) despite speaking in other situations" (American Psychiatric Association, 1994). Children develop this problem usually during preschool years, when they speak freely at home but not in other social contexts. Josephson and Porter (1979) report an incidence of less than .05% within the general population of school-aged children. The earliest reference in psychiatric literature was made in 1877, but the most commonly used term, elective mutism, was coined in 1934, when the condition was differentiated from language delays and various psychiatric conditions. The APA began using the phrase "selective mutism" in its most recent diagnostic manual.

Numerous theories have been offered regarding the origin of this phenomenon. Earlier models focused on an overly close mother-child relationship, in response to which children were thought to fear divulging maternal secrets if they spoke in public. Other theorists suggested the occurrence of a traumatic event during children's speech development.

Recent literature suggests that selective mutism is a form of more general social anxieties (Crumley, 1993; Boon, 1994). One author even draws a connection with dissociative identity disorder, or multiple personalities (Jacobsen, 1995). Many researchers, however, agree upon the manipulative quality of children's refusal to speak as a means to exert a sense of personal freedom in response to feeling overcontrolled by parents or other adults.

Treatment approaches usually focus on a student's speech in the school setting. A variety of rewards are given to students as they speak more frequently. Another approach focuses on changing the internal negative thought processes that inhibit speech. Children replace such thoughts with more positive self-talk that encourages externalized speech. Therapists frequently opt for a combination of treatment approaches, some even including the use of medication (Boon, 1994). In addition to counseling in the school setting, family-oriented therapy is often offered in order to diffuse manipulative struggles between children and adults.

References

American Psychiatric Association. (1994). *Diagnostic and statistical manual of mental disorders* (4th ed.). Washington, DC: Author.

Boon, F. (1994). The selective mutism controversy (continued). *Journal of the American Academy of Child and Adolescent Psychiatry, 33* (2), 283.

Crumley, F. E. (1993). Is elective mutism a social phobia? *Journal of the American Academy of Child and Adolescent Psychiatry, 32* (15), 1081–1082.

Jacobsen, T. (1995). Case study: Is selective mutism a manifestation of dissociative identity disorder? *Journal of the American Academy of Child and Adolescent Psychiatry, 34* (7), 863–866.

Josephson, M. M., & Porter, R. T. (Eds.). (1979). *Clinician's handbook of childhood psychopathology.* New York: Aronson.

E. K. SWEITZER

Self. The concept of the self is one of the most puzzling of all concepts. The self is in one respect the most familiar of all entities; I am constantly and pervasively aware of my self. Yet the self is also in some ways the most deeply mysterious of all the entities with which human beings deal.

One way of opening up the mystery of selfhood is to reflect on the way humans use the word *I.* When I say *I,* normally I am referring to a certain human person, Stephen Evans. However, the word *I* cannot be replaced by the name or other identifying label. For even if I became amnesiac, forgot my name, and no longer knew who I was, I would still in one sense know what I would be referring to by *I.* I would still be referring to *myself,* and it seems impossible for me to be mistaken about this. I am a self, a being who not only can say *I* but also can do so in this special manner. I can refer to myself as the self that I am conscious of being and that I cannot be mistaken in thinking myself to be, however mistaken my other beliefs about the self may be.

As many philosophers have argued (e.g., Bertocci, 1970), the concept of the self also seems essential to understanding human mental abilities, particularly cognitive functions. Knowing, particularly perceptual knowing, involves the unification of diverse elements. When a person hears a clock strike seven times and thereby comes to know that it is seven o'clock, the diverse experiences are in some way unified in her consciousness. An experience of succession is not the same as a succession of experiences. In order for a person to hear the seventh chime as the *seventh* chime, it would seem necessary for the person who hears the seventh chime to be the same person as the one who heard the first chime and to be aware of being the same person. In addition to the experience, then, it appears that there must exist a self that has these experiences, a self that persists over time (Castell, 1965).

The concept of a self that continues over time also seems essential for legal, moral, and religious practices. Unless the person who stands in the courtroom is in some sense the same person as the one who committed the crime, it would be unjust to punish the person. A person should not be convicted of doing what some other person did. Moral responsibility—praise and blame, reward and desert—similarly depend upon a continuing self. Morality may depend upon the self in a still stronger sense, for many people believe it illogical to hold a person morally responsible for an act unless that act is freely performed by the person. Freedom of this sort is often regarded as a distinctive ability of the self.

The Christian faith requires the concept of the self for the same reasons as moral and legal practices, since God is viewed by Christians as the Judge of all the earth who holds his creatures responsible for their actions and punishes them if they refuse to accept his mercy and forgiveness. Christianity also requires the self to make sense of life after death. Christians believe that after death believers will come to life again with new bodies and yet remain the same selves. Those Christians who do not deny the intermediate state between death and resurrection must also believe that people continue to exist as selves before the resurrection occurs.

The Rejection of the Self in Psychology. Despite the theoretical and practical significance of the concept of the self and the fundamental importance of the concept for common-sense psychology and ordinary experience, the concept of the self has been for long periods practically abandoned by psychologists. Psychologists who disagree among themselves about almost everything else have agreed that the concept of the self was neither needed nor useful in psychology.

The banishment of the self is most evident in behaviorism, which regarded the self as a vestige of the medieval concept of soul (Watson, 1925). Skinner insists that "the free inner man who is held responsible for the behavior of the external biological organism is only a prescientific substitute for the kinds of causes which are discovered in the course of scientific analysis" (Skinner, 1953, p. 447). Those causes are believed by the behaviorist to lie outside the organism, not in a self.

However, behaviorists are only the tip of the iceberg. Trait psychologists appear to be studying a self of sorts, but a psychometrically observable set of tendencies is hardly a self in the traditional sense.

An attenuated self seems to survive as the ego in Freudian psychology, but the ego does not look much like a self in orthodox Freudian theory. Rather, it is a derivative of unconscious forces, part of a deterministic, warring, three-part system, which is described from an objective third-person standpoint.

Even thinkers who are sympathetic to the self ultimately shy away from the self as a substantial, continuing entity. James (1890), for example, ultimately concludes that psychology can find no use for the self as a knowing entity, though he leaves open the possibility that for some other discipline it may be necessary to postulate a self as an entity. More than

60 years later Allport (1955) developed something that approximated the self in his concept of the proprium. However, he refused to say that the proprium is a true substantial self. Although, like James, he leaves open the necessity to postulate a self for theological and philosophical purposes, such an entity is not necessary for psychology.

Reasons for Rejecting the Self. There have been various reasons for rejecting the self. First, the concept of the self as a substantial agent, an enduring entity that originates actions, seems inherently obscure and mysterious to many. It is very difficult to say what is the self that has experiences, apart from those experiences; very difficult to say what is the self that performs actions, apart from a description of those actions.

Second, the self seems tied to introspective methods in psychology. The self is what I am aware of or fail to be aware of when I reflect on my own mental states. As psychology moved away from such methods as proper for science, the concept of the self fell into disuse.

Third, the self has also been ignored because of a conviction that science requires objectification. The self seems inherently subjective, something to be grasped and understood by participatory experience. Yet many psychologists believe that science requires objectivity, a third-person perspective, not a first-person perspective. This is why thinkers like Sigmund Freud, who postulate something like a self, seem to denude it of its selflike qualities.

Fourth, the self has been thought to be a *homonculus*, an explanation of a person's behavior by postulating a little person inside the person, whose behavior is left unexplained. The self is then an evasion of the quest for psychological explanations, in which all behavior is attributed to the choice or the will of the agent.

Fifth, it has been thought by some that a psychology of the self will necessarily be individualistic and foster selfishness. Some Christians especially have seen a psychology of the self as an expression of human pride (Vitz, 1977).

Sixth, it has been charged that the concept of the self implies that humans have free will, and many psychologists see determinism as an essential presupposition of scientific psychology.

Finally, the use of the concept of the self has seemed to some to be implicitly dualistic, since the self as a self-conscious entity does not appear to be identical with its body. Dualism in turn is thought to be an unscientific, religious way of viewing human beings.

These reasons make psychologists' aversion to the self understandable. Yet many of the reasons appear shaky, especially from a Christian perspective. Some brief criticisms of each of these points follow.

First, the fact that a self can be described only through its experiences and actions does not necessarily make it especially mysterious. Many entities (perhaps ultimately all entities) can be identified only by what they do. In any case, from a Christian perspective it seems plausible that there is something genuinely mysterious about selfhood. Must all mysteries be avoided?

Second, it also seems questionable as to whether introspection is an illegitimate method of gaining knowledge. Although introspection is certainly not infallible, it would seem to be a fact that we can and do learn things about ourselves by attending to our own stream of consciousness.

Third, the demand that the self be objectivized seems to be a question-begging assumption that the world consists entirely of things that can be understood completely in object terms, that no genuine subjects exist.

Fourth, to attribute an action to the choice of an agent is admittedly not to explain it. But the concept of the self is not necessarily a homonculus. The self is not a little person inside the person, but the person himself or herself considered as a subject. Psychologists can still attempt to understand the choices of agents and explain how the choices are made, so employing a concept of self does not mean psychologists will have nothing to do.

Fifth, the concept of the self is not inherently individualistic, since it is possible to see a self as essentially related to others. Nor does a psychology of the self necessarily foster selfism or selfishness. From a Christian perspective the meaning of selfhood is found in self-denying love.

Sixth, it is not true that determinism is a necessary presupposition of psychology. Psychologists do not have to assume there are determining causes for all behavior in order to look for what determining causes there are. The actual laws that psychologists discover are invariably statistical, probabilistic, and culture-based. Such empirical discoveries neither presuppose nor imply determinism. In any case it is possible to believe in the self and still embrace determinism. The issue of the self's existence should be separated from the question of its freedom.

Finally, it is by no means obvious that a psychology of the self must be dualistic, although it certainly will reject reductionistic materialism. A nonreductive monism or materialism may be adequate (Reichenbach, 1978). However, Christian psychologists have in some cases rejected dualism too quickly, and a good case can be made for a biblical dualism (Cooper, 1982a, 1982b).

Theories of the Self. Besides telling us what a self is, a theory of the self should explain why human beings are selves and how it is possible for them to be the same self over time while changing in various ways. Three major types of theories have emerged.

Materialistic Theories. A simple account of the self is to identify it with the body. This helps to solve the problem of the relation of self to body. It also provides a solution for the problem of continuity in change, since the identity of the self can be explained in the same way as the continuing identity of any living physical object can be explained.

However, it is hard to see how the body can account for the uniquely subjective aspects of myself as an *I*. The bodily theory cannot be squared with our conviction that we transcend our bodies. It seems possible to us that a person could gain a new body and yet remain the same self. Even if this is impossible, it is conceivable and intelligible; it happens constantly in fairy tales and science fiction. Out-of-body experiences are reported by near-death patients as well as Eastern mystics. If Christianity is true, having a new body is not just an abstract possibility but a future occurrence.

Certainly the human self is intimately related to the body and forms some kind of unity with it. But however close the union, it does not seem that it can be a strict identity.

Relational Theories. A variety of thinkers have rejected materialism while attempting to avoid a substantial self. In general such theories see the self as a set or bundle of experiences (Hume, 1739/1888) or more plausibly as a relation between experiences.

One candidate for this relation is memory. Perhaps a self is a set of experiences that includes among its later members' memory experiences of its earlier ones. Grice (1941) has developed a sophisticated version of this view, which goes back to John Locke. However, it is hard to see how remembering one of my past actions makes me the same person as the one who acted; rather, it seems that it is the fact that I am the same person that makes it possible for me to remember the action.

Another candidate for the relation is qualitative similarity of traits. This view sees the self or identity of the person to consist in a set of traits or dispositions that might collectively be described as a personality or character. It is because a person exhibits a relatively stable personality that we regard him or her as the same person over time. Thus the problem of the identity of the self becomes the same as the psychological problem of identity, in which the person tries to discover his or her true personality or character. However, a person can change his or her personality drastically and still remain the same self. Saul becomes Paul and is in one sense a new person. But he must also in some sense be the same person; otherwise we could not say Paul was the man who formerly persecuted Christians. A person can change her identity in the psychological sense and still remain the same self. Also, a person or self must be seen as transcending her character or personality if she is to be regarded as in any way responsible for forming or altering that personality.

A third type of relational view might be termed the existentialist view. This view, a very difficult one to understand, holds that the self consists of activities but there is no substantial agent to perform those activities. Rather, the self is constituted by its own activities. Acts of consciousness occur, some of which are acts of knowing. When such acts take themselves as objects, what is thus taken is a self. Besides existentialists such as Sartre (1957), this view has recently been defended by Nozick (1981).

Agent Theories. The traditional view is that the self is a continuing agent that has its experiences rather than simply being composed of them; that performs actions without consisting solely of those actions. Within this general framework, however, advocates of this view diverge sharply.

For example, advocates of the agent view disagree as to whether the self can be experienced. Some philosophers hold that all or at least many acts of consciousness include an awareness of the *I* that is conscious (Husserl, 1913/1962). Others agree that one can introspectively be aware of the self but that this involves an apprehension of (very recent) past acts of the *I;* the act of apprehending cannot take itself as object (Campbell, 1957). Still others hold that the self cannot be apprehended in experience at all, but rather it is an explanatory hypothesis, a necessary postulate to account for the unity of experience.

Advocates of the traditional view also disagree about the nature of the self. Some follow Kant in viewing the true self as a timeless noumenal ego, whose true nature cannot be known. Bertocci (1970), however, views the self as completely temporal and empirically describable. Campbell (1957) adopts an intermediate position in which the self is viewed as a temporal entity whose nature is truly expressed in its empirical activities and character but that is not completely reducible to those characteristics that are empirically describable. Campbell believes that in introspection, particularly in the situation of moral temptation, we are aware of the self as an entity that transcends its personality, or characteristic patterns of desiring and acting, so that it is possible for a self to at least try to oppose its own character.

The Return of the Self in Psychology. In psychology, after the initial banishment of the self, there seems to have been a slow, steady, and now massive return to the self, which is present in almost every tradition. This is perhaps most evident in third-force psychologies: humanistic psychology, existential psychology, and phenomenology. In these movements the person is clearly seen as a self-conscious, responsible being who not only is driven by urges but also is moved by meanings and values.

The self has also made a strong comeback in psychoanalysis. Indeed, the history of one strand of the psychoanalytic movement is really the history of ego psychology. In his later work Freud himself began the process of seeing the ego as more than a weak derivative product, a process continued by Anna Freud and others, culminating in Erik Erikson's vision of the self as a quest for identity. Perhaps closest of all to a true self is the British object relations theory pioneered by Fairbairn and popularized by Guntrip (1971). In this view the ego is not merely an object in a system but a true self, which participates in the formation of the unconscious.

Within the behavioristic tradition the cognitivization of psychology has been remarkable, and it is obvious that a psychology that emphasizes cognition must make room for a cognizer. In place of the empty organism that contains only its learning history, psychologists such as Mischel and Albert Bandura have developed social learning theories that recognize the importance of the self-system in understanding behavior. This cognitivization of psychology has even allowed for a rapprochement of sorts between Albert Ellis's rational-emotive therapy (RET) and behavioral therapists.

Mention should also be made of Allport's pioneering book on the self, *Becoming* (1955). Before it was popular to do so, Allport attempted to rehabilitate a concept of the self with his notion of the proprium and in the process showed how psychology is still haunted by philosophical questions.

The Self and Christian Faith. Since Christians believe that the ultimate reality is personal and that ultimately the existence of a person lies behind the existence of everything else, Christians have a strong interest in preserving the person (Evans, 1977). Reductionistic accounts must therefore be resisted. The Christian psychologist will recognize that the human self is dependent on God and is not autonomous and that the self is a part of the created order. The self is partially a product, and its activities are made possible by various impersonal processes. But there is a difference between explaining how selfhood is possible and explaining selfhood away. Psychology that is Christian must be a psychology that makes room for the concept of the self and related concepts, such as belief, desire, meaningful action, responsibility, and intention.

References

Allport, G. W. (1955). *Becoming.* New Haven, CT: Yale University Press.

Bertocci, P. (1970). *The person God is.* New York: Humanities Press.

Campbell, C. A. (1957). *On selfhood and godhood.* New York: Macmillan.

Castell, A. (1965). *The self in philosophy.* New York: Macmillan.

Cooper, J. (1982a). Dualism and the biblical view of human beings I. *Reformed Journal, 32,* 13–16.

Cooper, J. (1982b). Dualism and the biblical view of human beings II. *Reformed Journal, 32,* 16–18.

Evans, C. S. (1977). *Preserving the person.* Downers Grove, IL: InterVarsity Press.

Grice, H. P. (1941). Personal identity. *Mind, 50,* 330–350.

Guntrip, H. (1971). *Psychoanalytic theory, therapy, and the self.* New York: Basic.

Hume, D. (1888). *A treatise of human nature.* Oxford: Clarendon. (Original work published 1739)

Husserl, E. (1962). *Ideas: General introduction to pure phenomenology.* New York: Collier. (Original work published 1913)

James, W. (1890). *Principles of psychology* (Vol. 1). New York: Holt.

Nozick, R. (1981). *Philosophical explanations.* Cambridge, MA: Harvard University Press.

Reichenbach, B. (1978). *Is man the phoenix?* Grand Rapids, MI: Christian University Press.

Sartre, J. P. (1957). *The transcendence of the ego.* New York: Noonday.

Skinner, B. F. (1953). *Science and human behavior.* New York: Macmillan.

Vitz, P. C. (1977). *Psychology as religion: The cult of self-worship.* Grand Rapids, MI: Eerdmans.

Watson, J. B. (1925). *Behaviorism.* New York: People's Institute Publishing.

C. S. EVANS

See CONSCIOUSNESS; MIND-BRAIN RELATIONSHIP; PERSONHOOD.

Self Psychology. This term is most closely associated with the work of Kohut, a psychoanalyst, who developed a theory of psychological development based on the construct of the self. Originating in infancy, the self integrates and adequately develops to produce healthy relationships in adult life; or the self fragments and otherwise inadequately develops, producing the total range of adult psychopathologies. Kohut's work is presented in two volumes, *The Analysis of the Self* (1971) and *The Restoration of the Self* (1977).

Kohut asserted that the Freudian psychic apparatus (ego, id, superego) and the complexities surrounding this apparatus (castration fear, oedipal conflict, penis envy) are inadequate to describe the basic infantile psyche. Kohut proposed that the self, comprised of the total body of inner experiences, is the center of the psychological universe. The self is not a part of the psyche, as are the ego, superego, and id, but rather the sum of all these entities plus an unnamed integrating function.

Development of the Self. The development of a cohesive adult self has its beginning in the second year of life, when the "fragmentary cognitive precursors of the self" are consolidated into a nucleus, which Kohut called the infantile grandiose self. The child's natural tendencies at this stage are personal exhibitionism and idealization of its caretakers, who are perceived to be omnipotent. The infant has a natural psychic fusion with its caretakers and hence develops a belief in its own omnipotence. The archaic representations of mother and self, experienced as one object, are called self-objects. The absence of an experienced separation of self and others leads naturally to the infant's grandiosity. If the caretakers are adequately nurturing, this structure enhances the development of the grandiose self. In simple terms, the infant receives most of what he or she wants. Under such conditions the self-object is further idealized, leading gradually to idealized parental image. These two components, the grandiose self and the idealized parental image, represent the two basic elements of the infant's self. The grandiose self is the seed from which grow adult self-confidence, assertiveness, and ambition, while the idealized parental image matures into admiration and love.

A central characteristic of the self is its bipolar nature. One pole of the self is ambitions; the other is ideals. Connecting the two poles are the talents and skills of the individual. A person is driven by ambition and led by ideals. Ambition is the mature form of childhood aggressivity and leads to assertiveness. Ideals originate from childhood idealizing of parents and the subsequent inner and personal development of these ideals. Satisfying and productive life results from proper integration and cooperation of these parts of the bipolar self that allow a person to achieve and nurture as well as to follow and be nurtured.

Kohut's stages of development of the self may be summarized as follows: (1) narcissistic early infantile self-objects give way to (2) a developing sense of self along with control over self and the world followed by (3) early love and hatred, with some of the earlier omnipotence of self and other having been abandoned, and (4) a mature loving based on proper distinction between self and other and realization of personal and others' limitations. The progression can be expressed as "I am perfect," "You are perfect," "I am part of you and perfect," "We are separate and perfect," "We are separate and imperfect." From the proper development of the grandiose self and the idealized parental image grows the nuclear self, or mature personality.

A later elaboration that Kohut (1977) made to this basic structure of the healthy (nuclear) self is that psychological health results from the integration of the superficial and the deep. The superficial is that which is historical and factual; the deep is that which is creative and unique. The superficial results primarily from a loving relationship with the father, the deep from similar contact with the mother. The implication is that empathic mothering is the primary ingredient in moving infantile grandiosity to mature creativity, and good fathering moves the child's idealized parental image to proper admiration of others.

Psychopathology and Treatment. When the child does not receive adequate parenting, usually because of narcissistic and otherwise maladapted parents, the child remains fixated on archaic grandiose self and self-objects. Thus the self remains primitive and fails to develop adequately for satisfactory adult adjustment. The person remains impaired in loving and valuing. The adult personality is also deprived of the energies invested in maintaining these early structures, and adult realistic activities are hampered by intrusions of these early narcissistic needs into daily life. The immature adult expects too much both of self and of others.

In psychotic disturbances delusional ideations result from very early grandiose self or self-object representation that have failed to mature, thus leading to paranoia and delusional grandiosity. In narcissistic personality and behavior disorders the self is more developed but insufficiently so to avoid undue fears and inappropriate arrogance. Kohut identifies the following systems as all due to early narcissistic injury (lack of love): sexual perversions, inhibitions in work and play, oversensitivity, undue rage, lack of humor and empathy, poor impulse control, feelings of emptiness and depression, and feeling not fully real. What has happened when people experience such things, Kohut suggests, is that defensive structures cover the low self-esteem, depression, feelings of rejection, and incessant hunger for approval. Defenses against feelings include pseudovitality, undue romanticism, and hysterical features, and compensatory structures, essentially inadequate displacements, replace the desirable sublimation. Thus the narcissistically injured person engages in neurotic behavior or delinquency in place of achievement and creativity, the natural results of properly integrated early narcissism.

Kohut's principal interest was in narcissistic disorders; with people who in his view have had deficient experiences in two out of the three areas of the self (ambitions, ideals, and talents and skills). Such persons are vulnerable to narcissistic injuries, real or imagined, to which they respond with anxiety or fragmentation. They become easily hurt and defensive and are unable to sustain a good self-esteem under disappointment or rejections. They may become lonely and feel empty or become unduly aggressive.

Whereas narcissistic personalities have achieved a cohesive self, however vulnerable, borderline patients have not achieved such cohesiveness. Thus borderlines and lesser developed personalities such as schizoids, paranoids, and psychotics are not candidates for psychoanalysis. Neurotic persons can be dealt with primarily by attending to the fear of rejection and the inadequate self-supports.

Much of Kohut's work relates to the transference phenomenon occurring in analysis. If the therapist is empathic (loving) and distant without being disinterested, the patient projects his or her narcissistic injury on the therapist, allowing the basic analytic work to progress and resolve such injuries. The malfunctions associated with early damage are alleviated by the analyst allowing the patient freedom to be appropriately narcissistic. The therapist seeks to replace archaic self-object constructs with realistic appraisals of self and others. This is done by the therapist being empathic for the patient and concentrating on developing the person's ability to cope with disappointment. The therapist thus serves to encourage both poles of the self, ambitions and ideals, by serving first as the idealized parental image and then as a real person. Kohut has now been generally accepted as providing a hallmark way of understanding the development of the self as well as the importance of the therapist's role in helping persons with inadequate self-development.

References

Kohut, H. (1971). *The analysis of the self*. New York: International Universities Press.

Kohut, H. (1977). *The restoration of the self*. New York: International Universities Press.

R. B. JOHNSON

See PSYCHOANALYTIC PSYCHOLOGY.

Self Theory. Carl Rogers developed his self theory well after he had formulated his person-centered therapy. His view of personality grew out of his view of therapy, and the former can be understood only in the context of the latter.

In order to account for the personal changes that he observed clients going through in therapy, Rogers formulated his structural view of personality. Subsequently he formulated a statement on how personality evolves, which constitutes his theory of personality development. Finally, in answer to the question What sort of person would emerge as the end product of a growth experience of the person-centered type? he formulated his normative, or ideal, view of personality.

Structural Perspective. Rogers's earliest (structural) theory of personality (Rogers, 1951) coincides with the time when his overall thinking was still structure bound rather than process-oriented. He presented it in the form of 19 propositions.

The first seven propositions deal with the human organism and how it functions in its environment. According to Rogers, it functions as an organized whole, and as such it reacts to an experienced or perceived environment. It has only one motivating tendency: to actualize and enhance itself by fulfilling its experienced needs in a perceived world. This actualizing activity Rogers calls behavior.

The next five propositions deal with the development and function of the self. In accordance with the actualizing tendency the self differentiates out of the organism's total perceptual field. It becomes elaborated through the organism's interaction with its social environment, and it carries within itself values that are derived from both the organism and the social environment. The latter values are frequently perceived distortedly as coming from the organism rather than from the environment. Once the self has become established, it becomes that entity in relation to which all the experiences of a person become symbolized and perceived. The organism also tends to adopt only those ways of behaving that are consistent with this self-structure.

The next four propositions (13–16) deal with psychological maladjustment. Maladjustment occurs when certain organic experiences generate behaviors that are inconsistent with the self-structure. These may be significant experiences and thus need not be related to the self. But because of their inconsistency with the self they are not taken up into the self-structure. The result of this is psychological tension. Experiences that are inconsistent with the self come to be perceived as a threat to the self, and in defense against this the self-concept tends to become more rigid, thereby shutting out an increasing number of significant experiences. The final three propositions (17–19) describe how this trend can be reversed. Under certain conditions, when there is no external threat to the self-structure, these inconsistent experiences may be allowed into awareness to be assimilated into a revised self-structure. When this occurs, a person becomes more integrated within himself or herself and thus also more accepting of others. Finally, he or she will replace the present value system with a more fluid organismic valuing process as a guide for life.

Developmental Perspective. In his theory of the development of personality and the dynamics of behavior Rogers describes how the human infant develops into a full-fledged personality and how disintegrations and reintegrations can occur during this development. The characteristics of the human infant are essentially those of the human organism. For infants, experience is reality. They react to their experience in an organized, total fashion and in accordance with their tendency to actualize themselves. They value their experiences in terms of whether those experiences enhance their organism. They behave with adience toward those that do and with avoidance toward those that do not.

As infants mature, certain experiences related to themselves differentiate out of their total experiential world and become perceptually organized into a self-concept. Together with this newly developed awareness of self, growing infants also develop a need to be regarded positively by significant others in their surroundings. This is a potent force in their lives. Because of it growing children are no longer exclusively oriented toward their own organismic valuing process but become at least partially oriented to the values of others.

These positive-regard satisfactions and frustrations can also come to be experienced by children apart from the positive-regard transactions they may have with others around them. When this happens the children have, as it were, become their own significant social other. They have come to regard themselves positively or negatively, independent of what others say about them. This Rogers calls self-regard.

Whenever significant others selectively value some aspects of the child as more worthy of positive regard than others, the child tends to become similarly selective in his or her self-regard. The child then begins to avoid or seek out certain self-experiences solely in terms of whether they are worthy of self-regard. Whenever that occurs, the child is said to have acquired conditions of worth. If, however, the growing child were to experience only unconditional positive regard from others, then no conditions of worth would develop in him or her; self-regard would thus also be unconditional and the need for positive regard and self-regard would never be at variance with his or her organismic evaluation. For Rogers this would represent a fully functioning, psychologically well-adjusted individual.

However, this is not what happens in child development. More often than not development produces individuals who have conditions of worth. Because of their need for self-regard such individuals tend to perceive their experiences selectively, symbolizing those experiences that are consistent with their current self-concept and barring from awareness those experiences that are not. An incongruence thus arises between their selves and their experience. This tends to produce discrepancies in their behavior as well. Behaviors that enhance their self-concept will be at odds with behaviors that, while enhancing their total organism, are inconsistent with their self-concept.

If individuals have accumulated such a large degree of incongruence between self and experience that they can hardly keep it from coming to awareness, they become anxious. When their incongruence has increased to such proportions that they can no longer defend their self against it, the self disintegrates and the organism becomes disorganized. In such a state the organism may at one time behave in ways that are consistent with the self and at other times in ways that are not.

This confused regnancy in the individual's organism is the end result of the process of defense that started when individuals obtained their first conditions of worth. The process can be reversed by decreasing individuals' conditions of worth and by increasing their unconditional self-regard. The conditional positive regard of others gave individuals their conditions of worth and caused them to be conditional in their self-regard. By the same reasoning others can remove these by making their positive regard toward an individual unconditional. This effectively eliminates the threat against which individuals defend their self-concept. With the threat removed, the process of defense can begin to reverse itself. Individuals can symbolize more and more of their experiences into their awareness. They can revise and broaden their self-concept to include these new experiences and as a result can become more and more integrated. Thus they experience increased psychological adjustment and, like the infant, once again use their own organismic valuing process to regulate their behavior. The final result of this therapeutic process is that the individual becomes more and more of a fully functioning person.

Normative Perspective. The fully functioning person is the ultimate in actualization of the human organism. As a matter of fact, such a person does not exist. There are only persons moving in the direction of fully functioning without ever reaching it. Thus the description of a fully functioning person is pure form. It is an ideal or normative description of personality functioning (Rogers, 1969). Rogers's normative description coincides with that period in his development when his thinking had become fully dynamic and process-oriented. It asks the question What is an optimal person?

Such a person is fully open to his or her experience. Every stimulus originating in the organism or the environment is freely relayed through the nervous system without distortion. There are no barriers to fully experiencing whatever is organismically present.

Second, such a person lives in an existential fashion. Each moment is new to him or her. No one can predict what the person will do the next moment, since what he or she will do grows out of that moment. In such existential living the self and personality emerge from experience, rather than experience being twisted to fit a preconceived self-structure. This means that one becomes a participant in and an observer of the ongoing process of organismic experience rather than being in control over it.

Such living in the moment means an absence of rigidity, of tight organization, of the imposition of structure on experience. It means instead a maximum of adaptability, a discovery of structure in experience, a flowing, changing organization of self and personality, of which the most stable characteristics are openness to experience and the flexible resolution of one's existing needs in the existing environment.

Finally, such a person finds his or her organism a trustworthy means of arriving at the most satisfying behavior in each existential situation. He or she does what feels right in this immediate moment and generally finds this to be a competent and trustworthy guide for behavior.

Rogers compares the organism of such a person to a giant computer. Because such a person is open to experience, he or she has access to all the available data in the situation. Out of all these his or her organism comes up with the most economical avenue of need satisfaction in this existential situation. That is, it comes up with a way of behaving that feels right.

It is not infallible, however. Even the organism of a fully functioning person makes mistakes because at times some of the data will be missing. But this is not serious, since being open to experience, the fully functioning person can quickly spot that error and quickly correct it. The computations of such a person will always be in a process of being corrected, because they will be continually checked against resulting behavior.

The fully functioning person who emerges from a theoretically optimal experience of personal growth is able to live fully in and with each and all of his or her feelings and reactions. This person makes use of his or her organic equipment to sense as accurately as possible the existential situation within and without. He or she uses all of these data in awareness but recognizes that the total organism may be and often is wiser than his or her awareness. This person allows the total organism in all its complexity to select from the multitude of possibilities that behavior that in this moment of time will be most generally and genuinely satisfying. He or she trusts the organism in its functioning not because it is infallible but because he or she can be fully open to the consequences of each action and can correct those that prove to be less than satisfying.

Such persons can experience all of their feelings and are afraid of none. They are their own sifters of evidence but are open to evidence from all sources. They are completely engaged in the process of being and becoming themselves and thus discover that they are soundly and realistically social. They live completely in this moment but learn that this is the soundest living for all time. They are fully functioning organisms, and because of the awareness of self that flows freely in and through their experiences they are fully functioning persons.

In Rogers's view of personality organismic processes take preeminence over self-processes. In this respect also he oriented himself more to John Dewey's pragmatism than to existentialism or phenomenology. Thus his theory of personality is not a self theory but an organismic theory. Growth rather than self-consistency is the basic intent of his view of personality.

Rogers believes in the inherent goodness, or positive directedness, of the individual person. He localizes the origin of evil, or negative directedness, in the environment—that is, in the way significant others relate to the individual person. But he fails to explain how it is possible that inherently good persons become evil to each other when they relate to each other.

By identifying the problem of evil with a defect in one part of created human reality, Rogers fails to recognize that evil is sin: a matter of the human heart. He does not acknowledge that like redemption sin, and therefore evil, is total; that evil, like our deliverance from evil, affects the whole of created human reality. Because of his attitude he is driven to overvalue personality (our individual separateness) and to devalue communality (our membership in larger social wholes). This means that Rogers's view of personality cannot account for the positive effect of socialization on the growth and development of personality.

References

Rogers, C. R. (1951). *Client-centered therapy*. Boston: Houghton Mifflin.

Rogers, C. R. (1969). *Freedom to learn*. Columbus, OH: Merrill.

H. A. Van Belle

See Person-Centered Therapy.

Self-Actualization. A major concept in organismic theories of personality. Organismic theories emphasize the unity, integrity, and organization of the organism as opposed to theories that segregate mind and body. Organismic theories begin with the assumption that the individual is an organized whole. One drive provides the motivation for all behaviors. Self-actualization operates as the sovereign motive for a plethora of individual actions. Specialized drives (e.g., aggressive, consummatory, and sexual impulses) are surface manifestations of the generalized drive of self-actualization. Self-actualization, operating as a comprehensive motive, accounts for the individual's striving to fulfill inherent potentialities.

Kurt Goldstein first developed self-actualization as a major theoretical construct. Influenced by Gestalt psychology, he believed the primary psychological organization operating in personality is the figure-ground relation. The figure is the principal, dominant, or consistent behavior of the organism that appears against the backdrop (ground) of lesser behaviors and environmental processes.

Organisms prefer natural figures and manifest them in flexible, orderly responses to situations. Natural figures reflect the underlying potentials of the organism. Unnatural figures result when tasks are imposed upon the person by intense situations. As a consequence of unnatural figures the person's behavior may be rigid, inappropriate, and nonadapting. For Goldstein physical and psychological health requires natural figures.

New figures emerge as the fundamental tasks of life change. Behind various figures is the drive to achieve one's innate potentialities. This striving for achievement of one's potential is termed self-actualization, and it induces the organism to replenish any deficiency or deprivation. The organism achieves stability when energy is balanced throughout the organism.

Self-actualization is a universal, natural phenomenon that is expressed in various ways. The different expressions depend in part on the surrounding sociocultural milieu and the individual's potentialities. Goldstein maintained that the best method to define one's potentialities is to list one's preferences, especially as found in natural figures.

Although Goldstein favored organismic variables within the individual as the cause of behavior, he did not conceive of the organism as immune from the environment. Self-actualization depends on the organism coming to terms with the environment. In doing so, opportunities to self-actualize would be possible as the individual avoided or conquered obstructions, threats, and pressures.

A second organismic theory of personality was proposed by Andras Angyal, who conceived of the organism and its environment as a unit called the biosphere. The biosphere and other systems normally evolve into differentiated yet interdependent systems. A general principle in nature, which Angyal called self-expansion, integrates these tendencies. A system such as personality expands and differentiates so long as it does not endanger its unity. Although Angyal's terms are unique, the parallel to self-actualization is obvious.

Self-actualization is most closely associated with Abraham Maslow and Carl Rogers. Maslow's (1970) holistic-organismic theory asserts that human behavior is motivated by basic needs (deficiency or D motives) and metaneeds (being or B motives). Basic needs are arranged in a hierarchical manner in which fundamental needs must be satisfied before higher needs can exert their influence. If an organism has a deficiency need, it acts to remove the deficit. Basic needs are dominant over the metaneeds and are ordered in a hierarchy: physiological needs, safety needs, belongingness and love needs, self-esteem, and self-actualization. Metaneeds are growth needs related to justice, truth, goodness, beauty, law and order, and perfection.

In an attempt to develop a healthy psychology Maslow made an extensive study of self-actualizers, including Abraham Lincoln, Thomas Jefferson, Walt Whitman, Henry David Thoreau, Albert Einstein, and Eleanor Roosevelt. Unique attributes of self-actualizers include a realistic orientation to life; acceptance of self, others, and nature; spontaneity; problem-centeredness instead of self-centeredness; and an air of detachment. Self-actualizers need periodic privacy, show autonomy and independence, have a fresh appreciation of people and things, experience profound mystical or religious experiences, identify with the human race, develop deep and intimate relationships with a few specially loved people, and evidence democratic values and attitudes. Furthermore, self-actualizers distinguish between means and ends, have a philosophical sense of humor and a high degree of creativity, and resist enculturation. Peak experiences seem to be a focal point in self-actualizers (Maslow, 1964). Because basic needs are predominant self-actualization is expected only in some mature adults.

Rogers's personality theory has much in common with that of Maslow. A major similarity is the commitment to an organismic perspective that asserts one master life force. However, Rogers expresses a positive and optimistic view of human nature. Human nature is innately good; the individual becomes a free, independent, and purposive person when he or she is unencumbered by a restrictive environment. This Rousseaulike position reflects Rogers's therapeutic experience and religious orientation. Humans live up to their fullest potentialities when they are free to experience and free to satisfy their inner nature.

A central construct in Rogers's theory is the actualizing tendency, which manifests itself through self-maintenance, self-enhancement, self-actualization, and the organismic valuing process. As the only motivational construct the actualizing tendency is a biological force that motivates the individual to seek fulfillment of inborn tendencies. The actualizing tendency drives the person to become more fully human. For Rogers becoming fully human is the essence of life. The actualizing tendency is "the inherent tendency of the organism to develop all its capacities in ways which serve to maintain or enhance the person" (Rogers, 1959, p. 196).

The motives advocated by other theorists are held as surface evidences of the underlying actualizing tendency, which serves the individual by reducing tensions in response to deficiency needs by means of basic organismic maintenance processes. From a psychological perspective the individual possesses a sense of personal identity (i.e., self-concept) and is devoted to maintaining self-concept. Rogers termed this self-maintenance.

Other activities of the organism serve to increase tension for the purpose of enhancing the organism. Rather than maintaining an even distribution of energy (cf. homeostasis, tension reduction in Sigmund Freud, and entropy in Carl Gustav Jung), the individual actively concentrates energy upon an area of life. Self-enhancement is a similar process geared toward development of an area of self.

To Rogers self-actualization is a special case of the actualizing tendency applied to the portion of experience represented by the self-concept. To the extent that self-actualization is unified with the organismic valuing process, the individual is well-adjusted.

Rogers addressed the question of how an organism selects certain experiences to maintain or enhance itself while it avoids others not conducive to growth. The organismic valuing process, a special process within the actualizing tendency, serves to answer that question. Experiences are evaluated against a criterion. Experiences that are perceived as maintaining or enhancing the organism are valued and sought, while experiences that oppose maintenance or enhancement are devalued and avoided. The actualizing tendency assists the individual in becoming more adequate.

As Maslow studied self-actualized individuals, Rogers undertook a study of the fully functioning person. Individuals who are using their talents, realizing potentials, and moving toward a more complete knowledge and experience are described as fully functioning. Rogers (1961) listed the attributes of such an individual. The fully functioning individual is open to experience whereby the self is congruent with that experience and there is no need for defensiveness. Existential living describes the person who lives each moment to its fullest. In making decisions the fully functioning person relies on personal judgment and choice instead of social code or institutional convention. This concept of the good life also includes existential freedom, a subjective freedom in which one is free to live as one chooses and the individual accepts personal responsibility for actions. The optimally adjusted individual is also creative. The fully functioning individual is in tune with inborn potentialities, responds creatively and adaptively to changing environments, and is not a conformer or prisoner of society (cf. Maslow's self-actualizing personalities).

Some individuals point out similarities between the psychological concept of self-actualization and the theological doctrine of sanctification. Sanctification normally suggests the transformation of the person toward being more Christlike, becoming more the human God intends. Sanctification includes crises (cf. peak experiences with Wesleyan-Arminian entire sanctification) and process (cf. growth in grace). If God is the author of the actualizing tendency, it may well be that sanctification and self-actualization are essentially the same experience expressed in different terms.

References

Maslow, A. (1964). *Religions, values and peak experiences.* Columbus: Ohio State University Press.

Maslow, A. (1970). *Motivation and personality* (2nd ed.). New York: Harper & Row.

Rogers, C. R. (1959). A theory of therapy, personality and interpersonal relationships, as developed in the client-centered framework. In S. Koch (Ed.), *Psychology: A study of a science* (Vol. 3). New York: McGraw-Hill.

Rogers, C. R. (1961). *On becoming a person.* Boston: Houghton Mifflin.

R. L. Timpe

See Humanistic Psychology.

Self-Alienation. Alienation can be analyzed in terms of four ruptured relationships: between God and person, between persons, within a person, and between persons and nature. Self-alienation, the disharmony and divisiveness within an individual, is readily apparent from the extent of human maladaptive behavior (e.g., neuroses, psychoses, alcoholism, drug addiction, acts of violence, and suicide).

Many hypotheses are offered to explain the divisiveness within human nature. Sigmund Freud proposed a split between the conscious and the unconscious, wherein the larger part of human motivation is purported to lie beneath the surface of awareness. This accounts for the defense mechanisms that control human behavior and direct it in ways unknown to the individual. Other writers refer to the split between cerebral-intellectual and affective-emotional functions (Fromm, 1968) or the pitting of intellect against feeling, reason against passion, and head against heart (Roszak, 1969).

Personal meaninglessness in present times has been the theme of Frankl (1963) and his school of logotherapy. According to Frankl, inner emptiness and meaninglessness are elements of an existential vacuum, leading to frustration and neurosis. May (1967) sees self-alienation in terms of a loss of personal significance, contending that contemporary people are hollow, lacking a center of personal strength and values. In a brilliant analysis of the effects of accelerative change on people Toffler (1970) discusses the impact of overloading on sensory, cognitive, and decisional levels of personal functioning.

The Judeo-Christian tradition places self-alienation consequent to the rebellion of original humankind, as described in the Book of Genesis. Adam and Eve, because of their pride and disobedience, were punished by banishment from the garden of Eden, the state of perfect friendship with God. The resultant human condition, shared by all of Adam and Eve's descendants, is characterized by suffering, guilt, and death, as well as a darkened intelligence and weakened will (Hammes, 1978). Paul reflects on the internal divisiveness of human nature in his comment on the law of the spirit and the law of the flesh as being in conflict (Rom. 7:17–25).

References

Frankl, V. E. (1963). *Man's search for meaning.* Boston: Beacon.

Fromm, E. (1968). *The revolution of hope.* New York: Harper & Row.

Hammes, J. A. (1978). *Human destiny: Exploring today's value systems.* Huntington, IN: Our Sunday Visitor.

May, R. (1967). *Psychology and the human dilemma.* Princeton, NJ: Van Nostrand.

Roszak, T. (1969). *The making of a counter culture.* Garden City, NY: Doubleday.

Toffler, A. (1970). *Future shock.* New York: Random House.

J. A. Hammes

See Existential Psychology and Psychotherapy.

Self-Concept. The constellation of perceptions and attitudes that a person maintains with regard to himself or herself. To speak of the self-concept in the singular is somewhat misleading, since there are many different selves or more accurately aspects of the self that are perceived and evaluated. One particular self-concept measure, the Tennessee Self-Concept Scale (Fitts, 1965), has identified eight different aspects of the self: identity self, judging self, behavioral self, physical self, moral-ethical self, personal self, family self, and social self. This is not necessarily an exhaustive list, nor is it the only way in which the various parts of the self can be conceptualized, but it serves to illustrate the complexity of this psychological construct.

An aspect of the self-concept that is of great interest to counselors and psychotherapists is the personal self, or what is more commonly known as self-esteem. This is defined by Coopersmith (1967) as "the evaluation which the individual makes and customarily maintains with regard to himself: it expresses an attitude of approval or disapproval, and indicates the extent to which the individual believes himself to be capable, significant, successful, and worthy" (p. 5). Research studies have found that persons with low self-esteem are generally more influenced by pessimism and threat; are less capable of resisting pressures to conform; and are more burdened by fears, ambivalence, and self-doubt than persons with high self-esteem. In addition, individuals possessing high self-esteem tend to assume a more active role in social groups, to express their views more frequently, and are generally more creative than are their low self-esteem counterparts (Coopersmith, 1967).

Other research studies have found a positive correlation between high self-esteem (characterized by self-acceptance) and the acceptance of others. That is, those who feel positively about themselves tend to feel the same way toward others, while those who dislike themselves tend to express the same rejecting attitude toward those around them. A similar study found that those who are self-accepting also perceive others as being accepting, whereas those disliking themselves tend to see others as having a similar rejecting attitude.

This latter finding ties in well with research examining the relationship between self-esteem and concept of God. These studies found that persons with low self-esteem tend to conceive of God as critical, rejecting, and distant, whereas those with high self-esteem tend to see God as more loving, personal, and close (Bixler, 1979). Since children often attribute to God the characteristics of their parents (Nelson, 1971), it would be logical to assume that an abused or neglected child would simultaneously develop a poor self-concept and a negative God concept.

The negative effects of a poor self-concept on interpersonal and intrapsychic functioning are thus well researched and documented. In addition, most counselors could cite numerous case examples attesting to the destructiveness inherent in the self-condemning attitudes of their clients. For these reasons many Christian therapists have championed the notion that self-esteem is an important and necessary part of the healthy personality and is therefore to be cultivated in therapy.

This viewpoint is not, however, without its critics. Vitz (1977), for example, argues that the emphasis on self-love and self-realization is antithetical to the biblical idea of love and is a product of secular humanism. He further states that secular psychology promotes self-worship while disparaging or ignoring traditional Christian virtues such as humility, obedience, and self-sacrifice.

When it is examined closely, the apparent conflict between these two perspectives may be more apparent than real. The warnings against sinful pride and the advocacy of Christian self-esteem may be seen as complementary rather than contradictory once the semantic and theological ambiguities are cleared up.

Those who are critical of the Christian self-esteem movement tend to emphasize the doctrine of total depravity, which holds that in every respect humans are inherently exploitative and self-seeking. To these critics the notion of Christian self-love is not only a contradiction in terms; it implies that self-centeredness is the solution rather than the problem. The major strength of this critique lies in its faithfulness to the biblical witness regarding the inherent sinfulness of the human race. Since most theologians define root sin as pride or self-love, it would seem that this would eliminate any notion of Christian self-love. However, the force of this argument is mitigated by the fact that most advocates of Christian self-esteem mean self-acceptance when they speak of self-love.

Self-acceptance does not imply a denial of the doctrine of depravity; rather, it recognizes that something has been added to it. According to Hoekema (1975), this means that "since believers now belong to Christ's new creation, we are to see ourselves as new creatures in Christ, not just as depraved sinners. To be sure, apart from Christ, we are sinners, but we are no longer apart from Christ. In Christ we are now justified sinners, sinners who have the Holy Spirit dwelling within. Our way of looking at ourselves must not deny this newness, but affirm it" (p. 55).

Christians must continue to be wary of becoming prideful and self-centered, since the old nature continues to exist. In a real sense the self-concept must remain in the eschatological tension between the already and the not yet. Christians are new creatures in Christ who still must be wary of selfishness. It is this need for wariness that prompts the warnings from the critics of Christian self-esteem.

However, a positive self-concept grounded in God's unconditional, electing love in Christ does not lead to selfishness. Rather, it relieves Christians of the burden of having to generate feelings of self-worth based on performance. Since they need not be slaves to ego-enhancing behavior, they can be free to be unselfish and to manifest virtues such as sacrifice, obedience, and humility. But without a healthy self-acceptance the practice of these virtues can easily become a neurotic striving to gain God's approval.

Christian self-esteem, rightly understood, does not lead to exploitative self-centeredness but rather to an appreciation and acceptance of oneself and one's neighbor. This truth is beautifully expressed by Lewis (1942) in *The Screwtape Letters* when Screwtape writes: "The Enemy [God] wants him [man], in the end, to be so free from any bias in his own favor that he can rejoice in his own talents as frankly and gratefully as in his neighbor's talents. . . . He wants each man, in the long run, to be able to recognize all creatures (even himself) as glorious and excellent things. He wants to kill their animal self-love as soon as possible; but it is His long-term policy, I fear, to restore to them a new kind of self-love—a charity and gratitude for all selves, including their own; when they have really learned to love their neighbors as themselves, they will be allowed to love themselves as their neighbors" (pp. 64–65).

References

Bixler, W. G. (1979). *Self-concept/God-concept congruency as a function of differential need for esteem and consistency.* Unpublished doctoral dissertation, Fuller Theological Seminary Graduate School of Psychology.

Coopersmith, S. (1967). *The antecedents of self-esteem.* San Francisco: Freeman.

Fitts, W. (1965). *Tennessee self-concept scale: Manual.* Nashville: Counselor Recordings and Tests.

Hoekema, A. (1975). *The Christian looks at himself.* Grand Rapids, MI: Eerdmans.

Lewis, C. S. (1942). *The Screwtape letters.* London: Centenary.

Nelson, M. (1971). The concept of God and feelings toward parents. *Journal of Individual Psychology, 27,* 46–49.

Vitz, P. (1977). *Psychology as religion: The cult of self-worship.* Grand Rapids, MI: Eerdmans.

W. G. BIXLER

See SELF; SELF-CONSCIOUSNESS.

Self-Concept Tests. The measurement of self-concept has been complicated by the problems of defining this construct. There are at least 30 measures of self-esteem and self-concept (Robinson & Shaver, 1973). Psychotherapists are especially concerned with the measurement of self-esteem, since improvements in this area are often thought to be the most important measure of effective psychotherapy (Prochaska, 1979). What is needed is systematic validation work so that we can more accurately and meaningfully measure these constructs.

Of the available measures the Tennessee Self-Concept Scale (Fitts, 1965) and the Piers-Harris Children's Self-Concept Scale (Piers, 1969) are the most highly recommended. The tests are psychometrically superior to the many other scales available. A third measure, the Janis-Field Feelings of Inadequacy Scale (Eagly, 1967), is widely used. Two scales that were especially developed for children but have also been widely used with adults are the Self-Esteem Scale (Rosenberg, 1965) and the Self-Esteem Inventory (Coopersmith, 1967).

Finally, three scales that attempt to measure the discrepancy between the real and idealized self are the Index of Adjustment and Values (Bills, Vance, & McLean, 1951), the Butler-Haigh Q-Sort (Butler & Haigh, 1954), and the Miskimins Self-Goal-Other Discrepancy Scale (Miskimins & Braucht, 1971).

Self-esteem has also been informally assessed from such self-report inventories as the Minnesota Multiphasic Personality Inventory (MMPI), the Personality Research Form (PRF), the California Personality Inventory (CPI), and the Adjective Checklist, as well as the varied projective assessment measures. This approach is at best intuitive and highly dependent on the assessment skills of the examiner. It is not recommended from either a clinical or psychometric perspective, in light of the definitional confusion.

Self-concept and self-esteem are closely related constructs. Both are plagued with ambiguities. The eight scales mentioned are widely considered to be the best of the many current scales specifically designed to measure them. Clinicians who use these measures must realize the limitations of present tests due to the sparse data available about the validity of these theoretical constructs.

References

Bills, R. E., Vance, E. L., & McLean, O. S. (1951). An index of adjustment and values. *Journal of Consulting Psychology, 15,* 257–261.

Butler, J., & Haigh, G. (1954). Changes in the relation between self-concepts and ideal concepts consequent upon client-centered counseling. In C. R. Rogers & R. F. Dymond (Eds.), *Psychotherapy and personality change.* Chicago: University of Chicago Press.

Coopersmith, S. (1967). *The antecedents of self-esteem.* San Francisco: Freeman.

Eagly, A. H. (1967). Involvement as a determinant of response to favorable and unfavorable information. *Journal of Personality and Social Psychology, 7,* 1–5. (Monograph) (Whole No. 643).

Fitts, W. (1965). *Tennessee self-concept scale: Manual.* Nashville: Counselor Recordings and Tests.

Miskimins, R. W., & Braucht, G. (1971). *Description of the self.* Fort Collins, CO: Rocky Mountain Behavioral Sciences Institute.

Piers, E. (1969). *Manual for the Piers-Harris children's self-concept scale.* Nashville: Counselor Recordings and Tests.

Prochaska, J. O. (1979). *Systems of psychotherapy: A transtheoretical approach.* Homewood, IL: Dorsey.

Robinson, J. P., & Shaver, P. R. (1973). *Measures of social psychological attitudes* (Rev. ed.). Ann Arbor, MI: Survey Research Center.

Rosenberg, M. (1965). *Society and the adolescent self-image.* Princeton, NJ: Princeton University Press.

R. E. BUTMAN

See PSYCHOLOGICAL MEASUREMENT; PERSONALITY ASSESSMENT.

Self-Congruence. *See* CONGRUENCE.

Self-Consciousness. This term has two major meanings, both of which are of interest to psychologists. First, self-consciousness refers to the awareness that humans have of their own selves: their behaviors, feelings, and thoughts. The term implies that this awareness extends to knowing; that these thoughts, feelings, and acts originate in the self rather than in some source outside the self. This characteristic—the ability to reflect on and be aware of one's self—is a major factor separating humans from the animal kingdom.

Second, self-consciousness is an ill-at-ease feeling experienced by a person who is uncomfortably aware of self in social situations. This is probably a feeling universally experienced at some time or another, since shyness is a common phenomenon. The self-conscious person will approach a gathering of people, strangers or friends, and experience a painful rush of feelings that everyone in the room is staring at him or her. Furthermore, the self-conscious person will also be convinced that everyone is evaluating him or her and that rejection is imminent. Although it may appear quiet and subdued on the outside, the self-conscious person's internal life is "a maze of thought highways cluttered with head-on collisions of sensations and noisy traffic jams of frustrated desires" (Zimbardo, 1977, p. 29).

Researchers vary in how they categorize self-consciousness. Some see it as central to the concept of shyness. Buss (1980) describes self-consciousness as having two major manifestations: public (concern with the observable self and how others interact and react to it) and private (preoccupation with feelings, fantasies, and motives that are not seen by the public). The privately self-conscious person is concerned about the inadequacies and shortcomings of the self and thus is caught in a destructive mode of thinking. Buss feels that when public self-consciousness goes awry (i.e., when it becomes elaborate and extensive) social anxiety is the result. For Buss social anxiety is embarrassment, shame, audience anxiety, and shyness. Hence self-consciousness is a precursor of and an even larger concept than shyness.

To other researchers, however, self-consciousness is a part of the larger framework of shyness. Crozier (1979b) views self-consciousness as a part of shyness and sees it as related to deficient or nonexistent assertiveness. Crozier conceptualizes shyness as an anxious feeling in social situations that makes a person want to withdraw from interaction with others. Shyness is accompanied by feelings of unhappiness, preoccupation with self, inhibition, and self-consciousness. Crozier defines situations that provoke self-consciousness as those that make or are seen to make large demands on one's competence or that increase or seem to increase the possibility of being criticized.

Most researchers agree that shyness (tension and inhibition around others) and sociability (the desire to be with others) are separate personality factors (Cheek & Buss, 1981). A consensus also seems to exist that self-consciousness, reticence, and low self-esteem fit together and are related to one another (Crozier, 1979a). Therapy for shyness and self-consciousness is most effective when it consists of methods designed to improve social skills rather than methods seeking to stimulate insight.

References

Buss, A. H. (1980). *Self-consciousness and social anxiety.* San Francisco: Freeman.

Cheek, J. M., & Buss, A. H. (1981). Shyness and sociability. *Journal of Personality and Social Psychology, 41* (2), 330–339.

Crozier, W. R. (1979a). Shyness as anxious self-preoccupation. *Psychological Reports, 44* (3), 959–962.

Crozier, W. R. (1979b). Shyness as a dimension of personality. *British Journal of Social and Clinical Psychology, 18* (1), 121–128.

Zimbardo, P. G. (1977). *Shyness: What it is and what to do about it.* Reading, MA: Addison-Wesley.

J. R. Beck

See Self-Concept.

Self-Control. In its most limited definition the term refers to an individual lowering the probability that he or she will engage in an undesirable behavior by manipulating a controlling response. A controlling response is a behavior that changes the likelihood that the target behavior will occur. The target behavior is the response the person is trying to modify. In its broader definition self-control is a label for all forms of self-change, self-management, self-modification, and self-regulation. Self-control may include the use of controlling responses to weaken, to strengthen, or to maintain a target behavior.

Human reflection on self-control has a very long history. The Greeks wrote about methods of self-control four thousand years ago, and Paul encouraged temperance (a limited form of self-control) when writing to the early Christians (1 Cor. 9:24–27). In contrast to such early encouragements of self-control, a systematic exploration of how people can regulate their own behavior has a very short history.

Skinner (1953) played an important role in launching the contemporary research on self-regulation. He included a chapter on self-control in *Science and Human Behavior* (1953), a chapter that had a catalytic impact on laboratory studies of self-control during the 1960s. Perhaps the most prolific of such investigators during this period were F. H. Kanfer and his associates. Through an extensive series of laboratory studies they evaluated the effects of self-evaluation and self-reinforcement. This basic research was soon followed by applied research on self-administered psychological treatments in children, adolescents, and adults. Not long after the publication of the first research articles on the clinical applications of self-control procedures the first book telling people how to control their own behavior in a systematic, scientific fashion appeared (Watson & Tharp, 1972).

Two major developments promoted the wedding of experimental psychology and a personal self-control technology. First, behavior therapy, or behavior modification, began as a new movement within psychology and psychiatry during the late 1950s. In contrast to most forms of psychotherapy that had developed during the first half of the twentieth century, behavior therapy was presented as a describable, teachable, applied science rather than an elusive art. Increasing clarity in defining and describing treatment procedures facilitated teaching future therapists, and this new specificity stimulated early behavior therapists to instruct their patients to carry out some of the treatment procedures on themselves.

The second major development that accelerated the growth of self-control methods was biofeedback. In the 1960s laboratory scientists investigated the possibilities of instrumentally conditioning autonomic processes. Their work suggested that persons can learn to control responses that psychologists had traditionally assumed to be involuntary. For example, persons may be able to learn to raise or lower their own skin temperature or blood pressure on command.

The conceptual models underlying both behavior therapy and biofeedback supported the assumption that individuals control themselves through the same kinds of operations they use to influence other persons.

One procedure that may be used in self-control is the administration of setting events. Setting events are powerful factors that change a person's activity level or alter the individual's sensitivity to particular cues and consequences. The more common setting events are deprivation schedules, satiation schedules, psychotropic drugs, physical restraints, providing choices, pleasant stimulation, aversive stimulation, and providing a caring relationship.

Another self-control procedure is the use of cues (discriminative stimuli) and prods (unconditioned or conditioned stimuli). Whereas setting events alter the general state of the individual, cues and prods impact a relatively narrow band of behavior. Common self-regulation procedures based on cues or prods include choosing and defining a target behavior, presenting an immediate cue or prod for the target behavior, setting goals, setting performance standards for consequating the target behavior, writing a performance contract, choosing reinforcers in advance, and providing a behavioral model.

A third self-management strategy is primary behavior. Individuals hold a unique position as behavior modifiers; they can directly modify their own behavior by practicing a desired behavior, by engaging in a response that competes with an undesired behavior, or by withholding an undesired behavior. In contrast, there is no way one person can directly produce actions in another individual. Although counseling and psychotherapy have neglected the role of practice in changing human behavior, athletics and the performing arts have carefully attended to this aspect of the psychology of self-regulation.

Consequences and feedback are a fourth means of self-control. These interventions include self-observation, self-recording, comparing performance with a goal, and self-reinforcing or self-punishing.

All these various elements may be combined into self-administered treatment packages comparable to those administered by professional therapists in the past. The same kinds of strategies may be used to promote self-control in any person facing normal problems in living.

References

Skinner, B. F. (1953). *Science and human behavior.* New York: Macmillan.

Watson, D. L., & Tharp, R. G. (1972). *Self-directed behavior: Self-modification for personal adjustment.* Monterey, CA: Brooks/Cole.

P. W. CLEMENT

See SELF-MONITORING.

Self-Defeating Behavior. *See* SELF-HANDICAPPING.

Self-Denial. Narcissism is often glorified, and the media thrust such persons at us as role models. Yet this is also a time in which people struggle with a despairing sense of lost or undeveloped self. The teachings of Christ about self-denial are vital for people struggling with these paradoxical extremes.

Biblical Teachings about Self-Denial. The phrase *deny himself* occurs in only one event, although that is recorded in three Gospels (Matt. 16:24–25; Mark 8:34–37; Luke 9:23–24). Self-denial is described in other passages (Matt. 10:37–39; Luke 14:25–27; 17:33; John 12:25–26) in terms of our putting service to God first and giving up having self-needs as our highest priority. Jesus declared this to be his life purpose (John 4:34). The most profound description of self-denial is that in Philippians 2:5–11, which describes the example Jesus set for us in emptying himself of divine prerogatives in order to come to earth as a fully human person ready even to go to the cross. The wording *take up* declares that we are to take up the cross daily as a voluntary act, just as Jesus did. It is not something imposed upon us by God against our will.

Theology of Self-Denial. Jesus is the ultimate model of authentic life; that is, he lived life as it was created to be by the author of life for all humans to follow (Acts 3:15). Jesus did not glorify himself by becoming the center of an adoring cult of people who demeaned themselves in response to his demands. Instead he described himself as a suffering servant (Mark 9:35). Jesus was self-sacrificing and self-denying. This empowered him to be the ultimate giver of love to all humankind. He calls us to follow his supreme example so that we can fulfill our mission in life just as he did. Jesus took up his cross and became the Savior of the world, and he was taken up to glory (Acts 1:8–9). He has given us human hope that as we put God's work first, we too will have abundant life (John 10:10) as we fulfill our God-given mission on earth. Self-denial does not mean therefore that we become people of no consequence or value; instead it means that we become the very best that we can be. Because we love God, we trust that through service to God and to other people we may also have personal fulfillment.

Psychology of Self-Denial. From a cognitive theory perspective self-denial should not be confused with either self-rejection or self-centered thinking. In addition, by learning a form of positive self-talk, which affirms that we are valuable and so are the other people in our lives, we can avoid competitive or dominative patterns of thinking and behaving.

From a Gestalt theory perspective we may learn to share feelings in a trusting, open, and accountable community. In such a caring group we can enjoy putting the group's interests above our own and thereby reduce our tendencies toward the isolation inherent in hedonism. Through caring about the pleasure of others we may ourselves experience more delight in life. This integration will help us become ever more committed to the avoidance of pleasure gained at the expense of others.

From the perspective of family systems theory we are to be subject one to another (Eph. 5:21) rather than practice power and dominance. Children are not to be provoked into discouragement by parents (Eph. 6:4). Children are to obey their parents when they are minors (Eph. 6:1) and honor their parents when they become adults (Exod. 20:12). Thus parents are to help their children outgrow them rather than keep them subjugated throughout life. This is one form of parental self-denial.

Clinical Applications. Many people who have suffered trauma in childhood become self-rejecting and move into adulthood suffering from low self-esteem and depression. Others may have compensated for parental rejection by becoming self-centered, and they move into adulthood searching for those who will adore them. Yet another outcome may be that marital relationships are seriously impaired because the partners do not practice self-denial as they attempt to love each other. During inevitable conflicts they may seek to dominate the other as a self-protective strategy or evade the other because it feels too risky to make the self vulnerable. Other people suffering from childhood trauma may become codependent, which is a form of self-rejection rather than self-denial (*see* Codependency). The codependent individual sacrifices integrity in hope of pleasing the dominant person and thereby maintaining the relationship. Many people avoid these pathological outcomes by practicing self-denial in which they choose to take up the cross of suffering love.

In psychotherapy people may learn to value themselves more and at the same time become more self-denying. Self-esteem helps give deep meaning to self-denial. If a person believes he or she is of no value and yet volunteers to serve God, that person may not truly be an effective servant of God. The biblical way to build self-esteem is to do the best we can and be proud of what we have accomplished (Gal. 6:4). In biblical self-denial we seek to be good stewards of our talents by cultivating our God-given skills so that we will have even more to contribute to God's work (Matt. 25:14–30). Self-denial does not mean self-rejection. Jesus did not reject himself though in self-denial he did seek to do the work of his heavenly Father (Matt. 26:39). In Christian psychotherapy we may learn positive self-statements, identify personal skills, become motivated to gain further education for career advancement, and yet not in any way claim to be superior to someone else. We are not to make comparisons that are competitive with others (Gal. 6:4). We can practice self-denial by learning to think and act in terms of dedicating ourselves to doing God's will with this newly developed personhood.

Insight into childhood patterns may help individuals learn how they came to be self-rejecting or self-glorifying. These two errors are attempts to cover the serious distress of perceived parental rejection. People can increase self-esteem by celebrating personal growth with closest friends and then with others. They can grow in pride in personal accomplishments without claiming to be superior to anyone. Individuals can delight in accomplishments that are a partial fulfillment of God's will. Self-esteeming Christians can identify talents that have been given by God and identify possible new career paths, church service, and civic work that will fulfill those God-given gifts. These individuals will now have more capability for fulfilling God's call. Such Christians know that self-denial also leads to self-fulfillment.

H. Wahking

See Christian Growth; Religious Development.

Self-Destructive Behavior. Any of a number of stereotyped or repetitive behaviors by which an individual causes damage to his or her body. It is perhaps the most dramatic and extreme form of chronic human psychopathology. Baumeister and Rollings (1976) have called it "the most distressing and bizarre of all behavioral aberrations that people exhibit. . . . There are probably few among us . . . who do not experience a quickened sense of anguish upon witnessing a child beat and brutalize himself" (pp. 1–2).

Any analysis of this behavioral excess raises three fundamental questions: Why do some people repeatedly inflict injury upon themselves? Why does such behavior persist in the face of severe consequences? What can be done to modify such behavior? Consideration of these matters raises other complex issues, and answers are still only partial.

Self-injurious behavior is a serious problem with the mentally retarded in many institutionalized settings. Because of the possibility that the individual might inflict severe damage upon himself or herself, it is a problem that demands immediate attention on the part of the staff members. Such behavior forces people to respond. Like any other behavior, it increases with the presence of reinforcing consequences, and the attention of well-meaning adults is often precisely such a reinforcer. There are varied forms of self-injurious behavior, the most common being head banging, eye gouging, self-biting, self-scratching, tooth grinding, and rectal digging. These behaviors often occur in conjunction with other rhythmic stereotyped behaviors such as rocking, weaving, and finger flicking (Baumeister & Forehand, 1973). In certain cases the behavior appears to be part of the temporal pattern or topography of these stereotyped behaviors, whereas in other cases it appears to be under very specific stimulus control (Bachman, 1972). Some individuals will exhibit mild forms of self-injurious behavior that will be fairly stable and continuous, whereas others will show forms that occur in high-frequency bursts, resulting in serious tissue damage, only to cease once the injury has been inflicted. Shortly after the lesion heals, the individual will then exhibit another burst, and the cycle will be repeated, often for years.

There are five hypotheses about the etiology and/or maintenance of self-injurious behavior. The positive reinforcement hypothesis states that it is a learned operant, maintained by social reinforcement, which is delivered contingent upon the occurrence of the behavior. The negative reinforcement hypothesis suggests that at times it is maintained by the termination or avoidance of an aversive stimulus following the occurrence of a self-injurious act. The self-stimulation hypothesis contends that a certain amount of tactile, vestibular, and kinesthetic stimulation is necessary for the organism; and when it is not obtained, the organism will engage in activity that aims at increasing these levels of stimulation. The organic hypothesis states that self-injurious behavior is most often due to aberrant organic processes (e.g., brain damage, subseizures, metabolic or endocrine disorders). The final hypothesis, the psychodynamic, argues that the behavior is an infantile or fetal drive, a form of masochism, a rejection mechanism, displacement of anger or aggression, evidence of poor ego identity, or the search for body reality (Lester, 1972).

A review of research on treatment of self-injurious behavior (Butman, 1979) suggests that there are many effective means of suppressing it and replacing it with more adaptive behaviors. Of the treatments available, response contingent electrical shock, noxious odors, overcorrection, and certain types of reinforcement of other behavior strategies appear to produce the most durable changes in frequency and intensity. Certain legal, ethical, administrative, and procedural considerations make it incumbent upon researchers and clinicians to develop, refine, and evaluate other nonaversive alternatives to punishment for the treatment of this behavioral problem.

References

Bachman, J. A. (1972). Self-injurious behavior: A behavioral analysis. *Journal of Abnormal Psychology, 80,* 211–224.

Baumeister, A. A., & Forehand, R. (1973). Stereotyped acts. In N. R. Ellis (Ed.), *International review of research in mental retardation* (Vol. 5). New York: Academic Press.

Baumeister, A. A., & Rollings, J. (1976). Self-injurious behavior. In N. R. Ellis (Ed.), *International review of research in mental retardation.* (Vol. 8). New York: Academic Press.

Butman, R. E. (1979). *The non-aversive treatment of self-injurious behavior in severely and profoundly retarded children.* Unpublished doctoral dissertation. Fuller Theological Seminary.

Lester, D. (1972). Self-mutilating behavior. *Psychological Bulletin, 78,* 119–128.

R. E. BUTMAN

Self-Disclosure. To disclose is the ability to express in words and gestures what is private, on the inside, or not accessible to others. It is the act of making known what is hidden or kept in secret. Self-disclosure is the process of gradually communicating personal data to another individual (privately) or to a group of people (publicly). It is a subjective activity practiced at times for personal enjoyment, growth, and satisfaction. As two individuals become familiar with each other and closely interact over time, they begin to reveal more of themselves to each other.

Self-disclosure is a reflection of a positive and rather seasoned self-concept. It is a manifestation of an appropriate inner excavation toward better self-discovery and a confident and adequate self-presentation. People with a positive self-concept will be able to reveal more of themselves than will those with a negative self-view. Self-disclosure is a form of self-presentation and includes elements of self-display, which is the tendency to exhibit one's best qualities. It requires a good degree of self-evaluation (assessing strengths, weaknesses, needs), self-awareness (being in touch with deep emotions, thoughts, movements), and self-direction (judging for oneself what needs to be done).

The term *self-disclosure* was introduced by Jourard (1964). Later, prominent therapists, like Rogers and Maslow, promoted that personal disclosure is essential for healthy personality development, equilibrium, relational balance, and personal growth.

Self-disclosure is a fine skill that may be learned through modeling or imitation and is refined through practice. It is a function of a healthy personality and a sign of ego strength. It is the ability to bring into light what is invisible or unknown and to show plainly and without reservation what has not been previously uncovered or unveiled. Usually, before disclosing sensitive information, exposing private materials, or sharing intimate experiences, people make sure that enough trust, safety, and confidentiality have been established in the relationship. In addition, mutual respect and openness, empathy and support, and nonjudgmental attitudes are prerequisites for emotional expression and genuine transparency.

Self-disclosure is a bold activity during which individuals reveal certain intimate aspects about themselves only to the extent they actually know or understand themselves. However, to be "in touch" does not necessarily mean the person is able or "willing" to reveal himself or herself. Disclosures can be appropriate or inappropriate. Some people are high revealers (overdisclosing) while others are low revealers (underdisclosing). Inappropriate disclosure can be overwhelming, offensive, and at times damaging to relationships. A high revealer, for example, may disclose too much, too fast, too soon. A low revealer, on the other hand, is more highly reserved and may feel unsure or unable to reciprocate others' disclosure. Training in interpersonal and social skills is essential for both types. They need to learn sound judgment, use a measure of discrimination, and realize that there is a time for free sharing and a time for appropriate withholding. They need to acquire the art of listening, sharing, disclosing, and ultimately reciprocating. These functions are necessary for bonding and building intimate relationships. They require experience and discernment and reflect a good level of emotional maturity.

Healthy self-disclosure adheres to the "norm of reciprocity" with the expectation that partners exchange personal revelations and take turn in showing similar levels of intimacy. Self-disclosure is a major factor in close relationships and a central goal of intimate communication. It is an essential agent for improving and stabilizing significant relationships. Practicing self-disclosure will deepen one's self-knowledge, will enhance one's emotional life, will maximize one's potential and talents, and eventually will lead to better self-actualization.

In counseling and psychotherapy, self-disclosure on the part of the client is encouraged and actually well promoted, especially during the first phases of therapy. Disclosure is considered essential for the success of any counseling process. Most people have greater difficulty revealing themselves in front of a large group than on a one-on-one basis. There are many factors that determine the degree, timing, and manner of self-disclosure, including cultural background, ethnic group, family history, communication style, and past experience with disclosure (whether positive or negative). It is the therapist's challenge to facilitate disclosure by reducing tension, removing obstacles, addressing reluctance, and building enough safety and trust. Serious client-counselor differences can hinder the flow of disclosure and therapy, like differences in age, gender, education, faith, economic level, subculture, ethnicity, or worldview.

Disclosure on the part of the therapist is still somewhat controversial. Some theorists believe that it may contaminate the therapeutic process and minimize the representation or role of the therapist as an expert, analyst, or observant. They claim that the therapist ought to be subjectively removed from the immediacy and emotional struggles of the patient and maintain a distinct professional image or profile. Other theorists argue that the therapist's disclosure may actually enhance the counseling relationship, promote warmth and empathy, and increase the alliance, trust, and depth. When the therapist is more involved, naturally interactive, and at times directly and openly sharing from his or her own journey, clients sense, appreciate, and relate to the therapist's humanness. Consequently, the bonding and team work between them will grow and flourish.

The concepts of disclosure and revelation are enriched by the teachings of the Scriptures and the dynamics of the Christian faith. Gradually and systematically, God revealed divine nature as well as the human condition, according to the understanding, timing, and maturity of the people. Finally, in the fullness of time, when history and humankind were ready, Christ, through incarnation, became the full and complete revelation of God (Gal. 4:4). Christ disclosed the personhood of God which had been invisible. Christ is the full manifestation of the Trinity (John 1; Col. 1). That is a remarkable phenomenon of self-disclosure. The Logos (cf. Greek mythologies) became Sarx (flesh) and "dwelt among us, and we beheld his glory, full of grace and truth . . . and from his fullness we all received . . . No one has ever seen God; the only Son, who is in the bosom of the Father, he has made him known" (John 1:14, 16, 18). Furthermore, we are all called to cultivate intimacy with God which is manifested in deep sharing, mutual disclosure, active transparency, and a close and nurturing relationship.

N. Abi-Hashem

See Healthy Personality.

Self-Disclosure, Therapist. No clinician minimizes the value of appropriate self-disclosure. Rather, the controversy surrounds the question of what level and intensity of self-disclosure by the therapist best facilitates the helping process. Opinion varies considerably in the psychotherapeutic literature, especially between psychodynamically oriented and humanistically oriented practitioners. Further, what may be an appropriate level and intensity in individual therapy may be inappropriate in a group setting and vice versa (Corey, 1996). Researchers (e.g., Hammond, Hepworth, & Smith, 1977) have devoted considerable time and energy to exploring this issue and related matters in order to improve therapeutic communication.

Self-disclosure may be defined as giving access to one's private life or to one's secret thoughts, feelings, and attitudes (McLemore, 1978). It is the antithesis of concealing one's own feelings and personality. For the therapist, a high level of self-disclosure would be a setting in which nothing is held back, even at the risk of embarrassment. Further, when negative feelings are shared they would be used constructively, a process that Augsburger (1973) calls "care-fronting." Realizing how difficult it is for most persons to reveal their psychological problems, therapists need to recognize their own vulnerabilities and strive toward becoming healthy role models themselves (see Guy, 1987). Therapists then need to recognize and own their own personal conflicts. Through self-exploration and personal growth, they have the potential to find ways in which their own disclosure can facilitate rather than retard the psychotherapeutic process (see Corey & Corey, 1989).

As clients self-disclose, it is likely that the therapist's own deep feelings of pain and joy, love and hate, hurt and tenderness will be touched (see Copans & Singer, 1978). Recoiling from these reopened wounds, the therapist may choose to deal with the fears and anxieties by not sharing. At times this may be appropriate. At other times these feelings and reactions may be the substance that could facilitate the deepening of the helping relationship and the healing of old wounds. Learning to use personal experience in therapy and learning from therapy how to better conduct one's own life are parallel processes. Copans and Singer argue that experiencing one's own wounds in therapy does not mean that one necessarily exposes them but that one is open to them. The process of learning to do this is gradual and is facilitated by the therapist's fully experiencing the moment in therapy rather than by rigorously removing oneself from the process (see Evans, Hearn, Uhlemann, & Ivery, 1993).

Self-disclosure by the therapist can have a number of positive benefits. Appropriate levels and intensity of sharing can build therapeutic rapport and trust. Further, they can serve as excellent models of interpersonal openness (Jourard, 1971; Jourard & Landsman, 1980). They also can demonstrate to clients that their problems are not necessarily unique and that previously unacceptable feelings, thoughts, and actions are acceptable. Appropriate self-disclosure may moreover have a dyadic effect; that is, with good rapport and trust persons tend to reciprocate self-disclosure unless it is too intense or unexpected. Finally, for the Christian therapist, it may be one important expression of how we image God in therapy (see Jones & Butman, 1991). At all times, however, self-disclosure must not impede the therapeutic process by diverting the focus of the clients' awareness away from their own thoughts, actions, and feelings for prolonged periods of time. Inappropriate or excessive self-disclosure runs the risk of degenerating into listless sermons or personal narratives that are potentially irrelevant or even intrusive. Longitudinal research would suggest that experience potentially teaches the clinician about the need for timing, tact, and sensitivity when it comes to such important change variables as therapist self-disclosure (see Corey, 1996).

Self-disclosure properly used might also be used to challenge clients (Egan, 1982). It is appropriate if it helps clients to talk about themselves, if it helps them talk about their problems more concretely, if it helps them develop new frames of reference and perspectives, and if it helps them set realistic goals for themselves. Egan suggests that this is most likely to occur if self-sharing is selective and focused, is not a burden to the client, and is not used too often.

Self-disclosure in the therapeutic context is a risk. In spite of this, it is a skill that should be a natural part of the effective clinician's repertoire. A therapist who is willing and able to disclose when indicated is much more likely to be an effective agent of change than is one who is consistently aloof, distant, and inexpressive. Christian mental health professionals in particular are called to transparency rather than impression management. Our mandate is to be radically transparent to Christ and to reflect him in all that we do and say, including the clinical context (see Jones & Butman, 1991). Our commitment to truth seeking and truth telling ought to be evident in the quality and depth of our personal disclosure.

References

Augsburger, D. (1973). *Caring enough to confront.* Scottdale, PA: Herald.

Copans, S., & Singer, T. (1978). *Who's the patient here? Portraits of the young psychotherapist.* New York: Oxford University Press.

Corey, G. (1996). *Theory and practice of counseling and psychotherapy* (5th ed.). Pacific Grove, CA: Brooks/Cole.

Corey, M., & Corey, G. (1989). *Becoming a helper.* Pacific Grove, CA: Brooks/Cole.

Egan, G. (1982). *The skilled helper: Models, skills, and methods for effective helping* (2nd ed.). Monterey, CA: Brooks/Cole.

Evans, D., Hearn, M., Uhlemann, M., & Ivery, A. (1993). *Essential interviewing* (4th ed.). Pacific Grove, CA: Brooks /Cole.

Guy, J. (1987). *The personal life of the psychotherapist.* New York: Wiley Interscience.

Hammond, D., Hepworth, D., & Smith, V. (1977). *Improving therapeutic communication.* San Francisco: Jossey-Bass.

Jones, S., & Butman, R. (1991). *Modern psychotherapies.* Downers Grove, IL: InterVarsity Press.

Jourard, S. M. (1971). *The transparent self* (Rev. ed.). New York: Van Nostrand, Reinhold.

Jourard, S. M., & Landsman, T. (1980). *Healthy personality* (4th ed.). New York: Macmillan.

McLemore, C. (1978). *Clergyman's psychological handbook: Clinical information for pastoral counseling.* Grand Rapids, MI: Eerdmans.

R. E. BUTMAN

Self-Efficacy. People's beliefs in exercising control over their own functioning and over their environmental circumstances to produce at a self-designated level of performance. People with a strong sense of self-efficacy are more likely to perceive difficult tasks as hurdles to get over rather than as overwhelming challenges to be avoided. As a result the self-efficacious person is more likely to be focused and more committed in approaching a difficult task than is the person with a weaker sense of self-efficacy. Moreover, the person high in self-efficacy is more likely to react to failure with increased effort and reduced stress. In contrast, the low self-efficacious person is likely to avoid difficult tasks if that is possible or to approach such tasks by emphasizing their insurmountability and the individual's personal deficiencies. This orientation often results in lessened effort and perseverance, and the resulting poor performance may create a self-fulfilling prophecy.

Self-efficacy is clearly related to self-esteem, though the two are conceptually distinct. Self-esteem is the sense of personal worth associated with the self-concept and may influence as well as be influenced by one's self-efficacy beliefs.

Bandura (1986) suggests that the development of self-efficacy beliefs are influenced by four major sources. First, the extent of one's prior successes, or mastery experiences, especially those that require great effort and through which temporary setbacks along the way are experienced, help determine self-efficacy. Second, vicarious experiences through the success of social models, especially if those models are perceived to be similar to one's self, influence efficacy beliefs. Efficacy beliefs are also enhanced through social persuasion, that is, being told repeatedly by others of one's capabilities, and the perception of emotional states (e.g., positive mood, general physiological arousal) that facilitate performance.

The influence of self-efficacy on human functioning is mediated by four basic psychological processes: cognition, motivation, affect, and selection. The first process, cognition, suggests that self-efficacious beliefs influence the way we think about ourselves. The Olympic gymnast, for example, can visualize herself successfully completing the vault just prior to her attempt. The less efficacious individual may be able only to think about what can go wrong. Self-efficacy beliefs also influence motivational processes. The extent to which one expects a positive outcome will surely influence the degree to which the individual desires to engage in the activity, especially if the outcome is highly valued (*see* Achievement, Need for).

High self-efficacy beliefs also influence affective processes. The person who has confidence in his or her ability to produce a successful outcome is more likely to see the self in a positive light; this viewpoint can develop a greater sense of resiliency in the face of adversity. The person burdened with weak self-efficacy beliefs may experience depression through unfulfilled aspiration. Finally, self-efficacy beliefs can influence the types of experiences people select. Persons high in self-efficacy may choose those settings that require performances that test their capabilities but are still within the range of successful performance. Less self-efficacious individuals may choose tasks that are either obviously easy, thus protecting the self-image from failure but also not enhancing the sense of efficacy (i.e., "it is so easy anybody can do it"), or may choose tasks from which they expect to fail.

Research on the sources of self-efficacy has not considered the effect of religious experience. Depending on one's approach to religion as well as particular religious beliefs or doctrine, religious experience may either enhance (e.g., the sense of being personally empowered by the Holy Spirit) or hinder (e.g., an exclusive emphasis on the incompleteness and fallenness of human nature) self-efficacy beliefs.

Reference

Bandura, A. (1986). *Social foundations of thought and action: A social cognitive theory.* Englewood Cliffs, NJ: Prentice-Hall.

P. C. HILL

See BANDURA, ALBERT; LOCUS OF CONTROL.

Self-Esteem. To esteem someone or something is to value, respect, affirm, and give worth to that object or person. To esteem oneself is the ability to properly evaluate and accurately present oneself which involves a realistic assessment of personal strengths and weaknesses, positive and negative qualities, and true potentials and limitations.

Self-esteem is determined by the general feeling people have about themselves and by the global ideas, attitudes, or perceptions they create about themselves. It is a self-ranking activity based upon the individual's successes and failures. Self-esteem is an internal ability to assign attributes to oneself and conduct subjective appraisals and private judgments. This phenomenon may occur over a long period of time and involves complex affective and cognitive processes. The results can be positive or negative depending on the person's developmental history, childhood experiences and family background, mental reasoning and emotional stability, level of expectations and set of ideals, nature of current challenges and pressures, personal meaning and sense of direction, external appraisal and social feedback, and eventually existential outlook and spiritual faith.

Besides having a global rating about themselves, people usually develop separate ratings or levels of esteems for different domains of their lives. These include certain faculties, attributes, or traits, and several areas of functioning. As people act, react, and interact they typically create impressions about themselves, others, life, and ultimately God. Comparing oneself to others externally, and comparing real self to ideal self internally, are very common, yet subtle, daily practices. Some aspects of self-esteem appear to be fundamentally established and well set or concrete while others appear to be fluid, open, fragile, or progressive as the person's identity evolves and his or her life's journey unfolds.

Self-esteem may be thought of as the organized configurations, connotations, or impressions about the inner structure, value qualities, and relational personhood or selfhood which are accessible to the individual's awareness (cf. Rogers, 1951, p. 136). Self-esteem can be the product of several intrapsychic, interpersonal, and sociocultural phenomena and, more precisely, the product of certain cognitive assumptions on multiple levels. It can be temporal or permanent, internal or external, specific or global, and individual or communal. People may view themselves favorably in one area and unfavorably in another. Most probably, self-esteem is being always modified and adjusted, consciously or unconsciously, based upon the unmet emotional needs, surrounding events, outcomes of personal efforts, and reactions of significant others.

One of the first clear definitions of self-esteem was formulated by William James (1890) when he suggested that it equals success divided by pretensions. In other words, it results from the successes (or lack of) an individual actually achieves tempered by what he or she originally expected to achieve.

Some hold that self-esteem is composed of several elements and is an extension of at least three basic aspects of selfhood: 1) self-image, which refers to how people feel about their external shape, physical body, and public appearance; 2) self-concept, which refers to how people perceive their personality structure, skills, knowledge, and life experience; how competent and confident they generally feel; and how comfortable they are in their role, capacity, or potential for making meaningful contributions (self-definition and efficacy); 3) self-worth, which refers to whether a person feels any inherent value or internal significance and whether a person considers himself or herself as a unique and special individual.

The term self-esteem is broadly used and perhaps, like an umbrella, covers many similar yet not identical terms like: self-identity, self-perception, self-value, self-description, self-evaluation, self-acceptance, self-presentation, self-definition, self-confidence, self-affirmation, and self-efficacy. Some of these terms are more popular than others and, in many cases, are used interchangeably. Working against sound self-esteem are the feelings of inferiority, irrational self-ideals, negative messages, distorted views, unhealthy self-talk, self-criticism, self-deception, self-defeating behaviors, and negative self-fulfilling prophecies. These can easily generate helplessness, hopelessness, worthlessness, deep inner frustration, major dissatisfaction with life, and pessimism.

An average disappointment or a minor failure can be perceived and handled differently depending on the individual's level of self-confidence and emotional stability. For some, who are secure enough, the incident may be mildly disturbing. For others, who are more vulnerable, it may be greatly devastating and could reinforce their negative views about themselves and the world. Once these negative imprints have been established, they virtually perpetuate themselves into vicious cycles leading to increased downward spiral movements.

There are two common temptations that often lead to extreme positions: (a) overestimating oneself (grandiosity, self-preoccupation, pride, egocentricism) which can lead to narcissism and result in controlling and abusing others, or (b) underestimating oneself (self-doubt, self-depreciation, self-hatred) which can lead to pleasing others, addictive behaviors, perfectionism, anxieties, and depression. In addition, "giving" to the point of becoming depleted or "taking" to the point of being overly saturated are both signs of major insecurities and dysfunction. Invariably, the way we act upon the world shapes the way we perceive ourselves and, vice versa, the way we perceive ourselves shapes the way we act upon the world.

Numerous research studies have explored the subjective well-being (SWB) of people. For example, Myers and Diener (1995) found four inner traits which appear to mark happy people: self-esteem, sense of personal control, extraversion, and optimism. Better indications about well-being stem from knowing about one's personal traits, close relationships, work experience, spirituality, and culture.

A Theological Perspective. There has been much controversy around the notion of self-esteem in Christian circles. The attitudes range from totally rejecting, to moderately integrating, to completely embracing the concept. From a biblical point of view, believers are called to respect, nurture, give worth to, pray for, set value on, and have charity and care for others as well as themselves. The presence of God's image within us, along with the sinful nature, is a vivid example of the constant tension we feel. Like so many other apparent contradictions in the Christian faith, we are called to observe and integrate "both-and" instead of "either-or." This principle applies to other domains of life as well. Christian believers are called to carefully reconcile and accommodate many polarities, like truth and grace, acceptance and rejection, dignity and deprivation, love and hate, joy and sorrow, glory and shame. Since we live in a broken and fallen world, groaning for full redemption, we shall continue to attend to and experience such inevitable tensions. These forces are always at work within and without and truly are integral parts of our humanness.

Each individual believer is called to be a healthy self and become a well rounded and complete person. Self-esteem has been often mistaken for self-worship, misunderstood as arrogance or pride, and confused with self-centeredness. We clearly are not called to be "selfish beings" (with inflated ego), yet at the same time, we are not called to be "selfless beings" either (without sense of self). Both are unhealthy and could lead to serious disturbances and psychopathology.

The Christian faith fundamentally promotes both self-affirmation and self-denial, self-care and self-sacrifice, self-love and self-hate, self-presentation and self-preservation, and a natural balance between genuine receiving and authentic giving. This is not a mysterious paradox to resolve or an impossible task to accomplish. Rather, it is a positive tension needed for our mental creativity and emotional stability. It is essential for character development, integrative living, and relational maturity.

The Scriptures challenge us to be secure, humble, self-aware, and yet, at the same time remain open, well equipped, and highly motivated as we strive toward meaningful identity, personal growth, communal harmony, and productive service. Virtually, the resolution of paradoxes begins to emerge when the person accepts both realities and reconciles both polarities rather than splitting them or dwelling on one extreme. Individuals with a healthy sense of self have been and will continue to be more effective ministers of Christ and better disciples in God's kingdom.

Evidently, there is an element of fulfillment in self-sacrifice (Mark 8:35; John 12:25). According to Hardy (1986), Christian love is not totally free from self-regarding aspects, for "we are not indeed called on to renounce desire for our true welfare, but to find it in self-sacrificing love" (p. 571). After all, the New Testament does accept the Old Testament precept of loving our neighbor as ourselves as a natural fact (Lev. 19:18; Mark 12:31; Rom. 13:9).

Stott (1984) eloquently addressed this issue by emphasizing that we must "affirm" our true self, that is, who we are by creation, and we must contain, temper, and even "disown" our false self, that is, who we are by the fall. He added that true self-denial (denying the desires and wishes of our false and fallen self) is not the road to self-destruction but the road to self-discovery. We are to affirm and value everything within us that is compatible with Jesus Christ (p. 28). According to Ellison (1983), constructive humility (not pride) and true meekness (not weakness) are the biblical counterpart of positive self-esteem. True humility is based on God's approval and acceptance rather than on self-negation. Johnson (1989) also tried to outline a Christian understanding of proper self-esteem and suggested that it is an accurate response to knowing ourselves which evidently results from knowing God.

A Cultural Perspective. Certain cultures display a strong social cohesiveness to the degree that individuals are lost in the group. They place greater value on the communal harmony rather than on the individual uniqueness and therefore discourage a completely private or separate identity. Other cultures overemphasize the "individual" more than the "social" aspect of being to the degree that they glorify personal autonomy, total privacy, and a constant need for individual recognition.

In most Western societies, identity is individually achieved, while in most Eastern and non-Western cultures, it is communally ascribed. Western cultures greatly emphasize independence, autonomy, and achievement. They are characterized by "doing" and the "me" generation, that is, personal value is based upon "what you do or accomplish" more than on "who you are." Unfortunately, the industrial and technological revolutions have resulted in a glorification of individualism, competition, isolation, and self-gratification. At times, many who live in the current "post-Christian" era place the self in the same position that earlier traditional subcultures reserved for their gods (Johnson, 1989). There certainly is a danger in over-emphasizing the theoretical notion of "separation-individuation" (cf. psychodynamic literature) in cultures where personal space, rigid boundaries, strict privacy, self-sufficiency, and self-reliance are already highly praised. In addition, the present mass media and social climate keep reinforcing these values.

Both "I, me" and "us, we" are essential for survival and must be actively present in any balanced and functional human existence. When studying the biblical model of the community of faith, individual value, and spiritual culture we find a remarkable interplay and beautiful harmony between the "I" and "we," self and others. Accordingly, sound personal identity reflects solid connectedness, deep rootedness, rich belongingness, and prolonged heritage. It derives from and feeds into the communal identity which marvelously results in an interdependent, intimate, and meaningful existence.

Few recent studies have tried to explore the cross-cultural factors and dynamics of self-esteem and the effect of ethnic identity, age, and gender on self-rating (cf. Brooke, 1995; Karim, 1990; Martinez & Dukes, 1991; Phinney, 1991; Watkins & Cheung, 1995). New writings, observations, and research studies, which take into consideration the socio-cultural and religious aspects of self-esteem, are much needed.

Finally, the role of an experienced Christian therapist is to enhance the value of clients, especially the young and adolescents, and help them make realistic attributions of themselves, others, and the world. To break the deep-rooted and negative self-view cycles is perhaps one of the greatest challenges facing any counselor. For people to feel good about themselves, to know where they are coming from, what they represent, and where they are going, is essential for leading healthy, productive, and satisfied lives.

Practical Suggestions. The following suggestions can help those who struggle with low self-esteem, poor self-image, or some degree of worthlessness:

1. Watch any negative thoughts, disruptive ideas, unhealthy messages, self-defeating talks or habits, unrealistic inner dialogue, destructive mental scripts, or irrational expectations.

2. Learn good self-awareness skills and exercise self-monitoring, thought-stopping, and self-instruction techniques. Begin to unlearn the unhealthy patterns of behavior and consistently replace them by new, productive, and healthy ones.

3. Memorize and deeply meditate upon certain Scriptures and refined positive statements. They will help repair distorted concepts about self and others. Bible verses like "I thank thee because I am fearfully and wonderfully made" (Ps. 139:14), and also like Joshua 1:9, Exodus 33:14, Psalms 8:4–6, 90:17, 100:3, 138:3, Isaiah 40:28–31, Zephaniah 3:17, and 1 Timothy 1:12 are examples of the vast available resources and excellent therapeutic tools.

4. Practice self-affirmation by countering old negative thoughts and messages. Gradually reverse them with positive and constructive ones. For example, an extreme negative thought would be: "I am a failure! I can't do anything right." Changing it to a realistic positive, would become: "Although I make some mistakes at times, I know I can do so many things right, and I have proven that before." Furthermore, it is highly recommended to compliment or fortify the new statement by adding an appropriate and powerful Scripture verse like ". . . and I can do all things through Christ who strengthens me" (Phil. 4:13). Hopefully, this begins to repair the pathological cycles and allows the positive input to penetrate into deeper layers of the soul until it reaches the core of the person's being.

5. Seek affirmation from caring others and surround yourself with positive and mature people. That is extremely essential for any emotional healing, mental recovery, and spiritual stability. Receiving nurture can be difficult for some who are more comfortable giving and showing care. However, receiving openly as a skill needs to be learned and constantly practiced by reaching out to others and taking interpersonal risks. It requires courage, honesty, and humility. The results can be marvelously refreshing to the mind and deeply therapeutic to the soul.

References

Brooke, S. L. (1995). Critical analysis of the culture-free self-esteem inventories. *Measurement and Evaluation in Counseling and Development, 27,* 248–252.

Ellison, C. W. (Ed.). (1983). *Your better self: Christianity, psychology, and self-esteem.* San Francisco, CA: Harper & Row.

Hardy, E. R. (1986). Self-Denial. In J. F. Childress & J. Mac-Quarrie (Eds.), *The Westminster dictionary of Christian ethics.* Philadelphia, PA: Westminster.

James, W. (1890). *Principles of psychology* (Vol. 1). New York: Holt.

Johnson, E. L. (1989). Self-esteem in the presence of God. *Journal of Psychology and Theology, 17,* 226–235.

Karim, S. F. (1990). Self-concept: A cross-cultural study on adolescents. *Psychological Studies, 35,* 118–123.

Martinez, R., & Dukes, R. L. (1991). Ethnic and gender differences in self-esteem. *Youth and Society, 22,* 318–338.

Myers, D. G., & Diener, E. (1995). Who is happy? *Psychological Science, 6,* 10–19.

Phinney, J. S. (1991). Ethnic identity and self-esteem: A review and integration. *Hispanic Journal of Behavioral Sciences, 13,* 193–208.

Rogers, C. R. (1951). *Client-centered therapy.* Boston, MA: Houghton Mifflin.

Stott, J. (1984, April 20). Am I supposed to love myself or hate myself? *Christianity Today,* pp. 26–28.

Watkins, D., & Cheung, S. (1995). Culture, gender, and response bias. *Journal of Cross-Cultural Psychology, 26,* 490–504.

Additional Readings

Backus, W., & Chapian, M. (1980). *Telling yourself the truth.* Minneapolis, MN: Bethany.

Narramore, B. (1978). *You're someone special.* Grand Rapids, MI: Zondervan.

Hart, A. D. (1992). *Me, myself, & I.* Ann Arbor, MI: Vine.

Tournier, P. (1957). *The meaning of persons.* New York: Harper.

Wagner, M. E. (1975). *The sensation of being somebody.* Grand Rapids, MI: Zondervan.

N. ABI-HASHEM

See SELF; SELF-CONCEPT.

Self-Fulfilling Prophecy. A prediction or belief that serves to bring about its own fulfillment. The person believing it acts in such a way as to make the prophesied event more likely. It is sometimes called the Pygmalion effect after Ovid's and George Bernard Shaw's account of people who shape others to be what the creators want them to be. It is also called the experimenter expectancy effect because researchers may unintentionally cause their experiments to come out as expected. The concept of the self-fulfilling prophecy was developed by Merton (1948), but it has been developed extensively by Rosenthal. It is sometimes called the Rosenthal effect.

The classic studies involve rats and schoolchildren. Rosenthal and Fode (1963) randomly divided 60 rats among 12 experimenters who were to teach their rats to run to the darker arm of a T-maze. Although all the rats were the same, six of the experimenters were told that they had "maze-bright" rats and the other six were told that they had "maze-dull" rats. From the beginning of the experiment the rats believed to be smart became better performers. They showed a daily improvement in their scores throughout the experiment, while those believed to be dumb improved only through the third day, then did worse. The dull rats refused to move from the starting position 29% of the time, while the bright ones refused only 11% of the time. The experimenters with the bright rats viewed their animals as brighter, more pleasant, and more likable and were more relaxed with them. They described their own behavior as more pleasant, friendly, and enthusiastic and handled their rats more often and more gently than the experimenters with the dull rats.

Rosenthal and Jacobson (1968) did a similar experiment with teachers and schoolchildren. They gave all the children in a school an intelligence quotient (IQ) test and told the teachers it was a test that would predict intellectual blooming. They then randomly picked 20% of the students and told the teachers that these students would show a sudden spurt in intellectual growth. As with the rats, the only differences between the children were in the minds of the teachers. The children were tested eight months later, and it was found that the children randomly designated as bloomers increased in IQ scores by four more points than those not picked. Furthermore, the effect was greater in the lower grades than in the upper ones. The teachers may have paid greater attention to the bloomers, may have been more patient and more encouraging, and may have communicated that high standards were being set for them.

These experiments have been widely criticized, and literally hundreds of similar studies have been conducted. The effect is not always found, but it is found often enough for most people to believe it is real. Rosenthal (1976) reviewed all the studies he could locate, and 109 of the 311 studies found a statistically significant correlation. Thus self-fulfilling prophecy is found only about one-third of the time, indicating that we do not understand the factors producing it well enough to find the effect every time an experiment is run.

Rosenthal (1976) believes that four factors produce the effect. First, we tend to produce a warmer social-emotional climate for special people. Second, we give the special ones better feedback as to how they are doing. Third, we give them more material and more difficult material. Finally, we give the special ones more opportunities for responding.

Self-fulfilling prophecy is of concern not only in conducting experiments and in education but also in many other areas. People who believe they can produce only a little do so, while those who think they can do more actually do more. People taking surveys find the results they expect to find, influencing the responses. Hypnotists find that their success in hypnotizing a given person depends on whether or not they believe the person can be hypnotized. Psychotherapists have greater success if they believe the client can be helped.

The phenomenon of self-fulfilling prophecy has obvious implications for the church. Sunday school teachers who expect their children to misbehave may produce misbehavior. Pastors who expect trouble with their official board may elicit the trouble. Christian counselors who expect a patient to get worse may treat the patient in such a way that he or she actually does. Of course, if Christian workers expect the best from people, they will be more likely to get it.

References

Merton, R. K. (1948). The self-fulfilling prophecy. *Antioch Review, 8,* 193–210.

Rosenthal, R. (1976). *Experimenter effects in behavioral research* (Enl. ed.). New York: Irvington.

Rosenthal, R., & Fode, K. L. (1963). The effect of experimenter bias on the performance of the albino rat. *Behavioral Science, 8,* 183–189.

Rosenthal, R., & Jacobson, L. (1968). *Pygmalion in the classroom.* New York: Holt, Rinehart, & Winston.

R. L. KOTESKEY

Self-Handicapping. A self-presentation strategy that arranges in advance impediments that will hinder performance. Although it is a self-defeating behavior, the strategy is ironically used to protect an already fragile view of the self. By arranging, either consciously or unconsciously, impediments that prohibit successful performance, the individual is ensuring that failure will not threaten self-esteem. Common examples include partying the night before an exam, procrastinating to complete an assigned task such as a term paper, or using alcohol or drugs as one is about to engage in a crucial activity. Individuals also may rely on personal (e.g., test anxiety) or social (e.g., gender discrimination) factors as convenient impediments. Self-handicapping is but one of many self-presentational strategies to enhance the self-concept, but it has become an extremely well-researched topic.

A key to understanding the self-handicapping tendency is that the arranged cause of failure is not threatening to one's view of the self. For example, an early study of self-handicapping (Berglas & Jones, 1978) found that men who were told they were successful on tasks, regardless of whether they were successful (i.e., noncontingent success that was seemingly independent of their performance), chose a drug described as debilitating rather than a facilitative drug before performing similar upcoming tasks. Other men, given success feedback only when they were successful (i.e., contingent success that was seemingly dependent on their performance), were more likely to choose the facilitative drug prior to similar upcoming tasks. The experimenters maintained that those in the noncontingent success condition, who were surprised by their earlier good fortune but who were also less sure of their subsequent performance, could blame a future poor performance on the debilitative drug. Blaming the drug is far less threatening to one's esteem than admitting, for example, lack of ability.

Not everyone equally employs self-handicapping strategies. Whether a person self-handicaps is influenced by both personal characteristics and characteristics of the situation. Of personal characteristics, people low in self-esteem are more likely to self-handicap, although people high in self-esteem will use self-handicapping as a strategy if it is likely to make them appear outstanding or if the appearance of success is particularly meaningful and important to the individual. People who are more aware of themselves as social objects (public self-consciousness) are more likely to self-handicap. A self-handicapping scale has been developed (Rhodewalt, Morf, Hazlett, & Fairfield, 1991) to measure generalized preferences for self-handicapping behavior. Characteristics of the situation that foster self-handicapping include when an important aspect of the self is threatened with public disconfirmation, when a preexisting handicap is not available, and when the possibility of employing a handicap is highly plausible.

References

Berglas, S., & Jones, E. E. (1978). Drug choice as a self-handicapping strategy in response to noncontingent success. *Journal of Personality and Social Psychology, 36,* 405–417.

Rhodewalt, F., Morf, C., Hazlett, S., & Fairfield, M. (1991). Self-handicapping: The role of discounting and augmentation in the preservation of self-esteem. *Journal of Personality and Social Psychology, 61,* 122–131.

Additional Reading

Higgins, R. L., Snyder, C. R., & Berglas, S. (Eds.). (1990). *Self-handicapping: The paradox that isn't.* New York: Plenum.

P. C. Hill

See Excuse Making.

Self-Help Groups. *See* Mutual Help Groups.

Self-Help Psychology. *See* Popular Psychology.

Self-Instruction. A type of cognitive-behavioral intervention associated with Meichenbaum (1977), who first used the technique with impulsive hyperactive children. The problem-solving deficits that Meichenbaum discovered through studies of these children were that they did not analyze their experience in cognitive mediational terms and that they did not have rules formulated on the basis of this analysis to guide their actions. In developing a therapeutic intervention, therefore, Meichenbaum attempted to teach these children "(a) how to comprehend the task, (b) spontaneously produce mediators and strategies, and (c) use such mediators and strategies to guide, monitor, and control their performance" (1977, p. 31).

The treatment package that Meichenbaum and Goodman (1971) developed was called self-instructional training and consisted of five steps: the child observed the adult model performing the task as he talked out loud to himself; the child performed the task under the direction of the adult's instruction; the child performed the task using his own verbal instructions; the child performed the task while whispering the instructions to himself; and the child performed the task using covert instructions. This treatment package employs several intervention strategies common to many cognitive-behavioral interventions. During the first step the adult's instructions serve as a cognitive model for the child, an example of what his thoughts should be. The second step is a form of participant modeling, where the child and the adult model perform a task together. The actual self-instruction begins in step 3, in which the child guides his performance with overt verbal instruction. Step 4 is a fading of the instructions, and step 5 moves the self-instruction from an overt to a covert level.

When research using this treatment approach was supportive of its usefulness with children, Meichenbaum returned to a group of patients who had been the subject of his doctoral dissertation, adult schizophrenics. In his dissertation study (Meichenbaum, 1969) a group of hospitalized schizophrenics received an operant training program to engage in healthy talk (relevant and coherent talk). While test-

ing the schizophrenics Meichenbaum found that several spontaneously repeated the experimental instruction, "Give healthy talk; be coherent and relevant." A more elaborate self-instructional package for schizophrenics was then developed and tested by Meichenbaum and Cameron (1973), in which schizophrenic patients were taught to monitor and alter their own behavior and thinking. Meichenbaum and Cameron's results, replicated in a case study by Meyers, Mercatoris, and Sirota (1976), showed that such training significantly improved verbal and cognitive functioning among the schizophrenics.

More recently the use of self-instructional training has been expanded to treat a variety of adult as well as childhood disorders. For example, Genshaft and Hirt (1980) used self-instruction for the treatment of mathematics anxiety. Assertive deficits have also been treated with self-instructional training, either alone or in combination with behavioral rehearsal (Craighead, 1979). Self-instructional methods also have been incorporated into many coping-skill approaches.

While research evidence supports the usefulness of self-instruction, there are still several unanswered questions about this treatment approach. A primary concern is what self-instructions should be taught to clients: those that are specific to a certain task or those that are more general and conceptual? Also, the process by which self-instruction mediates behavior is poorly understood. Although Meichenbaum (1977) argues that thought is covert speech and that such covert speech regulates behavior, there is not agreement on this position. An additional question is how such Christian activities as prayer and Scripture memorization lend themselves to inclusion in such a treatment approach. However, in spite of these questions, self-instruction treatment approaches appear to have increasing acceptance as a way of modifying certain cognitive and behavioral responses.

References

Craighead, L. W. (1979). Self-instructional training for assertive-refusal behavior. *Behavior Therapy, 10,* 529–542.

Genshaft, J. L., & Hirt, M. L. (1980). The effectiveness of self-instructional training to enhance math achievement in women. *Cognitive Therapy and Research, 4,* 91–97.

Meichenbaum, D. (1969). The effects of instructions and reinforcement on thinking and language behavior of schizophrenics. *Behaviour Research and Therapy, 7,* 101–114.

Meichenbaum, D. (1977). *Cognitive-behavior modification.* New York: Plenum.

Meichenbaum, D., & Cameron, R. (1973). Training schizophrenics to talk to themselves. *Behavior Therapy, 4,* 515–534.

Meichenbaum D., & Goodman, J. (1971). Training impulsive children to talk to themselves. *Journal of Abnormal Psychology, 77,* 115–126.

Meyers, A., Mercatoris, M., & Sirota, A. (1976). Case study: Use of covert self-instruction for the elimination of psychotic speech. *Journal of Consulting and Clinical Psychology, 44,* 480–482.

E. M. ALTMAIER

See COGNITIVE-BEHAVIOR THERAPY.

Self-Monitoring. Self-monitoring is the extent to which individuals perceive and are influenced by environmental cues (Snyder, 1987). High self-monitoring individuals are sensitive to external cues and are willing to use these cues as guidelines for their behavior as they choose how to present themselves to others. Low self-monitoring individuals seem to be more internally controlled. They are less likely to notice and/or value external cues. Hence they are controlled more by internal states rather than by monitoring of the situation (Schlenker & Weigold, 1992). In reality, however, most people fall between the two extremes.

The concept of self-monitoring was developed by Snyder specifically to deal with individual differences in self-presentation and impression management. It seems as if some people are highly aware of and influenced by environmental pressure, while others are largely oblivious and immune to it. Those who are more immune are less concerned about controlling the impressions others form about them. Snyder developed the Self-Monitoring Scale as a way to assess this individual difference. His work has been extremely heuristic. Snyder's scale has stimulated more research on individual differences in impression management than has any other personality measure (Schlenker & Weigold, 1992).

There are strengths and weaknesses associated with both the high and low self-monitor. High self-monitors will evidence less consistency across situations. Because their behavior is influenced by situational cues, they will behave differently as their situational cues change. Although inconsistency has a negative connotation, the description also implies that high self-monitors will be better able to adapt to new situations.

High self-monitors will also evidence little consistency between their attitudes and their behavior. Attitudes tend to be more predictive of behavior when social pressures are minimized. Because high self-monitors are so quick to notice and be influenced by implied social pressure, they tend to experience social pressure in a stronger manner. As a result high self-monitors tend to be effective social participants who adapt their behavior to social expectations but pay a price of being less consistent (Schlenker & Weigold, 1992).

Low self-monitors evidence more consistency both across situations and between their attitudes and behavior. They also find it more difficult to develop healthy interpersonal skills because they are unlikely to notice the cues that are important in personal relationships. When low self-monitors do establish relationships, however, they tend to be more

committed to them. As a result the relationships tend to be more stable (Snyder & Simpson, 1987).

Snyder's work is not without its critics, however. Some critics have noted that his scale has a number of weak measurement properties. Others have suggested that the presence of low self-monitoring behavior might be interpreted as a motivated attempt to appear more autonomous and independent rather than as a feature of one's personality. That is, the low self-monitor may be playing a role and hiding self-monitoring practices in order to do so (Schlenker & Weigold, 1992).

Self-monitoring as an individual difference phenomenon might be a very useful concept to consider when one deals with family relationships and other conflict scenarios. For example, when spouses recognize that they have differences in their awareness of and influence by social cues, they might be better prepared to understand each other's strengths and weaknesses and be more empathic as a result.

References

Schlenker, B. R., & Weigold, M. F. (1992). Interpersonal processes involving impression regulation and management. *Annual Review of Psychology, 43,* 133–168.

Snyder, M. (1987). *Public appearances/private realities: The psychology of self-monitoring.* San Francisco: Freeman.

Snyder, M., & Simpson, J. A. (1987). Orientations toward romantic relationships. In D. Perlman & S. Duck (Eds.), *Intimate relationships: Development, dynamics, and deterioration.* Newbury Park, CA: Sage.

G. L. WELTON

See SELF-CONTROL.

Self-Perception Theory. Devised by Bem (1967) as a behavioral alternative to cognitive dissonance theory, self-perception theory hypothesizes that our attitudes are the result of observing our own behavior and then inferring our attitudes from these observations. This is similar to judgments we routinely make about others. For example, if you notice that a friend routinely volunteers to work with the kindergarten class in the Sunday school, you conclude that your friend enjoys working with young children. According to self-perception theory, if someone pointed out that you regularly volunteer to work with the young adults you might then conclude that since you work with teens that you must enjoy them.

While self-perception theory was proposed as an alternative to cognitive dissonance theory, it may instead be a compatible theory. According to cognitive dissonance theory, we experience tension (dissonance) when two of our cognitions (thoughts, beliefs, ideas) are in conflict. To reduce the tension we must change one of our cognitions or add a third that reconciles the other two. Unlike cognitive dissonance theory, self-perception theory assumes we have not already formed cognitions (e.g., beliefs) about some of our behaviors or that those cognitions are weak or uninterpretable. It is only when we observe something about our behavior that we form a cognition (belief) consistent with our observation. Therefore, if we have firm beliefs and behave in a fashion inconsistent with those beliefs, we will experience dissonance and must reconcile the two cognitions (cognitive dissonance theory). However, if we become aware of our behavior but have no beliefs that contradict the behavior, then we form beliefs based on the observed behavior (self-perception theory).

In some ways self-perception theory is similar to James's (1890) theory of emotion, which hypothesized that behavior precedes emotion. James said we are afraid because we run, not that we run because we are afraid. Self-perception theory argues that at least in some situations we believe because we behave, not that we behave because we believe.

References

Bem, D. J. (1967). Self-perception: An alternative interpretation of cognitive dissonance phenomena. *Psychological Review, 74,* 183–200.

James, W. (1890). *The principles of psychology* (Vol. 2). New York: Holt.

J. D. FOSTER

See ATTRIBUTION THEORY.

Self-Punishment. A self-control procedure in which individuals present or remove a stimulus following their own behavior, thus weakening it. Examples include saying, "Oh, that was dumb," slapping oneself on the hand, and administering an electric shock.

Self-punishment is especially helpful in situations where the undesirable behavior produces immediate reinforcement but also results in delayed aversive consequences. Examples include overeating, staying out too late, alcohol abuse, and going back to sleep in the morning after switching off the alarm. A portable shock apparatus has been developed that can be used to administer self-punishment. It has been used for a variety of undesirable behaviors, such as obsessive thoughts, homosexual fantasies, visiting adult bookstores, and dressing in clothes of the opposite sex.

A basic problem with self-punishment procedures is that their unpleasant nature results in little motivation to carry out the procedures. Only a person who is highly motivated to give up homosexual fantasies would consistently administer electric shock when these thoughts occur. Another disadvantage is that unlike self-reinforcement, the effectiveness of self-punishment is not well established.

Self-punishment is rarely used in a pure form. In those self-control procedures where self-punishment is used, it is generally used in conjunction with a self-reinforcement procedure. As with self-reinforcement, self-punishment carries connotations that are inconsistent with behavior theory unless it is clearly understood that the act of administering self-punishment is itself a learned response, which is maintained by the positively and negatively reinforcing consequences that the environment provides to support it.

R. K. BUFFORD

See PUNISHMENT; LEARNING.

Self-Reinforcement. *See* REINFORCEMENT, SELF.

Selye, Hans (1907–1982). Austrian physician best known to psychologists for his study of stress. Born in Vienna, he received his M.D. (1929) and Ph.D. (1931) from German University, Prague. He took a position at Johns Hopkins University in 1931; the following year he moved to McGill University in Montreal, where he remained from 1932 to 1945. In 1945 he moved to the University of Montreal, where he taught until his retirement in 1976.

According to Selye, stress is the body's response to demands made on it. Selye refers to these demands as stressors. Stress, then, is a biological state manifested by a syndrome, a set of symptoms. On the basis of a long series of experiments with animals, he concluded that bodily stress reactions follow a three-state general adaptation syndrome. The three stages of this syndrome are an alarm reaction, a stage of resistance, and a stage of exhaustion.

In the alarm reaction the body mobilizes its resources to cope with added stress. The adrenal glands step up their output of adrenaline and noradrenaline. As these hormones enter the bloodstream, some bodily processes are speeded up and others are slowed, to concentrate bodily resources where they are needed. Common physiological responses during this stage are increased cardiac rate and output, increased blood pressure, increased respiratory rate, decreased blood supply to the visceral organs, increased blood supply to the vital organs (heart, brain, liver, peripheral muscles), and dilation of the pupils. These responses constitute a physiological call to arms: the fight, flight, or fright responses to the stressors.

If the stress persists, the individual enters a second stage, resistance. During this stage the person seems to develop a resistance to the particular stressor that provoked the alarm reaction. The symptoms that occurred during the first stage of stress disappear, even though the disturbing stimulation continues, and the physiological processes that had been disturbed during the alarm reaction appear to resume normal functioning.

If the stress still continues, the stage of exhaustion comes about. In this stage the body's resources are exhausted and the stress hormones are depleted. Unless a way of alleviating stress is found, a psychosomatic disease, organ failure, serious loss of health, or death may occur.

Two ideas appear to be central to Selye's theory. The first is that the body's response is the same regardless of the source of the stress. The second is that a continued pattern of these reactions ultimately results in physical breakdown.

Selye's major works are *The Physiology and Pathology of Exposure to Stress* (1950), *The Stress of Life* (1956), *Stress in Health and Disease* (1976), and *The Stress of My Life* (1977).

S. N. BALLARD

See STRESS.

Sensation and Perception. The study of how we take in information about the world around us and the picture we create of that world. The term *sensation* refers to the processes that occur when physical energy in the environment (such as sound waves) is registered by a sense organ (such as the ear). The term *perception* refers to the conscious experience of the environment; how we interpret and label the information received through our senses. The loudness and pitch of a sequence of sounds are sensations; the experience of a melody is a perception.

Sensation and perception belong on a continuum; they are also interactive processes. Experience and expectations direct perceivers to select from the sensory information available and help organize that information into a particular precept, while sensory information influences which particular memories, labels, and expectations are selected from the mind.

Sensory and perceptual processes have been considered basic to an understanding of the human mind for many centuries by Greek philosophers, Arabic and Latin scholars, British empiricists (*see* Empiricism), and others. Founders of modern experimental psychology, such as Wilhelm Wundt and Granville Stanley Hall, focused their research primarily on the senses. The study of sensory and perceptual processes is now an active subdiscipline of psychology. The bulk of research has been on the visual system; David Hubel and Torsten Wiesel won the 1981 Nobel Prize in physiology and medicine for their research on the organization of the visual cortex. Other active areas include other human sensory systems, cross-species and cross-cultural comparative studies, and perceptual development.

All sensory systems contain the same basic elements. They differ only in the kinds of physical energy they register (light, sound waves, mechanical or chemical energy). Each system has a sense organ (such as eyes, ears, skin). Within each sense organ are receptors that register physical energy and transduce it into neural energy. For vision, these are the rods and cones of the retina; for hearing, the hair cells of the basilar membrane in the inner ear. How do we distinguish between seeing a tree, hearing music, or tasting an orange—qualitatively very different experiences—when we do not perceive these things directly but only as they have been transduced into neural activity? In the early nineteenth century Johannes Muller proposed the doctrine of specific nerve energies, which states that each neuron or set of neurons is specific to particular sensory experiences. If one neuron is active, then one has a visual experience. If another neuron is active, one has an auditory experience. The subsequent discovery of neural pathways specific to each sensory system up to the level of the cortex supports this doctrine.

After transduction the patterned neural activity that represents the physical stimulus is carried to the brain, where it is organized and integrated. Some of this organization occurs in the thalamus, a large structure deep in the forebrain; further organization occurs in the primary processing areas of the cerebral cortex, the large outer surface of the brain. From the cortex information is relayed to numerous other brain regions, where it is integrated with information from the other senses, memories, and emotions to produce a meaningful picture of the world.

Therefore, perception occurs in the brain, not in the sense organs. Direct stimulation of sensory receiving areas in the brain can create sensory experiences. For example, one "sees stars" after a blow to the back of the head, which stimulates the primary visual processing area of the occipital lobe. Also, different aspects of a stimulus are processed separately. For example, the perception of a blue jay flying past results from separate mechanisms that process color, contour, and movement; concepts like "blue jay" are retrieved and incorporated into the percept. We know these processes are separate because of the existence of cases where people have lost one specific aspect of perception, such as the ability to see color or movement. How our perceptions can be so unified when stimulus aspects are processed separately is known as the binding problem, and is the subject of much current research in psychology, neuroscience, and philosophy.

Since our perceptions result from the integration of sensory information with memories, emotions, and expectations, we do not perceive the world objectively. Numerous compelling examples demonstrate this, such as perceptual illusions and certain aftereffects. Strawberry and apple shapes cut out of orange-red construction paper are perceived as more red than mushroom or geometric shapes cut from the identical paper. Ambiguous shapes are perceived in different ways, depending on the context in which they are seen (Goldstein, 1996).

The fact that our picture of the world includes in a real way our personalities and experiences has implications for therapists and counselors. Clients do not function in objectively defined contexts; rather, their perceptions of their situations play an important role in their responses. There are also implications for the presumed objectivity of science. If science is based on the premise that valid knowledge about the world is obtained through the senses, then the observation that perception results from an interaction of beliefs, expectations, and motivations with sensory stimulation clearly challenges the assumption of objectivity.

Despite the implicit challenge to objectivity, perception is often reduced to mechanistic neurophysiological mechanisms that are partly genetically determined and partly shaped by environmental stimulation; in either case the perceiver is viewed as a passive responder. However, there are alternative voices. In the early 1900s the Gestalt psychologists argued against the idea that perceptions are the sum of units of sensation, coining the famous phrase: "The whole is different from the sum of its parts." Researchers from a cognitive perspective have clearly demonstrated the roles of memory, motivation, and context on perception. And the ecological approach describes the person as an active perceiver who becomes an expert in picking up the sensory information available in the environment (Gibson, 1979). Although the dominant paradigm remains reductionist, these persistent alternative voices reflect a more Christian view of human beings as active agents functioning in a dynamic context.

References

Gibson, J. J. (1979). *The ecological approach to visual perception*. Boston: Houghton Mifflin.

Goldstein, E. B. (1996). *Sensation and perception* (4th ed.). Pacific Grove, CA: Brooks/Cole.

H. LOOY

See PERCEPTUAL DEVELOPMENT.

Sensitive Period. Developing organisms, whether they are animal or human, encounter sensitive or critical periods when biological changes and environmental influences interact in such a way as to have a permanent effect. The earlier the period of influence, the more profound the consequences; damage to the fetus is greater in early pregnancy, and harm to the child is more severe during the first few years of life. If the expectant mother takes a drug such as Thalidomide or contracts a disease such as rubella (German measles) during the first three months of pregnancy, when the limb buds of the fetus are forming and the heart, eyes, ears, and other organs are taking shape, the damage to the child may be malformed arms and legs, an impaired heart, blindness, deafness, and in some cases mental retardation and even death. The fetus is less sensitive to these influences after the first trimester, although malnutrition of the mother, smoking, or excessive alcohol consumption may be harmful to the unborn at any time during the gestation period.

The human infant is more sensitive to becoming attached to the principal caretaker (usually the mother) during the first year of life than at any other time, and if this child is neglected or mistreated during this time he or she may become emotionally scarred. Studies of animals confirm the importance of early bonding; birds imprint on the first moving object within hours after hatching, and monkeys deprived of mothering are unable to relate to other monkeys and will engage in self-mutilation when they are under stress. A dog or a cat growing up wild will not make a good pet even though it is given care when it is mature. The critical period for learning to love and for receiving love has passed.

Even as there are sensitive periods for physical development and for emotional attachment, so there also are sensitive periods for the acquisition of personality traits needed for optimal psychological functioning (Erikson, 1980). The first and most important component of a healthy personality is a sense of trust acquired by the baby during the first year, followed by a sense of autonomy in the toddler, initiative in the preschooler, industry at the elementary school age, identity at the high school level, Intimacy in early adulthood, generativity in middle adulthood, and integrity in old age. Each component is sensitive to a particular time in the person's life and is dependent on the formation of the personality components preceding it.

Freud (1923/1961) believed that a sensitive or critical period exists for moral development. If a child has not acquired a superego or conscience before the age of six, it will be either more difficult or impossible to develop a sensitivity to right and wrong at a later time. There is also evidence for an optimal time for toilet training (Sears, Maccoby, & Levin, 1957), language acquisition (Bloom, 1970), intellectual performance (Piaget, 1971), and classroom learning.

Parents and educators are understandably concerned when a child does not proceed at the optimal rate for learning a particular skill. There is now increasing interest in the consequences to the child who is pushed into activities for which he or she is not prepared. Growing up too fast too soon is the theme of Elkind's *The Hurried Child* (1981), which shows that damage may be as great for the child who is hurried as for the child who proceeds too slowly. Either way the stage of growth has not been linked to its most sensitive period, resulting in less than optimal performance.

The Scriptures tell us to "train a child in the way he should go, and when he is old he will not turn from it" (Prov. 22:6, NIV). The sensitive period for training in appropriate behavior comes in childhood, and the effects of that training last for a lifetime.

References

Bloom, L. (1970). *Language development*. Cambridge, MA: MIT Press.

Elkind, D. (1981). *The hurried child*. Reading, MA: Addison-Wesley.

Erikson, E. H. (1980). *Identity and the life cycle*. New York: Norton.

Freud, S. (1923/1961). The ego and the id. In J. Strachey (Ed. and Trans.), *The standard edition of the complete psychological works of Sigmund Freud* (Vol. 19). London: Hogarth. (Original work published 1923)

Piaget, J. (1971). *Biology and knowledge*. Chicago: University of Chicago Press.

Sears, R. R., Maccoby, E. E., & Levin, H. (1957). *Patterns of child rearing*. Evanston, IL: Row-Peterson.

B. CLOUSE

See LIFE SPAN DEVELOPMENT; DEVELOPMENTAL PSYCHOLOGY.

Sensory Deprivation. Sensory deprivation (SD) is a state of depleted sensory input created by techniques devised to alter or drastically reduce the normal flow of sensory information reaching the brain. Prolonged sensory deprivation can alter brain activity, impair normal cognitive and perceptual functions, and produce hallucinations. Psychological interest was piqued by the effects of brainwashing techniques inflicted upon American prisoners during the Korean War. The prisoners were isolated for long periods of time in tiny, underground cubicles that restricted movement and shut out light and sound except for occasional propaganda messages. This harsh treatment produced hallucinations, confusion, and distortions in thinking in addition to incredible physical stress. A number of soldiers cracked under this treatment, ostensibly converting to communist beliefs and signing false confessions.

Interested researchers at McGill University in Canada (Bexton, Heron, & Scott, 1954), under the leadership of Donald O. Hebb, simulated some of these conditions with volunteers who were paid $20 per day for participation. Except for short bathroom breaks or meals, volunteers were asked to lie in bed, their eyes covered with translucent goggles, their arms and legs covered with padded cardboard cylinders to reduce tactile stimulation, and sound restricted to the monotonous hum of a fan. In spite of the pay (which was generous in the 1950s) and the fact that volunteers could sleep as much as they liked, all participants found the experience unpleasant and half quit before 48 hours. Those who remained reported visual hallucinations, an inability to concentrate, aimlessly drifting thoughts, and blank periods in which they could not tell if they were awake or asleep. Testing right after the sessions also revealed mild cognitive, perceptual, and motor impairments that disappeared in a few days.

Subsequent studies generally confirmed the McGill findings, although variations in techniques and procedures have inevitably produced some inconsistencies. (Researchers have also employed confinement to bed, an iron lung, a whole-body respirator previously used for polio victims, or submersion in a tank of water kept at body temperature in dark, soundproof rooms to produce sensory deprivation.) The most consistent findings are the cognitive impairments during sensory deprivation and hallucinations, although hallucinations may not be as frequent as the McGill studies seemed to indicate (Zubek, 1969).

The hallucinations produced by sensory deprivation have some intriguing features. They vary in complexity from the very simple (formless, meaningless, lights or sounds), to animated scenes that are very colorful and may incorporate voices or music, to complex visions that are organized and realistic. Observers are not able to control their onset, content, or termination and have engaged in conversation or physical exercise without disrupting them. They are similar to the hallucinations produced by LSD or mescaline in that they are primarily visual, often progress from diffuse perceptions of light or geometric forms (lattice work, cobwebs, or spirals) to complex, realistic images (Seigal, 1980). However, drug-induced hallucinations are usually much more vivid and realistic. SD-induced hallucinations bear some resemblance to dreams, and sensory deprivation can create an altered state of consciousness that resembles a twilight state of sleep. It is possible that the hallucinations are being created by the same brain mechanisms that bring forth the imagery of our dreams.

Sensory deprivation was extensively researched through the 1960s, but after that interest declined until the mid-1970s. Lilly (1972), a psychiatrist, reported some unusual results with his water immersion technique, which aroused immediate interest in early New Age circles. (New Agers are interested in any technique that alters consciousness because they believe that altered states provide access to spiritual realities; Hillstrom, 1995.) Lilly had experimented extensively upon himself, experiencing waking dreams, trancelike states, and even apparent mystical encounters in his tank. He reports that when he took LSD before entering the tank, he was able to leave his body, travel to other realms at will, and even meet with two spirit guides who had previously saved his life on a bad LSD trip.

Suedfeld (1980), who also believes that SD can be a powerful spiritual tool, suggested that one way to revive general interest in the process would be to change its name to restricted environmental stimulation technique (REST) to get rid of sensory deprivation's negative image. He and others also conducted studies that suggested that REST might be a valuable tool for some types of therapy. This strategy has worked, and sensory deprivation is back, reframed as REST, a possible adjunct to therapy and a tool that alters consciousness so discerning participants can use it to explore other (spiritual) realities.

From a Christian perspective there are two very real dangers in this kind of spiritual seeking. The Bible strongly forbids every practice (e.g., mediumship, spiritism, divination, casting spells) that is intended to establish contact with any spiritual being aside from God himself (see Deut. 17:9–13; Lev. 19:26, 31; 20:6, 27). The experiences encountered in altered states can be highly deceptive. Altered states interfere with normal perception, judgment, and critical thinking and at the same time can produce experiences that seem real, awe-inspiring, and significant, even though they are absolutely false (Hillstrom, 1995). The combination provides a powerful strategy for spiritual deception.

References

Bexton, W. H., Heron, W., & Scott, T. (1954). Effects of decreased variation in the sensory environment. *Canadian Journal of Psychology, 8,* 70–76.

Hillstrom, E. L. (1995). *Testing the spirits.* Downers Grove, IL: InterVarsity Press.

Lilly, J. C. (1972). *The center of the cyclone.* New York: Bantam.

Siegal, R. K. (1980). Hallucinations. In R. L. Atkinson & R. C. Atkinson (Eds.), *Mind and behavior* (Scientific American). San Francisco: Freeman.

Suedfeld, P. (1980). *Restricted environmental stimulation: Research and clinical applications.* New York: Wiley.

Zubek, J. P. (1969). *Sensory deprivation: Fifteen years of research.* New York: Appleton-Century-Crofts.

E. L. Hillstrom

See Consciousness.

Sentence-Completion Tests. Verbal projective techniques widely used in both clinical practice and research. Stimulus words or sentence stems that permit an almost unlimited variety of possible completions are given to the examinee. Examples might be Life is . . . ; The Bible . . . ; It is a terrible thing to be . . . ; God . . . ; It would be nice to forget . . . ; Fathers often . . . ; Most churches. . . . There are numerous published and unpublished forms of sentence completion tests, the most widely used one being the Rotter Incomplete Sentences Blank. Other prominent measures include the Bloom Sentence Completion Survey, Activity Completion Technique, Incomplete Sentences Task, Geriatric Sentence Completion Form, Washington University Sentence Completion Test, and Miner Sentence Completion Scale (see Gregory, 1996).

As with any projective technique, the assessor assumes that the completed sentences reflect the underlying motivations, conflicts, and fears of the assessee. Scoring tends to be subjective-intuitive, but more objective and standardized formats are available for widely used measures such as the Rotter Incomplete Sentences Blank. Very limited data are available on the more formal psychometric characteristics of these tests (i.e., reliability, norms, validity, standardization). This has certainly not diminished their perceived usefulness to therapists who appreciate their conceptual or clinical validity (i.e., they help therapists to develop a dynamic working model of the person).

Sentence-completion tests are almost always used in conjunction with a full battery of psychological tests (see Groth-Marnat, 1990). In this way the clinician or researcher can evaluate emotional, cognitive, or behavioral qualities of persons in as meaningful and reliable a way as possible. This is a challenge, since there is little agreement among personality theorists as to what personality is or what the terms means. The perspectives of theory, research, and testing have been relatively independent of one another, resulting in a great proliferation of tests and instruments intended to measure personality but without sufficient clarity about the core constructs (see Maloney & Ward, 1976). Models that are truly integrative are urgently needed in clinical assessment to help the clinician or researcher more accurately and logically evaluate an individual's overall intellectual and personality functioning.

The Rotter Incomplete Sentences Blank can be scored in a more objective fashion. A single adjustment score is calculated by summing the scores across all responses. Although this deceptively simple score can provide a quick and efficient index of daily functioning, it hardly does justice to rich and complex dimensions of personhood. As with all self-report measures, it is subject to response biases and expectancy effects. Unless the examinee is cooperative and truthful, the data may be of questionable validity.

The wise clinician must be careful not to overgeneralize from any single assessment measure. It is best to consider the results of a sentence-completion test as a small but not necessarily representative sample of behavior. When they are used in conjunction with such other highly regarded psychology tests as the Wechsler scales, the Minnesota Multiphasic Personality Inventory (MMPI), the California Psychological Inventory (CPI), the Rorschach Ink Blot Test, or the Thematic Apperception Test (TAT) they may prove to be useful tools for developing clinical inferences or hypotheses.

References

Gregory, R. (1996). *Psychological testing* (2nd ed.). Boston: Allyn & Bacon.

Groth-Marnat, G. (1990). *Handbook of psychological assessment* (2nd ed.). New York: Wiley Interscience.

Maloney, M., & Ward, M. (1976). *Psychological assessment: A conceptual approach.* New York: Oxford University Press.

R. E. Butman

See Personality Assessment; Psychological Measurement.

Sentiment. A word used by Allport (1950) to refer to interest, outlook, or system of beliefs. Sentiments spring from a person's course of development when stable units of personality begin to emerge. According to Allport, personality emerges as a product of motivation and organization. This system of readiness or motivated organization prepares the person for adaptive behavior that may be manifested as a habit, trait, neurosis, or sentiment. It becomes sentiment when the behavior represents an organization of feeling and thought directed toward a definable object of value, such as one's mother, son, keepsake, neighborhood, or fatherland.

Sentiment may also involve more abstract ideas of value, either positive or negative, such as the nature of beauty or religion. Thus an atheist may have a negative sentiment with regard to all things considered religious, while a Christian would have a positive sentiment. Allport discussed extensively the nature of mature religious sentiment. He viewed this as disposition built through experience that is able to respond favorably and in certain habitual ways to conceptual objects and principles that the person regards as of the utmost importance as well as to what is regarded as permanent or central in the nature of things.

Reference

Allport, G. W. (1950). *The individual and his religion.* New York: Macmillan.

J. H. ROBERTSON

See PERSONALITY; ALLPORT, GORDON WILLARD.

Separation. *See* DIVORCE; LOSS AND SEPARATION.

Separation Anxiety Disorder. Separation anxiety disorder is a childhood disorder that is developmentally inappropriate and involves excessive anxiety regarding separation from home or from major attachment figures. To be diagnosed, the patient must display at least three of the following symptoms for at least a four-week duration, independent of pervasive development disorder, schizophrenia, or other psychotic disorder: recurrent, excessive distress when separated from home or major attachment figures; persistent and excessive anxiety that a potentially disastrous event (i.e., getting lost or getting kidnapped) will lead to separation from major attachment figures; persistent reluctance or refusal to go to school or elsewhere because of fear of separation; persistent and excessive fear or reluctance to be alone or without major attachment figures at home or without significant adults in other settings; persistent reluctance or refusal to go to sleep away from home or even without being near a major attachment figure at home; repeated nightmares involving the theme of separation; and repeated complaints of physical symptoms such as headaches, stomachaches, nausea, and/or vomiting when separation from major attachment figures occurs or is anticipated.

Researchers have estimated the prevalence to be approximately 4% in children and young adolescents. According to the *DSM-IV* (American Psychiatric Association, 1994), this is purely an estimation due to the fact that the disorder often goes undiagnosed. The disorder seems to be equally common among boys and girls. However, this changes in adolescence, with females becoming three times more likely than males to be diagnosed with the disorder (Kendall & Hammen, 1995).

Many factors may contribute to the development of this disorder. Some studies suggest that traumatic experiences are the primary cause, while others suggest that prior learning experiences in the family make certain children more vulnerable to it. Infant-caregiver attachment plays an important part in development. If children do not form healthy attachments when they are very young, they may suffer from this anxiety later in their development (Bowlby, 1969; Kendall & Hammen, 1995).

In addition, supporting the diathesis-stress model, researchers have shown that separation anxiety disorder is more common in first-degree biological relatives of those who have had the disorder than in the general population. The disorder also appears to be more frequent in children of mothers with panic disorder (American Psychiatric Association, 1994). In some cases the anxiety truly is a learned response: children and their primary caregivers develop a mutually dependent relationship in which separation is distressing to both. These children tune into the anxiety of their parents when separated. These anxieties are transmitted unconsciously to the child, who is unequipped developmentally to discriminate between one's own fears and those of others; hence the learned response (Benner, 1985).

This disorder provides a clear illustration of the contrast between normal and abnormal behavior depending on one's age. Almost all children exhibit a form of separation anxiety toward the end of the first year of life, peaking around 12 months and then gradually disappearing. In some children, however, it does not disappear but persists well into their childhood years. In the most common patterns of the disorder, the anxiety disappears on schedule only to reappear at full intensity some later time in childhood or early adolescence after some type of life stress. For example, the death of someone close to the child, an illness, a move and/or change of schools, or another major change or stress may encourage the development of the disorder. Onset is rarely as late as adolescence, but this is not undocumented.

The anxiety concerning possible separation and the avoidance of situations involving separation may persist for several years. In some extreme cases, children with this disorder cannot be separated from the parents or other primary attachment figures by so much as a wall and will literally follow them from room to room. In most cases, however, the child prefers to stay at home with the parent or prefers to stay in close company to the major attachment figure. But even when the parent or attachment figure is close, the child may be haunted by fears of disaster, such as a kidnapping or fire, that may occur if they are ever apart. Children with this disorder generally exhibit sleeping problems as well, since sleep means separation. Consequently they may appear at their parents' door night after night, asking to crawl into bed with them. If the parents do not allow this, the children are likely to camp outside of their parents' door (American Psychiatric Association, 1994; Bootzin, Acocella, & Alloy, 1993).

Children with the disorder are often described as unusually conscientious, conforming, and eager to please. However, most of the children are typically viewed as demanding, intrusive, and needing constant attention, putting strain on parents (Benner, 1985). Therefore parent-child conflicts are common and serve only to exacerbate the problem, since the parents' annoyance and anger cause the children to become more fearful of abandonment and separation (American Psychiatric Association, 1994).

In Western society, where independence is so positively reinforced, individuals may suffer an extreme amount of stress in dealing with the fact that they have this disorder. Adolescents with the disorder will often deny their symptoms—especially males, perhaps contributing to the difference in prevalence of diagnoses among adolescent females and males. However, the disorder can manifest itself in their limited activity alone and reluctance to leave home. In older individuals suffering from separation anxiety disorder, we can often observe trouble handling changes in circumstances such as moving, college, and getting married. The few adults with the disorder tend to be overly concerned about their spouses and children and experience marked discomfort when separated from them (American Psychiatric Association, 1994).

Another concern demanding attention is the lack of social development if the disorder goes untreated. Children, in not wanting to go to school because of the separation, often fall away from any academic progress. They may stop doing homework and/or studying altogether, believing that they may not have to go to school any longer if they do not do the work required. Also, in not going to school, camp, or other children's houses to play, they do not get the opportunity to develop social skills. They do not make any new friends and easily lose the friends they once had (American Psychiatric Association, 1994).

Research regarding the optimal treatment for children with anxiety disorder such as separation anxiety disorder is minimal. Attention in the past has been given to behavioral problems that researchers deemed more disruptive. However, studies are beginning to appear regarding this issue (Kendall et al., 1992; Kendall & Hammen, 1995). Cognitive-behavior therapy seems to be the treatment of choice (Klein, Koplewicz, & Kanner, 1992). Therapists first teach the children about their emotional, cognitive, and behavioral fear reactions. Then they teach the children strategies to manage the arousal. Once the patients learn the skills, they practice them in the once-feared context—being alone, separated from the attachment figure. Therapists have also employed systematic desensitization, during which the therapist separates the child from the attachment figure while allowing him or her to remain in a safe environment with another adult the child likes and deems responsible. Eventually the child will learn that he or she can be safe without necessarily being with the attachment figure. Note that in treatment for this disorder, as in many forms of treatment, family support is needed.

Some medications such as clomipramine and imipramine have been used to treat the symptoms directly. However, due to the fact that medications treat only the symptoms, not the problem itself, and because of tolerance and withdrawal effects, therapists and physicians do not recommend medications for this disorder (Kendall & Hammen, 1995; Klein, Koplewicz, & Kanner, 1992).

References

American Psychiatric Association. (1994). *Diagnostic and statistical manual of mental disorders* (4th ed.). Washington, DC: Author.

Benner, D. G. (Ed.). (1985). *Baker encyclopedia of psychology.* Grand Rapids, MI: Baker.

Bootzin, R. R., Acocella, J. R., & Alloy, L. B. (1993). *Abnormal psychology: Current perspectives.* New York: McGraw-Hill.

Bowlby, J. (1969). *Attachment and loss: Attachment.* New York: Basic Books.

Kendall, P. C., Chansky, T. E., Kane, M. T., Kim, R., Kortlander, E., Ronan, K. R., Sessa, F. M., & Siqueland, L. (1992). *Anxiety disorders in youth: Cognitive-behavioral interventions.* Needham, MA: Allyn & Bacon.

Kendall, P. C., & Hammen, C. (1995). *Abnormal psychology.* Boston: Houghton Mifflin.

Klein, R. G., Koplewicz, H. S., & Kanner, A. (1992). Imipramine treatment of children with separation anxiety disorder. *Journal of American Academic Child Adolescent Psychiatry, 31* (1), 21–28.

K. J. HETRICK

See ATTACHMENT THEORY AND DISORDERS.

Separation-Individuation Process. *See* MAHLER, MARGARET.

Sex Differences. *See* MEN, PSYCHOLOGY OF; WOMEN, PSYCHOLOGY OF.

Sex Education. Although it appears that the childbearing rate in the United States for teenage women is down from its high point in the 1950s, it is down in spite of dramatic increases in the frequency of teenage intercourse experience and decreases in the age of first sexual experience. About 40% of high school students are nonvirgins by the end of the ninth grade; by the senior year about 72% are nonvirgins with 55% reporting having sex in the previous three months (the rates for women are slightly lower than for men). More than one million American teenage females get pregnant each year. It appears that the birthrate is down primarily because of increased use of abortion. An estimated 3.1% of women between 15 and 17 and 6.3% of women aged 18 and 19 have an abortion each year (compared to 2.8% of all women); about 400,000 abortions are performed annually on women between the ages of 15 and 19. Other major changes over time include increases in the frequency of teenage mothers keeping their children and decreases in the frequency of teenage parents marrying as a response to pregnancy (Jones & Jones, 1993; Venovskis, 1988).

Sex education is a frequent answer to the question of how to respond to the contemporary sexuality crisis. Christians face particular challenges with regard to sex education because important principles of a Christian sexual ethic and the broader vision of sexuality behind them are no longer widely shared in Western culture. Surveys are unanimous in indicating that premarital sexual intercourse is regarded as immoral by only a small percentage of the public, and there is widespread sympathy for tolerance and acceptance of homosexual practice. Most common is the moral view that any sexual acts that are consensual, that bring pleasure and do not inflict damage, and that are growth-enhancing for the participants are acceptable if not commendable.

Sex education programs vary widely on at least the following dimensions: context of intervention (school, church, community center or clinic, family); age at which instruction begins; comprehensiveness of the educational intervention; relative emphasis and prioritization of such program goals as inculcation of moral tradition, encouragement of abstinence, facilitation of long-term and/or short-term enjoyment of an enriching sexual life, prevention of pregnancy and sexually transmitted diseases (STDs), self-acceptance of sexual identity, or utilization of available family planning services such as abortion or emergency contraception (the term for postintercourse intervention to eliminate possible pregnancy); mode of intervention, including such methods as the provision of information, modification of attitudes, modification of values, or directly shaping desired behavior patterns (from developing refusal skills to training in purchasing condoms); and the assumptions behind the program, such as that sex is a natural bodily function, that pleasure or love or procreation are the purpose for sexual expression, or that a particular moral stand on such matters as contraception and abortion is correct.

As sex education programs vary on all these dimensions and more, simple conclusions about whether or not sex education works are difficult to draw. There are no objective studies of the effectiveness of programs offered in churches. For simplicity we might think of two prototypes of school-based sex education: Comprehensive programs that attempt to be value-neutral in providing information about the array of possible sexual choices, and either deemphasize abstinence or balance attention to abstinence with instruction in contraceptive methods, both on the assumption that a substantial percentage of students are going to become sexually active, and abstinence-oriented programs that deemphasize attention to contraceptive instruction and attempt to foster chastity.

The competent evaluation of whether a program works should minimally include comparisons against an appropriate control group, objective and valid measures of outcome that look at changes in behavior as well as attitudes, short- and long-term assessments of change, and an honest assessment of possible negative consequences of the program. Evaluations of program effectiveness have been plagued with problems. While abstinence-oriented programs are popular with moral conservatives, the empirical evidence of their effectiveness is meager, with most studies lacking comparisons to control groups and long-term follow-ups and plagued by too much reliance on assessments of attitudes (of uncertain validity) without accompanying rigorous scrutiny of behavior changes.

Comprehensive sex education programs have been more competently evaluated, but the results have been discouraging. We might summarize the goals of comprehensive programs as decreasing the incidence of sexually transmitted diseases, decreasing rates of irresponsible sexual experimentation among teenagers, increasing utilization of contraception by teenagers, decreasing teen pregnancy, and decreasing birth rates. We know that sexually transmitted disease rates for teens are not decreasing generally, and a few (e.g., HIV infection and chlamydia) are increasing steadily. The evidence suggests that rates of teenage sexual activity have gone up markedly since the 1950s. The last three goals of increasing contraceptive use, reducing teen pregnancy, and birth are where proponents often claim success. Flora and Thoresen (1988, p. 967), however, noted that although 80% of school districts offer some sort of sex education programming, the "effects of these education programs are unrelated to changes in sexual behavior, such as reduced frequency of 'unsafe' sexual intercourse or lower adolescent pregnancy rates." There is little evidence showing that these programs dramatically increase the reliable use of contraceptive methods above the effect of their general availability, though condom usage may be slowly increasing (effective contraceptive utilization seems more common among European adolescents). When they are asked whether school-based sex education programs decrease teen pregnancy, researchers often describe program results in terms of decreased fertility rates, a term that refers to the rate of live births. Any decreases or stabilization in live births to teenagers appears principally due to increased use of abortion. Thus only one goal of public sex education has been successfully achieved, a goal that is not often publicly stated: of decreasing live births by increasing the utilization of abortion by teenage women.

Comprehensive programs can also be faulted conceptually for attempting to make sex education value-neutral. There is no such thing as meaningless sex in any society. Sex always has meanings for relationships and for society that transcend its physical acts. At its worst value-neutral sex education takes a most meaningful human action and presents it to the student stripped of that meaning. Sex education is never value-neutral or meaning-neutral; rather, only certain meanings and values are removed (i.e., its moral and sacramental meanings) and others are presented as of equal value. Baumrind (1982) has suggested that children are reared to expect value judgments from authority figures such as teachers in such emotionally charged areas as sexuality. When values are not mentioned or when a string of possible different values are presented to students with no particular prioritization or emphasis, adolescents interpret this as an authoritative declaration that no one value is better than any other value.

Research on the four factors predicting sexual experimentation of teens is quite relevant to this topic (see Jones & Jones, 1993). First, the closer the child's relationship to the parents, particularly between mother and daughter, the less likely the child is to have sex. It seems that a close relationship between parent and child instills in the child the desire to want to live out the values and moral beliefs of the parents, personalizes the moral choices of the adolescent as issues of loyalty to the parent, and probably serves as a resource for meeting the child's emotional needs that might otherwise be addressed via the sexual experimentation. Second, the sexual activity of the teenager's peer group is a predictor of teen sexual activity; this finding may be both cause (teens influenced by the peer group) and effect (teens seeking peer groups that behave similarly). Third, religious faith influences sexual activity; adolescents who have a firm personal faith are less likely to be sexually active. Finally, the degree to which the child values academic achievement predicts early sexual involvement; teens who have academic goals, are confident in their academic skills, and who believe in the value of their school work are more likely to delay their sexual experimentation than academically discouraged adolescents. These predictive factors suggest the vital role of parents in shaping the sexual behavior of their children. Parents can cultivate their relationships to their children, guide their selection of peers, cultivate their religious faith, and encourage their sense of meaning and purpose in their future vocations. Churches have a vital role to play as well.

Complex questions remain: What should be done for children whose parents abdicate their sex education responsibility? What changes must occur in society (e.g., the media) to support change in adolescent behavior patterns? How should morality be taught in public schools in a pluralistic society? Should Christians support or at least not object to contraceptive availability and instruction for adolescents who decide to be sexually active?

References

Baumrind, D. (1982). Adolescent sexuality. *American Psychologist*, 37 (12), 1402–1403.

Flora, J., & Thoresen, C. (1988). Reducing the risk of AIDS in adolescents. *American Psychologist, 43,* 965–970.

Jones, S., & Jones, B. (1993). *How and when to tell your kids about sex: A lifelong approach to shaping your child's sexual character.* Colorado Springs, CO: NavPress.

Venovskis, M. A. (1988). *An "epidemic" of teenage pregnancies?* New York: Oxford.

S. L. JONES

See SEXUALITY.

Sex Identity. *See* GENDER IDENTITY.

Sex Therapy. Modern sex therapy was inaugurated with the landmark publication of Masters' and Johnson's *Human Sexual Inadequacy* in 1970 and enjoyed a period of great optimism about the effectiveness of the new techniques (LoPiccolo, 1994). Prior to Masters and Johnson, sexual problems were treated with little success, as they were conceptualized as manifestations of long-term intrapsychic pathology (Zilbergeld & Kilmann, 1984). Therapy was far from brief with psychoanalysis being the standard treatment focusing on resolution of unconscious conflicts (Leiblum & Rosen, 1989). Masters and Johnson (1970) and Kaplan (1974) revolutionized the treatment of sexual problems by introducing time-limited behavioral techniques oriented toward symptom resolution (Leiblum & Rosen, 1989). From the modern sex therapy perspective, problems were conceptualized as arising primarily from ignorance about sexual functioning and negative attitudes toward sexuality. Hence treatment focused upon improving sexual attitudes and increasing knowledge about sexual functioning. The aim was to reduce anxiety and to increase sexual arousal, which led to more satisfying sexual interactions. In contrast to psychoanalysis, modern sex therapists adopted a directive approach and actively facilitated couple interaction. Therapy was distinguished by the extensive use of homework assignments in which the couples practiced the behavioral techniques (e.g., sensate focus, communication exercises) they had learned in session (LoPiccolo, 1994).

Modern sex therapy was built upon Masters' and Johnson's approach, which had three basic tenets. First, the presenting destructive sexual system was altered. Couples were directed to engage in new experiences. Second, resolution of sexual conflict was facilitated when the couple did what they had previously avoided. Third, this process brought to the fore issues that could be addressed with traditional therapeutic techniques. This approach was effective, particularly with male premature ejaculation and female primary anagorsmia (Zilbergeld & Kilmann, 1984). Although they were embraced with enthusiasm, these new approaches were not useful for treating all types of sexual dysfunctions. Problems of sexual desire, despite being among the most common complaints among couples seeking therapy, remained the most difficult and demanding faced by therapists (LoPiccolo, 1994). Moreover, LoPiccolo (1994) noted that contemporary outcome research on the effectiveness of sex therapy has failed to achieve the success rates initially reported by Masters and Johnson. LoPiccolo (1994) speculated that changes within contemporary culture and within clients who present for treatment of sexual difficulty have led to the decreases in outcome effectiveness of traditional sex therapy approaches. Sex therapists and theorists attempted to deal with the more recalcitrant sexual difficulties by adopting less theoretically pure and more eclectic approaches. This movement toward a transtheoretical perspective has initiated a new era in treating sexual problems (LoPiccolo, 1992, 1994).

Postmodern Sex Therapy. Leiblum and Rosen (1989) identified four major trends in sex therapy that may have predicated the emergence of postmodern sex therapy. First, the role of biological factors in sexual dysfunction received greater appreciation. Organic factors are ruled out before couples engage in therapy. Second, pharmacological interventions, particularly in the treatment of erectile dysfunction, received more emphasis. Third, greater attention was given to the dilemma posed by desire disorders and by inhibition in the experience and expression of sexual interest. Desire disorders represent the new frontier in sex therapy. They are the most complex and multifarious of problems encountered by sex therapists. The last trend represented an amalgamation of approaches in which therapeutic attention was focused on interpersonal systems concepts and object relations therapy.

These changes within sex therapy reflect changes in contemporary culture and in the types of problems that couples present in therapy (LoPiccolo, 1994). LoPiccolo views the postmodern society as more open and accepting of sexuality. More favorable sexual attitudes combined with greater availability of information in self-help books have helped many couples resolve problems that were once treated in session with the aid of a sex therapist. Therefore, many of those who seek help in contemporary therapy present disorders of sexual desire, which have more complex etiologies.

LoPiccolo (1994) notes that a postmodern approach takes into account the reasons behind the client's resistance to change. His approach has psychoanalytic underpinnings. He believes that sexual problems have a positive adaptive value that must be addressed if change is to take place. These secondary gains have adaptive value in four possible areas. First, sexual dysfunction may maintain systemic homeostasis (balance between individuals) for the couple with problems with intimacy, closeness, vulnerability, trust, power, or sharing. Second, sexual problems may have individual psychodynamic value as an individual defends the self against a low self-esteem or awareness of unacceptable cognitions. Third, sexual problems may have

adaptive value for an individual with unresolved family of origin issues (e.g., from an alcoholic family or a history of sexual abuse). Finally, sexual dysfunctions may have operant reinforcing value. For example, one might receive promotions and praise from work colleagues for devoting extra energy to the job that might compete with focusing energy to the sexual relationship. Using these four areas as a framework, the task of the postmodern sex therapist is to assess accurately both primary dysfunction and the concomitant secondary payoffs. Treatment focuses on both symptom resolution, using traditional modern sex therapy techniques, and on providing means to have secondary gains met in ways more adaptive for the couple.

To understand who benefits most from sex therapy, Zilbergeld and Kilmann (1984) identified several positive predictors of positive outcomes. First, couples benefit from sex therapy most when they have more circumscribed problems (clearly identifiable and recent onset of the problem area) and a limited number of complaints. Couples who present with pervasive or numerous complaints do not obtain the most positive outcomes. Second, couples with strong and committed relationships obtain the most beneficial outcomes. Third, active participation in treatment leads to more favorable outcomes. Lastly, couples benefit most from sex therapy when they have stability in other life areas (e.g., work, extended family relationships). Effective sex therapy requires couples who demonstrate intimacy and stability (Penner & Penner, 1990).

Successful sex therapy depends upon precise assessment. Penner and Penner's *Counseling for Sexual Disorders* (1990) is a helpful resource for the sex therapist and provides useful materials and rationale for a detailed sexual assessment. The text is replete with forms that may be used as templates for evaluating a couple's presenting problem. Penner and Penner provide a framework for sexual counseling from a biblical perspective, and they include more than 30 out-of-session activities from which the sex therapist can tailor treatment to unique presenting problems of each couple.

Sexual Desire Disorders. Sexual desire disorders have remained recalcitrant to many treatment efforts and have received considerable attention in recent years. Because sexual desire disorders represent the new frontier in sexual treatment, they will be discussed in this article (see specific entries for treatment of other sexual dysfunctions). The *DSM-IV* denotes two types of sexual desire disorders: sexual aversion disorder and hypoactive sexual desire disorder (American Psychiatric Association, 1994). Less common than hypoactive sexual desire disorder, sexual aversion disorder is characterized by an aversion to or an active avoidance of genital sexual contact. The aversion disorder causes marked distress or disturbance in interpersonal functioning and cannot be accounted for by another Axis I disorder (except another sexual dysfunction). Hypoactive sexual desire is characterized by a recurrent or persistent or absent desire for sexual activity or fantasy. Lief (1977) was one of the first to identify the problem and described it as inhibited sexual desire. Kaplan (1977), utilizing her triphasic conceptualization of human sexual response, named the problem hypoactive sexual desire. The etiology of hypoactive sexual desire disorder is thought to be complex, as is evidenced by its resistance to traditional treatment efforts (Leiblum & Rosen, 1989). No theory currently dominates the field (Heimann, Epps, & Ellis, 1995). Approaches have broadened to incorporate biological, intrapsychic, and interpersonal factors and are no longer theoretically pure (LoPiccolo, 1994). The traditional boundary between sex therapy and marital therapy is being blurred (Leiblum & Rosen, 1989).

Heimann, Epps, and Ellis (1995) delineate numerous problems of the current status of research on sexual desire disorders with couples. None of the studies included in their review employed adequate control group methodology, and most follow-up data covered only limited time. Furthermore, the nature of the hypoactive sexual desire disorder makes it difficult to operationalize. For example, many researchers measure desire level by self-report or frequency of sexual activity (see Heimann, Epps, & Ellis, 1995, for a review). Several questions arise: How many times does one have desire for sexual activity and not act on it? How many times does one engage in sexual activity without desire? Do all participants define desire similarly? Even diagnostic criteria of the *DSM-IV* rely on the subjective appraisal of the clinician based upon factors of age, sex, and life context (American Psychiatric Association, 1994).

Summary. Sex therapy continues to evolve. As sex therapists pursue more effective treatment, they modify the techniques to ameliorate presenting problems of complex etiology. Masters and Johnson moved beyond ineffective psychoanalysis to behavioral techniques and inaugurated modern sex therapy. As society changed and problems of sexual desire persisted, the techniques of Masters and Johnson became less effective. With the emergence of postmodern sex therapy, treatment has become less theoretically pure and more eclectic to find effective therapy for problems of sexual desire.

References

American Psychiatric Association. (1994). *Diagnostic and statistical manual of mental disorders* (4th ed.). Washington, DC: Author.

Heimann, J. R., Epps, P. H., & Ellis, B. (1995). Treating sexual desire disorders in couples. In N. S. Jacobson & A. S. Gurman (Eds.), *Clinical handbook of couple therapy.* New York: Guilford.

Kaplan, H. S. (1974). *The new sex therapy.* New York: Brunner-Mazel.

Kaplan, H. S. (1977). Hypoactive sexual desire. *Journal of Sex and Marital Therapy, 3,* 3–9.

Leiblum, S. R., & Rosen, R. C. (1989). Introduction: Sex therapy in the age of AIDS. In S. R. Leiblum & R. C. Rosen (Eds.) *Principles and practices of sex therapy* (2nd ed.). New York: Guilford.

Lief, H. (1977). Inhibited sexual desire. *Medical Aspects of Human Sexuality, 7,* 94–95.

LoPiccolo, J. (1992). Post-modern sex therapy for erectile failure. In R. C. Rosen & S. R. Leiblum (Eds.) *Erectile failure: Assessment and treatment.* New York: Guilford.

LoPiccolo, J. (1994). The evolution of sex therapy. *Sexual and Marital Therapy, 9,* 5–7.

Masters, W. H., & Johnson, V. E. (1970). *Human sexual inadequacy.* Boston: Little, Brown.

Penner, J. J., & Penner, C. L. (1990). *Counseling for sexual disorders.* Dallas: Word.

Rosen, R. C., & Leiblum, S. R. (1989). Assessment and treatment of desire disorders. In S. R. Leiblum & R. C. Rosen (Eds.), *Principles and practices of sex therapy* (2nd ed.). New York: Guilford.

Zilbergeld, B., & Kilmann, P. R. (1984). The scope and effectiveness of sex therapy, *Psychotherapy, 21,* (3), 319–326.

Additional Readings

Penner, J. J., & Penner, C. L. (1981). *The gift of sex: A Christian guide to sexual fulfillment.* Waco, TX: Word. This invaluable work is directed to the layperson or couple with sexual problems. It is also suitable for couples in premarital counseling.

Rosen, R. C., & Leiblum, S. R. (1988). *Sexual desire disorders.* New York: Guilford.

T. L. HIGHT

See SEXUALITY.

Sexual Arousal Disorders. *DSM-IV* describes one sexual arousal disorder for each gender. Both describe problems that are significantly disturbing either to the people with the disorder or to their relationships. As with all of the sexual dysfunctions, a disorder is not diagnosed unless the problem is persistent or recurrent. Arousal disorders are not diagnosed if the partner fails to provide enjoyable stimulation.

About 10% of people have an arousal disorder. Older men and women are more likely to experience arousal difficulties, and about half of people who see a clinician for a sexual dysfunction primarily complain of arousal problems.

In female sexual arousal disorder (inaccurately called frigidity), women cannot develop the physical changes of sexual arousal: increased blood flow and lubrication of the genitals. Some women can produce these changes but lose them before completing sexual activity. Often they are unable to develop sexual desire or achieve orgasm, and they may lack a subjective feeling of sexual arousal. If intercourse is painful, they may avoid sexual activity, with negative consequences for marriage.

Symptoms of female sexual arousal disorder may accompany the physiological changes accompanying menopause, nursing, and certain medical disorders, including diabetes. Clinicians do not diagnose this disorder if the symptoms are due exclusively to physiological causes.

The male form of sexual arousal disorder is called male erectile disorder (formerly impotence), in which men are unable to produce an erection firm enough for sexual intercourse. Some men produce an erection but lose it either upon attempting to penetrate the vagina or during intercourse. Most men with this disorder are able to produce a reliable erection while masturbating, and nearly all have erections during REM dreams, although they may not be aware of it.

Erectile disorder may impair marriage, preventing consummation and causing infertility. It is associated with low sexual desire and premature ejaculation.

The overwhelming majority of men with erectile disorder have previously experienced no such difficulty, and many find that the problem occurs only in certain situations or when the relationship is poor. Others have problems only with women whom they deeply love. Symptoms may happen in episodes separated by periods of normal function. Between 15% and 30% of the time the symptoms disappear without treatment.

Medication for high blood pressure, diabetes, and chronic alcoholism may impair erections. Some form of physical or hormonal problem is suspected in the majority of men with erectile disorder, but psychological factors are nearly always involved. If the cause is purely physiological, the man will be unable to experience an erection even during REM sleep. Consequently, an erection during sleep indicates that psychological factors are involved. The simplest test for erection during sleep is to apply a moistened strip of postage stamps around the base of the penis before going to bed. An erection will break the perforations. Sometimes, the discovery that erections occur during sleep is sufficient to end the episode of erectile disorder.

Fear, anxiety, anger, hostility, and poor communication in the relationship all contribute to arousal disorders. A woman is particularly likely to experience problems that result from not experiencing enough variety of stimulation to learn what is most arousing for her. If she does not know her own sexual anatomy or is unwilling to tell her partner what she wants him to do, arousal problems are more probable.

Since the man's erection is essential for sexual intercourse, some theorists argue that the man is under considerable performance pressure. As long as erection occurs reliably the pressure is insignificant, but once erection fails, even for medical reasons, concern increases dramatically. Worry then interferes with erection, compounding the problem.

Treatment of sexual arousal disorders deals primarily with the relationship, after considering the possible role of physiological conditions or psychological depression. Therapists encourage the couple to communicate about sexual activity that each person finds pleasurable.

As ignorance about sexual anatomy and behavior often contributes to arousal problems, clinicians will typically provide information about effective sexual behavior to the couple. Education about female sexual anatomy and responsiveness is intended to help the woman communicate her needs and to enable the man to be a more effective and sensitive lover.

Behavioral therapists may recommend sensate focus, in which partners take turns touching each other without sexual arousal being expected. In order to develop sensitivity to nongenital stimulation and to reduce anxiety about sexuality, they do not touch genitals or breasts. A few days later the couple begins genital stimulation, with no expectation of an erection. Erections that do occur are allowed to subside before touching resumes, and the couple learns that they can produce an erection.

Older men with erectile difficulties may require a longer period of stimulation and no other treatment. Especially after menopause, women may find that a water-based lubricating jelly is an adequate solution.

Some interventions are effective when physical problems cause an arousal disorder. Hormone therapy or changes in medication may help.

For men, the drug yohimbine may be taken by mouth, and various medications may be injected directly into the penis to produce an erection. Microsurgery to repair constricted blood vessels is sometimes effective. Various surgical methods to produce erections through implants or pumps frequently work well, but they have drawbacks. None of the physical methods produce long-term success if the relationship is contributing to the disorder, so psychological factors must always be considered.

P. D. YOUNG

See SEXUAL DYSFUNCTIONS.

Sexual Aversion Disorder. *See* SEXUAL DESIRE DISORDERS.

Sexual Desire Disorders. Desire is the first phase of the sexual response cycle of desire—excitement—orgasm—resolution. It includes both fantasizing about sexual activity and wanting to engage in sex. Desire occurs prior to feeling sexual pleasure and before tumescence, the increase of blood flow into the genitals.

Men as well as women may experience two sexual desire disorders. Hypoactive sexual desire disorder is a lack of interest in sexual activity. People who actively avoid sexual contact with a partner suffer from sexual aversion disorder.

According to *DSM-IV* (American Psychiatric Association, 1994), hypoactive sexual desire disorder (previously called inhibited sexual desire disorder) should be diagnosed when the clinician judges the client to have too few or no sexual fantasies or no desire for sexual activity. Not only does such a person not seek occasions for sexual activity but also he or she does not take advantage of readily available opportunities. Since many people who meet this criterion are satisfied with the condition (one study suggests 20% of the population have the disorder), the diagnosis may be applied only if the low level of desire seriously troubles the individual or relationships.

Some people with low sexual desire may be interested in one form of sexual activity or one partner but not another, whereas others are generally uninterested in sexual expression. Hypoactive sexual desire disorder usually begins in adulthood, after a stage of normal desire. The disorder became more common after it was first listed in *DSM-III*, perhaps reflecting the higher levels of sexual activity that people came to expect in the 1980s, and 60% of people with the disorder are men. Some clinicians claim that more men complain of low sexual desire than of any other sexual problem, and low desire often accompanies other sexual problems.

As the level of sexual desire is always judged in the context of a relationship, one person's desire may be low only in contrast to a partner's sex drive. For example, a woman's sexual desire level typically reaches a maximum when she is in her late thirties. If her husband is of the same age, his sex drive is likely to be declining. Consequently, she may complain of his relative lack of interest when his desire level is normal.

People with sexual aversion disorder actively avoid genital contact with a partner and typically find that the idea of such contact produces anxiety, fear, or disgust. Some people with this disorder avoid only genital contact but enjoy kissing and cuddling. Others shun all actions that are remotely sexual in nature. To avoid sexual situations, they may evade a partner completely, neglect hygiene, or become intensely involved in work or social activities, including church. Sexual aversion is less common than hypoactive sexual desire and is more common in women than in men.

Some people with sexual aversion disorder may panic when they face a sexual situation, and the disorder frequently impairs a marriage relationship.

Both sexual desire disorders are explained by similar theories, but the studies on which the theories are based are often poorly designed and conflicting. Clinicians commonly point to emotional problems in the relationship, such as anger or fear, and argue that the desire problem is a symptom of a larger difficulty with the relationship. Others suggest that the low level of desire is causing the problems in the marriage, and perhaps both are correct.

Another explanation points to experiences in the past, suggesting such causes as parents who taught strongly negative attitudes toward sex, a repressive religious upbringing, sexual abuse, or rape.

Sexual desire may be inhibited by depression, obsessive-compulsive disorder, or various medications, including drugs used to treat high blood pres-

sure or anxiety. When such factors are the sole cause of low levels of interest in sex, the clinician should not diagnose a sexual desire disorder.

Some people have low sexual desire because of fear of the consequences of sexual activity, including pregnancy, appearing foolish, or contracting sexually transmitted diseases (STDs). The AIDS epidemic has increased sexual avoidance among college women in particular.

Where the sources of the disorder can be identified, changing the behavior of the partner or even the situation may reduce the severity of the symptoms. Some sexual desire problems are due to poor hygiene or insistent sexual demands from the spouse, both of which may be changed with some effort and improved communication. If the fears of negative consequences of sexual activity are unrealistic, education about likely outcomes of sexual interaction may be helpful. In many cases, however, it appears that therapy must be directed at uncovering the underlying, hidden causes of the disorder.

Cognitive behavior therapy, which works fairly well for other sexual dysfunctions, has not been as effective with desire problems. A common cognitive strategy of people with desire disorders is to begin thinking about negative situations and worries whenever they face a sexual opportunity. As this strategy usually reduces anxiety about possible sexual activity, it is reinforced and thus very difficult to eliminate. Further, by avoiding sexual activity, people with these disorders have few opportunities to learn that they may enjoy sex.

Christian counselors, teachers, pastors, and parents must be very careful as they advocate sexual purity so that they do not convey messages that sexual activity is inherently evil, dirty, or destructive, to be avoided in all situations. Children reared with a positive view of sexuality in marriage are less likely to develop sexual desire disorders.

Reference

American Psychiatric Association. (1994). *Diagnostic and statistical manual of mental disorders* (4th ed.). Washington, DC: Author.

P. D. YOUNG

See SEXUAL DYSFUNCTIONS.

Sexual Dysfunctions. Sexual dysfunctions involve the disruption of the normal sexual response cycle. The sexual response cycle begins with desire, then excitement, followed by orgasm, and finally resolution.

Male erectile disorder (formerly known as impotence) is an inability to achieve or maintain an erection during intercourse. The disorder may be primary, having never been able to achieve erection, or secondary, having achieved erection in the past. Physiological causes of male erectile disorder include alcohol and drug use, diabetes, vascular disease, and hormonal irregularities. This may be especially true of men after age 70 (Mohr & Beutler, 1990). Penile implants are often used for treatment of physiologically caused male erectile disorder. Mental health treatment sequences move progressively toward intercourse while remaining relaxed (Kaplan, 1987).

In premature ejaculation orgasm is reached quickly so that the experience of intercourse is unsatisfactory. This usually causes the woman to be unable to reach orgasm before the male has reached the resolution phase. Treatment usually includes a stop-start method of sexual arousal to stall the ejaculation. Young men usually learn to delay orgasm as they become more experienced sexually, and they may seek help for premature ejaculation *(DSM-IV)*.

Male orgasmic disorder (formerly inhibited male orgasm) is a delay or absence of orgasm after the excitement stage of sexual response. This disorder is rare; however, the most common type is the inability to experience orgasm during intercourse, although manually or orally stimulated orgasm can be achieved.

Female sexual arousal disorder is the inability to maintain lubrication and swelling during sexual excitement, which causes an upsetting disruption of sexual activities. It may be caused by medications, menopause, diabetes, lactation, or psychological difficulties. Therapy is recommended when psychological factors are associated.

Female orgasmic disorder (formerly known as frigidity) is characterized by difficulty reaching orgasm after reaching the excitement phase of sexual response. This is experienced along a continuum from total inability to experience orgasm, to orgasm experienced only under certain conditions, to occasional difficulties reaching orgasm. The vast differences that females experience in orgasm makes diagnosis of this disorder difficult and often subjective. The cause of female orgasmic disorder is believed to be anxiety, which produces defenses to prevent the woman from responding to her partner. Treatment involves arranging the sexual experience so that the woman can respond to nondemand coitus and increasing sexual stimulation while remaining relaxed.

Sexual pain disorder, or dyspareunia, is the experience of pain during intercourse. It is more common in females but also exists for males (Lazarus, 1989). This sexual dysfunction is likely to be caused by a physical problem such as infection, lack of lubrication, improperly positioned uterus or ovary, a rigid hymen in females, congenital penile curvature for males, or sexually transmitted diseases (STDs). Therefore, a physical examination of the client is usually recommended as the first course of treatment. Dyspareunia can also be caused by psychological difficulties such as guilt, anxiety, previous rape, or sexual abuse. If sexual pain is caused by psychological difficulties, then therapy is recommended.

Hypoactive sexual desire disorder is a type of sexual desire disorder in which males or females have little desire for sex. Etiology is believed to either be biological or psychological factors that block sexual motivation. Sexual aversion disorder is diagnosed when individuals have a complete lack of interest in sex and avoid sexual situations.

Sexual dysfunctions are often associated with erroneous learning, anxiety, and interpersonal problems within couples. All treatment of sexual dysfunctions is most effective when both members of the couple recognize the difficulty as a joint problem (whether the dysfunction is present in the male or female) and work together to overcome their sexual dysfunction.

References

Kaplan, H. S. (1987). *The illustrated manual of sex therapy* (2nd ed.). New York: Brunner.

Lazarus, A. A. (1989). Dyspareunia: A multi-modal psychotherapeutic perspective. In S. R. Leiblum & R. C. Rosen (Eds.), *Principles and practice of sex therapy* (2nd ed.). New York: Guilford.

Mohr, D. C., & Beutler, L. E. (1990). Erectile dysfunction: A review of diagnostic and treatment procedures. *Clinical Psychological Review, 10,* 123–150.

J. S. RIPLEY

See DYSPAREUNIA; PREMATURE EJACULATION; VAGINISMUS.

Sexual Masochism. Sexual excitement derived from personal suffering and pain. The term originated in the works of Leopold V. Sacher-Masoch, who wrote about fictional characters who received sexual pleasure from pain. Masochism has been broadened to include not only enduring pain for sexual excitement but also receiving gratification from self-denial and suffering in general.

Sexual masochists prefer or indulge exclusively in behavior such as being bound, beaten, spanked, stuck with pins, trampled, verbally abused, humiliated, or otherwise made to suffer in conjunction with the sexual act. Orgasm may be very difficult or impossible to achieve without such behavior.

The individual must take part in the behavior and not just fantasize it to be considered a sexual masochist. A sexual activity may not be harmful. However, the possibility of harm is frequently a part of the experience, and sometimes the risk taking is such that the activities may be life-threatening. The central feature of masochism is not the pain or injury but submission to power. In the height of masochistic sexual excitement the pain itself is not experienced but only the sensation of being overpowered.

In theory the masochist is less afraid of physical pain than of an imagined uncontrollable encounter. The pain and being overpowered are in a sense controllable and therefore the lesser of two threats. The masochist's behavior circumvents the sexual inhibition that comes from an uncontrollable pain and rejection and thus allows sexual arousal to develop. The powerful woman (usually a prostitute) is the controllable substitute for a feared father figure.

The essential difference between masochism and sadism is that masochism stresses subjection to power. Sadists must subject the victim to pain or injury. Both the sadist and masochist engage in their sexual perversion as either a prerequisite or a replacement for coitus.

Sexual masochism is a learned behavior from childhood. The child may have received attention from hostile or destructive parents only when he or she was injured, ill, or failing in some way. So the child develops masochistic coping behavior that is coupled to sex as he or she matures sexually.

Treatment of sexual masochism is up to the therapist's discretion; there is little definitive data on effective psychological treatment modalities. Behavioral and insight-oriented treatments are the major exclusively psychological treatment methods. Behavioral therapy includes assertive training and desensitization. Insight-oriented therapy focuses on the restructuring of sexual attitudes through insight into the masochist's developmental process.

Chemotherapy is also utilized to help control extremely dangerous self-destructive behavior. Drugs are usually used in conjunction with other treatment procedures.

M. A. CAMPION

See SEXUALITY.

Sexual Pain Disorders. Sexual pain disorders, or dyspareunia, is the experience of pain during intercourse. It is more common in females but also exists for males (Lazarus, 1989). This sexual dysfunction is likely to be caused by a physical problem such as infection, lack of lubrication, improperly positioned uterus or ovary, a rigid hymen in females, congenital penile curvature for males, or sexually transmitted diseases (STDs). Therefore, a physical examination of the client is usually recommended as the first course of treatment. Dyspareunia can also be caused by psychological difficulties such as guilt, anxiety, previous rape, or sexual abuse. If sexual pain is caused by psychological difficulties, then therapy is recommended.

Females. Sexual pain among females often manifests itself as vaginismus. Vaginismus occurs when the outer third of the vaginal opening constricts involuntarily. A conditioned response to impending penetration is believed to be the cause of vaginismus. Treatment includes progressive penetration by the woman of her fingers in her vagina while relaxing, until the woman is able to contain the penis.

Males. Although it is rare, some males suffer from postejaculatory pain because of genital muscle spasms associated with ejaculation or because of a psychological conflict over ejaculation (Kaplan, 1993). Treatment of this disorder involves relaxing the genital muscles to reduce cramping.

References

Kaplan, H. S. (1993). Post-ejaculatory pain syndrome. *Journal of Sex and Marital Therapy, 19,* 91–103.

Lazarus, A. A. (1989). Dyspareunia: A multi-modal psychotherapeutic perspective. In S. R. Leiblum & R. C. Rosen (Eds.), *Principles and practice of sex therapy* (2nd ed.). New York: Guilford.

J. S. RIPLEY

See DYSPAREUNIA; SEXUAL DYSFUNCTIONS; VAGINISMUS.

Sexual Response Psychology. The study of human sexual response has developed considerably in recent decades. Nosology of diagnosis and treatment of sexual dysfunctions has been refined accordingly. Prior to the pioneering efforts of Masters and Johnson, little research existed on the human sexual response (Allgier & Allgier, 1991). Until recently human sexual response was seen as a monolithic event that passed from lust to excitement and was climaxed by the orgasm. Sexual dysfunction similarly was seen as a single entity. Males with sexual problems were classified as impotent and females were frigid. Treatment, like the dysfunction, was undifferentiated (Kaplan, 1979).

Masters and Johnson were the first to regard human sexual response as a natural biological function and scientifically studied the human sexual response in both males and females (Kaplan, 1979). They revolutionized the study of human sexuality by systematically observing behavioral and physiological dimensions of sexual functioning in laboratory settings (Allgier & Allgier, 1991). Masters and Johnson classified the human sexual response into two phases based upon physiological alterations in genital organs: excitement and orgasm. Disorders of excitement and orgasm were seen as separate syndromes requiring different treatments. Their work led to major advances in sex therapy (Kaplan, 1974).

Both excitement and orgasm phases are served by reflex centers in the lower spinal cord. Vasocongestion, the physiological substrate of the excitement phase, involves the reflexive dilation of genital blood vessels during arousal. As vessels dilate genital organs become engorged with blood and change shape to adapt them to their reproductive functions. In the male the penis becomes large and hard to penetrate the vagina. The scrotum thickens and elevates partially. In the female the clitoris becomes engorged in a similar manner to the penis (Penner & Penner, 1990). The *labia minora* (inner lips) become engorged and extend outward, while the *labia majora* (outer lips) spread flat. The vagina balloons and the uterus begins to pull up and away from the vagina to prevent penile contact during thrusting. The inner two-thirds of the vagina lengthens and widens in a "tenting effect" (Allgier & Allgier, 1991). The outer third of the vagina narrows to produce the "orgasmic platform" (Masters & Johnson, 1966). Within 20 seconds of any form of stimulation, the vaginal barrel begins to lubricate with transudate from the blood to accommodate the penis.

Myotonia is the physiological substrate of the orgasm phase. Continued sexual stimulation triggers an orgasmic reflex and certain genital muscles contract. The orgasmic response is the shorter and more intense phase (Penner & Penner, 1990). For the male, muscle contractions during orgasm consist of two independent but coordinated reflexive subphases. Emission involves the contraction of the seminal duct system and moves ejaculate to the base of the penis. During ejaculation the seminal fluid is expelled by contractions of muscles at the base of the penis at eight-tenths of a second intervals. For the female, orgasm is the contraction of equivalent striated muscles at eight-tenths of a second intervals. These muscles are similar to those activated in the ejaculatory subphase of male orgasm without emission.

Masters and Johnson amplified their biphasic classification into a four-stage model of the human sexual response cycle: excitement, plateau, orgasm, and resolution. The excitement and plateau stages are under the control of the passive (parasympathetic) branch of the autonomic nervous system (Penner & Penner, 1990). Arousal is an automatic, involuntary response to pleasure. Anxiety interferes with normal sexual functioning; treatment of arousal disorders centers on reducing anxiety and increasing pleasurable sensations. Orgasm is under the control of the active (sympathetic) branch of the autonomic nervous system. Orgasm is a natural, unavoidable reflex to adequate stimulation. Treatment of orgasmic disorders centers on education of sexual functioning and mechanics to provide sufficient stimulation.

Believing Masters and Johnson's two-phase approach to be inadequate, Kaplan criticized and amplified it (Lief, 1985). Her formulation, based upon her clinical experience, places more emphasis on the psychological experience of human sexual response by the addition of an initial desire phase. The desire phase, like arousal and orgasm phases, has a separate physiology, a distinctive pattern of pathogenesis, and special therapeutic requirements (Kaplan, 1979). Kaplan's three phases are physiologically related but discrete. They are interconnected but governed by separate neurophysiological systems. Human sexual response is no longer monistic but is viewed as a dynamic interaction of biological, psychological, and sociocultural factors. Each factor has to be considered for effective treatment of sexual problems.

Kaplan's addition of the desire phase led to another revolution in diagnosis and treatment of sexual dysfunction. The study of the human sexual response and its disorders provided a catalyst for the integration and amalgamation of a wide spectrum of ideas and approaches from the psychoanalytically minded, the behaviorists, the family and cou-

ple therapists, and the physiologically oriented gynecologists and urologists (Kaplan, 1979).

Lief (1985) modified Kaplan's triphasic formulation to highlight relational components of the human sexual response. Leif's classification, DAVOS, includes five stages: desire, arousal, vasocongestion, orgasm, and satisfaction. Arousal and vasocongestion are two components of excitement. Arousal is psychological in nature, and vasocongestion is physiological in nature. Satisfaction refers to an individual's experience of the response.

Models of sexual problems and methods of treatment have developed with each refinement of the human sexual response cycle. Masters and Johnson revolutionized sex therapy, but with her addition of a desire phase Kaplan augmented the model of Masters and Johnson with a psychological component. Desire phase disorders now represent the new frontier in sex therapy (LoPiccolo, 1994). Each refinement of the human sexual response has contributed to more precise diagnosis and effective treatment of sexual problems.

References

Allgier, E. R., & Allgier, A. R. (1991). *Sexual interaction* (3rd ed.). Lexington, MA: Heath.

Kaplan, H. S. (1974). *The new sex therapy*. New York: Brunner/Mazel.

Kaplan, H. S. (1979). *Disorders of sexual desire*. New York: Simon & Schuster.

Lief, H. (1985). Evaluation of inhibited sexual desire: Relationship aspects. In H. S. Kaplan (Ed.), *Comprehensive evaluation of disorders of sexual desire*. Washington, DC: American Psychiatric Press.

LoPiccolo, J. (1994). The evolution of sex therapy. *Sexual and Marital Therapy, 9,* 5–7.

Masters, W. H., & Johnson, V. E. (1966). *Human sexual response*. Boston: Little, Brown.

Penner, J. J., & Penner, C. L. (1990). *Counseling for sexual disorders*. Dallas: Word.

T. L. Hight

See Sexuality.

Sexual Sadism. Behavior that inflicts suffering on the victim in order to produce sexual excitement. The term *sadism* is derived from the Marquis de Sade, who according to accounts in his autobiographical writings inflicted great cruelty on his victims for sexual pleasure.

The sadistic act may follow coitus for more gratification, be involved with enhancing sexual desire, or be used to produce orgasm without intercourse. Sadistic acts of violence can include sticking with needles, slashing with a razor, biting, beating, disembowelment, cutting off breasts, or defecating on the victim. The sadist may also derive sexual excitement from the odor or the taste of blood. The sadist derives little sexual satisfaction if the victim remains passive. There appears to be a need for power over the victim. The victim must be dominated, injured, or destroyed in order to achieve sexual fulfillment.

The sadist has a range of emotions during the sexual assaults, including anxiety, rage, vengeance, relief, and ecstasy that come from overpowering the victim. During the sadistic act the sadist appears to have little control over his behavior. Unless he is caught, he will continue to repeat the sadistic acts.

Sexual sadism covers a range of behavior. It is usually not considered pathological unless it brings marked physical harm to the victim. Much sadistic behavior goes unreported because the partners are cooperative and the sadistic acts are less life-threatening and violent.

The sexual sadistic behavior usually has its beginnings in adolescence and is found almost exclusively in males. During adolescence there are strong sexual emotions. If by chance they are paired with seeing someone receive physical pain such as being cut or beaten, then the adolescent may begin the conditioning process that results in sexual sadism. The sadist usually has a negative attitude toward sex and is feminine, undersexed, timid, and fearful of impotence. The sadistic behavior is designed to arouse strong emotion in the victim so that the sadist can peak his sexual mood, to achieve orgasm.

Sexual sadism is rarely encountered in psychological or psychiatric practice. Most clinical information of sadistic behavior is from accounts of prostitutes. The actual frequency of sexual sadistic behavior is not known.

Treatment may include insight-oriented psychotherapy, sex education, behavioral therapy, or chemotherapy. The use of drugs may produce sexual apathy that would diminish sexual arousal.

M. A. CAMPION

See SEXUALITY.

Sexuality. This term has been used in a variety of ways. At the broadest possible level, the term *gender sexuality* in this article will refer to "the way of being in, and relating to, the world as a *male* or *female* person" (Kosnick, Carroll, Cunningham, Modras, & Schulte, 1977, p. 82). A second type of sexuality, here termed *erotic sexuality,* is that of passionate desire for the other; the longing for completion through interaction with another, which possibly but not necessarily includes emotional, intellectual, spiritual, or physical interaction with the other (Thielicke, 1964). Finally, when physical sexual action is the focus, the term *genital sexuality* will be used, even though the sexual expression may not involve the genitals. When experience at all of the above levels is the focus, the unqualified term *sexuality* will be used.

Theological Perspectives. *History of Christian Thought.* The thinking of the early church in the West on the topic of sexuality was deeply influenced by hellenistic and gnostic thought forms (Bullough & Brundage, 1982; Kosnick et al., 1977). Departing from the historic Hebraic affirmation of body life and sexuality, many of the early church fathers (including Justin Martyr, Origen, Tertullian, Jerome, and Ambrose) viewed genital sexuality as at most acceptable only within marriage for procreation, while erotic passion was to be spurned at all costs. Virginity or chastity within an established marriage was viewed as a superior mode of life. Justin Martyr and others wrote approvingly of young people having themselves castrated for the kingdom; these acts were later declared self-mutilation and condemned by the church.

Augustine's writings were the central pillar of the thinking of the church until the Reformation. He argued that the conjugal act in marriage for procreation's sake is in itself sinless but paradoxically suggested that the pleasure attached to that act is a consequence of original sin and that erotic desire is a product of humanity's lower, fleshly nature. Other writers later attempted to remove the stigma from sexuality (e.g., Thomas Aquinas), but Roman Catholic thought until very recently continued to reflect Augustine's reasoning.

The Reformers, among their other amendments of Christian doctrine, rejected the Roman Catholic doctrine of clerical celibacy and its implicit asceticism on scriptural grounds. Luther, Calvin, and others esteemed marriage and sexual union as the gifts of God; to both, sexuality was a natural part of human existence. Luther dealt with the topic in an especially frank and earthly manner. Subsequent Protestant thought on this theme tended to vacillate between a latent asceticism and the healthier balance achieved by the Reformers (Feucht, Coiner, Saver, & Hansen, 1961).

Biblical Themes. Sexuality in all its forms was an intended part of the created order. Genesis 1:27 teaches that males and females were equally created in the image of God, and this gender differentiation and the institution of erotic and genital sexuality were hailed by God as very good. Genesis 2:24–25 persuasively refutes any notion that conjugal relations between husband and wife are in any way contrary to God's intended order.

The Old Testament also suggests that bodily existence, marriage, and sexual intercourse are all gifts from God. A major distinction between the Hebraic people and pagan cultures about them was their refusal to overly spiritualize sex by attributing genital sexuality to God or to degrade the gift of sexuality in general by attributing its origins to Satan or the fall. While genital sexuality in marriage is affirmed in the Old Testament, harsh condemnation is expressed for extramarital genital sexuality. At points in the Old Testament women are given radical equality with men; in other places the Scriptures portray a patriarchal society that does not reflect the equality of the sexes indicated to have been God's intent before the fall.

To understand the treatment of sexuality in the New Testament one must first realize that the Scriptures do not attempt to give systematic attention to the topic in the same way in which they treat the great doctrines of human depravity and divine grace. Rather, the broad themes are briefly noted in addressing specific problems of concern. Further, all New Testament writings are colored by the eschatology of the writers, who expected an imminent return of Christ. Most of Paul's writings that have been understood as antisexual (e.g., 1 Cor. 7) are better understood as being rooted in this view of eschatology. His positive, Hebraic affirmation of the place of sexuality in human existence is more clearly presented in Ephesians 5 and 1 Timothy 4:1–5. Other New Testament passages do seem to portray a more negative view of sexuality (e.g., Rev. 14:4) but cannot be dealt with here.

Theological Themes. In understanding our sexuality it is critical to affirm that human existence is inevitably an embodied, physical existence. The fact that sexuality in all its forms is intimately intertwined with physical processes cannot be used to denigrate that aspect of our being. "Thus does the 'biblical view' of man represent him as consisting of two principles, the cosmical and the holy, which unites the individual into a free and personal oneness of being" (McDonald, 1981, p. 78). While Scripture makes this differentiation, it never denigrates the physical at the expense of the immaterial, and it constantly emphasizes the unitive, integrated nature of our existence. It should be remembered that body life can be made spiritual or carnal; the term *flesh (sarx)* is in Scripture primarily an ethical term, and we can have a fleshly mind as well as a fleshly body. Three great theological doctrines support a Christian affirmation of embodied life: creation (God made us physical beings), incarnation (the Son of God took on embodied existence and yet remained perfect and sinless), and resurrection (believers, like Christ, will be raised from death to live as embodied beings for eternity).

Unlike classical Reformed theologians such as Charles Hodge and Louis Berkhof, the neoorthodox theologian Karl Barth viewed the gift of sexuality as fundamental to the image of God in humanity. Barth, and many since, have suggested that human sexuality reflects the differentiation of persons within the Godhead and God's intimately relational nature. "God created man in His own image, in correspondence with His own being and essence. . . . God is in relationship, and so too is the man created by Him" (Barth, cited in Small, 1974, pp. 131–132; see also Thielicke, 1964). Thus our sexual natures reflect the nature of the Creator of the universe.

It must be remembered that all our experience of sexual life is conditioned by the fall. Brunner (1939) has suggested that as a result of the fall a "vast rent . . . runs right through human nature" (p. 348). In the area of sexuality, according to Brunner, this rent has two results: "a shame which cannot be overcome, and a longing which cannot be satisfied" (p. 348). That is, a sense of shame reminiscent of the shame of Adam and Eve over their nakedness and a lack of fulfillment of our desire to know the

other (which results in an unsatisfied longing and personal isolation) are perpetually ours as a result of the fall. Further, Brunner points out that enmity between the sexes is the result of the fall. One result of this enmity is that in the agelong struggle between the sexes, in which males have largely been dominant, the original distinguishing characteristics of the sexes (aside from the obvious anatomical differences) have been blurred. We have little information about what God originally intended in differentiating male and female, as we have spent the eons since the creation recreating ourselves in our own images.

Sexual Ethics. Issues of sexual ethics are a battleground today for the Christian church, particularly the issue of homosexuality. Although it is not as hotly contested, there has been a substantial erosion of confidence in the traditional prohibition against premarital sexual intercourse. Turner (1993) has accurately described the fundamental divide in these debates as between two groups. Some people argue that the morality of any sexual act must be assessed by factors external to the acts themselves; all sexual acts, it is argued, are on a continuum of good to bad, with placement on that continuum depending upon certain qualities of the intentions before and results after (and hence external to) those acts. Such qualities as noncoerciveness, affection, expression of one's true personhood, faithfulness, growth enhancement, and the like are used to judge the morality of each act. In this view moral judgments about acts cannot be made on the basis of genders or marital status of the actors. Others argue that the internal nature of certain acts themselves determine their morality. They argue that the external factors do condition the moral status of many sexual acts (loving marital sex is better than unloving marital sex) and are helpful in adjudicating ambiguous cases in which Scripture is silent (such as petting) but nevertheless that sexual ethics are grounded in certain internal or intrinsic characteristics of sex acts, such as the gender and marital status of the participants. These people would argue that these intrinsic characteristics exist because of God's sovereign mandate and revelation of the purposes that are to be served by our genital sexuality as discussed next.

Purposes of Sexuality. Genesis 1:28 states clearly that procreation is a fundamental purpose of genital sexuality, and the Scriptures as a whole are so clear on this point that it needs no further elaboration.

Union is a clear purpose of sex presented in Scripture. Genesis 2:24 suggests that becoming "one flesh" is foundational to marriage and that genital sexuality is in some way fundamental to this process. The exact meaning of "one flesh" is a topic of some debate. Some scriptural passages suggest that becoming one flesh with another is in some sense an immediate and permanent result of sexual intercourse (e.g., 1 Cor. 6:16). Such a doctrine creates numerous philosophical and practical difficulties, including the question of the marital status of the person who has had intercourse with more than one person. Theologians generally conclude that becoming one flesh denotes a process of growth between married persons in which sexual intercourse is a necessary but not sufficient precondition. The end goal of the process is to be a unitary expression of fidelity, commitment, purpose, love, and ownership of the other (see Small, 1974).

Several biblical passages suggest a third purpose of sexuality, that of physical gratification and pleasure. Paul's discussion in 1 Corinthians 7 suggests that genital sexuality in marriage gratifies a passionate desire and that this function of marriage is not sinful. Proverbs 5:19 suggests that the exhilaration of physical love serves to enhance the stability of a marriage.

From a theological perspective, a group of broader purposes of sexuality emerge. Kosnick et al. (1977) broadened the terms *procreative* and *unitive* to *creative* and *integrative* better to describe the broadest purposes of sexuality. They argue that our potential for "shared existence" (p. 85) with persons of the opposite sex calls us to the task of creative completion of our personhood, to the realization of our unfulfilled potentials. Sexuality reminds us experientially of our relational natures and thus beckons us toward integration with others, including a nongenital integration or fellowship with others beside our spouses. Thielicke (1964) similarly argues that eros opens up the person to the experiences of greater levels of self-acceptance and growth. We might also argue that sexuality was divinely created to experimentally teach us important truths about the Godhead and our relationship thereunto. Gender differentiation reflects God's differentiated personhood, and sexual union in marriage reflects the complementary truth of union across differentiation within the Godhead and between God and humankind. Sexuality as a part of marriage is obviously a part of the symbolic representation in that institution of the relationship between Christ and his church (Eph. 5:21–33). This symbolism was obvious in the Old Testament as well, where sexual passion was a prime metaphor for the relationship of Israel to her God, both in positive, faithful sense (Song of Songs) and the negative, adulterous sense (e.g., Ezek. 23).

Physical Perspectives. Contemporary textbooks in human sexuality (e.g., Masters, Johnson, & Kolodny, 1995) provide excellent detailed presentations of the issues briefly presented here.

Sexual Anatomy. Genetic gender is fixed at the moment of conception. An embryo with a pair of XX sex-determining chromosomes is a genetic female; a genetic male possesses an XY pair of chromosomes. Some individuals are conceived with abnormal chromosomal arrangements that complicate the process of sexual differentiation.

Development of internal and external sexual anatomy is a function of hormonal levels in the developing fetus. The internal and external sexual anatomy of males and females is indistinguishable up until the sixth week or so after conception. Differentiation is practically complete around the fourteenth week of development. Under the influence of androgens (male hormones) the internal and external sexual anatomy of a male begins to develop. In the absence of these hormones, or when the target tissues are unresponsive to the hormones, female anatomy develops. These processes occur regardless of the genetic sex of the fetus. That is, a genetic female under the influence of androgens will develop testes, penis, and scrotum, while a genetic male not exposed to androgens develops ovaries, uterus, and vagina. Such conditions are called pseudohermaphroditism. The true hermaphrodite, which is very rare, is the infant born with true ovaries and testicular tissues and almost always with a uterus.

Sex hormones also influence the brain. The most well-documented gender differentiation is the hypothalamus, which plays a major controlling function in the regulation of sex hormones. The hypothalamus in the female is patterned for cyclical hormone production, resulting after puberty in the ovulatory/menstrual cycle, while the male hypothalamus maintains a relatively constant level of sex hormone production. Other possible brain differences between females and males have been sufficiently established to be firmly reported. It cannot be firmly asserted that the culturally stereotypical differences in aggressiveness, emotionality, or sexual responsiveness are rooted in stable brain deficiencies.

The next major stage of sexual development occurs at puberty. Under the influence of suddenly escalating hormone levels, changes begin to occur in the genitals and in other secondary sex characteristics. For both males and females puberty results in enlargement of the external genitalia, growth of pubic and other body hair, and an overall growth spurt. Females begin to experience breast enlargement, menarche (first menstruation), ovulation, vaginal secretion (including nocturnal lubrication), and development of feminine body form due to changes in bone structure and muscle/fat ratios. Males experience voice deepening (due to growth of the larynx), growth of facial hair, increased potential for muscle growth, increased incidence of erection, and nocturnal emissions. Puberty normally occurs between ages 10 and 16 (one to two years later for boys than for girls), though earlier and later dates can occur. Neither pregnancy nor impregnation is possible before puberty.

Adulthood is a fairly stable period of sexuality from a biological perspective. Menopause is the cessation of ovulation and menstruation for women, a condition that can be accompanied by discomfort and distress. A very small percentage of males experience a similar lessening of hormone production with resulting distress called the male climacteric. Most people, male and female, experience decrease in sexual desire with aging; but a cessation of desire or capacity for sexual response is no longer viewed as a normal aspect of aging.

The most important sex organs for the male are the penis, testicles, seminal vesicles, and prostate. The glans, or head of the penis, is richly enervated and is highly sensitive to tactile stimulation. The testicles, seminal vesicles, and prostate all contribute to ejaculation. For some men the penile foreskin is surgically removed at birth (circumcision). Presence or absence of the foreskin does not seem to affect sexual response. There is some evidence that the wives of uncircumcised men have slightly elevated risk for cervical cancer. The testes, along with the adrenal glands, produce the male sex hormone; the testes alone produce sperm.

The female sex organs are the *labia majora* and *minora*, clitoris, vagina, uterus, and ovaries. The clitoris is the most erotically sensitive area of the female body, followed by the outer one-third of the vagina and the *labia minora*. The clitoris, like the penis, has a glans or head, which is richly enervated and extremely sensitive to stimulation. The inner (deeper) two-thirds of the vagina seems to be less sensitive to stimulation. The ovaries produce the female sex hormones and the ova, which can be fertilized by sperm and implanted in the uterus for development and birth.

Sexual Physiology. The degree to which sexual drive is a biologically rooted phenomenon is unclear. Research suggests that there is some correlation between intensity of sexual drive and testosterone levels in males (produced in the testicles and adrenal glands) and androgen levels in females (produced in the adrenal glands). This relationship of hormone levels and sex drive is a complex one, however, in that sex drive is also a function of a number of psychological factors as well. Low sexual desire is not necessarily a function of lowered hormone levels, and hypersexual desire is not necessarily a function of elevated hormone levels. Hormones do nothing to direct sexual desire; there are no firmly established sex hormone differences between heterosexuals and homosexuals. While sexual response is closely regulated by female hormone levels in most animals, it appears that there is no such relationship for human females.

Sexual response is most commonly conceptualized as occurring in four stages: desire, excitement, orgasm, and resolution. The desire stage is thought to be biological, emotional, cognitive, and social/relational. There are many determinants of desire, including the experience of physical sex drive, desire for children, longing for emotional closeness, desire to be normal according to subcultural standards, striving to dominate or be dominated, thrill of the forbidden or unknown, or the pursuit of physical exhilaration and/or relaxation. Desire draws one toward sexual encounter, resulting in excitement.

The excitement stage results from effective sexual stimulation of any sort, physical or psychological. The two basic changes in the body during ex-

citement are vasocongestion (concentration of blood in the sexual organs) and muscular tension throughout the body, especially in the genital area. Males and females both begin to experience increased muscular tension, including the beginning of elevation of heart and respiration rates. Vasocongestion in the male results in erection of the penis. Erection is a hydraulic event resulting from engorgement of blood in the penis. Vasocongestion in females results in the beginning of swelling of the tissues in the genital area, including hardening (erection) of the clitoris and lubrication of the vagina, which results from seepage of the vaginal walls. Vaginal lubrication does not come from glands. Nipple erection from vasocongestion is typical in women and frequent in men. Testicular elevation begins in this stage. As the excitement stage continues, the same physiological reactions intensify for both sexes. In women the labia swell and deepen their color, the vagina expands, the uterus moves within the abdomen to become more erect, the clitoris continues to engorge with blood and become more sensitive, and the breasts swell. A flush on the skin of the chest is common. In men erection becomes complete, as does elevation of the testicles. A small amount of fluid may pass from the penile opening before ejaculation; this fluid may contain live sperm. This is a major reason why interruption of the coitus before ejaculation is not effective as a method of birth control. The length of the excitement and plateau stages varies widely.

Orgasm, frequently called climax or coming, is characterized for both sexes by a sharp peak of overall muscular tension but especially rhythmic muscular contractions of the genital area (for women, the outer third of the vagina and the uterus; for men, the penis, urethra, and prostate). Males typically experience a sensation of ejaculatory inevitability, which signals the beginning of orgasm but precedes ejaculation. After this point is reached, orgasm is begun and ejaculation is inevitable within seconds, even if stimulation ceases. For males, ejaculation and orgasm are usually parallel but differentiable events. Orgasm without ejaculation and the reverse are possible and have been documented.

There is some controversy about types of female orgasm. Sigmund Freud believed that there were two types of orgasm, clitoral and vaginal. The clitoral orgasm was deemed less mature and more autistic, while the vaginal orgasm (produced in coitus only) was viewed as more mature. The research of Masters and Johnson and others has demonstrated to the satisfaction of most of the scientific world that physiologically speaking there is only one type of orgasm, one that results from clitoral stimulation. They showed that the clitoris is stimulated indirectly during intercourse by penile thrusting and that there are no physiological difference between orgasm during masturbation and intercourse. Nevertheless, it is for these structural reasons that most women are not orgasmic by intercourse stimulation alone. Many women experience orgasm only with direct clitoral stimulation of some kind either before, during, or after intercourse.

The final stage of sexual response is that of resolution. For males and females the resolution stage is most often characterized by a rapid return to the unaroused resting state. The changes of the excitement states reverse themselves rapidly. If the person has reached a state of high excitement but has not experienced orgasm, resolution takes a much longer time to occur, and this can result in a variety of uncomfortable lingering sensations. In this phase a major difference between females and males emerges. Females are biologically capable of being multiorgasmic through the continuation of sexual stimulation. Not all women desire such an experience or find it pleasant, however. Males experience a refractory period following orgasm during which continued sexual stimulation does not result in a return of erection and capacity for sexual response. This refractory period is typically brief in young men (seconds or minutes) and gradually lengthens in duration with age (extending to hours or even days in later years).

Psychological Perspectives. *Sexual Development.* How do physical males or females become psychological males or females? Perhaps the two predominant models of gender differentiation are the psychodynamic model and the biosocial model. The latter enjoys the greatest acceptance today.

There are a number of psychodynamic models; the classical one is that of Freud. Freud believed sex (libido) to be the primary drive of human existence. He believed that around the ages of 4 to 5 young children come to have strong sexual/affectional longings for the opposite parent. In both sexes, well-focused genital sexual desire like that experienced in adolescence, but a more diffuse desire to possess all the attention and affection of the opposite-sex parent. For both sexes this affection is accompanied by a fear of the same sex parent, who is seen as a stronger, more competent competitor for the other parent's affection and who might hurt the child in the rivalry. This fear leads in normal development to identification with the same-sex parent (becoming like them, assuming their characteristics) as a way of vicariously having the special affection of the other parent. Gender identity develops through identification. This process can be complicated by disturbances in father-mother relationships, absence of either or both parents, and psychological disturbances of either or both parents.

The biosocial view of gender differentiation is primarily identified with John Money, who has conducted a great deal of research with cases of sexual deviancy, gender disturbance, and physical aberrations in sexual development (summarized in Masters, Johnson, & Kolodny, 1995). Money emphasizes the interaction of biological and learned or psychosocial factors in development. Biological factors determine genital appearance of the newborn child. Genital appearance at birth influences the manner in which parents and others interact with the developing child, influencing the child to accept the socially defined role behaviors of male or female. Money and his colleagues believe there is a critical period for gender identity development; gender identity is usually set by age three and is largely impervious to change. Thus children whose sex is misidentified at birth (e.g., the female misidentified as a male due to genital masculinization caused by high androgen levels during development) or children reared as the other sex due to parental psychological disturbance grow up with a relatively stable sense of themselves being the other sex than they are physically.

Psychodynamic and biosocial theorists agree that developments in childhood and adolescence, both physical development and the development of erotic feelings for the opposite sex, serve to further solidify the person's gender identity. The development of homosexual, bisexual, and other sexual orientations are poorly understood despite decades of debate and research. It is clear that genetic and other possible physical factors cannot be ignored, but there are good arguments against an exclusively biological hypothesis and in favor of interaction between biological and psychological/familial factors (Byne & Parsons, 1993).

Sexual Behavior. Sexual behavior occurs throughout the life cycle (see Masters, Johnson, & Kolodny, 1995 for summaries of relevant studies). Erection in male babies and vaginal lubrication in females have been demonstrated soon after birth. Children seem to naturally experience stimulation of the genital area pleasurable. Genital self-stimulation (masturbation) is common in young children. A variety of types of sexual play continues throughout childhood for many children. Orgasm is possible throughout the life cycle, even though maximal pleasure is not derived therefrom until after puberty. Prepubertal males do not ejaculate upon experience of orgasm.

Genital sexual activity is common in adolescence. Early studies suggested a large disparity between the occurrence of male and female masturbation in adolescence. This gap has been shrinking over the years, but males are still much more likely to masturbate. It can be said with some firmness that the large majority of adolescent males have masturbated to orgasm at least once by the age of 18. The number who regularly practice masturbation is thought to be overall somewhat below the overall incidence.

Erotic dreams and nocturnal emissions (together commonly called wet dreams) are almost universal in boys during adolescence. Erection is common throughout the life cycle as a correlate to the rapid eye movement (REM) stage of sleep, the stage when dreaming is most likely. Wet dreams may represent a mechanism for the release of sexual tensions. It is less commonly known that the female correlate of erection, vaginal lubrication, occurs regularly in sleep during REM periods. While it is not as common as nocturnal emissions in males, orgasm during erotic dreams is not unusual for women; up to 50% report this occurrence by adulthood.

Figures on homosexual experience in adolescence are difficult to interpret, given the common sampling problems and the differences across studies in how homosexual experience is defined. Some studies have inquired about homosexual stimulation to orgasm, while others have used a much broader definition that might incorporate any sort of same-sex sexual play, even in earliest childhood. The best summary of this data suggest that a substantial number of men and to a lesser degree women have fleeting homosexual experiences early in life. It appears that only about 2 to 3% of the male population and 1 to 2% of the females are exclusively homosexual in experience, with an additional 5 to 10% of each sex having at least one significant prolonged homosexual experience. Male homosexuals outnumber females three to one.

Intercourse before marriage is becoming more common and more accepted in American society. The consensus of a number of studies is that by the senior year of high school, more than 70% of teens are nonvirgins, with males only 6 to 8 percentage points ahead of females. These figures appear to represent a dramatic change in sexual behavior among females, who are becoming much more sexually active. These figures cannot be taken to indicate a complete swing toward promiscuity, however, as most adolescents do not report large numbers of sexual partners. Whereas in the 1950s many men reported first intercourse experience with a prostitute, most young men and women now report intercourse to occur in a caring relationship. Casual sex is perhaps only slightly more widespread today than in the past, but there is a much broader acceptance of sex with affection outside of marriage than was previously the case. Cohabitation is much more widespread today.

In adulthood most persons marry. The frequency of intercourse in marriage may have increased moderately over the past several decades. Frequency of coitus decreases steadily with age. In this the sexual desires of the male seem to predominate, in that it is commonly reported that males' sexual desire peaks in late adolescence and the early twenties, declining thereafter. Females' sexual desire is reported to peak in the thirties and forties. Estimates of the frequency of adultery vary widely, with the best recent studies suggesting lower incidences (ranging between 10 and 20% in a cross-sectional sample) than previously reported (*see* Affairs). Some studies suggest that a fairly high percentage (up to one-half) of married couples experience moderate to strong dissatisfaction with their sexual relationship with their spouses.

Factors Influencing Sexual Behavior. Research with adolescents and college students (Chilman, 1978) suggests that the following factors are associated with premarital coitus: increasing age, lower religiousness, greater permissiveness of peers, lessened influence of and communication with parents, higher self-esteem in boys but lower self-esteem in girls, lower academic achievement expectation, higher value of independence from family, permissiveness of parents, and basic sexual ideology or morality.

A number of factors that influence satisfaction with genital sexual experience have been identified in the clinical treatment literature. The factors that have been implicated in decreased sexual satisfaction include lack of information or misinformation about sexual response, deeply ingrained negative attitudes toward sex, anxiety due to fear of pregnancy or of intimacy, performance anxiety, fatigue or illness, and relationship disturbances. Many experts in the field who have advocated greater sexual enlightenment for our society are recognizing that the cost of sexual revolution has been greater emphasis on sexual performance relative to relational intimacy and subjective satisfaction. Some have suggested that the current trend emphasizing affection and relationship (but not necessarily marriage) before sex is a reaction against these trends. Possibly as another reaction to the cultural emphasis on sexual performance, sex therapists report an increasing number of persons seeking treatment for disorders of sexual desire. Increasingly people who find sex to be less important in life are viewed by themselves and others as abnormal.

Sexual dysfunctions must be differentiated from sexual deviations (or more commonly today, variations). Dysfunctions represent failures to perform adequately; deviations represent disorders in response to sexual objects. The most common sexual dysfunctions in women are disorders of arousal, orgasmic dysfunctions, vaginismus, and dyspareunia. Males experience disorders of arousal, erectile dysfunction, and premature or retarded ejaculation (*see* Sex Therapy).

Sexuality and Adjustment. What is the relationship between sexual functioning and personal adjustment? Views based on early dynamic formulations tended to link the two closely, so that sexual dysfunction was viewed as symptomatic of more deeply rooted personality disturbances; from these came the description of the sexually underresponsive woman as frigid. Some writers pushed this view further to conclude that sexual response is the best index of adjustment.

In the early stages of the development of sex therapy as a specialty within mental health practice, the opposite ideology seemed to be pressed. Sexual functioning was viewed as a learned phenomenon without necessary linkages to other aspects of personality functioning. This conception was supported by the rapid successes in treatment of sexual dysfunction reported by Masters and Johnson and others.

The current view among many prominent sex therapists (see Leiblum & Rosen, 1989) is that neither of these broad formulations is adequate. Rather, for some individuals sexual dysfunction represents a relatively simple problem amenable to brief intervention. For others the sexual disturbance is a problem for which more fundamental change is essential.

Integration. The interrelationships between the theological, biological, and psychological perspectives on sexuality are critical, but only a sampling can be explored. First, it should be stated that any definition of normality is conditioned by a priori assumptions regarding the nature of optimal human response and the purposes of that response. The implicit theory of most sex researchers and clinicians is that sexual functioning is, from an evolutionary perspective, intended for procreation, and has become endowed with tremendous pleasure-producing qualities as a spur to reproductive activity. Because species survival and pleasure are viewed as the highest human goods (with some theorists emphasizing the primacy of individual hedonistic gratification and others the importance of subsuming individual pleasure to the collective good), most writers in this field exhibit a broad acceptance of sexual behaviors. These writers would argue for a scientific basis for determination of normalcy based on empirical study of statistical frequency, pleasure derived, and harm/benefits produced by a particular behavior. Christians must recognize the implicit values behind such a scientific analysis and suggest alternatively that other purposes of sexuality must be considered in the determination of normalcy. Thus despite the high statistical frequency, reported pleasures derived from, and lack of empirical evidence showing harm produced by premarital sex, Christians can assert that such actions are statistically frequent but not normal, in the same sense that those actions violate the meaning and purpose for which the act of coitus was created by God. However, Christians must struggle with empirical and clinical evidences in areas that might be called borderline (Thielicke, 1964), since these areas are not clearly dealt with in Scripture.

Our consideration of the purposes and nature of sexuality affects our definition of optimum sexuality. Optimum sexuality cannot be defined in terms of physical performance standards only, since such standards omit reference to the broader purposes of unity and reflection of spiritual truth that are important to sexual relationship. Optimum sexuality will be that which is most in accord with the purposes of sex; thus optimum genital sexuality in marriage is appropriately open to procreation, is pleasurable, is promoting of interpersonal union, and in its wholeness and holiness mirrors the nature of God and of Christ's relationship to his church. Such formulations of optimum sexuality are critical to judging the effectiveness of sex therapy in treatment of sexual dysfunctions, which to this point has been largely judged by the criteria of frequency and speed of orgasm. Such purely functional criteria can be seen from an integrated perspective to be important to the purpose of pleasure but limited. True enhancement of sexual life must have in focus a broader view of the meaning and purpose of sexuality.

References

Brunner, E. (1939). *Man in revolt*. London: Lutterworth.

Bullough, V., & Brundage, J. (1982). *Sexual practices and the medieval church*. Buffalo, NY: Prometheus.

Byne, W., & Parsons, B. (1993). Human sexual orientation: The biologic theories reappraised. *Archives of General Psychiatry, 50,* 228–239.

Chilman, C. (1978). *Adolescent sexuality in changing American society*. Washington, DC: U.S. Government Printing Office.

Feucht, O., Coiner, H., Sauer, A., & Hansen, P. (Eds.). (1961). *Sex and the church*. St. Louis: Concordia.

Kosnick, A., Carroll, W., Cunningham, A., Modras, R., & Schulte, J. (1977). *Human sexuality: New directions in American Catholic thought*. New York: Paulist.

Leiblum, S., & Rosen, G. (Eds.). (1989). *Principles and practice of sex therapy* (2nd ed.). New York: Guilford.

Masters, W., Johnson, V., & Kolodny, R. (1995). *Human sexuality* (5th ed.). Boston: Little, Brown.

McDonald, H. D. (1981). *The Christian view of man*. Westchester, IL: Crossway.

Small, D. (1974). *Christian: Celebrate your sexuality*. Old Tappan, NJ: Revell.

Thielicke, H. (1964). *The ethics of sex*. New York: Harper & Row.

Turner, P. (May, 1993). Sex and the single life. *First Things*, 15–21.

S. L. Jones

See Sexual Response Psychology.

Sexually Transmitted Diseases. Sexually transmitted diseases (STDs) include eighteen or more specific conditions, varying dramatically in symptoms and cause but sharing a common mode of transmission that names the category: they are transmitted through sexual contact. Formerly known as venereal diseases, a title now restricted to those STDs that are transmitted only through sexual contact, STDs include a number of diseases that may be contracted through nonsexual means as well, such as sharing needles, sexual toys, and clothing. Many STDs may infect infants during childbirth, with potentially devastating effects.

Sexually transmitted diseases are most common among people who are sexually active with many partners, and each additional partner exponentially increases the risk. Unsafe sexual activities with an infected partner, such as intercourse or oral sexual activity without a condom or dental dam, or contact with menstrual or other blood, dramatically increases risk. Even with a condom, sexual activity with an infected partner is risky, as condoms may slip or tear.

Sexual activity with an uninfected partner carries very little risk of STD infection, but determining whether a potential partner is infected is difficult. Many STDs produce no observable symptoms, and surveys show that a distressingly high number of college students, especially men, say that they would lie about infection in order to engage in sexual intercourse. The surest way to prevent infection is to abstain from intimate sexual activity (intercourse, anal sex, oral sex) except within a mutually monogamous relationship with an uninfected partner.

The most common STDs are chlamydia, gonorrhea, genital warts, and genital herpes. Chlamydia is the most widely spread STD, affecting people in all strata of society. Most women infected with chlamydia have no symptoms before the serious consequences of pelvic inflammatory disease, including infertility and ectopic pregnancy. Men infected with chlamydia may be symptom-free, or they may experience a discharge from the penis, burning sensations when urinating, itching, painful testicles, and fever. The painful testicles and fever indicate an infection of the testes, which may produce infertility.

Symptoms of gonorrhea in men include a watery discharge from the penis, itching or burning, and pain when urinating. If gonorrhea is not treated, symptoms may get worse, but even if they subside the man is still infectious. The majority of women with gonorrhea have mild or no symptoms, but untreated gonorrhea, like chlamydia, can produce pelvic inflammatory disease.

Genital warts are caused by a virus that may be transmitted by people who have no symptoms. Although the warts themselves are merely a nuisance and are readily treated, the virus has been implicated in cervical cancer.

Genital herpes is caused by either of two strains of virus, one of which also produces the common cold sore. The virus is common, affecting perhaps one out of every seven adults. Symptoms include small, itchy bumps on the genitals, which progress to blisters and then, bursting, to ulcers. Some people also experience flulike symptoms. The symptoms subside within two weeks, but the virus remains and many more outbreaks may occur, usually lasting about five days. Some people with the virus are infectious even when they have no symptoms.

Syphilis is a bacterial infection that is transmitted only through intimate sexual contact or through the placenta. The first symptom of syphilis, which may not appear until 12 weeks after infection, is a red, pea-sized bump on the genitals, usually either inside the vagina or on the glans of the penis. Untreated syphilis progresses to a second stage, characterized by a skin rash, then, often years later, to a third stage, which may involve heart disease or brain damage (*see* General Paresis).

Hepatitis A and B may be transmitted sexually, as may various infections of the urinary tract and vagina. Parasitic infections, such as scabies and pubic lice, may be transmitted both sexually and through other close contact, including sharing clothing, bedding, or towels.

Most sexually transmitted diseases are readily treated medically. However, the infection may exact a psychological toll, with feelings of shame and guilt outlasting the course of the disease. Christian counselors should be prepared to provide support and encouragement and the assurance that through Christ, forgiveness is available.

Christian counselors may be especially helpful to victims of acquired immune deficiency syndrome (AIDS), caused by the human immunodeficiency virus (HIV). HIV is most commonly transmitted sexually, through either heterosexual or homosexual activity, and through needle sharing. Transmission also occurs from mother to baby either before or during birth or through breast milk. Infection from blood transfusions is now rare. Although the course of HIV infection varies, it appears to be uniformly fatal. People who test positive for HIV are usually referred to counseling to help them deal with the devastating verdict, and loving, supportive, and nonjudgmental counsel from Christians has been very effective.

P. D. YOUNG

See AIDS.

Shame. Shame is generally defined as "an unpleasant emotional reaction by an individual to an actual or presumed negative judgment of himself by others resulting in self-depreciation vis-à-vis the group" (Ausubel, 1955, p. 382). Contemporary psychologists focus less on shame than on other negative emotions, particularly anxiety, fear, and guilt.

Shame involves an objective act and a subjective feeling of the person. The objective act breaches a social convention and has as its consequence the subjective feeling of condemnation and derogation. Lynd (1958) noted that shame is experienced as "a wound to one's self-esteem, a painful feeling or sense of degradation excited by the consciousness of having done something unworthy of one's previous idea of one's own excellence" (p. 24). A sense of unworthiness or of being scorned originates in the breach of propriety. The individual engages in self-condemnation when modesty or another sentiment related to self-respect, especially in the eyes of another, has been violated.

Shame has its roots in Old English, where it meant to cover or hide an exposure. Covering up was a defense against being exposed, which wounded self-respect. Baldwin (1901) examined the historical development of shame and noted it involved two types of exposure. The more prominent occurred in situations in which the physical functions of elimination and sexuality were exposed. Sigmund Freud and Ruth Benedict viewed shame as a defense against exhibitionism and voyeurism; shame was an assurance that privacy would be maintained. When an individual says, "I feel ashamed," the meaning may be, "I do not want to be seen."

A second type of shame involves exposure in situations of an intellectual or moral nature. Baldwin maintained that in this form shame may reveal a simple weakness of the person (e.g., the presence of a physical handicap), a disappointment of social expectations (e.g., a bad judgment that led to embarrassment, an exposure of ignorance or incompetence), or a breach of social or moral prescription. Moral shame is a reaction to the negative moral evaluation of others and provides the major boundaries for acceptable behavior in shame cultures.

Several theorists have attempted to differentiate shame and guilt. It is commonly asserted that guilt is an internalized form of shame in which the individual judges himself or herself, while shame is externalized in a group's judgment. Freud (1923/1961) maintained that shame is more external than guilt. Shame is based on disapproval from the outside, from other persons, while guilt (i.e., self-reproach) comes from criticism within. Shame is a failure to live up to someone else's expectation, while guilt is the failure to live up to one's own expectation.

Alternate accounts have been offered by Piers and Singer (1971) and Alexander (1948). To Piers the essential difference is that guilt follows transgression of prohibitions, whereas failure to reach goals or ideals leads to shame. Alexander made a similar distinction. Guilt arises out of wrongdoing, whereas shame comes from inferiority. This distinction has been blurred in more recent writings. Ausubel (1955) writing on moral shame suggested that it is not necessary that the individual internalize and accept the values of the group but only that there be awareness of the group's value and a recognition that one's action has transgressed that value. If the individual had internalized and adopted the value and then acted contrary, guilt would accompany shame. In this latter case external sanctions are accompanied by internal ones.

Lynd (1958) summarized attempts to explain the underlying mechanisms of shame. Experiences of shame develop from exposure, particularly unexpected exposure to sensitive and intimate aspects of self. While the exposure may be to others (i.e., social), it is also personal. The emotion is particularly strong when the exposure is unexpected and the individual is powerless to prevent it. Blushing and hiding one's face are immediate reactions to unexpected exposure.

Pain of unexpected exposure is particularly acute when one's action is inappropriate to the situation or incongruous with a positive self-image. Discrepancy of action and the prevailing social convention initiates shame in cultures where social convention is highly prescriptive and clearly defined.

Shame may have origins in threats to trust. When trust is threatened or destroyed, the person may question the adequacy of his or her worldview. Trust makes an individual vulnerable, and exposure of that vulnerability is experienced as shame. Lynd concluded, "Shame over sudden uncovering of incongruity mounts when what is exposed is inappropriate positive expectation, happy and confident commitment to a world that proves to be alien or nonexistent" (1958, p. 43).

References

Alexander, F. (1948). *Fundamentals of psychoanalysis*. New York: Norton.

Ausubel, D. P. (1955). Relationships between shame and guilt in the socializing process. *Psychological Review, 62,* 378–390.

Baldwin, J. M. (1901). *Dictionary of philosophy and psychology* (Vol. 2). New York: Macmillan.

Freud, S. (1960). The ego and the id. In J. Strachey (Ed. and Trans.), *The standard edition of the complete psychological works of Sigmund Freud* (Vol. 19). London: Hogarth. (Original work published 1923)

Lynd, H. M. (1958). *On shame and the search for identity.* New York: Harcourt Brace.

Piers, G., & Singer, M. (1971). *Shame and guilt.* New York: Norton.

R. L. TIMPE

See GUILT; SUPEREGO; CONSCIENCE.

Shaping. A technique in operant psychology whereby a new response is developed through differentially reinforcing ever closer approximations of the desired end behavior. An example would be teaching simple language to an autistic, withdrawn child—specifically, teaching the child to say "mama." In his or her current state the child occasionally emits cries, grunts, and other nonverbal sounds in no apparent pattern. The clinician would first determine what would serve as a reinforcer for the child by observing the sorts of activities the child engages in freely. Raisins are picked as the reinforcer since the child consumes them as often as possible.

Since the child has never uttered "mama," the response must be shaped. The clinician decides on a first approximation of the target behavior. Since speech is most likely to be appropriate when the child attends to the people about him or her, the first approximation picked is for the child to look in the direction of the clinician. When the child does look toward the clinician, he or she is immediately given a raisin; when he or she is looking away, no raisins are given. This pattern is called differential reinforcement of desired behavior.

After looking toward the clinician has become a frequent response, the clinician makes a closer approximation of the target necessary for reinforcement; looking at the clinician's face is the next chosen response. Again this behavior is differentially reinforced. The process continues in this fashion through the painstaking gradual steps toward the desired end behavior. The following steps might be necessary: looking at the clinician's face, looking in her eyes, holding eye contact and making small lip movements, making any sound, making a sound at the loudness of normal speech, making a sound at least vaguely similar to "mm," closer approximations to "mm," approximations to "ma," articulating "ma," articulating "mama." Through this process the child might eventually be led to say "mama" in an appropriate manner. Other speech might be developed in a similar fashion. Prompting and modeling are other techniques that might be used to speed the learning process.

Shaping is used in developing specific desired patterns of animal behavior (a widely acclaimed example being that of the chicken playing a piano); in developing appropriate social behavior in the profoundly disturbed (the retarded, autistic, or psychotic); and in less formal forms in gradual skill development in normal persons.

S. L. JONES

See BEHAVIOR THERAPY; LEARNING.

Sheldon, William Herbert (1898–1977). Psychologist who worked out a relationship between physique and temperament. Born in Warwick, Rhode Island, he received an A.B. degree from Brown University in 1919 and an M.A. from the University of Colorado. He received a Ph.D. degree in psychology (1926) and an M.D. degree (1933) from the University of Chicago. Later he spent two years studying in Europe with Carl Gustav Jung, Sigmund Freud, and Kretschmer.

During his graduate work Sheldon taught at the University of Chicago, Northwestern University, and the University of Wisconsin. He became professor of psychology at the University of Chicago in 1936, then went to Harvard in 1938, Columbia in 1947, and the University of Oregon in 1959, where he remained until his retirement in 1970. At the time of his death he was associated with the Biological Humanics Center in Cambridge, Massachusetts.

After carefully examining standardized photographs of thousands of naked men, Sheldon concluded that the variations of physique could be accounted for by three primary components: endomorphy, mesomorphy, and ectomorphy. Endomorphs have a predominance of soft roundness throughout their bodies with the digestive organs dominant. Mesomorphs show strength, hardness, and toughness with a predominance of bone and muscle. Ectomorphs are thin, flat-chested, and fragile. Sheldon saw these as extensions of the early layers of the embryo.

Correlated with the basic physiques are three basic temperaments. Endomorphs typically show viscerotonia, a general love of comfort, relaxation, sociability, people, food, and affection. Mesomorphs show somatotonia, a love of physical adventure, risk taking, action, noise, courage, and aggression. Ectomorphs show cerebrotonia, a predominance of restraint, inhibition, and a desire for solitude and concealment. The correlations were quite high, with all of them at about $r = +.80$. Sheldon believed that both body build and temperament are primarily the result of heredity.

Most of Sheldon's writings represent attempts to identify and describe the major physiques and temperaments and then apply these to life. His major works are *The Varieties of Human Physique* (1940), *The Varieties of Temperament* (1942), *Varieties of Delinquent Youth* (1949), and *Atlas of Men* (1954). He began work on similar atlases of women and children but had greater difficulty in classifying them. Sheldon's emphasis on constitutional factors was not well received in an environment dominated by behaviorism. Furthermore, his studies were correlational, so he did not show the causal relationships between physique and temperament.

R. L. KOTESKEY

See CONSTITUTIONAL PERSONALITY THEORY.

Short-Term Anxiety-Provoking Psychotherapy. This brief, psychodynamically oriented psychotherapy was created by Sifneos (1972, 1979). In order for a client to be selected for inclusion in this therapy it must be clear that the individual has been able to establish and maintain at least one significant extrafamilial relationship in the past; has no recorded history of suicidal gestures or attempts; has not been nor currently is diagnosed psychotic or borderline psychotic; has sufficient ego strength to satisfactorily tolerate loss of important objects in the past without decompensating; and has a well-defined complaint. If the client does not meet these criteria, then he or she should be referred to an anxiety-suppressive brief therapy; it is primarily supportive and reeducative in nature, involving such tactics as environmental manipulation and reassurance along with the presentation of new information.

Sifneos has worked within the context of a university/medical complex in a major metropolitan area. Thus he has experienced little difficulty obtaining the highly select variety of clients appropriate to short-term anxiety-provoking psychotherapy.

Sifneos works from a traditional psychoanalytic framework. In his work he tends to focus primarily on oedipal issues, which he assumes to underlie most of his clients' complaints. Once these issues are worked through, along with the resistance that one typically encounters in dealing with them, it is time to terminate. It is integral to this method that the therapist not allow the client to dilute the therapeutic focus by free associating to other issues. When the client does begin to wander, it is the therapist's job to corral the subject and redirect the conversation to underlying oedipal material.

The major difference between short-term anxiety-provoking psychotherapy and traditional psychoanalysis is the activity level of the therapist. In a rather directive and active style the therapist first establishes a working therapeutic alliance with the client and then proceeds to clarify, interpret, and confront the various defenses the client uses to protect against the very real pain involved in facing oedipal material.

Sifneos's therapeutic style has been characterized as that of a benevolent senior lecturer (Mann & Goldman, 1982). He tends to channel the course of the therapy session much as if he were implementing a well-known, tried-and-true lesson plan he has been over many times. One particular area of predictability has to do with the typical stages through which a client passes.

The initial stage is characterized by a warm sense of optimism on the part of the client. Hopefulness that things will be better abounds. This stage, which lasts anywhere from one to eight or ten sessions, melts into a middle phase of therapy that is much less emotionally buoyant. The warm glow dissipates into a variety of colder, more conflictual feelings as the therapist's interpretations and confrontations begin to make an impact. This stage lasts anywhere from half a dozen sessions to 30 or more. The final phase of therapy is typically that of separation. Feelings that go with this stage are a mixture of the first two: the despair of being alone and responsible for oneself mixed with the optimism associated with experiencing one's own potency. This stage lasts from half a dozen sessions up to a dozen or more.

Sifneos does not put a specific time limit on the duration of psychotherapy. This practice is contrary to what other short-term psychodynamic theorists and therapists advise (e.g., Malan, 1976). He designs his treatment program based on the specific case. Using a predetermined termination date as a powerful metaphor for other inevitable separations in the client's life is a tactic that short-term anxiety-provoking psychotherapy does not utilize.

Critique. From Sifneos's writings it is difficult to learn how to use this approach. Much of the how-to technology is missing in comparison to other writers in the field (e.g., Davanloo, 1978). One can read many of the transcripts and be left to wonder about the principles involved and the timing for implementing them. This confusion is compounded further when anecdotes and illustrations seem to point primarily to the therapist rather than the therapy.

However, the approach does appear to be potentially quite valuable in helping a practitioner become more effective and efficient. The best prerequisite for using this technique is to have already engaged in a longer-term psychodynamic therapy oneself. The other primary requirement would seem to be one's willingness to explore with an open mind new and potentially risky ways of being with a client. It is recommended that before one begins the approach that a competent supervisor in the area be available for consultation.

References

Davanloo, H. (Ed.). (1978). *Basic principles and techniques in short-term dynamic psychotherapy.* New York: Spectrum.

Malan, D. H. (1976). *The frontier of brief psychotherapy.* New York: Plenum.

Mann, J., & Goldman, R. (1982). *A casebook in time-limited psychotherapy.* New York: McGraw-Hill.

Sifneos, P. E. (1972). *Short-term psychotherapy and emotional crisis.* Cambridge, MA: Harvard University Press.

Sifneos, P. E. (1979). *Short-term dynamic psychotherapy: Evaluation and technique.* New York: Plenum.

V. L. SHEPPERSON

See SHORT-TERM THERAPIES.

Short-Term Dynamic Psychotherapy. This article will describe the various patient selection criteria, assessment issues, and therapeutic approaches of D. H. Malan and Habib Davanloo. Other short-term dynamic approaches are described in Short-Term Anxiety-Provoking Psychotherapy and Short-Term Therapies.

Malan's systematic treatment and research work in the area of brief dynamic therapy began with Michael Balint at the Tavistock Clinic in 1955 and continued through the 1970s (Malan, 1976a, 1976b). During the latter part of this period Davanloo began exploring the limits of what was possible using this modality (Davanloo, 1978). His work built on Malan's foundational concepts and research; it has also gone beyond the frontiers that had been reached by Malan and his associates.

Both Malan and Davanloo have stretched the limits of patient selection criteria beyond limiting treatment solely to well-contained neurotics with circumscribed oedipal foci. They will also treat patients with more severe psychopathology: borderline, characterological, obsessional, phobic, and long-standing complex neuroses with less than clear, tidy limits to the disorder. Davanloo has also specified the following criteria: at least one meaningful relationship in the past; good ego strength that can withstand confrontation and moderate amounts of anxiety without psychotic decompensation; an intellectual and emotional capability to focus and circumscribe a specific issue on which to work; and a fair measure of insightfulness, flexibility, and motivation.

Initial assessment issues in the first several sessions for both of these theorists include the formulation of a situational conflict focus as well as the formulation of an underlying dynamic conflict focus. One typically would expect the presenting problem to be a muted reflection of underlying nuclear issues stemming from early traumatic events and repetitive early family constellations of behavior. It is essential that the therapist be able to formulate a central focus (among the many possible for any one patient) that is both workable for the therapist and acceptable to the patient. While actively focusing on this central issue the therapist also evaluates the patient's ego strength, defensive structure, psychological-mindedness, intellectual functioning, motivation, insight, and responsiveness to interpretation; Davanloo also looks for early signs of transference and countertransference. Concurrent with this initial evaluation period Davanloo advocates that the therapist contract with the patient for a short period of trial therapy. This trial period essentially consists of using the basic therapeutic techniques to be used throughout therapy in order to assess more thoroughly the patient's capability to withstand the stress of this anxiety-arousing therapy.

Both Davanloo and Malan tend to use interpretation as their primary therapeutic technique; they also make full use of traditional tools of suggestion, abreaction, clarification, confrontation, and manipulation (allowing the client free choice to manipulate his or her own environment and learn from these experiences). Both therapists tend to be much more active in the sessions than a traditional longer-term psychodynamic approach would dictate. Dependency of a passive variety is not encouraged; furthermore, one is encouraged to interpret both negative and symbiotic transference in order to prevent their development.

The most useful interpretations for Malan focus on making connections between the clients' reactions to the therapist and past reactions to parents (a transference-parent or T-P link). Davanloo's work represents a significant advance in this area. He posits two content triangles within which the therapist can make useful interpretations: the triangle of person and the triangle of conflict. The first involves interpersonal connections between the therapist, current significant others, and past significant others (T-C-P links); the second, intrapersonal connections between the client's impulses, defenses, and anxieties (I-D-A links). The degree to which a client can emotionally connect two or more points within and across these triangles is a good prognostic sign; the most useful connections tend to be T-C-P links by which the client is able to connect all points of the person triangle (e.g., "The anger you are experiencing toward me right now seems very similar to how you described being furious with your boss this week; it also reminds me of the rage you went into as a child with your father when he ignored you").

Davanloo tends to be more confrontive in his technique than any other short-term dynamic therapist. Gentle but relentless questioning and confrontation of defenses against true feelings are the order of the day. Vagueness, avoidance, passivity, and minimizing of feelings are actively confronted. The anger and defensiveness that this confrontation arouses are then fair grist for the therapy mill; if one fails to interpret, clarify, and support these negative reactive feelings, therapy is likely to be unsuccessful. In a similar vein one is encouraged to relentlessly push for early transference feelings; it is deemed critical to interpret these feelings as well as a variety of other unconscious material (e.g., fantasies, dreams, and oblique meanings of words). When these techniques are used, treatment can be expected to last anywhere from 10 to 40 sessions.

The need for brief therapy is growing. For those therapists trained in traditional theoretical orientations this form of brief therapy is an ideal modality to explore further.

References

Davanloo, H. (Ed.). (1978). *Basic principles and techniques in short-term dynamic psychotherapy*. New York: Spectrum.

Malan, D. H. (1976a). *The frontier of brief psychotherapy*. New York: Plenum.

Malan, D. H. (1976b). *Towards the validation of dynamic psychotherapy*. New York: Plenum.

V. L. SHEPPERSON

See PSYCHOANALYTIC PSYCHOTHERAPY; PSYCHOANALYSIS: TECHNIQUE.

Short-Term Therapies. Short-term therapy, or brief therapy, has gained a certain respectability. This type of therapy traditionally has been viewed as a sort of stopgap intervention that one resorts to if one does not have an adequate amount of time or expertise to do anything else. The current mainstream perspective has shifted. It is being recognized that significant intrapsychic and interpersonal change can be accomplished in a short time if one is willing to try something different.

Gurman (1981) adopts a perspective supportive of this new emphasis on briefer therapies. He maintains that a high percentage of all psychotherapy patients terminate treatment in fewer than 12 sessions, and thus the emphasis on briefer therapies is new only by design.

Brief therapies in general have a number of common ingredients. They tend to concentrate on just one or two salient issues or themes. They require the therapist to be relatively more active and directive than a traditional longer-term therapist would be. The therapist has to be willing to assume more responsibility for what happens during each session without infringing on the client's autonomy or treating him or her like an infant.

The therapies requiring a short time have a significant number of differences from each other. These differences center around basic theoretical assumptions regarding the mechanism of change, criteria for patient selection, and therapeutic style and strategy. Approaches to these differences can be reasonably grouped into two major camps: brief individual therapies (psychodynamic and behavioral) and brief systems therapies.

Brief Psychodynamic Therapies. *Theoretical Assumptions.* The basic curative element postulated by psychodynamic therapists practicing brief therapy is still insight. The client's insight into his or her own intrapsychic process is facilitated primarily by active clarification and interpretation of resistance and transference, in roughly that chronological order. A highly focused beam of emotional energy is brought to bear on the defined issue at hand. This issue will typically vary across patients and therapists. Sifneos (1979), Wolberg (1965), Malan (1976), and to a lesser degree Davanloo

(1978) tend to focus primarily on oedipal issues to the exclusion of what they view as themes of lesser importance. Particular attention is paid to evidence of oedipal struggles within the therapy relationship. Mann and Goldman (1982) take a distinctively different approach. They tend to pursue individuation-separation issues as a central theme. This pursuit is ensconced in a theoretical framework that is time conscious: the fact that one has so little time to work together is used as a powerful lever to push the client into the separation-individuation arena.

Criteria for Patient Selection. In general dynamic briefer therapists have relatively stringent requirements for allowing patients to work in a brief therapy format. Most of the theorists cited will require all of the following qualities in a patient: resilient ego strength, a focused presenting problem, fair to good capacities for attention, relatively high motivation, a history of at least one past successful relational attachment, a better than average capability for insight, no prior suicide attempts, and no evidence of psychosis or borderline psychiatric conditions. Mann and Goldman (1982) claim to have a much lower criterion; namely, good ego strength as demonstrated by the patient's ability to tolerate loss adequately in the past. If these criteria are not met, the therapist will tend to switch therapeutic modalities from dynamic to supportive therapy. Sifneos refers to this as moving from short-term anxiety-provoking therapy to short-term anxiety-suppressive therapy.

Treatment Strategy and Techniques. Most brief dynamic theorists are stage-oriented. The length of these stages is dependent on both therapist and client variables. The most important therapist variable is whether a predetermined termination date is part of the treatment plan (e.g., Mann sees all clients for only 12 sessions; the other theorists cited vary their treatment length from 8 to 40 sessions, with 12 to 15 weekly sessions being modal). Although different descriptive terminologies are used to define treatment stages, the concepts are relatively similar. The initial stage is characterized by a bright, optimistic expectancy, the establishment of a supportive alliance, and the development of a positive transference. The therapist is actively assessing, defining, and clarifying the central issue with the client while establishing a trust base that will support the negative effect aroused later in treatment. This phase typically lasts from one to three sessions.

The second phase of therapy is initiated by a higher frequency of confrontive interpretations on the part of the therapist. The client's defenses and transferences are actively confronted in such a way as to arouse anxiety; the client may also be challenged to engage in a variety of different therapeutic activities (e.g., Wolberg, 1965). This is followed by a shift in the client's mood from buoyant expectancy of magical change to a potpourri of negative emo-

tions. If the client does not leave treatment at this point, the prognosis for significant short-term change is enhanced. This stage lasts from 4 to 20 sessions, depending on the particular theorist's orientation and the severity of the client's disorder. The final stage of therapy finds the therapist pushing the client to integrate new ideas, feelings, and activities into his or her daily life. Most brief therapists will also work to help clients process their separation anxiety in a more healthy manner than they have been able to do in the past.

Brief Behavioral Therapy. *Theoretical Assumptions.* The subgroups within the behavioral school traditionally have emphasized the crucial importance of environmental factors in the change process. Classical and operant conditioning using a stimulus-response model was the accepted method of change. More recently cognitive behavior modification approaches have flourished. These approaches are more compatible with a social learning perspective in which cognitive mediating variables are accepted as causal in the change process. An excellent example of a broad-spectrum behavioral approach is the multimodal behavioral therapy of Lazarus (1976).

Criteria for Patient Selection. The primary benefit of brief behavior therapy is that one may tailor a particular behavioral approach to the level of intelligence, insight, judgment, and ego strength of each individual. The treatment door is wide open to the poor-functioning chronic schizophrenic as well as the bright, high-functioning neurotic (Wilson, 1981).

Treatment Strategy and Techniques. The initial step in this approach is to carry out a detailed behavioral assessment of a well-defined problem. The therapist then contracts with the client, either verbally or in writing, a specific agreement detailing the procedures they will follow, the number of sessions they will work together (most often 8–12 sessions to begin with for mild to moderately severe difficulties), and a contingency plan for dealing with any foreseeable difficulties. If the patient appears to have more than one problem, the least difficult will be addressed first. Along with establishing the rewarding feeling of mastering one difficulty the brief behavioral therapist will often arrange for external positive reinforcements in order to enhance motivation. Thus difficulties are addressed in a stepwise fashion, with the therapist functioning as a benevolent teacher-coach.

Brief Systems Therapies. *Theoretical Assumptions.* Brief systems (marital and family) therapists assume that change can and will take place even without insight if the system is willing to follow the therapist's prescriptions; change is cybernetic and follows principles of circular rather than linear causation (*see* Family Systems Theory); and many problems in living that individuals bring to therapists are the result of a lack of coping skill rather than an excess of backlogged emotional garbage; that is, most psychological problems have pedestrian origins.

Criteria for Patient Selection. The systems therapist will typically include all of the significant individuals within the identified patient's current primary social grouping, whether they are related biologically or not. A central concern for most brief systems therapists, regardless of the nature or severity of the presenting problem, is to redefine the problem in such a way that the therapeutic system (therapist and family) can avoid getting enmeshed in nonproductive interpersonal clutter. Depending on the aptitude, interests, and resilience of the particular systems therapist an extremely broad range of difficulties can be treated using this modality.

Treatment Strategy and Techniques. The primary tool of the strategic brief therapist is directive rather than interpretation (Haley, 1976). Directives typically focus on how members within the system interact with one another and the sequence and structure of their interactional process.

Directives can be either compliance-based or defiance-based (Papp, 1980). When working with a cooperative system the therapist will frequently exercise his or her expert authority to involve as many members of the family as possible in an activity. This activity can be either within or between sessions. The therapist can direct this activity based on a straightforward or more indirect, metaphoric conceptualization of the problem. The effect of this intervention is to relabel or redefine a few strategic areas of the system's sequence of interaction; eventually this change in sequence will calcify into a structural change in the system. When the oppositional tendencies within the system are such that compliance-based directives are rendered impotent, the brief strategic therapist will move toward the use of defiance-based directives. This has become known as paradoxical intervention, and the art of understanding and effecting such directives has received much attention.

Systems therapists are less stage-oriented than are dynamic brief therapists. Some will tend to conceptualize intermediate phases in therapy that are viewed as necessary halfway houses to the desired restructure of the system (Haley, 1980).

The average length of treatment is usually between 12 and 20 sessions. The Milan group conducts what they have referred to as long brief therapy; typically they see a family for only 12 sessions, but each session is one month apart (Palazzoli-Selvini, Boscolo, Cecchin, & Prata, 1978). They contend that the system requires that amount of time to digest their carefully planned strategic interventions. This group is also distinctive in that they have used a Greek chorus concept in which an anonymous panel observes through a one-way mirror and sends in interventions that the cotherapist team can choose to be puzzled by, disagree with, passively acknowledge, or actively applaud. This unique technique allows for a spatial representation of the ambivalence toward change present within most systems. The Greek chorus can push hard for transformation, while the cotherapists can express doubts and vote for homeostasis.

Summary. Some of the contrasts made between the major camps of brief therapy are in practice more theoretical than real, since many brief therapists are eclectic by disposition. For example, an individual might be seen alone, but treatment might flow from a systemic conceptualization of the client's problem, with both interpretations and directives being used as the therapist deems appropriate. The continued development of brief therapies is highly likely given the current economic and political climate. The use of these active, high-leverage treatment tactics is an area of conceptual and operational potency that the average clinician cannot afford to be without.

References

Davanloo, H. (Ed.). (1978). *Basic principles and techniques in short-term dynamic psychotherapy.* New York: Spectrum.

Gurman, A. (1981). Integrative marital therapy: Toward the development of an interpersonal approach. In S. H. Budman (Ed.), *Forms of brief therapy.* New York: Guilford.

Haley, J. (1976). *Problem solving therapy.* San Francisco: Jossey-Bass.

Haley, J. (1980). *Leaving home: The therapy of disturbed young people.* New York: McGraw-Hill.

Lazarus, A. A. (1976). *Multimodal behavior therapy.* New York: Springer.

Malan, D. H. (1976). *The frontier of brief psychotherapy.* New York: Plenum.

Mann, J., & Goldman, R. (1982). *A casebook in time-limited psychotherapy.* New York: McGraw-Hill.

Palazzoli-Selvini, M., Boscolo, L., Cecchin, G., & Prata, G. (1978). *Paradox and counterparadox: A new model in the therapy of the family in schizophrenic transaction.* New York: Aronson.

Papp, P. (1980). The Greek chorus and other techniques of paradoxical therapy. *Family Process, 19,* 45–57.

Sifneos, P. E. (1979). *Short-term dynamic psychotherapy: Evaluation and technique.* New York: Plenum.

Wilson, G. T. (1981). Behavior therapy as a short-term therapeutic approach. In S. Budman (Ed.), *Forms of brief therapy.* New York: Guilford.

Wolberg, L. R. (Ed.). (1965). *Short-term psychotherapy.* New York: Grune & Stratton.

V. L. SHEPPERSON

See PSYCHOTHERAPY, EFFECTIVENESS OF.

Shyness. Shyness is a form of social anxiety in which individuals are very self-conscious and worry about how others judge them. Over the years theorists and research gave little attention to shyness, even though it is a significant social phenomenon and a pressing personal problem. Zimbardo's (1977) work focused theorists' and therapists' attention on the concept, and now a rich literature exists. Shyness is one of only a handful of concepts that has phenomenological validity, in which the lay person's construct mirrors that of the professional. Its experience is universal, leading some writers to describe shyness as the common cold of social interaction.

Shyness affects personal comfort and inhibits normal behavior patterns. Self-identified shy people described seven types of interpersonal problems from shyness: problems in making friends, meeting new people, and enjoying new experiences; negative emotions, including anxiety, depression, and loneliness; difficulty in being assertive and offering one's opinion; difficulty in enabling others to appreciate the shy person's qualities; poor self-presentation; difficulty thinking and communicating in groups; and acute self-consciousness (Jones, Cheek, & Briggs, 1986).

Zimbardo (1977) found that more than 80% of one sample indicated feeling shy at a some point in life, while 40% considered themselves shy at the moment. He also noted that shyness is more prevalent in children than in adults. However, children who are shy are more shy as adults than children who are less shy. Shyness presents a debilitating effect on relationships through awkwardness, anxiety and self-doubt, and an inability to control shyness bouts. On the positive side, shyness carries favorable connotations of modesty, sophistication, and high class. Furthermore, shyness makes one appear selective, discreet, and introspective. It serves as a mask to prevent one from being noticed. In its origins and its consequences, shyness is a complex multidimensional concept.

At the physiological level shyness approximates other strong emotions. It causes sympathetic nervous system arousal with increased heart rate, elevated blood pressure, added perspiration, and butterflies in the stomach. But one physical sign normally is not involved in general arousal, one that shy people cannot hide: blushing. They tend to concentrate on these physical symptoms and may experience them before entering situations that bring on shyness (e.g., contact with strangers or the opposite sex, being the focal point of attention in a group, new social situations) in an anticipatory reaction. Blushing is accompanied by feelings of embarrassment. These feelings emanate from the chronic low self-esteem most shy persons experience. According to Zimbardo (1977), feelings of embarrassment are likely to occur when the individual believes that personal ineptness might be revealed, especially in a social context laden with evaluation possibilities.

Shyness is associated with Introversion and heightened self-consciousness, especially public self-consciousness. Chronically shy people engage in self-analysis and introspection to an almost obsessive degree. This led Hans Eysenck to note that one may be neurotically shy or simply prefer to be alone (i.e., introverted shyness). Zimbardo suggested that public shyness carries a greater burden than private shyness: "the publicly shy cannot readily communicate their fears, uncertainties, good qualities, and desires to the appropriate others. Putting themselves in these nonreturnable self-containers, they don't get the help, advice, recognition and love everyone needs at one time or another" (1977, p. 31).

Some research suggests that shy individuals are deficient in self-monitoring. In social situations the shy person focuses attention on self, monitoring the adequacy of social responses and physiological indicators of emotion. Excess public self-consciousness detracts from the ability to focus on the demands of the social events. Excess monitoring of self prevents adequate monitoring of the social situation and adapting to its subtle changes.

Trait descriptions of shyness find support in that many individuals are shy in a variety of social situations, and children who are shy demonstrate similar tendencies as adults. Shyness seems to be stable across time as a generalized social response. However, state descriptions of shyness also have utility. Shyness is more likely to occur in social situations wrought with the potential for social failure; hence the feeling of social anxiety. Those situations involve meeting new people in which the personal stakes are high and the fear of failure great.

Some theorists view shyness as a product of the labeling process, social programming, and Self-fulfilling prophecy. Social psychologists suggest that individuals are labeled as shy by self and others from specific social events. Individuals attribute shyness to personal inadequacy and then act in accord with the label on future occasions. Individuals may be programmed to be shy by the passive nature of television viewing and by the socialization training of children by parents. While research is unclear, there is some reason to predict that an overprotective style of parenting shields children from social and evaluative contexts and facilitates shyness.

The current research is rich with suggestions about therapeutic interventions, most of which employ behavior or cognitive-behavioral strategies to improve social skills. Behavioral strategies, especially modeling, role playing, and guided practice, improve the social skills in a variety of social environments. Cognitive-behavioral techniques focus on monitoring the social situation more and the self-reactions, especially the physiological indices of anxiety and embarrassment, less. Intervention strategies teach the person to attribute social anxiety to the external situation and to attribute effective performance to oneself. The final product is greater self-confidence and greater social competence.

References

Jones, W. H., Cheek, J. M., Briggs, S. R. (1986). *Shyness: Perspectives on research and treatment.* New York: Plenum.

Zimbardo, P. G. (1977). *Shyness: What it is, what to do about it.* Reading, MA: Addison-Wesley.

R. L. Timpe

See Personality.

Sibling Rivalry. Sibling rivalry is a phenomenon most people have experienced to one degree or another, since most people have siblings. The sibling relationship is often complicated and is influenced by such factors as parenting style, genetics, gender, life events, and other individuals outside the family. The quality of sibling relationships is a relevant topic for study because sibling relationships can be predictive of the quality of relationships with others outside the home. Within sibling interactions, either aggressive or cooperative behaviors develop.

Sibling rivalry first develops in early childhood, and it is not something we are programmed to experience. There may be environmental causes of sibling rivalry. Differential treatment of siblings on the part of the parents can trigger rivalry, especially in the "neglected" sibling. However, differential treatment by parents also causes hostility on the part of the "favored" child.

The differential treatment of siblings by mothers has been the subject of the most research and seems to be the most predictive of sibling rivalry. Differences in the amount of control and affection toward the siblings by the mother is associated with a competitive sibling relationship. Aggressive and punitive parenting styles are also linked with sibling aggression. Studies indicate that maternal control and physical punishment may be linked with sibling aggression. Nurturing behavior from the mother, however, can lead to positive sibling interaction. Recent studies (see Volling & Belsky, 1992) indicate that mothers who stress social rules and the feelings of others and who are sensitive to their children's needs tend to have children with positive sibling relationships.

The level of attachment a child has to his or her mother may also play a role in sibling rivalry. Children who as infants were insecurely attached to their mothers are less likely to respond in a positive way to a sibling in distress. Relations with their siblings are often aggressive. The situation is only aggravated if both siblings were insecurely attached to their mother. The results of such studies imply that much of the rivalry is related to getting attention from the parents; however, in studies where children themselves were asked about why they fight, the most common reason given was "bad moods" in two-parent homes where the father was present and tension over toys or their rooms in homes where the father was absent (Prochaska & Prochaska, 1985).

Different types of sibling pairs can trigger different levels of rivalry. Brother/brother pairs, who are most often the subjects of comparison by their families and by society, seem to trigger the most rivalry, with identical twin brothers having the most competitive relationship. Sister/sister pairs seem to be the closest type of sibling relationship. Brother/sister pairs trigger less rivalry because society is less likely to compare them with each other. In childhood, the comparisons are limited to things such as who walked or who talked first. As the siblings get older, the comparisons extend to grades and in adulthood to who makes the most money or who has the biggest house. This kind of comparison exacerbates the rivalry present in the relationship.

Dunn, Slomkowski, and Beardsall (1994) found that there is continuity in the quality of the sibling relationship between early childhood and early adolescence and that birth order has no effect on the stability of the relationship. However, there are some indications that significant life events can change the nature of the relationship. Events such as the death of a parent, marriage, or leaving home can change the quality of a sibling relationship. The effect of life-changing events can be either positive or negative. Sometimes the marriage of a sibling can adversely affect the sibling relationship as the new spouse can be seen as the outsider. The death of a parent can often drive siblings closer together as they try to cope with their grief.

References

Dunn, J., Slomkowski, C., & Beardsall, L. (1994). Sibling relationships from the preschool period through middle childhood and early adolescence. *Developmental Psychology, 30* (3), 315–324.

Prochaska, J. M., & Prochaska, J. O. (1985). Children's views of the causes and "cures" of sibling rivalry. *Child Welfare, 64* (4), 427–433.

Volling, B. L., & Belsky, J. (1992). The contribution of mother-child and father-child relationships to the quality of sibling interaction: A longitudinal study. *Child Development, 63,* 1209–1222.

M. L. Freeman

See Parenting.

Sick, Pastoral Care of. Pastoral care of the sick is one aspect of the multifaceted ministry of pastoral care, whose mandate for caring and compassion is rooted in the ministry and teaching of Jesus (*see* Pastoral Care). The pastoral functions of healing, guiding, and sustaining those in their care historically have been extended to the sick as pastors have exercised their right of initiative to visit those isolated from the community by illness. Little more than a generation ago pastors and chaplains visited the sick in their homes, while today the sick and dying are most often found in hospitals. The pastor, who feels less comfortable in the hospital than in the study, may question the significance of her role in the care of the hospitalized parishioner unless she understands that illness and hospitalization are almost always crisis-producing experiences and that the restoration of health means more than getting well. Medical services focus on the physical aspects of disease and distress, but the concern of pastoral care is for the care of the whole person, including the person whose spiritual pain sometimes transcends his or her physical pain.

The task of pastoral care of the sick is to witness to the certainty of God's presence and grace in the midst of the crisis that illness and hospitalization often bring. Pastoral care is offered as a faithful presence in crisis, as companionship in loneliness, grief, and discouragement and as a faithful reminder that the God who we worship is with us and for us in every human dilemma through Christ.

Pastoral care is a responsive ministry that is uniquely sensitive both to the parishioners' immediate physical situation and to their unique perception of it. The pastor's shepherding of the sick is focused on the one individual whose physical restoration may or may not be forthcoming but whose wholeness is nonetheless the pastor's continuing concern.

Effective pastoral care begins with attentive listening that leads to an accurate assessment of the parishioner's spiritual needs and concerns. The solicitous concern and attentive listening offered by the pastor communicates the reality that the pastor's presence represents the God who knows, cares about, and is available to the parishioner. In attentive listening the pastor may ascertain the patient's view of disease, suffering, and death and the degree to which the parishioner's faith informs his or her perceptions, hopes, and fears. Careful listening will ensure that the care that the pastor subsequently offers is indeed a response to the patient's concerns and will preclude any ill-fitting or predetermined words of comfort, no matter how well intended. The patient who has been heard by the pastor has already been cared for in a number of health-engendering ways, including experiencing himself or herself and feelings as valued and significant.

The psalmist speaks of Yahweh as the shepherd who restores souls and as the one whose presence sustains (Ps. 23). The need for the healing and sustaining ministry of pastoral care is particularly evident in hospitals, where aspects of medical care and treatment may bring significant stress. The impact of a new diagnosis or coping with a chronic condition can be so profound and confusing that even deeply religious patients can find themselves strangely disengaged from their faith. Treatments that consume physical and emotional energy leave little available for the religious patient's spiritual practice or reflection. The pastor's presence and prayer at the bedside serves as a reminder of the sustaining truths that the parishioner already knows; that God's concern and care for him or her is ongoing, independent of his or her strength or efforts. The pastor's willingness to be with her parishioner in the midst of the changes and challenges that illness brings incarnates the good news of which the psalmist spoke: that God does not abandon, forget, or forsake his people (Ps. 23).

Illness can be a time of searching for a deeper understanding of the meaning of faith and life. A patient searching for meaning in the midst of a difficult diagnosis may seek answers from his or her faith tradition. This search may raise theological questions, the answers to which have taken on a new and vital significance. When a parishioner brings these questions to the pastor it is because the patient wishes to have the perspective of faith applied to these. A parishioner who hopes to better understand his or her faith and how it speaks to the situation can be greatly helped by the theological perspective that the pastor can offer. This is especially true in a time when high-tech equipment is routinely used to prolong life and alert patients par-

ticipate fully in decision making regarding their care. In cases such as traumatic emergency or care at the end of life, fundamental attitudes about death and the meaning and quality of life become the basis of a patient's (or family's) decision about treatment options. Offering guidance from a theological perspective or providing guidelines and questions to facilitate the parishioner's own search for answers not only is helpful and comforting to the patient and family but also is appreciated by the medical team.

Healing is multifaceted. Physicians and health care teams recognize that the way pain or illness is perceived by a patient can influence that patient's therapeutic outcome. Major medical centers regularly employ psychiatrists, psychologists, clinical social workers, chaplains, and ethicists to address the emotional, social, spiritual, and moral aspects of patient care. Among these professional views, pastoral care alone seeks its roots in a theological worldview at the same time that it comes to terms with the forces and contending voices of the contemporary scene. For this reason its perspective and interventions continue to be an enduring and significant contribution to the care of the sick (*see* Clinical Pastoral Education).

Additional Readings

Pruyser, P. W. (1976). *The minister as diagnostician.* Philadelphia: Westminster.
Richmond, K., & Middleton, L. (1992). *The pastor and the patient.* Nashville: Abingdon.
Holst, L. E. (Ed.). (1985). *Hospital ministry.* New York: Crossroads.
Aden, L., & Ellens, J. H. (Eds.). (1988). *The church and pastoral care.* Grand Rapids, MI: Baker.

B. N. MITCHELL

See PASTORAL CARE; PASTORAL COUNSELING.

Signal Detection Theory. According to signal detection theory, the likelihood of persons indicating they have detected a stimulus depends on the sensitivity of the person and the person's decision-making strategy (criterion). Sensitivity is affected by two factors: the intensity of the stimulus and the ability of the person's sense receptors to detect the stimulus. A louder sound is easier to detect than a softer sound, and a person with normal hearing is more likely to hear a given sound than a person who is hearing-impaired. The criterion reflects the strategies used by the person in making a decision. Strategies are affected by factors such as potential reward or punishment associated with a response and the probability of the response occurring. For example, a person listening to a radio while working may not notice when a particular song is played. However, if the same song is the signal to call the radio station to win a desirable prize the person is much more likely to reach for the phone in response to even remotely similar melodies. Mothers are more likely to hear the cry of a baby than others in the same room and more likely to think they hear the cry of their baby even when they do not. The consequences of failing to hear the cry make them more willing to err than they would in other situations.

In a typical signal detection experiment a tone (signal) is presented intermittently at a low-intensity level near the detection threshold of the subject. There are then four possible responses: hit (correct detection of signal), correct rejection (no signal and no response), false alarm (response when there is no signal) and miss (signal but no response). By holding the sensitivity constant and manipulating the subject's criterion (e.g., varying the probability of the signal occurring) researchers plot the relationship between the probability of hits and false alarms. This plot is known as a receiver operating characteristic curve (ROC), and each point along the curve indicates a different criterion used by the subject.

J. D. FOSTER

See SENSATION AND PERCEPTION.

Sin, Psychological Consequences of. A biblical understanding of the psychological consequences of sin must begin with the fall and its disastrous effects for all of creation. The first three chapters of Genesis hold that all pain, suffering, and disorder stem not from God's good intentions but from the disobedience of Adam and Eve. In this sense it is right and proper to assert that all psychological disorder is the result of sin. However, this assertion must be qualified by the equally biblical notion that persons suffer psychologically not only because they are sinners and follow in Adam's train but also because they are victimized by a world infected by sin.

The third and fourth chapters of Genesis provide a vivid illustration of this. Adam and Eve commit the primal sin and are then made to suffer the consequences of their own actions as pain in childbirth and toiling by the sweat of one's brow. However, the next section of the narrative tells the story of the murder of Abel by his brother, Cain. The text makes it clear that Abel is killed because of his brother's jealous wrath and not because he had offended God. Abel is innocent of wrongdoing and thus becomes the victim of the sin of his brother.

The Scriptures are replete with this dual understanding of the consequences of sin, consequences that stem from one's own evil and consequences brought about by the evil of others. A major biblical theme is God's recognition and condemnation of the victimizing capacity of sin. As Berkouwer (1971) notes, "Nowhere does the Scripture take an easy view of our sin on the false presumption that it is merely a sin against our fellowman. The anger of the Lord rests on that man who sheds an innocent man's blood. An unimaginable guilt may show its ugliness in human affairs: but just as unimaginable is the judgment against the man who spurns his neighbor and does injury to his fellowman who was made in the image of God" (p. 243).

Injury to one's neighbor may take the form of physical abuse; however, the injury that can be inflicted on a person's mind and emotions is often more subtle and more damaging.

Another form of psychological damage can be attributed to the effects of the fall on the natural world. Paul alludes to this when he describes the entire creation as being subject to futility and enslaved to corruption so that it "groans and suffers" (Rom. 8:20–22). In essence the physical universe is injured and in turn can injure its inhabitants in such diverse ways as disease, flood, and famine. These distortions, or "injuries," of the physical creation are the result of sin, the first sin, and thus those who suffer psychological trauma due to these distortions may be said to be suffering, albeit indirectly, the psychological consequences of sin.

That these physical distortions can cause psychological trauma is beyond dispute. A great number of diseases and physical maladies may seriously disrupt the psychological functioning of an afflicted person. For example, brain lesions or tumors may cause symptoms ranging from depression to hallucinations to gross sexual misconduct. Hypothyroidism (underactivity of the thyroid gland) may cause delusions, hallucinations, apathy, and slowness of thought. Involuntary crying or laughing may occur with the onset of multiple sclerosis, while hypoglycemia (low blood sugar) may precipitate full-blown anxiety attacks (Bockar, 1975). Also, there is a good deal of recent research suggesting that certain mental disorders such as schizophrenia and bipolar disorder may have genetic components.

Both natural and manmade disasters leave victims not only physically battered but psychologically paralyzed. The effects of a disaster such as an earthquake on victims can include hysterical reactions, phobic reactions, nightmares, anxiety, social withdrawal, and concentration loss, among other symptoms.

There is also the psychological victimization of persons by their fellow human beings. Paul's solemn warning to fathers to avoid provoking their children to anger "lest they become discouraged" (Col. 3:21) carries with it an implicit recognition that psychological damage can result from poor parenting.

The psychological damage to young children who have been physically or sexually abused is sometimes irreparable. Victims of rape or incest can develop depression, anxiety, dissociations, or other symptoms as a means of coping with the shame, frustration, fear, and rage associated with the traumatic experiences. These and other more subtle attacks on an individual's dignity and worth may precipitate emotional problems.

That extensive and often permanent psychological damage can be inflicted on persons by the sins of others cannot be denied. Thus any counseling approach that wishes to take the concept of sin seriously must recognize that sin victimizes the innocent and that the psychological consequences of sin include the wounds and scars of the emotionally abused.

However, while affirming the biblical notion that sin victimizes, it must not be forgotten that the perpetrators of sin pay dearly, both spiritually and psychologically, for "missing the mark." To assume that sinning would have no psychological consequences would be to deny the holistic view of persons espoused by the Bible. "Scripture constantly makes it clear that sin is not something which corrupts relatively or partially, but a corruption which fully affects the radix, the root, of man's existence, and therefore man himself" (Berkouwer, 1962, p. 140).

The belief that persons suffer mental torment for their sins was until recently a belief firmly rooted in Western culture and reflected in the great literature—Shakespeare's Lady Macbeth. It is ironic that what was one of the most important themes in Western literature is now denied by many behavioral scientists who are attempting to understand the nature of human personality and existence while ignoring the insights of a Shakespeare or Dostoevski.

It should be noted that not all psychologists deny the existence of sin or the consequences stemming from sinning. Menninger (1973) attempts to salvage the concept of sin from the dustbin of the current era. He documents how our society has chosen to ignore or destroy the notion of sin and the price that has been paid for doing so.

Sin and guilt cannot be separated biblically or psychologically; thus it is guilt that most profoundly affects the psyche of those who sin. This idea has had an ardent spokesman in Mowrer (1961; Mowrer & Veszelovszky, 1980), who holds that a certain degree of mental illness stems not from psychological guilt feelings but from real, actual guilt brought on by misdeeds—sin. While his terminology, which includes words such as guilt, confession, and expiation, is not as theologically precise as one might hope, Mowrer has attempted to shed light on the role of conscience and morals in mental disorder.

One of Mowrer's students, Smrtic (1979), describes a number of cases of persons with psychological symptoms such as anxiety, suspiciousness, mania, and suicidal gestures, which he believe stem directly from wrong behavior and unconfessed sin. An exhaustive list of psychological symptoms related to actual sin in the life of individuals is not possible, due to the unique psychological makeup of each person. However, suffice it to say that feelings of meaninglessness, isolation, anxiety, and guilt may stem from the emptiness of being alienated from God by willful disobedience.

Neither Mowrer nor Smrtic would argue that unconfessed guilt is the cause of all psychological disturbance. However, they have provided a much-needed counterpoint to the idea that all mental disorder is the result of victimization and that none of it is caused by the disturbed person.

Thus it is apparent that psychological disorders may be rooted in the sin of victimization, the sinfulness of the distorted creation, or the personal sin of the disturbed individual. The biblical doctrine of the spiritual, mental, and psychological unity of the person allows for the possibility that all three causative factors could be operating simultaneously in one individual. In this situation a variety of interventions would need to be utilized. For example, confession and prayer, psychotherapy, and medication might all be needed to help a person overcome the debilitating effects of depression.

A truly biblical approach to counseling and psychotherapy recognizes that while sin is the root cause, a loving response to a suffering person would involve spiritual, psychological, and medical forms of treatment in concert. As Tournier (1962) has so perceptibly noted, "Every psychological confession has religious significance, and every religious confession, whether ritual and sacramental or free, has its psychological effects. It is perhaps in this fact that we perceive most clearly the unity of the human being, and how impossible it is to dissociate the physical, psychological and religious aspects of his life" (p. 204).

References

Berkouwer, G. C. (1962). *Man: The image of God.* Grand Rapids, MI: Eerdmans.

Berkouwer, G. C. (1971). *Sin.* Grand Rapids, MI: Eerdmans.

Bockar, J. A. (1975). *Primer for the nonmedical psychotherapist.* New York: Spectrum.

Menninger, K. A. (1973). *Whatever became of sin?* New York: Hawthorn.

Mowrer, O. H. (1961). *The crisis in psychiatry and religion.* Princeton, NJ: Van Nostrand.

Mowrer, O. H., & Veszelovszky, A. V. (1980). There indeed may be a "right way": Response to James D. Smrtic. *Psychotherapy: Theory, Research, and Practice, 17,* 440–447.

Smrtic, J. D. (1979). Time to remove our theoretical blinders: Integrity therapy may be the right way. *Psychotherapy: Theory, Research, and Practice, 16,* 185–189.

Tournier, P. (1962). *Guilt and grace.* New York: Harper & Row.

W. G. BIXLER

See RELIGION AND PERSONALITY.

Single Parents. Single parenting is the fastest-growing lifestyle in the United States. In 1970, 11% of the children under 18 lived with one parent. By 1979 this figure had risen to 19.3%. By 1990, nearly one-half of all children will spend time in a one-parent family (Bumpass, 1990), nearly one-fifth of which will be headed by a father (Bianche, 1995). The only other family lifestyle that is rapidly growing is the reconstituted family, which is often formed following life as a single-parent family.

The single-parent family is formed as a result of one of three events: divorce or separation, death of a parent, and birth or adoption of a child to an unmarried parent. Divorced parents constitute two-thirds of single parents, while never-married parents constitute one-fourth (Bilge & Kaufman, 1983).

Single Parents

In the 1980s and 1990s, delayed marriage and child-births outside of marriage contributed more than divorce to single-parent families (Bianche, 1995). Adoption by single parents, particularly of foreign-born children, is also rapidly growing. Of all one-parent families, most are still headed by working women. Seventy-three percent of divorced women work, while only 51% of married women work.

The single-parent family experiences five specific areas of stress that differentiate it from the two-parent family: lower income, more limited sense of power and control, diminished social support and involvement, reduced emotional support and physical assistance within the household, and often a traumatic event or series of events that began the new family lifestyle.

The traumas that began the majority of single-parent families add to the adjustment difficulties of the single parent. Where divorce has occurred, the tensions of the former marital relationship may linger on, creating special difficulties when decisions about the child require parental contact. Bitterness and resentment may remain, especially if the single parent did not want the divorce. Where the trauma was the death of a parent, the grief process complicates the adjustment. Where the trauma was an unplanned pregnancy, major adjustments of future plans are needed. Thus single parenting for most people is not a choice but an unwelcome consequence. This is one reason most single parents report a more limited sense of power and control over their lives (Smith, 1980). They also report a sense of alienation, helplessness, and victimization.

The reduction of adult physical assistance and emotional support within the household further reinforces the sense of less power and control. One person cannot do what two did before. The parent may consequently feel increasing inadequacy as a result of seeing more things not done and of having no one within the family to turn to for emotional support.

Less time is available for social activities and participation in community life. The single parent often feels the responsibility of picking up the roles and activities of the other parent. Thus the parenting role becomes dominant, and personal desires and activities with other adults take second or third place.

Research shows that 32% of single-parent families, as compared to 51% of two-parent families, know 20 or more neighbors (Smith, 1980). This may result from decreased time to spend with neighbors as well as the parent's response to the social stigma against one-parent families that is often found in American culture.

Cross-cultural research has shown that single-parent families are not unique to American society but exist in many cultures. Whether the single-parent family becomes a personal and social problem depends on the availability of supportive social networks as well as the cultural attitudes toward it (Bilge & Kaufman, 1983). American society seems to provide few of these resources. Single parents often need to find and create their own support networks, another stressful responsibility.

Three types of social networks have been identified among single parents (McLanahan, Wedemeyer, & Adelberg, 1981). The family of origin provides some single parents almost all of their support, with division of labor occurring along the lines of traditional roles. This type of network provides direct services, such as home repairs, and emotional support, especially security and a sense of worth. It does not provide much opportunity for intimacy and social integration.

A second type of support structure is the extended network, composed usually of new same-sex friends, especially other single parents. This structure is often large, with various clusters of relationships. Different individuals are depended on for different kinds of support. These relationships are often less durable and less intense than the family-of-origin relationships. A large majority of the women who establish this kind of network are attempting to reestablish their independence and have high career aspirations. This network may not provide a great deal of security or sense of worth, but it does provide intimacy and opportunity for social integration.

A third type is the conjugal network, which includes the presence of a key male or spouse equivalent. Here two subtypes parallel the previous two networks, depending on the parent's choice to focus on parent role or career role.

All these networks provide varying degrees and types of support to the single parent. The existence of such support networks is a critical variable in the functional character of the single-parent family. Where these are present, both parent and children gain support and assistance.

The single-parent family usually experiences financial stress. The income of families headed by women is about one-half that of two-parent families (Buehler & Hogan, 1980). A large number of wives and children experience downward economic mobility following divorce. Many wives are forced to work in order to maintain a standard of living close to what they and the children have come to enjoy. This often reduces their time with the children, their involvement with other adults, and their ability to keep things at home as they once were.

Considerable concern is often voiced by Christians and by married individuals about the effect of single parenting on the children. A widely read research study by Wallerstein (1989) added to those concerns, as it detailed the problems encountered by a select sample of children of divorce in their early adult years. The study did not have a control group of children from conflicted marriages, which would have been the likely situation for these children had the parents not divorced. It is still clear that two parents are better than one for both the parents' and the children's sake, but research on the effects of single parenting has not shown that if all other circumstances are equal, it is necessarily bad for the children. The presence of conflict is more determinative of negative effects. Children who perceive greater conflict in their single- or dual-parent families were found to have lower self-concepts (Bilge & Kaufman, 1983). The presence of a socially supportive network was also found to be important for the healthy development of children (McLanahan, Wedemeyer, & Adelberg, 1981). Cross-cultural research seems to support the conclusion that the family structure (one parent versus two parents) is not the most significant variable in assessing the consequences to the children (Bilge & Kaufman, 1983).

The number of single-parent families headed by fathers more than tripled between 1970 and 1990 (Greif, 1995). Research indicates that family well-being is the same for mother-headed and father-headed families. (Cohen, 1995). At the same time, males within American culture have the least opportunity to develop good parenting skills, especially in the area of meeting the emotional needs of the children. Research has shown that the effect of fathers spending more time with their children and having the sole responsibility for child rearing is that their approach to discipline moves away from authoritarian methods toward the use of more nurturing methods (Smith & Smith, 1981). Clearly fathers, both single and married, benefit from increased presence with their children and could benefit from more extensive child-rearing training.

Single parents do have unique stresses and challenges, but if they are given a supportive Christian network these parents can live a meaningful life for themselves and provide an effective, nurturing environment for their children.

References

Bianche, S. (1995). The changing demographic and socioeconomic characteristics of single parent families. *Marriage and Family Review, 20,* 71–97.

Bilge, B., & Kaufman, G. (1983). Children of divorce and one-parent families: Cross cultural perspectives. *Family Relations, 32* (1), 59–72.

Buehler, C. A., & Hogan, M. J. (1980). Managerial behavior and stress in families headed by divorced women: A proposed framework. *Family Relations, 29* (4), 525–532.

Bumpass, L. L. (1990). What is happening to the family? Interactions between demographic and institutional change. *Demography, 27,* 483–498.

Cohen, O. (1995). Divorced fathers raise their children by themselves. *Journal of Divorce and Remarriage, 23,* 55–73.

Greif, G. (1995). Single fathers with custody following separation and divorce. *Marriage and Family Review, 20,* 213–231.

McLanahan, S. S., Wedemeyer, N. V., & Adelberg, T. (1981). Network structure, social support and psychological well-being in the single parent family. *Journal of Marriage and the Family, 43* (3), 601–612.

Smith, M. J. (1980). The social consequences of single parenthood: A longitudinal perspective. *Family Relations, 29* (1), 75–81.

Smith, R. M., & Smith, C. W. (1981). Child rearing and single parent fathers. *Family Relations, 30* (3), 411–417.

Wallerstein, J. (1989). *Second chance: Men, women and children a decade after divorce.* New York: Tichnor & Fields.

A. D. COMPAAN

See CHILD CUSTODY; DIVORCE; PARENTING.

Singleness. This term includes four groups of people, each with some similar issues but also unique problems and areas of concern: the never-married, the separated, the divorced, and the widowed. Their numbers are increasing rapidly, from 4 million in 1950 to an estimated 20 million in 1982. Social factors influence this greatly. It is now more acceptable for women to pursue their own interests, including attending college (in 1960 there were 1.2 million women in college as compared with 3.5 million in 1972), which tends to delay marriage. Singleness as a lifestyle, though still carrying some social stigma, has become a more acceptable alternative, and freer sexual mores with less restrictive role constraints have had some influence on this.

A crucial element in the psychological health of the single person is his or her acceptance of the state of singleness, much as people can be happily or unhappily married. Whether the person is single by choice or not is a critical factor. One group of singles, such as the young or happily divorced, may plan to marry in the future but are contentedly single. There are those who have chosen singleness as a preferred lifestyle (e.g., priests), the once-married who choose not to remarry, and those who do not want to marry. These groups face some issues that married people in our society do not face. However, they seem to handle them much better than those who are single not by choice—through death of a spouse, termination of a marriage, or the lack of opportunity to marry when they would like to.

There are advantages to being single. Frequently there is an increased mobility, freedom, and psychological and social autonomy. Singles often build sustaining friendships and support structures. They generally have more time to devote to career opportunities and other interests. Adams (1976) cites three factors that determine healthy singleness: economic independence, social and psychological autonomy, and the preference to remain single.

There are also disadvantages to being single, not all of which are experienced by every single. Some have an unfulfilled desire for children and a family of their own. Others report isolation, loneliness, insecurity, or lack of social status. Peer and social pressures to marry abound. Some social policies favor the married, and marriage legitimizes sexual experiences.

Between ages 30 and 34, 12% of men and 7% of women have never married. That percentage decreases to 7.9% and 5.2% respectively in the age group 35 to 39; and by age 65 only 4% of men and

6% of women have never married (Stein, 1976). More than 60% of all singles live in large cities, and that number is increasing. Cities offer more single-oriented attractions, and over the last decade families have been drawn to the suburbs. The median age of first marriage has risen for both men and women, from 20.3 in 1960 to 22.3 in 1983 for women, and from 22.8 to 24.8 for men.

Life as a single in a marriage-oriented society frequently produces significant pressures. Singles cope with these pressures through one of several strategies. Some choose the professional route, throwing all of their time and energy into their careers. Others devote themselves to relationships. A segment opts for the individualistic route, stressing self-growth and development. Some take a supportive role in the lives of their friends, while others remain passive and isolated. Community activism is another available route. All of these strategies may of course be chosen by married persons, but they generally do not have the same time and freedom to devote as singles.

Single old people who have never married tend to be lifelong isolates, but they are not especially lonely, presumably having gotten used to being alone (Gubrium, 1976). They tend to be more positive than divorced or widowed old people and do not have to face the bereavement following a spouse's death that so affects most older people.

Men who are single tend to be less intimate in their friendships with other men than single women are in their friendships with other women. However, single women tend to be more isolated than single men. Isolation and lack of intimacy are often a result of a lack of support and care structures, combined with the stereotypes of society and role expectations.

Extensive analyses by Bernard (1972) reveal that single women tend to be happier than single men, who are more likely to show depression and phobic tendencies. Men who remain unmarried are not as successful as married men in terms of education, income, and occupation, but women who remain unmarried are higher achievers than married women. How much this relates to social pressures and role expectations and how much to other factors is unclear.

Problems that are brought to therapy by singles are often the same problems that married people may feel—loneliness, isolation, lack of support, insecurity. However, the single often has the added pressure of society's disapproval.

References

Adams, M. (1976). *Single blessedness*. New York: Basic Books.
Bernard, J. S. (1972). *The future of marriage*. New York: World.
Gubrium, J. F. (1976). Being single in old age. *International Journal of Aging and Human Development, 6* (1), 29–41.
Stein, P. J. (1976). *Single*. Englewood Cliffs, NJ: Prentice-Hall.

Additional Readings

Cargan, L., & Melko, M. (1982). *Singles: Myths and realities*. Beverly Hills, CA: Sage.
Simenauer, J., & Carroll, D. (1982). *Singles: The new Americans*. New York: Simon & Schuster.

D. L. SCHUURMAN

Sixteen Personality Factor Questionnaire. An objective instrument designed to measure the basic dimensions of normal personality. The self-administering test (16 PF) exists in five forms that vary according to the particular testing situation. The basic form consists of 187 multiple-choice items that are answered by selecting one of three responses and are easily scored. Sixteen is the lower age limit for the test. The primary developer, Raymond Bernard Cattell, saw factor analysis as the best method for personality test construction and used that technique to develop this test.

Names for the 16 personality factors (e.g., premsia and sizothymia) were created originally so that the meaning of common words would not interfere with understanding. This labeling was a fine attempt at clarity. However, these terms became a liability because jargon-laden clinicians lost interest, prompting the test publisher to use recognized words such as warmth, conformity, and dominance.

The 16 PF takes approximately 50 to 60 minutes to complete. Questions have to do with behavior, interests, and preferences. Norms are available for high school students, college students, and general population groups. The instrument has the same advantages as most other objective personality questionnaires: good reliability, ease of administration and scoring, low cost, and standardization that allows for high research potential.

While the factor analytic construction of this test promised pure factors without overlap, the scales are not as pure as was hoped. This, along with the highly technical development of the test, has caused it to fall a good deal short of the claims methodological purists made for it. The publisher, the Institute for Personality and Ability Testing, continues to produce many of the technical and clinical writings supporting the test, and a number of clinicians use it regularly. But it has disappointed its developers by not enjoying the widespread use it seemed destined to attain.

Assessing normal and mildly troubled people according to a wide range of traits will continue to be the strength of the Sixteen Personality Factor Questionnaire. As a part of a test battery or in vocational counseling the test complements other measures of nonpathological personality dimensions. Use in marital therapy may also hold some promise. Since some forms lack validity measures of test-taking attitudes, care should be used in evaluating the results without information on socially desirable response sets.

Now that computer scoring and interpretation is nearly routine in personality testing, the 16 PF has mated with a technology similar to the science that gave it birth. A primitive actuarial or probability-based interpretive system is available using computers to aid the clinician. The test will continue to be a good objective measure of normal personality traits. Even more likely is its continued use as a research tool helping psychologists uncover the dimensions and structure of personality. As the best factor-analytic personality questionnaire, Cattell's work will stand as a testimony to thoughtful psychological investigation.

Additional Readings

Cattell, R. B. (1973). *Personality and mood by questionnaire.* San Francisco: Jossey-Bass.

Cattell, R. B., Eber, H. W., & Tatsuoka, M. M. (1964). *Handbook for the Sixteen Personality Factor Questionnaire [16 PF].* Champaign, IL: Institute for Personality and Ability Testing.

Karson, S. E., & O'Dell, J. W. (1976). *Clinical use of the 16 PF.* Champaign, IL: Institute for Personality and Ability Testing.

Krug, S. E. (1981). *Interpreting 16 PF profile patterns.* Champaign, IL: Institute for Personality and Ability Testing.

D. SIMPSON

See PERSONALITY ASSESSMENT; PSYCHOLOGICAL MEASUREMENT; FACTOR THEORIES OF PERSONALITY; CATTELL, RAYMOND BERNARD.

Skinner, Burrhus Frederic (1904–1990). Considered to be the father of modern behavioral psychology. Son of a moderately prosperous lawyer, Skinner was born in Susquehanna, Pennsylvania, and grew up there in a middle-class Protestant family. He attended Hamilton College, completing his B.A. in 1926. Skinner planned on a literary career but quickly gave this up. He enrolled in psychology at Harvard in 1927, completing his M.A. in 1930 and his Ph.D. in 1931.

Skinner became a National Research Council Fellow (1931–1933) and then a Junior Fellow in the Society of Fellows (1933–1936) at Harvard; during this period he worked in the laboratory of W. J. Crozier, an experimental biologist. He taught at the University of Minnesota from 1930 to 1945, taking time out during 1942 and 1943 to conduct war research sponsored by General Mills, and for a Guggenheim Fellowship in 1944 and 1945. Skinner became chairperson of the department of psychology at Indiana University in 1945. He then went to Harvard as William James Lecturer in 1947, joined the Department of Psychology in 1948, and remained there for the balance of his career.

Skinner's most lasting contribution to psychology was his "demonstration that behavior could be studied as a self-sufficient subject matter, rather than as a reflection of inner mental events" (Holland, 1992, p. 665). The goal of Skinner's work was simple: the control, prediction, and interpretation of behavior. He showed that most animal and human

behavior is controlled by its consequences rather than its antecedents. Operant behavior, as Skinner termed it, acts on the environment. In contrast, respondent behavior is elicited by the environment.

Skinner played an important role in the development of behavioral research techniques and equipment; he developed the Skinner box, the cumulative recorder, and the first teaching machines. He disliked formal theory and emphasized single-subject rather than group research. While he was a graduate student at Harvard, Skinner developed a lifelong friendship with Fred Keller. Through his teaching at Columbia University, Keller was most influential in propagating Skinner's theory; it was Keller's students who popularized behavioral psychology in the 1950s and 1960s.

Among the many honors awarded to Skinner were the Warren Medal of the Society of Experimental Psychology in 1942; the Distinguished Scientific Contribution Award of the American Psychological Association in 1958; the Edward L. Thorndike Award in Education in 1966; the United States Air Force Hoyt-Vandenburg Trophy in 1967; the National Medal of Science in 1968; the Gold Medal of the American Psychological Foundation in 1971; the International Award of the Joseph P. Kennedy, Jr., Foundation for Mental Retardation in 1971; the Humanist of the Year Award of The American Humanist Society in 1972; the Creative Leadership Award for Distinguished Contributions to Educational Research and Development by the American Educational Research Association in 1976; the First Annual Award of the National Association for Retarded Citizens in 1978; and the American Psychological Association's Award for Outstanding Lifetime Contribution to Psychology in 1990. Skinner also received more than 20 honorary degrees.

The breadth of Skinner's intellectual interest is indicated by his many professional associations, including fellow of the American Psychological Association and the Royal Society of Arts; and member of the National Academy of Sciences, the American Philosophical Society, the American Academy of Arts and Sciences, and the New York Academy of Sciences.

A prolific writer, Skinner published 19 books dealing with a broad range of topics from technical aspects of operant behavior to mental illness, education, politics, and social policy. His most influential works in psychology include *The Behavior of Organisms* (1938), which outlined his basic theory and philosophy; *Science and Human Behavior* (1953), in which he applied his theory to everyday human activities; *Verbal Behavior* (1957), his account of private events and consciousness; and *Beyond Freedom and Dignity* (1971), applying his theory and philosophy to social systems, ethics, and religion. Skinner helped found the *Journal of the Experimental Analysis of Behavior* (1958–) and the Division of the Experimental Analysis of Behavior in the American Psychological Association.

Although he was tremendously influential and widely acclaimed, Skinner is also a controversial figure who frequently championed unpopular positions. Thus Skinner's critics are numerous. Among the criticisms are charges that Skinner reduces people to robots or automatons; dehumanizes people, destroying freedom and personal responsibility; denies the existence of the mind; undermines the basis for morals through rejection of all but empirical bases for ethical decisions; fosters totalitarianism by his emphasis on control of human behavior; and confuses his personal philosophy with his science, resulting in scientism rather than science (Bufford, 1981; Cosgrove, 1982; Wheeler, 1973). Skinner responded to these criticisms most extensively in *Answers for My Critics* (in Wheeler, 1973).

A signer of the *Humanist Manifesto II*, Skinner espouses materialistic humanism. In *Beyond Freedom and Dignity* (1971), Skinner articulates this philosophy. According to Skinner, people have no special moral sense; rather, environment has taught them to behave in certain ways. At times his humanistic views seem to shape Skinner's scientific conclusions (Cosgrove, 1982). For example, he concludes that punishment has harmful effects and does not work, that has been a view effectively challenged (Bufford, 1981).

Although he was a determinist, Skinner believed that humans can control their own destiny. "Man himself may be controlled by his environment, but it is an environment which is almost wholly of his own making" (Skinner, 1971, p. 196). Thus Skinner ends up discounting determinism and advocating a view similar to that of causality and responsible choice held by most Christians.

Because of Skinner's significant role in the development of modern behaviorism, many people have come to view Skinner's religious perspectives as central to behavior theory. However, Bufford (1981) contends that Skinner's worldview is not essential to behavior theory.

References

Bufford, R. K. (1981). *The human reflex: Behavioral psychology in biblical perspective*. New York: Harper & Row/CAPS.

Cosgrove, M. P. (1982). *B. F. Skinner's behaviorism*. Grand Rapids, MI: Zondervan.

Holland, J. G. (1992). B. F. Skinner (1904–1990). *The American Psychologist, 47*, 665–667.

Skinner, B. F. (1938). *The behavior of organisms: An experimental analysis*. New York: Appleton-Century-Crofts.

Skinner, B. F. (1953). *Science and human behavior*. New York: Macmillan.

Skinner, B. F. (1957). *Verbal behavior*. New York: Appleton-Century-Crofts.

Skinner, B. F. (1971). *Beyond freedom and dignity*. New York: Knopf.

Wheeler, H. (Ed.). (1973). *Beyond the punitive society*. San Francisco: Freeman.

R. K. BUFFORD

See BEHAVIORAL PSYCHOLOGY; CONDITIONING, OPERANT.

Sleep and Dreaming. Sleep is so familiar and universal that we seldom stop to think about its strangeness. Yet, when we sleep we enter a peculiar and vulnerable state in which we lose our awareness of the outside world and our ability to control our thoughts or actions. Mental events become surrealistic, distorted, and bizarre, and voluntary muscles are periodically paralyzed to prevent us from acting out our dreams and possibly injuring ourselves or others. Memory is altered, too. Most of the mental activity and vivid imagery of the night disappears without a trace, so insistently that it would seem that we are programmed to forget it. What is the purpose of this odd state called sleep? Scientists are still not sure, but they have discovered some fascinating information about it.

Early researchers were surprised to learn that sleep is not uniform. It consists of two different states: rapid-eye-movement sleep (REM) and slow-wave sleep (NREM), which is further subdivided into four stages. Research also revealed that most people follow a similar pattern of sleep throughout the night. Before sleep onset, their muscles relax and their brain waves (electroencephalograms or EEGs) shift from the rapid beta waves (13–40 Hertz or cycles per second) that are prominent during waking to the slower and higher amplitude alpha waves (8–12 Hz). As sleep commences EEGs slow, and theta (4–8 Hz) and later delta (1–4 Hz) become prominent as sleepers gradually move through stages 1–4 of NREM sleep. Meanwhile, heart rate, blood pressure, and muscle tension decrease and sleepers become progressively more difficult to awaken. In this first period sleepers spend considerable time in stage 4.

After about 90 minutes, the first bout of REM sleep appears. EEGs shift from high-amplitude delta to fast, low-voltage signals that are similar to waking EEGs. The sleepers' eyes begin to dart rapidly to and fro under closed eyelids as if they are watching some fast-moving event. Men often experience penile erections, and women, increased vaginal blood flow during REM (although this is not usually related to sexual themes in dreams). Breathing rate, heart rate, and blood pressure can increase significantly and become quite variable. Meanwhile, muscle tonus drops dramatically, leaving the voluntary muscles paralyzed except for brief twitchings in the hands or feet. After about 10 minutes, REM makes way for NREM and the cycle begins again. During the remainder of the night REM and NREM alternate approximately every 90 minutes, with REM periods getting longer and NREM becoming progressively lighter (more time in stages 1 and 2). When sleepers are awakened from REM, they report vivid, narrative dreams about 80 to 85% of the time. When awakened from NREM they occasionally report vivid dreams, but more frequently (60 to 70% of the time) they say they were "just thinking" or are aware of simple imagery.

Humans vary greatly, at different ages, in the amount of time they spend sleeping. Newborns sleep 14 to 18 hours per day (50% of this in REM), 5-year-olds average 11 hours (25% in REM), and adults average 7 to 9 hours (20% in REM), although a sizable number of people (7%) apparently need 6.5 hours or less to function normally. Sleep time and quality can change significantly with age. Among those who are 65 or older, nighttime awakenings increase, stage-4 NREM decreases (by 15 to 30%), and light sleep increases. Although no one has discovered why this occurs, most experts suspect it is due to a weakening of the brain mechanisms that control sleep.

Some of the physical mechanisms involved in sleep and waking have now been identified. Alert wakefulness apparently depends on neural activity in three systems of neurons in the brainstem that variously utilize acetylcholine, norepinephrine, and serotonin as transmitters. Slow-wave sleep begins when neurons in the basal forebrain (just in front of the hypothalamus) become active. REM sleep is apparently associated with the activity of acetylcholinergica neurons in the pons. Some of these neurons produce cortical arousal (reflected by the fast, low-voltage EEG patterns that occur in REM) and presumably dreams. Others fire in conjunction with rapid eye movements, and still others produce atonia, the muscle paralysis that prevents us from acting out our dreams. Additionally the suprachiasmatic nucleus of the hypothalamus, which receives neural input from the eyes, synchronizes sleep and waking (and a host of other functions) with daylight and darkness (Carlson, 1995; Kalat, 1995).

Some investigators have studied the effects of sleep deprivation to help them try to understand sleep. They have found that moderate or partial deprivation (2 to 3 days) produces surprisingly few deficits, aside from periodic sleepiness (which manifests most insistently at night). Prolonged deprivation (5 to 10 days) can produce fine hand tremors, droopy eyelids, occasional double vision, and lowered pain thresholds. It impairs tasks that require sustained attention, effort, or concentration and may also produce mild confusion, disorientation, irritability, or transitory visual or tactile hallucinations. A few individuals (5% or fewer) have shown more disturbed behaviors (vivid hallucinations, delusional thinking), but this is certainly not the norm (Webb, 1975). Deprivation studies with animals have produced more severe effects (in some cases, death). However, in animal studies the effects of loss of sleep are confounded with stress because the manipulations required to keep animals awake also produce stress. In such cases it may be stress rather than sleep loss that produces the damaging effects (Rechtschaffen, Bergmann, Everson, Kushida, & Gilliland, 1989).

Other researchers have studied the effects of selectively depriving people of REM or stages 1 to 4 of NREM. REM or stage-4 NREM deprivation (but not deprivation of stages 1, 2, or 3) consistently produces rebound effects. Volunteers thus deprived will spend increased amounts of time in REM or stage 4 when they are allowed to sleep normally, as if trying to make up the loss. These and other findings suggest that REM and stage-4 NREM may be the most helpful stages of sleep, possibly because they provide rest and restoration for the brain. (Other parts of the body are apparently able to restore themselves without sleep, just with rest.) The brain does appear to be resting in stage-4 NREM because it cools and its metabolism and blood flow drop by 75% in this stage (Bushbaum et al., 1989). Sleepers are also very unresponsive and groggy if awakened from stage 4. Some investigators believe that REM may help restore the brain, perhaps in memory consolidation or housekeeping functions.

Dreaming, like sleep, has been studied extensively but still remains a mystery. One very old explanation (still current in New Age thought and some older tribal cultures) is that dreaming allows one's spirit access to a realm beyond the physical plane. However, this view is difficult to reconcile with the finding that dreaming is not just a human activity. All mammals and some birds engage in REM sleep, and there is evidence that they dream. Cats whose brains have been lesioned to prevent atonia act out their dreams during REM.

From a Christian perspective, God has communicated with humans through dreams (e.g., Jacob, Joseph in Egypt, Joseph the earthly father of Jesus, Paul). More often, however, God communicated with humans directly, often providing tangible evidence of his presence (e.g., Moses and the burning bush, the miraculous events of the exodus, Abraham and Sarah, Paul on the road to Damascus, and so forth). God spoke through dreams infrequently (only to a few people and only once or at most a few times to each of them); each dream had a special purpose, so we should not construe such accounts to mean that God communicates regularly to humans through their dreams or that we can gain special access to God's will or spiritual things by recording and interpreting our dreams. If God had created dreams for this purpose, why would he also have programmed our brains to forget each night's activity so completely and insistently?

Sigmund Freud hypothesized that dreams are the subconscious mind's disguised attempts to satisfy its deep and socially unacceptable sexual urges. However, current understanding of the physiological controls on sleep and dreaming has modified Freudian thinking considerably. In addition, detailed studies of dream content (from dreams collected in the lab or at home) indicate that fewer than 5% of dreams are explicitly sexual (Snyder, 1970). Most dreams are rather prosaic. Fewer than 5% are in exotic or unusual settings. About 95% involve other persons, more than half known to the dreamer. The most frequent themes include misfortune, aggression, fear, failure, or anger rather than sex or positive themes.

Most of the current hypotheses about dreaming are physiologically based and assume that the physiological processes that occur during REM sleep are central, perhaps reflecting memory consolidation or even the purging of useless memories from the brain, whereas dreaming is primarily a byproduct of this activity (Crick & Mitchison, 1983). Dreams are presumably created by the brain (or mind) in its attempts to organize and interpret the random images, sensations, and memories stimulated by high levels of neural activity in REM. Such hypothesis might help explain why dreams can be so unrealistic, improbable, and disjoint and yet contain personal and sometimes meaningful elements. The disjoint, unrealistic aspects of dreams may be due to the randomness of the input, while personal and meaningful aspects are partly due to the fact that input is drawn from our personal store of memories and beliefs and partly due to the efforts of the mind/brain system to make sense of the input.

Whether such hypotheses are true is still an open question, because they all leave some data unaccounted for. Better explanations will probably require a more sophisticated understanding of the relationship among brain, mind, and self than that afforded by current materialistic models.

References

Buschsbaum, M. S., Gillin, J. C., Wu, J., Hazlett, E., Sicotte, N., Dupont, R. M., & Bunney, W. E. (1989). Regional cerebral glucose metabolic rate in human sleep assessed by positron emission tomography. *Life Sciences, 45,* 1349–1356.

Carlson, N. R. (1995). *Foundations of physiological psychology* (3rd ed.). Needham Heights, MA: Allyn & Bacon.

Crick, F., & Mitchison, G. (1983). The function of dream sleep. *Nature, 304,* 111–114.

Kalat, J. W. (1995). *Biological psychology* (5th ed.). Pacific Grove, CA: Brooks/Cole.

Rechtschaffen, A., Bergmann, B. M., Everson, C. A., Kushida, C. A., and Gilliland, M. A. (1989). Sleep deprivation in the rat: X. Integration and discussion of the findings. *Sleep, 12,* 68–87.

Snyder, F. (1970). The phenomenology of dreaming. In L. Madow and L. H. Snow (Eds.), *The psychodynamic implications of the physiological study of dreams.* Springfield, IL: Thomas.

Webb, W. B. (1975). *Sleep, the gentle tyrant.* Englewood Cliffs, NJ: Prentice-Hall.

E. L. Hillstrom

See Dreams, Therapeutic Use of.

Sleep Disorders. Humans are afflicted with a variety of sleep disorders. Some of the more serious include insomnia, sleep apnea, sudden infant death syndrome (SIDS), and narcolepsy. Nocturnal enuresis (bedwetting) is inconvenient and can be embarrassing to the enuretic, but it is usually outgrown by the age of 5 and seldom occurs beyond the age of 12. Sleep talking and sleepwalking also have been classified as sleep disorders, but these are usually of minor consequence.

Individuals with narcolepsy may manifest any or all of the following symptoms: excessive daytime sleepiness, hypnogogic hallucinations, sleep paralysis, and cataplexy. They are also subject to daytime sleep attacks, episodes of sleep that begin abruptly and that last from 1 to 30 minutes. These are most likely when those afflicted are bored, fatigued, or have just consumed a heavy meal.

Cataplexy is a sudden loss of muscle tonus or muscle control that can last for several minutes. The loss may be partial, creating feelings of weakness and fatigue, or virtually complete, causing the victim to collapse. Narcoleptics do not lose consciousness or become confused during these episodes, but they may lapse into REM sleep if the episode lasts longer than a few minutes. Cataplexic episodes are almost always triggered by strong emotion, particularly anger or elation. (In some cases the trigger is specific. One man suffered attacks only when he tried to pitch a ball to his young son.) The frequency of cataplexy varies greatly in different people. Attacks may occur daily, weekly, monthly, or only once or twice in a lifetime.

Sleep paralysis is a temporary inability to move that occurs in the twilight state between waking and sleeping, while one is still at least partly conscious. Sleep paralysis occurs infrequently in normal sleepers, but some 40% to 60% of those with narcolepsy report occasional incidents. Hypnogogic hallucinations are vivid, dreamlike episodes that also occur at the borders of sleep and are virtually always accompanied by sleep paralysis. This combination can be frightening (e.g., watching a terrifying man standing next to the bed or seeing and feeling snakes crawling all over one's body without being able to move). Such episodes may last up to 5 minutes but can often be interrupted by intense effort or by a touch or a word from another person.

Narcolepsy afflicts from 2 to 5 people out of every 1,000. Symptoms most frequently appear between the ages of 15 and 20 and remain a lifelong problem once they appear. This disorder also appears to have a genetic component. Kessler, Guilleminault, & Dement (1974) found that relatives of narcoleptics are 60 times more likely to have narcolepsy than people in the general population. The symptoms of narcolepsy are almost certainly produced by a brain abnormality that causes the neural mechanisms responsible for various aspects of REM sleep to become active at inappropriate times. Cataplexy and sleep paralysis are evidently produced by the same mechanism that normally paralyzes muscles during REM sleep to keep sleepers from acting out their dreams, and hypnogogic hallucinations are apparently brief dream episodes that intrude into wakefulness.

Narcolepsy is often debilitating. Persistent sleepiness and sleep attacks can be disruptive and are often poorly understood by family members, friends, or employers. In addition, cataplexy can also be dangerous, especially if it occurs while one is operating equipment or driving. Treatment strategies include both medication and education. People who have narcolepsy need to learn good sleep habits to optimize their sleep at night, that short naps can reduce daytime sleepiness, and that the symptoms are not their fault. Stimulants like methylphenidate, pemoline, or amphetamine can reduce sleepiness and cataplexy can be treated with imipramine (Anch, Browman, Mitler, & Walsh, 1988).

Sleep apnea syndrome is another incapacitating disorder. Apneas are temporary pauses in breathing that can become so frequent or so long that the lungs are unable to bring in an adequate supply of oxygen. Brief apneas (10 to 20 seconds long, occurring 5 to 10 times an hour) occur in people whose sleep is normal, but individuals with sleep apnea syndrome can have disruptive pauses that last from 15 to 60 seconds or even up to 2 minutes and occur hundreds of times a night. In these episodes, rising levels of carbon dioxide eventually stimulate emergency chemoreceptors and sleepers are aroused, gasping for air. This allows oxygen and carbon dioxide levels to return to normal and the cycle begins again. These repeated arousals severely alter normal sleep patterns and cause sufferers to feel excessively sleepy during the day. People who have this condition rarely recall these episodes and have little insight into their problem. They usually seek medical assistance for excessive sleepiness.

Sleep apnea varies from very mild to severe. It is often associated with snoring and it is more common in men than in women, in people who are overweight or obese, and in older adults. It is present in about 4% of the population between the ages of 14 and 65 and approximately 37% of the elderly. In central apnea, the pauses in breathing are due to a lack of effort to breathe (suggesting a malfunction in the brain mechanisms that control breathing). In obstructive apnea the pauses in breathing are due to a blockage of the airway rather than a lack of effort to breathe. Normally pharyngeal muscles keep upper airways open by dilating forcefully enough to balance the negative pressure created by drawing in a breath. These muscles need to exert even greater force if sleepers are lying flat on their backs (causing the weight of the neck to press down on the muscles), have extra weight on their necks, or have narrow or obstructed air passages. When the pharyngeal muscles relax during the deeper stages of sleep (as most muscles do), such factors apparently tip the balance. The muscles are no longer able to exert enough force to keep the airway passages open. When the sleeper is roused to waking or lighter stages of sleep in apneac episodes, the muscles regain their tone and air flow is restored.

Professionals use several strategies to treat obstructive apnea. Patients are advised to avoid alcohol and other central nervous system depressants like sleeping pills or tranquilizers because these aggravate sleep apnea. If patients are obese, losing weight can help. Episodes of apnea are most likely when people are flat on their backs, so sleeping in other positions or reclining diminishes the problem. If sufferers have airway obstructions, these can often be corrected by minor surgery. Patients can also wear a device that fits over the face and provides positive airway pressure, keeping airway passages open, even in deep sleep. This device works well once patients adapt to wearing it. Central apnea can sometimes be treated with respiratory stimulants (theophylline or medroxyprogesterone). It is important for individuals with moderate to severe apnea to seek medical help because the chronic shortages of oxygen in apneac episodes might eventually contribute to heart or brain damage or circulatory problems (Anch, Browman, Mitler, & Walsh, 1988).

Sudden infant death syndrome (SIDS) may be related to sleep apnea. In this syndrome, healthy infants die quietly in their sleep for no apparent reason. Studies of the siblings of SIDS babies and babies who have almost died from SIDS indicate that there is probably a genetic factor in this disorder because many of these children have disturbed sleep patterns as early as one week of age. SIDS babies apparently suffer episodes of apnea but fail to be aroused by rising levels of carbon dioxide in their bodies and die for lack of oxygen. Monitoring devices will signal parents or caretakers if a baby stops breathing so they can intervene and awaken the child.

Insomnia, the inability to obtain a satisfactory amount of sleep, afflicts many people. According to various surveys, 20% to 35% of all adults have occasional or frequent difficulties obtaining satisfactory sleep. In many cases insomnia is infrequent and transient; in others it is persistent. Persistent insomnia creates real problems because it affects mood, cognitive functioning, and many other aspects of life. Populations at greater risk include the elderly, women, and patients with medical or psychiatric disorders.

Many factors can contribute to insomnia. It can be precipitated by any situation that produces strong emotional upheaval (fear, sorrow, tension, worry) or stress. It can also be induced by shift work or by sleeping at irregular times during the day. Many bodily functions (sleep and waking, hormone secretion, body temperature, and others) vary regularly on a 24-hour cycle (circadian rhythms). These variations are controlled by an internal clock, the suprachiasmatic nucleus of the hypothalamus, which synchronizes all these events, timing them to correspond to the hours of daylight and darkness. Sleeping for long periods during the day or at irregular times desynchronizes the clock and can disrupt many functions, including mood, energy, the ability to think or function efficiently, and sleep. Jet lag, caused by traversing several time zones in a short time, produces similar symptoms. These symptoms persist for several days until the clock can reset to match local light-dark cycles. Caffeine (ubiquitous in coffee, soft drinks, and some aspirin-based pain relievers) and caffeinelike substances in tea and chocolate can also contribute to insomnia. Caffeine resets the internal clock, delaying sleep. Its consistent use can be disruptive, particularly in older individuals.

The prevalence of insomnia increases with age (up to 50% of those between the ages of 65 to 79 are troubled by insufficient sleep at least occasionally). Many factors contribute to this trend: diminished function in the brain mechanisms that control sleep, chronic physical problems that create disruptive pain and discomfort, increased use of medications, some of which interfere with sleep, sleep apnea, and the presence of periodic, vigorous, involuntary leg movements that disturb sleep.

Treatments for insomnia vary greatly. Since insomnia can have many causes, the most effective strategy is to try to identify specific causes and treat these. Common causes include chronic environmental or interpersonal stressors, irregular sleeping habits, overuse of caffeine, use of medications that interfere with sleep, alcohol or drug abuse, psychiatric disorders that involve depression or excessive anxiety, painful physical ailments, apnea, and involuntary periodic leg movements.

When the cause of insomnia is not apparent or cannot easily be changed, doctors often prescribe sleeping medications. The benzodiazapines are currently favored because they are safe, and they do help to induce and maintain sleep. However, they also have substantial drawbacks. They are not considered a permanent solution and are prescribed for limited amounts of time. They should not be used with other central nervous system depressants, like alcohol, because the combination could be lethal. They may also cause excessive sleepiness during the day or produce subtle impairments in driving or operating equipment that are not that apparent to the user. The continued use of benzodiazapines also creates tolerance (the need to increase the dosage after a few days to obtain the same effect) and withdrawal symptoms when medication is discontinued. Sleep disturbances that were present before starting the medication reexert themselves and may be exacerbated for a few days by rebound effects. (Benzodiazapines suppress REM sleep, and REM suppression can result in more time in REM and vivid nightmares when the suppression is removed.) Very gradual withdrawal can help minimize these symptoms.

Some people try to alleviate insomnia by ingesting alcohol or by taking over-the-counter sleep medications. Neither of these strategies is helpful. Alcohol reduces the amount of time it takes to fall asleep and promotes deeper sleep for two to three hours; however, it also increases awakenings and stage-1 NREM in the second half of the night. When it is used on a sustained basis, it creates more problems than it alleviates. Nonprescription sleep medications are generally ineffective and can create problems because they alter the structure of sleep, suppress REM sleep, and produce rapid tolerance.

Desperate users may escalate their dosages to compensate but then have a very difficult time stopping the medication because of withdrawal symptoms.

The best self-help for mild insomnia that is not related to medical problems is to practice good sleep hygiene. Keeping a regular sleep-waking cycle is important because irregularities can disturb circadian rhythms. The single most important factor is probably a consistent time of awakening. Sleeping in or prolonged napping should be avoided because these can decrease the next night's sleep. It is also important to get enough sleep each night. "Enough" is the amount that allows one to feel alert and energetic the next day, and this varies considerably. Some people function well on six hours or less, but most need seven to eight hours. Avoiding caffeine, nicotine, and alcohol or taking caffeine only in the morning can also help, because all of these can disturb sleep. Moderate exercise in the late afternoon or early evening may promote deep sleep, and engaging in a quiet activity, such as reading or handwork, 30 to 60 minutes prior to bedtime can also increase relaxation and encourage sleep.

References

Anch, M. A., Browman, C. P., Mitler, M. M., & Walsh, J. K. (1988). *Sleep: A scientific perspective*. Englewood Cliffs, NJ: Prentice Hall.

Kessler, S., Guilleminault, C., & Dement, W. C. (1974). A family study of 50 REM narcoleptics. *Acta Neurologica Scandinavica, 50*, 503–512.

E. L. HILLSTROM

See SLEEP AND DREAMING.

Sleepwalking. *See* SLEEP DISORDERS; SOMNAMBULISM.

Smoking. Tobacco users usually find it difficult to stop, even though smoking and smokeless tobacco constitute a major health problem. Smoking is an addiction that is hazardous to your health. It significantly increases your risk for developing heart disease, hypertension, and chronic obstructive lung disease. It has been shown to cause cancer of the lungs, mouth, larynx, and esophagus. Passive smoke (from being around people who are smoking cigarettes, cigars, or pipes) also increases a person's risk of developing heart disease. It increases a child's chances of developing bronchitis, pneumonia, middle ear infections and it worsens asthmatic conditions. Chewing tobacco (smokeless tobacco) carries similar health risks for those who use it. Pregnant women who smoke are more likely to have babies with health problems. Smoking is responsible for about 30% of all cancer deaths each year in the U.S. and it accounts for nearly 90% of all lung cancer deaths. Smokers die more frequently than nonsmokers from heart disease, strokes, lung cancer, and other lung ailments. The risk of smokers having heart attacks is three times greater than for developing lung cancer. Although an ex-smoker can have the same lower nonsmoker's risk of developing lung cancer or heart attack after 5 to 10 years of not smoking, damage from emphysema (a lung disease often caused by smoking) is irreversible.

One of the reasons people find it so difficult to stop smoking is because it affects physiological, psychological, and behavioral areas of one's life. The motives for smoking appear to be complex. The main reasons for continuing to smoke are thought to be: 1) smoking becomes a learned habit and such habits are resistant to change; 2) smokers become addicted to the nicotine in cigarettes; and 3) smoking is highly pleasurable at the beginning and the withdrawal symptoms associated with stopping are disagreeable.

People usually learn to smoke through friends who pressure them. Although it is not enjoyable at first, people learn to tolerate the discomfort with practice and then begin to enjoy smoking with their friends. When smoking becomes pleasant, people start to smoke in other situations and the habit spreads and becomes ingrained. Sometimes they smoke to cope with unpleasant feelings such as anger, tension, anxiety, or boredom.

Smoking may be difficult to stop because it provides such an immediate effect. The nicotine from an inhaled cigarette reaches the brain in seven seconds. A person who smokes a pack daily and takes 10 puffs on each cigarette will get more than 70,000 doses of nicotine per year. This is certainly a higher frequency of drug usage than that of an alcoholic or any other type of drug addict. There are few initial negative consequences of smoking. Health problems caused by smoking take years to develop. Furthermore, smoking does not interfere with work performance; some people say smoking improves their work productivity. No other type of drug user can make this claim.

Recent research has shown that people who stop smoking are those who not only realize that smoking can truly be bad for their health but they see themselves as personally susceptible to the serious consequences of continued smoking. Moderate smokers may know that smoking poses a serious threat to their health, but they do not see themselves as being personally vulnerable to health problems as a result of smoking.

There are several factors associated with heavy smoking, including age, sex, economic status, behavior of family and peers, school and athletic achievement, and psychological status. After leaving elementary school, students are more exposed to older drug using students and they have greater opportunity to smoke and use other drugs. White adolescents have the highest smoking rates and the smoking rate for high school students has risen over 20% in the past few years. Parents who smoke are more likely to have children who smoke. Since most people begin smoking with friends, possibly to appear more mature and independent, unassertive young people with low self-confidence or significant levels of anxiety are more susceptible to peer pressures to conform. Those who do well in school or athletics are less likely to smoke, as are those with a high sense of personal well-being.

The habit of smoking can be prevented when young people are supervised and when there is a positive value to not smoking. It is beneficial when youths who are leaders help their friends avoid situations that might lead to smoking. Educating people, so they can understand the consequences and resist pressures toward the use of tobacco, is helpful in prevention efforts. Young people can best overcome influence from others if they are taught the expected arguments and ways to refute them ahead of time. This method is sometimes referred to as psychological innoculation. Assertiveness training can be an aid to resisting influence from others, as can learning to respond to the persuasive comment that "smokers are more independent" with the remark that "they aren't if they're addicted to smoking."

Other methods that make people more resistant to smoking are learning to cope with anxiety and increasing confidence and self-esteem. Anxiety can be reduced through a wide variety of physical and psychological practices, ranging from sports to relaxation techniques and meditation or prayer. A belief in God, as the controller of the universe who is a helper available to all, can also reduce anxiety. Confidence and self-esteem usually increase when a person develops competence in skills or activities that others value or admire—such as athletic, academic, or work success. The rewards of these successes make the possible rewards of tobacco and other drugs less attractive.

It is never too soon or too late to stop smoking. There are many good programs for quitting smoking. Counselors, self-help books, and internet resources outline many effective ways to stop smoking. Some people are helped by using nicotine patches, under a doctor's supervision, to overcome their addiction to nicotine. One of the most successful methods to stop smoking is tapering off over time. The smoker who wants to quit can develop a plan which may include: (a) recognizing that smoking is harmful to the smoker and the smoker's companions who inhale secondhand smoke; (b) gaining support from friends; (c) keeping track of the circumstances where smoking seems most appealing and developing other ways of coping in these situations.

Many smokers worry about gaining weight after they stop smoking; however, the average weight gain for ex-smokers is usually only about three pounds and that is rarely permanent. Another concern of smokers who consider quitting is withdrawal symptoms from the body's physical addition to nicotine. Some people do experience increased irritability or lowered energy levels when they first stop smoking, but both disappear with time.

A person who is unsuccessful in the first or second attempt to stop smoking should not be deterred from the goal of becoming a former smoker. Continued efforts will bring success. Millions of people can attest to this. An ex-smoker saves several hundred dollars yearly by not buying cigarettes, cigars, or pipe tobacco and by receiving preferential non-smoker's insurance rates. Becoming an ex-smoker leads to an improved sense of well-being and a generally healthier, wealthier, and longer life.

M. A. NORFLEET

See HEALTH PSYCHOLOGY.

Social Cognition and Perception. See PERSON PERCEPTION.

Social Comparison Theory. Festinger's (1954) theory of social comparison asserts that human beings have a tendency to evaluate themselves. People want to know if their feelings, beliefs, and abilities are appropriate or correct. Sometimes physical reality can provide a standard for evaluation (e.g., a belief concerning someone's height can be confirmed using a tape measure). However, such physical standards are not always available; it is hard to find a yardstick for evaluating most attitudes. Under such conditions people often rely on social reality for evaluation; they compare themselves to the behavior and attitudes of others. Sometimes social comparisons are "upward"; we compare ourselves to people who are more successful, have finer possessions, or are more intelligent. Such comparisons may leave us feeling inadequate or dissatisfied. Sometimes social comparisons are "downward"; we compare ourselves to people who are less fortunate, less wealthy, or less bright. Such comparisons may lift our spirits and leave us with a sense of gratitude and relative good fortune.

However, social comparison can apply to more than just our feelings of satisfaction or dissatisfaction. Another example of social comparison might be conformity. Certainly people sometimes conform as a strategy for gaining acceptance from others. But people also conform simply to be right. Imagine someone attending an event at a local theater. During the intermission he or she discovers that the signs indicating the men's and women's restrooms are missing. Faced with such a dilemma, one's solution might be to observe the choices made by others and conform to the behavior of someone of the same sex. Such an example suggests we sometimes do social comparison so our actions will be appropriate and right.

Social comparison seems to be a pervasive human phenomenon. Thus it makes sense that God might take it into consideration when relating to people. Such a perspective sheds light on certain passages of Scripture. For example, there is God's command that the Israelites should destroy the nations inhabiting the promised land (Deut. 20:16–17). Certainly such a command represented a judgment upon the practices of those nations. But in addition such a command seems to have been an attempt to protect the integrity of the Israelites' faith (Deut. 20:18). Cohabitation with other nations would have led to social comparison along many dimensions, including beliefs. Pagan notions could have crept into the Israelites' faith. The seriousness of this threat was confirmed when the Israelites allowed other nations to live in the promised land.

A similar situation seems to be the marriage of Christians and non-Christians. The discrimination inherent in the command for Christians not to marry non-Christians (2 Cor. 6:14) becomes more understandable when the potential for social comparison with a non-Christian spouse is recognized. It is possible that the non-Christian spouse might drift toward the views of a Christian beloved, but it is also possible that the attitudinal currents might move in the opposite direction.

A significant issue in the discussion of social comparison and faith is the importance of the attribute being evaluated. When a belief is particularly significant, the result may be an attempt by the believer to persuade rather than to compromise (Gordon, 1966). Such a possibility is intriguing and deserves further exploration.

Another significant issue is the possibility that Christians are called not to perform social comparison. Galatians 6:4 encourages people to test their own actions and not compare themselves to others. Is this passage a general admonition to avoid social comparison or a warning against some forms of social comparison? Perhaps the latter is closer to the truth. Prejudice, which involves a downward comparison toward others, seems to be a clear example of social comparison that is detrimental. With this kind of comparison self is elevated because others are derogated. Yet, Christians are called to compare themselves to Christ and live as Christ lived. Social comparison may simply be a fact of life. The righteousness or sinfulness of social comparison may depend upon the motivation behind the comparison and the actions and thoughts that flow from the comparison.

References

Festinger, L. (1954). A theory of social comparison processes. *Human Relations, 7,* 117–140.
Gordon, B. F. (1966). Influence and social comparison as motives for affiliation. *Journal of Experimental Social Psychology,* Supplement 1, 55–65.

R. L. BASSETT

See ATTRIBUTION THEORY.

Social Development. See DEVELOPMENTAL PSYCHOLOGY.

Social Influence Therapy. Social influence therapy was developed out of the broad base of theory on the role of psychotherapist as influence agent. It emanated from the theoretical and empirical work of the 1960s and 1970s on the psychology of power, influence, demand characteristics, manipulation, suggestibility, and expectation effects in the psychotherapy relationship. Gillis (1974, 1979) first integrated and articulated the tactical implications that psychotherapist influence could have as a discrete body of psychotherapy technique.

The goal of this approach is to effect change by identifying, analyzing, and utilizing the many ways in which influence dynamics operate in psychotherapy. The approach is boldly manipulative in nature. It uses techniques of persuasion and tactics derived from strategies of attitude change, interpersonal attraction, cognitive dissonance, and placebo effect. Social influence therapy comprises four stages: enhancing the patient's belief in and commitment to treatment; establishing the psychotherapist's position of influence; using this position to deliver the therapeutic attitude-changing message; and providing evidence that change is taking place. For example, relying on cognitive dissonance reduction research that suggests individuals value highly those things they have worked hard to attain, this approach often requires patients to make considerable sacrifices to gain admission to treatment through substantial fees and extensive assessment workups. Or patients might be required to read outcome research studies to enhance their belief in the value and effectiveness of their therapy.

Although this approach has elements of a formal system of psychotherapy, it is probably more appropriately viewed as a specific conceptual and technical framework within which many forms of psychotherapy can be conducted. These techniques are compatible with any psychotherapy that relies heavily on the psychotherapist-patient relationship itself as the primary instrument of healing. The responsible use of therapist-controlled influence is desirable within any distinctively Christian values framework as long as appropriate ethical standards are met. For example, it would be most important to obtain truly informed consent for treatment with this approach and to refrain from trying to convince a patient that progress is being made when there is no objective evidence of improvement. Abuse of psychotherapist influence and power is possibly a heightened risk with this approach and should be carefully avoided.

References

Gillis, J. S. (1974, December). Therapist as manipulator. *Psychology Today*, 90–95.

Gillis, J. S. (1979). Social influence in psychotherapy: A description of the process and some tactical implications. *Counseling and Psychotherapy Monograph Series* (No. 1), Pilgrimage.

D. M. Cook

See COUNSELING AND PSYCHOTHERAPY: OVERVIEW.

Social Interest. Adler contended that human beings are essentially social, not merely sexual, beings. The central concept of his theory of personality is *Gemeinschaftsgefühl*, which has been translated as social interest. This translation leaves much to be desired. Social implies mores or collectivism. Interest implies something mild, cognitive, and ephemeral. Some of Adler's followers have contended that the ultimate concept is ineffable and cannot be reduced to words. Others have tried by offering humanistic identification or commitment to others. It involves feelings of brotherly love for other people in the present as well as a feeling of affinity for the whole human race past and future. The individual with social interest has integrated strivings for adjustment to reality, and these strivings enhance the strivings of others. A person motivated by social interest also has a commitment to understanding the psychic needs of other people and strives to become a significant other who can help fulfill those needs.

Brennan (1969) suggested that social interest involves both a phenomenological meaning and a transcendental meaning. The first involves the fact that I experience you as different (feeling), yet in a more fundamental way I experience our sameness as humans (social). The transcendental meaning refers to the fact that social interest cannot be understood through contemplation but only through action and being with others. With social interest the transcendence is transcendence of one's own fictions that impinge upon the reality of the other.

According to Adlerians, social interest also implies a rational and objective outlook. Individuals devoid of social interest become limited by idiosyncratic cognitive processes and private logic. These are fictions that protect against inferiority feelings at the expense of an accurate perception of reality. The participation in socially constructed reality is a commitment to learn what one's words and behavior mean to the other.

For Adler and his followers social interest is the essence of mental health. The individual is always unique but always involved with others. The healthy individual is one with a developing capacity to transcend his or her limitations and relate to others. The healthy individual is characterized by mutual striving for achievement (Lichtenberg, 1963). Neurosis is characterized either by achievement without mutuality (i.e., self-centeredness) or by mutual strivings without achievement (e.g., passive dependency, suicide). The purpose of therapy based on individual psychology is to help the patient develop social interest.

References

Brennan, J. F. (1969). Autoeroticism or social feeling as basis of human development. *Journal of Individual Psychology, 25*, 3–18.

Lichtenberg, P. (1963). Mutual achievement striving and social interest. *Journal of Individual Psychology, 19*, 148–160.

T. L. Brink

See ADLER, ALFRED; HEALTHY PERSONALITY.

Social Learning Theory. An approach to human behavior and personality that attempts to combine the principles of learning derived from behaviorism, including the influence of environmental factors, with the contributions of cognitive psychology. Like behaviorism, it focuses on observable behaviors rather than postulating inner dynamics and drives not readily amenable to empirical investigation. However, cognitive components such as the individual's expectations of outcomes and the values associated with behavioral performance are also considered. Thus psychological functioning is best understood as a continuous reciprocal interaction among behavioral, environmental, and cognitive factors. This interlocking perspective suggests that not only behavior is influenced by the environment but also the environment is also partly a product of the person's own making, and a measure of control over one's own behavior is therefore possible.

Julian Rotter and Albert Bandura have developed two separate formulations of social learning theory which, although somewhat different in their emphases, are complementary. Rotter focuses on psychological aspects while Bandura emphasizes the social components of behavior.

Rotter's theory (Rotter, Chance, & Phares, 1972) views human behavior as being actively directed toward particular goals rather than passively controlled by environmental influences. Rotter postulates that the probability that an individual will engage in a particular pattern of behaviors depends on the individual's expectancies concerning the outcomes to which those behaviors will lead (reinforcement expectancies), the likelihood of performing the behavior when certain environmental conditions are present (behavior potential), and the value placed by the person on those outcomes (reinforcement value). For example, a college student is likely to spend time studying and writing term papers if she expects that these actions will lead to good grades and if she places high value on good grades. The subjective expectancies of outcomes and the values placed on those outcomes are a function of prior learning experiences of the individual in similar situations.

Psychopathology may occur as a result of difficulties encountered in any of the three major components of Rotter's formula (i.e., behavior potential, expectancies of reinforcement, and reinforcement values). For example, the individual may persist in behaviors that are inadequate for attaining certain desired reinforcements; the person may have a very low expectancy of being able to attain desired outcomes (low freedom of movement); or the individual may place an excessively high need value on certain types of reinforcements. In addition, the person's minimal goal level, or the lowest outcome that he or she will accept as satisfactory, may be excessively high. As a result of such difficulties the individual is likely to engage in inappropriate (nongoal-oriented) behaviors that are commonly associated with anxiety, depression, and other forms of psychopathology.

The goal of psychotherapy, in Rotter's view, is to bring about a more gratifying level of functioning by revising expectancies to accord with the realities of the present situation, reducing minimal goal levels, learning to value alternate goals, and so on. Although behavior modification techniques may be used to alter behavior directly, the focus is placed on changing expectancies and values in order to indirectly change behavior.

Bandura's (1971, 1986) formulation of social learning theory may be viewed as a complement to Rotter's theory in that it explores the ways in which behaviors are learned and expectancies are developed. The most distinctive feature of Bandura's theory is the belief that most of our behavior is learned by observing other people and modeling our behavior after theirs. Thus Bandura emphasizes the importance of cognitive symbols in the process of personality development. Behaviors that are learned through observational attention are retained symbolically in the form of words and/or images in long-term memory until they are reproduced at a time when the individual is motivated to perform them.

Bandura furthermore asserts that behavior is learned not only through the direct experience of reinforcement but also, and more importantly, through vicarious reinforcement (i.e., observation of reinforcements obtained by others) and self-reinforcement (via self-observation, self-evaluation, and feelings of pride, satisfaction, guilt, etc.). A more recent development in Bandura's theory is the cognitive mechanism of self-efficacy, the belief or conviction on the part of individuals that they can produce certain effects or outcomes (Bandura, 1986). In Bandura's perspective, people who perform effectively have high yet realistic efficacy expectations that guide their behavior. Though modeling still plays an important role in Bandura's theory, it is seen as a means by which self-efficacy is developed.

Psychotherapeutic applications of Bandura's theory include the use of modeling to reduce phobic reactions and self-directed behavior change therapy (Mahoney & Thoresen, 1974). Much of the more recent research has investigated behavior following efforts at strengthening self-efficacy expectations through such experiences as graded mastery, vicarious modeling, and verbal persuasion. Research (e.g., Grembowski et al., 1993; O'Leary, 1992) shows that higher self-efficacy helps reduce depression and phobias in people who initially lacked confidence in their ability to overcome these disorders.

Social learning theory also has had a major influence on current techniques of cognitive-behavior therapy. Social learning theory has received wide acceptance among contemporary psychologists because of its combination of behavioristic and cognitive approaches, its firm grounding in empirical research, and its numerous applications to psychotherapy.

From a biblical perspective social learning theory is generally compatible with the Christian view of persons, with its emphasis on the importance of both cognitive factors (the heart or mind) and overt behavior in human experience. Like Scripture, social learning theory sees a person as an active, rational agent, responsible for actions and able to change behaviors yet ever subject to the influences of the social environment.

References

Bandura, A. (1971). *Social learning theory.* Morristown, NJ: General Learning Press.

Bandura, A. (1986). *Social foundations of thought and action: A social cognitive theory.* Englewood Cliffs, NJ: Prentice-Hall.

Grembowski, D., Patrick, D., Diehr, P., Durham, M., Beresford, S., Kay, E., & Hecht, J. (1993). Self-efficacy and health behavior among older adults. *Journal of Health and Social Behavior, 34,* 89–104.

Mahoney, M., & Thoresen, C. (1974). *Self-control: Power to the person.* Monterey, CA: Brooks/Cole.

O'Leary, A. (1992). Self-efficacy and health: Behavioral and stress-physiological mediation. *Cognitive Therapy and Research, 16,* 229–245.

Rotter, J. B., Chance, J. E., & Phares, E. J. (Eds.). (1972). *Applications of a social learning theory of personality.* New York: Holt, Rinehart, & Winston.

R. A. MARTIN AND P. C. HILL

See LEARNING; LOCUS OF CONTROL.

Social Maturity Tests. Social maturity testing, elsewhere termed social intelligence testing, is an older and by no means universal label for a small category of psychological testing instruments used primarily in the assessment of the developmentally disabled. These tests seek to quantify adaptive versus maladaptive behavior, especially social behavior, at the behavioral interface of personality and intellectual functioning. In general these tests attempt to measure the degree to which an individual has acquired the social and socialized behaviors that are thought to be normative for an individual's chronological age. This reference point has also been defined as the individual's age developmental status or as the social behavior characteristics of the supposedly typical age-cohort.

It is difficult to clearly define what behaviors are subsumed under the constructs of social maturity or social intelligence. Historically, therefore, social maturity testing has been a somewhat vague assessment endeavor. More recently this type of assessment has been subsumed under the broader category of behavioral testing, particularly with mentally retarded populations, where quantifying adaptive versus maladaptive behavior in general, inclusive of social behaviors, is so important to treatment planning and treatment outcomes measurement. By far the most widely known and utilized of this

category of tests is the Vineland Social Maturity Scale developed by E. A. Doll in the 1920s and 1930s and revised in the mid-1980s as the Vineland Adaptive Behavior Scales (VABS). The scales seek to compare individual levels of social and personal competence against normative reference points. The statistical unit of measure is a so-called chronological age that defines through standardized normative descriptors the adequacy of daily living tasks or skills that the individual usually and habitually performs. The VABS provides normative comparisons applicable from birth through 18 years and for low-functioning adults. The primary domains of behavior that the new Vineland evaluates include communication, daily living skills, socialization, motor skills, adaptive behavior composite (an amalgamation of the four domains previously listed), and maladaptive behavior. The psychometric properties of the test are good. Other instruments in this evolving class include the Adaptive Behavior Inventory for Children, the Adaptive Behavior Scale, the Caine-Levine Social Competency Scales, the Trainable Mentally Retarded School Competency Scales, and the Balthazar Scales of Adaptive Behavior. For detailed discussion of this area of assessment and related topics see Barnett (1983), Coulter and Morrow (1978), and Sattler (1992).

References

Barnett, D. W. (1983). *Nondiscriminatory multifactored assessment: A sourcebook.* New York: Human Science Press.

Coulter, W. A., & Morrow, H. W. (Eds.). (1978). *Adaptive behavior: Concepts and measurement.* Orlando, FL: Grune & Stratton.

Sattler, J. M. (1992). *Assessment of children's intelligence and special abilities* (3d ed. rev.). Boston: Allyn & Bacon.

D. M. COOK

See PSYCHOLOGICAL MEASUREMENT; PERSONALITY ASSESSMENT.

Social Network Intervention. In terms of social anthropology, social network is a construct of social relations. It involves an analysis of patterns of linkages between persons and the manner in which an individual is linked to the larger social structure. Three levels of analysis exist. The microlevel of analysis is linkage of the individual to intimates, family, extended kin, and close friends. The macrolevel is community, social, and cultural organization, analyzed in terms of impersonal collectives. The mezzolevel is social network analysis: the personal linkages between persons (direct linkages) and through persons to others (indirect linkages).

The social network paradigm (Leinhardt, 1977) represents a conceptual schemata for mapping the mezzolevel of social linkages. Consider a Persian rug. A macrolevel analysis considers the overall type of rug. A microlevel analysis involves the structure of any one square inch. A mezzolevel analysis traces how each color thread is tied to another thread to produce patterns. The threads are the content of social links; the knots are personal contacts.

Consider threads in terms of content (golf interest, political influence, dental skill). A dentist may be linked to persons in his life space who are dentists, politicians, golfers, or some of each, or people with all three themes (direct linkages). The same dentist may have a political interest but know no politicians. Yet he may influence politicians via conversation with his golf partners who have political connections (indirect linkages). If the person has single theme links (he only knows dentists), the network will be sparse and simple in content and have few interconnections. If a person embodies many themes, he will link directly and completely to more persons. At the same time there will be more interconnections among the people in the network, thus indirectly linking him to many others (e.g., the dentist has golf friends who know his political friends).

A community, like a rug, is composed of many intersecting social themes that link different people directly and indirectly to each other. Thus a person does not have one social network. Rather, she participates in many different social networks, which indirectly interconnect. Social network analysis may focus on themes: rumor networks, political networks, community assistance networks. Or analysis may focus on persons: the connections an individual has to others (egocentric analysis). Social network analysis is applied in mental health to both theme analysis, such as family or assistance networks, and to individual analysis (Gottlieb, 1981).

From the standpoint of individual analysis a person is linked to approximately 1,500 to 2,000 persons, the finite limits of one's personal community. These persons can be arranged in zones. Zone 1 (personal) consists of family you live with or who are most important (1–10 persons). Zone 2 (intimate) consists of close intimates (2–20). Zone 3 (extended) consists of those with whom you regularly interact but who are not as important to you (50–100). Zone 4 (nominal) consists of persons you know or interact with casually (around 500 persons). Zone 5 (extended) consists of people linked indirectly to you via persons in the other zones (around 1,000 persons).

The first two zones, called the intimate psychosocial network (25 persons), form a relatively stable social system that mediates the relationships between the person and his or her social world (Pattison, Llamas, & Hurd, 1979). There are significant correlations between disturbances in this intimate social network and psychiatric disorders. It is important to note that social networks may be constructive and supportive, neutral, or destructive and pathogenic. Therefore a social network system should not be labeled a support system, because it may not operate as such.

The application of social network theory and analysis has resulted in new mental health interventions (Pattison, 1981). First are thematic social network interventions: the construction of crisis information centers, the activation of mutual assistance programs, and the organization of informal community networks. The intent of such clinical programs is to activate latent and indirect social links into an active and direct linkage. The resulting social network can then assist persons in crisis, respond to emergencies, and provide sustaining emotional and material support.

A second intervention strategy is screening-planning-linking. The focus is on an individual in crisis who lacks good network resources. The network convener screens inactive, latent, or indirect links and convenes the personal network of the person to bring resources to his or her aid.

A third strategy is work with extended family, kin, and friend systems in which the social network is intact but dysfunctional. The network therapist, much as a family therapist, collates the network, identifies dysfunctional elements of the social system, and seeks to change the structure and function of the social network (Speck & Attneave, 1973).

A fourth strategy involves persons with pathological networks, such as drug and alcohol abusers, or inadequate networks, such as chronic schizophrenics. The task of the network therapist is to recruit new members for the social network of the patient, constructing a new and more viable ongoing network.

The methods of social analysis can be applied to church and parish social systems (Pattison, 1977). The pastor can analyze the various social network themes that link parish members as well as determine the social network resources available to an individual member. In turn social network interventions can be employed to improve utilization of parish resources to meet the needs of the membership.

References

Gottlieb, B. (Ed.). (1981). *Social networks and social support in community mental health.* Beverly Hills, CA: Sage.

Leinhardt, S. (Ed.). (1977). *Social networks: A developing paradigm.* New York: Academic.

Pattison, E. M. (Ed.). (1977). *Pastor and parish: A systems view.* Philadelphia: Fortress.

Pattison, E. M. (Ed.). (1981). *Clinical applications of social network theory.* New York: Human Sciences Press.

Pattison, E. M., Llamas, R., & Hurd, G. (1979). Social network mediation of anxiety. *Psychiatric Annual, 9,* 56–67,

Speck, R. V., & Attneave, C. L. (1973). *Family networks.* New York: Pantheon.

E. M. PATTISON

See FAMILY THERAPY: OVERVIEW; FAMILY SYSTEMS THEORY.

Social Psychology. Social psychology is a scientific inquiry of "how people think about, influence, and relate to one another" (Myers, 1996, p. 3). In a hierarchy of academic disciplines, social psychology lies midway between the holistic disciplines of theology and political science and the elemental disciplines of chemistry and physics. Both psychology and sociology lay claim to social psychology as one of their subdisciplines. Yet some social psychologists assert that it is neither's handmaiden but is its own discipline. Their argument centers on traditions that define sociology as the scientific inquiry of group structure and function and psychology as the science of the behavior, thoughts, and feelings of individuals. The fundamental unit of social psychological inquiry is the dyad, a person in the real or implied presence of another person. Because of a common level of explanation and similar content, social psychology allies more closely to personality psychology and the sociology of small groups than other divisions of psychology or sociology. The divisional organization of the American Psychological Association reflects this commonality, as does *The Journal of Personality and Social Psychology*.

Social psychology's essential questions are three-fold:

- By what processes do individuals perceive, conceive, and ascribe actions, feelings, and thoughts to others? How does a person describe and explain the actions of one's self and others?

- By what processes do individuals communicate and influence others? How does a person come to change or persuade others, alone and in groups?

- By what processes do groups operating as social environment exert influence on the individual? How does a group come to change the actions, affections, and attitudes of individuals?

These questions address social cognition, social influence, and social relations, respectively.

On the surface many social psychological theories seem like common sense in the problems analyzed and the concepts utilized. Heider's (1958) psychology of interpersonal relations sounds deceptively like common sense. Yet in this naive description of behavior, social psychologists have repeatedly demonstrated the fundamental attribution error. Observers of behavior tend to underestimate the potency of environmental or situational forces and to overestimate the potency of internal forces like traits, ability, or effort.

Social psychologists' theories organize themselves loosely about six fundamental themes: reward, cognitive consistency, causal explanation, social comparison and self-evaluation, achievement, and freedom and control.

Others affect the formation of attitudes, social behavior, and values. Family and peer influence socialization, especially self-concept, sex typing, and sex roles. Family and peers mediate rewards that encourage certain behaviors while discouraging others. On other fronts individuals learn by imita-

tion and modeling. In still other situations rewards are tokens of an exchange economy. Continuing relationships depends on bargaining, social exchange, and cooperation. When the norm of reciprocity fails or when costs outweigh benefits, relationships are terminated.

Several theories assert that individuals are motivated to maintain internal consistency of actions, affections, and ideas. When cognitions are dissonant, when interpersonal relations are imbalanced, when ideas and actions are logically inconsistent, these tensions motivate the change of dissonant cognitions, imbalanced commitments, or inconsistencies. This cognitive consistency theme centers on the person striving for consistency of behavior and belief.

The theme of causal explanations examines how the person perceives and interprets the other's acts and dispositions. The person's implicit personality theory influences what impressions are formed and what attributions are made. The person makes judgments about the causes of the other's behavior and evaluates the level of responsibility. Those judgments influence subsequent interactions between the person and others.

The person uses information about and from others to form, evaluate, and change attitudes, beliefs, and opinions. The person engages in social judgment and comparison to determine the nature of operating norms and reality. When fixed standards of performance are lacking, comparing one's self to others helps define reality. With fixed standards present, comparison informs one's self of competence and confidence.

Culture in the United States emphasizes individual achievement, so it is understandable that American personality and social psychologists focus attention on the antecedents and consequences of achievement, the conditions under which it is exercised, and the personality factors that provide the predisposition for action (*see* Achievement, Need for). The level and type of achievement motivation plays a role in the leadership style proffered.

In American culture individualism and achievement are closely tied to the sense of freedom and control. When the individual has an internal locus of control, achievement motivation is strong and the sense of freedom is high. If freedom is constrained, the individual is motivated to reassert the freedom by engaging the action that is banned. But individuals with external locus of control feel like victims of situations. When freedom is constrained, these individuals experience a sense of helplessness and hopelessness.

Social psychologists generally employ the scientific method through experimental, field, and survey techniques. A minority challenges its scientific nature, pointing to the difficulty of replicating findings. The rationale is that social interaction occurs within a fixed sociocultural context that cannot be duplicated; social psychology is therefore historical rather than experimental.

A unique feature of social psychological experimentation is that interpersonal techniques investigate interpersonal behavior. The researcher interested in interpersonal behavior must use interpersonal relationships. Elaborate strategies for sorting the effects of the experimenter from those under actual consideration have been proposed.

American interest in social psychology is a century old with Triplett's study of social facilitation in 1897. The first textbooks by William McDougall and Edward Ross appeared in 1908. Division 8 of the American Psychological Association began in 1945. *The Journal of Abnormal and Social Psychology* began in 1965. Most social psychologists look to Kurt Lewin as the discipline's founder; his applied and theoretical work in the 1930s and 1940s provided a great impetus for systematically investigating an individual's social behavior.

References

Heider, F. (1958). *The psychology of interpersonal relations.* New York: Wiley.

Myers, D. G. (1996). *Social psychology* (5th ed.). New York: McGraw-Hill.

R. L. Timpe

Social Work. A multifaceted profession historically related to the Judeo-Christian belief in meeting the financial needs of the poor. Beginning in the 1700s social work in America was a humanitarian effort by wealthy philanthropists who provided aid to persons unable to care for themselves. The misperception that social work is confined solely to the administration of financial relief is still common.

Modern social work practice is conducted by trained professionals concerned with the interactions between people and their social environment that affect the ability of people to accomplish their life tasks, alleviate distress, and realize their aspirations. The function of the social worker is therefore to enhance the problem-solving and coping capacities of people; link people with systems that provide them with resources, services, and opportunities; promote the effective and humane operation of these systems; contribute to the development and improvement of social policy; dispense material resources; and serve as agents of social control (Pincus & Minohan, 1973).

The field of social work has three levels of practitioner skills. The beginning level is the B.S.W. (Bachelor of Social Work), which entails graduation from an accredited undergraduate school of social work. The most common and the most nationally recognized level of practice competency is the M.S.W. (Master of Social Work), which requires two years of graduate training. The Doctor of Social Work is generally reserved for those individuals involved in research in academic settings.

The core practice methods within social work include casework, group work, and community organization. These serve to prevent and to remedy individual and environmental dysfunction. Social casework, more commonly referred to today as clinical social work, is an area of specialization that focuses primarily on individual psychotherapy and family treatment. The theoretical orientation was originally influenced by the psychoanalytic movement in the early 1920s but today draws from all major theories of personality development and treatment approaches. Common settings for casework include psychiatric hospitals, community mental health centers, probation and parole, family counseling agencies, schools, and private practice.

Social work educators have likened casework to restoring, reinforcing, and reshaping the psychosocial functioning of the individual and/or family that is having trouble in personal and social encounters. Social casework is viewed as an active form of psychotherapy that focuses on the study, diagnosis, and treatment of the social environment. The casework process is a problem-solving process designed to understand human behavior in light of environmental stresses and to bring appropriate material or psychological resources to bear on problem resolution (Perlman, 1977).

Group work is a way of serving individuals within and through small, face-to-face groups in order to bring about desired change. The group is viewed as a social system whose influences can be managed to develop client abilities, to modify self-images and perspectives, to resolve conflicts, and to inculcate new patterns of behavior (Vinter, 1965). Group work was traditionally practiced in national youth-serving agencies such as the YMCA and YWCA, settlement houses, and urban community centers. Today, however, group work is widely practiced in children's institutions, medical settings, rehabilitative centers, correctional centers, and facilities for both the mentally and physically disabled.

The third method of social practice, community organization, views the community as the identified client. Murphy (1954) defines this specialization as concerned chiefly with the work of the promotional and coordinating agencies aimed at raising money, seeking enactment of social legislation, or coordinating social welfare activities.

Regardless of which interventive method is utilized, the social work profession is built on scientific knowledge of human growth and behavior and ethical principles, the most crucial of which are the belief in the worth and dignity of every human being, a nonjudgmental attitude, and the protection of the right of each person to participate in all decisions concerning him or her.

Social work, like all helping professions, is confronted with many modern-day issues, problems, and trends that will greatly influence its future. Some of these issues include elimination of racism and poverty, development of workable and fair income-maintenance programs, helping to develop a better distribution of health care, reducing crime and delinquency, and the preservation of individual liberties in a mass society (Ferguson, 1975). Within the profession itself critical issues that must be addressed include personnel training and deployment. The continual expansion of societal needs and pressures for service delivery will require constant reevaluation of tasks performed by both B.S.W. and M.S.W. social workers. Another issue that has met with widespread disagreement within the profession has been the emergence of private practice. Many individuals perceive the focus upon individual and family psychotherapy, as opposed to broader societal issues such as income maintenance, as a departure from the traditional role and function of social work. A final issue is the national focus of the National Association of Social Workers and the National Federation of Clinical Social Work for legal regulation of social work practice, thereby upgrading practice standards and protecting consumer rights.

Regardless of society's problems, the profession of social work will continue its fight to ensure individual integrity, family unity, and social justice for all individuals.

References

Ferguson, E. (1975). *Social work: An introduction* (3rd ed.). Philadelphia: Lippincott.

Murphy, C. (1954). *Community organization practice.* Boston: Houghton Mifflin.

Perlman, H. (1977). Social casework. In R. Morris (Ed.), *Encyclopedia of social work* (17th ed.). New York: National Association of Social Workers.

Pincus, H., & Minohan, A. (1973). *Social work practice: Model and method.* Itasca, IL: Peacock.

Vinter, R. (1965). Social group work. In *Encyclopedia of social work* (15th ed.). New York: National Association of Social Workers.

R. WELSH AND P. PERRY

Society for the Exploration of Psychotherapy Integration (SEPI). The Society for the Exploration of Psychotherapy Integration was formed in 1983 to promote discussion among psychological researchers and practitioners from diverse theoretical and professional perspectives. The interdisciplinary membership consists of professionals from the fields of psychiatry, psychology, and social work and from specialties such as cognitive sciences, psychobiology, health psychology, and social psychology.

Professionals in SEPI come from many nations and represent the major schools of psychology theory: psychodynamic, cognitive-behavioral, and humanistic-existential. The goal of SEPI is to be a reference and educational group for professionals exploring the interface between divergent theoretical approaches to various psychological problems. So, for example, an attendee at a SEPI annual meeting or reader of the *Journal of Psychotherapy Integration* might hear an in-depth discussion of the etiology and treatment for borderline personality disorder from psychoanalytic, cognitive, and existential perspectives, followed by a discussion of the similarities and differences among approaches, and summarized by delineation of how the most effective techniques from each school might be integrated into ongoing treatment plans.

The question of eclecticism is at the center of SEPI debate. For many years professionals who approached theory or practice of psychotherapy through combining concepts from two or more schools of thought were considered poorly trained and/or hopelessly confused. For those same many years, however, psychotherapists have been increasingly confronted with the inadequacies of any one pure school of psychological theory to address complex and overlapping client pathologies. Cognitive-behavioral approaches offering success with anxiety disorders such as phobias are enhanced by concomitant use of existential imagery approaches, and both give way to the effectiveness of psychodynamic techniques when personality disorder is also present. SEPI leaders, an august group of recognized thinkers in their fields, seek to establish respectable and effective ways to improve psychotherapy outcomes without losing theoretical power.

For Further Information

SEPI, Dr. George Stricker, The Derner Institute, Adelphi University, Garden City, NY 11530.

K. M. LATTEA

Society for the Scientific Study of Religion (SSSR). The Society for the Scientific Study of Religion is a nonprofit education and research corporation founded in 1949 by students of social science and of religion. The purpose of the society "is to stimulate and communicate significant scientific research on religious institutions and experience." To this end the society not only publishes the *Journal for the Scientific Study of Religion* (*JSSR*, established in 1961) but also cosponsors an annual convention, usually during late October or early November, with its sister society, the Religious Research Association (RRA).

Membership in SSSR is open to anyone, regardless of religious identification, interested in the study of religion. The largest group of members are sociologists, though a number of psychologists, anthropologists, political scientists, and other social scientists are members. Nonsociologists are encouraged to join. The society maintains a nonsociological position on its executive board and on occasion will have a nonsociologist serve as editor of the *JSSR*.

The *JSSR* is the preeminent journal of the scientific study of religion and is provided as a benefit of membership to the society. Instructions regarding submissions to the journal are located inside the front cover. Also inside the front cover of each issue is the address of the society's executive office and business office.

P. C. HILL

See PSYCHOLOGY OF RELIGION; PSYCHOLOGISTS OF RELIGION; RELIGIOUS RESEARCH ASSOCIATION (RRA).

Sociobiology. Sociobiology is the descriptive name given to an interdisciplinary strategy for understanding behavior. The distinguishing characteristic of sociobiology is the assertion that genetic processes are the single important explanatory factor. Genes provide the key to understanding all aspects of organisms and their behavior. All characteristics of an organism, including size, shape, color, amount of hair, sensory abilities, and all behavior, from the most trivial to the most complex, result from genetic instructions. While various sciences study the genetics of the physical characteristics of organisms, sociobiology is singularly focused on understanding genes' effects on behavior.

The behavior triggered by genes is assumed to have one primary function: to ensure that an organism will have maximum probability of reproduction and thus that that organism's genetic lineage will survive into the next generation. Sociobiologists believe that social behavior persists in an organism's activity inventory for the sole purpose of increasing the odds that the organism will reproduce. Social behavior that fulfills this purpose will persist; behavior that does not increase the probability of survival to reproduce will fade from the species.

Sociobiologists have generated controversy due to their insistence that not only the behavior of ants and elephants but also the most special and precious of human behaviors (e.g., love, altruism, religion), are explained by genes' devotion to survival. Thus although humans may naively believe that some behavior serves high and noble purposes, such is not the case, since sociobiological analysis can demonstrate that all behavior is ultimately linked to the ebb and flow of survival and reproduction.

The controversy concerning sociobiology touches many issues, but two primary areas of disagreement may be identified that are of most concern to Christians. These are philosophical naturalism and research evidence.

The person committed to philosophical naturalism believes that the physical world and its inhabitants are all there is. The shape and activity of everything is guided by the unchanging laws of nature. No outside factor, such as God, is required to account for the origins of the universe or anything that has happened therein since time began. This assumption is a key component of the interpretations of behavior set forth by sociobiologists. For example, religious behavior is assumed to have flourished because it assisted survival and reproduction.

The controversy over research evidence builds on the foundation of philosophical naturalism. A large percentage of the interpretive data used by sociobiologists is based on studies of lower organisms, especially social insects such as ants and bees. Since the laws of nature generated both ants and humans, understanding the behavior of ants aids directly in the understanding of humans. Neither ants nor humans persist in the performance of behavior not directed by the genetic commitment to survival and reproduction.

Additional Reading

Dawkins, R. (1989). *The selfish gene* (Rev. ed.). New York: Oxford University Press.
Wilson, E. O. (1978). *On human nature*. Cambridge, MA: Harvard University Press.
Wilson, E. O. (1975). *Sociobiology: The new synthesis*. Cambridge, MA: Harvard University Press.

D. KAUFFMANN

See HEREDITY AND ENVIRONMENT IN HUMAN DEVELOPMENT.

Soiling. *See* ENCOPRESIS.

Solution-Focused Therapy. In the 1990s the revolution in mental health care has accelerated the popularity and growth of brief approaches to therapy. The publication of numerous books and the growing attendance at workshops worldwide indicate that the most popular brief therapies are those that are solution-focused rather than problem-focused.

Solution-focused brief therapy (SFBT) was developed by Steve de Shazer and Insoo Kim Berg (Berg & Miller, 1992) at the Brief Family Therapy Center in Milwaukee, Wisconsin. It has been expanded by O'Hanlon and Weiner-Davis (O'Hanlon & Weiner-Davis, 1989) and others (Walter & Peller, 1992; Selekman, 1993).

Solution-based approaches to change grew out of the brief and strategic therapy movements that gained prominence during the 1970s. Much of the early work was done at the Mental Research Institute (MRI) in Palo Alto, California. It was influenced by the therapeutic ideas of Milton H. Erickson, who emphasized the value of narrative (the stories people tell about themselves) in the change process. He believed that whatever patients brought to therapy—their language, beliefs, resources, and sense of humor—could be utilized by the therapist in constructing therapeutic tasks. Much of what solution-based therapists do is an application of Erickson's utilization principle.

Traditional approaches to psychotherapy are based on the assumption that the presenting problem is not the real problem but merely a symptom of a much deeper psychological or interpersonal problem that must be uncovered, interpreted, and processed. Effective therapy must be intensive and reconstructive and often requires much time.

Central to the SFBT approach is the hypothesis that no problem happens all of the time. There are always exceptions to the problem. Change can take place by helping patients capitalize on their existing strengths and resources. The basic principle appears simple: increase what works and decrease what does not work. What are the exceptions to the problem? What is the patient doing differently at those times when they are not anxious or depressed? What has worked before? What strengths can the patient apply? What would be a useful solution? How can they construct it?

However, SFBT is more than a collection of questions and techniques. Behind these simple tools is a fundamental paradigmatic shift as to ways in which people can change. The therapist and patient work on cocreating solutions for what is problematic in the here and now and what needs to happen so that the situation can improve. The therapist focuses more on the strengths and resources that patients bring to therapy than on their weaknesses or limitations.

Some of the key assumptions of SFBT include:

- Change is inevitable and small changes are all that are necessary. A change in one part of a system usually leads to change in other parts of the system.
- One need not know a lot about the problem to help people solve it.
- Patients define goals.
- Problems are solved; people are not cured.
- Effective therapy builds on patients' strengths rather than dwelling on their weaknesses.
- If something works, don't fix it.
- If something does work, do more of it.
- If something doesn't work, do something different.
- Keep it simple.
- There is no such thing as failure, only feedback.

The therapist stance is active, strategic, and solution-focused. One of the therapist's main tasks is to help a patient learn how to recognize and mark an exception to the problem that is already occurring. This is then used as the basis for developing a more enduring change.

The first session is an important part of successful SFBT. One of the therapist's first tasks is to determine the termination criteria. The answer to the question, What do you suppose needs to happen for you to no longer need to come for therapy? often contributes to the treatment plan.

Solution-based treatment begins by immediately delving into the discovery of solutions. The formation of realistic, achievable, and highly specific treatment goals is fundamental to SFBT. Goals are determined by patients. They decide for what they are customers. De Shazer (1991) believes that "in order for therapy to be brief and effective, both therapist and client need to know where they are going

and they need to know how to know when they get there. . . . Most simply, a picture of 'life after successful therapy' can guide the work of both therapist and client."

Well-formed goals are small, concrete, specific, and behavioral. They are in the here and now and are indicated by the presence of something rather than the absence of something. They emphasize what persons will do or think rather than what they will not do or think. Well-formed goals describe and encourage the first small steps the patient needs to take rather than the end of the journey.

Several interventions are unique to SFBT. Probably the most well-known is the miracle question. It is helpful for patients to imagine a future where their problem is solved: Suppose you were to go home tonight, and while you were asleep, a miracle happened and the problem that brought you here was solved. How will you and those around you know the miracle happened? What will be different? What would you do differently? What would your spouse notice you were doing differently?

Another intervention is the formula first-session task. At the end of the first session the therapist may say, "Between now and the next time we meet, I would like you to notice what is happening in your life that you would like to continue to happen." This encourages the patient to focus on the solutions that are already occurring.

Solution-based therapists also use scaling questions. The patient is asked to create a scale with 1 being when the problem was at its worst and 10 being when the miracle has occurred. They are then asked, Where are you now? That can be followed up with a question such as, What would need to happen for you to be .5 higher on your scale? Scaling uses language to create a kind of visual image, a spatial component that gives patients a way to notice change while reinforcing the idea that no change is too small or insignificant.

While there is a need for research to examine its strengths and limitations, the existing literature demonstrates that SFBT is a pragmatic approach to change that can be used in a variety of church and clinical settings. It can be especially helpful in situations in which the pastor or clinician has a limited amount of time. Proponents say the average number of sessions range from three to ten.

SFBT is both a way of looking at change as well as a way of doing therapy. In the hands of a well-trained therapist it can be an effective way for helping people change. However, therapists learning this approach must beware of becoming solution-forced rather than solution-focused. Even with patients where a pure solution-focused approach may not be the treatment of choice, solution-based insights can be an invaluable way to facilitate increased effectiveness in therapy.

References

Berg, I. K., & Miller, S. D. (1992). *Working with the problem drinker.* New York: Norton.

de Shazer, S. (1991). *Putting difference to work.* New York: Norton.

O'Hanlon, W., & Weiner-Davis, M. (1989). *In search of solutions.* New York: Norton.

Selekman, M. (1993). *Pathways to change.* New York: Guilford.

Walter, J. L., & Peller, J. E. (1992). *Becoming solution-focused in brief therapy.* New York: Brunner/Mazel.

G. J. OLIVER

See SHORT-TERM THERAPIES.

Somatization Disorder. Somatization disorder is predominantly seen in females, usually appearing before the age of 30. It is characterized by medically unexplainable recurrent or chronic ill health of multiple bodily systems. The patient typically has made numerous visits to physicians and may have had an inordinate amount of hospitalizations and surgeries that have been fruitless.

The disorder had existed since antiquity, but not until Briquet's *Treatise on Hysteria* in 1859 was there any clear elucidation and quantification of data. After studying 430 patients with hysteria over a 10-year period, Briquet concluded that in women the age of onset was either prepubertal or before the age of 20. It is now believed that the incidence of this polysymptomatic disorder is 10 to 20% of first-degree female relatives who suffer from the same disorder, whereas male relatives show an increased prevalence of sociopathy and substance-related disorders (Woerner & Guze, 1968).

New to the most recent edition of the *DSM-IV* criteria is a history of different pain sites (e.g., head, foot, back) or physical function (e.g., urination, sexual intercourse). In addition, diagnostic criteria include a history of the following: at least two gastrointestinal symptoms other than pain (e.g., nausea, bloating, food intolerance), one sexual or reproductive symptom other than pain (e.g., sexual indifference, irregular menses), and one pseudoneurological symptom or deficit not limited to pain (e.g., paralysis, weakness, hallucinations). Further, each of these symptom clusters cannot be explainable by a known medical condition or effects of substances.

The incidence in the general population is .2% to 2% among women and less than .2% for men. Individuals with this disorder frequently present with impulsiveness, antisocial behavior, difficulty controlling their impulses, personality disorders, and suicidal behavior.

The diagnostic criteria in *DSM-IV* require a history of physical symptoms of several years' duration beginning before the age of 30 and must be comprised of one of the following clinically significant complaints. These symptoms are grouped into four clusters: four pain symptoms, one pseudoneu-rological symptom, two gastrointestinal symptoms, and one sexual symptom.

There are still diverse opinions regarding the etiology of the somatization disorder. Maany (1981) postulates that such a disorder may be a subtype of a masked depression. He suggests that the diverse somatic symptoms are depressive equivalents. Liskow, Clayton, Woodruff, Guze, and Cloniger (1977) maintain that a somatization disorder arises primarily from a hysterical personality core. However, others speculate that such a disorder has its origins in a still unknown pathophysiological process.

References

Liskow, B. I., Clayton, P., Woodruff, R., Guze, S. B., & Cloninger, R. (1977). Briquet's syndrome, hysterical personality, and the MMPI. *American Journal of Psychiatry, 134,* 1137–1139.

Maany, I. (1981). Treatment of depression associated with Briquet's syndrome. *American Journal of Psychiatry, 138,* 373–376.

Woerner, P. I., & Guze, S. B. (1968). A family and marital study of hysteria. *British Journal of Psychiatry, 114,* 161–168.

K. R. KRACKE

Somatoform Disorders. In *DSM-IV* seven types of disorders that affect bodily function or perception have been classified as somatoform disorders. They are somatization disorder, undifferentiated somatoform disorder, conversion disorder, pain disorder, hypochondriasis, body dysmorphic disorder, and somatoform disorder not otherwise specified. These disorders frequently occur with physical symptoms without apparent or gross organic dysfunction. They are viewed as psychological in origin, since they are not under voluntary control and are not the result of pathophysiology.

In the past the somatization and conversion disorders were generally viewed as hysterical in nature. The somatization disorder is characteristic of multiple and diverse somatic symptomatology and history of chronic ill health. Conversion disorder is the impairment in one's voluntary motor or sensory functioning, and psychological sequalae are viewed critical to onset. Undifferentiated somatoform disorder manifests in one or more physical complaints not attributable to a medical condition and present for at least six months. Pain disorder is limited to localized pain without the presence of demonstrable organic etiology; psychological sequalae are viewed critical to onset, severity, or existence of the pain. Hypochondriasis occurs when an individual's hypervigilance to physical cues or functioning culminates in either overinterpreting or misinterpreting sensations as evidence of an ongoing disease entity. Body dysmorphic disorder is the languishing preoccupation of one's perceived bodily defect that its parts are functioning socially, occupationally, or in another area. The residual category of somatoform disorder not otherwise specified allows for a clinical identification when the criteria for one of the other somatoform disorders has not been clearly met.

K. R. KRACKE

Somnambulism. Habitual sleepwalking. It is a fairly common phenomenon, occurring in approximately 10 to 15% of the population. As a sleep disorder it primarily affects males, is generally associated with childhood and early adolescence, and tends to run in families. It is often associated with other sleep disorders. Sleepwalking movements are generally rather simplistic or automatic, with more extended and complex behaviors being the exception rather than the rule. For instance, a person may get up, stand for a short time or take a few steps, and then return to bed. There are no reports of anyone ever being injured during a sleepwalking episode. Awakening a person during a sleepwalking episode is usually difficult; when it occurs, the person is typically disoriented and will have no dream recall or memory of the preceding events. Episodes of sleepwalking are usually sporadic, occurring perhaps only a few times in a person's life.

Sleepwalking has been interpreted as being a hysterical recant, a dissociative reaction, or primarily an unconsciously motivated acting out of dreams. Scientific research indicates that sleepwalking occurs during slow-wave deep sleep (sleep stages 3 and 4) rather than during REM sleep, when dreaming takes place. Sleepwalking presently is interpreted more benignly and does not usually warrant professional intervention. In childhood, sleepwalking may be motivated by factors closer to the surface of consciousness rather than the unconscious. Discreet questioning will typically reveal such mental stressors as a worry about some aspect of home life or school. Childhood sleepwalking is usually developmental-phase specific and disappears with time. Chronic sleepwalking and sleepwalking in adulthood may be a manifestation of a personality disorder or may be indicative of more severe emotional distress.

D. S. McCULLOCH

See SLEEP DISORDERS.

Soul. In contemporary usage the term *soul* refers to the nonmaterial aspect or essence of a human being that confers individuality. It is often used synonymously with mind or self. In Christian theology the soul carries the further connotation of being that part of the individual that partakes of divinity and survives the death of the body.

The Greek word *psyche* is the parent word of soul in English. *Psyche* in its earliest origins means the breath that gives life to a person. The term occurs more than nine hundred times in the Old Testament and Apocrypha (as recorded in the Septuagint) and is distributed fairly equally among the various books. Most often it stands for the Hebrew

nepes (originally, throat, gullet; the breath, exhalation) but is also used to represent other Hebrew words that mean heart, inner person, or living thing (see Brown, 1978). Twice it is used to refer to *ruah* (spirit; Gen. 41:8; Exod. 35:21).

In the New Testament *psyche* corresponds to *nepes*, but its usage is relatively infrequent. Of the 101 New Testament occurrences 37 appear in the synoptic Gospels. It is used to communicate inner life, seat of life, or life itself. It is the life that we must lose in order to find life (Mark 8:35). According to Brown (1978), *psyche* can be seen as equivalent to ego, person, or personality (the whole inner being).

Modern scholarship has underscored the fact that Hebrew and Greek concepts of soul were not synonymous. While the Hebrew thought world distinguished soul from body (as material basis of life), there was no question of two separate, independent entities. A person did not have a body but was an animated body, a unit of life manifesting itself in fleshly form—a psychophysical organism (Buttrick, 1962).

Although Greek concepts of the soul varied widely according to the particular era and philosophical school, Greek thought often presented a view of the soul as a separate entity from body. Until recent decades Christian theology of the soul has been more reflective of Greek (compartmentalized) than Hebrew (unitive) ideas.

Viewing the soul as an entity different from the body has resulted in centuries of debate concerning its origin (see Wright, 1988). Three main options have been championed: preexistence, the Platonic-inspired belief that souls experience a higher existence prior to their entry into a human body; traducianism, the view that the soul is derived from our parents by the process of procreation; and creationism, the assertion that God creates a soul *ex nihilo* for each human being.

In the modern era biblical theology's large-scale rejection of dichotomist anthropologies appears to favor traducianism. However, in reality, Hebrew-inspired anthropologies overturn an assumption common to all traditions: the soul is not a part of human nature but characterizes it in its totality, just as flesh and spirit do.

If a distinction between body, spirit, and soul must be made, it may be helpful to view the body as the vehicle for sense-consciousness, the spirit as the means for God-consciousness, and the soul as the provider of self-consciousness. Through information made available by the body and spirit, the soul makes decisions of eternal significance.

In what may be one of the greatest ironies of the twentieth century, the term *soul* has become all but lost to modern-day *psyche*-ologists (literally one who studies the soul) and *psycho*therapists (servants of the soul). To William James, as to most modern psychologists, the soul as such does not exist at all but is merely a collection of psychic phenomena.

References

Brown, C. (1978). Soul. In C. Brown (Ed.), *The new international dictionary of New Testament theology.* Grand Rapids, MI: Zondervan.

Buttrick, G. A. (Ed.). (1962). *The interpreter's dictionary of the Bible.* Nashville: Abingdon.

Wright, D. F. (1988). Soul, origin of. In Sinclair, B. F., Wright, D. F., & Packer, J. I. (Eds.), *New dictionary of theology.* Downers Grove, IL: InterVarsity Press.

Additional Readings

Benner, D. G. (1988). *Psychotherapy and the spiritual quest.* Grand Rapids, MI: Baker.

Berkouwer, G. C. (1962). *Man: The image of God.* Grand Rapids, MI: Eerdmans.

Leech, K. (1977). *Soul friend.* San Francisco: Harper & Row.

May, G. (1982). *Care of mind care of spirit.* San Francisco: Harper & Row.

G. W. MOON

See BIBLICAL ANTHROPOLOGY; SPIRIT.

Spanking. *See* CHILD DISCIPLINE; PARENTING.

Spearman, Charles Edward (1863–1945). British psychologist who pioneered in factor analysis in testing. Born in London, he served as an officer in the British army from 1883 to 1897, when he decided that he wanted to study psychology. He received his Ph.D. degree in 1904 from the University of Leipzig, studying under Wilhelm Wundt, and did postdoctoral work with Kulpe at Würzburg and with Muller at Göttingen.

Spearman became reader (instructor) in experimental psychology at University College of the University of London in 1907. He was appointed professor of mind and logic in 1911 and professor of psychology in 1928, when the department of psychology was separated from the department of philosophy. He retired from the University of London in 1931 and held temporary teaching positions in the United States three times before his death.

In 1904, while he was still in Germany, Spearman published two papers that foreshadowed his most important contributions. Although he did not use the term *reliability coefficient* until 1907, one of his 1904 papers introduced the concept. He made many other contributions in the area of statistics and measurement. He developed a widely used rank-order correlation coefficient appropriate for use on data at the ordinal level of measurement. With one of his students, he proposed the Spearman-Brown prophecy formula as a method of estimating the reliability of a test when it is lengthened. These quantitative contributions have been lasting ones in psychology.

His second paper (1904) presented his two-factor theory of intelligence. He believed that all mental tasks involve both a general ability factor, g, and a specific ability factor, s. There is only one g, and it underlies every intellectual performance. However, there are as many s's as there are tasks, and they come into play only when doing one particular task. Thus one's performance is a combination of g and whatever s's are involved. This theory has been the subject of controversy for many years. Spearman later proposed possible group factors, such as verbal ability and spatial ability, and other general factors, such as perseveration, oscillation, and Will.

Spearman did not write many books. His best-known ones are *The Principles of Cognition and the Nature of Intelligence* (1924), *The Abilities of Man* (1927), and *Psychology Down the Ages* (1937). This last is not a history of psychology but of selected problems that led up to his two-factor theory.

R. L. KOTESKEY

See PSYCHOLOGY, METHODS OF.

Spence, Kenneth Wartenbee (1907–1967). Neobehaviorist psychologist who sought to develop a general theory of behavior through an analysis of learning. Born in Chicago, Spence moved to Montreal, Canada, at four years of age and received his education at McGill University (B.A., 1929; M.A., 1930). He received his Ph.D. from Yale in 1933 under Robert Yerkes. He then spent four years as a National Research Council fellow at the Yale Laboratories of Primate Biology in Orange Park, Florida, and one year teaching at the University of Virginia. In 1938 he went to the University of Iowa and remained there until 1964, when he went to the University of Texas.

Spence arrived at Yale as a student the year after Clark Leonard Hull became a research professor there. From then on their thinking was intertwined. Hull said that Spence had contributed generously and effectively with suggestions and criticisms to his *Principles of Behavior.* After Hull's death Spence carried on with the same type of thinking, so much so that by 1959 Frank Logan called it the Hull-Spence Approach. Spence remained in Hull's shadow for his whole career.

Shortly after completing his doctorate Spence published an analysis of discrimination learning to explain transposition, a phenomenon that had been an embarrassment to behaviorists for many years. His theory of discrimination learning set the battle lines for years to come with psychologists who followed the lines of Gestalt Psychology. He was primarily concerned with facts. Theory and methodology are justified in that they contribute to the gathering and ordering of facts. He placed an emphasis on fractional anticipatory goal responses, classically conditioned responses made as animals were responding in an experiment. For Spence motivation is complexly determined by several variables, and habit strength is a function of the number of stimulus-response pairings. Spence also served as an interpreter of the philosophy of science to psychologists.

Spence received many awards, including the American Psychological Association Distinguished Scientific Contribution Award in 1956, the first year it was given. He was the first psychologist invited to give the Silliman Lectures at Yale. The lectures were later published as *Behavior Theory and Conditioning* (1956) and show the relationship between his theorizing and his experimentation. He wrote many journal articles, some of which were gathered in *Behavior Theory and Learning* (1960).

R. L. KOTESKEY

See BEHAVIORAL PSYCHOLOGY.

Spirit. In current usage the word *spirit* can be described as the animating force within living beings. It is the will to live and survive. A defining quality of human beings, spirit is in this context the activating principle of the personality.

In prehellenic writings spirit is related to air. That people are alive as long as they breathe led to the conclusion that air was the bearer of life. In Aristotelian thought *pneuma* (spirit) was a force in the embryo that eventually produced a mature person (*see* Aristotle). Stoic philosophers related *pneuma* and *psyche* (soul or mind) at an intellectual level, attributing to *pneuma* certain of the functions of the *psyche* (i.e., thought and speech). In animism spirit was a presiding divinity inhabiting inanimate objects.

The Greek word for spirit and some of its cognates are *pneuma*, which is spirit or wind; *pheo*, to blow (e.g., a musical instrument); *ekpneo*, to breathe out; *empneo*, to pant; *pneumatikos*, spiritual; and *theoneustos*, God-breathed or inspired by God. The Greek root *pneu* refers to the movement of air. When the suffix *ma* is given to *pneu*, the resulting Greek word *pneuma* denotes air set in motion (Brown, 1978). This has significance in biblical thought: the air set in motion becomes a metaphor for activity of a divine origin.

The Hebrew equivalent of *pneuma* is *ruah*, which means blowing. This blowing comes from God; in one-third of the 377 instances of *ruah* in the Masoretic text, the use alludes to breathing, an outward expression of the life force that equates to being alive (Brown, 1978).

Biblical View of Spirit. Spirit is the word used from the earliest traditions to denote the mysterious invisible power of God. That power was manifested in the wind (Exod. 10:13, 19), in the breath of life (Gen. 6:3; Ps. 104:29–30), and in the power of charismatic leaders and prophets (Judg. 6:34; 13:25; Isa. 10:6, 10; Wakefield, 1983, p. 357).

In New Testament theology spirit is given those attributes that join humanity's spiritual existence to God through more personal experience. The spirit of the individual is the realm of human existence through which the spirit of God (Holy Spirit) communicates with people through God's presence (John 7:37–39). This divine presence opens the possibility of new dimensions in human awareness of and sensitivity to God. The spirit becomes essential to spiritual life, as air and water are necessary for physical life. This opens a pathway for God to express divine character through people and to change the life of people as they exist in the unique environment of God's presence. Moreover, the believer is given eternal life through the spiritual force with which God infuses.

The experience of the indwelling of the Holy Spirit is given prominence in the New Testament (e.g., John 14:16, 17; Acts 2:4, 38; 11:15–17; Rom. 8:9). Throughout church history, however, where the Spirit interacts with people of faith to impart special spiritual gifts (1 Cor. 12), that interaction creates a tension between older traditions and the immediacy of fresh inspiration (Wakefield, 1983, p. 358). Persons who have emphasized the work of the Spirit have always been looked upon with suspicion. The church has struggled with each wave of inspiration, whether human or divine. Orthodox faith responds to unorthodox movements like the presence of new wine in old containers. The resulting diversity has been tolerated only as both have matured. This tolerance usually exists where a dialog between the diverse viewpoints occurs, thereby creating an examination of the biblical basis for the new movement as well as an appreciation for the value of older tradition.

While the Holy Spirit is connected to one's spiritual vitality, it is separate from the human persona. The spirit is the creative energy of God bestowing that energy on a person but always keeping the recipient of the spirit separated from it in essence and ownership. The individual is not allowed to co-opt that cosmic power for personal use. Even though it is a gift, the Spirit still functions at the discretion of God (1 Cor. 14).

Conclusion. The concept of spirit as an animating force in humans may be understood as a personality quality that is distinct from the spirit as a personal indwelling force and channel of divine communication. In contemporary use spirit is viewed as the will to live and achieve, but the Spirit of God or Holy Spirit describes an energy of divine origin that creates the mysterious link between God and creation. The two ideas may be related, but the term *spirit* is more precisely defined when the personality construct is distinguished from the theological term.

References

Brown, C. (1978). Spirit. In C. Brown (Ed.), *The new international dictionary of New Testament theology*. Grand Rapids, MI: Zondervan.

Wakefield, G. S. (1983). *The Westminister dictionary of Christian spirituality*. Philadelphia: Westminister.

Additional Readings

Benner, D. G. (1988). *Psychotherapy and the spiritual quest.* Grand Rapids, MI: Baker.

Berkouwer, G. C. (1962). *Man: The image of God.* Grand Rapids, MI: Eerdmans.

May, G. (1982). *Care of mind care of spirit.* San Francisco: Harper & Row.

D. S. AULTMAN

See BIBLICAL ANTHROPOLOGY; PERSONALITY; SOUL.

Spiritual and Religious Issues in Psychotherapy. Before the advent of modern psychotherapies the care of souls was predominantly a function of religious communities. This has changed as scientific ways of knowing have gained momentum and contemporary clinical psychology has developed. Many of the pioneers of clinical psychology saw their methods as more scientific and objective than spiritual healing traditions—sometimes scorning religious explanations and practices. For example, Sigmund Freud referred to religion as an illusion, John Watson once criticized a colleague by suggesting he had returned to religious explanations, and Albert Ellis described the Judeo-Christian concept of sin as contributing to most forms of psychopathology. In recent decades, in the context of postmodern thought (Jones, 1994) and increasing scientific evidence that religion can coexist with psychological health (Gartner, 1996), the bifurcation between religion and science has softened and a renewed interest in spiritual healing methods has resulted.

Many pastors and other religious leaders attempt to incorporate psychological advances in their counseling work, and many psychologists and other mental health professionals attempt to sensitively address religious and spiritual issues in psychotherapy. This same trend is evidenced in graduate training programs. Many seminary programs include course work and practical training in counseling theory. Similarly, several colleges, university graduate schools, and seminaries have graduate programs in psychology with an emphasis on integrating Christianity and psychology.

The Need for Spiritually Informed Interventions. There are many reasons to consider religious and spiritual issues in psychotherapy, two of which are considered. First, both psychotherapy and religion focus on existential issues such as personal meaning, freedom, values, and suffering. To illustrate, one can imagine a depressed psychotherapy client with a troubled marriage being treated by an agnostic rational-emotive behavior therapist each week and also attending religious services at an evangelical Christian church each week. When he or she is at the therapist's office, the client learns that it is irrational and silly to put up with a marriage that makes one unhappy. At church the same person learns that divorce is wrong and that the suffering endured in a troubled marriage can build stronger character.

In this example, psychology and religion provide competing value prescriptions for similar domains of behavior. The counselor equipped to provide spiritually informed interventions may find value and truth in both perspectives, the psychological and the religious. In this example, it may be helpful to dispute some of client's beliefs, as rational-emotive behavior therapists do, while also recognizing and respecting the values of the religious community in which the client worships. A counselor trained in psychology, theology, and spirituality can provide an appropriate intervention based on an in-depth understanding of the person, the person's religious values, and the faith community in which the person functions.

Second, religious and spiritual issues are important to consider in psychotherapy because most people seeking counseling express a desire to discuss religious matters. Even in today's mental health marketplace, with a ubiquity of psychiatrists, psychologists, licensed professional counselors, marriage and family therapists, and licensed clinical social workers, many prefer to seek help first from clergy. Those in the general public—the potential consumers of psychotherapy—believe that religious values are important for therapists to consider (Quackenbos, Privette, & Klentz, 1985).

Christianity as an Anthropological Foundation for Psychotherapy. Spiritually sensitive counseling interventions require the therapist to understand the values implicit in a client's religious worldview, much as one might work to understand a client's cultural and ethnic background. However, most Christian counselors see the task of integrating psychology and Christianity as larger than this. Because all counseling flows out of worldview assumptions and beliefs about human nature, a Christian understanding of persons is an essential foundation for understanding religious issues in Christian forms of therapy. Although there is no widely accepted Christian personality theory, there are common elements in most Christian perspectives. These elements include the Christian's view of self, personal need, and healing relationships.

View of Self. Most mental health professionals and religious leaders agree that those who develop an accurate understanding and acceptance of themselves are freed to experience emotional and spiritual health. For example, there are striking similarities between the characteristics of self-actualizers described by Abraham Maslow and the fruit of the Spirit described by the apostle Paul in Galatians 5:22–23. Moreover, most practitioners would agree that a faulty sense of self as evidenced by the extremes of narcissism or self-hate detracts from both spiritual and psychological health.

Despite these similarities, there are ways in which a Christian understanding of self varies from those views prevalent among mental health professions. Whereas a psychological process of self-understanding might involve personal therapy and insight, a Christian process of self-understanding requires knowing God. John Calvin suggested that an accurate view of self is possible only when one knows God, and likewise an accurate view of God is possible only when one knows oneself. A purely psychological understanding of self, especially those of the cognitive and behavioral traditions, may tend to minimize the aspects of self that cause unwanted emotions. In stark contrast, a Christian view of self includes an awareness of human sin and depravity. Jonathan Edwards writes: "It is therefore not unreasonable to suppose that people should suffer deep distress and much mental apprehension when they see how great and manifold are their sins in the light of the infinite majesty of God" (Edwards, 1808/1984, p. 52). Rather than leading to depression and hopelessness, Edwards argues, this Christian view of self leads to personal tenderness and gratefulness to God.

View of Personal Need. Just as an accurate view of self leads to health, an accurate view of human fallenness and personal need fosters spiritual well-being. Foster (1988) puts it this way: "The closer we come to the heartbeat of God, the more we see our need and the more we desire to be conformed to Christ" (p. 33). Christian doctrine teaches us to view ourselves as participants in sin rather than as innocent victims, that sickness and need are parts of our nature, and that recognizing our spiritual condition is a prerequisite to healing. Thus the inner peace (*see* Peace, Inner) we yearn for can never come by our own efforts but only by admitting we are powerless to conquer our own self-centeredness and by turning over the rule of our lives to Christ. The Christian gospel gives hope for broken and needy people, but only after they recognize their brokenness. Israel's King David describes himself as "poor and needy" in numerous places throughout the psalms, then affirms God's grace by concluding, "but the Lord takes thought for me" (Ps. 40:17, NRSV).

The idea of admitting that one is needy is not popular in contemporary Western society. We see it as a sign of weakness and vulnerability. Some people build persuasive arguments that emotional health comes with autonomy and individuality. But to the Christian there is only one way to spiritual health, and that requires us to recognize that we need God. Spiritual leaders throughout history have written about their brokenness and hunger for God, describing an awareness of personal need as a prerequisite for spiritual growth.

View of Relationships. At the heart of Christian spirituality is a healing relationship with God. Christians see themselves as those who were spiritually dead when "God, who is rich in mercy, out of the great love with which he loved us even when we were dead through our trespasses, made us alive together with Christ" (Eph. 2:4–5, NRSV). The Christian who is psychologically and spiritually healthy enjoys balanced, healthy relationships with Christ and others.

Spiritually sensitive therapists recognize that therapy relationships often point clients toward a healthier view of God and stronger relationships with others. The counseling relationship is helpful when it displays aspects of God's character: compassion, hope, forgiveness, kindness, fairness, appropriately confrontive, and so on. The counseling relationship is harmful when it becomes a means of personal power, grandiosity, or self-gratification.

Intradisciplinary Integration. Recent trends in the integration of Christianity and psychology are moving away from theoretical model building, in which theological and psychological concepts are analyzed and synthesized, toward discussions of practical therapeutic strategies. This trend toward applied integration, which Worthington (1994) titled intradisciplinary integration, has appeal to the many religious therapists and counselors who seek practical methods of simultaneously enhancing faith and mental health in their clients. To illustrate some of the trends in intradisciplinary integration, a brief discussion of prayer, Scripture, and forgiveness is provided.

Prayer. Prayer is more than a therapy technique. It is the primary vehicle of growth in the spiritual life. Prayer is also effective in helping people cope with physical pain and medical problems, in reducing fears of death, and in promoting abstinence for those in alcohol treatment (McCullough, 1995). Based on survey data, prayer appears to be a frequent but not routine part of Christian counseling and psychotherapy (*see* Prayer, Use of in Counseling).

Despite the importance of prayer and its widespread use among religious therapists, bringing it into the therapy office is not a simple matter. Some insist that prayer is an essential part of all Christian experience and should routinely be included in counseling. Others assert that counseling should remain distinct from spiritual guidance and that prayer may have unintentionally harmful effects on many clients. When therapists focus too intently on the question of praying aloud with clients in therapy sessions, other important uses of prayer are sometimes overlooked. For example, how often do we pray for our clients outside of a therapy session? How often do we pray silently and covertly for our clients during a counseling session? What about devotional meditation as a spiritual and psychological tool for relaxation and anxiety management?

It is also important to recognize that not all prayer is good. Jesus was critical of public prayers offered by those thinking more about the social impact of their words than about God (Matt. 6:5). He also condemned prayers of empty repetitious phrases and prayers of smugness (Matt. 6:7; Luke 18:9–14). Religious therapists may effectively incorporate some forms of prayer in their work, but it is unwise to assume that more prayer is always better than less prayer. Should counselors pray with clients? is the wrong question to ask. Instead we ought to ask, Which forms of prayer should we use with which clients and under which circumstances?

The role of prayer in healing has become a topic of research in recent years. Initial studies of devotional meditation and religious imagery indicate that these forms of prayer can be useful in therapy, but most types of prayer have not yet been systematically evaluated. In addition to the research task, religious counselors need to define clear ethical guidelines for the use of prayer in counseling.

Scripture. From a Christian perspective, Scripture is an essential tool for knowing God. It is God's special revelation to humankind. The psalmist describes the godly as those whose "delight is in the law of the LORD, and on his law they meditate day and night" (Ps. 1:2, NRSV). Moreover, Scripture provides theological boundaries for spirituality and meditation. Foster (1988) writes, "For all the devotional masters the *meditatio Scripturarum*, the meditation upon Scripture, is the central reference point by which all other forms of meditation are kept in proper perspective" (p. 29). Similarly, Scripture can keep therapists focused on timeless truth in the midst of professions vulnerable to fads and shifting standards of right and wrong.

Survey research indicates that many religious counselors use and teach principles from Scripture in their professional work. However, the explicit use of Scripture in therapy is quite rare among Christian counselors. For counselors who choose to use Scripture in counseling, it is important to consider the specific effects it might have on a client, based on a careful assessment of the client's needs, the therapeutic relationship, and ethical standards. It is also important to balance a healthy respect for Scripture as God's special revelation with personal humility, recognizing that all interpretations of Scripture are limited by imperfect hermeneutic methods. Our knowledge of God, self, and Scripture are all interrelated, and our capacity to understand any one of these elements will add to our ability to understand the others.

Forgiveness. Between 1990 and 1994 there were 90 articles published about forgiveness in psychology journals—almost a 300% increase from the same period in the previous decade. Clearly forgiveness is an increasingly popular topic among psychotherapists. Although this is an encouraging trend for religious therapists, it is important to remember that a Christian understanding of forgiveness may differ from the ways others understand forgiveness. McCullough and Worthington (1994) correctly observed that "theological, philosophical, and psychological understandings of forgiveness have not been well integrated" (p. 3). Whereas many therapists may perceive forgiveness as a way to feel better by letting go of past hurts, Christian doctrine provides a richer and more compelling rationale: "Be kind to one another, tender-hearted, forgiving

one another, as God in Christ has forgiven you" (Eph. 4:32, NRSV). For the Christian, forgiveness is to be a quality of character that results from insight about Christ's redemptive work, not just an act of the will. Forgiveness is an act of Christian compassion that comes from one person identifying with another. It suggests that two people are equally fallible, one responding to the offense of the other in loving identification. Healing comes as we see ourselves in those who hurt us.

Religiously sensitive counselors recognize the potential damage of introducing forgiveness as a therapeutic goal too early in the treatment relationship. Further, they recognize a Christian duty to forgive but do not use that duty to coerce or manipulate clients. Finally, they see a connection among sin, confession, and forgiveness, understanding that forgiveness properly flows out of humble self-awareness and gratitude to a forgiving God.

Challenges for the Future. A number of personal and professional challenges face religiously sensitive therapists as they consider applied integration issues. First, there are challenges related to personal and professional preparation. Whereas many seminaries and graduate schools equip therapists in theology and psychology, intradisciplinary integration introduces a need for preparation in spirituality and spiritual formation. Unlike competence in psychology and theology, understanding spirituality does not lend itself to traditional educational methods. Spiritual training is experiential and often private. It is rarely found in the classroom or represented by graduate degrees, but it is found in private hours of prayer and devotional reflection, in church sanctuaries where religious communities worship, and in quiet disciplines of fasting and solitude. This suggests that training religiously sensitive therapists is not purely a professional matter but an endeavor in which the traditional distinctions between personal and professional life become blurred and indistinct.

Second, because most contemporary forms of religious counseling are relatively superficial adaptations of mainstream counseling techniques, many religious therapists are faced with the challenge of confronting dominant views of mental health. Intradisciplinary integration requires us to evaluate carefully the goals of therapy and to challenge some of the views of healing that surround us in the mental health professions. Whereas many popular presentations of mental health suggest that people are OK, that they should look out for their own needs, and get out of unfulfilling relationships, Christian teachings point a different direction. Every Christian must be a broken person who admits both personal inadequacy and a profound need for Christ.

Third, religious therapists face scientific challenges. Though religious interventions have been an important part of soul care for many centuries, they have not typically been scrutinized by the scientific methods of modernity. In order to communicate effectively with other mental health professions, religiously sensitive therapists face the challenges of obtaining scientific support for their interventions. This in turn raises ethical and epistemological challenges in an age where scientific support for therapeutic procedures is quickly becoming a professional standard.

Considering religious issues in psychotherapy requires the therapist to consider theological and spiritual perspectives at the same time as engaging in the interpersonal and psychological aspects of therapy. These multiple tasks require a basic working knowledge of Scripture, religious history, theological anthropology, spiritual disciplines, and the spiritual life of the client. As therapists become more interested in the applied aspects of integrating psychology and spirituality, they face various challenges related to training, values regarding mental health, and scientific standards.

References

Edwards, J. (1808/1984). *Religious affections: How man's will affects his character before God.* Portland, OR: Multnomah.

Foster, R. J. (1988). *Celebration of discipline: The path to spiritual growth.* San Francisco: HarperCollins.

Gartner, J. (1996). Religious commitment, mental health, and prosocial behavior: A review of the empirical literature. In E. P. Shafranske (Ed.), *Religion and the clinical practice of psychology.* Washington, DC: American Psychological Association.

Jones, S. L. (1994). A constructive relationship for religion with the science and profession of psychology: Perhaps the boldest model yet. *American Psychologist, 49,* 184–199.

McCullough, M. E. (1995). Prayer and health: Conceptual issues, research review, and research agenda. *Journal of Psychology and Theology, 23,* 15–29.

McCullough, M. E., & Worthington, E. L., Jr. (1994). Models of interpersonal forgiveness and their applications to counseling. *Counseling and Values, 39,* 2–14.

Quackenbos, S., Privette, G., & Klentz, B. (1985). Psychotherapy: Sacred or secular? *Journal of Counseling and Development, 63,* 290–293.

Worthington, E. L., Jr. (1994). A blueprint for intradisciplinary integration. *Journal of Psychology and Theology, 22,* 79–86.

Additional Readings

Collins, G. R. (1993). *The biblical basis of Christian counseling for people helpers.* Colorado Springs, CO: NavPress.

Jones, S. L., & Butman, R. E. (1991). *Modern psychotherapies: A comprehensive Christian appraisal.* Downers Grove, IL: InterVarsity Press.

McMinn, M. R. (1996). *Psychology, theology, and spirituality in Christian counseling.* Wheaton, IL: Tyndale House.

Worthington, E. L., Jr. (Ed.). (1993). *Psychotherapy and religious values.* Grand Rapids, MI: Baker.

M. R. McMinn

See Religious Resources in Psychotherapy; Religion and Personality.

Spiritual Well-Being. Spiritual well-being in some form has been a concern of spiritual communities of divergent traditions throughout the ages. As is the case with many other spiritual issues, however, spiritual well-being has been largely ignored in the psychology community and has often played a less than central role in sociological and other behavioral science endeavors.

Although there have been numerous attributions made for this relative neglect, Benner (1991) points out that the diverse and often conflicting ways in which the general concept of spirituality has been described and applied "suggests to some that the concept is hopelessly vague and thoroughly unsalvageable for scientific use" (p. 3). Questions of how to quantify spiritual issues, authority and diversity questions, and value-free definitions of modern science have appeared insurmountable to some. More recent interest in the areas of spirituality in general and spiritual well-being in particular nonetheless have blossomed due to the failure of strictly defined modern science paradigms in addressing human questions of meaning and ethical clinical issues regarding proper treatment of clients with religious issues by secularized practitioners.

Spiritual well-being does not exist in isolation, but it is thought to relate to persons' experiencing of their spiritual dimension, and it may be affected by and contribute to their psychological and physical health dimensions. Spiritual well-being is not directly observable, and evaluation of it is limited to self-report and observation of related behaviors. In contrast to objective and economically based life satisfaction measures, spiritual well-being is thought to involve transcendence of empirically derived correlates of the self to include a social-psychological component (horizontal dimension) and a religious component (vertical dimension).

Two major approaches have recently emerged regarding spiritual well-being. One major strand comes from pastoral and theological circles and represents a resurfacing of longstanding Christian community behavioral practices generally falling under the rubric of spiritual disciplines. Proponents such as Willard (1988) and Foster (1988) maintain that engaging in certain behavioral and mental patterns regularly with the proper motivation and goals is likely to increase one's actual spiritual well-being as well as one's internal perception and experience of it. These disciplines (e.g., prayer, fasting, silence, meditation, etc.) taken together include both internal (subjective) experiences and external (objective) behavioral events.

The second major approach, represented mainly in the research of Ellison and other researchers, focuses more narrowly on construction and application of self-report, subjective measures of spiritual well-being. This line of inquiry has primarily stemmed from quality of life concerns, in which attempts have been made to evaluate personal satisfaction in terms of objective, economically based indicators over the past three decades. Such happiness ratings and quality of life indices have increasingly revealed that higher income and social relatedness have not produced improved quality of life perceptions; in fact, just the opposite finding has frequently been reported by respondents. This unexpected trend has given impetus to more systematic study and measurement of subjective contributors to quality of life experience, with the prototypical instrument in this area to date being represented by the Spiritual Well-Being Scale (SWBS) (Ellison, 1983; Paloutzian & Ellison, 1982). Conceptualization of issues related to spiritual well-being led to subscales designed to tap Religious Well-Being (RWB) and Existential Well-Being (EWB). Attempts to refine quantitative aspects of this concept have included efforts to develop norms for the SWBS (Bufford, Paloutzian, & Ellison, 1991).

Spiritual well-being is part of a complex multidimensional picture that reflects but is not synonymous with such concepts as spiritual health, spiritual maturity, and hope. In relation to spiritual health, Ellison (1983) describes spiritual well-being measures as "more like the stethoscope than the heart itself" (p. 332); spiritual well-being, he further comments, may be experienced at any stage of spiritual maturity and would be commensurate with one's level of spiritual development. The relationship between hope and spiritual well-being has been investigated by Carson, Soeken, and Grimm (1988), who concluded that there is some overlap between the concepts but that hope could also have more secular basis, at least in relation to coping with chronic illness. It may be that hope has a more future orientation, while the satisfaction and spiritual well-being measures have been more focused on immediacy in self-report. Landis (1996) reported that higher SWBS scores were correlated with better prognosis for long-term physical health problems such as diabetes mellitus.

Some of the additional research with the SWBS has shown positive correlations of higher SWBS scores with tests measuring purpose in life; acceptance by and intimate communication with God; positive self-valuation; average number of Sunday services attended per month; and amount of time spent in daily devotions. Higher SWBS scores have been shown to be negatively correlated with measures of loneliness, death anxiety, and state anxiety in cancer patients. The SWBS appears to show some promise for diagnostic utility, especially in the lower score ranges where its low ceiling does not have as much effect on its discriminative function. Further work also needs to be accomplished in understanding the factor structure of the SWBS before more complex interpretive statements can be generated (Ledbetter, Smith, Fischer, & Vosler-Hunter, 1991).

The great majority of empirical work done regarding spiritual well-being has been in the subjective self-report arena. More traditional pastoral/theological models focusing on behavioral and mental habit patterns also have much to offer, and work relating the self-report and pastoral/theological approaches to each other as well as associated topics such as hope, physical and psychological health, and coping strategies could prove fruitful in the future. Basic work still needs to be accomplished in the areas of construct validity and factor structure of the conceptual aspects of spiritual well-being, but the accomplished research is a far cry from unsalvageable or nonquantifiable and irrelevant to social science research in the areas of life satisfaction and meaningful goal orientation.

References

Benner, D. G. (1991). Understanding, measuring, and facilitating spiritual well-being: Introduction to the Special Issue. *Journal of Psychology and Theology, 19* (1), 3–5.

Bufford, R. K., Paloutzian, R. F., & Ellison, C. W. (1991). Norms for the Spiritual Well-Being Scale. *Journal of Psychology and Theology, 19* (1), 56–70.

Carson, V., Soeken, K. L., & Grimm. (1988). Hope and its relationship to spiritual well-being. *Journal of Psychology and Theology, 16* (2), 159–167.

Ellison, C. W. (1983). Spiritual well-being: Conceptualization and measurement. *Journal of Psychology and Theology, 11* (4), 330–340.

Foster, R. J. (1988). *Celebration of discipline.* San Francisco: Harper & Row.

Landis, B. J. (1996). Uncertainty, spiritual well-being, and psychosocial adjustment to chronic illness. *Issues in Mental Health Nursing, 17* (3), 217–231.

Ledbetter, M. F., Smith, L. A., Fischer, J. D., & Vosler-Hunter, W. I. (1991). An evaluation of the construct validity of the Spiritual Well-Being Scale: A factor analytic approach. *Journal of Psychology and Theology, 19* (1), 94–102.

Paloutzian, R. F., & Ellison, C. W. (1982). Loneliness, spiritual well-being and quality of life. In L. A. Peplau and D. Perlman (Eds.), *Loneliness: A sourcebook of current theory, research and therapy.* New York: Wiley Interscience.

Willard, D. (1988). *The spirit of the disciplines.* San Francisco: Harper & Row.

J. A. Ingram

See Spirituality, Psychology of; Existential Psychology and Psychotherapy.

Spirituality, Psychology of. Spirituality seeks direct apprehension of what is ultimate, without admixture of thought or emotion. Spiritual practice can deepen one's relationship with God to the union for which Jesus prayed. Spirituality does not necessarily involve communal beliefs or practices. It does require morality, virtue, and usually some meditative discipline.

Consistent spiritual practice goes through systematic changes with related psychological states and functioning. Each stage also has pitfalls and their cures. Religions do not always encourage spiritual practice; it can make people hard to control. Traditions often persecute their living mystics, then revere them after they die.

Basic Understandings and Preparation. Spirituality seeks to know God as one understands God.

Like Christians, some others hold the ultimate reality to be a personal God. Some consider the ultimate reality impersonal, as *Brahman* or *nibbana* *(nirvana)*. Spirituality produces deep self-knowledge en route to knowledge of God. It usually brings fringe benefits such as improved physical and psychological health.

A capacity for commitment is necessary. Most practitioners commit to a religious tradition. Some people who are not conformed to religious demands attempt spiritual practice but tend to give up easily. They often seek what spiritual practice is not designed to give, such as high experiences, special powers of mind or body, or an easy way out of personal difficulties.

The time-honored traditions assume commitment to basic morality. Similarly assumed are the virtues of generosity (*see* Generosity and Greed), patience, kindness, perseverance, and honesty. The Christian fruit of the Holy Spirit describe these, as do Buddhist *paramis*, spiritual perfections. Spiritual practice greatly increases such characteristics.

Spiritual practitioners ordinarily inspect the subtle processes of mind and body with meditation. Many methods have not proven themselves; some are a waste of time; others are dangerous. A time-honored tradition is the wisest choice. Practice of either simple concentration or mindful awareness of experience typically produces faster progress than thinking meditation.

History of Spiritual Psychologies. The earliest psychologies come from India. Hindu yoga practice was in place by 1500 B.C. Patanjali's *Yoga Sutras* (see Prabhavananda & Isherwood, 1969), compiled around 500 B.C., describes practice methods and states of consciousness occurring in practice. Also around 500 B.C. the Buddha taught awareness practice. Scriptures date from several years after his death. The other major work of Buddhist psychology is Buddhaghosa's *The Path of Purification* (1979; it dates from the fifth century).

These spiritual psychologies were developed from introspective accounts of meditation experiences. For centuries meditators described their meditation to knowledgeable teachers who assessed it against existing knowledge. Developmental psychologies of the systematic alterations in consciousness effected by meditation practice resulted. These psychologies are so precise that twentieth-century meditators find these ancient tomes accurately describe their experiences.

Jewish mysticism has similar works. Muslim Sufism's most important psychology comes from Al-Ghazzali in the eleventh century. The twentieth-century Indian sage Sri Aurobindo gave detailed psychological explanations of Vedantic forms of yoga (Ghose, 1976).

Eastern Orthodoxy has the earliest Christian models. In later European Christianity, John of the Cross (1991) stands out, although less detailed psychologies, such as that of the Ignatian *Spiritual Exercises* (Fleming, 1978/1980), exist. A psychologically minded contemporary work is Arintero's *The Mystical Evolution* (1950/1951).

Stages of Spiritual Practice. Our model of spiritual practice has six major stages. It incorporates understandings from the resources mentioned.

Opening. People typically start spiritual practice with both enthusiasm and unrealistic expectations that moderate as spiritual discipline develops. Two early experiences are common. People learn how ungovernable their minds are and also realize that meditation is frequently painful. They must become accustomed to holding the body still. This makes them aware of bodily pain and tension from which attention is diverted in everyday life.

Meditation uncovers what is hidden, buried, pushed aside, tied up, knotted, closed, covered over. Slowly it starts revealing oneself: forgotten memories, traumas, losses, misdeeds, emotions, concerns, patterns of thought and behavior. Much of this is painful, for one already knows what one does not mind knowing about oneself. Meditation cannot make one feel angry, sad, bored, or lonely, but it reveals such feelings hidden beneath the surface. Developing concentration produces islands of peace and calm. Flashes of genuine understanding of self and others may occur in even early practice.

Some people become discouraged by the difficulty of establishing concentration and the unpleasantness of pain and self-knowledge. Others become emotionally dependent on their teachers or want a special position with them. Some become so fascinated with their own psyches that they wander about in this mental content instead of meditating. When meditators have important experiences, they may become inflated with self-importance and egoistically consider the experience a personal possession.

Self-Knowing. After some time of practicing virtue and inner prayer or meditation, a harrowing time occurs. Aspirants feel as if they cannot meditate, as if everything is falling apart. Ordinary mental processes break down, which brings a strong sense of personal helplessness. They find practice unsatisfying as their established skill and peace is disrupted. Meditators begin to see their interior unpleasantness in finer detail and can experience intense remorse. They also become unable to delight in the things of God, which formerly were a dependable source of happiness.

St. John of the Cross called this time of suffering "the passive dark night of sense." Spiritual psychologies detail signs of transition into this stage. The signs differ in different forms of practice, but outcomes are surprisingly common. This rugged period eventually greatly intensifies faith, brings considerable lucidity, and makes meditation practice easy.

Blissfulness. After this difficult confrontation one enters blissful delights, the Christian illuminative way. One need no longer work hard to meditate, but one attends to the work being done in one. Meditators typically experience so much ease, bliss, and delight that most make the error of believing nothing lies beyond this. Buddhists call this *pseudonirvana.* Most people become quite attached to their delights. They often interpret experiences in ways flattering to vanity and self-importance.

Some people experience subtle light and sounds. Some feel touched by their personal deity. Various powers and energies may manifest, such as the *kundalini* experience of yoga. Many psychosomatic ailments heal at this time, as people see through the psychological processes maintaining them. Healing of purely medical problems also sometimes occurs. Greatly increased psychological health and balance manifest.

This blissful ease usually lasts for many years. It is the terminal point in practice for some people. This period ends when one recognizes how much work remains to be done and willingly embarks on it.

Purification. Next comes a most harrowing purification called "the dark night of the spirit." One confronts deep, common, habitual tendencies and also faces cosmic issues. Meditators experience anguish, terror, impotence, vulnerability, threat, dread, cosmic sadness, sense of impending annihilation, hopelessness, terrible aloneness, disgust with self and life, personal emptiness, and feelings of being doomed or beyond any satisfaction of any kind. Spiritual motivation, meaning, purpose, and value seem to disappear. Physical pain, frequently more intense than any previously experienced, also occurs. In touching the archetypal level of reality one deals with the basic issues of human life and aspiration and must be purged of the very roots of self-centeredness.

There is only one solution: surrender of ego. This is truly a death experience, and many people shrink back as they feel it coming. Yet the habitual and repeated death of "I-ness" becomes the only way out. This life-and-death struggle may endure for years. Little islands of peace, lasting short periods of time, may occur during it. Christians finally surrender all to God.

Balance. One eventually breaks into pervasive equanimity, truly indifferent to all experience and equally unmoved by intense bliss or anguish. Remarkable purity and absence of self-seeking comes. This stage too may last for years.

Often one enjoys very great stillness, like the doorway to the Ultimate, where no things exist but only a vast immenseness that may be dark or light. It may feel like touching, being in, or encountering breaks into the oneness of God, of the Ultimate. These unitive experiences differ from the simple union that may occur earlier. They come only after the intense struggle of purifying mind and almost always have a paradoxical quality. They are not simply meditation experiences, but they leave a pervasive influence on ordinary perception during daily life.

Realization. From this balanced state of mind, remaining unmoved by whatever happens, one becomes able to see God. The experience is unstable at first, with regular falls back into both equanimity and harrowing purgation. Over time the presence of God becomes more stable, and as further purification occurs, this takes place more deeply and intensely.

References

Arintero, J. G. (1950/1951). *The mystical evolution in the development and vitality of the church* (2 vols.). St. Louis: Herder.

Buddhaghosa. (1979). (B. Nyanamoli, Trans.). *The path of purification (Visuddhi Magga): The classical manual of Buddhist doctrine and meditation* (4th ed.). Kandy, Sri Lanka: Buddhist Publication Society.

Fleming, D. L. (Trans.). (1978/1980). *The spiritual exercises of St. Ignatius: A literal translation and a contemporary reading.* St. Louis: The Institute of Jesuit Sources.

Ghose, S. A. (1976). *The synthesis of yoga.* Pondicherry, India: Sri Aurobindo Ashram.

John of the Cross (1991). (K. Kavanaugh, O.C.D., & O. Rodriguez, O.C.D., Trans.). *The collected works of St. John of the Cross* (Rev. ed.). Washington, DC: Institute of Carmelite Studies.

Prabhavananda, S., & Isherwood, C. (1969). *How to know God: The yoga aphorisms of Patanjali.* New York: Signet.

M. J. MEADOW

See PSYCHOLOGY OF RELIGION.

Spirituotherapy. A term referring to the work of Charles R. Solomon; though he advances no precise definition of the term, it is a registered trademark of Grace Fellowship International of Denver, Colorado. Grace Fellowship was founded in 1969 by Solomon, who holds a doctorate in education from the University of Northern Colorado. There are several branch offices in and outside the United States.

In his *Counseling with the Mind of Christ,* Solomon presents spirituotherapy as a counseling approach. He asserts that Christian counseling "endeavors, first of all, to lead a person to trust the Lord Jesus Christ as Savior and Lord and then to disciple him in spiritual growth" (p. 21); it also may be defined as witnessing.

The primary qualification for counselors is spiritual maturity, which includes belief in miracles and in the inerrancy of the Scriptures, and a life "where self has been dealt a death-blow." A Bible school education is highly recommended, whereas seminary training may be an asset or liability, "depending on the emphasis of the institution." Because, in Solomon's opinion, training is not yet available through a satisfactory wedding of theology and psychology, one must resort to home study, conferences, and workshops.

The process of spirituotherapy is cast in a simplified model of humanity. This model is presented to counselees through six elaborate charts. It stresses the conflict of the natural people with the spiritual person. Counseling deals with the obstacles to spiritual progress (e.g., unconfessed sin, lack of surrender, need for restitution, unforgiving spirit, fear, refusal to break sinful alliances, lack of faith, and refusal to suffer).

The initial hour is for creating trust and rapport; determining the counselee's stage of spiritual growth; understanding the presenting problem; gathering a personal history (35 questions are suggested); and exploring rejection in childhood as a uniquely powerful factor in emotional illness. It is important that by the end of the initial session the counselee be given a general view of the answer to his or her problem and be helped to see "psychological *symptoms* as *spiritual* problems" (p. 66). A prayer commitment (*see* Prayer, Use of in Counseling) may be sought in the first hour, in which will is more important than feelings. Counselees are urged to read Scripture and devotional literature selected by Solomon, primarily from the victorious life movement.

Succeeding interviews are less structured. The diagrams disclose what teaching needs to be repeated; any commitment made in the first interview is assessed; focus is on the underlying problem rather than on the symptoms described as the presenting problem. Major goals are self-understanding and acceptance of one's position in Christ, thus appropriating spiritual life and power. Solomon states that it is insufficient to use Scripture verses merely to gain victory over symptoms. They should be used to gain insight into the underlying problem, namely, the self-life.

It may be unfair to evaluate spirituotherapy from the perspective of psychology. Solomon's writing is more for "soul-winning" by "personal workers" (see p. 58). He states that the approach is best used in local churches and is straightforward about the fact that familiarity with particular doctrine, language, and literature is necessary. His bibliography is almost exclusively devotional. Many statements indicate a bias against psychology, medicine, and psychiatry. Solomon discredits experts in psychology as part of "this world's system" (p. 63); he admits, however, that there are extreme cases that should be referred to them, though these are a small minority and are not defined.

The influence of psychoanalysis is apparent. Insight is pursued, and there is repeated emphasis on rejection experiences of childhood as determinative of emotional problems (contradicting an otherwise radical reduction of all problems to spiritual). Human troubles as experienced in unemployment, marital stress, and depression are regarded as symptoms.

There is in addition a dualism between the created world and spirit. This derives more from Greek philosophy than from the Hebraic view of Old and New Testaments, in which the unity of the human person and race is affirmed as starkly as the solidarity of the people of God—all in the physical creation. From a Christian psychological perspective spirituotherapy appears too individual in emphasis. There is little recognition of the common grace of God in the healing helps of behavioral and clinical sciences. Also, grasping the cognitive content of spirituotherapy may well require literacy, intellectual ability, and reasonably good emotional health in addition to Christian commitment.

Reference

Solomon, C. R. (1977). *Counseling with the mind of Christ: The dynamics of spirituotherapy.* Old Tappan, NJ: Revell.

Additional Readings

Solomon, C. R. (1971). *Handbook to happiness.* Denver: Grace Fellowship Press.
Solomon, C. R. (1976). *The ins and outs of rejection.* Denver: Heritage House.
Solomon, C. R. (1982). *The rejection syndrome.* Wheaton, IL: Tyndale House.

H. KLINGBERG, JR.

See CHRISTIAN COUNSELING AND PSYCHOTHERAPY.

Split-Brain Research. *See* HEMISPHERIC SPECIALIZATION.

Splitting. One of the most primitive ego defense mechanisms. The term is used in a variety of ways by different psychoanalytic theorists but generally describes a way of organizing external reality on the basis of whether the experiences are "pleasurable good" or "painful bad," these two types of experiences being split or kept apart in psychic life. It is thus a mechanism of defense frequently employed against ambivalent feelings toward a person or an experience. Splitting is thought to be the predominant mechanism of defense in psychopathologies reflecting the earliest developmental arrest, such as schizophrenia or the borderline disorders.

D. G. BENNER

See DEFENSE MECHANISMS.

Sport Psychology. The branch of applied psychology that deals with athletes and athletic situations. Professional psychologists find this area to be a fertile arena for the study of motivation and human performance enhancement. The increased popularity of sports and the corresponding need for methods of enhancing human performance have created an increasing need for psychologists with expertise in this field.

Clinical psychologists originally entered the sports world to administer psychological tests and to counsel athletes who were not functioning at their expected level of performance. Sport psychologists presently serve as consultants to coaches and players by giving them information about behavioral techniques that should enhance every athlete's performance. Often along with medical doctors and ministers, licensed psychologists travel and live with professional athletes, teaching them game enhancement techniques such as the use of imagery, biofeedback, hypnosis, and relaxation techniques. They also counsel athletes in setting effective goals for themselves and dealing with personal problems.

As a branch of applied psychology sport psychology has its own organization, the North American Society for Sports and Physical Activity, which publishes a journal and acts as a forum on this subject of growing interest.

D. S. McCulloch

See Applied Psychology.

Spouse Abuse. *See* Abuse and Neglect; Domestic Violence.

Stages of Family Development. *See* Family Life Cycle.

Stanford-Binet Intelligence Scale. One of the main psychological tests currently used in the assessment of intellectual development. It is also the test that gave birth to the well-known concept of intelligence quotient (IQ) as the ratio of mental age to chronological age.

In 1905 Alfred Binet was asked by the Minister of Public Instruction for the Paris schools to develop a test that would identify mentally retarded children (*see* Mental Retardation). Binet and an associate, Theodore Simon, constructed a test of 30 items arranged in order of increasing difficulty. By 1908 a second scale had been developed. In 1911 a third revision, which included many more items and could be administered to a much broader age range, was published.

In the United States the first revision was completed by Lewis Terman at Stanford University in 1916. This translation resulted in such major changes that the test became known as the Stanford-Binet. In 1937 a second revision, which resulted in two equivalent forms (L and M) of the test, was completed. In 1960 a third revision, incorporating the best items from the two equivalent forms of 1937, was published as one test (L-M). In 1960 standard scores leading to a deviation IQ replaced the previously used ratio IQ. This major change makes it possible to compare scores across the age levels. The norms presently in use were published in 1972.

The Stanford-Binet is administered by a professional familiar with the testing instructions, materials, and scoring procedures. The test consists of a number of subtests grouped according to age level and takes approximately one hour to complete. For most age levels there are six different subtests. Some are verbal, such as a vocabulary test; the others are performance-oriented, requiring the manipulation of objects such as block design. The successful completion or failure of a subtest determines the course of further testing.

In determining the level of intellectual development the basal age is first found. This is the age level at which all subtests are passed. From this point testing is continued upward until all subtests are failed. This is known as the ceiling age. The mental age is determined by adding to the basal age a certain number of months for each subtest successfully completed beyond the basal age.

Theoretically the highest mental age possible on the Stanford-Binet is 22 years and 10 months. According to the 1972 norms the average adult mental age is 16 years and 8 months. At approximately 14 years the mean mental age as determined by the Stanford-Binet begins to fall behind the chronological age. For this reason it is recommended that this test not be used as the only measure when assessing normal and superior adult populations. To calculate one's intelligence quotient (IQ) the determined mental age is divided by one's chronological age and then multiplied by 100.

W. W. Austin

See Intellectual Assessment; Psychological Measurement.

Starbuck, Edwin Diller (1866–1947). A pioneering figure in the psychology of religion. He was born in Bridgeport, Indiana, a rural Quaker community where religion was simply lived. That simple piety forged his character and influenced one of the country's longest careers in the psychology of religion and religious education.

Starbuck attended Quaker academies and earned an A.B. in philosophy (Indiana University, 1890), A.M. in psychology (Harvard, 1895), and Ph.D. in psychology with Granville Stanley Hall (Clark University, 1897). Before going to Harvard, Starbuck taught Latin and mathematics in Indiana at Spiceland Academy and Vincennes University. After receiving his doctorate he taught education for seven years at Stanford University (1887–1904) and for two years at Earlham College (1904–1906). The longest span of his career was in the State University of Iowa philosophy and psychology department (1906–1930). He spent his last years at the University of Southern California—eight years as professor emeritus of psychology.

Starbuck was one of the few people to make a full career of psychology of religion and related studies. At Indiana University the new humanism shook his Quaker piety, but his interest in religion flared the brighter. In December 1892, his paper at the Indiana Teachers' Association outlined a science of psychology of religion. He chose Harvard for graduate study because it seemed most open to that pursuit.

By late 1893 Starbuck was circulating questionnaires on conversion, breaking habits, and religious development, seeking data on firsthand religious experience of individuals. After a year he began to notice consistencies in the conversion data—ages near puberty, similarity to habit breaking, and personality dissociation. He took his data and questionnaires to Clark and accumulated 1,265 cases of conversion, recorded on huge charts so that he could observe the commonalties. These questionnaire data formed the basis for *The Psychology of Religion* (1899), the first book-length study of the subject. Starbuck's psychology of religion was empirical and factual but rarely reductionistic. He gave psychology of religion courses at Stanford as well as an educational psychology course that he believed to be the first university course in that field.

Starbuck taught his first course in character education in 1898. He took an extended sabbatical (1912–1914) to work on a massive religious education curriculum project with the Unitarian Church; church traditionalism frustrated completion of that project. He was soon challenged by the offer of a $20,000 prize by the Character Education Institution of Washington, D.C., for the best statement of character education. The committee Starbuck chaired won that prize in 1921 with a proposal that emphasized not traditional indoctrination but arousal of the child's creative interest and imagination—"a more natural approach in which the integrity of the child's personality was wholly respected" (1937, p. 243). The award and attendant public interest in character education led the State University of Iowa to establish the Institute of Character Research, which Starbuck headed (1923–1930). He took essentially the same work to Southern California.

Starbuck lived to see interest in empirical psychology of religion wane, until by 1930 only his and a few of his students' studies were visible in the United States. His autobiography (1937) cites his eleven books and other principal publications.

References

Starbuck, E. D. (1899). *The psychology of religion.* London: Walter Scott.

Starbuck, E. D. (1937). Religion's use of me. In V. Ferm (Ed.), *Religion in transition.* New York: Macmillan.

R. D. KAHOE

See PSYCHOLOGY OF RELIGION.

Statistics. Researchers use the term *statistics* to summarize numerical data and estimate the likelihood that a group of subjects represents a population of interest. Methods summarizing data from a particular sample are descriptive statistics. The most common descriptive statistics are measures of central tendency (indices of the average score) and measures of variability (indices of variation between scores). The mean, or arithmetic average, is the most typical measure of central tendency, but occasionally researchers report the median (the score dividing the top 50% of scores from the bottom 50%) or the mode (the most frequently occurring score). The standard deviation, most easily conceptualized as the average amount that scores deviate from their mean, is the most common measure of variability.

The correlation coefficient is also a descriptive statistic. A correlation coefficient *(r)* assesses the connection between two variables and has a value ranging from -1.00 to $+1.00$. The value of *r* conveys information about the nature and strength of the relationship between two variables. The sign (+ or –) indicates whether a relationship is positive or negative. If two variables are positively related, as one increases, so will the other. For example, height and weight are positively related: those who are taller often weigh more than short people. When two variables are negatively related, as one increases, the other will decrease. Television viewing and high school grade point average (GPA) are probably negatively related: those watching more television may have lower GPAs.

As the relationship between two variables becomes stronger, *r* moves away from the value of 0.00 toward either -1.00 or $+1.00$, depending on the nature of the relationship, negative or positive. Therefore, two variables that have a correlation of $-.77$ are more closely connected than variables that have a correlation of $+.32$. Note that we usually cannot infer any cause-and-effect relationships from correlation coefficients. If two variables are correlated, it does not necessarily mean one variable causes the other. We can only say that these two variables demonstrate some connection to one another; why that connection exists is not answered by this type of analysis.

Researchers use inferential statistical procedures to assess the probability that a particular sample represents a larger population. Common inferential procedures include the t-test and analysis of variance (ANOVA), procedures that assess if different groups have different average scores on some measure of interest. For example, a researcher would use a t-test to assess differences in the average score on a depression measure for males and females. This scientist would measure depression in a group of males and a group of females and then use the results of the t-test analysis to infer male-female differences in the general population.

If researchers assess differences between more than two groups, they use an ANOVA. However, an ANOVA identifies only whether a difference between groups exists; it does not identify which groups are different from one another. Researchers often will use a multiple-comparison procedure (e.g., a Scheffe or Tukey test) to pinpoint where group differences lie.

Statistics play a major role in social scientific research. However, because statistics are based on the notion of probability, they only allow us to draw conclusions about what is probably the state of affairs in the world. In addition, statistical procedures shed no light on the usefulness, importance, or moral value of the work at hand.

Additional Reading

Gravetter, F. J., & Wallnau, L. B. (1992). *Statistics for the behavioral sciences: A first course for students of psychology and education.* New York: West.

E. A. GASSIN

See PSYCHOLOGY, METHODS OF.

Status. This important concept in the description and analysis of group structure has sometimes been used to refer to position in a social system (e.g., father, lawyer, student). More generally, however, psychologists use the term to refer to the respect or prestige that is accorded a person who occupies a particular position.

An individual's status influences the way in which that person acts and also how other group members react to him or her. For example, status differences affect both the pattern and content of communication in groups. Not only do high-status persons speak more, but more communication tends to be directed toward them. Research on the interactions of psychiatrists, psychologists, and social workers has shown that even these individuals direct a disproportionate share of their remarks to those with greater status. In addition, high-status persons tend to confine most of their conversations to others of equal status.

Brown (1965) has described a universal norm concerning status effects on communication. Familiar address, such as that between intimate friends, characterizes messages directed toward those of lower status; more formal address, like that occurring between strangers, characterizes messages directed toward one higher in status. Brown also observes that generally the person of higher status is the pacesetter in all steps toward greater intimacy.

Although several studies have shown that high-status group members typically conform more to group norms than do low-status persons, the group may permit high-status members greater latitude in deviating from the majority position. On the basis of their past contribution to the group's goals, those of higher status may be given idiosyncrasy credit, which permits greater nonconformity under certain circumstances (*see* Conformity). This seems particularly true when the success of the group may depend on granting the high-status person the necessary freedom to marshal resources for goal attainment. At the same time the high-status person may be judged more harshly for his or her actions. For example, in one study of destructive obedience, subjects held the superior officer who gave the order more responsible than the soldier who executed it.

A person's status may also affect how other group members perceive his or her competence. Research investigating the effects of status on problem solving found that groups more readily accepted correct answers from high-status than from low-status members. Thus the final product of a group may be influenced by the status of the member who has the best ideas.

Reference

Brown, R. W. (1965). *Social psychology.* New York: Free Press.

M. BOLT

See GROUP DYNAMICS.

STD. *See* SEXUALLY TRANSMITTED DISEASES.

Stealing, Compulsive. *See* KLEPTOMANIA.

Stepfamilies. *See* BLENDED FAMILY.

Stereotype. A belief about the personal attributes of a group of people (Myers, 1996). Stereotypes can be positive or negative, accurate or inaccurate. Early research on stereotypes (e.g., Katz & Braly, 1933) asked respondents to indicate whether a target group possessed a particular trait. More recent attempts to measure stereotypes have asked respondents to rate the extent to which a target group possesses certain traits or to estimate the percentage of people in the group who possess a particular trait. Although research indicates considerable reduction in the negative stereotyping of ethnic groups, a survey of three hundred communities in the United States reported that a majority of respondents continue to believe that African-Americans are less industrious, intelligent, and patriotic than white Americans (*The New York Times*, 1991). Research indicates that gender stereotypes are held even more strongly than ethnic stereotypes. Women are perceived as sensitive, compassionate, warm, and dependent whereas men are considered assertive, dominant, aggressive, and independent.

Psychologists have maintained that even though certain stereotypes may have a kernel of truth, they often produce a number of negative consequences. First, they result in an overestimation of differences between groups. Although the beliefs, values, and other characteristics of groups may be similar, stereotypes may result in those groups being viewed as vastly different. Second, stereotyping may result in an underestimation of the variation within groups. Individuals are prejudged on the basis of their category membership, and a large number of distinguishable persons may be treated as equivalent. Third, stereotypes typically have not only descriptive but also evaluative content. They are ethnocentric judgments by which members of other groups are evaluated on the basis of local standards. As negative generalizations, stereotypes may be used as a justification for inequalities and hostility, thereby providing a major mechanism by which prejudice is sustained.

Recent research suggests that stereotypes may be an inevitable consequence of normal perceptual and thought processes. The tendency to form categories and to make inferences on the basis of category membership reflects the need to simplify and find meaning in a complex world. It may be neither possible nor desirable for people to treat each entity they encounter as unique. Unless generalizations are made, they can neither anticipate the future nor adequately cope with the environment.

Once formed, stereotypes perpetuate themselves by influencing people's attention, interpretations, and memories. Individuals are more likely to notice instances that confirm rather than disconfirm their expectations. Moreover, the actions of others are likely to be interpreted in terms of stereotypes held of them. Research has also shown that memory is selective, and people best remember those facts that support their own beliefs.

Stereotypes may also be resistant to change because they constitute self-fulfilling prophecies, in which prior expectations confirm themselves. Stereotypes guide people's behavior, which in turn influences the response of others in ways that are consistent with prior expectations. Individuals' beliefs about themselves are also influenced by the expectations and reactions of others to them.

Stereotypes can change in the light of disconfirming information, particularly if it is repeated and involves many, typical group members. In addition, researchers have found that once people become acquainted with a member of another group they are often able to set aside their stereotypes and judge that person on the basis of his or her own merit.

References

Katz, D., & Braly, K. (1933). Racial stereotypes of one hundred college students. *Journal of Abnormal and Social Psychology, 28,* 280–290.

Myers, D. G. (1996). *Social psychology* (5th ed.). New York: McGraw-Hill.

Poll finds Whites use stereotypes. (1991, January 10). *The New York Times,* B10.

M. BOLT

Stereotypic Movement Disorder. Persons with stereotypic movement disorder move their bodies in ways that are nonfunctional, repetitive, and seemingly driven. This may include relatively benign movements such as rocking, hand waving, and twirling objects. However, it may also involve dangerous or even life-threatening behaviors such as head banging and self-biting.

To fit the criteria for this diagnosis, such behavior must substantially interfere with normal activities or result in serious bodily injury. If mental retardation is also present, which is often the case with this disorder, the behavior must be problematic enough to become a focus of treatment. The behavior must persist for at least four weeks and must not be caused by substance use (particularly am-

phetamines) or a general medical condition. Finally, the behavior must not be better accounted for by any of the following diagnoses: obsessive-compulsive disorder (for a compulsion), trichotillomania (for hair pulling), a pervasive developmental disorder, or a tic disorder. Note that in the latter diagnosis, tics are involuntary movements, whereas stereotyped movements are voluntary.

Stereotypic movement disorder appears to be caused chiefly by situations in which a person does not get an adequate amount of sensory stimulation. Such is the case with persons who are blind or deaf, who are more susceptible than average to this disorder. Institutionalized persons are even more susceptible to this disorder, perhaps because such settings are often environmentally impoverished with low stimulation. Approximately one-fourth of all adults with severe or profound mental retardation living in institutions are diagnosed with this disorder. While self-stimulation appears to be the goal of the repetitive behaviors for most persons with this disorder, in some cases it seems to be triggered by a stressful event or painful medical condition (for example, an ear infection leading to head banging in a person with severe mental retardation; *see* Pain; Stress).

The most effective treatment of stereotypic movement disorder involves use of standard techniques of behavior modification. Among these are extinction, overcorrection, positive reinforcement, and differential reinforcement for other behaviors. Treatment of this disorder should also include ongoing medical evaluation if symptoms involve self-injurious behaviors. In such cases treatment will likely need to include a means of protecting the person from self-harm (e.g., putting a helmet on a child who engages in head banging).

N. S. THURSTON

Stimulus Control. A concept usually associated with operant conditioning. Although operant conditioning emphasizes the role of consequences in shaping and maintaining actions, cues (discriminative stimuli) that precede the response that is reinforced also acquire controlling power. A stimulus controls a response whenever some dimension of responding (usually rate) varies as a function of whether that stimulus is present or absent.

For practical purposes if a person wishes to strengthen a behavior, the goal may be achieved by identifying a stimulus that is usually followed by the desired behavior and presenting that cue on the occasions when the behavior is desired. If a person wishes to weaken a behavior, the goal may be achieved by presenting a stimulus that is rarely followed by the undesired behavior, by removing cues that are usually followed by the undesired behavior, or by presenting a stimulus that is usually followed by a response that is incompatible with the undesired behavior.

An example of applying stimulus control procedures to weight reduction would be as follows: Jane was a 20-year-old college student who wished to lose 20 pounds. During an initial evaluation she and her psychologist identified the cues that were most commonly associated with her eating: the visual presence of almost any food, being in the kitchen for any reason, watching television, reading, talking to friends, the hours from 5:00 P.M. on Friday through bedtime on Sunday, inactivity, boredom, and nervousness. She and her therapist developed a plan that Jane initiated.

Jane agreed to eat only when she was seated at a table specifically designed for eating: the kitchen table at home or a dining table in the university cafeteria. Except for talking to persons who were eating with her, she would engage in no other activities while eating (no watching television while eating). She would take only one serving per sitting and would leave some of each serving uneaten in order to weaken the association between the mere presence of food and eating. After she had eaten solid foods, she recorded the time of day and would not eat again until at least three and a half hours had passed. Finally, she was to stay out of the kitchen unless she was preparing or eating a meal, and all foods were to be stored out of sight. No candy, cookies, crackers, nuts, or other munchies would be purchased or displayed in open dishes on the counter.

All of these procedures were carried out by Jane, not the therapist. There were other elements in her total weight-control program, but the items listed are those that are appropriately classified as stimulus control procedures.

Stimulus control is particularly appropriate as an intervention for persons who clearly want to change their behavior. Even when a therapist is not sure of a client's motivation to change, stimulus control procedures should be tested before attempting more difficult, complex, or time-consuming interventions. When they fit a person's situation, stimulus control procedures are often the most efficient treatment available.

Verbal instructions are a common form of stimulus control. From this perspective the Bible can be conceived as a complex of God-given stimuli that can control human behavior.

P. W. CLEMENT

See CONDITIONING, OPERANT; LEARNING.

Stimulus Generalization. *See* GENERALIZATION.

Storytelling. *See* MUTUAL STORYTELLING TECHNIQUE.

Strategic Pastoral Counseling. Strategic pastoral counseling is a model of pastoral counseling developed to fit the role, resources, and needs of the typical pastor who counsels. Information about this typical pastor was identified by means of a survey of more than four hundred clergy, described in the initial volume introducing this approach (Benner, 1992). Since the publication of this book the model has been applied to the ten most commonly encountered counseling needs presented to clergy in a series of ten books for pastors and ten corresponding books for their counselees.

Strategic pastoral counseling can be described as short-term, bibliotherapeutic, wholistic, structured, spiritually focused, and explicitly Christian. Each of these characteristics will be briefly described, followed by a discussion of the three stages of the counseling process.

Counseling can be brief (that is, conducted over a relatively few sessions) or time-limited (that is, conducted within an initially fixed number of total sessions), or both. Strategic pastoral counseling is both brief and time-limited, working within a suggested maximum of five sessions. This number of sessions was established because 87% of the pastoral counseling conducted by pastors in general ministry involves five sessions or less. The model suggests that the five-session limit be communicated by the pastor no later than the first session. This ensures that the parishioner is aware of the time limit from the beginning and can share responsibility in keeping the counseling sessions focused.

Bibliotherapy refers to the therapeutic use of reading, and strategic pastoral counseling builds this into the heart of its approach to pastoral caregiving. The Bible itself is a rich bibliotherapeutic resource, and the encouragement of and direction in its reading is an important part of strategic pastoral counseling. Its use must be disciplined and selective, and particular care must be taken to ensure that it is never employed in a mechanical or impersonal manner. However, when it is used appropriately it can unquestionably be one of the most dynamic and powerful resources available to the pastor who counsels. Another unique bibliotherapeutic resource of this approach is the set of books specifically designed for strategic pastoral counselees.

Wholistic counseling is counseling that is responsive to the totality of the complex psychospiritual dynamics that make up the life of persons. Strategic pastoral counseling provides a framework for ensuring that pastoral care is responsive to the behavioral (action), cognitive (thought), and affective (feeling) elements of personal functioning. This provides much of structure for the counseling.

The structured nature of strategic pastoral counseling enables its brevity, the structure ensuring that each of the sessions has a clear focus and that each builds upon the previous ones in contributing toward the accomplishment of the overall goals. The structure grows out of the goal of addressing the feelings, thoughts, and behaviors that are a part of the troubling experiences of the person seeking help. This structure is described in more detail later.

The fourth distinctive of strategic pastoral counseling is that it is spiritually focused. This does not mean that only religious matters are discussed. Our spirituality is our essential heart commitments, our basic life direction, and our fundamental allegiances. Strategic pastoral counselors place a primacy on listening to this underlying spiritual story.

But just as it is important to not confuse spirituality with religiosity, it is equally important to not confuse Christian spirituality with any of its imitations. In this regard strategic pastoral counseling seeks to be distinctively and explicitly Christian. While the approach begins with a focus on spiritual matters understood broadly, its master goal is to facilitate the other person's awareness of and response to the call of God to surrender and service. This distinctively Christian focus is maintained through the utilization of Christian theological language and concepts and the resources of prayer, Scriptures, the sacraments, and congregational life. These resources represent powerful ways of bringing the one seeking help more closely in touch with God, who is the source of all growth and healing.

Stages and Tasks. The three overall stages that organize strategic pastoral counseling are encounter, engagement, and disengagement. The first stage, encounter, corresponds to the initial session, in which the goal is to establish a personal contact with the person seeking help, set the boundaries for the counseling relationship, become acquainted with the individual and his or her central concerns, conduct a pastoral diagnosis, and develop a mutually acceptable focus for the subsequent sessions. The second stage, engagement, involves the pastor moving beyond the first contact and establishing a deeper working alliance with the person seeking help. This normally occupies the next one to three sessions and entails the exploration of the person's feelings, thoughts, and behavioral patterns associated with this problem area and the development of new perspectives and strategies for coping or change. The third and final stage, disengagement, describes the focus of the last one or possibly two sessions, which involve an evaluation of progress and an assessment of remaining concerns, the making of a referral for further help if this is needed, and the ending of the counseling relationship.

The Encounter Stage. The first task in the initial stage of strategic pastoral counseling is joining and boundary setting. Joining involves making a connection with the counselee. This may occur automatically or it may require a few moments of conversation. Once it is established, the pastor should briefly communicate the purpose of the session and the time frame for it and any subsequent work together. This should not normally require more than a sentence or two.

The exploration of central concerns and relevant history usually begins with an invitation for the parishioner to describe what led him or her to seek help. After the pastor hears these immediate concerns, it is usually helpful to get a brief historical perspective on them and the person. The organiz-ing thread for this section of the first interview should be the presenting problem. These matters will not be the only ones discussed, but this focus serves to give the session the necessary direction.

Stripped of its distracting medical connotations, diagnosis is problem definition, a fundamental part of any approach to counseling. Diagnoses involve judgments about the nature of the problem, and either implicitly or explicitly pastoral counselors make such judgments every time they commence a counseling relationship. But in order for diagnoses to be relevant they must guide the counseling that will follow. This means that the categories of pastoral assessment must be primarily related to the spiritual focus, which is foundational to any counseling that is appropriately called pastoral. Thus the diagnosis that is called for in the first stage of strategic pastoral counseling involves an assessment of the person's spiritual well-being.

The framework for pastoral diagnosis adopted by strategic pastoral counseling is that suggested by Malony (1988) and used as the basis of his Religious Status Interview. Malony proposed that the diagnosis of Christian religious well-being should involve the assessment of the person's awareness of God, acceptance of God's grace, repentance and responsibility, response to God's leadership and direction, involvement in the church, experience of fellowship, ethics, and openness in the faith experience.

The final task of the encounter stage of strategic pastoral counseling is achieving a mutually agreeable focus for counseling. Often this is self-evident, made immediately clear by the first expression of the parishioner. At other times parishioners will report a wide range of concerns in the first session and will have to be asked what should constitute the primary problem focus. The identification of the primary problem focus leads naturally to a formulation of goals for the counseling.

The Engagement Stage. The second stage of strategic pastoral counseling involves the further engagement of the pastor and the one seeking help around the problems and concerns that brought them together. This is the heart of the counseling process. The major tasks of this stage are the exploration of the person's feelings, thoughts, and behavioral patterns associated with the central concerns and the development of new perspectives and strategies for coping or change.

It is important to note that the work of this stage may well begin in the first session. If the goals of the first stage are completed with time remaining in the first session, one can very appropriately begin to move into the tasks of this next stage. If the full five sessions of strategic pastoral counseling are employed, this second stage normally provides the structure for sessions two, three, and four.

The central foci for the three sessions normally associated with this stage are respectively the feelings, thoughts, and behaviors associated with the problem presented by the person seeking help. Although these are usually intertwined, a selective focus on each ensures that each is adequately addressed and that all the crucial dynamics of the person's psychospiritual functioning are considered.

The reason for beginning with feelings is that this is where most people themselves begin when they come to a counselor. But this does not mean that most people know their feelings. The exploration of feelings involves encouraging persons to face and express whatever it is that they are feeling, to the end that these feelings can be known and then dealt with appropriately. The goal at this point is to listen and respond empathically to the feelings of the one seeking help, not to try to change them.

After an exploration of the major feelings being experienced by the person seeking help, the next task is an exploration of the thoughts associated with these feelings and the development of alternative ways of understanding present experiences. It is in this phase of strategic pastoral counseling that the explicit use of Scriptures is usually most appropriate. Bearing in mind the potential misuses and problems that can be associated with such use of religious resources, the pastoral counselor should nonetheless be open to a direct presentation of scriptural truths when they offer the possibility of a new and helpful perspective on one's situation.

The final task of the engagement stage of strategic pastoral counseling grows directly out of this work on understanding and involves the exploration of the behavioral components of the person's functioning. The pastor explores what concrete things the person is doing in the face of the problems or distressing situations being encountered and, together with the parishioner, begins to identify changes in behavior that may be desirable. The goal of this stage is to identify changes that both pastor and parishioner agree are important and to begin to establish concrete strategies for making these changes.

The Disengagement Stage. The last session or two involves preparation for the termination of counseling and includes two specific tasks, the evaluation of progress and assessment of remaining concerns as well as making arrangements regarding a referral if needed.

The evaluation of progress is usually a process that both pastor and parishioner will find to be rewarding. Some of this may be done during previous sessions. But even when this is the case, it is a good idea to use the last session to undertake a brief review of what has been learned from the counseling. Closely associated with this is an identification of remaining concerns. Seldom is everything resolved after five sessions. This means that the parishioner is preparing to leave counseling with some work yet to be done. But he or she does so with plans for the future and the development of such plans is an important task of the disengagement stage of strategic pastoral counseling.

If significant problems remain at this point, the last couple of sessions should also be used to make referral arrangements. Ideally these should be discussed in the second or third session and they should by now be all arranged. It might even be wise if by this point the parishioner has an initial session with the person whom he or she will be seeing.

Because this approach to pastoral counseling is relatively new, no research on its effectiveness has yet been reported. However, many clergy report finding it to be a good match with their time availability, counseling skills, and overall pastoral responsibilities.

References

Benner, D. G. (1992). *Strategic pastoral counseling: A short-term structured model*. Grand Rapids, MI: Baker.
Malony, H. N. (1988). The clinical assessment of optimal religious functioning. *Review of Religious Research*, *30*, 3–17.

D. G. BENNER

See PASTORAL COUNSELING; SHORT-TERM THERAPIES.

Strategic Therapy. Strategic therapists assume that it is the therapist's responsibility "to plan a strategy for solving the client's problems" (Madanes, 1981, p. 19), which are embedded in interpersonal behavior sequences. They assume that a symptom "analogically, or metaphorically, expresses a problem and is also a solution," although perhaps an unsatisfactory one (Madanes, 1981, p. 21). They acknowledge as basis for so-called resistance the fundamental interpersonal and homeostatic principle that "when one person indicates a change in relation to another, the other will act upon the first so as to diminish and modify that change" (Haley, 1963, p. 189), and the fact that the one-down position of clients leads them to resent and defy the therapist (Papp, 1983). Strategic therapists aim to prevent repetitive [interpersonal behavior] sequences and to enhance "complexity and alternatives" (Madanes, 1981, p. 21) by providing clients with directives or prescriptions. Strategic techniques may presume either compliance or defiance on the part of the client: compliance-based strategies work either because clients find they cannot follow the directive or because compliance creates an ordeal; defiance-based strategies maximize "resistance" and rebellion (Rohrbaugh, Tennen, Press, & White, 1981). Strategic therapy is typically used with couples and families rather than with individuals.

The contemporary strategic therapies are rooted in the work of Milton Erickson (Haley, 1973), who applied strategic methods across the family life span. Currently there are at least five identifiable schools of strategic therapy; other strategic therapists borrow from one or more of these schools. The first chronologically is the brief therapy approach of the Mental Research Institute (MRI) in Palo Alto, California, which in some way influenced all the later schools. The MRI approach avoids historical exploration and emphasizes that the client's attempted solutions in the present often become the problem brought to the therapist. Such unsuccessful solutions include the paradoxical demand for deliberately spontaneous action; the search for no-risk living; striving for accord through opposition; and confirming an accuser's suspicions by defending oneself (Fisch, Weakland, & Segal, 1982). Distinctive MRI techniques include the "Devil's pact," in which the client agrees in advance to do whatever is prescribed; "advertising instead of concealing," which diverts attention from the anxiety-provoking problem; symptom prescription (simple therapeutic paradox); the intentional design of self-fulfilling prophecies in a family interaction; the "reframing of incomprehensible behavior" to provide a new perspective; the "undermining of an existing suspicion by the planting of another and more desirable suspicion" (Bodin, in Gurman & Kniskern, 1981, pp. 297–298); and "benevolent sabotage," or feigned therapeutic incompetence.

A second strategic approach, which is more sensitive to family history, was developed at the Institute for Family Study in Milan. The original work of Selvini Palazzoli (1978) with the families of anorexics was followed by a team approach to schizophrenic families that focused on the relational paradoxes common in these families and how these paradoxes "can only be undone by counterparadoxes in the context of therapy" (Selvini Palazzoli, Cecchin, Prata, & Boscolo, 1978, p. 8). Distinctives of this approach include circular questioning, an interviewing method that poses "questions that are constantly making connections among actions, beliefs, and relationships of individuals within the system" (Campbell, Draper, & Crutchley, in Gurman & Kniskern, 1991, p. 346); hypothesizing, an assessment procedure that regards "therapy as a research operation engaged in conjointly with the family" (Boscolo, Cecchin, Hoffman, & Penn, 1987, p. 10); neutrality, a therapeutic attitude that leaves family members wondering whose side the therapist is on; the technique of positive connotation, which approves and confirms "the homeostatic behavior of all the members of the family" (Selvini Palazzoli, Cecchin, Prata, & Boscolo, 1978, p. 58) and their underlying intentions, thereby putting family members who are demanding change into a pragmatic paradox (p. 61); the prescription of family rituals in which every detail is designed to change the system; long intervals between sessions, which are bridged by written prescriptions.

The Milan group eventually split into two groups. The Milan Associates, Boscolo and Cecchin, illustrate an ecosystemic epistemology (Keeney, 1983): they ask how problem behaviors serve the family's meaning system, its "shared premise, value, or myth" (Boscolo, Cecchin, Hoffman, & Penn, 1987, p. 16); construct a "logical" rather than a "positive" connotation for the problem's function; and prescribe rituals that "explode" double-binding communications or put "the interaction bind, consisting of simultaneous, conflicting directives, into a sequence" (p. 16). Selvini Palazzoli and Prata shifted from the original strategic model to one that used invariant prescriptions and later to a "general model for psychotic processes occurring in families" (Campbell, Draper, & Crutchley, in Gurman & Kniskern, 1991, p. 330).

A third strategic approach was developed at the Institute of Family Therapy in Rome. Andolfi (1979) described a set of restructuring tasks that resemble closely the techniques of the MRI group, combined with structural family therapy; a set of paradoxical tasks that include prescribing the symptom and prescribing the rules; and metaphorical tasks that function by bringing about changes in behaviors that are analogous to the symptom. Andolfi, Angelo, Menghi, and Nicolò-Corigliano (1983) focus on the redefinition of the therapeutic relationship, the context, and the problem; on provocation as a therapeutic intervention; and on strategic denial as homeostatic reinforcement.

A fourth strategic approach was developed at the Ackerman Institute for Family Therapy. This group emphasizes that strategic therapy is warranted only for treatment-resistant families, those who have been unable to benefit from direct, compliance-based interventions such as advice, suggestions, interpretations, and tasks to be interpreted literally. These are replaced by defiance-based interventions such as paradoxical prescriptions and interventions that combine compliance and defiance, such as the reversal, "an intervention in which the therapist directs one family member to reverse his/her attitude or behavior around a crucial issue in the hope it will elicit a paradoxical response from another family member" (Papp, 1983, p. 37). The Ackerman group "classically uses a consultation team behind a two-way mirror as a Greek chorus that can offer support, disagree with the interviewer, express surprise and confusion, and form therapeutic triangles with family coalitions" (Hoffman, 1981, p. 29). They also make frequent use of family choreography (Papp, 1983) and of therapeutic metaphors and rituals (Bergman, 1985).

A fifth strategic school is found at the Washington Family Therapy Institute founded by Haley and Madanes. Haley is well known for his identification of classic therapeutic paradoxes (1963), his insistence that all therapy is manipulative (1963, 1976), his emphasis on hierarchy and power in the family (1976, 1980), and the prescription of therapeutic ordeals (1984). Madanes (1981) adds to the strategic armamentarium the playful pretend technique, which is not confrontational and does not rely on rebellion.

Strategic therapy is the focus of frequent ethical critique because it embraces "a managerial, contractual approach to therapeutic relationships" (Doherty & Boss, in Gurman & Kniskern, 1991, p. 614).

References

Andolfi, M. (1979). *Family therapy: An interactional approach.* (H. R. Cassin, Trans.). New York: Plenum.

Andolfi, M., Angelo, C., Menghi, P., & Nicolò-Corigliano, M. (1983). *Behind the family mask.* (C. L. Chodorkoff, Trans.). New York: Brunner/Mazel.

Bergman, J. S. (1985). *Fishing for barracuda.* New York: Norton.

Boscolo, L., Cecchin, G., Hoffman, L., & Penn, P. (1987). *Milan systemic family therapy.* New York: Basic Books.

Fisch, R., Weakland, J. J., & Segal, L. (1982). *The tactics of change: Doing therapy briefly.* San Francisco: Jossey-Bass.

Gurman, A. S., & Kniskern, D. P. (Eds.). (1981). *Handbook of family therapy.* New York: Brunner/Mazel.

Gurman, A. S., & Kniskern, D. P. (Eds.). (1991). *Handbook of family therapy, Vol. II.* New York: Brunner/Mazel.

Haley, J. (1963). *Strategies of psychotherapy.* New York: Grune & Stratton.

Haley, J. (1973). *Uncommon therapy: The psychiatric techniques of Milton H. Erickson, M.D.* New York: Norton.

Haley, J. (1976). *Problem-solving therapy.* San Francisco: Jossey-Bass.

Haley, J. (1980). *Leaving home.* New York: McGraw-Hill.

Haley, J. (1984). *Ordeal therapy.* New York: Jossey-Bass.

Hoffman, L. (1981). *Foundations of family therapy.* New York: Basic Books.

Keeney, B. (1983). *Aesthetics of change.* New York: Guilford.

Madanes, C. (1981). *Strategic family therapy.* New York: Jossey-Bass.

Papp, P. (1983). *The process of change.* New York: Guilford.

Rohrbaugh, M., Tennen, H., Press, S., & White, L. (1981). Compliance, defiance and therapeutic paradox: Guidelines for strategic use of paradoxical interventions. *American Journal of Orthopsychiatry, 51,* 454–467.

Selvini Palazzoli, M. (1978). *Self-starvation.* (A. Pomerans, Trans.). New York: Aronson.

Selvini Palazzoli, M., Cecchin, G., Prata, G., & Boscolo, L. (1978). *Paradox and counterparadox.* (E. V. Burt, Trans.). New York: Aronson.

H. Vande Kemp

See Short-Term Therapies; Family Communications Theory; Paradoxical Intervention.

Street Drugs. The use of drugs in the United States is widespread. We take drugs—chemical substances that affect physiological functions, mood, perception, and consciousness—to increase alertness, lose weight, eliminate pain, ease tension, fight depression, and prevent pregnancy. The typical American family has about 30 different drugs in its medicine cabinet. Physicians write about 1.5 billion prescriptions per year. More than 80% of Americans frequently consume caffeine, two-thirds of adults drink alcohol, and one-third of adults smoke regularly. Although the use of some of these drugs contributes to a number of personal and social problems, they are both legal and socially acceptable. The United States has declared other drugs—marijuana, cocaine, heroin, amphetamines, barbiturates, and hallucinogens—to be illegal because their use is thought to produce self-destructive, antisocial behavior. They are considered harmful in part because people frequently become addicted to them; habitual users develop a physical or psychological dependence on a drug that makes it very hard for them to stop taking it.

Since Ronald Reagan declared war on illegal drug traffic in the 1980s, reducing the supply and consumption of these drugs has been a major priority of the federal government. Despite the nation's growing alarm about street drugs, the use of illegal drugs has declined from a peak of 14% of Americans in 1979 to less than 6% by the mid-1990s. Nevertheless, despite spending billions of dollars to win this war and arresting millions of citizens for selling or possessing drugs, the United States has been unable to reduce the total volume of illegal drugs or to stem the tide of drug-related crime in its cities.

Types of Drugs. Marijuana is the most widely used illegal drug in the United States. It is popular in social settings because, like alcohol, it is thought to ease or enhance interaction. Extensively used since the 1960s, when many young people smoked marijuana (reefers) as an act of rebellion against the values of the middle-class society, it is today used by about 5% of Americans, mostly between 18 and 25. While researchers and policymakers have hotly debated marijuana's effects, the consensus is that it has few negative long-term consequences and does not lead to the use of stronger drugs. However, prolonged smoking of marijuana can cause cancer and other lung problems as well as harm a woman's unborn baby. Most users experience feelings of relaxation, well-being, distortion of time and distance, hunger, and eventual drowsiness. Because a marijuana high slows reaction time and impairs coordination, it can contribute to automobile accidents.

Heroin is the most frequently abused member of the opiate family, which includes opium, codeine, and morphine. These depressant drugs are highly addictive. Users quickly develop a tolerance for them and must continually use more of these drugs to achieve the same results. Withdrawal is very difficult because it usually involves nausea, chills, cramps, diarrhea, excessive sweating, and rapid weight loss. Heroin is popular because it produces feelings of elevated self-esteem, peacefulness, and euphoria, although only about 1 of every 1,000 adult Americans uses it regularly. This may be in part because heroin often costs users as much as $100 per day. More than 50% of the nation's heroin addicts live in New York, Los Angeles, and Chicago.

Cocaine, a drug derived from the leaves of the coca plant, has hooked millions of new users who are enthralled by the sense of alertness, power, and euphoria it provides. Sigmund Freud advocated its use as an antidepressant that increased energy and creativity, and many athletes and artists have taken the drug to enhance their performance. Usually snorted through the nasal passage, cocaine has been labeled the rich person's drug because of its high cost. Since the mid-1980s, however, crack, a much cheaper form of cocaine that is smoked and produces an instant and very powerful but short-lived rush, has been popular among the underclass. Tragically, in some poor communities many sickly, low-weight crack babies are being born with cocaine addictions formed in utero. Infrequent users of cocaine are often irritable and depressed after the drug wears off. Many daily users experience sleeplessness, loss of appetite, hallucinations, and a paranoid psychoses. Those addicted to the drug tend to have short attention spans, extreme mood swings, and low levels of productivity at work.

Amphetamines are a family of stimulant drugs that include benzedrine, dexedrine, and methedrine. These uppers are legal when they are prescribed by physicians and are used by many dieters and people who want to stay awake. Moderate doses of amphetamines such as speed may produce alertness and excitement, but this is usually followed by feelings of irritability and tension, insomnia, and even loss of reflective judgment. Repeated use of amphetamines may produce speech disturbances, brain damage, depression, and long-term personality disorders.

Barbiturates, which are typically used to enhance the effects of other drugs, depress the central nervous system. Prolonged usage can cause physical dependence, with symptoms similar to those of heroin addiction. An overdose of barbiturates, especially quaaludes, can cause convulsions, coma, and sometimes death.

LSD, mescaline, and other psychedelic drugs are called hallucinogens because when they are taken in large doses they produce hallucinations as well as sweeping psychological changes, including significant alterations in emotion, perception, and thought. LSD, the best-known hallucinogen, became popular with the counterculture of the 1960s and in the 1990s is widely used by affluent suburban teenagers. A small dose of this colorless, tasteless drug, usually licked from the back of a stamp, has profound results. An acid trip, which some users describe as intensely beautiful and others as incredibly frightening, scrambles the nervous impulses so that colors become kaleidoscopic, music becomes confused with smell, and objects appear to expand and contract. Large doses of hallucinogens, especially the very dangerous PCP (angel dust), can lead to panic attacks, nightmares, assaultive behavior, seizures, coma, and psychosis.

Theories of Why People Use Drugs. Researchers advance a number of theories to explain why people use drugs. From studies of identical twins, some researchers hypothesize that certain individuals have a genetic predisposition toward the use of particular drugs. It is clear, however, that the use of drugs is a learned behavior that is more prevalent in some societies, at certain historical periods, and among particular social groups. Other theorists consequently prefer psychological and sociological explanations for patterns of drug use. Behaviorists contend that people first take drugs because they provide a reward (pleasure, escape from stress) and continue to use them because withdrawal is unpleasant and painful. Convinced that personality characteristics are an important determinant in drug abuse and addiction, psychologists have classified addicts as narcissists, psychopaths, sociopaths, dependent personalities, schizophrenics, neurotics, and character-disordered individuals. While no consensus exists among psychologists, the most common theory is that drug addicts have weak personalities and low self-esteem and use drugs to try to escape their problems. These traits are typically thought to emerge as a result of having been overindulged or frustrated and not given clear behavioral standards during childhood. It is simplistic to assume that only certain personality types develop drug problems, but personality plays a significant role in an individual's decision to use a drug. Social psychologists argue that drug use, like other behaviors, is learned by interaction with other people. While the dominant culture encourages negative attitudes toward drug use, many people learn to use drugs by modeling the behavior of their parents, friends, or business associates. By interacting with people who take drugs, individuals develop a value system that defines drug use in a positive fashion. Other theorists contend that drug use is connected with a variety of social factors. Some people turn to drugs because they have difficulty fulfilling all their role obligations. Others do so because they cannot cope with the pressures of a society that so strongly emphasizes individual achievement. Rapid social change encourages drug use by making people confused about social norms and contributing to feelings of alienation, isolation, and misery.

Problems Associated with Drug Use. In addition to the physical, emotional, and mental problems drug use causes individuals, it also causes or contributes to many economic and social problems in America. The use of illegal drugs presently costs the United States as much as $100 billion dollars a year because of absenteeism from work, reduced productivity, the control and treatment of drug abuse, welfare funds to support unemployed drug abusers, and the expense of processing drug users through the criminal justice system. Drug use is highly correlated with other forms of crime, especially shoplifting, burglaries, muggings, and prostitution, which are often committed to provide money to buy drugs, as well as with poverty, unemployment, spouse and child abuse, marital instability, and divorce. AIDS is spreading among America's heterosexual population primarily through the sharing of needles and syringes by intravenous drug users. The drug traffic in many inner cities has led to many murders. It has supplied immense revenue for organized crime and has stimulated the rise of new crime syndicates among various ethnic communities.

Reducing Drug Abuse. Social scientists and policymakers argue over whether prevention, treatment, increased law enforcement, or greater social tolerance is the best way to deal with America's drug problems. Many insist that efforts to decrease drug use should focus on discouraging youth from trying drugs, but they disagree sharply about how to achieve this aim. Most experts contend that educational programs that present factual information about drugs are more effective than those that try to frighten youth by stressing the perils of use. Critics warn that drug education classes in the schools stimulate some teenagers to experiment with drugs. Debate also rages over whether prevention programs should stress total abstinence or moderate use of drugs, which many researchers claim does not usually cause serious psychological or physical problems.

A number of different treatment programs have been developed to enable addicts to stop using drugs. Individual psychotherapy has not been successful in helping people give up their use of drugs; strong social support usually is necessary for people to kick the habit. Aversive therapy, which associates the effects of a drug with an unpleasant sensation, has worked to discourage smoking but has rarely been effective with other drugs. Many hospital-based chemical dependence programs, based upon the same general principles as Alcoholics Anonymous (AA), opened during the 1980s, but they declined rapidly during the early 1990s largely because insurance companies refused to pay for such expensive treatment. Following the model developed by Synanon, founded in 1958, therapeutic communities, most notably Phoenix House, have been created to help addicts deal with their psychological and physical problems, accept responsibility for their own actions, and support one another in the recovery process.

Legal efforts to reduce drug use have focused on interdiction and prosecution. The United States has urged the governments of nations (primarily in Latin America) that supply drugs to America to increase their efforts to apprehend drug dealers. The federal government employs thousands of agents who work to stop the flow of drugs into America or to prevent the production and sale of drugs in the nation. Millions of Americans are arrested each year for drug offenses, more than 300,000 are in prison as a result, and the total cost of the nation's enforcement efforts is more than $20 billion a year. Critics object that these policies make drugs more expensive, thus encouraging more dealers to enter the trade, and that the methods of enforcement (wiretaps, undercover agents) pose a serious threat to civil liberties.

As a result some social scientists and politicians advocate increased social tolerance of drug use, with their proposals ranging from reduced penalties for some types of drug offenses to full legalization of all drugs. Proponents contend that this approach would remove the profit from drug distribution, make drugs less attractive as forbidden fruit, curb the power of organized crime, undermine drug cultures, remove some of the stigma from drug use, permit adults to choose their own behaviors, and probably reduce the amount of drug use in America. They argue further that this approach would be more compassionate because it would allow for the creation of more maintenance programs (the only legal one at present dispenses methadone to about 125,000 heroin addicts) to supply drugs to habitual users or addicts.

The extensive use of drugs in the United States testifies to the deep dissatisfaction many Americans feel with their lives. Because social conditions such as inadequate education, unemployment, discrimination, and poverty contribute to personal malaise, Christians must work to remedy these problems, whether they have structural or personal sources. At the same time, belief that only a personal relationship with Jesus Christ provides salvation from sin and power for living compels Christians to proclaim and embody the gospel as the principal means of helping those enslaved to drugs as well as those who feel tempted to try them. Denominations and congregations, however, also need to develop specific programs directed by distinctly biblical presuppositions and based primarily on the principles of group support to discourage youth from using drugs and to help users of all kinds, including addicts, cease their self-destructive and socially detrimental behavior.

Additional Readings

Goode, E. (1993). *Drugs in American society.* New York: McGraw-Hill.

Inciardi, J. A. (1992). *The war on drugs II: The continuing epic of heroin, cocaine, crack, crime, AIDS, and public policy.* Mountain View, CA: Mayfield.

Inciardi, J. A., & McElrath, K. (Eds.). (1995). *The American drug scene: An anthology.* Los Angeles: Roxbury.

Oakley, R., & Ksir, C. (1992). *Drugs, society, and human behavior.* St. Louis: Times-Mirror/Mosby.

G. S. SMITH

See SUBSTANCE-USE DISORDERS; PSYCHOPHARMACOLOGY; BRAIN AND HUMAN BEHAVIOR.

Street People. The United States has long had groups such as hobos and unemployed migrants for whom homelessness was either a preferred lifestyle or a temporary condition. In recent years, however, the number and variety of men, women, and children living on the streets of America's cities has grown substantially. Authorities disagree about the number of homeless people in the United States, with estimates ranging from 300,000 to 3,000,000. As many as 7,000,000 Americans may have experienced prolonged periods of homelessness during the first half of the 1990s. More than one-half of the nation's street people are African-Americans, about a quarter are European-Americans, and about one-seventh are Latinos. For a long time most of those living on the streets were single men; today about 50% of the homeless are families. Investigators believe that almost half of the homeless have some kind of a drug or alcohol problem.

People live on the streets for a variety of reasons. Some teenagers are put out of their homes by their parents; others run away. Some adults have been evicted by landlords because they failed to pay their rent; others lost their homes because of floods or fires. Some of the homeless lost jobs because of technological change; others have never developed job skills. Some of those living on the streets are too old or too infirm to work; others are demoralized because of a personal tragedy. Some people have small pensions that enable them to stay at cheap rooming houses part of each month but sleep on the streets when their funds run out. While most Americans who live on the streets do so because they have no other options, some choose to do so because it offers adventure, danger, and excitement.

Homeless people face a variety of problems. They are exposed to the heat of summer, the cold of winter, and all forms of precipitation. Finding enough food to eat is a continual struggle. Without jobs, insurance, or welfare payments (typically one must have an address to be eligible for welfare), they root through garbage for food, beg, do odd jobs, and collect aluminum cans in an effort to survive. Because they live on the streets, sleeping on park benches, on top of heating grates, in cardboard boxes in back alleys, or in abandoned cars, they are often victims of crime. They consequently suffer from a number of physical ailments and often receive inadequate medical attention. An estimated 15% of shelter residents are infected with the AIDS virus. Perhaps the greatest problem the homeless encounter, however, is that society seems to be largely unconcerned with their plight.

Several explanations are frequently offered for the recent rise in homelessness. The most popular one is the release from state mental hospitals during the 1960s and 1970s of large numbers of chronically disturbed patients who were not dangerous to themselves or others. This policy, aimed at enabling these people to live more normal lives in the community, supported by community mental health programs and aided by psychotropic drugs that greatly reduced their disruptive behavior, has allegedly produced a large population of severely disturbed people who wander the streets. Researchers estimate that about 30% of the homeless have mental problems. Mental illness, however, is frequently a consequence of instead of a factor producing homelessness. Those who lose their homes suffer severe stress as a result of hunger, lack of sleep, physical ailments, and feeling disorganized, depressed, and overwhelmed by fear. Other commonly cited causes of homelessness are the major reduction in the amount of federal monies spent on subsidized housing programs, the return of the affluent to certain central city neighborhoods (which displaces the poor), urban renewal, sharp increases in the cost of rental housing, the demolition of single-room

occupancy hotels and cheap rooming houses or their conversion into condominiums, and low-paying, dead-end jobs that do not give people sufficient income to pay for housing. Approximately one in five of those who live on the streets have a full-time or a part-time job but still cannot afford a place to live. Homelessness usually results from a long series of crises and a gradual process of disengagement from supportive relationships (family and friends) and institutions.

Some programs have been created to help those without homes. The National Coalition for the Homeless has worked since its founding in 1982 to collect and disseminate information, to conduct studies, and to pursue various legislative and judicial means to reduce homelessness. City governments and private organizations operate soup kitchens to provide meals for the homeless and shelters to provide them with a temporary place to sleep. Christian congregations have played a leading role in these activities. Habitat for Humanity, a nonprofit Christian ministry, has enlisted hundreds of thousands of volunteers to build or renovate homes for those without adequate accommodations. In light of God's great concern for the poor as it is evidenced in the Old and New Testament teachings, the gleaning laws and other provisions designed to help sojourners and the dispossessed in ancient Israel, and the policies of the first-century church, Christians should expand their efforts to aid the homeless. In addition to insuring that they receive adequate food, shelter, clothing, and medical attention, Christians need to help the homeless overcome their dependence on drugs and alcohol, improve their interpersonal relationships, strengthen their family life, receive counseling to deal with psychological, emotional, and spiritual problems, gain job training, find meaningful employment, and boost their self-esteem. This can be accomplished only if Christians make assisting the homeless a high priority and seek to change the institutional discrimination, poor schools, lack of decent jobs, and other social factors that keep some people mired in the underclass.

Other remedies have been suggested to help the homeless. Some people argue that churches and private charities do not have sufficient resources to deal with the problems of those without homes and therefore the federal government must take a greater initiative by creating more job training programs, providing work projects, increasing food assistance programs, and furnishing free housing. Some experts contend that the homeless who are mentally ill or children should be cared for in institutions. Others object that the government's current financial problems, coupled with the inefficiency and waste typically involved in government programs, make it impossible for the government to effectively assist the homeless.

Additional Readings

Blau, J. (1992). *The visible poor: Homelessness in the United States*. New York: Oxford University Press.

Howe, M., & Young, J. (1986). *The faces of homelessness*. Lexington, MA: Heath.

Jencks, C. (1994). *Homelessness*. Cambridge, MA: Harvard University Press.

Wright, J. D. (1988). The mentally ill homeless: What is myth and what is fact? *Social Problems, 35,* 182–191.

G. S. SMITH

Stress. It is ironic that as new technological conveniences have proliferated, stress has become an increasingly commonplace experience. This is less paradoxical, however, in light of current information-processing demands and increasing societal pluralism. With every new convenience come new choices, further complicating decision making. Communications constantly barrage individuals with multimedia exposure to stressors around the globe. Pluralism removes absolutes and frowns on generalizing, rendering each moral choice a novel situation without reference points. Thus it is not surprising that a vast research literature on stress, addressing a variety of perspectives, has accumulated since the 1950s.

Selye (1946, 1956) is typically credited with the first formal research on human stress, although his work focused on physiological responses (e.g., increased adrenaline output) to physical stressors (e.g., wounds). He based his research on the principle of homeostasis, the tendency for physiological systems (e.g., humans, animals) to respond to external disruptions with maintained internal balance via an orchestrated response of the subsystems. He demonstrated that physiological systems defensively reacted to noxious stimuli with a sequence of three responses: alert, resistance, and exhaustion when the first two responses fail. He called this sequence the general adaptation syndrome because he observed it as frequent and commonplace in living organisms.

A more psychological focus on stress was presented by Lindemann (1944) and Caplan (1964). Lindemann studied grief reactions of survivors and of families of those who were killed in the tragic Coconut Grove fire in Boston. He concluded that stressful life circumstances were at least as important in predicting human functioning as the individuals' characteristics (e.g., personality traits). He further proposed that clergy and other caretakers could facilitate healthy grief resolution.

Extending Lindemann's study of grief, Caplan (1964) developed crisis theory, a formal conceptual model for understanding stress reactions to crises in general. He proposed four phases. First, the individual confronted by perceived threat and increased tension attempts to restore psychological homeostasis with habitual problem-solving responses. Second, when these attempts fail, tension increases in the face of continued threat and the individual begins to feel ineffective and distressed. Third, distress further increases tension, habitual problem-solving responses are abandoned, and random, novel trial-and-error responses are enacted. If these are successful, homeostasis is restored and the individual may report personal growth. If they are not, major decompensation, the fourth phase, ensues, producing drastic effects (e.g., major psychopathology). Caplan's seminal work provided the foundation for current crisis intervention techniques.

Holmes and Raye (1967) focused on life events in defining stress. Using their Social Readjustment Rating Scale (SRRS) and Schedule of Recent Experiences (SRE), they empirically demonstrated that the cumulative effects of readjustment in response to life events are related to susceptibility to illness. They proposed that the amount of readjustment required by events, whether positive or negative, was crucial in predicting adjustment. Research since then has shown, however, that only those stressful events perceived as negative are crucial in predicting maladjustment (Cohen, 1988).

The correlation between stressful life events and maladjustment has been repeatedly demonstrated but is not strong, leading researchers to examine potential moderators of this relationship, such as coping skills. For example, a person with effective coping skills might successfully resolve a stressful situation with little distress, whereas an individual facing the same event with poor coping skills might experience crisis and decompensation. One theoretical model considering life events, coping, and adjustment was developed by Lazarus and his colleagues (e.g., Lazarus & Launier, 1978; Lazarus & Folkman, 1984; Lazarus, 1991). They propose an ongoing transaction between person and environment as the source of stress. They define stress as occurring when one comes to view one's transaction with the environment as involving threat, harm or loss, or challenge that strains personal resources. This perceptive process is labeled appraisal, and stress vulnerability is dependent upon it. Whereas negative life events and poor coping skills have often been cited as links to stress, this model attributes a more foundational role to appraisal. By definition, a life event is negative only when appraised as such; and unless an event is appraised as stressful, coping does not even begin.

Appraisal involves three phases (Lazarus & Folkman, 1984). In primary appraisal, the individual evaluates the extent to which an event is irrelevant, harmless, positive, or stressful. Stressful events are further appraised as potentially harmful (threatening), actually harmful (i.e., involving harm or loss), or potentially beneficial (challenging). When events are viewed as stressful, secondary appraisal follows, whereby adequacy of personal coping resources is assessed. Within this framework, distress is directly dependent upon these appraisals.

Lazarus and Folkman (1984) note that individual characteristics of the person also affect appraisal. For example, to the extent that one views a circumstance as important (resulting in more personal investment in outcome), stress will increase. Thus, a person who derives significant self-esteem from athletic prowess will experience more stress in athletic competitive events than someone less invested. Similarly, a perfectionistic individual will typically be more stressed (due to unrealistic expectations) than is someone willing to accept valid personal limitations. Personal beliefs are another relevant person factor. For example, Caucasian Protestants who strongly believe that God is in control of outcomes have been found to experience less depression in the face of negative life events than do those not holding such beliefs (Bjorck, Lee, & Cohen, 1997).

Situational factors such as event imminence, predictability, and probability can affect appraisal (Paterson & Neufeld, 1987). For example, the stress of an anticipated exam generally increases the closer one gets to taking it. Likewise, a predictable event can be less stressful than an unpredictable one because it is possible to prepare for it.

Successful stress interventions are primarily cognitive-behavioral, such as stress inoculation training (Meichenbaum, 1996), biofeedback, stress management programs, and relaxation training. All such techniques acknowledge, either tacitly or directly, that stress can be reduced by replacing maladaptive appraisals with adaptive ones. This coincides with the biblical exhortation to be transformed by the renewing of the mind (Rom. 12:2). Such techniques also encourage the realistic acceptance of healthy limits rather than attempts to maintain unrealistic levels of personal control (Bjorck, 1995). A biblical perspective can augment this significantly through the understanding that God is always completely in control and requests that Christians cast their anxieties upon him (1 Peter 5:7). Indeed, a deepening understanding of God's competence, together with an acceptance of human limits, can be foundational in reducing stress in the midst of modern society.

References

Bjorck, J. P. (1995). A self-centered perspective on McIntosh's religious schema. *International Journal for the Psychology of Religion, 5,* 23–29.

Bjorck, J. P., Lee, Y. S., & Cohen, L. H. (1997). Manuscript submitted for publication.

Caplan, G. (1964). *Principles of preventive psychiatry.* New York: Basic Books.

Cohen, L. (1988). Measurement of life events. In L. Cohen (Ed.), *Life events and psychological functioning: Theoretical and methodological issues.* Newbury Park, CA: Sage.

Holmes, T. H., & Raye, R. H. (1967). The social readjustment rating scale. *Journal of Psychosomatic Research, 11,* 213–218.

Lazarus, R. S. (1991). *Emotion and adaptation.* New York: Oxford University Press.

Lazarus, R. S., & Folkman, S. (1984). *Stress, appraisal, and coping.* New York: Springer.

Lazarus, R. S., & Launier, R. (1978). Stress-related transactions between person and environment. In L. A. Pervin & M. Lewis (Eds.), *Perspectives in interactional psychology.* New York: Plenum.

Lindemann, E. (1944). Symptomology and management of acute grief. *American Journal of Psychiatry, 101,* 141–148.

Meichenbaum, D. (1996). Stress inoculation training for coping with stressors. *The Clinical Psychologist, 49,* 4–7.

Paterson, R., & Neufeld, R. (1987). Clear danger: Situational determinants of the appraisal of threat. *Psychological Bulletin, 101,* 404–416.

Selye, H. (1946). The general adaptation syndrome and the diseases of adaptation. *Journal of Clinical Endocrinology, 6,* 117–230.

Selye, H. (1956). *The stress of life.* New York: McGraw-Hill.

J. P. BJORCK

See RELAXATION TRAINING; COPING SKILLS THERAPIES; HEALTH PSYCHOLOGY.

Stress Disorders. *See* ACUTE STRESS DISORDER; POSTTRAUMATIC STRESS DISORDER.

Stress Inoculation. *See* COPING SKILLS THERAPIES.

Strong, Edward Kellogg, Jr. (1884–1963). Author of the Strong-Campbell Interest Inventory. He was born in Syracuse, New York, the son of a Presbyterian minister. He received his M.S. from the University of California at Berkeley in 1909 and his Ph.D. from Columbia University in 1911. After postdoctoral research at Columbia, military service, and teaching at Carnegie Institute of Technology, Strong went to Stanford University in 1923 and remained there for the rest of his career.

Although he was interested in advertising and marketing, Strong's major contribution was in the study of vocational interests. He published the Strong Vocational Interest Blank in 1927 and revised it in 1938. It has undergone several more revisions. The test does not predict success in an occupation; it only compares a person's interests with those of people in that occupation.

Strong was the author of *Vocational Interests of Men and Women* (1943), *Vocational Interests Eighteen Years after College* (1955), and many articles on vocational interest.

R. L. KOTESKEY

See INTEREST MEASUREMENT; VOCATIONAL COUNSELING.

Strong-Campbell Interest Inventory. Widely acclaimed as the bellwether of career counseling and personnel selection, this test identifies an individual's interests and value patterns in order to provide an occupational orientation. Its authors, Edward Kellogg Strong, Jr., and David P. Campbell, asserted that these patterns, when compared to those in representative vocations, would predict job satisfaction, depending on how carefully they matched. The test has been in use for more than half a century, has gone through several revisions, and has been the object of several thousand research investigations. Millions of copies of the measure have been sold, and it has launched and sustained many careers.

The test is a paper-and-pencil inventory that usually takes about 30 minutes to complete. It is machine scored and interpreted by any one of several computer services for a fee. The current form of the test is a merging of the earlier Strong Vocational Interest Blanks for men and women. The test consists of 325 items that are checked "like," "dislike," or "indifferent." These items are constructed on six occupational themes, and scores on these clusters indicate the examinee's orientation toward realistic, investigative, artistic, social, enterprising, and conventional values. The responses are then analyzed for overall interest trends, degree of consistency of 23 basic interest areas, and degree of similarity to persons in a wide range of vocational pursuits.

The test asks the examinee to respond to a listing of more than 100 occupations, express interest in more than 50 behavioral activities and 39 amusements, and express preferences between 30 pairs of activities and 15 personal characteristics. Obviously such data can be valuable for course or career selection, employee counseling, personnel selection, research purposes, or assessing the many factors that influence decision making.

Many counselors believe the Strong-Campbell Interest Inventory to be the best vocational interest inventory available. It should not be interpreted in a rigid psychometric manner, but it should be used to generate hypotheses with regard to vocational issues. These should then be explored in depth both in the context of the counseling relationship and in the community. The test should never be used apart from more extensive psychological assessment that will help the person make the best possible decision with the data available. In addition, the Christian counselor ought to give careful thought to the perceived gifts and talents of the individual and the pressing needs of the community in making any recommendations about vocation, calling, or ministry. Multiple sources of feedback are likely to prove most helpful to the individual in making such difficult and important decisions. The Strong-Campbell Interest Inventory can be one useful source of such feedback.

R. E. BUTMAN

See VOCATIONAL COUNSELING; INTEREST MEASUREMENT.

Structural Analysis. The method used by transactional analysis to understand what is happening within the individual.

First-order structural analysis initially involves reflection on the gestures, words, and postures of the individual to ascertain whether the person is acting from within the judgmental (parent), the rational (adult), or the uninhibited (child) part of his or her personality. These are termed ego states and refer to conscious or preconscious sets of attitudes and feelings. More refined analyses include assessing which part of the parent (nurturing or controlling) and of the child (adapted or free) are dominant at a given moment.

Second-order structural analysis involves exploring the inner drama resulting from the dynamic interaction among the ego states as they vie for power in the individual as well as reflecting on the parental and situational influences that have determined the special character of the ego states within the person.

These types of analyses are undertaken in transactional analysis therapy in efforts to increase insight and self-understanding toward the end that the client may make enlightened decisions to change.

H. N. MALONY

See TRANSACTIONAL ANALYSIS.

Structural Family Therapy. Structural family therapy was developed by Salvador Minuchin and his colleagues at the Wiltwyck School for Boys, treating the underorganized families of juvenile delinquents (Minuchin, Montalvo, Guerney, Rosman, & Schumer, 1967), and at the Philadelphia Child Guidance Clinic, extending the focus to overorganized psychosomatic families (Minuchin, Rosman, & Baker, 1978). Regarded as highly culture-sensitive, structural family therapy reflects the rich ethnic history of its founder: the child of Russian Jews who immigrated to Argentina, Minuchin was jailed as an anti-Peronist revolutionary; he fought in the Israeli war for independence, then was a physician to a multilingual Israeli army regiment; in New York he developed a therapeutic milieu at a residential treatment center for children; in Israel he directed residential institutions for displaced children of the Holocaust and participated in kibbutz life; he studied interpersonal psychoanalysis at the William Alanson White Institute (Minuchin & Nichols, 1993). It was natural for Minuchin and his many ethnic minority colleagues to give cultural context a central role in human behavior.

Structural family therapy emphasizes that the unit of treatment, whether an individual, couple, nuclear or extended family, institution, or community, is always a *holon*, constituting both part and whole (Koestler, 1979). Family structure, or internal organization, is observable through behavioral transactions and reflects underlying rules. Structure varies qualitatively in terms of richness/paucity, flexibility/rigidity, and coherence/incoherence and has the three dimensions of boundaries, alignment, and power (Aponte & VanDeusen, 1981). Boundaries define participation in (sub)systems over time, with spouse, parent, sibling, and parent-child subsystems forming the primary within-family holons.

Boundaries are formed and internalized as experiences of belongingness and separateness alternate in family and culture and range in quality from disengaged through permeable to enmeshed. Therapy focuses on boundary making (when boundaries are inadequate) and boundary diffusing (when boundaries are overly rigid).

Alignment refers to the ways family members join or oppose each other and includes both healthy affiliation and the symptom-generating cross-generational coalitions labeled as triangulation, detouring, and stable coalitions.

Power denotes "the relative influence of each [family] member on the outcome of an activity" (Aponte, 1976, p. 434) and is always relative to a particular transaction. Therapy focuses on unbalancing coalitions and changing hierarchical relationships (i.e., those pertaining to decision-making power).

Family members share a reality, "a set of cognitive schemas that legitimate or validate the family organization" (Minuchin & Fishman, 1981, p. 207). Both structure and reality may at different stages of therapy be developed, validated (through joining), or challenged (Laird & Vande Kemp, 1987). The therapist reframes reality by emphasizing interconnectedness or complementarity, creating new family myths, and providing hope.

Families develop dysfunction when they are stressed by the community and social world through such forces as economic depression, poverty, racial and gender discrimination, and political unrest; by internal movement through the family life cycle (Carter & McGoldrick, 1989; Fishman, 1993; Minuchin & Nichols, 1993); or by individually based problems such as retardation, disability, unemployment, or physical illness. Structural family therapists address symptoms with a variety of techniques, many of which were developed in collaboration with Jay Haley and are also used by the problem-solving and strategic family therapists. Generally setting aside the historical origins of symptoms, the therapist bases assessment on enactment, constructing "an interpersonal scenario in the session in which dysfunctional transactions among family members are played out" (Minuchin & Fishman, 1981, p. 79). The therapist observes this interaction to generate hypotheses about the locus of the problem and the structures that sustain it, thus identifying structural deficiencies and planning possible restructuring and unbalancing interventions. The therapist must be a confirmer of persons and their competence, a leader of the therapeutic system, and an alert responder to systemic feedback, becoming a self-manipulator and accommodator. As the therapist monitors interpersonal distance, she becomes an active participant in the family transaction in facilitating engagement or draws family members away from each other into relationship with the therapist in centralizing engagement. The therapist modifies enactments by increasing their intensity, prolonging them, introducing or removing persons from the interaction, prescribing alternative transactions, or introducing experimental probes that test the system's flexibility and adaptability. The goal is always to modify structure so that the family can fulfill its developmental and cultural functions.

Structural family therapy, because of its sensitivity to cultural context, is regarded as more sensitive to gender issues than most family therapies (Luepnitz, 1988). Because of its explicit rejection of individualism and affirmation of self in context, it is also highly amenable to psychotheological integration.

References

Aponte, H. (1976). Underorganization in the poor family. In P. J. Guerin (Ed.), *Family therapy: Theory and practice* (pp. 432–448). New York: Gardner.

Aponte, H., & VanDeusen, J. M. (1981). Structural family therapy. In A. S. Gurman & D. P. Kniskern (Eds.), *Handbook of family therapy*. New York: Brunner/Mazel.

Carter, B., & McGoldrick, M. (1989). *The changing family life cycle: A framework for family therapy* (2nd ed.). Boston: Allyn & Bacon.

Fishman, H. C. (1993). *Intensive structural therapy: Treating families in their social context*. New York: Basic.

Koestler, A. (1979). *Janus: A summing up*. New York: Vintage.

Laird, H., & Vande Kemp, H. (1987). Complementarity as a function of stage in therapy: An analysis of Minuchin's structural family therapy. *Journal of Marriage and Family Therapy, 13*, 127–137.

Luepnitz, D. (1988). Salvador Minuchin: The matter of functionalism. In *The family interpreted: Feminist theory in clinical practice*. New York: Basic.

Minuchin, S., & Fishman, H. C. (1981). *Family therapy techniques*. Cambridge, MA: Harvard University Press.

Minuchin, S., Montalvo, B., Guerney, G., Rosman, B., & Schumer, F. (1967). *Families of the slums*. New York: Basic.

Minuchin, S., & Nichols, M. P. (1993). *Family healing: Tales of hope and renewal from family therapy*. Toronto: Maxwell/Macmillan.

Minuchin, S., Rosman, B. L., & Baker, L. (1978). *Psychosomatic families: Anorexia nervosa in context*. Cambridge, MA: Harvard University Press.

Additional Readings

Colapinto, J. (1991). Structural family therapy. In A. S. Gurman & D. P. Kniskern (Eds.), *Handbook of family therapy* (Vol. 2). New York: Brunner/Mazel.

Fishman, H. C., & Rosman, B. (Eds.). (1986). *Evolving models for family change: A volume in honor of Salvador Minuchin*. New York: Guilford.

Minuchin, S. (1974). *Families and family therapy*. Cambridge, MA: Harvard University Press.

Minuchin, S. (1984). *Family kaleidoscope: Images of violence and healing*. Cambridge, MA: Harvard University Press.

H. Vande Kemp

See Family Therapy: Overview.

Structural Integration. An approach to personality growth through working with the physical body and energy levels. It is also known as rolfing, after its creator, Ida Rolf. It is not strictly a technique or a psychotherapeutic process, yet psychological changes do occur through rolfing.

Rolf received the Ph.D. in biological chemistry from the College of Physicians and Surgeons of Columbia University. Building on homeopathy, yoga, and osteopathy, she began to develop a new approach to dealing with chronic situations in the body. Homeopathy is a branch of medicine that arouses the patient's own healing powers through increasing the symptoms, which leads to a healing crisis. In the early 1950s Rolf started teaching a 10-hour sequence of aligning the myofascial system. This came to be know as rolfing.

Rolfing, according to its followers, restructures the body. Based on the premise that individuality is shaped by experiences, environment, choices, goals, emotions, and intellect, rolfing suggests that just as our minds bear memories that have consequences on our emotional health, so do physical memories (injuries, anxieties) shape our physical bodies. These memories build up and result in posture problems, discomfort, depression, and susceptibility to illness and disease.

The goal of rolfing is to bring to the body a more resilient, higher energy system. It is an ongoing process. During the 10-hour cycle of work a rolfer uses physical pressure to stretch and guide the fascia to a place of easier movement. Fascia is the elastic tissue surrounding muscle in the body. It starts beneath the skin and positions muscles, bones, nerves, and organs. Also called the organ of structure, fascia makes up the shape of the individual and is abused through the normal process of living. Rolfing reverses this process, attempting to bring balance to the body.

In structural integration, the concept of balance is the key factor in determining the serenity of the body. The basic belief of rolfing is that one can add structure to the body, causing a change in function that transcends the physical. A human being is an energy field in the larger energy of earth and gravity; greater awareness releases energy and frees it to be more available for individual functioning. Rolfing frees that energy. The results of this body work reach into the emotional, behavioral, and spiritual life of the individual, since chronic tension or strain eventually develops into emotional problems such as irritability or dependence. When the physical energy is released, it releases the whole system, intellectually and emotionally. Because of this, some emotional and physical pain is often experienced through the 10-hour cycle. Sometimes deeply repressed memories are released in intense emotional experiences, often relating the experience itself to a particular part of the body.

Rolf's work was given increased exposure through Esalen in California, where she did some work with Fritz Perls and other contemporaries. In 1969 Esalen funded a research project to determine physiological effects of rolfing, including measurement of brain waves, blood, and urine, and psychological profiles. Testing was done before and after the 10-hour cycle, and significant changes were found in the clients (Rolf, 1971). In 1977 Rolf published a formal exposition of the nature of the human body complete with diagrams. The Rolf Institute in Boulder, Colorado, trains rolfers in the theory and practice of structural integration.

Reference

Rolf, I. P. (1977). *Rolfing.* Santa Monica, CA: Dennis-Landman.

D. L. SCHUURMAN

Structuralism. The school of psychology associated primarily with Edward Bradford Titchener. It is also referred to as introspectionism and existentialism. Through its definition of psychology and its prescription of a methodology, structuralism was the force that led psychology away from mental philosophy into the realm of science. Ultimately it was a system whose deficiencies inspired the rise of behaviorism and functionalism as well as the psychologies of the Würzburg school and the Gestaltists.

The roots of structuralism lie in the experimental psychology of Wundt, who expressed the fundamental conviction that "psychology is the study of mental contents and that it is a science which approaches these contents chiefly through introspection and experimentation" (Heidbreder, 1933, p. 93). Wundt differentiated between physics and psychology as sciences based on immediate and mediate experience, respectively. Both are, however, sciences based on experience rather than metaphysics.

Titchener also defined psychology as the science of mental life, distinguishing between mind and consciousness. Mind refers to the sum total of mental processes occurring in the lifetime of the individual (and thus cannot be studied introspectively), and consciousness to the sum total of mental processes occurring now, at any given present time. Like Wundt, Titchener held that all science is based in experience. But physics (or natural science) differs from psychology in that physics studies aspects of the world, or experience, without reference to persons; psychology studies the world from the perspective of the person experiencing it. Thus the subject matter of psychology became experience dependent on an experiencing person. Titchener further reduced the experiencing person to the nervous system, including the sense organs, thus adopting in theory Wundt's physiological psychology. This adoption created some conceptual problems in Titchener's system. The dependency he spoke of was not conceived as causality or any other direct relationship, since he subscribed to a psychophysical parallelism in which bodily processes and mental processes occur side by side, with no interaction between them.

The method of psychology was introspection, which Titchener contrasted with inspection, the observation of the physical world. Introspection, the observation of the contents of consciousness, must involve only description of mental contents, without interpretation or speculation or labeling of the stimulus. While ordinary habits and principles of common sense predispose persons to see objects and events, all the trained introspectionist is to report are the qualities of the stimulus. To do otherwise constitutes the stimulus error, which involves seeing things rather than conscious contents.

In order to train introspectionists and to understand the mind Titchener had to specify the elements constituting the mind. He settled on three elementary processes: sensation, affection, and images. Sensations are the elements of perception, images the elements of ideas, and affections the elements of emotions. Each of these elements is also assigned attributes. Sensations and images are characterized by quality, intensity, duration, and clearness (which is also an essential characteristic of attention); affection is characterized by the first three but lacks clearness. To these general attributes Titchener added particular attributes for some processes. The study of these attributes and processes constituted much of the experimental work completed by Titchener, his Cornell students, and his colleagues in the Society of Experimentalists. The study of mental processes also led Titchener to postulate what became known as the context theory of meaning, which holds that a new mental process (or core) acquires its meaning from the constellation of mental processes within which it occurs.

Mental processes involved in the activity of the psychologist are analysis and synthesis (both descriptive) and causality (explanatory). These addressed, respectively, the questions of what (by reducing the material to its elements and describing these), how (by showing how the elements are arranged and combined), and why. Motivating the psychologist's activity is the search for understanding of the generalized human mind. In this goal Titchener opposed both an emphasis on individual differences (differential psychology) and the focus on applied psychology that became especially prevalent in the United States after World War I.

While structuralism may clearly be considered psychology's first paradigm (Kirsch, 1977), psychology soon underwent a fundamental revolution. The various schools that emerged were all in one way or another critical of structuralism. The Würzburg school challenged the analysis of thought in terms of images, sensations, and conscious contents and modified the introspectionist method into a phenomenalist one. The behaviorists questioned the mentalist emphasis. The Gestalt psychologists objected to the analysis of wholes into elements. The functionalists introduced the study of individual differences and the use of animals and children as subjects (even though they could not be trained in introspection). The psychoanalytic psychologists questioned the focus on consciousness and the disinterest in change.

Because its method was a rigid one, setting narrow limits on the scope of psychology, structuralism effactually died with its founder. However, it left behind the rich legacy of inspiration for the later experimental psychologies of the twentieth century.

References

Heidbreder, E. (1933). *Seven psychologies*. New York: Appleton-Century-Crofts.
Kirsch, I. (1977). Psychology's first paradigm. *Journal of the History of the Behavioral Sciences, 13*, 317–325.

H. VANDE KEMP

See PSYCHOLOGY, HISTORY OF; WUNDT, WILHELM.

Stupor. A state in which the sensibilities are immobilized and the individual loses appreciation of his or her life and surroundings. In an organic sense it is synonymous with unconsciousness, as the person appears dazed and unresponsive. A benign stupor is associated with a disorder from which recovery may be expected. Malignant stupors, as in catatonic schizophrenia, carry little chance of recovery. A stupor may also occur as the result of severe panic reactions, as a response to a physical attack, or upon hearing bad news such as the loss of a job, friend, or relative. In most cases such stupors are temporary, although a prolonged immobility may lead to or indicate more serious problems.

D. L. SCHUURMAN

Stuttering. *See* COMMUNICATION DISORDERS.

Style of Life. One of the central concepts of Adler's system of individual psychology, along with inferiority feeling, social interest, and fictional goals. Alder's use of the term lacked precision, and at different times he described style of life in terms of personality structure, self, ego, unified coping system, and one's unique pattern of perceiving oneself and life's problems. The concept certainly overlaps the idea of fictional goals, but style of life is more general and includes one's characteristic behavior patterns as well as one's perception of goal.

Holism is a key aspect of the style of life. It is not a mere composite of separate characteristics but the dominant whole that transcends the parts and whose impact is seen within each part. All behavior springs from the style of life. A person may appear to have contradictory ideas or competing goals, but this illusion is due to our failure to comprehend the underlying, unifying Gestalt.

Although the style of life embraces all aspects of an individual's personality, the Adlerian view is that the cognitive elements are central. The individual perceives external reality through the fictions and then selects an appropriate behavior. People are not driven by emotions. Emotions are produced in order to help individuals maintain a certain style of life.

Other characteristics of the style of life are uniqueness, creativity, and stability. Although every human being strives toward feelings of perfection and superiority, each person operates with different fictions, conceives of his or her goal differently, and comes out with a unique pattern of characteristics and habits, a style of life. Although both heredity and environment have some influence, they furnish only the building blocks from which the individual fashions his or her style of life, the most creative and unique work of art. Although people can change their life styles, Adler believed that the period of early childhood is formative and that few people can change style of life without intensive psychotherapy.

Adler attributed all mental disorder to fundamental defects in the style of life. The entire clinical approach of individual psychology is geared to style of life: comprehending it, helping the patient to gain this insight, and then changing it.

The strongest critique of the style of life concept comes from empirical research on personality. In too many cases individuals have conflicting goals, behavior is counterproductive, interpersonal similarities outweigh the differences claimed by uniqueness, behaviors change according to the situational demands or stage of the life cycle. The concept of a stable, unique, consistent, and unified style of life appears to be more of an ideal than an accurate generalization. Nevertheless, the concept may be a relevant approach in clinical work or spiritual counseling, in which the goal is to change the individual's fundamental orientation.

T. L. BRINK

See INDIVIDUAL PSYCHOLOGY; ADLER, ALFRED.

Sublimation. The process by which socially acceptable gratification of instinctual drives or desires is obtained through substitute activity. Though an unconscious process generally classed with the defense mechanisms, it does not involve repression or ego opposition to the instinctual drive. Rather, it is a healthy function of the normal ego, deflecting an unconscious and otherwise consciously unacceptable impulse into socially acceptable expression, substituting the aim and/or object of the impulse while permitting adequate discharge of mental energy associated with that impulse. Examples of this would include sublimation of aggressive impulses through becoming a soldier, a football player, or a business executive.

R. LARKIN

See DEFENSE MECHANISMS.

Subliminal Perception. A process involving a response to stimulation that is too weak or too brief to be consciously reported. Subliminal perceptions result from stimuli that cause the sensory receptors to fire (sensory threshold) but are not strong enough to reach conscious awareness (perceptual threshold). They are perceptions, therefore, that are below (Latin *sub*, under) the threshold (Latin *limen*, threshold) of conscious awareness. A related term is subception, which is the reaction to an emotion-producing stimulus that is not perceived to the point of being reported but is detectable from a person's autonomic responses.

In experiments on subliminal perception weak stimuli of short duration are presented to subjects. The subjects report that they do not see the stimulus. However, if shock is paired with a subliminally presented stimulus, subjects will begin to show an emotional response to the presentation of the weak stimulus.

Subliminal perception is to be distinguished from discrimination without awareness. This phenomenon involves attending to only part of a stimulus field and not perceiving the unattended portions. This is not subliminal because subjects could sense the unattended things if they wanted to. In subliminal perception stimuli get into the brain but are not strong enough to cause conscious awareness.

One question asked by psychologists concerning subliminal perception is how much people can be affected by the subliminal stimulation. In the past some individuals in advertising suggested that people can be motivated to buy products as a result of subliminally presented advertising. In 1956 a false report surfaced that said movie audiences were being influenced by subliminal messages to buy soft drinks and eat popcorn. Pertinent questions about experimental procedures were not answered by the experimenters, however, and such results have not been considered reliable (Pratkanis, 1992). There continue to be unreliable reports that advertisers manipulate consumers by imperceptibly imbedding erotic images or words in advertising. Rock recordings are said to contain subliminal satanic messages that can be heard if the recordings are played backwards. There are also self-help tapes available for weight loss and smoking that contain subliminal messages such as I am thin or Smoke is bad. (See Greenwald, Spangenberg, Pratkanis, & Eskenazi, 1991, for research on the lack of effectiveness of such taped messages.)

Current research suggests that subliminal stimuli can trigger weak responses and feelings in subjects (Krosnick, Betz, Jussim, & Lynn, 1992; Murphy & Zajonc, 1993). The conclusion reached by researchers is that it is doubtful that subliminal cues could have a significant effect on people's attitudes or behaviors. It is felt that subliminal messages, which are weak stimuli, would not prove to be more effective than strong stimuli in changing attitudes.

References

Greenwald, A., Spangenberg, E., Pratkanis, A., & Eskenazi, J. (1991). Double-blind tests of subliminal self-help audiotapes. *Psychological Science, 2,* 119–122.

Krosnick, J., Betz, A., Jussim, L., & Lynn, A. (1992). Subliminal conditioning of attitudes. *Personality and Social Psychology Bulletin, 18,* 152–162.

Murphy, S., & Zajonc, R. (1993). Affect, cognition, and awareness: Affective priming with optimal and suboptimal stimulus exposures. *Journal of Personality and Social Psychology, 64,* 723–739.

Pratkanis, A. R. (1992). The cargo-cult science of subliminal persuasion. *Skeptical Inquirer, 16,* 260–272.

M. P. Cosgrove

See Sensation and Perception.

Substance-Induced Disorders. According to the *Diagnostic and Statistical Manual of Mental Disorders* (*DSM-IV*; American Psychiatric Association, 1994, p. 176), the substance-related disorders are comprised of two separate groups, the substance-use disorders (i.e., substance dependence and substance abuse) and the substance-induced disorders (i.e., substance intoxication; substance withdrawal; and substance-induced delirium, persisting dementia, persisting amnestic disorder, psychotic disorder, mood disorder, anxiety disorder, sexual dysfunction, and sleep disorder). Substance refers to any drug, medication, or toxin. The dosage of the drug or medication typically determines the symptoms of the disorder; however, some disorders can appear after a single administration of the drug. Examples of toxins that might cause a substance-induced disorder include aluminum, lead, pesticides, antifreeze, carbon monoxide, fuel, and paint. Symptoms of substance-induced disorder include cognitive and mood impairments, hallucinations, delusions, anxiety, and seizures.

The development of a reversible substance-specific syndrome due to the recent ingestion of or exposure to a substance is the essential feature of substance intoxication (American Psychiatric Association, 1994, p. 183). Symptoms are due to the substance's direct effect upon the central nervous system, and the most common symptoms include disturbances in perception, attention, thinking, psychomotor behavior, and interpersonal behavior. The exact clinical presentation of substance intoxication is influenced by the individual's tolerance for the substance, the setting of drug administration, and the dose and substance involved. In order to be classified as substance intoxication, exposure to the substance must lead to a maladaptive change in behavior. For example, tachycardia due to excessive caffeine use is a physiological sign of intoxication; but if this is the only symptom, a diagnosis of caffeine intoxication would not be made because of an absence of corresponding maladaptive behavior.

Intoxication typically develops within minutes of exposure to a sufficiently large dose and intensifies with repeated use. As blood levels of the substance decline, symptoms abate, but this may occur slowly over hours or days, depending on the pharmacology of the substance and the physiology of the individual.

Substance-specific maladaptive behavioral change with both cognitive and physiological concomitants seen when there is a cessation of or reduction in prolonged substance use, is the essential feature of substance withdrawal (American Psychiatric Association, 1994, p. 184). Maladaptive behavior includes social and/or occupational functioning, and the symptoms are not due to any general medical condition. Symptoms of substance withdrawal develop after doses are reduced or stopped; at the same time symptoms of intoxication improve when dosing stops. The more severe symptoms of substance withdrawal typically cease within a few days of cessation of use; however, some subtle symptoms of withdrawal might last for several weeks or months after substance use has ended.

Laboratory tests, such as blood and urine analyses, can help determine recent substance use. Just as a positive laboratory test by itself cannot establish a pattern of substance use, neither can a negative test rule out such a diagnosis. These tests can, however, help identify substance withdrawal and establish individual tolerance levels.

Substance intoxication and withdrawal are often associated with other physical and social problems. A decline in the general health of the user due to poor diet, inadequate hygiene, or other medical conditions is not uncommon. Traumas resulting from falls occurring during intoxication or withdrawal can also affect the overall health of the individual, as can diseases associated with substance use (e.g., HIV, hepatitis, tetanus). Violence, aggressive behavior, criminal activity, and automobile accidents are major complications of substance use as well. Also, because most of these substances cross the placenta, they represent a threat to the health of the fetus if they are taken by a woman during pregnancy.

Some symptoms of substance-induced disorder are similar to those of other mental disorders and must be differentiated from these conditions to make a correct diagnosis. For example, substance-induced psychotic disorder must be distinguished from schizophrenia and other psychotic disorders for correct treatment to be implemented. For a diagnosis of substance-induced mental disorder there must be evidence of intoxication or withdrawal that is obtained from laboratory analyses or physical examination. In addition, the relationship between onset of the mental disorder and substance use is critical in determining whether the mental disorder is a physiological effect of the substance. If symptoms of mental disorder persist during periods of abstinence from the substance or last for more than four weeks after intoxication or withdrawal symptoms have ended, a diagnosis of non-substance-induced mental disorder is usually appropriate.

Substances that are frequently used and that induce disorders include but are not limited to alcohol, amphetamine, caffeine, cocaine, inhalants, and nicotine. Alcohol intoxication requires recent ingestion of alcohol and is characterized by significant maladaptive behavioral or psychological changes as well as slurred speech, incoordination, impaired attention or memory, and/or unsteady gait. Alcohol withdrawal results from a cessation or reduction in heavy alcohol use and is identified by insomnia, nausea or vomiting, psychomotor agitation, anxiety, and/or autonomic hyperactivity.

Symptoms of caffeine intoxication include tachycardia or cardiac arrhythmia, excitement, insomnia diuresis, gastrointestinal disturbance, rambling flow of thought and speech, and psychomotor agitation. Amphetamine and cocaine intoxication has similar symptoms, which include tachycardia or bradycardia, pupillary dilation, changes in blood pressure, nausea or vomiting, and psychomotor agitation or retardation. Withdrawal for both substances is also similar and is distinguished by fatigue, insomnia or hypersomnia, vivid and unpleasant dreams, and increased appetite.

Nicotine withdrawal occurs within 24 hours of an abrupt cessation of or reduction in nicotine use, defined as a daily use of nicotine for at least several weeks (American Psychiatric Association, 1994, p. 244). Symptoms include insomnia, irritability, frustration or anger, anxiety, increased appetite, restlessness, decreased heart rate, difficulty in concentrating, and a depressed mood.

Finally, inhalant intoxication is characterized by a recent intentional exposure to an inhalant leading to dizziness, incoordination, lethargy, depressed reflexes, psychomotor retardation, muscle weakness, or euphoria. Examples of maladaptive behavior associated with inhalant intoxication include belligerence, assaultiveness, and apathy.

Reference

American Psychiatric Association. (1994). *Diagnostic and statistical manual of mental disorders* (4th ed.). Washington, DC: Author.

K. S. Seybold

Substance-Use Disorders. The abuse of drugs is not a new phenomenon, but the extent of abuse in the twentieth century has been remarkable. Drug abuse has become a major public health problem since the 1960s. Although alcohol consumption has declined in the 1980s and 1990s, "there are more deaths, illnesses and disabilities from substance abuse than from any other preventable health condition" (Horgan, 1993, p. 8). In the 1950s drug abuse

in the United States consisted mainly of heroin usage by persons in large metropolitan areas. Now a wide variety of drugs is available in most all parts of the country, and one can find users of these substances in all segments of society.

A substance-use disorder, according to the *DSM-IV* (American Psychiatric Association, 1994), consists either of substance dependence or substance abuse. The *DSM-IV* describes both dependence and abuse syndromes for nine substance classes (alcohol, amphetamines, cannabis, cocaine, hallucinogens, inhalants, opioids, phencyclidine, and sedatives) and dependence but not abuse for one substance class (nicotine). The *DSM-IV* describes neither an abuse nor a dependence syndrome for caffeine, however.

Dependence. The central feature of substance dependence is continued use in spite of serious problems stemming from use of that substance. A craving for the substance is a feature of dependence. One can make a diagnosis of substance dependence when any three of the following seven features are present during the same 12-month period: tolerance (a need for larger amounts of the substance to achieve the same effect); withdrawal (the specific pattern of which will vary according to the substance involved; *see* Substance-Induced Disorders); more extensive use than intended; desire to stop use or a lack of success in curtailing use; large amounts of time spent on acquisition of, use of, or recovery from the use of the substance; abandonment of important activities; or continued use despite awareness of its dangers. Tolerance and withdrawal (criteria 1 and 2) may or may not involve physiological dependence.

Abuse. The central feature of substance abuse is a "maladaptive pattern of substance use manifested by recurrent and significant adverse consequences" of that use (American Psychiatric Association, 1994, p. 182). The diagnosis of substance abuse is less severe than that of substance dependence and is not made if a person meets the criteria for substance dependence. A substance-abuse diagnosis is appropriate if one or more of the following have been present within the last 12 months: substance use resulting in a failure to fulfill other major obligations, substance use when it is physically hazardous, recurrent legal problems related to use of the substance, or ongoing use in spite of other serious problems associated with that use.

Attitudes toward substance-abuse problems can vary widely across various cultural groups. Substance dependence usually begins in the first half of adulthood. When it begins in adolescence, it is usually associated with other disorders of conduct, including school problems. Males predominate in substance-use disorder diagnoses. The pattern of substance dependence is variable and can include periods of total abstinence, heavy use, or nonproblematic use. High relapse rates occur in the first year after a substance-dependent user has entered a period of remission. Persons diagnosed with a substance-use disorder often suffer from accompanying medical disorders.

Major Drug Families. Amphetamines, including speed and appetite suppressants, are stimulants that one can take orally or by injection. Their use can lead to increased alertness and insomnia. The stimulant effect of amphetamines is longer-acting than that of cocaine. Aggressive and/or violent behavior is associated with amphetamine dependence. The amphetamines can have legitimate medical uses under the supervision of a physician for the treatment of obesity, narcolepsy, and other physical problems.

Cannabis (marijuana, hashish, THC) is a family of drugs derived from the cannabis plant. Its use is illegal in the United States but not in some other parts of the world. No known physiological dependence forms, but a moderate amount of psychological dependence can occur. Tolerance does form. The drug is taken orally or smoked. Cannabis euphoria includes a relaxation of inhibitions and some disoriented behavior.

Cocaine is a narcotic and a stimulant that can be either injected or sniffed. Freebase conversion allows the drug to be smoked. Cocaine produces powerful euphoric states and users can quickly become dependent on it.

Hallucinogens (LSD, ergot, mescaline) are mostly used for brief periods of time and are best known for the delusions and hallucinations that occur following their use. The use of hallucinogens is often accompanied by serious legal and interpersonal problems.

Inhalant-related disorders are induced by inhaling odors given off by various substances such as gasoline, glue, various paint products, and other volatile compounds. Because these products are readily available, large amounts of time and effort to obtain them are not necessary, as is the case with other substances discussed in this article.

Opioids (naturally occurring heroin, morphine, and synthetics such as methadone) are narcotics with high levels of physical and psychological dependence potential and with serious tolerance and withdrawal features. The drugs can be administered orally, smoked, or injected. Abuse and dependence of opioids usually go together. The annual death rate is high, often accompanied by violence or serious drug-induced health problems. Opioid users usually have a history of previous polydrug use.

Sedatives, including barbiturates, entail all prescription drugs for sleeping and most antianxiety medications. When they are taken at high doses and with alcohol, these drugs can be lethal. Dependence on these substances can be intense.

Nicotine dependence is physiologically and psychologically intense, probably due to the overlearned quality of the behavior, the ubiquitous presence of cues in the environment, and the unpleasant features of withdrawal.

Related Problems. Substance abusers frequently experience accompanying pathologies. For example, long-term use of cocaine can lead to paranoid ideation. The cost of obtaining illicit substances can lead to illegal actions and criminal behavior. If a drug abuser is trying to self-medicate for an anxiety or depressive disorder, the condition can worsen instead of improve due to incorrect administration and/or dosage levels. Drug abusers who experience extremely labile moods are also subject to violent outbursts. In addition to the accompanying pathologies, substance abusers can experience resulting psychopathologies such as the substance-induced organic mental disorders (intoxications, withdrawals, deliriums, hallucinosis, and amnestic disorders). Physical health often suffers and Depression is frequently a resulting mood disturbance, as is evidenced by high suicide rates among drug abusers.

Substance abuse often seems to occur in persons suffering from personality disorders, especially the antisocial personality disorder. Certain features of the antisocial personality (chronic violation of societal rules and expectations, delinquency, truancy, running away) may predispose the person to drug abuse. The most powerful predicator of future drug abuse are signs of behavioral deviance in elementary school. Some researchers have described a drug-dependent personality (not an official *DSM-IV* classification) that includes low self-esteem, low capacity for affection, and low frustration tolerance.

Treatment. The traditional individual psychotherapeutic interventions have not been very successful with substance-abuse problems. Other methods such as psychosurgery, electroconvulsive therapy (ECT), hypnosis, and psychodrama have had unremarkable success. The most successful approaches are group approaches using homogeneous populations in residential treatment. Group rules, isolation of the abuser from previous drug-filled settings, high levels of motivation, and gradual return of privileges as behavior becomes better socialized seem to be the key factors in successful treatment (Glasscote, Sussex, Jaffe, Ball, & Brill, 1972). Teen Challenge is one such nationwide program, which also includes the spiritual dimension and a strong call to drug abusers to reform by being spiritually regenerated. Methadone maintenance is used with some success in helping heroin addicts ease off addiction, improve their physical health, and cease their illegal activities. Ethnic and multicultural issues can have an important bearing on treatment planning (Gordon, 1994).

References

American Psychiatric Association. (1994). *Diagnostic and statistical manual of mental disorders* (4th ed.). Washington, DC: Author.

Glasscote, R. M., Sussex, J. N., Jaffe, J. H., Ball, J., & Brill, L. (1972). *The treatment of drug abuse: Programs, prob-*

lems, prospects. Washington, DC: Joint Information Service.

Gordon, J. U. (Ed.) (1994). *Managing multiculturalism in substance abuse services.* Thousand Oaks, CA: Sage.

Horgan, C. (1993). *The nation's number one health problem.* Princeton, NJ: The Robert Wood Johnson Foundation.

J. R. BECK

See ALCOHOL ABUSE AND DEPENDENCE; ALCOHOL-INDUCED DISORDERS.

Substitution. The process by which repressed impulses seek indirect discharge through substitute satisfactions in place of those originally desired. The psychic energy of the original instinct is displaced to any impulse connected by unconscious association with the repressed impulse. The substitute impulse, or derivative, then takes on increased intensity and perhaps altered emotional tone consistent with the original impulse. Most neurotic symptoms are such derivatives.

See DEFENSE MECHANISMS.

Sudden Infant Death Syndrome. In sudden infant death syndrome (SIDS), an infant, believed to be healthy, suddenly stops breathing during the night and dies silently without suffering. Each year SIDS kills approximately 10,000 North American infants between 1 and 12 months of age and represents the leading cause of infant death in industrialized nations. Its frequency peaks 2 to 4 months after birth, and it rarely occurs in infants younger than 1 month or older than 1 year. SIDS victims are more likely to be boys, to be a second- or third-born child, and be part of a multiple birth (Craig & Kermis, 1995; Kinney, 1994).

Although researchers do not know the cause(s) of SIDS, several hypotheses, based on information about the characteristics of SIDS victims, are being tested.

Infants who die of SIDS have higher rates of premature birth, low birth weight (less than 2,500 grams), low Apgar scores (less than 7 out of 10), limp muscle tone, abnormal heart rate and respiration, and delayed central nervous system development. At time of death more than half of the babies have colds or mild respiratory infections (Berk, 1994). This might explain why breast-fed babies are less vulnerable to SIDS than bottle-fed babies (breast milk provides some immunity to many viruses, making breast-fed babies more resistant to infections). Many victims have irregular respiratory patterns with frequent lengthy disruptions of breathing; therefore, doctors detecting a breathing difficulty should recommend a device that sounds an alarm if the baby stops breathing.

Infants whose mothers smoked during pregnancy are two to three times more likely to die from SIDS than are infants born to nonsmokers. The risk of SIDS is three to four times higher for infants occasionally exposed to smoke postnatally and up to 23 times higher in infants exposed postnatally to frequent smoke (21 cigarettes or more a day). Prenatal exposure to opiates and barbiturates, which depress central nervous system functioning, increases the risk of SIDS tenfold. Exposure to nicotine and other drugs strain the respiratory control system in the infant's brain (Kandall & Gaines, 1991; Klonoff-Cohen et al., 1995).

Infants born to unmarried teenage mothers receiving poor prenatal care are at a higher than normal risk. The risk is higher if the mother was ill during pregnancy, had a short interval between pregnancies, or had previously miscarried. Mothers in labor 16 hours or longer are more than twice as likely to have an infant die of SIDS than are mothers with shorter labors. There is a sevenfold increase in SIDS associated with a rare breech delivery: a single footling delivery, in which the baby emerges one foot first. More common forms of breech birth are not associated with SIDS (Berk, 1994).

Because research suggests that infants put to sleep in the prone position (on their stomachs) are at greater risk for SIDS, the American Academy of Pediatrics (1992) recommends putting infants to sleep on their backs or sides. One theory suggests that if an infant lies face-down in a blanket, a pocket of carbon dioxide from exhaled breath may accumulate around the baby's face, displacing all the oxygen. Babies vulnerable to SIDS may have a brain defect or muscular weakness that prevents them from responding to the carbon dioxide, so they do not wake up, cry, or turn their heads. Kinney (1994) concluded that a tiny part of the brain called the arcuate nucleus, located in the brainstem, is absent or defective in SIDS infants, making them insensitive to carbon dioxide build-up and oxygen deprivation.

There is a higher rate of SIDS during the colder months, and many SIDS victims are discovered sweating with a high body temperature (Berk, 1994). Parents consequently are encouraged to not overbundle babies and to keep the nursery at room temperature.

An infant's unexplained death devastates the family; their grief is mixed with guilt, anger, and frustration. The family must get as much information as possible as well as support. They must be reassured that SIDS is not caused by neglect or a problem with the baby's crib, that it is not hereditary, that there is a 98% likelihood that future children will not get SIDS, and that SIDS is nobody's fault.

References

American Academy of Pediatrics Task Force on Infant Positioning and SIDS. (1992). Positioning and SIDS. *Pediatrics, 89* (6), 1120–1126.

Berk, L. (1994). *Child development* (3rd ed.). Boston: Allyn & Bacon.

Craig, G. J., & Kermis, M. D. (1995). *Children today.* Englewood Cliffs, NJ: Prentice-Hall.

Kandall, S. R., & Gaines, J. (1991). Maternal substance use and subsequent sudden infant death syndrome

(SIDS) in offspring. *Neurotoxicology and Teratology, 13,* 235–240.

Kinney, H. (1994 October). Brain development and SIDS. Paper presented at the 1994 Canadian Foundation for the Study of Infant Deaths Baby's Breath Conference, Toronto.

Klonoff-Cohen, H. S., Edelstein, S. L., Lefkowitz, E. S., Srinivasan, I. P., Kaegi, D., Chang, J. C., & Wiley, K. (1995). The effect of passive smoke and tobacco exposure through breast milk on sudden infant death syndrome. *The Journal of the American Medical Association, 293,* 795–798.

D. NEEDHAM

Suffering. People suffer everywhere, every day, in settings as dramatic as genocidal war or as ordinary as a suburban household. In their pain they inevitably raise questions about God's role in the sometimes painful and even horrifying affairs of human life. These questions concern the issue of theodicy; that is, the attempt to explain how the power and goodness of God can be reconciled with the experience of evil. (For a technical theological discourse about theodicy, see Stone, 1996.)

How do we care for a grieving person who asks, Why did God let this happen? How could God allow someone so young to die? Where is God in this plane wreck? First, we must discern the true nature of the question. Many whys are poetic questions, symbolic ways to express the depth of one's misery. It may be easier to ask Why did God do this? than to say I feel devastated by my loss. It certainly is a mistake to engage in theological discussion when the person's question is not a question but a metaphoric way of expressing powerful emotions.

A helpful way for caregivers to determine whether the why is poetic or literal is to respond tentatively to persons' emotional hurt: Your son's death is an enormous loss for you. If they readily grasp onto the helper's empathetic responses, it is sensible to follow that tack and facilitate the expression of feelings, taking care not to pass over the why question altogether but return to it at a later time.

Other individuals may reply to the caregiver's empathy with a verbal or implied Yes, but . . . These people most likely are looking for a real answer to the why and may be unable to deal with their grief emotionally until they have first dealt with the theodicy question inherent in their plight. In any event the question seldom goes away by itself. As the intensity of the loss diminishes, the theodicy issue may arise even more forcefully, and a helper who reintroduces the question at a later time can provide an important opportunity for growth.

Caregivers have to prepare themselves to respond to suffering and to the theodicy questions of those who suffer. Vital to that preparation is a thorough, personal examination of theodicy in light of one's own faith.

Whether helpers respond to the vital issues of theodicy, neighbors and friends are likely to do so.

Simplistic and damaging answers flow from well-meaning individuals at a time when their hearers are vulnerable; many suffering people are left off balance by theological answers such as This has happened to bring you to the Lord, or God wanted her to be with him in heaven. They may also hear pop psychological answers to the theodicy issue: You are responsible for your feelings, or You are sick because of your destructive thoughts. Thoughtful guidance by the helper can help prevent or heal the hurts brought on by such misguided truisms.

It is also important to remember that many people who do not verbalize about theodicy questions are thinking about them just the same. The whys bubble up from the deepest well of one's being and should not be turned into casual ideological debate. Caregivers who have worked out their own views on theodicy will recognize the uniqueness of each person and each situation and frame their responses accordingly. Our task is to help suffering people find their own metaphors that convey the comfort and promise of our faith.

When we talk with persons about their understandings of suffering, it is best to begin by discovering their thoughts (however uncertain) rather than immediately verbalizing our own views, listening very carefully before responding. Sometimes it is helpful to ask direct questions: Is that how you've always thought about it? What's troubling or confusing you now? What answers have other people suggested to you? How has this loss [illness/divorce] affected your faith?

We need to be careful not to imply that those who are suffering ought to feel any particular way. People who already feel guilty for questioning the goodness of God may end up feeling doubly guilty if the caregiver asserts, for example, that one should view suffering as a blessing.

When communicating our own understanding of faith's response to theodicy in a care or counseling setting, we are not engaging in a technical theological discussion. It is important to speak personally and directly, without jargon, yet give suffering people the cognitive tools they need to begin making sense of their plight. Possibly the most helpful approach is to speak from our own experience of loss and our own struggle with the question of theodicy, sharing what has benefited us or others we know in times of pain. We also can share the message of Scripture—not citing isolated texts to prove a point but emphasizing its many stories of God's abiding presence and help in times of trouble.

Suffering is not a thing to be desired. It is a given—not good but inevitable, a part of our finitude that can lead to growth or despair. It may be that more people will survive the experience of evil, loss, and pain with the help of a believer's quiet assurance and the presence of God than with a religionist's critique of their theology. But in the midst of suffering God speaks both a verbal (literal) Word through the clear discussion of why questions and a visible (metaphoric) Word through the loving presence of the church embodied in the pastoral ministry of another.

Faced with tragedy, we may at times do little more than stammer a few inadequate words on the great enigma of a God who loves us yet allows us to suffer, perhaps excruciatingly. But as we mature in our faith, we arrive at ever-deeper understandings of the relationship between human suffering and God's power and love. We will find it possible to be with the sufferers, to cry and feel helpless with them, but also to speak confidently of the presence of a loving God who, though not the cause of their sorrow, can be their strength and their release.

Reference

Stone, H. (1996). *Word in deed.* New York: Haworth.

H. STONE

See PASTORAL CARE; SUPPORTIVE PSYCHOTHERAPY.

Suggestibility. The quality or state of being easily influenced by suggestion. Individuals may be influenced by others to change their attitudes, ideas, beliefs and/or behavior without critically analyzing the process. Suggestibility relates to the degree of susceptibility to being influenced by such suggestion. The current thoughts on suggestibility lean toward any type of personality being capable of being influenced by suggestion, although rigid individuals may be less likely to allow themselves to be so influenced. Perhaps that is why drugs, alcohol, and hypnosis are likely to play a part in facilitating the state of mind that is most open to being influenced by others' suggestions.

One vehicle through which a person may be open to suggestion is social influence by an appeal to conform (e.g., traditional or ceremonial ritual, political and business sales pitches). In most situations involving suggestibility, the person to be influenced must trust and/or respect the person or institution making the suggestion, since the idea and the communicator are easily associated. Therapists have some prestige, as do teachers and others in authoritative professions, and a parent-child situation often encourages and facilitates influencing others. The tendency to go along with the crowd most often occurs when situations are filled with feelings and are nonspecific or when people are unsure of themselves or of their decision-making ability.

In psychotherapy and counseling, suggestibility is a two-edged sword. Therapists should not suggest anything that may be detrimental at the time or later. Nor should anything be suggested that would better be part of the independent and mature decision-making processes of the patient or client. Some individuals in therapy or counseling may present themselves as quite dependent upon others, especially those in authoritative positions. They may in-

vite and encourage the therapist to make suggestions about a variety of issues. A very high level of suggestibility on the part of such persons may be apparent. While some suggestion may be helpful at certain junctures and may facilitate progress, overuse of this process may hamper the individual's growth to more independent behavior and thinking. Therapeutic suggestions are best when they are positively verbalized. Although presenting an idea in a negative fashion may be done for effect or may be aimed at a dramatic warning, the suggestion is more likely to be clear and understood in a positive formulation.

On the other end of how susceptible an individual is to the suggestions of another person are the possibilities for power plays, especially for exploitation and manipulation. Thus an authoritative person might seek to gain power over another person who is perceived as weaker or subordinate by the use of inequality and domination. By suggesting to someone who wants to be one of the crowd and to be well liked that most people engage in a specific behavior or share a particular thought greatly increases the probability that that suggestion will be accepted. Selling ideas and products often depends on this phenomenon.

Suggestibility may even be linked with competition, if the message of the suggestion is that some individuals within the subordinate group will be winners of a coveted position or honor (e.g., using perfume X and winning the attention of attractive members of the opposite sex) over those not wise enough to follow the suggestion (using perfume X). The suggestion that the product will bring about a desired effect may encourage competition among the users of this product to use it more often and in stronger intensity.

There is also much competition by various parties to suggest competing products to people. The strength of the appeal interacts with the suggestibility of the individuals, contributing to sales resistance of people. Therapists and counselors are not immune to selling their particular product, competing among themselves, and appealing to the suggestibility of potential patients and clients. This becomes an ethical issue; individuals should be protected from their own suggestibility whenever that tendency is not guided by thoughtful reflection and informed knowledge.

C. A. RAYBURN

See HYPNOSIS.

Suicide. Suicide is the deliberate taking of one's own life. Suicide violates the Sixth Commandment and is therefore a sin, usurping God's control over life and death. Because suicide is considered a sin and because faith helps endure a suicidal crisis, a religious person is less likely to commit suicide than a non-religious person.

Approximately 30,000 Americans commit suicide annually, although many suicidologists believe that figure underestimates the actual number of suicides because many suicides are misreported as accidents. Suicide is the eighth leading cause of death among American adults; it is the third leading cause of death among adolescents and young adults aged 15 to 24.

For every completed suicide, there are between eight and twenty attempts. At least five million living Americans have attempted to kill themselves. Suicide attempters are most likely aged 25 to 44, whereas suicide victims are most likely over 50. Between 40% and 80% of adults have considered suicide at least once during their lives. Of those who have committed suicide, approximately half had made at least one prior attempt, and two-thirds of those who attempt suicide and fail never try it again. Most people who attempt suicide and fail report relief and they promise never to try it again (Clark & Fawcett, 1992).

Approximately 70% of suicide victims satisfy the *DSM-IV* criteria for depression of some sort (but it is important to realize that the overwhelming majority of depressed people do not commit suicide). The risk of suicide is relatively low while the depressed person is experiencing the worst part of the depressive episode. At that point, the despair is the deepest, but so is the apathy; the person does not care or have the energy to design and implement a plan to end life. The risk increases as the person emerges from the worst part of the depressive episode; the person's mood is still bleak, but they have regained enough ability and energy to act. Many people who commit suicide were not depressed, but they were likely experiencing some other psychological problem. For example, among men, substance use disorder is related to a seventy-five-fold increase in the suicide rate. Schizophrenics are also more likely to commit suicide than is the general population.

Although suicide attempts are three times more common among women than men, men are three times more likely to kill themselves (Girard, 1993). This sex difference is attributable to the different ways that men and women use to commit suicide; men use more violent and more foolproof methods. For example, men are more likely to shoot themselves, whereas women are more likely to take an overdose of pills. Shooting oneself is the most common method of suicide in the United States.

The suicide rate among children and adolescents, while significantly below that of adults, is rising more rapidly than for any other age group. Approximately half of high-school students have contemplated suicide at least once, and 10% have attempted it. White and Native-American youths are more than twice as likely to commit suicide as African-American youths; however, in inner cities, the rate among young African-American men is twice as high as those among young white men. Suicidologists have recently reported an increase in the suicide rate among 75- to 84-year-olds. Being single, widowed, or divorced greatly increases suicide risk, presumably because the person's social-support network is smaller or non-existent.

Even though suicide occurs at all social and economic levels, rates are lower among employed persons than unemployed persons. Among the employed, the risk of suicide is higher in prestigious, high-pressure jobs. For example, suicide rates are higher among psychologists, psychiatrists, physicians, and lawyers (Wekstein, 1979).

Approximately 10,000 American college students attempt suicide each year and 10% succeed. The rate among college students is significantly higher than the rate among same-aged peers not attending college. It is believed that academic pressures are not responsible for the increased risk among college students; rather, loneliness and interpersonal problems are to blame. About 20% of college students consider suicide at least once during their college years.

Phillips (1974) suggested that suicides are more likely following a highly publicized suicide. For example, in the weeks after Marilyn Monroe's death, suicide rates increased by over 10%. Even highly publicized suicides of non-famous persons trigger other suicides. The suicide rate also increases in the weeks following the suicide of a television character.

Society continues to hold several misconceptions about suicide. Contrary to popular belief, suicides are not more common around holiday periods (with the exception of Independence Day), suicides are usually committed with some advance warning (approximately 80% of completed suicides are preceded by a warning of some sort), and the tendency to commit suicide is not inherited. Also, suicide is not related to the seasons, the weather, or days of the week.

Several researchers have attempted to categorize suicides and suicidal behavior. Farberow and Litman's (1970) classification is threefold. The "to be" group contains people who do not want to die, but instead want to communicate their distress to others. Their attempts usually involve methods that are less likely to work, and they may attempt suicide in such a way that intervention by others is probable. This group is disproportionately female and comprises two-thirds of the suicidal population. The "not to be" group (5% of the suicidal population) contains people who are determined to die; they seldom give warnings and they typically use very violent methods. The "to be or not to be" group (30% of the suicidal population) contains people who are ambivalent about dying and who leave the question of death to fate.

Maris (1992) suggested that suicides fit into five categories based on what motivates the person to act. The most common motivation for suicide is *escape;* the psychological pain is so intense that the person can no longer endure it. Maris estimated that 20% of suicides are motivated by *anger and re-*

venge. A suicide is considered *altruistic* if committed in dedication to higher goals (military suicide missions). Suicides may occur while engaging in *risky behavior;* the behavior is intended to stimulate, but instead it kills. Many suicides are *"mixed,"* motivated by a combination of the above factors.

Friends and relatives of suicide victims should obtain counseling to help them overcome their feelings of distress, bewilderment, anger, and guilt; however, most survivors do not obtain the help they need. Counselors and peer-support groups give survivors an outlet to express their feelings. Some survivors wonder why they had not predicted the suicide or what they could have done to have prevented it. Survivors have an especially high mortality rate in the year following their loved one's suicide. Especially in need of counseling are those survivors who were present (or on the telephone) when the suicide occurred; in 25% of suicides, someone other than the victim is present (or speaking with the victim).

Between 15% and 25% of suicide victims leave notes, usually addressed to friends or relatives. Researchers have compared genuine suicide notes with notes written by non-suicidal persons who were instructed to write a typical suicide note. Genuine suicide notes contain a greater number of instructions, such as suggestions about raising children and explicit orders about how to dispose of the body; they also contain evidence of great anguish. Lacking in the real notes is the general and philosophical content that characterizes those written by non-suicidal persons; for example, the comment "be good to others" is not likely to appear in a real suicide note (Baumeister, 1990; Shneidman & Farberow, 1970).

Theories of suicide are sociological, psychological, or biological. Durkheim (1897) proposed an early sociological theory in which he distinguished among three types: egoistic suicide, altruistic suicide, and anomic suicide. A person may commit egoistic suicide if they feel disconnected from society; they lack social supports to help them function normally. An altruistic suicide is sacrificial, committed for the betterment of society. An anomic suicide is a suicide caused by a sudden change in the victim's environment; for example, a person may commit suicide if they lose their prestigious job and realize that their standard of living will be significantly lowered. Durkheim's theory does not account for individual differences; for example, it cannot explain why one person who loses their job commits suicide, while another person who loses their job does not.

Shneidman (1987) has proposed a psychological theory of suicide which suggests that suicide is the only solution to a problem causing excruciating pain and suffering; suicide ends the pain. Shneidman noted that a suicidal person cannot formulate alternative solutions because they are so stressed. When the stress lessens, the person thinks of other solutions and suicide is not among them.

Critics contend that Shneidman's theory fails to account for the suicides which appear to be motivated by a desire to make someone feel guilty, a desire for reincarnation, or the desire to join a dead loved one.

Baumeister (1990) suggested that suicides occur because of an intense desire to escape from painful self-awareness. Therefore, a person aware of their shortcomings and failures suffers. When a person has established high goals and fails to achieve them, the painful awareness of their fallibility may trigger suicide.

Biological theories attempt to find a relationship between neurotransmitters and suicide. Research has revealed a relationship between serotonin and suicide. Suicide victims have abnormally low levels of serotonin's major metabolite (5-HIAA) and post-mortem examinations of suicide victims' brains reveal an increased number of serotonin receptors (in response to the low levels of serotonin) (Brown & Goodwin, 1986).

There is no guaranteed way to prevent someone from committing suicide. Being able to recognize the warning signs of suicide and knowing high-risk groups is crucial. Suicidologists note that few people really know what to do when dealing with a suicidal friend or relative (Wekstein, 1979). Experts agree that suicidal talk must be taken seriously; those who talk openly about suicide are a high-risk group. Some comments about suicide are vague; experts claim that the first step in prevention is to directly ask whether a person is seriously contemplating suicide.

A suicidal person needs empathy and immediate social support. There are over 200 suicide prevention centers throughout North America staffed with qualified personnel to provide the necessary support. Workers typically deal with potential suicide cases over the telephone, and their first task is usually to ascertain the degree of risk. Dew et al. (1987) reviewed five research projects on the effectiveness of suicide prevention centers and concluded that suicide rates did not drop after the centers opened. Another concern is that most people who use the centers do not return for more assistance as suggested and they do not obtain help elsewhere. However, because many people use the centers to weather a suicidal crisis, there is no logical reason to close them.

In addition to providing support, it is important that the crucial problem be identified. The suicidal person is confused and feels buried by their problems; they need help to isolate the crucial problem. Once it has been isolated, it may not seem so overwhelming and alternative courses of action can be suggested. If they have any doubts about ending their life, it is important to capitalize on these doubts; some experts claim that these may be the best arguments for life over death. Once support has been offered and alternative actions have been suggested, it is necessary to recommend professional treatment.

The goal of professional treatment is to prevent suicidal behavior. Prevention entails evaluating a client's risk factors and the seriousness of their intent. When an attempt, or further attempt, is judged to be likely, hospitalization in a psychiatric facility may be suggested. If the person refuses voluntary commitment, they may be involuntarily committed. The law allows involuntary commitment for a limited time (usually three days), but it requires certification from a psychologist or psychiatrist that the person is highly suicidal. If a clinician assesses the client's risk to be moderate or minimal, the client will be urged to get outpatient therapy, where the underlying problem is determined and problem-solving procedures are suggested. Cognitive-behavioral treatments and family and marital therapies may be involved.

There are several clinical and ethical issues pertaining to suicide. For example, professional organizations such as the American Psychological Association and the American Psychiatric Association allow a therapist to break therapist-client confidentiality if it means protecting the life of a suicidal client. If a therapist's client commits suicide, the client's family may file a malpractice suit against the therapist if they believe that the therapist failed to take reasonable precautions. Also, professionals will have to deal with the ethical issues surrounding doctor-assisted suicide, where severely ill patients enlist the help of their doctor to end their life. At the center of this debate is the question of whether people who do not want to live in pain have the right to end their life.

References

Baumeister, R. F. (1990). Suicide as escape from self. *Psychological Review, 97*, 90–113.

Brown, G. L., & Goodwin, F. K. (1986). Cerebrospinal fluid correlates of suicide attempts and aggression. *Annals of the New York Academy of Science, 487*, 175–188.

Clark, D. C., & Fawcett, J. (1992). Review of empirical risk factors for evaluation of the suicidal patient. In B. Bongar (Ed.), *Suicide: Guidelines for assessment, management, and treatment*. New York: Oxford University Press.

Dew, M. A., Bromet, E. J., Brent, D., & Greenhouse, J. (1987). A quantitative literature review of the effectiveness of suicide prevention centers. *Journal of Consulting and Clinical Psychology, 55*, 239–244.

Durkheim, E. (1951). Suicide (Trans.). J. A. Spaulding & G. Simpson. New York: Free Press. (Original work published 1897).

Farberow, N. L., & Litman, R. E. (1970). A comprehensive suicide prevention program. Suicide Prevention Center of Los Angeles, 1958–1969. Unpublished final report DHEW NIMH Grants No. MH 14946 & MH 00128. Los Angeles.

Girard, C. (1993). Age, gender, and suicide: A cross-national analysis. *American Sociological Review, 58*, 553–574.

Maris, R. W. (1992). How are suicides different? In R. Maris, A. L. Berman, J. T. Maltsberger, & R. I. Yufit (Eds.), *Assessment and prediction of suicide*. New York, London: Guilford Press.

Phillips, D. P. (1974). The influence of suggestion on suicide: Substantive and theoretical implications of the Werther effect. *American Sociological Review, 39*, 340–354.

Shneidman, E. S. (1987). A psychological approach to suicide. In G. R. VandenBos & B. K. Bryant (Eds.), *Cataclysms, crises, and catastrophes: Psychology in action*. Washington, DC: American Psychological Association.

Shneidman, E. S., & Farberow, N. L. (1970). A psychological approach to the study of suicide notes. In E. S. Shneidman, N. L. Farberow, & R. E. Littman (Eds.), *The psychology of suicide*. New York: Jason Aronson.

Wekstein, L. (1979). *Handbook of suicidology: Principles, problems, and practice*. New York: Brunner/Mazel.

D. NEEDHAM

See DEPRESSION; SELF-DESTRUCTIVE BEHAVIOR.

Sullivan, Harry Stack (1892–1949). American psychiatrist; the chief proponent of what is called the dynamic-cultural or interpersonal school of psychoanalysis. Along with Karen Horney, Erik Erikson, and Erich Fromm he is generally seen as one of the major neo-Freudians. Sullivan deemphasized the orthodox psychoanalytic stress on biology in favor of the view that most psychological troubles are engendered by life experiences. He suggested that it takes people to make people sick, and it takes people to make people well. He saw human relationships as both the cause of and the potential remedy for psychological disturbance.

Born in Norwich, New York, Sullivan was graduated in 1917 from the Chicago College of Medicine and Surgery. However, he was significantly influenced by both philosophers and anthropologists, and the breadth of his thinking made these influences apparent. Sullivan, more than anyone else of his era, made an intensive and lifelong study of the ways in which individual people affect one another. He argued that nonorganic psychological problems are at root faulty ways of relating to others. The psychotherapist's job, therefore, is to correct the patient's self-defeating interpersonal styles and maneuvers. Sullivan's key clinical question routinely was, What is this particular client trying to do to or with me in this situation; how is he or she attempting to structure our time together? While dynamically oriented therapists have stressed intrapsychic mental events and behaviorists have stressed overt actions, Sullivan advocated that both be carefully attended to, especially as they relate to past interpersonal experience.

Sullivan advocated the careful observation of exactly how the patient expresses himself or herself, how he or she gets along with other people outside of the consulting room, and what has gone on interpersonally in the past. He emphasized that other people are the most important aspects of anyone's environment, and he even went so far as to say that without interpersonal relationships a human being is hardly human at all. To Sullivan the very concept of personality had no meaning apart from a person's characteristic interpersonal relationships.

Sullivan believed that there is an essential continuity between psychological normality and abnormality. In this regard he was perhaps the earliest physician to reject the idea that psychological troubles are diseases. While recognizing that certain organic abnormalities, such as brain tumors, can radically alter behavior, he believed that most of the problems for which people consult therapists are essentially difficulties in living. Such difficulties center upon the specific human challenge of achieving and maintaining intimate relationships with others.

Although a number of books by Sullivan are available, most of these were put together from his clinical lecture notes and in certain cases from his students' notes. Sullivan was primarily a teacher of psychotherapeutic method and only secondarily a writer. Nevertheless, some of his posthumous volumes have earned the status of psychiatric classics, including *The Psychiatric Interview* (1954), *Clinical Studies in Psychiatry* (1956), and *Schizophrenia as a Human Process* (1962). He was a highly influential teacher in one of the most prestigious psychiatric hospitals in the country, St. Elizabeth's in Washington. He was also pivotal in the establishment of Chestnut Lodge, in Rockville, Maryland, another major treatment center and training institute.

From a theological point of view there is a great deal to commend in Sullivan's thought. If we have been made in God's image, as Christians maintain, this seems to imply that we are intrinsically relational beings—that we have been *made* to relate to God and our fellows. It seems only fitting, therefore, that Christian psychologists pay special attention to the nature of relationships. While Sullivan himself may not have been especially religious, his overall orientation appears compatible with the Christian worldview.

C. W. McLemore

See Interpersonal Psychology.

Superego. One of three psychic structures postulated by Sigmund Freud. In contrast to the id, which is seen as the seat of the individual's impulses and drives, and the ego, which includes the person's perceptual and judging functions, the superego is the source of morality and moral judgment. It functions as a kind of moral observer or watchman in the absence of parents and other socializing agents. It observes one's moral thoughts and actions and passes out self-punishment in the form of guilt for misbehavior and self-esteem for good behavior.

Roughly equivalent to the conscience, the superego is believed by psychoanalysts to develop largely during the first six years of life in the context of intimate parent-child relationships. Although later psychoanalysts have enlarged and altered some aspects of Freud's theory, the general understanding of the superego closely follows that laid down by Freud. He believed the superego develops out of the ego under the impact of the child's oedipus complex, which he assumed to be a universal psychological experience.

During the oedipal period (roughly four to six years of age) the male child is theorized to develop a growing love for his mother, a resentment toward his father, and a desire to replace his father as the sole source of his mother's affections. Fearing punishment from his father because of his murderous and incestuous wishes, the child is forced to repress and renounce his unacceptable desires. In the process he sets up within his personality an inner mental picture or representation of his parents' judgments and prohibitions. These images merge with the child's earlier parental introjects to form the special part of the ego known as the superego. The superego, built up by taking in these parental standards and punishments, then begins to function in place of external parental control. Much like the ego observes and evaluates the individual's wishes in light of external realities, the superego observes and evaluates one's wishes and desires in light of internalized moral standards.

Freud hypothesized that as a result of this process, the forbidden impulses of love (toward the mother) and hatred (toward the father) are redirected by the superego toward the child's own personality. Instead of experiencing love and anger toward his parents, the child directs his love and anger at himself in the form of self-esteem and guilt, respectively. Self-esteem is regulated by superego approval instead of the approval or disapproval of parents, and guilt over the violation of one's inner values replaces fear about the external consequences of one's behavior.

Although the main features of the superego are believed by psychoanalysts to be laid down in the first six years of life, the process of identifying with meaningful people and taking in both their standards and their corrective attitudes continues to shape one's superego throughout life, especially through the formative years of preadolescence and adolescence. Consciously chosen adult values also merge with internalized parental values to produce the unique form and content of the adult superego.

One interesting aspect of Freud's concept of the superego is his explanation of why the superego can be so harsh and punitive while in reality the parents may have been relatively loving and nonpunitive. Freud did not believe that the child's superego is simply an internalized version of parental prohibition. He believed that children project or attribute their own anger to their parents, so that when they take a mental picture of their parents into their superego, they take it not as the parents were but as the children have distorted them by their own anger. The strength of the superego's punishment, in other words, is not due simply to the parents' actual punitiveness but to the combined strength of the parents' punitiveness and the child's anger at the parents.

In therapy psychoanalytically oriented therapists attempt to help patients develop a superego that has realistic and necessary moral standards but is not punitive or overly restrictive. This is done by helping patients understand the early parent-child interactions that caused the superego to be either too lenient or too punitive, by assisting the patient in consciously selecting more appropriate or adult standards, and by modeling a responsible but accepting and nonpunitive approach to moral issues.

S. B. NARRAMORE

See PSYCHOANALYTIC PSYCHOLOGY.

Superstition. Unreasoning fear or awe of something mysterious or imaginary; religious belief or practice founded on fear or ignorance. The development of the modern concept of superstition and superstitious behavior has had a long history. From a Latin source meaning to stand over, perhaps in awe or amazement, our English word derives from the Old French word meaning to survive.

Prior to the twentieth century the religious emphasis in superstition was much more pronounced, some writers using religion and superstition interchangeably. With this in mind we might interpret the word *ignorance* in the definition to include those beliefs founded on misunderstanding or misinterpretation. However, we should avoid the once common usage that considered all non-Christian belief systems as superstition. Current usage largely reflects the general sense of an irrational belief or behavior, perhaps reflecting the widespread deemphasis of religious thought and practice in contemporary American society. However, the origins of most common superstitions are still to be found in religious contexts.

A speculation as to the exact meaning of the Old French source word for superstition is that this word refers to old, pre-Christian beliefs or practices that survived into the Christian era. While it is philologically unlikely, this interpretation provides a number of useful insights into superstitions in the Anglo-American culture. While a number of such pagan survivals exist, not all are considered superstitions. Determination of why some beliefs of non-Christian origin are superstitions and others are not illustrates an important feature of superstition: the superstitious belief is out of its original context and has not become integrated into a new context.

Examples of pagan elements in Anglo-American culture that are not considered superstitions are the mistletoe and holly wreaths used as Christmas decorations. These initially were central features of druidic rituals occurring around the winter solstice. Now they have been firmly incorporated into popular Christian practices and also greatly reduced in significance. Kissing under a sprig of mistletoe is but a faint echo of the salacious druidic fertility ritual from which this practice was derived. In contrast, the avoidance of black cats and the special significance given to the number 13, which originated in the amalgam of pagan and heretical Christian beliefs known as witchcraft, have not become integrated within alternate contexts. The relationship of these superstitious beliefs to their original context is for the most part severed, and it is difficult to eliminate them from the popular mind. Thus we find that superstitions are most often found expressed as isolated beliefs and actions that are removed from their original contexts or given greater emphasis and meaning than their current context can support.

There are important distinctions among magical thinking, weakly organized or obscure belief systems, and superstition. Magical thinking is an attribute of most of us, and in general it is based on drawing false causal links between unconnected events. An example is the belief that thoughts or wishes can alter the course of material events. While there is an element of magical thinking to be found in superstition, the use of this concept in psychology refers particularly to exaggerated instances of the example given here. Weakly organized belief systems and belief systems employed by various subcultures (e.g., hexing, voodoo, or root working) are not superstitions in the sense of our primary definition, although they are contexts for the origin of superstitions. The significance of these distinctions is found when evaluating superstition from a psychological and particularly a clinical viewpoint.

A particular problem encountered when superstitious beliefs complicate a clinical evaluation is that superstitiousness may be misinterpreted as psychopathology per se. Similarly the presence of superstitious beliefs may lead to an overestimation of the severity of psychopathology when it is present. This is due to the confusion of superstition and magical thinking found even in the current diagnostic criteria of the American Psychiatric Association. Conversely, pathology might be misinterpreted by some practitioners as merely manifestations of superstition. This is often complicated when psychologically disturbed individuals use symbols common to superstitions to express their psychopathology.

In order to determine the true state of affairs in a given case we must first ask: Is the patient's behavior motivated by an expressible belief that relates his or her behavior causally to a desired outcome? This addresses the issue of magical thinking versus a belief in magic. If such a belief is in force, the possibility of psychopathology need not be ruled out, but accepting the superstitious belief as direct evidence of psychopathology must be avoided. The appropriateness of such a belief for the individual should be evaluated. Is the belief commonly held by other people from similar backgrounds or traditions? If this is the case, we must again exercise caution in interpretation of the patient's superstitious behavior vis-à-vis the possibility of psychopathology. In a situation where conflicting experience would seem to invalidate a superstitious belief, the psychologically healthy individual will abandon or modify that belief. The psychologically ill person will be more likely to reinterpret his or her experience in order to minimize the apparent conflict between belief and experience or may even deny the validity of the experience.

Finally, the extent to which a belief interferes with an individual's daily life must be considered. The healthy individual is able to maintain normal activities regardless of his or her superstitious beliefs. The inability to do so, especially if there is a sudden onset of the superstitious behavior or avoidance of common activities, is highly suggestive of psychopathology, not superstition.

Additional Readings

Chrisman, N. J., & Maretzki, T. W. (1982). *Clinical applied anthropology*. Boston: D. Reidel.

Crapanzano, V., & Garrison, V. (Eds.). (1977). *Case studies in spirit possession*. New York: Wiley.

Kleinman, A. (1980). *Patients and healers in the context of culture*. Berkeley: University of California Press.

G. S. HURD

See MAGICAL THINKING.

Supervision in Psychotherapy. Supervision is fundamentally about training therapists or counselors in the knowledge, skills, and attitudes of the mental health professions. Students are supervised by well-trained therapists or counselors who model professionalism, guide the integration of knowledge and skill, and evaluate the student's progress. Most often students' therapeutic work is supervised during their graduate work through their licensure. Supervision may be provided through the faculty of their graduate program, through their training site, or through a combination of both. More and more therapists and counselors are also opting for postlicensure supervision by peers as part of their ongoing professional growth. Many training programs and states now require supervisors to have training in supervision.

Methods. Supervision may be conducted in a variety of ways. The most common method is one professional psychologist or counselor meeting with one student or a small group of students. Often a formal or informal contract prescribes the frequency, location, and specific focus of the meetings. It is not uncommon for students to have more than one supervisor, each with a different focus. For example, one supervisor may be responsible for monitoring paperwork and adherence to institutional procedures, another supervisor may focus on assessment or diagnosis, and another on case material.

Supervision is usually focused on case- or client-generated material. This may take the form of the student's verbal self-report, a written report or verbatim transcripts of a session, or an audio or videotape of a session. Live supervision occurs when the supervisor is either in session with the therapist or can monitor the session through a one-way mirror. The supervisor can assist the student by providing in vivo suggestions, phoning in suggestions, using a bug in the ear, or by arranging for breaks in the therapy.

Models. Supervision is often conducted according to the developmental needs of the student and/or according to the therapeutic orientation of the supervisor. Supervision research has focused on the developmental needs of student counselors. Although researchers disagree on the exact stages of development, most agree that the beginning therapist tends to be more anxious and dependent on the supervisor for technique training. The beginning therapist focuses on basic listening skills and the fundamentals of case assessment/formulation. The middle-stage therapist is learning orientations and theories and is practicing some independence from the supervisor. Student therapists are engaging in self-exploration of their own issues, values, and preferences. The supervisor models integration of learning with therapeutic intervention with clients. The end-phase student therapist engages the supervisor as a sounding board for increasingly complex theory and case formulations. The supervisor and nearly autonomous student are able to focus on finer points of technique, theory, and therapist self-awareness. The developmental approach looks overall at the changing needs of students in relation to their self-development as professionals, to their relational needs with the supervisor, and to their growing skill as therapists or counselors.

Another approach to supervision follows the principles and practices of the major schools of psychology. Just as each school has different theories and techniques, each school has different theories and techniques for supervision that parallel the basic assumptions held for clients. Dynamic supervision may focus on the transference/countertransference occurring between the therapist and client and between the therapist and the supervisor (also known as parallel process). Cognitive and behavioral supervision may be more focused on assessment of client behaviors and intervention skill development. Family systems or group supervision is focused on assessing the process dynamics of groups and interventions for the systems. Supervision may also focus on the therapist's role within the family system or group process. The therapies belonging to the third force or humanistic schools each have their own guiding principles for supervision. With increasing numbers of psychologists and counselors declaring an eclectic approach, supervision becomes more focused on developing guiding principles for choosing among the various schools of thought and technique.

Roles. Supervision calls for a variety of interpersonal roles and responsibilities: teacher, monitor of professional and ethical issues, role model, colleague, and so forth (Bernard & Goodyear, 1992). The supervisor must also act as evaluator of the students' learning, skills, and clinical suitability. In some supervision contexts the supervisor walks a fine line between exploring the students' issues with a client and doing therapy with the students. Although the supervisor may act as counselor on occasion, this is generally discouraged (Holloway, 1995). The needs of the students, demands of the clinical situation, and the preferences of the supervisor often determine which roles are employed.

Ethics. As with clients, ethical principles apply to supervision. These principles include providing due process, allowing informed consent of the client and informed consent of the supervisee, avoiding dual relationships, maintaining confidentiality, and monitoring competence. Counselors and therapists should abide by the appropriate ethical and legal codes of their professional alliances such as the American Psychological Association or the American Association of Counseling and Development.

Supervision is an important part of counselor and therapist development. Guest and Beutler (1988) suggest that early supervision experiences continue to exert influence throughout a therapist's or a counselor's professional life. The complexity of the mental health profession and the therapeutic task necessitates a well-balanced supervisory relationship.

References

Bernard, J., & Goodyear, R. (1992). *Fundamentals of clinical supervision.* Boston: Allyn & Bacon.

Guest, P. D., & Beutler, L. E. (1988). Impact of psychotherapy supervision on therapist orientation and values. *Journal of Consulting and Clinical Psychology, 56* (5), 653–658.

Holloway, E. (1995). *Clinical supervision: A systems approach.* Thousand Oaks, CA: Sage.

M. L. Dykstra

See Training in Counseling and Psychotherapy.

Supportive Psychotherapy. A type of psychological treatment that utilizes various techniques directed toward symptomatic improvement and reestablishment of a client's usual adaptive behaviors.

Distinctives and Objectives. Psychotherapy is a psychological treatment assisting people with emotional problems. The treatment may be one of three different kinds: supportive, reeducative, or reconstructive (Wolberg, 1977). The differences between these kinds of treatment center on their objectives and approaches. The many, varied schools of psychotherapy find their preference in one of these three kinds of treatment. An example of each is guidance (supportive), family therapy (reeducative), and psychoanalytic psychotherapy (reconstructive).

As suggested by its name, supportive therapy aims to support clients, strengthening their defenses and preventing them from getting worse during the healing process. This treatment works to bring a client to a place of emotional equilibrium as soon as possible; its intent is to bring about an improvement of the symptoms so that the client can resume a level of functioning close to his or her norm. This therapy has three goals: to strengthen existing defenses; to promote a level of functioning in the individual adequate to meet the demands of his or her environment; and to reduce or remove the detrimental external factors that prompt the stress. These somewhat modest goals are not intended to change personality structure, although sometimes constructive alterations occur on their own once restoration is made and the successful new adaptations have been achieved.

Supportive measures may be used in two ways: as a primary treatment or as an adjunct to reeducative or reconstructive psychotherapies. Wolberg (1977) suggests four reasons for using support: as a temporary necessity for basically sound personality structures that are momentarily overwhelmed by transient pressures the person is unable to handle; as a primary, extensive means of maintaining borderline and characterologically dependent clients in homeostasis; to promote ego building, so that an individual can subsequently lend his or her efforts to more reconstructive psychotherapeutic work; and as a temporary resting place during more intensive therapy when anxiety becomes too great for one to cope adequately.

Those who seem to benefit most from supportive psychotherapy are people who are experiencing an acute crisis and need temporary encouragement. Chronically disturbed individuals also can function quite adequately when receiving ongoing support.

Supportive therapy is contraindicated if authority issues are so predominant that the client becomes competitive and depreciating and seeks control of the therapeutic process by aggressive or hostile means. This form of therapy is also contraindicated if the client detaches and becomes helpless; in this instance, supportive therapy serves only to encourage the pathologic dependency.

Therapeutic Approach and Techniques. Supportive therapy views the client as an individual capable of change. Furthermore, it is not assumed that insight is necessary for such change to occur. A more crucial curative ingredient is hopefulness; an individual will weather the necessary difficult times when he or she believes there is hope, even if that hope must be temporarily borrowed from the therapist. Therapeutic optimism is therefore an important qualification for the supportive therapist. He or she should also have and be able to communicate a concern for and nonjudgmental acceptance of the client. The therapist should also be flexible, as supportive therapeutic work typically draws on a broad range of techniques.

Directive Guidance. The giving of advice or guidance is a technique that must be carefully regulated to the needs of the client. Specific recommendations are suitable for anxious and disorganized individuals but not for those capable of making their own decisions. Advising a client in areas of life changes that may be irreversible should be avoided.

Nondirective Guidance. This technique avoids some of the dangers of directive guidance yet provides guidance. The therapist listens carefully and offers the client a summary of the problems he or she has described along with several approaches for resolution. The therapist assumes the person is capable of good judgment and places the responsibility for decisions on the client.

Environmental Intervention. This technique consists of initiating stress-reducing changes in the environment when a client is unable to take action to improve his or her own situation. Examples might be a phone call to an employer or to a medical facility for an appointment, or suggesting a change of housing or a vacation. This technique must be used carefully with those clients who easily become dependent.

Ventilation. Allowing a client to express previously suppressed emotions and thoughts often results in a noticeable reduction of emotional tension and the capability to think more clearly. This method should be used selectively. It should not be employed if tension escalates rapidly or disorganized thinking and behavior increase.

Reassurance. Encouragement can often be beneficial, particularly after the client has thoroughly expressed his or her feelings concerning a situation. General, pat statements, such as "Everything will be all right" are not supportive and usually shut down further communication.

Education. After the client's problems are determined, the therapist's participation can often have an educative component. The focus may be on providing the client with the information and experience for learning better ways to solve problems.

Diversion. This tactic redirects a client's thinking and/or behavior away from disturbing topics to less intense and more therapeutic ones. Diversion is used primarily with clients who become so absorbed in personal problems that they neglect other important areas of their lives. It is particularly useful for those who are medically ill or experiencing chronic pain.

Other Techniques. Other supportive measures include tension control such as self-relaxation, self-hypnosis, meditation, and biofeedback; milieu therapy, which includes environmental manipulation, home treatment, day treatment, occupational therapy, music therapy, dance therapy, and social therapy; pressure and coercion; persuasion; confession; chemotherapy; and inspirational self-help group therapies such as Alcoholics Anonymous (AA) or Parents United.

Biblical Evaluation. A basic theme of Scripture is growth and restoration. Central to life is the phenomenon of growth, the capacity to change, and the restorative process. The biblical message is that while pain, hurt, pathology, and sin exist, there is still hope for healing and wholeness.

Christ teaches us through his parables and discerning dialogues that people hear and respond at varying levels, depending on their circumstances and personal development. Children, adults, men, women, disciples, and Pharisees all heard the same message, but each responded quite differently. Depending on the situation, Jesus used a variety of approaches, such as guidance, instruction, encouragement, acceptance, and protection.

There is a similarity between some approaches of supportive psychotherapy and the approaches Jesus took. The directive approach is clear in such passages as, "Go home to your people and report to them what great things the Lord has done for you, and how He had mercy on you" (Mark 5:19, NASB). Reassurance and encouragement are given as people hear a message of hope: "I am the way, and the truth, and the life" (John 14:6, NASB). Education is masterfully illustrated: "He who has seen Me has seen the Father" (John 14:9, NASB). "He who is without sin among you, let him be the first to throw a stone at her" (John 8:7, NASB) is a superb diversion tactic.

Supportive therapy therefore seems to be an important mode of psychological treatment, broadly compatible with Christ's own style of relating to people. Either as an adjunct or an alternative to more reconstructive approaches, supportive techniques are clearly the treatment of choice in many situations.

Reference

Wolberg, L. R. (1977). *The technique of psychotherapy* (Vol. 1) (3rd ed.). New York: Grune & Stratton.

B. J. SHEPPERSON

See SHORT-TERM THERAPIES.

Suppression. The conscious forcing of desires, thoughts, emotions, or impulses out of consciousness. This process of conscious inhibition differs from repression, which is an unconscious ego defense mechanism. It is possible, however, that material that the individual originally willfully removes from consciousness through suppression may eventually submit to unconscious repression, becoming unavailable to further conscious awareness, should it represent a sufficient threat to the ego. An example of suppression would be the person who is aware of feelings of strong hostility toward his boss but chooses to force hostile thoughts and feelings from his awareness and focus on necessary businesslike cooperation.

R. LARKIN

See DEFENSE MECHANISMS.

Surveys. *See* PSYCHOLOGY, METHODS OF.

Suspicion. Suspicion is a noun describing the adjective *suspicious*. Both words go back to the verb *to suspect*, which means to believe or to surmise. In social psychology suspicion is part of the larger topic of attribution: the process of making inferences about the behavior of others. Suspiciousness specifically deals with inferences made about the motives underlying the behavior of others. When a person is suspicious, he or she is surmising that the other person intends harm, deceit, or exploitation.

Some degree of suspiciousness is warranted, but it must be apportioned to the situation: the risks of a false positive judgment (to infer that someone intends evil when he or she is sincere) must be weighed against the risk of a false negative judgment (to assume that someone can be trusted when he or she is attempting to deceive). When one is dealing with known criminals, suspicion is often warranted. The same can be said for persons who are chemically dependent or who have other addictions (e.g., gambling) or who are overly zealous in their sales presentations. To accept their good will and promises of reform may be foolish. Their past behavior often provides enough evidence to make suspicion the most reasonable surmisal.

In many situations, however, suspiciousness leads to unfortunate results. A vicious cycle of dysfunctional interpersonal exchange may follow: each attempt to reassure the suspicious person may be perceived as a more strenuous attempt to deceive. A manager who is overly suspicious about an employee may engage in supervisory practices that sap motivation, discourage initiative, and drive that employee out of the company. A parent who is overly suspicious about a child and takes additional surveillance measures can lose the child's trust and effectively shut down communication between the generations.

Another area in which suspicion is rarely helpful is in a marital relationship. Many men and women are insecure in their own lovability and fear that a spouse may easily be wooed away by another suitor. This can lead to a persistent delusion that the spouse is in the midst of an affair.

In personality psychology suspiciousness is seen not as a temporary state that may or may not be justified by the situation but as an enduring trait that determines how the individual approaches all situations. Suspiciousness is one of the mainstays of William James's tough-minded personality type. Suspiciousness is also on one of Raymond Bernard Cattell's Sixteen Personality Factor Questionnaire scales. Research has shown that suspiciousness can be considered an enduring disposition to infer.

However, correlations with other traits are usually quite low. For example, among African-Americans religiosity is negatively correlated with suspiciousness, but the patterns are less consistent for other Americans. In some cults religiosity would go along with acceptance of a worldview that sees all outsiders as minions of Satan. Because of low cor-relations with other traits, it is not clear among industrial psychologists to what extent suspiciousness can be used to predict who will make a good airline pilot, police officer, entrepreneur, or psychotherapist.

In clinical psychology one looks beyond occasional or limited suspicion and seeks a generalized and excessive trait of suspiciousness. *DSM-IV* gives suspiciousness as criterion A for the diagnosis of paranoid personality disorder. In addition to the suspicion that others are exploiting, harming, deceiving, or plotting against one, suspiciousness can take the form of having doubts about the loyalty of friends, associates, and family. Suspicious people tend to be extremely guarded in their self-presentation and look for hidden meanings (i.e., confirmation of their suspicions) in events or the remarks and actions of others. Suspicious people are extremely sensitive to any slight or insult, responding quickly and excessively. Some of the signs of paranoia can also be found in suspicious patients: exaggerated concerns with self-sufficiency, autonomy, blaming others, or threats of legal action.

Suspiciousness is a trait firmly established by early adulthood, but two conditions seem to exacerbate it. One is the use of illegal drugs, especially amphetamines and cocaine (*see* Street Drugs). Another is the onset of dementia in later life. In the early stages of Alzheimer's disease, for example, patients may suspect that others are stealing things from them or replacing or moving objects rather than realize the failing powers of their own memories.

The great challenge in doing psychotherapy with a suspicious person is the construction of the therapeutic alliance. One tendency in psychotherapy with suspicious patients is that as the therapeutic alliance is created, a deepening depression may ensue. The suspiciousness and related symptoms of paranoia are defenses against self-blame, lack of self-acceptance. As a result suspicion and rigidity in general should not be directly attacked. Rather, to earn trust the therapist should respect the patient's autonomy and admire the patient's force of will.

T. L. BRINK

See PARANOIA; TRUST.

Symbolic-Experiential Family Therapy. Carl Whitaker, the originator of symbolic-experiential family therapy, describes this approach as more of a philosophy than a theory. He also views family therapy as an art rather than a scientific procedure.

Symbolic-experiential family therapy requires two therapists who serve as guides in resolving the family's problems. Additional therapists may serve as consultants if a particular problem arises. For example, if the two main therapists are males and a family member feels that males are biased, a female therapist may serve as consultant for as many sessions as necessary. Or parents may object to their daughter's dating a black male, and so a black therapist may be called as a consultant. The cotherapy model allows the family to learn from the therapist interaction and provides opportunity for the therapists to observe each other as well as the family process (Whitaker & Keith, 1981).

The focus of therapy is the here and now. The therapists teach the family that they can direct their own development in spite of the problems of the past. To facilitate this family members need to respect generational differences and form healthy boundaries, learn how to participate in a family, and learn to individuate from the family. Each family member is encouraged to be flexible in his or her family roles. The therapists model this process by joining the family and separating from them throughout the sessions.

Whitaker is emphatic that all family members must participate in the sessions. If one family member does not show up, the session may be cancelled until the missing person agrees to come. This procedure is explained in the initial setting up of an appointment. Not wanting to participate is a direct message about the ongoing family dynamics. Extended family members are invited to come as consultants to the family as often as they can. Participants may include a former spouse, pastors, or others deeply concerned about the family. Just as a therapist can call in consultants, the family has the same right to assistance by calling family consultants (Napier & Whitaker, 1978).

The therapists attempt to increase interpersonal stress in the family in order to examine the relational dynamics and patterns of interaction. Such techniques as paradoxical intervention or as if situations are frequently utilized. For example, a suicidal mother may be asked, "How long do you think your family will mourn if you killed yourself?" The additional stress facilitates examining family members' thoughts and feelings during the session. Homework is not encouraged; family members are encouraged not to discuss the session between appointments. This is designed to keep the sessions emotionally charged.

Every family begins therapy with a family assessment. The stressors on the family are examined. The purpose is to become acquainted so that a relationship can develop. The early expression of empathy and concern for areas of family concern becomes the cornerstone for working together. Every family has its own distinct story, and the therapists need to know the story in order to assist them. During this assessment process interaction dynamics are observed and process hypotheses are formed so that the family dynamics can be examined and clarified during the course of therapy. If the family wishes to stop, they are taking a risk and need to be encouraged to use their strengths. Keeping them in therapy would probably be for the therapists' needs and not for the family's. If they wish to return, they are welcome, and they may continue to develop at stages with intermittent breaks in therapy.

Whitaker is undoubtedly correct in not considering this a unique system of family therapy. It remains unresearched and largely untried except by Whitaker and his associates.

References

Napier, A. Y., & Whitaker, C. A. (1978). *The family crucible.* New York: Harper & Row.
Whitaker, C. A., & Keith, V. (1981). Symbolic-experiential family therapy. In A. S. Gurman & D. P. Kniskern (Eds.), *Handbook of family therapy.* New York: Brunner/Mazel.

Additional Readings

Whitaker, C. A. (1976a). A family is a four dimensional relationship. In P. J. Guerin, Jr. (Ed.), *Family therapy.* New York: Gardner.
Whitaker, C. A. (1976b). Hindrance of theory in clinical work. In P. J. Guerin, Jr. (Ed.), *Family therapy.* New York: Gardner.

T. M. JOHNSON

See FAMILY THERAPY: OVERVIEW.

Sympathy. A feeling of compassion for either a person or a group that is experiencing distress. It is also seen as a capacity for sharing the interests and concerns of another human being. Sympathy may arise even when there is no emotional attachment toward the person or group with whom one is sympathetic. Sympathy differs from empathy in that the feelings of the sympathetic person remain essentially internal and knowledge of what caused the other person's feelings is not necessary. Sympathetic responses are feelings resulting from the observation of an emotion displayed by another. The sympathetic person becomes an imitator, although the sympathetic feeling need not be similar to the feeling of the other person.

Sympathy is regarded as a complex emotion because it presupposes that a person has the ability to perceive and understand the misfortunes of others as well as the ability to express this feeling to others. People vary widely in their sensitivity to others. The emotional climate of the home is considered the greatest influence in the development of sympathetic feelings. If the parents are considerate of other people's feelings and are able to express them in a positive way, the children are more likely to adopt similar attitudes.

J. H. ROBERTSON

See EMPATHY.

Symptom Prescription. *See* PARADOXICAL INTERVENTION.

Syncope. The temporary loss of consciousness as a result of a failure in the supply of blood to the brain, as in fainting. It is sometimes a hysterical or conversion symptom but may also occur in psychosomatic disorders when emotional stress interferes with the circulation of blood to the brain.

Syndrome. A group or pattern of symptoms that occur concurrently and are indicative of a recognizable disease or condition. This term is similar to, but less specific than, *disease* or *disorder*.

Systematic Desensitization. A therapeutic procedure based on the framework of learning theory. Wolpe (1958) is generally credited for its development. The specific goal of treatment is to substitute relaxation responses for debilitating anxiety or fear responses in specific triggering situations. The approach assumes that anxiety and fear symptoms are learned or conditioned and therefore can be deconditioned. Therefore, systematic desensitization, together with most behavior therapy, has developed directly from the application of laboratory research in the behavioral sciences.

The history of desensitization dates to a model experiment by Jones (1924). She eliminated a young boy's fear responses to small animals by gradually exposing the boy to the feared animal, in this case a rabbit. The child sat in a high chair eating while the animal was introduced into the room a considerable distance away. Over a series of trials the rabbit was moved closer and closer to the boy, each time with the boy in his chair eating. After many such sessions the boy was able to hold the rabbit on his lap with no evidence of fear.

No one applied the results of Jones's research until Wolpe and his colleagues became interested in treating anxiety symptoms. From their work they formulated a four-step procedure that is generally still followed.

First, the therapist obtains a detailed account from the client of those situations triggering anxiety. From this information the therapist constructs one or more anxiety hierarchies. This is a list of situations ranked by the client from least to most anxiety-arousing. An example of a hierarchy used to treat a phobia about leaving the house might include the following, beginning with the situation arousing the least anxiety and ending with the one arousing the most: going to the door of the house; opening the front door of the house; going out on the porch; going down the steps; walking out to the front walk; going to the edge of the property; walking to the end of the block; walking down the second block.

Second, the therapist trains the client to relax. Wolpe favored Jacobson's (1938) progressive relaxation procedure for this purpose. The therapist systematically directs the client alternately to contract, then relax, each individual muscle group in his or her body. Through this exercise the client becomes progressively more relaxed and comfortable.

Third, the desensitization process begins. While the client relaxed in the comfortable state, the therapist has him or her vividly imagine each scene in the hierarchy. The presentation is done over several trials, each trial beginning with the least anxiety-producing event and continuing through the hierarchy until the client first notices muscle tension and/or anxiety. At that time the client signals the therapist, usually by lifting an index finger. The therapist then helps the client restore the relaxed state by visualizing a peaceful scene. When the client again relaxes and signals the therapist, a second trial on the hierarchy starts. Trials continue until the person can visualize going through each step of the hierarchy without feeling anxiety or muscle tension. At that point the hierarchy is considered deconditioned, and supposedly anxiety has been eliminated as a response to those visualized situations.

During the fourth step the client acts out the hierarchy behaviorally. A person deconditioned on the preceding hierarchy will go out of the house and walk down the block. If he or she is successfully desensitized, the person will experience a decrease in anxiety.

Compared to more dynamically oriented therapies the desensitization procedure is relatively brief. However, its effectiveness has been well documented both experimentally and therapeutically. Its value lies in the treatment of phobias and anxiety evoked by specific situations. This value is also the major limitation, as most anxiety conditions are not so easily connected to specific situations.

Some therapists claim the approach is naive, meaning that only symptoms are treated, while personality, the quality of the relationship, transference, and other important aspects of therapy are ignored. These are the major deficiencies in the approach. Some dynamically oriented theorists warn that disorder could become more severe. Neither has generally been found.

Finally, the approach in its extreme treats persons as mechanistic and reactive. No emphasis is placed on a relation to God as central to understanding human beings. However, this criticism is not aimed at the method as much as toward the philosophical reasoning underlying most behavioristic views of persons.

References

Jacobson, E. (1938). *Progressive relaxation* (2nd ed.). Chicago: University of Chicago Press.

Jones, M. C. (1924). The elimination of children's fears. *Journal of Experimental Psychology, 7,* 382–390.

Wolpe, J. (1958). *Psychotherapy by reciprocal inhibition.* Palo Alto, CA: Stanford University Press.

L. PARROTT III

See BEHAVIOR THERAPY; RELAXATION TRAINING; ANXIETY; PHOBIC DISORDERS.

Tt

TAT. *See* THEMATIC APPERCEPTION TEST.

Techniques of Christian Counseling. In counseling God is the ultimate change agent, and God works directly on the client's heart and through the counseling relationship. But how does change happen within a relationship? Counselor and client interact, and that interaction creates a different phenomenological experience for the client; that is, a change in the client. Some interactions are spontaneous and others are more scripted, planned, or repeatable across different clients. Those may be called counseling techniques. When the counseling techniques deal with Christian content, they may be called Christian counseling techniques.

Most Christian counseling techniques either have been derived from a religious tradition (called ecclesiastically based techniques) or have been adaptations of secular counseling approaches (called Christianized approaches), such as cognitive-behavior therapy with explicitly Christian content.

Ecclesiastically Based Techniques. Several investigators have studied the relative frequency of use of ecclesiastically based techniques in counseling (Ball & Goodyear, 1991, two studies; Jones, Watson, & Wolfram, 1992; Richards & Potts, 1995 [with Mormons], two studies; Worthington, Dupont, Berry, & Duncan, 1988). Three approaches generally are used to evaluate the prevalence of use of these techniques. First, clients and therapists have been asked after each session what they did (Worthington, Dupont, Berry, & Duncan, 1988). Second, people have been surveyed about what they do (Ball & Goodyear, 1991, study 1; Jones, Watson, & Wolfram, 1992; Richards & Potts, 1995, study 1). Third, therapists have described critical incidents producing change or negative effects (Ball & Goodyear, 1991, study 2; Richards & Potts, 1995, study 2).

On the basis of these studies we might draw several conclusions. First, the use of ecclesiastically based techniques is a function of individual therapists' preferences rather than a unitary approach to therapy. That conclusion is based on two observations: which techniques were studied differs in the various studies, and prevalence of use differs in the various studies.

Second, some techniques are used more frequently than are others, notably those that are often not obtrusive to clients (such as praying for a client, explaining a Christian concept, implicit Christian teaching, or teaching a scriptural concept) or those that are acceptable in secular therapy as well as explicitly Christian therapy (e.g., forgiveness). This raises two questions.

How openly do Christian counselors use ecclesiastically based techniques? For example, a counselor can use forgiveness, praying silently for the client, or teaching a Christian concept such as confessing wrongs without a client knowing that the counselor is using a Christian concept. Even interventions that sound Christian, such as confronting sin, might be done so that the client never realizes that the counselor is working from a Christian perspective.

Why are explicit techniques not used more often than they are? Counselors may be concerned about clients perceiving the counselor as too religious, confusing boundaries between professional and pastoral counseling, offending clients, or lack of effectiveness of ecclesiastically based techniques.

Third, the distribution for prevalence of use does not parallel the distribution for techniques involved in either positive or negative critical incidents in counseling. Some techniques are more potent than are others. Praying for clients, quoting Scripture, teaching scriptural concepts, and forgiveness apparently are thought to produce dramatic positive responses (and sometimes dramatic negative responses, especially teaching concepts and quoting Scripture).

In general we might adduce several guidelines for using ecclesiastically based techniques.

- Use ecclesiastically based techniques only when one is prompted by the Holy Spirit.
- Use them only when they are appropriate for the counseling context.
- Use them only in a trusting relationship.
- Base their use on a knowledge of the client's personality, values, and expectations.

- Match technique to client's values, level of spirituality (Worthington, Dupont, Berry, & Duncan, 1988), and seriousness of disturbance. Do not use them if religion is part of the problem, such as with religious delusions, feelings of persecution by God, or bad experiences with religion or church. Negative effects can arise. In cases of poor matching some clients may be driven away or may complain to supervisors, insurance companies, or managed-care companies.

- Use them carefully and infrequently (Jones, Watson, & Wolfram, 1992), weighing their religious and therapeutic impact against secular techniques.

- Investigate whether the techniques one uses are effective.

Much work is still needed. For example, what happens when a religious intervention occurs, and are ecclesiastically based techniques effective at producing change? Only for prayer (Finney & Malony, 1985) and forgiveness (Hebl & Enright, 1993; McCullough & Worthington, 1995) have any studies of effectiveness been done.

Integration of Religiosity into General Theoretical Approaches. *Cognitive Therapy.* Two versions of cognitive therapy have been tested. One version (Propst's) is more like Beck's and the other is more like Albert Ellis's. Propst, Ostrom, Watkins, Dean, and Mashburn (1992) conducted a clinical trial of Propst's (1980) therapy for depression with religious clients. Propst et al. compared nonreligious cognitive-behavioral therapy (NRCBT), religious CBT (RCBT), pastoral counseling treatment (PCT), and waiting-list clients. Therapy involved 18 one-hour sessions in both CBT groups. In PCT, 75% of each session was spent in nondirective listening and 25% was spent discussing Bible verses or religious themes of interest to the clients (what we might have described as ecclesiastically based techniques). By the end of treatment RCBT reduced depression more than waiting list; NRCBT and PCT did not. Nonreligious therapists using the religious CBT outperformed both the waiting list and nonreligious therapists with the NRCBT treatment. The religious therapists using the NRCBT treatment were superior to the waiting list but not to the RCBT treatment. Most effects were maintained at follow-up. In a separate study Richards, Owen, and Stein (1993) adapted Propst's treatment for use with perfectionistic Mormon clients. Clients reduced perfectionism and depression and increased self-esteem and sense of existential well-being but did not change their sense of religious well-being.

Three investigations of adaptations of rational-emotive therapy (RET) have shown it to be similarly effective. Johnson and Ridley (1992) compared RET and a Christian version of RET for ten mildly depressed Christian clients. Six 50-minute sessions were conducted within three weeks. Participants were tested pre- and postintervention for depression, automatic negative thoughts, and irrational ideas. Participants in both treatments improved in depression and automatic negative thoughts. Only Christian RET participants reduced their irrational ideas. Religious values did not change for either treatment. RET and Christian RET did not differ in the amount of change they produced. Johnson, Devries, Ridley, Pettorini, and Peterson (1994) replicated the study with 32 Christian clients. Similar findings were obtained by Pecheur and Edwards (1984), who provided eight hours of therapy over four weeks to mildly depressed Christian students. (For additional issues in RET with Christian clients, see Watson, 1994.)

Overall religiously adapted cognitive therapy has been found to be effective with mildly depressed religious clients (see Johnson, 1993, and Johnson & Ridley, 1992, for reviews). Christian versions of cognitive therapies have not affected religious orientation or religious behavior more than have the nonreligious versions.

Christian counseling techniques are important, but studies have shown that they are probably not the main therapeutic ingredient in a client's change. There is evidence that they are used but less evidence that they are very effective. It is incumbent on practitioners who use such techniques to determine how much they contribute to stimulating change and then to apply the techniques with Christian humility.

References

Ball, R. A., & Goodyear, R. K. (1991). Self-reported professional practices of Christian psychotherapists. *Journal of Psychology and Christianity, 10* (2), 144–153.

Finney, J. R., & Malony, H. N. (1985). An empirical study of contemplative prayer as an adjunct to psychotherapy. *Journal of Psychology and Theology, 13,* 284–290.

Hebl, J., & Enright, R. D. (1993). Forgiveness as a psychotherapeutic goal with elderly females. *Psychotherapy, 30,* 658–667.

Johnson, W. B. (1993). Christian rational-emotive therapy: A treatment protocol. *Journal of Psychology and Christianity, 12* (3), 254–261.

Johnson, W. B., Devries, R., Ridley, C. R., Pettorini, D., & Peterson, D. R. (1994). The comparative efficacy of Christian and secular rational-emotive therapy with Christian clients. *Journal of Psychology and Theology, 22,* 130–140.

Johnson, W. B., & Ridley, C. R. (1992). Brief Christian and non-Christian rational emotive therapy with depressed Christian clients: An exploratory study. *Counseling and Values, 36,* 220–228.

Jones, S. L., Watson, E. J., & Wolfram, T. J. (1992). Results of the Rech Conference survey on religious faith and professional psychology. *Journal of Psychology and Theology, 20,* 147–158.

McCullough, M. E., & Worthington, E. L., Jr. (1995). Promoting forgiveness: A comparison of two brief psychoeducational group interventions with a waiting-list control. *Counseling and Values, 40,* 55–68.

Pecheur, D. R., & Edwards, K. J. (1984). A comparison of secular and religious versions of cognitive therapy with depressed Christian college students. *Journal of Psychology and Theology, 12,* 45–54.

Propst, L. R. (1980). The comparative efficacy of religious and nonreligious imagery for the treatment of mild depression in religious individuals. *Cognitive Therapy and Research, 4,* 167–178.

Propst, L. R., Ostrom, R., Watkins, P., Dean, T., & Mashburn, D. (1992). Comparative efficacy of religious and nonreligious cognitive-behavioral therapy for the treatment of clinical depression in religious individuals. *Journal of Consulting and Clinical Psychology, 60,* 94–103.

Richards, P. S., Owen, L., & Stein, S. (1993). A religiously oriented group counseling intervention for self-defeating perfectionism: A pilot study. *Counseling and Values, 37,* 96–104.

Richards, P. S., & Potts, R. W. (1995). Using spiritual interventions in psychotherapy: Practices, successes, failures, and ethical concerns of Mormon psychotherapists. *Professional Psychology: Research and Practice, 26,* 163–170.

Watson, P. J. (Ed.). (1994). Rational-emotive therapy [Special issue]. *Journal of Psychology and Christianity, 13* (4).

Worthington, E. L., Jr., Dupont, P. D., Berry, J. T., & Duncan, L. A. (1988). Christian therapists' and clients' perceptions of religious psychotherapy in private and agency settings. *Journal of Psychology and Theology, 16,* 282–293.

E. L. WORTHINGTON, JR.

See COUNSELING AND PSYCHOTHERAPY: OVERVIEW.

Telephone Therapy. The primary use of the telephone in therapy is found in crisis hotlines, which are available in most urban areas. These centers are staffed by paraprofessional workers with various levels of training; most are given little initial instruction in crisis intervention and only a modicum of continuing education (Burns & Dixon, 1974). Due to the intrinsically stressing nature of this work and the lack of adequate preparatory or in-service training, turnover and burnout rates for this type of telephone therapy are high (Greenstone & Leviton, 1979).

The telephone can be used in other therapy modalities besides crisis intervention. Relationship-based therapies of all varieties can be done over the phone. This type of ongoing telephone therapy generally is the result of a person having begun work with a therapist in one location and then relocating in another area where a compatible therapist is not available. Almost always some initial or intermittent contact on a face-to-face basis is required, both for therapeutic maintenance of rapport and the safe release of repressed and often intense emotions, which are difficult to express on a sustained basis over the telephone.

While working with a client in this sort of on-going therapy the therapist should be acutely aware of several variables. The first has to do with the physical setting of the client on the other end of the line. It is good, particularly for visually oriented therapists, to inquire regarding the client's physical milieu. One can ask the client to close his or her eyes while talking with you, imagine you with them in the room, and then describe in detail what they see. It behooves the therapist to place himself or herself in that physical niche by using whatever imagery is at his or her command. This is necessary if one is striving to establish adequate levels of identification and empathy with the client.

The second variable, requiring the therapist's awareness, pertains to the use of language. In the absence of kinesthetic or visual stimuli one is required to extract every bit of meaning from the auditory information available. One should therefore endeavor to pace with or match the client's use of language. This use of neurolinguistic programming techniques is critical for the maintenance of rapport and empathy.

The final awareness needed by a telephone therapist pertains to the use of face-to-face booster sessions of intense therapeutic work as needed. If the therapist feels out of touch or puzzled with the course of treatment, he or she should ask that the client use an audiovisual telephone apparatus (particularly as this tool becomes more available) or request a face-to-face interview. The need for such adjunctive methods will obviously depend on the client, the therapist, and the quality and nature of their relationship.

References

Burns, J. L., & Dixon, M. C. (1974). Crisis theory, active learning and the training of telephone crisis volunteers. *Journal of Community Psychology, 2,* 120–125.

Greenstone, J. L., & Leviton, S. C. (1979). *The crisis intervener's handbook* (Vol. 2). Dallas: Crisis Management Workshops.

V. L. SHEPPERSON

See SUPPORTIVE PSYCHOTHERAPY; LAY COUNSELING; PARAPROFESSIONAL THERAPY.

Television Viewing, Effects of. Almost since its beginning, social critics have lamented the negative effects of television while mass media scholars searched for empirical evidence of such. Researchers' interest in television effects continues in part because of the increasing time spent with television. In the typical U.S. household, the television is on about seven hours per day. Further, most people watch at least two to three hours of television each day.

As viewing time increases, other activities are displaced. Typical findings in time use studies indicate that, as television viewing increases, work, sleep, outdoor activities, and other forms of recreation and relaxation decrease. Thus television directly affects behavior when viewers spend more time viewing and less time doing other things.

For some people, television viewing results in less social interaction when viewing displaces interpersonal conversation or other social activities. Sometimes social interaction is replaced with parasocial interaction when viewers become involved with television characters or personalities, speaking to and relating as if the viewer personally knows the television figures. For others, television viewing facilitates social interaction. Many discussions and/or arguments are based on televised sporting events, news reports, or even dramatic or comedy entertainment programs.

In addition to changing time use, people learn from television. Television viewing affects viewers' awareness, beliefs, attitudes, and values, as well as behavior. From news programming viewers learn about news events. From sports programming viewers form positive or negative attitudes toward players, coaches, teams, and cities. From entertainment programs viewers learn about characters, plots, and settings. From commercials viewers learn about the existence, availability, and claimed features of various products and services.

These learning effects may seem relatively inconsequential, the result of extended observation of any object, situation, or phenomenon. However, much of the current research centers on understanding the underlying significance and power of these and other apparently trivial influences.

Katz (1980) has described the history of "media effects research" in terms of the varying roles of selectivity and interpersonal relationships in understanding the nature and extent of media effects. Katz's analysis encompasses television. Selectivity is the tendency among audiences to select or choose (consciously or unconsciously) the extent to which they view particular television programs (selective exposure), give attention to specific television content (selective attention), perceive messages in particular ways (selective perception), and remember some or all of what they experience in watching television (selective retention). Selectivity is based primarily on preexisting attitudes, values, beliefs, and behaviors. Interpersonal relationships in this context refer to the extent to which interpersonal influences operate to facilitate or mitigate the effects of television.

Individual selectivity and the impact of interpersonal relationships on television viewers will vary. For example, selectivity in children develops and fluctuates concurrently with emerging behavior patterns, beliefs, attitudes, and values. The interpersonal influence of parents, teachers, family friends, siblings, and peers will also modify, negate, or amplify the impact of television on children. Among all audiences, characteristics such as age, education, family income, and social status and mobility in the larger society affect the way selectivity and interpersonal relationships function for each viewer.

Selectivity interacts with specific television content. The vast majority of programming is designed as entertainment. Even news and information programming must attract audiences to remain on the air. Programs possessing large audiences continue. When the audience shrinks programs are canceled. Thus in one sense the national television audience (at the lowest common denominator) gets the programs it wants. However, the economic basis of American broadcast television also insures that viewers will be regularly exposed to some messages they do not want such as, for example, commercial advertisements.

Prime time advertising slots can cost more than $200,000 for 30 seconds of air time. Advertisers pay these large sums for access to the television audience of potential buyers, clients, and voters. Thus the television audience is exposed to entertainment as well as persuasive messages. Selectivity and interpersonal influence help clarify the nature of television's impact through the combination of entertainment and persuasion content.

Research Findings. *Persuasion.* Attempts to persuade through television may be seen in political campaign ads, advertising campaigns for products or services, public service announcements, public health campaigns, and other prosocial campaigns. The consensus among communication scholars is that these kinds of persuasive messages have a minimal impact on target audiences in terms of the obvious intended persuasive goal (McGuire, 1986; Schudsen, 1984).

There is, however, substantial evidence that consumer advertising informs viewers of various products and services. Effective ad campaigns, including jingles or slogans, often become well-known. Yet evidence of dramatic increases in purchase decisions that result from persuasive messages within advertisements is largely absent from the published scientific literature.

One approach to theorizing about television viewing effects is known as uses and gratifications. This model emphasizes the motivations or intentions (uses) of the viewer as a limiting factor in the likely effects of television. Accordingly, audiences seek fairly specific gratifications from television. For example, when people use particular programs for purposes of personal entertainment (gratification), there is a strong resistance to the uninvited persuasive messages presented in commercials. Since television viewers want entertainment, it is no surprise that the commercial breaks are filled with product pitches that are designed primarily with entertainment as the goal (to capture attention and hold it for a few seconds) while secondarily promoting a product or service.

Age and experience influence the way television commercials affect children. Preschoolers typically do not understand the persuasive intent of commercials. Early elementary school children begin to understand and tend to believe the claims of ads. But even with relatively little consumer experience as they grow older, children develop a healthy skepticism toward television commercials. This resistance to the persuasive messages of commercials is one example of selectivity intervening in television effects.

Although television ads typically do not compel viewers to purchase products, they do promote consumerism, materialism, and other generally hedonistic values and lifestyles. Often the images presented in television ads encourage self-centeredness. Television ads are designed to appeal to powerful human emotions, desires, and needs. For example, personal security, belongingness, love and romance, sensuality and sex, wealth and riches, pride and power are often the prominent themes of modern television commercials. Many destructive, negative social attitudes, values, and beliefs are regularly reinforced in this way.

Socialization. By nature, modern television programs provide substantial information about social relationships that can and often does contribute to the socialization process of people newly introduced into a social system. Children who develop in the context of significant exposure to television may be socialized into the society presented in the world of television rather than the world outside television. For most individuals, socialization occurs over many years and results from many influences such as, for example, parents, siblings, peers, teachers, neighbors, religious leaders, counselors, and others. Television is one of many socializing influences.

However, the social information presented on television varies significantly across a broad spectrum of available programs. Social interaction shown in *Mister Rogers' Neighborhood* or on *Sesame Street* is quite different from that displayed by the Power Rangers or in typical Saturday morning cartoons. These portrayals are similarly distinct from the adult social interactions shown in daytime or evening soap operas, crime drama, adult-oriented situation comedies, or theatrical-release movies shown on television. Research points to a real danger that the portrayals of adult situations or graphic real-life violence may be observed, stored in memory, and mimicked by child viewers.

Bandura's (1977) social learning theory describes and elaborates mechanisms whereby the behavior patterns of television models may be observed, imitated, and repeated under conditions of subsequent reward contingencies. Simply stated: viewers can learn new behavior patterns by viewing models and then, through actual or vicarious rewards, imitate the learned behavior. Laboratory research efforts to test this theory have repeatedly demonstrated the power of a simple television presentation of violence to facilitate aggressive behavior in children. Children can learn aggressive behaviors from television, and given the right experimental situation, will imitate aggression toward others.

Findings from field research are more problematic for establishing the causal link between these variables. Part of the problem lies in the nature of selectivity and interpersonal relationships. A commonly reported finding from field research of violent television and aggression is that when statistical models control for previous levels of aggression in children, the relationship between viewing and subsequent aggression becomes quite small. However, an equally common finding is that children who are more aggressive watch more violent television programs. These children also tend to identify more closely with violent television characters. Thus, real-world selectivity confounds researchers' ability to isolate the independent and unique impact of televised violence on aggressive behavior.

In addition to selectivity, interpersonal influence from parents, peer groups, or others can either counteract or facilitate the negative effects of exposure to violent television images and content. Families or peer groups who discourage aggression minimize the negative impact of violent television on children. Families or peer groups who encourage aggression amplify the negative impact of television. Findings from numerous examples of field research, including natural experiments and other quasi-experimental designs, suggest that greater exposure to violent television facilitates aggression in children of all ages, especially boys who identify with violent television characters.

More disturbing perhaps is the consistent finding from experimental research that television images of violence can interact with preexisting viewer anger or frustration to elicit subsequent aggression directed at individuals or institutions that are similar in some way to those depicted in the television portrayal of violence. Thus the most vulnerable to the negative influence of television viewing are angry, frustrated people, adults and children, who through suggestion, imitation, and/or other mechanisms not fully understood initiate violence toward others or themselves (see, for example, Berkowitz & Rogers, 1986).

Television images of violence are probably the most researched category of content for negative effects. But the social learning mechanisms suggested by Bandura (1977) are equally applicable to images of social respect and politeness, dating relationships and behavior, marriage and family relationships, sexuality, work, interpersonal conflict, problem solving, and race relations. Research conducted on exposure to programs such as *Sesame Street*, where prosocial interaction is intentionally modeled, provides evidence that children will imitate the positive actions and attitudes they observe. When children are exposed to antisocial behavior and attitudes or immoral or deviant portrayals, social learning is equally likely if there is little or no strong opposing interpersonal influence from parents. Thus the socializing impact of television varies especially based on the level of selectivity (self-determined or other-determined) and interpersonal influence.

In the same way that young viewers may be socialized by the images and interactions portrayed in television, viewers may also form beliefs about themselves as a result of their experience with television. In fact, uses and gratifications researchers report that sometimes television is used by individuals to make sense of their own life experience, including the formation or strengthening of a self-concept. This happens through identification with fictional characters or television personalities.

Additional Findings. *Knowledge Gaps.* Television tends to increase knowledge gaps between the advantaged, educated segments of the audience and the disadvantaged, less educated segments of the viewing audience. Those who know more initially tend to learn more from prosocial information campaigns or programming (e.g., *Sesame Street*). Knowledge gaps have been reported for both children and adults; those who tend to know more typically gain more from exposure to information in television programs or advertising campaigns. Knowledge gaps vary depending on selectivity processes and interpersonal influence processes.

Agenda Setting. Agenda-setting effects result when certain stories or topics are prominently presented in television news stories to the relative exclusion of other news stories and topics. Those stories given the wider or more frequent coverage tend to increase in importance in the minds of audience members. Thus by focusing attention on certain issues or problems, viewers' judgments of the true importance of national or local problems are affected by the agenda-setting role of television news coverage. By overreporting certain news items, television can and has been shown to shift viewers' beliefs about which issues are truly important.

Ideological Formation. Ideological formation refers to the ability of television to shape and influence fundamental beliefs about reality. Cultivation theorists and researchers (Gerbner, Gross, Morgan, & Signorelli, 1986) study how the facts, images, and stories presented to the television audience are incorporated into viewer orientations, beliefs, and lifestyles. Although cultivation theorists are sometimes criticized for making claims beyond the data, it is clear from a number of studies that some viewer beliefs about reality are derived directly from television. When television viewing time is greater, the effects are greater. Finally, the cultivation effect is most striking when viewers do not have alternative sources of information concerning the reality beliefs at issue.

Media System Dependency. Media system dependency theory (Ball-Rokeach & DeFleur, 1976) adds the useful concept of individual dependency relationships for understanding television effects. Television is likely to have greater effects when the viewing audience is dependent on television for meeting personal goals in three general areas: for understanding and knowledge about self and the environment; for guidance about how to act or react in various situations; and for play or recreation. When individual dependence on television is higher, the effects are greater. Stated another way, when individuals turn to television to meet personal goals (conscious or unconscious) the effects are likely to be substantial.

References

Ball-Rokeach, S. J., & DeFleur, M. L. (1976). A dependency model of mass media effects. *Communication Research*, 3, 3–21.

Bandura, A. (1977). *Social learning theory.* Englewood Cliffs, NJ: Prentice-Hall.

Berkowitz, L., & Rogers, K. H. (1986). A priming effect analysis of media influence. In J. Bryant & D. Zillman (Eds.), *Perspectives on media effects.* Hillsdale, NJ: Erlbaum.

Gerbner, G., Gross, L., Morgan, M., & Signorelli, N. (1986). Living with television: The dynamics of the cultivation process. In J. Bryant & D. Zillman (Eds.), *Perspectives on media effects.* Hillsdale, NJ: Erlbaum.

Katz, E. (1980). On conceptualizing media effects. In T. McCormack (Ed.), *Studies in communications*, Vol. 1. Greenwich, CT: JAI Press.

McGuire, W. J. (1986). The myth of massive media impact: Savagings and salvagings. In G. Comstock (Ed.), *Public communication and behavior*, Vol. 1.

Schudsen, M. (1984). *Advertising, the uneasy persuasion.* New York: Basic Books.

M. D. COZZENS

See AGGRESSION; COGNITIVE DEVELOPMENT; MODELING; SOCIAL LEARNING THEORY.

Temper Tantrum. An excessive and inappropriate emotional outburst, such behavior can be seen throughout the life span but is most common during the preschool and early school years. In its most extreme form the behavior can be quite manipulative and coercive in that it demands a response. The important decision is whether to intervene, and if so, exactly how.

In its milder form the temper tantrum can be ignored, which will lead to what behaviorists call extinction. Competing and/or incompatible behaviors should be reinforced so that a large alternative behavioral repertoire is available. Positive reinforcement for good behavior is far more effective in the long run than punishment for inappropriate behavior. Attention by well-meaning adults can serve to reinforce and maintain such emotional outbursts.

With children, temper tantrums usually follow the consequences of breaking rules. All rules should be clearly explained in advance. The reasons behind the rules and the consequences of breaking them should be fully clarified. Temper tantrums at times appear to be ways of testing the limits.

If extinction and reinforcing incompatible or competing behaviors prove unsatisfactory, alternative forms of discipline should be used. Assertive, direct commands may prove to be effective (Canter & Canter, 1976), as may a time-out procedure (Patterson, 1971). Threats or verbal attacks on the child should be avoided. The parent or teacher should also consider that the inappropriate behavior may be modeled on a regular basis for the child by peers or adults.

If the temper tantrums are frequent, the possibility of a problem in some aspect of the home or school situation should be considered. The rules may be vague or too difficult; the commands may not be direct or sufficiently clear; the child may not be getting enough attention for appropriate behavior; the child may be sick or tired; or the parents may be under significant stress. Spanking as an intervention strategy is recommended by some as a last resort, given careful guidelines (Narramore, 1979).

As with all behavior or emotional disorders, the clinician must be sensitive to the total picture. The personalities of the teachers and parents, the school or home environment, the needs and abilities of the child, and the community environment may all influence a given incident. Whatever intervention is selected, one must be careful to implement it with sensitivity.

References

Canter, L., & Canter, M. (1976). *Assertive discipline: A take charge approach for today's educator.* Seal Beach, CA: Canter & Associates.

Narramore, B. (1979). *Parenting with love and limits.* Grand Rapids, MI: Zondervan.

Patterson, G. R. (1971). *Families.* Champaign, IL: Research Press.

R. E. BUTMAN

See DISRUPTIVE BEHAVIOR DISORDERS.

Temperament. As distinguished from personality more generally, temperament consists of individual differences viewed as predispositions rooted in biology but not immune from environmental influences. Temperament accounts more for the how of behavior than its why. It is usually applied to differences in emotion, attention, and activity levels that appear early in life, are relatively stable and enduring, and underlie the individual's reactions to stimulation.

The ancient physicians Hippocrates and Galen categorized four temperamental subtypes as choleric, melancholic, phlegmatic, and sanguine. These subtypes were thought to have emerged from differences in bodily humors. Different combinations of humors led to particular temperamental styles. Early in the twentieth century, scientific study of temperament emerged in eastern Europe with Ivan Pavlov's theorizing of the innate organization of the nervous system. In western Europe, Kretschmer's body type research and Hans Eysenck's work with central nervous system arousal and neuronal excitation continued the trend.

In the United States one of the earliest definitions of temperament was offered by Gordon Allport in 1937 and repeated in his 1961 revision: temperament is the "characteristic phenomena of an individual's nature, including his susceptibility to emotional stimulation, his customary strength and speed of response, the quality of his prevailing mood, and all the particularities of fluctuation and intensity of mood, these being regarded as dependent on constitutional make-up, and therefore largely hereditary in origin" (p. 34). W. H. Sheldon and S. S. Stevens gathered further support in the 1940s for the proposition that temperament is a function of at least an inherited body form or physique, if not the four cardinal humors.

Temperament study was relatively dormant for the next two decades because of its association with inherited characteristics, which ran counter to the prevailing psychoanalytic and behavioral theories. Due to a revival in the 1960s, and particularly using modern methods of longitudinal, twin, and adoptee/family studies, temperament research is enjoying significant attention as a viable contributor to our understanding of personality development.

Beginning in the 1960s, Chess and Thomas undertook a major longitudinal study examining temperamental differences in newborn infants (see Chess & Thomas, 1987). In this study, known as the New York Longitudinal Study (NYLS), the authors identified infant behavior patterns and categorized these along nine dimensions: activity level, rhythmicity, approach/withdrawal, adaptability, intensity, sensory threshold, mood, distractibility, and attention span/persistence. These nine dimensions clustered around three general types: easy temperament children (cheerful, relaxed, predictable behaviors), difficult temperament children (irritable, fussy, intense, unpredictable behaviors), and inhibited children (shy and socially withdrawn, high motoric activity, negative emotionality).

Parents will note distinctions in activity levels, reactivity to stimuli, and general emotionality among their children. However, what for one set of parents is difficulty may be to another set an endearing and manageable characteristic. Difficult or inhibited temperamental styles are not necessarily predisposing risk factors for maladjustment. Caregivers have the ability to reinforce or modify temperamentally based reaction. Although the tendency toward developing mild or significant psychopathology is invariably greater for difficult children, those children who lived within families described as superior in behavioral structure were more likely to have positive clinical outcomes (Maziade et al., 1990). Thus the key to managing difficult temperament children lay in identifying potential problems and using foresight and flexibility in dealing with them.

Other current models of infant and child temperament are offered by Bates, Freeland, and Lounsbury (1979) and Buss and Plomin (1984). All these researchers agree that temperament has biological, genetic, and emotional components. Despite lack of agreement on a set of temperament dimensions, most researchers agree on the viability of differences in reactivity, emotionality, sociability, distractibility, and activity. But the heritability of temperament should not imply a static quality from birth to death. Like intelligence and physique, temperament may be altered to some extent by medical, surgical, and nutritional influences as well as through learning.

Among the approaches most often used for assessing temperament are twin and adoptee studies, parent questionnaires, laboratory observation, and physiological assessment. Parents serve as a broad information base to report their child's usual behaviors under normal and in other circumstances. Laboratory studies plan interactions with the experimenter, the primary caregiver, or another child.

Observations may be quantified according to frequency, duration, and strength of response.

Physiological assessment provides information on the underlying biological mechanisms. Twin comparisons and general infant evaluations (Kagan, Snidman, & Arcus, 1992) using measures like electroencephalograms (EEGs), heart rate, and production levels of the hormone cortisol support the growing consensus that people begin life with biological differences and that predisposing temperaments play a role in our personality adjustment as adults.

New Christian believers are familiar with old temperamental tendencies even in the face of a strong and determined decision to be a different person. Nevertheless, selecting new environments, intentionally curbing old habit patterns, and finding useful and healthy outlets for our natural tendencies can reshape desirable patterns.

References

Allport, G. W. (1961). *Pattern and growth in personality.* New York: Holt, Rinehart, & Winston.

Bates, J., Freeland, C., & Lounsbury, M. (1979). Measurement of infant difficultness. *Child Development, 50,* 794–803.

Buss, A., & Plomin, R. (1984). *Temperament: Early developing personality traits.* Hillsdale, NJ: Erlbaum.

Chess, S., & Thomas, A. (1987). *Know your child: An authoritative guide for today's parents.* New York: Basic.

Kagan, J., Snidman, N., & Arcus, D. M. (1992). Initial reactions to unfamiliarity. *Current Directions in Psychological Science, 1,* 171–174.

Maziade, N., Carons, C., Cote, R., Merette, C., Bernier, H., Laplante, B., Boutin, P., & Thivierge, J. (1990). Psychiatric status of adolescents who had extreme temperaments at age seven. *American Journal of Psychiatry, 147,* 1531–1536.

D. H. Stevenson

See Personality; Heredity and Environment in Human Development.

Tension. Defined technically as a reaction or force produced by muscular contraction, tension also refers to a particular emotional state very similar to anxiety, with feelings of tightness or tautness, apprehension, increased alertness, inability to relax, and restlessness, or to mental strain.

There are many possible causes of tension. It may be due to some types of medical or organic disease (Jacobson, 1970) or to such biological or physical factors as insufficient sleep, inadequate nutrition, and effects of drugs or medications. However, tension is more commonly the result of psychological and religious stress or distress (Collins, 1977). Such stress may include personal or family conflicts, sexual incompatibility, divorce and separation, business or academic pressures, life changes, boredom, traumatic experiences, religious guilt due to sin, or false guilt. More fundamentally tension is often due to maladaptive ways of thinking (e.g., expecting perfection from oneself and others, dwelling only on the negative, jumping to premature and often wrong conclusions, catastrophizing or magnifying the problem). Such thinking can lead to maladaptive behaviors (e.g., overworking, avoiding work), which in turn may cause more tension.

Intense prolonged states of tension can have deleterious effects, similar to those produced by excessive stress or distress (Hart, 1989, 1995). Such effects may include states of fatigue, exhaustion, and insomnia (*see* Sleep Disorders); various types of nervousness and emotional maladjustment, particularly anxiety states; addiction to alcohol or drugs; increased susceptibility to high blood pressure, hardening of the arteries, heart attack, and stroke; headaches, ulcers, and a number of other physical disorders; and spiritual problems such as guilt, loss of faith, spiritual dryness, and bitterness. Tension can therefore produce negative physical, psychological, and spiritual effects. However, it can also draw our attention to significant problems in our lives that may have caused the tension and motivate us to deal with such problems or seek help for them. Tension is a danger signal that may lead to further growth and blessing if we respond appropriately.

There are a number of ways of overcoming excessive or prolonged tension. Spiritually the use of prayer with thanksgiving (Phil. 4:6–7; *see* Prayer, Psychological Effects of) and meditation on God's Word or Christian meditation (see Ray, 1977) are powerful means. Fellowship with a group of believers involving intimate and open sharing, confession, and prayer is also important (James 5:16). Psychologically a number of tension-reducing strategies aimed toward relaxation are available, including progressive relaxation (the alternate tensing and relaxing of different muscle groups), passive meditation, pleasant imagery, self-hypnosis, and autosuggestion (see Woolfolk & Richardson, 1978). Listening to soothing or uplifting music can also be helpful. Other psychological methods for coping with tension include stress-inoculation strategies (Meichenbaum, 1985), rational self-talk and other forms of cognitive restructuring, biofeedback, time management skills (including time for rest, recreation, and vacation), and realistic goal setting (see Collins, 1977; Woolfolk & Richardson, 1978). From a Christian perspective, cognitive restructuring or changing one's maladaptive thinking will require learning to think more biblically and truthfully (Phil. 4:8), using the Scriptures as the foundation (see Backus & Chapian, 1980). The use of passive meditation and self-hypnosis for relaxation has been questioned by Collins (1977) as perhaps being of dubious value, particularly for Christians. He points out that such techniques for escaping from stress or tension may dull our thinking, open our minds to harmful influences, desensitize the conscience, and promise happiness without dealing with the issue of sin.

Tension can be reduced physically by regular exercise, proper nutrition, and sufficient sleep. A physician should be consulted if organic or medical disease is suspected. Where necessary, medication can aid in reducing tension states. A professional counselor or psychotherapist may also be needed if tension continues to be experienced over a period of time with obvious deleterious effects.

References

Backus, W., & Chapian, M. (1980). *Telling yourself the truth.* Minneapolis, MN: Bethany Fellowship.

Collins, G. R. (1977). *You can profit from stress.* Santa Ana, CA: Vision House.

Hart, A. D. (1989). *Overcoming anxiety.* Dallas: Word.

Hart, A. D. (1995). *The hidden link between adrenalin and stress* (Rev. ed.). Dallas: Word.

Jacobson, E. (1970). *Modern treatment of tense patients.* Springfield, IL: Thomas.

Meichenbaum, D. (1985). *Stress inoculation training.* New York: Pergamon.

Ray, D. (1977). *The art of Christian meditation.* Wheaton, IL: Tyndale House.

Woolfolk, R., & Richardson, F. (1978). *Stress, sanity, and survival.* New York: Monarch.

S.-Y. TAN

See RELAXATION TRAINING; STRESS.

Terman, Lewis Madison (1877–1956). American psychologist best known for his work in intelligence testing. Born in Indiana, he grew up on a farm and entered Central Normal College in Danville in 1892. By the age of 21 he had three degrees from that institution. He became a high school principal but wanted to teach psychology and needed a degree from a recognized school. He entered Indiana University in 1901 and earned his A.B. and M.A. degrees within two years. He completed his Ph.D. at Clark University in 1905 in spite of ill health.

Because of a pulmonary hemorrhage Terman was advised to move to a warm climate. He served as principal of a high school in San Bernardino, California, for one year before beginning to teach at Los Angeles State Normal School. In 1910 he moved to Stanford University, where he remained until he retired in 1942. He remained active in research until his death.

Next to that of Alfred Binet, Terman's name is most frequently associated with the testing movement. Terman spent more time on the Binet test and became more of a specialist on it than Binet himself. Others had translated Binet's test, but Terman extensively revised it and standardized it on American children. Although he called it the Stanford Revision of the Binet-Simon Scale of Intelligence, it was essentially a new scale that bore only superficial resemblance to Binet's test. The scale, standardization information, and directions for administration were published in *Measurement of Intelligence* (1916), which immediately became the standard work on intelligence testing. Terman multiplied Stern's mental quotient by 100 to remove the decimal point and renamed it the Intelligence Quotient, or IQ. The Stanford-Binet was revised in 1937, 1960, and 1972 and is widely used.

Recognizing the need to identify intellectually gifted children, Terman began a comprehensive, long-term study of them in 1921. The subjects were 1,528 California children with IQs above 140 (*see* Genius). Initial results showed that these children were alert, eager, social, interested, and interesting. He followed them until his death 35 years later and found that they were healthier and more stable than average and kept their high ability into adulthood. These findings were reported in *Genetic Studies of Genius* (5 vols., 1926–1959). Terman was general editor of the series and principal author of all except one volume. He also attempted to estimate the IQs of three hundred major historical figures, many of whom compared as children with those in his study.

R. L. KOTESKEY

See INTELLECTUAL ASSESSMENT.

Thematic Apperception Test. A projective test used as a means to uncover and understand both the conscious and unconscious processes of an individual. The test was developed in 1934 by Henry Alexander Murray. The third revision, published in 1943, is widely used for diagnostic purposes in personality assessment and treatment planning.

The Thematic Apperception Test (TAT) may be administered to any person over the age of four. The test consists of 31 cards, 30 of which have a black-and-white picture. The remaining card is blank. Only between 10 and 20 cards are usually administered, depending on the sex and age of the individual being tested and the purposes for which the test is given. During administration the individual is shown one picture at a time and is asked to construct a story that tells what is happening, what led up to the event, what the people are thinking and feeling, and what will occur in the future. Hence the name *thematic*, referring to the themes elicited, and *apperceptive* for the perceptual-interpretive processes involved in constructing a story to the picture.

The underlying rationale for the test is that the spontaneous stories given in response to these pictures, many of which depict ambiguous human situations, require the individual to draw on past experiences and current needs and sentiments. The aim of the test is to confront the subject with a variety of pictured situations that will elicit indications about which of these situations are personally important or associated with conflict. Both conscious and unconscious processes are assumed to be influential in the individual's imaginative creations and affect both the content and manner in which the story is told.

The TAT is administered and interpreted by a psychologist who is familiar with the test materials, procedures, and norms. Findings from the interpretation are given after a careful synthesis and integration of all the test material and are reported as inferential statements. The TAT frequently is administered with other psychological tests, particularly the projective Rorschach Ink Blot Test. These two projective measures together provide the professional with complementary and relatively comprehensive data concerning the individual's personality functioning.

W. W. AUSTIN

See PERSONALITY.

Theme-Centered Interactional Groups. Model of group work that has as its most essential characteristic the setting of an explicit theme or focus for the group interaction. This theme is announced by the group leader at the beginning of each session. The goal is then to optimize, not maximize, the degree of theme-centeredness, bringing it into balance with the interactional and less task-centered aspects of the group experience. Because of this balancing of content and process, it has been suggested that the model is useful not just in group psychotherapy but also in group processes as diverse as the classroom, committee or other task group, or growth group. Another reason for its usefulness in such different types of groups is that it is primarily a model of group process and only secondarily a set of techniques for group leadership.

The theme-centered interactional approach was developed by Ruth Cohn, a European psychoanalyst and group psychotherapist. Trained at the Zurich Psychoanalytic Institute, she emigrated to the United States in 1941. It was in the context of her group supervision of psychotherapists that she developed the theme-centered approach; for a number of years the approach was primarily seen as a model of supervision of therapists. A common theme would be countertransference, and Cohn would seek to help therapists better understand the ways in which it operated both by discussing the concept theoretically and by examining its operation in the present experience of the group members. Later she became interested in applying the model to other types of groups, and its ties with psychotherapy supervision came to be a thing of the past.

Although Cohn did not see her model as strictly a psychoanalytic one, she did bring to it a number of psychoanalytic concepts and values. The most important of these is the precedence given in psychoanalysis to resistance. She stressed that resistances against the theme should always be given precedence over anything else, particularly over a rigid pursual of the theme. Thus any personal or collective distractions should be responded to: not analyzed but rather expressed. This also reflects the psychoanalytic principle of free association in that group members are encouraged to express whatever thoughts they have, without censoring or regard for slavish focus on the theme.

The approach also reflects the influence of the sensitivity group movement. While Cohn adopted some of the techniques of this tradition, she rejected its anti-intellectual bias. She argued that sensitivity is not enough. By this she meant that people need not only to sense and come to self-awareness but also to think. As a result of this, theme-centered interactional groups retain something of the flavor of sensitivity groups but additionally encourage thinking and rational discussion.

The most important of the philosophical concepts underlying the theme-centered approach are the related concepts of autonomy and interdependence. Cohn argued that sensitivity groups overemphasized autonomy at the expense of interdependence. Consequently the theme-centered approach elevates these two concepts to positions of equal emphasis, making it a task of the group leader to attempt a balance between the autonomy of group members and their interdependence. Other dimensions of group experience that the approach also sees as important to be kept in balance are emotional expression versus cognitive expression, focus on content versus process, focus on intropsychic experience versus interpersonal experience, and focus on the past versus the present.

Because there has been very little research done on the theme-centered interactional approach, it is difficult to speak with any confidence about its effectiveness. One study (Sheehan, 1977) demonstrated significant positive changes in both self-esteem and self-evaluation during theme-centered growth groups. However, much more research is necessary.

Although the model seems to have important implications for group psychotherapy, its greatest application seems to be as an approach to personal and professional growth. In 1966 Cohn founded her first training institute in the method and called it the Workshop Institute for Living-Learning. Since then branches have been established in a number of cities and countries in Europe and North America. These institutes offer groups for professionals as well as the public and also provide consultation to community groups interested in the method.

Reference

Sheehan, M. C. (1977). The effects of theme-centered growth groups on the self-concept, self-esteem, and interpersonal openness of adults (Doctoral dissertation, Columbia University Teachers College, 1977). *Dissertation Abstracts International, 38,* 5656–b. (University Microfilms No. 78–04,468)

Additional Readings

Shafer, J. B. P., & Galinsky, M. D. (1974). *Models of group therapy and sensitivity training.* Englewood Cliffs, NJ: Prentice-Hall.
Cohn, R. C. (1972). Style and spirit of the theme-centered interactional method. In C. J. Sager & H. S. Kaplan

(Eds.), *Progress in group and family therapy*. New York: Brunner/Mazel.

D. G. BENNER

See GROUP DYNAMICS; GROUP PSYCHOTHERAPY.

Therapeutic Community. A constant concern throughout history has been the development of effective and responsible ways of relating to members of society who, for whatever reason, deviate from the norms. We have passed through many reforms as definitions of deviance, and society's response to it has evolved. Therapeutic community stands as one example of a more humanitarian approach to mental illness that began in the late nineteenth century and gained momentum in the twentieth century.

Therapeutic community involves the self-conscious creation of a social organization within which the total resources of both patients and staff, as well as the total environment, will be used to their optimum potential to further treatment. The total organization is seen as a vital force in determining therapeutic outcome. Patients are involved in leadership and treatment. All relationships, whether patient-staff, patient-patient, or staff-staff, are seen as potentially therapeutic and are examined to maximize this potential. The emotional climate and the physical environment are created to facilitate treatment.

Origins and Development. The therapeutic community approach evolved in the historical context of psychiatry's pursuit of more humanitarian treatment of those suffering from mental illness. The humanitarian approach looked on mental illness as sickness and the sufferers as persons in need of care, comfort, and cleanliness in their surroundings. Other important influences were interpersonal psychology and psychiatry, milieu therapy, group therapeutic techniques, social psychiatry, and administrative therapy (Almond, 1974).

During the 1940s much research and analysis brought into perspective the psychiatric hospital as a small society, the dynamics of which could either facilitate or inhibit treatment. It was recognized that the institution was a hybrid form of society that disregarded family needs; the benefits and needs of relationships between the opposite sex and various age groups were ignored. Instead it created subcultures in which patients insulated themselves from staff and treatment personnel, who in turn insulated themselves from the controlling bureaucracy. These decision makers were removed from patients to such an extent as to be almost unaware of their needs.

Social and administrative therapies focused on the organizational, administrative, and sociocultural processes in terms of their role in treatment. Sullivan's emphasis on communication, the role of culture, the significance of the intensity and meaning of behavior, the role of the environment in determining the functional use of behavior, the defini-

tion of the role of the psychiatrist as a participant-observer, and the training of staff in interpersonal skills contributed to this new approach to mental illness (Sullivan, 1953, 1956).

Milieu therapy, with its focus on the physical environment and social structure, developed at the same time as the therapeutic community approach. It involved paying attention to and using the environment of the patient toward therapeutic goals. This concept was eventually expanded to include the role of all persons relating to the patient as significant in the treatment process.

Prior to 1935 psychopathology was usually understood in terms of intrapsychic conflict, even though social adjustment was the criterion most often used for measuring improvement. A new interest in the social relationships of patients led to the concept of group treatment techniques. Thus the treatment of individuals through the medium of the group developed and made a significant contribution to the therapeutic community approach.

The merging of psychiatric and sociological concepts of mental illness in social psychiatry led to a serious study of potentialities for treatment inherent within community relationships. This included staff-patient, patient-patient, and patient-administrator relationships. Interpersonal relations and environmental influences were considered important factors in etiology, diagnosis, and treatment (Greenblatt, York, & Brown, 1955; Freeman, 1965).

The term *administrative therapy* was used to describe an approach developed at this time that emphasized open doors, increased liberty and self-determination, a meaningful work program with appropriate incentives, and useful and healthy use of leisure time (Clark, 1964; Taylor, 1958). Those using this term distinguish between administrative therapy and therapeutic community. The lines of separation between the approaches are, however, sketchy.

From this brief historical sketch it can be seen how influential the various therapeutic developments of the day were in the evolution of the therapeutic community concept of treatment. This was a period of major advance in the treatment of mental illness, and therapeutic community was one dimension of that development.

Almond (1974) identifies the beginnings of therapeutic community in the work of Maxwell Jones at Belmont Hospital in England during 1947 to 1959. However, while Jones is definitely the individual most clearly identified with the development of therapeutic community, others were also involved in similar activities.

Bion and Rickman (Taylor, 1958) introduced and developed new principles of treatment at the Northfield Military Hospital Training Wing in 1943 to bring unruly soldiers under control. They used group methods and a reduction of the traditional authoritarian structure to create a feeling of belonging and a social environment. They felt this gave the men a sense of responsibility and enabled them to deal with their own problems and antisocial behavior. In 1946 Bion's methods were further developed in the second Northfield experiment. An open-door policy, more parole, improved nurse-patient relationships, gainful employment, and a general focus on interpersonal relationships was also being introduced in several other hospitals at the same time. As early as 1938 Bierer introduced therapeutic social clubs at Runwell Mental Hospital for inpatients.

Jones served at the Effort Syndrome Unit, Mill Hill, from 1939 to 1945. Several principles developed in this unit were later refined and modified to form the therapeutic community model. The authoritarian hierarchy was broken to permit free communications among all staff and patients, nurses were actively involved in treatment, and patients were educated concerning their symptomatology. Sociodrama and role playing as therapeutic techniques were practiced, treatment was defined as all-pervasive in the patient's total experience, and Problem solving through group discussion rather than appeal to authority was introduced. Many of these concepts were poorly developed and very much in an experimental stage.

From 1945 to 1947 Jones developed the Ex-Prisoner-of-War Unit at Dartford, Kent, England. Repatriated prisoners of war were the patients. The experimental nature of this unit allowed for the development of the principles introduced at Mill Hill, and an extensive work therapy program was an added feature. The use of psychodrama and group therapy was greatly developed. From 1947 to 1959 Jones was associated with the Neurosis Unit at Belmont Hospital. During these years the concept of therapeutic community matured and was articulated and refined through scholarly interaction. From 1959 to 1962 Jones served in several capacities in the United States, which served to make his work more widely known. He returned to Scotland in 1963 and there developed a therapeutic community at Melrose (Dingleton Hospital) that embodied the principles of therapeutic community.

Sullivan's early emphasis on the part played by the hospital environment and the role of nurses is a precursor to the use of the therapeutic community model in the United States and Canada. One of the best-known therapeutic community programs in the United States was the Yale–New Haven Community Hospital, which opened in January 1960. Under the medical direction of Thomas Detre this unit, known as Tompkins I, developed clearly as a therapeutic community. The consultation work carried on by Jones in North America during the 1960s and 1970s also assisted in the adoption of the principles of therapeutic community in numerous other psychiatric hospitals.

Principles of Therapeutic Community. Since the concepts of therapeutic community developed over a period of time, a description of its principles must specify the period being described. Because the most careful studies of therapeutic community were conducted on its application by Jones at Dingleton Hospital from 1963 onward, and because this program was the basis of many of Jones's own observations (Jones, 1966, 1968b), it is the basis of the following discussion.

The Total Community as Treatment Agent. Jones felt that the major distinctive of therapeutic community is the way in which an institution's total resources are self-consciously pooled to facilitate treatment (Jones, 1959). Administrators, clinicians, support staff, and patients were all viewed as a part of the total treatment team. All would also be involved in community meetings where the question of their positive or negative influence on treatment was discussed. These groups were designed to enhance the sensitivity of staff to their role in treatment.

This approach led to a redefining of the roles of those normally defined as treatment staff (i.e., psychiatrists, psychologists, and social workers) so as to permit the inclusion of nurses, administrators, maintenance staff, and recreational staff in the treatment team. This was accomplished through the blurring of role distinctions and the inclusion of all relevant staff in patient assessment and treatment groups. One of the ways this blurring was accomplished was through the discouragement of dress distinction perpetuated through uniforms or typical attire for various professional groups.

Perhaps the best example of this principle is the treatment role established for nurses. Jones began involving nurses in discussion groups with patients and as participants in sociodrama. They soon were referred to as social therapists and were recognized as important culture carriers. Because of their intensive involvement with patients they were accepted as key contributors to diagnosis and treatment discussion.

The role of the patient evolved from a passive role to one in which the patient was urged to assume all the responsibility he or she was capable of assuming for his or her own progress toward health and the improvement of fellow patients. Some emphasis on patients' learning to understand their problems began early. The patient was then expected to participate in discussion groups to help others to understand their problems. Patients were given opportunity and encouraged to provide meaningful feedback to fellow patients concerning their behavior and its effects. The patient's role was defined as that of a collaborator in treatment and later as that of a culture carrier in relation to the orientation of new patients.

It is obvious that to accomplish such a redefinition of role for nurses and patients a corresponding change of role for psychologists, social workers, and doctors was needed. The flattening of the traditional hierarchical structure and the facilitation of open communication was essential.

The Creation of Community. The concept of culture and the role it plays in therapy are crucial. Jones defined culture as "a cluster of socially determined attitudes and behavior patterns grouped and elaborated around structurally defined roles and relationships" (1952, p. 66). The culture was created with the intent of maximizing the resocialization of patients. In this context he spoke of doctors as social engineers. The staff and patients who had been in the institution for some time were described as culture carriers whose responsibility was to transmit the culture of the institution to new members. A treatment goal was to help the patient to adapt to the culture of the program and to learn to find new and satisfying roles in such a social context. The assumption was that he or she would then become more effective in adapting in the community after discharge. Psychopathology was expressed in relationships and could be dealt with through education, confrontation, and modeling by staff and patients.

An underlying principle was that of permissiveness. A pervasive attitude of permissiveness facilitated the patient's expression of symptomatology, which was dealt with through a supportive teaching of new behavior as the unacceptable behavior was confronted. The culture of the society was described in terms of permissiveness, understanding, helpfulness, mutual responsibility, inquiry, expression of feeling, democratic-equalitarian organization, and the facing of tensions, conflicts, or role confusion that arise (Rapoport, 1960). The redefinition of the patient in this culture gave him or her a strong sense of belonging and facilitated the patient's identification with the culture and motivation toward treatment.

The principle of open communication, which negated the traditional concept of lines of communication, was recognized early and developed to play an increasingly important role. The goal was to develop the freest communication possible between patients and staff. It was discovered that this eliminated much distortion that often occurred if communication was limited to formalized channels. Nonverbal communication was studied, and acting out was viewed as communication. Giving and receiving of feedback was encouraged. The question of confidentiality or privileged communication was dealt with by extending the circumference of confidentiality to include the total community, and the sharing of the most intimate material in the group became the norm (Jones, 1953).

Permissiveness coupled with open communication and the broader concept of confidentiality made it possible to deal with unacceptable deviation from the cultural norms in a group context. This reduced manipulation and the playing of one staff against another. In the context of an accepting group a person was encouraged and, if necessary, required to look at his or her behavior and its implications. Through group discussion the patient was helped to discuss his or her deviant behavior and to recognize its outcome for self and others (Jones, 1968a). This was spoken of as social learning.

All of this had implications for the role of leadership and the exercise of authority in the community. The hierarchical structure of the organization was flattened. Authority was dispersed through the community on a horizontal plane, with staff and patients assuming authority commensurate with their function. Authority was experienced as residing in the official leader only at times of crisis when it was necessary that he function decisively. Otherwise Jones described his function as leadership from behind or as a catalyst. This concept of latent leadership permitted the development of leadership skills and functions among staff and patients.

Programs and Techniques in Theory. A summary of approaches used in therapeutic community philosophy included learning theory, psychodrama, work therapy, and a problem-solving orientation, in addition to the more traditional use of drug therapy, psychoanalytic techniques, and group therapy. These more specific approaches were used in the context of a community designed for treatment.

General learning theory and the Gestalt theory of learning were used to explain the social learning approach practiced. The focus was on understanding and unlearning habitual patterns of behavior found to be ineffectual and the learning of new, more adequate, and satisfying ways of coping. Acknowledging and revising the emotional responses to behaviors was central, and for this reason there was a strong emphasis on the expression of feelings (Jones, 1968b).

Psychodrama was used to facilitate the expression and identification of feelings. Buried dynamics of behavior were explored through projective techniques. Work therapy was developed into a very useful approach with helpful outcomes in patient self-worth and constructive use of time. With the emphasis on treatment being the function of all staff, the personnel in the work therapy program took on real significance. Work therapy was also developed to contribute to a sense of community as well as training skills.

Decision making by consensus was one of the more radical focuses of therapeutic community. Any unilateral decision was seen as contradictory to its basic philosophy. A genuine attempt at reaching unanimity required providing rationale for decisions to patients and staff, which often involved sharing of information not traditionally available to either patients or frontline staff. However, the communication of respect and significance to members of the community proved to be of great benefit, especially to patients. The mutual education and learning that grew out of this approach was deemed to justify the large amount of time consumed in the process.

Out of this grew an approach to problem solving that became clearly defined. The approach was to solve community problems, which often involved a person's personal problems, by group discussion rather than through appeal to authority. Third-party intervention was not accepted as a way of resolving interpersonal or personal issues. Turning the community problem into what is referred to as a living-learning situation, the process involved bringing together all involved parties in the presence of a group facilitator and the airing of all feelings, interpretations, expectations, and accusations. The facilitator sought to create a social learning experience for participants as they moved toward resolution and reconciliation. The timing of these encounters and the skill of the therapists were crucial. The confrontation was sought as close to the experience as possible unless the situation was such as to suggest delay would be more effective. These concepts were applied to staff as well as to patients.

Another process developed was the postmortem meeting, which followed many activities and was intended to maximize the learning potential in each experience. The modeling provided by the more expert staff for other staff and patients in these activities was very helpful and educative.

Current Status. Since Jones's early work therapeutic communities have proliferated. Many applications of the concept, however, bear little resemblance to the original communities developed by Jones. Therapeutic community approaches have continued to be utilized in psychiatric hospitals and have also been adopted in a number of nonhospital drug treatment programs. Residential programs such as Synanon and Daytop Village are therapeutic community programs. Freudenberger (1972) has described an application of therapeutic community principles within a psychoanalytic private practice, and a number of other nonresidential applications have been described (e.g., Siroka & Siroka, 1971). While therapeutic community is certainly not a major contemporary treatment modality or approach, it has played an important role in shaping much current mental health philosophy.

References

Almond, R. (1974). *The healing community.* New York: Aronson.

Clark, D. H. (1964). *Administrative therapy.* Philadelphia: Lippincott.

Freeman, H. L. (Ed.). (1965). *Psychiatric hospital care.* London: Bailliere, Tindall, & Cassell.

Freudenberger, H. J. (1972). The therapeutic community in private practice. *Psychoanalytic Review, 59,* 375–388.

Greenblatt, M., York, R. H., & Brown, E. L. (1955). *From custodial to therapeutic care in mental hospitals.* New York: Russell Sage Foundation.

Jones, M. (1952). *Social psychiatry.* London: Tavistock.

Jones, M. (1953). *Therapeutic community.* New York: Basic.

Jones, M. (1959). Towards a clarification of the "therapeutic community" concept. *British Journal of Medical Psychology, 32,* 200–205.

Jones, M. (1966). Therapeutic community practice. *American Journal of Psychiatry, 122,* 1275–1279.

Jones, M. (1968a). *Beyond therapeutic community.* New Haven, CT: Yale University Press.

Jones, M. (1968b). *Social psychiatry in practice.* Hammondsworth, England: Penguin.

Rapoport, R. N. (1960). *Community as doctor.* Springfield, IL: Thomas.

Siroka, R. W., & Siroka, E. K. (1971). Psychodrama and the therapeutic community. In L. Plank, G. B. Gottsegen, & M. G. Gottsegen (Eds.), *Confrontation.* New York: Macmillan.

Sullivan, H. S. (1953). *The interpersonal theory of psychiatry.* In H. S. Perry & M. L. Gawel (Eds.). New York: Norton.

Sullivan, H. S. (1956). *Clinical studies in psychiatry.* In H. S. Perry, M. L. Gawel, & M. Gibbon (Eds.). New York: Norton.

Taylor, F. K. (1958). A history of group and administrative therapy in Great Britain. *British Journal of Medical Psychology, 31,* 153–173.

G. C. TAYLOR

Therapeutic Double Bind. Developed by Milton H. Erickson, this concept refers to the therapeutic tactic of placing the client in a situation facing two choices where either choice would be acceptable to the therapist and supportive of the therapy process. The therapist frames these choices in such a way as to place the client in a quandary, a benign double bind. These quandaries block or disrupt the client's habitual attitudes and responses and force change.

As an example, Erickson might say something like the following to a young child experiencing difficulty leaving his mother and going to school: "I think you will find that as you get older, leaving your mother will come quite easily. In fact, I think you will notice that it will happen soon. I wonder if you would like that good feeling of being able to go to school by yourself to come within one month or two." The obvious role of suggestion in this example shows the important role the therapeutic double bind plays in Erickson's approach to hypnosis, which is where this technique has been most perfected.

Additional Reading

Erickson, M. H., Rossi, E. L., & Rossi, S. I. (1976). *Hypnotic realities.* New York: Irvington.

D. G. BENNER

See HYPNOTHERAPY.

Therapeutic Recreation. Recreation, a basic human need, refreshes the mind and the body. It is a pleasurable activity which may be pursued for intrinsic motivation. The essence of recreation is subjective experience, not necessarily the activity itself, for that is what makes experiential recreations therapeutic. Re-creation is an act of renewal. It involves relaxation, amusement, kinship, and play. Leisure becomes more meaningful when it occurs after serious work, intense performance, or heavy duty. Some theorists believe that leisure and work should not be mutually exclusive. Certain people find enjoyment in their work. In fact, some organizations try to incorporate leisure time and playful activities during the busy work schedule.

Therapeutic recreation (TR) is defined as a process in which individuals are collectively engaged and during which recreational programs are employed as a method of intervention to help bring about desired mental, emotional, physical, and behavioral changes, with the ultimate goal of greater personal growth. TR consists of activities designed to relieve stress, promote socialization, develop cognitive skills, improve self-concept, and increase tolerance for authority figures. Furthermore, recreational activities trigger mental alertness, brighten mood, facilitate interaction, and increase self-disclosure and personal bonding.

TR can take place indoors or outdoors, one-on-one or in group setting. It is also utilized as a form of rehabilitation for those who have been disabled by an accident, injury, or illness. It expedites their recovery and helps them appropriately adjust. It provides them with opportunities to improve the quality of their lives and prepare to reenter the community or public living with more functional abilities. TR often increases self-confidence through mastery of skills and enhances self-care through learning to plan for one's own leisure and relaxation. Also, it can teach cooperation, reframe mental processes, release tension, diminish rigidity and defensiveness, and enhance emotional openness and spontaneity.

Behaviors as simple as practicing one's hobby or as complex and comprehensive as some sophisticated programs planned by a specialist can be highly beneficial and very therapeutic. They may have the remarkable effect of energizing and relaxing the whole organism or system. While play comes naturally for children, adults struggle with many barriers and inhibitions. However, once engaged, adults enjoy the same feelings evoked in child play (though adults like to dignify their play and call it recreation).

The role of the recreational therapist or "therapeutic recreator" is to educate, evaluate, set goals, model, design programs, and utilize techniques in order to meet the needs of a special population he or she is trying to serve. However, the level of satisfaction and enjoyment depends on the degree of participation. Higher involvement usually results in deeper satisfaction and more rewarding and meaningful experiences. Basically, the social stimulation and cultural factors shape the recreational forms and experiences of people. In order for a group to have a meaningful recreational experience, the activities must be socially appropriate, morally acceptable, and culturally relevant so that these activities are in harmony with the norms, values, and traditions of that particular people group.

Also called "recreational therapy," TR serves as an adjunct or supplement to the basic psychological and psychiatric clinical services. It is considered an important resource and an essential auxil-

iary to mainstream counseling techniques. Within the health and medical models, TR attempts to follow the "biopsychosocial" approach. It is similar to and has elements of many other sub-specialized fields like "art, play, music, drama, physical, plant (horticulture), poetry, dance, occupational, and sport" therapies. These fields have been and, still, are being developed to provide a better, more complete, and holistic approach to patient care.

This approach is consistent with the biblical teachings on the importance of "rest" after work and "enjoyment" of God's creation as well as of the communal life. The spiritual aspect of recreation has been often minimized or neglected. It can provide a unique and significant experience of joy, freedom, vitality, and genuine transcendence. The Christian view of the human nature and functioning strongly encourages a "creative expression" and promotes a "healthy integration" of mind, soul, body, and spirit.

N. ABI-HASHEM

Therapist-Induced Psychopathology. *See* IATRO-GENIC PSYCHOPATHOLOGY.

Thinking. It is widely considered that the three predominant modes of human existence are thinking, feeling, and behaving, although these three frequently overlap. Thinking encompasses a wide range of internal, symbolic processes, such problem solving, reasoning, and hypothesis testing. Most psychologists assume that such processes influence behavior, although not necessarily in any simple or direct way. Thinking is not the same as learning, which refers to the influences of past experiences on one's abilities or performances. Just as words symbolize or denote particular objects, events, or concepts, thinking apparently symbolizes external objects, events, or concepts with an internal process that we do not entirely understand.

Major Models of Thinking. Psychology has seen several distinct and important approaches to thinking. Watson (1930), a behaviorist, attempted to reduce thinking to internal speech, or talking to oneself, reasoning that when speech becomes internal, it becomes thought. Watson believed that thinking, like any other simple motor behavior, could be explained, and hence thinking would serve the laws of classical conditioning that were central to his view of human psychology (*see* Conditioning, Classical). Spoken words become substitutes for the situations to which they refer. Watson observed that certain words are integrally connected with observable reality and can elicit subtle responses. The word *fire* elicits a fear response in a human like that of a real fire, much as a bell, after being paired with meat powder, made Ivan Pavlov's dogs salivate. Watson failed to demonstrate that thought is subvocal speech because he could not detect traces of muscular movements, such as contractions of the larynx, during thought. Watsonian behaviorism continues to have influence in modern attempts to find objective ways to measure thought processes.

Gestalt theory (Kohler, 1947) radically challenged the behaviorist understanding of thinking. Gestalt theorists conceived of the thinker as actively discovering order and meaning that wait to be apprehended. Thinking was conceived as the capacity to find patterns and relationships, and as such it is far more than an accumulation of simple abilities to make more complex ones. For example, the discovery of a pattern in a string of digits to be recalled differs from rote memorization of the numbers serially, and the exercise of pattern finding can improve retention. Most importantly, Gestaltists recognized that thinking involves mental processes that cannot be explained in terms of motor behavior. While the Gestalt approach introduced provocative ideas to deal with complex processes, it was too vague as a theory to be tested directly, and it could not explain how the abilities to discover order and meaning arise during human development.

The cognitive-developmental approach of Piaget (1952) and others demonstrated that qualitative changes in thinking processes emerged in Western society in children between the ages of five to seven. Children of this age are able to conserve number, volume, weight, and mass (as noted in the ability to state that the number of coins has not changed when they are spread out rather than bunched together). Other kinds of conservation similarly show that the child no longer judges quantity to have changed when one noncrucial dimension changes. Piaget believed that there is a heavy interaction between a human being and its environment leading to the development of thinking. Others have challenged Piaget's analogical understanding of thinking as lacking biological substrate data (Bruner, 1973).

A blend of behavioral and cognitive understanding of thinking can be found in the information-processing theorists, who have been strongly influenced by developments in computer technology. The analogy of human thinking to the computer is based on the assumption that humans are processors of information. This has led to attempts by researchers to simulate human thinking processes by using computer programs. Continued research into computer "thinking" has revealed that computer processing and human thinking, although they show some similarities in problem solving (Newell & Simon, 1972), appear to be widely divergent.

Existing schools of psychology give us no clear understanding of thinking. It appears likely that each of these schools may contribute to our understanding of the human thinking process, but thinking itself must be a highly complex process that is far beyond our present ability to truly grasp.

Types of Thinking. Concept learning is the form of thinking that allows a person to group items according to a common element or dimension. A concept learning experiment asks a subject to determine the common element of several items (example: red circle—yes, red square—yes, green square—no; answer: redness). It has been discovered that subjects' concept learning occurs through their testing various hypotheses over the learning trials and eventually being able to match hypothesis with conclusion. Concept learning has been found to be no different from simple motor learning.

A second form of thinking is that conceptualized as meaning, as compared with rote learning. Meaningful learning involves acquiring new ideas and the ability to use them appropriately through relating them to one's previous concepts. For example, children might gain a meaningful understanding of the concept of probability by relating it to what they already know from their own experience regarding the likelihood of rain on a given day. Related to meaning is memory, namely, how people search their memories, store new concepts, and forget.

Problem solving and deductive reasoning are types of thinking that call the person to evaluate complex situations and problems and come up with possible solutions through an examination of probable outcomes. Somewhat in contrast to problem solving is creative thinking, which seems to require the thinker to go beyond or even against examining the available evidence to find something new, interesting, and possibly provocative. Some researchers have worked with techniques to enhance creative thinking (Arieti, 1976; Rothenberg, 1971). Some philosophers (Polanyi, 1958) have expanded the understanding of creative thinking to include a more cosmological approach of apprehending reality, or a way of grasping the world around us in a meaningful way.

From a biblical and Christian perspective the matter of thinking brings us many questions. The bulk of the scriptural references to thinking (e.g., 2 Chron. 13:8; Job 35:2; Ps. 10:6) are suggestions, often from God, that human thinking is limited and often selfish and self-limited. But Scripture does not go so far as to castigate thinking, and there is some reference to valuing human thinking, especially when thinking is compared to meditation or worship (Pss. 63:6; 119:52). Jesus often asks his followers or his antagonists what they think of him (Matt. 5:17) or what he says in his parables (Matt. 21:28; Luke 10:36), and Paul admonishes us to be mature in our thinking (1 Cor. 14:20) but to also guard thinking, particularly when we are inclined to think of ourselves as superior to other people (Gal. 6:3). Comparisons of thinking should be made with meditation, intuition, and feeling to get a full grasp of the concept.

References

Arieti, S. (1976). *Creativity: The magic synthesis*. New York: Basic.

Bruner, J. S. (1973). *Beyond the information given*. New York: Norton.

Kohler, W. (1947). *Gestalt psychology*. New York: Liveright.

Newell, A., & Simon, H. A. (1972). *Human problem solving.* Englewood Cliffs, NJ: Prentice-Hall.

Piaget, J. (1952). *The origins of intelligence in children.* New York: International Universities Press.

Polanyi, M. (1958). *Personal knowledge.* Chicago: University of Chicago Press.

Rothenberg, A. (1971). The process of Janusian thinking in creativity. *Archives of General Psychiatry, 24,* 195–205.

Watson, J. B. (1930). *Behaviorism* (Rev. ed.). New York: Norton.

R. B. Johnson

See Cognitive Psychology.

Thorndike, Edward Lee (1874–1949). Pioneer in learning theory. Born in Williamsburg, Massachusetts, where his father was a lawyer and later a clergyman, Thorndike graduated from Wesleyan University in 1895 and went to Harvard to study under William James. He earned another bachelor's degree at Harvard in 1896 and a master's degree in 1897. He transferred to Columbia, where he was awarded the Ph.D. in 1898. After one year of teaching at Western Reserve, he returned to Columbia in 1899 and remained there until his retirement in 1939.

Thorndike is sometimes called the founder of animal psychology because of his early work with chicks learning mazes and cats discovering how to get out of locked cages. However, shortly after his appointment to Columbia his major interests shifted to human learning and education. He developed psychological tests and a theory of intelligence. He studied individual differences, sex differences, fatigue, interests, attitudes, and vocabulary. As the most influential educational psychologist of his time he wrote leading college textbooks as well as texts for children.

His major contribution was in the area of learning. Thorndike created connectionism, an experimental approach to associationism. The older philosophical associationism was concerned with connections between ideas, but Thorndike was concerned with connections between stimuli and responses. Although he called this trial-and-accidental-success learning, it has more frequently been called trial-and-error learning. He formulated three laws to account for this learning. The law of readiness referred to the circumstance under which the learner would be satisfied or annoyed, a physiological matter determined by maturation. The law of exercise referred to the strengthening of connections through use of practice or their weakening through disuse. The law of effect stated that responses became "stamped in" or "stamped out" because of their consequences, a "satisfying state of affairs" or an "annoying state of affairs." He later modified the laws of exercise and effect but remained a connectionist.

Thorndike wrote 507 articles and books, a record equaled by few others. His doctoral dissertation, *Animal Intelligence,* was one of his most important works. It was published in 1898 and republished with other related studies in 1911. The first edition of *Educational Psychology* appeared in 1903 and *Introduction to the Theory of Mental and Social Measurements* in 1904. Thorndike has had a profound influence on modern learning theory. His emphasis on stimulus-response bonds and reinforcement are core concepts in most neobehavioristic theories.

R. L. Koteskey

See Learning.

Thought Stopping. A behavioral technique used to help persons troubled by recurring uncontrolled thoughts and worries. Examples include obsessive rumination about cleanliness that persists even after careful washing, excessive fear of riding in automobiles or planes, and extreme fearfulness about being robbed or assaulted.

The basic technique involves four steps. First, the individual is asked to describe recent experiences in which the troublesome thoughts occurred. As the patient begins to describe the troublesome thoughts, the therapist suddenly and emphatically says Stop. This process is repeated several times. Second, the person is asked to imagine himself or herself in the unpleasant situation and to signal when he or she begins thinking obsessive thoughts. Again there are several repetitions of the procedure. When this step is complete, the therapist has developed control over the unwanted thoughts by means of the stop commands.

Third, the client is taught to say Stop aloud to his or her own thoughts. Typically the client initially makes a feeble and unconvincing effort and must be encouraged to be emphatic. Finally the person is told to think Stop in response to the troublesome thoughts.

The individual gradually experiences difficulty in thinking the troublesome thoughts and must be encouraged to make a conscious effort to produce them to facilitate the therapy process. This process permits additional exposure to the Stop command and helps the person learn to produce and eliminate the thought at will. This is especially important where the troubling thoughts are exaggerated forms of normal concerns, such as checking to see that the doors are locked.

Thought stopping is a form of aversion therapy that uses contingent punishment. Procedural variations include use of electric shock in place of the word *stop,* use of similar procedure to stop unwanted visual images, and use of thought stopping together with covert assertion. Although research on thought stopping is fairly limited, preliminary results are promising.

R. K. Bufford

See Behavior Therapy; Cognitive-Behavior Therapy.

Thumb Sucking. The earliest form of habitual manipulation of the body and usually also the earliest form of self-stimulation. It is extremely common during the first two years of life and should be viewed with concern only if it persists after age six or seven. However, even then it is rarely sufficient reason for a psychological referral if it appears alone and is not part of a constellation of other behaviors and feelings that in aggregate constitute a problem.

Sucking the thumb appears to serve two possible purposes. First, it may be viewed as an expression of a basic sucking impulse designed to ensure survival. Although it may begin as a reflex, a second purpose or meaning is added when the child begins to use thumb sucking to produce comfort or body pleasuring. Sigmund Freud viewed the behavior as gratification of oral sexuality. Thus viewed, it is essential if the child's psychosexual development is to proceed beyond the oral stage toward more mature levels.

Whether or not thumb sucking is sexual, it is without question an absorbing and deeply satisfying behavior for the child. It has been suggested that parental anxiety over their children's thumb sucking not only is usually unnecessary but also may reflect parents' unconscious or conscious connection between thumb sucking and masturbatory activity. Thus their own early conflicts and concerns over masturbation may be reactivated when they observe their children's thumb sucking.

Attempts to eliminate thumb sucking through mechanical restraints or noxious substances are rarely effective and often counterproductive. The behavior usually will be outgrown and can be ignored. However, if it persists, behavior modification techniques are often helpful.

D. G. BENNER

See LIFE SPAN DEVELOPMENT.

Thurstone, Louis Leon (1887–1955). American psychologist best known for his work in measuring intelligence. Born in Chicago, he studied electrical engineering and received his M.E. from Cornell in 1912. For a year he served as an assistant to Thomas Edison and for a brief time taught mathematics. His growing interest in learning, especially the mathematical relationship between practice and improvement, led to graduate study at the University of Chicago, where he received his Ph.D. in 1917.

Thurstone taught psychology at the Carnegie Institute of Technology from 1915 to 1923, spent a year in government research in Washington, and then returned to teach at the University of Chicago. He remained at Chicago from 1924 until 1952, when he moved to the University of North Carolina.

Thurstone's lifelong interest in applying mathematics to psychology led to his contributions in the area of measurement. He attacked the concept of mental age, noting that it cannot be applied to adults because scores do not continue to increase with increasing age. He suggested using the individual's percentile rank in a given age group, but other psychologists thought that this would confuse teachers, so little was done. This is essentially how adult IQs are determined today.

He also did not think of intelligence as consisting of a single general factor. Thurstone introduced the technique of factor analysis into intelligence testing and concluded that measuring intelligence involves measuring several different primary abilities, such as verbal comprehension, word fluency, number manipulation, space visualization, associative memory, perceptual speed, and logical reasoning. His works on intelligence include *The Nature of Intelligence* (1924), *The Measurement of Intelligence* (1925), *The Vectors of the Mind* (1935), *Primary Mental Abilities* (1938), and *Multiple-Factor Analysis* (1947).

Thurstone's theoretical and experimental work in multiple factor analysis was initiated in 1929, although he had derived his original equation while he was still at Carnegie. In addition to applying it to intelligence, he applied it to other areas, such as perception. He is known for work on simple structure and other contributions to the development of multiple factor analysis. He also contributed to the construction of modern scaling techniques and their use in attitude measurement in *Measurement of Attitudes* (1929). His attitude scales were used to assess attitudes toward war, other races, communism, capital punishment, and so forth. Thurstone was among the founders of the Psychometric Society and its journal, *Psychometrika*.

R. L. KOTESKEY

See INTELLIGENCE; INTELLECTUAL ASSESSMENT; PSYCHOLOGICAL MEASUREMENT.

Tic Disorder. Tics are repetitive, involuntary, stereotyped movements or vocalizations. An individual will admit that he or she has the urge to make them, can consciously suppress them for a time, is aware of mounting tension with such suppression, and experiences a sense of relief after their execution.

Tics appear most commonly about the face and are usually manifested as blinking, grinning, smirking, lip licking, throat clearing, grunting, or nose and forehead wrinkling. Tics may be either simple or complex, based on the degree of involvement of motor or vocal behavior.

In the past tics were thought to have a hysterical component. However, tics occasionally appear in individuals who demonstrate obsessional and compulsive traits. A tic, regardless whether its origin is psychogenic or the result of brain injury or physiological malfunction, may be exacerbated by stress. Tics disappear during sleep and diminish when the individual is preoccupied.

Most tics are viewed as a behavior that was learned or had its origin in a past traumatic experience or stressful situation. Thus, the tic can be considered a truncated movement of withdrawal or aggression that may have been the only possible response. Children are more susceptible to tic disorders due to their less mature inhibitory controls. *DSM-IV* necessitates the onset prior to the age of 18 for all four of the tic disorders listed.

DSM-IV makes the most definitive classification of tics (stereotyped movement or vocal disorders). They are broken down into either Tourette's disorder, transient tic disorder, chronic motor or vocal tic disorder, or tic disorder not otherwise specified. Tourette's disorder (Gilles de la Tourette's syndrome) is characterized by multiple complicated and widespread motor and vocal tics.

Although it is generally assumed that there is a psychogenic origin in the transient tic disorder and chronic motor or vocal tics, no evidence has substantiated a psychogenic basis for Tourette's disorder. Most studies seem to implicate a genetic-familial predisposition or central nervous system pathology etiology. Tourette, who discovered the condition, believed that the disorder is inherited, since two of his nine patients had affected relatives. It is now believed that Tourette's and other related presentations are transmitted in an autosomal dominant pattern. Other research has shown that approximately 70% for female and 99% for male patients with Tourette's and other tics have positive family history of such a disorder.

While psychoanalytic treatment for the transient disorder and chronic motor and vocal tic disorders has been unsuccessful, most tic disorders are rather successfully treated through behavioral techniques. This form of treatment typically involves the use of an extinction program known as negative practice, or mass practice, wherein the individual is persuaded to repeat the undesired tic voluntarily until the point of exhaustion. Since negative practice is a tedious and time-consuming method, it has been combined with a form of anxiety-relief conditioning. The patient is administered an unpleasant stimulus while the tic is being repeated, and the unpleasant stimulus is terminated simultaneously with cessation of the tic. Negative practice and anxiety-relief conditioning used together have been found to be more successful than either one alone.

K. R. KRACKE

See TOURETTE'S DISORDER.

Time Out. This behavioral technique, literally time out from positive reinforcement, involves removal of a person from the opportunity to obtain positive reinforcement. It is the most popular form of negative punishment and is readily implemented in any behavior modification program. An example of a time-out procedure would be a teacher who places a misbehaving child in the hall until the child quiets down. While he or she is in the hall the child misses the opportunity to earn reinforcement (the attention of peers and the general stimulation of the classroom), and the disruptive behavior should decrease. In order for time out to be effective, the situation from which the individual is withdrawn must be enjoyable or reinforcing.

D. G. BENNER

See BEHAVIOR THERAPY.

Titchener, Edward Bradford (1867–1927). Founder of structuralism. He was born in Chichester, England, and attended Malvern College and Oxford, where he studied philosophy and the classics and later became a research assistant in physiology. He then went to Leipzig, where he studied for two years, receiving his doctorate in 1892. Although he actually saw little of Wilhelm Wundt, Wundt made a lifelong impression on him.

Titchener would have liked to remain in England, but the British were not ready for pioneering work in psychology. After a year as extension lecturer in biology at Oxford, he went to Cornell University in the United States. He remained at Cornell the rest of his life, teaching psychology, directing the laboratory, and directing more than 50 doctoral dissertations. He was a dogmatic individual who refused to change as American psychology did. Although he was elected a charter member of the American Psychological Association in 1892, he resigned a year later. He even refused to attend meetings when the convention was held in Ithaca. In 1904 he founded his own group, the experimentalists, and dominated the meetings.

Titchener's psychology was an extension of Wundt's structuralism. Psychology was defined as the study of conscious experience. There were three basic classes of the elements of consciousness. Sensations (sights, sounds, tastes, etc.) were the elements of perceptions, and Titchener claimed there were 42,415 possible ones. Images were the elements of ideas, and affective states were the elements of emotion. Each basic element could have the attributes of quality, intensity, duration, and clearness, and sometimes extensity.

Titchener also explored the problems of attention, the arrangement of conscious elements. Like Wundt, he accepted the principle of association. His context theory of meaning held that one mental process is the meaning of another. The context of related processes gives meaning to the core of sensation and images. Like Wundt, Titchener used introspection as his method of observation.

Titchener wrote 216 articles and notes and a dozen books. He also attempted to translate Wundt's *Principles of Physiological Psychology* several times, but Wundt always had a new edition out before

Titchener could get the previous one translated. His most important books are *An Outline of Psychology* (1896), *The Primer of Psychology* (1898), a four-volume *Experimental Psychology* (1901–1905), and *Textbook of Psychology* (1910). Most of his books were introductory and experimental texts but were significant in outlining his position.

R. L. KOTESKEY

See STRUCTURALISM; ATTENTION; PSYCHOLOGY, HISTORY OF.

Toilet Training. The process of acquiring control over bowels and bladder elimination presents a special challenge to many children and parents. If it is attempted too early or in an overly harsh or critical manner, it can be the occasion of a fierce battle of wills and can lead to a variety of maladaptive behaviors in the child. However, if it is approached with skill and understanding, it can be a satisfying experience for both parent and child.

Several approaches to toilet training have been developed in recent years. The best known and most widely used is that developed by Azrin and Foxx and described in *Toilet Training in Less Than a Day* (1974). Based on research done in toilet training profoundly retarded individuals, this highly effective approach eliminates the major frustrations that can accompany toilet training. This article will describe Azrin and Foxx's procedure.

Before beginning training, parents should determine that the child can perform the following tasks: imitate a simple action that is modeled by a parent; identify the major parts of the body by pointing to them; and follow simple instructions, such as Sit down, Follow me, Give me your cup. A child who is at least 20 months old and who can perform these tasks should be ready to be trained.

The parent who will do the training should plan to spend up to a full day and to ensure that he or she and the child will not be disturbed by external distractions. In advance of the training the trainer must identify all the specific skills the child will need to master, such as going to the potty chair, grasping and lowering pants, sitting down, urinating, wiping, pulling up pants, removing pot, carrying pot to toilet, emptying contents into toilet, flushing, and replacing pot.

The trainer uses a doll to model all these actions. As the doll carries out each task, the parent praises the doll's successes. When the parent finishes the modeling session, he or she asks the child to play the role of the trainer and to walk the doll through the same sequence of actions again. Next the parent models the desired behaviors without using the doll. Then the parent asks the child to play the role of trainer and to model for the parent the specified skills.

To cause a frequent need for urination the trainer gives the child something to drink about once every five minutes. These drinks are used along with food and treats as reinforcers for successful performance of skills by the child. These tangible reinforcers are accompanied by extensive praise, applause, hugs, and kisses. The program must include a large variety of reinforcers, immediate reinforcement following a success, and frequent reinforcement. The parent checks the child's pants about once every five minutes. If the pants are dry, the parent reinforces the child. If the pants are wet, the parent first reprimands the child and then ignores him or her for five minutes. Following this time out the trainer requires the child to come from different locations in the house to the bathroom and to engage in the prescribed sequence of toileting behaviors.

The trainer uses verbal prompts extensively. In early stages of training the parent can manually guide the child through desired actions until the child performs them in response to an oral request. Throughout training the parent states how pleased significant other persons will be when they hear of the child's successes. These persons include the absent parent, siblings, grandparents and other relatives, and characters from books and television.

During the course of training verbal prompts and frequent reinforcements are gradually stopped. By the end of the training session prompts are eliminated and reinforcement is delivered only for urinating in the potty chair. During subsequent days no reminders to urinate are given; however, the parent does check the child's pants before meals, naps, and bedtime. Dry pants produce praise. Wet pants lead to a reprimand and instructions to change his or her pants and to practice the actions of going to the bathroom.

The average length of the training session is 4 hours, with a range of one-half to 14 hours. Younger children take longer to train than older children, but almost all children who pass the readiness tests can be successfully trained.

Reference

Azrin, N. H., & Foxx, R. M. (1974). *Toilet training in less than a day.* New York: Simon & Schuster.

P. W. CLEMENT

See PARENTING.

Token Economy. A system of psychological treatment or intervention, based on the principles of operant conditioning (*see* Conditioning, Operant), in which tokens serve as the immediate consequences for the treated behaviors. These tokens are known as tangible conditioned reinforcers. They may consist of items such as points, poker chips, check marks, marbles, paper punches on a card, entries in a bank book, or literal tokens. Such items are linked to back-up consequences, which may be either reinforcing or punishing, in that the tokens are exchanged for these back-ups. Token economies usually emphasize the use of positive back-up reinforcers, which involve consequences such as money, food, access to activities, or other privileges. Less frequently tokens may be linked to punishing consequences. The most common punishing consequences are response costs such as fines.

The conceptual model underlying the token economy assumes that abnormal behaviors are influenced by the same variables that affect normal behaviors. The behaviors that get people into trouble in families, schools, or communities are actions. Actions are greatly modified by their consequences. Whereas certain environmental changes may produce reflexive responses, actions may produce changes in the actor's environment. Such changes are called consequences. B. F. Skinner and developers of the token economy have emphasized the use of positive consequences. When a token, such as a check mark on a card, can later be exchanged for a positive consequence, the token becomes an immediate positive reinforcer.

For example, John, a 33-year-old chronic schizophrenic, attended a day treatment program at a local church. One of John's problems was that he usually failed to make eye contact and appropriate social greetings when first encountering another person. He set a personal goal to increase the frequency of greeting other persons within the day treatment program. He carried a small card in his shirt pocket. Whenever a staff member observed John making a social greeting, the staff member punched John's card with a distinctive paper punch. Each hole constituted a token. Each day John could go to the program's reinforcer cafeteria and purchase such items as snacks, beverages, and toiletries. Each item had a cash value. Each punch on John's card was worth a specified amount.

Long before psychology became an identified discipline, various cultures had developed complex token economies. Their tokens became known as money. In most cases money had no inherent value. It derived its value from what it could purchase; thus money became the most pervasive tangible conditioned reinforcer.

In *Walden Two*, Skinner provided a grand design for an entire community that ran on a token economy based on the principles of operant conditioning. Skinner described an ideal community based on a science of behavior. One of the distinctive features of this fictitious community was that it ran without punishment. Skinner argued against aversive and coercive techniques to control people's behavior. In reference to social influences he wrote, "I insist that Jesus, who was apparently the first to discover the power of refusing to punish, must have hit upon the principle by accident. He certainly had none of the experimental evidence which is available to us today" (1948, p. 261).

Within contemporary psychology the token economy developed as part of the behavior modification movement. During the 1950s a limited number of psychologists began applying the concepts and procedures of operant conditioning to problems in living. They demonstrated that the approaches Skinner had developed in working with rats and pigeons could be applied to people. Over time clinical researchers demonstrated that operant procedures could alleviate various forms of serious psychological disturbances (Ayllon & Azrin, 1968; Kazdin, 1977).

The token economy involves paying people to do what is socially desirable. In contrast to the protests of some critics who argue that people should do what they are supposed to do without having to be paid, the Bible seems to give directions that are consistent with the token economy. For example, Jesus declared, "The worker deserves his wages" (Luke 10:7, NIV).

In the clinical example given earlier, offering social greetings was John's work in the day treatment program. Engaging in cooperative social play is the work of children in treatment for aggressive acts toward others. Performing academic assignments is the work of learning-disabled students in special classrooms. Putting on and buttoning their own pants is the work of retarded children in state hospitals. In each case the Bible and contemporary psychological technology seem to be in harmony.

References

Ayllon, T., & Azrin, N. H. (1968). *The token economy: A motivational system for therapy and rehabilitation.* New York: Appleton-Century-Crofts.

Kazdin, A. E. (1977). *The token economy: A review and evaluation.* New York: Plenum.

Skinner, B. F. (1948). *Walden two.* New York: Macmillan.

P. W. CLEMENT

See APPLIED BEHAVIORAL ANALYSIS; BEHAVIOR THERAPY.

Tolman, Edward Chace (1886–1959). American behavioral psychologist. Born in West Newton, Massachusetts, he was the son of a prosperous factory owner. At his father's urging he earned a bachelor's degree in electrochemistry in 1911 from the Massachusetts Institute of Technology. However, rather than entering the family business he entered Harvard to study philosophy and psychology. He received his M.A. in 1912 and his Ph.D. in 1915.

After serving as a psychology instructor at Northwestern University from 1915 to 1918, Tolman moved to the University of California at Berkeley, where he remained, with two brief interruptions, until his retirement in 1954. During World War II he served in the Office of Strategic Services. When he refused to sign a loyalty oath in California, he taught at Harvard and the University of Chicago (1950–1953). He led the successful fight against the oath and was reinstated by an order of the California Supreme Court.

Although he was trained in the structuralist tradition, during graduate school Tolman spent a month in Germany with Kurt Koffka and was introduced to behaviorism. He developed a system he called purposive behaviorism, a cross between behaviorism and Gestalt psychology. He believed that all behavior is goal-directed. He introduced the concept of intervening variables so that psychology would have a way of making statements about inner states and processes that cannot be observed.

Tolman's cognitive theory of learning was the major alternative to Clark Leonard Hull's theory of learning between 1930 and 1950. He postulated that repeated performance of a task builds up sign-Gestalts, learned relationships between cues in the environment and the organism's expectations. If a rat or person is put in a maze, expectancies are formed at each choice point. If the rat gets to the food, its expectancies are confirmed. Soon a pattern of sign-Gestalts, a cognitive map, is established. The organism gets to know something about its environment. Although Tolman never developed a fully integrated system, his experiments challenged Hull's theory.

Several times Tolman revised his system in articles, frequently renaming concepts, but he remained a purposive behaviorist. His success at achieving an integration of Gestalt psychology and behaviorism is shown in the fact that some historians classify him as a behaviorist and others as a Gestalt psychologist. He did his own thinking instead of fitting into an existing system. Tolman's major work was *Purposive Behavior in Animals and Men* (1932).

R. L. KOTESKEY

See LEARNING.

Touching, Use of in Therapy. See PHYSICAL CONTACT IN THERAPY.

Tourette's Disorder. Tourette's disorder is also known as Gilles de la Tourette's syndrome, Tourette syndrome, and *maladie des tics*. Multiple motor tics and one or more vocal tics are the primary criteria for making this diagnosis. Tics are sudden, spasmodic, involuntary motor movements or vocalizations. Examples of motor tics are blinking, touching, squatting, sniffing, or twirling. Examples of vocal tics are grunts, barks, snorts, coughs, and coprolalia (obscenities). These tics may appear concurrently or at different times. To qualify for this diagnosis they must occur many times a day during most days for at least one year and the person does not go longer than three consecutive months without having any tics. The first tics must appear before the patient reaches age 18, and the tics are not caused by a drug or another foreign substance or by a general medical illness.

Tourette's disorder appears in diverse racial and ethnic groups and is more common in males than in females. This disorder is relatively rare. Onset may be as early as age two. Half of all persons with the problem meet the diagnostic criteria by age seven. The disorder is usually lifelong, but there may be periods that are symptom-free, lasting from weeks to years. In most cases the symptoms decline during adolescence and adulthood. For some people the symptoms disappear by adulthood.

Obsessive-compulsive disorder, attention-deficit/hyperactivity disorder, and learning disorders may also be present. From 35% to 50% of people with Tourette's disorder also meet the criteria for obsessive-compulsive disorder. Tourette's disorder may be accompanied by hyperactivity, distractibility, impulsivity, social discomfort, shame, self-consciousness, depression, rejection by others, and impaired social, academic, or occupational functioning.

Chronic motor or vocal tic disorder is similar to Tourette's disorder, but the former diagnosis requires only motor or vocal tics; otherwise the diagnostic criteria for these two disorders are the same. Likewise, transient tic disorder may look like Tourette's disorder, but this diagnosis is used only when the tics have been present for up to 12 consecutive months.

Tourette's disorder runs in families. Although there has not been a convincing demonstration of a central nervous system abnormality in persons with Tourette's disorder, many experts agree that this is a neurobiologically mediated disorder. In contrast, although the tics are viewed as involuntary, the person usually has the ability to suppress them voluntarily for brief periods of time lasting up to several hours.

Haloperidol and pimozide are the most commonly used drugs in treating Tourette's disorder. Clinical researchers using these drugs have reported about a 50% to 60% reduction in tics. Clonidine has produced an average reduction of about 25%. The major disadvantages of drug treatment include negative side effects, failure to take the drug long-term, and the requirement for continuous use.

Controlled studies on the effectiveness of behavioral treatments for Tourette's disorder show about a 90% reduction in tics. Such treatments include habit reversal training (strengthening behaviors that are incompatible with the tics); massed or negative practice of the most socially offensive tics; relaxation training; self-monitoring and self-reinforcement; and contingency management, including group contingencies designed to focus the attention of other persons on appropriate behaviors in the patient. The major limitation of behavioral treatment is the large amount of time required to do the initial intervention.

Additional Readings

Comings, D. E. (1990). *Tourette syndrome and human behavior*. Duarte, CA: Hope Press.

Dornbush, M. P., & Pruitt, S. K. (1995). *Teaching the tiger: A handbook for individuals involved in the education of students with attention deficit disorders, Tourette syndrome, or obsessive-compulsive disorder.* Duarte, CA: Hope Press.

For Further Information

Tourette Syndrome Association, 42–40 Bell Boulevard, Bayside, NY 11361. (718) 224-2999

P. W. CLEMENT

See TIC DISORDER.

Tournier, Paul (1898-1986). French-speaking Swiss physician who pioneered a Christian "medicine of the whole person."

Biography. Tournier was born on 12 May1898 in Geneva, Switzerland, the son of a pious Calvinist pastor who died when Tournier was three months of age. He survived a serious illness in infancy but was orphaned at the age of six when his mother died of breast cancer; he and his older sister were reared by relatives. A family history of physical and emotional problems may have set the stage for his later career as physician and psychotherapist.

Tournier was a lonely introvert as a youth, but through the friendship of significant persons in his life he gradually recognized his intellectual ability and eventually his own worth as a person. As a young man he worked in the repatriation of Russian and Austrian prisoners of World War I. He founded an international child welfare organization and organized a famine relief effort for Russian children; invented calculating machines; cowrote and costaged a play. In 1923 he graduated from the University of Geneva Medical School, then completed internships in Paris and Geneva, and in 1928 established a general medical practice.

In 1924 Tournier married Nelly Bouvier, and the couple had two sons. In 1932 he was introduced to the Oxford Group movement, a pietistic group with emphases on personal conversion and small-group sharing, which made his nominally Calvinistic Christian faith real and prompted him to dedicate his life to a Christian view of medicine. (This same Oxford Group was influential in the founding of Alcoholics Anonymous.) As he listened to his patients, Tournier became interested in the personal and spiritual meaning of their illnesses, embarking on what would become his career as a psychotherapist. When his neutral country was hemmed in by the Nazis and the Fascists during World War II, he served in the medical corps.

In 1940 Tournier published his first book, on the medicine of the whole person, later translated into English as *The Healing of Persons* (1940/1965). Over the course of the next 44 years he wrote a total of 21 books (with translations into at least 13 languages) and numerous articles, and he lectured internationally. Theological influences reflected in his writings included Calvinism, neo-orthodoxy, evangelicalism, pietism, and ecumenism. Psycho-logical influences included classical psychoanalysis, existentialism, and personalism. Perhaps his best-known work and single best summary of his thought is *The Meaning of Persons* (1955/1957). His other books have addressed topics such as loneliness, existential weakness and fear, the Bible and medicine, true and false guilt, human development, human freedom, marital communication, life and career, retirement, violence and power, the role of women, suffering, and listening. In 1947 Tournier and others (later known as the Bossey Group) established the first, subsequently annual, International Conference on the Medicine of the Person to informally and prayerfully reflect on Christianity with a concern about the excessive specialization and depersonalization of medicine. The first parallel Conference on Medicine and Ministry of the Whole Person in the United States was held in 1972 in North Carolina.

Nelly Tournier died in 1974, and in 1984, at the age of 86, Tournier married Corinne O'Rama, a concert pianist some forty years his junior.

Personality Theory. Although Tournier's writing is anecdotal and unsystematic, a discernible theory of human personality may be gleaned from his writings (Collins, 1973; Houde, 1990).

Tournier viewed the human person structurally as a whole entity made up of two interrelated aspects: the natural personage and the supernatural person. The personage represents the external roles or means of expression of the person. It includes the body, the psyche (feelings, imagination), and the mind (thinking, reasoning), which may be observed or studied by science. The person is the authentic unadulterated self, the center of personal existence and decision making. It is identified as the human spirit, which is hidden and can be fully known only by God.

Tournier understood persons to be motivated on the natural level by physical drives, psychological unconscious and conscious feelings and reason, social suggestion, and one's practical situation or place. On the personal or spiritual level he emphasized the importance of human freedom, the vital instinct (competing drives for love and power), the moral conscience, and existential meaning. He also recognized the spiritual influences on human beings of God and the devil.

Tournier recognized two movements in the formation of the person: natural enrichment (self-fulfillment, self-assertion) and supernatural relinquishment (renunciation, self-denial). He noted an inherent rhythm of life between these successive and complementary movements. He spoke of human development in terms of the seasons of life: childhood (spring), adulthood (summer), old age (autumn), and death (winter).

Regarding individual differences, Tournier's early formulations focused on the classical temperaments of Hippocrates (choleric, melancholic, sanguine, phlegmatic). He later simplified his view to two primary temperaments: strong (optimistic, confident, active, and aggressive) and weak (doubtful, passive, contemplative, and fearful). He also considered the importance of gender for human personality. Tournier recognized ultimately the mystery of the person, which precluded artificial categories of classification.

Psychopathology and Psychotherapy. From Tournier's perspective the development of psychological illness results from a complex interaction of natural and supernatural factors. Natural factors include inborn temperament, accidental psychological trauma (such as parental discord and negative education), psychological complexes (false ideas and disturbed emotions; e.g., false guilt, violence, unhealthy fears), and mode of life, which ultimately result in a strong or weak reaction. Spiritual causes might also contribute toward psychopathology: sin and true guilt, the fundamental inner conflict (disabled liberty and an impaired moral conscience are unable to manage the vital instinct of power over love), and existential fears such as the "Paradise lost" complex.

Tournier recognized two movements in the healing of persons: psychology and religion. Psychological "salvation" involves exoneration from false guilt and appropriate self-assertion. Religious salvation involves convicting grace (God's love and severity), faith, repentance, saving grace (God's forgiveness of true guilt and God's guidance), and a reversal of attitude (involving true liberty, true morality, self-denial, inner harmony, true fellowship). Tournier envisioned an ideal person characterized by true strength—a balance of faith and realism, true morality versus moralism, self-assertion and self-denial.

Technical scientific treatment or advice might consist of recognized medical techniques, psychoanalytic technique (discovery of truth, expression of emotion), and positive or preventive health measures addressing healthy thinking, lifestyle, or social environment. The heart of psychotherapy, however, consists of dialogue. Tournier noted two parallel dialogues. The dialogue with persons consists of reciprocity (including appropriate therapist self-disclosure), listening for understanding (interest and patience), and nonjudgmental acceptance (respect and support). The dialogue with God consists of prayerful meditation, confession of sin (absolution and forgiveness), Bible reading, and church fellowship. An integrative medicine of the whole person consists of doctors of the whole personality who work as a team to integrate psychotherapy and soul healing in their lives and professional practice.

Contributions. Tournier's greatest legacy is his pioneering work in the integration of psychology and Christianity, including the practical application of biblical insights to counseling, and the reinterpretation of psychological theorists such as Sigmund Freud, Carl Gustav Jung, Alfred Adler, and others from a Christian perspective. His Christian personality theory presents a high view of the human person and the human capacities for freedom, conscience, and meaning. He promoted value and respect for the human person from conception beyond natural death. He acknowledged within a psychological theory the spiritual realities of sin, the longing for heaven, salvation through grace, forgiveness, and the ideal of virtuous living. Tournier encouraged the practice of interpersonal dialogue and prayer. He recognized that ultimate personal fulfillment comes from the free choice to sacrifice oneself for another. He advocated a balanced, whole-person approach to healing involving medicine, psychotherapy, and soul healing.

Tournier's most controversial thought was his theology of universal salvation even apart from a profession of Christian faith, which he explained as his attempt to be both orthodox and tolerant. His adoption of the language of instincts and drives may reflect the psychological climate of his day; however, terms such as needs and motives might be more faithful to the vision of the human person that he advanced.

References

Collins, G. R. (1973). *The Christian psychology of Paul Tournier.* Grand Rapids, MI: Baker.

Houde, K. A. (1990). The Christian personality theory of Paul Tournier (Doctoral dissertation, Fuller Theological Seminary, Graduate School of Psychology, 1990). *Dissertation Abstracts International, 51* (7B), 3603 (Publication No. 90-33538).

Tournier, P. (1940/1965). *The healing of persons.* (E. Hudson, Trans.). New York: Harper & Row. (Original work published 1940)

Tournier, P. (1955/1957). *The meaning of persons.* (E. Hudson, Trans.). New York: Harper & Row. (Original work published 1955)

Additional Reading

Peaston, M. (1972). *Personal living: An introduction to Paul Tournier.* New York: Harper & Row.

K. A. HOUDE

See CHRISTIAN PSYCHOLOGY; CHRISTIAN COUNSELING AND PSYCHOTHERAPY.

Tragedy. *See* GRIEF; LOSS AND SEPARATION; TRAUMA.

Training in Counseling and Psychotherapy. Training in counseling and psychotherapy occurs within several disciplinary contexts (e.g., social work, psychology, nursing, pastoral care, psychiatry, family therapy). While the discipline has varied, there has nonetheless been a remarkable consistency in training approaches across disciplines. Many of these approaches had their roots in psychological theory and research and have then been modified to suit the special needs of various settings or patient populations.

Training in Core Conditions. Perhaps the strongest influence on the process of training, and on specific interactional outcomes, was the work of Carl Rogers and his associates. Beginning in the 1960s, the client-centered orientation to counseling has influenced the training of practitioners by focusing on the necessary and sufficient ingredients of therapeutic change. Rogers defined these ingredients as empathic understanding, unconditional positive regard (warmth), and congruence (genuineness). Rogers suggested that these attitudes on the part of the therapist are both necessary and sufficient. That is, he believed that positive change in counseling would not occur without them and would invariably occur in their presence. As early as 1957 (Rogers, 1957), he described a method for training in core conditions where the student listened to audiotaped interviews, role played with other students, observed interviews with actual clients, conducted interviews with clients, and participated in personal therapy. These steps form the core of much of what occurs in training today.

Rogers's emphasis on core conditions was altered by Truax and Carkhuff (1967), who developed human relations training by focusing on observable therapist behaviors. Rather than considering abstract notions of empathy and warmth, Truax and Carkhuff attempted to develop a structured, didactic approach to training in which the focus was on teaching specific conversational responses that were assumed to be correlated with attitudinal variables. Most of the currently popular methods for training counselors build on this approach; even programs not meant to train counselors in the core conditions invariably include therapist response skills of warmth, genuineness, immediacy, and reflection of feelings, responses that formed the core of client-centered therapy.

Given the emphasis on training counselors to provide these core conditions, it would be expected that psychology has been able to demonstrate their effectiveness in therapy outcome. Reviews of the outcome literature do suggest, first, that some therapy overall is better than none and, second, that certain treatments appear to have empirical support for certain conditions (e.g., empirically validated treatments). Further, the core conditions form the basis for understanding how a counselor builds a relationship with a client, and this relationship, commonly termed the therapeutic alliance, appears to be critical in fostering client change. However, research evidence does not support the sufficiency of these core conditions in promoting client change.

Nonetheless, including these dimensions in training provides a facilitative context for counselors to consider their own personality and biases and the roles these can play in the therapeutic context. Rogers emphasized the importance of attitudes and not skills, and the attitudes he focused on were acceptance, understanding, and genuineness. Counselors in training would do well to consider themselves and their practice within these three dimensions irrespective of their actual therapeutic approaches.

Supervision. Supervision is a key element in training counselors. However, the term *supervision* has embodied a wide variety of definitions. Loganbill, Hardy, and Delworth (1982) defined supervision as "an intensive, interpersonally focused, one-to-one relationship in which one person is designated to facilitate the development of therapeutic competence in the other person" (p. 4). Within this definition, they saw four major functions for supervision: monitoring client welfare, enhancing the growth of the counselor, promoting transition between stages of growth, and evaluating trainee progress.

Their model, based on developmental theory, has informed much of supervision research and theorizing (Loganbill, Hardy, & Dellworth, 1982). Briefly, they suggest that trainees progress along predictable stages of growth in their development as counselors: stagnation, confusion, and integration. Further, eight key issues that face all counselors manifest themselves differently as a function of the different stages: competence, emotional awareness, autonomy, theoretical identity, respect for individual differences, purpose and direction, personal motivation, and professional ethics. Since this model is developmental, it proposes that counselors reapproach these issues throughout their professional lifetimes, resolving them in various ways.

It should be mentioned that other approaches to supervision (see Holloway, 1992 for a review) consider the processes and outcomes of supervision from other perspectives. One such perspective is by supervision roles, where the supervisor's role is comprised of a set of expectations on the part of the supervisee along dimensions of function and attitude, and combinations of met and unmet expectations influence the outcome and effectiveness of supervision. Another perspective is that of the practice of therapy, where a supervisor is conceived in terms akin to that of a therapist: providing understanding and warmth, provoking self-understanding, and increasing personal awareness. An additional perspective is that of education, where a supervisor functions as a teacher-coach, instructing the supervisee in relevant skills and critiquing their applications in counseling interactions.

Two additional considerations should be noted. First is that any supervisor must consider how well the trainee is performing along a specified set of performance indicators. Trainees typically are in educational settings where their acquisition of specific counseling skills is a goal, and the supervisor must provide feedback to the trainees both to improve their performance and as an summative evaluation. A second consideration is the assumption that supervision must occur in one-on-one settings. In contrast, group supervision is an efficient use of resources and provides the further benefit of trainees learning from each other as well as from the supervisor.

Overall, in supervision, there should be an emphasis on the supervisor understanding the needs and the dynamics of the trainee's clients and of the trainee and the interaction of these, particularly as these are in conflict (Mueller & Kell, 1971). Further, the trainee's level of development is important to keep in mind, whether the supervision is conceptualized from a developmental theory or not.

Use of Technology. With the advent of video and audio recording technology, new methods of supervision were developed. For example, the widespread use of audiotaping allows supervisors and trainees to process interviews more directly and more completely than via material presented by the trainee from memory. Several bugs in the ear devices let the supervisor speak directly to the trainee during an interview and actively influence the delivery of interventions. However, the training area has witnessed an important adoption of technology in two areas: microcounseling and interpersonal process recall.

Microcounseling. Ivey (1971) originally conceived of microcounseling as an adaptation of a training model applied to teaching. It emphasizes breaking down complex skills into small behavioral subunits that can be described, modeled, practiced, observed, and corrected through the use of videotape feedback. Ivey and his colleagues used this approach to teach three basic counseling skills: attentiveness, accurate reflection of feelings, and summarization of feelings. Other skills for which microcounseling methods have been used are giving direction to clients, expressing feelings by the counselor (immediacy), and interpretations.

Their training model consists of four steps. The first is a baseline interview, in which the trainee interviews a volunteer client in a videotaped interaction. The second stage is training, in which the trainee reads materials describing the desired skill, views the videotape with a supervisor, views filmed versions of models performing the desired skill, and compares his or her performance to the filmed models. The third step is reinterview, in which the trainee conducts a second filmed interview, emphasizing the desired counseling skill. The fourth step is review, in which the trainee reviews the second taped interview with the supervisor and critiques his or her acquisition of the skill.

The significance of the microcounseling approach is its flexibility and adaptability to teaching many counseling skills. It is suitable for beginning counselors and provides them with a supportive and instructional environment. It is equally suitable for more advanced counselors interested in updating their skills. This approach is important in its clear definition of desired interviewing behaviors and the use of videotape models to teach counselors the target skill in the context of an actual interview.

Interpersonal Process Recall. This is a structured method of video replay for counselors developed by Kagan and associates (Kagan, 1980). The four assumptions behind this approach are that people are the best source of knowledge about themselves, that we all have implicit theories about human behavior, that labeling interpersonal and intrapersonal processes provides order and structure, and that counselors must understand human interactions in order to be effective.

Based on these assumptions, interpersonal process recall is a structured training sequence in which the counselor views videotapes of his or her interviews with a supervisor who functions as an inquirer to guide the recall session. While the counselor trainee chooses where in the tape to stop to make observations, the inquirer's role is to facilitate the types of discussions that meet the above assumptions, namely, to help the trainee understand himself or herself better and to label the interpersonal processes occurring within the trainee and in the session. Thus, questions such as Do you recall what you were feeling? What thoughts were you having here about the client? and What did you want to happen after that? are meant to guide the discussion of the thoughts, feelings, and expectations of the counselor in the counseling session.

Interpersonal process recall has been evaluated in many contexts and appears to be an effective method of training. In particular it influences trainees to focus on their own affect and cognitions and to better understand the role of their own internal processes in the counseling session.

Issues in Training. In her recent review, Holloway (1992) notes three new directions in supervision. First is the idea that approaches to supervision that establish common themes, such as developmental models or supervisor role models, appear to have considerable research support and to enjoy wide applications in the educational arena. However, it is still unknown what effects the supervisor's objectives and strategies and the institutional setting have on the process of supervision. Researchers and clinicians should work together to articulate models of how these two facets work to enhance or detract from the effectiveness of training and supervision.

Second is the use of group supervision. Although there are no clearly articulated models of group supervision, the use of peer groups is a common practice. Again, supervisors and researchers need to consider the issues in group supervision and ways in which peer presence helps or hinders the work of learning to be a counselor. In addition, the ways in which the supervision group overlaps with the roles and functions of other related groups, such as support groups and therapy groups, is unknown.

Third is the issue of selection: what types of persons make good counselors. There seems to be a shared belief that certain people are better therapists; thus selection programs have attempted to measure personality variables such as warmth, perceptiveness, and so on and correlated these with success as a therapist. However, the research evidence to date does not indicate that any particular therapist characteristic is related to training outcome. As Matarazzo (1978) noted, since counseling is an intensely human endeavor, we should be safe in assuming that therapists who are flexible and open minded would do better. However, research showing that therapy can have deleterious effects suggests that selection remains a concern for educational programs that purport to train counselors.

It is important to remember that training beginning counselors and enhancing the skills of advanced therapists may well be two very different processes. Thus supervision must take differences of personality, abilities, skills, and clients into account. Issues such as these are important to psychology and to other disciplines for which training and supervision in psychotherapy are key components.

References

Holloway, E. L. (1992). Supervision: A way of teaching and learning. In S. D. Brown and R. W. Lent (Eds.), *Handbook of counseling psychology* (2nd ed.). New York: Wiley.

Ivey, A. E. (1971). *Microcounseling: Innovations in interviewing training*. Springfield, IL: Thomas.

Kagan, N. (1980). Influencing human interactions: Eighteen years with IPR. In A. K. Hess (Ed.), *Psychotherapy supervision: Theory, research, and practice*. New York: Wiley.

Loganbill, C., Hardy, E., & Delworth, U. (1982). Supervision: A conceptual model. *The Counseling Psychologist, 10*, 3–42.

Matarazzo, R. (1978). Research on the teaching and learning of psychotherapeutic skills. In S. L. Garfield and A. E. Bergin (Eds.), *Handbook of psychotherapy and behavior change* (2nd ed.). New York: Wiley.

Mueller, W. J., & Kell, B. L. (1971). *Coping with conflict: Supervising counselors and therapists*. New York: Appleton-Century-Crofts.

Rogers, C. R. (1957). The necessary and sufficient conditions of therapeutic personality change. *Journal of Consulting Psychology, 21*, 95–103.

Truax, C. B., & Carkhuff, R. R. (1967). *Toward effective counseling and psychotherapy: Training and practice*. Chicago: Aldine.

E. M. Altmaier

See Counseling and Psychotherapy: Overview; Psychotherapy, Effectiveness of.

Trait. Psychologists and biologists employ the term *trait* to refer to any relatively enduring characteristic describing a group or an individual. A trait's existence is inferred from repeated observations across a diverse range of circumstances. Some biologists reserve the term for genetic characteristics as opposed to environmentally induced ones.

If the trait is present in all members of a specific group, then it is a common trait. But if the trait reflects only one individual's consistency, it is termed a unique trait. The trait description may refer to behavioral or manifest consistency in diverse situations or may infer causation through underlying constructs. In the former case the trait is a surface trait, while in the latter case it is a source trait. As behavioral indicators surface traits are readily observed, but source traits are inferred, underlying structures. In Allport's (1961) analysis, traits are constructs that give rise to equivalent actions in response to diverse stimuli or to equivalent stimuli yielding related but distinct responses. Traits render stimuli and responses functionally equivalent. Thus there may be multiple indicators of a trait.

Based on multiple observations, a trait description is an abstraction of the common elements in those observations and a generalization of the pattern to other situations or individuals. A trait's relative strength is a probability statement of likely action.

Controversy exists as to whether traits are real characteristics of actors or the inferential products of observers. As an advocate of the first position, Allport conceived of traits as neuropsychic structures, while many personality and social psychologists view traits as attributions made by observers about persons. In the first case, traits are used as causal explanation for latent consistency in behavior, a consistency modified only slightly by environmental demand. In the latter position, traits are labels used by observers as descriptions of apparent consistency in behavior. The attribution of a label may initiate a filtering process that selectively ignores disconfirming evidence.

Although traits are ascribed to human intellect, most trait theories are concerned with emotional, social, or personality domains. The most prominent trait concepts (as causal structures) are found in the works of Gordon Willard Allport and Raymond Bernard Cattell. In addition, some theorists equate traits and types. However, a majority seem to follow the direction of Hans Eysenck, who placed them on a continuum of specificity-generality. Specific responses are organized into a habitual response, sets of habitual responses in a trait, and sets of traits into a type. As traits order diverse behaviors, types order traits.

Reference

Allport, G. W. (1961). *Pattern and growth in personality*. New York: Holt, Rinehart, and Winston.

R. L. Timpe

See Temperament; Personality; Type.

Tranquilizer. Any of a number of drugs used to reduce anxiety, tension, or agitation. The term technically refers to a group of phrenotropic compounds whose effects are primarily exerted at a subcortical level. This results in no interference with consciousness, in contrast to hypnotic and sedative drugs, which also have a calming effect. Common usage of the term distinguishes between minor tranquilizers (such as Valium, Miltown, and Librium), which are antianxiety agents, and major tranquilizers (such as chlorpromazine or Thorazine), which are antipsychotic agents. Minor tranquilizers are used principally in the treatment of anxiety, while major tranquilizers are used principally in the treatment of schizophrenia.

D. G. BENNER

See PSYCHOPHARMACOLOGY.

Transactional Analysis. A theory of personality, a view of psychopathology, a mode of psychotherapy, and a philosophy of life. In each of these the primary data for consideration are observable ways in which persons interact with each other. These interpersonal interactions are called transactions, and it is the belief of this approach that an analysis of these transactions is the prime means for understanding and changing persons.

As a theory of personality, transactional analysis assumes that those behaviors, attitudes, and styles that characterize persons are habits they have developed in efforts to obtain "strokes" from other persons with whom they interact. "Stimulus hunger" is seen as the basic motivation of life. This term refers to the innate desire to interact with the world and most of all the desire to interact with other people. Personality is therefore a style of interacting with others from whom one seeks recognition, status, and intimacy. Personality does not result, as Sigmund Freud suggested, from an individual need for pleasure but from a social need for others. In this regard transactional analysis is more like ego psychology than psychoanalysis.

As a view of psychopathology, transactional analysis assumes that persons are born innocent and trusting. They yearn for intimacy, and they reach out confidently to others. Over time two events commonly occur. People become stereotyped and they become defensive. They give up on experiencing intimacy, for which persons have a need, and settle for the types of interpersonal relationships, or transactions, that lead to isolation and negative self-images. These types of transactions are called games, and they always end in bad feelings for both persons involved. Games are those types of interactions that always result in negative endings and reinforce a person's bad feelings.

As a mode of psychotherapy, transactional analysis assumes that if persons become aware of the self-defeating, intimacy-destroying, isolation-producing ways in which they are interacting with others, and they decide to change these into more fulfilling manners of relating, they can. Transactional analysis affirms the capacity of people to recognize and analyze and alter their behavior. As contrasted with psychoanalysis, which is pessimistic about persons'

abilities to become aware of their dynamics because of its presumption that psychopathology is determined by the unconscious, transactional analysis is optimistic about the ability of persons to gain such insight because it presumes that the origins of these problems is in conscious and subconscious ego states that are available for introspection.

As a philosophy of life, transactional analysis affirms the potential and possibility of intimacy in human relationships. It is prescriptive, not just descriptive, of what human life ought to be, and it has ideal states toward which it feels society ought to be committed. For example, in Steiner's *Scripts People Live* (1974) a significant section is devoted to a critique of the type of society that promotes isolation and competition. Transactional analysis is optimistic and realistic at the same time. It is idealistic in terms of what human life was meant to be, and it works with persons and with institutions to make them more humane in the sense that they better induce intimacy among people.

Background. While transactional analysis includes a number of contemporary theorists (e.g., Harris, Steiner, Jongeward, James), it evolved from the ideas of one man, Eric Berne. Berne was a psychiatrist who practiced most of his life in the San Francisco area. He had gone through several years of training to be a psychoanalyst prior to being told he would not be approved (1956). It has often been assumed that because of this disappointing experience Berne decided to create his own theory in contrast to psychoanalysis. This is only partially true; Berne had begun much earlier to state his opinions about the need for a shorter form of treatment than psychoanalysis and for a view of personality that emphasized the ego rather than the id. These ideas germinated during his experience of growing up in the home of a father who was a physician to the poor in Toronto. While a United States army psychiatrist, Berne published five papers on clinical intuition.

In the late 1950s Berne began to conduct weekly seminars for professionals in his San Francisco office. This led to the publication of *Transactional Analysis in Psychotherapy* (1961), which is said to be the formal beginning of the movement. Many of the recent leaders of the International Transactional Analysis Association and writers in the *Transactional Analysis Journal* were participants in Berne's weekly seminars. There they became stimulated by his social psychiatry (a label often ascribed to transactional analysis) and went on to make significant theoretical contributions of their own.

In his seminars Berne placed great emphasis on simple language. He discounted fancy verbiage and cautioned professionals not to use incomprehensible technical jargon. He was interested in finding easy-to-understand terms that patients could fathom and could use in their own effort to get well. He reportedly said after listening patiently to an elaborate case presentation replete with jargon, "That is all well and good. All I know is the patient is not getting cured" (reported in Steiner, 1974, p. 14). In spite of the fact that some professionals criticized transactional analysis for its use of colloquial, folksy, undignified terms such as games, trading stamps, and fairy tales, Berne was unapologetic in his insistence that theory should be shareable and usable.

Basic Concepts. Among these terms were the ones used by Berne to denote ego states. It was his conviction that behavior is a function of the role persons perceive themselves to be playing in transactions with other persons. These perceived roles are determined by the state of mind, or ego state, of the person at a given time. Although he recognized that people's mental states are complex and unique, Berne suggested that they could be grouped under three major types: the parent, the adult, and the child ego states.

Parent ego states are those in which a person experiences directive, nurturing, critical, prescriptive, and/or protective inclinations. Transactional analysis distinguishes between critical and nurturing parent ego states and suggests that these attitudes and feelings are usually derivatives of people's experiences with their own parents.

Child ego states are those in which a person experiences impulsive, accommodating, fearful, enthusiastic, pleasureful, intuitive, hurtful, and/or gleeful inclinations. Transactional analysis distinguishes between the free and adapted child ego states and suggests that these feelings too are derivatives of people's experiences with others from whom they have learned these childlike attitudes. Further, transactional analysis sees the child ego state as the repository of natural, innate energy and self-affirmation. The little professor component of the child ego state is that unlearned wisdom with which children are endowed and upon which persons can draw for unlearned wisdom.

Adult ego states are those in which a person experiences pragmatic, rational, realistic, functional inclinations leading toward problem solving and cooperation. Transactional analysis perceives the adult ego state as energized by the child ego state and influenced by the parent ego state. It suggests that the adult should dominate life and that problems ensue when persons interact with each other on the basis of the prejudgments of the parent or the impulsiveness of the child. However, the hyperrationality characteristic of those who have blocked off their parent or their child ego states presents an equal problem. The optimal state of affairs is one in which there is a free-flowing relationship among the three ego states with the adult dominating.

Relationship to Psychoanalysis. This model of psychic structure illustrates transactional analysis's similarity to as well as its difference from psychoanalysis. Both theories contend that inner personality structure is important, although their terms for the components differ and their presumptions about levels of consciousness are dissimilar. The terms *id, ego,* and *superego* seem similar to *parent, adult,* and *child.* Psychoanalysis assumes that the id is unconscious and that the ego and superego operate in unconscious, preconscious, and conscious states. Transactional analysis contends that they are all conscious ego states.

Furthermore, whereas psychoanalysis concludes that the ego and superego are structures that evolve from the id, transactional analysis feels that the parent and adult ego states coexist with the child from an early time in a person's life. From this point of view the ego (of which the parent, adult, and child ego states are parts) exists as a psychic structure along with the id almost from the very beginning of life.

Moreover, these ego states exist in the conscious or preconscious mind and are available to the person for reflection. This is a critical difference from psychoanalysis, which believes that much of the personality is unconscious and available to awareness only through such procedures as free association and dream analysis. Transactional analysis is very hopeful about people's attempts to understand themselves. In this sense the psychoanalytic model of personality as an iceberg of which only a small part can be seen above the water is turned upside down by transactional analysis. Personality is like an inverted iceberg: most of the ice is above the water and can be seen.

Both psychoanalysis and transactional analysis assume that personality structure develops through life experiences. However, whereas psychoanalysis contends that memories become distorted and repressed, transactional analysis is convinced that past memories have been stored in the mind just as they happened and can be recalled. The mind is like a phonographic and photographic recorder that stores experiences and later expresses itself through the several ego states to which the person has access through introspection.

The final difference between psychoanalysis and transactional analysis regards the nature of neurotic behavior. Both are learning theories that emphasize habits. Both emphasize the uncanny tendency of persons to repeat behavior that is self-destructive and unproductive. Pathology for both is continuing to give old answers to present problems. Two emphases are distinctive in transactional analysis, however.

First, transactional analysis is larger in structure and in concept than psychoanalysis. Freud was primarily concerned with the tendency to repeat behavior that held down the repressed anxiety associated with anger and sex. Transactional analysis agrees with this but in addition is concerned with total life goals and the person's orientation to the world. Thus it talks of life positions that underlie the living out of life scripts that extend across a lifetime.

The second distinctive of transactional analysis is the nature of the motivation that underlies the repetition compulsion that characterizes psychopathology. The psychoanalytic understanding is grounded in the fear of a negative consequence (i.e., a repressed impulse getting out of control). In contrast, transactional analysis sees repeated unproductive behavior (i.e., games) as based on the avoidance of a positive consequence. Human behavior, as noted, is the result of the instinctive urge to relate to others. Optimal relating involves intimacy—free, spontaneous, trustful, energized transactions. However, intimate relationships are unpredictable, risky, and therefore frightening. Persons are attracted to intimacy and afraid of it at the same time. Because of the exhilaration it evokes, they long for it; but because of its lack of sureness, they settle for less than intimacy and construct games to guarantee it will not occur. They do not trust themselves to be intimate. This is quite different from the psychoanalytic point of view.

The Therapy Process. The transactional analyst works on a threefold model: analysis, experience, decision. The first step is structural analysis, in which clients are led into an analysis of the dominant ego states that characterize their interactions with others. Then they explore the genesis of these relative emphases in relationships with parents and in other significant experiences. They next attempt to analyze the transactions they are having with important persons to assess patterns and to ascertain the nature of games that may be present. Through depth reflection the person is led into intuitions about life scripts and basic life positions.

In the experience part of therapy the client is led through recreations of important events and significant interactions. Reexperiencing is encouraged because it is assumed that insight by itself is not healing. Insight provides the basis for change, but change comes through reexperiencing and redecision. Many procedures are utilized to facilitate such experiencing. The transactional analyst is an active therapist and engages in intentional interventions to evoke the involvement of the client emotionally as well as cognitively.

The transactional analyst is convinced that change comes by redecision. The therapist assumes the role of the nurturing parent and encourages the client in thinking that life can change. Although premature decision, which is not based in emotional reexperience, is abortive, change will never occur unless individuals determine to courageously try to be different. Transactional analysts believe that people can take control of their lives and that healing can occur provided such decisions are grounded in depth insight.

Evaluation. There are a number of underlying assumptions in transactional analysis that Christian counselors would do well to consider. Examples of such assumptions are that persons are born with a trusting, open, intimacy-seeking attitude (the I'm OK, You're OK life position) but lose it in the process of living and that healing means a redis-covery and reassertion of that basic attitude toward life. Christians would agree with this and would call it being created in the image of God. Yet Christians would not agree that other life positions (I'm OK, You're Not OK; I'm Not OK, You're OK; I'm Not OK, You're Not OK) are only misperceptions. They too are real. The issue for the Christian is not wrong attitudes or incorrect perceptions, but sin. The Christian assumes that the most correct statement of reality is I'm Not OK, You're Not OK. As the Bible states, "All have sinned and fall short of the glory of God" (Rom. 3:23, NIV). From the Christian point of view, transactional analysis does not have a serious enough doctrine of the human condition.

Another issue has to do with what happens when persons affirm their OK-ness. It is not simply a change of attitude or the making of a new decision, as transactional analysis would contend, but a recognition that sin is present and only God can make it right. No effort or insight can return persons to the I'm OK, You're OK position. The Christian gospel says that God in Christ has done this for us (cf. Rom. 8). He has forgiven our sin and restored us to a position of OK-ness. Thus the Christian corrective to transactional analysis is I'm Not OK, You're Not OK, but That's OK. This is redemption as well as healing.

Transactional analysis makes sound assumptions that can be used by Christian counselors if they keep in mind that it is based on humanistic presuppositions that need supplementing by the affirmations of the Christian faith.

References

Berne, E. (1961). *Transactional analysis in psychotherapy.* New York: Grove.

Steiner, C. (1974). *Scripts people live.* New York: Grove.

H. N. MALONY

See SCRIPT ANALYSIS.

Transcendental Meditation. *See* MEDITATION.

Transfer of Learning. The influence that learning in one situation has upon learning or behaving in other situations. The importance of transfer is evident in the assumption of most educational programs that whatever is learned in specific tasks will be retained and used appropriately outside of instructional settings.

It is often difficult to demonstrate whether learning in specific situations results in better performance on subsequent tasks. One problem is that while a distinct task (e.g., learning to play handball) may facilitate subsequent learning (e.g., playing tennis), this improved performance may not be due to the transfer of specific learned skills but also to what is called learning to learn. In such a situation of general or nonspecific transfer, learning skills are acquired through previous experience with a variety of learning situations. For example, practicing driving several types of automobiles may facilitate learning to drive a particular type of automobile. In this example the increased facility may be attributed to experience with the particular feature of one type of automobile, experience with general features shared by more than one type, or both.

The number of ways in which instances of transfer can differ reveals the complexity of these phenomena. First, transfer can be either positive or negative. Positive transfer occurs when prior learning facilitates or increases the learning in a subsequent task, as in the example of learning to drive. Negative transfer describes the case in which prior learning impedes or inhibits learning in a new task. A common example occurs whenever learning the sound system of one language (e.g., English) impedes learning the sound system of another, dissimilar language (e.g., Chinese).

Second, transfer can be either lateral or vertical. Lateral transfer is the influence of learning a task on learning other tasks at a similar level of complexity. Vertical transfer is the influence of learning a task on learning more complex tasks requiring a higher level of ability. This is particularly important for learning in any area in which tasks can be organized into a hierarchical order according to complexity, with the learning of the simplest tasks transferring to learning at higher levels.

Third, transfer can occur in many areas of learning, including the broad, distinct domains of cognitive, affective, and psychomotor learning.

Thus it is not surprising that there are currently no all-inclusive theories to explain transfer phenomena. Rather, the emphasis is on theories that explain only certain kinds of transfer. This modern approach is a radical departure from the assumption, widely held until the early twentieth century, that academic training in a few formal disciplines can positively affect all subsequent learning by training faculties of the mind. As faculty psychology declined and behaviorally oriented research on learning took its place, the earlier assumption was abandoned.

A key generalization in academic learning is that the major concepts and principles of a subject provide more positive transfer than does specific information. One application to Bible study is that emphasizing important themes and concepts throughout Scripture, rather than specific details, will facilitate students' study of unfamiliar books and passages.

D. R. RIDLEY

See LEARNING.

Transference. The term means literally to convey information or content from one person, place, or situation to another. The psychological usage expresses a special type of relationship with another person. The usual pattern is for a person in the present to be experienced as though he or she were a person in the past. Thus transference, from a psychoanalytic point of view, is a repetition of an old object relationship in which attitudes and feelings, either positive or negative, pertaining to a former relationship have been shifted onto a new person in the present. Another way of describing this is to say that a mode of perceiving and responding to the world that was developed in and appropriate to childhood is inappropriately transferred into the adult context (Peck, 1978).

Although when it is broadly defined transference can be seen to occur in all relationships to some degree, its role in therapy has been the focus of most attention. In therapy the patient displaces or transfers specific affective or cognitive contents that pertain to another person in an earlier developmental relationship onto the therapist.

Therapeutic Perspectives. Transference phenomena have long been a primary concern of psychoanalysts and psychoanalytic psychotherapists. Freudian theory asserts that the patient transfers to the therapist the attributes or images of significant persons from the past, usually the parents, and thus repeats the experiences of childhood in the process of psychotherapy (Freud, 1949). Furthermore, transference is assumed to be primarily unconscious and to take place in therapy without the patient having awareness of the distortion. Some therapists (Alexander, 1956) label the transference situation as irrational, due to the belief that the present responses made sense only in the past environment and are repeated in the therapeutic context. Yet transference is the sine qua non of dynamic psychotherapy in that it gives the opportunity to deal with unresolved conflicts of the past.

While other theoretical orientations recognize the existence of transference phenomena, none of them places such emphasis on the importance of transference or locates the emotionalized experiences so completely in the past. Jung (1968) understood transference to be a special case of projection, a psychological mechanism that carries over subjective contents from both the personal unconscious (shadow) and the collective unconscious (archetypes) to the object of the therapist. He maintained that transference is never voluntary and intentional; it takes place spontaneously and without provocation. The handling of transference may be a part of Jungian psychotherapy, but it is not essential.

Adlerian theory (Ansbacher & Ansbacher, 1964) presents transference as a special kind of social feeling in the development of social interest. The feelings that the patient has toward the therapist are to be accepted as valuable and genuine but need not be analyzed and interpreted as in psychoanalysis. Effective psychotherapy does not depend on working through a transference neurosis. Rather, the emotional exchanges between patient and therapist serve as a model for the patient's further growth in attaining a wholesome sense of social interest.

Adherents to transactional analysis consider transference to be the patient's attempt to substitute the therapist for the parent (Berne, 1961). This substitutionary tendency is easily observed in the transactions between patient and therapist. The transference situation happens when the therapist sends an adult-to-adult stimulus message but receives a child-to-parent response. This crossed transaction corresponds to the Freudian concept of transference. Very little attention is given to transference in transactional analysis; more concern is shown for learning how to make better contact with one's own ego states and to transact effectively and appropriately with other people.

Therapies that reflect existential, phenomenological, and perceptual perspectives tend to see the transference situation as real feelings in a here-and-now relationship (May, Angel, & Ellenberger, 1958). Boss (1963) has asserted that the patient does not transfer feelings that he or she had for a parent to the therapist; instead the patient presents to the therapist life data that never developed beyond a limited and restricted form of infantile experience. So the phenomena are to be understood in terms of perception and relatedness to the world rather than a displacement of detachable feelings from one person to another. Perls (1973) too observed that transference in therapy relates more to what has been missing in an individual's life than what has been experienced previously. Specifically transference stems from personal deficits instead of forgotten emotionalized childhood experiences. The person has introjected parts of the environment in an attempt to shortcut the growth process of self-realization. These introjections and deficits become unfinished Gestalts and must be completed in therapy.

One of the most practical approaches to understanding and dealing with transference comes from the behavioral orientation (Dollard & Miller, 1950). The behavioral view holds that transference is a special form of generalized learning. The therapist's presence provides a social situation much like those in which the patient has previously been punished or rewarded by significant other persons. The stimuli of the therapist provoke the same responses from the patient that were learned in earlier interactions with significant human figures. Either a negative or positive transference response will be provoked, depending on the specific therapist stimulus effect. The behavior therapist helps the client to resolve the transference situation by teaching him or her to discriminate between different sets of stimuli and then to learn how to respond appropriately.

Summary. Therapeutic approaches to transference range from scrutinizing all of the patient's reactions to the therapist for transference information, to viewing transference as nonessential and irrelevant to psychotherapy (Leites, 1979). The phenomena that characterize transference exist in virtually all object relationships and so are present in the therapeutic context. The most plausible position to take on this aspect of human behavior appears to be an integration of the existential and behavioral perspectives. Transference is then seen as involving genuine here-and-now feelings for the therapist that are generalized by the person from previous learning conditions. It is also reasonable to suppose that some of the dynamics of this generalization of past experiences lie somewhat out of the person's awareness.

References

Alexander, F. (1956). *Psychoanalysis and psychotherapy.* New York: Norton.

Ansbacher, H. L., & Ansbacher, R. R. (Eds.). (1964). *The individual psychology of Alfred Adler.* New York: Harper & Row.

Berne, E. (1961). *Transactional analysis.* New York: Grove.

Boss, M. (1963). *Psychoanalysis and deseinanalysis.* New York: Basic.

Dollard, J., & Miller, N. E. (1950). *Personality and psychotherapy.* New York: McGraw-Hill.

Freud, S. (1949). *An outline of psychoanalysis.* New York: Norton.

Jung, C. G. (1968). *Analytical psychology: Its theory and practice.* New York: Pantheon.

Leites, N. (1979). *Interpreting transference.* New York: Norton.

May, R., Angel, E., & Ellenberger, H. F. (1958). *Existence: A new dimension in psychiatry and psychology.* New York: Basic.

Peck, M. S. (1978). *The road less traveled.* New York: Simon & Schuster.

Perls, F. (1973). *The Gestalt approach and eyewitness to therapy.* Ben Lomond, CA: Science & Behavior Books.

D. SMITH

See PSYCHOANALYTIC PSYCHOLOGY; COUNTERTRANSFERENCE.

Transference Neurosis. An artificial neurosis appearing in psychoanalysis wherein the early oedipal situation is recreated in the transference relationship to the analyst. In this regressed state the patient relives the original infantile conflicts. Psychoanalysis usually has as its goal the creation and resolution of the transference neurosis. In contrast, psychoanalytic psychotherapy attempts to keep the transference from developing to this point.

See PSYCHOANALYSIS: TECHNIQUE.

Transient Situational Disturbance. *See* ADJUSTMENT DISORDERS.

Transpersonal Psychology. Transpersonal psychology posits a transcendent, nonmaterial reality that goes beyond the realm of individual personality. This reality underlies and binds together all phenomena. Transpersonal language and concepts differ somewhat from those of both conventional science and mainstream Christianity. Some scholars refer to the field, which has few unanimous premises, as spiritual psychology; others, the science of consciousness. Transpersonal psychology has been called the fourth force in psychology, after psychoanalysis, behaviorism, and humanistic psychology.

Philosophical Background. The underpinnings of transpersonal psychology are similar to those of Eastern (principally Indian) philosophy and the mystical traditions of Christianity and other world faiths. God is seen primarily as immanent in all things. Most theorists agree that individuals can directly experience the underlying transcendent reality, which is related to the spiritual dimension of human life and which some call God; and that such experience involves expansion of consciousness beyond ordinary conceptual thinking and ego awareness. Some transpersonal psychologists allege that traditional religions have lost sight of such self-transcendence, which is the heart of spirituality, by falling into legalism and dogmatism.

Transpersonal psychologists view the human person as more than a complicated machine, a higher animal, or even ordinary waking human consciousness. They often think of people in terms of levels or states of consciousness. Self-transcendence, the ultimate human goal, involves dissolving ego boundaries to experience a transformation or expansion of consciousness. Mystical awareness or insight is the most notable state of expanded consciousness. Transpersonal psychology encourages the pursuit of total health: body, emotions, mind, intellect, and spirit. Self-transcendence optimally is sought only in the context of social, moral, ethical, and psychological considerations. Before a healthy self-transcending expansion of consciousness can occur, one must have established a solid ego awareness or self-identity. Without a clear sense of self, loosening of ego boundaries may precipitate psychosis. Solidly established morality is also a prerequisite.

Some earlier psychologies relevant to transpersonal psychology are Carl Gustav Jung's ideas about the collective unconscious and similar notions in William James's writings. Some others include psychosynthesis (Assagioli, 1965), Victor Frankl's logotherapy, Gestalt thought, and various existential and phenomenological theories. The works of spiritual guides and mystics (Progoff, 1980) and interpreters of Hindu or Buddhist philosophy (e.g., Trungpa, 1973) figure prominently.

History. Transpersonal psychology grew out of humanistic psychology during the 1960s. Its leaders thought humanism failed to go far enough in its vision for human existence. Sutich (1976), who was almost completely paralyzed from youth, believed that mystical experiences cast doubt on basic humanistic understandings. Maslow's (1968, 1971) exploration of what he called the values of being, inherent in any truly transcendent experience, led him to a similar position. Maslow observed that these values are those characteristics by which religious people define God: love, truth, justice, beauty, and

so on. Inspired by Julian Huxley's transhumanism, Sutich first called the movement transhumanistic psychology. However, he and Maslow agreed on the term *transpersonal psychology.*

Miles Vich, editor of *The Journal of Transpersonal Psychology,* which was begun in 1969, and Grof (1979), known for work on LSD-induced states of awareness, also worked with Sutich in founding transpersonal psychology. Some of the most important other developmental work in the field was done by Ring (1980), Tart (1975), Walsh (Walsh & Vaughan, 1980), and Wilber (Wilber, Engler, & Brown, 1986).

The Association for Transpersonal Psychology was formed in 1971, with Alyce Green of the Menninger Foundation as its first president. The association managed the journal and provided a forum for scholars attracted to the movement. The first national and international transpersonal conferences were held in 1973 and have been regular events since then. In 1979 Mary Jo Meadow organized the Transpersonal Psychology Interest Group within the American Psychological Association.

Many regional and local transpersonal organizations have sprung up. Schools specializing in transpersonal psychology include the California Institute of Transpersonal Psychology, John F. Kennedy University, and the California Institute of Integral Studies. Transpersonal programs typically require students to be engaged in their own spiritual quests (see Fadiman & Frager, 1976), with programs comprehensive enough to include physical discipline or body work (such as *hatha yoga* or *tai chi*), emotional training, meditation, and other spiritual disciplines, as well as intellectual study.

Academic Study. Transpersonal psychologists usually avoid reductionistic methods of investigation. They see individuals, their behavior, and their experience as complex entities that are not to be reduced to lower levels of analysis. Occasionally, investigators use conventional scientific methods based on logical positivism; however, they make greater use of Gestalt, phenomenological, and existential methods. An experiential empiricism that relies on presumably self-validating experiences is the major method.

Transpersonal psychologists study various topics involving the alteration of consciousness and spiritual well-being in both individuals and society. The study of altered states includes dreams, imagery, hypnosis, autogenic states, meditation, mysticism, extrasensory perception, precognition (prophecy), out-of-body experiences, and drug-altered states of consciousness.

Subjects related to individuals include non-ego states of awareness, the role of various ego states in human development, transcendent experience, relationships between healthy (mysticism) and unhealthy (psychosis) transcendence of ego boundaries, personal transformation, creativity, full health, development of human potential, spiritual growth, and the achievement of liberation (*samadhi*, enlightenment, self-realization). Studies regarding society include building new relationships between science and the humanities, the transformation of society toward spiritual values, societal health, group or shared consciousness, the organic unity of all persons (related to such religious ideas as the mystical body of Christ or the Buddha-nature of all beings), and the application of transpersonal concepts to social structures: business, science, education, human services, and religion.

Several transpersonal scholars have tried to classify or map consciousness. Normal waking consciousness is only its most familiar form, with the psychoanalytic preconscious and unconscious relatively close to ordinary consciousness. The next layer is concerned with issues of personal finitude, birth, death, and suffering. More remote are the realms of deep dreamless sleep, Zen *satori*, the influence of good and evil spirits, and some religious ecstasy. Beyond those states lie layers of deepening mystical experience, including mystical experience with a content, such as an idea of God, and that without specific content, like Buddhist *nibbana* (*nirvana*) or Hindu *nirguna Brahman*. As a composite this map represents the view of no single transpersonal psychologist but illustrates some interests in the field.

While some transpersonal psychologists consider various parapsychological phenomena in their domain, others do not. Additional areas of study include spiritual disciplines, ways to achieve control over altered states, and the integration of Eastern and Western views of the person.

Transpersonal Therapy. Transpersonal therapists typically work at whatever level is needed to help clients integrate their lives. Most prefer to counsel those with some interest in and capacity for spiritual work. Starting with the client's existential realities, situation, and unique constellation of assets and liabilities, the therapist fosters a healthy interaction of all the person's functions. Such integration typically is viewed as a spiritual task in itself.

Transpersonal therapies deal most explicitly with spiritual pathologies. Typical problems include spiritual pride, prejudices, fanaticism, dogmatism, legalistic mentality, unproductive guilt, excessive introspection, blindness to value, hedonism, general ego-centeredness or self-preoccupation, fascination with the occult or cultism, overvaluing paranormal powers, seeking spiritual shortcuts or consolations, avoiding genuine and manifest life tasks for artificial ones, spiritual materialism, impatience for growth, difficulty in letting go, excessive rationality, and fixation on lower-level needs (pleasure, highs, power, good feelings, esteem of others).

Transpersonal therapists draw methods from logotherapy, psychosynthesis, Jungian analysis, Gestalt and existential therapies, music, dance, and art therapies, and various spiritual disciplines. Popular techniques include meditation, relaxation, centering exercises, focusing, breathing practices, physical disciplines of body work, guided imagery, autogenic training, hypnosis, sensory deprivation, biofeedback, dream logs and dreamwork, inner dialogues, music, art, and sports (Boorstein, 1980; Reynolds, 1980; Vaughan, 1979; Welwood, 1979).

Other Applications and Evaluation. Like other psychologies, transpersonal understandings can enrich Christian thought and practice. Although transpersonal psychology is open to various religious and spiritual traditions, it is not anti-Christian. Some Christians, however, are suspicious of transpersonal psychology's bases in non-Christian, Eastern religions. Like Christianity, the Eastern traditions emphasize the importance of morality and virtue as a basis for spiritual practice. In both principle and practice, Eastern meditative techniques and other disciplines are separable from the religious systems in which they originated.

Meditation and mystical experiences are also inherent in the history and practice of Christianity. They are found more in the Eastern Orthodox and Roman Catholic traditions than in the Protestant, but they are congruent with evangelical Christianity (e.g., Brandt, 1979). Eastern meditation techniques, which have been taught in the West from around the turn of the twentieth century, have become available in specifically Christian formats (see Culligan, Meadow, & Chowning, 1994; Meadow, 1994).

Transpersonal psychology also suggests a helpful corrective to rigidly materialistic science. However, the basic premises of the two approaches seems so different that rapprochement seems difficult. Few people trained in traditional science give credence to the nonmaterial as a scientific entity, even if they profess a personal religious faith. Nonetheless, some theoretical physicists suggest various forces or energies that might qualify as underlying transcendent realities. Others have pointed out that reports of mystical experiences are highly similar to the understanding and language of physics. Christian scientific, psychological, or religious practitioners can remain open to the possibilities in transpersonal approaches while holding to their own important personal values.

References

Assagioli, R. (1965). *Psychosynthesis*. New York: Nobbs, Dorman.

Boorstein, S. (Ed.). (1980). *Transpersonal psychotherapy*. Palo Alto, CA: Science & Behavior Books.

Brandt, P. (1979). *Two-way prayer*. Waco, TX: Word.

Culligan, K., Meadow, M. J., & Chowning, D. (1994). *Purifying the heart: Buddhist insight meditation for Christians*. New York: Crossroad.

Fadiman, J., & Frager, R. (1976). *Personality and personal growth*. New York: Harper & Row.

Grof, S. (1979). *The principles of LSD psychotherapy*. New York: Hunter House.

Maslow, A. H. (1968). *Toward a psychology of being* (2nd ed.). Princeton, NJ: Van Nostrand.

Maslow, A. H. (1971). *The farther reaches of human nature*. New York: Viking.

Meadow, M. J. (1994). *Gentling the heart: Buddhist loving-kindness practice for Christians*. New York: Crossroad.

Progoff, I. (1980). *The practice of process meditation*. New York: Dialogue House Library.

Reynolds, D. K. (1980). *The quiet therapies*. Honolulu: University Press of Hawaii.

Ring, K. (1980). *Life at death: A scientific investigation of the near-death experience*. New York: Coward, McCann & Geoghenan.

Sutich, A. J. (1976). *The founding of humanistic and transpersonal psychology: A personal account*. Unpublished doctoral dissertation, Humanistic Psychology Institute.

Tart, C. T. (1975). *Transpersonal psychologies*. New York: Harper & Row.

Trungpa, C. (1973). *Cutting through spiritual materialism*. Berkeley, CA: Shambhala.

Vaughan, F. (1979). *Awakening intuition*. Garden City, NY: Doubleday, Anchor Books.

Walsh, R. N., & Vaughan, F. (Eds.). (1980). *Beyond ego: Transpersonal dimensions in psychology*. New York: St. Martin's.

Welwood, J. (Ed.). (1979). *The meeting of the ways: Explorations in East-West psychology*. New York: Schocken.

Wilber, K., Engler, J., & Brown, D. (1986). *Transformations of consciousness: Conventional and contemplative perspectives on development*. Boston: Shambhala.

M. J. Meadow

See Humanistic Psychology.

Transsexualism. *See* Gender Identity Disorder.

Transvestic Fetishism. Transvestic fetishism is one of the paraphilias identified in *DSM-IV* (American Psychiatric Association, 1994). Men with transvestic fetishism (no women have been found with the disorder) combine elements of transvestism, or cross-dressing, and fetishism (obtaining sexual arousal from an object). They wear one or more articles of women's clothing in order to become sexually aroused.

Their arousal may include either masturbation or sex with a partner. More than two-thirds of men with this disorder marry, and the majority do not disclose their disorder but are discovered. Their wives are always distressed by the discovery, and they typically blame themselves for their husband's loss of masculinity. Some wives accommodate their husband's preferences, but many will terminate the marriage.

Not all transvestism is fetishistic. Some men dress as women, even in public, to cope with the stress of being male, and some of them report that they feel more sensitive when they are cross-dressed. Some men engage in both fetishistic and nonfetishistic transvestism, with the intensity of each varying with age and situation.

Men with gender identity disorder also engage in cross-dressing, but as their transvestism is not for the purposes of sexual excitement, they are not diagnosed with transvestic fetishism. Some men with transvestic fetishism may become unhappy with their maleness (known as gender dysphoria), but most are typically masculine. However, they may believe that they have both masculine and feminine components in their personalities.

Transvestic fetishism is diagnosed only in heterosexual men. They repeatedly engage in cross-dressing or experience intensely arousing sexual fantasies or urges about dressing in women's clothing for a period of at least six months. The diagnosis is applied only if the fetishism upsets the person or interferes with his job or relationships. Men with transvestic fetishism rarely seek treatment unless they are coerced to do so by their wives.

Some men with transvestic fetishism have occasionally engaged in homosexual acts, but their preference is heterosexual. If a man with a primary homosexual orientation cross-dresses to make a political statement or as part of prostitution, he is not diagnosed with transvestic fetishism.

Transvestic fetishism begins in childhood or adolescence. Many men with this disorder were praised as children for dressing in female clothing. Others were punished by being forced to dress as a girl in an attempt to induce humiliation. The disorder frequently begins when boys masturbate while examining or fondling lingerie. Donning feminine apparel then allows them to fantasize that they are the women to whom they are making love, a form of autoeroticism. This dual role contributes to the development of a sense that their personalities contain both masculine and feminine components.

Learning theorists argue that the fetish aspect of the disorder develops by conditioning, as the boy associates being cross-dressed with the sexual satisfaction produced by masturbation. While the sexual arousal and orgasm reinforce the cross-dressing behavior, guilt and humiliation may also result, and he may resolve repeatedly never to engage in the behavior again.

After discovery, the humiliation may be such a strong punisher that the sense of pressure to cross-dress dramatically diminishes, and the man believes himself cured. However, as stress and opportunity arise the compulsion to cross-dress typically returns, making him more miserable than before. The negative statements he makes to himself may play a role in sexual masochism, which often occurs in men with transvestic fetishism.

The meaning a man attributes to feminine clothing may contribute to the disorder. Becoming a woman by cross-dressing may lighten the sense of burden for a man who believes that his male role requires unbearable responsibilities. This idea may better explain nonfetishistic transvestism, however.

Along with the other paraphilias, transvestic fetishism is difficult to treat. It is illegal in some jurisdictions to appear in public cross-dressed, and some men steal women's clothing, but most men with this disorder do not break the law. As they typically come to therapy only at the insistence of their wives, they may resist treatment.

One helpful treatment is to learn the cues that start the cross-dressing behaviors and to avoid situations that trigger the urge to cross-dress. Another is to imagine drastically negative consequences if the disorder is exposed to the public.

Aversion therapy presents a noxious stimulus such as a shock, a nasty aroma, or a loud noise whenever the client becomes sexually aroused while fantasizing about cross-dressing. It may enable the client to control his urge to cross-dress, but it usually does not remove the desire.

Orgasmic reorientation therapies increase sexual arousal to appropriate stimuli, to compete with transvestic arousal. While this approach does increase the variety of stimuli that are arousing, it does not appear to remove the fetishism. Some clinicians combine orgasmic reorientation with aversion therapy.

Improved social skills and stress management sometimes help clients control the urge to cross-dress.

Reference

American Psychiatric Association (1994). *Diagnostic and statistical manual of mental disorders* (4th ed.). Washington, DC: Author.

P. D. YOUNG

Transvestism. *See* GENDER IDENTITY DISORDER; SEXUAL AROUSAL DISORDERS.

Trauma. A certain event, force, or mechanism that causes malfunction or severe personal damage. Trauma can be experienced on a physical, mental, behavioral, emotional, or communal level. It may be the result of deep injury, sudden shock, major violence, or significant loss. Trauma has elements of terror, humiliation, impairment, and pain. During the traumatic event, the person's thinking appears to stop and his or her emotions tend to freeze, as if time stands still. Usually, fear, disbelief, confusion, hurt, resentment, and marked helplessness engulf the whole system or organism.

Traumas can result from physical causes like bodily injuries, auto accidents, and serious illnesses, from natural disasters like earthquakes, fires, floods, famine, and storms, from social unrest like conflicts, violence, threats, and civil wars, or from personal life experience like multiple crises, persistent abuse (mental, physical, emotional, sexual), major stresses, and unexpected losses or tragedies.

Traumatic experiences often have a lasting psychological effect. The impact is usually substantial and chronic. Reactions to trauma range from mild and temporary symptoms to severe and long-term disturbances, like psychotic breaks (thought disorder, reality distortion, mental disintegration), affective disorders (clinical depression, phobias, anxieties, panic attacks), physiological malfunctions (aches, pains, multiple physical complaints), and behavioral and personality changes (acting out, addiction, aggression, or obsessive-compulsive, borderline, avoidant, dependent, paranoid tendencies). As a result of a bodily trauma, for example, people may die or suffer a permanent physical damage. It has been estimated that in the United States alone 150,000 people annually die due to accidents and traumatic events and about fifteen million become somewhat disabled.

The diagnosis known as post traumatic stress disorder (PTSD) carefully describes the common responses to trauma. It highlights the disturbances and behaviors most traumatized people experience or display. It is used by mental health professionals as a criterion for such conditions and includes a cluster of symptoms like: reexperiencing the fear; remembering and reliving certain aspects of the trauma; recurrent intrusive thoughts or flashbacks; persistent avoidance of any reminder associated with the event; inability to recall many important details; psychic numbness; restricted emotions; sleep disturbances and nightmares; increased arousal and hypervigilance; and exaggerated responses upon exposure to a situation that somewhat resembles the traumatic event. However, it is worthy to note here that a certain condition must be met before qualifying for the diagnosis. According to the *DSM-III-R* (APA, 1987), "the person has experienced an event that is outside the usual human experience and that would be markedly distressing to almost anyone" (p. 146). The *DSM-IV* (APA, 1994) went further to emphasize the person's exposure to an "actual or threatened death or serious injury, or a threat of physical integrity of self or others" and the person's emotional response which involves "intense fear, helplessness, or horror" (p. 427).

During and immediately after a traumatic event, people usually manifest severe anxiety symptoms, certain patterns of detachment or dissociation, and other reactions known as acute stress disorder. If not processed or resolved, the impact may linger and increase in severity leading eventually to PTSD and further psychological morbidity.

A tragic or traumatic moment can be painful for any individual, especially if the experience is associated with permanent environmental, familial, or personal changes. These changes are at times radical and foundational. From a dynamic or analytical perspective, psychic traumas may substantially alter the emotional stability, mental familiarity, and inner structure of the ego or core self. Trauma may cause the loss of the previously established safety, security, and means of psychological gratification. The unpleasant disturbances evoke, at times, a state of anxiety-aggression which can be negated, as some theorists believe, only by developing a counter-state of aggression-restoration. If reclaiming the lost stability and means of gratification is not possible, the individual will then develop inner defense mechanisms and different coping strategies. These can be healthy or unhealthy, mainly depending on the availability of resources, personal qualities, and the adaptive capacities of the survivor.

Recovery and stabilization of a traumatized individual or a family unit normally depend on several factors: nature of the trauma, preexisting conditions, emotional stability, support system during and after the crisis, past history of handling stressful events, age and gender of persons involved, and the spiritual faith or existential position on hope.

In counseling and psychotherapy, treatment depends largely on the approach, experience, and orientation of the therapist. However, some general guidelines and interventions may apply to all trauma victims (cf. Meichenbaum, 1994): Try to establish a therapeutic alliance and gently solicit accounts; educate clients about the nature of PTSD; insure each client's safety and survival; in the case of multiple traumas or victimizations, start with the most pressing one; address target symptoms and teach clients tension reduction and stress management; be careful when uncovering memories (memories can be constructed or reconstructed at times); help clients see their responses as self-protective measures and help them "reframe" their reactions rationally; commend clients on their survival abilities, strength, resiliency, and positive coping mechanisms; help them shift focus from being "victims" to "survivors" by restructuring the meaning and implications of the "trauma story"; apply desensitization and introduce reenactments in a safe environment; conduct grief therapy and facilitate the mourning process (PTSD and grief may overlap); collaboratively, discuss recovery measures and teach them how to reframe recurrent memories and possible future lapses; help them set new goals, mobilize fresh support, establish new relationships, and reinvest their psychic energy in broader interests and endeavors (clients will hopefully begin to transfer their "pain" into "purpose" and their "misery" into "mission"); finally, remain available for personal support, advice, and encouragement.

In a philosophical and clinical essay, Egendorf (1995) emphasized what it means to hear through other people's pain. Egendorf believed that the what, where, how, and whom shift focus and meaning as time progresses. The meaning of trauma itself virtually changes as the hearing deepens. Accordingly, one may hear 1) the psychophysical reactions to traumatic events, 2) the playing out of themes from a lifetime, 3) violations, whose inner message is a demand to awaken the soul and mind beyond self-protective ways of existence, and 4) a uniquely powerful opening for intimacy and communion with significant others.

References

American Psychiatric Association. (1987). *Quick reference to the diagnostic criteria from DSM-III-R*. Washington, DC: Author.

American Psychiatric Association. (1994). *Diagnostic and statistical manual of mental disorders* (4th ed.). Washington, DC: Author.

Egendorf, A. (1995). Hearing people through their pain. *Journal of Traumatic Stress, 8*, 5–28.

Meichenbaum, D. (1994). *A clinical handbook/Practical therapist manual for assessing and treating adults with PTSD*. Waterloo, Ontario: Institute Press.

N. ABI-HASHEM

See ABUSE AND NEGLECT; DEATH AND DYING; DISSOCIATION; DISSOCIATIVE DISORDERS; EMPATHY; GRIEF THERAPY; LOSS AND SEPARATION; LOSS OF FUNCTION; PAIN; POSTTRAUMATIC STRESS DISORDER; STRESS; SUFFERING; TRAGEDY.

Triadic-Based Family Therapy. The focus on an interpersonal triangle within the family cuts across most of the traditional schools of family therapy; this is true regardless of whether the theoretical orientation is psychoanalytic, structural, strategic, problem-solving, experiential, or communicational. Family therapy grew from an initial focus on dyads (e.g., the mother-child dyad, as exemplified in the schizophrenogenic mother notion of Fromm-Reichman, 1948). Since that time a major shift has taken place, and many individuals have focused on triads as opposed to individuals, dyads, or larger units of study. Ravich (1967) notes that there is a vast difference between a two-person and a three-person system.

Triadic-based family therapy is identified primarily with the work of Zuk (1969, 1971). Haley (1976, 1980) and Bowen (1966) have also made important contributions.

Theoretical Considerations. One of the best-known claims for the importance of triadic family therapy was made by Bowen: "The basic building block of any emotional system is the triangle. When emotional tension in a two person system exceeds a certain level it triangles in a third person, permitting the tension to shift around within the triangle. Any two in the original triangle can add a new member. An emotional system is composed of a series of interlocking triangles. It is a clinical fact that the original two person tension system will resolve itself automatically when contained within a three person system, one of whom remains emotionally detached" (1966, p. 368).

Haley (1967) has elaborated on this theoretical foundation by describing three primary characteristics of the perverse triangle. First, the members are not peers; one is in a different generation from the other two. Second, in the process of interaction one person forms a coalition with the single person from the other generation against the remaining third party. This coalition is not an alliance in which the two operate independently of the third; rather, it is a process of dual action against the third person. Third, the emotional coalition between the two persons is denied frequently, especially when the parties are queried regarding a specific act. This pattern is seen most frequently in a clinical situation when a family appears with a symptomatic child connected to one overinvolved parent and one emotionally detached parent. This particular pattern of family interaction has been intrapersonalized and institutionalized by psychoanalytic theory as the oedipal conflict.

When the typical family is broken down into triads, a staggering complexity of units for study is generated; in the average American family of two parents, two children, and two sets of grandparents, this group of eight people generates 56 possible triangles. Any one person in the family is involved in 21 different triangles concurrently, each of which has the potential for an intergenerational coalition of a perverse nature. Within this network no two individuals are in the same position relative to the overall context. These triangles are intimately related. Adaptive behavior within one triangle may have maladaptive repercussions in another triangle. When all triangles are amicable, no problems appear; but when one individual is the nexus for two triangles that are in conflict, tension is generated within that individual. If the tension exceeds a certain critical level, it may manifest itself in symptomatic behavior. This behavior is seen in this theoretical framework as both a cry for help and protection from the anxiety generated by the triadic conflict.

Treatment Considerations. High levels of therapist activity within this primarily brief treatment modality are almost always required for effective treatment. The primary role of the triadic therapist is to serve as a flexible mediator, challenger, positive reframer of transactions, and shifting coalition partner within the extant family triangles (Haley, 1976; Zuk, 1971). The goal is to shift the balance of pathogenic relating among family members so that newer, more constructive family hierarchies, composed of interlocking series of triangles, become possible. It is assumed that once the structure of the family is rearranged, communication patterns will be forced to change and individual symptomatic behavior will improve (Haley, 1980). Change comes about when families begin behaving differently, whether or not insight into their own interaction process occurs.

It is inevitable that the family will involve the therapist in their covert triangulations. It is therefore critical that the therapist take cognizance of his or her coalition status at any one point in time. An excellent method for maintaining coalition neutrality has been proposed by Palazzoli-Selvini, Boscolo, Cecchin, and Prata (1980). In this method the therapist, in front of the whole family, systematically queries each family member in turn regarding specific aspects of the relationship between any other two family members (e.g., "Johnny, can you tell me what Mommie and Suzie fight the most about?"). This method serves to make implicit family triangulations explicit and to keep the net coalition valence of the therapist neutral at the end of such a circular interview.

This intervention style and way of thinking about families constitutes a growing edge within the field.

It is highly likely that the focus on triads, combined with innovative therapeutic methods, will provide a cutting edge for continued growth and development within the mainstream of systems therapy.

References

Bowen, M. (1966). The use of family theory in clinical practice. *Comprehensive Psychiatry, 7,* 345–374.

Fromm-Reichman, F. (1948). Notes on the development of treatment of schizophrenics by psychoanalytic psychotherapy. *Psychiatry, 11,* 263–273.

Haley, J. (1967). Toward a theory of pathological systems. In G. Zuk & I. Boszormenyi-Nagy (Eds.), *Family therapy and disturbed families.* Palo Alto, CA: Science & Behavior Books.

Haley, J. (1976). *Problem solving therapy.* San Francisco: Jossey-Bass.

Haley, J. (1980). *Leaving home.* New York: McGraw-Hill.

Palazzoli-Selvini, M., Boscolo, L., Cecchin, G., & Prata, G. (1980). Hypothesizing, circularity, neutrality: Three guidelines for the conductor of the session. *Family Process, 19,* 3–12.

Ravich, R. (1967). Psychotherapy for the whole family. *American Journal of Psychotherapy, 21,* 132–134.

Zuk, G. H. (1969). Triadic-based family therapy. *International Journal of Psychiatry, 8,* 539–548.

Zuk, G. H. (1971). *Family therapy.* New York: Behavior Publications.

V. L. Shepperson

See Family Therapy: Overview.

Triangle. In the context of family therapy a triangle consists of three people stuck in repetitious, maladaptive patterns of interaction. Troubled families frequently contain a central triangle made up of the mother, father, and a problem child. This threesome becomes the primary focus of family therapy, which seeks to alleviate stress by transforming dysfunctional triangular interactions into adaptive transactions among the three.

Triangles create problems because they involve a breach of family or generational boundaries. For example, when unresolved conflict in marriage prompts spouse A to draw an outsider in for support, a triangle is formed. The support helps spouse A to feel better, but it siphons off energy from the marriage. Furthermore, spouse B resents the outsider, whose support hardens spouse A's position and deepens the marital polarization. Hence triangles not only feed on tension; they also produce conflict.

J. A. Larsen

See Family Systems Theory; Family Systems Therapy; Triadic-Based Family Therapy.

Trichotillomania. Trichotillomania is a disorder characterized by self-inflicted hair loss. According to the *DSM-IV,* trichotillomania is diagnosable when the hair pulling is preceded by tension and leads to obvious hair loss. In addition, individuals with trichotillomania experience a sense of pleasure, gratification, or relief when pulling hair. If the hair pulling is better explained by another mental disorder or a medical/dermatological problem, the diagnosis of trichotillomania does not apply. The *DSM-IV* indicates that this condition must also lead to significant problems in other life areas. Since trichotillomania has been linked to mood and psychotic disorders, there is some question as to whether a separate diagnostic category is merited.

Trichotillomania usually begins in childhood and may continue into adulthood or take a more episodic course. In adults the disorder is reported more in females, although this distinction may reflect the general acceptance of hair loss in males. While hair loss is typically noted on the scalp, other bodily areas may be affected. The individual may try to conceal or deny the hair loss and hair pulling. Individuals with trichotillomania often twirl their hair, mouth it, and/or ingest it. In extreme cases such behavior can lead to gastrointestinal disturbances.

While there are multiple causal factors for trichotillomania, stress is considered an important determinant in about 25% of the cases. Other therapists report disturbances in parent-child relationships, fear of being alone, and frustration as potential causes.

There is no consensus on treatment. Children generally improve spontaneously. Psychiatric or psychological evaluation is recommended for adolescents and adults. Some success has been reported for psychoanalytic therapies, hypnosis, and pharmacological interventions (e.g., antidepressants, antipsychotics). A myriad of behavioral interventions (e.g., habit reversal, thought stopping, self-monitoring, aversive conditioning) have also been employed. Assessing the efficacy of these treatments is difficult, since documented interventions have usually involved single cases.

J. P. GRIMM

Trust. An act of dependency upon another person for the fulfillment of biological, psychological, social, or spiritual needs that cannot be met independently. It is subjective confidence in the intentions and ability of another to promote and/or guard one's well-being that leads a person to risk possible harm or loss. Trust then involves both perceptual and behavioral dimensions. Perceiving another person as trustworthy does not constitute trust, nor does simply engaging in a risk-taking behavior without some positive expectancy about the response. Perceiving someone as trustworthy and placing oneself in a position of vulnerability due to the possibility of betrayal is trust. Trust may involve the vulnerability of one's self-concept and emotional well-being, relationships, possessions, social and economic position, or physical being.

Trust is not usually an all-or-none phenomenon. There are degrees of trust, which can be assessed by the level of positive expectancy about someone's trustworthiness together with the magnitude of damage involved if betrayal occurs. A process of observation and testing typically occurs before significant outcomes are entrusted. As confidence increases, subjective assessment of the risk involved tends to decrease and greater (objective) acts of trust occur. Interpersonal attraction and reciprocated acts of disclosure appear to facilitate the development of trust.

It seems that people differ in their general tendency to trust people. Some persons are so trusting they are called gullible. Others are so suspicious that they are called paranoid. Erikson (1963) suggests that this basic orientation is due to the adequacy with which basic needs of the infant were met during the helplessness of the first year of life. Two scales widely used to assess such a generalized trust orientation are the Philosophy of Human Nature Scale (Wrightsman, 1974) and the Interpersonal Trust Scale (Rotter, 1967).

Acts of trusting vary considerably. They may involve the safekeeping of property, acceptance of a persuasive communication, seeking help for problems, selection of a physician, or sharing confidential information. The diversity of trust acts may be categorized into three general types of trust: persuasive, functional, and personal. Persuasive trust involves a belief in the validity of a message and the integrity of a messenger so that an idea is accepted or a product is bought. Acceptance of the appeals of politicians, evangelists, and salespeople requires this kind of trust. Functional trust is confidence in the capacity and expertise of the one being trusted to competently fulfill a function, such as flying an airplane or doing surgery. Personal trust is the expectancy that another will accept voluntarily disclosed intimate information, treat it with value, and act in one's best interest. This is the trust of intimate friends. More than one kind of trust may be expressed toward another person. Trust of one type may facilitate the other types in certain situations.

The act of entrusting specific outcomes to a specific person at a given time involves a complex mixture of one's history of trust encounters in general and in similar situations; the level and kind of felt need; information about the other person's sincerity, capability, integrity, and intentions based on direct and indirect observation; the kind of relationship that exists; the kind and degree of trust required; and the situational context.

The phenomenon of trust has been studied by psychologists from the perspectives of laboratory experimentation in bargaining and negotiation (Deutsch, 1962), developmental theory (Erikson, 1963), encounter group therapy (Schutz, 1967), self-disclosure theory and research (Cozby, 1973), and measurement (Rotter, 1967; Wrightsman, 1974).

One of the most basic concepts in the Bible is that of faith. Faith is a perspective that affects both perception and practice. It involves a sense of confidence about the truth of biblical statements regarding the existence and nature of phenomena beyond immediate sensory experience, including God, and about the ultimate spiritual consequences of various decisions and behaviors. The Hebraic and early Christian understanding of faith merged belief and behavior in a manner that is synonymous with trust. Without actions that express belief, belief is not regarded as faith (James 2:14–26).

The Bible can be understood as a record of the qualities of God that encourage perception of him as absolutely trustworthy (1 John 4:9). The illustrations of his capabilities (Eph. 3:20), integrity (1 Peter 1:17), and love (1 John 4:9) revealed in historical accounts of his relationships with specific people are intended to enable all people to believe and entrust the direction and decisions of their lives to him. The incarnation of Christ further demonstrated the desire of God to act for the benefit of humanity through his redemptive act of self-sacrifice (Rom. 5:8).

In addition, the Scriptures repeatedly demonstrate the positive consequences of trusting God (Ps. 22:4–5; Rev. 21:3–7) and the negative results of failing to do so (1 Kings 21:21–25; Rev. 20:15) as means of motivating people throughout history to act on their biblically based perceptions of his character.

References

Cozby, P. C. (1973). Self-disclosure: A literature review. *Psychological Bulletin, 79*, 73–91.

Deutsch, M. (1962). Cooperation and trust: Some notes. In M. R. Jones (Ed.), *Nebraska symposium on motivation* (Vol. 10). Lincoln: University of Nebraska Press.

Erikson, E. H. (1963). *Childhood and society* (2nd ed.). New York: Norton.

Rotter, J. B. (1967). A new scale for the measurement of interpersonal trust. *Journal of Personality, 35*, 651–665.

Schutz, W. E. (1967). *Joy*. New York: Grove.

Wrightsman, L. S. (1974). *Assumptions about human nature: A social-psychological approach*. Monterey, CA: Brooks/Cole.

C. W. Ellison

See Psychosocial Development.

Twin Studies. *See* Heredity and Environment in Human Development.

Type. A type generally denotes an ideal specimen or exemplar for defining a category. In practice it refers to an individual who possesses most of the defining qualities. Personality typologies make prominent use of types. A type theory of personality links underlying biological processes to a small number of classification categories. Biological differences explain different personality types. Type theories usually embrace fewer explanatory categories than do trait theories.

Hippocrates developed the oldest typology, which was later systematized by Galen and formalized by Kant. This typology described four temperaments.

The sanguine type was even-dispositioned, warmhearted, optimistic, and energetic. The choleric was quick to action, assertive, and prone to hostility and anger. Depression, sadness, and anxiety characterized the melancholic. The phlegmatic type was listless and lethargic. These temperament types, it was hypothesized, resulted from the predominance of one of four body fluids: blood, yellow bile, black bile, or phlegm, respectively. Some popular Christian typologies have utilized this orientation.

Modern typologies are either psychological or physical. Jung's (1960) analytical psychology postulated two psychological or attitude types. Jung presumed but never fully described the underlying neurological mechanism. The introverted type was hesitant, reflective, withdrawn, living in an inner, subjective world. The extraverted type focused on the external, objective world and consequently was action-oriented, sociable, outgoing, and adaptable to situations. Jung supplemented the attitude types with four ego functions (i.e., functional types) of sensing, intuiting, thinking, and feeling. The former two were irrational functions, while the latter were rational. Attitude types combined with functional types to yield eight personality types (introverted sensing, extraverted sensing, introverted intuiting, etc.). The Myers-Briggs Type Indicators (MBTI) measure these personality characteristics.

Eysenck (1967) explained Jung's attitude types by referring to the arousal levels and excitability of the ascending reticular activating system (ARAS). Extraverts, including sanguine and choleric types, were low in ARAS arousal, while introverts (phlegmatic and melancholic types) exhibited high ARAS arousal. Emotional stability characterized the sanguine and phlegmatic types, while choleric and melancholic types are emotionally labile (i.e., high in neuroticism). ARAS arousal stimulated visceral (i.e., emotional) brain arousal, which was low in normals but high in neurotics. Thus Eysenck used the extraversion-introversion and emotional stability-neuroticism axes in a Cartesian coordinate system to explain the classical temperaments. The sanguine was a normal extravert, the choleric was a neurotic extravert, the melancholic was a neurotic introvert, and the phlegmatic was a normal introvert.

Physical typologies associated temperament with body type. Kretschmer (1925) developed a body typology postulating two normal temperament types: the schizoid and cycloid. The schizoid type was unsociable, quiet, and serious, while the cycloid was sociable, good-natured, humorous, and impulsive (cf. Jung's introversion and extraversion). Under psychotic attack schizoids became schizophrenic, while cycloids displayed manic depression. He noted that schizophrenics were normally tall and thin or athletic, but manic depressives were typically pyknic.

Sheldon (1954) modified this physical typology in which three temperament types were linked to physique (i.e., somatotype). Mesomorphy (highly developed skeleton and musculature) yielded a temperament type of somatotonia, a craving for activity and power, aggressiveness, ruthlessness, and risk taking. Endomorphy (massive viscera) was linked to viscerotonia, the love of comfort, gluttony, sociability, and affection. Ectomorphy (lanky, non-muscular, thin physique) corresponded to cerebrotonia, evidenced by excessive restraint, social inhibition, and intelligence.

References

Eysenck, H. J. (1967). *The biological basis of personality.* Springfield, IL: Thomas.

Jung, C. G. (1960). A psychological theory of types. In H. Read, M. Fordham, & G. Adler (Eds.), *Collected works* (Vol. 8). New York: Pantheon.

Kretschmer, E. (1925). *Physique and character.* New York: Harcourt.

Sheldon, W. H. (1954). *Atlas of men: A guide for somatotyping the adult male at all ages.* New York: Harper.

R. L. TIMPE

See PSYCHOLOGICAL TYPES: JUNG'S VIEW; FACTOR THEORIES OF PERSONALITY.

Ulcers. Open sores that can occur inside the body or on its outer surface. The latter are often referred to as pressure ulcers or bedsores, and they occur most often in people who are confined to bed or a wheelchair. The term is commonly used to refer to a peptic ulcer, which is an ulcer in the upper gastrointestinal tract. The two major forms of peptic ulcer are chronic duodenal ulcers, which occur in the part of the small intestine leading out of the stomach, and gastric ulcers, which occur in the upper part of the stomach. *Peptic* refers to the fact that these ulcers are caused partially by digestive juices, one of which is acid-pepsin.

Ulcers occur in approximately 10% of the population. They are much more common in men than in women. Duodenal ulcers occur four times more often than gastric ulcers. The highest incidence of gastric ulcers is from age 60 to 70, whereas it is highest for duodenal ulcers when a person is in the fifties.

The primary symptom of an ulcer is pain in the area between the navel and the breastbone. The pain may be a burning sensation or a continuous gnawing sensation; some people with ulcers are awakened at night by pain. The pain is often relieved by eating or by taking antacids. Some people with ulcers have no symptoms, or they experience a bloated sensation after eating. Other people with gastric ulcers lose weight because they develop an aversion to food; eating increases their discomfort. In more severe cases, ulcers may cause internal bleeding, which is passed as black, tarry stools or as red blood when bleeding is massive.

Treatment focuses on relieving pain and helping the ulcer heal. The most widely accepted treatment is the administration of medication that inhibits acid secretion. It is also common to give antacids, which are effective and less expensive but may require more frequent dosages. Blood tests may reveal the presence of an organism named *Helicobacter pylori* in some people with peptic ulcers. When this organism is present, standard antacid treatment is supplemented with a combination of bismuth and antibiotics that cure the *H. pylori* infection and prevent recurrence in the majority of patients.

Ulcer sufferers are instructed not to take aspirin and not to drink alcohol, since these substances irritate the stomach lining. In addition, drinks containing caffeine, such as coffee and tea, are omitted from the diet because these drinks stimulate the secretion of gastric acid. Greasy or spicy foods may also cause discomfort. Peptic ulcers usually heal within one to three months with active medical treatment. Surgery is indicated when there are complications such as unresponsiveness to medications, obstruction, or when the ulcer perforates and allows stomach acids to pass directly into the abdomen. These complications require immediate medical attention.

People who develop ulcers are often described as hard-driving, successful individuals who have strong needs to please and to receive attention from others. They are also characterized as stressed, tense, and conflicted between needs for dependence and independence. Ulcer sufferers seem to have an overactive digestive system in response to chronic stress. A person who is prone to gastric upset can take preventive action by avoiding aspirin, caffeine, and alcohol and by learning better relaxation and communication skills in order to cope with stress and to meet personal needs more effectively.

M. A. NORFLEET

See PSYCHOSOMATIC FACTORS IN HEALTH AND ILLNESS.

Unconditional Positive Regard. A term popularized by Carl Rogers. It is central to his theory of personality development and his person-centered therapy. The idea is not new with Rogers, but he utilized it more profoundly, consistently, and exhaustively than did others.

The roots of this idea may be seen in the Judeo-Christian concepts of the dignity of human persons as image bearers of God and of the unconditional quality of God's unmerited grace toward unworthy humans. Rogers's perspective was therefore shaped by his early upbringing in the Christian faith, though he tended to disavow the connection.

The Judeo-Christian notion of the dignity of humanness gives rise to concepts of human freedom and the inherent value of persons. Combined with the idea of imaging God, it implies a growth-oriented destiny, inherent in humanness, requiring freedom for self-actualization of all the potentials for human personality development with which God has endowed us. God's grace, moreover, guarantees a context of proximate and ultimate freedom within which humans may freely experiment and grow, confident that God's grace is always greater than all our inadequacies and spiritual or moral failure.

The unconditional positive regard of one human for another (e.g., a parent for a child or a therapist for a patient) frees the other to accept the challenge of his or her own potentials for growth and/or healing. Rogers, in adopting this perspective on personality formation and therapy, reflects the unconditional grace model of redemption as biblically expressed.

Influences on the Rogerian formulation of this concept can be traced from the Positive Thinking movement through John Dewey to Rogers. However, a crucial difference must be noted between Dewey and Rogers. Dewey romantically assumed the inherent goodness of humans, expecting permissiveness to enable the flourishing of positive native characteristics in human personality development. Rogers is not that kind of romantic. He recognizes the native human potential for pathology and evil and values the function of discipline, constraint, and guidance for personality development. His emphasis on unconditional positive regard for inciting growth and healing expresses his conviction that it is in that context of affirmation that humans flourish. Unconditional positive regard is an affirmation of a human person in his or her brokenness and distortions, as well as in his or her strengths and growth options. With that affirmation a person will be more receptive to the externally imposed disciplines that produce self-discipline and the positive growth options that will replace self-destructive ones.

J. H. Ellens

See Self Theory; Humanistic Psychology; Person-Centered Therapy; Rogers, Carl Ransom.

Unconscious. Thoughts, feelings, and other mental processes that are not currently in conscious awareness are considered unconscious. Three of the most obvious examples of unconscious processes are forgetting the name of a friend, slips of the tongue, and posthypnotic suggestion. In forgetting a friend's name we are aware that we know it but cannot bring it to consciousness. In slips of the tongue we accidentally say one word when we consciously intend to say another. We may say *loathe* instead of *love, hell* instead of *hail,* or *sex* instead of *six.*

A person under hypnosis may be given the suggestion to take off his watch, open the window, or unbutton his jacket at a specified time after coming out of hypnosis. He is also told that he will not remember the command. When the time comes, for no reason he is aware of he suddenly takes off his watch, unbuttons his jacket, or walks over and opens the window. Just as in accidental forgetting and slips of the tongue, mental processes that impact the person's actions are going on outside of conscious awareness.

Some people speak of the unconscious as if it were a concrete psychological entity or a location where unwanted thoughts and feelings are dispatched, a kind of psychological basement. More accurately unconscious refers to the current status of a thought or feeling. Either we are aware of it or we are not. The level of awareness varies along a continuum from complete awareness to total unawareness.

Although sensitive poets, artists, and thinkers had long been aware of the reality and power of unconscious psychological processes, Sigmund Freud was the first to systematically explore the nature and function of unconsciousness. He identified three levels of awareness. In addition to the conscious level he postulated preconscious and unconscious levels. Preconscious thoughts or feelings, while not being in immediate awareness, can be called to attention with relatively little effort. One's age, phone number, or address are good examples. Most of the time we are not consciously thinking about these things, but at any moment they can be recalled by turning our attention to them. Since a finite number of thoughts can occupy our conscious minds at any one time, most thoughts have to be out of awareness. But by turning our attention to them we can immediately bring many of these thoughts and feelings to mind. These readily available thoughts are called preconscious.

Unconscious thoughts are much less accessible to awareness. They typically become accessible only with much effort because they are purposely although unconsciously banned from awareness. The individual wants to avoid remembering because the repressed experience would be too painful. For example, people involved in a tragic accident who lose their sight (hysterical blindness) or those who cannot remember any of their life before age eight or ten are probably pushing unpleasant experiences and feelings from awareness. These thoughts and feelings may be very difficult to remember. One of the major goals of insight-oriented therapy is to help people overcome their repressions in order to face previously avoided painful memories, feelings, thoughts, or wishes.

Since preconscious thoughts are out of awareness because we are attending to other things, they are considered descriptively unconscious. Unconscious thoughts, however, are considered dynamically unconscious because they are actively kept from awareness in order to avoid the anxiety, guilt, or pain associated with them. It is the dynamic interaction of anxiety or guilt-producing thoughts or memories with defense mechanisms such as repression that results in truly unconscious, as opposed to preconscious, thoughts. This dynamic nature of unconscious thoughts also explains how they can continue to impact personality adjustment long after they are forgotten. If an individual has to expend a considerable amount of emotional energy keeping unconscious thoughts from awareness, this defensive process limits and impoverishes the personality and can be a key factor in causing personality maladjustment.

Unconscious thoughts also operate differently from conscious ones and are not necessarily rational. In dreams, for example, two or more people or ideas may be merged into one (condensation), and mutually contradictory or exclusive ideas (such as a dead person talking) may coexist.

Although few psychologists accept all of Freud's theorizing, his views on the presence of unconscious thoughts, wishes, and feelings are now nearly universally accepted. So too is the belief that these unconscious thoughts have meaning and influence our conscious choices and decisions. However, theorists still debate the content of the unconscious, and most would not agree with Freud's belief that the most important of these repressed thoughts are sexual in nature.

S. B. NARRAMORE

See PSYCHOANALYTIC PSYCHOLOGY; COLLECTIVE UNCONSCIOUS.

Underachiever. The belief that some students are underachieving has probably been suspected by parents and teachers for millennia. However, the study of underachievement (UA) within education and psychology began in the 1960s as a result of a growing body of research on students, especially secondary students, who were not performing up to their potential. Admittedly, the evaluative concept of underachievement includes the assumptions that Western, formal education is inherently valuable and that all students should be equally motivated to realize their academic potential. Nevertheless, most educators in the United States believe such a label is useful to describe the characteristics of some students. Underachievement has been operationally defined as a large discrepancy between a child's intellectual potential as measured by an intelligence test and its actual educational attainments as measured by grades or achievement tests (McCall, Evahn, & Kratzer, 1992).

Underachievers in general have been found to share certain characteristics: low perception of their abilities and poor self-concept; fear of failure (see Failure, Fear of); unrealistic, perfectionistic standards (see Perfectionism); poor peer relations; problems relating to authority; and an external locus of control (Bricklin & Bricklin, 1967; Whitmore, 1980). However, some researchers argue that underachievers are likely made up of a heterogeneous set of groups with some unique features. Mandel and Marcus (1988) distinguish five groups: those with overanxious disorder; those with conduct disorder; those with identity disorder who have low motivation due to a lack of purpose; those with oppositional defiant disorder; and those with academic problems. The last is the largest group of underachievers (40% to 50%).

Mandel and Marcus describe (1988) members of this last group as easygoing, well-liked, and without severe anxieties. However, the primary difficulty of these underachievers is that they appear to be strongly motivated to maintain performance at mediocre levels. They consistently do not take the necessary preparation and execution needed for increased success. They frequently engage in rationalization, often blaming others or their circumstances for their difficulties, and avoid the self-insight and the taking of responsibility required for improvement. Nor do underachievers necessarily grow out of their difficulties. Underachieving students examined later as adults were found to have been more likely to get divorced, obtain jobs with lower status, change jobs more frequently, and receive less income than their non-UA peers with the same ability (McCall, Evahn, & Kratzer, 1992). With regard to gender, most studies of underachieving students have found that boys outnumber girls, by a 2:1 or 3:1 ratio (McCall, Evahn, & Kratzer, 1992).

Hypothesized causes for UA are primarily social (biological causation distinguishes true learning disabilities from underachievement). Some parents of underachievers have been found to be indifferent to them, particularly their educational accomplishments. Others, however, communicated unrealistic expectations to their child (Butler-Por, 1987; Mandel & Marcus, 1988). Such apparently opposite parenting practices may have led to the same outcome because neither provided the optimal social support that fosters the internalization of healthy motivational or volitional structure. Teachers and schools have been faulted for providing competitive atmospheres that heighten fear of failure and self-awareness (Butler-Por, 1987). It has been noted that UA has features that resemble learned helplessness (McCall, Evahn, & Kratzer, 1992). Perhaps both parents and teachers can contribute to UA if task situations are created that are unattainable and that therefore lead to apathy and passivity. In addition, life stress such as family divorce (Dowdall & Colangelo, 1982), has been found to be related to UA.

At the same time an excessive clinical preoccupation with extrapersonal causes can unwittingly exacerbate feelings of helplessness. When such awarenesses are widely shared, as they are in American culture, the external locus of control beliefs of underachieving adolescents will likely be reinforced. A supportive emphasis on personal responsibility for their success or lack of it (the volitional dimension) would presumably be genuinely therapeutic.

Reviews of the benefits of traditional therapy for underachievement have not been very encouraging (Butler-Por, 1987; Mandel & Marcus, 1988; McCall, Evahn, & Kratzer, 1992). Benefits generally have been negligible to modest and when present were linked to the precise focus of intervention (e.g., self-concept). The mental, motivational, volitional, and social dynamics of underachievement make it a complex, challenging problem. However, Butler-Por found that the training of teachers in providing a supportive but structured environment that created success experiences resulted in significant changes in underachieving students in reduced fear of failure, increased internal locus of control, higher self-concept, and higher grades. Mandel and Marcus recommend the following program when working with an academic-problem underachiever: set a mutually agreed-upon specific goal (e.g., obtaining a B on the next history test); take a detailed stock of present study habits and preparation; focus on specific problems and isolate each excuse within that problem area (e.g., "I just can't seem to find the time to study"); make explicit links between each excuse and its natural consequences (underachievers often do not make such connections); request solutions from the student for each specific problem; call for specific action from the child; follow up on what happened the next day or week; repeat steps 3–7 for each excuse the child tends to make; gradually shift to a nondirective approach that fosters increased personal responsibility.

References

Bricklin, B., & Bricklin, P. M. (1967). *Bright child—poor grades: The psychology of underachievement.* New York: Delacorte.

Butler-Por, N. (1987). *Underachievers in school: Issues and intervention.* New York: Wiley.

Dowdall C. B., & Colangelo, J. P. (1982). Underachieving gifted students: Review and implications. *Gifted Child Quarterly, 26,* 179–184.

Mandel, H. P., & Marcus, S. I. (1988). *The psychology of underachievement.* New York: Wiley.

McCall, R. B., Evahn, C., & Kratzer, L. (1992). *High school underachievers.* Newbury Park, CA: Sage.

Whitmore, J. R. (1980). *Giftedness, conflict, and under-achievement.* Boston: Allyn & Bacon.

E. L. JOHNSON

See ACHIEVEMENT, NEED FOR; ACHIEVEMENT TESTS.

Undoing. An ego defense mechanism consisting of the performance of some activity perceived as the opposite of that against which the ego is seeking defense. This unconscious process is designed to undo, atone for, or otherwise annul an objectionable thought, behavior, or impulse. The undoing activity may be actually or only magically an opposite. Undoing frequently includes unconsciously motivated expiatory acts, apologizing or repenting, counter-compulsions, self-inflicted punishment or penance, and some compulsive ceremonials. Undoing is often seen in the obsessive-compulsive psychoneurosis. An example would be the compulsion to repeatedly wash one's hands in an unconscious attempt to undo and defend against the guilt and conflict associated with habitual masturbation.

R. LARKIN

See DEFENSE MECHANISMS.

Unemployment, Psychological Effects of. The first sociological and psychological studies of unemployment were made during the Great Depression in England, Europe, and North America. In the 1950s there was research on the impact of prolonged labor disputes and the periodic layoffs occasioned by the business cycle. More recent research has been done in the United States on the sluggish economy, mergers, downsizing, and the impact of plant closures in the last quarter of the twentieth century. Research done in Mexico during the early 1980s and mid-1990s has focused on widespread unemployment (mixed with rapid inflation and currency devaluation) occasioned by the interaction of foreign markets and political miscalculation.

Most of these studies have focused on one specific kind of worker. The portrait is that of the male head of household, about 40 years of age, with limited formal education and a blue-collar factory job. Such workers are seen as going through definable stages in their response to unemployment, not unlike the grief stages outlined by Elisabeth Kübler-Ross. The first stage may be denial: "the plant really won't close" or "this pink slip is a mistake" or "this is just temporary; they will call me back soon." The second stage seems to be shock and anger: "how could they do this to me?" or "the company [or the union, or the country] is unfair." Then comes a new resolve: the worker accepts his loss of the old position, but he now hopes that this will merely give him an opportunity to move on to something new and better. He optimistically redoubles his efforts to seek a new position or move into a new line of work. Occasionally this is accompanied by going back to school or moving geographically. Gradually the fourth stage emerges: frustration. His hopes are repeatedly dashed and he redefines success by lowering his expectations. At last he gives up and accepts resignation. He spends less time looking for work, considers only inferior jobs, and may even give up before he submits an application or goes for an interview. This is akin to the learned helplessness of depression. His self-concept has been altered: "No one wants me. I'm useless" and "Why bother filling out another application? I don't need any more rejection."

The clinical and social picture darkens in the latter stages. What we usually see are the symptoms of agitated depression, though in the third stage some obsessive-compulsive job search tendencies can be found, and in the last stage some phobic behavior is not uncommon. Suicide levels increase in the wake of mass unemployment, though most of the unemployed do not go this far. A more common complication is that by stage 4 and sometimes as early as stage 2 the individual may be vulnerable to chemical dependency. Some patients might report psychophysiologic reactions (e.g., ulcers) in stage 4 or somatoform reactions ("I can't work. My hand is paralyzed") in stage 5. Those with hypochondriacal or paranoid tendencies of personality will have these exacerbated in stage 5.

The social and interpersonal impact of prolonged unemployment interacts with the downward psychological spiral. Many unemployed people experience a creeping loneliness, especially if they relied upon work-related roles for their interactions with other people or had most of their socialization with comrades from the workplace. Diminished income can also reduce the amount of recreational activity that requires money (e.g., bowling, attendance at professional sports), leaving the unemployed individual with only the most economical of pastimes (hanging around the street corner or watching daytime television programs).

The impact on family life has also been noted. For the husband the loss of the role as bread winner may diminish his status in the home. If the wife returns to the labor force because of his unemployment, she may resent being forced to do so. Even if she does not respond in this way, the man may fear these changes in the relationship and become more withdrawn or demanding. The frequency of sexual contact with his wife decreases. The time they spend together in recreation and conversation decreases. Divorce and domestic violence become more likely.

One problem with the aforementioned picture is it assumes that all or most workers fit the profile. Many background variables moderate the individual's response to prolonged unemployment. Gender is the foremost. Women seem to cope better: it is more socially acceptable for them to be returning daytime students, homemakers, caregivers, and volunteers. Age is another variable: men from 30 to 60 have the worst time with prolonged unemployment. Older men may slowly accept their unemployment as a premature retirement, especially if they can qualify for some pension benefits. The younger man, especially if he is not the sole support of a family, can use the unemployment as an opportunity to move on and can go back to school or join the armed forces. Many younger adults seem to have a general expectation of poor economic times, so unemployment does not strike them as either unexpected or as a stamp of personal failure. The influence of variables such as education, socioeconomic status, and ethnicity are less clear.

Purely quantitative measures of unemployment and subsequent psychological reactions must be supplemented by qualitative research, especially interviews (focus group and ongoing in-depth personal). Researchers must focus not only on what happens to the unemployed, but how. What investigators need to track is the decision-making process of the unemployed person. Initial interviews will be unproductive, as the unemployed utilize various defense mechanisms: denial, reaction formation, repression, projection, displacement. However, researchers who are able to wade through the self-justifying prose and stay on the track that follows the process of decision making will be rewarded, gaining a glimpse of the private logic of the unemployed person moving from one stage to the next.

Intervention with this population should avoid the temptation of giving a basket of canned food at Christmas, a pep talk, and a list of jobs. That may be precisely what unemployed people want in stage 3, but it will not spare them from the emotional ravages of the later stages. Peer support and pastoral care can be most useful: they must talk about their experiences and recognize the stages they are going through.

Additional Reading

Feather, N. T. (1989). *The psychological impact of unemployment.* New York: Springer-Verlag.

T. L. BRINK

See POVERTY, PSYCHOLOGICAL EFFECTS AND COUNSELING; ACHIEVEMENT, NEED FOR.

Unpardonable Sin. The fear that one has committed the unpardonable sin can be an intrusive obsession of religious people who struggle with obsessive-compulsive cognitive styles. The major *DSM-IV* diagnosis characterized by such obsessions is the obsessive-compulsive disorder. Persons for whom this diagnosis is appropriate frequently obsess over a fearful or disturbing thought in spite of attempts not to think about the issue. The recurring obsession tends to intensify with rehearsal rather than to subside. A true obsession operates at levels far beyond normal concern or worry.

The fear of having committed the unpardonable sin often begins when a religious person with obsessional potential reads the New Testament passage referring to the sin for which forgiveness is not available: "But whoever blasphemes against the Holy Spirit will never be forgiven; he is guilty of an eternal sin" (Mark 3:29, NIV). An important component of the triggering capacity of this verse centers on the use of the concept of blasphemy. Blasphemy for the religious person is extremely ego-dystonic and represents one of the most reprehensible acts a religious person could perform. Hence, a fear of having committed the unpardonable sin takes on serious, profound, and deeply troubling features.

This severe statement of Jesus as recorded in the Gospel of Mark meets all of the criteria for an issue that serves as a good obsessional trigger: exclusivity, absoluteness, ambiguity, and impossibility (Beck, 1981). In other words, the obsessional person latches on to issues that by their very nature are ambiguous and issues that nonobsessing persons have difficulty explaining. Just as the paranoid person focuses on concerns that ultimately cannot be proved or disproved, the obsessional person ruminates on issues that are vague and unanswerable.

Nonetheless, a fear that one has committed the unpardonable sin is not a harmless or tepid issue. Those obsessed with this idea can be terrorized by the recurring thought. If people have already committed an act or indulged an idea that meets the criteria for these harsh words of Jesus, their fate is settled: eternal damnation without hope of remission or assuagement.

The reference Jesus makes to the unpardonable sin is normally classified by New Testament scholars as one of the hard sayings of Jesus (Bruce, 1983). Mark and Matthew both record for their readers the setting in which this statement first occurred: A delegation of religious officials traveled from Jerusalem to Galilee on an official mission to investigate the growing popularity of Jesus of Nazareth. The thorniest issue for the threatened religious leadership of the nation swirled around the power of Jesus to perform mighty signs and wonders such as casting out demons. The official verdict of this panel of investigators was that Jesus was using the power of Satan himself to cast out demons. The only other viable explanation was that Jesus was empowered by God himself, a conclusion they were hesitant to make. Jesus replied to the illogical conclusion of these religious leaders by saying, "How can Satan drive out Satan?" (Mark 3:23, NIV). Later in that same passage he describes the tragedy of committing the unpardonable sin. Those who blaspheme and sin can obtain forgiveness, but if they blaspheme against the Holy Spirit (i.e., by attributing to Satan a power that rightfully belongs to the Holy Spirit) they will find no forgiveness.

New Testament interpreters suggest two possible ways in which we can understand this saying of Jesus. First, we can define the unpardonable sin strictly by the contextual meaning in Mark and Matthew and in Luke. This approach to identifying the specific sin that Jesus had in mind would define the unpardonable sin as refusing to give due credit to the Holy Spirit when credit is due (Mark and Matthew) and as refusing the Spirit's help in avoiding denial of the Savior (Luke 12:10). These restricted meanings of the unforgivable sin address a very specific offense against the Holy Spirit. Second, we can define the unpardonable sin more broadly based on the whole counsel of Scripture. In this view the only sin that ultimately counts toward defining one's eternal destiny is the sin of refusing to believe in Jesus. "Everywhere (in Scripture) to reject Him is the sin of sins, and ultimately it is the only sin that counts" (Smith, 1953, p. 182). All of our other sins and blasphemies can be forgiven; but if we die refusing to give allegiance to Jesus as Lord and Savior, that sin cannot be forgiven.

References

Beck, J. R. (1981). Treatment of spiritual doubt among obsessing evangelicals. *Journal of Psychology and Theology, 9,* 224–231.

Bruce, F. F. (1983). *The hard sayings of Jesus.* Downers Grove, IL: InterVarsity Press.

Smith. C. R. (1953). *The Bible doctrine of sin.* London: Epworth.

J. R. BECK

See DOUBT; PASTORAL CARE; PASTORAL COUNSELING; SIN, PSYCHOLOGICAL CONSEQUENCES OF.

Vv

Vaginismus. *DSM-IV* (American Psychiatric Association, 1994) identifies two sexual pain disorders: dyspareunia (genital pain before, during, or after intercourse) and vaginismus, spasmodic contractions of the muscles around the vaginal opening that are triggered when the woman, her partner, or a physician attempts to insert anything into the vagina. The involuntary contractions of vaginismus make sexual intercourse impossible or at best very painful, and they interfere with insertion of tampons, fingers, or gynecological instruments.

By preventing intercourse vaginismus frequently interferes with sexual relationships and produces marital discord, lack of consummation, and infertility. However, there is no reliable evidence that women with vaginismus unconsciously reject their sexuality. They often enjoy sexual activity, as long as penetration is not attempted. With a cooperative partner or through masturbation, women with vaginismus are capable of orgasm.

Vaginismus is often diagnosed during the first gynecological examination, when the physician examining the genitals observes the spasms closing the vagina, although some women with vaginismus do not have problems during an examination.

Vaginismus is rare, affecting fewer than 2% of women. Often it is chronic, following either the first gynecological examination or the first attempt at sexual intercourse. Young women are more likely to have the disorder than older women, but the disorder may be acquired at any age after a sexual assault. Medical conditions such as endometriosis or a vaginal infection may trigger vaginismus. Even after the medical condition is treated, the acquired vaginismus may persist.

Women who develop vaginismus after being sexually assaulted, raped, or molested sometimes report negative attitudes toward sex. Such traumatic experiences may associate fear with sexual activity, contributing to vaginismus. In many respects vaginismus acts like a conditioned response, with an association between vaginal penetration and fear-induced spasms that prevent penetration. Since some women with vaginismus have experienced painful pelvic examinations or have been victims of gang rape, the conditioning explanation may be reasonable.

It appears that negative attitudes about sex rarely cause vaginismus by themselves, in the absence of any history of sexual or genital trauma. However, vaginismus was a common complaint during the Victorian era of the nineteenth century, when many women were taught that sexual activity was to be feared and avoided. If they approached sexual intercourse with great fear, it is likely that their first experiences were painful, with conditioned vaginismus a potential consequence.

The interaction of vaginismus and male erectile disorder demonstrates the complexity of sexual relationships. In some women vaginismus develops after their husbands experience erection problems, while some men develop erection problems following their wives' vaginismus. Sexual dysfunctions in one partner apparently can cause enough anxiety to trigger problems in the other.

According to some clinical reports, vaginismus may sometimes be traced to fear of becoming pregnant. Other reports suggest that vaginismus stems from an extremely repressive religious upbringing, one that not only forbids sexual behavior outside marriage but also prohibits looking at one's own body while bathing or talking with a family member about anything remotely connected with sex. Christian counselors may help such women to achieve a more positive view of their sexuality, but it is not known whether vaginismus will then be eliminated. It does not appear that normal religious teaching, which attempts to limit sexual expression to marriage, will produce vaginismus.

Vaginismus is readily treated through physical dilation of the vaginal opening in a gradual process similar to systematic desensitization. From a graduated set of plastic rods shaped like a penis, the woman inserts the smallest into her vagina overnight. She continues with the same dilator each night until she no longer experiences spasms upon inserting it, and then she proceeds to the next larger size, repeating the process until she is able to engage in intercourse without spasms. This process usually eliminates vaginismus.

Another popular method is to use either her own or her husband's fingers as dilators, following a similar process. The woman may prefer to guide her husband's hand and control the insertion of his finger, in order to minimize anxiety. As it is usually impossible to leave a finger in place overnight, plastic dilators are effective more quickly in most cases.

Reference

American Psychiatric Association. (1994). *Diagnostic and statistical manual of mental disorders* (4th ed.). Washington, DC: Author.

P. D. Young

See Sexual Pain Disorders.

Validity, Test. *See* Psychological Measurement.

Values and Psychotherapy. Although it has been long supposed by professionals to be value-neutral, psychotherapy involves a complicated interplay of the values and beliefs of clients, of therapists, and of their respective communities (Goldsmith & Hansen, 1991). For highly religious clients, their religious community is often their most important reference group, in which their values and beliefs are likely to be explicit and shared by most of their friends and family. Although most psychologists claim some religious preference, many are not actively involved in their faiths, and their religious views are not considered very important by most of their associates.

Beliefs are perceptions of what is; for example, "There is a God." Values are perceptions of what ought to be; for example, "I should pray more." Most values flow from beliefs, and the logical consistency of these is a key point upon which many therapists focus (Probst, 1996, p. 393). A life based on a consistent set of religious beliefs is just as emotionally healthy as a life based on any other consistent set, Probst claims. Accumulating evidence suggests a consistent religious life may be healthier, happier, and more resistant to stresses than a nonreligious one (e.g., Gartner, 1996).

Many academicians have been predicting a rapid increase in secularization in North America, similar to that in most parts of Europe and Israel, where typically less than 10% of the general population is actively religious. Although it has been predicted for decades, this secular trend has not appeared, and North American religious involvement is not much different than it was in 1950 (Hoge, 1996). Belief in God is affirmed by about 95% of the population, acceptance of the divinity of Jesus Christ by about 75%, and belief in an afterlife by about 75%. In 1991, 76% agreed that "the only assurance of eternal life is personal faith in Jesus Christ." In 1992, 87% said religion is important or very important to their daily

lives; only 12% said it is unimportant, figures that again are stable over time. In 1987, 44% of American Protestants and 13% of Roman Catholics said they have been born again. Some beliefs have changed, however. The percentage of those saying they believe the Bible to be the literal Word of God dropped from 65% in 1963 to 32% in 1991, although respect for the moral and spiritual teachings of the Bible remains high. Respect for religious authorities has also dropped off sharply, especially for younger Roman Catholics.

On moral or social issues, there is inconsistency. Most conservative Christians claim strong negative attitudes toward the use of alcohol and drugs. Highly religious Christians drink less, but there are few teetotalers. The correlations between degree of religious commitment and avoidance of alcohol are low (.10–.30), meaning almost as many highly religious people as nonreligious ones drink. Conservative, committed Protestants and Roman Catholics are the bedrock of opposition to unrestricted, legalized abortion, but a 1994–1995 survey of abortion patients estimates that one in five women who got abortions is born again or an evangelical Christian. Abortion rates among Roman Catholic women were 29% higher than among Protestants, partly due to a high abortion rate among Hispanics (Vobdja, 1996). Conservative Christians differ sharply from moderate and liberal Christians in their higher concern for national security issues. They also differ in strong disapproval of homosexuality, including gay rights and ordination, and in attitudes toward extramarital sex. Conservative religiosity does not predict conservative economics or views toward the poor, the environment, or other social issues, however. Hoge (1996, p. 39) sees three current religious trends that are relevant to psychotherapy: the decline in religious authority places a greater burden on individuals to make their own religious value decisions; increasing social tolerance for different religious viewpoints causes questioning of traditional (stereotyped) religious judgments, with weakening boundaries and consequent anxiety; and rapidly changing sexual mores will trouble many religious people and lead to more intergenerational conflict in families.

Studies show that troubled conservative Christians (evangelicals and fundamentalists) prefer to seek counseling from clergy than from mental health professionals, as do other groups, such as nonwhite Roman Catholics. Factors such as cost, shame, and fear of attack on religious values are given as reasons. These Christians do not, however, rate such clerical pastoral counseling as more effective than counseling by nonclerical therapists. Worthington (1993, pp. 131–132) proposes three value dimensions he feels are important to highly religious clients when they evaluate therapy: the "authority the person affords Scripture," the "authority the person affords . . . ecclesiastical leaders," and the "degree to which the person identifies with the norms of his/her religious group." If a counselor's values are perceived to lie outside a client's zone of toleration on these dimensions, therapy may fail due to premature termination, low trust, and high resistance. If a client closely identifies with a group whose norms hold that all emotional problems are due to sin and can be conquered by prayer, piety, and obedience, great shame may be felt for seeking therapeutic help. The very act of seeing a counselor may be seen as evidence of a spiritual failure, as Koltko (1990) has shown with Mormon clients.

In one study, 84% of respondents to a national survey said they attempt to live according to their religious beliefs. Lovinger (1996) gives an excellent summary of the beliefs and values of various major religions and denominations found in North America, including attitudes toward psychotherapy. He says, for example, that Jews feel comfortable with free association and other self-exploratory depth techniques. But fundamentalists and lower-socioeconomic Roman Catholics, among others, may be uncomfortable with such techniques and prefer direct advice from a counselor who is seen as an authority. Studies also show that when religious people live in accordance with their moral values, they score better on mental health measures, including self-esteem, purpose in life, sexual satisfaction, social consciousness, and spirituality. Those who deviate from their moral values report more depression, anxiety, substance abuse, and other symptoms.

Many religiously committed persons, chiefly religiously traditional Christians but also some mental health professionals, view psychology as representing a hostile and competing worldview. "Secular priests" was what London (1986) said the role of psychotherapists has become. Maher (1996, pp. 449ff.) says, "Most therapists are self-appointed police of their own lists of what they approve and disapprove" and are "sniffing out" disapproved client behaviors for change; that is, for treatment. In contrast to their credo, Maher finds, many therapists are "very judgmental" and "extremely quick to moralize." Maher adds that religious and spiritual counselors often also have similar hidden agendas for change presented as part of treatment. He advocates development of explicit directions of value change that are agreed to by both the therapist and client.

While many values therapists affirm are shared with their religious clients, some are not. Christians generally hold that the values revealed by God, such as the Ten Commandments, are the most important ones. Many therapists, however, hold that individual autonomy, personal growth, and individual responsibility are the major values that set the goals for therapy (Lovinger, 1996, p. 359). Many therapists are also uncomfortable with the supernatural.

According to Tan (1996, p. 366), recent surveys show that about 70% to 80% of clinical psychologists claim a religious preference, about 40% say they attend religious services, and 65% to 75% reported that spirituality is relevant to their own lives, although their spirituality is often nontraditional. Shafranske (1996b) reports that about 22% of a 1990 random sample of psychologists were Roman Catholic, 20% Jewish, and 30% to 40% mainline Protestants (led by 12% Methodists). But 85% of these psychologists said they had little or no training in how religion and psychology relate, 68% of them said they thought it is inappropriate for a therapist to pray with a client, 55% thought it is inappropriate to use Scripture or other religious texts in therapy, and 73% felt it would be appropriate to recommend a client leave a religion the therapist felt is hindering psychological growth. Gass (1984), however, found that orthodox Christians prefer the use of Scripture and prayer in therapy.

Clearly there are some major ethical problems in value differences between devout religious clients and less religious or less orthodox therapists. The 1992 revision (American Psychological Association, 1992) of the ethical guidelines of the American Psychological Association (APA), psychology's main professional body, now specifically includes religion along with age, race, gender, and other human differences that psychologists are to be sensitive to and receive training in. In part to promote such religious knowledge, the APA has recently sponsored training workshops for psychologists working with highly religious clients and has published the book (Shafranske, 1996a) from which many references have been taken. Shafranske (1996a) is by far the best source on the interaction of religious values and psychotherapy, so I have preferred to cite this one source. Worthington (1993) is the next best source; his work is a collection of essays specifically reflecting Christian viewpoints. Both sources deal extensively with ethics. Browning (1987) is the best source for a Christian analysis and critique of classical counseling theories.

In a broad sense, counseling deals with human meanings, morals, and goals. All these are shot through with religious concepts and values. In a narrower sense, counseling deals with the techniques and processes by which therapists treat their clients. Here the meanings are counselor/client interpretations of the clients' particular events, ideas, and feelings. The morals focus on counseling ethics, often governed by professional guidelines. The goals are specific intended improvements in the quality of clients' lives and functioning. Again, all are intertwined with religious views and values. An ethical therapist should be able to identify and use religious sources, including clergy, to support client processes and goals. Ethical therapists should also be aware of religious sources of therapeutic resistance (Bergin, Payne & Richards, 1996, p. 308). Tan (1996) discusses some specifics about how prayer, Scripture, and referrals can be used ethically and what constraints should be observed to prevent ethical risk to clients. Referrals to religious professionals, lay counselors, or groups (e.g., 12-step programs) by mental health professionals should be more frequent.

Tan (1996) also points out the danger of a religiously zealous counselor being ethically abusive in imposing particular religious viewpoints on his or her clients. He says (p. 369) it is ethical for therapists to share their faith if they are dealing with relevant clinical problems, working within the clients' belief system, and working with a well-defined therapy contract with fully informed consent to include religious or spiritual interventions. Within this ethical framework, healing ministries of prayer, forgiveness, deliverance, repentance, and even conversion may constitute an acceptable and desirable dimension of therapy. Also see McMinn and Meek (1996) for a survey of ethical beliefs and practices among Christian counselors. They conclude that unlicensed counselors with no graduate degrees are at greatest risk for ethical failure. Scanish and McMinn (1966) propose ten guidelines for assessing the ethical competence of Christian lay counselors.

References

American Psychological Association (1992). Ethical principles of psychologists and code of conduct. *American Psychologist, 47,* 1597–1611.

Bergin, A. E., Payne, I. R., & Richards, P. S. (1996). Values in psychotherapy. In E. P. Shafranske (Ed.), *Religion and the clinical practice of psychology* (pp. 297–325). Washington, DC: American Psychological Association.

Browning, D. (1987). *Religious thought and the modern psychologies: A critical conversation in the theology of culture.* Philadelphia: Fortress.

Gartner, J. (1996). Religious commitment, mental health and prosocial behavior: A review of the empirical literature. In E. P. Shafranske (Ed.), *Religion and the clinical practice of psychology.* Washington, DC: American Psychological Association.

Gass, C. S. (1984) Orthodox Christian values related to psychotherapy and mental health. *Journal of Psychology and Theology, 12,* 230–237.

Goldsmith, W. M., & Hansen, B. K. (1991). Boundary areas of religious clients' values: Target for therapy. *Journal of Psychology and Christianity, 10,* 224–236. (Also in Worthington [1993].)

Hoge, D. R. (1996). Religion in America: The demographics of belief and affiliation. In E. P. Shafranske (Ed.), *Religion and the clinical practice of psychology.* Washington, DC: American Psychological Association.

Koltko, M. E. (1990). How religious beliefs affect psychotherapy: The example of Mormonism. *Psychotherapy, 27,* 132–141.

London, P. (1986). *Modes and morals of psychotherapy* (2nd ed.). New York: Hemisphere.

Lovinger, R. J. (1996). Considering the religious dimension in assessment and treatment. In E. P. Shafranske (Ed.), *Religion and the clinical practice of psychology.* Washington, DC: American Psychological Association.

Maher, A. R. (1996). Existential-humanistic psychotherapy and the religious person. In E. P. Shafranske (Ed.), *Religion and the clinical practice of psychology.* Washington, DC: American Psychological Association.

McMinn, M. R., & Meek, K. R. (1966). Ethics among Christian counselors: A survey of beliefs and behaviors. *Journal of Psychology and Theology, 24,* 26–37.

Probst, L. R. (1996). Cognitive-behavioral therapy and the religious person. In E. P. Shafranske (Ed.), *Religion and the clinical practice of psychology.* Washington, DC: American Psychological Association.

Scanish, J. D., & McMinn, M. R. (1996). The competent lay Christian counselor. *Journal of Psychology and Christianity, 15,* 29–37.

Shafranske, E. P. (Ed.). (1996a). *Religion and the clinical practice of psychology.* Washington, DC: American Psychological Association.

Shafranske, E. P. (1996b). Religious beliefs, affiliations and practices of clinical psychologists. In E. P. Shafranske (Ed.), *Religion and the clinical practice of psychology.* Washington, DC: American Psychological Association.

Tan, S.-Y. (1996). Religion in clinical practice: Implicit and explicit integration. In E. P. Shafranske (Ed.), *Religion and the clinical practice of psychology.* Washington, DC: American Psychological Association.

Vobdja, B. (1996, August 8). Abortion reaches wide cross-section of American women. *The Washington Post,* p. A17.

Worthington, E. L., Jr. (Ed.) (1993). *Psychotherapy and religious values.* Grand Rapids, MI: Baker.

W. M. Goldsmith

See Psychology as Religion; Counseling and Psychotherapy: Overview.

Values Assessment. Numerous scales have been developed for the purpose of values assessment. Some are broad in scope and provide a comprehensive picture of one's interests, attitudes, and values, while others are more specific and inquire into only one or two areas. Two of the most widely used measures are the Allport-Vernon-Lindzey Study of Values and the Strong-Campbell Interest Inventory.

The Study of Values was developed by Gordon Allport, P. E. Vernon, and G. Lindzey in 1951. The inventory is designed to assess the relative strength of one's values and interests in six areas: theoretical, economic, aesthetic, social, political, and religious. The items were originally formulated on the basis of the theoretical framework of Spranger (1928), a German philosopher. The final item selection used in the measure was based on the internal consistency within the six areas assessed.

The Study of Values is one of the simpler psychological tests to take, score, and interpret. Items are grouped into either two or four statements representing different values. The individual is forced to choose between the alternative statements with little if any indication as to which value is being assessed. The forced choice format reveals the relative strength of the values in that if the individual scores high in any one value, some other values must therefore be lowered. Norms are available for high school and college students and for several occupational groups.

The Strong-Campbell Interest Inventory provides information about one's basic interests and the various vocational fields that best suit these interests. This inventory is the 1974 edition of the Strong Vocational Interest Blank and reflects the culmination of years of research by Edward Kellogg Strong, Jr., and D. P. Campbell on the original inventory constructed by Strong in 1927. Two major changes include the introduction of a theoretical framework to aid in the interpretation process and the combining of the men's and women's forms, with the elimination of sex-oriented items, into a single test booklet.

Through years of research Strong and Campbell found that one's basic interests are fairly well established by early adulthood and do not radically change for most people throughout the remainder of life. The inventory consists of 325 items that assess six general occupational themes (e.g., investigative, artistic); 23 basic interest scales (e.g., science, public speaking); and 124 occupational scales (e.g., banker, priest). In five sections of the inventory one marks "like," "dislike," or "indifferent" to indicate his or her preferences having to do with occupations, school subjects, activities, amusement, and day-to-day contact with various types of people. In the two remaining sections one marks "yes," "no," or "?" to self-descriptive statements and one's preferences between paired items. The inventory is scored by computer at designated agencies. Results are expressed in numerical scores with reference to the whole sample taking the test. Also, interpretive phrases such as "high," "moderately low," and "average" are used to help the individual better understand how he or she scored in comparison with others.

Reference

Spranger, E. (1928). *Types of men.* Halle: Niemeyer.

W. W. Austin

See Psychological Measurement.

Values Clarification. An approach to moral and values education developed by Raths and his associates in the mid-1960s. It was based on some of the conceptual ideas of John Dewey and Carl Rogers. Raths wanted to develop an approach to moral education that would help people deal positively with the many value-loaded issues of complex societies. It seemed that an approach to moral education was needed that would be an alternative to either indoctrinative moralizing or complete neglect of value areas of life.

Values and Valuing. The educational approach of values clarification is based on specific understandings of values and the valuing process. Values are defined as guidelines emerging from life experiences that guide behavior in future experiences. It is believed that a person's values emerge from that person's experiences and that it is therefore inappropriate to expect one person to have or adopt the same set of values as another person. Thus it seems inap-

propriate to base moral and values education on transmitting or imposing an external set of values. The values clarification solution is to build an educational approach upon the nature of the process by which values emerge rather than upon the content of a set of prescribed values. The valuing process is the way by which one comes to hold some particular values. It is believed that a person does not truly value something unless the value emerged through this process.

Criteria for Values. Seven specific criteria for a value are based on the following elements.

Choosing Freely. It is believed that if a person has been tricked or forced into believing something or acting in a certain way, it could not be said that the person values that idea or action. Choosing freely also implies some intellectual understanding.

Choosing among Alternatives. Unless a person is allowed to choose from among alternatives, it seems inadequate to say that a free choice has truly been made.

Choosing after Thoughtful Consideration of the Consequences of Each Alternative. The key word of this criterion is *consequences.* The goodness or badness of an alternative is based on pragmatic consequences. If one alternative is truly better than another, it ought to be evident to people doing the choosing.

Prizing and Cherishing. A value is not merely any choice but something that a person is positive about. A person may at times choose the lesser of two evils, but it would be wrong to say that the choice was a real guiding value.

Affirming. One should be willing to publicly affirm or to be publicly associated with a value statement or action.

Acting upon Choices. If one really values something, having chosen it after thoughtful consideration of its consequences, then one ought to be willing to live with the consequences by acting upon the value.

Repeating. Most people can find enough courage to try something once. Such acting does not represent a true value unless the action is repeated consistently in each situation that calls for the value.

Value Education. Such an understanding of the valuing process suggests a new purpose and methodology for value education. The purpose of moral and value education is not to impose a set of external values but to respect individual freedom by helping people become more aware of the values that guide their behavior. The new methodology is based on the necessity for a person to understand alternative values. It is also based on the idea that values are not merely verbal propositional statements to be learned and repeated but are freely chosen and consistently acted-upon guidelines for behavior. Thus values cannot adequately be understood as content of instruction but as conclusions from life.

The educational process of clarification involves reflective examination of life and its value-rich situations. Personal values are examined in light of the criteria of the valuing process. A value that does not satisfy the criteria is judged not to be a personal value. The role of the teacher becomes that of a nondirective facilitator who helps a student clarify the values.

The activities a teacher uses in values clarification primarily involve asking questions and other nondirective strategies. The most popular strategies include what are known as clarifying responses and a values continuum. Clarifying responses are questions asked by the teacher to get the learner to reflect upon a particular value and how well it fits the criteria of the valuing process. The values continuum strategy involves identifying the two extreme choices of a particular value issue and then asking students to place themselves somewhere on the continuum. Students are then asked to discuss among themselves how each one has made the decision and how one's decision compares with the criteria of the valuing process. In all cases it is inappropriate for the teacher or other students to impose a set of values or right answers on a student.

Values clarification has become a very popular educational approach in K–12 schools, in nonformal education, and in Christian ministry settings. Its popularity seems to rest on three factors. First, it is a simple instructional tool to use. It requires little expertise on the part of the instructor, especially in the area of moral philosophy and social ethics. Second, it is unoffensive and safe since it does not require a specific right answer to issues of moral and social values. This factor has been especially attractive to public education in pluralistic societies. Third, there is usually a positive feeling of accomplishment when it is used. Educators feel as though they have done something important, students feel affirmed in their own values and identity, and there is usually a better atmosphere of warmth and trust developed in the learning environment.

Because the primary focus of values clarification is on the nature of the valuing process itself and on avoiding indoctrination, proponents of values clarification have always been hesitant to suggest that any one set of values is more right than another set. They claim to be able to offer a value-free approach to moral education.

Criticisms and Evaluation. Because of the value-free orientation of values clarification its conceptual foundation has been strongly criticized as being ethically relativistic. It tends to send the message that it is acceptable to believe whatever one wants to as long as it was self-chosen from alternatives, is prized, and is consistently acted upon.

A second major criticism of the values clarification conceptual foundation is that it makes no distinction between personal preferences and tastes, social and cultural values, and ethical and moral values. The values clarification technique helps people feel good about their own identity and personal tastes, but it is then indiscriminately used when one approaches moral issues. Some critics believe that because values clarification does not make a distinction between personal preferences and moral values, it should not be used with reference to moral issues.

Criticisms of the educational procedures of values clarification rest on three points. First, it appears to be too conceptually abstract and too verbal to be appropriately used with preteenagers. Since preteenagers usually respect adult opinions and actions as authoritative, it may be that a teacher using values clarification instructional techniques is imposing a set of values—including the value that all things are equally acceptable and that there is no right and wrong. Second, it is claimed that the values clarification group instructional technique ignores the strong power of peer influence upon learners. It is suggested that in any kind of group discussion the opinion leaders of the group will have more influence on the values of others than is assumed by the clarification process. Values clarification technique, it is said, ignores the sociological interaction of a learning experience and focuses only on individualistic psychological factors.

Third, the outcomes of the values clarification educational process seem to be identified with such phrases as "it works," "warmth," "trust," "feeling good about oneself." These are similar to the general outcomes associated with nondirective therapy, upon which many of the values clarification educational ideas are based. Therefore it may be that the success of values clarification is not attributable to its concepts of value, ethics, or education but to its therapeutic power.

Since its introduction in the mid-1960s values clarification's major spokespersons have been Simon and Kirschenbaum. Simon has written several practical manuals and conducted many seminars and in-service training sessions for teachers. Kirschenbaum has kept alive the conceptual thinking about values clarification through his involvement with the National Humanistic Education Center. He has offered a revision of the previously stated seven criteria and the valuing process. He has suggested that the valuing process includes five dimensions: thinking, feeling, choosing, communicating, and acting. He does not suggest this as a new orientation for values clarification but as a more comprehensive analysis of the valuing process upon which the instructional techniques are based.

Additional Readings

Kirschenbaum, H., & Simon, S. B. (Eds.). (1973). *Readings in values clarification.* Minneapolis: Winston.

Raths, L. E., Harmin, M., & Simon, S. B. (1966). *Values and teaching: Working with values in the classroom.* Columbus: Merrill.

Simon, S. B., Howe, L., & Kirschenbaum, H. (1972). *Values clarification: A handbook of practical strategies for teachers and students.* New York: Hart.

R. B. McKean

Van Kaam, Adrian L. (1921). Born in the Netherlands and ordained a Roman Catholic priest (1947), Van Kaam came to the United States in 1953. He taught philosophy and psychology at a seminary in Holland and spiritual formation as related to psychological development at Duquesne University. He received a doctoral degree in psychology from Case Western University. In 1963 he founded the Institute of Formative Spirituality at Duquesne, where he and his colleagues continued work in the science of foundational human formation or formative spirituality and formation theology. Van Kaam had founded these disciplines in his homeland in 1944.

Van Kaam is the founder and editor of the journals *Studies in Formative Spirituality* and *Envoy*. He has written more than 24 books and more than 100 articles. He is co-founder of the Epiphany Association, where he develops resources in formative spirituality.

Basic to the science of human formation is distinguishing between informative thinking and formative thinking. Informative thinking is what is done in everyday life. It has resulted in, among many things, technological advance. Formative thinking relates directly to our formation. "We are always *giving or receiving form* in our life" (Van Kaam, 1983, p. xvii). As we dwell on such experiences, unique meaning for our formation may be revealed. These discoveries enable us to have insight into the structures, dimensions, conditions, and dynamics of the human formation process. Informational thinking tends to be detached from experiential implications. It seeks solutions.

Complete dependence on the informational does not seem to be sufficient for the full flowering of human life. Formative thinking is associated with the work of spiritual masters in Eastern and Western religions. It seeks to integrate art and science as well as the insights of philosophy and theology. It focuses on themes of formation. These may reveal the structures that make it possible to see patterns among differing points of experience.

Van Kaam sees all this as appropriate to any philosophical or theological tradition. However, he concentrates on a Christian formation theory of personality. Contributions from a wide variety of arts and sciences are deemed suitable grist for the formation theory mill.

Van Kaam has been a prolific writer. The series of four books in which he sets out his theory grew into six volumes between 1983 and 1995. Besides the length, they are very dense reading. Each page is packed with information. Since the vocabulary is often used in ways unique to formation theory, the reading cannot be done quickly. The table of contents for the first volume in the series covers over eight pages. However, it is all worth reading. Van Kaam may have developed an approach to integration that, especially if simplified, could be helpful to psychologists and to clergy and laity in the church.

Reference

Van Kaam, A. (1983). *Formative spirituality,* Volume 1: *Fundamental formation.* New York: Crossroad.

E. S. GIBBS

See EXISTENTIAL PSYCHOLOGY AND PSYCHOTHERAPY; CHRISTIAN PSYCHOLOGY.

Verbigeration. Also known as cataphasia, this is the monotonous or morbid repetition of sentences, words, or phrases, usually without any apparent meaning. It is common in schizophrenic reactions, where a patient will utter the same reply to any line of questioning.

Vertigo. A psychophysiologic reaction to internal stress or conflict in which an individual feels that he or the world around him is spinning. Vertigo is sometimes caused by conditions in the inner ear or other organic disease, but it may also be a psychosomatic reaction. In the latter case vertigo may serve as a defense against unacceptable impulses or as an escape from a threatening situation.

Victims of Violent Crimes. These persons are usually distinguished from victims of domestic violence, property crimes, and harm suffered from natural or accidental injury. Victims of violent crimes are those who have innocently suffered psychological and/or physical harm resulting from some illegal activity. For example, robbery, rape, homicide, and assault are proscribed behaviors for which laws provide penalties. There are also property crimes that may cause psychological stress but that are not considered to be violent. Burglary may occur when no victim is present, but it can generate a crisis as disruptive as robbery.

A determination of who is the victim can often be technical and should be considered carefully when an agency or a member of a helping profession decides to provide assistance. Too narrow a definition may leave persons with serious psychological, physical, or social needs without service.

The Victim and Services. Historically the victim has held a role outside the criminal justice and social service systems. The criminal justice system has traditionally been unconcerned with the problems and needs of such persons. To a considerable extent the victim still has no formal status within the criminal proceedings and as a result has no specific rights or access to goods and services. After the contact with law enforcement personnel, the victim becomes a witness for the prosecution whose sole benefits are limited to those of witnesses. For those who do not perform such a role, much of the process is limited to restitution, which has historically been uncollected, or to civil proceedings against persons who for the most part are judgment-proof. Social service systems also have traditionally not viewed victims as a special group with special needs.

Consideration of the victim has grown in recent decades. Interpretation of crime statistics through victim surveys and methods of compensating victims began during the 1960s in the United States. Services for victims began in early 1974, with greater development occurring in the last half of that decade. Numerous compensation programs were initiated, and research is increasingly being focused on the forgotten person within the system.

The criminal justice system, however, still functions to a great extent either in opposition to or secondary to the interests of the victim.

Victim Perceptions and Crisis Intervention. It has sometimes been assumed that different types of victimization require different types of intervention. While it is true, for example, that the intervention with a sexual assault victim may be procedurally different from that of a purse snatching, the crisis intervention process is functionally identical. Knudten, Meade, Knudten, and Doerner (1976) found great similarity in both the needs and responses of victims of varying crimes in a sample population of two thousand persons. Research by Denton (1979) confirmed that finding.

Perceptions or assessments of situations are assumed to strongly influence emotional responses to such situations. It has been noted that victims of crime may perceive the incident as threat, loss, or challenge, depending on the degree of stress involved (Golan, 1978). High-stress situations tend to produce a perception of threat and an emotional response of anxiety. Somewhat less stress in a situation is associated with a perception of loss and emotions of depression. Low-stress situations are perceived as challenge and are accompanied by anxiety plus resolve.

Therapeutic intervention will depend largely on which of the perceptions the victim uses to define the situation. Victims generally define the events as threat, regardless of crime type, with some secondary loss perceptions (Denton, 1979). These perceptions represent the initial interpretation of the experience and are subject to change over time. Some change occurs among those who initially define the experience as a low-stress event (challenge or no-impact) and who in time come to view the event as a high-stress experience. Such changes are important to therapeutic interventions.

The counselor should focus the intervention on establishing a rapport sufficient to offer support and allow assessment of and assistance with the victim's perceptions of the event, the victim's ability and methods of coping with what for most is a short-term crisis, and organization of the client's support system.

Awareness of the victim's perceptions of the event allows the intervenor to determine and assist in managing feelings of anxiety and depression. High-stress responses should direct the intervenor to build on an accurate understanding of the experience and utilize the victim's situational supports (family, friends, clergy). Victims with challenge perceptions more often require brief support and specific information about subsequent prevention, replacement of lost items, or claims and documents.

It is important to help manage the immediate social context. In many instances close friends and relatives are upset and may themselves require assistance. It should be noted that such disturbed relationships can be as serious a threat to the victim as the initial event.

The role of the client's faith should not be neglected. Religious commitment has been found to be an important variable in predictive studies, and as such it can be a legitimate and powerful tool in the therapeutic process. Clergy and other religious associates can lend considerable situational support. The role of faith and forgiveness can provide necessary release from attitudes that hinder the healing process.

Information about and assistance with the criminal justice process is often necessary. Questions about what will happen, where, and when are anxiety-producing. Support, particularly if the offense produced a formal crisis, may be critical. The normal healing process can begin within hours and is usually resolved within 24 hours to 4 weeks. Often this process is well under way when painful experiences must be recalled and relived. Many victims find the court experience more difficult than the original victimization.

The counselor should develop resources within the community to provide immediate access to and obtainment of specific social needs. This may best be facilitated by a local victim assistance program, rape crisis center, or crisis intervention agency. The intervenor should also make provision for cases for whom the brief nature of crisis intervention is not sufficient. Other short-term therapy or psychotherapy may be indicated. Information should be collected concerning available state compensation for various fiscal losses associated with medical costs or lost work resulting from the crime.

Research has consistently isolated one centrally important service activity upon which all intervenors should capitalize. In the words of the responders, "Someone cared about me."

References

Denton, R. (1979). *What they think/what they do: A study of the perceptions and service utilization of victims of violent crime.* Unpublished dissertation, School of Applied Social Sciences, Case Western Reserve University.

Golan, N. (1978). *Treatment in crisis situations.* New York: Free Press.

Knudten, R. D., Meade, A., Knudten, M., & Doerner, W. (1976). *Victims and witnesses: Their experiences with crime and the criminal justice system.* Washington, DC: National Institute of Law Enforcement and Criminal Justice, U.S. Department of Justice.

Additional Reading

Viano, E., & Drapkin, I. (1974–1975). *Victimology: A new focus* (5 vols.). Lexington, MA: Lexington.

A. R. DENTON

See DOMESTIC VIOLENCE.

Video Feedback in Therapy. The use of videotape techniques in therapeutic treatment has developed rapidly since the acceptance of this equipment in psychological healing. Berger (1970), a psychiatrist, was a pioneer in the innovative applications of video for many settings, including training and treatment.

Video feedback may take several forms. A particular session may be taped and instantly replayed to the client, the tape may be played back at a later time, or certain sections of it may be used. As a tool in a total plan of treatment, its adaptability for particular counselors and clients is nearly unlimited and should be geared to the needs of the client. Creative counselors can find many innovative uses for videotape, both for their own diagnostic role and for increasing awareness and encouraging change in their clients.

A rationale for the use of video feedback in therapy is based on the belief that what people report what they do and think, as in a typical counseling session, is not necessarily what they actually do. Video feedback allows the client to obtain a clearer picture of himself or herself. An increase in self-awareness and the understanding of one's impact on others and others on self often lead to change. Emotional and intellectual insights gained from observing oneself in relationship to others can lead to change in image, attitude, self-concept, reactions, and behavior. Videotape provides an undistorted reproduction of the situation in which the meaning and nuances can be open to interpretation but the actions cannot. Both verbal and nonverbal communication are important indicators of self, and incongruencies can be readily pointed out and recognized with the use of video. One is able to see and experience oneself more objectively through this tool than is usually possible through other methods.

As a diagnostic tool and also a springboard for the therapeutic process video can be a powerful therapeutic resource. Initial anxiety and self-criticism are natural, and often they are followed gradually by awareness of the need for change and avenues for making that happen. With groups video feedback can take many forms, including playback without sound to facilitate concentration on nonverbal signs, taping the group's reaction to an earlier tape, and instant replay requested by any member of the group. With the premise that self-image is based on how one perceives self and how one perceives others perceive him, video feedback is a tool that facilitates bringing this process to awareness. Consensual validation has a powerful effect on an individual. It is particularly beneficial for confronting denial, discrepancies between affect and content, and verbal and nonverbal differences. Feedback can focus on a specific action or behavior that is reinforced through what the person or group can see for themselves. The group process is therefore enhanced through feedback, self-image exposure, confrontation, and testing out of new behaviors. Video feedback is also effectively used in family therapy in similar situations and for similar reasons.

The use of video equipment in therapy raises ethical issues of privacy and confidentiality. However, these issues are not insurmountable and do not substantially differ from those involved in therapy that does not employ such techniques. Video feedback will not make an inadequate or ill-trained therapist a good therapist. It is a tool that, if it is used properly and in the right hands, can be a powerful force in the therapeutic process. Beyond the traditional uses video feedback has been used effectively with delinquents and drug addicts, multiple personalities, and terminal patients, and after suicide attempts (showing the survivor the steps he or she went through in the reviving process), as well as for sexual dysfunction problems.

Reference

Berger, M. (Ed.). (1970). *Videotape techniques in psychiatric training and treatment.* New York: Brunner/Mazel.

D. L. SCHUURMAN

See SUPERVISION IN PSYCHOTHERAPY; TRAINING IN COUNSELING AND PSYCHOTHERAPY.

Vineland Social Maturity Scale. *See* SOCIAL MATURITY TESTS.

Violence. *See* AGGRESSION; DOMESTIC VIOLENCE; VICTIMS OF VIOLENT CRIMES.

Violence, Causes of. Violence is physical force or fury used to injure or damage. It is traditionally thought of as being reserved for homicide, remarkable physical injury, and damage to property. Violence, because of the political ramifications, has been reduced to examining thoughts, intentions, and words. The definition of violence has broadened to include a wide range of assertive behavior such as domestic violence, disciplining children, and sports. Some commentators go as far as to characterize violence as a public health epidemic in the United States (Bell & Jenkins, 1993). The reported increase in violence may be a result of the broadening of the definition of violence and better reporting and recordkeeping.

The causes of violence have several theories, which include the evolutionary process of humankind, inherent chemical structure, basic social learning theory, and the sinful nature of humankind. The human race from an evolutionary standpoint is considered to be predatory with a natural instinct to kill with a weapon. The reason the human race advanced over its animal ancestors was the ability to use weapons. Human beings are able to stand upright and therefore have a superior capacity to swing a club and kill (Ardrey, 1967). The violent predators would survive and pass on their killer instinct; the less violent would become extinct. Males who fought and successfully gained territory were chosen by females because they were the best providers.

Rage and violent behavior reside in the physiology of humankind, according to other authors (Rosenfeld, 1968). In a laboratory experiment animals were able to be electrically or chemically stimulated to induce rage and violence in peaceful monkeys. Once the stimulation was removed the monkeys became peaceful again. It is theorized that the difference from person to person with regard to violent behavior is the result of genetic factors.

Pines-Maya (1985) found highly aggressive people to have lower levels of 5-HIAA, which is a result of the breakdown of the neurotransmitter serotonin. In laboratory experiments low levels of serotonin showed increased violence in animals. In humans high levels of testosterone correlated with highly aggressive behavior. Research indicates there may be a chemical aspect that contributes to violent behavior.

Social learning theory suggests that violence is a learned behavior. Aggressive behavior is learned from the environment in which the person was reared. Violence is learned when the child is in an abusive violent home or in a general environment in which violence is condoned or necessary for survival. The child does not subsequently learn socially acceptable ways to control stresses in life or to express emotions. The self-image of a child is also damaged from living in a dysfunctional family. The child is not able to accept criticism or difference of opinion without overreacting with violent behavior. Other ways of modeling violence may include gun ownership and watching violence on television or in movies.

From the traditional Judeo-Christian perspective, the fallen nature of the human race is sinful and self-destructive. The basic nature of humankind allows people to be open to a variety of maladaptive behavior, including violence (Ps. 51:5; Rom. 7:5; John 8:34; Rom. 3:23). The Bible does not condone violence except for self-defense or defending one's property or country in time of war.

The Bible takes a strong position against interpersonal violence. The fundamental biblical concept that Christ is the Son of God and died for humankind's sins provides the basis for forgiveness and reconciliation. The Holy Spirit gives believers power to love with a compassion that would preclude violent reaction (John 3:16; Matt. 5:43–44; 1 Cor. 13).

The treatment of violent interpersonal behavior is through counseling, education, chemotherapy, and spiritual healing. Marriage counseling, individual insight therapy, and group therapy are usually part of any treatment approach. Education that focuses on prevention and awareness of the cause of violence can lead to behavior change. There is some evidence that the drug lithium is effective in limiting outbursts. Chemotherapy must be carefully monitored and be part of a treatment plan and not the entire treatment approach. Spiritual healing through prayer, forgiveness, and reconciliation in the context of traditional family and community values may be part of treating violent behavior.

References

Ardrey, R. (1967). *African genesis*. New York: Dell.
Bell, C. C., & Jenkins, E. J. (1993). Community violence and children on Chicago's South Side. *Psychiatry, 56*, 46–54.
Pines-Maya, M. (1985). Aggression: The violence within. *Science Digest, 93*, 36–39.
Rosenfeld, A. (June 21, 1968). The psycho-biology of violence. *Life*, 67–71.

M. A. CAMPION

See AGGRESSION; DOMESTIC VIOLENCE; VICTIMS OF VIOLENT CRIMES.

Violence, Child Witnesses of. *See* DOMESTIC VIOLENCE.

Violence, Effects on Children. Children have always been exposed to violence, but the levels of community violence that children experience, witness, or hear about have never been higher. Community violence encompasses a wide range of behaviors, including chasings by gangs, drug deals, suicides, sexual assault, physical threats, muggings and beatings, stabbings, and shootings. Children may experience, witness, or hear about these behaviors in a variety of settings, including their homes, neighborhoods, and schools.

Research on the effects of violence on children began by focusing on how war interfered with children's normal development. Descriptive reports of children's responses to wartime stress began appearing in the 1940s. These responses included intrusive thoughts, fear of recurrence, anxieties (*see* Anxiety), difficulty concentrating, depression, and sleep disturbances (*see* Sleep Disorders), as well as more severe reactions. These descriptive reports highlighted adjustment problems faced by some children; however, it was impossible to determine whether the stress reactions observed were due to particular stressors associated with war, such as bombings, evacuations, or the death or absence of parents; to the unpredictable and chronic nature of the wartime violence; or to aspects of children's environments that are unrelated to war violence.

In the past several years focus has shifted to the chronic violent conditions many children face, particularly those living in the inner cities of the United States. Recent epidemiological surveys in a variety of neighborhoods, urban and suburban, have documented that 13% to 44% of adolescents report being slapped, hit, or punched at school, up to 22% reported being beaten up or mugged in their neighborhoods, up to 33% reported being shot at or shot, and up to 16% reported being attacked or stabbed with a knife. In terms of witnessing or hearing about violence, 11% to 67% of adolescents have seen someone being beaten up or mugged in the neighborhood and 24% to 82% have seen someone beaten up or mugged at school. Between 7% and 46% of adolescents have witnessed a knife attack, and 5% to 62% have seen someone being shot or shot at. Although prevalence rates of violence exposure for elementary school-age children are lower, they are still significantly high to evoke concern. For example, 3% of school-age children in a moderately violent Washington, D.C., neighborhood reported witnessing a murder. In general children witness two to four times the amount of violence than they experience.

There is some evidence that exposure to violence differs across gender. Physical victimization at home and sexual abuse or assault occur to females more often than to males. Other forms of victimization are higher among males. Parents tend to underestimate the amount of violence to which children have been exposed.

Children's responses to violence they witness or experience differs by age. Preschoolers are more likely than older children to become dependent and clingy, regress in their levels of social maturity, and withdraw. School-age children often experience somatic complaints, such as stomachaches or headaches. School-age children may develop learning difficulties and may have difficulty concentrating as a consequence of exposure to violence. Aggressive behavior is also a typical response in this age group. Adolescents may also act out in response to community violence (*see* Acting out). Other forms of problem behavior such as substance abuse, delinquency, and promiscuity are also seen.

Moral development may also be affected by long-term exposure to community violence. Jerome Kagan has argued that children do not lose the cognitive ability to distinguish right from wrong, but the emotions that accompany knowledge of morality—guilt, shame, pride, empathy—may become blunted with prolonged exposure to violence. Because both moral knowledge and moral emotions are necessary to produce moral behavior, long-term exposure to violence increases the chances that youth will lose their capacity to behave morally (*see* Moral Development).

A number of potential clinical responses to violence have been identified. One common response is posttraumatic stress disorder (PTSD), including intrusive thinking. Intrusive thinking occurs when unwanted images of the violence pop into children's minds. Children also may experience nightmares or other sleep problems. Intrusive thinking keeps children aware of the violence even when they would rather not think about it. Other symptoms experienced by children include anxiety, fear, depression, and the development of a sense of hopelessness or fatalism about their lives. Some children may become desensitized to the violence to the point where it no longer affects their well-being.

Not all children who experience or witness violence are at equal risk for developing problems. Children from families whose parents have not graduated from high school have more of a risk of developing symptoms of fear and anxiety than do children from more educated households. Other stressful experiences in the child's life may exacerbate the effects of community violence on children's psychological health. Children from families with high levels of support from parents who have opportunities to talk about their experiences with violence are less likely to develop adverse responses.

Additional Reading

Garbarino, J., Dubrow, N., Kostelny, K., & Pardo, C. (1992). *Children in danger. Coping with the consequences of community violence.* San Francisco: Jossey-Bass.

W. KLIEWER

See DOMESTIC VIOLENCE.

Virtue, Concept of. The concept of a virtue has been a prominent ethical and psychological concept since ancient times, and it is fair to say that ethics has always, with the exception of a period in the nineteenth and twentieth centuries, been virtue ethics. The ethics of Plato and Aristotle centered on the notion of the traits of a fully functioning, psychologically healthy, and morally good person (*see* Healthy Personality). The same was true of Stoicism, as well as of other Hellenistic schools such as the Epicureans and the Skeptics. The Bible is pervaded by such virtue concepts as faith, justice, hope, love, patience, compassion, and many others. The vast second part of St. Thomas Aquinas's *Summa Theologiae* (1948) is devoted almost entirely to moral psychology, and more than half of this is devoted to virtues and vices. René Descartes (1989), in the seventeenth century, thought of ethics as being about the good person; and David Hume (1983), in the eighteenth, focused his ethical inquiries on such major traits as justice and benevolence, as well as lesser ones such as discretion, industry, frugality, cheerfulness, greatness of mind, temperance, patience, considerateness, and courage. However, from the time of the Enlightenment until about 1970, the concept of a virtue fell into eclipse, and ethical inquiry centered on discrete acts and the principles or policies enjoining them, with little attention being paid to the psychology of the good person and his or her overall adjustment to the physical and social world (happiness).

In the late twentieth century the concept of a virtue has undergone revival in both Christian and non-Christian circles, to such an extent that in the mid-1990s the concept again dominates ethical inquiry. Anscombe's "Modern Moral Philosophy" (1958) gave the original impetus, and the works of MacIntyre (1981, 1988), have been crucial. This development, which focuses interest on the nature and conditions of proper personal formation, brings ethics much closer to the concerns of psychology, especially personality theory and psychotherapy, as well as the traditions and disciplines sometimes called Christian spirituality.

A human virtue can be defined as any trait that allows its possessor to live well that life which is distinctively human. But the question, What is it to live well as a human being? is answered in various ways by various moral and psychological traditions. Thus any list of the virtues, as well as the particular concept of any single virtue, is relative to some conception of human nature and the human good, and we get rival lists of the virtues and rival conceptions of the particular virtues. The utilitarian virtues that Franklin (1964) lists in his *Autobiography*, for example, differ vastly from the ones mentioned by the apostle Paul in his letters to the Ephesians, Colossians, and Galatians. And both lists differ from the virtues commended in the letters and essays of Seneca the Stoic.

We see the same diversity among contemporary psychotherapies as we see in the history of ethics. Each psychotherapy commends some set of personality traits as healthy, mature, and fulfilling of human nature, against the background of its own distinctive conception of human nature and the human good. Carl Rogers commends congruence, Carl Gustav Jung individuation, Albert Ellis rationality and nonmusturbation (something like Stoic apathy), Heinz Kohut healthy narcissism, Murray Bowen differentiation of self (which differs markedly from Jungian individuation), Ivan Boszormenyi-Nagy justice and mutuality and gratitude, and so on. Each of these is in significant ways incompatible with as well as similar to the Christian virtues, at which any Christian psychotherapy must aim. For this reason no non-Christian psychotherapy can be used authentically by Christians without careful and profound adaptation.

References

Anscombe, G. E. M. (1958). *Philosophy 33*, 1–19.

Aquinas, Thomas (1948). *Summa theologiae*. (The Fathers of the English Dominican Province, Trans.). Westminster, MD: Christian Classics.

Descartes, R. (1989). *The passions of the soul*. (S. Voss, Trans.). Indianapolis, IN: Hackett.

Franklin, B. (1964). *Autobiography*. New Haven, CT: Yale University Press.

Hume, D. (1983). *An enquiry concerning the principles of morals*. (J. B. Scheewind, Ed.). Indianapolis, IN: Hackett.

MacIntyre, A. (1981). *After virtue*. Notre Dame, IN: University of Notre Dame Press.

MacIntyre, A. (1988). *Whose justice? Which rationality?* Notre Dame, IN: University of Notre Dame Press.

MacIntyre, A. (1990). *Three rival versions of moral inquiry*. Notre Dame, IN: University of Notre Dame Press.

Additional Reading

Roberts, R. C. (1993). *Taking the word to heart: Self and other in an age of therapies*. Grand Rapids, MI: Eerdmans.

R. C. ROBERTS

See TRUST; LOVE; FAITH; HOPE.

Visions and Voices. These are sight or sound events that have a compelling sense of reality but are not attributable to external stimulation of sensory organs. These experiences are classified as hallucinations and understood as symptoms of a psychotic process except if they occur while falling asleep, dreaming or waking or during culturally sanctioned behaviors such as religious ceremonies. Visions and voices are experienced as true perceptions of the environment, and if they are not part of culturally sanctioned activities they often lead to confusion over what is real, fearfulness, distrust of others, and unusual behaviors.

The most common hallucination, voices, are experienced as speech from unseen sources. The *DSM-IV* (American Psychiatric Association, 1994) does not distinguish between voices from inside or outside the head, although some clinicians would include as hallucinatory only those voices referenced to outside sources. The initial experience of voices may feel like a special way of knowing and occasionally they are entertaining, but over time voices usually become insulting, demeaning, accusing, and condemning. They may command the performance of certain behaviors or the avoidance of certain behaviors to avoid catastrophic consequences. The voice's content may be linked to feelings, inner conflicts, fantasies, self-concept, or life events, but the person experiences and accepts it as from another.

Visions are experienced as defined or shadowy figures, often people, or as unformed images, such as flashes of light or movements in the periphery of sight. They differ from illusions, which are misperceptions or misinterpretations of actual external stimuli. Although visions are believed less frequent in psychotic disorders, research has indicated that between 8.4% and 22% of the population reports experiencing a vision (Lindal, Stefansson, & Stefansson, 1994).

Helpful responses to persons experiencing visions and voices is accepting the reality to them of their experience, responding to the feelings created, helping them to feel safe and back in control, and not arguing. Accepted treatment for psychotic hallucinations includes medications and therapy.

From the Old Testament prophets to John's writing of the Book of Revelation, visions and voices are part of the biblical heritage. As part of contemporary worship, visions and voices would be accepted as a normal part of the culture for those who practice them as part of their religious communities.

References

American Psychiatric Association. (1994). *Diagnostic and statistical manual of mental disorders* (4th ed.). Washington, DC: Author.

Lindal, E., Stefansson, J. G., & Stefansson, S. B. (1994). The qualitative difference of visions and visual hallucinations: A comparison of a general population and clinical sample. *Comprehensive Psychiatry, 35,* 405–408.

B. E. ECK

See HALLUCINATION.

Vocational Counseling. Vocational counseling historically has been organized around the premise that "social progress must be engineered more by the improvement of man as learner, worker, and citizen than by the improvement of man's physical technology" (Wrenn, 1964, p. xi). Although there is no general agreement on the precise origin of the vocational counseling movement (some would attribute it to Frank Parsons at the turn of the twentieth century), it emerged as an integral part of the ideological, industrial, urban transformation of America.

The human and the technological have become almost a unity in the world, but the vocational counseling movement has through the years developed more sophisticated theories and applications regarding the human side of the equation. Together theory and application represent vocational development and vocational counseling, each dependent on the other.

Theories of vocational development are the base upon which vocational counseling rests. Initially, vocational theories focused on occupations and, through descriptions of the characteristics of people successfully employed in them, merely matched people and positions. In the 1950s more dynamic theories of careers emerged that dealt with how people choose, enter, and progress in their vocations, which were conceived of in a broader sense than just a job. Instead of studying occupations as static entities, whereby prediction of success in an occupation is treated as though the position and the characteristics of the person filling it would remain the same throughout the person's lifetime, theorists began to look at the whole sequence (the career) of work experiences occurring during the course of a person's life (Super, 1969).

With the new emphasis on career as a sequence of changing personal characteristics and work experiences, theorists began to make use of the concept of life stages. Eli Ginzberg, Robert Havighurst, Anne Roe, Donald Super, and David Tiedeman made major contributions to the understanding of the lifelong process of decision making and the relationship of needs, values, interests, coping abilities, and self-concept to career decision making. In addition, Super and Crites have worked extensively on the concept of vocational maturity, noting the difference between the ability to plan and the ability to deal with realistic preferences.

It should be obvious that the applied side of the movement, vocational counseling, is much more involved than just matching a person to a specific job. Crites (1974) has reviewed the major approaches and contrasted them along the dimensions of diagnosis, process, outcomes, interview techniques, test interpretation, and use of occupational information. Diagnosis is the hallmark of the trait-and-factor approach, the first of five that Crites reviews. He caricatures it as "three interviews and a cloud of dust," or assigning a battery of tests (interview 1), interpreting the test results (interview 2), briefing the client on the use of the occupational information file (interview 3), and sending the client on his or her way (cloud of dust) without having tried or changed a thing.

According to Crites, the trait-and-factor approach does have enough assets to find expression in one form or another in most of the other approaches. The person-centered approach, while highlighting the importance of the client's participation throughout the entire decision-making process, has a hard time introducing information into the interview process. The psychodynamic approach broadens the process by including internal motivational factors, but at times it can be excessive. With its greater emphasis on maturational than motivational factors, the developmental approach, which is founded on Super's theory of vocational development, is favored by Crites as the most comprehensive and coherent of the various vocational counseling approaches. Finally, rather than focusing on the antecedents of vocational behavior, the behavioral approach focuses on the conditioning of vocational behavior by its consequences. This has the advantage of emphasizing the actual behaviors involved in the decision-making process.

A recent development has been to move away from the one-on-one interview to a group-oriented approach. This has helped to correct some of the sex bias and lack of information regarding career opportunities for women that can go undetected in the interview approach. Career decisions can be made anywhere, but learning God's will is going to occur more freely in the company of fellow believers. It is important that we seek first the kingdom of God as our calling, and within the context of the body of believers begin to select those work activities that bring honor and glory to the Lord and further his kingdom (Farnsworth & Lawhead, 1981). It is likely that by praying, studying the Bible, and utilizing whatever professional resources are available as a group of Christians committed to one another, each person will be more likely to relate the occupation he or she chooses to the needs of others. The Christian's career is not a personal possession but service to others.

References

Crites, J. O. (1974). Career counseling: A review of major approaches. *The Counseling Psychologist, 4* (3), 3–23.
Farnsworth, K. E., & Lawhead, W. H. (1981). *Life planning: A Christian approach to careers* (Rev. ed.). Downers Grove, IL: InterVarsity Press.
Super, D. E. (1969). Vocational development theory: persons, positions, and processes. *The Counseling Psychologist, 1* (1), 2–9.

Wrenn, C. G. (1964). Preface. In H. Borow (Ed.), *Man in a world at work*. Boston: Houghton Mifflin.

K. E. FARNSWORTH

See STRONG-CAMPBELL INTEREST INVENTORY; APPLIED PSYCHOLOGY.

Volition. *See* WILL.

Vows. Vows are solemn promises, pledging one's word of honor, entering a covenant, the taking of an oath before God to carry through a specific action or a particular lifestyle. These commitments might be done in private, between the individual and God only, or in public, most often in the community of believers or a group united by a common cause. Marriage vows or commitment to a religious lifestyle such as poverty, chastity, or celibacy have implications for society as well as being obligations to God. These promises then may take the form of a public declaration.

Vows connote a certain devotion and dedication to staying on a course of disciplined and steadfast quest to pursue one's ideals and the good and true, such as the teachings of Christ or God. Freely choosing to bring ourselves more in line with what we perceive to be the path in which God leads us brings us into a deeper relationship with God. Yet, precisely because we realize that such a choice may extend beyond our usual human abilities, we may find it necessary to enter a rigorous and precise contract with God and to acknowledge that only with God's help will we be able to keep it. Vows are not tests of individuals' ability to keep a solemn promise but rather a significant symbol and sign that inward longing for closeness to the Other takes on the more tangible semblance of a serious commitment and formal contract.

Under certain circumstances vows might be broken temporarily or permanently. Marriage vows might be broken if adultery or another serious breach of the marital relationship exists. A vow of silence might be nonbinding if speaking out saves lives. Vows may cease not only if integral conditions change but also if vows are time-related or if it is deemed by a religious body (as the Roman Catholic church has historically claimed) that serious impediments exist to the vow being fulfilled.

Vows have been found in paganism, Hinduism, Buddhism, Jainism, Judaism, Islam, Christianity, and other religions. Deuteronomy 23:21–23 warns that once made, a vow had to be fulfilled. First Samuel 14:24 speaks of the oaths invoking a curse upon those who did not fulfill a vow. Prophets often admonished people for casually taking vows and insincerely carrying them out. The connection between vows and consecration is evident in early Christian tradition, with Christians committing themselves to live in specific ways.

C. A. RAYBURN

See PROMISES.

Voyeurism. The act of achieving sexual pleasure by furtively watching others disrobing or in a state of nudity. The voyeur, or peeping Tom, is generally a young male who obtains sexual gratification by looking at the genitals of another or by observing sexual acts. To be able to see others in one of these states the voyeur will often peer in windows at night. While watching, or peeping, the individual may engage in masturbatory play, sometimes to orgasm (*see* Masturbation).

This desire to see by stealth is so intense that it surpasses in importance the normal sexual act. The voyeur is not interested in making contact with the person of his sexual desires. His primary interest is to achieve orgasmic expression by viewing others. If he is apprehended, it is for loitering and prowling. Rarely does he become a more serious sexual deviant.

Viewing others in various stages of undress occurs on a continuum from secretly looking at pornographic magazines or advertisements of female underclothing to going to peep shows or to bars where nude dancing is provided. These more legitimate forms of peeping are harmless to others. On the other extreme of the continuum is the socially isolated person who prowls the neighborhood looking for the opportunity to see something. He will often sneak around backyards and come up to bedroom windows, peering through cracks in the curtains. Although he is harmless, the threats imagined by the one watched are often traumatic.

This pattern of behavior may develop when the normal curiosity of youth is coupled with shyness, inadequate relations with the other sex, or experiences that titillate the curiosity, such as peep shows or magazines. Viewing the body of an attractive female is quite stimulating sexually for most males. The privacy and mystery that generally surround sexual activities tend to increase curiosity about them. Peeping satisfies some of the curiosity and to some extent meets the voyeur's sexual needs without the trauma of approaching a female and thus without the failure and lowered self-status that such an approach might bring. The suspense and danger associated with peeping may intensify the emotional excitement and sexual stimulation.

Liberalization of laws concerning adult movies and magazines have probably removed much of the secrecy from sexual behavior. They provide an alternative source of gratification for would-be peepers. However, the voyeur's need to spy on sexual behavior of unsuspecting couples is still met only in peeping.

L. N. FERGUSON

War, Psychological Effects of. Professional psychology in the United States regularly has mobilized in support of war efforts since the call for extensive mental testing of military personnel in World War I (WWI). Again during World War II (WWII), the American Psychological Association (APA) set up an Emergency Committee in Psychology, one subcommittee of which produced a popular book for soldiers entitled *Psychology for the Fighting Man.* Similarly in response to the Persian Gulf War APA organized a massive counseling assistance program for families of military personnel.

Sustained professional interest in the psychological effects of war trauma began to appear in the scholarly literature during WWII. Since that time research on war effects has grown in response to more than 120 additional wars, 22,000,000 war-related deaths, and many times that number of war-traumatized survivors, the large majority of whom have been civilians. Most data arising from war settings are descriptive, consisting of anecdotal evidence and clinical observations. Systematic quantitative data have been collected in a few conflict settings such as Northern Ireland, Israel, and South Africa, or in nonconflict settings in the West among refugee peoples who had fled wars. Only recently has the field of psychology begun to recognize that it has an additional role in analyzing war effects; that is, to counter the social psychology of armed conflict with nonviolent and cooperative responses. Two recently formed organizations are evidence of this recognition: The APA Division of Peace Psychology and the Committee for the Psychological Study of Peace of the International Union of Psychological Science.

Psychological effects of war trauma vary according to many factors. These include the immediacy, duration, and degree of violence; level of overall security; intrapersonal resources; social support systems; social and historical context, such as being a member of the politically disenfranchised or of a governing elite; socioeconomic context, such as employment status; and cognitive appraisal (i.e., the personal significance an individual places on the armed conflict). Within these various contexts the risk and extent of war-related stress can be predicted according to the degree of actual loss or threat of loss and the coping resources available to the individual.

Persons at risk for war-related stress include combatants and civilian adults and children in settings of active armed conflict; combatants and civilians outside of immediate danger zones but at risk for entering such settings; and persons outside of immediate danger zones but who are potential targets of terrorism. These combatants and civilians are at personal risk for death or injury or for the trauma of witnessing death or injury of others. Often separated from family, they have experienced multiple transitions in roles and activities in a very short time. In addition, civilian populations forced to flee their homes also face the stressors of community breakdown; inconsistent access to food, water, and shelter; atemporal attitudes (i.e., they long for the past; they have no investment in the present; they have little confidence in their uncertain future); and adaptation, even acculturation, in the eventual resettlement area. Also at risk for war-related stress are families or loved ones of members in any of the aforementioned groups. Families left behind are burdened with new and multiple roles, financial pressures, fear for the safety of their loved ones, and disruptions and negative reactions in their children's lives. Due to role changes, even reunions with their loved ones can be times of stress. Finally, persons living in safety but who are socially or psychologically fragile and thus particularly vulnerable to the instabilities and insecurities of a nation or community involved in conflict are also at risk for war-related stress.

The APA Task Force on War-Related Stress delineated a series of common stress reactions relevant to those affected by war. They include guilt about actions; shame over failure; excessive drinking or drug use; uncontrolled or frequent crying; sleep problems (*see* Sleep Disorders); depression, anxiety, and anger; stress-related physical illness, such as headaches or stomachaches; inability to forget scenes of horror from the war; difficulty concentrating or excessive ruminating; social isolation; blunting of emotions; suicidal thoughts and plans; and various signs of family stress. These may be evident singly or in a variety of combinations; likewise the severity of reaction may vary from brief and mild experiences to decades long, full-blown posttraumatic stress disorder (PTSD). General symptoms of PTSD include reexperiencing the traumatic event(s) through nightmares, flashbacks, or intrusive recollections; avoidance or withdrawal from the outside world; and increased arousal, such as exaggerated startle responses.

Children may provide additional patterns of responses. Since they are less likely to recognize their stress-related problems or to speak directly about them, effects may emerge indirectly in school work, relationships with peers and with family members, and in regression to behavior associated with earlier chronological ages. Reactions in young children in particular often mirror the reactions of their parents. Little is known about the effects on children of actual participation in armed conflict. Psychosocial outcomes appear related to cultural definitions of childhood and associated role expectations, social support, and degree of coercion in entering combat. For example, an Afghani boy praised by his community while fighting alongside family members in a war declared holy by the local mullah may show few signs of war-related stress. In contrast, a Mozambican boy forced by a guerrilla combat unit to commit violent murders against unarmed civilians both to desensitize and to initiate him may well suffer the full symptomatology of PTSD and more.

Many children thrive in spite of war traumas. This resilience in children is associated with good social skills, high internal locus of control, good problem-solving skills, social support from family and the wider community, and stable and healthy living conditions.

Communities also can experience resilience in the midst of war through participatory community development, even when they are forcibly displaced. This has been demonstrated around the globe particularly in communities whose members work cooperatively and share a common religious faith. Attributions of collective efficacy result when social systems are again established with known boundaries, social norms, and expectations; however, power and decision making are shared among the community's membership. This often results in changed gender roles and can have a particularly empowering effect on women.

Psychological effects of war are not limited to stress reactions to traumatic events. They also include social psychological responses that initiate, maintain, or reduce violent intergroup conflict. Psychological processes of perception, motivation, emotion, identity, and social interaction are all relevant. For instance, perceiving events from one's

societal point of view only permits misperception of adversaries' intentions and expectations, as was the case in the Cuban missile crisis or the Persian Gulf War. The social psychology of ingroup bias can lead to exaggerating the positive traits of one's own group while exaggerating the negative traits of one's adversaries. Stereotyping adversaries' perversities results in perceiving them as less than human, permitting one no longer to identify with them and consequently to treat them in ways one would never wish to be treated. This was clearly evident in the ethnic cleansing horrors in Bosnia. Likewise psychological processes can lead to nonviolent solutions to conflict. These include encouraging conflicting groups to work cooperatively for shared goals, nurturing realistic empathy to humanize and create a more complex view of one's perceived adversary, and creating larger shared or overlapping group identities, as are occurring today in Northern Ireland between Roman Catholic and Protestant communities.

Additional Readings

Cairns, E. (1996). *Children and political violence.* Oxford: Blackwell.

Hobfoll, S. E., Spielberger, C. D., Breznitz, S., Figley, C., Folkman, S., Lepper-Green, B., Meichenbaum, D., Milgram, N. A., Sandler, I., Sarason, I., & van der Kolk, B. (1991). War-related stress: Addressing the stress of war and other traumatic events. *American Psychologist, 46,* 848–855.

Wilson, J. P., & Raphael, B. (1993). *International handbook of traumatic stress syndromes.* New York: Plenum.

M. D. Roe

See Trauma.

Watson, John Broadus (1878–1958). Father of American behavioral psychology. Born and reared in Greenville, South Carolina, he received an M.A. from Furman University and then went to the University of Chicago, where he received his Ph.D. in 1903 and remained as an instructor. In 1908 Watson left Chicago for Johns Hopkins. Forced to resign from Johns Hopkins in 1920 due to adverse publicity about his divorce, he subsequently entered the advertising business.

While he was in Chicago, Watson began studying the relationship between animal and human behavior and helped found an animal laboratory. This work was continued at Johns Hopkins. The first published statement of his behaviorist views was in an article entitled "Psychology as the Behaviorist Views It" (1913). Watson's most important books include *Behavior, an Introduction to Comparative Psychology* (1914), *Psychology from the Standpoint of a Behaviorist* (1919), and a semipopular book, *Behaviorism* (1925).

Watson led the revolt against introspection, the study of conscious experience, which then dominated American psychology. He noted that introspection is not suited to the study of animals. An avowed materialist, he objected to concepts such as mind, consciousness, volition, and emotion, stating that psychology should be the science of directly observable behavior. Watson advocated direct observations of behavior and adopted the conditioned reflex method of Russian physiologist Ivan Pavlov.

A strong environmentalist, Watson believed that the conditioned reflex is the basic learning mechanism. His conditioned reflex method has come to be known as classical conditioning or respondant conditioning.

B. F. Skinner's research indicates that most behavior is operant rather than reflexive in nature and that the conditioned reflex plays a much more minor role than Watson believed. Genetic and other biological factors also clearly play a much larger role than Watson recognized. However, strict materialism and emphasis on the study of observable behavior continue to characterize modern behaviorism, and Watson's role as the founder of American behaviorism remains secure.

R. K. BUFFORD

See BEHAVIORAL PSYCHOLOGY; CONDITIONING, CLASSICAL.

Weber, Ernst Heinrich (1795–1878). German physiologist who laid the groundwork for experimental psychology. The son of a theology professor, he was born in Wittenberg. He completed his early studies at Wittenberg and was awarded the doctorate in 1815 at Leipzig, where he spent his entire career, teaching anatomy and physiology from 1817 until his retirement in 1871.

Weber made contributions to all areas of physiology. His publications include research on the physiology of the circulatory system, the ear, the eye, the liver, and especially the skin. He published a Latin monograph, *On Touch* (1834), and an article in Wagner's *Handbook of Physiology* (1846) in which he further elaborated his findings on the skin senses. Although both are now considered classics, his findings attracted little attention until the publication of *The Sense of Touch and the Common Sensibility* (1851).

In *On Touch* Weber announced his discovery of what came to be known as Weber's Law. This was a statement of the first quantitative law in psychology. Weber set out to determine the smallest difference between two weights that could just be discriminated, the just noticeable difference. He found this to be not a given value but a constant ratio. For example, if the ratio is 1:40, a weight of 41 grams is reported as being just noticeably different from one of 40 grams. Weber conducted experiments on other senses and found other ratios but generally found the ratio was a constant within any sense. Although he did not realize it at first, this was the beginning of psychophysics, later developed by Eachner.

Weber also determined the accuracy of the two-point threshold, the distance between two points needed before subjects report feeling two distinct sensations. If the distance is less than this threshold, subjects report feeling only one point; if more, they report two points. He found that the two-point threshold differs in various parts of the body, that it is very small for the fingertips and large for the back. This was the first systematic, experimental demonstration of the threshold, a concept widely used in psychology even today.

He also contributed articles on the improvement of medical education, emphasizing the need to adopt scientific methods. He urged the application of scientific findings and was a cofounder of the German Polytechnic Society.

R. L. KOTESKEY

See SENSATION AND PERCEPTION; EXPERIMENTAL PSYCHOLOGY.

Wechsler Intelligence Tests. The Wechsler Scales are a collection of intelligence tests for children and adults. Created by David Wechsler, these scales are the most commonly used instruments for providing intelligence quotients, or IQs. Three types of IQ scores are provided: a full-scale IQ, which is a measure of overall intellectual functioning; a verbal IQ, which represents auditory-vocal intelligence; and a performance IQ, which reflects visual-motor ability. To calculate IQs, examinees' scores are compared to persons of their age group, resulting in an average IQ score of 100.

The verbal IQ measures the overall ability to distinguish between subtle differences in verbal concepts and the ability to synthesize words so that they convey developed thought processes. There are six verbal subtests. The information subtest measures acquired knowledge and long-term memory, while the similarities subtest assesses abstract verbal reasoning ability. The vocabulary scale taps the ability to verbalize the meaning of words, and the comprehension subtest measures social judgment and common sense. The arithmetic scale focuses on the ability to concentrate and focus, and the digit span subtest measures immediate auditory memory, attention, and sequencing.

The performance IQ is determined by subjects' abilities to respond quickly to various tasks involving visual-motor skills and nonverbal reasoning. They include picture completion, which reflects the ability to detect visual detail; coding/digit symbol, a measure of visual-motor speed, attention, and concentration; picture arrangement, which focuses on perceptual organization and logical sequencing ability; block design, which measures logic and reasoning in spatial relationships; and object assembly, which taps the ability to synthesize concrete parts into meaningful wholes.

Clinicians routinely compare examinees' verbal IQ to their performance IQ to determine if the differences between them are large enough to be considered statistically relevant. Large differences typically indicate that examinees are more developed in either verbal or performance skills. IQ testing is helpful not only to compare intellectual functioning within an age group but also to compare persons' strengths and weaknesses relative to their own abilities. For example, verbal subtests are typically compared to determine if specific types of verbal abilities are a relative advantage or disadvantage for a person; performance subtests are also compared in this manner.

Adults ranging in age from 16 to 74 take the Wechsler Adult Intelligence Scale, Revised (WAIS-R). The WAIS-R is a descendent of the Wechsler-Bellevue Intelligence Scale (Form I), which was created in 1939. Children ranging in age from 6 to 16 take the Wechsler Intelligence Scale for Children, Third Edition (WISC-III). This scale can be traced to the Wechsler-Bellevue Intelligence Scale (Form II), developed in 1946. The WISC-III also contains two supplemental performance scales: mazes and symbol search, which are optional. The Wechsler Preschool and Primary Scale of Intelligence, Revised (WPPSI-R) is currently used in measuring the IQ of children ages 4 to 6. Several subtests on the WPPSI-R were modified from the other Wechsler scales to ensure their appropriateness for younger children.

All of the Wechsler scales require individual administration from trained examiners. The examiners follow specific instructions during the administration, which ensures that all examinees are tested under similar conditions. Clinicians often administer some type of achievement measure to determine if examinees have learned academically at a level consistent with their intellectual potential.

T. J. Aycock

See Intellectual Assessment; Intelligence; Psychological Measurement.

Wertheimer, Max (1880–1943). One of the three originators of Gestalt psychology. Born in Prague, Czechoslovakia, where his father directed a commercial school, he studied law at the university there. He later shifted to the study of philosophy and psychology, finally going to Würzburg, where he received a Ph.D. degree in 1904.

Little is known about Wertheimer's activities between 1904 and 1910, but he spent time in Prague, Vienna, and Berlin. In the summer of 1910, while on a train from Vienna to the Rhineland for a vacation, Wertheimer conceived a new way to deal with apparent movement. He got off the train at Frankfurt, bought a toy stroboscope, and began testing his hypothesis in his hotel room. He contacted an old friend at the University of Frankfurt who offered him a tachistoscope and introduced him to two new assistants at the Psychological Institute. These assistants, Wolfgang Köhler and Kurt Koffka, had completed their degrees within the last two years, and they became Wertheimer's first two subjects. From that time on their lives and work were intricately interwoven in Gestalt psychology.

Wertheimer lectured at Frankfurt until 1916, when he went to the University of Berlin. During World War I he conducted research of military value on listening devices. In 1929 he was granted a professorship at Frankfurt, but he stayed only until 1933, when he was among the first group of refugee scholars to arrive in New York. He joined the New School for Social Research in 1934 and remained there until his death.

Wertheimer's work on apparent movement, the phi phenomenon, led to the emphasis on the whole of experience rather than on the elementism of the structuralists. This emphasis on the whole is illustrated in his principles of organization describing how our perception is naturally organized. Objects near each other tend to be grouped together, as do objects that are similar. If certain parts of our perceptual organization are left out, we tend to complete it, to make the Gestalt complete.

Wertheimer's other major contribution is reflected in the title of his only book in English, *Productive Thinking* (1945). All of the cognitive processes are redefined in terms of the conception of Gestalt. His essential argument is that recentering takes place in problem solving so that new forms of figure-ground organization occur. Wertheimer was the least published of the Gestalt leaders, but his articles were pivotal.

R. L. Koteskey

See Gestalt Psychology.

Wholistic Health and Therapy. See Holistic Health and Therapy.

Will. Although we know by experience that we have the ability to commence or cease behavior and in so doing manifest the presence of a volitional component in our personality, the interest of psychologists in this subject has been minimal. This is rather surprising, since Wilhelm Wundt and William James, two of the key historical figures in psychology, contributed much to an understanding of the will. James, for example, argued that self-initiated behaviors are the consequence of mental images of the act that is to be performed. When we conceptualize a certain idea and when that moves us into an action we are capable of performing, will has been demonstrated. In contrast, a wish involves a similar process, but we are incapable of engaging in the conceptualized behavior. Wundt, an avowed determinist, posited that the problems of psychology are problems of volition, a position that led to his voluntarism movement.

As the discipline of psychology developed at the turn of the twentieth century, concern with volition waned and an antimentalistic approach came in vogue. Global concepts such as will, intention, and self-control were replaced by more scientifically credible terms such as drive, motive, conscious, and unconscious. Implicit in this movement was a deterministic model, which was epitomized in both the psychoanalytic and behavioristic traditions and which facilitated a rejection of the self-determined, self-directed person. This change in orientation is understood best in the context of the philosophical and scientific heritage of the field. Danziger (1979), for example, has argued that although Wundt is known for his structuralistic scientific approach to psychology, there is evidence to suggest that he never intended it to be other than a branch of philosophy. In essence the tension surrounding volition is a conflict between scientific respectability and philosophical integrity. Irwin (1942), referring to this issue, concludes that psychologists have avoided volition because of the importance of experimental methods, so that "problems have been determined by methods rather than methods by problems" (p. 115).

In 1968 a symposium at the American Psychological Association meetings entitled "Whatever Happened to the Will in American Psychology?" raised an important historical question and stimulated a renewed interest in volition (e.g., Gilbert, 1970; Kimble & Perlmuter, 1970), as did a conference in England on the philosophy of psychology in 1971 (Brown, 1974). However, the content and methodology of North American psychology is still not greatly concerned with the subject.

The Will in Psychology. One might best understand the current status of volition by considering it from five theoretical viewpoints: behavioristic, developmental, experimental, psychoanalytic, and humanistic psychology.

In *Beyond Freedom and Dignity* (1971) B. F. Skinner posits that a belief in an autonomous person who is responsible for self-directed action is fallacious and comes from a lack of understanding of the real cause of human behavior: the environment. This empty-box view of human beings precludes any investigation of volition. In contrast, both Erik Erikson and Jean Piaget stress the importance of volition in the development of the child.

Erikson, in outlining the autonomy versus shame and doubt stage of ages two to three, claims that an inevitable clash of wills occurs between parents and children. Ideally a firmly supportive atmosphere for the child will create a control of the will without a loss of self-esteem. In a slightly different vein Piaget conceptualizes the development of will as being based on self-identity and disequilibrium in moral conflicts. When a child leaves the early egocentric stages for growth, the expenditure of energy in decision making is based on the will reestablishing the priority of various values. As a result the child, faced with the conflict of watching television or doing homework, exercises the will and determines an appropriate course of action based on the internalized value system.

Westcott (1983) has suggested that will may be researched as an experience in and of itself rather than as an objective quantifiable entity. Although a body of experimental research looking at the issues of volition, control, and freedom does exist (Brehm & Brehm, 1981), he argues that an understanding of the phenomenology of volition is most appropriate. Rather than laboratory work, what is needed is dialectic and semantic investigation in terms of how people describe will when they are confronted with choices. Westcott perceives his sample not as subjects but as respondents or coinvestigators.

Sigmund Freud's first published case, Frau Emmy von N., raised the issue of will versus counterwill. He suggested that when we want to do something, a counterwill responds. In times of stress and fatigue we find ourselves following the defeating messages and go against our will. Shapiro (1981) similarly argues that although those people with rigid personalities describe a weakness of will in decision making, the reality is that they have underlying unrecognized wishes and intentions. Carl Gustav Jung followed a similar line of argument in claiming that will is part of consciousness and is influenced by unconscious instincts. Otto Rank, the neo-Freudian, saw the central problem of life as being the exercise of the will. The neurotic, in fleeing from responsibility, experiences defeat and a lack of will to independence. The therapeutic process is a reinforcing of the fact that in order to grow and develop, the patient needs to choose responsibly even to the extent of challenging the analyst and setting a time for termination.

Humanistic psychology, represented by Rollo May, Abraham Maslow, and others, reacted to the deterministic influence of psychoanalysis and behaviorism, claiming it undermined personal responsibility. A person always has the capacity to choose and experience freedom, and the will has the power to affect any environmental influence.

The Will in Theology. Although the biblical concept of heart is often stereotyped as the seat of the emotions, this captures only one component of its function. In actuality the heart is all that is within, including the cognitive, emotional, and volitional. Paul's appeal to "believe in your heart" (Rom. 10:9, NIV) is a holistic emphasis that touches all of who we are. Subsumed under this is the issue of choosing or willing. Similarly when Jesus, referring to the Jews, said, "You refuse to come to me" (John 5:40, NIV), he also stressed the fact that "You do not have the love of God in your hearts" (John 5:42, NIV). A lack of cognitive and emotional understanding produced a constraint of the will to choose correctly.

The Christian who understands "Rejoice in the Lord always" (Phil. 4:4, NIV) recognizes that this injunction is an appeal to the will, since it is a command; but the intent of the verse goes beyond the will into the cognitive and emotional. It is not a blind choice but a full appreciation and experience of the Lord and who he is. A careful reading of other New Testament commands shows that they also are an appeal to the whole person.

As to its origin, volition is usually seen by Christians as being part of the image of God in humans (Berkhof, 1939). As such it mirrors one of the characteristics of God. Although humankind's ability to choose in the right direction was marred by the fall, it did not deny one's capacity to choose.

Recognizing will as part of the image of God, much current popular Christian psychology has been influenced by the cognitive behavior modification tradition, in which freedom to choose one's thoughts and emotions is stressed. Rychlak (1979), in commenting on the popular psychologies, has suggested that one reason the self-help movement works is because of its stress on the power to choose and overcome one's circumstances. The potential problem for the Christian counselor, however, is that an excessive preoccupation with this approach will implicitly deny the holistic emphasis contained in the biblical concept of heart.

In sum, Christians in articulating their own position on the will need to remain loyal to the interrelatedness of all the components of the whole person.

References

Berkhof, L. (1939). *Systematic theology*. Grand Rapids, MI: Eerdmans.

Brehm, S., & Brehm, J. (1981). *Psychological reactance: A theory of freedom and control*. New York: Academic Press.

Brown, S. C. (Ed.). (1974). *Philosophy of psychology*. New York: Barnes & Noble.

Danziger, K. (1979). The social origins of modern psychology. In A. R. Buss (Ed.), *Psychology in social context*. New York: Irvington.

Gilbert, A. (1970). Whatever happened to the will in American psychology? *Journal of the History of the Behavioral Sciences, 6*, 52–58.

Irwin, F. W. (1942). The concept of volition in experimental psychology. In F. Clarke & M. Nahm (Eds.), *Philosophical essays in honor of Edgar Arthur Singer, Jr*. Philadelphia: University of Pennsylvania Press.

Kimble, G., & Perlmuter, L. (1970). The problem of volition. *Psychological Review, 77*, 361–384.

Rychlak, J. F. (1979). *Discovering free will and personal responsibility*. New York: Oxford University Press.

Shapiro, D. (1981). *Autonomy and rigid character*. New York: Basic.

Skinner, B. F. (1971). *Beyond freedom and dignity*. New York: Knopf.

Westcott, M. R. (1983). Volition is a nag. Paper presented at Research Conference in Honor of Richard L. Solomon, University of Pennsylvania.

R. WILSON

See DETERMINISM AND FREE WILL.

Will Therapy. A form of treatment associated with Otto Rank who assumed that the central element in neuroses was the birth trauma. He believed this trauma to lead to two basic desires: the desire to return to the womb and the desire to reenact separation and achieve a more satisfactory degree of independence. In will therapy patients are encouraged to assert themselves and strengthen their will, thereby moving toward independence.

Winnicott, Donald Woods (1896–1971). British pediatrician and psychoanalyst. In recent years his work has become increasingly popular among psychoanalysts and child psychiatrists throughout the world.

Winnicott differed from the pioneers in the field of psychoanalysis in two ways. First, he took the theory of emotional development back into earliest infancy, even before birth. Thus a large part of his work was devoted to the verbal exploration of what is preverbal in the history of the individual. The second difference was the way in which he presented his ideas and theories. He described himself as being nonintellectual. His thinking was shaped by his training in psychoanalysis, but his unique contribution to the general theory of psychoanalysis arose out of his clinical experience and observations.

Winnicott is best known for his therapeutic work with children. He did not always use psychoanalysis on the child but rather selected his mode of therapy according to the child's need. If he did choose to use psychoanalysis, the technique most often employed was the squiggle game—the drawing technique that he developed. This technique involves an impulsive line drawn by the therapist, which the child has to turn into something; then the child makes a squiggle that the therapist has to turn into something. After each squiggle is completed, the child free associates to it as a stimulus (*see* Free Association).

Winnicott did not attach any magical quality to the squiggle game, but he saw it as one way of getting into contact with the child so as to help the psychotherapeutic consultation come alive for both child and analyst. In this way the child's experiences as presented in the interview and the interaction between child and therapist help make the interpretation by the therapist more meaningful to the child.

Involving the parents in their child's treatment was important to Winnicott, and the squiggle game facilitated this. He would use the child's drawings in consultations with the parents to help them recognize themes and conflicts. In this way the parents could best support the child in the changes resulting from therapy.

Additional Readings

Davis, M., & Wallbridge, D. (1981). *Boundary and space: An introduction to the work of D. W. Winnicott*. New York: Brunner/Mazel.

Winnicott, D. W. (1971a). *Therapeutic consultations in child psychiatry*. New York: Basic.

Winnicott, D. W. (1971b). *Playing and reality.* New York: Basic.

B. JOSCELYNE

See CHILD THERAPY; PSYCHOANALYTIC PSYCHOLOGY; OBJECT RELATIONS THEORY; OBJECT RELATIONS THERAPY.

Women, Psychology of. The psychology of women has undergone many definitions. One recent definition that attempts to encompass earlier ones is this: "the study of behavior (not excluding male gender-role behavior) mediated by the variable of female sex . . . the psychology of women is also defined as that which includes all psychological issues pertaining to women and their experiences" (Denmark & Fernandez, 1993, p. 4). Why the formal study of woman and her experiences has emerged in the psychological discipline can be understood only from its historical roots.

Historical Context. Traditional beliefs about women significantly affected the lens by which scientists examined women's growth and experience (if they chose to examine her experiences at all). Woman as intellectually and morally inferior was the prevailing theme surrounding the discussions. Western views of woman as inferior originate in Judeo-Christian traditions and teaching. Common interpretations of the early biblical story cast woman as evil and responsible for introducing sin into the world (quotes cited from Gundry, 1986, p. 21).

Augustine: "The woman herself alone is not the image of God: whereas the man alone is the image of God as fully and completely as when the woman is joined with him."

Aquinas: "As regards the individual nature, woman is defective and misbegotten, for the active force in the male seed tends to the production of a perfect likeness in the masculine sex, while the production of women comes from a defect in the active force or from some material indisposition, or even from some external influence, such as that of a south wind."

Tertullian: "God's sentence hangs still over all your sex and his punishment weighs down upon you. You are the devil's gateway; you are she who first violated the forbidden tree and broke the law of God. It was you who coaxed your way around him whom the devil had not the force to attack. With what ease you shattered that image of God: Man! Because of the death you merited, the Son of God had to die."

These were authoritative words that have had profound impact on the views of women throughout history. Religion was the first source of knowledge for questions of human nature. Over time science has increasingly taken its place. And yet scientists approach their questions having already been shaped by their powerful cultural beliefs. Of important note as well is the fact that most of the scientists have come from the privileged class.

During the late nineteenth and early twentieth centuries two views of women influenced both scientific and popular thought.

Inferior Brains and Wombs. Early scientists searched primarily for the why of a behavior rather than question the assumptions behind the belief. This was certainly true for the research examining women's intellectual inferiority. Brain size was the popular view for determining intelligence: the larger the brain, the greater the intelligence. The faulty conclusion, therefore, was that women were less intelligent because their brains were smaller. Another view posited (albeit erroneously) that there were limiting vital forces available that had to serve both cognitive and reproductive functions. Women who diverted these vital forces to intellectual pursuits were thus limiting their reproductive capabilities. Potential sterility or at best deformity were the risks women were told they were taking if they explored intellectual ideas. Hence, the brain-womb conflict resulted, a biological argument attempting to explain women's intellectual inferiority.

Freud on Women. Sigmund Freud considered women a mystery. He even goes so far as to suggest that perhaps poets are the best source of information concerning femininity (Freud, 1961, p. 135). Freud follows his predecessors, however, in his best attempts at understanding this mystery by comparing the woman to the man. This comparison is most conspicuous when Freud attempts to explain the oedipus complex (that important psychic event that results in superego development) via the female's experience. When the female child discovers she has no penis—in effect she has already been castrated—she develops penis envy, which has many psychic consequences. The task during this phallic stage is twofold: transfer her love object (mother) to other men (initially the father) and most importantly, develop a strong superego (moral conscience). Freud asserts that upon discovering the "wound to her narcissism, she develops, like a scar, a sense of inferiority." Freud described a masculinity complex, which essentially is a contempt a woman begins to feel for her own sex, seeing it as inferior, and she insists on behaving as a man. Freud cautions that the woman must get over this masculinity complex for her to achieve "regular development towards femininity."

Freud charged that character traits that had been written about women throughout the centuries, such as women show less sense of justice and are more often influenced by feelings of affection or hostility, could be explained from this phallic period. Little girls are described as less aggressive, defiant, and self-sufficient than are boys. The reasons these little girls are so dependent and compliant is their great need for being shown affection. This affiliative need results in a large amount of narcissism. In addition, Freud regards shame to be a feminine characteristic par excellence, serving the purpose of concealing her genital deficiency. To some degree Freud alludes to the possibility that some of these distinctions may be due to social breeding rather than merely to sexual function.

The long-term consequence for superego development differs for women as opposed to men. For the boy, castration anxiety serves as an important motivator to identify with the father; in essence to introject the father and the father's values. The strength of the anxiety shapes the strength of the superego. The female child does not have that anxiety, since she perceives herself as already castrated. Hence the formation of her superego must suffer; it cannot attain the strength and independence needed for appropriate moral development. Freud knew the impact of his views when he wrote, "and feminists are not pleased when we point out to them the effects of this factor upon the average feminine character."

Freud discusses the sex differences that emerge from both instinctual dispositions and especially from the resolution of the oedipus complex. He argued that what is ethically normal for women is different than that for men because women's superegos are inexorably tied to their emotional center.

Freud's psychology of women resulted in the view that femininity, described as appropriate female development, is behavior that is passive, dependent, nurturant, and desiring motherhood. Femininity also requires a male's presence that will provide necessary strong moral guidance. These types of traits are readily apparent in the contemporary gender stereotypes: women are seen as concerned for the welfare of others (expressive or communal) and men as assertive and controlling (instrumental or agentic). Men are perceived to be stronger and more active, characterized by high needs for achievement and autonomy, and women are perceived as deferent, nurturant, and concerned with affiliation.

Early Women Psychologists. The presence of women psychologists in the history of the discipline has been rendered virtually invisible. It is the rare text that includes the contributions made by women in the formation of psychology as a scientific discipline. Both their writings and their personal experiences provide not only theoretical nuances but also the realities for women in psychology.

The entry of women into institutions of higher education was accomplished only with difficulty and by overcoming numerous obstacles. It is noteworthy that early women in psychology were attempting to work during the same time as women's role was being defined along a feminine attribution scale. These notions of femininity and the attendant role prescriptions most often prevented admission of women into graduate schools or, minimally, the allowance of women to take graduate courses for credit. This kept women from achieving the coveted and necessary Ph.D.

Family responsibilities also presented obstacles for women in their pursuit of higher education.

Women were most often expected to care for aging parents, and this responsibility is cited frequently in the historical accounts of women professionals. Not surprisingly, women found themselves caught in the conflict of choosing between marriage and career. They were advised that if they chose marriage they must use their heads rather than their hearts. In other words, they were cautioned to make decisions about marriage partners based on the ability of the two careers to mesh rather than from love.

In spite of the obstacles, early women psychologists wrote important texts, headed major departments, and held critical offices in organizations (Scarborough & Furumoto, 1987). Mary Whiton Calkins was the first woman to hold the office of president of the American Psychological Association in 1905 and the office of president of the American Philosophical Association in 1918; Milicent Shinn authored *Biography of a Baby* in 1893; Ethel Puffer Howes wrote *The Psychology of Beauty* in 1905, held academic positions at Radcliffe, Wellesley, and Simmons colleges, and became director of the Institute for the Coordination of Women's Interest at Smith College in 1925; Margaret Floy Washburn was the first woman to receive a Ph.D. in psychology from Cornell in 1894, was president of APA in 1921, was the second woman to be elected to the National Academy of Science in 1931, published more than 70 articles in the *American Journal of Psychology,* and wrote the text *The Animal Mind* in 1908; Christine Ladd-Franklin was widely known for her theory of color vision and was an international authority on the topic of vision; Kate Gordon Moore taught at Mount Holyoke, Teacher College, Columbia, Bryn Mawr, Carnegie Institute of Technology, and the University of California, eventually serving as chair at UC; Lillien Jane Martin served on the faculty at Stanford University, becoming the first woman to head a department in 1915; Naomi Norsworthy wrote the text *The Psychology of Children* in 1918.

This list of women includes only American psychologists. This does not, however, preclude the importance of early European women psychologists. Karen Horney and Anna Freud are among the better-known women who have contributed both theoretical and clinical knowledge to the field of psychology.

Current Themes in the Psychology of Women. Prior to the 1970s there was little mention of the psychology of women as an area of scientific investigation. Most psychological research included only animals or white male humans in the population sample. The irony of this lies in the importance the discipline places on generalizability. Research samples must be representative samples. Nevertheless, the idea of male as representative of the norm was so prevalent that principal investigators were unaware that 50% of the population had been excluded. Subsequent to the women's movement, the scientific investigation of gender has received increased attention and research. The American Psychological Association organized a new division in 1973 entitled The Psychology of Women (Division 35), which spawned new research methodologies and questions. Two weighty issues have guided much of the current research: sex difference and the development of gender identity.

Current Approaches Examining Sex Difference. The search for sex difference crosses almost all areas of human behavior. Whether it is to examine brain lateralization, spatial/verbal abilities, or mathematical/intuitive strengths, researchers have compared men to women in hopes of finding or not finding sex difference that can be substantiated with biological underpinnings. This search for sex difference has too frequently been replete with methodological errors and perceptual biases. Additionally, many psychologists concerned with gender question the utility of data collected on sex difference. Hare-Mustin and Marecek (1988) suggest that two types of biases frequently occur when scientists attempt to explain sex difference empirically. They discuss the alpha bias and the beta bias as the attendant result, depending upon whether one highlights or denies difference.

The alpha bias is the exaggeration of differences between groups. Researchers who hold this position work from a framework of celebrating differences, focusing on women's special qualities. This has the positive consequence of placing value on what has typically been undervalued in our society and labeled a feminine attribute (e.g., caring for others, relatedness). This has also fostered a sense of shared identity for women in addition to spawning new social ethics. The negative results have been to ignore within-group variability and particularly and perhaps most importantly deny dominant/subordinate explanations for group differences. For example, when one is in a subordinate position, one learns to place importance on relatedness, especially when it means being close to the one in power. Additionally, when one celebrates essentialism then one risks supporting the status quo. The argument becomes one of nature rather than human choice.

The beta bias is one of minimizing differences. The positive result from this position has been more equalized treatment between men and women, whether in the work force, academy, or courts. However, there are negative consequences as well. Perhaps the most critical is that this position assumes men and women are similarly situated; in other words, the playing field is level for both sexes. The realities are that there is a power and resource differential between women and men. Only women experience childbirth, and accommodating to this special need is essential and yet lost with beta bias. Another risk is that in denying difference and extolling similarity one may inadvertently reinforce the norm of the dominant group: women can and should become more like men.

Rhodes (1990) offers a third alternative that challenges centrality of gender difference and its organizing premises. Rather than merely comparing males and females as our primary way of analyzing data or even setting up our methodology, this view seeks to reformulate the hypotheses for testing to ones of social relations between and among women and to power distributions as they affect men and women.

Development of Gender Identity. How do we come to know what it means to be female? What forces shape our gender identity? Gender identity refers to a "fundamental, existential sense of one's maleness or femaleness, an acceptance of one's gender as a social-psychological construction that parallels acceptance of one's biological sex . . . it is inarguable . . . that gender is one of the earliest and most central components of the self-concept and serves as an organizing principle through which many experiences and perceptions of self and other are filtered" (Deaux & Major, 1990, p. 93). Two leading theories in the field are the feminist psychoanalytic view and the developmental gender schema theory.

Psychoanalytic Views. Chodorow (Lorder, Coser, Rossi, & Chodorow, 1981) argues that the process of being gendered is slow and that gender stereotypes are implanted in children before they are old enough to choose. She identifies the pre-oedipal stage as a critical time for gendering to occur. Due to the fact that mothers perform most of the caregiving functions, boys and girls have intense early relationships with their mothers. When the boy reaches the oedipal stage he realizes how other his mother is from himself. With identification with his father he introjects both the values and the prestige accorded to the male sex in Western society. Along with this awareness comes contempt for women as the boy learns to identify himself as separate. The mother-daughter relationship remains intense for a longer period of time because the daughter does not so readily recognize the otherness of her mother. The oedipal stage weakens the close bonds (symbiosis) but never truly severs the connection. Daughters generally stay in connection with their mothers and other women; identity formation does not require interruption. Therefore, due to the abrupt separation, boys are more prepared for the public arena, in which autonomy and independence is required. Girls are more prepared for the private arena, in which nurturance and closeness is required. Chodorow suggests that dual parenting would prepare boys and girls for competence in both arenas, public and private.

Gender Schema Theory. Developmental research shows that from birth, sex-typed behavior is imposed upon infants. Men and women view and describe female infants differently from male infants. Daughters are rated as smaller, with more fine features, softer, and less alert than sons. Sons are perceived as stronger and hardier than daughters, despite the fact that these infants do not differ by any physical attributes. Parents, particularly fathers, frequently attribute stereotypical characteristics to their infants solely as a function of infant gender. To illustrate this further, a study examining whether adults play differently with infants based on their gender found that adults offer dolls to a child they perceive to be a girl and male sex-typed toys (e.g., hammers) to a child they perceive to be a boy. The same child was used in both conditions; the researchers simply dressed the child as male or female, depending upon the condition. These studies assert that adult response is independent of differences in the child's behavior. The response was governed solely by perceived sex of the child.

When children are approximately two to three years of age they understand that they are a boy or girl and begin to organize information from the environment within their new gender schema. Around the age of four or five, the child experiences gender constancy, the realization that gender is a permanent characteristic. As the child organizes the information from the multiple sources in the environment, he or she translates the information into rules with which to conform. The child internalizes the gender lens embedded in the society, evaluates the different ways of behaving that the culture defines as appropriate, and rejects any behaviors that do not match his or her sex. Children learn very early that what parents, teachers, peers, and the church consider to be appropriate behavior varies as a function of sex; that toys, clothing, occupations, hobbies, domestic chores, even pronouns, vary as a function of sex. As children learn the contents of society's gender schema, they learn the selective attributes linked to their own sex. Children learn to apply the attributes selectively to the self, which in turn organizes their self-concept. In effect children learn to evaluate their adequacy as a person in terms of the gender schema. Cultural standards become internalized, prompting behavior to conform to the culture's definition of maleness and femaleness. Cultural myths become self-fulfilling prophecy.

Future Directions. The goal of the psychology of women should be to weave a redemptive vision for men and women in God's community. The psychology of women has challenged many of our prevailing notions of power and relationships. It has challenged our widely held beliefs concerning reason over emotion, the bifurcation of the mind and the body, the sacredness of autonomy over community and relationships. We are challenged to listen for the silent voices, to attempt to understand the devaluation that has diminished their voices. It has challenged us to listen to the angry voices, to the pain and hurt inflicted because of the differential power base. We are made aware how traditional male traits have served as the human norm.

Christians acknowledge that although we are made in God's image, we are fallen and desperately in need of Christ's redemptive vision for gender reconciliation (see Van Leeuwen, Knoppers, Koch, Schu-urman, & Sterk, 1990). Thoughtful research in the psychology of women can further the journey toward this reconciliation.

References

Deaux, K., & Major, B. (1990). A social-psychological model of gender. In D. L. Rhodes (Ed.), *Theoretical perspectives on sexual difference.* New Haven, CT: Yale University Press.

Denmark, F. L., & Fernandez, L. C. (1993). Historical development of psychology of women. In F. L. Denmark & M. A. Paludi (Eds.), *Psychology of women.* Westport, CT: Greenwood.

Freud, S. (1961). *The standard edition of the complete psychological works of Sigmund Freud* (Vol. 22). London: Hogarth. (Original work published 1923)

Gundry, P. (1986). Why we're here. In A. Mickelsen (Ed.), *Women, authority and the Bible.* Downers Grove, IL: InterVarsity Press.

Hare-Mustin, R. T., & Marecek, J. (1988). The meaning of difference: Gender theory, postmodernism, and psychology. *American Psychologist, 43* (6), 455–464.

Lorder, J., Coser, R., Rossi, A., and Chodorow, N. (1981). On *The reproduction of mothering: A methodological debate. Signs: Journal of Women in Culture and Society 6* (3), 482–514.

Scarborough, E., & Furumoto, L. (1987). *Untold lives: The first generation of American women psychologists.* New York: Columbia University Press.

Rhodes, D. L. (1990). *Theoretical perspectives on sexual difference.* New Haven, CT: Yale University Press.

Van Leeuwen, M., Knoppers, A., Koch, M., Schuurman, D., & Sterk, H. (1990). *After Eden: Facing the challenge of gender reconciliation.* Grand Rapids, MI: Eerdmans.

C. J. NEAL

See MEN, PSYCHOLOGY OF.

Woodworth, Robert Sessions (1869–1962). American experimental psychologist. After receiving his A.B. degree from Amherst College in 1891, Sessions taught high school science and college mathematics before studying psychology and philosophy at Harvard (M.A. 1897). After receiving his Ph.D. from Columbia in 1899, he taught physiology in New York City hospitals for three years and studied under Sherrington in Liverpool. In 1903 he returned to Columbia, where he remained until his first retirement in 1945. He continued teaching there until his second retirement in 1958 at 89 years of age. In 1956 he received the first Gold Medal Award of the American Psychological Foundation for his work as an integrator and organizer of psychology.

Woodworth did not belong to any school of psychology, such as behaviorism or functionalism, and he expressed his dislike for the constraints imposed by such schools. He came as near to being a truly general experimental psychologist as anyone ever did. He became a rallying point for the middle-of-the-road position in psychology.

According to Woodworth, psychology must begin by investigating the nature of the stimulus and the response. Then it must consider the organism as interpolated between the stimulus and the response. Rather than an S-R psychology, Woodworth wanted an S-O-R psychology. Psychology must study both consciousness and behavior. Observation, experimentation, and introspection are all valid methods for psychology. As early as 1897 Woodworth spoke of developing a motivology. He wanted a dynamic psychology, one concerned with the interpretations of the causal factors in change, concerned with motivation. His primary concern was with the driving forces that activate a person, with determining why people feel and act as they do.

Woodworth's list of publications is long, and his work has influenced many generations of students. His revision of Ladd's *Physiological Psychology* (1911) became a standard handbook for more than 20 years. *Dynamic Psychology* (1918) was a plea for a functional psychology that included the topic of motivation. His clear and simple introductory text, *Psychology* (1921), went through five editions by 1947 and outsold all other texts for 25 years. *Contemporary Schools of Psychology* (1931) was revised in 1948 and again in 1964. His *Experimental Psychology* (1938) was revised in 1954 and is a classic in the area. His last work, *Dynamics of Behavior,* was published when he was 89.

R. L. KOTESKEY

See PSYCHOLOGY, HISTORY OF.

Word Salad. A jumbled collection of words, expressed either vocally or in writing, that have no meaningful connection. It is caused by severe psychotic decompensation in certain thought disorders. In thought disorders looseness in associative or logical reasoning varies from occasional minor lapses in rational thought, termed cognitive slippage, to more disorderly reasoning, confusion, and incoherence. Word salad falls near the extreme of incoherence. Such difficulty represents serious disorganization in personality. It is found in some cases of acute schizophrenia, particularly hebephrenic schizophrenia. Autistic involvement and neologisms, or made-up words, usually add to the confusion of word salads.

The person expressing the word salad has little or no recognition of the incomprehensibility of his or her verbal exchange. Careful listening will sometimes allow the content to become intelligible, but only if other information about the speaker and his or her context is considered. Trying to communicate with the person in this state is futile. To reduce this symptom treatment for the psychotic condition with chemotherapy is necessary. As the intensity of the condition clears, the person will usually be able to communicate more reasonably.

M. R. NELSON

See SCHIZOPHRENIA.

Work and Play. From earliest times work and its complement, play, have been objects of human reflection. God had scarcely created the world before man got his first work assignment, to till and keep the garden of Eden (Gen. 2:15). But the first account of work predates even this, for God himself worked at creation and then rested at its completion (Gen. 2:2). These first references to work are positive. God freely chose and heartily approved of his own work (Gen. 1:31), and Adam's tasks were perfectly suited to the marvelous life of Eden.

It did not take long for this picture to change. The next chapter recounts the fall of humans and God's ensuing judgment. The ground was cursed, and man faced "toil . . . thorns and thistles . . . sweat" (Gen. 3:17–19). This is the base for the tradition that work is a curse, a penalty for sin. This view has enjoyed strong and extensive support, yet the earlier images of work as a desirable thing will not go away.

For people who see work as a curse, play is delicious shirking or an attempt to recoup one's powers for fresh work. The person who majors in play is a fool or a scoundrel. And he or she might be charged with impiety because he or she has so little regard for the force of the fall.

To say work is a curse is not to say that it serves no good purpose. If, as folk wisdom says, an idle mind is the devil's workshop, then people need someone to keep them busy at a worthwhile task such as survival. As they struggle to make ends meet, they come face to face with their own finitude, insecurity, and wretchedness. In this condition they are disposed to seek and depend on God. They may even come to see their toil as a form of expiation or purgative for evil thoughts and deeds.

The work-as-curse people stress the indignity rather than the dignity of work. Without awkward and back-breaking tasks people have room for vanity and indolence. The idle rich are too smooth and self-pleased. They need blisters and grime to acquaint or reacquaint them with their mortality and insufficiency.

Medieval monasticism did little to dignify ordinary work. The line between sacred and secular or profane activity was clear. One has only to glance at a typical monastery schedule to see that prayer and other worship were central. Rising at two in the morning, the typical eighth-century Benedictine attended his first service at two-thirty. Again and again he was recalled to worship until late-afternoon vespers signaled day's end. This was the sanctified life. All the others—the merchants, farmers, and craftsmen—went through their own dismal routines. They did not enjoy the high and peaceful callings of their more spiritual brothers. When work was to be done within the monasteries, simple, repetitive, manual labor was popular since it freed the mind for communion with God.

Martin Luther's disdain for this framework of thought is legendary. In his commentary on Genesis 13:13 he writes that mundane tasks have "no appearance of sanctity; and yet these very works in connection with the household are more desirable than all the works of all the monks and nuns" (1960, p. 349). His theological populism was infectious, and Christendom's view of work has never been the same. Luther contended that a man could be called by God to a station in the workaday world just as surely as to the traditional ministry.

As a spokesman for the dignity of ordinary work Luther was not alone. John Calvin developed this theme, and it is an integral part of Reformed thinking. Reference to Genesis 1:28 recurs in the literature. This cultural mandate generates the conviction that God's children are to bring all of creation under his blessed sovereignty. The fisherman has a part no less than the pastor. Colossians 1:15–20, with its reference to the reconciliation of all things on earth to Christ, underscores and renews the mandate in Genesis.

Max Weber's classic, *The Protestant Ethic and the Spirit of Capitalism* (1930), ties the thought of Luther and Calvin to the subsequent economic life of Europe. His work demonstrates the impact of theology on culture, and it stands over against the Marxist view that people are at base economically motivated.

Two centuries after Calvin's death the Industrial Revolution in England stimulated a fresh look at the nature of work. While there were important gains in productivity and economic vitality, the impact on men was often frightful. The predatory style of some enthusiastic capitalists left little room for worker dignity and welfare. Farmers and craftsmen laid aside their tools and trooped to the mills, where many suffered from the depersonalizing grind of factory work.

Victorian writers Thomas Carlyle and John Ruskin pinned a good deal of blame on laissez-faire economics and called for a rediscovery of the joys and honor of craftsmanship. Mass production by machine was in their estimation a life-denying institution.

Ruskin and Carlyle were upstaged by their fellow Victorian, Karl Marx. His forceful picture of oppression, with accompanying theory, prescription, and prophecy, has mustered forces of social change for the better part of a century. And at the center of this movement is a view of what human work should and should not be. A considerable body of current literature on alienation is one of his legacies, and his solution joins a host of utopian visions, including those of Plato, Tommaso Campanella, Sir Thomas More, B. F. Skinner, and millenarians.

If the nineteenth century was preoccupied with work, the twentieth has become fixed on leisure. In our time philosophers and theologians have given us a fresh understanding of and respect for play. Drawing on sources as old as Aristotle and as stolid as Immanuel Kant, they have psychologized the definitions of work and play. Whereas work was once understood in terms of physical compulsion, it is now tied to a sense of compulsion. The definition is more attitudinal than circumstantial.

On this model a person may be at play while he or she struggles to meet a business deadline. It is all in the person's perspective. If a person wholeheartedly gives himself or herself over to a task, relatively oblivious to payoffs or penalties, he or she is playing. The same person may, however, be working in the middle of a volleyball game. A frantic search for fun or uneasy attempts to gain peer approval can make volleyball work.

De Grazia (1962) in particular links work and play with time consciousness. A person at leisure and play is so preoccupied with the matter at hand that he or she loses a sense of time. Indeed, the expression *leisure time* is contradictory. The person at work is a clock-watcher, so dissatisfied with the present task that he or she constantly looks beyond it to a later, liberating moment. This person's time drags.

There has been something of a Counter-Reformation in this connection. Roman Catholic and secular thinkers alike have found fault with the Calvinistic attention to rectitude and service in every moment of life. Novak (1976) shows why play, the realm of ends rather than means, is so central to human well-being. Cox (1969) reaffirms the Roman Catholic regard for celebration. Alongside *homo faber* (man the worker) and *homo sapiens* (man the knower), Cox stands *homo festives* (man the celebrator) and *homo fantasia* (man the dreamer and mythmaker). De Grazia (1962) is naturally close to Roman Catholic sentiment, since he relies so heavily on Aquinas's favorite philosopher, Aristotle.

The controversy boils down to this: Do people work in order to play or play in order to work afresh? Calvinists are concerned that all of life become a stewardly act unto God. Play for them is essentially renewal for Christian service. The more Roman Catholic tradition gives the contemplative and celebrative life primacy, for this is our heavenly destiny. So play comes in our finest and not our furtive hours.

Each tradition counters the excesses of the other. And whether work or play is ultimate, the penultimate does not suffer dishonor, since the literature is so strongly supportive of both.

Jourard (1974), a humanistic psychologist, synthesizes the traditions in his account of the whole, healthy person. He stresses the value of work and provides guidelines for vocational satisfaction. But his counsel extends to leisure as well. The person who neglects either aspect faces turmoil and dissolution.

Virtually all Christian psychologists, theologians, and philosophers now argue that the proper Christian life, even with its suffering, should bear the marks of play. God, they reason, would have us whole, absorbed in life, and at peace. Crippling and dreary alienation is understood not as the price of Christian discipleship but as the mark of sub-Christian living.

References

Cox, H. (1969). *The feast of fools*. Cambridge: Harvard University Press.

de Grazia, S. (1962). *Of time, work, and leisure*. New York: Twentieth Century Fund.

Jourard, S. (1974). *Healthy personality: An approach from the viewpoint of humanistic psychology*. New York: Macmillan.

Luther, M. (1960). Lectures on Genesis. In J. Pelikan (Ed.), *Luther's Works* (Vol. 2). St. Louis: Concordia.

Novak, M. (1976). *The joy of sports*. New York: Basic.

Weber, M. (1930). *The Protestant ethic and the spirit of capitalism*. New York: Scribners.

Additional Readings

Gerber, E., & Morgan, W. (1979). *Sport and the body: A philosophical symposium*. Philadelphia: Lea and Febiger.

Huizinga, J. (1950). *Homo ludens: A study of the play-element in culture*. New York: Roy Publishers.

Ryken, L. (1979, October 19). Puritan work ethic: The dignity of life's labors. *Christianity Today*, 14–19.

M. Coppenger

See Healthy Personality.

Work Motivation. A worker's output, measured in either quantity or quality, can be conceptualized as the product of Ability x Motivation. Industrial/organizational psychologists dedicated to the improvement of output can accomplish this goal by improving ability (via selection and/or training of personnel) and/or by motivating workers to do more and better.

Research involving the correlations between specific motivations and specific worker-related behaviors (e.g., absenteeism, productivity) is not always informative. It is hard to quantify the strength of such motivations and in some situations, the target output variables as well. Even when precise measurement is possible, there are so many confounding variables (e.g., home life, prior experiences, the external job market) that the resulting correlations are usually low. It is not surprising that so many theories are chasing few or poor-quality data.

Universal Theories. MacGregor (1960) distilled work motivation theories into Theory X (workers are inherently lazy and need to be motivated by a combination of fear and financial gain) and Theory Y (workers are inherently social and creative and should be motivated by these higher, humanistic needs). Theory X was the assumption of the great efficiency expert Frederick W. Taylor at the turn of the twentieth century, and he has been followed by a variety of theories that make cognitive-behavioral assumptions.

B. F. Skinner's operant conditioning model (*see* Conditioning, Operant), although it developed primarily from animal research, can be applied to human employees. Such behaviorism would assume that greater rewards and rewards more intricately tied to worker efforts will motivate greater efforts.

Cognitive models also focus on workers' understanding of the link between their efforts and rewards. Equity theory and expectancy theories suggest that individual workers assess the value they bring to the position (in terms of education, experience, ability, effort) and what they get out of the job (in terms of job satisfaction, pay, benefits, prestige). If the worker thinks that what he or she is giving exceeds what he or she is getting, a likely result will be that the worker will decrease effort.

Kurt Lewin argued that the very process of making decisions can have an impact on motivation. If authoritarian management dictates a policy or goal, then the workers do not own it and have at best a limited stake in its attainment. Alternatively, when individuals have some input into the decision-making process, they will be more motivated to adhere to the resulting policies and pursue the agreed-upon goals.

Sigmund Freud is often quoted that love and work are the important aspects of life. Several of the more humanistic reinterpreters of psychoanalysis have been applied to motivation. Alfred Adler saw one's career as a way of reflecting and developing social interest; overcoming inferiority feeling through accomplishment and contribution to the larger society. Erich Fromm spoke of the productive personality as capable of mature interpersonal relationships.

Abraham Maslow's hierarchy of needs is really a hierarchy of motives. Since the lower, physiological needs have priority, they must be satisfied first. The implication for management is that workers first desire a living wage before considering safety, social interaction, esteem, or self-actualization. As each need is met, the next comes to the fore as the one that is the main motivation.

Individual Differences. Individual differences between workers can result in differences in the level or type of motivation. Adler said that each person has a different set of guiding fictions in his or her quest to overcome inferiority feelings. Three laborers on the same job site might view it differently: one conceives of the job as twenty bucks an hour, the second as a way to get out of the house and be with buddies, the third as building a cathedral. Fromm found that few individuals have the productive character, being fixated as oral-receptive, oral-exploitive, anal-retentive, or marketing types. Maslow thought that only about 2% of individuals could consistently function at the highest level of motivation: self-actualization (with the rest of us scurrying to meet our shifting lower levels of need).

Cardiologist Meyer Friedman attempted to construct a typology of different work motivations. Type-A individuals tended to be workaholics, pushing themselves and their subordinates very hard, even when there was little need to do so (*see* Workaholism). They would even keep score in their recreational activities. These fast-trackers got frustrated quickly while waiting in lines or being subjected to any delay beyond their control. By contrast, Type-B individuals were slower-paced, more relaxed, more able to enjoy leisure, and less emotionally invested in their careers. The Jenkins Activity Schedule is one test for assessing Type A/Type B personalities.

Jung's typology of introvert (I)–extrovert (E), intuitive (N)–sensate (S), thinking (T)–feeling (F), and judging (J)–perceptive (P) led to the development of the Myers-Briggs Type Indicator (MBTI). Extroverts are more motivated by group support and sanctions. Sensates are happiest when they are working on specific details, while intuitives always have to be oriented to the big picture. Thinkers like some problem-solving challenge in their work. Feelers want emotional gratification. Perceptives tolerate ambiguity. Judgers need clear standards and do not mind enforcing the rules.

One of the best personality theories for vocational counseling is John Holland's, which categorizes people into six vocationally related personality types: realistic, social, investigative, enterprising, conventional, and artistic. The realistic types prefer to work with things, but the social types want to help other people. The investigatives want to study a problem in a library or laboratory, while the enterprising types want to lead organizational action that will solve the problems. The conventionals want structured work environments (e.g., the post office, the assembly line), while the artistics want unstructured situations in which their creativity can flow.

David McClelland pointed out that different workers and managers might be higher or lower on different job-related motives, such as the needs for achievement (*see* Achievement, Need for), power, and affiliation. Those with high achievement needs prefer a task-oriented environment with moderate levels of risk and difficulty. Those with a power orientation want status, prestige, and influence over other people. Those with affiliation needs want the acceptance of co-workers and are more motivated by cooperative, as opposed to competitive, environments.

There are also individual differences associated with specific job-related priorities: salary, benefits, geographic stability, avoidance of stress, avoidance of boredom, prestige, opportunity for advancement, clean, comfortable, or safe working environment, interesting work, pleasant relations with co-workers, flexible scheduling, time off.

Other Differences. What motivates an individual worker can vary according to the life cycle or personal crises. In their twenties, many workers are motivated by money, promotions, and prestige. Workers who have hit a plateau of satisfaction with income and prestige may turn to motivators such as interesting nature of the work, flexible scheduling with time off for family duties (the so-called mommy track), pleasant working conditions, or the chance to contribute something enduring or significant to the human race (what Erik Erikson referred to as generativity). Personal crises such as a spouse who is unemployed, ill, or seeking divorce may cause many workers to rapidly reevaluate their job-related priorities: health care coverage may come to the fore, or it could be flexible hours to care for an infirm family member.

The greatest complication surrounding job-related motivation is that there may be different kinds of motivation associated with different job-related criteria (e.g., quantity of output, quality of output, absenteeism, safety, turnover). A policy that successfully motivates workers to show up for work every day is not necessarily going to be successful in getting those workers to meet production quotas or uphold standards of quality or safety. For example, piece work might be successful with increasing productivity and reducing absenteeism, but it may undermine quality and safety.

Herzberg's two-factor theory suggests that different parts of a job are related to different types of job satisfaction or dissatisfaction. He said that the physical environment of the work related to hygiene needs. If poor compensation, unacceptable policies or supervision, poor relations with co-workers, or other dissatisfactions with the physical work environment existed, the worker would become dissatisfied. If there are no problems in these aforementioned areas, the worker does not become satisfied with the job but avoids dissatisfaction. Other motivation needs, however, are more related to the content of the work: the opportunity for growth, achievement, responsibility, advancement. If these are met, the worker becomes satisfied, but if they are not met, dissatisfaction is not necessarily going to ensue.

Stress. Burnout is an emotional alienation and exhaustion often attributed to job-related stress or dissatisfaction. Individual differences are prevalent: some susceptible workers burn out while their hardier co-workers may find the same situation tolerable or even invigorating. In fields such as law enforcement, health care, social work, counseling, teaching, and the ministry, it is often the most dedicated and people-oriented workers who burn out, especially if they find that their position requires them to do a lot of paperwork and rule enforcement while providing little opportunity for meeting the needs of their clients one on one.

The assumption that excessive stress is the primary cause of burnout can be traced to the Yerkes-Dodson Law, which holds that there is an optimum level of environmental stimulation: below that point, workers get bored and performance declines, and above that point, workers get overly stressed and performance declines. It would be more appropriate to think of stress and boredom as two separate factors. Some jobs (e.g., tending a slow-paced station on the assembly line) are low stress and high boredom, while other jobs (e.g., emergency medical services) are definitely high stress and low bore-dom. However, a job can avoid both stress and bore-dom, as is known by those professionals who have managed to build a practice with their preferred clientele and those university professors and re-searchers who work in supportive environments. Some jobs can be both stressful and boring (e.g., tending a fast-paced station on an assembly line, military on full alert).

Burnout can be prevented and ameliorated in several ways. One is by using realistic job previews as a selection technique; that is, by telling appli-cants all the bad things about the position. Some applicants who are susceptible to burnout may then withdraw their candidacy. Those who persist through the job application process are inoculated and will not measure the everyday job frustrations against idyllic standards of what the job entails.

In dealing with workers who are subject to highly stressful situations, the good manager attempts to be as supportive as possible. One important aspect of this is to shield the individual front-line worker from bureaucratic hassles. Another strategy is to give the individual worker as much control as pos-sible over his or her own job flow, so that the worker can self-regulate the incoming stress. The last re-sort is to build emotional support for burned-out workers by creating empathic teams and also by being there as an individual when needed.

Advice. All of these theories merge, at least when it comes to offering advice to managers. When one describes what results one wants from workers, be clear, not subtle. When one distributes rewards, make sure that they are fair, or better yet, that they are perceived as fair by workers. Encourage work-ers to openly state what they want, and be prepared to listen. Most of the innovations in management, from management by objectives to quality circles, have attempted to incorporate these features in dif-ferent ways.

Reference

MacGregor, D. (1960). *The human side of management.* New York: McGraw-Hill.

Additional Readings

Aamodt, M. G. (1996). *Applied industrial organizational psychology* (2nd ed.). Pacific Grove, CA: Brooks/Cole.
Auerbach, A. (1996). *The world of work: An introduction to industrial/organizational psychology.* Madison, WI: Brown & Benchmark.

T. L. BRINK

See MOTIVATION.

Workaholism. The collective mythology of the American or Puritan work ethic on the culture is both astounding and frightening. As the twentieth century draws to a close, the residents of the United States contemplate a rich history of the work ethic in such characters as John D. Rockefeller, John Henry, and Billy Graham. Cultural changes are re-defining individual and family lives toward values of pleasure, self-worth, vacations, and comfortable work environments. The roles of males and females in the family have also changed as nearly 80% of mothers work outside the home. More than half of Americans are employed outside the home, and those who work within their homes have finally been accorded status. However, to nearly eight mil-lion workaholics, work is a craving, a compulsion for control and power, an addiction.

Workaholics work because they are addicted to their job. Workaholics mistake activity for produc-tivity. It is routine for them to work 60- to 70-hour weeks, even showing up on holidays or weekends. For the workaholic there is not a viable alternative to work; no other activity uses energy, demands at-tention, and provides regular social interaction around a visible outcome. Most workaholics (nearly 70%) are happy not only at work but also with the rest of their lives. Their lives are given credibility by the social approval and attention they receive for being at work. Workaholics work at relationships, at their spiritual lives, at play, at anything. Thus the process is never as valuable as the compulsion they have to gain approval and success. Workaholism is not about healthy work but addiction and the abuse of power and control at significant emotional cost to co-workers, spouses, and children.

Three significant concerns have been expressed by mental health professionals about the worka-holic. Is the compulsive addiction to work a neu-rotic, anxiety-coping strategy? Does work serve as a substitute for intimacy in family, marital, and in-terpersonal situations? Do the long hours invested in work lead to denial or other defense mechanisms characteristic of addictions? Is a workaholic dys-functional because of intrapsychic issues, or is a workaholic interpreting reality through his or her work ethic (Minirth, Meier, Wichern, Brewer, & Skipper, 1981)?

At present no psychopathology is directly at-tributed to being a workaholic. This may in part be due to the work habits of many professionals (psy-chiatrists and psychologists) who would formulate such a pathology. However, an increasing number of mental health professionals, prompted by the codependency movement (*see* Codependency), are concerned about the possibility of addiction to work and/or a personality disorder. Most often a range of behavioral and psychological dysfunctions, such as depression, anxiety, and anger, may be diagnosed when workaholism is the primary disorder. Denial is the primary defense mechanism.

Certain behaviors and attitudes that are tradi-tionally viewed as dysfunctional (e.g., poor self-image, rigidity, omniscience, and disturbed inti-macy) characterize the workaholic. Work may produce stress and pressure to succeed; however, workaholics appear to use these stressors to rise to the occasion. They seem to have internalized the conventional wisdom of "when the going gets tough, the tough get going" or "winners aren't quitters, and quitters aren't winners!" Thus it is suggested that this is a personality pattern whereby the person interprets reality by taking an active role in work. Feeling bad about self, loneliness, and internal stress become stimuli to bear down harder and not to seek comfort in realistic goals or relationships. The process of denial of internal discomfort becomes entrenched and resistive to external logic. As physiological symptoms emerge, workaholics resort to denial to defend against real health concerns. They now may live by the credo "no pain, no gain." The workaholic is defended from external logic and even resistant to dire physiological consequences. A patient of mine recently stated, "I'd rather burn out than rust out!"

The workaholic therefore may be curiously defended against his or her condition, but the family is not. The disturbance of intimacy function is well documented (Killinger, 1991). Workaholics are often the children of addicts, not realizing that work has become their drug of choice. They recreate the same dysfunctional family they came from. The workaholic places his or her family at a lower priority than attempts to gratify work cravings. This neglect if not abuse of the family is of great concern to therapists. Many workaholics ignore the demands of family and household duties under the guise of providing a better lifestyle for their loved ones. The substitution of being at work, even on a computer, for interpersonal contact, love, warmth, and nurturance needed by family members becomes habitual. The effect on these attachments is disastrous.

The absent parent or spouse presents conflict with biblical admonitions concerning the family. The Scriptures particularly address the role of the father, mother, and spouse as being representative of God's relationship with humans. The importance of interaction and stimulation of these relationships has direct effect on attitudes toward the family and even neurological development of children. The workaholic family is not safe. It is not acceptable to express feelings or share concerns. Children are taught that there is a right, good, or perfect way to do things, and above all they are to make their parents proud. Play is substituted for competition and winning. The workaholic family is much like the Pharisees: committed to the outward image of the law with little internal grace and forgiveness.

Christ dealt with a workaholic episode in his visit to the home of Mary and Martha (Luke 10:38–42). While Christ was teaching, Mary chose to enjoy the time with him. Mary had chosen the simple life of listening to Jesus. In contrast, Martha was anticipating the meal and working on the preparations. She became emotionally upset and distracted. Frustration over getting everything right overwhelmed her, and she complained directly to Jesus about Mary. Christ admonished her that she worried about so many things when only a few things are necessary. The workaholic becomes so engaged in many tasks that he or she truly loses sight of the simplicity of God's larger plan (Matt. 6:25–34).

The treatment of the workaholic must involve addressing the addiction to work and the use of denial to defend against failing to gain approval and success. Workaholics allow their perfectionistic work ethic to overpower their weaker love/grace ethic. They must understand the difference between conditional love and unconditional love. They can do this by realizing that their cognitive functions must be balanced by their feeling functions. He or she who understands loves and who feels understood, feels loved. Vulnerability, receptivity, nurturance, and the willingness to accept failure must replace being right, approval, and success. Workaholics must give up their need for control and power. They must also accept that they have recreated their family of origin and its addiction by replacing the old addictions with a new one: work. Finally they must grieve the loss of the old self and forgive themselves for all the wasted effort. The journey to discovering a new self based on love, enjoyment, and peace will truly be temporally and eternally worthwhile.

References

Killinger, B. (1991). *Workaholics: The respectable addicts.* New York: Simon & Schuster.

Minirth, F., Meier, P., Wichern, F., Brewer, B., & Skipper, S. (1981). *The workaholic and his family.* Grand Rapids, MI: Baker.

F. B. WICHERN, SR.

See STRESS; HEALTH PSYCHOLOGY.

Worship. An Anglo-Saxon term implying esteem, gratitude, and praise for someone who has demonstrated worthiness for such respect and adoration. It is derived from the Old English *worthship*, referring to the worthiness of the object of worship. The Latin word most used in reference to worship in the medieval church was *leiturgia*, from which the English word *liturgy* derives. Liturgy is a strategy or pattern for action toward a chosen goal. The pattern or strategy is derived from the goal to be achieved. Thus in liturgy form comes from the nature and shape of the content of the action. This is true in worship and in daily work. We may refer to the liturgy of work or of worship, but standard usage today is confined mainly to worship.

Christian worship is not mainly a program for teaching Christian truth nor an emotional pep rally where one can get one's spiritual batteries charged. Worship is the celebration of the historical facts that God was uniquely in Jesus of Nazareth, reconciling the world to himself, and that God has always and continues to maintain and shepherd his creation in gracious providence and eternal love.

The celebration of worship arises from the individual and communal delight and relief of knowing those two historical facts. Worship is therefore the celebration of gratitude and hope. It is the act and experience of taking profound and grateful account of God's nature and behavior: he is for us, not against us. He is not a threat but our consolation. The psychological principle undergirding worship's redemptive value is that people who can be grateful can be healthy and people who cannot be grateful cannot be healthy. The purpose of worship is to enhance spiritual wholeness, emotional health, and creatively holy life while expressing gratitude to God. Experiencing and celebrating the joy and relief of God's grace in forgiveness and providence produces the fulfillment of that purpose.

History. Christian worship is normally communal, an act and experience of persons in congregation. The Judeo-Christian worship tradition began in an individualistic pattern. The patriarchs from Adam to Jacob often worshiped alone. That pattern persisted during the era of the judges, although communal worship had been developed. Israel worshiped as a nation during Moses' leadership. Shiloh was a place of national communal worship during the early years in Canaan and was prominent in Israel's life by the era of Samuel. After a struggle with persisting individualism and tribalism in worship, Israel came to a unified communal worship when David brought the ark of the covenant to Jerusalem. This communal liturgical experience gave rise to the psalms of David, sung in Israel's worship. Communal worship came to full bloom with the building of Solomon's temple.

The believing community was split by Jeroboam between worship at Dan and Beersheba and after the exile between Samaria and Jerusalem. However, when Israel honored its communal worship ideal, assembling as congregation at the temple in Jerusalem, its life as a nation and as a worshiping community centered in the liturgy of the great day of atonement. After the exile this focus was sturdily maintained, while the rise of synagogues came into vogue in local communities. These were centers of religious instruction rather than worship centers as such.

The history of the Christian movement and its worship is equally meaningful. Early Christians seem to have gathered rather spontaneously for worship (Acts 2). They worshiped with emphasis upon communal celebration, in a free-form style, although they continued to practice the Israelite rituals and met in the synagogues. By the second century there was no uniform universal Christian liturgy but numerous strong liturgical movements. Professional clergy, sacraments, catechetical programs, and preaching lectionaries were already everywhere in use. The church as an institution was forming.

In the third century Hippolytus standardized the liturgy mainly on the form current in Justin's time. A considerable variety in forms of worship throughout the churches of Europe, Asia, and Africa persisted until the official promulgation of the first Roman rite in the seventh century. The liturgies of the Eastern churches tended to be less stereotyped and even more celebrational than those of the Western, or Roman, church. After Gregory the liturgies of the West have varied little from the first Roman rite, except those of the Reformation churches. The Roman Catholic church has simplified some elements for local convenience.

The liturgies of the Reformation churches were shaped by a radical reaction to the formalism of the Roman rite. This reaction took two directions. The mainstream of Anglican Catholicism under Henry VIII flows into contemporary Episcopal and Methodist usage and endeavors to preserve as much of the historic liturgy of Christendom as is theologically and practically possible in the present age in local usage. The mainstream of Reformed liturgy flows into contemporary Presbyterian, Reformed, Baptist, Congregational, and most fundamentalist and evangelical usage. It endeavors to dispense with as much of the Roman rite as it can without losing distinctive Christian character and gospel-centered meaning. Lutheranism preserves some of both these mainstreams, adhering in significant degree to the cardinal elements of the Roman form while endeavoring to inspire it with the biblical and evangelical spontaneity and vitality sought by the Reformers.

Large deficits unfortunately persist in Protestant liturgies. In their attempt to avoid the formalism into which the Roman rite had fallen by the sixteenth century, they have tended to become mere contexts for preaching. That would have been appropriate to the teaching sessions of the early church's synagogues but not to worship in the third-century churches or in the liturgy of Gregory the Great. Protestantism has so significantly lost its sense of worship and liturgy as celebration that its people go to sermon, not to worship. That is an excess deriving from the Reformation emphasis on the centrality of the Word at the expense of the sacraments. The result is a devaluing of the essential function of worship: the mediation to needy persons of the consolation of the gospel of grace, through the symbolic acts, elements, and sequences of the liturgy, for the psychological and spiritual healing of the congregation as individuals and as community.

Function and Structure. The function of worship is psychological and spiritual healing through the celebration of God's grace. Liturgy therefore must have the function of enacting the process of celebrating that grace. The psychospiritual dynamics of celebration involve symbolic elements such as bread and wine, the centrality of the pulpit, Bible, and the shape of the sanctuary; symbolic sequences such as opening greetings followed by God's law, congregational penitence, God's absolution, and eucharistic celebration of the gift of grace; psychospiritual growth in insight, anxiety reduction, relief from guilt, joy in God's peace, and comfort in Christian fellowship; and the reshaping of the worshipers' discipleship as they move from the sanctuary to renew the world.

The structure of liturgy should come from the demands of that function, as it did in the Old Testament temple rites and in the first Roman rite. In properly redemptive worship the worshiper moves from the world of work to the sanctuary, through the encounter with God to confession of sin, absolution, celebration of that absolution in the eucharist, expressions and gifts of gratitude, sermonic guidance for the life of grace in the world of work, and finally the benediction. The psychospiritual process recapitulates our personal conversion processes. We move from the world to God. Then we move through the psychospiritual stages of greeting, guilt, grace, gratitude, and guidance. Then we move back to the world as renewed persons, renewing God's world. That is the healing and redeeming process worship is intended to be, was in Scripture, and endeavored to be in the historic Christian church.

Protestantism, particularly its American products in fundamentalism and evangelicalism, uniformly lacks this psychospiritual understanding of true worship. The focus on didactic sermons as the center of worship has turned Protestant worship into an essentially cognitive process, largely oriented on the left hemisphere of the brain. But worship should be more of a right hemisphere celebration, a response of the heart as celebration of God's unconditional, radical, and universal grace.

J. H. ELLENS

See RITUAL; PSYCHOLOGY OF RELIGION; SPIRITUALITY, PSYCHOLOGY OF.

Wundt, Wilhelm (1832–1920). Commonly considered the founder of psychology. The son of a Lutheran pastor, he was born in the village of Neckarau (near Heidelberg), Germany. His early education was from a young vicar whom Wundt liked better than his parents. When the vicar was transferred to another village, Wundt went to live with him until he was ready for the university at 19. To earn a living and study science while practicing it, Wundt decided to become a physician, studying at Tübingen, Heidelberg, and Berlin. He received his doctorate from Heidelberg in 1855.

Wundt taught physiology at Heidelberg from 1857 to 1874. During these years his conception of psychology as an independent and experimental science began to emerge. After one year at Zurich, Wundt began the most important phase of his career, his years at Leipzig. He was appointed professor of philosophy in 1875 and worked there continuously for 45 years until his death.

Although there is much controversy over the exact date, some time soon after arriving at Leipzig Wundt established a psychological laboratory, of-

fered courses in experimental psychology, and began a journal *(Philosophical Studies)* to publish research originating in his laboratory. In 1879 one of his students published the first research with Wundt from the new laboratory. In 1979 the American Psychological Association had a celebration to recognize the century of psychology's existence.

Wundt was the founder of what is now called structuralism. The subject matter of psychology was immediate experience, which was studied using the method of introspection. Experience was to be broken down into its elements of sensations and feelings. Wundt's doctrine of apperception then accounted for unified conscious experience. Most of the research at his laboratory involved sensation, reaction time, attention, and feelings.

Wundt's most important work, perhaps the most important work in the history of psychology, is his *Principles of Physiological Psychology,* published in two parts in 1873 and 1874. This appeared in six editions over the next 37 years, establishing psychology as a laboratory science with its own problems and methods. Although structuralism died, Wundt's system was most important in the development of psychology. Functionalism, behaviorism, and Gestalt psychology emerged as direct criticisms of it. Wundt *was* psychology for nearly 20 years.

R. L. KOTESKEY

See PSYCHOLOGY, HISTORY OF; STRUCTURALISM.

Würzburg School. In Germany the Würzburg School helped to set up a clearer differentiation between act and content psychologies, parallelling the opposition between functionalism and structuralism in the United States. It also stressed purposiveness and wholeness, opposing the elementistic and atomistic approaches of structuralism and associationism. Chronologically the members of the Würzburg School are Oswald Külpe (who founded the laboratory in 1894), A. Mayer, J. Orth, Karl Marbe, H. J. Watt, Narziss Ach, August Messer, and Karl Bühler.

These psychologists employed the method of systematic experimental introspection, which involved the performance of a complex task such as judging or remembering, followed by a retrospective report of the subject's experiences during the original task. The whole experience was methodically described, time period by time period.

The contributions of Mayer and Orth demonstrated that a subject's responses depend on unanalyzable and indescribable conscious attitudes *(Bewusstseinslage)* having an affective tone, depending on internal as well as external stimuli. Marbe added such states as doubt, hesitation, and confidence, which were thought to be neither sensations, images, nor feelings. In his studies of judgments Marbe often found that subjects did not know how the judgments were made, thus shedding doubt on the theory that judgment involves the mental retention of the image of one object while comparing it with the impression of a second.

The research of Watt and Ach contributed the observation that a mental set or determining tendency *(Einstellung)* was often brought about by the task *(Aufgabe)* itself, so that the conscious work was done as soon as the instructions were comprehended. A good example of this is involved in the reading of music: the exact notes played are determined initially by the key signature and do not require a conscious judgment for each note read.

Messer and Bühler did most to develop the doctrine of imageless thought, the view that the actual thought processes, although they can be examined by introspection, are not sensory or imaginal in character. Thoughts are elements devoid of sensory quality or intensity but possessing clearness, assurance, and vividness. The controversy over the existence of thoughts apart from images continues to the present.

H. Vande Kemp

See Psychology, History of.

Yerkes, Robert Mearns (1876–1956). A pioneer in the development of comparative psychology. He was born in Breadysville, Pennsylvania, and studied at Ursinus College, intending to go into medicine. He went to Harvard in 1897 and became interested first in zoology, then in philosophy and psychology. At Harvard he earned another A.B. in 1898, an M.A. in 1899, and a Ph.D. in 1902.

Yerkes taught at Harvard from 1902 to 1917. During this time he collaborated with John B. Watson, who was making a comparative study of vision in animals. Although Yerkes was not a behaviorist, Watson was impressed with his work with animals. Yerkes also had just translated some of Ivan Pavlov's papers that reported the discovery of the conditioned reflex.

When the United States entered World War I in April 1917, Yerkes was asked to organize American psychologists to assist the military. As chairman of the General Committee on Psychology he directed work on such topics as the effects of high altitude, morale, and gas masks. However, he is most widely known for his work in developing intelligence tests to be used to classify recruits, to eliminate the unfit, and to identify the superior.

The development of these intelligence tests, the Army Alpha for literates and the Beta for illiterates, was an amazing feat. By 7 July 1917 his committee had developed a plan to test the entire military, prepared 10 forms of the group tests and 5 forms of the individual tests, written an examiner's guide, and validated their tests on 400 subjects. By 1 October 1917 testing was in progress to further evaluate the tests so that they could be revised. The revision was completed by April 1918, and by the end of 1918 tests had been given to 1,726,000 men.

After his military work during World War I and a brief stay at the University of Minnesota, Yerkes spent 1924 to 1944 as research professor at Yale.

Yerkes's other major contribution was the development of comparative psychology. He studied crabs, turtles, frogs, rats, mice, worms, crows, doves, pigs, monkeys, apes, and humans. His first book was *The Dancing Mouse* (1907) and his last was *Chimpanzees: A Laboratory Colony* (1943). Probably his most significant work was *The Great Apes* (1929). In 1929 he realized a long-time ambition by establishing the Yale Laboratories of Primate Biology in Orange Park, Florida. It was renamed the Yerkes Laboratories of Primate Biology when he retired from active administration in 1941.

R. L. KOTESKEY

See COMPARATIVE PSYCHOLOGY; INTELLECTUAL ASSESSMENT.

Yerkes-Dodson Law. In general the Yerkes-Dodson law (also called the Inverted-U law) suggests that there is an optimal level of arousal. Performance increases as the amount of stimulation (e.g., presence of others) approaches the optimal level of arousal. However, stimulating beyond the optimal level of arousal results in performance decrements. Further, the optimal level will vary with degree of learning and task difficulty. Well learned and easy tasks have a higher optimal level of arousal than do poorly learned and difficult tasks.

This conclusion results from three experiments that Yerkes and Dodson (1908) conducted using mice and a white-black discrimination task. The experiments differed in task difficulty and shock intensity. Overall they found that the optimal stimulus strength (shock) varied with task difficulty. Easy tasks required a more intense stimulus strength, whereas more difficult tasks required moderate strength stimuli.

The Yerkes-Dodson law is evidenced in a wide range of psychological findings. For example, Stennett (1957) found a U-shaped function when manipulating motivation in human maze learning. Broadhurst (1959) found that neurotic subjects learned more quickly than nonneurotic subjects on easy tasks but learned more slowly on difficult tasks. Pessin and Husband (1933) found that an audience slowed learning a maze and nonsense-syllable task. However, after the subjects had learned these tasks, the presence of an audience increased performance (cf. Zajonc, 1965).

Since Yerkes and Dodson (1908) did not tie the inverted-U relationship to any underlying concepts, researchers freely borrowed it. Broadhurst (1959) linked the Inverted-U law with motivation, claiming that the law described the optimum motivation level for learning a task. Easterbrook (1959) related the Inverted-U law to performance. Researchers concluded that an easy-to-perform task requires more drive or motivation in order for it to be performed well, but a difficult to perform task requires less drive or motivation. Finally, the Inverted-U law was linked with arousal (Easterbrook, 1959; Hebb, 1955). Arousal presumably reduces the number of cues utilized. Therefore, a certain level of arousal is necessary in order to concentrate on a task and utilize task-relevant cues. However, overarousal can result in a type of tunnel vision that prevents the use of relevant cues, thereby negatively impacting performance. The concept of arousal also allowed the Inverted-U law to be linked with personality types and physiological states (e.g., extraversion; see Matthews, 1985).

Thus the Yerkes-Dodson law provides a simple explanation for a variety of findings in a number of different areas within psychology. The Inverted-U law states that performance increases until an optimal level of arousal is reached, after which performance diminishes. However, the unique aspect of the law is that it also predicts that overmotiva-tion can decrease performance (cf. Teigen, 1994). Applications of the law exist in learning, memory, personality, and clinical psychology.

References

Broadhurst, P. L. (1959). The interaction of task difficulty and motivation: The Yerkes-Dodson law revived. *Acta Psychologica, 16*, 321–338.

Easterbrook, J. A. (1959). Emotion, cue utilization, and organization of behavior. *Psychological Review, 66*, 183–201.

Hebb, D. O. (1955). Drives and CNS. *Psychological Review, 62*, 243–254.

Matthews, G. (1985). The effects of extraversion and arousal on intelligence test performance. *British Journal of Psychology, 76*, 479–493.

Pessin, J., & Husband, R. (1933). Effects of social stimulation on human maze learning. *Journal of Abnormal and Social Psychology, 28*, 148–154.

Stennett, R. G. (1957). The relation of performance level to level of arousal. *Journal of Experimental Psychology, 54*, 54–61.

Teigen, K. H. (1994). Yerkes-Dodson: A law for all seasons. *Theory & Psychology, 4*, 525–547.

Yerkes, R. M., & Dodson, J. D. (1908). The relation of strength of stimulus to rapidity of habit-formation. *Journal of Comparative Neurology and Psychology, 18*, 459–482.

Zajonc, R. B. (1965). Social facilitation. *Science, 149*, 269–274.

C. KOCH

Zz

Zeigarnik Effect. A series of experiments conducted by Bluma Zeigarnik revealed that people tend to remember uncompleted tasks better than completed ones. This effect is thought to be due to the persistence of drive inherent in tasks left uncompleted, in that an intention to perform a task may create a sense of psychic tension that persists until the task is completed. In the initial experiments subjects were interrupted while performing a number of tasks. Unfinished tasks were subsequently recalled more frequently than finished ones. The intention to reach a set goal is said to correspond to a tension within the system of a person. The tension is released once the goal is reached.

This tendency is not necessarily unhealthy, but it may be carried to neurotic extremes if an individual becomes totally preoccupied with what he or she has left unfinished and fails to derive any sense of accomplishment from completion of goals. The theory corresponds to Sigmund Freud's basic assumptions about the persistence of unfulfilled wishes and suggests that memory is not just a matter of association bonds but rather involves motivation and emotion as well.

D. L. Schuurman

Zoophilia. The achievement of sexual pleasure or arousal through the use of animals. The range of behavior may be from sexual excitement in connection with stroking and fondling of animals to sexual intercourse. Kinsey's work showed about 1% of the males studied had been involved in one fashion or another with animals. The usual choices of animals were dogs, chickens, horses, or cows. The behavior is more frequent among males.

This behavior is most common in the preadolescent years and in rural areas. Although it is often associated with the upper educational level, it may be seen in persons with lower intellectual abilities or where the influence of alcohol is involved. It also sometimes occurs as a result of sexual isolation from females. Zoophilia is rare among adults.

Cases have been reported where sadistic attacks are made on animals in conjunction with sexual involvement. In many areas it is a crime to have sexual relations with an animal. The Levitical law states that lying with any animal is punishable by death for both males and females (Lev. 18:23; 20:15–16).

Treatment would involve teaching responsible behavior control and increasing social skills.

L. N. Ferguson